THE EBAY PRICE GUIDE

The eBAY

PRICE GUIDE

What Sells for What (in Every Category!)

Julia L. Wilkinson

**NO STARCH
PRESS**

San Francisco

THE EBAY PRICE GUIDE. Copyright © 2006 by Julia L. Wilkinson.

1 2 3 4 5 6 7 8 9 10 – 09 08 07 06

No Starch Press and the No Starch Press logo are registered trademarks of No Starch Press, Inc. Other product and company names mentioned herein may be the trademarks of their respective owners. Rather than use a trademark symbol with every occurrence of a trademarked name, we are using the names only in an editorial fashion and to the benefit of the trademark owner, with no intention of infringement of the trademark.

Publisher: William Pollock
Managing Editor: Elizabeth Campbell
Production Assistance: Christina Samuell
Cover Design: Octopod Studios
Copyeditor: Andy Carroll
Compositors: Riley Hoffman and Megan Dunchak
Proofreaders: Stephanie Provines, Megan Dunchak, Riley Hoffman, and Christina Samuell

For information on book distributors or translations, please contact No Starch Press, Inc. directly:

No Starch Press, Inc.
555 De Haro Street, Suite 250, San Francisco, CA 94107
phone: 415.863.9900; fax: 415.863.9950; info@nostarch.com; www.nostarch.com

The information in this book is distributed on an "As Is" basis, without warranty. While every precaution has been taken in the preparation of this work, neither the author nor No Starch Press, Inc. shall have any liability to any person or entity with respect to any loss or damage caused or alleged to be caused directly or indirectly by the information contained in it.

Library of Congress Cataloging-in-Publication Data

Wilkinson, Julia L.
 The eBay price guide : what sells for what (in every category!) / Julia L. Wilkinson.
     p. cm.
 ISBN 1-59327-055-0 (cd-rom)
1. eBay (Firm) 2. Internet auctions--Handbooks, manuals, etc. I. Title. HF5478.W548 2005
 381'.177--dc22
                                        2005025146

BRIEF CONTENTS

Acknowledgments xxvii

Introduction xxix

Chapter 1: Antiques 1

Chapter 2: Art 13

Chapter 3: Baby 19

Chapter 4: Boats 25

Chapter 5: Books 29

Chapter 6: Business & Industrial 45

Chapter 7: Cameras & Photo 63

Chapter 8: Cars, Parts & Vehicles (eBay Motors) 79

Chapter 9: Cell Phones 91

Chapter 10: Clothing, Shoes & Accessories 97

Chapter 11: Coins 111

Chapter 12: Collectibles 127

Chapter 13: Computers & Networking 165

Chapter 14: Consumer Electronics 177

Chapter 15: Crafts 195

Chapter 16: Dolls & Bears 211

Chapter 17: DVDs & Movies 219

Chapter 18: Entertainment Memorabilia 225

Chapter 19: Gift Certificates 239

Chapter 20: Health & Beauty 255

Chapter 21: Home & Garden 279

Chapter 22: Jewelry & Watches.. 299

Chapter 23: Music 315

Chapter 24: Musical Instruments 325

Chapter 25: Pottery & Glass 341

Chapter 26: Real Estate 363

Chapter 27: Specialty Services 373

Chapter 28: Sporting Goods 385

Chapter 29: Sports Memorabilia, Cards & Fan Shop.. 421

Chapter 30: Stamps 439

Chapter 31: Tickets 459

Chapter 32: Toys & Hobbies 467

Chapter 33: Travel 499

Chapter 34: Video Games 507

Chapter 35: Everything Else.. 531

Appendix: eBay Lists... 557

CONTENTS IN DETAIL

ACKNOWLEDGMENTS   **xxvii**

INTRODUCTION   **xxix**

Why an eBay Price Guide? xxix
Why Did It Sell for That? Analyzing Prices xxx
Methodology xxxi
Identical Items and "Dutch" Auctions xxxi
Low Prices xxxi
Quoting Auctions and People xxxi
In Conclusion xxxii

1
ANTIQUES   1

Beware of Fakes and Reproductions 1
Low Sellers and Bargains 2
High Flyers and Notables 3

Antiquities (Classical, Amer.) ▸ Egyptian 4	Furniture ▸ Beds 8
Antiquities (Classical, Amer.) ▸ The Americas 4	Furniture ▸ Cabinets, Armoires, Cupboards 8
Architectural & Garden ▸ Chandeliers, Fixtures, Sconces 4	Maps, Atlases, Globes ▸ Maps, Atlases 8
Architectural & Garden ▸ Garden 5	Maritime ▸ Sextants 8
Architectural & Garden ▸ Hardware 5	Maritime ▸ Anchors 9
Asian Antiques ▸ Chinese 5	Musical Instruments ▸ Keyboard 9
Asian Antiques ▸ Japanese 5	Musical Instruments ▸ String 9
Books, Manuscripts ▸ American 6	Rugs, Carpets ▸ Large (9x7–9x12) 9
Books, Manuscripts ▸ European 6	Rugs, Carpets ▸ Medium (4x2–9x6) 10
Decorative Arts ▸ Ceramics, Porcelain 6	Science & Medicine ▸ Medical 10
Decorative Arts ▸ Glass 6	Silver ▸ Silverplate 10
Decorative Arts ▸ Metalware 7	Silver ▸ Sterling 10
Decorative Arts ▸ Woodenware 7	Silver ▸ Sterling ▸ Flatware 11
Ethnographic ▸ African 7	Textiles, Linens ▸ Fabric 11
Ethnographic ▸ Native American 7	Textiles, Linens ▸ Quilts, Bedspreads 11

2
ART   13

Art Bargains 13
High Prices and the Integration of Live Art Auctions 14

Drawings ▸ Contemporary (1950–Now) 14	Prints ▸ Antique (Pre–1900) 16
Drawings ▸ Antique (Pre–1900) 15	Prints ▸ Contemporary (1950–Now) 17
Folk Art (Paintings) 15	Sculpture, Carvings 17
Mixed Media ▸ Contemporary (1950–Now) 15	Self-Representing Artists 17
Paintings ▸ Antique (Pre–1900) 15	Wholesale Lots ▸ Paintings 18
Paintings ▸ Contemporary (1950–Now) 16	Wholesale Lots ▸ Prints 18
Posters 16	

3
BABY   19

Car Safety Seats ▸ Booster to 80lbs 20	Nursery Bedding ▸ Quilts, Comforters, Duvets 22
Diapering 21	Nursery Decor 23
Diapering ▸ Diapers 21	Nursery Furniture 23
Feeding, Breast & Bottle 21	Safety 23
Memory Books, Keepsakes 21	Strollers 23
Nursery Bedding ▸ Blankets 22	Toys ▸ Rattles, Teethers 23
Nursery Bedding ▸ Sets 22	

4
BOATS 25

Bargains and Misplaced Items 25
    Fishing Boats 27   Sailboats 27
    Powerboats & Motorboats 27   Other Boats 28

5
BOOKS 29

Pricing to Sell 29
Best Categories 30
Buyers' Bargains 31
Magazines and Catalogs 31
Book and Magazine Accessories 31

    Accessories ▸ Address Books 32   Magazine Back Issues ▸ Home and Garden 38
    Accessories ▸ Blank Diaries, Journals ... 32   Magazine Back Issues ▸ News, General Interest ... 38
    Accessories ▸ Bookmarks 32   Magazine Subscriptions ▸ Celebrity 38
    Antiquarian & Collectible ▸ Americana 32   Magazine Subscriptions ▸ Cooking, Food, Wine .. 38
    Antiquarian & Collectible ▸ Children's 33   Magazine Subscriptions ▸ General Interest 38
    Antiquarian & Collectible ▸ History 33   Magazine Subscriptions ▸ Men 39
    Antiquarian & Collectible ▸ Literature 33   Magazine Subscriptions ▸ Movies & TV 39
    Audiobooks ▸ Fiction—Cassette 33   Magazine Subscriptions ▸ Sports & Outdoors 39
    Audiobooks ▸ Fiction—CD 34   Nonfiction ▸ Art & Photography 40
    Audiobooks ▸ Instructional—Cassette 34   Nonfiction ▸ Biography & Memoir 40
    Audiobooks ▸ Instructional—CD 34   Nonfiction ▸ Business & Economics 40
    Audiobooks ▸ Religion—Cassette 34   Nonfiction ▸ Computers & Internet 40
    Audiobooks ▸ Religion—CD 34   Nonfiction ▸ Cooking, Food, Wine 40
    Audiobooks ▸ Self-Help—Cassette 34   Nonfiction ▸ Health & Fitness 40
    Audiobooks ▸ Self-Help—CD 35   Nonfiction ▸ History 41
    Catalogs 35   Nonfiction ▸ Hobbies & Crafts 41
    Children's ▸ Classics 35   Nonfiction ▸ Home & Garden 41
    Children's ▸ Fiction 35   Nonfiction ▸ Military & War 41
    Children's ▸ Learning to Read 35   Nonfiction ▸ Reference 41
    Children's ▸ Picture Books 36   Nonfiction ▸ Religion 41
    Children's ▸ Series 36   Nonfiction ▸ Self-Help 42
    Fiction ▸ Action, Adventure 36   Nonfiction ▸ Sports, Recreation 42
    Fiction ▸ Classics 36   Nonfiction ▸ Transportation 42
    Fiction ▸ Fantasy 37   Nonfiction ▸ Travel, Geography, Exploration 42
    Fiction ▸ Horror 37   Nonfiction ▸ True Crime 42
    Fiction ▸ Mystery, Thriller 37   Textbooks, Education 42
    Fiction ▸ Romance 37   Wholesale, Bulk Lots ▸ Audiobooks 43
    Fiction ▸ Science Fiction 37   Wholesale, Bulk Lots ▸ Books 43
    Magazine Back Issues ▸ Celebrity 37   Wholesale, Bulk Lots ▸ Magazines 43

6
BUSINESS & INDUSTRIAL 45

Best Deals 46
    Agriculture & Forestry ▸ Antique Tractors &   Food Service & Retail ▸ Point of Sale,
      Equipment 46   POS Equipment 50
    Agriculture & Forestry ▸ Farm Implements &   Food Service & Retail ▸ Refrigeration &
      Attachments 46   Ice Machines 50
    Agriculture & Forestry ▸ Forestry Equipment &   Food Service & Retail ▸ Vending &
      Supplies 47   Tabletop Concessions 50
    Agriculture & Forestry ▸ Tractor Parts & Manuals ... 47   Food Service & Retail ▸ Wholesale Lots &
    Construction ▸ Building Materials & Supplies 48   Bulk Foods 51
    Construction ▸ Heavy Equipment & Trailers 48   Healthcare, Lab & Life Science ▸ Imaging &
    Food Service & Retail ▸ Bar & Beverage Equipment 48   Aesthetics Equipment 51
    Food Service & Retail ▸ Commercial Kitchen   Healthcare, Lab & Life Science ▸ Lab Equipment ... 51
      Equipment 49   Healthcare, Lab & Life Science ▸ Lab Supplies 52
    Food Service & Retail ▸ Furniture, Signs, Decor 49   Healthcare, Lab & Life Science ▸
    Food Service & Retail ▸ Furniture, Signs,   Medical Equipment 52
      Décor ▸ Display Cases 50

Healthcare, Lab & Life Science ▶
  Medical—Specialty 52
Healthcare, Lab & Life Science ▶ Medical
  Supplies & Disposables 52
Industrial Electrical & Test ▶ Circuit Breakers,
  Transformers 53
Industrial Electrical & Test ▶ Industrial Automation,
  Control 53
Industrial Electrical & Test ▶ Industrial Automation,
  Control ▶ Robotics 53
Industrial Electrical & Test ▶ Industrial Automation,
  Control ▶ Drives & Motion Control 53
Industrial Electrical & Test ▶ Motors &
  Transmissions 54
Industrial Electrical & Test ▶ Test Equipment 54
Industrial Electrical & Test ▶ Wholesale Lots 54
Industrial Supply, MRO ▶ Air Compressors 54
Industrial Supply, MRO ▶ Cleaning & Painting 55
Industrial Supply, MRO ▶ Commercial Radios 55
Industrial Supply, MRO ▶ Forklifts & Other Lifts .. 55
Industrial Supply, MRO ▶ HVAC 55
Industrial Supply, MRO ▶ Hydraulics &
  Pneumatics 56
Industrial Supply, MRO ▶ Pumps 56
Manufacturing & Metalworking ▶ Metalworking
  Equipment 56
Manufacturing & Metalworking ▶ Metalworking
  Supplies 57

Manufacturing & Metalworking ▶ Process
  Equipment 57
Manufacturing & Metalworking ▶
  Semiconductor & PCB Equipment 57
Manufacturing & Metalworking ▶ Woodworking ...57
Office, Printing & Shipping ▶ Copier Toner &
  Supplies 58
Office, Printing & Shipping ▶ Commercial
  Printing Presses 58
Office, Printing & Shipping ▶ Fax Machines &
  Supplies 58
Office, Printing & Shipping ▶ DVD-R, CD-R &
  Blank Media 59
Office, Printing & Shipping ▶ Office Furniture 59
Office, Printing & Shipping ▶ Printing &
  Graphic Arts 59
Office, Printing & Shipping ▶ Shipping &
  Packing Supplies 59
Office, Printing & Shipping ▶ Shredders 60
Office, Printing & Shipping ▶ Trade Show
  Displays 60
Office, Printing & Shipping ▶ Office—
  Wholesale Lots 60
Other Industries ▶ Dry Cleaning, Laundromat 61
Other Industries ▶ Oil & Gas 61
Other Industries ▶ Power & Utilities 61
Other Industries ▶ Websites & Businesses for Sale ..61

7
CAMERAS & PHOTO
63

Digital Cameras: Finding Your Range 63
Camcorders 64
Getting Your Props: Accessories and More 64
Binoculars & Telescopes ▶ Binoculars &
  Monoculars 64
Binoculars & Telescopes ▶ Telescopes 65
Camcorder Accessories ▶ Accessories 65
Camcorder Accessories ▶ Batteries & Chargers 65
Camcorder Accessories ▶ Blank Tapes & Memory .. 65
Camcorders ▶ 8mm, Hi8, VHS 66
Camcorders ▶ Digital 66
Camcorders ▶ Sony 66
Digital Camera Accessories ▶ Accessories 67
Digital Camera Accessories ▶ Batteries & Chargers . 67
Digital Camera Accessories ▶ Memory Cards 67
Digital Cameras ▶ Canon 68
Digital Cameras ▶ Nikon 68
Digital Cameras ▶ Sony 68
Digital Cameras ▶ Point & Shoot 69
Digital Cameras ▶ Digital SLR 69
Digital Cameras ▶ Specialty Digital Cameras 69
Film ▶ 35mm 69
Film ▶ Medium, Large Format 70
Film Camera Accessories ▶ Camera
  Body Accessories 70
Film Camera Accessories ▶ Other Film &
  Movie Accessories 70
Film Cameras ▶ 35mm Point & Shoot 70
Film Cameras ▶ 35mm Rangefinder 71
Film Cameras ▶ 35mm SLR 71
Film Cameras ▶ Instant Print, Polaroid 71

Film Cameras ▶ Movie 72
Film Processing & Darkroom ▶ Chemistry 72
Film Processing & Darkroom ▶ Enlargement
  Equip. & Supplies 72
Film Processing & Darkroom ▶ Hardware,
  Lighting & Setup 72
Film Processing & Darkroom ▶ Photographic Paper ...73
Lenses & Filters 73
Lighting & Studio Equipment ▶ Background
  Material & Equip 73
Lighting & Studio Equipment ▶ Light Controls &
  Modifiers 74
Lighting & Studio Equipment ▶ Portable
  Flash/Strobe 74
Lighting & Studio Equipment ▶ Props &
  Stage Equipment 74
Manuals, Guides & Books ▶ Camera Manuals 74
Manuals, Guides & Books ▶ How-To, Guides &
  Techniques 75
Photo Albums & Archive Items ▶ Archival &
  Mounting Materials 75
Photo Albums & Archive Items ▶ Photo Albums 75
Printers, Scanners & Supplies ▶ Photo Printers 75
Printers, Scanners & Supplies ▶ Printing
  Software & Supplies 76
Printers, Scanners & Supplies ▶ Scanners 76
Professional Video Equipment ▶ Cameras 76

Professional Video Equipment ▸ Editing,
   Post-Production 76
Professional Video Equipment ▸ Recorders &
   Players 77
Projection Equipment ▸ Accessories 77

Projection Equipment ▸ Projectors 77
Tripods, Monopods ▸ Monopods 77
Tripods, Monopods ▸ Tripods 78
Vintage ▸ Accessories 78
Vintage ▸ Cameras 78

8
CARS, PARTS & VEHICLES (EBAY MOTORS)   79

From Sky-High to Down-to-Earth: Price Ranges 80
Passenger Vehicles ▸ Acura 81
Passenger Vehicles ▸ BMW 81
Passenger Vehicles ▸ Cadillac 81
Passenger Vehicles ▸ Chevrolet 81
Passenger Vehicles ▸ Chrysler 82
Passenger Vehicles ▸ Dodge 82
Passenger Vehicles ▸ Ferrari 82
Passenger Vehicles ▸ Ford 82
Passenger Vehicles ▸ Honda 83
Passenger Vehicles ▸ Hummer 83
Passenger Vehicles ▸ Hyundai 83
Passenger Vehicles ▸ Infiniti 84
Passenger Vehicles ▸ Jaguar 84
Passenger Vehicles ▸ Jeep 84
Passenger Vehicles ▸ Lamborghini 84
Passenger Vehicles ▸ Land Rover 85
Passenger Vehicles ▸ Lexus 85
Passenger Vehicles ▸ Lincoln 85
Passenger Vehicles ▸ Mazda 85

Passenger Vehicles ▸ Mercedes-Benz 86
Passenger Vehicles ▸ Mitsubishi 86
Passenger Vehicles ▸ Nissan 86
Passenger Vehicles ▸ Oldsmobile 86
Passenger Vehicles ▸ Plymouth 87
Passenger Vehicles ▸ Pontiac 87
Passenger Vehicles ▸ Porsche 87
Passenger Vehicles ▸ Rolls-Royce 87
Passenger Vehicles ▸ Saab 88
Passenger Vehicles ▸ Saturn 88
Passenger Vehicles ▸ Shelby 88
Passenger Vehicles ▸ Subaru 88
Passenger Vehicles ▸ Toyota 89
Passenger Vehicles ▸ Volkswagen 89
Passenger Vehicles ▸ Volvo 89
Motorcycles ▸ Harley-Davidson 89
Motorcycles ▸ Honda 90
Car & Truck Parts 90
Other Vehicles ▸ Aircraft 90

9
CELL PHONES   91

Accessories, Parts ▸ Accessory Bundles, Packages .92
Accessories, Parts ▸ Batteries 92
Accessories, Parts ▸ Belt Clips, Holsters 93
Accessories, Parts ▸ Chargers, Cradle Chargers 93
Accessories, Parts ▸ Faceplates, Housings 93
Phones Only ▸ Nokia 94
Phones Only ▸ Motorola 94
Phones Only ▸ Samsung 94

Phones with New Plan Purchase ▸ Motorola 95
Phones with New Plan Purchase ▸ Nokia 95
Phones with New Plan Purchase ▸ Sony, Ericsson .. 96
Prepaid Phones & Cards ▸ Prepaid,
   No Contract Cards 96
Prepaid Phones & Cards ▸ Prepaid,
   No Contract Phones 96

10
CLOTHING, SHOES & ACCESSORIES   97

Paying Less—and More—Than Retail 98
Infants & Toddlers ▸ Custom, Handmade 98
Infants & Toddlers ▸ Boys' Clothing 99
Infants & Toddlers ▸ Girls' Clothing 99
Boys ▸ Clothing (Sz 4–7) 99
Boys ▸ Clothing (Sz 4–7) ▸ Pajamas 99
Boys ▸ Clothing (Sz 4–7) ▸ Swimwear 100
Boys ▸ Clothing (Sz 4–7) ▸ Underwear 100
Boys ▸ Clothing (Sz 8 and up) ▸ Jeans & Pants 100
Boys ▸ Clothing (Sz 8 and up) ▸ Outerwear 100
Boys ▸ Clothing (Sz 8 and up) ▸ Shirts & T-Shirts .. 101
Boys ▸ Shoes 101
Girls ▸ Accessories 101
Girls ▸ Clothing (Sz 4–6x) ▸ Dresses 101
Girls ▸ Clothing (Sz 4–6x) ▸ Outfits & Sets 102
Girls ▸ Clothing (Sz 4–6x) ▸ Sweaters 102
Girls ▸ Clothing (Sz 7 and up) ▸ Jeans & Pants 102
Girls ▸ Shoes 102
Men's Accessories ▸ Belts 103

Men's Accessories ▸ Hats 103
Men's Accessories ▸ Neckwear, Ties 103
Men's Accessories ▸ Wallets, Holders 103
Men's Clothing ▸ Blazers & Sport Coats 104
Men's Clothing ▸ Jeans 104
Men's Clothing ▸ Outerwear 104
Men's Clothing ▸ Pants 104
Men's Clothing ▸ Shirts 105
Men's Clothing ▸ Suits 105
Men's Clothing ▸ Men's Shoes 105
Uniforms ▸ Adult 106
Vintage ▸ Men's & Women's Accessories 106
Vintage ▸ Unisex & T-Shirts 106
Vintage ▸ Women's Clothing 106
Wedding Apparel ▸ Wedding Dresses 107
Women's Accessories, Handbags ▸
   Handbags, Bags 107

Women's Accessories, Handbags ▸
  Scarves, Wraps 107
Women's Accessories, Handbags ▸ Sunglasses .. 107
Women's Clothing ▸ Misses ▸ Dresses 108
Women's Clothing ▸ Jeans 108
Women's Clothing ▸ Outerwear 108
Women's Clothing ▸ Pants 108

Women's Clothing ▸ Skirts 109
Women's Clothing ▸ T-Shirts, Tank Tops 109
Women's Clothing ▸ Maternity 109
Women's Shoes 109
Wholesale, Large & Small Lots ▸ Men's Clothing .. 110
Wholesale, Large & Small Lots ▸
  Women's Clothing 110

11
COINS
111

Bullion ▸ Gold 113
Bullion ▸ Platinum 113
Coins: Ancient ▸ Byzantine 113
Coins: Ancient ▸ Celtic 113
Coins: Ancient ▸ China 114
Coins: Ancient ▸ Greek 114
Coins: Ancient ▸ Medieval 114
Coins: Ancient ▸ Roman: Imperial 114
Coins: Ancient ▸ Roman: Republic 115
Coins: US ▸ Collections, Lots 115
Coins: US ▸ Colonial 115
Coins: US ▸ Small Cents ▸ Lincoln
  Wheat (1909–1958) 116
Coins: US ▸ Dimes 116
Coins: US ▸ Quarters 116
Coins: US ▸ Halves 116
Coins: US ▸ Dollars 117
Coins: US ▸ Dollars ▸ Eisenhower (1971–78) 117
Coins: US ▸ Errors 117
Coins: US ▸ Gold 117
Coins: US ▸ Mint Sets 118
Coins: US ▸ Proof Sets 118
Coins: US ▸ Rolls 118
Coins: World ▸ Asia, Middle East 119

Coins: World ▸ Europe 119
Coins: World ▸ North, Central America 119
Coins: World ▸ Gold 120
Exonumia ▸ Elongated Coins 120
Exonumia ▸ Medals 120
Exonumia ▸ Tokens: Civil War 120
Exonumia ▸ Tokens: US Trade 121
Paper Money: US ▸ Colonial Currency 121
Paper Money: US ▸ Confederate Currency 121
Paper Money: US ▸ Large Size Notes 121
Paper Money: US ▸ Small Size Notes 122
Paper Money: US ▸ Obsolete Currency 122
Paper Money: World ▸ Africa 122
Paper Money: World ▸ Asia, Middle East 123
Paper Money: World ▸ Australia, Oceania 123
Paper Money: World ▸ North, Central America ... 123
Paper Money: World ▸ Europe 123
Paper Money: World ▸ South America 124
Publications & Supplies ▸ Supplies 124
Scripophily ▸ Airlines 124
Scripophily ▸ Autographs 125
Scripophily ▸ Communications 125
Scripophily ▸ Industrial 125

12
COLLECTIBLES
127

PEZ Dispensers and eBay-ana 129
Advertising ▸ Agriculture 129
Advertising ▸ Candy & Nuts 129
Advertising ▸ Cars 130
Advertising ▸ Clothing, Fashion 130
Advertising ▸ Coffee, Tea 130
Advertising ▸ Communication & Utilities 130
Advertising ▸ Computers, High Tech 131
Advertising ▸ Distillery 131
Advertising ▸ eBay-ana 131
Advertising ▸ Food & Restaurant 131
Advertising ▸ Gas & Oil 132
Advertising ▸ Health & Beauty 132
Advertising ▸ Household 132
Advertising ▸ Retail Establishments 133
Advertising ▸ Soda 133
Advertising ▸ Soda ▸ Coca-Cola 133
Animals ▸ Bear 133
Animals ▸ Bird 134
Animals ▸ Cat-Domestic 134
Animals ▸ Cow 134
Animals ▸ Deer 134
Animals ▸ Dog 135
Animals ▸ Dolphin 135
Animals ▸ Elephant 135

Animals ▸ Fish 135
Animals ▸ Frog 136
Animals ▸ Insect, Butterfly 136
Animals ▸ Monkey, Ape 136
Animation Art, Characters ▸ Animation Art 137
Animation Art, Characters ▸ Animation
  Characters 137
Animation Art, Characters ▸ Japanese, Anime 137
Arcade, Jukeboxes & Pinball ▸ Arcade 137
Arcade, Jukeboxes & Pinball ▸ Jukeboxes 138
Arcade, Jukeboxes & Pinball ▸ Pinball 138
Autographs ▸ Historical 138
Autographs ▸ Political 138
Banks, Registers & Vending ▸ Banks 139
Banks, Registers & Vending ▸ Vending 139
Barware ▸ Glasses, Cups, Mugs 139
Barware ▸ Shot Glasses 140
Bottles & Insulators ▸ Bottles 140
Breweriana, Beer ▸ Bottles 140
Breweriana, Beer ▸ Cans: US 140
Breweriana, Beer ▸ Cans: Non–US 141
Breweriana, Beer ▸ Drinkware, Steins 141
Casino ▸ Cards 141
Casino ▸ Chips 142

Clocks ▶ Antique (Pre–1930) 142
Clocks ▶ Vintage (1930–69) 142
Comics ▶ Golden Age (1938–55) 142
Comics ▶ Silver Age (1956–69) 143
Comics ▶ Bronze Age (1970–79) 143
Comics ▶ Modern Age (1980–Now) 143
Comics ▶ Graphic Novels, TPBs 144
Comics ▶ Newspaper Comics 144
Cultures, Ethnicities ▶ Asian (1900–Now) 144
Cultures, Ethnicities ▶ Black Americana 144
Cultures, Ethnicities ▶ European 145
Cultures, Ethnicities ▶ Hawaiiana 145
Cultures, Ethnicities ▶ Native Americana 145
Cultures, Ethnicities ▶ Western Americana 145
Decorative Collectibles ▶ Avon 146
Decorative Collectibles ▶ Boyds 146
Decorative Collectibles ▶ Christopher Radko 146
Decorative Collectibles ▶ Dept 56 146
Decorative Collectibles ▶ Enesco 147
Decorative Collectibles ▶ Hummel, Goebel 147
Decorative Collectibles ▶ Lladro 147
Decorative Collectibles ▶ Longaberger 148
Decorative Collectibles ▶ Swarovski 148
Decorative Collectibles ▶ Unbranded 148
Disneyana ▶ Vintage (Pre–1968) 148
Fantasy, Mythical & Magic ▶ Dragons 149
Fantasy, Mythical & Magic ▶ Fairies 149
Fantasy, Mythical & Magic ▶ Harry Potter 149
Fantasy, Mythical & Magic ▶ Lord of the Rings 149
Fantasy, Mythical & Magic ▶ Magic 150
Furniture, Appliances & Fans ▶ Electric Fans 150
Furniture, Appliances & Fans ▶ Furniture,
    Large Appliances 150
Historical Memorabilia ▶ Fairs, Expositions 150
Historical Memorabilia ▶ Flags 151
Historical Memorabilia ▶ Fraternal Groups 151
Historical Memorabilia ▶ Political 151
Historical Memorabilia ▶ Royal Memorabilia 151
Holiday, Seasonal ▶ Christmas:
    Vintage (Pre–1946) 152
Holiday, Seasonal ▶ Christmas:
    Modern (1946–90) 152

Holiday, Seasonal ▶ Christmas:
    Current (1991–Now) 153
Holiday, Seasonal ▶ Halloween 153
Housewares & Kitchenware ▶ Kitchenware 153
Housewares & Kitchenware ▶ Tableware 153
Knives, Swords & Blades ▶ Fixed Blade Knives 154
Knives, Swords & Blades ▶ Folding Knives 154
Knives, Swords & Blades ▶ Swords 154
Lamps, Lighting ▶ Lamps: Electric 154
Lamps, Lighting ▶ Lamps: Non-Electric 155
Linens, Fabric & Textiles ▶ Fabric 155
Linens, Fabric & Textiles ▶ Lace, Crochet, Doilies .. 155
Linens, Fabric & Textiles ▶ Quilts 155
Linens, Fabric & Textiles ▶ Table Linens 156
Metalware ▶ Brass 156
Metalware ▶ Pewter 156
Militaria ▶ Civil War (1861–65) 157
Militaria ▶ WW II (1939–45) 157
Pens & Writing Instruments ▶ Pens 157
Pez, Keychains, Promo Glasses ▶ Pez 157
Photographic Images ▶ Antique (Pre–1940) 158
Pinbacks, Nodders, Lunchboxes ▶
    Lunchboxes, Thermoses 158
Pinbacks, Nodders, Lunchboxes ▶ Pinbacks 158
Postcards & Paper ▶ Postcards 158
Postcards & Paper ▶ Matchbooks 159
Radio, Phonograph, TV, Phone ▶ Radios 159
Radio, Phonograph, TV, Phone ▶ Telephones 159
Religions, Spirituality ▶ Christianity 160
Rocks, Fossils, Minerals ▶ Fossils 160
Science Fiction ▶ Star Trek 160
Science Fiction ▶ Star Wars 160
Science, Medical ▶ Medicine, Dentistry 161
Tobacciana ▶ Ashtrays 161
Tobacciana ▶ Cigar 161
Trading Cards ▶ Animation 161
Trading Cards ▶ Animation ▶ Pokemon 162
Trading Cards ▶ Sci-Fi, Fantasy 162
Transportation ▶ Automobilia 162
Transportation ▶ Railroadiana, Trains 162
Vanity, Perfume & Shaving ▶ Perfumes 163
Vanity, Perfume & Shaving ▶ Shaving 163
Vintage Sewing ▶ Buttons 163

13

COMPUTERS & NETWORKING

165

Dells 165
Apples and Macs 166
Apple, Macintosh Computers ▶
    Apple Components 166
Apple, Macintosh Computers ▶ Apple Desktops ... 167
Apple, Macintosh Computers ▶ Apple Laptops,
    Notebooks 167
Apple, Macintosh Computers ▶ Apple Parts &
    Accessories 167
Desktop PCs ▶ 700 Mhz to 1 Ghz 168
Desktop PCs ▶ 1.1–2.0 Ghz, 1400+ to 2000+ ... 168
Desktop PCs ▶ 2.1–2.6 Ghz 168
Desktop PCs ▶ 2.7 Ghz 168
Desktop PCs ▶ 3.0+ Ghz 169
Desktop PC Components ▶ Cables,
    Adapter Cards 169

Desktop PC Components ▶ CPU 170
Desktop PC Components ▶ Memory 170
Desktop PC Components ▶ Motherboards 170
Desktop PC Components ▶ Speakers &
    Headphones 170
Desktop PC Components ▶ Video Cards 171
Desktop PC Components ▶ Web Cams 171
Laptops, Notebooks ▶ Dell 171
Laptops, Notebooks ▶ Gateway 171
Laptops, Notebooks ▶ HP, Compaq 172
Laptops, Notebooks ▶ IBM, Lenovo 172
Laptops, Notebooks ▶ Sony 172

Laptops, Notebooks ▸ Toshiba 173
Laptops, Notebooks ▸ Tablet PCs 173
Laptop Accessories ▸ Batteries 173
Laptop Accessories ▸ Cases, Bags 174
Laptop Accessories ▸ Drivers 174

Laptop Accessories ▸ Keyboards 174
Laptop Accessories ▸ Memory 175
Laptop Accessories ▸ Mice, Mouse 175
Laptop Accessories ▸ Other Parts 175

14
CONSUMER ELECTRONICS 177

iPod, You Pod, We All Pod 177
DVD Players 178
Big-Ticket and Heavy Items 178
Car Electronics ▸ Car Audio In-Dash Units 178
Car Electronics ▸ Car Speakers &
    Speaker Systems 179
DVD Players & Recorders ▸ Portable DVD Player .. 179
DVD Players & Recorders ▸ Single-Disc
    DVD Player 179
Digital Video Recorders, PVR ▸ Replay TV 179
Digital Video Recorders, PVR ▸ TiVo 180
Gadgets & Other Electronics ▸ Calculators 180
Gadgets & Other Electronics ▸ Home Automation 181
Gadgets & Other Electronics ▸ Surveillance 181
GPS Devices ▸ Accessories & Cables 181
GPS Devices ▸ Automotive GPS Devices 181
GPS Devices ▸ Recreational GPS Devices 182
GPS Devices ▸ Maps, Software 182
Home Audio ▸ Accessories & Cables 182
Home Audio ▸ Amplifiers 183
Home Audio ▸ Headphones, Headsets 183
Home Audio ▸ Receivers 183
Home Audio ▸ Speakers & Subwoofers 183
Home Theater in a Box ▸ With DVD Player 184
Home Theater in a Box ▸ Without DVD Player 184
Home Theater Projectors ▸ Projector
    Screens & Material 184
Home Theater Projectors ▸ Projectors 185
MP3 Players & Accessories ▸ MP3 Accessories ▸
    Apple iPod Accessories 185
MP3 Players & Accessories ▸ MP3 Accessories ▸
    Universal Accessories 185
MP3 Players ▸ Apple iPod 185
MP3 Players ▸ Apple iPod ▸ 20GB 186

MP3 Players ▸ Apple iPod ▸ Mini 186
MP3 Players ▸ Creative 187
MP3 Players ▸ iRiver 187
PDAs/Handheld PCs ▸ Accessories 187
PDAs/Handeld PCs ▸ Handheld Units 187
Portable Audio ▸ Accessories, Bags & Cases 188
Portable Audio ▸ Batteries & Charges 188
Portable Audio ▸ CD Players 188
Portable Audio ▸ Headphones 188
Radios ▸ CB Radio 189
Radios ▸ Ham Radio 189
Radios ▸ Scanners 189
Satellite, Cable TV ▸ Cable TV 189
Satellite, Cable TV ▸ Satellite TV 190
Telephone & Pagers ▸ Answering Machines 190
Telephone & Pagers ▸ Corded Telephones 190
Telephone & Pagers ▸ Cordless Telephones 191
Telephone & Pagers ▸ Headsets 191
Televisions ▸ Accessories & Cables 191
Televisions ▸ HDTVs, Direct-View 191
Televisions ▸ LCD Flat-Panel TVs 192
Televisions ▸ Plasma TVs 192
Televisions ▸ Portable TVs 192
VCRs ▸ Beta 192
VCRs ▸ VHS 193
Vintage Electronics ▸ 8 Track Players 193
Vintage Electronics ▸ Reel-to-Reel Tape 193
Vintage Electronics ▸ Speakers 193
Vintage Electronics ▸ Tubes 194
Wholesale Lots ▸ Gadgets 194
Wholesale Lots ▸ Other Consumer Electronics 194

15
CRAFTS 195

Crafters Supplies: eBay vs. Retail 196
Scrapbooking Savings 196
Bead Art ▸ Beads 196
Bead Art ▸ Kits, Instructions 197
Candle & Soap Making ▸ Molds 197
Candle & Soap Making ▸ Scents, Fragrances ... 197
Ceramics, Pottery ▸ Molds, Kits 197
Ceramics, Pottery ▸ Polymer Clay 198
Ceramics, Pottery ▸ Ready-to-Paint Pieces 198
Crocheting ▸ Hooks 198
Crocheting ▸ Patterns 198
Cross Stitch ▸ Kits 199
Cross Stitch ▸ Patterns 199
Decorative, Tole Painting ▸ Patterns, Instructions .. 199
Decorative, Tole Painting ▸ Transfers, Decals 199
Embroidery ▸ Hand Embroidery Thread, Floss 200
Embroidery ▸ Kits 200

Embroidery ▸ Patterns, Transfers 200
Fabric ▸ Cotton 200
Fabric ▸ Lace 201
Fabric ▸ Silk 201
Fabric ▸ Synthetics, Blends 201
Fabric Embellishments ▸ Appliques 202
Fabric Embellishments ▸ Trims 202
Floral Supplies ▸ Flowers, Foliage 202
Framing, Matting ▸ Frames, Kits 202
Framing, Matting ▸ Mats 203
General Art & Craft Supplies ▸ Adhesives,
    Glue Guns 203
General Art & Craft Supplies ▸ Other Supplies ... 203
Glass Art Supplies ▸ Stained Glass Supplies 203
Handcrafted Items ▸ Handcrafted Purses, Bags 204

Handcrafted Items ▸ Handpainted Items 204
Knitting ▸ Needles 205
Knitting ▸ Patterns 205
Latch, Rug Hooking ▸ Kits, Patterns 205
Leathercraft ▸ Hides, Leather 205
Macrame 206
Needlepoint ▸ Kits 206
Painting & Drawing ▸ Drawing 206
Painting & Drawing ▸ Painting 206
Paper Crafts, Origami 207
Quilting ▸ Tops, Blocks 207

Ribbon ▸ Grosgrain 207
Scrapbooking ▸ Albums 208
Scrapbooking ▸ Stickers 208
Sewing ▸ Machines, Sergers 208
Sewing ▸ Notions, Supplies, Tools 209
Spinning ▸ Roving, Wool, Fiber 209
Stamping ▸ Stamps 209
Weaving ▸ Looms 209
Woodworking ▸ Supplies 210
Yarn 210
Wall Decor, Tatouage 210

16
DOLLS & BEARS · 211

Antique Dolls 212
Barbies: Old to New 212
Antique Bears 212
Newer Bears 213

Bears ▸ Boyds 213
Bears ▸ Care Bears 214
Bears ▸ Steiff 214
Bears ▸ Antique 214
Dolls ▸ Antique (Pre–1930) 215
Dolls ▸ Barbie Contemporary (1973–Now) 215
Dolls ▸ Barbie Vintage (Pre–1973) 215
Dolls ▸ By Brand, Company, Character ▸
    American Girl 216
Dolls ▸ By Brand, Company, Character ▸
    Franklin Mint 216

Dolls ▸ By Brand, Company, Character ▸ Bratz ... 216
Dolls ▸ By Brand, Company, Character ▸
    Madame Alexander 216
Dolls ▸ Clothes, Accessories 217
Dolls ▸ Furniture 217
Paper Dolls ▸ Modern 217
Paper Dolls ▸ Vintage 217
Wholesale Lots ▸ Barbie 218
Wholesale Lots ▸ Dolls 218

17
DVDS & MOVIES · 219

TV on DVD 220
Selling Movies 220

DVDs ▸ Action, Adventure 221
DVDs ▸ Comedy 221
DVDs ▸ Drama 221
DVDs 222
DVDs ▸ Sets 222

Film 223
Laserdisc 223
VHS 223
VHS Non-US (PAL) ▸ Other 224

18
ENTERTAINMENT MEMORABILIA · 225

Music and Beatlemania 226
Television and Theater 227

Autographs ▸ Movies 228
Autographs ▸ Music 228
Autographs ▸ Television 228
Autographs ▸ Theater 228
Autographs ▸ Other 229
Movie Memorabilia ▸ Ads, Flyers 229
Movie Memorabilia ▸ Apparel 229
Movie Memorabilia ▸ Lobby Cards 230
Movie Memorabilia ▸ Photos 230
Movie Memorabilia ▸ Posters 230
Movie Memorabilia ▸ Pressbooks 230
Movie Memorabilia ▸ Programs 231
Movie Memorabilia ▸ Props 231
Movie Memorabilia ▸ Scripts 231
Music Memorabilia ▸ Country 231
Music Memorabilia ▸ Rock-n-Roll 232
Television Memorabilia ▸ Apparel 232
Television Memorabilia ▸ Photos 232

Television Memorabilia ▸ Pins, Buttons 233
Television Memorabilia ▸ Posters 233
Television Memorabilia ▸ Press Kits 233
Television Memorabilia ▸ Props 234
Television Memorabilia ▸ Scripts 234
Television Memorabilia ▸ Wardrobe 234
Television Memorabilia ▸ Other 234
Theatre Memorabilia ▸ Ads, Flyers 235
Theatre Memorabilia ▸ Playbills 235
Theatre Memorabilia ▸ Posters 235
Theatre Memorabilia ▸ Props, Wardrobe 235
Theatre Memorabilia ▸ Souvenir Programs 236
Theatre Memorabilia ▸ Window Cards 236
Theatre Memorabilia ▸ Other 236
Video Game Memorabilia ▸ XBox 236
Video Game Memorabilia ▸ Atari 237
Video Game Memorabilia ▸ Nintendo 237
Video Game Memorabilia ▸ Halo 237

19
GIFT CERTIFICATES 239

Clothing 240
General Merchandise and Restaurants 240
$300 Worth of Pizza? 241

Books, Music, Movies 241
Books, Music, Movies ▸ Barnes and Noble 241
Books, Music, Movies ▸ iTunes 242
Books, Music, Movies ▸ Amazon.com 242
Books, Music, Movies ▸ Entertainment 242
Books, Music, Movies ▸ Blockbuster 242
Books, Music, Movies ▸ Borders 243
Books, Music, Movies ▸ Circuit City 243
Books, Music, Movies ▸ Movies 243
Books, Music, Movies ▸ AMC Theatres 244
Books, Music, Movies ▸ Sam Goody 244
Books, Music, Movies ▸ Sony 244
Books, Music, Movies ▸ Best Buy 244
Books, Music, Movies ▸ Loews 244
Books, Music, Movies ▸ Hollywood 245
Clothing 245
Clothing ▸ Ann Taylor 245
Clothing ▸ Lane Bryant 245
Clothing ▸ Chico's 246
Clothing ▸ Old Navy 246
Clothing ▸ Saks 246
Clothing ▸ Gymboree 246
Clothing ▸ TJ Maxx 246
Clothing ▸ Land's End 247
Clothing ▸ Victoria's Secret 247
Clothing ▸ Macy's 247
Clothing ▸ Marshall Fields 247
Clothing ▸ Gap 247

Clothing ▸ Eddie Bauer 248
Clothing ▸ Abercrombie 248
Clothing ▸ Polo 248
Clothing ▸ Banana Republic 248
Clothing ▸ J Crew 249
Clothing ▸ Children's Place 249
Clothing ▸ Fashion Bug 249
Clothing ▸ Express 249
Home & Garden 249
Home & Garden ▸ Home Depot 250
Home & Garden ▸ Lowe's 250
Home & Garden ▸ Michaels 250
Home & Garden ▸ Pier 1 251
Home & Garden ▸ Bed Bath & Beyond 251
Home & Garden ▸ Pottery Barn 251
Restaurant 251
Restaurant ▸ Panera Bread 252
Restaurant ▸ Chuck E. Cheese's 252
Restaurant ▸ Starbucks 252
Restaurant ▸ Wine 253
Restaurant ▸ Pizza Hut 253
Restaurant ▸ Domino's 253
Restaurant ▸ Subway 253
Restaurant ▸ Morton's 253
Restaurant ▸ Red Lobster 254
Restaurant ▸ Taco Bell 254
Other Gift Certificates 254

20
HEALTH & BEAUTY 255

Outfit a Beauty Salon for $2,100.00 255
Hair Styling and Makeup 256

Bath & Body ▸ Bath Sets, Kits 257
Bath & Body ▸ Body Lotion 257
Bath & Body ▸ Body Wash 258
Bath & Body ▸ Cellulite Treatment 258
Bath & Body ▸ Soap 258
Coupons ▸ Health Care 258
Dietary Supplements, Nutrition ▸ Herbs,
    Botanicals 259
Dietary Supplements, Nutrition ▸ Nutrition Bars,
    Shakes 259
Dietary Supplements, Nutrition ▸ Sports
    Supplements 259
Dietary Supplements, Nutrition ▸ Vitamins,
    Minerals 259
Fragrances ▸ Men 260
Fragrances ▸ Women 260
Hair Care ▸ Brushes, Combs 261
Hair Care ▸ Conditioner 261
Hair Care ▸ Curling Irons 261
Hair Care ▸ Hair Color 261
Hair Care ▸ Hair Dryers 262
Hair Care ▸ Hair Loss 262
Hair Care ▸ Rollers, Curlers 262
Hair Care ▸ Salon Equipment 263

Hair Care ▸ Shampoo 263
Hair Care ▸ Straightening Irons 263
Hair Removal ▸ Epilators, Electrolysis 263
Hair Removal ▸ Shavers 264
Health Care ▸ Body Enhancers 264
Health Care ▸ Family Planning 264
Health Care ▸ First Aid 265
Health Care ▸ Sleeping Aids 265
Health Care ▸ Smoking Cessation 265
Health Care ▸ Other Health Care Items 265
Makeup ▸ Beauty Tools 266
Makeup ▸ Blush 266
Makeup ▸ Cases, Bags, Totes 266
Makeup ▸ Eyeliner 266
Makeup ▸ Eye Shadow 267
Makeup ▸ Face Powder 267
Makeup ▸ Foundation 267
Makeup ▸ Lipstick 268
Makeup ▸ Mascara 268
Makeup ▸ Mixed Brands 268
Makeup ▸ Sets & Kits 268
Nail ▸ Acrylic Nails, Tips 269
Nail ▸ Manicure Kits 269
Nail ▸ Nail Art 269

Nail ▸ Nail Polish 269
Nail ▸ Pedicure Kits 270
Massage ▸ Massagers 270
Medical, Special Needs ▸ Braces, Supports 271
Medical, Special Needs ▸ Mobility Equipment 271
Medical, Special Needs ▸ Monitoring, Testing 271
Natural Therapies ▸ Aromatherapy 271
Natural Therapies ▸ Herbal 272
Natural Therapies ▸ Other Natural Therapies 272
Oral Care ▸ Electric Toothbrushes 272
Over-the-Counter Medicine ▸ Cough, Cold, Flu 272
Over-the-Counter Medicine ▸ Pain Relief 273
Skin Care ▸ Acne, Blemish Control 273
Skin Care ▸ Anti-Aging Products 273

Skin Care ▸ Cleansers 273
Skin Care ▸ Moisturizers 274
Tanning Beds, Lamps 274
Tattoos, Body Art ▸ Flash 274
Tattoos, Body Art ▸ Piercing Supplies, Kits 275
Tattoos, Body Art ▸ Tattoo Machines, Guns 275
Tattoos, Body Art ▸ Tattoo Supplies 275
Vision Care ▸ Contact Lens Accessories 275
Vision Care ▸ Eyeglass Frames 276
Vision Care ▸ Reading Glasses 276
Weight Management ▸ Foods, Bars, Snacks 276
Weight Management ▸ Pills, Tablets, Capsules ... 277
Wholesale Lots ▸ Beauty & Personal Care 277

21
HOME & GARDEN   279

Big-Ticket Items and Major Appliances 280
Anyone for a Wine Cellar? 280
Furniture Prices 281
Bath ▸ Shower Curtains 281
Bath ▸ Towels, Washcloths 282
Bath ▸ Whirlpool, Spa 282
Bedding ▸ Comforters 282
Bedding ▸ Duvet Covers 282
Bedding ▸ Sheets 283
Building & Hardware ▸ Cabinets &
        Cabinet Hardware 283
Building & Hardware ▸ Doors & Door Hardware . 283
Building & Hardware ▸ Tile & Flooring 284
Dining & Bar ▸ Bar Tools & Accessories 284
Dining & Bar ▸ Dinnerware & Serving Pieces 284
Dining & Bar ▸ Flatware 284
Electrical & Solar ▸ Alternative & Solar Energy 285
Electrical & Solar ▸ Switches & Outlets 285
Food & Wine ▸ Beer & Wine Making 285
Food & Wine ▸ Candy & Chocolate 285
Food & Wine ▸ Spices, Seasonings & Extracts 286
Furniture ▸ Bedroom Furniture 286
Furniture ▸ Living Room, General Furniture 286
Gardening & Plants ▸ Garden Décor 286
Gardening & Plants ▸ Plants, Seeds & Bulbs 287
Health, Cooling & Air ▸ Air Conditioners 287
Health, Cooling & Air ▸ Furnaces,
        Heating Systems 287
Home Decor ▸ Candles, Candle Holders 288
Home Decor ▸ Photo Frame & Display 288
Home Decor ▸ Wall Décor 288
Home Security ▸ Security Systems 288
Home Security ▸ Sensors, Motion Detectors 289
Vacuum Cleaners & Housekeeping ▸
        Cleaning Supplies 289
Vacuum Cleaners & Housekeeping ▸
        Home Organization 289
Vacuum Cleaners & Housekeeping ▸
        Vacuum Cleaners 290

Kitchen ▸ Cookware & Bakeware 290
Kitchen ▸ Small Kitchen Appliances 290
Kitchen ▸ Tools & Gadgets 290
Lamps, Lighting, Ceiling Fans ▸ Chandeliers 291
Lamps, Lighting, Ceiling Fans ▸ Ceiling Fans 291
Lamps, Lighting, Ceiling Fans ▸ Table Lamps 291
Major Appliances ▸ Ranges, Cooking Appliances 291
Major Appliances ▸ Dishwashers 292
Major Appliances ▸ Refrigerators, Freezers 292
Major Appliances ▸ Washers, Dryer 292
Outdoor Power Equipment ▸ Chainsaws 292
Outdoor Power Equipment ▸ Lawn Mowers 293
Outdoor Power Equipment ▸ Leaf Blowers &
        Vacuums 293
Patio & Grilling ▸ Charcoal Grills & Accessories ... 293
Patio & Grilling ▸ Gas Grills & Accessories 294
Patio & Grilling ▸ Patio Sets & Picnic Tables 294
Pet Supplies ▸ Cats 294
Pet Supplies ▸ Dogs 294
Pet Supplies ▸ Fish 295
Plumbing & Fixtures ▸ Bathroom 295
Plumbing & Fixtures ▸ Kitchen 295
Plumbing & Fixtures ▸ Plumbing Parts &
        Accessories 295
Pools & Spas ▸ Pools 296
Pools & Spas ▸ Spas, Hot Tubs 296
Rugs & Carpets ▸ Area Rugs 296
Rugs & Carpets ▸ Throw Rugs 297
Tools ▸ Hand Tools 297
Tools ▸ Power Tools 297
Window Treatments ▸ Blinds 297
Window Treatments ▸ Curtain Rods, Hardware ... 298
Window Treatments ▸ Curtains, Drapes 298
Window Treatments ▸ Valances 298

22
JEWELRY & WATCHES   299

The Influence of Trends 300
Engagement Rings for Two Weeks' Salary? 300

Watches from Three to Six Figures 300
Findings . . . and Finds 301

Bracelets ▸ Bangle 301
Bracelets ▸ Beaded, Strands 302
Bracelets ▸ Link, Chain 302
Bracelets ▸ Tennis 302
Charms & Charm Bracelets ▸ Italian Modular 302
Charms & Charm Bracelets ▸ Traditional 303
Children's Jewelry ▸ Bracelets 303
Children's Jewelry ▸ Necklaces & Pendants 303
Designer Brands ▸ Brighton 303
Designer Brands ▸ Tiffany 304
Designer Brands ▸ David Yurman 304
Earrings ▸ Dangle, Chandelier (Chandelier) 304
Earrings ▸ Hoop, Huggie 305
Earrings ▸ Studs 305
Ethnic, Tribal Jewelry ▸ African 305
Ethnic, Tribal Jewelry ▸ Asian, East Indian 305
Ethnic, Tribal Jewelry ▸ Native American 306
Handcrafted, Artisan Jewelry ▸ Earrings 306
Handcrafted, Artisan Jewelry ▸ Necklaces &
    Pendants 306
Jewelry Boxes & Supplies ▸ Jewelry Boxes 307
Jewelry Boxes & Supplies ▸ Tools, Findings 307
Loose Beads ▸ Lampwork, Crystal & Glass 307
Loose Beads ▸ Stone 307
Loose Diamonds & Gemstones ▸ Diamonds 308

Loose Diamonds & Gemstones ▸
    Gemstones ▸ Ruby 308
Loose Diamonds & Gemstones ▸ Gemstones ▸
    Other Gemstones 308
Men's Jewelry ▸ Cufflinks 309
Men's Jewelry ▸ Rings 309
Necklaces & Pendants ▸ Chains 309
Necklaces & Pendants ▸ Pendants, Lockets 309
Necklaces & Pendants ▸ Strands/Strings 310
Pins, Brooches ▸ Cameos 310
Pins, Brooches ▸ Silver, Solid (w/o Stone) 310
Rings ▸ Bands, Wedding & Anniversary 310
Rings ▸ Cubic Zirconia & Moissanite 311
Rings ▸ Diamond Engagement/Anniversary 311
Rings ▸ Gemstone Rings 311
Sets ▸ Gold, Plate/Fill (w/o Stone) 311
Sets ▸ Gold, Solid (w/o Stone) 312
Sets ▸ Silver (w/o Stone) 312
Sets ▸ Other Stones, Materials 312
Vintage, Antique ▸ Costume 312
Vintage, Antique ▸ Fine 313
Jewelry & Watches ▸ Watches ▸ Pocket Watches ..313
Watches ▸ Wristwatches 313
Wholesale Lots ▸ Watches 314
Wholesale Lots ▸ Mixed Jewelry Lots 314

23
MUSIC   315

CDs vs. Vinyl vs. Cassettes 315
The UK Factor 317
Digital Music Downloads and the Future of eBay Music 317

Accessories 317
Cassettes 318
CDs 318
CDs ▸ Classical 318
CDs ▸ Country 318
CDs ▸ DJ, Dance 319
CDs ▸ Jazz 319
CDs ▸ Metal 319
CDs ▸ Pop 320
CDs ▸ Rap, Hip Hop 320
CDs ▸ Reggae, Ska 320
CDs ▸ Rock 321

CDs ▸ R&B 321
CDs ▸ Soundtrack, Theater 321
CDs ▸ World Music 322
Digital Music Downloads 322
DVD Audio 322
Records 323
Records ▸ Pop 323
Records ▸ Rock 323
Super Audio CDs 324
Other Formats (8 Track) 324
Wholesale Lots 324

24
MUSICAL INSTRUMENTS   325

Getting a Fair Discount 326
Guitars: Your Chance to Own Rock History? 326
Pianos and Local Pickup Auctions 327

Brass ▸ Baritone, Tuba 328
Brass ▸ Cornet, Trumpet 328
Brass ▸ French Horn 328
Brass ▸ Trombone 328
Electronic ▸ Drum Machines 329
Electronic ▸ Samples, Samplers 329
Electronic ▸ Synth 329
Equipment ▸ Cases 329
Equipment ▸ Instrument Stands 330
Equipment ▸ Music Stands 330
Equipment ▸ Tuners 330

Guitar ▸ Acoustic 330
Guitar ▸ Amplifiers 331
Guitar ▸ Bass 331
Guitar ▸ Electric 331
Guitar ▸ Parts, Accessories 332
Guitar ▸ Instruction Books, CDs, Videos 332
Harmonica ▸ Hohner 332
Harmonica ▸ Johnson Blues King 333
Harmonica ▸ Other 333
Keyboard, Piano ▸ Accordion, Concertina 333
Keyboard, Piano ▸ Electronic Keyboards 333

Keyboard, Piano ▸ Organ 334
Keyboard, Piano ▸ Piano 334
Keyboard, Piano ▸ Instruction Books, CDs, Videos .. 334
Percussion ▸ Cymbals 334
Percussion ▸ Drums 335
Percussion ▸ Parts, Accessories 335
Percussion ▸ Tambourines 335
Pro Audio ▸ Computer Recording 335
Pro Audio ▸ Mixers 336
Pro Audio ▸ Speakers 336
Pro Audio ▸ Multi-Track Recorders 336
Pro Audio ▸ Power Amplifiers 336
Pro Audio ▸ Rack Gear 337
Sheet Music, Song Books ▸ Sheet Music 337

Sheet Music, Song Books ▸ Song Books 337
String ▸ Bass 337
String ▸ Banjo 338
String ▸ Cello 338
String ▸ Harp, Dulcimer 338
String ▸ Violin 338
Woodwind ▸ Bagpipes 339
Woodwind ▸ Bassoon, Oboe 339
Woodwind ▸ Clarinet 339
Woodwind ▸ Flute 339
Woodwind ▸ Piccolo 340
Woodwind ▸ Recorder 340
Woodwind ▸ Saxophone 340

25
POTTERY & GLASS
341

Changes in Popularity over Time 342
$500.00 for a Burger King Mug? 342
Depression Glass 342
The Real McCoy 343
The Joys of Collecting Pottery and Glass 344

Glass ▸ Art Glass ▸ Bohemian/Czech 344
Glass ▸ Art Glass ▸ Italian 344
Glass ▸ Art Glass ▸ North American 345
Glass ▸ Art Glass ▸ Scandinavian 345
Glass ▸ Art Glass ▸ Paperweights 345
Glass ▸ Art Glass ▸ Stained Glass 346
Glass ▸ Glassware ▸ 40s, 50s, 60s 346
Glass ▸ Glassware ▸ Amethyst 346
Glass ▸ Glassware ▸ Carnival Glass 346
Glass ▸ Glassware ▸ Cobalt 347
Glass ▸ Glassware ▸ Contemporary Glass 347
Glass ▸ Glassware ▸ Crackle Glass 347
Glass ▸ Glassware ▸ Cut Glass 347
Glass ▸ Glassware ▸ Depression 348
Glass ▸ Glassware ▸ Early American
        Pattern Glass 348
Glass ▸ Glassware ▸ Kitchen Glassware 348
Glass ▸ Glassware ▸ Opalescent 348
Glass ▸ Glassware ▸ Opaque 349
Glass ▸ Glassware ▸ Pressed Glass 349
Glass ▸ Glassware ▸ Pyrex 349
Glass ▸ Glassware ▸ Ruby 349
Glass ▸ Glassware ▸ Waterford 350
Pottery & China ▸ Art Pottery ▸ American Art 350
Pottery & China ▸ Art Pottery ▸ Asian 350
Pottery & China ▸ Art Pottery ▸ Blue Mountain 350
Pottery & China ▸ Art Pottery ▸ Brush/
        Brush-McCoy 351
Pottery & China ▸ Art Pottery ▸ Delft 351
Pottery & China ▸ Art Pottery ▸ European Art 351
Pottery & China ▸ Art Pottery ▸ Folk 351
Pottery & China ▸ Art Pottery ▸ Made in Japan 352
Pottery & China ▸ Art Pottery ▸ Majolica 352
Pottery & China ▸ Art Pottery ▸ McCoy 352
Pottery & China ▸ Art Pottery ▸ Quimper 353
Pottery & China ▸ Art Pottery ▸ Roseville 353
Pottery & China ▸ Art Pottery ▸ Scandinavian Art ... 353
Pottery & China ▸ Art Pottery ▸ SEG/Paul Revere ... 353
Pottery & China ▸ Art Pottery ▸ Staffordshire 354
Pottery & China ▸ Art Pottery ▸ Stangl 354

Pottery & China ▸ China, Dinnerware ▸ Aynsley .. 354
Pottery & China ▸ China, Dinnerware ▸
        Blue Ridge 354
Pottery & China ▸ China, Dinnerware ▸
        Blue Willow 355
Pottery & China ▸ China, Dinnerware ▸ Chintz 355
Pottery & China ▸ China, Dinnerware ▸
        Commemorative 355
Pottery & China ▸ China, Dinnerware ▸ Crown
        Staffordshire 355
Pottery & China ▸ China, Dinnerware ▸ Dansk 356
Pottery & China ▸ China, Dinnerware ▸
        Decorative 356
Pottery & China ▸ China, Dinnerware ▸
        Dinnerware 356
Pottery & China ▸ China, Dinnerware ▸ Dresden . 356
Pottery & China ▸ China, Dinnerware ▸ Fiesta:
        Contemporary 357
Pottery & China ▸ China, Dinnerware ▸
        Franciscan 357
Pottery & China ▸ China, Dinnerware ▸ Gorham . 357
Pottery & China ▸ China, Dinnerware ▸ Hall 357
Pottery & China ▸ China, Dinnerware ▸
        Hummel, Goebel 358
Pottery & China ▸ China, Dinnerware ▸ Lenox 358
Pottery & China ▸ China, Dinnerware ▸ Limoges .. 358
Pottery & China ▸ China, Dinnerware ▸
        Made in Japan 358
Pottery & China ▸ China, Dinnerware ▸ Meissen ...359
Pottery & China ▸ China, Dinnerware ▸ Mikasa 359
Pottery & China ▸ China, Dinnerware ▸ Nippon 359
Pottery & China ▸ China, Dinnerware ▸ Noritake ...359
Pottery & China ▸ China, Dinnerware ▸
        Occupied Japan 360
Pottery & China ▸ China, Dinnerware ▸ Pfaltzgraff 360
Pottery & China ▸ China, Dinnerware ▸
        Red Wing, Rumrill 360
Pottery & China ▸ China, Dinnerware ▸
        Royal Doulton 360
Pottery & China ▸ China, Dinnerware ▸ Spode 361

Pottery & China ▸ China, Dinnerware ▸ Stangl ... 361
Pottery & China ▸ China, Dinnerware ▸
   Steubenville 361
Pottery & China ▸ China, Dinnerware ▸
   Stoneware 361

Pottery & China ▸ China, Dinnerware ▸ Tea Pots,
   Tea Sets 362
Pottery & China ▸ China, Dinnerware ▸
   Wedgwood 362

26
REAL ESTATE   363

Gold Mining Claim Rush? 364
Residential Homes 365
Take This Timeshare—Please! 365
Land ▸ Homesite, Lot 367
Land ▸ Recreation, Acreage 367
Land ▸ Other 368
Residential Homes 368
Commercial 369
Manufactured Homes 369

Timeshares for Sale ▸ Attractions/Theme Parks 369
Timeshares for Sale ▸ Beach/Ocean 370
Timeshares for Sale ▸ Lakefront 370
Timeshares for Sale ▸ Mountain/Skiing 370
Timeshares for Sale ▸ Other 371
Other Real Estate 371

27
SPECIALTY SERVICES   373

Pet Projects 373
Finding Your Voice 374
Your Business in a Blog? Web Services 374
Advice & Instruction ▸ Business & Computer 375
Advice & Instruction ▸ Diet & Fitness 375
Advice & Instruction ▸ Lessons, Tutoring 375
Advice & Instruction ▸ Other 375
Artistic Services ▸ Custom Crafts 376
Artistic Services ▸ Interior Design 376
Artistic Services ▸ Music Composition & Poetry .. 376
Artistic Services ▸ Painting & Drawing 376
Artistic Services ▸ Other 376
Custom Clothing & Jewelry 377
Custom Clothing & Jewelry ▸ Costumes 377
Custom Clothing & Jewelry ▸ Hats, Handbags,
   Accessories 377
Custom Clothing & Jewelry ▸ Jewelry 377
Custom Clothing & Jewelry ▸ Shirts 377
Custom Clothing & Jewelry ▸ Other 378
eBay Auction Services ▸ Listing Services 378
eBay Auction Services ▸ Packing & Shipping 378
eBay Auction Services ▸ Shopping Assistance 378
eBay Auction Services ▸ Other 378
Graphic & Logo Design 379
Media Editing & Duplication ▸ Music 379

Media Editing & Duplication ▸ Photo & Video 379
Media Editing & Duplication ▸ Other 379
Printing & Personalization ▸ Address Labels 379
Printing & Personalization ▸ Business Cards 380
Printing & Personalization ▸ Glasses, Mugs 380
Printing & Personalization ▸ Holiday Cards 380
Printing & Personalization ▸ Invitations,
   Announcements 380
Printing & Personalization ▸ Party Favors 380
Printing & Personalization ▸ Signs, Decals 381
Printing & Personalization ▸ Stationery 381
Printing & Personalization ▸ Other 381
Restoration & Repair ▸ Cars & Other Vehicles ...381
Restoration & Repair ▸ Jewelry & Watches 382
Restoration & Repair ▸ Computers & Electronics ...382
Restoration & Repair ▸ Musical Instruments 382
Restoration & Repair ▸ Other 382
Web & Computer Services ▸ Internet Promotion ...382
Web & Computer Services ▸ Web Design 383
Web & Computer Services ▸ Web Hosting 383
Web & Computer Services ▸ Other 383

28
SPORTING GOODS   385

Golf: Big Berthas and eBay Drop-Off Stores 386
Different Types of Prey: Paintball, Fishing, and Hunting 386
Indoor Sports 387
Airsoft ▸ Airsoft BBs 388
Airsoft ▸ Airsoft Guns 388
Archery ▸ Arrows 388
Archery ▸ Bow, Shooting Accessories 388
Archery ▸ Bows 389
Baseball & Softball ▸ Apparel & Footwear 389
Baseball & Softball ▸ Balls 389
Baseball & Softball ▸ Bats 389
Baseball & Softball ▸ Gloves & Mitts 390
Basketball ▸ Apparel & Footwear 390

Basketball ▸ Balls 390
Billiards ▸ Balls 390
Billiards ▸ Cues 391
Billiards ▸ Tables 391
Bowling ▸ Apparel & Footwear 391
Bowling ▸ Balls 392
Boxing ▸ Apparel 392
Boxing ▸ Gloves 392
Boxing ▸ Protection Gear 392

Camping, Hiking, Backpacking ▸
    Backpacks 392
Camping, Hiking, Backpacking ▸
    Canteens, Coolers 393
Camping, Hiking, Backpacking ▸
    Cookware, Stoves 393
Camping, Hiking, Backpacking ▸
    Sleeping Gear 393
Camping, Hiking, Backpacking ▸
    Tents, Canopies 394
Canoes, Kayaks, Rafts ▸ Canoes 394
Canoes, Kayaks, Rafts ▸ Inflatable
    Canoes, Kayaks 394
Canoes, Kayaks, Rafts ▸ Kayaks 394
Canoes, Kayaks, Rafts ▸ Paddles 395
Cycling ▸ Apparel 395
Cycling ▸ Helmets and Protection 395
Cycling ▸ Mountain Bikes & Parts 395
Cycling ▸ Road Bikes & Parts 396
Cycling ▸ Universal Parts & Accessories 396
Disc Golf ▸ Discs 396
Equestrian ▸ Riding—English 396
Equestrian ▸ Riding—Western 397
Exercise & Fitness ▸ Cardiovascular Equipment ... 397
Exercise & Fitness ▸ Exercise Monitors,
    Computers 397
Exercise & Fitness ▸ Strength Training 398
Fishing ▸ Freshwater 398
Fishing ▸ Fly Fishing 398
Fishing ▸ Saltwater 398
Fishing ▸ Tackle Boxes 399
Fishing ▸ Vintage 399
Football ▸ Apparel & Footwear 399
Football ▸ Balls 399
Football ▸ Protective Gear 400
Go-Karts, Recreational ▸ Complete
    Go-Karts & Frames 400
Golf ▸ Accessories 400
Golf ▸ Apparel 400
Golf ▸ Bags 401
Golf ▸ Balls 401
Golf ▸ Clubs ▸ Complete Club Set 401
Golf ▸ Clubs ▸ Driver 402
Golf ▸ Footwear 402
Golf ▸ Golf Carts, Cars 402
Golf ▸ Vintage 402
Hunting ▸ Apparel 403
Hunting ▸ Decoys 403
Hunting ▸ Game Calls 403
Hunting ▸ Gun Parts 404
Hunting ▸ Gun Accessories 404
Hunting ▸ Hunting Accessories 404
Hunting ▸ Knives 404
Hunting ▸ Taxidermy, Mounts, Antlers 405
Hunting ▸ Vintage 405
Ice, Roller Hockey ▸ Ice Hockey 405
Ice, Roller Hockey ▸ Roller Hockey 405
Ice Skating ▸ Apparel 406
Ice Skating ▸ Skates 406

Indoor Games ▸ Air Hockey 406
Indoor Games ▸ Darts 406
Indoor Games ▸ Foosball Tables & Combos 407
Indoor Games ▸ Shuffleboard 407
Inline, Roller Skating ▸ In-line Skates 407
Inline, Roller Skating ▸ Protective Gear 407
Inline, Roller Skating ▸ Roller Skates 407
Lacrosse ▸ Sticks 408
Martial Arts ▸ Apparel 408
Martial Arts ▸ Sticks & Swords 408
Paintball ▸ Air Systems & Accessories 409
Paintball ▸ Barrels 409
Paintball ▸ Paintballs 409
Racquetball & Squash ▸ Racquetball Racquets 409
Racquetball & Squash ▸ Squash Racquets 410
Running ▸ Apparel 410
Running ▸ Footwear 410
Scooters ▸ Electric 410
Scooters ▸ Gas 411
Scooters ▸ Kick Scooters 411
Scuba, Snorkeling ▸ Fins 411
Scuba, Snorkeling ▸ Masks 411
Scuba, Snorkeling ▸ Snorkels 412
Scuba, Snorkeling ▸ Tanks 412
Scuba, Snorkeling ▸ Wet Suits 412
Skateboarding ▸ Apparel & Shoes 412
Skateboarding ▸ Complete Skateboards 413
Skateboarding ▸ Decks 413
Skiing & Snowboarding ▸ Apparel 413
Skiing & Snowboarding ▸ Cross Country Skiing .. 413
Skiing & Snowboarding ▸ Downhill Skiing 414
Skiing & Snowboarding ▸ Snowboarding 414
Snowmobiling ▸ Parts & Accessories 414
Soccer ▸ Apparel & Footwear 414
Soccer ▸ Balls, Pumps 415
Soccer ▸ Gloves, Socks, Shin Guards 415
Surfing, Wind Surfing ▸ Apparel 415
Surfing, Wind Surfing ▸ Body Boards 416
Surfing, Wind Surfing ▸ Surfboards 416
Surfing, Wind Surfing ▸ Wetsuits 416
Surfing, Wind Surfing ▸ Windsurfing 416
Tennis ▸ Apparel & Footwear 417
Tennis ▸ Balls 417
Tennis ▸ Racquets 417
Triathlon ▸ Bike 417
Triathlon ▸ Run 418
Triathlon ▸ Swim 418
Wakeboarding, Waterskiing ▸
    Wakeboarding, Kneeboarding 418
Wakeboarding, Waterskiing ▸ Water Skiing 418
Other Sports ▸ Backyard Games 418
Other Sports ▸ Cricket 419
Other Sports ▸ Cheerleading 419
Other Sports ▸ Fencing 419
Other Sports ▸ Field Hockey 419
Other Sports ▸ Rugby 420
Other Sports ▸ Snowshoeing 420
Other Sports ▸ Volleyball 420
Other Sports ▸ Wrestling 420

29
SPORTS MEMORABILIA, CARDS & FAN SHOP   421

The Finer Points of Cards 422
How Much Can It Cost to Ship a Card? 422
Baseball, Golf, Hockey, and Racing 422
You Never Forget Your First Card: Favorites 423

Authenticator Pre-Certified ▸ Baseball-MLB 424
Authenticator Pre-Certified ▸ Basketball-NBA 424
Authenticator Pre-Certified ▸ Football-NFL 424
Autographs, Original ▸ Baseball-MLB 424
Autographs, Original ▸ Basketball-NBA 425
Autographs, Original ▸ Boxing 425
Autographs, Original ▸ College-NCAA 425
Autographs, Original ▸ Football-NFL 425
Autographs, Original ▸ Golf ▸ PGA 426
Autographs, Original ▸ Hockey-NHL 426
Autographs, Original ▸ Olympics 426
Autographs, Original ▸ Soccer 426
Autographs, Original ▸ Tennis 427
Autographs, Original ▸ Wrestling-WWE 427
Cards ▸ Baseball-MLB 427
Cards ▸ Basketball-NBA 427
Cards ▸ Boxing 428
Cards ▸ etopps 428
Cards ▸ Football-NFL 428
Cards ▸ Golf ▸ PGA 428
Cards ▸ Hockey-NHL 429
Cards ▸ Racing-NASCAR 429
Cards ▸ Soccer 429
Cards ▸ Tennis 429
Cards ▸ Wrestling-WWE 430
Cards ▸ Storage, Display Supplies 430
Fan Apparel & Souvenirs ▸ Baseball-MLB 430
Fan Apparel & Souvenirs ▸ Basketball-NBA 430
Fan Apparel & Souvenirs ▸ Boxing 431
Fan Apparel & Souvenirs ▸ College-NCAA 431

Fan Apparel & Souvenirs ▸ Cycling 431
Fan Apparel & Souvenirs ▸ Football-NFL 431
Fan Apparel & Souvenirs ▸ Golf-PGA 432
Fan Apparel & Souvenirs ▸ Hockey-NHL 432
Fan Apparel & Souvenirs ▸ Horse Racing 432
Fan Apparel & Souvenirs ▸ Olympics 432
Fan Apparel & Souvenirs ▸ Racing-Formula 1 433
Fan Apparel & Souvenirs ▸ Racing-NASCAR 433
Fan Apparel & Souvenirs ▸ Soccer-European 433
Fan Apparel & Souvenirs ▸ Soccer-World Cup 433
Fan Apparel & Souvenirs ▸ Tennis 434
Fan Apparel & Souvenirs ▸ Wrestling-Professional . 434
Game Used Memorabilia ▸ Baseball-MLB 434
Game Used Memorabilia ▸ Basketball-NBA 434
Game Used Memorabilia ▸ Football-NFL 435
Game Used Memorabilia ▸ Hockey-NHL 435
Game Used Memorabilia ▸ Racing-Auto 435
Vintage Sports Memorabilia ▸ Baseballs 435
Vintage Sports Memorabilia ▸ Bats 436
Vintage Sports Memorabilia ▸ Bobble Heads 436
Vintage Sports Memorabilia ▸ Cereal Boxes 436
Vintage Sports Memorabilia ▸ Gloves-Baseball 437
Vintage Sports Memorabilia ▸ Pennants, Flags 437
Vintage Sports Memorabilia ▸ Photos 437
Vintage Sports Memorabilia ▸ Pins 437
Vintage Sports Memorabilia ▸ Publications 438
Vintage Sports Memorabilia ▸ Shirts 438
Vintage Sports Memorabilia ▸ Ticket Stubs 438
Vintage Sports Memorabilia ▸ Other 438

30
STAMPS   439

What's It Worth? 439
Hot Stamps 440
European Stamps 441

United States ▸ 19th Century: Unused 441
United States ▸ 19th Century: Used 442
United States ▸ 1901–40: Unused 442
United States ▸ 1941–Now: Unused 442
United States ▸ 1901–Now: Used 442
United States ▸ Back of Book 443
United States ▸ Confederate States 443
United States ▸ Covers 443
United States ▸ Errors, Freaks, Oddities 444
United States ▸ Plate Blocks/Multiples 444
United States ▸ Possessions 444
United States ▸ Sheets 444
United States ▸ Collections, Lots 445
Australia ▸ Australian States 445
Australia ▸ Kangaroos 445
Australia ▸ Collections, Lots 445
Canada ▸ Covers 446
Canada ▸ Mint 446
Canada ▸ Provinces 446
Canada ▸ Used 446

Canada ▸ Collections, Lots 447
UK (Great Britain) ▸ Commemorative 447
UK (Great Britain) ▸ Covers 447
UK (Great Britain) ▸ Edward VII 447
UK (Great Britain) ▸ Elizabeth II 447
UK (Great Britain) ▸ FDCs 448
UK (Great Britain) ▸ George V 448
UK (Great Britain) ▸ George VI 448
UK (Great Britain) ▸ Victoria 448
UK (Great Britain) ▸ Collections, Lots 448
Asia ▸ China 449
Asia ▸ Japan 449
Asia ▸ Korea 449
Asia ▸ Thailand 450
Europe ▸ Austria 450
Europe ▸ Belgium & Colonies 450
Europe ▸ Czechoslovakia, Czech Republic 450
Europe ▸ Denmark & Faroe Islands 451
Europe ▸ France & Colonies 451
Europe ▸ Germany & Area 451

Europe ▶ Greece 451
Europe ▶ Hungary 452
Europe ▶ Ireland 452
Europe ▶ Italy & Area 452
Europe ▶ Netherlands & Colonies 452
Europe ▶ Norway 453
Europe ▶ Poland 453
Europe ▶ Portugal & Colonies 453
Europe ▶ Romania 453
Europe ▶ Russia & Area 454
Europe ▶ Spain & Colonies 454
Europe ▶ Sweden 454
Europe ▶ Switzerland & Liechtenstein 454

Latin America ▶ Caribbean 455
Latin America ▶ Central America 455
Latin America ▶ Mexico 455
Latin America ▶ South America 455
Publications & Supplies ▶ Publications 456
Publications & Supplies ▶ Supplies 456
Topical & Specialty ▶ Animation, Cartoons 456
Topical & Specialty ▶ Cinderellas & Fakes 456
Topical & Specialty ▶ Nature 457
Topical & Specialty ▶ People, Sports 457
Worldwide ▶ Philatelic Covers 457
Worldwide ▶ Postal History 457

31
TICKETS

459

The Most Overpriced Concert Ticket Ever Bought? 460
A Hot Lunch Date with Rupert Murdoch 460
Theme Parks and Sporting Events 461
Theater: I'll Take Manhattan 461

Event Tickets ▶ Concerts 461
Event Tickets ▶ Movies 462
Event Tickets ▶ Sporting Events 462
Event Tickets ▶ Theater 463
Event Tickets ▶ Other 463

Experiences ▶ Music 464
Experiences ▶ Sports 464
Experiences ▶ Theme Parks 465
Experiences ▶ Other 465

32
TOYS & HOBBIES

467

Vintage Power: Toys from Old to New 467
Do You Yo-Yo? Classic Toys 468
Un-Losing Your Marbles 468
Modern Toys 469

Action Figures ▶ Batman 469
Action Figures ▶ GI Joe 470
Action Figures ▶ Lord of the Rings 470
Action Figures ▶ Power Rangers 470
Action Figures ▶ Spider-Man 470
Action Figures ▶ Sports 471
Action Figures ▶ Star Trek 471
Action Figures ▶ Star Wars 471
Action Figures ▶ Superman 472
Action Figures ▶ Teenage Mutant Ninja Turtles ... 472
Action Figures ▶ Transformers 472
Action Figures ▶ X-Men 472
Action Figures ▶ Mixed Lots 473
Beanbag Plush, Beanie Babies ▶ Disney 473
Beanbag Plush, Beanie Babies ▶ Ty 473
Beanbag Plush, Beanie Babies ▶ Other 473
Building Toys ▶ Blocks 474
Building Toys ▶ Erector Sets 474
Building Toys ▶ LEGO 474
Building Toys ▶ Lincoln Logs 474
Building Toys ▶ Tinker Toys 475
Classic Toys ▶ Balls, Frisbees, Boomerangs 475
Classic Toys ▶ Colorforms 475
Classic Toys ▶ Etch A Sketch, Spirograph 476
Classic Toys ▶ Kites 476
Classic Toys ▶ Magic, Magician Supplies 476
Classic Toys ▶ Marbles 476
Classic Toys ▶ Rocking Horses 477
Classic Toys ▶ Slinky 477
Classic Toys ▶ Yo-Yos 477

Classic Toys ▶ Other 478
Diecast, Toy Vehicles ▶ Aircraft 478
Diecast, Toy Vehicles ▶ Bikes, Motorcycles 478
Diecast, Toy Vehicles ▶ Boats, Ships 478
Diecast, Toy Vehicles ▶ Cars, Trucks-Diecast 479
Diecast, Toy Vehicles ▶ Cars, Trucks-Plastic 479
Diecast, Toy Vehicles ▶ Cars, Trucks-Pressed Steel .. 479
Educational ▶ Alphabet 479
Educational ▶ Geography, History 480
Educational ▶ Mathematics 480
Educational ▶ Music, Art 480
Educational ▶ Reading, Writing 480
Educational ▶ Science, Nature 481
Electronic, Battery, Wind-Up ▶ Battery Operated . 481
Electronic, Battery, Wind-Up ▶ Electronic,
    Interactive 481
Electronic, Battery, Wind-Up ▶ Wind-Up,
    Walking Toys 482
Fast Food, Cereal Premiums ▶ Cereal &
    Other Premiums 482
Fast Food, Cereal Premiums ▶ Fast Food 482
Games ▶ Board, Traditional Games 482
Games ▶ Electronic 483
Games ▶ Miniatures, War Games 483
Games ▶ Role Playing 483
Model RR, Trains ▶ N Scale 483
Model RR, Trains ▶ HO Scale 484
Model RR, Trains ▶ O Scale 484
Model RR, Trains ▶ G Scale 484
Models, Kits ▶ Air 484

Models, Kits ▸ Automotive 485
Models, Kits ▸ Military 485
Outdoor Toys, Structures ▸ Ride-Ons, Tricycles 485
Outdoor Toys, Structures ▸ Sand, Water Toys 485
Outdoor Toys, Structures ▸ Swings, Slides, Gyms ... 486
Outdoor Toys, Structures ▸ Tents, Tunnels, Playhut .. 486
Pretend Play, Preschool ▸ Brio 486
Pretend Play, Preschool ▸ Brio Compatible 486
Pretend Play, Preschool ▸ Dishes, Tea Sets 487
Pretend Play, Preschool ▸ Dress-Up, Costumes 487
Pretend Play, Preschool ▸ Fisher Price 487
Pretend Play, Preschool ▸ Play-Doh,
       Modeling Clay 487
Pretend Play, Preschool ▸ Playmobil 488
Pretend Play, Preschool ▸ Playskool 488
Pretend Play, Preschool ▸ Puppets 488
Pretend Play, Preschool ▸ Wooden,
       Handcrafted Toys 488
Puzzles ▸ Modern (1970–Now) 489
Puzzles ▸ Vintage (Pre–1970) 489
Radio Control ▸ Vehicles 489
Robots, Monsters, Space Toys ▸ Monsters 489
Robots, Monsters, Space Toys ▸ Robots 490
Robots, Monsters, Space Toys ▸ Space Toys 490
Slot Cars ▸ Modern (1970–Now) 490
Slot Cars ▸ Vintage (Pre–1970) 490
Stuffed Animals ▸ Disney 491
Stuffed Animals ▸ Gund 491

Trading Card Games ▸ Magic the Gathering 491
Trading Card Games ▸ Star Wars 491
Trading Card Games ▸ Yu-Gi-Oh 492
TV, Movie, Character Toys ▸ Barney 492
TV, Movie, Character Toys ▸ Bob the Builder 492
TV, Movie, Character Toys ▸ Disney 493
TV, Movie, Character Toys ▸ Dora the Explorer ...493
TV, Movie, Character Toys ▸ Gumby 493
TV, Movie, Character Toys ▸ Harry Potter 493
TV, Movie, Character Toys ▸ Hello Kitty 494
TV, Movie, Character Toys ▸ Muppets,
       Sesame Street 494
TV, Movie, Character Toys ▸ My Little Pony 494
TV, Movie, Character Toys ▸ Pokemon 494
TV, Movie, Character Toys ▸ SpongeBob
       Squarepants 495
TV, Movie, Character Toys ▸ Teletubbies 495
TV, Movie, Character Toys ▸ Thomas the
       Tank Engine 495
TV, Movie, Character Toys ▸ Winnie the Pooh 495
Vintage, Antique Toys ▸ Cap Guns 496
Vintage, Antique Toys ▸ Cast Iron 496
Vintage, Antique Toys ▸ Cowboy, Western 496
Vintage, Antique Toys ▸ Play Sets 496
Vintage, Antique Toys ▸ Pull Toys 497
Vintage, Antique Toys ▸ Wind-up Toys 497
Vintage, Antique Toys ▸ Other Vintage Toys 497

33
TRAVEL
499

Good Experiences 500
Prices for Air, Land, and Sea 500
Start Packing 501
Airline 501
Cruises ▸ Alaska 501
Cruises ▸ Caribbean 502
Lodging ▸ Bed & Breakfast 502
Lodging ▸ Hotel 502
Lodging ▸ Vacation Rentals ▸ US ▸ California 502
Lodging ▸ Vacation Rentals ▸ US ▸ Florida 503
Lodging ▸ Vacation Rentals ▸ US ▸ Hawaii 503
Lodging ▸ Other 503
Luggage ▸ Backpacks 503
Luggage ▸ Business Cases 504

Luggage ▸ Carry-ons 504
Luggage ▸ Duffle Bags 504
Luggage ▸ Garment Bags 504
Luggage ▸ Sets 505
Luggage ▸ Suitcases 505
Luggage ▸ Other Luggage 505
Vacation Packages ▸ Florida 505
Vacation Packages ▸ Hawaii 506
Vacation Packages ▸ Caribbean 506
Vacation Packages ▸ Mexico 506

34
VIDEO GAMES
507

A Million-Dollar Xbox 360: Selling for a Premium 507
Popular Newer Systems 508
Nintendo and GameCube 508
Games for the Budget-Minded 509
Accessories ▸ 3DO 509
Accessories ▸ Atari 509
Accessories ▸ Colecovision 510
Accessories ▸ Commodore 510
Accessories ▸ Intellivision 510
Accessories ▸ Microsoft Xbox 510
Accessories ▸ Nintendo 64 511
Accessories ▸ Nintendo Game Boy 511
Accessories ▸ Nintendo Game Boy Advance 511
Accessories ▸ Nintendo GameCube 511

Accessories ▸ Nintendo NES 512
Accessories ▸ Nintendo, Super 512
Accessories ▸ PC Games 512
Accessories ▸ Sega CD 513
Accessories ▸ Sega Dreamcast 513
Accessories ▸ Sega Game Gear 513
Accessories ▸ Sega Genesis 513
Accessories ▸ Sega Master 514
Accessories ▸ Sega Pico 514
Accessories ▸ Sega Saturn 514

Accessories ▸ Sony PlayStation 514
Accessories ▸ Sony PlayStation 2 515
Accessories ▸ Other Accessories 515
Games ▸ 3DO 515
Games ▸ Apple 515
Games ▸ Atari 516
Games ▸ Colecovision 516
Games ▸ Commodore 516
Games ▸ Intellivision 516
Games ▸ Microsoft Xbox 360 517
Games ▸ Microsoft Xbox 517
Games ▸ Nintendo 64 517
Games ▸ Nintendo Game Boy 517
Games ▸ Nintendo Game Boy Advance 518
Games ▸ Nintendo Game Boy Advance SP 518
Games ▸ Nintendo Game Boy Color 518
Games ▸ Nintendo GameCube 518
Games ▸ Nintendo NES 519
Games ▸ Nintendo, Super 519
Games ▸ PC 519
Games ▸ Sega Dreamcast 520
Games ▸ Sega Game Gear 520
Games ▸ Sega Genesis 520
Games ▸ Sega Saturn 520
Games ▸ Sony PlayStation 521
Games ▸ Sony PlayStation 2 521
Games ▸ Sony PSP 521
Internet Games ▸ Anarchy Online 521
Internet Games ▸ DAOC 522
Internet Games ▸ Diablo, Diablo 2 522

Internet Games ▸ Eve Online 522
Internet Games ▸ Sims Online 523
Internet Games ▸ Ultima Online 523
Internet Games ▸ Other 523
Systems ▸ 3DO 523
Systems ▸ Atari 524
Systems ▸ Colecovision 524
Systems ▸ Commodore 524
Systems ▸ Intellivision 524
Systems ▸ Microsoft Xbox 360 525
Systems ▸ Microsoft Xbox 525
Systems ▸ Nintendo 64 525
Systems ▸ Nintendo DS 525
Systems ▸ Nintendo Game Boy 526
Systems ▸ Nintendo Game Boy Advance 526
Systems ▸ Nintendo Game Boy Advance SP 526
Systems ▸ Nintendo Game Boy Color 527
Systems ▸ Nintendo GameCube 527
Systems ▸ Nintendo NES 527
Systems ▸ Nintendo, Super 527
Systems ▸ Sega Dreamcast 528
Systems ▸ Sega Genesis 528
Systems ▸ Sony PlayStation 528
Systems ▸ Sony PlayStation 2 528
Systems ▸ Sony PSP 529
Vintage Games 529
Wholesale Lots ▸ Accessories 529
Wholesale Lots ▸ Console Systems 529
Wholesale Lots ▸ Games 530
Wholesale Lots ▸ Other 530

35
EVERYTHING ELSE

531

Unconventional Advertising 531
Getting the Most out of eBay 532
Learning New Tricks 533
A Tomb with a View: From Death to Life and Beyond 533
Hot Memberships and Costumes 534
Mature Audiences Only 534
Taking Your Chance on a Mystery Auction 534
Weird Stuff 534

Advertising Opportunities 535
eBay User Tools 535
Education & Learning ▸ Preschool–Kindergarten 536
Education & Learning ▸ Elementary School 536
Education & Learning ▸ High School 536
Education & Learning ▸ Adult & Career Education .. 536
Education & Learning ▸ School Supplies,
    Equipment 537
Education & Learning ▸ Teaching Supplies,
    Resources 537
Education & Learning ▸ Other 537
Funeral & Cemetery ▸ Caskets 538
Funeral & Cemetery ▸ Cemetery Plots 538
Funeral & Cemetery ▸ Cremation Urns 538
Funeral & Cemetery ▸ Mortuary Supplies 538
Genealogy ▸ Births, Marriages, Deaths 538
Genealogy ▸ Census Records 539
Genealogy ▸ City, State Directories 539
Genealogy ▸ Family Trees 539
Genealogy ▸ Military Records 539
Genealogy ▸ Other 540

Gifts & Occasions ▸ Costumes 540
Gifts & Occasions ▸ Gag Gifts 540
Gifts & Occasions ▸ Gift Baskets 541
Gifts & Occasions ▸ Greeting Cards .. 541
Gifts & Occasions ▸ Party Supplies ... 541
Gifts & Occasions ▸ Wedding Supplies .. 542
Gifts & Occasions ▸ Wholesale Lots .. 542
Information Products ▸ How-To Guides .. 542
Information Products ▸ Wholesale Lists .. 542
Information Products ▸ Other 543
Mature Audiences ▸ Adult Toys 543
Mature Audiences ▸ Animation & Comics 543
Mature Audiences ▸ Art: Nude 543
Mature Audiences ▸ Autographs 544
Mature Audiences ▸ Books 544
Mature Audiences ▸ Clothing, Accessories 544
Mature Audiences ▸ Domain Names ... 544
Mature Audiences ▸ Magazines 545
Mature Audiences ▸ Photographic 545
Mature Audiences ▸ Pin Up 546
Mature Audiences ▸ Risque Novelties ... 546

Mature Audiences ▸ Video 546
Mature Audiences ▸ Other 547
Memberships 547
Metaphysical ▸ Astrology 547
Metaphysical ▸ Crystal Healing 547
Metaphysical ▸ Feng Shui 548
Metaphysical ▸ Goth 548
Metaphysical ▸ Psychic, Paranormal 548
Metaphysical ▸ Reiki 548
Metaphysical ▸ Tarot 549
Metaphysical ▸ Wicca 549
Metaphysical ▸ Other 549
Mystery Auctions 549
Personal Security ▸ Alarms 550
Personal Security ▸ Body Armor 550
Personal Security ▸ Handcuffs 550
Personal Security ▸ Knuckle Dusters 551
Personal Security ▸ Locks 551
Personal Security ▸ Pepper Spray 551
Personal Security ▸ Safes 551
Personal Security ▸ Stun Guns 552

Personal Security ▸ Surveillance Cameras 552
Personal Security ▸ Other 552
Religious Products & Supplies ▸ Bibles Covers &
    Accessories 553
Religious Products & Supplies ▸ Clothing 553
Religious Products & Supplies ▸ Crosses 553
Religious Products & Supplies ▸ Educational
    Materials 553
Religious Products & Supplies ▸ Jewelry 554
Religious Products & Supplies ▸ Judaica 554
Religious Products & Supplies ▸ Rosaries 554
Religious Products & Supplies ▸ Other 555
Reward Pts, Incentive Progs ▸ Proof of
    Purchase, UPCs 555
Reward Pts, Incentive Progs ▸ Impressions,
    Ad Space 555
Reward Pts, Incentive Progs ▸ Other 555
Weird Stuff ▸ Slightly Unusual 556
Weird Stuff ▸ Really Weird 556
Weird Stuff ▸ Totally Bizarre 556
Other 556

APPENDIX
EBAY LISTS   557

Most Infamous eBay Auctions 557
Nine Auctions Inspired by the Virgin Mary Grilled-Cheese Sandwich 559
Twenty-Five Things You Can't Sell on eBay 561
Twelve Auctions That Became eBay Trading Cards 562
Five of the Weirdest Auctions according to eBay's Uncle Griff 563
Four Websites Devoted to eBay Auctions or eBayers 563
eBay Auction with the Most Hits 564
Three "Ghost" Auctions 564
Six of the Most Expensive Things Sold on eBay 564
Five Celebrity Home Auctions and a Door 564
Strange Human Auctions 565
Five Popular Collectibles Searches 566
Twelve eBay Categories That Delivered $1 Billion or More in Worldwide
    Annualized GMV (Gross Merchandise Volume) 566
Top Keywords from A-Z 567
Fifty Top eBayers with the Most Feedback 567
What Ten of the Top eBay Sellers Sell 568
Some Revenge Auctions 569

ACKNOWLEDGMENTS

Not everyone would be willing to tackle a project as huge in scope as an eBay price guide, which I've often reflected might just as well have been titled "A Price Guide to Everything." One person who was, and who I'd like to thank first for making this book possible, is Bill Pollock of No Starch Press. Bill is a man of innovation and risk-taking; a man on the cutting edge of just about anything; a man who always seems to be about to go under a tunnel during cell phone conversations.

My wonderful editor, Elizabeth Campbell, not only did not run kicking and screaming when she took on this massive project, but handled it with great cheerfulness and skill, and even put up with my email babblings throughout. I'd also like to thank editors Karol Jurado and Susan Berge for their contributions to the earlier phases of the project. And thanks to Riley Hoffman and Megan Dunchak for all of your layout expertise.

Copyeditor Andy Carroll made many suggestions and careful edits with much patience and good nature; I thank him for making it a much better book.

I am extremely grateful to all the folks at BrightBuilder/Hammertap, makers of the DeepAnalysis tool, which was used to obtain the lion's share of these prices—especially Russell Baird and Jen Cano for their advocacy and tolerance for all my questions.

Sujinder Pothula, Thom Downing, and Rebecca Thomas helped me out in a pinch, and I am very grateful to them all. As always, I must also thank Ina Steiner for many things; without her, this book would not be here in this form. Also thanks to David Steiner, who continues to be a great font of industry knowledge.

Both Ina Steiner and industry expert and eBay renaissance man Skip McGrath were willing to review the book for me and give me feedback; thank you both very much.

A big thanks to my whole family for their patience in letting me work on this book night and day.

Finally, I'd like to thank eBay for making this big, fascinating mass of data possible.

INTRODUCTION

There are more things in heaven and earth, Horatio,
Than are dreamt of in your philosophy.
—William Shakespeare, *Hamlet*, Act I, Scene V

Maria: When we entered the abbey, our worldly clothes were given to the poor.
Captain von Trapp: What about this one?
Maria: The poor didn't want this one.
—*The Sound of Music*

Why an eBay Price Guide?

Most of us love to talk about prices. How much the neighbor's house went for, or what that old painting in your attic might be worth—these are topics that interest just about anyone in our material-based society. Miss Manners may say not to discuss prices in public, but even if we refrain from bragging at a party about that bargain we got on a designer suit, many of us at least hash over the costs of things when we're at home, or with close friends and family. Whether it's that too-small pair of Levi's or that ancient vase that was collecting dust on a garage shelf for years, people are curious about how much their stuff is worth. And the gossip is not all about how we can make money; it's also about how we can get good stuff on the cheap.

eBay, sometimes dubbed "The World's Biggest Yard Sale," has changed the way many of us shop, as well as how we dispose of our unwanted or no-longer-needed items. We can search for exactly what we want without having to scour yard sales and thrift stores for months, or put up with things that were inexpensive but that were not what we would have chosen in a store. It has made whole new categories of merchandise available to people via online shopping. For example, people can now buy used clothing at a substantial discount from what they would pay for it new.

But there has been no guide that tells people how much they can expect to pay for such gently used items, or what they can reasonably expect to receive when selling such merchandise. And it isn't limited to used clothing. There are many other items for which it has previously been hard to gauge prices: used videos, CDs, DVDs, computers, electronics—

pretty much any type of consumer merchandise that exists is available on eBay. Because these items are not thought of as "collectibles," in many cases, price guides have not been created for them.

The very existence of eBay has affected the price of some types of items, because they are now more readily available than they may have been in the pre–online shopping days. For example, some say that the advent of eBay caused the prices of Depression glass to fall, because so many people were digging this popular collectible out of their basements and attics to list it on the popular online auction site. The supply increased dramatically, and hence the prices fell.

I wanted to write this book because I was fascinated with the range and scope of prices on eBay. I wanted to give the average person a way to quickly scan the huge variety of things now available, and the prices they might get for the things they have to sell.

eBay is a dynamic online price guide to everything, and the closing prices of auctions change over time as the markets for things change. Although it is easy enough for any one person to look up a few prices using eBay's Completed Listings feature, it is a much larger undertaking to review a wide variety of eBay's many categories, and to retrieve and analyze high and average prices for each.

Also, because there are so many categories on eBay, some people dwell only within a few sections and don't investigate the numerous nooks and crannies. For example, before I wrote this book, I didn't think of buying original art on eBay. While researching the self-representing artists subcategory, I came across some beautiful and colorful oil paintings perfect for a space I had been trying to decorate. I bought one for what seemed to me a song.

I envision a reader flipping through the book and thinking, "Used Levi's can go for that much? I hadn't thought of selling mine, but now I will," or, "I can get a three-year-old sedan for that little?" In some cases, the book may inspire the reader to see the value in some of their things: "Good thing I saved that stash of old '60s albums." And in other cases, it may inspire them to finally clear some clutter from their home: "Wow . . . it's time to get rid of that box of old '80s albums."

In still other cases, it may help the small business person acquire equipment at a discount—equipment they hadn't even realized was available on eBay: a John Deere tractor, the entire contents of a salon, an industrial-strength coffee maker? All here.

Why Did It Sell for That? Analyzing Prices

In the chapter introductions, I also sought to pull out key high and average (or median) price examples from each category and discuss why each one sold for the price it did. In some cases, I refer to examples of the lowest prices and analyze why they may have ended at such rock-bottom numbers, so you will know what types of items to avoid selling. (The original version of this book included low prices, but because so many of them were one cent, and also had disproportionately high shipping charges, they are not in the final version). Learning about the low sellers can also teach you how to get the best prices when buying.

Finally, in the "eBay Lists" appendix, I examine other types of eBay stats: We have seen many news articles about this or that bizarre eBay auction—the guy who tried to sell his friendship; another guy who listed his family. Larry Star, the guy who listed his ex-wife's wedding dress—complete with photos of him wearing it—was all over the media (the auction netted him $3,800.00).

Whether you are simply curious about selling or buying on eBay or are already doing so, *The eBay Price Guide* has something for you. The eBay curious may want to know how much they can expect to get for various types of items, and those already selling will want to know not only what other types of things they could be profitably selling, but also what kinds of prices they can expect to pay for things they want.

Although there are some generalists out there in the eBay selling world, most eBayers specialize in selling one type of item. They may have done some research about market prices in their area of focus, but probably have not taken the time to extensively research other areas, if for no other reason than that it is very time-consuming. If you are such a seller, *The eBay Price Guide* can give you a starting point for researching other products that you may want to start selling.

Methodology

How were the prices in this book obtained? The answer is, using various methods. But acquiring this large quantity of prices and sifting out the high, and especially the average, prices required the help of a tool, or the book would have taken much longer to complete. That tool is HammerTap's DeepAnalysis, a program that allows you to retrieve hundreds or thousands of prices from given subcategories, and to do specific keyword searches for certain types of items. In many cases, the prices in this book were obtained by using DeepAnalysis to cull 500 to 2,000 auction prices from each of many key eBay subcategories. The software calculates average prices for a given subcategory or keyword search. This book is accompanied by a CD, so if you want to look up more prices or details about the items within the book, you can. You can register for and download the software at www.hammertap.com/deepanalysis and try it out for yourself.

Identical Items and "Dutch" Auctions

In some cases, when bulk retrieval of prices was not possible, manual searches were conducted using eBay's Completed Listings feature. In those instances, such as in some of the Books subcategories, the method of price retrieval is noted before the price listings.

There are two types of price results that are denoted by comments in brackets within the price tables:

- Multiple identical items often sell for the exact same price. For example, seven red bookmarks, all with the exact same auction title, all sold for $2.00 each; this would be denoted with "[7 of these sold for $2.00 each]."
- A group of identical items are sometimes all sold in one single auction, known as a "multiple item" or "Dutch" auction. If, for example, the seven bookmarks all sold in a multiple-item auction, one single auction for seven bookmarks would be listed. The results for this type of auction would be denoted with "[7 of these sold in a multiple item ("Dutch") auction for $2.00 each]."

Low Prices

The initial draft of this book included samples of the lowest prices for the selected subcategories. However, as so many of them were "penny" items, listed for and often selling for $0.01, usually with higher shipping charges to make up for such a low price, those prices didn't seem to be as useful to include. However, in some chapters, some of those low prices are discussed, as well as what to watch out for in terms of inflated shipping and "gimmicky" low starting prices.

Quoting Auctions and People

Spelling and grammar aren't always the top priorities for people communicating online. I have quoted all sellers, buyers, and list participants verbatim. Misspellings, incorrect grammar, and multiple exclamation marks are property of their authors and are part of the fun!

In Conclusion

I hope that you will take away from this book a good sense of the huge breadth and depth of items available on eBay, along with useful information about why certain things sell for so much or so little. You will come away with many ideas about things to sell that you might not have thought of otherwise, about what you can buy to save money, and about how much you can save. You can return to the prices in the book again and again as your needs change, and the book should serve as a key reference tool in your eBay library. And hopefully, you will also be entertained by the more outlandish and unusual auctions, and the facts and trivia in the appendix, "eBay Lists."

eBay is many things to many people: For some, it has become their full-time business. For others, it is a way to supplement their income. Some people use it to find bargains and buy name-brand merchandise at deep discounts. Others use it to clear clutter from their homes. Whatever it is for you, I hope this book enhances your eBay experience and opens your eyes to some areas of the site you would not otherwise have discovered.

1

ANTIQUES

The Antiques category has greatly contributed to eBay's growth since the site's inception in 1995. In the early days of eBay, according to one longtime seller, half or more of all sales were from this category, which featured many one-of-a-kind items. But now, with the vast range of items available throughout the site, antiques and collectibles have dropped to about 12 percent of the total merchandise sold on the site.

Because older, rarer items are generally more valuable, it's not surprising that the items in the Antiques subcategories have higher average final sales prices than many other eBay categories. For example, in the Antiques ▶ Furniture ▶ Cabinets, Armoires, Cupboards subcategory, the average sales price is around $630, based on a sample of 1,000 auctions. Compare that with about $36.00 for, say, the Home & Garden ▶ Bedding ▶ Bedspreads, Coverlets category.

The Antiques category is like a microcosm of eBay, only with older, rarer versions of the items you can find in other categories. For that reason, if you are browsing and not searching, you may want to check the corresponding non-antique eBay category as well for what you seek; a seller may have listed an antique German beer stein, for example, in the Ceramics, Porcelain category under Decorative Arts, within Antiques, but also in Collectibles ▶ Breweriana, Beer Drinkware, Steins ▶ Steins ▶ Germany.

Beware of Fakes and Reproductions

Because antiques need to be genuinely old to be valuable (there was some discussion on the eBay Antiques discussion board as to how many years old something needs to be to be considered an "antique," with most agreeing around 100 years—although clearly there are exceptions to this throughout the category), buyers need to be very careful about purchasing in this category. Recently, a rash of items of questionable authenticity have come on the market, many of which are based in China, according to discussion on the eBay Antiques board. One seller said the Chinese antiques section was "perhaps the only site in the world where one can buy a 'genuine' T'ang dynasty bowl for less than the price of a Big Mac." He said the only true statements coming from these sellers is that the specimens are in excellent condition—"understandable since they were probably made last week!"

But another seller pointed out that some people like the reproductions for the high degree of artistic skill they often show: "Buy a $49 T'ang camel by all means, and enjoy it for what it is. But please don't bore us with your astonishment when you discover it isn't 1800 years old," he said.

Of course, fakes and reproductions are not limited to the Chinese antiques categories; they can be found in antiques from any subcategory, as well as in other main eBay categories, such as Clothing, Shoes & Accessories. One seller commented that it seemed like "every commode with a cabriole leg" was purporting to be French. So the bottom line for you as a buyer is "caveat emptor"—buyer beware; and do your homework. Thoroughly check a seller's feedback, and look for reputable dealers, if possible. If you can get a certificate of authenticity from the seller, great. (As a seller, bear in mind that offering such guarantees can net you a higher final sales price as well as good feedback from your buyers.)

Remember that, in general, genuine antiques are going to cost genuine money, as one seller put it. Look for a good return policy, and don't forget to check shipping charges, especially for items from foreign countries. Some sellers make most or all of their profits in this area. As an example, on the low end of the Antiques ▶ Rugs, Carpets subcategory, one rug that the seller says is 70 to 80 years old sold for $0.99, but with $55.00 shipping and handling. Of course, these rugs are heavy, and shipping will not be cheap, but be sure to look carefully at shipping costs to get an idea of your total cost.

Another thing to bear in mind when shopping for antiquities located in their native lands is that some countries have laws forbidding exporting of ancient artifacts if there is not an established owner. (In some cases the government's permission may be needed.)

In some cases, the items in the Antiques subcategories are not even presented as antiques, but replicas, such as the reproduction (albeit evidently high quality) sculpture of ancient Egyptian pharaoh Tutankhamen's burial mask, which sold for $4,900.00: "This extraordinary sculpture has been made using the very same ancient technique that was used by Egyptians centuries ago - polished graphite with the aspect of black basalt covered by layers of bronze," reads the description. The materials used for the piece were evidently expensive: the face of Tutankhamen was covered by a layer of 24-karat gold, and the blue finishes were created using a powder of blue lapis lazuli—"exactly as the ancient goldsmiths of Egypt did."

Low Sellers and Bargains

What sells for the lowest prices in the Antiques category? It varies, of course, but items of questionable age and bad condition are two such types of things. For example, an item in the Antiques category may not necessarily be an antique—the seller might not give the item's age, or perhaps doesn't know.

Some buyers find a bargain by betting on whether or not something is genuine or valuable when it is not clear. One seller in the Antiques ▶ Books, Manuscripts ▶ American subcategory offered up this cheeky teaser of an auction title: "Probably Not a Photo of WALT WHITMAN." The auction description reads, in part, "This is probably just an old guy with a big white beard sitting next to an open window. It probably is not an original mounted photograph of one of America's greatest poets. But there is that beard, and I have seen photos of Walt Whitman in a similar pose. There is no information anywhere on the photo or mount regarding subject, photographer, location, or date." Someone took a chance on this, and paid only $0.99.

Other items sell for a low price because they are, quite frankly, just not that attractive, or even odd. I once read a description of a long, orange, antique cylindrical light fixture that the seller characterized as "very unique . . . not sure of its purpose in life." It sold for $2.50.

But aside from the offbeat and the questionable, there are some great bargains to be found in the Antiques category if you look around carefully enough. I find that if you get past the prices that are so low as to be gimmicky, such as $0.01 to $0.99, with high shipping usually tacked on, you can find some interesting items that may not be from a famous maker but are nonetheless desirable. For example, some cool old maps, offered by a PowerSeller with a good feedback rating, sold for only $2.99: "2 Very Old Maps1589 Maris Pacifica/West Pacific might have been pages from old books mounted on boards unsure. Def. very early1589 and they don't appear to be repros," reads the description.

High Flyers and Notables

Of course, there is much more here than inexpensive artifacts. The category is chock-full of amazing, unique, and expensive items. There are two Civil War diaries in the Books, Manuscripts ▶ American subcategory. An "1862 CIVIL WAR SOLDIER DIARY BATTLE CONTENT MI 4TH REG" sold for $3,051.00 (there is a photo of the front page of the journal, on which, poignantly, "Remember me" is written in cursive). The other, "Authentic Civil War Diary Journal George W. Miller 1863," went for $699.00.

The Civil War, a popular flashpoint for items in many categories, pops up again with high prices in such Antiques subcategories as Science & Medicine, including an old Civil War–era "U.S. Hosp. Dept." bottle, a brown glass bottle that sold for $711.50. Other things in this subcategory, while being interesting from an academic (or morbid curiosity) stand-point, are a bit macabre: the "REAL HUMAN SKULL, RARE, MIXED DENTITION" ($600.00). As the seller wrote in the description, "This skull if from a child of approximately six years of age and has the best display of mixed dentition this seller has ever seen! As can be seen in the images, it has artfully dissected by a skilled doctor of German descent to reveal the presence of ALL OF THE PERMANENT TEETH ON THE LEFT SIDE!" If you want something a bit cheaper, there is the "NIGHTMARISH! Rare FREAKS Old GRAPHIC PHOTO MEDICAL BOOK" featuring "ALLIGATOR PEOPLE! PINHEADS! DWARFISM! DEFORMED LIMBS!" ($60.00).

But strangeness aside, there are truly some exquisite items throughout the Antiques category, especially on the high end of the price ranges. The Gorham "SHEAF OF WHEAT set for 12," which sold for $2,599.00; the "Elegant Empire French Crystal Chandelier" at $1,825.00; and the ancient Hindu stone statue ("museum piece 16th century") at $2,500.00. A Meissen centerpiece (a valuable German type of porcelain) sells for $2,950.00 in the Decorative Arts ▶ Ceramics, Porcelain subcategory, and a glance down the high column here reveals other famous old makers such as Wedgwood, Jacob Petit, and Boch & Catteau.

With larger items, such as furniture, the upper end of prices often goes even higher, with an American Renaissance bedroom set, circa 1875, being one of the highest here at $15,999.00, and a French Country armoire, circa 1850, going for $5,600.00.

But let's not forget the stuff in the middle—you don't have to be a millionaire to pick up items that fall into the average price range. Need a piece to complete your silver set? You can pick up a Reed & Barton Marlborough serving shell for $50.99, or a William & Mary place setting by Lunt for $58.99 (a new one will run you around $150.00 to $180.00, retail). And that's the fun of the Antiques category for many people: eBay did not, contrary to some contrarians, take away the thrill of the hunt for these old, rare items—it just moved a lot of it online. It made it more accessible for many people, but didn't remove all the challenges, since that perfect find for you may take several weeks or months and saved-searches for you to track down on eBay. So do be wary in this category, but, by all means, have fun.

Antiquities (Classical, Amer.) ▶ Egyptian

The average sales price in this subcategory is $116.46.

	HIGH		AVG
EGYPT_EXQUISITE_PHARAOH_TUTANKHAMEN_24carate_GOLD_LAPIS	$4,900.00	Ancient Egyptian Commemorative Scarab !	$142.50
EGYPT_EXQUISITE_PHARAOH_TUTANKHAMEN_24carate_GOLD_LAPIS	$3,500.00	Ancient Egyptian Canopic Jar, Late Period	$142.50
Ancient Egyptian Goddess Bastet Dynasty 26	$1,580.00	Ancient Egyptian Child Canopic Jar with Imsety headed	$137.50
Pfeiffer deluxe shippaquik	$1,440.00	Ancient Egyptian Third Intermediate Period Pharaoh	$133.50
EFTIS:EGYPTIAN GOLD FILIGREE Ring 14thC N/RES!	$1,225.00	Ancient Egyptian Anubis (New Kingdom)	$130.49
EFTIS: Egyptian Mummy Bead Mask 500 BC N/Res!	$1,034.00	ANCIENT EGYPT EGYPTIAN FAIENCE AMULET BEADS SCARAB 3	$129.95
4 Ancient Egyptian Canopic Jar, Late Period(715-332 B.C	$1,026.00	Ancient Egyptian Kohl Vessell I(332-30 B.C.E.)	$127.50
Rare Ancient Egyptian Statue Of "Ramses II"	$960.00	Medieval Kingdom Chess Box/Board *NEW COLLECTIBLES*	$125.95
Ancient Egyptian Stela of(Winged Isis,Winged Solar Disk	$910.00	Ancient Egyptian King Menkaura (Mankaure) As Sphinx	$122.50
Very old wood figure. Figurehead? Egyptian? Mystery!!	$903.00	Ancient Egyptian Carved Canopic Jar with jackal headed	$122.50
Ancient Egyptian(Dynasty 18) Relic Relief of Tutankhamun	$810.00	Ancient Egyptian Isis With Child Horus	$122.50
Treasuregate - Rare Egyptian silver cartouche ring	$600.00	Ancient Egyptian Large Ushabti !	$122.50
Ancient Egyptian Ramses the Great Offertory Relief	$510.00	Ancient Egyptian Horus panal From outer wooden coffin	$122.50
EFTIS:BRONZE Egyptian HORUS Statue 1000 BC N/RES!	$474.00	Ancient Egyptian(Dynasty18) Tutankhamun Big wooden bust	$122.50
Ancient Egyptian Tutankhamun Veneration Statue	$455.00	Rare Ancient Egyptian Head Of "Tutankhamen"?	$119.50

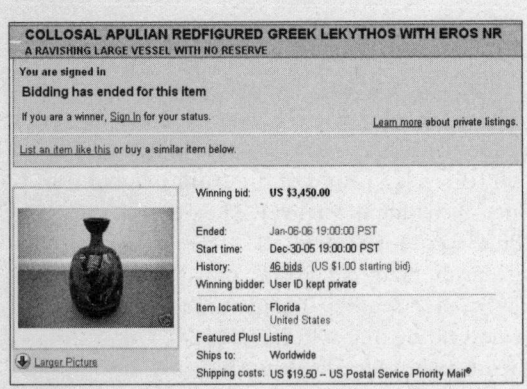

COLLOSAL APULIAN REDFIGURED GREEK LEKYTHOS WITH EROS NR
A RAVISHING LARGE VESSEL WITH NO RESERVE

You are signed in

Bidding has ended for this item

If you are a winner, Sign In for your status.

List an item like this or buy a similar item below.

Learn more about private listings.

Winning bid:	**US $3,450.00**
Ended:	Jan-06-06 19:00:00 PST
Start time:	Dec-30-05 19:00:00 PST
History:	46 bids (US $1.00 starting bid)
Winning bidder:	User ID kept private
Item location:	Florida United States
	Featured Plus! Listing
	Ships to: Worldwide
Larger Picture	Shipping costs: US $19.50 -- US Postal Service Priority Mail®

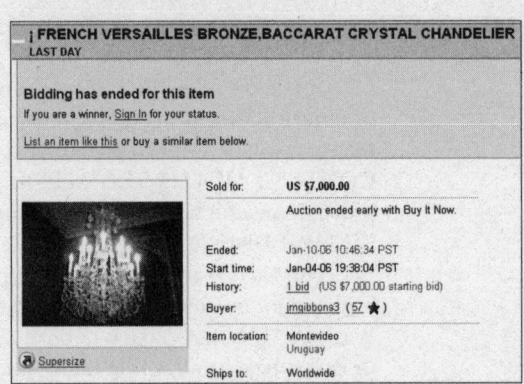

¡ FRENCH VERSAILLES BRONZE,BACCARAT CRYSTAL CHANDELIER
LAST DAY

Bidding has ended for this item

If you are a winner, Sign In for your status.

List an item like this or buy a similar item below.

Sold for:	**US $7,000.00**
	Auction ended early with Buy It Now.
Ended:	Jan-10-06 10:46:34 PST
Start time:	Jan-04-06 19:38:04 PST
History:	1 bid (US $7,000.00 starting bid)
Buyer:	jmgibbons3 (57 ★)
Item location:	Montevideo Uruguay
Supersize	Ships to: Worldwide

Antiquities (Classical, Amer.) ▶ The Americas

The average sales price in this subcategory is $104.06.

	HIGH		AVG
Antique tool -EZY-OUT set	$2,550.00	Native American Indian Antique Hand Forged Old Spear	$145.50
Paul Evans Dinning Table American Eames Era	$2,025.00	PRE COLUMBIAN ANCIENT VESSEL POTTERY COSTA RICA 1200AD	$137.79
Paul Evans Set of Six Chairs American Eames Era	$1,525.00	Hand Painted Buffalo Hide Sioux Style	$130.05
Hamilton Pocket watch	$1,500.00	Par Aide Golf Ball Washer	$130.00
Pre Columbian Huari matched pair of Dogs ca. 700AD	$1,475.00	Native American Indian Rare Old Soap Stone Oil Lamp	$129.00
RARE ORIGINAL 1937 NATIONAL JAMBOREE BANNER	$1,231.89	Native American Indian Antique Framed Print Drescher	$127.50
AUTHENTIC WHITE HOUSE WALL CLOCK EISENHOWER WWII	$1,225.00	Charles Doepke American LaFrance Ladder Truck -Vintage	$127.50
Fossils GIANT 43" TRICERATOPS DINOSAUR LEG BONE Fossil	$1,200.00	CONN 1915 LICENSE PLATE PAIR GREAT CONDITION	$127.50
six dinning room chairs with beautiful carved legs	$1,000.00	IMPORTANT & FINE/MICMAC TRIBAL COUNCIL BASKET	$125.00
Paul Evans Swivel Chair American Eames Era	$750.00	Antique pre-columbian pottery bowl super genuine	$125.00
EDISON HOOVER FORD SIGNED AUTOGRAPHED PICTURE PSA DNA	$669.99	Depression Glass- Child's Tea Set	$125.00
Pre-Columbian Mayan Zoomorphic Jade Plaque	$599.00	Antique Old Wood Fishing Tackle Box	$113.01
PRE-COLUMBIAN MASTER TAINO ZEMI Puerto Rico cemi	$560.24	Hamilton vintage watch	$112.50
1925 NICKEL WESTERN ELEC. 51AL DIAL CANDLESTICK PHONE	$500.00	Ancient Egyptian Faience Vessel with4 Sekhmet as handle	$111.99
Vintage twig table	$500.00	OLD GWTW LAMP WITH GREEN DECORATION ELECTRIFIED	$110.00

Architectural & Garden ▶ Chandeliers, Fixtures, Sconces

The average sales price in this subcategory is $117.28.

	HIGH		AVG
ELEGANT EMPIRE FRENCH CRYSTAL CHANDELIER /NO RESERVE	$1,825.00	ART DECO HANGING CHANDELIER CEILING FIXTURE N-SLIP SHAD	$127.50
Antique 18 Arm Brass Chandelier-Candleabra-vintage	$965.55	Milo Baughman Eames Era Chrome Chandelier Light Fixture	$127.50
ANTIQUE ITALIAN WROUGHT IRON HANGING LAMP CHANDELIER NR	$963.00	Antique Lightolier Solid Brass 5 Light Chandelier EC	$127.50
ANTIQUE GOTHIC FRENCH BRONZE CHANDELIER 12 LIGHTS	$960.10	~VINTAGE Ornate BRASS & CRYSTAL PRISM 6 Arm CHANDELIER~	$127.50
ANTIQUE HEAVY BRONZE CHANDELIER-ANGELS	$840.00	Antique 8 ARM Brass Chandelier w/Prisms~MADE IN SPAIN	$126.49
2 XLarge Antique ART DECO PENDANT FIXTURE GLOBES-17"T	$765.05	Arts & Crafts Copper Hanging Fixture Light Shade COPPER	$125.50
ART DECO LIGHT SLIP IN FIXTURE SHADE CHANDELIER HANGING	$699.00	Solid Brass and Crystal Chandelier - 17.5"	$125.00
BEAUTIFUL EMPIRE STYLE CRYSTAL CHANDELIER OLD	$696.00	Vintage Brass Chandelier-Cut Glass Prisms-Czech-Crystal	$125.00
ART DECO CEILING LIGHT FIXTURE VICTORIAN CHANDELIER 30s	$685.99	ITALIAN WROUGHT IRON HANGING WALL SCONCE LIGHT FIXTURE	$123.53
Empire Black & Bronze Cherub Elegant Vintage Chandelier	$650.00	Old Pair NAUTICAL SHIP'S WHEEL Sconces ~ Anchor ~ Stars	$123.50
ANTIQUE LARGE BRONZE & AMBER ALABASTER CHANDELIER.	$630.00	EARLY 1900's BRASS HANGING LIGHT FIXTURE	$122.50
Antique Art Noveau? Chandelier Light Fixture	$572.00	Antique Metal French Country Cottage Chandelier	$122.00
ART DECO NOT SLIP IN ON HANGING CEILING LIGHT FIXTURE S	$525.00	CHANDELIER 8 ARM , BOBECHES , PRISMS CEILING CANOPY	$120.00
~BEDAZZLING! Antique Brass CRYSTAL French Chandelier~	$517.99	Rare Antique European Gilded Metal Chandelier w/Prisms	$120.00
ANTIQUE WALL AMBER ALABASTER SCONCES (PAIR)	$510.00	NEW! High End Modern spider chandelier. contemporary	$117.51

Architectural & Garden ▸ Garden

The average sales price in this subcategory is $62.75.

	HIGH		AVG
Ancient Hindu Stone statue,museum piece 16th. Century	$2,500.00	1916 fancy garden photo history bk 341pgs!! ESTATE FIND	$89.88
Old Primitive Millstone,mill stone primitive	$1,500.00	ANTIQUE ROSEVILLE PLANTER AND FLOWER FROG	$86.00
1959 COPAR PANZER GARDEN TRACTOR W/ SNOWPLOW-NR!!!	$920.00	Shabby ORNATE Antique Cast Metal TABLE STAND~Chic White	$82.97
LAGARDO TACKETT ARCHITECTURAL POTTERY PLANTER-ORIG.	$909.00	~WAGON WHEEL-LARGE-WESTERN-SOLID WOOD AND STEEL~	$82.50
1959 COPAR PANZER GARDEN TRACTOR-NR!!!	$810.00	Ornate Bird Bath	$81.00
Antique Cider Press	$721.00	OLD Cast Iron Lion Head~ Part of OLD Water Fountain	$81.00
ANTIQUE IRON GARDEN BENCH W/ GRAPES MOTIF OLD!!	$699.00	Awesome Shabby Vintage Chic Cherub Cement Garden Statue	$78.77
Sunbeam Rain King sprinkler store display rack shelf	$542.99	Folk Art Ballard School Birdhouse Bird House	$75.00
Vintage wrought iron table with six chairs	$520.00	ANTIQUE ENAMELWARE BUCKET paris chic hp shabby roses	$74.99
Antique brass bell	$510.00	Windmill Wooden Handcrafted Yard Ornament	$71.00
Shabby Chic Antique Cast Iron Rose Vine Trellis Gazebo	$500.00	COVERED WAGON mail box- old and used	$70.95
LAGARDO TACKETT ARCHITECTURAL POTTERY PLANTER-BLACK	$499.99	Stainless Steel Drinking Water Fountain Sink, Park Type	$70.00
1800'S VICTORIAN GARDEN ARMILLARY SUN DIAL/ SUNDIAL	$456.61	46 INCH WROUGHT IRON WINDOW BOX PLANTER	$69.00
GIGANTIC VINTAGE CLAM SHELL 24 1/2" LONG, 45 PDS, NR	$451.00	Bound 1925 Full Year Garden & Home Builder Magazine	$66.99
GIGANTIC VINTAGE CLAM SHELL 24 1/2" LONG, 45 PDS, NR	$362.00	Vintage Garden Plaque Angels Music Among Trees 14"x13"	$66.02

Architectural & Garden ▸ Hardware

The average sales price in this subcategory is $31.39.

	HIGH		AVG
Train Bell Railroad School Church 1860s Old Lg Ex NR	$432.93	Antique Brass Horse Coat Hat Rack	$35.00
Rare Antique Annunciator Servants Doorbell Door Bell	$422.69	SOLID BRASS DOOR KNOCKER	$35.00
ANTIQUE DOORBELL DOOR BELL VICTORIAN KNOB	$393.00	GREAT Pair Antique Cast Iron Architectural LION HEAD'S	$34.99
OLD hand painted cast iron door knocker-ART NOUVEAU	$305.00	Victorian Style Brass Door Bell Unused with Key	$34.50
Connells Fancy Mechanical Door Bell & Twist 1891	$280.00	ANTIQUE SPRING LOADED BRASS FREE HANGIN DOOR BELL	$34.33
Rare annunciator door bell doorbell knob antique servan	$203.50	Arts & Crafts Brass Key & Key Hole Door Knocker NR	$34.02
ANTIQUE CAST IRON PARROT DOOR KNOCKER	$202.50	Unusual Cast Iron Tripple Prong Swivel Coat Hook	$34.00
Victorian Nickel Mechanical Door Bell and Twist	$192.50	Antique Set of 8 Eastlake Coat Hat Hooks Acorn Finials	$33.88
CAST IRON DOOR KNOCKER/GRATE 1930's TULIP DESIGN	$167.50	VICTORIAN BRASS DOOR BELL TURN KEY	$33.83
Antique Brass TWIST DOOR BELL - Victorian - Works!	$157.50	Tiny Vintage Fox Head Door Knocker Brass	$33.14
FABULOUS OLD SOLID BRASS LION HEAD DOOR KNOCKER	$153.50	VINTAGE ART DECO DOORBELL DOOR BELL NUTONE CHIME	$33.05
Neoclassical Brass Door Knocker No Reserve	$152.50	Early 1900's Cast Bronze Sargent Co. Doorbell Plate!	$33.00
Painted Cast Iron Door Knocker Rare Large Floral	$139.99	Antique Brass Door Bell Handle, Parts, Eastlake	$32.60
Antique Victorian Door Bell, Very Detailed 19th Century	$129.00	VINTAGE 1940'S NUTONE DOOR BELL-CHIME-MODEL K16,1061	$32.56
c 1880 Solid Brass Victorian-Eastlake Doorbell	$128.85	OLD GLASS CRYSTAL DOOR KNOBS WOW NR	$32.12

Asian Antiques ▸ Chinese

The average sales price in this subcategory is $77.07.

	HIGH		AVG
Chinese Export Blue & White Bowl Lotus Kangxi Signed NR	$4,002.00	Chinese Porcelain Bin Thuan Shipwreck Ming Swatow Bowl	$100.00
Qianlong Mark & Period Chinese Bowl w/ Bats	$1,735.00	Antique Chinese Cloisonne Bowl Dragon & Peach LARGE!	$99.00
~ca1840~ROSE MANDARIN~12inch Oval Dish~Chinese Export~	$809.00	Famille Rose Porcelain Big Bowl With Dragon&Fish Motif	$99.00
SUPER 1830' S EXPORT FRUIT BASKET WITH AMERICAN EAGLE	$647.51	RARE STONE AGE PAINTED NEOLITHIC POTTERY BIG BOWL	$98.00
LARGE CHINESE COPPER RED GLAZED BOWL	$540.00	5 Antique Chinese Export Elegant Ladies Bowls 1870	$96.80
Chinese Export Sterling Silver Basket Grape/Leaf WingOn	$520.00	AN 18C CHINESE IMARI BOWL - FLOWERS AND FOLIAGE	$92.00
A Fine Blue And White Bowl. Tianqi Mark. Kangxi	$510.00	4 Antique Chinese Export Elegant Ladies Tea Bowls 1870	$91.80
ANTIQUE-CHINESE EXPORT PAIR PLANTERS,MEIJI W/ U.S EAGLE	$510.00	Chinese Export 18thC Qianlong European Gilded Bowl	$90.00
Chinese Export Canton Famille Rose Punch Bowl 19th c	$496.01	Antique CHINESE EXPORT Blue & White BOWL Estate Found	$89.00
Fine Wanli Period Blue & White Shallow Bowl	$495.00	Beautiful Song Dynasty(960-1279) Celadon Glaze Bowl	$88.00
Matched Pr Antique 18thC Decorated Chinese Export Bowls	$489.99	16th Century Ming Dynasty Blue & White Big Bowl (S21)	$83.00
Blue White Early Canton Chinese Oriental Bowl	$474.99	ANTIQUE 19c CHINESE EXPORT BLUE & WHITE FOOTED BOWL	$81.00
Unusual Covered Bowl 19c Chinese Export Rose Mandarin	$405.00	Chinese 19TH C Export Canton B & W Chestnut Basket	$80.90
Antique Chinese Ornate Pewter Warming Bowl Server	$400.00	VINTAGE RUSSIAN ORIENTAL PLIQUE A JUR ENAMEL BOWL	$80.00
CHINESE YUAN DYNASTY JUN YAO PORCELAIN BOWL-HRTM	$305.00	LARGE 17" ANTIQUE BLUE WHITE PORCELAIN BOWL	$78.70

Asian Antiques ▸ Japanese

The average sales price in this subcategory is $79.51.

	HIGH		AVG
OLD Satsuma Meiji Ornate Signed Kinkozan Box Vase WOW!!	$1,502.00	Japanese 19thC Kutani Bowl	$91.51
Japanese Antique Nabeshima Porcelain Dish	$1,325.00	1631: Vintage Japanese Tea bowl. RAKU. Mt. Fuji. w/box.	$90.99
Japanese Ando cloisonne copper enamel writing box	$1,226.00	Beautiful Japanese Ko Imari Bowl, Bird/Bamboo 19c NRSV	$90.00
JAPANESE SILVER/GOLD Chrysanthemum~IMPERIAL BONBONNIERE	$1,125.00	Vintage Japanese Bronze Buddhist Gong Pillow Striker	$90.00
Japanese Teabowl Karatsu ware:Muan Nakazato #yO244	$1,104.00	INABA JAPANESE CLOISONNE ENAMEL BOX Butterflies Peonies	$89.88
BEAUTIFUL JAPANESE CLOISONNE BOX MEIJI 4 3/4" X 4"	$950.00	1818: Japanese Tea pot. MUSHIAKE ware. w/Signed box.	$88.55
Japanese Sterling Postcard & Poststamp Box, Miyamoto	$643.33	Fukagawa Koransha Bamboo Bowl Meiji Imari - Japanese	$85.00
OLD JAPANESE SILVER BOX Mt FUJI	$560.00	19th Century H.P. Brocade Imari Rice Bowl-Cranes-Signed	$83.54
Large Rare 19Th Japanese Imari Pair Double Fish Plates	$510.00	Vintage Japanese Silver Wire Cloisonne Box NR	$82.09
NR 1800's fantastic Large Japanese Cloisonne Ginger JAR	$500.00	NEW Asian NINGBO Cabinet -Antique Reproduction	$80.00
3 Fine Old JAPANESE LACQUER BOXES with Gold Flowers	$475.00	+ Very Fine OLD JAPANESE Gold LACQUER BOX with Cranes +	$80.00
SUPERB art deco JAPANESE SILVER SNUFF BOX KOI FISH 1920	$463.00	Antique Handpainted Japanese Imari Plate 12"	$80.00
AWESOME Japanese Kutani Meiji Figural Box Vase Enameled	$449.00	RARE 1800's COVERED BOX - EDO PERIOD - SATSUMA	$80.00
MAGNIFICENT LARGE JAPANESE MEIJI PERIOD IMARI BOWL.	$446.99	RARE JAPANESE IMARI BOWL, LATE EDO PERIOD, CIRCA 1850.	$80.00
Fine Antique Pair Japanese Imari Black Ship Bowls 10"	$395.00	1916: 5-set Japanese Teacup. HAGI. Famous DEIKA SAKATA.	$80.00

Books, Manuscripts ▸ American

The average sales price in this subcategory is $82.88.

	HIGH		AVG
Rare Robert Frost" New Hampshire" Limited Autographed	$3,500.00	Modern Library / The Sun Also Rises / Ernest Hemingway	$103.50
1862 CIVIL WAR SOLDIER DIARY BATTLE CONTENT MI 4TH REG	$3,051.00	MAPPLETHORPE, Robert Biography UNCORRECTED PROOF	$100.00
BEACON COVER ART LOVES OF A GIRL WRESTLER 1960 LOOK	$2,225.00	1874 Bound Volume NEWSPAPERS Philadelphia PENNSYLVANIA	$99.99
SUPER RARE 1800s 1st TEXAS AUTOBIO JOURNALS CROCKETT	$2,017.00	TEXAS ANNEXATION TX Texan Western Americana 1844 RARE	$98.77
The works of John Locke.	$800.00	Richard Brautigan's " Willard & His Bowling Trophies"	$95.00
Authentic Civil War Diary Journal George W Miller 1863	$699.00	1776,Rev. War group of supply documents signed	$93.00
1767 ORIGINAL MANUSCRIPT AMERICAN REVENUE CHAS TOWNSEND	$650.00	1804 newspaper ALEXANDER HAMILTON killed in duel w Burr	$92.00
1860 Autographed Bible Belonging to Clement Clark Moore	$500.00	ANDREW JACKSON AUTHENTIC HAIR PRESIDENT BRAVE GENERAL	$92.00
MILITARY HISTORY Revolutionary War Army 1794 VERY RARE	$436.00	1873 NEWBURYPORT MAGIC GHOST WITCHES WHITCHCRAFT BOOK	$91.13
1960s BEAT POET BUKOWSKI SIGNED RARE ART PRINT BOOK 65!	$405.00	1757,John Harvey,Antigua.;letter to Thomas Greenough	$90.00
1900 PHOTO DOCUMENTRY LIFE OF SOUTHERN BLACK SLAVES	$390.00	RARE 1849 LIVES OUTLAWS & DESPERADOES TEXAS & SOUTHWEST	$89.99
Ca. 1832 Anti-Jackson Broadside from Portland, Maine	$382.00	VINTAGE 1869 NYC MANUAL 50 PRINTS MANY IN COLOR, 2 MAPS	$87.88
Puddnhead Wilson Those Extraordinary Twins Mark Twain	$362.89	Mark Twain Collectors!!!!	$87.66
Antique German Bible	$335.00	Oration 4th of July 1860 inscribed by Edward Everett	$87.00
RARE 1833 LEATHER AMERICANS GUIDE 2000 COPIES ONLY	$312.78	1874 Architect Manuscript HOUSE SPECIFICATION Lowell MA	$85.00

Books, Manuscripts ▸ European

The average sales price in this subcategory is $196.00.

	HIGH		AVG
1518 BREVIARIUM w/ BRASS CORNERS / POST INCUNABULA II	$5,001.00	Illuminated Manuscript Leaf, Gold Initial,c.1390	$222.50
1544 Dante, Marcolini edition, splendid engravings!	$5,000.00	BLAEU: SCOTLAND - HC – 1640	$220.27
INCUNABULA: Gerson: OPERA: 1494: Albrecht Durer Woodcut	$4,410.00	Classic on COMMERCE & TRADING Le parfait n?ciant 1742	$215.50
SUPERB INCUNABULA Rubricated throughout MYSTIC 1494	$4,371.00	1587: Three law books, bound together - folio edition	$214.50
INCUNABULA - de Ausmo PISANELL?& de Nevo CONSILIÁ 1479	$4,260.00	1514 very rare book printed at Ferrara Bigo coelestes	$214.50
Rare Easton Press 100 Greatest Books Ever Written Set	$3,383.33	ITALIAN, LATIN MANUSCRIPT, PERGAMENA MANOSCRITTO 1200	$212.50
ORIG.HANDWRITTEN MANUSCRIPT,CONVENT TRAUNKIRCHEN1460/80	$3,329.00	9 FINE ANTIQUE LEATHER BOUND BOOKS/ BOOK SET - NR	$207.50
Corpus of Canon Law Post post incunabula 1505 Church	$3,000.00	1761 MANUSCRIPT. SPANISH INFANTRY REGULATIONS	$203.50
#001 BRAUN HOGENBERG Original city view LONDON 1572	$2,750.00	1728 - HORACE - Antique Leather Book - LATIN - NR	$202.50
INCUNABULA Valore Missarum 1493 Knoblochtzer Heidelberg	$2,650.00	1698 RARE Swiss CLASSIC by KOENIG on ZOOLOGY	$202.50
1719 LEEWENHOEK Microscope Letters v. Rare 1st edition	$2,627.77	13th Century Bible Leaf, GOSPEL of JOHN 8 - 10	$202.50
WAR AND PEACE, LEO TOLSTOY-1886*RARE FIRST EDITION	$2,550.00	Medieval Illumin. Vellum Leaf, Folio Bible, Grusch, ca1250	$202.50
1558 NEW TESTAMENT ILLUSTRATED w/ 107 WOODCUTS	$2,500.00	DIE REKLAME IHRE KUNSTUND WISSENSCHAFT 1914	$200.00
RARE INCUNABLE, BONAVENTURA, FOLIO,1500	$2,025.00	Bible - Biblia - German - Very Old – Large	$200.00
Boris Pasternak DOCTOR ZHIVAGO first edition in Russian	$1,689.00	9 FINE ANTIQUE LEATHER BOUND BOOKS/ BOOK SET - NR	$200.00

Decorative Arts ▸ Ceramics, Porcelain

The average sales price in this subcategory is $139.10.

	HIGH		AVG
Magnificent Meissen Centerpiece-NO RESERVE	$2,950.00	ENGLISH MAJOLICA BEGONIA LEAF TRAY, circa 1870	$170.17
EARLY 19TH C. PORCELAIN WORCESTER SPODE DERBY PLATE	$2,325.00	BEAUTIFUL SET OF ORIGINAL MEISSEN CHERUB CANDLESTICKS	$164.50
MUSEUM QUALITY BOCH KERAMIS CATTEAU ART DECO VASE #1	$1,950.00	A Set of 5 Chinese Cups 18th C. Kang-xi	$162.50
MUSEUM QUALITY BOCH KERAMIS CATTEAU ART DECO VASE #6	$1,776.00	RARE Beautiful Mason's American Marine china 8 pieces	$159.30
WEMYSS PIG	$1,640.09	Beautiful Red & Green Adams Staffordshire Cup Plate,	$157.50
FIGURAL sarreguemines MAN MAKING WINE, 3 pc set AMAZING	$1,625.00	White Ironstone 11 7/8" Cake Plate	$157.50
MUSEUM QUALITY BOCH KERAMIS CATTEAU ART DECO VASE #3	$1,525.00	MUSEUM ALERT A ONE OF A KIND ROSEVILLE FRUIT BOWL	$153.50
FINE C1920 WEDGWOOD CRIMSON JASPER DIP PITCHER / JUG	$1,525.00	A Superb Dutch Delft Tile Biblical 18th C. Text	$152.50
JACOB PETIT Old Paris Porcelain PAIR OF PITCHERS SIGNED	$1,490.00	Rare Porcelain of Paris Book by de Guillebon ~ Vase Urn	$152.50
porcelain painting antique signed art KPM ?	$1,458.00	Sargadelos JOAN MIRO Abstract Porcelain Sculpture	$152.49
PAIR Meissen Figurine Figural Sweetmeat Salt c.1890	$1,200.00	1800s REGIMENTAL PORCELAIN PIPE BOWL PORTRAIT MILITARY	$152.30
RARE FANTONI ANIMAL VESSEL,,gamboni italian	$1,005.00	Delft tile with bird, 17th century	$150.00
WEDGWOOD TRICOLOR JASPER BISCUIT BARREL	$985.00	SHAW TEA LEAF IRONSTONE BUTTER DISH & DRAINER C 1880	$149.49
1887 Wedgwood Calendar Tile	$891.00	BEAUTIFUL OLD ORIGINAL MEISSEN PORCELAIN FRUITBOWL	$149.00
S&V SCHAFER & VATER LARGE DECANTER FLASK " PROSIT "	$861.01	Staff. Pearlware Brown Transfer Set 8 Handless C/Ss-NR	$141.50

Decorative Arts ▸ Glass

The average sales price in this subcategory is $64.33.

	HIGH		AVG
Wavecrest Wall Plaque	$3,800.00	5 PIECES VINTAGE HALL AUTUMN LEAF JEWEL TEA NICE	$76.00
Frosted Glass Art Powder Box by Lalique	$1,645.00	HP Czechoslovakia Reverse Painted Ball Liquor Set LQQK	$75.00
ca1890 Mercury Glass Super Rare 8 Light Chandelier	$1,225.00	Fenton # 5158 BA Blue Satin Elephant ~~ EXCEPTIONAL ~~	$75.00
Cranberry Glass Bell w/ White Looping Wedding Bell	$665.00	Aqua South Jersey Lily - Pad Pitcher	$75.00
7 piece CRANBERRY epergne & metal base	$500.00	FLINT GLASS PILLAR MOLDED BAR BOTTLE c.1860	$73.00
Wavecrest Hinged Egg Crate Box~Hand Painted	$481.00	TS Victorian Moser Cobalt Cabochon Pin Tray!	$71.99
Beautiful Wavecrest Mt. Washington Cigar box 9" diag.	$455.99	OLD CRANBERRY GLASS BOWL FLUTED EDGE RIGAREE FEET	$70.97
Early Small Blown Flint Glass Whale Oil Lamp w/Burner	$380.35	Gorgeous Antique Mantel Luster With Prisms Flowers	$69.99
Exquisite Cranberry Glass Lustres Lusters W/Prisms	$364.09	VINTAGE~ AEROLUX *RARE* LIGHT BULB RED ROSE *LQQK!!!	$68.50
ANTIQUE CZECH MANTEL LUSTRES\LUSTERS ELECTRIC"GORGEOUS!	$339.00	VINTAGE JEWELRY CASKET w/ORMOLU & FLUER DE LIS PRONGS	$67.00
TS Victorian Mt. Washington Coralene Rose Bowl!	$331.52	TS Victorian Vaseline High Top Shoe Perfume Holder!	$66.00
Vintage Murano Green Glass Venetian Picture Frame NICE!	$330.00	1950s STEUBEN Signed Art Glass ASHTRAY	$66.00
ANTIQUE VICTORIAN PAIR MATCHED MANTLE COBALT LUSTERS	$326.00	Rare Hazel Atlas Cocktail Tumbler & Shaker Set Barware	$65.99
A Dutch/English Wine-Bottle Onion 17th C.	$275.00	Silhouette Picture - Curved glass front - late 1800's	$65.00
Serene Portrait Stained Glass	$265.00	EAPG Antique Victorian Cranberry Glass Pair Shakers	$64.51

Decorative Arts ▶ Metalware

The average sales price in this subcategory is $84.37.

	HIGH		AVG
RARE HARRY BERTOIA FIGURAL SCULPTURES	$3,050.00	1920's Art Deco Nude Lady Frankart ? Card Holder	$99.99
Beautiful Antique Art Nouveau Deco Sculpture Woman GR @	$1,785.00	STUNNING ARTIST SIGNED WHITE METAL BUST	$99.95
Art Nouveau Jardiniere WMF Quality	$1,150.00	ANTIQUE HAND CHASED TEA CADDY BOX HUNT SCENE	$99.00
Gorgeous Art Deco Frankart Type Vase w/nudes, NR!	$1,142.00	ART DECO GERMAN SHEPHERD DOG STATUE. SIGNED. 20S. RARE.	$99.00
1930 art deco LE VERRIER Book ends pair Bronze like	$899.00	Pair 18 3/4" Bradley and Hubbard Cast Candlesticks B&H	$96.99
FRENCH ENAMEL STERLING BOX (c. 1910) WITH ORIG. BOX	$860.00	russian constructivist avantgarde vase	$95.00
RARE FRANKART DECO FIGURAL NUDE FISH BOWL AQUARIUM	$850.00	ANTIQUE WHITE METAL RARE LION FIGURE STATUE	$93.25
RELIQUARY MONSTRANCE SAINT ANTHONY RELIC HOLDER 1785	$787.00	Metal Statue of Female 8 ? in. Tall	$91.99
Arne Jacobsen Cylinda Line Stelton Set 7 Retro Modern	$785.99	Frankart Owl bookends 1920's	$89.84
FRANKART ART DECO BOOKEND NYMPH SYLPH PAIR SIGNED NR	$618.00	Vintage Art Nouveau Women Bookend Busts L'Hiver	$89.09
Curtis Jere "Raindrops" Chrome Sculpture - eames era	$588.85	End Of The Trail Brozned/Enameled/Cast Iron Bookends	$89.00
Antique - Vancouver Breweries Limited Tray - RARE!	$515.05	Art Deco Semi Nude Lady Metal Figurine Statue Greist	$89.00
20s-30s deco cocktail shaker,glasses,bullet shaped	$492.87	FRANKART STYLE ART DECO NUDE CANDLESTICKS 1984	$89.00
KRENIT METAL FINE ART BOWL DANISH MODERN EAMES ERA see.	$480.00	BEAUTIFUL LARGE ART NOUVEAU CASKET JEWEL BOX!!	$86.00
Frankart Art Deco Nude Sculpture Candlestick Pair 1920	$475.00	Old French Vantines Incense Burner Lamp Complete	$86.00

Decorative Arts ▶ Woodenware

The average sales price in this subcategory is $70.50.

	HIGH		AVG
walnut carved eagle 1890 Brienz	$2,225.00	3 black forest carved wood antler mounts 1900-1920	$89.00
2 antique black forest carved wood ram head shelves	$1,407.77	ANTIQUE TREEN FERN LEAF CARVED BUTTER STAMP	$88.76
Chandelier Black forest hanging antlers light VINTAGE!!	$700.00	Swiss Black Forest Bear w/ Copper Bowl from Brienz	$88.00
Marked Black forest Eagle Inkwell detailed carving	$665.00	black forest wood target color print munich maid 1931	$87.00
2 antique black forest hunting plaques painted in oil	$636.77	Antique Oak Barley Twist Candlesticks	$85.00
Hippo Kay Bojesen danish design	$621.00	MINT ! Black forest Bear thermometer	$82.00
Large Antique Black Forest Lamp Quail Partridge Bird	$510.01	Old SOUVENIR MAUCHLINE WARE Napkin Ring & Trinket Box	$81.00
GREAT wood carved BLACK FOREST CUCKOO CLOCK at 1880	$510.00	2 OLD WOOD ARCHITECTURAL CARVINGS OF MAIDENS RARE 1900S	$76.00
carved Bear Tabacco-jar 1912	$510.00	MERGANSER DUCK DECOY by CHET LANGAN A+A+A+A+A+A+A+A+	$76.00
BEAUTIFUL ARMOIR STYLE EMPIRE NEW	$455.00	LARGE witco by westenhaver Garden Post TIKI Eames Era	$76.00
Oak Ice Box	$450.00	ANTIQUE TREEN BELL BUTTER MOLD STAMP STRAWBERRIES	$76.00
Fine period Bilston Battersea Enameled Box	$450.00	LARGE witco by westenhaver sword TIKI rare eames era	$75.00
Wildboar carved at Brienz	$425.00	Huge Victorian Turned Cocobolo Treen Urn	$75.00
18th C. Wooden candlestick with angelheads	$425.00	8 PC Miniature Carved Wood Marching Band Figures-Anri??	$72.05
Swiss Brienz Black Forest Platter GRINDELWALD Painting	$421.00	ANTIQUE BLACK FOREST WOOD BEAR INKER	$71.00

Ethnographic ▶ African

The average sales price this subcategory is $64.66.

	HIGH		AVG
Massive Yoruba BEADED Vest TUNIC African Art w/ Wear NR	$787.52	LWENA - AFRICAN CEREMONIAL DRUM - ANGOLA # 3791	$69.99
BAULE TREASURE POT - 3 PIECES	$650.00	CHOKWE - AFRICAN BOWL WITH COVER - ANGOLA # 3942	$69.99
Ethiopian Headrest - Boni	$560.00	LUBA - CALABASH WATER CONTAINER - CONGO # 4359	$69.99
GothamGallery Beautiful Ghana Asante Akuaba Doll	$395.00	Awesome African Bow,Arrows & Quiver-Authentic	$69.90
1936 primitive African tribal music 78 rpm record x6	$356.52	HAND FULL OF OLD KATANGA H-CROSSES CURRENCY	$69.75
#1 BEAUTIFUL ANTIQUE IVORY BRACELET-IFE, NIGERIA	$350.00	BEST BOOK THROWING KNIFE Weapon African Art Congo Gabon	$69.00
MUSEUM QUALITY ANTIQUE AFRICAN SLAVE TRADE SWORD	$340.00	Fantastic African Ebony Head - Kenya - FREE SHIPPING	$69.00
GothamGallery Magnificent Gabon Fang Judicial Ngil Mask	$326.00	Fine Older African Bwa Hawk Mask - 39" Wide	$69.00
Ethiopian Headrest - Boni	$319.00	Impressive African Dan Mask - Liberia - Abundant Dreads	$68.99
VERY ANCIENT AFRICAN MASK	$300.00	GothamGallery Fine-North Nguni KnobKerrie Tribal Weapon	$66.35
SUPERB ANTIQUE DYAK CANOE PADDLE	$290.00	Excellent old Yombe Fetish - The Best	$65.00
Rare Fang Carving - Bound Male Figure on Bed	$280.00	VINTAGE 1944 NEW GUINEA AFRICAN HUNT BOW & 3 ARROW LOT	$65.00
Boy prepared for the Circonstion ceremonies signed	$261.11	LOZI POT - OLD	$65.00
GothamGallery Superb Gabon Fang Byeri Reliquary Figure	$260.00	DOGON EQUESTRIAN METAL HAIRPIN * OLD	$65.00
Starkies Mechanical Bank Reg. #844290	$256.00	A pair off 19th Century Bronze Tribel African Bowls	$64.26

Ethnographic ▶ Native American

The average sales price in this subcategory is $123.86.

	HIGH		AVG
Large, 19th C. Apache Figural Polychrome Olla	$3,050.00	FINE NORTHWEST COAST HAIDA INDIAN LARGE SILVER PENDANT	$140.00
Large Antique Graphic Apache Indian Basket	$2,480.96	Vintage HOPI Indian KACHINA doll, WOLF Kweo c. 1940's	$137.50
Fine Nez Perce Cornhusk Bag, Large	$1,902.70	HUGE MUSEUM GRADE ESKIMO "WOMANS KNIFE" BLADE,	$134.05
Large Antique Figural Beaded Indian Plateau Bag	$1,625.00	Native American Indian Old Artifacts Arrowheads / Tools	$132.50
Fine and large Nez Perce Cornhusk Bag, Compex Design	$1,610.00	NATIVE AMERICAN INDIAN ARTIFACT ANTIQUE CALI BASKET!	$132.50
Large Antique Apache Indian Basket NICE!	$1,511.00	INDIAN ARTIFACTS COLLECTION 125+ ARROWHEADS 4.5 POUNDS	$131.53
Northwest Coast Killer Whale Totem Pole - NICE PAINT	$1,225.00	Old Native American Pocket Mirror Beaded Arround	$130.49
Giant SKOOKUM DOLL Indian WOMAN 34 in. RARE!	$999.00	Native American Indian Rare Old Soap Stone Oil Lamp	$129.00
Old Plains Sioux Beaded Moccasins	$960.00	Native American Indian Old Alaska Totem Silver Spoon	$129.00
GORGEOUS 1890's Large Navajo Hand Woven Rug	$935.99	Early INDIAN Made SNOWSHOES w/ POMPOMS RARE BEAUTIES!	$129.00
Northwest Coast Argillite Stone Carving - Haida?	$911.99	Native American Indian Old Antique Beaded Pouch 1890	$127.50
Old Unusual Plains Beaded Moccasins with Beaded Strap	$910.00	LOST LAKE,MISSOURI FLINT,FOUND IN STODDARD CO.MO.NR	$127.50
Native American Indian Huge Stone Hohokam Axe Artifact	$899.00	1903, 1941,1944 Books, Art Prints, Photos free shipping	$126.86
Antique Polychrome Native American Indian Basket	$898.00	FULL GROOVED HEMATITE AXE	$125.00
2 Fine CATLINITE EFFIGY PIPES Brass-Tacked Stem *NR*	$866.00	NAVAJO SILVER ASHTRAY, 1920s-40s, NR	$125.00

Furniture ▸ Beds

The average sales price in this subcategory is $542.97.

	HIGH		AVG
Incredible American Renaissance Bedroom Set c1875	$15,999.00	Beautiful Mahogany Rococo Bed	$700.00
1870-80s 3 PC MARBLE TOP VICTORIAN WALNUT BEDROOM SET	$6,925.00	ANTIQUE EMPIRE MAHOGANY KING SIZE BED BEDROOM SET FGTY	$677.00
Antique Furniture Magnificent 5' Knight/Lady 4PosterBed	$3,795.00	3 PIECE BEDROOM SET REFINISHED ANTIQUE***NR	$675.00
Sweet Decorated Victorian Cottage Bedroom Set~1890	$3,550.00	EXQUISITE PAINTED FRENCH BED CHIC - SHABBY	$661.01
NICE CHIPPENDALE ITALIAN BEDROOM SET	$3,500.00	2 DIE 4 INCREDIBLE EASTLAKE BED!!	$650.00
FANCY WALNUT VICTORIAN EASTLAKE BED Ca. 1890s's	$3,250.00	EXQUISITE ART NOUVEAU BED FRAME EARLY 1900s NR FRENCH	$616.00
Antique Carved Wood 4 poster King Bed w/ Nightstand set	$3,200.00	Antique Italian Wrap-Around BED Queen King Size Glamour	$605.00
Antique Victorian 3 pc. Walnut Marble Top Bedroom Set	$2,850.00	Incredible 1920s 3 Pc Burl Walnut Inlay Bedroom Set	$599.99
Danish Modern King Teak Floating Platform Bed Eames Era	$2,700.00	Pair Pennsylvania House Solid Cherry Twin Beds c1950's	$595.00
George II Four Post 4 Poster Canopy King or Queen Bed	$2,499.00	Pair Mahogany Sleigh Style Twin Beds John Stuart c1940s	$595.00
ORNATE 3PC VICTORIAN OAK BEDROOM SET HIGHBACK BED	$2,400.00	EXQUISITE BAROQUE ROCOCO CARVED MAHOGANY TWIN SIZE BED!	$585.00
ETHAN ALLEN CHERRY GEORGIAN COURT KING POSTER POSTS BED	$2,325.00	Antique French Carved Oak BED Queen Size, Full ROSES!	$570.00
FANTASTIC CARVED WALNUT BOMBE QUEEN BED FRAME	$2,276.00	Antique ART DECO 4 PC CARVED BEDROOM SET ARMOIRE NO RES	$560.00
FINE ETHAN ALLEN MAPLE BEDROOM SET 4 PC SUITE	$2,155.00	RARE ITALIAN VICTORIAN ROSES MAHOGANY CARVED TWIN BED !	$560.00
Rare & Romantic Victorian Brass and Iron Canopy Bed	$1,850.00	DANISH MODERN TEAK QUEEN BED W/ NIGHTSTANDS~ EAMES ERA!	$560.00

Furniture ▸ Cabinets, Armoires, Cupboards

The average sales price in this subcategory is $630.39.

NOTE *The very high prices on the high end in this subcategory skewed the average a bit so that there are many more prices below the average price than above it.*

	HIGH		AVG
Magnificent French Country Armoire circa 1850	$5,600.00	Hoosier Cabinet	$800.00
GREAT CARVED GRIFFIN SIDEBOARD	$5,500.00	Antique Victorian Buffet Hutch	$700.00
NICE CARVED MAN OF THE MOUNTAIN VITRINE	$4,750.00	Antique pie safe	$685.00
GREAT CARVED WALNUT ANTIQUE BOOKCASE VITRINE	$4,500.00	18thC Antique Spanish Box/Cabinet on Stand vargueno	$650.00
GREAT ANTIQUE CARVED OAK HUNT & STAINED GLASS CABINET	$4,250.00	19th C. ANTIQUE IRISH SIDEBOARD BUFFET DRESSER BAR	$611.00
A rosewood, ebonised and ivory inlaid cabinet, Italy	$3,958.00	Circa 1890 Diamond Dye Court Jester Cabinet	$605.00
c1820 Regency Mahogany Compendium Wardrobe / Armoire	$3,505.00	Antique Vintage Victorian Italian Walnut Server Buffet	$600.00
GORGEOUS CARVED OAK RENAISSANCE CABINET:26 CARVED FACES	$3,250.00	Ornate Carved 1800's Mirrored Hutch Bar Sideboard	$598.95
RARE Walnut Plantation Desk! Never seen another like it	$3,200.00	1850s Tennessee CHERRY JELLY CUPBOARD w/Turned Legs nr!	$596.00
FREE SHIP~LATE 1800's SOLID WALNUT STEP BACK CUPBOARD	$2,999.99	Armoire / Wardrobe - French Country Style Antique	$573.51
Antique Mahogany Bar	$2,500.00	RARE ANTIQUE LOUIS PHILIPPE ROSEWOOD MIRROR ARMOIRE !!!	$565.00
Biedermeier Armoire 1835	$2,500.00	Antique Furniture 8025 walnut side board sideboard	$558.00
SUMPTUOUS FRENCH EMPIRE BURL WALNUT MARBLE TOP BUFFET	$2,395.00	FABULOUS! QUARTERSAWN OAK BUFFET SIDEBOARD	$546.00
SCHOOL TABLE COMPAS TO JEAN PROUVE	$2,350.00	UNIQUE VICTORIAN ETAGERE with BEAUTIFUL BEVELED MIRROR	$511.00
Huge Antique Chippendale Burl Walnut Sideboard	$2,326.00	Antique Rosewood Hand Carved China Bookshelf Cabinet	$510.01

Maps, Atlases, Globes ▸ Maps, Atlases

The average sales price in this subcategory is $38.24.

NOTE *The very high prices on the high end in this subcategory and the relatively small number of auctions skewed the average so that there are many more prices below the average price than above it.*

	HIGH		AVG
The British Colonies by R. M. Martin and John Tallis	$1,525.00	1783 STEREOGRAPHIC WORLD MAP ORIGINAL ANTIQUE MAP	$49.99
JOHNSON'S WORLD ATLAS 1867 ANTIQUE MAPS RARE	$613.00	Rare Early German Handheld Astronomy Glass Planetarium	$48.99
1742 DOPPELMAYR Celestial Chart Constellation Figures!	$564.99	PURPLE LAPIS GEMSTONE GLOBE 330mm GOLD LASER LINE 37"	$48.95
1839 Julius Lẹwenberg large Folio Atlas +++RARE+++	$529.00	BLUE LAPIS GEMSTONE GLOBE 330mm COPPER LASER LINE 37"	$48.95
1783 Holy Bible w/6 Sacred PULL-OUT Topographical Maps	$499.99	#1807 rare Twin-Hemisphere Map of the World by Barlow	$46.00
VINTAGE WORLD MAP~Tooled LEATHER & WOOD Wall Decor ART~	$436.46	1875 HUGE ATLAS FOLIO Swinton RARE Illustrated NR	$44.75
1748 Le Rouge Map of WORLD in HEMISPHERES * NO RESERVE!	$360.00	SDUK Map Rivers of the World Dated 1834 Antique Orig	$41.00
1730 Map South Hemisphere S. America Australia Pacific	$350.66	Penobscot Bay Region Decorative Map	$37.00
Hẹsphẹ Occidental, De L'Isle / Buache, Paris 1760	$322.50	NEW GREEN QUARTZ 3" GEMSTONE GLOBE PAPERWEIGHT NEW	$32.95
Map of World 1839	$299.00	1854 FINDLAYS CLASSICAL ATLAS Hand Colored Maps	$31.01
Folio Rocque Map North Ireland Eire c1780 NiceCartouche	$262.00	Tallis Map of 1851-Tex.,Mex.,Calif.-Giclee on Canvas	$30.99
Anville Kitchin Wall Map Britain Ireland Poland 1794	$181.50	LOT OF 2 STEIFF TIGERS- SMALL AND LARGE! NO RESERVE!	$30.88
CENTURY ATLAS Complete with Fabulous maps	$158.05	Map of the Holy Land in Hebrew	$29.99
1782 WORLD IN HEMISPHERES ORIGINAL ANTIQUE MAP	$156.50	HUGE VINTAGE WORLD MAP PANORAMIC ART POSTER AIR FRANCE	$29.99
1851 Tallis Map of WORLD on MERCATORS * HAND COLOURED!	$149.99	Virginia John Smith Huge Map 1624	$29.95

Maritime ▸ Sextants

The average sales price in this subcategory is $150.57.

	HIGH		AVG
18th C - 1760 American Backstaff - King, Rhode Island	$6,700.00	Sextant by Spencer, Browning and Co., London	$189.50
AN-5851-1 Eclipse Pioneer sextant	$1,299.00	Sextant by Simex	$187.50
RARE EARLY ENGLISH SEXTANT	$627.00	WWII U.S. Navy B.U. Ships Stadimeter w/mahogoney box	$185.00
C. PLATH NAVISTAR PROFESSIONAL SEXTANT 5 STARS GUARANTY	$600.00	Sextant by Tamaya	$180.50
Octant, Brass. Marked "Depose G.F"	$587.00	8" Working Nautical Brass Micrometer Sextant In Box	$179.50
TAMAYA SEXTANT, AUTHENTIC, 1976	$525.00	Sextant, Surveyors by Tamaya	$177.50
Sextant, by The Forth Scientific Instrument Co., Leith	$521.11	WWII Bausch & Lomb Naval Sextant NR	$175.00

	HIGH		AVG
Circa 1825 OCTANT Brass Ivory Ebony, Elegant Instrument	$512.37	1942 Stadimeter Maritime Commission-Schick, Inc.Sextant	$170.39
Antique British Sextant w/ case Heath & Co. Cert 1914	$503.00	Link A-12 Sextant	$162.50
TAMAYA "JUPITER" (MS-833) SEXTANT	$500.00	RARE SOVIET CCCP USSR NAVY SEXTANT SNO-T IN BOX 1977	$159.00
ASTRA IIIB SEXTANT WITH ACCESSORIES	$500.00	RARE SOVIET CCCP GLOBE OF STAR SKY IN WOODEN BOX 1976	$157.50
Sextant by Cameron & Blakency (sp) Glasgow & Sunderland	$470.00	tamaya sextant authentic no583	$157.50
8 BILLION DEAD ANTS	$450.00	Davis Mark 25 Master Sextant	$154.48
ANTIQUE FRENCH VEDY Fⁱx BRASS SEXTANT	$450.00	Antique Fuji Sextant in Original Wood Box w Paper	$152.50
Tamaya Jupiter Sextant	$440.00	WWII US NAVY SEXTANT David White 1943 in WOOD CASE	$152.50

Maritime ▸ Anchors

The average sales price in this subcategory is $64.77.

	HIGH		AVG
MARITIME ANTIQUE SHIPS ANCHOR	$1,100.00	ANTIQUE IRON ANCHOR 16"LG X 16" W X 10 3/4. 5LBS NICE	$80.62
Antique 18th Cen. 1700s Iron Nautical Anchor, NR, RARE!	$400.00	Old Boat Anchor	$76.00
19th Cent Iron Anchor from Maine, hand wrought?	$156.05	LARGE SHIP'S ANCHOR, NAUTICAL, MARITIME, BOAT>	$66.00
Old Boat or Ship Anchor - 20lb.	$103.51	VINTAGE ANTIQUE BRASS ANCHOR 12LBS with STAND "NICE"	$61.09
18th-19th Cent Iron Anchor from Maine hand wrought 44"	$100.00	LARGE SHIP'S ANCHOR, NAUTICAL, MARITIME, BOAT>	$61.00
Small Brass Anchor Pat'd 1899 Salesman Sample?	$99.00	OLD UNIVERSITY OF WASHINGTON HUSKY BOAT ANCHOR *20 LBS.	$49.00

Musical Instruments ▸ Keyboard

The average sales price in this subcategory is $319.25.

	HIGH		AVG
1892 Steinway Piano Model A	$8,000.00	Original Ernst Birnstock Concertina Bandoneon	$510.00
1920s NELSON WIGGIN COIN OP NICKELODEON 5 INSTRUMENTS	$7,100.00	Antique Tournaphone Roller Organ	$483.00
9ft Chickering Grand Piano /antique carvings/Rosewood**	$6,499.00	RARE c1840 CHILDS HARMONIUM PUMP ORGAN IN ROSEWOOD CASE	$479.00
Circus Calliope band organ music box piano	$4,300.00	Melville & Clark Player Piano	$410.05
Waltham Ornate Antique Baby Grand Piano	$3,350.00	1800s? B. Shoninger-New Haven CT Pump Organ- NR	$405.00
Mission Oak Upright Piano C1910 FINAL REDUCTION	$3,200.00	Antique Melodian c. 1860	$399.99
Sohmer Grand Piano, handmade by Sohmer Bros in 1885!	$3,000.00	Bandoneon Sch?nherr & Matthes Bandonion	$368.00
FINEST VICTORIAN HAND PAINTED VICTORIAN PUMP ORGAN *	$2,850.00	UNIQUE MASON & HAMLIN MODEL GOLDEN OAK PUMP ORGAN-NR!	$355.99
1929 Christman 5 Feet Studio Baby Grand Piano! BestDeal	$2,400.00	Lovely Carved Antique Upright PIANO & Bench~Ludwig & Co	$350.00
1901 CHICKERING CONCERT GRAND PIANO 7' 6" VERY RARE	$1,599.00	Antique Player Piano - VERY Rare Tiger Oak Cabinet	$308.97
ANTIQUE SQUARE GRAND PIANO NO RESERVE	$1,580.00	VINTAGE Hammond Organ^^Vacuum Tube Type^^	$305.00
Antique 1908 Wing&Son Concert upright Grand Piano NICE	$1,325.00	Antique Piano in Good Condition	$300.00
Antique Handpainted Square Grand Piano - NO RESERVE	$1,222.99	Hohner Accordeon [Concertina]	$290.00
FENDER RHODES EIGHTY EIGHT 88 KEYS ELECTRIC PIANO	$1,025.00	original –M & H– Bandoneon Bandonion	$290.00
Vox Continental Vintage Combo Organ Works 100% N/R WOW!	$825.00	Flute. The end of 19 centuries. France.	$260.00

Musical Instruments ▸ String

The average sales price in this subcategory is $226.74.

	HIGH		AVG
Rare 1935 Martin F-7 #609XX - No Reserve	$4,750.00	ANTIQUE BERINI FRENCH VIOLIN W/ORIGINAL BOW ++	$256.00
Romantic Guitar by Panormo London 1850s	$3,200.00	1960s Silvertone Harmony Solidbody Electric Guitar	$255.00
Rare Vintage Gibson 1956 Country Western	$2,584.00	1900 SPRUCE WOOD STUDENT VIOLINCELLO	$255.00
1954 Les Paul Antique guitar**restoration project**	$2,550.00	Stella Harmony 12 String Guitar - BLUESY W/GREAT NECK	$255.00
Antique alte old LYRE guitar gitarre	$2,111.00	VAUILLAUME VIOLIN BOW	$255.00
Gibson S. S. Stewart Banjo	$2,014.89	2 Univox Les Paul Copy Lawsuit Vintage Black Beauty	$252.42
MARTIN UKALEILE	$1,680.00	19th-Century Cittern or Waldzither, 5-course guitar	$250.00
4/4 violin with label "N. Gusetto Cremona 1786" !!!!!!	$1,675.00	HOPF VIOLIN	$250.00
1853 Ashborn Parlor Guitar (Brazilian Rosewood) NR!	$1,624.00	3/4 Violin - excellent condition- 30+ years old	$250.00
Complete Viola Outfit!!!	$1,500.00	Vintage Antique Kay Archtop like Regal or Harmony	$249.00
Rare Antique Kamaka Pineapple Ukulele	$1,500.00	Vintage Roland G707 G-707 MIDI Guitar Electric	$233.59
1928 Eugen Meinel Violin	$1,500.00	Antique Jacobus Stainer Violin In Box Vintage Germany	$232.51
Italian Mandolin by De Cristofaro, Napoli 1900s	$1,400.00	Fine Old VIOLIN Copie JIOVAN PAOLO MAGINI BRESCIA 1715	$231.49
Vega Whyte Laydie Model R 5 String Banjo w/case	$1,395.00	Vintage 1960's Bacon 5-String Banjo "Folk Model"	$229.00
A VERY BEAUTIFUL OLD ESTATE VIOLIN	$1,375.00	vintage rickenbacher electro with matching amp and case	$227.50

Rugs, Carpets ▸ Large (9x7–9x12)

The average sales price in this subcategory is $202.54.

	HIGH		AVG
9x12 ANTIQUE 1890S PERSIAN MAHAL ORIENTAL RUG NR CARPET	$2,550.00	ANTIQUE BIDJAR 7x10 PERSIAN RUGS PH56 free shipping	$230.27
Gorgouse Persian Rug Silk Naein 8x11N/R	$1,650.00	Stunning Large Persian Kashan Rug 10x7	$230.00
11x11 Ghombad Design Chinese Silk 100% Rug Square 3143	$1,449.00	NAVY BLUE WOOL CHINESE 8x11 oriental area rug CARPET	$230.00
ECG PERSIAN 8'1"x11'0" TABRIZ 140 kpsi RUG	$1,275.05	BEAUTIFUL ANTIQUE ESTATE TURKISH SIVAS CARPET_ALLOVER	$228.76
7x11 FINE PERSIAN WOOL&SILK TABRIZ RUG*FREE PAD	$1,150.00	Stunning Large Persian Kashan Rug 10x7	$227.50
SIGNED Tabriz Handmade Oriental Persian Carpets - Rugs	$995.00	WONDERFUL! 9'7x7'10 GORAVAN PERSIAN RUGS CARPETS P-1421	$227.50
MIDNIGHT BLUE FRENCH AUBUSSON WEAVE RUG 9 X 12 RARE	$960.00	<-> ANTIQUE SAROUK 7x10 PERSIAN RUGS PC46 free shipping	$220.09
9x12 Genuine Bird of Paradise Whittall Wool Wilton Rug	$950.00	ANTIQUE IVORY HERIZ RUG 295x200 cm 6,6x9,7 ft	$220.00
Grand S.Antique Veg Dyed Armenian Kazak Rug 10 x 7	$910.00	Antique 11'1X8'0 Sabzevar Persian Rugs Carpets R-4362	$212.50
LIGHT BEIGE PINK FRENCH AUBUSSON WEAVE RUG 10 X 14	$910.00	Rare Vegetable Caucasian Kazak Large Rug 10x6	$209.50
10'ROUND SIGNED OUSHAK DESIGN ORIENTAL RUG NR CARPET	$850.00	2.3 x 11.9 Genuine Whittall Bird of Paradise Wilton Rug	$205.01
Pottery Barn Sunita 9x12 Rug, NEW & GORGEOUS!!	$780.01	Square 9'11X9'7 Mashad Persian Rugs Carpets R-779	$203.61
Rare Vegetable Afghan Chobi Large Rug 11x8	$617.55	OVERSIZED TURKOMAN 9X13 WOOL ON WOOL N/R (H207)	$202.50
Rare Vegetable Afghan Chobi Large Rug 12x9	$611.00	Signed Large Persian Kashan Rug 10x7	$202.50
Impressive 12'8x9'7 MASHAD PERSIAN RUGS CARPETS R-3963	$579.00	Stunning Large Persian Tabriz Rug 11x9	$202.50

Rugs, Carpets ▶ Medium (4x2–9x6)

The average sales price in this subcategory is $86.19.

	HIGH		AVG
19th C Facharlo Kazak Caucasian Rug. Fjaa	$2,700.00	ANTIQUE!!! 6'7x4'4 HERIZ PERSIAN RUGS CARPETS R-3777	$99.00
ANTIQUE CARPET WITH ARMENIAN "ZINANSHAN" EMBLEM 1918	$999.99	8X10 HANDTUFTED INDIA RUG BLACK&BURGUNDY	$99.00
Antique Outstanding Turkish Oushak Ushak Rug Size 6x8.4	$989.99	Antique Ghashghai, (qashqai)	$99.00
c1938 GRENFELL HUGE HOOKED RUG MAP of NEWFOUNDLAND #2	$811.01	S.Antique Afshar	$99.00
100% SILK PERSIAN ISFAHAN DESIGN HAND TIED RUG 4 X 6'8	$680.00	FREE SHIPPING HANDMADE 4X7 PERSIAN LILIHAN RUG	$99.00
Antique Beautiful Turkish Oushak Ushak Rug Size 4.3X6.8	$495.95	FREE SHIPPING PAIR OF ANTIQUE 2X3 TURKISH OUSHAK RUGS	$99.00
Karastan Rug...6.5 x 9 ft...Kirman Oriental Design..	$409.99	WOOL HUNTER ORIENTAL CARPET 6X8 PERSIAN AREA RUG CARVED	$95.89
NAVAJO RUG, VINTAGE-CRYSTAL 1890-1910	$405.00	IVORY 5X8 OVAL WOOL CHINESE AUBUSSON AREA RUG ORIENTAL	$95.00
8x8 CREAM ROUND TABRIZ DESIGN ORIENTAL RUG NR CARPET	$399.00	IVORY 5X8 WOOL ORIENTAL AUBUSSON AREA RUG HANDMADE SOFT	$95.00
Nice Pink Color @# Oriental Handknotted Silk Rug (6'	$369.99	Superb Veg Dyed S.Antique Uzbek kargai Rug 7 x 6	$93.60
4x10 ANTIQUE 1940 PERSIAN TABRIZ ORIENTAL RUG NR CARPET	$350.00	Antique mahal	$92.88
Antique Bakhtiar	$350.00	9.6X6.6 RSIZE C.1960 120KPSI PERSIAN JEWEL ISPAHAN RUG	$92.00
BEAUTIFUL ANTIQUE ERIVAN KARABAGH RUG__4x7	$320.00	Superb S.Antique Caucasian Sirki kargai Rug 7 x 4	$91.00
ESTATE ANTIQUE TURKISH OUSHAK RUG__SUBSTANTIAL	$306.00	Kashmir Silk & Wool Pile Cashmiri Rug 6x4	$89.88
HAND MADE SILK DECORE RUG ANTIQUE	$299.99	AMAZING! 9'9x4'11 BAKHTIAR PERSIAN RUGS CARPETS R-3171	$89.00

Science & Medicine ▶ Medical

The average sales price in this subcategory is $52.44.

	HIGH		AVG
Antique 1920 ELECTRIC LIGHTED EYE CHART /medical	$1,527.00	NIGHTMARISH! Rare FREAKS Old GRAPHIC PHOTO MEDICAL BOOK	$60.00
Civil War. US HOSP DEPT Bottle. RARE COLOR.	$711.50	COOPER'S FIRST LINE OF SURGERY. circa 1813	$60.00
post Civil War DOCTORS BAG/INSTRUMENTS/MEDS/SADDLE BAG	$610.00	THREE antique Violet Wand electrodes, European size	$59.99
REAL HUMAN SKULL, RARE, MIXED DENTITION	$600.00	VINTAGE HAND HELD OPTOMETRIST'S TRIAL LENS, OPTICAL	$58.00
Medical Device-Antique-Wood Case-Glass Cups?Hearing?	$535.00	ANTIQUE ATTRACTIVE SPHERICAL GREEN BOTTLE-MEDICAL? +B!	$57.99
OVER 100 Antique Medical & Surgical Instruments	$515.99	Antique Medical Sterilized Catgut Ligatures GLASS Tubes	$57.98
ANTIQUE OLD PHARMACY MEDICAL APOTHECARY PORCELAIN JAR	$499.00	1851 MEDICAL MIDWIFE MIDWIFERY FORCEPS USE LEATHER NR	$57.00
1899 DRUG STORE PHARMACY Book 5000 Recipes / Formulas	$405.00	180+YEAR OLD FOLDING SCALPEL	$57.00
Rare 1768 Materia Medica Pharmacy Medical Formulary!	$405.00	Display/descriptions sheet 46 Violet Ray Electrodes	$56.98
RARE ANTIQUE TRIAL LENS SET - OPTOMETRY NACHET & FILS	$400.00	rare blue poison bottle	$56.55
Antique Wax Portrait James Gregory M.D., Edinburgh U	$393.99	Antique VAPO-CRESOLENE Lamp Orig.Box, Bottle, Paper...	$56.00
E.RARE!1875 ANTIQUE MEDICAL INSTRUMENT-SPHYGMOMANOMETER	$390.00	VERY OLD ANTIQUE LEATHER MEDICINE BALL EXERCISE 1920'S	$54.51
Anesthesia Collin inhaler	$382.01	EARLY DOCTOR'S OFFICE GLASS NEEDLE AND PIN WASTE JAR	$54.50
Antique Oral Surgery Dental Instruments Wood Handles	$367.00	Antique Apothecary Jar Porcelain "Ung: Stirac:" Western	$53.99
White Cast Iron Dentist Chair 0571 Navy marked Antique	$365.00	Antique Medical Red Cross Boxed Aseptic Ligature CATGUT	$53.88

Silver ▶ Silverplate

The average sales price in this subcategory is $59.98.

	HIGH		AVG
Mint French Christofle Flatware Complete Set for 12	$2,000.00	WILCOX 2339 FLOWER-POT,SILVERPLATE.ART NOUVEAU	$76.90
BEAUTIFUL FIGURAL NAPKIN RING	$886.00	FAB SIGNED WMF ART NOUVEAU SILVERPLATE JEWEL CASKET	$76.00
Complete Victorian Silver Sewing Chatelaine * C1896	$785.00	LAKE PLACID CLUB NY NUTCRACKER NUT CRACKER ADIRONDACKS	$75.00
19th Century French Christofle Flatware for 5 Persons	$750.00	British Wood & Silver 2 Inkwell Inkstand - Excellent	$75.00
VICTORIAN SILVER NAPKIN RING-GIRLS SEATED	$586.30	Silver serving dome, elegant!	$71.01
RARE VICTORIAN CHERUB & BIRD SILVER MASTER SALT HOLDER	$565.99	Ca 1880 TUFTS ~SILVERPLATE~ART DECO~5 NUT DISHES	$71.00
Victorian AMBERINA Art Glass Bottles Castor Cruet Set	$560.00	Victorian Carved Pickle Castor Set Mary Gregory Insert	$69.99
Antique Toronto S.P. Cranberry Glass Pickle Castor	$430.99	7" PEARL NAUTILUS SEA SHELL Seashells Shells Seashell	$67.99
Antique Pickle Jar - Pressed Cranberry Glass - Fairies	$420.00	CRUET SET ANTIQUE ANTIQUES CASTOR	$67.01
BEAUTIFUL FIGURAL NAPKIN RING	$381.00	Antique Hvy Gorham AESTHETIC Silver Wine Bottle COASTER	$65.00
Marvelous WMF Art Nouveau Crystal Claret Jug C1890	$350.00	Antique c1900 SILVERPLATE INCENSE PERFUME Oil LAMP NR	$64.99
Antique Cobalt Brides Basket Bowl W/ Silver Stand *NR*	$348.00	ANTIQUE ENGRAVED SILVER PEDESTAL WINDUP CLOCK	$64.88
RARE Silverplate Napkin Ring - Cat w/ Glass Eyes / WOW!	$341.99	ROGERS BROS. TRIPLE PLATE SILVER BRIDE'S BASKET FRAME	$62.00
Rare Piedouche Thurible Censer Catholic Relic 19th C.	$330.00	ENGLISH SILVER COVERED DISH SUITE - CREST & NUMBERED	$61.50
GORGEOUS SILVER CRUET SET COMPLETE WITH BELL-MUST SEE!	$324.99	Pairpoint Aesthetic Silverplate Bowl - Spider Snail Vin	$61.00

Silver ▶ Sterling

The average sales price in this subcategory is $109.89.

	HIGH		AVG
BUCCELLATI SILVER. Irresistible unique piece.	$7,900.00	Fine English Hallmarked Sterling Silver Heart Ring Box	$124.27
ANTIQUE STERLING FIGURAL CORKSCREW/OPENER	$5,057.00	VINTAGE STERLING SILVER EARCLIPS GEORG JENSEN,NR!	$124.12
MECHANICAL CLOCK MALACHITE SILVER DIAMONDS - F. RUCKERT	$3,550.00	STUNNING 1889 ANTIQUE GORHAM REPOUSSE STERLING MIRROR	$124.00
Mint Condition 17th Century Seal Top Spoon	$1,675.00	#29 MINI SCROLLS & FLOWERS STERLING MATCH SAFE NR	$123.00
Cartier Sterling Silver with Lenox Porcelain Cup	$1,525.01	Vintage Sterling Vanity Set - Mirror, Brush, Comb, Exc.	$122.50
1886 GORHAM Sterling Repousse DOUBLE INKWELL- EXC! NR	$1,075.00	#18 ART NOUVEAU STERLING SILVER MATCH SAFE / HOLDER NR	$120.48
REPOUSSE BALTIMORE SILVER STERLING TEA CADDY A. JACOBI	$775.50	Vintage Sterling Tazza Scalloped Edge ? nr ? Estate	$120.00
Sterling KERR Art Nouveau Flask Nudes and Faces	$710.52	Sterling Corn Cob Holders	$115.50
ANTIQUE ENGLISH CHURCH SILVER TRAVELLING COMMUNION SET	$660.00	BEAUTIFUL STERLING SOVEREIGN CASE COIN HOLDER	$114.90
RARE STERLING SILVER COCONUT CUP BISLEY RIFLE PRIZE	$655.00	Cartier Sterling Silver Giraffe!!!	$113.50
LARGE ENGLISH STERLING SILVER TROPHY CUP FAT CATTLE	$562.00	#20 FLATWARE STYLE STERLING MATCH SAFE / HOLDER NR	$112.50
Antique sterling silver Tiffany makers tea caddy	$550.00	Antique Sterling Luggage Ticket BOSTON Fabulous Detail	$112.50
JUDAICA-ANTIQUE RUSSIAN SILVER WEDDING RING	$510.00	Duke of York sterling sardine fork Whiting	$112.49
VINTAGE GUCCI SILVER PICTURE PHOTO FRAME	$481.99	ANTIQUE STERLING SILVER DOUBLE SOVEREIGN CASE 1906	$111.38
Silver canteen of fish serving implements St.Petersburg	$450.00	Sterling Tiffany & Co. Art Deco Powder Compact	$110.50

Silver ▸ Sterling ▸ Flatware

The average sales price in this subcategory is $51.00.

	HIGH		AVG
Gorham SHEAF OF WHEAT set for 12 -NR	$2,599.00	CHICAGO ARTS & CRAFTS KALO STYLE SILVER SERVING SPOON	$66.77
Art Nouveau Tray 835 Silver. Halfmoon and Crown	$645.87	WALLACE SIR CHRISTOPHER STERLING 2 PLACE/OVAL	$66.50
GORHAM MELROSE STERLING 16 PCS 4 VINTAGE TRUE	$359.96	All Sterling Gravy Ladle Hester Bateman by C J Vander	$60.00
35 Pc 1891 Pat Ornate Sterling Silver Flatware Set NR	$345.00	Monkey Spoon Silver Tea Caddy 01 Hallmrk Justice /Bowl	$59.99
REED & BARTON FRENCH RENAISSANCE STERLING 16	$319.96	Monkey Spoon Silver Tea Caddy #02 Hallmark People /Bowl	$59.99
TOWLE OLD MASTER STERLING 16 PCS 4 SETS	$315.00	Monkey Spoon Silver Tea Caddy 07 Halmrk Servant In Bowl	$59.99
Tiffany ENGLISH KING dinner knives -NR	$308.11	European Silver Tea Caddy 08 Hallmarked Justice Figure	$59.99
INTERNATIONAL ROYAL DANISH STERLING 16 PCS 4	$265.00	Monkey Spoon Silver Tea Caddy #09 Hallmark Ship In Bowl	$59.99
GORHAM KING EDWARD STERLING 8 PCS 2 TRUE DINN	$227.50	Monkey Spoon Silver Tea Caddy 10 Hallmrk Windmill Scene	$59.99
1880 IMPERIAL RUSSIAN ENAMELED SILVER SPOON	$203.50	TOWLE OLD COLONIAL STERLING 4 TEASPOONS	$59.96
TOWLE LOUIS XIV STERLING 16 PCS 4 SETS	$195.00	8 STERLING CA 1846 WOOD@HUGHES VIOLIN SPOONS	$59.95
KIRK OLD MARYLAND STERLING 6 ICED TEA SPOONS	$179.99	LUNT WILLIAM AND MARY STERLING PLACE SETTING	$58.99
GORHAM STRASBOURG STERLING 8 PCS 2 SETS	$169.98	LUNT MODERN VICTORIAN STERLING PLACE SETTING	$58.99
GORHAM MELROSE STERLING VINTAGE SALAD SET	$159.99	8 Piece Sterling Silver Flatware Dinner Knives Set	$57.57
Large Sterling Silver Serving Fork Very Ornate MUST SEE	$158.38	STERLING ROSE POINT- WALLACE PUNCH LADLE NR	$54.99

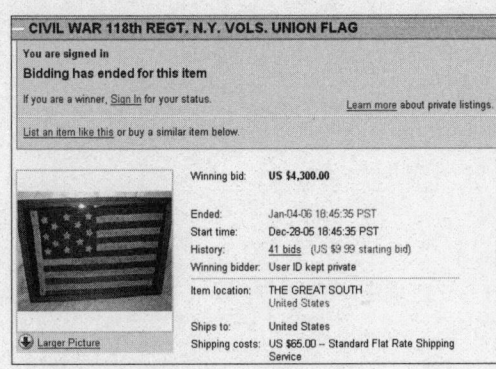

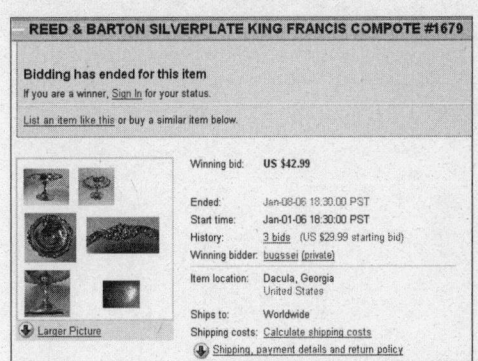

Textiles, Linens ▸ Fabric

The average sales price in this subcategory is $20.36.

	HIGH		AVG
ALICE IN WONDERLAND COTTON HANDKERCHIEFS GLADYS PETO	$556.00	RARE FRENCH BLANC DE CAMBRAI	$21.50
Antique vintage Rose PK Calico Quilt fabric 6 yds Mint	$350.00	VINTAGE 1890s 27"W STUNNING ROSES ON RED QUILT FABRIC	$21.50
ANTIQUE OLD VINTAGE 19C EARLY YELLOW /RED CALICO FABRIC	$223.49	2 OLD TICKING ZIPPERED COVERS FOR YOUR BENCHES, SEE!!!!	$21.28
19c PAISLEY TAPESTRY YARDS! Antique Fabric!	$212.50	Old Feedsack Feed Sack Novelty Floral Musical Note	$21.02
10 Vintage Full Size Feed Sacks-nice colorful prints	$200.00	Brunschwig Fils grospoint animal print fabric	$21.01
ANTIQUE GAUZE PATRIOTIC BUNTING BIG & LITTLE STARS!!!!!	$158.16	Pierre Frey cut velvet fabric	$21.00
6 yds+ Vintage 30s/40s ROMANTIC FLORAL Fabric ~Fabulous	$139.50	1800's Vintage Claret Cotton Fabric Girls Prairie Dress	$20.59
10 Lovely Full Size Vintage Feedsacks-Lots of Color!	$108.01	BEAUTIFUL VINTAGE CABBAGE ROSE NUBBY BARKCLOTH PANEL #2	$20.51
5yds Divine Stroheim & Romann Framed Neoclassical Print	$102.00	Antique~Old~Vintage~19C~Calico~fabrics~145pcs~	$20.50
French Country Yellow w/PINK ROSES 1940's w/SCROLLS	$99.99	Laura Ashley & Cyrus Clark Princess ~ GORGEOUS Lavender	$20.50
Gorgeous Vintage BARKCLOTH Nubby PINK ROSE Bouquets!	$99.99	AH-Vintage novelty cotton cottages/houses fabric-36"wid	$20.50
Rare Vintage SCALAMANDRE Plume de Paon PEACOCK Fabric!	$99.99	Very nice fabric made in French	$20.50
8 Fabulous Vintage Drape Panels Dramatic HUGE Roses	$99.00	Vintage Material Fabric Ecru Cotton w/ Crocheted Lace	$20.50
Beautiful Embroidered Edwardian White Lawn Fabric	$95.00	LOT OF VINTAGE 60's - 70's COTTON FABRIC SHAPES RETRO	$20.50
Antique Art Nouveau Deco Figural Drapes Curtains Panels	$92.88	ANTIQUE~VINTAGE~OLD~ 19C~Claret~FABRIC~	$20.49

Textiles, Linens ▸ Quilts, Bedspreads

The average sales price in this subcategory is $65.28.

	HIGH		AVG
Important 1850 Providence Rhode Island Album Quilt	$3,000.00	antique vintage hand made duck foot patern quilt	$72.00
Antique American Handmade Album Pattern Quilt	$850.00	VINTAGE HaNdStltChEd postage stamp pattern - NICE!	$71.00
Antique American Handmade North Carolina Lily Quilt	$710.00	VINTAGE HANDSTITCHED QUILTS W/SAILBOATS-NR	$70.56
Antique American Handmade Ocean Waves Variation Quilt	$595.00	Very beautiful old bedspread from 1900-20	$70.00
Antique Handmade American 19th Century Pinwheel Quilt	$575.00	VINTAGE YO-YO HANDSTITCHED QUILT	$70.00
Antique Vintage Nine Patch Variation Cotton Quilt	$500.00	HAND SEWN QUILT TOP-812 SQUARES-BEAUTIFUL PASTEL COLORS	$69.99
Antique American Handmade Irish Chain Quilt	$485.00	Amish Country Sleigh/Buggy Blanket	$69.99
Antique American Handmade Four Patch Quilt	$475.00	WOW 40 Double Wedding Ring Quilt Top -FEEDSACK-NR	$69.00
WELL-EXECUTED 30's Double Wedding Ring Quilt ~MINT!	$475.00	Antique VintageStar and Blocks, Quilt 1940"s Feedsack	$67.00
Spectacular IRIS FLOWERS Vintage HAND~APPLIQUE Quilt NR	$432.00	QUILT, FAMILY QUILT, HANDMADE, 1900'S	$66.51
BEST ANTIQUE BRASS QUILT RACK STAND ON EBAY MUST SEE NR	$412.00	Fabulous Vintage SARAH KAY QUILT Top ~DOLLS * GIRLS~	$66.50
ANTIQUE TREE OF LIFE HAND STITCHED QUILT	$410.00	OUTSTANDING_Never used CANDLE WICK BLANKET_73x102 Huge	$66.12
AA+ ELABORATE ANTIQUE FLORAL APPLIQUE QUILT c 1930s	$405.00	GORGEOUS BLUE AND WHITE DOUBLE IRISH CHAIN QUILT NO RES	$66.00
Lg. GORGEOUS 30's Poppy Applique Quilt ~MINT!	$400.00	1940 Antique Quilt, Multi-Colored Circles	$66.00
EARLY 1840s Carolina Lily QUILT ~ SUPER FABRICS	$399.00	Antique Nosegay Quilt	$66.00

2

ART

Art is a fascinating category on eBay, not just because some truly wonderful old masters now come up for sale regularly, but because it quietly houses a treasure trove of works of new artists whose pieces can sometimes be had for a song.

As an investment, original art of high caliber can be very profitable over the long haul. Stories of serendipitous finds in offbeat places titillate would-be art scouts. Consider the story featured on the Oprah Winfrey show about the man who, to his wife's chagrin, one day dragged home an old painting from a yard sale and added it to the huge heap of stuff he'd already accumulated. As it turned out, hidden behind that painting was another painting, an original oil by an American artist whose works had appreciated over time. He sold it for a bundle and was able to afford a new home, in which he prominently displayed a copy of the painting that had become his own personal winning lottery ticket. In a similar story, a 29-year-old man bought a garage-sale painting for $5.00, which turned out to be Joseph Decker's Ripening Pears. He sold it to a museum for $1 million.

Art Bargains

Those stories are obviously rare. However, although you may not be lucky enough to resell a painting for that kind of profit on eBay, the good news is that there are many art bargains to be had, especially when buying original art from self-representing or new artists. There are some wonderful, interesting pieces of art here by artists selling their own work. I purchased a vibrant oil painting of a mountain scene by a relatively unknown artist for only about $15.00.

In a discussion thread on the eBay boards, artists explain why they are sometimes willing to sell their stuff for a song: to get exposure, to get their feedback ratings up, to increase interest in their auctions, and to drive people to their other listings.

High Prices and the Integration of Live Art Auctions

On the other end of the scale, some of the highest art prices on eBay come from "live auctions." Through partnerships with various bricks-and-mortar auction houses, it is possible to bid on selected auctions via the eBay Live Auctions interface. To participate online, you need to sign up ahead of time via the Live Auctions area on eBay and agree to comply with the specific auction house's terms and conditions for the sale. You can cast an absentee bid ahead of time and also participate as the sale is happening via the Live Auctions interface. The winning bid may come from an online participant, the actual auction floor, or from private bidding.

There are some truly impressive items in the Live Auctions area of eBay. For example, in the price sampling in the Art ▶ Paintings ▶ Antique (Pre-1900) section of this chapter, the highest-priced item is "The Codex Stosch," a set of drawings of ancient Roman arches and temples from Rome and Cori by Giovanni Battista Da Sangallo, an artist who lived 1496–1548. It was listed by Scotland-based auction house Lyon & Turnbull, and sold for GBP 230,000.00 (about $403,029.00). Although the auction was open to eBay bidders via the Live Auctions format, the actual winner came from the real-life auction floor, and the bidder was there in person. But even when the winning bidders of these high-profile auctions are there in person holding a paddle, we get a glimpse at the often-glamorous world of fine art—and the sometimes dizzying final sales prices—via the electronic window of eBay Live Auctions.

There are plenty of quality items in the Art category at more down-to-earth prices. And art by famous names can be affordable, too, though sometimes you need to look at the current century. Consider the Jerry Garcia lithograph, *Never Swat a Fly*, which went for $275.00; or the original Peter Max drawing for $178.25—the final sales prices for each are in the average range in the Contemporary subcategory of Drawings.

Although you have less to worry about in terms of fraud in the Art category than in some other categories on eBay, it does happen occasionally. The most high-profile example came when a man bought a fake Richard Diebenkorn painting for $135,805.00 in 2000. The sellers eventually pled guilty to using made-up eBay IDs to run up the bidding on fake artwork (a practice known as "shill bidding"), and were ordered to pay $94,000.00 in restitution.

However, the occasional scandal aside, there are lots of beautiful pieces sold by honest and legitimate dealers and self-representing artists alike. Art is a category that you may never have considered checking out, but I urge you to look through it. You may find something that really grabs you. Who knows? That artist may become famous someday, and your original piece of art may be one of your soundest investments.

NOTE *This category seemed particularly flooded with items under a dollar, which brings the average prices down. However, as with other very low-priced items on eBay, it's important to check the shipping and handling charges; this will give you the real cost of acquiring the item. A penny starting price is often just a gimmick to get the bidder's attention—with many such listings, the seller was clearly making his or her profit through inflated shipping/handling fees.*

Drawings ▶ Contemporary (1950–Now)

The average sales price in this subcategory is $144.90.

	HIGH		AVG
ORIGINAL KEITH HARING SUBWAY DRAWING	$7,999.00	Robert Bateman Original 60's Lithograph	$299.99
R.C. GORMAN ** Original Oil Pastel ** Must Sell	$3,800.00	GRATEFUL DEAD/JERRY GARCIA Never Swat a Fly litho	$275.00
Peter Max "Liberty Head"...12' by 12' acrylic on canvas	$2,950.00	GRATEFUL DEAD/JERRY GARCIA Never Swat a Fly litho	$256.00
Attributed to Marc Chagall Painting with Expertise	$2,825.00	Snow Leopard	$250.00
Attributed to Pablo Picasso Painting with Expertise	$2,046.00	PICASSO TOROS TOREROS 1st Edition/W/DJ RARE NR	$203.51
Pablo Picasso Original Drawing	$1,900.00	busty CATWOMANN COLOR orig ART by DBLACK	$201.00
Attributed to Willem De Kooning Painting with Expertise	$1,775.00	SEXY casual JESSICA RABBIT COLOR orig ART by DBLACK	$184.50
Takashi Murakami DOB Drawing Signed	$1,699.00	Peter Max Original Drawing	$178.25
Attributed to Fernand Leger Painting with Expertise	$1,626.00	SCHLYER Orig. Male Nude Gay Interest Drawing/Painting	$177.50
ORIGINAL Aldo Luongo Painting Charlie Parker Bird Art	$1,499.99	Daniel Johnston Original Drawing	$164.12
WATERCOLOR PAINTING by GERALD COLLINS GLEESON	$1,000.00	Drawing in book Signed Picasso	$160.00
RARE DALI BY DALI 1ST ED DJ SIGNED EROTIC SKETCH	$967.00	Original Charcoal Drawing by Carrie Graber 1995	$152.50
Rauschenberg Status of Liberty Silk Screen 1963	$910.00	JESSICA RABBIT origART SKETCH by DBLACK	$150.00
Lee Godie - Chicago Outsider Artist - Dated Drawing	$800.00	Custom pencil drawn portrait of up to three subjects.	$150.00
LEE GODIE DRAWING - DOUBLE WOMAN - CHICAGO OUTSIDER ART	$730.00	Original Abstract Watercolor & Ink Drawing Signed Appel	$149.99

Drawings ▶ Antique (Pre–1900)

The average sales price in this subcategory is $107.78.

	HIGH		AVG
Original drawing by G. F. BARBIERI IL GUERCINO-1630	$4,550.00	18th Century Drawing of Resting Goat, Signed Bernet	$149.95
Heran Chaban " Sunset Glow " 1887- 1939 France	$2,295.00	Harvard - Drawings at Fogg Museum - by Mongan & Sachs	$149.50
RODIN Original Sketch drawing	$1,637.00	1830 Superb Genre Study, Important Listed Artist	$149.00
Pierre Auguste Renoir Signed Pencil Drawing of Girl	$1,602.87	VERY NICE OIL PANTING 2 OFF THEM L@@K L@@K DONT MISS	$147.50
18TH CENTURY BOOK - 300 W/C ARMOURIALS FOLIO SIZE	$1,594.00	Original L. Lucioni signed portrait: Route 7 in Vermont	$146.50
Pastel of a farmer in the country VAN GOGH??	$1,500.00	Impressionist Landscape Drawing Painting	$142.50
Exceptionally Fine 16th C. German Old Master Drawing	$1,025.00	EDWARD SEAGER 1809-1886 WELL LISTED SIGNED DATED 1848	$129.77
Edgar Degas1834 PENCIL DRAWING SIGNED NO RESERVE $999	$999.00	Portraits by Ingres -1896 Portfolio- Paris - Rothschild	$129.50
Van Gogh signed mixed media.	$898.00	Old Charcoal Drawing - Hunter W/Rifle - Jay Hambidge	$129.50
Samuel Prout (1783 1852) British Listed Artist	$860.00	Arthur W. Dow SIGNED book Composition 1st edition 1899	$127.50
La Dame aux Camellias Stamped Etching by Louis Icart	$845.00	OLD MASTER DRAWING - CLASSICAL STUDY OF A FACE	$126.00
Early Old Master Pen and Ink Drawing on Laid Paper	$810.00	France 1900 Excellent Study of a Bearded Man listed	$119.99
Pierre Auguste Renoir Signed Pencil Drawing of Woman	$787.78	RUSSIAN COSSACK. watercolor. 19c. Young Woman.	$117.80
Manet Original Drawing Signed	$717.77	REV JOHN L PETIT - NOTRE DAME LUSIGNAN FRANCE 1859	$112.50
Paul Cezanne Signed Detailed Sketch on Thick Page RARE	$687.77	Old Master Drawing	$112.50

Folk Art (Paintings)

The average sales price in this subcategory is $66.50.

NOTE *These results are based on a keyword search of the Folk Art subcategory for auctions with the word* painting *in the title.*

	HIGH		AVG
Antique 1820 Huge Folk American Painting	$6,000.00	BABAE Philippines Art 16X12 Filipino Oil Painting NR	$84.90
ORIGINAL THEOREM PAINTING BY DAVID ELLINGER	$3,500.00	R. Collins Mini Folk Art Raven Bird Painting, Crow	$83.00
HOWARD FINSTER earlyOriginal Painting Outsider Folk Art	$899.00	PAIGE KOOSED WATERCOLOR PAINTING	$78.99
Superb 19th C. Shadow Box of Ship, Painting Background	$700.00	Black Folk Art Oil Painting- Signed-"Pickin Cotton"	$78.77
Howard Finster Beast Leopard 1988 RARE BIG painting	$599.99	Folk Art-GROUPER-Kim McCoy Outer Banks Fish Painting #2	$78.00
UNSIGNED FOLK ART OIL ON BOARD WHALING PAINTING	$561.99	LUCKY WHITE HORSE fairy girl FOLK art painting TASCHA	$77.95
18thC Antique Folk Art *Pin Prick Painting* of Children	$490.00	Primitive Folk Art Original Painting Mix Media	$77.00
Rare BEAUTIFUL FLOWERS by WOODIE LONG,Original Painting	$425.51	PAIGE KOOSED WATERCOLOR PAINTING	$76.29
ISATIRICAL SCENE w FIGURES 18/19th C. Oil Painting	$404.00	Folk Art-MERMAID-Kim McCoy Painting Corolla Duck NC #1	$76.00
Victorian oil painting of children 19th century Antique	$389.89	Frida Kahlo Mexican Folk Art Original Girl Painting	$76.00
WONDERFUL 19th C. Folky Cats Painting!	$336.99	Primitive Folk Art Original Painting Animal Cow	$71.00
VINTAGE FOLK ART WITCH HALLOWEEN PAINTING LARGE SHELF	$316.00	EX LARGE PRIMITIVE FOLK ART PAINTING NR 24" X 20"	$70.89
Oh! MoseT George Washington Painting with Appraisal	$299.00	Primitive Folk Art Original Painting Animal Tiger	$68.00
Adam Maeroff >west PA Folk border collie sheep Painting	$282.99	Folk Art Cat Canvas Painting-Movie Theater Cats-Shelly	$68.00
ORIGINAL folk art painting cow country horse Criswell	$277.00	R. Collins Mini Folk Art Primitive Bird Painting, RVG	$67.00

Mixed Media ▶ Contemporary (1950–Now)

The average sales price in this subcategory is $91.90.

	HIGH		AVG
Peace On Earth, Peter Max, Mixed Media, Signed	$4,250.00	EAMES SWAG LIGHT MOD BURLAP WOOD	$102.50
Peter Max God Bless America mixed media 2001	$3,500.00	SALVADOR DALI "AUTHENTIC WOODCUT" W/COA NR!!	$102.50
STEPPIN' OUT ON BROADWAY C. FAZZINO Artist's proof	$2,243.18	HISASHI OTSUKA Sword of Loyalty MIXED MEDIA PRINT w/COA	$101.50
Peter MAX Bill MACK Original Painting Drawing Art	$1,826.00	MARGARET KILGALLEN BOOK 200+ Barry McGee GRAFFITI *MINT	$99.99
JAMES COIGNARD, TRIPTYCH, ORIG	$800.00	URI LIFSHITZ (2) two signed lithographs Jewish Israeli	$99.00
Taz and his Bride Tie the Knot! Bugs Bunny as Minister	$725.00	BEAST LOVER framed Canadian outsider/art J.Swinton	$96.00
50 PCS of ORIGINAL S/N ARTWORK-$15,000+ VALUE!	$495.00	HISASHI OTSUKA Sword of Strength MIXED MEDIA PRINT COA	$96.00
Sabzi S/N HE Giclee on Canvas "Night Falls"	$490.00	1972 New York City Subway Map Mint by Massimo Vignelli	$87.00
Charles Fazzino 3-D Art Kinda Kinky Erotic Pop-Art	$405.00	Alex Perez AP Serigraph on Paper "Winding River"	$87.00
RUFINO TAMAYO MIXOGRAPH MILITARY MAN	$405.00	CAPTAIN AMERICA 50TH B&W LITHO SIG JACK KIRBY AP 17/50	$86.99
RUFINO TAMAYO LITHOGRAPH HOWLING DOGS S/N	$390.00	PETER MAX signed Hard Rock Cafe Signature Series Shirt	$86.00
PICASSO LITHOGRAPH HAND SIGNED IN INK	$375.00	retro tiki neck face barry mcgee paris hilton pop folk	$86.00
RUFINO TAMAYO LITHOGRAPH JAZZ PLAYER	$370.00	Raymond Pettibon Book-"A CAN AT THE CROSSROADS"	$80.99
Sailor Sailor's Valentine Shell Art Mermaid	$360.00	50s 2 Retro Mod Modernist CAT Wall Art Japan Eames Era	$75.00
Raymond Pettibon's **TRIPPING CORPSE**LOOK!!!!!!	$306.00	Colored Pencil Comic Kidnapping - EtherNet	$75.00

Paintings ▶ Antique (Pre–1900)

The average sales price in this subcategory is $308.00.

	HIGH		AVG
1001: The Codex Stosch GIOVANNI BATTISTA DA SANGALLO	GBP 230,000.00	Original Peter Baumgras Painting *PORTRAIT* 1871	$499.99
758: Russian Painted Porcelain Genre Scene Plaque, Russ	$54,000.00	M.S. Laidman (American, 1956) , Original	$492.00
Alfred Sisley Painting, Inondation #497296	$27,000.00	EDM. H. OSTHAUS "STYLE" DOG/DUCK (DECOY)	$484.99
Early Maine Portrait of Child w/ Decorated Stoneware	$8,100.00	1839 MANUSCRIPT SPLENDID PAINTINGS Bright Bold Figures	$431.00
Antique 1820 Huge Folk American Painting	$6,000.00	ISATIRICAL SCENE w FIGURES 18/19th C. Oil Painting	$404.00
CLINTON LOVERIDGE b1824 American LISTED	$4,500.00	Rare c1850 Labeled Spotted Cove Antique Picture Frame	$400.00
Reynolds "Docks"	$4,450.00	Old Antique Primitive Folk Art Painting Niagara Falls	$396.00
Angel Espoy Painting Early American Artist	$3,100.00	Antique Primitive Mormon Painting Houses Landscape >NR<	$355.00
Jewish Art (SIGNED)- OIL ON WOOD PANEL	$2,550.00	Antique Hudson River School Campfire Landscape Painting	$355.00

Antique 1850 Folk American Painting	$2,550.00	2DIE4! Exquisite 19th C. Victorian Roses Oil Painting	$345.00
RARE EDWARD DODGE C1844 VIRGINIA PORTRAIT MINIATURES	$2,515.00	19th C Miniature Watercolor Portrait on Ivory Renniger	$331.01
THOMAS BIGELOW CRAIG A.N.A. 1849-1924 OCTOBER DAYS	$2,500.00	Antique Oil Painting with Frame Late 1800s ~ MUST SEE!	$305.00
Rare Oval KPM Victorian Lady Protrait Plaque By Muller	$2,252.03	NICE 19TH CENTURY O/C STILL LIFE OF STRAWBERRIES	$300.00
Montague-Black/White Oil Painting-1881-Yosemite Valley	$2,175.00	Florence Robinson watercolor New York, listed artist	$300.00
Original 1877 Oil Painting Clinton Loveridge Albany NY	$2,000.00	18th C. American Miniature Portrait of Sarah Champe	$300.00

Paintings ▶ Contemporary (1950–Now)

The average sales price in this subcategory is $45.64.

	HIGH		AVG
Hisashi Otsuka: Father & Son, Ltd Ed 154/300, Serigraph	$2,500.00	3rd Marine Div QUANG TRI Vietnam - Late 1960s PAINTING	$55.32
FINE AUSTRALIAN ABORIGINAL ART, by JEANNIE PETYARRE	$700.00	ART ORIGINAL OIL CANADIAN E. M. ELLIOTT Majolica" $9.99	$54.88
JEAN CLAUDE PICOT, Original Watercolor, NO RESERVE!!	$299.99	ART SALE ORIGINAL OIL CANADIAN E.M ELLIOTT MARINE $9.99	$52.01
ART OIL E.M. ELLIOTT "FAMOUS CHURCH STOWE VERMONT"$9.99	$270.00	Surf Art Original Hawaii Painting Surfing Canvas NEW~	$51.99
Chemiakin, Mihail. Mosaic Press. 2 Volumes. 1st.	$255.00	2 modern WATERFALL landscape paintings HUGE 30 X 40's	$49.99
Pair of Original Watercolor Chinese Landscapes	$199.99	asian zen cherry blossom art oil painting SET /3	$49.99
ORIG FLORAL Abstract Modern Art Iris Irises Painting NR	$177.50	Art Oil Canvas repro KANDINSKY ABSTRACT Circles Picture	$49.99
Abstract Original Oil- HUGE- 36x36x2-Color, Earthtones	$157.50	ORIGINAL OIL PAINTING LANDSCAPE	$49.99
GRAY DAVIS ORIGINAL WATER COLOR	$150.00	Two Painted Ceramic Tiles, signed Picasso? NR	$49.99
HUGE Original Abstract Painting red + Flowers Lawren	$149.00	Oil Painting - Nyc Manhattan Pop Art - R. Miller	$41.00
Set of 4 asian art bamboo zen oil paintings GREAT!	$101.78	36" Signed Oil Painting: Downfallen Frail-drug addict?	$41.00
Asian Vintage Lacquer Panel Vietnam 1969 War Inscribed	$100.00	ART ORIGINAL ACRYLIC Perth Ontario E.M ELLIOTT $9.99 NR	$40.00
ERYKAH BADU jazz R&B Pop Art painting not cd	$100.00	Original Portrait Painting Old Indian , Cottrelle	$36.57
Color_MasTer_G.V.ART_RED AND BLACK #50_3 PANELS_HUGE***	$99.99	Sweet Cat Cats Family Oil Painting Animal Art ~Cute	$36.00
Color MasTer_G.V.ART+INDEPENDANCE BEAUTY_ Abstract #422	$99.90	2 ORIGINAL Paintings for published CHILDREN'S BOOK	$35.00

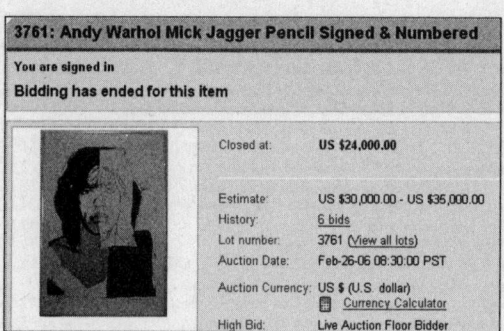

Posters

The average sales price in this subcategory is $26.29.

NOTE *These results are based on a keyword search of the Posters subcategory for auctions with the word* poster *in the title.*

	HIGH		AVG
Uncle Sam Poster World War I Awesome Genuine Antique!	$500.00	Peter Max 1993 CLINTON Inaugural Poster (B)	$32.04
1960 Air France Travel Poster "Roma" by Nathan	$455.00	SAN FRANTASIA by Albert Tolf Poster Photolithography	$31.89
1939 POSTER - WORLDS FAIR - GOLDEN GATE EXPO	$256.00	Emek Air/Stereolab S/N silkscreen poster"04"	$31.33
1960's Air France Travel Poster "Paris" P.Baudovin	$213.50	1970 HUNTER S THOMPSON FOR SHERIFF CAMPAIGN POSTER NR	$31.00
WWI Lithograph Poster Share the Victory Haskell Coffin	$204.00	Muhammad Ali IMPOSSIBLE IS NOTHING Adidas Poster 27x36	$30.00
1960 Air France Travel Poster "Europa" by Jean Carlu	$203.61	BEBE Sexy 4x6 Bus Shelter Poster - 6ft	$29.40
1950's Air France Travel Poster "Geece" by Guy Georget	$202.50	Vintage Braniff Poster - CONCORDE	$28.00
1939 POSTER - CALIFORNIA WORLDS FAIR VOLLMANN PRODUCTIO	$201.50	Sexy Olivia-bebe 4x6 ft Poster Ultra Rare+ Desirable	$28.00
1960 Air France Travel Poster "India" by Jean Carlu	$197.50	Vintage Ringling Bros & Barnum & Bailey Lion Poster	$27.36
Vintage World War 1 Poster by F. Strothmann - Beat Hun	$152.50	Peter Max 1993 CLINTON Inaugural Poster (A)	$26.00
1960 Air France Travel Poster "Africa" by Nathan	$152.50	ORIG. WORLD WAR I POSTER- FIGHT GERMANS w/LIBERTY BONDS	$26.00
OZ UNDERGROUND MAGAZINE ORIGINAL POSTER*FREE SHIPPING*	$146.00	Express Fashion Poster (8' x 5') —> L@@K!!!! <—	$26.00
1960 Air France Travel Poster "Japan" by Nathan	$126.50	OZ POSTER featuring L Frank Baum First Editions	$25.00
ORGINAL French poster SEM Goursat 1917	$108.60	Peter Max 1993 CLINTON Inaugural Poster (A)	$24.99
ORIGINAL Steinlen Poster Pendant Qu'ar 1917	$99.00	Peter Max 1993 CLINTON Inaugural Poster (B)	$24.99

Prints ▶ Antique (Pre–1900)

The average sales price in this subcategory is $77.33.

	HIGH		AVG
Durer, D?rer, Albrecht, Woodcut, Lifetime Impression	$2,750.00	FABULOUS ART DECO LITHOGRAPH WITH LADY AND DOG	$125.00
Laurencin, Marie, La Sir?, Original Signed Etching	$850.00	STUNNING ANTIQUE LITHOGRAPH	$125.00
1844 HENRY CLAY COLOR CAMPAIGN	$760.00	TIN PICTURE ~ LADY & ROSES	
ENGRAVING By NEAGLE		ANTIQUE VICTORIAN CHROMO PRINT ROSES PHOTO FRAME	$125.00
1912 Gamy-Montaut Motor Car Racing Touring Schneider	$760.00	1881 Book - Holland - Henry Havard - Maxime Lalanne	$109.50

1908 Gamy-Montaut Motor Car Racing Single Cylinder	$641.00	Neat 1897 Assorted Fruit 1028 Yard Long Dated	$100.00
Goya, Francisco, Framed Etching and Aquatint	$595.00	European Lithograph Tobacco Pipe Color Print Didot	$96.00
33 Volumes of Etchings - World's Best Etchers	$538.00	Interior View Of The House Of God By Cruikshank!	$88.99
1913 Gamy-Montaut Motor Car Racing France Aeillot Prix	$512.00	Lot of Very Old Engravings,,Etchings,Lithographs, RARE!!	$82.50
1913 Gamy-Montaut Motor Car Racing Tour France Unicorn	$511.00	-Huge- 1800's -Art Treasures of Germany- Book - Plates!	$80.00
1911 Gamy-Montaut Motor Car Racing Delage Indy 500	$511.00	2 ANTIQUE CURRIER & IVES PRINTS FRAMED "TO THE RESCUE"	$77.00
RARE 1888 PICTURESQUE CALIFORNIA VOL.1 - 55 PRINTS	$409.00	Old Yard Long #5101 Fruit James Lee Chicago	$75.00
1912 Gamy-Montaut Motor Car Racing Licorne Unicorn	$399.95	1859 Harper's Weekly w Mountain Meadows Massacre UTAH	$73.76
Antique Art Book Rembrandt Etching Etchings 1859 - NR	$399.00	EARLY NEWFOUNDLAND DOG ANTIQUE	$66.00
1800s FRANK LESLIE'S HARPER'S WEEKLY Vol. WINSLOW HOMER	$383.88	ENGRAVING LANDSEER 1892	
ANTIQUE CURRIER & IVES "VIEW	$306.01	1894 YALE Vs VASSAR COLLEGE FOOTBALL PRINT C. D. GIBSON	$66.00
OF NEW YORK" FRAMED WOW!		Kunisada Woodblock Print Books #9/10, circa 1850s	$60.00

Prints ▶ Contemporary (1950–Now)

The average sales price in this subcategory is $71.48.

	HIGH		AVG
RARE!!! RW18 FEDERAL DUCK STAMP PRINT-MAYNARD REECE	$1,345.00	Lithograph of All Winners #11 signed by Alex Schomburg!	$96.00
BEV DOOLITTLE "Whoo" Owl LE, SN 1980	$800.00	STERANKO Nick Fury classic cover reproduction	$91.00
Signed JIM CLARY 1:40 A.M. TITANIC TIME, APRIL 15, 1912	$525.00	Stephen Lyman Winter Shadows Black Wolf Art Print	$89.99
1979 FIRST OF STATE NEVADA DUCK STAMP & PRINT BY HAYDEN	$423.00	Sivard's "PRESIDENT CLEVELAND AT BROOKE AND HARRY 1894	$89.00
Rare limited edition Tucker Smith Great Northern print	$361.00	NEAL ADAMS CONAN SIGNED LTD #83/100 PRINT 1975 F+ NR!	$76.00
Frank CHO Cheesecake and Critters Portfolio with SKETCH	$345.00	VINTAGE ROBERT TAYLOR "STEAMING INTO WIND" FRAMED PRINT	$74.99
Charles Wysocki 4 Print Set Four Seasons PP #11/12	$295.00	Keith Mueller 1999 Rhode Island Duck Stamp Print	$61.00
FRIENDS OF THE NRA CIVIL WAR PRINT	$207.50	DISNEY FRAMED PINOCCHIO ON STAGE SERIGRAPH SERICEL CEL	$59.99
AMELIA EARHART ETCHING WITKOFF AVIATION LITHO ART PHOTO	$149.99	RARE Charles Burns Illustration Ltd Ed Print Duffy Grp	$52.00
Limited Edition Lithograph of SR-71 Blackbird	$138.19	Postal Commemorative Stamps John Deere Print	$51.00
Air Combat Legends by Nicolas Trudgian	$137.50	DAVE BARNHOUSE "YESTERDAY'S HERO" SN/AP	$51.00

Sculpture, Carvings

The average sales price in this subcategory is $85.71.

NOTE   *These results are based on a keyword search of the Sculpture, Carvings subcategory for auctions with the word sculpture in the title.*

	HIGH		AVG
BRONZE SCULPTURE - HENRY MOORE - THE WARRIOR	$1,500.00	MOUNTAIN GOAT~~Signed Wood Sculpture~~Bali Art	$123.85
PARDELL LEGENDS SCULPTURE "ESTEEMED WARRIOR"	$1,009.00	CARLOS ESTEVEZ SADDLEBRED HORSE SCULPTURE EQUINE ART	$122.50
WHITTEN LEGENDS "RAPTURE" GHOST DANCER SCULPTURE	$800.00	CARLOS ESTEVEZ STANDARDBRED HORSE SCULPTURE EQUINE ART	$120.50
Vintage Metal Modern Art Sculpture Marc C.Jere Era WOW!	$700.00	COLORFUL STEEL METAL MODERN ART SCULPTURE NR!	$119.99
ORIGINAL LIMITED sculpture SURREALIST SILENCE,BRONZE!	$610.00	KARG Signed Pucini Dichroic Art Glass Sculpture	$105.00
FAMILY SCULPTURE BY HENRY MOORE SIGNED & NUMERED	$510.00	BULL POWER~Bali Hand Carved Wood ART Sculpture~NEW	$103.51
JEFF KOONS 'BALLOON DOG' PORCELAIN SCULPTURE! MINT N/R!	$456.00	Louis Moreau Metal Sculpture Statue Vision de Mai	$103.50
RECLINING FIGURE BRONZE SCULPTURE HENRY MOORE SIGNED	$450.00	50s 1.5Ft Danish Modern Teak Sculpture Nude Eames Era	$102.50
Stunning Terracotta Sculpture WOMAN with Dog	$450.00	CARLOS ESTEVEZ, JUMPER, SCULPTURE EQUINE ART	$102.50
JEFF KOONS 'BALLOON DOG' PORCELAIN SCULPTURE! MINT N/R!	$425.00	BEAUTIFUL and UNIQUE EROTIC WOOD SCULPTURE	$101.12
[2 of these sold for $425.00 each]		ARTEMIS PAL LUCITE OWL 10 SCULPTURE PALATNIK BRAZIL	$100.97
Nice Absract Curtis Jere Wall Sculpture, Bertoia, eames	$420.53	Copper Rolling Ball Sculpture Marble Art!	$99.99
HENRY MOORE STRINGED WOMAN SCULPTURE SIGNED & NUM	$405.00	Contemporary Abstract Modern Metal Wall Art Sculpture!	$99.00
60s BRONZE Sculpture GOAT Modernist PICASSO Nambe Eames	$395.00	Unique Modern Contemporary Hanging Mobile Art Sculpture	$90.00
SENSATIONAL BRONZE SCULPTURE; MEPHISTO	$355.00	Unique Modern Contemporary Hanging Mobile Art Sculpture	$89.00

Self-Representing Artists

The average sales price in this subcategory is $53.78.

NOTE   *These results are based on a keyword search of the Self-Representing Artists subcategory for auctions with the word painting in the title.*

	HIGH		AVG
D. Hurd ROAD LESS TRAVELED LARGE Original Painting IBND	$895.00	Nude male painting modern figure ORIGINAL ANTOINE ART	$60.00
D.Hurd ABSTRACT JAZZ Original Oil Painting Art IBND	$585.00	ORIGINAL ART Painting MALE NUDE Nudes GLADSTONE eMOMA	$60.00
Westie Highland Terrier Dog Renaud Painting Petunias	$455.00	FIDOSTUDIO Abstract 4ART Original modern NUDES PAINTING	$60.00
Miniature 'Dance' Oil Painting-P.Saltarelli-NR	$355.00	Original Signed Acrylic Floral Painting	$60.00
THE RAW ARTIST spiritual biblical art painting IBND	$355.00	MODERN ABSTRACT PAINTING, "Warm Happiness"	$59.99
WOMAN KEELYART Original Oil Painting Portrait Large Art	$345.00	BLACK CAT PAINTING, TRICKY KITTY, gothic	$58.76
Wicked Faeries ORIGINAL PAINTING gothic fairy goth art	$318.00	Original Female Nude Art Painting WWAO 4is EBSQ KJ	$58.00
THE RAW ARTIST modern abstract art painting IBND	$306.00	NR Original Abstract Art Flower Painting by HORVATH	$56.00
W Hawkins Midwest impressionist plein air art PAINTING	$292.26	DADDY, LOOK UP! ORIGINAL HAYWARD PAINTING 14"x21"	$56.00
W Hawkins Western impressionist plein air art PAINTING	$273.00	IVES Original Painting: Bird Art - BLACK CROW - RED SKY	$56.00
ORIGINAL ART Painting MALE NUDE Nudes GLADSTONE eMOMA	$271.49	Painting by Zora Kader , Still Life With Birds ,NR	$56.00
HUGE abstract Modern Art FRESCO Painting RED POPPIES	$259.99	BOOTH-Original Modern Art Metallic Painting EBSQ	$55.00
VOSS-ART Huge ORIGINAL Abstract OIL Portrait PAINTING	$255.00	Boat on the Beach oil painting, 20" x 16"	$55.00
Hawkins Western impressionist vintage look art PAINTING	$255.00	ROUND WRAPPED CANVAS AMAZING COLORFUL ABSTRACT PAINTING	$55.00
KADLIC-French Country Red Poppies-ORIGINAL OIL Painting	$237.50	ORANGE CAT ON QUILTS folk art original painting TASCHA	$54.03

Wholesale Lots ▸ Paintings

The average sales price in this subcategory is $13.30.

	HIGH		AVG
IRISES 2 art paintings Van Gogh Repros HUGE 30X40's	$49.99	AVRIL LAVIGNE POP ART !!!!!!!!!!!!!!!! 3 PIECES 5x7	$14.95
BIG RARE Abstract Art Collection! 13 SIGNED Paintings !	$24.95	[2 of these sold for $14.95 each]	
Lot of 20 Egyptian High Quality PAPYRUS wholesale 8X12	$22.95	AVRIL LAVIGNE POP ART !!!!!!!!!!!!!!!! 3 PIECES 5x7	$14.95
		Lot Of 8 Ancient Egypt Papyrus Art Prints From Cairo NR	$10.49
		Lot Of 8 Ancient Egypt Papyrus Art Prints From Cairo NR	$9.99
		BIG RARE LOT of 8 MATCHING Abstract Paintings! Wow	$9.99
		Oil Painting on Canvas Beautiful Lady 24x36	$9.99
		Lot Of 8 Ancient Egypt Papyrus Art Prints From Cairo NR	$9.99

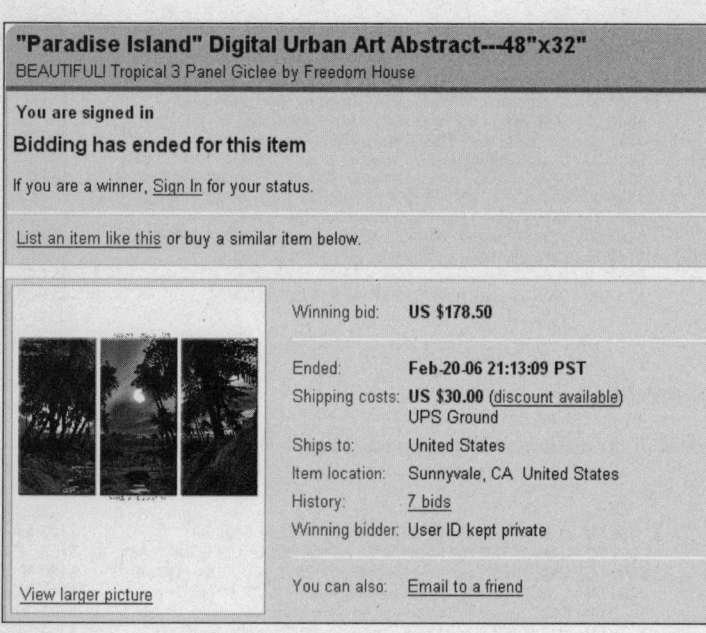

"Paradise Island" Digital Urban Art Abstract---48"x32"
BEAUTIFUL! Tropical 3 Panel Giclee by Freedom House

You are signed in

Bidding has ended for this item

If you are a winner, Sign In for your status.

List an item like this or buy a similar item below.

Winning bid:	**US $178.50**
Ended:	**Feb-20-06 21:13:09 PST**
Shipping costs:	**US $30.00** (discount available) UPS Ground
Ships to:	United States
Item location:	Sunnyvale, CA United States
History:	7 bids
Winning bidder:	User ID kept private

View larger picture

You can also: Email to a friend

Wholesale Lots ▸ Prints

The average sales price in this subcategory is $38.52.

	HIGH		AVG
Parrot Artwork from Beak Boutique; wholesale lot of 14	$60.00	Lot of 9 Matted & Framed Lovely Victorian Ladies	$39.95
WHOLESALE 60 ART NOUVEAU PRINTS MUCHA GREAT FOR RESALE	$59.95	CHARLES M RUSSELL 6 WESTERN ART PRINTS WHOLESALE LOT G	$34.99
[2 of these sold for $59.95 each]		magnolia pictures, arangements, and table ware	$32.13
WHOLESALE LOT 25 ANTIQUE 1920s ART NOUVEAU LITHOGRAPHS	$49.00	set of concave metal frames with pictures men and women	$32.00
Norman Rockwell Prints	$41.00	Lot of 30 Victorian Maud Humphrey Bogart Prints	$30.00
		[3 of these sold for $30.00 each]	
		Wholesale Lot of 15 New Framed Victorian Motto Prints	$28.00
		Lot 10 Beautiful Victorian Florals by Paul de Longpre	$25.75
		THE WOODSHED By Russell May	$25.00
		MAKING APPLE BUTTER By Russell May	$25.00
		Country Road By Russell May	$25.00
		FREDERIC REMINGTON 6 INDIAN ART PRINTS WHOLESALE LOT A	$24.99
		FREDERIC REMINGTON 6 WESTERN ART PRINTS $25 WHOLESALE	$24.99
		FREDERIC REMINGTON 6 INDIAN ART PRINTS WHOLESALE LOT A	$24.99
		Lot of 160 Beatiful Victorian Floral Bible Verse Prints	$24.95
		LOT of 21 VICTORIAN SAINT BERNARD PRINTS ELSLEY	$24.95
		[2 of these sold for $24.95 each]	

3

BABY

The Baby category is relatively new on eBay, and some of the items can be found in other similar categories. For example, you can find diaper bags in both Baby ▶ Diapering ▶ Diaper Bags and also in Clothing, Shoes & Accessories ▶ Infants & Toddlers ▶ Other Items.

Anyone who's had a baby knows how quickly you can go through supplies, and there are certainly plenty of bricks-and-mortar retail stores catering only to infants and toddlers, so it makes sense to pull all the subcategories related to babies and young children into one area.

Here you will find the gamut of prices, from luxury goods for fashion-conscious parents to rock-bottom wholesale lots. A Louis Vuitton Sharon Stone monogram diaper bag (described as in new condition) went for $305.00, included in a lot with a used Vuitton purse and briefcase (Vuitton bags sell on eLuxury.com for several hundred to several thousand dollars). With Vuitton products, fakes and replicas abound, so it is especially important to check a seller's feedback and the item description carefully. A Sharon Stone Vuitton diaper bag reportedly sells new for around $13,000.00, so it's easy to be skeptical about such a bargain, although, in this case, the seller did have a 100 percent positive feedback rating.

A new Coach-brand Scribble diaper bag (this has the colorful "C" Coach logos all over its exterior) went for $256.99. It wasn't completely clear from the pictures exactly which Scribble bag this was, but Scribble purses new from the Coach site can go from around $180.00 for a small tote to around $500.00 for a satchel. This particular seller had only a 75 percent positive feedback rating, however—not a good sign.

Although eBay is usually a good place to find bargains on everyday merchandise, occasionally you will see something go for more than its retail price. This is the case with the used (one-year-old) Chariot carrier bike trailer/jogger/stroller, which sold for $495.00 with

21 bids. New, this is $399.00, according to the seller. There can be various reasons for this price inflation: people may want an older model that has been discontinued, it may be sold out of stores, or it may simply be a case of an emotional bidding war, among other possible reasons.

Perhaps the most practical items in the Baby category are diapers, both cloth and disposable. Here, an example of a good deal is the lot of 17 new medium-size Fuzzi Bunz–brand cloth diapers, which retail for around $23.00 each. These sold for $204.50 with 12 bids, a savings of $175.50 over the $380.00 retail price for 17 of them. Shipping was only $5.95.

But sometimes, when you factor in an eBay seller's shipping fee, the savings comes out in the proverbial wash. A lot of 103 size 1 Huggies-brand diapers sold for $9.50, with 10 bids, and shipping of about $10.00. But a pack of 56 goes for $10.49 at an online drugstore that offers free shipping, so with everything factored in, you essentially get the same number of diapers per dollar.

At the low end of the Diapering subcategories you can find many coupons, which can save you a lot of money in the long run. A lot of 20 Pull-Ups Training Pants coupons, for $2.00 off any jumbo pack or larger can save you $40.00, according to the seller.

Aside from such everyday items, the Baby category is full of many unique items for the nursery that you may not find anywhere else: vintage birth announcements, a vintage crocheted baby blanket, a hand-pieced quilt, and so on. The bottom line for the Baby category is it can save you money and be a fun, alternative place for new parents and those buying them gifts to shop. And if your baby is grown up, this is the perfect place to make some money passing on those types of items.

Graco Turbo Booster Car Seat 8495COA BRAND NEW

Bidding has ended for this item
If you are a winner, Sign In for your status.

List an item like this or buy a similar item below.

Winning bid:	**US $29.99**
Ended:	**Mar-06-06 14:08:48 PST**
Shipping costs:	**US $20.00** Standard Flat Rate Shipping
Ships to:	United States
Item location:	New York, NY United States
History:	1 bid
Winning bidder:	tapbud (42 ☆)
You can also:	Email to a friend

View larger picture

Car Safety Seats ▶ Booster to 80lbs

The median sales price in this subcategory is $47.00.

NOTE   *The median price is the one with as many prices higher than it as below it. The median price is given here instead of the average price because of the method by which these prices were obtained.*

	HIGH		AVG
Britax Roadster	$200.00	NIB Graco TurboBooster/Coastal Print FREE SHIPPING!!!	$49.00
05 BRITAX MARATHON CONVERTIBLE CAR SEAT - 10 patterns	$194.99	New in Box ~ Eddie Bauer Booster Car Seat ~ No Reserve	$48.01
[2 of these sold for $194.99 each]		NEW EDDIE BAUER HIGHBACK CAR SEAT BLUE	$47.13
2005 Britax Marathon Convertible Car Seat BRAND NEW	$180.95	Cosco Summit High Back Booster Seat L@@K L/N	$47.00
[2 of these sold for $180.95 each]		Compass B500 INT1 Folding Booster Car Seat BRAND NEW	$46.99
EDDIE BAUER ELITE 3 IN 1 MANCHESTER BOOSTER CAR SEAT	$178.00	NEW EDDIE BAUER HIGH BACK BOOSTER CAR SEAT LATCH NR	$46.97
2005 Britax Marathon Convertible Car Seat BRAND NEW	$175.91	RARE COSCO Nascar Dale Earnhardt Car Seat For children 22 80 pounds GREAT SHAPE	$46.80

Diapering

The average sales price in this subcategory is $45.22.

	HIGH		AVG
Very CHIC Louis Vuitton Diaper Bag + PURSE + BRIEFCASE	$305.00	NWT Rocawear Roca Wear GIRLS 8pc DIAPER BAG SET 6-9m	$66.00
New Coach Scribble Diaper Bag..............NR	$256.99	NWT Vera Bradley Baby Bees Diaper Bag (RETIRED)	$66.00
COACH BRAND NEW AUTH BABY BLUE QUILTED DIAPER BAG	$230.00	SHANGHAI MOMMY BAG BY KECCI-NWT "NAVY"	$64.99
* BNWT Coach Laptop/Diaper Multi Tote Bag Black 6460 *	$220.00	SHANGHAI MOMMY BAG BY KECCI-NWT "CORNSILK"	$64.99
[2 of these sold for $220.00 each]		Almost New Coach Black Backpack / Purse / Diaper Bag	$64.99
Tylie Malibu Changing Diaper Bag Satchel No RSV NWOT	$190.50	New Vera Bradley French Blue Diaper Baby Bag w/pad	$62.00
Coach diaper bag purse combination	$177.70	SHANGHAI MOMMY BAG BY KECCI-NWT "FIREWORKS"	$59.99
Authentic Coach Pink Daisy Handbag/ Tote / Diaper Bag	$162.50	VINTAGE Summer Surprise OOAK boutique TOTE bag SWAKD	$50.57
Authentic Kate Spade Blue Dot Noel Tote NWT	$160.00	Raviani Zebra Calf Shopper Purse Diaper Bag $258 HOT	$50.56
Kate Spade Newbury navy large baby diaper bag NWT	$158.51	Kecci Mommy Bag	$50.00
NEW Authentic PINK COACH Diaper bag / Laptop Carryall	$154.50	NWT~RALPH LAUREN SIGNATURE DESIGNER DIAPER BAG PINK $75	$49.99
COACH BRAND NEW AUTH BABY PINK QUILTED DIAPER BAG	$152.50	Oilily Diaper Bag w/ Changing Pad NR NWOT	$47.50
**Brand NWT Hot Pink Medium Kate Spade Baby/Diaper Bag*	$137.64	Vera Bradley Diaper Bag - Citrus Floral Yellow - RARE!!	$46.00
Coach Multi Tote Diaper Bag	$127.50	KATE SPADE-AUTHENTIC DIAPER / MESSENGER BAG-USED	$46.00
JUICY COUTURE BLUE DIAPER MATERNITY BAG FAST SHIPPING*	$125.50	NWT ~ VeRa BRaDLeY BABY Diaper BAG ~ Anastasia BLACK	$45.00
NWT - Kate Spade Grass Green Nylon Diaper Bag-NR- $180	$122.50		

Diapering ▸ Diapers

The median sales price in this subcategory is $9.50.

NOTE *The median price is the price with as many prices higher than it as below it. The median price is given here instead of the average price because of the method by which these prices were obtained.*

	HIGH		AVG
Cotton Bottoms New All White Birth To Potty Pack+Bonus Peachy Cheeks Nappys	GBP 249.99	One Size Hemp Inserts 4 Cloth Pocket Diapers Lots of 4	$9.50
New Buy It Now Pay Later Scheme		Medium Firefly fFitted Diaper	$9.50
21 Wonderoos Diapers plus inserts!!!!!	$365.00	Little Lambs One Size AIO Lot of 2 Cloth Diapers	$9.50
Tots Bots Birth To Potty Pack ~ Peachycheeksnappies ~ The Whole Tots Bots Nappy	GBP 199.99	103 Huggies Diapers Size 1	$9.50
and Wrap Range Available		Sugarpeas Cloth Diaper ONE SIZE Sugarpeas Exec Cond	$9.50
Huge Name Brand Cloth Diaper Lot 58 Diapers Total	$242.51	Fuzzi Bunz Pocket Cloth Diaper	$9.50
18 SMALL Fuzzi Bunz +35 inserts +2 diaper pail liners Complete Starter Kit!!	$232.50		
23 Medium BUMKINS AIO Cloth Diapers, White,GREAT DEAL	$223.50		
Fuzzi Bunz 54 Piece LOT Kooshies AIO Cloth diapers	$212.52		
Fuzzi Bunz Cloth Diapers 17 NEW Sz Med NO RESERVE	$204.50		
Cloth Diaper Blowout! Diapers, Covers, All in One's	$202.50		
Ecobaby Organic Cotton Diapers	$201.06		
Motherease unbleached cotton nappies (20)with wraps(7)	GBP 100.00		
AIO's, Fitted, and Pocket Diaper Lot....Great Brands!!!	$174.00		
HUGE LOT OF 20 KISSALUVS 0 BRAND NEW	$172.50		

Feeding, Breast & Bottle

The average sales price in this subcategory is $14.81.

	HIGH		AVG
(120) 4cases Zevex Enteral Feeding Bags	$120.00	NWOT Goddess 511 Nursing Bra, size 34F softcup wht	$20.50
osco, acme, jewel, albertsons gift card $101.99	$91.00	*3* 36D NIP Nursing Bras,& 66 Nursing Pads NIP!!	$20.00
Similac Advance with Iron Lot of 9 12.9oz	$76.02	ANTQUE BABY BOTTLE IN ORIGINAL BOX (BECK'S)1927	$19.99
Similac Advance with Iron Lot of 9 12.9oz	$73.50	Cooler - Thermo Electric great for travel summer & baby	$17.72
Madame Lang's Perfected Nurser Turtle Baby Bottle 1890	$41.00	VINTAGE OLD MINI NURSER BABY BOTTLE 2 1/2 INCHES HIGH	$17.01
Babystyle Nursing Bra Size Medium	$31.01	Antique Acme Nursing/Baby Bottle	$16.49
Two Cases NIB Pediasure Enteral Formula - Vanilla	$31.00	Lot of Nursing Bras, Pads & Maternity Pantyhose 36D,42D	$12.50
##====>>>>Evenflo DOUBLE breast PUMP<<<<=====##	$26.00	Medela Soft-Cup Maternity and Extra Support Nursing Bra	$12.39
Boutique Burp Cloth Bundle* Yummy Colors!* Stylin' Baby	$22.00	Nursing/Breastfeeding Blanket, New!	$12.25
NWOT Goddess 511 Nursing Bra, size 34F softcup wht	$20.50	3 PERSONALIZED BURPCLOTHS/ADORABLE APPLIQUES!! MUST SEE	$12.00

Memory Books, Keepsakes

The average sales price in this subcategory is $14.06.

	HIGH		AVG
ANTIQUE STERLING SILVER BABY RATTLE BUNNY RABBIT nr	$154.49	VINTAGE BIRTH ANNOUNCEMENTS HUGE LOT INVITATIONS NWT	$20.00
Antique Sterling BABY SPOON CAT FIDDLE NURSERY RHYME	$93.98	Jeff Gordon/Nascar/Photo Album/Memory Book	$19.99
BNIB Tiffany & CO. Sterling Silver Baby Teething Ring!!	$75.22	*VINTAGE* baby book Cradle to College NIB how sweet	$17.26
Anne Geddes Authentic, Eight (8) Framed Pictures	$45.00	Peter Rabbit - Story dish, cup & bowl set - Wedgwood	$17.00
Boy's 0-3 months Carter's, Gap, New Balance Lot	$41.00	My Baby Book - personalized baby book	$16.50
DIVINE VINTAGE SCOTTISH SATIN AND LACE CHRISTENING GOWN	$39.99	THANK HEAVEN for LITTLE BOYS,12x12 SCRAPBOOK ALBUM	$16.49
Terra Traditions "Sleeping Baby" 4 x 6 photo album NEW	$29.00	THANK HEAVEN for LITTLE GIRLS, 12x12 SCRAPBOOK ALBUM	$14.99
The Story of ME - Baby Memories Keepsake memory book	$27.99	Reed & Barton Silverplate Heart Shaped Baby Bank	$12.95
Collage Baby Girl Frame - 1month to 1yr. photo mattings	$25.99	Irish Linen Christening Bonnet - 'The Magic Hanky' BNWT	$12.50
30 DUCK BATH FIZZIE BABY SHOWER BIRTHDAY FAVORS	$23.75	My Baby & Me by Judith Levy (1999)	$11.49
Vintage Real Limoges Hinged Box Pink Carriage - Pram	$23.06	SHARPER IMAGE TALKING PICTURE ALBUM BRAND NEW	$10.55
Gold and Ruby Child's Ring	$23.05	School Memories Keepsake Book	$10.50
Gold and Ruby Tiny Baby Ring	$21.50	I WILL TAKE CARE OF YOU	$9.99
Grandma's Brag Book Scrapbook with pre-made pages	$21.50	Madam Alexander HUG ME KITTY baby doll, MINT	$9.99
Terra Traditions "Angel Baby" 4 x 6 photo album NEW	$20.55	NEW PRECIOUS MOMENTS PILLOW (FOR YOUR NEW BABY)	$9.99

Nursery Bedding ▶ **Blankets**

The average sales price in this subcategory is $17.78.

	HIGH		AVG
NWT Carter's 19-piece Just Stay Little Set 3-6 months	$51.99	HAND PIECED PATCHWORK QUILT	$19.99
1979 FISHER PRICE BUNNY SECURITY BLANKET & BONUS BIBS!	$51.00	Gymboree APPLE BLOSSOM 4pc Blanket/Romper Set 3-6 3m 6m	$19.87
VINTAGE CROCHETED BABY CARRIAGE BLANKET SCOTTIE DOGS	$40.40	Pandolph~Moda Seaside Surf Chenille Baby Blanket~Sweet!	$18.50
VINTAGE BABY ESMOND BEACON BLANKET WITH ORIGINAL BOX	$36.50	GYMBOREE LITTLE SNAPPER BLANKET & BIB NEW NWT 0-3-6-12	$18.29
NWT Carter's Baby Bubbles Blanket & Sleep n' Play (3 m)	$36.00	Gymboree 2001 Mr Fix It Tools 5 pc HTF Lot INCL Blanket	$18.00
HTF purple JOHN LENNON Real Love 5 pc lot SHIP SPECIAL	$32.99	GYMBOREE LITTLE FIRETRUCK BABY BLANKET NEW NWT 0-3-6-12	$17.00
Handcrotched "Bambi" Blanket, NEW & BEAUTIFUL	$31.00	GYMBOREE BOYS LIGHTHOUSE ROMPER/BLANKET NEW NWT 3-6 MOS	$16.49
GYMBOREE COUNTRY PICNIC LADYBUG BLANKET NEW NWT 0-3-6	$28.01	Boys blue JOHN LENNON Real Love romper/blanket lot	$15.50
Gymboree 2000 Farm Friends 7pc lot w/ Blanket! 6 12 mo	$27.51	NWT Ralph Lauren Reversible Blanket Boys Blue Too CUTE	$15.50
GYMBOREE COUNTRY PICNIC LADYBUG BLANKET NEW NWT 0-3-6	$27.01	New, Hand Crochet Furry "BABY" Rug/Blanket	$15.49
GYMBOREE MERMAID GIRLS BLANKET NEW NWT 0-3-6-12-18 MOS	$27.00	GYMBOREE CHOO CHOO TRAIN BLANKET NWOT CUTE!	$14.99
Moses Basket	$26.00	GYMBOREE BOYS LION ZOO SAFARI BABY BLANKET NEW NWT	$14.56
GYMBOREE CHOMP ALIGATOR BLANKET NEW NWT 0-3-6-12 MOS	$26.00	NWT TOMMY HILFIGER Pink 2 RECEIVING BLANKETS/REV CAP	$13.00
HTF yellow JOHN LENNON Real love 4 piece lot blanket	$24.50	GYMBOREE BOY LAWN PARTY FROG GOLF BABY BLANKET 0-3-6-12	$12.50
NWOT girls JOHN LENNON pink blanket/sleepers/bib/romper	$22.50	GYMBOREE Zebra Blanket Romper Hat 0-3 3pc WOW	$12.49

Nursery Bedding ▶ **Sets**

The average sales price in this subcategory is $44.28.

	HIGH		AVG
NEW 9 Pc ~PRINCESS Nursery Crib Set Baby Girls ~$300.00	$178.50	GORGEOUS 9 PIECE CRIB/TODDLER SET (Shabby Chic Style)	$65.00
NEW 5pc DISNEY PRINCESS TWIN SHEET SET COMFORTER CANOPY	$164.24	PRECIOUS MOMENTS NOAH'S ARK COMPLETE CRIB SET 12 P	$55.00
Beatrix Potter's Peter Rabbit 4-piece crib bedding set	$103.50	Adorable Pottery Barn Kids Firetruck Shaped Rug 3' x 5'	$46.00
Yves Delorme Crib Bedding~ for a Special Baby Boy	$99.99	Bob the Builder Full Size Bedding Includes Curtains	$45.00
Pottery Barn KidS Cars & Doggy Quilt & sheet set TWiN	$97.56	Beatrix Potter Quiltex Crib Ensenble	$41.00
NEW 5pc DISNEY PRINCESS TWIN SHEET SET COMFORTER CANOPY	$86.00	Custom Boutique OOAK Nursery Crib Bedding Set 10 pcs.	$41.00
Lambs and Ivy 14 Piece Country Noah's Nursery Set	$80.50	NEW! 4PC DISNEY PRINCESS TODDLER BED - BEDDING SET	$39.00
~Pottery Barn Outer Space Rocket Lot~10 pcs	$72.01	NEW! 4PC DISNEY PRINCESS TODDLER BED - BEDDING SET	$37.00
8pc Kids Line Baby Denim Crib Set	$72.01	NEW! 4PC DISNEY PRINCESS TODDLER BED - BEDDING SET	$36.00
NEW! 4PC CARE BEARS TODDLER BED BEDDING SET	$70.00	NEW! 4PC CARE BEARS TODDLER BED BEDDING SET	$36.00

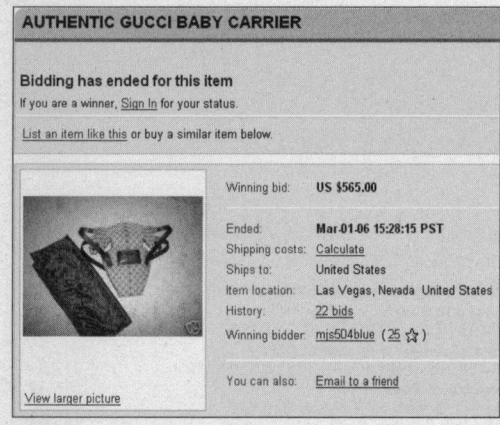

Nursery Bedding ▶ **Quilts, Comforters, Duvets**

The average sales price in this subcategory is $32.10.

	HIGH		AVG
Hand Made Baby Quilt	$280.00	Crib Size Cowboy Quilt	$49.22
A PAIR OF HAPPY DAISY POTTERY BARN KIDS QUILTS	$160.50	NIKKEN TRAVEL COMFORTER 49"X57"	$49.00
POTTERY BARN KIDS PINK ISLAND PATCHWORK TODDLER QUILT	$102.50	QUILT, TWIN SIZE, BEVERLY BLUE, RETAILED $100.00	$29.00
HANDMADE EMBROIDERED BABY QUILT - FLANNEL - BEAUTIFUL!	$79.99	Antique Vintage CHILDS BABY EMBROIDERED QUILT-PLAY TIME	$26.09
Pottery Barn Kids Kasey Stripe Toddler Quilt+Sham Blue	$67.00	New York Yankees Baby Quilt	$25.00
POTTERY BARN KIDS BLUE ISLAND PATCHWORK TODDLER QUILT	$61.00	Louisiana State University Baby Quilt	$24.00

Nursery Decor

The average sales price in this subcategory is $19.02.

	HIGH		AVG
Whimsical Shabby French Garden Bunny Chandelier	$249.50	8 Surf Board Beach drawer knobs pull match Pottery Barn	$23.99
[2 of these sold for $249.50]		CLASSIC POOH Hand Hooked Wool Round Area Rug	$23.74
Tree of Life with 7 OOAK Polymer Clay Babies	$220.26	18Cottage Chic VINTAGE plastic baby/child/doll hangers	$23.50
Pottery Barn Kids 5' Round Bunny Rug	$162.50	Restore & Restyle FLOWERS ETC. FLOWER POT shadow box	$22.50
Pottery Barn Kids 5' Round Bunny Rug	$147.50	8 Surf Board Beach drawer knobs pull match Pottery Barn	$22.50
KATHERINE'S HUMPTY DUMPTY JACK IN THE BOX DOLL HUGE!!	$125.00	Debbie Mumm Noah's Ark Drawer Pull Knobs Set of 6 NIB	$22.49
Boutique FAUX Cake & Plate Shabby HP Roses WDAS CBD	$112.59	Winnie the Pooh Character Stuff Animals!!	$21.86
Pottery Barn Kids 5' Round Bunny Rug	$99.99	Mickey Mouse Picture Frame Disney Store NEW!	$21.17
BEATRIX POTTER BOOKENDS - Peter Rabbit - NO RESERVE	$84.50	Irmi Vintage Kid's Giraffe Coat Rack	$20.50
Boutique Fairytale Tea for Two HP Shabby Roses WDAS	$81.11	Restore & Restyle FLOWERS ETC. trash can wooden square	$20.50
HERMES Scarf / Decor *AUTHENTIC ONE OF A KIND USA*	$81.00	Pepsin syrup advertising poster: Children and Cottage	$20.50
Boutique TEA SET & TRAY Shabby HP Roses WDAS CBD	$78.00	Restore & Restyle FLOWERS ETC. drawer pulls set of 10	$20.03
Like New 100% Wool Pottery Barn 5 x 8 ABC Rug	$68.85	NWOTStar Light Nursery Rug yellow, blue, baby, children	$20.01
VINTAGE CIRCUS CLOWN TABLE LAMP W/NIGHTLIGHT	$61.02	Over The Hill Diaper Wreath - adorable - unique - Gift	$20.00
KELLY RIGHTSELL BUNNY LAMP NEW!!!	$59.95	Classic Pooh Bear Picture Frames	$19.99
KELLY B RIGHTSELL "RABBIT WITH BEES" RUG NWT	$58.00	Cat's Meow 14 PIECES NURSERY RHYME RHYMES	$19.36

Nursery Furniture

The average sales price in this subcategory is $74.57.

	HIGH		AVG
Simmons Shaker Bureau, Hutch, Chest Baby furniture	$400.00	Glider and Ottoman in Excellent Condition - Local P/U	$102.50
Wicker Rocking Chair with Cushions	$305.00	Glider Rocker/Rocking Chair w/Ottoman NIB	$100.00
Bellini glider (rocker) and ottoman set	$200.00	Step 2 Fire Truck bed (toddler)	$100.00
Antique Baby Changing/Doctor's Exam Table	$199.00	Antique Oak Platform Rocker - Late 1800s Eastlake Style	$71.98
Step 2 fire truck firetruck toddler bed PLUS!!	$162.50	ANTIQUE BABY WOODEN ROCKING CHAIR,ROCKER,VINTAGE	$53.00
Rocker/Recliner - Tan (purchased at Foley's)	$150.00	Natural wood toddler bed with mattress	$52.01
NEW ARMS REACH CO SLEEPER BEDSIDE / PACK AND PLAY MINT	$116.00	Little Tikes Tykes Blue Race Car Corvette Bed &Mattress	$51.00

Safety

The average sales price in this subcategory is $24.97.

	HIGH		AVG
Sturdy, light weight PVC Exercise Pen Playpen Puppy pen	$91.00	Evenflo Wide Spaces Swing Gate Fits 42" - 60" Dog Baby	$28.00
Q-See 2.4 GHz Wireless B&W CCTV Camera and Monitor	$61.00	WIRELESS PINHOLE COLOR SPY CAMERA SECURITY NANNY CAM	$27.00
Richell Deluxe Pet Sitter - Wood/metal dog gate - NEW	$49.99	WIRELESS PINHOLE COLOR SPY CAMERA SECURITY NANNY CAM	$26.00
Home Security Camera & Monitor Baby Monitor(Brand New)	$49.01	WIRELESS PINHOLE COLOR SPY CAMERA SECURITY NANNY CAM	$25.45
Home Security Camera & Monitor Baby Monitor(Brand New)	$44.00	WIRELESS PINHOLE COLOR SPY CAMERA SECURITY NANNY CAM	$24.50
Home Security Camera & Monitor Baby Monitor(Brand New)	$43.00	WIRELESS PINHOLE COLOR SPY CAMERA SECURITY NANNY CAM	$22.50
Home Security Camera & Monitor Baby Monitor(Brand New)	$41.01	[2 of these sold for $22.50 each]	
Evenflo Wide Spaces Swing Gate Fits 42" - 60" Dog Baby	$40.00	WIRELESS PINHOLE COLOR SPY CAMERA SECURITY NANNY CAM	$21.56
WIRELESS PINHOLE COLOR SPY CAMERA SECURITY NANNY CAM	$33.00	WIRELESS PINHOLE COLOR SPY CAMERA SECURITY NANNY CAM	$20.56
First Years Hand Free Gate Fits 29" - 34" Dog Baby	$31.00	WIRELESS PINHOLE COLOR SPY CAMERA SECURITY NANNY CAM	$20.53

Strollers

The average sales price in this subcategory is $122.68.

	HIGH		AVG
CHARIOT CARRIER BIKE TRAILER, JOGGER OR STROLLER...USED	$495.00	Trek Rocket child trailer/ jogger Great Condition-NR	$147.50
Chariot Carrier Bike Trailer and Jogger Stroller	$330.00	PACIFIC CYCLE DOUBLE STROLLER/BICYCLE TRAILER W/BREAK	$125.00
ANTIQUE ROYALE PRAM BABY CARRIAGE BUGGY STROLLER	$317.00	Instep Duo Cruiser Bicycle Trailer Stroller DuoCruiser	$102.50
Burley D'Lite Bike Trailer with Walk 'n Roller Kit	$305.00	Healthrider Double Jogging Stroller - Free Shipping	$102.50
Burley 2 Seat Trailer - Excellent Condition	$280.00	BELL Multi-Seat Jogging Baby Stroller/BICYCLE TRAILER	$96.00
Burley D'Lite 1 or 2 Child Bicycle Trailer - Top Cond!	$225.00	ANTIQUE F.A. WHITNEY BABY BUGGY STROLLER CARRIAGE	$91.50
TREK Child Trailer - Experience lasting top quality	$202.50	NIB SAFER CHILD/BABY BICYCLE SEAT/CARRIER W/ACCESSORIES	$89.00
NIB NEW 2005 Double Bike Trailer / Stroller~ AWESOME !	$199.99	DOUBLE DECKER r Baby Stroller, Jogger, Frame	$81.00
Burley solo bike trailer w/stroller attachment	$160.00	Pacific Explorer Double Stroller Bike Trailer Combo	$76.00
ANTIQUE WICKER BABY BUGGY CARRIAGE Pristine/Full Sized	$152.50	Antique Vintage "GENUINE TAYLOR TOT" Baby Stroller	$76.00
		BRAND NEW IN THE BOX! LITTLE TIKES COZY CRUISER	$75.00

Toys ▸ Rattles, Teethers

The average sales price in this subcategory is $22.62.

	HIGH		AVG
Old Victorian Sterling & Mother of Pearl BABY RATTLE	$102.50	Vintage MOP Teething Ring with Sterling Silver Rattle	$17.38
Old Sterling & Pearl BABY RATTLE Nursery Rhyme RABBIT	$63.00	Vintage MOP Teething Ring with Sterling Silver Rattle	$11.06
		FISHER PRICE 1966 ROCKING HORSE CHIME BALL BEAUTIFUL!!	$10.50
		ANTIQUE BABY RATTLES & TEETHERS–THE COLLECTORS BIBLE!!	$9.99
		NWT PRECIOUS MOMENTS PRAYER DOLL W/BONUS BLANKET	$8.99

4

BOATS

Boats is a relatively new top-level category on eBay. It began as a subcategory of eBay Motors and can still be found within that main category as well.

Because boats are higher-dollar-value items than many other things on eBay, you need to be extra careful here when buying or selling. Some eBayers report that sellers of vehicles—be they boats or cars—are pressuring buyers to leave feedback for the transaction while they are still on the dealer's lot (or private premises of the seller). You're better off waiting until you get the vehicle home and can have it checked out. Or better yet, you may want to arrange to have an inspection of the vehicle before you complete the sale.

Sellers need to be wary, too. One man told of a buyer who purchased his boat, which he'd given a bath, hooked up, and tied down, and had ready to deliver at 5 AM the next day. At 3 AM he got a call from the buyer, who said his wife went nuts when she found out about his big-ticket purchase, and now he wanted to back out of the deal, plus get back his deposit.

Bargains and Misplaced Items

People buying even brand-new vessels can save thousands of dollars on boats. A new Skeeter SL180 fishing and skiing boat went for $15,100.00 on eBay, a savings of about $4,900.00 over the retail price of this model, as listed on sites such as iBoats.com. And if you're willing to dip back into previous decades for a used model, you can save thousands more. For example, a 1988 Skeeter "Fish & Ski Fresh 150" with a Mariner motor went for only $5,000.00.

Luxury yachts and sailboats have the loftiest prices in this category, not surprisingly. A couple of the most expensive boats in this sample include a 147-foot Camper & Nicholson luxury yacht, which sold for $175,000.00 with 19 bids; and a 1991 catamaran Outremer 40 went for $130,000.00 with 28 bids. (In comparison, a 1992 Outremer was listed for sale on yachtbroker.escapeartist.com for $165,000.00; and a 1999 Outremer was listed on another site for 225,000.00 euros).

In the middle of the price range in Boats ▶ Powerboats & Motorboats, a 2003 Sea Ray SRX sold for $12,100.00, and a 1995 Boston Whaler went for $14,100.00. Average sailboat prices here fell between about $2,900.00 and $3,500.00. Most of these were slightly older models, with many from the 1980s and fewer from the 1970s and 1960s.

The Other Boats subcategory has some interesting finds, including several houseboats ranging from about $5,600.00 all the way to $72,000.00 on the high end and one for $3,000.00 in the average range of prices.

As you get into the low range of prices for Boats ▶ Other Boats, you start to see a phenomenon that occurs frequently in the low end of prices for many eBay subcategories: the prices are very low, but they sometimes include items that don't really belong in that category. Therefore, in the low range of Boats ▶ Other Boats, you see things like boat motors for a couple hundred dollars, a wireless rotating spotlight for $65.00, a tabletop propane grill for $20.00, and even a "Nautical large framed sail picture" for $74.49.

But that doesn't mean you can't find actual boats for rock-bottom prices. Some of the least expensive vessels in the Other Boats subcategory include a rubber raft boat for $69.99, a riptide kayak for $150.00, and an antique wooden outboard boat for $200.00. Some are fixer-uppers: in the Sailboats subcategory, a Laser sailboat went for $159.50 with 36 bids. The description of this item certainly does not overpromise: "If you watch Dave Letterman—'will it sink or will it float?'—this is the condition of this sail boat . . . If you are just going out for the day to learn how to sail, this would be a great, fun boat for family outings—life jackets required!"

Not all the lowest-priced boats are in poor condition; a Snark Sea Skimmer sailboat in "excellent condition" sold for $300.00. The seller says it was only used six times in a freshwater lake, and "the 55 sq. ft. main and 15 sq. ft. jib make this a fast boat!"

Some only need minor tweaks: an AMF Alcort Sunfish from the 1980s went for $345.03 with 24 bids—it is billed as being in "working condition" other than the sail perhaps needing replacing; and an El Toro sailboat, complete and in "excellent condition" sold for $350.00. It was made in 1970 and is described as "ready to sail" except for one line stop that can be replaced "for about ten bucks at West Marine store."

All in all, you would be hard-pressed to find a wider variety of boats of all types in one location online, and savings of thousands of dollars are not uncommon. Just be sure to vet any potential purchase carefully, as always, and have a sound knowledge of eBay's policies and procedures for before and after the sale, in case anything should go wrong with the transaction.

2004 DONZI 35 ZFO W/ TRIPLE 250 MERCURY XS OPTIMAX & TRAILER

Bidding has ended for this item
If you are a winner, Sign In for your status.

List an item like this or buy a similar item below.

The seller ended this listing early to sell to the high bidder(s) at cu

Winning bid:	**US $95,000.00**
Ended:	Feb-21-06 17:24:25 PST
Shipping:	Buyer responsible for vehicle pick-up or shipping. Vehicle shipping quote is available.
Sells to:	Worldwide
Item location:	Saint Petersburg, Florida United States
History:	1 bid
Winning bidder:	millenniummarineservices (2)

Fishing Boats

The average sales price in this subcategory is $4,781.18.

	HIGH		AVG
2004 Stratos 201 Pro XLDC / Yamaha 250 VMAX HPDI	$28,500.00	b 20 boston whaler outrage	$4,999.99
21' Shallow Sport - Miller Lite Boat - Yamaha 150 VMax	$26,500.00	1989 KingFisher XL-179 FS Bass Boat w/Johnson GT150	$4,950.00
2003 Triton TR-21 bass boat with trailer	$25,600.00	1990 TRACKER NITRO 175 F 17 1/2 FT BASS BOAT!!!!	$4,950.00
2002 Bayliner 2452 Ciera Classic	$25,441.00	1989 KingFisher XL-179 FS Bass Boat w/Johnson GT 150	$4,950.00
Triton 2001 SF-21 Not Ranger Skeeter Lund	$20,499.00	1983 Ranger 350 V Bass Boat	$4,800.00
2005 Bass Cat Sabre **Brand New** Never put in water!	$19,500.00	1998 JAVELIN 389 B 19' BASS BOAT & TRAILER NO RESERVE!	$4,750.50
2004 NITRO 929 CDX FISHING 225HP MERCURY BASS BOAT NEW	$19,200.00	2004 tracker Grizzly 16 Bass " NO RESERVE"	$4,750.00
2005 Triton TR-186 Bass Boat, Mercury VMax 150 H.P.	$18,011.00	19.5 " BONITO FISHING BOAT 140 HP EVINRUDE SUPER NICE	$4,551.00
Skeeter TZX190 Bass Boat Only 100 Hours! Like New LOOK	$17,999.00	1999 PRINCECRAFT 162 DLX w/ 35hp /Trolling Motor&F.F.	$4,550.00
2001 DYNASTY 23' CENTER CONSOLE 02' 225 SALTWATER NICE!	$17,988.00	1995 Trophy 1703 CC with trailer and motor	$4,550.00
1997 Ranger 461 Comanche Bass Boat	$16,600.00	Tracker bass boat magna17 Convertible, 90HP Evinrude	$4,550.00
STRATOS 2004 BASS FISHING BOAT 285 150 HP LIKE NEW	$16,000.00	Tracker Super Guide V-16, 40 ELPT, close to new	$4,550.00
1999 TRITON TR21	$15,600.00	1985 RANGER 372V BASS BOAT 200 MERCURY	$4,550.00
VIPER COBRA 201 BASS BOAT	$15,500.00	1993 Sunbird 20ft. CENTER CONSOLE w/trailer NO RESERVE!	$4,509.99
NEW 2005 SKEETER SL180 FISH AND SKI	$15,100.00	16FT Lund Mr. Pike Boat with 40HP Johnson Motor	$4,501.00

Powerboats & Motorboats

The average sales price in this subcategory is $10,015.32.

	HIGH		AVG
147' Camper & Nicholson Luxury Yacht	$175,100.00	2003 Sea Ray SeaRay SRX 185 Fish & Ski w/WARR, 19 hrs!!	$12,100.00
1999 Sea Ray Sundancer 340 - Only 180 Hours!	$115,000.00	#6103 1993 29ft Wellcraft Prima 287	$11,600.00
43 foot Wellcraft Scarab SC Thunder Low Hours	$106,850.00	93 Lavey craft speed / ski boat	$11,150.00
2004 ELIMINATOR 28 DAYTONA TD TUNNEL CAT 100MPH SKATER	$100,000.00	40ft.OWENS 1947 "Classic"	$11,095.00
1995 Sea Ray 370 Sedan Bridge 200 Hours	$94,000.00	Yamaha XR1800 Limited Edition 2000 (GREAT LAKES) 310hp	$11,000.00
2005 Fountain 29 Fever Powerboat not Cigarette Formula	$81,999.00	Fishing Boat Procraft 180 Combo Fish and Ski	$10,550.00
- 28' BOSTON WHALER OUTRAGE-W/A -Fishing Legend!	$75,000.00	Great looking 1996 Red CrownLine 20' !	$10,101.00
Apache Powerboat, Not Fountain, Cigarette, Clean,	$73,600.00	28' Checkmate Speed Performance Boat NR	$10,000.00
2003 Cobalt 282 with Twin Mercruiser 350 Mag MPI	$71,000.00	Bayliner/US Marin 3250 Avanti Sunbridge NO RESERVE Boat	$10,000.00
BAJA 29 OUTLAW 2002 / NOT FOUNTAIN SCARAB DONZI SST	$69,490.00	Sea Ray Searay Express Cruiser 300SRV w//trailer NR	$9,900.00
1995 34FT MAGIC SORCERER	$68,000.00	Boston Whaler 17' with Honda 90 HP 4-Stroke OB 98 hrs	$9,500.00
BAJA 33 OUTLAW SST BOAT - No Reserve Auction	$65,000.00	33' 1974 Chris Craft Coho/FE All Fiberglass Cruiser	$9,457.00
- 28' BOSTON WHALER OUTRAGE-W/A -Fishing Legend!	$63,850.00	95 Celebrity Firestar, V8, Captains Call, Will Ship, NR	$9,000.00
NO RESERVE YACHT BOAT BURNS CRAFT 43 MOTORYACHT CLEAN	$63,360.00	Sea Ray 175 Bowrider Fish & Ski	$8,900.00
2002 Baja 29 Outlaw SST Boat with Trailer	$63,100.00	#6062 1982 29ft Wellcraft Scarab CC Cuddy	$8,700.00

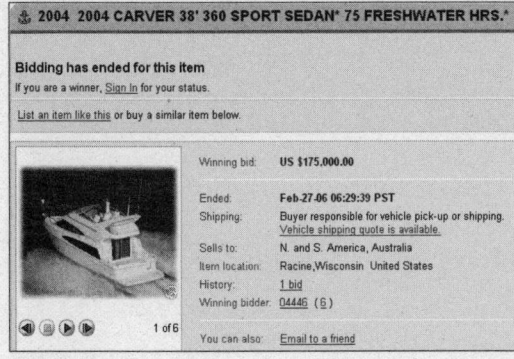

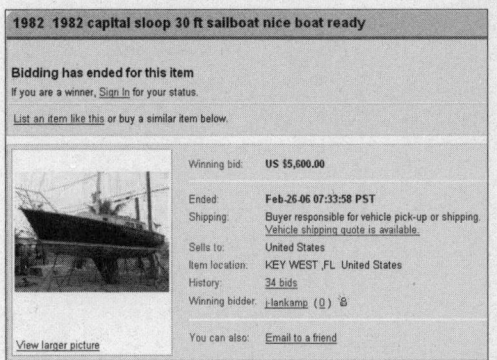

Sailboats

The average sales price in this subcategory is $3,113.74.

	HIGH		AVG
Fast sailing catamaran Outremer 40	$130,000.00	1976 26' SAILBOAT S2 YACHTS 8 METER WITH TRAILER	$3,360.51
Gemini 3400 catameran perfromance cruiser sailboat	$70,000.00	1983 MacGregor 25 Sailboat With Trailer	$3,300.00
FRESHWATER C&C 41' SAILBOAT IN VERY NICE CONDITION	$61,600.00	1968 Classic 23' Crocker Ketch Recent Inboard Diesel RI	$3,250.00
32' CATALINA SLOOP NO RESERVE AUCTION	$45,655.00	Hunter and '80 Luger Sail Boats both for 1 bid! HURRY!	$3,250.00
J/33 J-Boats 33' sailboat great for Racing or Cruising	$36,000.00	Catalina 22, with Trailer, New Sails, Rigging, Cushions	$3,226.75
SAILBOAT CANADIAN SAILCRAFT CS30 CLEAN SHARP 30 ft 1985	$25,700.00	29' Ericson Yacht tall rig	$3,200.50
#6096 1979 38ft Downeaster 38 Cutter	$25,475.00	22 foot trailerable daysailer weekender	$3,200.00
1974 Columbia 45' Sailmaster Sloop	$25,000.00	17' VENTURE SAILBOAT EXCELLENT CONDITION!!! MUST SEE!!!	$3,150.00
2004 MacGregor 26 M Sailboat with Motor and Trailer	$24,600.00	32 foot Sloop	$3,150.00
MacGregor Sailboat 26X trailer 4 stroke 50HP Suzuki	$17,500.00	WD Schock Co Sailboat Thistle 17_ Daysailer #2120	$3,065.00
32' Pearson Sailboat in Harbor in Charleston, SC	$15,300.00	26 ft. Chrysler Sloop/Trailer/Yamaha Motor WOW!!!	$3,050.00
MacGregor 26X 50-HP Powersailer (1999)	$13,300.00	Islander 37 Blue Water Cruiser Project boat Low Reser	$3,050.00
HUNTER 31 WheelTiller Ocean Sailboat South Carolina	$13,275.00	24 foot American Mariner Recently Rebuild	$3,050.00
TMI (Ticon) 30ft Sailboat	$13,000.00	1974 Balboa 26 Foot LOW RESERVE	$3,050.00
1976 Tartan 34 Take me to the Bahamas!	$12,000.00	Laser Sailboat In Great Condition With Trailer, Phili	$3,050.00

Other Boats

The average sales price in this subcategory is $3,114.50.

	HIGH		AVG
1998 Gibson Executive Houseboat 50'	$72,605.12	21" Maxum Runabout, 1990, Good shape and runs great	$3,650.00
LUXURY HOUSEBOAT - GREAT LIVEABOARD	$40,000.00	ZODIAC 15' INFLATABLE YAMAHA OUTBOARD 50	$3,620.00
2005 Yamaha SX 230 High Output, SX230HO, Jet Boat, New	$34,200.00	WAVERUNNER: 1997 YAMAHA GP1200	$3,250.00
1989 FORMULA 29' PC MINT WITH GENERATOR NO RESERVE	$25,200.00	1994 Four Winns Fling 14', trailer, cover,115HP Extras	$3,250.00
Catamaran Cruiser houseboat	$23,000.00	VA3208BE	$3,200.00
Boston Whaler "Revenge" Cuddy Cabin 200hp Dual trailer	$17,099.00	Scat II Hovercraft - Rescue Craft - 35 HP Cuyuna Engine	$3,150.03
Breau Bay Craft/Crew Boat/Work Boat/Aluminum Boat	$16,600.00	24' Pontoon, trailer, 40 HP Mercury Outboard, canopy	$3,150.00
1993 Aqua Cruiser Houseboat 30 ft	$15,000.00	1979 PENN YAN SPORT FISHING BOAT 26' MODEL 26SF - GREAT	$3,055.06
48' HOUSEBOAT at Lake Powell	$12,800.00	19' Cheyenne Picklefork Hydro/no jet boat/v drive drag	$3,050.00
Airboat 1997 Alumitech Airgator	$12,300.00	1969 26' Houseboat NO RESERVE	$3,000.00
PONTOON BOAT-2000 18 FT VOYAGER FISH & SPORT	$9,600.00	Marathon Florida Keys Houseboat 40' Fiberglass V Hull	$2,979.99
2004 BAYLINER,175 BR,W/TRAILER,BOAT,NICE,CLEAN,175,NO R	$9,100.00	SWITZER CRAFT	$2,949.00
1969 Nauta-Line 34' Houseboat on Lake Travis, TX !!!!!!	$8,500.00	Skeeter bass boat	$2,900.00
1997 SUN TRACKER 21FT. PARTY DECK BOAT	$8,500.00	Penn Yan restored rare vintage wood boat wooden canoe	$2,850.00
House Boat 42' Nautaline Fiberglass	$7,100.00	1989 Scatt Hovercraft Boat Kawasaki 440 with trailer	$2,764.97

5

BOOKS

Of all eBay categories, Books has the most competition from other online selling venues, including Amazon.com, Alibris, and Abebooks. Each of these selling venues has its pros and cons. Abebooks is the largest fixed-price online marketplace for books, with over 50 million books listed. But among some professional booksellers, there is also a perception that its prices can be too high. "For searching comps [sales prices for comparable books], the primary weakness of Abebooks is price inflation," says Craig Stark, editor of the bookselling resource newsletter "The BookThinker" (www.bookthink.com).

But knowing that your book is worth a lot of money and actually being able to sell it for a good amount are two different things. In that respect, because eBay simply has so many people shopping its virtual aisles, it's often the best place to unload that inventory. Unless, of course, you have lots of patience and shelf space, or can afford to wait for months until that perfect well-heeled buyer comes along.

One nice thing about buying books, as opposed to other items, is that sellers can ship your purchase using "media mail," aka "book rate," which is a lot cheaper than first-class or priority mail rates. However, it does take longer to arrive—usually seven to ten days.

Pricing to Sell

I picked up a paperback copy of *Fast Times at Ridgemont High* by Cameron Crowe at a yard sale for a dollar or so, buying it mainly because I'd seen the movie based on the book and thought it would be interesting to read the novel. What I didn't realize at the time was that this particular edition of the book had more value because it was published before the movie came out: on the cover was a blonde cheerleader—not one of the actresses from the movie—and a box that proclaimed "Soon to Be a Motion Picture." It was also in very nice condition for a vintage book, with no creases, rips, or stains.

I looked up the book's value on Abebooks and Amazon.com based on similar listings and came up with a value of $95.00, which sounded great, so I listed it on Amazon.com at that fixed price. Weeks passed, and nothing. So I decided I'd try my luck on eBay—there might be some Sean Penn or Cameron Crowe fans on there trolling for memorabilia. Sure enough, by the end of the week, the book sold. I got $43.00 for it—not quite the lofty $95.00, but not a bad return on my $1.00 investment. I started the bidding just under $10.00, to attract attention and to avoid the higher insertion fee for items started at higher than $9.99.

Sure, you might have better luck selling your books on the other sites. But eBay's Books category does offer sellers a huge number of potential buyers, and it offers buyers a vast selection. eBay's Fiction Books subcategory alone had listed well over 100,000 books as of this writing.

NOTE *If you've not yet tried your hand at it, selling books on eBay can be a lot easier than selling other items, because of eBay's increasingly integrated Pre-Filled Item Info feature. This allows you to enter an ISBN (International Standard Book Number) and let the eBay software fill in the item description and even a stock photo for you; you don't even have to fool around with a digital camera. Of course, with a rare and particularly valuable book, you will want to take your own pictures of the book, but for more moderately priced or everyday books, this expedited listing process can be the best choice.*

Best Categories

There aren't too many surprises in the Books category. Rare or antique books go for a lot more than common everyday books. The midrange of prices in the subcategories usually falls between about $4.00 and $10.00. On the low end, the actual final sales prices are often just pennies, plus a few dollars for shipping—sometimes $5.00 or a little more. In some cases, it looks like sellers are making their money on the shipping and handling fees, but even then, with their time factored in, some are probably losing money on these books. Certainly, as a buyer, you can pick up any number of mass-market paperback books by popular authors for very low prices: a 1996 Jonathan Kellerman title sells for $1.49 plus $3.00 shipping; *Cause of Death* by Patricia Cornwell sells for $1.99 plus $3.50 shipping.

Aside from lower-priced fare, the Antiquarian & Collectible subcategory houses some amazing items that fetch plenty of prices in the thousands. Some very interesting and historic books come up in the Antiquarian & Collectible ▶ Americana subcategory, for example. An 1852 first edition of Harriet Beecher Stowe's *Uncle Tom's Cabin* sold for $3,207.00, and a copy of *My Bondage and My Freedom* by abolitionist Frederick Douglass went for $1,125.00. With these old, rare books, the sellers are usually careful to include many different photos in the auction, with several different angles of the book, including the spine, cover, and inside pages and illustrations. (If you're selling a collectible book and don't want to include multiple pictures, at least try to take a single clear photo of the book at a slight angle, so its spine and cover are clearly visible.) For the Douglass book, a scanned title page and a page with Douglass's photo were included.

When selling books, the big buzzwords are *edition* and *condition*, but these aren't the only deciding factors in a final sales price. (The spine of the Frederick Douglass book was mostly worn away, but as the seller put it, it's in "good condition for its age.") Sometimes what draws people to a book is the art or the artist who did the illustrations—either interior or cover—so if your book features notable illustrations, be sure to include the artist's name in the auction title, so eBayers searching on that artist will find your item. Similarly, regional books can attract people who grew up or currently live in an area, or who have other strong ties to the place. One of the top sellers in the Antiquarian & Collectible ▶ Americana subcategory was a series of ten books from 1887 entitled *Picturesque California*, edited by John Muir, with 120 plates. This kind of book has strong regional appeal and is also full of many beautiful illustrations. It's rare, in great condition, and would appeal to naturalists and fans of California history alike, all of which help explain why it fetched $3,000.00.

The publishing phenomenon of Harry Potter pops up throughout the category, from a high of $2,060.00 for five "deluxe" first editions plus a couple of "bonus books" (about fantastic beasts and Quidditch) in the Antiquarian & Collectible ▶ Children's subcategory, to $455.50 for a set signed by J.K. Rowling. The low end goes down to $0.01 with $5.00 shipping for a used paperback (although the latter is not included in this sample). A typical Harry Potter book in gently used condition goes for around $11.00 with a few bucks shipping.

Audiobooks is a particularly hot subcategory in Books, with a midrange price of about $6.00 to $16.00. Many of the higher-priced titles include foreign-language instruction ("PIMSLEUR Learn to Speak Russian," for $445.00) and self-help ("Lucinda Bassett Attacking Anxiety and Depression CDs. 16 CDs-4 videos-workbook-2004 deluxe edition-Complete," for $305.00).

Buyers' Bargains

Sellers may do well with first editions and audiobooks, but there are plenty of bonanzas for buyers in this category as well. It's a great place to find inexpensive gifts, such as new address books or journals—a new Barbie spiral-bound journal went for only one cent plus shipping charges. And used or rare books can also make very special gifts for people because they can have sentimental value. One eBay seller recalls the reaction she got from a buyer of her circa 1968 Betty Crocker cookbook with a red background and a round design on the cover: "I opened the pages of this cookbook, and it was like time stood still. All of a sudden, my grown kids were little again, and they were trying to help me bake cookies in the kitchen," wrote the buyer.

Magazines and Catalogs

eBay currently includes magazines and catalogs in the Books category. This includes back issues of popular magazines (a copy of the very first *Playboy*, with Marilyn Monroe on its cover, sold for $2,800.00), and you can also find discounted magazine subscriptions here. A year's subscription to *People* went for $63.99, which, according to the auction description, is normally sold by one seller for $114.00—a savings of $50.01. Marilyn Monroe pops up again in the high prices of the Magazine Back Issues ▶ Celebrity subcategory, such as on a 1947 *Parade* magazine cover, which sold for $357.87. Among general interest bestsellers, old *National Geographic* issues tend to do very well, capturing two of the high price slots in this sample, including a set of a dozen 1964 reprints of 1899 issues for $314.99.

In terms of catalogs, the Princess Diana dress auction catalog regularly sells here for close to $500.00—in this sample it sold for $477.73. Abercrombie & Fitch Quarterly magazines sell well regularly in lots—here they fetched $425.00. Mid-century Sears catalogs and things like antique hardware and general goods catalogs often command high prices as well.

Book and Magazine Accessories

Unless you're selling high-end items like the Chanel agenda and planner book listed in this chapter, book accessories are not the highest-yielding items. This category is, however, a good place to search for gifts at low prices, like specialized bookmarks, or address books with a theme to match your gift recipient, such as the Baby & Sunflower address book that went for $3.50.

In sum, the Books category on eBay is a great place to pick up inexpensive common paperbacks and low-cost gifts, and it's a good place to sell rare and antique books, magazines, and catalogs, where millions of people can potentially be exposed to your listing. Selling common, everyday books can also be relatively easy and quick with eBay's Pre-Filled Item Info feature. Before you sell, though, it's wise to check completed prices for comparable versions of your specific book or magazine to make sure it will be worth your while.

Accessories ▸ Address Books

The average sales price in this subcategory is $6.01.

	HIGH		AVG
AUTHENTIC CHANEL GREEN CAVIAR LEATHER AGENDA	$125.00	@@ I LOVE LUCY FRIENDS STAY CONNECTED ADDRESS BOOK @@	$6.50
Levenger CIRCA LEATHER JACKET FOR ADDRESS BK espresso	$32.00	Red Hat Credit Card Holder Book "4 Society Lady"	$6.50
Telephone book1956 Fall River/Little Compton/TivertonRI	$30.00	GENUINE BLACK LEATHER ADDRESS BOOK - FLEUR DE LIS	$6.50
Levenger CIRCA LEATHER JACKET FOR ADDRESS BK toffee	$25.95	Vintage FANCY ADDRESS BOOK made in Japan NIB	$6.50
WHOLESALE MICKIE AND MINNIE MOUSE ADDRESS BOOKS LOT/24!	$24.99	Franklin Covey Business Binder with complete guts	$6.00
Wholesale 12 Magnetic Travel Size Address/Phone# Books	$24.51	Brand NEW Telephone and Address Book Gold Tone in Gift	$6.00
1940 Shenandoah, Iowa Telephone Book and Calendar	$23.95	FOUR Beautiful Address Books Flower Victorian and Asian	$5.99
NEW Levenger Circadex Leather Pocket Address Book Brown	$21.51	Address Birthday Anniv, Christmas card Gift list Book	$5.99
NIB Vintage Metal Address Phone Book ~Zephyr American~	$20.95	Vintage Bakelite Address/Phone Book	$5.99
Hallmark Maxine Refillable Address Book	$20.53	NEW gift idea Phone Address book vintage shoe	$5.99
ZIGGY'S ADDRESS BOOK............	$18.49	BUTTERFLY & HYDRANGEAS SPIRAL ADDRESS BOOK ~ NEW	$5.99
CALFSKIN LEATHER Ring Bound Desk ADDRESS BOOK NEW Gift	$16.39	LANG FOLK ART ADDRESS BOOK - NEW IN BOX	$5.95
Vintage Bates List Finder Metal Address Phone Book	$15.99	RED HAT LADIES ADDRESS BOOK ~ PURPLE AND RED ~ NEW	$5.95
DRAGONFLY PHONE ADDRESS BOOK NEW REAL NICE!	$15.50	ADDRESS BOOK Hard Cover Womens Art Deco Collection	$5.75
Vintage Bates Metal List Finder Phone Address Number Nw	$15.50	EMILY ADAMS COUTURE ADDRESS BOOK - NEW	$5.50

Accessories ▸ Blank Diaries, Journals

The average sales price in this subcategory is $8.38.

	HIGH		AVG
New Tumi Letter Pad Leather In Sealed Box 1779	$109.00	Journal with decorative leather, cover	$8.00
Italian Leather Journal LIKE Harry Potter LOTR 8x10 BIG	$99.00	Beautiful Hand Made Journal/Diary	$8.00
Vintage Italian Leather Diary drawings Pressed flowers	$80.00	[2 of these sold for $8.00 each]	
Italian Written Childs Leather	$50.00	2 New Laurel Burch Journal / Diary Fantasic Felines	$7.99
Diary & Art Work LOOK!!		Emily The Strange Morphing Journal Art Book	$7.99
Anthony Tony Robbins Results Coaching Journal NEW	$41.00	Wholesale 10 Monet Diaries Day Journal Diary Office New	$7.99
3 Graces Italian Handcrafted Leather Journal /Scrapbook	$40.01	[2 of these sold for $7.99 each]	
Toccata Italian leather journal / sketch / scrapbook	$40.00	NEW~Palm Tree~Boxed Gift Set~5 Pc. Set~Nice~	$7.99
Beautiful Handmade Leather Bound Journal Set	$35.99	Wholesale 10 Monet Diaries Day Journal Diary Office New	$7.99
Unique Handmade Leather Bound Journal Set	$35.99	3 MOLESKINE Cahier Pocket notebook/plain/ruled/squared	$7.95
Beautiful Handmade Leather Bound Journal Set	$32.99	NEW - VERA BRADLEY NEW HOPE JOURNAL	$7.03
Distressed Leather HANDMADE Pocket Sized journal CSS	$32.00	*NEW* CICELY MARY BARKER FLOWER FAIRY SET *FUCHSIA*	$7.00
Gold Deer Leather HAND-MADE travel journal CSS	$31.00	FIORENTINA - Copper Metallic Cork Journal	$7.00
Paris Hilton Leather Journal/	$30.00	WRITE TO REMEMBER MY VACATION JOURNAL GUIDED WRITING	$7.00
Hermes Orange Set/3 ~ WOW		Moleskine Diary 2005 380 pages, address+planner	$7.00
NWT KATE SPADE PINK LEATHER	$29.99	[2 of these sold in a multiple item ("Dutch") auction for $3.50 each]	
JOURNAL BOOK FOR PURSE		Experiences, Attitudes & Observations-A Golf Journal	$7.00
Vintage Diary 1886 EXCELSIOR	$29.42	BLACK CLOTH BLANK JOURNAL ~ DIARY ~ NEW	$6.95

Accessories ▸ Bookmarks

The average sales price in this subcategory is $45.22.

	HIGH		AVG
Paper Lace Punch Paper Bookmark w Scrap Love Token 1870	$103.00	Blue Suede Leather Bookmark with Sterling Silver Charms	$6.99
Unusual Mauchlinware Item Bookmark, Mt. Washington	$58.00	Royal Blue Suede Leather Bookmark with Fancy Cross	$6.99
English cameo top, brass page, book marker	$50.00	ASIAN SPICE BEADED BOOK THONG BOOKMARK	$6.99
Authentic TIFFANY sterling silver bookmark	$35.51	GO FISH! BEADED BOOK THONG BOOKMARK	$6.99
ATLANTIS STS-71 " FLOWN " In Space Beta Cloth Bookmark	$31.01	Sterling Silver .925 Pig Book Mark ff58	$6.99
Franklin EBC-530 Exhaustive Concordance of the Bible-	$31.00	BRIGHTON Chrome & Gold Metal Bookmark FREE SHIP BIN!	$6.99
Bear Bookmark Yosemite National Park 1940's Copper	$31.00	~ Silver FAIRY BOOKMARK Pewter Faery Fairies~	$6.99
FRANKLIN DICTIONARY & THESAURUS ELECTRONIC NEW IN PACKA	$31.00	Sterling Silver .925 Pig Book Mark ff58	$6.99
Early Blue Book Routes Celluloid Advertising Bookmark	$27.06	Jeweled Beaded Bookmark ~ PURSE LOVER ~ BHV	$6.99
Sterling Silver Bookmark Art Nouveau Lady & Flower NM	$25.01	Bookmark Hooks Silver	$6.53
Swiss Black Forest Handcarved Bookmark - Brienz c.1900	$24.99	(GG) NEW! GENUINE REED & BARTON	$6.08
ZELCO BOOKMARK DICTIONARY NEW NEVER USED	$22.75	STERLING BOOKMARK NR!	
ATLANTIS STS-71 " FLOWN " In Space Beta Cloth Bookmark	$22.50	1921 GIRL RESERVE-YWCA Bookmark with PLEDGE	$6.05
VATICAN COLLECTION Blue Enamel Gold Cross Bookmark	$19.99	Glass beaded bookmark - green glass	$6.00
[2 of these sold for $19.99 each]		HANDMADE felt bookmarks magnetic lot re-sell variety s	$5.99
Vintage Sterling Silver Millifiori Bookmark NR!	$19.99	Angel Thank You Book Thong/Book Mark	$5.99

Antiquarian & Collectible ▸ Americana

The median sales price in this subcategory is $9.99.

	HIGH		AVG
UNCLE TOM'S CABIN/1stEd/2VOL/HARRIET BEECHER STOWE/1852.	$3,207.00	MISS MINERVA ON THE OLD PLANTATION-1ST ED.	$9.99
ALL 18 FIRST PRINTING, 1st ISSUE PONTS for BOTH VOLUMES		HOUSEHOLD JOURNAL, 1861	$9.99
MUIR~PICTURESQUE CALIFORNIA~120 PLATES~10 VOLS~1887	$3,000.00	1947-48AAAM Research Equipment	$9.99
Mark Twain Rare Signed Book!	$1,899.99	Catalog - car&tools WWII	
1806 39 FANTASTIC HANDWRITTEN LEDGER LOT.	$1,730.00	1935 Whitman Famous Indian	$9.99
Baltimore Merchants; Quakers; Zoarites		Chiefs by Ben Ely #932	
1856 slave book MY BONDAGE & FREEDOM frederick douglass.	$1,125.00	Vintage VIOLETS IN THE KITCHEN	$9.99
Mark Twain LIFE ON THE MISSISSIPPI 1st/1st	$999.00	Cookbook SIGNED gourmet	

Antiquarian & Collectible ▸ Children's

The median sales price in this subcategory is $6.00.

	HIGH		AVG
Harry Potter 5 deluxe books 1st/1st plus extras! N/R.	$2,060.00	4 Vintage Dr Suess HC Books Fish Out Of Water +	$6.00
A total of 8 Bloomsbury 1st/1st books in mint condition		3 VINTAGE HARDY BOYS BOOKS....BROWN COVERS	$6.00
Kay Thompson, "Eloise" 1rst Prtng. First book of the Eloise series	$975.00	WINNIE THE POOH - by Milne –	$6.00
Harry Potter 1st Three Books Signed	$898.88	1971 - Children's Classic!	
TOAD HALL/Ltd.Ed/SIGNED A.A.MILNE KENNETH GRAHAME/1929	$865.00	Lot Of 6 Winnie The Pooh Books	$6.00
Harry Potter and the Philosopher's Stone (Signed).	$750.00	published in 1990 HB	
Bloomsbury, 1999, First Deluxe Edition, First Printing		THE LITTLE CHAP/1919-1ST EDITION	$6.00

Antiquarian & Collectible ▸ History

The median sales price in this subcategory is $9.99.

	HIGH		AVG
Abraham Lincoln - Autograph Endorsement Signed	$5,500.00	Valentine's Manual of the City of Old New York 1924 HB	$9.99
Voyages From Montreal, on the River St. Laurence, Throu	$4,227.00	1908 HARVARD UNIVERSITY BOOK	$9.99
Fine Early INCUNABLE from the Duke of Portland.	$3,717.00	RACISM RACE & CALIFORNIA	
Folio Rubricated- not after 1475.		Forty Years of American Life 1ST ED 1937 ,1821-1861	$9.99
WINSTON CHURCHILL 1st Edition WWII; LEATHER SET History Gift	$2,475.10	by Thomas Low Nichols, M.D. Stackpole Publishers	
Services. FLAWLESS Condition, MINT+! . 1st Edition EVER!! RARE!		Historia Documental de Puerto Rico	$9.99
27 volume Warren Commission JFK Assassination Report.	$1,251.99	Murga Sanz T.I 1956	
John Kennedy report by Earl Warren, et al.		10 Vol Books 1905 Story of the World 2000+illustr	$9.99

Antiquarian & Collectible ▸ Literature

The median sales price in this subcategory is $9.99.

	HIGH		AVG
E.R. Burroughs COMPLETE TRUE 1st ED/Printing MARS SET!!.	$4,638.00	Franklin Mint Library Charles Dickens Great Expectation	$9.99
5 1st state Dust Jackets incl. Thuvia, Fighting Man		FE Ned Rorem THE PARIS DIARY Composer 1st DJ gay int	$9.99
Franklin Library 100 GREATEST BOOKS OF ALL TIME + Notes	$3,506.00	the count of monte cristo-dumas vol. 2	$9.99
ON THE ROAD Jack Kerouac Viking 1st HC DJ SIGNED	$3,049.00	Pete Dexter DEADWOOD n/f 1st	$9.99
13 Signed Kurt Vonnegut Books; incl. SHV, 6 Easton, BOC.	$1,925.00	The Winthrop Woman 1958 Anya Seton	$9.99
Slaughterhouse Five and BOC (nf/nf) 1st Prngs w/ djs			
1ST EDITION! LEATHER Set: ALEXANDER POPE! Iliad,Odyssey Gift	$1,825.00		
Services. RARE, 1824: '"Roscoe's Pope"'! GORGEOUS FULL LEATHER!			

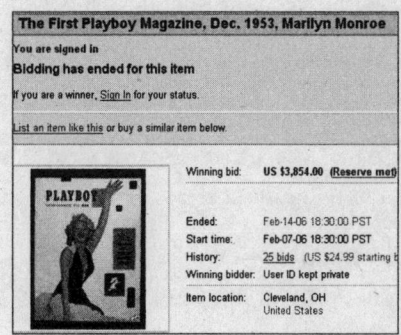

Audiobooks ▸ Fiction—Cassette

The median sales price in this subcategory is $7.00.

	HIGH		AVG
THE WORK AND THE GLORY AUDIO BOOK SERIES (All 9) LDS	$237.60	UNABRIDGED AUDIO BOOK	$7.00
47 Audio Books on Cassette, 1 on CD all unabridged.	$202.60	" JACKDAWS" by KEN FOLLETT	
J.K. Rowling, D. Koontz, S. King, N. Roberts, more!		Lot of Audiobooks-Novels	$7.00
HUGE LOT, GRISHAM, KING, CORNWELL, GRAFTON, 56 ON TAPE	$199.99	Mr. Murder, Dean Koontz, Audio book	$7.00
LEFT BEHIND BOOKS 1 - 12 UNABRIIDGED VERSION	$150.00	2 Tony Hillerman audiobook	$7.00
HUGE LOT 30 AUDIO BOOKS ON TAPE-FICTION/NON-FICTION.	$137.50	First Eagle/Hunting Badger	
Mystery-Thrillers-& Good Non-Fiction-Some Never Opened		The Lovely Bones by Alice Sebold (2002)	$7.00

Audiobooks ▶ Fiction—CD

The median sales price in this subcategory is $9.01.

	HIGH		AVG
Stephen King audiobook set Many titles, CD, cassette	$255.00	AUDIO BOOKS CD UNABRIDGED	$9.03
Stephen King Audio All 7 Dark Tower CD Audio Books	$222.50	THE CAT WHO TALKED TURKEY	
Harry Potter ALL 6 Audio BOOKS CD BRAND NEW Unabridged	$192.50	THE ART OF MENDING~Elizabeth Berg~Unabridged~CD Audiobk	$9.01
ALL 6 HARRY POTTER AUDIO CD BOOKS NEW No Reserve	$192.50	Bleachers By John Grisham	$9.01
ALL 6 HARRY POTTER AUDIOBOOKS ON UNABRIDGED CD.	$188.00	The Hobbit - J.R.R. Tolkien - Audio CDs	$9.00
new-factory sealed-reasonable shipping-NOT bootlegs!		"THE GREAT GATSBY" by F. Scott Fitzgerald- unabridged	$9.00

Audiobooks ▶ Instructional—Cassette

The median sales price in this subcategory is $9.51.

	HIGH		AVG
Robyn Thompson's Complete Rehabbing Courses	$430.51	Ultimate Italian by Ingeborg Lasting Ph.D. (1998).	$9.95
PIMSLEUR Learn To Speak RUSSIAN 1,2,3 Combo Set Cas NEW.	$385.00	448 Page Book + 8 Audio Cassettes	
Save With a Combo Set, Single Units Also Available Here		Mastering Spanish (1986) plus extras!	$9.51
PIMSLEUR Learn to Speak French 1,2,& 3 Combo Cass NEW.	$383.00	PIMSLEUR GERMAN LANGUAGE	$9.51
Save With a Combo Set, Single Units Also Available Here		LESSONS LANGUAGE PROGRAM	
Understanding Objectivism - Ayn Rand Tape Lecture.	$202.50	Dog Psychology audiotape set,	$9.50
Leonard Peikoff Lecture 22 Tapes Atlas Shrugged		DVM, 9 hours, Dodman dogs	
ROBYN THOMPSON'S RETAILING FOR ALL CASH - CASS/MANUAL	$153.43	VERBAL ADVANTAGE LEVAL ONE- 2 AUDIO CASSETTES	$9.38

Audiobooks ▶ Instructional—CD

The median sales price in this subcategory is $18.99.

	HIGH		AVG
PIMSLEUR Learn To Speak Russian 1,2,3 Full Set CDs NEW.	$445.00	Instant Immersion LEARN FRENCH 8 audio CDs NIB	$18.99
Save with a combo set! Single Units Also Available Here		NEW Learn to Speak Spanish Language	$18.99
PIMSLEUR Learn to Speak CHINESE MANDARIN 1,2,3 CDs NEW.	$433.00	Easy on 8 Audio CD	
Save With A Combo Set, Single Units Also Available Here		New 8 audio CD's Learn to Speak GERMAN Language	$18.99
Pimsleur Learn To Speak FRENCH Combo Set 1,2,3 Cd! FULL	$320.00	NEW Speak ADVANCED Spanish language	$18.97
Pimsleur Learn to Speak MANDARIN CHINESE vol. 1-3 on CD	$315.01	Easy on 8 Audio CD	
Learn an Accent, Acting w/ an Accent CD ALL 25 titles	$235.00	Teaching Company, Doctors: History of Medicine	$18.95

Audiobooks ▶ Religion—Cassette

The median sales price in this subcategory is $7.50.

	HIGH		AVG
HUGE LOT~Joyce Meyer Teaching Tapes ~Must See!	$335.00	Jack Boland STARTING OVER	$7.50
22 COMPLETE SETS !!! LIKE NEW CONDITION...GREAT DEAL!!		Audio Lecture 4 Lessons Mint!	
CREATION OF HUMAN ABILITY LECTURES SCIENTOLOGY HUBBARD	$179.60	~JAMES EARL JONES READS THE BIBLE~	$7.50
Joyce Meyer cassette tapes. 13 complete albums	$168.50	AUDIOBOOK LIKE NEW	
Work and the Glory Audiobooks vol. 2-9 new never used	$138.10	NICE! Great Mormon Women Dramatized LDS Audio Tapes	$7.50
17 KENNETH COPELAND CHRISTIAN AUDIO CASSETTE TAPE BOOKS	$121.76	Jack Deere, Demonic Inroads, 5 audiotapes.	$7.50
Collection of Kabbalah Class Tapes	$127.50	Charismatic Vineyard Theologian	
10 sets of Joyce Meyer teaching tapes! HUGE lot #3	$102.50	Audio Set: Joyce Meyer's Believing God! New, A255	$7.50

Audiobooks ▶ Religion—CD

The median sales price in this subcategory is $15.50.

	HIGH		AVG
Bible in Living Sound *COMPLETE* 75 CDs - $446 Reg NEW!	$266.00	Joyce Meyer CONTENTMENT AND SATUSFACTION CDS	$15.50
43 CD SERIES ON BOOK OF REVELATIONS BY DAVID JEREMIAH	$168.50	New International Version Audio Bible (2001) Dramatized	$15.50
NEW! Dramatized Left Behind CD Set - Sound and Drama!	$143.93	Teaching Company - Great World Religions - Christianity	$15.50
REMOTE VIEWING TRAINING COURSE David Morehouse	$120.50	Audio Set: Joyce Meyer's Believing God! New, C255	$15.49
The Teaching Company Understanding the Human Body DVDs	$105.53	T.D. Jakes Heirs of the Promise Boxed CD Set! New	$15.45

Audiobooks ▶ Self-Help—Cassette

The median sales price in this subcategory is $6.99.

	HIGH		AVG
Attacking Anxiety & Depression Complete Program- NIB!!.	$350.00	Zig Ziglar Top Performance	$6.99
Self Help Program for stress, anxiety & depression		Mega Speed Reading Kevin Trudeau&	$6.99
Attacking Anxiety and Depression, Lucinda Bassett! BNIB	$232.50	Howard Stephen Berg	
Attacking Anxiety & Depression Complete Program- NIB!!.	$225.00	Ed Forman,Fully Alive,6 audio cas-great wisdom	$6.99
Self Help Program for stress, anxiety & depression		Creating Love by John Bradshaw	$6.99
Attacking anxiety & depression by LUCINDA BASSETT. A SELF-HELP,	$223.50	(1992) Audiobook	
Lucinda Bassett's Attacking Anxiety and Depression NIB. complete set!	$200.00	31 SECRETS OF AN UN 4 GETABLE	$6.99
17 cassettes, 1 video, workbook , MORE !		WOMAN, MIKE MURDOCK	

Audiobooks ▸ Self-Help—CD

The median sales price in this subcategory is $15.95.

	HIGH		AVG
Lucinda Bassett Attacking Anxiety and Depression CDs. 16 CDs-4 videos-workbook-2004 deluxe edition-Complete	$305.00	New 2 CD FLOW Mihaly Csikszentmihalyi nlp	$15.95
Lucinda Bassett Attacking Anxiety & Depression program. Includes BOTH complete CD & Cassette sets for self help	$297.16	Get 10 Qualities of charisma NLP nightingale Conant CDs	$15.95
LUCINDA BASSETT ATTACKING ANXIETY–DELUXE NEW CD EDITION. 16 CDs, 4 COACHING VIDEOS, CURRENT VERSION WORKBOOK++++ [2 of these sold for $293.95 each]	$293.95	New 2 CD The Psychology of Achievement Brian Tracy nlp	$15.95
		Brian Tracy's 21 SECRETS TO SUCCESS	$15.89
Attacking Anxiety and Depression (Lucinda Bassett)	$227.50	8 Audio CD Set NEW	
LUCINDA BASSETT ATTACKING ANXIETY–DELUXE CD EDITION. 16 CDs, 4 COACHING VIDEOS, CURRENT VERSION WORKBOOK++++	$287.95	New 6 CD CHOOSING YOUR OWN GREATNESS Wayne Dyer	$15.69

Catalogs

The average sales price in this subcategory is $21.67.

NOTE *These results are based on a keyword search of the Catalogs subcategory for auctions with the word* catalog *in the title.*

	HIGH		AVG
Rare Princess Diana Dresses Auction Catalog Hardback	$477.73	Buescher Band Inst Catalog 1923 trumpet trombone horns	$25.99
Abercrombie A&F Quarterly Catalog Magazine Set	$425.00	1954 SEARS 68th. ANNIVERSARY CATALOG	$25.49
A.G. Spalding & Bros. Winter Sports Catalog Ca. 1889	$305.00	Skinner catalog glass canes walking stick whimseys	$23.53
OLD SHAPLEIGHS HARDWARE CO KEEN KUTTER CATALOG	$237.50	1920s Pathe phonograph player catalog w flyer	$23.50
OLD Lightolier Co. ART IN LIGHTING Catalog ART DECO	$229.49	JOHN PLAIN CATALOG Book+supplement 1942 BUDDY L LIONEL+	$23.39
1935 Hamilton Punch Board Gambling Board Color Catalog	$212.00	'06 Annual Seed Catalogue Catalog Ross Bros Worchester	$23.15
MODERN FIREFIGHTING EQUIPMENT Catalog 1926	$168.39	Spiegel Catalog,1946,Spring Summer,Complete	$23.00
1901 Farwell Ozmun Kirk HARDWARE CATALOG 1311 pages	$168.00	1953 Simpsons Sears Spring & Summer Catalog 1st	$22.50
1957 Sears Christmas Catalog Wish Book Vintage	$167.50	1927 PERFECTION STOVE Range Furnace CATALOG Orig	$22.50
1960 Sears CHRISTMAS Catalog - TOYS DOLLS PEDAL CARS	$150.50	1952 FREDERICK'S OF HOLLYWOOD HOLIDAY CATALOG VOL 5 #6	$22.49
1908 Storrs & Harrison seed catalog Painesville OHio	$130.07	1953 FREDERICK'S OF HOLLYWOOD HOLIDAY CATALOG VOL 6 #12	$22.49
EARLY Gebruder Marklin Miniature Railway Catalog c.1900	$114.50	1954 FREDERICK'S OF HOLLYWOOD SPRING CATALOG VOL 7 #15	$22.49
1966 ORIGINAL SIMPSONS-SEARS CHRISTMAS CATALOG NEAT! NR	$112.50	1954 FREDERICK'S OF HOLLYWOOD HOLIDAY CATALOG VOL 8 #19	$22.49
1960 Sears Christmas Book Catalog-Vintage Toys	$110.00	HEWLETT PACKARD CATALOG 1976 ELECTRONIC INST. & SYS	$22.45
Vintage Sears and Roebuck Catalog /1924-1925	$100.00	SEARS SPRING & SUMMER CATALOG 1973 IN PAPER WRAPPER!	$22.01

Children's ▸ Classics

The median sales price in this subcategory is $3.04.

	HIGH		AVG
Seuss Bartholomew and the Oobleck 1st Ed. 1949 200/200	$861.00	Madeline and the Bad Hat by Ludwig Bemelmans FREE SHIP	$3.20
1932 Ralston Purina Seckatary Hawkins Book	$522.00	12 Little Golden Books for Children- Poky Puppy -Heidi	$3.04
charlie and the chocolate factory- dahl-1st edition	$401.00	WALT DISNEYS BAMBI/BIG GOLDEN BOOK-1949	$3.03
The Adventures Of Pinocchio-Collodi-1926-1st Amer. Ed..ATTILIO MUSSINO ILLUSTRATIONS	$360.01	1967 Walt Disney Whitman Book Gnome Mobile #1577	$3.01
		RARE 1989 Disney DONALD IN	$3.00
OZ BOOK COLLECTION, BY L. FRANK BAUM, 14 HARD COVER BKS	$286.99	DISNEYLAND Large Boardbook	

Children's ▸ Fiction

The median sales price in this subcategory is $2.99.

	HIGH		AVG
HARRY POTTER-PRISONER OF AZKABAN-SIGNED UK DLX1ST ED #1 100% GENUINE SIGNATURE BY CLIFF WRIGHT-COVER ARTIST!!!	GBP 1,100.00	7 Goosebumps Childrens - Great Variety!	$3.00
		The MAGIC PUDDING Norman Lindsay	$2.99
WORK FROM HOME: LOT OF 338 PERSONALIZED CHILDRENS BOOKS. CREATE-A-BOOK LETS YOUR CHILD BE THE STAR OF THE STORY!	$627.89	RUDYARD KIPLING children's book AMAZON jaguar ARMADILLO	$2.99
Harry Potter and the Sorcerer's Stone by J. K. Rowli... Set of First 3 Books ~ First Printings~First Editions	$500.00	PONY PALS-LOT OF 4 [2 of these sold for $2.99 each]	$2.99
Paolini ERAGON: First U.S. Printing, MINT, SIGNED	$426.50	Children's Fiction The Boxcar Children	$2.99
HARRY POTTER BOOKS HAND SIGNED SET 1ST/ JK. ROWLING. COMES WITH ORIGINAL COA.	$381.99		
Tom Swift Jr Series Volumes 1 thru 29 Set	$340.00		

Children's ▸ Learning to Read

The median sales price in this subcategory is $3.13.

	HIGH		AVG
200 New books Scholastic,make good offer,retail $1000. all ages,picture,bestsellers,disney,newberry,award win-	$300.00	LG. LOT OF DISNEY/NICKELODEON BOOKS!! 16 BOOKS TOTAL!	$3.24
1946 Friends & Neighbors Dick and Jane Child Book	$283.99	Leap Pad Phonics Program Lesson 7, Mole's Huge Nose NIP	$3.14
Lot of Teacher Big Books	$200.00	Dr. Seuss B-32 SUMMER Children's Book HC Alice Low	$3.13
57 lot DR SEUSS Beginner Books Hardcovers NEW	$187.50	Group of 3 Early Reading Books	$3.09
22 Like New Dr. Suess Larger Size Books	$157.50	Mine, All Mine 1999 Ruth Heller Book about pronouns	$3.03

Children's ▸ Picture Books

The median sales price in this subcategory is $3.67.

	HIGH		AVG
Huge Lot of Childrens Books! Eric Carle, Dr Seuss...	$179.50	Amy Maura	$3.70
The Polar Express, Scholastic, over 80 books!!!		Lot 11 Vintage Wonder Books	$3.69
Huge Children's Book Lot Eric Carle Lois Ehlert Teacher.	$177.50	Very Good Shape	
74 GREAT BOOKS POPULAR AUTHORS INSTANT LIBRARY		SoftPlay NOAH'S ARK Bible	$3.67
Children's Book Lot Caldecott Eric Carle Teachers NEW.	$167.50	Story Cloth Book NEW NR	
60+Popular Authors&Titles INSTANT LIBRARY		My Mama Had a Dancing Heart	$3.58
Ultimate Lot of 65 DR. SEUSS HC BOOKS!!! NR!	$114.49	by Libba Moore Gray hb	
LARGE LOT OF 60 CHILDREN'S SPANISH BOOKS *NEW*.	$112.50	Berenstain Bears books -	$3.58
CLASSROOM K - GRADE 3 ESPANOLA/ENGLISH		various titles	

Children's ▸ Series

The median sales price in this subcategory is $3.99.

	HIGH		AVG
Harry Potter and the Philosopher's Stone (Signed).	$750.00	5 FRENCH BOOKS SERIE LIVRE D'ARGENT	$3.99
Bloomsbury, 1999, First Deluxe Edition, First Printing		4 FRENCH BOOKS CONTES ET FABLES D'ANIMAUX	$3.99
HARDY BOYS SINISTER SIGNPOST W/DJ, THICK, ORANGE EPS	$522.99	Phantom Stallion Softcover Books #1 #2 #8	$3.99
Sutton - Judy Bolton Lot of 33 Books Vintage! HB/DJ OOP	$499.00	NANCY DREW #12 MESSAGE IN	$3.99
Percy Fitzhugh: Pee Wee Harris Turns Detective HB DJ	$379.89	HOLLOW OAK Vintage Early PC	
Walter Farley 21 Vintage Black Stallion Books-HB/DJ OOP	$375.00	NANCY DREW #41 WHISTLING BAGPIPES Vintage BEAUTIFUL!	$3.99

Fiction ▸ Action, Adventure

The median sales price in this subcategory is $1.95.

	HIGH		AVG
SAUL BELLOW "Henderson the Rain King" SIGNED! 1959	$400.00	ONCE AN EAGLE, ANTON MYRER, 1968, FIRST EDITION	$1.95
LOT OF 15 ~ CLIVE CUSSLER ~ DIRK PITT NOVELS ++	$355.01	VOYAGE BY STERLING HAYDEN, 1976	$1.95
The Heat Islands by Randy Wayne White (1992)	$200.00	Skeleton Crew by Stephen King (1985)	$1.95
Wizard and Glass by Stephen King (1997)	$172.50	3rd Degree by Andrew Gross, James Patterson 2004 $3 S&H	$1.95
DEATHLANDS SERIES BOOKS 71 IN ALL	$170.00	ONCE AN EAGLE, ANTON MYRER, 1968, FIRST EDITION	$1.95

Fiction ▸ Classics

The median sales price in this subcategory is $2.99.

	HIGH		AVG
38 LEATHER HARD COVER BOUND CLASSIC NOVELS VICTORIAN NR	$810.00	LITTLE WOMEN - WWII Edition	$2.99
Gone With the Wind, First Edition, May 1936	$760.00	The Three Theban Plays by	$2.99
ALL 5 HARRY POTTER BOOKS 1ST Ed. SIGNED J.K. ROWLING. L	$455.50	Bernard MacGregor Walker K...	
IMITED EDITION, VERIFIED AUTHENTIC WITH COA'S ISSUED		HARRIET BEECHER STOWE.	$2.99
ALL 5 HARRY POTTER BOOKS 1ST Ed. SIGNED J.K. ROWLING	$354.99	UNCLE TOM'S CABIN - 1981	
LIMITED EDITION, VERIFIED AUTHENTIC WITH COA'S ISSUED		Pride and Prejudice by Jane Austen / & Cliff Notes	$2.99
30 VOLUMES TIME LIFE CLASSICS OF THE OLD WEST - - MINT!	$255.25	The Odyssey (Trojan War, Odysseus, Troy) Homer	$2.99

Fiction ▶ Fantasy

The median sales price in this subcategory is $4.00.

	HIGH		AVG
Colour of Magic Terry Pratchett HB 1/1 Signed	GBP 4,650.00	Ranma 1/2, Vol.7, Rumiko Takahashi,	$4.00
Ultra Rare 1983 Colin Smythe 1st Edition 1st Print		Viz Graphic, BR.NEW	
V.RARE-2 x SHADOWMANCER - 1/1 HB - Leather + Paintings	GBP 4,000.00	LOT OF 4 MYTH SERIES PB BOOKS	$4.00
The very first mount and faber copies, signed & No 1's		by ROBERT ASPRIN	
ROBOT SANTA - DEAN KOONTZ - SGNED - ORIG. PARKS DRAWING	$550.00	PIERS ANTHONY LOT OF 9-MIXED LOTS	$4.00
JK ROWLING SIGNED HARRY POTTER & THE SORCERER'S STONE.	$385.00	The Book of Lost Tales Part One	$4.00
obtained 04.21.05 : bonded COA : officially sponsored		by J. R. R. Tolkien	
* 1 UK ED 1/1 - GAME OF THRONES - GEORGE R.R. MARTIN*	$336.52	Key of Valor by Nora Roberts	$4.00
Wheel of Time Complete Set - HB - Robert Jordan	$167.50	Large Print Book	

Fiction ▶ Horror

The median sales price in this subcategory is $2.00.

	HIGH		AVG
Dean R Koontz Uncorrected Proof. Hanging On	$1,045.00	1 HC "MEMNOCH THE DEVIL"	$2.01
STEPHEN KING - SIGNED FIRST EDITION FIRESTARTER - 1980	$1,026.00	VAMPIRE CHRONICLES ANNE RICE	
Anne Rice Interview With The Vampire 1ST EDITION SIGNED.	$1,025.00	Flesh Gothic by Edward Edward Lee (2005)	$2.01
THE COMPLETE VAMPIRE CHRONICLES ALL SIGNED 1ST EDITIONS		Tarnished Gold by V. C. Andrews (1996)	$2.01
STEPHEN KING WIZARDS & GLASS SIGNED & NUMBERED #249	$910.00	HARDCOPY of THE STAND by STEVEN KING!!!!	$2.00
STEPHEN KING THE WASTELANDS SGND & #ED DARK TOWER #249	$835.00	MIDNIGHT WHISPERS by V. C. Andrews (1992)	$2.00

Fiction ▶ Mystery, Thriller

The median sales price in this subcategory is $1.99.

	HIGH		AVG
Agatha Christie TEN LITTLE NIGGERS 1st w/fdj 1939 RARE	$500.00	The Sinner by Tess Gerritsen (2004)Low Shipping!	$1.99
HUGE Lot of 3,000 Mixed FICTION PAPERBACKS !!!	$405.00	Sax Rohmer 33 titles eBooks on CD Dr. Fu Manchu	$1.99
Sanibel Flats by Randy Wayne White (1990)	$400.00	One False Move by Alex Kava (2005)Low Shipping!	$1.99
Set 85 Bantam Agatha Christie Mystery Collection Books	$399.80	LOT OF 2 LISA JACKSON PAPERBACKS	$1.99
AGATHA CHRISTIE MYSTERY COLLECTION ~80HB BOOKS~ LEATHER	$357.00	Cause of Death by Patricia Cornwell (1997)	$1.99

Fiction ▶ Romance

The median sales price in this subcategory is $1.78.

	HIGH		AVG
DIANA PALMER - -73 BOOKS	$223.50	Liana Merrill - MY RED SHOES - ONE NIGHT? SAY YES!!!	$1.78
OUTLANDER DIANA GABALDON RARE HB/DJ/1ST/1ST	$158.12	NORA ROBERTS-2 Books,The Calhouns,2005, Series	$1.78
Diana Gabaldon - A Breath of Snow and Ashes - ARC	$149.95	~ EXIT TO EDEN ~ by Anne Rice * Erotic * xltsp	$1.78
72 ROMANCE PAPERBACKS BY DIANA PALMER SOME HTF OOP	$127.50	The Gift by Nora Roberts (2004) New	$1.78
40PB Paranormal Vampire Time Travel Witch Ghost MAGIC	$125.05	Pleasure Garden by Regan Allen (2005)	$1.78

Fiction ▶ Science Fiction

The median sales price in this subcategory is $2.99.

	HIGH		AVG
V.I.E. The Vance Integral Edition Jack Vance	$3,650.00	2001 - Making of / Kubrick / Paperback / 1970	$2.99
ROGER ZELAZNY,NINE PRINCES IN AMBER,1HB,VF/F,SIGNED/VR	$1,535.11	Star Trek : Q-Space 1 – 3	$2.99
DARK TOWER GUNSLINGER TRUE 1st SIGNED BY STEPHEN KING.	$1,100.00	STAR WARS THE TRUCE AT BAKURA	$2.99
TRUE 1st/1 IN MINT CONDITION SIGNED BY STEPHEN KING		by Kathy Tyers (1994) 1st	
Stephen King The Dark Tower VII DELUXE LIMITED SIGNED.	$700.00	STAR WARS - DARKSABER by	$2.99
DELUXE EDITION # 484 IN PUBLISHERS SHRINKWRAP		Kevin J. Anderson (1995) 1st	
Easton Press Signed First Editions	$699.44	The Main Experiment PB Christopher Hodder-Williams	$2.99

Magazine Back Issues ▶ Celebrity

The median sales price in this subcategory is $4.99.

	HIGH		AVG
MARILYN MONROE(Parade)Norma Jeane_Cover 1947	$357.87	Big 8 HALLE BERRY MAGAZINE LOT MAGAZINES	$4.99
MARILYN MONROE (Fox)1954~the Dynamo_ Cover ~ Mint	$227.50	Allure May 2002 CHRISTINA AGUILERA cover NL	$4.99
MARILYN MONROE(Beautiful) Hit~ Cover~1949~Mint	$224.72	LA CONFIDENTIAL MAGAZINE -	$4.99
OZ TV WEEK MAGS 1969 COLLECTABLE SUPER RARE VOLUME 60's	AU $180.29	TOM CRUISE BEYONCE BRAD - PIC	
Extravaganza of TV & music history !! Very Cool Retro		Fleetwood Mac Joan Collins Will Rogers Jr. Peter Best	$4.98
RARE LAFF JAN 1953 MARILYN MONROE SEXY PIN-UP GIRLS	$137.50	Osbournes Lisa Marie Presley Tim McGraw Jerry Lewis	$4.98

Magazine Back Issues ▸ Home and Garden

The median sales price in this subcategory is $3.00.

	HIGH		AVG
HARROWSMITH MAGAZINE ISSUES #1-83 HB in Green Leather	$174.50	Victoria Magazine April 1996 good condition	$3.00
MARTHA BY MAIL CATALOG 17 ISSUES FROM MARTHA STEWART	$129.49	Victoria Magazine April 1995 Great Condition	$3.00
Martha Stewart Living #1 Winter 1990 Premier Issue	$127.50	LOT of 6-REAL SIMPLE- -FEB.-AUG.+OCT.2002- -FULL OF INFO!	$3.00
PREMIERE Issue Martha Stewart Living Magazine 1990	$120.49	Mother Earth News Back Issues - Lot of 4	$3.00
Mary Engelbreit's HOME COMPANION Magazines	$103.63	DEC. 1935 THE AMERICAN HOME Magazine NICE COND. XMAS	$3.00

Magazine Back Issues ▸ News, General Interest

The median sales price in this subcategory is $5.00.

	HIGH		AVG
Huge Lot Geographic News Bulletin 1925-1937	$1,026.05	LOT 11 VINTAGE LIFE MAGAZINES 1960'S	$5.00
1600 Time Magazines-1933 & Up -Rare- Great Ads & Covers	$799.99	LIFE MAGAZINE OCTOBER 29 1971 DAVID CASSIDY NICE NR	$5.00
National Geographic-1899 12 Issues 1964 Reprints	$314.99	LIFE MAGAZINE JANUARY 21 1972 A WEEKS DEAD IN VIETNAM	$5.00
National Geographic-1898 12 Issues 1964 Reprints	$280.00	COSMOPOLITAN BRIDGET BARDOT ISSUE NOVEMBER 1958	$5.00
WW1- HISTORY OF FIRST WORLD WAR (Purnell) Complete	GBP 142.00	2 Awesome Issues of Life Magazine June 9&October 8,1945	$5.00

Magazine Subscriptions ▸ Celebrity

The average sales price in this subcategory is $8.20.

	HIGH		AVG
RARE "V" 1948 french magazine Marilyn Monroe cover	$162.28	GISELE BUNDCHEN NEW FRENCH MAG PHOTO 2005 !!!	$9.75
MARIANNE FAITHFULL cover +8p, PATTIE & JENNY BOYD &more	$76.00	MARIAH CAREY NEW FRENCH SEXY MAG FHM COVER 2005 !!!	$9.75
yasmeen ghauri for Gianni Versace 1992! Rare photos	$59.10	GISELE BUNDCHEN NEW FRENCH	$9.50
MARILYN MONORE LIZ TAYLOR VIVIEN LEIGH JULIE LONDON	$49.99	GLAMOUR MAG 2005 COVER !!!	$9.50
MAGAZINE LAS VEGAS VOL 5	$49.95	Amazing Romola Garai clippings!!	$9.50
NO 12 DECEMBER 1954 XMAS EDIT.		CHAD MICHAEL MURRAY Magazine ONE TREE HILL PICS POSTERS	$9.50
PAMELA ANDERSON NUD* PL@YBOY	$39.99	2005 Mary-Kate Ashley Olsen Twins Magazine Poster Pics	$9.50
Mexican Magazine MEGA RARE		Jaguares, Caifanes Sonika 07/2005 HOT Mexican Magazine	$9.50
STAR Magazine Subscription - 52 ISSUES/1 YR - $0 S/H	$36.99	JOHNNY DEPP NEW FRENCH MAG	$9.50
MARILYN MONROE LANA TURNER 1953 COVER MAGAZINE	$34.99	PREMIERE 2005 SPECIAL ISSUE	
MARILYN- Her Tragic Life MAGAZINE by ESCAPE 1962 Monroe	$31.94	Jane Magazine 2 year Subscription 20 NEW issues NO S&H	$9.49
Antonio Lopez mag. Vanity 1983 illustred	$30.00	Amazing Michael Vartan clippings!!	$8.99
STAR Magazine Subscription - 52 ISSUES/1 YR - $0 S/H	$29.99	NY DAILY NEWS 25 HOURS-ANDERSON COOPER-4/10/2005	$8.50
STAR Magazine Subscription - 52 ISSUES(1 Yr)	$28.50	Maxim Magazine 4 years Subscription 48 NEW issues	$8.50
STAR Magazine Subscription - 52 ISSUES/1 YR - $0 S/H	$28.00	AFTER DARK GAY MAGAZINE JOSEPH	$8.50
RAGAZZA IN ASIA (BUGGLES)	$28.00	BOTTOMS MELINA MERCOURI	
TUTTO N.10/83 ASIA (BUGGLES)	$28.00	Takeshi Kaneshiro BRIDGE MAGAZINE w/Andy Lau Zhang Ziyi	$8.49
IAN THORPE - THE BIOGRAPHY HC Book Aussie NEW BE QUICK!	$28.00	Spin Magazine 3yr Subscription 36 NEW issues	$8.45

Magazine Subscriptions ▸ Cooking, Food, Wine

The average sales price in this subcategory is $13.07.

	HIGH		AVG
Wine Spectator 2 year subscription (34 issues)	$49.99	2yr Subscription COOKING LIGHT Magazine	$17.00
[4 of these sold for $49.99 each]		2yr Subscription COOKING LIGHT Magazine	$16.00
Wine Spectator 1 year subscription (17 issues) - $0 S/H	$29.99	Sunset Magazine Subscription Western Living at its Best	$15.00
Wine Spectator 1 year subscription (17 issues)	$29.99	WEIGHT WATCHERS MAGAZINE	$14.97
[4 of these sold for $29.99 each]		SUBSCRIPTION 2 YRS FREE SHIP	
Wine Spectator 1 year subscription (17 issues)	$28.99	Cooking Light & Gourmet Magazine Subscription 1 Year	$14.50
WINE SPECTATOR Magazine Subscription-17 ISSUES-$0 S/H	$25.49	BON APPETIT Magazine - 3yr Subscription {36 issues}	$13.98
WINE SPECTATOR Magazine Subscription-17 ISSUES-$0 S/H	$24.99	[4 of these sold for $13.98 each]	
GOURMET and BON APPETIT 3YRS Each FREE SHIPPING	$24.95	SAVEUR Magazine - 5yr SUBSCRIPTION {45 issues}	$13.98
4 COOKING MAGAZINES - Subscription {1yr Each}	$23.98	[4 of these sold for $13.98 each]	
COOKING LIGHT - 3yr SUBSCRIPTION {33 issues}	$20.98	Wine Spectator 1 year subscription ~ $0 S&H ~ NR!!!	$13.26
[4 of these sold for $20.98 each]		BON APPETIT Magazine - 3yr Subscription {36 issues}	$12.98
Wine Spectator 2 year subscription ~ $0 S&H ~ NR!!!	$20.50	Wine Enthusiast Magazine 1 yr. FREE S/H No Hidden Costs	$11.95

Magazine Subscriptions ▸ General Interest

The average sales price in this subcategory is $7.81.

	HIGH		AVG
The Economist Business News 1 Yr Subscription 51 Issues	$52.00	National Geographic Adventure	$9.99
THE ECONOMIST Magazine Subscription - - 1 year 51 issues	$48.51	Magazine 2Yr Sub +2 Bonus	
The Economist Business News 1 Yr Subscription 51 Issues	$47.95	Full year of Details magazine (1998)	$9.99
The Economist Business News 1 Yr Subscription 51 Issues	$44.95	Full year of Details magazine (1999)	$9.99
CONSUMER REPORTS w/BUYING GUIDE - 3yr Subscription	$39.98	Guitar One Magazine 3 Year Subscription w/ 2 Bonus	$9.99
CONSUMER REPORTS w/BUYING GUIDE - 2yr Subscription	$26.98	Guitar One Magazine 3 Year Subscription w/ 2 Bonus	$9.99
ENTERTAINMENT WEEKLY Magazine Subscription 1 Year	$26.97	FORBES MAGAZINE 3 Yr Sub NEW NR!	$8.99
NEW YORKER Magazine - 3yr **Special Sale**	$25.98	Invest Right *LOOK*	
[3 of these sold for $25.98 each]		MAD MAGAZINE 1YR(12 ISS)	$8.99

	HIGH		AVG
NEW YORKER Magazine - 3yr **Special Sale**	$24.98	MAGAZINE SUBSCRIPTION$8.99 WOW	
[2 of these sold for $24.98 each]		Golf World MAGAZINE 1Yr Sub 46new issue Free S/H	$7.69
FAMILY CIRCLE, WOMANS DAY, FAMILY FUN 3 YRS EACH NO S/H	$24.94	[3 of these sold for $7.69 each]	
O, Oprah Magazine-1 Year Subscription	$21.00	Parents magazine 3 yr subscription 36 NEW Issues	$7.49
NEWSWEEK 1YR (53 ISSUES) SUBSCRIPTION!!	$19.00	Runner's World magazine 2 yr subscription 24 NEW Issues	$7.49
NEW YORKER Magazine - 2yr **BEST BUY** {92 issues}	$17.98	Sunset 1 yr subscription 12 NEW Issues	$7.49
[6 of these sold for $17.98 each]		American Angler magazine 2 yr subscription 12 Issues	$7.49
Playboy Magazine 1 Year Subscription w/ 2 Bonus	$16.99	Parents Magazine 3 Year Subscription w/ 2 Bonus	$6.99
[2 of these sold for $16.99 each]		Ebony Magazine 1yr"FREE" S/H No Hidden Costs	$6.49
READER'S DIGEST - 4yr Subscription {48 issues}	$15.98	Rolling Stone magazine 2 yr subscription 24 NEW Issues	$6.49

Magazine Subscriptions ▸ Men

The average sales price in this subcategory is $24.58.

	HIGH		AVG
MARILYN MONROE DECEMBER 1953 PLAYBOY**	$3,950.00	Maxim Magazine 3 year Subscription 36 NEW issues	$6.97
ABSOLUTELY MINT!!		[3 of these sold for $6.97 each]	
Playboy Magazine, 1954 Volume 1, Number 2	$316.22	Playboy January 1964	$6.95
Ryan McGinness Bathing ape street art Skateboard deck	$133.50	Modern Man Magazine Jan 1958 Jayne Mansfield Pinup	$6.50
1957 PLAYBOY Magazines Complete Set (12 issues)	$111.45	Japanese Girls Photo Magazine "Beppin" K-Y-64z	$6.45
KAWS x BATHING APE COLETTE BENDY TRANSPARENT Limitd100	$85.99	LOT OF PENTHOUSE 1974 MENS MAGAZINES CENTER FOLD	$6.05
[2 of these sold for $85.99 each]		Japanese School Girls Photo Magazine Cream 10/03	$6.00
KAWS x BATHING APE COLETTE BENDY TRANSPARENT Limitd100	$82.00	Japanese School Girls Photo Magazine Cream 10/02	$6.00
ANN MARGRET, LAURA GEMSER, CATHERINE BACH and ++	$76.99	Japanese School Girls Photo Magazine Cream 08/04	$6.00
King Magazine Vida Guerra Mya Gloria Velez Beyonce	$41.00	Japanese School Girls Photo Magazine Cream 04/00	$6.00
11 issues of Playboy from 1958, no September	$41.00	Playboy Magazines August 1958 & March 1960 NR	$5.99
GQ Magazine 2004 Collection of Issues, All Good Cond	$37.00	Supreme Milk book w/ Michael Lau & Bathing ape x kaws !	$5.99
RAQUEL WELCH 70s - collectible of 54 photos	$35.00	VIDEO GIRLS Vol.3 Photo Magazine Japanese girl -DVD-	$5.99
Takashi Murakami DALEK signed 2002 first art Book Bape	$34.99	PLAYBOY AUG. 1977 PATTY MCGUIRE	$5.95
'50s FABULOUS FOTOS FEATURING BETTY PAGE Betty Page-c	$33.99	DA FONZ HENRY WINKLER	
ART PROSTITUTE BAPE Obey Giant Shepard Fairey Signed	$32.00	PLAYBOY MAY 1978 ANITA RUSSELL ANITA BRYANT	$5.95
Complete Set of Playboy Magazines from 1964	$32.00	LOUIS VUITTON x Takashi Murakami *june* LV bible bape	$5.74

Magazine Subscriptions ▸ Movies & TV

	HIGH		AVG
Star Magazine 1 Year Subscription w/ 2 Bonus	$39.99	SOAP OPERA DIGEST 1 YEAR	$6.99
US Weekly Magazine 1 Year Subscription w/ 2 Bonus	$36.00	MAGAZINE SUBSCRIPTION DEAL!!!!	
US Weekly Magazine 1 Year Subscription w/ 2 Bonus	$35.99	Rolling Stone Magazine 2 Year Subscription NO S/H	$6.99
US Weekly Magazine 1 Year Subscription w/ 2 Bonus	$34.99	MOVIELINE Magazine Subscription - 1 Year -FREE Shipping	$6.39
[3 of these sold for $34.99 each]		PREMIERE 3 YEAR MAGAZINE SUBSCRIPTION	$5.99
TV Guide 1 Year Magazine Subscription 52 New Issues	$29.98	BEST DEAL ON EBAY	
[13 of these sold for $29.98 each]		VIBE MAGAZINE 3 YEAR Subscription NO SHIPPING	$5.99
ENTERTAINMENT WEEKLY Magazine Subscription 1 YR -NO S/H	$27.29	ROAD AND TRACK 1 Year Magazine Subscription FREE SHIP!!	$5.99
[2 of these sold for $27.29 each]		WIRED MAGAZINE 3YR SUBSCRIPTION NO S/H	$5.89
Entertainment Weekly Subscription-- 1+ year / 57 issues	$26.97	GIANT 4 YEAR MAGAZINE SUBSCRIPTION	$4.99
NICKELODEON Magazine - 3yr SUBSCRIPTION {30 issues}	$11.48	GUIDE TO TV MOVIES++	
[3 of these sold for $11.48 each]		PREMIERE Magazine Subscription 1 Year - Free shipping!	$4.89
Rolling Stone Magazine 2 year Subscription 52 NEW Iss	$10.98	VIBE 1 YEAR MAGAZINE SUBSCRIPTION	$3.99
Rolling Stone Magazine 4 Year Subscription NO S/H	$9.99	12 ISSUES BEST DEAL!!	

Magazine Subscriptions ▸ Sports & Outdoors

The average sales price in this subcategory is $9.73.

	HIGH		AVG
FLEX 2 Year Magazine Subscription HOT FREE SHIPPING!	$25.99	National Geographic Kids Magazine 1yr Subscription 10is	$9.99
Golf Package Deal 3 Magazines One Low Price	$19.95	Sport Fishing 3 Year Subscription w/ 2 Bonus	$9.99
[3 of these sold for $19.95 each]		Trapper & Predator Caller 1 Yr. Subscription w/ 2 Bonus	$9.99
SPORTS ILLUSTRATED Magazine - 1 Year Subscription	$19.88	Golf World Magazine 3 Year Subscription w/ 2 Bonus	$9.99
the LOWEST PRICE on eBay! 56 ISSUES - SAVE $20!		[3 of these sold for $9.99 each]	
[3 of these sold for $19.88 each]		Trapper & Predator Caller 1 Yr. Subscription w/ 2 Bonus	$9.99
SPORTS ILLUSTRATED FOR KIDS 1YEAR MAGAZINE SUBSCRIPTION	$18.99	Golf World Magazine 3 Year Subscription w/ 2 Bonus	$9.99
4yr BACKPACKER Magazine - SUBSCRIPTION {36 issues}	$18.98	National Geographic Kids Magazine 1yr Subscription 10is	$9.99
[3 of these sold for $18.98 each]		Boating Magazine 2 year Subscription 24 NEW Issues	$9.99
THE SPORTING NEWS Subscription 3 YEARS - FREE Shipping!	$16.88	ESPN Magazine 3 Year Subscription w/ 2 Bonus	$9.99
The LOWEST PRICE on eBay! 180 ISSUES! Save $77!		Sport Fishing Magazine 2 year Subscription 18 NEW iss.	$9.95
[2 of these sold for $16.88 each]		Transworld Surf MAGAZINE 2Yr Sub 22new issue Free S/H	$8.99
Truckin' Magazine Subscription 1 Year Free S/H 13 Issue	$15.91	ESPN Magazine 2 year Subscription 52 NEW issues	$8.99
3yr Subscription FLORIDA SPORTSMAN Magazine	$15.50	SPORTING NEWS~NEARLY 4 YEARS	$8.99
RUNNING TIMES + RUNNERS WORLD Subscriptions~22 issues!	$14.97	MAGAZINE SUBSCRIPTION-NEW	
Golf World Magazine 2 yr Subscription 92 new issues	$13.95	Sporting News MAGAZINE 2Yr Sub 120new issue Free S/H	$8.99
[2 of these sold for $13.95 each]		Fly Rod & Reel Magazine 3 Year Subscription w/ 2 Bonus	$8.99

Nonfiction ▸ Art & Photography

The median sales price in this subcategory is $8.50.

	HIGH		AVG
A Way of Seeing-Photographs of New York by Helen Levitt.	$721.00	Barns / Nicolas S. Howe / 1998	$8.50
With an Essay by James Agee		PAINTING MORE THAN THE EYE	$8.50
Peter Beard Photos-STRESS AND DENSITY BOOK.	$560.00	CAN SEE ROBERT WADE BOOK	
Very rare book published in 1999- in original plastic		WATERCOLOR FLOWERS BOOK	$8.50
Bernard Buffet art book / Bernard Buffet: Lithographs 1	$511.89	PAINTING BOOKS LOT RILEY EASTON	
a day off: TONY RAY-JONES PHOTOS. Scarce 1st	$352.50	Norman Rockwell by Bob Hersey -A POP-UP BOOK	$8.50
DRAWINGS SIR WILLIAM RUSSELL FLINT BOOK*DJ*1950 1st ED	$330.00	The Artist's Way Creativity Kit ~ Cameron~ journal, etc	$8.50

Nonfiction ▸ Biography & Memoir

The median sales price in this subcategory is $3.95.

	HIGH		AVG
George Harrison Books - Set of 3 - Alike Numbered Titles:	$5,525.00	Pope in America (1979) A PICTORIAL	$3.95
"I Me Mine" "50 Years Adrift" "Songs"		RECORD JOHN PAUL III	
La Principaute de MONACO, signed by Prince Rainier III.	$1,200.00	The Last Knight by Norman F. Cantor (2004)	$3.95
Plates & history of Rainier's Limited Ed only 100 signd		Elvis World by Jane Stern, Michael Stern (1987)	$3.95
Winston Churchill Complete Speeches 1897-1963 8 Vol. HC	$775.55	"TO AMERICA: PERSONAL REFLECTIONS..."	$3.94
LSD My Problem Child by Albert Hofmann (Signed)	$650.00	--STEPHEN AMBROSE	
Memoirs by Harry S Truman 2 Vols. Both Autographed by Harry Truman	$355.00	[2 of these sold for $3.94 each]	

Nonfiction ▸ Business & Economics

The median sales price in this subcategory is $3.95.

	HIGH		AVG
Dan Kennedy's "MOTHER of all OFFERS" w/ CD's & DVD's!!!.	$697.77	Betty Crocker's 40th Anniversary	$3.95
MASSIVE Dan Kennedy Library all on CD & DVD!!		Edition Cook Book	
Paper Game 14 Video Bootcamp VHS John Behle, mortgage	$688.00	The Laws of Money, the Lessons of Life by Suze Orman...	$3.95
DAN KENNEDY - MOTHER OF ALL OFFERS - $2995 Value.	$547.00	Ultimate no B.S. business	$3.95
Sold By A TRUE Dan Kennedy Licensee - POWERSELLER		success book by Dan Kennedy	
E-MINI S & P Trading System Traders International E-Mini system	$510.00	The 9 Steps to Financial Freedom by Sue Orman, Suze ...	$3.95
Dan Kennedy's "DELUXE Copywriting Seminar" on CD & DVDI.	$299.77	NEW STRATEGIES FOR BUYING	$3.95
This ELITE package is now on CD & DVD!!		REAL ESTATE WITH NO CASH	

Nonfiction ▸ Computers & Internet

The median sales price in this subcategory is $5.00.

	HIGH		AVG
Video CBT Complete 18 Lab HD Set - Windows 2000/2003.	$875.00	Wario World by Prima Temp Authors (2003)	$5.00
Over 170 Hrs of CBT Training on an 80 GB USB Hard Drive		[2 of these sold for $5.00 each]	
Microsoft Visual Basic 6.0 Enterprise Edition Brand New	$400.00	PCs for Dummies by Dan Gookin (2003)	$5.00
Hellocomputer CCIE Voice Lab workbook with Solution	$400.00	PCs All-In-One Desk Reference	$5.00
Microsoft Visual Studio 6.0 Professional Edition *NEW*	$284.00	for Dummies by Mark L....	
Microsoft VISUAL STUDIO .NET Enterprise Developer	$167.50	Beginning Active Server Pages 3.0 ASP HTML	$5.00

Nonfiction ▸ Cooking, Food, Wine

The median sales price in this subcategory is $4.25.

	HIGH		AVG
Antique bartender bartending book cookbook 1887 recipes	$175.00	1936 Cookbook ~ Household Searchlight Recipe Book	$4.25
AMERICAN COOKERY 1831 BY AN ORPHAN	$174.95	3 HOMETOWN COLLECTION-AMERICA'S	$4.25
WOODSTOCK VT COLTON		BEST RECIPES- 92-94-95	
RARE PRESBYTERIAN COOKBOOK 1913 GOOD THINGS TO EAT	$158.49	Food Network Kitchens ~Making It Easy~ Cookbook NEW	$4.25
Time Life The Good Cook Cookbook Set of 27 Books	$152.50	Wilton Yearbook Cake Decorating 1978	$4.25
Time Life "THE GOOD COOK" Cookbooks~Complete 28 Vol.	$150.00	THE SOY ZONE DIET BARRY SEARS 101 RECIPES COOKBOOK	$4.25

Nonfiction ▸ Health & Fitness

The median sales price in this subcategory is $3.00.

	HIGH		AVG
1988 NARCOTICS ANONYMOUS BOOK	$202.50	What to Expect When You're	$3.00
COMMEMORATIVE EDITION 268		Expecting by Arlene Eisen...	
NARCOTICS ANONYMOUS - 2ND EDITION/1ST PRINTING W/ DJI	$189.99	Lot of 2 Fat-Burning Foods Plus Cookbook	$3.00
New First Place Weight Loss Program Starter Kit	$150.00	The Art of Sensual Massage by Inkeles & Todris	$3.00
ACE Personal Trainer Certification Exam Manual & More	$130.00	The Complete Book of Pregnancy & Childbirth by Sheil...	$3.00
This is Aikido by Koichi Tohei (10th Dan) 1972	$123.50	Woman An Intimate Geography by Natalie Angier	$3.00

Nonfiction ▸ History

The median sales price in this subcategory is $5.99.

	HIGH		AVG
Official Records of the War of Rebellion (O.R.). Complete 128-volume set in Near Fine condition	$999.00	Shelby Foote*Civil War*Vol. 1 *Time Life*NEW* 1st EDIT	$5.99
Encyclopaedia Britannica 24vol.set,1883,All original. By A & C Black, Edinburgh, Some foxing	$920.00	EDWARD ROWE SNOW BOOK 1984 HISTORY OF MIDDLE TENNESSEE	$5.99 $5.99
McKENNEY & HALL INDIAN TRIBES 120 COLOR PLATES	$515.00	THE ROYAL FAMILY~PIERRE BERTON	$5.99
SHELBY FOOTE - CIVIL WAR COMPLETE 14 VOLUME SET / NrMt	$349.99	~1954~1ST	
From PEENEMUNDE to OUTER SPACE * WERNHER von BRAUN 1962. NATIONAL AERONAUTICS & SPACE ADMINISTRATION	$295.00	Gracefully Insane ....by Alex Beam	$5.99

Nonfiction ▸ Hobbies & Crafts

The median sales price in this subcategory is $4.95.

	HIGH		AVG
Japanese Embroidery Examples & Techniques	$237.52	Ultimate Price Guide Fast Food Collectibles McDONALD's	$4.95
Lot 90 FINE WOODWORKING Magazine 1976-93 Taunton's NR	$203.50	AMERICA'S GLORIOUS QUILTS...HUGE COFFEE TABLE BOOK!!	$4.95
PRINCIPLES of KNITTING ~ HUGE CLASSIC REFERENCE	$202.50	30k WoodWorking PLANS Wood Working PROJECTS DIY CD BNHW	$4.95
Pacific Coast Highway by Alice Starmore - Like New!	$149.09	Folk Art Landscapes for Every Season by Judy Diephou...	$4.95
Spoken without a Word Elly Sienkiewicz Baltimore album	$123.69	A GARDEN OF QUILTS Mary Elizabeth Johnson	$4.95

Nonfiction ▸ Home & Garden

The median sales price in this subcategory is $4.24.

	HIGH		AVG
Native orchids united states & Canada c a luer 1975	$137.50	THE COMPLETE BOOK OF HOME INSPECTION, N. Becker	$4.24
FOXFIRE BOOKS 1, 2, 3, 4, 5, 6 7 8 9 10; 10 VOLUME SET	$132.50	Garden Pools Fountains & Waterfalls * Southern Living	$4.24
Bonsai Photos of Now Famous Minature Trees Book	$113.61	Jane Austen's Town and Country Style Decorating Design	$4.24
introduction to the orchids of mexico l a wiard rare	$104.50	THE RUTH STOUT NO-WORK GARDEN BOOK-YEAR ROUND!	$4.24
COLE, Lithops, flowering stones plants botany cacti	$99.95	OLD-TIME GARDENING WISDOM by Jerry Baker	$4.24

Nonfiction ▸ Military & War

The median sales price in this subcategory is $7.80.

	HIGH		AVG
Civil War-Official Records Naval-Complete & near-mint	$520.00	VIETNAM NONFICTION-THE PROUD	$7.85
CIVIL WAR by Shelby Foote 40th Anniversary 14 Vol. Set	$350.00	BASTARDS & INTO THE GREEN	
Virginia Civil War Battles and Leader Series, 17 vols. Bonus: 2 vols from Virginia Regimental Histories Series	$340.99	BOOK- "THE GRAND SCUTTLE"- SINKING OF THE GERMAN FLEET	$7.85
HISTORY OF THE 68th BOMB SQUADRON-44TH BOMB GROUP.	$330.00	United States Marine Corps History Book Gorgeous!!!!!!!	$7.84
THE FLYING EIGHTBALLS by WEBB C. TODD (8th Air Force)		Korean War: TRUCE TENT AND FIGHTING FRONT - Hermes	$7.80
Time Life, The Civil War: Complete Set, 28 Vol	$320.00	The Mosquito Log. the inside story of the much loved Mossie	$7.78

Nonfiction ▸ Reference

The median sales price in this subcategory is $4.99.

	HIGH		AVG
New 2005 ENCYCLOPEDIA BRITANNICA 32 volume set	$990.00	Free Goverment Grant Money,Money for Artist,Lesko Grant	$4.99
Encyclopaedia Britannica 24vol.set,1883,All original. By A & C Black, Edinburgh, Some foxing	$920.00	AMERICAN INDIAN PAINTERS: A Biographical Dictionary DUTCH WITH EASE (1995)	$4.99 $4.99
Oxford Dictionary of National Biography plus index (...	$455.00	Plat Book Buena Vista County Iowa 1973 Atlas History	$4.99
2003 World Book Encyclopedia LikeNew Teacher Homeschool	$400.00	1961 PIONEER South Jr. High School	$4.99
*Dictionary Of The Middle Medieval Ages 11-volume Set	$304.99	Yearbook, DOWNEY, CA	

Nonfiction ▸ Religion

The median sales price in this subcategory is $4.00.

	HIGH		AVG
Complete Biblical Library OT Full Set - 22 Volumes	$1,999.45	GOD WROTE ONLY ONE BIBLE Jasper Rayl	$4.00
Watchtower GREEN Bound Volumes 1879-1919 Complete	$1,225.00	+ How we got our	
Crowley's Equinox complete white 10 volume Weiser set.	$1,000.00	McGee Thru-the-Bible Romans Ch 1-8	$4.00
Equinox Magick Crowley OTO Thelema AA Gnostic 93 Tahuti		Freedom to Choose by Ernest Gruen (1976)	
Crowley's Equinox complete white 10 volume Weiser set.	$1,000.00	On the Brink by Rod Parsley (2000)	$4.00
Equinox Magick Crowley OTO Thelema AA Gnostic 93 Tahuti		From Mission To Madness,	$4.00
COMPLETE BIBLICAL LIBRARY - complete 17 vols set. Harmony, 9 vols Study Bible, 6 vols Dictionary, Grammar	$659.00	Last Son Of The Mormon Prophet	

Nonfiction ▸ Self-Help

The median sales price in this subcategory is $2.75.

	HIGH		AVG
ALCOHOLICS ANONYMOUS FIRST EDITION SIGNED BILL WILSON	$2,213.00	THE ULTIMATE WEIGHT SOLUTION BY DR PHIL MCGRAW	$2.75
ALCOHOLICS ANONYMOUS * 1ST EDITION 15TH PRINTING HB/DJ	$730.00	Who Moved My Cheese? by Spencer Johnson (1998) HB/DJ	$2.75
Alcoholics Anonymous 1st Ed 2nd Printing 1941	$700.00	The Ultimate Weight Solution by Dr. Phil McGraw (2003).	$2.75
Rare 1950 -Alcoholics Anonymous- 1st 13th Book w/DJ -AA	$511.00	The 7 Keys to Weight Loss Freedom	
Attacking Anxiety & Depression w/ Lucinda Bassett.	$262.00	Life Strategies by Phillip C. McGraw (2000)	$2.75
Midwest Center for Anxiety delux CD version!!!		IYANLA VANZANT * UNTIL TODAY * NEW *	$2.75

Nonfiction ▸ Sports, Recreation

The median sales price in this subcategory is $5.00.

	HIGH		AVG
personal Srapbooks J Stanley Reeve Sportsman Author	$1,026.00	MASTER FALCONRY: TRAINING THE APPRENTICE	$5.00
Colt .45 Service Pistols - - by Charles Clawson	$500.00	FALCONRY I: SURVEY COURSE	$5.00
RARE AND UNUSUAL FLY TYING MATERIALS, Vol 2.	$340.00	FOR THE NOVICE FALCONER	
New First Edition, SIGNED BY BOTH AUTHORS		MONTANA TROUT (Steam Fishing) GUIDE BOOK 1stED MAPS	$5.00
Traditional Aikido Volume 5 by Morihiro Saito	$306.00	Even Brook Trout Get the Blues by John Gierach (1993)	$5.00
"AUTOMOBILE RACING" BY RAY F. KUNS FIRST EDITION	$268.00	The Survival Handbook by Peter Darman (1996)	$5.00

Nonfiction ▸ Transportation

The median sales price in this subcategory is $6.99.

	HIGH		AVG
Automobile Quarterly. Quarterly hardcover automotive magazine	$511.00	Flying 89/4 Piper Malibu Mirage Poberezny team Dassault	$6.99
Ferrarissima Ferrari Magazine. semi annual magazine of Ferrari style	$385.00	EAA 95/12 B-25 Gee Bee RotorWay Exec Grumman Panther	$6.99
* Rare Signed & Numbered - Checkered Flag by Helck 1961	$356.00	This Old Harley - HARLEY DAVIDSON MOTORCYCLE BOOK MINT	$6.99
AUTOCOURSE 1968-69 Edition	$306.11	Forden FORD AIR TOURS 1925-1931 Aviation + pamphlet NEW	$6.99
AUTOCOURSE 1969-70 Edition	$290.45	Chilton's Chrysler Full-Size Trucks, 1989-96 Repair ...	$6.99

Nonfiction ▸ Travel, Geography, Exploration

The median sales price in this subcategory is $4.00.

	HIGH		AVG
Airstream * Vintage Book Trailer Travel by Byam HB/DJ	$201.00	Two on a Big Ocean by Hal Roth (1978)	$4.02
1914 Yellowstone Park Giude 178 Pages Plus Fold Out Map	$157.50	Rough Guide to New Orleans (2001)	$4.00
Hailstorm over Truk Lagoon by Klaus P. Lindemann (1982)	$157.44	Into the Heart of Borneo by Redmond O'Hanlon (1987)	$4.00
LASSOING WILD ANIMALS IN AFRICA, GUY H. SCULL 1911 1ST	$150.00	LONELY PLANET Costa Rica Travel Guide low ship	$4.00
1899, Our Islands and Their People, 2 Vol Pictorial	$150.00	Weird N.J. - NJ - New Jersey - Near Mint	$4.00

Nonfiction ▸ True Crime

The median sales price in this subcategory is $3.54.

	HIGH		AVG
Buford Pusser rare book and poster. Poster signed by author	$150.00	Jonbenet-Never Before Revealed Evidence & Photos**NEW	$3.56
Disco Bloodbath by James st James (1999)	$112.50	Lot #6 5 True Crime Paperbacks	$3.55
Inside the Mind of Scott Peterson by Keith Ablow (2005).	$102.50	BLOOD BROTHER - By SCOTT PETERSON'S SISTER, ANNE BIRD.	$3.55
PLUS+ (Lot of 14) True Crime Books, pb, new & lk-new NR		The acceptance: Scott was guilty of murder !! HB:DJ	
Disco Bloodbath by James st James (1999)	$102.50	Three true crime books	$3.54
Sins of the Mother by Maria Eftimiades (1995)	$100.00	[2 of these sold for $3.54 each]	

Textbooks, Education

The median sales price in this subcategory is $0.25.

	HIGH		AVG
INSTRUCTOR EDITION Human Anatomy & Physiology by Marieb	$3,550.00	Networking by Bruce Hallberg (2001) RARE COLLEGE BOOK	$0.25
PLI Patent Bar Review materials including audio & video	$1,395.00	Sports and Entertainment Marketing by Dotty B. Oelke...	$0.25
PATENT BAR EXAM PRG USPTO BAR REVIEW LAW	$1,125.00	Microsoft Frontpage 2000 by Stoney Gaddy (2002)	$0.25
Chiropractic WLP Mother Load. 31 Videos, Manual	$1,025.00	LOT OF 3 GREAT NOVELS / AUDIOBOOKS ON CD /2 UNABRIDGED	$0.25
Career Step - Medical Transcription ONLINE course	$1,002.00	LOT 4 MICHAEL CRICHTON AUDIOBOOKS AUDIO BOOKS ON TAPE	$0.25
RN Clept Books by The College Network 1-10 or 12	$910.00	LOT OF 4 HISTORY KNOWLEDGE PRODUCTS TAPES -	$0.25
Understanding Health Policy by Thomas S. Bodenheimer...	$900.00	WW2 REV WAR	
2006 California BarBri - Bar Review Study Materials	$895.00	old Arithmetic school textbook 1961 book 5 in a series	$0.25
The Complete (KAPLAN) ARE Learning System.	$840.56	GRADE 1 SCOTT FORESMAN CELEBRATE READ TEACHER EDITION	$0.25
Ingles sin Barreras 100% ORIGINAL NUEVO -DVD/CD 2006	$770.00	Bob Miller's Geometry for the Clueless by Bob Millel...	$0.25
OPORTUNIDAD UNICA!!! EL ORIGINAL, NUEVO DE PAQUETE!!		Introduction to Comparative Politics	$0.25
WISC-IV - psychology testing kit by psychorp (child)	$760.00	Math Practice Workbook: Spanish Edition	$0.25
Brand New CPA Review Materials for 2005/2006	$750.00	Public Speaking for Personal Success, Speech Book	$0.25
100% ORIGINAL DVD-INGLES SIN BARRERAS 2005-2006	$750.00	HTML for Dummies with cd rom helper	$0.25
2005 New York (NY) Barbri Bar Review Complete Set	$700.00	KINDERGARDEN WEEKLY READER SCIENCE SPIN W TEACHER GUI	$0.25
INGLES SIN BARRERAS DVD -NUEVO, SELLADO & ORIGINAL	$700.00	Kochar's Concise Textbook of Medicine, Internal Board R	$0.25

Wholesale, Bulk Lots ▸ Audiobooks

The average sales price in this subcategory is $22.40.

	HIGH		AVG
dent prep materials		3 uanbridged Dean Koontz audios on cassettes	$22.50
AUDIOBOOKS LOT OF 45	$250.00	Audio Books Lot of 17 NR Free Shipping Action/Adventure	$22.50
50 MYSTERIES AND ROMANCES ON CASSETTES & CD	$200.00	CD - Lot of 4 Unabridged and Abridged Fiction	$22.50
HUGE LOT 37 FICTION AUDIOBOOKS AUDIO BOOKS ON TAPE	$131.64	LOT OF 3 GREAT NOVELS / AUDIOBOOKS	$22.50
PIMSLEUR Learn to Speak GERMAN 1/I/one CD NEW	$119.06	ON CD /2 UNABRIDGED	
HUGE LOT 15 MICHAEL CRICHTON	$119.00	LOT 4 MICHAEL CRICHTON AUDIOBOOKS	$22.49
AUDIOBOOKS~UNABRIDGED	$102.50	AUDIO BOOKS ON TAPE	
WHOLESALE LOT OF 33 NEW AUDIOBOOKS BOOKS ON TAPE	$102.50	LOT OF 4 HISTORY KNOWLEDGE	$22.45
HUGE LOT 37 FICTION AUDIOBOOKS AUDIO BOOKS ON TAPE	$96.02	PRODUCTS TAPES - WW2 REV WAR	
Pimsleur FRENCH I, II, III series COMPLETE tapes	$90.26	Harry potter vidieo cassests	$22.05
Dan Brown Audio Book Lot CD's Unabridged Like NEW	$90.09	CD - Dark Tower III and IV by Stephen King	$22.02
HUGE LOT 10 UNABRIDGED AUDIOBOOKS	$88.87	CD - Lot of 3 Unabridged Novels on Audio	$22.00
AUDIO BOOKS ON TAPE		HUGE LOT of 6 UNABRIDGED DANIELLE STEEL AUDIOBOOKS	$21.77
HUGE LOT 37 FICTION AUDIOBOOKS AUDIO BOOKS ON TAPE	$87.56	CD - Lot of 3 Abridged and Unabridged Biographies	$21.76
W.E.B. Griffith 9 Audio Unabridged-The Corps series	$85.00	Lot of 8 Mystery/Thrillers: All UNABRIDGED	$21.59
HUGE LOT 10 UNABRIDGED AUDIOBOOKS	$84.56	8 audio book sets - unopened - unabridged – NEW	$21.59
AUDIO BOOKS ON TAPE		Lot of 8 Unabridged Mystery/Thriller Audiobooks	$21.50
HUGE LOT 8 LARGE UNABRIDGED AUDIOBOOKS AUDIO BOOKS	$83.71	5 Mary Higgins Clark 3 Tami Hoag audios on cassettes	$21.50

Wholesale, Bulk Lots ▸ Books

The average sales price in this subcategory is $13.90.

	HIGH		AVG
RARE VITA SACKVILLE-WEST COLLECTION INCLUDING AUTOGRAPH	$350.00	13 LOT OF DANIELLE STEEL HARDBACK ROMANCE NOVELS	$14.10
Wholesale lot of Readers Digest Condensed Books	$202.50	Lot of 20 Historical Romance Books	$14.05
LOT OF 32 ROBERT E. HOWARD BOOKS	$165.33	Popular Fiction 50 PB Book Lot Plain Coulter Steel +	$14.00
- CONAN , CORMAC ++++		HUGE BOOK LOT 50 NORA ROBERTS ROMANCE WOW!!!!!!!	$13.99
30 Postmodern Emerging Church Books / Ministry, McLaren	$143.71	ROMANCE BY SANDRA BROWN	$13.95
SET OF 17 NANCY DREW BOOKS	$137.50	Romance Books, Newer titles, popular authors	$13.86
MYSTERY CHILDRENS KEENE		40 Mystery-Thrillers Bookstore Overstock Shelf-ready	$13.56
FEARLESS Series of books by Francine Pascal (38 Books)	$110.50	MILITARY MILITARIA US WWII	$13.50
PATRICK O'BRIAN group of 20 - Aubrey / Maturin series.	$100.01	WORLD WAR II HISTORY BK LOT	
Lot of 31 First Edition Books all Signed by the Authors	$95.55	31 HEALTH+WELLNESS+DIET+	$13.50
Lot of 30 NEW LeapPad Leap Frog Phonics Books NR	$81.00	FITNESS BOOKS LOT+LARRY NORTH	
Lot Of 14 Hardback Edition Books Mixed Genre Mostly Law	$80.67	CHRISTIAN MAN MEN BOOK LOT LOVE MARRIAGE ARTERBURN	$13.50
True Crime Books pb-whole lot of evil here! (Lot of 50)	$78.00	23 Harlequin Historical Romance–Medieval, Western +	$13.50
21 Star Wars Books: Prequels w/ Revenge of the Sith +	$61.00	Nora Roberts/J D Robb-Lot of 20 Paperbacks-DEAL!!	$13.50
True Crime Books pb serious psycho, nice (Lot of 25)	$59.89	LOT 37 BABY TODDLER CHILDRENS BOOKS 32 HB 5 PB DAYCARE	$13.50
LOT OF 28 HOME IMPROVEMENT+	$54.00	Lof of 16 Historical Romances Goodman Hunter Ranney +	$13.02
DECORATING+GARDENING BOOKS		LOT OF 54 CHRISTIANITY BOOKS+	$13.00
Lot of 20 books by Clive Cussler, Mostly Hardcover	$51.00	CHRISTIAN LIVING+SELF HELP	

Wholesale, Bulk Lots ▸ Magazines

The average sales price in this subcategory is $20.00.

	HIGH		AVG
4-1962-63 SPIDERMAN + BATMAN COMICS	$283.66	Lot of 7 Alain Delon french magazine Paris Match	$20.50
4-1962-63 THE INCREDIABLE HULK & GREEN LANTERN COMICS	$255.52	Huge Lot of 65 WIZARD Magazines 1995-2002	$20.50
HUGE LOT OF FINE HOMEBUILDING MAGAZINES~NO RESERVE!	$199.99	Communication Arts Design Annuals + Bonus CD – NR	$20.50
Wrestling Magazines Collection 1976-1999 (525+ Issues)	$152.50	50 "LIFE " MAGAZINES mostly70's some 80's	$20.01
MAD MAGAZINE, 40 tight, bright issues, 1960-1968	$137.50	BEATLES NAGAZINE LOT..WITH BOOK...VINTAGE MINT CON..	$20.00
6-1962-63 'THE FLASH & THE FANTASTIC FOUR' COMICS	$119.16	VAN HALEN VINTAGE MAGAZINE LOT..MINT CON..	$20.00
9-1963 TALES TO ASTONISH + JUSTICE LEAGUE COMICS	$113.61	Analog Science Fiction LARGE LOT!! 1960's-1990's	$20.00
16-EARLY 1960'S SCI-FI COMICS (HOUSE OF SECRETS.....)	$109.16	vintage RAILROAD MAGAZINE - LOT / 18 issues* 1957-1963	$19.01
4-1963 JOURNEYS INTO MYSTERY COMICS	$109.16	Collection National Lampoon Magazines "1974-1981"	$18.95
PENTHOUSE MAGAZINE COLLECTION COMPLETE SEPT 1972 - 1979	$105.01	HEADPRESS peter sotos jim goad whitehouse blood axis	$17.00
vintage TRAINS MAGAZINE - LOT OF 30 issues * 1940's *	$67.70	Lot of Gear, Notorious, Stuff, FHM, & Maxim magazines	$16.29
6-1961-64 STRANGE ADVENTURES+STRANGE TALES COMICS	$53.66	Lot of 16 eBay magazines & 1 CD,Auctions,Make Money,How	$16.07
The Gregg Writer Old Magazines Lot of 10 1920's Issues	$51.00	HOUSE PLAN HOME PLAN MAGAZINES HUGE LOT/20!	$15.55
Sonic the Hedgehog Comic Comics Lot: THIRTY-FIVE Issues	$51.00	Old Muzzleloader Magazines and Books Lot	$15.50
Popular Mechanics The complete 1970's 120 issues	$50.00	(8)different NATIONAL GEOGRAPHICS/1918-1920/vintage	$15.25

6

BUSINESS & INDUSTRIAL

The Business & Industrial category is an especially growing one on eBay, as more small businesses find they can save money buying equipment and supplies in online auctions.

More than 724,000 Americans now derive all or part of their income by selling on the site. (Some say the number may be even larger than that, considering that business owners employ others to keep the operations going). And an additional 1.5 million people say they supplement their income via eBay, according to an ACNielsen international research study on behalf of eBay. Indeed, eBay, with its consistent policy of maintaining a "level playing field," has been a boon for many small businesses. eBay CEO and President Meg Whitman has said the Internet has fostered the growth of small business more than that of big brands. Although some eBay sellers have a "multichannel" strategy, also using their own stand-alone websites and other sites such as Amazon.com and uBid.com, eBay's millions of customers are difficult for many businesses to ignore.

A lot of those businesses are doing their buying and selling in this, the Business & Industrial category. Here, you can buy half a bridal store's inventory for $2,200.00, and pick up 72 stainless steel forks for your restaurant for about $20.00 including shipping. And all kinds of other things sell constantly: a piece of restaurant equipment sells every 20 minutes, an oscilloscope every 10 minutes, and a forklift every 4 hours, according to eBay. Julie Watts of Internet service provider Wyoming.com said she saves about $300,000.00 a year over standard purchases by buying through eBay (as recorded in "United States of eBay," a booklet distributed by eBay at the Small Business Summit, May 5, 2004). In one of her best deals, she bought $10,000.00 worth of networking cards for just $1,000.00.

Best Deals

You need to be careful when you compare prices in this category to other online sites, because some of the items are so unique that they can only be found on eBay. You also need to factor in things like whether the item is used or new; if it comes with any extras, such as a cartridge with a printer; and, of course, shipping costs. But for items you're buying new, you can compare prices to online venues, such as OfficeDepot.com.

In the Office, Printing & Shipping subcategory, one eBay buyer got a Brother 560 fax machine with toner for $36.00, plus $25.00 shipping, a total of $61.00. ("New one costs $113," touted the auction's subtitle.) A quick search on the Internet revealed another such machine for $89.99 plus $8.99 shipping, from a seller on Amazon.com, which totals $98.98. So in that case, eBay offered a better deal—a savings of about $29.00.

In other cases, the savings margin may be slimmer. A pack of 100 Tyvek mailers could be bought on eBay for $22.05 plus $6.00 shipping, for a total of $28.05. On OfficeDepot.com, you could get them for $29.99 with free shipping, so the difference between the two deals is less than a couple of dollars.

Some sellers find their customers in other eBay vendors. Because they are doing a lot of shipping, these vendors are a natural for products like bubble wrap and other office supplies. One seller capitalizing on this is Floridian Gary Neubert, whose business, GatorPack, offers things like packing peanuts, bubble wrap, and tape, and his company now supports three families and requires a 7,000-square-foot warehouse (also documented in "United States of eBay").

Of course, for bigger things, like building supplies, people often shop in person at bricks-and-mortar stores for obvious reasons: the shipping would be prohibitive or, in some cases, the items aren't available online. But even some massive items, like tractors, are traded over eBay—the buyer usually picks up such things in person.

In fact, tractors are some of the most popular items in this category, with "tractor" and "John Deere" appearing in the Top 10 List on the main screen of Business & Industrial. One man in Missouri bought at least six tractors on eBay, which he resold for as much as 200 percent profit.

But there is a lot more than just farm equipment and packing peanuts here: This category seems to have everything including the kitchen sink for businesses—the new Aero commercial kitchen stainless steel sink, for instance, which went for $308.10 with Buy It Now.

Agriculture & Forestry ▸ Antique Tractors & Equipment

The average sales price in this subcategory is $139.67.

	HIGH		AVG
1965 John Deere 4020 Gasoline Tractor	$3,900.00	David Bradley Antique Tractor Snow Plow-Pick Up OnlyA+	$150.00
JOHN DEERE 1500 NO-TILL DRILL 10 FOOT	$3,800.00	Avery Tractor 8-16 Cylinder Sleeves	$150.00
FARMALL 1935 F-12	$3,500.00	Wood running gear / Spoked wheels, John Deere? Case?	$148.50
RANSOME JAGUAR 4000 DIESEL TRACTOR LO HRS - NO RESERVE	$2,903.00	Frame/axle/transmission/controls David Bradley Tractor	$144.49
INTERNATIONAL 130 TRACTOR MOWER	$2,400.00	Early David Bradley Tractor - Briggs & Stratton	$142.50
FARMALL 1935 F-12	$2,250.00	OLD PLANET JR. CUT OUT FARM IMPLEMENT WRENCH # H 4	$141.26
1947 Ford gasoline Antique Farm Tractor, Runs Great	$2,000.00	ANTIQUE JARI SICKLE MOWER RUNS AND WORKS GOOD	$134.07
VINTAGE RARE TORO TRACTOR NOT JOHN DEERE	$1,925.00	57 pcs. of farm equipment,pamphlet,catalog,JD IH MF AC	$128.50
1948 Ford 8n tractor loaded with extras	$1,575.00	1909 Advance Tractor Thresher Catalog - Battle Creek	$127.59
1949 BF Avery Model A Antique Tractor in Nice Orig Cond	$1,500.00	1966 (not 1969)Sears Suburban Tractor Antique Collector	$125.00
1940 Silver King Tractor	$1,500.00	Bosch DU4 Magneto!! L@@K!!!	$125.00
HORSE DRAWN BUGGY VELIE CARRIAGE CO ALL ORIGINAL	$1,480.00	1951-1953 David Bradley Super Power Garden Tractor	$125.00
MINNIAPOLIS MOLINE ZTU 1944 TRACTOR	$1,475.00	Webster magneto not wico sumpter sumter hit miss	$125.00
SUPERIOR LOADER WITH 60" BUCKET - NO RESERVE	$1,450.00	LOWTHER C SAW W / WISCONSIN MOTOR LOT 776	$125.00
International Harvester TD6 Crawler Dozer Caterpillar	$1,330.00	2-Wheel trailer for David Bradley Walk BehindTractor	$115.01

Agriculture & Forestry ▸ Farm Implements & Attachments

The average sales price in this subcategory is $307.53.

	HIGH		AVG
Cornhusker Grain Hopper bottom trailer not John Deere	$6,852.50	AG-RAIN Irrigation Hose Reel W 505 Used Reel	$400.00
GEHL Mixer Feeder 7210 Excellent Condition	$4,450.00	Case 6 Ton Running Gear W 14 FT Hay Bed Nice	$386.28
Harley Pro-6 Power Rake Hydraulic just like new	$4,200.00	Southern 48" Rotary Cutter	$380.00
3 POINT BACK HOE / BACKHOE new! CAT 1 / 3 PT / 3PL	$2,550.00	SHAVER 3 POINT 7IN POST DRIVERHYDRAULIC NICE #8998	$355.00

3 POINT BACK HOE / BACKHOE new! CAT 1 / 3 PT / 3PL	$2,525.00	Adjusta Flex Tine Harrow 5ft wide [2 of these sold for $324.00 each]	$324.00
Bearcat Wood Chipper	$2,500.00	Tractor 6' York Rake	$315.00
NEW!! TOWABLE RIDE-ON TRENCHER/ Backhoe	$2,499.99	little giant hay and grain elevator 24' pto	$314.99
2004 John Deere 419 Front End Loader Like New	$2,200.00	PTO AND 3 POINT HOOKUP TERRAMITE	$306.00
3 POINT BACK HOE / BACKHOE new! CAT 1 / 3 PT / 3PL	$2,100.00	Bobcat Bucket Forks	$305.00
3 point hitch backhoe	$2,036.57	CASE 446 GARDEN TRACTOR	$305.00
Ditch Witch Brand Backhoe Attachment! NO RESERVE!	$2,025.00	York Rake 12ft with 3 point hookup	$300.00
Backhoe For Jinma Tractors Frame Mount WOWOWO Look	$1,800.00	Quick Link Disconnect Tractor Hitch - 3pt Kubota Deere [2 of these sold in a multiple item ("Dutch") auction for $145.00 each]	$290.00
FENCE POST DRIVER - HYDRAULIC - SHAVER	$1,750.00	Quick Implement Tractor Hitch - Deere Kubota more [2 of these sold in a multiple item ("Dutch") auction for $145.00 each]	$290.00
BAckhoe for Tractor, 3-point, Skidsteer!	$1,725.00	York Rake & Grader Blade	$281.99
KELLY 3PT BACKHOE FOR COMPACT TRACTORS LIKE KUBOTA	$1,675.00	King Kutter 60" Landscape/Yard Rake	$257.00

Agriculture & Forestry ▸ Forestry Equipment & Supplies

The average sales price in this subcategory is $426.56.

	HIGH		AVG
45 H.P CAT ENGINE SAWMILL W/ 30 INCH BAND WHEELS @LOADER	$33,000.00	066 stihl chainsaw new bar and chain 046 084 husqvarna	$585.00
45 H.P CAT ENGINE SAWMILL W/ 30 INCH BAND WHEELS @LOADER	$31,095.00	STUMP GRINDER WITH KOHLER MAGNUM 18	$560.00
John Deere 540A Log Skidder	$12,200.00	Spiegel Relaskop Forestry Tool	$515.99
2000 VERMEER WOODCHIPPER BC1230A	$12,000.00	COOKS BAND SAW SHARPENER	$500.00
Austin-Western 60 Ft. Rough, Terrain Crane, 17,000 LB.	$9,750.00	AUTOMATIC SAWMILL WOOD	
BRUSH BANDIT 12 INCH DIESEL CHIPPER	$8,000.02	ALASKAN MK III SAW MILL AND	$457.00
1993 VEMEER WOOD CHIIPER	$7,499.00	STIHL 056 SAW, SAWMILL	
Lucas Mill 8" 20hp saw mill sawmill 8.5 x 17 inch Dim	$6,750.00	Perkins T1004 4-cylinder Diesel engine	$430.00
JOHN DEERE 440B CABLE SKIDDER	$6,500.00	10,000 gallon collapsible, portable liquid storage tank	$425.00
VERMEER 4X4 LOADER TRACTOR/ TREE SPADE. NO RESERVE!!!	$5,225.00	Stihl 064 chainsaw w/new bar&chain like new rebuilt	$420.00
WARATAH TOOTH KIT CARBIDE NK F452111 FOR FELLING HEAD!! [10 of these sold in a multiple item ("Dutch") auction for $350.00 each]	$3,500.00	Stihl 064 chainsaw no bar and chain	$394.00
		stihl 066 28" bar no reserve	$370.98
Rigsby 24" nursery tree spade - tree planter	$3,000.00	BK Radio 2 way handheld radio	$365.00
HUD-SON PORTABLE 18" SAWMILL BEST BUY IN THE USA	$2,500.00	STANLEY CS26 HYDRAULIC CHAIN	$355.00
SAVE HUDSON PORTABLE SAWMILL SCRATCH & DENT LOG TOOL BN	$2,280.55	SAW WITH POLE & HOSES USED	
AgriMetal PTO LS Straw Mulcher - Bale Chopper NICE!	$1,999.99		

Agriculture & Forestry ▸ Tractor Parts & Manuals

The average sales price in this subcategory is $13.94.

	HIGH		AVG
IH Service Manual Chassis 3388 and 3588	$100.95	RARE - 1954 ROTOTILLER MODEL 2 ORIGINAL BROCHURE MANUAL	$14.99
IH Service Manual International 5088, 5288, 5488	$78.00	Minneapolis-Moline U Operating Manual S-119 C	$14.99
IH Service and Parts Manual 886, 986, 1086, 1486, 1586	$76.00	WISCONSIN MODEL VH4 ENGINE SERVICE MANUAL	$14.95
Hesston sales manual salesmens brochures insert lot	$68.76	Deutz Fahr 1980's Series 7 Tractor Service Bulletins	$14.76
THE GIBSON TRACTOR INSTRUCTIONS & PARTS LIST	$61.00	Allis Chalmers D14 D17 Tractor I&T Shop Service Manual	$14.50
Yanmar Tractor Manual Set CD	$29.00	International 666 IH 666 Tractor Parts Catalog OLD !	$14.50
2 Standard Garden Tractor Manual Manuals	$54.00	CONTINENTAL L HEAD ENGINE SERVICE MANUAL	$13.95
Steiger Microfiche Parts and Service Bulletin Assorted	$52.00	Case IH Operators Manual 1440, 1460, 1480	$13.60
IH Cub Cadet Tiller #2 Rotary Tiller Manual	$50.00	International Harvester 1440 combine parts manual	$13.50
NEW HOLLAND TRACTOR SQUARE/ ROUND HAY BALER FACTORY	$49.95	IH International 100 130 140 404 2404 tractor IT manual	$13.50
Mccormick Super MTA manual-1954 LOOK!	$46.50	John Deere 410 Loader Backhoe Orig. Op. Manual	$13.50
McCORMICK-DEERING F-30 TRACTOR PARTS CATALOG	$42.00	Chilton TRACTOR Journal Sept. 1/ 1918	$13.16
1928 Huber Super Four Parts & Operating Tractor Book	$41.00	Caterpillar D 7 Tractor 17A1- up Service Manual (Used)	$13.00
Power King Tractor Owner's Manual + Bonus Sections	$40.00	Allis Chalmers B - WF Tractor I&T Shop Service Manual	$13.00
VINTAGE FARMALL CUB 1940"S MANUAL	$39.83	Cub Cadet Service Manual Lawn Tractors Assorted	$13.00

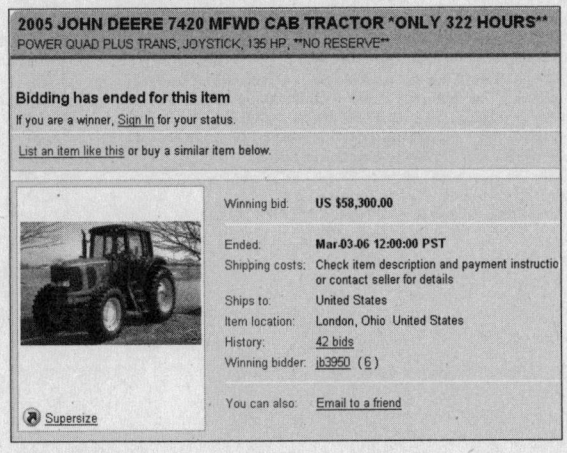

2005 JOHN DEERE 7420 MFWD CAB TRACTOR *ONLY 322 HOURS*
POWER QUAD PLUS TRANS, JOYSTICK, 135 HP, **NO RESERVE**

Bidding has ended for this item
If you are a winner, Sign In for your status.

List an item like this or buy a similar item below.

Winning bid:	US $58,300.00
Ended:	Mar-03-06 12:00:00 PST
Shipping costs:	Check item description and payment instructio or contact seller for details
Ships to:	United States
Item location:	London, Ohio United States
History:	42 bids
Winning bidder:	jb3950 (6)

You can also: Email to a friend

Supersize

Andersen Frenchwood Hinged Inswing Patio Door

Bidding has ended for this item
If you are a winner, Sign In for your status.

List an item like this or buy a similar item below.

Winning bid:	US $1,605.00
	No payments for 3 months
Ended:	Feb-27-06 11:25:42 PST
Shipping costs:	Pickup only - see item desc
Ships to:	Will arrange for local pickup
Item location:	SHELBY TOWNSHIP, MICH
History:	21 bids
Winning bidder:	rufus370 (42 ☆)

View larger picture

You can also: Email to a friend

Construction ▶ Building Materials & Supplies

The average sales price in this subcategory is $97.94.

	HIGH		AVG
50,000 sf of steel roof material r panel used	$6,100.00	3 Rolls Pinkwrap Home Wrap Tape Like Tyvek House Wrap	$101.01
24KW DIESEL GENERATOR - BRAND NEW - ENCLOSED 24 KW	$5,400.00	Stairway, Interior for home or building	$100.00
20KW DIESEL GENERATOR - BRAND NEW - ENCLOSED 24 KW	$4,395.02	Electric, Concrete - Mortar Mixer	$100.00
Onan RS 20000 Genset Generator - like new condition	$3,850.00	KEYLESS ELECTRONIC DOOR LOCK (DEADBOLT)	$99.99
Chain Link Fence NEW 1500 Feet 9 gauge	$2,500.00	216 SQ. FT. METROFLOR VINYL "HARVEST" PLANKS + ADHESIVE	$99.99
HONDA GENERATOR EU 3000 IS INVERTER EU3000is LIKE NEW	$1,400.00	TGI floor joists 14" wide & narrow flange cords NO RES	$99.00
New roll of luxury commercial broadloom carpet, 2460 sf	$911.00	Tyvek DrainWrap Two Brand New Rolls - Home Wrap	$96.00
New roll of luxury commercial broadloom carpet, 2034 sf	$875.00	BOSCH ROUTER BITS "NEW" UNUSED-21 NEW CARBIDE BITS 1/4"	$91.00
driveway pavement road reflectors nicholas rich	$425.00	Used Natural Gas Modine heater	$90.00
New roll of luxury commercial broadloom carpet, 966 sf	$411.00	2 MILITARY FENCE PROTECTION SYSTEMS (FPS) by PERIMETER	$86.00
CORRUGATED ROOFING OR SIDING.	$400.00	GAFFERS TAPE PREMIUM 12 ROLL CASE 7.42 PER ROLL USA !	$83.00
Rod Iron Sliding Gate	$399.99	[3 of these sold for $83.00 each]	
3/4" X 500' LARGE radiant heat tubing pipe	$275.00	MECHANIC TOOL BOX TOP CHEST TOOL BOXES FATHER'S DAY NEW	$81.00
BEAUTIFUL! DECORATIVE WOOD FLOOR MEDALLION NO RESERVE	$261.89	BOSCH Shaper Cutter "NEW" UNUSED- CARBIDE	$80.99
1 New Case (25) Hilti HY-150 epoxy anchoring system	$260.00	ARMSTRONG CEILIING TILES 24X48X3/4 NEW WHITE 9bxs.(72)	$79.00
		New Louisville Ceiling Folding Wood Attic Ladder	$78.50

Construction ▶ Heavy Equipment & Trailers

The median sales price in this subcategory is $6,500.00.

	HIGH		AVG
1999 CAT D6RXL NO RESERVE	$75,000.00	IHC T6 Widetrack Dozer,w/Winch/Canopy-"Monty"	$6,836.00
4 UNITS! 1999 BobCat 763 Skid Steer Loaders- Package		Crawler Chronicles-More Tails from "Moosey"-	
Cab+Heat+Installation/FTL Shipping/All Fees- Included	$58,099.60	Yanmar B08-3 small excavator	$6,750.50
2001 CATERPILLAR D5C XL III DOZER, LIKE NEW!	$52,000.00	MUSTANG 940 SKID STEER WITH ATTACHMENTS	$6,651.00
2003 Sky Trak 6036 Legacy extenda boom	$44,900.00	WITH DIRT BUCKET/ GRAPPLE BUCKET/ 8' FRONT RUNNER RAKE	
Bobcat 341 Excavator Less than 100 hours	$42,101.00	JCB BACKHOE, X POWER CO. MACHINE, 4 IN1 BUCKET, DIESEL	$6,600.00
1999 CASE 580 SUPER L SERIES II BACKHOE	$36,500.00	FORD 4500 TRACTOR LOADER BACKHOE... NICE MACHINE...	$6,600.00
New Holland LW 90 wheel loader	$35,100.00	ANOTHER NO RESERVE... WARMKA AUCTION CO.	
KENWORTH W900 DUMP TRUCK 1997	$34,100.00	Bobcat 743 diesel skid steer loader	$6,514.00
DOZER D4H CAT CATERPILLAR CAB LOW HOURS HIGH TRACK	$32,800.00	BOMAG BW120AD-3 Ride On Vibratory Roller	$6,510.00
HIGH TRACK 6 WAY LOW HOURS EXCELLENT CONDITION LOW COST		1999 Model Vermeer 5750 Trencher just 1341 HRS!!	$6,500.00
2005 CATERPILLAR 262B SKID STEER WITH CAB!	$30,000.00	TERRAMITE T5C MINI BACKHOE NOT ALLMAND OR BOBCAT	$6,500.00
1994 INTERNATIONAL 4900 D, WITH CRANE FERRARY 710	$30,000.00	BOBCAT 975 SKID STEER	$6,500.00
KOMATSU 120-6 WITH HYDRAULIC PROGRESSIVE LINK THUMB	$29,999.99	skid steer bobcat brand	
1996 MACHINE NICE		Excavator Smalley model 808	$6,500.00
2003 RAYCO C85L MINI TRACK LOADER----FREE SHIPPING	$29,900.00	L@@K! ..Big Backhoe...680 Case!.. Low Reserve! ..L@@K!	$6,500.00
MONEY BACK GUARANTEE		When you don't want to send a boy!	
1995 Manitou MVT1340L Rough Terrain Telescopic Forklift	$28,100.00	case 850 crawler dozer 6-way blade 90% undercairage	$6,500.00
1998 CAT TH103 RT TELESCOPIC FORKLIFT TELEHANDLER	$27,400.00	LEE BOY PAVER L900S DIESEL LOW HOURS GOOD CONDITION	$6,400.00
10,000# CAPACITY, ENCLOSED CAB, AIR CONDITIONING		KOMATSU 8000LB DIESEL Forklift	$6,350.00
		Local delivery. Call for other delivery	

Food Service & Retail ▶ Bar & Beverage Equipment

The average sales price in this subcategory is $71.51.

	HIGH		AVG
commercial coffee,espresso retail equipment and more	$3,999.00	Talking Computerized Alcohol Tester !! MONEY MAKER!!!	$87.55
CONTI ESPRESSO MACHINE PACKAGE & XTRAS	$3,400.00	3 hole adjustable cup dispenser	$86.00
Excellent Mahogany Pub Style Bar	$2,500.00	BUNN VPR COMMERCIAL COFFEE MAKER!!!!	$86.00
3 GROUP CHROME AUTOMATIC ESPRESSO COFFEE MACHINE	$1,325.00	EBCO COMMERCIAL WALL MOUNT WATER FOUNTAIN COOLER	$82.00
One group Commercial/Domestic Espresso?expresso machine	$1,195.00	BUNN VPR COMMERCIAL COFFEE MAKER!!!!	$80.03
SCOTSMAN Ice Maker/Dispenser (5052716)	$787.00	BAR STOOLS NO RESERVE	$80.00
19 Oak and Copper Bar and Bar Back.	$713.19	COMMERCIAL WAITRESS STATION	$80.00
Dynamo Silver Coin Op foosball commercial or home use	$601.00	BUNN COMMERCAIL VPR AUTOMATIC COFFEE BREWER MAKER	$79.99
Crathco Cold Beverage - 3 Bowl Drink Fountain Dispenser	$599.00	Bloomfield 3 Pot coffee Maker w /hot water faucet	$79.00
3 GROUP CHROME AUTOMATIC ESPRESSO COFFEE MACHINE	$525.00	4 SLOT STAINLESS STEEL CUP DISPENSER INDUSTRIAL	$77.00
Wilshire Quantum 4000 Juice Dispenser	$495.00	LOT OF 60 BEER EQUIPMENT VALVES,PUMPS EXC. COINDITION	$75.01
Scotsman Ice Machine	$430.00	Bunn VP17-2 Low Profile Pourover Coffee Brewer	$75.00
3 Compartment 83'' Underbar Under Bar Undercounter Sink	$380.00	BUNN VPR Pourover Coffee Brewer -NO RESERVE	$75.00
COMPACT RED COKE SODA MACHINE ~VERY RARE~ FREE SHIP	$345.00	Bunn VPS Commercial Coffee Brewer Maker	$75.00
PIONEER MARK-15 Smoke Eater Air Cleaner NICE!	$299.99	Talking Computerized Alcohol Tester !! MONEY MAKER!!!	$75.00

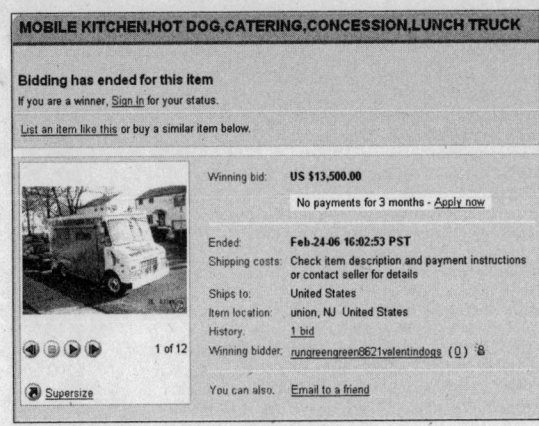

MOBILE KITCHEN,HOT DOG,CATERING,CONCESSION,LUNCH TRUCK

Bidding has ended for this item
If you are a winner, Sign In for your status.

List an item like this or buy a similar item below.

Winning bid:	**US $13,500.00**
	No payments for 3 months - Apply now
Ended:	**Feb-24-06 16:02:53 PST**
Shipping costs:	Check item description and payment instructions or contact seller for details
Ships to:	United States
Item location:	union, NJ United States
History:	1 bid
Winning bidder:	rungreengreen8621valentindogs (0)

1 of 12

Supersize

You can also: Email to a friend

10,000 METRIC TONS OF MID-VOL METALLURGICAL COAL!
GOOD QUALITY READY FOR LATE APRIL WORLD-WIDE DELIVERY!!

Bidding has ended for this item
If you are a winner, Sign In for your status.

List an item like this or buy a similar item below.

Sold for:	**US $1,500,000.00**
	Auction ended early with Buy It Now
	No payments for 3 months - Apply
Ended:	**Mar-07-06 13:36:10 PST**
Shipping costs:	Freight - see item description below
Ships to:	Worldwide
Item location:	Karthus, PA United States
History:	1 bid
Buyer:	humanomexicano (15 ☆)

1 of 5

Food Service & Retail ▸ Commercial Kitchen Equipment

The average sales price in this subcategory is $253.00.

	HIGH		AVG
Doboy Horizontal Wrapper	$6,000.00	Electric Countertop Deep Fat Fryer 2 Basket New 220v	$299.00
Autofry MTI-40 Hoodless Ventless Auto Fry Fryer "NEW"	$4,350.00	[3 of these sold for $299.00 each]	
MANDELBOX - The Original Gas Almond Nut Roaster	$4,200.00	Vulcan 6 Burner Gas Range With Oven - NO RESERVE	$299.00
TAYLOR MATE 168 /27 SOFT SERV /REAL NICE	$3,500.00	IMPERIAL GAS 6 BURNER RANGE WITH A CONVECTION OVEN	$294.99
Wolf Industrial Gas Range/Stove challenger/snorkler New	$2,284.00	Chester Fried Deep Fryer for Chicken Model MGF-50	$280.00
Scale-O-Matic Dough Divider	$2,000.00	GARLAND RANGE USED COMMERCIAL STOVE GAS ! !	$280.00
LATE MODEL ALTO-SHAAM COOK & HOLD WARMER / OVEN	$1,975.00	Electric Countertop Deep Fat Fryer 2 Basket New 220v	$279.00
Roscher-matic Dual Chamber Vacuum Packager	$1,802.00	Popcorn Machine *Good Condition NR*	$275.00
HENNY PENNY DEEP FAT PRESSURE FRYER COOKER	$1,525.00	IMPERIAL GAS 6 OPEN BURNER WITH LARGE OVEN BELOW	$274.99
KOCH COMMERCIAL VACUUM SEALER MODEL # X200 STAINLESS	$1,400.00	$880 Viking Professional Gas Double Side Burner NR	$270.50
HENNY PENNY GAS PRESURE FRYER	$1,280.00	MERCO CONVECTION ROTISSERIE CHICKEN TURKEY OVEN	$265.00
60" SS 4 Burner Grill & Dbl Oven Comm Gas Range - NU NR	$1,225.00	Robot Coupe Burre Mixer	$265.00
RHODES KOOK E KING COOKIE MACHINE / DEPOSITOR & 2 DIES	$1,225.00	PITCO FRIALATOR F34 DONUT FRYER	$255.01
AUTO FRY DEEP FRYER MTI-10 MACHINE *NICE* *NR*	$1,200.00	COUNTER TOP FOOD WARMER, FISH AND CHICKEN WARMER	$255.00
NEW Vulcan VG36 Six 6 Burner Stove Range Oven VG 36	$1,199.00	Robo Coupe Immersion Blender, Model MP450, No Reserve	$251.99
		DUKE AEROHOT2 COMPARTMENT GAS STEAM TABLE FOOD WARMER	$251.51

Food Service & Retail ▸ Furniture, Signs, Decor

The average sales price in this subcategory is $55.50.

	HIGH		AVG
BOOTHS "WAYMAR" USED FROM RESTAURANT OUT OF BUSINESS	$1,976.00	RED DOG BEER SIGN,PLANK ROAD BREWERY, NR	$90.00
26+ft of retail counter w/power for cash register	$843.33	ORDER A CARVED POINTING FINGER RESTROOM SIGN	$79.00
restaurant mahogany type chairs 100 available	$610.00	(2) RESTAURANT STYLE WOODEN HIGH CHAIRS - Brand NEW	$75.00
COMMERCIAL RESTAURANT BOOTH SEATING - BOOTHS	$585.00	NEW ANIMATE COFFEE OPEN SIGN LED, no neon, NO RESEVE	$69.95
NEW 30x30 Reversible Table Tops and Bases - 10 sets	$494.00	MICKEY'S FINE MALT LIQUOR BEER BAR MIRROR SIGN GLASS	$63.00
8 Restaurant Bistro Tables (w/ 36" Bases)	$242.50	USED SOLID OAK PEDESTAL TABLE, NO RESERVE!!!!	$60.00
Restaurant Quality Hard Wood 30x30 tables & Chairs	$220.00	[2 of these items sold in a multi-item ("Dutch") auction for $30.00 each]	
[4 of these items sold in a multi-item ("Dutch") auction for $55.00 each]		ELECTRIC "ATM" WINDOW SIGN -1/2 The Price of NEON Signs	$59.95
COMMERCIAL RESTAURANT BOOTH SEATING - BOOTHS	$202.50	PICNIC TABLE	$59.00
folding cafeteria table,with attached stools,krueger	$200.00	DINER SATURN ROCKET NEON BEER BAR SIGN RESTAURANT	$56.00
Restaurant Tables - GREAT DEAL!!!	$152.50	Nichol Kola Advertisment Signs Drink Soda Country Store	$55.00
SOLID OAK PEDESTAL TABLE 150 Years Old Antique	$152.50	15 Tables (30x30) & 30 Chairs - Lot Sale	$51.50
TONIGHTS SPORTSFARE PUBSIGN / CHALKBOARD	$119.00	36 Letter Size, 2 Panel, Cafe Style Menu Covers, NEW	$50.00
New 24"x49" STAINLESS STEEL Kitchen Work Prep TABLE	$115.00	Sale Sign Kit 22 asstd pieces KBK085-X1	$48.00
[6 of these sold for $115.00 each]		[2 of these sold in a multi-item ("Dutch") auction for $24.00 each]	
RESTAURANT BOOTS FAST FOOD SEATING FURNTURE	$100.00	Advertisement Moxie Sign Drink Coke Pepsi Glass Tin	$45.00
SOLID BRASS MEN RESTROOM SIGN ELEGANT	$99.99	2 Vehicle Magnetic Magnetics and 1 Yard Sign Signs	$45.00

Food Service & Retail ▸ Furniture, Signs, Décor ▸ Display Cases

The average sales price in this subcategory is $129.56.

	HIGH		AVG
NEW MCCALL 3 GLASS DOOR REVOLVING DISPLAY CASE COOLER MORE COOLERS AVAILABLE INSIDE	$6,340.16	Multi color LED scrolling display board fully customize	$149.95
		STORE RETAIL GLASS DISPLAY CASE 69" FIXTURE C	$149.00
Seasonal Retail Display Kiosk - Complete Business Pckg	$5,000.00	Store Display Counter - Antique	$149.00
76" REFRIGERATED AND DRY BAKERY SHOWCASE DISPLAY DUAL	$4,050.00	Motorized Turntable/Rotating Pedestal forRetail Display	$142.00
REGAL DUAL TEMP DUAL ZONE BAKERY DELI WOW 1 YEAR OLD !!		[2 of these sold in a multiple item ("Dutch") auction for $71.00 each]	
Hussmann 16' Refrigerated Display Case Cooler SEATTLE	$3,750.00	Glass Wood Retail Commercial Store Counter Display Case	$127.50
Barker 6 ft. Refrigerated Curved Glass Bakery Case	$3,499.99	Otis Spunkmeyer Cookie & Muffin Display Case	$127.50
JEWELRY DISPLAY CASES 10'x15' CUSTOM BUILT (3YRS OLD)	$3,000.00	Giorgio Armani Display Case	$127.50
Retail Candy Display Case - 4' Refrigerated	$2,800.00	Amish Milk Wagon Coffee Table Display Case	$125.00
[2 of these sold in a multiple item ("Dutch") auction for $1,400.00 each]		GRIDWALL DISPLAY PANELS - LOT OF 14 , 2 sizes	$125.00
Candy Display jelly belly gravity bins entire unit	$2,659.00	A Multiple Hat Display Rack	$117.50
retail unit, dispenser with stands racks brachs		Merco 2-Tier Sandwich Merchandiser	$115.99
Food stand, Food trailer, concession stand, fruit stand	$2,000.00	~ART DECO SPIKED HEEL CHAIR ~ PARIS APT CHIC ~NR	$109.99
Retail Displays Store Fixtures	$1,525.00	SMITH LIGHTED SUNGLASSES DISPLAY CASE W/ STORAGE	$102.50
LOCKING OAK DISPLAY CASES WITH GLASS SHELVES (SET OF 2)	$1,277.01	NICE MIRRORED GLASS SHELF DISPLAY MERCHANDISER	$102.50
5 retail display case	$1,000.00	72 Inch Wide Glass Sales Display Case Cabinet w/ 2 Shlf	$102.50
[4 of these sold in a multiple item ("Dutch") auction for $250.00 each]			
CABINETS AND DISPLAY CASES	$999.99		
dry bakery display case FEDERAL like new	$950.00		
Retail Pastry/Deli Display Case. 4' Dry w/curved glass	$910.00		

Food Service & Retail ▸ Point of Sale, POS Equipment

The average sales price in this subcategory is $130.15.

	HIGH		AVG
Gilbarco PC G-Site GSite GC-40 Register Single or Dual	$2,650.00	Sharp XEA302 1800PLU 99 Dept. Cash Register FREESHIP*	$139.00
MICROS 3700 POS SYSTEM W/7 TOUCH SCREENS	$2,500.00	ROYAL 600sc / 601sc CASH REGISTER + BAR CODE SCANNER :)	$137.50
WORKSTATIONS		ROYAL 115cx Battery Cash Register FREESHP*NEW	$134.99
VeriFone Ruby SuperSystem 24Mhz 8MB RAM	$1,995.00	[10 of these sold for $134.99 each]	
Verifone Ruby Supersystem II POS System Register	$1,700.00	Royal 583cx Cash Register 1000items PLU FREESHIP*	$134.99
MICROS 3700 POS TOUCH SCREEN WORKSTATION	$1,525.00	ROYAL 600sc / 601sc CASH REGISTER + BAR CODE SCANNER	$134.95
CASH REGISTER		[2 of these sold for $134.95 each]	
CRS 3000 POS SYSTEM 2 UNITS	$1,250.00	Adler-Royal Olivetti Alpha 9180SC Auto Cash Register	$133.51
VeriFone Ruby SUPERSYSTEM II POS SYSTEM REGISTER	$1,000.00	IBM POS 4614 System Including Cash Draw AS-IS	$132.50
micros eclipse pos refurbished 3700 no reserve	$609.99	Swintec SW20 Cash Register Portable Like New w/ Extras!	$127.50
SHARP UP-3300 POS TOUCH SCREEN CASH REGISTER	$600.00	ROYAL 600 SC POS CASH REGISTER MANAGEMENT SYSTEM *L@@k*	$127.50
Like new card/hologram tipper!hot stamp machine! w/foil	$515.00	LINK POINT 3000 CREDIT CARD MACHINE W/ PRINTER & CORDS	$127.50
Samsung ER-5240m P.O.S. Cash Register	$510.00	Micros Stand-alone Roll Printer clean,repaired,&painted	$125.00
5 MICROS USED SYSTEM UNITS	$505.00	IBM 4820 SurePoint POS Touchscreen LCD Computer Monitor	$125.00
2 Panasonic Workstation JS-510WS POS with Epson Printer	$500.00	Javelin Wedge ELO Touchscreen POS	$125.00
Samsung ER-5100 Cash Register	$499.00	Sable Technologies CT90 MK1.1 POS Terminal	$124.39
Casio TE-3000s cash register & drawer 5.2 in. color LCD	$449.00	ROYAL ALPHA 600SC 601SC CASH REGISTER SCANNER/WRTY!!	$124.00

Food Service & Retail ▸ Refrigeration & Ice Machines

The average sales price in this subcategory is $511.65.

	HIGH		AVG
Walk in Cooler/Freezer w/ glass doors L-shape	$6,100.00	BEAUTIFUL VICTORY 1 DOOR REFRIGERATOR ON CASTERS	$598.72
WALK-IN COOLER 8' x 12' - NEW - FREE SHIPPING	$4,125.00	True Glass Door Cooler Refrigerator Merchandiser	$595.00
[2 of these sold for $4,125.00 each]		Fridge double door Traulsen	$590.00
Brown Walk In Retail Freezer - No Reserve	$3,999.00	Dixie Narco Glass Door Merchandiser Cooler Refrigerator	$585.00
WALK-IN COOLER 8' X 8' - NEW - FREE SHIPPING	$3,525.00	[2 of these sold for $585.00 each]	
deli display case	$3,115.00	deli display case - refrigerated Hussmann or similar	$561.00
Vogt Model 4000 Ice Machine with bin - good condition	$2,551.00	SCOTSMAN ICE MAKER (ICE MACHINE)	$560.00
SERVICE/SELF SERVICE REFRIGERATED BAKERY CASE	$2,500.00	Manitowoc Cube Ice Machine Hoshizaki 600# Single phase	$550.00
Taylor Thick Milk shake freezer frosty 358-33 Machine	$2,480.55	RANDELL 48" REFRIGERATED WORKTOP UNDERCOUNTER	$545.00
Beverage air refrigerator display case, deli, cooler	$2,324.00	COMMERCIAL SCOTSMAN ICE MAKER HEAD W BIN & CART	$530.00
True Stainless Steel 3-Door Freezer-72 in Cu. Ft.	$2,300.00	Beverage Air KR48-1AS Reach-In Refrigerator	$526.99
Hussmann deli case meat case curved glass	$2,200.00	Used Scotsman 170-1B Ice Machine, Like New Condition	$525.00
9 Door Walk-In/Reach-In Cooler w/Compressor & Condenser	$2,025.00	Beverage Air FC49 Commercial Floral Refrigerator Cooler	$520.00
WALK-IN COOLER 8' X 10'	$2,000.00	PREP TABLE NEW 2003 NEVER USED REFRIGERATED S/S	$520.00
SERVICE/SELF SERVICE REFRIGERATED BAKERY CASE	$1,975.00	LEER Commercial Reach-In Ice Storage Freezer - NICE!	$515.00
Ice Cuběr Machine - Ice maker 800 lbs head & C-700 Bin	$1,950.00	2-Door Manitowoc AV2A Reach-In Freezer No-Reserve	$510.00

Food Service & Retail ▸ Vending & Tabletop Concessions

The median sales price in this subcategory is $63.00.

	HIGH		AVG
ATM PARTS (TIDEL,NCR,TBS,TRITON,GREENLINK & more...)		S.S.F COMMERCIAL BULK VENDING GUMBALL CANDY MACHINES	$65.00
ATM PARTS LIQUIDATION FINAL SALE!!!!	$38,000.00	Royal 200 Laundry Soap Vending Machine	$64.99
80 NEW VENDSTAR 3000 BULK CANDY MACHINES.	$7,000.00	VENDSTAR 3000 Bulk Candy Vending Machine - NR	$64.50
$12,000.00 CERTIFICATES FOR CANDY, YOU PAY SHIPPING !!!		NORTHWESTERN GUMBALL / CANDY	$64.50
ANTARES- NEW Vending Snack/Drink/Bill Changer	$5,250.00	VENDING MACHINE W/ STAND	

5 Antares Snack, Beverage Combo w/Coin Changer. All located and earning income!	$3,550.00	Very Interesting 1947 - 5 Cent Coin Dispenser Changer	$64.00
		LARGE HOT OIL KETTLE POPCORN	$64.00
HOTDOG CART (with grill, frier, and cooler built-in)	$3,100.00	POPPER MACHINE MAKER NEW	
38 nearly new Vendstar 3000 3-head candy machines	$3,000.00	32 ATM Paper Rolls for Triton 9600,9500,9100, Etc. ATMs	$63.95
Commercial Popcorn Popper & 2 Commercial Carmelizers	$2,999.00	DIXIE NARCO UP STACK ACCEPTOR MODEL USA-15 117 VOLTS	$63.88
Rowe Model 448EII Cold Food Vending Machine – Recond	$2,426.00	CASH CODE BILL ACCEPTOR AMZ USA PLUS FOR CHERRY MASTER	$63.00
Brand New Tranax 1500 MiniBank ATM Machine (not Triton)	$2,399.00	COINCO MAG50B 117V VALIDATOR	$62.00
$2,399 cash or $69/month includes ship and install		MAG-50 BILL ACCEPTOR NEW	
Tidel 3400 ATM	$2,300.00	Double Head Gumball Candy Bulk Vending Machine Extra $	$62.00
ATM Machine Triton 9100	$2,140.00	x-mas gift Classic Quiet Salesman/Kid's Savings Bank	
Gold Medal 32 oz. Popcorn Popper Machine 2011 FPE	$2,025.00	VINTAGE NATIONAL CIGARETTE	$62.00
Saeco 7P Plus Espresso, Coffee Vending Machine	$2,025.00	VENDING MACHINE LOOK NR !!!!	
U-Turn Vending Machines-Still in Box.	$2,025.00	Trivend Metal Triple Candy / Gumball Vending Machine	$61.75
10 U-Turn 8 Compartment Vending machines-Brand new		NEW ~Double Headed~ Bulk Gumball/Candy Vending Machine	$61.03
New F820 Fastcorp Frozen/Ice Cream Vending Machine	$2,000.00	DOLLAR BILL CHANGER CM-100 FOR PARTS	$61.02

Food Service & Retail ▶ Wholesale Lots & Bulk Foods

The average sales price in this subcategory is $20.99.

	HIGH		AVG
ZIPPO LIGHTER BUSINESS - 48 LIGHTERS $1300+ RETAIL	$709.99	100ct Wholesale Foods Jobber Lot Salsas Mustards NR	$24.42
Extreme Scents Candle Business + Website + Supplies +NR	$561.00	4 FAKE/DUMMY SECURITY CAMERA SCANNING MOTION, AMAZING	$23.99
Huge Lot 90 Symbol Hand Barcode Scanner C Photos Texlon	$511.01	[2 of these sold for $23.99 each]	
Flower shop- going out of bus- wholesale resale lot!	$350.00	9 Small Metal Cups Gold & Silver Trophy Parts Awards	$23.99
LOT * Drug Store STORAGE Tubs / Bins with Folding Lids	$265.00	Pemmican Sweet Mesquite Beef Jerky Case Lot	$23.76
Scrolling Message Electronic LED Badge Wholesale Lot 12	$252.60	1000 8" Glow Light Sticks Bracelets Favors + Free Bonus	$23.00
[2 of these sold for $252.60 each]		5 LB. Wholesale Lot CANDY Salt Water Taffy, Assorted	$22.95
18 Cases of KLEENEX C-Fold Towels 01500 - 40,000 towes	$150.00	[2 of these sold for $22.95 each]	
360 SNICKERS Marathon low carb Peanut Butter bars	$100.00	100 - 10oz New Clear Plastic Bottles and Lids	$22.50
500+ Asstd Greeting Cards w/envelopes & free display	$100.00	Dexatrim All in One Diet Bars - Lemon Crisp	$21.98
360 SNICKERS Marathon low carb Peanut Butter bars	$100.00	[2 of these sold in a multiple item ("Dutch") auction for $10.99 each]	
[3 of these sold for $100.00 each]		One Dozen Decorative Red Marble Apples W/Brass Stems	$21.96
Alligator Cajun JERKY Beef Buffalo Venison Elk HOT Lots	$89.00	Case of Magnum Capello W. Zinfandel Wine NR	$21.50
HUGE LOT OF HUNDREDS OF STORE PRICING SIGNS TAGS LABELS	$79.98	Case of 750ml Capello W. Zinfandel Wine NR	$21.50
[2 of these items sold for $39.99 each]		RYKOFF SEXTON restaurant salad - dessert plate * LOT *	$21.05
24 Red Hanes Stedman Short Sleeve Shirts Wholesale Lot	$75.00	LOT of 120 Jeweled Belly Tattoos/Retail Ready! HOT!!	$21.00
Lot Of 58 Waterfall Store Display Slatwall Fixtures	$69.00	5 LB. Wholesale Lot CANDY Salt Water Taffy, Assorted	$20.95
balloon inflating machine w/ free balloons	$66.99	[2 of these sold for $20.95 each]	
		Case of 1998 Merlot Clos Du Muriel Wine NR	$20.75

Healthcare, Lab & Life Science ▶ Imaging & Aesthetics Equipment

The average sales price in this subcategory is $1,364.72.

	HIGH		AVG
Hewlett Packard Image Point Hx Ultrasound Machine	$10,600.00	ATL Ultramark UM4A Ultrasound System NO RESERVE!	$2,375.00
Healthcare Equipment Supplier Web Site For Sale	$10,000.00	X-ray machine - KMA 300/125 complete system -	$2,324.99
[2 of these sold for $10,000.00 each]		ATL Ultramark 8 UM8 ultrasound system w/ 4 probes	$2,200.00
(2) Endermologie LPG Cellu M6 ES1 Machines & Exam Table	$9,000.00	AI Acoustic Imaging 5200S Ultrasound Envision Open TZ	$2,025.00
LPG CELLU M6 ES1 ENDERMOLOGIE MACHINE & TABLE?	$6,600.00	COMPLETE XRAY SYSTEM W/ KONICA DEVELOPER	$2,025.00
SHIMADZU 4500 C.T. SCANNER	$6,100.00	SONY UP-D70XR Digital Video Medical Printer	$1,999.95
SHIMADZU ULTRASOUND OB/GYN GREAT PRICE! S/H INCL*	$5,495.00	Amfit Digital Contour Digitizer model 350A footfax	$1,999.00
DIASONICS GATEWAY 2D ULTRASOUND WITH DICOM	$5,100.00	Non Surgical FaceLift Microcurrent Face Lift Computer	$1,699.00
1990 PHILLIPS BV-25 C-ARM CARM X-RAY C ARM NO RESERVE	$4,480.00	ATL UM4 PLUS ULTRASOUND MACHINE	$1,625.00
ACUSON XP 10, MODEL 128 ULTRASOUND SYSTEM	$4,050.00	GE Ultrasound Probe LA39 for Logic 700, 500, & 400	$1,625.00
Philip Mobile C-arm X-ray BV 29	$4,050.00	GE RT-3600 ULTRASOUND	$1,550.00
TOSHIBA SSA 270A Color Ultrasound+ 2 Monitors+PROBES!	$3,995.00	AGFA CP 1000 14" WIDE X-RAY	$1,501.00
Toshiba Capasee II Ultrasound system, Model SSA-22A	$3,800.00	FILM PROCESSOR AUTOMATIC	$1,500.00
ATL Ultramark UM9 HiDef Ultrasound System 5 DAY SALEn/r	$3,550.00	HOLOGIC X-RAY BONE DENSITOMETER ** NO RESERVE	$1,500.00
OB/GYN ACUSON 128 XP 10 ULTRASOUND 3 PROBES S/H INCL*	$3,500.00	Sony UP-51MDU Color Video Printer	$1,500.00
Keithley Traid X-Ray measuring system	$3,200.00	C-ARM TABLE BY MEDI MATIC	$1,475.00

Healthcare, Lab & Life Science ▶ Lab Equipment

The average sales price in this subcategory is $117.73.

	HIGH		AVG
Axioplan (Zeiss) Microscope	$3,000.00	Zeiss Microscope Classic Pumpkin ill. & CSI 250W Socket	$135.83
New Carl Zeiss Inclined Binocular + 10X Eyepieces OPMI	$1,250.00	_OLYMPUS MOTORIZED FIVE POSITION MICROSCOPE TURRET	$131.50
Phase Contrast Microscope Hund Wetzlar & Polarizer	$950.00	Zeiss Microscope MC63A Camera System w/Polaroid back	$130.37
Zeiss Microscope Universal Septuple Nosepiece Like New!	$889.00	B&L Phase Contrast Condenser, 10X Obj for DynaZoom	$129.50
ZEISS BINOCULAR OBSERVER TUBEOPMI	$857.00	ZEISS 125/16 BINOCULAR MICROSCOPE TUBE (HEAD)	$128.05
Metalurgic Microscope Hund Wetzlar Epi New	$850.00	Filar Microscope Eyepiece Micrometer	$127.00
Zeiss microscope objective Neofluar 40X/0.75 ICS	$761.00	Zeiss Microscope Polarizer for Vertical illumination	$126.50
Zeiss Axiomat Binocular Head	$698.00	Leitz Wetzlar Condenser with 0.55 S 15 Lens + Dovetail	$125.00
Zeiss 1880 OPMI Surgical Microscope Stand	$661.00	Zeiss Filterblock for Striking Light	$125.00
Microscope 100um Piezo Positioner Set, Ultra Precise!	$650.00	Leitz Trinocular Head for 30mm in diameter Oculars	$125.00
Zeiss Microscope Axio Optovar Magnification Changer	$647.77	OLYMPUS NOSEPIECE	$124.50
Olympus Microscope UMPLAN FL 100x/.95 Dry Infinity Lens	$595.50	Zeiss Microscope f=200 Auxiliary Lens (47 50 71)	$124.49
Olympus Microscope Trinocular for BH series Microscopes	$588.00	4 Turrets in One Deal	$119.50
ZEISS PHOTO ADAPTER F=74	$520.00	Leitz microscope Plezy adapter	$118.09
Zeiss microscope parts Axiotron Axioplan	$500.00	Zeiss Microscope Stage #47-33-56-9901	$118.01

Healthcare, Lab & Life Science ▸ Lab Supplies

The average sales price in this subcategory is $27.56.

	HIGH		AVG
tall PYREX GLASS STOPPERED BOTTLE. RUBY RED LONG NECK	$406.63	Special 60cm Distilling Column, Pyrex Lab Glass	$32.55
Lab Glass Vacuum Chamber Bell Jar 30"x 18-1/16"ODx 3/8"	$280.00	1 liter pressure-equalizing funnel	$32.51
Absolutely HUGE LOT Misc. Glass Lab Items! Must See !	$213.83	Glassware - 74 pieces-flasks, fleakers and cylinders	$31.01
Drykeeper Dessicator	$160.00	(2) SGA Allihn 400mm Condensers Pyrex Lab Glass	$31.00
Large Shott 3-Piece Vacuum Chamber or Fermenting Vessel	$145.00	Proportional Voltage Controller	$31.00
Huge Lot Kimble/Kimax/Pyrex Lab Glass/Glassware	$132.50	800ml Pyrex Beaker 6 pack	$30.05
Organic Chemistry Lab Glassware & More 100 Pieces!!!	$132.50	PYREX : 250ML BEAKERS - NEW - BOX OF 12	$29.99
GLASS VACUUM CHAMBER WITH PRESSURE GAUGE/VALVE	$125.00	Potassium Nitrate (KNO3) 22 lbs High Grade Extra Fine**	$29.95
New!!!, Large,Pyrex,Dome Reaction Chamber, Check it!!	$125.00	Lab Thermometers	$29.95
GLASS VACUUM CHAMBER WITH PRESSURE GAUGE/VALVES	$125.00	11 Piece Lab Glass Standard Taper Adapter Lot	$29.00
Bellco 15 Liter Overhead Drive Vessel 4 Arms Bioreactor	$125.00	4000 ml Beaker Lab Glass Beakers	$28.99
[2 of these sold for $125.00 each]		HUGE NEW! Borosilicate	
LabGlass new 2000ml Separatory Funnel	$110.00	Antique Pyrex Lab Glass Glassware	$28.50
[5 of these sold for $110.00 each]		Heavy Pyrex Vacuum Bell Jar with Aluminum Bottom	$28.00
10 MM x 8 " PYREX GLASS BOROSILICATE TUBING TEST TUBE	$108.00	3000ml Single Neck Pyrex ,	$28.00
[36 of these sold in a multiple item ("Dutch") auction for $3.00 each]		Round Bottom Flask!Like New!	
Lab Glass Vacuum Chamber Bell Jar 30"x 18-1/16"ODx 1/4"	$105.94	SYRINGE LOT BD YALE GLASS	$27.66
Kontes Universal Electrode Kit, Pyrex Lab Glass	$104.33	UNUSED ASST SIZES W/ NEEDLES	

Healthcare, Lab & Life Science ▸ Medical Equipment

The average sales price in this subcategory is $315.74.

	HIGH		AVG
QXCI EPFX Biofeedback Device QUANTUM Stress Detection	$8,500.00	COULTER ONYX (USED)	$500.00
Dynarad HF-110F Mobile Radiographic X-ray System	$4,050.00	CRYOMEDICS ZOOMSCOPE COLPOSCOPE 3001 OB GYN	$499.99
Gemini Chiropractic Table	$3,656.00	Airshields C200 Infant Incubator	$499.00
COHERENT XAM-SP SUPERPULSE AMBULASE CO2 MEDICAL LASER	$2,750.00	narkomed sevoflurane Vaporizer	$499.00
NEW Microderm Microdermabrasion Microdermabrador SH In	$2,495.00	G.E. Prucka Cardio-Lab Mac-Lab 2000/4000/7000 Combo	$495.00
Portable Ultrasound Machine Linear Transvaginal probes.	$2,417.00	Welch Allyn PanOptic Ophthalmoscope/Otoscope-Like NEW	$414.57
Ritter 75 Evolution Examination/Surgical Chair	$2,375.00	Ortho Regular X-Ray Cassettes Rare Earth Curix Screens	$400.00
Skin Science Microdermabrasion Unit NO RESERVE	$1,999.00	DEVILBISS 9055D SLEEP MACHINE WITH ACCESS!!!!	$400.00
Weck Surgical Microscope	$1,700.00	Lasersonics ND YAG Laser Optical deck complete HeNe	$375.00
PHILIPS MEDICAL (HP) DEFIBRILLATOR CODEMASTER XL PLUS	$1,195.00	HOMETRAC Cervical Traction Unit. Deluxe case.	$360.00
Digene Hybrid Capture System for Pathology Lab HPV DNA	$1,175.00	DEVILBISS 9001D SLEEP MACHINE WITH ACCESS!!!!	$350.00
HGM Portable Laser (Argon)	$1,100.00	Xomed-Treace MPS 2000 Micro-Craft Power System	$350.00
Stryker Rugged X FRAME Ambulance Stretcher Cot ferno NR	$1,075.00	chiropractic drop table	$346.00
SYNTHES SURGICAL DRILL SYSTEM	$1,026.00	Amrex Synchro Sonic U/50 Ultrasound Machine	$345.00
Stryker Rugged X Ambulance Stretcher NR 500LBS ferno	$1,001.00	GE 200MA X-Ray Unit Machine	$330.00

Healthcare, Lab & Life Science ▸ Medical—Specialty

The average sales price in this subcategory is $271.29.

	HIGH		AVG
Cerec 3D by Sirona	$55,500.00	EdenTrace II Plus Polysomnography BreathSensor	$395.00
MCC Cabinetry from Patterson Dental Like New L@@K!!!	$13,601.00	Dental Lab MICROSCOPE w/STAND & Light - New in Box*	$379.00
Sirona/Siemens Cerec 2 Chair-Side Dental Lab Mill II	$7,000.00	Dental Piezo Ultrasonic Scaler+3 tips! NEW!	$378.00
Insight Millennium Chiro Chiropractic 2nd Generation	$5,395.00	Manikin head for typodont by Columbia Dentoform Corp	$375.00
LifeStyle Portable Oxygen Concentrator! New! w/extras	$3,999.00	Aseptico AEU-17B Dental Surgimotor II	$375.00
NEW IN BOX MIDMARK/RITTER M9 AUTOCLAVE NR	$2,975.00	DENTAL DEMETRON OPTILUX CURING LIGHT AND ACCESSORIES	$365.00
KAVO DIAGNODENT NEW IN BOX WITH 2 TIPS	$2,650.80	Puritan Bennet Renaissance PB100 Spirometer	$360.00
Siemens 300 Ventilator without Graphics mon Respirator	$2,500.00	Puritan Bennett GoodKnight 420S CPAP w/extras	$350.00
Midmark M11 Sterilizer in Excellent Condition	$1,825.00	Puritan Bennett GoodKnight 418G CPAP Sleep Apnea System	$315.00
T-Bird Legacy Portable Ventilator	$1,599.00	SEAC Dental System	$306.00
VersaMed iVent 201 Ventilator for EMS SIMV PSV Oximetry	$1,595.00	Sullivan ResMed CPAP S6 Lightweight Sleep Apnea Machine	$305.00
Rebuilt Statim 2000 Autoclave Sterilizer NO RESERVE!!	$1,500.00	INVACARE MODEL 5 OXYGEN CONCENTRATOR	$300.00
Dental Cavitron SPS Item 610	$960.00	MACAN MD-9 Electrosurgical Unit dental electrosurgery	$299.95
Tuttnauer 2540 M Sterilizer in Excellent Condition	$881.01	Chad Oxymatic 411 Oxygen Regulator NEW	$296.99
DENTAL EQUIPMENT- INTRAORAL CAMERA/X RAY/IMAGING	$850.00	Respironics Aria LX CPAP System with all accessories	$280.00

Healthcare, Lab & Life Science ▸ Medical Supplies & Disposables

The average sales price in this subcategory is $34.05.

	HIGH		AVG
Huge lot of New Kendall sharps containers various sizes	$482.25	Case of 12 Surgical Gowns-Scrubs, new fabric surplus NR	$36.00
ETHICON SUTURE *FOUR* UNOPENED BOXES PDS II/ VICRYL	$403.67	Ethicon Suture-Vicryl,4-0, 27", 1/2,17 mm, J214H	$36.00
10000 Latex-Safe Vinyl Exam Gloves LARGE	$260.00	AUTO SUTURE ENDO GIA 30-3.5 RELOADS 030807L 11-05	$36.00
ETHICON Dermabond DHV12 Topical Skin Adhesive, NIB 1/07	$207.50	Biogel Latex Surgical Glove 50pr Sz 6.5 M13-6	$36.00
LARGE LOT of ETHICON and USS DG ophthalmic suture	$153.06	Ethicon Suture-Vicryl,3-0, 18", 1/2 36mm, J738D.Violet	$36.00
Dermabond Topical Skin Adhesive DHV12 *FREE SHIPPING*	$152.50	Ethicon Suture J944H NIB exp07-2008 3-0 OB/GYN VICRYL	$36.00
2 BOXES of ETHICON Dermabond DHV12	$150.00	[3 of these sold for $36.00 each]	
NEW ETHICON Dermabond Topical Skin Adhesive glue suture	$146.50	New Vicryl 2-0 Violet Suture J726D	$35.00
[2 of these sold for $146.50 each]		USSDG Suture Biosyn 4-0 18" P-13 NIB SM-3690	$35.00
NEW ETHICON Dermabond Topical Skin Adhesive glue suture	$146.50	SUTURE Vicryl 6-0 PS-3 J499G exp Jul 08 or later.	$35.00
Dermabond DB12 exp 2006-06 glue sutures suture	$142.50	Ethicon Suture 1677H NIB exp 07-2007 4-0 silk plastic	$35.00
3-0 VICRYL ...VC442H...EXPIRED JAN 2005...Sealed Box	$127.68	5 STAPLER GUNS - REFLEX ONE SURGICAL STAPLERS WIDE	$34.99

[3 of these sold in a multiple item ("Dutch") auction for $42.56 each]

Ethicon Suture Vicryl 3-0 27" PS-2 NIB J427H	$123.61	[2 of these sold for $34.99 each]	
Ethicon Suture Monocryl 3-0 27" PS-2 NIB Y427H	$123.50	SUTURE Prolene 5-0 PS-3 8681G exp Jul 08 or later.	$34.76
4-0 Ethilon Suture by Ethicon PS-2 1667 exp 1/10 3 doz	$122.50	D&G, 3-0, Maxon, T-5 Needle EXP 2005-01	$34.00
ETHICON DERMABOND SUTURE SKIN GLUE DHV12 1DOZ 2/07	$122.50	1000 Vacutainer Precisionglide Needles 21G x 1 ½	$34.00
		ETHICON 5-0 PDS II P-3 SUTURE Z493G 1/07 NIB	$34.00

Industrial Electrical & Test ▸ Circuit Breakers, Transformers

The average sales price in this subcategory is $82.38.

	HIGH		AVG
NEW!!! 300 KVA 480 DELTA TO 208 Y 3 PHASE TRANSFORMER	$2,490.00	New Square D 3 Phase Transformer	$125.00
SORGEL Three Phase Insulated TRANSFORMER 480V 300KVA	$2,000.00	EC-1465 POWERSTAT VARIABLE AUTOTRANSFORMER 56A	$122.50
GE Electrical Transformer 225 KVA Pri 208v sec 480/277	$1,675.00	4-Ratelco Constant Voltage Chargers	$109.00
Bailey Network90 Full MMU01 Rack complet with I/O cards	$1,000.00	Powerstat 1256D 240V Input, 0-280V Out, 28 KVA	$102.50
TRANSFORMERS,480-208-115 FOUR FOR ONE PRICE	$850.00	General Electric GE Transformer 3 Phase 30KVA Y Delta	$102.50
Jennings vacuum contactor, like-new	$750.00	General Electric Transformer Single Phase 3 KVA	$101.00
NEW!!! 15 KVA 480 DELTA TO 240 3 PHASE TRANSFORMER	$699.00	GENERAL SIGNAL HEVI-DUTY HS1F5AS 1 PH 5 KVA TRANSFORMER	$100.89
General Signal Dry Transformer, 3ph, 75 KVA, 480/240 II	$530.00	Oneac Model CSD23100 [Used]	$100.00
TRANSFORMER SQUARE D 112T6H	$500.00	SQ. D 30 KVA 3PH TRANSFORMER	$100.00
ITE Dry Transformer, 75 KVA, 480/240 delta-delta !!!!!!	$455.00	Q-TRAN QL SERIES QLM-600 24V NEW	$99.99
45 KVA OLSUN ELECTRICS 3 PHASE HV480 LV240/120 NEW!! NR	$450.00	Topaz 2.5 Kva Noise Isolator Power Supply Transformer	$99.00
GENERAL ELECTRIC 75 KVA TRANSFORMER	$430.00	GENERAL ELEC. VARIABLE TRANSFORMER VOLT PAC.!!!!!!!	$91.00
112.5 KVA TRANSFORMER ACME ELECTRIC CORP	$399.00	4-Ratelco Constant Voltage Chargers	$90.50
Solid State Tesla Coil ! SSTC ! 24" lightning	$399.00	STACO 3PN1510 Variable Autotransformer Variac	$90.07
FEDERAL PACIFIC 75 KVA 3 PHASE CLASS AA DRY TRANSFORMER	$375.00	Neon Sign Transformer, 15kv 60ma Good Condition!	$85.00

Industrial Electrical & Test ▸ Industrial Automation, Control

The average sales price in this subcategory is $96.44.

	HIGH		AVG
YASKAWA SERVO PACK DRIVE	$1,055.51	IDEC Power Supply 24 VDC 100 Watt- PS5R-E24 - 5 pcs.	$110.50
Fanuc Power Supply Module PSM-26 - A06B-6087-H126 NIB!	$970.00	Magnetek	$108.05
Baldor BSM90A-2150AA 10Nm AC Servo Motor & Drive, NR	$895.00	(2) CONTROL TECHNIQUES UNI1405 UNIDRIVE 5HP AC DRIVE	$104.49
Siemens Relcon 6SE85 AC Drive Board	$750.00	AC DRIVE MAGNETEK GPD 503 MOD DS316 H.P. 7.5-10	$103.50
Fanuc A06B-6087-H115 Alpha Power Supply ,New in Box	$660.00	Baldor AC Motor Adjustable Speed Drive Control Unit	$102.50
INDRAMAT TVD 1.3-08-03 MODULE POWER SUPPLY NIB	$650.00	Nordson power board, repair kit 3000 Vista series	$102.50
ALLEN BRADLEY CONTROLLOGIX 1756-A17/B RACK W/PS	$599.00	KB Genesis Adjustable Frequency AC Inverter KBE2 1101 P	$102.50
ABB 20HP ACH500 Variable Speed Drive, Bypass, Enclosure	$499.99	Sola Power Supply SDN10-24-100 24VDC 10A	$100.50
NEW AB Allen-Bradley 1336 PLUS II Adjustable Frequency	$456.25	Allen Bradley PowerFlex4 2HP AC Drive 3phase NEW!!	$100.00
Allen-Bradley 1756-PA75 Factory Sealed *No Reserve*	$405.00	AC TECH VARIABLE SPEED AC MOTOR DRIVE	$99.00
NEW SIEMENS MIDIMASTER 10 HP MOTOR DRIVE 6SE95228CG40	$399.00	(2) CONTROL TECHNIQUES UNI1405 UNIDRIVE 5HP AC DRIVE	$99.00
Fanuc power supply A16B-1211-0890 15M controls	$361.25	FANUC A16B 1210 0480 R PC BOARD NEW !!!	$99.00
Fanuc A14B-0061-B002 02 Power Unit for CNC or GMF - NR	$355.00	Allen Bradley Power Supply 1775-P1 Ser B	$99.00
Two Allen Bradley Power Flex 4 AC Drives Factory Sealed	$350.00	Nikki Denso Actus Power NPSA-20NN-50-E8 AC Servo Drive	$99.00
Allen Bradley 1336 Plus II 10 HP VFD, A/C Drive	$349.99	CUTLER HAMMER SIZE 3 MOTOR STARTER	$99.00

Industrial Electrical & Test ▸ Industrial Automation, Control ▸ Robotics

The average sales price in this subcategory is $318.17.

	HIGH		AVG
TORCHMATE II CNC Plazma/Routing/Tube Cutting	$14,005.02	FANUC A06B-6066-H006 SERVO AMPLIFIER AC	$410.00
GM FANUC 6 AXIS ROBOT ARC MATE SR. WELDING CENTER	$9,100.00	Yaskawa Robotic Arm / Linear Actuator	$405.00
Fanuc S-500 robot with RJ controller and pendant	$8,101.00	Parker Daedal BT100 Ballscrew Cross Roller Table	$400.00
MILLER (OTC DAIHEN) MRV-6 WELDING ROBOT	$6,000.00	Parker Daedal Rotary Table	$400.00
Fanuc Arc-Mate Welding Robot RG2	$2,750.00	Adept Model 440 Robotic Arm Industrial Robotics (2)	$399.00
Nachi 8608 Robot, AM10 Controller, 6 axis, NO RESERVE!!	$2,550.00	Fanuc Robotics 3000rpm Servo Motor NEW	$375.00
Brooks PRI WTM511-2-FWS02 Wet Robot Edge Grip Capable	$2,499.00	Equipe/PRI 7" B Robot Arm.	$350.00
SEIKO Epson D-TRAN SCARA Arm Robot and Controller.	$2,200.00	MICROBOT TEACHING ROBOT	$345.00
Equipe ESC-200 Robot Controller	$1,650.00	FANUC A06B-6066-H006 SERVO AMPLIFIER AC	$333.00
[2 of these sold for $1,650.00 each]		FANUC A06B-6066-H006 SERVO AMPLIFIER AC	$300.00
Adept Robots model 310 and 640	$1,600.00	Equipe/PRI 7" Robot Arm.	$300.00
PRI Brooks Automation ESC-201B Robot Controller * NR *	$1,575.00	G17408 Newport RV120CCHL Precision Rotational Stage	$299.99
Nordson 6 Axis Robotic Arm Robot Painter + Cntrl/Hyd	$999.99	5 AXIS SCORBOT-ER 3 ROBOT! EDUCATIONAL/INDUSTRIAL! GRIP	$299.99
Genmark Robot	$872.00	Fanuc Servo Amplifier Module	$255.00
Adept SIO (IDE) main controller board (NEW..NEVER USED)	$800.00	GALIL MOTION CONTROL DMC-1540, 4 AXIS	$250.00
Newport Kensington Track Robot Controller 4000 w Cables	$799.00	[4 of these sold for $250.00 each]	

Industrial Electrical & Test ▸ Industrial Automation, Control ▸ Drives & Motion Control

The average sales price in this subcategory is $89.02.

	HIGH		AVG
YASKAWA SERVO PACK DRIVE	$1,055.51	Allen Bradley Size 3 Motor Starter 509-DOD	$99.00
Baldor BSM90A-2150AA 10Nm AC Servo Motor & Drive, NR	$895.00	ALLEN BRADLEY 160 VARIABLE SPEED DRIVE	$99.00
Siemens Sikostart 3RW34, 75 hp soft start, complete	$800.00	Nikki Denso Actus Power NPSA-20NN-50-E8 AC Servo Drive	$99.00
Siemens Relcon 6SE85 AC Drive Board	$750.00	Cutler Hammer CN15DN3A Freedom Series Contactors ,3 NEW	$96.66
Fanuc A06B-6087-H115 Alpha Power Supply ,New in Box	$660.00	Furnas Heavy Duty Combination Starter/Breaker Size 1	$95.00
ABB SOFTSTART 75 HORSE POWER SOFT STARTER AC DRIVE	$511.00	Cutler Hammer Magnetic Starter A10CNOA 10 HP NEW	$94.00
ABB 20HP ACH500 Variable Speed Drive, Bypass, Enclosure	$499.99	Square-D Motor Starter Enclosure-30A 3-Phase 110V Coil	$91.72

NEW AB Allen-Bradley 1336 PLUS II Adjustable Frequency	$456.25	[2 of these sold in a multiple item ("Dutch") auction for $45.86 each]	
GE FANUC PCB BOARD	$456.00	1HP,230V, Inverter, Variable Speed Drive, VFD	$90.00
3-N.I.B.-CUTLER HAMMER COMBINATION STARTER	$450.00	New Allen-Bradley 505-BOD Size 1 Reversing AC Starter	$89.99
[3 of these sold in a multiple item ("Dutch") auction for $150.00 each]		EHB 34060 3 PHASE 3P - 60A - 480 / 240 VAC SQUARE D	$86.00
Allen-Bradley 150-B500NBD Series A Soft Starter	$449.00	Cutler Hammer Size 4 Motor Starter Series B1	$86.00
Telemecanique Contactor LC1FH43 3PH/220-600V/100-200HP	$410.00	Yaskawa Single Axis, SGDA-02AS + SGM-02A314B	$86.00
[2 of these sold in a multiple item ("Dutch") auction for $205.00 each]		NEW BOXED ALLEN-BRADLEY COMBINATION STARTER	$85.00
NEW SIEMENS MIDIMASTER 10 HP MOTOR DRIVE 6SE95228CG40	$399.00	Furnas-Size 2 Starter,w/Solid State Overload-22-45 Amps	$85.00
Two Allen Bradley Power Flex 4 AC Drives Factory Sealed	$350.00	**NEW** ALLEN BRADLEY 240V AC DRIVE, Powerflex 4	$84.88
Allen Bradley 1336 Plus II 10 HP VFD, A/C Drive	$349.99		

Industrial Electrical & Test ▸ Motors & Transmissions

The average sales price in this subcategory is $52.34.

	HIGH		AVG
GE Fanuc, Servo & Motor, New,	$1,365.00	NEW 2HP ELECTRIC MOTOR, SINGLE PHASE 115/ 230 VAC	$60.00
Ac3PH Motor TEFC	$1,000.00	NEW Treadmill Replacement Motor 130VDC 2.5HP 4500RPM	$60.00
Altivar Motor Controller with Motor	$355.00	[3 of these sold in a multiple item ("Dutch") auction for $20.00 each]	
New! 6.5hp Honda OHV Industrial engine-pump engine	$299.99	Siemens 2HP TEFC Electric Motor 3-Phase 230/460 V NEW	$59.99
5.5 HORSE Honda GX 160 Horizontal Shaft Motor (NEW)	$290.00	Baldor Electric Motor, 2 HP, VM3614, 208-230/460V, 3 Ph	$59.99
NEW 5 HP BALDOR AIR COMPRESSOR ELECTRIC MOTOR L1409T	$289.95	Antique Ritter laboratory motor model A dental motor	$58.00
NEW SURPLUS 5 HP ,1PHASE BALDOR ELECTRIC MOTOR	$265.00	US MOTOR 1HP ELECTRIC MOTOR - 1720 RPM - NOS!	$57.78
Franklin Deep Well Motor 5 hp single phase 230v NEW	$250.00	GE ELECTRIC 2 HP MOTOR	$57.50
Diesel fuel pumps and heater assemblie	$250.00	CHICAGO ELECTRIC 3 HP COMPRESSOR DUTY ELECTRIC MOTOR	$57.00
BALDOR 1 1/2 Hp MOTOR 145TC HAZ LOC & VACUUM PUMP	$244.18	2.5HP DC MOTOR, GO-CART, BATTLEBOT, ROBOT	$57.00
NEW SURPLUS 5 HP ,1PHASE BALDOR ELECTRIC MOTOR	$241.50	2-speed motor from leslie speaker cabinet for hammond	$56.01
NEW 5 HP BALDOR AIRCOMPRESSOR ELECTRIC MOTOR L1410T	$230.03	NIB RELIANCE P56H343439U 3 PH 60 HZ 1 HP 1725 RPM MOTOR	$56.00
NEW 5 HP BALDOR AIRCOMPRESSOR ELECTRIC MOTOR L1410T	$227.50	Consolidated Precision Ball Bearing NN3013 NR	$56.00
SKF OIL INJECTOR 226400/BEARING REMOVAL TOOL/BRAND NEW	$224.70	2.5HP DC MOTOR, GO-CART, BATTLEBOT, ROBOT	$56.00
NEW 5 HP BALDOR AIRCOMPRESSOR ELECTRIC MOTOR L1410T	$222.50	1 HP GENERAL ELECTRIC MOTOR NIB NEW	$55.00
		Tsubakimoto Recirculating ballscrews 46" CNC PLC	$54.10

Industrial Electrical & Test ▸ Test Equipment

The average sales price in this subcategory is $224.95.

	HIGH		AVG
Fujikura FSM-30S Fiber Arc Fusion Splicer 34 Test Arcs	$7,995.00	Dynatel 2273 Cable Locator Part	$250.00
Raytheon Palm IR 250 Thermal Camera	$5,200.00	SAGE INSTRUMENTS 930A COMMUNICATIONS TEST SET	$249.99
HP 70000 Series Spectrum Analyzer 50khz-26.5Ghz	$4,500.00	PTS 620 Frequency Synthesizer 1-620MHz 620R6N1X	$249.99
Audio Precision Portable One Plus Analog test unit	$4,494.00	3M DYNATEL 573A/P SHEATH CABLE FAULT LOCATOR	$249.99
Baker ST112S 3, 6 & 12 KV Surge / High Potential Tester	$4,050.00	Bio-Tek RF302 Electrosurgical Analyzer	$249.90
Audio Precision System One DSP+ SYS-222G	$4,000.00	Phillips PM 5515 Color TV Pattern Generator PAL & NTSC	$239.00
HP 4192A LF Impedance Analyzer NICE!	$3,215.00	PLL Down converter for Spectrum Analyzers and FSM CF285	$239.00
Radiodetection RD4000 Pipe & Cable Locator Set >10 Watt	$3,195.00	Sencore CM2000 Monitor TV Analyzer	$237.65
HP GSM / MS CELLULAR RADIO BASE STATION TESTER 8922F S	$2,875.25	HP 64700 EMULATOR / ANALYZER for 68302 CPU's w/ ADAPTER	$233.88
HP Agilent 4145B Semiconductor Parameter Analyzer	$2,650.00	HP 70205A Graphics Display 47.3W/1.2SLPS	$233.33
IFR FM/AM 1600s Service Monitor IFR1600s IFR1600 ,1600	$2,098.00	SCIENTIFIC ATLANTA	$232.50
AGEMA 510 THERMAL CAMERA	$2,025.00	Miteq AMF-40-005180-28-10P-K solid state amplifier NR	$230.50
3M Dynatel 2210 underground Cable Pipe Line Locator	$1,776.00	Hotip Resistance Soldering Unit - Like NEW	$229.49
Ocean Optics/RAMAN Systems R-2000 Spectrometer	$1,500.00	PLL Down converter for Spectrum Analyzers and FSM CF285	$229.00
STABILOCK SI 4015 COMMUNICATIONS MONITOR W/OPTIONS	$1,500.00	GUILDLINE /URRENT COMPARATOR RESISTANCE BRIDGE MOD:9975	$225.72

Industrial Electrical & Test ▸ Wholesale Lots

The average sales price in this subcategory is $52.50.

	HIGH		AVG
HUGE lot of Explosion Proof Electrical Inventory #2	$3,383.00	Huge Lot of New and Used Hardware $1 No Reserve	$90.00
Huge Lot of over 320,000 ICs, Mil Spec to Commercial!!!	$3,250.00	Huge Lot of Misc Industrial Hardware $1 No Reserve	$88.00
HUGE lot of Electrical Panels, Switches, Boxes	$3,225.00	lot of electrical tape	$79.96
Huge Lot of over 195,000 Connectors and ICs, Mil-Spec	$2,550.75	[4 of these sold in a multiple item ("Dutch") auction for $19.99 each]	
HUGE lot of Explosion Proof Electrical Inventory #1	$2,269.00	25 Amphenol Plug for jacketed cable 165-13 series	$78.88
CommScope #3227 / LMR 400 Equivalent -15 x 1000 ft roll	$2,250.00	MASSIVE LOT 26,900 pcs Asst. Radial Electrolytic Caps	$76.01
Large lot of Electrical Panels, Switches Disconnects 3	$1,675.00	IC CYPRESS 24PINS CY7C291A WHOLESALE LOT=77	$74.50
Lot 2 - Electrical Panels Switches, Disconns, Starters	$1,625.00	4500 +++ PCS Conectors & Headers Huge LOT	$68.99
LOT (500+) REELS Surface Mount Resistor/Capacitor SMT	$666.00	LARGE LOT 50 Reels Asst SMT Resistors Capacitors	$59.99
Lot of 10,983 ICs and Connectors, Valued over $20,000!	$660.00	Lab Transistor Tester, Multimeter & more	$57.78
ALLEN BRADLEY LOT.NR FREE SHIPPING	$600.00	TERMINAL LUG WHOLESALE LOT = *1398	$57.78
ELECTRONIC COMPONENTS, CONNECTORS, IC'S	$575.00	NEW IC'S NE555P LM555CN DIP TI $+500.00 VALUE	$56.76
LOT OF 31,949 ICs, 58 Diff Types NSC, MOT, TI, AND MORE	$510.00	Huge Lot of New and Used Electrical Components $1 NR	$54.00
NEW IC'S PBL3764A/4 PBL3764/4 R2 ERICSSON $6k HC5523IM	$499.00	MIXED LOT OF MOSTLY SIEMENS CONTACTORS, RELAYS, OVERLOA	$53.00
Large Lot of 40,202 ICs, Connectors, & Diodes, 53 Types	$380.00	LOT OF STAEFA CONTROL MODULES NIB!!	$52.99
		237 pcs lot BNC right angle conectors	$52.78

Industrial Supply, MRO ▸ Air Compressors

The average sales price in this subcategory is $76.92.

	HIGH		AVG
True Industrial grade 5 HP Air Compressor by Devair	$1,558.47	BASIC REPAIR KIT FOR A QUINCY COMPRESSOR QR-325	$138.50
EATON REFRIGERATED DRYER FOR 10-15 HP AIR COMPRESSORS	$799.00	Zurn refrigerant type air dryer	$134.49
[2 of these sold for $799.00 each]		164 FT SAE100R2AT 3/8" HYDRAULIC	$129.99
EATON REFRIGERATED DRYER FOR 10-15 HP AIR COMPRESSORS	$798.00	HOSE FLUID POWER NEW!!	

PLASMA ARC CUTTING THERMAL DYNAMICS PAK 50	$750.00
DELTECH I-R COMPRESSED AIR DRYER REFRIGERATED	$735.00
Refrigerated Air Dryer Ingersoll-Rand 50cfm TMS 50	$636.00
SAYLOR BEALL COMPRESSED AIR DRYER – AIR COMPRESSOR	$613.23
New Snap on 3/4 Drive Impact Gun IM75 W/Warrantee	$514.77
Hankison Compressed Air Dryer model HPR10-115	$500.00
BULLARD COMMANDAIR BREATHING FILTRATION SYSTEM NEW	$470.00
Speedaire Refrigerated Air Dryer 35 CFM 3YA52	$460.00
NEW 10HP AIR COMPRESSOR PUMP	$455.00
AIR COMPRESSOR PARTS (LOTS OF THEM) L@@K!!	$426.00
40 SCFM REFRIGERATED COMPRESSED AIR DRYER	$425.00
HUGE Brand New 3 THREE PHASE AIR COMPRESSOR PUMP	$415.00

GE 5 HP Single Phase Motor	$125.00
Like New Horizontal 120 gal Air Receiver Tank	$122.50
New Single Phase 5 HP Compressor Duty Motor	$122.50
NEW BAUER CAPITANO VALVE KIT 1ST 2ND 3RD STAGE VALVES	$112.50
NEW COOPER DOTCO END GRINDER	$112.50
WILKERSON DESSICANT AIR DRYER AND WATER SEPERATOR	$101.01
LUBRIQUIP TRABON MODU-FLOW LUBRICATOR W/AL-25 PUMP	$99.99
Ingersoll Rand Compressor Air Dryer	$90.00
100Ft Poly Flex Braided Air Hose 3/8"	$89.00
NICE ARO AIR REGULATOR FILTER LUBRICATOR 3/8" NPT	$85.00
Yellow Cloth cover Fire Hose 1" ID 300 ft	$82.09
ZEKS AIR COOLED AFTERCOOLER	$77.56

Industrial Supply, MRO ▶ Cleaning & Painting

The average sales price in this subcategory is $444.79.

	HIGH		AVG
Carpet Cleaning Van & Truck Mounted BluelineThermalWave	$40,000.00	OZONE GENERATOR - Pool Spa Powerful Corona Discharge	$569.95
Carpet Cleaning-Dynachem 310 TM w/ 96 Ford E350 Van	$16,500.00	Phoenix 200 Dehumidifier! 25 gal/day! N/R! L@@K!	$562.00
New Double wall insulated spray paint booth	$10,900.00	EBAC TRITON DEHUMIDIFIER NEW	$545.00
Pro Chem Performer 405 Truck Mount System	$6,600.00	Von Schrader MACH 12 VS12	$520.00
Hotsy Shark SSD-503067E/G Hot Water Pressure Washer NEW	$5,995.00	Dyson DC14 SS-COM Complete Steel Upright Vacuum NEW	$520.00
MINUTEMAN 3800 RIDER FLOOR SCRUBBER	$5,200.00	SAND BLASTER COMMERCIAL TYPE	$510.00
Only 32.7 hours of use!!!		Von Schrader VS1 Carpet Extractor	$510.00
Rotobrush & New Inspection Camera Package	$4,495.00	CLARKE FM 2000 FLOOR MAINT. BUFFER SCRUBBER	$500.00
Morantz 3 in 1 Ultrasonic Blind Cleaning Machine	$4,050.00	Carpet extractor	$500.00
STEAMWAY CARPET EXTRACTOR CARPET CLEANER	$3,599.99	US PRODUCTS COBRA 300H CARPET CLEANING EXTRACTOR	$500.00
89 gmc vandura carpet cleaning truck mount	$3,550.00	Nobles Concorde HP Carpet Extractor / Cleaner	$499.00
Rotobrush with Rotovision	$3,500.00	Host Dry Extraction Carpet Cleaning Machine Nice	$485.00
PRO CHEM PERFORMER "CUB" CARPET CLEANER/EXTRACTOR	$2,650.00	Brand New Dyson DC15 The Ball Upright Vacuum $650 NR	$465.03
commercial truck mount carpet cleaning machine kohler	$2,025.00	KARCHER HDS810 COMMERCIAL /	$450.00
HEPA-AIRE 6000 PORTABLE POWER VAC SYSTEM, DUCT CLEANING	$2,000.00	INDUSTRIAL STEAM CLEANER	
Car detailing trailer	$1,750.00	NEW Powr-Flite Cmcrl Ozone Generator Odor Neutralizer	$450.00

Industrial Supply, MRO ▶ Commercial Radios

The average sales price in this subcategory is $109.90.

	HIGH		AVG
DECIBEL UHF 6 CH COMBINER CLOSE FREQ-LOW LOSS	$1,595.00	Motorola , Jobcom, Johnson, GE Radios LOT OF 4	$125.27
TEFLON MIL SPEC COAX CABLE M17/128 RG400 QTY1050' -NEW-	$999.97	Motorola System Saber Full Keypad UHF Qty 2	$125.00
MOTOROLA XTS 3000 HAND HELD RADIO I THANK DIGITAL	$845.01	Motorola Saber II Vhf Radio	$125.00
(2) Motorola MTX838 HT1000 HT1000 MTX 838 MT 1000	$800.00	LOT OF (10) FEMALE N CONNECTOR FOR HELIAX, ANDREW L4PNF	$125.00
6 MOTOROLA MT1000 VHF LOW BAND RADIO 33 CH 42-50 MHZ	$760.00	Two motorola radius SP50 +, one charger only	$122.50
Motorola MTS2000 FLASHPORT Model III 160CH 800MHz H38	$611.00	Motorola MTS 2000 Flashport 900MHz MTS2000 2way Radio	$122.50
MOTOROLA MTS2000-MOD-2-FLASHPORT-800/W/ACC.LIKE NEW	$549.00	MOTOROLA MTS 2000 FLASHPORT HANDIE TALKIE FM RADIO	$120.00
Motorola MTS2000 800 Mhz SMARTZONE	$525.00	2x Motorola GTX 800MHz Portable Two-Way Radios	$120.00
Whelen 295HFSA6 Hands Free Siren BRAND NEW!!	$502.00	Philips Dodge Motorola Radio Repeater Ham UHF Duplexer	$119.95
Motorola MT2000 160 Ch VHF 136-178 MHz Handheld Radio	$499.00	Motorola MTX 8000 UHF Business Band Amateur Radio 800mz	$118.89
Motorola MTS2000 FLASHPORT Model III 160CH 800MHz H38	$495.00	Icom H 16 Portable radio/charger/RF Amp/Case/spk/mic	$115.00
Motorola MTS2000 Flashport 2 way Radio With Accessories	$480.00	Motorola MTS 2000 Model 11 SMARTNET FLASHport Radio's	$114.50
Motorola MTS2000 FLASHPORT Model III 160CH 800MHz	$477.77	Motorola HT1000 UHF handheld radio Jedi HT 1000 NR!!!!!	$113.50
Motorola MTS 2000 Type III 800 MHz Two-Way Radio	$475.00	Kenwood Response , Communication Radio VHF HI BAND	$113.49
MOTOROLA SECURENET KEYLOADER DES/DES-XL	$456.00	99 CHANNEL MT1000 VHF MOTOROLA RADIO FIRE RESCUE MURS	$112.50

Industrial Supply, MRO ▶ Forklifts & Other Lifts

The average sales price in this subcategory is $137.45.

	HIGH		AVG
2 TON COFFING CHAIN HOIST W/ELECTRIC WALKER, CRANE	$3,500.00	Electric Cable Winch Hoist 660/1320 lbs Heavy Lift Tool	$159.99
21' SPAN BRIDGE CRANE & CM LODESTAR 2 TON TROLLEY HOIST	$1,632.52	Shop Crane Engine Hoist Cherry Picker / Leveler / Stand	$159.99
Rotary SP 9000lb Hoist	$1,500.00	Electric Hoist 1100lb. Capacity	$157.50
3 Ton CM Electric Chain Hoist Loadstar	$1,450.00	LITTLE MULE LINEMAN STRAP HOIST! 4000 LB! NEW!	$153.26
NICE CM VALUSTAR ELECTRIC CHAIN HOIST 4000 LB 115volt!	$1,325.00	Rope Block Pulley-Hoisting Wheel-Skookum 8" A8	$152.50
2 Ton YALE Electric Hoist	$1,225.00	DAYTON 1/2 TON HOIST 1 HP Single Phase	$150.00
YALE INDUSTRIAL 3 TON BRIDGE CRANE	$1,200.00	YALE 1 TON AIR HOIST & TROLLY WITH CONTROLS	$150.00
Clark LP Forklift 31 Wide Fork Truck Propane LP Engine	$1,125.00	WRIGHT -WAY 1/2 TON ELECTRIC HOIST (USED)	$150.00
CM valuestar electric chain hoist 1ton 20ft lift *NEW*	$1,125.00	McKissick 15 TON Capacity – SNATCH BLOCK AND HOOK	$143.50
CM LODESTAR 1 TON ELECTRIC CHAIN HOIST NEW NIB	$1,100.00	Little Mule Cable Hoist 2 Ton Puller Hoist NEW	$142.55
CM Lodestar R 2 Ton 20' Electric Chain Hoist	$1,075.03	NEW FORKLIFT PROPANE TANK STEEL FREE SHIPPING	$139.00
ZIMMERMAN BALANCER LOAD POSITIONER hoist air cm	$995.00	[2 of these sold for $139.00 each]	
Budgit 2 ton electric chain hoist	$900.00	Chatillon TD-5 Force Gauge !!	$135.49
Electric Chain Hoist - IR 1 Ton "SP" Hook Mounted	$900.00	4 NEW CROSBY 17 TON SHACHLES	$135.43
NEW ALUMINUM FORKLIFT PROPANE TANK **FREE SHIPPING**	$175.00	CM 3/4 ton hand chain hoist / puller BRAND NEW!!!!!!!!!	$135.20
		CROSBY BLOCKS 10 TON SNATCH BLOCK W SWEIVEL HOOK NICE!	$132.00

Industrial Supply, MRO ▶ HVAC

The average sales price in this subcategory is $194.12.

	HIGH		AVG
Liebert System 3/Low Hours/60hz/30Tons/Glycol Upflow	$8,995.00	Radiant Floor Heat Manifold 5 circuit with flow gauges	$207.50
T-240 FRP Cooling Tower, 30 CTI/T, New, w/Warranty	$2,186.00	PROMAX RG5410A AC RECOVERY UNIT	$207.50

Denso MovinCool Classic 26 Spot Cooler 24HFU-1	$2,100.00	Evaporative cooler / NEW / AC / swamp cooler	$206.09
Denso MovinCool Classic 26 Spot Cooler	$2,000.00	[2 of these sold for $206.09 each]	
T-230 FRP Cooling Tower, 22.5 CTI/T, New, w/Warranty	$1,868.00	Radiant Floor Heat Manifold 5 circuit with flow gauges	$202.50
Portable 5 Ton Air Conditioner Unit, Over 10K new!	$1,774.00	Radiant Floor Heat Manifold 4 circuit with flow gauges	$202.50
Sanyo 36XLS32 Ductless split system air conditioner	$1,675.00	Copeland Scroll Compressor ZR34K3PFV930 BRAND NEW	$202.50
Port-A-Cool 2000 with reservoir	$1,124.99	NIB Friedrich Through the Wall A/C Elec Heat $720	$202.50
Buderus Oil Fired 4 Section Boiler (no burner)	$1,077.50	3 Ton Commercial Roof Top A/C HVAC Heat Pump	$202.50
SUSSMAN ELECTRIC BOILER MODEL MBA4	$1,009.00	CARRIER 4TON CONDENSING UNIT SEALEDNEW 38CKCO48560	$200.00
5 Ton Packaged Roof Top A/C HVAC Gas Furnace Pack	$1,000.00	YORK Refrigerant Storage/Recycling System	$200.00
TYLER REFRIGERATION RACK SYSTEM	$999.00	DATA AIRE INC (2 units) Liebert HVAC - No RES	$200.00
HEIL 3.5 TON 3 PH AIR CONDITIONER W/AIR HANDLER	$950.00	CARRIER 3.0 TON AIR CONDITIONER 3 PHASE, 208/230 VOLT	$200.00
HVAC Equipment	$950.00	New Carrier Air Handler	$200.00
T-210 FRP Cooling Tower, 7.5 CTI/T, New, w/Warranty	$911.00	Weil Mclain Natural Gas 3 Section Boiler	$199.00
		Radiant Floor Heat Manifold 4 circuit with flow gauges	$195.19

Industrial Supply, MRO ▶ Hydraulics & Pneumatics

The average sales price in this subcategory is $125.74.

	HIGH		AVG
ENERPAC, CYLINDERS,HYDRAULIC ,OVER $20,000.00, ALL NEW	$9,000.00	ENERPAC 20 TON HYDRAULIC LOW HEIGHT CYLINDER- NEW-	$142.50
4 Post Hydraulic Press 85 x 48 Hydraulic Pump	$3,250.00	100 ton industrial pancake jack	$138.61
EASTMAN KWIKRIMP SUPER 2 HYDRAULIC HOSE CRIMPER	$1,502.00	SPX POWER TEAM 17 1/2 TON RT172 HYDRAULIC JACK	$138.50
Greenlee model 940-M3 W/ control valve	$1,200.00	Enerpac Model P-80 Pump Tool with Hose	$133.50
ENERPAC HYDRAULIC BEARING PULLER 17 1/2 30 AND 50 TON	$911.01	GRACO FAST FLOW PNEUMATIC BARREL PUMP MOD 226-940	$133.25
Hydraulic Test / Learning Station	$699.99	ENERPAC 25 TON PORTAPOWER JACK HEAD	$132.50
ENERPAC RCH-603 hollow plunger 60 Ton cylinder NR	$660.55	John Barnes Corp hydraulic pump	$132.49
Power Team Hydraulic Pump/Stretcher PE554PT & 9628 D	$625.55	GAST AIR MOTOR# 4AM-NRV-70C WITH DAYTON GEAR BOX UNUSED	$130.33
Pneumatic Rivet Crimper Squeezer With Foot Control	$610.00	American Stainless Steel Pump 3/4 HP w/ clamps NEW	$130.27
Weatherhead Hydraluic Crimper T-460 "New"	$599.00	Heavy Duty Hydraulic Air PUmp ATD Premium Products New	$130.06
ENERPAC PUMP # 1200B	$565.55	10,000 psi hydraulic test set with digital readout	$129.50
HYDROLINE Hydraulic Cylinder NEW	$550.00	IVERY NICE! PETERSENS HEAVY DUTY 50 TON HYDRAULIC JACK	$127.51
Aeroquip FT1380 -115 Hydraulic Hose Crimp Machine	$535.00	ENERPAC MODEL # PA-133 AIR/HYDRAULIC PUMP	$127.50
Vickers PVB45 Variable Displacement hydraulic Pump	$516.00	ENERPAC Hydraulic CYLINDER 50 TON- L-502 NICE!!	$125.38
New Snap on 3/4 Drive Impact Gun IM75 W/Warrantee	$514.77	DeviceNet SMC EX230-SDN1 Serial Unit w/valves	$125.00

Industrial Supply, MRO ▶ Pumps

The average sales price in this subcategory is $140.22.

	HIGH		AVG
CUMMINS AUXILIARY HYDRAULIC POWER UNIT ENGINE DIESEL	$6,100.00	Enerpac electric hydraulic pump HUSHH PUP works great	$324.99
3 PCS VICKERS HYDRAULIC UNITS W/ LINCOLN 50 H.P. MOTOR	$1,500.00	REXROTH BRUENINGHAUS HYDROMATIC	$320.00
SPX Hydraulic Pump Valve Honda Engine Not Enerpac New	$1,499.99	Fenner 12VDC Double Acting Hydraulic Pump w/ remote	$319.25
HYTORC 10KPSI ELECTRIC HYDRAULIC PUMP PORTABLE115 V	$1,265.00	DENSION HYDRAULIC PUMP # T6 CCMB22 B22 1R00 D100 NEW	$315.88
HYTORC AIR 10KPSI 4 PORT HYDRAULIC PUMP PORTABLE	$1,225.00	DENSION HYDRAULIC PUMP # T6CC 022 022 1R03 NEW	$315.88
THOMAS&BETTS Color-Keyed PUMPAC. Battery powered pump	$999.99	Myers Rustler Submersible Well Pump 1 HP 20 GPM NIB	$309.00
HYDRATIGHT SWEENEY HYDRAULIC 1" DRIVE RATCHET	$999.00	Red Jacket Submersible Deep Well Pump 1HP 230V 25GPM	$309.00
Carr Lane Roemheld Swiftsure Electric Hydraulic Pump NR	$985.00	Enerpac Pump, 11/2 HP, 110 V , 5000 PSI , 5 GAL Tank	$307.99
REXROTH BRUENINGHAUS HYDROMATIK	$670.00	Brand New Vickers PVE 19R	$305.00
HYDRAULIC PUMP-NEW		NEW FLOTEC 1HP SUBMERSIBLE WELL WATER PUMP 230V 20 GPM	$304.00
Brueninghaus Hydromatik variable displacement axial	$630.00	DUMP PUMP 12V Hydraulic Pump Snow Sweep Splitter	$301.00
Myers Rustler Submersible Well Pump 1 HP 20 GPM NIB	$309.00	Denison Hydraulic Vane Pump T6EP-062-3R00-B1	$300.00
ENERPAC # PUJ-1200B ELECTRIC HYDRAULIC PUMP	$580.00	Hydraulic Piston Pump Tandem Cessna Eaton New	$299.99
Continental 4cyl Power Unit w/ Hydraulic Pump!	$565.55	Hydraulic Piston Pump Tandem Cessna Eaton New	$299.99
Stanley 8HP Honda Hydraulic Power Pack Unit 2000 PSI	$550.00	Lincoln 1242 12V Grease Gun Free Shipping	$149.00
LMI MILTON ROY CHEMICAL PUMP # M151- 35P - "USED"	$536.00	[2 of these sold for $149.00 each]	

Manufacturing & Metalworking ▶ Metalworking Equipment

The average sales price in this subcategory is $2,240.34.

	HIGH		AVG
2001 HITACHI SEIKI MS-400H Horiz Mach Center CNC Mill	$85,000.00	Burgmaster 6 Turret Drill Machine - Works Great!	$2,850.00
MONARCH MDL PMC-750 4 AXIS CNC	$52,000.00	LAGUN 9" x 42" VARIABLE SPEED VERTICAL MILLING MACHINE	$2,850.00
VERT MACHINING CENTER 98		J Head Bridgeport Vertical Mill SN#J149061 MPC109-1-4A	$2,800.00
HAAS TM-2 tool room mill LIKE NEW cost$39,500	$31,600.00	Bridgeport Series II CNC Vertical Mill Centroid ___ N/R	$2,750.00
FADAL VMC 5020A CNC VERTICAL MACHINING CENTER	$30,300.00	MAZAK V-5 CNC VERTICAL MACHINING CENTER w/FANUC 5M	$2,650.55
FADAL 4020 5 AXIS CNC MILLING MACHINE WITH PROBE	$29,500.00	ANAYAK Knee Milling Machine - Like Bridgeport Series II	$2,603.21
2002 FADAL VMC 15XT CNC VERTICAL MACHINING CENTER	$29,100.00	EMCO MAIER F1 CNC MILLING MACHINE LEVEL 4 CPU	$2,600.00
Haas Super Mini Mill , 2002 Low Hrs excellent condition	$26,050.00	WEBB 3HP VARIABLE SPEED VERTICAL KNEE MILL N BRIDGEPORT	$2,600.00
Cincinnati Gilbert Horizontal Boring Mill GREAT SHAPE	$16,700.00	LAGUN 9" x 48" VARIABLE SPEED VERTICAL MILLING MACHINE	$2,550.00
Bridgeport Series 1 EZ-TRAK CNC Vertical Mill, 2002	$16,200.00	BURGMASTER 6 SPINDLE AUTO INDEXING TURRET DRILL PRESS	$2,550.00
Haas VF-0 CNC VMC Rebuilt 2005 (VFO)	$16,100.00	Bridgeport Series I CNC Vertical Mach Center w/ TC	$2,500.00
LeBlond Makino Fnc 74 VMC	$15,200.00	CNC Mill 4-Axes SERVO Tabletop w/ Large X/Y table new	$2,499.00
Okuma & Howa 4VA	$14,500.00	[2 of these sold for $2,499 each]	
Bridgeport 308 CNC Machining Center FREE SHIPPING	$12,950.00	SUPERMAX 9" X 49" VARIABLE SPEED MILLING MACHINE	$2,400.00
SUPERMAX Max-3 CNC Mill 1993 Fanuc 0MC - $1 NO RESERVE!	$11,300.01	KEARNEY &TRECKER MILAWAUKEE MDL 307-S-12 VERTICAL MILL	$2,300.00
LUCAS HORIZONTAL BORING MILL	$10,898.00	Lagun FTV-2 Vertical Mill GOOD CONDITION	$2,235.23

Manufacturing & Metalworking ▶ Metalworking Supplies

The average sales price in this subcategory is $80.32.

	HIGH		AVG
Telesis Pinstamp TMP3100 Marking System	$3,200.00	BIJUR Spraymist coolant unit type UB	$110.00
VL/RAMPE Vibratory Tumbler	$2,500.00	6" TO 12" MICROMETER 1 SET NEW MICROMETERS	$109.95
Di-Acro diacro template controlled turret punch	$1,601.00	PRO PLATER Automotive Plating Kit GOLD Silver Chrome	$104.02
1" Titanium tube 18'9" Grade 2 welded .049 wall 36 pcs	$1,579.00	6" /150 MM ELECTRONIC DRO QUILL KIT NEW	$99.90
42 x 24 FT Sandblast blast cabinet NEW Made In USA	$1,299.00	[2 of these sold in a multiple item ("Dutch") auction for $49.95 each]	
Race Car Tube Tubing Bender Set New	$750.00	Race Car Tube Tubing Notcher NEW free shipping.	$99.00
DUMORE No. 5, 1/2 HP TOOL POST GRINDER No Resesrve	$670.00	STARRETT MACHINIST TOOL INDICATOR	$96.00
TAPCO PRO III C-10 SHEET METAL BRAKE	$610.00	6" MILLING MACHINE VISE NEW VISES	$89.95
Jet metal cutting band saw with coolant pump	$600.00	Union Machinist tool chest box oak	$86.33
New Hermes GTX Engraving Machine Engraver Engravers	$599.99	ALBRECHT KEYLESS DRILL CHUCK 1/32-1/2" R8 ARBOR	$86.00
Machinist tool Mitutoyo End Mill Drill Chuck Box Tools	$400.00	Martronics Etch-O-Matic Super Kit/WIth Free stencils	$86.00
Wire Cutter and Stripping Machine	$362.53	AVIATION UAT 90 DEGREE ANGLE DRILL -SURPLUS	$85.00
Numberall Model 40B Numbering & Lettering Press & More	$332.50	USED MILWAUKEE 2" DIE GRINDER	$82.51
24 ALUMINUM COPE & DRAGS	$310.00	Used Milwaukee 1/2" drill	$82.00
FOUNDRY EQUIPMENT CASTING		GREENERD NO.#3 ARBOR PRESS	$81.00
Aciera Drill Press for Watch, Clock, Instrument Making	$305.10	Oil Skimmer for Machine Tool Coolant Tanks (NEW)	$81.00

Manufacturing & Metalworking ▶ Process Equipment

The average sales price in this subcategory is $308.71.

	HIGH		AVG
Amada TimeSaver Wet 37" Deburr Machine	$8,500.00	SS Chromalox Electric Heat Exchanger(NEW)	$500.00
TY Sausage Linker - Model 90 ACL	$6,000.00	CAMCO ROLLER DIAL INDEX DRIVE, CNC	$480.99
700 Ton Marley Galvanized Cooling Tower (Dual Cell)	$5,150.00	OPTICAL TABLE / BREADBOARD 2' x 4' x 2"	$450.00
GYRA-VIB" MR "SERIES 60" STAINLESS STEEL SEPERATOR	$5,000.00	Alfa Laval stainless steel fittings valve dairy	$371.00
ITW GEMA POWDER COATING MANIPULATOR WITH 6 GUNS	$4,500.05	BV-1005 BROOKFIELD PROGRAMMABLE RHEOMETER RVDV III	$365.00
Hauser Auger Powder Filler New	$4,500.00	FISHER CONTROL VALVE 3'' 300 REPAIRED W/ ACTUATOR	$355.00
SCREW CONVEYOR - AUGER - Martin, Dodge - 150 feet - lot	$3,600.00	KASON VIBROSCREEN NO RESERVE	$332.00
ITW GEMA POWDER COATING MANIPULATOR WITH 6 GUNS	$3,050.00	Ferguson-Conveyor Model 926CDSF	$325.00
Elf 4 head filler	$1,525.00	SUTORBUILT BLOWER MOD# GACMBPA CAT# 4MP NEW	$310.00
Sweco 48" Stainless Screener	$1,525.00	Filter Housing, Pall Trinity 316L SS Cartridge	$305.00
TORIT / VOKES DALAMATIC REVERSE JET DUST COLLECTOR	$1,512.00	GILMAN HEAVY-DUTY MACHINE TOOL CARTRIDGE SPINDLE, CNC	$284.00
Custom Built Lab Pumping System w/ American Lewa Pumps	$1,500.00	NEW! Lab Size ASC Scientific PULVERIZER-Crusher Mill	$282.77
125 LIN/FT POWERED CASE CONVEYOR	$1,500.00	AXIFAN TUBEAXIAL FAN 21" DIAMETER 2 H.P.	$256.00
Tank, 50 gallon SS Pressure w/Lightnin Mixer 115 volt	$1,250.00	AXIFAN INLINE TUBEAXIAL FAN 24" DIAMETER 2 H.P.	$255.00
Coolant Wizard Junior	$1,150.00	AXIFAN INLINE TUBEAXIAL FAN 36" DIAMETER 10 H.P.	$255.00

Manufacturing & Metalworking ▶ Semiconductor & PCB Equipment

The average sales price in this subcategory is $272.28.

	HIGH		AVG
LEYBOLD HERAEUS PORTABLE LEAK DETECTOR. MOD: UL 200 DRY	$7,200.00	CAMMAX PRECIMA PULSE HEAT BONDER PPS60-P	$450.00
CTI Cryogenics On-Board IS 8F Cryopump 8185037G002	$3,600.00	AutoRoll Exactra 180 Screen Printer	$449.99
Branson / IPC 3000 Series Oxygen Etcher	$2,199.99	Leybold Inficon Transpector 1 RGA Electronics Head	$409.00
Advanced Energy RFG 2000-2V RF Generator 2 kW 13.56 MHz	$2,199.00	CTI CRYOPUMP Cyrotorr 10	$406.23
LEYBOLD MECHANICAL, UNITIZED, HIGH VACUUM PUMP. ? DRY ?	$1,726.00	Advanced Energy PE-1000 AC Plasma Power Source	$384.00
ENI - OEM-12B Solid State 13.56 MHz RF Generator	$1,524.00	ENI VPA-1987-21127 Power Amplier Meter 0-500 Watts	$355.00
LEYBOLD "TURBOVAC 50" TURBO PUMP	$1,380.00	Advanced Energy MDX-052 Remote Interface !!SEALED!!	$355.00
Keithley 595 Semiconductor Quasistatic CV Meter	$1,327.00	Applied Materials P5000 RF Match Phase IV 13.56MHz Etch	$315.00
NEW!!! High Vacuum 2" Dia Magnetron Sputtering Gun	$1,112.79	Hine Design Robot Elevator Reciever A94-016-03	$305.00
SolaMetrics 4 Bottle Resist Cabinet auto switching SVG	$1,050.00	KaVo 4052 USED SPINDLE	$300.00
Keithley 595 Semiconductor Quasistatic CV Meter	$1,045.00	12 INCH REFLOW FURNACE OVEN / SCREEN PRINT DRYING BELT	$299.99
ENI - OEM-12B Solid State 13.56 MHz RF Generator	$1,025.00	INFICON SENTINEL 200 DEPOSITION PROCESS CONTROLLER	$295.00
1 Lot of Fluorocarbon Spin Rinser Dryers Qty: 20 Units	$999.99	Advanced Energy MDX-052 Remote Interface	$293.88
Unitek Hughes Welder HRW250B & VTA-60 Welder Head Pedal	$999.99	Quintel Vari-Watt HA-5 Lamp Power Supply	$282.00
Advanced Energy HFV8000 5kW 2MHz Plasma Generator * NR	$999.00	C17364 Varian 921-0062 Vaclon Pump Control Unit	$270.00

Manufacturing & Metalworking ▶ Woodworking

The average sales price in this subcategory is $241.98.

	HIGH		AVG
TORCHMATE II CNC Plazma/Routing/Tube Cutting	$14,005.02	WOOD WORKING AUTOMATIC VERTICAL LATHE / SHAPER	$332.00
SAWMILLS - NEW 13HP NORWOOD LUMBERMATE BAND SAWMILL	$5,135.00	PORTER CABLE MODEL 550 POCKET CUTTER	$331.89
SIG PVC Oven - Model 22P-PVC/20	$4,800.00	Delta Stock Feeder - Industrial Quality	$330.00
SERVO CNC PLASMA CUTTER, ROUTER, ENGRAVER PARKER 12X5'	$4,400.00	Stock Feeder - Industrial Quality	$330.00
Virutex Edge bander Model EB-25	$4,000.00	Delta Stock Feeder - Industrial Quality	$306.00
pratt and whitney 12" slotter	$2,500.00	Stock Feeder - Industrial Quality	$305.02
Powermatic 5 HP Model 27S Shaper ~ No Reserve!	$2,451.52	ruvo overhead router, wood router	$300.00
Delta 20" Metal Cutting Band Saw	$2,150.00	Delta 14" Radial Arm Saw	$300.00
.............Torit Dust Collector<<NEW>>..............	$2,130.00	2" THOMSON 6' LINEAR ROD W/ PILLOW BLOCK BEARINGS CNC	$299.00

	HIGH		
Edgebander Holt-Her 1408	$2,000.00	NEW 2" THOMSON 5' LINEAR ROD W/ PACIFIC PILLOW BLOCKS	$299.00
MIDWEST AUTOMATION LAMINATE	$1,999.99	New Incra LS17 Wonder Fence System!	$289.00
PINCH ROLL MODEL PR 1300		Stock Feeder - Industrial Quality	$280.00
Trend CNC Smart Plus	$1,625.00	Stock Feeder - Industrial Quality	$270.00
Table Boring Machine	$1,400.00	[2 of these sold for $270.00 each]	
Terrco KSTAR 2 Spindle Carver with lots of carving bits	$1,199.00	1 hp Woodshop Dust Collector Cincinnati 100S New Unused	$255.00
Rockwell 20" Band Saw	$1,195.00	SHOPSMITH POWER STATION	$239.05

Office, Printing & Shipping ▸ Copier Toner & Supplies

The average sales price in this subcategory is $51.72.

	HIGH		AVG
Genuine Oce F10 Toner	$911.11	Kodak Image Source 110 Toner	$75.00
HP 4600 Toner Set Of 4 C9720A C9721A C9722A C9723	$525.00	KONICA ,7020.7025,7030 OEM TONER	$75.00
HP 4600 Toner Set Of 4 C9720A C9721A C9722A C9723	$511.00	[3 of these sold in a multiple item ("Dutch") auction for $25.00 each]	
HP 4600 Toner Set Of 4 C9720A C9721A C9722A C9723	$501.36	NEW CASE of 4 KODAK TONER HX 828 8581 BLACK NIB	$74.99
OEM HP 4600 Toner Set C9720A, C9721A, C9722A, C9723A	$499.00	HEWLETT PACKARD LASERJET TONER CARTRIDGE C4129X	$70.00
HP 4600 Toner Set Of 4 C9720A C9721A C9722A C9723	$490.00	Panasonic NEW KX-P6300 Process unit KX-PEP4	$69.99
Xerox Toner for models 2060,2045,6060,5252	$450.00	Kodak Black Hx Toner CAT 828.8581	$66.00
Xerox DocuColor 12 Toner Set - All 4 Colors	$250.00	MINOLTA QMS magicolor 6100 6110 $55.00	$65.00
OCE D4 DEVELOPER FOR 9400 SERIES LARGE FORMAT PRINTERS!	$240.50	Canon Copier CLC 1000 2400 3100 Manual Feed Assembly	$63.00
Muratec TS120 Toner Master carton of (6) New Genuine	$182.45	Canon PC 740 745 770 775 790 940 PC940 980 PC 981 toner	$62.55
Xerox Toner for Docucolor C-Y-B-M	$167.50	Pitney Bowes Printpowder 371-0 (6 cartridges)	$61.05
[2 of these sold for $167.50 each]		3 units Kodak IX toner - wlg	$61.00
Xerox Toner for Docucolor C-Y-B-M	$163.60	GESTETNER TONER 3222/3227/P7027/P7032 EPD CODE 885210	$60.99
Kyocera TK-60 toner kit, 1800,3800 series	$162.00	GPR-7 Toner Unit For Canon	$59.00
[4 of these sold in a multiple item ("Dutch") auction for $40.50 each]		BROTHER DR-200 DRUM UNIT	$55.99
PHOTO CONDUCTOR UNIT TYPE 1027 SAVIN , RICOH ,GESTERNER	$160.00	Kodak Image Source 85 Toner	$55.00
9 Imagistics & Pitney Bowes 469 Toner for CD2000/CD1500	$153.50		

Office, Printing & Shipping ▸ Commercial Printing Presses

The average sales price in this subcategory is $1,191.08.

	HIGH		AVG
Mark Andy Model 2100 Printing Press System	$65,000.00	Streamfeeder Friction Feeder ST-1250, like Longford	$2,175.00
Heidelberg GTOZ+ 2-color Perfector 14 x 20	$26,100.00	MULTI 1450 K 2-Color Press w/ KOMPAC! Swing-Away T-51	$2,000.00
Heidelburg SBG Diecutter Letterpress	$18,000.00	Automatic Pad Printer Like New	$1,999.00
Ryobi 3302, 2 Color Press, Excellent Condition	$15,000.00	AB DICK 375 13X18 PRINTING PRESS	$1,820.00
Ryobi AB Dick Bourg Printing Press Collator Equipment	$14,982.20	Heidelberg Windmill 10 x 15 Press S/N 103 673	$1,500.00
Heidelberg Quickmaster 46-2	$13,500.00	Kluge Letterpress Model N Auto feed & 4 Chases PERFECT!	$1,499.00
Indigo E-Print Pro+ Offset Digital Press	$12,900.00	305 Challenge Hyd. paper cutter	$1,295.00
KOMORI Two Color 37" - L237SII, Montakop, Adast cutter	$12,500.00	AB Dick 360 Pro (gray) 2 color	$1,250.00
KLUGE 13X19 EHD Hot Foil Stamp, Die Cut, & Emboss Press	$12,500.00	Hamada 661ECD	$1,225.00
HP DESIGNJET 815MFP PRINTER BRAND NEW COMPLETE	$11,500.00	AB Dick 9810 XCS Offset Printing Press	$1,225.00
HP / Indigo E-print 1000+ 4 Color Digital Offset Press	$11,500.00	AB Dick 9840 printing press similar to Ryobi Itek Multi	$1,200.00
HEIDELBERG KORD64-GREY MODEL	$11,000.00	Didde Apollo 2/C Roll to Sheet Web Press	$1,199.99
HP / Indigo E-print 1000+ 4 Color Digital Offset Press	$10,500.00	24 INCH NUMBERING MACHINES LOT OF 32 FOR PRINTING PRESS	$1,100.00
ENTIRE PRINTSHOP FOR SALE	$8,000.00	Heidleberg TOK Offset Sheet-fed Printing Press	$1,094.00
Miehle Favorite Offset Printing Press	$6,497.89	Die cutter, Kluge 12 X 18 Die cutting press	$1,025.00

Office, Printing & Shipping ▸ Fax Machines & Supplies

The average sales price in this subcategory is $35.05.

	HIGH		AVG
CANON LC3170 FAX MACHINE SUPER G3!!	$675.00	Sanyo fax machine #SFX-311 thermal paper	$40.00
RICOH 3900NF DIGITAL FAX MACHINE / 2 PAPER TRAYS, MINT!	$611.00	Pitney Bowes 9910 Fax Machine Used	$39.90
$6,000 Castelle Faxpress 5000 8-Port Fax Server NR	$493.88	Geniune BROTHER DR 400 DRUM UNIT	$39.01
Brother PPF5750E PPF-5750E Laser Fax "Factory Sealed"	$465.00	PANASONIC KXFPG376 FAX MACHINE/CORDLESS PHONE	$38.99
MURATEC F-110 PLAIN PAPER FAX MACHINE	$422.01	ComSwitch 5500 Fax/Line Share Switch Phone Modem	$37.99
[2 of these sold in a multiple item ("Dutch") auction for $211.01 each]		Savin 3720 Super G3 Excellent Used Condition NR!!!	$37.66
Sharp FO-5500 Professional Office Fax Machine	$355.00	Brother Intellifax 780MC Thermal Fax Machine	$37.15
Samsung SCX-4720F Laser Copier/Printer/Fax	$349.00	Canon CFX-L4000 Plain Paper Laser Fax Machine Copier NR	$37.00
Kyocera Mita LDC-870 Digital Laser Fax Machine	$339.90	$1,000 Toshiba DP80F Fax Machine NR	$36.56
BROTHER INTELLIFAX PPF-4750E PPF4750E W 1 YR USA WARNTY	$309.98	Used Samsung SF-531P Multi-Function Laser Fax	$36.00
Canon 9000 Laser Class Fax Machine/Copier-Exc Cond.	$309.00	Brother 560 Fax machine w/toner cartridge. NO RESERVE	$36.00
TOSHIBA DP120 toshiba fax LOW PRICE with extra cassette	$299.00	LEXMARK x4270 BUSINESS FAX	$36.00
MURATEC MFX-1600 FAX/COPIER/PRINTER/SCANNER FLATBED!	$299.00	MACHINE ALL IN ONE PRINTER $	
TOSHIBA DP120 toshiba fax LOW PRICE with extra cassette	$299.00	HEWLETT PACKARD FAX 1010	$36.00
BROTHER INTELLIFAX PPF-4750E PPF4750E W 1 YR USA WARNTY	$289.98	MACHINE COPY COPIER *IN BOX*	
[3 of these sold for $289.98 each]		ASAP TF300 Plus Phone Line Management Fax Switch	$35.99
Okidata Model 5650 Fax Machine	$203.50	BROTHER FAX MACHINE #1820	$35.85

Office, Printing & Shipping ▶ DVD-R, CD-R & Blank Media

The average sales price in this subcategory is $35.05.

	HIGH		AVG
FUJI SDLT Tape Media for 110/220 and 160/320 Drives	$1,495.00	Sony DVCAM (large size) 64 mins (Qty 6)	$32.50
FUJI DLT IV Media- 20 New Sealed, Lifetime	$369.00	250 SONY 2HD Floppy Disks Valued at $150+	$31.01
MAXELL DLT IV MEDIA QTY:20 PCS.	$335.00	5 Sony HMD-1G Hi-MD 1GB Media Mini Disc MZ-RH10 NH600D	$28.00
50 DLT IV 20/40GB Data Cartridge w/Cases	$203.50	500 New In Box Sealed 3.5" Floppy Diskettes	$27.99
[2 of these sold for $203.50 each]		40 Maxell 3.5" Floppy Disk New Sealed Box - No Reserve	$27.56
Sony AIT3 SDX3-100C 8MM 100/260GB Cartridges (5Pack)	$175.00	100 Certified IMATION 2DD Floppy Disks/Diskettes	$27.50
5 Brand New Sony AIT AIT3 AIT-3 Tapes SDX3-100C	$165.00	2 New Atari/Roland Portfolio 64K Memory RAM Disk Cards	$26.69
50 DLT IV 20/40GB Data Cartridge w/Cases	$153.50	Panasonic LM-AK60U DVD-RAM 2.8GB 60Min (Brand New)	$26.00
5 Brand New Sony AIT AIT3 AIT-3 Tapes SDX3-100C	$150.00	[4 of these sold in a multiple item ("Dutch") auction for $6.50 each]	
[2 of these sold for $150.00 each]		Lot of 8: HP 2.6GB Rewritable Optical Disk 92280F NEW	$26.00
2950 Blank 3.5 Inch High Density Floppy Disks	$150.00	PANASONIC DVDRAM DVD-RAM 2.8GB LM-AK60 DISC	$26.00
5 Brand New Sony AIT AIT2 AIT-2 Tapes SDX2-50C	$145.00	Shugart 8" floppy disks used 23	$25.67
4 Sony SDX2-50C AIT Data Cartridges New Sealed!!	$121.15	512 MB San Disk Compact Flash New Camera IPod PC Audio	$25.51
100-TDK DDS-2 4mm Data Storage Back Up Tapes NEW	$99.99	2x 10 packs of Maxell DDS-3/125 Tapes NIB	$25.00
Lot of 40 IMATION 120MB Super Disk Diskettes	$80.00	2 New Atari/Roland Portfolio 64K Memory RAM Disk Cards	$25.00
104 Shugart 8" floppy disks used	$76.00	Lot of 8: HP 2.6GB Rewritable Optical Disk 92280F NEW	$24.99
2 New Sony AIT2 AIT-2 Tapes SDX2-50C + Cleaning Tape	$70.00		

Office, Printing & Shipping ▶ Office Furniture

The average sales price in this subcategory is $93.12.

	HIGH		AVG
Conference Table & Chairs	$1,825.00	CHERRY WOOD VENEER FILING CABINET 4-DRAWER VERY NICE!!!	$102.00
Hon Work Stations In Dallas Very NICE N/R	$1,115.00	(2) Filecabinets for architect drawings	$100.01
George Nelson Omni Wall Work/Storage Sytem circa 1960	$999.00	Very Nice Custom Made Oak Drawer Storage Cabinet Hobby	$100.00
SPACESAVER MOBILE SHELVING UNIT VERY NICE	$900.00	FLAT FILES METAL priced to sell Great storage	$100.00
SAFCO BLUEPRINT ART MAP FLAT FILE CABINET CABINETS NRl	$849.99	OAK VENEER FILING CABINET 4-DRAWER VERY NICE!!!	$100.00
Fire File 4-Drw.Vertical legal by "Fire King"	$766.56	Four Drawer Lateral File Cabinet - Hon	$100.00
Flat File Cabinets, Artwork, Blueprints, Drawings	$760.00	FLAT FILES METAL priced to sell Great storage	$99.99
Flat File Cabinet	$739.00	Pottery Barn Kids Cameron Wall Cubby with Doors WHITE	$99.99
Fireking 22" Fireproof Turtle File Cabinets #4R1822-C	$675.00	MODERN 3 DRAWERS METAL HOME OFFICE FILE/FILING CABINET	$99.99
SAFCO BLUEPRINT ART MAP FLAT FILE CABINET CABINETS NRl	$660.00	Pottery Barn Kids Cameron ART Wall Cubby WHITE	$99.99
10 DRAWER METAL FLAT FILES MAP BLUEPRINT ART TOP & BASE	$550.00	BENSON STEEL 5 DRAWER LATERAL FILE FILING CABINET NRl	$99.99
* FireKing 4 Drawer Fire Proof File Filing Cabinet	$536.00	2-DRAWER LATERAL FILE FILING CABINET, ATLANTA	$99.99
Excellent Condition Fire Proof Shaw Walker File Cabinet	$500.00	STEELCASE 4 DRAW LATTERAL FILE CABINETS 42 INCH	$99.95
Map Blueprint Flat File Cabinet 10-Drawer	$499.99	Art Metal Blueprint Flat File Hanging Cabinet On Wheels	$99.00
FREE SHIP~KIMBALL OFFICE FURNITURE WALNUT FILE CABINET	$495.00	POTTERY BARN KIDS Postmans Hutch Honey NEW STILL IN BOX	$99.00

Office, Printing & Shipping ▶ Printing & Graphic Arts

The average sales price in this subcategory is $148.89.

	HIGH		AVG
SEAL IMAGE 62 PLUS LAMINATOR	$8,100.00	Videojet nozzle (New) P/N SP371675	$180.00
Heidelberg KORD62 Printing Press	$5,500.00	X-Rite DTP32R Auto Scan Densitometer Xrite	$177.50
VIDEOJET Excel 170i Printer NO RESERVE	$3,399.99	VINTAGE LETTER/PRINTING PRESS	$175.50
Hercules 4 up Imagesetter with Processor	$3,000.00	CABINET WITH MIXED TYPE	
Roland PC-12 Printer/Cutter	$3,000.00	KELSEY EXCELSIOR MERCURY MODEL U 5X8 PRINTING PRESS	$162.50
3D Systems Actua 2100 3D Concept Modeler/ Printer	$2,995.00	USED REVOLVING DARKROOM DOOR WORKS GREAT	$158.50
Videojet Excel High Resolution Printer 170 l Video jet	$2,500.00	LOOK!! FOILMAX LASER FOIL SYSTEM, DDA 900	$153.50
T Shirt Heat Transfer Press 11x15 NEW. Machine IRON-MP	$2,334.00	Business card slitter set	$152.50
[6 of these sold in a multiple item ("Dutch") auction for $389.00 each]		Richeson Model 695102 Baby Printing Press, New	$151.99
SN 4000 Numbering Machine	$2,025.01	Multigraphics Model 1650 master clamp # 13-1-195463 new	$150.00
Gretag Macbeth SPM 100 Densitometer / Spectrophotometer	$1,495.00	5 Videojet Pump Diaphragms w/oring	$150.00
Graphtec CE-3000-60 w/Software Ex Cond ~~NO RES.~~~~~	$1,435.00	Dictaphone 3740 ExpressWriter Micro Transcriber	$150.00
Videojet nozzle (New) P/N SP371675	$1,250.00	Videojet UHS nozzle (New) P/N SP356666	$150.00
[5 of these sold in a multiple item ("Dutch") auction for $250.00 each]		VIDEOJET PARTS LARGE LOT..........................N/R	$150.00
Presses - Ryobi 3200 w/T-Head & AB Dick 360	$1,135.00	LATERAL FLAT FILING / FILE / CABINET 5 DRAWER	$150.00
ELTRON_ZEBRA_P310_C_COLOR_ID_CARD_PRINTER_W/WARRANTY	$1,099.00	3Dies Grommet Machine Sign Cutter Vinyl Plot! NEW!	$149.99
HP LaserJet 4600dn Color Laser Printer	$999.99	[13 of these sold for $149.99 each]	

Office, Printing & Shipping ▶ Shipping & Packing Supplies

The average sales price in this subcategory is $22.55.

	HIGH		AVG
Commercial MailBoxes	$1,025.00	Pitney Bowes Online Postage Labels for eBay(R)-250 Sht	$27.00
Instapak 900 - Foam In Place Machine Model 901 - USED	$358.00	STANLEY BOSTITCH BOXLOK MODEL D14 BOX STAPLER	$25.25
KIRK-RUDY ENVELOPE LABLING MACHINE.NO RESERVE!!!!!!	$257.50	BRAND NEW 8" IMPULSE HEAT SEALER	$25.00
Cargo Net Heavy Duty Nylon Web 10 foot X 10 foot	$225.00	BRAND NEW 4" IMPULSE HEAT SEALER	$25.00
[3 of these sold in a multiple item ("Dutch") auction for $75.00 each]		Shipping Envelopes Bags 500 Dura Lite 14x17	$25.00
3 Lots of 10 Furniture Moving Pads Blankets Padding	$202.04	100 Photo mailers 9 3/4 X 12 1/4 Peel n Seal	$23.99
[4 of these sold in a multiple item ("Dutch") auction for $50.51 each]		51LB NEW DIGITAL SHIPPING POSTAL SCALE POSTAGE SCALES	$22.85
Viking Custom ATA Road Case (1/2" stucco Aluminum) - NR	$132.50	100 6x9 TYVEK PLAIN WHITE ENVELOPES THE VERY BEST	$22.05
Total Foam / Instamate Instapak Plastic Film NEW ROLL	$132.50	100 6"x9" TYVEK PLAIN WHITE ENVELOPES THE VERY BEST!!	$22.05

BOX STAPLER-FLOOR MODEL-HEAVY DUTY-LIKE NEW	$130.00
PNEUMATIC BOSTITCH D60 CARTON / BOX STAPLER	$127.72
Viking Custom ATA Road Case (1/2" stucco Aluminum) - NR	$102.50
BOSTITCH AIR PNEUMATIC BOX STAPLER P 50 CROWN	$96.00
New Adhesive Backed Packaging Foam - 320 Piece Pallet	$85.00
New In Box SONY Microcassette Transcriber BM-840T	$80.00
Eltron Zebra Thermal *5120* Labels UPS LP 2844 LP2844	$79.99
60 cu ft Woven Polyethylene Peanut Dispenser	$76.00

51LB NEW DIGITAL SHIPPING POSTAL SCALE POSTAGE SCALES	$21.95
40 Mailing Shipping Poster Tubes ANY SIZE YOU WANT	$20.73
qty 250 mailing / shipping tubes 2 x 7" w/cap	$20.05
SOFTWARE - Retail, Inventory, POS, Bar Code, Pick-Pack	$20.00
6 LIKE NEW HEAVY DUTY FURNITURE MOVING BLANKETS PADS	$19.99
KIP9900FAMILY(NEW)CLEANING BLADE	$19.95

Office, Printing & Shipping ▸ Shredders

The average sales price in this subcategory is $73.67.

	HIGH		AVG
SEM Disintegrator Model 1012	$1,624.99	New Fellowes Powershred PS70-2 Paper Shredder Heavyduty	$87.17
HSM commercial / industrial quality paper shredder NR	$801.01	[6 of these sold for $87.17 each]	
IDEAL DESTROYIT 4003 HIGH CAPACITY/SPEED PAPER SHREDDER	$599.99	New Fellowes Powershred PS70-2 Paper Shredder Heavyduty	$84.00
Fellowes Powershred 380CC Cross Cut Paper Shredder##	$599.95	ROYAL 1280MX CROSS CUT PAPER SHREDDER NEW	$79.77
GBC Shredmaster 2250X Cross Cut Paper Shredder	$465.00	[2 of these sold for $79.77 each]	
Fellowes PS420sc 42pg. Heavy Duty Shredder FREE SHIP*	$399.00	FBI DA312 Dual Anti Identity Theft Royal Paper Shredder	$69.97
SEM 2715 Cross Cut Shredder No Reserve!	$375.00	Achiever CCS1010 Crosscut Paper Shredder 10 sheet NEW	$69.97
Fellowes PS220c 15 page Confetti Shredder FREE SHIP*	$329.99	Fellowes PS60C-2 Cross Cut Paper Shredder	$67.51
ROYAL 1610X CROSS CUT PAPER SHREDDER **BRAND NEW**	$299.95	Royal 10X 10pg. CrossCut Shredder shreds cds FREESHIP*	$64.99
Fellowes PS220C-2 Cross Cut Paper Shredder##	$299.77	[2 of these sold for $64.99 each]	
COMMERCIAL/INDUSTRIAL CONFETTI PAPER SHREDDER cross cut	$299.00	Shredder, Cross Cut, GBC CC-85, NEW, 06601	$59.99
FELLOWES POWERSHRED 320C-2 PAPER SHREDDER	$290.00	Alera 240120 DVD CD Floppy Disk Paper Shredder CrCards	$59.97
Fellowes PS220 25 page Shredder FREE SHIP*	$289.99	80X Royal Confetti Crosscut Paper Shredder 8 Sheet NEW	$59.97
Fellowes PS220c 15 page Confetti Shredder FREE SHIP*	$249.99	Royal CC75 Crosscut Paper Shredder 7 Sheet & CC's	$59.97
DS240P Sentinel Stripcut Paper Shredder 24 Sht CD clips	$249.97	[4 of these sold for $59.97 each]	
		NEW VF1000MX Royal CD Staples Paper Shredder	$56.99
		ROYAL 85X CROSS CUT PAPER SHREDDER **BRAND NEW**	$56.00
		10X Royal Confetti Paper Shredder High Security	$55.01
		10X Royal Confetti Paper Shredder High Security	$54.59

Office, Printing & Shipping ▸ Trade Show Displays

The average sales price in this subcategory is $133.10.

	HIGH		AVG
10' Pop Up Display Booth, Tradeshow Exhibit, Trade Show	$2,796.00	EZ-E to Set Up TENT INSTANT CANOPY No R-Z-VE!	$152.50
[4 of these sold in a multiple item ("Dutch") auction for $699.00 each]		POWER POP-UP DISPLAY 36X150 - Sihl 3624	$150.00
10 X 20 TRADE SHOW BOOTH ($15,000 Value)	$1,775.00	[2 of these sold in a multiple item ("Dutch") auction for $75.00 each]	
SKYLINE 10' Mirage Tradeshow "Pop-Up" Booth with Extras	$1,300.00	New Trade Show Display Table Top Folding Display PopUp	$150.00
Custom Modular Trade Show Display	$995.00	[3 of these sold for $150.00 each]	
Skyline Mirage 10 Ft. Pop-Up Display. Top of the Line.	$895.00	New Trade Show Display Table Top Folding Display PopUp	$143.01
10' Nomadic Pop-Up Booth Display, light Skyline Frame	$850.00	Nomadic Instand Trade Show Display 10' No Reserve	$137.50
Skyline Trade Show Booth Tradeshow Display Red Backdrop	$810.00	Trade Show Booth Backdrop Frame-aluminum	$135.50
10' Pop Up Trade Show Displays, Exhibit Booth Display	$785.00	Skyline Mirage tabletop display	$127.50
[4 of these sold for $785.00 each]		Nomadic Instand Trade Show Display 10'	$127.49
TRADE SHOW EXHIBIT DISPLAY BOOTH 10' X 8'	$775.00	XM RADIO 10'x10' EZ UP Shelter Canopy	$126.50
Skyline Mirage 10x8 Pop-Up Trade Show Display Booth	$700.02	L&R Solid State Ultrasonic T28-b	$125.00
10' Pop Up Display Booth, Tradeshow Exhibit, Trade Show	$699.00	[2 of these sold for $125.00 each]	
[2 of these sold for $699.00 each]		Lot- Matching Wall Display Case / Cases, Metal, Glass	$125.00
20' Trade Show Display,4 Lights,2 Ship Cases!	$625.00	New Trade Show Display Table Top Folding Display PopUp	$123.50
[2 of these sold for $625.00 each]		Brand New 10'x10' EZ-to Set Up Canopy Sidewall	$121.35
Nomadic Instand Trade Show Display 6' No Reserve	$611.50	Trade Show Display Folding Display Exhibit pop up	$117.50
TRADE SHOW EXHIBIT BOOTH DISPLAY & TABLE POP UP N/R WOW	$590.00	Trade Show Display Folding Display Exhibit pop up	$115.00
Nomadic trade show display like new 10' x 8' w/ lights	$525.00		

Office, Printing & Shipping ▸ Office—Wholesale Lots

The average sales price in this subcategory is $17.77.

	HIGH		AVG
LOT OF 4- HERMAN MILLER AERON CHAIRS - LIKE NEW	$1,575.00	OFFICE CALCULATOR TI-5045 SV	$19.99
1000 Elegant Office Pens	$250.00	Legal Size 3 Ring Binders - New - Case of 36	$19.95
100 Clubhouse Metal-Rubber Grip Promotional Pen - Laser	$195.00	Legal Size 3 Ring Binders - New - Case of 18	$19.90
300 BIC Widebody Tri Stic Color Grip / FREE PRINTING	$175.00	[2 of these sold in a multiple item ("Dutch") auction for $9.95 each]	
HUGE Office Supply Lot - 60 LBS Of New/Shelf Pulls NR	$148.85	Case of 2500 Commercial Envelopes Bright White #10	$18.95
1000 Promotional Stick Pens Best Seller / FREE PRINTING	$140.00	260 CD Jewel Case Cases w/ Clear Inserts	$17.61
[2 of these sold for $140.00 each]		DYMO LETTER TAG LABELMAKER	$17.51
1000 Promotional Stick Pens Best Seller / FREE PRINTING	$135.00	200 PREMIUM MAGNETIC BUSINESS CARD MAGNETS /w Adhesive	$16.99
144 DOZEN BLACK PERMANENT MARKERS TOTAL OF 1728	$125.00	32 4PK (128) NEW Permanent Marker Black Color HUGE LOT	$16.95
LIGHTLY USED MONT BLANC MEISTERSTUCK GOLD LINE CLASSIQU	$100.00	260 CD Jewel Case Cases w/ Black Inserts	$16.50
6 Piece Desk Accessory Kit NEW 50 Sets	$100.00	[8 of these sold for $16.50 each]	
2"x165' CLEAR PACKING TAPE ONLY $0.59 (216 ROLLS)	$99.00	200 PREMIUM MAGNETIC BUSINESS CARD MAGNETS /w Adhesive	$16.49
50 PARKER JOTTER BALLPOINT PEN PENS SUPER SALE	$98.75	CASE LOT OF PAID STAMPS	$16.00
500 Promotional Stick Pen Personalized FREE PRINTING	$90.00	4 FAKE/DUMMY SECURITY CAMERA SCANNING MOTION, AMAZING.	$15.99
Better Pack 333 Gummed Tape Dispenser Machine	$67.00	200 PREMIUM MAGNETIC BUSINESS CARD MAGNETS /w Adhesive	$15.99
Certificate Diploma Display Plaque Cherry Finish	$59.50	Focus/Pentech Exec Tech Mechanical Pencils (1 Case/48 3	$15.70
[7 of these sold in a multiple item ("Dutch") auction for $8.50 each]		WHITE CUBICLE CLIPS WHOLESALE LOT OF 192	$15.50

Other Industries ▸ Dry Cleaning, Laundromat

The average sales price in this subcategory is $249.15.

	HIGH		AVG
Sears Coin Laundry Commercial Washer Dryer keyed alike	$5,990.00	CISSELL A PANTS TOPPER!! LIKE NEW! MINT!!! GREAT COND!!	$355.00
CHICAGO IRONER 24 INCH ROLL, GAS MODEL GA-24	$3,500.00	WHITE 760 SPACE CARROUSEL - DRY CLEANING	$325.00
CHICAGO Ironer, Model TG-14, 14" Roll Gas	$2,500.00	Maytag Washers and Dryers: Coin Laundry Equipment	$306.00
HUEBSCH LOADSTAR II 30EG	$1,800.00	PND 2000 HI STEAM HEATED PROFESSIONAL PRESS TABLE IRON	$305.00
[3 of these sold in a multiple item ("Dutch") auction for $600.00 each]		WASCOMAT DRYER, LOT OF 2	$262.70
Carpet Cleaning Equipment (In 78' GMC Van) With Tools	$1,676.61	Commercial Coin Laundry Equipment: Laundromat	$250.00
Ultrasonic ShineABlind Window Blind Cleaning Machine NR	$1,625.00	[2 of these sold for $250.00 each]	
85 POUND COMMERCIAL WASHER/HIGH SPEED EXTRACTOR COMBO	$1,499.99	Ecolab Porta Washer Model P High Pressure Cleaner Unit	$207.50
50 POUND COMMERCIAL WASHER/HIGH SPEED EXTRACTOR COMBO	$1,249.99	Laundry Detergent Bleach Soap Vending Machine Mat	$202.53
Multimatic Prince Dry Cleaner NO RESERVE! Good cond.	$1,135.00	NEW Never Been Used Commercial Dryer	$200.00
Minuteman Ambassador Carpet Cleaner/Extractor	$850.00	Coin-operated washers and dryers	$200.00
Money Maker!! Great Machine!!	$722.69	NEW Never Been Used Commercial Dryer	$200.00
DEXTER T400 WASHER	$660.00	Shirt folding machine - dry cleaner out of business	$199.00
Money Maker!! Great Machine!!	$601.00	GREENWALD ULTRA-GUARD COIN-OP BOXES (8)	$192.53
COIN-OP COMMERCIAL MAYTAG 3 Washers, 3 Dryers	$600.00	2 sets Double stacked Whirlpool dryers	$189.00
Huebsch Commercial On-Premises Dryer Natural Gas	$600.00		

Other Industries ▸ Oil & Gas

The average sales price in this subcategory is $143.85.

	HIGH		AVG
855 Cummins/Onan generator set	$8,000.00	GRACO 1" diaphram pump oil	$150.00
Tokheim Premier H426-B Dispensers	$6,200.00	Verifone (Ruby) Expanded PLU Memory card	$150.00
GILBARCO ADVANTAGE B7C 3+1 WITH VAC/MONOCHROME	$4,500.00	Veeder-Root TLS-350 Tank Monitor Module	$150.00
Gilbarco Advantage B79 Blender Dispenser	$3,800.00	[2 of these sold in a multiple item ("Dutch") auction for $75.00 each]	
[2 of these sold for $3,800 each]		Dresser Wayne Main CPU/ VISTA NEW IN BOX	$149.99
Oil Field ECHOMETER - Model D and Compact Gas Gun	$3,217.00	NEW Olivetti Wayne Dresser PR4 4/B (DR) Printer *WOW*	$147.50
Gilbarco Advantage B21 Single-product Dual Dispenser	$3,200.00	Graco electronic oil meter despensor nozzle	$147.50
Mobile Oil Change Equipment	$2,225.00	New OmegaFlex 250' Reel Gas Tubing TracPipe Pipe 1/2"	$144.47
VEEDER-ROOT TLS-350 PLUS W/ PRINTER	$1,986.00	Gilbarco T-17840-G2 CRIND Regulator/ WORKS	$140.00
VEEDER ROOT TLS-350 UST MONITORING SYSTEM	$1,685.66	[2 of these sold in a multiple item ("Dutch") auction for $70.00 each]	
GILBARCO G-SITE POINT OF SALE G SITE	$1,495.00	TRI CONE ROCK /OIL GAS DRILL BIT 6 1/8 IN.DIAMETER UKA	$137.50
Hydra Drill 2000 - Well drill	$1,392.00	New Heavy Duty Oil Drum-(Fuel Tank) Adj. Brass Faucet	$133.00
GILBARCO HIGHSPEED MASTER LC METERS WITH SATELLITE	$1,200.00	Dresser Wayne VISTA 883074-001CAT Annunciator Board	$132.00
[4 of these sold for $1,200 each]		[6 of these sold in a multiple item ("Dutch") auction for $22.00 each]	
Tokheim PREMIER B/C DPT CPU Board NEW IN BOX	$1,120.00	Gilbarco M00141-B002 ENCORE Keypad/ BRAND NEW	$128.49
[8 of these sold in a multiple item ("Dutch") auction for $140.00 each]		Tokheim PREMIER B Interface Board NEW IN BOX	$128.00
Veeder-Root TLS-300 Tank Monitor/ Mfr. 6/31/03	$970.00	Marconi/Gilbarco T19976-G3 Meter (New)	$127.50
DRESSER MEASUREMENT (ROOTS METERS)	$960.00	VEEDER-ROOT PLLD FOR FE PETRO	$127.50

Other Industries ▸ Power & Utilities

The average sales price in this subcategory is $107.16.

	HIGH		AVG
Concrete Imaging Sys. GPR Conquest by Sensors and SW	$9,800.00	Lot of 11 Lemco Econo-Block M-1070-1 Cable Blocks M1070	$113.05
PowerSaver	$3,500.00	Pole Tree Climbing Spurs Spikes Gaffs	$112.50
Ditch Witch Subsite 950 Cable and Pipe Locator	$1,526.00	DYNA LOCK SELF RETRACTING LANYARD PULLY SYSTEM	$112.50
GMP GENERAL - CABLE LASHER WITH CASE	$1,426.01	BASHLIN Aluminum Climbers Gaffs w/140-DS Pads	$112.50
RadioDetection Cable/Pipe Locator PXL2-BD1/RD400 LCTx	$1,275.00	Nice set of Pole Climbing spikes. With Harness & Belt	$109.00
Cable Lasher Type J With Case	$1,180.00	Pump & Valve Packing Garlock 1200 PBI	$108.09
GMP Lashers	$1,100.00	Klein Lineman climbing belt	$107.50
Radiodetection Cable Fault Locator System RD400	$1,075.00	LUG-ALL SRAP HOIST	$105.29
CABLE LASHER TYPE C	$1,025.00	Buckingham Pole Tree Climbing Spikes Gaffs nt klein LN	$105.15
Condux Lasher	$1,000.00	Klein Pole/Tree Climbing Spikes/Spurs	$105.00
REEL-O-MATIC MINI-PENTHOUSE COILING MACHINE	$1,000.00	Lot of 10 LEMCO L-381 Multiple Cable Blocks	$105.00
!! 2 ROSEMOUNT ANALYTICAL PT# 54EA-01-09 MODEL 54E *NEW	$754.00	Bashlin 130-D pads and aluminum adjustable gaffs	$104.49
[2 of these sold in a multiple item ("Dutch") auction for $377.00 each]		Bashlin Climbing Gaffs Used Good Condition	$104.00
RADIODETECTION RD400PXL CABLE LOCATOR RD400 FFTX	$670.00	3" Tree Climbing Spikes/Gaffs	$102.52
RADIODETECTION PIPE/CABLE LOCATOR RD432PDA/RD400LLTS	$660.00	KLEIN LINEMAN POLE/TREE CLIMBING BELT+POSITIONING STRAP	$102.51
GMP GENERAL 7992 F - CABLE LASHER WITH CASE	$625.00		

Other Industries ▸ Websites & Businesses for Sale

The average sales price in this subcategory is $47.75.

	HIGH		AVG
Huge established website making 30-40$ a day	$3,900.00	NEW! for 2005 Legacy V HOME INSPECTION REPORT SOFTWARE	$49.99
CampusWeekly.com College Print Newspaper Biz for sale!	$2,499.98	[2 of these sold for $49.99 each]	
Complete Nevada Incorporation: LLC or Corporation	$299.00	XLB 2005 Home, Commercial Inspection Report SW +Course	$49.99
Home Inspection Certification Course and Certification	$295.00	Summer Sale! XL Std 2005 Home & Comm Inspection Report	$49.99
3D Inspection Home Inspection Software version 4.0	$217.50	DIAMOND AND GEM JEWELRY ..BUY AT 10% RETAIL PRICE !!!	$49.95
Nevada Corporation or LLC with Book, Seal & Certs	$139.00	NEEDCLICKS.COM DOMAIN NAME!!! WORTH OVER $90,000!!!	$41.00
$700 Real Estate Marketing System For Sale$$$	$67.00	INSTANT BUSINESS - 15 Audio Titles - DUPLICATION RIGHTS	$37.00
BUSINESS DATABASE DIRECTORY OVER 28 MILLION COMPANIES	$59.00	Ultimate_Expired_Listing_System_For_Realtors!	$29.95
HEAD FOR SALE !!!	$56.00	Home Inspection Report Software - HIM 2.0	$27.99
NEW! for 2005 Legacy V HOME INSPECTION REPORT SOFTWARE	$49.99	Home Inspection Report Software. MSI's Legacy 2005 OOo	$24.99

7

CAMERAS & PHOTO

You can find all things photographic here, for everyone from the professional photographer to the amateur just looking to stock up on disposable cameras for vacations. In terms of volume, there are more digital cameras in this category than other types of cameras, and even more digital camera accessories. So it's no surprise that eBay chose to list digital, not film, cameras in its Top 10 List on the main page of the Cameras & Photo category. In the list are the Canon EOS Digital Rebel, the Kodak EasyShare, Nikon Coolpix, the Canon PowerShot S500, and the Sony Cyber-shot DSC-T1.

Digital Cameras: Finding Your Range

To compare prices for a popular digital camera, let's look at the Canon EOS Digital Rebel. One of the high eBay prices for a Canon Rebel XT 8 MP (megapixel) was $1,252.00 with 22 bids. The seller said the retail price is $1,359.00. On Amazon.com, however, a Canon EOS Digital Rebel XT 8 MP with an 18–55 mm lens has a retail price of $1,499.99 crossed out, and an actual price of $879.94 (this you don't get to see until you add it to your shopping cart). But you can also get a "NEW Canon EOS Digital Rebel XT SLR Camera wth Lens 350D," an 18–55 mm zoom lens, for $881.00 on eBay, and it comes with accessories such as a wide strap, battery charger, battery pack, two cables, and software. The Amazon.com camera does not appear to come with these accessories, and the battery pack alone is about $48.00, so overall, that eBay camera looks to be a little better deal.

What about the average price range for digital cameras? Several of the popular Canon PowerShot S500s landed in this range, from $299.99 to $305.00 in this price sample. The $299.99 camera had been used for about a year, but was billed as being in excellent condition and as having been kept in a leather case. On Amazon.com, you can find the

Canon PowerShot S500 5MP Digital Elph with 3x Optical Zoom for anywhere from $323.00 up to $406.90, all new. So eBay had the best deals, at least if you are willing to buy a camera that's a little used.

But you can pay a lot less for a digital camera if you are willing to buy an even older model. A "Canon Powershot 600 Vintage Digital Camera, Complete" went for only $39.99. According to the seller, this camera sold for $949.00 new in 1996. Okay, 1996 is quite a ways back, but if your needs are simple, this or a similar camera may do for you. There are also many less-souped-up new cameras that are around the $100.00 range.

Camcorders

How about camcorders? According to eBay's Top 10 List, Sony digital camcorders are popular. One of the best-selling camcorders on Amazon.com is the Sony DCR-DVD403 DVD Handycam Camcorder with 10x optical zoom, going for $1709.93 new, with used and new ones available from $818.00. The lowest price for that model camcorder on eBay during the time period researched was $565.55, and that was for a camera with less than 10 hours of usage, with no accessories. Several of the Sony DCR-DVD403 camcorders were available for around $740.00, with prices going up to $979.00 for a "Deluxe Kit" plus four-year warranty (this includes accessories such as straps, a battery, and chargers). So you can find both higher and lower prices on eBay than in other places, depending on what extras are included.

Getting Your Props: Accessories and More

Some of the lowest prices in Cameras & Photo are in the Accessories subcategories. But as in other categories, beware dirt-cheap prices: shipping on the one-cent blank camcorder tape— "3 Sony Mini DV Tape Digital Camcorder DV Cassette"—is $16.99, and it's coming from Hong Kong. A better deal would be the "TDK MiniDV Tape 60/90" for $1.99, whose seller advertises free shipping. However, the seller also has only a 91.7 percent feedback rating, which could be better. Another seller offers 5 Fuji mini-DV digital tapes for only $5.00 ("Tapes $7.99 each in the store. All 5, only $5 bucks with Buy It Now. Try and beat that."), and he doesn't seem to be charging anything above actual shipping cost.

There is plenty more to explore in Cameras & Photo: professional-quality cameras, film cameras, film, studio backdrops and lighting, and darkroom equipment. Check out the Lighting & Studio Equipment ▸ Props & Stage Equipment subcategory for fun items such as three large prop crayons, a children's Western gun set prop, and portrait costumes such as hats and dresses. There are great deals to be had here, and lots to choose from, but do your due diligence and comparison shop before you buy.

Binoculars & Telescopes ▸ Binoculars & Monoculars

The average sales price in this subcategory is $61.59.

	HIGH		AVG
Canon 10x42L IS WP Binoculars +Case 10x42 BRAND NEW USA	$1,299.95	OLYMPUS 10 x 25 Magellan Waterproof Binocular	$70.99
Canon 18x50 IS Binoculars + Case BRAND NEW USA	$1,029.95	OLYMPUS 10 x 25 Magellan Waterproof Binocular	$70.69
SWAROVSKI 7X42B SLC BINOCULAR	$575.00	NEW Carson Z-80S 80x25 SuperZoom Binoculars	$70.50
Canon 12x36 II IS Binoculars + Case BRAND NEW USA	$499.95	Pentax 7x50 PCF II Binoculars FREE SHIPPING!	$68.00
[4 of these sold for $499.05 each]		NEW! $165 NIKON TRAVELITE V 9 X 25CF BINOCULARS	$66.00
DOCTER 15x60 BINOCULARS	$485.00	Pentax 8x40PCF V Binoculars-New Demo	$65.00
Swarovski 10x25 pocket size binoculars	$470.00	NEW! $165 NIKON TRAVELITE V 9 X 25CF BINOCULARS	$62.50
PENTAX 10X43 DCF SP BINOCULARS W LIFETIME USA WARRANTY	$439.98	Barska Gladiator binoculars 12-60x70mm zoom	$60.66
Zeiss 10X40B Dialyt Binoculars....Leica, Steiner, Nikon	$431.00	Nikon 10x25 Sportstar III Binoculars 7492 NEW	$57.99
Zeiss Conquest 10x30 B T Binocular	$375.00	PENTAX 10X50 PCF WP BINOCULARS, NO RESERVE	$57.90
Zeiss Conquest 10x30 B T Binocular	$371.07	OLYMPUS 8-16 x 25 Zoom PC I Tracker Binocular	$56.55
CANON 12x36 IS II binocular Like New Binoculars 12X36IS	$355.00	NEW SUPERIOR 10x42 WATERPROOF	$54.99
LEICA 10X25 BCA COMPACT BINOCULARS NO RESERVE	$333.85	DELTA STYLE BINOCULARS	
Zeiss 10x25 ClassiC Compact Binoculars QUALITY OPTICS	$329.00	[2 of these sold for $54.99 each]	
[3 of these sold for $329.00 each]		WOW! MINOLTA AUTOFOCUS	$54.95
Canon 10x30 IS Binoculars + Case BRAND NEW USA	$319.95	COMPACT 10x23 BINOCULARS	
[2 of these sold for $319.95 each]		Nikon TRAVELITE IV 12 X 25CF (Like New Condition) L@@K!	$52.00
PERFECT LEICA 10X25 TRINOVID BINOCULARS -NO RESERVE	$295.00	Bushnell Featherlite instafocus Binocular 7x50 11-7504	$51.00

Binoculars & Telescopes ▸ Telescopes

The average sales price in this subcategory is $145.61.

	HIGH		AVG
TAKAHASHI EPSILON 300	$12,995.00	NEW WHITE 6" BAYTRONIX REFLECTOR TELESCOPE NO RESERVE	$151.57
TELESCOPE - ASTROGRAPH - RARE!!!		NEW BLUE 6" BAYTRONIX REFLECTOR TELESCOPE LOWEST PRICE	$151.00
MEADE SN-10 ON LOSMANDY G11	$2,500.00	BUSHNELL NORTHSTAR GOTO 525 X 3" TELESCOPE 78-8831 NEW	$150.00
Meade 10" in LX200 Telescope Mint condition	$2,095.00	MEADE DS-114 Reflector	$150.00
SWAROVSKI HABICHT AT 80	$1,051.50	MEADE 114EQ-DH4 STARFINDER TELESCOPE -box, manual,parts	$150.00
TELESCOPE SPOTTING SCOPE NR		BUSHNELL TELESCOPE GOTO 3IN W/ RVO 78-8831	$149.99
MEADE ETX-125AT Telescope with Tripod & AUTOSTAR	$1,049.95	3" x 525 Motorized Deep Star Telescope	$149.00
Meade LX-200 Telescope w/ SMART DRIVE	$960.05	NEW DARK GREEN 6" REFLECTOR	$147.50
Meade Telescope, ETX-125EC Brand New IN BOX!	$899.00	ASTRONOMICAL TELESCOPE NIB	
Meade ETX-125AT 125mm Relfector Telescope with AUTOSTAR	$709.95	CELESTRON 90 SPOTTING SCOPE with PORRO PRISM	$143.01
Meade ETX-125 EC With Tripod and Accessories	$695.00	BRAND NEW 6" NEWTONIAN REFLECTOR TELESCOPE	$140.50
MINT Meade Telescope ETX-125EC w/ Autostar & Tripod	$665.00	Rock Tumbler Thumlers Model B 15 Lb. Capacity New	$140.00
Meade ETX-125 Scope	$635.00	[2 of these sold for $140.00 each]	
Celestron SP-C8 - classic orange tube w/lots of extras	$631.55	CELESTRON HIGH POWER TABLETOP TELESCOPE NEW NR!	$140.00
MEADE ETX-90 TELESCOPE, AUTOSTAR,	$601.00	[2 of these sold in a multiple item ("Dutch") auction for $70.00 each]	
TRIPOD, 3-LENS & MORE		BUSHNELL NORTHSTAR GOTO 525 X 3" TELESCOPE 78-8830 W/tyl	$139.99
Orion XT10 10" Dobsonian Telescope with Object Finder	$600.00	Meade #884 Deluxe Tripod For ETX Telescope Like New	$139.00
MEADE ETX-90AT Telescope with Tripod & AUTOSTAR	$569.95	NEW 1400 6" NEWTONIAN TELESCOPE TELESCOPES	$138.50

Camcorder Accessories ▸ Accessories

The average sales price in this subcategory is $53.52.

	HIGH		AVG
MONITOR STEADICAM MASTER SERIES FILMS	$2,025.00	Dazzle DVD Creation Station 200, NEW IN BOX!	$64.00
Mako Uderwater Housing for Sony Handycam DCR PC100	$1,326.00	BeachTek DXA-4S Audio Adapter	$63.04
Sony DSR DU1 hard drive recorder+adapter dsr 370 570	$1,186.11	lightwave mm-xl-1 mic mount canon, xl1 xl1s, xl2 xl-1s	$60.00
Ocean Images Underwater Video Housing/free Sony camera	$500.00	4x4 glass filters Kenko ND.9	$56.86
Underwater Video w/ Sony Hi8 w/extras	$456.00	4x4 glass filters Formatt 6 point star filter	$56.00
Pioneer DJM-3000 4ch. Mixer w/ Effects.	$342.00	EWA MARINE HOUSING VMV	$55.99
Glidecam 4000 Pro & Forearm Brace - XL1, XL2, DVX100...	$333.00	CANON OPTURA DM-MV1 NEW	
Sony Handycam DCR HC21 camcorder 4 year warranty	$329.99	4x4 glass filters Scheider 4x4 clear	$52.00
Eyetop Color LCD Video Screen Glasses *NEW*	$329.95	SONY PRINT CARTRIDGE AND PHOTO PAPER 3 IN 1	$51.52
[3 of these sold for $329.95 each]		SIMA CT-2 Transfer DVD/VHS GoDVD DIGITAL VIDEO ENHANCER	$51.00
Sony EV-C100 Hi-8 VCR	$305.00	Mini-Steady Cam	$50.00
Varizoom VZ-Pro-L Lanc Controller	$285.09	Sony HVL-20DM Dual Video Light - lowest $	$50.00
*** Glidecam 2000 Pro - Brand New - FREE SHIPPING ***	$279.00	SONY MAVICAP MVC-FDR1E	$50.00
[12 of these sold for $279.00 each]		SIMA CT-2 Transfer DVD/VHS GoDVD DIGITAL VIDEO ENHANCER	$50.00
GlideCam 2000 Pro Camera stabilizer	$270.00	Studio1 (Sign Video) XLR PRO 2 inputs (Beachtek DXA)	$50.00
Glidecam 2000 Pro Like New!	$255.00	2 Large Ambico Bags Bag Digital SLR Camera s	$49.00
# VZPROL Varizoom Control-L Zoom Controller NEW	$232.51	[2 of these sold for $49.00 each]	

Camcorder Accessories ▸ Batteries & Chargers

The average sales price in this subcategory is $6.00.

	HIGH		AVG
lot of 10 GE/RCA EP096FL VHS VIDEO camcorder BATTERY	$39.99	MXP KODAK KLIC-5001 Battery DC Easyshare DX6490 7630	$6.49
[2 of these sold for $39.99 each]		BATTERY CHARGER SET FOR NIKON En-EL3 8700/5700/D70	$6.29
Archos Lithium-Ion Battery	$34.00	FOR NIKON EN-EL1 995/885/8700 BATTERY CHARGER SET	$6.29
Battery Charger Set+2 BP-522 FOR CANON ZR40+MORE	$30.99	BATTERY CHARGER SET FOR NIKON En-EL3 8700/5700/D70	$6.29
[2 of these sold for $30.99 each]		[2 of these sold for $6.29 each]	
Sony NPQM71D Rechargeable Battery Pack	$26.00	HITACHI VM-BPL13 VM-BPL27 VM-BPL13A VM-BPL27A BATTERY	$6.24
Battery Charger Set+2 Battery 4 CANON G1 G2 G3 G5 PRO1	$24.97	Lower SHIP! For JVC BN-V416/BN-V416U GR-DVL520U Battery	$6.00
Sanyo Li-10B Li10B 1200mAH for OLYMPUS C-50 STYLUS 300	$21.50	Battery for GR-DVL320U for JVC BN-V416U/BN-V416	$6.00
For Sony NP-F960 CAMCORDER BATTERY BEST REPLACE LOW SH	$19.95	Lower SHIP! For JVC BN-V416/BN-V416U GR-DVL520U Battery	$6.00
[2 of these sold for $19.95 each]		EN-EL1 ENEL1 Li-ION BATTERY	$5.99
Battery Charger Set+(2x) NB-2L 4 CANON S30 S40 S45	$19.00	NIKON COOLPIX NEW 4300 4500	$5.99
2 CASIO EXILIM NP-20 BATTERY EX-Z3 EX-S2 EX-S1PM EX-M1	$18.50	FAST CHARGER 4 Sony NP-F330 F550 F750 F960 {$6.99 SHIP}	$5.99
Battery Charger Set+BN-V416U Battery for JVC GR-DVL725U	$18.00	EN-EL1 ENEL1 Li-ION BATTERY	$5.99
NP-FM91 Battery for Sony TRV530 TRV240 TRV340 ~LOW SHIP	$17.90	NIKON COOLPIX NEW 4300 4500	$5.99
Sony NPQM71D Rechargeable Battery Pack	$17.49	6 Duracell 625A 1.5V Photo Medical Batteries NEW IN BOX	$5.99
Coolpix EN-EL1 Battery and MH-53 Charger NEW!!	$15.99	BATTERY CHARGER SET FOR NIKON En-EL3 8700/5700/D70	$5.99
2 RCA EPO96FS VIDEO CAMERA CAMCORDER BATTERIES EPO96FS	$14.99	For Sony BC-VM50 Battery Charger NP-FM50 FM70 FM90	$5.50
[2 of these sold for $14.99 each]		FAST CHARGER 4 Sony NP-F330	$5.50
SB-L220 BATTERY 4 SAMSUNG VP-D7L SCD80 SCD103 SB-LS220	$14.95	NP-F550 NP-F750 F960 LOW SH	

Camcorder Accessories ▸ Blank Tapes & Memory

The average sales price in this subcategory is $29.54.

	HIGH		AVG
Sony Handycam DCR TRV80	$425.00	10 JVC MiniDV Mini DV Digital Video Tape Tapes DVC NR	$30.00
100 Sony MiniDV Mini DV Video Tape Tapes DVC Free S/H	$320.00	10 Panasonic MiniDV Mini DV Digital Video Tape Tapes NR	$30.00
100 Sony MiniDV Mini DV Video Tape Tapes DVC Free S/\	$320.00	10 Panasonic MiniDV Mini DV Video Tape Tapes	$29.99
[2 of these sold for $320.00 each]		10 Panasonic MiniDV Mini DV Video Tape Tapes	$29.99
100 Panasonic MiniDV Mini DV Video Tape Tapes	$260.00	10 Panasonic MiniDV Mini DV Video Tape Tapes	$29.99
[3 of these sold for $260.00 each]		10 Panasonic MiniDV Mini DV Video Tape Tapes	$29.99

100 Panasonic MiniDV Mini DV Video Tape Tapes	$247.50	10 Panasonic MiniDV Mini DV Digital Video Tape Tapes NR	$29.56
100 Panasonic MiniDV Mini DV Video Tape Tapes	$245.00	10 Sony MiniDV Mini DV Digital Video Tape Tapes NEW NR	$29.51
[2 of these sold for $245.00 each]		10 Sony MiniDV Mini DV Digital Video Tape Tapes NEW NR	$29.33
100 Panasonic Mini DV Tape (100) MiniDV Tapes Brand New	$239.99	10 Sony MiniDV Mini DV Digital Video Tape Tapes NEW NR	$29.02
[2 of these sold for $239.00 each]		10 Panasonic MiniDV Mini DV Digital Video Tape Tapes NR	$29.01
50 MiniDv Tapes Mini Dv tape DVC Maxell Brand NEW	$154.19	10 Sony MiniDV Mini DV Digital Video Tape Tapes NEW NR	$29.01
50 pack NIP Panasonic Mini DV Tapes AY-DVM63PQ 63 min	$135.00	10 Panasonic MiniDV Mini DV Digital Video Tape Tapes NR	$29.00
[4 of these sold for $135.00 each]		10 Sony MiniDV Mini DV Digital Video Tape Tapes DVC	$29.00
50 MiniDv Tapes Mini Dv tape DVC Maxell Brand NEW	$128.01	2 Bryco MiniDV Tape Rack video Storage 50 tapes Sony	$28.99
50 MiniDv Tapes Mini Dv tape DVC Maxell Brand NEW	$119.99		
[3 of these sold for $119.99 each]			
30 SONY MINI DV TAPES	$112.50		
50 MiniDv Tapes Mini Dv tape DVC Maxell Brand NEW	$105.00		
50 MiniDv Tapes Mini Dv tape DVC Maxell Brand NEW	$104.06		
50 MiniDv Tapes Mini Dv tape DVC Maxell Brand NEW	$102.50		

Camcorders ▸ 8mm, Hi8, VHS

The average sales price in this subcategory is $78.99.

	HIGH		AVG
PANASONIC AG-455 S-VHS PROFESSIONAL CAMCORDER NR	$565.00	GE CG400 8mm Camcorder	$80.00
SONY SVO-2000 INDUSTRIAL S-VHS HI FI EDITTING SYSTEM	$500.00	JVC SUPER VHS CAMCORDER PACKAGE NO RESERVE	$79.99
Panasonic AG 456U	$485.00	Panasonic VHS Pro-Line AG-170 Professional Camcorder	$79.99
Panasonic AG SVHS 456U Pro Line CAMCORDER / CAMERA	$465.00	SONY HANDYCAM VISION 8MM CAMCORDER CCD-TRV22	$79.01
Canon L2 Hi 8mm Camcorder w/ 15x Macro Zoom/Accessories	$399.99	PANASONIC AG 170 CCD-PIEZO	$79.00
SONY HANDYCAM DCR-DVD92	$385.00	REPORTER VHS CAMCORDER MINT!	
DVD CAMCORDER AND ACCESSORIES		JVC Compact VHS-C Camcorder with 3" Color LCD	$79.00
JVC GY-X3U Professional SVHS Camcorder with EXTRAS	$375.00	JVC GR-AX760U 400x Zoom VHS-C Camcorder Video Camera	$78.77
2 CCD Panasonic AG-460 S-VHS Video Camcorder camera	$360.00	JVC GR-XM260U Super VHS-C Video Camcorder w/ 2.5in LCD	$78.66
PANASONIC AG-456 REPORTER CAMCORDER S-VHS PRO LINE!!	$356.00	Sony Handycam CCD TR416	$78.05
Panasonic Ag 456 SVHS Professional Video Camcorder	$355.00	JVC GR SXM330 video camera	$78.00
Modified B/W Pxl 2000 Pixel Camcorder Pxl2000 Camera	$350.00	JVC SUPER VHS CAMCORDER GR-SXM260U	$78.00
Fisher-Price PXL 2000 Deluxe Camcorder System	$345.00	Sharp VL-E720U 8mm camcorder	$78.00
Fisher Price Pxl 2000 Pixelvision 2000 Camera	$342.01	sony handycam video 8 CCD-TR83	$78.00
PANASONIC AG 456 UP VIDEO CAMERA CAMCORDER PROLINE	$340.00	SONY CCD-TRV16 8MM XR HANDYCAM NIGHTSHOT 180X ZOOM	$77.76
Panasonic AG 456U S-VHS Video Camera	$306.00	JVC GR-SXM260U SVHS-C SUPER VHS Video Camcorder NR!	$77.55

Camcorders ▸ Digital

The average sales price in this subcategory is $275.26.

	HIGH		AVG
Canon XL1 and XL1S, Bogen 3066, Sennheiser, Mackie Mix	$7,000.00	JVC GR-D250U Digital Video Camera Mini DV Camcorder	$279.99
JVC GY-HD100U 3 CCD PROHD CAMCORDER 16X PRO HD LENS	$4,500.00	Canon ZR 45 MC Brand New in Box (not refurbished)	$279.00
Canon XL2 - NR - Used Twice (NTSC)	$4,226.00	JVC GR-D90U DIGITAL DV CAMCORDER MINT WORKING	$279.00
Canon XL2, High End Extras, Miller, Sachtler, KATA,N.N.	$3,950.00	Canon ZR70 ZR70MC Digital Mini DV Camcorder NEW IN BOX!	$279.00
Canon XL2 Perfect condition Great Buy	$3,600.00	JVC GR-D270 MiniDV Camcorder w/25x Optical Zoom GRD270	$277.77
Panasonic AG-DVX100A Complete Editing Package!	$3,500.00	NEW! PANASONIC PV-GS32 DIGITAL PALMCORDER MINI DV GS32	$276.00
Canon XL2 Digital Video Camcorder Mini DV Package MINT!	$3,415.00	Brand New Panasonic Palmcorder Multicam PV-GS19 bundle	$275.51
Canon XL2 with accessories	$3,300.00	Canon ZR300 Digital Camcorder like new	$275.00
Canon XL2 MiniDV Camcorder w/Lens	$3,199.00	NEW**!!! Canon ZR 200 Digital Camcorder	$275.00
Canon XL2 PAL Digital Camcorder Mini DV in BOX w/ EXTRA	$3,185.00	Canon ZR200 -MiniDV -FREE 32MB sd card & Firewire cable	$275.00
Canon XL2 w/ Anton Bauer Gold Mount	$3,050.00	Canon Optura	$275.00
BRAND NEW Canon XL2 CCD Mini DV Camcorder NR	$3,049.00	Panasonic Palmcorder Multicam PV-GS31, New, Sealed	$275.00
Canon XL2 Mini DV Digital Camcorder	$3,010.00	11 MP MEGA PIXEL PMP DIGITAL	$275.00
Canon XL2 Like New!	$3,000.00	VIDEO CAMCORDER CAMERA MP3	
Panasonic AG-DVX100A P	$2,950.00	[2 of these sold for $137.50 each]	
MiniDV Digital Camcorder DVX100		Digital Panasonic PV-GS31 Palmcorder MultiCam Camcorder	$275.00

Camcorders ▸ Sony

The average sales price in this subcategory is $322.20.

	HIGH		AVG
Sony DSR-300A DVCam w/ Canon YH18x6.7 KRS-A SY14 Lens	$4,000.00	SONY DCR-HC32 MINIDV HANDYCAM CAMCORDER NEW IN BOX!!	$325.00
SONY HDR-FX1 HDV HANDYCAM	$2,825.00	Sony DCR-HC30 Mini DV HandyCam Camcorder New in Box	$325.00
CAMCORDER 1080i NEW IN BOX		Sony Handycam DCR HC21 NEW IN BOX!!!!!	$325.00
SONY DCR-VX2100e DIGITAL PAL CAMCORDER INCLUSIVE KIT	$2,549.99	SONY DCR-IP220 MICROMV CAMCORDER	$324.99
LIGHT & MOTION UNDERWATER HOUSING & Sony DCR TRV130	$2,500.00	BLUETOOTH TOUCH SCREEN	
Sony DCR-VX2100 Camcorder +$1500 EXTRAS!New	$2,328.00	SONY TOUCHPANEL DCR-HC21 WORRYFREE HANDYCAM (NIB)	$320.25
Sony DSR PD150 PD 150 Low Hours!!!	$2,325.00	SONY DCR-HC30 MINI-DV DIGITAL HANDYCAM CAMCORDER! WOW!	$320.00
Sony PD-150 DVCAM Camcorder pd150 mini dv not xl1	$2,078.00	SONY DCR-TRV480 DIGITAL-8 CAMCORDER *NEW* *USA*	$319.99
Sony Handycam DCR VX2000 Mint Condition + Extra's	$1,861.76	Sony Handycam DCR HC40 Digital Camcorder	$318.00
Sony DCR VX2000 - 8 Hours of Use - Comes with warranty!	$1,711.00	Sony DCR-HC32 MiniDV Handycam Camcorder + More NR	$311.89
Sony Handycam DCR VX2000 MiniDV Camera 3 CCD	$1,701.25	SONY DCR-TRV480 DIGITAL 8 HANDYCAM CAMCORDER SEALED	$310.00
Sony Handycam DCR VX2000	$1,700.00	Sony Handycam DCR IP5 with extras	$306.50
Sony Handycam DCR VX2000 - Great Condition and Extras!	$1,699.00	Sony Handycam DCR DVD201 Digital Camcorder and more	$305.76
Sony VX2000 mini dv camcorder Perfect Condition!	$1,685.00	SONY DCR-HC30 MINIDV DIGITAL HANDYCAM CAMCORDER! WOW!	$305.00
Sony DCR-VX1000 MiniDV 3CCD with Wide Angle Lens	$1,600.00	Sony DCR-PC110 minidv camcorder*GREAT CONDITION*	$302.50
Sony DCR-VX2000 - barely used - great deal!	$1,500.00	Sony Handycam DCR-HC20 camcorder recorder digital NR	$300.00

Digital Camera Accessories ▶ Accessories

The average sales price in this subcategory is $39.48.

	HIGH		AVG
IKELITE SUBSTROBE DS-125 DS 125 UNDERWATER STROBE	$1,026.53	CEIVA Digital Photo Receiver, New in Sealed Box	$50.00
Epson P-2000 Multimedia Storage Viewer (P2000)	$630.00	2x Teleconverter for Nikon AF	$50.00
Tokina AF ATX 12-24 Pro DX Zoom Lens Canon, Nikon NEW	$464.83	Fuji Finepix 6900 S602 S7000 Wide Angle Macro Lens 3 DA	$49.99
Tokina AF ATX 12-24 Pro DX Zoom Lens Canon, Nikon NEW	$459.83	NEW X-Drive PRO Image Tank MP3 Player + Battery Holder	$49.99
Canon EOS-DCS1c EF 28mm f/2.8 + 50mm f/2.5 Lens NR	$441.00	OLYMPUS E-1 CAMERA SPECIAL GRID FOCUSING SCREEN I	$49.00
Sigma AF-DC 18-200 Lens for Canon & Nikon Cameras NEW	$329.83	COLUMBIA SPORTING VEST (Fishing & Photo)	$46.00
Nikon 8800 8700 8400 5700 D70 D100 Color LCD Glasses	$319.95	ADOBE Photoshop 7.0 + Tutorial + Manual - Full version	$46.00
BOGEN MANFROTTO Panoramic VR Head for Professional Pano	$299.95	Canon EH17L / EH17-L Semi Hard Case EOS 20D DigitalSLR	$45.10
Nikon SF200 Slide Feeder for Coolscan 4000ED ; LS 2000	$270.00	New 1" Digital Picture Frame Keychain - Holds 56 Photos	$45.00
Nikon MSV01 Coolwalker Digital Storage Photo Viewer NEW	$264.83	Nikon ES-E28 Coolpix Slide Copying Adapter	$45.00
NEW 20GB FlashTrax, hard drive & Mp3 player	$249.00	Nikon MB-E5000 Battery Pack/Handgrip	$44.50
NR - Smartdisk Flashtrax 40gb multimedia player	$202.50	CANON CP-200 PORTABLE DIGITAL PHOTO PRINTER	$42.00
NEW 20GB EZDigiMagic Portable Hard Drive Card Reader	$199.00	Nikon SK-E900 Flash Bracket for Coolpix Digital Cameras	$41.00
Fisheye Converter FC-E8 FOR NIKON Coolpix BRAND NEW	$180.00	OLYMPUS E-1 CAMERA SPECIAL GRID FOCUSING SCREEN I	$41.00
Fuji Finepix S7000 S5100 S5000 Digital Picture Frame	$179.95	iPix rotator for Nikon Coolpix 990	$40.00

Digital Camera Accessories ▶ Batteries & Chargers

The average sales price in this subcategory is $12.92.

	HIGH		AVG
Quantum Turbo compact battery for digital camera/flash	$304.00	Panasonic Rechargeable Battery Lumix DMC-FX8 FX9 LX1	$12.99
Canon Powershot A75 w/ rechargable batteries and more..	$171.71	[2 of these sold for $12.99 each]	
Canon BG-E2 Battery Grip for EOS 20D *NEW USA*	$169.95	2 NP-80 1600MaH FOR FUJI RECHARGABLE BATTERIES +CHARGER	$12.99
Canon Battery Vertical Grip Pack BG-E2 BGE2 EOS 20D	$169.95	FOR CANON NB-1LH NB-1L CHARGER+BATTERY S500 S410 S400	$12.99
Canon BG-E2 Vertical Battery Grip 20D BGE2 EOS NEW	$155.51	12 AA 2300mAh RECHARGABLE BATTERIES + RAPID CHARGER	$12.99
JVC Camcorder; Model GR-D30U; 700x Digital Zoom Mini DV	$137.50	Compact Charger & 4 AA 2300mAh & 4 AAA 800mA Batteries	$12.99
SONY DSC T1 CYBERSHOT CRADLE MEMORY STICK & ACCESORIES	$112.50	CHARGER for GATEWAY DC-T50 DIGITAL CAMERA + BATTERY XK	$12.95
Sony DSC-T1 Camera USB Base Cradle Charger + Accessor	$112.50	Charger + Battery NB-4L For Canon Powershot SD200 SD300	$12.75
Quantum QB1 Compact digital SLR battery	$100.99	12 AA 2300mAh RECHARGABLE BATTERIES + RAPID CHARGER	$12.56
CANON BG-E1 BATTERY GRIP FOR CANON EOS DIGITAL REBEL	$100.00	12 AA 2300mAh RECHARGABLE BATTERIES + RAPID CHARGER	$12.50
AC-VF10 Charger For SONY NP-FS11/FS21/FS31 & 2BATTERIES	$92.00	SONY AC-LS5 AC Adapter Charger ACLS5 Cybershot Camera	$12.50
New Fisher FVDC1 3.2MP Digital Camcorder NO RESERVE	$85.00	12x 2500 mA NIMH AA BATTERIES-LATEST FREE CASES	$12.50
SONY AC-VQP10 DCR-HC20 HC40 HC65 HC85 DUAL CHARGER NEW	$84.99	12 AAA 1150mAh RECHARGEABLE BATTERIES + RAPID CHARGER	$12.50
Sony DSC-T1 Camera USB Base Cradle Charger and Acces..	$79.95	2 x NP-40 D-Li8 BATTERY 4 PENTAX OPTIO S FUJI 1500mah I	$12.50
SONY DSC T1 CYBERSHOT CRADLE	$75.00	12 AA 2300mAh RECHARGABLE BATTERIES + RAPID CHARGER	$12.50
MEMORY STICK & ACCESORIES		SONY AC-LS5 AC Adapter Charger ACLS5 Cybershot Camera	$12.50

Digital Camera Accessories ▶ Memory Cards

The average sales price in this subcategory is $26.06.

	HIGH		AVG
Nikon Coolwalker MSV-01 Image Storage Coolpix 8700 8800	$255.00	128mb RS-MMC REDUCED-SIZE MULTI-MEDIA CARD NOKIA 128 MB	$26.96
FlashTrax 20GB digital camera photo video viewer mp3 hd	$229.01	* SanDisk 512MB Compact Flash 512 mb CF memory Card *	$26.95
THEbox HP25OTG 80G Multi-media Storage & Player	$229.00	* SanDisk 512MB Compact Flash 512 mb CF memory Card *	$26.67
NIB 40GB EZDigiMagic Palm Size Hard Drive & Card Reader	$199.00	* SanDisk 512MB Compact Flash 512 mb CF memory Card *	$26.60
(20) Kodak 6C6692 Digital Science 520MB Data Transport	$152.51	Three (3) New LEGACY 64 MB SD Cards- Free Shipping!	$26.60
SONY MSX-M1GN 1gb,HIGH SPEED	$103.50	* SanDisk 512MB Compact Flash 512 mb CF memory Card *	$26.37
PRO DUO for PSP, DSC-T1		SANDISK 512MB SD MEMORY CARD (SDSDB512768)	$26.35
SANDISK 1GB MEMORY STICK PRO DUO SONY PSP	$99.00	* SanDisk 512MB Compact Flash 512 mb CF memory Card *	$26.28
1gb pro duo memory stick SANDISK	$96.00	* SanDisk 512MB Compact Flash 512 mb CF memory Card *	$26.05
Scandisk Memory Stick Pro Duo 1GB 1 GB	$96.00	SANDISK (SDSDB512768) 512MB SD MEMORY CARD	$26.01
Sandisk 1 gb pro duo card, ready to ship! PSP ready!!!	$94.50	PNY TECHNOLOGIES MEMORY CARD 1.0 GB	$26.00
SANDISK Memory Sticks; 1GB PRO Duo	$91.00	[2 of these sold for $26.00 each]	
NEW SANDISK 1GB GIG MEMORY STICK PRO DUO SONY	$89.00	SANDISK SDCFB-512-A10 512MB COMPACT FLASH CARD	$26.00
SANDISK Memory Sticks; 1GB PRO Duo	$86.00	Sony GENUINE 50 Pack Spindle Mini CD-R	$26.00
1.0MB Sandisk memory stick pro Magic Gate	$80.00	* SanDisk 512MB Compact Flash 512 mb CF memory Card *	$26.00
SONY DSC-P200 WIDE ANGLE & TELE LENS + SONY VAD-PHC	$79.00	SANDISK SDCFB-512-A10 512MB COMPACT FLASH CARD	$26.00

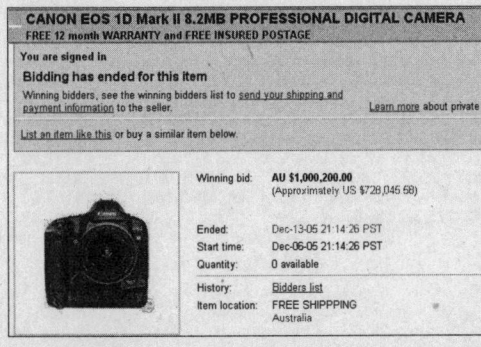

CANON EOS 1D Mark II 8.2MB PROFESSIONAL DIGITAL CAMERA
FREE 12 month WARRANTY and FREE INSURED POSTAGE

You are signed in
Bidding has ended for this item
Winning bidders, see the winning bidders list to send your shipping and payment information to the seller. Learn more about private

List an item like this or buy a similar item below.

Winning bid:	AU $1,000,200.00
	(Approximately US $728,045.58)
Ended:	Dec-13-05 21:14:26 PST
Start time:	Dec-06-05 21:14:26 PST
Quantity:	0 available
History:	Bidders list
Item location:	FREE SHIPPPING
	Australia

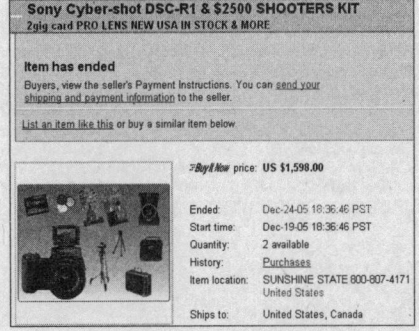

Sony Cyber-shot DSC-R1 & $2500 SHOOTERS KIT
2gig card PRO LENS NEW USA IN STOCK & MORE

Item has ended
Buyers, view the seller's Payment Instructions. You can send your shipping and payment information to the seller.

List an item like this or buy a similar item below.

Buy It Now price:	US $1,598.00
Ended:	Dec-24-05 18:36:46 PST
Start time:	Dec-19-05 18:36:46 PST
Quantity:	2 available
History:	Purchases
Item location:	SUNSHINE STATE 800-807-4171
	United States
Ships to:	United States, Canada

Digital Cameras ▶ Canon

The average sales price in this subcategory is $312.00.

NOTE *These results are based on a keyword search of the Digital Cameras subcategory for auctions with the word* Canon *in the title.*

	HIGH		AVG
Canon EOS-1DS Mark II, 16.7 Megapixel SLR	$7,100.00	NEW Canon PowerShot S500 5.0 MP DIGITAL Camera 12X Zoom	$320.00
Canon EOS 1Ds Mark II 16.7 MP New (not 1D)	$6,125.00	Canon SD400 Powershot Camera (5.0 Megapixel) New in Box	$320.00
Canon EOS 1DS, Low Actuations!	$4,000.00	NEW IN BOX! Canon PowerShot SD400 Digital ELPH 5.0 Mp	$320.00
Canon EOS 1Ds 11.1 Megapixel Camera EX condition	$3,650.00	Canon PowerShot SD400 5MP Digital Camera N0TSD200 SD500	$320.00
Canon EOS 20D NEW 1288 pic 17-40 L Lens 50mm L 1GB CF!	$2,000.00	CANON A95 DIGITAL CAMERA ALL INCLUSIVE PACKAGE	$319.99
CANON EOS 20D DIGITAL SLR + CANON 75-300MM 18-55MM LENS	$1,799.99	Canon PowerShot SD200 Digital Camera +512mb Kit NEW USA	$319.00
CANON EOS-20D DIGITAL CAMERA W/EF-S 17-85 LENS *NEW*USA	$1,799.83	~*BNIB Canon.PowerShot SD400 Digital ELPH/Low Ship*~	$316.00
Canon EOS 20D Digital SLR $2300 EXTRAS +2 EF LENSES+1GB	$1,749.99	!Brand NEW! Canon SD400 Digital ELPH 5.0MP + Free PS7.0	$315.75
Canon EOS 20D Digital SLR & 2 Lenses & 47st Pro Package	$1,589.95	BRAND NEW Canon PowerShot SD400 5.0MP Digital Camera NR	$315.75
Canon EOS 20D Digital SLR with 18-55mm & Deluxe Package	$1,469.95	New Canon PowerShot SD300 Digital Camera +512MB +MORE	$315.00
Canon EOS 1D - Digital SLR - in great condition	$1,425.99	NEW CANON POWERSHOT SD400 DIGITAL ELPH 5.0 MP SD500 !	$315.00
Canon EOS 20D 8.2 MP Camera 18-55mm Kit USA* NEW+NR!!!!	$1,275.11	~*BNIB Canon PowerShot SD400 Digital ELPH/Low Ship*~	$315.00
Canon EOS Digital Rebel XT 8 MP w/17-85mm Lens IS US	$1,252.00	Canon G3 4 Megapixel Camera Like New With Extras	$315.00
BRAND NEW Canon EOS 20D Digital SLR Camera * No Reserve	$1,250.00	Canon PowerShot A95 w/ PRO KIT	$314.99
Canon EOS Digital REBEL XT 350D SLR Camera +$2500 PKG	$1,239.99	Canon Powershot SD400 5MP Digital Elph Camera with 3x O	$310.00

Digital Cameras ▶ Nikon

The average sales price in this subcategory is $320.00.

NOTE *These results are based on a keyword search of the Digital Cameras subcategory for auctions with the word* Nikon *in the title.*

	HIGH		AVG
Nikon D2X 12.4 MP Digital SLR Camera 5 Lenses CASE ACC!	$4,700.00	Nikon Coolpix 4800 4MP Digital Camera+256MB Kit NEW USA	$328.80
Nikon D2X Digital SLR Camera Body 12.4MP & USA Wty NEW!	$4,557.00	[3 of these sold for $328.80 each]	
Nikon D2X Digital SLR Camera Body BRAND NEW USA	$4,431.00	Nikon Coolpix 5700 5.0 Megapixel-Like Brand New	$325.00
Nikon D2X Digital SLR Camera Body	$4,349.00	Nikon Coolpix 7900 7 MP Digital Camera with 3x Optical	$325.00
12.4MP & USA Wty NEW!		New Nikon Coolpix 5000 5MP Digital Camera - POWERSELLER	$325.00
Nikon D2X Digital SLR Camera Body	$4,301.00	Nikon Coolpix 4500 Digital Camera USA Warrnty	$320.00
12.4MP & USA Wty NEW!		[2 of these sold for $320.00 each]	
Nikon D2x 12mp.Camera USA Model	$4,102.00	NEW Nikon Coolpix 7600 7.1MP; 3X OPT ZOOM+BONUS 512 SD	$319.95
Nikon D2X 12.4 Megapixel Brand New	$3,551.00	Nikon Coolpix 7900 7.1 Megapixel Digital Camera NEW	$315.83
Nikon D2Hs SLR Digital Camera Body BRAND NEW USA D-2HS	$2,650.00	Nikon Coolpix 5700 Digital Camera USA 1yr Warranty	$315.00
Nikon D1X SLR Digital Camera with USA 1 Year Warranty	$2,299.95	Nikon Coolpix 7900 7 MP Digital Camera with 3x Optical	$314.99
Nikon D1x camera	$1,975.01	Nikon Coolpix 7900 7.1 Megapixel Digital Camera NEW	$312.83
NIKON D1X COMPLETE SET MINT/GREAT DEAL!	$1,950.00	Nikon Coolpix 7900 7 MP Digital Camera with 3x Optical	$312.00
Nikon D2H Body Kit (with US warranty Card)Not D1 D1X	$1,824.99	Nikon Coolpix 5700 5.0 Megapixel-Excellent Condition	$310.00
NIKON D1X DIGITAL SLR CAMERA plus extras	$1,800.00	Nikon Coolpix 7900 7.1 Megapixel Digital Camera NEW	$309.83
NIKON D2H EXCELLENT PLUS CONDITION CHECK IT OUT bn	$1,700.00	Nikon Coolpix 5900 Digital Camera 5MP USA + 256MB KIT!	$308.95
Very Clean NIKON D1x Body with 4 Batteries	$1,650.00	Nikon Coolpix 7900 7 MP Digital Camera with 3x Optical	$308.75

Digital Cameras ▶ Sony

The average sales price in this subcategory is $149.09.

NOTE *These results are based on a keyword search of the Digital Cameras subcategory for auctions with the word* Sony *in the title.*

	HIGH		AVG
SONY CYBERSHOT DSC-F828 PRO KIT & LOT MORE & USA WRTY	$999.99	SONY MVCFD100 FD MAVICA DIGITAL CAMERA W/3X ZOOM	$154.99
Sony Cyber-shot DSC-F828 8 Megapixel w/ 6 piece PRO KIT	$750.00	SONY MAVICA MVC-FD90 DIGITAL CAMERA	$154.50
BRAND NEW, FACTORY SEALED Sony Cyber-shot DSC-F828	$680.01	Sony DSC-F717 CyberShot Digital Camera REPAIR OR PARTS	$153.50
Sony DSC-F828 8.0	$680.00	SONY Cyber-Shot DSC-W1 Digital Camera 5.1MP WOW!!!	$153.50
Sony 717 Cyber-shot / Infrared Modified Digital	$600.00	Sony Mavica MVC FD91 0.85 Megapixel	$153.50
Sony Cyber-shot DSC-T7 512MB Kit +3 Years Warranty	$513.78	Sony Cyber-shot DSC-P93 5.0 Megapixel retail box	$152.51
SONY CYBERSHOT DSC-T7 DIGITAL CAMERA + $349 EX + 256M	$489.99	Sony Cyber-shot DSC-F505V 3.3 Megapixel CCD	$152.50
Sony Cyber-shot DSC-P200 Digital Camera Black+512MB Kit	$483.80	SONY CYBERSHOT DSC-F707 DIGITAL CAMERA 5.0MP	$152.50
Sony DSC-F828 8MP Digital Camera	$483.09	Sony WorryFreeDigital2 5.1 MP Cyber-Shot Digital Camera	$152.50
Sony DCR-TRV80 Handycam (Camcorder and digital camera)	$476.00	SONY CYBER-SHOT DSC-T1 DIGITAL CAMERA AS IS FOR PARTS	$152.50
Sony Cyber-shot DSC-P200 Digital Camera + 512MB Kit NEW	$474.95	Sony Mavica MVC CD350 3.2 Megapixel Factory Serviced	$152.50
Sony Cyber-shot DSC-T7 5.1 Megapixel New	$464.20	Sony Cyber-shot DSC-P41 4.1 Megapixel w/CASE and 512MB	$152.50
SONY CYBERSHOT DSC-F828 8.0MP DIGITAL CAMERA C@@L	$455.00	SONY CYBERSHOT DSC-P73 DIGITAL ZOOM CAMERA 4.1 MPXL *	$152.50
Brand NEW DSC F717 Sony Cyber-shot DSC-F717 5.0 MP	$430.01	SONY MAVICA MULTI-MEDIA DIGITAL CAMERA MVC-FD92 16X	$152.50
Sony Cybershot DSC-W5 5MP Digital Camera DSCW5+ 1GB	$429.80	Sony Cyber-shot DSC-P5 3.2 Megapixel	$151.69

Digital Cameras ▸ Point & Shoot

The average sales price in this subcategory is $24.39.

	HIGH		AVG
BRAN NEW JVC GZ-MC200US EVERIO IN THE BOX	$761.00	SLIMMEST CREDIT CARD SIZE DIGITAL CAMERA 209 PICS C-GR8	$24.95
JVC GR-DV3000U Digita Video Camcorder	$400.50	[12 of these sold for $24.95 each]	
Digital camera and DC200 housing Sealife Reafmaster	$250.00	1.3 M Pixels Digital Camera 3-in-1 PenCam PC webcam	$24.59
Panasonic DMC-FZ-1PPS 2MP Digital w/12x Leica Zoom!	$159.95	PHILIPS WEARABLE DIGITAL CAMERA 64MB NEW!	$24.50
Lot Of 10 Toshiba PDR-M11 Digital Camera #5650Z	$152.50	1.3 M Pixels Digital Camera 3-in-1 PenCam PC webcam	$24.50
panasonic SV-AV50 digital camera	$151.69	$100 Logitech 961305-0403 Pocket Digital 130 Camera NR	$24.49
Leica Digilux Digital Camera 1.5MP 8MB SmartMedia More!	$147.50	Philips 64MB Digital Camera KEY007817B Key Ring	$24.17
Sony Mavica MVC-FD92 1.2 Megapixel / 1.6 Megapixel (...	$139.53	OREGON SCIENTIFIC DS6628 1.3 MEGAPIXEL DIGITAL CAMERA	$24.09
050 / PENTAX OPTIO 50 5.0 MP DIGITAL CAMERA	$133.00	Che-ez! Foxz1 1.3 MP Mini Digital Camera Case Software	$23.99
Sony MVC-FD91 Digital Mavica Camera MPEG Movies 14X	$125.82	OLYMPUS D100 DIGITAL CAMERA IN BOX! COST $149.79!	$23.58
Minox / Leica M3 Digital Camera MINI CLASSIC!	$125.00	4 IN 1 300K Binoculars Digital Camera Video PC Cam	$23.00
Palm PalmOne Zire 71	$112.50	Agfa ePhoto 780c 0.35 Megapixel W/BAG + memory	$23.00
Canon PowerShot S330 2.0MP Digital Camera, Like New,NR	$112.50	1.3 M PIXELS DIGITAL STILL CAMERA w/ DISPLAY BRAND NEW	$22.72
OLYPUS CAMEDIA D-360L 1.3MP	$101.55	Brookstone Slimline Digital Camera	$22.50
DIGITAL CAMERA W/ 128MB MEM		JVC GC-A33 Dual Mode Digital Camera and accesories	$22.50
panasonic SV-AV50 digital camera	$100.66	Aiptek Pocket DV 2 1.3 Megapixel	$22.50

Digital Cameras ▸ Digital SLR

The average sales price in this subcategory is $514.49.

	HIGH		AVG
Contax N 6.2 MP SLR Digital Camera Warranty Retail Box	$3,650.00	Pentax *ist DS 6.1 Megapixel	$545.00
Kodak DCS Pro SLR Canon	$3,450.00	Pentax *ist DS 6.1 megapixel SLR camera; like new	$537.50
Kodak DCS Pro SLR/c Digital Camera - Excellent Demo !	$3,105.00	SIGMA SD9 DIGITAL CAMERA SD-9 - LIKE NEW! NO RESERVE!	$535.00
KODAK DCS PRO SLR/N DIGITAL	$3,100.00	Konica Minolta DiMAGE A2 8 Megapixel	$535.00
SLR CAMERA BODY - NIKON AF		Sigma SD9 SD 9 Digital SLR w/Power Pack	$525.00
Kodak DCS Pro SLR/n 13.9 Megapixel	$3,100.00	[2 of these sold for $525.00 each]	
Kodak DCS Pro 14n 14 Megapixel	$3,050.00	Almost new sigma sd9	$524.00
Kodak DCS Pro SLR/c 13.9 Megapixel	$2,975.00	Kodak DCS 520 Pro Digital SLR Camera Canon EOS 1N NR	$510.01
Kodak DCS Pro 14N Digital Camera with Sigma lens	$2,900.00	BR NEW PENTAX IST DS DIGITAL CAMERA 6.1 MP SLR CCD W/WT	$505.00
Kodak DCS Pro SLR/n 13.9Mpixel, Pocket Wizard, No Reser	$2,850.00	[2 of these sold for $505.00 each]	
Kodak Professional DCS Pro SLR/n Digital Camera Mint!	$2,670.00	Kodak DCS 520 Pro Digital SLR Camera Canon EOS 1N NR	$502.99
Kodak DCS Pro SLR/c 13.9 Megapixel, almost new!	$2,600.00	Sigma SD9 digital SLR w/2 lenses and accessories	$500.77
Kodak SLR/n 14 megapixels Nikon Mount	$2,560.00	SIGMA SD9. FULL KIT	$500.00
Kodak DCS Pro 14n 13.9 Megapixel (United states)	$2,550.00	Kodak DCS Pro SLR/n 13.9 Megapixel	$500.00
Kodak DCS Pro SLR/c 13.9 Megapixel	$2,500.00	PENTAX IST DS DIGITAL SLR WITH 18-55MM LENS KIT (18033)	$495.00
KODAK DCS Pro SLR/C 14 Megapixel	$2,495.00	Canon PowerShot S2 IS 5.0 Megapixel NIB LOW RESERVE	$460.05
Body, Canon Lens Mount		Sony Cyber-shot DSC-H1 5.1 Megapixel Brand New	$454.00

Digital Cameras ▸ Specialty Digital Cameras

The average sales price in this subcategory is $94.75.

	HIGH		AVG
Sony DCR-HC1000 HandyCam Mini DV Camcorder Digital NR	$1,025.00	HOT NEW LOOK! DC-8380 8MP Max Res DIGITAL CAMERA by SVP	$96.00
SONY DSC-F828 CYBER-SHOT CAMERA....L@@K NO RESERVE..!!	$607.01	VIDEO CAMCORDER DIGITAL CAMERA & MP3 -New! SVP DV6680	$96.00
Sony 717 Cyber-shot / Infrared Modified Digital	$600.00	NEW! 12MP Max DIGITAL CAMERA +RECs VIDEOS! +$200 BONUS!	$96.00
SONY CYBER-SHOT DSC/M1 W/MANY EXTRAS!!	$430.00	DXG 305v 5 in 1 - 3 MP Digital Camera NR $1.00 Start	$96.00
BRAND NEW Sanyo Xacti DMX-C5 / VPC-C5 Digital Camera **	$420.00	6MP DIGITAL CAMERA w/12X ZOOM & GIANT 2" LCD +REC VIDEO	$96.00
Sony Mavica MVC CD500 5.0 Megapixel	$363.00	12MP Max DIGITAL CAMERA +Records Videos! +$200 EXTRAS!	$94.00
Sony Mavica MVC CD500 5.0 Megapixel	$340.00	DIGITAL VIDEO CAMCORDER / CAMERA by GENESIS +MP3 Player	$93.00
Panasonic SV-AV100 D-Snap Video/Still SD digital camera	$330.00	8MP VIDEO CAMCORDER DIGITAL CAMERA & MP3 w/GIANT 2" TFT	$93.00
Sony Cybershot DSCP150 - 7.2 Megapixel Digital Camera	$320.00	6MP DIGITAL CAMERA w/3X OPTICAL ZOOM & GIANT 2" SCREEN	$92.50
Sony Cybershot DSCP150 - 7.2 Megapixel Digital Camera	$310.00	COMPACT 8MP DIGITAL VIDEO CAMERA / CAMCORDER DV-8530	$92.50
Sony Cybershot DSCP150 - 7.2 Megapixel Digital Camera	$295.00	NEW! DV-8230 6-1 DIGITAL VIDEO CAMERA / CAMCORDER & MP3	$92.00
PANASONIC CX-DH801U 8 DVD Changer BRAND NEW !!!	$275.00	COMPACT 8MP DIGITAL VIDEO CAMERA / CAMCORDER DV-8530	$92.00
Cube Style Digital Media Camera~~JVC	$272.00	6MP DIGITAL CAMERA with Panasonic CCD SENSOR +Rec Video	$92.00
DV6 Supacam 6.6Meg Camera Camcorder MP3 Player	$258.00	NEW! DIGITAL VIDEO CAMCORDER / CAMERA with MP3 Player	$92.00
Panasonic 5 in 1 camera/MP3 player- SV-AV30 / e-wear	$250.00	7-in-1 6.6 MP Digital Mpeg4 Camcorder Camera MP3 DV6307	$91.35

Film ▸ 35mm

The average sales price in this subcategory is $25.05.

	HIGH		AVG
35MM ONE TIME USE DISPOSABLE CAMERA W/ FLASH QTY 96	$279.99	Huge Lot of Kodak MAX 400 Speed 35 mm Film-New	$26.00
2 pks Kodak Technical Pan Film 35mm x 45.7 m	$272.52	Kodak Max Versatility 400 Speed 35 mm Film 24 rolls	$25.55
Technical Pan Tech Pan 25 150ft Roll-BEST FILM EVER!!	$242.50	Agfapan APX 400 Black and White 35mm Film 100 ft Bulk	$25.50
12 Rolls Kodachrome 25, 36 Exp, 10/01expirat. , frozen	$240.00	30 Rolls Kodak High Definition ISO 400 35mm Film	$25.45
150' 35mm HIE Kodak Infrared Film	$201.50	KODAK TMAX-400 - 24 exp. 35mm	$25.05
Fuji Pro Film 35mm NPS 100 rolls 36 exp. dated 3/05	$200.00	B&W FILM - 10 Fresh Rolls	
MINOLTA MAXXUM 3 SLR CAMERA 35-80 mm LENS	$170.00	KODAK PORTRA 160 NC 13 rolls, Expired But Still Good!	$25.00
Kodak Professional Supra 100, 35mm, 36 exp.- 20 pack	$168.32	20 ROLLS KODAK MAX 35MM 400 COLOR FILM 24 EXP.	$25.00
[16 of these sold in a multiple item ("Dutch") auction for $10.52 each]		KODAK MAX 400 35mm film, 25 24exp. rolls	$24.99
Technical Pan Tech Pan 25 150ft Roll-BEST FILM EVER!!	$152.50	10 Rolls - Kodak Elite Chrome 100/36 FRESH Exp 1/2007	$24.99

300 rolls Kodak EliteEktachrome Color Slide Film 24exp.	$150.00	Ilford HP5 Plus 135-24 B&W Film ISO 400 - 10 ROLLS	$24.99
MINOLTA 35MM X-370 CAMERA MANUAL FOCUS WITH LENSES	$140.00	Ilford Delta ISO 400 135-24 B&W Pro Film - 10 ROLLS	$24.99
NIKON FE 35MM SLR FILM CAMERA W/ NIKON FILTER BAG NR	$127.50	Lot 50 Rolls 24 exp 35 mm Color film 400 ISO 135 Camera	$24.99
ILFORD XP2 SUPER 36 EXP BW FILM 50 ROLL PRO PACK FRESH!	$125.00	KODAK GOLD 100 35mm film, 25 24exp. rolls	$24.99
100exp POLAROID TIME-ZERO SX-70 FILM FRESH DATE 03/2006	$124.45	20 Rolls of Fuji 800 Speed 36 Exposure Film	$24.99
60 Rolls Kodak 400 TMAX B&W film	$124.09	KODAK 400 FILM/24 EXP LOT OF 26 ROLLS..LOOK	$24.99

Film ▸ Medium, Large Format

The average sales price in this subcategory is $93.54.

	HIGH		AVG
Kodak Portra 400nc 220 *300 Rolls* Expired 8/04	$710.00	KODAK PORTRA 220 ,400 VC FILM 20 ROLLS NO RESERVE	$99.00
Kodak Pro Portra 160NC 120 240 Rolls Exp 3/2205	$362.00	LOT Polaroid 4x5 Sheet Film 52 53 54 55 57 59 72 79	$99.00
Kodak Professional Portra 160NC 220 *300 Rolls* NR	$355.00	KODAK portra 160vc 8x10 film C-41 2boxes FRESH	$98.69
150 ROLLS 120/220 FILM BLACK AND WHITE AND COLOR	$314.00	KODAK PORTRA 220 ,400 VC FILM 20 ROLLS NO RESERVE	$98.57
500 SHEETS OF PROVIA 100F 4X5 RDPIII FROZEN: 09/05!	$300.95	Kodak Ektachrome 100 Plus 4x5", 50 Sheet Box, Exp,08/06	$98.02
FP4 Ilford 4X5 14 boxes 50 sheets each	$272.00	[2 of these sold in a multiple item ("Dutch") auction for $49.01 each]	
Eclair ACL 400ft Magazine 16mm MP	$256.00	KODAK PORTRA 220 ,400 VC FILM 20 ROLLS NO RESERVE	$97.00
Kodak Portra NC 220 Professional Film	$230.00	20 Rolls PORTRA 160NC 220 Film 07/2005	$96.85
[2 of these sold in a multiple item ("Dutch") auction for $115.00 each]		20 ROLLS FUJI VELVIA 100F 120 FILM SUPER FRESH 8/2006	$92.95
5 KODAK PORTRA 70MM FILM 100ft Rolls	$227.00	[2 of these sold for $92.95 each]	
70mm 70 mm TriX film for Hasselblad etc	$220.05	B&W 10 rolls 120 FILM Agfa APX 25asa SEALED 0703	$92.78
Fujifilm 100F 120 Format Film (Case) 100 Rolls	$207.50	KODAK PORTRA 220 ,400 VC FILM 20 ROLLS NO RESERVE	$92.00
KODAK EPP 8x10-50pk- COLOR SLIDE	$202.50	M1 Case of Fuji MS 120 Slide Film RMS 100 Rolls	$89.99
FILM (04/2005 DATING)		FUJI PROVIA 100F/120-SLIDE FILM-12/04 DATING–50 rolls!	$89.00
KODAK VISION 500T 16mm Motion Picutre Film	$202.50	FUJI PROVIA 100F/120-SLIDE FILM-12/04 DATING–50 rolls!	$87.50
Fuji NPS 220 for Hasselblad Bronica Mamiya 100 roll lot	$199.95	Fuji film 3 velvia 50 sheet boxes refigerated	$87.02
381 rolls of 120 film Kodak and Fuji 160 400 LOOK!! NR	$193.50	Pelican flight case for arri or aaton cameras	$86.00

Film Camera Accessories ▸ Camera Body Accessories

The average sales price in this subcategory is $59.59.

	HIGH		AVG
LEICA M6 W/SUMMILUX F1.4 35MM LENS/BOX/MANUAL/EXC(01-10	$2,075.00	UNIVERSAL VIEWFINDER Attachment for Kiev Fed Cameras	$62.00
Leica Leitz MOTOR M	$551.99	Nikon MB-10 Multi-Power Vertical Grip for Nikon N90s	$61.01
LEICA LEICAVIT RAPID-WINDER FOR SCREW-MOUNT CAMERAS	$539.00	Nikon MD-15 not FA F4 F5 F6 MB-23	$61.00
Leica Motor M 14408 - NO RESERVE	$516.42	MINT CANON BP300 BP-300 Grip f EOS Elan 7 7e 7n 7ne NR	$60.01
Nikon DA-30 AE Action Finder for F5	$500.00	Zeiss Type Turret Finder (28mm,35mm,50mm,85mm,135mm)	$60.00
Hasselblad Xpan 90mm Lens	$430.00	NIKON MB-10 VERTICLE GRIP FOR N90s	$59.99
Vintage Voigtlander Prominent II Camera w/Accessories	$425.00	NIKON MB-16 BATTERY PACK FOR N80. LIKE NEW IN BOX ...	$59.95
Leica M 21mm Viewfinder with Case	$405.00	CONTAX RIGHT ANGLE FINDER EXC+ CONDITION	$59.00
LEITZ LEICA RAPIDWINDER-BLACK-CANADA-A-050-NEAT!!(02-68	$391.10	Nikon MB-10 MB10 Battery Grip for N90s/F90x SLR Camera	$59.00
Leica Leitz SKBOO 21mm Finder for Angulon Very Nice!	$350.00	Nikon Right Angle Viewing Attachment DR-3 DR3 + DK-7	$59.00
Leitz/Leica 35mm Viewfinder Silver Chrome Finder w/Case	$350.00	LEITZ LEICA IMARECT MULTI RANGE VIEWFINDER NR	$59.00
LEITZ LEICA 3.5CM(35MM)CHROME VIEWFINDER-#12010-(02-53)	$335.00	Original Black Metal M-Grip for the Leica M6	$58.77
LEITZ LEICA #12007 28MM VIEWFINDER IN BOX-EXCELL(02-56)	$324.00	Canon Rangefinder Camera Grip for the VT & VI-T	$57.10
LEICA 21MM SUPER ANGULON VINTAGE CHROME VIEWFINDER	$295.00	CONTAX PS-220 POWER PACK SET FOR TLA 360 FLASH	$57.00
Nikon MH-30 and NM-30 NiMh battery and charger for F5	$282.01	Canon BP-300 Battery Pack Grip EOS ELAN 7 E 7E	$57.00

Film Camera Accessories ▸ Other Film & Movie Accessories

The average sales price in this subcategory is $43.34.

	HIGH		AVG
MagiqCam II Camera Stabilizer , steadycam steadicam	$1,575.00	Leica take-up spool for M1 M2 M3 New In Box	$46.00
Ken-Lab Gyro Stabilizer Steadycam for Photo/Video	$1,225.00	Vivitar Instant Slide Printer	$46.00
Moy Geared Head	$1,000.00	Sankor Zoom Converter for Bell & Howell 16mm Projectors	$46.00
Angenieux 50mm(NEW),25mm,	$600.00	KODAK READYLOAD PACKED FILM HOLDER	$45.00
10mm"MINT"+extras Bolex B&H		Arri 2C High Hat/Friction Head	$45.00
8X10 WOODEN DEARDORFF VIEW CAMERA	$511.00	UNIVERSAL VIEWFINDER FOR ZORKI FED LEICA BOX	$44.00
NIKON AF NIKKOR 16MM F2.8/FISHEYE LENS	$355.00	Tamron Fotovix III-S	$41.50
Lumedyne #067X Power Pack, Flash Head & Battery 025	$354.99	SIGMA MIRROR-ULTRATEL- F-500MM CAMERA LENS	$41.00
Arri Arriflex Pistol grip?switch (hand grip)	$326.00	Polaroid 4x5 Film Holder Model 545	$41.00
Minolta Spotmeter F No Reserve	$317.00	Spiratone Rapid Rail Macrobel Bellows for Nikon Camera	$41.00
Sony Video Multi Color Corrector XV-C900	$290.00	Minolta Maxxum 5200i Flash Attachment & Cable	$41.00
HASSELBLAD PM45 PRISM FINDER	$284.00	BANANA REPUBLIC PHOTO JOURNALIST VEST SAFARI FISHING	$41.00
Alan Gordon Mark IV Director's Viewfinder	$260.51	Film Editing Equipment - 2 Spring Clamps for Rewinds	$40.56
MINOLTA MACRO AUTO BELLOWS I (ABI) ACCESSORY USED NR	$256.65	Sailwind Vignetter W/ Extension Bellows + 2 Vignettes	$39.00
Nikon Compartment Case FB-11A Rare Item Mint/Accesories	$250.00	NIKON MD-12 MOTOR DRIVE WINDER	$38.91

Film Cameras ▸ 35mm Point & Shoot

The average sales price in this subcategory is $51.93.

	HIGH		AVG
HASSELBLAD FILM CAMERA WITH ACCESSORIES AND HARD CASE	$872.62	BLACK YASHICA ELECTRO 35 GT CAMERA 35MM	$55.00
LEICA CM THE FINEST QUALITY 35mm CAMERA	$660.00	KONICA AUTO REFLEX 35mm CAMERA	$54.53
3 LOMO LC-A 35mm Russian Cameras Export NEW 2005 Box !	$519.00	Honeywell Pentax Spotmatic F with Lens 55mm 1:1.8 case	$54.00

Rollei 35S Anniversary Silver Excellent	$450.00	35mm Camera, Exakta, German Camera	$53.77
Konica Hexar Classic 120th Anniversary Edition	$437.00	LOT OF 6 NICE CAMERAS	$52.99
Konica Hexar Silver with HX-14 Flash and Silent Mode	$404.99	1 IS DIGITAL + ACCESSORIES	
LEICA MINILUX w/ LEICA SUMMARIT 40mm F2.4 w/WARRANTY	$379.99	OLYMPUS IS-2 35mm Camera	$51.00
NEW PROFESSIONAL STYLE 35 mm CAMERA ,W/ ZOOM LENS	$350.00	35mm camera outfit w/ telephoto lens	$49.99
[10 of these sold in a multiple item ("Dutch") auction for $35.00 each]		Chinon Genesis 35mm camera 35-80 zoom macro lens	$49.56
SONY CYBER-SHOT DSC-F717 5MP DIGITAL CAMERA for cheap	$345.00	Rollei 35 mm Point and Shoot Prego 90 Camera	$49.00
NEW PROFESSIONAL STYLE 35 mm CAMERA ,W/ ZOOM LENS	$369.90	Honeywell Pentax Spotmatic F with Lens 55mm 1:1.8 case	$48.00
[10 of these sold in a multiple item ("Dutch") auction for $36.99 each]		BRAND NIB COLORSPLASH	$48.00
Rollei AFM35 Auto Focus Camera LIKE NEW IN THE BOX	$312.00	CAMERA BY LOMOGRAPHY	
VINTAGE ROLLEI 35 MM HONEYWELL CAMERA GERMAN	$310.00	Orange Lomo Colorsplash camera color splash Lomography	$44.54
ROLLEI QZ 35W CAMERA F. A. PORSCHE DESIGN	$280.99	CHINON GENESIS III CAMERA, NO RESERVE	$42.00
LOMO LC-A Compact Automat 35mm Camera package	$222.50	LOMO's FISHEYE camera! only compact fisheye ever! fun!	$42.00
Rare Spirotechnique Aquamatic - Formaplex UW Camera	$201.50	Lomo Fisheye camera Lomography fish eye Holga	$41.07

Film Cameras ▸ 35mm Rangefinder

The average sales price in this subcategory is $117.97.

	HIGH		AVG
Nikon SP Rangefinder, 3 Nikkor RF lenses, Near Mint	$3,250.27	LOMO LC-A Compakt Automat 35mm camera, L. NEW, BOX, 12	$120.26
Nikon Rangefinder BLACK S3 2000 Brand New Box SP Leica	$2,950.00	LOMO COMPACT-A Russian Camera LC-A NIB NEW BOX	$120.00
Zuiho Honor S1, case box instructions, Leica copy minty	$2,233.00	[2 of these sold for $120.00 each]	
NIKON SP RANGEFINDER 35MM CAMERA + 50MM LENS	$2,004.00	Canon Canonet GIII QL17 G III QL 17 Rangefinder Camera	$120.00
Nikon SP 35mm rangefinder camera with two lenses.	$2,000.00	Minolta-35 model II	$120.00
Hasselblad XPAN with 45mm Lens (great kit with NR)	$1,580.60	LOMO Compact LC-A 35mm Film Camera	$119.99
Hasselblad Xpan with 45mm	$1,250.00	MINOX 35 ML + MINOX FLASH UNIT MF 35 ST + ACCESSORIES	$115.10
lens kit with box No Reserve!		NIKON RANGEFINDER NIPPON KOGAKU 13.5cm f3.5 NIKKOR	$113.61
Nikon Sp ~~NO RESERVE~~	$1,225.99	WOW! KODAK RETINA REFLEX CAMERA WITH TONS OF EXTRAS!!!	$113.51
hasselblad xpan & 45 mm lens	$1,220.00	VINTAGE ROLLEI 35 35MM COMPACT CAMERA ZEISS LENS + CASE	$113.50
Gorgeous Nikon S3 Rangefinder & 5cm (50mm) f/2 Nikkor-H	$1,136.00	ROLLEI 35 TE BACKPACKER !!	$112.50
Nikon S3 with NO S/N Body!! Not Limited Edition. NR	$1,082.88	Mamiya 35 Crown 35mm Rangefinder w/ 48mm f 1.9 Lens	$110.00
Konica Hexar RF Kit	$1,000.00	Lot of rangefinder cameras Hi-Matic FED QL17 Minox	$107.50
Nikon S2 rangefinder camera	$798.88	2 x Rollei B 35 black and chrome (B17)	$104.50
Gamma III camera body, Italian Leica copy, no. 10737	$798.88	SMENA-8M RARE?STEREO RANGEFINDRF RUSSIAN CAMERA	$103.50
NIKON S2 Rangefinder camera + Lens	$767.77	GORGEOUS VOIGTLANDER VITESSA N (TYPE 134) AND CASE	$102.50

Film Cameras ▸ 35mm SLR

The average sales price in this subcategory is $48.96.

	HIGH		AVG
Minolta High Speed AF APO 200mm	$835.00	KONICA TC AUTOREFLEX w SOLIGOR MC + Case & Manual NICE!	$49.95
Shift CA Rokkor 1:2.8 35mm Minolta Lens.	$815.56	New Vivitar Auto Extension Tube For Minolta MD / XG	$49.77
Konica Hexar with HX-14 Auto Flash	$396.00	Konica Auto Reflex T camera T- ring 1.25 Camera Adapter	$49.50
Bass Hound Fishing Boat	$370.01	LOT OF 6 KONICA AUTOREFLEX T BODIES FOR PARTS/REPAIR	$49.41
Konica T 4 + hexanon 57 / 1 1.2	$317.96	NICE KONICA Autoreflex TC 35MM 135mm, 50mm,tri-pod etc.	$49.00
GORGEOUS TOP-LEVEL MINOLTA MAXXUM 800Si BODY : EXC++	$268.75	MINOLTA SRT201 CAMERA WITH MD MINOLTA CELTIC LENS	$49.00
Beautiful Minolta SRT 202 Camera Body, EX++	$265.00	MINOLTA SRT SC-II CAMERA WITH 50MM MINOLTA LENS	$49.00
NIKON FE2 CAMERA KIT/55mm Micro NIKKOR/105mm NIKKOR	$247.50	MINOLTA XG1 35MM CAMERA w/45MM LENS + FLASH + EXTRAS	$48.00
Minolta XE-7 camera and lens	$237.06	Minolta SRT-102 35 MM Camera w/accessories	$47.51
2 MINOLTA SLR CAMERAS, LENSES & FLASHGUNS	$220.50	Minolta XG-M Camera Outfit	$47.50
KONICA AUTO REFLEX TC WITH LENSES	$202.50	Minolta SRT 202 35mm Camera and Accessories	$47.00
Konica FT-1 with 50mm Hexanon Lens, Near Mint!	$200.50	Konica FS-1 35 mm Cameria w/zoom lens	$46.67
Rokkor Minolta 58mm 58 mm f1:1.2 f1.2 Near Mint	$199.00	Minolta SR-1 Early SLR With 55mm 1.8 + Case + Book	$46.55
Minolta X-700 Complete Camera Outfit 4 lens & Case	$199.00	Professional Photographer Kit Minolta x-370s , More NR!	$46.00
Minolta Maxxum 700 si	$197.49	Minolta SRT101 35mm SLR with 58mm f1.4 Lens NR	$46.00

Film Cameras ▸ Instant Print, Polaroid

The average sales price in this subcategory is $34.41.

	HIGH		AVG
Polaroid 195 Land Camera Kit in case, mint	$710.00	VINTAGE POLAROID SX70	$34.95
NEW IN BOX POLAROID 690 CAMERA NIB INSTANT LIKE SX-70	$420.00	SX-70 BLACK TAN EXCELLENT !!	
Polaroid 195 Land Camera EX+ The Professional polaroid	$350.00	VINTAGE POLAROID SX70	$34.95
NEW IN BOX POLAROID 690 CAMERA NIB INSTANT	$325.00	SX-70 WHITE TAN EXCELLENT !!	
Polaroid 690, like sx-70 but better, as new, black AF	$295.00	POLAROID 600- 5 TWIN PACKS (100 SHOTS) 09/04 dating	$34.53
Polaroid 600SE 600 SE w/ Mamiya 127mm Lens	$255.01	Vintage Polaroid SX-70 Land Camera	$34.50
Polaroid Daylab II System w/ 3.25 x 4.25 base	$231.49	POLAROID CU-5 LAND CAMERA W/ HOOD N.R.	$34.33
Polaroid Instant Film Type 55 - pack of 20	$215.00	POLAROID SX-70 SONAR ONE STEP + CASE	$34.33
[10 of these sold in a multiple item ("Dutch") auction for $21.50 each]		VINTAGE SX-70 POLAROID LAND CAMERA WITH CASE	$34.00
POLAROID SLR 680 SE AUTOFOCUS LAND CAMERA MINT NR	$195.50	Black Polaroid SX 70 Sonar Onestep Land Camera	$33.80
Polaroid Portrait Kit #591 for 180 Land camera	$182.50	POLAROID 600- 5 TWIN PACKS (100 SHOTS) 09/04 dating	$33.00
Polaroid 195 Camera with Close-up accessory, No Reserve	$175.00	Vintage polaroid SX-70 Land camera ALPHA & leather case	$33.00
120/220 Rollfilm Back for Polaroid 600SE 600 SE Mamiya	$171.50	Polariod Camera SX - 70 Model 2	$32.55
Polaroid Instant Film Type 59 - pack of 20	$170.00	Polaroid SX-70 Land Camera Excellent Used Cond.	$32.55
[10 of these sold in a multiple item ("Dutch") auction for $17.00 each]		Polaroid SX-70 SX70 land camera SLR in working cond!	$32.50
polaroid instant passport & ID Camera not noritsu fuji	$162.50	Polaroid SX-70 Land Camera SONAR OneStep	$32.50
POLAROID 203 MINI PORTRAIT PASSPORT CAMERA	$160.25	Polaroid SX-70 Chrome with leather Case, needs help	$32.00

Film Cameras ▶ Movie

The average sales price in this subcategory is $156.72.

	HIGH		AVG
wilart 35mm Hand Crank Movie Camera With Cases & Tripod	$4,200.00	Kinoptik Apochromat lens	$760.00
Arriflex 16 BL Outfit w/ Angenieux 12-120mm Lens EXLNT	$4,050.00	ARRI 35 BL I , II - PL mount adapter , Arriflex	$750.00
Wescam Gyro-Stabilized Camera Mount Gyro	$3,383.00	KINOR CX-2M (16mm) MOTION PICTURE CAMERA (in USA)	$710.00
Worrel Geared Head Perfect Condition Suit Arriflex	$2,500.00	Angenieux 5.9mm lens for Arri Arriflex 16 SR PL	$700.00
Eclair NPR 16mm Camera Package with Glass, great shape.	$2,300.00	Zeiss 12mm Mk I Superspeed, Aaton mount, NRII	$670.00
Arriflex 16 mm Motion Picture Camera Package	$2,200.00	Bolex Rex 5 Camera w/ Motor and 400ft Magazine and Case	$646.23
16mm Movie Camera ECLAIR NPR Crystal Sync #1	$1,888.88	Chrosziel mattebox with adapter to Eclair ACL I camera	$630.00
GlideCam V-8 Movie/Video Camera Stabilization System	$1,750.00	Arriflex SR Eyepeice Adjustable Bracketry, Excellent	$99.00
Zeiss 11.5-115mm Super-16 Zoom Lens for Arri SR	$1,500.00	ARRIFLEX 35MM 2B/2C VARIABLE SPEED MOTOR	$99.00
Ken Lab KS-6 Gyro	$1,400.00	KRASNOGORSK-3 Russian 16mm Movie Camera	$96.00
Richter EMP camera not Arriflex,Aaton	$1,025.00	WOODEN TRIPOD LEGS - MINI TRIPOD LEGS	$96.00
Arriflex "M" 16mm Underwater Motion Picture Camera Set	$1,025.00	5x5 matte box for film cameras arri... others	$96.00
Arri (Arriflex)15mm 4"x 4" Studio Matte Box Kit w/Case	$1,000.00	THREE 100 Foot Rolls 16mm Kodachrome 25 Daylight Film	$92.56
Ronford Baker Heavy Duty Moy Legs Suit Arriflex	$1,000.00	ARRI/ARRIFLEX 1:3.4 SOM BERTHIOT ZOOM FOR 16 MM CAMERA!	$92.11
Ronford Baker Small Heavy Duty Moy Legs Suit Arriflex	$921.77	ARRIFLEX 35mm ARRITECHNO FILMCASSETTE AS NEW!!!!	$92.00

Film Processing & Darkroom ▶ Chemistry

The average sales price in this subcategory is $25.45.

	HIGH		AVG
Palladium Chloride ACS pure Photo 25g	$265.00	Potassium Iodide - ? lb !!!	$30.00
[4 of these sold for $265.00 each]		Potassium Iodide - ? lb !!!	$28.00
Palladium Chloride ACS pure Photo 25g	$245.00	DARKROOM CHEMICALS LOT	$28.00
ILFORD Ilfochrome / Cibachrome P-30 P30 Chemistry	$200.00	FIXER DEKTOL KODAK HC-110 NEW	
[10 of these sold in a multiple item ("Dutch") auction for $20.00 each]		Two boxes of Photographers Formulary #130 paper dev.	$27.76
Palladium Chloride ACS pure Photo 10g	$129.00	Metol (1 lb) + Hydroquinone (1 lb) - BARGAIN !!!	$27.00
Modern developer assortment 620051	$84.00	[2 of these sold for $27.00 each]	
P-Benzoquinone - Photograde ? kg !!!	$71.00	HUSTLER RAPID BATH HYPO CLEAR-16oz. SHIPPING DISCOUNTS!	$26.97
Palladium Chloride ACS pure Photo 5g	$70.00	[3 of these sold in a multiple item ("Dutch") auction for $8.99 each]	
P-Benzoquinone - Photograde ? kg !!!	$69.00	FUJI-HUNT COLOR FILM DEVELOPMENT STABLIZER	$26.00
Case of Kodak Fixer powder	$67.53	RA-4 Fresh Color Printing Kit - 6.5 Litres !!!	$25.60
KODAK T-MAX DEVELOPER! 1 Gal. - SHIPPING DISCOUNTS!	$66.50	4 liter Kit for C-41 Process, Color Film	$25.00
[7 of these sold in a multiple item ("Dutch") auction for $9.50 each]		Metol (1 lb) + Hydroquinone (1 lb) - BARGAIN !!!	$25.00
P-Benzoquinone - Photograde 500G	$65.00	Chemistry assortment 616051	$24.26
Palladium Chloride - 5 grams	$65.00	P30 PROCESSING KIT + MISC. ILFORD PAPER + inst. manual	$23.05
99.9% GOLD CHLORIDE for photo toner/glass/ceramics 3g	$62.50	(2) E-6 Chrome Dev. Kits, 500 ml by AGFA !!!	$23.00
99.9% GOLD CHLORIDE for photo toner/glass/ceramics 3g	$57.00	Chemistry assortment 617053	$22.26
Basic Darkroom equipment and chemistry	$56.00	C-41 / 1 gallon Developing Kit - BARGAIN !!!	$21.50

Film Processing & Darkroom ▶ Enlargement Equip. & Supplies

The average sales price in this subcategory is $105.59.

	HIGH		AVG
Beseler 8x10 MXT/ Aristo VCL 8100 Variable Head	$2,700.00	Beseler Enlarger & Photo Darkroom Equipment ***NR	$118.50
Beseler 23C II XL 23CII 23 C Ultra Complete Darkroom!	$1,425.00	Immaculate Durst 606 B&W/Color Enlarger- 35mm - 7X7	$112.55
SAUNDERS LPL 4 X5 COLOR ENLARGER OUTFIT	$1,375.99	OMEGA B-600 ENLARGER + BOGEN	$112.50
Beseler 23 II C XL Enlarger and Complete Darkroom Lot	$1,125.00	ENLARGER, + TONS OF EQUIP!	
Beseler 45V-XL Enlarger Motorized Chassis	$989.99	SALTHILL 11 X 14 5 BLADED PROFESSIONAL ENLARGING EASEL	$110.18
LEICA LEITZ FOCOMAT V35 ENLARGER WITH 40/2.8 FOCOTAR	$930.00	MINT LEITZ WETZLAR VALOY II ENLARGER,FOCOTAR LENS,LEICA	$106.27
Omega Enlarger, Enlargers, ProLab, D6, Lenses, Timer NR	$900.00	OMEGA C-700 ENLARGER C700 w/ 50mm Rodenstock & more!	$105.00
[3 of these sold in a multiple item ("Dutch") auction for $300.00 each]		PHOTO ENLARGER	$104.00
Beseler Universal Colorhead 45 MCRX enlarger & acc.	$900.00	Beseler 23c II Enlarger like new	$103.75
Durst 2200 8x10 Horizontal Enlarger, NO Reserve!!!!!!!!	$800.00	Darkroom Equipment Bundle	$103.50
COMPLETE DARKROOM w/Beseler 23CIII-XL, LOTS OF EXTRAS!	$711.00	OMEGA B22 Enlarger Photography Darkroom Lens & Board	$102.50
Leica V35 Auto-Focus 35mm Enlarger–No Reserve	$695.00	OMEGA SUPER CHROMEGA D DICHROIC PS COMPLETE!	$102.50
Saunders 4x5 Color Enlarger	$655.00	New and Unused Beseler Cadet II Enlarger w/ Xtras	$102.50
Omega D5 Enlarger w/Ilford 500H VC Head and Controller	$611.50	Durst 606 Enlarger Motorized+CopyLights Lens Easel MORE	$102.00
Leitz Focomat V 35 Autofocus Enlarger Includes Lens	$600.00	Beseler Darkroom Enlarger	$100.00
Saunders Super Dichroic 4500-II Enlarger w LENS & more	$600.00	OMEGA C700 ENLARGER WITH DICHROIC HEAD	$100.00

Film Processing & Darkroom ▶ Hardware, Lighting & Setup

The average sales price in this subcategory is $25.23.

	HIGH		AVG
Seal 210 Commercial Dry Mount Drymount Press 23"x18.5"	$355.00	Beseler Audible Repeating Enlarging Timer	$26.00
$14000 50 HX603/ Thorn 120v Clear Bulbs in a Box NR	$237.50	GRA-LAB Universal Timer Model 171 Mint Condition	$26.00
SAUNDERS 16x20 4 BLADED FOUR BLADE ENLARGING EASEL	$167.51	VINTAGE KODAK MODEL A DARKROOM	$26.00
BESELER HONEYWELL OMEGA KODAK CAMERA DARKROOM SETUP	$146.50	LAMP SAFELIGHT NEW! NIB	
$14000 50 HX603/ Thorn 120v Clear Bulbs in a Box NR	$143.50	GRALAB 450 DIGITAL DARKROOM TIMER	$26.00
SAUNDERS/LPL DIGITAL ENLARGING TIMER ET-500 LIKE NEW	$137.50	Graylab model 300 very nice darkroom timer	$26.00
NUARC VACUUM TABLE PHOTO LAB PROJECT SCANNER ENLARGER	$131.47	3 YANKEE DARKROOM SAFE LIGHTS W/FILTERS - LIKE NEW	$25.99
- Saunders Universal 11x14 4 Bladed easel. NIB	$127.50	GraLab Darkroom Timer Model 300 *NO RESERVE*	$25.00
BESELER DIGI-TIMER LIKE NEW WITH FOOT SWITCH	$126.50	Gra Lab Darkroom Timer	$25.00

	HIGH		AVG
ZONE 6 COMPENSATING TIMER	$122.50	Gra lab photo timer model 300 dark room timer clock	$24.99
ELC 250W 24V GE HALOGEN LIGHT BULBS-NIB	$120.80	Logan Desktop Light Box	$24.95
[20 of these sold in a multiple item ("Dutch") auction for $6.04 each]		Darkroom Timer by Gra-Lab - No Reserve	$24.95
Versalab "PARALLEL" laser alignment tool	$120.00	GRALAB DARKROOM TIMER- IN EXCELLENT CONDITION!	$24.50
Automated Temperature control unit. Water regulator	$114.52	Kearsarge 201 Electronic Darkroom Timer w/ 452 pedal	$24.49
DAYLAB 300 ENLARGER PROCESSOR CAMERA PHOTOGRAPHY FILM	$103.50	Gra Lab Darkroom Timer Model 300 with Buzzer (Used)	$24.00
Durst COLOLAMP Durst CLS 2000 Enlarger Quarts Lamp	$99.95	Kodak Darkroom Safelight 5 1/2" + OC Filter	$24.00

Film Processing & Darkroom ▶ Photographic Paper

The average sales price in this subcategory is $23.47.

	HIGH		AVG
Sony DCR PC105 HandyCam Mini-DV	$400.00	2 BOXES 100 SHEETS 8X10" KODAK PANALURE RC PHOTO PAPER	$24.95
Kodak Polycontrast IV RC F B/W Paper 50 pks x 25 sheets	$245.00	5 BOXES 10 SH. 16X20" KODAK POLYMAX II RC PHOTO PAPER	$24.95
Kodak Polycontrast IV RC F B/W Paper 50 pks x 25 sheets	$235.00	100 Sheets Kodak Polymax II RC 8x10 N Semimatte	$24.95
1000 sheets Ilford RC Multigrade IV Paper - No Reserve	$210.27	50 Sheets Kodak Polycontrast IV RC 11x14 F Glossy	$24.95
Ilfochrome (Cibachrome) paper 16x20 Medium Contrast	$177.50	Lot of 4 Canon Photo Paper Plus Glossy 50 Sheet 4x6	$24.53
KODAK PRO AZO RC 5X7, N2M Semimatt,100 sheet Exp01/06	$160.00	Kodak Polycontrast III RC F (Glossy) 25 sheet/PK, 8x10	$23.96
[2 of these sold in a multiple item ("Dutch") auction for $80.00 each]		[4 of these sold in a multiple item ("Dutch") auction for $5.99 each]	
Ilfochrome (Cibachrome) paper 16x20 High Contrast	$157.50	P30 PROCESSING KIT + MISC. ILFORD PAPER + inst. manual	$23.05
Kodak Professional Porta III Endura Paper.3.2" x 577	$156.00	Kodak Panalure Select RC 8x10 paper 250 ct - no reserve	$23.05
[8 of these sold in a multiple item ("Dutch") auction for $19.50 each]		Kodak Endura Professional Black & White Paper	$22.86
Expired fortezo 16 X 20 glossy paper	$150.00	Kodak Ektatherm Print Paper	$22.50
250 ILFORD MULTIGRADE 4 FIBER PAPER , 100 MULTIGRADE RC	$148.01	KODAK POLYCONTRAST 111 RC	$22.50
3 BOXES OF KODAK KODABROME II RC 8X10 PHOTO PAPER	$129.95	PROFESSIONAL PAPER 250 SHEETS	
Ilfochrome (Cibachrome) paper 16x20 Med Contrast Pearl	$127.50	Ilford MGIV Multigrade IV Photographic Paper MG4RC44M	$22.45
2 Rolls Kodak Royal Generations Photo Paper Matt	$127.50	(3) ROLLS MINILAB PHOTO PAPER FUJI KONICA DIGITAL NR!	$22.25
12 Rolls Fuji Paper Roll 5 inch by 575 Feet Photo Paper	$120.00	Kodak Kadobrome II RC paper 20x24 50 ct. No reserve	$22.17
** BRAND NEW Kodak Ektatherm 6800 6R Print Kit **	$120.00	Kodak Contrast Process ortho Paper 4x5 100 ct No rsrv	$22.07

Lenses & Filters

The average sales price in this subcategory is $54.04.

	HIGH		AVG
Contax Carl Zeiss 21mm 2.8 Distagon Lens	$4,200.00	Voigtlander Ultramatic & Bessamatic 2x Converter & acc.	$59.00
Leica Leicaflex SL Body - 4 Lenses -Fitted Leather Case	$1,100.00	500mm & 1000mm F8 Macro T-Mount Mirror Lens *NR*	$57.70
Sonnar 135/3.5 Zeiss M42 lens for PENTACON SUPER	$560.00	VIVITAR TELEPHOTO LENS 800mm IN CASE ~NICE!	$56.61
Alpa Retrofocus Angenieux R 11 28mm 3.5 Very Nice	$535.00	New Konica Hexanon 200mm F4 Lens *No Reserve*	$56.60
GORGEOUS STEINHEIL MACRO LENS for EXAKTA- NO RESERVE!!!	$481.67	Praktica MTL 5, Pentacon 1.8/50 lens, Vivitar 1:3.5/200	$56.00
Carl Zeiss 85mm f1.4 Planar Lens	$443.88	Nikon 200mm F.4 Nikkor Tele Lens	$56.00
Schneider Alpa Xenon 80 mm f1.2 lens fits Alpa 7 NR	$420.00	Steinheil Cassaron 40/3.5 lens for Exakta or Exa	$53.00
Exakta Zeiss Biotar 75mm f1.5 Lens THE BEST EXC+++	$369.95	400mm f6.3 Komura lens NEW in box with case - NR	$52.11
Tamron SP AF 28-105/f2.8 LD AF IF zoom lens Nikon Mount	$350.00	Canon Zoom Lens FD 70- 210mm with Skylight	$52.00
800mm f11 Vivitar Ser 1 Catadioptric T-Mount	$349.00	Fujica STX-1 35mm camera with 300mm Tamron SP Lens	$51.50
Kamerabau-anstalt Kilfitt 40 mm f3.5 macro lens Alpa NR	$326.50	400mm Promaster Telephoto Lens with Fujica STX-1 mount	$51.50
TAMRON SP CAMERA LENS 200 500 ZOOM 1:5.6	$306.03	5 Lens Minolta 28mm Canon 50mm Fish Eye 70 210 + MORE	$51.00
KONICA HEXANON VARIFOCAL F2.8 35-100MM	$306.00	Flektogon 35/2.8 lens for Exakta Exa	$51.00
Zeiss Chrome Biotar 75/1.5 for Exakta - Very Nice -	$305.00	Tamron 500mm f8 Nikon Minolta Pentax Canon Olympus	$51.00
MC Flektogon 2.8/20mm Zeiss lens for M42 Camera	$305.00	Vivitar 600mm Telephoto Lens	$51.00

Lighting & Studio Equipment ▶ Background Material & Equip.

The average sales price in this subcategory is $30.24.

	HIGH		AVG
AMVONA MUSLIN PHOTO BACKGROUND BACKDROP NEW	$184.50	JTL BACKGROUND & LIGHT SUPPORT FOR MUSLIN OR CANVAS	$32.01
SCENIC MUSLIN PHOTO BACKGROUND BACKDROP NEW	$183.50	AMVONA MUSLIN PHOTO BACKGROUND BACKDROP NEW	$31.59
AMVONA MUSLIN PHOTO BACKGROUND BACKDROP NEW	$170.50	AMVONA MUSLIN PHOTO BACKGROUND BACKDROP NEW	$31.55
AMVONA MUSLIN PHOTO BACKGROUND BACKDROP NEW	$156.26	6x9 Muslin Backdrop A102- New Background	$31.01
3x Chain Drive Background Set with Backdrop - New	$155.99	AMVONA MUSLIN PHOTO BACKGROUND BACKDROP NEW	$31.00
10X20 Studio Photography BACKDROP Muslin BACKGROUND	$152.50	10 ft x 15 ft JET BLACK MUSLIN BACKGROUND - NEW NR #W	$31.00
[2 of these sold for $152.50 each]		6x9 Muslin Backdrop W088 - New Background	$30.38
10X20 Photography BACKDROP Muslin Photo BACKGROUND	$147.50	ADJUSTABLE POSING STOOL With	$30.25
10X20 SILVERLAKE Backdrop Muslin Photo BACKGROUND	$142.50	PADDED SEAT *** NEW *** NR	
B&B 10x18 handpainted scenic muslin backdrop/background	$139.00	3x Chain Drive Background Set with Backdrop - New	$30.21
ADJUSTABLE SAVAGE POSING STOOL & TABLE NEW NR	$137.50	AMVONA MUSLIN PHOTO BACKGROUND BACKDROP NEW	$30.00
JP 10 x 20 ft SCENIC MUSLIN HAND-PAINTED BACKGROUND	$129.00	New 11x20 Photo Muslin Background Backdrop	$30.00
P.W. 11 X 21 ft SCENIC MUSLIN PHOTO BACKDROP/BACKGROUND	$123.50	10x12' Super White Seamless Photography Backdrop Muslin	$29.50
B&B 10x18 handpainted scenic muslin backdrop/background	$119.00	3x Chain Drive Background Set with Backdrop - New	$29.50
9x18 Muslin Backdrop A102- New Background	$117.99	10 ft x 15 ft JET BLACK MUSLIN BACKGROUND - NEW NR #W	$29.00
[2 of these sold for $117.99 each]		5CD Set DIGITAL PHOTO	$27.99
AMVONA SCENIC MUSLIN PHOTO BACKGROUND BACKDROP NEW	$109.49	BACKDROPS Photography Backgrounds	

Lighting & Studio Equipment ▶ Light Controls & Modifiers

The average sales price in this subcategory is $20.73.

	HIGH		AVG
Broncolor Satellite Reflector	$610.00	5 in 1 MULTI REFLECTOR LIGHT DISC 42" (110cm) NEW	$21.99
LITESTAGE MODEL 1600 Digital Photo Soft Light Box	$495.00	Larson Relectasol Square QC 42"	$21.50
Norman Tri-Lite: Optical Focusing Spotlight	$379.95	5 in 1 MULTI LIGHT REFLECTOR FLAG KIT 36 x 48 NEW	$21.50
Norman P800-D Power Pack w/LH 2000 Lamphead w/Fan	$250.00	5 in 1 Multi Reflecting Panel (40"x60") - NEW	$21.50
Norman 200C Outfit	$229.95	5 in 1 MULTI REFLECTOR LIGHT	$20.95
SMITH VICTOR KT900 3-500 WATT 3-Light Kit - Opened	$190.00	DISC LIGHTDISC 40 x 60 NEW	
LIGHT FX II LIGHT PAINTING SYSTEM, LIKE HOSEMASTER, NIB	$157.50	5 in 1 MULTI REFLECTOR LIGHT	$20.86
# 505541 Profoto Honeycomb Grid NEW	$149.99	DISC LIGHTDISC 36 x 48 NEW	
Profoto Narrow Beam Reflector	$127.50	5 in 1 MULTI REFLECTOR LIGHT	$20.74
WHITE BACKGROUND STUDIO	$119.99	DISC LIGHTDISC 32 NEW	
REFLECTOR PRODUCT PHOTOGRAPHY		5 in 1 Multi Reflector Disc (43") - NEW	$20.60
Bogen Lightform Windpanel P-22 Reflective White Fabric	$105.00	43" 5 in 1 Photo Light Disc Multi Reflector * NEW * NRI	$20.53
[5 of these sold in a multiple item ("Dutch") auction for $21.00 each]		5 in 1 MULTI REFLECTOR LIGHT DISC LIGHTDISC 36 x 48 NEW	$20.51
Norman P800-D Power Pack	$102.50	5 in 1 Multi Reflector Disc (43") - NEW	$20.51
Radio Slave Trigger kit for Studio Strobe hot shoe NEW	$100.50	43" Brand New Silver / Gold Reflector Disc.	$20.50
Radio Slave Trigger kit for Studio Strobe hot shoe NEW	$76.00	5 in 1 MULTI LIGHT REFLECTOR FLAG KIT 36 x 48 NEW	$20.50
Photoflex DL-1342WS Reflector - 42" Circular NEW	$74.00	Westcott Illuminator Reflector	$20.50
[2 of these sold in a multiple item ("Dutch") auction for $37.00 each]		5 in 1 MULTI REFLECTOR LIGHT DISC LIGHTDISC 36 x 48 NEW	$20.50

Lighting & Studio Equipment ▶ Portable Flash/Strobe

The average sales price in this subcategory is $81.15.

	HIGH		AVG
PORTABLE QUANTUM QFLASH	$910.00	Lumedyne 800 Watt Second Flash Head W/Long Coiled Cord	$90.09
X2 LIGHT STROBE W/ STAND		Samigon HALO-Light FRL-1 Fluorescent Ring Light	$89.99
Quantum T4D flash system almost new, warranty	$725.00	Norman LH2400 - 2400 Watt/Second Lamphead Flash	$84.99
Norman 200B portable strobe OUTFIT lots of EXTRAS NoRes	$660.00	PENTAX AF 280T TTL FLASHGUN Like New	$84.99
Lumedyne 067X 400w/s System – NR	$610.00	70mm Film Loader - Daylight ALDEN Bulk Film Loader	$84.99
Quantum Qflash T2 Camera flash w/Turbo battery	$520.00	Ring Light Macro Flash Minolta Maxxum i-series	$84.00
NEW QUANTUM Q-FLASH MODEL T4d, GREAT PRICE! NO RESERVE!	$485.00	Minolta A1 A2 7Hi 7i MACRO RING FLASH 3 days	$84.00
Quantum Qflash T4d NEW IN BOX	$477.00	Ring Light Macro Flash Minolta Maxxum i-series	$84.00
Elinchrom 500 EL500 Mono Photorgraphic Strobe Lighting	$461.00	Sunpak Auto 383 Super Thyristor Stobe non-dedicated	$83.11
Lumedyne Portable 244 Strobe System Cheap	$455.00	Nikon F90 N6006 N8008 N50 N60 N75 N90 MACRO RING FLASH	$81.50
dynalight studio set	$455.00	[3 of these sold for $81.50 each]	
Quantum Qflash T2D w/ Turbo battery	$450.00	Cool Lux Mini Lights - 2 complete units + extras	$77.01
TWO White Lightning Ultra 600 monolight strobe units	$443.25	Nice Sunpak Auto 522 Thyristor Flash Outfit LOOK!!	$77.00
QUANTUM Qflash Model T2 DIGITAL Camera flash Turbo Z	$441.00	Minolta Maxxum 3500xi Flash (7,9,7D,7xi,9xi,700si,800si	$76.95
Novatron PRO Portable Light Studio-Flash,Power Pack+ NR	$410.99	Quantum Battery 1+ w/ Charger & Original Box	$76.00
Elinchrom 500 EL500 Mono Photographic Strobe Lighting	$405.00	Lumedyne Flash Misc. Lot	$76.00

Lighting & Studio Equipment ▶ Props & Stage Equipment

The average sales price in this subcategory is $29.79.

	HIGH		AVG
Off The Wall Productions Mediterranean Studio Set	$2,500.00	NEW Ocean Mermaid Sea Shell Photo Photography Prop	$31.00
PHOTO PROPS OFF THE WALL- ROOMSIZE PORTABLE	$999.02	CUTE Photography Prop BUBBLES!!!	$31.00
Odessey 13' Aluminum circular lighting truss	$800.00	NEW Black HAND SHAPED Chair RETRO PoP 70s 60's FUN NRI	$31.00
OUTDOOR BRIDGE SET (OFF THE WALL)	$400.00	SPLIT LOG SWING * INDOOR / GARDEN OUTDOOR PHOTO PROP	$31.00
(2)Stage Lights NEW CONDITION source 4 750/50	$325.00	RICH MAPLE Studio Photography Backdrop, Photo Prop SALE	$30.96
Speedotron 8" Fresnesl Spot Flash Head	$306.01	22 black turtle neck shirts.	$30.76
FOG/SMOKE MACHINE ROSCO 1500 W/REMOTE CONTROL,	$215.00	Vintage Kliegel Bros. 2000 W Theater Follow Spot Light	$29.99
White Empire Columns & Four Balaster Balustrade	$202.50	Professional Infant/Baby Poser for Photography Studio	$29.99
Scenic Canvas Photo Background/Backdrop Used	$200.00	Studio Photography Photo Prop Children Posing Ladder	$29.59
10X20 Hand Painted BACKDROP Muslin BACKGROUND	$178.99	Childrens WHITE Studio Photography Backdrop Background	$29.45
10X20 Hand Painted BACKDROP Muslin BACKGROUND	$163.50	Photo prop child photography stage equipment chef pot	$29.00
Colortran Lee 6" 1KW Fresnel Stage Light & Barn Doors	$163.50	Photo Studio Prop 5" SPIKE STRETCH PATENT Dancer BOOTS	$29.00
10X20 Photography BACKDROP Muslin Photo BACKGROUND	$152.50	Childs Posing Bench Studio Photography Childrens Poser	$28.02
10X20 SILVERLAKE Backdrop Muslin Photo BACKGROUND	$142.50	Infant Baby Poser Photography Studio Posing Prop	$28.00
Colortran Lee 6" 1KW Fresnel Stage Light & Barn Doors	$140.27	SMALL MUSHROOM PROP BROWN	$27.99

Manuals, Guides & Books ▶ Camera Manuals

The average sales price in this subcategory is $8.92.

	HIGH		AVG
The Sinar System Handbook Plus Many Extras!	$66.00	Exakta RTL 1000 brochure original	$8.99
VOIGTLANDER GUIDE/BOOK VITO II & III, VITESSA, PROMINENT	$39.99	Canon Super 8 Zoom 518 318 movie cam manual original	$8.99
Original Photo Manual - Mamiya RB67 Lenses	$35.99	Bell Howell Specialist Filmosound 550 Projector manual	$8.99
Polaroid SX-70 Camera Repair Manual	$34.90	Original Photo Manual - Minolta X-570	$8.99
Contax,Zeiss,N1 Camera Color Brochure.Nice!	$33.00	[2 of these sold for $8.99 each]	
SONY CYBER- SHOT DSC-F707 CAMERA INSTRUCTION MANUAL	$29.50	Fuji F700 Instruction Owner's Manual & Software "New"	$8.95
Minox B Original Instruction Book	$25.00	Mamiya C3 Professional Instruction Manual	$8.90
ROLLEI ROLLEIFLEX SL66 CAMERA INSTRUCTION MANUAL BOOK	$24.99	Pentacon Six TL, Pentacon 6 TL (Praktisix) Inst. Manual	$8.90
Bronica S-2, Bronica C Repair Manual	$24.90	Rollei Rolleiflex 3.5F 2.8F 120-220 Instruction Manual	$8.90
Contax,Zeiss System Handbook for Contax	$22.00	Yashica MAT-124 Camera Instruction Manual, multi-lang.	$8.90
ORIGINAL MAMIYA SEKOR 1000DTL	$22.00	Mamiya C33 Professional Instruction Manual	$8.90
SERIES INSTRUCTION MANUAL		Mamiya M645 Super, Mamiya 645 Super Instruction Manual	$8.90

Contax,Zeiss System Handbook for Contax	$21.50	Novoflex Follow Focus Lens Instruction Manual	$8.90
SONY CYBER-SHOT DSC-P32 P52 P72 CAMERA MANUAL GUIDE	$20.50	Rollei Rolleiflex SL66 Instruction Manual	$8.90
ORIGINAL MAMIYA C330 INSTRUCTION MANUAL	$20.00	Mamiya 645 Pro TL, M645 Pro TL Instruction Manual	$8.90
ORIGINAL MAMIYA 645 M645 1000S INSTRUCTION MANUAL	$20.00	Rollei Rolleiflex SL66 Instruction Manual	$8.90

Manuals, Guides & Books ▸ How-To, Guides & Techniques

The average sales price in this subcategory is $13.21.

	HIGH		AVG
The Texture Screen by William Mortensen photo book	$179.09	Print Finishing by William Mortensen; a classic	$14.90
Craig Worshams Directing Commercials Seminar on DVD	$139.99	MAGIC LANTERN GUIDE BOOK	$14.50
Denis Reggie~6 Wedding Photography Videos~Complete Set	$138.49	FOR METZ FLASH SYSTEMS! NR!	
NYIP New York Institute of Photography VHS Tapes	$136.51	CREATIVE LANDSCAPE PHOTOGRAPHY by Benvie $ 29.95	$13.95
20 PORTRAIT and WEDDING PHOTOGRAPHY VHS TAPES	$120.27	3 PRO Glamour Nude Modeling Posing Guide Cards Poses	$13.50
NYIP New York Institute of Photography Course	$88.01	Athletes...Photographs...1860 to 1986	$13.49
10X20 High Key White Muslin PHOTO BACKGROUND	$86.00	Child's Play by JEFF LUBIN- Photography Video VHS	$13.45
6'6X9 Hand Painted BACKDROP Muslin BACKGROUND	$80.00	Professional Techniques for Digital Wedding Photography	$13.00
12 courses photography portrait studio lighting tips	$79.90	Johnny Stewart Wildlife Photographers Kit Varmint Call	$12.99
[2 of these sold in a multiple item ("Dutch") auction for $39.95 each]		Couples by Joyce Wilson - Photography Video VHS	$12.95
12 photography portrait studio lighting courses on CD	$79.90	Families by Joyce Wilson - Photography Video VHS	$12.95
[2 of these sold in a multiple item ("Dutch") auction for $39.95 each]		DIGITAL PHOTOGRAPHER'S HANDBOOK	$12.50
PHOTOVISION PHOTOGRAPHY 6 DVDs VOL 6	$76.99	Camera & Darkroom Photo Magazine (1994-95) 17 issues NR	$12.49
10X20 High Key White Muslin PHOTO BACKGROUND	$76.33	LOT OF TECHNICAL PHOTOGRAPHY	$12.49
A Day with Monte Zucker - 4 Photography Videos - VHS	$73.00	BOOKS WEDDING & MORE	
Charles Lewis - Professional Portraiture - VHS Tapes	$69.75	Pinhole Photography: Rediscovering a Historic Technique	$12.00
13 years of Zone VI Newsletters in a Zone VI Binder	$67.66	Innovative Techniques for Wedding Photography. N.R.I	$12.00

Photo Albums & Archive Items ▸ Archival & Mounting Materials

The average sales price in this subcategory is $23.76.

	HIGH		AVG
Fletcher 2100 Professional Mat Cutter 48"	$633.98	NEW PRINT FILE ARCHIVAL PRESERVER 600 PAGES 120-4B NR	$31.99
Seal Jumbo 150 Dry Mount / Laminating Press	$406.00	Print File Archival Preservers 45-8P	$31.50
Seal 200 commercial dry mount press. 16x20 format	$367.00	[9 of these sold in a multiple item ("Dutch") auction for $3.50 each]	
Seal 16 x 19 Jumbo 150 Dry Mount Mounting Press	$260.00	TAP Photo Folders PF-16 Assorted	$25.49
MOUNTING,LAMINATING &	$178.50	(500) 11x14 CLEAR SAVAGE POLY-VU SLEEVES	$25.00
TEXTURING PAPER~GREAT DEAL..		50 - 10M LETTER Laminator/LAMINATING POUCH NR	$22.50
NEW Black USB 6" LCD Digital Picture Photo Frame Viewer	$169.99	10-4Packs of Savage 16x20 Cut Size Mat Board 15404/1502	$22.05
NEW Black USB 6" LCD Digital Picture Photo Frame Viewer	$167.49	Optical Glass Proof Sheet Contact Printer by Print File	$21.72
NEW Black USB 6" LCD Digital Picture Photo Frame Viewer	$159.99	CREATIVE MEMORIES - Custom Cutting System Mat & Blades	$21.50
Wess Plastics Glass Slide mounts	$112.50	Logan Portable Light Box for slide viewing	$20.51
Pakon Slide Mounter and Imprinter	$99.99	MARSHALL'S Photo Coloring System-$65+ retail value!NEW!	$20.40

Photo Albums & Archive Items ▸ Photo Albums

The average sales price in this subcategory is $8.64.

	HIGH		AVG
TAKESHI KANESHIRO PHOTO ALBUM WITH VCD - NEW RELEASE!!!	$142.50	Talking Pictures photo album from Sharper Image	$9.25
fotos de vitor (DEGO) 1987 -2000	$100.00	Wedding Ring Bearers pillow, cake knife and photo album	$8.99
2845X SONY DIGITAL PHOTO FRAME PHD-A55	$78.77	New! Life Magazine Photo Album New! Glamourous	$8.99
3D-Album PicturePro Platinum 3.1 - Photo Software	$74.95	Lot of New Photo Albums HENZO 35 pgs 70 sides(2pcs.)	$8.95
3D-Album PicturePro Platinum 3.1 - Photo Software	$74.95	Sharper Image: Talking Pictures Photo Album NEW	$8.95
96 RED, BLUE, GREEN PHOTO ALBUMS LIQUIDATION! LOT!	$71.88	School Memories Keepsake Book	$8.72
3 NEW ITOYA 13x19 ART PORTFOLIO PRESENTATION DISPLAY	$56.95	Photo Album -Beautiful beaded with butterfly	$8.72
Bichon Decorated Photo Album	$56.00	10 Pioneer Panoramic Photo Albums, 4x12 Size	$8.57
8 Pioneer Photo Albums Full Size Memo Pocket Album	$50.43	SNUGGLE BUGS BABY'S FIRST PHOTO ALBUM BABY PICTURES	$8.50
PHOTOGRAPH ALBUM - circa 1910 BERGEN LINE NORWAY	$50.00	New Talking Photo Album ***holds 24 photos***	$8.50
COACH SOHO STRIPE PHOTO ID WALLET ALBUM CASE	$45.00	*FLEX PAGE* POST BOUND BINDER PHOTO ALBUM *180 PICS*	$8.28
NEW IN BOX! CEIVA DIGITAL PHOTO FRAME ALBUM CAMERA NR	$42.00	PHOTO ALBUM HALLMARK SAILBOATS	$8.01
Lightware soft portfolio case 11X14	$31.04	New pink flower photo album holds 200 pictures	$7.99
Photo Album 4 x 6 for 36 photos, Wholesale Lot 45 Girls	$31.00	PIONEER DIGITAL ACID-FREE CD PHOTO ALBUM - BRAND NEW	$7.99
Personalized Graduation Tassel Frame for 5x7 Photo NR	$30.95	New in Box Hallmark Stories Scrapbook Album Leopard	$7.99

Printers, Scanners & Supplies ▸ Photo Printers

The average sales price in this subcategory is $138.28.

	HIGH		AVG
Digital Photo Printing Kiosk - Pixel Magic 250	$6,117.00	*BRAND NEW* Canon CP-330 Compact Photo Printer	$142.50
Unused Fujifilm Pictrography 4500 Digital Color Printer	$3,600.00	Brand New Epson PictureMate Digital Photo Printer	$142.50
Fuji PrintPix Digital NC 1000	$2,550.00	Epson PictureMate Picture Mate Personal Photo Lab bonus	$142.50
Fuji Printpix NC-1000 Printer with IC-1000 Controller	$2,499.99	Epson Picture Mate personal photo lab. New in box	$142.50
Epson 4800 BRAND NEW with $150.00 gift for you!	$1,739.00	EPSON PICTUREMATE PHOTO PRINTER - NEW IN BOX	$142.50
Fujifilm Pictrography 4500 Digital Color Printer	$1,726.00	KODAK PRINTER DOCK 4000 Easyshare CX DX CAMERA PRINTER	$142.00
FARGO DTC515 ID card Printer with dual hopper	$1,525.00	EPSON PICTUREMATE PHOTO LAB BRAND NEW IN UN-OPENED BOX	$137.50
EPSON STYLUS PRO 4000, EPSON 4000	$1,475.00	*BRAND NEW* Canon CP-330 Compact Photo Printer	$137.50
Epson Stylus Pro 4000 Printer - LNIB	$1,445.00	NEW CANON PIXMA iP5000 PHOTO PRINTER -TOP PRODUCT/DEAL!	$137.50
EPSON STYLUS PRO 4000 PHOTO PRINTER, NEW WITH A $300 REBATE	$1,335.55	NEW CANON PIXMA iP5000 PHOTO PRINTER -TOP PRODUCT/DEAL!	$137.50
Roland Metaza Metal Photo Printer	$1,300.00	Canon Pixma iP6000D Photo Printer NEW IN BOX	$133.50
EPSON STYLUS PRO 4000	$1,225.00	NIB EPSON PICTUREMATE PHOTO PRINTER "NO RESERVE"	$132.51
Epson Stylus Pro 4000	$1,099.00	Epson Picturemate NIB USA 1st Generation	$132.50

Epson Stylus Pro 4000 Inkjet Printer	$1,000.00	NEW CANON PIXMA iP5000 PHOTO PRINTER -TOP PRODUCT/DEAL!	$132.50
Epson Stylus Pro4000	$899.00	EPSON PictureMate 4x6 Photo Printer	$130.06

Printers, Scanners & Supplies ▸ Printing Software & Supplies

The average sales price in this subcategory is $20.19.

	HIGH		AVG
(10) KODAK PH-40 PRINTER DOCK PAPER CASE FACTORY SEALED	$183.88	NEW KODAK PH-40 KIT PRINTER DOCK PHOTO PAPER CARTRIDGE	$20.50
Kodak Printer Dock Paper Kit PH40 4000 6000 Case of 10	$180.00	Kodak EasyShare PH40 Color Cartridge & Paper Kit PH-40	$20.50
Kodak Printer Dock Paper Kit PH40 4000 6000 Case of 10	$178.50	Genuine Canon Photo Paper Plus Glossy 4x6 120sheets NEW	$20.50
Kodak Printer Dock Paper Kit PH40 4000 6000 Case of 10	$177.50	2 PCKS KODAK HIGH GLOSS PHOTO PAPER 4x6 INKJET PRINTER	$20.05
(10) KODAK PH-40 PRINTER DOCK PAPER CASE FACTORY SEALED	$177.50	2 PCKS KODAK HIGH GLOSS PHOTO PAPER 4x6 INKJET PRINTER	$20.00
10 units (1 case) KODAK PH-40 CARTRIDGE & PHOTO PAPER	$152.50	NEW KODAK PH-40 Color Cartridge & Paper Kit PH-40	$20.00
(10) Kodak PH-40 Printer Dock media, Easy share paper	$152.50	420 SHEETS OF 4"X6" QUALITY, GLOSSY INKJET PHOTO PAPER	$20.00
Case of Kodak EasyShare printer dock Paper w/cartridge	$112.49	HP 4 / 100 SHEET 4X6 INKJET PHOTO PAPER SEMI-GLOSS	$20.00
PH-40 Kodak EasyShare Kit Cartridge & Paper 4x6 PH40	$108.00	NEW Kodak Picture Photo Paper 200 Sheet 4x6 High Gloss	$19.99
[6 of these sold for $108.00 each]		Kodak Premium Photo Paper 250 sheets–2 pk. of 125	$19.99
Case of Kodak EasyShare printer dock Paper w/cartridge	$105.00	NEW KODAK PH-40 KIT PRINTER	$19.91
[9 of these sold for $105.00 each]		DOCK PHOTO PAPER CARTRIDGE	
Case of Kodak EasyShare printer dock Paper w/cartridge	$100.00	NEW KODAK PH-40 PH-40 PRINTER	$19.90
[2 of these sold for $100.00 each]		DOCK PHOTO PAPER CARTRIDGE	
600 HP Premium Plus glossy photo paper 4 x 6 *	$96.00	[3 of these sold for $19.90 each]	
Kodak PH40 Media Kit for Printer Docks 4000/6000/plus,	$86.45	100 4x6 CANON PHOTO PAPER	$19.50
[5 of these sold in a multiple item ("Dutch") auction for $17.29 each]		PLUS GLOSSY 100 SHEETS NEW NR	
KODAK PH-40 COLOR CARTRIDGE & PHOTO PAPER KIT - 4 UNITS	$76.03	NEW KODAK PH-40 KIT PRINTER DOCK PHOTO PAPER CARTRIDGE	$19.01
KODAK PH-40 COLOR CARTRIDGE & PHOTO PAPER KIT - 4 UNITS	$75.01	KONICA INKJET PHOTO PAPER SPECIAL 4 PACK MIX	$19.00

Printers, Scanners & Supplies ▸ Scanners

The average sales price in this subcategory is $337.84.

	HIGH		AVG
Imacon Flextight 848 Scanner Mint	$10,150.00	SONY UY-S90 FILM SCANNER clean-nice shape-pro gear NR!	$355.00
Imacon FlexTight Precision II Drum Scanner 646 848 949	$4,550.00	Nikon LS-2000 SCSI Flim Scanner w/ SF-200 Auto Feed	$350.01
IMACON FLEXTIGHT PRECISION II DRUM SCANNER	$3,280.00	Nikon Coolscan IV ED (LS-40) Pro 35mm Film Scanner	$346.05
Professional Imacon Photo film Scanner, Exc, NR, boxes	$2,375.17	Nikon Coolscan IV ED, 2900 dpi, 35mm, Film Scanner	$345.78
Nikon Super Coolscan 9000 ED Scanner LS-9000 NEW USA	$1,999.95	Nikon Film Scanner LS-2000	$344.50
Nikon Super Coolscan 9000 Scanner LS-9000 USA 1yr Warr.	$1,875.01	Nikon Coolscan IV ED 2900 dpi 35mm Film Photo Scanner	$339.00
[2 of these sold for $1,875.00 each]		Nikon Slide Feeder SF-210 Coolscan SF210 4000 / 5000	$338.00
Nikon Super Coolscan 9000 Scanner LS-9000 USA 1yr Warr.	$1,871.00	[10 of these sold for $338.00 each]	
Nikon Super Coolscan 9000 Scanner LS-9000 USA 1yr Warr.	$1,825.01	Nikon Coolscan IV ED (LS-40) Film Scanner	$336.31
Nikon Super Coolscan 9000 Scanner LS-9000 USA 1yr Warr.	$1,805.89	Minolta Dimage Scan Elite II Film Scanner 2 5400	$330.21
Nikon Super Coolscan 9000 Scanner LS-9000 USA 1yr Warr.	$1,801.51	Nikon Coolscan IV ED (LS-40) - NO RESERVE!	$330.00
Nikon Super Coolscan 9000 Scanner LS-9000 USA 1yr Warr.	$1,801.01	Nikon Slide Feeder SF-210 Coolscan SF210 4000 / 5000	$329.95
Nikon Super Coolscan 9000 Scanner LS-9000 USA 1yr Warr.	$1,800.00	Minolta Dimage Scan Elite 5400 slide scanner	$325.00
[2 of these sold for $1,800.00 each]		Nikon Coolscan IV ED (LS-40) Film Scanner - Like New!	$325.00
Nikon Super Coolscan 9000 Scanner LS-9000 USA 1yr Warr.	$1,776.00	Pakon Impak F 12 Scanner System Film Processing	$315.00
Nikon Super Coolscan 9000 Scanner LS-9000 USA 1yr Warr.	$1,775.59	Nikon SF 200 (S) slide feeder	$306.00
Nikon Super Coolscan 9000 Scanner LS-9000 USA 1yr Warr.	$1,775.00	for LS 4000 NO RESERVE	

Professional Video Equipment ▸ Cameras

The average sales price in this subcategory is $529.80.

	HIGH		AVG
Sony DXC-D50WSL 16:9/4:3 Digital Video Camcorder	$18,295.00	Panasonic AG-EZ1 3CCD NTSC Digital Video Camcorder	$680.00
Sony DSR 570 WSL/2 DVCAM Camcorder, Mini DV	$14,000.00	Frezzi HMI Sun Gun MA24	$679.00
Sony DXC-D50WSL Camera DXC-D50, DXC-D50L, DXC-D50WS	$12,500.00	2 Panasonic WV-D5000 HD System Cameras, WV-CR12,WV-PH10	$610.00
3 PNEUMATIC VIDEO CAMERA STUDIO PEDESTAL W/ VINTEN HEAD	$8,645.00	Fujinon 2/3" B4 Wide Angle Lens NO RESERVE	$600.00
SONY DSR-390L DSR-390 Brand New in Box Camera w/lens	$6,690.00	Hitachi HV-C10 3 CCD Camera 1 good one bad	$570.00
JVC DY-90WU Native 16x9 Uncompressed Video Camera	$6,100.00	Canon Pistol Servo Zoom Controller, Excellent Cond.	$515.76
SONY DSR-390L DVCAM 3-CCD WARRANTY + FREE NEW FUJI LENS	$5,999.00	Panasonic AG-LA7200 Widescreen Lens Adapter, AG-DVX100	$513.00
SONY HVRZ1U 3CCD 1080i HDV NTSC CAMCORDER Z-1U HVR-Z1U	$4,995.00	Canon ZSG-200M Zoom Servo Grip like new	$511.00
Sony DXC 637 Camera with PVV3 Beta SP Recorder	$4,950.00	JVC KY 25 3CCD	$510.00
Ikegami Editcam 2- DNS 201W	$4,851.00	SONY DXF-50 ELECTRONIC VIEWFINDER	$501.00
IKEGAMI HL-V55 HLV55 BETACAM SP CAMCORDER MUST SEE–NR	$4,595.45	Fujinon FMM-6B, (5) Video Camera Focus Blocks	$472.99
HVRZ1U Sony HVR-Z1U 1/3-Inch 3-CCD HDV DVCAM NEW	$4,500.00	Bogen tripod 3066	$465.00
Sony HVR-Z1 1/3" HDV High Definition Camcorder NEW Z1	$4,450.00	Century Wide-Angle Video Lens Converter (.8 W8XCV)	$456.00
HVRZ1U Sony HVR-Z1U 1/3-Inch 3-CCD HDV DVCAM NEW	$4,400.00	JVC GY-X3U SVHS Video Camera	$455.00
HVRZ1U Sony HVR-Z1U 1/3-Inch 3-CCD HDV DVCAM NEW	$4,350.00	Sony VX3 Hi8 NTSC 3CCD CCD Video Camera & 12X Zoom Lens	$455.00

Professional Video Equipment ▸ Editing, Post-Production

The average sales price in this subcategory is $306.46.

	HIGH		AVG
Avid Unity LANshare EX System-MirroringRAID Almost NEW!	$31,000.00	SONY EVO-9700 DUAL HI8 8MM	$345.54
RCA KU-3A Ribbon Microphone ku3a	$3,000.00	EDITING VCR EVO9700 Complete	
Avid Media Composer 9000 AVR-77	$2,500.00	Avid DV Express 3.5 PC or Mac	$332.00
DSC1024HD SONY DSC-1024HD) Digital Scan Converter NEW	$2,499.99	PANASONIC AU 650/ reduced price player recorder	$325.00
Panasonic DVCPro AJ-D455	$2,400.00	SONY PVM-411 QUAD MONITORS EXCELLENT CONDITION	$323.00
Sony DSR-40 DVCAM Recorder/Player	$2,300.00	MAGMA 7 slot PCI Expansion Chassis – Works Great! NR!	$307.51
Primera Bravo Pro CD/DVD Printer / Duplicator - NEW!	$2,190.00	QTY 7 UTAH SCIENTIFIC RACK MOUNT VIDEO CHASSIS NR!	$306.09

SONY 1024HD BRAND NEW 1024 HD digital scan converter	$2,000.00	Panasonic WJ-AVE5 Digital Video & Audio Mixer	$305.00
KONA2 AJA KONA 2 12 Bit HD Capture Card BRAND New	$1,750.00	AMPEX ADO 100 ~ Digital Special Effects System	$305.00
Pinnacle Targa 3000 Card NEW in Box	$1,600.00	Matrox RT2500 / RT 2500 with G450 - RealTime Editing	$305.00
Sony C-500 Condenser Microphones PAIR c500	$1,600.00	AVID XPRESS DV 3.5 EDITING PACKAGE	$305.00
Sony DSR 11 DV Cam VCR	$1,595.00	Win XP / Mac OSX NR	
Primera Bravo II CD/DVD Printer / Duplicator - NEW!	$1,526.00	Targa 2000 RTX w/ Breakout Box like New in box!	$300.00
Huge Systems HMV-900 RAID Drive/Atto UL4D SCSI Card	$1,500.00	Huge Production Music Library!!	$300.00
SONY UVW 1600 BETACAM SP FULL EDIT PLAYER	$1,499.00	Pinnacle Liquid Edition PRO 5.5 with Breakout Box NEW	$299.00
TEKTRONIX 528A 1420 NTSC	$1,489.00	CEL Electronics P156-2 PAL to NTSC Standards Converter	$287.00
WAVEFORM MONITOR & VECTORSCOPE		Scan Do Pro Convertor	$283.78

Professional Video Equipment ▶ Recorders & Players

The average sales price in this subcategory is $485.77.

	HIGH		AVG
¡30 sdi Sony J-30SDI Compact Betacam Series Player New	$11,000.00	SONY CCD-V5000 Hi-8 Professional Video Camera Recorder	$520.00
SONY J30 SDI "brand new" in sealed box	$9,100.00	Sony SVP-5600 S-VHS Player	$515.00
JVC Professional D9 Video Recorder VTR	$5,100.00	Videonics FireStore FS-1 !!!	$510.00
Sony DXC 637 Camera with PVV3 Beta SP Recorder	$4,950.00	JVC HR-DVS3U MINI DV VHS DUAL PLAYER	$510.00
CHYRON INFINIT SCRIBE 2 CHANNEL W/601 VIDEO EXCELLENT	$4,221.00	Sony BVW-60 BetacamSP Player	$500.00
Panasonic AJ D950 DVCPRO50 VTR - DVC PRO AJD950	$4,000.00	SONY UVW 1200 RGB BETACAM SP VIDEO CASSETTE PLAYER	$499.00
Panasonic AJD 90 DVCPRO 50 Dockable VTR	$3,999.00	Videonics FireStore FS-1 !!!	$485.00
Betacam SX dockable recorder - Sony DNV-5	$3,900.00	RTS SYSTEMS MODEL 802 MASTER STATION W/GOOSENECK MIC	$468.00
SONY BVW70 Betacam SP edit recorder BVW 70	$3,900.00	JVC BR-DV3000 DV/Mini-DV Professional VTR Deck	$455.00
SONY DSR-70 DV CAM NTSC VIDEO CASSETTE RECORDER PLAYER	$3,850.00	SONY GV-D800 Digital Video Walkman Player / Recorder	$427.00
Sound Devices 744T 4-Channel Portable HD Recorder NEW!	$3,650.00	PANASONIC AG 1980 SVHS DESKTOP EDITOR VCR #1	$425.00
Sony UVW-1800 Betacam SP Video Cassette Recorder	$3,600.00	TEKTRONIX 1740 NTSC WAVEFORM VECTOR R-Y MONITOR EXCELLE	$423.00
SONY DSR 1500 DVCAM DV DVCPRO all in one DSR1500	$3,295.00	SONY EVV-9000 Hi8 CAMERA DOCKABLE VTR "NEW"	$414.00
SONY UVW 1400A Betacam SP recorder Low hours UVW1400A	$3,150.00	RTS SYSTEMS MODEL 802A-B3 MASTER STATION W/GOOSE MIC	$408.00
Sony BVW-75 Beta SP Broadcast Editor Four Channel Audio	$2,999.00	SONY GVD200 Digital8 8mm hi8 video player/recorder	$405.00

Projection Equipment ▶ Accessories

The average sales price in this subcategory is $52.93.

	HIGH		AVG
{Lot of 350+) Assorted Projection Lamps, 75w to 410w	$510.00	Sharp BQC-XGNV5XB/1 XG-NV5XB lamp unit LCD new	$58.68
Projection lamps Lot of 410	$472.00	GE Sylvania Assorted Slide Projector Lamps - 36 Bulbs	$58.00
PE "Cermax" Y1502 500W Xenon lamp - projector	$350.00	Infocus Replacement Bulb x350	$57.53
Panasonic ET-LA097NW (TWIN PACK) Projector Lamps (NEW	$345.00	10 EVD PROJECTOR LAMP BULB FOR	$56.95
New In Box InFocus LP340/350 Replacement Lamp	$335.00	3M APOLLO DUKANE KODAK +	
INFOCUS 340/350 REPLACEMENT BULB	$325.00	NEW IN BOX IN FOCUS LAMP-L25	$56.03
Sony LCD Projector Lamp LMP-P201	$325.00	IN FOCUS LITE PRO BULB (BRAND NEW)	$54.53
SHARP BQC - XVH37U//1 PROJECTOR LAMP LCD BRAND NEW UNIT	$306.00	LOT 33 SYLVANIA GE APOLLO DYS DYV BHC PROJECTION BULBS	$53.00
Sharp LCD projector lamp XG-NV6XU XV-DW100U bulb only	$295.00	PROJECTOR LAMPS - 150-W 120-V 4 unit in package Sylva	$51.00
[2 of these sold for $295.00 each]		~~ 46 LAMP LOT; ELC,EYK,EHA,FAL,DRA,FCS,FCR,ELE/ELT ~~	$51.00
LCD projector lamp Sharp XG-P10XU XG-V10XU bulb only	$295.00	Lot of 24 GE EJL PROJECTION LAMP 24V 200W MR-16 BULB NR	$49.99
NEC LT60LPK lamp for LT220 LT240 LT260 HT1000 NEW	$293.00	18 ENX PROJECTOR LAMP BULB FOR 3M APOLLO DUKANE ELMO +	$49.00
SHARP BQC - XVH37U//1 PROJECTOR LAMP LCD BRAND NEW UNIT	$291.00	2 Slide Projector Zoom Lenses KODAK	$48.50
NEC LT60LPK lamp for LT220 LT240 LT260 HT1000 NEW	$290.00	NEW IN BOX SANYO 5500 PROJECTION LAMP #PLC-LMP-12	$46.00
LCD lamp Sanyo PLC-XP17N XP18N XP20N XP21N bulb only	$280.00	LOT of 46 BSK PROJECTOR EXCITER LAMP BULBS NOS	$46.00
New Sharp LCD Projector Lamp BQC-PGC30XU/1 NEW IN BOX !	$269.99	?POA-LMP05 Projector Lamp Bulb? Proxima sanyo Eiki GE	$46.00

Projection Equipment ▶ Projectors

The average sales price in this subcategory is $89.13.

	HIGH		AVG
Westar/CFEC 105X 35mm Projection System NEW UNUSED!	$2,295.00	BELL & HOWELL Dual 8mm & Super 8 film PROJECTOR perfect	$99.00
Edison Home Kinetoscope silent movie projector not 35mm	$1,975.00	KODAK KEYSTONE DUAL SUPER 8 MM AND 8MM MOVIE PROJECTOR	$96.00
GOKO TC-302 R8 OVERHAULED @GOKO SERVICE IN NY	$1,525.00	KODAK EKTASOUND MODEL 285 MOVIEDECK FOR 8MM FILM	$95.00
Hitachi CP-X445 XGA 3200 Lumen Projector NEW	$1,357.50	Bell & Howell 456 super 8/8mm movie projector	$94.89
SIMPLEX 35MM XL PROJECTOR HEAD,MODEL PR1003	$1,247.22	Bell & Howell Super 8/8mm Autoload Movie Projector 471A	$91.01
PATHEOGRAPH c1915 SILENT FILM PROJECTOR	$1,200.00	EUMIG 610 SUPER 8/8MM PROJECTOR- AUTO THREADER	$89.88
Infocus LP600 business projector	$1,100.00	BELL & HOWELL DUAL AUTLOAD SUPER 8 8MM MOVIE PROJECTOR	$86.00
OPTOMA DIGITAL VIDEO PROJECTOR	$1,056.00	KODAK INSTAMTIC DUAL SUPER 8 MM AND 8MM MOVIE PROJECTOR	$85.00
2300 LUMENS HDTV NEW NR		GAF ANSCOVISION DUAL 8 Automatic Projector Super 8 8mm	$82.00
Hughes JVC D360SC Ultimate Projector Home Theatre	$1,000.00	Movie Projector Kodak Instamatic Super 8 & 8 mm	$81.00
Beaulieu 708EL Capstan Drive Super 8MM Projector	$988.69	KODAK KEYSTONE DUAL SUPER 8 MM	$79.97
Optoma H31	$910.00	AND 8MM MOVIE PROJECTOR	
CFEC/WESTAR 105 35mm Movie Projector Unused!	$801.00	Chinon 727 Whisper Dual 8mm Varible Speed Projector	$79.00
Epson Powerlite 730c Projector	$761.00	GAF 2788-Z Dual 8mm Super 8 Film Movie Projector	$78.00
Eiki Powerhouse One LC - X2 Projector Multimedia	$740.00	BELL AND HOWELL DUAL 8 WITH VARIABLE SPEED*MINT**	$77.00
HP vp6111 Digital Projector	$700.00	KODAK SOUND 8 MOVIE PROJECTOR Add Sound to 8mm Movies!	$76.00

Tripods, Monopods ▶ Monopods

The average sales price in this subcategory is $46.66.

	HIGH		AVG
VariZoom Flow Pod Ultimate Kit VZ-FP	$320.00	DYNATRAN PRO MONOPOD KIT W/BALL GRIP HEAD & CASE NEW	$49.00
LIKE NEW monopod GITZO CARBON FIBRE G1568	$152.50	[2 of these sold for $49.00 each]	
Regal Arkay Mono Studio Camera Stand w/ Geared Head	$149.00	72" MONOPOD 3WAY PAN HEAD QUICK RELEASE PLATE LEG	$49.00

[2 of these sold for $149.00 each]		DYNATRAN PRO MONOPOD KIT W/BALL GRIP HEAD & CASE NEW	$48.00
DYNATRAN PRO MONOPOD KIT W/BALL GRIP HEAD & CASE NEW	$129.00	Giottos Professional Monopod 5 section with case New	$47.88
PROFESSIONAL CAMERA TRIPOD KIT BALL GRIP HEAD & MONOPOD	$127.50	[2 of these sold for $47.88 each]	
[2 of these sold for $127.50 each]		CARBON FIBER MAGNESIUM ALLOY MONOPOD BALL HEAD NEW	$47.65
PROFESSIONAL CAMERA TRIPOD KIT BALL GRIP HEAD & MONOPOD	$127.49	DYNATRAN PRO MONOPOD KIT W/BALL GRIP HEAD & CASE NEW	$47.00
PROFESSIONAL CAMERA TRIPOD KIT BALL GRIP HEAD & MONOPOD	$122.50	74" SUPER LIGHTWEIGHT CARBON FIBER MONOPOD acfm	$46.99
UNI-LOC DuoPod pro MONOPOD Manfrotto #136 Fluid Head!	$122.50	DYNATRAN PRO MONOPOD KIT W/ BALL GRIP HEAD & CASE NEW	$45.12
PROFESSIONAL CAMERA TRIPOD KIT BALL GRIP HEAD & MONOPOD	$122.50	SLIK EZ-POD MONOPOD>>>NEVER USED!!!!!	$45.00
BOGEN 3249B MONOPOD, 361 BRACE,	$122.50	DYNATRAN PRO MONOPOD KIT W/ BALL GRIP HEAD & CASE NEW	$45.00
3292 POD, 3009 HEAD		PRO Monopod + Bag like Gitzo. New!	$44.99
CARBON FIBER MAGNESIUM ALLOY MONOPOD BALL HEAD NEW	$117.50	CARBON FIBER MAGNESIUM ALLOY MONOPOD BALL HEAD NEW	$44.05
PROFESSIONAL CAMERA TRIPOD KIT BALL GRIP HEAD & MONOPOD	$117.00	DYNATRAN PRO MONOPOD KIT W/BALL GRIP HEAD & CASE NEW	$44.01
Giottos MM 8970 3-Section Pro Carbon Fiber Monopod	$116.95	DYNATRAN PRO MONOPOD KIT W/BALL GRIP HEAD & CASE NEW	$44.00
Giottos MM 8970 3-Section Pro Carbon Fiber Monopod	$116.95	DYNATRAN PRO MONOPOD KIT W/BALL GRIP HEAD & CASE NEW	$43.00

Tripods, Monopods ▶ Tripods

The average sales price in this subcategory is $56.50.

	HIGH		AVG
O'Connor 35 tripod with a O'Connor 515 fluid head &Case	$1,125.00	QuickSet Camera Video Tripod - No Reserve	$61.00
VINTEN Vision 5 Fluid Head, Tripod, Spreader, Carry Bag	$1,025.99	PROFESSIONAL CAMERA TRIPOD KIT BALL GRIP HEAD NEW (858)	$61.00
BOGEN MANFROTTO 3191 Tripod &	$665.00	[2 of these sold for $61.00 each]	
3066 Video Head + Adapter		PROFESSIONAL CAMERA TRIPOD KIT 3 WAY PAN TILT HEAD NEW	$61.00
Bogen Manfrotto PRO Video Tripod w/Head,Bag Kit NEW!	$659.99	PROFESSIONAL CAMERA TRIPOD KIT 3 WAY PAN TILT HEAD NEW	$59.00
Miller 20 Fluid Head Tripod	$469.00	Sony VCT-D680RM Remote Control Tripod - NEW NR	$58.00
Gitzo G 2227 w/ Gitzo Ballhead 1277M & RRS Quickrelease	$425.00	PROFESSIONAL CAMERA TRIPOD KIT BALL GRIP HEAD NEW (828)	$57.55
Nikon F100 Mint condition - Body + original accessories	$425.00	SONY VCT-870RM 64" Photo / Video Tripod	$56.00
Sachtler 150mm Tripod, for Video 25, 30 or big Vinten	$399.00	PROFESSIONAL CAMERA TRIPOD KIT 3 WAY PAN TILT HEAD NEW	$55.00
O'CONNOR MODEL 50 FLUID HEAD TRIPOD (Nice Condition!)	$365.00	Velbon MAXi 347E Digital Tripod - NEW	$54.95
Bogen tripod 3051 with 3066 Head	$350.00	Bogen Manfrotto 3001 Tripod with Bogen #141 Head -NR-	$54.13
Gitzo G1128 MK2 carbon fiber tripod	$320.00	Wooden Camera Tripod U.S. Army Air Corps OLD/RARE/NEAT!	$54.01
Giottos MT-8170 Carbon Fiber Tripod BETTER THAN GITZO	$319.00	ANTIQUE BRASS TRIPOD FOR WW 2 RANGE FINDER	$53.99
Tripod: Bogen Manfrotto 3433 501 Fluid Head, 3001 Legs	$270.75	PROFESSIONAL CAMERA TRIPOD KIT 3 WAY PAN TILT HEAD NEW	$53.50
Professional Fluid Action Miller Head w/ Wooden Tripod	$256.50	PROFESSIONAL CAMERA TRIPOD KIT 3 WAY PAN HEAD NEW	$53.44
Manfrotto Bogen 4443D Carbon Tripod[not Gitzo]	$238.00	PROFESSIONAL CAMERA TRIPOD KIT 3 WAY PAN TILT HEAD NEW	$53.00

Vintage ▶ Accessories

The average sales price in this subcategory is $17.38.

	HIGH		AVG
Graflex , Crown Graphic camera outfit	$377.77	Fujica Leica 39MM - M42 Mount L —RARE—	$18.60
Carl Ziess 35mm Lens w/ Orig. Holder	$375.00	Leica 39mm MACRO Tubes	$18.50
Nikon F2 Photomic - Nice!	$199.99	Release transmission set for Exa Exakta	$18.50
NIKON F EYE-LEVEL PRISM - MINT ! no reserve	$187.50	FLASH BULBS #5B graflex other press cameras 24 BULBS	$18.50
Graflex 3 Cell Flash Handle for Star Wars Lightsaber	$178.50	Three Zeiss Ikon Contax 42mm Filters	$18.50
EXTREMELY RARE TOPCON METER for 35-L CAMERA	$152.50	Vivitar 130LX Meter	$18.27
Accurapid Wind film advance for Leica IIIc IIIf IIIg	$152.50	Fresnel focusing screen for Exa Exakta split image	$18.25
VIVITAR & MINOLTA BELLOWS FOCUS RAILS	$123.58	Leather Case for Early Canon Rangefinder Camera	$16.75
7 Vintage Camera Lenses-Old-Ilex Lense-Slide In-Optical	$113.61	STAR WARS LIGHT SABER - VINTAGE HEILAND SHUTTER WAND	$16.50
Westinghouse #5 flash bulbs	$112.05	Vintage 8" GE Mazda Foil #75 FlashBulb	$16.50
Pentacon 100/2.8 portrait lens for Exakta RTL	$102.50	OLD KATANA REFLEX 300MM F5.6 LENS (#19)	$16.05
Stereo Realist Red Button Viewer in Original Box	$92.00	Tin Kodak film canisters - 9	$15.75
Ernst Leitz Wetzlar Camera Acc. (f-stop pic previewer?)	$90.00	Rolleiflex Rolleicord 16 On Kit Cased	$15.62
Carl Ziess 85mm Lens w/ Holder	$89.00	FLASH BULBS #6 graflex other press cameras 24 BULBS	$15.50
Rare 5.8cm f1.4 Nikkor; The First Nikon F Normal Lens!	$89.00	Walz Self Timer For Rollei -type cameras w/ box & inst.	$15.50

Vintage ▶ Cameras

The average sales price in this subcategory is $86.31.

	HIGH		AVG
VERY NICE TAXIPHOTE 45 X 107	$2,235.00	STEREO 3D CAMERA & VIEWERS INSTRUCTION BOOKS	$89.00
Simon Wing New Gem 19th Century multi image wood camera	$1,599.00	ART DECO HANEEL TRIVISION CAMERA TRIVISION VIEWER FILM	$89.00
Contura 35mm Stereo Camera	$1,569.00	Very Nice Kodak Stereo Camera w/Case F3.5 Lens	$89.00
RARE 1800'S FRENCH FLOORSTANDING STEREOVIEWER	$1,250.00	REALIST STEREO CAMERA + BOOK + F FILTERS ILEX 3.5 LENS	$87.50
Boxed Widelux F7	$1,005.00	EX Kodak Kodaslide Stereo Viewer II w/Box & Slide AC/DC	$86.99
Stereo Viewer Educa French masterpiece	$865.00	Optineta, Meopta Czechoslovakia camera	$86.25
Custom Yashica Stereo camera	$799.99	Kodak #2 Stereo Wood Box Camera	$86.00
Viewmaster Camera, Cutter, Projector, mounts & viewer	$731.99	2005-06 McKeown's Cameras 12th Edition Guide	$86.00
Busch Verascope F40 - Fine French Stereo Camera 7p	$650.00	SPUTNIK LIKE?NEW RARE TLR STEREO RUSSIAN CAMERA	$86.00
ANSCO Camera w/ Universal Synchro 12" Lens & Case ++	$540.01	Vintage TOWER 35MM Stereo Camera Outfit and Rare Case	$86.00
Blair Stereo Hawk-Eye Camera	$500.00	Brumberger Stereo 3 D Viewer & 16 BSA, Ariel Cards 1953	$85.00
Excellent Busch f40 Verascope stereo camera -No reserve	$465.00	Kodak Stereo Camera with Field Case and Filters	$85.00
Museum Quality Conley Box Stereo Camera- Just aboutNEW	$450.00	Desirable ILEX Stereo REALIST by DrT - No reserve!	$84.00
WOLLENSAK 10 STEREO 35MM CAMERA CASE AND INSTRUCTIONS	$400.00	RARE VINTAGE MINIATURE CAMERA GOLDEN RICOH "16" & CASE	$82.00
Busch Verascope F40 -Rare stereo camera-Jules Richard	$399.00	Stereo Realist 35mm Camera by David White	$81.95

8

CARS, PARTS & VEHICLES (EBAY MOTORS)

The seed that became eBay Motors was planted in 1998 when eBay employee Simon Rothman was looking for a die-cast toy Ferrari and found a real Ferrari nestled within eBay's search results.[1] It turned out that there were many used cars being traded on eBay, even though there was no formal category for them at the time. (Indeed, many "meta," aka top-level, eBay categories are started when they grow organically from within the other eBay categories and it becomes clear they've earned a top slot of their own.)

eBay Motors was launched in April 2000, and today it's one of the most popular categories on the site, where an automobile sells every minute. Although some people might have cringed several years ago at the idea of buying a car online, some services and information eBay Motors offers takes a lot of the risk out of the transaction: certified vehicle inspections, vehicle history reports, and even a Financing Center. And eBay's own feedback system may be the most powerful tool for eBayers to use when vetting a potential buyer or seller.

Although there are still no guarantees something may not go wrong, the benefits to selling online are clear: sellers can often get more than they would from a dealer for a trade-in, and buyers can find a bargain by bypassing the middleman. eBay also opens up the marketplace for individuals far beyond the traditional newspaper classified ad: one woman who got 1,000 hits on her son-in-law's 2002 car figured only about 30 people would have come to see the car if she'd tried to sell it locally.

---

[1] eBay, *The Chatter* (newsletter), June 2005.

From Sky-High to Down-to-Earth: Price Ranges

So what kind of wheels are on the site today, and what are they going for? Let's take a look. On the high end, you can find just about every type of luxury car, including BMWs, Ferraris, and Lamborghinis. Top-selling Lamborghinis here include a 1997 black VT with 1,941 miles that went for $178,950.00. (It was over $275,000.00 new, according to the seller, and "worth every penny.")

One of the highest-priced BMWs included a 2004 7 Series 760Li that went for $75,200.00. This fits within the dealer retail range of $56,000.00 to $92,867.00 given for that year and model at resale car information site Edmunds.com. Factors that helped this sedan fetch a healthy sales price include lots of good-quality photos of every angle of the car's exterior, and several of the interior as well. (In general, when selling a car or other big-ticket item, you should include a lot more photos than you would with something inexpensive.) The seller gave a complete listing of the vehicle's many features, and from the pictures you can tell the car is clean and has been well cared for. It's also a popular color, black, with gray interior.

Want to pick up a Beemer on the cheap? One buyer got a 1992 5 Series for $2,950.00. It had 194,800 miles but was in "near perfect" condition and came with all the service records from its "two discriminating owners." If you get much cheaper here, though, you may be looking at a car with some damage, as in the 1992 3 Series 318is that went for $1,125.00 and ran great, but the left side was damaged. If you're a car fixer-upper, one of those deals may be perfect for you. You can even buy the parts you need within the Parts & Accessories sub-category, where you can find motors, fenders, door panels, and a host of other automotive pieces.

What about more everyday vehicles? One of the most popular cars in the United States is the Toyota Camry. One of the highest-priced Camrys in this sample was a 2005 silver XLE with 4,375 miles that went for $19,500.00. Interest was white-hot in this vehicle, as there were 41 bids. The auction was chock-full of photos from every conceivable angle, including inside the trunk and the front of the stereo.

A Camry from the average range of Toyota prices was a 1998 LE model with one previous owner and 96,000 miles that sold for $5,375.00. (The Kelley Blue Book, at KBB.com, puts the retail price for a similar model with 79,000 miles at $7,685.00, and the trade-in value at $4,175.00, so this Camry appears to be a pretty good deal for both buyer and seller.)

But there's more than just cars in the eBay Motors area: you can also find other vehicles such as motorcycles and even airplanes. In fact, one of the most expensive items ever auctioned on eBay was a Grumman Gulfstream II jet that sold for $4.9 million. In this sample, the aircraft go from a high of $197,501.00 for a 2001 Cirrus SR-22 down to $202.50 for an Easy Riser Motorized Hang Glider.

Whatever wheels (or wings) you're into, eBay Motors is a robust and growing community and worth considering for buyers and sellers alike.

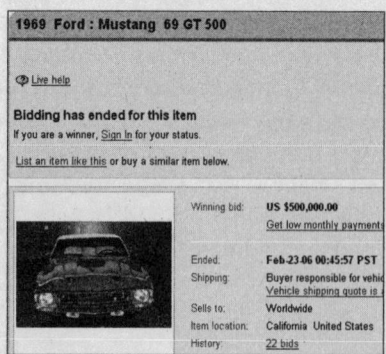

Passenger Vehicles ▶ Acura

The average sales price in this subcategory is $6,501.13.

	HIGH		AVG
Acura: : TL	$30,999.00	Acura: : Legend	$6,900.00
Acura: : TL	$28,900.00	Acura: : Legend	$6,900.00
Acura: : TL	$28,000.00	Acura: : Legend	$6,900.00
Acura: : TL	$27,700.00	Acura: : Integra	$6,699.00
Acura: : TL	$27,000.00	Acura: : Legend	$6,650.00
Acura: : CL	$19,105.00	Acura: : Integra	$6,600.00
Acura: : TL	$19,000.00	Acura: : Integra	$6,598.00
Acura: : RL	$18,950.00	Acura: : RL	$6,500.00
Acura: : RL	$18,600.00	Acura: : Integra	$6,500.00
Acura: : RL	$18,500.00	Acura: : TL	$6,500.00
Acura: : TL	$18,500.00	Acura: : Integra	$6,499.00
Acura: : TL	$18,000.00	Acura: : RL	$6,495.99
Acura: : TL	$17,995.00	Acura: : CL	$6,450.00
Acura: : TL	$17,950.00	Acura: : Legend	$6,450.00
Acura: : RL	$17,500.00	Acura: : Integra	$6,400.00

Passenger Vehicles ▶ BMW

The average sales price in this subcategory is $15,621.17.

	HIGH		AVG
BMW: 6-Series	$79,300.00	BMW: X-Series	$19,820.00
BMW: 6-Series	$77,000.00	BMW: 5-Series	$19,600.00
BMW: 7-Series	$75,200.00	BMW: Z3	$18,500.00
BMW: 7-Series	$73,601.00	BMW: 5-Series	$18,400.00
BMW: 7-Series	$68,651.00	BMW: 5-Series	$18,200.00
BMW: 6-Series	$62,500.00	BMW: 3-Series	$18,200.00
BMW: 3-Series	$53,300.00	BMW: 5-Series	$17,100.00
BMW: M-Series	$52,900.00	BMW: 7-Series	$17,000.00
BMW: M-Series	$52,888.00	BMW: 5-Series	$16,989.00
BMW: M-Series	$50,000.00	BMW: 7-Series	$16,500.00
BMW: M-Series	$49,800.00	BMW: 7-Series	$16,500.00
BMW: M-Series	$47,900.00	BMW: 3-Series	$16,101.00
BMW: 7-Series	$45,800.00	BMW: 5-Series	$15,995.00
BMW: 7-Series	$44,900.00	BMW: 3-Series	$15,990.00
BMW: 3-Series	$44,000.00	BMW: M-Series	$15,702.00

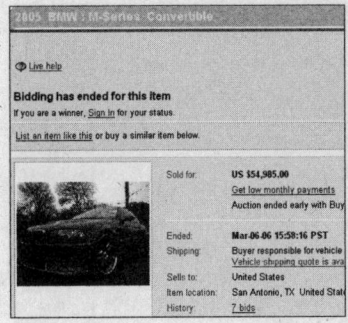

Passenger Vehicles ▶ Cadillac

The average sales price in this subcategory is $7,651.01.

	HIGH		AVG
Cadillac: Eldorado	$81,499.00	Cadillac: DeVille	$9,850.00
Cadillac: Escalade	$42,900.00	Cadillac: DeVille	$9,700.00
Cadillac: Escalade	$39,000.00	Cadillac: DeVille	$9,500.00
Cadillac: CTS	$36,480.00	Cadillac: Seville	$9,200.00
Cadillac: Escalade	$35,000.00	Cadillac: Allante	$8,750.00
Cadillac: Escalade	$34,900.00	Cadillac: Eldorado	$8,670.00
Cadillac: Escalade	$33,990.00	Cadillac: Seville	$8,500.00
Cadillac: Escalade	$33,900.00	Cadillac: DeVille	$8,125.00
Cadillac: Escalade	$30,600.00	[2 of these sold for $8,125.00 each]	
Cadillac: CTS	$30,500.00	Cadillac: DeVille	$8,100.00
Cadillac: Escalade	$29,300.00	Cadillac: Eldorado	$8,000.00
Cadillac: Seville	$28,688.08	Cadillac: Seville	$7,998.00
Cadillac: Escalade	$27,750.00	Cadillac: DeVille	$7,989.00
Cadillac: Escalade	$27,601.00	Cadillac: DeVille	$7,900.00
Cadillac: Escalade	$26,900.00	Cadillac: Allante	$7,800.00
		Cadillac	$7,600.00

Passenger Vehicles ▶ Chevrolet

The average sales price in this subcategory is $4,291.70.

	HIGH		AVG
Chevrolet: Other Pickups	$27,600.00	Chevrolet: El Camino	$5,000.00
Chevrolet: Other pickups	$26,900.00	[3 of these sold for $5,000.00 each]	
Chevrolet: El Camino	$23,100.00	Chevrolet: Other Pickups	$5,000.00
Chevrolet: El Camino	$19,900.00	Chevrolet: Other Pickups	$4,950.00
Chevrolet: Other Pickups	$19,000.00	Chevrolet: Other Pickups	$4,751.00
Chevrolet: Other Pickups	$18,800.00	Chevrolet: El Camino	$4,650.00
Chevrolet: Other Pickups	$17,500.00	Chevrolet: Other Pickups	$4,600.00
Chevrolet: El Camino	$17,000.00	Chevrolet: El Camino	$4,600.00
Chevrolet: Other Pickups	$16,500.00	Chevrolet: Other Pickups	$4,550.00
Chevrolet: El Camino	$15,975.00	Chevrolet: El Camino	$4,550.00
Chevrolet: Other Pickups	$15,600.00	Chevrolet: El Camino	$4,503.00
Chevrolet: Other Pickups	$15,300.00	Chevrolet: Blazer	$4,500.00
Chevrolet: Other Pickups	$15,000.00	Chevrolet: Other Pickups	$4,500.00
Chevrolet: El Camino	$14,700.00	Chevrolet: El Camino	$4,500.00
Chevrolet: Trailblazer	$14,699.00	Chevrolet: El Camino	$4,150.00
		Chevrolet: El Camino	$4,051.50

Passenger Vehicles ▸ Chrysler

The average sales price in this subcategory is $7,471.06.

	HIGH		AVG
Chrysler: 300 Series	$53,745.00	Chrysler: PT Cruiser	$8,600.00
Chrysler: 300 Series	$52,400.00	Chrysler: PT Cruiser	$8,500.00
Chrysler: 300 Series	$49,100.00	Chrysler: Town & Country	$8,448.61
Chrysler: Prowler	$34,100.00	Chrysler: PT Cruiser	$8,400.00
[2 of these sold for $34,100.00 each]		Chrysler: Sebring	$8,292.00
Chrysler: Prowler	$32,200.00	Chrysler: Sebring	$8,150.00
Chrysler: Prowler	$32,100.00	Chrysler: 300 Series	$8,101.10
Chrysler: 300 Series	$31,999.00	Chrysler: LHS	$8,077.44
Chrysler: Crossfire	$29,500.00	Chrysler: 300 Series	$8,000.00
Chrysler: 300 Series	$28,550.00	Chrysler: Town & Country	$8,000.00
Chrysler: Town & Country	$28,502.00	Chrysler: Sebring	$8,000.00
Chrysler: Crossfire	$26,840.00	Chrysler	$8,000.00
Chrysler: 300 Series	$25,000.00	Chrysler: Town & Country	$7,770.00
Chrysler: 300 Series	$24,800.00	Chrysler: PT Cruiser	$7,701.00
Chrysler: 300 Series	$24,600.00	Chrysler: Town & Country	$7,495.00
Chrysler: Crossfire	$23,995.00		

Passenger Vehicles ▸ Dodge

The average sales price in this subcategory is $8,510.52.

	HIGH		AVG
Dodge: Viper	$85,500.00	Dodge: Durango	$10,100.00
Dodge: Viper	$70,100.00	Dodge: Ram	$10,000.00
Dodge: Viper	$63,500.00	[2 of these sold for $10,000.00 each]	
Dodge: Viper	$60,001.00	Dodge: Ram	$9,900.00
Dodge: Viper	$45,300.00	Dodge: Ram	$9,875.00
Dodge: Viper	$44,500.00	Dodge: Ram	$9,750.00
Dodge: Grand Caravan	$34,800.00	Dodge: Coronet	$9,750.00
Dodge: Viper	$34,100.00	Dodge: Ram	$9,500.00
Dodge: Ram	$33,480.00	Dodge: Ram	$9,400.00
Dodge: Ram	$31,095.00	Dodge: Ram	$9,251.11
Dodge: Ram	$28,950.00	Dodge: Coronet	$9,200.00
Dodge: Charger	$27,900.00	Dodge: Ram	$9,000.00
Dodge: Viper	$27,100.00	Dodge: Durango	$8,800.00
Dodge: Ram	$26,902.00	Dodge: Dakota	$8,625.00
Dodge: Viper	$26,605.00	Dodge: Durango	$8,600.00
		Dodge: Ram	$8,500.00

Passenger Vehicles ▸ Ferrari

The average sales price in this subcategory is $107,426.01.

	HIGH		AVG
Ferrari : FXX SUPER ENZO New Ferrari FXX "Super Enzo" 1 of Only 20 for the World	$3,000,100.00	Ferrari: 360	$135,000.00
		[2 of these sold for $135,000.00 each]	
Ferrari	$1,085,000.00	Ferrari : 360 F1 Spider 2001 Ferrari 360	$132,500.00
Ferrari: Enzo	$820,500.00	F1 Spider **LOW RESERVE**	
Ferrari	$300,100.00	Ferrari: 360	$131,900.00
Ferrari	$253,000.00	Ferrari: 360	$123,100.00
Ferrari	$245,200.00	Ferrari: F430	$120,000.00
Ferrari	$225,100.00	Ferrari: 360	$115,888.00
Ferrari : 360 2005 FERRARI 360 SPYDER F1 FLY	$219,900.00	Ferrari: 360	$115,000.00
YELLOW LOOK @ PICS		Ferrari: 360	$105,002.00
Ferrari: 360	$219,500.00	Ferrari: Maranello 550	$94,999.00
Ferrari: 360	$215,000.00	Ferrari	$88,100.00
[2 of these sold for $215,000.00 each]		Ferrari: FERRARI F355 355 F1 SPIDER	$86,600.00
Ferrari: 360	$209,500.00	CONVERTIBLE	
[2 of these sold for $209,500.00 each]		Ferrari	$85,000.00
Ferrari: 360	$199,000.00	Ferrari	$82,100.00
Ferrari: 360	$173,500.00	Ferrari: 355	$80,100.00
Ferrari	$170,100.00	Ferrari: Ferrari	$76,100.00
Ferrari: 360	$167,500.00		

Passenger Vehicles ▸ Ford

The average sales price in this subcategory is $6,156.15.

	HIGH		AVG
Ford: Thunderbird	$38,600.00	Ford: Focus	$8,000.00
Ford: Excursion	$38,101.00	Ford: E-Series Van	$7,700.00
Ford: Escape	$33,815.00	Ford: Taurus	$7,500.00
Ford: F-350	$32,600.00	Ford: F-100	$7,500.00

Ford: F-150	$29,995.00	Ford: Ranger	$7,350.00
Ford: E-Series Van	$28,000.00	Ford: F-250	$7,100.00
Ford: Mustang	$26,999.00	Ford: Thunderbird	$7,051.01
Ford: Mustang	$26,000.00	Ford: Mustang	$7,000.00
Ford: F-350	$25,945.00	Ford: F-150	$6,851.09
Ford: Thunderbird	$24,600.00	Ford: Crown Victoria	$6,775.00
Ford: F-350	$24,101.00	Ford: E-Series Van	$6,600.00
Ford: F-350	$22,995.00	Ford: Mustang	$6,600.00
Ford: Mustang	$21,100.00	Ford: F-150	$6,500.00
Ford: F-350	$20,988.00	Ford: Explorer	$6,500.00
Ford: Mustang	$20,800.00	Ford: Windstar	$6,200.00

Passenger Vehicles ▶ Honda

The average sales price in this subcategory is $5,916.20.

	HIGH		AVG
Honda: Pilot	$27,900.00	Honda: Accord	$7,649.00
Honda: Accord	$27,130.00	Honda: CR-V	$7,600.00
Honda: S2000	$26,100.00	Honda: Civic	$7,500.00
Honda: S2000	$25,900.00	Honda: Accord	$7,490.00
Honda: S2000	$24,900.00	Honda: Accord	$7,401.00
Honda: S2000	$24,544.00	Honda: Accord	$7,345.00
Honda: S2000	$23,100.00	Honda: Accord	$7,150.25
Honda: Odyssey	$21,989.00	Honda: Civic	$7,100.00
Honda: Pilot	$21,900.00	[2 of these sold for $ 7,100.00 each]	
Honda: S2000	$20,100.00	Honda: Civic	$7,000.00
Honda: Element	$19,201.00	Honda: Accord	$7,000.00
Honda: Odyssey	$19,100.00	Honda: Accord	$6,900.00
Honda: Accord	$18,700.00	Honda: Accord	$6,800.00
Honda: Odyssey	$18,700.00	Honda: CRV	$6,700.00
Honda: Odyssey	$18,675.00	Honda: CRV	$6,302.99
		Honda: CRV	$6,250.00

Passenger Vehicles ▶ Hummer

The average sales price in this subcategory is $40,012.77.

	HIGH		AVG
Hummer: H1	$100,100.00	Hummer: H2	$45,000.00
Hummer: H1	$79,800.00	Hummer: H2	$44,477.00
Hummer: H1	$68,885.00	Hummer: H2	$44,000.00
Hummer: H1	$59,999.00	Hummer: H2	$42,000.00
Hummer: H1	$58,500.00	[2 of these sold for $42,000.00 each]	
Hummer: H1	$57,888.00	Hummer: H2	$42,000.00
Hummer: H1	$56,000.00	Hummer: H2	$41,899.98
Hummer: H2	$55,500.00	Hummer: H1	$41,500.00
Hummer: H1	$54,888.00	Hummer: H2	$41,000.00
Hummer: H2	$53,100.00	Hummer: H2	$41,000.00
Hummer: H2	$50,800.00	Hummer: H2	$40,999.00
Hummer: H2	$50,555.00	Hummer: H1	$40,900.00
Hummer: H1	$50,000.00	Hummer: H2	$40,500.00
[2 of these sold for $50,000.00 each]		Hummer: H2	$39,995.00
Hummer: H1	$49,900.00	Hummer: H2	$39,600.00
Hummer: H1	$49,500.00	Hummer: H2	$39,450.00

Passenger Vehicles ▶ Hyundai

The average sales price in this subcategory is $4,625.11.

	HIGH		AVG
Hyundai	$18,900.00	Hyundai: Tiburon	$5,995.00
Hyundai: Tiburon	$16,000.00	Hyundai: Tiburon	$5,888.00
Hyundai: Tucson	$15,500.00	Hyundai: Sonata	$5,800.00
Hyundai: Sonata	$14,900.00	Hyundai: Sonata	$5,800.00
Hyundai	$14,500.00	Hyundai: Accent	$5,695.00
Hyundai: Santa Fe	$14,000.00	Hyundai: Santa Fe	$5,600.00
Hyundai: Tiburon	$13,805.00	Hyundai: Elantra	$5,450.00
Hyundai: Santa Fe	$13,700.00	Hyundai: Elantra	$5,200.00
Hyundai: Sonata	$13,400.00	Hyundai: Sonata	$5,100.00
Hyundai: Santa Fe	$12,950.00	Hyundai: Elantra	$5,049.00
Hyundai: Tiburon	$12,700.00	Hyundai: Accent	$5,000.00
Hyundai: Sonata	$12,300.00	Hyundai: Elantra	$4,995.00
Hyundai: Sonata	$12,000.00	Hyundai: Elantra	$4,901.00
Hyundai: Santa Fe	$11,988.00	Hyundai: Tiburon	$4,700.00
Hyundai: Sonata	$11,100.00	Hyundai: Sonata	$4,650.00

Passenger Vehicles ▶ Infiniti

The average sales price in this subcategory is $12,575.24.

	HIGH		AVG
Infiniti: M45	$50,350.00	Infiniti: QX4	$16,100.00
Infiniti: QX56	$48,900.00	Infiniti: QX4	$15,501.01
Infiniti: QX 56	$43,100.01	Infiniti: QX4	$15,495.00
Infiniti: Q45	$42,000.00	Infiniti: G35	$15,400.00
Infiniti: Infinity QX56	$42,000.00	Infiniti: QX 56	$15,322.00
Infiniti: QX56 AWD	$41,900.00	Infiniti: QX4	$15,100.95
Infiniti: FX	$39,900.00	Infiniti: I30	$15,000.00
Infiniti: FX [	$33,900.00	Infiniti: QX4	$14,990.00
2 of these sold for $33,900.00 each]		Infiniti: QX4	$14,500.00
Infiniti: G35	$33,100.00	Infiniti: G20	$13,854.00
Infiniti: FX	$32,965.00	Infiniti: QX4	$13,800.00
Infiniti: G35	$32,900.00	Infiniti: QX4	$13,100.00
Infiniti: FX	$32,500.00	Infiniti: I30	$12,995.00
Infiniti: FX	$32,250.00	Infiniti: Q45	$12,950.00
Infiniti: FX	$31,999.99	Infiniti: QX4	$12,759.00
Infiniti: G35	$31,900.00		

Passenger Vehicles ▶ Jaguar

The average sales price in this subcategory is $11,870.72.

	HIGH		AVG
Jaguar	$92,777.00	Jaguar: E-Type	$13,500.00
Jaguar: XK8	$50,099.00	Jaguar: XJ8	$13,499.00
Jaguar: XK8	$49,051.00	Jaguar: XJ8	$13,495.00
Jaguar: XK8	$41,700.00	Jaguar: XJ	$13,401.00
Jaguar: XJR	$39,900.00	Jaguar: XJS	$13,350.00
Jaguar: E-Type	$38,211.00	Jaguar: Mark 2	$13,200.00
Jaguar: XK8	$34,950.00	Jaguar: XJS	$13,199.00
Jaguar: S-Type	$34,800.00	Jaguar: XJS	$13,100.00
Jaguar: E-Type	$33,600.00	Jaguar: XJ8	$13,000.00
Jaguar: S-Type	$32,500.00	Jaguar: XJ6	$13,000.00
Jaguar: XJR	$32,100.00	Jaguar	$12,999.00
Jaguar: E-Type	$30,000.00	Jaguar: XJS	$12,949.00
Jaguar: XK8	$29,988.00	Jaguar: XJS	$12,602.98
Jaguar: S-type	$28,985.00	Jaguar: E-Type	$12,600.00
Jaguar: XK8	$28,888.00	Jaguar: XJ	$12,100.00

Passenger Vehicles ▶ Jeep

The average sales price in this subcategory is $6,121.95.

	HIGH		AVG
Jeep: Wrangler	$28,358.53	Jeep: CJ	$6,850.00
Jeep: Wrangler	$28,000.00	Jeep: Wrangler	$6,801.00
Jeep: Grand Cherokee	$25,600.00	Jeep: Wrangler	$6,750.00
Jeep: Grand Cherokee	$24,500.00	Jeep: Grand Cherokee	$6,700.00
Jeep: Wrangler	$24,000.00	Jeep: Wrangler	$6,650.00
Jeep: Wrangler	$23,000.00	Jeep: Wrangler	$6,600.00
Jeep: Wrangler	$21,850.00	[2 of these sold for $6,600.00 each]	
Jeep: Grand Cherokee	$20,999.00	Jeep: Wagoneer	$6,600.00
Jeep: Wrangler	$19,500.00	Jeep: CJ	$6,600.00
Jeep: Grand Cherokee	$19,480.00	Jeep: Grand Cherokee	$6,600.00
Jeep: Wrangler	$19,200.00	Jeep: Cherokee	$6,500.00
Jeep: Grand Cherokee	$17,600.00	Jeep: CJ	$6,500.00
Jeep: Wrangler	$17,200.00	Jeep: Grand Cherokee	$6,495.00
Jeep: Grand Cherokee	$16,900.00	Jeep: Liberty	$6,200.00
Jeep: Liberty	$16,500.00	Jeep: Wrangler	$6,200.00
		Jeep: Grand Cherokee	$6,001.00

Passenger Vehicles ▶ Lamborghini

The average sales price in this subcategory is $87,484.32.

HIGH TO LOW

Lamborghini	$178,950.00	Lamborghini: Jalpa	$34,950.00
Lamborghini: Gallardo	$173,500.00	Lamborghini: lamborgini	$29,000.00
Lamborghini: Gallardo	$167,100.00	Lamborghini: Roadster	$26,100.00
Lamborghini: DIABLO VT	$150,000.00	Lamborghini: Lambghini	$14,600.00
Lamborghini	$147,000.00	Lamborghini	$14,000.00
Lamborghini	$145,700.00	Lamborghini	$1,250.00
Lamborghini	$142,500.00	Lamborghini: Lamborghini	$130.50

Passenger Vehicles ▸ Land Rover

The average sales price in this subcategory is $12,926.25.

	HIGH		AVG
Land Rover: Range Rover	$82,600.00	Land Rover: Range Rover	$13,400.00
Land Rover: Range Rover	$64,900.00	Land Rover: Defender	$13,100.00
Land Rover: Range Rover	$58,900.00	Land Rover: Discovery	$13,100.00
Land Rover: Range Rover	$58,299.00	Land Rover: Range Rover	$12,999.00
Land Rover: Range Rover	$56,900.00	Land Rover: Discovery	$12,995.00
Land Rover: Range Rover	$50,095.00	Land Rover: Range Rover	$12,900.00
Land Rover	$49,995.00	Land Rover: Discovery	$12,900.00
Land Rover: Defender	$46,550.00	Land Rover: Discovery	$12,900.00
Land Rover: Range Rover	$46,000.00	Land Rover: Discovery	$12,800.00
Land Rover: Defender	$44,700.00	Land Rover: Discovery	$12,711.00
Land Rover: Range Rover	$43,888.00	Land Rover: Discovery	$12,650.00
Land Rover: Range Rover	$41,995.00	Land Rover: Discovery	$12,500.00
Land Rover: Defender	$40,000.00	Land Rover: Discovery	$12,400.00
Land Rover: Defender	$35,005.00	[2 of these sold for $12,4000.00 each]	
Land Rover: Range Rover	$32,900.00	Land Rover: Freelander	$12,100.01
		Land Rover: Discovery	$12,100.00

Passenger Vehicles ▸ Lexus

The average sales price in this subcategory is $15,589.83.

	HIGH		AVG
Lexus: LX	$50,900.00	Lexus: RX	$16,000.00
Lexus: LS	$49,995.00	Lexus: IS	$15,995.00
Lexus: LS	$49,950.00	Lexus: RX	$15,988.00
Lexus: LS	$48,600.00	Lexus: RX	$15,973.00
Lexus: LX	$47,650.00	Lexus: RX	$15,850.00
Lexus: LX	$46,500.00	Lexus: ES	$15,500.00
Lexus: LX	$45,500.00	Lexus: ES	$15,350.00
Lexus: LX	$43,000.00	Lexus: RX	$14,985.00
Lexus: GX	$42,750.00	Lexus: GS	$14,900.00
Lexus: SC	$41,000.00	Lexus: ES	$14,877.00
Lexus: SC	$39,877.00	Lexus: GS	$14,750.00
Lexus: SC	$38,900.00	Lexus: RX	$14,500.00
Lexus: SC	$38,099.00	Lexus: ES	$14,400.00
Lexus: SC	$37,100.00	Lexus: SC	$14,100.00
Lexus: RX	$36,475.00	Lexus: GS	$13,999.00

Passenger Vehicles ▸ Lincoln

The average sales price in this subcategory is $7,961.08.

	HIGH		AVG
Lincoln: Navigator	$42,995.00	Lincoln: Town Car	$8,995.00
Lincoln: Navigator	$42,000.00	Lincoln: Town Car	$8,990.00
Lincoln: Continental	$40,100.00	Lincoln: Navigator	$8,900.00
Lincoln: Continental	$40,000.00	Lincoln: Town Car	$8,789.00
Lincoln: Navigator	$39,950.00	Lincoln: Navigator	$8,699.00
Lincoln: Town Car	$32,088.88	Lincoln: Mark Series	$8,500.00
Lincoln	$30,095.00	Lincoln: Town Car	$8,500.00
Lincoln: Town Car	$30,000.00	Lincoln: Mark Series	$8,500.00
Lincoln: Navigator	$29,900.00	Lincoln: Town Car	$8,299.00
Lincoln: Navigator	$29,742.00	Lincoln: Continental	$8,200.00
Lincoln: Navigator	$27,900.00	Lincoln: Town Car	$8,101.00
Lincoln: Navigator	$25,900.00	Lincoln: Town Car	$8,100.00
Lincoln: Navigator	$25,700.00	Lincoln: LINCOLN	$8,100.00
Lincoln: Continental	$25,405.00	Lincoln: Town Car	$8,000.00
Lincoln: Navigator	$25,301.00	Lincoln: Continental	$8,000.00

Passenger Vehicles ▸ Mazda

The average sales price in this subcategory is $4,928.22.

	HIGH		AVG
Mazda: RX-8	$28,000.00	Mazda: Miata	$5,700.00
Mazda: RX-8	$25,900.00	Mazda: RX 7	$5,650.00
Mazda: RX-8	$23,200.00	Mazda: 626	$5,600.00
Mazda: RX-8	$22,100.00	Mazda: MPV	$5,501.00
Mazda: RX-8	$21,500.00	Mazda: Miata	$5,500.00
Mazda: RX-8	$20,100.00	[2 of these sold for $5,500.00 each]	
Mazda: Miata	$19,995.00	Mazda: Millenia	$5,410.00
Mazda: RX-8	$19,850.00	Mazda: RX-7	$5,350.00
Mazda: Miata	$19,449.00	Mazda: B-Series Pickups	$5,250.00
Mazda: RX 7	$18,100.00	Mazda: Miata	$5,209.16
Mazda: Miata	$17,100.00	Mazda: Miata	$5,200.00
Mazda: Tribute	$17,100.00	Mazda	$5,100.00
Mazda: Mazda6	$16,950.00	Mazda: Miata	$5,000.00
Mazda: Miata	$15,750.00	Mazda: RX-7	$5,000.00
Mazda: Mazda3	$15,100.00	Mazda: Miata	$4,995.00
		Mazda: 626	$4,900.00

Passenger Vehicles ▶ Mercedes-Benz

The average sales price in this subcategory is $14,738.07.

	HIGH		AVG
Mercedes-Benz: 300-Series	$285,200.00	Mercedes-Benz : SL-Class	$16,500.00
Mercedes-Benz: SL-Class	$107,950.00	Mercedes-Benz : 500-Series	$16,000.00
Mercedes-Benz: S-Class	$71,777.00	Mercedes-Benz : C-Class	$15,600.00
Mercedes-Benz: CL-Class	$64,900.00	Mercedes-Benz : M-Class	$15,101.00
Mercedes-Benz: S-Class	$49,600.00	Mercedes-Benz : S-Class	$15,050.00
Mercedes-Benz: MercedesBenz	$47,101.00	Mercedes-Benz : SL-Class	$15,050.00
Mercedes-Benz: C-Class	$41,898.00	Mercedes-Benz : 500-Series	$15,000.00
Mercedes-Benz: S-Class	$39,999.00	Mercedes-Benz : S-Class	$14,900.00
Mercedes-Benz: CLK-Class	$38,500.00	Mercedes-Benz : S-Class	$14,100.00
Mercedes-Benz: S-Class	$37,925.00	Mercedes-Benz : M-Class	$13,999.00
Mercedes-Benz: M-Class	$35,500.00	Mercedes-Benz : M-Class	$13,725.00
Mercedes-Benz: E-Class	$34,400.00	Mercedes-Benz : CLK-Class	$13,601.00
Mercedes-Benz: S-Class	$34,000.00	Mercedes-Benz : M-Class	$13,500.00
Mercedes-Benz: M-Class	$33,700.00	Mercedes-Benz : E-Class	$13,500.00
Mercedes-Benz: SL-Class	$33,101.00	Mercedes-Benz : S-Class	$13,255.55

Passenger Vehicles ▶ Mitsubishi

The average sales price in this subcategory is $6,019.56.

	HIGH		AVG
Mitsubishi: Lancer	$28,900.00	Mitsubishi: Eclipse	$6,499.00
Mitsubishi: 3000GT	$25,200.00	Mitsubishi: Galant	$6,201.00
Mitsubishi: Lancer	$23,600.00	Mitsubishi: Eclipse	$6,200.00
Mitsubishi: Lancer	$23,000.00	Mitsubishi: 3000GT	$6,200.00
[2 of these sold for $23,000.00 each]		Mitsubishi: Eclipse	$6,100.00
Mitsubishi: Lancer	$22,999.99	[2 of these sold for $6,100.00 each]	
Mitsubishi: Lancer	$22,850.00	Mitsubishi: 3000GT	$6,100.00
Mitsubishi: Lancer	$21,500.00	Mitsubishi: Diamante	$6,099.00
Mitsubishi	$20,001.00	Mitsubishi: Eclipse	$6,000.00
Mitsubishi: Lancer	$19,600.00	Mitsubishi: 3000GT	$6,000.00
Mitsubishi: Lancer	$19,300.00	[2 of these sold for $6,000.00 each]	
Mitsubishi: Lancer	$18,000.00	Mitsubishi: Montero	$6,000.00
Mitsubishi: Montero	$18,000.00	Mitsubishi: 3000GT	$6,000.00
Mitsubishi: Montero	$17,600.00	Mitsubishi: Eclipse	$6,000.00
Mitsubishi: Lancer	$17,089.00	Mitsubishi: Galant	$5,999.99
Mitsubishi: Montero	$17,000.00	Mitsubishi: Eclipse	$5,999.00
		Mitsubishi: 3000GT	$5,995.00

Passenger Vehicles ▶ Nissan

The average sales price in this subcategory is $6,948.00.

	HIGH		AVG
Nissan: Armada	$40,000.00	Nissan: Maxima	$7,500.00
Nissan: 350Z	$33,499.00	Nissan: Pathfinder	$7,300.00
Nissan: Armada	$32,000.00	Nissan: 300ZX	$7,150.00
Nissan: 350Z	$31,900.00	Nissan: 240SX	$7,100.00
Nissan: 350Z	$30,720.00	Nissan: Frontier	$7,100.00
Nissan: Skyline GTR Vspec	$29,999.00	Nissan: Frontier	$7,000.00
Nissan: Armada	$29,900.00	Nissan: Pathfinder	$6,800.00
Nissan: Armada	$29,600.00	Nissan: Xterra	$6,800.00
Nissan: 350Z	$29,100.00	Nissan: Frontier	$6,702.36
Nissan: 350Z	$27,000.00	Nissan: 300ZX	$6,700.00
Nissan: Altima	$26,600.00	Nissan: Quest	$6,600.00
Nissan: Armada	$26,000.00	Nissan: 300ZX	$6,600.00
Nissan: 350Z	$25,000.00	Nissan: Xterra	$6,550.00
Nissan: 350Z	$24,900.00	Nissan: 240SX	$6,500.00
Nissan: 350Z	$24,500.00	Nissan: Xterra	$6,300.00

Passenger Vehicles ▶ Oldsmobile

The average sales price in this subcategory is $3,202.49.

	HIGH		AVG
Oldsmobile: Eighty-Eight	$30,000.00	Oldsmobile: Cutlass	$3,405.00
Oldsmobile: Cutlass	$22,000.00	Oldsmobile: Eighty-Eight	$3,400.00
Oldsmobile: Eighty-Eight	$17,100.00	[2 of these sold for $3,400.00 each]	
Oldsmobile: Cutlass	$15,600.00	Oldsmobile: Cutlass	$3,399.50
Oldsmobile: Ninety-Eight	$15,300.00	Oldsmobile: Cutlass	$3,350.00
Oldsmobile: Aurora	$14,999.00	[2 of these sold for $3,350.00 each]	
Oldsmobile: Starfire	$14,900.00	Oldsmobile: Aurora	$3,301.00
Oldsmobile: Eighty-Eight	$14,888.00	Oldsmobile: Cutlass	$3,300.00
Oldsmobile: Cutlass	$14,750.00	Oldsmobile: Cutlass	$3,175.00
Oldsmobile: Cutlass	$13,101.00	Oldsmobile: Eighty-Eight	$3,150.00
Oldsmobile: Ninety-Eight	$12,001.01	[2 of these sold for $3,150.00 each]	
Oldsmobile: Cutlass	$12,000.00	Oldsmobile: Cutlass	$3,080.00
Oldsmobile: F-33	$11,600.00	Oldsmobile: Cutlass	$3,051.00

Oldsmobile: Ninety-Eight	$10,000.00	Oldsmobile: Alero	$3,050.00
Oldsmobile: Cutlass	$9,999.00	Oldsmobile: Eighty-Eight	$3,050.00
		Oldsmobile: Aurora	$3,050.00
		Oldsmobile: Bravada	$3,050.00
		Oldsmobile: Cutlass	$3,050.00

Passenger Vehicles ▶ Plymouth

The average sales price in this subcategory is $6,201.95.

	HIGH		AVG
Plymouth: Barracuda	$68,000.00	Plymouth: Plymouth	$6,700.00
Plymouth: Barracuda	$54,900.00	Plymouth: Barracuda	$6,650.00
Plymouth: Barracuda	$42,500.00	Plymouth: Fury	$6,601.00
Plymouth: Barracuda	$40,100.00	Plymouth: Satellite	$6,500.00
Plymouth: Barracuda	$38,700.00	[2 of these sold for $6,500.00 each]	
Plymouth: Barracuda	$36,500.00	Plymouth: Duster	$6,499.00
Plymouth: Road Runner	$36,500.00	Plymouth: PT-81	$6,200.00
Plymouth: Prowler	$35,000.00	Plymouth: Fury	$6,100.00
Plymouth: Prowler	$34,999.00	Plymouth: Plymouth Deluxe	$6,000.00
Plymouth: Prowler	$34,995.00	Plymouth: Fury	$6,000.00
Plymouth: Prowler	$33,900.00	Plymouth: Road Runner	$6,000.00
Plymouth: Barracuda	$32,995.00	Plymouth: Custom	$6,000.00
Plymouth: Prowler	$32,895.00	Plymouth: GTX	$5,819.99
Plymouth: Barracuda	$29,100.00	Plymouth: Grand Voyager	$5,800.00
Plymouth: Barracuda	$29,000.00	Plymouth: Road Runner	$5,800.00
		Plymouth: Satellite	$5,750.00

Passenger Vehicles ▶ Pontiac

The average sales price in this subcategory is $6,198.50.

	HIGH		AVG
Pontiac: Trans Am	$47,600.00	Pontiac: Bonneville	$6,551.00
Pontiac: GTO	$42,600.00	Pontiac: Grand Prix	$6,400.00
Pontiac: GTO	$34,900.00	Pontiac: Firebird	$6,400.00
Pontiac: GTO	$32,900.00	Pontiac: PONTIAC	$6,200.00
Pontiac: GTO	$30,000.00	Pontiac: Montana	$6,200.00
Pontiac: Firebird	$27,995.00	Pontiac: Firebird	$6,100.00
Pontiac: GTO	$27,990.00	Pontiac: Trans Am	$6,100.00
Pontiac: GTO	$27,000.00	Pontiac: Grand Prix	$6,100.00
Pontiac: Firebird	$25,000.00	Pontiac: Le Mans	$6,000.00
Pontiac: Trans Am	$24,000.00	Pontiac: Catalina	$5,999.00
Pontiac: Firebird	$23,500.00	Pontiac: Grand Am	$5,900.00
Pontiac: GTO	$22,700.00	Pontiac: Trans Am	$5,899.00
Pontiac: GTO	$22,600.00	Pontiac: Grand Am	$5,598.00
Pontiac: GTO	$22,100.00	Pontiac: Firebird	$5,550.00
Pontiac: Firebird	$21,990.00	Pontiac: Catalina	$5,500.00

Passenger Vehicles ▶ Porsche

The average sales price in this subcategory is $20,379.19.

	HIGH		AVG
Porsche: 911	$149,900.00	Porsche: Boxster	$23,850.02
Porsche: 911	$115,900.00	Porsche: Boxster	$23,600.00
Porsche: 911	$92,100.00	Porsche: 911	$23,600.00
Porsche: 911	$86,900.00	Porsche: 356	$22,800.00
Porsche: Cayenne	$85,500.00	Porsche: 930	$22,596.00
Porsche: 911	$85,000.00	Porsche: Boxster	$20,050.00
Porsche: 911	$83,850.00	Porsche: Boxster	$19,995.00
Porsche: Cayenne	$80,500.00	Porsche: Boxster	$19,850.00
Porsche: 911	$75,850.00	Porsche: 911	$19,500.00
Porsche: 911	$74,975.00	Porsche: 911	$19,500.00
Porsche: Cayenne	$71,995.00	Porsche	$19,500.00
Porsche: 911	$69,000.00	Porsche	$19,100.00
Porsche: Cayenne	$65,600.00	Porsche: Boxster	$19,100.00
Porsche: 911	$64,100.00	Porsche: 911	$19,000.00
Porsche: 911	$57,900.00	Porsche: Boxster	$18,999.00

Passenger Vehicles ▶ Rolls-Royce

The average sales price in this subcategory is $25,416.75.

HIGH TO LOW			
Rolls-Royce	$275,000.00	Rolls-Royce: ROLLS-ROYCE	$29,850.00
Rolls-Royce	$105,000.00	Rolls-Royce	$27,500.00
[2 of these sold for $105,000.00 each]		Rolls-Royce: 1987.5 Silver Spirit	$27,000.00
Rolls-Royce	$39,600.00	Rolls-Royce: Silver Cloud II	$25,600.00
Rolls-Royce: Silver Shadow	$36,651.00	Rolls-Royce: Silver Spur	$19,900.00
Rolls-Royce: Corniche	$36,000.00	Rolls-Royce: SILVERWRAITH	$19,900.00
Rolls-Royce: CORNICHE CONVERTIBLE	$35,000.00	Rolls-Royce: CLOUD 2	$19,050.00
Rolls-Royce: 20hp	$31,300.00	Rolls-Royce	$19,000.00

Passenger Vehicles ▶ Saab

The average sales price in this subcategory is $6,005.39.

	HIGH		AVG
Saab: 9-3	$32,900.00	Saab: 9-5	$6,845.01
Saab: 9-3	$29,990.00	Saab: 900	$6,800.00
Saab: 9-3	$29,500.00	Saab: 9-3	$6,789.00
Saab: 9-5	$28,000.00	Saab: 9-3	$6,500.00
Saab: 9-3	$27,750.00	Saab: 900	$6,500.00
Saab: 9-3	$22,000.00	Saab: 900	$6,351.00
Saab: 9-3	$21,900.00	Saab: 9-3	$6,251.01
Saab: 9-3	$21,000.00	Saab: 900	$6,200.50
Saab: 9-3	$20,500.00	Saab: 900	$5,995.00
Saab: 9-5	$18,900.00	Saab: 900	$5,950.00
Saab: 9-3	$18,750.00	Saab: 9-5	$5,900.00
Saab: 9-3	$18,000.00	Saab: 900	$5,900.00
Saab: 9-3	$17,995.00	Saab: 900	$5,800.00
Saab: 9-5	$17,990.00	Saab: 9-3	$5,700.00
Saab: 9-5	$17,350.00	Saab: 9-5	$5,678.00

Passenger Vehicles ▶ Saturn

The average sales price in this subcategory is $2,358.02.

	HIGH		AVG
Saturn: Vue	$16,500.00	Saturn: S-Series	$2,869.00
Saturn: Vue	$14,000.00	Saturn: S-Series	$2,800.00
Saturn: Vue	$13,700.00	Saturn: S-Series	$2,795.00
Saturn: Vue	$11,000.00	Saturn: S-Series	$2,700.00
Saturn: Vue	$10,400.00	[2 of these sold for $2,700.00 each]	
Saturn	$9,500.00	Saturn: S-Series	$2,650.00
Saturn: Vue	$9,300.51	Saturn: S-Series	$2,602.00
Saturn: L-Series	$9,000.00	Saturn: S-Series	$2,583.33
Saturn	$8,400.00	Saturn: S-Series	$2,575.00
Saturn: Vue	$8,001.00	Saturn: S-Series	$2,572.00
Saturn: ION	$7,990.00	Saturn: S-Series	$2,550.00
Saturn: ION	$7,300.00	[2 of these sold for $2,550.00 each]	
Saturn: S-Series	$7,300.00	Saturn: S-Series	$2,500.00
Saturn: S-Series	$7,101.00	Saturn: S-Series	$2,499.00
Saturn: S-Series	$6,900.00	Saturn: S-Series	$2,425.00
		Saturn: S-Series	$2,358.33
		Saturn: S-Series	$2,350.00

Passenger Vehicles ▶ Shelby

The average sales price in this subcategory is $54,872.20.

HIGH TO LOW			
Shelby: SHELBY	$150,000.00	Shelby: Cobra	$38,500.00
Shelby	$136,600.00	Shelby: Shelby	$37,495.00
Shelby: GT-350	$88,888.00	Shelby: AC Cobra	$36,600.00
Shelby: GT500	$80,101.00	Shelby: Shelby: Cobra	$35,000.00
Shelby: Cobra GT 500	$72,950.00	Shelby	$35,000.00
Shelby: SHELBY	$62,500.00	Shelby: Cobra	$30,000.00
Shelby: SHELBY	$62,000.00	Shelby	$25,500.00
Shelby: 65 SHELBY CORBRA SUPER FORMANCE	$60,100.00	Shelby	$25,100.00
Shelby: SHELBY COBRA 289	$39,500.00	Shelby	$22,000.00
Shelby: Factory Five Cobra Replica	$39,500.00	Shelby: Cobra	$20,110.00

Passenger Vehicles ▶ Subaru

The average sales price in this subcategory is $7,590.02.

	HIGH		AVG
Subaru	$31,324.00	Subaru: Legacy	$7,877.77
Subaru: Impreza	$29,999.00	Subaru: Legacy	$7,850.00
Subaru: Impreza	$27,500.00	Subaru: Outback	$7,800.00
Subaru: Impreza	$26,999.00	Subaru: Legacy	$7,700.00
Subaru: Impreza	$26,589.00	Subaru: Forester	$7,700.00
Subaru: Impreza	$26,350.00	Subaru: SVX	$7,527.89
Subaru: Impreza	$26,100.00	Subaru: Impreza	$7,500.00
Subaru: Impreza	$26,000.00	Subaru: Legacy	$7,495.00
Subaru: Impreza	$25,650.00	Subaru: Forester	$7,203.00
Subaru: Impreza	$25,000.00	Subaru: Impreza	$7,200.00
Subaru: Impreza	$24,999.00	Subaru: Impreza	$7,132.00
Subaru: Impreza	$24,100.00	Subaru: Outback	$7,100.00
Subaru: Impreza	$24,000.00	Subaru: Impreza	$7,000.00
[3 of these sold for $24,000.00 each]		Subaru: Forester	$7,000.00
Subaru: Legacy	$22,101.00	Subaru: Forester	$6,995.00
Subaru	$20,995.00		

Passenger Vehicles ▸ Toyota

The average sales price in this subcategory is $5,671.07.

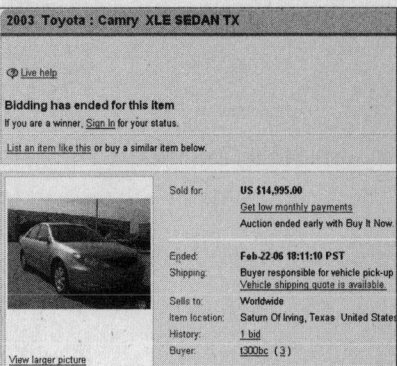

	HIGH		AVG
Toyota: Tacoma	$26,800.00	Toyota: Camry	$6,300.00
Toyota: Tacoma	$20,900.00	Toyota: Tacoma	$6,200.00
Toyota: Camry	$19,998.00	Toyota: Camry	$6,100.00
Toyota: Camry	$19,500.00	Toyota: Tacoma	$6,100.00
Toyota: Tacoma	$19,100.00	Toyota: Camry	$6,050.00
Toyota: Camry	$19,000.00	Toyota: Camry	$6,000.00
Toyota: Camry	$18,988.00	Toyota: Compact Truck	$5,995.00
Toyota: Tacoma	$18,900.00	Toyota: Camry	$5,900.00
Toyota: Camry	$18,100.00	[2 of these sold for $5,900.00 each]	
Toyota: Tacoma	$17,299.99	Toyota: Tacoma	$5,700.00
Toyota: Camry	$17,150.00	[2 of these sold for $5,700.00 each]	
Toyota: Tacoma	$17,000.00	Toyota: Camry	$5,699.99
[2 of these sold for $17,000.00 each]		Toyota: Compact Pickup	$5,526.00
Toyota: Tacoma	$16,995.00	Toyota: SR5 Pickup	$5,500.00
Toyota: Camry	$16,500.00	Toyota: Tacoma	$5,500.00
Toyota: Camry	$16,450.00	[2 of these sold for $5,500.00 each]	
		Toyota: Compact Truck	$5,499.00
		Toyota: Camry	$5,495.00

Passenger Vehicles ▸ Volkswagen

The average sales price in this subcategory is $4,758.87.

	HIGH		AVG
Volkswagen: Passat	$24,500.00	Volkswagen: Passat	$5,495.00
Volkswagen: Passat	$24,189.00	Volkswagen: Beetle (Pre-1998)	$5,401.99
Volkswagen: Passat	$22,750.00	Volkswagen: Beetle (Pre-1998)	$5,351.97
Volkswagen: Passat	$21,500.00	Volkswagen: Beetle (Pre-1998)	$5,299.00
Volkswagen: Passat	$19,650.00	Volkswagen: Beetle (Pre-1998)	$5,200.00
Volkswagen: Passat	$19,500.00	Volkswagen: Passat	$5,200.00
Volkswagen: Passat	$18,099.00	Volkswagen: Beetle (Pre-1998)	$5,200.00
Volkswagen: Passat	$16,559.00	Volkswagen: Passat	$5,101.00
Volkswagen: Passat	$16,500.00	Volkswagen: Beetle (Pre-1998)	$5,100.00
Volkswagen: Passat	$14,695.00	[2 of these sold for $5,100.00 each]	
Volkswagen: Passat	$14,500.00	Volkswagen: Passat	$5,085.00
Volkswagen: Passat	$14,300.00	Volkswagen: Beetle (Pre-1998)	$5,000.00
Volkswagen: Passat	$14,200.00	[4 of these sold for $5,000.00 each]	
Volkswagen: Beetle (Pre-1998)	$14,000.00	Volkswagen: Passat	$4,750.00
Volkswagen: Passat	$13,999.00	Volkswagen: Passat	$4,700.00
		Volkswagen: Passat	$4,699.00
		Volkswagen: Beetle (Pre-1998)	$4,550.00

Passenger Vehicles ▸ Volvo

The average sales price in this subcategory is $5,416.13.

	HIGH		AVG
Volvo: V70	$21,999.00	Volvo: V70	$6,100.01
Volvo: S40	$21,499.00	Volvo: V70	$6,100.00
Volvo: S80	$20,599.00	Volvo: S80	$6,061.00
Volvo: S40	$20,551.00	Volvo: P1800 S	$6,001.00
Volvo: S80	$20,210.00	Volvo: S70	$5,960.00
Volvo: S80	$19,000.00	Volvo: S70	$5,901.55
Volvo: S80	$18,700.00	Volvo: V70	$5,900.00
Volvo: S80	$18,500.00	Volvo: S70	$5,700.00
Volvo: V70	$18,450.00	Volvo: V70	$5,655.00
Volvo: V70	$18,000.00	Volvo: V70	$5,651.00
Volvo: S80	$17,900.00	Volvo: V70	$5,500.00
Volvo: S80	$17,060.00	[2 of these sold for $5,500.00 each]	
Volvo: S80	$16,900.00	Volvo: S70	$5,500.00
Volvo: V70	$16,900.00	Volvo: V70	$5,499.00
Volvo: V70	$15,900.00	Volvo: V70	$5,450.00
		Volvo: V70	$5,402.00

Motorcycles ▸ Harley-Davidson

The average sales price in this subcategory is $10,558.49.

NOTE   *These results are based on a keyword search of the Motorcycles subcategory for auctions with the words* Harley Davidson *in the title.*

	HIGH		AVG
Custom Built Motorcycles: Harley Davidson	$44,995.00	Harley-Davidson: Dyna / FXR	$11,830.93
Harley-Davidson: Softail	$25,000.00	Harley-Davidson: Dyna / FXR	$11,500.00
Harley-Davidson: Touring	$22,500.00	Harley-Davidson: Dyna / FXR	$11,350.00
Harley-Davidson: Softail	$21,600.00	Harley-Davidson: Touring	$11,301.00
Harley-Davidson: Softail	$21,500.00	Harley-Davidson: Touring	$11,100.00

Harley-Davidson: Touring	$21,103.00	Harley-Davidson: Softail	$11,000.00
Harley-Davidson: Touring	$20,100.00	Harley-Davidson: Softail	$10,701.00
Harley-Davidson: Softail	$19,801.00	Harley-Davidson: Softail	$10,700.00
Harley-Davidson: Touring	$19,500.00	Harley-Davidson: Softail	$10,600.00
Harley-Davidson: Touring	$19,433.00	Harley-Davidson: Dyna / FXR	$10,500.00
Harley-Davidson: Softail	$18,600.00	Harley-Davidson: Touring	$10,500.00
Harley-Davidson	$18,500.00	Harley-Davidson: Touring	$10,300.00
Harley-Davidson: Touring	$18,500.00	Harley-Davidson: Softail	$10,200.00
Harley-Davidson	$18,450.99	Harley-Davidson: Touring	$10,100.00
Harley-Davidson: Softail	$18,300.00	Harley-Davidson: ULTRA MC	$9,800.00

Motorcycles ▶ Honda

The average sales price in this subcategory is $3,194.38.

NOTE   *These results are based on a keyword search of the Motorcycles subcategory for auctions with the word* Honda *in the title.*

	HIGH		AVG
Honda: Gold Wing	$25,000.00	Honda: Shadow	$3,500.00
Honda: Gold Wing	$21,099.00	Honda: CBR	$3,500.00
Honda: RC45	$19,500.00	[2 of these sold for $3,500.00 each]	
Honda: Valkyrie	$19,100.00	Honda: CBR	$3,450.00
Honda: Valkyrie	$18,700.00	Honda: Gold Wing	$3,400.00
Honda: Gold Wing	$17,500.00	Honda: Honda	$3,400.00
Honda: Gold Wing	$16,499.99	Honda: Magna	$3,351.99
Honda: Gold Wing	$16,100.00	Honda: Shadow	$3,350.00
Honda: Gold Wing	$14,950.00	Honda: Gold Wing	$3,300.00
Honda: Gold Wing	$14,100.00	Honda: Shadow	$3,251.00
Honda: Gold Wing	$13,700.00	Honda: Nighthawk	$3,250.00
Honda: Gold Wing	$13,613.00	Honda: Shadow	$3,222.00
Honda: Gold Wing	$13,601.00	Honda: Shadow	$3,200.00
Honda: Gold Wing	$12,100.00	[2 of these sold for $3,200.00 each]	
Honda: VTX	$12,000.00	Honda: Magna	$3,200.00
		Honda: Magna	$3,199.00
		Honda: CBR	$3,150.00

Car & Truck Parts

The average sales price in this subcategory is $46.96.

	HIGH		AVG
MERCEDES CLK E CLASS COMMAND COMAND NAVIGATION MAP RDS	$1,000.00	1968-1982 CORVETTE HOOD RELEASE CABLE NEW GM	$53.00
		Land Rover Series-II,IIA,III Link Floor Mats	$52.00
1988 Jeep Comanche Truck 4x4 4.0L MJ NO RUST No Reserve	$710.00	vw cabriolet top boot	$52.00
Hard Top for 2002 Jeep Wrangler	$610.00	NEW WINCH FAIRLEAD FITS WARN RAMSEY SUPER 8000-9000LB	$51.00
Electric Dump Truck Tarp System	$499.00	VW Jetta & Golf 1985-92 Steering Rack & Pinion	$49.99
Porsche 914 2.0 Liter Engine and Transmission Complete	$499.00	Nash Metropolitan New Trunk Handle & Lock Assembly	$47.00
MGA MK2 complete grill NEW #995	$427.00	Dodge Ram billet hood strut covers	$46.79
wrecked 1996 ford mustang fast clean parts/fixme wow!!	$405.00	Land Rover Discovery Black Rubber Loadspace Mat	$46.00
Jeep Wrangler TJ Full Roof Rack	$390.00	porsche 914 door panels	$45.44
Honda, Acura b16a2 head	$365.00	porsche 914 alluminum threshold's	$45.00
2000 daewoo leganza rebuilt cylinder head	$300.00	FORD POWERSTROKE CRANKCASE VENT BYPASS MOD	$45.00
RAMSEY WINCH REP6000 "NEW" N/R	$295.00	HYUNDAI SANTA FE HOOD GUARD BRAND NEW PERFECT	$44.99
PORSCHE BOXSTER & S MANUALS FULL SET (NEW)	$280.00	1984-1996 Chevy Corvette New! Hatch support arms!	$44.00
1984 Pontiac fiero parts car complete with engine	$253.14	Early Ford Bronco Master Cylinder (NIB)	$43.99
eclipse tdo5h big 16g turbo MHI civic integra 90-99	$199.50	Warn Winch Remote Control, NIB!!	$42.66
BMW E65 Wood Steering Wheel for 7 Series 745i 745il 745	$199.00		

Other Vehicles ▶ Aircraft

The average sales price in this subcategory is $15,189.84.

	HIGH		AVG
2001 Cirrus SR-22 Low reserve is below wholesale	$197,501.00	1973 CESSNA 150L	$22,000.00
Bell UH-1H Huey Helicopter	$175,000.00	Beechcraft Musketeer airplane,aircraft,plane	$22,000.00
1981 Piper Aerostar 602P Machen Superstar, Low time	$130,500.00	1971 Grumman Yankee AA1A New Annual, All Logs SWEET!	$20,500.00
Cessna 206	$120,000.00	1975 CHEROKEE 140 CRUISER	$20,221.99
BELL 204B HELICOPTER	$119,500.00	BRAND NEW COMPLETE GLASTAR TAILDRAGGER KIT - AIRPLANE *	$19,950.00
2000 Cessna 172 Nav II KLN 94 color GPS 172SP 180 hp	$99,211.11	1966 CESSNA 150 F 1354TT HORTON STOL EXC. COND.	$19,700.00
Piper Turbo Lance II	$86,800.00	1961 Piper Pa 28 150 LYC. 0320 1350 SMOH	$19,204.01
1973 Cessna 182P SKYLANE Very Low TT	$78,700.00	Robinson Helicopter R22 Beta - PROJECT(Low Reserve)	$18,200.00
77 Piper Chieftain	$76,000.00	1950 Ercoupe 415G - Beautifully Restored	$18,100.00
1999 CITABRIA 7GCAA	$68,100.00	1969 Grumman AA-1 Yankee Clipper - FAST!	$17,990.00
1964 PA30 Twin Comanche! GREAT PLANE!! LOST MEDICAL!	$66,000.00	1978 Cessna 152 airplane GREAT PRICE!!!!! Waco Texas TX	$17,018.00
Piper Super Cub 1950 With EDO FLOATS/WINTER SKIS	$60,000.00	Piper PA38-112 Tomahawk	$16,700.00
GORGEOUS '72 Bellanca Super Viking - LOW RESERVE	$57,500.00	1973 Cessna 150 L TT 3180. SMOH 1975 STON 1198 IFR	$16,500.00
Robinson Helicopter R44 Clipper 2000 TT392 Project	$56,000.00	Dehavilland Dove	$16,000.00
1975 Piper Archer	$55,000.00	Cessna 150 4,140 TT 695 SMOH 600 STOH (not a 152)	$15,300.00

9

CELL PHONES

The cell phone category is very brand-driven; more so than some other eBay categories. And searches here can be defined by eBay's Item Specifics feature, which includes a "Phone Brand" option. In fact, all of the five most popular searches in the Cell Phones category (as provided by eBay on the main category page) include brand names, so people are clearly mostly searching by brand, and not so much by generic terms like *flip phone*. In order of popularity, those top searches are: *Nextel, Verizon, Nokia, Motorola,* and *Sprint.* Because of this, many price lists in this chapter are presented according to brand name.

One of the most popular cell phones in the high range is the Motorola Razr V3 special or limited edition. Designed to be "the thinnest flip phone ever," it includes a 4x digital zoom camera and a black anodized aluminum shell. Prices range on the high end from around $280.00 to $385.00.

But the Razr V3 also shows up in the average range of prices for Motorola phones, with two auctions ending at $102.50. Why? It turns out that these auctions are not for the actual phones, but for a link to a website that the seller claims "will tell you how you can get a Brand New Motorola Razr V3 for only $30." He claims that "there will be a waiting time for receiving this phone, and it may be long (2–3 months). However, I have personally used this site, and received my phone in 4 weeks. It is 100% legitimate." This "auction for a link to get an item" gimmick (as opposed to an auction for the actual item itself) is one you may find in a variety of eBay categories, so it goes without saying that you should proceed with caution.

Other Motorola phones in the average range include a "Motorola V600 PLUS ACCESSORIES!" that went for $100.00 with one bid; the seller says it sells for $400.00 in stores. He describes it as "rarely used," and it includes the battery, wall charger, and car charger. "The inner screen is perfect, the exterior has a few minor scratches, nothing that lowers the value of the phone. Works perfectly," according to the description.

Average prices for Nokia phones skewed a little lower than Motorolas: about $67.00 vs. the latter's $99.00. A Nokia 6560 (AT&T Wireless) color-screen TDMA went for $67.10 with five bids. The seller says it has a few small scratches from normal use, but that it "works perfectly. Great for anyone who still has a Cingular honored AT&T account." It includes a headset, home charger, and car charger.

On the low end, an AT&T Nokia 3560 color cell phone sold for $3.50. It had dings and scratches on the front cover and was missing the Nokia logo from the back cover, but, according to the seller, it was tested for basic functionality and "appeared to be in good working order."

Most low-end phones have some kind of flaw, or they are not actual working phones. Other lowest-priced Nokias include a dummy display phone (for use in stores) for $3.25, a phone with a broken screen "for parts," a link to a website (there's that pesky "auction for a link" gimmick again), and a few TDMA phones, as opposed to GSM phones (two different kinds of cell phone technologies—GSM is newer).

Don't forget to look in this category for accessories such as batteries, chargers, faceplates, and headsets. One auction on the low end included a bunch of faceplates in a wide array of colors. A new NEC 525 lithium ion replacement battery sold for $7.99; new, these can sell for $20.00 to $60.00. There are only a handful of chargers here, with prices ranging about $20.00 or greater; one is the Treo 650 1900 OEM Battery & OEM Car Charger, $36.79 with one bid. These sell for around $19.95 to $59.95 elsewhere.

Accessories, Parts ▶ Accessory Bundles, Packages

The average sales price in this subcategory is $8.84.

	HIGH		AVG
SMT5600 SMT 5600 ACCESSORY KIT RETAIL BOX LOT OF 25	$549.00	Audiovox VOX 8500 wall charger, car adapter, battery	$10.50
ENTIRE RETAIL BOX KIT COMPLETE–MINUS PHONE–GET IT ALL		ALL AUDIOVOX CDM-8610/8615 cell phone accessories	$9.00
Palm Treo 650 Sprint PCS PDA Phone Palmone Plus Extras!	$450.00	[6 of these sold for $9.00 each]	
Desktop cradle, 2nd battery, chargers, software, more!		7 Item PKG for Audiovox 8900 "Geniune Accessories	$7.99
TREO 650 WITH SUPER ACCESSORY PACKAGE	$415.00	{ Super Value *8*Item Phone PKG } Audiovox CDM-8900 NEW	$7.99
Keybrd, 512mb Crd, Car Chrg., Atlas Soft., Scrn Protec		7 Item PKG for Audiovox 8500 "Geniune Accessories	$7.99
LOT OF 15 OEM ACCESSORY PACKS/GIFT FOR MOTOROLA RAZR V3	$165.00	AUDIOVOX 8900 CELL PHONE CASE +CAR TRAVEL CHARGER +MORE	$7.95
pink razr / razor accessory kit SEALED inc BLUETOOTH	$160.00	brand new audiovox HF- 9100,9150,9155 install car kit	$7.49
Selling out fast get yours for Christmas be in the pink		6 AUDIOVOX CDM-8910 8910 CELL PHONE ACCESSORIES	$7.00
MOTOROLA PINK V3 RAZR Accessory Gift Set inc Bluetooth.	$129.99	[2 of these sold for $7.00 each]	
sexy, exclusive in UK, be the first in US to have it		6 AUDIOVOX CDM-8500 8500 CELL PHONE ACCESSORIES	$7.00
[6 of these sold for $129.99 each]		[3 of these sold for $7.00 each]	
MOTOROLA PINK V3 RAZR Accessory Gift Set inc Bluetooth	$122.50	6 AUDIOVOX CDM-8900 8900 CELL PHONE ACCESSORIES	$7.00
HUGE LOT of Mixed Cell Phone Accessories 141 Items	$120.05	[2 of these sold for $7.00 each]	
Motorola - Nokia - Siemens - LG - Mitubishi - Sony Eric		6 AUDIOVOX CDM-8100 8100 CELL PHONE ACCESSORIES	$7.00
MOTOROLA PINK V3 RAZR Accessory Gift Set inc Bluetooth	$120.00	6 AUDIOVOX CDM-8940 8940 CELL PHONE ACCESSORIES	$7.00
sexy, exclusive in UK, be the first in US to have it		[2 of these sold for $7.00 each]	
MOTOROLA PINK V3 RAZR Accessory Gift Set inc Bluetooth	$115.00	PRIMECO AUDIOVOX CELL PHONE W/CHARGER	$7.00
sexy, exclusive in UK, be the first in US to have it		6 AUDIOVOX CDM-9500 9500 CELL PHONE ACCESSORIES	$7.00
pink razr / razor accessory kit SEALED inc BLUETOOTH	$112.50	[2 of these sold for $7.00 each]	
Selling out fast get yours for Christmas be in the pink		NEW BATTERY+CAR+AC HOME CHARGER FOR KYOCERA 7135	$7.00
MOTOROLA BLUETOOTH HEADSET RARZ V3 PINK SPECIAL EDITION.	$105.00	[4 of these sold for $7.00 each]	
Has matching pink carry case & screen clean US WELCOME			
5pack Brand NEW Motorola H300 H 300 Bluetooth wireless	$103.00		
works with all bluetooth brands, v3 mpx220 hs850 h500			
pink razr / razor accessory kit SEALED inc BLUETOOTH	$102.50		
YOU HAVE GOT THE PHONE NOW LOOK "TOTALLY PINK"			
Motorola Bluetooth Wireless Handsfree Car Kit !!! NIB!!	$98.65		

Accessories, Parts ▶ Batteries

The average sales price in this subcategory is $8.42.

	HIGH		AVG
NEW NEVER USED PALM ONE HANDSPRING TREO 650 BATTERY	$26.02	*EXTENDED* Siemens S46 Battery **1200mAh**	$8.99
Audiovox cellular bag phone & battery model PRT 9200	$41.00	[2 of these sold for $8.99 each]	
PalmOne Treo 650 1900 mAh OEM Battery & OEM Car Charger	$32.99	Lithium Extended Battery Toshiba VM4050 4050	$8.99
PALMONE TREO 650 OEM 1900mAH LI-ION BATTERY *NEW*	$29.50	[2 of these sold for $8.99 each]	

Treo 650 Original OEM Battery 1900 mAh NEW	$26.99		*EXTENDED* Siemens S46 Battery **1200mAh**	$8.99
HITACHI G1000 SPARE BATTERY	$22.50		SIEMENS A56 SL56 M56 CT56 LI ION BATTERY MOBILE NIB	$8.99
NEC 525 Battery 800mAh	$22.00		DURACELL CR-V3 BATTERY 2 PACK LOW SHIP	$8.50
PalmOne Treo 650 1900 mAh OEM Battery NEW	$21.95		*** SLIM! *** Hitachi SH-P300 / P 300 BATTERY	$8.49
HANDSPRING PALMONE OEM ORIGINAL BATTERY TREO 650 3184WW	$20.99		NEC 515 525 LITHIUM-ION BATTERY - 700mAh - SILVER - NEW	$8.00
[2 of these sold for $20.99 each]			*NEW* NEXTEL i530 / i533 BATTERY *w/ YELLOW Back Cover*	$7.99
PalmOne Treo 650 1900 mAh OEM Battery NEW	$20.95		NEC 525 Lithium Ion Replacement Battery NEW	$7.99
[5 of these sold for $20.95 each]			[2 of these sold for $7.99 each]	
PalmOne Treo 180 or 300 battery & leather case pkg open	$20.49		Hitachi SH-P300/P-300 BATTERY Lithium-ION Standard New!!	$7.99
Treo 650 OEM Battery NEW	$20.00		[2 of these sold for $7.99 each]	
Original Blackberry OEM Battery 7100 7100t 7100v 7100r	$19.99		Lithium Extended Battery + 6 items Toshiba VM4050 4050	$7.99
SHARP TM 150 TM150 OEM BATTERY BONUS JABRA HEADSET @@	$18.85		BATTERY ** Panasonic GD87 / GD88 / GU87 / 87 / 88	$7.99
[2 of these sold for $18.85 each]			NEC 525 Lithium Ion Replacement Battery NEW	$7.99
SPRINT TREO 600 VEHICLE POWER ADAPTER NEW IN PACKAGE	$17.75		*** SLIM! *** Hitachi SH-P300 / P 300 BATTERY	$7.99
			NEW Siemens M46 ** Battery **	$7.99

Accessories, Parts ▶ Belt Clips, Holsters

The average sales price in this subcategory is $5.02.

Item	HIGH		Item	AVG
Lot of 2 Nextel i60 cell phones, holsters and chargers	$25.03		NEW PALMONE VERIZON TREO 650 PDA HOLSTER +SWIVEL CLIP	$5.99
MOBO BLACK LEATHER CASE Organizer TREO 600 650 $1 SHIP	$20.51		[5 of these sold for $5.99 each]	
Brighton Cambridge Phone Case Retail $54	$19.75		PalmOne/PALM ONE TREO-600 650 SWIVEL CLIP HOLSTER-BLACK	$5.98
MOBO BLACK LEATHER CASE Organizer TREO 600 650 $1 SHIP	$19.50		Timbuk2 Cell phone Holster Black	$5.55
New Treo 650 OEM Leather Latch Case Holster 470765	$18.99		MOBO BLACK LEATHER CASE Organizer TREO 600 650 .99 NR	$5.50
New Treo 650 OEM Leather Latch Case Holster 470765	$18.50		Sidekick II 2 ll Swivel belt clip Holster + car charger	$5.50
New Treo 650 OEM Leather Latch Case Holster 470765	$16.99		Body Glove Cell Phone Case / Universal Large - NEW	$5.25
MOBO BLACK LEATHER CASE Organizer TREO 600 650 .99 NR	$16.50		NOKIA 2260 3587i 3589i 3595 6010 6019i OEM BELT CLIP	$5.25
LOUIS VUITTON CELL PHONE CASE MONOGRAM DESIGN	$15.00		PHONE HOLSTER WITH CLIP AND EXTRA POCKETS - Motorola	$5.00
LOUIS VUITTON MURAHAMI DESIGN CELL PHONE CASE	$15.00		RIM Blackberry OEM Swivel Holster 6750 7730 7750 7780	$4.99
LOUIS VUITTON MONOGRAM DESIGN	$15.00		NEW PALMONE VERIZON TREO 650 PDA HOLSTER +SWIVEL CLIP	$4.99
CANDY BAR CELL PHONE-CASE			Sidekick II 2 Holster / Case / Swivel / Belt clip	$4.30
MOBO BLACK LEATHER CASE Organizer TREO 600 650 $1 SHIP	$14.85		BODY GLOVE UNIVERSAL BELT CLIP FOR NOKIA CLIP AND GO	$4.25
palmOne Treo 650 Original Leather Form Fit Case 3179WW	$13.99		MOBO BLACK LEATHER CASE Organizer TREO 600 650 .99 NR	$4.25
MOBO BLACK LEATHER CASE Organizer TREO 600 650 $1 SHIP	$13.35		TREO 270/300 phone SWIVEL HOLSTER OEM Quality	$3.99
MOBO BLACK LEATHER CASE Organizer TREO 600 650 $1 SHIP	$12.85		[7 of these sold for $3.99 each]	
			RIM BLACKBERRY T-MOBILE 7290 PDA CELL PHONE HOLSTER +I	$3.99
			[2 of these sold for $3.99 each]	

Accessories, Parts ▶ Chargers, Cradle Chargers

The average sales price in this subcategory is $6.10.

Item	HIGH		Item	AVG
T-Mobile Sidekick II (T-Mobile)	$152.50		Travel AC Charger Blackberry 7730 7750 7780	$6.99
MAPSOURCE METROGUIDE NORTH AMERICA VERSION 6 GPS Garmin	$70.00		Hitachi G1000 Travel Charger NEW Orig Pkg- Sprint PCS	$6.99
Treo 650 1900 OEM Battery & OEM Car Charger & Case-3	$36.79		HP IPAQ H6300/H6315 H-6315	$6.98
MOTOROLA WIRELESS BLUETOOTH ADAPTER DC 600	$28.00		HOME AC TRAVEL CHARGER OEM!	
TREO 600 CELL PHONE ACCESSORIES LOT HOLDER/USB/CHARGERS	$24.99		Hitachi G1000 Travel Charger NEW in Orig PKg–opened!!!	$6.50
[2 of these sold for $24.99 each]			palmOne Treo 650 Tungten T5 Premium Car Charger	$6.49
TREO 650 CELL PHONE ACCESSORIES LOT HOLDER CAR CHARGER	$19.99		HANDSPRING PALMONE OEM TREO	$6.45
New OEM Car Charger RIM Blackberry 6750 7730 7750 7780	$17.99		600 300 270 90 CAR CHARGER	
PALMONE OEM TUNGSTEN T5 TREO 650 TRAVEL CHARGER 3172WW	$14.99		TREO 650 CHARGER ACCESSORIES LOT CAR & TRAVEL CHARGERS	$6.25
New OEM RIM Blackberry Car Charger 7510 7280 7100 6280	$14.99		N OEM PLANTRONICS MX150 v400 t730 v600 i730 i95 + BONUS	$5.99
RIM Blackberry OEM Travel Charger 6750 7730 7750 7780	$14.99		NEW T-MOBILE SIDEKICK II 2 OEM HOME TRAVEL AC CHARGER!	$5.99
PALMONE TREO 650 OEM CAR CHARGER & LEATHER LATCH CASE	$14.99		Handspring Treo OEM Car Charger 300, 600, 270 and 180	$5.99
[4 of these sold for $14.99 each]			NEW T-MOBILE SIDEKICK II 2 OEM HOME TRAVEL AC CHARGER!	$5.99
* DESKTOP CRADLE CHARGER & 650mAh Battery for NEC 525 *	$14.99		[2 of these sold for $5.99 each]	
NEW BLACKBERRY TRAVEL CHARGER 7230/7280/7510/ @@BONUS@@	$13.33		$99 POWER-2-GO EMERGENCY CHARGER FOR LG (1 CASE) NR	$5.51
[2 of these sold for $13.33 each]			10 OEM T-MOBILE DANGER HIP TOP SIDEKICK2 HOME CHARGER	$5.50
Touchpoint 2100 2200 Desktop Charger w/Data !	$13.00		Handspring Treo OEM Car Charger 300, 600, 270 and 180	$5.24
Belkin F8V9995-B AC/DC Converter Car Plug to Wall	$13.00		Car Charger Blackberry 7730 7750 7780	$4.99

Accessories, Parts ▶ Faceplates, Housings

The average sales price in this subcategory is $5.24.

Item	HIGH		Item	AVG
Swarovski Crystals Cell Phone Bling Kit (400 crystals)	$34.99		LG vx4500 4500 faceplate cover Tigger SILVER DISNEY NEW	$5.49
LG VX6000 VX-6000 SOLID FULL HOUSING SET * HONEY BLACK	$29.99		LG vx4500 4500 faceplate cover Winnie the Pooh DISNEY	$5.49
LG VX6100 VX-6100 TRANS FULL HOUSING SET * SUPER CLEAR	$27.99		LG VX3200 VX 3200 INITIAL MONOGRAM A 3.50 SH Faceplate	$4.99
LG VX6100 VX-6100 FULL HOUSING SET * CLEAR PINK FLOWER	$27.99		LG VX3200 3200 phone FACEPLATE cover - MIDNIGHT BLUE	$4.95
LG VX6000 Full Complete Housing in ANY COLOR VX-6000	$26.99		LG VX3200 6100 phone FACEPLATE cover DARK FOREST GREEN	$4.95
LG VX6000 VX-6000 TRANS FULL HOUSING SET * SUPER CLEAR	$24.99		LG VX3200 3200 phone FACEPLATE cover DAISY FLOWER COLOR	$4.95
LG VX6000 FULL HOUSING SET - BLUE LASER-CUT DRAGON	$24.99		[3 of these sold for $4.95 each]	
lg vx6000 vx 6000 full housing set MONEY + FREE	$24.95		LG VX3200 3200 phone FACEPLATE cover - MOSSY OAK CAMO 6	$4.95
LG VX6000 BLACK FULL HOUSING+BATTERY+TOOL+F ANTENNA	$22.00		LG VX7000 7000 phone FACEPLATE cover - BABY PINK	$4.80
FOR LG C1300 G4015 FACEPLATE SET HOUSING PINK+ BATTERY	$21.95		LG VX7000 7000 phone FACEPLATE cover - HUNTER ORANGE	$4.80
(1) T-MOBILE SIDEKICK SK 2 II PHONE SKIN - ARGYLE PINK	$21.00		MOTOROLA V180 METAL CHOPPERS FACEPLATE	$3.99
LGVX6000 COMPLETE 6 PIECE COMBO SET BLACK	$19.99		SANYO 8200 BABY PHAT CAT BLACK FACEPLATE	$3.99
LGVX6000 COMPLETE 6 PIECE COMBO SET BABY PINK	$18.99		LG VX6100 FACEPLATE + BACK COVER *CLEAR PUR WATERDROP *	$3.99
(1) T-MOBILE SIDEKICK SK 2 II PHONE SKIN - ROCA JAY-Z	$15.50		LG VX6100 VX-6100 FACEPLATE + BACK COVER * PURPLE DROP	$3.99
nextel i730 face plate MONEY + FREE GIFTS	$11.95		LG VX6000 VX-6000 FACEPLATE FLASHING ANTENNA SIL_BUNNY	$3.29
			MOTOROLA FACEPLATE FLASHING ANTENNA V300 V600 SIL_S_MAN	$3.29

Phones Only ▶ Nokia

The average sales price in this subcategory is $66.92.

NOTE *These results are based on a keyword search of the Phones Only subcategory for auctions with the word* Nokia *in the title.*

	HIGH		AVG
Nokia 9500 Communicator Wi-Fi EDGE Bluetooth Camera Ph	$660.00	Nokia 3200 AT&T/Cingular w/ camera + orig. access/box	$69.00
Nokia 7710 Widescreen Smartphone	$650.00	New Nokia 6010 GSM unlocked Cingular T-mobile 3595	$69.00
Nokia 9500 Communicator	$650.00	UNLOCKED NOKIA 3100 WITH ALL ACCESSORIES	$68.00
New Nokia 9500 Communicator cell. Unlocked .	$620.00	Used Nokia 3650 GSM (AT&T Wireless) Camera/Video Phone	$67.50
Brand New Nokia 9300 Unlocked GSM Tri-Band	$594.99	Nokia 6560 (AT&T Wireless) Color Screen TDMA	$67.10
Nokia 9500 Communicator	$557.99	Nokia 6015 Cell Phone - Verizon - WEB, COLOR, NR!!!	$67.00
Nokia 6680 **Brand New**	$550.00	New Nokia 3100 3120 Color Cell phone Cingular NR	$67.00
99% New nokia 6680,3G smartphone,unlocked,SILVER BLUE	$500.00	Nokia 6340i phone NEW with FREE SIM CARD*EXTRAS*	$66.75
NEW UNLOCKED Nokia 6820 GSM Camera Phone	$160.00	LIKE NEW NOKIA 6800 GSM COLOR CELL PHONE UNLOCKED	$66.50
NOKIA 6260 WORLD PHONE VIDEO CAMERA GPS	$455.00	Nokia 3120 (Cingular Wireless) Like New	$66.26
Nokia 6680 3G Unlocked 1.3mpxl Digital Camera	$450.00	NEW Nokia 6800 GSM Messaging Phone	$66.00
BRAND NEW Nokia 7280 UNLOCKED LIPSTICK Cell Phone NR!!!	$425.00	NOKIA 2651 BRAND NEW 850/1900 UNLOCKED IN BOX	$65.01
Lot of 10 Brand New Nokia 6010 (T-Mobile) cell phones	$355.00	Nokia 3650 GSM Phone	$65.00
Nokia 7610 Tri-band GSM World Phone SIM Unlocked (Wht)	$347.00	ONE NEW Nokia 3587i CDMA ALLTEL & FREEBIES, FAST SHIP	$65.00
Nokia 7280 Unlocked HOT Lipstick VGA Camera Phone	$330.00	NOKIA N-GAGE QT ! NO ACTIVATION REQUIRED ! BLUETOOTH !	$65.00

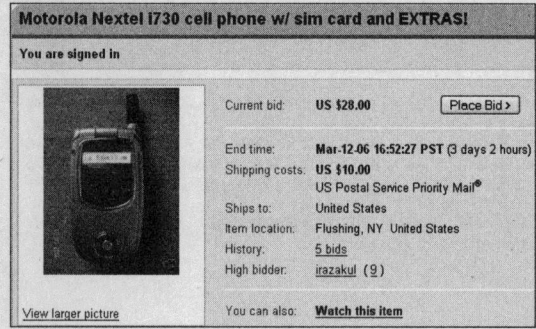

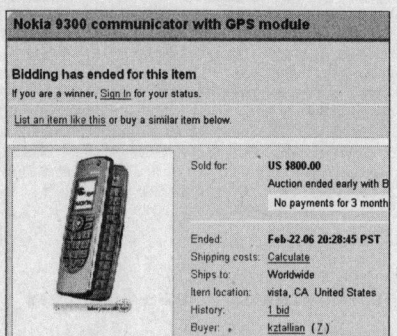

Phones Only ▶ Motorola

The average sales price in this subcategory is $98.67.

NOTE *These results are based on a keyword search of the Phones Only subcategory for auctions with the word* Motorola *in the title.*

	HIGH		AVG
Brand New Motorola V180 Cell Phone AT&T (No SIM)	$1,000.00	BRAND NEW MOTOROLA V60g V60 GSM UNLOCKED PHONE PACKAGE+	$99.99
MOTOROLA I860-CELL PHONE MOTOROLA I860 FOR NEXTEL I860	$550.00	MINT Motorola v60i, v60ci, v60 CDMA VERIZON cell phone	$99.99
Motorola A1000 Tri-Band GSM Camera Bluetooth PDA Phone	$425.00	BRAND NEW Motorola V188 T-mobile - color & speakerphone	$99.99
NEW MOTOROLA V3 RAZR LIMITED BLACK EDITION	$385.00	Motorola V60i(C) U.S. Cellular Brand New 1 year warr.	$99.95
NEW! MOTOROLA MOTO RAZR V3 LIMITED EDITION (Black)!NR	$377.95	Motorola V300 Camera Phone T-MOBILE CELL CELLPHONE LOOK	$99.01
Motorola Razr Razor V3 in Black	$355.00	Motorola V600 (Cingular Wireless)	$99.00
Motorola Razr BLACK V3 Unlocked and Unbranded NO LOGOS	$341.00	Motorola i730 used but mint condition	$98.00
NEW Motorola V3 RAZR Camera Phone BLACK EDITION! RARE!	$330.00	MOTOROLA ACCOMPLI 009 PERSONAL COMMUNICATOR #1	$97.00
MOTOROLA Moto Razr V3 Special Edition, Black(unlocked)	$325.00	Unlocked Motorola V188	$97.00
MOTOROLA RAZR V3 UNLOCKED RAZOR CELL PHONE NEW	$320.00	MOTOROLA 730C 730 VERIZON GPRS CDMA PHONE COLOR SCREEN	$96.25
MOTOROLA Razr V3 Low Reserve + Free Shipping (Cingular)	$320.00	Motorola V265 (Verizon Wireless)	$96.00
Motorola A630 camera bluetooth cell phone GSM qwert NEW	$315.00	Motorola V300 (T-Mobile)	$96.00
Motorola Moto Razr V3 Special Edition Black Unlocked	$315.00	Motorola V220 GSM Cell Phone - Unlocked	$95.00
NEXTEL I860 PHONE BRAND NEW PHONE MOTOROLA	$312.22	MOTOROLA V220 for Cingular - WORLD PHONE WITH CAMERA	$95.00
Motorola A630 * W/ HS850 BLUETOOTH HEADSET + MORE	$310.00	Motorola V400 v400 Camera Phone PINK UNLOCKED	$94.00

Phones Only ▶ Samsung

The average sales price in this subcategory is $105.11.

NOTE *These results are based on a keyword search of the Phones Only subcategory for auctions with the word* Samsung *in the title.*

	HIGH		AVG
Samsung SCH-i730 CDMA Verizon Cell Phone, SCH-I730	$710.00	Samsung A670 phone for Verizon	$117.50
BRAND NEW Samsung E335 Camera Phone!!	$660.00	SAMSUNG SGN E315	$115.00
Sprint PCS SP-i600 by Samsung	$405.00	Samsung Cdm8910 Brand New Phone Verizon Wireless	$115.00
Sprint PCS Samsung SPH-i600 Like New Extras NR	$400.00	Samsung SPH A660 (Sprint)PCS Vision Phone NIB!!!!!!!!	$114.99

NEW Samsung SGH-D500 TriBand Video Camera Phone	$365.00	** 2 ** Samsung SPH-A660 Cellphone Lot Sprint "Color"	$113.50
Samsung SGH P735 (T-Mobile) and RS-MMC Mem Card 32 MB	$350.00	Samsung SGH E316 (AT&T Wireless) Camera Cell Phone Sim	$113.50
New Samsung SGH P735 (T-Mobile)	$349.99	SAMSUNG E315	$112.65
Samsung SGH P735 (T-Mobile) NO RESERVE LIKE NEW	$342.00	Samsung E 715 Camera cell phone/ T-Mobile	$112.50
Samsung SGH P735 (T-Mobile)	$330.00	2 Samsung x427 Phones w/car charger Cingular	$110.99
Samsung i700 Verizon Phone & Pocket PC Camera PDA	$325.00	Samsung a670 phone for Verizon USED w/ accessories	$110.00
Samsung i700 Verizon Cell Phone & Pocket PC Camera PDA	$315.00	Samsung SGH E715 (T-Mobile)	$110.00
[2 of these sold for $315.00 each]		Samsung P107 (UNLOCKED)	$110.00
Samsung Sch-A890 Verizon High Picture Video phone	$306.00	Brand New Samsung E105 Color Phone(T-Mobile)	$110.00
NEW Samsung SGH-e720-BRAND NEW-UNLOCKED	$306.00	Samsung E715 T-Mobile GSM Cell Phone Camera #0499	$109.99
Sprint PCS Vision Smart Device SPH-i600 by Samsung	$305.00	LIKE NEW SAMSUNG V205 PHONE FOR T-MOBILE	$109.99
Samsung SGH D500 GSM Camera Cell Phone	$305.00		

Phones with New Plan Purchase ▶ Motorola

The average sales price in this subcategory is $84.33.

NOTE *These results are based on a keyword search of the Phones with New Plan Purchase subcategory for auctions with the word* Motorola *in the title.*

	HIGH		AVG
Brand New Motorola RAZR PHONES..FOUR RAZRS!!!..	$1,000.00	Motorola V70 (Cingular Wireless) new unlocked	$99.00
Brand New Motorola RAZR PHONES..FOUR RAZRS!!!..	$950.00	UNLOCKED Motorola V300 (T-Mobile)(Cingular)(Verizon)	$97.00
Brand New Motorola RAZR PHONES..FOUR RAZRS!!!..	$900.00	MOTOROLA V551 GSM CAMERA VIDEO PHONE NEW CONDITION	$97.00
BRAND NEW MOTOROLA RAZOR V3 CINGULAR CELL PHONE	$610.00	MOTOROLA V551 GSM CAMERA VIDEO PHONE NEW CONDITION	$96.00
nokia N91(no motorola,samsung,siemens,sony ericcson)	$510.00	*Motorola i730 Nextel phone w/sim & Extras*	$96.00
Motorola, Top Of the Line Cell Phone! Cheap! V-500	$399.00	$260 Motorola V80 Cellular Phone NR	$91.76
Motorola V3 UNLOCKED RAZOR CELL PHONE. F R E E	$345.07	MOTOROLA RAZR V3 NEW GSM CAMERA VIDEO WORLD PHONE	$86.00
BRAND NEW MOTOROLA RAZOR V3 CINGULAR CELL PHONE	$310.00	Motorola T720 Color Flip Phone T 720 *ALLTEL* L NEW	$85.00
MOTOROLA A925 * NEW* BLUETOOTH HEADSET*Unlocked	$299.00	Motorola T731 Color Flip Phone T720 mint *Qwest*	$81.00
FREE Motorola Nextel i860 Camera Phone + $50 (rebates)	$285.00	MOTOROLA V551 GSM CAMERA VIDEO PHONE NEW CONDITION	$81.00
MOTOROLA V3 RAZOR	$280.00	Cingular Motorola V180	$80.00
Motorola A 925 A925 like A1000 NEW	$276.00	MOTOROLA V300 (T-MOBILE) CAMERA, SPEAKERPHONE	$79.00
Motorola A 925 A925 like A1000 NEW	$270.00	Motorola V180 *GSM* Cell Phone Unlocked! *NICE*	$78.00
Motorola i860 NEW phone, Nextel NIB	$270.00	T-MOBILE CAMERA PHONE MOTOROLA V300 WITH ACCESSORIES	$76.00
MOTOROLA Moto Razr V3 Unlocked	$270.00	Motorola V300 (T-Mobile)	$76.00

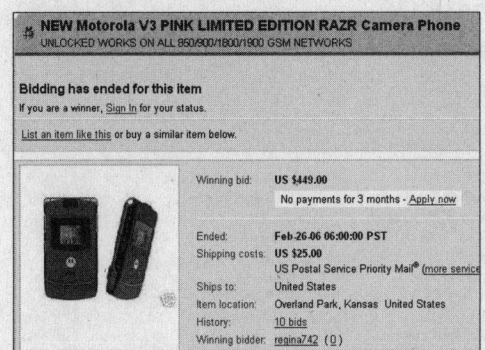

Phones with New Plan Purchase ▶ Nokia

The average sales price in this subcategory is $37.01.

NOTE *These results are based on a keyword search of the Phones with New Plan Purchase subcategory for auctions with the word* Nokia *in the title.*

	HIGH		AVG
nokia N91(no motorola,samsung,siemens,sony ericcson)	$510.00	Nokia 6225 (SprintPCS) CAMCORDER/CAMERA New in Box	$76.00
BRAND NEW NOKIA 8800 BLUETOOTH GSM VIDEO CAMERA CELL P	$510.00	NEW NOKIA 3220 VIDEO CELL PHONE	$69.00
[2 of these sold for $510.00 each]		Nokia 3100 *GSM* Color Screen Phone *Unlocked*	$66.01
10 x Nokia 6260 Brand New!!	$485.00	Nokia 6010 Cellular Phone Brand New Unopened	$65.00
Nokia 9500 Communicator	$430.00	Nokia 63401 Used Cell Phone Cingular	$52.00
Nokia 6260	$300.00	New Nokia 3200 Cell Phone Cellular AT&T Wireless & Box	$48.02
FREE KEYPADINOKIA 6600 PHONE'S RUBBER HOUSING/FACEPLATE	$207.50	Unlocked, Tri-Band GSM Nokia 3100b	$46.55
Nokia 6230 Cell Phone & Wireless Headset (BRAND NEW)	$204.00	nokia 6340i verry nice!!!!!!!!!!!!!!!!!!!!!!!!!!!!!!!	$37.83
Nokia,Web Phone, Yes tou can surf the web cheap, cheap	$199.00	Nokia 6010 *GSM* Color Screen Phone *Unlocked*	$36.00
Nokia 6230 cell phone NEW	$187.50	Two Nokia 3560 Color Phones L New *SunCom* AT&T	$35.00
Like New Nokia 9290 Communicator unlocked with EXTRAS!!	$177.50	Nokia 3595 Cell Phone Unopened!!!!!	$31.05
Nokia 6620 cellular	$175.01	NEW NOKIA 3220 VIDEO CELL PHONE	$31.00
Nokia 3620 Camera -Video Phone used	$173.49	Very nice NOKIA 6010 (T-Mobile) with CHARGERS used SEE	$29.99
NOKIA 6600 IN PERFECT CONDITIONS , AS NEW	$150.00	Tracfone Nokia 1221 with 120 minutes	$29.95
Nokia 3220 *GSM* Camera World Phone NEW *Unlocked*	$142.50	2 UNLOCKED NOKIA 3595 CELLPHONES	$29.00
Like New Nokia 9290 Communicator unlocked with EXTRAS!!	$142.50		

Phones with New Plan Purchase ▶ Sony, Ericsson

The average sales price in this subcategory is $122.93.

HIGH TO LOW

* BRAND NEW * Sony Ericsson S710 S710a w/ Accessories	$335.00	SONY ERICSSON Z500 LIKE NEW GSM CAMERA PHONE CINGULAR	$76.00
NEW and UNLOCKED Sony Ericsson K750i Cell Phone	$325.00	Sony Ericsson T237–Cingular (BRAND NEW IN A BOX!!)	$60.00
Sony Ericson P900 GSM 900/1800/1900 Used Good Cond.	$300.00	Ericsson R289LX (Cingular or AT&T) w/Charger like NEW!!	$59.97
Sony Ericsson V600i 3g umts phone - brand new	$227.50	[3 of these sold in a multiple-item ("Dutch") auction for $19.99 each]	
Sony Ericsson S700 i	$202.50	Sony Ericsson T206 (MetroPCS) cell phone NR	$46.50
SONY ERICSSON Z500 LIKE NEW GSM CAMERA PHONE CINGULAR	$127.50	[3 of these sold in a multiple-item ("Dutch") auction for $15.50 each]	
Sony Ericsson Z500a (Cingular Wireless)	$102.50	Sony Ericsson T206 (MetroPCS) cell phone NR	$35.31
SONY ERICSSON Z500 LIKE NEW GSM CAMERA PHONE CINGULAR	$95.00	[3 of these sold in a multiple-item ("Dutch") auction for $11.77 each]	
SONY ERICSSON Z500 LIKE NEW GSM CAMERA PHONE CINGULAR	$90.01	Brand New Sony Ericsson T237 With smart Card	$25.00
SONY ERICSSON Z500 LIKE NEW GSM CAMERA PHONE CINGULAR	$81.00		

Prepaid Phones & Cards ▶ Prepaid, No Contract Cards

The average sales price in this subcategory is $22.82.

	HIGH		AVG
Iridium Prepaid SIM Card 4989 Min remain, exp 9/2007	$2,000.00	Virgin $30.00 Phone Card for 25.00	$25.00
Iridium satellite prepaid phone card -500 minutes –new	$745.00	Verizon $30 Pay as You Go/Impulse Prepaid Card	$25.00
Iridium satellite prepaid phone card -500 minutes –new	$549.99	Net10 $30 Top Up Card/ BUY NOW!!!!!!!!!!!!	$25.00
THURAYA 7101 SATELLITE PHONE USED 3 WEEKS	$470.00	Long Distance International Prepaid Phone Calling Card	$25.00
SUPER SIM, LEATHER CASE, 2 BATTERIES, 40 UNITS CREDIT		Best Rechargeable Card from 1.9¢ with 473 Free Minutes!	
Iridium prepaid phone card ~600 US$ nearly 500 min left	$399.00	T-MOBILE Prepaid SIM CARD Up To 240 Min! Exp. Feb. 2006	$24.99
For Sattelite Phone,Worldwide shipping, fair conditions		[7 of these sold for $24.99 each]	
3000 MINS NET 10 PREPAID WIRELESS 1 YEAR OF SERVICE	$280.00	Boost Mobile 64K Sim Card Starter Kit W/$35 Credits NR	$24.99
SIDE KICK II T moBiLe PDA COLOr cELL pHOne MINT! MINT!	$255.00	FAST SHIPPING!! ANY AREA CODES AVAILABLE! HURRY !!!!!!!	
Iridium satellite prepaid phone card - 75min / 60days	$179.00	AT&T WIRELESS FREE 2 GO $50.00 CARD	$24.53
$10 AT&T Free2Go PREPAID AIRTIME CARD NEW SEALED NR!!	$165.22	***NEW Tracfone 100 minute card + 60 DAYS OF SERVICE***	$24.50
[22 of these sold in a multiple-item ("Dutch") auction for $7.51 each]		TRACFONE 100 Minutes Airtime Card + 40 Promo Minutes	$24.50
Lot of 25 Brand New T-Mobile SIM Cards	$142.51	Cingular / AT&T Prepaid Go Phone $15 Card Kic	$24.00
300 MINS DOUBLE MINUTE TRACFONE CARD 1 YEAR OF SERVICE	$130.00	[2 of these sold in a multiple-item ("Dutch") auction for $12.00 each]	
500 MINS DOUBLE MINUTE TRACFONE CARD 1 YEAR OF SERVICE	$127.50	T Mobile TO GO $25 Refill Prepaid Phone Card T-Mobile	$23.51
500 MINS DOUBLE MINUTE TRACFONE CARD 1 YEAR OF SERVICE	$125.05	Boost Mobile Kit - $10 Included - NEXTEL BOOST 64k Sim	$23.50
500 MINS DOUBLE MINUTE TRACFONE CARD 1 YEAR OF SERVICE	$124.99	T Mobile TO GO $25 Refill Prepaid Phone Card T-Mobile	$23.01
[6 of these sold for $124.99 each]		T Mobile TO GO $25 Refill Prepaid Phone Card Easy Speak	$22.99
300 MINS DOUBLE MINUTE TRACFONE CARD 1 YEAR OF SERVICE	$119.99	T Mobile TO GO $25 Refill Prepaid Phone Card T-Mobile	$22.52
[4 of these sold for $119.99 each]		[2 of these sold for $22.52 each]	

Prepaid Phones & Cards ▶ Prepaid, No Contract Phones

The average sales price in this subcategory is $28.86.

	HIGH		AVG
Satellite Phone with many Acc. 100% Planetary Coverage!	$629.99	Nokia 2285 PrePaid TracFone *Free 120 Minutes*	$29.50
PalmOne Treo 650 Sprint PCS Vision PDA Bluetooth Phone	$448.00	[2 of these sold for $29.50 each]	
Sony Ericsson S700i Unlocked Tri-Band GSM 1.3mp Camera	$305.00	Nokia 1221 TDMA PrePaid TracFone *With Free Minutes*	$29.50
MOTOROLA RAZOR V3 BLACK UNLOCKED!!!!!!!!!!!!!!!!!!	$300.00	Motorola120c CDMA PrePaid TracFone *With FREE 120 Minutes*	$29.50
Sony Ericsson S700i Unlocked Tri-Band GSM 1.3mp Camera	$280.00	Nokia 2285 PrePaid TracFone *Free 120 Minutes*	$29.50
NOKIA 6260/SMART PHONE/LOW RESERVE/FACTORY UNLOCKED	$232.50	MOTOROLA V120 WIRELESS DIGITAL CELLPHONE NEW TRACFONE	$29.02
BOOST MOBILE i 860 i860 TATOO FREE SHIPPING	$232.50	Tracfone Nokia 1100 Prepaid Cell Phone + 120 Minutes	$29.00
BOOST MOBILE i 860 i860 TATOO FREE SHIPPING	$214.50	Tracfone - Nokia 2285 cell phone 120 mins. + 4 months	$28.96
Boost Mobile Phone, Nextel, Boost, Camera Phone, i860	$202.50	Virgin Mobile AudioVox 8500 cell phone	$28.50
Samsung P777 UNLOCKED!!!!!	$200.00	Tracfone Nokia 2285 Prepaid Cell Phone +120 Minutes	$28.50
New Motorola V60 Tracfone FLIP Prepaid Phone w/120 mins	$199.96	SAMSUNG i300 PREPAID-EXCELLANT COVERAGE- PAY AS YOU GO	$28.00
[4 of these sold in a multiple-item ("Dutch") auction for $49.99 each]		NEW Motorola v120t TracFone +120 min. NOT RECONDITIONED	$28.00
BOOST i830 BRAND NEW	$159.99	NEW Tracfone Nokia 1100 FREE 120 min + CAR CHARGER	$28.00
Boost Mobile Motorola i830 Phone NEW IN BOX no reserve	$153.00	Tracfone - Nokia 1221 cell phone 120 minutes + 4 months	$27.85
Wow! Nokia Digital 5125 Tracfone with 1600+ Minutes	$152.51	Nokia 3585i Cell Phone PREPAID Simple Freedom "LKNEW"	$27.01
NOKIA 8910 TITANIUM WONDER	$152.50	TRACFONE NOKIA 1221/2285 PREPAID CELL PHONE + 120	$27.00

10

CLOTHING, SHOES & ACCESSORIES

Although all eBay categories are brand-driven to some extent, the Clothing, Shoes & Accessories category is even more so than others. The feature in the upper-right corner one day on the main page of this meta-category was "Top Ten Brands in Men's Clothing": Abercrombie & Fitch, Nike, Diesel, Prada, Gucci, Kenneth Cole, Banana Republic, Armani, Polo Ralph Lauren, and Sean John. The "Women's Accessories Top Ten Brands" share Prada and Gucci with the men's list; the other popular brands are Coach, Louis Vuitton, Chanel, Dooney & Bourke, Burberry, Kate Spade, Hermes, and Tod's.

Because of this focus on brand, it's not surprising that many of the highest prices in the Clothing subcategories are for luxury or high-end brand items. But the sellers of these items also have the onus of convincing prospective buyers that their wares are genuine, because some of the merchandise in this category is fake. For example, the top-selling men's tie in this sample is a "Very Rare 100% Real Hermes Tie," red with blue gliders. The seller assures buyers in the description that the tie is "guaranteed authentic . . . or your money back . . . this is not a fake like the Asian imports that have been flooding the eBay market." He goes on to say the tie is brand-new and still has the Hermes tags on it. (When buying high-end items, some of the things you can do to assure yourself they are genuine is to compare the picture of the tag in the auction to a real one, check for the serial number, and ask experts in the eBay Clothing community for advice.) It sold for $167.00 with two bids.

However, you don't necessarily have to dip into the high end of the price range to find a brand with cachet. A Jerry Garcia "Paris in the Rain Orange Neck Tie" sold for $15.00 in the middle range of the Neckwear, Ties subcategory. Other Garcia ties sold for $12.37 and

$13.79; new, these go for around $24.95 to $40.00. And a Giorgio Armani tie went for $15.50 with 11 bids, while a Tommy Bahama (a trendy brand known for its tropical designs) silk floral tie sold for $15.99.

Paying Less—and More—Than Retail

Depending on the item, you can score great savings over retail prices in the Clothing, Shoes & Accessories category, but for the right item, eBayers might pay more than retail price, too. For example, a Vera Wang wedding dress sold for $1,968.00, a huge savings from what the seller claims is the retail price of $28,000.00. (Many Vera Wang dresses are in the $6,000.00 to $12,000.00 range, according to one source.) But a pair of black patent Mary Jane Manolo Blahniks—the "urban myth" shoe of TV show *Sex and the City*, according to the seller—sold for a lofty $1,009.00, which was almost $500.00 over the retail price of $515.00. One thing that may explain the high price, claims the seller, is that the size selection in the black is "slim to none" in stores, and this shoe also features the harder-to-find 4.1-inch heel. This is also a case of a TV celebrity tie-in—Sarah Jessica Parker wore the shoes on the show.

You might see such tie-ins in other eBay items, such as "Oprah's earrings." Another pair of Manolo Blahniks tied to Sarah Jessica Parker and *Sex and the City*—the "Silver stolen shoes" from the "A Woman's Right to Shoes" episode in the original silver color (called the "Sedaraby D'Orsay" pump)—went for $799.99 ("The PERFECT Cinderella shoe, and an investment for all time—elegant beauty when you need that silver dress shoe [or even with your cool jeans!]," according to the description). This seller certainly appeals to the buyer's emotions and helps her to rationalize the purchase, a technique that can boost sales, as long as it's not too over the top.

Sometimes a seller's location may give him or her an edge in selling, and that may help explain the high final price of an item. For example, one seller scored a healthy price on an Oilily sweater, "new for the upcoming season," in bright colors. Oilily is a hot kids' brand based in Holland that often lands in the top range of prices in the children's categories. The seller was located in Switzerland and may have better or faster access to some items of this European brand. (Shipping was $14.00.)

There are a lot of children's clothes available here for very reasonable prices. For example, in the boys 4–7 clothing categories, the low end is full of items at about $1.00 to $2.00, including an Old Navy sweatshirt with hood for $1.52, and a Disney Donald Duck boy's football jersey for $1.04.

High-end kids' clothes often include such things as costumes, tuxedos, and pageant or dance wear, such as the girls' "National Pageant Western Wear" that went for $31.00 with three bids and the Disney Buzz Lightyear costume that sold for $38.51 with eight bids. But for garden-variety, everyday kids' clothes, average prices hover around $9.00 to $15.00, and as shipping is usually reasonable for clothing in general, buying clothes on eBay can save you lots of money, especially if you are willing to buy things "gently used."

Infants & Toddlers ▶ Custom, Handmade

The average sales price in this subcategory is $11.99.

	HIGH		AVG
ERIC CARLE Nursery Bedding Set	$355.00	Boutique Custom Minnie Dots Bracelet w/Polymer Charm	$12.27
Personalized Canvas Tote Bag Embroidered Great Gift !!!	$64.00	~M-A~Funky Flowers Boutique Toddler Fringe Bracelet	$12.22
[4 of these sold in a multiple item ("Dutch") auction for $16.00 each]		Personalized Burp Cloths -Great Newborn gift-Set of 3	$12.00
Boutique Winter fun Christmas 4p dress OOAK 2T-3T YAYAS	$60.50	3 Monogrammed Newborn Baby Hairbows/Bow/Bows Headbands	$12.00
AUTHENTIC COACH BLACK BACKPACK HANDBAG	$55.00	Personalized Burp Cloths -Great Newborn gift-Set of 3	$12.00
Roching Chair Cushions - Moon, Sun, Stars	$50.00	OYOD CUSTOM PATRIOTIC PAGEBOY HAT NB-ADULT	$12.00
Boutique~ADCB~ 3pc set Dress pants hat 2T 3T	$45.56	BOUTIQUE CLIPS! A TOTAL OF 10!	$11.65
Rocking chair cushions- SEA PRINT	$40.00	Boutique Bling SWIRLS & TWIRLS Hair Barrette SASAB	$11.49
Boutique~ADCB~ 3pc set Dress pants hat 2T 3T	$39.89	BOUTIQUE HOLIDAY CLIPS! A TOTAL OF 12!	$11.49
Custom Resell!! Frankenstein Halloween overalls! 24M!	$37.50	BB ~ boutique FRUITS OF SUMMER custom bracelet ~ BAM!	$11.00
MOther/Daughter Bracelet set for Domenica	$37.31	CUSTOM *12* HAIR BOWS INFANT	$11.00
D2MA GYMBOREE ALOHA WAHINE 3T SKIRT ,SHIRT, CUSTOM BOWS	$36.00	TODDLER BABY 39 COLORS WOW	
Miami GIA'S Teal Boutique Dolphin Charm Bracelet PBD	$35.95	HAND CROCHET/KNIT BABY HAT SCULL CAP BEANIE	$10.99
3 Monogrammed Baby/Infant Hairbows/Bow/Bows Headbands	$34.00	Custom Boutique Orange Yellow Baby Child Fall Bracelet	$10.99
BOUTIQUE CLIPS! A TOTAL OF 10!	$32.53	INFANTS COWBOY BOOTS 0-3M or 3-6M - Giddy Up!!! ODCM	$10.97
Boutique~studioE~INDIAN SUMMER~Toddler Bracelet~CUSTOM	$30.99	ADCB~BOUTIQUE Crochet TURTLE Hat CUSTOM	$10.59

Infants & Toddlers ▶ Boys' Clothing

The average sales price in this subcategory is $10.71.

	HIGH		AVG
Clovergirls Boutique *VINTAGE TOMBOY* Overalls O'alls	$120.27	LIKE NEW BOYS NIKE SPRING/SUMMER/FALL JACKET COAT 3T	$11.01
BOYS BEAUX ET BELLES CORDUROY "J" MONOGRAM JACKET 3 3T	$68.51	2 Baby Gap"Circus"Rompers Sz2xl Lion/Tiger Cute/Comfy	$11.00
GYMBOREE Boys FIREMAN coat Jacket fire man ~ SMALL 3T	$65.00	BOYS ECKO RED UNLTD HOODIE SWEATS TOPJACKET 3T	$11.00
Oilily Boys NWOT Sz 98/3 Blue/Grey Camo Jacket	$59.99	NWOT Baby Gap Plaid Jacket coat 2t 2 PREPPY	$10.75
OILILY FALL/WINTER COAT The Ice pack nwt sz 98	$59.00	Boy's Gray Velvet Jon Jon Swiss Vintage Christmas 2 3T	$10.75
NEW NWT Boys 4T COLUMBIA Hooded Winter SKI Jacket Parka	$49.99	BOYS 2XL 3XL GAP VEST/ HAT Outerwear 24-36mo	$10.73
SUPER Oilily dragon winter jacket size 3 or 98	$49.93	THOMAS THE TANK BATHTUB TOY BAG, NEW, SO CUTE!!!!	$10.55
Thomas the Tank Engine Train Denim Jacket Coat 4T EUC	$47.75	Boutique Brand Mondays Child 2 pc Button on Short Set 2	$10.55
Size 2/4, Boy/Girl Penguin Halloween Costume,4 pieces	$43.17	NEW BOYS SZ 2 2T POLO RALPH LAUREN NAVY JACKET NWT	$10.52
Polo by Ralph Lauren sport coat/jacket/blazer, 3T	$41.99	3T Carter's reversible Boys Jacket NWT Coat	$10.51
NWT LE TOP Boutique COWBOY Horse Cow Jacket 4T	$41.50	lot of 8 toddler boys size 4T clothing jeans jacket ++	$10.51
BEAUX ET BELLES 2 2T 3 Blue Corduroy Coat Gingham NWT	$41.00	KELLY'S KIDS firetruck longall initial G monogram 3T 3	$10.51
Boys Motorcycle Leather Jacket (2T)	$40.00	Boy's Ralph Lauren Logo Sweatshirt Hoodie- 2T	$10.50
Luli & Me Duuble breasted knit coat baby blue 3T boys	$37.68	Toddler SUPERMAN costume, size 2-4	$10.50
NWOT...ZACKALI*4*KIDS... BOYS ROMPER...SIZE 2	$36.00	NWT Gap boys size 2T windbreaker jacket NEW	$10.50

Infants & Toddlers ▶ Girls' Clothing

The average sales price in this subcategory is $9.10.

	HIGH		AVG
LIKE NEW BUZZY BUMBLE BEE HALLOWEEN COSTUME XXS 2 3 EUC	$55.00	LOT OF GIRLS DRESS UP/PLAY CLOTHES OR HALLOWEEN 2T-4T	$9.50
31 PIECE DANCE WEAR, LEOTARDS, 2/3/4, TAP, BALLET SHOES	$48.51	Toddler Girl's Gymnastics Leotard Size 2T *HOT*	$9.50
Gymboree 4 Gymbucks free shipping $100 off $200	$42.00	Ralph Lauren Dress Size 3/3T	$9.49
RefleXtions Ballet/Ballerina/Dance LEOTARD Pink 2T LN!	$41.00	OILILY Girls SOCKS Size 21 or 3 yrs. NWT 2 pr. Cute!	$9.29
NWT Ralph Lauren Girls Pink Corduroy Blazer Jacket 2/2T	$40.00	HANNA ANDERSSON Girls Fall Tights 90 100	$9.17
~~GYMBOREE~~ 7 PC LOT~~ DANDELION WISHES~~2T	$39.99	NWT Gymboree Grown with Love Girls Tights 2T 3 3T BTS	$9.15
National Level Pageant Sportswear/Casual Wear	$39.00	NEW Shimmery Unitard Leotard Dance Gymnastic 3T / 4T	$9.00
MINT ~ Baby Nay Princess Dress Set & Hairbows ~ 2T	$36.35	ELMO Handbag Plush Purse NWT ~ By Sesame Street	$9.00
BOUTIQUE GIGI GIRAFFE 2-4T	$35.66	NWT Gymboree Cute as a Button hat small-medium (3-4)	$9.00
LOT OF PRINCESS DRESS UP CLOTHES, GREAT DEAL	$34.98	Gymboree Cupcake leggins/sweater outfit 2t	$9.00
WOW BNWT Oilily Skort apron 92 98 104 2-4yrs RARE 2005	$33.75	Danskin Ballet Tutu Dress - Like New! 2t 3t 4t TOD	$8.99
National Pageant Western Wear	$31.00	GYMBOREE European Holiday BERET NWT 18m - 3T	$8.99
Pageant Western Wear State, Nat.Level Unique no reserve	$29.99	Dora the Explorer Cotton Toddler Wrap Robe, size 2/4T!	$8.99
Hanna Anderson Coat size 80/10-24 months	$27.00	GYMBOREE NWT Sunflowers Tights - 2T/3T	$8.76
Cute Toddler OILILY Green Sandals Shoes Sz 25	$26.52	NWT Girl Ballerina Pink Glove Tea Party Ballet Gymboree	$8.75

Boys ▶ Clothing (Sz 4–7)

The average sales price in this subcategory is $11.90.

	HIGH		AVG
Oilily NWT Boys Sz 104 VHTF Tractor Winter Jacket	$127.50	2 PAIR USA FLAG BOXING PUNCHING GLOVES GIFT KIDS 4ozNEW	$11.99
Huge 19 pc lot of boys (sz.7-8) OLD NAVY jeans & shirts	$115.50	Bratz Kids Pink bathrobe Rainbow Bath ROBE 4-5 Med NEW	$11.99
Thomas the Tank Engine Winter Coat Size 6	$64.33	Boys Leather Motorcycle Vest Medium $30 NWT	$11.99
Back to School! Huge Lot Boy's Clothing Size 7	$57.56	Boys Leather MotorcycleVest XSmall $30 NWT	$11.99
Columbia Tectonite Coat and Snowpants 4T Exc. Condition	$56.00	NIKE BLACK HOODED BASKETBALL SWEATSHIRT *NWT* SIZE 7	$11.99
New Boys Gymboree Halloween Pirate Costume NWT sz 4 M	$51.00	NIKE GREY HOODED BASKETBALL SWEATSHIRT *NWT* SIZE 6	$11.99
OILILY VELVET /JACKET FOREST COLLEGE nwt sz 116/128	$44.00	NWT CHILDS WINNIE THE POOH COSTUME SIZE 4-6T	$11.75
Designer Baby Magil Italy 2 Pc Outfit Plaid Wool Boy 5	$43.70	Boys sz 6 Black Tuxedo Tux w/ Tails	$11.56
School Uniform Boys Girls Childrens Size 4/5 Big Lot	$42.99	NEW nwt RALPH Lauren BOYS Polo SPORT Socks 4 4T 5 6 7	$11.51
GYMBOREE Boys Fireman COAT Jacket FIRE MAN ~ MEDIUM	$41.00	sz. 5 boys Tommy Hilfiger waist lenght winter coat	$11.50
Lot of Boys 4T Clothes for Fall Winter School NWT	$41.00	Boys Spongebob Squarepants Halloween Costume~size small	$11.50
Dinosaur Costume (Disney - Aladar)	$41.00	NWT Boys Nascar #3 D. Earnhardt Jacket..Size 5/6..$2.99	$11.50
FIREMAN Halloween Costume-Size 4-7-LIKE NEW!	$41.00	Falls Creek size 7 snowpants Boys	$11.50
Beaux et Belles 6 7 Blue Green Corduroy Coat Fall BTS	$40.99	Boys Rothschild Jacket Coat Size Small 7/8 Hooded ECI	$11.49
DISNEY STORE 4 PICE SIZ X-SMALL BUZZ LIGHTYEAR COSTUME	$38.51	Peter Pan or Robin Hood Child Costume Hand Made	$11.35

Boys ▶ Clothing (Sz 4–7) ▶ Pajamas

The average sales price in this subcategory is $10.62.

NOTE *These results are based on a keyword search of the Clothing (Sz 4–7) subcategory for auctions with the word pajamas in the title.*

	HIGH		AVG
HUGE NWT BOYS GAP GYMBOREE PAJAMAS RL FALL SCHOOL LOT 5	$130.00	Boys lot 4T Sleepwear Carter's Pajamas NWT EUC Fall	$11.01
Boys sz 6 BTS Lot 23 Pieces Shirts Pants Shorts Pajamas	$80.00	Disney Store Toy Story BUZZ LIGHTYEAR Pj's Pajamas 4/5	$11.00
GYMBOREE GAP 7 PAIRS BOYS PAJAMAS PJS 5 5T EUC	$61.00	GYMBOREE 5 Large L Zoo Gymmies Pajamas PJs RARE	$11.00
Lot of 8 pajamas size 5T/6-boys-Rugrats,Batman,Elmo++	$46.00	NWT Boys Buzz Lightyear Warning Pajamas Size 6 L.S.	$11.00
Lot of 8 Disney Boys 6-6X pajamas, pjs	$41.05	2 PAIR BOYS GAP PAJAMAS FLANNEL 6	$10.99
Lot of 5 Pair Boys Gap Pajamas 100% Cotton, Size 8	$41.00	BABY GAP HALLOWEEN JACK-O- LANTERN	$10.99
LOT BOYS CLOTHES 6 pair Fall Winter PAJAMAS Size 6	$37.00	PAJAMAS PJS 4 NWT	
Boys Size 6 Jeans, Pajamas & More! Huge Lot 14 pieces!	$32.00	NWT Baby Gap Boys Blue Swimming Bear Pajamas PJs 2T	$10.75
DISNEY BUZZ LIGHTYEAR Pajamas Boys 6 NEW	$32.00	NWT Boys sz 6/7 Fall Osh Kosh Flannel Pajamas PJ's!	$10.75
[2 of these sold in a multiple item ("Dutch") auction for $16.00 each]		3 Pairs Boys Pajamas in size 5/6 in very nice condition	$10.51
Thomas the Tank Engine Flannel Pajamas Size 6 Glows	$31.54	Lot of Boys Pajamas size 5 ~Disney - Buzz Lightyear~	$10.51
4 Pairs of Gap Pjs Pajamas size 5T 4/5	$30.09	Thomas The Tank Engine Pajamas PJ'S 5T	$10.51

	HIGH		AVG
Great Lot of 2 Sets Incredibles Pajamas; Size 5T	$30.01	New Boys Osh Kosh Halloween Pjs pajamas sz 4 4t $24.00!	$10.51
6prs Boys DISNEY STORE TOY STORY STITCH PAJAMAS 5/6 6X	$29.99	Lot of 4 Boys Pajamas PJs Long Sleeved Fall Winter 7 8	$10.51
BOYS 5T PAJAMAS CARTERS SPONGE BOB	$29.00	Thomas the Tank Engine Pajamas Size 4/5 NEW!	$10.50
HUGE LOT boys pajamas...carters, disney, N kids	$27.50	Power Rangers Short Pajamas PJ's Size 4 (special ship)	$10.50

Boys ▸ Clothing (Sz 4–7) ▸ Swimwear

The average sales price in this subcategory is $7.41.

	HIGH		AVG
TWO BOYS SPEEDO SWIM SUITS SIZE 24 NWT	$40.00	NWOT Disney Store Incredibles Dash Bathing Suit 4 4T 5	$7.99
MY POOL PAL SWIM BATHING SUIT FLOTATION BOY 50-70LB NW	$35.00	NWOT Disney Store Incredibles Dash Bathing Suit 7 8	$7.99
NWT NEW ECKO UNLTD Boys 2 PC Beach Short SET size 6	$31.00	ATLAN WET KIDZ WETSUIT 6-8 YRS MADE IN CANADA NICE!!	$7.99
*NEW Burberry swim shorts SOLD OUT size 4	$29.99	**LANDS END** Hawaiian SwimTrunks Cobalt Size 5-6 New!!	$7.99
*NEW Burberry swim shorts SOLD OUT size 5	$29.99	NWT Tommy Hilfiger Swimsuit Trunks Boys 4/4T	$7.99
NEW nwt *LILLY PULITZER* swimsuit/trunks sz 6 NASSAU	$29.51	NWT BOYS NIKE SWIM SHORTS / SWIM SUIT SIZE 7 NICE!!	$7.50
NWT NEW ECKO UNLTD Boys 2 PC Beach Short SET size 7	$27.99	Thomas the Tank Engine Swim Trunks	$7.50
TWO BOYS SPEEDO TYPE SWIM SUITS SIZE 24 NWT	$27.77	SIZE M(5/6) NWT-SEAN JOHN RED SWIM TRUNKS W/SIDE POCKET	$7.49
THOMAS THE TANK SWIM TRUNKS W/ T-SHIRT, 5/6 , NEW, HTF	$26.00	new with tags swimsuit boys clothes shorts size 6/7 !	$7.24
NEW nwt *LILLY PULITZER* swimsuit trunks sz 5 NUT HOUSE	$24.99	LARGE LOT BOYS SWIMMING TRUNKS	$7.03
FLORIANE Boys Babar Red and Tan Swimtrunks 5y $73 NWT	$24.59	NWT Chez Ami Patsy Aiken 2005 swim trunks sz 6	$7.01
Boys swim trunks 26 Waist~ 2 PAIR~SPEEDO AND DOLPHIN	$23.71	BOYS SIZE 7 SWIM TRUNKS–BLUE—NWT	$7.00
Green Patagonia Size Kid's 6 Nylon Swim Trunks!!	$21.05	[2 of these sold for $7.00 each]	
QUICKSILVER Boys Rash Guard Surf Shirt Wakeboard 6	$20.76	Thomas the Tank Engine Flip Flop Sandals Great 4 summer	$6.99
NEW FLOTATION BATHING FLOATATION SWIM SUIT 33-65 4 5 6	$20.75	Thomas & Friends Tank Engine ' NEW Swim Trunks 4T	$6.99
		DRAGONBALL GT SWIM TRUNKS NWT SZ X-SMALL 6/7	$6.99

Boys ▸ Clothing (Sz 4–7) ▸ Underwear

The average sales price in this subcategory is $7.12.

	HIGH		AVG
$180 Lot 28 Boys Hanes Underwear 3-8 Briefs NWT NR	$57.00	BOYS BOB THE BUILDER UNDERWEAR PACK OF THREE - SIZE 4	$7.50
$154 Lot 22 Boys Hanes Underwear 3-8 Briefs NWT NR	$53.06	NEW Osh Kosh OSHKOSH 3 Boys SHARKS Underwear 6	$7.50
HUGE 21 pc LOT Toddler BOYS UNDERWEAR Size 2-3-4 CHEAP	$31.00	NEW Boys MONSTER TRUCK underwear briefs 6 pair size 6-8	$7.50
NEW OLD NAVY 22PC BOYS UNDERWEAR BRIEF LOT SIZE 6	$26.50	6 New Pair Gap Briefs Underwear Boys Size 6-7	$7.49
HUGE LOT boys 4T underwear - spongebob, scooby, blue	$26.00	BOYS BOXER BRIEF by HANNA ANDERSSON~SZ SMALL~NIB	$7.49
NEW 4 GAP BOYS UNDERWEAR BOXER BRIEFS SIZE S 6 - 7	$24.01	BOYS BOXERS Fruit of the Loom Underwear Sz S(6/8) NIP	$7.49
12 pair boy's briefs underwear M 6-8 waist 22-23 NWT	$21.00	NWOT Disney Store Peter Pan Underwear 5 6 captain hook	$7.26
[3 of these sold in a multiple item ("Dutch") auction for $7.00 each]		TOY STORY BUZZ LIGHTYEAR BOYS	$7.01
NEW 4 GAP BOYS UNDERWEAR BOXER BRIEFS SIZE XS 4 - 5	$20.51	BRIEFS/UNDERWEAR~MUST SEE	
Lot of 15 Boys Briefs Children's Place &other Size 5/6	$20.50	NWT pack of 3 pairs TOMMY HILFIGER crew socks 4-7 years	$7.01
31 pr lot of boys underwear sz 6 Sponge Bob Hulk etc	$20.50	THOMAS THE TANK ENGINE SZ 4T THREE IN PACK UNDERWEAR	$7.00
NEW 4 GAP BOYS UNDERWEAR BOXER BRIEFS SIZE S 6 - 7	$19.38	Lot of 14 Pair of Boys Underwear Size 6	$7.00
NIP BATMAN + SPIDERMAN + SUPERMAN + HULK UNDEROOS SZ 6!	$19.00	NIP CHICAGO CUBS Boys Briefs 2 pairs sz 5-6 CUTE!!!!!!!	$7.00
Huge Lot 8 prs NWT Boys GYMBOREE BOXERS XL/XXL 6-7 NEW	$18.50	BOB THE BUILDER SZ 2-3T THREE IN PACK UNDERWEAR	$7.00
NEW 6 PAIRS GAP SIZE XS 4 - 5 BOYS UNDERWEAR BRIEFS	$18.32	THOMAS THE TANK ENGINE SZ 4T THREE IN PACK UNDERWEAR	$7.00
HUGE LOT boys 4T underwear - scooby, nemo & more	$16.73	2 PACKS OF BOYS SPIDERMAN SZ 6 UNDEROOS UNDERWEAR NEW	$7.00

Boys ▸ Clothing (Sz 8 and up) ▸ Jeans & Pants

The average sales price in this subcategory is $9.19.

	HIGH		AVG
BOYS 19 PC LOT SZ 16 BACK TO SCHOOL JEANS SHORTS TOPS	$75.50	NWT Inline Hockey Pants TOUR RAGE Large Youth	$9.50
MIXED LOT - BOYS PANTS - SIZE 12 - NWT - VALUE $288	$75.00	Bugle Boy, Rider, Rustler, L.L. Bean , Size 8 Pants	$9.50
Huge Lot 12 Pairs Boys Sz 12 Jeans, Pants NWT/Resale	$60.00	Land's End Denim Climber Pants Boys Husky size 18 !!	$9.49
Huge Lot boys 8 10 Back To School 37 pc JNCO Adidas	$57.00	OLD NAVY SIZE 8 SLIM.LOOK NEW	$9.49
boys boutique sz 12 school 33 pc lot jeans shirts look	$56.01	COLUMBIA BOYS CONVERTIBLE PANTS, SZ.10/12,NEW!	$9.45
NICE LOT OF BTS CLOTHES-GOOD CONDITION! SIZE 10	$54.00	5 PC. BOYS SZ 7/8 JEANS AND PANTS, LEVI, OLD NAVY	$9.39
Lands' End Boy's Cargo Climber Pants 16 Husky 6 pairs	$49.77	TONY HAWK skateboard Cargo Pants sz 10 slim 23"	$9.38
OILILY BOY'S PANTS 24 HRS SERVICE NWT HTF SZ 11 146	$49.00	NWT-Boys Size 16 JNCO Skateboard Pants!	$9.27
Lot of boys pants, size 8/10 , 12 pairs in all !!!	$42.02	Land's End Boys Denim Climber Pants Husky Size 20 mint!	$9.06
new abercrombie kids boys brown cameron cargo pants 14	$39.00	GAP camoflauge sz 14 pants. BRAND NWT! Many pockets! NR!	$9.01
Abercrombie Khaki Cargo Pants BOYS BOY'S 12 SLIM A&F	$38.00	Lot of boy's sz 8 jeans, pants NIKE, PLUGG, LEE	$9.00
LN LOT 4 ABERCROMBIE & GAP PANTS, SWEATS BOYS SIZE 10!	$36.51	Boys Black Dress Pants by John Henry - Size 14 Husky	$9.00
new abercrombie kids boys navy cameron cargo pants 10	$30.00	RALPH LAUREN POLO B SZ 8 CLASSIC CARPENTER PANT NWT	$9.00
Boys 12-14-16- HUGE lot Nautica Old Navy Nesi AG	$29.00	Levis SilverTab Boys Jeans 14 Reg Baggy fit (26x26.5)	$8.99
new abercrombie kids boys brown cameron cargo pants 14	$27.56	ABERCROMBIE NWT. BOYS CARGO FATIGUE PANTS LARGE	$8.99

Boys ▸ Clothing (Sz 8 and up) ▸ Outerwear

The average sales price in this subcategory is $15.74.

	HIGH		AVG
=NEW=OILILY GREAT BOMBER JACKET "BOSTA" SZ140(US9/10Y)	$122.50	NEW BOYS NIKE "NEW YORK METS" JACKET SIZE L (12/14)	$16.50
Sonia Rykiel Boy/Girls Black Winter Coat NWT (Sz. 8)	$99.00	BOYS L 14-16 *NWT* ZERO XPOSUR WINTER JACKET REVERSIBLE	$16.50
NASCAR Daytona 500 Goofy Disney Jacket Adult Size XL	$77.00	NWT Boys GAP Camo Camouflage Jacket/gloves M (8)	$16.49
NASCAR Daytona 500 Goofy Disney Jacket Adult Size L	$72.50	MAKAVELI TUPAC BOYS JACKET- SIZE 18/20-NWT	$16.00
3 Gucci GG Caps GRAY & BLACK & TAN /Brown Cap/Hat NEW	$68.90	Boys Abercrombie Jacket Size LARGE - Like NEW! LQQK!	$16.00
[6 of these sold for $68.90 each]		JNCO JEANS HOODIE BOYS L NWT	$15.99
Boys,size 12, Michael Jackson "Beat It" jacket,vintage	$62.51	NEW Childrens Leather coat Size 10	$15.99
HARLEY DAVIDSON BOYS RACING JACKET	$61.00	BOYS PITTSBURGH STEELERS REVERSIBLE COAT SIZE 8-10	$15.65
BNWT 100% AUTH. ARMANI JR. FALL JACKET SZ. 34/10 YEARS	$59.99	NWT SZ 20 BOYS RALPH LAUREN JACKET-RETAIL $65	$15.53

	HIGH		AVG
NASCAR Daytona 500 Goofy Disney Jacket Adult Size XL	$55.00	NASCAR Officially Licensed Boys Size 8 Jacket Coat NR	$15.50
NWT!! ~ Abercrombie Boys COAT ~ Small 7/8 ~ NIcE!!	$52.00	BOYS ABERCROMBIE LOGO HOODIE - XL	$15.50
POLO Ralph LAUREN Khaki Jacket Coat Boys Small 7-8-10	$51.01	Boys /Girls Tommy Hilfiger Jacket Lined Med coat	$15.50
CARHARTT INSULATED WORK HOODIE JACKET YOUTH MEDIUM	$51.00	NASCAR Daytona 500 Peg Leg Pete Disney Jacket Kids Sz M	$15.50
POLO RALPH LAUREN~BOYS KHAKI JACKET/COAT~SZ SMALL 8-10	$49.99	FUBU BLACK/GRAY BOYS JACKET- LARGE(14-16)NWT	$15.50
NWT/NEW Boys AND 1 WINTER COAT JACKET BTS Size 14/16	$48.95	PATAGONIA Nylon-Fleece Lined Jacket ~ Youth Large(12)	$15.00
Columbia Boy's 10/12 WINTER Coat Jacket NWT FREE SHIP	$47.00		

Boys ▶ Clothing (Sz 8 and up) ▶ Shirts & T-Shirts

The average sales price in this subcategory is $8.35.

	HIGH		AVG
WWE RAW	$50.00	Lot of 7 Boy's T-shirts SIZE 10-12	$8.50
NWT QUIKSILVER quicksilver l/s shirt L large to cool	$37.50	Houston Texans youth 10/12 NFL helmet football t-shirt!	$8.50
(6) Tommy Hilfiger Ralph Lauren SS T-shirts-Boys Large	$35.52	SPONGEBOB LONG SLEEVE T SHIRT SIZE 12/14 NEW	$8.50
3 Quicksilver O'Neill Boys Large Shirt L Shirt NEW lot	$32.99	SPONGEBOB LONG SLEEVE T SHIRT SIZE 4/5 NEW	$8.50
GAP POLO SHIRTS BOYS SIZE M 7-8 LOT OF 3	$29.00	LOT boys long sleeve shirts sz 8 OLD NAVY NWT	$8.50
NWT NIKE LEBRON JAMES #23 CLEVELAND CAVS JERSEY ~ MED	$28.07	Ralph Lauren Button Down shirt Boys size M 12-14	$8.50
BOYS JNCO "SKATER" HOODIE SIZE XL-BACK 2 SCHOOL	$27.51	BSA Official Uniform Shirt Boy Scout Youth Large Kahki	$8.50
youth medium texas longhorns football jersey shirt NWT	$26.06	EARNHARDT JR #8 NASCAR YOUTH T-SHIRT MED 10-12 NEW RED	$8.49
NEW NWT Abercrombie Boys Vintage Polo Shirt Size Large	$26.00	sz 10 Abercrobie lot **Boys** like new long sleeve	$8.27
Ralph Lauren MULTI STRIPE boy polo shirt L 16/18 NWT	$26.00	Ben sherman polo shirt sky blue medium mens	$8.19
UMBRO ENGLAND JERSEY SOCCER BOYS XL NWT 14/16 YRS	$25.21	BOYS SIZE MEDIUM 10/12 JNCO BLUE LOGO TSHIRT EAGLE	$8.09
NWT TOMMY BOYS S/S TEE SIZE XL-14/16 BACK TO SCHOOL	$25.08	Polo by Ralph Lauren Hawaiian Tropical Boys Shirt 20	$8.09
NWT $72.00 Blue Lacoste - Boys Size 16/18 (L) -Size 3	$25.03	~ GAP ~ BOYS NAVY BLUE POLO SHIRT, SIZE 12 XL	$8.05
NWT!! BOYS SKATER SKULL FLAMES SHIRT SIZE MEDIUM 10 12	$25.01	Ralph Lauren Boys Pink Check Dress Shirt w/pony 7/8	$8.05
NWT $72.00 White Lacoste - Boys Size 16/18 (L) - 3	$25.01	NEWwTAGS SOUTH POLE BACK 2 SCHOOL SHIRT BOYS CLOTHES 14	$8.03

Boys ▶ Shoes

The average sales price in this subcategory is $12.42.

	HIGH		AVG
Air Jordan 4 VI Retro 6y size sz 6 cool grey / chrome	$140.50	Boys New Patent Leather Bl. Oxfords Tap Shoe, size 3.0	$13.00
Air Jordan XI 11 Retro sz 9.5	$135.00	NWT GYMBOREE YACHT CLUB BROWN LEATHER SHOE BOYS 2	$12.99
Air Jordan 4 VI Retro 6y size sz 6 white chrome green	$127.50	Boys Nike Sunray swim sandals size 11	$12.99
Air Jordan XVI 16 sz 9.5	$75.00	Nike Air Rift (GS) size 5Y -BRAND NEW-	$12.71
The Beginings Jordans	$69.00	childs Merrell shoes boys or girls size 13 ; jungle moc	$12.50
New Nike Air Rift Trainer with Socks Gry/Wht Men Size 8	$61.00	DUFFS Boys Skateboard Shoe "The Kid" size 10 NEW UNWORN	$12.50
NIB Nike Air Force 1 (ones) Boys/Girls 4..Women 6	$51.00	Durango Child's Cowboy Boots size 11	$12.50
Nike Shox NZ (GS) size 4.5Y -BRAND NEW-	$51.00	New Boy's Tap Shoes by Leo's Black Size 3.5	$12.50
Air Jordan 2 II Retro 5y size sz 5 white / red / black	$51.00	NEW BOYS SPEEDO WATER SHOES SIZE 4	$12.00
NEW MENS ROCKPORT BLACK LACE SHOE SIZE 12 W	$50.00	New Boy's Leather Tap Shoes by Leo's Black Size 3.5	$12.00
~BK~ OILILY BLUE HIGH TOP SNEAKER SZ 29(US 12) BNIB	$49.00	NEW Elafenten Boys Andrew Navy / Jeans Shoe Sz 8.5 M	$12.00
Air Jordan 2 II Retro 6.5y size sz 6.5 white red black	$48.00	NEW Elafenten Boys Bradley Brown Nubuck Smooth Sz 9 M	$12.00
BRANNOCK DEVICE JUNIOR MODEL	$46.00	New Boy's or Girl's Tap Shoes White Size 5	$12.00
BRAND NEW BIRKENSTOCK COW SHOE SIZE 29 11 US	$45.99	Kids yellow/black Merrell Alpine Moc shoes 5.5	$11.10
NEW KIDS NIKE SHOX TURB OZ RUNNING SHOES BOYS 2.5	$45.01	Boys Shoes Sneakers Size 2 NEW Spiderman Light up	$11.10

Girls ▶ Accessories

The average sales price in this subcategory is $6.96.

	HIGH		AVG
Boutique Pixies Custom turquoise "rodeo" necklace	$57.51	Hilary Duff ~Butterflies & Gems~ Charm Necklace	$7.99
NEW STUFF HILARY DUFF LUNCH TOTE NOT BACKPACK LUNCHBOX	$38.00	Lizzie McGuire/Hilary Duff Mini Portable FM Radio NEW	$7.95
PRETTY IN PUNK Boutique PIXIES YuMmY FRINGE Bracelet	$31.59	volleyball shoes women sz 8	$7.83
HauteTOTS Euro Poppin' Posie Boutique Girls Necklace	$29.99	Limited Too BackPack Bag Tote Purse NWT Girls S M L XL	$7.76
Boutique STUDIOE SNOWMAN PINK CHRISTMAS Bracelet D2MA	$28.00	Silver & Gold Communion Baptism Cross Pendant #7132	$7.00
SPB*Boutique FUnkY Pink & Black CUfF Bracelet JEM*M2MA	$25.99	CARE BEARS Umbrella******NWT******	$7.00
MERMAID & BLOWFISH FUN Boutique PIXIES Child BRACELET	$25.50	GIGGLE GARDEN Boutique Beaded Socks * oh greta! * SASAB	$6.99
GYMBOREE FOLK SONG SNOW PANTS/hat/scarf/gloves XL XXL	$25.37	SCHOOL IS FUN Boutique Beaded Socks * oh greta!* SASAB	$6.99
Giggles Boutique Ladies Girl Fall Flora Fringe Bracelet	$24.99	NWT- Girls pink cord bucket hat David & Young - CoOll	$6.76
MUST HAVE! NWT DORA the EXPLORER SLEEPING BAG FUN!!	$24.99	*New* Pink Grass Hula Skirt Hawaiian Swimsuit Cover-Up	$2.00
NEW Girls Limited Too Justice "Monkey" Room Curtain	$24.00	CANDY LAND Queen Frostine Bracelet Hasbro Jewelry NEW	$6.00
2 New ~The Wiggles ~Backpacks ~Such a Deal !! L0()k	$22.49	BLUE TWILIGHT Boutique Beaded Socks * SASAB	$5.99
2 New ~The Wiggles ~Backpacks ~Such a Deal !! L0()k	$22.01	NWT Lot CARE BEARS * Toothbrush * Lip Balm * & MORE!!!!	$5.99
2 New ~The Wiggles ~Backpacks ~Such a Deal !! L0()k	$21.62	dance/drill team costume/uniform	$5.50
Icky Baby ARTIST SMOCK pink mermaids NWT art school	$21.50	Gold Chinese Dragon Folding Cloth Hand Fan Embroidered	$5.50

Girls ▶ Clothing (Sz 4–6x) ▶ Dresses

The average sales price in this subcategory is $14.37.

	HIGH		AVG
Brand New National Level Girls Pageant Dress 4 5 6 slim	$520.00	ANAVINI green check with smocked apples & worms size 6	$14.99
Orient Expressed Smocked Girls Holding Hands Bishop-2	$150.00	NWT Gymboree Tiger Love hooded dress sz 6	$14.99
Huge Lot DISNEY Princess Dress-up Dresses & Access!!!!!	$140.38	Girls Size 5 Gymboree Sweet Chic Denim Jumper Dress	$14.99
Raggedy Ann Exquisite Costume Dress 5 pc set	$115.00	Girls size 5 Polo Ralph Lauren dress size 5 NWOT	$14.99
Tiffany Designs Gown Pageant Dress Size 6 Winner	$102.50	NEW NAVY SUMMER~*DREAM*~FLOWER GIRL PAGEANT DRESS 6	$14.95
GIRLS PAGEANT DRESS LILAC SIZE 5	$67.00	Delicate white antique embroidered child's dress	$14.95
Boutique Dutch Jottum Dress Tulle New NWT 110 5 5y	$61.00	Gymboree Tiger Love Red Heart Dress/Tights Set 5	$14.52
BITTY BABY ROSY RED OUTFIT FOR GIRL (5) AND DOLL NIB	$49.99	NWT GAP GIRLS DENIM PINK BUTTERFLY SEQUIN DRESS 6-7	$14.50

Princess Tea Dress Up Suitcase and accessories	$49.99
BABY LULU~NWT$85~CHENILLE LAVENDER OVERALL SET~GIRLS 4T	$49.99
AMERICAN GIRL WINTER WONDERLAND BITTY BABY & GIRLS LOT	$49.88
NEW NATIONAL LEVEL WHITE PAGEANT DRESS sz 4	$48.00
Bitty Baby Ballerina With Girls Dress + Extras	$47.03
New DISNEY STORE Princess Belle Beauty costume dress up	$47.00
DISNEY PRINCESS ARIEL MERMAID PRESTIGE COSTUME DRESS 3-	$46.64

LAND'S END Girl Navy Corduroy School Jumper/Dress 6x/6	$14.08
Gymboree FOX TROT Dress 5 EUC Like NEW	$14.07
Girls 2 piece dress, size 6x. Very nice. like new:)	$14.06
Gymboree SWEET CUPCAKE Pink striped dress l/s HTF 4	$14.05
NWT BOUTIQUE BRAND ~ LIPSTIK ~ DRESS SIZE 4 $72	$14.00
Smocked Petit Ami dress & bloomer pants - size 4T	$14.00
NEW NAARTJIE Knit ripple Stripe Drift flower Dress L 6	$14.00

Girls ▸ Clothing (Sz 4–6x) ▸ Outfits & Sets

The average sales price in this subcategory is $21.23.

	HIGH		AVG
National Pageant Sportswear sz.4/5 "lets Rumba" TDF!!!	$405.00	Trendy~ BOHO Guess PATCHWORK Twirl Skirt and Top 4 -5-6	$21.71
~ HUGE LOT GIRLS CLOTHES ~ SIZE 5 / 6 CLOTHING GYMBOREE	$355.00	Precious Lilly Pulitzer skort sz 4 and top tee sz 6	$21.59
HUGE TRENDY SZ.6/6X LOT RALPH LAUREN TOMMY All NewWTags	$251.00	Cute BABY PHAT outfit jeans and shirt Sz 5-6	$21.51
GYMBOREE HUGE GIRL'S FALL/WINTER LOT! Sz. 6 and 7	$212.50	4pc School Uniform Lot Navy Skorts Sweater Jumper 5 / 6	$21.50
NWT BTS GIRLS SIZE 6 LOT OF 8 BOUTIQUE DESIGNER OUTFITS	$168.50	R/W/B Pageant wear"Boutique BTS outfit" LK.NEW sz.6X	$21.50
HUGE 53 pce Lot Girls BACK TO SCHOOL Clothes Sz 4,5,6	$162.50	Gymboree Mod Zebra Gogo Black Shirt/Pants Set 4	$21.48
HUGE 46 PC GIRLS LOT SIZE 6/6X SUMMER FALL SOME NWT!!	$154.25	NAARTJIE '04 2pc Arctic Linen Loom Dress NWT 6 ~OTTOP~	$21.38
~NWT~ New LOT Girls Fall Back-2-School Outfits Sz 6	$152.50	Funtasia Too Apples for Fall set, cute!! 4 4T	$21.19
Trendy Girls NWT,BTS Designer Lot sz.5, 5/6 SKECHERS	$147.50	Gymboree INDIAN SUMMER butterfly aline top 2pc set L 5	$21.11
Girls 26pc.NWT Fall BTS sz.6 6X,GAP, LIMITED TOO, O.N.	$142.50	NEW GAP NAVY BLUE RAINBOW 3PC TRACK SET SIZE 6-7	$21.00
Boutique Dutch Jottum 2 Piece Blouse Skirt 104 4y 4t	$112.39	LOT OF 6 FALL / WINTER OUTFITS GIRLS SIZE 6	$20.76
HUGE!! 59Pc. *TRENDY* GIRLS SZ 4/6 *BACK TO SCHOOL* LOT	$108.00	Gap Darling 4pc Set Skirt, Top, Sweater & Tights Sz 5	$20.59
16pc Gymboree BACK to SCHOOL Fall Lot, Size 5/6/7	$102.50	RED Poodle Skirt Set, 5 pcs.Girl's Sm.Homemade CUTE!	$20.55
HUGE LOT GIRLS girl boutique size 4 5 6 6X NEW NWT	$100.00	New Dance Outfit Youth Small Black/Pink/Red/Gold-Nice	$20.54
Sandi Henry Pageant Swim Suit 4/5	$100.00	NWT KEEDO 2 PC PANTS SET SIZE M (5 / 6)	$20.50

Girls ▸ Clothing (Sz 4–6x) ▸ Sweaters

The average sales price in this subcategory is $12.33.

	HIGH		AVG
OILILY NWT Fall 05/06 Gorgeous cardy KATCHIE 116 / 5-6	$159.00	Sale! NWT Cornelloki Girls Lime Green Sweater Size 4	$12.50
OiLiLY WINTER 04/05 K-BERYL SWEATER ~NEW~ SIZE 104	$93.99	Girl's Gymboree Folk Song butterfly sweater 5 EUC BTS	$12.50
OILILY NWT Fall 2005/2006 Great cardy KRAZE 116/5-6	$89.00	NWT Gymboree FOX TROT white criss cross sweater top 5	$12.50
New Juicy Couture Baby Cashmere Blue Sweater Girl Sz 6	$69.00	Gymboree Apple for the Teacher Red Cable Knit Sweater 4	$12.50
BURBERRY Girls Coral "B" Sweater 5y $108 NWT	$57.76	Gymboree Holiday Magic Cherries Hoodie sweater sz 5 BTS	$12.50
BURBERRY Girls Coral "B" Sweater 8y $116 NWT	$52.00	Gymboree Bubble Fun Ribbon Hooded Sweater 5 new NWT BTS	$12.50
BURBERRY Girls Coral "B" Sweater 6y $116 NWT	$51.00	Gymboree Sunflower Fields Sweater Size 6	$12.48
New Juicy Couture Baby Cashmere Pink Sweater Girl Sz 4	$49.00	Gymboree Mod Zebra Cardigan Sweater 5	$12.43
DISNEYLAND PRINCESS Sweat Jacket Girls Pink XS NEW	$48.00	GAP Kids Girls 4 Puppy Dog Pink Sweater	$12.06
[3 of these sold in a multiple item ("Dutch") auction for $16 each]		GYMBOREE Folk Song THE Fringe Sweater Size 4 NEW	$12.06
DISNEYLAND Tinker Bell Sweat Jacket Girls XS NEW	$48.00	NWT Gymboree SUNFLOWER FIELDS Navy Sweater Sz 4	$12.06
[4 of these sold in a multiple item ("Dutch") auction for $12.00 each]		Gymboree Bon Voyage Paris Kitty Cardigan Sweater L-5	$12.00
Oilily tie cardigan 104 4/5 girls great sweater LOOK	$46.01	RALPH LAUREN GIRLS 4/5 FALL/WINTER SWEATER	$12.00
SoldOut Worldwide OILILY GIRL FRIENDS SWEATER 4 5 6 116	$46.00	NWT GYMBOREE EUROPEAN HOLIDAY POODLE SWEATER SIZE 4	$11.99
Girls RALPH LAUREN SWEATER 6 6X BTS	$46.00	NWT GYMBOREE EUROPEAN HOLIDAY POODLE SWEATER SIZE 6	$11.99
RALPH LAUREN PANTS SHIRT SIZE 4T DRESS TOMMY SWEATER	$45.00		
~New WO Tags Oilily Sweater & Socks Sz 116 6/6x~	$42.99		

Girls ▸ Clothing (Sz 7 and up) ▸ Jeans & Pants

The average sales price in this subcategory is $9.07.

	HIGH		AVG
NWT 128 7/8 OILILY Denise Ole Ole Star Pants NR $$$	$59.99	GIRLS 10 MUDD MAD BLEACH PAINTED RIBBON JEANS	$9.50
Lot 7 girls pants, Pepe, Tommy, Mudd, abercrombie New	$52.00	MUDD CAMO PANTS w/TIE BOTTOMS - GIRLS SZ 14	$9.50
OILILY WINTER LAVENDER VELVET PANTS DUSSY NWT 122 CUTE	$50.02	sz 7 NWT gymboree MOD ZEBRA black FLARE PANTS NEW XXL	$9.50
GYMBOREE LOT Girls 6 7 XL XXL Bubble Gum Pant Jeans!!!!	$49.07	Girls Gap white cargo pants size 7	$9.50
BOUTIQUE JUICY COUTURE HEPBURN VELOUR PANT NWT 10	$43.00	Gymboree Bubble Fun Velour Yoga Pants 7 NWT	$9.38
DA NANG CAMOUFLAGE SILK PANTS NWT SZ M girls	$40.99	Gymboree NWT Sunflower Fields Sequin Yoga Pants ~8~ BTS	$9.37
MAKAVELI GIRLS PANT/ PANT SUIT; A+++++ BNWT; SIZE 8/10	$39.99	HANNA ANDERSSON RUFFLED PANTS SIZE 140 BTS!	$9.26
~Dickies~ 3 pairs Girls Pants size 1	$39.60	Gymboree puppy love mole skin pants girls 3x- 8 years	$9.05
NWT DA NANG silk camo pants M reg. price $94	$37.00	GAP Gapkids Girls black pants M 7 8 Adorable	$9.01
girls sz. 10 jeans / pants lot BTS	$36.04	NWT Gymboree 'TIGER LOVE' Velour Kitty Pants...Sz 9	$9.01
Flowers By Zoe~Crop Pant~Spandex~Pink Stitches Sz.10	$34.99	NWT Gymboree HIDE AND SEEK Mushroom Applique Pants 10	$9.00
~Gorgeous OILILY Velvet Pants Sz 128~ MUST SEE!	$33.01	Girls ABERCROMBIE Military Army Green Cargo Pants 12 **	$8.99
BOUTIQUE JUICY COUTURE PRINCESS VELOUR PANT NWT 10	$33.00	GIRLS ABERCROMBIE STUDDED HEART JEANS 10 EXC. COND. WOW	$8.99
BOUTIQUE JUICY COUTURE NEW WAVE VELOUR PANT NWT 10	$31.00	NEW Gap Kids/Girls Cargo Pants Size 12 Plus	$8.99
WOW ! DA-NANG Girls~ Silk Crop Pant/Sequins Sz.12~ NWT	$29.99	SO COOL GYMBOREE NWT MOD ZEBRA PANT 9 FSBIN	$8.99

Girls ▸ Shoes

The average sales price in this subcategory is $10.63.

	HIGH		AVG
Irish Dance Shoes: Boyne Walk Hard/Jig Shoes New!	$61.00	Girls Pink Golf Pond GYMBOREE Loafers Shoes Sz 8	$11.49
NEW - Antonio Pacelli Hard Shoes – Irish Dance	$56.00	Girls Shoes/Clothes, naartjie, size 2(youth)	$11.49
@ AWSOME@ RWB patriotic wear 5/6 pageant	$50.00	NIB! Splitsole Jazz Dance Shoes-Size 1M (Girl/Boy)	$11.29
Innisfree Irish Dance Shoes Jigs Sz 2 1/2 UK NWT	$49.99	MINT COND! RARE! Gymboree S.S. Dragonfly Clogs Sz. 9	$11.01
Innisfree Irish Dance Shoes Jigs Sz 2 UK NWT	$49.99	LOT OF 3 PAIRS OF DANCETIME TAP SHOES, 10, 11, & 11 1/2	$11.00
NEW GIRLS ETNIES CALLICUT PINK WHITE SKATE SHOES SIZE 5	$41.00	NEW IN BOX Girls Size 1 MUDD Brand Shoes, VERY NICE!	$10.99

	HIGH		AVG
NWT ~OILILY canvas tennis shoes flower power sz 32 US 2	$41.00	Stride Rite Baby Girls Leather Shoes 4.5 Wide W FREE	$10.99
Antonio Pacelli Child's Irish dance shoes - Hard shoe	$38.99	LOT OF 9 PAIRS OF GIRLS SIZE 10 SHOES - MANY STYLES	$10.50
NEW ETNIES CalliCut White/PkRose Girls Yth sz 6 shoes	$37.01	Gently Used Girls Tan Tap Shoes /Size 11	$10.50
New Agatha Ruiz De La Prada Girls Shoes 26/9	$37.00	BALLET POINTE SHOES BLOCH 5 1/2 XXX USED TOE	$10.50
New Pom D'api Girls Leather Boots Fuchsia 21/5	$36.00	LITTLE GIRL CANVAS SHOES/DENIM/ZIPPER/SIZE 10	$10.50
Girls boys dance tumbling shoes SZ 3 1/2 Bloch Capezio	$35.00	NWOB BLOCH TECHNO WHITE LEATHER TAP PINK HEART SHOES	$10.50
New Faro Girls Leather Shoes! 30/13 Spain	$31.89	New BLACK split sole jazz shoes...sz 4	$10.50
New Elefanten Girls Leather Shoes navy 28/10.5	$30.26	Dance Revolution Tan Boot Style Jazz Tap Shoe Sz 5	$10.49
New Pom D'api Girls Leather Boots Fuchsia 25/8	$29.99	NIP Gymboree Bubble Fun Shoes Big Girl Size 2 ~WOW~	$10.49

Men's Accessories ▶ Belts

The average sales price in this subcategory is $19.77.

	HIGH		AVG
DSQUARED NEW COLLECTION FW 05/06 !!! HIGHLIGHT BELT!!	$237.50	NEW! Kenneth Cole Reaction Men's Belt Size 36 Black	$20.01
NEW Peter Huber Alligator Crocodile Mens Belt Brown 38	$139.00	New Giorgio Armani Black Leather Belt w/ Gift Box A11	$20.00
NEW Peter Huber Alligator Crocodile Mens Belt Black 40	$139.00	DOLCE & GABBANA Leather belt D&G (sz 38-40)	$20.00
100 NEW LEATHER MENS BELTS with BUCKLES at WHOLESALE	$102.50	NEW GIORGIO ARMANI WHITE LEATHER BELT	$20.00
NEW! J .Lindeberg (White) Slater Pro Leather Belt (100)	$99.00	AX!! BLACK (M)33-35 free shipping buy NOW $20.00	$20.00
NEW! J .Lindeberg (White) Slater Pro Leather Belt (85)	$97.00	Ralph Lauren Polo Mens Size 36 38 or 40 Brown Belt $125	$19.99
J Lindeberg MIAMI Black Leather Golf Club Belt 34/95	$86.00	$125 POLO Ralph Lauren Black Ital. Leather Belt 36 NWT	$19.99
Exclusive Unisex GUCCI Double G Silver Buckle Belt 42	$85.00	RALPH LAUREN BLACK GENUINE LEATHER WIDE BELT MED AUTH	$19.99
Amazing Mens GUCCI Reversible Adjustable G Buckle Belt	$85.00	Perry Ellis Cordivan Leather Belt Silver Logo Buckle 34	$19.99
Mont Blanc Black Leather Mens Belt Oval Shaped Buckle	$81.51	POLO RALPH LAUREN MENS BLACK LEATHER BELT WOW $100 S 42	$19.99
NWT D&G, DOLCE&GABBANA, BELTs FOR MEN Sz STANDARD	$76.00	NEW DRESS GOLF BELT GATOR LEATHER BROWN 46 BIG & TALL	$19.95
ERMENEGILDO ZEGNA LEATHER BELT BROWN 36 RT $225 NWT NR	$69.99	NEW MEN'S GOLF BELT ALLIGATOR LEATHER SIZE 36 BROWN	$19.95
DSQUARED Keepin Me Hot : Mounties Belt szl(30-34) Tan	$69.00	new MEN'S GOLF belt ITALIAN ALLIGATOR LEATHER BROWN 36	$19.95
$285 VERSACE SS buckle Medusa leather belt 42 w/box	$64.99	Leather Belts WOLF SZ 30-60 HD New 11/2" Belt w/buckle	$19.95
New TOMMY BAHAMA What A Croc Brown Belt size 34 $185	$63.05	PUNK ROCK STAR WHITE SILVER STUDS LEATHER BELTS S/M	$19.95

Men's Accessories ▶ Hats

The average sales price in this subcategory is $16.00.

	HIGH		AVG
L-R-G lifted research group jean jacket L supreme hat	$142.50	RAFFIA COWBOY HAT WESTERN WEAR FRINGED RODEO HATS	$16.95
Bathing Ape BBC Hat Cap L white	$110.00	<>NEW<>PINK TEXAS LONGHORNS CAP HAT<>	$16.95
Genuine PITH HELMET Hat - India? Egypt?	$93.90	RAFFIA COWBOY HAT WESTERN WEAR FRINGED RODEO HATS	$16.95
NEW IN BOX - METRO PCS NOKIA 6015 6015i PHONE - NICE!!!	$89.99	GREG STRAW OUTBACK GAMBLER NORMAN HAT GOLF One Size	$16.51
Unofficial Flatpick-L Hat w/ Steve Kaufman Signature	$86.00	New Era Cap Hat - SF Giant (Black, 7 5/8)NE0004	$16.51
TOMMY BAHAMA HAND WOVEN STRAW/PANAMA HAT	$71.00	12 GREY Visor Visors caps cap hat hats Wholesale GRAY	$16.49
mint US NATIONAL PARK SERVICE hat Stratton 7 1/4	$64.00	Mens vintage German Tyrolean wool hat L	$16.45
NWT TILLEY ENDURABLE HAT T4 Khaki or Natural any size	$55.50	Evinrude Outboard Etec Fishing Cap Hat by Bombardier	$16.00
NWT TILLEY HEMP HAT TH4 Natural any size	$55.00	OCC ORANGE COUNTY CHOPPERS NAVY DAGGER HAT	$15.99
BRAND NEW TILLEY HAT LTM6 AIRFLO	$53.00	Straw Driving Cap- Men's Hats- New Item- Size XL	$15.99
Vintage 1960s Vietnam Thailand Korat Jungle Hat Ex!	$51.00	SHAPABLE COWBOY WESTERN HATS RAFFIA HAT COWBOYS	$15.99
FABULOUS PURPLE GLITZY XXXXX MEXICAN SOMBRERO HAT L@@K!	$49.99	BRAND NEW AUTHENTIC KANGOL 504 RED WOOL CAP HAT SZ LG	$15.99
VERSACE BASEBALL WHITE HAT CAP	$49.99	crushable raffia straw GOLF HAT new summer hats	$15.63
BLACK RAGING BULL LEATHER HAT WALKER COWBOY HATS	$49.99	crushable raffia straw GOLF HAT new summer hats	$15.61
COWBOY WESTERN WEAR HATS MOSSY OAK HAT COWBOYS HUNTING	$49.95	NJSP New Jersey State Police Hat FOP Trooper	$15.51

Men's Accessories ▶ Neckwear, Ties

The average sales price in this subcategory is $14.82.

	HIGH		AVG
VERY RARE 100% REAL HERMES TIE * RED w/ BLUE GLIDERS	$167.00	GIORGIO ARMANI SILK TIE MADE IN ITALY ORANGE	$15.50
100%Silk Brioni Tie Superb White Snow Special Occasions	$102.50	New D&G, DOLCE & GABBANA tie, White/Gold/Gray Stripe	$15.50
100 % Silk Brioni Tie Super Chic Living Red w/Blue Dots	$83.88	JERRY GARCIA PARIS IN THE RAIN ORANGE NECK TIE	$15.00
Authentic Hermes Silk Mens Tie	$75.00	New! Finest Italian Silk Tie Leveti of Hollywood! $159	$15.00
2005 Ribbons Vitaliano Pancaldi Silk Necktie Tie Ties	$74.00	JERRY GARCIA LE WIRED CROSSROADS NECK TIE- NWT	$15.00
NWT JERRY GARCIA SILK TIE/TIES NECKTIE COLLECTION #38	$65.52	NEW IKE BEHAR NEW YORK MEN SILK TIE $75 SILVER	$14.99
NWOT Blue Elephants Hermes Paris Suit Tie 7621 TA	$59.99	VALENTINO Italian Elegant Long Tie MUST SEE !!!	$14.99
HERMES 5019 EA 100% silk tie. Made in France	$56.00	LEAFY tie by JHANE BARNES ! Original Fabric	$14.99
100%Silk Brioni Tie Elegant White,Grey,Silver&Black Str	$54.99	NEW w/ Tag's TOMMY BAHAMA Off-Island Silk Tie 75.00	$14.50
BRAND NEW LEONARD PARIS SILK TIE. MADE IN ITALY.	$51.01	Men's $100. Stripe Silk Tie-IKE BEHAR (Golden Tan)	$14.00
100 % Silk Brioni Tie Superb Pink & Light Grey Stripes	$51.00	NWT - JERRY GARCIA TIE collection #38 $39.50	$13.79
New Kiton Style Luciano Soprani 7 Fold Tie MSRP $239	$49.95	EGON VON FURSTENBERG 100% silk tie. Made in Italy	$13.19
100%Silk Brioni Tie Superb White,Pink,Sky&Dark Navy Str	$46.00	TOMMY HILFIGER MENS WALLET WALLETS NEW BLACK TRIFOLD	$13.07
100%Silk Brioni Tie Light Pink Original Blue&Red Design	$45.00	LEATHER NECK TIE, Fathers Day Gift, men clothing;	$12.99
100%Silk Brioni Tie Elegant Snow White/Navy&Gold Stripe	$45.00	New GIANNI VERSACE tie, BLUE w/ Tan Stripe	$12.50

Men's Accessories ▶ Wallets, Holders

The average sales price in this subcategory is $29.83.

	HIGH		AVG
TRAVIS WALKER CUSTOM #00 CROSS WALLET & WALLET CHAIN	$2,310.00	Authentic Emporio Armani Mens Black Wallet (ABW1)	$29.99
NEW LOUIS VUITTON LV VERNIS GLACE BLACK DOUBLE WALLET	$330.00	NIB BEN SHERMAN EMBOSSED	$29.99
Louis Vuitton Men's CUIR GLACE PTE MONN POIGNEE Wallet	$297.00	BLACK WALLET w/ CUFF LINKS	
JP Tods TODS brown leather wallet for MEN wallets men's	$175.00	Prada Credit Card Holder Wallet Blue Saffiano	$29.99
NEW! LV LOUIS VUITTON MONOGRAM CANVAS MEN'S WALLET	$159.96	NEW Mens Black Lacoste Bi Fold Leather Wallet NIB	$29.95
[4 of these sold in a multiple item ("Dutch") auction for $39.99 each]		[2 of these sold for $29.95 each]	

Montblanc Mont Blanc Starwalker Fine Pen NEW 08485 NIB	$149.99	NEW RL Ralph Lauren Polo Leather Mens Wallet Black	$29.95
100% BEAUTIFUL AUTHENTIC PRADA UNISEX GYM/DUFFLE BAG	$142.50	NEW Mens Black Lacoste Bi Fold Leather Wallet NIB	$29.95
100% Brand New Louis Vuitton LV Vernis Glace Wallet Men	$136.02	Sporran Day /Evening Cantle Top	$29.95
[2 of these sold in a multiple item ("Dutch") auction for $68.01 each]		COACH ID &2 CARD HOLDERS & MONEY CLIP	$29.63
ACM AUTO CREDIT CARD HOLDER MANAGER MONEY CLIP WALLET	$107.94	3 NEW MEN'S LEATHER FOSSIL	$28.00
[6 of these sold in a multiple item ("Dutch") auction for $17.99 each]		WALLETS + MONEY CLIP - WOW!!	
BRAND NEW LOUIS VUITTON LV VERNIS GLACE BLACK WALLET	$100.00	NIB NEW LACOSTE Men's Black Bi Fold Leather Wallet	$28.00
AUTH Gucci GG Beige Monogram Wallet POWERSELLER RARE!	$99.95	NIB wTags Authentic Men's Coach BROWN Tri-fold Wallet	$28.00
AUTH Gucci GG Black Monogram Wallet *POWERSELLER*	$99.95	HUGO BOSS SOFT LEATHER BLACK	$26.99
GEUNINE CROCODILE (alligator) LEATHER WALLET TWO TONE	$99.00	BIFOLD WALLET NEW IN BOX	
NEW! Louis Vuitton Mens Monogram Wallet	$93.00	NWT COACH Men's Magnetic Money Clip #4643-MSRP $58	$26.09
[3 of these sold in a multiple item ("Dutch") auction for $31.00 each]		LOUIS VUITTON MONOGRAM SNAP WALLET NEW NR	$26.01
Auth. GUCCI brown monogram bi-fold wallet MEN's NEW BOX	$89.99	ARMANI MEN'S WALLET PURSE BLACK NR No.AW006	$26.00

Men's Clothing ▶ Blazers & Sport Coats

The average sales price in this subcategory is $41.35.

	HIGH		AVG
GORGEOUS $3795 KITON CASHMERE	$325.00	NWT Men's Dolce&Gabbana Sports Zip Jacket sz M, Blue	$46.99
SINCLAIR FREE TURNBULL OR BRIONI TIE INCLUDED	$304.11	NWT HOLLISTER VINTAGE SIR FETCHALOT JACKET BLAZER L	$46.00
Mint BRIONI 2 btn black blazer sportcoat 52L 52 L	$280.00	Men's D&G DOLCE GABBANA SPORTS JACKET sz M, Blue	$46.00
Brioni Blazer Sz. 44 Summer SALE !!!	$279.00	MANI BY GIORGIO ARMANI SPORTCOAT~*~SIZE 38-S~*~LQQK~*~	$46.00
Brioni Cashmere Blazer Sz. 44 Summer SALE !!!	$235.00	Hart Schaffner Marx Navy Wool Blazer 54L Nordstrom NEW	$45.50
MATSUDA Linen Jacket Comme des Garcons Issey Miyake	$200.00	Austrian Trachten Jacket/Janker4 Lederhosen 38 #6575	$45.00
DIESEL ZIP JACKET, MEN'S, ITALY, SIZE "L"	$186.00	$895 Joseph Abboud DB Blazer/Sport Coat BLACK 43R 43 R	$45.00
VSCT Miami loungejacket man dsquared ayor d&g	$169.00	mens velvet red blazer sport coat	$42.50
NWT AUTHENTIC GIANFRANCO FERRE $1320 BLAZER JACKET M	$149.99	$795 Samuelsohn Jacket Blazer 42 R Black Brown MINT	$41.00
Used $1495 Gucci Blazer 42/52	$149.00	LN Patagonia Mens Suit Jacket / Blazer, 42L	$41.00
ZARA SLIM CUT BLACK BLAZER Sz50 dior homme	$148.67	VINTAGE BLACK VELVET/SUEDE BLAZER/DINNER JACKET SZ 52 L	$41.00
FERRAGAMO SILK/CAMEL HR PLAID	$143.50	Vintage Yves Saint Laurent Cord Sport Jacket Coat 37	$41.00
BLAZER/SPORT COAT 42R NEW		Giorgio Armani grey 44R mens grey jacket blazer NR!	$41.00
Harley Davidson XXL Leather Eagle Jacket	$140.38	Gorgeous Mens BROOKS BROTHERS 3 Button Navy 52R NR!!!	$41.00
NEW $2700 VERSACE COUTURE 40 L SPORT COAT BLUE	$138.50	CANALI MENS BLACK WOOL SINGLE BREASTED BLAZER 42	$40.99

Men's Clothing ▶ Jeans

The average sales price in this subcategory is $20.82.

	HIGH		AVG
MOST WANTED DSQUARED RUNWAY F*CKER JEANS *52*	$349.00	44 x 30 OshKosh Bib Overalls Bibs Jeans New w Tags	$21.49
Dsquared "Engineered" (twisted) baggy jeans	$148.50	Akademiks Dark Stitch Jeans (W34 x L32) NWT	$21.49
NWT Diesel Levan 84J W29 32L not zathan zaf farco 29 30	$125.00	New Abercrombie & Fitch Mens Jeans 33/34	$21.01
RARE OG 50's VINTAGE LEVI'S BIG E 501 30 X 34 Redline	$121.50	NWT Hollister by Abercrombie Pacific Worker Jeans sz34	$21.00
New men's Versace jeans size 32x34 suede ornam lt blue	$102.50	Band New Marithe Francois short Girbaud jeans Sz 42	$21.00
LEVIS LVC 1933 EXPLOSION 501XX W36 L34- LIMITED VINTAGE	$91.00	MENS 34x30 5 PAIR LOT OF GAP AND OLD NAVY JEANS	$21.00
SEVEN ALL-MANKIND JEANS NWT Sz 33	$86.99	Brand New RocaWeaR Jean Sz. 34 Indigo, pants	$20.99
New Men's Versace Jeans Couture Sport Size 33	$83.00	NEW * 32 x 34 LEVI 529 LOW Straight Jeans * Levis NWT	$20.99
DIESEL BRAND NEW MEN'S ZATHAN JEANS 33-32	$79.99	LEVIS SILVERTAB JEANS 30 x 34 NWT LOW + LOOSE $48	$20.52
New AUTHENTIC Seven 7 For All Mankind Boot-Cut Jeans 32	$78.00	SKATEBOARD JEANS LOT-VOLCOM AWS,ZERO 32 WAIST	$20.50
SEVEN JEANS 7 - MENS JEANS - SIZE 36	$73.60	NWT Wrangler 13MWZ Cowboy Cut Sz. 31 x 38	$20.50
D&G New men's Dolce and Gabbana jeans sz 36	$71.00	NWT 20X Carpenter Jeans Sz. 28 x 36	$20.50
NEW 575 DENIM MEN'S BRANDON JEANS IN PLANTER WASH 30	$71.00	$62 BNWT Karl Kani Carpenter Jeans Pants 50 x 34	$20.50
BNWT Men's Destroyed DIESEL X-ROTUCK Jeans size 32 I	$70.01	Lucky Jeans Mens SZ 36	$20.50
MUST HAVE VERSACE JEAN COUTURE pants 38	$69.00	Band New Marithe Francois short Girbaud jeans Sz 32	$20.49

Men's Clothing ▶ Outerwear

The average sales price in this subcategory is $52.40.

	HIGH		AVG
VINTAGE BWL MALIBU CUSTOM BLACK MOTORCYCLE JACKET	$1,905.00	USMC Flak vest	$56.00
BWL MALIBU CUSTOM BLACK MOTORCYCLE JACKET VINTAGE BWL!!	$1,590.00	NEW HOLLISTER/ABERCROMBIE MAMMOTH RETRO JACKET/VEST L	$56.00
ROBERTO CAVALLI MENS $3354.00 LEATHER JACKET + BAG M	$1,158.00	The North Face -HydroSeal Men's Jacket LARGE	$55.00
gucci leather jacket BRAND NEW $5000.00	$499.99	VINTAGE USAF N-2B Flight Jacket Extreme Cold sz X-LARGE	$54.00
NEW Pelle Marc Buchanan Leather Jacket Size 62	$499.95	neW RuCA rvca HOODIE sweatshirt Large/Lg NWT	$54.00
Filson 252 Leather Field Satchel Unused With all tags	$405.00	Mens NWOT LEVIS VISIONAIRE BLUE Jean Jacket *Rare	$54.00
HARLEY DAVIDSON 100TH ANNIVERSARY LEATHER JACKET - MD	$350.00	Hollister Mens 2005 Hobson Ski Jacket, L	$53.43
HARLEY DAVIDSON 100th ANNIVERSARY LEATHER JACKET XL NEW	$280.00	NEW Goretex Jacket - XXXL 3XL	$51.59
New Feathered Friends FrontPoint Jacket	$250.00	old black leather jacket needs REPAIR! punk/ rockabilly	$51.50
Arc'teryx Alpha SV Jacket	$227.50	Corvette Black Leather Jacket - Size XL - Brand New	$51.02
NEW North Face Mens STEEP TECH APOGEE jacket Medium Red	$219.95	Oneill Snowboard/Ski Jacket 5000 MM Black NiceSick!!!!!	$51.00
AVIREX KING CASINO LEATHER JACKET	$215.00	NEW "SANYO-NEW YORK" Microfiber Jacket XL $195	$51.00
AVIREX LIMITED INSIGNIA LEATHER JACKET	$215.00	US GI Military ECWCS Gortex Desert Parka Medium Regular	$51.00
Arcteryx Gamma Mx Jacket Men's Medium New	$208.00	10X Gortex Realtree Camo Hooded Jacket Sz.XL Tall	$51.00
HARLEY-DAVIDSON black leather motorcycle jacket	$203.50	THE NORTHFACE GORE-TEX JACKET/COAT SZ: S	$51.00

Men's Clothing ▶ Pants

The average sales price in this subcategory is $19.25.

	HIGH		AVG
NEW! Arc'teryx Minuteman Gore-tex XCR Pants Bibs Men XL	$255.00	Brand New Adidas Pleated Front Stone Slacks w/ Tags	$19.99
NEW! Arc'teryx Arcteryx Minuteman Pants Bibs Men's M	$232.50	NEW 5.11 TACTICAL BLUE UNIFORM CLASS A PANTS SZ 34/34	$19.99

NEW Bavarian Lederhosen Knickers + Susp. XL - XXL	$174.00	NWT HOLLISTER ABERCROMBIE Oahu OpenTrack Active Pants L	$19.99
NEW! Arc'teryx Theta LT ski snowboard Pants Bib Men' S	$150.59	$145.00 Paradise Coves100% Twill SILK PLEAT SAND 38/30	$19.95
$650 DIOR HOMME HEDI SLIMANE BLACK PANTS TROUSERS HOT!	$150.00	Mens Kenneth Cole tan pants NWT!!! 36 x 34	$19.95
		BROOKS BROTHERS MENS DRESS SLACKS 36 NWT $118	$19.90
NEW! Arc'teryx Minuteman Gore-tex XCR Pants Bibs Men S	$122.50	NWT MENS DOCKERS CLASSIC FIT PLEATED PANTS / SIZE 52-32	$19.50
Men's Harley-Davidson Leather Pants Jeans - 38	$103.50	Mason's Distressed Cargo Pants from Bloomingdales Sz 32	$19.49
J. Lindeberg Troy mens zippered plum golf pants 34	$100.00	NEW MENS DOCKERS OLIVE KHAKI PANTS SLACKS W52 X L32	$19.03
AMAZING MEN'S GIANNI VERSACE PANTS 32	$91.00	NEW ABERCROMBIE MENS SCRUB PAJAMA PANTS M	$18.99
SEDITIONARIES,WESTWOOD ANGLOMANIA BONDAGE PANTS	$91.00	NEW ABERCROMBIE MENS SCRUB PAJAMA PANTS L	$18.99
C.C. FILSON WOOL PANTS/HUNTING PANTS SIZE 36	$88.77	$55 DOCKERS Mens Flat Front Dress Pants Black 38 x 30	$18.99
perfect BRIONI black slacks 46 x 30	$86.00	NWT $75 NIKE GOLF Mens Pleated Micro Fiber Pants 38X32	$18.99
perfect BRIONI tan slacks 44 46 x 30	$86.00	EMT/EMS, Fire, Rescue, Pants, New, Black, Large, Long	$18.95
Mens Authentic Prada Slacks/Pants Size Sm. 30W X 30L	$81.00	RALPH LAUREN SUPER 100'S GRAY DRESS PANTS MENS 36 X 32	$18.50
NWOT Hot Gucci Light Blue Flaired Slacks Sz.34 $325	$76.00	Dockers Premium Textured Microfiber Pants 42x30 NEW a	$18.50

Men's Clothing ▶ Shirts

The average sales price in this subcategory is $16.12.

	HIGH		AVG
Lot of 11 Mens Ralph Lauren Polo Mesh Shirts - Size M	$147.50	FANCY WESTERN LINEDANCING SHIRT	$62.99
brand new astros jersey with tags go for 170 normely	$112.50	3 New Ralph Lauren Polo sz Medium Pink Orange Aqua	$62.00
MATSUDA Gauze Shirt L Comme des Garcons Issey Miyake	$104.49	Filson Wool Shirt Straight Collar	$60.00
Authentic GUCCI Men's L/S Cotton Print SHIRT-NO RESERVE	$101.00	firsttastelatex - Latex Sleeveless Zip Shirt Mens L	$60.00
Kareem Abdul-Jabbar #33 LA Lakers pur-L	$79.99	Lot of 3 Lacoste Polo Shirts Men's New-Size 4 Sm Small	$56.00
$289 Auth Gucci men's navy blue chest logo polo shirt S	$75.99	NEW! Mens Tiger Woods Nike Short Sleeve Mock!! Last ONE	$54.50
Filson Wool Shirt Straight Collar	$71.00	Iron Maiden Jersey L Large Visions of the Beast #1	$53.52
Vintage Levi's Western Wear Black Cowboy Shirt Med.	$67.76	Kevin Garnett - Minnesota Timberwolves 1996 Home Jersey	$50.00
FANCY WESTERN LINEDANCING SHIRT	$62.99	NEW TOMMY BAHAMA SAND RIPPLE SILK TEE SHIRT XXL $95 NWT	$49.99
3 New Ralph Lauren Polo sz Medium Pink Orange Aqua	$62.00	NBA '84 JORDAN ROOKIE JERSEY 100% AUTHENTIC Sz.56	$49.00
Filson Wool Shirt Straight Collar	$60.00	NWT/NEW JAMS WORLD CRUISING BLACK SHIRT XL AWESOME!	$48.50
firsttastelatex - Latex Sleeveless Zip Shirt Mens L	$60.00	REYN JAMES DEAN MARLON BRANDO REBEL L HAWAIIAN SHIRT	$45.00
Lot of 3 Lacoste Polo Shirts Men's New-Size 4 Sm Small	$56.00	Insane Clown Posse lot	$41.00
NEW! Mens Tiger Woods Nike Short Sleeve Mock!! Last ONE	$54.50	Gsus Heren Shirt	$36.26
Iron Maiden Jersey L Large Visions of the Beast #1	$53.52	D & G Dolce Gabbana Mens Black/Orange V-Neck Shirt! M	$36.00

Men's Clothing ▶ Suits

The average sales price in this subcategory is $71.62.

	HIGH		AVG
New Men's Brown Pinstripe Suit Emporio Armani 40R 40 R	$400.00	NEW 2pc MEN'S DRESS SUIT 3-BUTTON NAVY PINSTRIPE 52L SG	$79.50
BRAND NEW VERSACE CLASSIC 3 buttoned light gray suit 44	$395.00	2pc MEN'S BUSINESS 3-BUTTON SUIT BLACK 40R NEW WITH TAG	$79.50
AMAZING men's 100% WOOL pin striped VALENTINO Suit 44R	$395.00	Boss Dark Green Suit	$79.00
Exclusive Mens VERSACE CASSIC 2 Tone Gray Wool Suit 44R	$385.00	MANI BY GIORGIO ARMANI SUIT~*~SIZE 44-L~*~ITALY~*~	$76.99
$2195 Gianni ITALY quality Mens Suits 100%Wool Tan 46L	$379.50	Boss Navy Pinstripe Suit	$76.00
Brioni Business Suit Sz. 44 Summer SALE !!!	$316.66	2pc MEN'S BUSINESS 3-BUTTON SUIT BLACK 36R NEW WITH TAG	$76.00
New Men's Brown Pinstripe Suit Emporio Armani 42R 42 R	$306.00	Mens Navy Pinstripe Dress Suit Size 44 R 44R New Suits	$75.00
ERMENEGILDO ZEGNA Suit 40R DARKBROWN new SU MISURA	$300.00	Hugo Boss Suit	$72.00
VALENTINO GREY MEN'S DOUBLE BREAST SUIT SZ 38 R NR NEW	$299.99	DAKS London Wool Suit 40R 40	$71.00
MISSONI BY VALENTINO ITALY WOOL BLACK SUIT 40 R $1200	$299.99	Steel Blue HUGO BOSS 2-btn Light Suit Jacket Men 44 R	$71.00
$1695 NWT E. ZEGNA Suit 36R Made In Italy & VERSACE Tie	$299.00	$929 BROOKS BROTHERS CHARCOAL + STRIPES MEN'S SUIT 48 R	$69.99
New ZEGNA Charcoal Pinstripe Wool Suit FREE SH 44R 44 R	$299.00	LIKE NEW BLUE 2-BUTTON RALPH LAUREN SUIT, 41T, WOW!!!	$69.99
GIORGIO ARMANI 2005 NEW MEN'S WOOL SUIT 44R	$288.00	2pc MEN'S BUSINESS 3-BUTTON SUIT BLACK 40R NEW WITH TAG	$69.50
Gucci 2pc men Black 44r 44 $$$$ 2000.00 Eur 56 46 suit	$280.00	$1400 CORNELIANI Suit 40S 40 S	$68.00
New! PALASSO SUIT $2195 (44S) REGAL BLACK W/ TAN STRIPE	$279.95	NWOT Tailored Flino For Americanmale 100's Suit 46R 46	$66.99

Men's Clothing ▶ Men's Shoes

The average sales price in this subcategory is $37.97.

NOTE *These results are based on a keyword search of the Men's Clothing subcategory for auctions with the word* shoes *in the title.*

	HIGH		AVG
Nike AIR JORDAN 2 Basketball Shoes NIB	$202.50	ECCO GOLF SHOES	$39.11
NEW PRADA AMERICA'S CUP MEN'S SHOES US 10,5 EU 44 #15	$170.00	NEW KENNETH COLE ITALIAN SUMMER	$39.00
[2 of these sold in a multiple item ("Dutch") auction for $85.00 each]		SHOES, LATEST SLIDES,10	
Authentic New PRADA Mens Dress Spazz Leather Shoes 7	$153.50	NIB Osiris Alter Skate Shoes Mens Sz. 10 Skateboard NEW	$39.00
Footjoy Foot Joy Classics Dry Premiere Golf Shoes 10 C	$152.50	NWT Timberland Boots Shoes #20062-gn (Green, US 10)	$38.90
Nike AIR JORDAN 2 Basketball Shoes NIB	$152.50	New adio Skateboard Shoes 88 Skate Sumner Men Size 11	$38.51
VINTAGE 1992 Nike Air max Jordan VIII 8 shoes sz. 12	$152.50	Brand new Diesel men's leather sneaker shoes size:11	$38.50
NIB AIR JORDAN IV (4) RETRO SHOES size 8.5 cool grey	$144.50	NEW mens DIESEL shoes sneakers leather 10 Euro 43 $89	$38.00
NEW $285 JIL SANDER PUMA SHOES NAVY BLUE 11 US	$133.50	Mens POLO R. Lauren Leather Casual Shoes Black – 11.5	$37.99
NIKE AIR JORDAN XX MENS BASKETBALL SHOES SIZE 10.5	$132.50	NEW TEVA men HYDRO water shoes US 10.5 EU 44 UK 9.5	$37.56
NEW $360 JIL SANDER PUMA SHOES BLACK 11 US	$125.00	STEVE MADDEN Mammbo Tan Shoes Mens Size 11.5 US 11 UK	$37.00
Danner? Hiking Boots Shoes Men's Size 8 1/2 BRAND NEW!	$123.51	Columbia Tan Leather Clogs, Shoes, Mocs, 10, 43, NIB	$36.99
NEW MENS MEPHISTO "ANGELO" BLACK DRESS SHOES RETAIL$350	$123.50	NWT Timberland Boots #10061-bk (Black, US 08)	$36.90
NEW Ferragamo Black Leather Tassel Loafers Shoes 10 D	$119.99	NEW Mens ADIDAS Response Sneakers Shoes Size 8 $85	$36.51
new COLE HAAN blk pinch tassel loafers 12 D shoes $165+	$114.99	Reebok Team Flare Size 12 Basketball Shoes	$36.00
Converse Batman Collection Hi Cut Tennis Shoes, Mens 10	$113.61	BLACK ZTRAXION STRIPE ADIDAS 11.5 MENS GOLF SHOES	$36.00

Uniforms ▸ Adult

The average sales price in this subcategory is $19.49.

	HIGH		AVG
USMC MARINE CORPS COL DECORATED DRESS BLUE XXL UNIFORM	$365.00	US NAVY EXTRA LARGE OFFICERS / CPO KHAKI UNIFORM	$19.99
USMC MARINE CORPS DRESS BLUE PARADE L DECORATED UNIFORM	$265.00	Brand new US army Class A enlisted mans uniform	$19.99
US NAVY PILOTS DECORATED 46R GULF WAR WHITE UNIFORM	$250.00	New UNIFORM scrubs/scrub DICKIES ELASTIC Set GRAY(L)	$19.99
US NAVY SEAL OFFICERS CHOKER WHITE DECORATED XL UNIFORM	$232.50	Dickies "Hip Flip" Black Scrub Set XL - Red Trim NWT	$19.99
US MARINE CORPS DRESS BLUE COMPLETE PARADE XL UNIFORM	$215.00	CUSTOM MADE NURSING SCRUB TOP SCOOBY DOO	$19.99
USMC MARINE CORPS DRESS BLUE COMPLETE PARADE UNIFORM	$172.50	LOT OF 4 NURSING SCRUB SETS AND JACKET	$19.99
Lot of size 5X women's scrubs 19 tops 7 pants	$138.49	BRAND NEW UNIFORM SCRUB SET FLOWERS CHEROKEE LIME XS	$19.50
US NAVY CAPTAINS DECORATED WWII MESS DRESS UNIFORM	$117.05	New UNIFORM scrubs/scrub DICKIES Set teal 2X	$19.49
US ARMY INFANTRY OFFICERS DECORATED DRESS BLUES UNIFORM	$103.73	3 Piece Cheerleader CHEERLEADING Uniform W/Sweater	$19.00
USMC MARINE CORPS KOREA & WWII DECORATED CAPTs UNIFORM	$102.50	NWT AUTHENTIC BOSTON RED SOX BALL CAP HAT CAPS MLB	$18.99
US NAVY SEALs COMMANDERS DECORATED GULF WAR UNIFORM	$102.50	NEW UNIFORM SCRUB SET FLOWERS DICKIES BLACK MEDIUM	$18.50
CLOWN COSTUME for working clown LARGE # 0053	$102.50	New UNIFORM scrubs/scrub DICKIES Set DARK PINK LARGE	$18.50
Star Wars Costume Snowtrooper softparts	$100.00	Cherokee Snoopy Scrubs Top Sz 2X Large NWT	$18.50
USMC MARINE CORPS MAJORS DECORATED WHITE CHOKER UNIFORM	$96.00	NURSING UNIFORMS/SCRUBS 2pc. sz.MED.~VERYCUTE~ NEW	$18.50
FOX RACING MOTOCROSS NEW GEAR BAG BOOTS HELMET 2005	$91.00	3 "New" Edith Bunker style Coverall Aprons 3X/4X	$18.00

Vintage ▸ Men's & Women's Accessories

The average sales price in this subcategory is $20.21.

	HIGH		AVG
19TH C STERLING SILVER POSEY POSY HOLDER TUSSIE MUSSIE	$1,925.00	Vintage Shoe Buckles & Collar Clips - Rhinestone Silver	$20.50
Antique Fan & Perfume Dance Chatelaine c 1890	$213.50	Vintage"The Police" Synchronicity 83-84 concert shirt	$20.50
SERGE MANZON EDITE PAR MABILLE BRACELET NR	$201.65	OLD VINTAGE WOODEN DUCK HEAD CLOTHES BRUSH	$20.50
STEPHEN DWECK-SILVER & BLACK AGATE EARRINGS -NEVER WORN	$189.00	1900 Christmas Give-Away tray from Rubles Dry Goods Sto	$20.49
ADIDAS Leather Vintage 60's 70's Suitcase France rare	$123.50	VINTAGE LEATHER DOCUMENT CASE/BRIEFCASE ATTACHE BRIEF	$20.49
Vintage GUCCI Mens Black Leather Travel Toiletry Case	$100.00	Vintage Wooden Hat Stand	$20.49
Vintage Schiaparelli Brocade Book Cover (s) 2	$99.98	Vintage Wooden Tulip Hat Stand	$20.49
Star Brand Shoe Boot Display Victorian Wooden	$85.00	Ladie's Gruen Wrist Watch - vintage SS/White gold	$20.00
LOUIS VUITTON TRAVEL LINGERIE CASE	$84.77	Vintage Shine Butler shoe holder for shoe shines	$20.00
VINTAGE VANS SHOES ILLUMINATED SIGN SURF,SKATEBOARD,BMX	$80.99	VINTAGE SCOTTIE DOG SHOE HORN BAKELITE	$20.00
Vintage Humming Bird buckle & belt, wear w/Kippy belt	$80.00	Mod 60's Vintage dress flower power suit case luggage	$19.99
GOTHIC VICTORIAN Huge STERLING BUCKLE ORNATE Silver	$79.88	BEAUTIFUL 50's "RAM'E" Copper Bracelet	$19.99
VINTAGE ANTIQUE NECKLACE LOCKET PENDANT JEWELRY GOLD	$78.00	VINTAGE STERLING BELT BUCKLES TURQUOISE AGATE + MORE	$19.99
LOT OF 25 WOOD WOODEN MARKED HANGERS	$76.00	VINTAGE COACH BROWN LEATHER FLAP SHOULDER BAG PURSE	$19.99
VUITTON - VINTAGE Man's Billfold	$72.00	Vintage Art Deco Cigarette Lighters Dunhill?	$19.95

Vintage ▸ Unisex & T-Shirts

The average sales price in this subcategory is $16.17.

	HIGH		AVG
VINTAGE BOSTON U.S. TOUR 1979 CONCERT T SHIRT	$263.55	TEENAGE MUTANT NINJA TURTLES coolest vintage t shirt	$17.01
VINTAGE ULTRA RARE PINK FLOYD ANIMALS TOUR 1977	$256.00	DUKES OF HAZZARD T SHIRT GENERAL LEE 1980'S WOMENS SMAL	$16.95
VINTAGE BLONDIE U.S. TOUR 1979 CONCERT T SHIRT	$192.49	Vintage Scottie Pippen USA Basketball Jersey Sz L	$16.75
ViNTAGE IRON MAIDEN 83 UK WORLD PIECE TOUR T-SHiRT	$137.50	vintage George Michael girls t-shirt S/XS 1989 Faith	$16.51
VINTAGE GRATEFUL DEAD ON THE ROAD 1978 CONCERT SHIRT	$135.83	VINTAGE THE CURE TOUR T-SHIRT VERY RARE	$16.51
VINTAGE ZZ TOP DEGULLO 1980 TOUR T SHIRT	$118.50	vintage EMBRACE ME BRACES soft 80s funny rad t-shirt L	$16.50
VINTAGE DAVID BOWIE 1978 WORLD TOUR CONCERT T SHIRT	$105.50	Vintage Disney Mickey Mouse Grey Sweatshirt Shirt	$16.50
VINTAGE BAD CO. BURNING THROUGH U.S TOUR 1977 T SHIRT	$92.55	vintage COUNTRY WESTERN PEARL SNAP t shirt emo rad M	$16.00
VINTAGE AC/DC BACK IN BLACK USA TOUR 1980	$91.00	*SOFT* vintage-retro 80s NEW YORK JETS football t-shirt	$16.00
VINTAGE ROLLING STONES 1981 DRAGON CONCERT T SHIRT	$91.00	vintage MOTLEY CRUE Dr. Feelgood concert t-shirt LOOK	$15.78
BLACK SABBATH U.S. TOUR 1978 CONCERT T SHIRT	$89.88	vintage MEMBERS ONLY JACKET black retro 80's size 40	$15.51
VINTAGE ALLMAN BROTHERS LIVE CONCERT T SHIRT	$89.88	CERVEZA IMPERIAL vintage COSTA RICA BEER promo t shirt	$15.50
COOL 1970s Advertising JOLLY GREEN GIANT Denim SHIRT!	$88.00	Vintage YES 1984 European Tour T-Shirt Soft Emo Retro	$15.50
vintage 80s FRESH IZOD LACOSTE STRIPED POLO rugby shirt	$86.00	vintage RALPH LAUREN POLO shirt PINK LOGO Small S emo	$15.50
Vintage U2 1985 TOUR JERSEY T-Shirt Unforgettable Fire	$79.00	vintage 80's JC PENNY TRANSPORTATION FAIR t-shirt SOFT!	$15.50

Vintage ▸ Women's Clothing

The average sales price in this subcategory is $23.92.

	HIGH		AVG
BEAUTIFUL VINTAGE 40's 50's Authentic Pastel Mink Stol	$469.99	Vintage Antique Pink Silk and Lace Camisole - Size 44	$26.00
Vintage Genuine Louis Vuitton carry-all,duffel bag	$255.00	VINTAGE LILLY PULITZER AQUA FLORAL/LACE SUN DRESS SZ 8	$26.00
Vintage European Ladies Night cotton Dress Lot, 25 pcs	$250.00	Four Moschino Collectors Original Gold Faucet Buttons	$25.00
Gorgeous Chinese jacket - shearling lined	$250.00	Vintage 70s sexy black JOY STEVENS SLIT WRAP dress	$25.00
Vintage CHINESE WEDDING SKIRT early 1900's	$208.50	Blue Satin Dress 14T	$24.99
Vintage CHINESE WEDDING SHIRT or JACKET, early 1900's	$208.50	WHITE Poet shirt/SCA/RENN/Pirate/costume	$24.99
FABULOUS VINTAGE MINK JACKET COAT~RUFFLED COLLAR	$200.00	5 PR VINTAGE NYLON HOSIERY STOCKINGS 9 1/2 NEW IN PKGS	$24.90
Wool & Vinyl JUNYA WATANABEE COMME DES GARCONS Jacket	$190.50	VINTAGE COTTON HAND CROCHET TOP or VEST Large WHITE	$24.00
Vintage Gucci Handbag	$152.50	VINTAGE (?) LILLY PULITZER DRESS SIZE 6	$23.51
Vintage St John Collection by Marie Gray Coat + Skirt	$141.04	Sexy Vintage Lilly Pulitzer Long Dress with Side Splits	$23.25
Vintage Diane Von Furstenberg Jungle Dress Size 6	$114.49	rockabilly vintage party prom dress 50's retro goth 50s	$22.72
Designer Natasha Gan Top/Skirt	$105.00	Vintage Fashions Magazines - 11 Back Issues	$22.49
1920s-1940s Silk Floral Print Kimono Style Robe	$102.50	VINTAGE BELT BUCKLES LOT OF 20 BAKELITE RHINESTONE	$22.49
VINTAGE 70s DISCO SEXY SPANDEX PEPPER SKINS HOT PANTS	$100.00	GORGEOUS DOUBLE LAYER TIENDA HO BLACK SKIRT!	$22.00
SHEEPSKIN SHEARLING Fur Coat Vintage? Like New	$100.00	BLACK ST JOHN MARIE GRAY SANTANA KNIT DRESS M-LG NR	$21.53

Wedding Apparel ▶ Wedding Dresses

The average sales price in this subcategory is $86.62.

	HIGH		AVG
PURE GLAMOUR!**EXQUISITE $28K VERA WANG WEDDING DRESS*4	$1,968.00	NR* NWT PRINCESS TULLE WHITE WEDDING GOWN DRESS SIZE 10	$94.57
		NEW WITH TAGS! GORGEOUS MOONLIGHT WEDDING BALL GOWN! NR	$93.99
EVE OF MILADY 2005 Valued at 4,000$ asking 1,200$	$1,200.00		
ALVINA VALENTA Authentic BRIDAL GOWN new! #AV8049	$900.00	Delicate Shimmering ClearLace New 14 white NR!!!!	$92.36
Romona Keveza Wedding Gown Dress - Size 10 - New	$860.00	Ginnis White 12 Informal Wedding Dress Bridal Gown	$92.00
Wedding dresses gowns dress gown Ivory-10 Moonlight	$710.00	Custom Made Chiffon Wedding Dress _NO RESERVE!!	$91.00
PALOMA BLANCA Authentic BRIDAL GOWN new! #3470	$599.00	Brand New Sexy Wedding Dress Wedding Gown	$90.99
Ulla Maija Wedding/ Bridal Gown NR	$599.00	Custom New Brand Sexy Wedding Gowns / Dresses Size 4-28	$87.50
NEW Maggie Sottero "SARCHI" Wedding Gown - never worn	$575.00	NWT ALFRED ANGELO IVORY WEDDING GOWN PLUS 18W $615 NR	$86.73
Eve of Milady Strapless Wedding Gown	$500.00	Vintage Wedding Dress	$84.13
BCBG Tulle Wedding Dress-Antique White-NWT-SZ 4	$320.00	Precious Moments Bride and Groom Doll wedding decor.	$81.00
NEW! Bridal Originals White Wedding Dress GO2AL Sz 14	$300.00	OLEG CASSINI WEDDING GOWN NWT $3,400 NR	$80.99
SPECTACULAR COUTURE SHEATH	$280.00	NWT EVE OF MILADY BEADED TULLE WEDDING DRESS 10 $2700	$80.00
*SAISON BLANCHE $1,200 NWT		Custom Redesigned Wedding Dresses/Bridal Gown 2-26 9205	$79.99
Lot of Wedding Gowns Bridal Dresses Wholesale Lot	$255.01	[3 of these sold for $79.99 each]	
Lot of 10 New Designer Wedding & Bridal Gowns	$255.00	6x the most gorgeous dress ever pearls & lace 68/64/66	$79.00
Wedding dress White Jacquelin style 9218 Size 6	$250.00	Ivory wedding dress sz 14 unaltered	$77.00

Women's Accessories, Handbags ▶ Handbags, Bags

The average sales price in this subcategory is $81.21.

	HIGH		AVG
Authentic LOUIS VUITTON COSMETIC TRAIN CASE & KEY	$1,614.00	Longaberger Mother's Day Tote Liner, Protector & mirror	$90.00
Gorgeous 18K Gold & Diamond Louis Vuitton Heart Locket	$912.00	TUMI messenger sling BAG green pink briefcase NWT $175	$89.95
Authentic LOUIS VUITTON SUITCASE & KEY ~ Brevete 1920s	$910.00	Auth GUCCI Mini Brown Tote Bag / Purse - 39888	$89.00
Vintage Hermes Cigarette Box	$812.00	Coach Studio Scribble Watch	$86.00
FANTASTIC CHANEL SPRING/SUMMER 05 TWEED BAG NWT	$805.00	MYSTERY BOX COACH PURSE PLUS MUCH MORE! LOOK !	$86.00
Hermes Mystery box " LOOK WHAT IS INSIDE!!!!!!!!!!!!!!	$799.00	COACH DUFFLE BAG "NEW" LARGE "C" black/black	$86.00
100% AUTHENTIC LOUIS VUITTON TRUNK–Brilliant Vintage!!	$760.00	COACH DUFFLE BAG "NEW" LARGE "C" black/black	$82.00
AUTH LOUIS VUITTON KEEPALL 45 TRAVEL BAG LUGGAGE NEW	$720.00	LV Garment Bag	$81.00
Louis Vuitton Pegase 60 Rolling Suitcase	$710.00	COACH SOHO BELTED BUCKLE BAGS PURES TOTES LIKE NEW	$81.00
LOUIS VUITTON MONOGRAM GARMENT BAG	$650.00	Brighton "CAROLINE" Black leather Bag w/ Box & felt bag	$81.00
GUCCI pink leather HOBO BAG bamboo rings NWT	$600.00	Diane Von Furstenberg Private Jet Rolling City Bag BLK	$80.00
100% Authentic LOUIS VUITTON Rare Trunk PLUS-Inner Tray	$585.00	VERA BRADLEY GARMENT &TOTE BAG SET BLK QUILTED FLORAL	$77.19
Hermes mystery box"NEW ITEM ADDED	$555.56	VERA BRADLEY MYSTERY WALLET<>< CASH INSIDE><>	$77.00
Louis Vuitton Vintage Trunk Suitcase	$512.99	NWT!!!! Liz Claiborne mystery purse. SUPER SHARP!	$77.00
Hermes mystery box 3 GIFTS INSIDE	$510.00	MYSTERY BOX COACH PURSE PLUS MUCH MORE!GET IT NOW	$77.00

Women's Accessories, Handbags ▶ Scarves, Wraps

The average sales price in this subcategory is $13.47.

	HIGH		AVG
Auth. HERMES XXL cashmere SHAWL Scarf BLACK/NEW	$775.00	Indonesia:Bali Rayon Sarong/Shawl/Fabric, Pink/Green	$15.00
BEAD & I - Beaded Scarf; Necklace; Lariat	$100.00	NEW BLACK/PINK SIGNATURE COACH SCARF	$14.99
NEW PRIMP Turquoise Ice Cream Hoodie Set Size : Medium	$90.00	Gray Velvet Choli Belly Dance Bellydance 60	$14.99
NEW PRIMP Turquoise Ice Cream Hoodie Set Size : Small	$90.00	Floral Sequin & Bead Georgette PROM WRAP Shawl, Black 8	$14.95
NEW PRIMP Pink Unicorn Hoodie Set * Size : Large*	$90.00	Hot Red Lotus Sequins Georgette Shawl Hipscarf	$14.50
NEW PRIMP Ice Cream Hoodie Set **** Size : Small ***	$89.00	$160 Lot 3 Ladies Acrylic Ponchos OSFM Outerwear NWT NR	$14.25
BELLY DANCE TRIBAL TASSEL BELT & BRA SET, PLUS SIZE	$86.25	NEW HANDMADE CROCHET CROCHETED HAT & SCARF SET	$13.50
NEW PRIMP Black Ice Cream Hoodie Set Size : medium	$85.00	Burberry logos neck scarf bandana in BEIGE NR	$13.50
LORO PIANA SCARF , IVORY CREAM , NWT	$73.00	LUCKY LADYBUG*YELLOW SCARF*SILKY WRAP *LADY BUG*free sh	$12.99
[2 of these sold for $73.00 each]		LARGE Vintage Wool/Silk TIGER HEAD SCARF	$12.95
LORO PIANA SCARF , RED , NWT	$73.00	MAROON BELLY DANCE DANCER DANCING COIN HIP SCARF BELT	$12.50
LORO PIANA SCARF , Soft Pink , NWT	$73.00	M Royal Blue Iris Hip Scarf Belly Dance Bellydance 45	$12.50
COACH JUMBO patchwork SIGNATURE SILK Scarf NWT	$62.99	MAKE YOUR OWN COOL- HOT	$12.49
100% New, Authentic Burberry Camel Cashmere Scarf, NR!	$60.00	BANDANA TIE HEADBAND Kit for 12	
100% Authentic Burberry Baby Pink Cashmere Scarf, NR!	$52.00	Burberry logos neck scarf bandana in PINK NR	$12.09
Veil * Skirt * Hip Scarf Belly Dance Bellydance 59	$49.99	Awesome BLACK EMBROIDED FRINGED SHAWL	$12.03

Women's Accessories, Handbags ▶ Sunglasses

The average sales price in this subcategory is $18.23.

	HIGH		AVG
OLIVER PEOPLES Aero	$295.00	*bebe* COTTAGE PINK W/ CHERRIES SUNGLASSES/CLEAR LNSE	$19.99
Vintage CARTIER Sunglasses EXCELLENT CONDITION!	$237.50	*bebe* NEW* SHABBY YELLOW FRAMES & CHERRIES SUNGLASSES	$19.99
Lot 28 Pairs Sunglasses Sun Glasses Ray-Ban Gucci CK	$153.50	NEW Womens Spy Isis Tortoise Sunglasses,NO RESERVE!! un	$19.95
New Maui Jim Sunglasses Malia	$140.50	Vintage *RAY BAN* B&L Tortoise Sunglasses	$19.29
AUTHENTIC Coach Black Onyx Samantha Sunglasses JEWEL	$130.51	women's vuarnet sunglasses	$19.01
NEW LULU GUINNESS L409 VINTAGE 50'S STYLE SUNGLASSES	$125.00	Authentic CHLOE sunglasses rhinestone heart, McCartney	$19.00
Maui Jim Womens Sunglasses Gold Rim Tortoise Shell+Case	$122.50	BN LOUIS VUITTON SUNGLASSES W/ RHINESTONE FRAMES!	$18.50
BLACK (ONYX) COACH SAMANTHA SUNGLASSES	$112.50	80's Vintage Sunglasses Celebrity Style Olsen Twins NOS	$18.38
KIESELSTEIN-CORD TITANIUM SUPER STAR SUNGLASSES	$100.00	BRIGHTON AUTH. "Passion Flower" Bracelet Sil Plated NEW	$17.50
COACH CHELSEA - S426 - ONYX SUNGLASSES	$96.00	BRIGHTON AUTH. "TITANIA" Bracelet Sil Plated NEW	$17.50
Womens Oliver Peoples sunglasses 57013 Jackie O - Rave	$89.60	BRIGHTON AUTH. "Flower Power" Bangle Sil/Lav/Lime NEW	$17.50
OAKLEY SUNGLASSES EYE JACKET VINTAGE	$75.00	BRIGHTON AUTH. "Spring Biouquet" Bracelet Silver NEW	$17.50

Roberto Cavalli Sunglasses. Ecuba 97S Col. F19	$71.00 Bausch & Lomb I's Series W2445Sunglasses NEW NR	$16.99
Chloe Asymmetrical Sunglasses - Clear Frames	$71.00 BOLLE MAMBA SUNGLASSES NIB SPORT WRAPS WHITE	$16.50
NEW SMITH VOODOO SKY BLUE FADE SWITCH LENS SUNGLASSES	$71.00 BN LOUIS VUITTON SUNGLASSES W/ RHINESTONE FRAMES!	$16.50

Women's Clothing ▶ Misses ▶ Dresses

The average sales price in this subcategory is $28.06.

	HIGH		AVG
CHANEL WOMEN'S PLUM SILK BOTANICAL DRESS sz 38	$500.00	NWOT Worthington Slinky Travellers Dress & Top Set 16	$30.00
$889 BCBG COLLECTION WHITE SILK TIER HALTER DRESS NEW 4	$389.95	Viva Purple Dress Red Hat Roses Sz L NWT Society	$29.99
Lovely$1,530. CHANEL flowery silk dress for marni dries	$302.00	As NEW SHOSHANNA Silk STRAPLESS Halter Party Dress 2	$29.99
Karen Alexander - Lovely Tan Damask Sundress - Size 6/8	$202.73	Women's Plus Size Dress - Silk - Green - 22W	$29.99
MARC BOUWER Red One-Shoulder Cocktail Dress sz10 New	$199.99	BCBG Paris Blue Purple V-neck Dress Sz. M NWT $164 NEW	$29.98
New MARNI summer Dress 42 ribbon Detail. Last One!	$177.50	UNIQUESSENTIALS NEW SARI FABRIC THROW DRAPES CURTAIN NR	$29.88
SAVE THE QUEEN flared sleeves RED HEARTS dress JPG NWT	$159.99	NEW $88 Victoria's Secret Black Ruched Mini Dress LARGE	$29.34
NEW! $2,020.00 MISSONI CARDI-COAT NEW, Sz 4	$137.50	August Silk~ Long Black/White Dress Size 14 – NICE!!	$27.02
Vintage Diane Von Furstenberg Art Deco Wrap Dress 12/14	$124.50	LILLY PULITZER SZ 10 BEAUTIFUL LILLY PRINT DRESS	$27.01
Cap Sleeve V Neck Tie Ella Moss Stretchy Cherry Dress L	$116.49	LAUNDRY Dress, Size 8, Retail $195, NWT, NO RESERVE	$27.00
BIG BEAUTY Sexy Green ISOLA Dirndl HEAVY Embroi BUST46"	$110.50	Laundry Ladies Dress Size 6 NWT Retail $195.00	$26.99
NWT CHETTA B silk cream long feather dress 6	$103.05	BOUTIQUE ROMANTIC TEA & SCONES NEIL & DAVID DRESS SZ S	$26.00
DIANE VON FURSTENBERG Smocked BOHO Strapless Dress 0/2	$91.00	NEW Juicy Couture Green Ruffle Terry Dress $98 SOLD OUT	$26.00
NEW! $2,020.00 MISSONI CARDI-COAT NEW, Sz 8	$91.00	VINTAGE DRESS hippie boho peasant 70's scene indie M	$26.00
$238 BCBG BLACK&WHITE SILK CHIFFON HALTER DRESS NEW 4	$82.00	BETSEY JOHNSON VINTAGE 80'S DRESS TOP SIZE SMALL	$25.52

Women's Clothing ▶ Jeans

The average sales price in this subcategory is $21.34.

	HIGH		AVG
NWT ROCK AND REPUBLIC VICTORIA BECKHAM JEANS 50 LOT	$2,200.00	new POLO ralph lauren LOW RISE summer jeans NWT Sz 8	$22.99
Wholesale LOT of SEVEN Jeans 36 pair NWT Pink Swarovski	$1,375.00	Pacsun Tilt Jeans - Size 00 Short	$22.50
"Seven Type" Low Rise HOT designer jeans 48 pairs sonnyblack trendy pair of jeans - sizes 24-30	$864.00	Signature Abercrombie and Fitch Vintage Destroyed Denim	$22.50
		NEW Abercrombie SUPER Destroyed Jeans 2 PAINTED	$22.50
100%AUTH CHANEL JEANS W PEARL LOGO CCI 36 MUST SEE! MOST BEAUTIFUL JEANS !!! STRETCH DENIM	$650.00	Lot of 9 pairs of Jeans -"TOMMY, POLO, LUCKY, LEVI"	$22.01
		$229 NEW Womens Costume National Straight Leg Jeans 10	$21.50
NWT $998 Roberto Cavalli Black Embrd. Jeans Small S New	$329.99	Women's Eckored Engine Power Plant Diamond Wash Jeans 5	$21.50
NWT Habitual Koi Placebo Jeans *RARE* 29	$285.00	NWT JUICY COUTURE GLITTER JEANS SIZE 26	$21.50
ROCK AND & REPUBLIC JEANS ROTH VAPOR W/ CRYS $249 SZ 29	$185.00	ABERCROMBIE & FITCH CHELSEA FLARE JEANS TINT 6 S	$21.01
Rock and Republic Roth Crystal Pocket Jean Addict Sz 28	$145.95	Levi's Jeans Women's 27 low rise Premium Distressed	$20.99
ROCK AND & REPUBLIC JEANS STEVIE ADDICT $189 Sz 30	$122.50	Seven For All Mankind Jeans Womens Boycut Sz 26 SEXY	$20.50
Rock and Republic Victoria Beckham London Crown Jean 30	$102.50	Size 12 ABERCROMBIE & FITCH buttonfly boot cut jeans	$20.50
Rock and Republic Roth Crystal Pocket Jean Addict Sz 27	$100.99	Levi's Dark Wash Nouveau Boot Cut 515 Jeans 8 HOT!	$20.50
100% AUTH Roberto Cavalli Leather pockets jeans SZ S	$100.00	Lucky brand peanut pant size 4/27 brand new with tags!!	$20.50
Rock and Republic Roth Crystal Pocket Jean Addict Sz 26	$99.88	Halogen size 4 long 33" flare low rise jeans lk nu #172	$20.49
NWT Citizens of Humanity Jeans size 28 retail $158.00	$93.02		
$158 NEW HUDSON TRIANGLE FLAP POCKET JEANS SZ 28	$91.00		

Women's Clothing ▶ Outerwear

The average sales price in this subcategory is $55.91.

	HIGH		AVG
SUPER STUNNING GOLDEN ISLAND FOX FUR COAT 54" LONG	$1,125.00	NWT Abercrombie & Fitch Ezra Fitch Cashmere Cardigan	$58.50
AMAZING QUALITY SUPERIOR SILVER FOX FUR COAT 52" LONG	$810.00	FRANKIE B JEANS DENIM JACKET TOP SZ M RARE PINK LOGO NR	$57.00
BLACKGLAMA Cassini FULL LENGTH DARK RANCH MINK Coat NR	$665.00	The North Face HyVent Gore Tex Shell Pants full zip	$56.11
Natural Ranch Mink Stroller	$400.00	~~Patagonia Burmese Fleece Quilted Jacket~~Medium~~	$56.00
Beautiful Saga Fox Fur Coat - Size M-L	$399.00	EILEEN FISHER PETITE Silk Quilted Oriental Jacket sz PL	$56.00
RALPH RUPLEY FUR COAT RICH BROWN MINK 1970'S ERA GREAT!	$388.00	NORTH FACE Pink/Gray Youth L	$56.00
LOVELY LARGE BROWN MINK FUR WOMEN COAT LIKE NEW	$370.01	100%Authentic Juicy Couture Royalty Set Baby Blue Sz M	$56.00
3/4 Length Gorgeous Chevron Mink Fur Coat L/XL	$363.05	100%Authentic Juicy Couture Royalty Set Black Sz S	$54.00
D81 VIVACIOUS Ladies Plush Red Fox Fur Stroller Coat -M	$345.00	Bold CHRISTIAN LACROIX Red Denim Jacket W/Lion Rear	$53.00
Mink Jacket, Black, SUPERB, baby mink w/zip closure	$307.02	Womens white & Blue Adidas winter jacket	$53.00
Vintage WHITE Mink Fur BOLERO Jacket COAT Stole Capelet	$305.00	J.Jill Linen Darcy Jacket ~ 10 ~ NWT $128	$52.00
NEW WOMEN HUSSEIN CHALAYAN MILITARY GREEN JACKET 6	$305.00	Paul Smith Womens Black leather Coat *Jacket	$51.60
STUNNING Genuine Female Mink Fur 1/2 Coat Jacket M	$300.00	Saga Grey White Fox Fur Coat Jacket Ladies Beautiful!	$51.01
ELEGANT PEARL MINK FUR COAT ~ 10-12	$266.99	Columbia Ski/ Snow Jacket +Bonus Eddie Bauer Ski Pants!	$51.00
Woman's Burberry's trench rain coat with winter lining	$255.50	NEW ROCAWEAR WOMENS DENIM JEANS JACKET LARGE $92	$51.00

Women's Clothing ▶ Pants

The average sales price in this subcategory is $17.89.

	HIGH		AVG
$1890 CHRISTIAN DIOR Tatoo Stretchy Leggings Pants 8 40	$586.00	TOMMY BAHAMA CROPPED / CAPRI PANTS Sz 6 SILK PANTS	$19.49
Emilio Pucci Wide Leg Printed Pants *NWT*	$299.00	bebe CONTRAST RIBBED WAISTBAND CAPRI szM NWT NoRESERVE	$18.99
***SEXY, SKINNY DOLCE & GABBANA CLASSIC BLACK PANTS*42	$270.00	S BLACK LOW RISE GAUCHO PANTS CROPPED WIDE LEG BOHO	$18.99
Eskandar 100% Linen GRN/GREY Pants-Sz 2 fr Bergdorf	$159.08	NEW EXPRESS BLACK EDITOR PANTS SZ 2 R	$18.38
SHAMASK Luscious Steel Gray Velvet Trousers NEW "2"	$139.99	BLACK*GAUCHO PANTS Cropped Capri Low Rise Wide Leg*M	$18.00
L.A.M.B Sweat Pants TAUPE M NWT Gwen Stefani Lamb	$115.00	KHAKI* GAUCHO PANTS Cropped Capri Low Rise Wide Leg * S	$18.00
LUCKY BRAND TATOO /CHINA GIRL /SWEAT PANTS	$82.63	$180 BCBG MAHOGANY PINSTRIPES FLARE DRESS PANTS NEW 6	$18.00
FABULOUS GIORGIO ARMANI BLACK LABEL PANTS	$80.00	Talbots Pants/Olive and Floral/14	$17.87

	HIGH		AVG
ST JOHN BASICS BLACK PLEATED SANTANA KNIT PANTS 10	$79.99	Oilily Cargo "Fish Scale" Pants SZ 36/6	$17.50
Blue Fish Simple Pants "Jasmine" Summer 97 Great Paint	$70.99	NWT BeBe black pants size 4p	$17.50
THEORY PRESTON PANTS. CAMEL. 12. NWT	$69.99	CP SHADES PANTS Small olive green Linen	$17.28
Banana Republic Linen-Blend Martin Pants 8	$69.00	aeropostale capris,size 11/12.NWT	$17.09
DA NANG Black Pants w/ Dragon Embroidery, Medium, NWT	$66.00	LIGHT BLUE GAUCHO PANTS Cropped Capri Low Rise Wide S	$17.00
7 Prs of Designer Jeans/Pants 7, Earl, Juicy sz 25	$64.17	NEW CELEBRITY CROP GAUCHO WIDE LEG KIMONO PANT-L-	$17.00
NWT Juicy Couture WHITE Linen Drawstring Pants MEDIUM	$61.00	New MODA $59 Marisa Fit Stretch Linen Pants 10 White	$16.99

Women's Clothing ▶ Skirts

The average sales price in this subcategory is $18.19.

	HIGH		AVG
Stunning Alexander McQueen Runway Pompom Skirt NWT	$899.00	SHIMMERING SILVER~VICTORIAN SKIRT~RAINBOW BLUE~S/M/L/XL	$19.99
BRAND NEW CHANEL O5A FLOWER DETAIL A LINE SKIRT SZ 36	$799.99	NWT J Crew Broken in chino skirt 6 IVY NEW!!!	$19.99
NWT $1,030 Marni Flower Embroidered Skirt Beige 38	$515.00	ABERCROMBIE Destroyed Cheyanne Denim Skirt- Size 6	$19.99
NWT $625 Marni Flower Printed Skirt White/Red 42	$318.00	$98 NWT Free People Green Boho Skirt 2	$19.99
$798 New RALPH LAUREN Blue Velvet Silk Ruffle Skirt 10	$149.99	Women's Black 100% Leather Skirt / Size 16	$19.38
ROZAE NICHOLS silk metalic thread fairy cat skirt P S	$122.50	New $69 ANN TAYLOR Black Floral Skirt 6P FLIRTY buySAFE	$18.99
NWT ISABEL DE PEDRO BLACK AND WHITE SKIRT SIZE 4	$115.20	Lot of Trina Turk, Bebe, Arden B! $420 Value	$18.49
DOUBLE D RANCHWEAR dress medium broomstick skirt	$113.39	NWT NEW April Cornell Hippie Bohemian Skirt L 12	$18.00
NWT MANDALAY maroon silk sheer flair skirt 4	$99.99	NWT ROCA WEAR One-piece Skirt - Ding (Black, L)RW0066	$17.90
Oilily skirt NWT!! Size 36 or 6 US! FAB! LQQK!!	$91.00	Steven Stolman Cotton Skirt-Sz 6-Excellent Cond.	$17.00
BOHEMIAN BEADED MISS ME SKIRT WITH BEADED BELT	$89.99	NEW Abercrombie ~FLIRT~ Mini Skirt, White, (Size Small)	$17.00
EILEEN FISHER Ink Silk Charmeuse Fluted Skirt XL - NWT	$89.95	NWT Chico's White House Black Market Short Buckle Skirt	$16.99
Burning Torch Long Hawaiian Style Cotton Skirt Sz P	$72.00	*MICHAEL KORS* BLACK&LEATHER SKIRT 12 $ 129 NWT*	$16.75
Marc Jacobs Cafe De Paris Printed Skirt 2 Green&Purple	$69.90	Lilly Pulitzer party long skirt	$16.50
JL-Marc Jacobs Floral Skirt 6 only 1	$61.00	CYNTHIA STEFFE Brown Tulle Tiered Embroidered Skirt L	$16.49

Women's Clothing ▶ T-Shirts, Tank Tops

The average sales price in this subcategory is $12.49.

	HIGH		AVG
Darling Louis Vuitton Chiffon Shoulder Strap Tank Top	$349.00	NWOT Quacker Factory Size 3x American Flag Tee & Bag	$13.00
Great China Wall gun T shirt tee with crystals	$275.00	NWT Urban Outfitters boho lolita Cute Blue Heart Tank M	$13.00
MARNI TERRA T Shirt (42).	$135.00	New Abercrombie Womens White Olivia East Coast Tee S	$13.00
L.A.M.B. Boudoir Baby Pink Tank Gwen Stefani Rare Lamb	$76.00	Christian Dior Tank Tops - J'adore Print Yellow 46	$13.00
L.A.M.B. GWEN STEFANI SWAROVSKI RHINESTONE T SHIRT TOP	$61.00	Custom Womens NEBRASKA HOTTIE T-Shirt S/M/L/XL NWT	$12.99
AUTH Marc Jacobs Flounce Silk Coffee Top/ Sz8	$52.00	NWT Ralph Lauren Pink Pony T-Shirt White X-Large	$12.99
Auth Theory CATARINA Tubular Tank Halter Top NEW $100!	$49.99	New BROWN Bebe Rhinestone Logo Tank Top Shirt sz LARGE	$12.95
NWOT C&C California Regular tank, 2 PCS, Size: S	$46.00	~NWT SKINNY MINNIE SUNLIGHT CAFE HORSES TANK SIZE M NR~	$12.50
Harley-Davidson NWOT **3** AWESOME Tank Tops - M	$45.99	NEW Prada Front Logo Back Pocket Tank Top Blk XL	$11.99
NEW '05 Women's BEIGE LOGO D&G Dolce&Gabbana T-SHIRT M	$44.99	NEW Prada Front Logo Back Pocket Tank Top Wht M	$11.99
BLUE CULT GWYNETH PALTROW POCKETS JEANS 26 NWT	$42.00	NEW Prada Front Logo Back Pocket Tank Top Wht XL	$11.99
NIB L.A.M.B. LAMB GWEN STEFANI WHAT COLOR IS LOVE SHIRT	$40.55	New Abercrombie Women's Olive Shelly Sheer Logo Tee S	$11.50
2 B FREE seafoam green fleur de lis tank top size XL	$37.00	Women's purple Abercrombie T-shirt, size XL (slim fit)	$11.50
authentic PEACE NOW shirt gothic lolita fruits jrock	$36.27	TOP VERSACE JEANS COUTURE WHITE T-SHIRT (G05671) Sz.M	$11.50
LOUIS VUITTON WOMAN'S SHIRT WHITE	$33.00	New Dolce & Gabbana EmbroseHollywoodMickey SSlvT BlkM	$11.50

Women's Clothing ▶ Maternity

The average sales price in this subcategory is $11.88.

	HIGH		AVG
SEVEN 7 FOR ALL MANKIND MATERNITY JEANS SIZE 28	$120.50	ADORABLE! MOTHERHOOD MATERNITY GINGHAM SUMMER OUTFIT M	$12.95
LQQK!! Huge Lot Maternity Clothes: Gap/Old Navy & MORE	$91.00	~EUC~Majamas For Babystyle RARE SATURDAY Nursing Top(S)	$12.53
new NICOLE MILLER & CO. maternity BACKPACK DIAPER BAG	$76.90	The Snoozer Pregnancy Nursing Body Pillow	$12.52
LQQK!! Maternity Clothes: Gap/Old Navy & MORE	$75.00	Lot of 9 Maternity Underwear Panties NR Like New!!	$12.51
Pea in the Pod, Mimi Maternity Gift Card!! LOOK! $90	$71.01	Plus Size 2x 3x Take Nine Maternity Panties Lot NWT	$12.50
New Snoogle Pregnancy Body Pillow (Maternity, Baby)	$56.00	Motherhood Maternity Support Belt Size XXL/2XL	$12.50
new NICOLE MILLER A PEA IN THE POD maternity DIAPER BAG	$49.00	NEW NIP Maternity Brief Cotton Panties underwear 6 pair	$12.00
Gorgeous Black Mimi Maternity 2 pc Pantsuit Size M	$43.50	Old Navy Maternity Panties Underwear Large Thongs	$12.00
Original SNOOGLE full body pregnancy pillow- used 2X	$42.00	~EUC~Motherhood Maternity Sheghetti Nursing Tank(S) SEE	$11.53
OLIAN-Silk Shantung Outfit-NEW	$39.99	Mama-T's Nursing sundress NWT Size XL	$11.49
NWT Maternity Clothes Size Medium-8 Items	$39.99	$152 Lot 4 Ladies Dax Coe Maternity Loungewear M NWT NR	$11.49
Maternity / Size Small Olian Lingerie 2pc. Set	$36.00	NWT Mums & Blossums Maternity Ivory Full Slip Sz Large	$11.00
Maternity / Size Medium Olian Lingerie 2pc. Set	$36.00	MOTHERHOOD MATERNITY SUPPORT BELT, SIZE L	$11.00
Snoogle Pregnancy Maternity Pillow LN Blue full body	$35.75	Medela Maternity Support Belt size S/M used one week	$10.99
~EUC~Majamas For Babystyle ORIGINAL Nursing Top(M)SEE	$35.00	$152 Lot 4 Ladies Dax Coe Maternity Loungewear M NWT NR	$10.94

Women's Shoes

The average sales price in this subcategory is $21.80.

NOTE *These results are based on a keyword search of the Women's Shoes subcategory for auctions with the word* shoes *in the title.*

	HIGH		AVG
Manolo Blahnik Campari black patent mary jane-4.1" heel Harder-to-find 105mm (4.1 inch) heel.	$1009.00	Brown Velvet JEWELED Peep Toe Wedge Pump Heels Shoe 8.5	$22.99
		Tan Beige Camel Brown High Heel Mule Clog Shoe Size 9	$22.99
MANOLO BLAHNIK ALLIGATOR PUMP SHOE 9B NEW $3,100.00	$939.00	EGGPLANT HIGH HEEL SHOE CHAIR	$22.50
NGG MANOLO BLAHNIK SILVER SATC STOLEN SHOES! 39.5/9.5	$799.99	VINTAGE ETIENNE AIGNER Horsebit Loafer Heel Shoe 9 M 9M	$22.50

4 INCH HEEL!!! RARE! RARE! ONE TIME CHANCE!!!	
Gucci Gold Chain Shoes Spring/Summer 2005 Size 39/9	$700.00
Stunning Christian Louboutin Platform Pump Shoe 38	$615.50
MYSTERY WHY AM I AUCTIONING OFF MY PRADA HEELS/MULES	$600.00
New 100% Authentic Louis Vuitton Murakami heels 7.5 - 8	$600.00
Sandals Size 7.5 - 8 With RECEIPT!! RARE SOLD OUT!!	
RENE CAOVILLA JEWELED SANDAL HEELS SHOE 6B $895.00	$399.00
Gucci Runway Shoe size 8 retails for $495.00	$300.00
MICHAEL KORS CROSBY boot shoe CAMEL whiskey 8	$269.95
MICHAEL KORS CROSBY boot shoe CAMEL whiskey 8.5	$269.95
MICHAEL KORS CROSBY boot shoe whiskey CHOCOLATE 7	$249.99
MICHAEL KORS CROSBY boot shoe whiskey CHOCOLATE 7.5	$249.99
Ballroom Dance Evening Dress shoe Drag Queen Costume	$202.50
NIB MANOLO BLAHNIK DALO PINK SUEDE SANDAL HEELS SHOE 38	$200.00

M 7-8 BANANA REPUBLIC CASHMERE	$22.50
HOUSE SLIPPER SHOE NEW	
ARIAT EQUIPPED Black/Brown Clog Mule Shoe Size 9 B	$22.00
Womens Vasque Velocity Trail Running shoe us 9.5 NIB	$22.00
Escada Red Suede Wedge Womans Shoe Sz 9B NWT.	$21.71
NEW BORN BLACK LEATHER LOAFER	$21.50
SHOE WOMEN 37 6.5/7 NICE!	
NEW ICE WHITE HIGH HEEL MOCCASIN	$21.50
WOMENS SHOE SIZE 8.5	
Clarks Val Comfort Walking shoe Black size 10 M	$21.50
NEW SEXY CLASSY PINK HIGH HEEL PUMP WOMEN SHOE SIZE 9	$21.50
Born Oxford Loafer Women shoe size 7 or 38 *Exc. cond*	$21.01
Anywears Pink Clog Soft Jelly Shoe Size Large 8 9 New	$21.00
Wanted Brand, W's STATIC Fun Sport Shoe 8.5 M $50 NEW	$20.99

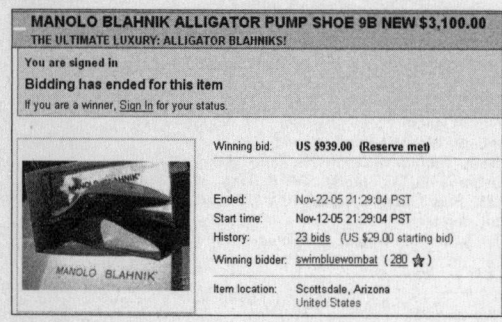

Wholesale, Large & Small Lots ▶ Men's Clothing

The average sales price in this subcategory is $127.99.

	HIGH		AVG
100 NWT Ralph Lauren Polo Shirts S/S S,M,L,XL,XXL	$1,200.00	WHOLESALE LOT OF 24 ADIDAS NEW MENS TREFOIL	$149.95
WHOLESALE LOT OF 50 MENS LACOSTE STRIPE POLO SHIRTS NWT	$1,050.00	WHOLESALE LOT - 10 New Men's Nike Tiger Woods Polo's	$144.99
100 RALPH LAUREN CLASSIC MESH SHIRTS WHOLESALE	$1,000.00	24 JON LAUREN LONG SLEEVE DENIM SHIRTS MIXED SIZES	$143.99
WHOLESALE LOT ABERCROMBIE Mens 9 Oz Recon Cargo Pants	$975.00	47 New Tommy Hilfiger shirts !! Great money maker NR !!	$139.95
WHOLESALE LOT ABERCROMBIE Mens 9 Oz Recon Cargo Pants	$949.99	WhoLeSale ChOpPeRS SUnGlASsES 7 DoZEn BiKeR NEW OCC	$137.50
LOT OF 50 RALPH LAUREN BIG PONY POLOS FOR MEN BRAND NEW	$912.00	Case Lot of COLOR T-SHIRTS S, M, L, XL Blank	$133.84
Abercrombie & Fitch Mountain Field Division Jacket 20PC	$900.00	Lot of 15 Mens Fubu Fleece Sweatshirts - New	$130.00
LOT OF 24 NEW ABERCROMBIE MENS VINTAGE TRACK JACKETS	$810.00	14NWT - POLO by RALPH LAUREN CLASSIC BUTTON DOWN SHIRT	$127.52
Auth Abercrombie Kilburn Destroyed Jeans lot of 25	$795.00	25 Pair Levis 501 Blue Jeans Levi's Pants Wholesale Lot	$125.09
WHOLESALE LOT ABERCROMBIE Mens Lejeune Cargo Pants NWT	$774.95	10 wholesale G Unit The Game Shirts FREE SHIPPING!	$125.00
WHOLESALE LOT ABERCROMBIE Mens Lejeune Cargo Pants NWT	$749.95	10 Wholesale Quicksilver Mens Sweatshirts FREE SHIPPING	$122.50
(50) Mens or Womens Lacoste polo shirts FREE SHIPPING	$743.00	BNWT 10 RALPH LAUREN POLO MEN SHIRTS WHOLESALE	$110.00
100% AUTHENTIC 50 MEN'S LACOSTE POLO SHIRTS NEW W/TAGS	$725.00	10 NEW RALPH LAUREN POLO MESH MENS SHIRTS WHOLESALE !!	$105.04
WHOLESALE LOT - New Hugo Boss Mens Polo Shirts 50 pc	$697.99	10 Wholesale Armani Men's T Shirts Free Shipping!!!	$102.50
50 LACOSTE Men's Pique Polos *Made in Peru* NWT	$676.66	Lee Ultraweight Fleece Crewneck Sweatshirts, Ash Color	$102.50

Wholesale, Large & Small Lots ▶ Women's Clothing

The average sales price in this subcategory is $30.50.

	HIGH		AVG
110+ Vintage Chuck Taylor Converse All Star Sneakers	$1,051.00	8 Pc Jrs Clothing Cute Skirts & Tops Size 13/XL NWT	$33.75
147 PC WHOLESALE LOT DEPT STORE NT RT 10,070.00 NR LOOK	$610.00	63 pc HUGE LOT LADIES SIZE SMALL 3 4 5 6 casual career	$33.00
100 WHOLESALE womens UPSCALE DESIGNER clothes NWT $7K	$595.00	MJR LOT OF 25 ASSORTED ITEMS	$32.00
VICTORIA SECRET 50 PC WHOLESALE LOT NEW ITEMS	$450.00	Chico's Top Jacket Skirt M / L Chicos 3 pc Lot	$31.99
100 PC Wholesale Lot SILHOUETTES Plus Size XL - 4X NEW	$400.00	Womens Exercise Gear Clothes Tops Bottoms Lot 26 M L	$31.98
NEW 100pc Wholesale Designer Womens Clothing Lot	$355.00	Wholesale Lot of 32 Woman's Designer Boutique Clothing	$31.09
WHOLESALE LOT 10 SETS JUICY COUTURE CROCHET HOODIE&PANT	$355.00	MATERNITY BABY STYLE GAP LOT COOL HIP CLOTHES SZ S or P	$31.00
50NWT WHOLESALE womens clothes OLD NAVY DKNY SEVEN7 LEI	$349.99	10 piece lot HIGH END DESIGNER CLOTHING all NWT !!!	$31.00
Lot of 18 Juicy Couture Pants and Jacket	$306.00	SZ M/L LOT WOMENS CLOTHING GOTHIC CLUBBING PUNK	$30.00
NWT WHOLESALE LOT 22 ITEMS JUICY COUTURE PANT &HOODIE	$290.00	HUGE LOT OVER 30 PIECES ALL NAME BRANDS!!!!!	$30.00
NWT Lot of 334 Woman's Designer Boutique Clothing	$285.00	NWT size 6 women's clothing lot, $161.00 retail	$29.99
NWT WOMENS WHOLSALE EBAY STARTER LOT $1000 TOMMY POLO +	$260.00	LOT 20+ items womens clothing size 14 16	$28.45
75 Piece Designer Womens Clothing Lot Juicy Tahari Gap	$255.00	American Eagle, Abercrombie 18 Piece Lot Sz. XS, S	$28.00
NWT Huge Lot of 54 Womens / Plus Size Clothes TRENDY Lg	$255.00	YEA BABY GOTHIC WIG n/R AUCTION SEXY DIVA WIGS	$27.59
50 PC DESIGNER NAME CASUAL/FORMAL WEAR L 12 resale lot	$255.00	NEW Junior 23 pc lot American Eagle Gap Old Navy & more	$27.40

11

COINS

The Coins category on eBay has a lot more than just, well, coins. There are mediums of exchange of all types, including gold bullion and paper money. There is even pseudo-money, as well as money-related items, such as exonumia (tokens, medals, elongated coins, and the like) and scripophily (stock certificates, autographs, and so on).

Far and away, the Coins: US subcategory contains the most listings of all the Coins subcategories—about 100,000. Within that subcategory, the most auctions can be found in Dollars (about 19,000), Halves (half dollars—about 12,500), and Quarters (about 12,000). But that doesn't mean there isn't a healthy load of coins from all over the world here—you can find everything from South African Krugerrands to Iraqi dinars to Japanese yen.

The most popular searches in Coins include the words *silver, gold, silver dollars, morgan, platinum, proof sets,* and *quarters.* They also include the acronyms *pcgs,* which stands for Professional Coin Grading Service, and *ngc,* the Numismatic Guaranty Corporation. eBayers searching on those terms are looking for coins that have been graded by those professional services.

Each type of coin or money has niche experts and followers who understand the nuances of what makes a particular piece valuable. However, that is not to say that you cannot do well selling coins here without a large base of knowledge. It's possible to research your specific item of money, compare final sales prices of similar items, and also tap the resources of the many helpful experts on the Coins discussion board in the eBay Community area. In fact, a recent highlighted discussion on the Coins discussion board was entitled "Best way to

Represent and sell coins without 'coin' knowledge?" It turns out there were many specialists willing to help this seller, who had bought a box of coins from Republicana Mexicana, Nederlands, Romania, and so on, at an estate sale. (Among the suggestions: use clear, good pictures; describe the best you can, "and the coin will sell itself." Another offered to help out this bewildered seller with ballpark values if he or she would post to the board the dates and denominations of the coins. ("If they are common world coins, they won't get a lot, and will sell at whatever the going rate is despite your asking price.")

Within the Bullion ▶ Gold subcategory, the highest price was for a large collection of graded US coins that the seller claimed was worth over $260,000.00. These went for $40,100.00 with 22 bids. The most expensive single item of gold here was a "rare huge 5.37 ounce Randsburg California gold nugget," which went for $3,500.00 with three bids. Average prices in this subcategory hover around $250.00 to $430.00, with several gold nuggets and older gold coins, such as an 1850 $10.00 Liberty US gold coin, being available. At the low end, there are many listings for "stocking stuffer" or novelty items, such as vials of gold flake leaf, which sold for a penny to $1.36.

Among the ancient coins subcategories sampled in the following tables, the Greek coins yielded the highest average sales price: $62.64. There are some fascinating items here, many of which date back more than 2,000 years. For example, an Alexander the Great–era coin, 336–323 BC, displaying the helmeted head of Athena, sold for $1,025.00. This "very nice coin comes from a hoard of gold staters from the times of Philip II, Alexander the Great and Lysimachos," says the seller in his description. This seller has 100 percent feedback and over 1,000 transactions, so prospective bidders could be reassured it was genuine.

US dimes have a higher average sales price than US quarters; about $62.00 vs. about $39.00. A couple of the highest-priced dimes here were both old and had minting process errors or other unusual features that made them rare: an "1889 Liberty Seated Dime MS66 Doubled Die" went for $566.00 with 13 bids, and an "1833 Bust Dime MS-61++ RAINBOW BEAUTY!!" sold for $561.00 with 22 bids.

Halves' high prices here tend to be quite a bit higher than either dimes or quarters, with five selling at $1,000.00 or more each, and the highest selling at almost $5,000.00: an 1859 Cameo Pattern Half that had been NGC graded. Their average sales price is high, too: $104.96. The Kennedy half dollars show up at the lower end, with three of them selling between $1.00 and $2.00 each.

Several of the high auctions for pennies are of "unsearched" lots, meaning the buyer has an opportunity to sort through them for truly valuable coins. The highest-priced lot in the Lincoln Wheat pennies subcategory was from a coin store, with 65,000 pennies in the lot. According to the seller, "there could be literally anything inside this collection! We have not searched this lot for key dates, gem grades, errors or double dies! Yes, there will be steel cents, yes there will be p, d, and s mint coins, no we have not searched these coins!" Lincoln Wheat pennies are the most voluminous of all the US pennies on eBay, at around 6,000 listings, followed by Indian Head (1859–1909) pennies at around 3,000, and then Lincoln Memorial (1959–Now) pennies, around 2000.

The high-selling penny auctions are for lots, and not individual coins. The most expensive single Wheat penny here went for $45.00, a "C-USA 1912 D Lincoln Cent EF45."

For some casual observers, it may seem odd to spend almost $50.00 for a penny, but coin lovers know better and get plenty of joy out of their hobby. As one numismatic enthusiast joked in an intriguing thread on the eBay Coins discussion board entitled "What has been your best coin buy?" his mother was baffled by his purchase in 1972 of an 1894-P Morgan Dollar BU for $50.00, with money he'd made from his paper route. She "couldn't understand buying a dollar for fifty dollars!"

Bullion ▶ Gold

The average sales price in this subcategory is $312.08.

	HIGH		AVG
HUGE COLLECTION OF GRADED US GOLD COINS OVER $260,000!	$40,100.00	31.3 GRAMS OF PURE GOLD NUGGETS. 1 OZ+	$405.01
50 Canadian Maple Leaf 1 ounce 2005 GOLD COIN/COINS	$21,300.00	two 10 gram gold bars	$405.00
CANADIAN MAPLE LEAF PURE GOLD COINS (10)	$4,400.00	California Gold Nuggets 1 Troy Ounce Nuggets Nugget NR	$390.00
10 Pack US Mint AMERICAN EAGLE GOLD COINS!	$4,371.52	18Karat solid tricolor necklace new condition	$379.99
10 Canadian Maple Leaf 1 ounce 2005 GOLD COIN/COINS	$4,350.00	1909-D $5 Gold Indian NGC MS-61	$375.00
SOUTH AFRICA KRUGERRAND GOLD COINS (10 Pack)	$4,315.00	$25 Gold Coin 1986	$355.01
CANADIAN MAPLE LEAF PURE GOLD COINS (10)	$4,300.00	HUGE GOLD NUGGET! Nuggets Golden NO RESERVE	$352.43
10 Vienna Philharmonic 1 ounce GOLD COIN/COINS	$4,280.11	1/2 oz + natural gold nugget 17 grams 99? no reserve	$300.10
SOUTH AFRICA KRUGERRAND GOLD COINS (10 Pack)	$4,272.13	33.7 Grams of Dental Scrap 18K Gold Caps	$300.03
RARE HUGE 5.37 OUNCE	$3,500.00	11.65 GRAM ENORMOUS!! BRIGHT!!	$296.25
RANDSBURG CALIFORNIA GOLD NUGGET		CA GOLD NUGGET/NUGGETS	
JOHNSON-MATTHEY (JM) PURE SILVER BARS 100OZ.	$2,176.22	NORWAY - 20 KRONER 1875	$275.00
(3) ENGELHARD PURE SILVER BARS - 100 oz. ea.	$2,159.67	1850 $10 Liberty US Gold Coin	$270.65
(3) ENGELHARD PURE SILVER BARS - 100 oz. ea.	$2,157.89	1994 PEOPLES REPUBLIC OF CHINA GOLD UNICORN SET PROOF	$270.00
Five one ounce Krugerrand's.	$2,100.00	Scrap Gold jewelry 35.5 grams 14kt 14K k kt scrap	$265.22
Large Gold Nugget	$1,874.00	NEW 2005 Chinese GOLD Panda MINT Coin Yuan Coins	$265.00

Bullion ▶ Platinum

The average sales price in this subcategory is $470.84.

	HIGH		AVG
10 One Ounce Engelhard Platinum Bar with Certificate#'s	$8,399.00	2004 $50 Dollar Platinum PCGS69	$480.00
2001 WTC Ground Zero 1 oz. Platinum Eagle 1 of 190 PCGS	$4,300.00	1990 1/2 oz Proof Platinum Chinese Panda	$479.00
2001 $100 WORLD TRADE CENTER PLATINUM LIBERTY EAGLE	$4,200.00	1998 W $50 1/2 OUNCE PLATINUM EAGLE PROOF NO RESERVE	$475.00
PLATINUM $50. MAPLE LEAF "WTC GROUND ZERO RECOVERY"	$3,651.00	2004 NGC MS69 $50 Platinum Eagle Coin Coins NO RESERVE!	$471.00
9-11 Ground Zero Recovery $100 Platinum Eagle PCGS	$3,549.99	2004 NGC MS69 $50 Platinum Eagle Coin Coins NO RESERVE!	$461.78
9-11 Ground Zero Recovery $100 Platinum Eagle PCGS	$3,400.00	(4) 2004 NGC MS69 $10 Platinum Eagle Coins NO RESERVE!!	$460.00
1999 PLATINUM Proof 4-Coin Complete Set No Reserv	$2,758.00	2002 $50 Platinum Eagle - 1/2 oz.	$460.00
2005-W Platinum Eagle Set All NGC Proof 69 Ultra Cameo	$2,650.00	1999 PCGS MS69 Platinum $50.00 1/2 oz. Eagle	$455.00
1997 AMERICAN EAGLE PROOF PLATINUM FOUR COIN SET	$2,499.99	MS-70 * 2004 $10 PLATINUM EAGLE * PCGS MS-70 !!!	$449.44
2004 Canada 4-Coin Proof Platinum Grizzly Bear Set RARE	$2,200.00	MS-70 * 2004 $10 PLATINUM EAGLE * PCGS MS-70 !!!	$443.66
y2001-W 4 PC. PROOF PLATINUM AMERICAN EAGLE SET!	$2,151.00	VINTAGE LADIES HAMILTON, PLATINUM & DIAMONDS WRISTWATCH	$440.00
2001AMERICAN EAGLE PROOF PLATINUM BULLION FOUR COINSET	$2,100.00	2003 * $10 PLATINUM * PCGS MS-69 * ONLY 22,007 MADE!	$109.99
2001-W American Eagle Platinum PROOF Four-Coin Set	$2,050.00	2003 Platinum $25 PCGS MS70 - Perfect Platinum!	$434.09
2002-W PLATINUM PROOF 4 COIN SET 6TH YR ONLY 6,782 SETS	$2,050.00	(4) 2003 NGC MS69 $10 Platinum Eagle Coins NO RESERVE!!	$431.30
2002 PLATINUM EAGLE Proof 4-Coin Complete Set No Reserv	$2,036.99	VERYRARE PURE PLATINUM P.Vincze medal "David & Goliath"	$425.00

Coins: Ancient ▶ Byzantine

The average sales price in this subcategory is $36.25.

	HIGH		AVG
Roman Empire Honorius 395 423 Gold Solidus Milan	$625.00	BYZ-JUSTIN 1-AE FOLLIS-ANTX	$37.70
Gold cup coin of Constantine IX, Christ, Byzantine, EF+	$580.00	Syracuse, Nicephorus I 802-811 AD ?follis	$37.55
Constantine VII 913-59 A.D. Gold Solidus-No Reserve!	$525.99	John II Comnenus 1/2 Tetarteron * Christ *	$37.30
Byzantine Solidus Portrait of Christ AD 945	$525.00	Tiberius II Constantine AE Follis VF ++	$37.00
Constantine VII Constantinople CHRIST gold solidus	$525.00	3 DAY! Lot of 2:ANASTATIUS, Ae 34 Follis & 1/2 Follis!	$37.00
Byzatine Gold Coin	$500.00	Syracuse, Constans II 641-668 AD ?half follis	$36.53
984/ byzantine gold coin FDC condition EX rare	$446.00	Syracuse, Michael I 811-813 AD ?follis	$36.52
Byzantine Portrait of Christ 1028 Romanus III	$399.00	3 DAY! Lot of 2: BASIL II&Constantine VIII, ANONYMOUS!	$36.26
Roman Byzantine solidus Gold coin FDC 20 MM XF++ancient	$380.00	Byzantine Coin, Dynasty of the Palaeologoi Palaeologi	$36.00
Byzantine Gold Solidus of Emperor Heraclius, 610-641 AD	$362.00	BYZANTINE EMPIRE 802 A.D. _ FOLLIS _ GOOD _ NICEFORO I	$36.00
Byzantine 2 Venice zecchini Gold solidus coins XF 20 MM	$340.00	Byzantine jesus 2 Bronze coins 24M XF ancient	$35.00
Justinian I (527 - 565 AD)- AV Solidus - Constantinople	$324.56	D. RAZMOSKA-BACEVA. CIRCULATION OF THE PALEOLOGI COINS	$34.00
Sogdian imitation of Byzantine solidus	$311.89	Byzantine FDC jesus rare bronze coin XF 27 MM see	$34.00
Genuine Greek Byzantine Gold Coin	$305.00	*AAH* Maurice Tiberius Follis "M" Cyzicus VI	$33.56
EFTIS: GOLD Focas Solidus coin 602 AD N/R!	$300.00	Maurice Tiberius Follis, Year 20	$33.01

Coins: Ancient ▶ Celtic

The average sales price in this subcategory is $26.43.

	HIGH		AVG
CELTIC GOLD STATER DOMINO CORIELTAUVI 50 BC.	$412.76	ANCIENT CELTIC SILVER COIN DUROTRIGES	$33.00
2100 Year Old CELTIC Silver Coin - God of WINE and LUST	$237.50	Billon-tetradrachm from the east-celts in Dacia	$29.00
CELTIC GOLD COIN - circa 45 B.C.	$179.00	ANCIENT CELTIC SILVER COIN	$28.81
AAH Celtic AR tetradrachm of Alexander III	$140.00	ANCIENT CELTIC BRONZE COINS 6X LOT	$28.00
AAH BEAUTIFUL Celtic 4drachm of THASOS	$116.66	*AAH* Celtic AR drachm of Philip III.	$27.53
Rare Celtic Propeller Money Bronze Coin 2000+ Years Old	$61.00	ANCIENT CELTIC COINS 4X LOT BRITAIN	$26.76
Celtic (?) 13mm,1.6gm	$58.76	B5.Celtic ring money La Tene period lot of 15	$26.01
British Iron Age Coins in British Museum	$49.00	ANCIENT CELTIC COPY AR GREEK COIN	$26.00
ANCIENT CELTIC SILVER COIN RHINELAND AR10	$48.76	ANCIENT CELTIC COPY AR GREEK COIN	$23.00
ANCIENT CELTIC SILVER COIN DUROTRIGES	$47.00	3 BRONZE CELTIC VOTIVES / RING MONEY ___Nice Lot !!!!!	$22.50
Ancient Celtic Triple Goddess Votive Ring Money! :)	$46.77	Nice lot,3 Bronze Ancient Celtic ring money,800-500B.C.	$21.25
L25.Celtic bronze ring money lot of 15 La Tene period	$45.89	Nice lot,3 Bronze Ancient Celtic ring money,800-500B.C	$21.00

Coins: Ancient ▶ China

The average sales price in this subcategory is $12.59.

	HIGH		AVG
China(Qing) Tien-cung han-chien in Manchu v-10 VS F-VF	$300.00	AD1038-1039 Chinese Coin HuangSongTongBao-Complicated S	$13.50
AD1821-1851 Chinese Coin XianFengYuanBao=200?w Moon Sun	$130.00	Rare Tang Dy"Tong Zheng yuan Bao"***XF**Rev:Stars& moon.	$13.50
Unknown China Big Coin Yi-kuo yen-chang 41.8mm VF	$122.50	AD1528 Ming Dy Chinese Coin 'Jia Jing An Bao'.	$13.50
Big AD845?Tang Dy Chinese Coin 'KAI YUAN TONG BAO'	$103.59	Cheng Bai (300-250 BC) Knife Coin	$13.16
Six Dynasties Dragon & Tiger High-relief Bronze Mirror	$78.77	RI Southern Han 907-971Qian Heng ZB Lead,Rev.Top.YI VF	$13.10
China(Five Dy.) Shun-tien yuan-pao Very Scarce Type	$51.00	BC221 Empire Yan Chinese Initial Coin??'YI 4 HUA'	$13.00
China(N.Song) Chih-ho chung-pao v-2 Iron Mother VScarce	$49.80	AD947 Liao Dy Chinese Coin?'TIAN LU TONG BAO'	$13.00
China(Ming) Hung-wu t-p 5 Cash Rev.Pei-ping V.Scarce	$48.00	Open Charm 58mm - 2 Dragon	$12.50
China(Yuan) Ta-yuan t-p Mongol Leg. Rev.Yi V.Scarce VF	$48.00	Charm 44x67 mm (O)	$12.50
China(Ming) Tien-chi t-p Rev.Fu Bing v-10 Scarce VF	$48.00	Two Charm 33.5x49 mm (Q)	$12.50
Rare Spring & Autumn Period SQUARE Bronze Mirror	$47.77	AD1204 Jin Chinese Coin TaiHeZhongBao-Moon Star&Flowers	$12.50
S. Ming/ Da Ming TB 26.2mm - Shuai on top	$47.54	AD995-1008 Korea Coin?JI YUAN ZHONG BAO??'Dong Guo'	$12.38
BC338-288 Chinese Double Loop Coin? 'East Zhou'	$46.88	7 psc Different Qing Dynasty/ Shun Zhi TB (A)	$12.05
AD1488-1505 Ming Dy Chinese coin HONG ZHI TONG BAO	$46.09	Unknown Very Rare Han Dy Coin ***XF***	$12.03
T1697 Antique Ancient Silver Ingot Yuan Bao Cube Coin	$46.00	fb Wang Mang Ta-ch'uan wu-shih lot(5pcs) S-120-31 F-VF	$12.00

Coins: Ancient ▶ Greek

The average sales price in this subcategory is $62.64.

	HIGH		AVG
Thrace-Lysimachos 297-81 B.C. Gold Stater-No Reserve!	$1,451.10	Greek-Thessaly Hemidrachm 5th Century B.C. W/COA	$65.00
Alexander the Great. 336-323 BC. Gold Stater, Athena	$1,025.00	Two Southern Italy fractions	$65.00
Kings of. Philip II. 359-336 BC. Gold Stater, SUPERB	$935.00	Moesia, ISTROS. Circa 4th Century BC. Silver Stater	$64.20
GOLD STATER ALEXANDER THE GREAT ANCIENT COIN ATHENA N/R	$861.00	Greek Istros Inverted Heads / Eagle on Dolphin 1Drachma	$63.00
Kings of Pontos-Mithradates VI 120-63 BC Gold Stater-XF	$510.15	SYRACUSE SICILY Silver TETRAS___406 BC___Rare !!!!!!!	$62.99
Alexander III of Macedonia Greek silver Tetradrachm VF	$490.00	Athens Silver Tetradrachm Athena/ Owl	$62.89
Silver Greek CoinTenedos Troas Tetradrachm 2nd cent BC	$433.00	MAGNA GRAECIA AND SICILY, MUSEUM BASEL INCR COINS & PHO	$62.85
Philip II Tetradrachm 359 - 336 BC	$425.00	Athens Silver Tetradrachm Athena/ Owl	$62.01
Ancient GREEK Coin ATTIC Athens ATHENA/OWl Silver Tdrm.	$399.00	Lot of 5 Macedon Ae's of Alexander the Great.	$61.50
EF Tarsus, Cilicia Mazaeus AR stater	$391.50	p11 Colophon Greek Silver Drachm 450 BC rare	$61.00
Alexander III, 336-323 BC, Silver Tetradrachm, 16.55 gr	$390.00	Lovely Greek silver coin	$61.00
EFTIS: GREEK Silver Babylon Tetradrachm coin 331BC N/R!	$356.01	*F* Parthia, VOLOGASES IV, Tetradrachm. aVF	$60.00
Illyria Epidamnos-Dyrrachium Silver Corinthian Stater	$350.00	GREECE 38BC PARTHIANS PHRAATES IV SILVER TETRADRACHM	$59.99
LUCANIA Metapontion DEMETER Ancient GREEK AR Coin 400BC	$329.00	INDO-SCYTHIANS. AZES AR. TETRADRACHM. XF.	$59.99
Athens Tetradrachm Athena/ Owl ca 375 BC	$299.99	50 Uncleaned Ancient Roman Holy Land Coins Lot 0706a	$59.00

Coins: Ancient ▶ Medieval

The average sales price in this subcategory is $36.09.

	HIGH		AVG
EFTIS:GOLD HALF-LAUREL James I Hammered Coin N/R!	$1,026.00	POLaND-KRAKoW Alexander Silver Coin Polgrosz XVI c.*	$37.99
NUESTRA SENORA DE ATOCHA, SHIPWRECK COIN	$615.88	Transylvania, Johann Zapolya, 1530 AR denar	$37.01
Venetian Gold Ducat abt. Extr. Fine SCARE	$450.00	BOHEMiA - Lot of 2 Medieval Coins XIV, XVI c. *	$37.00
DENMARK KRONE 1620 for the East India Trade	$411.00	Cologne Archbishops, Adolf I von Altena denar c 1200	$36.51
Byzantine - Medieval silver coin.Mint condition.	$356.00	6 Medieval coins - 4 Venice, 1 Cyprus and 1 ? NR	$36.50
CRUSADERS 1275 COUNTY OF TRIPOLI BOHEMOND VIII RARE RRR	$316.10	700+ Year Old Silver Coin - CRUSADER Knight of FRANCE	$36.28
Austrian-German-Silver-Friesacher Pfeninge-No date-	$260.00	Crusades, Achaia, Guillaume de Villehardouin denier	$36.00
Odo(Eudes) 887-898 AD - AR Denier - Limoges Mint	$250.00	Medieval silver coin.	$36.00
800+ Yr Old Silver CRUSADER Coin RICHARD the LIONHEART	$227.50	Halfpenny of Eawig Seaby 1128	$36.00
13 UNIDENTIFIED EUROPEAN? COINS CIRCA 1500-1800, NO RES	$219.50	500 Yr Old GERMAN Silver Coin ORDER of Teutonic KNIGHTS	$36.00
Genuine 500+ Year Old SILVER Coin of the DRACULA Family	$207.50	Levon I copper tank, BEARDED FACE Armenian 1198-1219 AD	$36.00
Crusades, Tripoli, Bohemond VII AR gros c. 1280	$204.06	CRUSADER ATHENS GUY II de la Roche,(1287-1308AD) Denier	$36.00
Alfred The Great Offering Penny	$203.51	Salzburg - archbishop Adalbertus III. - Appr.1170-1200	$36.00
CYPRUS,CRUSADER STATES.PETER II AR GROS	$195.00	Medieval D - Slavonia (13-14th cent.) - High Grade	$35.71
Wallachia, Mircea the Old, AR ducat c 1400	$189.50	3 DAY! Venetian Ar SOLDI, Andrea GRITI, 1523-1538AD!	$35.01

Coins: Ancient ▶ Roman: Imperial

The average sales price in this subcategory is $33.55.

	HIGH		AVG
VESPASIAN. 69-79 AD. GOLD Aureus	$1,699.00	PHILIP II Ancient ROMAN Coin Silver Anton.245AD JUPITER	$35.00
CONSTANTINE the Great. 307-337 AD. Gold Solidus EF rare	$1,475.00	Theodosius II<? >VOT MVLT X in laurel wreath.	$35.00
RARE ROMAN SESTERTIUS OF MACRINUS VF!!	$755.50	AE-37 of GETA from Mylasa in Karia tetrastyle temple	$35.00
THE BEST UNCLEANED ROMAN COINS ON EBAY!!	$726.15	*AAH* Lot of 3 Denarii, Septimius Severus	$34.99
SEPTIMUS SEVERUS SESTERTIUS GREAT PORTRAIT	$560.00	Nerva Dupondius.Great portrait. Green patina. 96-98 A.D	$34.50
Galerius as Caesar 293-305 AD AR Argenteus-Uncirculated	$480.00	Roman augustus caiser Heliopolis coin SESTERTIUS 24 MM	$34.00
Book: Cohen Monnaies Sous L?Empire Romain 8 Volumes	$400.00	Constantine I AE 18 mm. VF !!!! RARE !!!!	$33.55
Roman very rare King tetradrachm silver coin 27 MM FDC	$375.00	25 Ancient Premium Uncleaned Roman Bronze Coins 0729a	$33.55
200 HIGH GRADE ROMAN COINS FROM JORDAN.*UNOPENED BAG*	$360.99	AUGUSTUS AS. RARE.	$33.00
RRRR Majorian Ae 4 Roman coin	$306.00	Trajan AD 98-117 Silver Denarius "Fortuna COS VI" GREAT	$33.00
OTHO DENARIUS , 69 AD	$280.01	Julian II the Apostate. 360-363 AD, AE 1. VF	$33.00
Tiberius "Tribute Penny" 17/37AD Denarius ICG VF35	$275.00	Roman Silver Tetradrachm #6	$33.00
Maxentius AE Follis.	$271.00	Civil War countermarked sestertius VF	$33.00
Ext. RARE Swedish Plate Money Coin 2 Daler 1744 N/R	$249.50	*IC* VERY FINE AR DENARIUS OF ANTONINUS PIUS 138-161AD	$33.00
SUPERB SESTERTIUS OF CRISPINA. GREAT STRIKE!!	$245.00	*AAH* Gordian III Den "Jupiter" RARE	$32.99

Coins: Ancient ▶ Roman: Republic

The average sales price in this subcategory is $47.04.

	HIGH		AVG
Twelve Caesars ,Galba 68-69 AD Rome Oct. 68 Sestertius	$395.00	L13.Lot of 6 Roman republic AR denarius VF	$49.99
Julius Caesar AR Denarius, Roman silver coin, 50 BC	$393.00	ROMAN REPUBLIC SILVER COIN IN 14K GOLD PENDANT 100 BC	$49.00
1000 Ancient, Uncleaned Roman Coins	$305.00	VIBIA 2 DENARIUS____90 BC____Beautiful Apollo !!!!!!!!!	$49.00
Roman Republic Denarius Q. Caecilius Metellus Pius	$210.00	4 ANCIENT ROMAN REPUBLIC SILVER DENARIUS 100 BC	$49.00
Roman Republic Denarius L. Aurelius Cotta	$199.99	C Allius Bala Denarius. 92 BC., VF	$49.00
M. JUNIUS BRUTUS Denarius, B.C.55	$198.50	Q.f. Tampilus. 137 BC. AR Denarius, Roman Republic	$48.00
Silver Roman Coin M Antony & Octavia 39 BC.	$180.36	VERY NICE DENARIUS ""M.FURIUS L.f.PHILUS"" SEE ""	$47.78
VOLTEIA 4 AR DENARIUS____78 BC____Biga of Lions !!!!!!!	$171.47	Pair of Ancient Silver Coinage ANACS certified	$46.77
ROMAN 42 BC DENARIUS.	$165.13	C. Naevius Balbus 79 B.C. AR Denarius Serratus	$46.00
200+UNCLEANED ANCIENT ROMAN COINS& ARTIFACTS 100-400AD	$157.55	02527- Rare Denarius, C. Censorius, 88BC, Juggate, WOW	$46.00
ANCIENT ROME-SESTERTIUS-COMMODUS-SUPERB GREEN COLOR	$150.00	VERY NICE DENARIUS ""L.PISO FRUGI"" SEE SCAN	$46.00
RARE Caesar & Marc Antony 43 BC Denarius	$150.00	Roman Republic. Fabius Labeo. 124 B.C. AR Denarius	$45.00
CNE* MARC ANTHONY & CLEOPATRA. WEAK BUT RARE DENAR !!!!	$145.00	Junius Silanus Denarius. 116-115 BC, Roman Republic	$45.00
VIBIA 18 DENARIUS____48 BC____Adherent of Caesar !!!!!!	$133.49	L CALPURNIUS PISO & Q SERVILIUS CAEPIO	$45.00
Roman Republic AE Semis 130 BC M. Varguneius	$127.25	VERY NICE DENARIUS ""L. RUTILIUS FLACCUS""""RARE"""""	$44.78

Coins: US ▶ Collections, Lots

The average sales price in this subcategory is $117.01.

	HIGH		AVG
624-BU/CHOICE GEM MS-63 TO MS-67 MORGAN SILVER DOLLARS	$21,211.00	WHITES COINMASTER 5000/D Metal Detector COMPLETE	$143.50
OVER *50,000 MIXED OBSOLETE US COINS & SILVER	$12,999.99	NobleSpirit~ Exciting 1896-S ANACS XF40 = $160!	$142.50
45,000+OBSOLETE U.S. COINS,GOLD,SILVER,CARSON CITY SALE	$7,600.00	1878 8 TAIL FEATHERS MORGAN MS64 *$450* NO RESERVE!	$142.50
Collection of Great Morgan,s	$1,155.00	NGC CERTIFIED 1969-S KENNEDY HALF PR69 ULTRA CAMEO!	$141.00
36 PCGS+NGC SLABS MORGAN GOLD ROLLS PF+MINT SETL@@K NR	$899.52	POP'S LINCOLN SET 1940-49 PDS MS65 MS66 MS67 GEM BU RED	$139.50
MASSIVE ESTATE COIN COLLECTION! VALUE OVER $5000!	$819.09	NobleSpirit~ SEMI -KEY 1879-CC ANACS VF VAM-3 TOP 100!	$137.50
OLD COINS - SILVER, GOLD, & COPPER - SETTLING ESTATE	$785.03	1909 - 1982 LINCOLN CENTS ALBUM - NEARLY COMPLETE	$137.50
JEFFERSON NICKEL SET 1938-2005 CH/GEM BU/PROOF	$535.00	9 DIFFERENT DATED MORGANS SUPER NICE NO 1921	$132.71
UNSEARCHED WOODEN CIGAR	$520.00	COMPLETE 1937-1947 WALKING LIB. COLL;NICE;NR	$127.50
BOX OF COINS 70-75 COINS IN BOX		1883s BU KEY DATE MORGAN DOLLAR LISTS $500 NO RESERVE!	$126.55
[4 of these sold in a multiple item ("Dutch") auction for $130.00 each]		UNSEARCHED-MISC-TYPE BOX OF U.S.COIN 70-75 COINS IN BOX	$125.00
NGC CERTIFIED 1956 WASHINGTON QUARTER PR69 ULTRA CAMEO!	$511.00	[2 of these sold for $125.00 each]	
COIN COLLECTION ESTATE LOT PCGS VALUE $4032 + MORE ~ NR	$473.98	World War II Boxed Set of Silver Coins 1941 1945	$125.00
500 MIXED OBSOLETE US COINS /SILVER -CONTAINS NO WHEATS	$405.00	CIGAR BOX OF RARE US COINS-ESTATE-SILVER-GOLD-80 COINS	$119.00
Rare 1916/16 Buffalo Nickel Error Coin	$405.00	[2 of these sold for $119.00 each]	
Washington Quarters in Dansco Album 1932-1998 NO RESERV	$401.00	(130) SILVER CLAD HALVES $65 face - All KENNEDEY'S	$114.50
ESTATE LOT:COLLECTION,SILVER+GOLD+SETS,1,064+ OLD COINS	$395.00	5 Major Type, 2c, 3c,Seated Dime and Quarter, SLQ	$112.00

Coins: US ▶ Colonial

The average sales price in this subcategory is $69.98.

	HIGH		AVG
NEVIS"Counterstamped"9 Black Dogs (Lima 1 Real)Ex-Rare	$2,450.00	DESIRABLE! 1779 SPANISH COLONIAL 8 REALES!	$74.99
St. Patrick Farthing	$1,425.00	1786 Connecticut Coin- 3day-no reserve	$74.00
1772 British Geo.III Halfpenny Fine As Circulated In 13	$1,246.00	FANTASTIC! 1796 SAILING SHIP DRAGONSLAYER HALFPENNY!	$73.00
1789 MOTT Co. uncirculated - NGC Mint State 60 Brown	$1,195.00	TUSCANY ITALY SILVER PIASTRE CIRCA 1680 GOOD PIX NO RES	$72.00
1788 Vermont Cent, R-20, Sharp VF	$860.00	1721 BRUNSWICK GERMANY THALER MISTREATED WILDMAN NO RES	$70.99
1787 Fugio Cent, 8 Pointed Star on Label, Nice VF/XF	$836.00	Hawaii Quarter dollar coin 1883 colonial US hapara	$70.00
1787 Connecticut Cent, Horned Bust, Early Die State, XF	$790.00	PW: 1793 MIDDLESEX NATIONAL DH-995a CONDER TOKEN	$70.00
1788 Massachusetts Half Cent	$762.77	Historical Mexico 2 Reales 1776	$69.01
1794 Franklin Press Token	$610.00	KILLER! 1559 KNIGHT on HORSEBACK SILVER HALF GROSCHEN !	$68.77
A SUPERB! PERU 8 REALES 1772 CAROLUS III PILLAR DOLLAR!	$550.00	1787 Connecticut Cent F no reserve.	$68.77
1787 MA MASSACHUSETTS HALF CENT RARE COLONIAL COIN nr !	$535.00	FRENCH COLONIAL LOUISIANNE DOUBLE TOURNOIS ____ 1592	$67.88
1787 Fugio Cent, PCI VF-20	$528.00	1691-1700 FRENCH 4 SOLS SILVER COLONIAL COIN	$67.66
1787 New Jersey Cent, V.F., Breen #928, US Coins	$525.00	1723 Woods Hibernia Halfpenny, Choice Fine	$67.02
1787 Connecticut, Miller 34-ff.1, R-5 variety	$500.00	Very NIce 1692 IRELAND William & Mary Half Penny	$66.78
Washington Double Head Cent	$500.00	PW: 1795 BRITANNIA W/ THE 3 THOMAS'S: PAINE MORE SPENCE	$66.77

Coins: US ▶ Small Cents ▶ Lincoln Wheat (1909–1958)

The average sales price in this subcategory is $40.09.

	HIGH		AVG
COIN STORE BLOWOUT 65,000 UNSEARCHED LINCOLN WHEATS NR	$2,175.00	1,000 UNSEARCHED WHEAT CENTS	$42.09
1910-S Lincoln Cent NNC MS67 RED RARE!	$481.86	Big Lot Rolled 530 Wheat Pennies 1910s thru 1950s	$42.00
Unsearched Wheat Cent Penny Bag Bank Sealed Rare	$375.51	10 POUNDS OF LINCOLN WHEAT CENTS 30's 40's 50's	$41.01
Unsearched Wheat Cent Penny Bag Bank Sealed Rare	$355.00	steel penny war issue 1943 ngc mint state 65 philly wow	$41.00
1914D UNSEARCHED BANK ROLL LINCOLN WHEAT CENTS	$320.00	1000 WHEAT PENNIES UNSEARCHED!!! NO RESERVE!!!!	$41.00
1922-D Lincoln Cent NNC MS66 RED RARE!!	$308.98	1,000 UNSEARCHED WHEAT CENTS	$41.00
BEAUTIFUL NEAR COMPLETE SET LINCOLN WHEAT 1909 - 2005	$299.99	250 1943 STEEL LINCOLN WHEAT CENTS *5 FULL ROLLS*	$40.02
5000 COUNT UNSEARCHED WHEATIES BAG FROM HUGE HOARD!!	$290.00	1,000 UNSEARCHED WHEAT CENTS	$40.00
[2 of these sold for $290.00 each]		(((((21))))) ROLLS >>>WHEAT PENNIES<<< MIXED DATES NICE	$39.24
OVER 1 FULL BAG 1909-1958 WHEAT CENTS 112+ ROLLS	$255.00	1955 Lincoln Cent NGC PR67 RED	$36.00
5000 WHEAT CENTS 1909-1958 UNSEARCHED TAKE A LOOK!	$250.50	300 UNSEARCHED WHEAT PENNY SUPER HORDE DEAL	$35.90
5,000 Wheat Cents BANK BAG, Unsearched!!!!!! N.R.	$242.50	1952 Lincoln Cent NGC PR66 RED	$35.10
5000 + EXTRA 2000=TOTAL 7000+/- WHEAT CENTS! 46+POUNDS	$230.09	LOT OF 28 DIFF AU LINCOLN CENTS BETWEEN 36-P & 55-D	$35.05
45 pound wheat collection	$229.05	[5 of these sold in a multiple item ("Dutch") auction for $7.01 each]	
Unsearched bag 5000 Wheats from Estate Sale - nice one	$227.75	1935 S Lincoln 1c, NGC MS-65 RD, RARCOA	$35.00
5000 (34 lbs.) 1909-1958 HOARD of Mixed Wheat Pennies	$227.51	1000 Unsearched Wheat Cents	$34.99

Coins: US ▶ Dimes

The average sales price in this subcategory is $62.08.

	HIGH		AVG
1870 J-843 Pattern Dime NGC Graded PF 63	$1,299.99	1856 Seated Dime AU-53 NR	$69.89
1832 BUST HALF DIME (H10C) MS64 PCGS	$1,226.00	1876 AND 1878 SEATED LIBERTY DIMES "BEAUTIFUL COINS"	$68.87
RARE United States Seated Liberty Dime Coin 1865 VF	$822.55	1830 - Capped Bust Dime - NGC VF30	$68.76
1807 Draped Bust Dime Clashed Dies Solid/Solid AU55	$789.00	1830 Capped Bust Dime XF Trends $240	$66.00
1833 CAPPED BUST US COINS EARLY SILVER DIME .10c MS63	$604.99	1835 (VF) BUST DIME (CHEAP) HIGHGRADE	$65.99
BU/MS-63 1836 Capped Bust Dime $9.95 No Reserve! PQ PQ!	$581.01	Bust~ VERY OLD COINS 5-Dimes-1 Half Dollar	$63.00
1889 Liberty Seated Dime MS66 Doubled Die!!!	$566.00	United States One Dime Silver Coin 1853 XF	$62.77
1833 Bust Dime MS-61++ RAINBOW BEAUTY!!	$561.00	1889 Seated Liberty Dime MS-63, FLAHSY & TONING!!!	$62.00
1831 Bust Dime NGC au/58 JR-5 Sharp!	$500.00	1837 Capped Bust Dime XF Trends 240	$61.00
1834 Bust Dime MS-62/63 *** BEAUTIFUL!!	$455.00	1870 Seated Dime in XF condition	$60.99
1829 Small 10 Capped Bust Dime JR-3 AU55 in NGC holder	$450.00	1835 CAPPED BUST Dime (Original-VERY FINE) Nice!!	$59.15
1805 DRAPED BUST DIME **VG-8** 4 BERRIES VARIETY!!	$419.95	1835 Capped Bust Dime XF Trends $240	$58.57
1835 Capped Bust Dime MS65+ Super Original Toning	$410.00	1883 HAWAII DIME COIN ~RARE~	$58.00
1887 US Seated Liberty Dime PCGS MS64 0621	$392.00	1883 Hawaii 10C VF Detail Cleaned	$57.99
1891 Seated Liberty Dime MS67 Trends 3800	$380.00	1853 Seated Liberty Dime w/Arrows AU Trends $175	$56.01

Coins: US ▶ Quarters

The average sales price in this subcategory is $38.67.

	HIGH		AVG
4000 Quarters - Mixed Date / Mixed Grade	$999.00	MISSISSIPPI U S MINT P&D 2 ROLL SET STATE QUARTERS	$45.96
120 quarter set 1999-04 pds& silver certified perfect	$726.00	INDIANA U S MINT P&D 2 ROLL SET STATE QUARTERS	$43.01
1834 Bust Pattern Quarter Similar to J-50 Very Rare	$561.00	ARKANSAS U S MINT P&D 2 ROLL SET STATE QUARTERS	$43.00
Set of 3 Wisconsin Quarters High MS64 Low MS64 Reg MS65	$400.00	1883 Hawaii Quarter, Silver, Hawaiian. Beautiful	$42.55
1893 ISABELLA / MS-63 / DBL SHARP / NR / C9164	$356.50	Wisconnsin Quarter, with extra leaf: High leaf	$42.51
31 Rolls of State Quarters 1 roll of each state.	$325.00	LOT OF 8 QUARTERS~1898,1898,1906,08,27-S,37-S,47,53	$42.50
1917 Ty. 1 Standing 25c GEM MS-64+ 100% ORIGINAL!!!!!	$284.00	Washington Head Quarter Whitman 1932 1945 W/34 Quarters	$42.50
1883 EXTREMELY RARE HAWAII	$280.00	1999-2000 MIXED STATE QUARTER UNOPENED MINT BAG	$42.50
QUARTER PF/MS TREND $10,000		99 - 04 P&D UNCIRCULATED STATE QUARTER SET W/ BOOK	$41.00
2004 BU Wisconsin Down Leaf Error Variety End of Roll	$264.01	1999 NEW JERSEY BU P&D Rolls	$41.00
Wisconsin Quarter Extra Leaf High PCGS MS64	$250.00	[2 of these sold for $41.00 each]	
STATUE OF LIBERTY GRADED PCGS MS69 2003 $25	$231.50	INDIANA US MINT State Quarter 2 roll set R31	$41.00
Wisconsin Quarter Set- high. low. normal- RARE!	$207.51	LOUISIANA U S MINT P&D 2 ROLL SET STATE QUARTERS	$40.50
2004 BU Wisconsin Down Leaf Error Variety End of Roll	$180.07	MISSOURI U S MINT P&D 2 ROLL SET STATE QUARTERS	$39.50
NGC Mint State 62	$177.92	COMPLETE STATE QUARTER SET 99' DEL p&d thru 05 ORE p&d	$39.50
Wisconsin quarter low leaf PCGS MS64	$177.51	2003-S Clad PF Set St. 25cs, PF69 Ultra Cameo	$38.00

Coins: US ▶ Halves

The average sales price in this subcategory is $104.96.

	HIGH		AVG
1859 50c NGC PF65CAM Cameo Pattern Half J-241	$4,800.00	1830 CAPPED BUST SILVER HALF DOLLAR	$108.50
1870 Pattern Half Dollar MS66+ J-953 R.7	$2,025.00	1827 O-110 Bust Half EF-45+ R-4 VERY SCARCE VARIETY!!!	$108.50
1795 BUST HALF VF Cleaned	$1,350.00	1812 BUST HALF DOLLAR(VF-EF GREAT COIN!)	$107.70
1821 Bust Half Dollar SOLID MS-65 PQ PQ PQ	$1,175.00	1823 BUST HALF DOLLAR <> SUPER NICE!	$107.50
US COIN 1838 SILVER BUST HALF ANACS MS61 OLD REEDED EDG	$1,000.09	1831 Capped Bust Half Dollar!!** AU55 **EYE-APPEAL!!!!!	$105.01
Wonderful 1813 Capped Bust 50C NTC MS-62 Pristine!	$815.00	1838 Bust Half Dollar, XF +, NR	$105.00
1806 Draped Bust Half Dollar, Pointed 6, Stemless, XF	$800.00	1836/1336 VF/XF Capped Bust Half Dollar (O-108)	$104.03
1839 Capped Bust Half Dollar MS66 Very Nice	$785.00	1883 Half Dollar Hawaii	$103.59
1795 FLOWING hair HALF dollar Coin VG DETAILS	$740.00	34 Jefferson & 10 Kennedy Half Dollars Nice Lot	$103.51
1795 FLOWING HAIR 50c NNC F15 SCARCE!	$710.00	1818 Capped Bust Half Dollar FINE++	$103.49
1837 Capped Bust Half MS63 Trends $2250	$621.00	BUST HALF DOL. 1838 REEDED EDGE TYPE VF30 SOLID	$103.00

	HIGH		AVG
1836 Early Capped Bust Half 0-115 ltr edge MS63 Rainbow	$609.00	1834 Capped Bust Half AU	$102.50
1812 50C NGC AU55	$575.00	1834 Capped Bust Half Dollar Coin	$102.50
1806 DRAPED BUST HALF DOLLAR IN F-VF CONDITION	$567.99	1822 O-104 Cap. Bust Half EF-40 NICE ALBUM TONING!!!	$102.50
1803 draped BUST half DOLLAR lg3 EF DETAILS	$560.98	1926 Sesquicentennial Commemorative Silver Half Dollar	$102.50

Coins: US ▶ Dollars

The average sales price in this subcategory is $53.43.

	HIGH		AVG
1901 LESHER REFERENDEM SC $1 NGC-ms61 SILVER DOLLAR	$1,719.00	1998 MINT BOX/COA SILVER PROOF AMERICAN EAGLE	$58.95
1879 PATTERN J-1626 GOLOID DOLLAR PCGS-PR60 $1	$1,490.00	[2 of these sold for $58.95 each]	
1883 NGC Kingdom of Hawaii Dollar $ NGC AU-55	$1,275.00	POPE BENEDICT XVI 2005 U.S. 1oz. Pure SILVER EAGLE Coin	$57.00
u.s proof silver eagles	$960.00	[3 of these sold in a multiple item ("Dutch") auction for $19.00 each]	
$100FACE PEACE& MORGAN	$849.99	1988-Proof Silver American.	$55.00
SILVER DOLLARS MIXED DATE/MINTS		1988 Proof Silver Eagle origianl box and COA	$55.00
1890 cc NGC MS63 1890cc White Undergraded 2 Points	$799.00	1994 WOMEN IN MILITARY SERVICE $ NGC MS-69	$54.99
1996 AMERICAN SILVER EAGLE DOLLAR ROLL UNC MINT TUBE	$740.00	1986 AMERICAN SILVER EAGLE DOLLAR COIN (Air -Tite)	$52.80
Bullion Silver Dollar 2001W Proof Eagle PCGS 70 DCAM	$615.00	Huge lot of coin collections!!!! Don't Miss This!!!!	$51.01
1995 AMERICAN EAGLE SILVER DOLLAR ROLL BU/GEM	$512.99	1996 AMERICAN SILVER EAGLE DOLLAR COIN NGC MS 69	$51.00
1991 AMERICAN LIBERTY/ EAGLE	$455.00	DOLLAR BILL PAPERWEIGHT, 1969	$51.00
$50, 1 OUNCE GOLD COIN		1996 AMERICAN SILVER EAGLE DOLLAR COIN NGC MS68	$51.00
1883 Dollar Hawaii	$419.00	1 lb. Real Silver 1878 Silver Dollar Replica	$51.00
10 - 2005 W PROOF SILVER EAGLES NGC PF69 ULTRA CAMEO	$395.00	1996 AMERICAN SILVER EAGLE DOLLAR COIN NGC MS68	$50.51
10 - 2005 W PROOF SILVER EAGLES NGC PF69 ULTRA CAMEO	$381.78	Walking Liberty 1oz fine Silver ONE DOLLAR, Collection	$50.00
1997 AMERICAN SILVER EAGLE DOLLAR ROLL UNC MINT TUBE	$340.00	US Marine Corps 230th Anniversary Silver Dollar Proof	$50.00
2001 BUFFALO 2 COIN PROOF & BU DOLLAR SET BONUS	$329.00	1996 AMERICAN SILVER EAGLE DOLLAR COIN NGC MS68	$49.00

Coins: US ▶ Dollars ▶ Eisenhower (1971–78)

The average sales price in this subcategory is $53.43.

	HIGH		AVG
1000 Average Circulated Eisenhower Ike Dollars $1 - NR	$1,250.00	1977 - P (Unc. Roll) 20 coins Eisenhower dollars	$61.00
1974 EISENHOWER DOLLAR. PCGS MS66. POP 67! NO FINER!	$944.00	1976-S PCGS PR 69 DCAM CLAD Type2 IKE $ List=$175 *N/R*	$59.99
Lot of 4 1972 P Type 2 Ike Dollars $1 TY 2 PCGS Graded	$850.00	1976-S PCGS PR69DCAM TYPE 1	$58.10
Complete set, Silver & Clad Proof Ikes PCGS PR69 DCAM	$384.00	CLAD EISENHOWER DOLLAR	
1971-1978-S Ike $ Proof Set PCGS PR69DCAM PR69 w/box	$379.99	1976-D Type 1 Eisenhower Dollar PCGS MS65	$57.00
EISENHOWER DOLLAR SET 1971-1978 GEM BU AND PROOFS	$275.00	EISENHOWER IKE DOLLAR BU ROLL 1971 D 1971D	$56.99
COMPLETE SET EISENHOWER DOLLARS GEM BU/PROOF	$242.50	1972 EISENHOWER DOLLAR TYPE 2 AU-58	$56.55
1990-W Eisenhower GREEN PCGS Slab MS 69-RARE!	$227.50	NGC CERTIFIED 1976-D TYPE 1 IKE DOLLAR GRADED MS65!!	$56.00
EXTREMELY HIGH GRADE 1971-1978 IKE COLLECTION - NR!	$222.50	EISENHOWER IKE DOLLAR BU ROLL 1978 P 1978P	$52.99
1973 S - 1978 S Clad Ike Set, PCGS PR69 DCAM *Deal Week	$199.99	1972-P Uncirculated Ike Dollar Roll NO RESERVE	$51.51
[2 of these sold for $199.99 each]		SILVER UNCIRCULATED IKE DOLLARS STILL SEALED-LOT	$50.00
COMPLETE SET EISENHOWER DOLLARS GEM BU/PROOF	$197.50	12 Uncirculated Eisenhower Silver Dollars 1971/72/73	$49.99
1977 PCGS MS66 IKE DOLLAR RARE	$197.50	1974-S * SILVER * EISENHOWER $1 * PCGS PR-69 DCAM $9.99	$49.90
COMPLETE SET EISENHOWER DOLLARS GEM BU/PROOF	$187.50	UNC roll 1971 Eisenhower Dollars	$49.00
COMPLETE EISENHOWER DOLLAR COLLECTION NICE!!!	$179.52	Lot 36 Eisenhower Dollars Silver Dollar 1971-78 Mixed	$48.79
COMPLETE EISENHOWER COLLECTION IN DANSCO 32 COINS	$173.57	1978 D BANK WRAPPED ROLL IKE $1.00 SUPERB GEM BU	$47.99

Coins: US ▶ Errors

The average sales price in this subcategory is $60.09.

	HIGH		AVG
1990 NO "S" PROOF SET (RARE)	$6,900.00	estate 1876 /1876 VF30 Shield Nickel Breen 2506 59g	$64.75
H132) 1851-O NGC AU-55 $10 GOLD EAGLE	$2,150.00	1935-S/S RPM#2 ANACS EF45 BUFFALO 5c POP 1/5, 7 TOT NR!	$63.26
1955 LINCOLN CENT DOUBLE DIE OBVERSE PCGS AU58	$1,550.00	1945-D/D RPM#5 ANACS MS66FS JEFFERSON TOP 100 & TOP POP	$63.00
1922 Lincoln Cent Die #2 Plain No D Rare Key Error!	$1,225.00	1957 P/D MINT SET – INCL. DOUBLED DIE REVERSE NICKEL	$62.01
1999-W ERROR $10 GOLD AMERICAN EAGLE PCGS MS69 (NR)	$1,159.99	1939 REV OF 40 JEFFERSON NGC Mint State 66	$61.22
1999 W error 10$ gold eagle PCGS ms 69	$711.01	1953-S/S RPM#16 ANACS MS65RD LINCOLN CENT POP 1/2 URS-2	$61.00
RARE OREGON ERROR ON REV NO CLAD BEAUTY	$647.89	GRADED ANACS MS66 2001 P SACAGAWEA $1 RIM CLIP ERROR!	$61.00
**ORIGINAL WISCONSIN 3 COIN SET **MS66*65*65*NGC	$555.00	1909-VDB DDO-002 MS 64++ or ms-65	$58.44
1863 ERROR Brockage Civil War Token	$496.00	OREGON STATE QUARTER ERROR - REVERSE COPPER NOT SILVER	$57.89
2004-D WISCONSIN EXTRA LEAF QUARTER SET NGC MS 65 GEM	$495.00	1966 DDO-010 ICG MS67 Doubled Die Kennedy NR	$56.55
1999-W $5 Gold Eagle Error - Unfinished Proof Die MS69	$365.00	1796 Gallery Mint Half Cent Flip Over Brockage Strike	$56.00
ANACS CERTIFIED VG 8/8 1922 LINCOLN WHEAT CENT E-3011-H	$342.89	1941 1? FS-018.1/CONECA 2-O-I Bold Dbld. Die Obv N/R	$56.00
1984 DOUBLED DIE OBVERSE FS-037 NGC MS66RD LINCOLN CENT	$332.00	1921 MORGAN MS 65/66! PCGS REGISTRY HOT 50 VAM!	$56.00
1983 Lincoln Cent DDR Double Die #1 Rare Error PCGS !	$317.00	1946-S/S RPM#11 ANACS MS65RD LINCOLN CENT POP 1/3 URS-4	$55.01
613 FULL DATE BUFFALO NICKELS TEENS TWENTIES &THIRTIES	$304.00		

Coins: US ▶ Gold

The average sales price in this subcategory is $275.38.

	HIGH		AVG
1924-D-$20-PCGS MS63 *hucky*()	$6,000.00	$50 Gold Eagle 2005 1oz pure gold uncirculated	$457.50
14 Piece set $2.50 Indians " 1911-D Incuded " 3 Days	$5,600.00	1904-S Gold $20, ANACS EF-45, RARCOA	$450.00
$1000 Face-US Mint 90% SILVER COINS (PRE1965)	$5,040.00	1878-S Gold $20, ANACS EF-45, RARCOA	$445.00
CANADIAN MAPLE LEAF PURE GOLD COINS (10)	$4,610.00	1998 1 OZ GOLD American Eagle $50 Coin BU, .999 US Gold	$440.00

SOUTH AFRICA KRUGERRAND GOLD COINS (10 Pack)	$4,501.00	1898 $2.50 Quarter Eagle (PCGS MS62)	$350.00
10 Pack US Mint AMERICAN EAGLE GOLD COINS!	$4,500.00	1994-25 GOLD EAGLE NGC MS 69 NO RES	$288.00
10 Pack US Mint AMERICAN EAGLE GOLD COINS!	$4,413.00	1843-$5-PCGS AU53-1 DAY only! *hucky*()	$271.75
CANADIAN MAPLE LEAF PURE GOLD COINS (10)	$4,400.00	1907-$5-ANACS MS62-1 DAY only! *hucky*()	$270.99
10 Pack US Mint AMERICAN EAGLE GOLD COINS!	$4,371.52	A+ 1988 US $25 PURE GOLD COIN MOUNTED AS A PENDANT 21g	$266.00
SOUTH AFRICA KRUGERRAND GOLD COINS (10 Pack)	$4,315.00	2003 PCGS MS 69 1/2 Ounce Gold American Eagle Coin	$255.00
CANADIAN MAPLE LEAF PURE GOLD COINS (10)	$4,300.00	1855/56/59 ~ 4 x US Gold Coin Indian Head / LOOK!!!!!	$250.00
SOUTH AFRICA KRUGERRAND GOLD COINS (10 Pack)	$4,250.01	2003 - $25 Gold Eagle - NO RESERVE	$248.50
$20GOLD&COIN COLLECTION FOR SALE	$4,000.00	2004 1/2 OUNCE GOLD $25. EAGLE	$247.50
1 DAY ONLY NO RESERVE!		NGC GRADED MS69 GEM N/R	
NobleSpirit~ValuableSuitcase CoinCollection Inheritance	$3,000.00	1912 Gold $5 Indian, ANCAS AU-58, RARCOA	$240.00
$2.5 Gold 1848 PCGS 53 NACTcoin PayPal	$2,460.00	Five 1999 1/10th ounce uncirculated MS 70 gold coins	$238.15

Coins: US ▶ Mint Sets

The average sales price in this subcategory is $18.64.

	HIGH		AVG
US MINT PROOF SETS	$425.00	2005 US MINT UNCIRCULATED SET 22 COINS SEALED BOX	$19.49
US MINT UNCIRCULATED COIN SETS 1972-1981-1984-04	$299.00	1922 PEACE DOLLAR PCI MS65	$19.09
ORIGINAL 1957 DOUBLE MINT SET WITH ENVELOPE.	$215.00	2003 Uncircluated Coin Sets (D and P)	$19.05
1950 UNCIRCULATED SET P,D,S MINT COINS	$189.99	1995 US Mint Uncirculated Set	$19.01
1999-2004 MINT SETS TOP QUALITY	$187.50	2001 UNITED STATES MINT UNCIRCULATED COIN SET P & D	$18.99
2004 & 2005 Westward Journey Proof Coin & Medal Set	$175.00	1986 US Mint Uncirculated 10 Coin Set NICE!	$18.99
1999-2005 US MINT UNCIRCULATED P&D COIN SETS & MINT BOX	$167.50	1963 MINT SET - SILVER - (10 Unc. P&D Coins)	$18.70
3SETS 1999-NEVER OPENED US MINT BOX UNCIRC.P D	$164.19	1960 P SMALL DATE MS70 LINCOLN CENT GRADED SGS	$18.55
1881, 1882,1883, 1884 & 1885 Silver Dollar Collection	$162.50	2001 US P&D MINT 20 COIN UNCIRCULATED SET LIKE PROOF	$18.50
1958 Original Mint set	$155.00	HUGE GROUP OF MINT SET COINS!!! 50 MIXED MINT LOT!!!	$18.50
1883, 1884,1885, 1888 & 1889 Silver Dollar Collection	$144.00	[3 of these sold for $18.50 each]	
1988 CANADIAN CALGARY OLYMPIC	$129.95	2001 US Mint Uncirculated coin Set W/Statehood Quarters	$18.48
PROOF SILVER 10 COIN SET		1966 5 COIN US SPECIAL MINT SET LIKE PROOF	$18.28
(4) 1970 & (5) 1994 U.S. MINT SETS ALL UNOPENED!	$112.55	OLD US COINS 1967 MINT SET	$17.99
1983 P & D US Souvenir Mint Sets RARE!!!	$95.00	2005 United States Mint Uncirculated Coin Set. 22 Coins	$17.95
1983 SOUVENIR SET (P & D Mints) - RARE	$94.95	^^1962, UNITED STATES MINT SET-10 COIN^^	$17.56

Coins: US ▶ Proof Sets

The average sales price in this subcategory is $81.36.

	HIGH		AVG
10 proof 1 oz american eaglr gold coins	$5,700.00	NobleSpirit~ SUPERB GEM 1954 Fresh FROSTED PROOF Set!	$86.00
MASSIVE PROOF SET BLOWOUT!	$4,475.00	COMPLETE Black Box PROOF SETS 1973 - 1982	$84.99
TONS OF PROOF COINS! 5 DAYS!		5-1971 Unopened box of Proof sets *hucky*()	$84.00
1959 - 2005 US Mint PROOF SET Run +52 more -Total 100 !	$1,780.55	2003 & 2004 COMPLETE US MINT SILVER PROOF SETS	$83.95
1959 - 2005 US Mint PROOF SET Run +52 more -Total 100 !	$1,475.00	[2 of these sold for $83.95 each]	
PROOF RUN 1960 - 2005 SILVER PROOFS 1999 - 2005 US COIN	$1,375.00	Beautiful Lot Of 85 U.S. Coins In GREAT Condition	$82.05
COMPLETE 53 SET PROOF COLLECTION 1954 thru 2005	$1,325.00	1955 U.S. PROOF SET	$81.00
22 COINS! Proof/ NGS-PCGS SILVER EAGLE COLLECTION	$1,095.00	US COINS 1999 9 PC PROOF SET W/QUARTERS !!	$75.23
Complete set of American Eagle Proofs 1986-2005	$950.00	2005 Silver Proof Set, 2005 Mint Set and Free Bonuses	$75.00
US MINT PROOF SETS 1955-1998 - SILVER - NR!!!	$880.00	US COINS 1999 9 PC PROOF SET W/QUARTERS !!	$75.00
10 - 2005 W PROOF SILVER EAGLES NGC PF70 ULTRA CAMEO	$843.69	(5) 1976 40% SILVER U.S. MINT GEM BU IN MINT RED PACK	$74.99
10 - 2005 PROOF SILVER EAGLES NGC PF70 ULTRA CAMEO	$822.80	US COINS 1957 UNOPENED SILVER PROOF Set **RARE COINS**?	$71.99
10 - 2005 W PROOF SILVER EAGLES NGC PF70 ULTRA CAMEO	$813.33	LARGE lot of PROOF MINT SETS with COA	$71.00
10 - 2005 W PROOF SILVER EAGLES NGC PF70 ULTRA CAMEO	$811.05	1979 S Proof Set w/ Scarce Type 2 Clear S Cent	$68.05
41 YEARS 1960-2000 PROOF SET COLLECTION	$799.00	US COINS 1957 UNOPENED SILVER PROOF Set **RARE COINS**?	$67.99
1999 - 2005 Complete Silver Proof Sets W State Quarters	$725.00	1999-S (9) COINS PROOF SET	$67.00

Coins: US ▶ Rolls

The average sales price in this subcategory is $73.08.

	HIGH		AVG
2005 AMERICAN EAGLE SILVER COINS - US MINT SEALED CRATE	$4,556.00	1915-D Roll of Lincolns	$77.55
2005 AMERICAN EAGLE SILVER COINS - US MINT SEALED CRATE	$4,318.00	1968-S Proof Kennedy Half Dollar Roll	$77.05
2005 AMERICAN EAGLE SILVER COINS - US MINT SEALED CRATE	$4,150.00	1883-1912-D "V" NICKEL ROLL(UNUSUAL) 99C/NO RESERVE	$77.00
100 SEALED BANK ROLLS 2004 -D -WISCONSIN– EXTRA LEAF??	$1,325.00	2000 P&D SACAGAWEA DOLLAR US MINT ROLLS	$75.00
1 2004 P PEACE NICKEL 50 ROLL BOX NO RESERVE	$861.01	12 Mixed Circulated Rolls NO DATE Buffalo Nickels NR	$74.37
2001-2004 P & D $10 MINT ROLLS STATE QUARTERS	$754.66	2004-S SILVER Proof Kennedy Half Dollar Roll (20-Coin)	$73.45
ROLL OF 1938 D UNC BUFFALO NICKELS L@@K	$710.00	2005 D BISON BUFFALO SATIN FINISH ROLL 40 COINS NICKEL	$72.77
Nice BU roll of 1996 SAE $ *hucky*()	$696.00	GEM BU ROLL 1958-P WASHINGTON QUARTERS 25c	$72.76
ORIGINAL ROLL 1896-P MORGAN DOLLARS CH/GEM BU...	$661.00	BU Original roll of 1958-P Washington Quarter	$70.76
ROLL 1945 WALKING LIBERTY HALVES ..CH/GEM BU	$635.00	2004 PEACE NICKELS P & D Rolls in MINT SEAL BOX	$69.75
ORIGINAL ROLL 1889-P MORGAN DOLLARS CH/GEM BU.....	$560.00	2004 Westward Journey Peace Medal Nickel US Mint Rolls	$68.00
1884-O ROLL OF TWENTY GEM MORGAN DOLLARS BU- MS+ L@@K	$548.10	GEM BU ROLL 1959-D WASHINGTON QUARTERS 10c	$67.00
Unclaimed Property Liquidation-Unsearched Morgan Roll	$475.00	ROLL (20) WHITE UNC 1964 SILVER HALVES-NO/RSV	$66.51
1923 P PEACE DOLLARS - BU ORIGINAL ROLL- MINT MS+ NICE!	$420.50	GEM BU ROLL 1962-D WASHINGTON QUARTERS 25c	$66.00
2004-S Proof ** Peace Medal ** Nickel Roll (40-Coin)	$420.00	Original Bank Wrapped Roll 1955-S Roosevelt Dimes OBW	$66.00

Coins: World ▶ Asia, Middle East

The average sales price in this subcategory is $20.91.

	HIGH		AVG
1871 Japan Meiji i Yen Gold Coin, extremely rare	$404.00	NAGORNO-KARABAKH 2003 1000 Drams Van Lake Mint=300	$24.50
Iraqi Dinar	$400.00	British North Borneo 1929 25 cents silver UNC	$24.50
[2 of these sold for $400.00 each]		Taiwan NTD 20 Bimetal 5 Coin set in red wood case	$24.00
1883 Straits Settlement 1/2 Cents(Very Rare Date) XF	$399.00	Palestine Fifty Mils 1934	$22.50
Israel Gold Proof Coin David Ben Gurion 1974 500 Lirot	$321.78	Vietnamese Coins Indochine Vietnam 1815-1975 Zinc $1 NR	$22.50
Rare Saudi Arabia Hejaz al-Husayn AH1334 Gold Coin	$299.00	Thailand, leaf money, 58 gm , Ca 1100 ad, EF Nice	$21.99
Rare Salah Al Din Yusuf I H564-H589 Islamic Gold Coin !	$203.50	French Indo China Piastre 1895 (27,215 GR) superbe	$21.05
USA Error x 5	$201.99	Lot of 6 British North Borneo coins, 1894-1929	$20.55
RARE Tripoli ~ Libya AH1223 Yr-2 1808-10 Billon 30 Para	$199.99	STRAITS SETTLEMENTS, 1908 FIFTY CENTS FINE	$20.50
1995 INDONESIA PATTERN COIN SET, Rp.850000 & Rp.300000	$195.00	1939 Palestine 10 MILS - Nice Example	$20.50
CRUSADER KINGDOM JERUSALEM AMAURY 2 1197-1205AD Denier	$180.01	Palestine One Mil 1940	$20.50
Saudi Arabia AH 1370 (1950) Gold Guinea, Gem BU MS-66	$167.00	Strange Chien-lung Tung-pao?? found in Java, Indonesia	$20.50
Annam Silver 3 Tien Tu Duc Thong Bao 1848-83 aXF Scarce	$165.70	CEYLON: SRI LANKA: 1957	$20.49
N. Vietnam 1946 5 Hao PCGS MS65	$165.00	5 RUPEES GEM BU Animals	
Singapore 1988 12 ounce proof silver round	$127.00	Iraq 1937 50 Fils BU	$20.00
Straits Settlements 1903 1 Dollar F-VF Raised Letters	$117.50	CEYLON 1/2 STIVER 1815	$20.00

Coins: World ▶ Europe

The average sales price in this subcategory is $38.35.

	HIGH		AVG
Philip & Mary Shilling 1554-1558, EF	$1,780.00	FRANCE 1975 9 Piece FDC Set - In Original Box	$40.10
1881-A Francais Gold 100 Franc AU France Gold Angel	$710.00	1797 GEORGE III CARTWHEEL TWOPENCE AVF	$40.00
1860-61 (ND) GB 100% Obverse Brockage 1d. NGC AU55	$699.00	Great Britain 1485-1509 - Henry VII	$40.00
1852 Great Britain Sovereign NGC MS63 Choice	$599.00	1909 Trade Dollar in Beautiful Uncirculated Condition	$40.00
1859-BB Francais Gold 100 Franc AU France Napoleon III	$510.00	~ FRANCE 5 FRANCS 1828-W VF++ LARGE SILVER COIN	$39.99
France 1829T 1/4F AU	$449.00	FRANCE 1813L 5 Francs Napoleon Silver Crown Fine	$39.02
1893 Great Britain LVI Crown NGC MS63 PQ+	$375.00	COIN GB GEORGE V TRADE DOLLAR 1930 B KMT5 EF	$38.00
FRANCE Olympic Coin Set 10 SILVER & GOLD PROOF COINS	$315.00	UNKNOWN 1/2 PENNY 1793	$37.66
1812 GOLD 40 FRANCS FRANCE = NAPOLEON - STUNNING COIN=	$302.77	France 1782A 12 Sols UNC	$37.58
1900 Maundy Money Coin Set & Box~Queen Victoria~1905	$275.00	Great Britain Ch. England 1883 Silver 2 Pence & 4 Pence	$36.54
JACK NICKLAUS 10 ?5 FIVE POUND NOTES . Rare Numbers	$275.00	France 1888A 1F UNC	$36.51
France 1815M 5 Francs Napoleon "100 Days" KM-704.6	$273.88	SILVER HAMMERED COIN EDWIG / EDWIN ??	$36.06
1887 Great Britain 1/2 Sovereign NGC MS65	$261.00	FRANCE 1965 7 Piece FDC Set - In Original Box	$36.00
Great Britain Maundy Set 1898 NGC High Grade	$255.00	GREAT BRITIAN 1852 1/4 FARTHING FOR USE IN CEYLON	$35.99
Great Britain 1900 Maudy Set w/colourful toning	$222.50	England 1/2 crown 1909,6d1902,06,4d 1903,1d 1909	$35.00

Coins: World ▶ North, Central America

The average sales price in this subcategory is $18.73.

	HIGH		AVG
1980 Canadian Maple Leaf $50 coin1 OZ Gold	$451.00	5 1978 100 PESO SILVER COINS MEXICO .6429OZ EA.	$19.99
1858 20C PCGS AU55	$390.00	COLONIAL TOKEN ? PENNY 1854 BRETON 912 NB-1B, VF	$19.53
RARE 1870 5c Newfoundland FIVE CENT 40K mint VF C$325	$311.00	1990 CANADIAN MAPLE LEAF 1 OZ .9999 FINE SILVER	$19.50
c1850 HBC Hudson Bay Co. Brass Token 1 Made Beaver VF+	$280.77	Nova Scoria 1843 One Penny Token Copper	$19.49
c1850 HBC Hudson Bay Co. Brass Token 1/2 Made Beaver EF	$230.27	1844 Province of Canada half Penny, Coin is in Good con	$19.00
c1850 HBC Hudson Bay Co. Brass Token 1/4 Made Beaver EF	$230.27	Inventory Software AND Catalogue for Canadian Coins	$18.99
Canada, Newfoundland 1888 10 Cents ~ Queen Victoria	$202.50	1837 Canada Colonial Half Penny BankToken VF30 C$30	$18.95
HUDSONS BAY FUR TRADE TOKENS - EASTERN ARCTIC SET OF 5	$199.99	2002 CANADA $5 MAPLE LEAF HORSE PRIVY MARK	$18.50
CANADA $20 1967 GOLD COIN MONUMENT SUDBURY	$154.00	1881 NEWFOUNDLAND 50 CENTS	$18.50
VERY SCARCE 1919 5c Newfoundland FIVE CENT AU50 C$600	$153.50	NEW BRUNSWICK 1843 Penny Token NB-2A HRN	$18.49
(22) PC. MIXED LOT UNC/PROOF SILVER CANADIAN DOLLARS!	$124.63	Newfoundland 10 cent 1894 VF	$18.38
1862 New Brunswick Victorian Ten Cents - ICCS	$124.49	1856 NS 5A 1/2 CT BR# 876 TOKEN NICE PATINA XF. ***	$18.37
1858-Canadian 20 Cent Coin In VF+INR!	$111.08	FRENCH COLONIAL NEW FRANCE__ COUNTER STAMPED__1640___VG	$18.27
Superb and Rare Blacksmith BL-40 (EF condition)	$110.00	LOWER CANADA Bouquet Sou LC-37 HRN	$18.00
Set of 9 Canadian $5 .999 silver BU Coins	$109.48	BANK UPPER CANADA COIN TOKEN PENNY 1857 HIGH GRADE	$17.60

Coins: World ▸ Gold

The average sales price in this subcategory is $233.69.

	HIGH		AVG
Hungary 1966 1000 Forint 2.44 oz. Gold	$5,950.00	Byzantine Histamenon Nomisma 1028 - 34	$242.50
SOUTH AFRICA KRUGERRAND GOLD COINS (10 Pack)	$4,272.13	1/2oz Chinese .999 Gold Panda Bullion Coin 1988	$241.60
Israel HUGE GOLD medal: "OPERATION JONATHAN" mintage=90	$2,050.00	1809 GOLD FRANCE 20 FRANC-NAPOLEON HEAD-NICE	$241.19
Israel HUGE GOLD medal: "DAKAR SUBMARINE", mintage=150	$1,994.00	DETAILED 1747 SPANISH GOLD ESCUDO DOUBLOON !	$240.27
RARE P.Vincze Judaic HUGE GOLD medal: ISRAEL IN FREEDOM	$1,973.00	1982 Half Krugerrand Gold Bullion Coin	$235.50
Israel HUGE GOLD medal: "DAKAR SUBMARINE", mintage=150	$1,926.00	RUSSIA 1901 GOLD 5 RUBLES NGC MS-67, WOW!	$235.50
Lot of 4 Gibraltar Royal Cherubs 4 oz pure gold BU	$1,925.00	US $25 Gold Eagle 1/2 OZ Gold Coin	$234.01
RARE P.Vincze Judaica HUGE GOLD medal "Vision & Way"	$1,925.00	Israel 1980 GOLD coin "ZE'EV JABOTINSKY" ? oz CV = $265	$231.50
1984 & 1985 Isle of Man Platinum 1 oz Nobles BU 2 oz pl	$1,775.00	Mexico-Israel Exhibition 1979 GOLD medal, 17.3 grams	$231.50
SOUTH AFRICA KRUGERRAND GOLD COINS	$1,718.05	Mexican 1918 20 Peso Gold Coin; AU - UNC.	$228.10
SOUTH AFRICA KRUGERRAND GOLD COINS	$1,710.00	1998 MAGNIFICENT SEVEN IN GOLD COLLECTION	$227.50
Lot of 3 Gibraltar Royal Cherubs 3 oz pure gold BU	$1,485.00	Gorgeous ! Cuba $5 Pesos Gold Coin 1916 Unc.	$225.00
RARE 1979 MARC CHAGALL 3 oz. GOLD ART MEDAL! BEAUTIFUL!	$1,426.00	1982 Dominican Republic 200 Peso KM#58 ANACS Graded	$225.00
RARE 1979 MARC CHAGALL 3 oz. GOLD ART MEDAL! BEAUTIFUL!	$1,402.00	POPE JOHN PAUL II 2500 PISO GOLD COIN , POBJOY MINT	$225.00
RUSSIA 1989 1 oz gold Rouble NGC Proof 69 Rare!	$1,225.00	Canadian 22K $100 Gold Coin (1/2 troy ounce)	$224.72

Exonumia ▸ Elongated Coins

The average sales price in this subcategory is $5.35.

	HIGH		AVG
UNUSUAL ELONGATED 1908 PENNY WITH PRESIDENT TAFT 1909	$86.00	FAMILY WATCHING FIREWORKS Elongated Copper Penny	$5.50
SCARCE ELONGATE. Cardinal Stritch. OFP-12.	$57.00	Indianapolis Speedway Elongated Penny Cent Set of 5	$5.50
DISNEY 50TH ANNIVERSARY PRESSED PENNY COLLECTION & BOOK	$51.00	President John F. Kennedy Set of 2 elongated pennies	$5.50
Disneyland 50th Anniversary Elongated Penny Set +Extras	$50.55	SOUVENIR OF FLORIDA THE SUNSHINE	$5.50
Disneyland 50th COPPER penny SET & JULY 17 2005 MAP	$50.00	STATE ELONGATED PENNY	
Columbian Exposition Elongated Seated Liberty Dime- 6	$40.83	Great American Race, 1990, Terre Haute, Elongated Penny	$5.50
FIRST EDITION ELONGATED PENNY COLLECTOR BOOK W/PENNIES	$37.00	U.S.S. Arizona, Pearl Harbor, Hawaii Elongated Penny	$5.50
Columbian Exposition Elongated Liberty Head Nickel-5	$36.03	CA San Francisco 1939-40 GGIE Bridge Treas Is Elongated	$5.50
CANADA ELONGATED LARGE CENT 1910 MONTREAL CARNIVAL RARE	$35.00	Awesome Starter Lot Of 25 Elongated Coins	$5.24
Columbian Exposition Elongated Indian Head Penny	$33.01	CA SF GGIE 1939 Golden Gate Int Expo Elongated Cent	$5.01
Four (4) Birth Place of Pepsi Store Pressed Pennies	$31.55	Four (4) Birth Place of Pepsi Store Pressed Pennies	$5.00
1893 Columbian Exposition Elongated Cent	$28.88	Beam Bottle ELONGATED penny Royal Porcelain WOW DC	$5.00
Lot of 50 different ELONGATED Pennies	$28.00	Beam Bottle ELONGATED penny YELLOW KATZ wow DC	$5.00
Columbian Exposition Elongated Liberty Head Nickel-4	$25.03	Beam Bottle ELONGATED penny BLUE CHERUB wow DC	$5.00
4 Elongated pennies NEW! Zephyr Cove, Lake Tahoe, NV	$25.00	Beam Bottle ELONGATED penny Royal Di Monte WOW dc	$5.00
[2 of these sold in a multiple item ("Dutch") auction for $12.50 each]		Beam Bottle ELONGATED penny Zimmerman Two Headed Jug	$5.00

Exonumia ▸ Medals

The average sales price in this subcategory is $35.71.

	HIGH		AVG
1933 HUNGARY WORLD JAMBOREE BOY SCOUT MEDAL W/ PROGRAM	$785.00	Antique Railroad Locomotive Bronze Ad.Medal\Paperweight	$36.51
original order for personal courage - USSR	$560.00	1972 Richard Nixon Bronze Silver 2 Medal Set SCARCE	$36.51
GREAT SET FRANKLIN MINT COINS OF ALL NATIONS 3 COMPLETE	$473.53	Bronze Old Ironsides Medal	$36.50
Homage to Israel 25th Anivsry Silver Coin Set by Dali	$465.00	JAPANESE 7th CLASS ORDER OF THE SACRED TREASURE MEDAL	$36.00
VERY RARE 14K GOLD RUBY & CLAW SHRINERS SCIMITAR	$412.21	RAOB Medal - Millennium 2000	$36.00
VATICAN: GRAND CROSS - ORDER OF HOLY GREGOR THE GREAT	$355.00	G.B.Large 1937 Bronze Coronation Medal. Edward V111.	$36.00
Silver Medal La. Purchase Exposition (Olympics) 1904	$325.00	MEDALLIC ART CIVIL WAR GENERALS SILVER MEDAL ORIG BOX	$35.99
Gold Medal Louisiana Purchase Exposition 1904	$325.00	Large Civil War Centennial Bronze Medal Antietam	$35.00
36 FRANKLIN MINT PRESIDENTIAL SILVER MEDALS	$265.00	Large Civil War Centennial Bronze Medal Bull Run	$35.00
1959-1978 So Called Commemorative Half Dollar BU Set	$244.30	Large Civil War Centennial Bronze Medal Gettysburg	$35.00
Pair of JFK Kennedy gold medals .4141 ounce pure gold	$227.50	1976 Bicentennial 5oz. silver TENNESSEE (& bronze 1oz.)	$35.00
ANTIQUE JAPANESE 1930 CAPITAL REHABILITATION COMM MEDAL	$225.50	1876 Centennial Medal Coin Token Worlds Fair Bronze	$34.77
Ohio Veterans Civil War Medal 1861-1865 Tiffany Co.	$212.50	Military Medal Ft. Riley, Kansas 1908 / #1275	$33.75
Canada North West Mounted Police medal and ribbon	$210.28	Bronze 1886 City Of Albany 2 Hundred Anniversary Medal	$33.55
1933 Colorado Pedley-Ryan So-Called Dollar, NGC MS-63	$207.00	*PD*VINTAGE DUTCH DOG-MEDAL	$33.16
RARE Civil War Veteran MEDAL & Cuff Buttons MOLLUS	$202.50	with MINIATURE PINSCHER	

Exonumia ▸ Tokens: Civil War

The average sales price in this subcategory is $71.18.

	HIGH		AVG
V. RARE Hillsdale Mich Book/Stationery Cwt 450A-2b R-8	$1,700.00	Hartford Conn "Wide Awakes" Token Silvered Brass AU++	$76.00
RARE Memphis Tn "Steamer Lancaster" 600E-4a MS-64! NR	$1,580.55	The Federal Union Patriotic 178/267a MS-65! No Reserv	$74.00
RARE Cincinnati Ice Cream Saloon 165GX-3a R-9! MS-65!	$1,246.00	1863 Civil War Token United Country R3 or R5	$73.88
RARE R-9 White Metal Patriotic 359/436e MS-63 No Resv	$1,075.01	SCARCE R-5 Jackson Mich Staples Dealer 525B-1a NR	$73.77
RARE Detroit Female Venereal Diseases Doctor 225BL-2a	$935.00	CIVIL WAR TOKEN CWT PATRIOTIC-GEM RED UNC	$73.00
RARE Dowagic Mich Wallpaper Merchant 250A-1a MS-64!	$872.00	Almont Mich Druggist Dr. Richardson 35A-2a VF-25 No Res	$72.77
Boston Mass DIESINKER Cwt Jos. Merriam MS-66RB! NR	$845.00	Maumee City Ohio Toll Bridge Co. 540B-1a R-6 XF No Resv	$72.01
RARE John Bell/Presidents House Cwt 509A/510ab R-9! NR!	$785.00	SCARCE PATRIOTIC CIVIL WAR TOKEN 154/218a	$69.99
RARE R-7 Paw Paw Michigan "Flouring Mills" AU-58 NR	$736.55	1863 Civil War Token Not One Cent R4	$69.88
Boston Mass Die Sinker/Medalist Cwt 115E-2b MS-65! NR	$645.00	1863 Craig & Foy Birmingham, OH Civil War Token-XF+	$69.45

	HIGH		AVG
Original 1862 Merrimac Ironclad Ship MEDAL or TOKEN	$636.50	Cincinnati MEAT MARKET 165GC-3a MS-63 No Reserve	$69.00
Jackson Mich S. Holland & Son Druggists 525A-1a R-81 NR	$601.00	Female Merchant "Mrs. Reed" Ravenna Oh 765D-1a VF/XF	$68.79
Marshall Wisc Stoves/Tin G.W.Vosburgh 435B-1a MS-65 NR	$536.00	Nice Old Civil War Token Our Cent R5	$68.09
RARE R-9 ZINC Cincinnati Vest Mfgr Cwt 165DJ-12i MS-64	$535.05	1863 Redfield Beaver Dam, Wisconsin Civil War Token	$68.00
R-10! Columbus Ohio Eating House 200D-8a MS-64RB NR	$512.77	UNION Draped Flags Patriotic MS-64 Brown No Reserve	$66.67

Exonumia ▸ Tokens: US Trade

The average sales price in this subcategory is $22.55.

	HIGH		AVG
FAIRBANK, ARIZONA TERRITORY GHOST TOWN SALOON token	$1,175.00	Rochester, Montana Trade Token Foster Erickson Mont MT	$24.25
5TH OHIO REGT. O. VOL. SUTLER TOKEN	$307.60	IONE ALLEYS 5 CENT TRADE TOKEN IONE, WASHINGTON	$24.00
S. WHITED & CO. 97TH ILL. VOL. SUTLER TOKEN	$255.00	***SET LUMBER SCRIP-HONAKER, VIRGINIA	$24.00
Good For ONE BEER Token J.F.Leach & Co Kerrville Texas	$202.50	(ORANGE CITY, IOWA) - JOHN OEHLERICH (COW) - MILK TOKEN	$22.95
Alaska token - Butterhorn Bakery 1 lge. loaf, Ketchikan	$195.00	Hammond, Ind. VFW 802 old 5 cent trade token	$22.72
Fort Yates Dakota Territory Military Token	$187.50	South Louisiana Plantation Token 10? (J-10)	$22.72
ANCHORAGE ALASKA - ANCHORAGE CHAPTER No 3 MASONIC PENNY	$177.50	Lot 22 1940's Beer Chits Or Tokens Upstate New York NR	$22.50
5 CENT-C.S. COLEMAN-CHECOTAH	$177.50	Graceys Barber Shop Incused Kansas Token Maker	$22.39
JEROME, ARIZONA OTTO'S SALOON	$174.50	2 Fairfax Oklahoma tokens, SHAF'S #845, 846	$22.05
Vintage Anthony, Florida FL Fla. 10c Token Hard to Find	$162.49	1916 BAR - (Stites, Idaho) - GF 5c IT	$22.01
RENO NEVADA - SAGEBRUSH SALOON - TOKEN	$160.27	New Jersey Good For Token	$21.59
Alaska token - Spicketts Smokehouse 12 1/2c Juneau	$157.50	1837 Token Center Market, NY,NY. F+	$21.50
RARE PARK CITY UTAH TOKEN COIN ONTARIO CHAPTER 1882	$154.75	G.L. NATHLICH GOOD FOR FIVE CENTS TOKEN MAPLETON IOWA	$21.05
RARE R-10 LUMBER & COAL TOKEN HENRYETTA OKLAHOMA OK	$153.50	WVU Token-Morgantown, WV-1949 Football Schedule!	$21.05
MODEL CONFECTIONERY 5 CENT TRADE TOKEN, IDAHO	$152.50	Coal Scrip $5.00 Wasatch Store-Castle Gate-Utah-Carbon	$20.95

Paper Money: US ▸ Colonial Currency

The average sales price in this subcategory is $170.18.

	HIGH		AVG
PENNSYLVANIA 8/10/1739 20 Shilling EF NEWMAN PLATE NOTE	$10,001.00	COLONIAL May 10, 1775 CONTINENTAL CURRENCY $5 EF	$198.05
COLONIAL CURRENCY-NORTH CAROLINA-3 NOTE SHEET 1771	$1,495.00	1775 $5 Dollar Continental Currency	$197.50
New Jersey 4/12/1760 6Pounds CH Crisp EF	$1,290.30	COLONIAL Nov 29, 1775 CONTINENTAL CURRENCY $5 EF	$197.05
COLONIAL CURRENCY-NORTH CAROLINA-3 NOTE SHEET 1771	$995.00	1775 Continental Congress Currency $8 Dollar Note	$190.50
Pennsylvania 5/1/1760 50Shillings EF	$900.00	CONTINENTAL CURRENCY 1777 SIGNED BY DANIEL CARROLL	$178.58
RARE NEW JERSEY 1776 THREE POUND CONTINENTAL NOTE	$850.00	1777 Massachusetts Committee War 10 Pounds Note	$177.50
Two Shilling South Carolina Note 7/6/1789	$698.00	OBSOLETE 1776 SIX SPANISH MILLED DOLLARS NICE	$173.51
Delaware 5/1/1758 20Shillings Good	$400.00	Continental Currency - $65 dated 14 Jan 1779	$170.00
Scarce 1777 30 Pounds Massachusetts Treasury Cert.	$340.90	1776 Three Shillings King George Burlington New Jersey	$162.49
Colonial Currency New Jersey One Shilling 1776 NJ-175	$320.00	COLONIAL June 19,1776 CONNECTICUT CURRENCY 6 pence	$161.00
Uncirculated 1776 Continental Currency Note	$299.00	NORTH CAROLINA 20 SHILLINGS DEC. 1768	$157.00
$6 Continental Congress, CC-28, Choice AU	$250.00	1777 Delaware 10 Shillings Note EF N/R	$152.50
NOV 2,1776 THIRTY DOLLARS CONTINENTAL CURRENCY L@@K	$234.50	COLONIAL NOTE - TWENTY SHILLINGS - DELAWARE 1759	$152.50
3 Dollar Continental Currency, 1776 - AU	$210.50	1778 4 Shilling Note Colonial Currency Mass MA	$151.38
COLONIAL May 10, 1775 CONTINENTAL CURRENCY $7 VF+	$205.96	NORTH CAROLINA 5 POUND NOTE DECEMBER 1768 RARE ISSUE	$149.00

Paper Money: US ▸ Confederate Currency

The average sales price in this subcategory is $63.22.

	HIGH		AVG
CONFEDERATE CURRENCY 1861 $50	$2,276.00	AUTHENTIC CONFEDERATE 50 DOLLAR BILL WITH PALMETTO TREE	$71.03
T 6 $50 Confederate Nice!	$1,325.00	1862 $ 5 BANK OF LOUISIANA NEW ORLEANS FORCE ISSUE LQQK	$69.99
Rare Stack of Confederate 1863 $5 [Approx 89 notes]	$961.66	1862 $ 5 BATON ROUGE LOUISIANA LAZY FIVE NOTE SCARCE	$69.99
Type 17 Confederate $20 note, 1861	$699.00	CONFEDERATE $100 1864 CURRENCY PAPER MONEY AUTHENTIC	$68.76
CHOICE UNCIRCULATED $3 Florida Railroad Banknote	$661.99	Consec #'s Confederate Money Civil War $10 Artillery	$67.54
THIBODAUX LOUISIANA CIVIL WAR NOTE 1862 SUPER RARE	$638.99	$500 Confederate Bond> 1863> Cr. 59	$67.00
CSA Paper Money T-52 Trans-Mississippi	$595.00	1861, $1 Augusta Insur. & Banking Co. No. 872	$66.99
MELANCON NAPOLEONVILLE LOUISIANA CIVIL WAR ERA NOTE	$535.25	Rare 1861 Corp. of Richmond $2. Ctft. w/Upham Clause NR	$66.56
Authentic Confederate Currency: 9 Bills, Includes $500	$516.77	1862 CSA,Confederate GEORGIA $5 BILL,BANKNOTE,CURRENCY	$66.00
1861 $50 Confederate Note 2nd Series CRISP UNCIRCULATED	$510.99	$500 CONFEDERATE NOTE WITH EASTERN AIR LINE BACKSTAMP	$66.00
LOT of 25 1864 $10 CONFEDERATE NOTE CURRENCY VF-AU NR	$477.89	1864 Confederate Civil War Savings Bond C.S. C.S.A. NR	$65.00
RARE PAIR of Confederates...T-8 and T-10	$470.65	1860 $5 Five Dollar Bill Indian Miners Planters Bank	$65.00
Pair of Citizens'Bank of LA...includes Famous DIX note	$462.00	1864 CONFEDERATE Civil War Newspaper JEFFERSON DAVIS !	$64.33
LOT 20 1864 $10 CONFEDERATE NOTE CURRENCY AU-UNC NR	$461.00	1862 Confederate Currency $100 Note	$64.00
1864 $500 Confederate Note - Choice AU	$440.99	Rare Confederate $50	$63.50

Paper Money: US ▸ Large Size Notes

The average sales price in this subcategory is $280.90.

	HIGH		AVG
1899 $5 SILVER CERTIFICATE *** CHIEF *** NR THE FINEST	$11,950.99	TT 1917 $1 LEGAL TENDER FR# 37 PCGS 64	$286.00
1899 $1 EAGLE SERIAL # A9999999 A RARE FIND VERY CH CU	$5,000.00	1922 $10.00 Gold Certificate PMG Choice Very Fine 35	$285.02
TT 1896 $5 SC "EDUCATIONAL" PCGS 40 PPQ	$4,550.00	***1922 $20 GOLD CERTIFICATE***-Very nice note!! (C631)	$285.00
Capitalist Gods & Connoisseurs '37 $1000 Bank of Canada	$4,058.00	1880 $1 F-30 *LARGE BROWN SEAL* CGA VF35	$284.00
FR. 281 1899 $ 5 CGA 66 GEM UNCIRCULATED CHIEF	$3,838.88	1914 10 Dollar Federal Reserve Note,Blue, Burke Glass	$282.99

TT 1886 $2 SILVER CERT "HANCOCK" FR# 242 CGA 66 GEM	$3,675.00
P.A. 1896 $ 1 THE REAL FINEST KNOWN EDUCATIONAL NOTE	$3,551.00
TT 1886 $5 MORGAN DOLLAR BACK 71 KNOWN PCGS 25 FR# 260	$3,280.00
1880 $20 United States Note CGA CU 67	$2,987.00
1891 $50.00 Silver Solid VF —Strong colors	$2,750.00
$50 1880 Legal Tender Note VF+ FR 164 RARE & Nice	$2,700.00
TT 1896 $2 SC EDUCATIONAL FR# 247 PMG / NGC 45	$2,618.00
TT 1896 $2 SC "EDUCATIONAL" FR# 247 PCGS 45	$2,412.00
D.I. 1899$1 FR-233 BLACK EAGLE NEW GEM	$2,250.00
P.A. 1918 $5 FRBN "" J WHITNEY WALTER "" CGA GEM 67	$2,247.00

TC *STUNNING/GEM* $100 1861 WASHINGTON,D.C. RCGS/66	$280.01
1899 $1 Black Eagle Silver Cert FR-236 CGA AU-58	$280.00
1918 $2.00 BOSTON BATTLESHIP	$275.00
1923 FR-238 $1 SILVER CERTIFICATE CGC CU64	$275.00
1902 $10 "SAN FRANCISCO" Large Size National Currency	$274.50
ROSECRANS/NEBECKER 1891 MARTHA WASHINGTON $1.00	$273.00
BEAUTIFUL $2 1899 "SILVER CERTIFICATE" RCGS VF/25	$270.52
CB-$1.00 1896 FR.225 EDUCATIONAL SERIES, FINE TYPE NOTE	$270.20
1899 $2 SILVER CERTIFICATE NOTE	$270.00
1914 $5 RICHMOND DISTRICT VERY RARE NOTE	$270.00

Paper Money: US ▶ Small Size Notes

The average sales price in this subcategory is $89.59.

	HIGH		AVG
1934 A $500 FIVE HUNDRED DOLLAR BILL FRN NOTE CURRENCY	$2,325.00	1996 ONE HUNDRED DOLLAR BILL STAR NOTE	$93.88
1000 $2.00 FRN BEP SEALED 2003 TEN 100 ea.Unc. SEQ.#s	$2,323.23	1999 ONE HUNDRED DOLLAR BILL STAR NOTE	$93.63
P.A. 1934 $500 FRN CGA UNCIRCULATED ONLY 4 DIGIT LGS	$2,241.10	(5) 2004 $20 DOLLAR BILL STAR NOTES	$93.63
BRICK OF UNOPENED $2 BILLS	$2,025.00	1950 C $50 Chicago FRN	$92.05
$1000.00 FEDERAL RESERVE NOTE SERIES OF 1934	$2,025.00	TT 1928 B $10 FRN CHICAGO "LGS" PCGS 66 PPQ GEM 1/2	$90.99
TT 1934 $500 FRN SAN FRANCISCO, CA CGA 58	$1,250.00	TT 1993 $1 FRN ALMOST SOLID "64666666" CGA 67 GEM 2/2	$89.99
1934 A $500 FIVE HUNDRED DOLLAR BILL NOTE FRN CURRENCY	$1,250.00	CB- 6 $2.00 1976 MIXED STAR BICENTENENNIAL NOTES	$89.55
1000 $1.00 FRN BEP SEALED 2003 TEN 100 ea.Unc. SEQ.#s	$1,125.00	1929 $20-$10 "BOSTON" Small Size National Currency	$87.50
2001 CU $1 PHILA **SEALED BEP BRICK** 1000 Note Brick	$1,100.00	1928 A $50.00 Federal Reserve Note	$86.99
$10.00 FRN 1995 Full BEP 100 notes Unc. SEQ.#s	$1,065.00	ONE DOLLAR SILVER CERTIFICATES/CONSECUTIVE 1935s..NICE!	$86.00
1934 $500 note G-7 Fully XF+ BUY IT NOW! 3-Day only	$985.00	1928 B $10 FEDERAL RESERVE NOTE CU-GEM	$84.55
2001 $1 STAR * Note Pack 100 #00001201 LOW # FRN	$943.70	2001 $50 New York STAR AU RARE	$83.00
!!!!!!!!! $500 Bill 1934 Excellent Condition !!!!!!!!!!	$910.00	1996 $50 Federal Reserve Star Note - Crisp Uncirculated	$82.00
1928 $500 FIVE HUNDRED DOLLAR BILL GOLD NOTE FRN	$890.00	1935A-ONE DOLLAR SILVER CERTIFICATES/CONSECUTIVE NICE!!	$81.00
$500 Federal Reserve Note: XF Condition: 1934-A: Phil.	$875.00	TT 1969 $20 FRN STAR NEW YORK, NY CGA 65 GEM 3/3	$81.00

Paper Money: US ▶ Obsolete Currency

The average sales price in this subcategory is $52.73.

	HIGH		AVG
James Haxby United States Obsolete Bank Notes All 4 vol	$750.00	1933 OCEAN CITY - NEW JERSEY FIVE DOLLAR SCRIP	$56.00
CHOICE UNCIRCULATED $3 Florida Railroad Banknote	$661.99	Sterling, CO. 1933 Depression Scrip. Lion In Flight!	$55.00
Arkansas,Cincy-Little Rock Slate Co.	$481.76	$2 The Sussex Bank - Newton NEW JERSEY note CU!	$55.00
SANTA CLAUS ARRIVES IN JULY	$450.00	1863 15c B.G.Steever Millersburg PENNSYLVANIA Civil War	$53.76
*A.B.N.C. * $4 1800'S "PROOF" CHARLESTON,S.C. RCGS66	$438.00	Broken Bank Note Bank Central Bank of Montgomery, AL	$53.56
Canal Bank of Lockport, New York, $5, July 1, 1844	$366.95	Virginia $5 Obsolete Bank Note	$53.34
$2 Tallahassee Railroad Co. FLORIDA note COLORFUL CU!	$331.99	Hawaii $10 Note 1934A Great Shape NR L@@K	$53.01
Hi-Grade/SCARCE Utah MORMON issued Banknote	$316.27	// $2.50 Hillsville Savings Bank-Virginia-High Rarity//	$52.00
FLORIDA BANK OF COMMERCE $20 INTO 3 STATE 10? NOTES CU	$305.00	1835 $5 Washington County Bank - Calais MAINE!	$52.00
TC *STUNNING/GEM* $100 1861 WASHINGTON,D.C. RCGS/66	$280.01	2 Clear Lake Iowa Corn Exchange Trade Certificates	$52.00
1856 $2 OBSOLETE ARCADE BANK OF RHODE ISLAND NOTE NR	$257.00	FARMERS BANK of SANDSTONE BARRY, MICH 1838 $10	$52.00
Danville Bank - Virginia Obsolete Bank Note	$229.45	1853 Bank of South Carolina $10 Banknote EX-F	$51.01
Pair of PA Proof Notes...Pittston Bank $5 & $10.00	$224.50	1862 $5 OBSOLETE MANUFACTURERS BANK GEORGIA NOTE NR	$51.01
CHOICE DeWitt, IOWA Civil War SOLDIERS BOUNTY WARRANT	$212.52	Dunkirk, New York, Montanye & Co., 10 Cents, 1862	$49.99
1862 $5 OBSOLETE PEOPLES BANK RHODE ISLAND NOTE VF NR	$211.51	Cincinnatus, New York, D. Smith & Son, 25 Cents, 1862	$49.99

Paper Money: World ▶ Africa

The average sales price in this subcategory is $20.25.

	HIGH		AVG
Banque du Congo Belge 1000 Franc Bank Note, 10/04/47	$849.00	Egypt:P-163, 5 Piastres,1940 *Aswan Dam * RARE **	$21.71
SEYCHELLES NOTE 10 RUPEES 1954 PICK # 12 XF+.	$600.00	Djibouti 1000 Francs Tresor Public Bank Note NR! L@@K!	$21.40
Burundi 1968 5000 Francs Specimen-Rare!	$416.13	MALI P-12e 100 F (sign 8) soldier Crisp Unc	$20.50
Morocco 1943 1000 Francs Specimen-Uncirculated-Scarce!	$380.00	AFRICA - MADAGASCAR - ANIMAL 10 NEW NOTES. UNC.	$20.50
Belgian Congo 1948 50 Francs Specimen-No Res!	$255.00	French West Africa 1943 25 Francs P-38	$20.50
ANGOLA 500 KWANZAS 1991 P127 SCARCE	$212.50	BURUNDI 1964 5 FRANCS BANKNOTE CURRENCY P8 CHOICE UNC	$20.40
EQUATORIAL AFRICAN STATES 500 Francs ND 1963 UNC N/R	$203.50	LOT OF 5 SEYCHELLES P.32 - 10 RUPEES 1989 UNC BANKNOTES	$20.00
EXTREMELY LOW SERIAL # 000000 EYGPT P-167 SUPERB GEM!	$195.00	Nigeria 20 naira P11 #26a UNC	$20.00
ETHIOPIA 2 Thalers 1933 UNC Scarce Note NO RESERVE	$188.50	AFRICA - MADAGASCAR - ANIMAL 2 NOTES OF 5,000 FRANCS	$20.00
RHODESIA & NYASALAND 1957 1 POUND BANKNOTE CURRENCY AU	$186.25	French Algeria (Tunisia?) 5000 Francs P 42a - Scarce	$20.00
MALAWI 1 Pound 1964 UNC NO RESERVE	$181.25	Morocco - 100 Francs - 1944 - Du Maroc	$20.00
BELGIAN CONGO 1,000 Francs 1000 Francs 1959 NO RESERVE	$179.50	SOUTH AFRICA R50 BANKNOTES!	$19.99
GB UK QEII BRITISH POSTAL ORDER OVPT 'EAST AFRICA'	$152.50	Guinea set of 4 notes	$19.99
TUNEZ BANKNOTE 1960_5 DINAR_UNC	$145.00	AFRICA - ZAIRE - MOBUTU 4 NOTES OF 500 ZAIRES 1985.UNC	$19.50
RWANDA & BURUNDI 1963 5 FRANCS BANKNOTE CURRENCY CH UNC	$139.50	EQUATORIAL GUINEA P.17 - 5.000 BIPKWELE 1979 UNC BANKN.	$19.25

Paper Money: World ▶ Asia, Middle East

The average sales price in this subcategory is $46.79.

	HIGH		AVG
Hong Kong China - Hong Kong Bank $50 1923 Spec. aunc	$2,008.00	China ND (1939) 1 Sen, Japanese Military, Unc lot of 25	$49.99
The Chartered Bank of India, Aust. & China $100 1909? U	$1,800.00	P-477 The Farmers Bk Of China $100 1941 SP CU	$49.99
Hong Kong China - Hong Kong Bank $10 1923 Spec. AUNC	$1,400.00	China one old note	$49.00
Hong Kong - Hong Kong Bank $500 1930 GVF	$1,325.00	1898 Imperial Bank Of China 50TAELS A49 VG	$49.00
Hong Kong China - Hong Kong Bank $5 nd (1923) Spec. unc	$1,025.00	Wow 1956 Perfect UNC Hong Kong People Bank China $5 x 2	$49.00
Banque Industrielle de Chine 5 dollars 1914 Peking UNC	$698.00	1953 CHINA 5000 YUAN P859 (WEI HE Bridge)	$47.55
P-S541 Russo-Chines Bk $1 1909 VERY RARE UNC	$470.00	Provincial Bank of Sinkiang 6000000 yuan 1948 VF+ S178	$46.88
Extremely Rare 1999 CHINA100YUAN 88888888 P901 UNC10PIC	$456.00	Hong Kong - The Chartered Bank $5 nd (1970-75) 5 pc unc	$46.00
P-S383H Indust./Comm. Bk Ltd $10 1923 VERY RARE SP CU	$349.00	P-S3013 Fu-Tien Bk $1/2 ND SP CU	$46.00
1950 CHINA 50000 Chinese government palace P856 XF-UNC	$305.00	Rare 1977 Hong Kong Chartered Bank $10 x 8	$45.00
Hong Kong - The Chartered Bank $50 nd (1970-75) UNC	$305.00	1 lot of 3000 Antique China 1953 Rare! NR	$44.68
Extremely Rare 1990 CHINA 100YUAN P889b NO99999999 UNC	$285.00	Rare Tibet 25 Srang	$43.00
P-S153F The Bk Of Canton $1 1922 Rare SP CU	$240.50	Wow Last Set Same no.000092 Hong Kong HSBC Banknotes x4	$43.00
P-130 Bk Of Communications $10 1920 RARE SP CU	$236.50	1962 CHINA 1Jiao SPECIMEN Back green P877a	$42.80
Extremely Rare 1999 CHINA 100YUAN 33333333 P901 UNC	$236.16	Rare Prefix ZZ Replacement 1994 Hong Kong Bank100 50 20	$42.00

Paper Money: World ▶ Australia, Oceania

The average sales price in this subcategory is $36.81.

	HIGH		AVG
AUSTRALIA 1 POUND 1923(MILLER - COLLINS) CERTIFIED VF32	$898.00	1992 Uncut Block 4 x Australian $5 Banknotes NPA Folder	$41.05
AUSTRALIA $10 STAR NOTE 1968	$510.00	>>> AUSTRALIA 10 SHILLING EF 1954 - 1960 <<<	$41.00
NEW ZEALAND POSTAL NOTE FOR 2 POUNDS, RARE!	$455.00	*AWSOME* 2 PESO "VICTORY" PHILIPPINES AU	$40.01
WESTERN SAMOA 10 SHILLINGS NOTE 1944 CH EF/AU RARE	$430.55	Australia Gem Unc Phillips Wheeler $2 Note & $2 Stamp	$39.99
New Zealand postal note for 1 shilling	$373.00	1992 Uncut Block 4 x Australian $5 Notes Sydney Folder	$39.95
AUSTRALIA - 1933 One Pound - King George V` - VF+	$365.00	'42 Commonwealth of Australia 10 Shilling Note	$38.76
Australia Postal Note for 2'6	$343.00	Australia one old note	$37.00
AUSTRALIA - Ten Shillings Note 1939 - XF++ !!!	$300.00	1942 Commonweath of Australia 10 Shillings Note XF	$36.00
R402 $20 COOMBS/RANDALL 1967 NOTE VF CV=$850	$271.88	Australia Fifty Dollars Bank Note !!!	$36.00
Australian $100 Banknote Portfolio First Polymer Issue	$270.00	Fiji : Beautiful 1961 10 Shilling. L@@K!	$35.00
1,000 mint wrapped Japanese WWII Tien Gulden Notes	$256.90	100 1988 World Expo $5.00 Bills CU	$35.00
1994 Uncut Block 4 Australian $50 Banknotes NPA Folder	$249.00	[2 of these sold for $35.00 each]	$35.00
FRANCE NEW HEBRIDES @ RARE	$235.00	NEW CALEDONIA 50 Centimes 43 Pick 54 UNC (nec 194)	$35.00
@ 1943 EMERGENCY ISSUE		100 1988 World Expo $5.00 Bills CU	$35.00
AUSTRALIA -Ten Shillings Note 1939 - XF+ CV=$900 !!!	$231.38	Australia one old note	$34.88
Rare Australia KGVI 5 pounds 1941 XF No Reserve	$223.50	Scarce Australia 10 shillings 1961 XF No Reserve	$34.75

Paper Money: World ▶ North, Central America

The average sales price in this subcategory is $90.81.

	HIGH		AVG
Canada $2 1954 G/R test note EXTREMELY RARE!	$6,651.99	VF QUEEN ELIZABETH II 1954 DEVIL'S FACE $100 NOTE	$99.95
Capitalist Gods & Connoisseurs '37 $1000 Bank of Canada	$4,058.00	Bank Of Canada 1975 $100 very fine , clean	$99.00
Canada $1000. Bill 1954 Lawson Bouey - 3 consec #s	$3,150.00	CANADA 1937 $100.00 NOTE IN VF CONDITION (BJ)	$91.52
TWO CONSEC $1000 1988 Thiessen-Crow GEM UNC	$2,111.00	Superb Devil Beattie Coyne 2.00$ AU++/UNC	$91.50
VERY RARE!! 1914 $5 The Sterling Bank of Canada Note	$1,999.99	1935 BANK OF CANADA $5 NOTE	$91.00
RARE 1902 $4 Dominion of Canada DC-17a C/V $3000 "Fine"	$1,742.17	$20 1979 THIESSEN-CROW, 3	$91.00
Rare: 1914 $5 Bank of Hamilton Note. "TheMonetaryMan"	$1,150.80	CONSECUTIVE NOTES, CRISP UNC	
NICE $2 1935 Banque Du Canada QUEEN MARY FRENCH Version	$1,033.00	1935 Bank of Nova Scotia Canada $10 bill note	$90.00
CANADA 1988 $1000 NOTE IN UNC CONDITION (EKA)	$1,000.00	BANKNOTES 1923 to 1986__18 banknotes__Face value $63.25	$89.99
[2 of these sold for $1,000.00 each]		CANADA $25 Revenue (bond) original essay	$89.00
The Gore Bank Hamiton Upper Canada $1.00 Authentic	$837.99	CANADA $30 Revenue (bond) original essay	$89.00
1954 $20 REPLACEMENT UNC	$786.51	The Royal Bank Of Canada $5.00 1913	$89.00
Banque Canadienne $1.00 August 23rd 1836 Rare	$612.99	$20 1979 THIESSEN-CROW, 3 CONSECUTIVE NOTES, CRISP UNC	$86.00
2 Consecutive 1917 Canadian Bank of Commerce $5 Large	$450.00	1935 Bank of Montreal $5 Bill. No/Res. "TheMonetaryMan"	$84.99
The Imperial Bank Of Canada $4.00 1875 Rare	$431.89	1917 $10 CDN Bank of Commerce. Early Large Sized CIBC.	$83.00
The Mechanics Bank $10.00 1872 Very Rare	$426.88	Canada:Agricultural Bank 1834 Toronto. Fine. No problem	$82.51

Paper Money: World ▶ Europe

The average sales price in this subcategory is $45.53.

	HIGH		AVG
99 consecutively numbered JACK NICKLAUS ?5 notes(bills)	$2,500.00	2 BRAND NEW Jack Nicklaus Limited Edition ?5 Notes!	$49.00
Very Rare Romania 1920 2000 Lei Specimen-No Res!	$1,277.00	Jack Nicklaus ?5 Note Bill Five Pound mint condition	$49.00
Scarce Romania 1920 200 Lei Specimen-No Reserve!	$1,125.00	HUNGARY -P78- 1923 25,000 KORONA BANKNOTE - GRADE VG	$47.00
1000 SWISS FRANCS, CURRENT	$790.00	NATIONAL COMMERCIAL BANK OF SCOTLAND LTD 20 POUND NOTE	$46.66
NOTE, CRISP UNCIRCULATED!!!		Jack Nicholas Scottish Five Pound Note (Bill)	$46.00
Latvia: Jelgava (Mitau), issued in 20.10.1915., RR, VF	$725.24	14th JULY ROYAL BANK SCOTLAND JACK NICKLAUS ?5 NOTE	$45.00
riotis item:GREECE ONE DRACHMA NOTE HERMES 1885 UNC	$565.00	[3 of these sold in a multiple item ("Dutch") auction for $15.00 each]	

riotis item:GREECE TWO DRACHMAI NOTE HERMES 1885 HG	$491.00	riotis item:ITALY 100 AMC LIRE SERIES 1943 CRISP AU	$44.00
riotis item:GREECE 5 DRS NOTE 1897 RRR	$455.00	Two Jack Nicklaus UK Five pound notes	$43.00
riotis item:GREECE 20 DRS NOTE 1926 . VERY NICE!!!!!!	$416.11	ITALY - 1000 ITL AMC-SERIES 1943-A VERY RARE NOTE	$43.00
Bulgaria 1922 1000 Leva Specimen-No Reserve!	$405.00	Belgium 1948 100 Francs-Original XF-No Reserve!	$42.75
20 X RBS JACK NICKLAUS 5 POUND NOTES IN SEQUENCE	$400.00	PRE NICKLAUS ST ANDREWS TOM MORRIS GOLF ₤5 NOTE BOOKLET	$42.56
riotis item:GREECE 20 DRS 1955 GEM CRISP UNC	$333.00	1946 SPAIN 25 PESETAS (CH AU)	$42.50
Malta 1939 5 Shillings Specimen-Scarce!	$330.00	EURO, SPECIMEN OVERPRINT SET OF 7 NOTES (10 SETS)	$42.00
riotis item:GREECE 500 DRS 1955 GEM CRISP UNC	$308.00	Bulgaria 1922 5 Leva Specimen-No Reserve!	$42.00
G.B. PRISONERS OF WAR POW CAMPS 2s.6d. CAMP 89, FINE	$305.00	Bank Of Ireland ₤5.00 1935	$41.00

Paper Money: World ▶ South America

The average sales price in this subcategory is $21.00.

	HIGH		AVG
4 PERU - BANCO DE TACNA -10 SOLES - 4 BANKNOTE UNCUTED	$999.99	Uruguay One old note with columbus	$21.71
Rare Banco Del Ecuador 100 Peso Specimen	$535.00	ARGENTINA 10 NOTES 100 PESOS 272c UNC	$21.71
NETHERLAND ANTILLES CURACAO 250 GOULDEN 1967 BANK NOTE	$438.00	1923 10 DEZ MIL REIS BRAZIL PAPER MONEY	$21.50
NETHERLAND ANTILLES CURACAO 100 GOULDEN 1981 BANK NOTE	$349.00	1893 BRAZIL 100 REIS RARE ANTONIA LOCAL ISSUE BRASIL	$21.50
Chile 1899-1914 50 Pesos Specimen-Uncirculated!	$247.60	SURINAME 20 NOTES 2 1/2 GULDEN P-119 UNC	$21.01
VINTAGE 100 CEM MIL REIS BRAZIL PAPER MONEY	$230.50	SURINAME 20 NOTES 100 GULDEN PICK 133b UNC	$21.01
VINTAGE 50 CINCOENTA MIL REIS BRAZIL PAPER MONEY	$167.50	Peru - 100 Soles 1879 G/VG PIC9 VERY LOW NBR VERY RARE	$20.99
Peru : Stunning 1879 20 Soles Note. Unc.	$155.00	1913 BRAZIL P-24 CINCO 5 MIL REIS BRASIL ABNCo	$20.71
3 FALKLAND ISLAND ₤1 DIFFERENT DATES MINT UNC, RARE	$129.00	VENEZUELA SPECIMEN (MUESTRA) 50 BS BANK NOTES	$20.70
COLOMBIA 5 NOTES 500 PESOS ORO 7.8.1973 PICK 416 UNC	$99.99	5 UNCIRCULATED COLOMBIA NOTES bpo	$20.59
Venezuela 20000 Bs Banknote MUESTRA SIN VALOR	$99.00	Uruguay one old large size note	$20.50
Venezuela 50000 Bs Banknote ESPECIMEN SIN VALOR	$99.00	1925 BRAZIL P-81 DUZENTOS (200) MIL REIS BRASIL ABNCo	$20.50
NICARAGUA 50 Centavos 1894 ** RARE **	$89.97	BRAZIL 1960's UNC LOT - 1 to 1000 Cruzeiros!! ~LQQK!!~	$20.50
1880 200 REIS BRAZIL TROLLYCAR NOTE ~ TRULY UNUSUAL !!	$89.00	1942 BRAZIL P-127 VENTE MIL REIS/ 20 CRUZEIROS BRASIL	$20.50
VENEZUELA P-233R1 ND (1929) 100 BOLIVARES UNC #D100	$86.00	1942 BRAZIL P-126 DEZ MIL REIS/ 10 CRUZEIROS BRASIL	$20.50

Publications & Supplies ▶ Supplies

The average sales price in this subcategory is $18.40.

	HIGH		AVG
Pro-Coin 2006 - Coin Collecting Software. PCGS values	$329.89	5X 10X 15X 20X 30X COIN LOUPE COMBINATION $SAVE$	$19.99
[11 of these sold in a multiple item ("Dutch") auction for $29.99 each]		11 Used Elongated Penny Folders - The Penny Passport	$19.95
U.S. Mint GSA Certificate for 1879-CC Silver Dollar	$211.00	CoinsPlus! Professional Edition #1 Numismatic Software!	$19.95
DIGITAL MOTORIZED CHANGE COUNTER COIN SORTER NEW	$191.94	Coin & Stamp Acrylic Easel Stand Holder 2.5	$19.00
[6 of these sold in a multiple item ("Dutch") auction for $31.99 each]		[10 of these sold in a multiple item ("Dutch") auction for $1.90 each]	
DIGITAL MOTORIZED CHANGE COUNTER COIN SORTER NEW NR	$179.94	NGC COIN BOXES-2 NEW STYLE BOXES-EXCELLENT!!!!	$19.00
[6 of these sold in a multiple item ("Dutch") auction for $29.99 each]		Silica Gel Reusable Dehumidifier 900 gm Covers 66 Cu Ft	$18.95
KLOPP Model CE PORTABLE manual coin counter	$167.50	20 Pocket 2x2 Coin Pages (supplies) Lot of 200 Pages	$18.59
#1 DIGITAL LCD COIN SORTER & 100 WRAPPERS NEW NR DUTCH	$149.95	Electronic Motorized Coin Sorter Double Capacity !NEW!!	$18.00
[5 of these sold in a multiple item ("Dutch") auction for $29.99 each]		Electronic Motorized Coin Sorter Double Capacity	$18.00
# 1 MOTORIZED CHANGE COUNTER COIN SORTER FREE 100	$131.94	Electronic Motorized Coin Sorter Double Capacity	$18.00
[6 of these sold in a multiple item ("Dutch") auction for $21.99 each]		Electronic Motorized Coin Sorter Double Capacity !NEW!!	$18.00
#1 DIGITAL LCD COIN SORTER & 100 WRAPPERS NEW	$127.96	Electronic Motorized Coin Sorter Double Capacity	$18.00
[4 of these sold in a multiple item ("Dutch") auction for $31.99 each]		10X 15X Eye Loupes Headband Magnifier Opti Tools	$17.99
CC mint 1887 Morgan Silver dollar wooden box	$125.00	2x2 20 Pocket Coin Pages - lots of 200 NEW NIB archival	$17.99
MIZAR GOLD TESTER M24 ***USED***	$110.00	2x2 20 Pocket Coin Pages - lots of 200 NEW NIB archival	$17.99
#1 DIGITAL LCD COIN SORTER & 100 WRAPPERS NEW	$95.97		
[3 of these sold in a multiple item ("Dutch") auction for $31.99 each]			
#1 DIGITAL LCD COIN SORTER & 100 WRAPPERS NEW NR DUTCH	$89.97		
[3 of these sold in a multiple item ("Dutch") auction for $29.99 each]			
NGC DELUXE COIN BOXES–LOT OF 10	$89.90		
5000 NICKEL PAPER FLIPS CASE (BOXES of 100)	$89.50		
5000 HALF DOLLAR 2X2 INCH PAPER COIN FLIPS (IN BOXES)	$89.50		
Pro-Coin 2006 - Coin Collecting Software. PCGS values	$29.99		

Scripophily ▶ Airlines

The average sales price in this subcategory is $7.85.

HIGH TO LOW			
100 PAN AM WORLD AIRWAYS CAPITAL STOCK CERTIFICATES!	$52.00	OLD Pan Am American Airlines Airplane Vintage Stock RED	$4.95
FRAMED Pan Am Airline Stock Certificate!	$34.99	3 DIFFERENT PAN AMERICAN AIRWAYS STOCK CERTIFICATES!	$3.95
AIR CANADA STOCK CERTIFICATE	$19.99	Pan Am Corporation Stock Certificate Lady in Clouds	$2.99
1928-A silver certificate funny	$18.50	[2 of these sold for $2.99 each]	
back woods mellon blue+		Pan American World Airways, Inc. 1959	$2.99
25 Pan American World Airways Certificates 1954-1959	$10.51	OLD PAN AM WORLD AIRLINES STOCK CERTIFICATE 1964	$2.99
National Airlines Stock Certificate	$10.50	OLD PAN AM WORLD AIRLINES STOCK CERTIFICATE	$2.75
LOT OF 6 trans world airlines bonds	$8.99	OLD PAN AM WORLD AIRLINES STOCK CERTIFICATE	$2.25
Ten (10) Pan American Airways Certificates (4) Colors	$7.50	OLD PAN AM WORLD AIRLINES STOCK CERTIFICATE	$2.24
20 Pan American World Airways Certificates 1963-1979	$6.51	[2 of these sold for $2.24 each]	
big blue seal high grade AU	$6.50	OLD PAN AM WORLD AIRLINES STOCK CERTIFICATE	$1.99
nice 1934-D ONE DOLL FRED++		[4 of these sold for $1.99 each]	
UNITED TECHNOLOGIES (Sikorsky Helicopters)	$5.95	Pan Am Corporation 1991. Nice vignette!	$1.99
** FRAPORT ** the airport company, stock certificate	$5.50	LOT 3 Bankrupt stocks Vanderbilt Pan Am Penn Central RR	$1.25
big blue seal high grade UNC? nice 1934-A ONE DOLL FRED	$5.33	[2 of these sold for $1.25 each]	

Scripophily ▸ Autographs

The average sales price in this subcategory is $335.64.

HIGH TO LOW

Standard Oil Trust, 1882 - signed JOHN D. ROCKEFELLER	$4,600.00	early 1821 New York City hand signed payment check	$14.50
1884 Fred PABST SIGNED Brewing Stock Certificate/ GREEN	$399.99	early 1821 New York City hand signed payment check	$14.50
NYSE NEW YORK STOCK EXCHANGE MEMBER CERTIFICATE OLD NR	$362.00	RARE CHRYSLER STOCK w LEE IACOCCA SIG! FINEST CONDITION	$12.99
Benjamin F. "The Beast" Butler - Stock Certificate 1891	$100.00	[3 of these sold for $12.99 each]	
Stock Certificate signed by G.W. Bush Great Grandfather	$51.00	1868 The Doylestown National Bank Stock Cert	$12.50
THE CUBA RAILROAD COMPANY	$31.12	BEATLES RECORD CO. STOCK w MANAGER ALLEN KLEIN'S SIG!!!	$11.01
1892 Upstate NY RR Bond Signed by William Webb	$24.95	BEATLES RECORD CO. STOCK w MANAGER ALLEN KLEIN'S SIG!!!	$10.51
Louisiana Bond 1892 s/Foster $1,000 Bond	$24.88	BEATLES RECORD CO. STOCK w MANAGER ALLEN KLEIN'S SIG!!!	$9.99

Scripophily ▸ Communications

The average sales price in this subcategory is $13.95.

HIGH TO LOW

Postal Telegraph and Cable Co. (1884)	$125.95	Marconi Wireless Telegraph Co. Stock Certificate 1928	$9.95
SECRET TELEGRAPH COMPANY 1917 stock certificate	$103.50	40 CINERAMA: 100 SHARE COMMON STOCK CERTIFICATES!	$9.95
RCA RADIO CORPORATION STOCK CERTIFICATE 1946 SARNOFF	$45.00	IBM International Business Machines BLUE stock certific	$9.95
1913 Telephone Vignette Stock Certificate, Maine	$38.00	1963-b barr green seal high grade AU+? ONE DOLL FRED+++	$9.25
Worldcom Stock Certificate Bernard(Bernie)Ebbers Signed	$31.00	University Computing Bond - Sam Wyly	$9.19
Worldcom Stock Certificate Bernard(Bernie)Ebbers Signed	$30.00	GREENWOOD & CANISTEO, N.Y. TELEPHONE CO. Stock Certif.	$9.00
Worldcom Stock Certificate Bernard(Bernie)Ebbers Signed	$19.95	WORLDCOM STOCK CERTIFICATE MINT UNFOLDED	$8.70
[4 of these sold for $19.95 each]		LOYALSOCK, PA. TELEPHONE CO. Stock Certificate. Old!	$8.50
Worldcom Stock Cert. Sullivan / Ebbers Signed	$19.95	WORLDCOM STOCK CERTIFICATE MINT UNFOLDED	$8.36
3 Dif Stock Certs from Telepost Company, same owner, NR	$19.07	Majestic Radio & Television Corp. 1947	$6.99
Columbia Pictures Corporation - HOLLYWOOD	$17.77	RARE 1852 METROPOLITAL INSURANCE	$6.50
PFAFFTOWN TELE.CO STOCK CERT. WINSTON - SALEM, NC 1918	$17.50	CO 108 BROADWAY NY	
PFAFFTOWN TELE.CO STOCK CERT. WINSTON - SALEM, NC 1918	$16.50	Ulysses Telephone Co. stock - Ulysses, New York	$5.99
WORLDCOM STOCK CERTIFICATE-EBBERS-MINT UNFOLDED-L@@K	$14.61	Stock Certificate - AT & T Telephone Co. Shares	$5.75
ALEXANDER GRAHAM BELL AT&T STOCK CERTIFICATE	$10.62	Admiral Corporation Stock Certificate	$4.79
Antique IT&T Telephone & Telegraph Stock Certificate	$10.25	25 shares of GENERAL MOTORS stocks old nice	$4.00

Scripophily ▸ Industrial

The average sales price in this subcategory is $11.46.

	HIGH		AVG
Pabst Brewing Company 1893 Stock Certificate	$265.00	G.M. Stock Certificate - 2000 Common Shares - 1982	$15.50
Philip Best Pabst 1000 Shares Stock Certificate	$129.02	Merrill Lynch Stock - Old Quotron Vignette	$14.00
PERFECTION TIRE and RUBBER CO STOCK CERTIFCATE 1919	$47.65	1923 GOLD 100 LEVA TOBACCO SAVINGS STOCK CERTIFICATE	$13.39
		INDIA Share Certificate'23 Central India Spinning.Tata	$12.52
1925 Stock Certificate Daniel Boone Woolen Mills Issued	$45.00	Stock, bond, revenue certificate, Gainesville Florida	$12.50
EDISON CEMENT CORPORATION 1931	$40.90	BABCOCK & WILCOX - old stock certificate dd 1970s	$12.50
(3) Four Wheel Drive Company Stock Certificates 1918	$37.77	SCHUYLKILL FORGE CO., Shuylkill PA Iron STOCK BOOK 1939	$11.61
PERFECTION TIRE and RUBBER CO STOCK CERTIFCATE 1919\	$37.75	Consolidated Steel Corporation Name Badge ID NR	$11.50
		1967 Stock Certificate 1 Share Farmington Farmers Union	$10.50
Empire State Gas Improvement Co. (1889)	$36.65	Federal Power and Light stock certificate	$10.48
Pressman Tire and Rubber Company Stock Certificate	$36.52	Lot of -10 Pieces- "The American Tobacco Company"	$9.99
SIGNED HENRY CLEWS WHITE STAR I.M.M. PREFERRED STOCK	$29.95	INDIA Share Certificate Bararee Coke Co. Waterlow &Sons	$9.99
		1924 TOBACCO PRODUCTS CORP STOCK CERTIFICATE	$9.99
National Gas Investment Co. (1890)	$27.65	Rare Stock Certificate & Letter 1922 - Boston Co.	$9.99
MATHIESON ALKALI WORKS 1925 stock certificate	$25.75	Howe Sewing Machine Co Bank Note Rental Receipt 1873	$9.99

12

COLLECTIBLES

The Collectibles category is one of the oldest on eBay, and in terms of the number of listings, it is the largest. In 1995, in the earliest days of eBay (or "auctionweb" as it was then known), there were only a handful of categories, and one of them was "Antiques and Collectibles." In fact, the number for the Collectibles category is still 1. (Every eBay category and subcategory is assigned a number, with new categories now getting numbers in the tens of thousands.)

A few of the earliest Collectibles listings, as documented in Adam Cohen's book, *The Perfect Store*, included a Superman metal lunchbox, an autographed Michael Jackson poster, and a Hubley #520 cast iron hook and ladder truck. Collectibles such as Beanie Babies (which were created only shortly before eBay itself) were also key drivers of the early activity on the site.

Today the Collectibles category is a world in and of itself, listing around 2.8 million items—about 17 percent of the items on the eBay site, according to recent statistics. It has around 18,000 subcategories, some of which grew so much that they became entire meta-level categories themselves on eBay, such as Stamps.

One person's collectible is another person's throwaway, and the scope of the category is vast, but some areas do stand out. Some of the most popular recent searches within Collectibles include *Star Wars*, *Precious Moments*, *Coca-Cola*, *Harley Davidson*, *Harry Potter*, *Swarovski*, and *Avon*.

Pinball machines and jukeboxes are some of the highest-priced items overall in this sample: a "CRUISN EXOTICA 31" TWIN DRIVING GAMES by Midway" sold for $4,200.00, and an Orchestrion coin jukebox sold for $17,950.00.

Nostalgia drives a lot of purchases here. Scrolling though pages of old products, bottles, lunch boxes, and the like, is a stroll down the memory lane of American culture (and increasingly of other cultures as well). An eBay Collectibles purchase has become one way to grab a piece of our past.

Other purchases are all about aesthetics or the thrill of acquisition for the collector. To that end, some of the most beautiful items are within the Decorative Collectibles subcategory, and are listed by manufacturer rather than type of item. One notable high seller was a lovely sculpture by the figurine maker Lladro: a "Father Sun" Greek god statue that sold for $999.00 (the seller said it was $1,750.00 new). Other popular figurine and sculpture makers within this category are Hummel/Goebel (which also makes items such as ornaments and collector plates), Department 56, and Hallmark. High prices for Hummels, made by a German company called the Goebel Porcelain Factory, are mostly around $100.00, but go as high as $870.00 (for a 1959 salt and pepper shaker set in the form of a woman in a wintry outfit with a fur muff). Average prices for Hummels are around $34.00, with many of them being newer statues from the 1980s or 90s. Hummels (named for Maria Innocentia–aka "M.I." Hummel, the artist who designed them) inspire great devotion in their collectors, who are savvy about the nuances of figurines from different eras. If you list one, therefore, you should show a photo of the bottom of the item, or wherever the maker's mark and/or signature has been incised, because these logos or trademarks changed over the years. (That goes for a lot of collectibles, as well—people want to know when the item was made and what identifying marks are on the item.)

Another very popular type of decorative collectible here are Longaberger baskets. Longaberger makes other items, like pottery, but the baskets are the most popular. A high price here is $235.00 for a mint condition "Longaberger Hostess Housekeeper Basket Set."

Science fiction and fantasy items show up a lot in various forms throughout Collectibles—in comics, advertising, figurines, and the like. For example, Star Wars pops up in all these places: Collectibles ▶ Advertising ▶ Computers, High Tech, where a "Star Wars 1985 Tri Logo Anakin Carded Figure Vintage" sold for $46.00; Collectibles ▶ Advertising ▶ Gas & Oil, where a "LEGO 10019 Star Wars REBEL BLOCKADE RUNNER / TANTIVE IV" went for $280.00; and Collectibles ▶ Arcade, Jukeboxes & Pinball ▶ Pinball, where an "Atari Star Wars Video Arcade Game Extra Nice Shape" fetched $1,255.00. In the Comics subcategory, a "Marvel Star Wars Comics 21 issue lot" brought in $15.50; and a "Christopher Radko STAR WARS ornament * NIB * NR!!!" got $28.01 in Collectibles Decorative Collectibles ▶ Christopher Radko. One Star Wars item—a "Sideshow Star Wars Han Solo 1/4 Scale SOLD OUT"—was listed in the wrong category (Collectibles ▶ Fantasy, Mythical & Magic ▶ Lord of the Rings), which is one reason why it's important to do keyword searches as well as browse. It went for $212.00. There was even a "STAR WARS DEATH STAR PEZ CANDY DISPENSER 2004 NR!!," which sold for $0.99 in Collectibles ▸ Pez, Keychains, Promo Glasses. And there are more: Star Wars lunch boxes, die-cast toys, fiberglass props, beverage coolers, and so on.

PEZ Dispensers and eBay-ana

A persistent legend about how eBay was started is that eBay's founder, Pierre Omidyar, created eBay as a venue for his fiancée, Pam, to trade PEZ dispensers, which she collected. That is the "romantic" version of the story of eBay's founding, said Omidyar, and not the real reason he started this company, which had more to do with simply experimenting with the interesting market mechanism of an auction and the then-hot new medium called the Internet.

But in any case, PEZ dispensers do trade on the site, and you can find them there now. The highest-selling single dispenser listed in this chapter is a "Scary Green Head Monster Footless PEZ," which sold for $124.72. The seller didn't appear to know what he had, but seemed to get an okay price for the PEZ dispenser anyway. His description was cryptic: "Up for auction in good condition is a footless PEZ made in the USA. I don't know the actual name so if you do, please let me know. The pat No. is 3,845,882. There is no damage to note." One helpful soul posted a question to his auction, explaining, "That is a 'Creature From the Black Lagoon' pez. You should add this title to your description to attract more viewers." (Finding a valuable item whose seller does not seem to understand what he has on his hands, by the way, is a favorite pastime of eBay treasure hunters, but it requires some digging and creative searching, not to mention just plain dumb luck.)

Fittingly, the company that made collectibles take off on the Internet now has its own collectible subcategory—Collectibles ▸ Advertising ▸ eBay-ana—chock full of eBay pins, T-shirts, hats, and yes, PEZ dispensers, among other things, ranging in price from $0.99 up to $129.99.

The Collectibles category on eBay has something for everyone. Vast and deep, it houses the mammoth and the tiny, the whimsical as well as the scientific, the old and the new—kind of like eBay itself.

Advertising ▸ Agriculture

The average sales price in this subcategory is $28.67.

	HIGH		AVG
Old Advance Rumely Oil Pull Tractor Shop Poster Add	$1,100.01	1940's CALIFORNIA PRODUCE CRATE LABELS LOT ORIGINALS	$31.52
vintage dairy flange sign CASH FOR CREAM nr auction	$296.81	LARGE LOT NEW HOLLAND FARM EQUIPMENT BROCHURES / BINDER	$31.25
FLUE COVER / DOOR Old NICHOLS SHEPARD & CO STEAM ENGINE	$275.00	DeLaval CREAM SEPARATOR 1/7TH SCALE ...ERTL	$31.00
OLD ROUND FANCY CAST IRON FARM PLANTER SEAT	$260.60	1899 Woodhouse Agricultural Implements Farm Catalogue	$31.00
Cockshutt D1690 91 Cast Iron Grain Drill Ends Ornate	$260.00	PA Advertising Farm Book West Chester County 1914	$31.00
MYERS HAND WELL PUMP w BRACE from ASHLAND, OHIO -OLD!	$234.50	OLD McCORMICK-DEERING FARM MACHINES TIN SIGN TRACTOR	$29.00
Antique All Brass Grain Tester Sample Probe Pat. 1912	$217.50	ADVERTISING KNIFE SHARPENER LIVE STOCK SALESMEN CATTLE	$28.63
American Gasoline Engines Since 1872 Book - Hit & Miss	$183.50	ANTIQUE DEERING TRACTOR SEAT CAST IRON.	$28.00
Old All Brass Grain Tester Sample Probe	$173.50	Vintage Farm Bureau South Carolina Embossed Tin Sign	$28.00
Displaymasters True-Type Holstein-Friesian Cow	$163.75	1887 Esterly Harvester Mower Binder Whitewater WI Ad	$28.00
GUARANTEED OLD Horse Windmill Weight FOLK ART	$159.38	OLD REX CO. WIRE STRETCHER for FENCE	$27.98
1941 Illinois CORN HUSKING Contest Pin BAKELITE	$159.27	Gas Energy early gas engine magazine July, 1912	$27.77
Antique 1931 "Bucyrus-Erie" 37-B Shovel-Crane Catalog RARE!	$152.50	Celluloid Pin Back Button Crown Mfg. Co. Phelps NY	$27.59
Antique 1931 "Bucyrus-Erie" 43-B Shovel-Crane Catalog RARE!	$152.50	Brochure, Massey-Harris #3 Rake & Tedder, c1920s	$27.01
American Gasoline Engines since 1872 (C.H Wendel)	$152.50	OLD VINTAGE FENCING TOOL??OR LINEMAN S TOOL? NEED HELP	$26.55

Advertising ▸ Candy & Nuts

The average sales price in this subcategory is $32.99.

	HIGH		AVG
Rare German Young George Washington Candy Container	$973.00	Vintage Robinson Crusoe Tin Peanut Can	$35.50
AMOS AND ANDY GLASS CANDY CONTAINER VICTORY GLASS	$504.99	Fire Engine Glass Candy Container sgnd. Avor 2 Oz. NR	$35.38
Uncle Sam Candy Container/Bank	$475.00	Rabbit Candy Container	$34.69
Ziegler Marshmallow can Tin Milwaukee Wis Marshmallows	$469.64	VINTAGE POPEYE & HIS PALS CANDIES & TOY CANDY BOX	$33.99
C1909 Milk Glass Polychrome Drum Mug Candy Container	$464.99	GLASS BABY CARRAGE Candy Container ?? GC No Reserve OLD	$33.01
RARE ~ GLASS CANDY JAR ~ SPIRIT ST. LOUIS ~ LINDBERGH	$294.99	super clean UNCLE SAM Fanny Farmer CANDY FIGURE W/ HAT	$33.00
Early 20thC CREAM DOVE PEANUTS Country STORE GLASS JAR	$240.39	ORIG. HOLLOWAY_S MILK DUDS CANDY BOX CIRCA 1930_S	$32.55
G.O.P. Elephant Candy Container	$238.50	FANNY FARMER CANDY BABY BUGGY OLD ANTIQUE BOX STROLLER!	$32.31

large Buffalo Brand salted peanuts lithographed tin can	$214.50	Tom's Peanuts - Old Glass Counter Jar- Great Condition	$32.00
Marx Buddy Bank Candy Container	$204.25	20'S FLAPPER GIRL ON PHONE EMBOSSED LARGE CANDY BOX NR	$32.00
5 BEATLES 1964 LICORICE CANDY RECORDS FROM DISPLAY BOX	$199.99	1913 Electric Coupe Glass Candy Container	$32.00
Pre- WW II TOM'S TOASTED PEANUTS Display Jars	$175.00	1938 MARS CANDY BAR Factory Booklet MILKY WAY snickers	$31.99
TOMS PEANUTS OAK AND GLASS DISPLAY CASE	$175.00	Vintage MIDGET WASHER Glass Washboard / Candy Container	$31.67
Candy Container - Don't Park Here	$166.49	Tom's Peanut jar Red Nob LID (only) not lance candy	$31.15
VINTAGE LANCE COOKIE CRACKER JAR WITH LID & LANCE BASE	$162.50	Gordon's Snack / cookie jar Counter Gordons chips	$31.00

Advertising ▸ Cars

The average sales price in this subcategory is $18.95.

	HIGH		AVG
NOS 1934-1935 Buick Script Dash Clock In Original Box	$255.00	ELECTRIC VEHICLE PARKING sign * street car	$16.95
PORSCHE 1956 356 A & 550 SPYDER BROCHURE	$227.50	BUICK 1950 ROADMASTER, SUPER & SPECIAL BROCHURE	$15.50
Collect. Series 5 - Auto Companies of Europe 4400E	$150.00	STANDARD 1954 EIGHT BROCHURE LOT/2	$15.29
ASTON MARTIN 1956 DB3S COMPETITION CAR BROCHURE	$150.00	ADVERTISING CHRISTMAS CARD, HANCOCK BUICK FINDLAY OHIO	$15.08
1955 BUICK FACTS MANUAL BROCHURE	$128.38	1972 Moskvitch 408IE Brochure German Russia	$14.99
FERRARI 1968 356 GT 2+2 BROCHURE·	$128.01	1966 Moskvitch 408 Sales Brochure Russia	$14.99
1963 Buick Rivera Promo Model Car	$127.50	1969 Holden Torana Sales Brochure Australia	$14.99
SIATA 1952 208 S BROCHURE + LETTER	$122.49	A.C. 1954 ACE 2-SEATER SPORTS CAR + LETTER	$14.99
1940s Buick Fireball Eight Advertising Metal Bank NR	$103.61	NICE PORSCHE LETTER OPENER & SCISSORS DESK SET W/ CASE	$14.99
ASTON MARTIN 1959 DAVID BROWN DB4 BROCHURE	$92.11	LANCIA @1959 APPIA SEDAN 3RD SERIES BROCHURE	$14.99
Harley Davidson 1996 H. O. Train Set	$80.00	MASERATI @1984 DLX BROCHURE	$14.99
LANCIA 1954 OPEN SPORT CAR PHOTO + LETTER	$78.00	1972 ? Volga M24 Sales Brochure Russia Dutch	$14.99
ASTON MARTIN 1963 DAVID BROWN DB4 VANTAGE BROCHURE	$76.51	1965 Volga Sedan Sales Brochure Russia Norway	$14.99
FERRARI 250 GT PININFARINA & SCAGLIETTI BROCHURE	$76.51	Buick 1958 Accessories Brochure	$14.49
5' X 12' VINYL BANNER HERBIE FULLY LOADED.RARE.	$75.00	1955 BUICK OWNERS GUIDE MANUAL	$14.00

Advertising ▸ Clothing, Fashion

The average sales price in this subcategory is $23.38.

	HIGH		AVG
rare RED GOOSE SHOES Wall Light Up Pam Clock	$680.00	Rare antique shoe clothing advertising sign Gibson girl	$24.99
RED GOOSE SHOES METAL GOOSE STRING HOLDER 16"	$410.00	1904 BUSTER BROWN POND'S EXTRACT BOOKLET	$24.99
Cat's paw clock OLD antique Cats Paw Works	$372.00	John Bradshaw Crandell Buster Brown '28 calendar Eupora	$24.99
WEATHER-BIRD SHOES ROOSTER CHALK DISPLAY	$270.99	4 KEDS 70's STORE DISPLAY SIGNS~FRISBEE~RED/WHITE/BLUE	$24.99
VINTAGE TIN DOUBLE SIDE/FLANGE BEACON SHOES AD SIGN	$143.50	1930s POLL PARROT Shoes Para-Shooter PARACHUTE ·	$24.99
ANTIQUE RED GOOSE SHOES Advertising Pencil Box	$143.15	1929 CATALOG LAYING THE GHOST EDUCATOR SHOES ART DECO	$24.50
1920 Vintage Hamilton Brown Hardware Shoe Flange Sign	$103.55	Vintage Porcelain or China Advertising Shoe or Boot	$24.50
RED GOOSE SHOES lighted sign*vintage footwear*boots*	$100.00	UNIQUE MARBLE KENNY SHOES ADVERTISING POCKET KNIFE	$24.38
JULY 1919 ENDICOTT JOHNSON WORKERS REVIEW SOLDIERS	$97.69	VINTAGE PETERS DIAMOND BRAND SHOES ADVERTISE SIGN	$23.01
1922 CHRISTMAS ED. ENDICOTT JOHNSON CO. WORKERS	$92.31	1954 ADVERTISING CALENDAR POLL PARROT SHOES BARABOO WI.	$23.00
Early 1900's Outdoor Angle Sign For Shoes, Mint Cond.	$87.89	Early Pingree Shoe Girl Advertising Stickpin Premium!!!	$21.71
WOW! HUGE SHOWROOM DISPLAY REAL TENNIS SHOE	$79.00	Vintage Peters Shoes Paper Fan Edgerton WI Weatherbird	$21.50
Ecko Rhino Red Advertising Display Set Plastic Rhinos	$78.00	Vintage Weather Bird Shoes Tin Toy Clicker	$21.01
Stetson SALESMAN SAMPLE Miniature Hat Box Santa Hat	$76.13	1955 R H Palenske Print Advertising Calander, Complete	$21.00
SCARCE 1912 Buster Brown's Book of Travels SHOE ADS	$76.00	OLD WEATHERBIRD SHOES PLASTIC WHISTLE	$21.00

Advertising ▸ Coffee, Tea

The average sales price in this subcategory is $39.21.

	HIGH		AVG
Golden West Coffee Cowgirl Cloth Poster Advertisement	$6,766.00	OLD ACME COFFEE American Stores Phila 1lb Tin Can Steel	$38.77
Watt Pottery Parkway C.D. Kenny Co. Iced Tea Dispenser	$432.77	old Canajoharie, NY unopened coffee tin can, BEECH-NUT	$37.80
VERY RARE BLANKE'S JERSEY CREAM COFFEE TIN MILK PAIL	$360.99	Vintage Red Spot Coffee Door Sign - Coshocton Ohio	$37.69
VERY RARE 1# PRY TOP FARMERS PRIDE BRAND COFFEE TIN	$275.00	HALL MCCORMICK TEA LIGHT BLUE TEAPOT W/INFUSER	$36.51
Early 2lb Tin Canister Tabernacle Old Government Coffee	$272.89	Folger's Coffee Can 1946 GREAT CONDITION~MUST SEE!!!	$36.23
GOLDEN RULE ARCADE WALL MOUNTED COFFEE GRINDER N/R	$255.00	RARE EARLY 1900'S "BLANKE'S & FAUST" COFFEE BOOKLET	$36.00
Large DIE-CUT WOMAN ON SWING ad for HY-QUALITY COFFEE	$224.72	rare 1930s Tea Tin Trunk BROOKE BOND Farm Cows Grazing	$36.00
Cape May New Jersey Photo Book Circa 1888	$212.49	Celestial Seasoning Tea Advertising Tins 8 pc/set Nice!	$36.00
VERY RARE 3# WAMPUM BRAND COFFEE TIN (SUPER GRAPHICS)	$204.49	1964 AD FOR JEWEL FOOD STORE in Chicago Tribune TV Week	$35.99
Peek Frean Shaped Dragon Image Biscuit Tin c1890s	$197.50	OLD VINTAGE 1 POUND POLAR BEAR COFFEE TIN CAN MUSKOGEE	$34.64
NESTLE WORLD GLOBE GLASSWARE **HUGE** 76 PIECE SET	$195.00	BEN HUR COFFEE ENAMEL DINER COFFEE URN	$33.00
SILVER BABY SPOON FOR JEWEL TEA SALESMANS NEW BABY	$179.50	Vintage Wish Bone Coffee Tin can 1 lb keywind Org Lid	$32.99
AUSTRALIAN EMBOSSED GRIFFITHS TEA TIN - EX/COND.	$177.50	#2 Vintage BREAKFAST CALL COFFEE TIN, * TEA *	$32.66
ILLY COLLECTION artist JEFF KOONS--12 pc Cups & Saucers	$154.50	Early Tetley Tea Advertising Booklet Springfield, Mass	$32.65
GREAT OLD ADVERTISING TIN FORBES GOLDEN CUP COFFEE	$153.50	LOT OF 6 VINTAGE 1# COFFEE CANS- FOLGERS, BEECH-NUT, ET	$32.51

Advertising ▸ Communication & Utilities

The average sales price in this subcategory is $26.86.

	HIGH		AVG
COLUMBIA GRAFNOLA Ad Sign reverse painted phonograph NR	$663.36	1930's LINEMANS, ELECTRICIANS, WIRE SPLICING TOOL	$30.00
NIPPER RCA Dog Store Display- Large 36" plastic--Rare!	$331.66	Verd A Ray Verdaray Vintage Wooden Light Bulb Sign-RARE	$29.99
Victor Phonograph	$261.88	Baseball Tips From The Stars Complete Set!! Mars 1962	$29.14
RARE 1920s 3 PC METAL DEALER SIGN RCA RADIO TUBES	$195.00	Vintage Lot-13 "WLS FAMILY ALBUM" Magazines 1930's-50's	$29.00
Emerson Radio & TV 1940s Countertop Store Display Sign	$158.49	RARE! 8 WLAG "Listnin'in Radio News-Programs" 1923	$27.76
[2 of these sold for $158.49 each]		1934 RCA RADIOTRON ADVERTISING PUZZLE GAME IN BOX	$27.55
MURPHY RADIO METAL ENAMEL SIGN,ANTIQUE ORIGINAL	$157.50	RARE LIMITED EDITION SARSAPARILLA # 706 NIPPER DOG MINT	$26.65

::: KSFO Radio Mic Advertising NEON LIGHT BULB ~ Unique	$156.50	LOT - RCA NIPPER DOGS ITEMS - BUTTON PINS PATCH	$26.50
OLD RCA RADIO TUBES ADVERTISING SIGN MOTION LAMP !	$150.49	RADIO JINGLES, JAM PRODUCTIONS, 1220 WGAR, CLEVELAND	$26.00
* LIMITED EDITION NIPPER * ANTHONY VISCO * SCULPTURE *	$149.00	RADIO STATION WTAM 1923 EKKO STAMPS RECEPTION LETTER	$26.00
Real Prop Telegraphone w/ Union Carbide Advertisement	$134.49	Nice Nipper His Master's Voice Latch Hook Wall Hanging	$26.00
VINTAGE RCA TIN AUTHORIZED DEALER SIGN - A MUST SEE	$133.51	BEAUTIFUL RARE FENTON RCA * HIS MASTERS VOICE * BELL	$25.49
MAXFIELD PARRISH art~ 1921 GE/ Edison Mazda price list	$129.50	MAGNAVOX 10K GOLD & PEARL 10 YEAR SERVICE PIN	$24.99
RCA NIPPER DOG 18 INCHES TALL INJECTION MOLDED PLASTIC	$124.50	[3 of these sold for $24.99 each]	
VINTAGE SYLVANIA RADIO/TV SERVICE TIN SIGN - RARE SHAPE	$121.50	One RCA Victor Dog with Original Box	$22.72
VINTAGE SONY BOY ADVERTISING FIGURE/SONY BOY COIN BANK	$106.50	PACKARD BELL Lighter NOS/w/box TV/RADIO/STEREO HI-FI	$21.50

Advertising ▶ Computers, High Tech

The average sales price in this subcategory is $17.05.

	HIGH		AVG
1987 MacUser Editors Choice Award Trophy - vry large	$750.00	NEW MICROSOFT WINDOWS XP PROFESSIONAL POLYESTER SHIRT	$18.50
Apple Macintosh Picasso Flourescent Lighted Sign	$255.00	MICROSOFT WINDOWS HEALTHCARE POLO GOLF SHIRT L	$18.50
CRAY X1 paperweight in VELVET lined box VERY NICE	$188.00	NEW MICROSOFT WINDOWS SERVER 2003 VISUAL STUDIO SHIRT L	$18.50
PDR Folder, design by Paul Rand, featuring NeXT logo	$182.50	MICROSOFT SIGNATURE CUTTER & BUCK POLO SHIRT XL	$18.49
2~14K Schlumberger Pins with Coloured Stones~Orig.Boxes	$162.50	NEW MICROSOFT WINDOWS SQL SERVER BASEBALL HAT CAP	$17.99
IBM THINK SIGN - Wood Advertising Computer Collectable	$123.50	Lot of Four (4) Apple Think Different 8x10 Prints	$17.99
IBM THINK SIGN - Authentic 60's Era Desk Sign (Yellow)	$117.50	1992 MICROSOFT WINDOWS 3.1 LAUNCH PRODUCTION CREW SHIRT	$17.49
1960 IBM Annual Report, Paul Rand	$114.50	BRAND NEW BOEING AIRCRAFT COMPANY LAPTOP COMPUTER CASE	$17.29
Vintage & Rare IBM paperweight, Sphere CPU components.	$100.99	NEW RARE MICROSOFT WINDOWS V NECK PULLOVER SHIRT L	$16.50
IBM paperweight, Rare German Collectible	$100.99	NEW HEWLETT PACKARD HP INVENT JERSEY KNIT POLO SHIFT L	$16.50
RARE Honeywell Pewter Owl, 1960s, electronic parts	$100.00	NEW RARE DELL COMPUTER PIQUE POLO GOLF SHIRT L	$16.50
Brass CRAY sundial PAPERWEIGHT super computer	$91.00	NEW RARE MICROSOFT OFFICE JERSEY KNIT POLO GOLF SHIRT L	$16.50
RARE CISCO SYSTEMS INTERNET EMPLOYEE SHIRT XL	$81.00	SUN MICROSYSTEMS PURPLE WHITE CHEVRON HERRINGBONE SHIRT	$16.50
set of CRAY RESEARCH YMP bookends 1990 nice SOLID WOOD	$78.00	NEW MICROSOFT DEVELOPER NETWORK MSDN MICROFIBER JACKET	$16.50
Vintage 50s Orginal IBM "THINK" Wooden Desk Plaque	$78.00	2 New IPOD Posters: 1 Blue / 1 Yellow - Perfect - NRI	$16.50

Advertising ▶ Distillery

The average sales price in this subcategory is $16.02.

	HIGH		AVG
MUST SEE YELLOWSTONE Kentucky Bourbon BEAR AD Figure	$242.50	ABERLOUR SINGLE MALT SCOTCH WOOD BOTTLE STAND	$17.50
COINTREAU LIQUEUR ADVERTISING DISPLAY FIGURE	$205.50	Jagermeister Inflatable Shark New In Package	$17.50
Early 1900s Maryland Club Whiskey Promo Original Frame	$201.50	Jagermeister Lanyards Lot Of 20 New In Package	$17.50
VINT COLUMBINE PURE RYE	$155.00	Mellwood Antique Bourbon Whiskey Crate - Tongue/Groove	$16.99
METAL/BRASS CORKSCREW! NR!		JOSE CUERVO BAR~PARTY~RV~PATIO LIQUOR LIGHTS~AWSOME!!!	$16.99
Havana Club Cuban Barrel Proof Rum 1 Litre	$151.60	[2 of these sold for $16.99 each]	
CASPER WHISKEY JUG	$125.00	Brand New!!! Jagermeister Flag!!!!!!	$16.50
Old Deck PLAYING CARDS Adv GREEN RIVER WHISKEY	$123.50	ASHTRAY Advertising BLACK & WHITE Scotch Whiskey DOGS	$15.75
ADORABLE! Black & White Scotch Barking Scottie Dogs	$122.50	Crown Royal Coach with Bottle	$15.55
HUNTER WHISKEY FIRST OVER THE BARS METAL STATUE	$117.50	Wine rum whiskey Marquisat silver tasting cup on chain	$15.50
W.C. FIELDS KY BOURBON WHISKEY GIFT SET FULL, SEALED	$100.00	Jagermeister Lite-Up Buttons Lot Of 40 New	$15.50
Makers Mark " SPLASH " Display * BLUE & WHITE * UK KY	$91.00	Antique DUFFYS PURE MALT WHISKEY Celluloid Advertising	$15.50
VINTAGE ROMA WINE CHALKWARE OR PLASTER STATUE	$82.00	OLD WHITE HORSE SCOTCH WHISKEY BAR ADVERTISEMENT	$15.02
BLACK & WHITE SCOTCH WHISKY BACK BAR DISPLAY 1940's	$78.79	Big Jagermeister Blow Up	$15.01
Vintage Straight Whiskey Tray Sign Green River	$78.77	1916 Kentucky Favorite Whiisky/Favorite Distrib. Boston	$15.00
whiskey statue Old Kentucky Tavern vintage original	$78.00	BEEFEATER Imported GIN Advertising English Guard Figure	$14.99

Advertising ▶ eBay-ana

The average sales price in this subcategory is $8.75.

	HIGH		AVG
eBay Live 2005 PIN SET #211 LITHOGRAPH #211 STAFF SHIRT	$129.99	EBAY LIVE 2004 RARE AUCTIVA PIN SET~RED & ORANGE	$9.39
Ebay Live 2005 Lithograph Limited Edition w Pin NIB NR	$100.00	eBay Logo Baseball Cap Hat Adjustable Black New NR	$9.05
rare watch from ebay's Korean auction company	$77.76	2005 NEW EBAY THE POWER OF ALL OF US COFFEE MUG	$9.01
Kodak NonCurling Film Sign cira 1905 ish	$75.00	EBAY - Canada - WHT T Shirt -L	$9.00
2005 eBay Live Limited Edition Pin Set + Extras	$67.00	Ebay POWERSELLER pens mints magnet post its 2005 LIVE!	$8.99
Yoder Hollywood Wolf Whistle - Original NOS In Box	$56.01	Two Old Convention Pins - American Legion 1946 SF	$8.99
ONE & ONLY Autographed "Ghost Cane" trading card!	$52.27	eBay Flip Flops Beach Sandals Mint in Bag NEW eBay Logo	$8.99
eBay Live 2004 Pin Parade #109 out of 250	$51.00	EBAY Live 2005 Rubber Bracelets Red Blue New Collector	$8.97
EBAY LIVE 2005 35 PIN SET CARDS CLAPPER GALA LOT NEW	$50.00	eBay Live! 2005 USPS Nevada Special Issue Cover	$8.56
Ebay LIVE 2003 Orlando FL COMPLETE PIN SET WITH TIN	$49.99	Ebay Live Merchandise Shirts Pins Buttons Pamphlets NR	$8.50
eBay and PayPal Integration T-shirt t shirt adult large	$49.51	eBay LIVE 2004 RARE CONSUMER ELECTRONICS TRADING PIN NR	$8.50
Lot of 13 2003 Ebay Live Pins Live Event issued only	$46.99	I DIDN'T LOSE MY MIND, I SOLD IT ON EBAY!	$8.50
EBAY LIVE 2005 COMMEMORATIVE SILVER COIN LIMITED ED #50	$45.00	eBay Live 2005 Power Seller Tote	$8.50
SET of 4 LIMITED EDITION EBAY PEZ HEARTS	$45.00	eBay White Sweatshirt size L BRAND NEW	$8.50
EBAY LOGO MESSENGER BLUE BAG PACK REFLECTORS	$39.99	NEW eBay Stores Blue Collectible Photo Picture Frame	$8.49

Advertising ▶ Food & Restaurant

The average sales price in this subcategory is $54.28.

	HIGH		AVG
Soft Ice Cream Truck WORKS GREAT. GOOD MONEY MAKER LOOK	$15,099.00	Restaurant Creamer Rack, Holds 24 Creamers, Rare!	$59.99
1876 Salesman's Sample Ferguson Icebox/Cooler-Essex, VT	$2,550.00	BORDENS ANIMATED VINTAGE GERMANY ALARM CLOCK	$56.55
Borden's Dairy Elsie the Cow Fisher Price Pull Toy	$455.00	Borden's Elsie & Elmer the Cow Salt and Pepper Shakers	$56.00
Boise, Idaho (Pic) TRPQ Milk Bottle	$203.50	Vintage Dixie Dairy CO Miss Dixie CookBook Gary, In	$56.00

Borden's Malted Milk Porcelain Sign C. 1900	$189.98	4 mini pyro DAIRY creamer MILK BOTTLE with CARRIER	$52.99
BORDENS ELSIE THE COW AND BEAUREGARD LAMP	$177.50	GALLON ELSIE BORDEN MILK BOTTLE JUG WITH HANDLE	$52.00
Rare Wallace Restaurant China Borden Elsie the Cow Bowl	$147.50	3 pc LOT Cream Top Milk Spoon CreamTop Seperator bottle	$52.00
Rare Horlick's Store Jar with Reverse Glass Label	$143.50	ERTL Borden's Elsie the Cow Die Cast Truck Metal Bank	$51.00
SOUTHERN BELLE DAIRY FOOD ADVERTISING MILK CLOCK CLOCKS	$135.00	Large Good Humor Ice Cream Umbrella	$49.55
Vintage Clock Advertising Foremost Icecream	$132.49	VINTAGE BORDENS ELSIE THE COW TABLECLOTH ~ NICE!!!	$47.15
National Dairy Malted Milk tin canister	$127.55		
Pioneer United (Pic) Washington TRPQ Milk Bottle	$127.50		
1926 Hanfords Ice Cream Fountain Celluloid Hinged MENU	$122.50		
California Disney TRPQ Milk Bottle	$113.61		
BORDENS ELSIE ZIPPO LIGHTER 1960's VINTAGE	$105.49		

Advertising ▸ Gas & Oil

The average sales price in this subcategory is $53.28.

	HIGH		AVG
tokheim antique immaculate gas pump	$2,135.00	Porcelain Light Fixture Globe Shade Old Vintage	$59.99
Old Original Richfield Gasoline Gas Globe GILL BODY	$1,225.00	1920'S UNION OIL OF CALIFORNIA GAS / GASOLINE ROAD MAP	$57.06
RUSH VISIBLE ANTIQUE GAS PUMP	$1,075.00	Oilfield decals, stickers Red Adair	$57.00
Rare Wayne Gas Pump Clock Face	$1,009.99	Vintage Tide Water Associated Oil Co. Badge	$56.99
SHELL GAS PUMP	$875.00	CA 1940's CASITE GAS OIL SIGN ROUND GLASS THERMOMETER	$56.00
OLD 4 WAY TRAFFIC LIGHT SMILEY LENSES A MUST NO RESERVE	$778.89	Wayne 100 nozzle receiver	$56.00
INDIAN MOTORCYCLES ALL GLASS GAS PUMP GLOBE ORIGINAL !!	$566.00	VINTAGE CITIES SERVICE BOX DISPLAY ADV. FRICTION TAPE	$54.15
Original Sunoco Script Top M&S Wayne 80 Gas Pump Top !	$545.00	2 GREAT VINTAGE PORCELAIN GAS STATION/STORE LIGHTS	$53.25
air meter	$535.51	1930s JOHNSON OIL Highway Map of OKLAHOMA	$52.99
SOUTHWEST GULF PUMP	$510.00	SET OF 2 VINTAGE PANOLENE MOTOR OIL CANS	$52.08
ECO # 97 TIREFLATOR AIR METER REFURBISHED WITH LIGHT	$500.00	MINT c1930 EXIDE GLASS BATTERY CELL ACID WATER JAR	$52.00
Wayne Model 80 Vintage Gas Pump	$454.50	OIL BOTTLE SAFEGUARD PENNSYLVANIA SUPERIOR OIL 1920'S	$51.99
OLD 4 WAY TRAFFIC LIGHT CROUSE & HINDS (NICE)!!!!!!!	$428.46	Porcelain Gas Station Light/Sign/Pump	$51.91
PAIR OF ORIGINAL ELRECO GASOLINE GAS PUMP GLOBE LENSES	$406.00	Porcelain Gas Station Light/Sign/Pump	$51.01
gilbarco restored gas pump harley davidson theme	$375.00	Porcelain Light Fixture Globe Shade Old Vintage	$51.00

Advertising ▸ Health & Beauty

The average sales price in this subcategory is $13.57.

	HIGH		AVG
RARE Minty's Toothpaste Advertising Figure chalkware	$261.66	Cast iron advertising "Key To Success Use Eclipse Soap"	$14.95
Vintage Rexall Drugs glass tube thermometer No Reserve!	$147.50	NEW 2005 Siminar Beach Towel/Back Pack - FUN FOR ALL!!	$14.50
Vintage porcelain "Barber Shop" sign. 1940's to 1950's	$146.49	NEW! Mary Kay Girlfriends Umbrella _ Rare & Beautiful	$14.49
5 Little Girls Baby Northern Tissue Ad Prints Picture N	$102.50	Lifebuoy Health Soap Bath Size Old Vintage Soap	$14.27
Mary Kay 1988 statue...full size is at Headquarters	$102.50	SIOUX INDIAN OINTMENT TIN	$14.25
$248 Dermapower Home Microdermabrasion System NR	$82.01	BROWNSVILLE PA CHIEF DEERFOOT	
old box of face powder by LaBara	$68.76	PERSONALIZED BARBER SHOP SIGN Custom Retro Signs	$13.80
OLD GOLDEN PHEASANT PROPHYLACTIC CONDOM TIN	$67.00	[2 of these sold for $13.80 each]	
Vintage Alka-Seltzer Dispenser and Bottle	$66.66	RARE & HTF NEW MARY KAY '04 PRIZE GIRLFRIENDS UMBRELLA	$13.51
SALESMAN SAMPLE LOT	$66.37	NEW 2005 Mary Kay Seminar 2 in 1 Bag! Wonderful Item!!	$13.51
Mary Kay Cosmetics New Black and Pink Briefcase-Only 1!	$61.00	NEW 2005 Mary Kay Seminar PINK Cadilac Pillow!! FUN!!	$13.50
EVERSWEET Tip Tray Toilet Necessity for Refined People	$54.75	Black America - Darkie -Toothpaste - collectable	$13.45
LOT OF 3 VINTAGE UNUSED RAMSES CONDOMS IN TINS LOOK!!	$51.00	NEW 2005 Mary Kay Seminar Unique Round Mug!!	$13.39
Large Store Display Dr.West 18" Toothbrush "Think BIG"	$50.98	Mary Kay Collectible Star Box! Director Prize!	$13.13
ANTIQUE OLD PORCELAIN WOODS	$49.99	Vintage WWII era - COLGATE RIBBON DENTAL CREME - FULL!!	$13.03
TOOTH PASTE TOOTHPASTE JAR		Mary Kay Cadillac Pillow Seminar 2005	$12.99
RARE Coppertone Ad Girl and Dog Doll set	$43.77	NEW 2005 Mary Kay Seminar Logo T-Shirt size 'M'!!	$12.99

Advertising ▸ Household

The average sales price in this subcategory is $15.45.

	HIGH		AVG
SUNLIGHT SOAP Enamel Sign : LEVER BROS LTD : Early&RaRe	$169.00	vOld Pre-1940 Ivory Soap Bar in Orig Wrapper	$17.50
Vintage 40s Unopened BOX DREFT LAUNDRY DETERGENT-MINT!!	$152.50	Old Boraxo Can, Still Full of Soap	$17.16
Not a porcelain or enamel sign but a pressed metal one.	$128.50	VINTAGE 1940 FAB SOAP POWDER UNOPENED FULL DISPLAY BOX	$16.51
Vintage Wrights Coal Tar Soap Enamel Sign Exc!	$108.10	Old Advertising Tip Tray, Round, Fairy Soap Detergent	$16.50
Vintage Crazy Foam Superman/Batman Dispensers	$108.05	1953 Box of All Washing Soap Unopened	$16.13
VINTAGE OXYDOL LAUNDRY SOAP DETERGENT UNOPEN	$105.00	***Proctor and Gamble Advertising Picnic Basket***	$15.50
NOS TIN SIGN,- WHITE KING WASHING MACHINE SOAP -1920's	$100.99	Small Magazine Basket with Lid Ivory Soap 125 years	$15.50
Nice Vintage Unopened Box Bold Laundry Detergent 60's	$100.00	1940's LUX Laundry Soap FLAKES~Unopened Box~Neat	$15.50
VINTAGE 1972~IVORY SNOW IN BOX~MARILYN CHAMBERS ~	$91.00	2 ANTIQUE MONARCH Black & White Our Baby SOAP w/ BOXES	$15.10
Nice Vintage Unopened Box Tide Laundry Detergent 60's	$80.01	Set of 4. Ivory Soap Ads Nude Males. Gay Interest!	$15.00
Vintage 1920s Tin Soap Sign White King Washing Machine	$79.78	Pears Soap Book Mark Colorful Early	$15.00
UNUSED VINTAGE WHITE BORAXO HOLDER WITH BOX	$75.01	1919 Ivory Ad - naked men bathing - gay int.	$14.99
Antique SWIFT & Co. Soap Christmas Sampler Box.	$64.99	Vintage Unopened Ivory Flakes Laundry Soap 1937	$14.99
VINTAGE GOLD DUST TWINS WASHING POWDER TELECHRON CLOCK	$64.00	Antique Vintage Soap Collection ~ Rare Find~ Swift Wool	$14.49
Proctor & Gamble Ivory Soap Wooden Crate/Staten Island	$62.00	BLACK MEMORABILIA GOLD DUST TWINS	$14.42

Advertising ▶ Retail Establishments

The average sales price in this subcategory is $15.45.

	HIGH		AVG
HUGE !!! Antique Greek key Apothecary Jar Candy Counter	$2,550.01	Antique Drugstore Display Bell Jar	$42.00
LG RARE Banjo/Exposition Drugstore Apothecary Candy Jar	$2,195.00	1925 Drug Store Showcase Fixture Drug Business Catalog	$42.00
Hispac III Electronic Prescription Pill Counter	$995.00	VINTAGE? GLASS HUDSON BAY APOTHECARY JAR	$41.99
Original Antique Gold Leaf Flake Drug Store Trade Sign	$610.00	Apothecary Pharmacy Drug Store Jar - Opium	$41.00
2 STACKING DRUGSTORE APOTHECARY SHOW GLOBES CANDY JARS	$565.55	HUGE DELFT GREEN LIDDED APOTHECARY JAR!	$41.00
ANTIQUE APOTHECARY CANDY JAR 23 3/4" TALL	$388.99	Old Vintage Walgreens Copper Apothecary Jar Dr. Olson	$41.00
19TH CENTURY BLOWN GLASS CANDY JAR, APOTHECARY, ETCHED	$366.00	2 Vintage Pharmacy Apothecary Jars Candy Show Globes	$40.99
CANDY JAR VERY VINTAGE	$356.66	OLD DRUG STORE APOTHECARY 12" THUMBPRINT DAKOTA JAR	$40.76
1930'S "OWLS" CONDOM TIN - VERY RARE!	$310.66	Antique Apothecary bottles	$40.00
Old HIRES ROOTBEER Marble Soda Fountain Counter Plaque	$309.00	2 Eli Lilly Fish Bottles Pharmacy Drugstore Apothecary	$39.99
Duble-Tip Prophylactic / Condom Tin - L@@K	$294.00	Dakota Candy Apothecary Jar	$39.99
EXCELLENT 19thC DRUGSTORE Glass WINDOW SIGN	$280.00	Glass country store jar (blue tin lid)	$39.00
Rare Puritan Drugstore Apothecary Candy Glass Jar	$279.99	Large glass country store jar(green painted tin lid)	$38.95
Vintage 5 Spindle Milkshake Mixer / Machine	$256.00	VINTAGE EMBOSSED COLGANS TAFFY CANDY JAR DRUGSTORE	$38.00
DRUG STORE 23" CYLINDER CANDY JAR - OLD - EXCELLENT	$255.00	Pair Of Vintage Apothacary Pharmacy Show Globes	$37.89

Advertising ▶ Soda

The average sales price in this subcategory is $20.61.

	HIGH		AVG
ANTIQUE HOWEL'S ORANGE JULEP SODA FOUNTAIN SYRUP DISP	$1,358.00	Jones soda Skate with BAM standup	$21.50
ORIGINAL NESBITT'S THERMOMETER 12" ROUND WORKS NICE OLD	$538.78	VINTAGE "DOUBLE COLA" ALUMINUM SODA POP COOLER LOOK! NR	$21.50
Nugrape Bottle Shaped Thermometer Sign.. WOW..Nu Grape	$319.00	Large Coke Bottles Advertising Pepsi Soda Sign	$21.49
Nesbitt's Orange Soda Pop Antique Pam Clock Co REAL	$272.00	Jones Soda Skate with BAM stand-up	$21.00
KIST BOTTLE TOPPER RARE TOPPER W/ GIRL	$250.00	KICKAPOO joy juice 1965 6-pack carrier	$20.51
1930s SMILE ORANGE SODA Figural Menu Holder	$185.00	MOUNTAIN STATE AROMATIC GINGER ALE	$20.50
VINTAGE VESS SODA LOT CLOCK ADVERTISING MERCHANDISE NR	$180.00	Old Vintage FIZZIES Orange Soft Drink Tablets Package	$20.50
Rare Sodal Vintage Double Cola Metal Carrier 6 Bottle	$160.50	Vintage Metal Vernors Ginger Soda Cooler!	$20.49
VINTAGE ORIGINAL SUNCREST SODA LIGHT UP WALL CLOCK -NR-	$160.37	original brass grapette safety marker	$20.00
ORIGINAL NESBITT'S THERMOMETER SIGN WORKS NICE	$154.05	100 DIF CORK LINED UNUSED OLD SODA BOTTLE CAP CAPS	$19.99
NuGrape soda thermometer tin bottle sign good condition	$149.99	CLEO COLA THERMOMETER	$19.99
VINTAGE GREEN RIVER SODA FOUNTAIN DISPENSER	$127.54	It's Cott To Be Good vintage Wood Soda Crate	$19.99
MUG BUG PEDAL CAR	$102.55	Utica Club wooden crate old soda case	$19.69
AWESOME 1950'S B-1 LEMON LIME TIN THERMOMETER MINT NO R	$102.45	2 DRINK SMILE SODA KEWPIE HANGING SIGNS NR	$19.30
Jackson's Napa Soda Bottle Opener - Napa Valley Adver.	$100.69	100 DIF UNUSED OLD SODA BOTTLE CAPS	$18.45

Advertising ▶ Soda ▶ Coca-Cola

The average sales price in this subcategory is $13.51.

	HIGH		AVG
VINTAGE FLOOR MODEL COCA-COLA COOLER (ALL ORIGINAL)	$199.00	Coca Cola SOLID WOOD COAT / KEY RACK coke new mint	$14.99
DALE EARNHARDT Coke COCA COLA VENDING MACHINE FRONT	$125.01	COCA COLA COKE NASCAR WELCOME RACE FANS VINYL BANNER	$14.99
Near Mint 12 Pack Metal Coca Cola Carrier With Bottles!	$123.50	Coke Cola Tin Match Holder	$14.99
COCA COLA Illuminated Village Christmas Tree ~ LIMITED	$99.99	ATTENTION COCA COLA COLLECTORS 4 COKE ITEMS EARLY 90'S	$14.99
Vintage Drink Coca-Cola Zippo Lighter	$99.00	Coke Coca-Cola Jakes Service Station Frame NIB	$14.98
Coca Cola Japanese LIMITED EDITION 70's YO-YO set of 9	$91.01	Coca Cola Coatrack Coke Sold Here	$14.50
Vintage Coca Cola League Bowling Ball No Holes	$90.05	LOT OF (20) PIECES OLD DRINK COCA-COLA WOODEN NICKELS	$14.38
Coca Cola Light up Tree over 13 in tall	$89.99	Coke Coca Cola Wooden Bottle Carrier Vintage Case	$13.50
vintage 1940 wooden coca cola carrier w/6 empty bottles	$88.00	COKE TV COMMERCIALS SUPER 2 DVD SET COCA COLA 2 1/2 HRS	$13.49
aluminum 12 pack coca cola carrier. vintage 1940s	$69.02	Coca-Cola Wireless Remote-Contol Train Set, New	$13.00
COCA COLA NAPKIN & STRAW HOLDER & SALT & PEPPER SHAKERS	$66.00	COCA COLA COKE SODA SPORT STYLE DUFFEL GYM BAG TOTE	$12.99
Wow Mint 6 for 25 cents Coca Cola Carrier...COKE !!!!!!	$63.00	19996 Coca Cola History In Photographs book 1930-69	$12.99
Coca Cola Collection Lot of 33 Vintage Old Items Soda	$56.00	5 Mcdonalds Coca Cola Coins (VERY RARE 1983)	$12.50
1950s Coca-Cola Cooler (slight rust) w/ plastic shelf!	$52.00	NEW Lot 2 Coca-Cola Advertising Trash Cans Coke	$12.50
Coca Cola Vintage 1960's Aluminum Picnic Cooler	$51.00	Vintage Drink Bottled Coca-Cola Bottle opener	$12.50

Animals ▶ Bear

The average sales price in this subcategory is $15.45.

	HIGH		AVG
STEIFF ARK with Noah and Wife Limited Edition	$167.50	PARENT BEAR WARNING SIGN BLACK GRIZZLY TRAP	$18.01
1958 Sun Rubber Co. Brown Bear Squeaky Squeak Squeek	$133.50	Cherished Teddies 1993 bear of the month collection w/b	$16.50
Green Granite Bear Figurine from Canada Eskimo Art	$129.72	Lodge Camp Cabin Decor Black Bear Bearfootin Cookie Jar	$16.50
LOST SCULPTURES of Philip R. Goodwin - Sitting Bear	$101.00	BEAR WELCOME SIGN HOLDERS LOG HOME CABIN LODGE DEER	$16.49
MYSTERY Carving ARTIST SIGNED Chainsaw Carving BEAR NR	$95.00	Adirondack Bear Fish Pinetree Rustic Picture Decor Art	$15.95
Wee Forest Folk Just a Peek BB-6	$85.00	Large Hand (chain-saw)Carved Wooden Bear	$15.50
Bearfoots Bear Carvings LIL BEAR ~NEW~	$84.95	WESTERN LODGE CABIN METAL BEAR MOOSE ELK HUNTING ART	$15.50
ON SALE! 2005 BEARFOOTS "TRILOGY" THREE BEARS BOOKENDS	$64.99	CARVED WOODEN MECHANICAL BEAR FROM RUSSIA	$15.41
Large Walking Black Bear Statue Gorgeous	$59.00	Bearfootin' Salt & Pepper LODGE NORTHWOODS DECOR	$14.99
Singing Boyz II Men Teddy Bear "Limited Edition"	$56.00	CHAINSAW CARVED WOOD BEAR - INDOOR - OUTDOOR - 11"	$14.99
VINTAGE HAND CARVED WOODEN BEAR HUNTING SALMON STATUE	$51.00	Big Sky Bears "DYLAN IN LOG" - A delightful character!	$14.99

NY Mets Build A Bear 7/23	$49.99	Alaska Bear Excursion T-Shirt Paw Marks Bite Me 2XL	$14.99
Wee forest folk Welcome Home bear	$49.99	RaRe Pottery Pigeon Forge Bear	$14.99
HAGEN RENAKER MINI MICHAELS TEDDY BEAR DISNEY STICKER	$46.00	Bearfoots Mini Bear COWBEAR Cowboy Bear NEW	$11.95
Steiff Growler Teddy Bear	$38.00	GOEBEL Panda Bear Cubs	$11.50

Animals ▶ Bird

The average sales price in this subcategory is $20.05.

	HIGH		AVG
BOEHM GREATDANE DOG FIGURINE LARGE PIECE	$177.50	Bank Swallow Original Bird Wood Carving	$27.02
Greater Roadrunner original bird carving-Marty	$175.00	Andrea Sadek SCISSOR TAILED FLYCATCHER	$27.00
Black-capped Chickadee Original Bird Wood Carving	$150.00	FREE SHIPPING House Wren Bird Carving/Birdhug	$26.12
Original Wood Carving Common Crow	$122.50	Artesania Rinconada Ostrich #01 Mint In Box	$26.01
Common Nighthawk Original Bird Wood Carving	$76.11	House Finch Original Bird Carvings/Birdhug	$26.00
FOLK ART SHORE BIRD/DECOY	$76.00	50 Cigarette Cards,YOUNG BIRD,	$26.00
VINTAGE HAND CARVED IVORY BIRD. STUNNING EXAMPLE.	$75.00	ORNITHOLOGY,TWITCHER,1937	
16-Unit Purple Martin Bird House Barn w/ Pole	$73.44	Bridled Titmouse Original Bird Wood Carving	$25.53
[2 of these sold for $73.44 each]		GOEBEL ORIOLE BIRD FIGURINE CV 62 1962 ~ MINT	$24.99
12-Unit Purple Martin Bird House w/ 15' Pole	$73.44	FREE SHIPPING Birdhug Bird CarvingChimney Swift	$24.66
20-Unit Purple Martin Bird House w/ Pole	$72.41	Red-breasted Nuthatch Original Bird Wood Carving	$24.61
FREE SHIPPING Chickadee Orig Bird Carving/Birdhug	$71.10	Vintage A. R. Pigeon News Qty. 12 Books for Pigeons	$24.51
Vintage c.1950's Blue Heron Murano Glass Bird Figure	$66.00	Vintage Racing Pigeon Review Qty. 12 Books on Pigeons	$24.51
Stunning Porcelain Seagull in flight Rosenthal Germany	$65.00	FREE SHIPPING Kentucky Warbler Bird Carving/Birdhug	$24.50
VERY FINE BOEHM BIRDS from the LOCAL ESTATE SALE	$63.50	Brown-headed Nuthatch Original Bird Wood Carving	$24.02
PAIR OF ART DECO BRONZE BIRD FIGURE DESK ORNAMENTS	$62.00	ANDREA BY SADEK BIRD FIGURINES CARDINAL AND BLUE JAY	$23.49

Animals ▶ Cat—Domestic

The average sales price in this subcategory is $20.05.

	HIGH		AVG
Franklin Mint CAT ADVERTISING THIMBLE x20 Set + Shelf	$223.50	Kliban Cat / Dog Address Labels	$29.70
KLIBAN CAT IN TUB CANDY DISH	$125.00	Vintage 20's Cat Advertising Crumber Set	$28.67
Holt Howard Pink Cat & White Poodle Snack Trays L@@K	$78.77	Collectable Bill KLIBAN Blk/Wt Cat w/red boots PLATE	$27.97
MOTHER/KITTEN SIAMESE CATS 50's TV LAMP	$66.51	2004 Isle of Man GEM PROOF Silver Tonkinese Cat Coin	$27.95
STERLING SILVER PERSIAN CAT BROOCH/ PENDENT & EARRINGS	$63.62	2005 Isle of Man GEM PROOF Silver Himalayan Cat Coin	$27.95
Victorian Tin Cat Family Tray - Kitten Bouncing on Papa	$59.00	GUMPS CAT WITH MOUSE CACHEPOT POTPOURRI PORTUGAL SIGNED	$26.00
Tiki Mug by Munktiki . Maneki Neko 124 of 150	$49.00	OTAGIRI HANDCRAFTED BLUE CHINTZ CAT SUGAR SHAKER	$26.00
TY beanie baby babies Cool Cat Garfield cat 6 1/2"neat	$41.00	NEW RUSSIAN BLUE CAT LOVER'S WRIST WATCH! CATS	$26.00
Vintage Black CAT 3.75" x 4.75" Glass Vanity Pin Tray	$36.00	Inside painted cat snuff bottle with ornate lid & spoon	$23.19
Otagiri Blue Chintz Cat Wall Plaque Ktchn Towel Holder	$35.23	VINTAGE AVANTI PLUSH HIMALAYAN CAT & KITTEN 1983	$22.79
CAT,SCULPTURE,A BREED APART,SMUDGE,NEW	$35.00	Laurel Burch Lamp Shade	$22.50
c1930 FIGURAL chalkware KITTEN STRING HOLDER cat SUPER!	$34.50	VINTAGE CAT STRING HOLDER BABBACOMBE ENGLAND NR L@@K	$21.50
Vintage Kliban Cat in Roses Throw (?) Sleeping Bag (?)	$31.27	MULTI CAT TABBY BIRMAN ABBY & FLOWERS 11.5" WOOD CLOCK	$21.00
Kliban Cat / Dog Address Labels	$29.70	Bengal Cat Decal Sticker - GET FREE SHIPPING!	$20.00
Vintage 20's Cat Advertising Crumber Set	$28.67	Cat Kitten Hooked Rug - 2' x 3' New with Tag Tuxedo Cat	$19.99

Animals ▶ Cow

The average sales price in this subcategory is $18.54.

	HIGH		AVG
Cow Parade Collection	$2,000.00	COW Quartz Watch Leather TWO TONE Dairy	$18.95
HAGEN RENAKER DESIGNER WORKSHOP JERSEY COW #95	$417.00	UK London Cow Parade AELBERTA Mint w/Box/Tag 2002	$18.95
COW PARADE Black Tie Dog #9155 RETIRED! NO RESERVE!!	$408.00	COW CREAMER	$18.85
Cow Parade Black Tie Dogs, Retired Hard to Find	$350.00	COW Parade 2001 Retired Fun Seeker 9199 MIB Tag Box NR	$18.78
COW PARADE Diamonds are a Cows Best Friend 9122 RETIRED	$335.00	COWS ON PARADE LOLLIPOP MUNCHKIN COW MINT IN THE BOX	$18.75
COW PARADE Handsome #9153 RETIRED! NO RESERVE!!	$280.00	COWS ON PARADE THE WIZARD OF OZ COW MINT IN THE BOX	$18.75
COW PARADE~HANDSOME COW~retired~#9153 TAG & BOX	$276.05	Lot of 16 Mary Moo Moos	$18.58
COW PARADE piOWsso #9156 RETIRED! NO RESERVE!!	$257.00	Retired COWS ON PARADE ***MOOMAID*** #9139	$18.50
COW PARADE Uncle Sam #9119 RETIRED!! NO RESERVE!!	$255.59	Whimsical Hand Painted Italian Vintage COW CREAMER	$18.50
COW PARADE Udder Romace #9152 RETIRED! NO RESERVE!!	$255.00	Cow Parade - Glinda the Good Witch Cow Figurine 7723	$18.49
HOLSTEIN - FRIESIAN WHITE METAL TRUE TYPE COW TROPHY	$224.50	Breyer Texas Longhorn Bull & America Bison vintage lot	$18.45
Cows on Parade Milky Way NIB w/tag	$202.50	COWS ON PARADE SAM-MOO-RAI MINT IN THE BOX	$18.25
Beautiful RED ANGUS ? FULL BODY TAXIDERMY Baby COW CALF	$201.50	PRINCESS HOUSE LEAD CRYSTAL COW	$18.01
COW PARADE Out of Cow Towner #9121 RETIRED NO RESERVE!	$199.99	JOHN M. BROWNING - A WIZARD WITH GUNS	$18.00
COW PARADE~piCOWsso~mint condition~RARE COW	$190.50	COW PARADE ~ GRAPE BOVINE cows figurine NIB ready 2ship	$18.00

Animals ▶ Deer

The average sales price in this subcategory is $13.37.

	HIGH		AVG
Bradford Williams "The Duel" bronze deer sculpture	$250.00	NEW ! HIGH MOUNTAIN ELK, LICENSE PLATE W/NAME	$15.00
WHITETAIL DEER ANTLER ANTLERS SHEDS RACK LOT HORN	$162.50	Made in England Bambi Deer figurines Plichta Lenox?	$14.99
[2 of these sold for $162.50 each]		NEW CARIBOU REINDEER ETCHED GLASS SERVING PLATE	$14.99
WHITETAIL DEER MOUNT/ANTLERS/TAXIDERMY/BEDDING HUNTING	$102.50	Bull Moose Head Mount Buckle	$14.10
HOME INTERIOR BUCK DEER FAMILY STATUE DOE FIGURINE NIB	$56.00	Custom Steel Elk Caribou Deer ADDRESS SIGN Steel Metal	$13.99
Nippon Scenic Deer/Buck Footed Vase	$54.33	Retired 1984 HOMCO ANTLER RACK BUCK DEER SCULPTURE	$13.99
3 for1 DEER , BUCK, DOE, & FAWN for Home Interior	$52.99	NEW Deer Family Wind Chimes Windchimes (27)	$13.50

Item	HIGH	Item	AVG
WHITETAIL DEER ANTLER ANTLERS SHEDS RACK LOT HORN	$52.00	A Deer with A Big Deer Head	$13.50
Whitetail deer enthusiest great hand painted sculptures	$51.00	CUTE PORCELAIN FAWN STATUE, DE LEE ART CO. MEXICO	$12.51
Two Heissner Deer Yard Art Garden Figures, OLD Doe Fawn	$46.00	3 VINTAGE HARD-PLASTIC DEER "BREYER C"	$12.51
Great Escape Whitetail Deer Sculpture	$44.50	OLD Heissner Garden Figure FAWN DEER Orig Label GERMANY	$12.50
RETIRED 1984 HOMCO~ANTLER RACK BUCK~DEER SCULPTURE	$40.99	Russian Art Blown Glass Figurines-figurine-animals:DEER	$11.50
Ceramic Hand-Painted WHITETAIL DEER Figurine WCS	$40.00	OLD LEAD TOY DEER FIGURINE - LEAD TOY STAG FIGURINE	$11.50
Hagen Renaker**DISNEY-BAMBI, style two**W@W**L@@K**	$36.00	VINTAGE POTTERY DEER DOE	$11.49
Home Interiors Deer family/Set of 3/NR	$35.89	w 2 FAWNS ON CHAIN JAPAN	
H L Deaton 6th American Wilderness Figurine Elk, NR	$34.33	Erzgebirge Miniature Carved Wood Deer Fawn Germany	$11.48

Animals ▶ Dog

The average sales price in this subcategory is $21.55.

Item	HIGH	Item	AVG
Airedale Terrier Beach Jar by Nan Hamilton	$493.84	Airedale Welsh Lakeland Terrier etched glass platter	$20.51
Bedlington Terrier Figurine Dhal Jensen Copenhagen	$275.01	Goebel Airedale Terrier Dog Figurine	$20.50
VINTAGE DOG WIRE-HAIRED FOX TERRIER ETCHING SIGNED	$128.92	AIREDALE TERRIER-DOG-SHOW-BUCKLE-NEW-GREAT GIFT	$20.00
Papier M??iredale Terrier Wall Clock ~Unique~	$110.00	AIREDALE Terrier with Mummy Handsculpted Clay Original	$19.95
Wire Fox/Lakeland/Airedale TERRIER Bookends ENGLAND	$77.01	@ Handmade Pewter Figurine.@ Airedale Terrier	$19.90
VINTAGE AIREDALE FOX TERRIER DOG BOOKENDS	$66.00	AIREDALE TERRIER DOG SIGN terriers airedales	$19.50
Art Deco Sterling Silver Etched Glass Bracelet Airedale	$65.80	Furry Animal Dogs Goat Fur AIREDALE TERRIER PUPPY DOG	$19.47
SCARCE 1938 Airedale Terrier Morgan Dennis Dog Art Book	$57.78	AIREDALE Terrier Gooming can be FUN Sculpture	$19.45
Needle Felted Airedale Terrier by Wooliedales	$56.55	Vintage Airedale Kerry Blue Irish Terrier wine bar cork	$19.39
WELSH Airedale roller coaster original art painting ABB	$56.00	Vintage Completed Cross Stitch Wire Fox Terrier Airdale	$19.08
BEAUTIFUL CUSTOM PORTRAIT OF YOUR AIREDALE TERRIER DOG	$55.00	*TERRIER ANGEL PIN* Airedale Irish Welsh Fox Lakeland	$18.99
Vintage Framed AIREDALE TERRIER PAINTING-Signed	$52.00	CHRISTMAS IN JULY Airedale Terrier Angel Ornament Sally	$18.99
PHOTO LOCKET NECKLACE*Airedale Irish Welsh Terrier	$50.77	Furry Plush Stuffed Animal AIREDALE TERRIER PUPPY DOG	$18.97
Old Chalk Lady & Airedale Terrier Dog Doorstop / Statue	$49.00	AIREDALE TERRIER SNOWMAN Greeting Cards by Renaud	$18.95
Airedale Green Straw Hand Bag!! Hand Painted	$46.99	French Porcelain Knife Rest, 2 Terrier dogs, CUTE dog	$18.51

Animals ▶ Dolphin

The average sales price in this subcategory is $23.62.

Item	HIGH	Item	AVG
DOLPHIN 6' BRONZE FOUNTAIN sculpture beach Pool Art	$1,050.00	Dolphin Pair Night Shirt The Mountain Adult One Size	$22.99
Wyland Dolphin & Baby Prothole,Limited Edition AP-10.	$1,000.00	Romancing the Moon Dolphins Adult Nightshirt Mountain	$22.99
DOLPHIN VOYAGE~Balinese Carved Wood Wall Panels~ART	$87.50	NEON JUMPING DOLPHIN/FISH LIGHT SIGN,WALL/TABLE/BAR,E1	$22.99
New Large Dolphin 30" Lamp 3 Dolphins	$49.99	* DOLPHIN Heaven Sea WYLAND Bath / BEACH TOWEL New Gift	$20.50
DOLPHIN FLEECE JACKET THICK DOLPHINS SIZE XL BEAUTIFUL	$38.00	Bountiful Reef DOLPHIN & Sealife WALL CLOCK Dolphins	$20.45
Lassen Dolphin Whale figurine Limited Music Box	$37.99	DOLPHIN Bath/ Area Rug 51" CM Brand NEW Bathroom Mat	$20.00
DOLPHIN FISH CAR SEAT COVERS NEW GREY SEATCOVERS pp	$37.95	3 LARGE 50X60 DOLPHIN BEACH BLANKET THROW TOWEL NEW	$20.00
Lassen Dolphin A Perfect World Lucite figurine Limited	$32.01	NEW! XLG DOLPHIN DOLPHINS	$19.99
MANATEE and PUP ~ COPPER METAL FIGURINE Statue	$29.99	FISH OCEAN SEA FLEECE BLANKET	$19.99
Dolphin Patchwork Bags ~ Dolphins in Moonlight Purse ~	$26.50	3 LARGE 50X60 DOLPHIN BEACH BLANKET THROW TOWEL NEW	$19.99
[2 of these sold for $26.50 each]		dolphins Wallclock ! cool * clock	$17.49
Dolphin Gift Set Tea Light Snow Globe Oil Burner NIB	$25.89	BEAUTIFUL DOLPHINS Wall Clock Dolphin Clocks	$16.95
'AFRICAN ART:SHONA (ZIMBABWE) - DETAILED VERDITE DOLPHIN	$24.99	Robert Wyland Dolphin & Reef Afghan Blanket	$15.51
DOLPHINS /OCEAN ~ BAMBOO BEADED CURTAIN #43	$24.95	Dolphin snow globe music box	$14.99
Wyland Ocean Life Deluxe Snowdome Snowglobe plus+...MIB	$24.90	SET OF 4 FIGURINES DOLPHINS PLAY ON ACRYLIC SEA WAVES	$14.99
NEON JUMPING DOLPHIN/FISH LIGHT SIGN,WALL/TABLE/BAR,E1	$24.75	Lassen Dolphin Pair Leaping Clear Resin - 9861	$14.99

Animals ▶ Elephant

The average sales price in this subcategory is $21.17.

Item	HIGH	Item	AVG
ANTIQUE HUGE ELEPHANT IVORY TUSK SCULPTURE TAXIDERMY 24	$754.00	Elephant Lovers Collector Fitz & Floyd Ceramic Shelf NR	$22.83
Rare Elephant Statue Limited Edition	$299.00	Early Harmony Kingdom 1995 Box ED's SAFARI Signed MIB	$22.72
Rinconada Elephant Candy / Cookie Jar - *AP VHTF	$273.99	LENOX JEWELED ELEPHANT SALT AND PEPPER SHAKER NIB	$22.50
African Elephant Ivory Antique Carved Tusk (NO RESERVE!	$256.99	ELEPHANT TAPESTRY THROW AFGHAN BLANKET NEW	$22.45
GENUINE ELEPHANT EAR BIG FIVE PAINTING LION LEOPARD	$180.00	Pair of Artesania Rinconada Elephants #9	$22.27
ELEPHANT TEAPOT VERY RARE 1920, BEAUTIFUL !!!	$180.00	LENOX JEWELED ELEPHANT SALT AND PEPPER SHAKER NIB	$22.00
Milk Glass Elephant Covered Dish	$157.77	~Tina's Song~ Memorial Tribute Book Edition Four	$21.50
UNIQUE HAND CARVED 5 PIECE ELEPHANT TABLE- TEAK WOOD	$125.00	The Herd BEAU (retired) Elephant by Marty Martha Carey	$21.50
7 J.H. Miller Waxy Plastic Hut Natives Rhino Gorilla ++	$100.99	Arthur Court Elephant Picture Frame 5" x 7"	$20.50
HUGE STUFFED ELEPHANT GIGANTIC JUMBO BRAND NEW PLUSH	$99.00	RARE ELEPHANT ZIPPO LIGHTER?	$20.50
ELEPHANT HEAD WITH TUSK SCULPTURE BY TOSCANO, resin	$88.00	CUTE MCCOY POTTERY GREEN ELEPHANT CREAMER PITCHER	$20.50
HUGE STUFFED ELEPHANT GIGANTIC JUMBO BRAND NEW PLUSH	$61.00	THE HERD BY MARTHA CAREY BLUE IS RETIRED	$20.07
RUCINNI ELEPHANT BOX,SWAROVSKI CRYSTALS,RB24	$59.99	Set of 10 Note Cards ~Shirley by Jac~ TES	$20.00
? 1970s? Large Brass Elephant Dail Telephone (NEAT)	$57.95	*OUTRAGIOUS BIG BATIK ELEPHANT TAPESTRY~GOOD LUCK~!*	$20.00
OLD BRASS FIGURAL ELEPHANT DESK BELL FOR HOTEL SERVICE	$51.00	Vintage Cast Iron Elephant Book Ends ~ Estate ~	$19.99

Animals ▶ Fish

The average sales price in this subcategory is $19.91.

Item	HIGH	Item	AVG
60 inch Sailfish Taxidermy Fish Mount Replica	$250.00	Beautiful Rainbow Trout Wall Mt .Taxidermy App. fish	$21.21
60 inch Sailfish Taxidermy Fish Mount Replica	$200.00	Abalone & sterling jointed fish bottle opener, 7-1/4"	$21.06

	HIGH		AVG
TROPHY 2 BASS TREE—TROUT-BLUEGILL-CRAPPIE-TAXIDERMY	$200.00	9PC./FISH NET SET/FISHING NETS/NAUTICAL DECOR/#2	$21.02
		1954 Miller Studio Chalkware Fish, Seahorse, Shell, Ect	$20.50
Flying Fish Figurine made in Denmark Royal Copenhagen	$173.50	Tiny Bronze Goldfish. Signed.	$20.50
58 inch Wahoo Taxidermy Fish Mount Replica Art	$169.00	NEW - BIG MOUTH BILLY BASS – BATTERY OR 120V - LOOK	$20.50
Ancient Treasur HAND CUT Wooden	$110.01	Unique Vintage "Fish" Creamer, Germany	$20.50
Jigsaw Puzzle - ROUND!		SNOOK REDFISH 28" replicas Wall Mount pair fish	$19.99
Rare Live Coral Blastomussa Welsi - 02 colony	$106.00	MAHI MAHI 28" Taxidermy Plaque Wall Mount dorado fish	$19.98
Rare Live Coral Blastomussa Welsi - 02 colony	$105.00	[2 of these sold in a multiple item ("Dutch") auction for $9.99 each]	
Huge Lot of Vintage Chalkware Fish Miller Studio	$103.50	MANATEES manatee Wall plaque 3pack ocean seacows	$19.98
Stealhead Trout Salmon chainsaw carving fishing art NR	$100.99	[2 of these sold in a multiple item ("Dutch") auction for $9.99 each]	
Live Coral Blastomussa Merleti Colony	$96.01	Trout Fish Cattails Fishing Rod Rustic Cabin Decor Art	$19.95
Gorgeous purple tang live saltwater fish lrg 4.5"-5.5"	$79.00	SET CERAMICRAFT VINTAGE WALL POCKET FISH BIG EYE	$19.19
Pretty Fish Figurine made in Denmark Royal Copenhagen	$78.00	Vintage Miller Studio Chalk Bathroom Fish Wall Plaques	$19.05
Live Coral Large Acropora Efforescens Colony	$70.00	FISH MEASURING SPOON COFFEE SCOOP PEWTER W/HOOK	$18.50
primitive huge carved rustic fish garden or cabin decor	$69.99	Rustic Trout Wood Plaque Lodge Cabin Fisherman DecorNEW	$18.50

Animals ▶ Frog

The average sales price in this subcategory is $10.45.

	HIGH		AVG
Sigi Animal Jewelry & Sculptures, Silver Frog Ring	$95.95	Frog Haitian oil drum metal frogs decor art tropical	$12.50
Metlox Poppytrail Frog with Tie Cookie Jar	$66.15	3 Green Glass Frog Figures - CUTE	$12.50
Frog Goose Egg Swarovski /Pearl Bejeweled Keepsake Box	$64.99	Cobalt Blue Glass Frog Figurine - Made in USA Mosser	$10.99
New Frog Poker Chip Card Game Set Frogs Games Chips	$49.99	FROG PRINCE STATUE FOR SHELF MONITOR / GARDEN	$10.99
NICE Bronze TIFFANY STUDIOS	$45.88	TROPICAL RAINFOREST TREE FROG WALL CLOCK	$10.95
NEW YORK FROG PAPERWEIGHT		KOOKY FROG Windchimes Wind Chimes Welcome Frogs	$10.65
Blue Sky Clayworks GIRAFFE Tealight Holder	$38.00	2 Cast Iron Frog Hook Coat Hanger Rack Frogs Wall Hooks	$10.50
SIGNED BRONZE TIFFANY FROG	$36.00	VINTAGE THREE CAST IRON DANCING FROGS FROG OLD GARDEN	$10.49
FROM THE HEREND'S MEADOW COLLECTION	$33.85	TREE FROG CERAMIC PLANTER POT VASE STONE GLAZED W/ROPE	$10.00
Pink angelskin Coral Carved FROG on Black Coral Log	$33.00	Laser Cut Pewter Charm: FROG PAIR ON Crystal	$10.00
2 Axius Seat cover Covers TREE FROG Frogs NEW	$31.00	[2 of these sold in a multiple item ("Dutch") auction for $5.00 each]	
^ TREE FROG FROGS 4 INSULATED TERVIS TUMBLERS 16OZ	$29.99	Real Cane Toad Coin Purse! Amphibian Taxidermy	$9.99
RARE Vintage Sears NEIL THE FROG Pair Window Curtains	$28.77	FROG POND FLOATER- SITTING ROWING ON LOTUS LEAF!	$9.99
New Tiffany Style Stained Glass Lamp Frog with Umbrella	$28.55	FROG PARTY LIGHTS STRING FROGS PATIO LIGHT PRIMAL	$9.99
Vintage FROG Flip Phone Telephone w Croaking Sound CUTE	$28.00	VINTAGE FROG PLANTER MCCOY?	$9.99
JEANETTE ADAMS SILVESTRI MAJOLICA STYLE FROG TEAPOT	$27.00	FROGS AND DRAGONFLIES BANNER NEW W/NR!!	$9.99

Animals ▶ Insect, Butterfly

The average sales price in this subcategory is $11.30.

	HIGH		AVG
INSECTS/BEETLES/LARGE FRAMED COLLECTION OF BEETLES 2	$89.98	6 HUGE Insects Bugs for Garden, Science Lab.. Etc......	$11.50
Bald-Faced Hornet Wasp Nest	$84.00	Beetles Insects PHYLIUM PULCHRIFOLIUM leaf mimic	$11.02
RARE REAL PINK ORCHID MANTID FLOWER MIMIC ONLY ONE 2301	$56.00	INSECT I.D.CARDS~1962~MCGRAW HILL~WITH BOX	$11.01
14KT SOLID GOLD BEE JEWELRY PIN / PENDANT WITH DIAMOND	$49.00	Beetles Insects PHYLIUM Sp Brown Form Leaf mimic	$11.00
Exotic 21 Specimen Insect Collection with Scorpion **	$47.99	Russian blown glass animal figurine ART SPIDER! #03	$10.99
RARE REAL STRANGE DEAD LEAF MIMIC MANTID ONLY ONE 2302	$47.57	Russian Glass Blown Animals Figurine ART Insect SNAIL	$10.52
26 Exotic Beetles/Walking Stick/Lanternfly	$45.01	Russian Glass Blown Animals Figurine ART GRASSHOPPER	$10.50
Framed Insect: Long Legged Walking Stick (Taxidermy)	$43.00	2 Vintage Enameled House Fly Scatter Pins MintCond	$10.49
TARANTULA spider Beveled Glass FrameTaxidermy	$42.00	Italian 92.5 Sterling Silver SCORPION Ring size 8.5	$10.49
Framed insects - 7 pcs Exotic Insects - Thorny stick	$39.99	Russian Glass Blown Animals Figurine INSECT BUTTERFLY	$10.45
Framed Insect: Giant Spider (Aplopelma minax)	$39.99	*SPIDER* RUSSIAN ART BLOWN GLASS FIGURINE #662	$10.00
Walking Stick Insect, male, winged	$39.99	Vintage Grasshopper Japan Figurine Jiminy Cricket	$9.99
Framed Butterflies: Blue Menelaus & Assorted(Taxderimy)	$39.99	LARGE FRAMED CENTIPEDE SE ASIA Insect spiny	$9.99
FRAMED TARANTULA - PERU	$34.95	*SPIDER* RUSSIAN ART BLOWN GLASS FIGURINE #667	$9.99
Insect Collection display Box 16 x 20 inches	$32.00	INSECT Family Phasmatidae Female Walking Stick beetle	$9.99

Animals ▶ Monkey, Ape

The average sales price in this subcategory is $11.63.

	HIGH		AVG
AWESOME GORILLA BRONZE SCULPTURES!!! FANTASTIC DETAIL!!	$118.50	MONKEY WITH GEM- Necklace Jewelry	$12.88
KONGDOM SLOT MACHINES King Kong Gorilla theme!	$109.50	*MO's MONKEYS* SoCk MoNkEy " VINTAGE SOCK GAL"	$12.83
HOWARD PIERCE PORCELAIN MONKEYS	$77.09	Micro Foam Bead -Monkey- Soft Pillow Stuff Animal Ape	$12.51
HUGE GORILLA ! JUMBO GIGANTIC PLUSH STUFFED APE MONKEY	$69.99	OLD JADE OR ALABASTER FIGURINE OF 3 MONKEYS	$12.50
13" JIMBY Plush Monkey Beanbag Russ Berrie NICE	$52.00	Fine Metal See Hear Speak No Evil Monkey Trio Figurine	$12.06
VINTAGE TOY MONKEY GIRL TIPPY RUSHTON COMPANY	$49.65	Apes MONKEYS SPEAK NO SEE NO	$12.00
Vint Big Brother Sock Monkey 23" w/21" Tail and Levis	$42.09	HEAR NO EVIL VISOR CAP HAT	
Musical Jolly Chimp Daishin Toy	$40.00	BIG GEORGE The GORILLA~~by TY~~26"~~MWT~~Gorgeous~	$12.00
HUGE KING KONG MOVIE (1932) PROMO POSTER WOW!	$39.99	QUARRY CRITTERS~GORILLA~GUMBO	$11.99
[2 of these sold for $39.99 each]		Vintage sock monkey 17 1/2 inches stuffed w/ nylons	$11.76
Vintage Zip Zippy Monkey / Chimp Rushton Co. 1960s	$38.50	Rinconada JJC Carbajales Japanese Blue Monkey Baby NEW	$11.51
MINT JIMBY MONKEY BY RUSSI STILL HAS TAGS! 14 1/2"	$36.65	Beach Sock Monkey Stuffed Doll Sand $ and Crabs	$11.50
Fragile World Worried Monkey~Limited Edition NIB	$35.00	monkey ape chimp plush pillow too cute new fur trim	$11.49
Rushton, Howdy Doody Zippy Zip Chimp Monkey, no resv	$29.01	Unique Monkey Banana Holder Kitchen Houseware Ape	$11.00
A1730 3D Crystal Laser Art Animal Figure MONKEY GORILLA	$26.00	BRASS MONKEY Desktop BUSINESS CARD HOLDER	$10.99
SOCK MONKEY SET OF 5 ORNAMENTS MIDWEST of CANNON FALLS	$26.00	Monkeys - Monkey Hawaiin Palm Tree Electric Table Lamp	$10.88

Animation Art, Characters ▶ Animation Art

The average sales price in this subcategory is $35.12.

	HIGH		AVG
Dr. Seuss Signed Color Drawing of the Grinch on Page	$630.88	signed ===== Winnie the Pooh === cel =======	$46.55
Superpowers cel Batman Superman WW Robin others	$615.25	The Racoons - Animation Sequence #2	$45.00
Dr. Seuss Signed Color Drawing of Fish from Cat in Hat	$585.00	WB BOB KANE BATMAN FRAMED LITHO ·LAST PIECE	$44.99
LOONEY TUNES WARNER BROS ANIMATION ART OF FRIZ FRELENG	$506.61	10 "MY LITTLE PONY CELS" "$20"~Free Shipping~1 DAY ONLY	$40.00
Villains of Gotham City I and II Animation Cel Sericel	$500.00	[2 of these sold in a multiple item ("Dutch") auction for $20.00 each]	
Bob Kane, Charles Schulz & Jim Davis Signed Sketches	$460.00	Shade Tree Cowboy Collectible 211	$39.99
Jim Henson Signed Color Drawing of Kermit the Frog	$382.00	Rare Shadow Box Batman Original Art (not statue) NR	$39.95
Dr. Seuss, Charles Schulz & Bob Kane Signed Sketches	$355.00	Space Ghost full cast pencil drawing NICE 1980	$34.99
Bad Girls of Gotham Animation Cel Sericel	$350.00	HANNA & BARBERA SKETCH SIGNED AUTOGRAPH FLINTSTONE	$34.00
Original Aladdin Animation Cel - Disney 1992	$312.00	WB Scooby Doo Batman Superman lithograph WOW	$31.01
Framed Walt Disney Lumicels Mickey Mouse Picture	$285.00	Bugs Bunny Matted animation cel awesome	$31.00
WARNER BROTHERS SHERWOOD	$281.11	Archie Comics Wall Art Collectible Veronica Betty Rare	$30.99
FOREST II ANIMATION CEL NR!!!!		1987 Vintage Bill the Cat Bloom County Dakin Plush	$28.75
George Herriman Signed Amazing Drawing on Onion Paper	$170.27	Barney Bear from "Impossible Possum"	$27.99
Bill Hanna & Joe Barbera Signed Flintstones Drawing	$160.27	Bugs Bunny "Jack Wabbit & the Beanstalk"	$27.87
Gary Trudeau Signed Doonesbury Drawing on Card	$159.28	Two Vintage Woody WoodPecker Walter Lantz	$27.76

Animation Art, Characters ▶ Animation Characters

The average sales price in this subcategory is $15.97.

	HIGH		AVG
UNCLE SCROOGE MCDUCK SPORT	$1,499.99	1969 P&G Pogo figure - "Pogo Possum"	$17.99
OF TYCOONS BRONZE SCULPTURE		1969 P&G Pogo figure - "Porky Pine"	$17.99
Classic Pooh Calendar with Collectible Plates	$200.00	Aqua Teen Hunger Force Series 1 MASTER SHAKE Figure!	$17.00
Electric Tiki MIGHTY MOUSE Maquette Statue NOT Bowen	$183.49	*CUTE*-"Happy Bunny-All about me" bag/backpack	$16.49
Bellywashers	$120.00	SEALAB 2021 Series 1 Debbie Dupree \ Dr Quinn Figures!	$16.00
Taarna Heavy Metal Production Cel #1	$102.50	Rainbow Brite & Strawberry Shortcake Series (3 DVD) Set	$16.00
MEN IN BLACK MIB - WORM ALIEN - MOVIE prop -19 INCH	$18.00	[2 of these sold for $16.00 each]	
Wallace and Gromit Lot Watch Clock Magnet totes ec	$52.00	Rainbow Brite & Strawberry Shortcake Series (3 DVD) Set	$16.00
Vintage The Bonzo Book (Bonzo on the Film) by Studdy	$51.01	Wallace & Gromit Clock Tower Alarm Clock	$15.85
Avatar The Last Airbender San Diego Comic Con Cards	$43.00	Nightmare Before Christmas Sally Doll Hot Topic NWT	$15.50
Beatrix Potter Figurines, Lot of 4, great condition!	$42.36	DISNEY 1988 MICKEY MOUSE ANIMATION CELL	$15.50
ULTIMATE X-MEN #61 RETAILER Variant COIPEL SKETCH COVER	$39.99	Comic Con items V for Vendetta, Corpse Bride and more	$15.39
EMILY THE STRANGE SABBATH KITTY RAG DOLL PLUSH (NEW)	$39.99	Wallace and Gromit set of 4 magnets	$15.00
Rat Fink boxed action figure mint ! red jersey.	$36.65	8 TINKERBELL DIARIES / DIARY- PARTY FAVORS	$14.99
VINTAGE 1987 BILL THE CAT PLUSH FROM BLOOM COUNTY	$36.00	MICKEY MOUSE DESK COASTER (NEW)	$14.99
HUGE LOT LISA FRANK 31 SHEETS COLLECTIBLE STICKERS MINT	$36.00	G.I.Joe Baroness mini bust Palisades NEW MINT IN BOX	$14.99

Animation Art, Characters ▶ Japanese, Anime

The average sales price in this subcategory is $18.26.

	HIGH		AVG
Mazinger Z and Gran Mazinger DVD Spanish Complete Saga	$330.00	Naruto Rock Lee Cushion W/Wristband [Brand New] Rare!	$19.99
[6 of these sold in a multiple item ("Dutch") auction for $55.00 each]		MIB Space Channel 5 ACTION FIGURES! PUDDING and EVILA!	$19.99
Takatoku GOSHOGUN Diecast Combat Action MIB Popy	$275.00	DRAGONBALL Z COMICS MANGA VIZ VOLS 5-20	$19.99
ComBattler V Soul of Chogokin GX-01 BANDAI Die cast	$127.50	Initial D model Car figure (AE86 FC3S WRX)	$19.99
Weiss kreuz anime Ken Model Goggles - collector's item!	$120.00	Lucky Cat Baby - Hidamari no Tami Maneki Neko RARE ITEM	$19.00
Full Moon wo sagashite Mitsuki Dress cosplay anime	$109.99	3CD SILENT HILL 1,2,3 ORIGINAL SOUNDTRACK Game Music CD	$18.99
Dirty Pair Flash Completed PVC Statue Figure Anime RARE	$84.99	SAMURAI JACK Warrior Action Figure Cartoon Network NEW!	$18.50
Anime Girls Bravo Miharu 1/8 PVC girl Figure Hentai	$79.99	JAPAN MARIO PARTY "#5,YOSHI PLUSH Doll"	$18.49
Mazinger Z Sexy Sayaka GREAT Figure RARE Mazinkaiser	$71.00	3 CD GRAN TURISMO 4 OST/Classic/	$17.99
Bandai 1/850 Star Trek USS Voyager Model Kit	$71.00	Inspired SOUNDTRACK NEW	
PLEASE TEACHER MIZUHO KAZAMI RESIN STATUE 1/6 SC NEW	$69.99	Silent Hill Navigation Book Famitsu Konami Jp PSX 1999	$17.75
LEGEND of ZELDA GAME MUSIC COMPLETE 11 CD+DVD US Seller	$65.99	Pinky:st Pinky Street Captain ANIMATE ver.2 limited	$17.50
Japan Anime FUSHIGINO UMINO NADIA LD W/OBI HIDEAK/0804O	$61.00	MINT Gravitation Shuichi and Yuki BABY DOLL T-SHIRT!	$17.15
MAZINGER Z Soul of Chogokin GX-01 BANDAI Die cast Popy	$59.00	Gundam Seed Destiny Japan Photo Collection Vol. 2 - 3pk	$17.00
Pia Carrot Takako Kinoshita Figure by Kotobukiya in US	$58.99	Legend of Zelda GBA Import Famicom Mini Version	$17.00
Robotech VFA-6Z Sue Graham Shadow Masterpiece Macross	$55.52	YAMATO G-TASTE REN HAUMI 8" STORY! IMAGE! FIGURE! SEXY	$16.99

Arcade, Jukeboxes & Pinball ▶ Arcade

The average sales price in this subcategory is $250.31.

	HIGH		AVG
CRUISN EXOTICA 31" TWIN DRIVING GAMES by midway	$4,200.00	Mortal Combat II Video arcade game	$255.00
Monster Bash Pinball	$3,747.82	Sega Wave Runner full arcade game Works! Nice Shape	$255.00
LARGE WAREHOUSE OF ARCADE GAMES**NO RESERVE**	$3,000.00	NEOGEO AERO FIGHTERS/SAMURAI	$250.00
Video Arcade Cabinet Compatible with MAME(TM) XBOX, PS2	$2,895.00	SHOWDOWN ARCADE VIDEO GAME	$250.00
Gold Zone by Benchmark Arcade Redemption Game Coin-Op	$2,695.00	Neo Geo MVS 2 slot Video arcade game w/ Bust a move 25"	$250.00
CRUISN WORLD TWIN S/D DRIVING GAMES by midway	$2,200.00	SEGA Naomi Wild Rider Arcade	$250.00
Merit Megatouch Slim Maxx	$2,050.00	Choplifter CHOPPER 1 Coin-op VIDEO Arcade MACHINE	$250.00
Sapphire 2 Arcade Game DBV NR		SAMMY ATOMISWAVE King of Fighters: NEOWAVE Working 100%	$250.00
GOLDEN TEE 2005 EXTRA-LIKE NEW-MAKE OFFER NOW!!	$1,875.00	ARCADE SPY HUNTER STAND UP GAME COIN OPERATED	$250.00
Pot O Silver Quarter Coin/Pusher/Slider*Money Maker	$1,795.00	SPY HUNTER Full Size Arcade Game ~RARE~	$249.99
Ms Pac Man Galaga Arcade Game Cocktail Table $1	$1,699.00	Duck Hunt Stand Up Arcade Video Game Coin Op NO RESERVE	$237.50

[2 of these sold for $1,699.00 each]		LOT OF 100 JUKEBOX CD'S / WITH TITLE STRIPS	$237.50
Hydro Thunder sit down Boat racing Game	$1,525.00	GLADIATOR ~ VIDEO ARCADE GAME BY TAITO ~ NO RESERVE!!!	$234.50
Claim Jumper Coin-Op Redemption Arcade Game NO RESERVE	$1,355.55	Dragon's Lair / Space Ace Complete Harness - NEW	$230.00
GALAGA ARCADE GAME	$1,349.99	[2 of these sold in a multiple item ("Dutch") auction for $115.00 each]	
Pot-O-Silver Quarter Coin Pusher/Slider Money Maker	$1,311.00	1915 Vintage Watling Penny Scale Antique	$228.86
ARCADE PHOTOBOOTH PHOTO BOOTH	$1,300.00	GALAXIAN Arcade Machine Classic by Midway **working**	$227.50

Arcade, Jukeboxes & Pinball ▶ Jukeboxes

The average sales price in this subcategory is $572.61.

	HIGH		AVG
Orchestrion coin juke box music arcade guitar banjo	$17,950.00	Rowe Jukebox CD s & Records 45 s Very Nice Oldies	$660.03
Orchestrion coin juke box music arcade guitar banjo	$10,200.00	Vintage 1951 Wurlitzer 1450 Custom Jukebox	$660.00
VINTAGE 1946 WURLITZER MODEL #1015 BUBBLE JUKE BOX	$9,249.99	JUKEBOX ROCKOLA Ultra 437 (45's)	$610.00
Wurlitzer 800 Jukebox Excellent unrestored condition	$8,100.00	ROCKOLA 1936 SERIES B JUKEBOX	$600.00
Original 1947 WURLITZER 1015!!!!! PERFECT SHAPE!!!!!	$7,600.00	1952 AMI Model D-80 Jukebox	$600.00
Rock-Ola "Bubbler" CD Jukebox - IN OAK!!	$5,595.00	Rockola Wurlitzer Style Full Size Neon Jukebox Juke Box	$584.99
Vint 1956 Wurlitzer Juke Box THE CENTENNIAL 100 records	$5,584.84	AMI Rowe R 92 6 CD 100 45's Combo Jukebox Works Great!!	$576.66
NEW WURLITZER 1015 CD FULL SIZE JUKEBOX W/REMOTE	$5,400.00	Seeburg STD3 "Sunstar" Jukebox	$537.99
nickelodeon player piano music box jukebox arcade coin	$5,250.00	1959 WURLITZER 2300	$535.00
Restored Seeburg VL-200 Jukebox Absolutely Beautiful !	$5,995.00	ROCK-OLA MODEL 1484 WALL 1958 JUKEBOX /WITH RECORDS	$510.00
Seeburg Select-O-Matic 100 Jukebox	$4,250.00	WURLITZER 600 JUKEBOX - MULTI SELECTOR 1939	$499.99
Packard Manhatten	$4,000.00	Rockola 1448 Icicle 1955	$499.00
Early Wurlitzer Jutebox #1015 Restoration Project	$3,845.00	THE BEST 45 JUKEBOX , Rock Ola 459 Juke Box,	$495.00
WURLITZER 1100 JUKEBOX	$3,805.00	AMI ROWE JUKEBOX MODEL D80 Year 1951/1952	$460.00
Wurlitzer One More Time 45's Jukebox	$3,500.00	Rowe AMI R-87 45 RPM Jukebox Working	$455.00

Arcade, Jukeboxes & Pinball ▶ Pinball

The average sales price in this subcategory is $487.32.

	HIGH		AVG
WILLIAMS MONSTER BASH 1998 PINBALL MACHINE ~LIKE NEW!~	$4,500.01	Williams WINNER Pinball -Vintage 1972	$524.00
Nascar Pinball Machine manufactured br Stern !	$3,999.00	Monte Carlo Pinball Machine By Bally	$520.00
[3 of these sold for $3,999.00 each]		STELLAR WARS Pinball Machine by Williams, NR!	$500.00
NEW! NASCAR pinball from STERN pre-sale	$3,995.00	Working 1979 Stern Meteor Pinball Machine!!	$500.00
Sharper Image: The Simpsons Pinball Party	$3,700.00	BALLY Western FLIP FLOP Pinball 1975 Vintage Works !!!	$499.00
Twilight Zone Williams Pinball Machine EXCELLENT	$3,550.00	DRAGON PINBALL GOTTLIEB GREAT CONDITION	$499.00
Addam's Family Pinball - BEST ON EBAY- Addams Arcade	$3,495.00	Williams 3 Coins Pinball Machine Bally Gottlieb	$499.00
LORD OF THE RINGS PINBALL by STERN, Like New Demo Unit	$3,495.00	Gottliebs DERBY DAY pinball machine 1956 L@@K	$488.98
South Park Pinball Machine Sega Pin Southpark Arcade	$3,450.00	MR & MS PACMAN COIN PINBALL	$480.00
ADDAMS FAMILY PINBALL by BALLY ~ COLLECTIBLE GAME & NR!	$3,350.00	ARCADE GAME-- NO RESERVE!!	
THEATRE OF MAGIC PINBALL BY BALLY	$2,999.99	Bally MOTORDOME Pinball Great Shape Low Reserve	$476.75
BALLY WILLIAMS THE ADDAMS FAMILY PINBALL MACHINE	$2,999.00	SURE SHOT Pinball Machine....GREAT Backglass	$475.00
1993 BALLY TWILIGHT ZONE PINBALL MACHINE	$2,995.00	Williams Taxi Project Pinball Machine	$455.00
WILLIAMS INDIANA JONES PINBALL MACHINE VERY NICE!!	$2,948.00	Gotlieb Time Line Pinball Machine Very Nice Low reserv	$450.00
Theatre of Magic Pinball Machine Theater	$2,790.00	JackPot Pin Ball Machine by Williams - Vintage Works	$450.00
CREATURE FROM THE BLACK LAGOON PINBALL ~SUPER BALLY ~NR	$2,700.00	VINTAGE 1975 D. GOTTLIEB TOP SCORE 3 BALL PINBALL GAME	$446.00

Autographs ▶ Historical

The average sales price in this subcategory is $166.19.

	HIGH		AVG
Standard Oil Trust, 1882 - signed JOHN D. ROCKEFELLER	$4,600.00	Harry Houdini Signed Cut - Magical Item	$177.50
JOHN COLTRANE Pot For Four handwritten music	$4,250.00	Thomas Nast Signed Fantastic Drawing - Very Rare	$172.61
GEORGE WASHINGTON AUTOGRAPH LETTER !!! No Reserve	$2,275.00	VMF-214 Black Sheep Squadron WOW 8 signatures	$172.50
Pierre Auguste Renoir Signed Drawing of Female Nude	$1,526.00	Enola Gay signed Corgi 1:144 scale model Paul Tibbets	$171.38
Horatio Alger holograph of Carving A Name	$1,500.00	CALVIN COOLIDGE, TLS; RE: 1924 ELECTION	$170.48
DAVID "DAVY" CROCKET SIGNED PARTIAL DOCUMENT 1832	$1,199.00	Rare ENOLA GAY 24"x30" AUTOGRAPHED BY FOUR OF THE CREW!	$170.00
CIVIL WAR LADY DOCTOR, MARY E. WALKER POW/MOH, ALS.	$1,125.00	Apollo 11 Crew autographs	$168.38
WRIGHT BROTHERS WILBUR AND ORVILLE WRIGHT SIGNED	$1,121.00	Rare 1950s Bobby Fischer signed Lasker's chess book!	$165.50
Charles Bukowski poem letter signed with autograph	$1,052.00	Oliver Wendell Holmes Jr.- Supreme Court Justice- ANSI	$164.99
Chester W Nimitz ADMIRAL HISTORICAL SIGNED PHOTO SANDER	$957.50	AMERICAN NOVELIST JACK KEROUAC CUT SIGNATURE	$159.50
Leland Stanford signed Central Pacific deed 1885	$950.00	Generals Signed Pic Omar Bradley, Powell & Schwarzkopf	$156.12
PRESIDENT ABRAHAM LINCOLN CUT SIGNATURE	$950.00	Amelia Earhart, Amy Johnson, James Mollison Signed Pic	$154.01
Autograph, Charles Guiteau, Assassin of Pres. Garfield	$949.00	Jimmy Doolittle Signed Autographed Photo/Letter NR	$152.50
President John Kennedy Signed Card X5 + Kennedy Family	$937.99	SUPREME COURT CARDS EARL WARREN & WILLIAM O.DOUGLAS	$152.50
AUTOGRAPH ED 8 x 10 Sepia Photo of THOMAS EDISON	$930.00	DAVID BOWIE signed Document	$150.00

Autographs ▶ Political

The average sales price in this subcategory is $34.48.

	HIGH		AVG
1936 AUTOGRAPH SHEET w/ ALL 9 SUPREME COURT JUSTICES	$668.98	RUDY GIULIANI Signed Auto LEADERSHIP BOOK PSA/DNA	$37.12
Puerto Rico Signature Signed Letter Emeterio Betances	$499.00	Civil War BURTON signed receipts & misc. letters LOT +	$36.87
Politician Judson W. Lyons Hand Signed Cut Signature	$494.05	1944 Orig. Autographed Letter F. LaGuardia Mayor NY	$36.25
Representative Bob Mathias Hand Signed Political Photo	$483.05	Supreme Court Justice Sandra Day O'Connor signed FDC	$36.07
Representative Jim McCord Hand Signed 1943 Letter	$456.02	George W. Bush & George Bush hand-sign Autograph + COA	$36.00

Senator Edward Costigan Hand Signed Vintage Letter Head	$449.25
Mayor William Mayberry Signed 1903 Letter- Michigan	$426.02
U. S. Congressman Edward Miller Signed Political Photo	$403.52
Ambassador Chester Bowles Hand Signed 1967 Letter	$373.96
US Congressman John McCollister Signed Political Photo	$357.69
Ronald Reagan Autograph & Signing Photo of A B #1-1968	$314.99
LS-G.W.McCRARY(Sec/War)Request Military Capture Outlaws	$250.00
Saddam Hussein autograph signature signed document	$215.07
Saddam Hussein autograph signature signed document	$212.59
Robert F. Kennedy Signed Letters Photo Special Forces	$210.27

J C MCREYNOLDS Hand Signed Card Att General 1913-14	$36.00
Henry Kissinger Signed 8x10 (Nixon Secretary of State)	$36.00
William Owsley Governor of Kentucky - 1845	$36.00
Shah of Iran M.R.Pahlavi signed 1958 United Nations FDC	$34.99
WOMENS SUFFRAGE GOVERNOR COLORADO SIGNED DOCUMENT 1895!	$34.33
Dalai Lama Hand signed Autograph + COA	$32.89
Nixon-Ford Sec.of State Henry Kissinger signed BIG Book	$32.00
John McCain signed 1999 First Edition Vietnam book!	$31.01
Charles S. Morehead Governor of Ky. 1855-1859	$31.00
RUDY GIULIANI Hand Signed Autograph Autographed Photo	$30.51

Banks, Registers & Vending ▸ Banks

The average sales price in this subcategory is $64.68.

	HIGH		AVG
ANTIQUE DARKTOWN BATTERY IRON MECHANICAL BANK	$4,570.00	DURO SOUTHERN COMFORT MECHANICAL COIN SHOOTING BANK	$69.99
Antique Darktown Battery Cast Iron Mechanical Bank, NR!	$3,000.00	1950'S Book of Knowledge Indian shooting BEAR	$69.98
1890 J&E Stevens CLOWN ON GLOBE BANK *100% Original*	$2,500.00	WORKING CAST IRON "TRICK PONY" BANK. SUPERB! NR	$69.00
ALL ORIGINAL 1893 WORLD'S FAIR BANK (COLUMBUS BANK).	$1,490.00	Starkies Jolly N.	$69.00
SENTRY Tin Litho Mechanical Bank 1930s Germany 9"	$1,146.00	CAST IRON MECHANICAL BASEBALL BANK - HOMETOWN BATTERY	$67.62
SUPERB Vintage 1890 William Tell Mechanical Steven Bank	$850.00	Book Of Knowledge U.S. Spain Cannon Bank	$66.00
Original Shepard Hardware. Uncle Sam Bank!	$660.00	BOOK OF KNOWLEDGE TEDDY AND THE BEAR BANK B.O.K	$66.00
CAST IRON EAGLE & EAGLETS	$607.00	BOOK OF KNOWLEDGE INDIAN SHOOTING BEAR BANK B.O.K	$65.32
MECHANICAL BANK 1883 ORIGINAL		6 Antique Brass Post Office Box Doors	$65.00
Superb Antique Original Humpty Dumpty Mechanical Bank!!	$600.00	TRICK DOG BANK	$61.00
VINTAGE ANTIQUE CAST IRON MECHANICAL BANK _ WILLIAM TELL	$585.00	Spinaround planet coin bank Astro's Vacumet 1960's	$61.00
Mule Entering Barn Bank , Original (Grey) 1/6/1880	$550.00	Antique Clown Cast Iron Mechanical Bank	$60.00
J & E STEVENS TEDDY and THE BEAR	$550.00	UNCLE WIGGILY~RABBIT TOY TIN MECHANICAL BANK~J CHEIN	$59.99
Original Humpty Dumpty Cast Iron Mechanical Bank NO RE	$546.00	MECHANICAL OWL MONEY BANK "OWL TURNS HEAD"	$59.50
William Tell Mechanical Bank Guaranteed Old n Original	$531.00	251Original Mechanical Banks Full Color-BOOK	$59.00
Organ Grinder Cast Iron Mechanical Bank	$500.00	[3 of these sold for $59.00 each]	

Banks, Registers & Vending ▸ Vending

The average sales price in this subcategory is $72.81.

	HIGH		AVG
HOLCOMB & HOKE POPCORN CO. BUTTER-KIST PEANUT ROASTER	$2,550.00	VINTAGE VENDING MACHINE, 1 CENT	$76.00
[2 of these sold for $2,550.00 each]		1940's 1CENT GUM MACHINE!!!	$76.00
Antique EARLY Brass iron Matches VENDOR Vending MACHINE	$1,177.89	Vintage MI-CO Parking Meter	$76.00
1913 RELIABLE POSTAGE STAMP VENDING MACHINE	$1,026.00	WORKING MAKA NB -11B-400 DOLLAR BILL VALIDATOR	$76.00
Snack Vending Machine/ Rowe 4900	$999.00	Gumball , Simmons Coin Machine	$75.00
Soda/Juice Vending Machine Coke/Pepsi/Pop	$800.00	VINTAGE ANTIQUE STAMP MACHINE/ STAMP VENDING MACHINE	$74.99
VENDO COIN CHANGER Antique	$760.00	Telephone Pay phone Payphone p1	$74.99
Vendo Coca Cola Coke Machine		MAGIC FINGERS Motel Bed Vibrator NICE!!	$72.95
50's Vintage Candy Coin-op Vending Machine - Works!	$713.73	[3 of these sold for $72.95 each]	
Coin Changer by Vendo Company	$706.01	VINTAGE BEECH-NUT SOURS * CANDY DISPENSER MACHINE	$69.00
Watling Penny Scale with Fortune Arcade	$620.00	COIN MECH Nickel \ Dime STONER Gum Candy Machine Vendo	$68.87
1 Cent Pocket Lighter Fluid Dispenser-NO RESERVE!	$565.00	American Scale Mfg. Your Wate Your Fate Machine NR	$66.50
Van-Lite Early Lighter Fluid Coin Opp Dispenser	$515.55	STAATS MONEY CHANGER VINTAGE FEB, 25. 1890	$66.00
NORTHWESTERN SATURN 2000 ROCKETSHIP w/stand	$400.00	COIN CHANGER - IDEAL FOR OLDER COKE AND PEPSI MACHINES	$65.00
Art Deco 5¢ & 10¢ Stamp Vending Machine Counter Top	$366.00	[4 of these sold for $65.00 each]	
Pair Antique Coin Op STAMP VENDING MACHINE S Porcelain	$350.00	Coinco CT 48 Can Dispensing Mechanism - soda	$65.00
Original Condition Cigarette Vending Machine	$350.00	COIN CHANGER - IDEAL FOR OLDER COKE AND PEPSI MACHINES	$65.00

Barware ▸ Glasses, Cups, Mugs

The average sales price in this subcategory is $11.84.

	HIGH		AVG
Tiki Mug by Munktiki . Poison Mug # 141 of 150	$153.50	Makers Mark Kentucky Derby 131 Glasses - Set of Three	$14.50
VINTAGE GLASSES, *NAME YOUR POISON* SET OF *8* GOTHIC	$133.00	4 Red Wings Glasses Retired & Traded players- *MINT*	$14.50
naughty nude woman pin up girl bar glass set	$91.00	Set of 4 Western Ranch Brands Pilsner Glasses	$13.19
Kosta Boda Epoque Wine Glass in Gold by Anna Ehrner	$75.00	Guinness Pint Glasses	$13.10
MacKenzie Childs Low Ball Glass, BEAUTIFUL, COLLECTORS!	$61.00	McDonalds/Coke/Topps All Star Baseball Glasses (8)	$13.05
Pontarlier Absinthe Glasses - Hand Blown Antique Repro	$60.00	STAR TREK etched pilsner beer glasses (3) NR!!	$12.99
[3 of these sold in a multiple item ("Dutch") auction for $20.00 each]		NIB MICHELANGELO MASTERPIECE BEER MUGS~LUIGI BORMIOLI	$12.95
Vintage Drinking Glasses Set 9 Naked Hawaiian Lady Nude	$58.01	Wine glasses from Master's golf tournament	$12.73
MacKenzie Childs Low Ball Glass, BEAUTIFUL, COLLECTORS!	$54.88	Nude/Nudes/Nudie Girl Mugs-Vintage	$12.50
naughty nude woman pin up girl bar glass set	$53.01	8 Copper Beer Mugs	$12.50
NAME YOUR POISON 6 Glasses Goth Punk kitsch halloween *	$52.00	Vintage Opalescent Wine Glasses	$11.55
ANTIQUE HORN CUP DRINKING VESSEL STERLING RIMMED	$51.00	EAMES ERA 12 oz GOLD Decorated Glasses TUMBLERS Set 4	$11.51
COLECTIABLE BEER STEINS!!!! INCLUDING BUDMAN 3!!!	$50.00	~ 8 ~ Vintage Souvenir Drinking Glasses	$10.92
Peek-A-Boo Cocktail Glasses	$49.99	JAGERMEISTER 1.75LT HAND PUMP TAP NEW IN PACKAGE RARE	$10.70
Arizona Cactus Glasses Set of 8	$49.07	~VINTAGE~4.75" GLASS ~PINK MUSICAL PIGS~	$10.51
vintage tumblers cartoon devil, Negro gamblers barware	$49.00	[8 of these sold for $10.51 each]	

Barware ▸ Shot Glasses

The average sales price in this subcategory is $8.64.

	HIGH		AVG
VINTAGE HAZEL-ATLAS PINK ELEPHANT BEER MUG	$120.00	12 BLACK LIGHT CLEAR CLASSIC SHOT GLASSES - BAR LOT SET	$9.50
[2 of these sold in a multiple item ("Dutch") auction for $60.00 each]		US POSTAL SERVICE SQUARE FROSTED SHOT GLASS NEW	$9.50
72 shot glass display case, solid wood, glass door	$119.95	Lot Of 6 Shot Glasses Barbados-Bahamas-St.John-P Rico	$9.50
13 Shot Glasses Pikes Peak Knotts Berry Farm Culver ..	$100.00	Set of 4 Goldschlager Ruby Stem Triple Shot Glasses	$9.50
57 UNIQUE SHOT GLASS COLLECTION	$67.05	RED STRIPE BEER JAMAICA SHOT GLASS	$9.05
Vintage Nude Pinup Girls Shot Glasses	$66.00	24 Flashing LED shot glasses In assorted colors	$9.00
NEW Jack Daniels Chaser Jigger Shot Glasses (Set of 12)	$59.00	12 JUNIPER DEISGNER SHOT	$9.00
Old Kentucky Whiskey Shot Glass.	$57.66	GLASSES NEW BARWARE SET BAR	
40 Shooter / Shot Glass Display Case Cabinet -Hardwood	$49.95	BOTTOMS UP NUDE SHOT GLASS Vaseline Glass Deco A6570	$8.95
6 SPANISCHE HOFREITSCHUTE PIROUETTE LIPIZZAN HORSE	$42.83	HARD ROCK CAFE SHOT GLASS * CABO SAN LUCAS + OTHER	$8.50
Lot 35 Collectible Shot Glasses +2 Waterford Crystal NR	$41.00	NEW SET-6 ROYAL COPENHAGEN	$8.50
SHOT GLASS BOARD CHESS SET SHOTGLASS GAME *NEW NR	$39.96	CORDIALS/SHOT GLASSES W/BOX	
[4 of these sold in a multiple item ("Dutch") auction for $9.99 each]		Hard Rock Cafe Shot Glass - TOKYO	$8.50
2 JAGERMEISTER PEWTER STAG/ ELK SHOT GLASS / ELK HUNT	$32.00	Hand Blown Del Dueno Tequila Jade Green Shot Glass (4)	$8.50
72 COBALT BLUE DEISGNER SHOT GLASSES NEW BARWARE LOT	$32.00	4 Germany made metal shot glasses and leather case	$8.50
Shot Glasses a Rare and Unique Collection	$29.50	Vintage Cowboy Cattle/Ranch Brands Shot Glass w/Leather	$8.50
72 Brand New Shot Glasses w/"Tequila Rose" Logo	$28.99	VINTAGE 7 PIECE SHOT GLASS SET MADE IN JAPAN - ESTATE	$8.50

Bottles & Insulators ▸ Bottles

The average sales price in this subcategory is $27.36.

	HIGH		AVG
REMY MARTIN LOUIS XIII Cognac 700ml.	$1,150.00	Tequila DoN MaX Blanco SMOKE COLOR BOTTLE TALL 1.0 Ltr.	$29.99
Tres Cuatro Cinco Anejo Tequila	$400.00	Tequila DoN MaX Reposado GREEN COLOR BOTTLE TALL 1.0 Lt	$29.99
VINTAGE BACARDI SUPERIOR CARTA BLANCA RUM SPAIN*	$313.64	Tequila DoN MaX AᴺJO RED COLOR BOTTLE TALL 1.0 Litre	$29.99
Jack Daniel's UNIQUE SET OF GOLD MEDAL	$233.51	The Samson Battery Jar No 3 With Label	$29.10
Antique Larsen Cognanc Bottle and Contents circa 1960'3	$153.50	White House Vinegar Bottle (Mickey Mouse)	$29.00
Old Glass candy container rabbit running on log gold	$140.00	VARI-TONE GOLDEN AMBER VIOLIN BOTTLE	$28.00
Johnnie Johnny Walker Blue Label Scotch Whisky Rare	$137.50	COURVOISIER Very Special Cognac~Full/Sealed 375ml	$27.66
Royal Lochnagar Selected Reserve Malt Whisky Box Bottle	$132.38	Clorox Half Gallon Bottle with Label 1940's	$27.00
White House Vinegar Jar with Original Label - RARE	$117.53	VINTAGE TAYLOR FLADGATE 1ST ESTATE RESERVE PORT WINE	$27.00
1978 Glenmorangie Tain L'Hermitage Single Malt Whisky	$110.50	VINTAGE PERFECTION OIL DISPENSER CO. GLASS / LID RARE!	$26.75
TEQUILA DON JULIO 1942 ANEJO 100% blue agave 750ml.	$110.00	RARE VINTAGE FULL "FOUNT-O-INK" INK BOTTLE MINT!!	$26.50
Arizona Territory A.T. Seltzer Bottle Prescott	$106.37	VINTAGE COCKBURNS 20 YR OLD TAWNY PORT WINE BOTTLE	$26.00
RARE MILK GLASS VIOLIN BOTTLE	$103.50	Tequila Cuerno De Chivo Reposado 750ml Classic Bottle!!	$26.00
VINTAGE CHARTREUSE DIGESTIF ETCHED BOTTLE 1969	$103.50	VINTAGE 5 GALLON GLASS WATER COOLER BOTTLE JUG OLD	$25.49
VINTAGE GRAND CAMA DE LOBOS MADEIRA WINE BOTTLE	$102.50	Vintage Glass Baby Bottle	$25.00

Breweriana, Beer ▸ Bottles

The average sales price in this subcategory is $24.04.

	HIGH		AVG
Sam Adams Utopias '05 (4 NIB) '95(2)&'97(1) Triple Bock	$752.50	SPANGLER BREWING LIGHT AMBER BEER BOTTLE SPANGLER,PA.	$28.09
2001 SAM SAMUEL ADAMS UTOPIAS UTOPIA MMII	$356.26	BUDWEISER 2L BOTTLE, OKLAHOMA UNIVERSITY	$26.13
PORFIDIO ANEJO GUAJE GOURD MINT 750 ML. !!!!!!!!!!!!!!!	$350.00	LEISY'S BOCK BEER BOTTLE	$26.03
VINTAGE - POTOSI MINI BEER BOTTLE SALT & PEPPER SHAKERS	$305.00	SET 2 Lord Calvert Canadian Ceramic Whiskey Bottle Jug	$26.00
JOSEPH J. TERRIS LIGHTNING GINGER BEER	$255.00	**** 6 VINTAGE 1950's MINI BEER BOTTLES w/ CAPS ****	$26.00
1916 Coors Cereal Beverage Near Beer Bottle	$229.50	1893 Lembecks & Betz Beer Bottle - Jersey City NJ	$26.00
Sam Adams Samuel Adams Utopia Utopias 2005 edition NIB!	$189.99	Scarce BUTTE SPECIAL BEER Bottle, N/mint	$24.95
Rare 1880's G. Zeisler, La Crosse Wis. Applied top Beer	$177.77	Georgia Tech Liqueur Bottle	$24.00
SAMUEL ADAMS UTOPIAS - VERY DESIRABLE 2003 EDITION	$153.50	1930's Zoller's Pilsner Beer Bottle - Davenport, IA	$23.75
JOHNNIE WALKER 4 PK GREEN, BLUE, BLACK, GOLD JOHNNY N/R	$152.50	UNOPENED HAMMS IRTP 8OZ IN EXCELLENT CONDITION	$23.50
Sam Adams Utopia Utopias 2005 SEALED #1666/8000	$142.50	Sholtz Old Style Beer Bottle Brewed in Milan Ohio	$22.50
Sam Samuel Adams Utopia Utopias 2005 Collectable Bottle	$140.08	Fredericksburg Bottling Co. San Francisco Beer Bottle	$22.49
Sam Samuel Adams Utopia Utopias 2005 Collectable Bottle	$135.00	4 Mini Beer Bottle Shakers-Schlitz/Eastside/Acme/Pabst	$22.01
Sam Samuel Adams Utopia Utopias 2005 NIB (NO RESERVE!!)	$132.50	RARE BIG MAC 8 INCH BROWN BEER BOTTLE	$22.01
Limited Edition Sam Adams 2005 Utopias New In Box	$129.50	green CLARKE & WHITE advertising bottle, NEW YORK	$21.83

Breweriana, Beer ▸ Cans: US

The average sales price in this subcategory is $56.54.

	HIGH		AVG
King's Taste Beer - Nice Can!	$3,306.00	CANADIAN ACE IRTP CONE SUPER TUFF AND UNDERATED SWEET	$63.00
Silver Bar Beer Cone Top	$1,500.00	Duquesne Can-O-Beer Cone top - excellent condition	$62.88
Blatz Ale Low Profile Conetop - Nice Can!	$1,087.00	1949 BRAUMEISTER CONE TOP Beer Can - Nice!	$62.01
1940's - OLD TOPPER "Quart" SNAPPY ALE - A1+!!!	$821.59	Muehlebach's Pilsener Beer Can	$61.00
Ortlieb's Lager J-spout conetop - Nice Can!	$755.00	Royal Bohemian Cone Top Beer Can	$60.09
OLD TOPPER ALE 12 oz CROWNTAINER *RARE-WHITE*	$710.88	Schmidt's Beer Cone Top	$60.05
MUG ALE 12 oz Cone Top Can! CLASSIC GRAPHIC OHIO CAN!!!	$620.00	National Bohemian cone top beer can	$58.51
RARE EBLING'S White Head Ale 12 oz HP Cone Top*L@@K!*	$609.00	BIG COLLECTION OF 230 BEER CANS + 4 FULL + 12 BOTTLES	$58.00
EBLING WHITE HEAD ALE 12 oz CROWNTAINER *RARE*	$512.00	ROYAL BOHEMIAN Cone Top beer can *MN.* *SHARP!*	$56.51
Nice KOENIG BRAU Cone Top Beer Can	$500.00	cone top beer can Gold Metal Stegmaier Wilkes barre Pa.	$55.69
@Super Clean@ BUB'S STRONG Cone Top Beer Can	$470.57	OLD TOPPER SNAPPY ALE CONE TOP BEER CAN	$55.15
1940's - OLD TOPPER "Lager" BEER - A1+!!!	$459.00	Ballantine quart cone top beer can - unlisted version	$53.59

COOK'S GOLDBLUME BEER CONE TOP - COLLECTORS MUST HAVE	$447.05	Eand B Special Beer Cone Top	$52.03
RARE NICE PILSER'S PILSERS CROWNTAINER CONETOP BEER CAN	$443.88	Indoor Burger Beer Cone Top, Cincinnati, Ohio	$51.02
Ortlieb's Premium Lager Quart Cone	$405.00	4 ONE GALLON HUDEPOHL DRAFT BEER CANS	$51.00

Breweriana, Beer ▶ Cans: Non–US

The average sales price in this subcategory is $16.78.

	HIGH		AVG
MAC MAHON 2M EXPORT BEER, FT - 12 OZ - MOZAMBIQUE	$350.00	COMPLETE SET OF "MADAGASCAR" movie edition	$19.95
HOLSTEN-PILSENER 35cl Flat Top BEER CAN *MY-OH-MY!*	$321.06	17 DIFF. GUINNESS EXTRA STOUT 9 2/3OZ. PULL TAB CANS	$18.56
Very Rare - Takara Lager Beer SS - Japan	$300.00	LOWENBRAU Premium (Picure Lions) gallon from GERMANY	$18.50
MAC MAHON 2M ESPECIAL PRETA, SS - 12 OZ - MOZAMBIQUE	$266.00	Sapporo Lager Beer - München 1972 SS - # 614 - Japan	$18.50
McEWAN'S INDIA PALE ALE - STEEL FLAT TOP BEER CAN	$263.00	Red Stripe 4 Different 275ml beer cans	$18.06
MAC MAHON 2M SPECIAL, SS - 12 OZ - MOZAMBIQUE	$200.00	BRAHMA CHOPP TOUGH DIFFERENT VARIETY CAN LOOK	$17.50
9 Different Straight Steel South American Pull Tabs	$133.50	MALT 90 PERFECT SS BRAZIL TOUGH CAN B.O. WOW	$17.50
BOCA JUNIORS BY GENESSE SOCCER 12 CANS SET ARGENTINA	$114.50	4 SPECIAL STELLA ARTOIS : TAKE A LOOK !	$16.00
TENNENTS PIPER BEER CANS 15.5 OZ. PULL TAB CS	$104.05	6 DIF. SAINSBURY'S ALE/LAGER/	$15.50
Very Rare - Millers Taverners Ale SS - Australia	$87.06	STOUT 9 2/3OZ. P TAB CANS	
TENNENTS SWEET STOUT BEER CANS 15.5 OZ PULL TAB CS	$78.77	Vintage Bombers' Pin-up Beer bottle can WWII imported	$15.50
The first Catalogue of Venezuelan beer cans....	$60.00	18 Beer Cans Anchor San Miguel SP Knight Steinlager	$15.50
[2 of these sold for $60.00 each]		EINSIEDLER Landbier gallon from GERMANY	$15.00
Suntory Beer FRUIT AND BEER CAN Japan Cans COMPLETE SET	$60.00	Very nice SOCCER gallon from RUSSIA	$15.00
4 Diff Sweden Lys OL Porn 16 Oz Pull Tab Beer Can Cans	$57.00	Kirin Beer Suntory BEER CAN Japan Japanese 180ml	$15.00
Old Milwaukee - 71st Anniversary Set of 4 Lovely Ladies	$56.00	Asahi Beer Sapporo Kirin BEER CAN Japan Japanese MINI	$15.00

Breweriana, Beer ▶ Drinkware, Steins

The average sales price in this subcategory is $13.26.

	HIGH		AVG
OLD MCHENRY IL BEER BREWERY ETCHED ADVERTISING GLASS	$430.01	2 Vintage LONE STAR BEER Barrel Glasses COWBOY Logo	$13.65
BUDWEISER BUD MAN ORIGINAL	$222.50	ca 1910 Moerlein Footed Beer Glass~VERY RARE	$13.51
BUDMAN S&P SHAKERS MINT 1976		[2 of these sold for $13.51 each]	
Jack Daniels Shot Glass Complete Set 99cent No Reserve	$156.50	2 Vintage LONE STAR BEER Barrel Glasses COWBOY Logo	$13.50
RARE VINTAGE HOLANDA DECANTER SET CERAMARTE	$132.49	Jack Daniel's Key Chain Flask	$13.50
Fehr's XL Beer Drinking Cup Race Horse Can 1940 NM	$92.00	VINTAGE DONALD PISMER WHISKEY CROCK-EDINBURGH	$13.50
John Grafs Fine Weiss Beer 1889 Glass Tumbler Milwaukee	$66.00	VINTAGE HAMMS BEER 6 LONG STEM GLASSES VERY NICE	$13.49
Schmidt's Beer City Club St Paul MN Beer glass RARE	$64.00	1956 THUNDERBIRD 40A LIQUOR BOTTLE.NR	$13.29
unique impala drinking horn SCA renaissance festival	$61.01	Guinness Pint Glasses	$13.10
Old Style Beer Chicago Cubs 4 color pint glasses 4	$61.00	VINTAGE EFFINGER BEER GLASS	$13.00
JAX Beer small Glass Juice Drink JAX Best Beer in Town	$58.58	DALE EARNHARDT #8 NASCAR 4 PUB TULIP GLASSES NEW BUD	$12.99
VINTAGE GLASS & STERLING FLASK SWIRL PATTERN	$56.85	(4) Deschutes - Mirror Pond Pale Ale Pint Glasses	$12.95
Pabst Milwaukee Acid Etched Glass Beer Shell Pre-Pro	$56.00	Budweiser. Bud Man, Bud Bash IV on Coffee Mug!	$12.50
W J LEMP BREWING COMPANY GLASS ST LOUIS MO, EX	$51.00	YUENGLING LAGER 4 BAR BEER PINT PUB GLASSES GLASS NEW	$12.50
Lenox Budweiser Anheuser Busch Cup & Saucer	$50.00	6 RHINELANDER PILSNER TALL BEER GLASSES BY LIBBY	$12.50
Elvis Limited 1st Edition Music Box Decanter '77	$41.00	Guinness Pint Glasses (4) NIB New Never Used	$12.45

Casino ▶ Cards

The average sales price in this subcategory is $13.94.

	HIGH		AVG
2 New Decks Red/Blue KEM Arrow Wide Size Poker Cards SI	$192.50	KEM cards CASINO CLUB SI 2 Decks Dealer Button Set OOP	$13.99
KEM ARROW WIDE SI New condition red/blue sealed	$112.50	13 DECKS OF BELLAGIO CASINO CARDS	$13.95
Lot of 12 Decks of Sands Casino Playing Cards Unopened!	$103.61	[13 of these sold for $13.95 each]	
Double deck KEM cards/bridge/poker/casino NR NO	$76.00	Dal Negro PVC Plastic playing cards Freedom +free	$13.95
JERRY'S NUGGET CASINO PLAYING CARDS- SEALED/MINT/RARE	$68.00	[2 of these sold for $ 13.95 each]	
VINTAGE BEE PLAYING CARDS	$61.00	Dal Negro PVC Plastic poker cards r/b royal style +free	$13.95
12 DECKS CLUB SPECIAL 92 "NEW		13 DECKS OF BELLAGIO CASINO CARDS	$13.95
50 DECKS OF LAS VEGAS CASINO PLAYING CARDS ASSORTED	$49.95	25 Decks Used Nevada Casinos Playing Cards	$13.75
Texas Hold 'Em Golden 43MM Lucky Coin Poker Card Guard	$10.00	KEM cards CASINO CLUB SI 2 Decks Dealer Button Set OOP	$13.49
KEM- WIDE POKER Red/Blue KEM Arrow Back (RI)	$40.00	PLAYBOY ATLANTIC CITY PLAYING CARDS 2 DECKS MUST CI	$13.20
Vintage Kem Playing Cards, Fantasy Design, Sealed	$39.90	30 DECKS LAS VEGAS VINTAGE HOTEL CASINO USED CARDS LOT	$13.04
[2 of these sold in a multiple item ("Dutch") auction for $19.95 each]		NEW 4 Wood Curve Playing Card Holder Bridge Poker	$12.99

KEM Playing Card 4 Decks Narrow Arrow Bridge Size	$38.99	NEW 6 DECK CARD SHUFFLER POKER BRIDGE BLACKJACK	$12.99
KEM WINDROSE New condition-sealed-all original	$36.03	GOLDEN NUGGET PLAYING CARDS VINTAGE DECK UNOPENED GREEN	$12.50
Vintage Kem Playing Cards w/ Bakelite Case 1935/Birds	$34.00	1947 Kem Cards Paisley Two Decks	$12.50
101 Decks of Cards NEVADA CASINOS Used Playing Cards	$32.55	12 New Decks Gemaco Playing Cards Casino logo poker	$12.50
101 Decks of Cards NEVADA CASINOS Used Playing Cards	$32.00	Deck of Professionally Marked Cards - Not Poker Table	$12.50

Casino ▶ Chips

The average sales price in this subcategory is $5.48.

	HIGH		AVG
La Rue Casino, Las Vegas $1.00 Chip - Scarce Chip !!	$268.50	Sands Casino Dollar Casino Chip Las Vegas Nevada	$5.99
HUGE COLLECTION 70 $1 LAS VEGAS	$113.49	PALMS 2005 $1 CHIP SET OF 4 CASINO CHIPS	$5.79
CASINO POKER CHIPS NR!		$1.00 KINGS CASTLE	$5.77
53 Different Actual Las Vegas $1 Casino Chips	$101.00	RARE $1 CLUB FOREST - ILLEGAL 1930'S CASINO LOUISIANA	$5.75
Doc Holliday, Paulson, cane and hat $1 poker chips	$91.00	Little Caesars $1.00 Casino Chip Las Vegas	$5.74
SILVER SLIPPER Original $1 CASINO CHIP 1967 1968	$87.35	OLD ATLANTIC CITY GOLDEN NUGGET CASINO CHIP-LAS VEGAS	$5.53
100 $1 Nevada Jacks Casino Poker Chips + Paulson Cards	$61.00	LAS VEGAS CAESARS PALACE $1 CASINO CHIP TOKEN NICE	$5.51
Las Vegas Casino Chip Group, 18 Different, with $$ Cash	$58.85	VERY SPECIAL CELEBRITY CRUISES MILLENIUM $1 CHIP	$5.50
1860-1870 ONE DOLLAR IVORY SCRIMSHAW POKER CHIP	$47.00	WORLD SERIES OF POKER CASINO CHIPS $1 HARVEYS CHIP WSOP	$5.25
1967 Silver Slipper Casino Chip $ 1 Edmonton Canada	$43.51	Hacienda Las Vegas Obsolete $1.00 Casino Chip	$5.24
15 $1 Casino Gaming Chips	$43.27	Hooters Owl Club Casino $1.00 chip	$5.00
20 $1 casino chips	$41.11	[2 of these sold for $5.00 each]	
15 $1.00 Casino Gaming Chips	$39.50	FOUR $1.00 NEVADA GAMING CHIPS	$5.00
1860-1870 ONE DOLLAR IVORY SCRIMSHAW POKER CHIP	$37.65	BOOMTOWN RIVEBOAT CASINO BILOXI MISSISSIPPI $1 CHIP	$5.00
SILVER SLIPPER Original $1 CASINO CHIP 1967 1968	$37.01	RARE- PALMS 2001 $1 CHIP SET OF 4 CASINO CHIPS	$4.99
2 $2.50 & 13 $1 + 1 50 Cent Casino Gaming Chips	$34.00	$1 Antllean Casino Corp. Curacao chip	$4.99

Clocks ▶ Antique (Pre–1930)

The average sales price in this subcategory is $152.69.

	HIGH		AVG
Simon Willard Grandfather Clock Movement and Dial	$4,999.00	40" Hope Goddess Mystery Swinger Clock	$162.50
E.N. WELCH #3? CALENDAR CLOCK, RARE PARTS?	$2,822.99	antique spool J&P cotton advertising office wall clock	$162.49
Norris North East West Wood Works Column Clock 1820's	$2,550.99	Rare Seth Thomas Carved Oak Kitchen Clock w/ Bell Alarm	$158.15
CHELSEA CLOCK SOLID BRASS SHIP'S BELL W/BAROMETER	$1,725.00	NELSON TRAFALGAR VICTORIAN FRETWORK CLOCK RARE	$156.25
1WT ONE MONTH BIEDERMEIER VIENNA PREZISIONS REGULATOR	$1,600.00	SETH THOMAS ADAMATINE ANTIQUE CLOCK	$155.50
E. Howard Tower Street Clock Movement Watch	$1,482.79	United Anniversary Type Clock Dancing Figures Model 990	$155.00
Oak Seth Thoms No 2 Wall Regulator	$1,430.99	1885 Ansonia Longdrop Round Top Schoolhouse Clock	$154.49
Large Fancy French Morbier Wall Clock 4 Bells 3 Weights	$1,425.00	GERMAN PLATO FLIP NUMBER ROUND CARRIAGE CLOCK	$152.50
Waltham Banjo Clock George Washington Mount Vernon 1920	$1,392.99	ANTIQUE Large Telechron Neon AD CLOCK Nice pice	$152.50
Samuel Terry Pillar and Scroll Mantle Clock	$1,376.01	Victorian China Clock Case Signed Lion Profiles W Flowe	$152.49
ADVERTISING IRON (BAIRD?) CLOCK CASE STRAUSS CHICAGO	$1,375.00	ANSONIA 8 DAY DROP OCTAGON REGULATOR CLOCK	$147.50
Ithaca Calendar Clock - Solid Walnut Case Circa 1865	$1,050.00	ANTIQUE CARVED SIDE LONG DROP CALENDAR WALL CLOCK - NR	$145.50
ANTIQUE OAK WALL CLOCK (WEIGHT DRIVEN)	$1,010.00	ANIMATED SAMBO WINKER BLINKING EYE NOVELTY CLOCK	$142.50
VIENNA 58" EAGLE 3 WEIGHT REGULATOR WALL CLOCK - "3.wt"	$986.11	ANTIQUE CARVED TWISTS LONG DROP CALENDAR WALL CLOCK	$141.00
Diamond Head Banjo Clock by Wayne Cline Key Wind Mvmt	$950.00	NR! EARLY 1900 GERMAN PENDULUM MANTLE BLACK FOREST -86	$140.00

Clocks ▶ Vintage (1930–69)

The average sales price in this subcategory is $68.40.

	HIGH		AVG
Hamilton Chronometer ship's Deck Clock Watch Model 22	$1,250.00	RC (Royal Crown) Cola Pam Clock	$74.00
ORIGINAL OLD 1950s ELECTRIC NEON CLOCK CO. PINWHEEL	$1,235.00	LUX VINTAGE CHALET CUCKOO CLOCK-RED,	$72.99
VINTAGE FRENCH CARRIAGE CLOCK BRASS SIGNED	$1,143.00	CREAM COLORS,NICE	
ORIGINAL 1950s ELECTRIC NEON	$921.99	VINTAGE 9" ENGRAVED BRASS	$70.99
CLOCK CO. PINWHEEL CLOCK		W/ CRYSTAL GLASS HOUR GLASS	
Chelsea Boston Ships Clock and Barometer Set Stands	$700.00	Minneapolis Milwaukee Time-O-Stat Thermostat Clock +key	$69.99
NEOLITE / ATTENTIONEER NEON NUMBERS CLOCK	$687.00	NICE OLD AAA AUTOMOBILIA POCKET WATCH	$69.95
MATTHEW NORMAN CORNICHE	$635.75	Table Angel Clock .Special design!	$69.90
MOONPHASE CARRIAGE CLOCKJESSOPS		Russian NAVY 5CM-2 Military Boat/Submarine Clock	$69.00
Breitling/Wakmann USAF Military Aircraft Chronograph	$535.00	Vintage Unusual Kundo 6 Jewel Clock Round See Through	$68.87
Antique Neon Electric Clock LEWIS	$504.67	1935 Swiss Wooden Blinking Eye Scotty Clock	$66.85
Electric neon clock co. Cleveland Bubble clock Restored	$500.00	Nice Vintage Iron Fireman Clock, Thermostat, And Alarm	$66.02
RARE! ATMOS Le Coultre Perpetual Motion clock #47845	$471.00	USAF BULOVA AIRCRAFT CLOCK WORLD WAR II	$66.00
Vintage Le Coultre ATMOS Perpetual Motion Clock # 33731	$465.00	AIRCRAFT CLOCK PARTS, WITTNAUER 63 MODEL	$66.00
LE COULTRE & CIE ATMOS HERITAGE PERPETUAL MOTION CLOCK	$449.00	Vintage United Dancing Ballerina Mantle Clock	$66.00
Vintage Jaegar-LeCoultre Rue De La Paix Lamp-Post Clock	$446.00	ANTIQUE SESSIONS MANTLE CLOCK MANTEL	$62.99
jaeger le coultre geneva atmos clock	$440.00	Kit Cat Klock Rare Avocado Jeweled ELECTRIC	$62.77

Comics ▶ Golden Age (1938–55)

The average sales price in this subcategory is $38.36.

	HIGH		AVG
All Winners Comics V2#1 (Timely, 1948) CGC VF+ 8.5	$2,225.00	2449 - Adventures In Romances - No.1 -Comic Book	$41.02
ROY ROGERS ANNUAL, 1947. GIANT SIZE. RARE,PREMIUM COMIC	$985.00	CONTACT COMICS #9 1945 WW II Black Venus!!	$41.01
2456 - Sugar & Spike - No.1 -Comic Book	$955.00	MAD #13 (1954) Glossy sharp FN- 5.5, "Prince Violent"	$41.00
2446 - Mickey Mouse Magazine-No.9-Comic Book	$711.87	JACKIE & JANE LEARN THE STORY OF ICE CREAM-1950s Comic	$40.65

POPULAR COMICS #1 /1936/ DICK TRACY/1ST DELL COMIC!	$407.33	1951 SANTA CLAUS PARADE #1 Ziff-Davis 116pgs BV$320 VG+ $40.50
OVER 150 10 AND 12 CENT COVER PRICED COMICS	$405.01	Lot #112 Four Color 18 books $39.99
Great Fantagraphics Prince Valiant Lot: Volumes 1-16	$400.00	CAMERA COMICS #1-1944 World War II Cover $39.89
Two (2) 1940's Illustrated Stories of the Opera	$355.00	2042 - Dr. Fu Manchu - No.1-Comic Book $37.99
*ATOMIC COMICS #1, CLASSIC COVER, NICE FINE+ BOOK, 1946	$316.00	1961 MISS SUNBEAM IN BAKERSLAND GIVEAWAY COMIC - WEIRD $37.99
2451 - Teen-Age Romances - No.9 - Matt Baker-Comic Book	$315.00	2450 - Trail Blazers - No.1 - Jack Dempsy -Comic Book $37.78
SEVEN SEAS COMICS #6 VG-FINE GGA FOX	$304.00	TARZAN FC #161 (1947) * DELL GOLDEN AGE COMIC! GD/VG! $37.00
1942 #34 All American Comics Comic Book.	$304.00	3-D Romance #1 Comic $36.96
2443 - Teen-Age Romances - No.11 -Matt Baker-Comic Book	$291.00	SHEENA QUEEN OF THE JUNGLE # 1 Simba MEXICAN COMIC 1954 $36.80
The Adventures of Bob Hope #1 1950 Golden Age	$232.66	TARZAN #9 * DELL GOLDEN AGE COMIC! MID-GRADE FN! $36.50
2472 - Air Ace - Vol.2 No.2 -Comic Book	$204.50	1945 * Star Spangled Comics #43 * Simon & Kirby $36.05

Comics ▶ Silver Age (1956–69)

The average sales price in this subcategory is $35.86.

	HIGH		AVG
TALES OF SUSPENSE #39 UNRESTORED FN/VF	$2,000.00	10 PS PREVENTIVE MAINTENANCE MONTHLY WILL EISNER #5,14+	$37.00
Amazing Spider Man 10 1st Inforcers VF/NM 9.0 1964	$810.00	Astonishing Tales 1-9 Avg VG/F, NO RSV	$37.00
Uncanny X-Men 94 9.2/9.4 NM Wolverine White pages!	$560.00	** AMAZING SPIDER-MAN #43 ** Rhino on the Rampage	$36.50
Incredible Hulk 180 VG/F, 181 & 182 F+ 6.5, NO RSV	$535.00	Pogo Mobile, Walt Kelly	$36.00
Amazing Spider Man 14 1st Green Goblin VF 8.0 1964	$512.52	Uncanny X-Men 124 9.8 NM/MT White pages!	$36.00
Avengers 4 VG/F, NO RSV	$310.22	Uncanny X-Men 132 9.6/9.8 NM+/NMMT White pages!	$36.00
Amazing Spiderman 13 & 14 G/VG, NO RSV	$307.99	Doctor Strange 177-181 & 183 VG/F to F, NO RSV	$36.00
Daredevil 1 G, NO RSV	$232.49	1957 THE ADVENTURES OF REX THE WONDER DOG #31	$35.05
Iron Fist 1-13 & 15 Avg VF- 7.0/8.0, NO RSV	$224.50	Uncanny X-Men 127 9.8 NM/MT White pages!	$35.00
Daredevil 2-4 VG+, NO RSV	$205.50	BRAVE and the BOLD #23 Viking Prince origin by Kubert	$34.77
Uncanny X-Men 100 9.6/9.8 NM+/NMM White pages!	$204.50	Mixed lot of 26 Comics, 70's	$34.33
Captain America 101-105 F/F+ 6.0/6.5, NO RSV	$200.39	Astonishing Tales 9-24 VG/F to F, NO RSV	$34.03
Showcase #1 1959 DC-National Comics - Fire Fighters	$190.00	11 PS PREVENTIVE MAINTENANCE MONTHLY WILL EISNER _65_66	$34.00
Amazing Spider Man 18 Sandman VF+ 8.5	$189.50	BRAVE and the BOLD #21 Silent Knight & Viking Prince	$34.00
Uncanny X-Men 121 9.8 NM/MT White pages!	$177.50	BRAVE and the BOLD #31 1st app. Cave Carson	$33.00

Comics ▶ Bronze Age (1970–79)

The average sales price in this subcategory is $18.96.

	HIGH		AVG
Morse's Funnies, R.Crumb Cover, Scarce, second version	$999.99	1972 BIJOU FUNNIES #2 UNDERGROUND COMIC 1st PRINT NM+	$19.59
ALL-STAR WESTERN #10 (DC,1972) CGC NM- 9.2	$510.00	[2 of these sold for $19.59 each]	$19.38
Cerebus 1 no CGC 1977 Dave Sim not a counterfeit	$327.00	Lot of 29 Comic Books from the Silver & Bronze Age	$19.26
Cerebus the Aardvark # 1, Original 1st printing!!!	$242.50	Lot of four Sears March of Comics comic books	$18.50
PLANET OF THE APES #1 (MARVEL,1974) CGC NM/MT 9.8	$202.50	ASTONISHING TALES #31 (MARVEL,1975) CGC NM- 9.2	$18.50
EVEL KNIEVEL #1 MARVEL COMICS 1974 Giveaway CGC 9.6	$149.99	Black and White Comics 1st Print (VF) by R. Crumb	$18.50
YOUNG ROMANCE # 180 / CGC 9.4 ! DOUBLE-SIZE SCARCE 9.4	$129.99	Mr. Natural Comic #1 3rd Printing (VF) By R. Crumb	$18.09
Astonishing Tales #25 CGC 9.2	$128.49	FREEDOM FIGHTERS #3 (DC,1976) CGC NM 9.4	$18.00
TWO GUN KID 59 COMIC COLLECTION LOT 43-136 SHARP	$127.50	1974 INSIDE COMICS #1 R.CRUMB FANZINE UNDERGROUND	$17.50
Swamp Thing Ghosts Sgt Rock 6 1974 DC Comics Sealed	$112.52	Showcase #95 (DC, 1977) CGC NM+ 9.6 White pages	$16.79
RINGO KID 31 COMIC LOT COLLECTION 1-30 AND 1957 #20 !!	$112.50	MAN-THING #7 (MARVEL,1974) CGC NM+ 9.6	$16.50
TARZAN, the golden age of .. 1939/1942 . Lim. Ed. 1977	$110.05	The Man Thing #1 (1973) NEAR MINT, GREAT book !!!!!!!!!	$15.99
DC WEIRD WESTERN TALES #15 - CGC 9.4 - GEM!!	$104.11	JUNGLE ACTION MARVEL COMICS VOL. 1,2,3	$15.71
Underground Comic Flabby Thighs and Butter No.1	$100.00	SUPERNATURAL THRILLERS #15 (MARVEL,1975) CGC NM 9.4	$15.51
DC WEIRD WESTERN TALES #13 - CGC 9.2 - WHITE PAGES	$91.13	The Spirit #1 and #2 both NM 9.4 Kitchen Sink 1973	$15.50
Doomsday + 1 #4 (Charlton, 1976) CGC NM+ 9.6	$50.00	Marvel Star Wars Comics 21 issue lot	

Comics ▶ Modern Age (1980–Now)

The average sales price in this subcategory is $9.84.

	HIGH		AVG
RED SONJA #0 RRP SET (1 IN 1000) VARIANT! NO RESERVE!	$160.99	Space Ghost 1-6 COMPLETE Set Kelly Olivetti DC Comics	$9.99
RED SONJA #1 RRP EDITION (1 IN 300) + COMPLETE SET!	$158.49	MODESTY BLAISE #s 1, 3 American Edition O'Donnell	$9.99
Y The Last Man 1 - 34 Complete Series to Date	$102.72	Uncanny X-Men #94 Wizard Ace edition NM+!	$9.99
Daredevil Marvel Knights 1-75 Smith Quesada Bendis COMP	$102.50	Udon Comics Darkstalkers #3 Power Foil Madureira NM/M	$9.99
Complete Preacher Comic Book Series	$76.00	LINSNER-10 books;Dawn,Portable Dawn,Villain & Hero/more	$9.99
Lot of 30 Groo comics- issues 91-120	$73.01	Justice League Elite 1-12 COMPLETE Set DC Kelly Mahnke	$9.99
2 Long Boxes Comic Collection. 100% Marvel Titles! FUN!	$59.00	[2 of these sold for $9.99 each]	
Huge Lot Fables Y The Last Man Smax 50+ Comics	$57.00	Crux 1-33 Near Complete Set CrossGen Waid Epting Dixon	$9.99
MNT Verotik Frank FRAZETTA	$56.00	Global Frequency 1,2,3,4,5,6,7,8,9 WS Warren Ellis VF	$9.95
Illustration ARCANUM FANTASY		The League of Extraordinary Gentlemen 1-6 (6) Comics	$9.95
60 Dreadstar - Marvel/Epic and First Comics	$51.00	Jack T.Chick Christian Comics "The Crusaders"13 Issues"	$9.50
200+ Mutant Comics X-Men, Wolverine Great Collection	$51.00	THE SAVIOUR lot 1-6 Early Mark Millar work Trident UK	$9.50
LARGE LOT of WITCHBLADE COMIC BOOKS?made by Image	$50.50	Chaos! Jersey	$9.00
Eric Powell THE GOON 1-4 + COLOR SPECIAL + vol. 2 #1-13	$49.63	CHICKS AND MONSTERS Bill Bronson Art Sketch Book HOT!	$9.00
NYX 1-7 COMPLETE Quesada Middleton 3 1st X-23 Teranishi	$49.00	FATHOM #9 / 2 books - Midwest variant and Foil covers	$9.00
Seth Green and Hugh Sterbakov's Freshmen #1 signed!!!	$46.00	FRIDAY THE 13TH FOUR #1 ISSUES NM/MT	$8.99

Comics ▸ Graphic Novels, TPBs

The average sales price in this subcategory is $14.28.

	HIGH		AVG
THORN TALES FROM THE LANTERN (BONE 1983 JEFF SMITH RARE	$405.99	6 TPB/GNs Lot : Witchblade, Cla$$war, Tomb Raider, Dark	$14.95
P Craig Russell Ring of the Nibelung S&N HC	$162.50	Hiroaki Samura - Blade of the Immortal - Vol. 6 and 7	$14.95
RARE HUGE WRIGHTSON HARDCOVER " A LOOK BACK" 1979	$150.00	Hiroaki Samura - Blade of the Immortal - Vol. 8 and 9	$14.95
Frank miller sin city complete series vol 1 2 3 4 5 6 7	$100.00	WARLANDS TP 1, 2, 3 ARTRELEGIS, AGE OF ICE, DARKLYTE	$14.95
RARE WRIGHTSON HARDCOVER BACK FOR MORE S/N 213 OF 500	$100.00	BASIL WOLVERTON READER VOL. 2 TPB W/ POWERHOUSE PEPPER	$14.50
Usagi Yojimbo Travels with Jotaro Hardcover HC SIGNED	$91.06	Lot: 3 anime Graphic Novels ARIA manga vls 1-3	$14.50
SIN CITY 7 TPB SET FRANK MILLER 2 3 4 5 6 DARK HORSE!	$82.99	8 No Need for Tenchi Anime books volumes 1-8 set	$14.49
SANDMAN Trade Paperbacks #1-7 & #9/ TPB	$80.00	THE ART OF JOHN BYRNE VOLUME ONE * 1980 FIRST EDITION!	$14.48
PREACHER VOLS 1-9 FULL RUN TPB ENNIS Free Shipping	$79.99	STEVE DITKO READER TP VOL 3 NEW!	$13.99
Frank Cho Sketches & Scribbles! Signed Book! Rare!	$76.00	TRANSMETROPOLITAN - YEAR OF THE BASTARD TPB	$13.53
Overstreet Comic book Price Guides #4 - #15 Set	$75.02	Wizard World Frank Millers SIN CITY Handcuffs Key Chain	$13.50
Lot: 10 anime Graphic Novels Peach Girl Series 2 manga	$71.00	Dick Tracy by Chester Gould 1931-1951 HC like new	$13.00
Mars Vol 1-15(complete series) GN manga comic books	$70.99	STEVE DITKO READER TP VOL 3 NEW!	$12.99
$112 DANCE TILL TOMORROW Vol 1-7 Manga Yamamoto $0 Ship	$69.99	SIMON BISLEY'S ILLUSTRATIONS FROM THE BIBLE HC	$12.99
Lone Wolf and Cub #1-28 and Samurai Executioner any 10	$64.99	How to Draw Art for Comic Books Lessons Masters $15	$12.50

Comics ▸ Newspaper Comics

The average sales price in this subcategory is $14.20.

	HIGH		AVG
Prince Valiant - The 1980's Complete - Over 520 Pages	$305.00	L@@K NEW 2006 "LOVE IS" box CALENDAR...by Kim Casali	$14.99
WALT KELLY POGO PUCE STAMPS FRAMED	$249.00	COMIC PEANUTS SCHROEDER at GRAND PIANO DOORSTOP	$14.95
2 FANTAGRAPHICS PRINCE VALIANT COMIC V 40 41 + SKINDEEP	$193.40	NEWSPAPER COLOR COMICS 1922 ELMER PETER RABBIT GUMPS	$14.95
FANTAGRAPHICS PRINCE VALIANT VOL 39-KNIGHT'S BLOOD	$186.50	VINTAGE COMIC STRIP LOT 1930s MICKEY MOUSE Sappo CH987	$14.50
Fantagraphics PRINCE VALIANT Vol. 34 Mordred's Revenge	$179.50	VINTAGE COMIC STRIP LOT Howdy Doody LITTLE DEBBIE CH985	$14.50
BIG lot 160+ pages 1943 SUNDAY FUNNIES Comics	$146.50	VINTAGE COMIC STRIP LOT Red Barry THIMBLE THEATER CH984	$14.50
FANTAGRAPHICS PRINCE VALIANT # 38 PRINCE ARN'S EXPLOITI	$108.00	Wally And The Major "Army Boys" By Stan Cross	$14.50
NEWSPAPER COMICS DAILIES 1921	$88.00	Wally And The Major "Cane Cutters" by Stan Cross	$14.50
KRAZY KAT US BOYS GUMPS		NEW YORK CARTOON NEWS 12-Pg Cartoonist Newsletter, 1958	$14.27
Calvin & Hobbes-2 Promo Header Cards-Watterson	$78.00	Terry and the Pirates Hardcov. Storybook Milton Caniff	$13.49
Vintage Steve Canyon lunch box excellent NR	$72.69	Prince Valiant Flash Gordon Puck Comic Weekly 4/19/59	$13.38
FOSSIL, "SNOOPY FLOWERS" WATCH set with wooden case	$69.99	Superman Joe Palooka + Sunday Mirror Comics 11/17/46	$13.35
1934 Katzenjammer Kids in the Mountains Comic Book	$67.00	Batman Superman + Sunday Mirror Comics 9/1/1946	$13.35
Cathy Guisewite signed LMT ED Cookie Jar - RARE & MINT	$66.00	Superman Li'l Abner + Sunday Mirror Comics 12/1/46	$13.35
Calvin and Hobbes - set of 16 books - NR!	$66.00	DICK TRACY/LITTLE ORPHAN ANNIE/BEETLE BAILEY 1974 STRIP	$13.30
Calvin & Hobbes Lazy Sunday Bk Promo Header	$59.00	[2 of these sold for $13.30 each]	

Cultures, Ethnicities ▸ Asian (1900–Now)

The average sales price in this subcategory is $29.23.

	HIGH		AVG
KARAKALPAK WOOL WIDE LONG COMPLETE NOMAD'S TENT BAND	$900.00	Inlay Mahogany Pop Up Cigarette Box VINTAGE 1950s L@@K	$35.00
KARAKALPAK WOOL WIDE LONG COMPLETE NOMAD'S TENT BAND	$898.00	Uzbek Wool Woven Tent Band for Nomad's yurt	$35.00
OLD MORO CHESS PIECES UP FOR GRABS!!! NO RESERVE!!!	$825.00	Rajasthan India Old Shisha Embroidery Choli Front SALE	$32.99
Old Asian Textile Coat Jacket Taiwan Clothing Costume	$307.00	ASIAN antler carving DEMON DEVIL vintage statue	$31.01
Antique Timor Tribal Ritual Mask	$207.50	Vintage Chinese Japanese Incense Burner	$31.00
OLD UZBEK WOOL WEAVED WIDE LONG NOMAD'S TENT BAND	$170.39	VINTAGE AUTHENTIC ORIENTAL COOLIE HAT	$30.01
OLD ORIGINAL MORO DAGGER WITH IVORY POMMEL!!! N/R!!!	$152.50	Unique Hand Made Pouch Philippines Made From Bark	$29.99
16 Pairs Special Different Brass Earring Dayak, Borneo	$125.00	NEW HMONG/LAOTIAN SILK SHAWL/SCARF TEXTILE FABRIC K2	$29.01
MONGOLIAN~~ANTIQUE FLINT POUCH~~BRASS~~COW LEATHER	$99.99	SET OF 2 OLD BRONZE BRASS SINGH LION STATUES	$29.00
Old Uzbek Home Spun Cotton printed Fabric from Bukhara	$99.00	SOLID BRONZE SCULPTURE FAT LADY THAILAND UNIQUE 1	$28.00
OLD UZBEK WOOL WEAVED WIDE LONG NOMAD'S TENT BAND	$99.00	SOLID BRONZE SCULPTURE FAT LADY THAILAND UNIQUE 3	$28.00
OLD UZBEK WOOL PILE HANDMADE SADDLE BAG – KHURJINY	$99.00	SOLID BRONZE TURTLE TORTOISE SCULPTURE OLD THAILAND	$28.00
UZBEK WOOL WOVEN COMPLETE NOMAD'S TENT BAND	$99.00	YOGA MAT CARRY BAG - HANDMADE BY TIBETAN REFUGEES	$26.99
Naga Headhunter Tooth Teeth tribal Necklace – CREEPY	$99.00	OLD SMALL SOLID BRONZE LIZARD GECKO SCULPTURE	$26.00
Borneo dayak Headhunter tribal boar tusk necklace	$91.00	ASIAN MASK LONG	$26.00

Cultures, Ethnicities ▸ Black Americana

The average sales price in this subcategory is $27.52.

	HIGH		AVG
1890s BLACK AMERICANA TOBACCO JAR BLACK MAN w/ CIGAR	$406.00	black americana infamous CHICKEN INN 2 sided church fan	$28.75
Antique Black Americana Framed Oil on Canvas	$325.00	RARE Dixie Recipes Mammy Cook book Black Americana	$28.56
RARE 1852 UNCLE TOM'S CABIN 1st EDITION MATCHED SET 2vo	$255.03	TAR BABY AND GATOR FISHING LURE IN BOX FLORIDA SOUVENIR	$28.50
Rare Cast Iron Mammy Clock With Moving Eyes	$227.50	The Black Panther, Newspaper, February 26, 1972	$28.50
1838 Bill of Sale for Negroe woman named Mason, 18yrs	$208.65	Mammy SHORT'NIN' BREAD 1928 Black Americana Sheet Music	$28.00
NYC Jimi Hendrix Experience Rock Concert Ticket Stub 68	$205.50	GREAT NEGRO DANCE BANDS BLACK AMERICANA HISTORY HB/DJ	$28.00
THE UNCALLED by PAUL LAURENCE DUNBAR 1898 1st Ed	$202.50	VINTAGE BLACK AMERICANA SALT & PEPPER SHAKERS JAPAN	$27.99
Brownsville Affray-Court Martial Report-25th Inf-1907	$199.99	1843 Negro Estate Receipt Document Signed	$27.00
Old Figural Black Golliwog Vigny French Perfume Bottle	$198.50	Kembo A little girl of Africa The Nursery series 1925	$26.99
Black Americana waiter decanter bottle	$185.00	1923 Maxie Jones King ofthe Saxiephones Black Americana	$26.65
Vin Childs Guitar Ha-Ha the Laffing Black Man by Regal	$160.49	1960'S MARTIN LUTHER KING I HAVE A DREAM FOB PIN	$26.50

	HIGH		
Glycerole Shoe Dressing Tin Black Americana Trunk	$159.06	BLACK AMERICANA KITCHEN TOWEL, [BEAUTY]	$26.50
Rare BLACK HOBO WHISTLER BATTERY OP TOY 1960'S	$158.50	SAMBO JOLLY JIGGER FISHING LURE SOUVENIR LAKE MONROE FL	$26.25
Black americana orange crate original old	$151.50	BLACK AMERICANA MAMMY'S PRIDE CAKE SOAP ADVERTISING FAN	$26.00
The Best McCoy Jadite MAMMY Cookie Jar	$139.50	Black Americana Set Of Salt And Pepper Shakers	$26.00

Cultures, Ethnicities ▶ European

The average sales price in this subcategory is $33.65.

	HIGH		AVG
Authentic AMAN Romanian Oas folk dance costumes	$2,750.00	EUROPEAN EIFFEL TOWER CLOCK black WIRE PARISIAN french	$41.00
Authentic AMAN Croatian Baranja folk dance costumes	$1,676.00	Old W K Flower Girl Blumenkinder Erzgebirge German Wood	$41.00
Maurice Lacroix tour et nuit men's watch	$635.01	Spanish mud doll people spain- Bull Fight Set-figurines	$37.05
Vintage Frank Meisler Figurine, Klezmer Fiddler Rare!	$407.00	OLD ROMAN RINGS (DUG FIND)	$36.00
Authentic AMAN Croatian Baranja fancy dress costume	$406.10	East German Erzgebirge Set of 5 Angels With Gifts	$36.00
Arabia Finland Valencia tureen with lid	$245.00	1898 Photo Book Florence Naples Rome Italy 100's Photos	$34.99
W@W! Black Oktoberfest Lederhosen Leather Shorts W32"	$203.50	East German Erzgebirge Santa Music Box	$34.99
Pair Black Forest Germany Drechsestube Boy & Girl NR	$199.00	Porcelain Rosenthal BOY AND LAMB Figurine (GERMANY)	$33.00
16th CENTURY BRASS COOKING POT	$115.77	Old W K Flower Girl Blumenkinder Erzgebirge German Wood	$32.50
Oktoberfest Trachten Bavarian Hat Lot - 25 Alpine Hats!	$107.50	Lot of 2 ERZGEBIRGE Figures - SANTA, TOY MAKER/PEDDLER	$32.24
Boiled Wool Sweater Lot 20 Felted Wool Austrian Jackets	$100.00	GERMAN BAVARIAN OCTOBERFEST HAT WITH 9 HAT PINS NR...	$32.08
VINTAGE PLASTER FRAMES PORCELAIN FIGURINE LOVERS	$100.00	French Frolics 1925 Vol.1 No.1 First Erotica American	$32.01
Wood Wooden Bridal Spoon Chain Hallingdal Oslo Norway	$89.88	Childs wooden dutch shoes + Anri music box	$31.00
UKRAINIAN / UKRAINE Mens NIKE HOCKEY JERSEY	$78.77	Ukrainian Hand Carved Wooden Display - Tryzub Trident	$31.00
German Smoker, great shape, Artist, easel, collectible!	$76.26	#NAME?	$29.99

Cultures, Ethnicities ▶ Hawaiiana

The average sales price in this subcategory is $31.73.

	HIGH		AVG
Rare Antique LEONARDO NUNES UKULELE-UKE-Koa-Hawaii NR!	$257.50	HONOLULU Sterling Silver Souvenir Spoon 1890s HAWAII	$36.09
Hale Pua Airbrushed Painting ~PINK ORCHID~ Framed	$248.50	Barber_s Point TH Naval Air Station Employee Pin Hawaii	$36.00
1930s Hawaiian Grill Plaque Surfer Duke Kahanamoku	$224.72	NWT Boutique Hawaiian Blanket Sz: 63" x 84" HUGE!	$35.00
Hawaii Wood Carving Handcarved Wall Art Flowers Eames	$222.50	HAWAIIANA RARE MATSON LINE HAWAII MAP & BROCHURE 1928	$32.75
1871 BOUND VOLUME HONOLULU HAWAII NEWSPAPER THE FRIEND	$202.50	vintage 1950s Hawaiian Mermaid porcelain no reserve	$32.00
Hawaiian Pounder Pre-Turn wooden with human hair	$202.50	TROPICAL WALL CLOCK, carved pineapple, tiki hut / bar	$31.99
JEAN CHARLOT HAWAII KAHUNA TIKI ORIGINAL LITHO BEAUT	$165.00	CERAMIC DRUMMER-DANCER FIGURINE - 40s-50s - KREISS	$31.99
VINTAGE HAWAII KOA WOOD UKULELE UKELELE NO RESERVE	$152.50	Vintage Hawaii Hawaiian Hula Grass Skirt Dancer Bobber	$31.77
HAWAIIAN FIGURINE. VINTAGE. 1960'S	$150.00	Hawaiian, Hawaii Teak Wooden Pineapple Lazy Susan	$31.00
Kim Taylor Reece Photo Print / Solid Koa Frame	$147.50	Vintage HAWAIIAN Hawaii TABLECLOTH Hibiscus TROPICAL	$30.99
Frank Schirman 1971 Black Coral Male & Female Figurines	$145.84	PARADISE ISLAND Retro Bamboo Vintage Style Island SIGN	$30.00
RARE HAWAII RAILROAD STOCK CERTIFICATE ETC	$141.08	RARE OLD REGAL UKULELE	$30.00
Frank Oda HAWAIIAN ANTHURIUM Etched Glass Block Vase	$136.38	GILL LEI DANCER~~HAWAIIAN BAMBOO CURTAIN	$29.95
3 Vintage Hawaiian Koa Wood Trays Blair Of Hawaii	$130.27	FRANK SCHIRMAN BLACK CORAL KEHONI THE KISS SCULPTURE	$29.00
VINTAGE HAWAIIAN PEACOCK FEATHER HAT BAND-EXCELLENT	$127.50	Vintage Pewter Ashtray / High Relief Design	$29.00

Cultures, Ethnicities ▶ Native Americana

The average sales price in this subcategory is $43.67.

	HIGH		AVG
HISTORIC HOPI SEED JAR. N.R.	$6,600.00	GREAT KNIFE WITH ZUNI INLAY HANDLE–NR!!	$50.00
Perfect Museum NW COAST Cedar Bent Wood Chest	$787.77	Native CREE Indian Dancing Moccasins -ladys 7	$49.99
18-FOOT CROW STYLE TIPI-TEEPEE	$380.00	RARE! VINTAGE HOPI INDIAN CEREMONIAL SASH BELT	$49.99
GENUINE ESKIMO HARPOON INUPIAT WALRUS TUSK IVORY	$379.00	Pease pipe. Vintage/old	$49.99
Native American Porcupine Hair Roach Powwow Regalia 20"	$275.00	OLD INUIT ESKIMO seal on rock signed E9 1116	$49.00
Large Hand Painted Plains Indian War Shield W/ Feathers	$237.50	Pipestone Like Catlinite Pipe Peace Pipe	$46.00
Peyote Fan-Scarlet, Military, Blue & Gold-MACAW	$197.50	Trail of Painted Ponies "Blue Medicine" 1E First	$45.00
ESKIMO WALRUS TUSK SHAMAN	$185.00	PENDLETON BEAVER STATE INDIAN BLANKET PURSE BAG	$43.87
CARVING TRANSFORMATION ALASKA		Set of 2 American Indian Figures Sculptures Cornhusk	$41.00
NATIVE ALASKA FOSSIL BOWHEAD WHALE CARVING WALRUS IVORY	$182.00	NATIVE ALASKAN SOLID WALRUS IVORY HARPOON TIP INUPIAT	$40.99
Sebastian miniatures Nanepaashhemet\Webcowit\SML17A-18A	$154.49	VINTAGE SEWING TAPE MEASURE,	$40.77
Limited Edition Pendleton Blanket	$150.00	NATIVE AMERICAN,SKOOKUM ?	
Native American Western Beaded Dance Bustle Regalia	$140.00	NATIVE AMERICAN INDIAN CERIMONIAL PEACE PIPE peacepipe	$40.00
Native American Star Quilt NR	$138.50	CANVAS & WOODEN W/ BAMBOO PAPOOSE	$39.99
Spirit Quest ~PENDLETON~ Blanket *NEW*	$138.00	Rare Alaskan Whale Baleen Frond 33" Length	$38.00
Pendleton Beaver State Indian Style Wool Blanket Brown	$133.50	OGLALA LAKOTA PAINTED RABBIT HIDE–MERLE LOCKE	$37.99

Cultures, Ethnicities ▶ Western Americana

The average sales price in this subcategory is $91.91.

	HIGH		AVG
RARE -FOLDING MINER'S CANDLESTICK- CLEAVES	$3,775.00	horse hames and collar	$100.00
1860's DANCE HALL GIRL'S BEADED DERRINGER THIGH HOLSTER	$3,500.00	DEPUTY U.S. MARSHAL, OKLAHOMA TERRITORY 1895	$100.00
OLD WILL & FINCK DAGGER WITH SILVER SHEATH no bowie	$1,270.00	ANTIQUE WESTERN GUN PISTOL HOLSTER TOOLED STUDDED	$99.38
VINTAGE VISALIA A- FORK SADDLE , and BREASTCOLLAR	$1,228.00	Ideal's Roy Rogers Fix it Stagecoach	$99.00
Fantastic Sioux BEADED SADDLE THROW / DRAPE 10' *NR*	$1,225.00	TOOLED,STUDDED COWBOY SINGLE ACTION HOLSTER,NR	$99.00
Fine 1830-1850 American Made Bowie Knife-New Orleans ?	$1,136.00	Antique COWBOY/WESTERN Bent-Branch HORSESHOE HAT RACK	$95.00
Antique Wells Fargo Strong Box Lock Padlock with Chain	$900.00	Sheriff's Fine Leather Blackjack	$95.00

	HIGH		
Famous U.S. Deputy Marshal BILL TILGHMAN Signed Display	$899.00	ANTIQUE DOUBLE LOOP CARTRIDGE BELT	$88.00
PAWNEE BILL INDIAN/NOT COWBOY RODEO POSTER/WILD WEST	$837.00	Monterrey Western Ware Large Enamel Cowboy Platter	$87.00
15_ VINTAGE BONA ALLEN SADDLE,	$786.00	H BOKER ~ Buffalo HIDE SCALE ~ VERY RARE ~ Nice	$86.00
1899 Buffalo Bill Tickets Mixed Group of 5	$708.00	L.A. Huffman - _A CROW SCOUT - FT. KEOGH MT. 1879_	$82.81
SUNDAY MAGAZINE COWGIRL/NOT COWBOY COPY ORIGINAL OIL	$701.00	vintage unusual horse bit ? silver designs .. small ...	$82.75
1800's Wooly Buffalo Western Cowboy Chaps, MUSEUM	$600.00	5 MONTERREY WESTERN WARE 7 1/4" BOWLS CHUCK WAGON	$81.00
R.H. Ruana Bonner Montana Hatchet	$483.78	Antique Old West City Marshal Police Badge	$81.00
MONTERREY WESTERN WARE RARE VEGGIE BOWL PLATTER	$410.00	Cowboy Wrist Cuffs	$81.00

Decorative Collectibles ▶ Avon

The average sales price in this subcategory is $10.19.

	HIGH		AVG
1920-1923 VOLUME CALIF PERF. CO. OUTLOOKS-ONE OF A KIND	$227.50	6 Avon Lady Collectible Thimbles 1982-1984 Fancy Hats	$10.51
Set of 8 Ruby Red Avon Cape Cod Napkin Rings/Mint!!!	$96.00	Avon Porcelain 4 Spoons Collection with Rack-NIB	$10.50
Avon Hummingbird Crystal Dinner Plate Set	$91.00	AVON CAPE COD CANDLESTICK HOLDERS, BELL, VASE + MORE	$10.50
31 Pieces of Avon Cape Cod Pattern Glassware	$75.00	AVON - Pearls and Lace Cologne Spray - NEW	$10.50
Avon 2004 Mrs Albee President's Club Full Size Figurine	$51.00	Avon Hummingbird Crystal Cup and Saucer MIB	$10.50
Blue Cape Cod Royal Sapphire 12 dinner plates	$49.99	Avon Albee 1996 Bonnie Holden Print in Frame	$10.49
Avon Hummingbird Crystal Soup/Salad Plate/Bowl Set	$46.00	AVON RED CAPE COD LARGE PITCHER "GORGEOUS"	$10.49
Avon 1876 Ruby Cape Cod Collection Cake Pedestal Plate	$45.00	Lot of 13 Pcs. Avon Jewelry - Rings / Necklaces	$10.05
AVON MRS. ALBEE FULL-SIZE AWARD ~2004~ MIB	$36.20	AVON Nutcracker Anniversary Clock in Original Box 1997	$10.00
AVON CAPE COD CUPS,SAUCERS,WINE GLASSES/DECANTER +	$36.00	Avon Cape Cod Pie/Cake Knife	$10.00
Avon 2002 Mrs ALBEE President's Club Full size Doll	$34.61	RUBY RED AVON 1876 CAPE COD PIE PLATE SERVER	$9.99
Avon 1876 Cape Cod Ruby Red Pitcher & 6 Tumblers	$32.13	Pair Avon Ruby Cape Cod Oil/Vinegar Cruets	$9.99
Set of 8 Avon Lady THIMBLES w/Mahogany Display Rack	$32.09	2 Ruby Red Cape Cod Champagne Glass	$9.99
AVON RUBY RED CAPE CODE NAPKIN RINGS (4)	$31.52	AVON Royal Sapphire Cape Cod BAKER NEW	$9.99
AVON CAPE COD 1876 COLLECTION NAPKIN RINGS NIB	$31.52	AVON Royal Sapphire Cape Cod SERVING BOWL NEW	$9.99

Decorative Collectibles ▶ Boyds

The average sales price in this subcategory is $12.88.

	HIGH		AVG
SEVEN DIFFERENT BOYDS GNOME HOMES FIGURINES	$147.50	LISA T. BEARRINGER Boyds Bear Investment Archive NR	$13.27
LOT BOYD BEARS 12 PLUSH	$125.89	NEW!! AUGUSTA Boyds Bear Investment Collectables NIB NR	$13.05
11 FIGURINES SOME RETIRED TAGS		BOYDS~ EASTER EGG BEAR TREASURE BOX~RETIRED 2001	$13.00
2002 Longaberger/Boyds Woven Memories Basket/Cat Combo	$106.50	Boyds Bears Lot Of Americana Items LOOK Cute	$13.00
BOYDS Peeker of the Month set of 12 Calendar bears	$65.99	Boyds 1E Opie's Creel Basket w/McNibble Treasure Box	$12.99
DANBURY MINT BOYDS BEARS LIGHTED CHRISTMAS TREE	$65.00	Boyds 1E Lizzies Berry Basket w/McNibble Treasure Box	$12.99
Boyds Bear Country exclusive "MASON" throw afghan	$63.25	BOYDS BEARS TAPESTRY PILLOW! A Sister Is A Born Friend!	$12.53
BOYDS BEARS PLUSH WIZARD OF OZ 6-PC SET NEW IN BOX***	$61.00	Boyds Verna's Teapot w/McNibble IE Treasure Box MIB	$12.50
Boyds Bear Bailey HUGE 21" Americana Look a Must Have!	$60.00	Boyds Uncle Bean's Treasure Granny's Icebox w Frosty 1E	$12.50
Boyds Laura B. Bearyproud Plush	$56.00	[2 of these sold for $12.50 each]	
BOYD'S BEARS "Noah & The Ark" Musical Globe Ltd Edition	$54.00	Boyds Uncle Bean's Miss MacIntosh's Apple w/ Corey 1E	$12.50
10 Piece Boyd Bear Set	$49.00	Boyds Bears Wall Hanging Tapestry SHIPMATES Nautical	$12.50
BOYDS BEARS PLUSH WIZARD OF OZ 6-PC SET NEW IN BOX***	$46.00	BOYDS TREASURE BOX WILSON'S TYPEWRITER	$12.50
Boyds Carvers Choice Apple Harvest Stand LIKE NEW	$45.99	Boyds Bears Huck, Mandy & Zach Americana Set w/wagon	$12.50
BOYDS BAILEY BEAR ON SUITCASE COOKIE JAR-NIB-MINT COND.	$41.00	MINT AMBER B. OAKLEY BOYDS BEAR W/ TAGS	$12.00
Boyds First Ever Treasure Box Laurel Bearibean MIB	$41.00	BOYDS BEARS WITCHY BOOS BREW HALLOWEEN CANDLE HOLDER 1E	$11.99

Decorative Collectibles ▶ Christopher Radko

The average sales price in this subcategory is $27.75.

	HIGH		AVG
Signed Christopher Radko, Anniversary Disney Castle	$300.00	FROSTY TWIST RETIRED 2000 RADKO SNOWMAN ORNAMENT	$29.95
NWT Christopher Radko Pink Santa Ornament	$202.50	CHRISTOPHER RADKO 4.5" FROSTY-GO-ROUND-SNOWMAN	$29.95
Christopher Radko 2001 Caroling Snowmen Cookie Jar Mint	$159.99	MICKEY MOUSE CHRISTOPHER RADKO ORNAMENT DISNEY NR!!!!!!	$29.80
Christopher Radko Commemorative Bear Cookie Jar Mint	$149.99	Christopher Radko Santa in Car Ornament	$29.00
Christopher Radko 1995 Santa - St Nick	$139.28	RADKO 96-212-0 "FESTIVA" 6" TEARDROP BALL	$28.50
New Christopher Radko, Disney 50th Anniversary Castle	$130.99	RADKO TOY CHEST ORNAMENT	$28.09
Radko Santa in Car Rolls Royce Cookie Jar	$130.00	christopher radko STAR WARS ornament * NIB * NR!!	$28.01
Disney Radko Flora, Flauna & Meriweather Prototype 2000	$128.45	2003 Christopher Radko Surf & Sun, Tropical Tunes,	$27.99
Five (5) Christopher Radko Patriotic Ornaments	$127.50	Christopher Radko~ SEBASTIAN-The Little Mermaid-1997	$27.00
HTF L.E. Radko Disney 1997 BAMBI *THUMPER* ornament NR!	$127.50	RADKO SANTA SWIFT ORNAMENT	$26.99
Haunted Mansion, Nightmare, Christopher Radko, Disney	$127.50	Radko *MERRY MERLIN* NEW FOR 2005 1011588 (RED)	$26.99
Radko, Three French Hens - Twelve Days of Christmas	$124.95	Radko *MERRY MERLIN* NEW FOR 2005 1011588 (BLUE)	$26.99
Christopher Radko Signed Three French Hens in Box 1995	$122.50	(?'`_.? ~ 1999 RADKO ~ A Multitude of Angels ~ ?._'??)	$26.99
Christopher Radko Three French Hens New In Box 1995	$112.50	RADKO WIZARD OF WISHES CHRISTMAS ORNAMENT	$26.57
RADKO KOOKY SPOOKY HALLOWEEN FINIAL	$112.50	Christopher Radko-Holly Power Bells1011866 new NR	$26.51

Decorative Collectibles ▶ Dept 56

The average sales price in this subcategory is $23.84.

	HIGH		AVG
DEPARTMENT 56 BIRCH BARK SOUP TERRAIN	$351.50	Department 56 Wizard of OZ WE'RE NOT IN KANSAS ANYMORE	$24.99
Dept 56 Disney Park Village- Complete Set	$285.50	Dept 56 Halloween KRINKLES RAGGEDY WITCH FIGURE 13 INCH	$24.99
DEPT56 SEASONS BAY "KITE OF SPRING" RETIRED2002! MIB!	$162.51	DEPT 56 FIBER OPTIC SITTING BLACK CAT HALLOWEEN ADORABL	$24.99

	HIGH		
D56 Farfingle's Department Store Dr Seuss & Grinch NIB	$131.99	DEPT 56 HAUNTED FRONT YARD	$24.99
Dept 56 "WELCOME CHRISTMAS" LIGHTED TREE Grinch NR	$128.01	Dept 56 KRINKLES POINSETTIA CHRISTMAS STOCKING NEW	$24.99
Dept.56 RETIRED Haunted Barn Gift Set MIB-Paypal ONLY	$127.50	DEPT. 56 Folk Art Chicken Collectible Figurine McNutt 7	$24.72
DEPT 56 HALLOWEEN 7NEW piecesIN BOX!!!!!!!	$117.50	DEPT 56 NORTH POLE WOODS	$24.50
Dept 56 -Dickens Christmas Carol plate #3-1993 orig box	$103.52	Harley-Davidson Sign/Happy Harley Day/Two for the Road	$24.02
Dept 56 HERKY JERKY WHOMOBILE Grinch Dr Seuss NR	$100.89	Dept 56 Fall / Halloween - WINDMILL BY THE CHICKEN COOP	$23.54
DEPARTMENT 56 KENILWORTH CASTLE DICKENS VILLAGE	$100.00	Lot of (4) Department 56 Seasons Bay Accessories MIB	$23.50
HALLOWEEN DEPT 56 SNOW VILLAGE *HELGA'S FORTUNES SC@RCE	$93.99	Dept 56 Merry Makers Godfrey the Gatherer (MIB)	$23.48
Dept 56 FARFINGLE'S DEPARTMENT STORE Grinch Dr Seuss NR	$90.00	D56 PEANUTS COLLECTION "PEANUTS TRICK OR TREATS" New	$22.99
DEPARTMENT 56 CANDLE CROWNS- WIZARD OF OZ! SET 4!	$86.00	Dept. 56 - M&M'S Haunted Mine~Lighted~~2005	$22.99
Dept 56 Halloween PUNCH BOWL Black Cats & Pumpkins New	$86.00	Dept 56 General Village Stone Trestle Bridge	$22.99
Department Dept 56 Halloween Pumpkin Lit Haunted Scene	$82.02	NEW 2005 D.56 CHRISTMAS KRINKLES "NUTCRACKER" FIGURE	$22.89

Decorative Collectibles ▸ Enesco

The average sales price in this subcategory is $14.34.

	HIGH		AVG
Pink Sprinkler Bottle - Prayer Lady	$960.99	Enesco Ornament Chimer 4th wee trim	$14.99
ENESCO MAJESTIC MUSICAL FERRIS WHEEL EXCELLENT!!!	$137.53	Enesco Ornament "Happily Ever After" Snow White & 7 dw	$14.99
PARTY LINE ENESCO ANIMATED MUSIC BOX MOUSE PAY PHONE	$100.64	HEAVENLY KINGDOM "IN BOAT" # 612855 Enesco 1995–NR	$14.99
3 ENESCO MUSIC BOXES THE MAJESTIC, TEA FOR TWO, WHISTLE	$82.88	THOMAS KINKADE COTTAGE BY BROOKE MUSIC BOX NEW!!!	$14.95
PINK PRAY LADY CANDLE HOLDER	$75.00	Vintage Enesco Prayer Lady Toothpick holder pink mint	$14.50
Vintage Enesco Pink PRAYER LADY Air Freshener Holder	$62.00	GROWING UP birthday girl 16 by Enesco	$14.50
LOT 13 ENESCO CHRISTMAS ORNAMENTS ALL MOUSE MICE NR	$61.87	Enesco Kitchen Fairy "Birthday Cake"(New) Low S/H $4.00	$14.49
WAGGIN TAILS ENESCO MOUSE ANIMATED MUSIC BOX WESTERN	$57.56	Enesco Ornament Have A Soup-er Christmas 1st Campbell	$14.27
1992 I MADE IT WITH MY OWN HANDS by Laura's Attic	$54.99	Enesco Treasured Memories "Dressing Warm" 1981 Mom/Girl	$14.26
Enesco Kitchen Prayer Lady Planter	$53.01	ENESCO ORNAMENT PLAY IT AGAIN SANTA (AFRICAN -AMERICAN)	$14.05
BEDFORD FALLS BRIDGE MIB ITS A WONDERFUL LIFE LIGHT UP	$46.75	Kitchen Fairy onTeapot by Enesco NIB	$14.00
Cherished Teddies Santas workshop display	$46.00	Enesco Ornament Tinkertoy Joy	$13.83
KITCHEN PRAYER LADIES CRUMB TRAY OR DUST PAN NO.RES.	$43.50	2002 ENESCO FOUNDATIONS ANGEL/LOVE FIGURINE	$13.63
Circle of Love "Forever Bride & Groom" by Kim Lawrence	$41.00	Enesco Ornament "Mistle-Toast" 1st Christmas together	$13.57
Vintage Enesco Snappy Snail Teapot	$40.77	Enesco mitey-nice schoolhouse multi-action musical	$13.50

Decorative Collectibles ▸ Hummel, Goebel

The average sales price in this subcategory is $33.76.

	HIGH		AVG
1959 Goebel Salt & Pepper Woman w/ Muff	$870.00	RARE Hummel Goebel Angel Plaque TM1 CROWN MARK	$50.50
MI HUMMEL - TROUBLEMAKER, NEW FOR 2005, MINT/BOXED	$549.99	Hummel Feeding Time 199/0 1948	$50.00
1995 Olszewski "Dashing through the Snow" Signed MINT	$281.00	Goebel 1992 The Mail Is Here Clock Tower	$49.99
HUMMEL FIGURINE - "TRAVELING TRIO"	$275.00	HUMMEL GOEBEL 4" BIRD DUET #169 TMK 6	$49.95
HUMMEL GOEBEL FIGURINE CRYSTAL WINE GLASS FULL SET LNIB	$250.00	Hummel Figurine-For Father-Beautiful condition-NR	$47.00
Hummel Table Lamp 234 Birthday Serenade TMK-4	$203.50	2 1957 HUMMEL WERK VINYL DOLLS CHARLOT BYI IRISH	$46.00
Berta Hummel Christmas Village - Set of 8	$200.00	Beautiful Hummel Figurine-Farewell-Final Issue-Mint-NR	$45.99
RARE Terra Cotta Fawn Master Sculptors CE 15 Hummel	$199.99	1987 HUMMEL 21 SPICE JARS & RACK	$45.00
Beautiful Hummel Figurine-Coquettes-Mint cond.-NR	$158.50	Hummel STORE PLAQUE figurine 187 1947 W.Germany	$44.89
Hummel lamp. Out of Danger	$158.22	6 Hummel Music Boxes Feeding Time Apple Tree Girl Boy +	$42.99
HUMMEL GOEBEL GERMANY FRIAR TUCK STEIN mug	$153.00	Hummel Annual Bell 1991 "Favorite Pet" 14th in series	$42.51
Hummel Table Lamp 225/I Just Resting TMK-4	$152.50	MI HUMMEL - THE BOTANIST, NO.351/4/0, NEW, MINT & BOXED	$42.50
Hummel Figurines-Apple Tree Boy & Girl-Full Bee-Mint-NR	$152.50	VINTAGE HUMMEL OUT OF DANGER TABLE LAMP 44B	$42.00
Adorable Hummel Figurine-Blessed Event-Mint-NR	$152.50	M.J.Hummel HANDPAINTED GLASS /ARS #1451 Bernhardt NIB	$41.99
hummel #2135/C "precious pianist" tm8 3.75" nib $219	$150.00	Vintage Hummel Goebel Merry Wanderer Dealer Plaque	$40.99

Decorative Collectibles ▸ Lladro

The average sales price in this subcategory is $100.28.

	HIGH		AVG
Retired LLADRO FATHER SUN Greek GOD WAS $1750 SUPERB!!	$999.00	Very Nice LLADRO Oriental Geisha Lady w/ fan over face	$102.50
RETIRED Lladro The BLESSING John The Baptist SUPERB!!	$995.00	Retired Lladro - Prissy / Coiffure - Girl w/ Straw Hat	$102.50
Lladro " YOUNG MOZART " #5915G @LIMITED EDITION@	$880.00	Huge LLADRO #5611 Clown figure	$102.50
BEAUTIFUL LLADRO PAIR OF SIAMESE DANCER	$805.56	RARE LLADRO 4970# " SKIER PUPPET " RTD 85	$102.50
Lladro Summer, Fall, Winter, Spring Eggs	$760.00	Lladro " GARDEN TREASURES " #5591G @@RETIRED@@	$102.50
LLADRO "VICTORIAN LADY ON SWING " #1297G @ RETIRED@	$635.00	LLADRO #1071 SAD PUPPY DOG FIGURINE MINT $5NR!	$100.99
LLADRO Loving Mother Figurine #12409	$600.00	BEAUTIFUL LLADRO GIRL WITH GEESE NO RESERVE!	$100.75
LLADRO "LADY ON A HORSE" MINT CONDITION	$570.01	LLADRO Nun Catholic Nuns RETIRED #04611 Christianity	$100.01
Here Comes the Bride LLadro Figurine - Retired 1997	$511.00	1996 Lladro egg - herd of deer decoration Mint w box	$100.00
Lladro 6842 - You're Everything To - Figurines BNIB	$455.00	Lladro #5595 - Joy in a Basket	$100.00
LLADRO DANCE OF THE NYMPHS #1844 FIGURINE NIB SIGNED NR	$430.57	lladro "Wandering Minstrel"	$100.00
Lladro Pharmacist Figurine # 0100484 Retired	$404.99	BALLERINA STATUE HAND-MADE in SPAIN, 1979	$99.99
Lladro Figurine Medieval Girl #1381 -Retired-RARE-MINT!	$400.00	Lladro Girl with Milk Pail (Retired 1991)	$99.99
Lladro Couple on a Horse 18'' Porcelain Figurine	$400.00	Lladro porcelain figure, Bar Mitzvah Boy Reading Books	$99.00
Lladro THE HAPPIEST DAY New In Box!	$399.00	Lladro Astrology figurine Gemini 9 1/2" With Twins	$97.50

Decorative Collectibles ▸ Longaberger

The average sales price in this subcategory is $22.42.

	HIGH		AVG
Longaberger Queen Garden Splendor Bedding! NR!	$295.00	Longaberger Small Key 1st Basket	$24.00
LONGABERGER NEW WOVEN PANEL CHEST	$250.00	LONGABERGER BOYDS BASKET	$23.99
[2 of these sold for $250.00 each]		HANGER SITTER PATRICIA RARE NR	
Longaberger Hostess Housekeeper Basket Set! MINT	$235.00	Longaberger 1998 Sweetheart Basket	$23.38
LONGABERGER Butcher Block Wood Table with 3 Shelves	$214.50	LONGABERGER PEWTER PIE MAGNET & RESIN RECIPE BASKET	$23.00
LONGABERGER 1990 VIOLET BASKET SET MAY SERIES - RARE!	$207.50	LONGABERGER At Home Garden Vine Rug NEW	$23.00
LONGABERGER COMFORTER MINT COTTAGE TRELLIS SHAMS FREE	$199.99	Longaberger WW Whitewash Framed Kitchen Print Picture	$22.50
Longaberger Mini Resin Baskets & Pottery Signed & Dated	$185.50	Longaberger / Boyds Bears / Lucky O'Beary	$22.50
LONGABERGER Generations Wrought Iron Stand w/ Baskets	$157.76	Longaberger WoodCrafts Classic 11" Measuring Basket Lid	$22.49
Longaberger Picinic Basket Combo, LOADED	$152.50	1998 Small Purse w/ protector	$22.05
Retired Longaberger Generations Table	$127.50	Longaberger Basket CHERRY Fruit Medley Matted Print	$22.01
Longaberger Wrought Iron Envelope Rack - Retired	$95.00	Longaberger Green Toothpick & Sweetner Set - NEW-	$22.00
Longaberger Extra-Large Oval Picnic Basket Second	$89.99	Lngbrgr WINDOWBOX BSKT & WI STAND 3 Votive Holder NEW!	$21.99
Longaberger Wrought Iron Snowman and 2 Faces	$87.00	Longaberger Umbrella Protector - NEW-	$21.53
Longaberger Lots of Luck/Lucky You Sets NR!!!	$80.04	Longaberger - HEARTLAND - 1996 Medium Chore Basket	$21.50
Longaberger BOTANICAL FIELDS Shower Curtain	$79.99	Longaberger Little Market Basket Second	$21.50

Decorative Collectibles ▸ Swarovski

The average sales price in this subcategory is $85.19.

	HIGH		AVG
Swarovski 1995 SCS Limited Edition Eagle	$4,995.00	SWAROVSKI CRYSTAL DECOR OLIVINE NAPKIN RINGS	$94.99
SWAROVSKI ELEPHANT _ 1993 COLLECTOR'S SOCIETY PIECE	$700.00	Swarovski Crystal SOUTH SEA SHELL	$92.00
SWAROVSKI CRYSTAL GREEN MACAW - #685824	$685.00	Swarovski Crystal Christmas Tree Topper, mib	$91.06
NEW RETIRED SWAROVSKI APOLLO BOWL NO RESERVE!!!	$679.99	Swarovski Crystal SOUTH SEA SHELL	$91.00
NEW RETIRED SWAROVSKI APOLLO	$674.99	Swarovski ADENA LIGHT SIAM BUTTERFLY	$87.06
BOWL 206-212 NO RESERVE!!!		BLUE TULIP - SWAROVSKI CRYSTAL COLLECTOR'S SOCIETY	$86.00
Swarovski 2004 Retired Maxi Dolphin MINT in Box New !	$568.00	Swarovski CHILIPI aquamarine seahorse	$86.00
SCS limited edition 1989 Swarovski Turtledoves	$534.09	JAY STRONGWATER FOX FIGURINE $175.00	$85.00
SWAROVSKI RARE 1990 COLLECT. SOC.. LMTD ED "LEAD ME"	$480.00	[3 of these sold for $85.00 each]	
SWAROVSKI Crystal SOLIFLOR Bud Vase 0168000 RETIRED	$379.99	Swarovski Prince Frog	$84.85
SWAROVSKI.PEGASUS COLLECT" STAND FREE WITH BUY NOW"	$355.00	SWAROVSKI SCS KUDU STAND W/ BOX	$84.69
Swarovski - #118 CANDLEHOLDER ** Rare **	$355.00	Swarovski 2003 Retired Replica Set Cat Mouse Hedgehog	$82.01
Jay Strongwater Atlantis Fish Clock NIB Bargain!!	$350.00	Swarovski CELAYA Waikiki Blue seahorse brooch/pin	$80.99
Swarovski crystal Wonders of the Sea COLOR brand NITB	$340.89	Swarovski Crystal PEAR	$80.00
12 -Swarovski * 2003 Xmas ORNAMENTS * MINT Never Open	$329.00	JAY STRONGWATER SPANIEL FIGURINE $195.00	$80.00
JAY STRONGWATER LILY OF THE VALLY BOUQUET OBJECT	$317.00	SWAROVSKI CRYSTAL FLACON NAPOLEON (PERFUME BOTTLE)	$79.99

Decorative Collectibles ▸ Unbranded

The average sales price in this subcategory is $17.54.

	HIGH		AVG
John Deere Precision Classic	$400.00	McCoy SMILEY FACE HAPPY DAY Bowl-Mug-Plate Set	$24.95
4 BMW 16" Rims Michelin Alpine Tires 5 & 7 series 735i	$385.00	ART NOUVEAU 3 PIECE DESK SET	$24.50
John Deere Precision Classic	$305.05	ELIGANT ALIFORMS NEW BUTTERFLY W/ ADD-ON- LIFE-LIKE	$24.50
Real Mueller Fire Hydrant	$127.50	Elvis printed on bottle of razor relief 2.5 oz full	$24.00
National Maritime Historical Society Collectible Set	$127.00	Primitive Wood Antique Miniature Vintage Hope Chest Box	$21.52
Real Mueller Fire Hydrant	$122.50	Ghirardelli Replica Stagecoach Carriage	$20.50
Replica Wood Airplane Propeller - Two Tone Large	$90.00	Miniature Great Vintage Blue Bicycle with Front Basket	$20.02
SIGNED J STRONGWATER FOR ESTEE LAUDER 2002	$89.95	Squirrel Fountain	$20.00
Victorian Lady Face Mask wall Decor Hanging	$69.00	DEZINE FAIRIES "BUBBLE FAIRY" RETIRED	$19.99
IVOREX Osbourne plaque Canadian War Memorial Vimy Ridge	$66.65	Halloween Party MINIATURE TEA SET	$15.99
Victorian Lady Face Mask wall Decor Hanging	$59.50	Ceramic Windmill Light and Dutch Shoe	$15.76
VINTAGE RAILROAD STATION LAKEWOOD NEW JERSEY DISH	$58.76	Four SHERLOCK HOLMES Lapel Pins Attractive!	$15.55
Butterfly wing bird picture	$51.01	ELEPHANT LOVER MINIATURE TEA SET	$15.50
Victorian Lady Face Mask wall Decor Hanging	$49.50	Cloisonne 6 1/4" Oriental Ginger Jar	$15.50
Vintage Cowboy/Cowgirl Silhouette - Ex. Cond.	$47.88	VINTAGE JADITE GREEN APPLE DISH WITH COVER L@@K	$15.49

Disneyana ▸ Vintage (Pre–1968)

The average sales price in this subcategory is $41.21.

	HIGH		AVG
Original Walt Disney Autograph and Check	$1,120.00	DISNEY GOLDEN HORSESHOE REVUE ORIGINAL BINDER W/ PHOTO'	$45.44
RARE Huge MIB 16" A/O 1930's Mickey Mouse	$775.00	1964 MARY POPPINS *Disneyware* Melmac Child's Set-MIP	$45.11
Schuco Disneyland Monorail; 6333 Set with silver train	$590.00	1955 Disneyland Walt Disney 1st Postcard P Series RARE	$45.05
VINTAGE MICKEY MOUSE ZIPPO LIGHTER !! MINT CONDITION !!	$570.00	7 Vintage Gund Disney Squeaky Hand Puppet Set Lot	$43.52
MARX BOXED TIN MECHANICAL PLUTO MINT IN BOX	$510.00	Snow White Planter (Vintage)	$43.00
Rare Walt Disney Vernon Kilns Painted Mushroom Bowl	$495.00	VINTAGE WALT DISNEY BABY INFANT CRIB RECEIVING BLANKET	$42.99
1938 Ferdinand & Matador Marx Tin Wind Up Disney Toy	$409.48	VINTAGE 1930 DISNEY THREE LITTLE PIG MUG SEBRING CHINA	$42.99
VINTAGE MICKEY MOUSE	$406.88	DIME BANK-DISNEY-SNOW WHITE AND THE SEVEN DWARFS	$42.55
1939 Vintage Disney Golden Gate Exposition Map Poster	$395.00	1963 MICKEY MOUSE CLUB METAL LUNCHBOX W / THERMOS	$41.00
1960s VINTAGE MICKEY MOUSE DISNEY GOLD ZIPPO wBOX NR!	$348.55	Vintage Davy Crockett Pencil Box ı1954 Disney	$41.00
Vintage Bakelite Figural Snow White Napkin Ring	$312.00	Fantasia mixing bowl Disney Vernon Kilns	$40.00

THE 1930S MICKEY MOUSE WATERING CAN OHIO ART.	$310.75	VINTAGE MICKEY MOUSE WALT DISNEY ENT. WRITING TABLET $40.00
1959 Sleeping Beauty Cell	$306.00	Disney Mickey Bandleader Drum major rug carpet mat $40.00
Vintage Mickey Mouse Enamel Chrome Compact Powder Box	$293.99	DISNEY CINDERELLA GLASSES SET 6 VINTAGE $39.99
Vintage Celluloid Donald Duck Nodder	$273.09	Mouseketeer Handbag by Coleco #1633 $38.99

Fantasy, Mythical & Magic ▶ Dragons

The average sales price in this subcategory is $21.82.

	HIGH		AVG
High quality Dragon Holding Light globe Lamp	$235.00	Mythical Dragon Bookends! MINT! Medieval Gothic	$24.99
WINDSTONE EDITIONS PEARL DRAGON $9.99	$182.51	Dragon Gargoyle Demon On The Loose Wall 15"	$24.99
Enchantica _Snowthorn & Wargren_ EN2062	$152.50	KRYSTONIA - #3961 "THE PROPOSAL" - MIB - 2001 HARD FIND	$24.00
Windstone Editions, Pena, Retired White Male Dragon	$132.50	Luree tiny FANTASY DRAGON painting art ACEO atc CARD NR	$22.50
Medieval Knight Standing Lamp lighting globe	$117.50	Visions Of The Sorcerer Bradford Exchange Plates (4) NR	$22.49
Enchantica Summer Dragon 'Arangast' 1st Edition EN2026	$110.00	Rinconada Baby Dragon Rincababy~#1723 LE piece NIB	$21.94
Mysteric Standing Dragon with Fire Pot Lamp Night Light	$109.99	*HUGE BEAUTIFUL GREEN DRAGON TAPESTRY~WOW!*	$21.73
WINDSTONE EDITIONS PEARL DRAGON $9.99	$102.51	*HUGE BLUE YIN YANG DRAGON TAPESTRY~AWESOME!*	$20.50
Enchantica _Pia'Sharn_ EN2162	$100.00	New Set Of Two 14" Dragon Touch Lamps Dragons Lamp Set	$20.50
Enchantica 5th Anniversary Piece _Escape_ EN2110	$100.00	MYSTICAL CREATIONS GOTHIC METAL DRAGON TABLE LAMP LIGHT	$20.49
Amazing Flying Dragon Glass table with lid box	$89.99	Dragon Gargoyle Lamp With Globe 9 3/4" Tall-MIB	$19.99
Special design black dragon Sitting Dragon Lamp	$84.99	Celtic Wiccan Gothic Dragon Soap Dish 8''	$19.99
Enchantica Rattajack _With Snail_ EN2102	$76.00	Vintage Bronze Brass Dragon Hinged Ashtray Monster	$19.00
Krystonia figurine ~ TAG (signed piece)	$76.00	*AWESOME CELTIC DRAGON CURTAIN/DOOR PANEL~WOW!*	$18.81
Enchantica _Kirrock_ EN2159	$76.00	Hand-made Dragon mobile-used	$18.50

Fantasy, Mythical & Magic ▶ Fairies

The average sales price in this subcategory is $11.20.

	HIGH		AVG
Complete Set AMY BROWN ATTITUDE Diva Ornaments Fairies	$92.00	Fairy Dreaming Pill Box...So Cute..	$12.95
Tibetan ShamanS WEE LITTLE WATER FAIRY ELFIN MAGIC	$77.00	Amy Brown Purple Fairy Letter Boxed Gift Set New	$12.52
The Art of Amy Brown Hard Cover Book Faery Fairy Fae	$30.00	10 Fairy Magnets ~ Faerie Magic ~ Cicely Mary Barker	$12.50
[2 of these sold for $30.00 each]		Phantom of the Opera Compact/Pocket Mirror	$12.50
Man in Moon Porcelain Lithophane Night Light Delamare	$29.99	AMY BROWN FAIRY ART BELIEVE	$12.00
Fairy & Unicorn Patchwork Bag ~* Fairies Purse ~*	$26.50	12 NOTE CARDS IN PHOTO TIN	
Angel & Dove Patchwork Bag *~ Fairy Purse ~*	$26.50	Autumn Magic Faery Fairy Amy Brown Cuppa Mug Fey Fae	$11.99
Absinthe Patchwork Bag *~ Green Fairy Purse ~	$26.50	MARK ROBERTS SUNFLOWER FAIRY PRINCESS	$11.99
Gnome & Mushrooms Patchwork Bag / Purse ~* Fairy	$26.50	~ TRIO FAIRY SLAVE BRACELET~	$11.49
Fairy Patchwork Bag *~ Fairies Purse ~*	$26.50	>>Two Flying Sky Dancer Dolls & Crescent Moon Base<<	$10.51
Willow Fairy Patchwork Bag ~ Cicely Mary Barker Purse	$26.50	The Faeries Oracle Fairies Book Fantasy Mystical Estate	$10.50
Phantom of the Opera Compact/Pocket Mirror	$26.00	LADY COTTINGTON PRESSED FAIRY BOOK TERRY JONES ~MINTY ~	$9.99
DEZINE FAIRY DISPLAY Faerie Glen for FIGURINES Flowers	$26.00	Fairy Pewter Gallo 1997 Stepping into Water	$9.99
FAIRY TABLE CLOCK SO BEAUTIFUL	$25.00	NEW ITEM! Amy Brown NAUGHTY FAERY REFILLABLE LIGHTER!	$9.99
Fairy VASE Art Nouveau woman antique ivory gold deco	$25.00	NEW ITEM! Amy Brown GLAMOUR Fairy REFILLABLE LIGHTER!	$9.99
Parting the Veil Art of Nene Thomas Soft Cover Book	$25.00	Amy Brown Moon Fairy large Patch New Fairie	$9.99

Fantasy, Mythical & Magic ▶ Harry Potter

The average sales price in this subcategory is $16.96.

	HIGH		AVG
Burlon "B.B." Craig Face Jug	$410.00	HARRY POTTER QUIDDITCH COLLECTORS WATCH HT0P15	$17.00
HARRY POTTER Wizard's Watch-Honor Dumbledore! NEW! NR!	$208.49	HARRY POTTER QUIDDITCH LUNCHBOX LUNCH BOX NEW w/ Tags	$17.00
Harry Potter Wizard Watch, Dumbledore Watch NEW NIB	$202.50	Harry Potter Playing Cards in Unique Book-Shaped Tin	$17.00
HARRY POTTER - RARE PROMO WAND FROM THE HP1 PREMIER	$200.00	HARRY POTTER QUIDDITCH COLLECTORS WATCH HT0P15	$17.00
New Harry Potter Dumbledore Wizard Wrist Watch Seiko	$174.99	Harry Potter Hogwarts Printed Banner	$16.99
Harry Potter DUMBLEDORE wizard WATCH ~ LIMITED EDITION	$165.26	Harry Potter w/Hedwig & HERMIONE w/Crookshanks Bookends	$16.95
Harry Potter Marauders Map prop replica Azkaban	$162.25	[2 of these sold for $16.95 each]	
ULTRA RARE HARRY POTTER DUMBLEDORE	$147.50	Harry Potter w/Hedwig & HERMIONE w/Crookshanks Bookends	$16.95
WIZARD WRIST WATCH!!		HARRY POTTER HALF-BLOOD PRINCE HAT CAP PROMO ITEMS	$16.50
Harry Potter, Ron, Hermione Wand Set by Noble	$132.50	HARRY POTTER CATCHES THE SNITCH BACKPACK NWT back pack	$16.49
HARRY POTTER- GREAT PIECE OF MEMORABILIA	$125.00	DANIEL RADCLIFFE HARRY POTTER HANDSIGNED AUTOGRAPH	$15.50
Harry Potter Hard Cover 1-5 books BRAND NEW	$105.00	Harry Potter Half Blood Prince Rare Promo Hat !!!	$15.50
Harry Potter Legos! Castle 4709, 4705, 4728, 4712,4708	$102.50	Harry Potter Childs Comforter and sleeping bag	$15.50
Harry Potter POA Style Robe Choose Your House - ooak	$100.00	Licensed HARRY POTTER Backpack HOGWARTS GRYFFINDOR	$15.49
Harry Potter Collector Stones 72 Boxes and Display!!	$92.13	Harry Potter One Crown Coin (Real Money) NR	$15.27
HARRY POTTER RETIRED POA REMOTE CONTROLLED KNIGHT BUS	$90.00	Set of 2 Harry Potter Secret Trinket Box/ Uno Game	$15.02

Fantasy, Mythical & Magic ▶ Lord of the Rings

The average sales price in this subcategory is $49.09.

	HIGH		AVG
LOTR-Sideshow Weta ORTHANC Statue "ARTIST PROOF" MIB	$1,675.00	LORD OF THE RINGS UC. OFFICIAL STAFF OF SARUMAN INSTOCK	$62.00
Ringwraith Steed Statue Sideshow Weta Lord of the Rings	$530.00	`UC1417BL Glamdring Sword of Gandalf Scabbard~Blue	$61.00
SAURON 24" statue Sideshow WETA LORD OF THE RINGS	$438.88	GANDALF Sir Ian McKellen Lord of the Rings ORIGINAL ART	$60.00
[2 of these sold for $438.88 each]		SIDESHOW WETA LOTR (KING ELENDIL) BUST / STATUE	$56.50
SAURON 24" statue Sideshow WETA LORD OF THE RINGS	$438.88	SIDESHOW WETA 'CROWN OF	$51.00
LORD RINGS DARK LORD SAURON SIDESHOW WETA STATUE	$400.00	KING ELESSAR' LORD OF THE RINGS	

	HIGH		AVG
Sideshow Star Wars General Grevous 1/4 Scale SOLD OUT	$399.00	LORD RINGS CROWN KING ELESSAR HELM SIDESHOW EXCLUSIVE	$50.00
Galadhrim Archer Statue Lord of the Rings Sideshow Weta	$306.00	Lord of the Rings ARAGORN FINE Pewter STATUE	$49.99
Sideshow Weta Legolas and Gimli on Arod	$275.00	Sideshow WETA No ADMITTANCE BOOKENDS _ Gandalf & Bilbo	$49.00
#2063 Helm of the Dark Lord Sauron~Lord Of The Rings	$267.00	LOTR Silver Arwens Pendant and Earrings Evenstar	$44.99
`UC1411 Gauntlet of Sauron~Lord Of The Rings	$255.00	Lord of the Rings ARGONATH Bookends Statues NEW IN BOX!	$44.99
LOTR Rings GANDALF SHADOWFAX Statue Sideshow WETA	$255.00	SIDESHOW SAURON'S MACE LOTR Lord of Rings In Stock !!	$43.95
LORD OF THE RINGS-SAURON LIMITED EDITION GAUNTLET	$250.00	SIDESHOW WETA LOTR (NAZGUL STEED) BUST / STATUE	$43.00
Sideshow Weta Aragorn at the Black Gate	$245.00	SIDESHOW WETA LOTR (LEGOLAS GREENLEAF) BUST	$42.00
Sideshow Weta Minas Tirith & Minas Morgul "SOLD OUT"	$242.51	?MER (Karl Urban) Lord of the Rings ORIGINAL ART	$39.99
LOTR Sideshow Gondorian Helm Set Lord Rings #61	$239.95	RARE LOTR ROTK FELL BEAST w/ RIDER 3 FT WINGSPAN LOT NR	$38.11

Fantasy, Mythical & Magic ▸ Magic

The average sales price in this subcategory is $25.82.

	HIGH		AVG
Modern Art Stage Illusion	$605.00	Early 1900s Odd Fellows Ceremonial Costume	$28.00
Richard Himber's Fifth Dimension - Like New	$405.00	MAGIC / MENTALISM - TIME TRAVEL_Retail $79.99	$27.78
THE UNMASKING OF ROBERT-HOUDIN by Harry Houdini!!	$350.67	Max Maven's Videomind	$27.51
P&L Six Shot Lota and Hindu Jug (Prayer Vase)	$250.00	MAGIC TRICKS- FIRE FROM PALMS -AS SEEN ON TV MAGIC	$26.99
HARRY LORAYNE!! Personal Collection!!!!	$229.99	Shoot Ogawa Ninja Rings DVD + Linking Rings	$26.00
John Pomeroy Gem Magic Watch Grinder - Great Prop!	$227.50	Super Silk Transport	$26.00
Apocalypse Magazine COMPLETE FILE Harry Lorayne	$202.50	Torn DVD by Daniel Garcia	$26.00
FLYING CARPET ILLUSION	$200.00	The Silk Worm	$26.00
RARE!!! KEN BROOKE! Improved Fred Lowe's Coin Cylinder!	$185.00	SEANCE MENTALISM EUGENE BURGER SPIRIT MAGIC DVD	$25.49
Milton professional ventriloquist dummy puppet	$177.50	Gilligan's Prediction! BRAND NEW! SUPER SALE PRICED!	$25.45
Mikame Craft Magician's Chest - Gorgeous Utility Prop!	$147.50	Gigantic Lot of Vintage Books - Bargain Price!	$25.00
Sealed Jerrys Nugget cards	$105.49	3 Pr REAL DOUBLE LOCKING HANDCUFFS - CHAINED KEYS GIFT	$24.99
MENTALISM MAGIC PSYCHIC Q&A RICHARD WEBSTER RARE	$103.50	MONDO MAGIC TRICKS FLAMING BOOK FIRE TRICK & free gift	$24.99
Electric Balloon Pump, Balloon Animals	$99.99	56223217 Collapsible Child Top Hat Black New	$24.99
Collector Edition: ERDNASE The Expert at the Card Table	$99.99	The Classic Force DVD from Paul Green! Brand New!	$24.95

Furniture, Appliances & Fans ▸ Electric Fans

The average sales price in this subcategory is $56.68.

	HIGH		AVG
RARE Robbins & Myers STANDARD Electric FAN Oscilator	$1,583.98	VINTAGE ART DECO FRESH'ND AIRE ELECTRIC FAN EAMES ERA	$60.99
Rare Kerosene Powered Desk Fan Lake Breeze Motor LQQK!!	$1,511.00	Vintage Sears Woodgrain Hassock Fan (4-Speed) in Box	$60.00
A+ ANTIQUE EMERSON Oscillating Fan MARKED BRASS Blades	$970.00	VINTAGE DAYTON BRASS BLADE OSCELATING FAN	$60.00
Vintage Hot Air Fan Radio or Jost Germany	$749.99	VINTAGE VORNADO JR. ELECTRIC FAN - GREAT CONDITION	$58.97
Early Menominee Brass Blade Electric Fan	$735.00	OLD ANTIQUE BRASS CHANDELIER	$58.86
Vintage GE Brass Electric Fan Prepayment Motor NoRes!	$610.00	Vintage Northwind Brass Electric House Fan.	$57.01
Emerson Ceiling Fan Vintage Old Antique	$540.00	Fitzgerald Co. Starrite Chrome Electric 3-Speed Fan	$57.00
ADAMS-BAGNALL ELECTRIC CO.brass blade electric fan	$520.00	General Electric GE Copper Cast Iron Ceiling Fan NR!	$57.00
EMERSON SILVER SWAN VINTAGE ART DECO FAN ON STAND	$490.00	ANTIQUE CENTURY Electric FAN BRASS Blades Pat. 1914	$56.55
Early 1900's Ornate Westinghouse Ceiling Fan -BEAUTIFUL	$450.00	Vintage, Port A temp, Air Conditioner, Unique	$56.00
Antique Electric Cast Iron Fan 1897 Ornate GE Brass	$428.00	VINTAGE HASSOCK FLOOR FAN KENMORE 3 SPEED EAMES	$56.00
HOMART belt driven window fan - 1950's vintage	$415.27	Vintage LASKO Electric Window Fan all Metal	$55.09
Early Emerson Induction Motor Fan Brass Plated Blades	$404.00	Vintage Robbins & Myers Working Brass Blade Fan # 3600	$55.00
Trojan Emerson Electric Mfg Brass Fan Vintage No. 53644	$382.00	Vintage Robbins & Meyers Brass Blade & 17" Cage Fan	$53.58
Very nice 1901 GE GENERAL ELECTRIC 3 Speed BRASS FAN	$381.99	ROBBINS&MYERS VINTAGE , SMALL FAN BRASS BLADES!!	$53.22

Furniture, Appliances & Fans ▸ Furniture, Large Appliances

The average sales price in this subcategory is $170.26.

	HIGH		AVG
2 Edward Wormley for Dunbar Brass & Woven Front Cabinet	$5,902.00	ANTIQUE GE GENERAL ELECTRIC MONITOR TOP REFRIGERATOR	$192.50
FRANK LLOYD WRIGHT VINTAGE PRICE TOWER CHAIR- IMPORTANT	$5,800.00	TWO VINTAGE EAMES HERMAN MILLER SHELL CHAIRS	$188.50
Eero Aarnio Ball Globe Chair 'The Genuine Article'	$2,025.01	Vintage Antique Maytag Wringer Washer Model E2LS	$187.50
MILO BAUGHMAN Sideboard CREDENZA	$1,925.00	Vintage- Maple Butcher Block	$185.00
BAR Chrome Wood Eames		3 Lovely BAR STOOLS for $134.99 - only 3 months old	$182.50
1930'S GE MONITOR TOP 3 DOOR REFRIGERATOR NR	$1,775.00	VINTAGE WORKING MAYTAG WRINGER	$180.27
8 Vintage Eames Chairs w/ Original Bikini pads 60's	$1,625.00	WASHER WASHING MACHINE	
Western Furniture, Leather Sleigh Bed, Nailhead Trim	$1,300.00	1949 Herman Miller Eames Nelson Noguchi Book	$177.50
Rare 1960's Marcel Breuer Thonet B35 Chair: Eames Era	$1,150.00	Retro Vintage Chrome Dinette Chairs Red Silver Spartan	$175.00
Lislet COMMANDER Wood Burning Cook Stove	$1,100.00	Herman Miller La Fonda Shell Chair on casters	$160.00
OKEEFE & MERRITT COOK STOVE OVEN 1940/1950 salt&pepper	$860.00	Mackintosh Hill House Chair	$154.79
MONT BLANC #40 FOUNTAIN PEN . RARE.	$800.00	VintageThonet plywood chair-(Eames Heywood Wakefield)	$152.50
ORIGINAL BOMBO STOOLS DESIGNED BY STEFANO GIOVANNONI	$799.00	MODERN EAMES ERA PAUL MCCOBB CHAIRS by WINCHENDON	$152.50
6 MILO BAUGHMAN Chrome Cube DINING Conference CHAIRS	$795.00	ANNA CASTELLI KARTELL PLASTIC ROUND UP STORAGE SYSTEM	$152.50
OKEEFE & MERRITT COOK STOVE OVEN 1940/1950 salt&pepper	$795.00	Vintage Hoover Upright Vacuum 1940's Works! NR!	$151.75
HEYWOOD WAKEFIELD KNEEHOLE DESK M320 EX COND	$791.00	Pair Eames Era Danish Modern Lane Dovetail End Tables	$150.00

Historical Memorabilia ▸ Fairs, Expositions

The average sales price in this subcategory is $27.61.

	HIGH		AVG
1939 Golden Gate International Exposition road sign	$2,024.00	Souvenir badge&Coin Jamestown Exposition Ter-Centenial	$30.89
Original 1958 Brussels Worlds Fair Flag Flags - Huge	$335.00	PPIE PAN PACIFIC HARDBACK BOOK /PLATES '15 WORLD'S FAIR	$29.99
PPIE TOWER OF JEWELS OFFICIAL'S PIN 1915	$305.00	1915 PANAMA PACIFIC WORLD'S FAIR GOLD MEDAL COIN	$29.99

EXPO 58 BRUSSELS WORLD'S FAIR MINIATURE BUILDING 1958	$226.49	Tower American '68 World's Fair Texas Metal Building.	$29.59
1898 McKinley Trans Mississippi Expo dinner menu	$203.50	1939 Golden Gate Exposition Souvenir Spoon-Deco Nude La	$28.67
1937 INTERNATIONAL PARIS EXPO COLOR GORSKY PHOTOGRAPHY	$170.00	Aluminum Coin / Token 1894 San Francisco Midwinter Fair	$28.49
San Francisco PPIE Grnd Breaking 1911 Golden Gate Park	$159.06	ACE: VINTAGE SOUVENIR BUILDING WORLDS FAIR ATOMIUM BRUX	$27.99
FAIR AND EXPO tickets and "oddments"	$158.50	1907 Jamestown Exposition Historical Events Guide w/Map	$27.88
PANAMA PACIFIC EXPO SILVER ENAMEL COIN CASE 1915	$140.27	1934 Rio de Janeiro International Exposition (Brazil)	$27.00
San Francisco Panama Pacific Plate PPIE Cliff House	$138.49	SAN FRANCISCO WORLD'S FAIR 1939 PORTFOLIO OF 12 IMAGES	$27.00
LEWIS & CLARK EXPOSITION 1905 HAND MIRROR	$129.16	Jamestown Tercent 1907/Champion Potato Mach Near EF	$27.00
BEAUTIFUL 1907 INDIAN MAIDEN JAMESTOWN SOUVENIR SPOON	$125.50	1937 PARIS INTERNATIONAL EXPOSITION-20 PC BOOKLET	$26.99
1915 PANAMA PACIFIC EXPO SOUVENIR $50 GOLD SLUG	$110.27	1926 CELLULOID Mirror~SESQUI-CENTENNIAL EXPO~ Phila PA	$26.01
1910 London-Japan/British Exhibition Guide w/Map	$109.50	EXPO 92 Pin WORLD SONG General Motors 1992 WORLD'S FAIR	$26.00
Texas Centennial 1936 Kellogg's Jr. Ranger Certificate	$103.51	San Antonio"Hemisfair 68"Poster-Official -BIG	$26.00

Historical Memorabilia ▶ Flags

The average sales price in this subcategory is $7.90.

	HIGH		AVG
WWI Medical Field Hospital Guidon Flag	$204.49	MILLER LITE BEER FLAG FLAGS SUPER POLYESTER 3 X 5	$8.50
Michigan State Police FLAG	$76.00	GUATEMALA FLAG GUATEMALAN FLAG SHOPPING BEACH BAG TOTE	$8.50
WORLD WAR TWO OR ONE WW2	$39.99	JOLLY ROGER PIRATES 3'X5' FLAG CARIBBEAN Swords NEW	$7.99
WWI COLLAPSABLE FLAG POLE		New 3'x5' State Flag of Georgia 1956-2001	$7.99
RARE SEWN 34 STAR US UNION CIVIL WAR FLAG COTTON FLAGS!	$38.90	REBEL REDNECK FLAG - - - Confederate Flag - - 3x5ft	$7.99
2 OLD 48 STAR US FLAGS - PRINTED STARS/SEWN STRIPES	$29.75	Denmark Flag 36X60" NEW Flags 3X5'	$7.99
CSA REBEL BATTLE COTTON EMBROIDERED 3X5 FLAG	$28.95	Nova Scotia Flag 36X60" NEW Flags 3X5'	$7.99
69th IRISH BRIGADE REGIMENT EMBROIDERED 3X5 FLAG	$28.95	Ontario Flag 36X60" NEW Flags 3X5'	$7.99
COTTON SONS OF ERIN EMBROIDERED 3X5 FLAG	$28.95	3X5 AMERICAN BETSY ROSS FLAG 13 STAR FLAGS	$7.99
IRISH AMERICAN ERIN GO BRAGH EMBROIDERED 3X5 FLAG	$28.95	3X5 USA AMERICAN FLAG! 50 STARS! FLAGS NEW	$7.99

Historical Memorabilia ▶ Fraternal Groups

The average sales price in this subcategory is $21.23.

	HIGH		AVG
Beta Theta Pi gold fraternal pin badge dated 1854	$1,245.00	RAOB Medal - Buffaloes Together Summer Gala 2001	$23.01
Gold DAR Daughters American Revolution Pin Set 9 Pins	$382.99	TOTE Totem of The Eagle Improved Order Red Men Pin OLD	$22.50
1907 PC-Red Men Coming To Rehoboth Beach, Delaware-NR	$311.90	[2 of these sold for $22.50 each]	
Diamond 14KWG Cufflinks+ J Bonanno Mafia Godfather	$305.00	3 Vintage ILLINOIS BELL TELEPHONE CO Service Pins 10K	$22.27
SAR Sons Of The Revolution Member Badge Medal Pin	$213.07	1930's Improved Order of Red Men license plate TIN SIGN	$21.59
Night Riders of Reelfoot Lake Hooded Robe early 1900's	$200.00	LOT NH OLD GRANGE HUSBANDY FARMING EPHEMERA MEMORABLIA	$21.50
L.V. RONSON 1922 KIWANIS INTERNATIONAL BOOKENDS	$159.06	2 American Legion Past President Pins 10K Gold	$21.50
Motorcycle Club patch, biker patches,	$150.00	1914 Societa Columbus Washington Sons Pin Franklin Mass	$21.00
14k DAUGHTERS OF THE AMERICAN REVOLUTION D A R PIN NR	$135.00	CERTIFIED PUBLIC ACCOUNTANT w/ CPA Stamp	$20.95
1939 RITUAL BOOK ORDER OF THE RAINBOW FOR GIRLS	$132.50	LAWYER - LIBERTY & JUSTICE - with the ABA Stamp	$20.95
1907 PC-Red Men on Boardwalk-Rehoboth Beach, Del-NR	$108.47	1911 National Grange Convention Columbus, Ohio medal	$20.76
1875 MASONIC MEDAL OR FOB - 14KT - TRINITY CHAPTER	$106.49	SHRINERS 14K WHITE GOLD & DIAMOND LAPEL PIN NR !	$20.60
SONS OF THE AMERICAN REVOLUTION	$103.50	Bethlehem 53 Commandery Mount Vernon Drill Corps Medal	$20.55
NECK MEDAL #'d V -RARE		VINTAGE NAVAL ACADEMY MIDDIES FELT BANNER	$20.50
JUBILEE BOOK OF THE UKRANIAN	$99.99	Vintage EASTERN STAR Hanky Handkerchief	$20.50
NATIONAL ASSOCIATION 1936		Lot of 27 mixed fraternal pins and stuff - cool!	$20.50
ORIG ANTIQUE KNIGHTS OF PYTHIAS SWORD HENDERSON-AMES	$82.99	VINTAGE Shriners HAT BOX Clean Mint Condition	$20.50

Historical Memorabilia ▶ Political

The average sales price in this subcategory is $38.69.

	HIGH		AVG
++1793 US CENT CERTIFIED VERY FINE PCI,PCGS,ANCS	$3,100.00	1927 NY Times newspaper Sacco & Vanzetti executed	$66.00
Autographed Martin Luther King Jr Photo	$1,000.00	WILLIAM O. DOUGLAS SIGNED LETTER SUPREME COURT 1972	$58.79
VINTAGE WOMAN SUFFRAGE PARTY 1910's Banner VG NR!!!	$546.90	Official CIA Award Plaque The Real Deal	$56.05
JACK SMITH's WHITE HOUSE NEWS PHOTOGRAPHERS BADGE- RARE!	$424.99	1896 WJ Bryan's No Cross of Gold Sheet music	$53.96
Fran Hopkinson, Declaration of Independence	$410.00	Rare Unused Eugene Debs Stamp from 1920 while in Prison	$53.58
1853 WOMENS RIGHTS SONG - KATE HORN BALLAD	$363.99	++1803 US CENT CERTIFIED VG08 PCI,PCGS,ANCS,NGC++	$52.18
Justice Sandra Day O'Connor Bobblehead Doll Green Bag	$345.69	LESTER MADDOX - LUDOWICI, Ga. SPEED TRAP License Plate	$51.00
Antique Campaign Pins(2), Chas. Evans Hughes	$330.16	73 OLDER POLITICAL CAMPAIGN AND OTHER BUTTONS & PINS NR	$46.99
CURRIER PRINT WHIG TICKET-CLAY & FRELINGHUYSEN 1844	$300.00	New Historical US Congressional Holiday Ornament lot 9	$46.00
1900- McKinley / Roosevelt POLITICAL PIN/BUTTON	$294.00	George Wallace 1968 Presidential Campaign License Plate	$45.44
++1795 US CENT CERTIFIED VERYGOOD8 PCI,PCGS,ANCS	$280.08	CIA ZIPPERED SMALL PORTFOLIO EMBOSSED SEAL	$44.99
25 Unpublished Robert F. Kennedy Assassination Photos	$250.00	++1798 US CENT CERTIFIED FR2 PCI,PCGS,ANCS,NGC++	$43.00
GEORGE WALLACE MEMORABILIA INCLUDING ELVIS PICTURE WOW!	$153.43	Ted Kennedy anti-campaign 1980; Chappaquiddick reminder	$37.91
wm h murray for president pocket mirror	$127.50	VINTAGE Raphael & Tuck Postcards 18 PRESIDENTS	$36.95
++1794 US CENT CERTIFIED VERY FAIR2 PCI,PCGS,ANCS	$123.50	Antique Civil War Poster 1861 Paper Vintage Collectible	$36.00

Historical Memorabilia ▶ Royal Memorabilia

The average sales price in this subcategory is $108.46.

	HIGH		AVG
ROMANOV Tsar PHOTOGRAPH Duchess Anastasia & sisters	$12,000.99	Russian Genealogy - History and Families - Book	$298.00
ROMANOV Tsar PHOTOGRAPH Duchess Anastasia & Alexis	$5,800.00	Princess Caroline of Monaco Magnificent Clippings!!!!!	$229.00
Romanovs. Nicholas II. Alexandra. A.N.S., 1904.	$1,650.00	VICTORIA & ALBERT WEDDING JUG	$152.50

Imperial Russian officer's sword-shashka model 1909.	$1,225.00	Japanese Showa Hirohito Emperor Banzai Medal WW1 WWI	$135.01
ROMANOV Tsar DINNER Serving PLATE Russian Imperial Chin	$785.00	Russian Tsar Nicholas II Oil Painting Victorian style	$125.00
ROMANOV Tsar PHOTOGRAPH Alexi son of Nicholas	$770.00	RARE King Edward VIII Abdication Mug - Hammersley	$119.00
ROMANOV Tsar PHOTOGRAPH Nicholas officers 1st Squadron	$760.00	Ethiopian Military Academy Silver Medal Haile Selassie	$115.00
ROMANOV Tsar SOUP BOWL China 1893 Russian Imperial	$499.99	MINIATURE PORTRAIT OIL PAINTING ADMIRAL NELSON	$103.50
ROMANOV Tsar DINNER PLATE China Russian Imperial #1	$499.99	1840 Queen Victoria Coronation Pressed Glass Plate	$102.50
CZAR NICHOLAS II CORONATION 1896 CUP OF SORROW SUPERB!!	$489.00	Plaque History England English Battles Knights Medieval	$100.69
Ethiopia Order of Menelik Commander. Selassie w/Sash	$450.00	Plaque History England Jousting Knights Medieval Gothic	$100.69
TSAR czar NICHOLAS II CORONATION Cup Of Sorrows 1896	$450.00	The Russian State Coat-of-Arms: 500 Years - Book	$100.00
King Edward VIII Limited Edition Commemorative Box	$394.89	RUSSIAN ROMANOV Tsar bakelite or wood SNUFF TOBACCO BOX	$99.99
1885 ROYALTY RUSSIA GREAT PRINCE P.N AUTOGRAPH PORTRAIT	$375.00	UK Britain England Lawyers Judges Legal Court CDV # 29	$99.98
Russian coronation cup Nicholas & Alexandra 1896	$350.00	Haile Selassie Era Order of Solomons Seal Higher Grade	$95.99

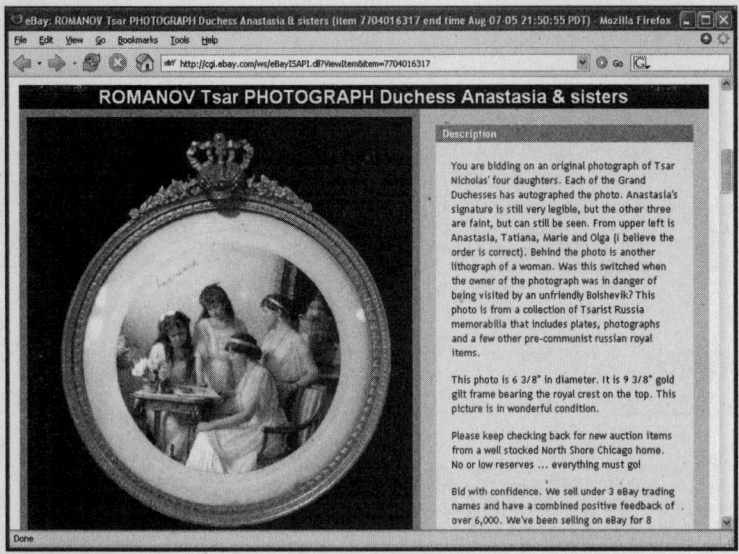

Holiday, Seasonal ▸ Christmas: Vintage (Pre–1946)

The average sales price in this subcategory is $26.66.

	HIGH		AVG
Rare Antique Stick Leg Sheep Platform Toy Christmas	$425.00	CHRISTMAS CANDY BOX, 1920's	$27.00
very rare super HEUBACH bisque snowbaby winter scene	$400.00	14 Vintage CHRITMAS COOKIE / BISCUIT / CAKE MOLDS	$26.99
Antique Sleigh Bells Old Horse Leather Strap Christmas	$282.77	5 VINTAGE LEAD FIGURES OF COWS AND PIGS FOR PUTZ SCENE	$26.51
NUTCRACKER VINTAGE WODDEN MAN SUPERB	$260.55	VINTAGE BARCLAY LEAD SANTA FIGURE ON SKIS!	$26.51
8 ANTIQUE FOLK ART PUTZ VILLAGE HOUSE CHURCH WINDMILL	$260.00	ANTIQUE TIN LIGHT UP CHRISTMAS STAR VERY UNIQUE!	$26.08
AUTHENTIC! BEAR ON SKI'S GERMAN SNOW BABIES	$211.67	LARGE PRESSED CARDBOARD SNOWMAN CANDY CONTAINER	$26.01
FANTASTIC VINTAGE MECHANICAL CHRISTMAS DISPLAY	$188.50	Wonderful Vintage Putz Camel Composition Stick Legs #11	$26.01
LOT 3 VINTAGE CHILDREN'S CHRISTMAS BOOKS NO RESERVE	$180.50	100 Vintage 1930's Christmas Stickers	$26.00
31 OLD GERMANY lead WINTER SCENE FIGURES Must See!!!	$170.27	PAPER-MACHE PIG CANDY CONTAINER VERY OLD	$26.00
Sweet 1880's Santa Claus Autograph Album, Hanover MA	$169.26	Vintage Decorated Bottle Brush Tree w/Garland + Beads	$26.00
TRAIN FIGURES LEAD CAST IRON SKIERS SKATERS SLEDDERS	$147.77	8 Walt Disney Celluloid Christmas Light Shades	$25.99
Dennison's 1912 Christmas Book	$130.50	VINTAGE SANTA NODDER CANDY CONTAINER - W GERMANY	$25.67
c. 1905 RAPHAEL TUCK NIGHT BEFORE CHRISTMAS STORY BOOK	$127.50	Lot 200+ 1930's Unused Christmas Gift Tags Santa, Kids	$25.49
RARE HUGE 5 1/2" GERMAN WOOLY STICK LEG ANTIQUE SHEEP	$127.50	Wonderful Vintage Putz Wooly Sheep Stick Legs #3	$25.49
AUTHENTIC! VINTAGE GERMAN SNOW BABIES, 2 WITH SLED	$125.00	Lots of Little Vintage Christmas items!	$25.00

Holiday, Seasonal ▸ Christmas: Modern (1946–90)

The average sales price in this subcategory is $16.37.

	HIGH		AVG
17 NY METROPOLITAN MUSEUM OF ART STERLING SNOWFLAKES NR	$357.00	Old 1930 Santa Papier Mache Japan Christmas	$17.62
14 SILVER PLATE SNOWFLAKES FROM NY MET MUSEUM OF ART NR	$158.48	1950's Felt Drummer Christmas Elf / Pixie - Set of 2	$17.50
NAPCO CHRISTMAS PLANTER GIRL WITH DOG ON LEASH	$147.50	Christmas Story Book by Woolworth's from 1953	$17.25
49" TALL VINTAGE CHRISTMAS LAWN ILLUMINATED CAROLER	$102.50	50'S FANNY FARMER SANTA SLEIGH CHRISTMAS DISPLAY, NO RS	$17.00
1958 Holt Howard "NOEL" Pixie Candle Stick Holders L@@K	$102.50	2 1950s Christmas decorations Christmas tree 5.5 inch	$16.76
Vintage Toy Japan Elf -Pixie Pair- 1940's Special Dolls	$89.99	Vintage Blume Christmas Carolers Candle Holders	$16.75
Vintage Aluminum Christmas tree–7 foot+	$78.54	RARE Vintage HOLT - HOWARD Elves - Pixies -EC - 12"	$16.50
VINTAGE NAPCO CHRISTMAS LADY HEAD VASE, 1956	$76.55	Old Glow In Dark ICICLES 7+ Dozen	$16.49
8 Vintage West Germany Christmas Pine Cone Elves	$66.75	VINTAGE CHRISTMAS FIREPLACE FULL SIZE FIREGLOW EFFECT	$16.27
2 Large Animated Illuminated Vintage Christmas Figures	$63.50	Sterling Christmas Medallions Towle Silversmiths; Vint.	$16.11
A Cup of Christmas Tea 2- 8" COOKIE PLATES w/Serv Rack	$63.00	Old Vintage Spun Cotton Penguin-Made in Japan	$16.05
60+feet of glass bead old christmas garland	$61.00	Vintage 1950's Made in Sweden Christmas Advent Calendar	$15.65
Vintage Relpo Christmas Girl Motorcycle Spaghetti 1960	$60.99	Vintage Pink 7 in Bottle Brush Christmas Tree	$15.51
Pottery Barn Rudolph Platter	$59.00	Vintage Turkey Candy Container Germany	$15.51
1951 Sears Christmas Book Catalog Toys Trains Capguns	$57.00	1951 FROSTY THE SNOWMAN Whitman Frame Tray Puzzle	$15.50

Holiday, Seasonal ▶ Christmas: Current (1991–Now)

The average sales price in this subcategory is $12.29.

	HIGH		AVG
1999 Carlton Ornament ~The Phantom Of The Opera~ #1	$296.99	Lenox/Disney: "IVORY DOPEY ORNAMENT" W/COA	$14.95
2000 Carlton Ornament ~The Phantom Of The Opera~ #2	$113.03	New Disney's Snow White Dopey christmas ornament	$14.03
Carlton Cards 1995 Opus 'n Bill ornament - HTF	$91.00	Radko Ornament Santa Fireman Stack	$13.49
3 New Waterford Times Square Ball Ornaments 00, 01, 04	$89.60	2004 ELOISE & SKIPPERDEE Carlton Ornament NEW	$12.99
Tiffany Sterling & Crystal Christmas ornament w/box!	$83.28	KATHERINE'S beanbag caucasion mermaid..$93.00 value	$12.95
Victorian Dollhouse #1 in Nostalgic Houses & Shops '84	$71.00	KATHERINE'S beanbag caucasion mermaids 2...$93.00 value	$12.95
Old World Inge Glass - Snow White and the 7 Dwarfs	$59.99	CHRISTMAS GINGERBREAD PORCELAIN ORNAMENTS-SET OF 4-NEW	$12.50
Set of 3 Orrefors Christmas Ornaments 1992 through 1994	$54.00	Lot Vintage Jeweled Beaded Sequin Ornaments	$12.00
NIB A PAIR (2) TOMMY BAHAMA	$49.99	Santa and Flamingo glass ornament	$12.00
CHRISTMAS ORNAMENTS - $130		Ballerina CAT glass ornament	$12.00
Breen Store Exclusive Holly Santa Ornament MWT NR	$48.99	HAND MADE IN POLAND CHRISTMAS ORNAMENT FREE SHIPPING	$12.00
Breen- Topping the Tannebaum, CATZ exclusive color	$45.00	Waterford Holiday Heirloom Festive Crystal Cut Ornament	$11.50
Breen Nordstrom Exclusive Santa Ornament MWT NR	$43.99	Wizard of Oz Polonaise Ornament	$11.00
Vintage 1977 Tiffany Hallmark Christmas Ornament NIB	$41.00	Wallace Candy Cane Ornament 2002 Christmas Cardinal MIB	$10.59
P. BUCKLEY MOSS 1st in Series - Signed & #'d ORNAMENT	$39.99	Radko "Ready for Sea" Donald Duck Ornament	$10.50
RARE Radko LTD 300 Green	$38.99	Wholesale 12 Dough Look Christmas Ornaments Santa	$10.50
Russian Santa Ornament MWT NR		Mrs. Claus riding a pig glass ornament	$10.38

Holiday, Seasonal ▶ Halloween

The average sales price in this subcategory is $24.28.

	HIGH		AVG
Star Wars Darth Vader Costume NEW Voice module & LED	$650.00	Sick Melting Severed Head Halloween Prop	$25.00
Life Size Dobson the Animatronic Butler Halloween Prop	$306.99	LUNA MOTH HALLOWEEN BLUE DEVIL HEAD #1823	$24.99
Life Size Count Dracula Hollywood Halloween Prop	$265.00	WITCH FROG w/ Pumpkin~ Halloween Yard Art Decoration	$24.99
Halloween Prop Haunted Lighted SKull Door Frame	$199.99	Witch Standing Haunt Halloween Accessories	$24.99
Flying Crank Ghost Halloween Prop	$197.50	LEMAX-SPOOKY TOWN-SPOOKIEST HOUSE ON THE BLOCK-LIKE NEW	$24.99
Life-Size Standing Pirate Captain Halloween Prop	$158.75	Halloween Candy Corn Geometric Polka Dot Compote Cake	$24.99
NEW Zombie Halloween Props Monster Life Size 6 FT TALL	$122.50	Witch Standing Haunt Halloween Accessories	$24.99
Life-Size Standing Screaming Mummy Halloween Prop	$122.50	Pirate Skeleton Skull Halloween Mask Hair Hat Prop NEW	$24.05
Life-Size Standing Pirate Captain Halloween Prop	$112.50	New Evil Ancient Mummy Halloween Mask Or Prop	$24.01
RARE GEMMY AIRBLOWN INFLATABLE GRIM REAPER TENT	$99.95	Sick Rotted Corpse Halloween Mask Or Prop	$24.00
Life-Size Hanging Flying Witch Halloween Prop	$86.00	*72 MINIATURE PLASTIC SKULLS* HALLOWEEN PROP	$23.51
98" BEWARE BANNER SIGN POST HALLOWEEN PROP	$84.95	Sick Screaming Faces Apron Halloween Prop	$23.27
HALLOWEEN MASK(ALBINO DRAGON MASK/PROP)	$81.00	LEMAX-SPOOKY TOWN-HALLOWEEN FESTIVAL-LIKE NEW COND.	$23.22
Life-Size Hanging Flying Witch Halloween Prop	$81.00	Sick Screaming Faces Apron Halloween Prop	$23.09
Life-Size Standing Old Witch Halloween Prop	$81.00	NEW CLASSIC CHIODO GHOUL HALLOWEEN MASK OR PROP	$22.95

Housewares & Kitchenware ▶ Kitchenware

The average sales price in this subcategory is $15.01.

	HIGH		AVG
Rooster and Rose NM/M Cookie Jar w/ PY marking in	$331.51	WADE MINIATURE HAPPY CHRISTMAS ENGLISH LIFE TEAPOT	$15.60
WINNIE THE POOH KRUEGER JUICE REAMER - NR	$168.49	1976 Sears Merry Mushroom Teapot	$15.53
LOT OF 4 CHALKWARE CHEF	$135.00	Campbell's Baked Beans Pot	$15.50
STRINGHOLDERS STRING HOLDER		CORNPOPPER OF COPPER- FOR THE FIRESIDE-VINTAGE/GORGEOUS	$15.49
HOLT HOWARD PIXIE HORS d'oeuvre DISH - 1959 pixieware	$130.48	SET OF VINTAGE BRONZE FLORAL BOOKENDS BOOKEND BOOK END	$15.49
1960~Holt Howard Jeeves Decanter~EXC VINTAGE CONDITION!	$105.00	HANG HOT PADS/TOWELS ON THIS PILLSBURY DOUGHBOY RACK	$15.49
IHQ Early Quistgaard Dansk Teak Tray, Modern Danish	$99.95	5 PC. TIARA PEACH PLATTER AND COFFEE/TEA CUPS SET	$15.49
VINTAGE ALL ALUMINUM LAUNDRY SPRINKLER W/ LABELS	$86.00	New Pillsbury Doughboy Paper Towel Holder 13" High	$15.00
Holt Howard Pixie Ware Cocktail Olives 1958	$83.00	Vintage set of Super Cute Cups Drink Glasses 50's 60's	$15.00
Green Depression Glass Small Egg-Beater Rare!	$76.00	[2 of these sold for $15.00 each]	
Decorative Vintage Old Oak and Iron Wine Press!!	$75.11	2 Vintage Wire Mesh BASKETS-Red Handles-Market-Kitchen	$15.00
Nambe Tri Corner Bowl 1QT #530	$67.00	VINTAGE YELLOW ENAMEL SOUP TUREEN VERY NICE	$14.50
Rooster and Rose Mint Bell with UCAGCO Mark - RARE	$66.55	RED WHITE CHECKS AND CHERRIES BANANA HOLDER	$14.50
vintage HOLT HOWARD Merry Mouse Desk message holder	$62.61	OLD B & W Dutch Boy Laundry Sprinkler Bottle Stopper	$14.00
HOLT HOWARD? KETCHUP~PIXIEWARE~JAR~CONTAINER	$61.00	VINTAGE PHILCO REFRIGERATOR ICE TRAYS / INSERTS	$13.50
Baileys Coffee Cup and Accessory Collection~ LE!!	$57.49	VINTAGE ENESCO CAT KITTY RECIPE HOLDER THERMOMETER	$13.08

Housewares & Kitchenware ▶ Tableware

The average sales price in this subcategory is $16.28.

	HIGH		AVG
RUBY STAINED ANTIQUE BERRY BOWL ZIPPER PATTERN	$432.00	LOVELY HAND PAINTED PORCELAIN OPEN SALT	$17.11
CZECH INTAGLIO JEWELED ORMOLU OPEN SALT CELLAR	$167.82	Sparkly, Clear Glass Open Salt Dip w/Cherries!	$17.05
Fine Sterling Silver Salt Cellars with Cobalt Liners	$145.00	GERMAN LUSTER BASKET OPEN SALT CELLAR DISH DIP 1900	$16.95
Huge Collection of (104) Open Salt Dips, No Reserve!	$122.50	DIAMOND POINT OVAL PEDESTAL OPEN SALT DIP / SALT CELLAR	$16.50
EARLY PRESSED SANDWICH FLINT GLASS LACY SALT	$114.50	Blue China Salt Dip w/Gold Handle-Gravy Boat shape	$16.50
BOSTON & SANDWICH LACY SALT BF-1b SCARCE	$109.26	4 Glass Salt Cellars Crystal 1 Glass Spoon 1 Pin Tray	$16.49
VINTAGE ANTIQUE GLASS SALT CELLAR MASTER SALT!	$85.00	Beautiful Intaglio Open Salt Ferns Amber	$16.49
HUGE LOT Open Salts Salt Dip Collection + Spoons 30+pcs	$78.77	LOVELY ETCHED _WINGED_ OVAL OPEN SALT DIP / SALT CELLAR	$16.48
6 Open MASTER SALTS Depression CUT CRYSTAL Late 1800's	$77.51	Gorham sterling silver open salt and pepper shaker set	$16.28
Collection of 74 Salt dips, open cellars, whatever!	$76.00	Victorian Shell Art MOP Mother of Pearl Open Salt	$16.27
EARLY PRESSED SANDWICH FLINT GLASS LACY SALT	$67.00	STERLING SALT CELLAR 3 LEGS WITH SPOON & HALLMARKS	$16.03

Cranberry Handblown Glass Open Salt Berry Pontil	$66.00	Noritake Peach Lustre Swan Open Salt	$16.00
LIMOGES w/Swags of Pink Roses & Silver Rim Open Salt	$62.00	PATTERN GLASS LIDS...TOTAL OF FIVE!!!!!	$15.99
EARLY PRESSED SANDWICH FLINT GLASS LACY SALT	$62.00	Beautiful Intaglio Open Salt Wreath Of Roses Amber	$15.72
VINTAGE TORTOISE ART GLASS FOOTED MASTER SALT	$60.00	SET of 4 SQUARE OPEN SALT CELLAR DIPS with SPOONS	$15.60

Knives, Swords & Blades ▸ Fixed Blade Knives

The average sales price in this subcategory is $37.37.

	HIGH		AVG
Busse Steel Heart II Knife w/ Sheath ** Great Condition	$525.55	Ka-bar #1255 3/4 Black Serrated Tactical Tanto Knife	$40.99
EK Commando Model # 4 1 Of 50 Made Limited Edition	$407.00	Tops Covert Anti-Terrorism Knife New Skeleton	$39.99
STRIDER EB-AC AIR WING TACTICAL KNIFE MILITARY LAW NEW	$275.00	Marbles IDEAL HUNTING KNIFE Game Getter Handle NIB NR	$39.99
CHRIS REEVE GREEN BERET 7" KNIFE KNIVES NEW IN BOX	$255.00	Marbles WOODCRAFT KNIFE Game Getter Handle NIB NR	$39.99
EK Presentation Throwers 1 Of 50 Made Limited Ed.	$227.75	Marbles FIELDCRAFT KNIFE Game Getter Handle NIB NR	$39.99
Blackjack Mamba (Mint condition w/sheath & box)	$215.00	Marbles GUT HOOK KNIFE Stacked Leather Handle NIB NR	$39.99
EK Commerative Marine Recon Fighting Knife Model 3	$211.50	Blackjack Warrior-new In The Box	$39.67
EK Comm.Army Special Forces Fighting Knife Model 3	$177.50	BOKER 519-HH STAG FIXED BLADE HUNTING KNIFE +	$39.00
EK Commerative U.S.Airborne Forc Fighting Knife Model 3	$164.55	BARKER S AUTO SWITCH BLADE KNIFE KNIVES	$38.00
Chris Reeve Shadow IV 4 *NO RESERVE* 5.5" A2 Excellent	$160.25	Bear Knife MGC Gentleman's Knife Genuine India Stag	$36.00
BLACKJACK CLASSIC MODEL #5 KNIFE	$160.00	SILVER SCORPION KNIFE-Steel Blades-Dagger-Display Stand	$35.95
EK Commerative Army Rangers Fighting Knife Model 3	$159.06	Russian Survival Knife HB-4 Exp.	$34.99
NEW HATTORI CLASSIC DROP POINT BOWIE HUNTING KNIFE	$152.50	CELTIC/VIKING BATTLE SWORD-Sharp Steel-Solid	$34.95
EK Commerative Air Special Ops. Fighting Knife Model 3	$143.75	Rambo First Blood Part II	$34.50
Tarani Karambit Journeyman knife and Trainer	$140.15	NEW IN BOX Cold Steel SRK Survival Rescue Knife	$33.05

Knives, Swords & Blades ▸ Folding Knives

The average sales price in this subcategory is $39.77.

	HIGH		AVG
G MULLER CUSTOM MAMMOTH IVORY DAMASCUS LL KNIFE KNIVES	$500.00	Beltrame. Snakewood handles Bayonet blade Brass bolster	$42.99
Rare 1st Generation Bulldog Knives	$375.00	Case XX 62009 Barlow Knife Red Red Bone 1940/1964	$42.00
David Yellowhorse Buck 501 Dall sheep	$336.00	BULLDOG BRAND PEARL STOCKMAN (KCA YOUTH KNIFE)-NEW	$41.78
David Yellowhorse Buck 501 Big Horn sheep	$325.50	CASE XX KNIFE 61050 BONE COKE BOTTLE WINSTON CUP 1991	$41.01
Case Stag Classic Knife 51094 Texas Toothpick 1994 NR	$304.00	Schrade Imitation Ivory Sharpfinger knife	$41.00
4 SPYDERCO KNIFE/KNIVES NIB! RARE, DISCONTINUED! LOOK!!	$296.00	Smith Wesson custom switchblade knife knives automatic	$40.50
Case Classic Sowbelly Knife PROTO NR	$286.00	Case XX Knife Congress Case XX Color Flag Shield NR	$40.09
Case Classic Knife Carolina Blue Proto Case Tested NR	$284.99	Kershaw Rainbow Leek	$39.88
Case Classic Genuine Pearl Doctors Knife PROTO NR	$280.00	john wayne collectible knife and lighter (zippo)	$39.00
CASE XX KNIFE 52050 STAG CLASSIC #09 SUNFISH 1994 NIB	$260.98	Case Rattlesnake bone Baby Dr Knife	$38.89
Damascus and Ivory Gents Folding Knife, Dagger	$222.53	BOKER automatic Knife Knives Switchblade auto	$38.00
Case Classic Gunboat Canoe Knife Green Bone PROTO NR	$202.50	KA-BAR KABAR KNIFE GENUINE STAG CANOE OLEAN UNUSED	$37.99
Case XX 5254 Trapper Stag Knife 1965/1969 Muskrat Blade	$168.05	CASE XX TRAPPER 2000 ROSEWOOD SREATED BLADNEW!!!E	$37.95
Case Classic Rogers Bone Muskrat Knife PROTO NR	$164.49	Case Knife Centennial Redbone Lockback 61059L wBox NR	$37.00
Puma Setter Lockback Knife 220 765 NR	$162.50	Kershaw 1660 Leek Knife Ken Onion Speed Safe Assited	$37.00

Knives, Swords & Blades ▸ Swords

The average sales price in this subcategory is $40.52.

	HIGH		AVG
IMPERIAL RUSSIAN DRAGOON OFFICER SABRE SWORD	$610.00	Old vintage Islamic Jambiya Dagger, no sword , NR	$49.99
Cold Steel 88W Japanese Wakazashi Imperial Sword NEW	$379.99	STEEL SWEPT HILT RAPIER Renaissance Sword Scabbard A018	$49.95
American Civil War Infantry officer's sword	$330.00	[2 of these sold for $49.95 each]	
Cold Steel Japanese 88BOK O Katana Warrior Sword	$319.99	Huge GRIFFIN TRIDENT SPEAR-Halberd-Steel-Knight 66-Inch	$47.96
German Prussian NCO Artillery sword/saber	$300.00	Medieval Sword of Richard the Lionheart Plus One Free!	$46.00
Ottoman yataghan (aka yatagan) very old !	$292.98	52 Inch Conan the Barbarian Sword	$45.00
Antique British Cavalry Sword with Scabbard and Knot	$280.00	1860 US Cavalry Saber 42" Civil War Swords, Authentic!	$42.00
Standard Green Metal Saya Military Sword for Japanese	$255.00	40 " GOD OF FIRE MEDIEVAL SAMURAI NINJA SWORD Weapon	$40.55
US army sword saber model 1902 m	$242.50	Very Old Short Sword. Must See!!!! N/R	$40.00
ANTIQUE MILITARY DRESS SWORD	$232.50	45" BARBARIAN SWORD II w/display HUGE LOOK!	$39.99
US ARMY 1860 CALVARY SABER		Barbary Pirate Cutlass 34" Scimitar Sword, Swords	$39.99
Cold Steel Small Sword 88SMS New Release Now Available	$229.99	Scottish Basket Claymore back sword	$39.00
Late 18th Century English Sword	$220.50	Achilles Sword w/Plaque - Troy Sword	$36.00
Antique Sword - c.1800 French & Indian War	$202.50	45" Rapier Style Sword swords knives and axes	$35.99
MODEL 1860 UNION OFFICERS SWORD	$202.50	CALVARY SWORD REPLICA	$35.95
WWII GERMAN POLICE OFFICER SWORD WITH SCABBARD BLACK	$182.49	4 pc WHITE SAMURAI SWORDS SET NEW RARE sword	$34.99

Lamps, Lighting ▸ Lamps: Electric

The average sales price in this subcategory is $45.42.

	HIGH		AVG
Antique Victorian Organ / Piano Oil Lamp - Beautiful!	$1,175.00	Vintage RETRO Eames Era Green Lucite Swag Hanging Lamp	$49.00
ART DECO Haley CONSOLIDATED Slip Shade GLASS CHANDELIER	$810.00	RETRO VINTAGE GOLD GLASS BALL HANGING SWAG LIGHT LAMP	$49.00
MACHINE AGE DECO HTF MUTUAL SUNSET LAMP ROHDE PFISTERER	$660.05	RETRO '60s SWAG LIGHT IRIDESCENT FLORAL HANGING LAMP	$48.99
Counterweight anglepoise typ desk lamp eames era light	$449.00	Vintage BELLOVA MCFADDEN & CO. METAL DESK LAMP	$47.02
OLD ART DECO GLASS FOYER CHANDELIER HALEY CONSOLIDATED	$405.00	Modern Deco Industrial Out Side Sconces	$47.00
O. C. WHITE INDUSTRIAL WORK LAMP EARLY BRASS	$315.00	VINTAGE BEAUTIFUL HANGING SWAG LAMP WITH CRYSTALS	$46.99

George Nelson Bubble Cigar Light Fixture Eames Knoll 34	$303.99
O. C. WHITE INDUSTRIAL WORK LAMP EARLY	$295.00
1950's Delux electric EXIT sign glass 2 sided Art Deco	$281.50
WOW! Atomic Sputnik Lamp/Clock Eames Arteluce era	$262.13
VINTAGE beer BUDWEISER ROTATING Ext RARE LIGHT SIGN 5Os	$260.00
Antique Very Old Bronze Dragon Wall Lamp/3 Arms RARE	$255.00
VICTORIAN Banquet Lamp, Metallic Gold Globe	$240.27
ART DECO CHROME FLOOR ASHTRAY SMOKING STAND WITH LIGHT	$227.50
SMALL ARTS & CRAFTS CANDLESTICK BOUDIOR LAMP W/SHADE	$221.38

Green Porcelain Gas station light with GE socket	$46.51
Antique Hand Blown Light Bulb #2 - Cobalt Blue- Works!!	$45.50
Edison Commemorative Light Bulb	$45.00
Beautiful Vintage Hand Painted Peachblow Wall Lamp	$43.98
Very unusual antique lamp EDISON stamped on rim 1890	$43.00
Vintage Pressed Glass Electric Wall Lamp and Globe	$43.00
Tiffany Style Leaded Slag Glass Swag Lamp Tans & Orange	$42.99
VINTAGE PALE CRANBERRY SWIRL GLASS HANGING SWAG LAMP	$42.00
BRASS MAP LIGHT Nautical lamp fixture Marine RED LAMP	$41.88

Lamps, Lighting ▸ Lamps: Non-Electric

The average sales price in this subcategory is $58.13.

	HIGH		AVG
Four 19th C. Frosted & Etched 2 5/8 Cameo Gas Shades	$3,550.00	ANTIQUE WV COLE MINE SAFETY LAMP LANTERN MINING LIGHT N	$61.00
Lovely Set of Four 19th C. Frosted Ball Gas Shades N/R	$921.00	NICE OLD CAST IRON HANGING CANDLE LAMP LIGHT	$60.59
RARE WOLF SAFETY CARBIDE LAMP/LANTERN/LIGHT	$680.00	OLD AMERICAN GAS MACHINE FIXTURE CATALOG ALBERT LEA MN	$60.00
RARE BRASS COLEMAN ARC LANTERN NEEDS REPAIR NRI	$676.00	ANTIQUE GAS BRASS VICTORIAN CEILING FIXTURE	$59.88
OLD RARE SOLID BRASS OIL CONTAINER - US LIGHT HOUSE NY	$616.98	FLORAL Decorated Glass Lamp Shade fits Aladdin Oil 10"	$58.89
Coleman Lamp shade #335 with fringe	$488.00	ANTIQUE VICTORIAN KEROSENE BANQUET LAMP part	$58.87
ANTIQUE COBALT BLUE FINGER KEROSENE LAMP	$461.00	OLD Mission Style Brass Hanging Gas Fixture Parts NR	$58.37
1880'S PORCELAIN 2-PANEL LITHOPHANE FAIRY LAMP	$455.52	OLD ANTIQUE GAS LAMP BASE (609)	$58.00
DIETZ Prison Lantern Reflector Chimney New York C 1890	$434.99	VINTAGE JUSTRITE CARBIDE MINING / CAVING LAMP	$58.00
CRANBERRY NAILSEA SATIN GLASS FINGER LAMP HAND-BLOWN	$403.00	VINTAGE POLISHED BRASS COLEMAN LANTERN	$57.75
Old Vintage Antique Light Bulb(Swan Patents)	$382.00	Coleman Lamp Not Lantern QL Quick Lite Original Shade	$57.00
FROSTED FONT GREEN STEM QUEEN HEART KEROSENE OIL LAMP	$325.00	1919 Coleman Gas Lamp Brass with White Shade 10"	$57.00
Antique Aladdin Model 5 Brass Hanging Lamp w/Shade	$311.05	Coleman/ Fiesta GI Pocket Stove ? NEW NEVER USED!!	$56.88
OLD Aladdin lamp drape Whip-o-lite Paper Shade	$297.00	Baker Street Solar Lamp Black Post $129 NR	$56.77
Kerosene Oil Library Hanging Lamp Font and Shade Match	$284.99	BRASS KEROSENE BANQUET LAMP FONT no res	$56.50

Linens, Fabric & Textiles ▸ Fabric

The average sales price in this subcategory is $19.66.

	HIGH		AVG
16+Y ROBERT ALLEN PLUSH BLACK VELVET Upholstery Fabric	$182.50	VINTAGE KIMONO FABRIC:Country Kasuri Cotton	$20.50
18Y ROBERT ALLEN PURPLE RIB VELVET Upholstery Fabric	$153.50	Designer Fabric Samples-15 Pounds	$20.31
7+Y SCALAMANDRE SILK FLORAL DAMASK UPHOLSTERY Fabric	$140.00	VINTAGE KIMONO FABRIC:Silk Gorgeous Flower	$20.00
21y STROHEIM ROMANN ARGENT KILIM Upholstery Fabric	$130.00	** 40 PIECES LOT ** VINTAGE SILK	$19.99
Great Vintage Marimekko and Isola panel/fabric 1960s	$129.41	KIMONO FABRICS #33	
5+y SCHUMACHER GLD FLEUR DE LI DAMASK UPHOLSTERY Fabric	$118.49	VINTAGE KIMONO FABRIC:Lovely Orange Flower	$19.57
7Y BRUNSCHWIG FILS SILK FLORAL DAMASK UPHOLSTERY FABRIC	$111.00	Hawaiian Tropical Sailboat Palm Trees Sunset Fabric 4Y	$19.52
18y SCHUMACHER GOLD FLORAL DAMASK UPHOLSTERY FABRIC	$110.00	Hand Printed Vintage Floral Pattern 1950's	$19.47
17y ROBERT ALLEN WHITE LEAF DAMASK UPHOLSTERY FABRIC	$99.00	VINTAGE KIMONO FABRIC:Yukata Cotton Bamboo	$19.00
19y LOVELY RICHLOOM BEIGE BROWN PLAID UPHOLSTERY FABRIC	$83.33	4.33Y! Kokopelli Surf Hawaiian Palm Tree Pink Fabric NR	$18.88
3+y SCHUMACHER SILVER LINEN VELVET Upholstery Fabric	$67.00	3Y Floral Foliage Blue Green Cream Decorator Fabric NR!	$18.88
20Y ROBERT ALLEN RED FLORAL VELVET Upholstery Fabric	$66.00	Red Hat Society Purple Red Cotton Fabric 4 1/2 Y	$18.61
CROSCILL COTSWOLD 3 yards X 93" W $32.99	$65.01	Raggedy Ann & Andy Wallhanging / Quilt Fabric	$18.51
[2 of these sold for $65.01 each]		Vintage 60's Black Sheer Striped Fabric	$18.50
9+Y WAVERLY SWEETWATER RED STRIPE UPHOLSTERY FABRIC	$62.99	Shimmering Purple Floral Brocade Fabric	$18.50
4+y SAMARCAND CHAMPAGNE SILK PLAID UPHOLSTERY FABRIC	$62.02	VINTAGE KIMONO FABRIC:Men's Yukata Cotton	$18.50

Linens, Fabric & Textiles ▸ Lace, Crochet, Doilies

The average sales price in this subcategory is $9.87.

	HIGH		AVG
VINTAGE LINENS LOT 50'S TABLECLOTHS DOILIES 170 PCS++++	$104.52	14 PC FASHION PINK RAYON VENISE YOKE APPLIQUE	$9.99
VINTAGE DOILIE DOILIES HUGE LOT 113 CROCHETED GORGEOUS	$80.99	LOVELY CROWN SCALLOPED WHITE RAYON VENISE LACE	$9.99
VINTAGE LINENS LOT -26 PIECES - MOSTLY CUTTERS	$57.00	I SET PILLOW COVERS & 4 SCARFS BATTENBURG LACE TRIM	$9.97
Psalm 23, filet crochet,wall hanging, bible verse,Bible	$55.00	~ 8 ~ Vintage Crocheted Doilies- Varies Sizes	$9.95
Estate Linens - HUGE LOT - Over 100 Doilys - All Sizes	$54.60	3 *charming* PINK Crochet DOILIES *perfect for dresser*	$9.95
60" Pretty Vintage 20s Silk Ribbon Flowers Trim 4 Dress	$52.50	HERITAGE LACE Doily "Heirloom" Design ~ White	$9.90
Victorian 70" x 19" Ecru Homespun Linen Runner	$46.00	[2 of these sold in a multiple item ("Dutch") auction for $4.95 each]	
Vintage cotton Doll fabric GOLDEN ROSE dotted swiss	$45.44	MINT Unused Vintage Hand Embroidered Dresser Scarf WOW!	$9.50
LOVELY IVORY RAYON VENISE EDGING LACE	$43.01	Doily;Doilies;Heart Shaped;Lot of 120;NIP;2" ea;white	$9.25
ANTIQUE HAND CROCHET WKD DOILIES	$36.89	Large Lot Vintage Unused Lace Trim~45 yds.+~Beautiful C	$9.25
+ TABLE TOPPER 35P LOT		1915 Home Needlework Magazine-Linens-Crochet 90 yr old	$9.25
New hand crocheted oval ROSE DELIGHT doily	$36.00	16 Pcs Vintage Linens Tablecloths Runners Etc f/Cutters	$9.15
set of 4 vintage crocheted corn on the cob pot holders	$36.00	Victorian and Vintage Lace Insets : Bon Marche Stock	$9.00
Handmade Crochet Pink Roses Doily	$32.99	BEAUTIFUL VINTAGE DUTCH HANDCROCHETED RUNNER!	$9.00
VINTAGE crochet chair back sofa set -4 pieces Doilies	$32.50	ELEPHANTS TWO MATCHING VINT DUTCH LACY CAFE TRIMS	$9.00
7 pcs Vintage Linens Gorgeous Embroidery & Crochet	$31.88	LOVELY LOT OLDER DUTCH BIGGER HANDCROCHETED DOILIES	$9.00

Linens, Fabric & Textiles ▸ Quilts

The average sales price in this subcategory is $40.03.

	HIGH		AVG
AMISH OLD ORDER LONESTAR QUILT MADE BY HAND	$475.00	CRYSTAL BLUE QUILT-KING SIZE QUILTS NEW HANDMADE	$41.99
Vintage Cathedral Window Quilt Hand Made Mint	$428.99	Vintage HOMEMADE Quilt ~ SUNBONNET SUE & SAM ~ PINK NR	$41.00

COLORFUL GRANDMA 'S FAN DESIGN AMISH QUILT	$400.00	Vintage Yo-Yo Quilt, Coverlet, Bedspread	$41.00
Handmade Oregon Quilt	$400.00	Antique 30's Feedsack Quilt MUST SEE!!!!! Bright Colors	$41.00
Amish Hand Made "PLANNED SAMPLER" QUEEN QUILT	$360.00	Beautiful Hand Made Queen Size Quilt 85" x 85" No Res	$41.00
NEW Full/Double Sized Hand-Sewn Amish Patchwork Quilt	$300.00	ANtIQue VINtAgE QUILT TOP MULTI-COLORED BLOCKS NR	$41.00
Exquisite Hand Assembled & Hand Quilted Vintage Quilt!	$282.00	Vintage Red & Blue 1900's TRIANGLE QUILT-Cutter	$40.66
Mennonite Hand Stiched Quilt	$250.00	Hand-pieced and Quilted: Redwork Sun Bonnet Sue 33x36	$40.00
Old Pa. Hand Made Quilt	$243.59	LOVELY VINTAGE/ANTIQUE SHABBY ROSE RING QUILT-FULL/TWI	$40.00
Unique-Vintage YOYO YO YO Penny Quilt Top-Hand Stitched	$242.37	Hand Quilted Large Dalhia Pattern Quilt	$39.99
ANTIQUE/VINTAGE QUILT ~ SOFT PASTEL COLOURS	$230.00	COLLECTIBLE BEAUTIFUL AFRICAN AMERICAN THEME QUILT	$39.99
ANTIQUE Hand sewn Quilt Snow Ball Pattern NO RESERVE	$200.00	VINTAGE LG RED WHITE & BLUE HAND STITCHED QUILT ESTATE	$39.99
Margaret Cavigga Collection - Blue & White King Quilt	$200.00	Old 40s or 50s Hand Quilted Hummingbird Pattern Quilt	$39.99
Vint Red Yellow Green & White Applique Quilt 87X 68 N/R	$188.50	Beautiful Embroider on Pieced Bars & Blocks Quilt	$39.99
Stunning Handmade Quilt Wedding Ring Pinwheel Yellow	$167.50	GORGEOUS NEW FRENCH COUNTRY STRIPED QUILT,BLUE&YELLOW	$39.99

Linens, Fabric & Textiles ▸ Table Linens

The average sales price in this subcategory is $18.41.

	HIGH		AVG
Unbeliavable 146" Luxurious cutwork tablecloth +12 napk	$499.00	Antique Linen TABLECLOTH & Napkin Set NEW in Box! Italy	$19.00
Vintage Hungarian Kalocsa Tablecloth Hand Embroidered	$144.50	CHIC~PINK~SOUTHERN BELLE~CHAIR DOILY~SHABBY~MINT	$18.99
Vintage Retro Never Used 1950's Texas Map Tablecloth	$121.75	VINTAGE LINEN TABLECLOTH~4 NAPKINS~SCANDINAVIAN DESIGN	$18.54
EXQUISITE VINTAGE ORGANDY MADEIRA TABLECLOTH-12 NAPKIN	$114.50	VINTAGE DEEP RED TABLECLOTH W/ WHITE CHERRIES NICE	$18.51
Gorgeous vintage round crocheted tablecloth - estate	$102.50	64" x 50" Vintage Pink Kitchenware Cotton Tablecloth	$18.50
Vintage Gourmet Picnic BBQ Tablecloth 63" x 52" Unused	$100.00	Vintage Tablecloth Embroidery Hydrangea	$18.50
DAMASK LINEN TABLECLOTH 62"x108"-12 NAPKINS-MIB-NR	$96.00	VINTAGE COTTON TABLE CLOTH-WHITE W/ KITCHEN PRINT	$18.49
JIANGSU CHINA HAND EMBROIDERED TABLE CLOTH & 14 NAPKINS	$94.00	Scarce Startex Fabric Folder w Tablecloth Samples 1940s	$18.49
4 vintage 1950's Tablecloths Butterfly Fruits Teatime	$79.88	Spectacular Vintage Linen Damask Tablecloth, Blue Plaid	$18.00
Vintage Tablecloth Lot 40's 50's Fruit & Floral 16PC's	$75.00	Vintage Tablecloth Pantry Novelty Unused w Label	$18.00
VINTAGE PORSGRUND FARMERS ROSE STYLE LACE TABLECLOTH	$72.11	Vintage PRINTS DU JOUR Tablecloth BARNYARD FUN ROOSTER	$17.57
Vintage State of Florida Tablecloth Bright Colors	$68.99	VINTAGE 60'S-PURE IVORY LINEN TABLECLOTH- GOLDEN WHEAT	$17.49
PR Vintage Yellow VERBENA BridgeTablecloth WILENDUR New	$66.00	Handmade Belgian lace IVORY wedding umbrella parasol	$17.49
VINTAGE STARTEX GOOD LUCK CHARMS TABLECLOTH Shamrocks	$63.53	Vintage Applique & Embroider Christmas Table Cloth	$17.27
Vintage Big Red Apples Apple Blossoms Cotton Tablecloth	$55.04	Romantic Vintage Tablecloth, Dreamy Pink Blossoms PEEK!	$17.16

Metalware ▸ Brass

The average sales price in this subcategory is $22.92.

	HIGH		AVG
Art Deco Oscar Bach Compote frankl rohde chase era	$1,681.00	50's Vintage Oppenheim Covered Dish Hand Made in Israel	$26.00
Vintage Tiffany Studios Clip New York	$247.50	Antique Brass Pump	$25.66
Vintage Brass Dolphin Andirons - Owen Mfg Co- Norfolk	$227.50	Vintage Post Office Mailbox Mail Box Combination Door	$25.66
Rare OPTIMUS Campingo stove Made in Sweden 1930's ?	$203.50	BRASS FIGURE OF A COAL MINER-SOLID - ENGLAND 6 1/2H X 6	$25.00
40 QT. (20 Gal.) Antique Brass Milk Can	$200.00	3VINTAGE BRASS PIECES-HANGING BELL,CANDLE SNUFFER,CAMEL	$24.99
OLD HAMMERED BRASS SIGNED ARTS & CRAFTS BOOKLENDS	$180.50	Old Art Nouveau Brass Owl Book Holder Rest	$24.95
OLD MEXICAN BRASS TILE MOSAIC TRAY SALVADOR TERAN	$141.28	Vintage German Art Nouveau Large Brass Bowl	$24.95
14" Brass Charger plate with Copper and Silver Inlay	$124.50	VINTAGE NUMBERED BRASS TAGS * MINER FACTORY CATTLE TRAP	$23.21
Navy ship engineroom siren / alarm	$122.50	ART-TOOL CONTE NYC Brass Glass Mold #4	$22.72
VERY OLD PAINTED BRASS BUNNY RABBIT PAPERWEIGHT	$111.00	Vintage, handforged, ladle, dipper, brass, set of 3	$21.96
Horse Brass 24 Total Vintage on Leather	$100.00	HAMMERED SPOON ARTS & CRAFTS MISSION STYLE STAR SAFFIRE	$21.66
SOLID BRASS PLANT STAND,VINTAGE,RARE	$91.00	3 Brass Trivet Williamsburg Thomas Jefferson King Queen	$21.50
10 post office brass box doors 3 1/2x 5" combination	$88.50	6 Vintage Post Office Doors & Frames W/combo	$21.07
VIRGINIA METALCRAFTERS-2 Pr. Brass Medallion Tieback	$83.59	BALDWIN BRASS NAPKIN RINGS ~8 DEVON PATTERN NEW IN BOX~	$20.56
Brass Grizzly Bear Paper Weight	$77.89	Lot Of Vintage Horse Brass - 7 Different	$20.50

Metalware ▸ Pewter

The average sales price in this subcategory is $21.39.

	HIGH		AVG
Antique Pewter Canister made by "Liberty & Co"	$870.21	METAWA HOLLAND PEWTER PITCHER VINTAGE/ANTIQUE NICE	$24.95
CASED50 PIECES OF" GORHAM'S PEWTER OCTETTE" FLATWARE	$540.01	Wilton Armetale Candleholder Sconce, rWp, Queen Anne	$24.59
Chilmark Pewter-Barnum-Lee at Antietam-Signed	$209.22	6 Pewter Jefferson Cups, Birmingham Pewter Collection	$24.51
HUGE ARTHUR COURT PEWTER ARMADILLO BASKET FRUIT BOWL	$181.37	2 Wilton PEWTER DINNER PLATES	$22.02
Chilmark-Petitto-Two Horse Racers	$162.50	VINTAGE KENT PEWTER COFFEE TEA POT CREAMER & SUGAR SET	$22.00
BIG LOT FULL THRUST PEWTER MINIATURE SPACESHIP STARSHIP	$153.50	TROUT PEWTER SERVING PLATTER	$21.99
5 PIECE ROYAL HOLLAND PEWTER CHOCOLATE POT SET	$152.50	VINTAGE ENGLISH SHEFFIELD PEWTER TANKARD	$21.61
Wilton Armetale Pewter Scalloped Plates, Bowls, 12 pc	$134.49	2 WILTON PEWTER SALAD DINNER CHARGER PLATES * 10?"	$21.50
Wilton Armetale Pewter Goblets (4)	$125.00	Danbury Mint classic car 1934 Duesenberg SJ	$21.00
Shirley Pewter: Pair Whale ? Oil Lamps	$116.45	Large Newer Wilton Armatale Platter Stately ? Gorgeous	$20.95
Noahs Ark Asian/Chinese Animal Figures, Pewter	$112.50	Danbury Mint classic car 1930 Packard Convertible	$20.50
Boy & Girl Pewter Candle Holders by Walli for Hudson	$105.00	Danbury Mint classic car 1937 Cord 812	$20.50
LE Pewter Figure of Arvin Statue Columbus Indiana	$86.00	Vintage Wilton Tray Pewter Southwest Theme	$20.49
4 PEWTER Antique Marked Spoon / Spoons w/Hallmarks	$84.00	Vintage Wilton Bowl Pewter Southwest Theme	$20.49
Chilmark "War Party" Pewter Sculpture by Polland	$81.99	Nice Pair of Vintage Pewter Candlestick Holders, Signed	$20.00

Militaria ▶ Civil War (1861–65)

The average sales price in this subcategory is $47.53.

	HIGH		AVG
Early, Pre C.W. Pigeon Eagle Head Officers Sword/Scb.	$1,700.00	C..S. PISTOL Civil War	$51.00
CIVIL WAR SOLDIER'S DIARY 8th PENN. INFANTRY 1862	$936.69	1902 GAR G A R GRAND ARMY CUT GLASS CIVIL WAR VETERANS	$50.01
CIVIL WAR FLAG 2nd NATIONAL CONFEDERATE SOUTH CAROLINA	$810.00	Aug 1862 military register company E 121st. regiment .	$50.00
Civil War Style Ammunition Bullet Pouch Cartridge	$612.00	ANTIQUE CIVIL WAR GUTTA PERCHA TINTYPE PHOTO WALL FRAME	$50.00
RARE CIVIL WAR NAPOLEON CANNON MOLD 6 POUNDER	$610.00	Civil War Confederate Hope Saddle Texas Crescent Star	$49.98
CIVIL WAR SWORD WITH SCABBARD	$560.00	Rebel Confederate Flag Full Queen Quilt / 2 Pillow Sham	$49.95
Vintage Tobacco Silk - Robert E. Lee - no reserve	$350.00	1864 CIVIL WAR OHIO VOLUNTEER SERVICE DOCUMENT	$48.57
Civil War Neck Stock, or "Leather Neck", Marines	$350.00	1889 GAR 23RD NAT'L ENCAMPMENT MILWAUKEE WIS TOKEN NR	$47.00
civil war plank and salute cannon, signal authentic	$305.00	CIVIL WAR SOLDIER LETTER 46TH PENNSYLVANIA	$47.00
Huge Model of Mountain Howitzer BLACK POWDER Cannon	$255.00	LE MAT REVOLVER REPLICA	$47.00
Civil War Dug Buckle & Belt (Crater Find)	$250.00	Sons of Confederate Veterans – License Plate	$46.05
Confederate Veterans Farmville VA Reunion Ribbon -1926	$178.49	GAR G A R GRAND ARMY CIVIL WAR VETERAN CABINET BUCK	$46.00
China Trade-Augustine Heard Co-Hongkong,1861-Fine ALS	$177.50	Civil War Veterans,2 Pc.Metal GAR Hat Badge,Gold Wreath	$45.02
United Confederate Veterans,Lg.Button,1904 Nashville,TN	$169.49	CIVIL WAR MEDAL	$45.00
Huge Model of 6 lb. BLACK POWDER Cannon over 18"	$154.00	[2 of these sold for $45.00 each]	
Franklin Mint Civil War Chess Set	$152.50	Large Lot Dug Relics from Ft. Fillmore, New Mexico	$44.00

Militaria ▶ WW II (1939–45)

The average sales price in this subcategory is $38.10.

	HIGH		AVG
M1 Carbine Original Paratrooper M1A1 Stock	$1,700.00	WW2 M1 CARBINE RECOIL PLATE FOR SAGINAW GEAR S'G'	$42.00
Wooden Military Airplane Propeller, WWII , 6 ft	$500.00	M1 GARAND NM GAS CYLINDER SCREW	$41.11
SUPER RARE 77th div PATCH W/OD BORDER-MINT!!!!!!!	$400.00	Typwriter, Remington - Rand, Model Seventeen	$41.00
M18 reflex sight for Quad mount on M16 Halftrack	$341.00	HUGE Book WWII Bombers SIGNED by 49 PILOTS!!	$40.00
M1 Garand Winchester stock WRA/GHD + crossed cannons	$332.78	WWII 1st Ranger BN Cheesecloth Back Uniform Patch Arch	$39.99
SETH THOMAS SHIPS BELL CLOCK	$317.00	1940's U.S. Naval Air station Alameda, CA yearbook	$39.99
Orig 509th Composite Group Unit History 1945 Printing	$280.00	U.S. G.I. WWII Mesh Netting	$39.95
CHELSEA SHIPS CLOCK	$250.00	WWII ARMY WATER JERRY CAN JEEP MB GPW DODGE CCKW WW2	$38.50
GERMAN POW ITEMS /CHITS LOT#3	$224.50	S&W Military Revolver Pistol Lanyard Ring Gun Parts	$37.03
US Military WWII Blood Chit Shuttle Mission n Russia	$202.78	Complete Springfield Made M1 Garand Rifle Bolt	$37.00
MODEL 1903 SPRINGFIELD BAYONET	$202.50	WORLD WAR II (2) Five Newspapers End of War - Lot 2	$36.50
4-VINTAGE- SEXTANT- CIRCA 1940 -AIR FORCES - U.S. ARMY!	$199.99	Vintage World War 2 MINES SIGN Old Skull WWII	$36.00
WWII FIGHTING FORTY FIFTH	$184.48	Collectible US Army Airbase Pueblo CO Pillow - Mother	$35.68
INFANTRY DIV. COMBAT REPORT		Lot of 1903 springfield rifle cut offs seriff cut off	$35.01
1903 1903A3 Springfield rifle stock	$152.51	South Sea Island Ethnic Child Sucks Nude Mom Photo	$34.99

Pens & Writing Instruments ▶ Pens

The average sales price in this subcategory is $26.26.

	HIGH		AVG
BRAND NEW! MONT BLANC BOHEME LEATHER / RHODOLITE, R/B	$799.99	EAGLE PENCIL CO NY,CRESENT FILL BLK CS GOLD BAND	$27.78
Mont Blanc LeGrand Rollerball Gold Vermeil "NIB"	$611.11	$125 Spanish CROCODILE Bidente Leather Pen Case - SPAIN	$27.30
NEW Montegrappa 70th Anniversary Fountain Pen MINT	$446.00	INTERESTING OLD PEN NIB TIN, NAVAL OFFICER, ANCHORS	$26.99
Incredible LUS Giubileo adjustable nib MINT Italy 1953	$431.00	Antique 19th C. John Holland Gold Nib Pen & Case	$26.62
Tiffany & Co 14K Pen & Pencil Combo (2 in 1) Signed NR	$385.00	HAND MADE TURNED AMBOYNA BURL BROKER PEN	$26.50
PRIVATE AUCTION FOR ROEL	$255.00	DRUG REP HUGE LOT 60 PENS CUPS CLIPS CALC PAPER MORE	$26.35
BRAND NEW! MONT BLANC BOHEME GREEN PLATINUM R/B	$209.99	VINTAGE 10K GOLD CROSS PEN AND PENCIL SET	$26.01
BRAND NEW! MONT BLANC BOHEME BLEU (BLUE) R/B	$199.99	Vintage 1970s BIC BANANA pen marker STORE DISPLAY BOX	$26.00
OLD BIG Gorham Sterling Silver Twist Dip Pen 1890s	$192.50	Kow Wood Clutch Machanical Pencil (Super Curly)	$26.00
OMAS Green Celluloid Rolling Ball Pen	$178.75	Antique Mother of Pearl Dip Pen with Original Case	$26.00
Unusual Antique Gold & Mother of Pearl Dip Pen	$167.50	Mont Blanc Pen - Skywalker Black Róller Ball- Checkered	$25.25
Montblanc Meisterstuck Platinum Le Grande Rollerball	$155.02	SENSA Zephyr Manhattan Red Rollerball NEW Roller Ball	$24.99
New Old Stock Namiki Burgundy Vanishing Point FP	$150.00	$139 UNIQUE Levenger Author's Back Cushion BLACK	$24.99
BRAND NEW MONT BLANC ROLLERBALL HIGHLIGHTER PEN B+P	$145.00	VINTAGE QUILL DIP PEN WITH GOLD COLORED NIB	$24.50
ROLLERBALL PEN (GENEVE) "Roberge" NEW "LooK"	$134.95	LOT 10 VINTAGE FOUNTAIN PENS, PENCILS, SHEAFFER, PARKER	$23.00

Pez, Keychains, Promo Glasses ▶ Pez

The average sales price in this subcategory is $9.91.

	HIGH		AVG
PEZ MISFIT TRUCK SET - ALL 32	$139.99	12 PEZ Pal Pilots no bp RARE & HARD TO FIND	$9.99
VARIATIONS! GLOW IN DARK!		15 Webby Pez dispensers Disney ducktales	$9.99
Scary Green Head Monster Footless PEZ	$124.72	[2 of these sold for $9.99 each]	
Lot of 83 Pez Candy Dispensers	$92.77	2002 Cubs CHARLIE BROWN Pez Dispenser + Commemorative	$9.99
COMPLETE set Barky Brown Pez LIMITED only 10,000 made	$55.00	Giant Texas Rangers Charlie Brown Pez Dispenser	$9.99
Old Ninja Turtles Pez 12 Count Display Box Never Opened	$52.01	Lot 6 Candy Pez Dispensers MOC MIB Sponge Bob Bart	$9.99
Large Pez Collection	$51.01	2005 COMPLETE SET of 6 Whistle Pez New Coach Whistles	$9.98
PEZ Collection (Over 130 Different Items) READ	$50.00	PEZ Gray Hair Shell Playworld MOC RARE & HARD TO FIND	$9.90
EBAY LIMITED EDITION PEZ SET OF 4!	$46.00	6 Aral gas & 6 Pilot pez pals no body parts DISPENSERS	$9.50

ALL MOC! $.99! NR!		
LOT OF 80 PEZ DISPENSERS LOOSE AND IN PACKAGE	$42.00	
Madagascar Fantasy PEZ Penguin	$41.00	
Huge lot of PEZ most NIB lot of 86	$40.00	
Asst. PEZ Pineapple Cop Fireman Panda Lamb Star Lot.	$38.00	
SMURF PEZ 5 PEICE SET MOC	$37.00	
MN Pez Costume for Charity	$32.00	
Madagascar Fantasy PEZ Penguin	$31.00	

LIMTED Edition BARKY BROWN pez fr Australia orange stem	$9.50
Madagascar pez set EUROPEAN Release Not same as US	$9.49
PEZ Six Great Flavors A Great Tin Sign	$9.43
4x3dif Smurfs S2 PEZ RETIRED Euro dispensers smurf	$9.25
12 Pez 6 Psyduck & 6 Mew Pokemon Disps loose	$9.00
2 x 4 dif Pink Panther Pez mint loose retired	$9.00
12 Pez 6 Psyduck & 6 Mew Pokemon Disps loose	$9.00
[2 of these sold for $9.00 each]	

Photographic Images ▸ Antique (Pre–1940)

The average sales price in this subcategory is $93.16.

	HIGH		AVG
EARLY AMERICAN VILLAGE SCENE, c.1841. PAPER MAT	$2,617.89	RARE HALVORSON CASE with 1/9 PLATE DAG of a LADY	$99.00
1/2 PLATE POLYCHROME COLOR DAGUERREOTYPE DATED 1849	$1,836.01	QUARTER PLATE HALFCASE DAGUERREOTYPE LOVELY FAMILY	$97.00
1/9 PLATE DAGUERREOTYPE - LADY IN UNIQUE CASE	$1,525.84	AMBROTYPE OF 2 BEAUTIFUL CHILDREN TINTED 4TH PLATE	$96.00
Identified/Published Confederate Ruby Ambro -NO RESERVE	$1,126.00	ANTIQUE DAGUERREOTYPE YOUNG GIRL	$96.00
Beautiful, Early Half Plate Dag in Rare Case	$1,113.88	Daguerreotype - Calmady Union Case - Id'd. Engraver	$95.99
PEWTER MAKER; WITH APRON, HAMMER+ COFFEE POT, c.1850	$871.75	Antique Gutta Percha Union Case 1/6 Plate EAGLE CANNON	$95.99
RARE ENGLISH STEREO DAGUERREOTYPE BY T. R. WILLIAMS	$850.00	Leather Photo Daguerreotype Case Gold Velvet WOW!	$94.00
Mix Collection of 28 Daguerreotypes, tin types & more	$850.00	early blue tones. daguerreotype.	$93.00
Antique Daguerrotype (LARGE 1/2 PLATE	$811.00	Daguerreotype 1/4 SOO CUTE Young Pair of Sisters! Oh My	$92.99
ANTIQUE COLLECTORS PHOTOCARD ALBUM (DAGURRATYPE PHOTOS)	$785.00	1/6 PLATE DAGUERREOTYPE - GIRL WITH BRAIDS	$92.00
superb 1840s MAN READING BOOK by AMERICAN DAG.	$735.00	1/6th Plate PHOTOGLASS OUTDOOR /ed/Ferrier & Soulier	$91.75
CIVIL WAR-Large albumen photo-Matthew Brady	$710.00	RARE HALVORSON CASE - BLIND MAN ? 1/6 PLATE DAG	$90.00
1860s CDV PHOTO ALBUM OF NEW BEDFORD MASS SEA CAPTAINS	$685.53	Dag - Dressed to the 9s	$90.00
1/4 PLATE DAGUERREOTYPE OF FARM HOUSE WITH FENCE	$666.86	ANTIQUE DAGUERREOTYPE PHOTO LOT = 6	$90.00
MUST SEE STUNNING!! HALF PLATE FULLCASE DAGUERREOTYPE	$570.00	Civil War Gutta Percha Anchor Navy Sweetheart Locket	$89.99

Pinbacks, Nodders, Lunchboxes ▸ Lunchboxes, Thermoses

The average sales price in this subcategory is $15.79.

	HIGH		AVG
OLD CARNIVAL SCENE LUNCHBOX AND THERMOS	$416.98	AWESOME NEW 2 PC NASCAR LUNCH	$16.99
1978 Vintage 'Little House' Lunch box & thermos	$361.99	BOX LUNCHBOX RACE CAR	$16.99
DEPUTY DAWG VINYL LUNCHBOX	$155.50	THE SIMPSONS HALLOWEEN LUNCH BOX LUNCHBOX W/ THERMOS	$16.99
1977 KISS METAL LUNCHBOX & THERMOS RARE EXCELLENT COND!	$128.26	1976 SUPER FRIENDS LUNCH BOX AND THERMOS	$16.51
VINTAGE LUNCHBOX	$105.46	Version 2.0 Lunchbox Collectors Software	$16.50
RARE 1962 ALADDIN AIRLINES THE STEWARDESS LUNCHBOX	$102.50	1981THE FALL GUY LUNCH BOX AND THERMOS	$16.25
Aladdin Beverly Hillbillies Lunch box Pail W/ Thermos	$101.51	1979 SESAME STREET LUNCH BOX AND THERMOS	$16.00
1974 Evel Knievel Vintage Metal Lunchbox	$99.98	VINTAGE - Girl Scout Soft LunchBag W/Metal Thermos	$15.95
VINTAGE 1962-64 TAMMY VINYL LUNCHBOX & THERMOS/ IDEAL	$91.00	HAWAIIAN HAWAII PINK LUNCHBOX LUNCH BOX BAG INSULATED	$15.65
WONDER WOMAN VINYL LUNCH BOX BY ALADDIN 1970'S	$89.00	1974 THE SIX MILLION DOLLAR MAN LUNCHBOX AND THERMOS	$15.61
Disney Firetruck Lunch Box-Mickey,Donald,Goofy,Pluto	$86.00	NWT Old Navy Lunch Box Zebra/pink design Girl's	$15.51
1977 WELCOME BACK KOTTER LUNCH BOX AND THERMOS	$71.00	Star Wars Darth Vader Dual Compartment Lunch Kit.Box	$15.50
Pink Vinyl Malt Soda Shop Groovy Lunch Box 1950s Hip	$69.87	Vintage Retro Wicker Thermos	$15.50
Disney School Bus Lunch Box-Mickey,Donald,Goofy,Pluto	$64.95	HARDY BOYS MYSTERIES LUNCH BOX & THERMOS FROM 1977	$15.50
RAGGEDY ANN AND ANDY RARE LUNCH BOX collectors	$60.00	METAL POPEYE LUNCHBOX with THERMOS	$15.50
vintage 1974 evel knievel metal lunch box	$56.00	1983 SESAME STREET LUNCH BOX AND THERMOS	$15.50

Pinbacks, Nodders, Lunchboxes ▸ Pinbacks

The average sales price in this subcategory is $7.20.

	HIGH		AVG
Disney Pins 50th Anniversary Castle set of 5	$110.00	THIERRY MUGLER A*MEN 1" BUTTONS Badges pins B*MEN RARE	$7.50
HR Giger pin set . 3 collector pins , limited 666	$100.00	TWIST ~BARRY MCGEE GRAFFITI ART BUTTONS Pins/Pin/Button	$7.50
Vintage Corn Carnival, Vandalia, Mo. Advertising Pin	$89.00	YOSHITOMO NARA - Japan art set 2 BUTTONS Pins Badges	$7.50
RARE Boomerang Harmonica Best Mouth Organs Pinback	$89.00	YVES SAINT LAURENT 1" BUTTONS Badges pins button YSL	$7.50
Signed Marilyn Manson T-shirt by all members Holywood	$61.00	World Cup USA 94 Soccer Football - 7 Pin Set	$7.50
13 different hot air balloon pins pin some shapes	$56.00	Disney Pins * Lanyard Mickey and Donald Baby Set **	$7.45
Rare 1955 MUSKY FESTIVAL Hayward, WI fishing pinback NM	$49.50	DHL FEDEX UPS 1" Buttons Pins Badges Pin Button Badge	$7.00
SEATTLE SEAFAIR , MISS BARDAHL AND WHITE GOAT? PINS	$45.00	COLLECTION of 14 TRAVEL PINS, MOSTLY GERMANY? NEAT , NR	$7.00
1925 American Bowling Congress Pin Back Button Scarce	$43.50	IRON WORKER TRAINING FUND PIN	$6.99
ANTIQUE MEDAL ELK NATIONAL CONVENTION BPOE 1899	$42.00	GRATEFUL DEAD 1" Buttons JERRY GARCIA Pins Badges SET1	$6.99
Remington UMC Pinback Pin	$39.13	Disney Pins Disneyland Security Officer Mini Badge	$6.99
1912 Columbus Ohio Centennial Pin Back Button Scarce	$37.99	FUNKO WACKY WOBBLER SMOKEY BEAR NODDER BOBBLE HEAD DOLL	$6.99
Vintage Statue of Liberty No Beer No Work Pinback	$37.51	ANCAM - 1974 WOODEN - SOUVENIER MUG	$6.99
C.I.O.(Lumber And Sawmill Workers)PinBack Buttons1930's	$36.05	*THE BEST* - SCREAMO LOT PINS/BUTTONS PUNK/EMO/INDIE/DC	$6.99
NEW! HILARY DUFF 1" BUTTONS Badges pins Hillary SET #1	$32.00	*THE BEST* - SUPER NINTENDO LOT PINS/BUTTONS PUNK/EMO	$6.99

Postcards & Paper ▸ Postcards

The average sales price in this subcategory is $8.80.

	HIGH		AVG
Early Postcard Album With 100 Nice Old Postcards	$130.50	North Georgia College Parade Band Atlanta Postcard +NEG	$9.25
Night Softball ACL YMCA Rocky Mount NC Postcard +NEG	$82.56	West Campus Enter Upper Iowa University Fayette IA +NEG	$9.25
BOX OF 600 POSTCARDS	$67.13	Horseback Camp Occoneechee Lake Lure NC Postcard +NEG	$9.25

Large Dealer Lot of 1000 Assorted Continental Postcards	$59.99	3554/ Montreal St Jean de Dieu Insane Asylum c1910	$9.00
LOT 180 Town City Scenic View Antique Vintage Postcards	$53.01	3592/ Mass. Williamstown Zeta Psi Fraternity House Will	$9.00
ALBUM FULL OF 200 OLD POST CARDS	$50.00	Vintage Grocery Store Interior, Kewanee, Illinois	$8.99
UK EDWARDIAN ACTRESS EDNA MAY 1907 POSTCARD	$46.90	Multi-view Hotel Fresno Hwy 99 CA Postcard +NEG	$8.75
Large Lot of 100 Beautiful Christmas Greeting Postcards	$45.99	Multi-view Tracy Inn Sacramento,Frisco CA Postcard +NEG	$8.75
1000 Chrome US and Foreign Postcards Postcard Lot	$42.15	Jolly Boat of the Anglo Saxon Mystic Seaport CT +NEG	$8.75
ANTIQUE~42 OLD POSTCARDS/ALBUM~ DATED 1907-1908	$42.00	Pleasant View On Shore West Haven CT Postcard +NEG	$8.75
100 ANTIQUE & VINTAGE POSTCARD LOT POSTCARDS	$39.99	St Mary's Catholic Church Lakeville CT Postcard +NEG	$8.75
LOT 74 PRE-1920 Town City Scenic View Vintage Postcards	$39.88	The New Southern Hotel Miami Beach FL Postcard +NEG	$8.75
Drayer Dorm Dickinson College Carlisle PA Postcard +NEG	$32.51	Pan American Int'l AirportTerminal Miami FL Postcd +NEG	$8.75
OLD 'For Auld Lang Syne' Iris Postcard made in Germany	$27.00	St Cyril Methodius Church Lemont IL Postcard +NEG	$8.75
Antique RARE Photo Post Card Bohemian Club CA. 1904	$26.00	St John Rectory Loogootee IN Postcard +NEG	$8.75

Postcards & Paper ▸ Matchbooks

The average sales price in this subcategory is $8.57.

	HIGH		AVG
Girlie Bar vintage matchbooks 1940's Box of 50	$172.49	2 VINTAGE DISNEYLAND KNOTT'S BERRY FARM MATCHBOOKS	$9.58
10 VINTAGE POMONA CALIFORNIA MATCHBOOK	$150.85	34 Diff Hillbilly Matchcovers (All FS)	$9.55
12 MATCHBOOK COVERS of SPORTS PERSONALITIES	$119.87	Lot of 30 American Ace match box - # 8445 - # 8481	$9.50
WWII HILTER MATCH STRIKER & WAR BOND MATCHES MATCHBOOK	$106.49	3 SCARCE INDIAN MATCHBOX LABELS.	$9.50
Osama Bin Laden Reward Matches	$75.00	74 CHINESE RESTAURANTS MATCHCOVERS	$9.38
HUGE LOT MATCHBOOKS 40'S 50'S & UP 8 -1/2 POUNDS OLD	$66.00	(49) Older MATCHBOOK Match Book LOT Wow! L@@K!	$9.25
5 WHITE SOX and 7 RED SOX MATCHBOOK COVERS	$61.11	Lot 100 Vintage Matchbooks Matches Las Vegas Casinos	$9.01
30 CASINO / GAMBLING F/S MATCHBOOKS Vintage Las Vegas	$58.77	Matchbook Matches	$8.59
1940s Superior Matchbook Salesman's Catalog	$45.44	VINTAGE MANNERS BIG BOY MATCHES ~ THESE ARE REALLY KQQL	$8.50
MATCHBOOK SAMPLES FOLDER - SALESMAN'S SAMPLES	$44.99	SCARCE JAPANESE MATCHBOX LABEL.	$8.50
USS Indianapolis Full Diamond Matchbook 1930s	$36.99	16 OLD MATCHBOOKS & 1940 PAPER FROM CHICAGO TRIBUNE	$8.50
Antique Vicks Advertising Matchbooks 3 boxes MIB	$36.85	10 ST. LOUIS CARDINALS MATCHBOOK COVERS	$8.19
165 Rare Vintage Automobile Matchbook Cover Collection	$36.50	Vintage American Express Matchbook Unused	$7.99
USS New Mexico Diamond Matchbook 1930s	$36.34	Two Old Panama Canal Zone Match Boxes Matches	$7.99
1 CARTON & 1 LOOSE WOODEN BOX OF CONGRESS MATCHES	$36.00	100 PLUS HAWAIIAN MATCHBOOKS	$7.95

Radio, Phonograph, TV, Phone ▸ Radios

The average sales price in this subcategory is $30.78.

	HIGH		AVG
RCA BAKERLITE VINTAGE TABLE MODEL RADIO CASE	$587.77	Vintage RCA Victor RADIO 68R3: ca. 1955 Works Great	$31.00
Rotary Spark Gap, Spring motor powered, induction coil!	$399.00	RCA SIGN Painted/Glass RCA TUBES Nice & OLD	$31.00
Old Antique Crystal Radio Mutual Bank Advertising Promo	$304.99	Crystal Radio Reproduction - Wired & Tested	$31.00
KENT ATWATER MODEL 49 VERY RARE XCELLENT++ SPEAKER !!!	$302.00	Beautiful Vintage wood speaker	$30.84
OTR massive Old Time Radio collection, 690+ shows	$299.00	Houston Texas Radio K-NUZ Radio Sales Brochures 50s	$30.00
NEW Tesla coil Ham Radio transformer winding machine	$299.00	RCA VICTOR GLOBE TROTTER AM RADIO - DIRECTIONAL ANTENNA	$29.99
[2 of these sold for $299.00 each]		RADIO PHILLIPS PHILCO CATHEDRAL BOOKENDS ANTIQUE REPO	$29.99
Vintage ATWATER KENT MODEL L Radio Horn Speaker MINT	$272.00	Antique Collectible Ritz Cracker Radio Cassette	$29.95
Vintage Crystal Radio Set w/ Dual Tap Switches Bakelite	$259.00	Miniature crystal radio kit -	$29.90
Eames Space Age Stereo Speakers Weltron Kartell b w	$239.50	[2 of these sold in a multiple item ("Dutch") auction for $14.95 each]	
Vintage RCA Basketweave Loop Ariel For Radiola 25 And ?	$228.48	VINTAGE 1915 BALDWIN RADIO HEADPHONES TYPE C !!	$28.99
Four Early 1920's & 30's Microphones "Must L@@K"	$225.00	RARE! 8 WLAG "Listnin'in Radio News-Programs" 1923	$27.76
MINT 1920's STEINITE CRYSTAL RADIO w/WAVE TRAP	$212.50	CHILDRENS TOY RADIO EARLY PLASTIC LIGHT GREEN	$27.01
Vintage Crystal Radio Set. Open Frame w/ Catwhisker	$190.50	Vintage Practical Radio & Electronics Course 1951 VGC	$27.00
Mod Eames Retro Space Age Stereo Radio Weltron Kartell	$159.00	ANTIQUE windup MORSE CODE telegraph ham radio device	$26.99
ULTRA RARE ZENITH ROYAL 500 ARE YOU READY IN PINK !!!!!	$153.50	GE-74100J Replica 30's Vintage Cathedral Radio AM/FM	$26.57

Radio, Phonograph, TV, Phone ▸ Telephones

The average sales price in this subcategory is $25.38.

	HIGH		AVG
5 NEW!!! PAY PHONE PROTEL 7000 BOARDS	$511.00	VINTAGE RED HIGH HEEL NOVELTY TELEPHONE- 1987	$26.00
Sevres China "Candlestick" Telephone	$455.00	VINTAGE BLUE ROTARY DIAL DESK PHONE	$26.00
vintage rotary wall phone pink	$251.40	1919 ANTIQUE REPLICA CANDLESTICK TELEPHONE	$26.00
T-REX DINOSAUR DINO PHONE telephone WORKS GREAT!	$156.00	Vintage ITT Beige Rotary Dial Desk Telephone	$26.00
Vialta Beamer Phone Video Station BM - 80	$148.19	AT & T BELL TT PRINCESS PHONE LK NEW - WHITE - NR	$26.00
MOD Western Electric SPEAKERPHONE pink-2500 TELEPHONE	$142.50	1970's Vintage Donut Telephone-Western Electric	$25.49
VINTAGE PINK PRINCESS ROTARY PHONE DIAL LIGHTS NR	$129.99	Black Tower Wine PROMO 1983 Novelty Phone	$25.40
Vintage Airplane Rotary Telephone Panton Eames phone	$127.63	VINTAGE ROTARY PHONE	$25.27
PRE OWNED PAY PHONE & SIGN WALL PHONE TELEPHONE KEYS	$127.50	Vintage Red Touch Tone Wall Phone Model 2554	$25.00
Vintage Telequest Hot Lips Pink Phone. Lip shape Panton	$127.50	COLLECTIBLE AND ANTIQUE FRENCH VINTAGE PHONE	$25.00
WESTERN ELECTRIC ROSE PINK ROTARY PRINCESS PHONE	$118.00	Coca Cola-Tiffany Style Light up Telephone NEW IN BOX	$25.00
PRE OWNED PAY PHONE & SIGN WALL PHONE TELEPHONE KEYS	$115.49	SO CHIC! French Style Ivory & Brass Telephone PHONE	$25.00
Bell System Western Electric 6 button TAM-32 w/Spkrphon	$113.50	NIB - Scooby Doo Talking Animated Telephone	$25.00
W.E. PAYPHONE W/ LOCKS W.E/ BELL SYS. LOGO *NICE*	$102.50	Vintage Snoopy & Woodstock Telephone 1976 With BONUS	$24.99
PAYPHONE - PROTEL ELCOTEL	$102.50	CLASSIC VINTAGE 1972 BLACK ROTARY DIAL TELEPHONE PHONE.	$24.99

Religions, Spirituality ▶ Christianity

The average sales price in this subcategory is $27.03.

	HIGH		AVG
Beautiful French Sterling chalice with Porcelain	$620.00	LARGE PIETA CHRIST BY BOUGUEREAU ON CANVAS REPRO	$29.00
Set of two Antique Gothic Altar Candelabra	$400.00	VINTAGE CLOISONNE ENAMEL HOLY WATER FONT GERMANY	$28.00
Bronze TABERNACLE DOOR AND FRAME, C1920 BELGUIM	$375.00	OLD 1933 BOOK 50 CHALK TALK PROGRAMS W.A. BIXLER NR	$27.99
ILLUMINATED VATICAN HOLY BIBLE 900 ILL. Vatican Library	$350.00	Crystal Lourdes Water Rosary BLESS BY POPE JOHN PAUL II	$27.99
RELIC ST. MARGARET MARY ALACOQUE RELIQUARY W/AUTHENTIC	$255.01	MY SUNDAY MISSAL - CATHOLIC MISSAL - NEVER USED	$27.57
Priest Liturgical Pallium Stole Mass Vestment Gold/Grey	$194.50	BEAUTIFUL PAIR RELIGIOUS VINTAGE BRASS CANDLESTICKS 19"	$26.99
SLABBINCK Liturgy Priest Mass Vestment Chasuble & Stole	$178.49	Rare Passion of Christ Mini Flip TV Viewer Souvenir	$26.61
Altar Vestment: Set of Six Brass Candlesticks	$177.50	NUNS-CARMELITES OF THE MOST SACRED HEART-PHOTOS	$26.00
2 Saint St Francis of Assisi Reliquary Relic	$152.50	MOST UNUSUAL* Stations of the Cross* Rosary	$26.00
Pair of Antique Nickle Plated Brass Coffin Stands.	$129.95	OUR LADY OF GUADALUPE MeXiCaN TiN CRoSS	$25.00
6 Catholic Books MEDITATION FOR SEMINARIANS PRIESTS SET	$112.50	EXQUISITE VIRGIN MARY PICTURE BRACELET RARE BEAUTIFUL	$25.00
Rare Dominican Relic St. Maria Reliquary	$104.49	8-SET~GORGEOUS ANTIQ PC's~LORD'S PRAYER~ANGELS~GOLD ACC	$24.99
Trappist Holy Rood Monastic Cowl Priest Alb Vestment	$104.49	NEW! Roman Catholic Tridentine TRAVEL Altar Cards	$24.99
Altar Chalice: Sterling Silver Ciborium	$103.50	MADONNA & CHILD diamond PYX priest deacon mass	$24.99
GORGEOUS SILVERPLATED HOLY WATER FONT 1900's. SUPERB	$99.99	ANTQ. 1900 WHITE LUTHERN CHURCH/HYMNAL PRAYERBOOK	$23.95

Rocks, Fossils, Minerals ▶ Fossils

The average sales price in this subcategory is $32.97.

	HIGH		AVG
Excellent Bird,Confuciusornis Bird Fossil,Museum Qualit	$5,110.00	4 3/4 in Megalodon Fossil Shark Tooth	$34.55
Rare Bird,Confuciusornis bird,Fossil	$2,025.00	Fossil Bone Petrified Wood? S.C. Shore Find	$34.00
Bird,Liaoxiornis Delicates Fossil,Museum Quality	$1,475.00	3 13/16 in Megalodon Fossil Shark Tooth	$33.75
EURYPTERID EURYPTERIS REMIPES FOSSIL	$310.50	4 5/16 in Megalodon Fossil Shark Tooth	$33.50
Mazon Creek, a rare Fully Clawed Tully Monster...!	$299.99	4 15/16 in Megalodon Fossil Shark Tooth	$33.50
Frogs,Rana Basaltica in Matrix Fossil,Museum Quality	$289.00	4 5/16 in Megalodon Fossil Shark Tooth	$33.00
Rare Young Frog Fossil,No Repair	$199.00	X-RARE FOSSIL GIANT MASTODON BABY TOOTH FOSSILS MAMMOTH	$33.00
Frogs,Rana Basaltica in Matrix Fossil	$199.00	Large Fossil / Claw? Tooth? Horn? Found in Kansas	$33.00
Fossil Crab in Matrix, Nice Specimen, NR	$179.17	4 5/16 in Megalodon Fossil Shark Tooth	$32.50
Fossil Crab in Matrix, Interesting Specimen, NR	$154.00	46 PETRIFIED ITEMS, 38 CLAWS	$31.51
SABER TOOTH TIGER SKULL, FLAWLESS!!!	$151.00	35 Brachiopod Fossils, Science, Geology Teachers, LOOK!	$31.00
@-@RARE*16"-XL SINOCERAS(ORDOVICIAN) FOSSIL – CHINA!	$142.50	Fossil cretaceous Avitelmessus crab, fossils, crabs	$31.00
5 1/2 in Megalodon Fossil Shark Tooth	$132.39	5 in Megalodon Fossil Shark Tooth	$31.00
5 9/16 in Megalodon Fossil Shark Tooth	$112.50	PS: Green Mary Ellen Jasper Fossil Slab Rough	$30.99
VEN17- NEMIANA SIMPLEX – EDIACARAN - EXTREMELY RARE!!	$107.50	Fossil cretaceous Avitelmessus crab, fossils, crabs	$30.01

Science Fiction ▶ Star Trek

The average sales price in this subcategory is $21.51.

	HIGH		AVG
Star Trek TOS Hero Communicator Prop–Unique Piece!	$431.00	STAR TREK NEXT GENERATION DIE CAST METAL REPLICA 1701D	$24.99
Star Trek COLLECTION Set Games Figures Plate MORE NR	$222.83	STAR TREK ORIGINAL SERIES TRICORDER PROP PLAYMATES	$24.50
=/\=Star Trek PHASER RIFLE prop kit NO RESERVE=/\=	$220.00	Star Trek 1999 Metal LUNCHBOX ~ Hallmark	$22.51
STAR TREK USS EXCELSIOR PEWTER MODEL NIB COA NR	$182.50	2002 Hallmark Star Trek Delta Flyer Ornament NIB	$22.50
STAR TREK 30 YEARS PLATE-RARE ENGINEERS TRIBUTE ...	$179.50	STAR TREK: ORIGINAL EPISODES PLATE- GOLD BORDER -MINT	$21.52
Star Trek Prop : Transporter command console	$162.50	Micromachines & Next Gen Board Game	$21.50
STAR TREK PROP : TACTICAL COMMAND CONSOLE	$158.38	STAR TREK: ORIGINAL EPISODES PLATE- GOLD BORDER -MINT	$21.38
Franklin mint Star Trek 25th anniversary chess board	$154.80	FASA Star Trek ROMULAN NOVA BATTLESHIP, 1/3900 NIP	$20.54
star trek TR-590 Tricorder prop replica with door LED's	$150.00	FASA Star Trek KLINGON L-24 BATTLESHIP, 1/3900 NIP	$20.54
12 Star Trek Badges Original Series	$145.00	STAR TREK: ORIGINAL EPISODES PLATE- GOLD BORDER -MINT	$20.52
STAR TREK Communicator Replica NEW IN BOX Prop	$135.49	Star Trek = KLINGON DAHAR MASTER Badge = Prop	$20.50
franklin mint 25th anniversary edtion enterprise	$130.00	STAR TREK NEMESIS BLANKET THROW BRAND NEW! MUST HAVE	$20.50
Star Trek Tridimensional Chess Set	$125.00	STAR TREK : THE MOTION PICTURE PLATE MINT COA	$20.50
Star Trek Klingon Coin Ship Miniature Franklin Mint NR	$108.16	Star Trek The Next Generation Romulan Warbird New/Box	$20.50
Star Trek Tri-dimensional Chess Set - New	$107.23	NOS Star Trek Enterprise POOL FLOAT Raft Lounge in Box	$20.50

Science Fiction ▶ Star Wars

The average sales price in this subcategory is $18.97.

	HIGH		AVG
C-3PO HELMET - fiberglass Head SW Prop C3PO	$308.90	Star Wars Original Trilogy Edition Monopoly Set	$20.00
Star Wars Fan made Boba Fett fiberglass armor prop	$175.00	9 COMIC CON PROMO & EXCLUSIVE STAR WARS CARDS FIGURES	$20.00
LEGO R2D2 LARGE TARGET SWEEPSTAKES	$157.50	VINTAGE roll STAR WARS wallpaper wall paper WOW !!!!!	$19.99
STAR WARS R2D2 BEVERAGE COOLER *BRAND NEW*	$150.00	Star Wars Hamilton Collector's Plates-Imperial Shuttle	$19.99
Star Wars: Mace Windu Lightsaber FX	$124.00	STAR WARS JAPAN PEPSI CANS 12 FULE SET - EP III	$19.90
Star Wars: Mace Windu Lightsaber FX	$119.00	Orig. 1977 STAR WARS Movie Program-Mint Cond.	$19.49
1977 STAR WARS R2 D2 COOKIE JAR MINT IN BOX !!	$117.50	STAR WARS 12 INCH ELECTRONIC DARTH VADER TALKS! MISB	$19.00
Star Wars Biker Scout Helmet Don Post Prop Armor	$106.02	STAR WARS Clone Strike QUINLAN VOS Jedi RARE Miniature	$18.50
Star Wars: Anakin Skywalker Episode III Lightsaber FX	$103.50	STAR WARS RANCOR STATUE LTD AND SOLD OUT	$18.50
Vintage Star Wars Lot Ships Playsets 19 Figures	$102.50	STAR WARS Clone Strike DESTROYER DROID RARE Miniature	$18.01
Star Wars Anakin Jedi Costume, Custom Made Tunics	$102.50	Star Wars Posters (Set of 4) Burger Chef & Coke 1977	$18.00

	HIGH		AVG
Star Wars: Anakin Skywalker Episode III Lightsaber FX	$99.99	Star Wars Micro Collection Xwing Fighter	$17.57
Star Wars: Darth Vader Episode V Lightsaber FX IN STOCK	$99.99	STAR WARS 12 INCH ELECTRONIC BOBA FETT TALKS! MISB	$17.50
Star Wars: Darth Vader Episode V Lightsaber FX IN STOCK	$99.99	Star Wars **MINT** Hamilton Collectors Plate 24K gold	$17.00
Star Wars Revenge of the Sith NEW FOSSIL DROIDS WATCH	$99.00	Star Wars Coins: 10 Sets (60 Coins Total)	$17.00

Science, Medical ▸ Medicine, Dentistry

The average sales price in this subcategory is $58.93.

	HIGH		AVG
Very unusual, fully fitted Homeopathic seed & grain box	$760.00	A T Still Founder Of Osteopathy Cast Copper Statue	$61.00
$2,900 Mertz WLP I.D.E.A.L. RETENTION Chiropractic DVDs	$699.00	Welch Allyn Otoscope 25020~Head Only~ NEW~~SAVE 50%~~	$60.00
Real human skull - bone - medical - echter Sch?l	$635.00	Antique Leather Doctor's Bag/Satchel	$60.00
REAL HUMAN SKULL MEDICAL GRADE EXCELLENT SHAPE	$550.00	1957 BJ Palmer Chiropractic Grn Book History in Making	$59.99
Real Human Skull For Medical Study -C50	$381.99	1927 The Art of Chiropractic Palmer Grn Bk Author Steph	$59.95
Real Human Skull For Medical Study -Great Dentitio/E33	$365.00	Vintage BRAIN/HEAD/ANATOMICAL/Medical/Model/NASCO	$58.00
Real Human Skull For Medical Study -C35	$346.26	Antique Medical Doctors Book-All Latin-Signed 1847-NR	$56.00
REAL HUMAN SKULL for medical use NO RESERVE B9	$330.00	Eli Lilly Pharmacy Graduation Spatulas	$56.00
Real Human Skull For Medical Study -F6, Full Dention	$325.00	Charity Hospital New Orleans 10K Gold Pin 1962 Award?	$52.50
Real Human Skull For Medical Study -C015/NR	$305.00	VINTAGE LEATHER DOCTOR BAG BY "PROFESSIONAL CASE,INC.	$51.00
Real Human Skull For Medical Study -F11, Full Dentition	$305.00	3 BOXES that Hold Glass Slides for MICROSCOPE w/SLIDES	$51.00
Scarce1920 Spirit of PSC BJ Palmer Chiropractic GreenBk	$300.00	Vintage Medco-sonlator Ultrasound Electro-therapy Unit	$50.00
Quack medical tesla coil diathermy Electro-therapy	$290.99	10k GOLD SOLDIERS HOME CHELSEA, MA MEDICAL/DOCTOR RING	$49.99
FAB ILL INTERNATIONAL STOCK FOOD CO POSTER VETERINARY	$260.00	ROUGH ON RATS MEDICINE TEACHING VETERINARY TRADE CARD	$47.00
Real Human Skull For Medical Study -C9	$258.00	Chester W Nimitz Battle of Midway MACO 2oz Silver Medal	$47.00

Tobacciana ▸ Ashtrays

The average sales price in this subcategory is $11.44.

	HIGH		AVG
OLD ART DECO Ashtray MARBLE Stand GREAT WOW @!	$162.49	Advertising The Sea Gull Hotel Miami Beach Ash Tray	$12.50
Old cast iron Dragon pedestal Ashtray Scroll Art Mfg Co	$147.50	VERY RETRO~VERY LARGE~SILVER ASHTRAY~COOL!!	$12.50
NATIVE nodder ashtray	$127.50	VINTAGE 1940'S? COPPER *COWBOY HAT* ASHTRAY?	$12.50
LARGE DAVIDOFF PORCELAIN CIGAR ASHTRAY IN BLACK/GOLD	$125.51	1950's Jake & Dorothy's (cafe) ash tray	$12.50
VINTAGE DUNHILL DECO WOOD STEEL ASHTRAY!! MINT UNUSED!	$99.99	Norwegian Pewter gothic pattern ashtray Vintage	$12.00
Standing Angelic Cherub Brass Ashtray	$82.00	THE CITADEL MILITARY COLLEGE OF SO. CAROLINA ASHTRAY	$11.77
ART DECO CHROME FLOOR ASHTRAY SMOKING STAND & LIGHTER	$78.00	Vintage Advertisement Ashtray Funeral Director L@@K	$11.50
OLD STORK CLUB NEW YORK NIGHTSPOT STONEWARE ASHTRAY	$63.26	Rare Ashtray, Alaska, Fairbanks, Richardson, Road House	$11.49
OLD ART DECO Ashtray Stand GREAT WOW @!	$63.00	Advertising: Camp Wishon. Springville, California.	$11.26
GENUINE NEW YORK CITY STORK CLUB ASHTRAY	$56.00	Vintage The Playboy Club Ashtrays Orange 6	$11.00
Vintage ashtray Stand with light, DKBRN glass ash tray	$51.00	NEW ORLEANS MICHELS BAR SEMI- NUDE LADY ASHTRAY	$11.00
DANISH-MODERN PANTON ERA SPACE AGE MOD STANDING ASHTRAY	$49.99	NEW Smokeless Ashtray w/ Carbon Filter Cigar Cigarette	$10.95
VINTAGE AGATE SLAG GLASS ART DECO LIGHTED SMOKE STAND	$46.00	ashtrays ATLANTIC CITY NEW JERSEY glass	$10.83
AMERICAN NURSES ASSOCIATION 1954 ASH TRAY	$42.99	Old Ashtray, Hotel Drake Wiltshire San Francisco	$10.51
Vintage Ashtray from Harry_s Bar Venice	$42.00	Nambe 563 Ashtray	$10.51

Tobacciana ▸ Cigar

The average sales price in this subcategory is $27.06.

	HIGH		AVG
angel cigar lighter saloon or newel post gas lamp	$712.02	1930s REAL Bakelite Club Meerschaum Cigar Holder Case	$30.00
Wooden Cigar Store Indian	$575.00	Bush Victory Cigar matches Makers Mark Inaug. Cigar	$30.00
Vintage Cigar Store Indian Statue	$510.00	MACBETH MALCOM Cigars	$29.89
1920'S ANTIQUE MIDLAND JUMP SPARK CIGAR COUNTER LIGHTER	$455.00	Tommy Bahama CIGAR Ashtray Splash Dance w/Sailfish NEW!	$28.50
CIGAR STORE INDIAN 6' WOOD Carving Geronimo Western	$449.00	ART NOUVEAU antique CIGAR HOLDER w/case BAKELITE	$28.00
ANTIQUE & EXTREMLY LIMITED ROMEO Y JULIETA HUMIDOR	$441.50	Old General Bunte Glass Display Jar And Lid	$28.00
Opus X Fuente Crystal Hand Carved and Painted Ashtray	$345.00	Box 25 cigar robt Burns Imperials	$27.66
5ft Wooden Cigar Store Indian Chief American Flag	$305.00	VINTAGE old MEERSCHAUM bakelite CIGAR HOLDER w CASE	$27.54
5ft Wooden STAINED Cigar Store Indian Chief ONLY 1!!	$230.00	Antique wooden cigar press	$26.60
1880-1900" Cigar Lighter/ Gas Lamp-Wall Mount-Nr	$228.50	OLD Cigar Advertising Glass Jar WHITE HOUSE CIGARS WIS	$26.51
4ft Wooden STAINED Cigar Store Indian CHIEF LAST ONE	$175.00	TRUMPS ROI TAN CIGARS ASSORTED UNOPENED PACKS	$26.00
Big Lot of Vintage Novelty AMERICAN FLAG Cigars	$159.30	RadioShack Wireless Thermometer Hygrometer	$26.00
Maker's Mark Cigars - Box of 25	$155.00	Vintage Leather Cigar case–AGME SWITZERLAND	$25.02
FULL COLLECTABLE BOX OF GURKHA 101 SIGNATURE COLLECTION	$122.50	2 NEW AUTHORIZED LIMITED FUENTE OPUS X CAP HAT $58 VAL	$25.00
ANTIQUE ALLIGATOR LEATHER HUMIDOR	$120.50	AVO Uvezian Cigar Ashtray Porcelain by Design Rare NR!	$25.00

Trading Cards ▸ Animation

The average sales price in this subcategory is $25.47.

	HIGH		AVG
1973 Topps Wacky Packages Posters Original Art. KODUCK	$7,900.00	Topps 16th Series Wacky Packages Puzzle Piece #6 M-R 16	$26.00
1973 Topps Wacky Packages Posters Orig. Art. NEVEREADY	$5,048.00	GARBAGE PAIL KIDS CARDS SERIES 6 FULL 48 PACK BOX MIB	$26.00
1974 Topps UK Version WACKY PACKAGES 48-Pack FULL BOX	$4,250.00	Wacky Packages/Mutt's/1st series/Wacky Packs	$26.00
1985 Topps Series 1 Garbage Pail Kids Art. KING KONG	$2,726.66	Spellfire, Forgotten Realms Complete set (1-100)	$26.00
2005 Topps Wacky Package Original Card Art. ALBERTO BO5	$1,461.00	Pokemon card lots, 11,000+++ on SALE charizard, kyogre	$26.00
Sslips Wacky Packages ORIGINAL ART! 1st series! package	$1,250.00	Pokemon card lots, 11,000+++ on SALE charizard, kyogre	$26.00
Magic MTG CE Beta Set Collectors Edition International	$999.00	GARBAGE PAIL KIDS 8TH SERIES Wax Box 1987 Topps	$25.53
1973 Topps Wacky Package Series 1 RARE Production Sheet	$910.00	1985 WACKY PACKAGES STICKERS SET 1 thru 44	$25.49

1973 Topps Wacky Packages Series 2 Production Sheet	$670.00	REN & STIMPY Wax Box 1993 Topps	$25.49
WACKY PACKAGES 1st SERIES COMPLETE 1st BAND-ACHE ETC.	$650.00	1986 Topps Garbage Pail Kids MINI Acetate Proof Set 165	$25.40
Wacky Packages Original Art 9th Series Hookey Topps	$475.00	Wacky Packages 1969 Wacky Ad #3 MINUTE MUD - Near Mint	$25.40
1974 Topps Wacky Packages Series 13 Production Sheet	$462.00	1973 Wacky Packs series 3 complete	$25.39
MTG Card lot and Box, Dual Lands, Library of Alexandra	$453.00	UNOPENED GARBAGE PAIL KID CARDS WITH GUM!!!	$25.00
1974 Topps Wacky Packages Series 11 Production Sheet	$430.01	Magic The Gathering MTG 5 decks unopened 200 cards Mint	$25.00
1986 Topps Garbage Pail Kids Series 5 Art. GASSY GUS	$417.00	Yu-Gi-Oh 2005 Collectible Tin - Vorse Raider	$25.00

Trading Cards ▸ Animation ▸ Pokemon

The average sales price in this subcategory is $12.15.

	HIGH		AVG
NETRUNNER CCG PROTEUS SEALED 36 BOOSTER PACKS BOX	$159.40	Tyranitar RARE HOLOFOIL Pokemon cards Expedition dark	$13.50
1056 Pokemon cards L@@k	$150.00	HUGE lot of pokemon cards. incl. CHARIZARD	$13.50
NETRUNNER CCG FACTORY SEALED 36 BOOSTER PACKS BOX	$144.50	150 POKEMON CARDS - INCLUDES 15 HOLOS - 1ST EDITION	$12.60
3,290 Pokemon cards PLUS! Includes 144 holos...	$127.50	BC $$$FROM AN ESTATE L@@K <> pokemon cards	$12.50
NETRUNNER CCG FACTORY SEALED 12 STARTER DECK BOX	$103.50	Pokemon Happy Birthday Pikachu Holo #24 Promo + Bonus	$12.50
NETRUNNER CCG FACTORY SEALED 36 BOOSTER PACKS BOX	$102.50	POKEMON SINGLE HOLO CARD EMERALD RARE CANDY AND 2 KYOGR	$12.50
POKEMON COLLECTION OF CARDS+GIFT	$85.00	Ax $$$FROM AN ESTATE L@@K <> pokemon cards	$12.49
//FREE SH. BUY IT NOW		Pokemon Limited Edition 23K Gold Plated Trading Cards	$12.49
MTG FIFTH EDITION FACTORY SEALED 36 BOOSTER PACK BOX	$80.05	WHOLESALE LOT~CASE OF ONE DOZEN POKEMON CARD BINDERS	$11.95
HUGE lot of 2900+ Pokemon Cards / MANY foils / OLD	$77.51	[4 of these sold for $11.95 each]	
POKEMON HOLOGRAPHIC TRADING CARDS, OVER 145	$71.00	LOTS of pokemon cards OVER 8,000 in lots BUY NOW!!!!	$11.50
52 Pokemon Marbles Pokeball and Marble Shooter Rare	$71.00	A x$$$FROM AN ESTATE L@@K <> pokemon cards	$11.49
CCG JYHAD VAMPIRE ANCIENT HEARTS SEALED 45 BOOSTER	$70.01	POKEMON CARD LOTS 11,000+ cards for sale	$11.00
MTG FIFTH EDITION FACTORY SEALED 12 STARTER DECK BOX	$66.10	3 ULTRA RARE CARDS deoxys ex, typhlosion ex, raichu ex	$11.00
PERU:52 ORIGINALS TAZOS (POGS) POKEMON WINTERS	$66.00	BC $$$FROM AN ESTATE L@@K <> pokemon cards	$10.99
POKEMON E3 PIKACHU(Red Cheeks)Cool Porygon Meowth Promo	$65.88	POKEMON CHARIZARD GOLD COLLECTORS CARD	$10.99

Trading Cards ▸ Sci-Fi, Fantasy

The average sales price in this subcategory is $16.19.

	HIGH		AVG
1998 Skybox Star Trek TOS James Doohan A32 Auto Card	$180.00	Star Trek 35th anniversary Julie Newmar A3 auto card	$18.52
Star Trek Quotable William Shatner auto QA1 card	$148.27	Star Trek Enterprise autograph card Gary Graham BBA11	$18.50
Star Trek Voyager CTH JERI RYAN autograph card!!!!!	$144.92	Star Trek Voyager Profiles McKean autograph card!	$17.50
Star Trek Voyager CTH KATE MULGREW autograph card!!!!!!	$100.00	STAR TREK ENTERPRISE 4 Anthony Montgomery Auto CARD	$17.21
ENTERPRISE SEASON 4 MULTI-CASE L.PARK/E.HOSHI	$99.95	Star Trek 35th anniversary Sally Kellerman"Dr. Dehner"	$16.51
Star Trek Original Series A26 SHERRY JACKSON Autograph	$87.00	Babylon 5 Special Edition Hologram H2	$16.50
Star Trek CCG BB/premier. COMPLETE SET, 363 cards	$86.00	1999 Skybox Star Trek TOS Ron Soble A66 Auto Card	$16.50
Star Trek Voyager CTH Garrett Wang autograph card	$86.00	Babylon 5: Complete: Tamlyn Tomita auto A4	$16.06
Star Trek Voyager CTH Robert D. McNeill autograph card	$86.00	QUOTABLE STAR TREK TNG ROSALINO CHAO AUTOGRAPH	$15.65
LOT SKETCHAFEX STAR TREK NEXT	$76.00	STAR TREK ENTERPRISE 4 T'Pol C3 COSTUME CARD	$15.51
GENERATION QUOTABLE CARDS		Original 1960's Star Trek Series 33 VHS 67 Episodes	$15.50
Babylon 5 Season Five Dual Auto A10 Tallman & Willerth	$74.95	BABYLON 5 CCG Card Collection 3 full Binders MINT!	$15.50
Star Trek Original Series A3 NICHELLE NICHOLS Autograph	$74.11	1999 Skybox Star Trek TOS Tony Young A67 Auto Card	$15.50
RARE! StarTrek VOYAGER Dual AutoCard NEELIX/KES #DA2	$68.75	Star Trek CCG The Motion Pictures Booster Box	$15.00
Star Trek Original Series A9 ROBERT BROWN Autograph	$68.67	[2 of these sold for $15.00 each]	
Skybox Star Trek TOS Clint Howard A13 Autograph Card	$67.66	Star Trek 35th anniversary Best of Bones 9 card set	$15.00

Transportation ▸ Automobilia

The average sales price in this subcategory is $25.19.

	HIGH		AVG
MINERVA GODDESS MASCOT HOOD ORNAMENT -1920s- FABULOUS!	$710.00	Ford Model A , Screwdriver , Nice	$30.76
AA CAR BADGE 1906/1907 EARLIEST STENSON COOKE -BRASS!.	$515.00	Old Moneybox LINCOLN from FELLESBANKEN - NORWAY	$29.00
BENTLEY 3-LITRE WINGED-B MASCOT HOOD ORNAMENT AEL-1920s	$510.01	Scrapbook of "AUTO ALBUM" panels by Tad Burness	$28.44
OLD BILL MASCOT HOOD ORNAMENT WW1 SIGNED :SUPERB: LOOK!	$500.00	Vintage Tel-Tru Cub automobile thermometer~suction cup	$26.13
DODGE SUPERBEE SCAT PACK SHOP LIGHT	$280.00	~LIKE NEW ~MILTON DRIVEWAY SIGNAL 1959 BELL~ DING,DING~	$26.00
Land Range Rover - LR3 - Sport 2005 - 2006 Hitch NEW NR	$192.49	Vintage Studebaker Phinney Walker Eight Days Car Clock	$25.50
OLD FRENCH AUTOMOBILE ADVERTISING TIN TRAY	$152.50	Dodge Superbee 1969 Green Wall Clock N027	$25.00
Porsche 356 912 Kolbenschmidt 1700 Pistons & Cylinders	$137.50	Ford Mustang SVT Cobra 2004 Speedo Clock D029	$25.00
Antique Thermos Brand Picnic Set for Auto Running Board	$100.00	BMW 2002 Tii Clock A018	$25.00
Early Chevrolet Oak Box	$99.99	Nash 1950 Wall Clock P082	$25.00
Ferrari Tools - Jack Bag Tool Kit Roll - $1 No Reserve!	$99.00	Plymouth 1968 Roadrunner Blue Wall Clock Q007	$25.00
CGS CGSs VINTAGE AMILCAR NEW CLUTCH SPRING SET	$99.00	Wix 1959 Chevy El Camino Car & Trailer & Tow Truck!!!	$24.99
Old Antique Cadillac Oil Can	$92.98	EVANSVILLE,IN..HARTMETZ BROS. DODGE..CA. 1930 PROMO CAR	$24.99
Vintage Metal Sign/Thermometer FRAM Filter,MONROE Shock	$80.00	KEVIN HARVICK #29 GOODWRENCH BLACK BRUSHED METAL QVC	$24.95
Franklin Mint CENTENNIAL CAR mini-ingot collection L@@k	$76.00	HURST WHEEL AND HURST MEMORABILIA BOOK	$24.95

Transportation ▸ Railroadiana, Trains

The average sales price in this subcategory is $32.81.

	HIGH		AVG
Old B&O Railroad China Pitcher by Lamberton, Trenton NJ	$2,703.53	AMTRAK CONDUCTOR'S DUTY BELT	$34.00
RARE, railroad, train depot ,bullentin board 1877	$1,500.00	Old Northern Pacific railroad kentucky whisky bottle	$33.76
3 Antique Steam Whistles	$922.00	BRASS A. BUTIN LANTERRN MADE IN PARIS NICE AND OLD WOW!	$33.32

ORIGINAL HEAD LIGHT LOCOMOTIVE LAMP	$599.00	6 ROCK ISLAND RAILROAD HIGHBALL GLASSES	$33.02
NEW YORK CENTRAL RAILROAD CAST IRON SIGN Thornwood NY	$370.00	WILLERS' STREAMLINE YOUR DIET DRINK MILK DAILY 1/2 GAL	$32.99
MARKLIN TIN PLATE HO TRAIN COLLECTION AND TRACKS	$203.50	Vintage railroad SPITTING ON THE FLOOR sign 1907	$32.99
Antique Switch - Stand Lamp	$162.00	Wooden Union Pacific Overland sign	$32.98
Southern Pacific 5 Tracks Porcelain Sign w/ reflectors	$155.00	Antique LIONEL railroad STOCKHOLDER PINBACK PIN BUTTON	$32.56
Old B&O Railroad China Serving Platter by Lamberton	$128.01	FJ&G RR. SIGN,Fonda-J'town-G'ville/Sacandaga/Adirondack	$32.00
Amtrak Years of Service Ring	$125.00	Art Deco Replica Fossil Express Train Book End? NEATO	$31.00
3 Vintage 1960s Great Northern Railway Railroad Pinback	$120.00	RARE VINTAGE ZIPPO LIGHTER FROM NYC SSC. NIB	$31.00
2 GLASS NUMBER PLATES FROM ERIE RR 4-6-2 #2541	$113.50	UP & SP safety/training tapes, diesel locomotive manual	$31.00
Monon Railroad Station Rossville Indiana Plate	$113.41	Burlington Route Railroad RR China Cup Saucer MARKED	$30.99
CHESSIE Railroad Cat / Kitten 50th Ann Plate 1983 NR	$113.25	6 ROMANTIC AGE OF STEAM RAILROAD TRAIN SERIES PLATES	$30.01
Cigarette Cards CONSTRUCTION OF RAILWAY TRAINS 1930	$112.50	Wabash Railroad Advertising Egg Timer	$30.00

Vanity, Perfume & Shaving ▶ Perfumes

The average sales price in this subcategory is $24.83.

	HIGH		AVG
1983 SILVER SENTIMENT Estee Lauder Compact Perfume BOX	$273.88	Lot of 9 Miniature Perfume Funnels Very Old!	$26.00
Lovely Vintage Czech. Perfume Bottle - Figural Stopper	$258.02	Vintage Art Deco FABERGETTE Encased Perfume Bottle	$26.00
Estee Lauder Solid Perfume Compact "Mischievous Monkey"	$258.00	LALIQUE Pour Homme "Mascots" Collection	$25.99
Vintage FAME by Corday Factice Perfume Bottle - WoW!	$229.50	LOT 2 ADVENTURER EDDIE BAUER COLOGNE + A/S DISCONTINUED	$24.99
Vintage NIB Miss Dior Diorama Diorissimo Perfumes	$224.20	ESTEE LAUDER WHITE RABBIT COMPACT	$24.99
Mini Miniature Perfume Bottle Collection	$212.50	Stunning! Aquamrian CZECH ART DECO PERFUME BOTTLE	$24.90
VERY RARE COTY AMBRE ANTIQUE FLACON 1995 perfume	$207.50	RARE SET OF 2 CZECH ART DECO PERFUME BOTTLEs	$24.90
13" tall CHANEL ALLURE CRYSTAL FACTICE PERFUME BOTTLE	$200.00	[2 of these sold for $24.90 each]	
FABULOUS VINTAGE CARON POIVRE PERFUME WITH BOX	$192.50	Estee Lauder Aliage Solid Perfume Pendant/Necklace	$24.55
2004 ESTEE LAUDER PAMPERED	$171.48	VICTORIAN PEARL & BRASS SNUFF PERFUME BOTTLE ON CHAIN	$24.50
KITTY COMPACT SOLID PERFUME		LOT2 ROYAL DOULTON PERFUME ULTRA BODY RICH CREAM SEALED	$24.00
Estee Lauder BEAUTIFUL Solid Perfume - LE BUSTIER	$165.00	Vintage Ivory Perfume Bottle	$23.39
Estee Lauder Solid Compact ~Lily Bouquet~ MIB	$159.99	Faberge Tigress Bath Powder Unopened Box 10 oz.	$23.02
Beautiful Estee Lauder "VIOLIN" Solid Perfum	$140.38	Coty IMPREVU Perfume BIG 1.8oz Spray FULL	$22.59
Schiaparelli Shocking perfume bottle	$125.00	WILD STRAWBERRY MUSK perfume 1/2 oz. MAX FACTOR	$22.01
Huge 12" - RALPH LAUREN - Factice Perfume Display	$122.50	TARTINE ET CHOCOLAT PTISENBON PERFUME 3.3oz SPRAY FULL	$21.99

Vanity, Perfume & Shaving ▶ Shaving

The average sales price in this subcategory is $25.17.

	HIGH		AVG
Antique Barber Chair/40'-50'-era	$1,300.00	Vintage / Repro (?) Blood Bowl - used with bleeding	$27.26
Antique Limoges Occupational Brick Layer Shaving Mug	$430.99	OLD Razor Blades in Box Gilt-Edge NR!	$27.00
Vintage Oster Hot Lather Shaving Barber Shop	$407.52	100 DIFFERENT VINTAGE RAZOR BLADES	$27.00
Vintage 1940's KOKEN Barber Chair!	$300.00	VINTAGE CERAMIC FROG HOLDS USED RAZOR BLADES	$26.99
Vintage Koken Barber Chair	$299.99	6 Old straight razors Germany Hamburg Settles NR lot	$26.51
1920s ___ BARBER SHOP catalog ___ poles, chairs, cases	$270.00	barber shop cabinet Sterilizer 1930 razor strap	$26.36
STRAIGHT RAZOR WITH CRACKED ICE HANDLES	$265.00	Prof.John H. Meyer Barbering Book Plainville, Ohio 1914	$26.00
Beautiful Cranberry Glass Barber Bottle w/ Stopper LOOK	$152.50	Vintage Red Imp Razor Strap State Barber School Balt	$26.00
antique blue satin glass barber bottle NR	$151.50	MARVY STERILIZER STATION GERMICIDAL DISINFECTANT	$25.00
Antique Amethyst Glass Mary Gregory Barber Bottle	$144.44	SHAVING POT W/ MIRROR 1883 RODGERS QUADRUPLE SILVER	$25.00
Rich RUBY / CRANBERRY Daisy & Fern Barber Bottle	$133.58	270 New Double Edge Safety Razor Blades Vintage 30Packs	$24.99
ANTIQUE BULLDOG DOG RAZOR BLADE COIN BANK from AUSTRIA	$128.50	ROLLS RAZOR THE TRAVELER W/CASE 1930 ENGLAND MINT	$24.50
Rare mini electric barber pole electric lights	$122.50	1967 Remington 300 Selectro Vintage Electric Shaver MIB	$24.50
VINTAGE CHROME CAMPBELL LATHER KING HOT LATHER MACHINE	$112.50	Glasharp Razor Holder Old Barbershop Item	$24.38
Vintage SR Droescher Hone Razor Sharpener Germany	$104.00	VINTAGE REMINGTON ROLLECTRIC AUTO HOME SHAVER	$24.05

Vintage Sewing ▶ Buttons

The average sales price in this subcategory is $11.64.

	HIGH		AVG
OVAL 2 1/4" GAY NINETIES ART GLASS JEWEL BUTTON/S	$410.00	COUPLE GREETING ON THE STREET-HATS-FRENCH-MAN,WOMAN	$12.49
2 VINTAGE BAKELITE BUTTON'S SHOES VANITY SEWING GREAT!!	$260.55	Three Hand Painted China Porcelain Lapel Buttons	$12.49
The Big Book of Buttons by Elizabeth Hughes (1992)	$225.25	VINTAGE HALF MOON BUTTON Rhinestones on black plastic	$12.43
Deluxe Antique Button Carved Japanese Ivory Family	$122.50	~ OLD ANTIQUE BLACK GLASS H.P. PORCELAIN rare BUTTON~	$12.39
*OLD*GORGEOUS SM SET OF SEVEN SATSUMA GOD BUTTONS	$103.00	NICE LOT OF ANTIQUE BONE BUTTONS 2. 4 AND 5 HOLE	$12.37
17th CENTURY Austro Hungarian Silver RUBY Pearl Button	$86.00	Czech White AB Glass Snowberry Buttons 12pc FREESHIPPI	$12.00
old SCOTTISH Agate FANCY Button Hook over 13" long	$84.50	XL Czech Glass Chunky Crinkle Mauve Nugget Buttons 12	$12.00
332 WONDERFUL CZECH VINTAGE GLASS BUTTONS	$76.00	24 VINTAGE DECO PAINTED WOOD BUTTONS FLORAL MOTIF	$12.00
FABULOUS FULLY DIMENSIONAL CARVED CHINESE BONE BUTTON	$76.00	Carved Button Sleeping Labrador Retreiver Tagua Nut	$11.51
445 WONDERFUL CZECH VINTAGE GLASS BUTTONS BLACK	$73.65	K127-AWESOME MEDIUM PORCELAIN W/LADY TRANSFER BUTTON	$11.50
MATCHED SET OF 4 ANTIQUE CINNABAR BUTTONS BIRD MOTIF	$61.00	~ 1940's REALISTIC CASEIN CARVED ARROWS 4 BUTTONS~	$11.50
Vintage Floral Celluloid Button In Tinted Metal Frame	$57.99	7 VINTAGE METAL AND RHINESTONE BUTTONS LOT 2470	$11.50
SPLENDID 2" DEEPLY CARVED CHINESE BONE TILE BUTTON	$56.00	Pearl Button Flower Blossom	$11.50
FABULOUS ENGRAVED & INKED BONE and WOOD BUTTON	$52.51	LARGE RIVETED FACETED CUT STEEL OPEN OLD FLOWER BUTTON	$11.50
GORGEOUS ANTIQUE SILK GARTER BUTTON!!! HAND PAINTED!!!	$51.00	Lot of 100+ Antique Shoe Buttons	$11.26

13

COMPUTERS & NETWORKING

Computers & Networking is one of the highest-grossing categories on eBay; according to recent statistics released by the company, its $2.9 billion GMV (gross merchandise volume, the total value of all successfully closed listings) is the fourth largest on the site.

Laptops and brand names are some of the things that stand out as popular in this category. Among the most frequent searches in here are: *dell, laptops, computers, dell laptop, pda, hard drive, apple, hp, desktop,* and *software.*

Dells

Because the most-used search terms show that Dell laptops are so sought-after here, let's take a look at some of the closed listings for that brand. On the high end, a "LOADED Dell Latitude C600 Laptop, PIII 750, 512 MB, 40G" sold for $430.00 with 16 bids. This is a refurbished computer, less than one year old. There are several other Dell Latitude laptops, from $430.00 up to $504.00 on the high end. Many of these top sellers are refurbished computers, suggesting eBay buyers don't mind getting something a little older and not in brand-new condition in order to save money. (New Dell Latitudes run from "starting" around $700.00 to $1,778.00 after rebate offers.)

Beyond the individual Dell laptops, though, what fetched the highest prices here are lots of multiple laptops, like the "LOT of 11 Dell Latitude Laptops C600, C640, C840" that sold for $2,424.00 with 36 bids. People are most likely buying these lots to refurbish and resell individually, as the seller suggests in the listing. Or, they may use them for parts, or sell the parts individually. In the case of the lot of 5 Dell Latitude C640s, P4 1.2Ghz DVD, selling at $1,725.00, the units need hard drives.

Not all the laptops in the lots need work, though. The two auctions for the "Lot of 5 DELL LATITUDE C600 PIII 700MHZ FREE LAPTOP BAG. DVD PLAYER 256MB RAM, 10GB Hard Drive, AC Adapter" both specify that these "corporate take-out laptops" were tested and in working condition.

The average price for Dell laptops is around $287.00. A typical computer here is a Dell P3 (Pentium 3) laptop, like the one that sold for $290.00 with 21 bids. Many of these garner over 10 bids, and some sellers throw in perks like a free laptop bag. The specs on this model are "750 MHZ/LAN/56K/FLOPPY/WINXP/OFF03/CDROM/LOADED 4SCHOOL." You have to pay an extra $25.00 for a wireless card, nor is a network or modem card included; the seller offers those as extras.

Apples and Macs

One of the most amazing things about the Apple computers here is the numbers of bids they can generate. A 1.42 GHz Mini Mac 100GB (gigabyte) Airport Bluetooth racked up 75, 93, and 96 bids in different auctions for $610.01, $620.75, and $600.00, respectively. This system, in the Power Mac G4 product family, is brand-new and customized to order, according to the seller. Elsewhere on the Web, you could find a Mac for $533.00 to $999.00, but with less memory and hard drive capacity (80GB vs. 100GB) according to Shopzilla.com.

Average prices for Apple/Mac desktops are around $259.00, with some of the most common auctions being for an Apple Mac Mini 1.2 GHz, and an Apple G4 Cube 400 and 500 MHz, 30GB hard drive. The "Apple G4 Cube 500 mHz 30 gig 512 meg DVD-rom" that sold for $244.53 with 15 bids "works but has issues," according to the seller: the hard drive is noisy, the DVD-ROM drive is slow to eject a disc, and "the cube sometimes goes into sleep mode or turns itself off."

The low end of this subcategory, as with many of the Computers subcategories, is cluttered with accessories that don't necessarily belong here, and computers that are old and/or are fixer-uppers. One of the lowest-selling items here that is an actual computer is a Macintosh Power PC 5500/225 ("Complete Working NR! $10!!") that went for only $4.99. The seller says it's been tested and is working "100%" . . . it features 2MB RAM, a 2GB hard drive, a 250 MHz processor, and a screen size of 15 inches. Its operating system is Mac OS 9. This system is probably around seven years old, as the Mac Power PC 5500/225 was introduced in 1997 and discontinued in 1998, according to EveryMac.com. The shipping alone is $53.00, but it shows that for less that $60.00, if your needs are fairly simple, you can buy a working PC from eBay.

Don't forget to look at computer accessories in this category, as many of these are bargains. For example, a Lamborghini hard-shell aluminum laptop case sold for $155.00, down from its retail price of $229.00, and $10.00 cheaper than the discounted $165.00 price that can be found on another website.

Apple, Macintosh Computers ▸ Apple Components

The average sales price in this subcategory is $49.57.

	HIGH		AVG
SEALED! TOSHIBA SATELLITE M35X-S311 Intel Centrino!!	$716.00	Powerbook G3 Pismo Logic Board Motherboard No Reserve	$60.00
Powerbook G4 Aluminum 867MHZ 12 inch Logic Board.	$348.00	Apple iMac G3 400Mhz FIREWIRE Motherboard/Logic Board	$59.99
Mac G4 Quicksilver 2002 Motherboard/Logic 820-1342-B	$285.00	2 Apple G4 Sawtooth Graphite Motheboards 850-1094-A	$57.99
Apple MDD Motherboard 867 MHz logic board Mac	$276.00	ibook G3 Clamshell 366MHz Motherboard	$56.00
Apple PowerMac G5 Motherboard Mother Board Low Ship!	$265.00	Apple G3 Motherboard & Processor 820-1049-A Lot of 5	$55.00
Apple Mac iBook 12 " Dual USB 900 mhz logic board	$260.00	APPLE G4 AGP MOTHERBOARD LOGIC BOARD 128MB	$51.00
G4 Powerbook Titanium 667 logic mother board	$260.00	Apple Imac G3 400mhz Motherboard/Logic board w/56k mdm	$50.99
Good 800mhz iBook Dual USB Logic Motherboard	$227.51	MACINTOSH POWER 9600 /300 MHZ	$50.00
Mac G4 Quicksilver Motherboard/Logic Board 820-1276-A	$225.00	Apple G4 Yikes Motherboard/Logic board Rev 2 w/FW	$49.99
[2 of these sold for $225.00 each]		B&W G3 Motherboard/Logic board Rev 2 w/FW & 400mhz cpu	$49.99
Apple G4 QuickSilver MotherBoard 820-1276-04I ! !	$214.26	[2 of these sold for $49.99 each]	
Mac G4 Quicksilver Motherboard/Logic Board 820-1276-A	$212.50	Apple G4 Quicksilver Logic Board (PN-661-2503)	$49.99
Apple Quicksilver G4 Logic Board/Motherboard 820-1342-B	$205.00	Apple iMac G3 400Mhz FIREWIRE Motherboard/Logic Board	$49.99
QuickSilver Dual 1Ghz G4 Motherboard	$201.50	G4 Digital Audio Front Control Panel	$49.99
Apple G4 QuickSilver 867MHz MotherBoard	$200.00	B&W G3 Motherboard/Logic board Rev 2 w/FW & 400mhz cpu	$49.99
Apple Quicksilver G4 Logic Board/	$199.99	56k Modem Apple Macintosh Beige G3/6400/6500 COMM Slot	$49.99
		[2 of these sold for $49.99 each]	

Apple, Macintosh Computers ▸ Apple Desktops

The average sales price in this subcategory is $258.74.

	HIGH		AVG
Power Mac G5 Quad 2.5GHz, 16GB ram, 1000GB hdd NO EQUAL. $12400 Retail! LOADED! 100% Feedbk Free Shipping!	$6,901.00	GRAPHITE/WHITE iBOOk,466MHZ 10GB,320MB DVD FIREWIRE,USB	$309.00
APPLE XSERVE RAID 3.5 TB REFURBISHED FACTORY SEALED. COMES WITH 14 BY 250 GIG HARD DRIVES	$5,499.99	Apple G4 Cube 500 mHz 30 gig 512 meg DVD-rom PowerMac 9600/350 Custom 512MB 18GBHD	$308.00 $300.00
Power Mac G5 Quad 2.5GHz, 4GB of ram, 500GB hdd, 7800GT	$3,650.00	Twentieth Anniversary Macintosh - 20th Mac TAM	$299.99
NEW Apple Powermac G5 2.7 DP 2GB RAM 20" Display. FREE SHIPPING!!	$3,599.00	Apple G4 Cube 500 mHz 30 gig 512 meg DVD-rom	$297.00
APPLE Power Mac G5 Quad Desktop Computer M9592LL/A* NEW	$2,900.00	Apple iMac G3 600 /256/40GB/CD-RW OS Keyboard&Mouse	$285.00
Apple Power Mac G5 Dual 2.0 + 23" Apple Cinema Display Poweer mac g5 and display	$2,601.00	Twentieth Anniversary Macintosh - 20th Mac TAM Apple G4 400MHz , 448 Mb Ram Desktop CPU	$275.00 $256.00
NEW Imac intel duo 2ghz/1Gb/250GB logic, Office,Adobe iwork, CS2, Toast, Office, CS2, more	$2,400.00	Apple G4 Cube 500 mHz 30 gig 512 meg DVD-rom Non Working TAM	$244.53 $232.50
APPLE POWERMAC G5 DUAL 1.8 GHZ 512 160 HD 23" DISPLAY	$2,275.00	Apple iMac G3 600 /256/40GB/CD-RW OS Keyboard&Mouse	$228.27
Almost New Apple PowerPC G5 DP 2 Ghz/1.5G RAM/SD/160HD	$1,995.00	Apple Macintosh Mac TV	$205.03
PowerMac G5 2.0 Dual LOADED ATi 9800 Pro 1.5GB/350GB	$1,850.00	PS Apple Macintosh Power Mac G4 Computer Desktop M5183	$202.50
NEW Apple 20" iMac 2.1 250GB 1.5GB RA	$1,750.00	PowerMac 9500/150 with Media 100 xe Audio/Video Editing	$200.00
20" iMac G5 Power PC 1.5 GB-RAM, 500GB HD. 90 Days Old! Built-in iSight + Front Row! FEDEX SHIPPING.	$1,699.95	iMac PowerPC G3 400MHz 10GB 128MB Mac OS 9.2	$199.99
Apple iMac G5 20" 2.0 GHz/1GB/400GB/AirBT UPGRADED L@@K	$1,577.98		
New MAC MINI w/ 17" FLAT LCD MONITOR, Complete Setup!!	$1,075.00		
1.42 Ghz Mac mini 512/80GB 20in LCD tons of extras!	$1,025.00		

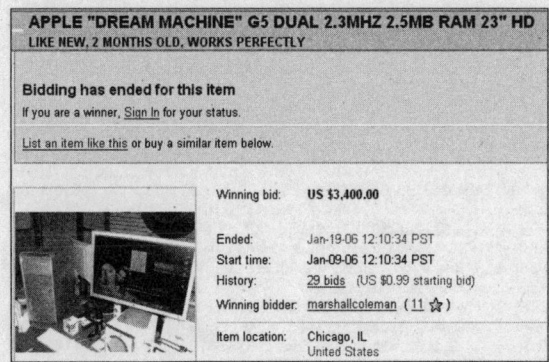

APPLE "DREAM MACHINE" G5 DUAL 2.3MHZ 2.5MB RAM 23" HD
LIKE NEW, 2 MONTHS OLD, WORKS PERFECTLY

Bidding has ended for this item
If you are a winner, Sign In for your status.

List an item like this or buy a similar item below.

Winning bid: US $3,400.00

Ended: Jan-19-06 12:10:34 PST
Start time: Jan-09-06 12:10:34 PST
History: 29 bids (US $0.99 starting bid)
Winning bidder: marshallcoleman (11 ☆)

Item location: Chicago, IL
United States

Mac Macintosh Color Classic Vintage Collectible !!!

Bidding has ended for this item
If you are a winner, Sign In for your status.

List an item like this or buy a similar item below.

Winning bid: US $187.50 (Reserve met)

Ended: Jan-16-06 23:45:00 PST
Start time: Jan-09-06 23:45:00 PST
History: 25 bids (US $1.00 starting b
Winning bidder: fabio1062 (5)

Item location: Alberta
Canada

Apple, Macintosh Computers ▸ Apple Laptops, Notebooks

The average sales price in this subcategory is $627.14

	HIGH		AVG
POWERBOOK G4 1.67 GHZ 512MB 100GB 17" SCREEN NEW	$2,225.00	Apple Ibook G4 w/ Airport Extreme!!!	$650.00
POWERBOOK G4 1.67 GHZ 512 MB RAM 80 GB 15" SCREEN NEW	$2,065.01	IBOOK,900MZ,14.1,256MG,30G,CDRW-DVD,OSX10.4	$647.00
POWERBOOK G4 , 15 - Inch, Super DVD-Rom/CD-RW, 1.5 GHz	$1,876.75	Excellent Condition I BOOK G4	$640.00
Powerbook G4 12" 1.5 Ghz 1.25GB RAM/AP/BT/80G HD/DVD?RW	$1,626.00	Apple 12" iBook G4 1.07Ghz 30g 256 RAM AplCare option	$635.00
14" iBook 1.33/COMBO/60GBHD/512MB/APcard/WARRANTY	$1,599.00	Apple ibook G4	$635.00
14" iBook 1.33/COMBO/60GBHD/768MB RAM/APcard + WARRANTY	$1,550.00	IBOOK,900MZ,14.1,256MG,30G,CDRW-DVD,OSX10.4	$630.00
14" iBook 1.33/COMBO/60GBHD/768MB RAM/APcard + WARRANTY	$1,550.00	Apple Ibook Notebook	$630.00
14" iBook 1.07/60GB/APcard/768MB/SuperDrive & APPLECARE	$1,550.00	iBook from Apple!	$630.00
Apple G4 1.33GHz ibook Super Drive + Bonus Save $1000	$1,500.00	Apple iBook G4 12" 1GHz 30GB hard drive 712MB RAM	$625.00
iBook, 60GB, 512 RAM, Office w/CD, Applecare and more..	$1,500.00	Apple iBook G4 Tiger, Airport, Carrying Case, extras	$621.00
NEW Apple iBook G4 Notebook 1.33 GHz 14" 60GB M9628LL/A	$1,439.00	Mac iBook G4 1.07 GHz 256 RAM Mac OS X	$620.00
APPLE 12" POWERBOOK G4 M9690 1.5 512 60 COMBO NEW NR	$1,439.00	APPLE iBOOK G4 933MHZ 256MB 40GB 15" COMBO DRIVE	$611.01
NEW Apple iBook G4 1.33GHz Superdrive14" 60GB M9628LL/A	$1,429.00	Mac ibook G4	$611.00
APPLE MAC iBOOK G4 LAPTOP OS X MS OFFICE VIRTUAL PC +++	$1,425.00	Apple Ibook G4 800MHz 30GB 768mb 14 LCD Combo Drive	$610.00
Apple iBook G4,Laptop 14 inch (Brand New)	$1,425.00	iBook G3 14" 900MHZ 640MB 40GB CDRW/DVD-ROM GREAT!	$610.00

Apple, Macintosh Computers ▸ Apple Parts & Accessories

The average sales price in this subcategory is $37.58.

	HIGH		AVG
Apple PowerBook G4 12.1" COMPLETE LCD Assembly TESTED	$449.00	Apple Wireless Keyboard, Brand new!	$43.00
Apple PowerBook G4 12" 1GHz Logic Board	$360.98	Lot of 5 Atto ExpressPCI PSC UW Mac scsi cards	$42.41
Marathon G-Rack Mac 6u G4 Rackmount Ears for 19" Rack	$280.00	Apple PowerMac G4 Power Supply! No Reserve!	$41.00
Logic board 800 Mhz for Apple G4 Titanium DVI PowerBook	$251.00	Apple 16/600 FAX CARD (PLUG AND PLAY)	$39.99
eMac G4 700mhz for parts - no reserve	$247.51	Apple 12 inch iBook G3 Dual USB Keyboard free ship	$39.99
nVidia GeForce 3 ADC video card for Apple Mac CUBE G4 [2 of these sold for $239.99 each]	$239.99	Apple PowerBook G4 12" PalmRest TouchPad Assembly BookEndz Pismo Docking Station	$39.00 $38.55
PowerMac G5 Enclosure 922-5952	$238.00	Griffin iMic USB External Sound Card + Lapel Mic PC/Mac	$37.99
G4 Dual 1.25ghz processor card board	$230.00	[2 of these sold for $37.99 each]	
Marathon G-Rack Mac 6u G4 Rackmount Ears for 19" Rack	$227.50	APPLE WIRELESS KEYBOARD... LIKE NEW!!!!	$37.00

Marathon IRack-DV Rack Mount Solution for iMac...I	$227.50
Raindesign Rain Design iGo Sitting Model for iMac G5	$207.50
Apple 15.2 in LCD SCREEN Powerbook G4 LTN152W3-L01 NEW	$200.00
Apple iMac G4 Motherboard Mainboard P79 800MHZ 820-1386	$199.45
Apple 15.2 in LCD SCREEN Powerbook G4 LTN152W3-L01 NEW	$199.00
Apple 15.2 in LCD SCREEN Powerbook G4 LTN152W3-L01 NEW	$190.00

Misc Apple Parts for Case for PowerMac G4 AGP Sawtooth	$36.76
VST UltraTek/66 Ultra-ATA/66 RAID PCI Card MAC	$36.00
Apple Macintosh Pro Keyboard CLEAR WHITE USB BRAND NEW	$36.00
Contour ShuttlePro Audio & Video Editing- Mac & PC	$36.00
Lk NEW Apple Wireless Bluetooth mouse for G5, PowerBook	$36.00
Powerbook G4 12" Case Parts Bottom and Top VGA	$36.00

Desktop PCs ▶ 700 Mhz to 1 Ghz

The average sales price in this subcategory is $93.08.

	HIGH		AVG
HUGE LOT OF 500 PCS 466 mhz -950 mhz Computers	$5,450.50	COMPAQ DESKPRO EN COMPUTER 1GHZ DESKTOP PC PENTIUM 3	$99.00
Lot of 25 HP E-PC PIII 933MHz, 256MB, 20GB, CDRW P4258T	$2,400.00	HP VECTRA VL 400SF 866 MHZ 10GB CD DESKTOP COMPUTER PC	$99.00
4 Shuttle XPC SV25 mini-computers	$510.11	Dell GX150 P3 1.0 GHZ, 256MB, CDRW, AGP	$99.00
Lot of 5 HP E-PC PIII 866MHz, 256MB, 20GB, CDROM P2795T	$475.00	[2 of these sold $99.00 each]	
Dual (2) P3 1000MHz Processor Dell Poweredge 1400SC	$450.00	3 lot ,Compaq Celeron, 850 Mhz, 128 mem, 10 G HD, SFF	$96.00
Dual (2) P3 1000MHz Processor Dell Poweredge 1400	$450.00	IBM P3 933Mhz/128MB/20GB Drive Win 2000 WARRANTY!	$95.00
LOT of 7 Compaq iPAQ Celeron 700/128/10 W2K Workstation	$405.00	PENTIUM III 3 COMPUTER PC TOWER 866MHZ/128MB/20GB	$94.99
OLD DELL Desktop Celeron 700 GHZ	$399.00	HP MINI e-PC 40 1GHZ 256MB 20GB Win98+drivers NR	$93.50
Sony Vaio PCV LX900 Slimtop	$338.33	Dell Dimension 4100/933P3/128/cdrw/dvd/30gb hdd/ more	$91.01
4 Shuttle XPC SV25 mini-computers	$330.00	IBM Desktop Computer PENTIUM III 728mhz	$91.00
LOT 3 DELL OPTIPLEX GX110 COMPUTER 933MHZ/128MB/20GB	$269.99	Pentium III P3 733MHz Desktop Tower 256MB/10GB P 3 NR+	$90.00
		Emachines E-Tower 700 mHz Computer	$89.99
Very fast computer!!! Hardly every used	$255.00	PIII 1GHz System, 256mb, 20GB, NIC, AGP - GREAT!!!	$89.99
Sony Slimtop PCV-LX700 Computer	$250.00	LOT of 2 Compaq iPAQ Celeron 700/128/10 W2K Workstation	$89.97
Dell Poweredge 2400 866 Mhz, 512 MB RAM, 18.2 GB SCSI	$250.00	DELL Optiplex GX110 PIII 933mhz SFF Slim Desktop	$89.95
Lot of 3 HP e-pc Pentium III 866 MHz 128MB Ram	$249.00	DELL PRECISION 620 TOWER 866X2 XEON PROCESSOR	$89.00

Desktop PCs ▶ 1.1–2.0 Ghz, 1400+ to 2000+

The average sales price in this subcategory is $142.99.

	HIGH		AVG
ALIENWARE AURORA 1GB 1.0 FULL TOWER SYSTEM BLACK	$1,236.77	NEW AMD DURON 1.8 WITH CDRW	$150.00
DELL Inspiron 6000 Notebook, New!	$670.10	AMD Athlon 1.1Ghz/256DDR/64MB Radeon/30G HD/CDRW/more	$149.99
HP laptop 1.4 GHz 512 ram 60 gig hard drive	$660.00	Compaq Presario 6312us 6000 AMD Athlon XP 2000+ 256 40G	$148.50
BSI FieldGo N9 Portable Lunchbox Computer	$636.09	HP Pavilion XT938 Athlon 1.3GHz 60GB 128MB CD-RW/DVD	$148.25
ULTIMATE GAMING COMPUTER WITH NO RES WORTH OVER $2K!	$560.00	EMACHINES T1840 INTEL CELERON 1.80GHZ DESKTOP PC AS-IS	$147.50
Custom Desktop Computer DVDRW w 19" TFT Flat Panel	$540.00	Dell Dimension 2350 desktop computer	$144.00
Desktop PC AMD Athlon XP 2400, 1GB RAM, 240GB HDD	$510.00	DELL DESKTOP WINXP Optiplex GX50/SDT 1.2 GHz 128MB 48X	$143.51
1.25 GHZ, 640MB Computer with monitor and desk!	$510.00	HP Pavillion AMD1600/256MB/30GB/CDR/XP Home	$143.49
SONY VAIO PCV-W10 with WIRELESS LAN	$504.00	AMD Duron 1.8 GHz PC with DVD-RW and DVD-ROM	$142.55
HP ZE4400 AMD ATHLON XP 1.6GHZ 256 MB 15" 20GB LAPTOP	$485.00	AMD Athlon XP1900+, 512DDR, 128MB Radeon	$142.50
CUSTOM PC ASUS A8V DELUXE AMD64 3200+ 2GB Ram SATA HDD	$455.00	GATEWAY 1.2GHZ 896MB 40GIG 64MB VIDEO CARD CD-RW	$142.50
E Machines T6212 AMD 64 bit processor	$444.78	Custom AMD Athlon XP 1800+ Desktop 256Mb 30Gb CDRW NIC	$142.50
New eMachines D6405 Desktop 512MB 80GB DVD?RW 15" LCD	$435.00	Hewlett Packard 503N Desktop Computer 1.7 Ghz Celeron	$142.50
Modded Watercooled Computer Custom built neon etc..	$425.00	Desktop PC - AMD Athlon 1.2Ghz, 512MB, ATI Radeon	$140.00
AMD XP1700+, Gigabyte, Supermicro, Server 2003 w/25 CAL	$410.00	Compaq D300v Evo Desktop Computer - 1.3GHz loaded!	$139.95

Desktop PCs ▶ 2.1–2.6 Ghz

The average sales price in this subcategory is $247.59.

	HIGH		AVG
*NEW*Alienware Aurora 5500 AMD 64 FX 55 6800 GT Black	$2,200.00	Dell Dimension 2400	$250.00
ALIENWARE AURORA 1.5 1GB FULL TOWER SYSTEM BLACK	$1,382.00	NEW DELL DIMENSION 3000 DESKTOP PC 2.4GHz 512MB 40GB @@	$250.00
AMD XP 2500+ Geforce 6800GT Moded Gaming Comuter	$1,200.00	Brand New Dell Dimension 3000+15" LCD 2.4GHz	$250.00
ATHLON XP SYSTEM - AWESOME GAMING PC	$1,200.00	Custom Whitebox,AMD XP2400+.512Ram,DVD,CD-RW,More	$250.00
Ultra Dragon Series ATX Case with Clear Side 2.4 GHz	$1,130.00	DELL Optiplex GX270 Small Form Factor PC	$249.99
Custom built AMD 2500XP With 17" LCD 1024mb90gig fx5200	$899.99	Dell Dimension 3000 2.4GHz Desktop Computer NEW	$249.95
Audio/Video/Gaming Computer Athlon 2600+ Adobe Software	$810.00	[2 of these sold for $249.95 each]	
AMD XP 2500+ Geforce 6800GT Moded Gaming Comuter	$730.00	2.0 GHZ COMPUTER COMPLETE W/ ACCESSORIES...NEW!!!	$249.00
Dell Dimension 4700 2.8Ghz 17" LCD 160GB 512MB DDR2	$680.00	Dell Dimension 3000 Desktop, BRAND NEW	$247.50
ASUS AMD K8V SE DELUXE 3200 CPU PC TOWER	$647.50	Dell Dimension 3000 Desktop Computer 2.4GHz/256M/40G HD	$245.00
HP Pavilion Desktop PC	$600.00	Dell Dimension 2400 Desktop Computer 2.6Ghz + Bonus!	$243.50
Home Desktop PC, 2.1 GHz, 1 GIG DDR Ram, DVD Dual Layer	$600.00	Desktop PC- AMD 2400+ Athlon XP- computer system	$242.99
HP a810n Athlon 64 3300+ Gaming PC 1GB Nvidia 6600 GT	$579.00	Black Computer AMD AthlonXP 2600+ with 512 MB	$242.50
AMD CUSTOM GAMING COMPUTER BFG	$560.00	NEW DELL DIMENSION 3000 COMPUTER+LCD FLAT PANEL MONITOR	$242.50
6800 DELL MONITOR +MORE		AMD XP2200 Super Fast Complete PC NO RESERVE!! 1.8ghz	$242.50
COMPAQ PRESARIO SR1030NX + 18 VIEWSONIC LCD	$555.00	NEW Dell Dimension 2400 2.4 80GB 48X 256mb Windows XP	$242.50

Desktop PCs ▶ 2.7 Ghz

The average sales price in this subcategory is $346.80.

	HIGH		AVG
POWEREDGE 1600SC 2*2.8ghz, 4GB,	$3,000.00	New Custom-built 2.8 GHZ Petium IV desktop computer	$350.00
4*73gb 1800 1850 2600		Compaq HP SR1430NX P4 2.93 GHz	$349.99
Athlon 64 X2 4800 Dual Core, ASUS A8N-SLI Deluxe	$2,400.00	Desktop DVDRW 160gb 512m	
POWEREDGE 400SC 3.4ghz 2gb	$1,401.00	New custom PC Sempron 2800+ 512 Mb,	$349.95

500GB RAID DVD-RW+ 8400 4700		160Gb 16x DVD-RW DL	
ALIENWARE AURORA 1GB 1.5	$1,337.00	NEW eMachine Desktop 2.8GHz	$349.88
FULL TOWER BLACK CASE		80G WIRELESS 768MB RAM	
NEW Dell Dimension 8400 Media	$1,275.00	NEW DELL Dimension3000+15"LCD	$349.00
Center PC + 20" 2005FPW		Monitor + Dell720 printer	
SONY PCV - RS 410 Desktop PC Computer Electronics VAIO	$1,200.00	Dell Dimension 4700, 2.8, 512MB,	$348.00
NEW Sony VAIO PCV-V300G	$1,200.00	80GB SATA, CDRW & DVD	
Desktop PC 2.8GHZ PENTIUM 4		*NEW* DELL DIMENSION 3000 DESKTOP	$346.00
Dell Dimension 4700 Desktop	$1,086.00	PC COMPUTER + MONITOR	
Computer DVD RW 1GB RAM		DELL 4500 Desktop Computer	$345.00
IBM Intellistation Z Pro Dual 2.8GHz/2GB/36.4GB/CDRW	$1,085.00	Flatscreen Monitor keyboard	
Dell Dimension 5100 Desktop	$1,065.00	NEW Dell 3000 P4 2.8GHz 15" LCD Monitor+720 Printer	$344.00
P4 2.8GHz HT 17" FP monitor		Dell Dimension 4700 computer 2.8Ghz P4 +BONUS 5100	$342.00
BRAND NEW Dell Dimension 9100	$999.99	*New* Dell Dimension 4700 P4+	$340.01
19" LCD 3.0GHz 8400 XPS		17" LCD E173FP Monitor HT	
$1700 Sony VAIO PCV-W700G Desktop PC NR	$987.00	IBM S50 8184-36U 2.8GHz HT	$340.00
Dell Dimension 4700 Desktop	$911.00	512mb 40G 8183 Thinkcentre	
Computer DVD RW 1GB RAM		New Dell Dimension 3000 P4 2.8G	$339.99
DELL P4 NEW DIMENSION 3000		512MB 80GB 48xCDRW 4700	
DESKTOP COMPUTER LCD MONITOR	$910.00	Dell Optiplex GX270 P4 2.8GHz PC with 120GB HD	$337.00
$2000SonyVAIO 2.8GHz Pentium4	$901.00	Dell Optiplex GX280 SFF P4 2.8G /	$335.01
PersonalComputerw/dvd NR		800Mhz FSB / 1Mb L2	

Desktop PCs ▶ 3.0+ Ghz

The average sales price in this subcategory is $346.80.

	HIGH		AVG
Fast PC Combo AMD Athlon64FX57	$4,200.00	FREE SHIPPING!! AMD 3200+ PC. 400W PS, 512MB RAM	$350.00
w/17" LCD Monitor & More		DELL Dimension 3000 Desktop PC	$350.00
AMD Athlon 64-bit X2 DUAL-CORE 4800+ TWO VIDEO CARD	$3,450.01	P4 3GHz HT 512MB *NEW*	$350.00
ALIENWARE AMD 4000+ 1GIG	$3,000.00	New Compaq? Presario SR1430NX/2.93G/	$350.00
RADEON 800 XT Plat Edl LOOK!!!		DL DVD?RW/160G/512M	
HTPC - Windows XP Media Center Edition 2005, 7" TFT LCD	$2,499.00	* AMD Athlon 64 3500+ 939 CPU + MB + Memory *	$350.00
ATHLON-64 X2 COMPUTER CUSTOM	$2,099.00	Compaq AMD64 3400+ LOADED w/ 5.1-Speakers - NEW	$349.99
COMPUTER GAMING PC DESKTOP		Bio Hazard ,AMD3000 ,512 Ram,120GbHD,52x CD burner	$349.00
[2 of these sold for $2,099.00 each]		HP Hewlett Packard Pavillion a1020n Desktop PC P4 NEW	$346.65
AMD XP 64 4000+ 3GB DDR 2x GeForce 6800 Ultra PCI-X SLI	$1,800.00	HP Pavillion a800n AMD XP 2.2GHz	$345.00
Alienware Area 51 Extreme Edition 3.2GHZ MINT	$1,750.00	512MB CD-RW 160GBHD/XP	
XPS GEN 4 * 250G * DVD+/-RW * ATI X850 XT *	$1,726.50	AMD ATHLON 64 3000+ 120GB HD	$342.50
AMD Athlon 64 3800+ Gaming PC	$1,699.00	1GB PC3200 ATI EXPRESS	
CUSTOM HARDCORE GAMING	$1,681.00	New Compaq Presario SR1010Z PC Desktop Computer AMD 64	$342.50
SYSTEM P4 DUAL, 320GB 4GB RAM		NEW Dell Dimension 4700 P4 3.0GHz	$342.07
NEW Sony VAIO 250GB All-In-One	$1,675.00	New Compaq Presario SR1010Z PC Desktop Computer AMD 64	$340.00
TV-PC P4 3.2E GHz DVD?RW		HOT Dell Dimension 3000 3.0Ghz, 512MB DDR, 15" LCD more	$339.00
Dell Dimension 9100 GAMING 830 DC 3Ghz + 2GB + X850 XT	$1,621.00	New Compaq Desktop PC, AMD 3100+,	$335.00
Shuttle SN25P Athlon FX-55 EVGA Geforce 7800GTX 256MB	$1,600.00	512MB,160GB, DVD?R/RW	
HP wx6200 Xeon Dual 3.4GHz /2GB Ram /70GB Drive/DVD	$1,577.00	NEW eMachines D6405 Athlon 64 3000+	$335.00
AMD 64 3500+ GAMING COMPUTER	$1,549.00	512MB 80GB DVD+/-RW	
TWO VIDEO CARDS INSTALLED!			

Desktop PC Components ▶ Cables, Adapter Cards

The average sales price in this subcategory is $7.88.

	HIGH		AVG
ASylum BFG Geforce FX 5950 Ultra OC [With ARTIC cooler]	$180.38	Box of Various PC Cables USB Printer Parallel Serial	$7.99
Digi 16EM Digiboard Acceleport ISA Card 70000749 NEW	$99.00	75 Foot Patch Cable Cat5e Cat5 RJ45 Network ETHERNET	$7.84
SGI Silicon Graphics VMR Module P/N 073-20742-30 Rev E	$66.70	Belkin FireWire 800/400 9 to 6 Pin 6ft Cable Mac or PC	$7.55
MONSTER ULTRA COMPONENT VIDEO 1000	$65.00	PC desktop parts, cables, pci cards, motherboard, case	$7.50
PLUGS ULT V1000 CV-8		24 pin Power supply Cable adapter for new INTEL P4 MB	$7.49
Monster Cable Ultra Series THX 1000 8 Foot Component	$61.00	[2 of these sold for $7.49 each]	
MONSTER ULTRA COMPONENT VIDEO	$60.00	20 > 24 PIN CABLE SERVER S775 MB	$7.49
1000 PLUGS ULT V1000 CV-8		TO ATX PSU DELL HP IBM	
MONSTER ULTRA COMPONENT VIDEO	$60.00	MAGIC I/O High Speed ECP Parallel	$7.49
1000 PLUGS ULT V1000 CV-8		port PCI CARD * NEW *	
QUATECH EPP PARALLEL PCMCIA CARD SPP-100	$52.00	ASUS P5GD2 Accessories - USB, SATA, IDE, Firewire	$7.16
nVidia Geforce Fx 5600 / 256MB Video Card /8x DVI & AGP	$41.01	[2 of these sold for $7.16 each]	
COMCAST CABLE MODEM ~NWOB~ 1 DAY ONLY!!	$33.00	National Instruments AT-GPIB/Tnt Ieee 488.2 Working	$7.00
MONSTER CABLE PGL400CVAA	$31.00	Vantec CSK-80-GR Cable Sleeving Kit (Green) Retail	$6.99
10 COMPONENT CABLE FOR PS2		Belkin Pro Series USB Extension 10ft Cable F3U134-10	$6.99
NEW LOT OF 3 CORDS FOR COMTROL	$27.99	Belkin FireWire 800/400 9 to 6 Pin 6ft Cable Mac or PC	$6.99
ROCKETPORT MULTIPORT		10 LOT 6' POWER CORDS COMPUTER/MONITOR/ETC	$6.99
D-Link AirPlus G Wireless PCI Adapter 54Mbps (DWL-G510)	$26.00	Belkin FireWire 800/400 9 to 6 Pin 6ft Cable Mac or PC	$6.99
NEW COMTROL ROCKETPORT MULTIPORT	$20.49	50 Foot Patch Cable Cat5e Cat5 RJ45 Network ETHERNET	$5.84
SERIAL CONTROLLER CARD		[2 of these sold for $5.84 each]	

Desktop PC Components ▸ CPU

The average sales price in this subcategory is $47.26.

	HIGH		AVG
AMD ATHLON 64 X2 DC 4400+ PGA939 2.2GHZ	$510.00	Athlon XP-M Mobile XP 1800+ 35W Processor CPU Laptop	$49.76
AMD Athlon 64 X2 4200 and Asus A8N-SLI Deluxe Combo NR!	$500.00	AMD Sempron 2800+ OEM CPU – NEW	$49.55
AMD Athlon 64 X2 4200+ Dual Core CPU	$465.00	[3 of these sold for $49.55 each]	
Unused Matched Pair Opteron 2.0GHz 246 Socket 940	$450.00	5 Pounds of CPUs for Recovery	$49.00
5 HP JetDirect en3700	$425.00	[2 of these sold for $49.00 each]	
[3 of these sold for $425.00 each]		AMD Sempron 2800+ OEM CPU - NEW	$48.99
TWO NEW 3ghz Xeon P4 CPUs Nocona 3.0 1MB 800 fsb D0	$415.00	AMD Sempron 2800+ OEM CPU - NEW	$48.50
SGI Silicon Graphics 02 Computers/Edgemark Workstation	$405.01	AMD Sempron 2600+ OEM CPU - NEW	$47.99
Angels vs. Devil Rays Diamond Club this Weekend!!	$380.00	AMD Sempron 2600+ OEM CPU - NEW	$47.10
5 HP JetDirect en3700	$377.55	AMD Sempron 2600+ OEM CPU - NEW	$46.99
Huge LOT of GOLD Scrap CPU's 200+ Chips Recovery	$340.00	AMD Sempron 2600+ OEM CPU - NEW	$46.01
Intel Pentium D 830 3 GHz DUAL CORE LGA 775	$310.00	2.93ghz celeron d 2930mhz 512/800 800mhz fsb	$46.00
Intel CPU 48 CPUs 1Ghz , 933Mhz , etc. Complete LOT	$300.55	AMD Sempron 2600+ OEM CPU - NEW	$45.99
10 Pounds Gold-Faced CPUs for Recovery	$299.00	Scrap Gold Processors LOT OF 50 - 5lbs.	$45.77
Intel Pentium D 830 DC 3.0 GHz /800FSB/2x1MB Cache	$295.00	AMD Sempron 2600+ OEM CPU - NEW	$45.00
Dual athlon MP 2200+ GA7dpxdw	$256.00	65 Computer CPUs for Gold Recovery / Salvage	$44.77
1GB DDR Volcano7 heatsink		AMD Sempron 2600+ OEM CPU - NEW	$44.55

Desktop PC Components ▸ Memory

The average sales price in this subcategory is $50.01.

	HIGH		AVG
HP 4GB PC3200 400Mhz DDR2 CL3 ECC P/N 345113-051	$899.00	256MB RAM for Dell Dimension XPS T 168 Pin SDRAM PC100	$54.99
IBM 4GB PC2-3200-CL3 MEMORY DIMM FRU 23P2871	$500.00	1GB PC2100 266Mhz 184PIN DDR MEMORY SINGLE STICK	$54.50
NEW IBM 73P2866 2GB KIT 2 X 1GB ECC REG DDR2 PC3200 CL3	$454.00	MICRON GATEWAY 1024MB DDR2 PC3200 1GB 240PIN MEMORY	$52.00
IBM 2GB(2x1gb) PC2-3200 CL3 ECC DDR2 Memory Kit NEW!	$440.00	SGI Silicon Graphics 320 540 512mb Ram (12) piec + More	$51.00
NEW IBM 73P2866 2GB KIT 2 X 1GB ECC REG DDR2 PC3200 CL3	$432.00	KINGSTON 512MB DDR SD RAM PC2100	$51.00
NEW IBM 73P2866 2GB KIT 2 X 1GB ECC REG DDR2 PC3200 CL3	$425.00	VIKING PC133U-333-542-B1 512MB 2 X 256MB	$50.00
HP PZ576UA 2.8GHZ 256MB 40GB CDROM PC NEW	$413.00	NEW Tone 2.2GB USB 2.0 1-Inch Micro Drive (Silver) NR	$49.00
NEW IBM 73P2866 2GB KIT 2 X 1GB ECC REG DDR2 PC3200 CL3	$315.00	HERCULES Gun Powder Pamphlets 1930s Group of 19 NR	$49.00
OCZ Dual Channel 2GB PC3200 EL Platinum DDR Memory	$304.00	Two Samsung 512 MB PC2-3200u RAM	$47.55
8 X 512 MB Hp/Compaq Server memory PC2100 4GB Combined	$265.00	BRAND NEW - 1GB DDR 2100/2700/ - 266/333Mhz	$46.00
Infineon 1GB Memory Rambus RIMM PC800-45 ECC (2 X 512)	$255.00	New SAMSUNG 512MB PC100 ECC Server Memory SDRam	$46.00
corsair 2 gbyte twinX matched memory pair	$250.00	VIKING MEMORY (5) 128 MB PC100 DIMS NON-ECC 168 PIN	$46.00
Lot Of Ten (10) 256Mb Sync PC-133 Avant SDRAM Memory	$232.50	SAMSUNG 240 pin 1GB DDR2 PC2-3200 - 333 MEMORY STICK	$46.00
Dell Dimension 8250 RAM memory 1 GB PC800-40	$219.95	K540 Lot of 42 Aopen 64MB SD PC100	$46.00
	$217.50	256MB OF RAMBUS MEMORY	$46.00

Desktop PC Components ▸ Motherboards

The average sales price in this subcategory is $55.51.

	HIGH		AVG
ASUS P5LD2 D - P4 630 3.0 GHz CPU 1 GB PC5400 DDR2	$524.00	New Dell Dimension 3000 Mainboard Motherboard	$59.99
Leadtek GeForce 7800 GTX 256MB	$430.00	DELL DIMENSION 4700 MOTHERBOARD M3918 P4 LGA775	$59.95
DDR3/PCI-E/VIVO/Dual-DVI		DELL DIMENSION 3000 MOTHERBOARD N6381 D865GV P4 S.478	$59.95
Intel P4 550 3.4GHZ + Intel D915PBL MB + XP Pro SP2 NIB	$350.00	[7 of these sold for $59.95 each]	
AMD athlon 64 3700+ w/K8N4-e Delux motherboard combo	$330.00	DELL DIMENSION 4700 MOTHERBOARD M3918 P4 LGA775	$59.95
Sun Axi Motherboard Model 501-4559	$300.00	[2 of these sold for $59.95 each]	
INTEL BAF2HPBB SERVER BOARD - SE7520AF2	$299.00	DELL DIMENSION 3000 MOTHERBOARD N6381 D865GV P4 S.478	$59.32
ASUS P5WD2 Premium WiFi TV Socket T (LGA 775) Intel 95	$277.99	ABIT Motherboard NF7 Series	$58.00
VIA EPIA mini-itx M10000, 512mb	$255.00	Sony INTEL MOBO D915GAG supports Pentium LGA775 Proc	$56.00
RAM, M1ATX CARPC CAR PC		Intel P4 SE7221BA1-E-Server board Socket T LGA 775 ATX	$56.00
Shuttle XPC SB83G5 Silver Intel 915 Barebone	$250.00	New Dell Dimension 3000 Mainboard Motherboard	$55.75
Brand New Intel Desktop Board D955XBK socket LGA775	$245.00	Dell Optiplex GX280 Motherboard LGA775 SATA 128MB Video	$55.00
Asus P5WD2 Premium WiFi-TV edition bundle	$239.00	Abit KA7-100 Slot A Raid Motherboard +AMD Athlon 800Mhz	$54.95
ABIT "Fatal1ty AA8XE" 925XE Chipset Motherboard For Int	$234.99	Dell XPS GENERATION 1 MOTHERBOARD f2905 NEW!!	$53.99
ASUS P5WD2 Premium Socket T	$223.99	ASUS P5GD1-VM 915G MB LGA775 MOTHERBOARD	$53.22
(LGA 775) Intel 955X ATX MB		Soyo SY-5EHM Super Socket 7 Motherboard open box	$53.17
ASUS P5LD2 DELUXE WiFi TV 945P DDR2 1066FSB SATA II	$222.99	DELL DIMENSION 3000 MOTHERBOARD N6381 D865GV P4 S.478	$52.00
Intel D955XBKLKR Desktop	$219.00	Motherboard, Sound & Video card, & 256 of Ram + amd Cpu	$51.50
Motherboard ATX 955 Board BOX		Intel BTX 915G DDR400 LGA775 Motherboard	$51.00

Desktop PC Components ▸ Speakers & Headphones

The average sales price in this subcategory is $38.64.

	HIGH		AVG
HOME STERO SYSTEM	$2,499.00	Boston Acoustics BA745 Speaker System **NEW** NR	$41.00
HP PAVILION 17 INCH WIDESCREEN NOTEBOOK COMPUTER,	$755.61	BOSTON ACOUSTICS 3 PC SPEAKER SYSTEM SUBWOOFER	$41.00
NEW! Klipsch SWS Subwoofer,& FREE 2.1 Subwoofer.KLIPSCH	$390.55	IBM THINKPAD 760 EL LAPTOP COMPUTER	$40.00
KLIPSCH PROMEDIA ULTRA 5.1	$244.99	Creative Labs DVD Player	$40.00
DIGITAL SURROUND SPEAKERS		Deluxe 1500W DVD Game PC Home Theater Ipod Speaker	$40.00
Klipsch ProMedia Ultra 5.1 Speaker System NR!!	$243.50	[2 of these sold for $40.00 each]	
Klipsch Promedia Ultra 5.1 Speaker System (moving)	$227.50	NEW DELL 5650 5.1 SURROUND SOUND SPEAKERS 100 WATTS	$40.00
Klipsch ProMedia Ultra 5.1 Computer Speakers System	$202.50	Deluxe 1500W DVD Game PC Home Theater Ipod Speaker	$39.99
Surround system, amp, 6 speakers,dvd,cd,mp3 player in 1	$195.76	New 5.1 Channel 7pcs Surround Sound Speaker System ~4	$39.95
BOSE? COMPANION 3? SPEAKERS - NEW	$195.00	[2 of these sold for $39.95 each]	

BOSE Companion 3 Multi-Media Speakers	$195.00	JBL Invader 4.1 Surround Multimedia Speaker System	$38.00
Klipsch ProMedia Ultra 5.1 Computer Speakers System	$185.65	Boston Acoustics computer speakers complete system	$36.00
BOSE? COMPANION 3? SPEAKERS – NEW	$185.00	NEC PC Theater. Includes Amp/Equalizer/Speakers NEW	$35.99
BOSE? COMPANION 3? SPEAKERS – NEW	$180.00	SILVER 3D LED LIGHT Computer Multimedia 2.1 PC Speakers	$35.00
[4 of these sold for $180.00 each]		ADVENT AW870 WIRELESS POWERED SPEAKERS 900 MHZ ACOUSTIC	$33.87
Boston Acoustics BA7900 5.1 Speakers	$178.57	Acoustic Research 900MHz Wireless Stereo Speakers AW871	$33.52
Altec Lansing 641 Digital Speaker System like NEW!	$158.93	Sony Vaio Desktop Speaker System with Woofer	$32.03

Desktop PC Components ▸ Video Cards

The average sales price in this subcategory is $40.70.

	HIGH		AVG
HP NVIDIA QUADRO FX3000 256MB AGP PN DL488B	$607.57	Gigabyte GV-N68128DH GeForce 6800 128MB AGP Video Card	$51.00
BFG 7800 GTX Nvidia card, brand new, used only once!	$510.01	3DLabs WILDCAT VP760	$50.84
BFG Geforce 7800 GTX OC - open box new	$506.00	4 REEL TIME RGB BOARD LOT 7	$50.00
BFG geforce 7800GTX OC like New! No reserve PCI EXPRESS	$440.00	LOT OF 50 –> VIDEO CARD BLOW-OUT AGP / PCI CARDS	$49.99
Leadtek GeForce 7800 GTX 256MB DDR3/PCI-E/VIVO/Dual-DVI	$430.00	ViewGraphics (Optibase) MediaPump MP503 PCI Adapter	$49.99
BFG Geforce 6800 Ultra OC 512MB PCIe	$400.00	ATI RADEON 256 MB VIDEO CARD	$46.00
BFG Geforce 6800 Ultra OC 512MB PCIe	$395.00	NVidia GeForce FX 5500 128MB DDR Video Card! wow	$41.00
BFG Geforce 6800 Ultra OC PCI-E x 16 256m Nvidia SLI	$365.00	2 Brand New Shure PS40 In-Line 15V 600ma Power Supply	$40.00
BFG NVidia GeForce 6800 Ulta OC 256MB AGP!!!	$355.00	New Apollo NVIDIA GeForce FX 6200TC video card 128 MB	$40.00
NVIDIA GeForce 6800 Ultra 256MB DDR3 Dual DVI 8X AGP	$340.00	HP Visualize FX5 Pro Graphics Card 64bit PCI A1262A	$39.99
GeForce 6800 Ultra OC 256 Meg AGP	$338.00	ABIT ATI Radeon X300SE 128MB TV/DVI PCI Video Card	$36.00
NEW eVGA nVidia GeForce 6800 Ultra 256MB PCI-E	$325.00	BFG Tech Geforce 4 Ti 4200 128mb DDR NOT ati	$36.00
BFG Geforce FX 6800 Ultra OC w/ 256 MB GDDR3	$325.00	Nvidia GeForce 4 4600 128mb	$36.00
Pinnacle Genie Plus 3D Digital Effects Editing System	$314.00	ABIT ATI Radeon X300SE 128MB TV/DVI PCI Video Card	$35.00
BFG Geforce 6800 Ultra OC watercooled	$305.00	Lot of 6 AGP Video Cards, ATI, Nvivia, Asus, etc	$32.51

Desktop PC Components ▸ Web Cams

The average sales price in this subcategory is $18.03.

	HIGH		AVG
New D-Link DCS-5300 Webcam 10/100 Fast Ethernet	$235.00	Logitech QuickCam, WebCam, ~~BRAND NEW~~ FREE SHIPPING	$19.95
4 Four Veo Observer Network Cameras LAST FEW BID NOW	$218.29	Logitech ClickSmart 420 Digital Camera & Video WebCam	$19.00
NIB*~ INTELLINET NETWORK IP CAMERA Prof. FACT SEALED	$199.99	Logitech QuickCam Web, New In Box, No Reserve	$18.99
Linksys Wireless-G Internet Video Camera (Model WVC54G)	$152.63	Logitech QuickCam Zoom Webcam	$18.51
NEW D-Link DCS-1000 Internet Camera	$150.00	Logitech ClickSmart 510 USB WebCam Digital Camera	$18.51
USB WIRELESS Webcam–Night Vision + Weatherproof	$149.99	Intel Pro PC Video Camera	$18.51
NEW. SEALED APPLE iSight	$119.50	New Logitech QuickCam Communicate - WEBCAM	$18.50
mannyeagle@aol.com	$110.00	Philips Funcam, BRAND NEW DMVC300K, WEBCAM	$18.07
[2 of these sold for $110.00 each]		Logitech QuickCam Zoom Video	$17.75
Panasonic BL-C10A Remote Video Monitoring Net Web Cam	$105.00	Web Camera W/ Mic WEBCAM	
PANASONIC BL-C10A NETWORK REMOTE MONITORING SYSTEM!	$104.99	Logitech QuickCam Zoom USB Webcam Web Camera Microphone	$17.00
DCS-1000W D-Link Fast 2.4 GHz Wireless Internet Camera	$104.50	Logitech ClickSmart 510 USB WebCam Digital Camera	$16.66
PANASONIC BL-C10A NETWORK REMOTE MONITORING SYSTEM!	$103.50	Logitech QuickCam Zoom Video Web Camera W/ Mic WEBCAM	$16.50
CCTV 8 Channel Digital Video Color Quad Processor	$99.99	Logitech Pocket Digital 130 Slim 1.3 MP Digital Camera	$16.07
Logitech Quickcam Orbit	$85.00	Philips Vesta Webcam 675k w/Mic - USB PCVC675k	$16.02
D-LINK DCS-900W 802.11b WIRELESS INTERNET CAMERA	$81.00	**NEW** INTEL USB WEB CAM small computer camera	$15.51

Laptops, Notebooks ▸ Dell

The average sales price in this subcategory is $286.21.

	HIGH		AVG
LOT of 11 Dell Latitude Laptops C600, C640, C840	$2,424.00	DELL LATITUDE C600 750 MHz LAPTOP LAPTOPS LAP WIRELESS	$290.00
Dell Latitude C640 P4 1.2Ghz DVD Lot of (5)	$1,782.00	DELL LATITUDE C600 PIII 700MHZ FREE LAPTOP BAG	$290.00
LOT OF 5 DELL LATITUDE C600 PIII-750 LAPTOPS DVD !!!!!	$1,725.00	[2 of these sold for $290.00 each]	
Dell Latitude C640 P4 1.2Ghz Lot of (4)	$1,590.11	DELL P3 W2K C600 LAPTOP COMPUTER NOTEBOOK WARRANTY	$290.00
Lot of 5 DELL LATITUDE C600 PIII 700MHZ FREE LAPTOP BAG	$1,425.00	[2 of these sold for $290.00 each]	
[2 of these sold for $1,425.00 each]		WIRELESS DELL LAPTOP~P3 500~256RAM~LAPTOPS~6.HD~1DAY~NR	$289.00
LOT OF 5 DELL LATITUDE C600 PIII-750 LAPTOPS DVD !!!!!	$1,329.53	Dell Latitude L400 PIII 700 - MINT - vaio hp sony	$287.00
LOT OF 5 DELL LATITUDE C600 PIII-750 LAPTOPS DVD !!!!!	$1,300.00	DELL LATITUDE PIII P3 LAPTOP LAPTOPS COMPUTER WINXP	$286.00
LOT OF 5 COMPAQ ARMADA M700 PIII-700 LAPTOPS DVD !!!!!	$1,299.00	DELL LATITUDE PIII 701Mhz/256RAM/20GIG/14" LAPTOP	$285.00
LOT OF 5 COMPAQ ARMADA M700 PIII-700 LAPTOPS DVD !!!!!	$1,260.01	Dell Latitude C600 Laptop lap top 750MHz 512MB CDRW/DVD	$285.00
LOT OF 5 COMPAQ ARMADA M700 PIII-700 LAPTOPS DVD !!!!!	$1,125.00	DELL LATITUDE C600 LAPTOP PIII 750 MHz 12G 128MB CD-ROM	$285.00
Lot of 7 Dell Latitude L400 / LS Laptop 400Mhz - 700Mhz	$1,026.05	DELL PIII WIFI XPPRO C600 LAPTOP COMPUTER LAPTOPS 750MZ	$285.00
DELL C600 FAST P3 DVD LAPTOP	$999.99	DELL LATITUDE CPX PIII, 750MHZ, 128MB, 18GIG, CD/ROM	$285.00
UPGRADEABLE TO WIRELESS NR		Awesome Dell C600 Laptop Lap Top Windows XP Laptops NR	$285.00
MINT Dell Inspiron 600m, Intel Pentium MProcessor 725	$749.00	DELL LATITUDE C600 PIII 750 128/20 CD Net 56k PR 2000*	$285.00
Karaoke DJ Computer System MP3+G CDG Burner & PLAYER	$650.00	Dell Latitude Laptop L400 P3 700 128MB 10gb SLIM!!!	$285.00
Dell Latitude C600 laptop P3/750Mhz Ram 128/20GB	$504.00	DELL LATITUDE C600 P3 750 MHz LAPTOP LAP TOPS COMPUTER	$285.00

Laptops, Notebooks ▸ Gateway

The average sales price in this subcategory is $117.86.

	HIGH		AVG
Gateway / MotionComputing M1200 Slate Tablet PC w/WIFI	$760.00	Gateway Solo 3350 PIII 700Mhz 128MB Ram	$131.50
Gateway 400SD4 Laptop Computer / Windows XP Home	$710.00	~GATEWAY 2000 SOLO LAPTOP~ MINT SHAPE~GREAT BARGAIN~	$127.50
Gateway M1200 Tablet PC with Keyboard, Flexdock, Cover	$660.00	Gateway Solo 5300, 900MHz, 128MB, CDROM, win XP !!!!	$124.99

Gateway 400SD4 Laptop Computer / Windows XP Home	$610.00	Gateway Solo 9300 Pentium III 750MHz 32MB	$124.50
Gateway 9500 P3 1.06ghz 128m-20HD-15"LCD-DVD/CDRW-1 DAY	$375.00	GATEWAY SOLO 9300 LAPTOP PIII W/15.7" SCRN PARTS/REPAIR	$124.50
Gateway SOLO 5300 PIII Laptop :: College Special!	$355.00	Gateway Laptop Computer Solo Pro 9300	$123.50
GATEWAY 200STM LAPTOP 2 BATTRIES WIFI AND 40 GIG	$355.00	GATEWAY 200STM 3450 EXTENDED BATTERY 6500641 ~ADEAL~	$119.00
Gateway Solo 5300 CL, 900MHz, 256MB, Laptop Notebook!	$355.00	Gateway Solo 1400 - 900MHz - Needs Bcklight or Inverter	$117.50
GATEWAY P-III LAPTOP WITH 256 RAM	$349.95	Compaq Armada E500 Good Condition Pentium III 600 Mhz	$113.61
GATEWAY P-III LAPTOP WITH 256 RAM	$349.95	GATEWAY SOLO 9300 LAPTOP LI-ION BATTERY 6500358 ~ADEAL~	$107.50
Gateway Solo 9500 P3 ,15.7LCD,20gbHD,DVD/CD_RW drive	$320.00	GATEWAY SOLO 9300 LAPTOP LI-ION BATTERY 6500358 ~ADEAL~	$102.50
Gateway Solo Pentium III 850MHz Laptop Computer/1day NR	$315.00	NEW GATEWAY SOLO 1450 LI-ION BATTERY 6500665 ~ADEAL~	$99.00
Gateway 9500 PIII 900 900mhz Laptop + 15 LCD & XP	$310.00	NEW GATEWAY SOLO 1450 LI-ION BATTERY 6500665 ~ADEAL~	$90.00
Gateway Solo 5300 - Pentium 3 with DVD - NICE!!!	$300.00	SOLO 5300 14.1" LCD BEZEL (FRONT+ BACK+ CLUTCH) ~ADEAL~	$86.00
Gateway Solo 5300 PIII 700 256MB 20GB Laptop Win XP	$300.00	GATEWAY PROFILE 3 AC POWER ADAPTER 6500504 ~ADEAL~	$82.00

Laptops, Notebooks ▶ HP, Compaq

The average sales price in this subcategory is $116.38.

	HIGH		AVG
NEW Compaq Presario Laptop w/Mobile AMD Athlon XP 2200+	$770.50	COMPAQ ARMADA 1750 LAPTOP	$119.99
NEW Compaq Presario Laptop w/Mobile AMD Athlon XP 2200+	$650.00	366MHz/64MB/6GB NOTEBOOK	
NEW Compaq Presario Laptop w/Mobile AMD Athlon XP 2200+	$640.00	COMPAQ ARMADA 1700 CHEAP	$119.27
Compaq Presario 2575 Laptop great condition	$400.00	TOUCHPAD WORKING LAPTOP NR	
COMPAQ Laptop Notebook Computer FULLY LOADED ~1DAY SALE	$400.00	COMPAQ ARMADA 1700 300MHZ	$118.50
COMPAQ Laptop Notebook Computer FULLY LOADED ~1DAY SALE	$385.00	CHEAP TOUCHPAD WORKING NR	
HP LAPTOP COMPUTER LAPTOPS LAP	$365.00	SLIM HP OMNIBOOK PII P2 300MHz	$118.26
COMPUTERS NOTEBOOK NEW		LAPTOP COMPUTER NOTEBOOK	
COMPAQ Laptop Notebook Computer FULLY LOADED ~1DAY SALE	$355.00	Compaq Armada 7400 P2 300MHz 128MB 6.4GB Laptop	$117.50
COMPAQ LAPTOP COMPUTER LAPTOPS	$355.00	Compaq Armada 1750 PII366Mhz/128MB/6GB/CD/Floppy	$117.50
COMPUTERS NOTEBOOK NEW		Compaq Armada 7800 Laptop Computer Notebook 8GB - NR!	$117.50
COMPAQ ARMADA LAPTOP NOTEBOOK	$325.00	Compaq Armada Laptop P2 266 mhz	$116.50
COMPUTER LAPTOPS WIRELESS		COMPAQ ARMADA 7400 LAPTOP	$116.00
COMPAQ Laptop Notebook Computer FULLY LOADED * 1DAY SAL	$315.00	PII 333 LOADED WITH SOFTWARE	
COMPAQ ARMADA LAPTOP NOTEBOOK	$310.00	COMPAQ ARMADA 7800 LAPTOP	$115.05
COMPUTER LAPTOPS WIRELESS		Compaq Armada M300 Laptop and Docking Station	$115.00
Compaq Armada Laptop Notebook Windows XP & Office 2003	$305.00	Compaq Armada Laptop 1700 PII 300Mhz 96Mb - GREAT PRICE	$114.99
COMPAQ ARMADA LAPTOP COMPUTER	$305.00	HP Omnibook 4150 PII 300MHz Laptop notebook Awesome	$113.45
NOTEBOOK LAPTOPS WIRELESS		COMPAQ PRESARIO 1235 LAPTOP COMPUTER	$112.50
COMPAQ Laptop Notebook Computer FULLY LOADED ~1DAY SALE	$300.00	Compaq Armada M700 laptop PII 366mhz 128mb 4GB	$112.50

Laptops, Notebooks ▶ IBM, Lenovo

The average sales price in this subcategory is $138.53.

	HIGH		AVG
Lot Of 185 IBM ThinkPad Laptop Laptops Notebooks LOOK!!	$7,155.00	IBM thinkpad P II chip, dvd player, Free Shipping,works	$143.49
@NEW!!! ***Acer TravelMate 8104*** RETAIL $2099!!!!!@	$1,534.00	NO RESERVE IBM 570 LAPTOP PII 366/192/6.5 CD FDD USB	$142.50
IBM Thinkpad 600x Laptop - Lot of 4	$810.00	IBM ThinkPad A20m - Perfect for Students!	$142.50
DELL LATITUDE CPX LAPTOP COMPUTER PENTIUM WIRLESS	$430.00	IBM ThinkPad 600E PII 366Mhz/128Mb/6.4Gb Laptops (2)	$141.27
IBM THINKPAD 600x Pentium III 500 Laptop - Like New!	$369.99	IBM Thinkpad 600X Laptop	$140.00
IBM THINKPAD 240X 500 MHz P3 Ultra-Compact Win 2000	$356.05	IBM ThinkPad 600E PII 366Mhz\128MB	$138.41
IBM THINKPAD T30*2366-86U*PARTS OR REPAIR	$355.00	IBM ThinkPad A20m Working Laptop for Parts or Build 15"	$138.01
IBM ThinkPad 600X 192MB 12GB CDROM	$349.00	ibm thinkpad 600e, new screen, 256mb, 6gb, great shape!	$137.53
DELL PENTIUM 3 LAPTOP COMPUTERS with DVD-ROM	$325.00	IBM LAPTOPS ThinkPad 600E LOADED 366MHz CHEAP LAPTOP $9	$137.50
DELL PENTIUM 3 LAPTOP COMPUTERS with DVD-ROM	$315.00	IBM THINKPAD 600e LAPTOP PIII 366MHz 6GB DVD 128	$137.50
600X IBM thinkpad-576RAM 500mhz 40GB HDD Loaded + More	$301.00	IBM ThinkPad 600X PIII 500 Mhz! NR!	$137.50
IBM Thinkpad 600x Laptop, P III, W / NEW BATTERY.	$299.99	IBM ThinkPad 570E P3 500MHz/192MB/56K/13.3" Ultra Thin	$135.50
IBM THINKPAD 600X PIII 500MHz - PRICE REDUCED- LAST ONE	$299.00	ThinkPad A20m 500 MHz 12GB 128MB 10x 56k SND NIC	$134.52
COMPLETE IBM THINKPAD COMPUTER LAPTOPS NOTEBOOK WIFI	$295.00	VERY NICE IBM 570E,PENTIUM III,500mhz.ALL READY TO GO.	$134.06
IBM Thinkpad 600x PIII P3 500 mhz Laptop Win2K Warranty	$290.00	IBM THINKPAD 600E LAPTOP TYPE 2645 - P2 - 366/200/6.4	$134.06

Laptops, Notebooks ▶ Sony

The average sales price in this subcategory is $287.99.

	HIGH		AVG
SONY VAIO VGN-U8G (Not U750P, U71P) EngWinXP and DVDRW	$2,000.00	Sony VAIO PCG-R505JL Laptop Win XP Home COMPACT!!!	$290.01
[2 of these sold for $2,000.00 each]		Sony PCG-Z505JE VAIO SuperSlim Pro Notebook / Laptop	$290.00
SONY VAIO VGN-U8G (Not U750P, U71P) EngWinXP and DVDRW	$1,850.00	Sony Vaio PCG-XG19 Laptop P3-650, 128MB, DVD/CDRW	$290.00
[2 of these sold for $1,850.00 each]		Sony VAIO Laptop PCG-955A. FREE SHIPPING.	$290.00
SONY VAIO VGN-U8G (Not U750P, U71P) EngWinXP and DVDRW	$1,800.00	Z505R Sony Superslim Laptop, less than 4 lbs	$290.00
SONY U101 .. 7.1" XGA / 60G UP / Small & Performance	$1,790.00	SUPERLOADED Sony PCG 610 Laptop DVD-RW No Reserve	$288.92
SONY U3 ... Full of CD-RW, 60G HDD, Two battery, WLAN!!	$1,690.00	SONY VAIO PCG-SR7K Laptop	$287.00
Sony PCG-C1MZX Picturebook in Excellent Condition -u101	$1,550.00	Sony VAIO? All-in-One Notebook PCG-F650	$285.00
Sony PCG-C1MZX Picturebook in Excellent Condition -u101	$1,535.00	SONY VAIO LAPTOP PCG-FX120	$285.00
SONY VAIO NOTEBOOK LAPTOP PCG-V505EC 100Gb 1Gb Ram	$1,500.00	PIII-700 128 Ram 10GB HD	
Sony VAIO TR3A,TR3AP2 Like New, Case, 1 Gb Ram, 40GB HD	$1,300.00	SONY VAIO LAPTOP IN GREAT CONDITION	$285.00
Sony Vaio PCG- U3/P SubNotebook Laptop!~ u1 u101 u3 u50	$1,299.95	Sony Vaio Laptop, PCG-R505-TSK, With DVD Dock!!	$282.77
SONY VAIO VGN-U50 HANDHELD COMPUTER MINT IN BOX EXTRAS	$1,251.01	Sony Vaio PCG 505G Laptop Notebook PCG-505G -new battry	$281.01
Sony Vaio U50 and additional long life battery included	$1,250.00	Used Sony Vio PCG-707 Notebook Laptop w/ Accesories NR	$280.00
SONY VAIO A190 LAPTOP NOTEBOOK + ACCESSORIES **NR**	$1,225.50	Sony Vaio XG500 (PCG-XG500) PC Notebook Computer	$280.00
Sony VGN-U50	$1,200.00	Sony VAIO PCG-FX210 800 MHz DVD-ROM Laptop Notebook	$279.99
Sony Vaio PCG- U3 SubNotebook Laptop!~ u1 u101 u3 u50	$1,199.95	[2 of these sold for $279.99 each]	

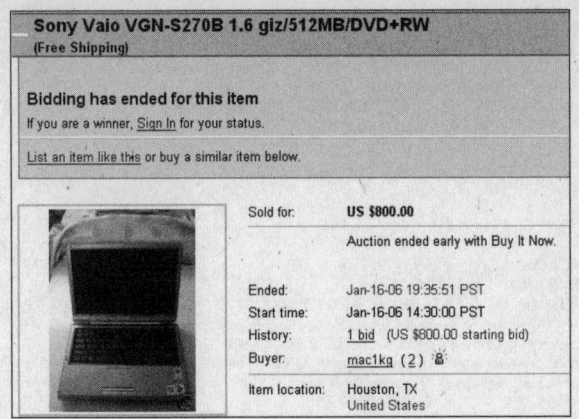

Laptops, Notebooks ▸ Toshiba

The average sales price in this subcategory is $232.63.

	HIGH		AVG
LOT of 8 Toshiba Tecra 8100 Laptops	$1,451.51	Toshiba Tecra 8100 P3 750MHz/DVD/20GB/256MB/56K/14" TFT	$237.50
LOT of 3) Toshiba Portege 4010 Laptop 933MHz/768MB/30GB	$1,250.00	Toshiba Satellite Pro 4600	$237.50
Toshiba Tecra A4 Laptop Computer - 512 MB + Wireless	$870.00	Toshiba Tecra 8100 Laptop PIII 700mhz 3.7gigHD 128mhz	$235.35
TOSHIBA LIBRETTO L5W	$760.00	Toshiba Satellite 2805-S503 Laptop, with case & camera	$235.00
TOSHIBA PORTEGE 4010 PIII LAPTOP COMPUTER + ACCESSORIES	$708.00	Toshiba Tecra 8100 P3 750MHz/DVD/12GB/128MB/56K/14.1"	$234.50
Toshiba Satellite Pen M 1.5 GHz 60 GB 512 MB Win xp Pro	$635.00	TOSHIBA SATELLITE 1755 DVD-ROM WINDOWS XP CELERON NR!!	$233.99
2 Toshiba Tecra 8100 Laptop computers with Spare Parts	$600.00	TOSHIBA PORTEGE 3480CT PIII 600 192MB 12GB DVD 2.5LBS	$232.50
Toshiba Libretto L1 & Cassiopeia E-200-Excellent Combo	$580.00	TOSHIBA TECRA 8100 Laptop PIII	$232.50
Toshiba Portege 2000 Laptop WiFi\DVD\WinXP\750mhz	$555.00	800MHz/12GB/256MB/CD-ROM	
Toshiba Satellite Laptop - Like New!	$550.00	Toshiba Tecra 8100 P3 750MHz/DVD/12GB/128MB/56K/14.1"	$232.50
[3 of these sold for $550.00 each]		Toshiba Tecra 8100 Laptop P3 700 12Gb 128MB DVD/CD-ROM	$232.50
TOSHIBA PORTEGE 2010 ....LIKE THE 2000 BUT BETTER	$550.00	TOSHIBA SATELLITE 1755 DVD-ROM WINDOWS XP CELERON NR!!	$232.50
Toshiba Portege 4010 Ultraslim & Light Laptop Warranty	$525.00	Toshiba Tecra 8100 700 Mhz PIII w/DVD Player!	$232.00
TOSHIBA PORTEGE 2010 LAPTOP LIKE THE 2000 BUT BETTER	$515.00	Toshiba Tecra 8100 P3 750MHz/DVD/10GB/128MB/56K/14.1"	$230.50
Toshiba Intel Pentium 3 850 MHz Laptop with 256 MB RAM	$515.00	Toshiba Satellite 1735 Laptop 700Mhz, 10GB, 128MB Ram	$230.50
Toshiba Satellite Laptop - Like New!	$510.00	Toshiba Satellite Pro 4200 Laptop Notebook Pentium III	$230.27

Laptops, Notebooks ▸ Tablet PCs

The average sales price in this subcategory is $559.22.

	HIGH		AVG
Tablet PC M1400 VA View Anywhere Motion M 1400 EXTRAS!	$2,375.00	ViewSonic Tablet/Laptop PC V1100 866mhz	$600.00
NEW! SONY VAIO T240P CENT PM 1.2ghz 512mb 60GB DVD/CDRW	$2,350.00	Compaq/HP Tablet PC TC1000	$599.00
FLYBOOK Tablet PC with TPC2005 512 MB RAM 80 GB HDD	$2,325.00	1GHz/256M/30G/WiFi/XGA/NR!!	
Sony U71 (U70 and U50 like) VAIO Tablet Handheld PC NR	$2,136.00	ECS Tablet Notebook 800 MHz 512MB 40GB DVD CDRW WiFi	$595.00
Motion Computing M1400 Tablet PC View Anywhere NEW!	$2,074.99	HP/Compaq TC1000 Tablet PC 512MB 60GB WiFi	$585.00
motion computing m1400	$1,861.00	Viewsonic Viewpad 1000 Tablet PC "NEW"!	$579.00
HP TC1100 TABLET PC W/ MULTIBAY II AND DVD BURNER!!!!!	$1,851.01	Great Value!! HP/Compaq TC1000 Tablet PC	$566.00
HP TC1100 TABLET PC W/ MULTIBAY II AND DVD BURNER!!!!!	$1,824.00	FUJITSU ST4110 TABLET PC GOOD	$560.00
***HP TC1100 TABLET PC W/ MULTIBAY II AND DVD BURNER	$1,814.00	CONDITION + EXTRAS LAPTOP	
MOTION TABLET M1400 - GREAT VALUE LIKE NEW	$1,800.00	Viewsonic Tablet notebook	$560.00
Motion Computing M1400 Tablet PC with a Ton of Extras!	$1,800.00	Viewsonic Tablet PC V1100 Laptop	$550.00
HP TC1100 TABLET PC W/ MULTIBAY II AND DVD BURNER!!!!!	$1,799.00	Panasonic Toughbook CF-48 P4 Mobile 1.6-CD-512RAM	$549.00
[3 of these sold for $1,799.00 each]		Xybernaut MA 5 Wearable mobile Computer w/ Touch Screen	$536.15
***HP TC1100 TABLET PC W/ MULTIBAY II AND DVD BURNER	$1,789.00	Acer Tablet PC - FREE SHIPPING!	$510.00
[3 of these sold for $1,789.00 each]		Tablet PC Electrovaya Scribbler SC300	$500.00
Motion Computing M1400 Tablet PC - - EXTRAS!	$1,780.00	Viewsonic Viewpad 1000	$495.00
Panasonic Toughbook 18 CF-18 Tablet PC Mobile 1.1GHz	$1,766.00	ViewSonic Viewpad 1000 tablet PC + Extra *NR*	$485.00

Laptop Accessories ▸ Batteries

The average sales price in this subcategory is $46.77.

	HIGH		AVG
Sharp CE-BL17 Standard Lithium Ion Battery for PC-UM PC	$143.73	APPLE MAC POWERBOOK G3 PISMO LOMBARD Li-Ion BATTERY	$49.99
Panasonic Toughbook CF-27 CF27 Battery CF-VZSU04W NEW!!	$129.95	VPR MATRIX 120 170B4 180B5 Li-iON BATTERY VPRN-BA200	$49.99
Gateway Solo 9550 Battery *Brand New* 9500 Primary	$122.50	BRAND NEW Battery for Apple iBook M6392 M7426 M7621G	$49.50
2 Batteries for a Gateway Solo 9300 Series Laptop	$122.50	Gateway M675 Li-Ion Notebook Battery 6500839 6500853	$49.00
Gateway M275 Convertible Tablet Battery 6500821	$109.00	BRAND NEW GATEWAY SOLO 1400/1450 LI ION BATTERY	$48.00
ECS EM-929L, EM929L Li-Ion BATTERY FOR A929 A928 NEW!	$109.00	Fujitsu LifeBook Laptop Battery FPCP65 New 4400 mAh	$47.95
Gateway Solo 9500/9550 Li-Ion Battery PN#6500600	$105.00	Gateway Solo 9500 Secondary Battery 6500518	$47.00
EMACHINES BATTERY FOR M2352 EMACHINES LAPTOP BATTERY	$103.50	BTP-37D1 New Acer Travelmate 610 611 612 614 Battery	$46.88
Gateway SOLO 9300 6500358 Replacement Battery NEW!	$103.50	PANASONIC TOUGHBOOK CF-71	$46.50
gateway battery 6500363 original bag 2150 cgr-b/625 AE	$103.50	BATTERY (CF-VZSU09, USED/REF)	

	HIGH		AVG
Gateway Notebook M500 M505 Li-Ion Battery 6500855	$100.01	Averatec 3100 3120 3150 3200 3250 3300 Battery, New	$46.25
Sharp Actius MM10 MM20 Laptop 9 Hour Battery Extended	$99.99	GATEWAY SOLO 9100 9150 2300 2550 2500 LAPTOP BATTERY	$46.00
Panasonic Toughbook CF28 CF48 CF50 Battery NEW!!	$99.95	Averatec 3000 3120 3150 3200 Li-ion Battery, * NEW *	$46.00
EMACHINES LAPTOP BATTERY FOR M6811 M6810 M6809 M6805	$99.00	NIB: 15" MAC POWERBOOK G4 RECHARGEABLE BATTERY	$46.00
Gateway Notebook M500 M505 Li-Ion Battery 6500855	$99.00	BATTERY FOR GATEWAY 400 /450 SERIES LAPTOP	$46.00
[2 of these sold for $99.00 each]		Averatec 3100 3120 3150 3200 3250 3300 Battery, New	$46.00

Laptop Accessories ▶ Cases, Bags

The average sales price in this subcategory is $33.86.

	HIGH		AVG
Compac Presario 2209CL Laptop TOP *	$435.00	NEW SAMSONITE NEW JACK COMPUTER	$32.99
Otterbox rugged tablet pc case fujitsu st4000 st5000	$233.50	BACKPACK SCHOOL BOOKBAG	
Tumi NWT Compact Computer Briefpack Backpack 96081	$195.00	LIKE NEW JANSPORT OPTIMIZER LAPTOP BACKPACK	$32.99
ACME MADE Designer laptop computer case/tote bag	$182.50	NEW Computer Samsonite? Executive Laptop Backpack	$32.99
CRUMPLER THE KARACHI OUTPOST 17" LAPTOP CAMERA BACKPACK	$159.99	Laptop Magazine #1 of 05' COMPUTER BACKPACK BAG CASE **	$32.79
Lamborghini?LM-PCC-102 Hard Shell Aluminum Laptop Case	$159.95	Wilsons Messenger Style Laptop Bag BNWOT! Leather!!	$32.00
Lamborghini?LM-PCC-102 Hard Shell Aluminum Laptop Case	$155.00	Sleek Luxurious ITALIAN Leather Briefcase	$31.99
Laptop leather upright expandable briefcase, backpack	$154.59	NEW!! BLACK OGIO METRO LAPTOP	$31.01
CRUMPLER WHICKEY AND COX LAPTOP PHOTO CAMERA BACKPACK !	$152.49	BACKPACK w/ MOTOROLA LOGO	
CRUMPLER WHICKEY AND COX	$149.99	New Computer Notebook Backpack Case / by Samsonite?	$31.01
LAPTOP PHOTO CAMERA BACKPACK !		Italian Leather Laptop Briefcase / LEGAL	$31.00
MINI motion Carpack Laptop bag	$149.50	Red Bull Energy Drink Laptop Computer Bag Carrier O'gio	$31.00
New Oakley Computer Bag, Apple, Sony, Dell, G5	$137.50	SAMSONITE COMPUTER NOTEBOOK LAPTOP BACKPACK CASE BAG	$31.00
CRUMPLER THE KARACHI OUTPOST 17" LAPTOP CAMERA BACKPACK	$129.99	[2 of these sold for $31.00 each]	
[4 of these sold for $129.99 each]		Mobile Edge Deluxe Backpack for Dell Inspiron Notebook	$31.00
New Silver Tumi Laptop Backpack	$129.28	JanSport Moby (Black/Black) Rolling Laptop Backpack	$31.00
CRUMPLER WHICKEY AND COX LAPTOP	$122.49	Dell XPS Inspiron Laptop BACKPACK Case NEW Bag!	$31.00
PHOTO CAMERA BACKPACK !		Super Soft Brown Leather Briefcase	$30.54

Laptop Accessories ▶ Drivers

The average sales price in this subcategory is $33.16.

	HIGH		AVG
20 Pieces New Toshiba Tecra 8000 Series Harddrive Caddy	$440.00	Toshiba 40gb Laptop Hard Disk Drive HDD	$36.88
hp ipaq pocket PC Hx 4700 + Bonus Leather Case	$422.61	Toshiba 1.8" HDD 5.0 GB Type II PC Card	$36.55
Gateway M675 DVD-RW DVD Burner Toshiba SD-R6112	$199.00	HP OmniBook 900 900B External Sleeve for Floppy/CD-ROM	$36.00
Lot Of Laptop Hard Drives 20,30,40 Gig	$160.00	[2 of these sold for $36.00 each]	
UJ-811B dvd-rw/cd-rw combo drive	$150.00	Dell Inspiron 2500 8000 8100 8200 8x DVD/CD-ROM Drive !	$35.95
Lot Of 7 12 Gig Hard Drives	$140.00	SUPERDISK IMATION LS-120 LS120 LAPTOP FLOPPY PCMCIA	$34.95
New OEM Gateway 450 600 Series DVD+/-RW Writer 5502891	$137.50	Lot of 29 Various Laptop Media Drives NEC,Micron,IBM	$34.33
SONY VAIO/ Laptop DVD/CDRW Combo Drive Toshiba SD-R2412	$132.50	Fujitsu MHS2020AT 20GB Laptop Hard Drive	$34.33
Toshiba External CD-RW/DVD USB 2.0 Drive PA3352U-1CD2	$130.00	Dell 2nd 20GB Laptop Hard Drive (9.5mm/ 2.5) - 0C777	$33.01
CF-27 CF-28 CF-29 DVD/CD-RW combo drive w/ caddy	$129.50	2 GB PCMCIA HARD DRIVE	$33.01
5 Pieces New Toshiba Tecra 8000 Series Harddrive Caddy	$120.00	SANDISK CRUZER MINI 1.0 GB	$33.00
[2 of these sold for $120.00 each]		Emachines M5305 M5310 DVD/CD-RW/CD-ROM Drive Combo	$32.00
One used Toughbook DVD ROM & CD-R/RW Drive Pack	$115.49	IBM TavelStar USB 2.0 Laptop Mobile Hard Drive - 20GB	$31.51
Panasonic (CF-VDD285M) Plug-In Module DVD Drive CF-29	$115.00	Toshiba DVD-R,RW Writer SD-R6012	$31.50
Mac Powerbook G4 15" titanium superdrive	$108.05	Sony CD-R/W/DVD-Rom Drive for Laptop - model CRX830E	$31.20
NEW TOSHIBA SD-R6472 DVD?RW DUAL LAYER COMBO SLIM DRIVE	$108.00	ABS PLUS 20.0 Laptop Automatic Backup System	$31.01

Laptop Accessories ▶ Keyboards

The average sales price in this subcategory is $22.45.

	HIGH		AVG
Panasonic Toughbook CF28 CF-28 Rubber Backlit Keyboard	$198.49	Toshiba Keyboard UE2010P02 Removed From 7220CTe	$24.99
Panasonic Toughbook CF29 CF-29 Rubber Backlit Keyboard	$190.50	Toshiba Satellite Keyboard NSK-8560P K000816640 TESTED	$24.99
Panasonic Toughbook CF29 CF-29 Rubber Backlit Keyboard	$152.50	UE2010P02 TOSHIBA TECRA 8100 8200 1800 1805 KEYBOARD	$24.95
Panasonic Toughbook Backlit Keyboard CF29 WKB291M	$152.50	[3 of these sold for $24.95 each]	
Panasonic Toughbook Backlit Keyboard CF29 WKB291M	$149.00	Toshiba Satellite 1605CDS 1675CDS Keyboard NSK-8560P	$24.00
Panasonic Toughbook CF28 CF-28 Rubber Backlit Keyboard	$127.99	HP Pavilion N5450 Keyboard like NEW PK1332N1000	$24.00
SONY VAIO PCG GRX GRV GRZ NVR FRV KEYBOARD	$75.99	HP Pavilion N5450 N5310 Keyboard PK1332N1000	$24.00
Averatec 3000 3120 3150 3200 Series Laptop Keyboard	$70.00	TOSHIBA SATELLITE PRO 4200 KEYBOARD	$23.99
1-478-0862-1 SONY VAIO PCG GRX GRV GRZ FRV NVR KEYBOARD	$70.00	Gateway Solo 5300 Laptop - CD Rom Drive	$22.50
1-478-0862-1 SONY VAIO PCG	$70.00	TOSHIBA SATELLITE 5000 seris KEYBOARD, just like NEW	$22.50
GRX GRV GRZ FRV NVR KEYBOARD		Toshiba A40 A45 A55 Series keyboard	$22.50
Acer TravelMate C100 parts - NEW KEYBOARD 99.N2982.001	$67.00	toshiba satellite pro 6100 keyboard NEW with warranty	$22.50
Acer TravelMate 200 210 220 260 520 730 740 KEYBOARD	$67.00	Sony Vaio Laptop Keyboard NSK-S2001 99.N1782.001	$22.00
Acer TM 650 660 800 6000 8000 Ferrari 3000 NEW KEYBOARD	$67.00	Sony GRX GRX500 GRX600 GRV Keyboard 147728521 FAST SHIP	$21.99
Acer TravelMate C110 parts - NEW KEYBOARD KB.T2707.001	$67.00	New Fujitsu C Series Laptop Keyboard CP098158-02	$21.50
Acer TM 650 660 800 6000 8000 Ferrari 3000 NEW KEYBOARD	$67.00	TOSHIBA SATELLITE A45 KEYBOARD G83C0003G110	$21.49

Laptop Accessories ▶ Memory

The average sales price in this subcategory is $23.75.

	HIGH		AVG
Lot of 1000 New 2 mb Flash IBM PCMCIA memory cards	$572.00	512MB (2x256MB) DDR2 400mhz Dell Inspiron Laptop Memory	$26.01
Lot of 100 Dell XPi 32MB Memory Upgrade - Simple Tech	$355.09	Kingston 256MB PC100 SDRAM Notebook Memory	$26.00
Huge Lot of Laptop Memories(32-256)	$237.50	HP Omnibook 800 800CT 800CS 32MB RAM Memory Module	$25.51
512MB PC133 Memory IBM Thinkpad A30 R30 R31 T23 X22 RAM	$104.99	Compaq LTE 5300 HDD/CD/FDD/DOCK/RAM WIN98! L@@K!!!	$25.47
[2 of these sold for $104.99 each]		Corsair System RAM - 512 MB PC 3200 200-Pin DDR SO-DIMM	$25.00
Samsung 1GB 200 pin PC2700 for laptop	$101.01	[2 of these sold for $25.00 each]	
30 boxes of 20 each ibm 64mb /10 each Kingston 64mb	$100.75	32Mb Ram Memory NEC Versa 4000 P/75 M/75 M/100 V/50	$25.00
512MB PC133 Memory IBM Thinkpad A30 R30 R31 T23 X22 RAM	$99.99	100pcs Lot Orignal Compaq SODIMM 144pins 3.3v 16MB EDO	$25.00
[2 of these sold for $99.99 each]		32MB memory upgrade for HP Omnibook 2000 or 5000 laptop	$25.00
1GB Kit (2)512MB Modules Dell Dimension 2400/4550/4600	$99.00	Toshiba Portege 3110CT 3480CT	$24.99
Lot Of (17) 64MB Notebook Memory Modules- Mix!!	$86.00	3490CT 64Mb Memory Module	
LOT 12 IBM 144pin 64mb 60ns laptop memory ram	$82.11	64MB RAM Memory IBM Thinkpad 380 380D 385 385D 535X	$24.95
Lot of Laptop Memory PC2100 DDR 512 256	$75.00	128MB memory Compaq Presario 1200 1600 1700 1800 12xl	$24.00
512MB DDR Dell Inspiron 9100 XPS Memory PC3200 512 MB	$74.99	[4 of these sold for $24.00 each]	
[2 of these sold for $74.99 each]		64MB MEMORY TOSHIBA SATELLITE PRO 480CDT 480 CDT RAM	$23.95
512MB DDR IBM Thinkpad A31 R32 T30 X31 512 MB Memory	$74.99	64MB RAM MEMORY TOSHIBA SATELLITE	$23.95
[2 of these sold for $74.99 each]		320CDS 325CDS 335CDS	
512MB DDR Dell Inspiron 9100 XPS Memory PC3200 512 MB	$74.99	64MB RAM MEMORY COMPAQ ARMADA	$23.95
512MB DDR TOSHIBA Laptop Memory 512 MB RAM NEW!	$74.99	1585DMT 1598DMT 7362DMT +	
[3 of these sold for $74.99 each]		64MB RAM COMPAQ ARMADA 1590 1590DMT 1590DT MEMORY	$23.95

Laptop Accessories ▶ Mice, Mouse

The average sales price in this subcategory is $6.25.

	HIGH		AVG
Mini Wireless Optical Mouse - 10 pc Lot @Factory Price	$69.00	Kensington 72212 PocketMouse Mini	$7.39
Kensington PilotMouse Bluetooth Optical MiniMouse 72414	$51.00	Mini USB Laptop Optical Mouse Sony Blue Red LED Scroll	$7.00
NEW Bluetooth STOWAWAY Travel Mouse PDA PC Mac	$49.99	Kensington PocketMouse Mini Wireless Optical Mouse	$6.99
[2 of these sold for $49.99 each]		[2 of these sold for $6.99 each]	
NEW Bluetooth STOWAWAY Travel Mouse PDA PC Mac	$48.00	Touchpad for Dell inspiron 8000 series Alps Glidepoint	$6.99
APPLE POWERBOOK G4 M5884	$45.00	Kensington Pocket Mouse Mini OPTICAL Wireless w/ NO RES	$6.75
PALMREST & TOUCHPAD MOUSE		MICRO INOVATIONS WIRELESS OPTICAL TRAVEL MOUSE	$6.50
NEW LOGITECH V500 CORDLESS NOTEBOOK MOUSE 2.4 GHZ	$40.03	MICRO TRAC BY FELLOWES MOUSE FOR LAPTOPS	$6.28
Apple Wireless Pro Mouse- Bluetooth	$40.00	NEW! Belkin MiniWireless Optical Mouse Mini Mouse	$6.01
SAMSUNG 512MB 200-pin DDR333 SO-DIMM PC2700 Notebook	$40.00	New Kensington 72214 Pocket Mouse Mini Wireless NR	$6.00
BRAND NEW i-Pen Mouse (Digital Pen)!!	$39.00	NEW Official Dell brand mouse pad black	$5.99
NEW Targus Wireless Mouse & Keypad Combo PAKP003U	$38.00	1 BLACK USB OPTICAL MOUSE – *NEWEST SHINING STYLE*	$5.52
Apple Wireless Blue Tooth Mouse BT A1015	$36.00	Kensington PocketMouse Mini Wireless Optical Mouse	$5.51
Apple Wireless Mouse, new	$35.09	NEW Logitech Cordless Optical Mouse W/ USB Receiver	$5.50
BT 500 Mobile Mini Blue Tooth Mouse BT-500	$32.00	[2 of these sold for $5.50 each]	
Wireless powerpoint Presentation Laser Pointer	$31.01	New Logitech Cordless Optical Mouseman Wireless Mouse	$5.50
NEW PORTABLE Targus Wireless Remote Presenter PAUM30U	$31.00	NEW USB Snake LED Light for Laptop notebook Torch Mini	$5.50

Laptop Accessories ▶ Other Parts

The average sales price in this subcategory is $16.32.

	HIGH		AVG
Compaq Armada 110 Notebook	$202.50	Dell 1100 5100 and 5150 Base Kit	$18.50
DELL INSPIRON 4100 Notebook Parts Lot	$177.50	Dell Latitude CPX/3700/3800/CPt Cpu Fan Heatsink NEW	$17.99
Compaq Presario 1700 Laptop for Parts ONLY!	$152.50	DELL C600 Mini PCI Ethernet - 56K Modem Card	$17.99
Compaq HP Evo N115 Notebook PC non-working	$142.50	Lap Desk Solid Ash (Board, Tray, Table) New!	$16.99
Compaq N1020v Laptop PARTS ONLY	$127.50	Laptop USB NOTEBOOK COOLER with Temp. LCD Display – NEW	$16.99
Adjustable Vehicle Laptop Computer Mount. Police EMS	$112.50	[2 of these sold for $16.99 each]	
LIKE NEW SOLIS TS280M LAPTOP COMPUTER PLUS EXTRAS!!!!!!	$100.00	Jumbo LAP DESK gr8 for laptop computer writing NEW	$16.00
Compaq Laptop Computer for Parts	$86.12	2 pc Sunon 12V DC Fan 30 x 10mm Laptop Replacement NEW	$15.95
DELL INSPIRON 7500 PPI LAPTOP FOR PARTS MONITOR	$81.00	New Lap Tray w/Light lap desk lapdesk laptop top bed	$15.50
NEW SEALED Logitech QuickCam	$57.01	Jumbo LAP DESK gr8 for homework laptop computer NEW	$15.00
Pro 4000 WebCam Web Cam		NEW COMPAQ ARMADA M700 14" LCD INVERTER FOR LT141X7-124	$15.00
IBM ThinkPad Case Plastics Kit for T20, T21 or T22	$56.45	Dell Inspiron 5000 parts:BACK TOP LID COVER SAMSUNG B+	$14.99
Japanese style folding laptop desk play lego lap table	$54.95	Dell Neon Sign Dealer Advertise Display Light Signs 342	$14.99
Dell Latitude CPi Laptop, A-Series\Model#:PPL	$51.00	INTEL Mini PCI internal wireless network card 2200BG bg	$14.13
Lot of 10 IBM 08K6086 Thinkpad T20 LCD Cover Kit NIB!	$49.99	Toshiba Satellite 1405-S171 CPU HeatSink + Cooling FAN	$14.00
USB GPS Receiver 4 Laptop Notebook Pocket PC WAAS 12-ch	$49.95	The iRac - Apple Titanium Powerbook G4 Laptop Stand	$13.45

14

CONSUMER ELECTRONICS

Consumer Electronics comes in at just ahead of the Computers category in terms of GMV (gross merchandise volume): with $3.2 billion in one recent quarter. It was third overall, just after eBay Motors and Clothing & Accessories.

iPod, You Pod, We All Pod

Car stereos, TVs, and home stereos all have a home here, but some of the hottest items in the category are a lot smaller and lighter than those: the Apple iPod and iPod Mini portable music player. Two of the most popular searches here are for *ipod* (#1) and *ipod mini* (#3).

A 15GB iPod billed as the "iPod Package from Hell with Free Shipping" went for $325.00. It is a third-generation iPod that comes with a docking station, speakers, earphones, and a charging adapter.

But what about the average-priced iPod you can buy on eBay? How new is it, and how does it compare to a retail price? A few Apple iPod 10GB third-generation MP3 players sold for around $132.00 to $133.00. I couldn't find any other 10GB third-generation iPods on sale to compare this one to; but a 40GB third-generation iPod was selling for $399.00 from Crutchfield.com, so the $132.00 price sounds pretty good if you don't mind getting a slightly older model.

And new iPods? Let's look at the auctions for the 20GB iPod, which holds 5,000 songs. On the high end, one sold for $300.00 with 14 bids; it comes with the earbud headphones, AC adapter, and a USB 2.0 cable. Several other "20 GB Photo Color" iPods sold around that price point; between $290.00 and $316.00. But there were also some that sold for less: from about $270.00 all the way down to $240.00 (not visible in this sample because the price fell between the high and average samples). At the Apple Store (www.applestore.com), an iPod

20GB goes for $299.00, so the prices seem to be comparable. The bottom line seems to be you can save money on a new iPod, but you can also buy one at close to retail, depending on your auction-digging skills.

DVD Players

A Pioneer Elite DV-47Ai DVD-Audio and SACD DVD Player is selling brand-new from one vendor on Amazon.com for $699.00; it sold here on eBay for $369.99 and $349.99. In terms of average prices, a Magnavox "MDV450 DVD/MP3 Player Region Free" sold for $34.99. It was described as new in box, with a universal remote. Shipping is $24.99. A "Sony NS725P DVD Player Minty" ("minty" referring to the color, I assume) went for $43.50. This is a DVD player that was released in 2003, so it is a little bit old. In general, the items in the average price range are very affordable and a little bit older technology, without being so old as to be considered truly "vintage."

Big-Ticket and Heavy Items

What about some truly large items, such as home theater systems? Do many of them sell on eBay, or is the shipping too prohibitive? There are some of them, but not as many as the smaller, lightweight items like iPods. There are around 1,400 Home Theater in a Box sub-category listings at one time, compared to about 5,700 iPod auctions. A top seller here was a Kenwood Fineline Networked 7.1 Home Theater System, $1,050.00, and a refurbished Cambridge SoundWorks Newton Theater MC300.5, $999.00. According to the seller, the Cambridge system sells normally for $1499.99. Shipping is around $50.00 for UPS ground, so even with the shipping you can get a bargain on a unit like this.

One thing you may notice more than in other eBay categories is the number of duplicate items that show up here, and that sell at duplicate prices. For example, there were four "Jeep Tweeters / Jeep Speakers / Grand Cherokee" listings that all closed at $49.99. This may be due to more people selling in bulk here, and a good number of people who refurbish and then resell electronics. Also, a lot of eBay stores sell electronic goods. In fact, there are links to some of the major eBay electronics stores from the Consumer Electronics main page.

It may also be due to some major companies that sell electronics on eBay. Motorola reportedly started selling cell phones, accessories, and two-way radios in 2002, and now it operates an eBay Store at www.motorola.com/ebay. Other companies have gotten in the act as a way to get rid of old or overstock merchandise. Because there are so many duplicate items throughout this category, if you're going to sell here, check out the competition in your subcategory and the completed auction prices to make sure the market isn't glutted and that profit margins aren't too slim.

Car Electronics ▸ Car Audio In-Dash Units

The average sales price in this subcategory is $40.91.

	HIGH		AVG
Nakamichi TD-1200II New!! Dragon for your car!!	$910.00	Kenwood KRC-335 am/fm cassette car stereo receiver	$41.00
Mcintosh MCD 410 changer No Reserve	$417.00	KENWOOD ,KRC-2005 "shaft style" Am/Fm, cassette player	$41.00
Nakamichi TD-800	$330.00	Honda AM/FM CD Player Car Stereo w/ Anti Theft Nice	$41.00
Eclipse CD8454 2 months old	$330.00	Like New ALPINE TDM-7582 No Reserve! Current Model!	$41.00
SUPER Nakamichi "CD 700 MOBILE TUNER/CD PLAYER" NR	$328.91	SONY XR - C900 CASS. PLAYER HI-END XES	$41.00
ALPINE 7400 am fm cassette car stereo 2 KNOB RADIO	$227.50	SONY CDX-CA810X CD Receiver	$41.00
ALPINE 7256, "shaft style" Am/Fm Cassette Player	$212.50	Nakamichi Mobile Reciever/Cassette Deck TD-35	$40.99
Pioneer KEH-P8800R (European) & CDX-P650 6 CD Changer	$202.50	kenwood krc-235 cassette player	$40.99
Audiobahn A3351 Car Stereo AM FM CD MP3 Remote NIB NR	$202.50	KENWOOD KRC 335 CASSETTE PLAYER W/REMOTE WORKS GOOD	$40.00
Alpine Deck,FM-AM,CD,MXMP3,XM Ready/Remote	$182.50	Alpine TDA-7564 Cassette Receiver w/ CD changer Control	$40.00
Car Stereo NAKAMICHI TD-500 In Dash	$165.00	Dual XD5110 In Dash CD Player Car Electronics Players	$37.00
New HONDA In dash CD Player CD-R MP3 Compatbile	$158.99	Denon DCR-7290 AM/FM/Cassette/CD Ctrl Car Stereo	$36.07
Kenwood Excelon in-dash cassette & cd changer combo	$156.05	NEW in box JVC in dash cassette receiver ks-fx430	$36.00
Eclipse In-Dash CD Head End Unit	$155.00	ROCKFORD FOSGATE RFX9000 AM/FM RADIO CD MP3 CAR STEREO	$36.00
Model CD5442 W/Remote		Sony CDX-4000x Xplod Tape Deck CD Ready	$36.00
Pioneer In-Dash Car Stereo and Pioneer 12-CD Changer	$150.00		

Car Electronics ▸ Car Speakers & Speaker Systems

The average sales price in this subcategory is $39.28.

	HIGH		AVG
Memphis Car Audio 15" 4 Ohm Subwoofers,1 PAIR, lot	$300.00	Jeep Grand Cherokee Dash Tweeters / Dash Speakers	$49.99
2 Sub kicker comp. 12" and Amplifier of 1500 W	$290.00	[4 of these sold for $49.99 each]	
Dynaudio MW170 MW-170 speakers 8" no reserve	$260.00	Jeep Tweeters / Jeep Speakers / Grand Cherokee	$49.99
ALTEC 604-E2 15 inch Duplex Loudspeaker	$255.00	[4 of these sold for $49.99 each]	
Dynaudio MW180 MW-180 9" speakers brand new	$252.51	Better than Jeep Infinity Dash Speakers / Dash Tweeters	$49.99
Dynaudio MD140/2 3" Midrange PAIR excellent NR	$229.55	[2 of these sold for $49.99 each]	
Memphis Car Audio 15" 4 Ohm Subwoofers,1 PAIR, lot	$205.00	ALPINE Type R 10 Inch Car Subwoofer SWR-1042D BASS	$46.00
Audio Development MM4 Midrange Speakers Sinfoni	$205.00	[2 of these sold for $46.00 each]	
FOSGATE 301M AMP AND * NEW	$177.50	CAR/TRUCK SPEAKERS CARPETED GREAT SOUND	$41.05
ALPINE 12 TYPE R SYSTEM		KICKER R19 RESOLUTION TWEETER	$41.00
INFINITY BASSLINK X 10" POWERED SUBWOOFER	$170.51	9603i INFINITY Reference 6x9 3-way Speakers 6x9 300W	$39.00
IMAGE DYNAMICS COMPRESSION HORNS	$168.00	NEW LANZAR VX830 3-WAY 8" CAR SPEAKERS 400W $35	$38.00
Two 12" RockFord Fosgate Sub Woofers. No Reserve Price	$167.50	POLK MOMO 12" SUBWOOFER MM2124 400WATT RMS 800WATT MAX	$36.67
DYNAUDIO MW170 8-INCH WOOFERS	$164.40	INFINITY SOUND SYSTEM 7 SPEAKERS-REFERENCE STANDARD	$36.00
WITH GRILLS NO RESERVE !!		SONY XPLOD XS-T250 Car Tweeter Speakers...Brand New!	$36.00
Dynaudio MD140/2 MD-140/2	$164.09	AURA PRO SERIES BASS SHAKER (PAIR)	$35.00
mid-range speakers no reserve		ALPINE TYPE E SWE-1242 12 750w COMPONENT SUBWOOFER SUB	$34.01
2002 CORVETTE Z06 FOUR BOSE	$156.00	Bose factory speakers from Acura Legend 91-95	$33.00
SPEAKERS 2 W BUILT IN AMP		LOT OF CAR SPEAKERS INFINITY KENWOOD POLK AUDIO 6x9 5x7	$31.00

DVD Players & Recorders ▸ Portable DVD Player

The average sales price in this subcategory is $79.49.

	HIGH		AVG
Mobile DVD/CD Player, Car, Mp301, Micro Pace	$319.95	Insignia 7" 16:9 Widescreen Portable DVD Player	$86.00
Sanyo CDV-7004 Mobile Video Entertainment System Roof .	$310.00	$230 MEMOREX PORTABLE DVD PLAYER 7 IN. TFT LCD MONITOR!	$85.05
AV-297 7" TFT LCD CAR IN-DASH MONITOR W & DVD PLAYER	$266.00	Insignia 7" 16:9 Widescreen Portable DVD Player	$82.10
CyberHome CH-LDV 700B Portable DVD Player	$244.71	Magnavox MPD820 Portable 8" Widescreen DVD Player 820	$82.00
[3 of these sold in a multiple item ("Dutch") auction for $81.57 each]		Venturer 7" Portable Dual Screen DVD System PVS1977	$82.00
BRAND NEW PORTABLE 5-IN-1 7" DVD+VCD+CD+MP3+MP4 PLAYER	$239.00	Insignia Model I-PD720 7-inch Portable DVD PlAYER	$82.00
10.2" Portable DVD Player For Less!!!!	$232.50	Insignia 7" 16:9 Widescreen Portable DVD Player	$81.00
New Kawasaki PVS1965 Mobile Dvd System w/(2)6.5"Screens	$230.00	[2 of these sold for $81.00 each]	
7"LCD TABLET PORTABLE DVD/MP4 Player WIRELESS TV/FM NEW	$225.00	INSIGNIA WIDE SCREEN 7" PORTABLE DVD PLAYER	$81.00
Audiovox 5.6" LCD monitor and portable dvd player / MP3	$224.95	All Region VGA Progressive DivX 5 MEPG4 Xvid DVD Player	$79.99
Kawasaki PVS1965 Mobile Dvd System * * NEW * * L@@k*	$224.50	CyberHome Portable DVD Player with 7" color screen.	$78.00
7" Dual Screen Portable DVD Player w/Car Kit	$222.50	Liquid Video Portable DVD Player (LIDM830)	$77.58
New Mustek Portable 10" Widescreen DVD - Music Player	$222.00	NEW Initial Technology IDM-1731 Portable DVD Player LCD	$77.00
Portable DVD *Mintek* Widescreen Monitor 10.2' MDP-1020	$202.50	PROTRON PORTABLE 7" DVD PLAYER W/REMOTE NEW!!	$77.00
Portable DVD Player 8" TV 400+ games remote 2-joysticks	$202.50	LIQUIDVIDEO 8" PORTABLE DVD PLAYER(LIDM830)	$76.00
8.4" DVD+MP3 6in1 PORTABLE PLAYER+JOYSTICK+TV+300 GAMES	$199.99	Initial IDM-1731 Portable DVD Player	$76.00

DVD Players & Recorders ▸ Single-Disc DVD Player

The average sales price in this subcategory is $38.38.

	HIGH		AVG
PIONEER ELITE DV-47Ai/B DVD/CD/SACD PLAYER 47A	$369.99	AKAI ZONE FREE DVD PLAYER! NEW!!!	$42.00
Pioneer Elite DV-45A Region Free DVD Player	$350.00	Philips DVP642 Ultra Slim Code Free DVD Player	$42.00
PIONEER ELITE DV-47Ai/B DVD/CD/SACD PLAYER 47A	$349.99	Denon 2800 dvd player	$42.00
Cambridge Audio Azur 540 D DVD player, MINT IN BOX	$289.00	DAEWOO REGION 1 2 3456 CODEFREE PAL/NTSC/ANY TV 110/220	$42.00
Momitsu V880n Networked DVD Player Region Free!!!	$275.00	Yamaha Natural Sound 5-Disk cdc705 RS, FREE DVD & TUNER	$41.00
Dish Network DVR 921 Receiver PVR DishDVR * NO RESERVE*	$247.50	DAEWOO DVD PLAYER, MULTISYSTEM, MULTIREGION, NR	$40.95
Lanzar DVD player, monitor & tv tuner	$119.50	New Sealed Philips DVP642DVD player (plays all formats)	$40.00
Home Theater system 5.1ChW/Dvd Player-Karaoke (NEW !)	$99.99	Multi-System DVD Player - APEX AD-600A	$40.00
REGION FREE Multisystem Prog Scan DVD Player PAL NTSC	$99.00	Philips DVP642 Ultra Slim Code Free DVD Player	$40.00
RJ TECH 1800 VCD CDG DIVX	$99.00	DAEWOO REGION 1 2 3456 CODEFREE PAL/NTSC/ANY TV 110/220	$39.98
KARAOKE SINGING MACHINE		AUDIOPHASE XM SKYBOX SATELLITE RADIO AP-XM101 MP3 FM	$39.00
RJTECH RJ-1800 DVX DVD VCD CDG DIVX MP3 KARAOKE PLAYER	$99.00	[2 of these sold for $39.00 each]	
[2 of these sold for $99.00 each]		Region Code Free PAL/NTSC PROGRESSIVE SCAN DVD PLAYER	$38.00
Samsung HD-841 UNLOCKED REGION FREE	$91.00	[4 of these sold for $38.00 each]	
NO HDCP DVD CD NR!		ALL MULTI REGION CODE ZONE FREE DVD PLAYER NTSC/PAL NEW	$36.00
APEX 1500 DVD PLAYER MULTI-REGION CODE FREE UPGRADED	$90.00	Daewoo Code Region Free DVD 5900	$35.99
AXION 7 INCH WIDE SCREEN	$86.00	Region Code Free PAL/NTSC PROGRESSIVE SCAN DVD PLAYER	$35.00
PORTABLE DVD PLAYER MP3 *NIB*		ALL MULTI REGION CODE ZONE FREE DVD PLAYER NTSC/PAL NEW	$35.00
RJ Tech RJ-1500DVXII Divx DVD Player - Play avi mpg dvd	$84.01	[4 of these sold for $35.00 each]	

Digital Video Recorders, PVR ▸ Replay TV

The average sales price in this subcategory is $134.29.

	HIGH		AVG
SONY DHG-HDD500 Digital Video Recorder NEW	$710.01	ReplayTV Panasonic Showstopper PV-HS3000 60Hrs + Extras	$143.81
DISH NETWORK 942 HD/ DVR RECEIVER	$610.00	ReplayTV 5040 DVR Commercial-skip,tons o features Mint!	$142.50
DISH NETWORK 942 HD/ DVR RECEIVER	$600.00	NEW! ReplayTV 5040 DVR Commercial Advance/Skip! BIN!	$139.49
Universal Remote MX3000 No Reserve!!!	$566.50	ReplayTV 5060 Commercial advance, download to you PC	$137.50
ReplayTV 5516 w/ Lifetime Service + $100 Rebate - NEW!	$471.00	ReplayTV 5504 - Upgraded to 200 Hrs Brand New - RTV5504	$137.50
Universal Remote MX3000 No Reserve!!!	$457.00	SONIC/BLUE RTV4508 ReplayTv Better than Tivo NO RESERVE	$136.20

Universal Remote MX3000 No Reserve!!!	$432.00	ReplayTV 2000 Replay TV TIVO PVR Upgraded w/ Remote	$134.49
Replaytv 5040 with Lifetime / 200 hours of recording	$431.00	** New Replaytv 4508 Replay TV Like 5040 Not TIVO ***	$133.99
MINT ReplayTV 5000 NEW quiet 160 gb disk just installed	$429.00	ReplayTV 5040 DVR Commercial Skip *LIKE NEW*	$132.50
ReplayTV 4532 320-hour PVR -like Tivo, Lifetime paid	$421.05	ReplayTV RTV2020 Lifetime Subscription Paid, No fees!	$132.50
ReplayTV 5516 w/ Lifetime Service + $100 Rebate - NEW!	$420.00	Replay TV 5508 80HR Digital Video Recorder DVR w/box-LN	$129.99
ReplayTV 5080 DVR Like 5040 *LIFETIME ACTIVATION*	$400.00	Panasonic Showstopper ReplayTV PVR w/ LIFETIME SUBSCRIP	$129.99
Refurbished ReplayTV 5160 + Lifetime Subscription	$396.11	Panasonic PV-HS2000 Showstopper ReplayTV	$128.51
DISH NETWORK HIGH DEFINITION RECEIVER 921 LIKE NEW	$390.00	Replay TV unit	$127.19
ReplayTV 4505 lifetime sub, never used, like 5040 5080	$380.00	Replay TV 5040 Digital Video Recorder	$125.99

40-Hour TiVo Series2 Brand New in Box

Bidding has ended for this item
If you are a winner, Sign In for your status.

List an item like this or buy a similar item below.

Winning bid:	**US $82.00**	(Reserve met)
Ended:	Feb-02-06 07:04:45 PST	
Start time:	Jan-26-06 07:04:45 PST	
History:	8 bids (US $40.00 starting bid)	
Winning bidder:	rschwartz2005 (88 ★)	
Item location:	Jericho, New York United States	
Ships to:	United States	
Shipping costs:	US $25.00 -- UPS Ground	

↓ Larger Picture

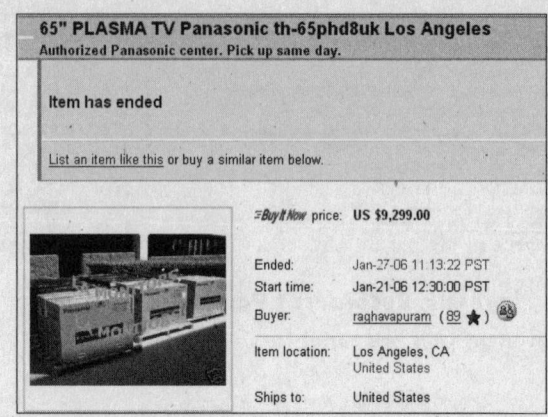

65" PLASMA TV Panasonic th-65phd8uk Los Angeles
Authorized Panasonic center. Pick up same day.

Item has ended

List an item like this or buy a similar item below.

≡Buy It Now price:	**US $9,299.00**	
Ended:	Jan-27-06 11:13:22 PST	
Start time:	Jan-21-06 12:30:00 PST	
Buyer:	raghavapuram (89 ★)	
Item location:	Los Angeles, CA United States	
Ships to:	United States	

Digital Video Recorders, PVR ▶ TiVo

The average sales price in this subcategory is $67.16.

	HIGH		AVG
NEW DIRECTV HDTV Receiver 250GB TiVo Recorder HR10-250	$495.00	HDR212 Philips Series 1 Tivo Excellent Condition	$71.00
NEW DIRECTV HDTV Receiver 250GB TiVo Recorder HR10-250	$485.00	RCA DVD Recorder VCD/MP3/CD DRC8005N PLAYPER SEALed+WTY	$71.00
ReplayTV 5516 w/ Lifetime Service + $100 Rebate - NEW!	$471.00	[2 of these sold for $71.00 each]	
NEW DIRECTV HDTV Receiver 250GB TiVo Recorder HR10-250	$455.05	TIVO SERIES 2 DIGITAL VIDEO RECORDER DVR "BRAND NEW"	$71.00
NEW DIRECTV HDTV Receiver	$430.00	PHILIPS TIVO RECORDER AND HARDWARE	$69.02
250GB TiVo Recorder HR10-250		Tivo Series 1 30 hours by Phillips	$69.00
Pioneer Elite DVR-57H Tivo DVD Recorder Hard Drive	$427.84	Sony Tivo DVR svr-2000 with remote	$68.00
ReplayTV 5516 w/ Lifetime Service + $100 Rebate - NEW!	$420.00	TIVO DVR Phillips Personal TV Receiver PTV 300 +Remote	$67.99
Pioneer Elite DVR-57H Tivo DVD Recorder Hard Drive	$395.00	RCA Scenium DRS7000 DVR and DVD Player – Used	$66.00
REPLAY TV 5040 WITH LIFETIME ACTIVATION	$370.00	TIVO TCD140060 Series 2 60 hour Digital Video Recorder	$66.00
Dish Network 921 DVR HD Satellite Receiver	$350.00	TIVO TurboNET Ethernet Adapter	$64.51
Philips HDR312 TIVO 198+ Hour Unit w/ LIFETIME SERVICE	$319.99	Philips TiVo series 1 14 hours DVR	$64.00
Pioneer DVR-531H-s DVD Recorder Player New 80 GB NIB	$289.99	Sony TiVo Model SVR-2000 Series 1 (with Remote)	$63.50
TiVo DVR with 298 hours + lifetime life time service NR	$280.00	Hughes DirecTV DVR Tivo SD-DVR40	$61.00
Sony SVR-2000 140 HRS LIFETIME TiVo subscription ($299!	$275.00	TiVo series 1 Ethernet network card	$56.00
Sony SVR-2000 DVR with Lifetime TiVo subscription	$269.99	Sony Tivo SVR-2000 SVR2000 With Remote	$56.00

Gadgets & Other Electronics ▶ Calculators

The average sales price in this subcategory is $22.09.

	HIGH		AVG
ICAL-100R Inventory Calculator	$275.00	** HP/Hewlett-Packard 12C Financial Calculator w/Case	$31.00
5 TEXAS INSTRUMENTS TI 83 PLUS CALCULATORS	$182.50	HP 10B BUSINESS CALCULATOR + OWNERS MANUAL. NEW!!	$29.00
Hewlett Packard HP-41CV calculator & accessories	$177.50	Sharp EL-620 Voice Synthesized Talking Calculator NICE	$25.49
3 TEXAS INSTRUMENTS TI 83 PLUS SILVER ED. CALCULATORS	$162.50	Sharp EL-1197P III Desk Top Printing Calculator NIB	$25.01
Texas Instruments TI-89 TITANIUM Graphing Calculator	$125.00	CalcInd Real Estate Master IIx Finance Calculator NEW	$25.00
Texas Instruments TI-89 TITANIUM Graphing Calculator	$124.50	TRW BUSINESS CARD HOLDER 3 GEM	$24.99
TI BA II Plus Professional Financial Calculator	$124.32	STONES & CALCULATOR	
[4 of these sold in a multiple item ("Dutch") auction for $31.08 each]		Texas Instruments TI-15 Explorer Calculator - NEW!	$24.45
NEW!! TI-89 TITANIUM ADVANCED GRAPHING CALCULATOR!!	$119.99	Sharp EL-2192R II Desk Top Printing Calculator NIB	$24.35
[2 of these sold for $119.99 each]		LOT OF 6 CALCULATORS GRAPHIC	$23.02
Texas Instruments TI-89 TITANIUM Graphing Calculator	$119.50	FINANCIAL SCIENTIFIC BASIC	
TI-84 PLUS-Silver edition-Graphing Calculator NEW!	$109.00	New WIreless Calculator Keypad Never used Targus Sealed	$23.00
NEW!! TI-84 PLUS SILVER EDITION GRAPHING CALCULATOR!!	$106.00	Sharp EL-1197P III Desk Top Printing Calculator NIB	$22.51
NEW!! TI-84 PLUS SILVER EDITION GRAPHING CALCULATOR!!	$97.00	CASIO FX-9750G PLUS Power Graphic Calculator Like TI-84	$22.50
NEW!! TI-84 PLUS SILVER EDITION GRAPHING CALCULATOR!!	$92.99	Sharp EL-1197P III Desk Top Printing Calculator NIB	$21.55
NEW!! TI-84 PLUS GRAPHING CALCULATOR!!	$86.00	CALCULATOR CANON P200-DH Heavy Duty desktop printing	$21.50
TEXAS INSTRUMENTS TI 84 PLUS SILVER ED. CALCULATOR	$86.00	Sharp EL-2192R II Desk Top Printing Calculator NIB	$20.91

Gadgets & Other Electronics ▶ Home Automation

The average sales price in this subcategory is $80.15.

	HIGH		AVG
M & S INTERCOM SYSTEM AND SUPPLIES	$1,049.95	Nutone Standard Intercom Master Unit - White (IM3204WH)	$131.00
NUTONE IMA4406WH INTERCOM + COMPONENTS–NEW!	$989.95	Working Nutone intercom speaker music Vintage? Radio NR	$109.50
NUTONE IMA4406WH INTERCOM +3 ROOM STATIONS, ETC.	$879.95	4 GE HOME OFFICE WIRELESS INTERCOMS NEW BABY MONITOR	$102.50
Nutone Intercom IMA3303WH KIT 9 ROOMS ,COMPLETE SYSTEM	$749.00	8 UNIT COMLITE SYSTEM 2000 HOME OFFICE INTERCOM SYSTEM	$99.99
Nutone Intercom IMA3303WH KIT 9 ROOMS ,COMPLETE SYSTEM	$715.00	4ch wireless intercom home/office(4 units)New	$94.00
NUTONE IMA4406 INTERCOM + ROUGH IN—NEW	$639.77	Lot 10 WIRELESS INTERCOM Unit Radio Shack 3-Channel NR!	$89.00
[2 of these sold for $639.77 each]		NUTONE INTERCOM MASTER UNIT IM-3103 NOS	$87.69
NuTone IMA4406 Intercom/CD Master w/Rough-In NEW!!!!	$620.00	Video Door Answering System NEW NR	$82.00
NuTone IMA4406 Intercom/CD Master w/Rough-In NEW!!!!	$599.99	4 GE HOME OFFICE WIRELESS	$81.00
NUTONE IMA3303WH INTERCOM AND COMPONENTS	$589.77	INTERCOMS NEW BABY MONITOR	
NUTONE IMA3303WH INTERCOM AND COMPONENTS	$579.99	Wireless Intercom Transmits Up To 1,000 Feet	$80.00
NU TONE NUTONE IMA4406 IMA 4406 INTERCOM	$575.00	4 GE HOME OFFICE WIRELESS INTERCOMS NEW BABY MONITOR	$77.01
A HOME RADIO-INTERCOM SYSTEM/ NUTONE	$427.00	4 GE HOME OFFICE WIRELESS INTERCOMS NEW BABY MONITOR	$77.00
M&S MUSIC & INTERCOM SYSTEM MC602-NEW IN BOX	$395.00	Nady Motorcycle Intercom/FM Radio PMC-3X "CHECK IT OUT"	$76.99
VD-520 New Generation Video Door Phone & Intercom	$389.00	Westinghouse Wireless Home Intercom System	$73.01
IM-4006 Nu Tone Intercom Master Station Nutone	$355.00	INTERCOMS, NOVI WIRELESS INTERCOMS	$73.00

Gadgets & Other Electronics ▶ Surveillance

The average sales price in this subcategory is $64.33.

	HIGH		AVG
PC Based Coaxial Security Surveillance System - camera	$406.00	Color Sony CCD CCTV Security Camera 480tv	$79.00
NEW JV-TV2070 12" QUAD OBSERVATION	$299.00	[4 of these sold for $79.00 each]	
SYSTEM W/4 CCD CAM		Color Security CCTV Car Wash Camera New!	$78.00
4 camera video security system, night vision, boxed	$285.00	Three Hundred Foot Cable with RJ-11e Connectors EXXIS	$71.00
4 camera video security system, night vision, boxed	$217.51	5 BURLE CAMERAS TC652EA +AUTO IRIS LENS TESTED	$70.00
Sony XC-003P CCD Color Video Camera Module	$209.50	Sanyo B/W CCD Camera M/N VCB-3524	$69.00
Sony XC-003P CCD Color Video Camera Module w/ lens	$209.50	MOTION SENSOR PIR SECURITY SPY CAMERA CCTV	$69.00
Panasonic WV-BP334 570 lines	$203.52	Lot of 17 Sony Acuilty Pulnix CCD Video Camera Modules	$67.00
Low Lux B/W Camera W/Lens		SSC12 SAMSUNG Weather resistant Camera with 2-Way Audio	$65.00
4 camera video security system, night vision, boxed	$203.50	SURVEILLANCE CAMERA MOTION DETECT A/V ALERT NIGHTVISION	$64.99
7" LCD Color TV Monitor 2.4 GHZ Wireless Camera New	$199.95	Panasonic B/W camera, Low Lux, 570 lines, WV-BP334 CCTV	$59.95
Lorex Time Lapse VCR#SG7964 N.I.B. LOW start NO res	$191.50	Color Weatherproof Bullet Security Camera Spy	$59.00
1280 Hour Daewoo Time Lapse cctv VCR recorder	$179.00	4 BURLE CAMERAS TC652EA MANUAL IRIS LENS TESTED	$57.75
[5 of these sold for $179.00 each]		NAVCO~4800~1/3~Color~DSP~Mini~Camera~L@@K	$57.51
1280 Hour Daewoo Time Lapse cctv VCR recorder	$178.49	Panasonic B/W camera, Low Lux, 570 lines, WV-BP334 CCTV	$56.00
1280 Hour Daewoo Time Lapse cctv VCR recorder	$167.50	COLOR WATERPROOF BULLET CCTV SECURITY CAMERA	$55.00
4 camera video security system, night vision, boxed	$159.50	PEEPHOLE REVERSER DOOR VIEWER NEW SALE SPY	$52.77
Samsung SSC-12 12" Monitor Surveillance Camera System	$157.50	Sony XC-75 CCD Video Camera Module w/ lens	$52.00

GPS Devices ▶ Accessories & Cables

The average sales price in this subcategory is $23.23.

	HIGH		AVG
Garmin eTrex Legend 8 MB GPS with PC Cable	$127.50	Garmin MCX9-180 Antenna iQue, Quest, StreetPilot 2610	$27.99
Garmin eTrex Legend 8 MB GPS with PC Cable	$121.88	Garmin MCX9-90 GPS Ant iQue, Quest, StreetPilot 2610	$27.99
GENUINE Garmin GA 29 GPS	$70.00	New Garmin GA 26C low-profile GPS Antenna	$26.00
Antenna GA29 176C 276C 182		GARMIN REPLACEMENT ANTENNA	$26.00
[4 of these sold for $70.00 each]		GPS111+/STP 010-10299-01!!!!	
GENUINE Garmin GA 29 low profile remote marine antenna	$66.55	Garmin iQue 3600 HotSync cradle w/USB connection	$24.99
GENUINE Garmin GA 29 GPS Antenna GA29 176C 276C 182	$65.00	Gilsson Amplified GPS Antenna with 90 degree MCX connec	$24.99
Garmin 010-10052-05 Low-Profile Remote Antenna GA 27C	$64.93	8 BATTERIES & FAST CHARGER FOR GARMIN RINO 110 120 GPS	$24.99
Garmin GA 27C Low Profile GPS Antenna *NEW*	$63.77	8 BATTERIES & FAST CHARGER FOR GARMIN RINO 110 120 GPS	$23.99
Garmin 010-10052-05 Low-Profile Remote Antenna GA 27C	$56.13	GARMIN ETREX LEGEND GPS BATTERIES & CHARGER 110-220V	$19.99
Garmin GA 27C Low Profile GPS Antenna, Rail Mount, etc.	$51.00	Garmin Motorcycle Power Audio Cable GPSMAP 276 C	$19.95
Garmin GPS to HP iPAQ Data	$44.95	GPS antenna Garmin 2,3,5,StreetPilot III,176,V,182,276C	$19.50
Connectivity Cable w/ POWER		GPS antenna Garmin eMap 60 76C 12xl iQue 3200 3600 M5	$19.50
NEW–GARMIN MAPSOURCE	$39.75	GPS antenna Garmin 60 76CS 76 2610 2620 iQue Rino PDA	$19.50
U.S.A. POINTS OF INTEREST		USB to RS232 converter adapter for Garmin GPS Cable	$19.50
Garmin AC/PC USA Adapter, 18 Pin 010-10276-00 New	$39.00	Garmin Rino 110 120 130 Cig Power PC Data Cable NEW	$18.50

GPS Devices ▶ Automotive GPS Devices

The average sales price in this subcategory is $240.44.

	HIGH		AVG
Pioneer AVIC-N2 In-Dash DVD & Navigation System	$1,156.00	Navman PiN 100 portable GPS Pocket PC Navigation PDA	$265.00
ECLIPSE AVN2454, AVN 2454 GPS navigation, DVD MP3	$1,100.00	Alpine GPS NVA-N751A\AS and Monitor TME-M006SA	$260.58
ECLIPSE AVN2454, in dash GPS navigation, DVD, MP3	$1,059.23	Alpine (NVEN852A) DVD Vehicle Navigation System	$257.00
Hands Free / Eyes Free Vehicle GPS Navigation	$771.00	NIB NavMate 2.0 GPS Vehicle Navigation System	$255.00
NEW! TOM TOM TOMTOM GO 700	$745.00	NEW NavMate 2.0 GPS Vehicle Navigation System	$250.00
AUTO VOICE GPS +EVERYTHING!		Navman Pin w/256mb SD & Car charger	$250.00

NEW! TOM TOM TOMTOM GO 700	$740.52	HP iPAQ Navigation System GPS Bluetooth Pocket PC NIB	$247.50
AUTO VOICE GPS +EVERYTHING!		Garmin Streetpilot GPS Street Pilot w/ Motorcycle Mount	$242.69
NEW! TOM TOM TOMTOM GO 700	$723.00	Pharos GPS with Dell Axim X5	$232.50
AUTO VOICE GPS +EVERYTHING!		HORIZON NAVMATE 2.0 NAV SYSTEM	$230.00
Jeep/Chrysler/Dodge RB1 GPS Navigation Radio!	$707.00	W/9 MAP CD'S "BRAND NEW"	
TomTom GO 700 Automotive GPS - Bluetooth Capability	$700.00	Horizon Navmate 2.0 GPS Navigation System w/ 9 Map CDs	$227.50
Kenwood GPS DVD In Dash With Motorized Screen	$699.99	Cobra 1000 DXL GPS/Navigation/Mcnally Streetfinder Sftw	$225.99
TomTom GO 700 Automotive GPS - Bluetooth Capability	$686.00	NEW NAVMATE HORIZON 2.0 CAR	$223.50
TomTom GO 700 Vehicle GPS Navigation (GO700) car truck	$685.01	AUTO GPS NAVIGATION SYSTEM!	
Horizon NAVMATE GPS Car Navigation System NEW +WARRANTY	$221.00	Brand New Medion PPC150 GPS PDA Pocket PC	$222.50
TOMTOM GO 700 GPS NAVIGATOR U.S. Version(LIKE NEW)	$655.00	NEW NAVMATE HORIZON 2.0 CAR AUTO	$222.50
tom tom go 700	$650.00	GPS NAVIGATION SYSTEM!	$265.00

GPS Devices ▸ Recreational GPS Devices

The average sales price in this subcategory is $61.50.

	HIGH		AVG
DELPHI NA10000-11B1 CAR	$350.00	Holux GR 231 bluetooth & USB GPS receiver 4 laptop PDA	$73.00
GPS NAVIGATION SYSTEM		Holux GR 231 bluetooth & USB GPS receiver 4 laptop PDA	$71.56
NEW Sky Golf SG2 GPS Rangefinder Digital Caddie	$335.00	Holux GR 231 bluetooth & USB GPS receiver 4 laptop PDA	$71.00
Delphi NA10000 Mobile Navigation In-Car GPS Receiver	$305.00	[2 of these sold for $71.00 each]	
Toshiba E755 Loaded GPS Wi-Fi ATI Presentation Pack!	$300.00	BC-307 CF GPS Receiver + Antenna & PCMCIA BC307 PDA	$69.95
HP iPaq Navigation System	$285.00	[2 of these sold for $69.95 each]	
Magellan eXplorist 500	$275.00	Holux XTrac Bluetooth GPS Receiver for Palm/Pocket PC	$67.00
TomTom NAVIGATOR 5	$265.00	Eagle Explorer GPS	$66.00
Wireless GPS Bluetooth for PDA		Holux GR 231 bluetooth & USB GPS receiver 4 laptop PDA	$66.00
TomTom NAVIGATOR 5	$262.00	[2 of these sold for $66.00 each]	
Wireless GPS Bluetooth for PDA		NEW Holux GM 213 USB PS2 GPS receiver laptop PDA	$66.00
TomTom NAVIGATOR 5	$257.50	Holux GR 231 bluetooth & USB GPS receiver 4 laptop PDA	$65.50
Wireless GPS Bluetooth for PDA		SDIO GPS Receiver iPAQ PDA SiRF WAAS Navigation	$64.23
iPAQ 4155 PDA With Belkin Bluetooth GPS	$255.00	Microsoft Streets & Trips 2005 + Holux USB GPS locator	$63.00
TomTom NAVIGATOR 5	$250.00	Auidovox GMR-GPS hand held Gps & Fm Transceiver LOOK!!	$62.03
Wireless GPS Bluetooth for PDA		NEW Holux GM 213 USB PS2 GPS receiver laptop PDA	$61.05
Standard Horizon GPS 150	$212.50	Microsoft Streets & Trips 2005 + Holux USB GPS locator	$61.00
Pharos SD SDIO GPS /OSTIA Navigation Software	$202.50	GPS GARMIN MAPSOURCE 128MB 128 MB DATA CARD	$60.99
FURUNO GP 31 NAVIGATOR GPS with antenna	$202.50	Microsoft Streets & Trips 2005 + Holux USB GPS locator	$60.95
Raytheon Raystar 198 GPS,Chart plotter,Marine GPS	$200.00	Holux GM 270 CF compact flash GPS receiver 4 laptop PDA	$60.00

GPS Devices ▸ Maps, Software

The average sales price in this subcategory is $75.39.

	HIGH		AVG
GARMIN 295 COLOR AVIATION GPS	$577.00	GPS GARMIN MAPSOURCE US ROADS AND RECREATION	$64.00
Garmin G chart Offshore Green Bay, Ws. #GUS275SS WGS84	$355.00	Brand New Magellan MapSend WorldWide Basemap	$64.00
GARMIN Quest Portable GPS L@@K NO RESERVE!!!	$324.01	Mapsource Bluechart Data Card MUS012R Tampa- New Orlean	$63.01
Garmin Street Pilot Color Map+ metro guide v3 map+ more	$287.00	Mapsource Bluechart Data Card MUS011R SW Florida	$63.00
GARMIN MAPSOURCE CITY SELECT EUROPE v 7 010-10359-00	$286.00	Mapsource Bluechart Data Card MUS011R SW Florida	$62.03
GARMIN MAPSOURCE CITY SELECT EUROPE v 7 010-10359-00	$280.51	Garmin MetroGuide North America ver. 6	$61.88
Garmin Quest Navigation	$275.00	Mapsource Rec Lakes FHS Garmin Brand Data Card GFH020R	$61.01
Garmin MapSource BlueChart Atlantic v7 CD-ROM New	$178.50	Garmin Mapsource Rec Lakes w/fishing HotSpots East V5cd	$61.00
Garmin Offshore G-Chart New York to Block Island	$175.00	Garmin Recreational Lakes and Fishing Hot Spots CD East	$61.00
AM FM & XM Radio CD Cassette (Factory GM 2005 Stereo)	$162.50	Garmin MapSource U.S. Topo CD-ROM	$61.00
Mapsource Bluechart Data Card MUS505L Gulf of Mexico-La	$158.52	NEW Garmin Mapsource BlueChart Deluxe Package	$61.00
~New Garmin Mapsource City Europe City Select v.7 New~~	$157.50	Mapsource Bluechart Data Card MUS010R SE Florida	$61.00
Mapsource Bluechart Garmin Data Card MUS504L Chesapeake	$152.52	Garmin MapSource MetroGuide CANADA v4	$61.00
garmin g chart (gps chip) for offshore gulf islands	$152.50	Mapsource Bluechart Data Card MUS003R Cape Cod	$61.00
GARMIN GPS 90 AVIATION HANDHELD NAVIGATION - W@W	$143.75	GARMIN MapSource MetroGuide U.S.A. Map CD-ROM Ver. 5.0	$60.01

Home Audio ▸ Accessories & Cables

The average sales price in this subcategory is $24.81.

	HIGH		AVG
Maxell Metal Vertex 3-Audio Cassette Tapes New Sealed	$202.50	Art-Glass (Sunflower) Perfume Bottle	$35.00
SONY METAL MASTER CASSETTE 90 MINUTES (10)	$194.49	2 NIP TDK SA-XG Cassette Tapes	$33.00
New 17 Maxell Capsule Metal Audio Cassette 90 Nakamichi	$192.50	CART TAPE FIDELIPAC BROADCAST	$16.00
SONY METAL MASTER CASSETTE 90 (10)	$174.49	100 SEC.MODEL 300 NEW!	
16 Maxell UDI 10.5 REEL TO REEL Tape Pioneer Teac Akai	$152.50	4 BASF LP35 SEALED REEL TO REEL TAPE Pioneer Teac $9NR	$31.00
RARE Teac CRC-90 CRC90 Case of (10) Metal Reel Tapes	$123.50	10? 3M Scotch #226 Master Recording Tape Reel-to-Reel	$30.05
6 Ampex 444 411 406 REEL TO REEL TAPE PIONEER TEAC 10.5	$122.50	New Nakamichi Metal ZX-C90 Audio Cassette RX CR Dragon	$29.00
6 Ampex 10.5" Grand Master 456 Reel to Reel CLEAN 1PASS	$119.50	10 Panasonic DV tapes Mini Dv video for SONY JVC CANON	$27.99
TDK MA-XG 90 Metal TYPE IV Cassettes for Nakamichi	$100.00	20 Sony Mini discs MD 80 min FREE MD case minidiscs MD	$27.99
[5 of these sold in a multiple item ("Dutch") auction for $20.00 each]		TDK SA-X 90 Cassette Tapes Qty 10 - IECII/TypeII - NEW!	$26.00
TEAC Reel Type Cassette Tapes - SIX COLORS LOT	$99.99	TDK MA-R C60 AND D60 VINTAGE CASSETTE TAPES (SEALED)	$24.27
TDK SA100 100-min Cassettes High Bias CD Quality - NIB!	$95.94	(4) AMPEX 7" Reel to Reel Recording Tape NEW!! 1800 ft.	$24.02
[6 of these sold in a multiple item ("Dutch") auction for $15.99 each]		100 DIGITAL AUDIO CDR-DA	$23.50
3M BLACK WATCH-CASE of 14 METAL Cassettes-74 min-SEALED	$81.00	74MIN f/PHILIPS CD-R 74 MIN	
SONY SR90 SR-90 MINUTE METAL TAPE AUDIO CASSETTE 10 PCS	$78.00	Maxell XLI 50-120B Reel To Reel Tape-NIB (NOS)	$20.50
TDK SA-X 90 Cassette Tapes, LOT OF 27 * NEW	$76.00	JVC BUNDLE OF 34 VIDEO CASSETTE 8 MM	$20.50
10 3M Blackwatch 4040 Metal Cassette Tapes (NIB)	$75.00	DENON HD-8 100 VINTAGE CASSETTE TAPES (SEALED)	$20.50

Home Audio ▶ Amplifiers

The average sales price in this subcategory is $178.32.

	HIGH		AVG
MCINTOSH MC7205, MC 7205 AMP	$2,500.00	SAE 2400-L Power Amplifier	$229.75
AMPLIFIER 5 CH.WITH METERS		ONKYO INTEGRA A-809 Integrated Amplifier (like new)	$225.00
MCINTOSH MA6500 – no reserve	$1,826.00	YAMAHA AX 596 INTEGRATED AMP LIKE NEW!	$220.00
Graaf GM50 Integrated valve amplifier	$1,575.00	LUXMAN STEREO INTEGRATED TUBE AMPLIFIER LV-103 AMP	$214.50
Niles ZR-4630 and 6 Solo IR Keypads "like Russound"	$1,500.00	Acoustic Research, AR Model AU Amplifier. Stunning.	$213.61
CARY SLI-80 SIGNITURE INT. TUBE AMP	$1,355.00	Yamaha CA-2010	$207.50
tube amp by manley labs EveAnna design intergated	$1,250.00	SCOTT 200 B STEREOMASTER TUBE INTEGRATED AMP	$200.00
Krell KAV 300i	$1,175.00	Super Rare AKAI Mini Componet Stack System w/ Speakers	$199.99
Primare A30.1 Integrated Amplifier - Like New!	$1,159.00	YAMAHA AMP/PREAMP DSP-A2070 & HARMAN KARDON TU909 NR	$193.50
ROTEL RSX-1065 LIKE NEW!!! With remote and manuals	$1,075.00	DBX BX-3 STEREO POWER AMPLIFIER WITH METER	$191.38
METAXAS AUDIO IKARUS 21 INTEGRATED MINT	$1,000.00	Yamaha HTR 5590 Receiver, Like New with Remote, Warrant	$189.72
FAMOUS CYRUS 8 INTEGRATED AMPLIFIER BOXED NR-MINT BIN	$999.99	Knight-Allied TUBE amp fact wired, ,like Fisher-Scott	$187.50
Silver Series NAD S300 Integrated Amp with Warranty	$949.00	NILES SI-245 SYSTEMS INTEGRATION AMPLIFIER NIOB MANUAL	$182.50
Beautiful Musical Fidelity A3.2 Integrated Amplifier	$895.00	Studer REVOX B150 Amplifier - Stainless front/LCD disp	$180.49
Musical Fidelity X 150 Integrated Amp New IN BOX	$830.00	PILOT 240 TUBE STEREO INTEGRATED AMP	$180.00
Musical Fidelity X 150 Integrated Amp store demo	$810.00	CROWN PS-400 STEREO AMP RACK MOUNT & HANDLES	$179.95

Home Audio ▶ Headphones, Headsets

The average sales price in this subcategory is $25.15.

	HIGH		AVG
Brand New Pioneer SE-DIR800C Wireless Headphones	$258.00	ACOUSTIC RESEARCH AW721 WIRELESS HEADPHONES BRAND NEW	$24.99
Shure E4c: Sound Isolating In Ear Earphones	$167.50	AW-811 900MHz Wireless Indoor/Outdoor Speaker(Open Box)	$24.99
NEW BLUETOOTH IPOD WIRELESS	$164.99	[2 of these sold for $24.99 each]	
HEADPHONES iCOMBI AP11 MP3		RCA Wireless 900Mhz WHP140 HEADPHONES New / FREE SHIP!	$24.98
SONY MDR-V900 STUDIO MONITOR HEADPHONES $129	$135.00	[4 of these sold for $24.98 each]	
SONY MDR-V900 STUDIO MONITOR HEADPHONES $129	$129.00	Wireless Headphones, Noise Suppression Stereo Headset	$24.95
[2 of these sold for $129.00]		[2 of these sold for $24.95 each]	
NEW BLUETOOTH IPOD WIRELESS	$102.50	Sharper Image: 900Mhz Wireless Headphones	$24.95
HEADPHONES iCOMBI AP11 MP3		Wireless Headphones, Noise Suppression Stereo Headset	$24.95
YAMAHA STEREO RECEIVER MODEL RX550	$100.00	New Acoustic Research AW791 900MHz Wireless Headphones	$24.50
SONY MDR-V700DJ HEADPHONES - NEW MDR-V700 DJ NR	$91.99	Wireless Headphones 900 MHz Personal Stereo RCA	$23.00
SONY MDR-V700DJ HEADPHONES - NEW MDR-V700 DJ	$89.95	Sharper Image: 900Mhz Wireless Headphones	$22.55
SONY MDR-V700DJ HEADPHONES - NEW MDR-V700 DJ NR	$86.00	Sharper Image: 900Mhz Wireless Headphones	$22.51
SONY MDR-V700DJ HEADPHONES - NEW MDR-V700 DJ NR	$85.00	SONY MDR-IF140 IR WIRELESS HEADPHONES/WEGA/VEGA XBR/DVD	$22.00
SONY MDR-V700DJ HEADPHONES - NEW MDR-V700 DJ NR	$81.00	Wireless Sterio Headphones. "brand new" NICE !!	$22.00
SONY MDR-V700DJ HEADPHONES - NEW MDR-V700 DJ NR	$79.01	Radio Shack 900Mhz Wireless Stereo Headphones NIB	$21.97
SONY MDR-V700DJ HEADPHONES - NEW MDR-V700 DJ NR	$76.00	Recoton Wireless Stereo Headphones W500	$21.50
NEW BLUETOOTH IPOD WIRELESS HEADPHONES iCOMBI AP11 MP3	$76.00	Sharper Image: 900Mhz Wireless Headphones	$21.50

Home Audio ▶ Receivers

The average sales price in this subcategory is $147.04.

	HIGH		AVG
New Bang & Olufsen Beosound 9000 6CD/Beo4 $4600	$3,650.00	ONKYO INTEGRA DTM-5.3 STEREO 3 ZONE 2 SOURCE RECEIVER	$155.38
[3 of these sold for $3,650.00 each]		Luxman R-115 Digital Synthesized AM/FM Stereo Receiver	$154.50
Bang & Olufsen BeoSound 9000 Stereo Receiver, 6 CD Plyr	$2,550.00	NAD 705 Stereo Receiver – excellent	$154.49
Krell KAV-300r stereo receiver	$1,876.00	CARVER "The Receiver" Magnetic Field 150 watts per !!	$152.50
NILES ZR-4630 MULTIZONE RECEIVER / MINT / NR	$1,125.00	70'S NAD 3080 INTERGRATED AMPLIFIER AMP STEREO NICE NR	$152.50
BANG & OLUFSEN BEOCENTER 9500+ STEREO SYSTEM	$950.00	Sansui Eight AM/FM Stereo Receiver - Sansui Model Eight	$150.00
McIntosh Mac 1500 Tube Receiver. A Classic!	$787.99	VECTOR RESEARCH VR-7000 1980 PRISTINE !! L@@K@ NR	$147.50
McIntosh MAC 1900 Solid State Audiophile Receiver	$775.00	Carver HR-732 A / V AM-FM Stereo Receiver	$145.00
MCINTOSH 1900 RECEIVER(PERFECT-MUSEUM QUALITY)!!!L@@K!!	$760.99	ONKYO TX-8511 STEREO, SUBWOOFER,	$143.05
MARANTZ SR 8400 AV SURROUND RECEIVER	$655.00	SPEAKERS & STANDS, NR!	
[2 of these sold for $655.00 each]		Carver HR-732 A / V AM-FM Stereo Receiver Very Clean!!	$140.50
Mcintosh Mac1500 Tube receiver. A true Classic!	$587.77	ADCOM GTP-450 STEREO RECEIVER	$139.99
MCINTOSH 4100 STEREO RECEIVER	$560.57	LUXMAN STEREO RECEIVER RX-101	$137.50
CONCEPT 16.5 MONSTER RECEIVER 165WPC BEAUTY	$534.99	D-940 PROTON AM/FM HOME RECIEVER	$132.50
Bang & Olufsen Beomaster 2000 complete Audio System	$500.00	SCHOLTZ TUNER NEW BOX	
NAD T743 A/V Receiver	$455.00	VINTAGE REALISTIC STA-2000D STEREO RECEIVER(DOLBY)	$129.00
B&K AVR 202 Stereo Receiver-Like New MSRP $2500	$437.98	Bang & Olufsen Beomaster 5500 Receiver w/Control Panel	$127.51

Home Audio ▶ Speakers & Subwoofers

The average sales price in this subcategory is $174.24.

	HIGH		AVG
Martin Logan - Descent Sub , Support Down Syndrome	$1,857.00	New Sonance In-Wall iPod iPort Docking System iPod	$199.00
CARVER SUNFIRE TRUE SIGNATURE EQ SUBWOOFER	$1,529.00	BRAND NEW YAMAHA YST-SW315 HOME THEATER SUBWOOFER	$184.95
McIntosh PS112 Subwoofer, New, No Reserve!	$1,350.00	VELODYNE VRP-12 12" VRP-SERIES POWERED SUBWOOFER	$182.50
New Definitive Technology SuperCube Reference Sub	$1,300.00	POLK PSW 450 POWERFUL SUBWOLFER 8 MONTHS OUT OF STORE	$180.00
New Definitive Technology SuperCube Reference Sub	$1,275.76	BRAND NEW YAMAHA YST-SW315 HOME THEATER SUBWOOFER	$179.95
Sunfire Subwoofer *PERFECT COND* TRUE SIGNATURE *NR*	$1,226.00	YAMAHA YST-SW315 10" HOME THEATER SUBWOOFER YSTSW315	$178.00
New Pair Definitive Technology Mythos One $1,800	$1,125.00	B&W AS1 POWERED SUBWOOFER, NEW OPEN BOX!	$176.70
New! M&K Miller & Kreisel MX-150 MK II THX Subwoofer	$1,025.00	YAMAHA YST-SW315 10" HOME THEATER SUBWOOFER YSTSW315	$175.00
Sunfire Subwoofer *BRAND NEW* MK IV **NO RESERVE**	$866.98	[2 of these sold for $175.00 each]	

Earthquake Supernova MkV-15BV remote control	$799.00	Klipsch KSW12 Subwoofer Gently Used	$174.88
Sunfire True Subwoofer Signature 2700-watt amplifier	$785.56	YAMAHA YST-SW315 10" HOME THEATER SUBWOOFER YSTSW315	$170.00
Klipsch RSW 12 Subwoofer	$780.00	YAMAHA YST-SW315 10" 270 WATT SUBWOOFER NIB	$169.99
BOSE ACCOUSTIMASS 10 SERIES II HOMETHEATER SYSTEM	$682.05	BOSE Acoustimass 5 Ser III Subwoofer+Freestyle Speakers	$168.29
Klipsch RSW-12 Reference 2400	$669.99	Infinity PS 10 10" 250-watt Powered Subwoofer Speaker	$163.16
Watt Subwoofer W/ Z Cable		M&K - Miller & Kreisel VX-4 12" Subwoofer	$162.50
Velodyne SPL-1000 Series II 10" Sub Subwoofer Black NEW	$664.00	VELODYNE DUAL 8 INCH HOME SUBWOOFER EXCELLENT CONDITION	$162.50

Home Theater in a Box ▶ With DVD Player

The average sales price in this subcategory is $107.01.

	HIGH		AVG
Kenwood Fineline Networked 7.1 Home Theater System	$1,050.00	NEW JVC DVD/MP3 HOME THEATER SYSTEM DOLBY PROLOG II DTS	$119.51
Cambridge SoundWorks Newton Theater MC300.5	$999.00	Insignia1,000W 6.1-Ch. Home Theater System w/DVD/CD/MP3	$119.50
Nakamichi SoundSpace 8.5 8 1/2 Home Theater System	$699.95	home theater system 5 dvd player philips mx 3950d	$118.00
Bose 321 Home Theater System DVD/CD/FM/AM	$658.23	Samsung Home Theater w/ 5 Disc Progressive Scan DVD	$113.50
NAKAMICHI 8 1/2 , 8.5 HOME THEATER -BETTER THAN BOSE!!!	$610.00	JSI Home Theater System with Progressive Scan DVD 300W	$112.50
COMPLETE ENTERTAINMENT SYSTEM-Klipsch, Onkyo, Yamaha!!!	$580.00	Philips Home Cinema Receiver Package MX1055D3799	$109.95
Theater Innovations TI-5150t Surround sound Home Audio	$515.50	YAMAHA RX-V630 6.1 Channel 450 Watt Receiver	$107.50
Philips MX6000i Streamium entertainment system Phillips	$485.00	Insignia1,000W 6.1-Ch. Home Theater System w/DVD/CD/MP3	$106.00
Nakamichi Soundspace 8 1/2 Home Theater System[used]	$465.00	Koss KS5192 Home Theater System w/Progressive Scan DVD	$105.00
Pioneer HTD-540DV-600 Watt Home Theater System	$399.99	Motorola DCP501 5.1 500W Home Theater DVD System -NEW-	$103.50
Denon M51 Home Theater. Display Unit. Perfect.	$399.00	Insignia1,000W 6.1-Ch. Home Theater System w/DVD/CD/MP3	$103.50
PANASONIC HOME THEATER SYSTEM SC-HT930 W/DVD MP3 NIB!!	$369.00	Audiovox VD1400HT DVD/VCR Home Theater System NICE!	$102.50
Philips Streamium MX6000i Home Theater 5DVD Speakers NR	$340.00	Toshiba DVD / VCR Player, Home Theater System SD-V55HT	$102.50
Yamaha Digital Home Theater YHT-760 with XM Tuner NEW	$325.00	Insignia1,000W 6.1-Ch. Home Theater System w/DVD/CD/MP3	$101.00
YAMAHA DVXS150B HOME THEATER CINEMA DVXS150	$299.99	Koss KS5192 Home Theater System w/DVD 6.1 Dolby 1000Wat	$100.99

Home Theater in a Box ▶ Without DVD Player

The average sales price in this subcategory is $240.64.

	HIGH		AVG
BLACK BOSE LYFESTYLE 48 SYSTEM NEW FACTORY SEALED BOX	$2,699.99	Bose Acoustimass Module & Subwoofer System	$256.00
BLACK BOSE LYFESTYLE 48 SYSTEM NEW FACTORY SEALED BOX	$2,650.00	Sony Home Theater in a Box 840W Total Power	$255.50
BLACK BOSE LYFESTYLE 38 SYSTEM NEW FACTORY SEALED BOX	$2,030.00	BOSE ACOUSTIMASS 5 SERIES IV II LIKE NEW, POWERED SPKR	$255.00
BOSE LIFESTYLE 50 HOME THEATER SYSTEM 5.1	$2,001.50	BOSE Aoustimass 6 Speaker System	$255.00
BOSE LIFESTYLE 50II EXCELLENT CONDITION	$1,800.00	6-Piece Home Theater Speaker System for Dolby 5.1 Bose	$255.00
[2 of these sold for $1,800.00 each]		Bose subwoofer, receiver, control + cabes- NO RESERVE!!	$255.00
NEW BOSE LIFESTYLE 50 HOME THEATER SYSTEM *NEW*	$1,600.00	*Like New* JBL SCS300.7 Surround Sound System	$249.99
BOSE LIFESTYLE 50 SYSTEM BLACK..... 48..38..28	$1,500.00	Bose Acoustimass 10 Series III Subwoofer NR	$247.50
Bose Lifestyle 25 Series II Home Theater Surround Sound	$1,351.00	NEW 2005 YAMAHA YHT-160 HOME THEATER REPLACES YHT-150	$235.00
LIFESTYLE 30 BOSE HOME THEATER SYSTEM	$1,250.00	[4 of these sold for $235.00 each]	
Bose Lifestyle 30 Home Theatre System II	$1,182.67	Pioneer Htd-540dv 600w Home Theater System 5.1 DTS	$232.50
BOSE LIFESTYLE 50- HOME THEATER SYSTEM 5.1	$1,180.00	BOSE LIFESTYLE CD MUSIC CENTER & RC5 REMOTE	$230.00
Bose Lifestyle 25 Series II Home Theater Surround Sound	$1,156.00	Yamaha Home Theater System YHT-160 650W 5.1 CH NIB!	$223.50
BOSE LIFESTYLE 25 SERIES II W/ REAR SPEAKER STANDS!!!	$1,150.00	*BRAND NEW IN BOX* SONY HT-DDW750 HOME THEATER SYSTEM	$222.50
Bose Lifestyle 30 Series II Home Audio System complete	$1,100.10	BOSE LIFE STYLE 18 SUBWOOFER ONLY WORKS PERFECT	$212.50
NEW Bose Lifestyle 50 Home Theater System LOOK! NICE	$1,100.00	SONY HOME THEATER SYSTEM-NO RESERVE! INCLUDES SUBWOOFER	$210.00

Home Theater Projectors ▶ Projector Screens & Material

The average sales price in this subcategory is $130.63.

	HIGH		AVG
Stewart Luxus Deluxe FireHawk 16:9 100" Screen	$1,036.00	NEW ELECTRIC MOTORIZED PROJECTOR SCREEN 96" x 96" NR!	$172.50
DALITE 45"X80" CINEMA CONTOUR	$845.00	1.3 Gain 100" Electric Projector Screen,Matte White 4:3	$160.99
HC CINEMA VISION PROTRIM		NEW DALITE 52"X 92" MODEL B MANUAL SCREEN HIGH CONTRAST	$158.00
epson PowerLite S3 Projector free sh+two-year warranty	$642.50	NEW DALITE 52"X 92" MODEL B MANUAL SCREEN HIGH CONTRAST	$157.50
Epson PowerLite Multimedia Projector & 76" Screen	$525.00	120" Pull Down Projector Screen, Matte White 4:3	$151.00
NEW HUGE 120" X 120" ELECTRIC	$524.00	DA-LITE 96x96 MANUAL WALL PROJECTOR SCREEN DALITE NEW	$151.00
SCREEN WITH REMOTE KIT		DA-LITE 72x96 HIGH CONTRAST PROJECTOR SCREEN DALITE NEW	$150.10
NEW 52" X 92" FIXED CINEMA	$450.00	[2 of these sold for $150.10 each]	
SCREEN HIGH CONTRAST+VELVET		DA-LITE 72x96 PROJECTOR SCREEN 1.5 GAIN DALITE NEW	$150.10
NEW 116" X 87" ELECTRIC SCREEN WITH FREE REMOTE KIT	$449.00	New! InFocus 50" Tabletop Table Top Projector Screen	$149.99
NEW 116" X 65" ELECTRIC SCREEN	$422.00	[2 of these sold for $149.99 each]	
W/FREE REMOTE KIT HDTV		NEW 59" X 106" HOME THEATRE MANUAL VIDEO SCREEN	$139.00
NEW 84"X 84" ELECTRIC SCREEN WITH FREE REMOTE KIT	$399.00	[3 of these sold for $139.00 each]	
49"X 87" ELECTRIC SCREEN	$349.00	NEW DALITE 96"X 96" MODEL B MANUAL SCREEN HIGH GAIN 2.5	$132.00
w/REMOTE KIT FREE SHIP HDTV		NEW 96" X 96" MANUAL PROJECTOR SCREEN MATTE WHITE	$128.00
[2 of these sold for $349.00]		[2 of these sold for $128.00 each]	
NEW ELECTRIC MOTORIZED PROJECTOR SCREEN 96" x 96" nrl	$305.00	NEW 96" X 96" MANUAL PROJECTOR SCREEN MATTE WHITE	$125.00
NEW ELECTRIC MOTORIZED PROJECTOR	$305.00	[4 of these sold for $125.00 each]	
SCREEN 120" 16:9 NR!		NEW ELITE 96"X 96" TRIPOD SCREEN W/KEYSTONE ELIMINATOR!	$125.00
1.3 Gain 100" Electric Projector Screen,Matte White 4:3	$299.95	[2 of these sold for $125.00 each]	
NEW 55"X 73" ELECTRIC SCREEN WITH FREE REMOTE KIT	$299.00	NEW DALITE 72"X 96" MODEL B MANUAL SCREEN HIGH GAIN 2.5	$123.00
[2 of these sold for $299.00]		NEW 72" X 96" MANUAL PROJECTOR SCREEN MATTE WHITE	$122.00
The Screen Works 13x17, E-Z Fold Truss Screen Frame	$273.00	[2 of these sold for $122.00 each]	

Home Theater Projectors ▶ Projectors

The average sales price in this subcategory is $788.10.

	HIGH		AVG
Vidikron Vision One CRT Projector	$7,650.00	BRAND NEW Gateway 210 DLP Projector HDTV, XGA	$800.00
Yamaha DPX-1100 DLP home theater projector.	$7,000.00	NEW BenQ PB6110 DLP 1600 LUMENS+FREE LAMP+ SCREEN	$799.00
Sim2 HT300+ high end DLP projector - like new low hours	$6,500.00	[2 of these sold for $799.00 each]	
Sharp XV-Z12000 Projector - NEW USA Model	$5,000.00	BenQ PB6110 DLP HDTV 1500 LUMEN 3YR WTY+84" SCREEN+LAMP	$799.00
[2 of these sold for $5,000.00 each]		IBM C400 DLP PROJECTOR BRAND NEW W/FREE BONUS PACKAGE	$799.00
Acer PD525 2600 Lumen XGA DLP Projector	$1,250.00	INFOCUS SCREENPLAY 4805 DLP PROJECTOR 16:9 WITH WTY.	$795.00
Yamaha DPX-1100 DLP home theater projector.	$3,250.00	[2 of these sold for $795.00 each]	
Sanyo PLC-XT16 Multimedia Projector	$3,200.00	Toshiba TDP 90U 2200 Lumens DLP Projector	$790.01
[3 of these sold for $3,200.00 each]		Like new HP MP3220 projector	$767.00
Ampro 4600HD 9"LC HDTV projector	$3,000.00	NEC XG-135 CRT Projector	$766.00
NEW BenQ PE8700+ DLP HOME THEATRE 16:9+ 2500:1 CONTRAST	$2,295.00	Toshiba TLP-671 LCD Projector w/ Document Camera	$765.50
Crystalio VPS 2300 – brandnew unit	$2,249.00	BenQ PB6100 DLP HDTV 1500 LUMEN 1YR WTY+52"X 69" SCREEN	$745.00
NEW! MITSUBISHI XD450U PROJECTOR DLP XGA 2600 LUMENS	$2,245.00	Hewlett Packard XB31(L1511A) DLP XGA Digital Projector	$736.05
INFOCUS SCREENPLAY 5000 PROJECTOR+SCREEN+$100 REBATE	$1,695.00	Like New HP VP6111 DLP Digital Projector 1500 lumens	$700.00
Faroudja DVP1000 Video Processor New No Reserve	$1,675.99	NEC XG 110 LC	$660.00
HP Digital HDTV Home Theater DLP Multimedia Projector	$1,599.99	HP VP6111 DIGITAL PROJECTOR	$650.00
Runco VX-1 DLP Projector. Mint. Mount. Motoriz Screen	$1,500.00	Hewlett Packard HP Digital Home Theater Projector XB31	$630.00

MP3 Players & Accessories ▶ MP3 Accessories ▶ Apple iPod Accessories

The average sales price in this subcategory is $12.40.

	HIGH		AVG
Logitech for iPod Wireless Headphones Bluetooth MP3	$125.00	Belkin Digital Camera Link for iPod	$15.00
[2 of these sold for $125.00 each]		Battery for *2200mAh Apple iPod 1, 2 Generation	$14.25
iPod /mp3 player / music enthusiast ultimate accessory	$113.00	Official iPod USB Power Adaptor m9837LL/a Fits all iPod	$13.85
Apple iPod 10GB MP3 Player	$112.50	New Nyko iPod Stereo Link Dock Connector to RCA	$12.99
New Louis Vuitton LV Monogram MP3 IPOD Case	$79.00	New NYKO iPod Universal Car Mount 3G 4G mini Photo	$12.99
Altec Lansing inMotion iM3 Portable Audio MaxxBass NR	$75.97	Apple iPod Power Adapter + Firewire Cable USB	$12.52
ALTEC LANSING inMotion iM3 iPOD Portable Speakers	$73.99	Apple iPod Power Adapter + Firewire Cable USB	$12.50
Altec Lansing INMOTION IMplus Ipod Portable Speakers g	$59.00	850mAh BATTERY for IPOD 3rd GENERATION 3G 3Gen +TOOLS	$11.95
20gb Apple Ipod Hard drive as is Harddrive ipod parts	$56.00	ALTEC LANSING IM3 IN MOTION PORTABLE AUDIO SYSTEM ipod	$11.49
Sony ECM-MS907 digital stereo microphone NEW NR	$51.00	850mAh BATTERY for IPOD 3 3rd GENERATION 3G 3Gen +TOOLS	$10.95
ALTEC LANSING INMOTION PORTABLE AUDIO SYSTEM SPEAKERS	$51.00	NEW iPod/Mini/MP3 Compact Portable Stereo Speakers Dock	$9.99
ALTEC LANSING INMOTION PORTABLE AUDIO SYSTEM SPEAKERS	$47.00	[2 of these sold for $9.99 each]	
@ iPOD &Mini &MP3 UFO SPEAKER ON STAGE DOCKING STATION	$46.01	APPLE IPOD 60GB PHOTO MINI AC HOME I POD CHARGER WHITE	$9.99
@ iPOD &Mini &MP3 UFO SPEAKER ON STAGE DOCKING STATION	$45.00	APPLE IPOD 4GB 3G 4G MINI WALL TRAVEL I POD CHARGER WH	$9.99
NEW 2 Year AppleCare Protection Plan for iPod	$40.00	APPLE IPOD 15GB 20GB 40GB AC HOME I POD CHARGER WHITE	$9.99
Dock for all iPod Photo Mini - Video Out + 3 Cables	$40.00	WIRELESS 2 SET MICROPHONE SYSTEM KARAOKE 2 MIC NEW 984	$9.95

MP3 Players & Accessories ▶ MP3 Accessories ▶ Universal Accessories

The average sales price in this subcategory is $10.92.

	HIGH		AVG
Dell Pocket DJ - 5GB	$184.40	IPOD ACCESSORIES (88065)	$14.27
Creative Labs Nomad Jukebox Zen Xtra 30GB	$150.00	Monster Cable RadioPlay Car Wireless FM MP3 Transmiter	$13.48
Dell Digital Jukebox 20 GB Generation 1 Package!	$150.00	Creative Nomad Jukebox mp3 Player CASE ADAPTER CABLE	$11.50
Nyko Universal Car Mount for the iPod Brand New	$65.00	FOR CREATIVE ZEN MICRO CAR+TRAVEL CHARGER+Y AUDIO CABLE	$10.99
Dell DJ Pocket DJ DJ20 DJ30 etc complete car kit, NEW!!	$61.00	[4 of these sold for $10.99 each]	
iRiver iHP-120 Accessories Brand New!!!!!	$55.00	Stereo Y Cable+Car+Travel Charger 4 CREATIVE ZEN MICRO	$10.99
Dell DJ Gen 1 Car Kit Charger Loading Dock Everything	$46.00	[2 of these sold for $10.99 each]	
Dell DJ Belkin? FM Transmitter Auto Kit	$41.00	For Creative Zen Micro Travel+Car Charger+Audio Y Cable	$10.99
Creative Zen Micro Wired Remote and Extra Battery	$39.99	BELKIN CAR CHARGER FOR DELL DJ NEW F8D0001-DL	$10.50
Samsung YH-820 Accessories lot	$39.00	Car Audio Cassette Adaptor for Apple iPod Mini CD MD	$10.00
Monster Cable RadioPlay Car	$35.00	FOR CREATIVE ZEN MICRO CAR+TRAVEL CHARGER+Y AUDIO CABLE	$9.99
Wireless FM MP3 Transmiter		Stereo Y Cable+Car+Travel Charger 4 CREATIVE ZEN MICRO	$9.99
Dell DJ 20 (Gen 2)/DJ 30-Docking Station w/ Accessories	$33.01	Belkin DELL DJ II Digital Jukebox?Car Cup Holder K8799	$9.51
Archos Multimedia Jukebox Player accesories	$31.82	FOR CREATIVE ZEN (MICRO) Car Charger+Travel Charger	$8.99
Creative Nomad Jukebox 3 Car Kit NIB	$23.00	Monster MP3 Music Connect cable MPC MCON-2m	$6.01
Belkin Auto Kit Cassette Adapter	$22.51	Retracting USB Cable+Car Charger for CREATIVE ZEN MICRO	$5.99
Case iPOD MP3 COMBO		For CREATIVE ZEN (MICRO) Car Charger+USB Retract Cable	$5.99

MP3 Players ▶ Apple iPod

The average sales price in this subcategory is $129.10.

	HIGH		AVG
IPOD'S 60 GIG AND 40 GIG COLOR WITH CASES	$920.00	Apple 10GB 3rd Gen iPod (c950318)	$132.50
IPOD'S 60 GIG AND 40 GIG COLOR WITH CASES	$910.00	10gb 2nd generation apple ipod w/extras	$132.50
IPOD'S 60 GIG AND 40 GIG COLOR WITH CASES	$545.00	**BARELY USED APPLE IPOD-10 GB** DIRT CHEAP	$131.50
IPOD'S 4GIG AND 40 GIG COLOR WITH CASES	$280.00	Apple iPod 5GB MP3 Player - 5 GB + Free iSkin Case	$130.75
IPOD fr Apple/HP $NO RESERVE$ BNIB + EXTRAS! 5000 SONGS	$255.00	Apple 10GB 3rd Gen. iPod Great Condition NO RESERVE!	$130.02
Apple iPOD 10GB MP3 Player 3rd Gen 10 GB SEALED+WARANTY	$250.00	Apple iPod 10 GB	$130.00

IPOD fr Apple/HP $NO RESERVE$ BNIB + EXTRAS! 5000 SONGS	$246.50
IPOD fr Apple/HP $NO RESERVE$ BNIB + EXTRAS! 5000 SONGS	$232.50
Apple iPOD 10GB MP3 Player 3rd Gen 10 GB SEALED+WARANTY	$222.50
[2 of these sold for $222.50 each]	
IPOD fr Apple/HP $NO RESERVE$ BNIB + EXTRAS! 5000 SONGS	$220.05
B/NEW Apple iPod Mini 6GB (6GB) MP3 **GREEN*** 2nd Gen	$215.00
B/NEW Apple iPod Mini 6GB (6GB) MP3 **GREEN*** 2nd Gen	$213.01
Apple iPod 10GB MP3 Player 3rd Gen sealed +1yr warranty	$212.50
Apple iPOD 10GB MP3 Player 3rd Gen 10 GB SEALED+WARANTY	$212.50
Apple iPOD 10GB MP3 Player 3rd Gen 10 GB SEALED+WARANTY	$212.00

Apple 10 GB iPod (M8976LL/A)	$129.99
Apple 3rd Gen iPod 10 Gig Very Clean	$128.50
iPod - 10 GB + Sony Travel Speakers - Great Cond - NR	$128.50
iPod - 1st Generation - 10GB	$127.50
10GB Apple iPod MP3 Player w/	$127.50
Phones & Charger USB Fire	
Apple iPod 10GB MP3 Player 2003 M8976LL/A	$127.50
Like-New, Collectors 5GB 1st Generation Apple iPod #142	$127.50
Apple 10GB 3rd Gen iPod (c950331)	$127.50
Apple iPod 10GB 3rd Gen, Works Great! Fast Ship—NR!	$127.50

---

50 X 4GB APPLE IPOD NANO BLACK OR WHITE

Bidding has ended for this item

If you are a winner, Sign In for your status.

List an item like this or buy a similar item below.

Winning bid:	**GBP 7,169.99 (Reserve met)**
	(Approximately US $12,748.96)
Ended:	Jan-20-06 12:30:27 PST
Start time:	Jan-17-06 12:30:27 PST
History:	42 bids (GBP 1.00 starting bid)
Winning bidder:	sfag5 (private) Not a registered user
Item location:	Leeds, West Yorkshire United Kingdom

MP3 Players ▶ Apple iPod ▶ 20GB

The average sales price in this subcategory is $177.34.

	HIGH		AVG
Apple 20GB U2 Special Edition Photo iPod MP3 Player NEW	$340.00	Apple iPod 20GB 4th Generation Portable MP3 Players wOW	$180.00
Apple iPod 20G & MORE -- FREE Shipping w/BIN	$330.00	Apple Ipod 20GB 4 Gen MP3 Player Great Con. nt Photo	$180.00
APPLE IPOD 20GB MP3 PLAYER 4TH GEN 20 GB FACTORY SEALED	$320.65	APPLE iPod 20GB MP3 Player for Mac and Windows	$178.50
::B/New iPod U2 COLOR :: FREE FEDEX OVERNITE shipping.:	$317.00	Apple 20GB iPod+HP MP3 Player With Click Wheel	$178.50
IPOD U2 EDITION 20GB USED MP3 PLAYER 4000 SONGS!!!!	$315.00	Samsung YH-925GS 20GB MP3 Player +Photo/Voice Recording	$178.50
BRAND NEW 20 GB iPOD	$310.00	RIO KARMA 20GB MP3/WMA/OGG PLAYER (LIKE IPOD 20 GB)	$177.50
Apple COLOR IPOD U2 20 GB NIB NR! 5,000 songs MP3	$305.00	New Apple iPod Mini 4GB MP3 Player 4 M9802LL/A BLUE	$177.50
Apple iPod 20GB Photo Color Brand New & Ready to Ship	$300.00	Apple iPod 20GB Digital Music Player MP3 4th Generation	$177.50
New Factory Sealed Apple iPod 30gb 30 gb Photo + HP	$300.00	New Apple iPod Mini 4GB MP3 Player 4 M9802LL/A BLUE	$176.50
Apple iPod 20GB Photo Color Brand New & Ready To Ship	$300.00	Ipod 20 GB , mp3 Player	$175.50
Apple iPod 20GB Photo Color Brand New & Ready to Ship	$290.00	APPLE 20GB iPOD (M9282LLA)	$175.03
NEW 20 GB Color Apple iPod - Never used	$288.00	Apple 20 GB iPod - Model No. A1059	$174.02
U2 iPod 20 GB; BRAND NEW, SEALED IN ORIGINAL BOX	$285.00	3rd Generation Apple 20GB iPod with Accessories	$172.61
New Apple iPod 20GB COLOR MP3 Player 20 MA079LL/A	$285.00	Ipod *like new*	$172.50
Apple iPod 20GB Color Photo Brand New In Box low ship	$283.43	Very Nice 20GB 3g Apple iPod w/ USB 2.0 for PC & Mac 99	$170.38

MP3 Players ▶ Apple iPod ▶ Mini

The average sales price in this subcategory is $165.42.

	HIGH		AVG
SEALED APPLE IPOD MINI 4GB PORTABLE MP3 PLAYER BLUE WTY	$305.00	Apple IPOD MINI BLUE 4GB BRAND NEW SEALED!! MINT!!!	$167.50
APPLE iPod 20GB MP3 PLAYER 4TH GENERATION 20 GB *NIB*	$242.50	SEALED APPLE IPOD MINI 4GB PORTABLE MP3 PLAYER BLUE WTY	$167.50
[2 of these sold for $242.50 each]		Apple ipod Mini 4gb silver mint in box	$167.01
APPLE iPod 20GB MP3 PLAYER 4TH GENERATION 20 GB *NIB*	$231.50	Apple iPod Mini BLUE 4GB Brand New & Ready To Ship	$167.00
APPLE iPOD 40GB PORTABLE 4TH GEN GENERATION MP3 PLAYER	$230.00	Apple Ipod Mini 4GB Blue	$166.72
NEW APPLE iPOD MINI 4GB BLUE WITH iTRIP & CASE	$228.51	SEALED APPLE IPOD MINI 4GB	$166.51
APPLE iPod 20GB MP3 PORTABLE PC/MAC PLAYER *IN BOX*	$222.52	PORTABLE MP3 PLAYER BLUE WTY	
APPLE iPod 20GB MP3 Player 4th Generation	$222.50	Brand New - Never Opened! Blue Apple Ipod Mini	$166.49
APPLE iPOD 40GB PORTABLE 4TH GENERATION MP3 PLAYER	$217.50	Apple IPod Mini 4Gig - Blue (NO RESERVE)	$166.45
NEW iPOD mini BLUE/AQUA, 6GB, 1500 songs,	$215.00	SEALED APPLE IPOD MINI 4GB PORTABLE MP3 PLAYER PINK WTY	$166.00
Brand New Apple iPod Mini BLUE 4GB 4 GB G i-pod Player	$212.55	Brand New Sealed In Box IPOD Mini SILVER 1000 SongS	$165.78
APPLE iPOD 40GB MP3 PLAYER 3RD GENERATION 3 GEN 40 GB *	$208.00	Apple Ipod 4GB Mini Blue MP3 + Warranty M9436LL/A	$165.50
APPLE iPod 20GB MP3 PLAYER 4TH GENERATION 20 GB *NIB*	$205.02	SEALED APPLE IPOD MINI 4GB PORTABLE MP3 PLAYER BLUE WTY	$165.50
APPLE iPOD 40GB PORTABLE 4TH GEN GENERATION MP3 PLAYER	$202.68	Blue 4GB Apple iPod Mini, Brand New w/ Warranty	$165.50
APPLE iPod Mini 4GB MP3 Player - BLUE Sealed w/Warranty	$202.51	SEALED Apple Ipod Mini MP3 4gb Blue WTY+Accessories!!!	$165.50
BRAND NEW!!! Apple Ipod Mini 4GB MP3 Player - BLUE	$202.50	Apple 4GB iPod Mini Blue MP3 Player !1 YEAR WARRANTY!	$165.50

MP3 Players ▸ Creative

The average sales price in this subcategory is $124.53.

	HIGH		AVG
Archos AV400 20 GB Video Player / Recorder MP3	$356.00	Creative Labs Zen Micro-With Songs-Beats iPod's Sound!!	$130.00
Creative Labs Zen Portable	$346.76	Creative Zen Nano Plus 1GB Purple MP3 Player nr NEW	$129.98
Media Center 20GB BRAND NEW		Creative Zen Nano Plus 1GB Orange MP3 Player nr NEW	$129.98
NEW Creative Zen Portable Media Center MP3 Video Player	$330.00	[2 of these sold for $129.98 each each]	
20GB Creative Zen Portable Media Center (PMC) * MP3	$320.00	Creative Zen Nano Plus 1GB Black MP3 Player nr NEW	$129.98
CREATIVE ZEN 20GB PORTABLE MEDIA CENTER ..NEW	$305.00	Creative Zen Micro 5GB MP3 Player (C 938494)	$128.50
Creative Labs Zen Portable Media Center 20GB BRAND NEW	$304.99	Creative Zen Micro 5 GB	$128.50
Archos AV400 20 GB Video Player / Recorder MP3	$304.00	Creative Zen Nano Plus 1 GB NEW SEALED MP3 WMA USB2	$127.50
Creative Zen Portable Media Center	$304.00	Creative Zen Nano Plus 1GB Orange MP3 Player nr NEW	$127.14
Archos AV400 20 GB Video Player / Recorder MP3	$300.00	Creative 5 GB Zen Micro MP3 Player (Silver)	$125.29
new Creative Zen 20GB Portable Media Center video,music	$299.00	USED Creative Zen Micro 5 GB White MP3 Player	$125.00
Creative Zen Portable Media Center	$299.00	Creative Labs Zen Micro 5 gb gig RED	$122.50
Creative 20 GB Zen Portable Media Center	$295.00	Creative Zen Micro 5GB MP3 Player (c949851)	$122.00
Creative Portable Media Center MINT CONDITION!!!!!	$285.00	Creative 5 GB Zen Micro MP3 Player, Dark Blue	$120.51
Archos AV400 20 GB Video Player / Recorder MP3	$283.09	CREATIVE NOMAD JUKEBOX ZEN NX 30GB NR	$117.50
Creative Zen Digital Media Center MP3 Player Portable	$281.99	CREATIVE ZEN MICRO 4gb MP3 PLAYER w/FM RADIO - LOOK!	$117.50

MP3 Players ▸ iRiver

The average sales price in this subcategory is $126.55.

	HIGH		AVG
New iRiver H340 40GB MP3 Digital Music Player NR!!!	$370.00	IRIVER H10 5GB MP3 FM-TUNER PHOTOS 90 DAY WARRANTY NR	$137.49
(NEW) 40GB iRiver PMP-140 PORTABLE MP3/VIDEO/FM PLAYER!	$355.00	IRIVER H10 5GB MP3 FM-TUNER PHOTOS 90 DAY WARRANTY NR	$137.00
IRiver H340 - 40 gb - color display	$355.00	iRiver 5GB H10 MP3 PLAYER VOICE *FM PLAYER *COLOR LCD	$131.00
40GB iRiver H340 JUKEBOX PHOTO	$350.00	iRiver iFP-799T 1GB iFP-799 MP3/FM Player Line-In Rec	$129.99
MP3/FM PLAYER *COLOR LCD		SEALED iRiver *1GB* iFP-899 PORTABLE MP3/FM PLAYER 899T	$129.95
Iriver PMP-140 Portable Media Player 40 GB New+Bonus	$337.00	[2 of these sold for $129.95 each]	
(NEW) 40GB iRiver PMP-140 PORTABLE MP3/VIDEO/FM PLAYER!	$334.95	iRiver H10 5GB Digital MP3 Player (Remix Blue)	$129.50
NEW Iriver PMP-140 40GB MP3 Video Player +FM PMP140	$330.00	20 GIG MP3 PLAYER W/ SOFTWARE & ALL CABLES	$125.00
Iriver Ifp-890 MP3 Player 256MB Genuine+SEALED	$325.00	iRiver H10 5GB MP3 Player - Triple Platinum	$122.50
Iriver PMP-140 Portable Media Player 40 GB New+Bonus	$316.03	SEALED iRiver *1GB* iFP-899 PORTABLE MP3/FM PLAYER 899T	$120.00
Iriver PMP-140 Portable Media Player 40 GB New+Bonus	$311.00	Iriver IFP-995 MP3 Player 512 mb COLOR ifp995 NEW	$119.99
NEW Iriver PMP-140 40GB MP3 Video Player +FM PMP140	$310.00	Iriver IFP899 MP3 Player "1GB" w/FM ifp-899	$118.50
(NEW) 40GB iRiver PMP-140 PORTABLE MP3/VIDEO/FM PLAYER!	$305.00	iRiver *1GB* MP3 PLAYER IFP899 +VOICE RECORDER+FM RADIO	$116.02
Iriver PMP-140 Portable Media Player 40 GB New+Bonus	$305.00	Iriver IFP899 MP3 Player "1GB" w/FM ifp-899	$116.00
NEW 40GB iRiver PMP-140 PORTABLE MP3/VIDEO/FM PLAYER!	$305.00	Iriver IFP-995 MP3 Player 512mb 512 mb COLOR ifp995 NEW	$114.00
(NEW) 40GB iRiver PMP-140 PORTABLE MP3/VIDEO/FM PLAYER!	$301.00	iRiver *1GB* MP3 PLAYER IFP899 +VOICE RECORDER+FM RADIO	$112.50

PDAs/Handheld PCs ▸ Accessories

The average sales price in this subcategory is $20.85.

	HIGH		AVG
IPC PP 55 Palm Treo 600 Thermal printer Mag Card Reader	$168.10	SOCKET LOW POWER ETHERNET CARD FOR POCKET PC NEW IN PAK	$25.00
FREE SHIPPING! UNLOCKED AUDIOVOX RTM-8000 CF GPRS CARD	$142.50	[2 of these sold for $25.00 each]	
Audiovox Toshiba RTM-8000 RTM-8000D GSM/GPRS CF Card	$119.00	BELKIN Bluetooth Wireless POCKET PC Adapter CF & PCMCIA	$24.95
LifeView FlyCAM CF 1.3MF w/flash digital video camera	$100.00	[2 of these sold for $24.95 each]	
PALM PILOT M130 HANDHELD COLOR PDA + WARRANTY	$85.00	Network LAN Card for NEC MobilePRO 780 790 880 900 900c	$23.95
Sandisk 256mb SD Card with WiFi	$85.00	[3 of these sold for $23.95 each]	
Used Symbol TRG3000 Trigger Handle for SPT/PPT Series	$71.00	New Battery for T Mobile HTC Pocket PC	$21.50
EZShow EZ2TV SVGA/NTSC/PAL Graphics Palmtops Notebooks	$71.00	Siemens 802.11b wireless CF card PDA Compact Flash PPC	$21.03
HP IPAQ BLUETOOTH WIRELESS STEREO HEADPHONES 2200 6300	$68.95	Wireless Wi-Fi card 4 NEC MobilePRO 780 790 880 900	$19.95
Pocket PC	$56.00	[4 of these solkd for $19.95 each]	
Socket SDiO wireless 802.11b card for PDA	$51.00	4in1 Handspring Palm Treo 600 Car Wall Charger Hotsync	$17.95
SAMSUNG I600 NEW ACCESSORIES	$43.00	* 8 ITEM PKG * TOSHIBA e310 e330 e335 e350 e355	$16.99
CF LAN ETHERNET COMPACT FLASH IPAQ DELL HP	$37.99	[2 of these sold for $16.99 each]	
Coach Deluxe Black Leather PDA Case	$34.00	Network 10/100 LAN Card 4 NEC MobilePRO 770 800 780 880	$16.95
Symbol Compact Flash WiFi 802.11b Ipaq Pocket PC PDA CF	$33.50	[3 of these sold for $16.95 each]	

PDAs/Handeld PCs ▸ Handheld Units

The average sales price in this subcategory is $144.78.

	HIGH		AVG
SONY Clie PEG-UX50 PERSONAL ENTERTAINMENT ORGANIZER	$536.00	Toshiba Pocket PC E740 plus 2 extra batteries	$152.49
Axim X50v + GPS – 624MHz, 128MB ROM 64MB RAM, 3.7" VGA	$490.02	Dell Axim X5 400 MHz 64MB with accessories NICE!!	$149.50
NEW HP iPAQ POCKET PC hx4700/hx4705 - 4700/4705 Sealed	$485.00	Brand New Palm PalmOne Tungsten E	$148.75
SPRINT PCS VISION SMART DEVICE PPC-6600 PDA & HEADSET	$475.00	NEW DELL Axim X30 32MB 312 MHz PDA Handheld PC 312MHz	$147.50
Palm 4GB LifeDrive w/ 1GB Card, Aluminum Case, & More!	$455.00	Compaq iPAQ Pocket PC H3955	$145.00
HP iPAQ POCKET PC hx4700/hx4705 - 4700/4705 SEALED	$409.00	TREO 600 PDA COLOR CAMERA PHONE FOR SPRINT + BATTERY	$143.55
NEW Palm LifeDrive Mobile Manager	$403.01	Palm PalmOne Zire 71 LIKE NEW	$142.50
HP iPAQ hx4705 - Pocket PC	$402.50	IPAQ 6315 MILD WATER DAMAGE / WITH ACCESSORIES	$142.50
HP iPAQ Pocket PC H6315 UNLOCKED	$399.00	HP IPAQ H2215 64MB COLOR POCKET PC	$142.50
Siemens SX66 Pocket PC/Cell Phone - New!!!	$396.28	BNIB Brand New Dell Axim X30 w/ 512 SD Card!	$140.00
HP iPAQ Pocket PC Hx4705	$392.77	Dell Axim X5 with 256mb SD card	$139.50
HP iPAQ Pocket PC H6315	$385.00	Samsung i600 Verizon Flip Cell Phone & Pocket PC PDA	$138.00
HP iPAQ Pocket PC hx4705 - 4700 series	$384.00	Toshiba e740 WiFi Pocket PC PDA 64MB	$137.50
PalmOne LifeDrive Mobile Manager	$380.00	HP iPAQ H2215 PDA	$137.50
Brand New HP iPAQ Pocket PC H6315 PDA Phone NR HURRY!!!	$377.00	*NEW* PALM PalmOne Tungsten E - OUTLOOK AND MP3	$134.50

Portable Audio ▶ Accessories, Bags & Cases

The average sales price in this subcategory is $6.33.

	HIGH		AVG
Brand New! Boostaroo Portable Audio Accessory	$24.95	New iPod 4th Silicone Skin Case With ArmBand (Clear)	$6.99
[2 of these sold for $24.95 each]		NEW iPod mini Transparent skin case with ArmBand	$6.99
Brand New! Boostaroo Portable Audio Accessory	$22.51	[2 of these sold for $6.99 each]	
Case Logic RBNW-280 280 DVD CD LEATHER WALLET HOLDER	$21.95	Ipod leather case w/ 360º belt clip NEW! 20GB 40GB	$6.99
Sumdex POM-444PB 96 CD / DVD Wallet Carrying Case NEW	$19.95	20 PIECE MINIDISC MD PSP UMD CASE FROM OZEN AUDIO New!	$6.72
CD, DVD Organizer "Case It"304 NEW $49 Value! Nice Gift	$17.99	Petite Sophistcate Top & Sweater Sz. SM & P	$6.51
Lot of 30 Memorex Mini Disks / Disk (recorded on once)	$16.51	FREE ARMBAND+SWIVEL! BLACK IPOD 4G SILICONE SKIN CASE	$6.50
48 Piece Minidisc Case from oZen Audio Brand New!	$16.50	24 Piece Minidisc MD PSP UMD Case From oZen Audio New!	$6.50
CASE LOGIC - Neoprene Portable DVD Player Shuttle Case	$15.56	Authentic Neiman Marcus floppy disc wallet NIB	$6.49
Sumdex POM-443PB 64 CD / DVD	$15.50	eXo3 4th Gen 40GB iPod case CARIBBEAN BLUE + iShade	$6.25
Wallet Carrying Case Pouch		LOT OF 15 CASE LOGIC 10/20 CAPACITY CD CASES/VISORS	$6.19
CASE LOGIC - Neoprene Portable DVD Player Shuttle Case	$15.49	24 Piece Minidisc MD PSP UMD Case From oZen Audio New!	$6.05
MIB~Automotive TV Case~suspension system for 9" TV	$15.00	BLUE neoprene CD jogging belt MP3 pocket sport case	$6.00
48 Piece Minidisc MD PSP UMD Case From oZen Audio. New	$10.83	[2 of these sold for $6.00 each]	
New iPod 4th Silicone Skin Case With ArmBand (Clear)	$10.50	*White Travel AC Charger Adapter Apple iPod Mini 4G 3G	$6.00
Belkin Portable Music TuneCast II FM Transmitter (F8V30	$10.50	Case Logic CD/DVD case	$5.50
SONY MINIDISC ARMBAND NET MD BRAND NEW!	$10.00	cow cd player case - new in box	$5.50

Portable Audio ▶ Batteries & Charges

The average sales price in this subcategory is $6.23.

	HIGH		AVG
SAFT Lithium Battery AA 3.6V 80pc Lot	$59.95	Energizer Rechargeable Batteries AAA 4-pack	$7.51
50 NEW DURACELL (#123) ULTRA 3 VOLT BATTIRES $1.00	$36.00	20 SONY 3 VOLT CR2016 BATTERIES FREE SHIPPING	$7.50
Brand New Battery 4 SHARP BT-21 BT-22 BT-21/2	$22.74	[2 of these sold for $7.50 each]	
[2 of these sold for $22.74]		NEW BATTERY STICK FOR STREAMLIGHT STINGER	$6.95
New Panasonic PV-BP88 VHS-C Camcorder Battery	$22.74	[10 of these sold for $6.95 each]	
Battery for Panasonic PV-BP50 AG-456 AG-455	$22.74	Hearing Aid Batteries Rayovac #10 , 24 pac	$6.51
Lead Acid Battery 6V 3400 mAh for SHARP BT- 30N VL-L95U	$22.74	Energizer Rechargeable Batteries AA 4-pack	$6.29
2 SOLAR PANEL 12 VOLT BATTERY	$21.90	Hearing Aid Batteries Walgreens #675 , 48 Pac Exp 2007!	$6.25
CHARGER CAR TRUCK BOAT RV		Panasonic AAA Battery Heavy Duty 60 pack	$6.05
Duracell 6 volt 245 / 2CR5 Lithium Batteries 6pc.	$21.06	Energizer Rechargeable Batteries AAA 4-pack	$6.01
New UPS SLA Sealed Lead Acid BATTERY 12 Volt 9Ah	$20.70	12 NEW 9 VOLT ALKALINE BATTERIES - EXP 2010	$6.00
50 NEW DURACELL (#123)	$20.50	[3 of these sold for $6.00 each]	
ULTRA 3 VOLT BATTIRES $1.00		5 BATTERIES - PANASONIC BATTERY CR2330 3V LITHIUM COIN	$5.00
Battery for Panasonic PV-BP50 AG-456 AG-455	$19.99	Energizer Rechargeable Batteries AA 4-pack	$5.00
20 Pack of CR123A Batteries for Camera, Etc.	$19.95	Duracell Ultra CR2 Lithium Camera batteries 8 pcs.	$5.00
hc1221w NEW CSB APC ups battery RBC21 bf500	$19.95	5 New CR 2016 lithium CR2016 battery WOW !!!	$4.99
[3 of these sold for $19.95 each]		[3 of these sold for $4.99 each]	
NEW RBC10 CSB hc1217w APC ups battery RBC 10	$19.95	5 CR 2032 lithium CR2016 battery NEW IN SEAL!	$4.99
[9 of these sold for $19.95 each]		100 AG13 357A A76 LR44 CX44 BATTERY *NEW*	$4.85
Duracell Ultra 123 Lithium Camera batteries 8 pcs.	$17.66	[2 of these sold for $4.85 each]	

Portable Audio ▶ CD Players

The average sales price in this subcategory is $19.31.

	HIGH		AVG
HP APPLE IPOD 40GB 40 GB MP3 PLAYER PE436A LQQK NR	$196.50	NEW ~ CRAIG PERSONAL CD PLAYER / MP3 / STEREO / REMOTE	$22.51
APPLE MINI IPOD BLUE 6GB 6 GB MP3 PLAYER A1051 NR WOW	$182.50	$70 DISNEY CLASSIC DCD6000-C PORTABLE CD PLAYER/RADIO!!	$21.50
APPLE IPOD MINI GREEN MAC PC 4GB MP3 PLAYER IN BOX	$167.50	Wilson/Power Brand Jeep Z Case Titanium Silver cd am/fm	$20.50
APPLE IPOD MINI 4GB PORTABLE MP3 PLAYER BLUE	$167.50	RCA LYRA RD1071A PORTABLE DIGITAL MP3 128MB	$20.49
CREATIVE NOMAD JUKEBOX ZEN XTRA 40GB 40 GB MP3 PLAYER	$142.50	Portable CD Player with Car Kit, Medion 7954 - Silver	$20.00
20GB RCA LYRA RD2780 JUKEBOX VIDEO MP3/WMA PLAYER w/LCD	$137.50	NEW CD Player Shower Radio with LCD Clock-Great Gift!	$19.50
Rio Karma (20 GB) USB 2.0 MP3 Player LQQK 90260461 NR	$137.50	Brand New Curtis CD Player & Radio for the shower	$19.50
BLUE APPLE MINI IPOD 4GB 4 GB MP3 PLAYER LQQK NR WOW	$122.50	Rio Volt SP90 Personal CD CDR CDRW MP3 WMA Player	$18.51
APPLE IPOD 20GB 20 GB MP3 PLAYER SPECIAL EDITION U2 WOW	$113.50	SONY D-NE710 ATRAC 3 PLUS SLIM BODY DESIGN WALKMAN MP3	$18.50
APPLE IPOD 3RD GENERATION 40 GB 40GB MP3 PLAYER NR WOW	$102.51	Craig Portable CD Player with AM/FM Radio & 5" B/W TV	$18.00
BROOKSTONE HUMMER PORTABLE AUDIO SYSTEM CD MP3 COMPATIB	$94.99	Shower/office CD Player and AM/FM clock Radio	$17.50
PINK APPLE IPOD MINI 4GB 4 GB MP3 PLAYER LQQK NR	$91.00	CD PLAYER / REMOTE / CAR KIT / FM RADIO NR	$17.50
SILVER APPLE MINI IPOD 4GB 4 GB MP3 PLAYER NR WOW!!!!!!	$89.00	VENTURER PERSONAL CD PLAYER W/ CAR KIT PORTABLE NR	$17.00
20GB RCA Lyra RD2850 20GB MP3/WMA PLAYER FM TUNER NR **	$87.00	Rio Volt Portable MP3 CD Player SP50 - NO RESERVE	$16.51
BLUE APPLE IPOD MINI 4GB 4 GB MP3 PLAYER LQQK NR WOW	$86.00	GPX HM3034 30 WATT STERO 3 DICS CD CASSETTE	$16.51

Portable Audio ▶ Headphones

The average sales price in this subcategory is $32.10.

	HIGH		AVG
SENNHEISER HD-650 HEADPHONES BRAND NEW NO RESERVE	$285.00	AUDIO TECHNICA ATH-M40FS ATHM40FS ATHM40 ATH-M40	$59.99
Shure E5c Headphones Brand New NIB use w/ Ipod E5 $0.99	$315.00	Etymotic ER6 In Ear isolating headphone monitors.	$51.00
Brand New Shure E5C Earphone	$300.00	Sigtronics Pilot Headset	$51.00
Shure E5 Headphones...AS NEW	$300.00	High end SONY MDR-E888LP MDR-E888SP earphone	$43.00
Shure E5c Headphones Brand New NIB use w/ Ipod E5 $0.99	$297.00	NEW SONY FONTOPIA MDR-EX71SL IPOD HEADPHONES WHITE NR	$41.00
Shure E5c Headphones Brand New NIB use w/ Ipod E5 $0.99	$295.00	Sony HiFi Studio Monitor Headphones MDR-V300	$38.95
Sony MDR-E888 HiFi Earbuds Headphones w/ Case Like NEW	$275.00	Sony MDR-EX71SL High Performance Headphones!	$34.49
BOSE QuietComfort 2 Acoustic NoiseCancelling Headphones	$274.00	SKULLCANDY SKULLCRUSHERS SKULL CRUSHERS HEADPHONES NEW!	$30.99

Bose Quiet Comfort 2 HeadPhones BRAND NEW!!!!!!!!!!!!!	$267.00	Sony MDR-EX71SL/WK Ear Bud Headphones... NEW ...	$30.00
sennheiser hd650 hd 650 hd-650 headphones	$263.88	NEW SKULLCANDY SKULL CRUSHERS HEADPHONE NEW	$30.00
Headroom Little Headphone Amp with Premium Module	$227.50	Sony Studio Monitor Foldable Headphone MDR-V300	$29.99
Sennheiser HD 600 USED Only one Month WOW !	$200.00	NEW! Skullcandy Crushers Headphones w/ Subwoofer SCS-SC	$29.90
NEW/SEALED! SHURE E4C SOUND ISOLATING EARPHONES	$180.50	NEW SONY FONTOPIA MDR-EX71SL IPOD HEADPHONES WHITE NR	$29.00
Etymotic research headphones ER-4P ER4P ER4-P	$158.00	SKULLCANDY SKULLCRUSHERS SKULL CRUSHERS HEADPHONES NEW!	$28.99
NIB! BANG & OLUFSEN A8 EARPHONES FOR IPOD ETC. NEW!!!!!	$137.51	New Sony Fontopia EarBud Headphones MDR-EX81LP/B Black	$27.55

Radios ▶ CB Radio

The average sales price in this subcategory is $42.57.

	HIGH		AVG
Browning Golden Eagle Mark III CB	$405.00	CITIZENS JIL 40 CHANNEL MOBILE/BASE CB TRANSCEIVER	$49.99
GALAXY SATURN **EXCELENT CONDITION**	$360.00	Pearce-Simpson Gladding Carib 55 Marine Radio WS1	$49.98
Browning Mark 2 4 piece with Golden eagle mic!	$355.00	Wilson 1000 Trunk Mt. Ant.	$47.50
General Grant CB Radio-Never Used-Free Shipping	$306.56	Royce 619 40 Channel Base / Mobile CB "NIB"	$46.99
Browning Golden Eagle Mark III CB	$300.66	Lot of (13) Vintage CB Radio Accessories...Take a Look!	$45.52
RCI 2970 (Used)	$275.00	HUSTLER CB Radio Antenna Short Shaft HiPower LongRange	$42.99
NEW IN BOX NORTH POINT NT9HP 10 METER RADIO	$257.00	2 Whiteface Johnson CB Radios Vintage Antique	$41.00
RARE COLLECTOR TUBE TYPE SONAR FS-2340	$250.00	Vintage Base/Mob CB radio Teaberry T CONTROL model 4009	$41.00
Cherokee CBS-1000 CB Base Station with Extras	$217.50	THE ORIGINAL DOCZY (WORKS GREAT)	$41.00
CPI CP400 CB RADIO & CP300 BASE AM/SSB NICE MUST SEE	$217.50	HUSTLER CB Radio Antenna Short Shaft HiPower LongRange	$39.99
Tram D201A	$200.00	40 Channel Handheld CB Radio/Radios & DC Power Cord	$39.99
HAM INTERNATIONAL "JUMBO" CB RADIO & D-104 MIKE !!!	$200.00	2 JOHNSON MESSENGER WALKIE TALKIES VINTAGE	$39.95
superstar cb radio black face with gold knobs	$177.50	Sears Roadtalker 40 SSB base station CB SIDE BAND	$39.66
Galaxy 959 SSB CB Radio, New Cond! Tuned up & TALKS!!!	$175.00	ASTATIC R D104 E ROAD DEVIL POWER Mic Cobra Galaxy	$38.88
CB(RANGER) PLUS 2 ANTENNAS 3 MICS COAX	$170.00	MAXON MCB 45 W CB RADIO WITH MIC	$38.00

Radios ▶ Ham Radio

The average sales price in this subcategory is $58.61.

	HIGH		AVG
Watkins-Johnson MJ-8608/FE Frequency Extender	$1,025.00	Hy-gain Tailtwister Antenna Direction Control Unit	$66.00
HARRIS RF AM-7223/URC AMPLIFIER ??? RT-1446 TRANSCEIVER	$500.00	Motorola Bulk Pack External Speakers QTY. 10 in case	$65.00
YAESU FT 101ZD TRANSCEIVER WITH EXTRAS RADIO	$360.50	COBRA sound tracker CB radio	$61.81
Varian TWTA Power Supply Model # 01008290-01	$316.11	Bird part number 4230-053 transmitter coupler block	$61.01
W3FF Buddipole Portable Antenna	$301.00	MFJ 1270B Packet Radio Controller	$61.01
HARRIS RF AM-7223/URC AMPLIFIER	$299.99	Bird Element 250W 2-30MHz	$60.00
Motorola CDM-1250 /450-520 Mhz/50W/ UHF Mobil Radio	$295.00	MFJ-418 Morse Code Tutor	$56.01
BEAUTIFUL REPRO FACEPLATE FOR COLLINS SC-301	$284.00	MFJ-461 Pocket Size Morse Code Reader	$54.00
Icom 745 HF Transceiver W/ External Speaker LOW RESERVE	$250.00	Hammarlund - (9) Small Variable Capacitors - 80-300 pF	$53.00
Collins 312B-4 Station Monitor NICE	$225.00	In Line SWR unit	$52.00
Motorola HT750 VHF 16 Channels	$224.00	HEATHKIT SB 600 POWER SUPPLY	$51.50
Motorola HT750 VHF 16 Channels	$210.00	Lot of 614 QSL Card Pictures Excell Condit 50s thru 90s	$51.01
motorola radios	$203.52	Ham Radio Items	$51.00
Motorola HT750 VHF 16 Channels	$202.62	2.5W TG2118 VHF 150-170Mhz WALKIE TALKIE 2 WAY RADIO	$25.00
ICOM Duel Band Transceiver IC-W32A	$197.50	Comet SBB-7 Dual Band 2M/70cm Amateur Antenna	$50.00

Radios ▶ Scanners

The average sales price in this subcategory is $68.17.

	HIGH		AVG
AOR AR 8200 Mk 3 Wide Band Scanner Receiver **MINT **	$717.00	RADIO SHACK PRO94 1000 CHANNEL	$80.99
AOR AR 3000A SCANNING RECEIVER 100KHZ-2036 MHZ	$490.00	DUAL TRUNKING SCANNER	
New Optoelectronics Digital Scout Frequency Recorder	$430.00	Uniden Bearcat bc200xlt scanner	$76.00
New!! Alinco DJ-X2000 Wide Band Receiver- latest ver.	$429.00	Minitor II Fire/ EMS Pagers- 2 Complete & Parts & Acces	$75.00
AR 8000 WIDE RANGE RECEIVER and Model 40 Opto Scout	$385.00	In Ear Scanner headphones headset 'USED ONCE	$72.00
NEW ICOM IC-R3 IC-R3ss Wide Band Receiver	$369.00	Icom ic-v8 vhf transmitter	$72.00
[3 of these sold for $369.00 each]		radio shack pro-90 300 channel trunk tracker scanner	$71.01
Cubic VHF UHF Receiver Multicoupler Distribution Amps	$349.50	Race Scanner Raceceiver 1600	$69.00
Yaesu Ft-840	$331.00	Radio Shack PRO-46 100 channel progammable Scanner	$66.13
Alinco DJ-X2000 Wide Band Police Scanner Portable SWEET	$325.00	Optoelectronics Optolinx	$66.00
Mint Condition Mod Realistic Pro 2006 Reciever	$300.00	Regency HX 1500 HX 1500 Scanner	$65.00
ICOM ~ IC-R3 ~ Handheld Audio / Video Receiver	$287.00	PRO-43 hyperscan 200 channel Scanner. Works Great!!	$63.85
Icom IC-R3 Audio Video Receiver Scanner	$280.00	REALISTIC PROGRAMMABLE POLICE SCANNER / RADIO PRO-2011	$63.62
Icom IC-R3 Wideband Audio and Video Receiver	$270.00	SWEET AOR AR 950 SCANNER - WOW - L@@K!	$62.01
AOR 8200B Scanner	$261.12	Bearcat 300	$62.00
AOR 8000 Non blocked UK version	$255.00	Minitor II Fire Pager Voice Pager Toner Motorola	$62.00

Satellite, Cable TV ▶ Cable TV

The median sales price in this subcategory is $19.99.

	HIGH		AVG
Motorola DSR 4402X Digital Receiver - NO RESERVE	$665.00	Cable Drop Amp electroline EDA 2400	$19.99
Motorola DSR 4402X Digital Receiver - NO RESERVE	$615.00	NEW VIEWSONICS PROFORMANCE VSA-604C 4 OUTPUT AMPLIFIER	$19.99
Scientific Atlanta PowerVu D9850 Receiver * NR*	$615.00	ELECTROLINE 1-PORT CABLE TV HDTV SPLITTER/AMPLIFIER	$19.99
Sadelco DisplayMax 800	$600.00	Dish Network/DP301 Receiver w/ Remote, Card Like New	$19.99
Scientific Atlanta PowerVu D9850 Receiver	$598.88	A21095 Blonder Tongue ZBPF Single Channel Bandpass	$19.99
MythTV	$595.00	[2 of these sold for $19.99 each]	

Scientific Atlanta PowerVu D9850 Receiver * NR*	$560.00	TIMELESS PRODUCTS CABLE BOX/DESCRAMBLER	$19.99
Motorola DSR 4402X Commercial Integrated Receiver	$535.00	A21096 Blonder Tongue ZHC-12 Passive Headend Combiner	$19.99
Motorola DSR 4402X Commercial Integrated Receiver	$525.50	A21097 Blonder Tongue SMR-1600 16 Port Multiswitch	$19.99
ACTERNA DSAM-100 Digital service activation meter	$510.00	1000' White RG6 Coax DSS Satellite Cable	$19.99
Motorola DSR 4500 X Digital Receiver *NR*	$500.99	[8 of these sold in a multiple item ("Dutch") auction for $19.99 each]	
ACTERNA DSAM-100 Digital service activation meter	$500.00	36 PCS THOMAS & BETTS SNAP & SEAL SNS11 COAX CONNECTORS	$19.99
MOTOROLA DSR-4500X DIGICYPHER II	$470.00	[2 of these sold for $19.99 each]	
SATELLITE RECEIVER		JERROLD IMPULSE CABLE CONVERTER BOX MODEL DPBB7312/V5	$19.99
Birdog Digital Satellite Finder Birddog Bird Dog PANSAT	$409.00	Philips RC19335004/01 TV QuadraSurf Remote Control FAST	$19.99
[3 of these sold for $409.00 each]		A21155 Pico Macom CEF/550 Channel 2 Elimination Filter	$19.99
Motorola DSR 4410X Digital Receiver - NO RESERVE	$405.00	A21157 Pico Macom CEF/550 Channel 10 Filter	$19.99
		MOTOROLA DCT2224/1661/ACDEG CATV Converter NR	$19.99

Satellite, Cable TV ▶ Satellite TV

The average sales price in this subcategory is $36.94.

	HIGH		AVG
HD-DVR DirecTv model HR10-250 Tivo New in Box	$450.00	Radio Shack Audio Video Home Network NIB	$49.99
DISH 921 high definition DVR receiver	$350.00	CBAND VIDEOCIPHER DECODER BLACK CAGE 018	$46.00
BRAND NEW DISHNETWORK DVR 625 DSS RECEIVER	$255.01	MOTECK SG2100 SG-2100 Dish Motor - FTA PANSAT FORTEC	$45.95
2 COOLSAT 4000 PRO! FREE FREE EXPRESS SHIPPING	$232.50	[2 of these sold for $45.95 each]	
2 COOLSAT 4000 PRO! FREE FREE EXPRESS SHIPPING	$232.01	SIRIUS SATELLITE RADIO ANTENNA (TERK SIR6)	$45.00
BRAND NEW DISHNETWORK DVR 625 DSS RECEIVER	$220.00	HU H Card Reader Sureshot No Reserve Like New	$41.00
COOLSAT 4000 PRO & CARD READER	$220.00	COMPRESSION TOOL, COAXIAL STRIPPER, 50 DIGICON FITTINGS	$38.50
WITH X-CRYPT SMART CARD		[3 of these sold for $38.50 each]	
2 COOLSAT 4000 PRO! FREE FREE EXPRESS SHIPPING	$216.00	COMPRESSION TOOL, COAXIAL STRIPPER, 50 DIGICON FITTINGS	$36.50
2 COOLSAT 4000 PRO! FREE FREE EXPRESS SHIPPING	$198.50	TERK TV44 VHF/UHF AMPLIFIED OUTDOOR TV ANTENNA! WOW!	$30.00
COOLSAT 4000 PRO & CARD READER	$192.50	CableTronix Digital Single Channel Modulator	$30.00
WITH X-CRYPT SMART CARD		INVACOM LNB SUPER LOW NOISE .3dB Horn SNH-031	$28.95
2 COOLSAT 4000 PRO! FREE EXPRESS SHIPPING	$192.00	video cipher	$28.05
COOLSAT 4000 PRO & CARD READER WITH X-CRYPT SMART CARD	$184.00	The Sky Peaker / Satellite Signal Finder / Meter	$27.00
COOLSAT 4000 PRO & CARD READER WITH X-CRYPT SMART CARD	$179.00	DSS H Cards Reader Writer Satellite TV Directv Dish	$26.00
Chaparral Corotor II+ WideBand C & Ku Feedhorn !!NEW!!	$154.49	Ku band Single LNB Model No. NJR2184F NEW/BIN	$25.99
COOLSAT 4000 PRO! FREE FREE EXPRESS SHIPPING	$127.53	1000' 75 OHM rg6 coax cable perfect vision	$25.00

Telephone & Pagers ▶ Answering Machines

The average sales price in this subcategory is $19.39.

	HIGH		AVG
music on hold phone system with 2-line speaker phone.	$285.00	GE 2.4 Ghz TELEPHONE ANSWERING MACHINE EXPANDABLE	$28.88
Bogen Friday FR-2000 Personal / Office Receptionist	$190.00	AT&T Remote Telephone Answering Machine Model #1527	$26.00
NEVERUSED2yrwarranty Bang &	$159.50	Panasonic Digital Answering System KX-TM100B	$25.00
Olufsen B & O BeoTalk 1200		GE Speakerphone Answering Machine w/ Cordless CI BLK	$24.99
Bogen Friday FR-2000 2-Line Digital Answ. machine, used	$152.50	[4 of these sold for $24.99 each]	
NEW Panasonic KXT2740 2 line answering machine	$123.05	GE Phone Answering System, Good Cond. NO RESERVE	$20.72
AT&T TWO LINE DIGITAL ANSWERING	$112.50	AT&T 900 MHZ CORDLESS TELEPHONE/ANSWERING MACHINE 9350	$20.50
MACHINE, CALLER ID		NEW IN BOX CODE-A-PHONE ANSWERING MACHINE	$19.99
Bogen Friday FR-2000 2-line Digital Answering Machine	$81.00	Brand New AT&T 1722 Digital Answering System**Free/Sh	$19.99
Telephone answering machine 5.8	$81.00	GE Answering Machine Cordless Speakerphone w/CID 27959	$19.99
2 handsets vtech i5881		[3 of these sold for $19.99 each]	
Bang & Olufsen BEOTALK 1100 Answering Machine	$73.00	GE 2.4 Ghz TELEPHONE ANSWERING MACHINE EXPANDABLE	$19.95
Bang & Olufsen BEOTALK 1100 Answering Machine	$70.00	Line Sharing Device TC-4000 Voice/ Fax /Modem	$19.00
Bogen TR 1000 Friday Office	$67.99	TELEPHONE TWO WAY RECORDER TR-200 NEW	$17.50
Answering Machine buySAFE		AUDIOVOX 900 MHz DIGITAL CORDLESS TELEPHONE NEW	$15.50
New! AT&T 2375 Cordless Phone System W/DAS	$63.77	2 line answering machine	$15.02
Radio Shack Voice Activated Telephone Recorder TCR-200	$61.00	Practically New VTECH cordless phone w/answering machin	$15.00
[2 of these sold for $61.00]		GE Answering Machine 4 Mailboxes Digital Recording NR	$15.00
NEW IN BOX AMERIPHONE EASY	$58.99	[2 of these sold for $15.00 each].	
RECALL ANSWERING MACHINE		CELL PHONE MICROPHONE PHONE RECORDING SPY NEW	$14.99
Telephone Answering Machine - AT&T Model 1337	$56.00	[2 of these sold for $14.99 each]	

Telephone & Pagers ▶ Corded Telephones

The average sales price in this subcategory is $50.24.

	HIGH		AVG
PBX 20X40 NORTEL MERIDIAN USED OFFICE PHONE SYSTEM	$1,426.17	New Walker W1100 amplified Telephone Hearing Impaired	$65.99
Phone System- Bizfon	$860.00	JACOB JENSEN phone vintage NIB danish design panton	$61.55
Six Nortel T7316E phones	$425.00	AT&T 954 Four Line Intercom Speaker Phones (Lot of 4)	$59.99
LOT OF (17) LUCENT 8410B TELEPHONES	$425.00	LUCENT PARTNER MLS18 DISPLAY	$59.95
LUCENT PARTNER ACS BUSINESS 4 PHONE SYSTEM PC ACCESS	$285.00	Payphone Pedestal	$56.00
AT&T Partner Phone System w/phones and main Processor	$280.51	GE 4-line Intercom Corded Phone w/instructions #29487	$56.00
5 SBC 410 4 line Telephones w/ Caller ID in orig. boxes	$250.00	Panasonic kx-t7135 Speakerphone w/Backlit LCD Avaya	$54.53
Panasonic KX-TG4000B 4 Line Phone Telephone System REF	$242.50	Ameriphone XL-40 Phone for Hearing Impaired —	$52.00
FIBERFONE FIBER OPTIC TALK SET BUTTSET	$225.00	Phone By Bang Olufsen Designer John & Lund,Jacob Jensen	$52.00
PANASONIC KXT7135W SYSTEM PHONES QTY OF 3##	$185.00	Lot of 3 Elcotel Series 5 Payphone Board	$49.99
Radio Shack System 612 4-Line Phone w. Intercom-NICE	$180.00	PHOTO PHONE ~ BIG BUTTON AMPLIFIED CORDED TELEPHONE	$49.75
(5) Plantronics A100 Headset+ Amplifer for Office Phone	$165.00	Pottery Barn GRAND WALL PHONE~BLACK~NEW OUT OF BOX!	$47.00
BANG & OLUFSEN - BEOCOM 2500 – B&O PHONE	$162.50	2 Sprint Two-Line Phones- EXCELLENT FEATURES- GRT COND!	$46.00
Radio Shack System 612 4-Line Phone w. Intercom-NICE	$162.50	TIMEX T488 AM/FM ALARM CLOCK RADIO/PHONE w/CID~NEW!!	$42.49
Radio Shack System 612 4-Line Phone w. Intercom-NICE	$152.50	4 MEI Mars MS16 Payphone Electronic Coin Mechanism	$41.00

Telephone & Pagers ▸ Cordless Telephones

The average sales price in this subcategory is $41.41.

	HIGH		AVG
Engenius 4-line cordless phone sys EP-490 w/4 handsets	$1,000.00	CT12 Plantronics WIRELESS Phone 2.4Ghz W-Headset	$50.00
B&O Bang & Olufsen Yellow BeoCom 2 Telephone.OBM.MINT-	$685.00	CYBERGENIE CY-DG2400 2.4GHZ PC TELEPHONE - WORKS GREAT	$50.00
Design wireless Phone Jacob Jensen T6 , B&O *NEW*	$325.00	CT12 Plantronics WIRELESS Phone 2.4Ghz W-Headset	$49.99
PHONE CORDLESS BANG & OLUFSEN BEO 600 NEW!!!	$310.00	NEWIN UNIDEN DCT6465-2 2,4GHZ CID	$49.98
BANG & OLUFSEN B&O BEOCOM 6000 XTRA HANDSET	$187.50	SPK 2 HANDSETS W/WNTY	
BANG & OLUFSEN B&O BEOCOM 6000 XTRA HANDSET	$185.00	New Plantronics CT11 2.5GHz Cordless Headset Telephone	$49.95
Cybergenie Full Phone System	$150.00	2-Line 2.4GHz Digital Spread Spectrum Cordless Phone	$49.00
New Ameriphone CLS45i Cordless Amplified Speakerphone	$149.95	Plantronics CT11 2.4 GHz Cordless Headset Telephone	$47.00
NEW SHARP UX-CD600 FAX/2.4GHZ/DSS/CID CORDLESS PHONE	$129.98	Sanyo 2.4GHz Cordless Phone Extra Handset Charger	$45.00
AT&T 2462 HOME PHONE, NO RESERVE	$119.49	2.4 GHz Cordless PHONE System Caller ID BRAND NEW!	$45.00
Long Range Cordless Phone SN-358	$108.50	Olympia 2.4 GHz CORDLESS PHONE SYSTEM w/THREE Handsets	$41.00
Long Range Cordless Phone SN-358	$104.50	CYBERGENIE ERICSSON 2.4GHz PC PHONE SYSTEM NEW	$41.00
New Clarity C440 Amplified Cordless Phone w/ Caller ID	$99.99	Olympia 2.4 GHz CORDLESS PHONE SYSTEM w/THREE Handsets	$41.00
[2 of these sold for $99.99 each]		Panasonic KX-TGA270s Add-on Cordless Handset / CallerID	$41.00
New Clarity C600 Amplified Cordless Phone w/ Caller ID	$91.99	Japanese PIONEER Multi-Handset Cordless Phone System	$39.99
NEWIN UNIDEN DCT6485-3 2.4GHZ CORDLESS PHONE/3 HANDSETS	$90.52	TWO CYBERGENIE Ericsson DG 200 Cygnion Phones 39New	$39.95

Telephone & Pagers ▸ Headsets

The average sales price in this subcategory is $51.12.

	HIGH		AVG
LOT OF 20 PLANTRONICS M12 Vista Universal Amplifier	$750.00	(3) PLANTRONICS A100 Headset System NORSTAR M7208 M7324	$105.00
20 Plantronics M12 Amplifiers with Executive Headsets	$565.00	PLANTRONICS / 4 LOT / VISTA M12 PHONE MODULAR AMPLIFIER	$97.00
LUCENT PARTNER ACS BUSINESS 4 PHONE SYSTEM PC ACCESS	$285.00	CT12 Plantronics WIRELESS Phone 2.4Ghz w-Headset	$80.99
LOT (5) Plantronics M12 Amplifiers & Supra H51 Headsets	$199.99	Plantronics CA10 Cordless Wireless 900mhz Headset	$79.95
LOT (4) Plantronics M12 Amplifier & Supra H51N Headset	$189.99	(5) PLANTRONICS T100 Headset f/ M7208, M2616, M2008	$69.99
CS50 Plantronics Headset Solution 100% Wireless	$185.00	Plantronics H81N TriStar Headsets, Lot of 2	$66.50
CS50 Plantronics Newest Wireless Headset, 100% Wireless	$184.00	PLANTRONICS S12 Telephone Headset and Amplifier	$51.00
CS50 Plantronics Newest Wireless Headset, 100% Wireless	$183.00	PLANTRONICS Telephone Headset System S12	$50.80
CS50 Plantronics Headset Solution 100% Wireless	$183.00	Plantronics M12 Amplifier with headset Like new	$50.00
LOT (4) Plantronics Vista M12 Amp & Mirage H41 Headset	$181.00	NEW Plantronics H81 headset M12 Amp combo H81-M12	$50.00
PLANTRONICS Used CS50 WIRELESS HEADSET w/ Lifter	$179.99	NEW Plantornics H161 headset M12 Amp combo H161-M12	$50.00
(5) Plantronics A100 Headset+ Amplifier for Office Phone	$178.18	Plantronics H-171 DouPro Convertible Headsets, Lot of 2	$50.00
Lot of 19 Plantronics M12 Vista Telephone Amplifier	$165.00	PLANTRONICS DSP-500 PC USB Gaming/Multimedia Headset !	$49.95
Plantronics WIRELESS Office Headset System CS50	$152.50	Plantronics TRISTAR H81N Noise Cancel Headset *Exclnt.	$49.00
	$152.50	Plantronics M12 UNIVERSAL AMPLIFIER with H91 headset	$46.00

Televisions ▸ Accessories & Cables

The average sales price in this subcategory is $9.10.

	HIGH		AVG
Plextor ConvertX PX-AV100U Digital Video Converter	$51.00	(NEW) 20ft. S-Video cable for DVD, SAT, CAB	$11.95
NEW! 75' FOOT S-VIDEO CABLE 24K GOLD ENDS HDTV/PLASMA	$39.95	Lot of 4 S-Video Female Couplers & a 25 Ft SVideo Cable	$11.95
[2 of these sold for $39.95 each]		002-02100 - 25' Composite+4 pin S-Video+RCA Audio CBL	$11.49
MONSTER M500v S - Video Cable x 10 Meter or 33 Feet	$36.00	S-Video 5-ft. Monster Cable - LOW SHIPPING	$10.51
High End Z500 S-Video Cable 13.2' SVHS THX Certified	$30.00	Monster S Video 3 Cable 1M - DVD HDTV	$10.50
002-02110 - 100' Composite+4 pin S-Video+RCA Audio CBL	$29.99	Monster Video2, S-Video 2m cable, 6.6ft, model MVSV2	$10.49
NEW! 50 FOOT S-VIDEO CABLE 24K GOLD ENDS HDTV/PLASMA	$28.95	Monster S Video 3 NEW - DVD Maxium Clarity 4M High End	$10.00
[3 of these sold for $28.95 each]		Monster Mseries M500v S-video cable	$10.00
Monster Cable S-VIDEO Audio Video Kit 4' THX V100 AVS-4	$26.95	Brand New MIT S-LinQ S-Video Cable No reserve	$9.99
High End Liberty S-Video Cable 6.6' SVHS THX Certified	$25.00	Monster Cable 8' THX S-Video CABLE(ULTRA 600)	$9.99
NEW! 35 FOOT S-VIDEO CABLE 24K GOLD ENDS HDTV/PLASMA	$24.95	12 ft. PREMIUM 24k Gold S-Video Cable 12'	$7.25
[5 of these sold for $24.95 each]		[2 of these sold for $7.25 each]	
Monster Video 3 High End S Video Cable - 13 FT 4M	$24.50	002-02095 - 12' Composite+4 pin S-Video+RCA Audio CBL	$6.99
Acoustic Research Pro II PR123 S-Video Cable 25 ft	$23.00	Acoustic Research Video/Audio Cable 6 Feet.. AP061 NEW	$6.99
NEW! 25 FOOT S-VIDEO CABLE 24K GOLD ENDS HDTV/PLASMA	$22.95	ACOUSTIC RESEARCH AP021 6 FT S-VIDEO CABLE	$6.99
[2 of these sold for $22.95 each]		002-02095 - 12' Composite+4 pin S-Video+RCA Audio CBL	$6.99

Televisions ▸ HDTVs, Direct-View

The average sales price in this subcategory is $505.17.

	HIGH		AVG
LOEWE $15,000 NEW FLOOR MODEL HOME SYSTEM!! ONE NIGHT	$6,235.00	Sony 32 HDTV KV-32HS510 Perfect condition - NR	$540.01
SONY 70" XBR LCD TV	$4,550.00	SONY KV-30HS510 30" Hi-Scan FD Trinitron WEGA HDTV	$536.01
Hitachi 60VS810 60"LCD HDTV Projection TV Brandnew	$2,655.01	Philips 34PW9819 34" High Definition Widescreen	$536.00
62" Mitsubishi DLP and Entertainment CTR! #WD62725 +wty	$2,600.00	SAMSUNG HCM422W TANTUS 42" HDTV	$525.00
73" Mitsubishi HDTV WS-73513?	$2,500.00	1080i MONITOR PIP &MORE	
NEW Sony KDP-65XBR2 65" XBR HDTV no reserve 65 SEATTLE	$2,076.00	Philips 34" WideScreen HDTV - Model 34PW850	$522.09
Toshiba HDTV 65" Wide Theatre Screen	$1,850.00	Sony 36XBR400 36" HD flat screen CRT w/ stand	$521.89
RCA HD61LPW42 - 61" Inch Widescreen 16:9 HD DLP TV	$1,780.00	Apex Digital AVL2776 27" HDTV Monitor - NEW IN BOX!!	$510.01
[2 of these sold for $1,780.00 each]		40" Sony HD Ready KV-40XBR700 TV	$510.00
SONY KV-40XBR700 40 INCH TRINITRON WEGA FLAT SCREEN TV	$1,524.00	36" Panasonic Tau Pureflat HDTV	$500.00
Philips Hi-Def 60" TV Bought 1 Year Ago	$1,225.00	Mitsubishi 55 inch HDTV ready wide screen	$500.00
Sony 51" HDTV, 2yr Warranty, Free Entertainment Center	$1,200.00	HITACHI 43UWX10B 43" INCH HDTV REAR PROJECTION TV	$490.01

MITSUBISHI 65" HIGH DEF Wide-Screen TV (Philadelphia)	$1,150.00	NEW Samsung 32" DynaFlat HD-Ready TV Monitor TXN3275HF	$489.99
SONY KV40XBR800 WEGA HDTV Beautiful 40" Flat Screen CRT	$1,125.00	JVC's l'Art PRO AV32S575 1080i Digital HDTV 32"Monitor	$465.00
SONY 42' LCD HDTV and 5 Disc DVD PLAYER ..NO RESERVE!!!	$1,100.00	SONY FD TRINITRON WEGA 32 INCH FLAT SCREEN KV-32XBR450	$465.00
Sony 34" XS955 KD-34xs955 Widescreen HDTV TV xbr tube	$1,075.00	Sony kv-36hs510 36in FD Trinitron WEGA HDTV Television	$457.00

Televisions ▶ LCD Flat-Panel TVs

The average sales price in this subcategory is $230.23.

	HIGH		AVG
Samsung LN-R237W 23" Widescreen HDTV-Ready LCD TV New!	$685.00	New!! Real 17" LCD TV Monitor Flat Screen!!	$240.00
NEW Viewsonic 30" WIDESCREEN LCD TV	$999.99	PANASONIC TC-17LA2D 17" LCD TV (slr)	$240.00
27" Norcent HDTV LCD TV-Monitor (NEW) Factory Seal	$650.00	COBY 15" FLAT PANEL TV/MONITOR with BUILT IN DVD PLAYER	$238.00
Magnavox 15MF200V 15" LCD Flat Screen TV with NTSC Tune	$449.99	SAMSUNG LTN1765 17" COLOR TFT LCD MONITOR + HDTV NEW !	$237.51
Sharp LC-20B6U-S 20" LCD HDTV TV LC-20B6US REFURBISHED	$425.00	Sanyo 15" LCD EDTV CLT1554 NEW IN THE BOX	$237.50
17" INITIAL HD LCD TV w/ built in DVD player DTV-171	$405.00	New 17" LCD TV Monitor Flat Screen Black Foldable!	$235.50
CYBERHOME 17" HDTV-READY LCD	$400.00	PHILIPS MAGNAVOX-LIKE NEW-15" FLAT LCD TV #15MF050V	$233.05
TV/DVD MONITOR CH-HGL1710		Foldable 17" LCD TV Monitor Flat Screen Silver!!	$232.50
VIEWSONIC 17IN 16:9 LCD/TV/HDTVCOMPATIBLE MONITOR	$400.00	Magnavox 15MF200V 15" LCD Flat Screen TV with NTSC Tune	$230.00
NEW Audiovox FP1500 15" LCD Flat-Panel Television TV	$399.99	Real 15.2" LCD TV Monitor Flat Panel Black! NEW!!	$229.99
ZENITH L17W36 17" 16:9 HD LCD TV LCDs TVs NEW	$390.00	[3 of these sold for $229.99 each]	
ZENITH L17W36 17" 16:9 HD Widescreen LCD TV LCDs TVs	$389.00	Sanyo 15" Flat panel TV Flat screen LCD TV New, Boxed	$229.00
Samsung LT-P1795W 17" 600:1 Contrast LCD HD TV	$385.20	SYLVANIA 15" FLATPANEL LCD DISPLAY	$225.00
Gateway 18" LCD TV Television Flat Panel Monitor	$380.55	WESTINGHOUSE 15" LCD TV-NEVER USED	$224.72
Sony 15" LCD WEGA TV Progressive Reverse 3:2 Pulldown	$380.50	New 15" Sylvania LCD HDTV Flat Panel TV Cheap Fast Ship	$224.72
15" TFT LCD FLAT PANEL BUILT-IN TV/DVD/MP3/DIVX PLAYER	$375.00	Foldable 17" LCD TV Monitor Flat Screen Silver NR	$222.50

Televisions ▶ Plasma TVs

The average sales price in this subcategory is $962.78.

	HIGH		AVG
50" Philips High Definition Plasma TV	$3,750.00	Akai PDP4298 42" Plasma w/ Stand/Spks/Tuner Refurb	$1,123.50
Akai PDP4298 42" Plasma w/ Stand/Spks/Tuner Refurb	$1,125.78	AKAI PDP4295ED 42" 16:9 WIDESCREEN	$1,105.00
PANASONIC 42" TH-42PHD7UY PLASMATV W/5YRS WARRANTY	$2,795.00	PLASMA EDTV! WOW!	
SONY PLASMA KDE-37XS955 & SONY SURROUND SOUND SYSTEM	$2,631.00	42" NEC PLASMA SYNC 4205W	$1,100.00
PHILIPS 42PF9976 42" 16:9 PLASMA HDTV	$2,499.00	NEW ~~~42 " PLASMA TV~~~ + WARRANTY & STAND	$1,050.00
DELL 42" PLASMA TV W4200 *HDTV* **BRAND NEW**	$2,425.00	ZENITH P42W46X 42" Plasma TV Plasmas TVs	$1,025.00
Philips 42" Pixel Plus 2 Plasma TV 42PF9976/37B	$2,424.95	[2 of these sold for $1,025.00 each]	
Philips 42" HD-Ready Plasma TV 42PF9966/37B w/ TUNER	$2,324.99	Great Plasma TV!	$1,000.00
Philips 42PF9956/37B 42" Flat Panel Plasma TV	$2,269.95	SVA HD4208U-II 42in PLASMA DISPLAY ED TV TELEVISION	$965.00
NEW AKAI 42" WIDESCREEN DIGITAL PLASMA TV with SPEAKERS	$2,200.00	SVA HD4208U-II 42in PLASMA DISPLAY ED TV TELEVISION	$950.00
DELL 42" PLASMA TV W4200 *HDTV* BEST PRICE! *BRAND NEW*	$2,149.99	Daewoo DP-42SM 42" Inch Flat Plasma Panel HDTV $2500	$925.00
[3 of these sold for $2,149.00 each]		Hitachi Plasma 42" TV Display HDTV Ready. Low Reserve!	$870.00
DELL 42" PLASMA TV W4200 *HDTV* BEST PRICE! *BRAND NEW*	$2,098.99	Used 42 inch Philips 42PW9962 Plasma TV	$780.00
[2 of these sold for $2,089.99 each]		TECH-VIEW 42" EDTV PLASMA HOT PRICE !!!! L@@K NR	$775.00
Philips 42FD993299 42" Widescreen Plasma TV	$2,094.95	Fujitsu PDS4221W-H Plasma Tv * NO RESERVE *	$770.00
NEW PHILIPS 42" HDTV FLAT PANEL PLASMA TV 42PF9956	$2,075.00	Hitachi 42" Plasma HDTV No Reserve!!!	$718.00
Philips 42FD995499 42" Plasma Display Television TV	$2,069.95	NEC 42" Sync Master Plasma Display Model PX-42VM2A	$710.00

Televisions ▶ Portable TVs

The average sales price in this subcategory is $45.55.

	HIGH		AVG
Sony Location Free 12.1" LCD TV & Web Browser	$700.00	sony 9" inch trinitron tv television white kv-9pt50	$48.91
Audiovox VE1040 10.4" Under Counter TV with DVD NEW!!	$405.51	CASIO EV-670 Handheld THREE INCH TFT PORTABLE COLOR TV	$48.51
Sony glasstron PLM-A35 Virutal Reality Portable TV LCD	$305.00	Innovatek Sp700 7" TFT LCD CAR MONITOR TV TUNER FOR DVD	$48.00
SONY GLASSTRON PLM-A35 PERSONAL LCD MONITOR	$227.50	Casio EV-660B Color Handheld Portable LCD TV	$47.00
AUDIO VOX 9" INCH LCD TV/DVD	$201.00	Radio Shack Portavision Color TV Monitor	$46.45
Casio Handheld Color TV 4" LCD #EV-4500 Brand New	$172.50	Sony Watchman B & W Battery Plug Adaptor Case FD-210	$46.20
Audiovox 7" Under-Counter Flip TV/Radio/Phone NEW!	$163.10	MAGNAVOX 5 INCH PORTABLE COLOR TV 5" TELEVISION MOBILE	$46.00
Casio Handheld Color TV 4" LCD #EV-4500 Brand New	$150.00	Casio EV-570 2.5" LCD TFT portable TV	$45.56
BIG SCREEN 46" TV - RCA Television	$150.00	Sony Watchman Portable TV Model FD-42A	$45.00
Brand New Casio EV4500 4-in. Handheld Color TV w/stand	$149.99	NEW!! CASIO HANDHELD LCD COLOR TELEVISION	$45.00
Audiovox VBP50 portable DVD player~ NEW!!	$145.00	NEW Casio portable COLOR TV 2.7"	$44.00
30 inch Flat Screen Television	$135.51	CURTIS MATHIS 13" COLOR TV/VCR COMBO, EUC!!	$43.00
CASIO PORTABLE COLOR TV EV-4500 LCD CRYSTAL VISION	$134.50	NEW TV SONY WATCHMAN 2.2 INCH COLOR LCD 1/3 Off Price!	$43.00
Toshiba Portable 9 Inch DVD Player with Bag Like New	$130.00	SPECTRA 5" COLOR PORTABLE TV	$43.00
Sony Trinitron 9" KV-9PT60 with Case and yoke	$127.50	CASIO WATER/SHOCK RESISTANT LCD COLOR TV 2.7"	$42.99

VCRs ▶ Beta

The average sales price in this subcategory is $93.37.

	HIGH		AVG
SONY UVW-1400 BETACAM SP RECORDER	$2,000.00	SONY BETAMAX HOME THEATRE SL-HFT7 SUPERBETA HIFI VCR	$99.99
Sony Beta SP UVW-1600 low hrs great condition NTSC	$1,000.00	ZENITH VCR (BETA FORMAT) MODEL VR8900W	$99.99
Sony Beta SP UVW-1600 low hrs great condition NTSC	$900.00	SONY SL-HF400 SUPER BETA HI-FI WITH REMOTE MIB	$99.99
SONY BETA PLAYER SL-HF2100 NO RESERVE!	$765.75	ZENITH VCR (BETA FORMAT) MODEL VR8500PT	$99.00
SONY BETA VCR SL-HF1000 EXCELLENT CONDITION!!!	$586.91	Sanyo Beta Betamax VCR 4590/4500+Manual SERVICED = Sony	$99.00
Sony Betamax SL-HF1000 Super Beta Hi-Fi Stereo VCR	$516.57	SONY SLO-325 BETAMAX PROFESSIONAL VIDEO RECORDER * VCR	$96.00
SONY BETA VCR EDV-7500 &	$485.00	SONY SLO-325 BETAMAX PROFESSIONAL VIDEO RECORDER * VCR	$91.00

LOT OF 150 UNOPENED MOVIES!	
SONY BETA VCR EDV-7500 & LOT OF 350 UNOPENED MOVIES!	$436.99
Sony SL-HF900 Super Beta Hi-Fi Betamax VCR MINT !!	$430.00
SONY BETA RECORDER SL-HF870D	$390.00
SONY SL-HF870D SUPER BETA HI-FI-MANUAL-REMOTE-PRISTINE	$375.00
SONY SL-HF870D BETA VCR SUPER BETA HI FI DIGITAL EFFECT	$365.00
SONY BETA VCR SL-HF900 EXCELLENT CONDITION!!	$355.03
SONY SL-HF750 SUPER BETA HI-FI VCR, DREAM MACHINE!!!	$341.00
SONY SL-HF 360 SUPERBETA HI-FI VCR IN THE BOX	$325.00

SANYO SUPER BETA HI-FI TAPE PLAYER TESTED IN GOOD SHAPE	$91.00
Sony Super Betamax Beta VCR SL-HFR70 No Reserve	$90.00
Quality Sony Betamax SL-HF 300 Play/Record VCR + REMOTE	$90.00
[2 of these sold for $90.00 each]	
SANYO BETA VCR 4020 BETACORD BII BETAMAX MACHINE	$89.95
Sanyo Beta Betachord VCR 4000 BII / BIII good cond !!	$86.00
SANYO VCR-4400 Top-Loading BETA II/III Video Recorder	$86.00
Sanyo Beta VCR #4590 with remote and manual..Like NEW!!	$86.00
Sanyo Beta HI FI / Super Beta VCR Model 7250	$82.76

VCRs ▸ VHS

The average sales price in this subcategory is $25.41.

	HIGH		AVG
Samsung SV-5000W Multisystem VCR NTSC/PAL/SECAM N/R	$265.00	GoVideo GV3000 Dual Deck VHS VCR	$26.51
SONIC BLUE GO VIDEO DDV3110 VCR DUEL DECK PLAYER/RECORD	$224.51	Audiovox VBP2000 portable VCR with 5 inch LCD screen	$26.00
$9,375 Pallet of 125 RCA AccuSearch 4-Head VCRs NR	$212.50	Hitachi MX828E VCR European Model! Dual Voltage!!	$26.00
Go Video DDV9485 Dual Deck 4 Head VCR Nice!	$211.38	Sylvania VCR	$26.00
GO VIDEO DDV3110 VCR WITH VCR DUAL DECK	$210.78	ORION VCR - W/ REMOTE -	$25.76
Samsung SV-5000W Worldwide PAL/NTSC/SECAM VCR	$182.50	IN EXCELLENT CONDITION!!!	
Go Video Dual Deck System Model 4010 & Remote VHS VCR	$177.50	VCRs and DVDs Players CHEAP	$25.00
JVC HM-DH30000U D-VHS DIGITAL HDTV RECORDER	$175.05	RCA VCR	$25.00
JVC HM-DH30000U D-VHS VCR HDTV DVHS *NR* Digital Player	$159.01	TDK VHS-C Video Adapter to watch VHS - C Tapes in VCR	$24.99
RCA VR800HF 8mm HiFi Stereo VCR w/Remote like new	$156.00	EXTRA LONG SONY BETA Head CLEANER-New 2005	$23.00
RIO GO VIDEO DDV9550 DUAL VHS VCR WITH REMOTE NR!	$152.50	Audiovox VBP2000 portable VCR with 5 inch LCD screen	$22.86
SONY VIDEO8 VCR	$139.02	Samsung HQ VCR w/remote, excellent working condition	$22.50
NEW 2005 JVC HR-V410 MULTISYSTEM VCR PAL SECAM $125	$129.00	VCR player, Funai w/remote	$22.50
[2 of these sold for $129.00 each]		Emerson EV598 4-Head VCR with Remote	$20.50
NEW JVC HR-V400AG MULTISYSTEM VCR PAL SECAM $115	$119.00	Complete VCR repair tools in zippered case.	$20.50
[2 of these sold for $119.00 each]		Sanyo 72H Real Time Video Cassette	$20.50
Nice HITACHI Multi-System VCR, NTSC PAL SECAM VHS	$113.49	Recorder SRT-7072	

Vintage Electronics ▸ 8 Track Players

The average sales price in this subcategory is $30.61.

	HIGH		AVG
Vintage WELTRON Space Helmet 8 TRACK/ Radio MOD	$326.00	AMFM EIGHT 8 TRACK PLAYER/RECORDER STEREO ELECTROPHONIC	$31.00
WOW! Pioneer TP-900 Car Radio 8-Track..MINT IN BOX!!!!!	$260.00	Vintage MGA SA-48 QUADRAPHONIC Stereo 8-TRACK RECEIVER	$31.00
**** RARE CRAIG 8 TRACK-FM MODEL 3142 NOS BOX MANUAL	$201.48	VINTAGE PIONEER H-R100 8-TRACK 8TRACK STEREO TAPE DECK	$31.00
Weltron Space Helmet 8 Track Player Radio RETRO 2001 NR	$182.50	WELTRON 2001 SPACE HELMET 8 TRACK PLAYER WORKS LOOK!!!!	$31.00
WOW!!! pioneer tp 900 8 track player/tuner mint in pack	$162.50	TOP OF THE LINE SEARS 8 TRACK /CASSETTE /AM/FM RECEIVER	$31.00
* NEW IN ORIG BOX * VINTAGE PORTABLE 8 TRACK PLAYER	$156.56	Centrex by Pioneer 8 track tape deck player	$31.00
Retro Weltron Model #2001 Space Helmet 8 Track/Radio	$131.22	GE PORTABLE 8 TRACK PLAYER POWER SOUND RED	$30.00
* NEW IN ORIG BOX * VINTAGE PORTABLE 8 TRACK PLAYER	$128.51	8 track panasonic player AM-FM stereo vintage records	$30.00
VINTAGE AKAI CR-83D 8-TRACK STEREO PLAYER & RECORDER NR	$128.51	Vintage Panasonic RS808 RS 808 8 Track Player Recorder	$30.00
Vintage - PANASONIC RS-838S Port. 8 Track RECORDER NIB!	$122.50	8 track tape splicing kit & 10' sensing foil	$29.95
VINTAGE RED 1970s PANASONIC TNT 8 TRACK PLAYER RQ-830S	$122.50	Toyo 8 Track Player Recorder Model CHR-335	$29.26
Pioneer Centrex 8 Track Tape Player Recorder Dolby 70's	$112.50	AUDIOTEX 8-TRACK TAPE PLAYER ALIGNMENT TAPE-VINTAGE-$$$	$29.00
Panasonic 8 Track Tape Player Recorder Home Deck	$110.00	Stereo 8 Eight Track Tape Cartridge Player/Recorder	$29.00
1967 Pioneer 8 Track Tape Player Recorder	$110.00	Pioneer QT 2100 8 Track Quad Quadraphonic Player	$28.75
Panasonic Blue TNT 8 Track Tape Player	$105.00	PANASONIC RQ-831A PORTABLE AM/FM RADIO 8 TRACK PLAYER	$28.12

Vintage Electronics ▸ Reel-to-Reel Tape

The average sales price in this subcategory is $40.98.

	HIGH		AVG
Stellavox SP7 Professional?Audio Tape Recorder / Player	$1,577.77	AKAI DC-250 GX-280D REEL TO REEL DUST COVER + BOX !	$45.00
CROWN CX844 4 TRACK RECORDER REEL TO REEL	$549.99	CAPITOL MAGNETIC PRODUCTS TYPE 605 AUDIO TAPE	$45.00
TEAC X 10 R REEL TO REEL DECK #15	$459.00	Vintage Wollensak 1520AV Reel To Reel Tape Recorder!	$44.67
Teac X-1000R	$404.00	(Lot of 6) Quantegy 456 audio tape 7" reel NIB NEW	$42.00
TASCAM 34 - 4 TRACK - REEL TO REEL RECORDER	$315.00	Lot of 36 Reel To Reel Recording Tapes -Most 1800 Feet	$42.00
Ross Reel to Reel Tape Recorder Player MINT CONDITION	$305.00	Roberts Reel to Reel Recorder 720, Great Condition	$41.00
Nagra III Reel to Reel Portable Tape Recorder	$300.00	Vintage Wollensak 1520AV Reel To Reel Tape Recorder	$41.00
VINTAGE NAGRA III REEL TO REEL PORTABLE TAPE RECORDER	$299.99	TASCAM TEAC 32 34 34B PINCH ROLLER NEW	$40.50
Technics 1500 Professional 10.5" Reel to Reel Deck Nice	$299.95	Ampex 456 Quantegy Grand Master 1 inch Tape Reel	$40.00
NAGRA PORTABLE SPEAKER AMPLIFIER IN EXC COND	$299.00	Scotch 10.5" reels, spare hub caps, & boxes! vintage	$39.50
TEAC X 7 R REEL TO REEL DECK	$214.95	Lot of 12 Scotch Reel To Reel Recording Tapes MIS New	$37.01
Maxell Metal Vertex 3-Audio Cassette Tapes New Sealed	$202.50	Mint condition REALISTIC 909 recorder	$36.09
RARE DUAL TG28 REEL TO REEL	$199.99	3 REEL TO REEL TAPES 2 BASF 1 SONY 10" REEL 3" HUB	$36.01
WOODBASE 1229 DUSTCOVER		MAXELL XLI 35-180B 10 1/2" RTR TAPE NIOB	$35.35
KYBE Series 440 tape cleaner	$177.50	[2 of these sold for $35.35 each]	
Vintage Tascam 22-4 reel to reel professional recorder	$162.50	Wollensak T-1616 Stereo Reel to Reel Tape Deck Recorder	$35.00

Vintage Electronics ▸ Speakers

The average sales price in this subcategory is $148.46.

	HIGH		AVG
Tannoy Super Gold 15" SGM 3000 Professional Series	$3,000.00	Pair Altec Lansing crossovers – N801-8A	$152.50
Infinity SIGMA Floor Stand Speakers Audiophile Quality	$2,225.50	Pair Match ALTEC Model 14 Compression Horn Drivers	$152.50

WESTERN ELECTRIC 728B SPEAKER NEAR MINT!!	$1,777.00	1 VINTAGE PHILIPS 8" DUALCONE ALNICO FULLRANGE SPEAKER	$150.49
VINTAGE ACOUSTIC RESEARCH AR-1 SPEAKERS REAL NICE	$1,600.00	UNIVERSITY 312 COAXIAL DIFFAXIAL 12" SPEAKERS VINTAGE	$149.99
VINTAGE JBL SIGNATURE HARLAN SPEAKER SYSTEM Jim Lansing	$1,278.80	ALTEC LANSING 601-A Duplex Speaker,Crossover.alnico	$149.50
McIntosh Labratory XRT18 Speaker Set Vintage NR	$1,143.22	one pair Siemens 2-way baffles Sf. L 6.4 AlNiCo	$149.00
RCA MI-9462 Vintage Speaker Cabinet - Rialto theater	$1,080.00	PAIR VINTAGE EV E-V ELECTRO-VOICE MODEL PRO-12 SPEAKERS	$149.00
JBL AQUARIUS IV TYPE S109 LOUDSPEAKERS CIRCA 1970	$999.95	Vintage Electro-Voice T350 Speaker (used)	$140.50
Altec 802B Horn Driver with Multi Cell Horn	$891.02	Pair INFINITY RS 6 Kappa Loudspeakers Speakers $1 NR!	$138.06
Vintage JENSEN Theater Horn & Driver XP-101 K4-244	$861.00	Vintage Electro Voice Horn Speaker=PA LOUD SPEAKER	$130.50
Altec 515 8gHP (one pair)	$750.00	2 VAC 1950's ALNICO SPEAKERS GERMANY 7' FULLRANGE !!!!	$130.50
PIONEER HPM-1500 SPEAKERS *ORIG BXS* HPM-150 *NICE*	$695.00	1 VINTAGE PHILIPS 8" DUALCONE ALNICO FULLRANGE SPEAKER	$130.49
TANNOY LGM Little Gold Monitors 12" Pair.	$660.00	VINTAGE BOZAK CROSSOVERS MODEL N-10102 3 WAY NICE!!	$129.50
Ampex 620 vintage tube amplifier & speaker set JBL	$575.00	Vintage Pair of Jensen P12 NF Like P12 N Speakers Nice	$127.50
GOODMANS MAXIMUS 1 2- WAY SPEAKER MONITORS /ROGER BBC	$560.00	Altec 416-8B 15" Woofer-needs reconed	$127.50

Vintage Electronics ▶ Tubes

The average sales price in this subcategory is $53.33.

	HIGH		AVG
DEFOREST SPHERICAL AUDION 1st TRIODE TUBE EVER!!!!!!	$2,708.00	Tubes, 12AU7A, HP, Amperex, Holland, Tested, 7 tubes	$72.00
12 B7971/B-7971 NIXIE Tubes w/Sockets + GeekKock/FLW	$590.00	Tubes, 6SN7, 6SN7WGT, Raytheon, Sylvania, 3 Tubes	$71.00
2 Tubes Siemens Halske CCa (6922 E88CC) d-getter	$536.00	Conar Model 223 Vintage Tube Tester ***EXCELLENT***	$69.89
MagneQuest FS-030 HQ output transformer for 300B, pair	$435.00	A matched pair 5AR4/GZ34 tubes	$69.00
4 <> Tubes Telefunken CCa Lorenz 6922	$407.99	NOS GZ34/5AR4 Amperex "Bugle Boy" Radio Vacuum Tube	$69.00
GEC KT88 Gold Lion - Matched Pair	$350.00	Telefunken Philips KC3 3 pcs.	$67.00
2 <> Tubes Telefunken E188CC 6922 7308	$326.00	7591A EH electro-harmonix tubes NEW QUAD	$65.00
Quad of Mullard EL34/6CA7 tubes	$215.28	[2 of these sold for $65.00 each]	
1 NOS Rectifier Tubes Telefunken RGN2004 mesh	$214.50	B & K Model 700 Dynamic Mutual Conductance Tube Tester	$63.00
(6) 5842, 417A tubes, Western Electric, NOS, NIB, NR	$207.49	TUBE TESTER DYNA JET MODEL 606	$60.00
(4) P Q Amperex 6922/61-47 Electronic Tubes	$203.50	3-WESTERN ELECTRIC 328A TUBES-STRONG	$59.99
2 NOS <> Tubes Telefunken E88CC 6922	$190.88	Vintage Supreme Model 589-A Tube Tester NICE!	$57.60
(8) 5691 & 5692 (6SL7/6SN7) tubes, used	$189.10	BIG BAG OF UNTESTED LOW VOLTAGE TUBES-TRANSOCEANIC TYPE	$57.50
QUAD TELEFUNKEN ECC808 ECC-808 Tubes NOS	$183.50	Jan VT-4-C / 211 power tube	$56.00
raytheon radio tv tubes light up pam clock sign C9+	$167.50	One Western Electric 421A duotriode tube, tubes	$56.00

Wholesale Lots ▶ Gadgets

The average sales price in this subcategory is $12.06.

	HIGH		AVG
PSP DVD/RW Drive 2.4 GHz Cordless PC Grab Box	$102.50	Acoustic Research Power Conditioner+Grab Bag	$15.55
NEXXTECH & CENTRIOS LOT OF 46 GADGETS & ELECTRONICS	$92.00	Electromagnetic Field Detector	$15.00
12 pieces BATTERY CHARGER, ALKALINE or NiCad switchable	$75.00	LOT 72 ALKALINE POWER BUY AAA BATTERIES BEST BY 2006	$15.00
UNCLAIMED FREIGHT MEGA DEAL! NO RESERVE!	$69.00	Lot of 10 White LED Keychain & Switchblade knife Gadget	$14.99
NEXXTECH LOT OF 65 GADGETS & ELECTRONICS	$63.00	2! 97-02 Ford Expedition Transponder keys key	$13.95
48 Shocking Pen Great GaG & Prank Items Wholesale Price	$57.01	Lot of 40 Beuler 12 Volt 40/50 Amp 5 pin Relays New!!!	$13.38
NEXXTECH & CENTRIOS LOT OF 45 GADGETS & ELECTRONICS	$55.00	Lot Novelty Gifts 27 Pedometer Binoculars Wallet Scan R	$12.49
UNCLAIMED FREIGHT MEGA DEAL! NO RESERVE!	$52.01	Lot of (1,200) 6"x6" Anti-Static Wipes NEW IN BOX!!	$11.61
UNCLAIMED FREIGHT MEGA DEAL! NO RESERVE!	$51.01	Lot of (1,200) 6"x6" Anti-Static Wipes NEW IN BOX!!	$11.49
UNCLAIMED FREIGHT MEGA DEAL! NO RESERVE!	$51.00	4 Brand New 6V 2CR5 Lithium Photo battery Olympus	$11.00
NEXXTECH WHOLESALE LOTS OF 70 ASSORTED CLOCKS/RADIOS	$50.00	30 PCS CR2450 CR 2450 WATCH Lithium Ion BATTERY	$11.00
COLLECTIBLE REMOTE CONTROL OSCAR MAYER WIENERMOBILE	$50.00	GRAB BOX: SONY, MEMOREX, DVD, CD, HP Cartridges, ++more	$10.85
UNCLAIMED FREIGHT MEGA DEAL! NO RESERVE!	$49.08	WHOLESALE LOT BOX 18 FELLOWES	$10.51
60 AA 2250mAh NiMH Rechargeable battery w 15 holders	$45.99	BODY GLOVE VEHICLE POWER	
[2 of these sold for $45.99 each]		25 PCS CR2430 CR 2430 WATCH Lithium Ion BATTERY	$10.50
NEXXTECH LOT OF 59 GADGETS & ELECTRONICS	$42.75	Lot of Stepper Motors Big & small DC Motors Gears belts	$10.08

Wholesale Lots ▶ Other Consumer Electronics

The average sales price in this subcategory is $35.25.

	HIGH		AVG
Ipod 60GP PHOTO lot of 3	$1,000.00	WHOLESALE LOT BOX 18 STREETGLOW RADIO BARS NEON BLUE	$36.01
Electronic test equipment,Oscilloscopes,multimeters,etc	$430.00	X10 SR227 Qty 4 Outlet Module No Reserve New	$36.01
Iriver Ifp-890 MP3 Player 256MB Genuine+SEALED	$325.00	WHOLESALE LOT BOX 24 STREETGLOW RADIO BARS NEON RED	$36.00
SQUARE D NEMA SIZE 6 STARTER MOTOR CONTACTOR	$304.00	WHOLESALE LOT BOX 15 MIXED	$36.00
WHOLESALE LOT OF 50 BRAND NEW 2 WAY RADIOS	$300.00	BOX OF PORTABLE CD PLAYERS	
[2 of these sold for $300.00 each]		SINGING MACHINE STVG-988 MTV	$36.00
MIX WHOLESALE ELECTRONICS – L@@K!!	$299.99	KARAOKE STATION W/MIC	
[2 of these sold for $299.99 each]		X10 WS467 Qty 5 Wall Switch Module. No Reserve New	$35.50
Wholesale Pallet Electronics Speakers DVD VCR CD Radio	$229.50	WHOLESALE LOT OF 10 MD/CD/MP3 PLAYERS	$33.00
BULK PALLET OF ELECTRONICS DEAL FOR YOU !!	$225.00	WHOLESALE LOT BOX 23 STREETGLOW	$31.05
Ademco 998 PI PIR/Aurora PIR Motion Detectors	$200.00	RADIO BARS NEON GREEN	
Wholesale Pallet Customer Returns Electronics Lot $2500	$200.00	Vector Sony Dynex Monster Cable RCA Grab Box NR	$31.05
3 Nortel Contivity 100 VPN Switch II DM1401E67 NIB!!	$180.00	Westell VersaLink Wireless Modem/Gateway Router (New)	$31.00
WHOLESALE LOT OF 122 ASSORTED CD/MP3 PLAYERS	$176.56	WHOLESALE LOT BOX 18 STREETGLOW XENON WHITE BULBS H7	$31.00
ELECTRONICS BULK LOT DEAL WOW LOOK $350 MSRP	$175.00	NEW $149 lot of ten AM/FM radio pens	$31.00
2 Kicker Solo Baric L5 12" subwoofers like new	$162.50	WHOLESALE LOT VARIOUS ELECTRONICS GRAB BAG - LOOK!	$30.09
wholesale nextel list i860 starting at $150,i836- $125	$160.76	GE Consumer Electronics Products Spacemaker radio	$29.99

15

CRAFTS

It is possible to buy everything you need to make your crafts, as well as sell your made crafts, here on eBay. But aside from doing business, eBay has given crafters across the country (and even in other countries) a chance to interact with others that share their sometimes arcane passions. The crafting community on eBay is a thriving and tight-knit one, if you'll pardon the pun.

Some crafters share the stories of how they got into selling supplies by accident. One man began selling the classic canes he made on eBay, and his customers started asking if he would sell them the raw materials to make their own canes. He then began selling cane blanks—handles and shafts—and now he runs a business selling small pieces of rare and exotic wood. "I began selling my scraps.....now I cut and sell specific standard sizes of rare wood," he says on the discussion boards.

Another eBay crafter sells sewing supplies. She has an offline sewing business, and had discovered she could sell the samples on eBay as a way of clearing space in her store room. Now she sells sequin and bead appliques, embroidery trims, Chinese frogs, and fabric swatches.

Among the advantages eBay has brought crafters is that it's given them a place to purchase supplies that may have been previously difficult to find in their local areas. "Unless you live in a big city, where there is a fabric district, it is just about impossible to find nice apparel fabric in the stores," said one crafter on the eBay Hobbies & Crafts discussion boards. She owns a small chain of women's apparel boutiques and lists her company's leftover fabric and trim.

Another boon is the ability to find the obsolete, discontinued, and vintage. An eBayer named Bonnie writes on the board that she sells mostly discontinued sewing patterns. "I have a huge inventory of at least 10,000 patterns from the 1980s to 2002," she said.

Crafters Supplies: eBay vs. Retail

So what about what we're most interested in here: prices? How do they compare to buying these supplies at the store (assuming that buying them from a store is an option for you)? Let's look at some reasonably common craft items and how they compare to retail.

Sculpey is a popular type of craft clay that can be used to make beads for jewelry. A 10-piece multi-color pack sold for $12.00 in the average price range in the Crafts ▸ Ceramics, Pottery ▸ Polymer Clay subcategory; a similar pack is available on MisterArt.com for $13.11, not taking into account shipping differences. So there's not a big difference there. But you might be able to save more by buying a bigger lot; for example, the "huge" lot of Fimo clay, 5 1-pounders and 78 packs, sold for $73.77, which works out to $0.88 per pack, vs. the retail price for a 2-oz pack at $1.49.

Beads are popular on eBay, but it can be difficult to compare prices because the quality of the beads is important, and it's harder to judge this online. Let's look at a brand name, the popular Swarovski crystal beads. A set of 12 8mm "CRYSTAL AB SWAROVSKI® 3700 Crystal Beads" went for $0.99, plus $2.00 shipping; a package of 12 similar Swarovski beads sells for $2.57 at FireMountainGems.com (shipping is based on weight, but there is a $2.65 handling fee per order).

Scrapbooking Savings

Scrapbooking has enjoyed a resurgence lately, and companies like Creative Memories, which sponsor house parties where people gather and work on their photo projects (and buy supplies), have helped fuel it. You'll find a lot of Creative Memories brand products in the Crafts ▸ Scrapbooking subcategory, with the lowest-priced album of this brand selling at $31.00. But if you look for other brands or no-name albums, you can pick up a scrapbook for as little as $0.99, with average prices around $14.00.

Some of the highest prices in the category overall are for sewing and other crafting machines. The top seller, a Gammill Quilting Machine, sold for $8,100.00. But most prices are in the hundreds, not thousands, of dollars. A new Janome 4618 LE machine went for $289.00. I found another one online for the same price, and they both have free shipping. Some Singer machines showed up in the average price range between $89.00 and $95.00; the $89.00 is a refurbished model but comes with a 30-day guarantee. At $239.00 suggested retail, according to the seller, this looks like more of a bargain.

There is a whole cornucopia of different arts available here—pottery, soapmaking, crocheting, cross-stitching, tole painting, not to mention woodworking, weaving, and tatouage. In short, you can save money here, but the big advantage may be in the sheer variety of items and types of lots available.

Bead Art ▸ Beads

The average sales price in this subcategory is $11.51.

	HIGH		AVG
REDMAX LAMPWORK GLASS TORCH	$350.00	20 glass pendant beads BABY PUFFER FISH D1	$14.15
Ten pounds of A to AAA beads and sterling silver	$295.00	TCS LAMPWORK BEADS 7 LENTILS "SAVOR THE MOMENT" BHV	$13.99
100 Packs Bali Sterling Silver Pendants, Chains Beads +	$192.50	Swarovski Crystals 46 10MM FACET HEART BEADS	$13.64
100 Packs Bali Sterling Silver Pendants, Chains Beads +	$127.50	24 Czech GREYHOUND Glass Beads, 20x13mm, Color: Rose	$13.51
100 Packs Bali Sterling Silver Pendants, Chains Beads +	$104.06	Misc. Hematite beads	$13.50
100 Packs Bali Sterling Silver Pendants, Chains Beads +	$102.50	LG LOT OF SILVER BALLENTINE TINY BEADS EGG ART SUPPLIES	$13.00
Seed & Bugle Beads Lot - 81 Bags - 2+ Pounds	$102.50	A GREAT VARIETY OF BEADS in ONE BOX!	$13.00
BEAD STORE INVENTORY CLOSEOUT LOT free shipping	$91.00	Swarovski Crystals 30 TEARDROPS	$12.50
BEAD STORE INVENTORY CLOSEOUT LOT free shipping	$90.99	V. RARE Swarovski Vitrail Med Disco Drop Beads 6002 1p	$12.49
32 Pkgs ALLURE Swarovski Crystal Sliders Crystals Watch	$86.61	100 STERLING SILVER ROUND BRILLIANT 5MM SEAMLESS BEADS	$12.49
100 Packs Bali Sterling Silver Pendants, Chains Beads +	$86.00	150+ small assorted funky polymer clay beads	$12.25
*HUGE LOT*BLUE MOON GLASS BEADS,FINDINGS,CHAINS+MORE	$70.00		
45 loose handmade polymer clay STACKER beads	$69.53	100pcs Swarovski #5301 6mm Bicone Mix 51 Colors Lot!!	$12.00
LOT 20 Bulk Packs Pure Allure Swarovski Crystal Beads	$66.68	Designer ROSE shades # 3Swarovski crystal beads 120p	$11.99
630+ PIECE SWAROVSKI CRYSTAL	$60.99	8 Petoskey Stone Beads 6 Small & 2 Larger	$11.87
ASSORTED LOT! GORGEOUS BHV		LOT - 10 Strands Druk Glass Beads 6mm Asst. Colors	$11.75

Bead Art ▶ Kits, Instructions

The average sales price in this subcategory is $8.73.

	HIGH		AVG
BeadPad Platinum Image-Pattern+Design Software	$37.00	Black Dragon! Very Detailed! Peyote or Loom!	$8.99
FACETED FIRE POLISHED Vintage CZECH GLASS Beads LOT! NR	$34.99	MILL HILL JEWELED BAR PIN BEADING KIT	$8.99
JAPANESE BEADED FLOWERS-Glass Bead/Beading Craft Book 3	$32.99	[4 of these sold for $8.99 each]	
5 Vintage Bead Pattern Books 4 Christmas Ornaments DIY	$31.01	BEADED FLOWERS Russian MAGAZINE GREAT bead book	$8.95
Fast & Easy-SEED BEAD SPINNER / STRINGER Tool	$31.00	B EAD BOOK CROCHET BEADED BAGS	$8.79
HUGE LOT of BEADS HAMMERED FLAT PENDANT DROP ELEMENTS	$30.00	Beaded Ornament Kit Set of 8 Christmas Packages	$8.79
LOT 3 VINTAGE BEAD & SEQUINS ORNAMENT KITS 12 ORNAMENTS	$29.75	DEB'S BEADS "A TOUCH OF THE BLUES" POLYMER CLAY FIMO	$8.78
Fabulous Set of Mill Hill Bead Kits!! - #15	$29.06	NEW OOP Mill Hill Delights Kit - An Apple a Day - MHD4	$8.72
12 Unopened Sequin & Pearl Art Kits - Looney Tunes+++	$29.00	NEW OOP Mill Hill Spring Simple Treasure Kit MHST20	$8.50
1924 Bead Work Emma Post Barbour Purses Jewelry Flapper	$29.00	NEW OOP Mill Hill Holiday Simple Treasure Kit MHST14	$8.49
Fast & Easy-SEED BEAD SPINNER / STRINGER Tool	$28.00	NEW OOP Mill Hill Holiday Sampler Kit - Tree - MHTS32	$8.49
NATIVE AMERICAN BEAD WEAVING LOOM KIT W/DOUBLE BONUS	$27.00	DEB'S BEADS "FAIRY CHARMS" POLYMER CLAY SCULPEY	$8.49
[3 of these sold in a multiple item ("Dutch") auction for $9.00 each]		DEB'S BEADS "PUPPIES EVERYWHERE" POLYMER CLAY	$8.49
BEAD PARTY KIT for 10! BEADS, TOOLS+++ for 40 PROJECTS!	$24.99	DEB'S BEADS "SWEET KITTENS CATS" POLYMER CLAY	$8.49
Lot of 6 Wire Jewelry and Bead Jewelry How-To Books	$24.99	Mill Hill Bead Kits - Drummer Boy & Candy Cane Santa	$8.28
9 BEAD & BUTTON MAGAZINE LOT beading	$24.52	Beaded Amulet Purses Instruction & Inspiration Book	$8.02

Candle & Soap Making ▶ Molds

The average sales price in this subcategory is $8.64.

	HIGH		AVG
Soap Cutter, Bar Cutter, Soapmaking Tool	$150.00	3 diff. BEAUTIFUL WOMAN Fine Art Soap Molds	$8.95
Commercial Quick Soap Cutter	$109.09	3 LIGHTHOUSE & DOLPHINS Fine Art Soap Molds	$8.95
Wood Soap Mold-18 bar	$52.00	Makes 9 guest LIGHTHOUSE Soap Tray Mold Molds	$8.95
NEW SUPER KIT 16 BAR WOODEN SOAP MOLD KIT WOOD SUPPLIES	$49.00	2 DOLPHIN, 1 WHALE, 1 SEALION Soap mold Molds	$8.95
OAK 36 BAR wood wooden SOAP MAKING supplies CUTTER MOLD	$45.00	5 BABY GUEST HEART Fine Art Soap Molds	$8.95
[3 of these sold for $45.00 each]		FLIP FLOPS SANDAL Soap Candy Mold Molds 4 Cavity NEW	$8.54
HUGE LOT SOAP SUPPLIES! molds colors oils pumice tubes	$39.00	GREAT DANE DOG marmaduke flex soap mold FREE scent oil	$8.51
LOT OF SOAP/CANDY MOLDS - ALL OCCASIONS - NEW & USED	$36.50	CINNI RED HEARTS Candle/Soap/Candy Silicone Mold 2nds	$8.50
15 BAR 5# LOAF Soap Making Mold, Cutter Box & Blade 3N1	$36.00	FLIP FLOPS SANDAL Soap Candy Mold Molds 4 Cavity NEW	$8.50
NEW WOODEN 16 BAR SOAP MOLD KIT WOOD W/KNIFE SUPPLIES b	$32.00	CHIHUAHUA CHI CHIWAWA TOY	$8.50
[2 of these sold for $32.00 each]		DOG flex soap mold FREE oil	
HUGE LOT 82 CANDY MOLDS AND "BE MINE" CANDY BOX KIT NR	$31.00	BLESSED BE wiccan wicca soap mold molds chocolate	$8.50
12-15 Pound/4 Compartment Vertical Soap Mold	$31.00	FLOWER BOUQUET Chase FLEX soap mold FREE fragrance oil	$8.50
Huge lot of Soap Making, Embeds, Flavor, Scents, Molds	$31.00	Mold Builder - Liquid Latex Rubber, New & Sealed	$8.50
Lot of 14 Tray Molds for Soap making (various)	$29.00	4 SLEEPING CAT martin Soap	$8.49
Big Lot of 17 Holiday Molds!	$28.77	Molds FREE FRAGRANCE OIL!	
FLEXIBLE SILICONE SOAP MOLD FLORAL FLOWER GIFT	$26.98	3 LIGHTHOUSE & DOLPHINS Fine Art Soap Molds	$8.45

Candle & Soap Making ▶ Scents, Fragrances

The average sales price in this subcategory is $6.25.

	HIGH		AVG
Huge Lot of Candle & Soap Making Fragrance Oil	$89.88	16 oz. Candle/Soap Fragrance Oil (BEACH BREEZE)	$6.49
HUGE LOT 162+ total oz candle scent fragrance 20 bottle	$63.00	16 oz. Candle/Soap Fragrance Oil (BUTTERSCOTCH)	$6.49
Fragrance Oils Clearance * 48 Bottles $9.99 Bid (C)	$52.25	16 oz. Candle/Soap Fragrance Oil (ETERNAL ROSE)	$6.49
Fragrance Oils Clearance - 50 Bottles $9.99 Bid (D)	$50.98	16 oz. Candle/Soap Fragrance Oil (CINNAPEAR)	$6.49
Large Lot of Candle Scents!!!	$45.00	16 oz. Candle/Soap Fragrance Oil (ENCHANTING APPLE)	$6.49
Candle Fragrance Oil Lot Candlemaking Clearance Sale !	$42.09	Lot of 10 Candle Making Fragrance Oils ~1 oz. ea~	$6.45
Lot of 15 Candle/Soap Fragrances 50 oz 4 candle making	$40.03	[2 of these sold for $6.45 each]	
HUGE LOT of 35 Fragrance Oils Soap & Candle Supplies	$40.00	Celtic Moonspice Fragrance Oil candlemaking soy	$6.26
Lot Fragrance Oils #5	$39.99	FRAGRANCE OIL BY CANDLE FACTORY	$6.25
Lot Fragrance Oils #4	$39.99	ROSE GERANIUM Premium Fragrance Candle Soap Soy Body	$6.00
**GINORMOUS SOAP & LIP BALM	$35.00	WHITE TEA ORIGINS Premium Fragrance Candle Soy Soap	$6.00
LOT**PACKAGING**FRAGRANCE		Lot of Candle/Fragrance Oils	$6.00
Wholesale lot - 20 candle soap fragrance scent oils	$31.00	8 oz. Angel Kissed Fragrance Oil Candle Soap Making	$5.99
Large Lot #6 Candle fragrance Oil Rain Cinaberry Hollyb	$31.00	Lot Fragrance Oils #1	$5.99
Big fragrance oil lot dyes mica, soap making bath bombs	$31.00	MADAGASCAR SPICE Premium Fragrance Candle Soap Soy	$5.78
Lot of Fragrance Oils for Candles! 63oz's - 28 bottles	$30.00	LOT of 8 Fragrance Oils-1oz ea.	$5.50
		[2 of these sold for $5.50 each]	

Ceramics, Pottery ▶ Molds, Kits

The average sales price in this subcategory is $12.13.

	HIGH		AVG
ENTIRE DISCONTINUED CERAMIC MOLD/MOLDS BUSINESS	$1,050.00	SUNDANCE CERAMIC MOLD - SNOWMAN ISICLES	$13.25
Aluminum Concrete / Cement Swan Planter Mold	$102.50	Jumping Fish Border Edger Mold Concrete Cement New!	$13.09
NATIVITY BETHLEHEM VILLAGE 6 Ceramic Mold Scioto 784 78	$91.00	Ceramic Mold Anchor 401 Dinosaur	$12.50
CERAMIC MOLD/ LG. SANTA MICKEY MOUSE	$76.00	Ceramic Mold Teddy Bear Ornaments	$12.50
Large Rabbit Aluminum Concrete / Cement Mold 11"	$66.00	Clay Magic _ Ceramic Mold Catalog _ 7th Edition _ 1993	$12.49
Aluminum Concrete / Cement Duck Mold 13"	$62.00	Ceramic Mold Dinosaur Anchor mold 403	$12.27
Large Chicken / Hen Aluminum Concrete / Cement Mold 14"	$56.55	12" ROOSTER w TALL FANCY TAIL Ceramic Mold Arnel 384	$12.00
Large Rooster Aluminum Concrete / Cement Mold 19"	$52.00	3 SUGARPLUM GIRL ORNAMENTS Ceramic Mold Dona's D 485	$11.90
Aluminum Duck Concrete / Cement Mold 7"	$46.00	GORGEOUS HORSE HEAD w/LONG MANE POLYMER CLAY MOLD!	$11.13
Concrete Mold, Cocker Spaniel, Rubber w/Plaster Backing	$40.98	Ceramic Mold Nowell 1888 Dinosaur	$11.05
BIG PUMPKINS & GHOSTS Ceramic Mold Kimple 1565	$38.88	Ceramic Mold Dona 1581 3 crackpot snowmen ornaments.	$11.05

Duckling / Duck Aluminum Concrete / Cement Mold 4-1/2"	$36.00	SANTA IN CHIMNEY DETAILED! Ceramic Mold Mayco M 1025	$11.00
Ceramic Mold Alberta 1116 Carousel horse & reindeer orn	$30.97	CERAMIC CASTING MOLD/MOLDS LRG POPPY FLOWER DISH W DIP	$10.55
Ceramic Mold Scioto 2104 2 frogs	$27.79	Ceramic Mold Mikes 273 Elephant	$10.53
Ceramic Mold Climbing Tree Frog Scioto 3217	$26.97	Cat Dish With Fish In Bottom Cats On Side CERAMIC MOLD	$10.51

Ceramics, Pottery ▸ Polymer Clay

The average sales price in this subcategory is $10.67.

	HIGH		AVG
NEW - HUGE LOT FIMO CLAY / 5 - 1pounders + 78 Packs	$73.77	Female Fairy Torso - Polymer Clay - Handmade Mold	$11.26
Fimo Premo Granitex Sculpey Huge Clay Set New	$67.76	jflo boutique butterfly polymer clay cane	$11.06
HUGE 27 LOT! Sculpey Fimo Polymer Clay ! NR!!! BHV	$61.00	Polymer Clay by Irene Dean, Irene Semanchuk Dean (2000)	$11.00
OOAK Troll Monkey Orangutan Baby Jolie (Becky's QT's))	$57.50	Two Polymer Clay Cane Ends (Canes#85)	$10.78
Sculpey III & FIMO Poly Clay / PREMO Shapelets & MORE +	$52.55	Autumn Tones In These Polymer Clay Cane Ends (Canes#75)	$10.77
7 In. Lady Fairy Push Mold 4 Polymer Clay - Press Mold	$49.99	FUSCHIA MILLEFIORI FLORAL UNCURED POLYMER CLAY CANE	$10.76
NEW ORIGINAL ATLAS 180 PASTA MAKER MACHINE	$49.95	Fantastic Figures by Susanna Oroyan (1994)	$10.54
SCULPTURING WITH JACK JOHNSTON-ADVANCE-VOL.4 VHS	$45.00	Polymer Clay Extravaganza by Lisa Pavelka (2003)	$10.50
NEW ORIGINAL ATLAS 180 PASTA MAKER MACHINE	$44.95	Sculpey III polymer clay lot 2oz packages	$10.50
LOT POLYMER CLAY, TOOLS, BK, PASTA MACH MOLDS + MORE	$42.00	[2 of these sold for $10.50 each]	$10.50
HUGE Mixed LOT Polymer Clay Beads Pins figures + More	$41.00	Lot of 12 Sculpey III polymer clay 2 oz	$10.50
HUGE LOT Polymer clay polymerclay dark colors 2oz bars	$41.00	Clay wraped polymer clay pens	$10.50
6 In. Girl Fairy Push Mold - Press Mold 4 Polymer clay	$39.99	POLYMERCAFE SUMMER 2004 DID YOU MISS THIS ISSUE?	$10.50
Girl Fairy Push Mold - being discontinued shortly	$39.99	WHITECATCRAFTS POLYMER CLAY	$10.50
[2 of these sold for $39.99 each]		GITD DRAGONFLY CANE SET	
7 In. Lady Fairy Push Mold 4 Polymer Clay - Press Mold	$39.99	Polymer clay polymerclay Lot of 10 1 oz bars	$10.50
[3 of these sold for $39.99 each]		Kringle and Snowman Polymer Clay Flexible Sculpey mold	$10.50

Ceramics, Pottery ▸ Ready-to-Paint Pieces

The average sales price in this subcategory is $6.84.

	HIGH		AVG
Unfinished Mermaid Ship's Head Shelf Bracket	$30.05	CERAMIC BISQUE- U PAINT-DOG OR PUPPY WELCOME PLAQUE	$7.00
CERAMIC BISQUE DRAGON/CASTLE INCENSE SMOKER (unpainted)	$32.50	2 Crackpot Cow Pots / Planters Ceramic Bisque U Paint	$6.99
TERRA COTTA TOAD HOUSE & FROG	$31.00	Large Mouth Bass Fish - Wall Mount - Ceramic Bisque	$6.99
Horse - Chicken - Cow Friends Welcome Ceramic Bisque	$29.95	READY TO PAINT CERAMIC BISQUE FAIRY 14" TALL FAIRIES	$6.99
TERRA COTTA ST. FRANCIS W/ DEER & BUNNY RABBIT STATUE	$24.99	MOOSE WEARING KNITTED SWEATER- CERAMIC BISQUE	$6.98
TERRA COTTA ST. FRANCIS HOLDING A DOVE STATUE	$20.50	Frog Crackpot Pot / Planter Ceramic Bisque U Paint	$6.88
Large Driftwood Wolf Pack - U-Paint Ceramic Bisque	$20.25	READY TO PAINT~CERAMIC BISQUE~EAGLE BUST~	$6.85
U YOU PAINT IT GREAT DANE DOG WALL BUST	$20.00	Box of ceramic bisque bears unicorns christmas & angel	$6.50
[2 of these sold in a multiple item ("Dutch") auction for $10.00 each]		4 PC. Baby Dragon SET(bisque)	$6.49
READY TO PAINT CERAMIC BISQUE LAYING PUG DOG CERAMICS	$18.58	Ceramic Bisque—Let It Snow	$6.00
Ceramic Bisque - ENT Tree Planter for Yard or Garden	$16.95	CERAMIC READY TO PAINT BISQUE	$6.00
Ceramic Bisque - Mare & Foal Horse - NEW ITEM	$16.95	COCKATOOS COCKATOO BIRDS	
Lg Lying Gnome Reading , Ceramic Bisque, Ready to Paint	$16.49	12" frogula FROG -SALE-UNPAINTED Ceramic Bisque	$6.00
XMAS FROG HO HO HO -SALE-UNPAINTED Ceramic Bisque	$15.50	Ceramic Bisque - Summer Fairy on Mushroom	$6.00
11" SNOW FROG -SALE-UNPAINTED Ceramic Bisque	$15.50	Small Ent (tree people)	$6.00
GAZEBO-LIGHTSCENE/WITH NATIVITY-CERAMIC BISQUE by EL	$14.99	READY TO PAINT CERAMIC BISQUE FAIRY LAYING FAIRIES CUTE	$6.00

Crocheting ▸ Hooks

The average sales price in this subcategory is $26.32.

	HIGH		AVG
GRAYDOG Crochet Hook MAMMOTH IVORY ~Flame Spiral ~ I	$355.00	SHARKY'S Crochet Hook/Hooks Vineyard Sz K	$26.62
GRAYDOG Crochet Hook: EBONY LAPIS TIGEREYE CARNELIAN, I	$265.00	19 Boye Steel or Aluminum Crochet Hooks	$26.60
GRAYDOG Crochet Hook EBONY DEER ANTLER ~FLAME~ SPIRAL Q	$264.99	New Lovely Wood Crochet Hooks 7 Sizes	$26.51
GRAYDOG Crochet Hook: ~AMETHYST~ & VENETIAN GLASS, I	$218.00	OZARKTWIST Crochet Hook Hooks PURPLE PEARL M	$26.51
NEW!! HUGE LOT CLOVER TAKUMI KNITTING NEEDLES!! WOW!!	$208.07	OZARKTWIST Roll Crochet Hook Hooks SOUTHWEST H	$26.50
GRAYDOG Crochet Hook: EBONY, ROSE QUARTZ, PEARL & CZ, G	$202.50	SHARKY'S Crochet Hook/Hooks Tapestry Sz P	$26.47
GRAYDOG Crochet Hook: EBONY, ~ROSE~ HEART & CRYSTALS, H	$202.50	SHARKY'S Crochet Hook/Hooks Passion Fruit Sz I	$26.01
GRAYDOG Crochet Hook ~PURPLEWOOD~ HEART PEARL CRYSTAL H	$200.49	Rock Maple "Bamboo" w/Japanese Characters - "P" Hook I	$26.00
GRAYDOG Crochet Hook: EBONY, AFZELIA BURL & BLOODWOOD K	$200.00	BRITTANY BLACK WALNUT CROCHET HOOK NEW! SZ F	$26.00
GRAYDOG Crochet Hook AFRICAN EBONY ~Jingle Rings ~ J	$191.50	Vintage Lot of Crochet Hooks and Wood Box	$26.00
GRAYDOG Crochet Hook YEW/REDWOOD BURL ~Flow Hook~ S	$187.50	OZARKTWIST Crochet Hook Hooks FLAMINGO ROYAL BLUE H	$26.00
GRAYDOG Crochet Hook: EBONY & VIOLET-BURL ~FLOW HOOK~ J	$187.50	SHARKY'S Crochet Hook/Hooks Blue Indigo Sz I	$26.00
GRAYDOG Crochet Hook EBONY/AFZELIA BURL ~Flow Hook~ N	$182.50	AJ's Bocote Rosewood Crochet Hook Size K	$26.00
GRAYDOG Crochet Hook LIGNUM VITAE SMOKETREE BURL FLOW N	$167.49	VINTAGE "BOYE" - COMPLETE CROCHET HOOK SET WITH CASE	$26.00
GRAYDOG Crochet Hook EBONY TAGUA NUT TURQUOISE ~FLOW~ L	$167.49	GRAYDOG Crochet Hook EMERALD PEARL ~Flow Hook~ J	$26.00

Crocheting ▸ Patterns

The average sales price in this subcategory is $4.16.

	HIGH		AVG
Crafters Crochet Pattern Patterns Jewelry Irish Filigre	$46.00	Lot of 13 CROCHET Leaflets Magazines HOOKED ON CROCHET!	$4.27
CROCHET BARBIE COMPLETE SET ROYAL COURT COLLECTION~NEW	$35.99	CROCHET * TUNISIAN BABY AFGHANS * 5 PATTERNS	$4.25
ANNIE'S FAVORITE BABY PROJECTS 49 DESIGNS 160PG HB	$35.47	CROCHET * HEIRLOOM AFGHANS FOR BABY * 6 PTNS	$4.25
CROCHET * ANNIE'S ATTIC * BABY BOOTIE BOUTIQUE * 10 PTN	$21.50	CROCHET * CUTE & COZY AFGHANS * SCOTTY DOG + 8 PTNS	$4.25
22 Crochet World Premier Issues; '90-'96; 570 + pattern	$17.50	KNIT/CROCHET * DOG SWEATERS * 10 DESIGNS	$4.25
German LACE CROCHET magazine FILET CROCHET	$16.02	CROCHET * ABSOLUTELY GORGEOUS BABY AFGHANS * BK 2 * 6	$4.25
VINTAGE 1945 PURSE HAND BAGS Crochet Knit Patterns (16)	$16.00	Crochet Cow Toaster Cover/Bed Doll	$4.25
book-200 Crochet blocks byJan Eaton	$16.00	LOT OF 33 "GOLD LOOK" CHARMS `KEYS ~WATCHES ~CATS ~ ++	$4.25
GREAT ! German LACE CROCHET book Hälspitzen120 patter	$15.50	CROCHET * LEARN NEEDLE TATTING STEP-BY-STEP	$4.25

	HIGH		AVG
Antique Victorian Crochet Beaded Purse Patterns CD '00!	$14.99	CROCHET * KEEPSAKE BABY AFGHANS * 7 PATTERNS	$4.25
ANNIE'S ATTIC NATIVE AMERICAN BARBIE CROCHET PATTERNS!	$14.50	CROCHET * IN THE BAG * 12 PATTERNS FOR BAGS	$4.25
Lot of 4 White Crochet Magazines	$14.37	CROCHET * PRECIOUS MOMENTS * DOLLS * BOOK 2	$4.25
Vintage Priscilla Irish Crochet Book #2 1912 - RARE!	$14.00	Set of 7 Rhapsody in Black Crochet Jewelry Patterns	$4.24
ASN1280 CROCHET LITTLE AMULET BAGS BOOK	$13.56	Annie's Crochet Newsletter No.33	$4.20
CROCHET SANTA'S WORKSHOP 12 ADORABLE PATTERNS RUDOLPH!	$13.47	Annie's Crochet Newsletter No.52	$4.20

Cross Stitch ▶ Kits

The average sales price in this subcategory is $7.80.

	HIGH		AVG
Rare MONOPOLY counted cross stitch kit Retired	$26.00	TASHA TUDOR ~AMPLE PANTRY~Counted Cross Stitch Kit	$7.99
PARTIALLY COMPLETED CROSS STITCH TABLECLOTH & NAPKINS	$26.00	FOOTPRINTS ~ Bucilla Counted Cross Stitch Kit	$7.99
2 1983 PARAGON NEEDLEPOINT CRIB COVERLETS<BAMBI	$26.00	MARY ENGELBREIT~Love, Home, Family~Ctd Cross Stitch	$7.99
SHEPHERD'S BUSH Checkered Sheep Cross Stitch SUPPLIES	$24.99	Dimensions Counted cross stitch kit "One Will Never Do"	$7.95
Sudberry House Bezel Clock Kit - Sudberry House	$24.01	Stamped Cross Stitch Inspirational Craft Kit New NR	$7.90
LOT OF 3 CROSS STITCH KITS NEW IN PACKAGE	$23.50	Sleepy Bears Janlynn Counted Cross Stitch Kit	$7.75
Disney Cinderella Cross Stitch Kit	$23.01	Four Seasons Doors Janlynn Counted Cross Stitch Kit	$7.74
DISNEY WINNIE THE POOH CROSS STITCH BABY AFGHAN, HUGE!	$22.50	COUNTRY & WESTERN Music Cross Stitch Kit ~ NIP	$7.59
New — "English Cottage Sampler" cross stitch kit	$22.50	Snowed in Kitten Cross Stitch Kit ornament L@@K	$7.56
PURSE COLLECTION COUNTED CROSS STITCH KIT	$21.55	Santa on the Rooftop stocking kit NIP	$7.50
KIT - Shepherd's Bush - LITTLE WITCH	$21.52	Merry Christmas Bear stocking kit by Bucilla NIP	$7.50
LOT OF 2 CROSS STITCH KITS THOMAS KINKADE NIP	$21.06	NEW! SUNSET "IN THE GARDEN" CROSS STITCH KIT	$7.49
Stamped Cross Stitch Quilt Blocks Sunbonnet Sue	$20.50	ROSE BOUQUET QUILT BLOCKS Stamped BUCILLA xs kit NEW	$7.49
Mirabilia THE DREAMER with linen, floss, beads	$20.50	sunset VICTORIAN SHELF counted cross stitch KIT pretty	$7.48
BRAZILIAN VIEW CROSS STITCH KIT - PARATY / RJ - NEW!!!	$20.00	Stitch 'N Quilt Sewing with Mama Cross Stitch Kit- NEW!	$7.00

Cross Stitch ▶ Patterns

The average sales price in this subcategory is $4.25.

	HIGH		AVG
C. A. Wells Acorn Scissors Purse	$89.00	The Big Book of Holidays by Good Natured Girls	$4.95
C. A. Wells Peacocks Silk Sewing Case	$77.86	Prairie Schooler WNR #3 NOAH'S ARK CROSS STITCH PATTERN	$4.95
Cross stitch Epoque Nouveau Russ Egg RARE Ltd Dimples	$45.00	Stitched For Comfort 4 Aghan Patterns NEW	$4.80
OOP "Mountain Lodge" P. Buckley Moss	$35.98	101 Clothespin Angels Cross Stitch Pattern	$4.52
Coca-Cola Coke Cross Stitch Pattern Book 1986	$31.00	Sports–Cross Stitch–Windsurf/Kayak/ATV/Climbing/++	$4.50
PC STITCH 7 CROSS ST PATTERN Fact-Sealed BOX+Prior.Shpg	$26.49	AUTHENTIC HUMMEL CROSS STITCH BOOK VOL. 1	$4.26
PC STITCH v.7 CROSS STITCH PATTERN SOFTWARE~ BRAND NEW!	$26.49	Southwestern/Native American cross-stitch pattern/kit	$4.25
Picanini Can Can - Cross Stitch Originals	$26.00	HERFORDSHIRE England Village Cross Stitch Import OOP	$4.24
BSA Boy Scouts Cross Stitch Patt Emblems Patches Badges	$21.00	COUNTRY GALLERY CROSS STITCH LEAFLET	$4.19
PFALTZGRAFF (Grapevine)Cross Stitch Pattern Book	$20.95	October 1923 Needlecraft Magazine	$4.00
Quilts of the Bible Cross Stitch Book Paula Vaughan	$20.50	July 1921 Needlecraft Magazine	$4.00
OOP "Heavenly Grace" P. Buckley Moss	$20.03	April 1922 Needlecraft Magazine	$4.00
Native American Designs in Cross-Stitch Book	$20.00	March 1921 Needlecraft Magazine	$4.00
Emblems Patches Badges BSA Boy Scouts Cross Stitch Patt	$18.50	Ewe & Eye Black Sheep Valentine Wren Cross Stitch	$4.00
GREAT! EUROPE germ. BURDA mag. cross stitch	$16.00	Alma Lynne "I Love Cross Stitch"	$4.00

Decorative, Tole Painting ▶ Patterns, Instructions

The average sales price in this subcategory is $9.91.

	HIGH		AVG
Shabby Cottage Folk Art by Artist Catherine Holman	$127.50	Oils Tole Book The Heart Of Nature - Jo Hollingsworth	$9.99
95 Decorative Painting Books	$119.50	Bible verse painting by Artist Catherine Holman	$9.95
THE DECORATIVE PAINTER 25 Tole Painting Bks 1997 - 2000	$104.50	JO SONJA FOLK ART SAMPLER VOL 1-2-3 TOLE PAINTING BOOKS	$9.95
Huge Donna Dewberry One Stroke Lot w\Binder! Must see!!	$85.00	ALMOST HEAVEN - 5 Books - Tole Painting - Oil - Angels	$9.95
THE DECORATIVE PAINTER 21 Tole Painting Bks 1991 - 1996	$80.00	COUNTRY SAMPLER Folk Art Tole Painting Vol 1-3 JoSonja	$9.95
6 Ros Stallcup books	$79.00	Donna Dewberry Binder for One Stroke RTG's - Rare!	$9.95
3 JOYCE HOWARD BOOKS	$77.68	ONE STROKE PEACEFUL LANDSCAPES BY DONNA DEWBERRY	$9.95
Terrie Cordray Opinery Folk Art Pattern Circle of Life	$59.99	The Big Book of Decorative Borders by Jodie Bushman ...	$9.80
Michele Walton Folk Art Tole Pattern Wood Cabinet LOOK!	$52.26	Kenna Reynolds & Donna Malone Cuddles & Critters	$9.76
DONNA DEWBERRY FOLK ART ONE STROKE PAINT BRUSHES LOT	$51.00	Shiny Ts & Other Fun Things Lindy Brown Susan Jill Hall	$9.50
JOY OF COUNTRY PAINTING VIDEO LANDSCAPE DOROTHY DENT	$47.56	Lot of 9 TOLE PAINTING BOOKS~Christmas,Victorian,Folk	$9.50
Country Village Victorian scene TOLE Pattern Cochrane	$43.99	ROSEMARY WEST "STRAWBERRY SANTA" PACKET	$9.49
THE DECORATIVE PAINTER 16 Tole Painting Bks 2001 - 2003	$41.00	ROSEMARY WEST "THOSE WHO GIVE LOVE, GATHER LOVE" PACKET	$9.25
24 Decorative Artist's Workbook Tole Painting Magazines	$41.00	Country Collection of Precious Folk , Helen Cavin, 1988	$9.06
MAGIC OF FLORAL PAINTING VIDEO GARY JENKINS	$41.00	Strokework Basics Video with Jo Sonja	$9.00

Decorative, Tole Painting ▶ Transfers, Decals

The average sales price in this subcategory is $7.52.

	HIGH		AVG
Tatouage~Fan Palm ~ NEW DESIGN~FREE SHIPPING	$59.99	SETS VINTAGE MEYERCORD DECALS - siesta fiesta	$8.00
[2 of these sold for $59.99 each]		Vintage small bubble dancer decals - Meyercord 6 diff	$8.00
Tatouage~Banana Tree W/bananas~Free shipping	$49.99	Italian Gold Leaf Sheets	$8.00
Vintage Meyercord Lg Mermaid Decal in Package	$41.00	12 Iron-On T-Shirt Transfers Avery Personalized Ink Jet	$7.99
ISLAND PALM TREES INSTANT STENCIL LUV TATOUAGE	$36.00	Rub-On Transfers - WORDS & GREETINGS - 6 pcs	$7.99
[6 of these sold in a multiple item ("Dutch") auction for $6.55 each]		Vintage Meyercord Floral Decals Bright Colors! 2 Pkgs	$7.99
Lot of 21 Sheets Meyercord Eagle Flag USA 60+ Decals	$36.99	VINTAGE MEYERCORD DECALS (2) KITCHEN DECOR Lot 2	$7.99
5 vintage travel decals	$35.75	BIRDS NEST/BUTTERFLIES INSTANT	$7.76
4 Old Meyercord Pin Up Risque Girl Bubbles Decals	$33.99	STENCIL LUV TATOUAGE	

CHOPPERS INC ** PINUP GIRL STICKERS ** RARE**	$31.00	ME & MY BIG IDEAS ALPHABET RUB-ON	$7.51
Tatouage~CITY WINDOW~NEW DESIGN~.99 shipping	$29.99	TRANSFERS-RV $25-NEW	
Tatouage~Lemon & Rose Tree~ NEW CONFIGURATION~3.00 Ship	$29.99	DECALS ~ Vintage CHERRY Kitchen CHERRIES ~ 24	$7.50
Decals ~HUGE LOT~ Roses Lilacs Perfume Baby Shabby&Chic	$28.89	VINTAGE MEYERCORD DECALS (2) KITCHEN DECOR Lot 1	$7.50
Vintage Meyercord 1960's HUGE Vinyl Mermaid Decal	$26.00	WOW ~ HUGE lot of 48 ~ ROSES Decals~ GORGEOUS~	$7.49
Cute 50s Meyercord Vanity Items w Winged Cherubs Decal	$26.00	12 Iron-On T-Shirt Transfers Avery Personalized Ink Jet	$6.99
Tatouage~Faries~*~BUY ONE GET ONE FREE	$24.99	[4 of these sold for $6.99 each]	
[2 of these sold for $24.99 each]		How To Paint Early American Folk Art!	$6.75
3 Old Meyercord Pin Up Risque Silhouette Decals	$22.50	VINTAGE MEYERCORD DECALS-ROSES	$6.52

Embroidery ▸ Hand Embroidery Thread, Floss

The average sales price in this subcategory is $20.20.

	HIGH		AVG
EMBROIDERY THREAD-SULKY 48 VIVID FALL COLOR KIT	$135.00	Punch Embroidery Yarn Lot of 136	$20.51
120 Large Spools Embroidery Machine Thread with RACK	$128.00	16 cards Rainbow Gallery TWEED 4-PLY Needlepoint Thread	$20.50
Isacord 100% Polyester Embroidery Thread	$125.00	10 cards Rainbow Gallery ANGORA Needlepoint Thread	$20.50
[3 of these sold for $125.00 each]		CUTE BOTTONS EMBROIDERY COLLECTION 4" x 4" hoop	$20.50
Isacord 100% Polyester Embroidery Thread	$122.82	Embroidery Sewing Thread Robison Anton 20 Spools New	$20.49
120 Large Spools Embroidery Machine Thread with RACK	$120.00	BOY BUTTONS EMBROIDERY COLLECTION 4" x 4" hoop	$20.05
350 Spools Embroidery Machine Thread ~NEW~	$118.00	NEW Holiday Embroidery Thread/Threads Brother Machine	$20.00
Isacord 100% Polyester Embroidery Thread	$115.00	DMC EMBROIDERY FLOSS (191)Thread ORGANIZER CASES	$19.99
50 Cones Isacord Polyester Embroidery Thread	$113.49	EMBROIDERY FLOSS 135+Skeins,	$19.99
50 Cones Isacord Polyester Embroidery Thread	$112.50	InPlanoCraftBox-New,NiceLot	$19.99
427 SKEINS DMC EMBROIDERY FLOSS 427 COLORS NEW STOCK	$102.00	120 Spool Mega Rack II for Embroidery Machine Thread	$19.99
120 Large Spools Rayon Embroidery Machine Thread	$99.00	20 cards Rainbow Gallery MATTE 18 Needlepoint Thread	$19.98
401 SKEINS 401 COLORS DMC EMBROIDERY FLOSS NEW STOCK 4U	$97.00	110 Skeins NEW DMC embroidery floss	$19.76
LARGE 100 Poly Machine Embroidery Thread Threads NEW	$96.00	140 skeins of embroidery floss ~ UNOPENED ~many colors	$19.51
LARGE 100 Poly Machine Embroidery Thread Threads NEW	$95.00	**20 SPARKLE METALLIC Machine Embroidery THREAD Threads	$19.50
LARGE 100 Poly Machine Embroidery Thread Threads NEW	$92.01	18 Skeins NEEDLE NECESSITIES French Wool Overdye Thread	$19.27

Embroidery ▸ Kits

The average sales price in this subcategory is $9.36.

	HIGH		AVG
Bucilla FELT Ornament Kit + 14 CHRISTMAS MUST SEE	$117.50	Bucilla "Noah's Ark" Lap Quilt/Baby Blanket Embroidery	$9.75
Awesome Hand Done Estate Crewel ? Vintage Pillow Top?	$56.55	Vintage Lighthouse Crewel Paragon Kit Blue Line	$9.70
Vintage Bucilla Jeweled Ornaments~Cinderella~Kit	$51.99	Erica Wilson Crewel Kit "Wildflower" Pillow Kit #7203	$9.50
Scenic "Forest Reborn" Crewel Embroidery Kit, Lg. 18X40	$46.00	Embroidery Kit Hoop Dancer Kachina Indian Dancer	$9.50
Vintage Bucilla Jeweled Ornaments~Noah's Ark~Kit	$46.00	Adorable Bucilla Santa & Friends Felt Tree Skirt Kit	$9.50
Lot of 4 - VINTAGE Christmas FELT Stocking Kits #9	$43.18	Bucilla Crewel Chorus Line Birds Embroidery Kit	$9.38
American Indian Cross Stitch Kit NIP Eagle Dance	$39.99	STORYBOOK FELT STOCKING KIT-NEW-HOBBY KRAFT	$9.38
Bucilla vntg NIP Alice In Wonderland felt ornaments kit	$38.78	THE GARDEN WREATH Crewel Embroidery BUCILLA 1994 NEW	$9.26
Vintage Beatrix Potter Crewel Kit & Wooden Stand Hoop	$36.10	Crewel Kit NEW Teddy Bear Bus Each with personality	$9.25
Doves Wedding Record - Crewel Embroidery Picture	$36.10	*Bucilla* Santa & Animals Stocking Kit	$9.15
Grandma Moses Goes To The Big City Paragon Crewel	$35.00	DOWN THE CHIMNEY FELT STOCKING KIT-NEW	$9.05
Grandma Moses In Harvest Time Vintage Paragon Crewel	$35.00	Bucilla Jeweled Holiday Ornament Kit rag-a-muffins	$9.00
Bucilla - Fishing Santa Stocking - 1997	$35.00	Vintage Crewel embroidery kit made in Germany	$9.00
Paragon Crewel Kit - Winter's Delight-Adele Veres RARE	$35.00	HISTORICAL FLAGS Crewel Embroidery Kit	$8.99
Bucilla Felt Applique Santa & Frosty 28"Jumbo Stocking	$34.00	1978 Sunset Embroidery Crewel Kit Fall Water Mill Pond	$8.99

Embroidery ▸ Patterns, Transfers

The average sales price in this subcategory is $8.23.

	HIGH		AVG
Simplicity Smart Box Design Transfer System	$75.00	Smocking Plate "SNORKEL BEAR" Kit with Floss & Insert	$8.99
4 VINTAGE APRONS-TRANSFER PRINT TO EMBROIDER 30'S-40'S	$50.00	Smocking Plate "DAZZLING DRAGONFLIES "Kit Floss&Insert	$8.99
HUGE ASST. OF EMBROIDERY TRANSFERS—8 POUNDS !!!!	$40.00	Smocking Plate "MAKE A LADYBUG WISH" Kit Floss&Insert	$8.99
Embroider a Garden by Diana Lampe (1994)	$34.03	Painting with Thread - Embroidery Book	$8.50
11PKGs. VINTAGE VOGART TRANSFER PATTERNS AND MUCH MORE!	$33.87	WOW ~Vintage Embroidery Transfer Patterns ~ HUGE Lot	$8.49
Vintage SUNBONNET GIRLS Embroidery TRANSFER Patterns	$32.88	Lot of 29 older Aunt Martha TRANSFER Pattern VARIETY	$8.30
Redwork CD 5-Vintage Designs 350+ Machine Embroidery	$28.95	Adorable ELEPHANTS 1946 Simplicity Embroidery Transfers	$8.12
HUGE LOT 1940's 50's Workbasket EMBROIDERY TRANSFERS	$28.60	Machine Embroidery Kittens Design	$7.99
HALLOWEEN DAY APPLIQUE EMBROIDERY COLLECTION 4X4 HOOP	$26.89	Machine Embroidery Sail Boat Design	$7.99
Machine Embroidery Teacup Designs (9)	$22.99	Lot of Five Embroidery Stamped Pure Linen Table Scarf	$7.99
3 Big Transfer Collection Books Embroidery Paint Punch	$20.50	HARDANGER Embroidery TEMPLATES BOOK Norwegian CD	$7.99
4 VINTAGE PILLOWCASES- PRINTED TO EMBROIDER 30'S-40'S	$20.45	Lighthouses #1 Machine Embroidery Designs	$7.99
I WANT TO BE... GIRLS EMBROIDERY COLLECTION - 4X4 HOOP	$20.00	Vintage Embroidery Quilt Pattern Cowboys & Indians	$7.99
I WANT TO BE... GIRLS EMBROIDERY COLLECTION - 4X4 HOOP	$19.00	Machine Embroidery Oriental Design	$7.99
Southern Belles/Bonnet Vint Mach Embroidery Designs CD	$18.95	Machine Embroidery Vintage Lady Design	$7.99

Fabric ▸ Cotton

The average sales price in this subcategory is $7.24.

	HIGH		AVG
MODA Robyn Pandolph collection 45 pieces quilt fabric	$87.00	ASST 1930's PRINTS BUNDLE - 12 FAT QUARTERS #B2	$7.99
Shabby Moda Seaside Rose Plaid Fat Quarter Bundle FQ	$51.00	M&M'S RACING TEAM Pillow Panel Fabric # 36-BONUS	$7.99
AUNT GRACE 2005 REPRODUCTION FABRIC-36 FATS-NEW LINE	$49.50	Autunm Quilter's Fabric-8 FQs-Debbie Mumm Etc.!!	$7.99
36 THIMBLEBERRIES Fat Quarters	$47.89	6 Everyday Angels Quilt Fabric FQ's S Winget	$7.99
15 LAUREL BURCH Fat Quarters-NEW FABRICS 7/23/05	$46.56	Laurel Burch Cat Fabric ~ 1/2 YD ~ Clearance Sale!	$7.90

90 Fat Quarters, 100% Cotton, Quilt Fabric 1/4 yard FQs	$45.99	[2 of these sold in a multiple item ("Dutch") auction for $3.95 each]	
150 Quality Fat Quarters	$41.00	M&M's Candy quilt fabric Novelty Red M & M Rare	$7.58
24 Assorted Kaffe Fassett Prints fabric Fat Quarters	$39.00	10 Black & White Fat Quarters # 10	$7.50
NEW! MODA GARDEN MAGIC QUILT	$37.99	Thimbleberries holiday fat quarters fabric quilting~6	$7.49
FABRIC 29 FAT QUARTERS		2 Yards Hawaiian Tropical Shirts Quilt Fabric	$7.17
20 PURPLE/LAVENDAR Fat Quarters	$34.95	Pink Angel Pig Wings Star Quilting Fabric Spy FQ Pigs	$7.00
THIMBLEBERRIES Q3 2005 Quilt Club '05 Quilt Fat 1/4's	$33.00	[2 of these sold in a multiple item ("Dutch") auction for $3.50 each]	
20 DIFFERENT HALF YARD CUTS OF HAND-DYED BATIK FABRIC	$32.99	8 Quilting Fat Quarters: Colonial Browns	$7.00
[2 of these sold for $32.99 each]		Cowboy Western Rodeo Toile Flannel Fabric FQ	$7.00
18 ROMANTIC FLORAL IMPRESSIONS fat quarters NEW	$32.75	[2 of these sold in a multiple item ("Dutch") auction for $3.50 each]	
CHECK IT OUT QUILT FABRIC 25 FAT QUARTERS FQ	$31.25	Nature's Delight !!! Quilt Fabric -6 Fat Quarters	$6.99
Hoffman Floral Fabric 15 Fat Quarters Roses	$31.00	Fall Leaves Autumn Bittersweet 1 Y Fabric Quilting	$6.99
NEW! Moda SEASONS by KTQ 16 Fat Quarters Quilt Fabric	$28.20	Pink Flamingo Polka Dot Umbrella FQ Quilt Fabric I Spy	$6.98

Fabric ▶ Lace

The average sales price in this subcategory is $12.16.

	HIGH		AVG
50"w ALENCON LACE french bridal victorian chic shabby	$78.99	Lace by the Roll 9 1/8 Wide Craft Tropical Peach 99 yrd	$14.21
50"w BEADED LACE bridal chic shabby victorian french IV	$53.53	10Yds Daisy Kingdom 1 1/4" Wagon-Wheel Eyelet Lace	$14.00
Alencon Ivory Lace 5" wide with pearls & sequins Bridal	$44.12	[2 of these sold in a multiple item ("Dutch") auction for $7.00 each]	
[4 of these sold in a multiple item ("Dutch") auction for $11.03 each]		CRAFT SUPPLIES - HUGE LOT OF LACE TRIM - WOW!!!	$13.99
5 Different Embroidered Lgt Colored Metallic Tulle Pcs.	$41.59	1/2" loop Trim Royal/Kelly/Turq. Craft Vintage 144 yds	$13.50
14" EMB NET LACE bridal pageant ballet heirloom 5y SALE	$40.00	Rusty/Orange Tassel Fringe Craft Vintage Retro Trim 33y	$13.49
30 Yds Assorted Lace Fabric	$40.00	Blk Sheer Tulle w/Delicate Metallic	$13.49
Alencon Ivory Pearl/Sequin Wedding Lace Applique 3x5	$40.00	Gold Embroidery 2+y	
[10 of these sold in a multiple item ("Dutch") auction for $4.00 each]		2 1/2" Wide White Lace Trim 15 yards LOOK!!	$13.30
Scalloped Ivory Bridal Alencon Lace Trim 9" wide	$37.70	Dark orange 1" Ball Fringe Craft Vintage Retro Trim	$13.00
[5 of these sold in a multiple item ("Dutch") auction for $7.54 each]		20 Yds White "Palm Tree" Lace 2 Inches Wide - Charming!	$13.00
LG. LOT of VINT. LACE & TRIM!! fascinating lot! Must C>	$37.21	[2 of these sold in a multiple item ("Dutch") auction for $6.50 each]	
Lot of10 Pink Pearl/Sequin Embr Lingerie Lace Appliques	$35.97	Embroidered Black/White Tulle	$12.99
[3 of these sold in a multiple item ("Dutch") auction for $11.99 each]		Latticed Bows & Florettes	
Bullit Sakal Surfboard 72" Swallowtail Trifin Wingtail	$34.00	Embroidered Royal Blue Sequined Tulle Floral Vines	$12.99
EMBR ORGANZA bridal lace victorian chic shabby 2.5y PH	$33.56	Embroidered Crimson Red Sequined Tulle Floral Vines	$12.99
LACE CURTAIN DRAPERY Fabric 9 1/2 ydsx 60" UNUSED!	$31.01	Black Butterfly Motif Stretch Lace Fabric 2yds.	$12.80
16"w EMBR TULLE LACE wh/g victorian pageant bridal veil	$31.00	Embroidered Sage "Fish Scales" Tulle Opal Sequins	$12.71
7" PEARLS/LACE victorian pageant boutique bridal IVO 7Y	$31.00	Chainette fringe navy blue Vintage Retro Trim 24 yds	$12.50

Fabric ▶ Silk

The average sales price in this subcategory is $22.71.

	HIGH		AVG
New Thai or China Dupioni Silk Fabric	$299.00	Coordinating Silks, Brocade & Dupioni Silk	$25.09
EMBROIDERED ITALIAN SILK SHEER CURTAIN FABRIC	$280.00	SCALAMANDRE SILK TAFFETA	$25.00
40 YARDS OF RED SILK SATIN FABRIC @ $3.00 A YARD	$120.00	BEAUTIFUL WILD ROSES SILK DUPIONI FABRIC 3 3/8 YDS	$25.00
High End 100% Silk, Unique Leaf Green 54" 10 yds	$108.50	2 1/2 Yards Beautiful Blue Praline Striped Silk Taffeta	$25.00
High End 100% Silk Brocade Fabric 54" 10 yds	$102.50	Gorgeous Blue/Multi colored woven silk matka fabric	$24.99
SCALAMANDRE BLUE SILK DAMASK	$102.50	5Y ANIMAL SKIN SILK TAFFETA FABRIC	$24.99
50 YARDS OF BLACK SILK ORGANZA FABRIC @ $2.00 YARD.	$100.00	2 YARDS GOLD EMBROIDERED SILK DUPIONI FABRIC	$24.99
Beautiful Blue Praline Striped Silk Taffeta	$100.00	Bronze Copper Gold Silk Poly Sheer Fabric 138" x 58.5"	$24.99
High End 100% Silk Fabric 54" Icy Sage green 10 yards	$89.00	6 Y GORGEOUS FAUX SILK DRAPERY	$24.99
10 Yards Off White 100% SILK Doupioni Fabric Heavy	$87.99	FABRIC PRETTY PERIWINKLE	
CHAMPAGNE 100% SILK DUPIONI FABRIC 10 YARDS NEW	$84.99	Vintage Hand Beaded 100% Pure Silk Saree Sari INDIA	$24.99
[3 of these sold for $84.99 each]		4 YDS BRIGHT ORANGE DUPIONI!	$24.50
PALE YELLOW 100% SILK DUPIONI FABRIC 10 YARDS NEW	$84.99	SILK 54" WIDE NO RESERVE	
10YD COPPER 54" SILK DUPIONI CURTAIN DRAPES	$84.99	Vintage kimono silk fabric-Iris 1252A	$24.00
SUNSET GOLD 100% SILK DUPIONI FABRIC 10 YARDS NEW	$84.99	Silk Fabric Thai CLASSIC GOLD 4 Yards 2 Ply	$23.99
5 YDS GOLD DUPIONI SILK 54" WIDE NO RESERVE!	$84.20	China Silk HABOTAI Fabric CREAM IVORY 4 Yards	$23.75
[2 of these sold in a multiple item ("Dutch") auction for $42.10 each]		Vintage kimono silk fabric-Gorgeous 1201E	$23.50

Fabric ▶ Synthetics, Blends

The average sales price in this subcategory is $10.83.

	HIGH		AVG
35 - 40 YARDS OF INSULATED SYNTHETIC DRAPERY FABRIC	$110.00	BEAUTIFUL LIGHT BLUE NYLON SHEER, 15 DENIER, 10 YARDS	$11.00
[2 of these sold in a multiple item ("Dutch") auction for $55.00 each]		BLUE SURFBOARD, HIBISCUS, PALMS HAWAIIAN PRINT FABRIC	$11.00
12 Y PACIFIC BLUE BOAT SEAT COVER MARINE AWNING FABRIC	$105.00	PINK SURFBOARD & HIBISCUS HAWAIIAN PRINT FABRIC 2 YDS	$11.00
8 yards of Cotton Lycra Knit 60" wide Fabrics	$44.83	[2 of these sold for $11.00 each]	
COUTURE EMBROIDERED SEQUINED FABRIC FUSCHAI 3 YDS Rose	$39.99	BLUE SURFBOARD & HIBISCUS HAWAIIAN FABRIC 58" X 2 YDS	$11.00
COUTURE EMBROIDERED SEQUINED FABRIC BLACK 3 Yards	$39.99	PINK ROXY LOOKING HAWAIIAN PRINT FABRIC 59" x 2 YDS	$11.00
COUTURE EMBROIDERED SEQUINED FABRIC T-Blue 3 Yards Rose	$39.99	SEA TURTLES ON BRIGHT BLUE HAWAIIAN FABRIC 2 YDS	$11.00
New 10 Yards 60" Sand Polyester Bridal Satin Fabric	$38.99	6 yards of Crushed Stretch Velvet Knit 60" wide Fabrics	$10.80
New 9 Yard Kelly Green Polyester Bridal Satin Fabric	$37.99	CHINESE SILK BROCADE FABRIC	$10.55
8 yards of Cotton Lycra Knit 60" wide Fabrics	$35.30	TURQUOISE BLUE DRAGON 3YARD	
PURPLE WHITE & PINK POODLE & HEART FLANNEL BACK FABRIC	$35.00	BREAST CANCER PINK RIBBON HEARTS FLANNEL BACK FABRIC	$10.50
[5 of these sold in a multiple item ("Dutch") auction for $7.00 each]		UNIQUESSENTIALS SALWAR KAMEEZ	$10.50
20 YD BOLT REMNENT-SYNTHETIC DRAPERY/UPHOLSTRY FABRIC	$30.00	FABRIC UNSTICHED W/ SHAWL	
New 10 Yd Royal Blue Nylon Fabric WATER REPELLANT!	$29.99	2 YD RED ROSES ROSE FLEECE FABRIC BLANKETS	$10.50
New 10 yards Ivory Shiny Bridal Satin Fabric BEAUTIFUL!	$29.99	RED WILD WEST COWGIRL, HORSE, RODEO FABRIC 58" x 2 YDS	$10.49
BEAUTIFUL PINK NYLON SHEER, 15 DENIER, 10 YARDS	$29.76	SHEER CURTAIN FABRIC MINT GREEN 6 YARDS X 118" WIDE	$10.49
New 10 Yd Celery Green Linen Look Polyester Fabric	$28.99	3 1/2 YD PURPLE GRAPE FLOWER POLY DBL KNIT FABRIC 54	$10.20

Fabric Embellishments ▸ Appliques

The average sales price in this subcategory is $96.97.

	HIGH		AVG
Lot of 100 Vintage Flower Appliques Quilt Scrapbook	$30.57	Organza Flower Appliques* 60 pcs/ Pink* Bridal	$6.50
HUGE 720 PC LOT 5MM 20SS CRYSTAL AB FACETED RHINESTONES	$29.99	C122 Organza Flower Appliques with Rhinestone (Trim)	$6.50
BLACK VELVET FLOWERS/RHINESTONE victorian quilt 144c	$22.37	Ribbon/Organza Flower Appliques*60PCS* Red	$6.50
Lot of 100 Vintage Flower Appliques Quilt Scrapbook	$21.49	Padded Felt dog Appliques x 40 (2 colors) - Kids/Craft	$6.50
Lot of 100 Ivory Crochet Lace Flower Appliques Quilt	$20.50	50 PCS. BEDAZZLER SILVER STARS STUDS NEW 1" WIDE	$6.49
120 Silver Heart Iron-On Studs; 3 5/8"	$20.50	~Satin Ribbon RED CABBAGE w/Leaf ROSES*CRAFTS*LOT/100~	$6.15
Adorable Fuzzy Bear Applique Pair	$20.50	Ribbon Cabbage Rose Appliques*60 pcs*Pink*Wedding	$6.00
ASSORTED BURGUNDY FRENCH WIRE ROSES 100 VICTORIAN	$20.34	8 DISNEY PRINCESS IRON ON APPLIQUE / NO SEW	$6.00
[3 of these sold in a multiple item ("Dutch") auction for $6.78 each]		Large Lot of White Lace Appliques - EMB-W-5	$5.99
HUGE 720 PC LOT 5MM 20SS SMOKED TOPAZ RHINESTONES	$17.99	4MM 16SS AMETHYST RHINESTONES HOT FIX 1 GROSS 144 PC	$5.99
48 pc White Cross Appliques	$17.99	4MM SS16 PINK FACETED METAL	$5.99
HUGE 720 PC LOT 5MM 20SS SUN ORANGE FACETED RHINESTONES	$17.99	RHINESTUDS HOT FIX 1 GROSS	$5.99
HUGE 720 PC LOT 4MM SS16 AB CRYSTAL FACETED RHINESTONES	$17.99	5MM 20SS JET - BLACK FACET RHINESTONES HOT FIX 1 GROSS	$5.99
30 Yards 3/8" **Tiny Swiss Dots**Grosgrain Ribbon~	$16.49	5MM 20SS EMERALD GREEN FACETED RHINESTONES 1 GROSS	$5.99
SaLe ASSORTED ROSE MAUV FRENCH WIRE ROSES 100 VICTORIAN	$16.04	5MM 20SS SMOKED TOPAZ RHINESTONES	$5.99
[4 of these sold in a multiple item ("Dutch") auction for $4.01 each]		HOT FIX 1 GROSS 144 P	
NAILHEADS SPOTS 1000 PCS GRAB BAG Assorted!	$16.00	Lace Flower w/ Satin rose Appliques x 60 Green - Craft	$5.99

Fabric Embellishments ▸ Trims

The average sales price in this subcategory is $9.48.

	HIGH		AVG
5 Yards SCALAMANDRE Gold SCROLL Tassel FRINGE	$219.10	BOLT YARDS AND YARDS OF 3" SATIN BRAID RED EMBROIDERED	$9.99
250 packages of lace, brand new in packages of 10 yds	$150.00	VICTORIAN ROSE SPRAY shabby french chic IV millinery 12	$9.99
Lace Trim Assortment Lot White (Over 1,600 Yards)	$75.00	VELVET LILIES BUNCH shabby millinery victorian chic PK	$9.99
18y KRAVET MOSS GREEN CORDING FABRIC TRIM OR CRAFTS	$60.99	450 Yards 3/4" Lace Trim Crafts Sewing Curtains Pillows	$9.99
Brown sm Ball Fringe 3/4" Craft Vintage Retro Trim144yd	$55.50	BEADS PEARLS DROPS BRIDAL DRESS TRIM EXQUISITE QUALITY!	$9.67
Huge Lot - NEW VENICE LACE,TRIMEX, Legend Trim-35+YARDS	$51.01	1-1/2y HOULES PARIS ROSE SILK FLAT FABRIC TRIM OR CRAFT	$9.50
21+y ALLEN DECORATIVE ANTIQUE GOLD GIMP FABRIC TRIM	$48.67	ELEGANT RICH IVORY 4" BULLION	$9.49
500 YARDS OF ASSORTED SILVER TRIMS	$43.00	FRINGE/6 YARDS/TRIM ~NEW~	
chic vintage Pink Tassel TRIM ~shabby cottage 18+yds	$41.00	5 YARDS LAVENDER SATIN BUTTERFLY RIBBON BABY, BRIDAL	$9.47
1000 YARDS OF ASSORTED METALLIC TWIST CORDS	$41.00	GOLD METALLIC ELASTIC 1500 ft 1/16	$9.38
TINY BABY DOLL SATIN ROSES/BUDS ASST'D COLORS 100	$40.00	White Sunset Lace Trim Wedding 12 yard x 5 inch	$9.00
[20 of these sold in a multiple item ("Dutch") auction for $2.00 each]		Vintage GOLD big POM POMS fringe10 yds.	$9.00
Houles Paris ~ Gold & Yellow Banding TRIM*15+yards*NR	$36.99	3" Chainette Light Gold Fringe 8 Yards of New FUN Trim	$8.99
BLACK GIMP~BRAID UPHOLSTERY TRIM 70+YD ROLL	$36.99	1/2" OMBRE ROSETTE W/pearls rococo Trim 5 Y- victorian	$8.99
Lot of Wide Gold TRIMEX VENICE LACE TRIM 25+ Yards	$34.99	18 YARDS WHITE COTTON EMB. EYELET 1 1/2" WIDE	$8.99
6+y HOULES PARIS WHITE TASSEL SILK FABRIC TRIM OR CRAFT	$34.00	6 YARDS OF A 5" WINE FRINGE	$8.99

Floral Supplies ▸ Flowers, Foliage

The average sales price in this subcategory is $34.68.

	HIGH		AVG
200 POPPY POD HEADS 14 " 13' 10" GIGANTHEUMS	$300.00	200 DRIED POPPY PODS HEADS BROKEN 7" 6" 5"	$40.00
300 DRIED POPPY PODS HEADS 13" 12" 10" 9"	$291.00	[4 of these sold for $40.00 each]	
450 DRIED POPPY PODS HEADS 8" 7" 6" 5" 4"	$230.00	36 DRIED POPPY PODS HEADS 13" 10" BIGGEST PODS	$40.00
[4 of these sold for $230.00 each]		[2 of these sold for $40.00 each]	
300 DRIED POPPY PODS HEADS 8" 7"6" HUGE JUMBOS	$200.00	30 DRIED POPPY PODS WITH LONG STEMS Papaver somniferum!	$39.99
250 DRIED POPPY PODS OVALS SUPER PODS	$190.00	25 Jumbo poppy pod heads +30 medium pods 55 Total PODS!	$39.99
200 DRIED POPPY PODS JUMBOS	$190.00	dried flowers: POPPY PODS BY THE POUND!	$39.00
GIGANTHEUMS 13"10 " 7"		DRIED LAVENDER BUDS sachets, weddings, pillows - 5 lbs.	$38.73
200 DRIED POPPY PODS GIGANTHEUMS ROUND	$160.00	dried flowers: POPPY PODS BY THE POUND!	$37.00
1000 POPPY PODS HEADS 2" 3" 4" 5" SEEDS NEW PODS	$160.00	35 DRIED POPPY PODS HEADS JUMBO 10" 7" 6"5	$35.00
[3 of these sold for $160.00 each]		[3 of these sold for $35.00 each]	
300 DRIED POPPY PODS HEADS VERY LARGE 7" 6" 5"	$150.00	200 POPPY PODS 3" 4'" 5" FRESH GREEN NEW SUPER	$35.00
100 DRIED POPPY PODS HEADS JUMBO 10" 9"	$140.00	[7 of these sold for $35.00 each]	
200 DRIED POPPY PODS HEADS JUMBO 10" 8"'7" 6"	$135.00	DRIED LAVENDER BUDS sachets, weddings, pillows - 5 lbs.	$35.00
200 DRIED POPPY PODS HEADS	$135.00	50 POPPY PODS HEADS JUMBO 8"7"6 " ROUND@ OVALS	$35.00
JUMBO 14" 10" 8"'7" 6"		[5 of these sold for $35.00 each]	
150 DRIED POPPY PODS 8" 7" NEW ROUND SHAPE	$130.00	DRIED LAVENDER BUDS sachets, weddings, pillows - 5 lbs.	$35.00
100 DRIED POPPY PODS HEADS MAMMOTH SIZE 12"10"	$130.00	53 DRIED POPPY PODS HEADS BROKEN	$34.92
[3 of these sold for $130.00 each]		100 + COLORFUL FALL LEAVES /PRESSED/DRIED	$34.00
100 DRIED POPPY PODS HEADS	$130.00	[2 of these sold in a multiple item ("Dutch") auction for $17.00 each]	
MAMMOUTH SIZE 12"10"		DRIED LAVENDER BUDS sachets, weddings, pillows - 5 lbs.	$34.00

Framing, Matting ▸ Frames, Kits

The average sales price in this subcategory is $21.50.

	HIGH		AVG
logan pro joiner	$185.00	3-16x20 Black Solid Oak Picture Frames with Glass	$22.49
Altos EZ Mat Cutting System Big Package 2 4505 360 Oval	$124.99	14 FT-ANTIQUE GOLD ORNATE PICTURE FRAME MOULDING	$21.95
PICTURE FRAMING SUPPLIES / FLETCHER POINT DRIVER	$79.00	4-8x10-Scrolled Pewter Picture Frames-Solid Wood	$21.60
4-12x16 Black Barnwood Style Solid Wood Picture Frames	$53.22	4-11x14-Distressed Black Picture Frames-Solid Wood-New	$21.50
4-11x14- Studio Black Picture Frames- Solid Wood- New	$52.20	3-16x20 Deluxe Flat Solid Wood Picture Frames-New	$21.50
6-16x20 Solid Oak Picture Frames with Glass	$52.00	LOT OF 5 NEW ELEGANT CHERRY WOODEN FRAMES 16x20	$21.49
16x20/16 x 20 White/Art/Picture/Wedding FRAME B2 WL	$52.00	4-11x14-Ornate Black Picture Frames-Solid Wood-New	$21.09
4-11x17 Black Solid Oak Picture Frames with Glass	$51.26	16x20/16 x 20 Brown Wood Picture/Photo/Wedding FRAME	$21.00

6-16x20 Solid Oak Picture Frames with Glass	$51.00	4-8x10 Black Primitive Solid Wood Picture Frames-Grungy	$20.80
6-8x10 Black Solid Oak Picture Frames with Glass	$49.51	4-12x16 Solid Oak Picture Frames with Glass	$20.60
Great Picture Framing Tool - Easy to Use	$49.00	12x16 GOLD WOOD PICTURE FRAME LIKE NEW NEVER USED	$20.55
[3 of these sold for $49.00 each]		4-8x10 Black Primitive Solid Wood Picture Frames-Grungy	$20.55
4-11x14-Scrolled Pewter Picture Frames-Solid Wood	$48.35	3-16x20 Solid Oak Picture Frames with Glass	$20.54
NEW FRAME MAKING & HANGING KIT - PROFESSIONAL TOOL	$46.99	OAK / ASH Picture Frame Moulding antique white	$20.51
6-16x20 Solid Oak Picture Frames with Glass	$46.53	4-12x16 Solid Oak Picture Frames with Glass	$20.51

Framing, Matting ▸ Mats

The average sales price in this subcategory is $12.05.

	HIGH		AVG
100 11 X 14 mat board whites/ivory	$60.00	15-8x10 Presentation Mats-Black/White Core	$13.25
[2 of these sold in a multiple item ("Dutch") auction for $30.00 each]		15-8x10 Presentation Mats-White/Black Core	$13.25
$MATBOARD~ Sea Gull,Olde Tan,Rose ~Crescent 32x40 (25)	$59.95	Mats for picture and needleart framing	$13.00
$MATBOARD~ Grey,Lilac,Russet ~Crescent 32x40 (25)	$59.95	NEW 50 of 5x7 picture frame Mat Board Matting mats	$13.00
$MATBOARD~ 7 Colors Variety Pack! ~Crescent 32x40 (19)	$56.00	(25) 8x10 MATBOARD, MAT BOARD, MAT MATS, ACID FREE	$13.00
$MATBOARD~ White,Topaz,Crimson ~Crescent 32x40 (22)	$53.95	14x18 Fruitwood Wooden Frame Photo or Picture	$12.99
$MATBOARD~ Purple,Green,Stone ++ ~Crescent 32x40 (21)	$52.58	20 16X20 Uncut Picture Framing Mats	$12.99
$MATBOARD~ Rubia,Green,Peach + ~Crescent 32x40 (21)	$51.95	[2 of these sold for $12.99 each]	
$MATBOARD~ 3-Sheet Variety Colors! ~Crescent 32x40 (21)	$51.95	10 16x20 Matboard Mat Board Blanks-ASSORTMENT	$12.52
$MATBOARD~ Black,Sage,Cranberry ~Crescent 32x40 (20)	$49.95	12-11x14 picture/photo mats, matting for 8x10	$12.50
Custom Mat up to 16x20 For your poster, print or art	$48.00	10~11X14 MATS MATTING Mattes 4 picture frames framing	$12.50
[24 of these sold in a multiple item ("Dutch") auction for $2.00 each]		Lot of 48 – 5X7 Mat Board Blanks { NO RESERVE}	$12.50
$MATBOARD~ Grey,Blue,Red,Nutmeg ~Crescent 32x40 (21)	$46.00	(18) 11x14 MATBOARD, MAT BOARD, MAT MATS, ACID FREE 01	$12.09
$MATBOARD~ Maroon,White,Garnet ~Crescent 32x40 (20)	$40.00	20-5x7 picture/photo mats, matting for 4x6 assorted	$12.05
$MATBOARD~ Cream,Purple,Mauve,Blue ~Crescent 32x40 (25)	$39.99	20 16x20 uncut/cut picture mats/mattes, Bainbridge	$12.00
$MATBOARD~ Blue,Cream,Black,Grey ~Crescent 32x40 (25)	$39.99	24 count 8x10 double mats with two openings – heart	$12.00
$MATBOARD~ Gold,Black,Cream + ~Crescent 32x40 (25)	$39.99	[2 of these sold for $12.00 each]	

General Art & Craft Supplies ▸ Adhesives, Glue Guns

The average sales price in this subcategory is $8.97.

	HIGH		AVG
POLYGUN II LT Glue Gun with New Box of Glue	$152.50	NEW Cordless/Rechargeable GLUE GUN Crafts	$12.00
Dexter Hysol 4000 Air Powered Hot Glue Gun	$100.00	GLASS BEAD MICRO BALLOONS for epoxy	$12.00
2 QUART HIDE GLUE POT HOLD HEET NEW	$70.87	[4 of these sold in a multiple item ("Dutch") auction for $3.00 each]	
XYRON 850 TWO-SIDED LAMINATION REFILL CARTRIDGE *NEW*	$43.00	Weller Portasol self igniting cordless glue gun	$12.00
SCRAPBOOKING - XYRON 1200 2-SIDED LAMINATION REFILL	$41.00	Duzzit Handy Hanger System	$11.99
Unused Hold Heet 2 qt Glue Pot Dbl Boiler Copper lined!	$33.05	XYRON 510 REPOSITIONABLE REFILL CARTRIDGE *NEW*	$11.00
WELLER Cordless GLUE GUN Butane Powered New	$32.99	Battery Operated Hot Melt Glue Gun BRAND NEW ITEM	$10.95
Bag of 500 Very High Bond Adhesive Circles!!!	$31.00	XYRON 900 LAMINATE / REPOSITIONABLE CARTRIDGE *NEW*	$10.55
XYRON 1200 Refill Cartridge - Brand New in Box!	$27.76	5 LBS. of 4" mini hi-temp glue sticks!	$10.51
XYRON 850 TWO-SIDED LAMINATION REFILL CARTRIDGE *NEW*	$26.99	Tear Mender Fabric/Craft Adhesive Leather/Clothes Glue	$10.50
DOTTO REMOVABLE REFILL'S LOT OF 8	$24.52	Large lot 3M Hot Melt adhesive Applicator parts NIP	$9.99
XYRON 900 80' PERMANENT ADHESIVE	$23.50	Twelve Pound Bag of Hot Melt Glue Chips	$9.99
REFILL CARTRIDGES NEW		9 NIP Low Temp Glue Guns & 9 New Bottles Styrofoam Glue	$9.99
XYRON 850 ACID-FREE PERMANENT ADHESIVE REFILL *NEW*	$23.00	9 3M SUPER 77 SPRAY ADHESIVE CONTACT CEMENT 2.3 OZ	$9.99
XYRON 850 ACID-FREE PERMANENT ADHESIVE REFILL *NEW*	$22.50	Tear Mender Fabric & Craft Adhesive /w Applicator	$9.75
Scotch 924 Adhesive Transfer Tape 12 Rolls 1/2in x36yds	$21.01	Lot of 20 Mini Glue Guns in Case	$9.55

General Art & Craft Supplies ▸ Other Supplies

The average sales price in this subcategory is $9.30.

	HIGH		AVG
STIMPSON MODEL 405 EYELET RIVET GROMMET SNAP TOOL	$181.50	Copper Leaf Sheets - Not Gold	$9.60
GRAPHIC ARTS - 92 Tria Markers plus extras.	$150.00	6 Blue Ball 1/2 Pint Canning Jars Glass Lids	$9.51
ARTOGRAPH AG100 Opaque Projector/Enlarger	$79.00	25 - 3-7/8" Brown Wooden Gingerbread Craft Supplies	$9.51
NEW - Vision Max Full-Spectrum Crafters Lamp	$69.99	36 BRAND NEW WHITE ORGANZA BAGS FOR WEDDING OR PARTY	$9.50
[2 of these sold for $69.99 each]		EXECUTIVE FOLDING CRAFT KNIFE/BOX CUTTER/ MATTE CUTTER	$9.50
LEATHER TOOL, BUTTON PRESS, HEAVY DUTY, UNIT,	$66.05	100 1/4" SMALL PYRAMID SPOTS/STUDS-PRONG SET-HI QUALITY	$9.50
VINTAGE Typewriter Key Bracelet KIT..Makes 4 bracelets!	$59.95	Pure Silver Leaf Sheets - Not Gold	$9.50
46 VINTAGE GLASS FACE REMINGTON TYPEWRITER KEYS	$52.05	Lot of 20 Miniature Tin Stencils ~ Seasoned With Love	$9.49
101 - Rare Vintage Typewriter Keys - Underwood	$49.68	* 144 Primitive Rusty Tin Jingle Bells - 10mm **	$9.01
BRAND NEW QUILLING FRINGER	$45.07	Large Oval Set of Paper Mache Boxes Craft Supplies	$9.00
500 IMITATION SILVER LEAF MADE IN ITALY FREE SHIPPING	$44.95	UNIQUE ROSE PINK CRAFT GAR (FISH) SCALES -DÉCOR	$9.00
Block Printing Press, Speedball Model B	$43.00	[3 of these sold in a multiple item ("Dutch") auction for $3.00 each]	
VINTAGE Typewriter Key Bracelet KIT..Makes 4 bracelets!	$42.91	Pearl Ex Powdered pigments by Jacquard	$9.00
VINTAGE EMESCO HOBBY DRIL WITH ARM AND HANDPIECE (Q53)	$37.00	Large Oval Set of Paper Mache Boxes Craft Supplies	$9.00
One Dozen Boars Teeth or Tusks	$36.09	Large Square Set of Paper Mache Boxes Craft Supplies	$9.00
COLLAGE EPHEMERA Lot ATC ACEO Altered Book Scrapbook	$36.00	KRAFT Zig Fill Shred - 10lb Box - NEW!!!	$8.99

Glass Art Supplies ▸ Stained Glass Supplies

The average sales price in this subcategory is $19.84.

	HIGH		AVG
Best Glass Kiln for Fusing and Bead Making by Jen-Ken	$520.00	Instant Peel and Stick Window Coverings Film VICTORIAN	$19.99
Best Glass Kiln for Fusing and Bead Making by Jen-Ken	$490.00	46 bottles ``~~Gallery Glass window color paint~`~`~	$19.99
Best Glass Kiln for Fusing and Bead Making by Jen-Ken	$470.00	2 NEW FINE FUSING CABOCHON STAINED GLASS GRINDER BIT	$19.99

Jen-Ken Fused Glass Fusing Kiln - SHIPS NOW!	$344.00	Toyo Brass Handle Supercutter Stained Glass Cutter NIP	$19.95
Jen-Ken Fused Glass Fusing Kiln - TLGC	$310.00	Stained Glass Supplies: Drill Bits @ Glass/Tool/Tools	$19.95
New Taurus 3 Ring Saw W/ DVD Stained Glass Supplies	$304.99	Glass Scraps for Mosaic Projects 12+lb FREE SHIPPING	$19.95
Jen-Ken Fused Glass Fusing Kiln - TLGC	$269.00	GALLERY GLASS Fabulous Florals Kit ~ HUGE! ~ MUST SEE!	$19.95
Jen-Ken Fused Glass Fusing Kiln - TLGC	$269.00	1/2 lb coe 96 Dichroic Fusing Glass Scrap	$19.52
NEW INLAND WET DRY STAINED GLASS DIAMOND BAND SAW DB100	$165.00	TAURUS 3 "HOW-TO" DVD + BEVEL ACCESSORY KIT 57107	$19.50
INLAND TWIN SPIN STAINED GLASS GRINDER ROUTER	$137.50	Book: Introduction to Stained Glass-Step by Step Manual	$19.38
NEW INLAND WIZARD IV PROFESSIONAL STAINED GLASS GRINDER	$132.75	Stained Glass Inland Work Station Organizer BEST DEAL	$19.00
Stained Glass,Grinder, Glass, Cutter, Huge Lot "LooK"	$126.15	2 NEW 3/4" STAINED GLASS GRINDER BIT HEAD SUPPLIES	$19.00
diamond band saw -stained glass. DIAMOND LASER 300	$107.50	Stained Glass Worden FlatDesignLoon Pattern w/filigree	$18.99
STAINED GLASS PREMIUM SAMPLE BOX Mixed Sheets PTTZS	$98.53	16 SQ Savoy Studios CLEAR patterns dichroic COE 90 AQI	$18.75
Stained Glass Starter Kit	$91.00	2 NEW STAINED GLASS GRINDER RIPPLE BIT HEAD SUPPLIES	$18.50

Handcrafted Items ▸ Handcrafted Purses, Bags

The average sales price in this subcategory is $14.85.

	HIGH		AVG
Handles Lot Handbag Purse bamboo wood beaded more	$100.00	Antiqued Brass Metal Purse Handbag Frame ~ 7" x 3"	$15.02
Boutique - Teacher School fabric purse tote bag	$56.00	25 Empty Cigar Boxes - Arturo Fuente, Avo, Davidoff etc	$15.00
AUBURN TIGER HANDMADE PURSE	$48.30	~~TEACHER TOTE/PURSE/HANDBAG~BRAND NEW!!~~~	$15.00
Mexican Prison Art Cute Handmade Original Woven Purse	$45.00	~~CAT LOVERS TOTE/HANDBAG/PURSE~NEW~~	$15.00
Barkcloth Tote ~ Violin, Music, Rose & Book Lovers !	$45.00	~~TEACHER TOTE/HANDBAG/PURSE~NEW!!~~	$15.00
Pig Farm Apple Timeless Treasures Fabric Tote Bag Purse	$42.50	PENGUIN fabric Handbag PURSE tote bag + checkbook cover	$15.00
25 Empty Cigar Boxes - Avo, Davidoff, CAO, Zino, etc...	$41.00	~~ELEMENTARY TEACHER TOTE BAG~NEW~~	$15.00
YELLOW DUCK TOTE BAG PURSE	$41.00	Wonderful Black/floral cigar box purse,very chic	$15.00
Shabby Pink Roses Chic Barkcloth Tote Bag Ruffle Purse	$40.33	PENGUIN fabric Handbag PURSE tote bag + checkbook cover	$14.49
From 64 Yogini, Chamunda handpainted on leather purse	$39.95	PERSONALIZED COLORING BOOK/CRAYON TOTE BAG - PRINCESS	$14.00
Butterfly Jean purse Handmade	$38.00	New ! DONKEY fabric TOTE bag - handbag PURSE Mules !	$13.72
Medical Scrub Doctor Nurse LPN RN Fabric Tote bag purse	$37.00	TOTE BAG~Hot Pink & Black~Vntg Pink Rhinestones	$13.59
Breast Cancer AWARENESS fabric purse tote bag Handbag	$36.00	TOTE BAG~Barkcloth Era~Paris Flea Market~Rhinestones	$13.50
Breast Cancer AWARENESS Handbag for Shannan	$35.00	HANDMADE FALL PUMPKIN POCKETBOOK /TOTE/HANDBAG	$13.49
Lilly Pulitzer PINK ROLLS ROYCE Handmade Purse Tote Bag	$34.00	Tote / Purse / Diaper bag / Handbag / Black Quilted	$12.99

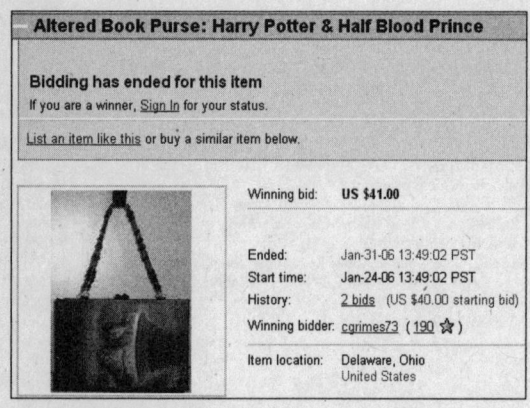

Altered Book Purse: Harry Potter & Half Blood Prince

Bidding has ended for this item

If you are a winner, Sign In for your status.

List an item like this or buy a similar item below.

Winning bid:	**US $41.00**
Ended:	Jan-31-06 13:49:02 PST
Start time:	Jan-24-06 13:49:02 PST
History:	2 bids (US $40.00 starting bid)
Winning bidder:	cgrimes73 (190 ☆)
Item location:	Delaware, Ohio United States

ENORMOUS 10,000+ pc. bead & finding lot JEWELRY MAKING
Beads, findings, containers, sales products, books

Bidding has ended for this item

If you are a winner, Sign In for your status.

List an item like this or buy a similar item below.

Winning bid:	**US $360.00**
Ended:	Jan-23-06 12:42:17 PST
Start time:	Jan-18-06 12:42:17 PST
History:	38 bids (US $0.99 starting bid)
Winning bidder:	recoupere (287 ☆)
Item location:	Denver, Pennsylvania United States

Handcrafted Items ▸ Handpainted Items

The average sales price in this subcategory is $14.27.

	HIGH		AVG
Shabby HP Chic Cathedral Radio General Electric Roses	$103.50	HAND PAINTED SNOWMAN BASKET@LOOK@	$14.99
Russian Lacquer Box - Man w/ Birdcage	$100.00	[2 of these sold for $14.99 each]	
Eickholt Glass handblown perfume vase	$68.00	Vintage Flag Picnic Basket Handpainted by JaNae	$14.99
Shabby HP Chic Ladies Lap Desk Organizer Roses	$66.10	~GINGERBREAD BAKER with RUFFLES & COVERED IN FLOUR~	$14.99
GINGERBREAD VINTAGE BUCKET FOR COOKIES SUPER CUTE PEEK!	$58.57	Pumpkin Crow Birdhouse Cattails HP Wood Firkin/Bucket	$14.51
Vintage Candle Keep~Primitive Pip Berry Vines~Candle~	$54.00	Recipe box~HP Primitive Folk Art~Stars~Sheep	$14.49
HP Primitive angel Lamp ! Sheep, pear, key	$53.75	Hand Painted Gourd Thirzaella the WITCH & stuff	$14.37
ALL ABOARD RAGGEDY EXPRESS WOOD	$53.30	Beautiful old Primitive Painted Tall Wood Candlesticks	$14.01
ANNIE LETTER TRAIN CUTE		victorian chic~hp roses~glass vase/candle holder ~large	$14.00
HP~Raggedy Ann and Andy with Toys	$52.00	HP*Jack-O-Lantern Treat Bowl*4 PM JOL Round Boxes*Tag*	$13.99
Wood cat litterbox screen - Handpainted violets WDAS	$49.50	HP Grape and Raspberry Gourd Set by Allyne	$13.99
Gingerbread sleeping in a pile of yummy frosting clay	$48.57	PRIMITIVE PAINTED WOOD PEAR BOWL ~ ARTIST M. HOWE	$13.51
HP Primitive Folk Art Vintage Westbend Canister Set	$47.01	HP Wood BookEnds~Primitive Saltbox~Folk Art~SSODS	$13.51
HP Primitive Folk Art Vintage Cake Saver glass dish	$47.00	Sweet Country French WATERING CAN Shabby hp ROSES ChiC	$13.50
HP Primitive 4 Folk Art Plates~Saltbox~Sheep~Willow	$45.00	Gingerbread chefs sitting on rolling pin clay handmade	$13.00
Table Lamp & Doily~ Saltbox~Swan~HP Primitive~Folk Art	$42.95	COLONIAL WILLIAMSBURG FIFE AND DRUM MEN GOURD ART	$13.00

Knitting ▶ Needles

The average sales price in this subcategory is $19.25.

	HIGH		AVG
1909 Boye needles shuttles bobbins keys display case	$197.50	HUGE LOT OF KNITTING NEEDLES	$19.99
NEW!LOT CLOVER BAMBOO KNITTING NEEDLES & ACCESSORIES!!!	$167.28	TOTES CIRCULAR DOUBLE LQQK	$19.95
Addi turbo SET 24" circular knitting needles 11 pair NR	$152.50	Bamboo 16" Cir Knitting Needles 11 & 15	$19.95
Addi turbo SET 12" circular knitting needles 10 pair NR	$141.00	Clover Takumi Bamboo Premium Circular Knitting Needles	$19.95
33 CLOVER Takumi CIRCULAR KNITTING NEEDLES MUST SEE!!!!	$122.50	Vintage circular knitting pins/knitting needles	$19.50
CLOVER TAKUMI BAMBOO KNITTING NEEDLES HUGE LOT! NIP	$83.99	Bamboo Knitting Needle US 1-11,10 prs NEW and Improved	$19.50
Clover Takumi Bamboo Knitting Needles Lrg. Asst.	$76.00	New Circular Bamboo Knitting Needles 29" x 5/8/10/10.5	$19.49
CLOVER TAKUMI BAMBOO KNITTING NEEDLES HUGE LOT *UNUSED*	$75.55	THREE BAMBOO CIRCULAR KNITTING NEEDLES	$19.06
Bamboo Interchangeable circular Knitting Needle set	$74.99	BIG Lot 56 KNITTING NEEDLES for YARN Bates Boye Hero	$18.53
[2 of these sold for $74.99 each]		VINTAGE BOYE KNITTING NEEDLE MASTER KIT KNIT CASE LOOK	$18.51
NEW!LOT CLOVER BAMBOO KNITTING NEEDLES & ACCESSORIES!!!		Knifty Knitter Round Loom Set W/ Hook,Bag,Patterns NEW!	$18.50
CLOVER TAKUMI BAMBOO KNITTING NEEDLES! 36 L@@K!!	$74.50	OVER 100 VINTAGE KNITTING NEEDLES KNIT AND MORE !	$18.50
CLOVER TAKUMI BAMBOO KNITTING NEEDLES HUGE LOT! NIP	$73.01	New Bamboo Knitting Needles Size US 1-11 Needle 10 prs	$18.50
Addi turbo SET 40" circular knitting needles 4 pair NR	$69.00	SALE NEW 29" Circular Knitting Needles 13, 15 & 17	$18.50
BRITTANY WHITE BIRCH KNITTING NEEDLES (SET OF 10)	$67.66	Bamboo Knitting Needle US 1-11,10 prs NEW and Improved	$18.50
Brittany 9 Walnut Knitting Needles New Never Used	$66.00	HUGE HUGE LOT KNITTING NEEDLES CIRCULAR + OTHERS	$18.50
	$65.00		

Knitting ▶ Patterns

The average sales price in this subcategory is $7.05.

	HIGH		AVG
Vintage Royal Baby Knitting Patterns Adorable Coats+++	$202.50	Book: Minnow Knits by Jil Eaton	$7.50
385+ AFGHAN PATTERN BOOK CROCHET KNITTING VINTAGE LOT	$128.49	Truely Rare! Antique Delicate Knit Afghan Lovely 1800's	$7.49
Easy Knitting Pattern Book Babies Kids Children	$71.00	15 Knitting Crochet Patterns Babies Toddlers Dresses++	$7.49
Heirloom Knitting - New Lace Knitting Book	$57.02	CABLED ACCESSORIES ~ KNITTING PATTERNS ~ NEW FOR 2005	$7.45
Pingouin 126 BABY CLOTHES & LAYETTES Knitting Book	$49.00	50+ Baby Items To Knit - Inc Preemies + Toys	$7.38
44 VINTAGE BABY CLOTHES knit/crochet patterns pattern	$46.56	Handmade Afghan	$7.00
Beautiful Baby Knitting Pattern Book Patterns Adorable!	$41.00	7 day afghans ` 60 patterns to knit and crochet` book	$7.00
300+ AFGHAN PATTERN BOOK CROCHET KNITTING VINTAGE LOT	$41.00	ROWAN - Miss Bea's Colours by Louisa Harding	$6.99
Baby Knitting Crochet Smocking Sew Quilt Needlepoint++	$32.65	PINGOUIN PATTERN BOOK #62 Fall/Winter Childrens Pattern	$6.99
PINGOUIN Baby Knitting Patterns Book # 150 Christmas +	$31.00	Vintage BABY Knitting Crochet PATTERNS Christening ++	$6.99
L@@K-12 skeins worsted yarn & 12 babies &kids books	$24.51	4 Baby Children KNITTING PATTERN BOOKS Cute & Adorable!	$6.99
Sirdar 22 Baby Knitting Patterns for DK Weight Yarn	$24.17	AARLAN KNIT BOOK in 4 different languages	$6.99
Irish Hand Knit Aran Children's Sweater, cream w/lambs	$24.01	KATIA #32 BABY SUMMER crochet/knit patterns pattern	$6.99
Baby Clothes 23 Knitting Patterns Fingering-Bulky Wt	$20.70	Fiber Trends Pattern A Berry Cute Baby Hat Adorable	$6.99
PINGOUIN Baby Layette Clothes Knitting Patterns Book	$20.51	PENGUOIN MAGAZINE – MOST POPULAR PATTERNS - EXCELLENT	$6.66

Latch, Rug Hooking ▶ Kits, Patterns

The average sales price in this subcategory is $12.24.

	HIGH		AVG
BERNAT German Shepherd LATCH HOOK RUG KIT 24x34 NEW!	$225.01	Lg. 20"x 30" Horse Latch Hook Rug Kit NIB	$12.75
CHESSIE CAT LATCH HOOK RUG KIT - NIP	$129.50	BUCILLA ARTICHOKE LATCH HOOK RUG KIT NEW Sealed	$12.62
1950's Rug Hooking Wool Cutter w/blades and Patterns	$80.99	LATCH HOOK RUG COMPLETE KIT RAGGEDY ANN & ANDY	$12.57
Magnificent BIG VINTAGE PEARL McGOWN HOOKED RUG Project	$66.51	Snowman Mitten Rug Hooking Pattern-So Cute!	$12.50
raggedy ann andy latch hook sewing lot 8 different ones	$65.00	Kris Kringle Latch Hook Kit	$12.50
Oriental Rug Design, punch/shear method	$58.00	DAISIES Latch Hook Rug Kit 16x32 CARON WonderArt Craft	$12.50
Moshimer Primitive Rug Hooking Pattern Aurora Rose	$57.51	PIANO KEYES AND ROSE LATCH HOOK KIT	$12.00
Large 30"x 50" Mountain High Latch Hook Rug Kit NIB	$56.67	covered bridge latch hook rug	$12.00
RUG HOOKING PATTERN FOR WOOL ON MONKS CLOTH	$51.03	KIDDIE KOMFIES Latch Hook KIT LOT + QUILT RAGGEDY ANN	$11.99
Vintage Cushing's Perfection Dyes rug hooking HUGE LOT	$51.01	WINTER WONDERLAND RAGGEDY ANN & ANDY LATCH HOOK KIT RUG	$11.86
LATCH-HOOK RUG KIT-QUILT LOOK RUG-PASTEL-5' X 3'	$51.00	Punch Embroidery Kit With Punch Needle Thread Hoop +NIP	$11.63
Pre-printed TURKOMAN Oriental rug KIT 4' X 6'	$51.00	BUCILLA Latch Hook Kit w Yarn HARLEQUIN #13046 Clown	$11.51
primitive rug hooking pattern-Ewe and Lamb	$49.50	Natl Yarn Crafts Latch Hook Rug Kit Elegance Flowers	$11.50
Shillcraft Pfaltzgraff Garden Party Latch Hook Kit	$48.99	Persian Hearts Latch Hook Kit NIB Rug or Wall Hanging	$11.50
Primitive Rug Hooking Pattern - Dog Walk	$45.99	Lion King Simba Nala Latch Hook Rug Kit MIB RARE	$11.50

Leathercraft ▶ Hides, Leather

The average sales price in this subcategory is $29.59.

	HIGH		AVG
Brand New Leather Cowhide Wing Chair	$549.99	LEATHER HIDE, REAL WATER BUFFALO, VEGETAL TAN 7-7.5 oun	$29.99
BISON BUFFALO HIDE - SKIN - SOUTH DAKOTA @ONE CENT!!	$458.77	LEATHER Pillow,Real cowhide!Embroidered Art,moose,COOL!	$29.99
061 Saddle! Leather Upholstery Hides/Hide/Cowhide/skins	$162.00	LEATHER Pillow,Real cowhide!Embroidered Art, Deer, UNIQUE	$29.99
LEATHER HIDE/HIDES UPHOLSTERY, CREAM COLOR 48 SF.	$129.00	LEATHER Pillow,Real cowhide!Embroidered Art,elk,UNIQUE	$29.99
Large Cowhide Rug Wall Hanging Western Ranch Decor	$125.00	[2 of these sold for $29.99 each]	
Buffalo hide rug, antique	$124.03	LEATHER Pillow,Real cowhide!Embroidered Art,Bear,COOL!	$29.99
3 LARGE Black Leather/Hide/Scrap/Pieces	$122.50	(324-4) Side Of Damaged Firm Off White Leather 4-5 oz.	$29.95
COWHIDES, SHORT HAIR, BLACK & WHITE, 34 SQUARE FEET	$120.00	BEAUTIFUL LEATHER HIDE SCHMIDT MAMUT HUNTER GREEN	$29.50
BROWN SEMI-ANILINE LEATHER HIDE 57.3 SQ FT	$99.00	(437-1) - Side of Brown Trim Cow leather	$29.50
Leather Chocolate Back Approx. 98x28in. 10oz.	$95.00	10+lbs Black Leather/Hide/Scrap/Pieces	$29.00
K27 Rich! Leather Upholstery fabric Hides/Hide/cowhide	$95.00	A-1 BLACK UPHOLSTERY LEATHER 3-4 OZ MEDIUM WEIGHT14SF	$29.00
LEATHER HIDE AUTO HARLEY DAVISON ORANGE 47 SQ. FT. 593	$89.99	BEAUTIFUL LEATHER HIDE SCHMIDT MAMUT DOE	$29.00
A-1 UPHOLSTERY LEATHER COWHIDE	$85.00	LEATHER HIDE PIECE TAN 35 SQ. FT. (p6)	$28.00
DK BROWN CROC PRINT 43SF		Scrap Saddle Skirting Leather - Large Piece	$28.00
(350-2) - Full Hide of Brown Bison - Buffalo Leather	$74.95	BRIGHT PINK LIZARD PRINT COW HIDE LEATHER SKIN	$27.50
(381-2) Quarter Hide Of Heavy Tooling Leather 13-15oz	$73.50	(432) Black Split Suede Chap Leather Hide 4 -5 oz.	$27.00

Macrame

The average sales price in this subcategory is $29.59.

NOTE *The below results were obtained by doing a keyword search on the word* macramé *in this subcategory.*

	HIGH		AVG
HUGE LOT - 80 MACRAME MAGAZINES PATTERNS HOW TO CRAFTS!	$45.52	Macrame SOUTHWEST Patio Chairs Pattern Book - Stools	$6.52
6 LBS. BIG GLASS MACRAME BEADS — LG. HOLES	$30.00	LOT OF SEVEN VINTAGE MACRAME BOOKS	$6.50
[2 of these sold in a multiple item ("Dutch") auction for $15.00 each]		LARGE LOT MACRAME ROUND METAL	$6.50
11 Spools of Vintage "Wii" Macrame Cord ...4800 Feet!!	$32.59	RINGS BEAD PURSE HANDLE	
6 LBS. BIG GLASS MACRAME BEADS — LG. HOLES	$30.00	Vintage Macrame Furniture Lawn Chair Pattern Book 1982	$6.50
[2 of these sold in a multiple item ("Dutch") auction for $15.00 each]		MACRAME/ CRAFT WOODEN BEADS - LOT OF OVER 200 !!	$6.50
10 Pounds Macrame Cord, Boards and Such	$26.00	50 Craft Art Wood Macrame/Cigar Box Handle Loose Beads	$6.49
3 - 210ft. rolls - Macrame Cord - White	$23.53	[2 of these sold for $6.49 each]	
Lot 400+ 2" Round & Square Macrame Rings/Hoops/Handles	$23.50	MACRAME PATTERNS FOR LAWN CHAIR REPAIRS	$6.11
MACRAME! Lot of 21 instruction booklets & hippie bag	$22.00	Mixed Lot of Macrame Cord Elefant Tan Brown Green Red	$6.04
LARGE LOT MACRAME SQUARE PLASTIC RINGS PURSE HANDLES	$22.00	macrame, purses, instruction books. patterns, crafts	$6.01
Macrame Beads Lot of 300+ with Case Jewelry NR	$21.50	NEW-4 ROLLS OF MACRAME CORD-JUTE-TWINE-ASSORTED	$5.99
Lot of 7 Skeins of Different Sized Macrame Never Used	$20.50	3 - 210ft. rolls -Macrame Cord- Golden Yellow	$5.99
10 MACRAME PATTERN BOOKS > OVER 125 PATTERNS	$20.50	3 - 210ft. rolls - Macrame Cord - Dk. Blue	$5.99
3 rolls macrame cord 6mm 100 yds. each Blues	$20.50	Mixed lot of macrame supplies cord beads rings booklets	$5.99
FOUR MACRAME CORD and SIX MACRAME CHAIR PATTERNS	$20.02	7 NEW Pkgs of Macrame Braid - Assorted Colors	$5.99
3 Macrame Booklets Lawn Chairs Furniture Crochet Hooks	$20.00	MACRAME AND BEADING Craft Books 1970-80	$5.99

Needlepoint ▸ Kits

The average sales price in this category is $15.74.

	HIGH		AVG
Beth Russell Acanthus Needlepoint Rug Kit Canvas Ehrman	$515.00	NIP Bucilla Petitpoint Le Paradis des Iris Iris Pardise	$17.95
William Morris Tapestry Needlepoint Canvas wools needle	$290.00	Dimensions 2486 Needlepoint Kit Magnolia Serenade	$17.50
Interlock 12 point canvas Brand New w/ striated wools		NEW Iris Paradise Needlepoint Pillow Kit Bucilla NIP	$17.37
ehrman tapestry needlepoint kit tortoiseshell cat new	GBP 102.00	DIMENSIONS NEEDLEPOINT KIT~"GEESE IN THE GARDEN" 1987	$17.00
Classical Animal Tapestry Needlepoint Canvas needle	$167.50	BETTER HOMES/GARDENS NEEDLEPOINT COMPLETE PILLOW KIT	$16.75
Interlocking 12 point mesh Brand New w/ striated wools		Gorgeous LOT of 4 Sets Of Vintage Needle Point NIB	$16.62
VEGETABLE STAND NEEDLEPOINT KIT! Charles Wysocki NEW!	$152.50	LONGSTITCH NEEDLEPOINT KIT ~LITTLE LION CUB~EMBROIDERY	$16.50
Ehrman Kaffe Fassett Needlepoint Kit Basket of Flowers	$149.95	Bucilla Needlepoint Kit-Angora Cat	$16.38
NIP WHITE HOUSE INN NEEDLEPOINT KIT! Dimensions NEW!	$137.50	DIMENSIONS NEEDLEPOINT KIT "WINTER SEASCAPE"	$16.08
MEDIEVIAL TAPESTRY KIT 31"X16" INCHES NEW &COMPLETE	GBP 77.77	New Vervaco Needlepoint Kit: Chicken w/Babies	$16.00
Elizabeth Bradley PANSY Needlepoint KIT	$135.00	Dimensions Needlepoint "Flower Basket" Dawna Barton	$16.00
NEW EHRMAN Cherries Tapestry needlepoint Kaffe Fassett	GBP 74.00	Vintage "The Humbug Stocking " by: Needle Treasures	$16.00
Old Time Shoppes- Dimensions Needlepoint Kit	$129.50	Dimensions Needlepoint ~Ribbon'N Roses~ Beautiful	$16.00
Elizabeth Bradley Camellia Needlepoint KIT New Flower	129.00	Needlepoint Kit, Magnolia Grandiflora, Bucilla	$15.99
Ehrman Bahouth Needlepoint Canvas Kit Starry Night	$103.61	KITTIES ALL BURNED OUT Needlepoint Kit	$15.99
Charles Wysocki 1981 Needlepoint Kit "Village Shopping"	$102.50		
Nantucket Winds 1982 Dimensions Needlepoint Kit	$100.99		

Painting & Drawing ▸ Drawing

The average sales price in this subcategory is $20.98.

	HIGH		AVG
Sennelier FULL SET OF JUMBO Soft Pastels 49 Set AMAZING	$435.00	Antique Drafting Tools in Original case NR!!	$22.00
Rembrandt Woodbox Pastel Set Complete 225 Sticks	$269.00	NEW REMBRANDT 30ct SOFT PASTELS~GENERAL SELECTION~WOW!	$22.00
DISNEY ANIMATION DISC Cel Drawing Disk for Artist Desk	$227.50	NEW # 78147 PANTOGRAPH	$22.00
EXCEPTIONAL VALUE:SET OF 225 SENNELIER OIL PASTELS +++	$214.49	CARRE NOUVEL HARD PASTEL STICKS IN BOX	$21.51
EXCEPTIONAL VALUE:SET OF 225 SENNELIER OIL PASTELS +++	$205.00	water color pencils, pastels, rulers, x-acto	$21.00
DISNEY ANIMATION DISC Cel Drawing Disk for Artist Desk	$203.47	REMBRANDT set 30 Soft Pastels *NEW art	$21.00
12 Field Animation Disc Disk Drawing / Cel Painting	$200.00	1950-58 KEUFFEL & ESSER CO.LEROY LETTERING SET	$20.50
Unison Soft Pastels Set-LandscpeSpecial Collection+Dark	$185.00	CRAYOLA State Your Color~Limited Ed. 64 Crayons~2 BOXES	$20.50
Unison Soft Pastels 72 Landscape Pastel set Professionl	$177.50	Painting with Pastels Instructional Video	$20.50
Unison Soft Pastels 72 Landscape Pastel set Professionl	$174.99	NEW! SET OF 2 PRISMACOLOR SOFT PASTELS 48 COLOR SET	$20.50
NEW:DELUXE ARTIST PORTRAIT PASTELS SET,100 IN WOOD BOX!	$174.49	2 Old Wood Boxes of Vintage Artist's Drawing Chalk	$20.50
Sennelier 100 Landscape Pastels in Unopened Wood Box	$165.00	Painting with Pastels Instructional Video	$20.45
NEW:DELUXE ARTIST PORTRAIT PASTELS SET,100 IN WOOD BOX!	$149.00	REMBRANDT set of 30 Extra Fine Soft Pastels BRAND NEW!	$20.01
ARTOGRAPH DB300 OPAQUE PROJECTOR	$132.50	NEW RAPIDOGRAPH Professional pens	$20.00
NEW,DELUXE SENNELIER 36 GIANT OIL PASTELS SET,WOOD BOX!	$127.50	REMBRANDT set 30 Soft Pastels *NEW art	$20.00

Painting & Drawing ▸ Painting

The average sales price in this subcategory is $13.96.

	HIGH		AVG
1950'S WESTERN PAINT BY NUMBER PAINTING DESERT MOUNTAIN	$128.50	2 BOOKS, PAINTING INSTRUCTION,	$14.50
Vintage Cowboy w/ covered wagons Paint-by-number (frame	$127.00	JERRY YARNELL, VANGOGH	
Vintage Wagon Train Western Paint by Number	$100.50	Paint By Number still life Eames era items 1 of 3 RETRO	$14.50
Vintage Framed Paint By Numbers Knight Oil Painting	$85.00	Vintage Framed Paint-By-Number Amsterdam Canal Scene #2	$14.49
Vintage Paris Scene PBN Paint by Number painting	$81.00	NEW Dimensions PAINT-BY-NUMBER STONEHEDGE BRIDGE	$14.49
Lg Framed Vintage COWBOY Horse WESTERN PAINT BY NUMBER	$78.77	Paint by Number Kit New Dimensions BLUE BIRDS IN SPRING	$14.00

Vintage Pair Paint by Numbers Framed Streetscenes ^	$76.00
Vintage PAINT BY NUMBER Fly Fisherman Picture Frame	$61.00
2 BOOKS,PAINTING LIGHT & SHADOW, KEYS TO FACES &FIGURES	$57.00
2 Vintage 50_s Paint by Number PBN Hawaii Tiki Painting	$56.00
Vintage Paint by Number, BEAR & FISH Mountain Scene	$52.95
PAINT A PHOTO	$25.76
1950's/60's Vintage Paint By Numbers,Western,Old West I	$51.00
[2 of these sold for $51.00 each]	
SPUMCO ARTS & CRAFTS: Paints; Books; Kits	$50.73
PAINT BY NUMBER POPPIES VINTAGE 40'S 50'S FLORAL RARE	$49.99

DEEP SEA PAIR 2 watercolor paint by number SHIPS TODAY	$13.95
Paint by Number Kit New Dimensions NORTHERN RAILS	$13.75
VINTAGE CHILDS PAINT SET	$13.12
Pair of Vintage Paint by Number Pictures *NR	$13.09
20" x 16" Moonlight Cabin Paint-by-Number NIB	$13.01
Vintage Paint by Number Pair Spanish Senorita Flamenco	$12.99
LADY JESSICA paint by number CAN SHIP TODAY	$12.95
Paint by Number Kit New Dimensions CALL THE WILDERNESS	$12.95
Paint by Number Kit New Dimensions "MOONLIT CABIN" L@@K	$12.95
Clowns-Paint By Number Set by The Art Award Co. Inc.	$12.83

Paper Crafts, Origami

The average sales price in this subcategory is $6.90.

NOTE *The below results were obtained by doing a keyword search on the word* paper *in this subcategory.*

	HIGH		AVG
Lot of parchment craft items PAINTS VHS PAPER ++++	$66.00	ORIGAMI PAPER HANDMADE JAPANESE SHINWAZOME WASHI	$7.50
GERMANY-"FOLIA" TRANSPARENT PAPER & PAPER STAR BOOKS	$43.44	Vintage Dennison Crepe Paper - Great Colors!!	$7.50
BEST 5x8 &TIN CAN PAPER MAKING KIT Papermaking DEAL YES	$41.00	VICTORIAN PAPER CUTTING DATED &	$7.50
Martha Stewart by Mail ~CREPE PAPER FLOWERS KIT ~	$40.50	SIGNED/SCHERENSCHNITTE	
Paper Punch Set (40 punches)	$36.00	WEAVING WITH PAPER by Malinda Johnston PAPER QUILLING	$7.50
FISKARS 12" PAPER TRIMMER W/EXTRA BLADE 9598 NEW	$34.99	SCRAPBOOKING TEA BAG ORIGAMI PAPER 1000 SHEET 2"SQ.	$7.25
Quilling Board Kits - Tools - Paper - LOW SHIP	$31.00	ORIGAMI PAPER HANDMADE YUZEN WASHI 30 SHEET GORGEOUS!	$7.25
45 pocket display rack for 8.5x11 paper or literature	$27.50	FUN MIX PACK ORIGAMI PAPER 80 SHEETS WITH FOILS 6X6	$7.25
Craft PATTERN BOOK bGM - Beautiful PAPER QUILLING	$21.00	2X JAPANESE CHINESE CALLIGRAPHY RICE PAPER 160s TOTAL	$6.99
ORIGAMI PAPER 6" 50 COLORS 550 SHEETS w/ FOIL	$20.50	ORIGAMI PAPER SAKURA FLOWERS 3 COLORS 60 SHEETS 6X6	$6.85
Southworth Onionskin Typewriter Paper LEGAL SIZE	$20.50	1000 SHEETS WITH PEARL COLORS ORIGAMI PAPER 2X2	$6.60
Arnold Grummer's PAPERMILL PRO Paper Making Kit, IN BOX	$20.50	1949 Dennison PARTIES WITH PURPOSE Crepe Paper Book	$6.51
ORIGAMI PAPER 6" 50 COLORS 550 SHEETS w/ FOIL	$20.00	ORIGAMI PAPER 6" GOLD FOIL 100 SHEETS	$6.50
[4 of these sold for $20.00 each]		ORIGAMI PAPER 6" GOLD FOIL 100 SHEETS	$6.50
Quilling Board Tool Kits Watercolor,Touch of Gold Paper	$20.00	ORIGAMI PAPER 1004 STARS PASTEL/FLUORESCENT STAR SET	$6.50
ORIGAMI PAPER 6" 50 COLORS 550 SHEETS w/ FOIL	$19.50	[3 of these sold for $6.50 each]	
ORIGAMI PAPER 6" 50 COLORS 550 SHEETS w/ FOIL	$19.00	ORIGAMI PAPER 300 SHEETS 3" SOLID MIX COLOR	$6.50

Quilting ▸ Tops, Blocks

The average sales price in this subcategory is $16.51.

	HIGH		AVG
APPLIQUE BALTIMORE ALBUM BOM KIT	$203.50	FAIRY MOUNTAIN Fabric Kaleidoscope Quilt Block Kit	$17.00
Scrappy DOUBLE IRISH CHAIN Quilt Top "Black and White"	$172.73	Set 9 Vintage Santa Christmas Quilt Blocks Fabric	$16.99
Vintage 9-patch QUILT TOP 5" blocks & sashing 90 x103	$140.50	Hampton Gardens KALEIDOSCOPE Quilt Block Kit	$16.99
Vintage 50 States Quilt Top ~ Embroidered & Handsewn	$127.50	GISELLE Kaleidoscope Quilt Blocks KIT Fabric	$16.99
1930's PINEAPPLE QUILT TOP	$100.99	FLORAL IRISH CHAIN QUILT TOP	$16.95
NEW Dresden Plate Quilt Top Blocks 1930s Vintage Pastel	$20.99	30 bluework snowmen quilt blocks	$16.50
Vintage 30s Flower Garden 42"x27"Quilt top and157 Piece	$82.50	GRAPES VINEYARD Fabric Kaleidoscope Quilt Block Kit	$16.50
Magnificent 30's Reproduction Quilt Top	$78.00	Vintage Harrison Fisher LIPSTICK LADY Fabric Square	$16.29
handmade quilt 86x86	$76.00	SUMMER ROSE Kaleidoscope Quilt Blocks KIT Rose Fabric	$16.25
Vintage Hand Sewn Grandmother's Flower Garden Quilt Top	$76.00	~16~Thimbleberries~Pumpkins~Quilt Blocks~Fall~	$16.10
VINTAGE FEEDSACK, FEED SACK Mushrooms & Birds - Cute!	$74.01	Unique Grandmother's Fan Quilt Blocks Bali Prints QUALI	$16.03
VINTAGE FEEDSACK, FEED SACK Mushrooms & Birds - Cute!	$73.01	MINI "STAR" Quilt Blocks w/ THIMBLEBERRIES FABRICS	$16.01
Kaleidoscope - Unfinished Patchwork QUILT TOP	$71.00	Purple and Green Floral Churn Dash Quilt Blocks/Top	$16.01
12 vintage embroidered quilt blocks	$66.83	Quilt Top, Block, or Wallhanging, Unfinished, Baby	$16.01
Vintage quilt top -Blue T-block pattern & extra fabric	$66.00	Cowboy~Western~Rodeo Quilt Blocks * Quilt Top	$16.00

Ribbon ▸ Grosgrain

The average sales price in this subcategory is $9.23.

	HIGH		AVG
LOT Striped GROSGRAIN Satins Ribbon Assorted 1200+ Yds	$99.17	Bright Colors!! 5/8 " Grosgrain Ribbon!! 30 Yards!!!	$9.48
94 yd roll of PINK WHALES PREPPY NOVELTY JACQUARD	$61.02	20 YARDS GROSGRAIN RIBBON-7/8" & 1.5" BRIGHT STRIPES!	$9.43
70 yd roll PINK TENNIS RACKET PREPPY NOVELTY JACQUARD	$55.56	Grosgrain Ribbon 14 yards 7/8" BRIGHT STRIPES	$9.40
70 yd roll PINK & WHITE WHALES PREPPY NOVELTY JACQUARD	$53.02	BRIGHT PINK W/DOTS GROSGRAIN RIBBON (7/8) 100FT	$9.38
LOT GROSGRAIN Ribbon Craft Supplies 600+ Yds	$51.01	Pastel Colors! 7/8 " Grosgrain Ribbon! 42+ Yards!	$9.26
LOT OF 5/8" GROSGRAIN RIBBON -VARIOUS BRIGHT COLORS	$35.00	20 YARDS GROSGRAIN RIBBON - DOTS AND STRIPES	$9.24
NOVELTY RIBBON -7/8" - 1 1/8" 2yards + = 32 yards min.	$31.04	10 yds 1 1/2" BROWN & WHITE Polka Dot Grosgrain Ribbon	$9.06
Stampin Up New Grosgrain Ribbons 125 yds 25 colors	$31.00	MUSIC NOTE COLORFUL GROSGRAIN RIBBON (7/8") 100 FT	$9.02
MIX 1.5 & 7/8" Stripe GROSGRAIN RIBBON 70 yd Stripes	$31.00	50 YARD ROLL GROSGRAIN 1" RIBBON CREAM	$9.01
70 yards of 7/8" Swiss Dot Grosgrain Ribbon	$29.99	10 yds Lime Juice & Hot Pink Polka Dot Grosgrain Ribbon	$9.01
55 yd roll PINK & BROWN WHALE PREPPY NOVELTY JACQUARD	$29.99	Jacquard with Flowers + Swirls + Grosgrain Ribbon Mix	$9.00
GROSGRAIN RIBBON - 7/8" SOLID TOTAL 100 YARDS L@@K	$29.89	Grosgrain Ribbon 40 yards 3/8" Swiss Dots and Solids	$9.00
Huge lot of grosgrain korker ribbon and barrettes	$28.00	20 YD HALLOWEEN KORKER RIBBON	$9.00
450 YARDS Grosgrain Ribbon NOT SO PERFECT 1.5"	$26.58	COMBO, BLACK & ORANGE	$9.00
Grosgrain Ribbon 18+ yards 7/8" Embroidered Daisies	$26.00	Belt Maker EXTRORDINAIRE! 7 Grosgrain Ribbons 1.5" 21yd	$9.00
25 Yards Brand New JACQUARD Whale Alligator Crab Ribbon	$26.00	LEOPARD & ZEBRA ANIMAL GROSGRAIN RIBBON (7/8") 73 FT	$8.99

Scrapbooking ▸ Albums

The average sales price in this subcategory is $13.78.

	HIGH		AVG
Florentia Heirloom Leather Scrapbook Album, NR	$121.48	8x8 COLORBOK PRE-DESIGNED SCRAPBOOK ALBUM- WEDDING	$14.95
UNIVERSAL 3/4 scrapbook POST EXTENDERS NEW	$50.00	CI - Sports Album - Soccer - 8x8	$14.12
Creative Memories 8 x 10 burgundy album & page protect	$35.50	New SEI 8x8 Friends / Groovy Gal Scrapbook in a Bag Kit	$14.01
Creative Memories 12x15 BIG Evergreen Album w refils	$55.52	you are our little girl Paper Bag Album!!! Mod	$14.00
K&CO BASIC GREY 6x6 SUBLIME ALBUMS Scrapbook Kit Paper	$51.00	8x8 COLORBOK PRE-DESIGNED SCRAPBOOK ALBUM-ALL OCCASION	$13.99
Creative Memories Lot 12 x 15 Big Scrapbook Book NIP ++	$51.00	CHILD KID SCHOOL MEMORIES KEEPSAKE ALBUM BOOK K-12 NEW	$13.99
Creative Memories Discontinued Making Waves 7x7 Album	$16.55	8x8 COLORBOK PRE-DESIGNED SCRAPBOOK ALBUM- BABY GIRL	$13.99
3-School Days Memory Books Albums-New!!	$46.01	K & Co. 6X6 Scrapbook & Paper Pad-Garden Collage 2004	$13.99
Creative Memories 12x15 Mahogany Album + Extras	$44.00	NIP Child School Year Memories Book Album K-12	$13.95
Creative Memories 8x10 MAUVE	$42.90	[2 of these sold for $13.95 each]	
Album, NLA, NEW, RARE		Disney Vacation Paper Bag Album 6x6	$13.50
Rollabind Crafters Kit Create A Book NIP	$41.02	FRIENDSHIP paper bag album	$13.50
Baby's First Book by Rag and Bone - NIB	$40.00	happy birthday paper bag scrapbook album	$13.50
Tim Coffey Travel Scrapbook	$39.99	Southern Living at Home SCHOOL PICTURES MEMORIES BOOK	$13.50
DOGGONE CUTE Paper Bag Album ** Larger Size**	$39.50	BACK TO SCHOOL premade paper bag album - MUST SEE!	$13.50
12x15 Creative Memories Sapphire album w/protectors	$39.00	Friends Paper Bag Scrapbook Album & Journal	$12.99

Scrapbooking ▸ Stickers

The average sales price in this subcategory is $3.80.

	HIGH		AVG
NEW MAKING MEMORIES SCRAPBOOKING	$76.00	Jolee's DOCTOR & NURSE ~Great Combined Shipping~	$3.99
ITEMS @ $260.00		Cute set of Stickers from Me & My Big Ideas scrapbook	$3.99
WOW K&CO 3D XL Scrapbook Stickers (Nice LOT)	$31.51	Marco Almera - Clear Charger Babe Vinyl Sticker RARE!	$3.99
Stickopotamus Binder & 155 Stickopotamus Sticker Sheets	$31.00	Marco Almera - Clear Flirt Nude Babe Vinyl Sticker RARE	$3.99
Brenda Walton Tim Coffey K&Company Lot of 14	$27.00	Marco Almera - Clear Seated Babe HOT Vinyl Sticker RARE	$3.99
WOW K&CO 3D XL Scrapbook Stickers (Nice LOT)	$26.00	Marco Almera -Clear Super Sport SEXY Vinyl Sticker RARE	$3.99
100 PACKS STICKERS INCLUDES PHRASE CAFE & VELLUM	$26.00	Jolee's Boutique Mexico Cinco De Mayo~2 pkgs	$3.99
creative memories lot - nice	$22.27	CREATIVE MEMORIES STICKERS HOLIDAY GRANDMA'S KITCHEN	$3.76
NEW DECORATIVE ART PENS - GELLY ROLL GLAZE - SET/10	$10.00	Scrapbooking CM Boy's First Years Stickers + More	$3.76
Jolee's Nostalgiques (5) LADY THEMES - BABY, WEDDING	$19.03	*NEW RELEASE* Jolee's True Faith NATIVITY 1	$3.75
HARLEY DAVIDSON SCRAPBOOK LOT–5 ITEMS–ALL NEW!!	$18.50	Pearly SNOWMAN WINTER Theme Sandylion Stickers	$3.75
Creative Memories Lot of 15 Page Completion kits HTF	$16.75	Creative Memories "Holiday Tree Decoration " Stickers	$3.75
Lot of 400 stickers Cars, girls, sayings, dragons +	$16.01	BBQ picnic USA PATRIOTIC & alphabet scrapbook stickers	$3.50
14 PACKS BEAUTIFUL DISNEY 3-D STICKERS-NEW!	$15.99	CREATIVE MEMORIES STICKERS~CAMPING ~FOREST~ NEW	$3.50
100 Packs of Assorted Stickers by Hallmark & more	$15.50	CREATIVE MEMORIES STICKERS~MARINE PRIDE ~NEW	$3.50
Creative Memories Sticker Assortment	$15.00	[3 of these sold for $3.50 each]	

Sewing ▸ Machines, Sergers

The average sales price in this subcategory is $95.18.

	HIGH		AVG
Gammill Quilting Machine	$8,100.00	NECCHI Omega 6011 Free Arm Sewing Machine -Used	$99.99
NEW Janome Memory Craft 9500 Sewing\Embroidery Machine	$1,499.00	Euro-Pro 6130 Deluxe Denim & Silk Sewing Machine $NR	$99.99
Bernina Artista 170 Sewing Machine	$1,000.00	4 Thread SERGER,OVERLOCK Sewing Machine, SERGERS, *NEW*	$99.00
NEW JANOME Memory Craft 4800QC Computer Sewing Machine	$849.00	[2 of these solld for $99.00 each]	
[2 of these sold for $849.00 each]		3 Thread SERGER, OverLock SEWING Machines, SERGERS, NIB	$99.00
Husqvarna Viking Rose Sewing Machine & Embroidery	$810.00	[2 of these sold for $99.00 each]	
National Carpet Binding Brute Carpet Binder	$667.00	4 Thread SERGER,OVERLOCK Sewing Machine, SERGERS,*NEW*	$99.00
Grace machine quilter	$650.00	Singer Model 1525 Sewing Machine - DEALER for 33 Years	$95.00
Husqvarna Viking 1003LCD 2, 3, 4 and 5 Thread Serger	$632.22	Necchi Lydia 544 Burnt Orange Sewing Machine Freearm	$93.75
Bernina 1080 Quilters Edition computerized sewing mach	$500.00	Singer Model 1525 Sewing Machine - DEALER for 33 Years	$91.00
* Industrial Feather Down Filling Machine sewing *	$500.00	Singer 4830 Sewing Machine 32 Stitch	$90.99
BLE 1 BLE1 BABYLOCK ECLIPSE SERGER SERGING MACHINE	$467.99	Brother 12x12 GIANT Hoop-It-All With Extension Table	$89.99
Quantum XL 100 W/many accessories Sewing Machine NR	$456.01	Singer Model 1525 Sewing Machine - DEALER for 33 Years	$89.00
US Industrial Hemmer Machine Blind Stich Blindstitch	$450.00	New 4 THREAD ,SERGER ,overlock ,sewing machine and more	$89.00
Elna 9000 Diva Sewing Machine	$400.00	ALL METAL SEWING MACHINE W/ INDUSTRIAL HANDWHEEL	$89.00
INDUSTRIAL STRENGTH SEWING MACHINE,	$400.00	Bernina Walking Foot–Brand NEW–125-200	$82.50
GREAT FOR LEATHER		Excellent Riccar Sewing Machine w/ Embroider Cams	$81.00

Sewing ▸ Notions, Supplies, Tools

The average sales price in this subcategory is $17.52.

	HIGH		AVG
NEW Singer Seam Ripper	$105.00	Clover Mini Iron NEW IN BOX	$18.75
NEW professional DRESS FORM mannequin-Size 8 w HIP	$300.50	Sewing notions grab bag! What fun!	$18.50
Professional DRESS FORM mannequins-Size 10 w/ HIP - NEW	$242.50	Husqvarna Viking Circular Attachment #412602645	$18.50
NEW professional DRESS FORM mannequin-Size 8 w HIP	$241.00	Box full of sewing material NR	$18.27
new RALF professional dress form mannequin-Size6 w HIP	$239.00	SEWING ROOM CRAFT MOUSE VINTAGE	$18.00
Amazing Designs II Box For Janome Embroidery	$189.00	MACHINE SIGN WALL CLOCK	
[2 of these sold for $189.00 each]		Making Handbags & Purses- Softcover Book	$17.38
THREAD WINDING ROLLING MACHINE	$149.00	3 doz(36) Nickel Swivel Snap Hooks (1/2in circle loop)	$16.99
Sewing dress form, mannequin, adjustable	$133.49	Threads Magazine - 2002	$16.60
Amanda Jane Smocking-Pleater Like New	$125.00	Velcro Brand Hook and Loop Black 2 inch Sew-on 50 yds	$16.52
Dress Makers Form Excellent Cond.	$105.99	EURO-PRO SEWING ACCESSORY BOX SPOOLS THREAD NEEDLES PIN	$15.61
military snap grommet eyelet canvas scovill mfg. dies	$89.00	TIMTEX Interfacing Stabilizer Hat Brims - 3 yards 13" W	$15.51
Heavy Duty Snap Press: Table top/interchangeable head	$87.50	Fasturn Sewing & Quilting Tool -Buy it Now for Free S&H	$15.50
Fabric Press, Singer Magic Press 4	$75.00	INDUSTRIAL SHORTCUTS FOR HOME SEWING -VHS-	$15.50
VINTAGE SINGER PINKER	$75.00	Nancy Zieman - Serger Feet On The Go VHS Video	$15.09
Wholesale Lot 800 Black Nylon Zippers 8" to 26"	$66.00	Lot of 125+ Thread Bias Hem Tape New Zippers	$15.05

Spinning ▸ Roving, Wool, Fiber

The average sales price in this subcategory is $13.17.

	HIGH		AVG
PRISTINE WHITE 2 Alpaca Fleece Fiber RawClean 10 lbs	$75.17	Faerie Wings Roving - Romney, Blue du Maine & Mohair	$14.00
20 pounds of nice raw alpaca fiber carmel and black	$75.00	Winter Moon roving - Romney Wool and Mohair	$14.00
Euroflax Originals LINEN 100 gm skeins CEDAR WOOD	$70.00	Bleached White Tussah Silk Top Spinning Fiber Roving	$13.95
[5 of these sold in a multiple item ("Dutch") auction for $14.00 each]		Bleached White Tussah Silk Top Spinning Fiber Roving	$13.95
WHISPER WHITE Alpaca Fleece Fiber RawClean 5 lbs	$66.54	MERINO Top CORAL 8 oz Lovely solid color ready to SPIN	$13.75
[2 of these sold in a multiple item ("Dutch") auction for $33.27 each]		Hand-dyed Romney Top-8 oz in Blue Lagoon!	$13.50
Corriedale Wool Roving, White, Washed 4.0 Pound Batch	$65.04	Sandalwood Merino Multi Blend Top roving Fiber 4 oz NR	$13.50
PRISTINE WHITE Alpaca Fleece Fiber RawClean 10 lbs	$55.00	[2 of these sold in a multiple item ("Dutch") auction for $6.75 each]	
[2 of these sold for $55.00 each]		OOAK Needle Felted Spinning	$12.99
Tassah Silk Fiber Sliver Roving Spin Top 32 oz	$51.00	Buddy CRF Handspun Roving	
Alpaca Wool/Raw/Unwashed/CreamBeige/10 lb/4H Fundraiser	$46.01	Wool roving, spin, needle felt, knit, merino	$12.99
Tussah Silk Roving Spin Felting Fiber 32 oz	$46.00	11+ oz. of kid mohair	$12.99
3 LBS. 2.5 OZ OF CVM & DYED SHEEP WOOL ROVING	$45.53	Bleached White Tussah Silk Top Spinning Fiber Roving	$12.95
HANDMADE SHEEP MADE FROM VINTAGE QUILTS (3 SHEEP)	$45.00	[2 of these sold for $12.95 each]	
10 lb Mohair Fleece	$45.00	Loose Yak Down Spinning Fiber Roving Wool Felting	$12.95
SPRING SALE: 1# of Supreme Softness: 100% Angora Top!	$42.50	Soft Merino Wool Spinning Roving Fiber 8oz Rosewood	$12.50
ORIGINAL KAREN TRAUB BASKET (Full of Surprizes!) NR	$42.02	6.5 lb spinning wool white fleece	$12.50
EXCEPTIONAL Lincoln Lamb fleece 5-6" staple low VW	$42.00	Loose Yak Down Spinning Fiber Roving Wool Felting	$12.45

Stamping ▸ Stamps

The average sales price in this subcategory is $10.46.

	HIGH		AVG
Lot of 10 Wood Scenes and Landscapes	$87.55	STAMPIN' UP! QUICK AND CUTE SET OF 8	$10.50
Stampin Up 11 Rubber Stamp Sets New Discontinued Lot	$82.79	STAMPIN' UP! *WATERCOLOR MINIS* SET OF 12	$10.50
HUGE Lot Handmade Cards 180, Stampin Up, CTMH, TAC	$81.00	Retired Stampin' Up "Easter Egg" NLA	$10.49
1932 Classroom Printer Rubber Stamp Set in wooden box	$66.00	WINE COLLAGE RUBBER STAMP	$10.49
DREAMS AND DRAGONS - RETIRED, RARE STAMPIN UP	$48.01	Stampin' Up! Retired SKETCH A PARTY Stamp Set NR	$10.49
NEW STAMPIN UP LOT! With Bounes	$45.00	Stampin Up Nice & Easy Notes	$10.49
Stampin' Up! Fruit Medley, Phrases + clsy brass RETIRED	$41.99	Stampin Up GOING SOMEWHERE Mounted Stamp Set	$10.45
CTMH ~Close to my Heart ~ ACRYLIC STAMPS~ MY MOM	$41.00	Stampin' Up -A Little Love ~ Mounted	$10.33
PSX 1997-1998 Catalog of rubber stamp images & samples	$41.00	Stampin' Up-Rose Rhapsody-Retired	$10.29
Lot of 16 Oriental Rubber Stamps	$40.89	Stampin up +others lot of Halloween stamps many HTF	$10.15
STAMPIN_ UP! _WHAT_S BREWIN__ SET/9 NLA RETIRED	$39.02	New Stampin Up color coach with the 12 new colors	$10.05
STAMPIN' UP "All Around Alphabet	$37.00	Stampin Up ROSE RHAPSODY two step stampin	$10.03
stampin' up Sketches	$36.05	Stampscapes BOULDER / ROCK RIDGE Rubber Stamp	$10.02
Spcl. BS Stamp Cache-Bill Hillcourt sig.-Camp Delmont	$36.00	STAMPIN' UP! TWO DIFFERENT STAMP SETS	$10.02
RETIRED Stampin Up "Garden Seeds" Set Never Been Used!	$36.00	Stampin' Up! Frame & Flourishes	$10.01

Weaving ▸ Looms

The average sales price in this subcategory is $53.21.

	HIGH		AVG
8-Shaft Macomber loom + many accessories	$1,200.00	Wooden Rug Hooking Loom /Rack + Yarn for Latch Hook Rug	$61.00
46" Gilmore Maple Floor Weaving Loom, Bench, & Access.	$1,000.00	Lot Weaving Flat Shuttle Pick Up Sticks Varied Sizes 8	$61.00
WEAVING LOOM, 8 HARNESS WITH STAND	$850.00	TABLE TOP LOOM FOR WEAVING CRAFT	$61.00
Like New SCHACHT Baby Wolf 4 Harness Loom + Extras	$850.00	Weaving loom shuttles & spools	$59.07
Like New Oak High Castle Floor Weaving Loom	$810.00	Like new Easy Weaver Hardwood Weaving Loom with everyth	$59.00
Sachet Baby Wolf 4 now/4 later Loom - Never Used	$800.00	TABLE TOP FRAME-LOOM WEAVING and book	$58.92
Leclerc Artistat 36" floor loom ..bench..extras weaving	$785.00	Easy Weaver - 18" X 10" A Friendly Loom Product (Wood)	$53.00
WEAVING LOOM NORWOOD 50" 8 HARNESS NR	$610.00	Large Adjustable Maple LOOM BENCH For Baby Wolf Loom	$51.00
50"(48"weaving width) Norwood Cherry 4 Shaft classic	$565.55	Small Table Top Loom	$49.00
Nilus Leclerc Folding 22" Maple Floor Weaving Loom- NR!	$511.00	Vintage 10" wood KAYanEE table top weaving loom w/box	$46.82
MACOMBER AD-A-HARNESS FOLDING FLOOR LOOM	$481.64	EASY WEAVER HARDWOOD WEAVING LOOM LIKE NEW HARRISVILLE	$46.00

Norwood 22" Workshop Loom	$455.00	RIGID HEDDLE LOOM	$46.00
Glimakra "Victoria" 27" Floor/Table Weaving Loom	$380.00	CONE HOLDER FOR WINDING WARP YARN WEAVING	$45.00
HARRISVILLE 4 HARNESS 4 TREADLE FOLDING FLOOR LOOM 36"	$350.00	Schacht Inkle Loom w/shuttle	$45.00
Bergman Loom Co. Loom	$330.96	HIGH CASTLE TRAY For SCHACHT Baby Wolf Loom NEW IN BOX	$44.95

Woodworking ▸ Supplies

The average sales price in this subcategory is $13.63.

	HIGH		AVG
Freud Rail And Style Door System # RS2000	$256.00	(250) Wooden wood shaker pegs 3 1/2 inch x 1/2 diam.	$14.70
Incra Ultra Jig -FINE-	$153.50	NEW MOISTURE BEARING ANALYZER for Wood , Etc. SALE NR	$14.49
20 GENUINE ELEPHANT IVORY TUSK Long Blocks, 1 Lb.	$150.00	100 Rectangle Sign Wood Cutouts, Craft Supplies / Items	$14.22
GRAFTED CLARO WALNUT Dry LUTHIER WOOD	$125.00	FOUR BARS BROWN POLISHING COMPOUND JEWELERS ROUGE	$13.99
Nora Hall Essential European Woodcarving video series	$107.02	5 New 48" Ratchet/Spreader BAR CLAMPS woodworking Clamp	$13.99
Lg. Victorian Horse Pull Toy c.1890 Needs Restoration!	$93.99	4 PCS KILN DRIED SPANISH CEDAR (561)	$13.50
Woodstock Rebel Cast Metal Router Table -FINE-	$82.50	1/16" Thick cut Walnut Veneer. 24 Sqft. No Res.	$13.50
Jet Table Saw Fence	$77.00	WAGON WHEELS - Toy Wood 6", 5", 4", 3?", 3 or 2" size	$13.09
GENUINE ELEPHANT IVORY TUSK Piano Key shafts, 1 Lb	$75.00	Compare to Anchorseal -> Wood sealer lathe seal wax	$13.03
Lenox 10 pc plumber's hole saw with Lenox vari-bit	$66.00	Exotic Hardwood Chitswood Snakewood Inlay H23	$13.00
Veritas Stone Pond and Grinder Rest	$66.00	Mortise and Tenon Joints Frank Klausz TAUNTON VHS Video	$13.00
80 rolls of 1 inch wood veneer - 8 foot rolls	$65.00	HIGH PRESSURE AIR SPRAY GUN NEW PAINT STAIN FAN PATTERN	$12.99
Freud Raised Panel Set #RP1000	$62.00	NEW MOISTURE BEARING ANALYZER for Wood , Etc. SALE NR	$12.99
12 ANTIQUE PIE SAFE TINS LOT 937	$61.00	FOUR BARS BROWN POLISHING COMPOUND JEWELERS ROUGE	$12.99
3/16" Veneer Plywood, 2 pallets of assorted sizes	$59.99	NEW MOISTURE BEARING ANALYZER for Wood , Etc. SALE NR	$12.99

Yarn

The average sales price in this subcategory is $18.39.

NOTE *The below results were obtained by doing a keyword search on the word* yarn *in this subcategory.*

	HIGH		AVG
11413 Skeins of Springer / Orchidee, Tapestry Wool Yarn	$350.00	MOUNTAIN COLORS "MOUNTAIN GOAT" HAND-DYED SOCK YARN	$19.00
120 SKEINS EYELASH YARN & ALDEMIR METALLIC 50g / 100gm	$192.48	Draped Poncho Knitting Kit Novelty Yarn Midnight Blue	$18.99
99 SKEINS IMPORTED EYELASH YARN! 20-25 DIFFERENT COLORS	$168.71	Yarn Knitting Wool lb 2,000 Yds Fisherman Aran	$18.73
Alice Starmore Scottish Fleet Yarn 12 Skeins Blue NEW	$168.50	Island Lime New Zealand Wool Yarn 3lb 9oz	$18.50
10 Skeins Noro Hana Silk Yarn #8 "Copper" Lot F	$162.50	Red Heart Tweed Yarn 11 skeins	$18.50
20 Skeins Apple Green Koigu Kersti Merino Yarn	$155.32	TAHKI Yarn 6 NEW Rolls ~WILLOW~ Crochet/Knit NICE BLUE	$18.26
70 SKEINS EYELASH YARN+ALDEMIR+100g+50g+2 SIZES+	$140.49	handspun hand dyed wool pretty pastel yarn ~bambino~	$18.00
10 Skeins Noro Hana Silk Yarn #43 Violet Purple	$125.00	DEBBIE BLISS BABY CASHMERINO YARN COLOR #503	$18.00
50 SKEINS EYELASH YARN+ALDEMIR+100g+50g+2 SIZES+	$105.99	Bright Red New Zealand Wool Yarn 2lb 10oz	$18.00
10 skeins Noro Silk Garden Yarn/knitting/crafts	$89.50	INTERLACEMENTS "TOASTY TOES" HAND-DYED SOCK YARN	$18.00
27 SKEINS EYELASH YARN=ALDEMIR=ALL 100 GRAMS!!! L@@K!!	$81.99	*** KOALA ** Handpainted Eyelash Ribbon COMBO Yarn Kit	$17.99
*** AUTUMN SUNSET *** Magic Poncho Novelty Yarn Kit	$69.99	EASY KNIT SHAWL KIT ~ Yarn Blend ~ Pattern ~ Brooch ~	$17.99
Debbie Bliss cashmerino superchunky yarn, Meino wool	$66.00	Stashbuilder! Novelty Euro yarn Sampler BLACK/GRAY	$17.51
HUGE MIXED LOT CROCHET KNITTING YARN 81 SKEINS N/R!	$66.00	Artisan NZ Merino Lace Weight Yarn Scarf Kit	$17.51
10 Skeins Noro Silk-Chenille Yarn #4 Green	$63.22	Henna New Zealand Wool Yarn 2lb 15oz	$17.50

Wall Decor, Tatouage

The average sales price in this subcategory is $13.03.

NOTE *The below results were obtained by doing a keyword search on the word* tatouage *in this subcategory.*

	HIGH		AVG
Tatouage Rainforest Collection! New Configuration $189	$129.95	Basket Garden Flowers Roses Sunflowers Love Tatouage ?	$14.95
Tatouage Country Garden Huge Set * Free Ship	$59.98	[2 of these sold for $14.95 each]	
Tatouage Jungle Mural w/ Leopard & Bird * Free Shipping	$56.98	Tatouage Pink Rose Tree * Free Ship Offer	$14.95
TATOUAGE ARTWORK, COMPLETE MURAL/SUMMER GARDEN	$51.00	Tatouage Sea Birds & Sea Oats	$14.95
TATOUAGE COMPLETE JUNGLE MURAL ~$4 SHIPPING~	$48.00	Large Garden Flowers White Picket Fence Love Tatouage ?	$14.60
Tatouage Tropical Door Mural * Free Ship Offer	$47.98	Large Country Basket Apple Jug & Shelf Love Tatouage ?	$13.99
TATOUAGE 6 Foot ~Tropical~ Door Mural $3.50 SH	$43.00	Large Fairies Butterflies Fairy Flowers Love Tatouage ?	$13.99
Tatouage Banana Tree * Free Ship Offer	$42.98	Large Country Basket Apple Jug & Shelf Love Tatouage ?	$13.99
Tatouage Fan Palm Tree NEW $3.90 Priority Ship	$41.00	Tatouage Bunnies & Squirrels * Free Ship Offer	$13.98
Tatouage Grape Vine Set	$20.00	Seashells Seahorse Starfish Shell Vine Love Tatouage ?	$13.95
Tatouage Lily Pond w/Ducks * Free Ship Offer	$39.98	Tatouage Fern Stalks Five Large Ferns Four Sheets	$12.99
Tatouage Pine Tree * Free Ship Offer	$39.98	Tatouage Mouse in Pot * Free Ship Offer	$12.98
Tatouage Lily Pond w/Ducks * Free Ship Offer	$39.98	Tatouage Pink Rose Tree * Free Ship Offer	$12.98
[2 of these sold for $39.98 each]		Picket Fence Rabbit Sunflowers Garden + Love Tatouage ?	$12.95
Tatouage Symmetrical Vines, Blue JaFlowers&Butterflies	$39.95	Tatouage Lion's Head Fountain * Free Ship Offer	$12.50
Tatouage Grape and Grapevine Border 32 Linear Feet New	$39.95	Tatouage Vegetables & Basket NEW Beautiful Kitchen	$12.50

16

DOLLS & BEARS

The Dolls & Bears category on eBay shows that you don't have to be a child to be fanatical about a certain kind of toy; certainly, there are all sorts of adults devoted to their doll or bear passion and knowledgeable about the nuances of their chosen type of collectible. Indeed, some of these toys command very grown-up prices.

If you want to sell a doll here but aren't sure what you have, the niche doll experts on the eBay boards would no doubt be happy to help you learn about the features and value of your prized toy. And enlist the aid of your spouse at your own risk. Doll collector Denise Van Patten, who writes about Doll Collecting for About.com, said she created a monster when she trained her husband to sell dolls—now he eyes her not-for-sale dolls and says things like, "Did you know we could get over $500 for R. John Wright's Musette on eBay?" or, "You CANNOT keep the Robert Tonner Matt/Sean doll! They are selling for over $400 now!" and even, "Would you LOOK at the messy hair on this doll? How do you expect me to sell this!"

And if you want to buy a doll at a bargain price or to resell, you may want to browse categories regularly for items that are underpriced because the seller doesn't know what he or she has (this is actually a strategy you can use in any eBay category). One savvy eBayer did this and found a 1945 Georgene Raggedy (made by Georgene Novelties, one of the earliest makers of the doll) with a 1970s Knickerbocker Andy for only $5.50. They were described only as "Old Raggedy Ann and Andy Dolls," and they were listed in the wrong category: Dolls & Bears ▶ Dolls ▶ By Brand, Company, Character ▶ Other Brands. They were a bit stained, but she cleaned them up and put Andy's proper outfit on him, and they were good to go. (A mint condition 1946 Original Georgine Novelties Raggedy doll recently sold for $735.00 on eBay.)

Antique Dolls

The top two sellers in Dolls & Bears ▶ Dolls ▶ Antique Dolls were both "Skookum" dolls, described by one seller as a type of doll first created by Mary McAboy in 1913 that became a popular tourist collectible. The most expensive one is a three-foot-tall (as size that is very hard to find, according to the seller) antique Skookum doll of a Native American chief. He is circa 1920–30, and "can stand alone."

He appears to be in very good condition, with details like "a composition head with expressive face, mohair braids with wraps, beaded (red/turquoise/white) brown leather moccasins, ivory felt shirt, and fringed ivory felt pants, which are decorated with leather appliqués and wooden beads," per the seller's description. He is wrapped in a traditional white, blue, yellow, green, and beige wool blanket and is wearing a headdress of white and red feathers. He is not without slight flaws: a couple of the feathers are broken, as are a couple of the wooden beads, says the seller. But overall, he is in very good condition.

The other high-selling Skookum doll is of an old woman, a Mary Frances Woods Indian Squaw Doll in very good condition. "She also has a composition head, this one covered by crepe paper and molded to display great age and authentic personality with hand painted features." Other fine details include eyes of black bead-headed pins, a mohair grey wig, an early–20th century print cotton skirt, and a necklace of assorted beads and pearls. The seller thinks she was patterned after a Cayuse squaw that was living in the era of the Lewis & Clark Expedition to the Pacific Northwest (1804). (This kind of historical detail is good to throw in and may help you attract bidders searching on related terms that wouldn't otherwise find your auction.)

Barbies: Old to New

It's hard to talk about dolls without mentioning that all-American classic, the Barbie doll. In terms of Barbies, pre–1973 is considered "vintage." The top seller here was a "Twist 'n' Turn" (TNT) Barbie from 1966, selling at a lofty $2,551.00 with 22 bids. She is dressed in black velvet, especially rare, per the seller, because these dolls are usually dressed in a bathing suit.

Two "Color Magic" Barbie auctions were also high sellers; notable because they were only Barbie torsos, and also because the second high seller was actually a "Dutch" (multiple item) auction of seven of the torsos, each at $150.00. The first was a single torso, and sold for $638.00 with 16 bids, and was especially desirable because her hair color was the rarer "lemon blonde" and not the more common "golden blonde." Color Magic Barbies were dolls from the 1960s whose hair could change from colors like "golden blonde" to "scarlet flame" and "midnight black" to "ruby red."

Although average prices for vintage Barbies are around $58.00, contemporary Barbies average around a more affordable $19.00, which is not far from what some of the dolls sell for new. In fact, some of the Barbies in the Dolls ▶ Barbie Contemporary subcategory are new in box dolls, such as Barbie as Harley Quinn, selling at $19.99.

Antique Bears

One of the highest-selling antique bears in this sample is a "magnificent" Strunz teddy bear, circa 1912, that sold for $1,889.88. He is in very good condition for such an old bear—with clean, fluffy yellow-brown fur of 90 percent mohair—which, of course, is a factor in fetching a high price. The seller was based in Germany, which is not surprising, because Strunz was a German company. In fact, German companies, such as Steiff, Bing, Cramer, and Schuco, make or made several of the most collectible bears and teddy bears.

"Teddy" bears are named for President "Teddy" Roosevelt, who was one of the hunters on a 1902 bear hunt that set off the teddy bear craze. Therefore, the oldest "teddy bears" are going to be 1902 and later. Looking through the list of high prices for antique bears, several of the aforementioned old brand names come up, such as Bing ($920.00), Schuco ($611.00), and one possible Steiff ($728.89).

The seller of the Schuco doll is very careful in her description to mention any flaws. "Constance is all original, with a few replaced nose stitches. . .her paw pads having been replaced years ago with old ticking material. . .I left them alone as they give her a very pleasing look and match her VINTAGE coat. . .She also has an old growler which no longer makes noise." This is something that is important for you to do, too, especially if you are selling a particularly valuable bear. It's hard to find a truly old bear or doll in perfect condition, and buyers don't like to be surprised, so it is best to be thorough about any imperfections in your listing.

Perhaps the best-known brand of the collectible bears is Steiff. According to auction house Christie's, this is because they are so well-made. One way to tell if a bear is vintage is to look for a seam across the top of the head from ear to ear. In later years, a button with the name *Steiff* on it was attached to the bear's ear.[1]

Newer Bears

You don't have to dip back to 1902 to find a bear that will sell well, though. They may not be bringing in prices in the thousands, but there are several Boyds bears in this sampling that went for $30.00. Boyds Bears started making bears in 1984 and specializes in antique reproductions. The bears are quality but not overly expensive. Current brand-new bears featured on the front of one Boyds-selling website range from $30.99 to $199.99 for a 40" tall "Big Jake." And in keeping with those prices, you can find a new-with-tag "Boyds Bear Country BBBC Exclusive Rosemarie Bearsley" bear for $36.00, one of the highest-selling single Boyds bears in the below sample.

Another modern type of collectible bear, the Care Bears, first showed up on greeting cards and then made their way into plush toys. In the words of their maker, American Greetings, they are "a group of adorable, furry friends each with a special caring mission. They help teach people how to care. Every Care Bear wears a bright-colored tummy picture that tells the world who they are and what is their special area of caring."

Most of the highest-priced Care Bear auctions are for lots of multiple bears; the highest-selling single bear here was a "vintage RARE True Heart Care Bear" for $152.50, one of the earliest bears, and released in the United Kingdom only. After that, the next-highest single Care Bear sold for a more affordable $61.00, a "1980s MIB [mint in box] CHAMP POSEABLE W/ TROPHY CARE BEARS." And average Care Bear prices are around a lower-still $12.00.

The Care Bears example shows that, just as the Boyds Bears company founder G.M. Lowenthal espoused, you can get "collectible" items without having to pay outrageous prices. Certainly you can find plenty of affordable collectible bears and dolls in this eBay category.

Bears ▶ Boyds

The average sales price in this subcategory is $13.67.

	HIGH		AVG
Danbury Mint Boyd's Bears Garden Shop Clock	$91.00	7 collectible Boyds Bears	$14.51
Danbury Mint Boyd's Bears Wooden Display Calendar +	$91.00	Boyds JILL STRAUSBAUGH Wood Ornament Ret RARE	$14.00
Boyds Glory B America #94390 CH	$86.05	Boyds JILL STRAUSBAUGH WOOD ORNAMENT RET RARE	$14.00
9 BOYDS Winter Items~Pooh, Piglet, Tiger, Eeyore+EXTRAS	$61.00	BOYDS VILLAGE TOWN GAS & ELECTRIC LAMP POSTS SET OF 4	$14.00
Danbury Mint Boyd's Bears Farmers Market Clock	$56.00	BACKYARD GARDEN boyd's wallhanging 478990530	$14.00
Boyd's Bears BoydsXpress Christmas Train, Danbury Mint	$55.01	Boyds JILL STRAUSBAUGH WOOD ORNAMENT RET RARE	$14.00
Boyd's Bears Collector Clock "Beary Lodge" Danbury Mint	$53.00	BOYDS KRINGLE'S VILLAGE CANDY CANE LAMP POST SET	$13.00
Boyds Bear Country Barn Exclusive Treasure Box	$25.59	Lot of 10 BOYDS Bears Animals~Frog, Lion, Truffles...NR	$12.99
Boyds 1st ed NIB Molly & Cricket. Yesterdays Child Doll	$49.00	Boyds EDDIE BEAN BAUER bear (1995)RARE	$12.99
Boyd's Bears "Santa Bear Special" Train, Danbury Mint	$48.05	Boyds Bears NASCAR Racing Bear 14" BOBBY LABONTE #18	$12.51
Boyd's Bears "Bearatone Railway" Train, Danbury Mint	$42.57	Boyd's Bear Angel Christmas Tree Topper	$12.45
Ten Cute & Cuddly BOYDS BEARS. ~ Great Collection! ~ NR	$41.00	The Boyds Collection - ROWENA'S TWIG CHAIRS - 2 Chairs	$12.01
Boyds Bear Country BBC EXCLUSIVE I C CRYSTALFROST NWT	$39.00	BEARINGTON BEAR and Hat box, BRAND NEW	$12.00
BOYDS PLUSH LOT OF 18 PLUS 1 NON-BOYDS	$38.00	Boyds Yesterday's Child MADELYNE retired MIB!!!!	$12.00
Boyds Longaberger 2005 HOH CancerBear ROSEBUD BEARYWELL	$38.00	6-Drawer Little Cabinet, Boyd's Bears?, Neat!!	$11.85

---

[1] Source: Christie's website, www.christies.com.

Bears ▸ Care Bears

The average sales price in this subcategory is $11.60.

	HIGH		AVG
RARE! Vintage Complete Set of 48 Care Bear Mini's	$170.00	Vintage 36" Tenderheart Care Bear	$12.50
Carebears: RARE Vintage TRUE HEART UK ONLY Care Bear	$152.50	LOT 1 VINTAGE CARE BEARS FUNSHINE CHEER GOOD LUCK BEARS	$12.50
RARE Complete Set of 1984 Care Bear Pedestal Glasses	$125.00	Grumpy and Baby Hugs Plush Care Bears 1983	$12.00
Huge Lot of 14 Care Bears 1980's w/ tags & booklets LOOK	$88.25	6 Vintage Care Bear Books - 5 Near Mint - 1983-5	$12.00
12 Original Butterick Care Bear Patterns from 1985	$67.99	Vintage Care Bears Good Luck Bear Glass 1985	$11.99
CARE BEARS LOT OF 10...Orginal	$67.00	Vintage 1983, Baby Hugs & Baby Tugs Care Bears	$11.50
Vintage Lot of 3 -1983 Care Bears in boxes - MINT	$61.48	Love-A-Lot Care Bear Mint in Box with Tag Bears MIB	$11.50
1980s MIB CHAMP POSEABLE W/ TROPHY CARE BEARS	$61.00	Vintage Care Bear Glasses 1983 Pizza Hut Lot of 4 Cute!	$11.50
Huge Lot Vintage 1980's Care Bears + extras care alot	$61.00	Care Bears 1980"s Vintage "Fill your day" Mug	$11.50
9 assorted CARE BEAR POSEABLE accessory vintage mint	$56.01	CARE BEAR GRUMPY BEAR BRAND NEW WITH TAGS VHTF	$11.05
CARE BEARS CARE-A-LOT CASE WITH 10 FIGURINES 3" - 1983	$56.00	18-INCH PLUSH CARE BEAR - BIRTHDAY BEAR	$11.00
Assorted lot of 8 vintage CARE BEAR POSEABLE mint	$52.14	CARE BEAR BEARS COUSINS GENTLE HEART LAMB VHTF NEW TAGS	$10.99
Lot of 8 Vintage Care Bears & Cousins-13"- 1983-84	$51.00	Care Bears 1984 (2) 1984 Bear Cousins Lamb & Elephant	$10.52
Lot of 10 Poseable Care Bears	$50.52	Care Bear Prof. Cold Heart w/Frostie Mug - NIB	$10.52
Lot Of 21 Vintage 1980's Care Bears & Cousins +++	$46.02	VINTAGE CARE BEARS CARE BEAR BRAVE HEART LION 1984 12"	$10.51

Bears ▸ Steiff

The average sales price in this subcategory is $85.88.

	HIGH		AVG
Steiff Japan BABY MASAKO bear HTFD	$790.00	Steiff Doll Baseball Player w/bat	$89.88
Steiff Disney Convention Minnie bear ~MINT~	$750.00	Steiff Rare 51cm Teddy Baby 1930 Replica Bear MINT!!!	$89.88
STEIFF PETSY BICOLOR 1927 LIMITED EDITION	$667.00	1994/1995 Steiff Club Edition Blue 35 Teddy Bear 1908	$89.00
Steiff Theodor Lmt. ed. Teddy Bear 2005	$525.00	Steiff 13" Dicky Bear 1985 Ltd. Edition	$89.00
ALFONZO STEIFF BEAR RED RARE REPLICA 00678 of 5000	$515.00	STEIFF ROLY POLY CLOWN Mint With Tags.	$88.99
STEIFF 2000 MEISSEN BEAR # 1269	$500.00	Steiff Teddy Bear with Gun	$86.00
Lot 6 Steiff 0300 5507 Bears mohair Zotty NO RESERVE!	$383.00	1994/1995 STEIFF CLUB BLUE TEDDY BEAR 1908 BLAU 35	$86.00
Lot 6 Steiff Bears 0172/32 0202/51,41 0150/32 0170/32	$355.00	Steiff Original Teddy 14 inch model 1907	$85.56
1983 Steiff White Tag Chocolate Brown Four Bear Set MIB	$355.00	NEW 2005 STEIFF NORTH AMERICAN CHRISTMAS "TEDDY SKATER"	$85.00
?STEIFF ?KUDDEL BEAR	$350.00	Steiff Mohair Chocolate Teddy Bear 20" Growler 0206/51	$85.00
Lot 2 Steiff Bridled Bridle Bears 0174/60,46 Lt. Ed. NR	$330.00	Steiff BERRYMAN BEAR, Ltd. Ed., QVC Exclusive	$85.00
Lot 2 Steiff Clemens Bears mohair replica 1909 0165/51	$310.99	Nr Mint '80s Steiff Mask Faced Original Teddy TALKS!	$85.00
Steiff Hudson Bay Voyageur Bear Canadian Stieff N/R	$299.00	STEIFF Bear, Chocolate Brown 0160/26	$85.00
Steiff Mr Vanilla Bear NR	$281.57	Steiff 7" Mohair Circus Band Dog Bandsman MIB	$83.50
Set of Steiff Four Seasons Bears Limited Edition NR	$280.55	84 LE White Tag 9.5" Steiff Original Teddy 0156/26 Mint	$82.57

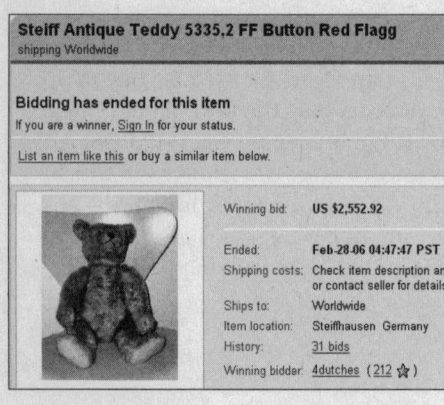

Steiff Antique Teddy 5335,2 FF Button Red Flagg
shipping Worldwide

Bidding has ended for this item
If you are a winner, Sign In for your status.

List an item like this or buy a similar item below.

Winning bid:	**US $2,552.92**
Ended:	**Feb-28-06 04:47:47 PST**
Shipping costs:	Check item description an or contact seller for details
Ships to:	Worldwide
Item location:	Steiffhausen Germany
History:	31 bids
Winning bidder:	4dutches (212 ☆)

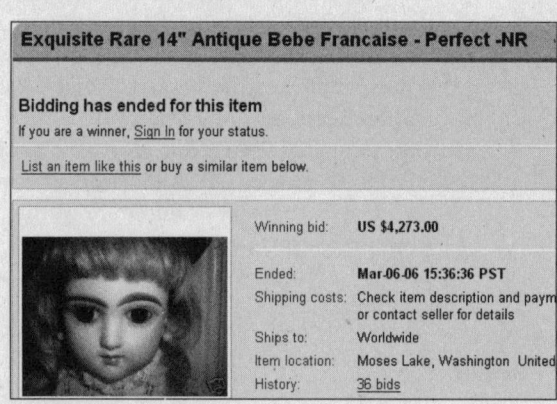

Exquisite Rare 14" Antique Bebe Francaise - Perfect -NR

Bidding has ended for this item
If you are a winner, Sign In for your status.

List an item like this or buy a similar item below.

Winning bid:	**US $4,273.00**
Ended:	**Mar-06-06 15:36:36 PST**
Shipping costs:	Check item description and paym or contact seller for details
Ships to:	Worldwide
Item location:	Moses Lake, Washington United
History:	36 bids

Bears ▸ Antique

The average sales price in this subcategory is $102.00.

	HIGH		AVG
Teddy Bear large Drawing by creator C.K. Berryman/ NR !	$3,650.00	miniature bear vintage STEIFF with button VGC	$115.00
MAGNIFICENT ANTIQUE STRUNZ TEDDY BEAR ca.1912 *	$1,889.88	Antique white mohair jointed 17" teddy bear-sweet!	$107.79
Raymond Weil Parsifal Womens Watch- $2995 Retail N/R	$1,299.00	ANTIQUE TEDDY BEAR	$104.49
RARITY ** ANTIQUE RED MOHAIR BEAR 20s **	$1,247.22	Antique German 1920'sTeddy Bear w/Huge Hump NR	$103.61
GEORGEOUS LARGE FARNELL TEDDY BEAR	$950.00	Strawbeary Creme *Craddle Cub Bear* By Mechel Lang	$102.50
EARLY BING~~ WHAT A BEAR!!! NO RESERVE	$920.00	RARE ANTIQUE BISQUE TEDDY BEARS circa 1900	$102.50
Small blonde bear #12-210	$835.56	c1920 Cute Little Girl w/ DOLL & TEDDY BEAR photo pc	$102.50
ANTIQUE VINTAGE TEDDY BEAR JOINTED STEIFF? 10in NR	$728.89	Large Knickerbocker or Gund ? bear on wheels NR	$100.50
Early 1915 Schuco Bear~15"~~NO RESERVE!	$611.00	Jointed Old Teddy Bear 1920's 25" Tall	$100.00
Sweet Antique c1905 American Ideal Mohair Teddy Bear NR	$566.00	Cute antique Mohair Teddy Bear ca. 1920*	$99.00
Vintage bear with original clothes	$521.00	Beautiful Old Hermann Teddy Bear 50s	$99.00
Rare Antique 16" American Aetna Mohair Bear	$504.21	1930's 12" Knickerbocker Cutie	$99.00
Emily Anne, Rare Very Early American Bear, 9.5" Tall	$495.00	C1920 24" Ideal Mohair Teddy Bear w/Hump Strawstuffing	$99.00
Cinnamon bear early 1900's odd nose stitchery 9-303	$410.00	27" antique teddy bear.mohair.excelsior.hardboard joint	$98.76
SALE! A Rare Schuco Roller Skating Bear w/Key	$399.00	ANTIQUE GERMAN STEIFF GRISLY MOHAIR TOY BEAR W/GROWLER	$98.00

Dolls ▶ Antique (Pre-1930)

The average sales price in this subcategory is $45.13.

	HIGH		AVG
Vintage SKOOKUM Indian Chief Doll - large 36"	$911.00	LOVELY PINK FELT DOLL HAT SALEMAN'S SAMPLE	$46.00
Mary Frances Woods Skookum Indian Doll RARE OLD	$587.77	c1920 Cute Little Girl w/ DOLL & TEDDY BEAR photo pc	$46.00
ANTIQUE style DOLL pram stroller TOY RABBIT glass eyes	$560.00	Pair of Skookum Bully Good 7" Indian Dolls *VERY NICE*	$46.00
19C 26" English Wax Doll Orig Garb & Shaker Bonnet	$445.00	AMERICAN INDIAN DOLL COLLECTION	$46.00
Antique Humpback Litho Childs Doll Trunk W/Antq Dolls!!	$431.00	Unusual Antique Straw Filled/Mohair Eskimo Doll	$45.99
Large All Bisque 150/6 Kestner	$415.00	Very Old Papier Mache or Composition Doll, Glass Eyes	$45.00
Antique All Original Papier-Mache Doll-No Restoration	$394.00	Composition doll what a grin	$43.99
Fantastic Kid Leather Body Doll w/Bisque Head Must See!	$308.99	Sweet 17" Antique Child Ichimatsu Japanese Gofun Doll	$43.97
Antique 18"Victorian Wax/Cloth Child Doll w Old Clothes	$305.00	Early 14 ? China Head Doll w/ Painted Shoes Germany	$43.52
Antique Rabbit, Mo Hair Fur, Muslin Body Raggedy Rabbit	$300.00	SOOKUM ANTIQUE INDIAN DOLL - 9 1/2"	$43.00
Antique Wood Doll Trunk W/Antq German Dolls & Toys!!	$290.02	TERRIFIC ANTIQUE 11" ALL METAL DOLL! SPRING STRUNG	$42.00
RARE MINT Large 20" A/O 1930's Lenci Cricket NR	$280.00	1915 SUNSHINE PAPER DOLLS, Uncut, from the Boston Ameri	$41.00
ORIGINAL TINY TEARS BABY IN BOX A MUST SEE BABY DOLL	$277.99	ANTIQUE DOLLS (6+) W/ VINTAGE	$41.00
VINTAGE ANTIQUE HALF DOLL PINCUSHION DOLL BY GOEBEL	$270.50	CLOTHES, VERY OLD, NICE!	
Rare/Antique Hand Painted Wooden Peg Doll Toy German ?	$262.77	SET OF ANTIQUE FLIRTY EYE WALKER DOLLS THAT TALK, NR	$40.99
ANTIQUE VINTAGE PRE 1940'S BABY DOLL MOVES NO RESV:>)	$249.36	LARGE OLD BOY DOLL. NEW YORK DOLL SHOE CO.	$40.75

Dolls ▶ Barbie Contemporary (1973–Now)

The average sales price in this subcategory is $19.37.

	HIGH		AVG
Limited Edition "Pink Splendor" Barbie	$280.00	EXOTIC BEAUTY BARBIE-2002-STYLE SET COLLECTION	$19.99
RARE MIMB Rita Hayworth as "Gilda" 14" doll	$200.00	Barbie as Harley Quinn New in box	$19.99
Selena Collection 3 Doll Set. Never opened.	$157.00	3- GET REAL GIRL (SPEC PRICE) SKYLAR SNOWBOARDING MIB	$19.99
LOT OF 5 BARBIES - MY FAIR LADY - NRFB COMPLETE SET	$138.49	Barbie as Harley Quinn New in box	$19.99
HARD ROCK CAFE BARBIE DOLL #1 NRFB	$135.00	DRAG QUEEN BARBIE TYPE MARILYN MONROE STYLE !	$19.99
LORD OF THE RINGS COLLECTORS BARBIE SEALED ARWEN NIB	$112.50	BARBIE AS SWAN BALLERINA FROM SWAN LAKE	$19.06
CRYSTAL JUBILEE BARBIE N.R.F.B.	$112.49	Barbie Mr. Christmas Animated Holiday Carriage 1998	$19.05
THE LORD OF THE RINGS FELLOWSHIP OF THE KING	$80.00	SPECIAL EDITION ELIZABETH TAYLOR BARBIE DOLL 2000	$19.05
MINT DELPHIEN SILKSTONE BARBIE NRFB	$77.00	1997 POLISH BARBIE DOLLS OF THE WORLD MINT	$18.50
Disney Flying Peter Pan, Wendy, Tinkerbell Doll Dolls	$77.00	Wheelchair Becky, Friend of Barbie	$18.50
2005 Inuit Legend Barbie Doll CANADIAN EXCLUSIVE	$69.00	1995 TYCO Kitchen Littles Barbies BARBEQUE SET-NRFP	$18.01
HARLEY DAVIDSON BARBIE #5, RED HAIR	$67.01	BARBIE LOVES FRANKIE SINATRA DOLLS Gift Set Mattel MIB	$18.00
2005 Inuit Legend Barbie Doll CANADIAN EXCLUSIVE	$65.00	Malibu Barbie-Reproduction-2001	$18.00
Duchess of Diamonds Barbie Swarovski Crystals 2001	$61.00	Barbie Doll Lot of DOLLS, EXTRA CLOTHES & STYLING HEAD	$17.75
NOLAN MILLER SHEER ILLUSION BARBIE	$61.00	Elizabeth Taylor White Diamonds Doll~NRFB ex	$17.55

Dolls ▶ Barbie Vintage (Pre–1973)

The average sales price in this subcategory is $58.14.

	HIGH		AVG
PRISTINE TNT BARBIE * BLACK VELVET SUIT * MINT IN BOX!	$2,551.00	BLACK BARBIE 1979 HARD TO FIND	$61.00
VINTAGE BARBIE FASHION CENTER "STORE DISPLAY"	$1,347.94	Vintage Barbie MISS BARBIE Doll w/ Orig. Swimsuit	$61.00
Gay Parisienne T.M. Barbie Outfit #964 Complete	$900.00	NOS Chickie the Fashion Model Vintage Doll New in Box	$61.00
AMERICAN GIRL SIDE PART VERY NICE!!	$800.00	1958-1965 AMERICAN GIRL BRUNETTE HEAD	$61.00
RARE BILD LILLI NO RESERVE!!!!	$743.00	1961 Barbie ken doll blonde EXCEPTIONAL conditi w/ box	$60.00
COLOR MAGIC Barbie Torso- Light Lemon Hair Color ?	$637.00	TALKING BARBIE/Buffy/Small Talk Family REPAIR KIT	$59.85
VINTAGE BLONDE AMERICAN GIRL	$548.00	[3 of these sold in a multiple item ("Dutch") auction for $19.95 each]	
BARBIE DOLL PRISTINE COND.		60s BRUNETTE TNT BENDABLE KNEE BARBIE IN JUMP INTO LACE	$57.00
# 2 Vintage Ponytail Barbie 1959 Red Hair	$525.00	Drop dead Gorgeous Platinum TNT barbie~Vintage TNT	$56.97
LOVELY LONG HAIR HIGH COLOUR BRUNETTE AM GIRL BARBIE	$460.00	KEN DOLL in BOX 1960 (Barbie Collection)	$56.00
COLOR MAGIC TORSOS "FACTORY MINT" 1 TO 10	$150.00	Vintage Bend-leg Midge ! Beautiful !	$56.00
VINTAGE OLD AMERICAN GIRL BARBIE? Flawless Face	$430.56	Vintage Barbie Doll American Girl Head Brunette	$55.77
Vintage 1st ISSUE HIGH COLOR COLORMAGIC BARBIE!!	$402.99	1962 Midge MIB	$55.00
MATTEL BARBIE DOLL 1958 + CLOTHING + CATALOGUE	$382.88	1962 Red Head Barbie & Outfit in Super Condition	$54.99
1965 GOLD 'n GLAMOUR Outfit #1647 Mint & Complete	$355.00	1960's Barbie Francie & Skipper doll & clothes accessor	$54.88
Twist N Turn TNT Barbie 1966 Mint Vintage NRFB	$341.66	1963 Barbie Skipper doll EXCEPTIONAL conditi w/ box	$53.98

MIB / NRFB #1 Blonde Ponytail Barbie Doll
Early Doll with Handpainted Eyebrows!

Bidding has ended for this item
If you are a winner, Sign In for your status.

List an item like this or buy a similar item below.

Winning bid:	US $13,988.00
Ended:	Mar-01-06 14:52:07 P!
Shipping costs:	Check item description or contact seller for de
Ships to:	N. and S. America, Eu
Item location:	Raleigh, North Carolina
History:	54 bids
Winning bidder:	mamabunkley (182

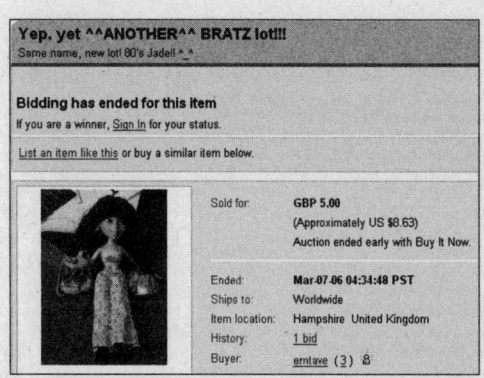

Yep. yet ^^ANOTHER^^ BRATZ lot!!!
Same name, new lot! 80's Jadell ^_^

Bidding has ended for this item
If you are a winner, Sign In for your status.

List an item like this or buy a similar item below.

Sold for:	GBP 5.00
	(Approximately US $8.63)
	Auction ended early with Buy It Now.
Ended:	Mar-07-06 04:34:48 PST
Ships to:	Worldwide
Item location:	Hampshire United Kingdom
History:	1 bid
Buyer:	erntave (3)

Dolls ▸ By Brand, Company, Character ▸ American Girl

The average sales price in this subcategory is $24.30.

	HIGH		AVG
American Girl Felicity & Elizabeth 2 Dolls, Books, Acc.	$245.00	AMERICAN GIRL ANGELINA BALLERINA BED & BEDDING SET NIB	$24.99
RETIRED AMERICAN GIRL LINDSEY- MINT, HARD TO FIND	$225.00	AMERICAN GIRL TODAY BIRTHDAY OUTFIT	$24.95
Pre-Mattel Pleasant Company American Girl Doll Clothes	$211.51	Doll Bike fits American Girls Size Doll or My Twinn	$24.95
American Girl Trunk Closet with Accessories and Clothes	$202.50	Pleasant Co American Girl Josefina School Set~RET/MIB	$24.50
NIB AMERICAN GIRL DOLL KAILEY & ACCESSORIES+BONUS	$202.11	18" 1992 W. GERMANY SHANNON & BONUS SASHA ARTICLE!	$24.50
American Girl Doll of Today, outfits, bunk bed, RETIRED	$177.50	Outfits to fit American Girl Dolls + picnic basket NR	$24.50
TWO American Girl Dolls	$167.50	American Girl Retired Urban Outfit NR	$24.38
NIB AMERICAN GIRL DOLL KAILEY & ACCESSORIES+BONUSES	$157.50	AMERICAN GIRL NELLIE'S PAJAMAS PLEASANT COMPANY	$24.04
American Girl Kirsten 1986 White Body - Rare!	$155.00	AMERICAN 18" GIRL DOLL VINYL (267) W/ OUTFIT & STAND	$24.00
American Girl Kailey Doll and Book New in Box!!	$150.00	Battat 18" OUR GENERATION Doll~1998~GORGEOUS BRUNETTE	$23.98
NIB American Girl 3 in 1 Dream Big 3 in 1 Murphy Bed	$134.50	American Girl RETIRED Pre-Mattel Cheerleader Outfit	$23.55
American Girl Doll w/ 3 Outfits, Bed, & Baseball!!!!!!	$127.82	YELLOW COLONIAL NIGHTGOWN & CAP made 4 American Girl	$23.50
AG MINIS AMERICAN GIRL COMPLETE GROOVY ROOM	$124.49	American Girl Cecile (France) Girls of Many Lands NIB	$23.50
AMERICAN GIRL ELIZABETH W/ ACCESSORIES & BOOK FELICITY	$119.00	American Girl Samantha Valentine Craft new	$23.04
American Girl DOLL ELIZABETH Doll +book BRAND-NEW! NRFB	$119.00	CUSTOM MADE PJ&BLANKET 4 American Girl YourDollsName	$22.99

Dolls ▸ By Brand, Company, Character ▸ Franklin Mint

The average sales price in this subcategory is $70.95.

	HIGH		AVG
Franklin Mint Complete Set Scarlett O'Hare Vinyl Doll	$1,012.00	Franklin Mint Scarlett O'Hara Black Dress Green Hat	$72.89
Franklin Mint Set Scarlett O'Hare Vinyl Doll W/Trunk	$510.00	FRANKLIN MINT HEIRLOOM FABERGE BRIDE DOLL ALEKSANDRA	$71.02
Franklin Mint Scarlett O' Hara Vinyl Doll Set GWTW	$455.00	Jackie Kennedy Doll-With Two Outfits-Franklin Mint	$71.00
JFK & JACKIE KENNEDY DOLL FRANKLIN MINT 13 OUTFIT TRUNK	$399.99	Queen Guinevere 16" Vinyl Doll by Franklin Mint	$71.00
FRANKLIN MINT Ultimate Marilyn Monroe 24" doll limited	$399.99	PRINCESS DIANA 16" VINYL DOLL - FRANKLIN MINT	$71.00
Lot 38 Cocktail Suit- Franklin Mint Princess Diana Doll	$334.99	Franklin Mint Southern Belle Outfit - Elizabeth Taylor	$71.00
Monroe Doll Bruno Rossellini GADCO	$312.57	Morgan Le Fay from The Franklin Mint Rare	$70.55
FM GIBSON GIRL DOLL TRUNK AND WARDROBE	$300.00	Franklin Mint SCARLETT O'HARA Gone With The Wind DRESS	$70.00
Pearl The Gibson Debutante Porcelain Doll	$298.00	Franklin Mint TITANIC Red & Black Rose Doll 1st Meeting	$69.99
Empress Faberge' Franklin Mint Porcelain Heirloom Doll	$296.91	Glittering Aqua Gown for 16" FM Princess Diana Doll	$69.99
ALL 6 QUEEN OF ENGLAND DOLLS Franklin Mint w/ COE & Box	$294.00	ELIZABETH TAYLOR DOLL Mint & NRFB COA Franklin Mint	$69.99
Franklin Mint - Marilyn Monroe "Love Marilyn" Doll	$275.00	FM~Harley "Dakota" Vinyl Fashion Doll & 2 Outfits MIB	$69.00
VANITY & CHAIR-FOR 16" VINYL ROSE/TITANIC-FRANKLIN MINT	$249.99	Gorgous Franklin Mint Porcelain & 24k Gold Gypsy Doll	$68.83
THE FRANKLIN MINT EVENING STAR PORCELAIN DOLL MIB	$230.00	FRANKLIN MINT ROSE White Gown with box RARE	$68.50
Rare Gray & White Suite for Princess Diana FranklinMint	$227.50	MIB Franklin Mint Scarlet O'Hara in Gone with the Wind	$67.66

Dolls ▸ By Brand, Company, Character ▸ Bratz

The average sales price in this subcategory is $13.75.

	HIGH		AVG
SetAll5 NIB BRATZ Secret Date w/ Boyz Dolls Cloe Jade +	$119.99	Bratz Slumber Party Jade New in box	$14.50
HUGE LOT OF BRATZ DOLLS AND ACCESSORIES!!!!!	$109.26	Bratz Yasmin New Year's CeleBratztion 2004 doll NRFB	$14.00
HUGE LOT OF 11 BRATZ DOLLS + COOL BRATZ CARRYING CASE!	$83.07	New In Box LIVIN Bratz Strut N Style DOOR BEADS	$13.99
Huge Lot of Bratz Dolls, Clothes, Shoes, Accessories	$81.00	NEW LiL BratZ Rock star Concert Cruiser bonus LilBratz	$13.99
Bratz Doll NEW NIB & house/pad used GREAT DEAL clothes+	$76.57	NIB BRATZ Boyz Boys CADE Motorcycle Electronic RETIRED	$13.99
HUGE lot BRATZ dolls, clothes, cases, car, spa!	$70.00	NEW BRATZ BABYZ PONYZ "CELESTE"~HARD TO FIND~NIB	$13.99
Bratz WILD LIFE SAFARI - 2004 Set of 5 BOYZ- NIB	$68.95	NEW BRATZ BABYZ PONYZ "PURSIA"-HARD TO FIND-NIB	$13.99
Bratz Ooh la la All 3 - Cloe, Dana, Kumi- NIB! Int Ship	$68.95	BNIB Bratz Ooh La La Dana Doll	$13.55
HUGE LOT of Bratz Dolls clothes accessories over 200	$67.00	BRATZ BOYZ BOYS BOY DOLL KOBY FUNK OUT FASHION CLOTHES+	$13.49
LARGE~LOT~11~BRATZ~DOLLS~4~BOYZ~EXTRAS	$66.00	New Bratz Lip Lamp with am/fm radio and alarm clock New	$13.33
LOT BRATZ DOLLS OVER 90 PIECES+ TRAVEL BAG+ ACCESSORIES	$66.00	LIL BRATZ FABRIC HANDMADE LAMP! Nightlight Size!	$13.25
HUGE LOT OF BRATZ DOLLS & CLOTHES! ORIGINAL 61 NR HURRY	$66.00	Hollywood Dolls	$13.00
Excl BratZ Tokyo MAY LIN +Winter Ball CLOE Doll $100.00	$65.55	Bratz Nighty Nite Sasha Brat Doll Brand New	$12.99
15 BRATZ DOLLS LOT PLUS MUCH MORE	$64.76	Bratz Babyz Rockin' Wagon Fits Baby and Her Pet!	$12.99
Huge Lot of Bratz Dolls and Accessories	$63.00	Bratz Funky Furniture Lounge Chill Out Lounge NRFB	$12.99

Dolls ▸ By Brand, Company, Character ▸ Madame Alexander

The average sales price in this subcategory is $29.04.

	HIGH		AVG
MADAME ALEXANDER 1993 LTD. ED. TRICK OR TREAT SET MIB	$164.98	Wendy Loves The Southwest Doll	$31.00
Lot of Eleven Madame Alexander Dolls That Need TLC	$204.49	Madame Alexander Doll Disney Pinocchio Jiminy Cricket	$31.00
Madame Alexander Guatemala 8 " Doll MIB Rare!	$204.18	Madame Alexander Doll Little Love My First Huggums NIB	$31.00
MADAME ALEXANDER DIONNE QUINTS & CAROUSEL	$182.50	Madame Alex 8 " Joseph's Coat 1995 only Doll NIB	$30.99
MADAME ALEXANDER Wizard w/ State Fair Balloon #13280 NR	$162.50	Madame Alex 8 " Calamity Jane 1994 only Doll NIB	$30.99
Lot of 7 Madame Alexander Collectible dolls	$148.50	Beautiful Madame Alexander Doll ~ Daddy's My Hero MIB	$30.99
MADAME ALEXANDER BRIDE DOLL, circa 1955	$135.50	BEAUTIFUL MADAME ALEXANDER RED RIDING HOOD DOLL ESTATE	$30.99
Faire~ality "The Fashion Collection" Trunk Set	$120.00	Madame Alexander Doll ~ Little Miss Muffet ~ NIB	$30.50
Madame Alexander Snow White Doll RARE	$112.50	Madam Alexander Fairy Godmother	$30.01
Madame Alexander Inventory Sale 2/four Clowns /MIB/NR	$112.50	1997 Madame Alexander Cinderella Doll NIB #13400	$30.00
MADAME ALEXANDER " SAMANTHA" 8" MIB	$102.50	VINTAGE 8 INCH ALEXANDER LITTLE WOMEN **BO PEEP **	$29.99
Madame Alexander 8" Wendy DOLL Black Grand PIANO MIB	$99.99	ICE SKATING GIRL 8" Madame Alexander doll	$29.99
Alexander Tea Time with Muffy 8" LOOK NEW	$99.00	Evil Sorceress - 8 inch	$29.75
ELOISE @ PLAZA Overnight Kit MIB & TONS of ELOISE ITEMS	$93.00	8 In Madame Alexander Miniature Bride Doll	$29.51
Madame Alexander Little Women Dolls	$89.96	Madame Alexander 8 " 1997 Ireland Doll Cute !	$29.28

Dolls ▶ Clothes, Accessories

The average sales price in this subcategory is $30.60.

	HIGH		AVG
Original Jumeau Couture 4-Pc. Ensemble, Bee Pin on Hat	$3,050.00	WYANDOTTE Vintage Doll Buggy Pram Stroller 1940's	$32.00
ORIGINAL Tagged Antique Ideal Shirley Temple Doll Coat	$2,916.68	4 pc. Doll Clothes Will Fit 8" Doll Ginny Alex-kin	$31.30
Vogue Doll Vintage Clothes Outfits L@@K NO RESERVE	$402.79	Lot of Vintage Doll Clothing Baby Secret ect 50+ Pcs	$31.00
Most ELEGANT 1909 ENSEMBLE for Bleuette ! Silk/lace	$350.00	HUGE LOT-100+++ Vintage Dollhouse,Doll Accessories-OLD	$31.00
1930 S Tagged SHIRLEY TEMPLE Sailor Dress 18 inch	$257.00	OLD DOLL feedsack BABY CLOTHES VINTAGE ANTIQUE dress	$30.99
Six 6 Million Dollar Man Bionic Steve Austin Kenner	$171.50	VINTAGE IDEAL TONI DOLL WEDDING DRESS & VEIL NICE	$30.95
R&B FACTORY wardrobe for the 11" composition DEBU-TEEN!	$168.59	Vintage Doll Dress Fits 8" Ginny Alex-kins 2 Pc. 1 Tag	$30.30
Dolllightful ~ Doll Dress & Bonnet & Parasol	$154.49	BABY DOLL ANTIQUE SILVER PLATES CUPS SAUCERS COFFEE POT	$30.00
14" P-90 Ideal Toni with original Play Wave Set	$144.49	5 Vintage Dresses, Penny Brite, store stock, tags	$30.00
Fantastic Antique Wool Doll Hat Bonnet	$127.50	7 Vintage Days of The Week Doll Panties	$29.99
Antique Outfit for Bisque Head Boy Doll	$123.50	VINTAGE VOGUE GINNY DOLL WEDDING DRESS & VEIL NICE	$29.95
50s Vogue Jill Matching Ginny Doll Wedding Gown MIB	$123.50	Vintage Doll Dress Fit 8" Ginny Alexander-kins Yellow	$29.28
MARY HOYER TAGGED SUMMER OUTFIT (14"DOLL)	$110.00	BLACK DOLLS ID/value book 1ST ISSUE tons pics/info HUGE	$29.00
COSTUME DE MARIEE 1908 DRESS F BLEUETTE B BINKILICIOUS	$102.50	20" CHERRY WOOD DOLL TRUNK FOR AMERICAN GIRL DOLL NEW	$29.00
Vintage 8" Doll Dress fits Ginny Or Alexanderkins	$100.99	5 Pairs High Heel Shoes Nancy Ann Revlon Dolls	$28.55

Dolls ▶ Furniture

The average sales price in this subcategory is $16.32.

	HIGH		AVG
FRANKLIN MINT GUINEVERE VINYL WARDROBE TRUNK -18"	$158.05	Adorable Overstuffed Bear/Doll Sofa/Chair~Bear fabric	$17.25
American Girl Furniture Lot Of (6) - Excellent Cond.	$139.05	White Rocking Chair with Sailboat painted on seat	$17.15
American Girl "Angelina Ballerina" Sofa - Chair & Otto	$127.50	My Twinn Wicker Chair and Table fits American Girl	$17.00
BEST Shabby Ornate White Chic Ashwell Fabric Doll Chair	$127.49	doll armoire/wardrobe handpainted 16" fits 5" hanger	$17.00
MY TWINN BRAND DOLL ARMOIRE	$123.05	BUNK BED SET - for 18 inch dolls	$17.00
FITS AMERICAN DOLL CLOTHES		White Wicker Hooded Doll Buggy Wheels Turn Very Nice!	$16.50
Doll bunk/trundle bed fits American Girl Doll	$101.99	Bed + Comforter Set For OAAK Polymer Mini Baby Must C	$16.49
Gotz *STROLLER* Pram Buggy Fits up to 22" dolls - NEW!	$100.00	COLLECTIBLE BRITISH TELEPHONE BOOTH PHONE DOLL RARE NR	$16.49
Lot of 100+ Doll House Furniture Wood, cast iron extras	$76.00	Mama & Papas Junior Collection Stroller for dolls. Very	$16.09
DELUXE DOLL WARDROBE ARMIORE for AMERICAN GIRL	$75.00	VERY NICE DOLL HIGH CHAIR	$15.99
Pottery Barn Kids Wooden Toy Doll SLEIGH BED & BEDDING	$69.95	SOLID WOOD DOLL CLOTHES RACK FOR 8" - 10" DOLL	$15.95
21" DOLL ARMOIRE, AMERICAN GIRL, CUSTOM KIT, + BONUS	$23.00	[2 of these sold $15.95 each]	
American Girl Bitty Baby HUGE lot of 4 RETIRED sets !!!	$69.00	Toy Bunk Bed Perfect For Your Childs Dolls	$15.75
BARBIE KEN DOLL PEPSI COLA FOUNTAIN DINER DIORAMA	$67.75	1988 Maxie Day Dreaming Bed Still In Box (Sold As Is)	$15.67
NEW CABBAGE PATCH 3 IN ONE STROLLER BED CRADLE 1983	$61.00	BEAUTY SALON CHAIR PERFECT SIZE FOR AMERICAN GIRL DOLL	$15.50
American Girl Samantha Brass Bed with Nightgown	$56.06	*Ornate White Metal Doll Bed w/Mattress/Cover/& Pillow*	$15.50

Paper Dolls ▶ Modern

The average sales price in this subcategory is $7.47.

	HIGH		AVG
Charles Ventura Paper Dolls	$102.50	AMERICAN GIRL SAMANTHA'S PASTIMES SET SEALED 1991	$7.99
Charles Ventura Paper Dolls	$51.57	BRENDA STARR MAGIC PAPERDOLLS NEW TOO COOL... L@@K	$7.99
Little House Paper Dolls Day on the Prairie New Uncut	$46.00	3 sets of Paper Doll Books	$7.99
Collector's Paper Doll Book of Robert Tonner Dolls	$46.00	128 Page Gay Paper Doll Book - Funny - Like New	$7.95
KATY KEENE (DEDICATION) Paper Dolls	$37.15	QUEEN HOLDEN'S BABY SHOWER	$7.50
Vintage Mary Engelbreit Magnetic Paper Dolls Boy Girl	$32.00	Paris the Heiress..Paper Dolls/Paris Hilton Parody NEW	$7.50
BRIGITTE BARDOT "Paper Dolls" Collection	$30.00	3 Boxes of Paper Dolls	$7.47
SET OF 5 DIONNE QUINTS PAPER DOLL BOOKS	$29.95	American Girl Samantha's Paper Dolls MIB - Theater Kit	$7.45
SCARLETT / Vivien Leigh Paper Dolls	$28.00	10 sets of Paper Dolls	$7.02
Katy and Gloria Paper Doll Book Katy Keene Uncut	$26.52	EMPRESSES AND QUEENS Paper Dolls Tom Tierney	$7.00
4 Sets of Gingham Paper Dolls	$23.33	carmen miranda paper dolls! never been used!	$7.00
1978 KISS Rock Group Paper Dolls-Pat Frey	$23.00	LOU RATHJENS Paper Doll Book of BRIDES	$7.00
Little House Christmas Paper Dolls Prairie Book Uncut	$21.01	Felicity American girl Paper Doll Uncut	$7.00
USBORNE CUT-OUT "MAKE THIS MODEL DOLL'S HOUSE", NEW	$20.55	Molly American Girl Paper Doll Uncut	$7.00
1997 LITTLE HOUSE ON THE PRAIRIE PAPER DOLLS-MINT	$20.50	Black American Heritage Paper Dolls - Lt Ed. -	$6.99

Paper Dolls ▶ Vintage

The average sales price in this subcategory is $21.08.

	HIGH		AVG
1941 HOLLYWOOD PERSONALITIES HOLIDAY INN PAPER DOLLS	$406.99	Cut Boston Herald Paper Doll Costume - DemiToilette	$21.51
1857 Paper dolls, 2 dolls, many outfits and 2 envelopes	$355.00	1916 MILTON BRADLEYS TRU-LIFE PAPER DOLLS	$21.50
Uncut Boston Globe Interchangeable President Candidates	$227.50	Uncut "Animal World" Cut Outs of Dogs, c1930s	$21.50
ESTHER WILLIAMS 1950 UNCUT PAPER DOLLS MERRILL	$209.49	Walt Disney's 101 Dalmations 1960	$21.27
Fine Victorian Scrap Angel White Winter Wear w Mica ++	$184.49	PAPER DOLLS, By Tom Tierney	$21.00
VINTAGE 1954 OZZIE & HARRIET & DAVID & RICKY UNCUT	$180.02	VINTAGE SAALFIELD LITTLE WOMEN PAPER DOLLS UNCUT	$21.00
Rare Early Hand made Family- French?1800's	$165.00	DINAH SHORE PAPER DOLLS 1954—NEARLY COMPLETE	$20.99
1935 Book YOUR OWN QUINTUPLETS Paper Dolls Babies	$157.50	Vintage Bridal Party 6 Bride Paper Dolls Clothes Folder	$20.60
Vintage Paper Dolls/ Here Comes The Bride/ Lowe/ Un-Cut	$152.50	2 Skater/1 Fashion Doll lot (1940's)	$20.55
1951 Saalfield Here Comes Bride UNCUT Paper Doll Box Se	$148.50	AVA GARDNER PAPER DOLLS 1952	$20.53
1940S/50S PAPER DOLLS/CLOTHES 6 DOLLS	$137.59	Vintage Paper Dolls/ We Love/ Gladys Rourke Blackwood	$20.50
COLLECTOR'S ALBUM HALLMARK STORY BOOK PAPER DOLL CARDS	$128.49	3 Vintage Shirley Temple Paper Dolls w/ Lots of Outfits	$20.50
Four Ideal Dolls	$123.49	GINNY 1984 2 doll set, paper dolls UNCUT Near mint!!!	$20.50
1954 Betsy McCall Paper Doll Story Book	$104.07	VINTAGE PAPER DOLL & CLOTHES=CA 1950	$20.50
MUST SEE - 1943 VINTAGE - PHOTO FASHIONS Paper Dolls	$100.00	Lucille Ball B&W Paper Doll Coloring Book!!! Gorgeous!	$20.50

Wholesale Lots ▸ Barbie

The average sales price in this subcategory is $21.33.

	HIGH		AVG
6 vintage barbie's + tonz of cloths	$166.07	WHOLESALE! LOT OF (20) BARBIE'S!!!!!	$38.94
BARBIE..LARGE LOT OF 33 Dolls, Clothes, Car, Van..ACC	$59.00	1992 holiday Barbie	$26.00
HUGE lot of Barbies, cloths and accessories. NR	$51.00	A HUGE LOT OF BARBIE'S & MORE!!!!!	$25.00
Juicy Couture Barbies BNIB, & Juicy Couture beach Towel	$46.00	WOW! OVER 165 PIECES OF BARBIE CLOTHING, SOME VINTAGE	$23.50
Barbie American Stories Collection 6 Doll Lot Zuckerman	$41.00	25 Pieces of Barbie Vintage Clothing & Accessories	$21.99

Wholesale Lots ▸ Dolls

The average sales price in this subcategory is $16.79.

	HIGH		AVG
Huge 52 Vintage Doll Lot from the 1930's- 1980's	$445.00	DOLLSTORE CLOSEDOWN! My loss, YOUR GAIN! LOT #24!	$20.50
AMERICAN GIRL MARISOL STARTER COLLECTION	$255.01	28 ASSORTED DOLLS & SQUEAK TOYS-SOME VINTAGE	$20.49
HUGE AMERICAN GIRL PLEASANT CO. FELICITY LOT NR MIB	$165.00	Wholesale Case of 12 New Modern Times Sisters Dolls NIB	$20.16
Lot of 29 Bride Dolls-Danbury Mint-CHEAP	$81.56	HUGE DOLL LOT SALE.....still adding	$20.00
WHOLESALE lot of 24 Porcelain Dolls	$72.99	Like Baby Face...here they are	$20.00
HUGE LOT 1970'S DAWN DOLLS AND MORE	$66.00	huge vintage lot elves santa christmas doll ornaments	$19.99
LOT OF 10 VINTAGE 1950'S, 1960'S DOLLS - DRESSED	$63.76	4 X-LG PORCELIN CLOWNS W SWING dolls clown gifts gift	$19.99
Lot of 6 Vintage Dolls,Ginny by Vogue,Malibu PJ,Rosebud	$60.99	DOLLSTORE CLOSEDOWN! My loss, YOUR GAIN! LOTS OF DOLLS!	$18.50
NWT~ LOT 20 of Ballerina FAIRY DOLLS Delton Products	$58.33	3 Goebel Dolls - Dingle Angel Bumble Charmer Cat +Bonus	$17.55
3 american girl dolls of many lands-cecil,saba,isabel	$50.99	LOT OF CLASSIC COLLECTIBLE BABY DOLLS//SOLD AS IS	$16.99
WHOLESALE LOT OF DOLLS- "NIB"	$49.99	Doll Lot Of (6) BEAUTIFUL ASSORTED 16" DOLLS New In Box	$16.90
-24 Pieces- Assorted 16" Victorian Collector Dolls NIB	$49.99	[5 of these sold for $16.90 each]	
Vintage OLD DOLLS - BABY DOLL LOT & DISNEY TRAY	$46.10	LOT of Vintage DOLLS Doll Porcelain	$16.50
1960s 70s LOT- 4 DOLLS, VOGUE, HORSMAN, COLLETTE, EEGEE	$46.01	Vintage Red Metal Case, Dolls Miss Curity Kewpie Sailor	$16.01
		WHOLESALE CASE 6 LOT KAREN COTTON RAG DOLL DOLLS	$15.87
VINTAGE CABBAGE PATCH DOLLS LOT +DOLL CLOTHES+ACCESORIES	$46.00	WHOLESALE lot of 48 jointed mini Porcelain Dolls	$15.50

17

DVDS & MOVIES

Most of the highest-selling auctions for DVDs and other movies in this category are for big lots—100 or more movies, or in some cases, box sets. For example, the ten highest prices in the DVDs & Movies ▶ DVDs ▶ Action, Adventure subcategory are all $500.00 and up, but many of them are for 100 or more movies. The highest is for a lot of someone's personal collection of 184 new-release DVDs that went for $1,110.00. The second-highest auction contained 225 titles, "super titles and condition," for $1,051.00. This is a mixed bag of "guy" flicks and children's movies, but popular ones: *The Terminator*, *Dragon: The Bruce Lee Story*, *Star Wars I: The Phantom Menace*, Disney's *Atlantis*, Disney's *The Lion King*, Disney's *Peter Pan*, and so on. (In my experience, Walt Disney movies sell very well, and usually for more than other children's movies.)

A number of *Star Trek* series or set DVDs sold for several hundred dollars. Some of the high-priced *Star Treks* show up under the DVDs ▶ Sets table below, but some didn't come up in the sample because the word "set" wasn't in the title; for example, "New Star Trek The Next Generation Seasons 1 Thru 7" ($406.00, 11 bids); "New Star Trek Deep Space Nine Seasons 1 Thru 7!" ($405.00, 16 bids); or "NEW DVD Star Trek Voyager Seasons 1 2 3 4 5 6 7 USA 1-7 Region 1 Authentic US Version All Season Complete 1-7" ($404.99, 2 bids). Suffice to say, if you're selling a series or set of DVDs, you should do well with it.

In terms of individual DVDs, the highest-priced was a copy of *Beauty and the Beast* from 2002 that sold for a whopping $835.00. Actually, this was a two-disc set, but I included it with individual DVDs because it's a single movie. Why did this one go for so much? It's hard to say, but it did go out of print (or on "moratorium," as the listing specifies), as Disney movies on video are wont to do, which created greater demand. That, and the combination of being new and still sealed helps. Still, the winning bidder had a feedback rating of −1, so one wonders if something went amiss in this auction; that price does seem a bit fishy.

What was the next highest-selling individual DVD? I had to laugh at this one because I had a metal lunchbox with these cartoon characters on it as a child: "Help, the HAIR BEAR BUNCH Cartoon series ALL Episodes," a single DVD, went for $510.00. *My Name Is Tanino*, a rare unrated DVD, went for $305.00. "This is the most highly sought-after film featuring Rachel McAdams from 'The Notebook,'" writes the seller in his description. "This 2 DVD edition is exceptionally rare in nearly all parts of the world and does not have any regional coding restrictions." The film does contain nudity, per the seller.

eBay's own Top 10 List for DVDs includes the keywords *Harry Potter, TV on DVD, Star Wars, Box Sets, The Incredibles, Disney DVDs, The Sopranos, The Little Mermaid, Million Dollar Baby,* and *Toy Story*.

TV on DVD

In terms of Comedy, TV series on DVD like *Friends* (GBP 196.00) and *Seinfeld* (GBP 139.99; around $257.70), both including all seasons, do very well. A DVD with all 10 seasons of *Friends* on Amazon.com is listed for $245.99, but it was not to be released for a couple of months. The average prices in the DVDs & Movies ▶ DVDs ▶ Comedy subcategory hover around $7.00, and include big-screen comedies like *Meet the Fockers*.

A fascinating subcategory here is older media, like 16mm film. To view those titles is to take a walk down memory lane—movies like *Abbot and Costello Meet Frankenstein* ($710.00), the original *Sabrina* with Humphrey Bogart and Audrey Hepburn ($404.45), and the 1960s original *Cape Fear* ($380.00). Average prices there are around a healthy $34.00, and include lesser-known titles as well as non–feature film fare like ads, trailers, and a travel documentary.

Jumping forward in time to laserdiscs, we find an eclectic bunch at the high end. A *Star Wars* trilogy for $311.00; "Song of the South BANNED JAPANESE DISNEY'S LASERDISC LD," $108.49; a rock LD, "Twisted Sister, Stay Hungry," $56.00; and a couple of anime/animation LDs, "Anime Laserdisc Collection - Like New - 20 Discs," $51.75; and "The Art Of Tom & Jerry Vol 1 -5 Disc Laserdisc Box Set," $49.99. But there are so many fewer laserdiscs on eBay than DVDs—at this writing, there were about 5,100 LDs compared to about 328,000 DVDs, and about 108,000 VHS tapes.

High prices for VHS tapes in this sample are considerably lower than the now more-common DVD, a sign that the former is moving even closer to obsolescence. They range from about $25.00 to about $145.00, with average VHS prices around $9.00.

Selling Movies

If you're new to selling movies on eBay, you may want to check out the Movies & Memorabilia discussion board. There is some interesting discussion there about selling, rare and out-of-print films, and plenty of griping about illegal copies some report seeing on eBay. But as one eBayer on the board said, "EBay cannot be the judge as an item's authenticity." eBay does have a page with links to a large number of media companies and their anti-piracy pages where you can report abuse that you see on eBay: http://pages.ebay.com/help/community/vero-aboutme.html#movies. It is then the media company's responsibility to tell eBay, "Hey! This item is a fake!" eBay can then pull the listing.

One regular online seller, Richard Grady, author of "The Trader Online" newsletter, thinks selling DVDs—at least new ones that buyers can find in multiple retail venues—is tough. He writes that most people think that DVDs are excellent products to resell on eBay because they are very popular, not particularly expensive, and easy to package and ship. But, he says, the DVD market is "one of the most competitive that there is . . . At any one time there will only be a certain number of buyers wanting to purchase a particular DVD, and if you take into account the numerous different places there are that each buyer could purchase from, it is likely that in general there will be more copies of an individual DVD available than there are buyers to purchase them. This situation causes prices to fall."

With a wholesale discount of just about $2.00 or $3.00 in the United States, says Grady, "when you take into account the fact that the large retail chains can purchase thousands of DVDs at a time and receive a bigger discount than individual traders, you soon see why it is very difficult for a small business to compete in such a competitive industry."

Still, some people seem to be getting good prices by selling movies, but these are often for rare ones. So if you're good at scouting these out, you may be able to flip them profitably. Or, you may want to do like many people are doing here and sell your entire movie collection at once. Obtaining DVDs new and competing with other retail outlets will probably be more difficult.

DVDs ▸ Action, Adventure

The median sales price in this subcategory is $6.07.

	HIGH		AVG
DVD'S,POPULAR MOVIES,SEASON SERIES,COMPLETE SERIES.	$1,775.00	Foxfire DVD Angelina Jolie lesbian jenny shimizu sexy !	$6.19
LOT MY PERSONAL COLLECTION, ALL GREAT CONDITION, SELLING ALL		Pearl Harbor (2001, DVD)	$6.19
184 DVDS MOVIES NEW RELEASES PERSONAL COLLECTION	$1,110.00	The Italian Job (DVD 2004)	GBP 3.49
FREE SHIPPING WITH BUY IT NOW .....SMOKE FREE HOME		HOW THE WEST WAS WON	GBP 3.49
HUGE LOT 225 DVDS ..SUPER TITLES AND CONDITION	$1,051.10	Voyage Of The Unicorn R2 DVD	GBP 3.49
217 DVDs Personal Lot Boxset Criterion Disney Movies	$942.00	DVD Battle of Britain	GBP 3.38
HUGE LOT 225 DVDS ....SUPER TITLES AND CONDITION	$925.00	War Movie Collection No. 13	
200+ DVD Private Colection. Instant Movie Library 4 U	$750.00	In the Army Now Pauly Shore	$6.07
200 dvds mainly geezer films action the odd comedy	GBP 410.00	DVD NEW SEALED	
James Bond 007 SE collection boxset 20 Dvds Rare new!	$650.00	Star Wars Episode I: The Phantom Menace	$6.07
153 DVD lot. All original.. excellent condition	$635.01	Brand New DVD	
ACTION DVD ULTIMATE COLLECTION	GBP 350.00	The One Jet Li R4 DVD	AU 8.00
140 DVD dvds Star Wars Action lot New Used	$610.00	Dances with Wolves (2004, DVD) Kevin Costner	$6.07
All In Great Shape Many Unopened		OCEAN'S TWELVE 12 DVD BRAND NEW IN BOX	AU $8.00
007 James Bond Collection SE boxset Vol1,2&3 New Sealed	$600.00	Desperado (2003, WS/DVD)	$6.07
Warner Bros. 100 Movie Dvd Collection New "A" Titles	$599.00	Quentin Tarantino, Salma Hayek	
100 Brand New Factory Sealed DVDs Major Studio Titles		ROAD HOUSE Patrick Swayze	$6.07
The James Bond Collection SE boxset Vol1,2&3 New Sealed	$500.00	Slayers: The Book of Spells (2005, DVD)	$6.07
JAMES BOND 007 Collection Out Of Print Vol 1,2,3 + FREE SHIPPING!!!!!	$425.00	12 Monkeys (1998, DVD)	$6.07

DVDs ▸ Comedy

The median sales price in this subcategory is $6.99.

	HIGH		AVG
THE BEST OF THE DEAN MARTIN VARIETY SHOW 20 DVD SET + 1	$425.00	DVD Meet the Fockers (2005, DVD) FULLSCREEN	$6.99
GUARANTEED - FAST & LOW SHIPPING - NO RESERVE - NEW !!!		DVD The Terminal (2004, DVD) FULLSCREEN	$6.99
A collection of Comedy DVDs	$400.00	DVD The Life Aquatic With Steve Zissou (2005, DVD)	$6.99
ONLY FOOLS AND HORSES THE LOT (25 GB Comedy DVDs)	GBP 210.49	Speed Racer Collector's Edition DVD 100% Guarantee!	$6.99
Friends – Complete – Series 1 – 10, DVD (2004)	GBP 196.00	Bad DER Santa WIDESCREEN DVD	$6.99
The Complete Only Fools and Horses Box Set	GBP 170.00	YOURS MINE AND OURS –Lucille Ball-New DVD	$6.99
Best of the Muppet Show complete 15 disc sealed DVD set. Complete	$300.00	HEARTBREAKERS - Special Edition - NEW DVD - SEALED	$6.99
15 disc OOP set. No Reserve / Free Insurance!!		Bustin' Loose CICELY TYSON RICHARD PRYOR FS DVD	$6.99
Newhart Inn Series (184 episodes; 1982-1990)	$300.00	BRAND NEW DVD - WHERE THE	
Three Stooges Entire Shorts DVD Collection! 40 DVD's! 3	$291.00	BUFFALO ROAM - Bill Murray	$6.99
ONLY FOOLS AND HORSES THE LOT	GBP 160.00	IT COULD HAPPEN TO YOU	$6.99
Sex and the City Gift Collection DVD Series Seasons 1-6	$265.00	Nicolas Cage Comedy MINT DVD	
BRAND NEW! 6 SEASONS... 94 EPISODES... 20 DISCS! NR!		Bad Santa [Badder Santa] (2003 NR) Bernie Mac	$6.99
CATHERINE COOKSON THE COMPLETE COLLECTION 23 DVD'S NEW	$261.15	The Object Of My Affection	$6.99
Futurama Seasons 1-4-Complete Box Set	GBP 142.00	NEW DVD JENNIFER ANISTON	
Friends Complete Series 10 Rare Skyline Boxset GBP 140.00	GBP 140.00	City Slickers DVD DVDs - Billy Crystal, Jack Palance	$6.99
Seinfeld DVD Brand New, Never Opened Very Rare 10 DVD's.	GBP 139.99	HONEYMOONERS Mike Epps, Regina Hall DVD NEW	$6.99
Includes all 9 Seasons (180 episode) BONUS BLOOPERS DVD		WHERE THE BUFFALO ROAM *DVD NEW!* Bill Murray	$6.99
Friends 1-10 complete series – 30 DVD Box Set	GBP 133.00	ARTHUR 2: ON THE ROCKS Dudley Moore NEW R1 WS DVD	$6.99

DVDs ▸ Drama

The median sales price in this subcategory is $6.07.

	HIGH		AVG
The Transporter (2003 DVD)	$609.00	Cat People DVD Nastassia Kinski	$6.50
78 DVD MOVIES IN ORIGINAL BOXES	$400.00	Malcolm McDowell NEW R1	
THE TAKEN ORIGINAL SCI-FI MINI-SERIES IN BOX SET		ROW YOUR BOAT! DVD! STARRING	$6.50
LOT OF 100 NEW AND VIEWED DVD'S DRAMA, ACTION,	$395.00	JON BON JOVI! UNOPENIL@@K	
COMEDY, ADVENTURE,SCIENCE FICTION, SPACE		3 DVD LOT- SUPERCROSS, UNDERCLASSMAN,	$6.50
SALO PIER PAOLO PASOLINI CRITERION RARE DVD	$394.05	TWO FOR MONEY	
Huge Personal DVD Collection Lot FREE SHIPPING 90+ @@@FREE	$364.96	American History X DVD *NEW* Edward Norton	$6.50
SHIPPING to US , NO Junk , NO RESERVE@@@		Latter Days (2004) Unrated Gay	$6.50
100 DVD LOT WITH NEW RELEASES FROM PERSONAL COLLECTION	$350.00	Interest Brand New DVD	

USED – BUY IT NOW AND RECEIVE FREE SHIPPING!!!	
McLeod's Daughters SERIES 1,2,3,4 DVDS BRAND NEW R4 $1	AU $451.01
RRP over $500! BRAND NEW AND SEALED	
BEVERLY HILLS 90210 ALL 10 SEASONS ON DVD + GREAT BONUS	GBP 190.00
THE FUGITIVE TV DVD COMPLETE L@@K!!	$326.50
COMPLETE SERIES DVD BOXSET UPSTAIRS DOWNSTAIRS	GBP 166.00
POIROT – David Suchet – 31 DVD Box Set	GBP 155.00
OZ complete season 1 to 6 (30 disc) BN Sealed dvd	$254.58
Mcleod's Daughters S1,2,3 DVD(all 3 box sets brand new)	AU $341.00
Upstairs Downstairs Series 1 to 5 (DVD 2003)	GBP 145.95
Brand New Sealed Soprano Seasons 1,2,3,4, & 5!!!!!!	$250.00

Crash (2005 New DVD) Sandra Bullock	$6.50
Kalifornia (DVD)Brad Pitt/Duchovny/	$6.50
Juliet Lewis UNRATED	
Crash (2005 New DVD) Sandra Bullock	$6.50
BONE COLLECTOR, THE (DVD)BRAND NEW	$6.49
BASIC INSTINCT (DVD S.E.) BRAND NEW	$6.49
Schindler's List, Collector Series, Widescreen (DVD)	$6.49
Paradise (1982) Phoebe Cates nudity	$6.49
Hallmark Classics CLEOPATRA DVD Valera Dalton NEW	$6.49
NEW SEALED DVD BELOVED – Danny Glover, Oprah	$6.49
Patch Adams DVD Collector's Edition robin williams MINT	$6.49

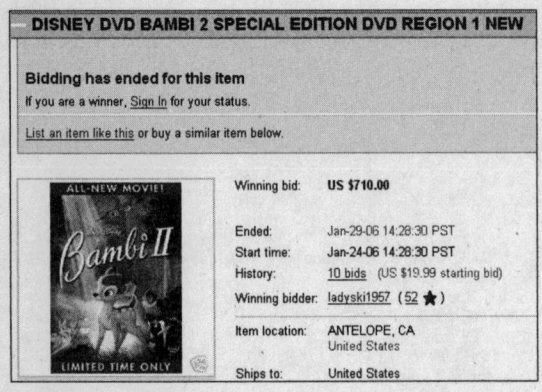

DISNEY DVD BAMBI 2 SPECIAL EDITION DVD REGION 1 NEW

Bidding has ended for this item
If you are a winner, Sign In for your status.
List an item like this or buy a similar item below.

Winning bid:	**US $710.00**
Ended:	Jan-29-06 14:28:30 PST
Start time:	Jan-24-06 14:28:30 PST
History:	10 bids (US $19.99 starting bid)
Winning bidder:	ladyski1957 (52 ★)
Item location:	ANTELOPE, CA United States
Ships to:	United States

Personal DVD Collection - 572 Separate Titles
Includes many Boxsets and Television Series

Bidding has ended for this item
If you are a winner, Sign In for your status.
List an item like this or buy a similar item below.

Sold for:	**US $3,000.00**
	Auction ended early with Buy It Now.
Ended:	Feb-01-06 10:37:19 PST
Start time:	Feb-01-06 10:18:56 PST
History:	1 bid (US $3,000.00 starting bid)
Buyer:	thenoizemusic (20 ☆)
Item location:	Vienna, West Virginia

DVDs

The average sales price in this subcategory is $20.10.

NOTE *The below prices were obtained by doing a keyword search on the word* DVD.

	HIGH		AVG
Sealed Beauty and the Beast DVD 2002 DISNEY	$835.00	The best of the Dean Martin Variety Show Vol. 1	$20.11
[2 of these sold for $835.00 each]		Bonnie Raitt - Road Tested (DVD)New Sealed	$20.11
Help, the HAIR BEAR BUNCH Cartoon series ALL Episodes	$510.00	Pat Benatar - Choice Cuts: The Complete Video Coll	$20.11
dvd wholesale movie lot	$416.00	DEAN MARTIN VARIETY SHOW NEW CD VOL 3	$20.10
My Name Is Tanino DVD Rachel McAdams Nude 2002 Unrated	$305.00	NOW AND THEN HERE AND THERE COLLECTIO DVD NEW SEALED	$20.10
CELINE DION Falling Into You Live DVD! Montreal 1996!!	$208.02	LIFE AS WE KNOW IT THE COMPLETE SERIES ON DVD	$20.10
SALO 120 DAYS CRITERION OOP FREE SHIPPING AUTHENTIC.	$202.50	Sinbad 3-Pack (Golden Voyage, Eye of Tiger, 7th Voyage)	$20.10
WHITE RING RARE NEW 100% POSITIVE FEEDBACK NO RESERVE		24 Season One	$20.10
The Nanny Complete 6 Seasons on 17 DVD Box Set RARE	$199.00	The Little Mermaid (1999, DVD)	$20.10
SHARPE'S COMPLETE DVD 15 DISC BOX SET LIMITED EDITION	$179.99	Japanese DVD - Zenra Challenger 108 Girls Special Asian	$20.10
Smurf Dvd Set	$154.00	3 Ninjas Trilogy DVD - FAST SHIP!!!	$20.10
ACLAND'S HUMAN ANATOMY ATLAS COMPLETE DVD, STEP 1 USMLE	$127.50	HOOSIERS GENE HACKMAN HICKORY XXXL BASKETBALL JACKET	$20.10
ACLAND'S HUMAN ANATOMY ATLAS COMPLETE DVD, STEP 1 USMLE	$122.50	Sky High, Shark Boy and Lava Girl, Hitchhikers - 3 DVDs	$20.10
ACLAND'S HUMAN ANATOMY ATLAS COMPLETE DVD, STEP 1 USMLE	$111.51	Lord of the Rings: The Fellowship o DVD - FAST SHIP!!!	$20.10
ACLAND'S HUMAN ANATOMY ATLAS COMPLETE DVD, STEP 1 USMLE	$111.50	Eerie Indiana -The Complete Series (2004, DVD) MINT!	$20.10
ACLAND'S HUMAN ANATOMY ATLAS COMPLETE DVD, STEP 1 USMLE	$102.50	SIGMUND AND THE SEA MONSTERS -	$20.10
TRANSFORMERS G2-HEADMASTERS/MASTERFORCE/VICTORY 30 DVD!	$100.00	SEASON 1 DVD NEW SEALED	

DVDs ▸ Sets

The average sales price in this subcategory is $27.78.

NOTE *The below prices were obtained by doing a keyword search on the word* set.

	HIGH		AVG
Prince - Royal Vision DVD SET : Volume 1_2_3_4	$207.50	Alien 1,2,3,4 Quadrilogy DVD Box Set Brand New Sealed	$28.03
JUST IN..THE SOPRANOS 5 SEASON 22DVD COLLECTORS BOX SET	$205.00	GILMORE GIRLS: SECOND SEASON (TWO 2) NEW USA 6-DVD SET	$28.00
The Nanny Complete 6 Seasons on 17 DVD Box Set RARE	$199.00	Dawson's Creek (The Complete 4TH Season) DVD SET	$28.00
SHARPE'S COMPLETE DVD 15 DISC BOX SET LIMITED EDITION	$179.99	DISNEY BABY EINSTEIN 17 DVD BOX SET - R1 BRAND NEW	$28.00
Smurf Dvd Set	$154.00	[2 of these sold for $28.00 each]	
JUST IN..THE SOPRANOS 5 SEASON	$152.50	DISNEY BABY EINSTEIN 16 DVD BOX SET - R1 + BONUS MONET	$28.00
22DVD COLLECTORS BOX SET		BUFFY COMPLETE SEASON 6 NEW 6 DVD-SET U.S. MADE	$27.77
Gnomon Workshop: Fluid effects 3 DVD set	$132.50	The Andy Griffith Show - The Complete Season 3 DVD Set	$27.60
James Bond Collection 007 Gift Set - Vol. 3 (2000, DVD)	$131.50	TALES OF THE CITY - Complete Unedited 3-disc set OOP	$27.59
THREE'S COMPANY, DVD SET, COMPLETE	$125.00	ANGEL SEASON 3,BRAND NEW DVD SET,,U.S MADE	$27.56
InuYasha Part 1234 &5 Eps 1-90 15 DVD Set EngDub $0 S/H	$122.50	Sopranos complete first season dvd 1st HBO box set	$27.50
SIMPSONS SEASON 1 2 3 4 5 SET 19 DVD NOT ASIAN IMPORT	$114.95	THE MUPPET SHOW SEASON ONE 4 - DVD SET *** SEALED ***	$27.03
Star Trek "The Original Series Season" 1-3 DVD Box Set	$100.00	NEW! 2005 Harry Potter 6 DISC Special Trilogy DVD Set	$27.02
Baby Einstein AUTHENTIC USA Disney Version 17 DVD SET	$99.00	Benny Hill: The Naughty Early Years - Set 3 (2005, DVD)	$27.00
New Star Trek Voyager Fourth Season 4 DVD Box Set	$91.00	Dawson's Creek Season Five DVD Box Set SEALED	$27.00
Star Trek - The Motion Pictures Collection 15 DVD SET	$90.99	DISNEY BABY EINSTEIN 15 DVD BOX SET +BONUS NOAH & MONET	$27.00

Film

The average sales price in this subcategory is $33.53.

NOTE *The below prices were obtained by doing a keyword search on the word* film.

	HIGH		AVG
Old 16mm FEATURE SOUND FILM Abbot&Costello/FRANKENSTEIN	$710.00	DANIEL BOONE 16mm FILM TV FESS PARKER	$35.50
16mm ORIG. FEATURE FILM "SABRINA" A. HEPBURN & BOGART	$409.45	16MM Film 6 HOPALONG CASSIDY THEATRICAL TRAILERS 9 MINS	$35.00
16mm ORIG. FEATURE FILM "CURSE OF THE DEMON" 50s HORROR	$399.00	16mm film HOME MOVIES OF EUROPE	$35.00
16mm ORIG. FEATURE FILM "CAPE FEAR" 1960s MOVIE CLASSIC	$380.00	ONE RUN ELMER (1935) 16mm FILM - BUSTER KEATON	$35.00
16mm Film - THE SIN OF HAROLD DIDDLEBOCK NR	$364.00	16mm Film '79 MASH - Private Finance Rare LPP	$34.99
16mm Film CAPTAIN MARVEL SERIAL 12 CHAPTERS	$336.00	16MM / THE CAT / Family Aadventure Film	$34.95
16mm FEATURE FILM "THE CAT & THE CANARY" BOB HOPE MOVIE	$331.00	1950's 16mm Color Film Linde Air Metal Joining	$34.00
8 Reels of 35mm Feature Film "RAJAKUMARUDU" (Telugu)	$295.00	Old 16mm CHARLIE CHAPLIN Film-THE BOXER	$33.03
8mm 16mm 35mm FILM SPLICER Metric Splicer & Flim Co	$260.00	WWI Red Baron Triplane Flight 50ft 8mm Film	$33.00
16mm Feature Film A Hard Day's Night	$225.00	Sananguagat Inuit Masterworks 16 mm film 25 Min. Long	$33.00
16mm comedy feature film SPIES LIKE US (1985)	$201.09	16MM FILM: I'M NO FOOL WITH ELECTRICITY-Walt Disney	$32.00
16MM FEATURE FILM - "MAGNUM FORCE" - THEATRICAL - AGFA	$183.50	Old Anheuser Busch BEER 16mm movie film DON'T GET DRUNK	$31.75
16mm film - DOBIE GILLIS tv show with Robby the Robot	$177.00	8 mm A MUST SEE B&W-No Sound Film	$31.59
16MM GEORGE MELIES SILENT FANTASY FILM	$162.50	Old 16mm movie film Pathe News World in Review England	$31.01
16MM GEORGE MELIES SILENT FANTASY FILM	$162.50	1950's 16mm Film Let's Visit The British Isles	$31.00

Laserdisc

The average sales price in this subcategory is $14.83.

NOTE *The below prices were obtained by doing a keyword search on the word* laserdisc.

	HIGH		AVG
Boxed laserdisc STAR WARS TRILOGY ~SEALED!! retail $250	$311.00	LAURENCE OLIVIER IN "WUTHERING HEIGHTS" on Laserdisc	$20.50
SONG OF THE SOUTH BANNED JAPANESE DISNEY'S LASERDISC LD	$108.49	COMPULSION - Orson Welles - RM WS Rare Laserdisc	$20.50
SALO Uncut LASERDISC Pasolini RARE ld DVD Criterion 120	$73.00	CARY GRANT, FAIRBANKS IN "GUNGA DIN" on Laserdisc	$20.01
Pioneer CLD-D501 Laserdisc / Jurassic Park, Star Trek	$66.00	PIONEER CLD-2080 LASERDISC PLAYER	$20.00
Twisted Sister, Stay Hungry, Laserdisc	$56.00	Criterion Beatles A Hard Days Night CAV Laserdisc OOP	$20.00
LASERDISC ANIMATION DISNEY ANIME & OTHERS	$56.00	TOY STORY THX DELUXE CAV LASERDISC BOX SET NEW	$20.00
Anime Laserdisc Collection - Like New - 20 Discs	$51.75	Laserdisc Howling Karloff Lugosi Frankenstein Gone Wind	$19.99
The Art Of Tom & Jerry Vol 1 -5 Disc Laserdisc Box Set	$49.99	SECRET LIFE OF WALTER MITTY on Laserdisc DANNY KAYE	$19.00
THE FLINTSTONES 1ST 14 EPISODES LASERDISC BOX SET RARE	$49.99	THE NEIGHBOR - Rod Steiger NEW! Laserdisc	$17.38
Lot of 22 LaserDisc Collection - Terminator, Lion King!	$49.00	A Fistful Of Dynamite Laserdisc DLX LTR-box Uncut OOP	$16.50
Metallica Cliff 'em All JAPAN/Japanese LD/Laserdisc+Obi	$48.00	FANTASTIC PLANET. RENE LALOUX. LD. LASERDISC.	$16.49
Art of Tom & Jerry -77 cartoons / 5 disc LASERDISC set	$46.55	THX 1138 LASERDISC GEORGE LUCAS LD LASER DISC	$16.49
STAR WARS ORIGINAL TRILOGY LASERDISC SET FULLSCREEN	$44.50	THE MAN WHO COULD WORKED MIRACLES on Laserdisc	$16.01
Looney Tunes Vol 3 Laserdisc Family Fun!!!	$44.04	Views Of A Vanishing Frontier Laserdisc Museum Of Art	$16.01
The Golden Age of Looney Tunes Vol 1 Laserdisc	$42.05	Boxed laserdisc set of THE BEATLES ANTHOLOGY awesome!	$16.01

FANTASTIC COLLECTION OF 57 MUSICAL VHS MOVIES!

Click to view supersized image

VHS

The average sales price in this subcategory is $9.05.

NOTE *The below prices were obtained by doing a keyword search on the word* VHS.

	HIGH		AVG
HUGE BARNEY SCHOOL HOUSE+23 VIDEOS VHS+22 BOOKS+MORE	$144.50	FELICITY (UNCUT) - GLORY ANNEN - VHS	$9.99
Lot of 30 Classic Videos & Cliffhangers VHS Video Movie	$90.00	FIVE - WILLIAM PHIPPS - VHS	$9.99
BBC Muzzy Spanish Language Course for Children, VHS	$88.90	2 VHS WHERE THERE'S A WILL THERE'S AN A Grade School	$9.95
Beauty of Japan D-VHS D-Theater Ultra Rare HDTV Tape!	$81.00	TURN OF THE SCREW vhs ntsc Lynn Redgrave, Jasper Jacobs	$9.95
Best of Saturday Night Live SNL 23 VHS Videos 1975-1993	$68.00	Four Seasons In Polish Cooking VHS Polish in English	$9.95
FREEDOM IS PARADISE... COMING OF AGE.. USED VHS	$46.00	The Beatles - Let It Be VHS Video	$9.50
The FIRM VHS Videos Set of 8 NEW	$41.00	CLOSE ENCOUNTER OF THE VAMPIRE vhs Horror HK LBX OOP JP	$9.45
3 JULIA CHILD VHS Videos COOKING POULTRY Desserts Soups	$40.00	Space Camp (1989, VHS) MINT CONDITION!	$9.06

32 VHS CFI Renewal Program Training Course	$40.00
Larry Williams 3 VHS Videos Secrets To Stock Investing	$37.00
Lots Wholesale VHS Videos Video Lot, 62 Movies + 5 DVDs	$35.42
VITO AND THE OTHERS... COMING OF AGE.. USED VHS	$34.00
Disney Dinosaurs Jim Henson TV show lot of 4 VHS	$34.00
The Sandpiper 1965 (VHS)Elizabeth Taylor Richard Burton	$33.00
Math Made EASY-Tutorial Videos -VHS (5 VHS Tapes)	$31.00

Atomic Journey bomb filmmaker Trinity Beyond 3-VHS NEW	$8.99
GOLDEN KAT VHS GKC-7 MIXED WRESTLING	$8.50
Dora the Explorer - Cowgirl Dora - VHS - New	$8.49
With Six You Get Eggroll DORIS DAY VHS *Free Shipping*	$8.49
Disney MARY POPPINS VHS video Original Clamshell SEALED	$8.49
BACK STREET vhs IRENE DUNNE / RARE	$8.39
Anne of Avonlea (1996, VHS)	$8.00

VHS Non-US (PAL) ▶ Other

The average sales price in this subcategory is $9.27.

NOTE   *The below prices were obtained by doing a keyword search on the word* PAL.

	HIGH
DAY-O vhs PAL format Elijah Wood	$112.50
TOUCH THE SUN - Devil's Hill vhs PAL format	$109.50
THE GREAT BRAIN vhs PAL fomrat Jimmy Osmond	$51.00
NOT OF THIS WORLD vhs PAL format Luke Edwards	$46.00
STAR OF INDIA CORNEL WILDE vhs PAL	$43.99
GARY SWEET POLICE RESCUE MATES / HOSTAGE PAL VIDEO	$41.60
THE GIFT vhs PAL format	$41.00
BAD ATTITUDES vhs PAL format Ethan Randall	$38.00
AND THE SEA WILL TELL COMPLETE TV MINI SERIES vhs PAL	$36.00
THE BUCCANEERS BBC TV MINI SERIES vhs PAL	$31.00
Female Real Action Wrestling - 3 matches - PAL format	$29.95
1993 Mr Olympia Bodybuilding PAL Format	$26.00
LEGEND OF RUBY SILVER vhs PAL format Jonathan Jackson	$23.49
DAVID vhs PAL format Matthew Lawrence	$22.50
LES GRANGES BRUL?S Alain Delon Simone Signoret VHS PAL	$22.49

	AVG
RACING THE PAST ROBERT URICH vhs PAL	$9.99
STANLEY AND LIVINGSTONE SPENCER TRACEY vhs PAL	$9.99
THE RICHEST CAT IN THE WORLD WALT DISNEY vhs PAL	$9.99
SOUTH OF ST LOUIS JOEL McRAE/DOROTHY MALONE vhs PAL	$9.50
Lou Ferrigno Stand Tall Bodybuilding PAL Format	$9.50
1999 Men of Muscle Bodybuilding PAL Format	$9.25
GOLD BUG vhs PAL format Anthony Michael Hall	$8.95
LAST ELECTRIC KNIGHT + 2 1/2 DADS vhs PAL format	$8.95
SLIM DUSTY ERIC BOGLE OTHERS A BIG COUNTRY PAL VIDEO	$8.50
1994 Mr. Olympia PAL Format	$8.50
FOREVER AND BEYOND vhs PAL format John Snee	$8.49
JOAN SUTHERLAND JEFFREY RUSH ON OUR SELECTION PAL VIDEO	$7.90
RIVALS vhs PAL format Scott Jacoby	$7.50
1989 Mr. Olympia Bodybuilding PAL Format	$7.50
DO YOU KNOW THE MUFFIN MAN vhs PAL format	$6.95

18

ENTERTAINMENT MEMORABILIA

Many subcategories in the Entertainment Memorabilia main category have not only robust high prices, but healthy average prices as well, of $30.00, $40.00, and up. If you're lucky enough to have a trove of entertainment memorabilia, whether inherited, collected, or purchased for resale, you might want to check out the "Want It Now" board on eBay as well as completed auction prices to see where the demand is. Sometimes these finds come from odd places. I remember reading about a man who was doing construction on his house and found that vintage movie posters had been used as insulation by someone who had worked in a theater; they were in good condition, having been shielded from light and other wear and tear over the years. In fact, it was not uncommon for builders in the 1910s and 1920s (and some in the 1930s) to "hook up with poster exchanges" to use posters as insulation, according to Bruce Hershenson in his article, "A History of Movie Posters," on Reel Classics (http://reelclassics.com). "Sometimes they are moldy and mildewed and require large amounts of restoration, but sometimes they are so tightly pressed together that they survive in relatively excellent condition," he writes.

Sometimes with movie memorabilia, it's more about the movie star than the movie. For example, an eBayer who was asking for advice on selling a stash of lobby cards (those big, stand-alone cardboard film ads you see in the lobbies of movie theaters) was advised to switch the name of the "unknown, forgettable" movie in his auction title with the name of its star, Hayley Mills, "since there are avid HM collectors." A bestseller among lobby cards, incidentally, is John Wayne: a couple of his cards sold for $300.00 and $150.00, respectively.

In terms of autographs, old-time/classic Hollywood stars seem to fetch the best prices, with many from the 1950s: a handwritten letter from Audrey Hepburn to her doctor fetched $710.00, a signed Marilyn Monroe contract got $510.00, and an original James Dean signature brought in $460.55. The Monroe contract is framed along with a publicity photo and signed by her and her first agent, Harry Lipton, according to the seller, who says the document dates between 1946 and 1949. The seller did not know what the contract was for, saying it was "obviously regarding something in the business" and that it was rare to find an artifact from Monroe's early days in movies.

The average prices in Entertainment Memorabilia ▶ Autographs ▶ Movies are around $33.00, and include some more modern actresses and actors such as Scarlett Johansson, Olivia Newton-John, and Mel Gibson, all of whose signatures sold for $35.00 each. Low prices here are around $1.00, and shipping varies from a reasonable $1.00 to a slightly higher $3.00 to $5.00, but as most of these items are simply pieces of paper or cardboard, such as signed checks, index cards, or publicity stills, it would be hard for sellers to justify gouging too much on postage for these items.

Disney remains a key flashpoint: one of the highest prices in the whole Entertainment Memorabilia category was signed by the man himself: a "WALT DISNEY Signed LADY AND THE TRAMP Book 1953" that sold for $4,150.00. This is a first-printing copy of the book on which the movie was based, Ward Greene's 1953 *Lady and the Tramp: The Story of Two Dogs*. It's autographed on the title page by Walt Disney, who also contributed a foreword to the book describing how the story came to be written, according to the seller. Other Disney items in the category include a 78 rpm Mouseketeers record signed by both Walt Disney and Annette Funicello that sold for $393.88.

Music and Beatlemania

In the Rock, Pop subcategory of Entertainment Memorabilia ▶ Music, only a handful of bands command the high end of prices, and one in particular far and away reigns supreme. It's no surprise that this band is The Beatles. (Beatles items of all kinds tend to sell very well in general on eBay.) The top price there is one of the highest in the whole Entertainment Memorabilia main category: $10,850.00 for a set of White Albums signed by each Beatle. One of only a few sets in existence, according to the seller, this one seems to have taken over ten years to put together; each Beatle signed his corresponding photo on the White Album at different times. "Ringo has signed in black ball point pen and dates from the early 1980s," explains the item description. "Paul has signed in dark blue ball point pen. His autograph dates from the early 1970s. John Lennon has signed in blue ball point pen. His signature was obtained in 1975. And George's signature dates from the mid-1980s."

The rest of the high price sample from Entertainment Memorabilia ▶ Music Memorabilia ▶ Rock-n-Roll is also dominated by The Beatles; ten other items are Beatles-related, including the second-highest priced item, a Beatles Rockola Jukebox. Other artists whose items made it into the high end here are The Grateful Dead, The Rolling Stones, Elvis, Neil Young, Jimi Hendrix, and Incubus.

The average price range of Rock-n-Roll memorabilia brings a wider swath of artists—a mix of old and new—and prices around $10.00: Led Zeppelin, Lee Ann Womack, Motley Crue, the Doors, Madonna, and so on.

The Entertainment Memorabilia ▶ Autographs ▶ Music subcategory seems dominated by other factors, such as who is currently touring; several "guest list ticket" packages of a single band, System of a Down, sold for between $200.00 and $677.00. (In other months you will, no doubt, find other touring bands.) Although these items may seem misplaced in this subcategory, the auctions do include a signed copy of their latest CD, *Mezmerize*, along with the VIP ticket package, so they technically belong here, although they are also listed in the Tickets ▶ Experiences subcategory.

Music autographs in the average range are a robust $58.40, with a mix of old and new artists such as Bobby Darin, George Harrison, and *American Idol* stars Bo Bice and Carrie Underwood. Sometimes the price simply depends more on the item signed than the artist; a certificate of authenticity (COA) and other guarantees help, of course. Meat Loaf shows up both in the average and low range, with a signed/framed CD with COA going for $59.00; and a signed card selling for a more down-to-earth $4.99.

Television and Theater

What about TV? Shows with die-hard fan bases pop up regularly, *Star Trek* being one of the key "classic" ones; a new one, cable TV's *Queer as Folk*, has spawned many a listing in the Entertainment Memorabilia ▶ Television Memorabilia ▶ Props and Television Memorabilia ▶ Wardrobe subcategories. Science fiction TV does well overall in the Television Memorabilia subcategories; in addition to *Star Trek*, you can find items from *Battlestar Galactica* ($57.50 for a "BATTLESTAR GALACTICA 4x6 Bus Shelter Poster 6ft," one of two posters that sold on the high end here); *Babylon 5* ($205.71 for a "Babylon 5 (S4) Media Press Kit ~ 26 Photos & 26 Slides"); and *The X Files* ($70.00 for 13 *X Files* pilot 35mm slides). A *Lost in Space* script shows up as the highest price in the Entertainment Memorabilia ▶ Television Memorabilia ▶ Scripts subcategory. But many TV shows of various genres and from several decades show up through the Television subcategories.

Theater does not seem to command the same lofty prices that the other media do, whether this is because its audience is smaller, it's more obscure, or for other reasons. High prices here are more likely to be in the hundreds rather than thousands of dollars. A couple of exceptions are the "ARENA DE VERONA 1952 PROGRAM MARIA CALLAS," $1,044.00; and the window card from *Prettybelle* (Angela Lansbury/Gower Champion), $1,576.50.

The Callas *Verona* program is notable because the opera star spent early years of her career there, from 1947 to 1954. (Incidentally, it's technically "Arena *di* Verona" and not "*de* Verona," but as with many eBay items, the misspelling has not necessarily brought its price down). The Angela Lansbury *Prettybelle* item may have gone for so much because the show was so short-lived and its programs are therefore rare; it lasted only a month in 1947 due to some controversy over its depiction of Southerners. But you can pick up many an old playbill for only around $15.00, and there are all sorts of affordable pieces of theatre history available in these subcategories, from the late nineteenth century to the present day.

The bottom line is, whether you're into opera or Xbox, Entertainment Memorabilia is a fun category for fans that can bring back memories for people in every generation.

Autographs ▶ Movies

The average sales price in this subcategory is $33.32.

	HIGH		AVG
Handwritten Letter from AUDREY HEPBURN to her Doctor	$710.03	FLORENCE HENDERSON - THE BRADY BUNCH - SIGNED PHOTO	$35.00
Marilyn Monroe Signed Contract & Photo (RARE!!)	$510.00	American Graffiti menu signed by Paul LeMat	$35.00
James Dean orig ink signature	$460.55	OLIVIA NEWTON-JOHN SIGNED CANDID 8X10 PHOTO PIC PROOF	$35.00
NATALIE WOOD-AUTOGRAPHED MOVIE LP- PROPERTY-CONDEMNED	$361.99	BRAVEHEART MEL GIBSON AUTO 8X10-COA	$35.00
The Devil's Rejects signed promo skull by 18 in person	$355.00	AN AUTOGRAPHED CREATURE FROM THE BLACK LAGOON DVD – NR	$34.33
Liza Minnelli,Dudley Moore & John Gielgud signed!!!!	$255.00	ROBERT WAGNER original autograph 1964 KISS BEFORE DYING	$34.00
RARE 1938 JUDY GARLAND Autograph The Wizard of Oz	$249.00	James Darren Autographed Gidget Collection DVD	$33.00
JOHN WAYNE ORIGINAL AUTOGRAPH DISPLAY SIGNED "THE DUKE"	$235.50	CHARLIE CHAPLIN SIGNED MAGAZINE PAGE AUTOGRAPHED	$32.57
Stan Laurel Signed Check	$231.11	Norma Shearer Autograph card	$32.00
GRETA GARBO RARE SIGNED 1ST EDITION BOOK 1955	$207.50	CHEECH & CHONG-SIGNED 45 RPM PIC SLV-PROMO-RARE	$31.00
HARRY POTTER AUTOGRAPH/SIGNED CHAMBER BOOK BY 7!!!	$207.50	Its A Wonderful Life SILVER PLATED BELL	$31.00
DRACULA STAR BELA LUGOSI HAND SIGNED MEMO PAGE	$202.50	RAY HARRYHAUSEN SIGNED THE 7th VOYAGE OF SINBAD 3	$30.00
BORIS KARLOFF LELAND HAYWARD HAND SIGNED MEMO PAGE	$192.50	John Travolta Autographed 1976 endorsed check	$30.00
** BRUCE LEE AUTOGRAPH SIGNED 3x5 INDEX AUTO COA NR *	$164.47	MEL BROOKS & CARL REINER autographed book!	$29.99
JAYNE MANSFIELD-SIGNED 10 INCH-MUSIC TO REMEMBER-SEXY !	$143.28	KING KONG & SON OF KONG 1930's STAR rare Guide $75	$29.50

Autographs ▶ Music

The average sales price in this subcategory is $58.40.

	HIGH		AVG
System Of A Down Guest List Ticket Package Minneapolis	$677.00	GEORGE HARRISON SIGNED CUT	$61.00
System Of A Down Guest List Ticket Package Chicago, IL	$625.00	SIGNED DOLLY PARTON CD + FRAMED + COA - SUPERB !	$60.00
MIKE SMITH BENEFIT – DONOVAN	$565.99	THE WHO HAND SIGNED LP BY4 FACE	$59.99
System Of A Down Guest List Ticket Package Columbus, OH	$560.00	DANCES BETTER YOU BET	$59.99
System Of A Down Guest List Ticket Package Cleveland	$550.00	AWESOME JIMMY BUFFETT HAND SIGNED ALBUM COVER	$59.99
System Of A Down Guest List Ticket Package Seattle, WA	$510.00	MEATLOAF SIGNED CD + FRAMED + COA	$59.00
CHECK IT SIGNED AUTOGRAPH	$510.00	VELVET REVOLVER– GNR AUTOGRAPH COLLECTION!!!!COA	$59.00
BEACH BOYS NO BEATLES PSA DNA		DUKES OF HAZZARD cast SIGNED cowboy HAT *PROOF	$56.55
PiNk FlOyD signed GUITAR ******** All 4	$510.00	Judy Garland Hand Signed Paper Cut wizard of oz	$56.00
System Of A Down Guest List Ticket Package Denver, CO	$444.77	ANGUS YOUNG AC/DC SIGNED SKETCH W/ COA	$52.00
System Of A Down Guest List Ticket Package Oakland, CA	$440.00	JIM MORRISON SIGNED CARD WITH C.O.A	$52.00
System Of A Down Guest List Ticket Package Edmonton	$425.00	Green Day Greenday GUITAR STRAP Autographed SIGNED! COA	$51.08
System Of A Down Guest List Ticket Package Hamilton, ON	$405.00	WAYLON JENNINGS HAND SIGNED LP HONKY TONK HEROES LEGEND	$51.00
MIKE SMITH BENEFIT - NANCY SINATRA BOOTS!	$361.00	BO BICE , CARRIE & VONZELL SIGNED 8X10 PHOTO IDOL PROOF	$51.00
System Of A Down Guest List Ticket Package Portland, OR	$330.88	THE WHO Signed Auto. Album LP - Rare 4 sig MOON + 3	$51.00
System Of A Down Guest List Ticket Package Detroit, MI	$315.01	Priscilla Lisa Presley sign ElvisbyPresleys bDVD + pics	$51.00

Autographs ▶ Television

The average sales price in this subcategory is $19.18.

	HIGH		AVG
MIKE SMITH BENEFIT - LATE SHOW with D LETTERMAN	$1,102.50	The Cast of THE O.C. - Cool 8X10 SIGNED X8 PHOTO *COA*	$19.99
WALT DISNEY-ANNETTE-MOUSEKETEERS-AUTOGRAPHED-78 RPM	$393.88	TOM SELLECK Magnum P.I. - SEXY 8X10 SIGNED PHOTO *COA*	$19.99
I LOVE LUCY ,LUCILLE BALL, DESI ARNAZ CAST SIGNED	$300.00	Ellen DeGeneres Autographed 8x10 Photo w/COA	$19.95
AUTOGRAPHED STARGATE ATLANTIS SCRIPT	$224.82	KELLY CLARKSON Gorgeous Signed Photo - Autograph	$19.90
Star Trek Autographs -Gene Roddenberry, D.C Fontana	$206.85	Kathleen Turner autographed 8x10 photo COA	$19.76
FAMILY GUY - SETH MCFARLANE SIGNED SCRIPT	$205.00	Erik Estrada autographed 8x10 photo COA	$19.50
BUFFY JOHN RITTER AUTOGRAPH AS TED A7	$199.00	BILL SHATNER & LEONARD NIMOY AUTOGRAPHED BOOK	$19.49
Peter Jennings Signed In SEARCH of AMERICA! Autographed	$169.00	Eva Mendes autographed 8x10 photo COA	$19.15
TERRIFIC Peter Jennings Signed THE CENTURY! Autographed	$150.98	Autographed PATRICIA HEATON In"EVERYBODY LOVES RAYMOND"	$18.99
DAVID MANN OCC AMERICAN CHOPPER SIGNED TRIBUTE PRINT!!!	$149.99	Hulk Hogan autographed 8x10 photo COA	$18.50
70s Mego Star Trek 8" Mr Scott MOC-JAMES DOOHAN SIGNED	$149.95	Jerry O'Connell autographed 8x10 photo COA	$18.50
THE SHIELD - SEASON 4 CAST SIGNED PHOTO	$146.54	CLINT HOWARD...Signed 8x10..ANDY GRIFFITH PIC AS LEON!!	$18.50
ROY ROGERS 1955 Framed COMIC with Orig. Autograph L@@K!	$142.50	Kelly Carlson autographed 8x10 photo COA	$18.47
GUNSMOKE Cast Signed James Arness Ken Curtis Photo	$130.49	Paris Hilton autographed 8x10 photo COA	$18.01
PLAYBOY ELKE JEINSEN TV MOVIE OUTFIT direct	$124.50	~*Lk. New ~Green Acres *The Complete first season DVD	$17.75

Autographs ▶ Theater

The average sales price in this subcategory is $25.84.

	HIGH		AVG
LINDA EDER SIGNED CONCERT POSTER	$260.00	Hirschfeld Signed Richard Kiley Man of La Mancha Poster	$27.78
RAYMOND HITCHCOCK -INK signed "HITCH" photo 1923	$250.00	Kristin Chenoweth 8x10 SIGNED Wicked Bdway Photo Glinda	$26.00
ELIZABETH TAYLOR RICHARD BURTON SIGNED VINTAGE PLAYBILL	$221.00	WICKED Idina MENZEL Jennifer THOMPSON Joe MANTELLO RARE	$26.00
BROADWAY'S ZERO MOSTEL WRITES FROM BOOT CAMP WWII	$202.50	WICKED Farewell FOR GOOD Idina MENZEL Jennifer THOMPSON	$26.00
MOSS HART GEORGE S. KAUFMAN SIGNED AUTOGRAPH 1931	$169.50	HELEN FORD AUTOGRAPHED RARE 1920s PORTRAIT PHOTO	$26.00
THEATRICAL PRODUCER BILLY ROSE LETER FROM FORT WORTH	$169.37	ACTESS CATHLEEN NESBITT RELATES TRIALS TO TONY AWARDS	$26.00
WICKED Sign BEST FRIENDS Kristin CHENOWETH Idina MENZEL	$162.50	Bebe Neuwirth & Juliet Prowse (signed 8x10) Chicago	$26.00
Idina Menzel SIGNED COLOR Photo Wicked Broadway Elphaba	$152.50	RENT - Playbill ORIGINAL CAST AUTOGRAPHS 1998	$25.00
Rare, Mint UP FOR GRABS Flyer Signed by Madonna!	$150.00	KATHARINE CORNELL SIGNED AUTOGRAPH 1931 PROGRAM BARRETT	$24.99
25TH ANNUAL PUTNAM COUNTY SPELLING BEE SIGNED POSTER	$149.99	EMILY SKINNER ALICE RIPLEY SIGNED SIDE SHOW PLAYBILL	$24.99
WICKED Signed POPULAR! Kristin CHENOWETH & Idina MENZEL	$137.50	AMELIE RIVES SIGNED AUTOGRAPH THEATRE PROGRAM 1920	$24.99
SARAH BERNHARDT SIGNED AUTOGRAPH THEATRE PROGRAM 1916	$128.50	SPAMALOT SIGNED SPAM FOOD W/COA+PROOF..WOW!!!!	$24.99
OTIS SKINNER MAUDE ADAMS SIGNED AUTOGRAPH PROGRAM 1931	$123.51	WICKED Signed Norbert & Kristin CHENOWETH Idina MENZEL	$24.99
COLE PORTER SIGNED 1950 PLAYBILL RARE AUTOGRAPHED W/COA	$112.50	JERRY HERMAN RARE SIGNED 'MILK&HONEY' MUSIC SHEET W/COA	$24.95
LILLIAN GISH REPORTS TO COLUMNIST FROM CHICAGO LENGTHY	$112.50	Liza Minnelli Signed Note c-1965 TORCHIA ESTATE	$24.95

Autographs ▶ Other

The average sales price in this subcategory is $44.62.

	HIGH		AVG
WALT DISNEY Signed LADY AND THE TRAMP Book 1953	$4,150.00	MIA HAMM AUTOGRAPHED SIGNED PHOTO HOT SEXY	$51.01
DENNIS THE MENACE-1957 Orig. Art-Signed Hank Ketchum	$998.00	John F. Kennedy Jr. Signed Framed Glass Display+COA	$51.00
Hank William Jr signed never player Washburn Guitar	$650.00	ANDY WARHOL AUTOGRAPH SIGNED 3X5 CARD	$51.00
Armstrong, Collins, Aldrin, Jr.: Apollo 11 Autographs	$621.00	hat signed by loretta lynn	$50.00
1970 Topps WAY OUT WHEELS FULL WAX PACK BOX 48ct !!	$610.00	BETTIE PAGE SIGNED ORIGINAL VINTAGE SEXY COLOR 8x10 PIC	$49.99
BEATLES-SOMETIME IN N.Y.C.-JOHN LENNON-genesis pub.	$350.00	Joe E Brown (1892-1973), Comic Star, Letter	$49.95
Eminem Autographed Brick from 8 Mile Road (24th of 30)	$304.00	Authentic Signed Photo of Dalai Lama with Envelope	$45.00
HOWARD HUGHES FABRIC AND NAILS FROM SPRUCE GOOSE	$207.51	President Gerald Ford Signed 8 x 10	$45.00
Frank Sinatra Scrapbooks, Autograph, Photos, Tickets...	$182.50	RINGO STARR SIGNED ALBUM "ROTOGRAVURE" THE BEATLES	$42.69
LANCE ARMSTRONG SIGNED 2005 8X10 PHOTO W/PROOF	$182.50	Slaughterhouse Five author Kurt Vonnegut signed book!	$42.00
FRANK SINATRA SIGNED AUTOGRAPH RAT PACK	$180.27	STAN LEE MARVEL X-MEN SPIDERMAN "RARE" SIGNED CARD	$41.03
Steve Perry Signed Gallery Print (Autographed Journey)	$150.00	WTQR Autographed Shirt - Angie Ward!!	$41.00
Kurt Vonnegut art prints - unique art created by author	$137.50	One2One–Hal Sparks on Cover, signed by Hal Sparks	$40.00
(Hollywood) John Ford, Signed Postcard, 1957	$122.50	MARISA MILLER Signed 8x10 TINY HOTPANTS - SEXY BUTT	$40.00
Helmut Newton They are coming NUDE original signed	$117.50	HOT! SEXY! FISHNETS ASIA ARGENTO AUTO 8X10-COA!	$40.00

Movie Memorabilia ▶ Ads, Flyers

The average sales price in this subcategory is $7.24.

	HIGH		AVG
Rare 1936 Lucille Ball RC Royal Crown Cola Sign 28" NR	$149.99	DAKOTA FANNING Venice mag Billy Corgan Ioan Gruffudd	$7.95
FANTASTIC Four 4 Jessica Alba HOT Movie Banner HUGE NEW	$99.99	GLADIATOR Connie Nielson lounging Russell Crowe ad	$7.95
LOT OF (10) GENE AUTRY PHOTO POSTCARD STURDIBOY SHIRTS	$62.98	GLADIATOR Russell Crowe washes hands Best Actor OscarAd	$7.95
rare MEL BROOKS YOUNG FRANKENSTEIN Promo	$45.00	GLADIATOR Russell Crowe Coliseum crowd Ridley Scott ad	$7.95
LORD OF THE RINGS Fellowship Arwen Frodo ringwraiths ad	$24.15	FRASIER KELSEY GRAMMER JANE LEEVES EMMY RECORD AD	$7.90
LORD OF THE RINGS FELLOWSHIP river horse Ringwraiths ad	$19.95	FRASIER KELSEY GRAMMER JANE LEEVES EMMY WIN AD	$7.90
LILO AND STITCH book with ducks Best Animated Oscar ad	$17.00	CHARLIE AND THE CHOCOLATE FACTORY Johnny Depp ad Willy	$7.75
JAG DAVID JAMES ELLIOTT CATHERINE BELL EMMY AD LARGE	$15.00	40s HOLLYWOOD CANTEEN movie ad SHICKSHINNY PA 62 STARS	$7.00
Biohazard Neon Sign Danger Evil Display Light Signs 385	$14.99	[2 of these sold for $7.00 each]	
The Aristocrats Movie Poster UNRATED 27x40 Rare NEW	$14.95	LILO AND STITCH w/ jar & bottle Oscar ad Best Animated	$6.95
Godfather Two Men Portrait Painting Poster 22x34	$13.95	PHANTOM OF THE OPERA Emmy Rossum Best Actress Oscar ad	$6.95
HUGE LOT OF MOVIE ADS FROM 1936 and 1938!	$12.50	FINDING NEVERLAND Johnny Depp Freddie Highmore Oscar ad	$6.95
FRASIER KELSEY GRAMMER JANE LEEVES	$12.00	GLADIATOR Crowe Joaquin Phoenix Connie Nelson Oscar ad	$6.95
FAREWELL AD+BONUS 5		GLADIATOR Russell Crowe w/ King Best Art Direction ad	$6.95
LOT OF (10) MINT ORIGINAL HOPALONG CASSIDY FAN LETTER	$11.01	GLADIATOR Russell Crowe Ridley Scott Best Director ad	$6.95
SIDEWAYS Virginia Madsen Thomas Hayden Church cast ad	$11.00	GONE WITH THE WIND - FRAMED PRINT – MUST SEE !!!!!	$6.49

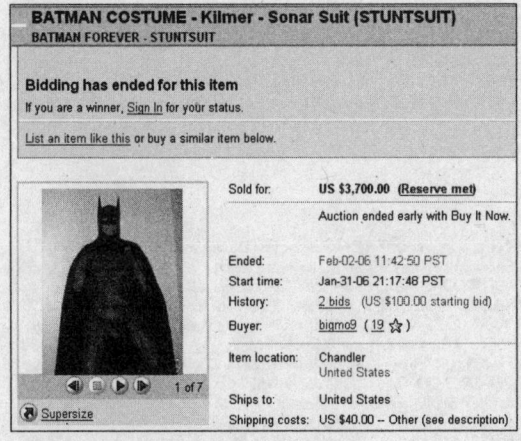

BATMAN COSTUME - Kilmer - Sonar Suit (STUNTSUIT)
BATMAN FOREVER - STUNTSUIT

Bidding has ended for this item
If you are a winner, Sign In for your status.

List an item like this or buy a similar item below.

Sold for:	**US $3,700.00** (Reserve met)
	Auction ended early with Buy It Now.
Ended:	Feb-02-06 11:42:50 PST
Start time:	Jan-31-06 21:17:48 PST
History:	2 bids (US $100.00 starting bid)
Buyer:	bigmo9 (19 ☆)
Item location:	Chandler, United States
Ships to:	United States
Shipping costs:	US $40.00 -- Other (see description)

1 of 7 | Supersize

Framed Phantom mask, Gerard Butler +autographs: Phantom
Lloyd Webber's The Phantom of the Opera Official Sale

Bidding has ended for this item
If you are a winner, Sign In for your status.

List an item like this or buy a similar item below.

Winning bid:	**GBP 4,800.00** (Approximately US $8,370.24)
Ended:	Feb-02-06 14:00:00 PST
Start time:	Jan-30-06 14:00:00 PST
History:	38 bids (GBP 1.00 starting bid)
Winning bidder:	felene (664 ☆)
Item location:	London, United Kingdom

Movie Memorabilia ▶ Apparel

The average sales price in this subcategory is $30.53.

	HIGH		AVG
Gone With the Wind Black Velvet Coat Jacket Robe	$1,036.12	Must Love Dogs purse+soundtrack+ 3 gift cards!!	$36.00
SPIDERMAN 2 COSTUME W/ SILK SCREENED WEBS AND ACRYLIC!!	$674.99	Fat Bastard Inflatable Costume/Austin Powers	$36.00
Russell Crowe's Boxing Glove from movie Cinderella Man	$610.00	TV ROOM glasses WONKA Charlie	$35.00
C.G.P. "Warlock" Michael Myers Mask Not Jason Or Freddy	$595.00	Chocolate Factory GOGGLES	
Phantom of the Opera ~ Swarovski Mask Pendant Necklace	$335.99	Matrix Reloaded Messenger Bag, NR!	$35.00
[2 of these sold for $335.99 each]		SCARFACE CLOTHING TRUST NO ONE POLO SHIRT XL	$34.99
Light Bat Cape Latex professional real look for costume	$299.99	TV ROOM glasses WONKA Charlie Chocolate Factory GOGGLES	$31.50
Phantom of the Opera ~ Swarovski Mask Pendant Necklace	$285.99	Limited Edition Wizard of Oz Fossil Watch	$31.00
Phantom of the Opera movie Swarovski Emmy Rossum's pin	$185.99	Prisoner of Azkaban, Sirius Black work shirt	$31.00
Elektra w Jennifer Garner Movie Promo Item Karate Outfit	$167.50	Willy Wonka TV Room Goggles (Charlie Chocolate Factory)	$30.00
Star Trek Movie Uniform Costume - Star Trek II – VI	$162.50	goggles Riddick and Pitch Black style, Vin Diesel	$30.00
matrix golf umbrella NEW! VERY RARE! keanu reeves	$160.00	Sky High Backpack, T-Shirt & School Supplies Promo Item	$30.00

	$150.00	goggles Riddick and Pitch Black style, Vin Diesel	$30.00
Star Trek Movie Uniform Costume - Star Trek II – VI	$150.00	goggles Riddick and Pitch Black style, Vin Diesel	$30.00
CAPTAIN AMERICA EASY RIDER NOS 1970'S HELMET	$129.99	Bat Costume Suit Utility Belt Gold Resin Buckle Prop	$29.99
Star Trek Movie Uniform Costume - Star Trek II – VI	$124.95	The Devil's Rejects Last Supper Promo Beach Towel L@@K	$28.50
Charlie and the Chocolate Factory Wonka Jacket BLACK	$120.00	Willy Wonka Goggles Glasses Charlie Chocolate Factory	$28.00

Movie Memorabilia ▶ Lobby Cards

The average sales price in this subcategory is $18.76.

	HIGH		AVG
INCREDIBLE SHRINKING MAN, 1957 Giant Cat Lobby Card #5	$320.00	GENE AUTRY & SMILEY SUNSET IN WYOMING	$20.00
JOHN WAYNE FLYING TIGERS MINT TC	$300.00	WILLIAM BOYD HOPALONG RIDES AGAIN	$20.00
Abbott and Costello Meet The Killer, Boris Karloff TC	$193.50	BATMAN Adam West ORIGINAL Lobby Card MEXICO NR!!	$19.99
JOHN WAYNE SHE WORE A YELLOW RIBBON	$150.00	THE THING FROM ANOTHER WORLD Classic SCI-FI Lobby Card	$19.99
JUNGLE CAPTIVE—Rondo Hatton and Paula the Ape Woman!	$150.00	BOB STEELE DOOMED AT SUNDOWN	$19.95
MONSTER THAT CHALLENGED WORLD, Orig 1957 Monster LC #8	$122.50	SERIAL MAN WITH THE STEEL WHIP 2 LC color	$19.95
I MARRIED A MONSTER FROM OUTER SPACE, 1958 Alien LC #8	$99.99	ROY ROGERS SUSANNA PASS 2 LC	$19.95
MONSTER THAT CHALLENGED WORLD, Orig 1957 Monster LC #2	$99.99	GENE AUTRY " RED RIVER VALLEY "1936 RARE	$18.60
PHANTOM OF THE OPERA, Orig 1962 Hammer LC #5, Best Card	$85.85	Clint Eastwood PLAY MISTY FOR ME 2LC	$17.49
SPIDER, Original 1958 AIP Sci-Fi LC #7, Monster Card	$76.59	John Wayne Fort Apache Mexican Lobby Card	$16.51
CARY GRANT / IRENE DUNNE PENNY SERENADE	$76.00	VINCENT PRICE "THE MAD MAGICIAN" 1954 ORG LOBBY CARD	$16.05
INVADERS FROM MARS, Orig 1953 Classic Sci-fi Lobby Card	$74.99	ALIEN Original SIGOURNEY WEAVER Sci-Fi SEXXY Lobby Card	$15.99
DINOSAURUS, Original 1960 Sci-Fi LC #8, Monster Card	$71.00	SAUCER MEN Horror THE SHIP OF MONSTERS Lobby Card LOOK!	$15.71
INCREDIBLE SHRINKING MAN, Orig '57 Sci-Fi Lobby Card #3	$69.00	ROY ROGERS IDAHO	$15.50
Ultra Rare CASABLANCA Original MEXICAN Lobby Card NR!!!	$64.73	TIM HOLT ARIZONA RANGER	$15.45

Movie Memorabilia ▶ Photos

The average sales price in this subcategory is $10.81.

	HIGH		AVG
Rare James Bond You Only Live Twice Photo	$58.00	Rare James Bond You Only Live Twice Photo	$12.49
'93 LOT OF 8 "RETURN OF THE LIVING DEAD III" PR PIX	$46.00	[2 of these sold for $12.49 each]	
Rare James Bond You Only Live Twice Photo	$45.50	Rare Original Steely Dan Promotional Photo	$12.25
Rare James Bond Thunderball Photo	$44.50	Rare Original Dorothy Lee Photo	$11.61
Rare Original Nat King Cole Trio Photo	$40.00	Jeffrey Chandler Roberta Tovey High Wind In Jamaica Pic	$11.50
[2 of these sold for $40.00 each]		TANE MCCLURE Agency Photo LEGALLY BLONDE	$11.50
Rare Hayley Mills The Parent Trap Photo	$38.55	SKEET ULRICH Agent Photo SCREAM	$11.15
RARE PHOTO of MARILYN MONROE - at JFK gala	$37.00	ERIC BRAEDEN Agent Photo RAT PATROL, YOUNG & RESTLESS	$11.06
Rare Edward Mulhare Photo The Ghost and Mrs. Muir	$36.00	RACHAEL DAYNE Agency Photo THE BLUE ROOM	$11.00
Rare Edward Mulhare Photo The Ghost and Mrs. Muir	$35.00	Rare Rita Hayworth Photo	$10.59
31130 SANDRA OH Photo AGENCY Portrait 1990s	$34.99	Rare James Bond Thunderball Photo	$10.50
RARE PHOTO of MARILYN MONROE - at JFK gala	$32.56	[2 of these sold for $10.50 each]	
CHRISTOPHER McDANIEL	$31.00	Jeffrey Chandler Roberta Tovey High Wind In Jamaica Pic	$10.50
Agency Photo 2001 MANIACS		[3 of these sold for $10.50 each]	
TODD CAHOON Agency Photo	$31.00	Rare Original Cliff Richard Promo Photo	$10.50
PACKING HEAT, LADDER 49		lenticular Schwartzenegger TERMINATOR 2	$10.50
Rare Original Norma Shearer Photo	$30.00	Rare Johnny Depp P Photo	$10.50
Kevin Sorbo Karina Lombard Kull the Conqueror Photo	$30.00	Rare Nicholas Clay Night Digger Photo	$10.50

Movie Memorabilia ▶ Posters

The average sales price in this subcategory is $15.12.

	HIGH		AVG
ORG Movie Mylars/Posters 299 All Genres 5"x25" NO Res.	$204.47	GOLDENEYE brosnan 007 BOND high gloss DS poster ROLLED	$17.50
Tim Burton "CORPSE BRIDE"-set of 2 vinyl banner. MINT.	$101.98	Adam Sandler BILLY MADISON Movie Poster Mint!	$17.50
DAY THE EARTH STOOD STILL SCI-FI ONE SHEET MOVIE POSTER	$99.99	HIGH FIDELITY Orig Movie Poster John Cusack Jack Black	$17.49
THE CHRONICALS OF NARNIA HUGE MOVIE BANNER L@@K	$99.00	RareClassic STAND BY ME Movie Poster River Phoenix Mint	$16.99
d423 RUSHMORE linen 1sheet '98 Schwartzman, Bill Murray	$91.00	Classic FAST TIMES AT RIDGEMONT HIGH Movie Poster Mint!	$16.99
THE CORPSE BRIDE MOVIE BANNER SET JOHNNY DEPP AND BRIDE	$81.00	Classic HOOSIERS Movie Poster Basketball Mint	$16.98
SNOW WHITE deluxe mirror mylar 93R POSTER rolled	$78.00	COOL HAND LUKE film poster PAUL NEWMAN 27x40	$16.00
ENDLESS SUMMER II D/S Original Movie Poster 1994	$77.00	STAR TREK FIRST CONTACT LOBBY CARD SET OF 8 1996	$15.52
The Matrix Movie Poster	$68.51	Cool BAD BOYS II Orig Movie Poster Will Smith Mint!	$14.99
d382 JACKIE BROWN linen teaser 1sh97 sexy Bridget Fonda	$66.00	Cool DIE ANOTHER DAY Orig Gun Movie Poster	$14.99
NIGHTMARE BEFORE CHRISTMAS burton DS poster ROLLED	$56.00	WHEN WE WERE KINGS ORIGINAL MOVIE POSTER / M. ALI	$14.99
LITTLE MERMAID animation DISNEY ariel DS poster ROLLED	$51.00	Tarantino's PULP FICTION Movie Poster Uma Thurman Mint!	$14.98
100 ORIGINAL MAINSTREAM MOVIE & VIDEO POSTERS! (4 lots)	$49.95	Cool Schindler's List Movie Poster Mint!	$14.98
A WOMAN UNDER THE INFLUENCE Film Poster John Cassavetes	$45.44	CHARLIE AND THE CHOCOLATE FACTORY Movie Poster Mint!	$14.98
SILENCE OF THE LAMBS foster HOPKINS ds POSTER adv.	$41.57	BIG FISH Orig Movie Poster Tim Burton Ewan McGregor	$14.98

Movie Memorabilia ▶ Pressbooks

The average sales price in this subcategory is $20.77.

	HIGH		AVG
THE HUSTLER;CUE BALL & STICK STYLE:US ONE SHEET	$461.00	VINTAGE D W GRIFFITH SOUVENIR PRESSBOOK LILLIAN GISH	$22.51
EXHIBITOR YEARBOOK 1933-34 MAJESTIC PICTURES	$225.00	1953 Marilyn Monroe Niagara Movie Pressbook	$22.50
THE LITTLE PRINCESS:SHIRLEY TEMPLE:BRIT CAMPAIGN BOOK	$202.49	Lake Placid Serenade Movie Program 1944 Promo Booklet?	$21.50
CIMARRON:RICHARD DIX:US PRESS BOOK	$162.50	JAMES BOND Dr. No and Goldfinger 1966 RR Pressbook!	$21.50
KARLOFF/BEFORE I HANG/u.s.pressbook	$160.00	Man Bait - Bad Blonde pressbook DIANA DORS Payton 1953	$21.50
Toys McCoy GI Jane Marilyn Monroe Troops Korea Barbie	$150.00	GRAUMANS CHINESE THEATRE Souvenir Book 1946 Signed	$20.73
1936 Tarzan Escapes Publicity Campaign Book	$140.58	2001 A Space Odyssey Facts For Editorial Reference Book	$20.60

1939 Tarzan Finds a Son Publicity Campaign Book	$140.58	'56=WAR AND PEACE=Pressbook=Audrey Hepburn, Henry Fonda	$20.51
BUCK JONES~PRESS BOOK~1932~ WHITE EAGLE*	$139.50	Girls on the Beach pressbook BEACH BOYS Lesley Gore 65	$20.50
THE UNHOLY NIGHT:ROLAND YOUNG:BRITISH PRESS	$124.72	GIRLS IN PRISON / HOT-ROD GIRL, Combo Pressbook	$20.41
1953= 5000 FINGERS OF DR. T =Pressbook=Hayes, Healy	$113.61	I'D RATHER BE RICH:SANDRA DEE/ANDY WILLIAMS:US PRESS	$20.05
ALICE ADAMS:K HEPBURN:ORIGINAL USA PRESS BOOK	$111.50	ANGELICA MARIA IN LOVE & ENGAGED Original Pressbook	$20.00
LITTLE MISS BROADWAY:SHIRLEY TEMPLE: BRITISH PRESS BOOK	$103.51	ANGELICA MARIA SOMEONE WANTS TO KILL US Origi Pressbook	$20.00
1932 TRADE ANNUAL. United Artists Mickey Mouse brochure	$100.00	LANA TURNER THE BIG CUBE Original Pressbook	$20.00
1949 Marilyn Monroe Marx Bros. Movie Pressbook	$100.00	Fastest Guitar Alive pressbook ROY ORBISON Joan Freeman	$20.00

Movie Memorabilia ▸ Programs

The average sales price in this subcategory is $17.03.

	HIGH		AVG
HOWARD HUGHES AUTOGRAPH W/COA HELLS ANGELS	$214.45	RITA HAYWORTH FRENCH MAGAZINE	$18.01
MARILYN MONROE EARLY MAGAZINE 1951	$129.12	75th Acadamy Awards Board of Governors Ball Program	$18.00
ORIGINAL MOVIE PROGRAM Dealers Lot DAWN OF DEAD NR CH56	$106.27	ACADEMY AWARDS 57TH PRESENTATION PROGRAM 1969	$17.88
7 VINTAGE MOTION PICTURE MOVIE THEATRE PROGRAMS 1920s	$102.50	ACADEMY AWARDS 58TH PRESENTATION PROGRAM 1969	$17.87
Japanese STAR WARS 6 PROGRAM BOX very limited edition!	$100.00	ORIGINAL MOVIE PROGRAM Romeo & Juliet OLIVIA HUSSEY xx	$17.30
ABBA the Movie Japan SET	$86.00	THE LONGEST DAY Great Movie Pictorial 140 Photos 1962	$17.00
5 Different Signed Sports Tickets -Hockey Canada v USSR	$77.52	DOC SAVAGE George Pal Kenneth Robeson Ron Ely Japan Pgm	$16.99
ORIGINAL PROGRAM Dealers Lot DAWN OF DEAD NR CR72 xx	$76.58	ORIGINAL MOVIE PROGRAM LOT Grease ANNIE CE265 xx	$16.78
ORIGINAL PROGRAM Dealers Lot DAWN OF DEAD NR CR77 xx	$76.08	ORIGINAL MOVIE PROGRAM LOT Conformist GODFATHER CR55 xx	$16.58
BACK TO THE FUTURE Panini sticker book and 180 stickers	$67.00	ORIGINAL MOVIE PROGRAM LOT Glory Boy HOLMES CR65 xx	$16.58
All Quiet on the Western Front World Premiere Program	$65.00	THE SISTERS:ERROL FLYNN/BETTE DAVIS:CINEGRAM	$16.50
1959 ACADEMY AWARD WINNERS AND ACTORS DIRECTORY #83	$60.95	BRIGITTE BARDOT VINTAGE POSTCARD	$16.50
Dean Martin Jerry Lewis 1955 concert program book	$56.00	The Prince and the Pauper~Orig 1937 Movie Book~Twain	$16.50
RARE! Hugh Jackman Oklahoma London Theatre Program	$51.00	Story of Motion Pictures Book Fox theatre corp. 1929	$16.49
Gone With The Wind 1939 Movie Premier Program	$51.00	SYD CHAPLIN GALLOPING FISH ORIG PROGRAM 1924 CONKLIN	$16.01

Movie Memorabilia ▸ Props

The average sales price in this subcategory is $95.71.

	HIGH		AVG
LIFE SIZE DON POST STAR WARS STORMTROOPER STATUE PROP	$3,550.50	LATEX COSTUME MASK SUPERHERO CAPTAIN AMERICA	$100.00
Life Size Swimming Alien Warrior Lifesize hanging Prop	$2,661.11	HIGHLANDER AUTOGRAPHED SWORD!!!!!	$100.00
ORGINAL 1975 Don Post Studios Captain Kirk Mask Myers	$1,000.00	Star Wars DARTH NIHILUS MASK Old Republic II - LATEX -	$100.00
James Bond 007 1965 Attache Case	$899.99	Lord of the Rings: The One Ring Sterling Silver & Gold	$99.99
SERIES 2 HELLRAISER GAME,	$837.00	[3 of these sold for $99.99 each]	
MONOPOLY, PINHEAD RARE!		PREDATOR COSTUME MASK movie prop with HELMET Wearable	$99.00
RARE CHARLIE AND THE CHOCOLATE	$799.99	THOR/ Hammer of Thor, Metal prop	$99.00
FACTORY WONKA CANE		Freddy Krueger Latex Mask! not Jason myers prop NEW!	$96.00
Star Wars Life Size Jabba The Hutt Bust 1:1 Lifesize	$750.00	Blank Firing Replica CZ75 Pistol Prop Gun CZ-75, nickel	$94.95
SDS Imperial Stormtrooper Helmet!	$580.78	[2 of these sold for $94.95 each]	
Stormtrooper Armor Prop Kit	$576.00	Arwen's Evenstar Pendant Necklace NEW Licensed	$92.00
Stormtrooper Armor Prop Kit	$575.00	45" Red Rider Leg Lamp A Christmas Story	$91.00
David Morgan Ten-Foot Bullwhip #455	$550.00	GLADIATOR movie-Statue of MAXIMUS	$89.99
Mad Lab Atomic Brain Life Support 14 Lights Prop	$515.00	Blank Firing Replica Beretta Cougar Pistol Gun	$89.95
Richard Coyle Blade Runner C&S Blaster Movie Prop	$455.00	BLANK FIRING COLT MILITARY 1911 SEMI-AUTO GUN	$88.00
DARTH VADER ESB FIBERGLASS HELMET STAR WARS PROP	$449.00	WALKER TEXAS RANGER JACKET WORN ON SHOW BY CHUCK NORRIS	$87.50
Crypt Keeper Life Size Tales From the Crypt	$420.00	Blank Firing Replica Beretta 92F Compact Pistol Gun	$86.95

Movie Memorabilia ▸ Scripts

The average sales price in this subcategory is $26.92.

	HIGH		AVG
HARRY POTTER Script Chamber of Secrets COA Signed by 7	$455.00	THE GODFATHER MOVIE SCRIPT 7 AUTOGRAPHS - MARLON BRANDO	$29.00
Twilight Zone Rod Serling Original TV Television Script	$406.99	HOUSE OF 1000 CORPSES SCRIPT SIGNED ZOMBIE AND MORE!	$29.00
HARRY POTTER SIGNED BY 9 SORCERERS STONE MOVIE SCRIPT	$356.00	EDWARD SCISSORHANDS MOVIE SCRIPT SIGNED X7 *JOHNNY DEPP	$28.01
HARRY POTTER PRISONER OF AZKABAN SIGNED MOVIE SCRIPT	$265.00	THE CROW MOVIE SCRIPT SIGNED BRANDON LEE!	$28.00
Autographed Stealth Script - Jamie Foxx, Jessica Biel	$255.16	SEABISCUIT SIGNED MOVIE SCRIPT	$27.50
HARRY POTTER SIGNED BY 9 CHAMBER SECRETS MOVIE SCRIPT	$227.75	KATE JACKSON WORKING SCRIPT MAKING LOVE CHARLIES ANGELS	$27.00
HITCHHIKERS GUIDE ORIGINAL USED SCRIPT COMPLETE	$217.55	HOUSE OF 1000 CORPSES SIGNED SCRIPT BY 5 *ROB ZOMBIE	$27.00
SIGNED HARRY POTTER SORCERERS STONE SCRIPT x12 wCOA	$202.50	NATIONAL TREASURE SIGNED SCRIPT CAGE+VOIGHT+KEITEL +6X	$26.51
LORD OF THE RINGS SIGNED BY 8 MOVIE SCRIPT	$152.50	PIRATES OF THE CARIBBEAN - SIGNED SCRIPT 6X DEPP BLOOM	$26.00
CHARLEY CHASE Hal Roach Studios 1925 original script	$128.50	STAR TREK THE WRATH OF KHAN SIGNED *JAMES DOOHAN SCOTTY	$26.00
The Devil's Rejects Original Script Rob Zombie Rare!!	$128.02	Real CAST SIGNED Mr. and Mrs. Smith SCRIPT Brad Pitt	$26.00
Ken Kesey, Unpublished Screenplay, Last Go 'Round, Rare	$103.49	EDWARD SCISSORHANDS SCRIPT SIGNED DEPP BURTON RYDER	$26.00
1966 Elvis Presley Double Trouble MGM Script	$102.50	Lupe Velez Estate Morning, Noon and Night ~ Script	$26.00
MASH THE FINAL TV EPISODE SCRIPT SIGNED BY 6 ALAN ALDA!	$86.00	PIRATES OF THE CARIBBEAN CAST SIGNED SCRIPT JOHNNY DEPP	$26.00
HEAT MOVIE SCRIPT - ROBERT DE NIRO, AL PACINO	$80.85	Star Wars: All three original movie scripts	$25.00

Music Memorabilia ▸ Country

The average sales price in this subcategory is $10.14.

	HIGH		AVG
MELISSA ETHERIDGE ROAD LESS TRAVELED 4 PIC PHOTO SET	$35.00	Jessica Andrews 17 HOT CMAFEST 2005 PHOTOS	$12.00
MELISSA ETHERIDGE ROAD LESS TRAVELED 4 PIC PHOTO SET	$34.55	MARTINA McBRIDE GUITAR PICK + LOCAL CREW BONUS	$10.50
RARE MARTINA McBRIDE 2005 UPDATE PRESS KIT w5COLOR PICS	$29.99	Dixie Chicks local crew shirt XL George Bush	$9.99
MELISSA ETHERIDGE ROAD LESS TRAVELED 4 PIC PHOTO SET	$29.99	DIXIE CHICKS! TOP OF THE WORLD 2003 TOUR BLACK SHIRT LG	$8.99

Martina McBride 2'x1' Photo Poster Concert Limited Ed.	$26.00	DIXIE CHICKS set(6) MAGNETS, music	$8.50
Rare Early MARTINA McBRIDE 1992 PROMO Album Flat Poster	$24.95	WWF Dixie Chicks Guitar Pick Lot 10 Unused	$7.50
REAL Travis Barker Rock Concert Band Drum Stick	$19.99	Beautiful MARTINA McBRIDE Casino Promo Ad $.99 NR	$7.39
NEW Gorgeous Martina McBride 8.5x11 Very Sexy Woman,WOW	$15.75	NEW Martina McBride 8.5x11 Gorgeous Closeup...WOW	$6.50
Jessica Andrews 17 HOT CMAFEST 2005 PHOTOS	$14.94	Huge MARTINA MCBRIDE Promo Poster Ad $.99 NR	$6.39
Jessica Andrews 17 HOT CMAFEST 2005 PHOTOS	$12.00	NEW Gorgeous Martina McBride 8.5x11 Very Sexy Woman,WOW	$6.00

Music Memorabilia ▶ Rock-n-Roll

NOTE *There is no average price statement for this subcategory because the prices were obtained using eBay's Completed Items feature.*

	HIGH		AVG
Beatles SET OF WHITE ALBUM PHOTOS SIGNED BY EACH BEATLE. INCREDIBLY RARE AND THE ONLY SET I'VE OFFERED EVER!	$10,850.00	MADONNA RARE **4** Candid 8x10 Hot PHOTO SET	$9.90
EXTREMELY RARE~BEATLES ROCKOLA JUKEBOX~1 OF 100~COA~NR.	$7,750.50	THE GRATEFUL DEAD JIGSAW PUZZLE 1000 PIECE~RARE	$9.90
YELLOW SUBMARINE~CD BUBBLER~MINT~LIMITED AUTH. EDITION		Michael BUBLE RaRE *3* PIC 8X10 PHOTO SET press pics	$9.90
Grateful Dead Toronto BG74 Postcard Fillmore RARE!!!	$5,101.67	ELVIS PRESLEY *HAMPTON ROADS* VCD/DVD	$9.90
Beatles NEMs Record Player Ultra Rare - Plays- Fine Shape	$4,950.00	Alan Parsons Project PYRAMID original Presskit w/photos	$9.90
Incubus Autographed DW Drumkit	$3,550.00	RARE! Every FASTER PUSSYCAT Footage on 1 VHS Tape	$9.89
Beatles OUTSTANDING ORIG 68 WHITE ALBUM FACTORY SEALED!.	$2,837.99	Johnny Rotten sex pistols Rare promotional poster 1984	$9.88
ONE OF THE BEST EXAMPLES I'VE OFFERED! NUMBERED!		BLACK CROWES, Backstage Pass (Laminated)	$9.88
Hofner President 'Stu Sutcliffe model' bass guitar	$2,599.68	BTO, Backstage Pass (Laminated) 1985 All Access	$9.88
"California Mission" signed Jerry Garcia lithograph	$2,500.00	Hard Rock Cafe MYRTLE BCH 04 City T-Shirt 4" SHOT GLASS	$9.88
Rolling Stones *K & S* Records 8 LP *LOT* . MULTI-COLOR. ORIGINAL	$2,500.00	DOORS, Backstage Pass	$9.88
US K & S RECS RELEASES - EXTREMELY LTD EDITION		THE MOTLEY CRUE, Backstage Pass (Laminated)87-88 World Tour	$9.88
BUFFALO NY ORIGINAL POSTERS ROLLING STONES 14X22 POSTER	$2,250.00	MOTLEY CRUE, Backstage Pass (Laminated)VIP	$9.88
BEATLES-SIGNED ORIGINAL AUTOGRAPHS.	$2,200.00	LED ZEPPELIN, Backstage Pass (Laminated)ALL ACCESS	$9.88
2 original singles and COA Included		GUNS N ROSES,Rare unique ORIGINAL POSTER	$9.88
RARE 1971 NEIL YOUNG WINNIPEG CONCERT POSTER BOARD	$2,151.32		
The Best Beatles Mono Butcher Cover On EBay Awesome!	$1,804.00		
Complete With Removed Trunk Slick And Mono Disc			
JIMI HENDRIX- ARE YOU EXPERIENCED-SIGNED & FRAMED ALBUM	$1,650.00		
1970's Kiss Pinball Machine	$1,525.00		

Television Memorabilia ▶ Apparel

The average sales price in this subcategory is $20.69.

	HIGH		AVG
Hilary Duff - Embroidered Jacket	$455.50	SURVIVOR 7 - Black Pearl Islands Balboa Tribe Buff –NEW	$24.95
The Adventures of Superboy (1990) Superboy's Boots	$300.00	DRAGONBALL Z BLUE BASEBALL JERSEY Size XXL	$22.99
Queer as Folk-Emmet's Pink outfit from Mikey's party	$204.50	[2 of these sold for $22.99 each]	
MARISKA HARGITAY LAW AND ORDER SVU WARDROBE/APPAREL	$202.50	The SOPRANOS HBO Hockey Jersey! Vintage CABLE SHOW	$22.49
Queer as Folk-Justin's Shirt from 401 REAL PROP SALE!	$163.50	Dukes of Hazzard Underoos SEALED Box, Long u-wear	$22.02
CATHERINE BELL/JAG WARDROBE/APPAREL	$162.50	GUINNESS BEER SOCCER STYLE 1759 IRISH SHIRT XL	$21.50
CATHERINE BELL/JAG WARDROBE/APPAREL	$152.50	Survivor PEARL ISLANDS Buff - Light Blue, Rupert's Team	$21.00
Roy Rogers Leather Chaps & Vest - Kids Vintage antique!	$150.01	the west wing Tshirt XL NEW	$20.55
RARE Roy Rogers Felt Chaps & Vest Western Suit sz10 Box	$129.00	*** DUKES OF HAZZARD ROSCO ENOS SHERIFF DEPT. PATCH ***	$20.51
Buffy - Sarah Michelle Gellar Studio Wardrobe w/ C.O.A.	$127.50	Set of 3 Three Stooges watches c 1990	$20.50
NIKKI COX LAS VEGAS WARDROBE/APPAREL	$105.35	6 million dollar man steve austin metal lunchbox +	$20.50
Actual Morrigan Costume worn on the TV show Hercules	$100.00	Aqua teen hunger force socks ADULT SWIM comic con RARE!	$20.50
[2 of these sold for $100.00 each]		Rare WWF Hulkamania Bandana	$20.50
BATGIRL BIRDS OF PREY GLOVES	$100.00	JOAN OF ARCADIA YELLOW HIGHSCHOOL FOOTBALL UNIFORM NR	$20.50
NIKKI COX LAS VEGAS WARDROBE/APPAREL	$82.45	ADULT SWIM MESSENGER BAG - courier bag - NEW	$20.50
MARISKA HARGITAY LAW AND ORDER SVU WARDROBE/APPAREL	$79.00	SURVIVOR SEASON 1 - BORNEO BUFF + TOTEM DISPLAY - NEW	$20.50

Television Memorabilia ▶ Photos

The average sales price in this subcategory is $12.83.

	HIGH		AVG
Photograph & old negative- JAMES STACY - Lancer	$172.46	GARY COLE GORGEOUS WANTED 8 X 10 PHOTO	$14.99
JAG, 1 NEW T-SHIRT SEASON 10TH	$112.50	STAR TREK SHATNER/NIMOY ON THE SET CANDID RARE PHOTO	$14.99
1 JAG SCRIPT EPISODE #200 "WHAT IF?" ORIGINAL	$110.00	NEWHART CAST FINAL EPISODE ORIGINAL 1990 CBS TV PHOTO	$14.99
Photograph & old negative - PERNELL ROBERTS	$102.60	General Hospital Steve Burton Jason Morgan GHFCW	$14.00
JAG, CAST AND CREW PICTURE 5TH SEASON 1999-2000	$102.50	General Hospital Rebecca Herbst Liz Webber Ted King	$13.16
Photograph & old negative- Wayne Maunder-James Stacy-	$92.05	General Hospital Kelly Monaco Autographed Photo	$13.01
JAG ALL EPISODE CAST LIST ALPHABETICALLY BY ACTOR	$91.00	COMBAT! Vic Morrow as Sgt Saunders 8x10	$12.50
The SOPRANOS mafia mob entire cast framed dinner photo	$79.00	OLIVIA WILDE blonde agency photo THE OC O.C. Alex Kelly	$12.50
VINTAGE 7 B&W PHOTO HOGANS HEROES COLLECTOR SPORTS CARD	$68.85	Bonanza - Lorne Greene and Pernell Roberts	$11.99
Photograph & old negative- WAYNE MAUNDER -Andrew Duggan	$60.00	THE DUKES OF HAZZARD CAST ALL 8 SIGNED AUTOGRAPHED 8x10	$11.50
KATE MULGREW agency headshot photo VOYAGER: STAR TREK	$53.00	JULIET LANDAU Agency Photo	$11.00
VLADIMIR KULICH Celebrity Photo ANGEL	$49.00	BRIGITTE BAKO head shot RED SHOE DIARIES	$11.00
General Hospital Kelly Monaco Dancing With The Stars	$46.00	STAR TREK CAST SPACE SHUTTLE ENTERPRISE 8x10 PHOTO	$10.99
Photograph & old negative - WAYNE MAUNDER	$46.00	LYDIE DENIER agency headshot photo TARZAN ACAPULCO HEAT	$10.62
1 JAG SCRIPT EP. #100 "BOOMERANG" (PART 1) ORIGINAL	$41.00	General Hospital Tamara Braun/Rick Hearst Color Photo	$10.50

Television Memorabilia ▶ Pins, Buttons

The average sales price in this subcategory is $5.95.

	HIGH		AVG
WAREHOUSE FIND (6) HOPALONG		THE LONE RANGER T V PIN ——— L@@K	$5.95
CASSIDY 6 POINT METAL BADGE	$64.00	ROY ROGERS and TRIGGER PIN ——— L@@K	$5.95
GHOULARDI VINTAGE PIN	$64.00	GET SMART T V RING ——— L@@K	$5.95
the Man from UNCLE original studio U.N.C.L.E Agent pin	$41.07	GET SMART TV SHOW RING ——— L@@K	$5.95
1950's Rocky Jones Space Ranger Wings	$39.98	ROY ROGERS and TRIGGER PIN ——— L@@K	$5.95
LOT OF (12) ORIGINAL 1940's SUPERMAN PINBACK BUTTONS !	$36.00	THE LONE RANGER T V PIN ——— L@@K	$5.95
QUEER AS FOLK 10 - 1" Magnets gay lesbian	$34.00	[3 of these sold for $5.95 each]	
COMBAT TV, RECON 2000 Button, dog tags, Patch set.	$31.01	LAGUNA BEACH Pins/Buttons MTV OC SURF CLUB BADGE RARE	$5.80
9 CBC AWG (arctic winter games) NWT 2002 pin/pins	$29.00	Vintage Dale Evans Pin Pinback Button Badge	$5.75
Three Stooges Vintage Pin back Button Larry Curly Moe	$26.99	10 Alf 1" Buttons Retro Emo A.L.F. 80's DVD	$5.75
1950 Space Captain Jet CBS TV Show Channel 2 Pinback	$24.99	1955 Robin Hood Iron on patch	$5.61
Ten Vintage Western Collectible Pins Hopalong Cassidy	$22.28	AGem SALE 1ct emerald BLUE TOPAZ PENDANT$.99	$5.50
3 CBC AWG (arctic winter games) NWT 2000 pin/pins	$21.75	DARIA PINS/BUTTONS PUNK ROCK BADGES MTV	$5.50
ACADEMY AWARDS OSCARS PIN BLK/GOLD	$21.50	THE OC PINS/BUTTONS 7 NEW RARE I HEART SETH COHEN BADGE	$5.50
PEN HOLDER FROM HIT SERIES	$20.50	CARNIVALE 5 - 1" buttons pins dvd indie punk nick stahl	$5.50
BARBER SHOP PENS INCLUDED		LOST Pins/Buttons Complete First Season Badges GET LOST	$5.50

1974 Topps The Six Million Dollar Man Partial Pack BOX

Bidding has ended for this item

If you are a winner, Sign In for your status.

List an item like this or buy a similar item below.

Winning bid:	**US $6,600.00**
Ended:	Feb-08-06 20:06:15 PST
Start time:	Feb-01-06 20:06:15 PST
History:	37 bids (US $9.95 starting bid)
Winning bidder:	member9290453 (454 ⭐)
Item location:	New York
United States

Television Memorabilia ▶ Posters

The average sales price in this subcategory is $9.93.

	HIGH		AVG
ROBERT LANSING TWELVE O'CLOCK HIGH POSTER TV GUIDE 60?S	$91.99	CARTOON NETWORK TEEN TITANS SUBWAY BANNER XL	$9.99
ALIAS 4x6 Bus Shelter Poster 6ft Jennifer Garner	$81.00	Everwood Original Promotional Poster!!	$9.99
PETER JENNINGS POSTER	$81.00	CAT CHOPPER / ORANGE COUNTY CHOPPERS POSTER	$9.99
[2 of these sold for $81.00 each]		SEX & THE CITY SARAH JESSICA PARKER BUS POSTER 4 X 6	$9.99
GIANT 6 FT 70'S FARRAH FAWCETT/ CHARLIES ANGELS POSTER	$76.00	ANDY WARHOL 15 MINUTES OF FAME B/W 24x37 POSTER	$9.99
The OC 4x6 Bus Shelter Poster 6ft	$71.00	1996 Friends Soda Shop Poster Courtney Cox	$9.99
BATTLESTAR GALACTICA 4x6 Bus Shelter Poster 6ft	$57.50	SMASHING PUMPKINS SIAMESE DREAM 24x37 POSTER	$9.99
ROBERT LANSING TWELVE O'CLOCK HIGH ARG. POSTER 60'S	$51.50	GET SMART "CONTROL Wants You!" Poster *	$9.99
PETER JENNINGS - ABC WORLD NEWS TONIGHT POSTER	$51.00	[2 of these sold for $9.99 each]	
1991 Lonesome Dove Movie Poster Robert Duvall	$49.99	George on Sofa Poster from Seinfeld Art Print Poster	$9.99
QUEER AS FOLK THIRD SEASON POSTER	$48.00	HI HI PUFFY AMIYUMI SHOW - XXL BUS SHELTER POSTER	$9.99
BATTLESTAR GALACTICA 4x6 Bus Shelter Poster 6ft	$46.00	LAPD LOS ANGELES POLICE NEWTON DIVISION T-SHIRT *NEW*	$9.99
QUEER AS FOLK THIRD SEASON POSTER	$43.50	CARTOON NETWORK TEEN TITANS SUBWAY BANNER XL	$9.99
SIX FEET UNDER HBO - LIMITED - SEASON FINALE POSTER	$39.76	QUEER EYE BOSTON RED SOX 5FT POSTER HUGE RARE 5FT	$9.99
SIX FEET UNDER everything ends CADILAC HERSE poster	$36.00	RARE Vintage '77 LEIF GARRETT in SKATEBOARD Poster 9x10	$9.95
NEW GILMORE GIRLS PROMO POSTER GILMORE GIRLS AND GUYS	$35.00	DENIS LEARY - FX - RESCUE ME- 2005 POSTER - 22X33	$9.95

Television Memorabilia ▶ Press Kits

The average sales price in this subcategory is $22.92.

	HIGH		AVG
Scarecrow And Mrs.King - Press Kit + Photos	$255.00	Dead Like Me Season 1Press Kit slides/photo Ellen Muth	$26.00
Babylon 5 (S4) Media Press Kit ~ 26 Photos & 26 Slides	$205.71	BECKER tv series PRESS KIT & COLOR SLIDES	$24.99
BATMAN+MR SMITH+WOW+LORDS+STEALTH+KINGDOM 20 PRESS KITS	$199.99	RELIC HUNTER v series PRESS KIT & COLOR SLIDES	$24.99
Battlestar Galactica, Stargate SG-1 PRESS KIT w/2dvds	$158.05	NASH BRIDGES tv PRESS KIT & COLOR SLIDES - DON JOHNSON	$24.99
The Golden Palace - Premiere TV Press Kit 1992	$105.00	STAR TREK Deep Space Nine 1999 Season	$24.95
TNT INTO THE WEST PRESS+3 DVD EPS 4, 5, 6 + PROMO CARDS	$100.01	BAYWATCH 1999 Press Kit - Photos & Color Slides	$24.95
RARE, Tales From The Crypt (LEATHER PROMOTIONAL KIT)	$100.00	THE CLOSER Kyra Sedgwick Presskit + 3 DVDs (3 episodes)	$24.95
LAND OF DEAD+RING+WAX+AMITYVILLE+DARK+PRESS KITS HORROR	$79.99	JAG 2001 - 2002 Season Digital Media Kit	$24.50
OVER THERE PRESS KIT BOOK STEVEN BOCHCO FX	$77.99	Almost Home - Rare Touchstone TV Press Kit 1992	$24.38
National Geographic Channel INSIDE 9/11 911 Press Kit	$76.02	SCI FI GHOST HUNTERS SEASON 2 PRESS GIFT BOX DVD + TOY	$24.00

ABC PIZZA MY HEART PRESS KIT + VHS SHIRI APPLEBY	$76.00	WEST WING 2005 EMMY DVD "2162 VOTES" FINAL SMITS, ALDA	$23.51
Stargate Atlantis TV series press kit with DVD holder	$71.01	TNT 2005 EMMY DVD SET LIBRARIAN, GRID, SALEMS LOT, WOOL	$23.00
HBO CARNIVALE FUN KIT FERRIS WHEEL RADIO SNOW CONE MAKE	$71.00	HISTORY CHANNEL 05 EMMY SEALED BOX DVDS DAVINCI CODE ++	$22.86
13 X-Files Pilot 35MM slides	$70.00	That '70s Show press kit - DVDs, poster, key chain, etc	$21.59
20 X-Files 35MM Slides from Season 4 (#3)	$70.00	BEACH GIRLS - ROB LOWE - Press Kit, Beach towel, Video	$20.51

Television Memorabilia ▶ Props

The average sales price in this subcategory is $98.21.

	HIGH		AVG
Star Trek Orig Prop TRICORDER Wah Chang TV Series TOS	$4,950.00	FRIENDS USED PROPS FROM MONICA'S APARTMENT UNIQUE	$103.75
Queer As Folk Props Liberty Ave/Barkers Pl street signs	$3,050.00	Blade Runner Cop 357 Gun Movie Prop Replica Blaster	$102.50
Queer As Folk- Rage backdrop	$2,850.00	BUFFY THE VAMPIRE SLAYER Orig. PROP WEAPON w/COA! See!	$102.50
Queer As Folk Props Gale Harold "Brian"'s ashtray	$2,025.00	JOAN OF ARCADIA PROP BRUSH ART SCULPTURE STATUE NO RES!	$102.50
ANGEL - CORDELIA'S "MOST IN VOGUE" SCREEN USED TROPHY	$1,325.00	THE SHIELD - STRIKE TEAM ROOM'S BOWLING PIN	$102.50
Queer As Folk Props Liberty Diner Menu	$1,275.00	MUPPETS' WIZARD OF OZ Costume Sunglasses Dorothy	$102.50
Queer As Folk Props Gale Harold "Brian" candleholders	$1,025.00	Stargate SG-1 Zat gun Licensed Lightspeed prop w/stand	$100.00
MUPPETS' WIZARD OF OZ Prop Book with Puppeteer Handles	$787.77	THE SHIELD - STRIKE TEAM ROOM'S FRAMED BASEBALLS	$93.75
Bandleader DESI Arnaz His Personal Cuban Gourd Maracas	$725.00	Replica Winchester M1892 Loop-Lever John Wayne Rifle	$92.95
Babylon 5 orig rubber stunt prop PPG rifle	$700.00	HAND PAINTED I DREAM OF JEANNIE GENIE BOTTLE	$92.02
RARE Star Trek Communicator Official Prop Replica	$650.00	Star Trek Voyager WORKING Cortical Stimulator Prop	$91.00
ANGEL - FRED'S SCREEN WORN WARDROBE - "DESTINY"	$627.55	Replica Winchester M1892 Loop-Lever John Wayne Rifle	$89.95
Queer as folk Brian's loft Jar showtime prop qaf gay	$611.60	MAN FROM UNCLE COMMUNICATOR PEN EXACT REPLICA PROP	$86.55
Queer As Folk- Fetch Sign	$610.00	HAND PAINTED I DREAM OF JEANNIE GENIE BOTTLE	$86.00
XENA Caesar's helmet. Original prop / wardrobe	$571.99	MAN FROM UNCLE (U.N.C.L.E.) COMMUNICATOR PEN PROP	$85.00

Television Memorabilia ▶ Scripts

The average sales price in this subcategory is $22.94.

	HIGH		AVG
TV Show "Lost in Space" Original script w/ 8x10 photo	$809.99	THAT'S MY BUSH TV 2001 SCRIPT (TREY PARKER SOUTH PARK)	$24.95
JAG, SERIES BIBLE, EPISODE #1- #158.- (1995-2002)	$401.00	CHEYENNE Old Western ORIGNAL SCRIPT Clint Walker	$24.00
DOLLY PARTON TV SERIES ORIGINAL SCRIPTS	$307.00	THAT 70'S SHOW..HAND SIGNED SCRIPT "ICE SHACK"	$24.00
THIRD WATCH–Autographed Script from First Episode	$144.40	THE SIMPSONS TV SCRIPT - AUTHENTIC - NOT A COPY	$23.50
HOT! SIGNED WEST WING "IN EXCELSIS DEO" SCRIPT x6 W/COA	$114.99	RARE! Genuine QUEER AS FOLK "SEASON 2" TV SCRIPT Look!	$23.50
BIG PINK REMCO SHOWBOAT THEATRE W/ PUPPETS SCRIPTS	$102.50	Autographed script from TV show: The King of Queens	$22.50
THE WEST WING Script w/7 Autographs, Sheen Janney Lowe	$102.50	LA FEMME NIKITA SIGNED DAILIES #220 "In Between" DVD	$22.50
DESPERATE HOUSEWIVES SIGNED BY 5 EPISODE SCRIPT	$100.99	SIX FEET UNDER..geniune show script.."The Plan"	$22.38
ORIGINAL SCRIPT FROM THE TV SERIES BONANZA	$93.00	CAST Signed BUFFY The Vampire Slayer PILOT Script!! WOW	$21.93
Star Trek orig 19 pg story O/L "In Essense–Nothing"	$90.00	Cast SIGNED x6 CSI TV Show Season FINALE Script!	$21.53
Night Stalker Lord of Smoking Mirror Original Script	$88.99	M*A*S*H* TV SCRIPT SIGNED BY ALAN ALDA!!!!!!	$21.50
THE SIMPSONS SIGNED "LISA'S...DENSITY" SCRIPT x4 W/COA	$85.99	HOT! Cast SIGNED X14 DESPERATE HOUSEWIVES Pilot Script!	$21.50
NCIS SIGNED SCRIPT & PHOTO ALL ORIGINAL SIGNATURES	$82.88	Starsky & Hutch script (copy)-The Heroes	$21.50
Gilligan's Island original 1964 script signed by	$81.00	MORK AND MINDY TV SCRIPT - AUTHENTIC - NOT A COPY	$21.50
THE DUKES OF HAZZARD Original SCRIPT GRANNY ANNIE	$80.00	NEW! Cast Signed LAW AND ORDER SCRIPT! Jerry Orbach &	$21.35

Television Memorabilia ▶ Wardrobe

The average sales price in this subcategory is $96.97.

	HIGH		AVG
QUEER AS FOLK BRIAN'S LEATHER COAT!	$4,049.00	Dolres Claiborne wardrobe shoes from film	$100.00
WORN ALL 5 SEASONS		[2 of these sold for $50.00 each]	
BUFFY- SPIKE'S SCREEN WORN LEATHER JACKET	$3,350.00	JOAN OF ARCADIA JOAN (TAMBLYN) OUTFIT TANK TOP JEANS NR	$100.00
BUFFY- SPIKE'S SCREEN WORN PANTS FROM "CRUSH"	$2,850.00	BAYWATCH Original LIFEGUARD TRUNKS with SHOW PLACARD!	$99.00
ANGEL - FRED'S SCREEN WORN WARDROBE FROM SEASON 5	$2,212.00	TOS Star Trek Uniform Tunic Shirt "Scotty"	$99.00
MUPPETS' WIZARD OF OZ Hero Costume Cloak and Hat Wizard	$1,528.00	Original Superman Worn Cape Christopher Reeve	$97.03
ANGEL - CORDELIA'S SCREEN WORN SHIRT - "YOU'RE WELCOME"	$1,225.00	JOAN OF ARCADIA JOAN (A. TAMBLYN) OUTFIT SHIRT PANTS NR	$96.00
Queer As Folk Wardrobe Gale Harold Brian flowered shirt	$985.00	JOAN OF ARCADIA TAMBLYN ABERCROMBIE TOP PANTS OUTFIT	$94.00
Queer As Folk Wardrobe Gale Harold "Brian"'s shirt	$909.96	North Shore Erica's Makika Dominczky Wardrobe Bikini S	$93.50
Queer As Folk Randy Harrison "Justin"'s "Scenester" tee	$810.00	# 1 Day Auction # Britney Spears Owned bra & thong set	$92.00
Queer As Folk Wardrobe "Brian" Gale Harold Bertoni Suit	$760.00	Catherine Zeta Jones INTOLERABLE CRUELTY Emanuel Blouse	$89.99
Queer As Folk Gale Harold "Brian"s Kenneth Cole shirt	$760.00	* CHARMED *Alyssa Milano *worn BRA + COA* WARDROBE *	$89.11
Queer As Folk Hal Sparks "Michael" Captain Astro Tshirt	$665.00	Genuine XENA Prop SUPERB Leather Gauntlet Set 4pc	$89.00
ANGEL - FRED'S SCREEN WORN WARDROBE - "DESTINY"	$627.55	MUPPETS' WIZARD OF OZ Hero Costume Biker's Cap Dorothy	$86.09
MUPPETS' WIZARD OF OZ Hero Costume Silver Shoes Dorothy	$547.28	ANGEL - JASMINE'S SCREEN WORN SWEATER	$86.00
North Shore Cary Brittany Daniel Wardrobe La Perla Bra	$521.99	JOAN OF ARCADIA JOAN (AMBER TAMBLYN) BED HEAD ROBE NR!	$85.99

Television Memorabilia ▶ Other

The average sales price in this subcategory is $34.25.

	HIGH		AVG
1966 THE GREEN HORNET STICKERS FULL WAX PACK BOX 24ct	$813.00	DUKE ELLINGTON Black Brown & Beige 1958 FIRST PRESS LP	$38.50
1966 Philly DAKTARI FULL WAX PACK DISPLAY BOX 24 ct	$711.00	Set of 5 Sailor Moon Plushies/UFO Dolls -still in box-	$38.00
VINTAGE CAPTAIN MIDNIGHT 1955-56 MANUAL, DECODER & MORE	$576.25	05 Wizard Comic Con Angel Vegas Lorne House Always Wins	$37.66
I Love Lucy Barbie Doll Collection Set Of (8) Dolls MIB	$526.99	Dukes of Hazard 1981 Vintage Metal lunch box	$36.75
1965 Topps SOUPY SALES FULL WAX PACK BOX 24ct	$525.00	2005 Wizard Comic Con ANGEL T1 Unpainted LORNE 103/500	$36.00
Vintage 1970 Orson Vulture Pufnstuf Puppet +Orig. Box	$460.55	Lancelot Link Secret Chimp complete series dvd Apes	$34.57
I Love Lucy Barbie Doll Collection Set Of (8) Dolls Lot	$405.50	Monogram The U.F.O. The Invaders 1/72 Model Kit #856012	$33.50
Hartland Davy Crockett Mint !!!!! RARE!!!!!	$305.00	GREEN ACRES TV Hooterville Handbook 1993 Out of print!	$32.38

For Your Consideration DVD's and VHS Tapes	$305.00	NBC Deck of Cards w/Photos Top Shows Friends, ER, ET	$32.01
1949 FAIRFAX CA High School Yearbook - DAVID JANSSEN	$286.00	Lancelot Link Secret Chimp complete series dvd Apes	$32.00
Hartland # 805 Tonto From The Lone Ranger MINT!	$256.99	LITTLE RASCALS LIMITED EDITION BOBBLE HEADS, ALL MINT	$32.00
Hartland # 801 Clayton Moore From The Lone Ranger MINT	$256.99	Saturday Morning With Sid & Marty Krofft	$31.54
LA FEMME NIKITA Custom BARBIE MINT ..Peta Wilson	$232.50	I DREAM OF JEANNIE BARBIE DOLL FROM TV SHOW CUTE! MINT	$31.01
Dukes of Hazzard NOS Vanity Fair Super Arm Phonograph	$205.00	1958 TV GUIDE Lucille Ball I Love Lucy	$31.00
Gilligans Island Packard Bell Transistor Radio C@@L	$191.38	INTO THE WEST:Episode # 1 "Wheel To The Stars" rare DVD	$31.00

Theatre Memorabilia ▶ Ads, Flyers

The average sales price in this subcategory is $8.13.

	HIGH		AVG
Antique Broadside Edwin Booth (1833-1893) Actor	$92.00	Movie Pressbooks	$8.52
Antique Broadside Edwin Booth (1833-1893) Actor	$88.00	victorian actress "maude fealy" color photo postcard	$8.50
BURLESQUE Detroit Vaudville ads LILI ST. CYR vintage	$51.32	PHANTOM OF THE OPERA Poster Size Ad #3 P. Karrie 8th	$8.50
1930 Ad Gus Arnheim at Cocoanut Grove w/ Bing Crosby	$43.42	PHANTOM OF THE OPERA Poster Size Ad #4 Holiday Season	$8.50
1926 Souvenir Program JEANNE EAGELS In 'RAIN' LOOK!!	$36.00	PHANTOM OF THE OPERA Huge Ultimate Phantasy Colm!	$8.50
ORIGINAL THEATER FLYER WITH WIZARD OF OZ AD-1939	$34.00	PHANTOM OF THE OPERA Broadway 11th Birthday	$8.50
1914 Bowdoin Sq. Theatre Boston Broadside - Nice!	$32.89	Two FIDDLER ON THE ROOF Handbills - Alfred Molina & OC	$8.00
RARE BROADWAY WICKED FLYER + 3 FREE 8x10 COLOR PHOTOS	$30.00	THE BOYS IN AUTUMN WALTER KOENIG MARK LENARD STAR TREK!	$7.99
1952 Audrey Hepburn Theater Flyer GiGi Harris, Chicago	$29.00	1930 Ad Pom-Pom Club Hollywood CA near nude dancers	$7.99
Wicked Fan Pack Idina Menzel Kristin Chenoweth Items ++	$26.99	1952 GUYS AND DOLLS VIVIANE BLAINE SAM LEVENE AD	$7.99
COLIN FIRTH/ALAN RICKMAN RARE Love Actually Movie MAP!	$26.00	1932 Ad GRAND HOTEL Graumans Garbo Barrymore Crawford	$7.89
1955 Charles Addams art The Matchmaker B'way play ad	$26.00	Broadway Bears pamphlet Hugh Jackman Chenoweth Wicked	$7.50
RARE BROADWAY WICKED FLYER + 3 FREE 8x10 COLOR PHOTOS	$26.00	HOLLYWOOD BOWL PROGRAM BRENDA LEE & POSTCARD 1960's	$7.50
1960s-80s Theatre Heralds - Mini Poster Style - 35	$24.99	Rare SERIOUS MONEY Handbill - Alfred Molina	$7.50
DE WOLF HOPPER WILLIAM A BRADY GILBERT & SULLIVAN 1915	$22.02	1931 Ad "NINE O'CLOCK REVUE" Gorgeous Girls $0 s/h	$7.25

Theatre Memorabilia ▶ Playbills

The average sales price in this subcategory is $15.47.

	HIGH		AVG
Rent Signed Poster Playbill Broadway OBC Idina Menzel	$312.00	Vivien Leigh "STREETCAR" Tennessee Williams 1949 London	$15.50
Sweet Charity Signed Poster Broadway Playbill Applegate	$249.99	Old & Unusual Collection of Chicago Theatre Play Bills	$15.50
Pre-Bdwy "GLASS MENAGERIE" Laurette Taylor '45 Playbill	$221.50	Orpheum Vaudville THOMAS EDISON Talking Pictures 1913	$15.50
LOT OF OVER 200 PLAYBILLS FROM '50s-'80s.	$182.51	1945 Theatre Playbill: I Remember Mama - Marlon Brando	$15.50
Kurt Weill "THE ETERNAL ROAD" Lotte Lenya 1937 Program	$145.51	Playbill WICKED WP K Chenoweth I Menzel Robert Morse Oz	$15.50
Noel Coward "DESIGN FOR LIVING" Lunt & Fontanne 1933	$104.01	WWII and Theater: 1945 UNITED NATIONS THEATER Lot of 2	$15.50
1877 Edwin Booth theater program, King Richard II	$104.00	Columbus Ohio Hartman Theatre Program	$15.05
Doubt Signed Poster broadway Cherry Jones Tony Awards	$99.99	PLAYBILL CARDS *1999-2000* BROADWAY AIDA-RIVERDANCE+++	$15.00
Over 100 PlayBills 1940's to 1960's	$99.00	PLAYBILL CARD *2001-2002* BROADWAY MAMMA MIA-GRADUATE++	$15.00
Playbill, 1938-SIGNED BY GEORGE M. COHAN	$78.00	a little night music	$15.00
George Gershwin "LET 'EM EAT CAKE" 1933 Broadway Flyer	$77.55	Fifty+ Count Theatre Lot (Over 8 lbs) Vintage Playbills	$15.00
1890 Gilbert-Sullivan/DOyly Carte program	$77.52	Lot of 4 1927 1928 Broadway Theatre Playbill Programs	$14.51
PLAYBILL - ORIGINAL - ELFRIDA OPERA - KINGS THEATRE	$73.00	CHRISTMAS CAROL Playbill Tim Curry (SPAMALOT, ROCKY HPS	$14.50
Fifth Edition Cotton Club Program Cotton Club Parade	$71.00	9 Philadelphia Pa Shubert Theater Playbill '28 LOT 2	$14.19
Lot of 100 Playbills	$67.00	Playbill Musical "ZIEGFELD FOLLIES" Fannie Brice 1936	$14.06

Theatre Memorabilia ▶ Posters

The average sales price in this subcategory is $35.50.

	HIGH		AVG
Broadway Boy From OZ Hugh Jackman cast signed poster	$401.56	BROADWAY SHOW POSTER NINE RAUL JULIA FRAMED	$41.00
Star Wars, A New Hope, Episode IV, Original NSS Poster	$381.00	THE DAY AFTER TOMORROW LENTICULAR 3D MOVIE POSTER –RARE	$40.06
Bway Producers Lane Broderick Beach stars sign poster	$324.01	DISNEYLAND Space Mountain 4x6 Bus Shelter Poster 6ft	$38.00
Broadway original cast Wicked leads signed poster	$295.00	THE NIGHTMARE BEFORE CHRISTMAS orginal one sheet poster	$36.00
Bway Sondheim Frogs Lane Bart cast signed window card	$261.76	Official DOLBY DIGITAL Home Theater Wall Plaque Sign	$36.00
Bway Barks 6 Moore Peters and many celebs sign poster	$256.00	NICOLE KIDMAN CHANEL No 5 - 4x6 Bus Shelter Poster 6ft	$35.99
HARRY POTTER AND THE SORCERER'S STONE Movie Banner!	$250.00	BETTY BUCKLEY TRIUMPH OF LOVE HUGE COLOR POSTER 14"x22"	$35.00
Broadway Nine revival Banderas and cast signed poster	$217.50	DISNEYLAND 50th Anniversary 4x6 Bus Shelter Poster 6ft	$33.00
Batman Begins vinyl movie banner LARGE	$207.50	serenity joss whedon D/S original Movie poster 27 x 40	$32.99
Bway Steel Magnolias Burke Ebersole cast signed poster	$190.50	Beauty and the Beast – Original Movie Poster	$32.60
Lord of The Rings III OVERSIZED Theatrical Banner	$189.50	Cirque du Soleil—Poster-O–24x36	$31.00
Broadway Bombay Dreams signed original cast poster	$178.19	DISNEYLAND Space Mountain 4x6 Bus Shelter Poster 6ft	$31.00
SWEET CHARITY Broadway Cast Signed Poster with Credits	$164.08	STAR WARS 1977 SUPER RARE HUGE POSTER LUCAS DARTH YODA	$31.00
Broadway Caroline Or Change orig cast signed poster	$152.50	0408#Jurassic Park Sign Lights Neon Movie Signs Light	$30.99
Broadway Henry IV Hawke cast signed poster	$152.50	Rent the Musical Framed Poster For Time Magzine	$30.00

Theatre Memorabilia ▶ Props, Wardrobe

The average sales price in this subcategory is $52.80.

	HIGH		AVG
Nightmare 5 Freddy Krueger prop mask	$821.11	Hairspray Prop Handsigned Bruce Vilanch Marissa Winokur	$60.00
L VRBA French Antique NECKLACE NO RESERVE	$430.00	Egyptian Dress Costume	$55.00
Broadway Boy From Oz Hugh Jackman signed vest	$325.00	HIGH POWER PREDATOR LASER FOR BIO HELMET MASK LOOK!	$54.99
FREDERICK NIHDA WIZARD OF OZ	$299.99	[2 of these sold for $54.99 each]	
LION MASK COSTUME MGM GRAN		Cirque Du Soleil Mystere Mask Feathers Masquerade Ball	$53.86
Marushin Israeli Replica Prop UZI Neil Simon Theater	$275.01	GLENGARRY GLEN ROSS - Rio Rancho Banner	$52.00
GLENGARRY GLEN ROSS - Ricky Roma's briefcase	$227.50	Vintage Red Exit Sign Globe Light Unique Theater Prop	$52.00

GLENGARRY GLEN ROSS - Ricky Roma's chair	$207.50	VINTAGE THEATER BRASS STANCHIONS W/RED ROPE	$51.00
RARE*PHANTOM OF THE OPERA REPLICA MOVIE MASK*RARE	$201.01	GLENGARRY GLEN ROSS - Williamson's lamp	$51.00
2 OLD 1888 DUMMY MAUSER STAGE GUN PROP RIFLE WOOD PARTS	$164.00	New Goldberg 16mm Film Reel Clock Home Cinema Theater	$49.95
GLENGARRY GLEN ROSS - Shelly Levene's desk	$162.50	Broadway Sweet Smell Of Success Lithgow signed prop	$48.00
THEATER STANCHIONS RED VELVET ROPES, HOME THEATER PROP!	$158.00	GLENGARRY GLEN ROSS - Dave Moss' rolodex	$47.00
Broadway Bares authentic Tim Curry signed Dr. lab coat	$157.53	3 Vintage Movie Reels/Den Decoration/Hollywood/Movies	$46.00
PROFESSIONAL MR PUNCH PUPPET * PUNCH AND JUDY *	$150.00	New Goldberg 16mm Film Reel Clock Home Cinema Theater	$45.00
VERY RARE SIGNED JOEL GREY FLASK BROADWAY WICKED NR	$129.50	PEACEMAKER PISTOL-Gold Engraved Finish-1280L	$44.96
Predator Latex Mask/Head Movie Prop/Costume	$125.55	OLD WEST PEACEMAKER PISTOL-Iron Grey-1186g	$44.96

Theatre Memorabilia ▶ Souvenir Programs

The average sales price in this subcategory is $17.24.

	HIGH		AVG
ARENA DE VERONA 1952 PROGRAM MARIA CALLAS	$1,044.00	London 1998 A.L. Webber 50th Birthday Celebration	$19.99
70+ Programs of Pittsburgh Theaters - 1920s & 1930s	$209.01	THEATRE PROGRAM 1888 GRAND OPERA HOUSE CHICAGO II	$19.99
Original Conan TV Sword	$209.00	THEATRE PROGRAM 1891 CASINO THEATER NEW YORK CITY I	$19.99
1922 Isadora Duncan Dance Program Carnegie Hall	$202.50	THEATRE PROGRAM 1893 COLUMBIA THEATER NEW YORK BROOKLYN	$19.99
BORIS KARLOFF PROGRAM & AUTOGRAPH HOLLYWOOD HORROR	$130.26	Barbra Streisand "FUNNY GIRL" Jule Styne 1964 Program	$17.51
1921 Anna Pavlova Palais du Trocadero Ballet Program #1	$102.50	1961 JEWEL BOX REVUE Program Female Impersonators NY	$17.49
Ted Shawn & His Men Dancers Program / 1930s / Ballet	$102.50	Rocky Horror Picture Show Press Kit With Photos!	$17.29
WICKED Cast Signed Souvenir Program -- Idina Menzel	$96.00	PASSION Early Bway Musical SCRIPT Stephen Sondheim	$17.00
John Cullum "1491" Chita Rivera * Meredith Willson FLOP	$77.78	CHESS Broadway Program & LIVE 2 CD Cast Recording! LOOK	$16.75
Julie Andrews "CAMELOT" Lerner & Loewe 1960 Program	$66.50	Mia Slavenska Frederic Franklin Ballet Program 1953 #2	$16.51
1933 University of Pennsylvania MASK & WIG Club Program	$52.00	Burlesque Program~Queen of Radiana & Startzman~1929~NR	$16.50
PHANTOM of the OPERA THE MAJESTIC THEATRE NEW YORK	$52.00	1923 Eddie Cantor Kid Boots Souvenir Theatre Program	$16.49
1940s SCRAPBOOK FULL OF PLAYBILLS & PROGRAMS 65+	$51.00	Ballet Theater 1953 Program Inside Illus Pablo Picasso	$16.49
HUGH JACKMAN - SUNSET BLVD PROG at the MIGHTY REGENT	$49.75	Seussical Souvenir Program - Cathy Rigby	$16.00
Orig. 1939 Gone With The Wind program with theater menu	$48.00	BALLET THEATRE 1949-50 / VERTES / GEORGE PLATT LYNES	$15.50

Theatre Memorabilia ▶ Window Cards

The average sales price in this subcategory is $39.32.

	HIGH		AVG
ANGELA LANSBURY-GOWER CHAMPION "PRETTYBELLE" W/CARD	$1,576.50	OOP! Broadway Poster ~WICKED~ Idina Menzel & Joel Grey	$45.00
Broadway Original Theatre Play Posters LOT 1st Print Ed	$462.50	[2 of these sold for $45.00 each]	
ORIGINAL GOLD FOIL RED RARE	$375.50	RARE! Original Broadway Poster ~RENT~ HOT!	$45.00
WINDOW CARD"ROTHSCHILDS"		Brooklyn Broadway Cast SIGNED Window Card	$45.00
Lennon Broadway Cast Signed Posters! 2 For 1!	$295.00	RARE! Original Broadway Poster ~RENT~ HOT!	$45.00
BROADWAY Theatre Play/Musical HUGE 100 TOUR POSTER LOT	$202.50	Broadway Poster ~WICKED~ Idina Menzel & George Hearn	$45.00
Dirty Rotten Scoundrels Broadway Cast Signed Poster	$201.00	[2 of these sold for $45.00 each]	
RARE PHANTOM OF THE OPERA W/	$188.49	Broadway Poster ~WICKED~ Idina Menzel & Joey McIntyre	$45.00
TWIN TOWERS WIDOW CARD NR		Thou Shalt Not Signed Window Card - Norbert Leo Butz	$39.99
Sweet Charity Broadway Cast Signed Poster	$185.00	Signed WICKED Poster	$39.00
The Light In The Piazza Broadway Cast Signed Poster!	$185.00	SUNSET BOULEVARD, ANDREW LLOYD WEBBER, FAITH BROWN	$36.00
1920s LITTLE NELLIE KELLY Theater Window Card LOU MAYER	$178.95	OOP! Broadway Poster~WICKED~Kristin Chenoweth~Joel Grey	$36.00
URINETOWN ORIGINAL CAST WC SIGNED	$177.50	Rare! Broadway Poster ~Cat~ Ashley Judd & Jason Patric	$36.00
The Paris Letter Broadway Cast Signed Poster	$165.00	Original Broadway Cast Poster ~Sweeney Todd~ Sondheim	$35.00
Obsession Broadway Cast Signed Poster! Rare!	$165.00	Rare! Broadway Poster ~Urinetown~ Charles Shaughnessy	$35.00
THOROUGHLY MODERN MILLIE ORIGINAL CAST WC SIGNED	$150.00	New! Broadway Poster~LA CAGE~Gary Beach & Daniel Davis	$35.00
1920s LITTLE JESSE JAMES Theatre Window Card LOU MAYER	$98.69	OOP! Broadway Poster ~WICKED~ Idina Menzel & Joel Grey	$35.00

Theatre Memorabilia ▶ Other

The average sales price in this subcategory is $26.01.

	HIGH		AVG
Photo Album of a Vaudeville Actress and Model	$393.00	CABARET Alan Cumming & Jane Horrocks DVD (video) rare	$30.00
37 volumes Folio Press Complete Shakespeare Plays	$375.00	Broadway's WICKED PRESS CLIPS DVD original cast FREE CD	$30.00
Vaudeville Magician Memorabilia Huge Old Paper Lot!	$369.00	BROADWAY WHO'S AFRAID OF VIRGINIA WOOLF PRESS KIT +3PIC	$29.99
Wicked Broadway Idina Menzel Elphaba MAC make up sheet	$325.99	LILLIAN HELLMAN: Montserrat *1STwDJ* 1950	$27.88
RARE Hairspray Lunch Box Filled w/ Collectables	$305.00	The Pajama Game - Vocal/Piano score	$27.52
THEATRICAL STAGE CURTAIN - WITH TRACK - 2 panels -green	$299.00	1964 Tina Louise Broadway Theatre Press Photo #2 g113	$27.01
2 PHANTOM OF THE OPERA TICKETS - SAT MAT - OCT 15 - NYC	$210.00	Exclusive Signed First Lady Suite Tote Bag	$27.00
Original Conan TV Sword	$209.00	Gone With The Wind Scarlett O'Hara World Doll MIB	$26.55
JOHN WAYNE FRANKLIN MINT BOWIE KNIFE	$208.50	Vintage Heywood Wakefield theater seats	$26.01
2 PHANTOM OF THE OPERA TICKETS - SAT MAT - OCT 8 - NYC	$185.00	San Fran. Music Box Company Phantom Snow Globe	$26.00
MIB 2002 2003 Carlton 2 Ornaments PHANTOM OF THE OPERA	$167.50	Idina Menzel Still I Cant Be Still CD Great Condition!	$26.00
THE MAGIC SHOW Original Set Rendering David Chapman	$150.00	Pink Panther Lamp – Genuine	$26.00
Opening Night Invite for Unopened Farrah Fawcett Play	$130.00	Lupe Velez Estate Morning, Noon and Night ~ Script	$26.00
7th Annual Edition of the Theater Catalogue, 1947-48 ed	$128.16	RARE VINTAGE PHANTOM OF THE OPERA SWEAT SHIRT JACKET XL	$26.00
Aerial Photographer's Camera US Army Air Force WWII	$127.50	Wicked the musical Stephanie j.Block Photo Set!!!	$26.00

Video Game Memorabilia ▶ XBox

The average sales price in this subcategory is $14.43.

	HIGH		AVG
Xbox Halo CORTANA MIP with 3 Bonus series 1 figures 2	$152.50	HALO 2 Trophy Crest black Medium M Shirt NEW XBOX	$15.00
Xbox Halo Series 3 figures lot of 5 - RARE and MINT 2	$122.50	HALO 2 Distressed Helmet Medium M Shirt NEW XBOX	$15.00
HUGE AND RARE OFFICIAL XBOX MAGAZINEs and DVDs	$101.01	HALO 2 Trophy Crest black Large L Shirt NEW XBOX	$15.00

	HIGH		AVG
Xbox Halo Series 2 figures lot of 4 - RARE and MINT	$62.05	HALO 2 XL Faux Longsleeve Shirt NEW XBOX	$14.99
Xbox Halo 2 II Master Chief Standee Promo Standup L@@K!	$51.00	NEW Microsoft XBOX Black Hooded Sweatshirt Shirt Small	$14.99
MICROSOFT XBOX GAME CONSOLE	$40.33	RARE XBOX RETAIL LOGO WINDOW / WALL SIGN	$14.99
HALO 2 Oval XXL Hooded Sweatshirt Shirt NEW XBOX	$35.00	HALO 2 logo embroidered Beanie Cap Hat NEW XBOX	$14.99
grand theft auto san andreas (factory sealed) xbox	$35.00	HALO 2 L Faux Longsleeve Shirt NEW XBOX	$14.99
MICROSOFT XBOX GAME CONSOLE	$34.75	HALO 2 XBOX BASEBALL SHIRT MED LOGO 3/4 sleeve	$14.95
RARE XBOX RETAIL DISPLAY - STAINLESS AND XBOX GREEN	$31.00	6 XBOX games NFL Blitz WF Raw 007 Night Fire LOT oF 6	$14.51
SEALED XBOX ODDWORLD STRANGER'S WRATH PREORDER DVD	$31.00	RARE & NEW XBOX RETAIL LOGO	$14.51
HALO 2 Oval L Hooded Sweatshirt Shirt NEW XBOX	$29.99	WINDOW / WALL SIGN	
HALO 2 Oval XL Hooded Sweatshirt Shirt NEW XBOX		HALO 2 Trophy Crest black XL Shirt NEW XBOX	$13.99
[2 of these sold for $29.99 each]		HALO 2 XBOX LONGSLEEVE SHIRT MED LOGO	$13.50
HALO 2 Oval M Hooded Sweatshirt Shirt NEW XBOX	$29.99	Large Lot of 23 Video Game Lanyards Xbox PS2 Gamecube	$13.00
[2 of these sold for $29.99 each]		HALO 2 PS2 XBOX GAME SET OF 2 POSTERS #1	$12.99
Bungie Xbox HALO 2 ~MASTER CHIEF~ GIANT DOOR POSTER	$26.00	[2 of these sold for $12.99 each]	

Video Game Memorabilia ▶ Atari

The average sales price in this subcategory is $38.74.

	HIGH		AVG
ATARI TRON VIDEO GAME PROMOTIONAL CARDBOARD STAND UP	$295.00	ATARI TENNIS VIDEO GAME PROMOTIONAL CARDBOARD STAND UP	$54.00
ATARI TRON VIDEO GAME PROMOTIONAL CARDBOARD STAND UP	$164.35	STAR WARS EMPIRE STRIKES PROMO VIDEO GAME POSTER ATARI	$54.00
ATARI 400 HOME COMPUTER REBATE CARDBOARD STAND UP 1983	$108.50	Tron Joystick & (2) Games for Atari 2600 Vintage 1983	$46.00
ATARI BUY 2 CARTRIDGES GET 1 FREE CARDBOARD STAND UP 82	$108.50	Lot of 19 Atari Activision Catalogs Brochures Computer	$38.00
DEALER LOT OF 10 MINT ATARI STOCKS a cult classicl RARE	$79.95	ATARI LOOPING VIDEO GAME PROMOTIONAL POSTER COLECO 1983	$37.50
ATARI ACTIVISION PROMOTIONAL CARDBOARD STAND UP 1982	$79.00	ATARI PEPPER 2 VIDEO GAME PROMO POSTER COLECO 1983	$37.50
ATARI DRAGONFIRE VIDEO GAME PROMO CARDBOARD STAND UP	$75.00	ATARI TARZAN VIDEO GAME PROMOTIONAL POSTER COLECO 1983	$37.50
ATARI G.I. JOE COBRA STRIKE PROMO CARDBOARD STAND UP 83	$71.26	ATARI TIME PILOT VIDEO GAME PROMO POSTER COLECO 1983	$37.50
ATARI ACTIVISION PROMOTIONAL CARDBOARD STAND UP 1982	$69.00	ATARI TURBO VIDEO GAME PROMOTIONAL POSTER COLECO 1983	$37.50
ATARI G.I. JOE COBRA STRIKE PROMO CARDBOARD STAND UP 83	$65.00	ATARI JAGUAR 64 BIT INTUATIVE MUTLIMEDIA SYSTEM	$37.00
ATARI RIVER RAID VIDEO GAME PROMO CARDBOARD STAND UP	$65.00	Pooyan by Konami for Atari 2600 Vintage 1982	$33.56
ATARI APOLLO GAMES PROMOTIONAL CARDBOARD STAND UP 1983	$65.00	1979 ATARI 400/800 GAME CONSOLE PERSONAL COMPUTER VTG	$26.67
ATARI SPACE CAVERN VIDEO GAME PROMO CARDBOARD STAND UP	$65.00	ATARI 5200 SYSTEM PROMOTIONAL CARDBOARD STAND UP 1982	$26.02
Atari Star Wars arcade game poster	$62.77	Strategy X by Konami for Atari 2600 Vintage 1982	$26.00
ATARI SPIDER FIGHTER VIDEO GAME PROMO CARDBOARD STANDUP	$61.06	LOT 5 ATARI 2600 RARE PHOENIX STORE PROMO POSTER GAME	$24.45

Video Game Memorabilia ▶ Nintendo

The average sales price in this subcategory is $16.22.

	HIGH		AVG
NEW! Nintendo DS with 4 Games FREE SHIPPING!	$180.00	Zelda 1 & 2 Gold + manual nes nintendo + bonus if BIN	$18.00
Nintendo Dolphin NPDP-GDEV kit NPDP-ODEM card GAMECUBE	$149.00	SDCC 2005 Nintendo Zelda Princess Exclusive Promo Coin	$17.50
NINTENDO GAMECUBE & MORE II (LIKE NEW!!) CLICK HERE!!	$124.33	PROMO Nintendo STARFOX Assault BIG CANVAS Banner Poster	$17.38
LARGE NEON SIGN NINTENDO GAME BOY STORE ADVERTISEMENT	$82.02	Metal Gear 1 + 2 snakes Revenge nes Nintendo bonuSifBIN	$17.00
Samus Metroid Action Figure Nintendo Power + 20 FREE	$81.00	PROMO Nintendo Gamecube METROID Prime SUNGLASSES +Bonus	$16.88
NES Nintendo w/Joystick & 9 Games (COLLECTIBLE!!!)	$76.24	Nintendo Gamecube system promo display NEW RARE	$16.39
OOC Earthbound Ness Plushie Plush Super Nintendo SNES	$61.00	RARE! NINTENDO GAMECUBE POKEMON	$15.99
Timbuk2 Nintendo E3 2004 Messanger Bag	$60.00	COLOSSEUM BONUS DISC	
Japanese Nintendo Famicom NES Poster - Metroid	$58.97	PROMO Nintendo GBA Donkey Kong Country 2 CANVAS Poster	$15.50
Nintendo Mario Bros Black YOSHI Bean Bag Plush MWT Wow!	$54.50	Nintendo 64	$15.50
Digimon Rumble Arena 2 Nintendo GameCube	$54.00	Nintendo VERY RARE Mario Golf promotional GOLF TOOL MIB	$15.50
Nintendo Super Mario Sunshine & FLUDD Plush Toy	$46.00	WALLPAPER Super Mario Brothers 3 Nintendo Game trim NES	$15.50
Nintendo Mario Bros Red YOSHI Bean Bag Plush WOW!	$46.00	Nintendo Nes System with 5 games WOW GREAT DEAL!	$15.00
Huge Lot of NES Nintendo Games 37 Games No Reserve!	$41.00	RARE Galaxy 5000 nes nintendo + bonus games if use BIN	$15.00
Vintage Nintendo Black ZELDA Game Watch MIB Store Stock	$39.99	1942 & 1943 RARE nes nintendo + bonus games if use BIN	$15.00
[2 of these sold for $39.99 each]		Nintendo Nes System with 5 games WOW GREAT DEAL!	$15.00

Video Game Memorabilia ▶ Halo

The average sales price in this subcategory is $23.07.

	HIGH		AVG
HALO 2 MASTER CHIEF STATUE 72" TALL	$610.01	HALO 2 Oval L Hooded Sweatshirt Shirt NEW XBOX	$29.99
Halo 2 Master Chief Prop/Costume SMGs Pair	$321.88	HALO 2 Oval XL Hooded Sweatshirt Shirt NEW XBOX	$29.99
Halo 2 Master Chief Prop/Costume SMGs Pair	$301.00	[2 of these sold for $29.99 each]	
HALO 2 MASTER CHIEF-4FT- VERY RARE-N/R	$242.00	HALO 2 Oval M Hooded Sweatshirt Shirt NEW XBOX	$29.99
HALO 2 MASTER CHIEF STATUE	$177.50	[2 of these sold for $29.99 each]	
HALO 2 Red Spartan Armor Vest Costume	$165.00	Bungie Xbox HALO 2 ~MASTER CHIEF~ GIANT DOOR POSTER	$26.00
Xbox Halo CORTANA MIP with 3 Bonus series 1 figures 2	$152.50	Vintage Nelsonic PLANES & TANKS Game Watch Store Stock	$24.95
MASTER CHIEF RED HALO HELMET SUIT COSTUME	$129.50	Odyssey Adventure "Killer Bees!" Vintage Spring 1983	$23.50
Xbox Halo Series 3 figures lot of 5 - RARE and MINT 2	$122.50	THUNDERCATS 3-D logo SIGN RARE II home , office	$22.99
Autographed Halo 2 poster. Signed by Frank O'Connor!	$103.08	The Legend of Zelda Twilight Princess Promo Coin SDCC	$22.55
Xbox Halo Series 2 figures lot of 4 - RARE and MINT	$62.05	BATTLESTAR GALACTICA SPACE ALERT HAND HELD BY MATTEL	$22.50
Big Rare Halo 2 and Grand Theft Auto San Andreas Poster	$61.00	Nintendo Super Mario Sunshine & FLUDD Plush Toy	$22.00
Halo 2 3-D Standee	$51.00	Who is Aragorn Legolas or Frodo w/out Evil Lord Sauron?	$22.00
Xbox Halo 2 II Master Chief Standee Promo Standup L@@K!	$51.00	HE WAS MASTER OF THE ONE RING THAT RULED THEM ALL	
HALO 2 Oval XXL Hooded Sweatshirt Shirt NEW XBOX	$35.00	Resident Evil Standee New in Box!! Unassembled	$21.50
		HALO2 HALO 2 SET OF 4 NEW POSTER XBOX PS2	$19.99
		[5 of these sold for $19.99 each]	
		OFFICIAL HALO 2 TROPHY CREST BLACK SHIRT MED	$18.99
		HALO 2 XL Faux Longsleeve Shirt NEW XBOX	$18.00

19

GIFT CERTIFICATES

It doesn't occur to many people to look for gift certificates on eBay, and yet this is one of the best categories in which to realize everyday savings. Although you can browse the gift certificates available to your local region (eBay offers options for all 50 states, and a non–United States category for outside the country), we'll take a look at gift certificates across all regions to get a broader view of specific types of gift certificates—Books, Music, Movies, Clothing, Home & Garden, Restaurant, and Other—and for major stores and brand names.

This category does not have as many listings, overall, as many other eBay categories, but it's a fun place to scope out savings on a variety of items and even some travel discounts. (Most of the travel certificates are listed in the Other Gift Certificates subcategory, and some are for a series of smaller-value certificates. For example, the $1,000.00 worth of Hyatt hotel certificates that sold for $800.00 consisted of a group of 10 certificates for $100.00 each.) And, of course, it's a good place to shop for gifts when you have no other ideas, although some people receiving these gift certificates as gifts are clearly turning them around on eBay, or many of them wouldn't be here. So there's a chance the gift certificate you buy on eBay to give to someone may come full circle and get listed here later.

From the looks of the highest final sales prices, people will spend a lot of money to realize only modest savings, such as spending $470.00 for a $500.00 Amazon.com gift certificate, allowing them to save only $30.00. Another person won about $47.00 worth of free books by paying $162.50 for a $211.00 Borders gift card.

Some of the largest savings in this category are on higher-dollar value certificates. For example, a $307.95 Barnes & Noble bookstore card was won for $256.05, providing savings of $51.50 for the buyer. (The odd amounts on some gift cards, by the way, are usually due to the seller offering a gift card that has been partially used; the amount is the dollar value remaining on the card, not the original amount of money the card was worth.) Contrast that with the lower value $73.63 Barnes & Noble certificate, which sold for $63.03, giving the buyer a net value of only $13.60.

Similarly, a $350.00 Borders gift card went for $232.50 (a $117.50 savings for the buyer), while a $75.00 Borders gift card went for $65.00, which is only a $10.00 savings for the buyer. This phenomenon may be explained by there simply being a smaller number of people willing to bid on these more expensive gift certificates. After all, to realize the savings, you do need to buy some $200.00 to $300.00 worth of merchandise, and many people may not want that many new books (or other items) in the near future.

For other types of items, such as electronics, it's easier to spend several hundred dollars at once; this is probably why many of the $500.00 Circuit City gift certificates sell for between $445.00 and $474.00 or so. Several people were even willing to spend close to the actual dollar value of a Circuit City gift certificate to realize only a $5.00 to $10.00 savings.

At the low end of prices in this category, the gift certificates were often more like coupons, offering deals where if you spent a certain amount of money in the store, you could save money, such as the Lane Bryant (women's clothing) store coupon offering "$50.00 off your purchase of $150.00 or more, or $25.00 off your purchase of $75.00 or more."

Interestingly, this was the first category I encountered that was not rife with penny auctions on the low end. This may be because people are more sensitive to shipping costs for these items. After all, how much can it cost to mail a small, lightweight gift card or paper gift certificate? The one-cent price with a five dollar shipping fee gimmick doesn't work in this category.

Clothing

What about gift certificates for clothing? What kind of money are people spending here, and how much savings are they getting out of the gift certificates? A couple of the biggest savings were for the Gap and Eddie Bauer: one buyer paid $411.15 for a $500.00 Gap gift card, a savings of $88.85; another paid $400.00 for a $500.00 Eddie Bauer card. More typical savings for Gap clothing, in the average price range, were about $10.00 to $25.00 for $50.00 to $100.00 gift cards. The purchaser of a $500.00 Abercrombie & Fitch gift card got a good value, paying only $380.05, for savings of $120.00. However, most Abercrombie & Fitch gift cards in the average price range yielded $25.00 to $45.00 in savings.

Other good values in the Clothing subcategory included savings of $127.98 on a $500.00 Banana Republic gift card, bought for $372.02; savings of $111.00 on a $450.00 J.Crew gift card, bought for $339.00; and savings of $100.85 on a $370.00 Express gift card, bought for $269.15.

People also bought coupons for money off, for example, for the Gap and the Children's Place. The items for the Children's Place in this sample were all for coupons, such as a 20 percent off coupon with free shipping that went for only $0.99.

General Merchandise and Restaurants

Big home-improvement stores, such as Home Depot and Lowe's, show up with a variety of gift cards ranging in value from about $10.00 up to $500.00. The savings here don't seem to be as great as in the other categories—they ranged from about $15.00 to $45.00 for the $500.00 gift certificates, and from $5.00 to $15.00 for the $50.00 to $100.00 certificates.

People fared a little better with cards from home furnishing and decor stores, such as Michaels, Pier 1, and Pottery Barn. The winning bidder for a $500.00 Pier 1 gift card realized a $118.25 value after paying $381.75 for the card. Good values for Pottery Barn included $97.00 for the purchaser of a $452.00 Pottery Barn gift card, bought for $355.00. For Michaels, a buyer got a $77.70 value, paying $180.78 for a $258.48 card. Other gift cards on the high end for Michaels yielded values of about $35.00 to $65.00.

In the restaurant world, most of the gift certificates are from big chain restaurants that offer relatively inexpensive fare, such as Pizza Hut, Subway, Panera Bread, and Starbucks, although the occasional higher-end restaurant, such as Morton's steak house, can be found. The availability of gift certificates for local restaurants will, of course, vary based on your region, so if you're looking for a nice restaurant, select your state in the Valid Locations drop-down menu in the Gift Certificates ▸ Restaurant subcategory. When I did a search for certificates in the District of Columbia, where I live, I found several $10.00 certificates listed for a variety of nice restaurants in my area. Two of the highest final prices for the D.C. area were $81.01 for a $125.00 Clyde's of Georgetown certificate, and $69.99 for a $100.00 Shula's Steak House certificate.

$300 Worth of Pizza?

At first glance, some of the highest value savings for the Restaurant subcategory seem to be in the pizza world: a $320.00 Domino's gift certificate sells for $14.99; a $360.00 Pizza Hut card for $6.00. Upon closer inspection, however, these deals are actually combination offers, where you can, for example, buy one and get one free on one visit, and get a free side order with the purchase of a large or extra-large pizza on another visit. These types of certificates would be best for the frequent pizza buyer. But there are deals for the more modest consumer of this popular food: several people are willing to bid enough to save a few bucks for a single Pizza Hut pie.

Books, Music, Movies

NOTE *There is no average price statement for this subcategory because the prices were obtained using eBay's Completed Items feature.*

	HIGH		AVG
$500 Amazon.com Gift Certificate Coupon Card Ship Free	$479.99	$25 Blockbuster Gift Card / Certificate	$23.00
$500.00 Best Buy Gift Card - Buy Now and Save $	$475.00	$25 BARNES & NOBLE GIFT CARD	$23.00
WAL MART GIFT CARD $500.00 VALUE, ONE DAY ONLY!!!	$467.00	$25 Circuit City Gift Card!! FREE SHIPPING!!!!	$22.72
WAL MART GIFT CARD $500.00 VALUE, ONE DAY ONLY!!!	$466.21	60 music downloads from Sony Connect	$22.61
Best Buy $500 Gift Card Certificate No Expiration NR	$455.01	Barnes and Nobel $25 Gift Certificate	$22.51
BEST BUY GIFT CARD $500.00, ONE DAY AUCTION	$452.50	$25 AMC Theatres Gift Card	$22.50
$500 circuit city gift card	$450.00	4 FANDANGO Movie Tickets, $48 Value, Free Shipping	$22.50
BEST BUY GIFT CARD	$402.99	Best Buy Gift Card $25 FREE SHIPPING!!!	$22.50
$428 Circuit City Gift Card Certificate NO Reserve	$381.38	25 AMC Theatres Entertainment Card MOVIEs GIFT CARD	$22.50
400$ Amazon Gift Certificate by email	$380.00	Barnes & Noble gift card with $25.00! Free Shipping!	$22.50
www.amazon.com online gift certificate	$366.53	~~~~100 Sony Connect Music Downloads Worth $100!~~~~~	$22.50
for sale Gift Services can be used on amazon.com and amazon.co.uk		AMC movie gift card, $25 - free shipping!	$22.48
Amazon Gift Certificate for $350	$336.01	$25 AMC THEATRES ENTERTAINMENT	$22.30
350.00 BEST BUY GIFT CARD	$321.00	GIFT CERTIFICATE CARD	
$350.00 CIRCUIT CITY GIFT CARD	$301.00	$25 Amazon.com Gift Certificate - Instant Delivery	$22.00
$200 Dollar Amazon.com Gift Certificate!	$300.02	Blockbuster Gift card* 2 movies, 2 drinks, pocorn+bonus	$22.00

Books, Music, Movies ▸ Barnes and Noble

The average sales price in this subcategory is $56.72.

NOTE *These results are based on a search in this subcategory using the keywords* Barnes and Noble.

	HIGH		AVG
Barnes and Noble Store Credit Gift Card $307.95	$256.05	BARNES AND NOBLE Gift Cert Store Credit $76.63 w Bonus	$63.03
$250. Barnes and Noble STORE CREDIT BN GIFT CARD	$202.52	$75 Barnes and Noble Gift Card	$62.52
BARNES AND NOBLE $200.00 GIFT CARD FREE SHIPPING!!NR!!!	$164.50	BARNES AND NOBLE Gift Cert Store Credit $80.30 w Bonus	$62.33
BARNES AND NOBLE Gift Certificate $230 Value low price	$152.50	BARNES AND NOBLE STORE CREDIT GIFT CARD FREE SHIPPING!!	$60.13
Barnes and noble gift cards 131.12	$107.70	BARNES and & NOBLE Store Credit Gift Card Certificate	$57.49
Barnes and Noble gift Card value 131.07	$100.00	BARNES AND NOBLE GIFT CARD $62.01 value Free ship!	$52.70
$117 Barnes and Noble Starbucks Gift Certificate Card	$97.45	Barnes and Noble $60.00 gift card - FREE SHIPPING	$52.50
NEW $109.06 BARNES AND NOBLE GIFT CARD/STORE CREDIT	$95.55	$63 Barnes and Noble Gift Card B&N giftcard	$50.13
$100 Barnes and Noble Gift Card B&N – FREE SHIPPING!!!	$89.00	Barnes and Noble gift card $56.49 value FREE SHIP	$48.22
BARNES AND NOBLE Gift Cert Store Credit $105.37 w Bonus	$88.08	BARNES AND NOBLE $59.70 Store Credit /Gift Card	$48.20

Books, Music, Movies ▶ iTunes

The average sales price in this subcategory is $24.28.

NOTE *These results are based on a search in this subcategory using the keyword* iTunes.

	HIGH		AVG
$200 Two Hundred iTunes Gift Certificate	$127.50	iTunes Music Store Card and Song Certificate	$29.00
$200 iTunes Apple Store Online Gift Certificate Card	$119.99	50 iTunes Download Codes IMMEDIATE DELIVERY Apple iPod	$28.77
[4 of these sold for $119.99 each]		30 iTunes Download codes Apple iPod FREE Shipping	$26.99
iTunes gift cards totaling $120 FREE SHIPPING!!	$91.00	2x $15 iTunes Gift Card Certificate * Free Shipping *	$26.00
iTunes gift cards totaling $105	$88.08	Apple iTunes $30 (30 Songs) Gift Card Certificate iPod	$25.49
iTunes music Store Card totaling $100	$81.00	Apple iTunes $32 (30 Songs) Gift Card Certificate	$25.49
60 iTunes Music Store Song Downloads-CHEAP! Best Deal!!	$71.50	33 iTunes songs	$24.99
[2 of these sold in a multiple item ("Dutch") auction for $35.75 each]		Apple iTunes $32 (30 Songs) Gift Card Certificate	$24.87
60 iTunes Music Store Song Downloads-CHEAP! Best Deal!!	$70.10	39 iTunes iTune music store download cards !!	$24.50
[2 of these sold in a multiple item ("Dutch") auction for $35.05 each]		30 iTunes Download codes Apple iPod FREE Shipping	$24.19
iTunes Music Store Card Gift Card $50.00 iPod Gift Card	$44.29	$100 Marriott Bonus Bucks Coupon	$24.10
$50.00 APPLE ITUNES GIFT CARD FOR IPODS	$44.00	Exp 03/21/2006 +iTunes	
$45 iTunes Gift Card – Free Shipping!	$43.00	Apple iTunes $32 (30 Songs) Gift Card Certificate	$23.00
60 iTunes Music Store Song Downloads-CHEAP! Best Deal!!	$42.00	[2 of these sold for $23.00 each]	
60 iTunes CHEAP! Apple iPod! Free Shipping!!	$39.99	30 iTunes songs	$22.99
Apple iTunes iPod Music Store Gift Card $50 !NEW!	$38.00	[2 of these sold for $22.99 each]	
iTunes Music Store Cards $50	$37.25	30 iTunes Download codes Apple iPod FREE Shipping	$22.59
iTunes Music Store Gift Card Certificate $50 NR	$37.00	Apple iTunes $30 (30 Songs) Gift Card Certificate iPod	$22.55

Books, Music, Movies ▶ Amazon.com

The average sales price in this subcategory is $93.35.

NOTE *These results are based on a search in this subcategory using the keyword* Amazon.com.

	HIGH		AVG
$500 Amazon gift certificate-free shipping, no reserve	$471.53	$100 Amazon.com Gift Certificate	$95.00
Amazon Gift Certificate $500 Amazon.com No Shipping	$455.00	$100 Amazon.com Gift Certificate - Instant Email	$94.61
500 DOLLAR AMAZON.COM GIFT CERTIFICATE FREE SHIPPING	$450.00	AMAZON.COM $100 GIFT CERTIFICATE free shipping	$94.61
$450 Amazon Gift Certificate- Instant-Free delivery	$425.01	amazon.com Gift Certificate! $100 (4 x $25) Free ship!	$94.61
$200 AMAZON Gift certificate / card FREE SHIP no emails	$410.00	$100 AMAZON.COM E-MAILABLE GIFT CERTIFICATE!!!!!	$94.56
[2 of these sold in a multiple item ("Dutch") auction for $205.00 each]		$100 Amazon Gift Certificate Instant Email Delievery !!	$94.56
$400 amazon gift certificate credit pay not coupon card	$370.00	$100 AMAZON.COM GIFT CARD	$94.53
$400 Amazon Gift Card Certificate	$360.00	CERTIFICATE (FREE SHIPPING)	
AMAZON.COM $325 Gift Certificates FREE DELIVERY	$310.00	$100 AMAZON.com GIFT card CERTIFICATE exp 6/07 FREE SH	$94.53
$100 AMAZON Gift certificate / card FREE SHIP no emails	$285.00	$100 Amazon Gift Certificate Instant Email Delievery !!	$94.53
[3 of these sold in a multiple item ("Dutch") auction for $95.00 each]		AMAZON.COM $100 GIFT CERTIFICATE free shipping	$94.43
Amazon.com Gift Certificate $300- Free Shipping	$265.00	AMAZON.COM GIFT CERTIFICATE! $100	$94.11
$263 AMAZON Gift Certificate INSTANT Email DELIVERY !	$250.00	(4X$25)-INSTANT EMAIL	
$250 Amazon.com Gift Certificate FREE email delivery	$245.02	$100 Amazon Gift Certificate Instant Email Delievery !!	$94.00
$250 Amazon Gift Certificate FREE email delivery	$242.54	$100 Amazon.com Gift Certificate Card *No Reserve*	$94.00
$250 Amazon gift certificate FREE SHIPPING exp 04/2007!	$233.50	AMAZON.COM $100 GIFT CERTIFICATE FREE SHIPPING!!!	$93.57
$240 Amazon Gift Certificate- Instant-Free delivery	$228.01	$100 Amazon Gift Certificate Instant Email Delievery !!	$93.56

Books, Music, Movies ▶ Entertainment

The average sales price in this subcategory is $13.75.

NOTE *These results are based on a search in this subcategory using the keyword* entertainment.

	HIGH		AVG
ENTERTAINMENT 2006 COUPON BOOK BOSTON AND MASSACHUSETTS	$74.97	$20.00 in Regal Entertainment Group Gift Certificates	$18.55
[3 of these sold in a multiple item ("Dutch") auction for $24.99 each]		2005 ENTERTAINMENT BOOK GTR VICTORIA	$15.50
2006 Brand New ENTERTAINMENT BOOK for Phoenix, AZ	$50.00	& MID VANCOUVER IS	
[2 of these sold in a multiple item ("Dutch") auction for $25.00 each]		IA/ND/NE/SD Omaha - Lincoln Boul $500 Entertainment Pkg	$10.49
AMC Entertainment Gift Card $50 Certified Mail ++Bonus	$42.08	FL Orlando Boardwalk Entertainme $250 Entertainment Pkg	$9.99
Regal Entertainment Gift Card $45 Free Shipping +Bonus	$40.02	NY New York City Rascals Comedy $360 Entertainment Pkg	$9.99
AMC THEATRES $40 ENTERTAINMENT CARD, MOVIES, POPCORN!	$34.00		

Books, Music, Movies ▶ Blockbuster

The average sales price in this subcategory is $17.45.

NOTE *These results are based on a search in this subcategory using the keyword* Blockbuster.

	HIGH		AVG
$250 Blockbuster Gift Card + Free Ship + Bonus + NR!	$237.50	$25 Blockbuster $5 Toys R Us Gift Card Cards Giftcard	$20.00
$ 150 Blockbuster Gift Card FREE SHIPPING	$140.00	10 Blockbuster FREE Rental Coupons MOVIE DVD or VHS	$19.50
Blockbuster Value Card	$110.00	10 BLOCKBUSTER FREE Rental Coupons Gift MOVIE DVD GAME	$19.50
$111.31 Blockbuster store credit gift card	$85.00	Blockbuster Gift Card $25	$19.50

Blockbuster Video $100 GIFT CARD	$83.50	12 FREE Blockbuster Gift Certificates	$19.00
Blockbuster Gift Card $100 *Free Shipping*	$82.10	Blockbuster Free Rentals DVD 20 Free Rental Certificate	$18.99
$100 BLOCKBUSTER GIFT CARD- FREE SHIPPING	$80.00	10 BLOCKBUSTER FREE Rental Coupons Gift MOVIE DVD GAME	$18.99
$100 Blockbuster Gift Card - Free Shipping!	$76.00	$20 Blockbuster Gift Card - Free shipping and handling	$18.52
$70 Blockbuster Gift Card Free Shipping!!!	$60.50	10 BLOCKBUSTER FREE Rental Coupons Gift MOVIE DVD GAME	$18.51
$50 Blockbuster Gift Card.......Free shipping w/bin	$45.00	BLOCKBUSTER $20 Giftcard $20 Gift Card NR Free Shipping	$18.50
BLOCKBUSTER GIFT CARDS $50 - FREE S/H	$43.01	10 FREE BLOCKBUSTER Rentals Coupons Gift MOVIE/DVD/GAME	$17.75
Blockbuster Gift Card $50 Free Shipping	$42.55	$25.00 Gift Card for Blockbuster Movie Store	$17.61
$50 BLOCKBUSTER GIFT CERTIFICATE CARD 1/31/08, LOW S/H	$42.25	$20 Blockbuster Gift Card - Free Shipping	$17.51
$50 Blockbuster Gift Card Certificate. FREE shipping!	$42.06	$20 Blockbuster Gift Card GiftCard - FREE shipping*	$17.51
$50.00 Blockbuster Gift Card - Free Shipping	$41.02	10 FREE BLOCKBUSTER Rentals Coupons Gift MOVIE/DVD/GAME	$17.50

Books, Music, Movies ▶ Borders

The average sales price in this subcategory is $49.33.

NOTE *These results are based on a search in this subcategory using the keyword* Borders.

	HIGH		AVG
Borders Gift Card $350 Great Gift!	$232.50	BORDERS/ Waldenbooks/Brentano's Gift Card Credit $81.17	$68.01
Borders Gift Card $211.06 Free Shipping!!	$162.50	$75 BORDERS BOOK STORE GIFT CARD Free Shipping NEW	$65.00
Borders Gift Card $211.06 Free Shipping!!	$152.50	$75 Borders Gift Card with Free Shipping	$62.51
BORDERS WALDENBOOKS GIFT CARD $175.70	$143.06	$71.93 Borders / Waldenbooks Return Gift Card- Free S/H	$62.14
Borders Waldens Brentano's Gift Card $157.95 FREE SHIP!	$128.90	$75 BORDERS Gift card, No Exp. Free Shipping, NR	$61.00
Borders Gift Card $173.18 Free Shipping!!	$122.50	Borders and/or Walden Books Gift Card $75!	$60.00
Borders Bretano's gift card $141.01 certificate Free SH	$118.26	$74 Borders/ Amazon.com gift card certificate Free S/H	$56.13
$130 BORDERS Books Gift Card FREE SHIPPING! No Reserve!	$107.00	BORDERS/ Waldenbooks/Brentano's Gift Card Credit $70.34	$56.01
126.00 BORDERS GIFT CARD W/ FREE S/H AND CONFIRMATION!!	$103.50	Borders Gift Card - FREE SHIPPING!	$53.05
$100 Amazon/borders E-gift certificate! exp 2007!!	$96.00	BORDERS BOOKS STORE GIFT CARD / CERTIFICATE ~53.86 BOOK	$46.01
Gift Card for Borders or Waldenbooks valued at $105.95	$91.90	$52.95 Borders / Waldenbooks Gift Card- Free S/H	$46.00
$100 Borders/ Amazon.com gift card certificate Free S/H	$91.00	$58.25 Borders / Waldenbooks Gift Card- Free S/H	$46.00
Borders Waldenbooks $100 Gift card certificate Border's	$82.01	Borders $50 Gift Card. Unused.	$45.00
Borders Return Gift Card $98.27 Free S/H	$82.00	BORDERS $55 Gift Card no exp date	$44.01
$100 BORDERS STORE GIFT CARD with Free Shipping !!!	$81.01	$57.10 Borders / Waldenbooks Gift Card- Free S/H	$43.83

Books, Music, Movies ▶ Circuit City

The average sales price in this subcategory is $84.04.

NOTE *These results are based on a search in this subcategory using the keywords* Circuit City.

	HIGH		AVG
Circuit City $500 Gift Card worth & coupon target bonus	$473.89	$129.28 Circuit City Gift Card NR	$115.00
$500 CIRCUIT CITY GIFT CARD CERTIFICATE FREE SHIPPING	$472.67	CIRCUIT CITY GIFT CARD Value $114.47 FREE SHIPPING L@@K	$102.61
$500 Circuit City Gift Card No Reserve!	$470.02	Circuit City Gift Card $110 No Expiration Free Shipping	$98.00
$500 Circuit City Gift Card FREE SHIPPING!!!	$465.01	CIRCUIT CITY $100 GIFT CERTIFICATE CARD FREE SHIPPING !	$94.09
$500 Circuit City Gift Card Certificate	$450.00	Circuit City CC $100 Gift Card Certificate FREE S & H	$93.01
$500 Circuit City Gift Cards - Certificate Credit !!!!!	$445.00	$105.00 circuit city gift merchandise card	$92.00
$476.88 circuit city gift merchandise card	$426.52	$100 Circuit City Gift Card Plus $30 OFF Coupons	$91.00
$450 Circuit City Gift Certificate FREE SHIPPING!!!	$425.00	$100 + Gift Card Certificate Mystery Maybe Circuit City	$75.00
$394 Circuit City Gift Card with Free Priority Shipping	$370.00	CIRCUIT CITY GIFT CARD $75 VALUE FREE SHIPPING IN U.S.!	$69.09
$425 Circuit City (CC) Gift Card FAST FREE SHIP!	$345.00	$75 circuit city gift card FREE SHIPPING $75	$67.02
$300 Circuit City Gift Card with Free Priority Shipping	$275.00	$73.49 circuit city gift merchandise card	$63.73
$326.39 Circuit City Gift Card - $s Off Electronics	$275.00	$65 Circuit City Gift Card Get it during their sale!	$60.09
$286.74 circuit city gift merchandise card	$260.01	$500 in Blank Circuit City Store Manager GC + Bonus!	$50.00
$257.03 circuit city gift card giftcard N/R	$233.50	$50 Circuit City Gift Certificate	$46.02
$252.25 circuit city gift merchandise card	$231.87	$50 Circuit City Gift Card. **will ship for free**	$45.50

Books, Music, Movies ▶ Movies

The average sales price in this subcategory is $11.80.

NOTE *These results are based on a search in this subcategory using the keyword* movies.

HIGH TO LOW			
(10) AMC MOVIE PASSES! Free Movies!! Comp tickets	$47.05	2 AMC THEATRE Movie Tickets Gen Adm FREE MOVIES #3	$11.01
(10) AMC MOVIE PASSES! Free Movies!! Comp tickets	$46.55	Best Buy Gift Card music, music, and more	$8.00
AMC THEATRES $40 ENTERTAINMENT CARD, MOVIES, POPCORN!	$34.00	$10 BLOCKBUSTER gift card movies games FREE shipping	$7.61
AMC THEATRES $25.00 GIFT CARD MOVIES POPCORN COKES	$19.62	Borders Books,Music,Movies (2) $10 off Coupons	$7.50
$20 AMC Movies Gift Card for Tickets or Consessions	$17.55	$21 Movie Cash Certificates Coupons FREE movies	$5.05
fye Gift Card $$$ music, movies, games, more	$15.51	AMC Theatres Movies Save a Ton!!!	$5.00
2 AMC THEATRE Movie Tickets Gen Adm FREE MOVIES	$12.01	BLOCKBUSTER Coupons 2 Free Rentals and 5-$1 OFF Movies	$3.25
[2 of these sold for $12.01 each]		Free 4 small Popcorns at Loews Cineplex Movies	$2.24

Books, Music, Movies ▸ AMC Theatres

The average sales price in this subcategory is $11.80.

NOTE *These results are based on a search in this subcategory using the keywords* AMC Theatres.

HIGH TO LOW

2 Gift Certificates $25 each ($50) AMC Movie Theatres	$41.40	4 AMC Movie Theatres Tickets worth over $30	$20.00
AMC THEATRES $40 ENTERTAINMENT CARD, MOVIES, POPCORN!	$34.00	4 AMC Movie Theatres Tickets worth over $30	$20.00
		AMC THEATRES $25.00 GIFT CARD MOVIES POPCORN COKES	$19.62
$30.00 AMC Theatres gift card....NO RESERVE!	$25.02	2 AMC Theatres Movie Tickets Passes, valued up to $21	$9.57
AMC Theatres $25 Gift Certificate	$21.49	2 AMC Theatres Movie Tickets Passes, valued up to $21	$9.50
AMC THEATRES $25.00 GIFT CARD	$20.52	AMC Theatres Movies Save a Ton!!!	$5.00
AMC THEATRES $25.00 GIFT CARD	$20.50	amc theatres coupon one free small popcorn no reserve!!	$1.54

Books, Music, Movies ▸ Sam Goody

The average sales price in this subcategory is $13.20.

NOTE *These results are based on a search in this subcategory using the keywords* Sam Goody.

HIGH TO LOW

Suncoast Sam Goody $50 Fifty Dollar Gift Card	$35.00	Suncoast Sam Goody On Cue Media	$6.50
SAM GOODY GIFT CARD FREE SHIPPING!!	$15.00	Play $10.00 Gift Card	
Suncoast Sam Goody On Cue Media Play Gift Card	$7.50	Sam Goody Gift Card – FREE SHIPPING	$2.00

Books, Music, Movies ▸ Sony

The average sales price in this subcategory is $11.80.

NOTE *These results are based on a search in this subcategory using the keyword* Sony.

HIGH TO LOW

50 FREE Sony Connect Music Store Downloads! NOT USED!	$15.49	10 Sony Connect downloads code	$2.99
36 FREE SONY CONNECT MUSIC STORE DOWNLOADS	$11.61	[2 of these sold for $2.99 each]	
30 Song DOWNLOAD SONY CONNECT POSSIBLE FREE SHIPPING NR	$10.00	Sony Picturebook PCG-C1VPK Laptop Motherboard Coupon	$2.99
GET 20 MUSIC SONG DOWNLOADS WITH SONY CONNECT	$6.05	15 FREE DOWNLOADS FROM THE SONY CONNECT MUSIC STORE	$2.50
25 FREE Sony Connect Music Store Downloads! NOT USED!	$4.25	Sony Connect 4 songs download **FREE SHIPPING w/BIN**	$2.49
Sony Connect - Coupon Codes for 10 Song Downloads	$3.50	Connect Sony 10 music downloads until 03/31/2006	$2.25
10 Sony Connect Music Downloads Free Shipping	$3.47	10 FREE Sony Connect Music Store Downloads	$1.00

Books, Music, Movies ▸ Best Buy

The average sales price in this subcategory is $111.14.

NOTE *These results are based on a search in this subcategory using the keywords* Best Buy.

	HIGH		AVG
$200 BESTBUY BEST BUY GIFT CARD NO EXP. FREE SHIPPING	$543.00	$200... BEST BUY GIFT CARD CERTIFICATE...NO EXPIRATION	$178.50
[3 of these sold in a multiple item ("Dutch") auction for $181.00 each]		$200 Best Buy Gift Card Certificate	$177.77
$500 Best Buy Gift Certificate Card No Reserve!!!	$492.00	$200 BESTBUY BEST BUY GIFT CARD	$177.50
$500 Best Buy Gift Cards - FREE FAST SHIPPING- no exp.	$475.00	NO EXP. FREE SHIPPING	
$500.00 BEST BUY GIFT CARD!!!	$474.99	$200 Best Buy gift card NEVER EXPIRES, Free Shipping!!!	$177.50
BEST BUY GIFT CARD $500	$469.00	BEST BUY $200.00 GIFT CARDs	$163.49
[2 of these sold for $469.00 each]		BEST BUY GIFT CARD $ 188.99 FREE SHIPPING!! NR!!	$162.51
Best Buy Gift Card $500	$465.00	$175 Best Buy Gift Card. Buy it Now. Don't Miss Out!	$157.50
$500 Best Buy Gift Card - Good Anywhere in the US!	$465.00	$174.94 Best Buy Gift Card Free Shipping No Reserve	$154.00
Best Buy $500 Gift Card No Expiration	$465.00	Best Buy gift certificates $160	$145.05
$500 Best Buy Gift Card - no expiration date	$464.00	$150 Best Buy gift card	$135.50
BEST BUY GIFT CARD-$500.00!	$456.00	$ 150 BEST BUY GIFT CARD N/R NO	$135.00
Best Buy Gift Cards $500 - Free Shipping - No Reserve	$455.00	EXP DATE FREE SHIPPING	
$500.00 Best Buy gift certificate, free ship	$452.09	$150 Best Buy Gift Certificate	$135.00
Best Buy Gift Card $500	$451.87	$150 Best Buy Gift Cards Never Expires Free Shipping!!!	$134.50
BEST BUY GIFT CARD $500.00 NO EXPIRATION N/R	$450.00	Best Buy Gift Card/Voucher	$131.02
BEST BUY GIFT CARD $500.00 NO EXPIRATION N/R	$442.50	$135 Best Buy Gift Certificate Cards! Free Shipping!	$120.00

Books, Music, Movies ▸ Loews

The average sales price in this subcategory is $12.93.

NOTE *These results are based on a search in this subcategory using the keyword* Loews.

HIGH TO LOW

$40 LOEWS CINEPLEX REEL DOLLARS MAGIC JOHNSON, STAR	$36.99	2 Loews/Star Theatre Movie Passes	$10.00
$25 Loews Cineplex Gift Card Reel Dollars FREE SHIPPING	$22.55	Loews Cineplex Movie Gift Certificates	$8.51
4 FREE Loews Movie Tickets/Passes	$22.51	1 Loews Movie Gift Certificate + Free Popcorn Coupon	$6.50

4 FREE Loews Movie Tickets/Passes	$20.10	Free 4 small Popcorns at Loews Cineplex Movies	$2.24
4 FREE Loews Movie Tickets/Passes	$20.01	Free 4 small Popcorns at Loews Cineplex Movies	$2.24
4 FREE Loews Movie Tickets/Passes	$19.80	Discount Movie Tickets to Loews, Cineplex Odeon, Star	$0.99
Two (2) Loews/Cineplex Free Admission Movie Tickets	$10.51	FOUR (4) LOEWS/CINEPLEX FANDANGO	$0.99
Two (2) Loews/Cineplex Free Admission Movie Tickets	$10.01	FREE MOVIE TICKETS	

Books, Music, Movies ▶ Hollywood

The average sales price in this subcategory is $11.51.

NOTE *These results are based on a search in this subcategory using the keyword* Hollywood.

	HIGH		AVG
JAMES TAYLOR /HOLLYWOOD BWL/ CLOSE/ BEST SUMMER NIGHT!	$127.50	10 FREE HOLLYWOOD VIDEO DVD / GAME COUPONS SAVE $59.90!	$12.56
$180.77 Gift card certificate Fredericks of Hollywood	$120.50	4 HOLLYWOOD MOVIE MONEY GIFT CERTIFICATE	$12.54
DINNER FOR TWO YAMASHIRO RESTAURANT HOLLYWOOD, CA	$82.95	10 FREE HOLLYWOOD VIDEO DVD / GAME COUPONS SAVE $59.90!	$12.29
6 HOLLYWOOD MOVIE CASH MOVIE MONEY TICKETS - $63 VALUE	$39.50	10 FREE HOLLYWOOD VIDEO DVD / GAME COUPONS SAVE $59.90!	$12.27
$48 Hollywood Movie Money (4- $12 tickets) FREE SHIP	$37.52	10 FREE HOLLYWOOD VIDEO DVD / GAME COUPONS SAVE $59.90!	$12.00
$40 Hollywood Video Gift Cards	$33.10	10 FREE HOLLYWOOD VIDEO DVD / GAME COUPONS SAVE $59.90!	$11.58
Trastevere Restaurant Hollywood CA $60Gift Certificate	$31.87	10 FREE HOLLYWOOD VIDEO DVD / GAME COUPONS SAVE $59.90!	$11.57
$40 PLANET HOLLYWOOD GIFT CERTIFICATES - ANY LOCATION!	$26.15	10 FREE HOLLYWOOD VIDEO DVD / GAME COUPONS SAVE $59.90!	$11.09
12 FREE HOLLYWOOD VIDEO Game or Movie Rental Coupons	$22.01	10 FREE HOLLYWOOD VIDEO DVD / GAME COUPONS SAVE $59.90!	$11.06
$25 Gift Certificate - Planet Hollywood D'town Disney	$22.00	[2 of these sold for $11.06 each]	
12 Free Rentals at Hollywood Video!	$20.00	10 FREE HOLLYWOOD VIDEO DVD / GAME COUPONS SAVE $BIG	$11.03
Hollywood Movie Tickets Passes (3) $31.50 value	$20.00	10 FREE HOLLYWOOD VIDEO DVD / GAME COUPONS SAVE $59.90!	$11.03
12 Free Rentals at Hollywood Video!	$18.01	10 Free Hollywood Video DVD or Game Rentals	$11.00
2 Hollywood Movie Money certificates $24 value tickets	$16.61	10 FREE HOLLYWOOD VIDEO DVD / GAME COUPONS SAVE $59.90!	$11.00
Hollywood Movie Money Tickets - $24 Value	$16.38	10 FREE HOLLYWOOD VIDEO DVD / GAME COUPONS SAVE $59.90!	$10.51

Clothing

NOTE *There is no average price statement for this subcategory because the prices were obtained using eBay's Completed Items feature.*

	HIGH		AVG
Abercrombie & Fitch $500 Gift Card	$495.00	$60 off at Gap/Old Navy/Banana Republic.com gift card	$25.00
Victoria's Secret Certificates $625 for only $525	$461.32	$50 Banana Republic Online LUXE Reward Gift Card	$25.00
$500 Kohl's Gift Card!!! Low Shipping!	$450.22	GYMBOREE GYMBUCKS $50 OFF $100 PURCHASE FREE SHIPPING!	$25.00
NORDSTROM NORDSTROMS $500 GIFT CARD! FREE SHIP!	$450.00	Victoria's Secret Gift Card- $30 Value- No Reserve	$25.00
Goldsmith's Macy's Gift Card Certificate Worth $500.00	$447.00	$50 Banana Republic Online LUXE Reward Gift Card	$25.00
$500 Macy's Gift Card - - Shop; Shop; Shop!!!	$445.00	$50 Banana Republic Online Reward Gift Card + FREE S/H	$25.00
$500.00 Dillard's Gift Card, Dillards	$436.00	$50 Banana Republic Online LUXE Reward Gift Card	$25.00
Free Shipping NR! Gift Services		$50 Gap Online Reward Gift Card + FREE S/H!	$25.00
$500 NEIMAN MARCUS Gift Certificate	$431.99	$50 Banana Republic Online Reward Gift Card	$25.00
Saks 5th Ave Gift Card- -face value $500	$430.00	$50 Gap Online Reward Gift Card + FREE S/H!	$25.00
+++++ MACY'S $ 500 Gift Card MACYS +++++	$430.00	COACH COUPON FOR YOUR PURSE/	$24.99
$500 JC PENNY GIFT CARD !! gift cards WOW HOT!!	$430.00	BAG OR WALLET SAVE 25%	
BANANA REPUBLIC GIFT CARD $499.16 FREE S/H.	$427.00	$30 Abercrombie and Fitch Gift Certificate	$24.56
I am the Cheapest on eBay gauranteed. NO PAYPAL.		Victoria's Secret Gift Certificate $29 - FREE SHIPPING	$24.50
$500 TJ MAXX GIFT CARD NR W/ FREE SHIPPING	$425.02	$25.00 GIFT CARD - Kohl's - FREE SHIPPING - Kohls	$24.25
$500 Banana Republic gift card	$425.00	JC Penney merchandise certificate $35.90	$24.16

Clothing ▶ Ann Taylor

The average sales price in this subcategory is $28.09.

NOTE *These results are based on a search in this subcategory using the keywords* Ann Taylor.

HIGH TO LOW			
$150 Ann Taylor gift card, FREE SHIPPING	$142.00	ANN TAYLOR COUPON 15-20% OFF – IN-STORE or ONLINE	$5.05
NEW Ann Taylor Store Gift Certificate Card Merchandise	$19.65	(4) Ann Taylor Loft coupons - 15% and 20% off purchase	$5.00
$27 ANN TAYLOR GIFT CARD GUARANTEED AUTHENTIC!	$19.00	ANN TAYLOR COUPON 15-20% OFF – IN-STORE or ONLINE	$4.01
Ann Taylor $20 Gift Card - Loft, Factory Store, Online	$16.00	ANN TAYLOR COUPON DISCOUNT CARD	$2.26
ANN TAYLOR LOFT Coupon ~ 15% or 20% ~ store, online	$8.01	SAVE 15%-20%OFF CLOTHES	

Clothing ▶ Lane Bryant

The average sales price in this subcategory is $11.51.

NOTE *These results are based on a search in this subcategory using the keywords* Lane Bryant.

	HIGH		AVG
LANE BRYANT GIFTCARD WORTH $85.26 W/RECEIPT	$65.00	5 Lane Bryant gift cheques (coupons) $15/$15 & $50/$150	$10.63
Lane Bryant Gift Card 60$ No Exp.	$51.02	Save up to $75 off at Lane Bryant - Online or Store	$10.00
(20) Lane Bryant cheques (coupons)	$38.07	[2 of these sold in a multiple item ("Dutch") auction for $5.00 each]	
$15/$15 & $50/$150		2 Lane Bryant $15.00 Gift Cheque exp. Aug.31 2005	$7.55

Clothing ▶ Chico's

The average sales price in this subcategory is $11.51.

NOTE *These results are based on a search in this subcategory using the keyword* Chico's.

HIGH TO LOW

10 Coupons El Chico Free Top Shelf Queso	$9.99	Chico Chicos $25 off $100 purchase coupon–good til 9/5	$0.99

Clothing ▶ Old Navy

The average sales price in this subcategory is $38.72.

NOTE *These results are based on a search in this subcategory using the keywords* Old Navy.

	HIGH		AVG
OLD NAVY GIFT CARD $500.00 NO EXPIRATION N/R	$378.08	OLD NAVY $75.00 Gift Card w/ free shipping!!!	$65.65
OLD NAVY $250 Gift Card Back to School BTS 4 5 6 7 8	$216.50	Old Navy $75.00 gift certificate	$63.35
old navy giftcard	$200.00	$50 GAP Old Navy Banana Republic Gift Certificates	$50.01
old navy gift card merchandise credit $158	$113.61	THREE- $20 Reward Cards For Banana Rep, Gap, old navy	$45.00
THREE- $50 Reward Cards For Banana Rep, Gap, old navy	$96.51	Old Navy $50.00 Giftcard! Free Shipping!	$42.56
$100 Old Navy gift card certificate FREE shipping!!	$93.52	$50 off Gap/Old Navy/Banana Republic.com gift card	$36.00
2 X $50 Old Navy Gift Card for Stores/Online FREE SHIP!	$93.00	OLD NAVY gift card $40.00 giftcard Old Navy FREE SHIP	$31.00
[2 of these sold for $46.00 each]		$30 OLD NAVY GIFT CARD w/ FREE shipping!!!	$27.01
$100 Old Navy gift certificate card Free shipping!!!	$92.40	Old Navy/Old Navy Outlet $25 Gift Card - Free Shipping!	$26.31
$100 OLD NAVY GIFT CERTIFICATE CARD	$92.00	$30 Old Navy Gift Card - Free Shipping!	$25.63
**$100.00~OLD NAVY~Gift Card Certificate 4/$25 Free S/H	$90.00	Old Navy Gift Card Credit $28.00 Free Shipping!!	$24.50
OLD NAVY 100.00 GIFT CARD, FREE SHIPPING TO US	$89.00	$25 OLD NAVY GIFT CARD –free shipping	$23.50
Never Used Old Navy $100 Gift Card banana republic gap	$83.00	$50 off & Free Shipping at Old Navy/Gap.com gift card	$23.00
$100.00 OLD NAVY Gift Certificate	$82.02	Old Navy/Old Navy Outlet $25 Gift Card - Free Shipping!	$22.76
$100 Old Navy / Gap /Banana Republic Reward / Gift Card	$81.00	Old Navy/Old Navy Outlet $25 Gift Card - Free Shipping!	$22.26

Clothing ▶ Saks

The average sales price in this subcategory is $207.94.

NOTE *These results are based on a search in this subcategory using the keyword* Saks.

HIGH TO LOW

SAKS FIFTH AVENUE GIFT CERTIFICATE CARD $500 VALUE	$485.00	Amex gift certificate SAKS FIFTH AVENUE $200.00	$150.00
SAKS FIFTH AVENUE GIFT CARD- $500 VALUE	$422.99	Saks Fifth Avenue Gift Card - $100 value - Free Ship	$91.00
SAKS FIFTH AVENUE GIFT CERTIFICATE CARD $450 VALUE	$410.00	$100 Saks Fifth Avenue Gift Card	$89.01
Saks Fifth Avenue $500 Gift Card Fully Transferable	$400.00	SAKS FIFTH AVENUE $100 GIFT CARD	$89.01
saks 5th ave gift card $400	$355.01	Qty 2 $50 SAKS FIFTH AVENUE Gift Certificates exp:02/06	$82.02
$387.63 SAKS 5TH AVE. GIFT CARD	$340.00	SAKS FIFTH AVENUE $35 GIFT CARD CERTIFICATE	$30.00
SAKS FIFTH AVENUE (5th Avenue) $200 Gift card	$181.00	SAKS FIFTH AVENUE $25.00 GIFT CARD / GIFT CERTIFICATE	$19.51
Saks Fifth Ave*Store Credit/Gift Card* $187.60 Free Shp	$172.00	SAKS FIFTH AVENUE GIFT CARD GIFT CERTIFICATE $35	$10.50

Clothing ▶ Gymboree

The average sales price in this subcategory is $88.22.

NOTE *These results are based on a search in this subcategory using the keyword* Gymboree.

	HIGH		AVG
Gymboree Merchandise credit gift card $376	$305.00	$130 Gymboree Gift Certificate Card	$109.50
GYMBOREE GIFT CARD CERTIFICATE~MERCH CREDIT~$208.40~WOW	$185.00	NWT Gymboree Fox Trot barette & FREE $120 CREDIT	$94.00
GYMBOREE MERCHANDISE CREDIT ~~~~~~$199.41	$170.01	GYMBOREE gift card $ 95 CREDIT MERCHANISE $ 95	$86.00
Gymboree Merchandise Credit / Gift Card $204.78 SAVE!!!	$167.50	$61.89 Gymboree Merchandise Credit	$48.00
$168 Gymboree Gift Certificate Card	$152.50	Gymboree coupon 25% off total sale. Expires July 2006.	$45.44

Clothing ▶ TJ Maxx

The average sales price in this subcategory is $118.69.

NOTE *These results are based on a search in this subcategory using the keywords* TJ Maxx.

	HIGH		AVG
$500 TJ MAXX GIFT CARD NR W/ FREE SHIPPING	$455.06	TJ MAXX GIFT CARD-SAME AS CASH! VALUE $209.- NO RESERVE	$176.52
$492.00 TJ Maxx -Merchandise Credit	$418.00	TJ Maxx Merchandise Credit/ Gift Card T.J. Max $146	$127.00
$398.00 Tj MAXX GIFT CARD	$350.01	TJ MAXX Gift Certificate Card Merchandise Credit $ 117	$104.70
TJ Maxx TJMaxx Gift Card Certificate $398.31	$347.99	TJ MAXX GIFT CARD	$102.51
400.00 TJ MAXX GIFTCARD	$340.98	*TJ MAXX* STORE CREDIT/GIFT CARD $107.95!! free ship	$93.02

Clothing ▶ Land's End

The average sales price in this subcategory is $12.55.

NOTE *These results are based on a search in this subcategory using the keywords* Land's End.

HIGH TO LOW

$25 Land's End Gift Card	$17.60 $10.00 LAND'S END GIFT CARD (GOOD @ SEARS ALSO) NO EXPI	$7.50

Clothing ▶ Victoria's Secret

The average sales price in this subcategory is $20.49.

NOTE *These results are based on a search in this subcategory using the keywords* Victoria's Secret.

	HIGH		AVG
Victoria's Secret clothing Gift card, certificate 276$	$248.82	Victoria's Secret Gift Card FREE SHIPPING	$35.00
Victoria's Secret Gift Card $250	$244.65	Victoria's Secret Credit $41.29..No Expiration.	$34.00
Victoria's Secret clothing Gift card, certificate 276$	$237.50	*WOW* VICTORIA'S SECRET $38.57 GIFT CARD W/FREE GIFT!!	$27.01
$215 Victoria's Victorias Secret Gift Certificate Card	$187.50	Victoria's Secret $33.98 Certificate	$25.55
VICTORIA'S SECRET GIFT CARD $189.16	$160.26	Victoria's Secret Gift Card of $30.85 - giftcard	$23.53
$150.00 - Victoria's Secret Gift Card	$153.50	$25 Victoria's secret gift certificate Free Shipping	$21.50
Victoria's Secret Merchandise Gift Certificate $192.50	$145.00	THE LIMITED + VICTORIA'S SECRET STORE CREDITS	$21.50
$160 VICTORIA'S SECRET GIFT CARD~STORE~ONLINE~FREE S&H	$133.50	Victoria's Secret $25 Gift Card Certificate FREE S/H	$21.00
Victoria's Secret Gift Card	$132.50	Victoria's Secret Gift Card $25.00...NR	$20.56
VICTORIA'S SECRET $ 100 STORE CREDIT GIFT CARD free s	$89.50	Victoria's Secret Angel Reward Gift Card FREE SHIPPING	$20.50
$100 Victoria's Secret Gift Card	$85.00	Victoria's Secret Gift Card VALUE $25.00	$20.08
Victoria's Secret Gift Card $90.51 NO RESERVE!!	$76.00	VICTORIA'S SECRET GIFT CARD	$20.00
VICTORIA'S SECRET GIFT CARD !!! NO RESERVE !!!	$74.06	Victoria's Secret Gift Card $25	$20.00
$100 VICTORIA'S SECRET GIFT CARD	$71.07	Victoria's Secret $25 Angel Reward Card - Gift Card	$19.77
$85 VICTORIA'S SECRET GIFT CARD GUARANTEED AUTHENTIC!	$71.02	VICTORIA'S SECRET GIFT CARD $20.00 - FREE SHIPPING	$18.72

Clothing ▶ Macy's

The average sales price in this subcategory is $87.42.

NOTE *These results are based on a search in this subcategory using the keyword* Macy's.

HIGH TO LOW

MACY MACYS MACY'S $500 GIFT CARD NEW FAST Shipping	$447.23	Macy*s $50 Gift Card - Free shipping if sold for $45	$42.00
MACY MACYS MACY'S $400 GIFT	$338.00	Macy "Friends & Family" Coupon for 15-20% OFF	$2.44
CARD NEW FAST Shipping		Macy*s 20% OFF Discount Coupons	$2.25
Macy*s $219.14 Gift Card	$174.50	$10 off a $50 storewide purchase at Macy*s - exp 12/05	$1.04
$100 Macy*s Gift Certificate	$83.01	$10 off a $50 storewide purchase at Macy*s - exp 12/05	$0.99
Macy*s $50 Gift Card - Free shipping if sold for $45	$42.01	[4 of these sold for $0.99 each]	

Clothing ▶ Marshall Fields

The average sales price in this subcategory is $100.42.

NOTE *These results are based on a search in this subcategory using the keywords* Marshall Fields.

HIGH TO LOW

$250 Marshall Fields Card! **Free Fast Shipping**	$207.50	2 $50.00 Marshall Fields Gift Cards FREE SHIPPING	$86.99
$200 Marshall Fields Gift Card Free Ship! NO RESERVE!	$187.39	MARSHALL FIELD'S $100 Gift	$86.00
$100 Marshall Fields Gift Certificate Card Free s/h	$92.50	Card~NR & FREE SHIPPING	
$100 Marshall Fields Field's gift card FREE SHIPPING	$92.50	Marshall Fields Gift Card No Reserve/With Receipt	$39.01
Marshall Field's Gift Card $100 , NO EXPIRATION	$91.00	$25.79 in gift cards to marshall fields	$20.89

Clothing ▶ Gap

The average sales price in this subcategory is $61.75.

NOTE *These results are based on a search in this subcategory using the keyword* Gap.

	HIGH		AVG
$500 Gap Gift Card Certificate & free shipping	$411.15	$100 Old Navy / Gap /Banana Republic Reward / Gift Card	$80.75
$310 Gap Gift Certificate Card	$290.00	$100 Old Navy / Gap /Banana Republic Reward / Gift Card	$80.30
GAP GIFT CARD CERTIFICATE $100 GAP.COM KIDS free ship	$264.00	$100 Old Navy / Gap /Banana Republic Reward / Gift Card	$80.20
[3 of these sold in a multiple item ("Dutch") auction for $88.00 each]		$100.00 Gap/Old Navy Bucks Back Coupons/gift card	$79.55
$290 Gap Gift Certificate Card	$256.01	$100.00 Gap/Old Navy Bucks Back Coupons/gift card	$79.00
$290 Gap Gift Certificate Card	$245.00	[2 of these sold for $79.00 each]	
$300 Gap Card - Back to School Special	$236.49	GAP GIFT CARD CERTIFICATE $100 GAP.COM BABY KIDS	$76.00
$275 GAP gift card - Free Shipping - No Expiration	$223.52	[2 of these sold for $76.00 each]	

	HIGH		AVG
$250 The Gap gift card certificate ***free shipping****	$221.00	GAP GIFT CARD CERTIFICATE $100 GAP.COM BABY KIDS	$72.01
$250. GAP/GAP KIDS/BABY/GAP.COM/	$209.37	GAP GIFT CARD CERTIFICATE $100 GAP.COM BABY KIDS	$72.00
GAP OUTLET GIFT CARD		GAP GIFT CARD CERTIFICATE $100 GAP.COM BABY KIDS	$71.01
$250 Gap Gift Card	$201.05	GAP GIFT CARD $75.00	$66.01
~GAP $200 Gift Card Gift Certificate~	$183.51	Gap Gift Cards $75	$65.65
$200 GAP GIFT CARD!!	$176.50	New Gap gift certificate cards $75 (25+50) Free Ship	$64.00
GAP GIFT CARD!! 200 DOLLAR VALUE!!!!!! FREE SHIPPING!	$176.50	$75 in GAP gift cards	$64.00
Gap Gift Card	$175.00	$75 GAP GIFT CARD *FREE SHIPPING*	$63.00
GAP Gift Card $186.88 plus FREE SHIPPING!!	$164.00	GAP $25 GIFT CARD FREE SHIPPING	$20.01

Clothing ▶ Eddie Bauer

The average sales price in this subcategory is $200.50.

NOTE *These results are based on a search in this subcategory using the keywords* Eddie Bauer.

HIGH TO LOW

$500 Eddie Bauer Gift Card Certificate Free Shipping	$400.00	Eddie Bauer Free Shipping Code	$0.99

Clothing ▶ Abercrombie

The average sales price in this subcategory is $141.84.

NOTE *These results are based on a search in this subcategory using the keyword* Abercrombie.

	HIGH		AVG
ABERCROMBIE and FITCH Gift Card A & F $500 only $.99	$490.00	$210 Abercrombie GIFT CARD credit $210 NO RESERVE	$172.52
*** ABERCROMBIE AND FITCH Gift Card A & F **** L@@K	$435.00	Abercrombie & Fitch Merchandise Credit - $212.36	$170.02
$500 Abercrombie & Fitch Gift Card FREE SHIPPING NO RES	$425.00	BRaND NeW $200 ABeRCRoMBie FiTCH GiFT CaRD - FREE SHiP	$168.16
Abercrombie & Fitch $500.00 Gift Card!!! FOR > .99?<	$415.25	ABERCROMBIE MERCHANDISE CREDIT GIFT CARD $214.34	$167.50
$500 ABERCROMBIE & FITCH Gift Card Certificate	$405.00	$210 abercrombie&fitch gift card	$165.61
Abercrombie and Fitch Gift Card $482.25	$385.00	(($197.75)) Abercrombie Fitch Gift Card FREE SHIPPING!	$163.50
$500 abercrombie gift card	$380.05	ABERCROMBIE & FITCH GIFT CARD CREDIT $222.00	$163.49
Abercrombie & Fitch Gift Card for $457.30 -Free Postage	$380.00	Abercrombie & Fitch Gift Card	$157.50
**ABERCROMBIE & FITCH Gift Card/Store Credit $443.83 **	$370.55	ABERCROMBIE AND FITCH GIFTCARD WORTH OVER $178	$154.51
Abercrombie and Fitch Gift Card $391.62	$320.01	Abercrombie & Fitch $200 gift card...FREE SHIPPING!!!	$153.52
Abercrombie and Fitch Gift Card $375.09- Save at A&F!	$305.00	$200 NEW Abercrombie & Fitch Gift Card - Free Shipping	$152.60
Abercrombie and Fitch Gift Card $375.09- Save at A&F!	$301.51	$178 Abercrombie GIFT CARD credit $178 FREE SHIPPING	$150.50
Abercrombie and Fitch Gift Card 367.64 Free Shipping	$299.11	ABERCROMBIE and FITCH $168.54 Gift Card/Merch Credit	$143.55
Abercrombie and Fitch Gift Card $364.26	$292.00	Abercrombie & Fitch Merchandise Card 173.86 Ezra Fitch	$142.94
Abercrombie and Fitch Gift Card 352.62 Free Shipping	$285.11	ABERCROMBIE AND FITCH GIFTCARD WORTH OVER $160	$142.50

Clothing ▶ Polo

The average sales price in this subcategory is $135.22.

NOTE *These results are based on a search in this subcategory using the keyword* Polo.

HIGH TO LOW

$300 POLO.COM Gift Certificate FREE SHIPPING	$240.50	Ralph Lauren Polo $152 Gift Card/ Store Credit	$130.00
$200 POLO.COM Gift Certificate FREE SHIPPING	$141.38	POLO.COM GIFT CARD $40	$29.00

Clothing ▶ Banana Republic

The average sales price in this subcategory is $106.77.

NOTE *These results are based on a search in this subcategory using the keywords* Banana Republic.

	HIGH		AVG
$500 dollar Banana Republic Gift Card (never expires)	$430.00	Banana Republic Gift Card - $261.08 Free Shipping	$203.50
Banana Republic Gift Card - $500 NR, Free Shipping!!	$430.00	$214 Banana Republic Gift Card	$184.50
Banana Republic Gift Card - $479.40 Free Shipping	$386.00	$192 Banana Republic Gift Certificate Card No Exp.	$155.06
BANANA REPUBLIC Gift Card - $470 Value - Free Shipping	$380.00	$200 Banana Republic Gift Certificate	$152.51
BANANA REPUBLIC GIFT CARD $ 500	$372.02	Banana Republic Gift Certificate Card Worth $118.51 NR!	$91.00
Banana Republic Gift Card - $425.86 Free Shipping	$355.99	BANANA REPUBLIC GIFT CARD $100 (no shipping charges)	$91.00
Banana Republic Gift Card Certificate $404 – FREE SHIP	$329.95	Never Used Old Navy $100 Gift Card banana republic gap	$83.00
BANANA REPUBLIC GIFT CARD CERTIFICATE BR $400 CREDIT	$326.01	Banana Republic $100 Gift Card Never Used Free Shipping	$81.03
BANANA REPUBLIC GIFT CARD $400.00 N/R Free Shipping!	$315.99	Banana Republic Gift Card $101.77	$81.03
$450 Banana Republic Gift Card NO EXPIRATON NR!!!	$299.00	$100 Old Navy / Gap /Banana Republic Reward / Gift Card	$81.00

Clothing ▶ J Crew

The average sales price in this subcategory is $169.80.

NOTE *These results are based on a search in this subcategory using the keywords* J Crew.

	HIGH		AVG
J Crew Giftcard $450	$366.00	$300 J. Crew Gift Card (FREE Priority Shipping)	$242.50
$405 J.Crew Gift Card Store Credit FREE SHIPPING !!	$349.95	J. Crew Gift Certificate $243.33 NO RESERVE, FREE SHIP!	$194.52
$450 J Crew Gift Card NO EXPIRATON NR!!!	$339.00	J. Crew $197 Gift Card/ Store Credit (merchandise)	$164.50
$400.00 - J. CREW GIFT CARD	$327.00	J. Crew $170 Gift Card/ Store Credit (merchandise)	$150.00
J Crew Gift Card $336.09 Free Shipping, Free Insured.	$275.00	J Crew Gift Certificate Card Credit $146.28 NR No Exp	$116.51

Clothing ▶ Children's Place

The average sales price in this subcategory is $0.78.

NOTE *These results are based on a search in this subcategory using the keywords* Children's Place.

	HIGH		AVG
2- The Children's Place 15% Off Coupons -FREE SHIPPING!	$3.84	CHILDREN'S PLACE (2)15%OFF COUPONS 2,4,6,8,10,12,14,16	$0.99
The Children's Place childrens coupon FREE SHIPPING 15%	$1.05	THE CHILDREN'S PLACE Coupons -10% +15% off all purchase	$0.99
Children's Place 15% Off Coupon	$1.04	$50 The Children's Place Coupons 3 6 9 12 18 24 No exp	$0.99
CHILDREN'S PLACE 20% OFF PURCHASE	$1.04	CHILDREN'S PLACE (5) $10OFF COUPONS 3,6,12,18,24	$0.99
The Children's Place 15% off all Purchases Season Pass	$0.99	$10 off at The Children's Place Store or On-Line .40s/h	$0.60
$50 The Children's Place coupons 3 6 9 12 18 No Expiry	$0.99	The Children's Place Gift Card Clothing 15%off School	$0.55
CHILDREN'S PLACE (5) $10OFF COUPONS 3,6,12,18,24	$0.99	The Children's Place Gift Card Clothing 15%off School	$0.54
CHILDREN'S PLACE (2)15%OFF COUPONS 2,4,6,8,10,12,14,16	$0.99	Children's Place 15% Off coupon Childrens	$0.50
THE CHILDREN'S PLACE 20% off IN STORE!! Exp 9/12	$0.99	15% Off @Children's Place Coupon / 10% Off Sears Coupon	$0.50
THE CHILDREN'S PLACE 20% off online coupon - FREE SHIP!	$0.99	15% Off @ Children's Place Coupon (New Season Pass)	$0.50

Clothing ▶ Fashion Bug

The average sales price in this subcategory is $14.15.

NOTE *These results are based on a search in this subcategory using the keywords* Fashion Bug.

HIGH TO LOW			
FASHION BUG GIFT CARD $100 buy jeans, shirts etc. BTS!	$75.00	Fashion Bug $20 off Coupon Expires Sept 10th	$2.50
FASHION BUG 100.00 GIFT CARDS GIFTCARDS	$74.75	2 FASHION BUG SAVE $10 OFF $25 PURCHASE COUPONS	$2.25
Fashion Bug Coupon Gift Card $20.00 free s/h	$5.00	WOW FASHION BUG $10 OFF $25!! 1 Cent Starting Bid! N/R	$2.11
Fashion Bug Coupon Gift Card $20.00 free s/h	$2.99	2 FASHION BUG coupon (s) , each is $10 off 25 , $1 ship	$2.00
[2 of these sold for $2.99 each]		4-$5 OFF $30 FASHION BUG COUPON GIFT CERTIFICATES 12/31	$1.25
$100 FASHION BUG GIFT CARD (5)	$3.75	4-$5 OFF $30 FASHION BUG COUPON GIFT CERTIFICATES 12/31	$0.99
$20 Coupons Exp 10/31/05		Coupons Old Navy Lane Bryant Dicks Reebok Fashion Bug	$0.99
$10 off $25 Purchase Fashion Bug Coupon Certificate	$2.78	2 FASHION BUG SAVE $10 OFF $25 PURCHASE COUPONS	$0.99

Clothing ▶ Express

The average sales price in this subcategory is $68.67.

NOTE *These results are based on a search in this subcategory using the keyword* Express.

	HIGH		AVG
American Express Prepaid $500 GIFT CARD	$490.00	New express GIFT CARD $121.98	$92.05
EXPRESS GIFT CARD $375.24	$275.00	$100 EXPRESS GIFT CARD! No Expiration date. FREE SHIP!!	$90.00
$370 express gift card	$269.15	$112 EXPRESS GIFT CARD, NO EXP, FREE SHIP	$86.00
EXPRESS GIFT CARD ($271) MENS WOMENS STRUCTURE DUAL	$227.50	EXPRESS $100.00 GIFT CARD NO RESERVE	$76.00
EXPRESS Gift Card certificate 300.00	$227.50	Express Gift/Merchandise Card $86 Value! FREE SHIP	$70.00
$300 Express Gift Card (Free Shipping)	$222.55	Express Gift/Merchandise Card $75.00 value*Free Ship	$64.00
EXPRESS GIFT CARD $279.03	$210.99	Express Gift/Merchandise Card $75.00 value*Free Ship	$62.95
Limited Express $250 Gift Card	$187.50	Express Gift/Merchandise Card $75.00 value*Free Ship	$62.01
Express Gift/Merchandise Card $213 Value! FREE SHIP	$182.50	$72 EXPRESS GIFT CARD GUARANTEED AUTHENTIC!	$60.92
United Airlines/United Express Travel Certificates $300	$175.00	$75 Express Women or Express Men Gift Card Certificate	$59.00

Home & Garden

NOTE *There is no average price statement for this subcategory because the prices were obtained using eBay's Completed Items feature.*

	HIGH		AVG
Thos Moser fine furniture Gift Certificate $2500 Gift Services	$2,121.00	4 - 10% OFF Home Depot Coupons, No Expiration	$6.14
$500 Home Depot / Expo Gift Card BUY 1 GET 3 FREE!!!!!!	$1,825.09	* 5 * LOWES 10% OFF COUPONS, EXPIRES OCT 20 AT LOWE'S	$6.13
$628.57 Restoration Hardware Merchandise credit	$520.77	2 Home Depot 10% Coupons $400 Off NO EXP	$6.10
WALMART GIFT CARD $500.00 BRAND NEW	$475.00	2 Home Depot Stores 10% Discount Certificate NO EXP	$6.10
LOWES MERCHANDISE GIFT CARD STORE CREDIT WORTH $496.65	$470.00	(5) Lowe's 10% Discount Coupons at Lowes! FAST Shipping	$6.07

POTTERY BARN & Williams Sonoma, William Gift Card__	$470.00	4 - 10% Off Home Depot Coupons, NO EXP	$6.07
$500 FREE SHIPPING- - - - No Reserve !!!		4 HOME DEPOT 10% OFF COUPONS **L@@K**!!	$6.06
$500 Home Depot Gift Card - No Reserve + Bonus	$470.00	4 Home Depot 10% off coupons, No Expiration Date	$6.06
$500 LOWES Home Improvement Gift Cards No Expiration	$470.00	4 - 10% Off Home Depot Coupons Coupon NO EXP	$6.06
Walmart gift card 500 dollars FREE shipping!	$469.95	[2 of these sold for $6.06 each]	
LOWES Merchandise Credit Store Gift Card Worth $ 495.58 Free Shipping !!!!!	$468.91	4 - 10% OFF Home Depot Coupons, No Expiration	$6.05
HOME DEPOT $500 Gift Card on hand LOW SHIP! Cards	$468.09	4 HOME DEPOT 10% OFF COUPONS **L@@K**!!	$6.05
Home Depot gift card	$468.00	2 Home Depot Stores 10% Discount Certificate NO EXP	$6.05
LOWE'S GIFT CERTIFICATES $492.42!!!! FREE SHIPPING!!!!	$467.51	(10) Lowe's 10% Discount Coupons at Lowes! FAST Ship!	$6.04
Lowes $500.00 Gift Card Certificate NO RESERVE	$466.01	2 10% OFF COUPON FOR HOME DEPOT STORES NO EXP	$6.03
$500 HOME DEPOT GIFT CARD Free UPS Next Day Shipping!	$460.01	4 - 10% Off Home Depot Coupons Coupon NO EXP	$6.03

Home & Garden ▸ Home Depot

The average sales price in this subcategory is $52.01.

NOTE *These results are based on a search in this subcategory using the keywords* Home Depot.

	HIGH		AVG
HOME DEPOT STORE CREDIT $530.00 WITH RECEIPT!	$485.00	$100 Home Depot Gift Card Gift Certificate	$88.55
$500.00 Home Depot Gift Card, No Reserve! Free Shipping	$485.00	$100 Home Depot Gift Certificate Brand New!	$87.01
$500 Home Depot Gift Card No Lowes NR!! Free Shipping	$477.01	HOME DEPOT $100 GIFT CARD	$87.00
$500.00 EXPO Design Center or Home Depot Gift Card, NR!	$471.00	$100 HOME DEPOT GIFT CARD	$86.23
500.00 Home Depot Gift Card Free Shipping NR!!!	$469.00	[2 of these sold for $86.23 each]	
$500 Home Depot Gift Card No Lowes NR!! Free Shipping	$466.55	$100 Gift Card to Home Depot	$85.00
500$ HOME DEPOT/EXPO gift card certificate Free ship	$466.07	HOME DEPOT GIFT CARD $100 GIFT CARD FREE SHIPPING	$84.00
$500 HOME DEPOT GIFT CARDFREE SHIPPING!!	$465.00	[3 of these sold for $84.00 each]	
$500-Home Depot Gift Card Certificate! w/ bonus coupon!	$465.00	$100 HOME DEPOT STORE CREDIT GIFT CARD OR EXPO DESIGN	$83.00
Home Depot Gift Card **$499.00**No Exp.***Plus 10% off	$465.00	$89.00 HOME DEPOT Gift Card	$81.00
$500.00 Home Depot Gift Card/Store Credit, No Reserve!	$461.10	HOME DEPOT GIFT CARD $85.00 FREE SHIPPING	$77.50
$100 Home Depot Gift Cards w/free shipping	$460.10	12 Home Depot coupons Contractor pack never expires !!!	$76.00
[5 of these sold in a multiple item ("Dutch") auction for $92.02 each]		HOME DEPOT GIFT CARD / STORE CREDIT VALUED AT $ 79.12	$68.25
HOME DEPOT $500 GIFT CARD FREE SHIPPING!!!!!!	$460.07	HOME DEPOT **$75 GIFT CARD** NO RESERVE! FREE SHIPPING!	$66.66
$500 Home Depot Gift Card No Lowes NR!! Free Shipping	$460.02	Home Depot Gift Card/Store Credit $60.44 Free ship	$55.53
$500 HOME DEPOT GIFT CARD Free UPS	$460.00	$52.56 Home Depot Gift Card Certificate + BONUS !!!!	$47.50
Next Day Shipping!		$50.00 Home Depot Gift Card Free Ship. NR!!!!!!!	$46.00

Home & Garden ▸ Lowe's

The average sales price in this subcategory is $31.39.

NOTE *These results are based on a search in this subcategory using the keyword* Lowe's.

	HIGH		AVG
$500 Home Depot Gift Card No Lowes NR!! Free Shipping	$477.01	Lowes-$103.63-NR-Free Shipping-Store Receipt	$86.11
$500.00 LOWES Gift Card Certificate FREE SHIPPING	$475.00	Lowes Store Credit For $102.90 With The Receipt N/R	$85.06
$500 LOWE'S LOWES GIFT CARD NO EXPIRATION	$471.57	Lowes Gift Card $100.00 w/receipt , NR	$84.50
$500 Home Depot Gift Card No Lowes NR!! Free Shipping	$466.55	Lowes Gift Card $100.00 w/receipt , Buy it now SAVE	$80.00
Lowe's Lowes Gift Card Store Credit $500 SHIPNOW	$465.99	[3 of these sold for $80.00 each]	
500$ LOWE'S LOWES gift card certificate Free ship	$465.09	Lowes Store Credit For $92.89 With The Receipt N/R	$79.61
$500 Lowe's Gift Card Certificate Lowes	$462.33	Lowe's gift certificate card to Lowes HIW Value @88.10	$79.01
$500 LOWE'S LOWES GIFT CARD NO EXPIRATION	$461.55	LOWES HOME IMPROVEMENT STORE GIFT CERTIFICATE $84.07	$73.00
$500 Home Depot Gift Card No Lowes NR!! Free Shipping	$460.02	$75.00 Lowes Gift Card-1 DAY ONLY! Ships Free!	$64.99
$500 Home Depot Gift Card No Lowes NR!! Free Shipping	$458.28	Lowes-$60.16-NR-Free Shipping-Store Receipt	$55.69
$500 Home Depot Gift Card No Lowes NR!! Free Shipping	$458.00	Lowes-$56.92-NR-Free Shipping-Store Receipt	$50.99
Lowes Gift Cards $500.00 Value No Expiration Date	$457.00	Lowes-$57.71-NR-Free Shipping-Store Receipt	$50.99
$500 LOWES Home Improvement	$451.00	Lowes Gift Card	$36.00
Gift Cards No Expiration		lowes merchandise credit $41.89	$33.77
500$ LOWE'S LOWES gift card certificate Free ship	$450.00	LOWES GIFT CARD*$34.07*FREE SHIPPING	$31.00
Lowes Gift Card – $485.42 – Free shipping w/ BIN!!	$450.00	Lowes-$34.92-NR-Free Shipping-Store Receipt	$30.00

Home & Garden ▸ Michaels

The average sales price in this subcategory is $87.65.

NOTE *These results are based on a search in this subcategory using the keyword* Michaels.

	HIGH		AVG
1DAY MICHAEL'S MICHAELS STORE CREDIT GIFT CARD $269.67	$203.73	Michaels Arts & Crafts gift card/store credit $143.09	$109.99
Michaels Gift card (store credit) $ 248.26!!!! U.S.D.	$184.50	MICHAELS ARTS AND CRAFTS gift card $122.00 (sizzix)	$96.00
1DAY MICHAEL'S MICHAELS STORE CREDIT GIFT CARD $258.48	$180.78	$129.52 MICHAELS GIFT CARD / STORE CREDIT	$94.71
Michaels Gift card (store credit) $ 242.39 U.S.D.	$174.89	Michaels Arts and Crafts Store Credit $134 FreeShipping	$89.99
Michaels gift card $195.06	$160.00	MICHAELS ARTS AND CRAFTS gift card $105.30 (sizzix)	$86.00
MICHAELS ARTS AND CRAFTS gift card $208.99 (sizzix)	$154.83	$104 Michaels Gift Card FREE SHIPPING!	$81.26
MICHAELS ARTS AND CRAFTS gift card $214.44	$153.57	$94.57 MICHAELS ARTS & CRAFTS STORE GIFT CARD SAVE~!	$72.67
Michaels Arts & Crafts gift card/store credit $190.79	$151.04	$98.74 MICHAELS store credit / return card	$71.00
$200.00 MICHAELS GIFT CARD	$142.61	$93.58 MICHAELS Gift / Return Card FREE SHIPPING	$68.02
MICHAELS ARTS AND CRAFTS gift card $169.27 (sizzix)	$130.68	MICHAELS GIFT CARD 101.11 STORE CREDIT N/R	$67.99

Home & Garden ▸ Pier 1

The average sales price in this subcategory is $53.54.

NOTE *These results are based on a search in this subcategory using the keywords* Pier 1.

	HIGH		AVG
500$ PIER 1 IMPORTS gift card certificate Pier1	$381.75	Pier 1 One Imports Gift Card $75.98- FREE SHIPPING!!!!	$60.00
Pier 1 imports GIFT CARD- VALUE $426.97 Free Shipping!	$356.02	NEW! PIER 1 IMPORTS GIFT CARD VALUE $85.00 NO EXP	$60.00
$292.28 PIER ONE pier 1 gift card!! NR & free ship!!	$234.51	[3 of these sold for $60.00 each]	
$254.40 Pier 1 One Imports Gift Card Gift Certificate	$203.50	pier 1 imports gift card	$51.20
$212.00 Pier 1 One Imports Gift Card Gift Certificate	$173.50	$50.00 Pier ONE 1 Gift Card Credit *FREE SHIPPING!!*	$43.00
$212.00 Pier 1 One Imports Gift Card Gift free S&H	$169.98	$50 Pier 1 Imports Gift Card	$42.00
$212.00 Pier 1 One Imports Gift Card Gift Certificate	$160.50	$50.00 PIER 1 IMPORTS GIFT	$41.02
~*$134.69 PIER 1 IMPORTS GIFT CERTIFICATE- FREE SHIP!*~	$107.51	CARD, N/R, FREE S+H!!	
Pier 1 Imports Gift Card $124.40	$104.49	$50 Pier 1 Imports Gift Card	$41.00
PIER ONE/ PIER 1 GIFT CARD FOR $125.00/ FREE SHIPPING!!	$99.78	[2 of these sold for $41.00 each]	

Home & Garden ▸ Bed Bath & Beyond

The average sales price in this subcategory is $15.70.

NOTE *These results are based on a search in this subcategory using the keywords* Bed Bath & Beyond.

	HIGH		AVG
BED BATH & BEYOND GIFT CERTIFICATE $281.76	$248.58	Bed Bath & Beyond $25 Gift Card - Free Shipping!	$22.75
$200 BED BATH & AND BEYOND GIFT CARD FREE S/H & COUPON	$187.50	$25.00 BED BATH & BEYOND GIFT CARD CERTIFICATE	$21.95
$200 Bed Bath & Beyond gift card / gift certificate	$180.00	85.00 Bed Bath & Beyond plus 20% off coupon! FREE SHIP	$21.50
$200 Bed Bath & Beyond gift card / gift certificate	$176.00	Bed Bath & and Beyond Coupon coupons LOT OF 30 FREE Shp	$19.99
Bed Bath Beyond Gift Card $200	$173.06	$20.00 Bed Bath & Beyond Gift Card No Exp! FREE SHIP!	$17.00
BED BATH & BEYOND $203 GIFT CERTIFICATE CREDIT & BONUS	$157.50	3 DAYS ONLY! $15 target & $5 bed bath & beyond +cpn	$16.63
* Bed Bath & Beyond Gift Card/ Store Credit ($184.07) *	$143.01	Pier 1 imports $20 Gift Card not Bed Bath & Beyond- NR!	$16.55
BED BATH & BEYOND gift card valued $130.00	$111.11	Bed Bath and Beyond $17.89 Gift Card (relisted)	$16.12
$120 Bed Bath & and Beyond Gift Card + 20% Off Coupon	$104.38	Theatre Arlington: $20 GC to Bed, Bath & Beyond	$15.51
Bed Bath & Beyond Gift Card $100 dollar Free Shipping	$91.00	20% off ENTIRE purchase Bed Bath and Beyond	$15.50
$100 in Bed Bath and Beyond Gift Cards! !	$89.25	BED BATH BEYOND $15 GIFT CERTIFICATE CARD AND % COUPON	$13.12
BED BATH BEYOND $100 GIFT CERTIFICATE CARD & COUPON	$83.00	Bed Bath & Beyond 20 % off ENTIRE PURCHASE COUPON	$10.51
$95.00 BED BATH & BEYOND Gift Card/Store Credit Fr Shpg	$80.50	20% OFF COUPON ON ENTIRE PURCHASE AT BED BATH & BEYOND	$10.50
Bed Bath & Beyond Gift Card! $88.70 Balance! Like cash!	$75.10	7 -33% $5 off $15 Bed Bath & and Beyond Coupons Coupon	$10.50
Linens-N-Things $85 Gift Card not Bed Bath & Beyond -NR	$75.01	~20~ 20% OFF BED BATH & BEYOND COUPONS Save $$$$$$$$	$10.00

Home & Garden ▸ Pottery Barn

The average sales price in this subcategory is $144.40.

NOTE *These results are based on a search in this subcategory using the keywords* Pottery Barn.

	HIGH		AVG
Pottery Barn / Williams Sonoma $500 Gift Card	$480.00	$226.18 POTTERY BARN KIDS MERCHANDISE CREDIT CARD	$192.50
$500.00 – POTTERY BARN GIFT CARD – $500.00	$465.00	$215.00 Williams Sonoma Gift Card Pottery Barn AVE~~>	$185.00
Pottery Barn, Williams Sonoma $500 Gift Certificate	$457.00	$200 POTTERY BARN GIFT CARD- free shipping!	$180.66
*** $500 POTTERY BARN GIFT CARD ***	$457.00	$200 POTTERY BARN GIFT CARD FREE SHIPPING	$180.00
500.00 Pottery Barn Gift Card	$455.00	Pottery Barn Gift Card $200 Verified Free Shipping NR*	$177.51
500.00 Pottery Barn Gift Card	$450.00	Pottery Barn Gift Merchandise Card!! $202	$176.00
$500.00 – POTTERY BARN GIFT CARD – $500.00	$441.20	Pottery Barn Gift Card Credit Certificate $206.26 (2)	$175.32
Pottery Barn, Williams Sonoma $500 Gift Certificate	$436.00	*** $200 POTTERY BARN GIFT CARD ***	$175.06
$500.00 Pottery Barn Kids Merchandise Cards	$420.00	$200 POTTERY BARN GIFT CARD- free shipping!	$173.71
POTTERY BARN KIDS Store Credit Gift Certificate $467.64	$415.00	$150 Pottery Barn Williams Sonoma Gift Card Certificate	$134.22
POTTERY BARN Store Credit Gift Certificate $469.81	$410.00	$150 Pottery Barn Gift Card & Certificate	$129.51
Pottery Barn Gift Card worth $450.00	$397.00	pottery barn gift card worth $150	$123.51
WILLIAMS-SONOMA GIFT CARD CREDIT POTTERY BARN $430.00	$380.00	$112.99 Pottery Barn Gift Card	$98.48
$500.00 Pottery Barn Kids Merchandise Cards	$380.00	POTTERY BARN WILLIAMS SONOMA $100 GIFT CERTIFICATE	$90.50
WILLIAMS-SONOMA GIFT CARD CREDIT POTTERY BARN $430.00	$375.02	$100.00 Pottery Barn Gift Card	$90.26

Restaurant

The average sales price in this subcategory is $23.17.

NOTE *These results are based on a search in this subcategory using the keyword* Restaurant.

	HIGH		AVG
WTHR-TV DINNER & OVERNIGHT ACCOMMODATIONS AT VILLA INN	$397.56	FLORIDA-APPLEBEE'S RESTAURANT COUPONS - $60 VALUE	$10.00
$400.00 Gift Card Certificate Red Lobster Olive Garden	$355.10	TEXAS ROAD HOUSE FREE KID MEAL	$10.00
$325.00 Gift Card Certificate Red Lobster Olive Garden	$291.23	COINS 20 ROADHOUSE COINS	
$325Gift Card for Red Lobster Olive Garden FREESHIPPING	$275.00	TEXAS ROAD HOUSE FREE KID MEAL	$10.00
Office gifts -family! save money and time!13giftcards=325		COINS 20 ROADHOUSE COINS	
$269 Olive Garden Red Lobster Gift Card Certificate NR	$251.49	San Jose CA Habana Cuba-$25 Gift Certificate	$10.00
2 FULL ROLLS SUBWAY SUB CLUB STAMPS !!/ WITH CARDS	$242.50	Missoula MT Encore-$25 Gift Certificates	$10.00

2 full rolls/ 10,000 stamps		Clio MI Spirit Restaurant-$25 Gift Certificate	$10.00
HOOTERS Gift Cards $250 Worth! Domestic FREE SHIPPING	$227.65	Pizza Gift Certificate....4 Aces Pizza...Ashley, PA	$10.00
$200.00 Gift Card CHILI'S MACARONI GRILL NO RESERVE!!!	$193.06	La Jolla CA La Dolce Vita Ristorante-$25 Gift Cert	$10.00
$200 Starbucks gift card certificate - NO RESERVE!!	$192.50	Falmouth ME Patti's Restaurant-$25 Gift Certificate	$10.00
Boston Market Gift certificates- $225 (one certificate)	$189.95	San Antonio TX Rita's On The River-$25 Gift Certificate	$10.00
$200.00 STARBUCKS CELEBRATION GIFT CARD *FREE SHIPPING	$189.50	Warrenton VA Tippy's Taco House-$25 Gift Certificate	$10.00
$210 CHILI'S GIFT CARD, ALSO MACARONI GRILL, ETC...	$188.53	Bellingham WA Wild Garlic-$25 Gift Restaurant Cert	$10.00
$200 OUTBACK STEAKHOUSE GIFT CARD CERTIFICATE	$185.99	Brookville PA DJ's Restaurant-$25 Gift Certificate	$10.00
Red Lobster Olive Garden Smokey Bones Gift Card $200	$185.00	Truckee CA The Truckee Diner-$25 Gift Certificate	$10.00
$200 RED LOBSTER / OLIVE GARDEN GIFT CARD GIFTCARD	$185.00	Wilkes-Barre PA The Chicken Coop-$25 Gift Certificate	$10.00

Restaurant ▶ Panera Bread

The average sales price in this subcategory is $22.92.

NOTE *These results are based on a search in this subcategory using the keywords* Panera Bread.

	HIGH		AVG
PANERA BREAD GIFT CERTIFICATE BAGELS/CREAM CHEESE >$100	$51.00	Coupons for 5 (yes FIVE) Bagel Packs @ Panera Bread $60	$23.92
$60 in Panera Bread Gift Cards (4 cards x $15) NEW!!!	$50.00	5 Panera bagel pack/expresso beverage coupon cards	$23.09
PANERA BREAD $50 Gift Card, NEW, Never Used	$45.01	4 Panera Bread Bagel/Coffee cards	$23.00
PANERA BREAD $50 Gift Card, NEW, Never Used	$44.88	5 Panera bagel pack/expresso beverage coupon cards	$23.00
Panera Bread Bagel Card (10 cards) (ONE DAY AUCTION)	$44.09	4 Panera Bread Bagel/Coffee cards	$22.94
Coupons for 5 (yes FIVE) Bagel Packs @ Panera Bread $60	$41.05	PANERA bread bagel pack coupon cards Set of 4 ONE DAY	$22.50
Panera Coupon Gift Certificate for 5 free bagel pack &.	$36.50	5 FREE Bagel Packs @ Panera Bread ($60 retail) +free	$21.67
Panera Bread Bagel Card (10 cards) (ONE DAY AUCTION)	$33.00	Coupons for 5 (yes FIVE) Bagel Packs @ Panera Bread $60	$21.52
Coupons for 5 (yes FIVE) Bagel Packs @ Panera Bread $60	$32.01	Coupons for 5 (yes FIVE) Bagel Packs @ Panera Bread $60	$21.23
LOT 5 Panera Bread FREE Bagel Pack coupons NR $75 value	$32.00	Coupons for 5 (yes FIVE) Bagel Packs @ Panera Bread $60	$21.00

Restaurant ▶ Chuck E Cheese

The average sales price in this subcategory is $12.55.

NOTE *These results are based on a search in this subcategory using the keywords* Chuck E Cheese.

	HIGH		AVG
1000 Chuck E. Cheese Actual Game Tokens	$142.50	chuck e cheese gift card guest pass pizza 4 soda token	$17.05
1000 CHUCK E. CHEESE TOKENS - $250 DOLLAR VALUE	$118.49	200 Chuck E. Cheese Arcade Tokens	$15.00
Chuck E Cheese Gift Certificate Card Free Ship Chucky	$43.01	1,000 Chuck E Cheese Tickets plus 10 free Tokens	$14.02
CHUCK E CHEESE GAME TOKENS - 250	$32.00	[2 of these sold in a multiple item ("Dutch") auction for $7.01 each]	
5,000 Chuck E Cheese tickets in receipts FREE shipping	$28.01	Chuck E Cheese Coupon 35 Free Tokens 8.75 Value	$13.86
250 Actual Chuck E. Cheese Tokens - $62.50 VALUE	$27.50	[11 of these sold in a multiple item ("Dutch") auction for $1.26 each]	
250 Actual Chuck E. Cheese Tokens-$62.50 VALUE	$27.00	100 NEW 2005 Chuck E Cheese Tokens and pizza coupon	$12.76
CHUCK E CHEESE GAME TOKENS – 250	$26.00	70 Chuck E. Cheese Game Tokens & 4 Pizza Cpns-$44 Value	$10.50
[2 of these sold for $26.00 each]		1,000 Chuck E Cheese Tickets plus 10 free Tokens	$10.49
CHUCK E CHEESE GAME TOKENS (250)	$25.49	106 Chuck E Cheese Game Tokens& 4 Pizza Cpns-$56 Value	$10.01
		80 CHUCK E CHEESE GAME TOKENS ++++++ BONUS	$9.99
		1,000 Chuck E Cheese Tickets plus 10 free Tokens	$8.95

Restaurant ▶ Starbucks

The average sales price in this subcategory is $23.17.

NOTE *These results are based on a search in this subcategory using the keyword* Starbucks.

	HIGH		AVG
Starbucks Drink Coupons Any Drink Any Size	$166.49	$30.00 STARBUCKS GIFT CARD! FREE SHIPPING! NO RESERVE!	$27.07
50 STARBUCKS FREE DRINK COUPONS --- NO RESERVE !!	$164.50	STARBUCKS gift card. $30.00. NR. No expiration.	$27.05
50 STARBUCKS FREE DRINK COUPONS (Any Drink, Any Size)	$163.44	$30 Starbucks Gift Cards (free coffee!!)	$26.08
50 STARBUCKS FREE DRINK COUPONS (Any Drink, Any Size)	$157.67	25 Starbucks FREE BREAKFAST SANDWICH COUPONS!!	$26.00
STARBUCKS FREE DRINK COUPONS Any Drink,Any Size, Extras	$157.54	Hawaiian Starbucks Gift Card + Hawaii Beanie Baby RARE	$26.00
STARBUCKS CARD $ 130	$111.00	Starbucks Gift Card $30	$25.08
25 Brand New Free Drink Coupons from Starbucks! NR!	$102.51	$30.00 STARBUCKS GIFT CARD *AND* 1/2 POUND BAG COFFEE!!	$24.77
$117 Barnes and Noble Starbucks Gift Certificate Card	$97.45	$25 STARBUCKS GIFT CARD & (1) 'FREE' STARBUCKS COUPON	$24.50
$100 Starbucks Coffee Gift Card Certificate 25 50 75	$95.56	$25.10 Starbucks Gift Card	$24.50
$100 Starbucks Card Free Shipping NR!!	$91.88	$30 Starbucks Coffee Gift Certificate Cards	$24.50
$97.85 STARBUCKS STORE CREDIT GIFT CARD *FREE SHIPPING*	$91.01	$25 STARBUCKS GIFT CARD & (1) 'FREE' STARBUCKS COUPON	$24.06
$94.24 STARBUCKS STORE CREDIT GIFT CARD *FREE SHIPPING*	$90.17	$25 STARBUCKS GIFT CARD No Reserve!! Free Shipping!!	$24.02
$100 Starbucks Gift Card	$87.01	Starbuck Starbucks Starbuckscard coffee $25 gift card	$23.50
25 Brand New Free Drink Coupons from Starbucks! NR!	$82.00	$25 STARBUCKS Gift Card-No Exp.-FREE SHIPPING!!!!	$23.10
25 STARBUCKS FREE DRINKS ANY KIND ANY SIZE	$81.50	$25 STARBUCKS Gift Card - No Minimum FREE Shipping	$23.06

Restaurant ▸ Wine

The average sales price in this subcategory is $79.29.

NOTE *These results are based on a search in this subcategory using the keyword* wine.

HIGH TO LOW

Embassy Suites Temecula CA Wine Country 2 NTS	$222.50	Total Wine & More Gift Certificate Card $25	$13.50
Hot Air Balloon Ride Temecula CA Wine Country 2 PL	$133.00	Wine Tasting at Napa Valley PEJU Winery - BEAUTIFUL	$6.96
WINE TASTING & TOUR FOR 4 AT ARROWOOD VINEYARDS, CA	$20.50		

Restaurant ▸ Pizza Hut

The average sales price in this subcategory is $8.40.

NOTE *These results are based on a search in this subcategory using the keywords* Pizza Hut.

	HIGH		AVG
10 PIZZA HUT LUNCH BUFFET BUY1GET1 FREE COUPONS 12/05	$20.50	20 FREE PERSONAL PAN PIZZAS PIZZA HUT	$9.80
10 PIZZA HUT LUNCH BUFFET BUY1GET1 FREE COUPONS 12/05	$19.41	*10 PIZZA HUT PERSONAL PAN BUY1GET1 FREE COUPONS 12/05*	$9.51
VA Pizza Hut $375 Gift Certificate	$16.50	*10 PIZZA HUT PERSONAL PAN BUY1GET1 FREE COUPONS 12/05*	$9.03
Pizza Hut $20.00 Gift Card	$15.99	$10 (2-$5) Pizza Hut Gift Cards	$8.91
Starbucks, Pizza Hut, and Burger King Gift Cards!!!	$15.50	*10 PIZZA HUT PERSONAL PAN BUY1GET1 FREE COUPONS 12/05*	$8.26
CO Denver Pizza Hut $250 Gift Certificate	$14.99	Pizza Hut gift card $360 value. Free shipping	$6.00
FL Florida YUM Pizza Hut $300 Gift Certificate	$14.99	*20 PIZZA HUT BUY 1 GET 1 FREE COUPON COMBO #2 12/31*	$5.59
Pizza Hut Discount Cards	$14.19	PIZZA HUT (10) Coupons Buy 1 Get 1 FREE! Exp 11/05	$5.50
Pizza Hut Discount Cards	$14.00	PIZZA HUT 3 FREE PERSONAL PAN PIZZAS	$4.50
$17 Pizza Hut gift card/certificate	$13.50	PIZZA HUT 3 FREE PERSONAL PAN PIZZAS	$4.26

Restaurant ▸ Domino's

The average sales price in this subcategory is $11.39.

NOTE *These results are based on a search in this subcategory using the keyword* Domino's.

HIGH TO LOW

2 Tickets + 2 Hospitality Passes	$89.88	OH Domino's Pizza $250 Gift Certificate	$14.99
Domino's Pizza 250 MIS		OH Domino's Pizza $250 Gift Certificate	$14.99
OH Domino's Pizza $250 Gift Certificate	$15.99	*20 DOMINO'S PIZZA BUY1/GET1 FREE COUPONS 12/31*	$3.25
OH Domino's Pizza $250 Gift Certificate	$14.99	*20 DOMINO'S PIZZA BUY1/GET1 FREE COUPONS 12/31*	$2.25
$250 Domino's Pizza INDY Pizza Pkg – IN	$14.99	*20 DOMINO'S PIZZA BUY1/GET1 FREE COUPONS 12/31*	$2.01
WV Domino's Pizza $320 Gift Certificate	$14.99	*20 DOMINO'S PIZZA BUY1/GET1 FREE COUPONS 12/31*	$1.75
VA Domino's Pizza $320 Gift Certificate	$14.99	*20 DOMINO'S PIZZA BUY1/GET1 FREE COUPONS 12/31*	$1.50
IN Indiana Domino's Pizza $250 Gift Certificate	$14.99	*20 DOMINO'S PIZZA BUY1/GET1 FREE COUPONS 12/31*	$1.29

Restaurant ▸ Subway

The average sales price in this subcategory is $12.78.

NOTE *These results are based on a search in this subcategory using the keyword* Subway.

	HIGH		AVG
1165 SUBWAY stamps + 25 Blank SUBCLUB Cards + Bonus	$127.65	25 SUBWAY Sandwich Cards!!	$15.50
1000 Subway stamps- FREE SHIPPING	$65.00	80 SUBWAY STAMPS 10 FULL CARDS FREE SUBS SUB	$15.50
[2 of these sold for $65.00 each]		10 Full Subway Club Card Coupons 80 Stamps 10 Free Subs	$15.01
100 Full Subway Sub Club Cards Organized in Packs of 10	$51.00	20 full subway cards 160 subway stamps	$15.00
50 Full Subway Sub Club Cards (400 Stamps)Free Subs!	$49.99	[2 of these sold for $15.00 each]	
50 SUBWAY SUB CARDS COUPONS	$49.95	LOT of 25 Subway Sub Club Cards WITH Stamps REAL DEAL	$15.00
- 50 FREE SUBS - FREE SHIP		CT Hartford Subway $250 Gift Certificate	$14.99
100 Full Subway Sub Club Cards Organized in Packs of 10	$45.09	[2 of these sold for $14.99 each]	
100 Full Subway Sub Club Cards Organized in Packs of 10	$44.99	10 FULL Subway Sub Club Cards Coupons 10 free subs!	$14.50
50 Subway Sub Club Stamps with cards Coupon Free	$44.60	120 SUBWAY stamps + 15 Blank Cards For 15 Free Subs	$14.48
600 Subway Stamps! FREE Subs! 600 Stamps! Coupon (2005)	$44.21	88 SUBWAY SUB CLUB STAMPS/11 SUB CLUB CARDS/FREE SUBS!!	$14.03
400 SUBWAY stamps + 50 Blank Cards to put them on!	$43.00	80 SUBWAY STAMPS 10 FULL CARDS FREE SUBS SUB	$14.00
50 Subway Club Cards (filled with stamps) 50 Free SUBS!	$41.11	88 SUBWAY SUB CLUB STAMPS/11 SUB CLUB CARDS/FREE SUBS!!	$13.60
500 Subway Stamps! FREE Subs! 500 Stamps! Coupon (2005)	$41.05	152 SUBWAY SUB CLUB STAMPS/19 SUB CLUB CARDS/FREE SUBS!	$13.45
500 Subway stamps- FREE SHIPPING	$41.00	152 SUBWAY SUB CLUB STAMPS/19 SUB CLUB CARDS/FREE SUBS!	$12.95
50 SUBWAY SUB CLUB CARDS + 400 STAMPS (card + stamp)	$37.05	*20 SUBWAY SUBS BUY1/GET1 FREE SUB COUPONS THRU 12/31*	$12.51
400 SUBWAY stamps + 50 Blank Cards to put them on!	$37.00	120 SUBWAY stamps + 15 Blank Cards For 15 Free Subs	$12.50

Restaurant ▸ Morton's

The average sales price in this subcategory is $95.04.

NOTE *These results are based on a search in this subcategory using the keyword* Morton's.

HIGH TO LOW

MORTON'S STEAKHOUSE 2 Gift Certificates, $225 Value	$187.50	Morton's Steakhouse Gift Card - $100.00	$85.00
Morton's Steakhouse 2 Gift Certificate Cards $200 Value	$181.03	Morton's Steakhouse $100 Gift Card	$79.20

$200 MORTON'S STEAKHOUSE GIFT CARD	$170.11	$75 MORTON's steakhouse Gift Card MORTONS	$69.99
$200 MORTON'S STEAKHOUSE GIFT CARD	$167.51	Morton's Steakhouse Gift Certificate	$40.00
Morton's Steakhouse $150 Giftcard	$125.52	MORTON'S STEAKHOUSE $25 Certificate (Indianapolis Only)	$10.50
$150.00 Gift Cert. To Any Morton's, The Steakhouse!!!!	$117.08	Morton's of Chicago - $25 GC for Louisville, KY	$3.25
MORTON'S "THE STEAKHOUSE" $100.00 GIFT CARD	$92.00	Morton's of Chicago - $25 GC for Louisville, KY	$2.26

Restaurant ▸ Red Lobster

The average sales price in this subcategory is $55.06.

NOTE *These results are based on a search in this subcategory using the keywords* Red Lobster.

	HIGH		AVG
$500 RED LOBSTER OLIVE GARDEN GIFT CARD CERTIFICATE	$480.00	Olive Garden Red Lobster $75 gift card. Free Shipping	$70.00
$500.00 GIFT CARD FOR RED LOBSTER AND MORE!	$475.00	[2 of these sold for $70.00 each]	
$250 RED LOBSTER/OLIVE GARDEN GIFT CARDS/FREE SHIPPING	$232.51	Olive Garden Red Lobster $75.00 Gift Card Free Shipping	$69.00
250 DOLLAR OLIVE GARDEN RED LOBSTER GIFT CARD	$227.50	OLIVE GDN, RED LOBSTER DARDEN GIFT CARDS- $75.00	$68.23
$250-RED LOBSTER/OLIVE GARDEN GIFT CARDS/FREE SHIPPING	$225.01	Olive Garden Red Lobster $75.00 Gift Card Free Shipping	$67.11
$250-RED LOBSTER/OLIVE GARDEN GIFT CARDS/FREE SHIPPING	$215.01	Olive Garden, Red Lobster, Darden gift card	$67.01
$250-RED LOBSTER/OLIVE GARDEN GIFT CARDS/FREE SHIPPING	$205.02	$75 + $4 Olive Garden RED LOBSTER GIFT CARD Certificate	$66.25
$200.00 Gift Card Certificate Red Lobster Olive Garden	$192.50	$75 Red Lobster/Olive Garden Gift Card + $7 in COUPONS!	$62.00
$200 Red Lobster/Olive Garden Gift Cards *No reserve*	$172.57	Red Lobster/Olive Garden $55.00 Gift Card.FREE SHIPPING	$50.56
$175 Olive Garden, Red Lobster gift card +$9 coupon	$172.50	$57 Red Lobster, Olive Garden gift card	$50.00
$175 Olive Garden, Red Lobster gift card +$9 coupon	$168.50	$50 Olive Garden Red Lobster Gift Cards $0 S/H	$48.00
Red Lobster, Olive Garden Gift Card	$167.51	OLIVE GDN, RED LOBSTER DARDEN GIFT CARDS- $50.00	$45.66
$175 Olive Garden, Red Lobster gift card +$15 coupon	$156.59	OLIVE GARDEN RED LOBSTER GIFT CARD $50.00	$45.00
$150 Olive Garden/Red Lobster gift card + $12 RL coupon	$145.00	$50 Red Lobster Gift Card. Never Expires	$45.00
$100 Gift card Red Lobster, Olive Garden, Smokey Bones	$95.00	[2 of these sold for $45.00 each]	
$100 Gift Card RED LOBSTER OLIVE GARDEN SMOKEY BAHAMA	$92.89	$50 RED LOBSTER OLIVE GARDEN GIFT CARDS No Reserve	$44.03
$100 GIFT CARD RED LOBSTER OLIVE GARDEN SMOKEY BONES ++	$92.08	$50 Red Lobster Or Olive Garden Gift Certificate	$44.00
$100 Olive Garden, Red Lobster, Smokey Bones Gift Card	$91.01		
$100 GIFT CARDS RED LOBSTER,OLIVE GARDEN, CERTIFICATE	$91.00		
$100 Gift Card RED LOBSTER OLIVE GARDEN SMOKEY BONES	$90.00		

Restaurant ▸ Taco Bell

The average sales price in this subcategory is $9.21.

NOTE *These results are based on a search in this subcategory using the keywords* Taco Bell.

HIGH TO LOW			
20 TACO BELL BURRITO BUY1GET1 FREE COUPONS 12/05	$17.00	*20 TACO BELL CHALUPA BUY1GET1 FREE COUPONS 12/05*	$10.05
*20 TACO BELL BORDER BOWL BUY1	$15.03	TACO BELL- QUIXNOS SUBS- CARL'S JR.(HARDEE'S)$5.00 EACH	$10.00
GET1 FREE COUPONS 12/05*		*20 TACO BELL BORDER BOWL BUY1GET1 FREE COUPONS 12/05*	$4.69
20 TACO BELL CHALUPA BUY1GET1 FREE COUPONS 12/05	$13.03	3 Taco Bell coupons from Entertainment Book; exp. 11/05	$1.75
20 TACO BELL CHALUPA BUY1GET1 FREE COUPONS 12/05	$11.07	Chicago TACO BELL (6) Coupons FREE Food! Exp 10/31/05	$0.30

Other Gift Certificates

NOTE *There is no average price statement for this subcategory because the prices were obtained using eBay's Completed Items feature.*

	HIGH		AVG
$2,500 of Ritz Carlton Gift Certificates 5 x $500 gift certificates	$2,174.99	GolfLand Big Surf/Sunsplash/WaterWorld Water Park	$20.50
$1,000 worth of Hyatt Hotel Certificates	$800.00	$1000 Gift Certificate - Help Katrina's pet victims Giving Works Item	$20.50
$1000 Polo Gift Certificate Nationwide Low Reserve !!	$621.00	$100 Marriott Bonus Bucks - Valid Until 04/02/2006!	$20.50
$700.00 SouthWest Airlines Gift Certificates Vouchers	$600.00	5 x Lowes 10% OFF Coupons, Fast Shipping, EXPIRES 11/03	$20.50
Marriott Hotel Charity 5 nts. West Palm Beach	$511.17	Jiffy Lube $30.00 Gift Certificate	$20.50
$500 COSTCO Wholesale Gift Card Certificate *FREE S/H*	$500.01	$500.00 Shopping Spree (Support Hurricane Katrina)	$20.50
Tiger Mania Gift Certificate	$500.00	Giving Works Item	
$500 BP/Amoco Gas Card + Free Gift Card IF BUY IT NOW	$500.00	400 Kellogg's AA American Airlines AAdvantage Miles	$20.50
GURNEYS INN RESORT SPA MONTALK NY 750 GIFTCARD	$500.00	500 DOLLAR Gift Card to mystery website online mall !	
2 round trip American Airlines Travel Certificates	$500.00	BEST BUY MYSTERY GIFT CARD	$20.50
no blackout dates, anywhere in lower 48 and Canada		$100 MARRIOTT BONUS BUCKS GIFT CERTIFICATE Mar 13, 2006	$20.50
Marriott Fairfield Inn Award voucher 5 nts +$75 cheque	$495.01	Walmart Mystery Gift Card****L@@K 1 DAY ONLY!!*****	$20.50
$500 Walmart Gift Card, Sam's Wal-Mart, FREE SHIPPING	$495.00	12 Blockbuster FREE Rental Coupons MOVIE GAME DVD GIFT	$20.50
* WAL-MART walmart GIFT CARD $497.57 sams SAM'S CLUB *	$492.61	$1000 Gift Certificate. Help Katrina's victims.	$20.50
Costco Wholesale Card - Value at $500 !Great Deal!	$492.01	$0 s/h Giving Works Item	
WAL-MART/SAM'S CLUB GIFT CARD $500 Free SHipping!	$490.00	$1000 Gift Certificate. Help Katrina's victims.	$20.49
STAPLES $551.16 Gift Card Certificate Free Shipping	$490.00	$0 s/h Giving Works Item	
Walmart Gift Card - 500.00 USD Gift Services Free Shipping!!	$485.10	2 TICKETS TO THE FASHIONISTAS SHOW IN LAS VEGAS	$20.49
$500 WalMart Gift Card/Certificate!!! Added extra card as BONUS!!!!	$485.00		
Speedway SuperAmerica Super America Gift Card $500	$480.01		
$500 Amazon Gift Certificate Card for $480 Amazon.com	$480.00		

20

HEALTH & BEAUTY

Cosmetics are a big business: Americans alone spend some $8 billion a year on them. eBay sellers are angling to get their share of that pie in the Health & Beauty category, while buyers are looking to cut down a bit on their personal care tab. One of the best things about this category, in my mind, is that it gives you access to items you otherwise would not normally be able to buy, at least not easily: large lots of Mary Kay products, for example, or the palette of 88 MAC brand eye shadow colors meant to be displayed in a salon. (Or even the entire contents of a salon.) Tired of schlepping to an Aveda boutique to buy their lipsticks? Pick up a set of four different shades here for $33.00.

But beyond just makeup and other relatively small things, hot items throughout Health & Beauty include tanning beds, Sonicare electric toothbrushes, Farouk CHI hair-straightening irons, Braun electric shavers, diabetic test strips, and tattoo machines.

Outfit a Beauty Salon for $2,100.00

Some of the big-ticket items, including one of the aforementioned tanning beds ($2,500.00), were listed in the Salon Equipment subcategory under Health & Beauty ▶ Hair Care. The Salon Equipment top seller in this sample was a lot of ten salon stations and other salon furniture and equipment for $6,100.00. The furniture was black leather and was from an upscale salon undergoing a renovation and unloading its old stuff. As the listing said, "A deal like this doesn't happen every day. An upscale beauty salon is undergoing a complete renovation and is selling the salon's entire contents." And they weren't kidding—a four-piece reception desk, jewelry case, storage and file cabinets, black leather couch and loveseat, black lacquer "Euro" coffee and end tables, 19" color TVs with remote, a Pioneer receiver, a CD player and speakers, a Coke machine, water machine, and an HP printer. "All in great shape for a great deal."

A lot of six "like new" beauty stations went for $3,200.00. The six stations were of a beautiful light wood color, with modern styling, and a reception desk was included. According to the seller, she originally paid close to $30,000.00 for the equipment, so this does seem to have been an amazing deal for some lucky beauty shop owner.

Looking for more than beauty stations? How about the contents of an entire salon for only $2,100.00? It includes hydraulic chairs, sinks, dryers, oval mirrors, a pedicure station and stool, a rolling cart, a manicure table on wheels, a glass and mirror shelving system, and five styling and two shampoo stations.

If you're a salon owner who only needs bits and pieces, you can find wall-mounted hair dryers for $200.00, beauty salon chairs for $201.00, and a single double-sided styling station for $158.00. All of these items were in the average price range of the Salon Equipment subcategory.

Other professional spa and aesthetic equipment sold in Health & Beauty include a "Photo Rejuvenation Skin Care Machine, DERMA MASTER 8000," for $749.50, and tattooing equipment ("TATTOO GEAR. Full Professional setup! Guns/Aclave/More!") for $1,225.00. But one of the highest-priced items in the whole category was an Endermologie machine ("LPG Endermologie Key6 Module"), which sold for $21,102.99. (Endermologie is a French technique of mechanical massage, purporting to smooth skin and reduce the appearance of cellulite.) If you want to try the technique yourself, you could buy an "Endermologie Like Cellulite Roller Massage System" for $69.99, which falls in the average price range of the Health & Beauty ▸ Bath & Body ▸ Cellulite Treatment subcategory.

Hair Styling and Makeup

Currently the big buzzword in the hair-styling world is "tourmaline." Tourmaline is a precious stone known to have ionic properties, and products using it are touted as being gentler to hair. Several of the top-selling hair dryers, for example, are "T3" models from HairArt, ranging in price from $144.00 to $205.49. Other popular sellers are the Farouk CHI 1,800 watt dryers, going for $143.08 to $167.50. (These CHI dryers are available from Misikko.com for $160.00 with free shipping, so these prices are pretty close to retail.) In the average price range for hair dryers, you can find a Sharper Image Salon Pro Ionic Conditioning hair dryer for $37.00 (they sell for approximately $69.95 retail), or a RevoStyler Rotating Hot Air Brush for $36.00 ("as seen on tv"—this is a hair brush/dryer that rotates as you use it, for a straightening effect).

Straightening irons are also here, with the same brands dominating the top range—T3 irons going for $117.50 to $177.50 in the high range of this sample, and CHI irons selling for $137.50 to $140.50. I also found some CHI 2-inch irons for as little as $81.00 for a used model, so be sure you look at all the available items before bidding. (CHI irons retail for around $144.99, though I found one on sale for $129.99 from Misikko.com).

Some of the best savings on everyday makeup and toiletries can be found under subcategories for mixed or wholesale lots. For example, a big lot of Arbonne brand makeup in a tote went for $300.00, which was $700.00 less than the $1,000.00 retail price. People are buying items in huge quantities to either resell individually, or, in some cases, to use themselves. With the bigger lots, such as the aforementioned Arbonne auction, or the "HUGE $8100.00 RETAIL LOT - Mary Kay" (selling for $2,025.00), they're most likely reselling it. As to the items in the average price range in Health & Beauty ▸ Wholesale Lots ▸ Beauty and Personal Care, such as the lot of five Bobbi Brown lip glosses (selling for $33.75 each), they may have been bought for personal use.

If you're a seller, you'll do better with the higher-end and hard-to-find brands, which will probably not come as a surprise. Luxury brands tend to sell for closer to retail value, and in some cases, if a product has been discontinued, or is vintage, will sell for a premium over retail. For example, a conditioner called Vaseline Hair Tonic, which its manufacturer recently decided to stop making, showed up several times throughout the Hair Care ▸ Conditioner subcategory. A lot of ten bottles of the tonic sold for $200.00; at $20.00 a bottle, this is a lot more than the $4.09 regular retail price for which the bottles were selling.

The health and beauty world is somewhat fickle, and trends and favored brands come and go, so sellers need to be aware of this. Right now some of the hottest brands seem to be MAC, Arbonne, Mary Kay, and Shu Uemura in the Makeup subcategory, and Ojon, PureOlogy, Paul Mitchell, Kerastase, and Bumble and Bumble in the Health & Beauty ▶ Hair Care ▶ Shampoo and Conditioner subcategories.

The brands you see most will depend on what subcategory you're looking at. Brands that show up frequently in the Health & Beauty ▶ Makeup ▶ Lipstick subcategory, for example, include Shu Uemura (a makeup artist who started his own line of cosmetics), Nars, Aveda, and Max Factor. A Shu Uemura Lolishine Reflects lipstick can be had for $9.00, $11.00 off the $20.00 retail price, and this is in the average price range of lipsticks, which hovers around $8.00. Several Max Factor Lipfinitys and a Nars frosted lilac lipstick are also here for around $9.00. The highest-priced single lipstick in this sample was a LipFusion Lip Plump in sheer natural baby pink for $33.51; it currently retails for $36.00 at Sephora.com.

When you look at the Health & Beauty ▶ Makeup ▶ Eye Shadow subcategory, there is some overlap in the brand names with the Health & Beauty ▶ Makeup ▶ Lipstick subcategory, but there are also many different ones. Shu Uemura shows up again, with a "Sables D'ete HIKARI Summer Lights Palette" for $61.00, but there are also several palettes of MAC eye shadow—a set of 88 colors that were previously only available in a spa or salon, selling for $49.00 to $61.00 in the high price range. In the average range for eye shadow, you can find Nars, Bare Escentuals, Almay, Trucco, and other brands of eye shadow, all for around $12.00.

There are plenty of other types of items in Health & Beauty, too—professional hair color, shavers, wheelchairs, glucose test strips, diet bars, and even plenty of pills purporting to enhance certain body parts. You may not find every shade, color, size, or flavor of item here, but you'll find many of them, and save on most. And with $45 billion a year spent on cosmetics by women in the United States alone, there is plenty of room to save money in this category of products. If you're a seller, on the other hand, stick to the hottest brands, styles, and gadgets, and you'll get closest to retail prices.

Bath & Body ▶ Bath Sets, Kits

The average sales price in this subcategory is $13.91.

	HIGH		AVG
ARBONNE RE9 ANTI AGING SKIN CARE SET RETAILS $266 NIB!	$154.50	Victoria's Secret Bath & Body set with Purse	$15.75
HUGE HUGE LOT OF JOHNSON & JOHNSON	$102.50	Philosophy's Surprise Party Gift Set	$15.60
BABY CARE PRODUCT'S		New L'occitane Shaving Set Cream Alum Stick After Shave	$15.50
Laura Mercier Creme Brulee Honey Bath Scrub Set New	$86.00	A complete collection of Shea Butter skincare	$15.50
Warm Spirit Lot! Incl. Body Butter, Candles & More!	$73.00	Arbonne Travel Size Ginger Citrus, Wash, Scrub & Butter	$15.50
38 Piece Borghese Bath and Skin care Set	$71.00	AWAKEN SEA SALT SCRUB FROM ARBONNE	$15.50
ARBONNE RE9 ANIT AGING SKIN CARE PRODUCTS EYE CREAM +	$71.00	Elizabeth Arden Green Tea - 5 Piece Set - NIB!!!	$15.37
05 NWT Juicy Couture Velour Cargo Collar Set bag BLUE L	$69.99	BeautiControl Platinum Regeneration Skin Renewing Serum	$15.00
Arbonne RE9 Travel Set	$62.00	Molton Brown London Set New!!!	$15.00
05 NWT Juicy Couture Velour Cargo Collar Set bag BLUE M	$58.09	bath and body "Casa Bella" gift basket	$15.00
Arbonne RE9 Travel Set	$56.01	6 PIECE BLISS BATH SET IN ZIPPERED POUCH-AWESOME!!!	$15.00
QVC PHILOSOPHY 3 PC SET SOUFFLE, BATH CREME, PURE GRACE	$55.00	[2 of these sold for $15.00 each]	
Stevie Nicks GOLD DUST TOUR BOOK	$51.01	NEW~30 OZ Jean Nate BATH SPLASH + 6 OZ BODY POWDER	$15.00
Laura Mercier Creme Brulee Souflee Bath & Scrub Set @NR	$51.00	NEW SONOMA BATH CO. 'HOTTIE' GIFT SET BODY WASH, LOTION	$14.99
Body Therapy & Solace Spa Package	$50.00	Annie Oakley Indulgence Set- "Indian Musk"	$14.00
05 NWT Juicy Couture Velour Cargo Collar Set bag BLUE S	$49.99	Bath Body Works Le Couvent Des Minimes HONEY & SHEA X4	$13.99

Bath & Body ▶ Body Lotion

The average sales price in this subcategory is $11.87.

	HIGH		AVG
EPICUREN MID-SIZE KIT*NEW*6 STEPS TO GREAT SKIN!	$155.00	Jessica Simpson Dessert whipped cream JUICY NEW 34+ NR!	$12.99
New La Prairie Silver Rain Perfumed Body Cream 7 oz	$88.50	Lancome Tresor Shower Gel 6.7 oz	$12.95
AVEDA 64fl oz HYDRATING FORMULA BODY LOTION	$73.05	MIMOSA BODY MILK BY LAURA MERCIER ~NEW~	$12.95
OPI AVOJUICE LOTION 8 X-LARGE 20oz BOTTLES WOW!	$70.00	white Musk by Alyssa Ashley bubble bath shower gel body	$12.50
Elemis Aromapure Skin Nurishing Milk Bath 14 oz 400 ml	$56.99	Emu Oil Hand & Body Lotion, 8oz. Bottle - FREE Shipping	$12.50
AVEDA Rosemary Mint - Body Lotion	$56.25	[2 of these sold for $12.50 each]	
LADY PRIMROSE 3pc Set- ROYAL EXTRCT Lotion/BathGel/Tray	$53.00	Melaleuca Renew Intensive Skin Therapy 8 oz	$12.50
Jessica Simpson 41 Piece Dessert BEAUTY & Treats Set	$51.00	Ray of Light LOOK 10lb slimmer Tanning Lotion $58r $1m	$12.50
JO Malone 154 BODY CREAM creme full size in box	$50.00	Supre Tattoo Dark Tanning Lotion $45r $1m No Res	$12.50
Kiehl's Creme de Corps Body Lotion& Body Wash Cream NEW	$41.00	? WEI EAST HAND & BODY PERFECTION?NEW	$12.50
HEMPZ HERBAL GALLON moist tanning lotion $1m	$40.01	DUWOP HANDS2HAIR 1.5 OZ NEW STYLING CREAM & LOTION	$12.16
BABOR Body Care 3 FULL Size Item Set w/case NEW! RV $78	$39.99	Jilsander No. 4 Moisturizing Body Balm Women (Tester)	$12.09
Body Bling Bronze By Scott Barnes (New/Unused) 4oz	$37.09	Matahari Dark Sexy Tan tanning lotion $1m NR	$12.00

CREATIVE SCENTSATIONS LOTION & WASH SET OF 6	$37.02	SHISEIDO energizing fragrance body cream New with Box
I Coloniali Deep Massage Body Cream	$36.00	PURE by ALFRED SUNG CONDITIONING BODY LOTION 6.8 FL.OZ.
w/Myrrh BRAND NEW		40 BRAND NEW Suave Naturals Body Lotion $50 Value!

SHISEIDO energizing fragrance body cream New with Box	$12.00
PURE by ALFRED SUNG CONDITIONING BODY LOTION 6.8 FL.OZ.	$11.99
40 BRAND NEW Suave Naturals Body Lotion $50 Value!	$11.99

Bath & Body ▸ Body Wash

The average sales price in this subcategory is $10.04.

	HIGH		AVG
VITABATH ORIGINAL SPRING GREEN BATH GELEE 128OZ NEW	$64.05	AUTHENTIC SHALIMAR LOTION 6.8OZ RETAILS $47+	$10.50
AVEDA 64 FL OZ ENERGIZING BODY CLEANSER	$63.00	Philosophy CRUMB BERRY PIE body wash 16 oz. w/BONUS puf	$10.50
1 Gallon of Miracle Aloe Vesta 3-N-1 Body Wash Foam	$59.95	(NEW) BURBERRY BRIT ENERGIZING BODY WASH	$10.50
AVEDA Energizing Body Cleanser ~ 1/2 gallon size!	$57.00	Philosophy pure grace bath cream 8oz+ fragrance samples	$10.50
AVEDA Calming Body Cleanser ~ 1/2 gallon size!	$55.79	PHILOSOPHY CINNAMON BUNS	$10.50
AXE 10x ANTI-HANGOVER shower gel body wash	$54.00	~PREMONITION~ By Mary Kay Foaming Bath & Shower Gel 8oz	$10.50
20 Estee Lauder SeaFoam Wash Gel Cleansers 2.5oz new	$49.95	New 16 oz Philosophy STRAWBERRY MILKSHAKE 3-in-1	$10.50
Dermalogica Conditioning Body Wash Prof 32ozFree sample	$49.00	New Origins Perfect World Body Cleanser White Tea HUGE	$10.50
6 OLD SPICE RED ZONE 8 HOUR BODY WASH	$46.00	Philosophy AMAZING GRACE FIRMING body emuls 4oz w/BO	$10.50
dermalogica conditioning body wash 32 oz. PRO SIZE	$36.01	Victoria's Secret HALO body wash Brand NEW	$10.50
NIB 3 16 OZ PHILOSOPHY SHOWER GEL/SHAMPOO/BUBBLE BATH	$36.00	NEW 16 OZ PHILOSOPHY SHOWER GEL/SHAMPOO/BUBBLE BATH	$10.49
Philosophy Sugar Cookie, Lemon Custard, Berries & Cream	$34.00	ADIDAS MOVES For Her BODY POLISH WASH (6) Big	$10.49
NIB 3 16 OZ PHILOSOPHY SHOWER GEL/SHAMPOO/BUBBLE BATH	$33.00	BATH & BODY WORKS PLUMERIA SPLASH, GEL, BODY CREAM LOT3	$10.49
New *Aveda* Caribbean Therapy Bath & Body *LOT of 3*	$32.99	THE THYMES EUCALYPTUS BODY WASH 8.75 FL OZ	$10.49
Philosophy LEMON CUSTARD & SUGAR COOKIE bath & gel NEW!	$30.99	Clarins Eau Dynamisante Shower Gel 5.3 oz $40	$10.49

Bath & Body ▸ Cellulite Treatment

The average sales price in this subcategory is $61.85.

	HIGH		AVG
LPG Endermologie Key6 Module	$21,102.99	Endermologie Like Cellulite Roller Massage System	$69.99
G5 Gx-99 Subdermal Therapy Cellulite Removal System	$800.00	AVON CelluSculpt/Cellu-Sculpt, NIP, Lot 10, FREE SHIP!!	$65.00
SYBARITIC Cellulite Mach Get rid of unsightly dimples!	$162.50	Endermologie Like Cellulite Roller Massage System	$61.22
LOT OF 30 AVON CELLU-SCULPT TREATMENT WITH FREE EXTRAS	$150.00	BODY SHAPE, Cellulite Reduction Cream	$56.00
MEDICAL THERAPY/A+ CELLULITE REMOVER/MASSAGER/THIGH/LEG	$103.50	Elemis Silhouette - Body Contouring 60 Capsules	$56.00

Bath & Body ▸ Soap

The average sales price in this subcategory is $7.65.

	HIGH		AVG
Redken AMINO PON BEAUTY BAR *NIB*	$78.00	Lot 3 New Melaleuca French Milled Bath Soap Bars	$8.27
12 Convatec 325208 Aloe Vesta 3-n-1 Cleansing Foam 8 oz	$49.95	Lot 3 New Melaleuca Platinun Bath Bar Soap French Mill	$8.26
CASE OF IVORY SOAP BARS! Stock up for Y3K!!!!	$40.99	LOT 3 New MELALEUCA Gold Bath Bar Soap (French Milled)	$8.26
SEAWEED ALGAESSAGE SOAP AND TONING GELS. 2 TOWEL BONUS	$38.00	FIDJI by Guy Laroche Paris 4-25grams Soap Bars	$8.09
Lot of 4 Miracle II Products -Neutralizer, gel,soap etc	$33.50	Elariia Perlier Double Latte liquid soap sensitive skin	$8.00
Tatiana Hand & Body Soaps by Diane Von Furstenberg	$31.28	50 Cool Moisture Dove Samples Soap Beauty Bar green tea	$8.00
Wholesale 12 Magno by Henkel Bath Soap 4.4 oz./125gr	$31.00	Crabtree and Evelyn Lavender Hand Wash, FULL SIZE!	$8.00
SEAWEED ALGAESSAGE SOAP AND TONING GELS. 2 TOWEL BONUS	$29.50	VICTORIA'S SECRET passionate kisses LIQUID SOAP	$7.99
LUSH 5 Soaps! Alkmaar,Demon,Noriko,Sandstone,Coco! N/R	$29.00	3 AHAVA Dead Sea Mud Cleansing Bar	$7.99
12 FULL SIZE BARS of WE LIVE LIKE THIS VEGETABLE SOAP	$28.00	NEW CRABTREE & EVELYN ROSEWATER W/ COLD CREAM SOAP SET	$3.99
BOX OF MINT TIFFANY SCENTED SOAPS - FOUR BARS	$28.00	SEA SPA , DEAD SEA SALT SOAPS ,LOT OF 4 , HEALING !!!	$7.98
HERMES 10 MINI Eau D'Orange VERTE Hand Soaps	$26.00	10 Purell 8oz Instant Hand Sanitizers Puffs Tissues NEW	$7.95
ERNO LASZLO special skin soap 3 trial size bars/kit	$26.00	TWO - L'Occitane 20% Shea Butter MILK SOAP 3.5 oz NR	$7.90
HERMES 10 MINI Eau D'Orange VERTE Hand Soaps	$25.00	Lush lot of 2 Golden Moon soaps, discontinued!	$7.87
NEW - HOTEL SOAP BY THE CASE	$25.00	L'Occitane Verbena shea butter soap 3.5 oz. TWO BARS	$7.85

Coupons ▸ Health Care

The average sales price in this subcategory is $5.15.

	HIGH		AVG
NYSC New York Sports Club FREE 30 day trial membership	$30.99	2 coupons for FREE Bayer product = $30.00 Value	$7.52
2 - COUPONS - FREE ADVIL - $29.98 VALUE.	$15.02	2 - COUPONS - FREE BAYER PRODUCT - $31.98 VALUE	$7.50
2-COUPONS-GILLETTE-$10 OFF ANY PRODUCT-$20 VALUE!!	$12.54	15 *COUPONS BUY HUGGIES BABY WIPES GET BATH ITEM FREE!!	$7.50
Four $5.00 FLONASE COUPONS	$12.00	2 coupons for FREE Bayer product = $30.00 Value	$6.66
2 - COUPONS - FREE BOUNTY 8 ROLL PACK - $17.98 VALUE	$12.00	IMITREX $10 COUPON/CHECK migraine care	$6.58
[2 of these sold for $12.00 each]		2-COUPONS-GILLETTE-$10 OFF ANY PRODUCT-$20 VALUE!!	$6.55
2 - COUPONS - FREE CHARMIN ULTRA BATHROOM TISSUE	$11.70	15 *COUPONS BUY HUGGIES BABY WIPES GET BATH ITEM FREE!!	$6.50
2 - COUPONS - FREE ADVIL - $29.98 VALUE.	$11.53	FLONASE $10.00!!!!!!!!!!!!!!!! coupon/check exp 9/9/05	$6.42
4 CVS Coupons Get $30 Gift Cefiticates w/ Transfer RX	$11.50	Pure Protein High Protein Bar Coupons—Free Bars!!!	$6.09
4 CVS $30 Coupons - Gift Certificates w/transfer RX	$11.06	Pure Protein High Protein Bar Coupons—Free Bars!!!	$6.01
2 - COUPONS - FREE CHARMIN ULTRA BATHROOM TISSUE	$10.70	Two $5.00 FLONASE COUPONS	$6.00
2 - COUPONS - GILLETTE M3Power RAZOR CARTRIDGE REFILLS	$10.50	ZonePerfect Nutrition Bar Coupons—Free Bars!!!	$5.76
2 - COUPONS - FREE BAYER PRODUCT - $31.98 VALUE	$10.50	Pure Protein High Protein Bar Coupons—Free Bars!!!	$5.51
2 - COUPONS - GILLETTE M3Power RAZOR CARTRIDGE REFILLS	$10.50	[2 of these sold for $5.51 each]	
2 - COUPONS - FREE CHARMIN ULTRA BATHROOM TISSUE	$9.03	2-COUPONS-GILLETTE-$10 OFF ANY PRODUCT-$20 VALUE!!	$5.50
2-COUPONS-GILLETTE-$10 OFF ANY PRODUCT-$20 VALUE!!	$9.02	SAVE UP TO $90 ON YOUR NEXIUM PRESCRIPTION	$5.25

Dietary Supplements, Nutrition ▸ Herbs, Botanicals

The average sales price in this subcategory is $31.98.

	HIGH		AVG
HERB GRINDER - Herbal & Food Grinding Processor NEW	$349.00	2 bottles TrimSpa EF X32, 120 capsules, Free Shipping!	$40.00
4 Bottles Extagen Penis Enlargement Pills!	$175.00	1lb Strong Organic Hawaiian Kava, Sakau -Free shipping!	$39.99
4 Bottles Extagen Penis Enlargement Pills!	$165.00	Libidus for Better Penis Enhancement	$39.95
[8 of these sold for $165.00 each]		**SIX** STEVIA LIQUID BOTTLEs 250 ML EACH ONE	$39.90
4 Bottles Extagen Penis Enlargement Pills!	$152.00	Spirulina 1,000 Tabs 500 mg Shipping FREE World Wide!	$39.00
3 Bottles Extagen Penis Enlargement Pills!	$150.00	2-mon SUPPLY PENIS ENLARGEMENT SEX PILLS THAT WORK!	$39.00
[3 of these sold for $150.00 each]		Bach Flower Essences Rescue Remedy FREE SHP	$37.99
4 Bottles Extagen Penis Enlargement Pills!	$145.00	2 brand new bottles of Zantrex-3 Free Ship!	$35.00
[5 of these sold for $145.00 each]		[2 of these sold for $35.00 each]	
3 Months Supply Extagen Penis Enlargement!	$110.00	Bloussant 2 month Supply!! Factory Sealed!	$35.00
[5 of these sold for $110.00 each]		Original TAHITIAN NONI JUICE New Sealed Bottle!	$35.00
3 Months Supply Extagen Penis Enlargement!	$102.50	Lose Your Weight Fast w/ Hoodia 500 with Green Tea	$34.99
[2 of these sold for $102.50 each]		[2 of these sold for $34.99 each]	
3 Months Supply Extagen Penis Enlargement!	$96.00	ORIGINAL BLACK ARROW SPANISH FLY SEX DROPS	$31.99
Original TAHITIAN NONI JUICE	$93.27	[3 of these sold for $31.99 each]	
New Sealed Case!		2 Month Supply ProMagnum-XL Penis Enlargement Sex Pills	$31.95
3 Months Supply Extagen Penis Enlargement!	$91.00	2 Month Supply ProMagnum-XL Penis Enlargement Sex Pills	$30.95
[4 of these sold for $91.00 each]		6 boxes PANAX GINSENG EXTRACT SUPER STRENGTH *22* YR	$30.00
		[2 of these sold for $30.00 each]	

Dietary Supplements, Nutrition ▸ Nutrition Bars, Shakes

The average sales price in this subcategory is $25.90.

	HIGH		AVG
OPTIFAST 800 VANILLA sealed case 12 boxes(84 packets)	$319.99	OPTIFAST 70 Chocolate Shakes: Unopened Box	$28.00
[2 of these sold for $319.99 each]		3 Boxes MEDIFAST Chai Latte, Cappuccino & Hot Cocoa NR	$28.00
CHOCOLATE CASE OPTIFAST 800 12 boxes (84 packets)	$319.99	NEW Reliv Classic 17.7 oz	$27.50
OAKWORKS AURORA PORTABLE	$299.00	60 Protein LUNA CLIF BARS Dulce de Leche Women 02/06	$27.00
FOLDING MASSAGE TABLE MINT!		NEW 48 Energy Bars CLIF Chocolate Brownie Protein	$27.00
Quick Weight Loss Center Products LA - Lot of 44 boxes	$280.00	FIVE 4 packs Nitro-Tech Fruit Punch Protein Shakes 45g!	$26.99
OPTIFAST-70 Low Cal: "120 VANILLA SHAKES"	$265.00	MLO PROTEIN BARS 21 GRAMS LOT OF 50 HUGE BARS !!!!	$26.89
LA Weight loss BARS	$263.00	72 LUNA LEMON ZEST BARS FOR WOMEN	$26.55
VANILLA OPTIFAST 800 10 BOXES (70PKTS) EXP 11/2006	$258.00	60 LUNA S'mores Smores Energy Protein Bars	$26.49
LA WEIGHT LOSS - Case 168 bars Chocolate Peanut Butter	$256.00	Optifast 800 Strawberry shake powder	$26.01
VANILLA OPTIFAST 800 10 BOXES (70PKTS) EXP 11/2006	$250.00	ISAGENIX Isalean Vanilla Shake WEIGHT LOSS nutrition	$26.00
OPTIFAST 800 CHOCOLATE ready to drink 2 CASES	$240.00	1 can Reliv Classic. -also selling Innergize Fibrestore	$26.00
OPTIFAST 800 Chocolate Powder	$238.50	36 ct. Lot ~ Snickers MARATHON Protein bars	$26.00
OPTIFAST 70 12 BOXES. 120 ORANGE SHAKES	$212.50	Xango Dietary Supplement- Mangosteen	$25.99
6 cans Reliv Classic -fresh + 2 free shaker cups	$197.50	[3 of these sold for $25.99 each]	
HMR HUGE LOT WEIGHT LOSS well over 100 items!!!!	$192.50	100 CHOCOLATE DELUXE PURE PROTEIN BARS NEW	$25.00
288 Prostyle Protein Bars 30Gr Protein/1g Sugar/5 Carbs	$189.95	[6 of these sold for $25.00 each]	

Dietary Supplements, Nutrition ▸ Sports Supplements

The average sales price in this subcategory is $31.90.

	HIGH		AVG
Growth Hormone Capsules-Triple Strength *Anti-Aging*	$1,257.60	MUSCLETECH PUMP TECH 200	$36.00
[20 of these sold in a multiple item ("Dutch") auction for $12.88 each]		CAPLETS NEW 08/08	
Reliv Innergize Sports Drink ~ Orange Flavor ~ 12 cans	$185.19	2 Containers Cytodyne Myo-Blast CSP3 120 count	$35.95
Reliv Innergize Sports Drink ~ Lemon ~ 12 ~ Expire 1/07	$162.00	New-Sealed.. Methyl-D- 90 Count -Free Shipping	$35.00
NO2 & CE2 Stack	$152.51	BSN Nitrix - 1 New, 1 Opened	$34.99
VPX, 1-TU, Ergopharm	$150.00	MHP's T-Bomb II Maximum Strength Testosterone Booster	$34.99
Super-oxygenate your water for total Health & Energy!	$149.95	M1T2 new legal hormone replacement. not m1t, 1-ad 4-ad	$34.99
LEGAL GEAR METHYL 1-P 75 CAPSULES (Sealed in bottle)	$138.20	thermo shred by muscletech set of 3 *factory sealed*	$34.52
[4 of these sold in a multiple item ("Dutch") auction for $34.55 each]		NutraSport CUTTING GEL - EPIDRIL	$33.99
Vale Detox Drink - 19 Vitamins - Clean Your System!!	$130.00	Full Size-New, Sealed!	
[2 of these sold in a multiple item ("Dutch") auction for $65.00 each]		pump tech by muscletech set of 3 *factory sealed*	$33.01
Michael Thurmond Thurmon Provida 6 Week Body Makeover	$130.00	[2 of these sold for $33.01 each]	
Nutrex 1-TU Mass/Strength builder	$127.50	thermo shred by muscletech, set of 3 *factory sealed*	$33.00
1 case/12 GNC Pro Performance HMB 120 tabs. NEW!	$123.45	3 Containers MuscleTech Creatine 6000-ES 510grams	$33.00
(3) MHP T-Bomb II Maximum Strength Testosterone 168 ct.	$120.50	NUTRACEUTICS Symbiotropin	$32.77
1 case/12 GNC Pro Performance HMB 120 tabs. NEW!	$120.12	Instone FORZA-T 60 capsules New Sealed	$32.00
1 case/12 GNC Pro Performance HMB 120 tabs. NEW!	$120.00	T-BOMB II, 168 tablets,brand new, sealed, EXP 11/07	$31.99
MRI NO2 1500 MG 180 & 300 CAPLETS Combo NEW	$115.00	Enduramax- Not Optygen	$31.95

Dietary Supplements, Nutrition ▸ Vitamins, Minerals

The average sales price in this subcategory is $23.06.

	HIGH		AVG
Juice Plus++++ 8 month Supply 16 FACTORY SEALED BOTTLES	$260.00	2 New NUTRIBIOTIC GRAPEFRUIT SEED	$25.06
MANNATECH*ADVANCED AMBROTOSE* 150 gr	$207.50	EXTRACT CONCENTRATE	
BRAND NEW!!! ADVOCARE MNS Maximum Energy 6 boxes	$179.99	Juice Plus Factory Seald No Reserve 1	$25.00
3 SETs OF USANA HEALTHPAK 100 W/OLIVOL save on shipping	$175.00	MONTH SUPPLY WOW!	
3 SETs OF USANA HEALTHPAK 100 W/OLIVOL save on shipping	$174.19	50 US NAVY Military Patch lot USN Brand NEW Patch !	$24.99
3 SETs OF USANA HEALTHPAK 100 W/OLIVOL save on shipping	$167.52	SAM-e (2 X 100 Tablets) 200mg	$24.99

3 SETs OF USANA HEALTHPAK 100 W/OLIVOL save on shipping	$147.45	*** THERALOGIX Prostate Dietary Supplement 120 Caps ***	$24.99
4 SETS OF USANA ESSENTIALS - Exp 4/07- SAVE ON SHIPPING	$133.00	Pharmanex G3 2Pak Gac NuSkin Nu Skin noni xango vitamin	$24.99
2 BOXES OF USANA ESSENTIALS EXP 06/2006 LOW shipping	$125.96	POTEN B-150 PHARMASSURE B VITAMIN MULTI LOT OF 10	$24.99
[2 of these sold in a multiple item ("Dutch") auction for $62.98 each]		BRUSH UPS ORAL B ** ON THE GO BRUSHING** LOT OF 100	$24.99
USANA SENSE FACIAL CARE DELUXE PACK	$123.45	Mannatech Plus 90 Capsules	$24.52
LOT 2 Jars Mannatech ADVANCED Ambrotose 75 gr !!	$116.00	Advocare Spark Energy Drink Grape	$24.38
LOT 2 Jars Mannatech ADVANCED Ambrotose 75 gr !!	$112.50	SAM-e 400mg. 80 TABLETS. DOUBLE STRENGTH. NEW LOOK	$24.37
2 BOXES OF USANA ESSENTIALS EXP 06/2006 LOW shipping	$110.00	Two new sealed bottles Isotonix Calcium Value Size	$24.25
[2 of these sold in a multiple item ("Dutch") auction for $55.00 each]		METAMUCIL CAPSULES HUGE LOT OF 500...LOOKIE...CHEAP!!	$23.50
Mannatech Advanced Ambrotose Complex Powder - 150g	$108.50	2 SEALED TRIM SPA X32-120 TABLETS EXP.12/07 & 5/06	$23.50
2 Jars of New Ambrotose Complex Powder Bulk 100g. NR!!	$107.50	ADVOCARE - COREPLEX (Brand New, Factory Sealed)	$23.16

Fragrances ▶ Men

The average sales price in this subcategory is $16.80.

	HIGH		AVG
AMOUAGE *GOLD* MEN 1.7oz EDT spr. $215.00 perfume	$105.50	ROYAL COPENHAGEN 3.3 EDC COLOGNE SPRAY 4 HIM SEALED NIB	$18.95
CARRINGTON COLOGNE FOR MEN 3.4oz ** RARE **	$110.00	HEI ~ Alfred Sung 3.4 oz edt Cologne for Men Spray NIB	$18.65
[3 of these sold in a multiple item ("Dutch") auction for $55.00 each]		CERRUTI IMAGE AFTER SHAVE BALM lot of (6) 3.3 z d	$18.53
Z Zegna 3.3oz Spray For Men - Ermenegildo Zegna	$83.70	* DESIRE BLUE * Alfred Dunhill ?Cologne 1.7 oz * NIB *	$18.50
[2 of these sold in a multiple item ("Dutch") auction for $41.85 each]		Hollister Co. 1.7 oz Mens Drift Cologne, NEW ! men's	$18.25
MIRACLE HOMME BY LANCOME 3.4 OZ. EDT SEALED IN BOX	$81.95	* FCUK HIM * French Connection * Men Cologne 3.4 oz NIB	$17.95
* ANGEL A*MEN * Thierry Mugler Cologne 3.4 * METAL CASE	$75.99	[2 of these sold for $17.95 each]	
2 Yohji Yamamoto Cologne Homme 100ml 3.4 OZ. NR	$66.00	Premium by Phat Farm 3.3oz /100ml COL Sp New/Retail	$17.90
VERA WANG Eau de Perfume for Women 3.4 oz NEW!	$58.00	Clinique Happy for men 1.7oz	$17.50
*SILVER MOUNTAIN WATER CREED 4.0 PERFUME	$57.50	ROYAL COPENHAGEN EAU DE COLOGNE	$17.50
FEELING MAN JILL SANDERS MEN EAU DE TOILETTE 1.7oz	$49.99	large 8 oz SIZE new 8oz	
* A MEN *?Thierry Mugler Cologne 3.4 oz * RECHARGE *	$49.50	CERRUTI IMAGE pour homme 3.4 oz edt Cologne NIB Sealed	$17.25
ORGANZA INDECENCE Givenchy Perfume 3.3 oz edp NEW	$47.99	MICHAEL KORS 4.2 oz. edt Cologne Huge * New In Box *	$16.99
NEW Burt's Bees Mens Bay Rum Cologne *Full 4 oz* Burts	$47.56	WINGS for men ,Giorgio Beverly Hills, 3.4oz mint in box	$16.99
TOMMY BAHAMA COLOGNE FOR MEN 3.4 SPRAY (MIB) LQQK<<<<<	$47.00	HEI by Alfred Sung 3.4 oz edt Cologne for Men * NEW *	$16.95
Chanel Allure Sport men's .EDT Spray 3.4 fl. oz.	$46.00	CANDIES by Liz Claiborne 3.4 oz edt COLOGNE for Men NEW	$16.95
Floris of London "Pink Grapefruit" Eau de Toilette RARE	$46.00	DOMINICA BAY RUM LIME COLOGNE CARIBBEAN IMPORT	$16.75

Fragrances ▶ Women

The average sales price in this subcategory is $15.59.

	HIGH		AVG
MISHA MIKHAIL BARYSHNIKOV 3.3oz EDT SPRAY FOR WOMEN	$129.99	Faberge Kiki Cologne Spray 3.5 oz New In Box	$19.95
LA PRAIRIE TRAVEL BAG " CAVIAR INDULGENCE"	$84.99	L'OCCITANE LAVENDER EAU DE LA	$19.50
CHARLES OF THE RITZ 1.9oz EDT SPRAY	$66.00	RECOLTE BLEUE NEW SAVE50%	
Abercrombie & Fitch "8" Fragrance for Women 3.4oz	$63.00	Serge Lutens MIEL DE BOIS 1/6oz decant	$18.99
[2 of these sold in a multiple item ("Dutch") auction for $31.50 each]		*** JOOP *** Perfume for Women * 3.4 oz * New In Box!	$18.95
Abercrombie & Fitch Signature Fragrance for Women 3.4oz	$60.00	Estate Eau De Joy Perfume, Jean Patou Paris France	$18.01
[2 of these sold in a multiple item ("Dutch") auction for $30.00 each]		KATE SPADE Beauty eau de Parfum spray	$18.00
Jo Malone 100 ml 3.4 oz Cologne Perfume Big	$59.09	JOOP * Womens Perfume 3.4 * GREAT PRICE***** NIB 3.3	$17.99
TOMMY BAHAMA for Her HUGE Perfume and Lotion - IN BOXES	$54.33	Trish McEvoy #9 Blackberry Vanilla Musk 3 pc Travel Set	$17.49
Vintage Faberge Babe Cologne Spray Huge! 4 oz Tester	$53.01	VINTAGE JOY PERFUME BY JEAN PATOU PARIS - NEVER USED	$17.40
Montaigne by Caron - Perfume edt 1.7 oz Spray - RARE	$47.51	Susanne Lang Honeysuckle - 1/8 oz. EDP Roll-On NEW	$17.02
Floris of London "Pink Grapefruit" Eau de Toilette RARE	$46.00	Boucheron Summer fragrance 3.4 oz	$17.00
CROWN PERFUMERY: Court Bouquet 3.4FL.OZ/100ml	$45.00	* 273 INDIGO * Fred Hayman * Perfume	$16.99
MILLER HARRIS terre de bois EDP NEW IN BOX $98	$45.00	2.5 oz EDP SEALED$	
Vivre Parfum Molyneux Paris .47 fl oz Perfume	$45.00	CERRUTI IMAGE POUR FEMME EDT 2.5 oz "FREE GIFT"	$16.50
Stila Midnight Bloom Eau De Parfum NIB 50ml $50.00!	$45.00	Demeter Honeysuckle Cologne Spray Large size - 4oz.	$16.25
i Profumi di Firenze Limone Di Sicilia 50ml 95% Full	$44.99	Brand New (2) Realities 1.7 EDP Sealed	$16.07

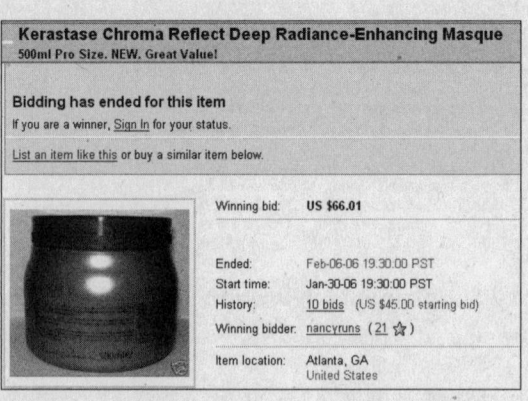

RARE VINTAGE GUERLAIN Sealed/ Signed Baccarat Bottle		**Kerastase Chroma Reflect Deep Radiance-Enhancing Masque**
		500ml Pro Size. NEW. Great Value!
Bidding has ended for this item		**Bidding has ended for this item**
If you are a winner, Sign In for your status.		If you are a winner, Sign In for your status.
List an item like this or buy a similar item below.		List an item like this or buy a similar item below.

Winning bid:	**US $351.00**	Winning bid:	**US $66.01**
Ended:	Feb-06-06 16:15:52 PST	Ended:	Feb-06-06 19:30:00 PST
Start time:	Jan-30-06 16:15:52 PST	Start time:	Jan-30-06 19:30:00 PST
History:	11 bids (US $25.00 starting bid)	History:	10 bids (US $45.00 starting bid)
Winning bidder:	azile (187 ☆)	Winning bidder:	nancyruns (21 ☆)
Item location:	White Sulphur Springs, New York United States	Item location:	Atlanta, GA United States

Hair Care ▶ Brushes, Combs

The average sales price in this subcategory is $22.07.

	HIGH		AVG
LEXINGTON HAIRMAX LASERCOMB	$378.00	BRAND NEW HOT AIR BRUSH BY REVOSTYLER–AS SEEN ON TV	$27.00
NEW CENTRIX CUTTING SHEARS	$200.00	Mason Pearson Popular Handy Pocket Brush GENERIC	$26.99
MODEL 6575 W/ BAG & COMBS!		BRAND NEW HOT AIR BRUSH BY REVOSTYLER–AS SEEN ON TV	$26.50
MASON PEARSON LARGE EXTRA PURE BRISTLE HAIR BRUSH B1	$149.95	Set of 4 Chi Farouk Ceramic Round Brushes!! *BRAND NEW*	$26.00
MASON PEARSON Large Extra Pure Boar Bristle Hair Brush	$127.00	[2 of these sold for $26.00 each]	
MASON PEARSON Handy Pure Bristle - Fine Hair Brush - B3	$106.00	T3 Brushes Set of 3 Tourmaline Ionic / Ceramic NIB L@@K	$25.00
Mason Pearson Hair Brush - POPULAR (B3)	$92.00	[2 of these sold for $25.00 each]	
MASON PEARSON SENSITIVE PURE BRISTLE HAIR BRUSH SB3	$89.95	FREDERIC FEKKAI TRAVEL BRUSH IN BOX UNUSED	$25.00
[2 of these sold for $89.95 each]		Mason Pearson Popular Junior Handy Pocket Brush GENERIC	$24.99
MASON PEARSON Lg Popular Bristle&Nylon-Normal HairBrush	$89.00	BRAND NEW HOT AIR BRUSH BY REVOSTYLER–AS SEEN ON TV	$24.99
[2 of these sold for $89.00 each]		[4 of these sold for $24.99 each]	
MASON PEARSON Handy Sensitive Bristle - Fine Hair Brush	$89.00	REVO STYLER ROTATING HAIR BRUSH STYLING SYSTEM	$22.50
MASON PEARSON Handy Pure Bristle-Fine Hair Brush - NIB!	$87.00	new unique RevoStyler Rotating Hair Brush revo seen tv	$22.50
Mason Pearson Hair Brush - POPULAR (B3)	$87.00	Betty Boop Hair Brush with Red Car Stand NIB	$21.99
MASON PEARSON BRUSH POPULAR Bristle & Nylon BN1 ~ NEW	$84.50	[2 of these sold for $21.99 each]	
[3 of these sold for $84.50 each]		Tourmaline Ionic (T3)Bristle Hair Brush 2.5" dia.	$21.50
MASON PEARSON BRUSH POPULAR Bristle & Nylon BN1 ~ NEW	$82.00	[2 of these sold for $21.50 each]	
MASON PEARSON BLACK POPULAR	$81.00	Tourmaline Ionic T3 Bristle Hair Brush 2" diameter	$21.50
BRISTLE NYLON BRUSH (BN1)		Tourmaline Ionic (T3)Bristle Hair Brush 3.75" dia.	$21.50
Mason Pearson Hair Brush - POPULAR (BN1)	$77.00	Tourmaline Ionic T3 Hair Brush 2.5" diameter new	$21.50

Hair Care ▶ Conditioner

The average sales price in this subcategory is $14.38.

	HIGH		AVG
10 Bottles Vaseline Hair Tonic NEW Scalp Conditioner	$200.00	American Crew Citrus Mint Cooling Conditioner Liter	$15.00
16oz OJON Restorative Hair Treatment *NEW* PLUS BONUS**	$147.50	PUREOLOGY HYDRATE CONDITIONER 8.5 FL OZ	$15.00
6 Bottles VASELINE HAIR TONIC & SCALP CONDITIONER Suave	$117.50	Frederic Fekkai technician shampoo 8 fl oz	$15.00
5 New Matrix Biolage Conditioning Balm 8.5 oz	$99.96	J.F Lazartigue Vita Cream W/ Milk Proteins - Retail $43	$14.99
[4 of these sold in a multiple item ("Dutch") auction for $24.99 each]		Triple Play. Montage Head Games Final Answer Cond.	$14.99
Full Case Of Senscience Inner Conditioner. Medium Hair.	$71.00	3 ~*~NEW~*~Redken Glass Smoothing Serum 2oz each	$14.99
[2 of these sold for $71.00 each]		OPI Two Tones Nail Polish + Rapidry Set NEW	$14.99
Crede ER Treatment (xlarge) 35.3 oz. 1,000g Refill size	$65.00	18 piece BACK TO BASICS POMEGRANATE	$14.99
Vaseline Hair Tonic NOW DISCONTINUED!!! 3 Available	$60.00	PEACH LOT new	
[3 of these sold in a multiple item ("Dutch") auction for $20.00 each]		3 Vidal Sassoon VS Balanced Daily Therapy Conditioner	$14.99
OJON Restorative hair treatment 4 pc lot Oprah's pick!	$55.01	Nioxin Protectives Moisturizing Scalp Therapy	$14.99
Crede ER Treatment (xlarge) 35.3 oz. 1,000g Refill size	$54.99	John Frieda Sheer Blonde Conditioner Lot Honey/Caramel	$14.97
33.8 oz Bumble & Bumble Curl Conscious Conditioner. NEW	$49.99	[3 of these sold in a multiple item ("Dutch") auction for $4.99 each]	
Full Case Of Joico K-Pak Leave-In Protectant. NEW. NR.	$48.01	Lancome Hair Sensation Rich Conditioning Mask ,NIB $24	$14.50
OJON ULTRA HYDRATING CONDITIONER 33.8 OZ * W/ FREE GIFT	$46.99	PHYTO 9 LEAVE IN CONDITIONER REG SIZE 1.7 OZ NIB	$14.50
Bumble and Bumble Alojoba Conditioner Liter 33.8oz	$45.00	Frederic Fekkai Full volume conditioner 8 fl oz	$14.50
GOLDWELL KERASILK ** ULTRA RICH CARE**–LTR PAIR (NEW)	$43.00	(5) L'oreal Loreal Preference Care Supreme conditioner	$14.50
pureology shampoo and conditioner for colour enhanced	$41.57		

Hair Care ▶ Curling Irons

The average sales price in this subcategory is $18.05.

	HIGH		AVG
OAKLEY THUMP MP3 SUNGLASSES 512 MB	$361.00	NEW CONAIR Triple Barrel Styling / Curling Iron	$20.50
CHI Flat Iron/Straightener 1" Priority shipping $7.00NIB	$91.00	BaByliss PRO Ceramic Curling Iron 3/4" NEW #BABC75M	$19.99
CHI SPRING 1 1/2 " CERAMIC CURLING IRON by FAROUK "NIB"	$87.25	jilbere Ceramic Tools Pro Hot Air Brush 1 1/4" NEW!	$19.99
Chi Farouk Spring 1" Curling Iron. N I B!	$85.55	jilbere Ceramic Tools Pro Curling Iron 1 1/4" NEW	$19.99
CHI Flat Iron/Straightener 1" Priority shipping $7.00NIB	$85.00	CONAIR 1 1/4" Curling Brush Combo	$19.99
CHI FAROUK Spring Grip Curling Iron 1 1/2 inch	$79.99	NEW-Gold N Hot Ceramic Triple Barrel Waver	$19.99
[3 of these sold for $79.99 each]		NIB VHTF Helen of Troy Super Mega 1 1/2 " Curling Brush	$19.99
CHI SPRING 1 1/2 " CERAMIC CURLING IRON by FAROUK "NIB"	$76.00	Conair BC167R 1 1/4" Hot Air Thermal Brush & Dryer NEW	$19.99
Ceramic InfraShine 1" Salon Model Flat Iron	$71.00	NEW REVLON HAIR CARE CORDLESS	$19.95
CHI Spring Professional Ceramic Curling Irons 1"	$70.00	RECHARGEABLE CURLING IRON	
13 PIECE SET CURLING IRONS SALON IRONS W/STAND & POUCH	$64.00	Braun Cordless Curling Iron Styler +Steam NEW	$19.95
CHI FAROUK Spring Grip Curling Iron 3/4 inch	$63.99	CONAIR CORDLESS BIG CURLS 1 1/8"	$19.75
[3 of these sold for $63.99 each]		CURLING IRON BRAND NEW	
CHI FAROUK Spring Grip Curling Iron 3/4 inch	$63.95	Hot Tools 1181 Pro Spring Curling Iron 1"	$19.09
Thermal Elite Oven w/ 3-Marcel Style Curling Irons	$53.00	Gold N Hot Triple Barrel Waver	$19.00
Jet Aire Pro Styling System - Hot Air Curling Iron RARE	$51.00	Braun C20 Cordless Curling Iron Styler - NEW!	$18.95
NEW HAI 3-In-One INTERCHANGEABLE CERAMIC CURLING IRON	$51.00	Hot Tools 1110 Pro Spring Curling Iron 1-1/4" NEW	$18.51

Hair Care ▶ Hair Color

The average sales price in this subcategory is $14.79.

	HIGH		AVG
Schwarzkopf Igora Royal & Personality Hair Color	$340.00	FUDGE PAINTBOX HAIR COLOR-LOT OF 4-ORANGE-YELLOW	$15.50
LOREAL LUCOLOR LOT OF 117 COLORS, 10 DEVELOPERS, CHART	$202.50	NEXXUS SIMPLY SILVER SHAMPOO 10.1OZ (3 BOTTLES)	$15.50
Matrix Color Sync Hair Color	$187.31	4 Loreal L'oreal Feria 72 Caramel Kiss Dark Blonde	$15.49
Matrix COLOR SYNC Hair Color 41 Tubes New & Swatch Book	$114.02	GIGA HOLD FREEZE HAIR PUTTY ultimate control ! 1 CASE!	$15.45
Goldwell top chic hair color package deal 12 items	$112.50	NEXXUS SIMPLY SILVER SHAMPOO 10.1OZ (3 BOTTLES)	$15.00

8 GOLDWELL CANNISTERS TOPCHIC HAIR COLOR	$85.99	Matrix Hair Color Color Sync Salon Swatch Book& more	$15.00
20 GOLDWELL HAIRCOLOR COLORANCE ACID COLOR TUBES	$82.34	Your new Lot 2x Redken Shades Eq color enhncing shampoo	$15.00
14 GOLDWELL CANNISTERS COLORANCE	$76.00	John Frieda BEACH BLONDE SUN STREAKS	$15.00
ACID COLOR HAIR COLOR		6 BOXES LOREAL PREFERENCE LB02 EX LIGHT NATURAL BLONDE	$15.00
MATRIX SOCOLOR Haircolor hair color LOT NEW!!!!!!	$75.01	6 PKGS CLAIROL HERBAL ESSENCES 24 ICY WHISPER BNIB	$15.00
21 TUBES GOLDWELL TOPCHIC HAIRCOLOR	$72.01	Matrix PRIZMS Clear Color Gloss 12 FL OZ	$14.99
~AVEDA~New unopened~Professional Hair Color~	$70.00	Matrix Prizms Clear Color Gloss	$14.99
8 GOLDWELL CANNISTERS TOPCHIC HAIR COLOR	$69.00	[2 of these sold for $14.99 each]	
John Frieda *Sun Streaks Highlighter* - 2 Tubes	$66.00	Lot of 12 Vicious Violet Hair Dye Raw Color Purple New	$14.95
18 TUBES REDKEN COLOR FUSION	$63.99	[3 of these sold for $14.95 each]	
HAIR COLOR NATURAL BALANCE		WELLA Koleston Perfect Hair Color LOT of 6 NEW!	$14.25
25 TUBES GOLDWELL TOPCHIC HAIR COLOR	$62.21	NEW JOHN FRIEDA blonde hair repair SHEER BLONDE (5)	$14.16

Hair Care ▸ Hair Dryers

The average sales price in this subcategory is $33.81.

	HIGH		AVG
TOURMALINE T3 IONIC HAIR DRYER W/ 3 FREE T3 BRUSHES!!!	$205.49	Sharper Image: Salon Pro Ionic Hairdryer	$38.01
TOURMALINE T3 IONIC HAIR DRYER W/ 3 FREE T3 BRUSHES!!!	$202.50	TWIN TURBO 2600 PROFESSIONAL HAIR DRYER	$38.00
NEW FROM CHI ROCKET HAIR DRYER	$167.50	SUNBEAM HAIR DRYER WALL-MOUNT 1628-050 + NIGHT LIGHT	$37.89
NIB 1800 WATTS AUTHENTIC		Sharper Image: Salon Pro Ionic Hairdryer	$37.00
FAROUK CHI HAIR/BLOW DRYER NEW ROCKET 1800 WATT	$159.00	Sunbeam Oster Wall Mount Hair Dryer 1626-020	$36.75
FAROUK CHI HAIR/BLOW DRYER NEW ROCKET 1800 WATT	$156.00	Hot Tools 1035 Pro Ion Dryer 1875 watt NEW	$36.65
T3 TOURMALINE IONIC HAIR DRYER 1800 WATTS -NEW!	$152.55	RUSK Speed Freak Pro 1600 W Ceramic Hair Dryer NEW !	$36.50
NEW CHI ROCKET PROFESSIONAL HAIR DRYER	$151.99	NEW Revo Styler Hot Air Brush Revostyler AS SEEN ON TV	$36.00
FAROUK CHI HAIR/BLOW DRYER NEW ROCKET 1800 WATT	$151.00	Revo Styler Rotating Hot Air Brush NEW	$36.00
Hairart T3 Tourmaline Dryer.+ Diffuser + FREE SHIP !!!	$151.00	BABYLISS PRO DOES SIZE MATTER HAIR BLOW DRYER 1875WATTS	$36.00
Hairart T3 Tourmaline Dryer.+ Diffuser + FREE SHIP !!!	$150.00	CONAIR Bonnet Pro Style Hair Dryer	$34.99
1800 WATT TOURMALINE II IONIC DRYER ~ NIB!! ~	$149.00	[2 of these sold for $34.99 each]	
T3 Hair Dryer with FREE T3Diffuser both NIB	$145.76	SUNBEAM HAIR DRYER WALL-MOUNT 1628-050 + NIGHT LIGHT	$34.95
TOURMALINE T3 IONIC HAIR DRYER	$144.00	Sharper Image: Salon Pro Ionic Hairdryer	$34.95
W/ 3 FREE T3 BRUSHES!!!		[2 of these sold for $34.95 each]	
FAROUK CHI HAIR/BLOW DRYER NEW ROCKET 1800 WATT	$143.48	TIGI Linea beadhead hardcore bionic ionic dryer $100	$34.01
FAROUK CHI HAIR/BLOW DRYER NEW ROCKET 1800 WATT	$143.08	SUNBEAM wall mount hair dryer night lite 1626-40, new!	$33.14

Hair Care ▸ Hair Loss

The average sales price in this subcategory is $66.61.

	HIGH		AVG
Anagen 50XLT Laser Hair Therapy Unit	$5,559.00	PROCERIN POWER COMBO 6 MONTH REGROWTH stop hair loss	$106.99
Authentic HairMax Laser Comb with Full Warranty!	$575.00	[3 of these sold for $106.99 each]	
Authentic HairMax Laser Comb with Full Warranty!	$540.00	PROCERIN POWER COMBO 6 MONTH REGROWTH stop hair loss	$103.99
Authentic HairMax Laser Comb with Full Warranty!	$535.00	[3 of these sold for $103.99 each]	
BRAND NEW Hairmax laser comb lasercomb	$520.00	EXT Hair therapy from Hair Club For Men NEW	$86.01
BRAND NEW Lexington Hairmax	$510.00	AVACOR	$82.00
LaserComb laser comb + DVD		Kevis European Hair & Scalp Lotion-3 boxes/36 vials	$76.25
BRAND NEW! UNUSED! LEXINGTON	$502.00	AVACOR 2 MONTHS SUPPLY SEALED 2-3 DAY SHIPPING	$74.95
HAIRMAX LASER COMB!		AVACOR hair growth formula, SAVE$$	$73.77
Hairmax laser Comb -brand new I Low Reserve	$501.00	HAIR FOLLICLE STIMULATOR (Magic Comb)	$73.00
Authentic HairMax LaserComb with Full Warranty!	$500.00	4MONTH PROCERIN HAIR LOSS REGROWTH 100% FEEDBACK ship$3	$69.99
New and Authentic Hairmax LaserComb w/ Full Warranty!!!	$500.00	4MONTH PROCERIN HAIR LOSS REGROWTH 100% FEEDBACK ship$3	$67.99
NEW!!! Leimo Laser Comb Stimulates Hair Regrowth!	$498.00	[2 of these sold for $67.99 each]	
[2 of these sold in a multiple item ("Dutch") auction for $249.00 each]		HAIR FOLLICLE STIMULATOR (Magic Comb)	$66.00
HAIRMAX lasercomb hair loss max laser comb + BONUS	$493.00	4MONTH PROCERIN HAIR LOSS REGROWTH 100% FEEDBACK ship$3	$65.99
Authentic HairMax Laser Comb	$485.00	GALLON - NIOXIN PROTECTIVES SCALP THERAPY W/PUMP	$64.00
BRAND NEW Lexington Hairmax LaserComb laser comb +DVD	$476.01	GALLON NIOXIN BIONUTRIENT PROTECTIVES CLEANSER W/PUMP	$61.00
BRAND NEW Lexington Hairmax LaserComb laser comb + DVD	$475.00	3 MONTH PROCERIN POWER COMBO REGROWTH stops hair loss!	$60.99
		[9 of these sold for $60.99 each]	

Hair Care ▸ Rollers, Curlers

The average sales price in this subcategory is $13.99.

	HIGH		AVG
ZOTOS Professional hot sticks with 80 rollers must have	$126.00	CONAIR BIG CURLS ELECTRIC HAIR ROLLERS CURLERS W/CLIPS	$14.99
Vintage Clairol Electric Rollers Hot Curlers PTC-20	$103.50	[2 of these sold for $14.99 each]	
Conair Professional Hot Sticks with 60 Rollers - NEW	$86.00	Conair BIG CURLS 5 Velvet Lg Hot Rollers-+5 xtraCurlers	$14.83
LA SALON CONAIR HOT STICKS.60 ROLLERS INCLUDED\ NEW!	$78.77	CLAIROL HOT ROLLERS (20 INSTANT HAIRSETTER)	$14.75
Conair Professional Hot Sticks with 60 Rollers - NEW	$76.03	CLAIROL HEATED 20 VELVET ROLLERS & CLIPS MODEL FH-20	$14.51
LA SALON CONAIR HOT STICKS.60 ROLLERS INCLUDED\ NEW!	$71.51	4 Salon Permanent Permanents and 84 Perm Rods NIB	$14.51
Conair Professional Hot Sticks with 60 Rollers - NEW	$71.00	REMINGTON express set travel hot rollers pins NEW dorm	$14.50
LA SALON CONAIR HOT STICKS.60 ROLLERS INCLUDED\ NEW!	$71.00	31 VINTAGE BRUSH HAIR CURLERS ROLLERS Pick & Fasteners	$14.50
ZOTOS Professional hot sticks with 60 rollers must have	$70.00	Clairol Kindness Instant Hairsetter - Hot Roller Kit	$14.49
60 Hot Sticks Spiral Rollers Conair Professional NEW	$66.00	Richard Caruso Molecular Steam 29 Curlers Hot Rollers	$14.40
60 Hot Sticks Spiral Rollers Conair Professional NEW	$66.00	RICHARD CARUSO TRAVELER MOLECULAR STEAM HAIRSETTER SET	$14.07
CLAIROL 20 INSTANT HAIRSETTER HOT ROLLERS W/CLIPS	$62.75	CONAIR ** HOT STICKS ** ROLLER SET	$14.01
MIB CLAIROL 20 INSTANT HAIRSETTER HOT ROLLERS W/CLIPS	$61.00	Clairol Lock n Roll With Instructions	$14.00
Zotos Wave Conductors 60 Spiral Hot Sticks, SUPER	$59.00	Vintage Lady Schick Lasting Curls Hairsetter Hot Roller	$14.00
GE Mist Condition Hairsetter-Steam Curlers/Rollers	$52.21	CARUSO NO-SALT MOLECULAR STEAM HAIRSETTING SYSTEM	$14.00
CLAIROL HOT ROLLERS CURLERS TRAVELER SET. RARE! MIB	$41.00	Clairol Lock n Roll With Instructions	$14.00

Hair Care ▸ Salon Equipment

The average sales price in this subcategory is $190.10.

	HIGH		AVG
Beauty Salon Equipment 10 Stations, Complete Package	$6,100.00	2 Electric Shampoo Joy Barber Hair Beauty Salon Chairs	$201.00
SALON STYLING STATION	$5,000.00	Wall Mounted Hair Dryers - used	$200.00
[5 of these sold in a multiple item ("Dutch") auction for $1,000.00 each]		*NEW* CENTRIX CUTTING SHEARS MODEL 6575 W/ BAG & COMBS!	$200.00
SALON STYLING STATION	$3,625.00	Toni & Guy Classic Cuts 2 - training video collection	$200.00
[5 of these sold in a multiple item ("Dutch") auction for $725.00 each]		NEW TAKARA BELMONT ELECTRIC HYDRALIC BASE	$199.97
Salon equiptment 6 Like new styling stations & desk	$3,200.00	[4 of these sold for $199.97 each]	
FULL SET PACKAGE DEAL BEAUTY SALON EQUIPMENT FREE S/H!	$2,788.00	SKIN & SPA SALON EQUIPMENT SHAMPOO CHAIR+SHAMPOO BOWL	$199.00
FULL SET PACKAGE DEAL BEAUTY SALON EQUIPMENT FREE S/H!	$2,598.00	[4 of these sold for $199.00 each]	
Orion Dr Muller 2000 model tanning bed 15 min bed	$2,500.00	Hydraulic BABY Chair Beauty Salon Skin Spa Equipment!!	$198.00
ENTIRE BEAUTY SALON- CHAIRS SINKS DRYER STATIONS +++	$2,100.00	SKIN & SPA BEAUTY SALON EQUIPMENT SET OF STEAMER NEW!!!	$198.00
Styling stations, salon chairs, dryers and mirrors	$2,081.00	[2 of these sold for $198.00 each]	
FULL SET PACKAGE DEAL BEAUTY SALON EQUIPMENT FREE S/H!	$1,398.00	NEW Shampoo Bowl &Chair Leg Rest BeautySalon Equipment	$189.00
FULL SET PACKAGE DEAL BEAUTY SALON EQUIPMENT FREE S/H!	$1,338.00	Top of the Line Dryer and Dryer Chair "lot"	$180.50
FULL SET SKIN & SPA BEAUTY PACKAGE	$1,288.00	BELVEDERE COLOR CARTS	$180.00
SALON EQUIPMENT NEW! [		[6 of these sold in a multiple item ("Dutch") auction for $30.00 each]	
[2 of these sold for $1,288.00 each]		Salon Reception Desk by Belvedere	$177.50
European Touch Pedicure Chair - NEW!!!!	$1,225.00	Styling Chair Beauty Salon Equipment WOOD !!	$158.00
Belmont 901 Men's Moterized Barber Hairstyling Chair	$1,025.00	Double Sided Styling Station	$158.00
SET OF HYDRAULIC STYLING CHAIR	$850.00	Shampoo Bowl Beauty Salon Skin Day Spa Equipment New !!	$158.00
BEAUTY SALON EQUIPMENT		[2 of these sold for $158.00 each]	

Hair Care ▸ Shampoo

The average sales price in this subcategory is $15.65.

	HIGH		AVG
Gee Your Hair Smells Terrific Shampoo CASE of 10-375 ml	$150.00	BUMBLE AND BUMBLE - "STRAIGHT" MUST HAVE	$16.76
[2 of these sold in a multiple item ("Dutch") auction for $75.00 each]		Pantene Pro-V Shampoo and Conditioner, total 6	$16.50
Ojon Restorative Hair Treatment HUGE 16oz Size	$142.50	PAUL MITCHELL INSTANT MOISTURE SHAMPOO 33.8FL.OZ.	$16.50
Ojon Ultra Hydrating Shampoo & Conditioner 33oz Sealed	$104.99	GRAHAM WEBB BODACIOUS SHAMPOO &	$16.50
NEW PUREOLOGY HYDRATE SHAMPOO & CONDITIONER	$92.63	CONDITIONER 8.5 OZ	
KERASTASE BAIN SATIN 2 SHAMPOO 1 LITER PRO SIZE !!	$69.00	Kerastase Bain Satin #1 Shampoo (8.5 fl.oz)	$16.50
Full Case Of Senscience Energy Shampoo. Normal.	$61.00	33.8 oz. Frederic Fekkai Du Jour Shampoo. NEW. NR.	$16.49
Ojon Ultra Hydrating Shampoo with Pump 33.8oz NEW	$57.00	KERASTASE Bain ELASTO CURL Shampoo Curly Hair!	$16.11
PureOlogy Hydrate Shampoo & Conditioner 32oz (1 Litre)	$54.00	BUMBLE AND BUMBLE CREME DE COCO SHAMPOO *NEW*	$16.01
Paul Mitchell Tea Tree Shampoo Gal-Free Ship	$52.95	KERASTASE OLEO RELAX SHAMPOO FREE SHIP BIN 8.4 oz	$16.01
Paul Mitchell Tea Tree Shampoo Gal-Free Ship	$49.95	Kerastase Bain Oleo-Relax Shampoo (8.5 fl.oz/250ml)	$16.00
10 Thierry Mugler Angel MEN Shampooing Integral 7oz new	$49.95	NEW!!! GRAHAM WEBB DAILY STRENGTH 3 PC. COMBO	$15.99
HEMPZ Hydrating Shampoo and Conditioner (Liters)	$47.50	HUGE Modern Organic Products MIXED GREENS SHAMPOO	$15.99
PUREOLOGY HYDRATE SHAMPOO & CONDITIONER 33.8 OZ EACH	$46.99	Malibu 2000 Just For Swimmers Hair Care System	$15.99
PUREOLOGY PURE VOLUME COLLECTION	$46.00	LUSH Plantational Henna Shampoo Discontinued 250g	$15.87
OLEO RELAX HUGE 34 0Z SHAMPOO PROFESSIONAL 1 liter	$45.00	Ojon Ultra Hydrating Shampoo 8.44oz NEW	$15.75

Hair Care ▸ Straightening Irons

The average sales price in this subcategory is $39.96.

	HIGH		AVG
T3 TOURMALINE 1 3/4 WET TO DRY IRON W/3 FREE T3 BRUSHES	$177.50	Hairart Ceramic Straightening Iron with box	$39.99
T3 TOURMALINE 1 3/4 WET TO DRY IRON W/3 FREE T3 BRUSHES	$153.50	NEW JDL Ceramic Digital LCD Hair Straightener IRON	$39.99
T3 tourmaline wet to dry straightening flat iron	$152.50	[4 of these sold for $39.99 each]	
T3 TOURMALINE 1 3/4 WET TO DRY	$148.50	New Tourmaline Ceramic Ionic Hair Iron T3 CHI True	$39.99
IRON W/3 FREE T3 BRUSHES		[4 of these sold for $39.99 each]	
CHI TURBO HAIR FLAT IRON STRAIGHTENER 2" AUTHENTIC!!!!	$140.50	NEW JDL Ceramic Digital LCD Hair Straightener IRON	$39.99
CHI TURBO HAIR FLAT IRON STRAIGHTENER 2" AUTHENTIC!!!!	$140.00	ER GO 2"MINI IRON CERAMIC PLATE,TO STRAIGHTEN HAIR.NIB.	$39.99
CHI TURBO HAIR FLAT IRON STRAIGHTENER 2" AUTHENTIC!!!!	$137.50	NEW JDL Ceramic Digital LCD Hair Straightener IRON	$39.99
T3 WET TO DRY TOURMALINE IONIC HAIR STRAIGHTNERS	$135.00	ION PRO MAXI FLAT IRON CERAMIC GLIDE HAIR STRAIGHTENER	$39.95
Hairart T3 Tourmaline 1 3/4 Inch Wet-To-Dry Iron	$132.50	[2 of these sold for $39.95 each]	
T3 TOURMALINE Wet - To - Dry IRON by HAIRART 1 3/4" NIB	$132.46	STRAIGHT CRAZY X2 CERAMIC STRAIGHTNING IRON~NEW~	$39.95
T3 WET TO DRY FLAT IRON 1/34 ***BEST PRICE ON EBAY***	$130.00	ION PRO MAXI FLAT IRON CERAMIC GLIDE HAIR STRAIGHTENER	$39.95
FHI 1" Limited Edition 100% True Ceramic Flat Iron	$129.99	PRO CERAMIC ION FLAT IRON WIDE, HAIR ACC, NR, NIB	$39.89
T3 TOURMALINE Wet - To - Dry IRON by HAIRART 1 3/4" NIB	$122.51	NEW FHI 1 1/4" CERAMIC IONIC FLAT IRON IRONS RFI 302	$38.99
T3 Tourmaline Wet-to-Dry Iron	$122.50	new chi p PRO TOURMALINE TRUE CERAMIC HAIR STRAIGHTENER	$38.00
HAIRART T3 TOURMALINE 1" CERAMIC	$118.50	CERAMIC FLAT IRON 1" Andis Gold Irons 395 F 20 Settings	$37.95
FLAT HAIR IRON *NEW*NR		STRAIGHT CRAZY X2 NEW!! Straightening Iron PLUS MORE	$37.25
Hairart T3 Tourmaline 1 3/4 Inch Wet-To-Dry Iron	$117.50	NEW Tourmaline Ceramic Hair Straightener / Flat Iron NR	$36.00

Hair Removal ▸ Epilators, Electrolysis

The average sales price in this subcategory is $42.06.

	HIGH		AVG
* NEW * Professional Laser Hair Tatoo Remover DMD4000lp	$1,575.00	PHILIPS SATINELLE EPILATOR-NEW MODEL!!	$43.95
LASER HAIR REMOVAL DMD2000LP TATTOO REMOVAL	$1,350.00	[3 of these sold for $43.95 each]	
Fischer Compu-blend Electrolysis Epilator Thermolysis	$988.32	EPILADY ULTRA EPILATOR 3 SPEED SETTINGS, W/CARRYING BAG	$43.57
Apilus Senior Professional Electrolysis Machine	$960.00	EPILADY TRIO Cordless Epilator + Adapter Charger Ultra	$43.15
Fischer CBX Epilator Pro Electrolysis Machine w/ MN!	$725.25	Sharper Image: E-Pen Electrolysis System	$43.00
Aavexx 500 Deluxe Electrolysis Hair Removal System	$429.99	Sharper Image: E-Pen Electrolysis System	$42.95

V2R-G Electrolysis Hair Removal System	$199.99	[8 of these sold for $42.95 each]
ELECTROLISIS REMOVER PERMANENT HAIR REMOVAL TOOL KIT	$199.95	Braun Silk-Epil Soft Perfection Body System	$42.51
HOME ELECTROLYSIS PERMANENT HAIR REMOVAL MACHINE KIT	$199.95	Emjoi Gently Gold Caress Hair Removal Epilator	$42.00
NEW DELUXE VECTOR HAIR REMOVAL ELECTROLYSIS SYSTEM	$199.95	Emjoi Gently Gold Leg & Body Hair Removal Epilator	$41.00
Aavexx 300 Electrolysis Hair Removal System	$192.50	Epilady Trio Hair Removal System - Like new!!!	$41.00
PROFESSIONAL EPILA PERMANENT LASER HAIR REMOVAL SYSTEM!	$189.99	New Epilady Discrete Plus Hair Removal System NIB	$41.00
[4 of these sold for $189.99 each]		EPILADY TRIO Hair Remover Epilator with Cordless Option	$41.00
PROFESSIONAL EPILA PERMANENT	$184.99	NEW in Package Epilady Trio CORDLESS Hair Remover	$40.03
LASER HAIR REMOVAL SYSTEM!		Emjoi Gently Gold Leg & Body Hair Removal Epilator	$40.03
Deluxe Aavexx 400 Electrolysis Hair Removal System	$152.50	Verseo 2-in-1 Epilator + Shaver Hair Removal System NEW	$39.99
Aavexx 500 electrolysis unit w/deluxe kit NR! Best Deal	$152.01	Epilady Legend - Brand New!!!	$39.99

Hair Removal ▸ Shavers

The average sales price in this subcategory is $36.75.

	HIGH		AVG
Panasonic ES8163 Pro-Curve Wet/Dry Shaver NEW!!!!	$180.50	GILLETTE MACH 3 RAZOR BLADES 40 CT. NEW SEALED	$41.01
Intimate Shaver-Hair Removal-Pubic/Bikini/Head Shaving	$179.55	BRAUN 7526 SYNCRO SYSTEM SHAVER ALL ITEMS WITH IT "NICE	$41.00
[9 of these sold in a multiple item ("Dutch") auction for $19.95 each]		Braun Synchro 7570 Complete electric razor rechargable	$41.00
New In Box Braun 8595 Activator System Shaver + extras	$156.00	Brand New Izumi IS-2430 Electric Shaver	$40.95
BRAUN 8595 ACTIVATOR ELECTRIC RAZOR SHAVER NEW SEALED	$150.00	BRAND NEW BRAUN FREEGLIDER 6680	$40.51
Braun Activator 8595 Rechargeable/Cord shaver. NEW!!!	$150.00	MEN'S ELECTRIC SHAVER	
Braun 8595 Cordless Shaver Activator System NEW+ Refill	$142.80	Braun Precision Styling and Shaping Shaver cruZer3 2865	$40.00
FACTORY SEALED BRAUN 8595 ACTIVATOR ELECTRIC RAZOR	$142.50	Grundig GS 6798 Electric Razor DESIGNO FX3	$40.00
Factory sealed Braun 8595 Electric Razor **BRAND NEW**	$141.02	Braun Flex XP 5612 Electric Shaver NEW SEALED	$39.99
Braun 8595 Cordless Shaver Activator Sys w/Refill -NEW	$140.00	Remington TITANIUM Ultra Shaver R-9500	$39.99
Braun Activator 8595 Electric Shaver BRAND NEW IN BOX!	$139.49	Wahl BEST 5000 Custom Electric Shaver PLUS BONUSES NEW	$39.95
Brand New Braun 8595 Activator Self Cleaning Shaver	$138.29	32 Gillette MACH 3 Razor Blades NEW	$39.00
NEW Braun Activator 8595 Self Cleaning Cordless Razor	$135.00	GILLETTE MACH 3 TURBO RAZOR BLADES 40 CT. NEW SEALED	$38.96
BRAUN ACTIVATOR SYSTEM MODEL #8595 NIB!!! NR!!!	$133.54	Like New Braun 5775 Flex XP II Rechargeable Razor/Shaver	$38.89
New Braun 8595 Shaver	$132.50	GILLETTE MACH 3 RAZOR BLADES 40 CT. NEW SEALED	$37.27
NEW Braun Activator 8595 shaver system Razor w/LCD	$132.00	Braun Precision Styling and Shaping Shaver cruZer3 2865	$37.03

Health Care ▸ Body Enhancers

The average sales price in this subcategory is $26.19.

	HIGH		AVG
Penis Enlargement - KIT- Extender NOT Pills or Pumps	$156.95	60 tabs ENZYTE (Factory Sealed) 2 Month supply	$30.00
[4 of these sold for $156.95 each]		1 Herbalife Prelox Blue Performance Enhancer PRE LOX NR	$29.99
Med. proven PENIS Enlargement Traction Device, Extender	$152.95	GALACTICA VIBRATNG MALE PENIS ENLARGER ENLARGEMENT PUMP	$29.99
AndroMedical Penis Enlarger, No More Penis Pumps	$150.00	2 Month Supply ProMagnum-XL Penis Enlargement Sex Pills	$29.95
PENILE ENLARGMENT PROGRAM DEVICE PRODUCT PENIS #1	$149.95	U NEED A PORN STAR'S 12 INCH PENIS! PUMP / PUMPS	$29.75
Penis Enlargement Extender NOT Pills or Pump Enlargment	$149.95	New HFR Nitric Oxide Gel Formula	$28.66
[2 of these sold for $149.95 each]		MAGNA-RX 60 TABLETS–SEALED	$28.12
AndroMedical Penis Enlarger, Not a Pump, FREE SHIPPING!	$107.50	[2 of these sold in a multiple item ("Dutch") auction for $14.06 each]	
Dr Joel's KAPLAN Penis ENLARGEMENT ENLARGER Pump KIT	$99.99	BIG MAN'S FULL 12" w/3 SLEEVES PENIS PUMP ENLARGER NEW!	$27.95
[5 of these sold for $99.99 each]		PENIS ENLARGEMENT & MUSCLE GROWTH	$27.95
NEW The Beast Anabolic Activator case of 12 2oz Bottles	$96.00	[3 of these sold for $27.95 each]	
Viacyn Penis Enlargement, 3 Month Supply, Free Shipping	$87.95	Enzyte Dietary Supplement	$27.60
120 Day Supply ProMagnum-XL Penis Enlargement Sex Pills	$79.95	Prolong-Rx 96 pills travel pack sex stamina male female	$27.50
Penis enlargement, enlarger, stretcher, penile !! Red	$75.00	MAX-XTENDER MALE PENIS ENLARGER STRETCHER ENLARGEMENT !	$27.01
AndroMedical Penis Enlarger, No More Penis Pumps	$75.00	VPRX Oil - Male Penile Enhancement Penis Enlargement	$27.00
NEW The Beast Anabolic Activator case of 12 2oz Bottles	$71.00	Penis Enlargement Pills 6 Mo.Supply FREE S/H-better sex	$26.00
Gents Penis Enlarger/Enlargement -Wear Anywhere-Anytime	$69.95	Penis Enlargement Pills 6 Mo.Supply FREE S/H-better sex	$25.00
DOC JOHNSON PROFESSIONAL TITAN PENIS ENLARGER PUMP	$69.95	[2 of these sold for $25.00 each]	

Health Care ▸ Family Planning

The average sales price in this subcategory is $41.92.

	HIGH		AVG
OvaCue Saliva Fertility Monitor by Zetek- Almost New!	$280.01	Clear Plan Clearplan Easy Fertility Monitor+BONUS!!!	$52.99
BRAND NEW CLEARBLUE EASY MONITOR+COMPLETE OVULATION KIT	$194.00	CLEARBLUE / CLEAR BLUE FERTILITY MONITOR TEST STICKS-NR	$51.09
NEW CLEAR BLUE EASY FERTILITY MONITOR & 30 TEST STICKS	$164.75	58ct CLEARBLUE CLEARPLAN FERTILITY MONITOR TEST STICKS	$51.00
Clearblue Easy Fertility Kit (New in Box)	$161.50	Clear Blue Fertility Monitor	$51.00
NEW Clear Blue Fertility Monitor and ClearBlue Sticks	$161.00	Clear Plan Fertility Monitor with Instructions	$51.00
Clearblue Easy Fertility Monitor & 30 Test Sticks NIB	$159.50	CLEARBLUE / CLEAR BLUE FERTILITY MONITOR TEST STICKS-NR	$51.00
NEW Clear Blue Fertility Monitor and ClearBlue Sticks	$152.60	Clearblue Easy Fertility Monitor 30 Test Sticks Sealed	$47.00
*NEW *CLEARBLUE DIGITAL FERTILITY MONITOR-OVULATION	$152.50	CLEARBLUE / CLEAR BLUE FERTILITY MONITOR TEST STICKS-NR	$46.75
Clear Blue Easy Plan Fertility Monitor + 29 test strips	$152.50	Clear Plan Easy - FERTIILITY MONITOR- It worked for Us	$46.00
GREAT CLEARPLAN EASY MONITOR + COMPLETE OVULATION KIT+	$152.50	CLEAR PLAN FERTILITY MONITOR	$46.00
NEW Clear Blue Fertility Monitor and ClearBlue Sticks	$150.27	W/EVERYTHING,FREE SHIP/BIN	
Clearblue Fertility Monitor + 30 STRIPS	$150.00	Clear Plan Easy Fertility Monitor	$46.00
CLEARBLUE EASY FERTILITY MONITOR & 30 CT. TEST STICKS!!	$150.00	ClearBlue Easy Fertility Monitor w/6 test sticks!!	$46.00
[2 of these sold for $150.00 each]		Clearblue Easy Fertility Monitor Test Sticks 30 test.	$46.00
NEW Clear Blue Fertility Monitor and ClearBlue Sticks	$147.50	CLEAR BLUE EASY FERTILITY MONITOR TEST STICKS *SEALED*	$44.52
NEW Clear Blue Fertility Monitor and ClearBlue Sticks	$142.50	Clear Plan Fertility Monitor	$44.00

Health Care ▸ First Aid

The average sales price in this subcategory is $23.20.

	HIGH		AVG
LAERDAL HEARTSTART MODEL FR - AED - DEFIBRILLATOR	$810.00	WHEEL CHAIR CUSHIONS - LOT OF 10 DIFFERENT NEW	$26.02
Chiropractic/Pettibon Adjusting Instrument	$405.00	Ever Ready Steel First Aid kit /supplies/$150.00	$26.00
New Cpr Prompt Manikin kit (6 manikin kits available)	$390.00	DuoDERM Extra Thin (((10))) sheets 4 x 4 "	$26.00
NIP Medtronic Physio AED Trainer-CPR Manikin-Laerdal	$305.02	3M Tegaderm Dressing #1626W - Quantity = 50 NIB	$26.00
Laerdal AED Trainer CPR Manikin Ambu Simulaids Prompt	$301.71	EMT EMS FIRE RESCUE MEDICAL STOCKED FANNY TRAUMA BAG	$25.49
LIFEPAK CR PLUS AED TRAINER BY MEDTRONIC	$242.50	Brand New Tegaderm transparent dressings box of 50	$25.00
LIFEPAK CR PLUS AED TRAINER BY MEDTRONIC	$200.00	OSHA CERTIFIED 205 PC FIRST AID KIT FOR HOME/OFFICE	$24.99
NEW-Laerdal Ambu Simulaids Nasco MPL Adult CPR Manikin!	$157.50	ALL PURPOSE & OUTDOOR FIRST AID KIT 204pc+26pc BONUS NW	$24.99
Dermabond DHV12 Sealed Box of 12 Skin Adhesive Suture	$148.50	EMT EMS FIRE RESCUE MEDICAL STOCKED FANNY TRAUMA BAG	$24.99
[2 of these sold for $148.50 each]		205 PC *OSHA CERTIFIED* FIRST AID KIT ~WHOLESALE~ NR!	$24.99
LAERDAL Resusci Anne CPR manikin w/accessories, LQQK!	$142.50	EMT WATCH - MEDIC EMS Doctor 911 HEALTH Star of life	$24.97
Military Medics First Aid 200+ Items NEW PRO Black M17	$129.99	[2 of these sold for $24.97 each]	
CPR Prompt training kit manikin infant adult in bag	$101.00	First Aid supplies/800 items/$250.00	$24.50
W.P.A. FIRST AID KIT WITH CONTENTS	$91.01	ConvaTec Moldable Wafers&Ostomy Bags. Medical supplies	$24.49
4 boxes of BD Vacutainer Brand blood sets 23G 3/4 -NR	$83.50	205 PC *OSHA CERTIFIED* FIRST AID KIT ~WHOLESALE~ NR!	$23.50
MagBoy Nikken MagCreator magnetic rolling massage NEW	$81.01	Nikken Magnetic Pillow new 20"x12"	$23.26

Health Care ▸ Sleeping Aids

The average sales price in this subcategory is $16.43.

	HIGH		AVG
RESMED AUTOSET T UNIT + ACC. CLINICIAN GUIDE+SOFTWARE	$400.00	BREATHE RIGHT NASAL STRIPS - 6 BOXES OF 12 LARGE.	$17.99
SLEEP Apnea HEALTHDYNE SNORE No MORE	$250.00	[6 of these sold for $17.99 each]	
DENTAL ANTI-SNORE/SNORING CONTROL, CLINICALLY PROVEN!	$149.00	Breathe Right SNORE RELIEF THROAT SPRAY - 2 boxes - NEW	$17.55
Respironics Remstar Heated Humidifier	$102.51	Homedics Sleep Sound Machine w/Adapter	$17.50
(5) Boxes Breathe Right Nasal Strips 60 Large TAN	$75.00	Sharper Image Heart & Sound Soother w/timer	$17.50
Sharper Image: Sound Soother 20 Light Wood	$74.95	60 BREATHE RIGHT NASAL STRIPS	$17.50
respironics comfortfull full face mask medium	$67.55	LARGE TAN 2 BOXES 30 NEW	$17.50
GOOD KNIGHT 418A SLEEP MACHINE WITH ALL ASSESSORIES	$66.00	OM Sound Machine - 6 soothing sounds NEW NR!	$17.15
New Respironics Comfortfull Full facemask SZ. M	$65.00	TWO SPEAKER SLEEP MACHINE - NICE!!!	$17.05
World's Best Inflatable Travel Neck Support Pillow!!	$62.00	72 BREATHE RIGHT STRIPS.... LARGE	$17.00
[5 of these sold in a multiple item ("Dutch") auction for $12.00 each]		60 BREATHE RIGHT NASAL STRIPS LARGE CLEAR 2 BOX 30 NEW	$17.00
BUY 1 GET 1 FREE NEW Neck Support Contour Memory Pillow	$59.99	Nap Alert Sleep Relaxation Task Timer FREE POUCH NEW	$16.95
Sharper Image: Sound Soother 20 Light Wood	$59.95	SILK BROCADE SLEEP MASK Blindfold CHOOSE YOUR COLOUR!	$16.50
[2 of these sold for $59.95 each]		Homedics Sound Spa White Noise Machine	$16.01
New Respironics Comfortfull Full facemask SZ. M	$56.00	World's Best Inflatable Travel Neck Support Pillow!!	$16.00
BREATHE RIGHT NASAL STRIPS SM/MED TAN 180 CT FREE SHIP	$55.00	[2 of these sold in a multiple item ("Dutch") auction for $8.00 each]	
[2 of these sold for $55.00 each]		SILK BROCADE SLEEP MASK Blindfold CHOOSE YOUR COLOUR!	$16.00
New Respironics Comfortfull Full facemask SZ. M	$51.00	Snore Gone Sleep Aid -Electronic Impulse Ultrasound	$15.99

Health Care ▸ Smoking Cessation

The average sales price in this subcategory is $43.84.

	HIGH		AVG
NICOTROL Nicotine Gum - 4mg CLASSIC - 24 box/2520 piece	$386.00	220 NICORETTE 2 MG MINT STOP SMOKE GUM SALE	$46.99
[2 of these sold for $386.00 each]		[2 of these sold for $46.99 each]	
NICOTROL GUM - 4mg MINT - 24 boxes/2520 pieces	$386.00	NICODERM CQ 7mg &14mg STEP 2 & STEP 3 TWO 14 patch kits	$45.99
NICOTROL Nicotine Gum - 4mg CLASSIC - 24 box/2520 piece	$362.00	Nicotine NICOTROL 42 Patches Sealed STEP 1, 2 & 3	$45.00
NICOTROL GUM - 4mg MINT - 24 boxes/2520 pieces	$362.00	14 NICODERM CQ CLEAR STEP 1 + 14 STEP 2 CLEAR PATCHS	$44.99
1620 Nicorette 2MG Orange Gum FREE FREE FREE	$360.00	NEW!! NICODERM CQ step 1 + 2 CLEAR THINFLEXX 28patches	$44.83
NICOTROL Nicotine Gum - 4mg CLASSIC - 24 box/2520 piece	$354.00	NICODERM CQ 7mg &14mg STEP 2 & STEP 3 TWO 14 patch kits	$44.00
1188 Nicorette 2MG Orange Gum FREE FREE FREE	$310.00	14 NICODERM CQ STEP 1 + 14 STEP 2 STOP SMOKE PATCHS	$43.99
NICOTROL GUM - 2mg CLASSIC - 24 boxes/2520 pieces	$308.00	[9 of these sold for $43.99 each]	
[3 of these sold for $308.00 each]		NICODERM PATCHES QUIT SMOKING AID 3 WEEKS SUPPLY	$43.02
NICOTROL GUM - 2mg MINT - 24 boxes/2520 pieces	$308.00	Tobacco Vaporizer and VaporMaker	$43.00
NICOTROL GUM - 2mg MINT - 24 boxes/2520 pieces	$284.00	NICOTINELL Nicotine gum 3 boxes FRUIT 2mg/288	$42.99
[4 of these sold for $284.00 each]		Nicorette Orange 2mg, 48 pcs ea, 5 boxes, 240 pcs gum	$42.60
Nicorette 2mg MINT (12 box/1260 pieces) + Sample Box	$266.00	Nicorette Commit 2 Mg Stop Smoking Aid 96 Lozenges	$42.01
Nicorette 2mg CLASSIC (12 box/1260 piece) + Bonus Box	$254.00	14 NICODERM CQ STEP 1 + 14 STEP 2 STOP SMOKE PATCHS	$41.99
Nicorette 2mg MINT (12 box/1260 pieces) + Sample Box	$254.00	[2 of these sold for $41.99 each]	
950 + 105 Nicorette 4mg Mint gum FREE	$240.00	28 NICODERM CQ STEP 2 STOP SMOKE PATCHS NEW SEALED	$41.99
NICOTROL GUM - 4mg CLASSIC - 12 box/1260 piece	$206.00	SMOKE AWAY Complete Stop Smoking Support Program NEW	$41.50

Health Care ▸ Other Health Care Items

The average sales price in this subcategory is $39.63.

	HIGH		AVG
Harvest Smartprep2 Centrifuge	$1,595.00	ONE TOUCH ULTRA SMART IN DUO TEST STRIPS 100	$48.20
CoaguChek S System	$640.00	2 INTERPLAK POWER TOOTHBRUSHES SEALED $48	$48.00
REMstar Pro Respironics with C-Flex system/CPAP	$600.00	Omron R7 Wrist Blood Pressure Monitor - BRAND NEW	$47.56
Alternating Pressure Air Mattress - HOSPITAL GRADE	$521.00	OMRON WRIST BLOOD PRESSURE MONITOR WITH A.P.S.	$47.00
SUUNTO X9 CROSS SPORT WRISTOP COMPUTER WATCH MEN NEW	$429.00	CD-27 EXPERT CARDIOLOGY STETHOSCOPE medical equipment	$46.00
[2 of these sold for $429.00 each]		Dual Action Cleanse II / Cellular Research Formula	$45.00
Bally Total Fitness Premier Plus Membership $9.50 p/mth	$355.00	Mark Of Fitness Automatic Blood Pressure Monitor MF-46	$44.85
RS MUSCLE STIMULATOR LIKE NEW RS4i	$327.00	Silent Knight Pill Crusher	$42.05

Saunders Cervical Hometrac Deluxe, Head n Neck Traction	$306.00	SADELITE THERAPY MOOD LIGHT (FLUORESCENT SUN)	$42.00
Saunders Hometrac Deluxe - Cervical Traction Unit	$290.00	2 HIV AIDS 10 MIN.HOME TEST DIY KIT(VALUE PACK)-SEALED	$41.99
OXYGEN CONCENTRATOR-Airsep Newlife Elite/Like New!!!!!	$260.00	EMS 2000 Muscle Stimulator	$41.00
OXYGEN CONCENTRATOR-Airsep Newlife Elite/Like New!!!!!	$257.50	NEW Lifestream Cholesterol Test Kit w/Video *HEALTH	$40.58
Pronex Cervical Traction - Neck Pain *No Reserve*	$230.02	Dental Night Guards/Custom fit	$39.99
DeVilbiss Five Liter Concentrator 5LPM Oxygen Like NEW	$227.50	2 BOTTLES OF MASON CO Q-10/COENZYME	$39.99
Hydrocollold water jacket impression trays	$225.00	Q10/300MG/60 CAPS	$39.99
INVACARE 5 LITER OXYGEN CONCENTRATOR	$213.00	Lifesource AND Medical Blood pressure monitor UB-328	$39.99

Makeup ▸ Beauty Tools

The average sales price in this subcategory is $13.28.

	HIGH		AVG
Lot MAC Makeup Brushes 116 150 190 224 213 209 face eye	$138.25	LANCOME FOUNDATION BRUSH # 2	$13.75
16 Pcs CHANEL Face/Eye/Lip Makeup Brush Set RV$515+Bag	$125.00	MAC makeup BRUSH CLEANSER HUGE NIB 235 ml	$13.75
NEW MAC PRO tool brush belt and 14 piece brush set$399	$102.50	Bare Escentuals Minerals FLAWLESS APPLICATION BRUSH New	$13.62
Huge Lot of Mary Kay Makeup Brushes and Applicators	$100.07	Bobbi Brown New, Desert Eyeshadow BRAND NEW IN BOX!	$13.51
NEW MAC PRO tool brush belt and 14 piece brush set$399	$99.00	brand new TWEEZERMAN Powerful 12X Magnified Mirror	$13.50
NEW MAC PRO tool brush belt and 14 piece brush set$399	$95.00	Bobbi Brown, CONCEALER BRUSH w/ CAP (Travel Size, 5").	$13.50
NEW MAC PRO tool brush belt and 14 piece brush set$399	$91.00	NEW MAC PRO tool brush belt and FREE mac pigment	$13.50
NEW MAC PRO tool brush belt and 14 piece brush set$399	$81.00	Bare Escentuals Minerals FLAWLESS APPLICATION BRUSH New	$13.50
MAC Tailormade Pinstriped Bag Brush Set 6 PRO Brushes	$79.00	Bare Escentuals Magic Wand Brushless Mascara	$13.50
NEW MAC PRO tool brush belt and 14 piece brush set$399	$61.00	Chanel Blush Brush #7	$13.50
BNIB MAC Tailormade PInstripe Brush Set	$60.00	4 CLINIQUE MAKE-UP BRUSHES PLUS TRAVEL SIZE SOAP - NR	$13.50
New 16 Sable StudioSeries Makeup Brush Brushes make up	$55.99	Jerome Alexander 5 Professional Make Up Brushes PRO NEW	$13.49
[2 of these sold for $55.99 each]		[2 of these sold for $13.49 each]	
Make up Brush Set with Case w/ Louis Vuitton Monogramm	$53.00	New NR Makeup Cosmetic Brush Roll Pouch tote bag	$13.45
NEW MAC BRUSHES MIXED LOT of 5 NO S/H FEES Worldwide	$51.01	New in Plastic Mary Kay Platinum Brush Set	$13.42
Italian Badger Series Makeup Brush Brushes Set make up	$51.00	BOBBI BROWN * SHORT HANDLE : EYE LINER BRUSH * NEW !	$13.00

Makeup ▸ Blush

The average sales price in this subcategory is $10.46.

	HIGH		AVG
Chanel Ruban Perle SUNLIGHT Creme Illuminator	$40.99	NIB Stila Sun Highlighter, Summer Collection!	$10.62
SCOTT BARNES - Chic Palette Blush in HONEY!	$38.00	SIB Becca Loose Shimmer Powder in Mermaid	$10.61
Bobbi Brown - Apricot Shimmer Brick Shimmerbrick - NIB	$37.50	Merle Norman Luxiva Creme Blush "Spice Chiffon"	$10.60
BOBBI BROWN PINK SHIMMER BRICK COMPACT NIB $35 blush	$36.99	NEW Chanel Triple Colour Crayon TAQUINE - BRONZE	$10.53
NEW CHANEL Makeup CHEEK LIPS COMPACT blush lipstick	$35.99	New Senegence BlushSense Rose Blush	$10.50
Bobbi Brown SHIMMER BRICK COMPACT in APRICOT–NIB	$35.00	BORGHESE BLUSH MILANO "ROSA BRILLIANTE" (DEEP PINK)	$10.50
Bobbi Brown SHIMMER BRICK COMPACT in BEIGE–NIB	$35.00	~BRAND New Smashbox ~GOLDEN BEIGE/RAY~ XL Blush Duo~NR~	$10.50
BOBBI BROWN BRICK COMPACT - FALL, 2005 -"APRICOT"	$34.92	tarte cheek stain for cheeks	$10.50
CHANEL Powder Blush ORCHID ROSE Brand NEW Color NIB	$34.25	BARE NECESSITIES MINERAL BLUSH-YOU "GLOW" GIRL!!!	$10.50
NEW!!! CHANEL CHEEKY ATTITUDE BLUSH ORCHARD ROSE	$34.17	ARTEMISIA Cheret Collage Bronzer Face Powder	$10.50
BOBBI BROWN SHIMMERBRICK COMPACT IN APRICOT ***NEW***!!	$31.00	Brand New in BOX SHU UEMURA P Pink 30 Blush	$10.49
BOBBI BROWN ROSE SHIMMER BRICK COMPACT NIB $35 blush	$31.00	NEW,SEALED ELIZABETH ARDEN POWDER BLUSH TERRAROSE (10)	$10.49
Bobbi Brown SHIMMER BRICK Compact Full Size NIB - ROSE	$30.00	Guerlain Bubble Blush - rose chamallow	$10.49
BOBBI BROWN ROSE SHIMMER BRICK COMPACT NIB $35 blush	$30.00	L'Oreal loreal Translucide Blush* Blushing/Rouge Glow*	$10.49
CHANEL JOUES CONTRASTE BLUSH MOCHA	$30.00	NEW,SEALED ELIZABETH ARDEN POWDER BLUSH TERRAROSE (10)	$10.49

Makeup ▸ Cases, Bags, Totes

The average sales price in this subcategory is $11.21.

	HIGH		AVG
220+ pc. Mary Kay Products & Consultant Supplies	$265.00	NEW ALUMINUM MAKEUP CASES / COSMETICS TRAIN CASE 4 MAC	$12.50
Louis Vuitton Brown Monogram Alma Handbag Auth NR	$199.99	MARY KAY GIRLFRIENDS COLLECTION UMBRELLA, NIP	$12.50
CHRISTIAN DIOR EYESHADOW + MORE MIXED LOT OF 20	$99.99	Mary Kay Seminar Water Bottle!!! Truly Awesome NEW!!!	$12.50
126pc vanity train case makeup kit $335 value make up	$89.00	NEW ALUMINUM MAKEUP CASES / COSMETICS TRAIN CASE 4 MAC	$12.50
Mary Kay 2005 Seminar Black & Pink Tote/Briefcase	$86.00	[3 of these sold for $12.50 each]	
COACH Embossed Leather Beauty Case~HUGE~FUSCHIA~NWT~WOW	$73.99	ALUMINUM PRO BLACK MAKEUP CASES TRAIN CASE Make Up	$12.01
New MARY KAY GLAM CASE limited edition - free samples!	$72.00	mary kay color pallete compact NIB holds tons of stuff	$12.00
[2 of these sold in a multiple item ("Dutch") auction for $36.00 each]		CHRISTIAN DIOR LIGHT AND LASTING EYESHADOW LOT OF 3	$11.99
MAC Pro Tool Brush Belt ** BRAND NEW **	$63.00	CHRISTIAN DIOR HIGHLIGHTS FOR HAIR LOT OF 3	$11.99
CHRISTIAN DIOR MASCARA LOT OF 10	$59.99	ALUMINUM PRO BLACK MAKEUP CASES TRAIN CASE Make Up	$11.50
New MARY KAY GLAM CASE limited edition - free samples!	$54.00	CHRISTIAN DIOR Clutch Makeup Bag Pink SUPER LOW PRICE!	$11.50
[2 of these sold in a multiple item ("Dutch") auction for $27.00 each]		[2 of these sold for $11.50 each]	
Mary Kay - Cool Wheels - Insulated Tote/Case On Wheels	$51.00	New Cosmetic Train cases Jewelry box Make up cases MAC	$11.49
ALUMINUM PRO MAKEUP COSMETIC TRAIN BEAUTY CASE for MAC	$50.00	MARY KAY MK DIVA SUNGLASSES LTD EDITION	$11.49
NEW ALUMINUM MAKEUP CASES / COSMETICS TRAIN CASE 4 MAC	$48.00	NEW ALUMINUM MAKEUP CASES / COSMETICS TRAIN CASE 4 MAC	$11.11
MAC Matt Murphy Bag as seen on OPRAH! NEW!!	$48.00	Mary Kay Roll-Up Tote Travel Bag	$11.01
ALUMINUM PRO MAKEUP COSMETIC TRAIN BEAUTY CASE for MAC	$47.00	ALUMINUM PRO BLACK MAKEUP CASES TRAIN CASE Make Up	$11.01

Makeup ▸ Eyeliner

The average sales price in this subcategory is $11.63.

	HIGH		AVG
LOT of SEVEN TONY & TINA HERBAL GLITTER EYE LINERS	$81.10	BOBBI BROWN - Sapphire Shimmer Ink	$12.50
Chanel Professional Eyeliner CHARCOAL / PLUM	$80.50	NEW Laura Geller Bubble Blush~RUM	$12.50
[7 of these sold in a multiple item ("Dutch") auction for $11.50 each]		ICE~w/ MIRROR COMPACT	

Chanel Professional Eyeliner BLACK / NAVY	$75.00	CHANEL BLACK WATERPROOF EYELINER NEW	$12.40
[6 of these sold in a multiple item ("Dutch") auction for $12.50 each]		NEW smashbox EYE Pencil DUO - Deep PURPLE and TAUPE	$12.38
Lot of 4 TONY&TINA Herbal Glitter and Eye Pencil	$56.00	MAC Glitter Eye Liner, MERCURIC, sold out, DISCONTINUED	$12.27
TONY TINA HERBAL GLITTER EYE LINER NIB GREEN/GREEN	$54.00	MAC COSMETICS FLUIDLINE EYELINER GEL SHADE *NEW*	$12.07
[2 of these sold in a multiple item ("Dutch") auction for $27.00 each]		HUGE Makeup Lot Eye Lip Body Art Goth Punk	$12.01
CHANEL PROFESSIONAL EYELINER COMPACT~VERY RARE TO FIND!	$43.99	MAC FLUIDLINE GEL EYELINER EYE LINER fullsize WAVELINE	$12.00
SKINMARKET SHIMMY POWDER SEX FULL SIZE (PINK)	$41.00	Lip Ink Semi Permanent Smudge Proof Eyeliner - Smoke	$12.00
TONY & TINA eyeliners-pink/gold, blue/silver,clear/slvr	$39.00	La Prairie Eye Contour Pencil BRUN	$12.00
Anna Sui 6 Liquid Eye Liner Eyeliner Assortment!!	$39.00	CHANEL PRECISION EYEBROW	$12.00
TONY & AND TINA HERBAL GLITTER PENCIL, LOT OF 3, NIB	$37.00	PENCIL- BROW DEFINER- AUBURN	
New Tony&Tina Herbal Glitter eyeliner/eye pencil brown	$36.55	NIB TONY TINA HERBAL GLITTER EYELINER GREEN/GREEN	$12.00
Anna Sui 6 Liquid Eye Liner Eyeliner Assortment!!	$36.00	TONY & TINA Herbal Glitter Eye Pencil ROYAL BLUE ~ NIB	$11.99
WHOLESALE LOT of 37 Cover Girl CG Smoothers Eyeliners	$34.95	TONY & TINA Herbal Glitter Eye Pencil GREEN /GREEN ~NIB	$11.99
Clinique Quick Eyes Eye Pencil Eye Powder 04 Wheat NIB	$34.00	MAC Glitter Eye Liner, SAUCEPOT, sold out, DISCONTINUED	$11.72
NIB Stephane marais eye kohl VIOLET	$32.50		

Makeup ▸ Eye Shadow

The average sales price in this subcategory is $11.28.

	HIGH		AVG
175+ Rimmel Metallic Stars Roller Eyeshadow Mixed Color	$113.50	Loreal Powder on the Loose~ Mystified~ Discontinued!	$12.00
Shu Uemura Sables D'ete HIKARI Summer Lights Palette	$61.00	PRESCRIPTIVES 2 SHIMMER EYESHADOW	$12.00
88 Shade Spa Eyeshadow #2 Pallet Including MAC Pigment	$61.00	PEPPERMINT&SPUN SUGAR	
78 Professional SPA Eyeshadow / Blush Palette Free MAC	$59.99	Rocket City Flip Palette Planetary Prima Don	$12.00
88 Shade Spa Eyeshadow #2 Pallet Including MAC Pigment	$57.55	JAFRA Eye shdw/Blush/Mattifier - BIN=Free S&H #314	$12.00
SHEER COVER EYE COLLECTION / FREE MASCARA	$56.00	Trucco Sebastian Pro Suede Eye Color eyeshadow	$12.00
88 Shade Spa Eyeshadow #2 Pallet Including MAC Pigment	$52.00	Tony & Tina EyeShadow Quad, Source Energy, NEW IN BOX!!	$12.00
[2 of these sold for $52.00 each]		EYEMAX FALL stack Eye Shadow shimmer NEW LOOSE POWDER,	$11.99
88 Shade Spa Eyeshadow #2 Pallet Including MAC Pigment	$51.00	Prescriptives Pick 2 Eye Shadow Refill * Venus New	$11.99
WOW ProSPA 88 Eyeshadow make up pallet-BONUS MAC Sample	$49.99	Bare Escentuals Luxe Liner/Shadow Full Sz New	$11.75
NEW 78 PRO Eye Shadow & Blush PALETTE + Mac Pigment	$49.99	NARS MOULIN ROUGE Eyeshadow, #2015	$11.72
88 Shade Spa Eyeshadow #2 Pallet Including MAC Pigment	$49.00	NEW Sealed Bare Escentuals Essentials Giggle Eye Shadow	$11.50
Valerie Beverly Hills New Wholesale 35pc Fullsized	$48.02	Mixed Lot of 8 Eyeshadow Trio by L.A. Girls	$11.50
SHEER COVER EYE COLLECTION / FREE MASCARA	$44.56	NARS Eyeshadow in CAIRO New and Unused	$11.50
SHEER COVER EYE COLLECTION / FREE MASCARA	$42.00	Almay Intense I-Color Trio for Blue Eyes	$11.50
CHANTECAILLE Apr?- Ski in St. Moritz	$41.99	YSL PARFUMES EYE SHADOW #2 "BLACKGOLD"~NIB LTD ED.	$11.48

Makeup ▸ Face Powder

The average sales price in this subcategory is $13.99.

	HIGH		AVG
150 Rimmel Pressed Powder Compacts Wholesale Lot Makeup	$127.50	Laura Mercier Foundation Powder # 5 New Boxed.	$14.99
Guerlain Meteorites Voyage Compact for Face Powder new	$89.95	My Minerals TruFinish Bare Finishing Powder NEW Lg	$14.99
URBAN DECAY Flavored Body Powder LOT OF SIX full size!	$72.00	Guerlain Les Voilettes Pressed Powder Perlee No.2 new	$14.95
T. LeClerc PRESSED POWDER BANANE NEW & SEALED 0.34 oz	$40.99	[3 of these sold for $14.95 each]	
Chanel RUBAN PERLE SUNLIGHT NIB	$40.00	Guerlain Les Voilettes Pressed Powder Azalee No.3 new	$14.95
CHANEL NATURAL FINISH PRESSED POWDER- TRANSLUCENT 2	$39.99	[2 of these sold for $14.95 each]	
Chanel PRECISION RECTIFIANCE INTENSE FLUIDE NIB	$39.99	2 LANCOME JUICY ROUGE LIPSTICK SUGAR ROSE FULL SZ~NEW	$14.50
Chanel PRECISION ECLAT ORIGINEL	$39.99	Models Prefer FLAWLESS NEUTRALIZING POWDER - NEW !	$14.50
RADIANCE REVEALING SRM		Chanel IRREELLE OMBRES MULTI-EFFECT EYESHADOW 23 SPHINX	$14.49
Chanel Double Perfection Compact TENDER BISQUE	$39.00	Chanel IRREELLE OMBRES MULTI-EFFECT EYESHADOW 26 NEON	$14.49
SHEER COVER EYE COLLECTION	$37.01	Chanel IRREELLE OMBRES MULTI-EFFECT EYESHADOW 21 FUSION	$13.99
[2 of these sold for $37.01 each]		PRESCRIPTIVES ALL SKINS POWDER-LEVEL 2-FULL SIZE *NIB*	$13.99
IMAN LUXURY PRESS POWDER MEDIUM DARK (LOT OF 4)	$37.00	[2 of these sold for $13.99 each]	
NEW CHANEL SOLD OUTPOUDRE COROMANDEL	$36.51	Chanel PRECISION BROW DEFINER BISTRE SOFT BROWN NIB	$13.99
CREAMY FACE POWDER		Bobbi Brown Face Powder Pale Yellow #1	$13.62
SHEER COVER NUDE *PRESSED POWDER*	$36.00	Origins Silk Screen Powder Caramel Mousse 06	$13.57
Chanel RUBAN PERLE SUNLIGHT NIB	$35.99	GIVENCHY SUN PRISM COMPACT *NEW IN BOX*	$13.50
Chanel RUBAN PERLE MOONLIGHT NIB	$35.99	Elizabeth Arden Flawless Finish Loose Powder LIGHT 2-03	$13.50

Makeup ▸ Foundation

The average sales price in this subcategory is $16.02.

	HIGH		AVG
CHANTECAILLE FUTURE SKIN IN NUDE NEW $58	$89.76	Laura Geller Matte Maker Invisible Oil Blotting Powder	$17.37
[2 of these sold in a multiple item ("Dutch") auction for $44.88 each]		NIB Merle Norman Luxiva Lasting Foundation SPF 12	$17.11
CLE DE PEAU BEAUTE LIQUID FOUNDATION - $110 RET- NEW-NR	$67.68	* NEW Sealed Bare Escentuals Essentials Bisque Powder *	$17.00
LIGHT SHADE TONE SHEER COVER MAKEUP KIT - BRAND NEW	$62.00	LOREAL CASHMERE PERFECT MAKEUP	$17.00
Giorgio Armani Cosmetics Jewel Palette	$61.00	NATURAL BEIGE -SET OF 2	
Sheer Cover Mineral System NIB 8 Pc Med/Tan- 90 day kit	$60.00	Nars foundation*Deauville * oil free 1 oz	$17.00
Bare Northern Minerals FULL SIZE 30 Piece Complete Set	$49.99	ALEXANDRA de MARKOFF LIQUID FOUNDATION 91 1/2 NEW	$16.99
1 POUND MINERAL MAKEUP FOUNDATION BIZ STARTER KIT	$49.00	ALEXANDRA de MARKOFF FACE SHAPERS	$16.99
SHEER COVER MINERAL FOUNDATION/FINISHING POWDER Medium	$48.00	CONTOURING COLOR	
Merle Norman Luxiva Lasting Foundation SPF 12	$46.99	CHANEL VOILE SHEER MAKEUP/FOUNDATION VANILLE NEW	$16.99
Bare Northern Minerals FULL SIZE 30 Piece Complete Set	$46.99	SHEER COVER Light/Medium Duo Concealer + Sponge - New!	$16.85
[3 of these sold for $46.99 each]		New BeautiControl Perfecting Wet Dry Finish - Nude	$16.51
CLE DE PEAU BEAUT?Cream Foundation - NEW!	$46.01	Stila Illuminating Powder Foundation Refill - 40 Watts	$16.51
SMASHBOX FOUNDATION- STICK LIQUID & PHOTOMATTE-LIGHT	$44.99	++ LANCOME COLOR ID PRECISE MATCH MAKEUP ID II-20(W)big	$16.50
CLE DE PEAU BEAUTE LIQUID FOUNDATION - $110 RET- NEW-NR	$44.51	Aveda Beechwood Tinted Moisture SPF15	$16.50
Bare Northern Minerals FULL SIZE 30 Piece Complete Set	$43.78	Nars foundation*Barcelona *balanced 1 oz	$16.50
Bare Northern Minerals FULL SIZE 30 Piece Complete Set	$41.00	NIB Merle Norman Luxiva Smart Finish Compact Makeup	$16.05

Makeup ▶ Lipstick

The average sales price in this subcategory is $8.03.

	HIGH		AVG
BUY 10 GET 11 FREE! MAX FACTOR LIPFINITY!!! LOT OF 21!!	$41.05	3 MAX FACTOR LIPFINITY EVERLITES Lipstick! MUST SEE!	$9.29
NARS FAME 12 LIPSTICK PALETTE--$65 new! huge palette!	$36.00	Shu Uemura Lolishine Reflects Lipstick #33!	$9.00
LipFusion Lip Plumper (Blush) [sheer natural baby pink]	$33.51	MAX FACTOR LIPFINITY LIP STICK W/MOISTURIZING 1 free	$9.00
Aveda Lipstick LOT Sheer Pomelo Sun Kola Nut Wild Plum!	$33.00	3 MAX FACTOR LIPFINITY LIP STICKS W/MOISTURIZING 1 free	$9.00
LipFusion Lip Plumper (Clear)	$31.99	New Senegence - Shell Gloss	$9.00
CLE DE PEAU BEAUTE LIPSTICK - $55 RET- NEW-NR	$31.00	Signature Club A Lipsticks, Lip Plumper, Plus Extras	$8.99
3 L'OREAL COLOUR ENDURE +"HOT FUDGE	$30.00	NARS LIPSTICK-KLUTE-NEW IN BOX-SEPHORA-FROSTED LILAC-NR	$8.99
Aveda Lipstick LOT Sheer Pomelo Sun Kola Nut Wild Plum!	$26.75	SeneGence Auburn BrowSense. New!	$8.99
SHEER COVER LIP COLLECTION BRAND NEW	$26.00	Marilyn Miglin Magic Perfume Spray	$8.99
10 BOURJOIS ASSORTED LIPSTICK COLLECTION GREAT DEAL NEW	$24.95	YSL PURE SHINE SHEER LIPSTICK SPF15 # 8-PLUM FUSION-NIB	$8.99
TRISH McEVOY LIP & GLOSS COMPACT NEW 10 COLORS BOXED	$24.50	YSL PURE SHINE SHEER LIPSTICK SPF15-PINK DIAMOND#11-NIB	$8.99
NIB Stephane marais lipstick no.5	$23.50	LipSense by Senegence Long Lasting NEW ! BRONZE	$8.99
AUBE rouge aquacrysty #RS101 & BE 108	$22.51	Burt's Bees Wings of Love Lipsticks (3)	$8.76
2 Max Factor 1260 Pink Gold Lipstick Lip Color	$22.50	YSL ROUGE PUR SHINE **NEW** RED STRASS #1 - IN BOX	$8.55
10 Mary-Kate and Ashley Replenishing Conditioners	$21.99	4 COVERGIRL OUTLAST LIPCOLOR Lipstick-Brand New! GREAT	$8.50

Makeup ▶ Mascara

The average sales price in this subcategory is $10.48.

	HIGH		AVG
ARTISTRY WATERPROOF MASCARA BLACK LOT OF 3 NIB LOW SHIP	$69.33	New Tony & Tina Herbal Eye Mascara - Black	$10.50
[7 of these sold in a multiple item ("Dutch") auction for $9.99 each]		CHANEL CILS A CILS LASH BUILDING	$10.50
BOURJOIS CHANEL (20) CIL A CIL DOUCEUR MASCARA NEW m	$65.99	MASCARA #30 MARINE~NIB	$10.50
12x Bourjois Longueur Sublime Mascara Noir Velours26	$48.95	#NAME?	$10.50
ARTISTRY WATERPROOF MASCARA MICA LOT OF 3 NIB LOW SHIP	$39.96	Longcils Boncza Paris Professional Makeup Lash Extender	$10.50
[4 of these sold in a multiple item ("Dutch") auction for $9.99 each]		LashSense by Senegence - Waterproof - Black - NEW!	$10.50
BEYOND LONG MASCARA Prescriptives 3-Pack BROWN/BrandNEW	$38.00	LAURA GELLER SPACKLE PRIMER FOR FACE 1OZ NEW	$10.50
SMASHBOX PHOTOFINISH Primer in Color Blend	$35.00	#NAME?	$10.50
10 Givenchy Mascara Volumateur Miroir Dark Blue 22 new	$34.95	TONY & AND TINA HERBAL MASCARA, NAVY BLUE	$10.50
MD FORMULATIONS ADVANCED HYDRATING COMPLEX gel formula	$33.56	#NAME?	$10.49
DR. DENESE FIRMING FACIAL PADS 60 PADS NEW	$33.00	Revlon Lash Fantasy Mascara 3-Piece Package $24 Value!	$10.49
LOT OF 12 MAX FACTOR LASHFINITY 502 MASCARA	$33.00	BOURJOIS CHANEL (3) CIL ACIL DOUCEUR	$10.49
LOT OF 8 MAX FACTOR LASHFINITY ASSORTED COLORS	$32.00	MASCARA 'AUBURN'	$10.49
SMASHBOX PHOTOFINISH foundation Primer	$31.00	SMASHBOX LIP GLOSS 35MM	$10.49
Benefit Bad Gal Gear - mascara, liner, false lashes	$31.00	BOURJOIS /CHANEL MASCARA (3) BLACK NEW m	$10.49
SMASHBOX PHOTOFINISH Primer in Color Adjust	$30.99	Kiss Me Mascara's Grand Lash Primer NEW IN BOX	$10.49
3 Lancome FLEXTENCILS Mascara ~ BLACK ~FULLSIZE	$30.99	Laura Geller Mascara Sealer BRAND NEW Free Shipping	$10.49

Makeup ▶ Mixed Brands

The average sales price in this subcategory is $15.06.

	HIGH		AVG
Lot 200 /46 Full size Lancome Clinique Estee lauder +++	$237.50	Four new Merle Norman definitive eye pincil Duo	$16.49
HUGE LOT OF 42 MAC,ESTEE LAUDER,CLINIQUE&BENEFIT +BONUS	$230.00	tommy bahama 6.7 oz body lotion/womans-new	$16.49
Wholesale Lot of 100 Lancome, Borghese, Clinique, More	$155.00	LOT 10 VICTORIA SECRET ESTEE LAUDER LANCOME BATH & BODY	$16.25
HUGE LOT! 100+ ESTEE LAUDER LANCOME ARDEN CLINIQUE MORE	$152.53	Three Merle Norman NEW Ultra Lipcolor	$16.00
TRAINCASE~SMASHBOX MAKE UP LOT~ 29pcs~low reserve~LQQK!	$152.49	borghese fango delicato mud 17.6 oz jar retail 48.00	$16.00
Wholesale Lot of 75 Lancome, Borghese, Clinique, More	$116.05	[2 of these sold for $16.00 each]	
Huge 30+ URBAN DECAY HARD CANDY TONY & TINA SUGAR LOT	$100.99	Cosmetics Lot - Clinique/L'Occitane/Marc Jacobs/Stila	$15.56
HUGE LOT OF MAKEUP NEW & UNUSED	$73.00	12 Piece Mary Kay , Eye Color, Eyeliner& Lipstick	$15.51
47-pc. Maybelline Mixed Makeup Lot ~Wholesale~	$66.00	AVON 36 pc Mixed Lot Makeup, beComing, Mark, Naturals +	$15.50
10 Lot Hard Candy Sephora Urban Decay Bloom Sugar *NEW*	$59.99	Sebastian Trucco POWDERS Fall Collection 2005	$15.50
Makeup by Vincent Longo	$53.51	borghese gel delicato/makeup remover 8.4 oz pump-new	$15.50
Lot Lancome, Estee, Clinique, Arden GWP items	$51.00	Prescriptives Arden Poppy Burts Bees Murad Lot $100+	$15.50
HUGE MIXED LOT CHANEL AVON	$51.00	Merle Norman Glow Getters NIB	$15.50
CLINIQUE PHILOSOPHY & MORE!		CHANEL BOBBI STILA SHISEIDO MURAD CLARINS 17 sample lot	$15.50
Huge lot of Cosmetics: Benefit, Urban Decay, Stila, MAC	$48.73	Huge 27 pc lot Cargo Hard Candy Urban Decay NIB Ret 140	$15.00
Stila Tarte Lancome MORE Goody bag-over 30 items!	$47.78	15-pc. Maybelline Eyeliner Pencil Makeup Lot ~Wholesale	$15.00

Makeup ▶ Sets & Kits

The average sales price in this subcategory is $20.36.

	HIGH		AVG
Arbonne - About Face Color Bonanza with makeup case	$415.00	Smashbox Runway Compact Studio NEW in box	$20.51
HUGE LOT ARBONNE MAKEUP IN NEW TOTE OVER $1000 RETAIL	$300.00	Helena Rubinstein Palette Mascara+Blush+Lipstick+Gloss	$20.51
SmaShBoX 36 pieces retail value $750	$153.50	Lorac 'Beach Bag' includes Lip Gloss Polish & Bronzer	$20.50
HUGE LOT! 100+ ESTEE LAUDER LANCOME ARDEN CLINIQUE MORE	$152.53	38 MAKE UP ITEMS IN A BURGANDY LEATHER ?TRUNK	$20.50
Chanel Makeup Cosmetic Kit - Limited Edition w/ Bonus	$152.50	Benefit Gorgeous Georgia Pallete Set NEW So PRETTY	$20.50
Eyelash Extensions Kit Cosmetic Makeup Lash Lashes	$149.95	Stila Palette Set Legally Blonde2 2003! Very Rare	$20.50
BIG LOT SMASHBOX COSMETICS , NO RESERVE!!!	$130.00	NARS MINI LIP LACQUER PALETTE/COMPACT-BEST SELLERS!	$20.50
OASIS Premium Eyelash Extensions Refill Kit	$107.50	IMAN - Shades of Paradise - Colors and Bamboo Tray	$20.50
New CHANEL 12 Pcs brush set + 10 free mask ~ USD370	$99.99	14PC TOVA SECRETS EYE MAKEUP PERFUME LIPSTICK BRUSH SET	$20.50
New ALEXIS VOGEL Makeup Complete Kit Light	$98.09	Benefit Decked Out Dandelion Palette	$20.50
NARS Palette in American Beauty NEW ! $65	$90.00	SHEER COVER ~Duo Concealer-Light/Medium~ BRAND NEW	$20.50
[2 of these sold in a multiple item ("Dutch") auction for $45.00 each]		Origins Lot of 5 Shadow Gloss Body Wash & More All New	$20.50

Trish Mcevoy Eyeshadow Lip Gloss Eyelashes... 16 items	$85.99	SHEER COVER ~Pressed Mineral Found W/Clutch~ New	$20.50
Arbonne CASTAWAY color set, new, never used	$75.99	SHEER COVER ~ MINERAL FOUNDATION~	$20.49
Trish McEvoy Makeup Sample Set; Mini Planner;travel bag	$73.58	BUFF BRAND NEW 4g	
BOBBI BROWN Clay Collection Nord Anniv Set NEW	$69.99	BOBBI BROWN DEEP LIP AND EYE PALETTE-NIB!!! STUNNING!	$20.49

Nail ▸ Acrylic Nails, Tips

The average sales price in this subcategory is $12.17.

	HIGH		AVG
OPI -"Absolute" student acrylic nail kit w/travel case	$217.50	LARGE LOT OF NAILENE DELUXE SALON ACRYLIC NAIL KITS !!	$14.99
Creative/Brisa UV Gel lamp kit with salon gel supplies	$163.25	LARGE LOT OF REVLON ACRYLIC NAIL POWDER 18 JARS!!!!!!!	$14.99
Brisa Gel Nail Lamp and Products	$116.53	[2 of these sold for $14.99 each]	
IBD Professional Gel Kit, Brand New.....................	$104.49	LARGE LOT OF NAILENE DELUXE SALON ACRYLIC NAIL KITS !!	$14.99
Lot of 3 IBD Intro Gel Kit plus Free UV Light, All New.	$100.78	REVLON INSTANT MANICURE FOR NAILS SET OF 4 BNIB e	$14.51
IBD THE PROFESSIONAL GEL KIT- BRAND NEW	$95.00	Lot of 6- Acrylic Nail Liquid-Powder-Nails-Oil-NR-A4	$14.50
Creative Nail Design...Brisa Gel Professional Kit	$92.00	A3-Lot of 36-Alpha 9 Acrylic Nail Liquid Brushes-Etc-NR	$14.50
Creative Nail Design...Brisa Gel Professional Kit	$90.00	EZFLOW COLORED ACRYLIC PASTEL FLOWER COLLECTION EZFLOW!	$13.51
Lot of 3 IBD Intro Gel Kit plus Free UV Light, All New.	$80.00	Acrylic purple liquid-8oz+4 oz pink powder+.5 primer!!	$13.50
Professional UV Gel & Acrylic Nail Kit w/UV Light	$71.01	NP2-Lot of 48-Revlon Repair Kits-Nail Kits-Powder-EtcNR	$13.50
CREATIVE NAIL DESIGN Perfect Color 3 - 3.7oz(105gm)NEW	$61.00	Nailene French Express Glue On Nails 4 sets Item77283	$13.29
NAILENE 100 SCULPTUREADY ACTIVE SQUARE NAILS LOT OF 5	$61.00	PROFESSIONAL EZ-FLOW Q-MONOMER 4 Oz EZ FLOW BRAND NEW	$12.99
LOT OF 5 LG SIZE CREATIVE NAIL ACRYLIC PRODUCTS	$55.00	EZFLOW Precision French Tips 100ct	$12.99
NAILENE SCULPTUREADY MEDIUM	$53.00	NEW Lot of Fing'rs Artifical Nails! French Polish++++	$12.99
SQUARE NAILS LARGE LOT WOW		Alpha 9 Pro Acrylic Nail Liquid & White Powder & Bonus	$12.75
Massive Lot of OPI Nail powders, buffers, file & MORE	$52.99	EZ FLOW COLORED ACRYLIC RAINBOW CANDY COLLECTION KIT !	$12.13

Nail ▸ Manicure Kits

The average sales price in this subcategory is $8.91.

	HIGH		AVG
Etre' Natural Beauty Complete Nail Care Kit	$75.00	Fabulous Fingers Vintage General Electric Manicure Set	$9.99
[10 of these sold in a multiple item ("Dutch") auction for $7.50 each]		Sensation Nail Kit $35 Hand/Body Lotion Love Spell ~NEW	$9.98
ProStrong Complete Nail Therapy 14 piece Collection	$68.00	5.5 in PROF. S/S CLIPPER FOR INGROWN NAILS	$9.95
NSI ATTRACTION PROFESSIONAL KIT - ACRYLIC NAILS	$63.00	Obey Your Body Nail Care Kit	$9.51
OPI PRODUCTS NAIL POLISH LIQUID L- 3000	$48.69	Barielle 60 Second Manicure	$9.50
$125 5 Pc SOLINGEN Python Manicure Set - GERMANY - NR!	$43.99	NEW SUPERNAIL PROF. DELUXE MANICURE	$9.50
LOTS OF 20, 12 PIECE MANICURE SET, L@@K!!!!!!!!!	$41.00	MACHINE SET 4 NAIL	
ProStrong Caring Hands 8-piece Nail Care Collection	$38.00	Beauticontrol Show of Hands Instant Manicure	$9.49
VINTAGE- PFEILRING –10 PIECE MANICURE SET NIB	$35.56	18 Pc. Salon Quality Manicure & Makeup Brush Set NEW	$9.00
NIB-HOMEDICS FACIAL SPA ULTRA- MICRODERMABRASION SYSTEM	$34.99	18 Pc. Professional Manicure & Makeup Brush Set NEW	$9.00
New Creative Spa Pedicure *Marine Masque 77oz*	$32.95	Sharper Image Nail Care System - Manicures & Pedicures!	$9.00
LIGHT ELEGANCE PROFESSIONAL NAIL PRODUCTS KIT	$32.01	18 Pc. Salon Quality Manicure & Makeup Brush Set NEW	$9.00
OPI PRODUCTS NAIL POLISH LIQUID	$30.00	Beauticontrol Show of Hands Instant Manicure	$8.99
NAIL ART - LUXURY MANICURE KIT (new)	$29.95	Zeepk Manicure set 4 pe.cuticle nipper cuticle pusher	$8.99
2 Etre nail care kits with LIGHT ALMOND scented lotion	$29.95	Conair 3700AXA Elegant Nails	$8.99
NAIL ART - LUXURY MANICURE KIT (new)	$29.95	Manicure Pedicure Set NEW	$8.99
Two Etre nail care kits with FREESIA scented lotion	$29.95	(2) IBD XTREME SEAL 100% UV DRY 14ml EACH BOTTLE	$8.99

Nail ▸ Nail Art

The average sales price in this subcategory is $7.19.

	HIGH		AVG
800 sheets of Gem Nail Tip Stickers (10 on each sheet)	$120.00	Chrome Crosses - Vinyl Sticker Decals	$10.00
PROFESSIONAL ELECTRIC NAIL DRILL - SINA MERCEDES 2000	$69.90	[2 of these sold in a multiple item ("Dutch") auction for $5.00 each]	
NEW! Badger 200-13 Fingernail Airbrush Painting Set	$68.00	48 pr Toe Separators A MUST for Nail ART. Polish Whole$	$9.99
NEW! Paasche Fingernail Airbrush Painting Kit	$55.00	8 KONAD Nail Art LOT Nail Polish + Stencil IMAGE PLATES	$9.99
NAIL JAZZ STAR DUTCH AUCTION!!!!!!!	$51.96	DIY PRINT A NAIL ART MACHINE WITH NAIL POLISH *L@@K*	$9.99
[4 of these sold in a multiple item ("Dutch") auction for $12.99 each]		48 pr Toe Separators A MUST for Nail ART. Polish Whole$	$9.99
NAIL ART - LUXURY MANICURE KIT (new)	$29.95	DIY PRINT A NAIL ART MACHINE WITH NAIL POLISH *L@@K*	$9.99
[2 of these sold for $29.95 each]		600 Pcs Rhinestones TEARDROPS Nail Art Jewelry Crafts	$9.98
KONAD Nail Art Design Set B. It's Magic!!!!!	$25.00	[2 of these sold in a multiple item ("Dutch") auction for $4.99 each]	
Konad Stamping Nail Art Set - Pick 3 Plate n 3 Polish	$22.00	wholesale lots of 50 sheets glitter nail arts	$9.60
Nail Dazzle Polish Paint All 10 Colors Retails $24.99	$20.37	WHOLESALE LOT OF "WHITE LINE"	$8.99
NEW NAIL ART AIRBRUSH MANICURE SYSTEM-HELEN OF TROY	$20.00	COLLECTION NAIL ART	
2 NAIL DAZZLE Kits FRENCH + REGULAR TV NEW Buy NOWSAVE	$17.99	KISS 1 Step Stick-On Acrylic French Nails 6 KITS $60	$8.99
[2 of these sold for $17.99 each]		UNIQUE Airbrush Large STENCIL Designs Nail art #P4	$8.60
Nail Dazzle Polish Paint All 10 Colors Retails $24.99	$17.50	KONAD Nail Art Design 8 pcs Set WoW	$8.50
144 NAIL ART NAIL STENCIL AIR BRUSH CRAFT DECAL LOT	$16.02	KISS 1 Step Stick-On Acrylic French Nails 6 KITS $60	$7.99
15 COLORS ULTRA FINE Sparkle STARDUST	$15.99	Nail Art-Make Glow in the dark NAILS-6 colors	$7.50
Nail Dazzle Polish Paint All 10 Colors Retails $24.99	$15.95	SIZE 18 ACRYLIC NAIL BRUSH KOLINSKY SABLE	$7.49

Nail ▸ Nail Polish

The average sales price in this subcategory is $7.69.

	HIGH		AVG
150 Rimmel Fingernail Polish Wholesale Lot Makeup NEW	$79.89	EZ FLOW COPPER TONES LACQUER COLLECTION 12 NAIL POLISH	$8.99
WHOLESALE nail polish LOT 250 pcs FREE Acrylic Display	$71.00	Develop 10 Calcium Gel Nail Hardener Strengthener BONUS	$8.99
10x Bourjois Vernis Anti-Choc Nailpolish Giftset new	$49.95	2 CLINIQUE NAIL POLISH,GAUZE AND BUFFY	$8.99
OPI-AVON- NUBAR Paint Set With Extras	$46.01	Lot of 6 Stila Nail Polishes RARE	$8.99

auth CHANEL nail polish lot (6) & chanel makeup bag	$41.00	FANTASY FUN Toma Nail polish collection	$8.95
Manicure Magic! Nail Polish French Manicure Kit 10 pcs.	$39.95	12 NUTRA NAIL 60 SECOND FRENCH MANICURE POLISH LOT NR	$8.74
WHOLESALE Misc. Lot - Nail Polish, Votives, Bracelets	$36.50	Pro Strong ProStrong Nail Enamel-NEW-CAMEO LUSTRE	$8.50
Manicure Magic! Nail Polish French Manicure Kit 10 pcs.	$36.01	[2 of these sold for $8.50 each]	
Pro Strong ProStrong 3-pc INSTANT NAIL BONDING KIT-NEW!	$30.10	lot sally hansen diamond strength nail top coat base	$8.00
Manicure Magic! Nail Polish French Manicure Kit 10 pcs.	$29.95	NEW CHANEL NAIL COLOUR NAIL POLISH - SURPRISE	$7.99
[2 of these sold for $29.95 each]		Huge Lot 24 Petites Nail Polish*all diff. colors*NEW*	$7.99
Manicure Magic! Nail Polish French Manicure Kit 10 pcs.	$29.95	2 BOBBI BROWN NAIL POLISH VELVET AND BASE COAT	$7.99
CHINA GLAZE MONTE CARLO 9PC DISPLAY NEW	$26.99	LANCOME NAIL POLISH VERNIS ABSOLU=SILKY SAND= LOT OF 10	$7.99
CHINA GLAZE FASHION LOUNGE 9 PIECE DISPLAY~NEW~	$26.99	LANCOME NAIL POLISH VERNIS ABSOLU ₌ ALLOY ₌ LOT OF 10	$7.99
Lot New Sephora Nail Polish	$25.00	REFILLABLE AEROSOL SPRAY CAN COMPRESSED AIR AIRBRUSH	$7.90
Brand New Lot Of 75 Nail Polishes All Colors! CoverGirl	$25.00	Pro Strong ProStrong Nail Enamel-NEW-BALLET NUDE	$7.68

Nail ▸ Pedicure Kits

The average sales price in this subcategory is $8.83.

	HIGH		AVG
Lord & Taylor Manicure & Pedicure Kit w/ Folding Case	$31.00	brand new! TWEEZERMAN Callus Shaver & Rasp Pedicure	$9.95
CREATIVE SPA SPA PEDICURE MARINE MASQUE MASK 77-oz	$30.00	MUNDIAL SPRING BARREL NIPPERS	$9.50
*New*Creative Spa Pedicure*Sea Salt Glow - 76 oz.*	$29.99	MANICURE PEDICURE KIT 4	
[2 of these sold for $29.99 each]		MaryKay "Private Spa MINT BLISS Pedicure Set"	$9.50
New*Creative Nail, Spa Pedicure - Callus Smoother	$29.98	NEW Tan Softening Skin Moisturizing Gel Lined Socks	$9.50
[2 of these sold in a multiple item ("Dutch") auction for $14.99 each]		Mary Kay Mint Bliss Pedicure Set-Limited Edition!	$9.49
*New*Creative Spa Pedicure - SEA SERUM - 4 fl oz.*	$24.95	NEW Mary Kay Pedicure Kit	$9.49
[5 of these sold in a multiple item ("Dutch") auction for $4.99 each]		[3 of these sold for $9.49 each]	
Huge Origins Lot-Perfect World Guardian, Ginger Twist	$22.49	NEW $29 Callous Remover	$9.38
PROFESSIONAL PEDICURE SET/*GIGANTIC!*/COSMETICS/MAKE UP	$21.00	Barielle Total Foot Care Cream - NIB	$9.25
Creative Spa Pedicure Sea Serum 4 oz.	$20.00	HOMEDICS SOLEMATE PORTABLE PEDICURE KIT NEW SEALED	$9.00
[2 of these sold in a multiple item ("Dutch") auction for $10.00 each]		REVLON SPRING BARREL NAIL NIPPERS	$9.00
brand new! TWEEZERMAN 6-Piece Pedicure KIT huge value!	$19.95	MANICURE PEDICURE KIT	
LOT of 2 - Mary Kay Private Spa Pedicure kits sets	$18.00	MaryKay Mint Bliss Spa Pedicure Set & Nail Polish NEW	$9.00
CREATIVE SPA SPA PEDICURE MARINE MASQUE MASK 77-oz	$18.00	REVLON ~TOENAIL NIPPER~PEDICURE CLIPPER~NEW	$9.00
Homedics Electric Manicure/Pedicure kit	$17.50	BEAUTICONTROL Save Your Sole Foot & Leg Scrub	$9.00
Mary Kay Priivate Spa Pedicure Set	$15.99	Avon PLANET SPA Dead Sea PEDICURE SALT SCRUB Set of 2	$8.99
BeautiControl Pedicure Kit and Aromatherapy Neck Wrap	$15.50	BeautiControl SPA PEDICURE SET/	$8.55
MaryKay Mint Bliss Spa Pedicure Set & Nail Polish NEW	$15.50	HOSTESS GIFT/ BRAND NEW	

Huge Mary Kay lot! Over $3,000 retail.
Anti aging, skin care, foundations, concealers, color

Bidding has ended for this item
If you are a winner, Sign In for your status.
List an item like this or buy a similar item below.

Winning bid:	US $1,000.00
Ended:	Feb-01-06 09:13:09 PST
Start time:	Jan-25-06 09:13:09 PST
History:	17 bids (US $500.00 starting bid)
Winning bidder:	aimed-2-please (74 ★)
Item location:	Lewisville, TX United States

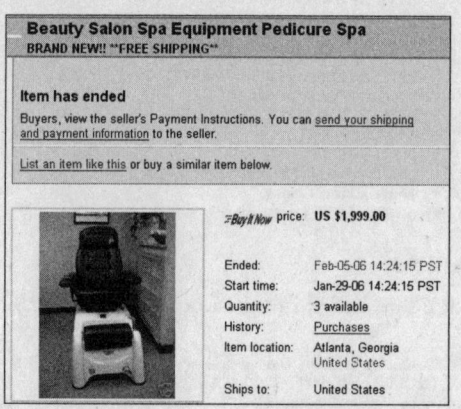

Beauty Salon Spa Equipment Pedicure Spa
BRAND NEW!! **FREE SHIPPING**

Item has ended
Buyers, view the seller's Payment Instructions. You can send your shipping and payment information to the seller.
List an item like this or buy a similar item below.

Buy It Now price:	US $1,999.00
Ended:	Feb-05-06 14:24:15 PST
Start time:	Jan-29-06 14:24:15 PST
Quantity:	3 available
History:	Purchases
Item location:	Atlanta, Georgia United States
Ships to:	United States

Massage ▸ Massagers

The average sales price in this subcategory is $29.43.

	HIGH		AVG
Health CHI MACHINE ORIGINAL SUN HARMONY	$349.00	NEW Vibrating Memory Foam Lumbar Back Cushion massage	$31.01
Perfect Touch - Shaitsu Massage Chair Recliner - New	$247.50	Like new Shiatsu Massaging Cushion	$31.00
Perfect Touch - Shaitsu Massage Chair Recliner - New	$242.50	OBUSFORME BACK THERAPY DRIVER'S SEAT"OBUS 92" - NIB!	$31.00
Perfect Touch - Shaitsu Massage Chair Recliner - New	$203.50	1/2 CASE NUKKLES MASSAGER NUCKLES NUKKLE FREE SHIPPING	$31.00
Homedics Shiatsu Massaging Cushion	$180.00	Conair Remote Control Foot Spa	$31.00
[3 of these sold in a multiple item ("Dutch") auction for $60.00 each]		Massager Electro Acupuncture Muscle Stimulator 4 Pads	$31.00
Ottoman 2.0 Foot and Ankle Massage Sharper Image NR	$178.72	MASSAGER HOMEDICS THERAPIST SELECT ELITE BRAND NEW	$30.24
iJoy Ottoman 2.0 Foot/Calf Massager NEW in Box	$177.50	MASSAGING SEAT TOPPER W/ SOOTHING HEAT/RELAXOR THERAPY!	$30.01
Medi-Rub Massager 2000 PLUS Brand NEW IN BOX!!!	$174.16	Massager Electro Acupuncture Muscle Stimulator 4 Pads	$30.00
BRAND NEW! IJOY OTTOMAN CALF FOOT MASSAGER	$169.99	[2 of these sold for $30.00 each]	
Brookstone Ottoman 2.0 robotic calf	$153.50	Brand New Dr. Scholl's Foot Spa Massage Heat Water Jet	$30.00
& Foot massager NEW		Body-Back-Buddy Massager - New	$30.00
Brookstone Foot Massager Ottoman Kneading ijoy rolling	$150.60	Massager Electro Acupuncture Muscle Stimulator 4 Pads	$30.00
Interactive Health Ottoman 2.0 Calf and Foot Massager	$150.00	[2 of these sold for $30.00 each]	
Evergain Chi Swing Massage Aerobic Exerciser 308DL	$145.00	Cushion Lounger With Massage Heater Light Brand New	$29.95
Jeanie Rub Variable-Speed Oscillating Massager New	$144.95	HoMedics Back Rejuvenator Massager	$29.65
Brookstone Programmable Personal Back Massager Masseuse	$129.99	3 Pair Dr Scholls Massaging Gel Insoles Mens 8-13	$27.00

Medical, Special Needs ▶ Braces, Supports

The average sales price in this subcategory is $21.68.

	HIGH		AVG
* Saunders Cervical Hometrac Neck Traction Unit *	$400.00	EBI, Plantar Fasciitis Night Foot / Ankle Support	$29.00
Halo for spine injury recovery - Halloween costume S&M	$380.00	Maternity Support Belt - Comfortable & Lightweight NEW	$27.99
OTTO BOCK PROSTHETIC LEG 3R45 TITAN 9227 PLUS SOCK NR	$338.00	WEIGHTED VESTS FOR AUTISTIC	$27.99
!! SAUNDERS CERVICAL HOMETRAC !! NECK TRACTION UNIT !!	$330.00	CHILDREN SPECIAL NEEDS	
Prosthetic 2 Alpha XL 6mm Locking Liners OWW	$215.00	Tuli's GAITors 3/4 Arch Supports LG Mns 8-10 Wmn 10-12	$27.95
PROSTHETIC LEG FLEX- FOOT PROSTESIS LEFT LEG	$202.50	CORFLEX_____Plantar Faciitis Night Splint__Foot Brace	$27.00
Chiropractic JTECH Activator Adjusting Tool Spinal New	$159.95	*NEW* Posture Support Back Brace! Straighten!	$24.99
[2 of these sold for $159.95 each]		Aspen Cervical Collar, Adjustable, Extra Pads	$24.99
Leg Brace Lot of Dynacast Extra Orthopedic Casting Tape	$137.50	Surgical Binder /Abdominal Support-LOT OF 12	$24.98
Prosthetic Leg / Artificial Leg / False Leg / Leg Brace	$127.50	Heel Spur Relief, Plantar Fasciitis arch support....NEW	$23.99
Custom Made Orthotics arch supports	$85.00	Tuli's GAITors 3/4 Arch Supports XL Mns 11-14 Wmn 13-16	$22.95
[2 of these sold for $85.00 each]		___Plantar Faciitis Night Splint____	$22.55
KAFO Right Leg Brace Knee Ankle Foot Plastic/Metal NR	$81.01	Fake left prosthetic leg / artificial limb prosthesis	$22.50
Miami J Hard Cervical Collar Brace- Like NEW!!	$81.00	FOOT BRACE for Achilles Tendinitis, Plantar Fasciitis	$22.01
custom orthotics arch supports inserts insoles orthotic	$79.00	McDAVID LIGHT WEIGHT ANKLE	$22.00
K AFO Leg Brace ~~Leather and Metal Leg Brace	$66.00	BRACE FITS EITHER FOOT	
custom orthotics arch supports inserts insoles orthotic	$65.00	Walk Fit Phase 4 Orthotics WalkFit Insole Size C NEW	$21.99
[9 of these sold for $65.00 each]			

Medical, Special Needs ▶ Mobility Equipment

The average sales price in this subcategory is $70.39.

	HIGH		AVG
JAZZY 1120 ELECTRIC POWER WHEEL CHAIR**NEW**	$1,600.00	4 Wheel Rollator, Aluminum Wheel Walker	$79.00
Tempurpedic Mattress.....(NO RESERVE)	$602.79	4 Wheel Adult Rollator Walker - Wheel Walkers	$79.00
Small Rifton Gait Trainer Walker Child Special Needs	$600.00	EMS belt w/handles lift assist, wheelchairs, etc	$77.00
Convaid Cruiser CX16 Child Adult wheelchair stroller	$570.00	Roho High Profile Wheelchair Cushion 4 inch cells	$76.00
NEW!!! SENSUS DELUXE QUEEN SIZE	$510.00	WHEELCHAIR CUSHION - ROHO LOW PROFILE 22 X 22	$76.00
MEMORY FOAM MATTRESS!!!		QUICKIE, INVACARE WHEELCHAIR CUSHION RETAIL OVER $500.	$76.00
Sunrise Med. Electric Wheelchair/Scooter Quickie G-424	$499.00	NEW Lightweight Travel 18" Wheelchairs Wheel chairs	$75.00
Brand New Scooter Pride Go-Go Ultra	$386.00	[5 of these sold for $75.00 each]	
Lightly used Roll-a-Bout	$385.00	HUGO WALKER, USED, BLACK, GLIDING SEAT WALKER	$75.00
Scooter wheelchair carrier lift. New. Custom drawbar.	$375.00	Transporte Wheelchair Lightweight 19" or 17" BRAND NEW	$74.99
Invacare Top End Eliminator RACING WHEELCHAIR SPORT	$365.00	24 Volt Invacare Wheelchair Battery Charger	$73.03
Scooter wheelchair carrier lift. New. Custom drawbar.	$365.00	FOUR wheeled HEAVY duty ROLLING walker rollator 2005	$70.95
Scooter wheelchair carrier lift. New. Custom drawbar.	$330.00	ROHO High Profile Dry Flotation Cushion-LIKE NEW	$70.51
EVEREST & JENNINGS SHOWER TOILET WHEELCHAIR	$330.00	Deep contour J 2 cussion, similar to Roho Dry Flotation	$70.00
Scooter wheelchair carrier lift. New. Custom drawbar.	$310.00	24NF 12 Volt 75AH Battery Electric Wheelchair Scooter	$69.95
Maclaren Special Needs Stroller - Pediatric Wheelchair	$308.01	[2 of these sold for $69.95 each]	
		FOUR wheeled HEAVY duty ROLLING walker rollator 2005	$69.95
		[2 of these sold for $69.95 each]	

Medical, Special Needs ▶ Monitoring, Testing

The average sales price in this subcategory is $46.24.

	HIGH		AVG
Quinton 4500 Stress Test Monitor & Treadmill -LIKE NEW!	$4,500.00	Palco Wet Stop 2 Bedwetting/Bed Wetting Alarm - *NEW*	$48.99
Coaguchek Roche Labs Blood Monitor Prothrombin Tester	$535.05	[2 of these sold for $48.99 each]	
Nellcor n 595 pulse oximeter, o2 sat monitor	$405.00	omron wrist blood pressure monitor (hem 637) NEW!	$48.02
One Touch Ultra Glucose test strips smart InDuo 600 NEW	$355.00	Omron Wrist Blood Pressure Monitor With APS HEM-637BX	$48.00
One Touch Ultra Glucose test strips smart InDuo 600 NEW	$343.00	New Omron Wrist Blood Pressure Monitor HEM-637 A.P.S.	$48.00
One Touch Ultra Glucose test strips smart InDuo 600 NEW	$325.00	Palco Wet Stop 2 Bedwetting/Bed Wetting Alarm - *NEW*	$47.85
Brand new BCI 3301 Handheld Pulse Oximeter	$325.00	Omron Wrist Blood Pressure Monitor With APS BRAND NEW	$47.50
[2 of these sold for $325.00 each]		OMRON HEM-637 WRIST BLOOD	$47.50
Nellcor "OxiMax" NPB-40 Handheld Pulse Oximeter	$320.95	PRESSURE MONITOR NO Box	
Criticare pulse oximeter 504DX NO RESERVE	$310.00	Accu Chek Check Comfort Curve Test Strips 100	$47.07
600 ONE TOUCH ULTRA SMART INDUO TEST STRIPS EXP 10/06	$310.00	$$$_ONE_TOUCH_ULTRA_TEST_STRIPS_$$$	$47.02
IVAC III Medisystem Infusion Pump	$305.00	New Omron Wrist Blood Pressure Monitor HEM-637 A.P.S.	$47.01
ISHIHARAS TEST FOR COLOR DEFICIENCY 38 PLATES 99 3	$297.00	omron wrist blood pressure monitor (hem 637) NEW!	$47.00
[3 of these sold in a multiple item ("Dutch") auction for $99.00 each]		New Omron Wrist Blood Pressure Monitor HEM-637 A.P.S.	$47.00
BCI 3301 PORTABE PULSE OXIMETER W/ 2 PROBES NR!	$290.00	New Omron Wrist Blood Pressure Monitor HEM-637 A.P.S.	$46.52
COAGUCHEK PT TEST STRIPS, 48/BOX	$204.00	One Touch Ultra Test Strips 2 boxes of 50,NEW	$46.15
[4 of these sold in a multiple item ("Dutch") auction for $51.00 each]		100 ONE TOUCH ULTRA SMART INDUO	$46.02
Nonin 9500 Pulse Oximeter Brand New In Box	$209.00	TEST STRIPS 2 NEW BOXES	

Natural Therapies ▶ Aromatherapy

The average sales price in this subcategory is $10.36.

	HIGH		AVG
YOUNG LIVING ESSENTIAL OILS SOLID OAK DISPLAY STAND	$119.00	24 6ml Essential Oils for Aromatherapy	$12.49
VAPOR BROTHERS VAPORIZER (LIKE NEW)	$115.00	BeautiControl Herbal Serenity Show of Hands Manicure	$12.00
YOUNG LIVING ESSENTIAL OILS ROSE 5ML ON SALE !!!	$100.00	24 6ml Essential Oils for Aromatherapy	$11.99
[2 of these sold for $100.00 each]		[3 of these sold for $11.99 each]	
Young Living Oil Diffuser - BRONZE- FREE GLASS PIECE	$79.00	4 oz Patchouli essential oil 100% pure SHIPPING OFFER	$11.00
New Young Living Essential Oil Diffuser - BLUE	$74.00	Twelve 10ml Essential Oils for Aromatherapy	$10.99

New Young Living Essential Oil Diffuser - GREEN	$72.50	[4 of these sold for $10.99 each]	
Lot Of Young Living Oils - Nine Bottles plus Ortho Ease	$72.00	Bath & and Body Works BERGAMOT CORIANDER Lotion	$10.99
large Dual Herbal defuser, vaporizer by AromaCare	$71.00	EUCALYPTUS 100% PURE Essential Oil Aromatherapy 8 oz	$10.99
BRAND NEW YOUNG LIVING STYLE OIL DIFFUSER BRONZE	$65.00	4 oz Patchouli essential oil 100% pure SHIPPING OFFER	$10.65
[3 of these sold for $65.00 each]		Arbonne Anti-Aging RE9 Facial Scrub	$10.50
ESSENTIAL OIL Young Living Style DIFFUSER New imperfect	$56.50	TANGERINETHERAPY HEALING GARDEN SPRAY	$10.49
Aromatherapy Kit_ Essential Oils_Lavender Patchouli NR	$51.00	CLARY SAGE ESSENTIAL OIL 2 oz PURE SHIPPING OFFER	$10.45
AromaCare II, Herbal vaporizer and defuser & VaoprMaker	$46.00	15ml Neroli Essential Oil	$10.00
Aromatherapy Essential Oil 27 Oil-Kit Lemon Lime Ginger	$44.01	Bulgarian Rose Oil in a traditional wooden container	$10.00
AromaCare II, Herbal vaporizer and defuser & VaoprMaker	$43.00	TRIPLE GINGERLILY SET / BUY 2 GET 1 FREE	$9.99
[2 of these sold for $43.00 each]		Salvia Divinorum PSYCHEDELIC EXPERIENCE	$9.99
AromaCare II, Herbal vaporizer and defuser & VaoprMaker	$43.00	Lecture on 2 CD	

Natural Therapies ▸ Herbal

The average sales price in this subcategory is $27.38.

	HIGH		AVG
Vapir Corded Herbal Vaporizer by Air2 - Nicohale	$86.00	AromaCare II, Herbal vaporizer and defuser & VaoprMaker	$43.00
large Dual Herbal defuser, vaporizer by AromaCare	$71.00	[2 of these sold for $43.00 each]	
AromaCare 1 large Herbal defuser, vaporizer	$71.00	Herbal Aromatherapy Essential Oil Kit 10 Oils	$19.95
[2 of these sold for $71.00 each]		Qty of *3* Herbal Heating Pads/Icepacks #1 on eBay!	$15.50
AromaCare 1 large Herbal defuser, vaporizer	$61.00	HERBAL THERAPY BUCKWHEAT HULL PILLOW	$13.00

Natural Therapies ▸ Other Natural Therapies

The average sales price in this subcategory is $29.67.

	HIGH		AVG
Brand New Ion Cleanse Detoxification Machine	$719.00	PHITEN TITANIUM BRACELET 8.25" Blk	$44.00
Deep Discounts on New Home Type Colonic Enema Board	$592.65	[4 of these sold in a multiple item ("Dutch") auction for $11.00 each]	
[3 of these sold in a multiple item ("Dutch") auction for $197.55 each]		2 Bottles wheatgrass -Freeze Dried Wheat Grass Juice NR	$41.01
Body Balance System Pro Detox Footbath	$450.00	Light Force Therapy Red LED IR Pain Relief No Reserve	$40.00
[2 of these sold for $450.00 each]		$145 USD MULTIMEDIA QIGONG FOR HEALTH SET!	$39.99
BioEnergizer Aqua Detox SPA SYSTEM - Full Kit	$299.00	PHITEN TITANIUM NECKLACE 26" Blue Gray	$39.98
[2 of these sold for $299.00 each]		[2 of these sold in a multiple item ("Dutch") auction for $19.99 each]	
Nikken Kenko Dream Queen Comforter	$281.81	PHITEN TITANIUM NECKLACE 26" Black	$39.98
Light Force Therapy Infrared LED Super Pain Relief IR	$255.00	[2 of these sold in a multiple item ("Dutch") auction for $19.99 each]	
Sam Biser's Save Your Life Collection 3 Volumes 12Tapes	$232.50	Cool-Aid Donjoy Cold Therapy Cooler	$39.00
DEVILBLISS 5 LITER OXYGEN	$225.00	TheraBreath Starter Kit	$36.00
CONCENTRATOR W/OSD		Happy PMS Progesterone Cream, 2 Bottles/FREE SHIPPING	$35.00
NEW DELUXE COLEMA BOARD KIT WITH	$204.95	18 Helga's Scented Eye Pillows LOT *New In Box*	$35.00
VIDEO /ENEMA/COLONIC		TheraBreath Starter Kit	$33.98
HOT TOWEL CABINET WITH UV BULB - BRAND NEW!	$145.00	TESTOSTERONE CREAM 5% LEGAL DOCTOR PRESCRIBED	$32.99
Bio Brain Tuner	$141.50	[2 of these sold for $32.99 each]	
23 Tuning Forks Holographic Repatterning Forks Set SALE	$139.99	HOMEOPATHIC TESTOSTERONE CREAM 5% LEGAL	$32.99
Don Croft Orgone parasite zapper, Chiropractic Holistic	$124.35	Light Force Therapy Red LED IR Pain Relief No Reserve	$31.00
Don Croft Orgone parasite zapper, Chiropractic Holistic	$123.50	Standard Cupping Set With 10	$29.99
PX Energized Shower Filter - Chrome - Complete	$120.00	Cups and 8 Magnets New	

Oral Care ▸ Electric Toothbrushes

The average sales price in this subcategory is $27.38.

	HIGH		AVG
Case of 6 Cool Mint LISTERINE Pocket paks oralcare stps	$800.00	Braun Oral-B ProfessionalCare D17511 Electri Toothbrush	$29.99
2 ROTA-DENT SPECIAL PURCHASE ROTADENT	$126.00	Oral-B Pro 7850 DLX Toothbrush w/ 8 Spare Heads	$29.99
[2 of these sold for $126.00 each]		BRAND NEW CYBERSONIC ELECTRIC TOOTHBRUSH	$29.99
6 CREST SPINBRUSH PRO WHITENING TOOTHBRUSHES + 12 HEADS	$97.00	Cybersonic Electric Toothbrush NEW FACTORY SEALED	$29.88
Oral B Professional Care 8850Dlx. (2) Handle New	$86.01	Cybersonic 2 As Seen On TV New In Box FACTORY SEALED!!	$29.56
Sealed, New, Lot of 5 Crest Spinbrush Pro Whitening	$84.08	Cybersonic 2 Complete Oral Care System -New-	$29.00
[4 of these sold in a multiple item ("Dutch") auction for $21.02 each]		[2 of these sold for $29.00 each]	
BRAND NEW PHILLIPS SONICARE ELITE 7500 DENTAL	$83.10	Cybersonic 2 As Seen On TV New In Box FACTORY SEALED!!	$29.00
Braun Oral B 8850 DLX Family pack! 2 Handles!	$82.50	Oral-B Sonic Complete S-200 Rechargeable Toothbrush New	$29.00
1 CENT OPENING BID ROTA-DENT NEW ROTADENT 1 EXTRA HEAD	$81.00	New Braun Oral B Professional Care 7000 w/ $10 Rebate	$28.99
NEW PHILIPS Sonicare 8800 Crest IntelliClean SYSTEM	$79.50	[2 of these sold for $28.99 each]	
NEW SONICARE ELITE PRO SERIES MODEL 7800	$77.25	Four New Rotadent One Step Replacement Brush Heads	$28.00
LOT OF 30 NEW BRAUN ORAL-B FLEXISOFT TOOTHBRUSH HEADS	$76.25	OralB 3D Excel Toothbrush, NIB, NR	$28.00
NIB Rotadent Electric Toothbrush	$76.01	BRAUN ORAL B 3D EXCEL PROFESSIONAL CARE TOOTHBRUSH	$28.00
PHILIPS SONICARE i8500 TOOTHBRUSH INTELLICLEAN NEW	$76.00	ORAL-B PROFESSIONAL CARE 7000 by Braun **NEW**	$27.59
16 Crest SpinBrush Pro Replacement Brush Heads	$76.00	NEW!! Cybersonic 2 Oral Care System ASOTV $99 value	$27.02
NEW PHILIPS Sonicare 8800 Crest IntelliClean SYSTEM	$75.00	BRAUN ORAL-B (9 REPLACEMENT HEADS)	$27.01
[3 of these sold for $75.00 each]		NEW FREE SHIPPING	

Over-the-Counter Medicine ▸ Cough, Cold, Flu

The average sales price in this subcategory is $18.84.

	HIGH		AVG
Airborne Cold & Flu Formula Orange 240 Tablets	$77.78	DAYQUIL/NYQUIL HUGE LOT OF 14 ITEMS...CHEAP..LOOK!!!!!	$24.99
Advil Cold and Sinus with PSEUDOEPHEDRINE HCl 30MG	$76.00	BREATHE RIGHT NASAL CONGESTION SM/MED TAN 90 CT	$23.38
Airborne Cold & Flu Formula Orange 240 Tablets	$75.00	BREATHE RIGHT NASAL CONGESTION STRIPS TAN LARGE 72 CT	$21.49
Airborne Cold & Flu Formula Orange 240 Tablets	$58.00	BREATHE RIGHT NASAL CONGESTION SM/MED TAN 90 CT	$20.15

Airborne Cold & Flu Formula Orange 240 Tablets [6 of these sold for $50.00 each]	$50.00	BREATHE RIGHT NASAL CONGESTION SM/MED CLEAR 72 CT	$19.50
		BREATHE RIGHT NASAL CONGESTION STRIPS TAN LARGE 72 CT	$16.00
		150 packets Advil Cold & and Sinus in dispensing boxes	$15.51
		3 ABREVA Cold Sore Treatment FACTORY SEALED	$14.99
		MUCINEX 600MG EXTENDED RELEASE EXPECTORANT FLU/COLD	$14.85
		60 CT MUCINEX DM EXPECTORANT COUGH SUPPRESSANT	$12.48

Over-the-Counter Medicine ▶ Pain Relief

The average sales price in this subcategory is $11.00.

	HIGH		AVG
Light Force Therapy Infrared LED Super Pain Relief IR	$265.00	16 Oz. BIOFREEZE Pain Relieving Gel w/ ILEX - Pump	$12.50
Orudis KT (Ketoprofen) 12.5 mg. 100 ct ~10 Boxes~	$230.00	LOT OF 6 BOXES ECOTRIN 81mg LOW STRENGTH	$12.50
Light Force Therapy Infrared LED Super Pain Relief IR	$207.50	400 Aleve Easy Open Arthritis Cap Pain Reliever	$12.00
Orudis KT (Ketoprofen) 12.5 mg. 500 Ct. 5 Boxes -Sealed	$125.00	3 new Excedrin QuickTabs 16 tabs/box SPEARMINT	$12.00
[2 of these sold for $125.00 each]		1,000 TABS, IBUPROFEN, GENERIC ADVIL, 200 MG	$11.99
500 ORUDIS KT 12.5 mg Tablets 100 ct. boxes (5) SEALED	$125.00	[2 of these sold for $11.99 each]	
500 TABLETS ORUDIS KT 12.5 mg. 100 ct. BOXES (5) SEALED	$118.00	2 NEW LARGE TUBES JOINTFLEX JOINT FLEX IRON MAN PAIN	$11.99
[2 of these sold for $118.00 each]		Flexium JOINT COMFOT 200 mg sam e 5 boxes of 20	$11.53
5 FRESH 100 TABLET BOXES OF ORUDIS KT 12.5mg FREE SHIPP	$105.00	300 ADVIL GEL CAPLETS PAIN RELIEF EXP 2/07 ~ SEALED	$11.50
Light Force Therapy Red IR LFT 9000 Pain Relief On TV	$52.00	DISPLAY BOX OF 24 - BC FAST PAIN RELEIF POWDERS	$11.50
BRAND NEW!! LIGHT RELIEF *AS SEEN ON TV*+EXTRA BONUSES!	$51.00	PRILOSEC OTC	$11.39
ORUDIS 12.5 mg. 100 Count * 2 Sealed Boxes	$49.99	Tiger Balm Red 50gm	$11.29
NICORETTE 4 MG GUM 170 PIECES MINT	$49.88	300 TYLENOL EXTRA STRENGTH GEL TABLETS	$11.11
Orudis KT 12.5mg 24 count box 10 box lot	$47.23	LOT OF 6 BAYER: ASPIRIN EXTRA	$11.02
BRAND NEW IN BOX LIGHT RELIEF LR150 AS SEEN ON TV	$47.00	STRENGTH STOMACH GUARD	
Orudis KT 12.5mg 24 count box 10 box lot	$46.55	TYLENOL XTRA STRENGTH 150 EACH BOTTLE 500 MG	$11.01
NICORETTE 4 MG GUM 170 PIECES ORIGINAL	$45.01	96 ALEVE ALL DAY STRONG TABLETS	$11.01

Skin Care ▶ Acne, Blemish Control

The average sales price in this subcategory is $13.00.

	HIGH		AVG
NEW EPICLEAR LOT OF 6 1.36OZ WOW LOOK!!	$137.50	LaRoche Posay Effaclar Foaming Gel Acne FREE SAMPLES	$13.99
DERMAFINA ACNE MEDICATION 6 MONTH SUPPLY (3 KITS)	$104.49	Biomedic AntiBac Acne Wash + FREE SAMPLES	$13.99
Biomedic 21 Day Intensive Acne Treatment New	$99.00	MURAD ~ APS PERFECTING DAY CREAM	$13.53
Verilux HappySkin Acne Light - helps control acne	$93.89	SPF 15 ~ 1.0 oz ~ NEW	
Bioelements Acne Clearing System	$91.00	SEALED Philosophy ON A CLEAR DAY H2o2 acne cream 1 oz	$13.50
Verilux HappySkin Acne Light	$90.00	NIB benefit BOO BOO ZAP acne blemish treatment ZAPPER!!	$13.50
Murad Acne kit with Bonus 30 day supply	$82.00	B Kamins MEDICATED ACNE GEL VOTED MVP - NEW	$13.49
[4 of these sold in a multiple item ("Dutch") auction for $20.50 each]		Neutrogena Advanced Solutions Acne Therapy System!	$13.27
Skin Medica - Uplifting Eye Serum 0.5 fl. oz.	$60.00	MURAD ~ Exfoliating ACNE Treatment Gel ~ 1.0 oz ~ NEW	$13.07
[2 of these sold in a multiple item ("Dutch") auction for $30.00 each]		MURAD Clarifying Cleanser 4.5 fl oz bottle *NEW	$13.01
Benzoyl Peroxide 10% Gran/Gel Acne Control / 128 ozs.	$59.02	NEW! MURAD Skin Perfecting Lotion ~ 1.0 fl oz ~	$13.00
2 *SEALED* MURAD PURE SKIN ACNE CLARIFYING SUPPLEMENT!!	$56.00	NIB Erno Laszlo Medicated Acne Treatment 2.5 oz	$13.00
ARBONNE Clear Advantage ACNE CONTROL Set	$54.00	NIB BeneFit *BOO BOO ZAP* acne pimple spot treatment	$13.00
Arbonne Clear Advantage Anti-Acne Set + Eye Cream	$53.00	MURAD Exfoliating Acne Treatment Gel *NEW*	$13.00
VICHY NORMADERM $45! 4-pack KIT Imperfect skin w/BONUS	$49.00	NIB Erno Laszlo Medicated Acne Treatment 2.5 oz	$13.00
302 Protein Drops, #1 for Acne Scarring, FREE SHIPPING!	$44.95	G.M. COLLIN ISOTONIC LOTION	$13.00

Skin Care ▶ Anti-Aging Products

The average sales price in this subcategory is $26.31.

	HIGH		AVG
Photo Rejuvenation Skin Care Machine, DERMA MASTER 8000	$749.50	OBAGI HEALTHY SKIN PROTECTION SPF 35	$28.25
NATURA BISSE Inhibit - Dermafill	$169.50	SK-II Signs Treatment 80G Brand New in Original Box!!	$28.01
Arbonne's Re9 Set Brand NEW in Gold Bag	$141.09	NIB Merle Norman Luxiva Changing Skin Treatment SPF 15	$28.01
LA MER THE LIFTING FACE SERUM 1 OZ , NEW	$127.50	MD FORTE Facial Cleanser I NEW	$28.00
TNS Recovery Complex Vitamin C and Retinol Free Ship	$121.50	[2 of these sold in a multiple item ("Dutch") auction for $14.00 each]	
Z. Bigatti Re- Storation Good Night Facial Cream 2 oz	$119.00	DHC Botanical Plakoenta *New In Box* ~Retail $48	$28.00
Chantal - Ethocyn Essence - 3 Vials - 3 Month Supply!	$117.50	DERMALOGICA TOTAL EYE CARE .75 oz Retail $37	$28.00
Obagi MAINTENANCE KIT Foam Gel Toner Exfoderm SPF 35	$111.99	StriVectin-SD EYE CREAM Brand NEW!	$27.99
LA THERAPIE GRAINES DE JEUNESSE- PINK CAPSULES ProSz NR	$104.00	~New~Dr Denese~SKIN RECOVERY SERUM~1oz~FULL SIZE~NR~	$27.51
SK-II Facial Treatment Care Set Brand New!!	$99.99	CHRISTIAN DIOR MODEL LIFT FIRMING CREME 1.7	$27.50
Obagi Foaming gel, Toner, Exfoderm, eye crm NEW	$99.00	SK-II De Wrinkle Active 25g /0.8 oz Brand New!!!!!!!	$27.00
TNS Recovery Complex Skin Medica New Larger Size	$91.99	Skin Medica Rejuvenative Moisturizer	$27.00
[3 of these sold for $91.99 each]		NEW Charles of the Ritz Revenescence Renewal Serum 2 oz	$27.00
TNS Recovery Complex Skin Medica .63 oz New Large Size	$90.00	NEW~Prescriptives~SUPER LINE PREVENTOR INTENSIVE EYE~NR	$27.00
BABOR HSR Lifting Cream Rich HUGE 200ml New/Sealed Jar	$89.99	OBAGI-C RX SYSTEM, C-EXFOLIATING DAY LOTION SPF 12,	$26.99
PREVAGE Antioxidant Creme 1.0 oz	$88.00	OBAGI EXFODERM AM #4	$26.50

Skin Care ▶ Cleansers

The average sales price in this subcategory is $14.89.

	HIGH		AVG
PEVONIA~ ENZYMO-SPHERIDES PEELING CREAM PROSIZE	$62.00	Christian Dior full size Refreshing Water and Toner	$15.50
Redken Amino Pon Conditioning Beauty Bar	$59.99	TIGI BEDHEAD FACIAL CLEANSER 8.5OZ. (2 BOTTLES) NO RESV	$15.50
Repechage Hydra Refine Cleansing Mousse Prof. Spa Size	$56.03	New SeneDerm by SeneGence 3 in 1 Cleanser Normal to Dry	$15.50
@@ SK II SKII FACIAL CLEAR SOLUTION SK-2 SK2 100ML @@@@	$54.00	DDF Sensitive Skin Cleansing Gel New/Untested @ Sephora	$15.50

PHILOSOPHY PURITY 32 Ounce Pump Cleanser New	$52.99	Beauticontrol Combo Skin Lot of 3 Toner Cleansing Scrub	$15.09
Philosophy's 32 oz. Purity Cleanser	$51.00	LA ROCHE POSAY - EFFACLAR FOAMING GEL 5.1 OZ.	$15.05
La Prairie Cellular Night Cream 1 oz New in Box	$49.99	Toleriane Foaming Cream Cleanser NEW 4.22ozFREE SAMPLES	$15.00
DHC Deep Cleansing Oil, Lot of 2, full size, New!	$49.00	ARBONNE BLACK MASCARA .15 OZ. - NEW	$15.00
philosophy 32 oz Purity w/pump + bonuses - NEW & SEALED	$48.68	Philosophy 8 oz. Purity Made Simple-New	$15.00
philosophy purity made simple (32 oz.) -HUGE BOTTLE	$47.00	MD SKINCARE All in One Facial Cleanser with Toner-NEW!!	$15.00
Obagi Gentle Cleanser & Toner New & Full Sz	$45.95	SENEGENCE SENEDERM 3 in 1 Cleanser Nor/dry	$15.00
SkinCeuticals Simply Clean Prof 750ml NEW	$45.00	Glytone Skin Rejuvenation System Step 1 Normal Skin	$15.00
Obagi Cffectives 10% High Potency Serum for Face Neck	$44.00	LA ROCHE POSAY - TOLERIANE FOAMING CREAM 4.22 FL. OZ.	$15.00
Yonka Gel Nettoyant Cleanser HUGE 13.5 OZ PROF SIZE	$44.00	La Roche-Posay TOLERIANE Gentle Dermo-Cleanser 200 ml	$15.00
YonKa Lait Nettoyant Cleanser HUGE 16 oz New!	$41.99	ERNO LASZLO *ACTIVE PHELITYL SOAP* 6OZ/1.7G NEW/SEALED	$14.99

Skin Care ▸ Moisturizers

The average sales price in this subcategory is $19.38.

	HIGH		AVG
CREME DE LA MER MOISTURIZING CREAM 2oz BOXED	$169.99	RE VIVE 4 Piece set	$19.99
[2 of these sold for $169.99 each]		AVEDA Tourmaline Charged Protecting Lotion $38 -NEW-	$19.99
Z. BIGATTI RE-STORATION GOODNIGHT FACIAL CREAM NEW $295	$138.50	ChanTal Ethocyn Moisturizer TWO Jars	$19.99
Natura Bisse Diamond Cream 1.7oz Full Size - NIB NR	$127.50	Orlane B21 Oligo Light Smoothing Cream 50ml/1.7oz	$19.99
NR! Le Mirador 11-pc set of skincare products – NEW	$119.35	JUICE BEAUTY Quench Oil Free Moisturizer NEW $40	$19.99
Sisley All Day All Year- Brand new	$103.00	NEUTROGENA VISIBLY EVEN & FIRM SKIN CARE LOT OF 7	$19.99
CHANEL MICROSOLUTIONS REFINING PEEL PROGRAM	$102.50	PHYTOMER ACCEPT NEUTRALIZING CREAM sensitive 10 tubes	$19.99
NR! Dr. Denese Deluxe Skin Care Items - 12 Pieces NEW	$92.25	NIB ANNEMARIE BORLIND NAT. LL REGENERATION night cream	$19.99
AVEDA ALL SENSITIVE MOISTURIZER 16.9 fl oz	$81.00	AHAVA Advanced Eye Cream	$19.99
Revive Moisturizing Renewal Cream	$80.00	2 NEW L'Occitane 20% Shea Butter Hand Cream 5.2 oz NIB	$19.99
Creme de LA MER Moisturizing CREAM 1oz NEW IN BOX NR	$80.00	H2O+ FACE OASIS HYDRATING TREATMENT,	$19.96
philosophy hope in a jar moisturizer, 8 oz. -BRAND NEW	$76.52	WHOLESALE AUCTION!	
RE VIVE SENSITIF OIL FREE LOTION SPF 15 SELLS $180	$71.56	[4 of these sold in a multiple item ("Dutch") auction for $4.99 each]	
PHYTOMER ACCEPT SOOTHING SKIN CREAM 100ML PROF SIZE NEW	$66.00	Vichy Oligo 25 Anti-Dull Skin Hydrating Care 1.7oz new	$19.95
SOTHYS HYDROPTIMALE CREME normal/dry PROF SIZE HUGE	$65.00	Jafra Royal Jelly Milk Balm Moisture Lotion Original	$19.95
PHILOSOPHY amazing grace firming body emulsion 16 oz.	$64.00	TRISH MCEVOY INTENSE EYE TREATMENT NEW FULL SIZE	$19.59
[2 of these sold in a multiple item ("Dutch") auction for $32.00 each]		Laura Mercier Intensive Moisture Mask New Sealed	$19.51

Tanning Beds, Lamps

The median sales price in this subcategory is $249.00.

	HIGH		AVG
Matrix L22 - Commercial Tanning Bed *BRAND NEW*	$12,100.00	SUNQUEST PRO 16SE WOLFF SYSTEM TANNING BED	$287.99
Mystic Tan Sunless Tanning Booth * not Tanning Bed NR!	$9,699.00	Tanning Bed - New Bulbs - Works Great	$284.00
Starpower 548 Tanning Bed Wolff Commercial Tanning Equipment	$7,533.00	SUNQUEST 2000 SH CANOPY TANNING	$280.00
THE NEW ERGOLINE AVANTGARDE 600 **BRAND NEW IN BOX**	$6,200.00	BED XLNT CONDITION NR	
Sontegra Baby X! 30-15 200 watt tanning bed	$4,500.00	24 New F71 Diamond Sun Tanning Lamps	$263.99
SOLARIS 423F ,Tanning bed,almost new,NO RESERVE\	$4,100.00	Tanning Bulbs-16 New Bronze Twister 9.5 Bulb Lamps F71	$260.00
COMPLETE TANNING SALON: 4 BEDS, 1 STANDUP MUCH MORE!!	$4,050.00	Lamps ship Free! Delivery Insurance Included!	
Powersun by ACN 32 lamps 2002 model tanning bed	$3,650.00	[5 of these sold for $260.00 each]	
TANNING BED MEGA EUROPA COMMERCIAL UPGRADE BED! VHR HOT	$3,576.47	24 Lamp Tanning Bed	$255.00
BRAND NEW LAMPS INCLUDED WITH BED!! $800.00 Value!!		Tanning Bed Timer ,T-Max Manager Pro	$250.00
SUNDOME TANNING BED MEGA BOOTH	$3,500.00	FST 16 Station Manager Tanning Bed Timer Free Shipping!!!	$249.00
STANDUP 10 MINUTE MAX		SUNTEGRA SUNBRELLA ARUBA 10	$237.50
SUPER SHAPE! NO RESERVE! BID NOW !		TANNING BED NEW JERSEY	
New 2006 28 LE Wolff Tanning Bed	$3,300.00	24 TANNING BED LAMPS / REPLACEMENT	$235.00
Beds 28 tanning bulbs Offers Welcome!		BULBS / NEW IN BOX	
1 Standup Tanning BOOTH 2 SunDash Tanning beds	$3,300.00	T-Max Tanning Bed Timer The Manager series	$232.50
REPO: ERGOLINE 52 Bulb VHR CYBERDOME TANNING BED	$3,050.00	Sunvision Pro 28LXT Tanning Bed May 2000	$227.50
SUNERGOLINE UPGRADE BED Was $12,900 new NO RESERVE		HEX BOOTH WITH REMOVABLE CHANGING AREA, NO RESERVE	$225.00
v600 wolfe stand-up tanning bed	$3,000.00	SUNQUEST WOLFF TANNING BED CANOPY MODEL 1000S N/R	$224.50
Used Dr. Muller Orbit 36/3 VHP Tanning Bed	$3,000.00	16 NEW Miracle Sun Extreme F71 9.5 Tanning Bulbs Lamps	$209.00

Tattoos, Body Art ▸ Flash

The average sales price in this subcategory is $29.80.

	HIGH		AVG
TATTOO FLASH RACKS!!!!!! ("FLOOR UNIT") 2 TIER SYSTEM!!	$369.00	Sailor Jerry GEISHA GIRLS Pin Ups Tattoo Flash Frame	$31.05
Vintage 1940s Tattoo Flash Rock of Ages	$305.00	tattoo ultrasonic cleaner	$31.00
*****new tattoo machine AUTOCLAVE FREE FLASH!!!!!!	$300.00	Ryan Downie Tattoo Flash 5pgs(machine gun machines art	$31.00
ANTIQUE TATTOO FLASH SHEET,CARD,ORIGINAL ART,PATRIOTIC	$300.00	Sailor Jerry RISE N SHINE Custom Tattoo Flash Frame	$31.00
Tattoo Flash Lot tatoo Set Machine rack gun	$243.49	TATTOO BODY SUIT POSTER	$31.00
Vintage 40s Tattoo Flash "No Reserve"	$212.50	HAND PAINTED TATTOO FLASH 8 SHEETS WITH LINES	$30.00
100 - 11 x 14 sheets of tattoo flash w/ lines	$210.00	10 tattoo flash thugs cross clowns skull neddle flag &	$30.00
Custom Rogers/Waters Tattoo Machine Flash Gun	$200.00	NEW line book by ryan downie tattoo machine flash	$30.00
TATTOO FLASH RACKS!!!!!! ("FLOOR UNIT")!!!!! LOWEST $$	$174.99	Paul Booth Tattoo Flash 5 sheets	$30.00
[2 of these sold for $174.99 each]		NEW line book by ryan downie tattoo machine flash	$30.00
TATTOO SUPPLIES. Great starter kit, everything you need	$172.50	8 tattoo flash dragon cross aztec skull lady w/lines	$30.00
TATTOO FLASH RACKS!!!!!! ("WALLMOUNT")!!!!! LOWEST $$	$157.51	10 tattoo flash thugs cross clowns skull neddle flag &	$30.00
Vintage 40s Tattoo Flash "No Reserve"	$142.50	Custom Tattoo Flash on CD's (set1, 2 & 3)	$30.00
Sailor Jerry Tattoo Flash Volume 2 Back in Print	$132.50	TATTOO FLASH LOT TIMMYTATTS PIN UP SAILOR FLAPPER	$29.99
Sailor Jerry Tattoo Flash Volume 1 ,back in print.	$127.50	TATTOO TUBES!! DIAMOND 4-8!!	$29.99
TATTOO FLASH	$102.50	("DISPOSABLE")!! 100 PACK!	

Tattoos, Body Art ▶ Piercing Supplies, Kits

The average sales price in this subcategory is $14.60.

	HIGH		AVG
TATTOO KIT* TRIBAL * Ink * Gun * Machine FREE SHIPPING	$199.95	50 Body Piercing Needles 18 gauge	$15.99
Spaulding Professional Body Piercing Kit Body Jewelry	$177.50	[2 of these sold for $15.99 each]	
Complete Body Piercing Kit Will Make You $2,000 #12	$169.99	50 Body Piercing Needles 16 gauge	$15.99
PIERCING KITS!!! PRO KIT # 2!! LOWEST PRICE!!	$129.99	[2 of these sold for $15.99 each]	
PIERCING KITS!!! STARTER KIT # 1!! LOWEST PRICE!!	$100.00	50 Body Piercing Needles 14 gauge	$15.99
Studex Ear Piercing Gun & 36 Pr. Piercing Studs #26	$89.99	[5 of these sold for $15.99 each]	
25 Piercing Body Piercing Kit with Forceps jewelry	$79.99	1 black GAUGE WHEEL measurement tool piercing tools NEW	$15.50
POWER SUPPLY For TATTOO MACHINE	$79.95	WHOLESALE LOT OF 100 14G STERILE BODY PIERCING NEEDLES	$15.50
GUN FREE SHIPPING		Pro TOOLS Open & Close for Body Piercing Ring Jewelry!	$15.49
Pro 16 Piece Body Piercing Tool Kit with Case!4 Jewelry	$74.99	WHOLESALE LOT OF *50* 12G STERILE BODY PIERCING NEEDLES	$15.00
[2 of these sold for $74.99 each]		PIERCING KIT BODY PIERCING TECHNIQUES BOOKLET	$14.99
PIERCING KITS!!! STARTER KIT # 1!! LOWEST PRICE!!	$71.00	Pro TOOLS Open & Close for Body Piercing Ring Jewelry!	$14.99
Pro 16 Piece Body Piercing Tool Kit with Case!4 Jewelry	$69.99	[2 of these sold for $14.99 each]	
POWER SUPPLY For TATTOO MACHINE GUN FREE SHIPPING	$67.00	PIERCING KIT 14G SS LABRET(CHIN/LIP) COMPLETE W/FORCEPS	$14.99
PIERCING KITS!!! STARTER KIT # 1!! LOWEST PRICE!!	$64.90	Body Piercing Tools Regular Ring Opener & Closer	$14.99
PIERCING KIT TOOLS PRO SET 8 PC	$49.95	PIERCING KITS 14G SS BANANA NAVEL COMPLETE W/FORCEPS	$12.99
W/ CASE BRAND NEW		PIERCING KIT BODY PIERCING TECHNIQUES BOOKLET	$12.99
[2 of these sold for $49.95 each]		50 Body Piercing Needles 14 gauge	$12.99
PIERCING KITS 50 PC W/ FORCEPS 14G SS BB 5 SETS	$39.99	50 Body Piercing Needles 16 gauge	$12.99
Pro 8 Piece Body Piercing Tool Kit with Case! 4 Jewelry	$39.99	[4 of these sold for $16.99 each]	

Tattoos, Body Art ▶ Tattoo Machines, Guns

The average sales price in this subcategory is $89.83.

	HIGH		AVG
Tattoo Equipment	$800.00	TATTOO MACHINE!! PITTSBURGH LIGHTNING!!	$99.99
Professional Tattoo Gun Machine Complete Kit	$583.50	LOWEST PRICE!!	
[3 of these sold in a multiple item ("Dutch") auction for $194.50 each]		TATTOO MACHINE!! THE GRAND DRAGON!! LOWEST PRICE!!	$99.99
NEWEST EBAY TATTOO KIT & TATTOO MACHINE!!	$575.00	Zeis New Modern Model Replica Tattoo Machine	$99.99
Mickey Sharpz,Tattoo,Tattoo Machine,Tattoo Gun,Flash	$520.00	NEW #1 HARLEY DAVIDSON GOLD TATTOO MACHINE L@@K	$99.98
Tattoo Kit!! Danny Fowler Machine, Sterilizer, Etc.!!!	$520.00	DRAGON CIRCLE TATTOO MACHINE GUN Ink Needle FREE STUFF	$99.95
Professional TATTOO KIT,W/ MICKEY SHARPZ Machine	$499.00	TATTOO ARM/ LEG REST!! IRON CROSS CHAIN!! LOW $$	$99.00
spaulding rogers tattoo kit with ink and colors	$461.00	TATTOO FLASH ART DESIGNS	$99.00
3M Thermofax 'The Secretary' Transparency Maker	$425.00	8 BRASS HAND CARVED GRIPS	$99.00
3-M TRANSPARENCY MAKER MODEL # 45FGA - TATTOO	$410.00	NEW HOOLIGAN MEAN GREEN TATTOO MACHINE	$92.99
seth c. aluminum liner, tattoo machine.1 of 5 made.	$400.00	NEW 3-SLOT RED METALLIC TATTOO MACHINE L@@K	$92.98
COMPLETE TATTOO KIT- 2 GUNS, POWER SUP, PEDAL/CLIPCORD	$395.00	SIDE BY SIDE SXS TATTOO MACHINE / Gun Jeff Hughes	$91.00
Tattoo Supply Sterilizer / Autoclave Fisher 750	$360.50	Tattoo Gun, Superior Soft Touch,power supply included!	$91.00
Paul Rogers by Micky Sharpz #378 Tattoo Machine 1996	$350.00	50+ photos tattoo machine P Rogers Sailor Jerry	$91.00
COMPLETE TATTOO KIT- 2 GUNS, POWER SUP, PEDAL/CLIPCORD	$350.00	Handmade Bronze Owen Jensen "Special" Tattoo Machine	$91.00
[2 of these sold for $350.00 each]		TREADLITE II WITH SUPERIOR VIPER	$91.00
3M Transparency Maker "The Secretary" GUARANTEED! NICE	$349.99	TATOO MACHINE GUN *N/R	

Tattoos, Body Art ▶ Tattoo Supplies

The average sales price in this subcategory is $83.33.

	HIGH		AVG
TATTOO GEAR.Full Professional setup! Guns/Aclave/More!	$1,225.00	*NEW* SCREAM BRAND TATTOO INK KIT 10 4-oz bottles!!!	$119.99
tuttnauer 2340M autoclave.mfg.1997 excellent condition	$1,000.00	High Quality Tattoo Machines	$110.00
TATTOO KITS!! PRO KIT!! # 5!! LOWEST PRICE! 2 MACHINES!	$939.00	[2 of these sold for $110.00 each]	
[6 of these sold for $939.00 each]		tattoo kit great price	$102.51
Tattoo Equipment	$800.00	*******TATTOO MACHINE****** RUNS GREAT	$102.50
3M Transparency Maker AGA ThermoFax Stencil Tattoo	$700.00	tattoo kit great price	$102.50
3M TRANSPARENCY FLASH MAKER	$650.00	NEW STERILIZED 100 Tattoo Needles + 100 Matching Tubes	$100.00
THERMOFAX TATTOO THERMO FAX		DENTAL, TATTOO ,PIERCING CHAIR GREAT FOR TATTOO SHOPS	$100.00
3M Transparency Maker TATTOO Stencil ThermoFax FLASH	$645.00	[2 of these sold for $100.00 each]	
3M Transparency Maker TATTOO Stencil ThermoFax FLASH	$600.00	NEW STERILIZED 100 Tattoo Needles + 100 Matching Tubes	$100.00
Lot of 2 3M Transparency Makers Maker 45DG	$576.75	TATTOO STENCIL MAKER "L@@K"	$99.00
3M TRANSPARENCY FLASH MAKER	$560.00	Tattoo Gun, Superior Soft Touch,power supply included!	$91.00
THERMOFAX TATTOO THERMO FAX		TATTOO INK KITS!!! BASIC KIT 2!!! 2oz BOTTLES!! LOW $$	$89.99
PELTON AND CRANE AUTOCLAVE/STERILIZER/TATTOO/VET	$560.00	Tattoo Machine Brass (Complete Machine) ::Maltese Cross	$89.95
TATTOO KITS!!! INTERMEDIATE PLUS!! # 4!! LOWEST PRICE!!	$489.00	Permanent Make-up/Tattoo Pigment Color $300.00 VALUE	$86.00
3m Thermofax Transparency maker 45 fga stencil tattoo	$479.00	TATTOO INK KIT!!! BASIC KIT # 1!!! LOWEST $$	$84.99
3M TRANSPARENCY MAKER THERMOFAX STENCIL TATTOO FLASH	$462.00	40 Tattoo Pigment Dispersion Colors / Tattooing Inks	$81.00
spaulding rogers tattoo kit with ink and colors	$461.00	[2 of these sold for $81.00 each]	

Vision Care ▶ Contact Lens Accessories

The average sales price in this subcategory is $10.62.

	HIGH		AVG
BOSTON- ADVANCE COMFORT FORMULA CARE SYSTEMS 12 SYSTEMS	$40.00	LOT OF 4- CLEAR EYES REDNESS RELIEF DROPS- .02 FL. OZ.	$15.00
Freshlook colored contacts pacific blue	$39.95	6 CIBA Clear Care Contact Lens Solutions and Cases	$15.00
REFRESH ENDURA LUBRICANT EYE DROPS (3) BOX SINGLE-USE	$31.00	3 Bottles - 1 oz. BOSTON ADVANCED exp. 08/2007	$14.67
ULTRASONIC CONTACT LENS CLEANER new version super clean	$29.95	30 Sterile Brand New Contact Lense Cases Free Ship	$14.50
$99 BRAND NEW ULTRASONIC CONTACT LENS LENSES CLEANER NR	$29.95	BOSTON CONDITIONING SOLUTION	$14.01

ULTRASONIC CONTACT LENS CLEANER new version super clean	$29.95	~ (3)ORIGINAL - CONTACTS	
[4 of these sold for $29.95 each]		BOSTON SIMPLUS CONTACT SOLUTION	$13.50
$99 BRAND NEW ULTRASONIC CONTACT LENS LENSES CLEANER NR	$29.95	12 BOTTLES 12 CASES NEW	
ULTRASONIC CONTACT LENS CLEANER new version super clean	$29.95	LOT OF 50 NEW BAUSCH & LOMB WHITE CONTACT CASES	$13.00
Lot of 74 Brand New Designer Eyeglass Cases	$29.03	NEW! LIZ CLAIBORNE Contact Lens Travel Storage Case Bag	$12.51
Clensatron Contact Lens Cleaning Unit NIB NR	$28.31	12 Bausch & Lomb Renu MultiPlus Contact Lens Free Ship	$12.50
27 CONTACT LENS CASES -NEW	$28.00	Boston SIMPLUS GP contact lens solution - 3 bottles	$12.50
Expressions Colored Contacts Aqua Cooper Vision	$27.99	Boston SIMPLUS GP contact lens solution - 3 bottles	$12.38
BOSTON- ADVANCE COMFORT FORMULA CARE SYSTEMS 12 SYSTEMS	$27.00	BOSTON ADVANCE COMFORT contact solution - 3 bottles	$11.38
Non-prescription Acuvue 2 Sapphire blue contacts	$25.00	Boston SIMPLUS GP contact lens solution - 3 bottles	$11.25
[2 of these sold for $25.00 each]		20 Bausch & Lomb RENU Contact Lens Solution + Cases	$11.13
Colored contacts	$25.00	Boston SIMPLUS GP contact lens solution - 3 bottles	$11.05

Vision Care ▸ Eyeglass Frames

The average sales price in this subcategory is $28.01.

	HIGH		AVG
BRAND NEW GUCCI GG 2568 EYEGLASSES SUNGLASSES FRAMES	$165.00	Nike Flexon Unisex Black Chrome Opthalmic Frame	$39.95
PRADA PR 08FV RHINESTONES EYEGLASSES FRAMES $279 VPR	$155.00	HOT NEW AUTHENTIC GUCCI 1668 EYEGLASSES SUNGLASSES	$39.95
NIB Oakley Blender 2.0 Gunmetal 50/19 RX Frame	$147.50	49 19 140 rare NEOSTYLE modern fashion eyeglasses FRAME	$39.00
PRADA PR 07E EYEGLASSES FRAMES $239 RETAIL VPR	$145.00	New CAROLINA HERRERA Eyeglasses PLASTIC TORTOISE	$37.50
PRADA PR 07E EYEGLASSES FRAMES $239 RETAIL VPR	$142.50	Designer Okio eyeglass frames with clip-on sunglasses	$35.00
AUTHENTIC PRADA VPR52E 1BC-101 RIMLESS EYEGLASS 51MM	$130.00	Gianfranco Ferre Eyeglasses GF 00102 Red Brand New	$34.99
AUTH OAKLEY EYEGLASSES THREAD 4.0 BLACK 11-839	$119.00	KARMA 100% TITANIUM FULL ROUND "VINTAGE" LOOK!!	$32.75
CHRISTIAN DIOR CD 3052 OPTICAL FRAMES EYEGLASSES BLACK	$114.00	versace eyeglass frames,new genuine,made in italy	$32.00
HOT SEXY GUCCI 1444 EYEGLASSES SUNGLASSES	$109.95	round special RODENSTOCK eyeglasses frame 45 27 140	$31.50
Oakley O2 Prescription Eyewear, Eyeglass Frame	$99.20	New, Coach women's eyeglasses, Greenwich, with case, NR	$31.01
BLACK LUNOR GERMAN MODEL 211 FRAMES MINT!	$93.00	Christian Dior glasses frames eyewear w/case	$29.99
JP Gaultier Designer Eyeglass Glass Frames	$92.01	Lot of 6 Cadore Moda Studio Designer Eyeglass Frames	$29.99
DIOR Eyeglasses Chestnut/Metallic Brown New CD7569J-Che	$79.99	Ellen Tracy Magnetic Clip On Eyeglass Frames #276	$29.99
GIORGIO ARMANI GA 254 EYEGLASSES FRAMES STONES KN5	$74.95	GUESS Designer Eyeglass Frames w/clip-on 461	$29.99
New, Coach women's eyeglasses, Joanna, with case, NR	$72.00	New Coach Eye Glass Frame Holly 504 Toffee 49-16-135	$29.00

Vision Care ▸ Reading Glasses

The average sales price in this subcategory is $11.19.

	HIGH		AVG
VIDEO MAGNIFIER - READING AND LOW VISION AID CCTV	$189.00	A LOT OF 10 PAIRS OF READING GLASSES(FREE SHIPPING)	$13.99
Wiley X (SG-1) Red & Clear lenses FREE SHIP	$75.00	Bifocal Reading Sunglasses BLUE BLOCKER LENSES +2.00	$13.99
RAY BAN B&L SUNGLASSES CLASSIC COLLECTION 3 W2184	$67.95	[2 of these sold for $13.99 each]	
Jimmy Crystal Reading Glasses w/Swarovski Crystals+1.50	$64.99	Bifocal Reading Sunglasses BLUE BLOCKER LENSES +1.50	$13.99
READING GLASS 550 600 MACULAR DEGENERATION 83	$60.96	EXTRA LARGE MAGNIFIER 5" MAGNIFYING GLASS	$13.00
[4 of these sold in a multiple item ("Dutch") auction for $14.99 each]		+1.25 Rhinestone READING SUNGLASSES Glasses BLACK	$12.99
RAY BAN B&L SUNGLASSES ROUND PLASTIC TORTOISE	$59.00	Art Wear Rimless Red Reading Glasses +3.00 MSRP $29	$12.99
Ladies Progressive Reading Glasses! Look Young!!!	$52.21	[2 of these sold for $12.99 each]	
Vintage Antique Glasses Bug Eye Fly 1/10 12KGF NR	$51.00	Art Wear Rimless Pink Reading Glasses +2.50 MSRP $29	$12.99
RAY BAN B&L SMALL WAYFARER ST. NEAT PEARL GREY/BLACK	$45.99	Art Wear Rimless Black Reading Glasses +1.75 MSRP $29	$12.99
RHINESTONE READING GLASSES MADE FROM SWAROVSKI CRYSTALS	$35.00	~**Quality Reading Glasses Ex-strong up +5.00	$12.99
Swarovski Crystal Reading Glasses +1.00	$34.00	LOT OF 17 READING GLASS 1.0 TO 3.25 NEW!!!!!!!!!!!!	$12.52
Brighton Reading Glasses +2.0	$30.00	Brand New foldable reading glasses +375 with case	$12.00
[2 of these sold in a multiple item ("Dutch") auction for $15.00 each]		CHIC Plaid READING GLASSES 2.0 white,tan, black and red	$12.00
Brighton Reading Glasses +2.0 28	$29.32	LOT OF 12 NEW READING GLASSES	$11.99
[2 of these sold in a multiple item ("Dutch") auction for $14.66 each]		+2.00 ASSORTED UNISEX	
REM Eyewear "Suspense" Reading Glasses - BRAND NEW!!!	$29.00	Jimmy Crystal Reading Glasses w/Swarovski Crystals+2.0	$11.00
Swarovski Crystal Reading Glasses +1.50	$27.95	+2.50 HAND PAINTED Quality Reading SUNGLASSES Glasses	$10.99

Weight Management ▸ Foods, Bars, Snacks

The average sales price in this subcategory is $32.36.

	HIGH		AVG
HUGE lot of Nutrisystem food nutri system	$315.00	Medifast Protein Bars - 3 Boxes of Lemon Fantasy !	$33.00
Quick Weight Loss Center Products LA - Lot of 44 boxes	$280.00	Medifast Protein Bars - 3 Boxes of S'More Granola !	$33.00
LA WEIGHT LOSS BARS ONE CASE	$265.00	[2 of these sold for $33.00 each]	
HUGE LOT OF NUTRISYSTEMS Food~158 MEALS	$255.00	Medifast Tropical Punch! - 3 Boxes - Refreshing!!	$33.00
HUGE!! 133 Piece NutriSystem	$251.03	Medifast Protein Bars - 3 Boxes of S'More Granola !	$33.00
Weightloss Food Program!!		Medifast Protein Bars 3 Boxes of Fruit and Nut Granola	$33.00
1 Month Supply- Nutri-System Food, Snacks and all Meals	$215.99	Medifast Oatmeal - 3 Boxes of Vanilla Berry ! [	$33.00
Nutrisystem 28 days 112 meals Nutri System	$215.00	2 of these sold for $33.00 each]	
HUGE NutriSystem FOOD LOT	$205.00	Medifast Oatmeal - 3 Boxes of Maple & Brown Sugar !	$33.00
exp. dates 2006-07 104 ITEMS		[2 of these sold for $33.00 each]	
Nutri System Nourish for Women-28 Month Supply- CHEAP!	$199.01	Medifast Protein Bars 3 Boxes of Fruit and Nut Granola	$33.00
Lot of 101 Nutrisystem Nourish Meals Nutri System Food	$189.04	[4 of these sold for $33.00 each]	
1 Case of La Weightloss Lite Bars - ANY FLAVOR!!	$182.50	LA Lites 4 boxes Peanut butter/Carmel LA Weightloss	$32.49
1 CASE of LA WEIGHTLOSS Lite Bars - Any Flavor	$180.95	Medifast Oatmeal - 3 Boxes of Vanilla Berry !	$32.00
12 Sealed Double boxes of LA Lites Peanut Butter Bars	$180.50	Medifast Pudding - 3 Boxes of Banana Pudding !	$32.00
NutriSystem Nourish Program Food	$179.50	Medifast Pudding - 3 Boxes of Chocolate Pudding !	$32.00
1 CASE of LA WEIGHTLOSS Lite Bars - Any Flavor	$177.50	[2 of these sold for $32.00 each]	
		WHAT A DEAL! 2 Boxes LA Weightloss Peanut Butter Bars	$31.87
		Suzanne Somers Somersize Bake & Fry Kit	$31.59
		63 CLIF BUILDER'S PROTEIN BARS, 3 FLAVORS	$31.50

Weight Management ▸ Pills, Tablets, Capsules

The average sales price in this subcategory is $24.26.

	HIGH		AVG
2 UT Tennessee Vols season football tickets great seat	$665.00	LEPTOPRIL Stimulant/Non-Ephedra 95 CAPSULES Brand New	$24.99
ADVOCARE MNS ORANGE 2 BOXES ,1 BOX PEAK TEA	$202.50	[2 of these sold for $24.99 each]	
Emagrece SIM from Brazil, ORIGINAL - ALL LEVELS	$185.00	2 bot HOT-ROX fat loss phenom completely EPHEDRA FREE	$24.99
Emagrece SIM from Brazil, ORIGINAL	$182.50	LEPTOPRIL Stimulant/Non-Ephedra 95 CAPSULES Brand New	$24.99
Emagrece SIM from Brazil, ORIGINAL - ALL LEVELS	$170.00	Propolene Diet Pills Weight Loss Pills 2 Sealed Bottles	$24.99
[2 of these sold for $170.00 each]		LEPTOPRIL Stimulant/Non-Ephedra 95 CAPSULES Brand New	$24.99
BRAND NEW LA WEIGHT LOSS 2	$164.26	[5 of these sold for $24.99 each]	
EXCEL AND CARB ENDERS SUPPS		HoodiaXtra Hoodia Gordonii 1000mg. 90 Diet Pills.	$24.99
Emagrece SIM from Brazil, ORIGINAL - ALL LEVELS	$152.50	5 BOTTLES CarboZyne CARB BLOCKER EXTREME DIET PILLS LOT	$24.95
Lipovarin 3 WEEK RAPID WEIGHT LOSS SYSTEM	$122.50	5 BOTTLES FAT BURNER ~ METABO ULTRA-MAX DIET PILLS LOT	$24.95
4 Sealed Bottles 95ct Leptopril (Leptoprin -SD generic)	$104.00	3 Bottles - HOODIA DIET MAX PILLS Gordonii Cactus Pill	$24.94
500g (1,1lb's) Pure Dried HOODIA POWDER Fast Shipping	$99.00	3 Lean Balance Weight, Fat loss and Calcium support	$24.51
Release Weight Loss Program w/Censor, New and Sealed	$96.00	Leptopril 95ct (Leptoprin-SD generic) SEALED 1/08 exp	$24.06
RELACORE–5 BOXES OF 110 CAPSULES EACH	$96.00	Hoodia Diet Max -Weight Loss System 500mg	$23.85
Release Weight Loss (UNOPENED) Plus Censor	$86.00	[3 of these sold in a multiple item ("Dutch") auction for $7.95 each]	
RELEASE WEIGHT LOSS PROGRAM	$77.00	Leptopril non-ephedra 95ct dietary supplement	$23.50
WITH CENSOR NEW SEALED		VPX REDLINE BY EVOBURN & CAMP 120 CAPS NEW 05/07	$23.04
AG Waterhouse Leptoprin-SD Unopened, Not Anorex	$76.00	Fahrenheit metabolism breakthrough for women exp 2/08	$23.00

Wholesale Lots ▸ Beauty & Personal Care

The average sales price in this subcategory is $57.50.

	HIGH		AVG
Over $10,000 MARY KAY Products Cosmetics WHOLESALE LOT!	$3,550.00	100 PIECE WHOLESALE MAYBELLINE ASSORTED MAKEUP	$71.00
HUGE $8,100 RETAIL LOT - Mary Kay! NO RESERVE!!!	$2,025.00	Bobbi Brown Lip Gloss Creamy Nectarine Lot of (5) NIB	$67.50
Huge MARY KAY Makeup Wholesale Lot $4,800 NR	$1,131.00	[2 of these sold in a multiple item ("Dutch") auction for $33.75 each]	
Mary Kay Wholesale Lot OVER $3,700 Retail, NR	$1,026.67	150 Bon Bons Lip Gloss Globes Wholesale Makeup Lot NEW!	$67.00
Huge MARY KAY Makeup Wholesale Lot $3,400 NR	$990.00	47-pc. Maybelline Mixed Makeup Lot ~Wholesale~	$66.00
Mary Kay Wholesale Lot over $1600	$864.16	100 Rimmel Eye Shine Eyeshadow Cream Wholesale Lot NEW!	$66.00
100 pc MAC *HUGE WHOLESALE LOT* -NEW IN BOX	$795.77	HUGE LOT LIPSTICK!!!! OVER 100 Pieces! 3 DARK Colors	$64.00
MARY KAY COSMETIC MAKEUP	$737.99	Mary Kay Sample Organizer with 400 + Samples	$63.51
WHOLESALE LOT $3000.00 WORTH		*100* Rimmel Hydrasense Flawless Hydrating Make-up Mix	$61.00
Mary Kay $1800.00 wholesale Lot	$675.00	MARY KAY SUPPLIES DIRECTOR & CONSULTANT	$61.00
****HUGE lot of MARY KAY- with FREEBIES*****over $2500	$667.58	$160 RETAIL MARY KAY WHOLESALE LOT 6 PARTY BAG KITS!!!	$61.00
MARY KAY MAKEUP & SKIN CARE LOT WORTH $2300+	$504.99	ERNO LASZLO CONCEALER LOT OF 10 RARE! NEW!	$60.00
HUGE Mary Kay Lot	$494.42	[2 of these sold for $60.00 each]	
HUGE Mary Kay Wholesale Lot - OVER $1900 RETAIL	$492.00	~LOT OF 35~MARY KAY~MK~HIPNOTICS	$56.00
HUGE LOT OF MARY KAY PRODUCTS	$467.57	~LIP~WHOLESALE~LOW S/H~	
OVER $1650 RETAIL ALL NIB		Mary Kay Wholesale LOT 107 items! Timewise! Lipstick!	$56.00
MAC MAKE-UP WHOLESALE LOT 70 ITEMS, NEW W/ BOXES!	$415.50	Bourjois 3D Effet Lip Gloss BEIGE ELASTIC Lot of 8	$55.98
		[2 of these sold in a multiple item ("Dutch") auction for $27.99 each]	
		Wholesale lot Christian Dior Basic Foundation Teint New	$55.00

21

HOME & GARDEN

The Home & Garden category delivered the fifth-largest gross merchandise volume (GMV) of all the eBay categories, $2.5 billion, and it is one of 12 eBay categories to deliver $1 billion or more in GMV. Here buyers can get many everyday items for the house at considerable discounts. And while many buyers are getting good deals here, sellers are doing well too. Many sellers offer discontinued and overstock merchandise, some obtaining their stock directly from a company, and others buying wholesale and reselling items individually. Casual sellers are also getting a lot more for that unused china or no-longer-needed furniture than they would at a yard sale.

But while there are many bargains to be found, not everything comes at a deep discount, particularly the popular newer items. For example, in the high range of prices in the Home & Garden ▶ Bath ▶ Shower Curtains subcategory, an "Elizabeth Paisley shower curtain" by Pottery Barn, new in the package, sold for $56.99; the Pottery Barn website was offering it for $59.00. A better deal could be found in the average price range: A Nicole Miller raffia shower curtain sold for $16.99; this was $37.95 elsewhere online.

Not everything is cheaper on eBay, though. I found a Tommy Hilfiger "surf" twin down comforter for $59.99 at Shop.com; one of these went for $81.99 and another for $100.00 in the high price range in the Home & Garden ▶ Bedding ▶ Comforters subcategory. But a Hilfiger "hula" twin comforter sold for $34.99 in the average price range, which appears to be a very good price, as similar Hilfiger comforters sell new on Macys.com for $94.99 ("lowest price of the season") to $125.00 (on sale) to $165.00 (full price). Again, bear in mind that these items may not be fresh from the factory—they may be a season or more old. As patterns and styles are discontinued, you can often get them cheaper from merchants like eBay sellers who buy them at closeout prices.

Number crunching aside, my favorite thing about the Home & Garden category is that you can find good deals on so many things you need to keep a household running. These are not "just for fun" items like collectible lunch boxes, but everyday things like sheets, towels, and pillows.

Speaking of sheets, anyone who's bought new ones, which is just about all of us, knows how expensive they can be, depending on thread count and brand. In this sample, I found that there are usually better values in the average price range than in the high range. For example, a set of Ralph Lauren gingham sheets sold for $24.99 on eBay, while a similar set cost around $65.00 for a fitted sheet, flat sheet, and one pillowcase from Polo.com. In the high end, the savings didn't seem as great. A Pottery Barn Kids "Chloe" twin sheet set and sham went for $71.50; I found a price of $78.00 for the same set elsewhere online, a difference of only $6.50. (There are, of course, exceptions to that rule of thumb.)

Big-Ticket Items and Major Appliances

With home remodeling being so hot, eBay is a great place to scout out things like appliances, cabinetry, and other large items, like above-ground pools and home spas. For example, several Koral steam shower/spa/whirlpool saunas sold for between $1,750.00 and $2,200.00 (the manufacturer's suggested retail price is $9,999.00, according to the seller).

Luxury as well as more moderately priced brands are here. A Sub-Zero refrigerator/freezer (a high-end brand known for keeping food very fresh) went for $5,500.00 (albeit with a $200.00 crating and handling fee); according to the seller, this unit (model 632/S) retails for over $7,000.00. Quite a bit cheaper, but still in the high range of prices in this subcategory, a new Frigidaire top-mount stainless refrigerator sold for $809.00; this sells for $849.00 from the Frigidaire.com website, so that's a $40.00 savings. In the average range for refrigerators and freezers, there are more substantial savings to be had, with two Frigidaire units selling for around $200.00. One, a fridge with a freezer on top, was white and in "barely used" condition (it was bought in 2003 but kept in the garage for two years). The seller says it was bought for $800.00 at Lowe's. The other was a Frigidaire refrigerator less than a year old, and still under warranty.

A large, cream-colored Aga brand stove that was several years old but in "like new" condition sold for $5,200.00. (Agas are large, high-end stoves popular in England, and they retail for several thousands of dollars, sometimes over $10,000.00, depending on the model.) Another stove, a Jenn-Air stainless steel model, was purchased for $1,026.50, a savings of about $1,052.00 over what the seller says is the retail price of $2,079.00.

Anyone for a Wine Cellar?

One of the most interesting items in this sample from the Home & Garden category is the redwood stand-alone wine cellar (which holds 2,500 bottles) that sold for $1,782.18 in Home & Garden ▶ Food & Wine ▶ Beer & Wine Making. Another listing that stands out is the "entire contents of a 5 bedroom home – WHAT A DEAL!" that went for $2,500.00 in the Home & Garden ▶ Furniture ▶ Living Room, General Use subcategory. This one has a somewhat bizarre backstory—it's a daughter selling her mother's things that were in storage. The mother apparently had a financially irresponsible history and disappeared with some shady friends, leaving the daughter with responsibility for the storage facility. The whole history of the relationship is laid out in the listing's description: "I must make it clear that we are not doing this for retaliation, we are doing it because the moving company is going to auction everything off everything anyhow—at least this way we can hopefully make enough money to make good on the things that she had promised to do for us—even if it is only enough to pay our daughters' tuition, we will be so grateful," wrote the seller. The auction includes a photo of the front of the house the things were taken from, and a scan of a hand-written inventory of the items, including two beds, an armoire, a headboard, a footboard, two nightstands, a dresser, sinks, TV stands, a TV, a baker rack, and a table.

More typical listings in that subcategory include a chair with ottoman ($425.00) and a child's computer desk ($109.95). But then again, there is also a "stripper pole with stage DOES NOT BOLT TO CEILING" ($365.00).

Furniture Prices

How does furniture in Home & Garden compare to retail prices? A Ballard Designs "shabby chic" bed canopy/crown (a half-moon-shaped crown that affixes to the wall behind the bed, and from which fabric hangs on either side, making a "canopy" of sorts) sold for $77.00, down from $129.00 retail, per the seller. This was one of the average prices. A similar discount could be had for a funky, curved, and cushy "retro rocker" from Pottery Barn Teen: it sold for $76.00, as compared to $139.00 in the PB Teen catalog.

Among the high prices in bedroom furniture, a Pottery Barn cream "Francisco" (a dark, clean-lined style) armoire/cabinet in like-new condition went for $406.01. I couldn't find this exact model on the Pottery Barn website (probably because it has been discontinued), but some larger Francisco armoires retail for $1,599.00 to $1,899.00 (or $599.00 for a TV stand alone), so this seems to be a very good deal.

Of course, it's not all name brand stuff here: there are no-name and vintage items, like a lovely cedar chest with a decorative carving in front that the seller appears to have painted white and then distressed. This sold for $219.00. A "new white tall pine bookcase" with an attractive bead-board back and round knob feet sold for $189.00.

Some of the antique pieces here are really special and not necessarily expensive, such as the charming antique gentleman's chifforobe (wardrobe with drawers), a very solid-looking armoire-like piece complete with a mirror and doors. It would need refinishing to look perfect, but at $102.50, do you really care?

This category is also home not only to living things (with many orchids and other plants to be had for $10.00 to $30.00) and edible things (chocolate and spices), but to industrial-type items like air conditioners, furnaces, and power tools such as leaf blowers. There are also things that home builders use, like doors and flooring. In fact, the Home & Garden ▶ Building & Hardware subcategories are good places to poke around if you're remodeling—you can get things like kitchen cabinets, faucets, and tile here.

If you've ever remodeled a kitchen, you know that new, solid wood cabinets can run $10,000.00 or more. And indeed, one auction for custom-made wood cabinets (available in a variety of real wood types, such as maple, oak, and cherry) that would retail for $9,000.00, according to the seller, went for $2,650.00. ("You choose any style and size of cabinets you want up to $9,000.00 SRP from our price list!") The same seller, who also sold most of the other cabinets in the high-price sample, sold an auction for 30 lineal feet of standard base cabinets and 30 lineal feet of 30" high wall cabinets for $2,970.00 ($99.00 per lineal foot), which is almost 40 percent off the regular selling price of $4,847.70 ($161.59 per lineal foot). This seller seems to have carved a very good niche for himself in the kitchen cabinet area; he's the main seller in the upper end of that subcategory, and his listings are very professional and lay out a good case for buying from him instead of a big-box store.

To sum up, the Home & Garden category on eBay houses a cornucopia of items both large and small. If you want the latest, newest style, you may not find it here at a big discount, but if you're willing to accept something a season or so past its prime, you may snag a wonderful deal. Certainly, a wide range of attractive and useful things for the home are here, including, literally, the kitchen sink.

Bath ▶ Shower Curtains

The average sales price in this subcategory is $16.77.

	HIGH		AVG
POTTERY BARN CHANTAL TOILE SHOWER CURTAIN & TOWEL SET 6	$109.99	Lace Shower Curtain FABRIC with Valance White - New	$17.99
[3 of these sold for $109.99 each]		Waverly Blossom Hill Sh. Curtain, NIP, MSR $39.99Nice	$17.99
wyland shower curtains and hooks -brand new -orig pkg	$79.99	BLUE DIAMOND BEADED VALANCE SHOWER CURTAIN SET	$17.99
Pottery Barn Kids Froggy Frog Bath Mat & Shower Curtain	$59.00	BIG BROWN BEAR IN WOODS LODGE	$17.99
Pottery Barn Elizabeth Paisley Shower Curtain~NIP	$56.99	CABIN SHOWER CURTAIN NEW!	
Pottery Barn Spring Stripe Shower Curtain~NIP	$51.00	HAPPY BUNNY "ITS ALL ABOUT ME" SHOWER CURTAIN NEW	$17.50
NIP Restoration Hardware Cabana Stripe	$41.00	DEAN MILLER SHOWER CURTAIN	$17.49
Mountain Retreat Shower Curtain Set	$40.00	Dale Earnhardt Sr. 3 Nascar Shower Curtain NIB	$17.49
NEW! Butterfly SHOWER CURTAIN & HOOKS~White~Blue~Purple	$40.00	MIRABELLA SHOWER CURTAIN	$16.99
Croscill Lafayette Napoleon Shower Curtain Blue New	$39.99	[7 of these sold for $16.99 each]	
[2 of these sold for $39.99 each]		NICOLE MILLER RAFFIA BLUE SHOWER CURTAIN	$16.99
Curved shower curtain rod Adjusts up to 5ft 7in! NIB	$39.01	Thalia Sodi Peacock Feathers Fabric Shower Curtain NEW	$16.95

	HIGH		AVG
Ralph Lauren Polo Terry Cloth shower curtain-Cream-NIP	$36.00	RED FLAMES SHOWER CURTAIN NEW HOT TOPIC	$16.76
Curved shower curtain rod Adjusts from 4 FT - 6 FT long	$35.95	FISH Fabric Shower Curtain Rainbow TROUT BASS curtains	$15.99
Croscill Lafayette Napoleon Shower Curtain Blue New	$34.99	Silver Curved Shower Rod – New	$15.99
Nicole Miller Evening Glamour Shower Curtain NEW	$34.99	[5 of these sold for $15.99 each]	
[2 of these sold for $34.99 each]		Betty Boop Shower Curtain-the KISS-New!	$15.75
Nicole Miller Evening Glamour Shower Curtain NEW	$34.99	Betty Boop Film Strip Shower Curtain - New	$15.75

Bath ▸ Towels, Washcloths

The average sales price in this subcategory is $15.65.

	HIGH		AVG
$210 Lot 6 Ralph Lauren Polo White Cotton Towels NR	$104.49	Lot of 12 Egyptian Cotton Wash Cloths In Pink Dogwood	$19.27
$422 Lot 37 Madison & Max Cotton Bath & Hand Towels NR	$51.00	WAVERLY FIELD OF FLOWERS BATH TOWEL LOT TOWELS 2 NEW	$18.99
DISNEY MICKEY MOUSE Jacquard Bath Towel NEW	$49.95	WAVERLY VINTAGE ROSE BATH TOWEL LOT TOWELS NEW 2	$18.99
[5 of these sold in a multiple item ("Dutch") auction for $9.99 each]		Kokopelli Embroidered Towels Stunning	$18.99
SPA BATHROOM SHEETS/TOWELS	$48.47	$175 Lot 10 Revere Mills Blue Bath & Hand Towels NR	$18.50
NWT NAUTICA 4 Large BATH Towel Set Nautica White $100+	$43.50	Springmaid Royal Paisley 3-piece luxury towel set	$18.00
$175 Lot 10 Revere Mills Cotton Hand & Bath Towels NR	$42.11	NEW Waverly Country Life Black Toile Bathroom Towel Set	$18.00
$226 Lot 23 White Bathroom Towels Madison & Max NR	$41.05	PINK PRINCESS + CROWN BATH TOWELS	$17.00
$420 Lot 34 Towels Madison & Max Santens Circulon NR	$41.00	26" X 50" LOT 2 NEW	
Tower of Blue Bath Towels - 4 Bath - 4 Hand - 4 Wash	$40.99	Lot of 42 Pure Cotton Wash Cloths in assorted Colors	$16.53
Four Ralph Lauren Shower Towels, New with Tags	$40.63	AQUIS MICROFIBER WAFFLE WEAVE HAIR TOWEL WHITE	$16.50
$303 Lot 24 Cotton Towels Royal Velvet Utica Hilasal NR	$39.00	Waverly Country Life Toile Fingertip Towels (2) NWT	$16.08
Tower of White Bath Towels - 4 Bath - 4 Hand - 4 Wash	$37.97	14 50x23 white bath towels washclothes pool utility car	$16.00
[5 of these sold for $37.97]		NEW! AQUIS MICROFIBER HAIR TOWEL BLUEBERRY	$16.00
$200 Lot 20 Madison & Max Bath Towels & Washcloths NR	$37.50	TOWEL SET 12 PC BATH HND WSH BURG	$16.00
$167 Lot 10 Revere Mills Bath Bathroom Towels NR	$37.00	SALESMAN SAMPLES NEW!	
$238 Lot 21 Revere Mills 2 Cotton Bath & Hand Towels NR	$36.61	New DENA DESIGNS Glamour Girl GUEST TOWELS Paris / NYC	$15.99

Bath ▸ Whirlpool, Spa

The average sales price in this subcategory is $367.54.

	HIGH		AVG
KORAL-Luxury Steam Shower Spa WHIRLPOOL, Sauna, KL- B308	$2,200.00	Steam Shower Whirlpool w/ Massage Jacuzzi Hot tub Sauna	$999.00
[2 of these sold for $2,200.00 each]		ANOTHER BEAUTIFULL UNIT AT EXCELLENT PRICE	$950.00
KORAL-Steam Shower SPA,Massage,Sauna,WHIRLPOOL KC9007	$2,075.00	Whirlpool Steam Shower w/ Massage Hot Tub Sauna	$911.01
Whirlpool Steam Shower w/ Massage Jacuzzi Hot tub Sauna	$2,026.00	Jacuzzi Whirlpool Bath - Este Vistelle - NEW - 33% OFF	$879.00
Wet Steam, Jet Bath Tub Jacuzzii & Shower Enclosure	$2,001.00	K1384-N1 Biscuit Watersilk whirlpool	$839.00
Whirlpool Steam Shower w/ Massage Jacuzzi Hot tub Sauna	$2,000.00	KORRAL VICHY SHOWER UNIT+MASSAGE	$750.00
Steam Shower Bath Sauna Jacuzzi Whirlpool Bathtub	$1,925.00	+Steam Shower+KLBF1108	
Steam Shower Bath Sauna Jacuzzi Whirlpool Bathtub	$1,875.00	Steam Shower Bath Whirlpool Hot Tub + Sauna + Massage	$702.00
Steam Shower Bath Whirlpool Jacuzzi + Sauna + Hot Tub	$1,826.00	Steam Shower Bath Whirlpool Hot Tub + Sauna + Massage	$685.98
Whirlpool Steam Shower w/ Massage Jacuzzi Hot tub Sauna	$1,825.00	60X 60 WHIRLPOOL TUB!!!! BRAND NEW!!!!!!!	$550.00
[2 of these sold for $1,825.00 each]		jacuzzi whirlpool bath tub riva 6 oyster NEW IN BOX	$500.00
KORAL-Steam Shower SPA,Massage,Sauna,WHIRLPOOL KC9007	$1,750.00	KORRAL Vichy Aluminum Shower Panel,	$499.00
Whirlpool Steam Shower w/ Massage Jacuzzi Hot tub Sauna	$1,728.00	SEAT+ FOOT MASSAGE	
Whirlpool Steam Shower w/ Massage Jacuzzi Hot tub Sauna	$1,700.00	$2,280 Jacuzzi Whirlpool Bath - New 1$ No Reserve!	$480.00
Steam Shower Bath Whirlpool Jacuzzi + Sauna + Hot Tub	$1,675.00	Kohler Sojourn drop-in corner 60x60 whirlpool 5 jets NR	$475.00
Whirlpool Steam Shower w/ Massage Jacuzzi Hot tub Sauna	$1,625.00	Whirlpool Bath Tub	$435.00
Steam Shower Bath Whirlpool Jacuzzi + Sauna + Hot Tub	$1,601.00	MR STEAM, 6KW STEAM BATH GENERATOR, MS 150	$385.00

Bedding ▸ Comforters

The average sales price in this subcategory is $34.96.

	HIGH		AVG
700TC Hungarian Goose Down Comforter TWIN	$123.99	Beige Twin Goose Down Feather Comforter & Pillow Set	$39.99
NEW LUXURY FULL QUEEN WHITE GOOSE DOWN COMFORTER 44OZ	$117.50	Pottery Barn Teen Parka Twin Comforter Blue NEW	$39.95
Glacier Luxury Twin Winter White Goose Down Comforter 3	$109.99	Twin Size Simmons Down Comforter/Hunter Green/NIP!	$39.95
Tommy Hilfiger Twin Surf Surfs Up Down Comforter NIP	$100.00	4Pc Twin Size Shark Tale Comforter Set !! Brand New !!	$38.00
Glacier Luxury All Season Goose Down Comforter 2	$99.99	Simmons Beautyrest Feather Down Comforter Twin size	$37.00
Charter Club Mount Fuji Goose Down TWIN Comforter NEW	$99.99	Simmons Beautyrest Feather Down Comforter Twin, Navy	$37.00
Comforter Twin w/ canopy & Curtains Pink Roses	$96.00	Simmons Beautyrest Down & Feather Comforter Queen/Full	$37.00
Tommy Hilfiger - SURF SURFBOARD TWIN DOWN COMFORTER	$95.00	CHARTER CLUB MATTERHORN FULL/QUEEN DOWN COMFORTER	$35.00
Charter Club Mount Fuji Goose Down TWIN Comforter NEW	$92.99	NEW TWIN WHITE DOWN BED COMFORTER COMFORTERS BEDDING	$35.00
[3 of these sold for $92.99 each]		3Pc Twin Size TEEN TITANS Comforter Set !! Brand New !!	$35.00
Tommy Hilfiger Surf 's Up - Down Comforter New! - Queen	$92.99	[2 of these sold for $35.00 each]	
Tommy Hilfiger Twin Plaid Navy Down Comforter NIP 1ST!	$92.00	DISNEY FINDING NEMO TWIN 100%COTTON BEDDING COMFORTER	$34.99
Tommy Hilfiger Surf Comforter Twin Size Down Comforter	$89.00	Tommy Hilfiger Twin Hula Red Blue Down Comforter NEW	$34.99
RALPH LAUREN BEACHSIDE PREPPY TWIN COMFORTER &BEDSKIRT	$88.00	Twin Luxury White Down Alternative Comforter 300 TC	$34.99
Tommy Hilfiger Lavender Plaid Down Comforter NEW King	$83.07	4Pc Twin Size Shark Tale Comforter Set !! Brand New !!	$34.99
Tommy Hilfiger Twin Surf Surfs Up Down Comforter NEW	$81.99	CHATEAU WHITE DOWN COMFORTER W/ 4 FEATHER PILLOWS- TWIN	$34.95

Bedding ▸ Duvet Covers

The average sales price in this subcategory is $38.24.

	HIGH		AVG
POTTERY BARN TEEN PIQUE GREEN DUVET TWIN NEW SOLD OUT	$262.00	Pottery Barn Kids MVP Baseball Twin Duvet NEW!	$39.99
POTTERY BARN KIDS JULIANA PINK TWIN QUILT & SHAM	$169.99	POTTERY BARN Lafayette Duvet, BLUE/WHITE, Twin, NEW	$39.99

Hilfiger Nate Comforter Cover Twin XL Sheets DORM More	$162.00	RALPH LAUREN ALLISON COMFORTER COVER TWIN NIB	$39.99
Pottery Barn Kids Yellow Happy Bugs Twin Duvet NIP	$120.50	White King Duvet & Pillow cover Set Egyptian Cotton 420	$39.99
Pottery Barn Kids Mia Duvet & Sheet Set & Sham Twin New	$119.99	POTTERY BARN TEEN LUXE RIBBON DUVET COVER (TWIN)	$39.99
Pottery Barn PB Teen Puravida Stripe Duvet~Twin~+ Sham	$108.72	Hilfiger Twin Comforter/Duvet Cover & Sham Set -TYLER-	$39.99
POTTERY BARN ISLAND SURF sheet set pink queen	$108.00	Pottery Barn My First Car Brandon Twin Duvet	$39.99
Pottery Barn Under the sea twin duvet and sham pink	$99.99	NEW NAUTICA MARINERS MARINER'S CORD OLIVE TWIN DUVETED	$39.99
Pottery Barn Kids JULIANA LINEN DUVET & SHAM TWIN NEW	$99.00	NIB! RALPH LAUREN WEST HIGHLAND OLIVE TWIN DUVET	$39.99
SET SAIL TWIN DUVET COVER*Pottery Barn Kids*NEW IN PKG!	$97.01	White Queen Duvet & Pillow Cover Egyptian Cotton 420TC	$39.99
Pottery Barn Kids Juliana twin duvet cover floral linen	$92.00	POTTERY BARN KIDS EXPLORER DUVET COVER TWIN NIP	$39.99
Pottery Barn Kids Moon and Stars Duvet~Twin~+ Sham!	$90.99	Pottery Barn Explorer Sheet Set Twin & Case New	$39.99
Ralph Lauren - ISABELLE SCALLOPED WHITE KING DUVET	$85.00	WATERBURY TWIN Duvet 2pc Ensemble Set RED Brand New	$39.99
Pottery Barn Red Paisley Twin Duvet Cover & Sham	$83.00	PB Pottery Barn TEEN Cord Cargo Duvet TWIN PURPLE NIP	$39.99
AMISH HANDMADE QUEEN QUILT	$81.00	POTTERY BARN KIDS PINK GINGHAM CHAMBRAY TWIN DUVET NEW	$39.00

Bedding ▶ Sheets

The average sales price in this subcategory is $24.43.

	HIGH		AVG
Charisma Parchment Supima Cotton Queen Sheets Set	$145.00	NEW!! Jessica McClintock Emily QUEEN Flannel Sheet Set	$25.49
DISNEY TINKERBELL TINKER BELL SHEET SET NIP FULL	$128.56	DISNEY PRINCESS LACE Full Sheets SHEET SET New	$24.99
1000TC Organic Egyptian Cotton Bed Sheets FULL SIZE	$107.50	Ralph Lauren PINK twin gingham sheets NIP	$24.99
HIGHGATE MANOR EGYPTIAN COTTON	$79.88	Dean Miller - SURF SAFARI QUEEN SHEET SET - NEW	$24.99
SHEET SET 1000TC Q DIJON		BRAND NEW 320TC FULL SIZE SHEET SET 100% COTTONSATIN	$24.99
NWT POTTERY BARN KIDS CHLOE TWIN SHEET SET & SHAM	$71.50	NEW VIBRANT YELLOW SATIN TWIN SHEET SET NICE!	$24.99
TWIN CHERRY CHERRIES COMFORTER/SHEETS BED IN A BAG	$69.99	TWIN BRILLANT ORANGE ~ TIE/TYE DYE SHEETS/sheet Jersey	$24.99
TIE TYE/ DYE BRIGHT TWIN COMFORTER	$65.99	NIP 3 PC SET TWIN SATIN SHEETS LILAC PURPLE / SILVER	$24.99
SHEETS BED IN A BAG		BRAND NEW 320TC FULL SIZE SHEET SET 100% COTTONSATIN	$24.99
TIE TYE/ DYE BRIGHT TWIN COMFORTER SHEETS BED IN A BAG	$64.99	[3 of these sold for $24.99 each]	
LAURA ASHLEY~Emilie~QUEEN SHEET SET~Blue Flower~NIPnr	$64.99	DISNEY PRINCESS LACE Full Sheets SHEET SET New	$24.99
SAFARI ANIMALS QUILT & SHEET SET TWIN -COMPANY KIDS	$64.99	Dean Miller - SURF SAFARI QUEEN SHEET SET - NEW	$24.99
EGYPTIAN COTTON 500 TC BEDDING ENSEMBLE QUEEN BRICK	$57.86	BRAND NEW 320TC FULL SIZE SHEET SET 100% COTTONSATIN	$24.99
Tommy Hilfiger ELIZABETH ANNE Full Sheet Set 1stQual	$57.10	[2 of these sold for $24.99 each]	
Pottery Barn Kids Island surf Sheet set Twin - new	$56.50	NIP 3 PC SET TWIN SATIN SHEETS HOT SEXY SHOCKING PINK	$24.50
Pottery barn BRIGHT TOILE TWIN SHEET SET NEW	$55.00	waverly sweet violets twin sheet set FREE SHIPPING WITH	$24.00
RALPH LAUREN 4PC FULL SHEET SET/ POLO BEARS	$54.99	Disney Princess Sleeping Beauty Aurora FULL SHEETS	$23.99

Building & Hardware ▶ Cabinets & Cabinet Hardware

The average sales price in this subcategory is $203.07.

	HIGH		AVG
Complete Kitchen: Cabinets, Corian, Sub Zero, Dacor etc	$11,600.00	All Wood Kitchen Cabinets Vanity Bath Cabinet RTA NR	$710.00
Custom Built Wood Kitchen Cabinets Bath Vanity Cabinet	$2,970.00	NEW! All-Wood Kitchen Cabinets: MANUFACTURER DIRECT	$200.00
All Wood Kitchen Cabinets Vanity Bath Cabinet RTA NR	$2,850.00	Custom Built Wood Kitchen Cabinets Bath Vanity Cabinet	$495.00
All Wood Kitchen Cabinets Vanity Bath Cabinet RTA NR	$2,650.00	All Wood Kitchen Cabinets Vanity Bath Cabinet RTA NR	$255.00
All Wood Kitchen Cabinets Vanity Bath Cabinet RTA NR	$2,600.00	NEW! All-Wood Kitchen Cabinets: MANUFACTURER DIRECT	$200.00
All Wood Kitchen Cabinets Vanity Bath Cabinet RTA NR	$2,475.00	Konig wood touch up kit 662 B-box w 2 training video's	$175.00
Custom Built Wood Kitchen Cabinets Bath Vanity Cabinet	$1,540.00	KRAFTMAID CABINETRY BRAID CORBELS GINGER GLAZE MAPLE	$152.50
All Wood Kitchen Cabinets Vanity Bath Cabinet RTA NR	$1,306.00	Accuride CB3832-24" Black Drawer Slides New In Box	$142.50
All Wood Kitchen Cabinets Vanity Bath Cabinet RTA NR	$1,125.00	[10 of these sold in a multiple item ("Dutch") auction for $14.25 each]	
Custom Built Wood Kitchen Cabinets Bath Vanity Cabinet	$990.00	KRAFTMAID CABINETRY VANILLA GLAZE CORBELS	$94.00
		Oak Kitchen & Bath Cabinet All Wood Fully Assembled	$75.00

Building & Hardware ▶ Doors & Door Hardware

The average sales price in this subcategory is $26.18.

	HIGH		AVG
Andersen 400 Series Frenchwood? Outswing Patio Doors	$1,310.00	5 oak french cabinet doors 12 7/8 x 15 7/8 A11	$29.99
WEISER LOCK POWERBOLT 3000 ULTIMATE 3 DOOR LOCK PKG	$222.50	New Genie Garage Door Opener Photocell Set	$28.00
Von Duprin 6211 US32D 24VDC FSE Electric Strike NIB	$220.00	[3 of these sold for $28.00 each]	
[2 of these sold in a multiple item ("Dutch") auction for $110.00 each]		Schlage Antique Brass Artisan Handle Set	$27.89
WEISER LOCK POWERBOLT 3000 ULTIMATE 3 DOOR LOCK PKG	$195.00	Vintage Metal door peep hole	$26.00
Wireless Design Doorbell Jacob Jensen B&O **NEW**	$135.00	WESIER LOCK POWERBOLT 3000 LOCK	$26.00
[2 of these sold for $135.00 each]		AND KEYPAD PACKAGE	
pella aluminum clad 5 ft patio slider.	$129.02	Baldwin Nickel Plated Brass Door Knocker, mint & old	$23.98
4.0" all brass door hinge, door hinges	$117.00	[2 of these sold in a multiple item ("Dutch") auction for $11.99 each]	
[39 of these sold in a multiple item ("Dutch") auction for $3.00 each]		6 Brass Baldwin Entry Latches Locksmith L@@K NEW	$23.50
Newbury Gliding Patio Door Hardware by Anderson	$101.33	Solid Brass - Bronze MANATEE Door Bell & Cover	$22.00
ORIGINAL KWIKSET CHANGE KEYS - LOCKSMITH DEAL!!	$99.90	Solid Brass - Bronze DRAGONFLY Door Bell and Cover	$22.00
[10 of these sold in a multiple item ("Dutch") auction for $9.99 each]		RODAN AV-100 ELECTRONIC EYE	$21.71
WEISER LOCK POWERBOLT 3000 ULTIMATE 3 DOOR LOCK PKG	$92.00	DOOR ANNOUNCER NIB	
3.5" all brass door hinge, door hinges !!	$80.00	New Box of 2 BARON Style DOORBELLS Doorbell	$21.51
[32 of these sold in a multiple item ("Dutch") auction for $2.50 each]		Baldwin Nickel Plated Brass Door Knocker, mint & old	$21.00
Von Duprin 99ALK US28 36" w/RX Switch	$69.88	[2 of these sold in a multiple item ("Dutch") auction for $10.50 each]	
VINTAGE GRISWOLD(?) DOOR KNOCKER PEEP HOLE	$68.05	6 Brass Baldwin Passage Latches Locksmith L@@K NEW	$20.50
NEW Anderson Brass Sliding patio Door hardware wlockset	$52.02		

Building & Hardware ▸ Tile & Flooring

The average sales price in this subcategory is $203.07.

	HIGH		AVG
Brazilian Soapstone Tile 18"x18" !!	$2,800.00	50 assorted TALAVERA CERAMIC TILE	$132.50
[800 of these sold in a multiple item ("Dutch") auction for $3.50 each]		MEXICO MEXICAN 4" 4x4	
Brazilian Soapstone Tile 12"x12"	$2,100.00	TalaveraTile Mosaic FLOWERS	$96.20
[700 of these sold in a multiple item ("Dutch") auction for $3.50 each]		Handpaint Mexican Mural	
Glass Mosaic Tile blend KISMET *20 sheets*	$600.00	Daylily Tile Panel for Victorian Style Fireplace #1	$85.00
[8 of these sold in a multiple item ("Dutch") auction for $75.00 each]		Talavera Tile Mosaic FLOWERS VASE	$75.00
SUPER Saltillo Tile 12x12 One Pallet Low Shipping 336ft	$400.00	NIB Easy Heat ft1048 warm tile system	$74.50
Kitchen Tile mural handmade for stone marble ceramic	$399.99		

Dining & Bar ▸ Bar Tools & Accessories

The average sales price in this subcategory is $12.56.

	HIGH		AVG
Chateau Laguiole Sommelier BEAUMARD Corkscrew wine	$119.95	Pomerantz Wine Tabletop Wine Opener - Black/Chrome	$16.00
NIB ROGAR ESTATE WINE OPENER	$107.50	NEW QUALITY PROFESSIONAL CORKSCREW WINE OPENER KIT *	$15.99
BRONZE GRAPE CORKSCREW NR		[2 of these sold for $15.99 each]	
Chateau Laguiole Olive Wood GRAND CRU Corkscrew wine	$99.95	NEW POMERANTZ WIZARD TABLETOP WINE OPENER BLACK/CHROME	$15.50
Chateau Laguiole Black Horn Corkscrew wine opener	$84.95	3? Pulltap Wine Corkscrew Opener Key, Appears New	$15.50
[2 of these sold for $84.95 each]		Williams and Sonoma: Vigneto Wine Bottle Opener	$15.50
LAGUIOLE SOMMELIER G.DAVID /CORKSCREW/	$75.00	NEW POMERANTZ WIZARD TABLETOP	$15.50
WINE /FRANCE		WINE OPENER BLACK/CHROME	
Rogar Estate Vintage Silver Wine Opener Granite Table	$62.99	Rabbit & Company 6-Piece Wine Tool Collection Corkscrew	$15.00
Metrokane 6015 Rabbit Wine Corkscrew Took Kit (6-Piece)	$59.00	TIRE BOUCHON MANCHE BUI Lesprit & Levin Wine Opener	$15.00
Modernist Animal Horn Bottle Opener Eames Era	$53.77	CORK-POPS WINE BOTTLE OPENER BLACK CORKSCREW	$14.49
Metrokane SILVER Rabbit Corkscrew Wine TOOL KIT NEW	$49.95	WINE COMPANION CORKSCREW BOTTLE OPENER SET NEW LEEDS	$14.00
Screwpull-Lever Model	$39.00	[2 of these sold in a multiple item ("Dutch") auction for $7.00 each]	
Premium Pulltap Wine Corkscrew Bottle Opener Key 3?	$36.00	2 Rabit Style Corkscrew Wine Bottle Openers(Brand New)	$13.99
Mother of All Corkscrews! Estate Wine Cork Remover	$35.98	Metrokane Rabbit Corkscrew & Foil Cutter Like NIB	$13.72
WineMaster Corkscrew by Vacu Vin	$35.00	WINE COMPANION CORKSCREW BOTTLE OPENER! NEW LEEDS	$13.25
Metrokane Silver Rabbit Wine Corkscrew BONUS	$34.95	5-PC. WINE BOTTLE OPENER TOOL KIT CORKSCREW SET BAR SET	$12.95
Metrokane Silver Rabbit Wine Corkscrew BONUS	$32.95	Collectible Cadillac 3pc Wine Tool Kit in Walnut Box	$12.55

Dining & Bar ▸ Dinnerware & Serving Pieces

The average sales price in this subcategory is $14.95.

	HIGH		AVG
New Banana Republic 5-Piece Bamboo Flatware, 10 Sets	$280.00	Deca Dukes of Hazzard plate and cup good shape! daisey	$19.99
8-4 PIECE TROPICAL PINEAPPLE DINNERWARE-DISHES	$152.45	Lenox, Poppies on Blue, Salt and Pepper Shaker	$19.99
Williams Sonoma Spode Transferware Stilton Keeper	$99.99	SHABBY Cottage Chic CAKE Plate / Footed * X LARGE	$18.99
NEW Set 4 Silver Plated Chargers Plates *3 Available*	$30.09	Williams Sonoma BLUE Oval Bread Warming Ceramic Basket	$18.99
Slice of Life Dinnerware Plates-222 Fifth Collection NR	$86.00	New Banana Republic Natural Bamboo Salad Serving Set	$18.73
Tiffany & Co. White Wicker Basket	$61.00	Blue Enamelware Coffee Pot With Percolator 12 Cup	$18.00
NASH METROPOLITAN AIRSTREAM ENAMELWARE , 12 PIECE	$59.99	Four Fiesta Cappuccino Mugs Rose Color	$18.00
Villeroy and Boch Knife Rests- Botanica Pattern	$58.98	Blue Willow butter dish	$16.49
VINTAGE RARE ART DECO KNIFE REST, MULTI COLOUR GLASS	$56.55	SUPER CUTE WATERMELON BOWL, PITCHER	$15.99
Johnson Brothers Coffee mugs & Creamer	$56.00	& CUP-USED ONCE!	
2 Vintage Woody Woodpecker Cereal Bowl and Mug Sets	$50.99	MINT! Bernardaud **FRUTTI FIORI** tea saucer!	$15.95
MIXED LOT OF BROWN TRANSFERWARE-THE MEADOW-BEAUTIFUL!	$45.00	Southern Living at Home Toscana Tidbet Set Celery	$15.55
4 PEWTER PLATES CHARGERS COLONIAL DESIGNS ENGRAVED NR	$42.00	JOY MANGANO PIATTO GIFT SET	$15.50
Waverly Sweet Violets Tall Cake Stand NEW	$41.01	PFALTZGRAFF 220 G 3 PIECE SALAD SET BROWN DRIP STONEWAR	$15.50
Fly Fish Dishes~Angler~Rainbow Trout~Dinnerware~Rustic	$39.95	Five Fiesta Jumbo / Chili Bowls Rose Color	$15.00
[2 of these sold for $39.95 each]		Spode Christmas Tree pair of Candle Holders	$14.99

Dining & Bar ▸ Flatware

The average sales price in this subcategory is $36.99.

	HIGH		AVG
CHRISTOFLE HOTEL Sterling Silver Silverware Utensils VG	$2,850.00	NEW Wood Flatware Box Silverwear Case Felt Lined Drawer	$43.01
Dansk Germany Flatware Teak Handles 38 Pcs. 446	$407.00	SILVERWARE HOLIDAY GOLD 71 PC FLATWARE SET WITH CHEST	$42.50
Bestecke SOLINGEN 24KT Gold Flatware 72 Pc. Set in Case	$142.50	Anant Ebony Bronze Flatware 142 pieces w/wood case	$41.00
65 PC BAROQUE GOLD PLATED FLATWARE SET & CHEST -NEW	$125.00	Bronze flatware by James Quality Jewellers	$41.00
4 Drawer Maple Flatware or Silverware Chest	$122.83	ROGERS & BRO. 63 Piece Goldplate Flatware Set NEW	$40.57
SILVERWARE CHEST/BOX, WILLIAM	$112.50	LARGER WOODEN SILVERWARE STORAGE CHEST BOX	$40.00
ROGERS & SON, WALNUT		ELEGANT 144pc. NICKEL BRONZE FLATWARE SET FROM THAILAND	$40.00
NEW in Box Reed & Barton Mahogany Flatware Chest !	$102.50	SILVER SILVERWARE FLATWARE STORAGE CHEST BOX ONEIDA NEW	$38.99
Vintage Thai Bronze Flatware 169 Piece Service for 12	$100.00	[3 of these sold for $38.99]	
4 Five-piece International Pewter Flatware Settings NEW	$99.99	vintage NAKEN S SILVERWARE storage CHEST / BOX for 12	$37.22
SILVERWARE STORAGE CHEST- ROSE OAK NEW	$99.99	Set of 11 Silver and Nickel Forks \ flatware	$37.00
Reed & Barton Mahogany Silverware Flatware Chest Drawer	$99.00	Williams Sonoma Expandable Drawer Tray w/Knife Rack	$36.00
VINTAGE 105 PCS Y THAILAND BRONZE	$99.00	Golden rose fork spoon Renaissance feast gear SCA	$36.00
SERVING FLATWARE NR		[6 of these sold in a multiple item ("Dutch") auction for $6.00 each]	
Best Mod Flatware-Lucite Stainless Stanley Roberts 43pc	$99.00	WALNUT STAINED SILVER FLATWARE CHEST, HINGED LID DRAWER	$36.00
Reed & Barton Mahogany Silverware Flatware Chest Drawer	$99.00	Lunt Sterling Dk Walnut Wooden Flatware Box.	$34.00
Spode Christmas Tree Flatware Chest *NEW!*	$78.54	6 oldfashioned soda fountain spoons nickel silver 7-1/2	$33.25

Electrical & Solar ▶ Alternative & Solar Energy

The average sales price in this subcategory is $79.07.

	HIGH		AVG
4000 Watt Wind Turbine Generator WIND FARM 12, 24, 48 V	$999.95	Wind turbine generator blade propeller 3 rotor BIG 86"	$162.50
OutBack MX60 MPPT Charge Controller	$958.00	GLOBAL SUN OVEN (SOLAR POWER)	$154.50
[2 of these sold in a multiple item ("Dutch") auction for $479.00 each]		10" Tubular Skylight, solar tube skylights NEW NR	$152.50
AIR-X MARINE 400W WIND GENERATOR	$650.00	GAS POWER SUBMERSIBLE HOT TUB	$131.50
400W AIR-X Wind Generator, Tripod & 25' 10ga POWER CORD	$645.00	HOT WATER HEATER NR	
BRAND NEW RHEEM SOLAR 80 GALLON TANK WITH ELEMENT	$595.00	TRACE PHOTOVOLTAIC GROUND FAULT	$127.50
Air X Marine 400 watt 24 volt wind generator	$510.00	PROTECTION-SOLAR USE	
NIB AIR 403 12 VOLT WIND GENERATOR - SELLS FOR $600.00+	$500.00	Solar Panel 24 watt	$117.50
Air X 400 watt wind generator, (NIB) 12 volt DC	$499.00	50–NOS– Round Solar Cells ..	$104.49
[2 of these sold for $499.00 each]		REPLACEMENT PROP FOR THE 403 WIND GENERATOR	$94.95
AIR-X LAND 400W WIND GENERATOR	$495.00	Solar Panel 24 watt	$83.00
Wind turbine generator / 24 volt. / 1000 Watt max!	$450.00	Wind Turbine Generator / Tower / Pole / Mount KIT	$81.00
Wind Turbine Generator 12 volt SLOW WIND TYPE 7'	$449.95	Solar Power 30 yr batteries with EQUALIZER desulfator	$72.00
800 Watt 12 volt Wind Generator windmill	$389.00	Wind turbine generator blade propeller 6 rotor 1/2" hub	$71.00
Wind turbine generator / 48 volt / 1000 Watt max!	$380.00	Wind Turbine Generator Blades/Propeller/3 rotor	$68.00
Bio Diesel Biodiesel Kit / Fuel for 10 cents a gallon	$369.95	TRACE PHOTOVOLTAIC GROUND FAULT	$66.00
[2 of these sold for $369.95 each]		PROTECTION-SOLAR USE	
HAWK Wind Turbine Generator 12, 24, 48 V 2300 Watts	$366.98	12V Briefcase Solar Panel Generator *	$65.99

Electrical & Solar ▶ Switches & Outlets

The average sales price in this subcategory is $24.75.

	HIGH		AVG
Lutron GRX-3106 Grafik Eye 6 Zone 2000W Black/Ivory	$406.26	Lutron White Faedra Multi-Location Smart Dimmer 2 pcs	$26.00
Lutron Grafik Eye (GRX-2404) Dimmer - 4 Zone	$312.50	LUTRON CENTURION C-1500 WATT	$26.00
Lutron GRX-3103 Grafik Eye 3 Zone 1500W Black/Ivory	$252.00	ROTARY INCANDESCENT DIMMER	$26.00
100 amp 240 volt Manual Transfer Switch	$250.00	LOT 5 LEVITON 1755 IVORY DECORA TRIPLE ROCKER SWITCH	$26.00
LUTRON GRAFIK EYE 3000 SERIES HI POWER 4 DIMMING MODULE	$228.50	GENERAL ELECTRIC Low Voltage Switches RS 2-37 NICE!	$26.00
Lightolier Insight Dimmer & Switch Wholesale LOT NIB	$199.99	Intermatic T104 Heavy-Duty Contractor Grade Time Switch	$25.51
LUTRON GRX-RS232 GRAFIK EYE RS232 CONTROL INTERFACE!	$182.50	(LOT OF 10)LEVITON QUIET/LIGHT SWITCH+COVER(WHITE)	$25.50
LEVITON 3-WAY DECOR SWITCHES**NIB**	$110.50	White Lightolier Sunrise Low Voltage Inductive Dimmer	$24.95
Lutron RadioRA RAS-8L Single Location Dimmer Control	$102.50	10 Leviton Trimatron S P Toggle Dimmer Switches Ivory	$24.95
amerock carriage house outlet cover in antique brass	$98.00	Ivory Lightolier Onset Rocker Dimmer Preset 1000W	$24.95
[7 of these sold in a multiple item ("Dutch") auction for $14.00 each]		NEW DIGITAL TIMER U8 15-Amp AC Wall Outlet All Purpose	$24.89
LEVITON 3-WAY DECOR SWITCHES**NIB**	$91.00	Leviton Decora 3 Way Sure Slide Dimmer Switches Almond	$24.51
LEVITON SINGLE POLE DECOR SWITCHES**NIB**	$89.00	LOT 5 IVORY 4-WAY 20A 120-277V GRDNG DESIGNER SWITCH	$23.39
NEW 1129 Sylvania z-wave Delux starter kit x-10	$80.00	New GE Dimmer Touch Switch Wall Switch Plate 6 Pc light	$22.99
RadioRA RA-1000LM Multi-Loc. Dimmer	$79.00	Leviton Decora Ceiling Fan Speed Control Switches White	$22.55
RadioRA RALV-1000L Single Pole Dimmer w/LEDs	$76.00	USB 1.1 4 PORT KVM SWITCH	$22.50

Food & Wine ▶ Beer & Wine Making

The average sales price in this subcategory is $41.71.

	HIGH		AVG
Wine Cellar Room-2500 Bottles	$1,782.18	4QT WRIGHT HDWE WINE PRESS/LARD/SAUSAGE/FRUIT/CIDER	$51.00
CORRELL APPLE CIDER FRUIT PRESS	$504.00	TIN GRAPE FRUIT APPLE WINE CIDER CRUSHER GRINDER PRESS	$51.00
All Grain Lager Homebrewing starter equipment	$490.00	Cabo Wabo Tequila Barrel Keg - Sammy Hagar - Van Halen	$49.95
HOMEBREW STAINLESS STEEL BREWING SYSTEM (NEW)	$195.00	Wine Bottle Corker - Heavy Duty made in Portugul - NEW	$46.99
22.5 Gal. Wine Barrel - New ReCooped French Oak Barrel	$190.00	Vintage Grinder Grapes Apples Fruit Wine Cider Antique	$46.07
Le Nez du Vin Wine Education Kit - Jean Lenoir - Scents	$175.00	Delux Absinthe Brew Kit With Wormwood, Spoon and Glass	$46.00
Grape / Wine / Cider / Fruit Press	$172.50	Tri-Clover - 3/4" Sanitary Fittings,Tee,Elbows,Clamps++	$46.00
GRAPE FRUIT APPLE WINE CIDER CRUSHER GRINDER PRESS BERY	$170.52	Beer Machine. Your Personal Micro Brewery - nr	$46.00
New APPLE / CIDER / WINE / GRAPE / FRUIT PRESS.	$167.50	Delux Absinthe Brew Kit With Wormwood, Spoon and Glass	$45.00
New Hard/Apple/Cider/Wine/Fruit/Juice Press. No Reserve	$165.00	[6 of these sold for $45.00 each]	
APPLE CIDER/WINE/FRUIT JUICE PRESS!	$142.50	Home Beer Making Kit (Homebrewing, Homebrew, Home Brew)	$42.00
Vintage Oak & Metal Wine/Cider Press	$130.38	2QT ENTERPRISE WINE PRESS/LARD/SAUSAGE/FRUIT/CIDER	$42.00
Cornelius Keg Kit for Homebrew Beer w/o Keg - 10# CO2	$128.31	<>NEW 'MR. BEER' KIT w/ 5 CANS MIX	$41.00
KEGERATOR KIT FOR HOMEBREW BEER	$127.50	3" Single Tap Beer Tower & Becks tap handle	$41.00
KEG CO2 TAP GAUGES !!		BRAND NEW! Mr Beer Premium Brew Kit !!FREE SHIPPING!!	$39.99
8 QT ENTERPRISE WINE PRESS/LARD/SAUSAGE/FRUIT/CIDER	$122.50	ATC 0-25% Alcohol 0-40% Brix Refractometer 4 wine beer	$39.99

Food & Wine ▶ Candy & Chocolate

The average sales price in this subcategory is $10.15.

	HIGH		AVG
STAINLESS STEEL CHOCOLATE FONDUE FONDU FOUNTAIN MAKER	$75.89	ORIGINAL CHOCOLATE FACTORY 92 Piece Kit AS SEEN ON TV	$11.99
NIB - Stainless Steel Chocolate Fondue Fountain	$63.00	LOWEST PRICE 5 FULL CASES OF CANDY	$11.99
6lbs. JAMAICAN BLUE MOUNTAIN COFFEE NO RESRV	$58.00	CIGARETTES FRESHEST	
HERSHEY BUTTER TOFFEE SKOR BITS-COOKING- RECIPE-FOOD	$43.96	Soft Diamond Salt Licorice candy - 2.2 lbs - Zout	$11.99
[4 of these sold in a multiple item ("Dutch") auction for $10.99 each]		LOWEST PRICE 5 FULL CASES OF CANDY	$11.99
Jelly Belly Jelly Beans: 49 Flavor Assortment / 10lbs	$45.00	CIGARETTES FRESHEST	
Assorted 5lbs of CANDY/ SNACKS + FREE SHIPPING!!	$31.98	Soft Diamond Salt Licorice candy - 2.2 lbs - Zout	$11.99
[2 of these sold in a multiple item ("Dutch") auction for $15.99 each]		1# Delicious PURE maple sugar candy/ $4 ship /50 states	$11.70
TWIX CARAMEL CANDY BAR 36 COUNT NEW FRESH	$29.99	1# Delicious PURE maple sugar candy/ $4 ship /50 states	$11.51
Godiva Chocolatiers Truffles Poids Net 347g 2 Packs	$28.00	Sugar Free Candy Go Lighty Allen Wertz Chocolate Mix	$11.00
1 Box of Willy Wonka Candy Bars - 36 UK Chocolate Bars	$26.00	HARRY POTTER Bertie Botts Every Flavor Bean Jelly Belly	$10.51

la pipette black licorice pipes 60CT Indivally wrapped	$24.99	LorAnn Candy Flavoring Oil 12 Different New1dr Bottles	$10.50
LICORICE ALTOIDS 10 TINS $24.99 liquorice LOW SHIPPING	$24.99	THE ORIGINAL CHOCOLATE FACTORY	$10.50
Lindt assorted Chocolate Truffle balls 96ct.	$24.00	As Seen on TV 92 pc NIB	$10.50
Velamints Chocolate Sugar Free Fat Free 2 tins per !!!!	$22.00	3 Boxes of Wonka Nerds Rope 24 Per Box - NIB	$10.50
[8 of these sold in a multiple item ("Dutch") auction for $2.75 each]		THE ORIGINAL 99PC CHOCOLATE FACTORY KIT !!!	$10.50
GODIVA PREMIUM ASSORTED CHOCOLATES 16OZ SEALED BOX	$21.97	ORIGINAL CHOCOLATE FACTORY 92 Piece Kit AS SEEN ON TV	$10.49
MARZIPAN PASTE FOR MOLDING: 5 lbs.	$21.00	THE ORIGINAL CHOCOLATE FACTORY - NEW, AS SEEN ON TV	$10.45

Food & Wine ▶ Spices, Seasonings & Extracts

The average sales price in this subcategory is $9.71.

	HIGH		AVG
Blair's 16 Million Reserve #172 of 999	$132.50	1/4 lbs 100% Certified Organic Madagascar Vanilla Beans	$10.51
5 Kgs GOURMET ORGANIC	$50.99	***NEW***TASTEFULLY SIMPLE***GARLIC GARLIC***	$10.50
VANILLA TAHITENSIS A BEANS		1,000 GOURMET TAHITENSIS A VANILLA BEANS	$10.50
1 lb. ORGANIC TAHITENSIS VANILLA BEANS 5" to 6" long!	$36.00	25 ORGANIC GOURMET VANILLA BEANS - 5" to 6" long	$10.50
Sea Salt, Spice, Herb, Pepper Mill Grinder - FREE Ship	$33.00	RIB RUB~AWARD WINNING BBQ RECIPE~ PORK RIBS	$10.50
1 lb ORGANIC GOURMET VANILLA - 6" to 7" long	$32.00	Watkins - Original Double Strength Vanilla - 11 oz	$10.07
1 lb ORGANIC TAHITENSIS VANILLA BEANS 6" to 7" long!!	$31.00	Homemade Gourmet Distributor Goodies/supplies	$10.01
12 empty new spice bottles 4" clear glass	$28.53	Elephant Garlic, 2 Pounds, Food Grade Bulbs	$10.00
Homemade Gourmet Pantry Staples Set of 4 new	$28.00	HANGING MULTI COLORED RED HOT CHILI PEPPER DECORATION	$9.99
1 lb. ORGANIC TAHITENSIS VANILLA BEANS 5" to 6" long!	$26.59	Pure Cap Pepper Extract!! Hotter Than Hot Sauce!! NEW!!	$9.99
1 lb ORGANIC TAHITENSIS VANILLA BEANS 6" to 7" long!!	$26.10	1 CASE OF DANNCY VANILLA EXTRACT. DIRECT FROM MEXICO!!!	$9.99
1 lb ORGANIC GOURMET VANILLA BEANS - 5" to 6" long	$26.00	Watkins Original Vanilla FREE SHIPPING!	$9.99
ZATARAIN'S ROOT BEER EXTRACT 12 / 4 OZ BOTTLES	$25.50	MEXICAN VANILLA EXTRACT DARK & CLEAR BOTTLES	$9.99
Smokin' In The Dark BBQ Rub - 5 lb. - Barbecue Barbeque	$24.49	[2 of these sold for $9.99 each]	
Smokin' In The Dark Spicy Rub - 5 lb- Barbecue Barbeque	$23.99	Watkins Original Vanilla - FREE SHIPPING!	$9.99
Smokin' In The Dark BBQ Rub - 5 lb. - Barbecue Barbeque	$23.99	Tastefully Simple Lot-corn salsa,fiesta mix, &more	$9.89

Furniture ▶ Bedroom Furniture

The average sales price in this subcategory is $63.59.

	HIGH		AVG
MACKENZIE CHILDS SIDE TABLE DESK W/DRAWER HAND PAINTED	$934.04	BALLARD DESIGNS SHABBY CHIC CROWN BED CANOPY CORNICE	$77.00
NEW FULL SIZE MURPHY BED CABINET, FRAME & FOUNDATION!	$799.00	POTTERY BARN RED SINGLE RETRO ROCKER PRECIOUS!	$76.00
LOVESAC SUPERSAC 6 ft and the 3ft KIDSAC!	$431.97	Powell Headboard Queen size metal White Victoria New	$76.00
STRONGEST QUEEN SIZE MURPHY WALL BED FRAME & FOUNDATION	$425.00	MAHOGANY BED STEPS STOOL LIBRARY/KITCHEN STEP VICTORIAN	$74.33
POTTERY BARN CREAM FRANCISCO ARMOIRE CABINET	$406.01	Pier One 1 Imports WICKER DESK PLUS WICKER CHAIR	$70.99
FURNITURE COLLECTION-BAMBOO COUCH-HAND CARVED BED LAMP	$385.12	MAHOGANY BED STEPS STOOL LIBRARY/KITCHEN STEP VICTORIAN	$69.95
FULL or QUEEN size Murphy bed / wall bed frame - NEW	$369.00	POTTERY BARN PINK PASTEL SINGLE RETRO ROCKER PRECIOUS!	$69.45
Chic and Shabby White Trunk - Cedar Chest	$219.00	VINTAGE~SUITCASE~LUGGAGE SCHEIBE RACK~STAND~ROSE STRAP	$68.00
NEW WHITE PINE WIDE BOOKCASE / BOOK SHELF / BOOK CASE	$209.00	POTTERY BARN PINK PASTEL SINGLE RETRO ROCKER PRECIOUS!	$68.00
Beautiful Ikea Bedroom Glass Door Wardrobe Closet	$202.50	NEW! VERMONT White & Natural Maple HEADBOARD 54/60"	$64.00
NEW WHITE PINE TALL BOOKCASE / BOOK SHELF / BOOK CASE	$189.00	ANTIQUE VINTAGE COMMODE WASH STAND TABLE NIGHT STAND	$61.00
NEW WHITE PINE TALL BOOKCASE / BOOK SHELF / BOOK CASE	$189.00	POTTERY BARN GREEN PASTEL SINGLE RETRO ROCKER PRECIOUS!	$60.00
Carson Bed Mahogany Queen NR	$175.99	MAHOGANY VICTORIAN BED STEP	$60.00
Pottery Barn Kids Cameron Wall Cubby & base WHITE	$167.92	VICTORIAN SOLID MAHOGANY BED STEP STOOL	$59.00
REVOLVING JEWELRY BOX ARMOIRE WOOD IN OAK FINISH	$159.00	New Portable Closet wardrobe organizer dorm guest room	$56.00

Furniture ▶ Living Room, General Furniture

The average sales price in this subcategory is $119.20.

	HIGH		AVG
Entire contents of a 5 bedroom home - WHAT A DEAL!!	$2,500.00	Oversized / Overstuffed Leather Chair	$150.00
Georgian Lane 3 seater Leather Sofa Chesterfield NR	$2,012.00	Harley Davidson Custom Pool / Billiard Ball Set - SALE!	$149.37
8' 11" Putnam Rolling Library Ladder Pantry Wine Cellar	$1,000.00	XXX Removable 8' Stripper pole *UV* COLORS !!!	$147.50
[2 of these sold in a multiple item ("Dutch") auction for $500.00 each]		Brinks Anti-Theft Wall Safe .43 Cu Ft.	$143.18
bamboo tiki bar and bar stools	$810.00	Brinks Anti-Theft Wall Safe .43 Cu Ft.	$140.68
NEW 100% Leather WINSTON Recliner Pottery Barn Throw	$799.99	Jack Daniels Swivel Bar Stool with Backrest	$131.50
GORGEOUS CHERRY BAR WINE AND LIQUOR WALL UNIT	$699.00	*2* BLACK SUEDE LIKE/BRUSHED SILVER BAR STOOLS CHAIRS	$129.95
CLASSIC CHERRY HOME BAR WITH SINK, WINE RACK, FOOTRAIL	$669.00	CHIMING WALNUT Tambour Mantel Mantle Clock!!!	$127.50
Root Furniture Teak Set Garden Tree Rustic Nakashima	$595.00	Leather and wood Spanish sling back chairs (2)	$125.00
Mahagony Cherry Hall Tree w/ Brass, Mirror & Marble	$595.00	AUTHENTIC MEXICAN RUSTIC CHIMINEA	$120.00
Inlaid Syrian Large Game Table Chess, Poker, mosaic	$550.00	FIREPLACE LOS ANGELES	
Home Theater Seats, 1 Row of 5 Theatre Chairs	$250.00	Childs computer desk for kids 2 - 6 yrs old	$109.95
Gaming Accent Side Occasional Card Ornate Table Burled	$499.00	Childs computer desk for kids 2 - 6 yrs old	$109.95
Double Sized Chair with Ottoman. Great Shape, Still New	$425.00	Girlie Pinkish Salmon Leather Sofa Loveseat	$102.50
FURNITURE COLLECTION-BAMBOO COUCH-HAND CARVED BED LAMP	$385.12	Cool Vintage leopard print Chairs Very Cool MUST SEE!	$100.00
Stripper Pole with Stage DOES NOT BOLT TO CEILING	$365.00	Fluke 77 III Multimeter w/case & Instructions	$98.66

Gardening & Plants ▶ Garden Décor

The average sales price in this subcategory is $22.27.

	HIGH		AVG
Lighthouse 4' Painted lighted Garden or Yard Decoration	$264.00	SCOTTIE DOG Weathervane	$24.95
[3 of these sold in a multiple item ("Dutch") auction for $88.00 each]		BICYCLE Weathervane	$24.95
Set of 5 Genuine Giant Tridacna Gigas Clam Shells	$203.05	New Wrought Iron Happy Sun! Very Modern and Beautiful	$24.95

KOI Pond Laguna Pressure Filter W/UV PT 1502	$180.31	SNOWMOBILE Weathervane	$24.95
Lighthouse 4' Painted lighted Garden or Yard Decoration	$159.00	RUNNING HORSE Weathervane.	$24.95
KOI Pond Laguna Pressure Filter W/UV PT 1500	$132.50	CAIRN TERRIER DOG Weathervane	$24.95
2 Lighted Palm Trees 7 Ft. Yard/Home/Party/Luau HOT	$105.47	WITCH Weathervane	$24.95
SWEET Lady Slipper Watercolor MAINE ARTIST Janet Conrad	$74.99	TRIKE ULTRALIGHT Weathervane	$24.95
Wooden wagon wheel 36" hardwood- Set of 2	$50.00	NEW TERRA COTTA OUTDOOR PLANTER FEEDER THERMOMETER	$24.95
UNIQUE 3D 4' FOOT LIGHTED PALM TREE TREES G568	$49.99	DANCING DRAGONFLIES GARDEN PLAQUE cast iron DRAGONFLY	$22.01
Wizard of Oz Play Set	$45.45	Beautiful 12-1/2" VERDIGRIS BRASS ARMILLARY SPHERE	$20.49
NEW OUTDOOR ROCK SPEAKERS	$41.55	VINTAGE AERO MODEL 12-B MINIATURE	$20.49
Filigree Water Hose Holder NIB - Holds 100' of Hose	$41.50	WINDMILL, GENEVA NEBR	
Frog Water Hose Holder NIB - Holds 100' of Hose	$39.50	Western Decor Real Working Med Pitcher Hand Water Pump	$20.26
box of o/d decor/garden WORTH OVER $200/ALL ITEMS NEW	$36.99	GOTHIC /GREENMAN-Wall Hanging L@@K~ copr	$20.00
Medium Glass Bell Jar/Cloche/Dome w/Knob	$34.99	Slag Glass Rock Aquarium / Garden Decoration Yard Art	$19.99

Gardening & Plants ▸ Plants, Seeds & Bulbs

The average sales price in this subcategory is $9.52.

	HIGH		AVG
Rare variegated Monstera d. 'Thai Constellation' plant	$102.50	...HRD-2-FND...'Snake' Plant...MOONSHINE...	$11.00
Philodendron Willsonii Huge gigantic plant	$100.00	NEW Chia Pet Chia PUPPY Planter New In Sealed Box	$10.50
Orchid Flask Paph Species Sanderianum - only two left	$99.99	..hrd-2-fnd..SANSEVIERIA..Hahnii.. 'Pearl Young'..	$10.50
Monstera marmorata Yellow variegated philodendron	$96.00	African Violet~BABY BRIAN TRAIL	$10.50
Orchid Flask Paph Species Praestans v. Bodegomii	$59.99	African Violet~Rainy Nights	$10.50
OASIS SELF-WATERING SYSTEM *BRAND NEW*	$50.00	African Violet - NYMPH FLY * Dates Semimini Wasp	$10.50
Orchid Paph fairrieanum X niveum BS	$35.99	Hoya bella - miniature fragrant Hoya species	$10.50
Paph Gratrixianum Species Orchid	$35.99	Streptocarpus Leaf - ICED ICE BABY * Variegated Strep	$10.50
Eipremnum pinnatum skeleton key philodendron cousin	$31.01	KALANCHOE PREGNANT PLANT	$10.49
Orchid Paph druryii SPECIES PLANT BS	$31.00	African Violet - SNOW WASP *Frilly White Dates Wasp SM	$10.01
Orchid Phrag Caudatum - SPECIES	$29.99	RARE EASTER CACTUS__2_PLANTS__MUST HAVE	$9.99
Orchid Phrag wallisii - SPECIES	$29.99	ROOTED PLANT! Dracaena marginata DRAGON TREE COLORAMA	$9.99
Epipremnum pinnatum blue Cebu blue + philodendron	$29.02	LUCKY BAMBOO - 30 Plants (4"-6"-8" Ten Each) - 1 Price	$9.99
Philodendron Silver blue spear leaves collected	$29.00	ANT PLANT Caudiciform Hydnophytum formicarium-Seedlings	$9.95
African Violet 400 MINI THUMB POTS 1 1/2" Terra Cotta	$28.00	GOLD TOOTH ALOE NOBILIS PLANT WITH OFFSETS SUCCULENT	$9.95

Health, Cooling & Air ▸ Air Conditioners

The average sales price in this subcategory is $179.57.

	HIGH		AVG
CENTRAL HEAT AIR CONDITIONER VARIABLE A/H 14 SEER 5 TON	$1,895.00	Fedders 8000 BTU Portable Air Conditioner in the box	$265.00
New in box 2.5 ton Goodman 15 seer heat and air system	$1,699.00	Fedders 8000 BTU Portable Air Conditioner in the box	$255.00
4 Ton Electric/Gas Heat Package System 10.4 SEER	$1,151.00	SOLEUS PORTABLE A/C 9000 BTU	$249.00
HEAT PUMP & AIR CONDITIONER NEW IN BOX 2 TON 12 SEER	$1,040.00	w/remote - #MA-9000AH	
Marine Air: Coolmate Air Conditioner - 12,000 260466	$999.99	MobilAir 9000 BTU Portable Air Conditioner with Heater	$247.50
CENTRAL HEAT AND AIR CONDITIONER NEW PACKAGE UNIT 3 TON	$980.00	MobilAir 9000 BTU Portable Air Conditioner with Heater	$242.51
Marine Air: Coolmate Air Conditioner - 12,000 260466	$960.00	A/C Split Unit 18000BTU Power V220 - Remote Control	$235.00
New 1 1/2 ton Goodman heat and air conditioning system	$799.00	PORTABLE EVAPORATIVE SWAMP	$231.50
CENTRAL HEAT AND AIR CONDITIONER NEW IN BOX 2 TON	$790.00	COOLER (Air Conditioner)	
1 Ton mini split ductless air Conditioner 12000 B T U	$549.00	A/C Split Unit 18000BTU Power V220 - Remote Control	$229.99
[2 of these sold for $549.00 each]		Kenstar TurboCool Portable Evaporative Cooler 1000 CFM	$229.00
1 Ton mini split ductless air Conditioner 12000 B T U	$549.00	[2 of these sold for $229.00 each]	
3 /4Ton mini split ductless air Conditioner 9000 B T U	$499.00	9000 BTU SUNPENTOWN PORTABLE AIR CONDITIONER	$228.50
Soleus Air KY-36 Portable Air Conditioner 14000 BTU	$445.00	DeLonghi Pinguino Portable Air Conditioner	$204.50
NEW CARRIER AC WITH HEAT 13,5BTU RV BOAT MOTORHOME	$419.00	Soleus Air KY-28U 9000 BTU Mobile Air Conditioner &Heat	$202.51
[5 of these sold for $419.00 each]		Champion WCM28 Evaporative swamp cooler window unit	$183.83
Amcor 12,000 BTU Portable Air Conditioner (ALD-12000E)	$409.00	PORTABLE EVAPORATIVE SWAMP COOLER (Air Conditioner)	$182.50
[4 of these sold for $409.00 each]		Soleus Air KY-28U 9000 BTU Mobile Air Conditioner &Heat	$175.00

Health, Cooling & Air ▸ Furnaces, Heating Systems

The average sales price in this subcategory is $187.46.

	HIGH		AVG
280,000 BTUs CLEAN BURN Waste Oil Furnace heater	$2,026.00	wood stove fisher...like new ...insert or free standing	$300.00
Lanair Waste Oil Furnace heater-140,000 BTU's	$1,975.00	York Split System Heat Pump	$261.00
175,000 BTU's SHENANDOAH Waste Oil Furnace heater	$1,925.00	WOOD BURNING STOVE WITH POWER FAN	$255.00
CLAYTON #1800 WOOD & COAL FURNACE	$1,900.00	Superior Natural Gas Fireplace Insert	$250.00
Ducane 100,000 BTU Gas Furnace w/ 3 Ton AC Package	$1,375.00	Coal & flame effect electric fire and beech surround	$244.50
2.5 Ton AC air cond Package w/ 75,000 BTU Gas Furnace	$1,325.00	NIB DIMPLEX 23" ELECTRIC FIREPLACE INSERT DF12309 W846	$120.00
Corn Stove-Brand New Factory Second-PreTested!!SAVE$$NR	$1,255.03	[2 of these sold for $120.00 each]	
TimberRidge Pellet Stove	$1,076.00	Wood Stove Fireplace Insert Circulator NICE COND.!	$225.84
Reliant Industries Pellet Stove	$1,046.00	VERMONT CASTINGS Vigilant Woodburning Stove	$203.50
Vermont Castings Defiant Encore #2140 Wood Stove NR!	$1,020.00	Vermont Castings Intrepid II Catalytic Wood Stove	$203.50
WEATHERKING 120K BTU 90+ GAS UPFLOW FURNACE	$870.00	New~ 23" ELECTRIC FIREPLACE INSERT W/ REMOTE ~ Dimplex	$199.95
Corn Stove-Brand New Factory Second-PreTested!!SAVE$$NR	$845.22	High End Dual Blower Fireplace Insert Glass Door NEW NR	$199.00
Corn Stove-Brand New Factory Second-PreTested!!SAVE$$NR	$815.00	DAYTON PROPANE 30K UNIT HEATER	$199.00
NEW VERMONT CASTING VENT FREE	$800.00	Wood Burning Stove, New,	$195.00
GAS STOVE (1/2 NEW COST)		beckett af oil burner	$191.50
Corn Stove-Brand New Factory Second-PreTested!!SAVE$$NR	$731.22	BRAND NEW BECKETT OIL BURNER	$190.00

Home Decor ▸ Candles, Candle Holders

The average sales price in this subcategory is $6.66.

	HIGH		AVG
STERLING TIFFANY&CO CANDLE SNUFFER w/ wood handle NIB	$51.00	Stay On Top Candle Topper – HOME SWEET HOME	$8.00
100 Smokeless Candle Wick Dippers USA NR wire snuffer	$28.88	Home Interior Fresh Fruit Candle Capper *NEW*	$8.00
[2 of these sold for $28.88 each]		SONOMA CANDLE SHADE FRUIT home interior	$7.99
Stay on Top Candle Capper Topper Snuffer Farm BARNYARD	$26.00	Ornate Bronze Candle Snuffer NIB!	$7.99
Stay on Top Candle Capper Topper Snuffer Daisy DAISIES	$21.50	WILDFLOWER ROMANCE CANDLE SHADE home interior	$7.99
VINTAGE GORHAM STERLING SILVER CANDLE SNUFFER	$21.50	SONOMA CANDLE SHADE FRUIT home interior	$7.99
Old Virginia Candle Co. Candy Corn Witch & Cat Topper	$21.50	OLD VIRGINIA CANDLE CAPPER—SPRINGTIME ANIMAL	$7.99
PARTYLITE ENCHANTMENT SNUFFER	$20.50	Ornate Bronze Candle Snuffer NIB!	$7.99
Old Virginia Candle Company Wine & Private Reserve	$20.50	Candle Capper (S'topper) Bonnie	$7.99
85 Smokeless Candle Wick Dippers USA NR wire snuffer	$20.50	BRASS CANDLE SNUFFERS / NEW/ASSORTED DESIGNS	$7.98
Old Virginia Candle Company Pumpkin Almond & Scarecrow	$19.99	[2 of these sold in a multiple item ("Dutch") auction for $3.99 each]	
1800's SCISSORS CANDLE SNUFFER WICK TRIMMER	$19.00	Beautiful Jeweled Silver Look Candle Snuffer - NEW	$7.50
European Victorian Italian Brass Candle Snuffer	$17.50	MIKASA CANDLE SNUFFER - BRAND NEW	$7.49
VINTAGE CANDLE SNUFFER-IVY	$16.50	Wholesale 12 Americana Heart Candle Capper Lid Topper	$7.38
Partylite Paris Retro Pillar Tray	$16.23	Pewter BUTTERFLY Candle Snuffer w Crystals Butterflies	$6.95
STERLING SILVER CANDLE SNUFFER	$16.01	Pewter with Enamel Sun Moon & Stars Candle Snuffer	$6.95

Home Decor ▸ Photo Frame & Display

The average sales price in this subcategory is $10.32.

	HIGH		AVG
Sterling Silver Antique Vintage Picture Frame	$237.50	FISHING POLE PHOTO FRAME picture lures photograph rod	$11.99
VINTAGE SHELL FRAME, GREAT MIRROR FRAME, PICTURE FRAME	$37.50	24X30 Handcrafted Gold Leaf Picture Frame w/Liner	$11.09
Brand New Enameled Mike + Ally 3x3 Photo Frame	$35.00	LIBERTY OF LONDON PICTURE FRAME	$10.50
ROUND DAZZLING JEWELED PHOTO CROWN PRINCESS FRAME	$35.00	16 x 20 Antique Gold Leaf Black Wood Picture Frame	$10.50
VINTAGE ART DECO REVERSE PAINTED FOIL GEOMETRIC FRAME	$24.50	Classic Winnie the Pooh Matted Framed Picture 5 x 7	$10.50
LARGE ORNATE GOLD FINISH PICTURE FRAME	$21.05	Beautiful & Crystal Mikasa Frame (12 1/2 X 15)	$10.49
NEW BVLGARI BULGARI ROUND CRYSTAL PICTURE FRAME	$20.50	$299 Lot 11 Burnes of Boston Picture Photo Frames NR	$10.00
VINTAGE ART DECO REVERSE PAINTED FOIL FRAME	$17.05	PINK AND BLACK PICTURE FRAME POLKA DOTS AND DRESS	$9.99
SOUTHWEST KOKOPELLI PICTURE FRAME-BRAND NEW!	$17.01	Seagull Pewter frame - new - 3 1/2 x 5"- floral design	$9.99
LAUNDRY room rules home decor picture framed	$16.95	Your Dog's Name-Personalized Dog Bone Picture Frame 4x6	$9.99
Chippy Shabby Peely Picture Frame 5 x 7", Klein Roses~	$16.50	PICTURE FRAME 4X4 RND LION HEADS/RHINESTONES	$9.99
$230 Lot 11 Picture Photo Frames Burnes of Boston NR	$16.49	ANY SIZE WOOD FRAME, FRAMES up to 11x14 PINE	$9.99
16 x 20 Antique Gold Leaf Fine Art Picture Frame	$16.03	LOT OF 18 CUTE FUN PICTURE FRAMES AND FUZZY MIRROR	$9.95
Seagull Pewter frame - new in box - 4x6"	$15.50	Unusual ~8 x 30 Vintage Wooden Divided Picture Frame	$9.55

Home Decor ▸ Wall Décor

The average sales price in this subcategory is $6.89.

	HIGH		AVG
Cast Iron swiveled Round Hanging Wall / Door D?r	$47.00	NEW Sun Moon Star Celestial Cosmos Double Switch Plate	$7.98
LOT 8 ANTIQUE LOOKING WALL PLATES OUTLET/ SWITCH COVERS	$29.50	[2 of these sold in a multiple item ("Dutch") auction for $3.99 each]	
Lot 3 Shabby Vintage Style Rose Plate Outlet Cover Chic	$21.49	WIZARD OF OZ (set) light switch cover	$7.98
SHABBY HP ROSES DOUBLE SWITCH PLATE OUTLET COVER CHIC	$15.99	Raggedy Ann and Andy Outlet Cover on White set of 2	$7.49
CHILI PEPPER PEPPERS DOUBLE SWITCHPLATE COVER	$15.99	Rubber Ducky Duck SINGLE SWITCHPLATE Switch Plate Cover	$7.49
BALDWIN BRONZE 4752-112 CLASSIC	$15.50	Amerock Carriage House Antique Brass Outlet Plate	$7.00
DUPLEX OUTLET COVER LOT		Switchplate - Peter Max - Umbrella Man	$7.00
HELLO KITTY DOUBLE SWITCH PLATE COVER	$15.22	Eeyore Light Switch Cover Plate Cute DBL New design	$7.00
John Lennon light switch cover real love BABY newborn	$14.00	~THOMAS KINKADE~A NEW DAY DAWNING~JMBO SGL SWITCHPLATE~	$7.00
SOUTHWESTERN KOKOPELLI SGL LIGHT SWITCH PLATE	$12.99	Switchplate - Piter Max-Blushing Beauty	$7.00
Blue Jean Teddy Bear Outlet Cover Plate SET of 2	$12.00	BALLOONING OVER PARIS SWITCH PLATE COVER	$6.99
Horse Cowboy BOOT cactus SWITCHPLATE cover Outlet	$11.99	CURIOUS GEORGE PAINTS SWITCH PLATE COVER	$6.99
Hillary Duff light switch cover Lizzie McGuire	$11.58	Zebra Skin Print - Light Switch Plate Cover	$6.35
Amerock Carriage House Antique Brass Switch/Outle Plate	$11.00	Hillary Duff Lizzy McGuire Switchplate Switch Plate	$5.99
Amerock Carriage House Antique Brass Dual Switch Plate	$10.00	Baseball New York Yankees lightswitch cover	$5.99
OUTHOUSE redneck SWITCHPLATE COVER wall switch DOUBLE 1	$9.99	Twilight Zone Rod Serling lightswitch cover	$5.99

Home Security ▸ Security Systems

The median sales price in this subcategory is $12.95.

	HIGH		AVG
GE Simon 3 Alarm kits LOT OF 30 Brand New in Box	$3,249.00	Home Security Keypad Alarm System Window Door lock	$13.00
NEW 6kw SILENT DIESEL GENERATOR 6000 Watts 6 kw	$1,275.00	Lot of 10 ADT Home Security Stickers Decals Authentic	$12.99
ATS INCLUDED + Exclusive!! + NO RESERVE		Radionics D220AW Fixed Keypad NIB	$12.99
NEW 6kw SILENT DIESEL GENERATOR 6000 Watts 6 kw	$1,149.00	(ADEMCO) HONEYWELL MAGNETIC	$12.99
ATS INCLUDED + Exclusive!! + NO RESERVE		CONTACTS NEW	
OmniTouch Omni Touch 32A00-1 HAI Console New	$565.00	Lot of 10 ADT Home Security Stickers Decals Authentic	$12.99
F64 NEW GSM AUTODIAL WIRELESS BURGLAR & FIRE ALARM	$468.54	DRIVEWAY PATROL ALARM SYSTEM ~NEW~	$12.95
[3 of these sold for $468.54 each]		Ademco 5881L Wireless Reciever NIB	$12.95
F64 NEW GSM AUTODIAL WIRELESS BURGLAR & FIRE ALARM	$468.54	1,ADT,HOME,SECURITY,BURGLAR,	$12.50
[2 of these sold for $468.54 each]		ALARM,YARD,SIGN,&STICKERS	
Ademco 5816 wireless transmitters *LOT OF 25* 1.00 S/H	$459.99	ADEMCO VISTA 10 6128 NO RESERVE !!!!!!!	$12.50
[2 of these sold for $459.99 each]		DSC 2 Wire Smoke Detector.New In Box	$12.50
NORTHERN COMPUTERS N1000IV-X ACCESS CONTROL PANEL	$425.00	Computar VARI FOCAL 3.5 - 8MM F1.4 TV LENS New	$12.50

HONEYWELL ACCESS SYSTEMS
20 ADEMCO 5816 WIRELESS D/W TRANSMITTER WHITE LYNX $399.79
[2 of these sold for $399.79 each]
door lock home security system dead bolt keyless entry $369.95
NEVER GET LOCKED OUT AGAIN LOOK INSIDE!! LOOK INSIDE!!
NEW GSM AUTODIAL BURGLAR & FIRE ALARM WIRELESS+WIREFREE $366.17
10 sensors+4 remotes,Calls+Texts**Now Works Worldwide**
ESP INFINITE (complete wireless home alarm system) $359.23
SIMPLY THE BEST WIRELESS HOME SECURITY SYSTEM AND MORE!
7 Wireless Security Alarm System & 3 loud Strobe Sirens One of the best $347.06
systems on the market, comes complete!

Alarm Strobe! Alarm! Security Light! Burglar Alarm!	$12.50
ADT ademco 5804 4-button keyfob remote	$12.50
LOW TEMP CONTACT SWITCH SURF	$12.49
MT 40* ADEMCO VISTA LYNX	
X-10 Security PIR Motion Detector MS10A + BONUS	$12.49

Home Security ▶ Sensors, Motion Detectors

The median sales price in this subcategory is $14.99.

	HIGH		AVG
ADEMCO 5890PI WIRELESS MOTION DETECTOR QTY 5	$325.00	BOX OF 6 CORAL PLUS X INFARED DETECTORS AS A LOT	$15.00
ADEMCO 5816 WIRELESS CONTACTS QTY 10	$162.51	BRAND NEW INTELECTRON MOTION DETECTOR SECURITY LIGHT	$15.00
GE ITI WIRELESS MOTION SENSORS LOT OF 2 NEW	$142.49	PROTEC ELECTRONIC BURGLAR ALARM	$15.00
Hope/Zuni Mustard Sensual Lights Just For Volcano	$142.00	Safe-T-Alert Intruder Alarm RV/Motorcoach - Brand New!	$15.00
20 DSC Digital Bravo 3P Pet Immune-PIR Motion detectors	$122.50	Motion Sensor Singing Owl	$15.00
ADEMCO 998 PIR MOTION DETECTORS (lot of 10)	$107.50	FREE SHIPPING Heath/Zenith Motion Sensor Security Light	$15.00
LOT OF TWO ADEMCO 5890PI MOTION DETECTORS NEW	$105.51	New Alarm Driveway Sidewalk Patrol Alert System NR	$15.00
LOT OF 2 GE/ITI WIRELESS MOTION SENSOR DETECTORS -SIMON	$103.50	BOX OF 6 CORAL PLUS X INFARED DETECTORS AS A LOT	$15.00
ADEMCO 5890PI WIRELESS MOTION DETECTOR QTY 5	$100.00	Outdoor Motion Activated SURVEILLANCE light lantern wow	$14.99
LOT OF 2 GE/ITI WIRELESS MOTION SENSOR DETECTORS -SIMON	$100.00	SALE X10 3-PK DS10A SECURITY DOOR WINDOW SENSORS X-10	$14.99
ADEMCO 5890 MOTION DETECTORS (2) NEW	$92.00	[3 of these sold for $14.99 each]	
27 Home Security Sensors ShockTec RK600S00000A NIB *	$90.00	Heath Zenith Wireless Command Alert System NEW	$14.99
LOT OF 2 GE/ITI WIRELESS MOTION	$85.37	Heath/Zenith wireless motion sensor security light kit	$14.99
SENSOR DETECTORS -SIMON		GE/ITI Supervised Wireless Interior Siren Simon/Concord	$14.95
Ademco wireless motion detector 5890 (2) NEW alarm	$83.00	LOT OF 3 REGENT #MS180 Bronze Motion Sensor Replacement	$14.76
Ademco wireless motion detector 5890 (2) NEW alarm	$82.00	New Alarm Driveway Sidewalk Patrol Alert System NR	$14.75

Vacuum Cleaners & Housekeeping ▶ Cleaning Supplies

The average sales price in this subcategory is $10.62.

	HIGH		AVG
NUTONE DELUXE POWER NOZZLE CT-600-NEW	$134.95	Williams Sonoma LAVENDAR Liquid Dish Soap 16oz NEW!	$16.21
Eureka Bathroom Kitchen Steam Cleaner w/ FLOOR Tools	$57.00	BARE HARD FLOOR TOOL VACUUM CLEANER BRUSH ANY	$15.90
BISSELL	$50.00	[2 of these sold in a multiple item ("Dutch") auction for $7.90 each]	
Scunci Steamer Steam Cleaner No Reserve	$47.00	FLOWTHRU WATER FED BRUSH CAR WASH WINDOW CLEANING	$15.00
NEW Scunci Steamer w/bonuses LOW SHIPPING	$41.00	LUCASOL Tanning Bed Cleaner BUY IT NOW	$14.95
NEW!-Easy-Off Microwave Wipes -76520RC	$37.14	MUSTC BRAND NEW HANDY SPRAY BOTTLE-TOWEL HOLDER IN ONE!	$13.90
BRAND NEW STEAM BUGGY POWER STEAM CLEANER	$35.00	[2 of these sold in a multiple item ("Dutch") auction for $6.95 each]	
Smell Killer HGTV Deodorizer Ferret Cat Odor Remover NR	$34.95	~HUGE Lot of Potpourri ~ * 15 BAGS* Seasons, Int. NR	$13.50
Smell Killer HGTV Deodorizer Ferret Cat Odor Remover NR	$34.95	BLACK & DECKER SCUMBUSTER HARD TO FIND ACCESSORIES	$12.75
Carpet Cleaning Tool-Lift Buddy	$31.99	RoboMaid 48 PC Electrostatic Pad Set; RoboMaid Pads	$12.50
Smell Killer Classic HGTV Metal Disk Odor Deodorizer	$29.95	Smell Killer Shoe Foot Boot Odor Deodorizer Freshener	$11.95
Scunci Steamer Lk New In Box	$29.00	Professor Amos 25 piece Turbo Pad Cleaning Erasers New	$11.48
SHARK HAND HELD STEAMER Euro-pro brand new	$27.00	Giant Window Washer Set *2ND STORY* OUTDOOR CLEANING	$11.09
COMMERCIAL GRADE LARGE RUBBERMAID MOP BUCKET	$26.00	BLACK & DECKER SCUMBUSTER - JUMBO 14 PIECE SET!	$11.06
Eureka Enviro Steam Cleaner - Hot Shot	$26.00	UV CLEAN HOME URINE CLEANING SUPPLIES PET Dog Cat	$11.06
NEW DYSON DC14 ANIMAL WAND AND HANDLE PART	$24.99	Deluxe Window Washer Set In Original Box - No Reserve!	$11.01
		Fuller Brush 27-1/2" Dryer Vent Cleaning Brush	$11.00

Vacuum Cleaners & Housekeeping ▶ Home Organization

The average sales price in this subcategory is $17.32.

	HIGH		AVG
2-Die-4 1940s Wood Brunswick Bowling Lockers	$305.00	New 12 Pack CLEAR PLASTIC Shoe Box STORAGE BINS w/ Lids	$20.95
2 ProStor HeavyLift Garage Overhead Storage Racks (NEW)	$265.00	10 Drawer Rolling Cart Storage Organizer NEW	$20.55
2 ProStor HeavyLift Garage Overhead Storage Racks (NEW)	$240.50	JOY MANGANO HUGGABLE HANGERS DUST	$20.50
POTTERY BARN DAILY SYSTEM ORGANIZER 5 units, WHITE	$177.50	COVERS NEW NR 24PC MV	
Rowenta DG-580 DG580 Steam Generator Iron Irons 1745W	$149.99	JOY MANGANO HUGGABLE HANGER DUST COVERS MAUVE	$20.00
POTTERY BARN DAILY SYSTEM ORGANIZER 4 units, WHITE	$117.50	THE STYLESTATION PERSONAL ORGANIZER	$19.99
ProStor Heavy Lift Garage Overhead Storage Rack (NEW)	$110.00	Storage Organizer - 20 Pair Shoe Rack - Lynk	$19.99
ProStor Heavy Lift Garage Overhead Storage Rack (NEW)	$99.50	IKEA 3 Drawer file/storage chest!! NEW!! "ALVE"	$19.99
8 Brand New Space Bags, Extra Large Size 26.5" X 39.5"	$52.55	JOY MANGANO HUGGABLE HANGERS CLIPS & HOOKS - MAUVE	$19.99
overhead garage CEILING STORAGE SHELF shelves rack!	$52.22	4 Space Saving Storage Bags -Vacuum Seal Bag! +Bonus!	$19.99
Pottery Barn Multistripe Canvas Totes Set/2 NEW	$49.95	6 Quilted Zippered Covers for China Dishes * he2	$19.50
Pottery Barn MULTISTRIPE Canvas Tote/2 TOTES Large ~NIB	$47.99	CLOTHING RACK LAUNDRY IRONING	$19.04
[2 of these sold for $47.99 each]		CAMPING EQUIPMENT RV	
Pottery Barn MULTISTRIPE Canvas Tote/2 TOTES Large ~NIB	$47.99	4 IKEA CD DVD STORAGE BOXES LEATHER L@@KING- BLACK	$18.50
POTTERY BARN DAILY SYSTEM ORGANIZER CALENDAR, BLACK	$41.00	Chrome Laundry Kitchen Cart Wheels Two Shelf Home	$17.99
NEW 5 DRAWER ORGANIZER AND STORAGE UNIT	$40.00	JOY MANGANO 24 HUGGABLE HANGERS DUST COVERS - MAUVE	$17.02
[2 of these sold for $40.00 each]		Overhead Rack - No Reserve Auction - .01 Start	$17.01

Vacuum Cleaners & Housekeeping ▸ Vacuum Cleaners

The average sales price in this subcategory is $126.84.

	HIGH		AVG
HYLA NST VACUUMM MINT 5 YAER WARRANTY!!	$898.00	HOOVER VACUUM S3646-020 CANISTER	$154.99
Miele Red velvet vacuum cleaner like new with book	$798.00	FILTER QUEEN CANISTER VACUUM CLEANER 70 ANNIVERSARY ED	$150.27
BIG POWER 6 SPD 6YR WRNTY L/ RAINBOW VACUUM	$678.00	Kenmore Progressive Canister Vacuum 23812/23813	$144.49
Filter Queen Majestic Vacuum Cleaner 360 + Defender 360	$630.00	HOOVER S3641 WIND TUNNEL CANISTER VACUUM	$142.50
Dyson DC11 canister vacuum NEW Full Gear	$625.00	Tri Star Tristar Vacuum Very Nice Clean Condition SAVE	$139.99
[2 of these sold for $625.00 each]		White Kenmore Progressive Canister Vacuum 25614/25615	$137.50
One Month Used Filter Queen 360 magestic vacuum w/atach	$599.00	Hoover S3755 WindTunnel Bagless Hepa Canister Vacuum NR	$133.50
FILTER QUEEN 75 -04 VACUUM L-NEWnBOX DEMO SAMEas 360	$599.00	NEW IN BOX Shop-Vac? Professional Wet/Dry Vac	$130.00
Famous HYLA NST w/accessories, Very Nice, No Reserve	$590.00	COMPACT TRI STAR VORTECH VACUUM	$129.99
Dyson DC11 All Floors Brand new canister model	$575.00	CLEANER MINT POWERHEAD	$129.99
KIRBY ULTIMATE "G" DIAMOND EDITION	$550.00	Brand New !!! Hoover L2310 Garage Vacuum	$129.99
FILTER QUEEN MAJESTIC 360 VACUUM-3 MOS. OLD!	$549.00	EUREKA CANISTER VACUUM 6982D W/POWER HEAD	$129.99
MIELE S514i Solaris Turbo Plus Vacuum Cleaner	$511.00	Brand New !!! Hoover L2310 Garage Vacuum	$129.99
FILTER QUEEN MAJESTIC "LE" VACUUM ELECTROLUX 5 YR WRNTY	$488.00	KENMORE PROGRESSIVE CANISTER VACUUM, #1 RATED	$129.00
MIELE CANISTER VACUUM S514 + STB TURBO BRUSH LIGHT BLUE	$479.00	Vintage 1950s Style Aqua Airway Air Way Vacuum Cleaner	$128.95
TRISTAR TRI STAR EXL -02 VACUUM SAMEas MG2 FACTORYBOX!	$475.00	KENMORE 25513 CANISTER VACUUM POWERMATE LNIB	$127.54

Kitchen ▸ Cookware & Bakeware

The average sales price in this subcategory is $12.60.

	HIGH		AVG
PINK Enamel Kitchen ROASTER PAN (Kitchenaid look alike)	$141.09	ALPHABET cookie cutters SET LARGE NEW	$14.99
Corning Ware 10 Pc. Harvest Range Topper Set with Lids	$98.77	Pampered Chef Deep Dish Baker- Hunter Green NIB	$14.99
WEAREVER COOKIE SHEET NONSTICK AIRBAKE lot 9	$56.55	Pampered Chef Stoneware Loaf Pan * NEW/NR *	$14.50
Arepa Maker Oster Family Size South America style	$46.01	CORNING WARE CORNFLOWER 10X10 HIGH DONE HARD TO FIND	$14.50
CHANTAL BAKEWARE KITCHENAID PINK MIXING BATTER BOWLS	$44.99	NEW Le Creuset 9 1/4" Square Baking Dish Pan Cherry Red	$13.99
Pyrex Daisy & Butterfly Nesting Bowls - Set of 4	$36.00	SONOMA Le Creuset CitrusYelow 10.5x7 RECTANGULAR BAKER	$13.95
LE CREUSET Heart 2.5 Quart Covered Baking Dish! NIB!!	$35.00	BAKE AND SERV stainless steel Au-Gratin Dishes SET 6	$13.51
WILLIAMS-SONOMA LE CREUSET FLAME RECTANGULAR BAKER	$35.00	Set / 2 Exopat Silicone Baking Liners LIKE Silpat 12X17	$13.38
5 AirBake 15-1/2" X 20" Mega Baking Sheets NEW!	$32.00	New In Box Pampered Chef Deep Dish Pie Plate Cranberry	$13.03
PANS: VILLAWARE STAINLESS ROASTING	$29.60	Pampered Chef Stackable Cooling Rack - (NIB)	$13.00
LASAGNA PAN w/ rack		Set of 3 10'x14' stackable Cooling Racks – NIP	$13.00
RARE! CORNING WARE CORNFLOWER 6PC CUTLERY W/RACK	$28.50	[2 of these sold in a multiple item ("Dutch") auction for $6.50 each]	
ROMERTOPF CLAY POT TERRA COTTA #110 2-3LBS	$27.95	Pampered Chef ~ PINK QUICK STIR PITCHER ~ NIB	$13.00
2 NEW MADELEINE/MADELAINE PANS/MOLDS MADELINE	$27.01	NIB - SET of 6 Round Porcelain Ramekins - Custard Cups	$12.99
Williams-Sonoma Big Red Pottery Bread Warmer Basket	$26.99	NIB Cuisinart Ramekins 5OZ - Creme Brulee Set of 4 RED	$12.99
6 LARGE Teflon Non Stick Baking Mats Oven or Pan Liners	$26.00	Pampered Chef Baking Bowl Dish Pan	$12.72

Kitchen ▸ Small Kitchen Appliances

The average sales price in this subcategory is $44.90.

	HIGH		AVG
Blendtec Space Saver	$515.54	NEW IN BOX CUISINART CHROME	$50.75
[2 of these sold in a multiple item ("Dutch") auction for $257.77 each]		DUET BLENDER/FOOD PROCESSOR	
Vita-Mix Super 5000 w/all contents	$411.00	KitchenAid Custom Metallic 5 Speed Ultra Power KSB5NK	$50.00
Vita-Mix/Vitamix 5000 total nutrition center blender	$369.99	KitchenAid Ultra-Power 5-Speed Blender KSB5MY	$50.00
K-Tec Champ hp3 KTec 3 horsepower blender FREE SHIPPING	$330.00	NEW ! Hamilton Beach Commercial Bar Blender Model 901	$49.99
Brand New K-Tec HP3 Champ Blender KTEC	$330.00	Villaware Smoothie Machine Maker NIB NR not refurbished	$49.00
[2 of these sold for $330.00 each]		~New DELUXE Magic Bullet FAST SHIP @MoneyBack Guarantee	$48.95
Vitamix Vita-mix Turbo Blender Never Used 4500 Gourmet	$305.00	~NEW~DELUXE~ Magic Bullet Blender Processor FAST SHIP	$48.95
NEW!! Waring MX1000R Professional 3-Horsepower Blender	$290.00	New DUO SMOOTHIE MAKER Blender & Two Bonus Containers	$47.90
Vita-Mix Power Turbo Blender 4500 BRAND NEW Sealed	$288.00	[2 of these sold for $47.90 each]	
[2 of these sold for $288.00 each]		NEW!!! Braun MX2050 PowerMax Jug Blender	$47.01
Brand New Vitamix 4500 Turbo Blender Vita-mix w/ Extras	$284.99	~NEW~DELUXE~ Magic Bullet Blender Processor FAST SHIP	$46.99
Vita-Mix 5000 Total Nutrition Center Vitamix &recipe bk	$282.00	KitchenAid ultra 5 speed blender, retails for over $120	$46.89
NEW! Vita-Mix 1300 TurboBlend 4500 Blender NO RES!	$275.00	NEW!!! Braun MX2050 PowerMax Jug Blender	$46.00
VITA-MIX MAXI 4000 COMPLETE VITAMIX VITAMIXER-EXCELLENT	$270.00	Magic Bullet Blender	$45.00
Brand New Vitamix 4500 Turbo Blender Vita-mix w/ Extras	$269.99	Delux MAGIC BULLET Blender/Juicer NIB 21 PC SET New	$45.00

Kitchen ▸ Tools & Gadgets

The average sales price in this subcategory is $18.26.

	HIGH		AVG
TOMATO FOOD MILL SQUEEZO STRAINER 1991 Linmar Int.	$120.77	GARDEN WAY SQUEEZO STRAINER - Model 400TS	$31.00
SQUEEZO II ALL METAL STRAINER w/ 3 SCREENS GARDEN WAY	$112.50	3 1/2 QUART FOOD MILL*NIB*	$30.99
SQUEEZO II All Metal Strainer w/ 3 Screens Garden Way	$107.10	3 1/2 QUART FOOD MILL*NIB*	$29.99
Garden Way Squeezo, All Metal, 3 screens	$101.99	VITANTONIO VICTORIO FOOD MILL / TOMATO STRAINER # 200	$29.00
ORIGINAL ALL-METAL 3 SCREEN SQUEEZO STRAINER BRAND NEW	$100.95	FOOD STRAINER AND SAUCE MAKER	$28.50
STRAINER BRAND NEW		NORPRO JUICEMATE,VEGETABLE&FRUIT STRAINER...NIB	$28.50
LEMRA ALL METAL SQUEEZO STRAINER - FOOD MILL	$96.00	Pampered Chef Colander and Bowl Set with Lids New	$26.00
Squeezo Strainer by Garden Way , All-metal, 3 screens	$91.00	Wearever Conical Strainer Sieve Chinois w/Stand,Pestle	$26.00
ROSLE Stainless Steel Food Mill with 3mm Sieve Disc	$83.00	New Foley Food Mill Colander Strainer Stainless Steel	$25.49
Garden Way's Squeezo Strainer 3 Screens All Metal	$68.26	FOLEY FOOD MILL SIEVE CANNING # 101 LIKE NEW NO RUST	$24.50
Victorio Food Strainer 200 Berry/Tomato/Pumpkin Juicer	$63.00	COLANDER STAINLESS STEEL 5 QT COLANDERS BRAND NEW	$22.00
Squeezo Plus with 3 Screens Not Complete	$60.00	[4 of these sold in a multiple item ("Dutch") auction for $5.50 each]	
Williams Sonoma CHINOIS, PESTLE & STAND Brand NEW	$59.99	$90 Housewerks Stainless Steel Colander 3-piece Set NR	$20.70

	HIGH		AVG
~ GARDEN WAY ALL METAL SQUEEZO II JUICER STRAINER NIB ~	$59.99	COLANDER 5 QUART STAINLESS STEEL 0-8mm*NIB*	$20.50
SQUEEZO TOMATO STRAINER - ALL METAL - SUPER	$58.00	NWT KITCHENAID COLANDER KITCHEN AID STRAINER RED	$20.50
WILLIAMS-SONOMA MAUVIEL COPPER COLANDER (NEW	$54.99	Oxo Good Grips Salad Spinner - BRAND NEW IN BOX	$19.54

Lamps, Lighting, Ceiling Fans ▶ Chandeliers

The average sales price in this subcategory is $146.81.

	HIGH		AVG
REAL ANTLER MULE DEER CHANDELIER BY CDN 28"x25"	$990.00	8lt Crystal Chandelier see Photo * Teardrop Crystals !*	$199.95
CHANDELIER CRYSTAL LIGHTING CHANDELIERS 46X52	$849.00	8lt French Crystal Chandelier Lighting New!!	$199.95
1960'S SCIOLARI CHROME & LUCITE CHANDELIER 15 BULBS	$665.00	Whitetail ANTLER Chandelier log Furniture cabin hunting	$199.00
MONTH SPECIAL ANTLER CHANDELIER BY CDN	$572.00	[2 of these sold for $199.00 each]	
large victorian hand carved candle stick chandelier	$500.00	Hall & Foyer La Serena Large Cage Chandelier	$179.99
CHANDELIER U DROPS CHANDELIERS WATERFALL	$497.00	Hall & Foyer La Serena Large Cage Chandelier	$179.99
ANTIQUE 29"W BRONZE 8 ARM	$450.00	ORNATE 12 Light Chandelier OLDE WORLD Sovereign GOLD	$178.27
CHANDELIER W/CRYSTAL PRISMS		Vintage Glass Chandelier Floral Design fixture	$170.00
MULE DEER ANTLER CHANDELIER BY CDN 38x20 CAST	$448.00	HUGE NEW BRASS CHANDELIER BEAUTIFUL NEVER USED	$159.00
Fantastic French Brass & Crystal Chandelier Bronze Lamp	$440.00	Brass and crystal Basket chandelier light fixtures NR	$158.45
EXQUISITE PINEAPPLE Antique French Brass Chandelier	$425.00	Brass and crystal Basket chandelier light fixtures NR	$157.50
MULE DEER ANTLER CHANDELIER MADE FROM REAL ANTLERS	$405.00	Vintage 8 Light Chandelier Crystal Baroque Star Prisms	$154.50
30 % lead crystal chandelier,Retail $1900.00 NR	$399.99	5L MURANO VENETIAN style CRYSTAL CHANDELIER NR	$145.06
Vintage Dainty Sliverado Cherub chandelier	$395.00	Antique Bronze French Chandelier 6LT	$140.00
Rare Vintage New Orleans Crystal and Brass Chandelier	$381.00	KALCO LIGHTING PALM/WICKER 9 LT CHANDELIER LIGHT FIXTUR	$122.50
Real Whitetail Shed Antler Chandelier (antlers elk)	$378.33	Old Brass & Crystal Chandelier 8 Lights	$113.50

Lamps, Lighting, Ceiling Fans ▶ Ceiling Fans

The average sales price in this subcategory is $58.88.

	HIGH		AVG
Casablanca Stealth ceiling fan, top of line motor	$355.01	HUNTER 52" Ceiling Fan w/ Light & REMOTE WHITE HR 21526	$69.99
Ellington Palladin Ceiling Fan, 56" Bronze, Beautiful	$339.00	New OHIO STATE BUCKEYES FOOTBALL Ceiling Fan 42"	$68.00
Minka Aire F529-BS/CH Special Edition	$305.00	HUNTER 44" CEILING FAN W/3 LIGHTS WHITE HR 20466	$68.00
Gyro Ceiling Fan Minka Aire Nickel Restoration Hardware	$300.00	Palm Frond Ceiling Fan Blades Burl 15" Blade Set	$68.00
Woodland 52" Ceiling Fan-With Antler Chandelier	$285.00	New Hunter Ceiling Fan 52" Belle Meade Weathered Bronze	$68.00
Minka Aire Gyro Ceiling Fan with Light	$256.00	NICOR 52" CEILING FAN INDOOR OUTDOOR LITE KIT INLCLUDED	$68.00
MINKA AIRE FLYTE f-531 brushed nickel maple blades	$250.00	HUNTER 52" Ceiling Fan w/ Light ANTIQUE PEWTER HR 21545	$67.99
Antique Vintage Robbins Myers Ceiling Fan Old	$213.61	HUNTER 52" Ceiling Fan OUTDOOR ALUMINUM HR 23577	$67.00
NEW AND SEALED MINKA AIRE ACERO	$209.95	HUNTER 52" Ceiling Fan OUTDOOR ALUMINUM HR 23577	$66.99
FAN MODEL F601-BS/BN		BRAND NEW HAMPTON BAY INDUSTRIAL CEILING FAN 60" WHITE	$66.20
2 Tier Ceiling Fan! Craftmade Twin Air Brand New Rustic	$181.50	New Hunter Ceiling Fan 52" Brunswick - Antique Brass	$65.00
Casablanca Ceiling Fan Santorini Oil Rubbed Bronze	$179.00	New Hunter Ceiling Fan 52" Dominion - French Vanilla	$65.00
Emerson Odyssey Ceiling Fan Maple Blades	$168.05	New Hunter Ceiling Fan 52" Brunswick - Antique Brass	$65.00
Tropical Ceiling Fan Palm Leaf Design Blades Islander	$152.50	Mickey & Minnie Mouse ceiling fan and light NIB	$62.00
Seagull Long Beach Bronze Finish INDOOR/OUTDOOR 52" Fan	$136.32	PALM /BANANA LEAF PASTEL CEILING FAN BLADES (5)	$59.99

Lamps, Lighting, Ceiling Fans ▶ Table Lamps

The average sales price in this subcategory is $27.57.

	HIGH		AVG
Waterford Lamp 18" Tall Never Used Perfect	$162.50	ROCK SALT CRYSTAL LAMP ~	$39.99
Solid Brass Whimsical Frog Lamp Rare	$95.00	16-22 LBS ~ NATURAL IONIZER	
2 Nickel and Cherry Contemporary Table Lamps - NIB	$90.00	TOY STORY SPINNING LAMP- RARE	$36.00
DISNEY MICKEY MOUSE Wooden Shelf NEW	$90.00	LICENSED OHIO STATE BUCKEYES TOUCH LAMP	$36.00
[6 of these sold in a multiple item ("Dutch") auction for $15.00 each]		Cleveland Indians TOUCH LAMP (CUSTOM)	$35.99
NEW - Mission Style Tiffany Table Lamp	$79.00	Pair of Cambridge 36" Swirl Urn Table Lamps with Shade	$34.33
NEW - Quoizel Tiffany Dragonfly Table Lamp	$79.00	JOSE CUERVO TABLE LAMP	$33.00
Pottery Barn Kids AIRPLANE LAMP New In Box	$69.99	Set of 2 "Orient Express" Brass Lamps	$30.00
Ott-Lite Lexington Series 118Y42 Captiva Table Lamp New	$69.00	3PC AGED IRON LAMPS FLOOR LAMP	$30.00
DISNEY MICKEY MOUSE Wooden Shelf NEW	$60.00	TABLE LIGHTS NEW	
[4 of these sold in a multiple item ("Dutch") auction for $15.00 each]		DISNEY EEYORE Lavender Lamp NEW	$29.99
DISNEY TINKER BELL Garden Lamp NEW	$60.00	Teen/Girl's/Tween/Dorm Acrylic Lamp & Night Light Pink	$27.97
[2 of these sold in a multiple item ("Dutch") auction for $30.00 each]		Brass Candlestick Table Lamp with Off White Linen Shade	$27.00
STUNNING SHABBY~RACHEL ASHWELL ROSES BOUDOIR LAMP~CHIC	$59.89	EGYPTIAN - Egypt King's Throne *Gorgeous Golden*	$26.95
TABLE LAMPS: 2 NEW Antique Look Lamp/Shade $160/NR	$56.95	Lamps-BEAUTIF Antique Baroque	$26.50
ROCK SALT CRYSTAL LAMP ~ 16-22 LBS ~ NATURAL IONIZER	$53.11	Gold Style Table Lamp NEW	
Paper Hat Table Lamp, Isamu Noguchi, 1950s	$51.29	Metal Eiffel Tower Lamp	$26.03
BRAND NEW DISNEY PRINCESS ANIMATED TALKING LAMP	$51.00	Touch Lamp 24 inch Jimmie Johnson # 48	$26.00

Major Appliances ▶ Ranges, Cooking Appliances

The average sales price in this subcategory is $278.93.

	HIGH		AVG
Wolf 48" Dual Fuel Range	$7,900.00	Italian Style 30" Stainless Steel Range Hood 198B2-30	$389.95
AGA Cooker Stove	$5,200.00	NEW! VIKING DEV900 EXTERIOR VENTILATOR 900CFM	$388.00
Stainless Steel Kitchen with double wall oven, #1	$2,500.00	NEW! DACOR 30" BLACK WARMING DRAWER OVEN PWO30B	$367.00
30" Kitchenaid Combo Microwave/Convection Oven in S/S	$2,100.00	NEW! DACOR REMP3 1000 CFM REMOTE BLOWER	$364.00
36" SS Moon Crystal ISLAND Range Hood, MADE IN ITALY!	$1,295.00	NEW! GE MONOGRAM 27" BLACK WARMING DRAWER OVEN	$363.00
[3 of these sold for $1,295.00 each]		BOSCH GAS COOKTOP 5 BURNER	$350.00
36" Jenn-Air electric ceramic cooktop JEC0536ADS	$1,151.08	SHOWROOM MODEL NHT922A	

- JENN-AIR STAINLESS STEEL SINGLE WALL OVEN -	$1,026.50	36 Inch White Glass Gas Cooktop 5 Burners New	$349.95
36" GLASS - ISLAND RANGE HOOD. Chimney - Vent Stove.	$950.00	KENMORE 30" PROFESSIONAL STAINLESS RANGE HOOD 57800	$325.00
36" GLASS- ISLAND Range Chimney Vent Stove Hood	$935.00	IWATANI INDUCTION COMMERCIAL COOKER MODEL-US 9000	$300.01
36" GLASS- ISLAND Range Chimney Vent Stove Hood	$925.00	36 Inch White Glass Gas Cooktop 5 Burners New	$299.95
36" GLASS- ISLAND KITCHEN RANGE HOOD, GLA-090, 900cfm	$921.00	New Jenn Air Cartridge A122B/JEA8120ADB w/ FREE SHIP!	$297.99
36" ISLAND-GLASS, HOOD RANGE, LA-90 CVD ISL	$920.00	KENMORE 30" PROFESSIONAL STAINLESS RANGE HOOD 57800	$294.00
36" GLASS - ISLAND RANGE HOOD, GLA-090, 900cfm	$900.00	NEW WHITE JENN AIR RADIANT ELEMENT CARTRIDGE JEA8120ADW	$284.95
36 S.Steel, Island Range Hood "OCTAGONAL"	$875.00	NEW BLACK JENN AIR RADIANT ELEMENT CARTRIDGE JEA8120ADB	$284.95
36 S.Steel Kitchen, Island Range Hood "OCTAGONAL"	$850.00	KITCHENAID 15" ELECTRIC COOKTOP BLACK KECC051HWH BNIB	$283.89

Major Appliances ▸ Dishwashers

The average sales price in this subcategory is $184.26.

	HIGH		AVG
Fisher Paykel Double Dishdrawer Stainless Dishwasher	$1,429.00	New Frigidaire Stainless Steel w black Dishwasher #837	$300.95
Gaggenau Dishwasher Stainless Interior NO Reserve	$930.00	EQUATOR'S 72 SERIES FULL-SIZE REFURB DISHWASHERS- WHITE	$299.95
Dishwasher - KitchenAid KUDS01FLSS New in original box	$925.00	18" Built - in Dishwasher Frigidaire Model FDR251 NEW	$266.67
New Thermador Stainless Steel Curved Handle Dishwasher	$899.00	Kitchen Aid KUDS01DJ Stainless Steel Dishwasher NICE!	$255.00
New Thermador Stainless Steel Curved Handle Dishwasher	$849.00	FISHER & PAYKEL Single Dishdrawer Black Dishwasher	$251.50
NEW~JENN-AIR PRO-STYLE DISHWASHER MODEL JDB2150AWP	$835.00	NEW Bosch SHU33A02 White 24" Dishwasher 3-Cycle QUIET	$250.00
Dishwasher - KitchenAid KUDS01DJSS New in original box	$776.00	Eurotech by ASKO EDW174E White 24" Dishwasher Warranty	$249.00
GE MONOGRAM INTEGRATED STAINLESS DISHWASHER@ $1 RESERVE	$760.00	Frigidaire FDB510LCS 24" Built-In Dishwasher White	$245.59
NEW! BOSCH DISHWASHER STAINLESS SHX46L05UC	$759.00	Brand New NIB High Quality EQUATOR compact dishwasher	$227.51
NEW! BOSCH DISHWASHER STAINLESS SHX46L05UC	$749.00	Brand New NIB High Quality EQUATOR compact dishwasher	$225.00
Bosch Fully Integrated Dishwasher Stainless Interior	$710.00	Eurotech by ASKO EDW174E Black 24" Dishwasher	$224.72
Miele Touchtronic Dishwasher - Great condition	$700.00	24" UltraWash QuietGuard 3 Stainless Steel Dishwasher	$222.50
NEW 24" Stainless Inside&Out BOSCH Dishwasher NO RESERV	$695.00	KENMORE 24" PORTABLE DISHWASHER - LIKE NEW!	$203.51
Fisher & Paykel in Dishwasher	$635.00	Kenmore Portable Dishwasher with Wood Counter Top	$202.50
New Bosch Integra White Dishwasher Stainless Interior	$629.99	New Kenmore Black Dishwasher w/ Adjust. Racks #865	$202.50

Major Appliances ▸ Refrigerators, Freezers

The average sales price in this subcategory is $181.53.

	HIGH		AVG
Sub Zero 632 Side By Side Classic Stainless Steel	$5,500.00	MICROFRIDGE Refrigerator & Microwave combo LOW PRICE!!!	$236.00
NORCOLD mod. 1082 Propane Refrigerator - Freezer	$886.54	MICROFRIDGE Refrigerator & Microwave combo FOR COLLEGE	$227.50
Danby Propane Gas Refrigerator 7.8 c.f.	$869.00	MICROFRIDGE FOR COLLEGE Refrigerator & Microwave combo	$227.50
Frigidaire GLRT188WDS Top Mount Stainless Refrigerator	$809.00	MICROFRIDGE Refrigerator & Microwave combo LOW PRICE!!!	$227.50
Frigidaire GLRT212IDW Top Mount Refrigerator White	$539.00	KENMORE 18 cu.ft. Top Freezer Refrigerator w/ Ice Maker	$225.00
Frigidaire FRT21HS6DQ Top Mount Refrigerator Bisque	$529.00	Whirlpool Custrom Series Refrigerator Almond NICE!	$207.50
Frigidaire FRT18IS6CB Top Mount Refrigerator Black	$469.00	MICROFRIDGE Refrigerator & Microwave	$207.00
Kenmore Refrigerator White in "like New" condition	$449.00	combo FOR COLLEGE	
BRAND NEW MICROFRIDGE FREE SHIP* with "buy it now"	$425.00	Ge FRIDGE REFRIDGERATOR White, 59x27x23 Near new	$203.51
[5 of these sold for $425.00 each]		MICROFRIDGE Refrigerator & Microwave	$202.50
BRAND NEW MICROFRIDGE FREE SHIP* with "buy it now"	$415.00	combo FOR COLLEGE	
[5 of these sold for $415.00 each]		FRIGIDAIRE REFRIGERATOR W/ FREEZER ON TOP NEW $800	$201.50
AMANA Stainless Steel Refrigerator Bottom Freezer 21.9'	$405.00	New Frigidair refrigerator under manufacturers warranty	$200.00
BRAND NEW MICROFRIDGE FREE SHIP* with "buy it now"	$401.00	Refrigerator	$200.00
BRAND NEW MICROFRIDGE FREE SHIP* with "buy it now" NR	$397.50	MICROFRIDGE-fridge, freezer, & microwave. FOR COLLEGE!!	$200.00
BRAND NEW MICROFRIDGE FREE SHIP* with "buy it now"	$390.00	Vintage Kelvinator Refridgerator Red Works Like New	$185.00
BRAND NEW MICROFRIDGE FREE SHIP* with "buy it now"	$385.00	Maytag refrigerator in great used condition- CLEAN!	$182.70

Major Appliances ▸ Washers, Dryer

The average sales price in this subcategory is $24.48.

	HIGH		AVG
maytag fruit jar casting parts(not finished)	$310.89	OVER 2000 APPLIANCE REPAIR AND PARTS LIST MICRO FILM	$33.86
Maytag Neptune Electric Dryer - 3 Years New!	$275.00	WHIRLPOOL WASHER TIMER 3351744	$33.01
Whirlpool Duet Stand/Pedestal Pair New	$152.50	INVENSYS FSB NEW IN BOX	$31.01
Filtrol 160 Septic System Lint Filter as seen on TV	$125.00	MAYTAG NEPTUNE WASHER CIRCUIT BOARD MAH3000	$31.01
WHIRLPOOL DUET WASHER/DRYER	$112.29	Maytag Washer Stem & Boot Seal Repair Kit 22204012	$30.05
STAND/PEDESTAL PAIR NEW		Maytag Washing Machine Motor # S68PXMAJ-1012	$30.00
Kenmore Elite White HE3 Pedestal 42842	$107.50	Kenmore 46062 White 12 in. Laundry Pedestal	$29.99
Kenmore Elite White HE3 Pedestal 42842	$104.50	Center Seal and Tub Bearing Kit	$29.95
Maytag Neptune Conversion Kit 12002039	$102.50	Center Seal and Tub Bearing Kit	$29.95
Maytag Neptune Front Loader Washer Motor Rework Kit	$96.00	new rod for a 1/2 horse upright maytag	$29.00
Kenmore, Whirlpool, circuit board 8546229	$89.99	MAYTAG NEPTUNE WASHER CIRCUIT BOARD MAH4000AWW	$27.50
MAYTAG NEPTUNE MachineControl Board MAH4000	$85.00	Antique Manual Hand Crank Universal Clothes Wringer	$26.00
$180 BRANDNAME WHITE ELITE HE3 WASHER DRYER PEDESTAL	$82.00	Antique Washing Machine Wringer, Bicycle No. 740, NICE!	$26.00
MAYTAG NEPTUNE WASHER CONTROL BOARD. NEW!	$80.00	New Whirlpool Kenmore Dryer Timer Switch 3976569N	$25.00
HE4 Pedestal, Graphite for washing machine /dryer	$79.99	Whirlpool Kenmore DRYER MOTOR #279827	$24.99
[2 of these sold for $79.99 each]		WASHER TIMER KENMORE RECYCLED PART 3951166	$24.95

Outdoor Power Equipment ▸ Chainsaws

The average sales price in this subcategory is $58.80.

	HIGH		AVG
STIHL MS 880 MAGNUM VERY VERY NICE	$990.00	Husqvarna 51 Parts or Repair	$67.66
New Oregon 511-A Chain Saw Sharpener / Grinder	$780.00	Sears Craftsman Chain Saw, 18" Bar, Fine Cond.	$66.56

[3 of these sold in a multiple item ("Dutch") auction for $260.00 each]	
STIHL 088 MAGNUM CHAINSAW 36" STIHL BAR MS880	$630.00
*New * Stihl 044 chainsaw with 20" bar & chain	$502.50
STIHL 044 MAGNUM CHAINSAW	$475.00
STIHL 038AV SUPER PRO CHAINSAW MAGNUM CLEAN & POWERFUL	$375.00
STIHL MS-260 18" CHAIN SAW (NEVER USED OR GASSED)	$356.98
Antique Chain Saw – Mall Model 12A with Bow Bar	$345.00
Stihl MS 200 chainsaw w/14" bar & chain	$330.00
Stihl 066 magnum, run nice-sthil -chainsaw	$315.00
IEL Super Pioneer 52 Chainsaw Chain Saw 50's Vintage	$308.33
394 HUSQVARNA CHAINSAWS	$256.00
Stihl 029 Farm Boss Chainsaw 24" chain and bar	$230.00
VINTAGE REMINGTON SUPER 660 CHAINSAW OLD USED	$224.72
NEW PRO MAC 700 GAS CHAINSAW	$214.53

Poulan 2375 WILDTHING 18" Chainsaw 30 day warranty	$65.00
Poulan WILDTHING 18" 42cc Chainsaw 30 DAY WARRANTY.	$65.00
POULON 306 CHAIN SAW WITH 24 INCH BAR	$64.00
Jonsered 52 E OLD Chainsaw Collectable Vintage NR!! saw	$63.57
Craftsman 18 in. 42cc Gas Chain Saw Red	$63.00
ELECTRIC CHAIN SAW SHARPENER 13303	$63.00
CRAFTSMAN 20" / 46cc Gas Chainsaw	$62.26
Partner P70 Chainsaw Chain Saw— NICE RUNNING SAW!!	$62.00
john deere	$61.88
Early Clinton D35 6 HP Gas Chain Saw w 21" Bar	$61.03
CRAFTSMAN 18" GASOLINE CHAINSAW	$61.00
40cc GAS CHAIN SAW	$60.00
STIHL CHAINSAW PARTS MS290 CYLINDER PISTON CRANK	$60.00
Stihl Chainsaw Model 026 Pro	$59.99

Outdoor Power Equipment ▸ Lawn Mowers

The average sales price in this subcategory is $36.01.

	HIGH		AVG
16.5HP OHV BRIGGS & STRATTON	$275.00	Early Briggs A Carbureator Antique Vintage Old	$46.00
Kawasaki 12.5hp vertical shaft engine——Z-1184	$275.00	8HP BRIGGS & STRATTON ENGINE REBUILD CUSTOM SIZES	$46.00
BRIGGS AND STRATTON 9.5 HP OHV INTEK SNOW ENGINE	$249.99	NEW Briggs And Stratton "Quantum35" engine 3.5 hp NR	$44.95
Briggs 16 HP OHV VTwin Horiz. Cub Cadet 2165	$247.50	MTD complete service manuals with microfiche	$44.05
NEW Briggs And Stratton 11 HP vert. shaft engine NR!	$212.50	dealer lot of briggs and stratton pistons & misc 18pcs	$42.00
Briggs and Stratton 16.5hp overhead Valve motor	$205.00	HUGE LOT BRIGGS & STRATTON ENGINE MOTOR HEAD GASKETS 2B	$41.00
Briggs & Stratton 12.5HP I/C Lawn Mower Engine	$204.52	Starter - Briggs & Stratton, Brand New	$40.03
Briggs & Stratton 22 HP Twin OHV	$202.50	briggs&stratton carb,new,12 hp-12.5 -others??	$39.99
Briggs & Stratton 18 hp Engine	$200.03	Wheel Horse Electric Clutch for WheelHorse Tractor	$38.55
BRIGGS AND STRATTON 18 HP BOTTOM SHAFT RUNS GREAT	$200.00	Briggs & Stratton 12 volt electric starter #497596 twin	$38.45
COMPLETE 18 HP TWIN BRIGGS & STRATTON ENGINE	$199.00	David Bradley Air Breather Tube and Cleaner - Briggs	$37.99
BRIGGS AND STRATTON 12 HP 10 11 ENGINE MOWER TRACTOR	$193.49	dealer lot of briggs and stratton parts 20+pieces	$37.99
Briggs 15hp OHV Gold engine 15 hp Craftsman vertical	$162.50	Briggs & Stratton Engine Starter Generator & Regulator	$37.26
12 HP Briggs Stratton Signature Series Engine 42 inch	$159.95	briggs stratton carburetor brand new	$36.50
USED 17.5 HORSEPOWER TWIN CYLINDER I/C BRIGGS ENGINE	$150.00	dealer lot of briggs and tecumseh parts 50+pieces	$36.02

Outdoor Power Equipment ▸ Leaf Blowers & Vacuums

The average sales price in this subcategory is $163.27.

	HIGH		AVG
CYCLONE RAKE by Woodland Power Products, Lawn Vacuum	$965.00	STIHL BR420C BACKPACK LEAF BLOWER TOOL "NR"	$177.50
Cyclone Rake Mulcher/ Vacuum/Collecter	$940.00	STIHL BR420c COMMERCIAL GAS BACKPACK BLOWER BR 420c	$177.50
Cyclone Rake Leaf Vacuum and Mulcher	$851.00	Dethatcher for Walker Mower, Heavy Duty New Tines	$175.00
3-Stihl BR400 Backpack Blowers	$700.00	NEW IN THE BOX HUSQVARNA 125BT BACKPACK LEAF BLOWER	$172.75
Billy-Goat self propelled vac, not giant vac or troy	$615.50	Nice Echo BackPack Blower PB6000	$172.50
2-Tempest Power Blowers	$529.05	REDMAX EB7000 GAS POWERED BACKPACK LEAF BLOWER NR	$172.50
BILLY GOAT VACUUM BILLYGOAT KD511/C w/HOSE	$500.00	Echo PB-260i Start Back Pack Blower - NIB!! - NR!!	$172.50
New Stihl BR 550 PRO Backpack Blower Super Nice!!!!!!!	$420.99	Echo PB-403T Gas Professional Backpack Blower PB403T~NR	$171.55
Backpack blower Echo PB751	$410.72	JOHN DEERE 4600BP BACKPACK LEAF BLOWER GAS POWERED	$170.00
Backpack blower Echo PB751	$404.99	HUSQVARNA 145BT BACKPACK BLOWER 145 BT LIKE NEW	$169.99
ECHO COMMERCIAL BACKPACK BLOWER PROFESSIONAL PB-651T	$399.00	Shindaiwa Backpack Blower	$168.50
little wonder 9hp walk behind blower	$380.00	ECHO PB-261L BACKPACK BLOWER	$167.50
Redmax EBZ 8000 Backpack Blower	$380.00	ECHO PB-260L ProLite Gas powered blower **Brand new*	$166.49
MOSQUITO MAGNET CORDLESS LIBERTY PLUS BRAND NEW NR!	$365.00	L@@K!!!! Stihl Backpack Blower BR400 No Reserve !!!!	$165.50
~New Echo PB-650 Gas Backpack blower w/ 2 yr. warr.~	$356.00	HUSQVARNA 125BT Backpack Blower - NEW	$165.00

Patio & Grilling ▸ Charcoal Grills & Accessories

The average sales price in this subcategory is $74.46.

	HIGH		AVG
CUS.MADE BBQ PIT SMOKER GRILL BARBEQUE TRAILER NEW!	$4,050.00	25 Spring Handles for BBQ Grill, Pit, Smoker, Fireplace	$92.00
CUS.MADE BBQ PIT SMOKER GRILL BARBEQUE TRAILER NEW!	$1,200.00	COBB GRILL	$90.95
COOKSHACK ELECTRIC SMOKER	$1,025.00	Lodge Round Cast Iron Hibachi Charcoal Grill L510 - New	$90.57
Chester Smoked BBQ Cooker / Smoker	$1,000.00	Char Broil American Gourmet Smoker Grill BBQ NIB $249!	$90.10
Komodo Kamado Refractory BBQ	$960.00	NEW CHAR-BROIL AMERICAN GOURMET SMOKER BBQ GRILL !!!!	$82.99
Weber Ranch Kettle New in Box	$635.00	[3 of these sold for $82.99 each]	
Big Green Egg MHDA Medium Barbecue BBQ Grill - 15"	$569.00	Weber Performer Charcoal Grill with Gas Ignition	$82.84
Used Large Big Green Egg Smoker, Atlanta Area	$475.00	Weber Charcoal Grill NIB!	$76.25
LARGE BBQ/SMOKER/GRILL MOUNTED ON TRAILER	$399.99	25 Spring Handles for BBQ Grill, Pit, Smoker, Fireplace	$76.01
Big Green Egg Long Cypress Table for LHDA BBQ Grill	$299.00	Brinkman Vertical Charcoal BBQ Smoker New In Box!	$70.00
Big Green Egg LGE Heavy Duty Mini Barbecue - 9.5" Grid	$209.00	Brinkman Vertical Charcoal BBQ Smoker New In Box!	$64.50
Apollo Charcoal Grill w/ Cart and Free Cover & Shipping	$199.00	New Weber 741001 One Touch Silver Grill 22.5	$63.00
COWBOY STYLE FIREPIT & GRILL BARBEQUE, Bar-B-Q FIRE PIT	$199.00	WEBER KETTLE ROTISSERIE Turkey BBQ Grilling Grill	$59.75
VINTAGE CHARCOAL GRILL, BBQ,	$192.50	WEBER Summit Built In Side Burner BBQ Grill Grilling	$55.01
BARBECUE, EAMES MUSTC !!!		WEBER PERFORMER CHARCOAL GRILL 841001	$53.67
The Holland Portable Gas Grill BBQ outside camping	$184.50	Homer's Smokey Joe Weber Simpsons Grill NIB	$52.55

Patio & Grilling ▸ Gas Grills & Accessories

The average sales price in this subcategory is $35.98.

	HIGH		AVG
New Stainless Steel Barbecue Grill BBQ	$1,000.00	portable propane gas stove range-camping	$45.00
Broilmaster Super P3 Black, 3 Shelves & PC Cart	$959.00	Vintage Sunbeam Party Grill Sandwich Maker Near Mint	$44.00
New Charcoal Barbecue Grill	$299.00	PROPANE SAFETY gauge for gas grills boats Rv tanks ++	$38.98
New Stainless Steel BBQ Grill Side Burner / Sideburner	$250.00	[2 of these sold in a multiple item ("Dutch") auction for $19.49 each]	
Broil King Crown 2 Gas Grill - LP or Natural Gas	$239.00	NEW IN THE BOX CHAR-BROIL ELECTRIC ROTISSERIE	$38.00
New Stainless Steel BBQ Grill Side Burner / Sideburner	$225.00	NEW WEBER FOLDING CART FOR Q & BABY Q GRILLS 41429	$37.99
Outdoor Kitchen BBQ Island Stainless Utility Drawer	$152.50	Coleman RoadTrip Portable Propane Grill	$37.80
NIB Coleman Propane Roadtrip Road Trip Grill Complete	$148.49	Ducane rotisserie motor shaft forks tray & wood chips	$37.55
NIB Coleman Propane Roadtrip Road Trip Grill Complete	$138.99	THE HOLLAND GRILL HALF GRID	$37.25
NIB Coleman Propane Roadtrip	$138.99	WEBER REPLACEMENT FLAVORIZER BARS #9813 **NEW**	$36.99
LX Grill w/Wheels&Handle		WEBER GAS GRILL REPLACEMENT FLAVORIZER BARS 9816 *NEW!*	$36.01
NIB Coleman Red Propane Roadtrip LXE Road Trip Grill	$138.00	WEBER SILVER A COOKING GRATES SS #9885 **NEW**	$34.99
NIB Coleman Red Propane Roadtrip LXE Road Trip Grill	$129.99	[2 of these sold for $34.99 each]	
[2 of these sold for $129.99 each]		Char-broil grill replacement hose	$34.39
NIB Coleman Propane Outpost	$112.50	WEBER GAS GRILL BURNER TUBE SET NEW #3609	$34.00
200,000BTU Stove &CarryCase		[2 of these sold in a multiple item ("Dutch") auction for $17.00 each]	
DCS Stainless Storage Doors	$102.50	WEBER GAS GRILL REPLACEMENT FLAVORIZER BARS 9816 *NEW!*	$33.99
		Great Outdoors Grill Co. 34" Wide Body Smoker	$32.22

Patio & Grilling ▸ Patio Sets & Picnic Tables

The average sales price in this subcategory is $117.74.

	HIGH		AVG
7PC OVAL TEAK WOOD FURNITURE TABLE (94-71" L)*FREE SHP	$1,899.00	Pottery Barn Kids CHESAPEAKE PICNIC TABLE W/ BENCHES	$149.99
6 PC TEAK WOOD GARDEN OUTDOOR PATIO SOFA SET BRAND NEW	$1,500.00	2 Pottery Barn Chesapeake Chaise Cushions Multistripe	$147.95
[2 of these sold for $1,500.00 each]		LIFETIME 6FT FOLDING PICNIC/OUTDOOR	$146.00
7 PC TEAK SET GARDEN OUTDOOR PATIO FURNITURE NEW	$1,034.99	TABLE BRAND NEW !	
7 PC TEAK SET GARDEN OUTDOOR PATIO FURNITURE NEW	$999.99	[2 of these sold for $146.00 each]	
[3 of these sold for $999.99 each]		NEW IN BOX! LIFETIME 6 FOOT FOLDING PICNIC TABLE	$144.98
7 PC TEAK SET GARDEN OUTDOOR PATIO FURNITIURE NEW	$850.00	60"x40" Oval Dining Table and 6 Chairs	$140.08
Wrought Iron Outdoor Patio Set 8 Chairs Umbrella Bar +	$650.00	Pottery Barn Kids CHESAPEAKE PICNIC TABLE W/ BENCHES	$129.50
Multi Piece Wicker Furniture Set Outdoor/Patio	$510.00	POTTERY BARN CHESAPEAKE CHAISE	$125.00
Mexican Style Tiki Bar / Patio Furniture - Hand Made!	$510.00	CUSHION MULTISTRIPE DOUB	
Multi Piece Wicker Furniture Set Outdoor/Patio	$479.00	TEAK WOOD FURNITURE MINI TABLE (18") ***FREE SHIP***	$119.00
5-Piece Wicker Patio Furniture Set - New!	$456.75	60"x36" Dining Buffet Table and 6 Chairs	$103.50
PATIO/LANAI SET TABLE MARBLE TILE/SWIVEL CHAIRS SET 4	$399.00	40" Round Dining Table and 4 Chairs	$102.50
4-Piece Mexican Style Patio Furniture Set - Hand Made!	$367.90	Patio Furniture Set	$100.00
8pc metal/glass outdoor patio furniture table & chairs	$331.00	Outdoor Patio or Poolside White Fiber-Resin Bar Set	$100.00
Coleman Backhome Roll-Away Outdoor Patio Furniture Set	$295.00	Outdoor Patio Console Table~NIB~Faux Marble~Holds wine	$86.99
5 pc.Outdoor Patio Chat Set Tile Table and Four Chairs	$265.00	Vineyard Bronze Bistro Patio Barista Set - 3Pcs	$80.00

Pet Supplies ▸ Cats

The average sales price in this subcategory is $21.86.

	HIGH		AVG
Littermaid LM900+Tent+Drinkwell Foun+70ozRES	$184.95	Feliway Comfort Zone Plug-In brandnew in box	$25.99
Littermaid LM900+Drinkwell Foun+70ozRES+1yr Filters	$172.50	[4 of these sold for $25.99 each]	
Littermaid MEGA LM900+Petmate Pet Fountain	$141.95	72 POUND PETS PET GREETING CARDS CAT CATS W CAPT. L2	$24.99
Kittywalk Pet Stroller (NEW IN BOX - NO RESERVE)	$126.00	2II FELINE SHED STOP FOR CATS SHEDDING / FREE Shipping	$24.99
NEW Littermaid MEGA LM900-Oldest Seller Since 1999	$119.75	2 Brand NEW Feliway Comfort Zone Plug In Diffusers	$24.99
Feliway Comfort Zone Plug In brandnew with 4 Xtra refill	$79.99	Complete Pet Dental Care Kit from Oxyfresh Pet Products	$24.00
Bold Chartreuse (Pet) Personal Companion Stroller	$77.79	Cat Scram-Train Cats Stay off Counters, Out of Rooms!	$24.00
LitterMaid LM500 - Automatic cat litter box - NIB!	$72.00	SOFA SCRAM - Sonic Mat for pets	$22.97
Miniature Display Camping Tent - Salesmans Sample	$67.00	Travel Pet Carrier - Backpack w/ WHEELS for Cat – Dog	$22.72
[2 of these sold for $67.00 each]		Scat Mat Extension 48x20	$22.55
Drinkwell Pet Fountain+70 oz Res+Brush Kit+1 Yr Filters	$57.45	Advantage Flea 4 Pk Orange Kitten 0-9lbs FREE SHIPPING!	$22.50
Scat Mat Cat Training Mat for Cats & Dogs! New 48x20!	$56.95	Drinkwell Pet Fountain 50 oz Accessory Kit With Brushes	$22.50
Large CAT PLAYPEN CAGE	$56.00	NEW! CALMATIVE COMFORT ZONE PLUG-IN W/FELIWAY & REFILL	$22.40
COMFORT ZONE~FELIWAY~REFILLS,LOT OF 4 BOTTLES!NEW!	$52.99	NIB Feliway Behavior Modification Spray 75 mL	$21.99
Scat Mat Cat Training Mat for Cats & Dogs! New 30x16!	$47.95	Frontline Top Spot Feline 3 Pack Free Shipping	$21.50
Drinkwell Pet Fountain+70oz Reservoir+FREE Fat Cat Toy!	$46.95	Frontline Top Spot Feline 3 Pack Free Shipping	$21.00

Pet Supplies ▸ Dogs

The average sales price in this subcategory is $31.21.

	HIGH		AVG
DOORMATE Auto PATIO DOOR Sys & PETMATE	$325.00	PETS PET 4 STEP FOR DOGS & CATS MAKE CLIMBING EASIER	$42.99
Dog door, pet door, wall mounted dog door	$244.04	Autographed Pic Animal Precinct Greyhound Donation	$41.00
[4 of these sold in a multiple item ("Dutch") auction for $61.01 each]		New PetStep II Half step Pet Dog Ramp NR Small Ramp	$39.99
Bichon Frise 36"x48" Pop Art Painting	$200.00	NEW BED-COUCH DOG/CAT RAMP-	$39.99
Elegant Solid Wood Dog/Cat Pet Steps, Stairs MUST SEE	$199.99	CARPETED FURNITURE PET RAMPS	
Petsafe Instant Fence PIF-300 Wireless Dog Fence	$197.50	Dog 4 Step Pet steps cat dogs stairs ramp Couch ***	$37.88
NEW PetSafe XL DOG PET DOOR for SLIDING PATIO DOOR **	$147.50	SMART DOG Basic In-ground Pet Fencing System	$36.00
Large STAYWELL 861 INFRA RED DOG DOOR	$142.50	PET DOG BIKE BICYCLE SEAT BASKET dogs up to 14 lbs	$34.95
IDEAL PET Sliding Pet Patio Dog Doggy Doggie Door	$109.51	PET DOG BIKE BICYCLE SEAT BASKET dogs up to 14 lbs	$34.95

IDEAL PET Sliding Doggie Door Pet Patio Dog Doggy	$109.50	Green Um 1200 count. Protects lawns from pet urine burn	$33.99
PETSAFE DELUXE DOG patio door dog sliding door	$109.00	Pet cat or dog wicker toy chest box......NEW	$33.00
NR NIB Luxury Pet Stroller / Carrier for Dogs or Cats	$104.25	Green Um 1200 count. Protects lawns from pet urine burn	$33.00
**NEW PetSafe EXTRA LARGE Classic Model DOG PET DOOR *	$96.00	New Dog Johnson Pet Door Large NR 2 way No Reserve NIP	$31.99
PETSTEP 2 HD PORTABLE FOLDING DOG pet step II ramp	$95.00	NIB Pet / Dog / Doggy Door!! SIZE LARGE!!! MAGNADOR!!	$31.98
EXTRA WIDE TELESCOPING DOG/CAT RAMP-CARPETED PET RAMPS	$94.99	Pet Car Seat - Comfort Ride	$31.00
EXTRA WIDE TELESCOPING DOG/CAT RAMP-CARPETED PET RAMPS	$94.99	Ideal Large Pet Door 9 X 15 - NEW IN BOX	$27.95

Pet Supplies ▶ Fish

The average sales price in this subcategory is $41.88.

	HIGH		AVG
11,000 GPH Water Pump!! Fish Pond Waterfall e	$393.00	12-13" SANKE LIVE KOI POND FISH	$56.00
BIG MAX Lg. Fish Pond Lake Aerator aeration System	$345.00	Live Koi Fish 10" Garden Pond Imported Japan	$56.00
Fish Pond Aerator Aeration - COMPLETE SYSTEM	$329.00	700 GAL. POND PUMP PROFESSIONAL SERIES	$53.77
20" SHIRO UTSURI LIVE KOI FROM JAPAN	$295.00	Set of Two 11" Doitsu Hariwake Live Koi	$53.01
BEAUTIFUL 14-15" SELECT AKA BEKKO BUTTERFLY LIVE KOI	$242.51	@NEW 55 GAL. AQUARIUM STAND MADE BY PENN-PLAX	$52.51
15-16" SHOWA LIVE KOI FROM JAPAN	$225.00	The Pond Guardian - Electric fence protects fish NEW	$51.01
LIVE KOI POND GARDEN FISH 11-12" 3 STEP KOHAKU IMPORTED	$202.02	LOT OF 5 7-8" LIVE KOI - POND JAPANESE KOI - GORGEOUS!	$51.01
Live koi fish Genjiro Farm 16 inch AKA Ginrin Sanke	$199.99	11"-12" High Quality Live Butterfly Koi Garden Pond	$51.00
Live Koi Fish Tazawa Farm 16" Sparkling Female Ginrin	$199.99	25 domestic 1-3 inch koi fry from Japanese Koi Parents	$25.00
FISH MATE POND FILTER 25W NEW UV POND FILTER	$181.00	LIVE SEAHORSE (H.reidi) Brazillian snowflake 3"	$50.00
10-11" (LARGE TOSAI) SHOWA LIVE KOI FROM JAPAN	$175.00	Live Koi Fish 10-11" Garden Pond Imported Japan	$49.95
10-12" GIN RIN SHOWA LIVE KOI FROM JAPAN	$175.00	10" Kin Kikokuryu Live Koi	$47.00
Milwaukee *SMS125* pH/ORP Controller	$169.95	BEAUTIFUL 9" KI UTSURI BUTTERFLY LIVE KOI POND FISH	$46.00
Milwaukee SMS122 pH Controller / MA957 Regulator Combo	$159.00	11" Beni Kin Kikokuryu Live Koi	$46.00
50 LBS of Carribbean Live Rock FREE SHIPPING	$155.00	Turbo-Twist 3X Pond/Tank U.V. Sterilizer	$41.99

Plumbing & Fixtures ▶ Bathroom

The average sales price in this subcategory is $91.76.

	HIGH		AVG
EVERYTHING For Your Clawfoot Tub in 1 PKG1000	$719.12	Delta Venetian Bronze Roman Tub Faucet 2755RB-616RB NE	$128.49
60X 60 WHIRLPOOL TUB!!!! BRAND NEW!!!!!!!	$550.00	Price Pfister Georgetown Roman Tub Faucet RT6-GXMB	$127.50
Clawfoot Tub Shower Enclosure Set with Gooseneck Faucet	$409.00	DELTA 2555 VICTORIAN RUBBED BRONZE LAV FAUCET	$121.51
KOHLER "Finial" K 331-4m Clawfoot Bath Tub Faucet NEW!	$366.05	Antique Brass & Porcelain Cast Iron Tub Faucets plus	$121.38
PIONEER BRUSHED NICKEL ROMAN TUB SHOWER SINK FAUCETS	$355.00	OIL RUBBED BRONZE CLAWFOOT TUB FAUCET w/HANDSHOWER$400+	$109.99
Moen 263WR Vertical Spa Shower Set in Wrought Iron	$325.00	NEW KOHLER SHOWER FAUCET BRUSHED CHROME-VALVE INCLUDED!	$109.50
Satin Waterfall Collection Bathroom Faucets Combo Set	$299.99	New MOEN 82240 Tub Shower Platinum Posi-Temp FREE S&H	$109.00
3 Gold Jacuzzi Roman Bath Tub Sink Faucets Combo Set	$279.99	[2 of these sold for $109.00 each]	
DELTA 156 VICTORIAN RUBBED	$267.00	Delta Venetian Bronze 2555RB-216RB NEW!!!!!!!!!	$105.06
BRONZE KITCHEN FAUCET 156RB		Tub Mounted Bathroom Faucet With Hand Shower "Copper"	$99.99
Gold Jacuzzi Roman Bath Tub + Sink Faucets Combo Set	$247.50	Ant. COPPER Roman Tub Set C Spout Fontaine Faucet	$99.99
JACUZZI RAINBOW FAUCET BRASS 6690	$228.90	Wall or Tub Mounted Bathroom Faucet w Hand Held Shower	$99.99
Danze Opulence Antique Copper Tub Shower Faucet Faucets	$227.99	Tub Mounted Bathroom Faucet With Hand Shower "Copper"	$99.99
Satin Sink + Tub Waterfall Bathroom Faucets Combo Set	$219.99	Ant. COPPER Roman Tub Set C Spout Fontaine Faucet	$99.99
Gold Jacuzzi Roman Bath Tub + Sink Faucets Combo Set	$209.99	Tub Waterfall Faucet with Hand Shower Set M-124	$99.95
Chrome Clawfoot Tub Drain & Water Supply Set w/Stops	$209.00	Price Pfister Treviso 806-DK00 Roman Tub Faucet NEW	$91.00

Plumbing & Fixtures ▶ Kitchen

The average sales price in this subcategory is $229.74.

	HIGH		AVG
PORCELAIN FIRE CLAY DOUBLE FARM / APRON KITCHEN SINK!	$808.00	SINKS -22"x16" APRON FARMHOUSE	$285.00
[2 of these sold in a multiple item ("Dutch") auction for $404.00 each]		(KITCHEN) COPPER SINK #1	
35"x22" DOUBLE BOWL APRON FARMHOUSE KITCHEN COPPER SINK	$780.00	Blanco 511-967 Undermount Stainless Steel Kitchen Sink	$269.00
SINKS - 33"x22" APRON FARMHOUSE (KITCHEN) COPPER SINK	$725.00	Blanco 511-707 Silgranit Double Kitchen Sink-Anthracite	$269.00
[2 of these sold for $725.00 each]		Blanco 510-876 Undermount Stainless Steel Kitchen Sink	$269.00
SINKS - 33"x22" APRON FARMHOUSE (KITCHEN) COPPER SINK	$720.00	Bathroom Glass Sink with Top Lavatory on Pedestal CB12	$255.00
Elkay ELUH3920 Undermount Stainless Kitchen Sink	$699.00	Blanco 511-607 Silgranit Double Kitchen Sink-Anthracite	$249.00
Blanco 512-750 Undermount Stainless Steel Kitchen Sink	$609.00	BEAUTIFUL BLACK VESSEL SINK! FLOWERS!	$245.00
BLANCO PRECISION KITCHEN SINK 1 & 1/2 Bowl Mode#512-749	$580.00	FHP Franke Granite Hi Lo 33x22 kitchen sink 3 colors!	$239.00
KOHLER 3356 undercounter kitchen sink	$580.00	SWANSTONE Kitchen Sink NEW 33x22 Single Bowl list $525	$239.00
Stone Sinks, Niche Mosaic Onix & Marble Vessel Sink S46	$550.00	Blanco 511-607 Silgranit Double Kitchen Sink-Anthracite	$239.00
FRANKE sink TRIPLE compartments with drainboard S.S.	$549.00	Blanco 511-605 Silgranit Double Kitchen Sink - Biscuit	$239.00
PORECLAIN LARGE WHITE FIRE CLAY FARM/APRON KITCHEN SINK	$535.00	SWANSTONE Kitchen Sink NEW 33x22	$239.00
Blanco 512-747 Undermount Stainless Steel Kitchen Sink	$526.13	super SALE! list $470+	
Kohler 3356 Stainless Steel Undermount Sink	$510.00	Blanco 511-607 Silgranit Double Kitchen Sink-Anthracite	$239.00
APRON FARMHOUSE KITCHEN SINK COPPER 33" x 22"	$499.99	Kindred US1930/90L/E (KSS5U) Undermount Kitchen Sink	$237.50
PORECLAIN LARGE WHITE FIRE CLAY FARM/APRON KITCHEN SINK	$499.00	Kindred US1930/90L/E (KSS5U) Undermount Kitchen Sink	$232.50

Plumbing & Fixtures ▶ Plumbing Parts & Accessories

The average sales price in this subcategory is $84.21.

	HIGH		AVG
Basement WatchdogA/C-D/C Battery Backup Sump Pump Sys	$360.00	RAND 1.4 HP WATER PUMP/Shallow Well/Irrigation/Fountain	$99.95
Grohe 35.253.000 Grohsafe Pressure Balance Shower Valve	$343.00	[6 of these sold for $99.95 each]	

	HIGH/left		AVG
[7 of these sold in a multiple item ("Dutch") auction for $49.00 each]		Flotec Floodmate 7000 3/4 HP Sump Pump NEW	$97.70
BUR CAM EASYFLUSH SYSTEM FOR BATH ROOM ADD ON	$338.00	Laing Circulating pump NEW SMT-303-BS	$96.00
BASEMENT WATCHDOG A/C-D/C SUMP PUMP Model BWD12-120C	$315.00	NEW ZOELLER SUBMERSIBLE SUMP PUMP	$92.67
[6 of these sold for $315.00 each]		*New* Wayne Portable Pump 1450 GPH, 1/2 HP	$91.01
Basement WatchdogA/C-D/C Battery Backup Sump Pump Sys	$313.36	Flotec FP4012-08 1/2 HP Shallow	$91.00
Basement WatchdogA/C-D/C Battery Backup Sump Pump Sys	$306.78	Well Jet Pump NEW InBOX	
CRAFTSMAN 2 HP 3-WIRE DEEP WELL SUBMERSIBLE PUMP	$300.00	Flotec Sewage Pump FPSE 3200A	$90.01
BASEMENT WATCHDOG A/C-D/C SUMP PUMP Model BWD12-120C	$299.00	Craftsman Professional 3/4 hp Hydro-Glass Shallow Well	$90.00
[2 of these sold for $299.00 each]		NEW 1/2 HP SUMP PUMP 3050 &	$89.99
Basement WatchdogA/C-D/C Battery Backup Sump Pump Sys	$297.56	INSTALLATION KIT FREE SHIP	
Basement WatchdogA/C-D/C Battery Backup Sump Pump Sys	$296.83	Craftsman Pro 1/2 HP Stainless Submersible Sump Pump	$86.00
Basement WatchdogA/C-D/C Battery Backup Sump Pump Sys	$296.82	Craftsman Professional 3/4 Hp Shallow Well Jet Pump	$84.00
Basement WatchdogA/C-D/C Battery Backup Sump Pump Sys	$295.85	Flotec Sewage Pump FPSE 3200A	$83.94
Basement WatchdogA/C-D/C Battery Backup Sump Pump Sys	$285.00	Craftsman 1/2 hp Hydro-Glass Well Jet Pump 2514-1133	$81.25
Basement WatchdogA/C-D/C Battery Backup Sump Pump Sys	$283.00	Laguna WG 10,000 Power Jet Waterfall Pump	$81.00
Home Water Pressure System Flotec FP4815	$280.00	Basement Watchdog Emergency Sump Pump System NIB	$80.53

Pools & Spas ▸ Pools

The average sales price in this subcategory is $217.46.

	HIGH		AVG
Endless Pool 8' x 14' With Accessories	$10,800.00	NEW SANDSTONE 18' R Above Ground Swimming Pool Pools	$365.00
Endless Swimming Pool Only 2 years old!! NO RESERVE	$8,876.78	18' x 4' Easy Quick Set Swimming Pool W/Ladder & Pump	$300.50
DOUGHBOY POOL 15 x 25 above ground	$2,700.00	NEW Intex EasySet 15'x3.5' Portable Swimming Pool Pools	$289.00
New 18' x 33' x 52" Oval AboveGround Swimming Pool Kit	$2,241.00	18' x 42" Quick Up? Above Ground Swimming Pool Kit	$285.00
2 Person 7'- 14 Jet Spa / Hot Tub	$1,995.00	NEW 18' X 48" Easy Set Intex swimming Pool! FULL SET	$279.00
New 27' x 52" Round Above Ground Swimming Pool Kit VLR	$1,525.00	Intex 18' x 42" Easy Set Pool Brand New!!	$278.00
12 jets, 2 person whirlpool bathtub bath tub	$1,499.95	Sand N Sun EasySet 18' x 48" Portable Pool - New in Box	$250.00
ABOVE GROUND SWIMMING POOL 12'x32'x48" BRAND NEW	$1,249.00	24 Foot Round Cedar Ridge Doughboy Pool	$250.00
Eldorado 52"Above ground pool Deluxe Equipment Package	$935.00	BRAND NEW GOLDLINE POOL COOLING CONTROL COMBO	$225.00
NEW Oval 24'x12'x48" Swimming Pool Package pools COOL	$899.01	Aqua Leisure 18' x 4' Deep Simple-Set Swimming Pool	$207.50
Above Ground Portable Pool 9ftx17ftx48in Quick Pool	$789.99	18'x4' EASY SET POOL	$200.00
Above ground pool 15' x 30'	$722.00	AERO FAMILY QUICK POOL W/ PUMP! NEW!! HUGE 11' x 6' !!	$199.99
NEW SANDSTONE 18' R Above Ground Swimming Pool Pools	$610.00	INTEX 15'x42" METAL FRAME POOL SET EASY SETUP KIT 56948	$199.99
New 21' Round Above Ground Swimming Pool	$608.25	15' 42" Easy Quick Set Swimming Pool W/Ladder & Pump	$190.00
NEW IN BOX KD Royalty Swimming Pool 16' Rd	$579.69	Swimming pool	$182.50

Pools & Spas ▸ Spas, Hot Tubs

The average sales price in this subcategory is $1,581.54.

	HIGH		AVG
Portable hot tub 12 person trailered propane heated	$7,000.00	NEW Essential Spas AURORA SPA 38 Jets Hot Tub Tubs	$2,375.00
NEW SIBERIAN ELITE 7 Person 13HP,4 Pump 67 Jet Spa Spas	$5,000.00	Essential Spas 10HP ALEXANDRIA Spa 59 Jet Hot Tub Tubs	$2,300.00
NEW MONTREAL ELITE 13HP, 4 Pump 64 Jet Spa Spas	$4,950.00	NEW Essential Spas AURORA SPA 38 Jets Hot Tub Tubs	$2,275.00
New Spas: 48Jet SupraDeluxe Hot Tub Therapy Spa w/Wrnty	$4,645.00	NEW BAYSIDE 6 -7 PERSON HOT TUB SPA 50 JETS TUBS SPAS	$2,150.00
NEW SPA HOT TUB 2005 VAIL 52 JETS SPAS TUBS 7 PERSON	$4,499.00	NEW Essential Spas AURORA SPA 38 Jets Hot Tub Tubs	$2,125.00
15HP Essential Spas INFINITY SPA 108 Jet Hot Tub Tubs	$4,300.00	BIG 6 person FIR infrared SAUNA w/ CD player + AM/FM	$2,051.00
New Spas: 6seat 37Jet Hot Tub Therapy Spa w/Warranty!	$4,195.00	NEW Essential Spas MONACO 31 Jets Spa Hot Tub Tubs	$2,025.00
15HP Essential Spas INFINITY SPA 108 Jet Hot Tub Tubs	$3,905.00	NEW Essential Spas MONACO 31 Jets Spa Hot Tub Tubs	$2,025.00
NEW 2005 TAHITIAN 6 Per Hot Tub Spa 10 Colors Spas Tubs	$3,900.00	NEW Essential Spas MONACO 31 Jets Spa Hot Tub Tubs	$2,006.00
New Spas: 8seat 37Jet Hot Tub Therapy Spa w/Warranty!	$3,790.00	Vita Spa Nearly New Hot Tub Jacuzzi not Hot Springs	$1,890.10
NEW 10HP Essential Spas NEPTUNE SPA 80 Jet Hot Tub Tubs	$3,550.00	NEW BAYSIDE 6 -7 PERSON HOT TUB SPA 50 JETS TUBS SPAS	$1,826.00
NEW 10HP Essential Spas NEPTUNE SPA 80 Jet Hot Tub Tubs	$3,511.11	NEW Essential Spas 25 Jets SEABROOK SPA Hot Tub Tubs	$1,800.00
NEW 10HP Essential Spas NEPTUNE SPA 80 Jet Hot Tub Tubs	$3,501.00	NEW Essential Spas 25 Jets SEABROOK SPA Hot Tub Tubs	$1,725.00
NEW 2005 TAHITIAN 6 Per Hot Tub Spa 10 Colors Spas Tubs	$3,500.00	92 x 92 Hot Tub - 7 adult seating - like new(Houtson)	$1,601.00
NEW 10HP Essential Spas NEPTUNE SPA 80 Jet Hot Tub Tubs	$3,500.00	Softub T-220 Softtub Soft tub Sof tub portable hot tub	$1,600.00

Rugs & Carpets ▸ Area Rugs

The average sales price in this subcategory is $103.06.

	HIGH		AVG
ITALIAN MASTERPIECE RUG RUGS PURE SILK HAND MADE	$1,995.00	$550 Handtuffted Green Woolen Pile Carpet NR	$140.50
Pottery Barn Colette Rug ~9 x 12~	$821.00	Pottery Barn Teen Pink Flokati 6' Round Rug New!	$139.99
POTTERY BARN FRANKLIN PERSIAN WOOL 9 X 12 RUG	$749.99	Pottery Barn Desiree Area Runner Rug, 2.5 x 9	$137.50
Pottery Barn 9 x 12 Felted SHAG Rug - Taupe - New	$579.99	6'Octagon Rug Traditional Persian Oreintal Burgundy 6x6	$135.50
Pottery Barn Monelle Rug ~9 x 12~	$549.99	cow hide South America GIANTcow skin area rug cow hides	$132.50
Pottery Barn RED Logan Gabbeh Rug ~ 9' x 12'~	$529.99	IKEA LISTED large 9'10" x 6'7" modern, neutral rug	$127.27
Pottery Barn HENLEY LINCHEN GREEN Area Rug 9X12	$404.99	New Pottery Barn Kids Alphabet Soup Rug 5' Round	$109.99
Sealed Pottery Barn Tara Soumak Rug 8x10 (like Alina)	$379.00	Two Karastan Mini Rugs 2' x 1'6"	$107.50
Pottery Barn Sophie Wool Rug 9x12	$370.52	BRAND NEW Pottery Barn Kids Animal Animals Rug 5' Round	$99.99
Pottery Barn Kingston Chenille 9x12 Rug	$299.99	Unique Room Size CONTEMPORARY 8x11 Modern Area Rug NEW!	$99.95
POTTERY BARN BABY BUTTERFLY RUG 5' X 8'	$250.99	Royal Palace, Antique Bouquet 5'x8'6" Rug, Eggplant	$98.00
BEAUTIFUL BIDJAR AREA WOOL RUG 9x12 NEW RETAILS $2599	$202.50	[2 of these sold in a multiple item ("Dutch") auction for $49.00 each]	
$600 Hand-tufted Sarouk Beige/Tan Rug 6' octagon NR	$202.00	POTTERY BARN 7X9 Hailey Rug Pink Baby Blue	$89.99
$5,000 AREA RUG CUSTOM LEATHER N	$200.00	KIDS SPORTS BASKETBALL SOCCER FOOTBALL AREA 5X7 RUG	$85.00
WOOL DESIGNER MODERN		NEW! 6x9 Naturals - Sisal Area Rugs Genuine Carpets	$82.00
Enjjoyable 14'0x9'10 Kilim Persian Rugs Carpets ZA491	$199.00	POTTERY BARN TEEN ROUND FLOKATI RUG 6 FT LAVENDER	$81.02

Rugs & Carpets ▸ Throw Rugs

The average sales price in this subcategory is $23.66.

	HIGH		AVG
+NEW COWHIDE STEER RUG LEATHER HAIR COW HIDE #13T+	$204.00	TROPICAL FISH 3 Piece BATH RUG SET *NEW*	$24.99
NEW COWHIDE RUG COW HIDE	$187.50	Fire Engine Child Shape Kids Rug Nursery-Brand New!	$24.99
RUGS SKIN LEATHER STEER B78		LAMBS WOOL rug hide 2 X 3 natural GC for floor or wall	$24.99
NEW COWHIDE RUG COW HIDE RUGS SKIN LEATHER STEER B69	$185.54	GIRAFFE - Soft 100% Alpaca Rug ! PERU ART - NR - Unique	$24.99
COWHIDE tricolor STEER RUG COW HIDE #tm34	$160.00	HORSE 40"X60" THROW/AREA RUG DOOR FLOOR KITCHEN MAT	$24.99
+COWHIDE STEER RUG LEATHER HAIR COW HIDE #56+	$160.00	Daisy PINK Kids RUG 25x28 Nursery Decor Wall Art	$24.98
+COWHIDE STEER RUG LEATHER HAIR COW HIDE #26+	$160.00	Sports Balls Shape Kids Shape Rug-Fun Rug, Children's	$24.50
2ft X 3ft Sheepskin Raccoon Rug	$137.50	AMERICAN PATRIOTIC RUG stars braided hooked cotton 36"	$24.49
hand hooked wool rug pink floral antique 2 x 6 runner	$127.50	POTTERY BARN STINSON/MULTI-COLORED THROW RUG / 3X5'	$24.49
Longhorn Steer Rug Brindle Tiger Stripe NEW HIDE Huge	$102.50	Royal Palace Rug "Artistry" 30"x50" Sage Oval Throw Rug	$22.83
NEW!!! $350 4X6 Brown Leather Suede Shag Rug	$89.00	French Country Rose Runner Throw Rug OH So Shabby Chic	$22.50
Kelly Rightsell area rug ~Precious for childs room!	$82.00	2 MAUVE PINK & CREAM CHENILLE FLORAL AREA THROW RUGS NR	$22.49
HUGE Cowhide Rug Cow Hide Rugs Skin - Lovely brown L5	$79.00	27 X 45 Blue Jean Rag Rug	$22.00
Vintage Floral Oval Hooked Rug	$57.00	New Disney Finding Nemo Bath Mat Area Throw Rug Fish	$20.99
Pottery Barn Elephant Walking Round Rug ·	$57.00	Hooked, Hook, Rug	$20.50
LUXURIOUS SHEEPSKIN RUG FUR SHEEP SKIN PELT RUGS	$54.95	BEAUTIFUL THROW RUG 10 ' X 14'	$20.50

Tools ▸ Hand Tools

The average sales price in this subcategory is $22.77.

	HIGH		AVG
S&K Socket Sets	$600.00	NEW - Xcelite nut driver set	$27.50
SNAP-ON TOOLS NEW PNEUMATIC CV BOOT INSTALLER	$202.50	Stanley 4Pc Mm Reverse Gear Wrench Set -New Box of 4	$26.98
10 Drawer Tool Chest – New	$202.49	KLEIN TOOLS - WIRE STRIPPERS - REAMER - UNIBIT	$26.72
SNAP-ON TOOLS 1/2-DR 6-PT IMPACT SOCKET SET	$152.50	Kenworth Tow Pin K143-C-122	$26.55
SNAP ON 1/2 DRIVE METRIC SOCKETS	$152.50	Stanley 5M X 3/4" Metric Tape Rule-Box of 36	$26.11
SNAP-ON Tap & Die Set TDM117A TDM-117A (41) PCS..NEW!!	$108.09	6000 Grit KING Waterstone	$26.00
CRAFTSMAN 22" GAS BUSHWACKER HEDGE TRIMMER 25CC	$101.00	Snap On Adjustable Pliers NEW	$26.00
Craftsman Torque Wrench 1/2 in. Drive #44597 NEW IN BOX	$100.00	NEW Dale Earnhardt Snap-On Tools Breaker Bar	$25.49
INGERSOLRAND 1/4 AIR DRILL	$96.01	NEW STEEL POLYURETHANE FOAM GUN / DISPENSER	$25.00
114 Back Spot Facers / Back Countersinks w/ Arbors	$88.77	LEATHERMAN TOOL as NEW nr	$24.77
SNAP-ON TOOLS NEW 8PC SREWDRIVER SET	$86.50	SNAP-ON HAND VACUUM PUMP/TESTER USED WITH CASE	$24.28
SNAP ON 3/8 IMPACT DRIVER 208EPIT 8 PCS	$82.81	INNER TIE ROD TOOL FOR RACK AND PINION	$23.50
matco deluxe pro stud welding kit SS5150	$80.95	2-Vise Grip Locking C-Clamps Model 11R	$23.50
GB electrical KOW-520 ratcheting knockout punch set	$79.95	TAP & DIE SET ACE #614 MADE BY HANSON CO.	$23.19
SNAP-ON TOOLS MATCO MAC TOOLS 1/2-DR IMPACT SOCKET SET	$76.00	MAKITA DC1410 CORDLESS TOOL BATT., CHARGER	$23.00

Tools ▸ Power Tools

The average sales price in this subcategory is $77.87.

	HIGH		AVG
Shopsmith Mark V with Accessory Tools	$1,701.00	MILWAUKEE 1/2" ELECTRIC IMPACT WRENCH MODEL 9070-20	$100.01
SHOPSMITH MARK V with many ACCESSORIES	$1,200.00	NEW RAND MORTISING MACHINE W/ MORTISE BITS/MORTISER	$99.95
SHOPSMITH MARK 5 # 510 HOME WORKSHOP SYSTEM	$1,025.00	EXOTIC WOOD ~ FIGURED AFRICAN BOSSE LUMBER 6/4	$99.00
Paint Shaver Pro w/5" Sanding Kit 10580	$695.00	NEW! DEWALT DC500 2 GALLON VACUUM CORD/CORDLESS	$93.00
Paint Shaver Pro w/5" Sanding Kit 10580	$675.00	Milwaukee 1/2" Right Angle Drill	$91.03
Dewalt HeavyDuty SDS Max Demolition Hammer Kit D25900K	$508.00	Dewalt DW911R Jobsite Radio / Battery Charger	$87.58
TITAN INDUSTRIAL TRASH PUMP 3x3 never used	$500.00	NEW RAND 12 TON HYDRAULIC SHOP PRESS/TOOL	$84.95
dewalt dw073kd rotarey laser 18 volt cordless level	$306.56	WOOD ~ X-FANCY FIDDLEBACK MYRTLE LUMBER	$81.00
dewalt 18 Gauge 18V Cordless Swivel Shear dc490ka	$285.00	Shopsmith 10E/ER Caster Set NO RESERVE	$81.00
BRAND NEW KARCHER K 2400 2400PSI GAS PRESSURE WASHER	$281.00	Dewalt DC011 Heavy Duty Work Radio/Charger	$81.00
EXOTIC WOOD ~ INCREDIBLY FIGURED BUBINGA LUMBER	$279.00	KARCHER 1500 PSI ELECTRIC PRESSURE WASHER	$80.99
Hilti GX100 gas-driven fastening system~nailer/NR!	$275.00	NIB dewalt heavy duty 2 gallon wet dry vac dc500	$80.00
WYCO Concrete Vibrator 8'shaft W/ 12"X 1.5"Square Head	$245.99	Dewalt DW321 5.8amp Jig Saw NEW IN BOX	$80.00
Snap On Cordless Impact Wrench 1/2" 2 Battery Snapon	$232.50	24V POWER CORDLESS IMPACT WRENCH	$79.99
Dewalt Heavy Duty 16 Gauge Nibbler - DW896	$227.50	GUN DRIVER 1/2" SOCKET	
EXOTIC WOOD ~ INCREDIBLY FIGURED ZIRICOTE LUMBER	$202.50	RAM MDL R-100 HEAVY DUTY ELECTRIC	$78.00
BOSCH NIBBLER 1529B 20 GA STAINLESS / 16GA STEEL "NEW"	$199.00	METAL CUTTING SHEARS	

Window Treatments ▸ Blinds

The average sales price in this subcategory is $24.89.

	HIGH		AVG
Nanik Vertical Wood Blinds in Walnut BRAND NEW	$305.00	NEW POWER EASE Blind Remote Master and Add On	$28.88
HUNTER DOUGLAS VERTICAL BLINDS - NO RESERVE	$127.50	2" Genuine wood blinds - 46" Wide - Brite White	$28.76
Pottery Barn 2 Paxton Roller Shades 35 X 72 Cranberry	$99.99	BEAUTIFUL~NEW~ WOODEN WINDOW BLIND! (70x59) WOW!	$28.00
Remote Control Electric Rolling Blind System to 6.5 FT	$99.00	7 x 6' BAMBOO Canton roll-up BLINDS	$27.99
VERTICAL BLINDS 127"W X 73"H like new center opening	$95.00	30-3/4x71-3/4 Wood Blinds, White, 2"	$27.99
Premium 2" Wood Blinds - Custom Made To Order	$85.00	4'x 7' BAMBOO Roman SHADES / BLINDS w/valance	$27.99
Wood Window BLINDS 29" x 70" Window - Beautiful!!	$75.00	NEW POWER EASE Blind Remote Master and Add On	$27.78
[3 of these sold in a multiple item ("Dutch") auction for $25.00 each]		NEW HUNTER DOUGLAS NANTUCKET	$27.50
Beautiful 94" Levolor Horizontal Blinds	$70.00	WHITE SHADES/BLINDS 34X21	
Oak Wood Blinds 28" x 58" 2 inch slats ~Like New	$68.66	New Pottery Barn WHITE Sausalito Shade 32" X 63" WOW	$26.00
[2 of these sold in a multiple item ("Dutch") auction for $34.33 each]		84"x72" New "Slat" Bamboo Blinds Shades	$24.99
Wood Blinds - Wood Blind - Your Color Choice	$57.00	IKEA NEW 2 White Roman Cotton Blinds/Shades 39.25 X 67	$24.40
Pottery Barn PAXTON ROLLER SHADE NATURAL 22 x 72	$46.00	BEAUTIFUL~New~ WOODEN WINDOW	$24.00

34-3/4x63 Wood Blinds, Wood Color, 2"	$45.00	BLINDS! (34x70x2) WOW!	
84"x72" New "Toro" Bamboo blinds shades	$43.99	2" Genuine wood blinds - 36" Wide - Brite White	$23.26
POTTERY BARN KIDS ROMAN SHADE 32 x 63 BLUE GINGHAM	$41.00	NEW IKEA 2 Bamboo Roll-Up Window Blind Shades 31"x64"	$22.95
NEW!! 2" Faux Wood White Blinds 46" x 64"	$41.00	2" Genuine wood blinds - 36" Wide - Brite White	$21.50

Window Treatments ▸ Curtain Rods, Hardware

The average sales price in this subcategory is $18.80.

	HIGH		AVG
Remote Control Electric Curtain Track System 3-13 FT	$109.00	POTTERY BARN TEEN DOUBLE BRACKET ROD 24-48 BLACK	$22.00
Remote Control RC Motorized Window Drapery Curtain Rod	$109.00	Pottery Barn Curtain Rod with 2 Hold Backs 108"-60"	$21.72
Remote Control Electric Curtain Track System 3-13 FT	$109.00	Rustic Cast Iron Star Curtain Rod Holders	$20.99
Remote Control Electric Curtain Track System 3-13 FT	$100.00	35 Levolor Gold Drapery-Curtain clip rings New NR	$20.51
Remote Control Electric Curtain Track System 3-13 FT	$99.00	Pottery Barn Kids Star Architectural Hardware Holdbacks	$20.49
Pottery Barn MEDIUM BRASS Scroll Rod Set New	$64.00	Column Off White Window Curtain Sconces - Pkg 4	$19.99
2 All SPORTSs SPORT CURTAIN DRAPES TIEBACKS Tie backs	$60.00	Pottery Barn Universal Single Drapery Rod BRASS 28-48	$19.99
[3 of these sold in a multiple item ("Dutch") auction for $20 each]		DECORATIVE CURTAIN RODS FAN TAIL FINIAL	$19.99
2 IKEA Dignitet CABLE WIRE CURTAIN ROD Systems! NEW!	$54.99	2 IKEA Cable Wire CURTAIN ROD Systems with Clips! NEW!	$19.99
POTTERY BARN DOUBLE SCROLL ROD XL BLACK NEW	$52.09	NIB POTTERY BARN PARKER URN HOLDBACK ROD FINIAL SET 2	$19.99
Pottery Barn UNIVERSAL XLg std SINGLE DRAPE ROD BRONZE	$49.99	[2 of these sold for $19.99 each]	
DISNEY ARIEL Drapes NEW	$49.98	NWT - POTTERY BARN "PARKER URN" FINIAL PEWTER SET/2	$19.99
[2 of these sold in a multiple item ("Dutch") auction for $24.99 each]		NWT - POTTERY BARN "PARKER BALL" FINIAL PEWTER SET/2	$19.99
POTTERY BARN SMALL BRASS Scroll Rod Set NEW	$46.00	POTTERY BARN KIDS DOUBLE ROD ADD-ON KIT–WHITE 96-120"	$19.95
Pottery Barn DRAPERY ROD 48-88" w/ PARKER BALL FINIALS	$43.95	POTTERY BARN DARK BRONZE COMPONENT	$19.05
NIB Pottery Barn Cast Iron Square Drapery Rod. 60-108"	$42.00	CURTAIN ROD 48-88"	
Pottery Barn Curtain Drape Rod and Finials	$41.50	2 Horseshoe CURTAIN ROD HOLDERS (Real Horse Shoe)	$18.99

Window Treatments ▸ Curtains, Drapes

The average sales price in this subcategory is $24.89.

	HIGH		AVG
NOBILIS SILK TRIMMING TASSEL 17 YARDS	$380.00	Waverly Floral Manor Fruit Double Layer Valances	$32.33
10 PIECE CUSTOM DRAPERY KIAWAH HOME MAKEOVER	$150.00	Restoration Hardware	$31.00
Pottery Barn 2 Paxton Roller Shades 27 X 72 Natural	$119.99	DECORATIVE TRIMMING TASSEL 8.5 YARDS	$29.99
Pottery Barn 1 Dupioni Silk Drape 50 X 84 Pole Pebble	$79.99	POTTERY BARN LINEN APPLIQUE PANELS two 63" PINK	$29.99
English Style Off-White Lace Curtains - 3 sets	$61.00	POTTERY BARN SILK DUPIONI VALANCE BRIGHT PINK 2	$29.99
Pottery Barn Morgan Stripe Cafe Curtain S/2 44x24" New	$59.99	2 Pottery Barn Kids Butterfly Sheers 44x96" NIP	$28.99
Waverly *TAHITI* Palm Tree Tab Top Curtains 42x84 Pair	$49.99	Exotic Door Deco Toran/Drape Valance Sari India	$26.99
Pottery Barn Pair Grommet Drape Bottom border Maize 96"	$49.99	SUPER LAVENDER EMBR SARI CURTAIN DRAPES THROW	$25.00
NWT Pottery Barn Curtains 63" Ivory Linen & Cotton x4	$45.00	NEW CURTAINS Hunter Green Ruffled Priscillas Drapes	$24.98
Pottery Barn 1 Dupioni Silk Drape 50 X 63 Pole Pebble	$44.99	[2 of these sold in a multiple item ("Dutch") auction for $12.49 each]	
POTTERY BARN CORDUROY PANEL DRAPE BLUE NAVY 2 63"	$44.99	Birdhouse Swag Curtain Valance/Window/Kitchen/Bath/Bird	$24.10
SAGE JACQUARD BROCADE CURTAINS/DRAPES CURTAIN 8 PC SET	$44.99	[2 of these sold in a multiple item ("Dutch") auction for $12.05 each]	
Pottery Barn 1 Dupioni Silk Drape 50 X 63 Pole Wine	$44.99	VINTAGE BROCADE PURPLE SARI CURTAINS FABRIC	$24.00
[2 of these sold for $44.99 each]		MAROON EMBR SARI CURTAINS DRAPES THROW FABRIC	$24.00
POTTERY BARN CORDUROY PANEL DRAPE BLUE NAVY 2 63"	$39.99	IKEA White Tab Curtains Drapes sheer 2 panels NEW Wilma	$23.95
[2 of these sold for $39.99 each]		IKEA Blue Tab Curtains Drapes sheer panels 2 NEW Wilma	$22.95
POTTERY BARN CORDUROY PANEL DRAPE red 2 63"	$39.99	TOMMY HILFIGER CURTAINS - 2 PANELS W/ TIEBACKS	$22.75

Window Treatments ▸ Valances

The average sales price in this subcategory is $13.91.

	HIGH		AVG
NEW 2 Pottery Barn MORGAN STRIPE Cafe Valance 44x13	$74.00	Two Formal Window Valances Capulet Stripe New NR	$15.50
OUTHOUSE Curtain VALANCE Linda Spivey Out House NEW!	$53.00	Waverly Country French Cabernet Valance ROSES	$15.49
7 HOME DEKOR VALANCES BY CROSCILL, BEAUTIFUL TAPESTRY	$51.00	Lovely Pair of Laura Ashley Bramble Window Valances (2)	$15.05
2 Croscill Fragrance Ascot Valances NIP 1st Quality	$49.99	NEW Pottery Barn Kids ALPHABET SOUP VALANCE 18x44	$15.00
CROSCILL PATRIOT VALANCE MERCURY SAGE GREEN NIP	$46.00	Primitive Country Homespun Americana Valance	$15.00
JC Penney Mustique Swag Valance	$43.00	POTTERY BARN KIDS BUTTER GINGHAM VALANCE 50"X 18"	$14.99
One Pottery Barn Morgan Stripe Cafe Curtain 44x36"	$39.95	NIP ~ WAVERLY ROMANTICA IN CRIMSON YORK VALANCE	$14.99
Custom box pleated valance - palm trees - beige w/ sage	$39.00	[2 of these sold for $14.99 each]	
Waverly Tahiti Sage Fairfield Valance NEW! Palm Tree	$36.05	WAVERLY ROSETTE IN ONYX BALLOON VALANCE ~ NIP	$14.99
Leather Valance Sage Rustic Log Cabin Bear Western New	$36.00	Country Cabin Swag NEW Valances 2 Burgandy Plaid	$14.99
Custom Laura Ashley Quartet Valance Cottage Chic Roses	$35.36	The Cow Jumped Over The Moon Valance Set of 2 NEW	$14.99
[2 of these sold in a multiple item ("Dutch") auction for $17.68 each]		2 RED VIGNETTE VICTORIAN TOILE VALANCES CURTAINS	$14.99
2 NEW Croscill Jewel/Gemstone ASCOT Valances 1st	$34.99	Green or Pink Central Park Toile Valance NEW nursery	$14.99
WAVERLY*GARDEN ROOM*VINTAGE ROSE DOUBLE LAYER VALANCE	$33.00	NEW DENIM BLUE JEAN TAB VALANCE LOT OF 2 60 x 16" NIP	$14.50
Tommy Hilfiger JENNA Blousson Valance 1stQual NEW	$32.95	2 BLACK ENGLISH COUNTRY TOILE FABRIC VALANCES CURTAINS	$13.99
NEW CROSCILL TOWNHOUSE ASCOT VALANCE 1ST QUALITY	$32.00		

22

JEWELRY & WATCHES

The Jewelry & Watches category is similar to the Art category on eBay in that big names—in this case, brand names as opposed to famous artists—at very high prices tend to dominate the high end (many of which sell via eBay's live auction format), but many quality items are also available at affordable prices. Artisans with small businesses peddle many nice pieces at reasonable to low prices. In fact, many jewelry makers purchase their supplies as well as sell their wares in the Jewelry & Watches category—findings, such as hooks, rings, and many types of beads are available here.

One example of an item in the high price range is the "French Harmer Platinum Diamond/Ruby Bracelet" that sold for $8,000.00 in the Jewelry & Watches ▸ Bracelets ▸ Bangle subcategory. Although $8,000.00 may seem like a lot of money, the "estimate" on this auction was US $157,500.00 to $167,500.00. (Live auctions on eBay usually feature this "estimate," which, as defined by the site, is the "expected price for a lot set by the auction house based on previous sales of similar items.") The bracelet weighed 42.6 g, was about 6.5 inches long, and featured about eight total karats of diamond (which are in F color, VVS clarity) and five total karats of ruby. Other high sellers were two 18-carat gold and lapis lazuli bracelets with diamonds that sold for $6,200.00.

As evidence that luxury brand names hold up well over time (often true for everything from jewelry to clothing to cars), a Cartier white gold and diamond bracelet sold for $4,500.00. The seller said she bought it at her local Seattle, Washington, Cartier retail store in 2002 for about $6,000.00, and the photos in the auction clearly show the Cartier signature. She also gave the serial number of the bracelet, which came in its original red Cartier box. All these factors, along with the seller's positive feedback rating of 100 percent and an included Cartier certificate, helped this eBayer fetch a healthy resale price for her gently used item.

If you're looking for a bangle that doesn't cost thousands of dollars, however, you can choose from a variety of bracelets in this subcategory that sold for around $9.00, the approximate median price. Many of these are "Indian ethnic glass" bracelets, traditional round bracelets that Indian women often wear with saris.

The Influence of Trends

Speaking of Indian bracelets, the whole nouveau hippie look has helped sales of such jewelry, and many sellers include keywords such as *ethnic* and *boho* in the titles of their listings to capitalize on this movement. Ethnic jewelry is one trend that influences listings here; others are the Italian modular charm bracelet, dangly "chandelier" style earrings, and silver Tiffany bracelets (the latter having spawned many cheaper imitations).

The whole modular bracelet trend was started by an Italian company called "Nomination," which created "composable" bracelets of cube-like charms with letters, numbers, images, and other designs on them; the charms could be arranged and rearranged in bracelets to reflect a person's individuality. Now these Italian bracelets have a whole subcategory on eBay: Jewelry & Watches ▶ Charms & Charm Bracelets ▶ Italian Modular. A high seller here was a lot of "14 Charms for Deb"—a series of modular charms that featured photos and images of flowers and the Golden Gate Bridge that sold for $83.86 with free shipping. Most of the other highest sellers in this subcategory were for wholesale lots, such as the auction for 2,500 photo charms that sold for $588.00, or as the seller put it, "about $0.235 each."

How do the prices here compare to retail prices? Let's look at another trendy item, the silver Tiffany heart-tag toggle bracelet. On the Tiffany website, it sells for $195.00 with the toggle clasp. (The simpler heart-tag charm bracelet, without the larger toggle clasp, is $175.00 retail.) On eBay, Tiffany silver heart-tag toggle bracelets sold in this sample for $152.50 and $145.00 (which was in the average price range for the Tiffany brand subcategory), a savings of up to $50.00. In each case, the sellers claimed the bracelets were authentic.

Engagement Rings for Two Weeks' Salary?

People are also buying engagement rings on eBay. There were about 14,000 diamond engagement or anniversary rings listed on one recent date. The top seller in this sample went for about $9,000.00, followed by some in the $3,000.00 to $5,000.00 range, but I have seen diamond rings sell for $35,000.00 on eBay (an "$85,000.00 PLATINUM 6.13 ct FANCY LIGHT YELLOW DIAMOND RING" that featured a 5.03 carat "oval-cut natural fancy light yellow diamond" of VS1 clarity in the center).

But how much is your average, garden-variety diamond engagement ring? A search of a thousand completed auctions for "14k gold 1 ct diamond ring" brings an average price of $322.02. Some of these are actually 0.5 carats, but some are also 1.2 to 1.9 carats, so it may all come out in the wash; certainly many rings in that sample are at least 1 carat. As a comparison, a 14-karat white gold solitaire engagement ring with a 1 carat princess-cut diamond in a 4-prong setting sold for $2,999.00 on Zales.com. Suffice to say you can find plenty of diamond rings on eBay for hundreds rather than thousands of dollars. (Of course, diamonds are going to vary in color, cut, and clarity, which affects their price, but there are many good deals out there.) eBay even has an informational section devoted to choosing a diamond engagement ring at http://pages.ebay.com/buy/guides/engagement-rings-buying-guide.

Watches from Three to Six Figures

Ask most people in the United States to name a luxury watch brand, and they'll say Rolex. And yet, among the highest-selling wristwatches in this sample, other names such as Blancpain, Piaget, Patek Philippe, Audemars Piguet, and Roger Dubuis show up. Indeed, the most expensive watch in this sample is a Blancpain 18-karat gold diamond dress watch, truly an exquisite timepiece, which sold for $65,000.00. That's actually a bargain, according to the seller, who says its approximate retail price is $215,000.00 plus tax, although there is the curious qualifier that "the retail price provided is based solely upon our past knowledge and should not be relied upon as fact." If that retail price sounds exorbitant to you, know that there are indeed watches out there that cost into the six figures, so it's not outside the realm of imagination!

Other high prices here include $41,000.00 for a Piaget 18-karat gold diamond and emerald watch, $25,999.00 for a Rolex Daytona 18-karat white gold bracelet watch, and $24,600.00 for a Patek Philippe 18-karat yellow gold watch. Interestingly, quite a few of the most expensive luxury watches here do go unsold—in the completed prices results for this subcategory, there are several pages of unsold watch listings priced from $695,000.00 (there are those six figures) for a rare Patek Philippe platinum "Minute Repeater" (billed as new and with the "GREATEST COMPLICATION EVER"), to $100,000.00 and $90,000.00 watches, and on down to $10,000.00 watches and below.

The average price in Jewelry & Watches ▶ Watches ▶ Wristwatches is quite a bit more down to earth; it's around $150.00, with familiar names such as Timex, Seiko, and Movado being nearer this mark.

Findings . . . and Finds

The Jewelry category is about selling as well as buying, but, as mentioned before, while many people sell their wares here, they also can buy what they need to make them here. In the Jewelry & Watches ▶ Jewelry Boxes & Supplies ▶ Tools, Findings subcategory, you can find everything from industrial casting and engraving machines for making jewelry (such as an induction casting machine for $3,251.00) to the tiny rings, hooks, and thin wire used to make necklaces (like the hundred 5mm sterling silver open jump rings for $5.49). If you combine those items with the wide variety of beads and loose gemstones, you'd never need to leave your house to create and sell jewelry on eBay.

Some sellers don't make the stuff they sell—they buy it wholesale, either here or via another venue. And some of them go on online treasure hunts in the mixed lot subcategories to see if there are unassuming gems lurking within—literally as well as figuratively—that may have been overlooked. That big lot of grandma's costume jewelry may contain a valuable signed Trifari pin, say, or other special pieces that stand out to a knowledgeable jeweler's or collector's eye. If you're in a lucky mood, try your hand at it; otherwise you should find plenty of real and simulated gems throughout the entire Jewelry & Watches category to cover your gift list.

Bracelets ▶ Bangle

The average sales price in this subcategory is $10.03.

	HIGH		AVG
4348 French Harmer Platinum Diamond/Ruby Bracelet	$8,000.00	Indian Glass Bangles 2.4 Gypsy Belly Dance Sari Charms	$8.99
6327 French Harmer Platinum Diamond/Ruby Bracelet	$8,000.00	DL-14 Silver Floral Design Bangle Cuff Bracelet	$8.99
3872 de GRISOGONO 18K Gold-Lapis-lazuli Bracelet w/Dia	$6,200.00	Lot of 3 Wooden BANGLES Octagonal Rnd Bracelets *BOHO	$8.99
6236 de GRISOGONO 18K Gold Lapis-lazuli Bracelet w/Dia	$6,200.00	Indian Ethnic GLASS SARI BANGLE BoHo Bracelets Brown L	$8.99
4684 BUCCELLATI 18K Gold Bangle	$4,800.00	Indian Glass Bangles 2.5 Gypsy Belly Dance Sari Charms	$8.99
Authentic Cartier Love Bracelet. 18 carats white gold with 6 diamonds	$4,500.00	New Authentic Alligator Bangle Bracelet /Cuff	$8.99
6854 BUCCELLATI 18K Gold Leaf Shape Bangle	$4,300.00	[2 of these sold for $8.99 each]	
5072 BUCCELLATI 18K Gold Leaf Shape Bangle	$4,200.00	Beautiful Black Jade & Gold "Fortune" Bracelet- BG17	$8.99
18K WG 5Ct Diamond Bangle	$4,100.00	Indian Ethnic GLASS SARI BANGLES BoHo Chic Bracelets M	$8.99
4696 MARINA B 18K Gold Diamonds Open Bangle	$3,800.00	NIB MENS STAINLESS STEEL BANGLE BRACELET BLACK RUBBER	$8.99
6819 18k Gold Bangle Bracelet with Round & Marquise Dia	$2,200.00	Pittsburg Steelers Spirit GLASS SARI BANGLE Bracelets L	$8.99
4393 MARINA B 18K Gold Bangle	$2,100.00	DANGLE BRACELET Simulated Pearls & Swarovski Cryst 107S	$8.99
3848 CHANTECLER 18K Gold Pearls Bangle w/Dia/Ruby/Sapp	$2,000.00	BEAUTIFUL 14KT GOLD OVERLAY DIAMOND	$8.99
[2 of these sold for $2,000 each]		CUT BANGLE BRACELET	
2.04 CT ROUND DIAMOND BANGLE BRACELET 18 K	$1,833.00	3 ROW RHINESTONE & DARK WOOD BANGLE BRACELET - NEW	$8.99
WHITE GOLD RETAIL APPRAISAL IS $ 4069.00!!!!!!		WOOD & RHINESTONE BOHEMIAN	$8.99
1.54 CT PRINCESS DIAMOND BANGLE BRACELET 18K	$1,719.00	BANGLE BRACELET- GREAT GIFT	
WHITE GOLD		STUNNING 14KT GOLD OVERLAY	$8.99
ALL DIAMONDS ARE 100% NATURAL!!		DIAMOND CUT BANGLE BRACELET	

Bracelets ▶ Beaded, Strands

The average sales price in this subcategory is $27.32.

	HIGH		AVG
456: 18ct white gold necklet with a central curved sect	GBP 1,800.00	14KT GOLD TIN CUP GENUINE PEARL BRACELET 14K	$31.00
Antique Estate Slide Diamond&Pearl Bracelet	$1,400.50	NO RESERVE* GENUINE TAHITIAN	$29.95
5212 14KY Gold Bracelet w/ Emerald/ Diamond	$1,300.00	PEARL BRACELET 14K Y/GOLD	$28.99
7206 14KY Gold Bracelet w/ Emerald/ Diamond	$1,300.00	$299 white pearl & gold bead bracelet. 9mm pearls!!!	$28.99
Mikimoto Strand of 5 mm Pearls of the Highest Quality.	$1,000.00	Beautiful BlackOnyx/ MOP Sterling Silver Bracelet	$27.99
Mikimoto Clasp, Mikimoto Gold M charm, 22 inches long		V $5100 DOUBLE AKOYA PEARLS BRACELET 14K 7.5"	$26.00
7842 MARIA MENARINI 18KW Gold Bracelet w/ Diamond/ Mult	$900.00	HONORA Pearl Leather Bracelet w/Pink Strap Sterling S	$25.99
LADIES 14K WHITE GOLD & DIAMOND BRACELET	$800.00	PRECIOUS AAA+ WHITE&YELLOW	$24.99
7" 14K GOLD RUBY AND DIAMOND BAR BRACELET #625023	$800.00	SALTWATE PEARLS BRACELET	
4118 18K White Gold Bracelet w/ Diamond/ Onyx	$650.00	Pearl Silver Mother of Pearl Heart Charm Bracelet 2 ROW	$24.99
6154 18K White Gold Bracelet w/ Diamond/ Onyx	$650.00	Pearl & Silver HONORA Bracelet 3 ROWS	$24.99
3803 18k White Gold Bracelet with Diamonds and Turquois	$600.00	Opal Solid Gold Ring Size 7 NR	$24.05

Bracelets ▶ Link, Chain

The average sales price in this subcategory is $25.85.

	HIGH		AVG
JUDITH RIPKA 925 & 18k CHAIN BRACELET	$457.75	NEW Brighton Twinkle Toes Bracelet Hard to find!	$28.00
CHROME HEARTS STERLING FLORAL CROSS ID BRACELET 9.5"	$400.00	SS Bracelet - 12+ Cts. Emerald Cut Amethysts!	$27.50
JOHN HARDY ARMADILLO LINK BRACELET	$360.00	BRIGHTON SILVER PEDIGREE DOG CHARM BRACELET ADORABLE	$27.00
Authentic JOHN HARDY Sterling Silver Bracelet-Woven	$235.00	Brighton Bracelet"Memory Lane" Silver nwt	$26.49
Authentic Tiffany & Co Heart Link Gold/Silver Bracelet	$232.50	Mens Womens Silver Harley Davidson bikers Cuff bracelet	$26.03
Designer Don Lucas Sterling charm bracelet ret. $399	$212.50	PAMPERED CHEF CONSULTANT CHARM BRACELET WITH 5 CHARMS	$26.00
Tiffany Heart Clasp bracelet	$155.00	STERLING SILVER HEART & OVAL LINK TOGGLE BRACELET $1NR	$26.00
Tiffany & Co. Graduated bead necklace/bracelet set!	$151.00	HANDMADE SOLID S/S .925 WESTIE LINK BRACELET. L@@K!	$26.00
245.6 Grams HEAVY CURB LINK BRACELET-Sterling Silver-MX	$149.99	B305 Silver 7.5" Double Square Byzantine Bali Bracelet	$25.49
CHROME HEARTS GABOUR STYLE SILVER 925 BRACELET NEW!!	$149.00	7 inch Sterling Silver Medical ID Alert Bracelet ss	$25.00
Authentic Tiffany & Co heart bracelet worth $1295	$147.50	Genuine Diamond Necklace	$24.99
Tiffany Heart Link Bracelet	$142.51	Mens Silver Tone STAINLESS STEEL MAGNETIC GOLF BRACELET	$24.99
Chrome Hearts Dagger ID Fancy Chain Bracelet w/ Clip	$139.99	New STAINLESS STEEL Mens MAGNETIC Therapy BRACELET	$24.99
Harley Davidson Bracelet 100 th Anniversary Siver	$130.00	DAZZLING Silver w/ Marcasite Heart Bracelet	$24.99
Gucci .925 Sterling Silver Link Bracelet	$125.00	CLASSIC Vintage STERLING SILVER Bangle Hinged Bracelet	$24.32

Bracelets ▶ Tennis

The average sales price in this subcategory is $82.25.

	HIGH		AVG
Authen TIFFANY & CO. 18K YG DIAMOND & SAPPHIRE BRACELET	$2,750.00	Blass Night & Day Sapphire Bracelet 14kt- Franklin Mint	$90.50
$8500 7.00CT SAPPHIRE & DIAMOND BRACELET	$870.00	$1090.03 8.4 CT SAPPHIRE & DIAMOND BRACELET SOLID GOLD	$86.00
USGL certified sapphire and diamond bracelet / earrings	$810.00	20 CT. 86 MARQUIS GENUINE SAPPHIRE BRACELET- NO RESERVE	$84.05
Vintage Gold Sapphire Diamond Locket Picture Bracelet	$800.00	7.6" Princess Blue Sapphire & Round Platinum Bracelet	$82.30
BEAUTIFUL SAPPHIRE DIAMOND BANGLE 14K $.01	$700.00	sapphire & diamond tennis bracelet w/ earrings to match	$82.03
NR 13.37ct Nat. MultiColor Sapphire Bracelet 14kWG	$610.00	14K WHITE GOLD SAPPHIRE & DIAMOND BRACELET...7"L	$81.01
14K Gold Bracelet with 63 Princess Cut Sapphires	$500.00	$2,500 1.85CT SAPHIRE BRACELET	$76.10
7 CT PRINCESS CUT SAPPHIRE TENNIS BRACELET	$400.00	$3000 4.20CT BLUE SAPPHIRE & DIAMOND BRACLET	$76.01
QUALITY-14K YG-SAPPHIRE/DIAMOND BRACELET-7 IN.-12.30 GR	$325.00	NO RESERVE * NATURAL SAPPHIRE & DIAMONDS BRACELET	$76.00
9.55ct RAINBOW SAPPHIRE TENNIS BRACELET	$249.99	ASTONISHING 10K SAPPHIRE & DIAMOND TENNIS BRACELET	$76.00

Charms & Charm Bracelets ▶ Italian Modular

The average sales price in this subcategory is $1.98.

	HIGH		AVG
0135: Charm bracelet 18kt yellow gold (acid tested not Live Auctions!	$825.00	Black Chow Chow Dog Custom Photo Italian Charm Charms	$3.24
WHOLESALE LOT OF 2,500 PCS PHOTO ITALIAN CHARMS - PW82.	$588.00	free s/h* LADYBUG NOAH ITALIAN CHARM/CHARMS FIT ZOPPINI	$2.99
About US$0.235 each ! 50pcs or 100 pcs Per Design!		PUGSTER Charms ENAMEL TURTLE BRACELET Jewelry New Hot	$2.99
ESTATE AWESOME 14K GOLD STARTER CHARM BRACELET NR	$426.79	BETTA #1 FISH CUSTOM ITALIAN CHARM/CHARMS Munchy	$2.99
WHOLESALE 100 PCS ITALIAN CHARM WATCHS - LW100	$400.00	MONARCH BUTTERFLY CUSTOM ITALIAN CHARM, CHARMS	$2.99
About US$4.00 each ! Over 100 Designs To Choose.		PUGSTER Italian Charms FAIRY WITH RHINESTONE WINGS X2	$2.99
WHOLESALE 100 PCS ITALIAN CHARM WATCHS - SRDW LW100	$371.01	DETAILED SHAR PEI DOG ITALIAN	$2.98
*RARE ESTATE 14K GOLD MECHANICAL "RING BOX" CHARM NRv	$355.00	CHARM/CHARMS FOR ZOPPINI	
VINTAGE 750/18K GOLD CHARM BRACELET 5 CHARMS 28.6 GRAM	$350.00	PUGSTER Italian Charms CHIHUAHUA BROWN Bracelet Jewelry	$2.35
NEW ITALIAN Charms LOT. More than 600 pieces! SS/18K	$338.00	RUNNING HORSE GLITTER GOLD	$2.34
NOMINATION, Made in Italy Stainless Steel & 18K CHARMS		NEW ITALIAN CHARM CHARMS	
WHOLESALE 100 PCS ITALIAN CHARM WATCHS - SRDW LW100	$326.89	AMETHYST FEB BUTTERFLY SPARKLE Italian Enamel Charm	$2.28
433: RELIGIOUS VINTAGE NEEDLEWORK SIGNED Live Auctions!	$325.00	BUTTERFLY ON DAISY & Blue Sparkle Italian Charm Moth	$2.28
WHOLESALE LOT 5600 ITALIAN CHARMS 18K PLATED	$309.63	Yellow Lab Labrador Retriever Italian Charm~Cute!	$2.25
0219: Free Land Overalls kickplate Live Auctions!	$275.00	American Eskimo Photo Italian Charm~Lot of 2!	$2.00
WHOLESALE 100 PCS ITALIAN CHARM WATCHS - SRDW LW100	$250.00	PUGSTER Italian Charms WESTERN COWBOY	$2.00
WHOLESALE 100 PCS ITALIAN CHARM WATCHS - SRDW LW100	$226.00	HAT SNAKESKIN New	
WHOLESALE LOT 170 AUTHENTIC DISNEY ITALIAN CHARMS - NEW	$199.99	MONKEY w/ BANANA Italian Charm Bracelet Link charms new	$1.99

Charms & Charm Bracelets ▸ Traditional

The average sales price in this subcategory is $10.13.

	HIGH		AVG
14k Vintage Plique ?our Charm ~ Paris, France!	$213.50	CUTE NEW! PALM TREE W/ FLORIDA SIGN 14K GOLD CHARM 330	$13.95
14k GOLD STUNNING 3D BLACKAMOOR PRINCESS CHARM PENDANT	$103.50	STERLING Silver 3-D Charm SPLIT OAK BASKET with Bee	$13.77
14K GOLD 3D HAPPY BIRTHDAY CAKE CHARM - Opens to candle	$59.99	Sterling ENAMEL BLUE BIRD Perched on BIRD BATH Charm	$11.77
14k GOLD 3D LADIES PURSE HANDBAG CHARM enamel	$34.99	14k Yellow Gold Baby Toy ABC Blocks Charm for Bracelet	$10.56
NEW! 3D REVOLVER PISTOL HAND GUN CHARM 14K GOLD 689	$31.95	10k Yellow Gold Baby Boot / Shoe Charm for Bracelet! NR	$10.56
NEW* 14K SOLID GOLD CHRISTMAS TREE CHARM PENDENT NR	$30.00	VINTAGE SILVER HEAVY HORSE AND CARRIAGE CHARM	$10.50
Vintage sterling silver blue ENAMEL USA map charm	$25.99	James Avery Sterling Silver Dancing Shoes Charm	$10.50
14k GOLD 3D MOVEABLE DUTCH WINDMILL CHARM PENDANT	$25.49	Hand-Crafted SKYE Yorkie Terrier Charm Bracelet "B"	$9.99
14K Y/G ORNATE BEER STEIN CHARM/PENDENT W/OPENING COVER	$24.50	DOUBLE DECKER BUS Vintage Sterling Silver Charm	$9.99
capitol records sterling enameled charm	$23.50	Sterling & Enamel MONARCH BUTTERFLY charm	$9.99
10k Tri Color Rose Color Solid Gold Clown Charm Cute NR	$16.99	LOT OF 12 MIXED STYLE PEWTER CHARMS	$9.99
Vintage Sterling Silver Erotic Woman Moon Rider Charm	$15.95	Vintage INTAGLIO BUBBLE Enamel Horses Sterling Charm	$9.49
Darling Miniature SHAKER BASKET STERLING Silver CHARM	$15.50	FAIRY CHARM sterling silver winged faery enamel	$9.40
UNIQUE GIRL SCOUT PENDANT/CHARM	$15.50	Free S/H G181 Sterling Silver Charms Schnauzer + Bone	$8.99
Vintage Sterling Fountain Square Cincinnati Ohio Charm	$15.45	Free S/H G184 Sterling Silver Charms Shar-Pei + Bone	$8.99

Children's Jewelry ▸ Bracelets

The average sales price in this subcategory is $8.83.

	HIGH		AVG
$330 14k Yellow Gold Girl Heart Id Bracelet HIGH POLISH	$66.00	~Sun~ 18K White Gold BABY BANGLE Bracelet GF 9-24 Mnths	$9.99
GeNuiNe WhiTe PearL BabY BraCeLeT by Gucci	$61.00	BABY BANGLE BRACELET LEAF FLOWER SILVER	$9.99
Darling Baby I.D. Tag Bracelet in 10k Solid Gold .99 NR	$41.00	~Snowflake~ 18KT Gold BABY BANGLE Bracelet GF 0-9 Mnth	$9.99
18K GF GeNuiNe WhiTe PearL BabY BraCeLeT by Gucci	$39.76	Child's Rolled Gold Bangle Bracelet	$9.99
Darling Baby figaro I.D. Tag Bracelet in solid 10k gold	$36.00	~Butterfly 18K Gold GF TEEN CHAIN BRACELET Charm Sz 4-5	$9.99
Boutique UPTOWNGIRLS pink and brown fringe bracelet CBD	$32.00	~Mistletoe~ 18KT Gold BABY BANGLE Bracelet GF 9-24 Mnth	$9.99
PRIVATE Auction For Our Wonderful Customer~Deanna!~	$30.00	~Curve~ 18KT Gold BIG GIRL BANGLE Bracelet GF 5-12 Yrs	$9.99
10kt & 14kt Solid Gold Bracelets,3 for 1!!!!!!!!!! NR!	$26.99	STUNNING Sterling Silver Pearl Baby / Child Bracelet	$9.99
Girls Bracelet Boutique~Candy Land Lollipop Girl~	$26.50	Vintage Child's 4 Lucky Charm Bracelet	$9.99
Boutique Rubber Duck Swarovski & Polymer Clay Bracelet	$25.00	Goldilocks & 3 Bears! Strlng Slvr Swarovski by LRS BHV	$9.99
Custom Auction for Rene'- m2m boutique bracelets	$25.00	VINTAGE GIRL SCOUT BROWNIE BRACELET	$9.99
Boutique PRIDDY Unicorn Baby Bracelet	$22.99	~Waves~ 18K White Gold GIRL BANGLE Bracelet Age 5-12	$9.99
Sterling Silver BABY ID Cuff Bracelet ENGRAVEABLE .925	$21.55	~Starlet~ 18K White Gold BABY BANGLE GF Bracelet 9-24 Mn	$9.99
~New Moon~ 18KT Gold BABY BANGLE Bracelet GF 0-9 Months	$21.00	Child Bracelet, Lovely PINK Swarovski Crystals, 6", NR!	$9.95
Girls Bracelet Boutique ~Very Cherry Butterfly~ Sweet!	$20.50	Etched Baby / Child Sterling Silver Bangle Bracelet 302	$9.95

Children's Jewelry ▸ Necklaces & Pendants

The average sales price in this subcategory is $9.68.

	HIGH		AVG
Baby Add-A-Pearl Necklace MIB 3 pearls; VINTAGE	$245.51	Little Orphan Annie On Top of World Charm	$9.99
DAVID YURMAN CABLE KIDS 18K GOLD CROSS PENDANT NECKLACE	$180.00	Little Orphan Annie Skating Charm	$9.99
~ My First Pearls 14" Genuine Pearl Necklace ~ Dutch!	$120.00	Sterling Silver Baby/Child Pendant FREE ENGRAVING	$9.99
[12 of these sold in a multiple item ("Dutch") auction for $10.00 each]		Boutique Belles "Calvin" Dragon Necklace BHV winipoo	$9.99
~ My First Pearls 14" Genuine Pearl Necklace ~ Dutch!	$96.00	Boutique Belles "Kenny" Dragon Necklace BHV winipoo	$9.99
[12 of these sold in a multiple item ("Dutch") auction for $8.00 each]		LANDSTROMS BLACK HILLS GOLD KIDS	$9.99
Childrens or Baby 14K Gold Cross 15" 14K Gold Necklace	$52.99	X-MAS NECKLACE 50% off	
COMPLETE 36pc UNIT-ENCHANTED FAIRY DUST NECKLACES-df01	$52.51	STERLING SILVER CROSS W/ IMITATION PEARLS PENDANT	$9.95
NEW GENUINE DIAMOND PENDANT .32 CTW NECKLACE!	$46.00	KIDS BLUE & PINK CROSS CHARM PENDANT STERLING SILVER	$9.95
Lot of 40 Plastic Clip on Charms from the 80's	$41.00	SWAROVSKI CRYSTAL MOVABLE TEDDY BEAR NECKLACE	$9.00
TEEN #1 FRIEND PENDANT 14K YELLOW GOLD	$36.64	Childrens Kids Flip Flop Shoe Earring Necklace Set	$9.00
LOTS<>VINTAGE CHILDRENS PLASTIC CHARM NECKLACE	$35.00	italian solid sterling silver anchor necklace chain 24'	$8.99
BAPTISM MEDAL 14K SOLID GOLD ITALY CHARM PENDANT	$32.99	FUN GIRLS JEWELRY W/ WINNIE THE POOH	$8.99
PRECIOUS NEW 16" ITALIAN 14 K.Y.GOLD NECKLACE+NoRESERVE	$30.00	MUSIC JEWELRY BOX	
NEW 14K GOLD PINK BABY SHOES PENDANT	$29.99	Colorful PLASTIC CHARM Chain Link Necklace + DAISY snap	$8.55
boutique STITCHINCHICKS custom THANKFUL FALL necklace	$28.00	University of Missouri, Mizzou Tigers Charm Bracelet	$8.50
C9D WDAS Boutique Clay Unicorn Necklace Custom CBD BHV	$26.00	BEAUTIFUL CRYSTAL DOUBLE HEART NECKLACE COOKIE LEE	$7.99

Designer Brands ▸ Brighton

The average sales price in this subcategory is $5.55.

	HIGH		AVG
Brighton 2003 Think Pink Event Charm Bracelet MIB	$177.50	BRIGHTON ELIZA BRACELET	$25.00
NWT! Complete Set Brighton LOVE BUG Collection! NR!!	$130.00	BRIGHTON ELLINGTON HEART	$25.00
Complete Love Bug Set! All NWT! Reg. $195.00!! WOW!!		(SILVER) BRACELET - -NEW	
Brighton"Hopi Dreams"Necklace,Bracelet & Earrings NWT	$125.63	BRIGHTON ENCHANTED HEART BRACELET	$25.00
Brighton 2003 Breast Cancer Awareness Bracelet View similar	$124.52	BRIGHTON LUCKY CLOVER BRACELET	$25.00
Brighton " Power of Pink" Bracelet/ Watch, Limited Qty.	$117.50	BRIGHTON LUTECE BRACELET	$25.00
NWT! Brighton GLASS MOUNTAIN Necklace Bracelet Earrings	$109.48	BRIGHTON PARK AVE HEART	$25.00
Brighton"Aries"Necklace Bracelet & Earrings NWT	$107.99	CHARM BRACELET-RED-NEW	
Brighton Glass Mountain Set! NWT! Swarovski Crystals!	$106.56	BRIGHTON PICADILLY BRACELET	$25.00
Brighton"Portabello" Necklace,Bracelet & Earrings NWT	$103.00	BRIGHTON 7" HEART BRACELET	$25.00
From the New Fall Line!		BRIGHTON BOHEMIAN FLOWER BRACELET	$25.00
Brighton Portabello Necklace, Earrings & Bracelet! New!	$102.50	BRIGHTON CENTRAL PARK BRACELET	$25.00

Brighton"Aries"Necklace Bracelet & Earrings NWT	$100.01	BRIGHTON DOLCE VITA BRACELET	$25.00
Brighton "Wild Heart" Necklace,Bracelet & Earrings NWT	$98.79	BRIGHTON ELLINGTON HEART (GOLD) BRACELET	$25.00
Brighton "Garden of Eden" Bracelet Necklace Earrings	$98.51	BRIGHTON ENCHANTED HEART BRACELET	$25.00
Brighton"Central Park"Necklace,Bracelet & Earrings NWT	$92.82	BRIGHTON LUCKY CLOVER BRACELET	$25.00
RARE Brighton HAWAII charm bracelet **NEW w/tag	$92.00	BRIGHTON LUTECE BRACELET --NEW	$25.00

Designer Brands ▶ Tiffany

The average sales price in this subcategory is $142.64.

	HIGH		AVG
New Lady 18k Tiffany & Co. Full Diamond Dress Watch NR	$5,101.24	Tiffany & Co. Graduated bead necklace/bracelet set!	$151.00
New Men's 18k Tiffany & Co. Full Diamond Dress Watch NR	$5,100.00	AUTHENTIC TIFFANY&CO OVAL TAG	$151.00
1 CT Heart Diamond Engagement Tiffany Style Ring	$2,950.00	NECKLACE & ROUND BRACELET	
HUGE TIFFANY PLATINUM ROUND CUT	$2,750.00	Authentic Tiffany Double Knots Sterling Cuff Links	$150.00
DIAMOND ENGAGEMENT RING		Tag necklace from the RETURN TO TIFFANY Collection. Ste	$150.00
TIFFANY & Co - Girard Perregaux Chronometer 18K GOLD	$2,335.00	Authentic Tiffany & Co heart bracelet worth $1295	$147.50
NEW TIFFANY PLATINUM ROUND CUT	$2,325.00	AUTHENTIC TIFFANY & CO TOGGLE LINK HEART NECKLACE &	$145.00
DIAMOND ENGAGEMENT RING		TIFFANY & COMPANY STERLING EARRINGS WITH BOX	$144.50
VINTAGE TIFFANY & CO. 14K RUBY DIAMOND NECKLACE CHOKER	$2,275.00	Tiffany Heart Link Bracelet	$142.51
Vintage Tiffany Duo Dial Doctor's Watch	$2,125.00	Authentic Tiffany & Co Mesh Necklace Heart Pendant	$142.50
NEW Tiffany & Co. Platinum Diamond Solitaire Ring VS1 G	$1,999.00	Tiffany Heart Link Necklace	$140.49
1.54 CT TIFFANY CERT. DIAMOND ENGAGEMENT RING RINGS	$1,915.00	Authentic Tiffany & Co. 14kt Y/G Shell Charm Pendant	$140.00
1956 TIFFANY & Co, OMEGA Waterproof Automatic, 14k Gold	$1,875.50	AUTHENTIC TIFFANY AND CO. OVAL	$140.00
AUTH MEN'S TIFFANY & CO ATLAS 18K GOLD QUARTZ WATCH	$1,500.00	TAG NECKLACE & BRACELET	
CERT~TIFFANY & CO~PLATINUM ASSCHER~E-VVS DIAMOND~RING	$1,324.99	Tiffany and Co. Sterling Silver/Pearl Bracelet	$139.49
Tiffany & Co. Diamond Platinum Wedding Band	$1,200.00	Authentic Tiffany & Co Hook & Eye Ring/Excellent!!/7.5	$137.50
NEW 1.25CT TIFFANY ROUND CUT DIAMOND ENGAGEMENT RING NR	$1,000.00	authentic tiffany co heart tag necklace & bracelet	$136.20

Designer Brands ▶ David Yurman

The average sales price in this subcategory is $399.53.

	HIGH		AVG
David Yurman Ladies Full Diamond Thoroughbred-NR	$3,650.00	DAVID YURMAN HAMPTON 14K GOLD	$415.00
David Yurman Sterling Diamond Ladies Cable Watch-NR	$2,575.25	STERLING & ONYX NECKLACE	
DAVID YURMAN DIAMOND BEZEL	$2,250.00	Authentic David Yurman Hampton Necklace w/Black Onyx	$411.53
STERLING SILVER WRISTWATCH		DAVID YURMAN DOUBLE CABLE DOUBLE	$410.00
DAVID YURMAN PAVE DIAMOND	$2,250.00	X BANGLE 14K/STERLING	
BEZEL&THOROUGHBRED&WATCH		David Yurman Amethyst 7mm Cuff Bracelet - Like New!	$405.00
DAVID YURMAN DIAMOND BEZEL	$2,250.00	DAVID YURMAN 7mm GOLD Metro SILVER Cable Bracelet - NR	$405.00
STERLING SILVER WRISTWATCH		DAVID YURMAN 14K GOLD & STERLING	$400.00
David Yurman Midsize SS Sterling Diamond Thorougbred-NR	$2,025.00	ONYX ALBION EARRINGS	
DAVID YURMAN RHODOLITE GARNET STERLING CABLE WATCH	$1,875.00	Woman's David Yurman Sterling and Gold Ring "New"	$400.00
David Yurman Sterling Stainless Ladies Dia Thoroughbred	$1,800.00	David Yurman Thoroughbred Cuff Bracelet	$399.00
DAVID YURMAN AUTHENTIC SILVER, GOLD & PAVE NECKLACE	$1,700.00	Impressive David Yurman Diamond/18K Gold Star of David	$399.00
David Yurman 14K Gold & Sterling DY Logo Pearl Necklace	$1,650.00	David Yurman Thoroughbred Cuff Bracelet	$399.00
[6 of these sold in a multiple item ("Dutch") auction for approx. $300.00 each]		Authentic David Yurman 925 14K Pink Tourmaline Ring	$395.00
David Yurman Mens Stainless Chrono Thoroughbred-NR	$1,525.00	DAVID YURMAN?AMETHYST?AND	$395.00
Stunning David Yurman Gold/SS Mixed Chain Necklace	$1,525.00	14K?GOLD ALBION?EARRINGS	
DAVID YURMAN PAVE DIAMOND BEZEL THOROUGHBRED WATCH	$1,520.00	Authentic David Yurman 925 14K Chalcedony Pendant	$382.77
David Yurman Ladies Sapphire Diamond Thoroughbred-NR	$1,425.00	David Yurman Quatrefoil Earrings Diamond Silver	$382.39
David Yurman Chelsea Collection Ladies Wrist Watch	$1,350.00	DAVID YURMAN 14K GOLD SILVER	$381.99
		CHALCEDONY CABLE BRACELET	

Earrings ▶ Dangle, Chandelier (Chandelier)

The average sales price in this subcategory is $10.77.

NOTE *These results are based on a keyword search of the Dangle, Chandelier subcategory for auctions with the word chandelier in the title.*

	HIGH		AVG
18K White Gold Chandelier Diamond Earrings 2.25" Long	$425.00	MULTI COLOR SHELL CRYSTAL CHANDELIER EARRINGS-New	$11.50
ELEGANT 2 CT GENUINE DIAMOND CHANDELIER EARRINGS $1 NR!	$218.05	Blue With Long Seashell Chandelier Earrings	$11.50
14K WHTE GOLD .50 ROUND DIAMOND CHANDELIER EARRINGS NR	$200.99	Gypsy Red Ruby Simulated Chandelier Hoop Earrings 1235	$11.05
Two Tone 14kt Gold Chandelier Diamond Earrings .50ctw	$142.53	EXQUISITE PERIDOT CRYSTAL CHANDELIER EARRINGS - WOW!	$10.99
TIGER LILY ClipOn LUNCH AT THE RITZ Chandelier Earrings	$112.38	EXQUISITE TOPAZ CRYSTAL CHANDELIER EARRINGS - WOW!	$10.99
NEW 14-kt. Gold BLUE Topaz Chandelier Earrings	$110.00	LAKH CZ BLUE CHANDELIER EARRINGS SARI INDIA BELLY DANCE	$10.99
6-7.5mm White Pearl + Diamond Solid Gold Chandelier	$62.00	Victorian Turquoise Synthetic Chandelier Earrings 1120	$10.84
New 10 KT Two Tone Gold CHANDELIER Ladies Earrings $299	$36.99	5 Inches Long! CHANDELIER EARRINGS Beads, Crystals	$10.50
GENUINE DIAMOND 14KT WHITE GOLD CHANDELIER EARRINGS NR	$36.00	RAINBOW MOTHER OF PEARL LIKE CHANDELIER FASHION earring	$10.50
Long 18K GOLD GP Shoulder Duster Chandelier Earrings	$32.00	Chandelier Earring Earrings SWAROVSKY RHINESTONE BRIDAL	$10.50
3.60 CARAT GENUINE CITRINE CHANDELIER EARRINGS	$30.59	PINK MOTHER OF PEARL LIKE SHELL CHANDELIER earrings	$10.50
Turquoise Charms Seashell Chandelier Cluster Earrings	$26.00	NEW EXOTIC BRASS TONE BEADED CHANDELIER EARRINGS	$10.49
NEW Sorrelli clip CRYSTAL Chandelier earrings	$25.00	COLLECTION OF 9 PAIRS OF CHANDELIER/DANGLING EARRINGS	$10.49
SWAROVSKI CRYSTAL*CHANDELIER/DANGLE/DUSTER EARRINGS*3IN	$24.99	RAINBOW MOTHER OF PEARL SHELL CHANDELIER EARRINGS	$10.49
14K Gold Chandelier Diamond-Cut Heart Earrings E250	$24.95	Austrian Crystal Hoop Chandelier Earrings Gold 5.0 cm	$10.49

Earrings ▸ Hoop, Huggie

The average sales price in this subcategory is $22.69.

	HIGH		AVG
CHAUMET 18K GOLD EARRINGS	$405.00	$189 14K GOLD DIAMOND CUT HOOP EARRINGS LARGE BRAND NEW	$29.53
18KT YELLOW GOLD GORGEOUS HALF HOOP!...	$112.50	RHODOLITE GARNET AND DIAMOND GOLD 9K EARRING $1 NR	$29.26
14K VERY LARGE yellow GOLD 14KT HOOP EARRINGS HOOPS	$94.99	WHITE GOLD plumeria STUDS post earrings	$29.00
14K Gold Fancy Hoop Earrings	$78.00	10K GREAT PLAIN THICK GOLD 10KT HOOP EARRINGS HOOPS	$28.99
Glitter Opal Gold Leverback Earrings	$76.00	$115 14k Yellow Gold Hoop Earring Diamond CUT LOVELY	$28.99
Estate 14K " X " Earrings white & yellow gold CARLA	$75.00	10K GREAT PLAIN THICK GOLD 10KT HOOP EARRINGS HOOPS	$28.99
10K VERY VERY LARGE GOLD 10KT 2 5/8 HOOP EARRINGS HOOPS	$72.99	14K GOLD HOOPS 4.3 GRAMS YELLOW GOLD N/R	$27.00
UGLY JEWELRY$599 14K Gold Two-Tone Hoop Earrings *NR*	$69.99	BLUE SAPPHIRE AND DIAMOND GOLD 14K EARRING $1 NR	$26.95
14K White Gold Extra Large "Runway" Hoop Earrings	$64.00	14 KT Yellow Gold French Back Earrings	$26.60
14K VERY LARGE white GOLD 14KT HOOP EARRINGS HOOPS	$62.99	IMPERIAL TOPAZ AND PINK TOURMALINE 9K EARRING $1 NR	$26.00
14K Gold Extra Large "Runway" Hoop Earrings	$61.00	10k Gold Elephant Design Hoop Earrings Hoops *w51	$26.00
14K GOLD @@ QVC EternaGold LARGE HOOP EARRINGS 5 Grams	$55.55	Textured & Polished Twisted Design Earrings 14K Hoop	$26.00
10K LARGE GOLD RAMS 10KT HOOP RAM EARRINGS HOOPS @$319	$54.99	beautiful 14k gold mesh and hoop earrings	$25.00
Large 14K Hoop Earrings-Pierced Omega Back-6.7 Grams	$53.00	14 kt Yellow Gold Hoops Nice Intricate Design LOOK	$24.99
$237 New 14K White Yellow Gold Square Huggie Earring NR	$51.00	BLUE SAPPHIRE AND DIAMOND GOLD 9K EARRING $1 NR	$23.10

Earrings ▸ Studs

The average sales price in this subcategory is $22.68.

	HIGH		AVG
18K Gold 7.5mm Mikimoto Pearl Earrings w/Box NR	$275.00	Gorgeous AA 20mm blue mabe pearl silver earring	$32.00
$4750 GEOR.14K WG DIAMOND S.S.WT.	$130.50	14K LOVE KNOT CULTURED DROP PEARL EARRINGS	$31.01
PEARL EARRINGS $1~NR		$1650RARE BLUE/BLACK AKOYA AAA+ PEARL EARRINGS 18K NR	$31.00
Beautiful pink pearl and diamond earrings $4680.	$100.00	BEAUTIFUL JEWELRY SET Silver Pearl Necklace & Earrings	$27.00
$4750 GEOR.14K WG DIAMOND S.S.WT. PEARL EARRINGS $1~NR	$91.00	Gorgeous AA 18mm blue mabe pearl sterling silver earrin	$26.00
GENINUE JAPANESE AKOYA 7MM EARRINGS 14K NR	$90.00	10MM CULTURED CORAL ROSE PEARL	$24.99
14K YG. PEACOCK BLUE AKOYA PEARL 8MM EARRINGS NR$	$75.00	STUD EARRINGS, 14K NR	
$1200 RARE COPPER AKOYA PEARL 18K DIA.EARS.$1 NR	$56.90	big champagne sea shell pearls earrings 925sc 14mm	$20.50
RARE COPPER BROWN AKOYA PEARL 14K STUD STYLE EARRINGS	$52.99	Pearl Stud Earrings, Solid 14kt Yellow Gold, 9mm Pearls	$20.01
STUNNING 8.4 mm Black South Sea Pearl Earrings 14K Gold	$51.99	Gorgeous Genuine Golden Pearl & 14K Solid Gold Earrings	$19.99
$4100 DIAMOND 14K YG AKOYA COPPER BROWN PEARL EARS NR	$51.02	Lot of 4 Colorful Genuine Pearl Earrings 18K Gold RARE!	$19.99
ES~RARE~GENINUE TAHITIA SILVER GRAY PEARL 14K STUD NR$1	$50.99	Genuine Bright Purple Pearl & 14K Gold Earring Studs	$19.99
14K YG 10-11mm Tahitian Cultured Pearl Stud Earrings	$50.01	Gorgeous AA 20mm mabe pearl sterling silver earring	$19.99
RARE COPPER BROWN AKOYA PEARL 14K STUD STYLE EARRINGS	$49.99	Lot of 4 Colorful Genuine Pearl Earrings 18K Gold RARE!	$19.99
RARE COPPER BROWN AKOYA PEARL 14K STUD STYLE EARRINGS	$49.99	[2 of these sold for $19.99 each]	
14K GOLDEN-YELLOW PEARL EARRINGS 7MM NR	$49.99	14K YG 9-10mm Cultured Pearl Earrings - Set of 3	$19.00

Ethnic, Tribal Jewelry ▸ African

The average sales price in this subcategory is $15.44.

	HIGH		AVG
IVORY ELEPHANT HAND CARVED NECKLACE JEWELRY ANIMAL	$226.00	Tibetan necklace- Sacred chank shell	$19.99
UNIQUE DOGON Bronze Amulet Ring - Mali	$125.00	Old Style Aluminum Tuareg Bracelet Mali - Africa	$19.95
MASAI MAASI WARRIOR AFRICAN	$103.50	30.75"Long & 1.75" Width Masai Beautiful Bead Belt # 14	$19.50
BEADED BRACELET HANDMADE		Exquisitely Tuareg Silver Earrings - Mali - Africa	$19.50
African Trade Beads -Antique Bead Necklace	$76.00	TUAREG RING CARNELIAN	$18.60
AFRICA ADORNED - Angela Fisher - beads/jewelry/history	$60.00	African - Hand Made Genuine Elephant Hair Bracelet, New	$18.24
Tuareg ID Silver Bracelet - Mali Africa	$53.99	Nice strand turquoise white heart trade beads	$18.00
African Jewelry - Small "Fulani Gold" Ethnic Earrings	$52.01	Nice old red white blue stripe Trade Beads	$18.00
Tuareg Silver Ingall Earrings (Blue) Mali - Africa	$44.00	African Jewelry - Small "Fulani Gold" Ethnic Earrings	$17.00
Sterling Silver FERTILITY GODDESS Pendant ROLO Necklace	$40.00	20 Metal Ethiopian Beads: Bug Shaped! Tribal African	$16.49
Gorgeous - Moroccan Cuff Bracelet - Africa	$39.95	African Beads -60 Forest Green Melon Beads	$16.00
Old shell necklace from Africa.	$39.00	African Beads -40 Big Ivory Cow Bone Beads	$16.00
African Jewelry - Small "Fulani Gold" Ethnic Earrings	$38.00	SALE! TEN BEAUTIFUL LG ETHIOPIAN-AFRICAN SILVER BEADS	$15.99
Beautiful African Jewelry Tuareg Silver Bracelet Mali	$37.99	African Jewelry Necklace Earrings Vintage Fashion	$15.50
Rare Chinese Miao Folk Silver Garment Ornament	$36.99	African Ethnic Jewelry - Tuareg Silver Diamond Earrings	$15.50
STERLING SILVER ELEPHANT HAIR 2 KNOT SAFARI BRACELET	$36.00	[2 of these sold for $15.50 each]	

Ethnic, Tribal Jewelry ▸ Asian, East Indian

The average sales price in this subcategory is $6.64.

	HIGH		AVG
Belly Dance KUCHI tribal BIG BIG Choker Necklace 811p1	$68.00	Gold RUBY RED Kundan Belly Dance Gypsy Art 17	$8.95
Stunning DAZZLING CHECKERBOARD CUT ROYAL AMETHYST Ring	$47.39	UNIQUESSENTIALS ETHNIC INDIAN JEWELRY SET BELLY DANCE	$8.75
VINTAGE ANTIQUE SIAM NIELLO STERLING SILVER PIN 1930's	$46.99	UNIQUESSENTIALS 24kt GOLD PLATED JEWELRY salwar kameez	$8.50
ANTIQUE SIAM NIELLO STERLING SILVER CUFFLINKS 1930's	$41.00	ETHNIC Sari KUNDAN Kameez BELLYDANCE Jewelry Set NEW	$8.50
TRIBAL Banjara BELLY DANCE Belt COWRIE TASSEL MIRROR CB	$34.99	Tibet Tibetan Tribal Jewelry Red Yak Bone Bracelet	$8.50
ETHNIC Kundan LENGHA Sari BRIDAL India JEWELRY SET SALE	$34.99	(v45a) gorgeous 18" jade necklace/$1	$8.47
Amazing DAZZLING TOP GRADE PRINCESS CUT BLUE TOPAZ Ring	$34.89	UNIQUESSENTIALS JEWELRY SET BELLY DANCE SALWAR KAMEEZ	$8.07
Fantastic Golden Stripe TOP GRADE ABSTRACT JASPER Ring	$28.43	ETHNIC Sari KUNDAN Kameez BELLYDANCE Jewelry Set NEW	$8.00
UNIQUESSENTIALS MIXED SLAVE BRACELET WHOLESALE LOT 10pc	$28.09	GOLD HAIR~FOREHEAD TIKKA belly dance wedding sari GYPSY	$7.99
Handcrafted India Lakh Necklace. Travel Jewelry	$26.00	UNIQUESSENTIALS JEWELRY SET BELLY DANCE SALWAR KAMEEZ	$7.51
Designer Craftmanship Floral STERLING SILVER Pendant	$23.69	UNIQUESSENTIALS BRASS FINGER CYMBOLS ZILLS BELLY DANCE	$7.36
SAREE SARI ETHNIC INDIAN JEWELRY SET BELLY DANCE	$19.99	(503l) rare yellow turquoise necklace//no reserve	$7.26
Necklace. Discover Traditional India Lakh Jewelry	$19.99	Tibet Solid Sterling Silver Om Ghau Pendant	$7.00
Discover A Jewelry Tradition. Lakh Necklace	$19.99	UNIQUESSENTIALS JEWELRY SET BELLY	$6.75
[2 of these sold for $19.99 each]		DANCE SALWAR KAMEEZ	
AWESOME SILVER RHINESTONE ANKLETS fr SARI	$17.00	UNIQUESSENTIALS PAYAL ANKLET SET BELLY DANCE JEWELRY NR	$6.75

Ethnic, Tribal Jewelry ▶ Native American

The average sales price in this subcategory is $66.80.

	HIGH		AVG
CHARLES LOLOMA Hopi Legendary - Jewelry Master	$1,800.00	MASSIVE OLD KINGMAN TURQUOISE NECKLACE	$81.00
Quality Vintage Navajo silver Concho belt,1935-40,NR	$587.77	ANTIQUE NAVAJO SILVER & TURQUOISE ICE TEA SPOON 1920s	$79.99
ROCKI TURQUOISE Navajo STERLING Designer Necklace NR	$349.95	Dead Pawn Navajo Concho Belt 16 Turq Cabs	$77.00
60'S "RARE" "LAVENDER PIT- BISBEE TURQ." NECKLACE, N/R	$255.00	VINTAGE SILVER CONCHO BELT THUNDERBIRD DESIGN	$76.56
LARRY MOSES BEGAY Navajo SUGILITE CLUSTER Bracelet NR	$233.50	BIG Old Pawn 1950s Navajo Real Coral Sterling Ring 7	$76.00
VINTAGE NAVAJO SILVER & TURQUOISE CAKE/PIE SERVER	$229.50	Antique – Navajo Whirling Wind Bolo - 1940's	$74.99
Huge Old Pawn Navajo Turquoise Bracelet	$208.50	SUGILITE CORAL TURQUOISE 2-SIDED INLAY BEAR BRACELET	$70.00
Vintage Navajo Link style concho belt,20s/30s,NR	$202.50	GORGEOUS NAVAJO MADE SPINNEY/TURQUOISE DANGLE EARRINGS	$69.99
ROCKI GORMAN Navajo GASPEITE Sterling Necklace DOUBLE D	$199.95	A+ LARGE Navajo S Silver Wild Horse Ring Size 8?	$69.95
Traditional Santo Domingo Turquoise Necklace 2 Jaclas	$194.95	Gorgeous HUGE Navajo Cuff 10 Sleeping Beauty Turq Nugg	$65.00
LG Old Pawn 30s Zuni Green Turquoise Ster Row Ring 11.5	$187.00	OLD ZUNI DISHTA FLUSH SET 5 TURQUOISE ROW RING 1950s	$60.00
HUGE AWESOME D Pawn Green Turquoise Sterling Bracelet	$178.49	Navajo Hand Made Sterling Silver Lapis Heart Pendant	$57.99
Sterling Silver Concho Belt	$159.06	Gorgeous HUGE Navajo Cuff 10 Sleeping Beauty Turq Nugg	$55.00
OLD PAWN - Royal Blue Lapis Concho Belt - 1970's Estate	$159.00	Buffalo Ring - One-Of-A-Kind Size 12 - Carved Turquoise	$54.00
GORGEOUS CARVED TURQUOISE EAGLE STERLING RING	$157.50	REAL GASPEITE Navajo STERLING Silver Pendant No Reserve	$51.00

Handcrafted, Artisan Jewelry ▶ Earrings

The average sales price in this subcategory is $9.63.

	HIGH		AVG
Amy Kahn Russell Ocean Jasper Earrings!!	$60.00	EP~GODDESS~WHITE PEARL-AMYTHEST FREEFORM EARRINGS	$9.99
20 PLUS Pair Interchangeable Earrings,Gems,Beads,SS,BHV	$51.00	DSS Green Mojave Turquoise Dangle Earrings	$9.99
SUZANNE SOMERS YELLOW CZ FLOWER EARRINGS LIMITED EDITIO	$49.99	DSS Carnelian Hoop Earrings	$9.99
AYALA BAR RETIRED ROSE PINK BEADED PIERCED EARRINGS NEW	$49.99	AMAZING WHITE TURQU CHANDLIER S SILVER EARRINGS AnnieD	$9.99
AYALA BAR Is Art Jewelry - Earrings NWT Gold Lever Back	$49.00	Handcarved Cinnabar and crystal earring	$9.99
Lois Hill Granulated Drop Earring Sterling Silver New	$46.00	SHIANA Thai Karen Silver Swirl Earrings 24mm	$9.99
SALE Coral Pink Opal Briolette Gem Hoop Earrings IDG	$45.00	AMAZING FLUORITE CHANDLIER S SILVER EARRINGS AnnieD	$9.99
6 PAIRS* SS earrings EAR threaders THREAD lot WHOLESALE	$42.51	SHIANA Thai Karen Silver Swirl Earrings 24mm	$9.99
LONDON BLUE TOPAZ LABADORITE LINEAR EARRINGS BY V. WIL	$39.00	Chandelier Earrings RED HEARTS and SILVER	$9.95
Rhodochrosite Silver Wire Wrap Earrings - Free S&H!	$36.00	blue quartz teardop bead earrings sterling silver wires	$9.95
.925 SS SILLMANITE ROSE QUARTZ EAR THREADER EARRINGS	$34.99	Green Jade, Peridot Quartz Earrings - SWris	$9.95
Boro Dangle Earrings Swarovski Crystals Sterling sil	$33.99	Teal-Red-Blue Lampwork, Red Jade Earrings - SWris	$9.95
Handcarved clip-on earrings by ALEXIS BITTAR-lt gold	$33.87	Chandelier Earrings RED HEARTS and GOLD	$9.95
30 PAIR LOT HANDCRAFTED BEAD MURANO GLASS EARRINGS PERU	$32.10	Chandelier Earrings GOLD/SATIN/OPAL White	$9.95
BUTTERFLIES ARE FREE!	$29.99	Beaded Earrings AMBER and GREEN Rainbow	$9.95

Handcrafted, Artisan Jewelry ▶ Necklaces & Pendants

The average sales price in this subcategory is $18.51.

	HIGH		AVG
GENUINE AAA LARIMAR LARGE HAND-MADE NUGGETS Necklace	$399.95	AAA Peach Moon Stone & Pink Chalcedony SS Necklace	$19.99
Amy Kahn Russell Black Onyx & Mother Of Pearl Bracelet	$225.00	14k GF Pink Candy-Jade & Aventurine Necklace	$19.99
SUZANNE SOMERS PINK CZ HEART NECKLACE LIMITED EDITION	$121.50	Necklace Blue Turquoise Chips Knit Choker Collar	$19.99
SALE 14K GOLD Kyanite Blue Topaz Gemstone Necklace IDG	$110.00	Necklace Rose Pink Quartz Huge 50mm Rose Pendant	$19.99
Pearl Citrin Calcite Necklace - SOFT GLOW	$109.16	STUNNING AMAZONITE & STERLING SILVER TASSEL NKL	$19.98
BD Jewelry - Eeyore's Sunflower Lampwork Necklace	$99.00	HAND-PAINTED 'MINI PORTRAIT' FACETED CITRINE~AMETHYST	$19.95
Vintage Murano Glass Beads Millefiori necklace MULTI C	$93.00	Black Czech Glass, Silver Flower Necklace - DANGLES!	$19.52
C~ ALL STERLING & CRYSTAL NCKL NEW PRICE! LOW RESERVE!	$89.95	Rhinestone Watch/Pendant Joan Rivers Frog Watch Garnets	$19.50
Italian Gold Mounted Cameo Pendant	$80.00	Smoky Quartz, Czech Glass Necklace -CARVED JADE PENDANT	$19.50
Vintage Rosenthal Porcelain Hand Painted Floral Pendant	$76.00	Turquoise, Smoky Quartz, Pearl Necklace - LAUGH OFTEN	$19.40
handcrafted ceramic flower basket necklace Flying Color	$72.71	A-Z Green Leaf Jasper African Turquoise Necklace Choker	$19.39
N04362APPLE GREEN TURQUOISE	$71.00	18" BLUE & LIME GREEN TURQUOISE BRIOLETTE NECKLACE C&L	$19.39
CRYSTAL COIN PEARL NECKLACE		Sterling Silver CARVED BONE MOON FACE Pendant FREE SHIP	$19.37
Michal Golan Petite Hamsa Necklace NEW NR, Black Enamel	$68.00	LILLY PULITZER coral quartz turquoise jade NECKLACE 145	$19.00
ZARA ~MERMAID ON LILYPAD~RARE SHATTUCKITE-LAPIS 14K NK	$65.00	N0349??NATURAL? OCEAN JASPER NUGGETS? NECKLACE	$18.50

Jewelry Boxes & Supplies ▶ Jewelry Boxes

The average sales price in this subcategory is $20.71.

	HIGH		AVG
Greiner MIRROR Jewelry w/ Lock WHITE Safekeeper NEW	$227.50	EARRING HOLDER TREE STANDING 15x12 HOLD 40 PR	$22.35
Steinhausen Burl-wood Quad Automatic Watch Winder Case	$179.95	EAMES ERA ,3 TIER MENS WOOD & BRASS JEWELRY BOX,	$22.10
Hannah Jane Jewelry Armoire Cabinet NEW WHOLESALE	$150.00	96 Jewelry Gift Boxes Showcase Countertop Ring Displays	$21.99
Gold & Silver 4' Safekeeper Jewelry Armoire ~NO DAMAGE	$122.50	VINTAGE JAPAN MUSIC JEWELRY BOX HANDPAINTED	$21.52
Large Vintage Ornate Syroco Wall Jewelry Box w/ Mirror	$102.50	PreZerve GREEN Jewelry Organizer w/ FlexZorb	$21.50
CHERRY STANDING JEWELRY CHEST BOX ARMOIRE HOLDER CASE	$99.00	OLD JUNGLE TIGER ANIMAL JEWELRY BOX CHEST STOOL BENCH	$21.00
Syrian Arabian Mosaic Inlaid Bombe Jewelry Box NO RSV	$98.00	100 WHITE RING JEWELRY BOXES 3.5"x3.5"x1"	$20.99
ART DECO BAKELITE GREEN&BLACK ROUND BOX-PERFECT	$92.00	Gorgeous Jewelry Box from Anthropologie	$20.51
OAK 12 WATCH CASE JEWELRY BOX DISPLAY ORGANIZER GIFT	$89.00	Lot of Tiffany Boxes, Bags, Pouch, Ribbons	$20.50
Beautiful Victorian Laquer Jewelry Box with inlay	$88.00	WHOLESALE LOT OF 50 MUSICAL JEWELRY BOXES	$20.50
CHERRY BOMBAY JEWELRY ARMOIRES ARMOIRE CHEST CHESTS BOX	$85.95	TWO VINTAGE PLASTIC RING BOXES FOR ONE PRICE	$20.01
BOMBAY JEWELRY BOX ARMOIRE CHEST CHERRY QUEEN ANNE	$84.00	Musical Jewelry Box-Ballerina Tower-MELE 829	$20.00
AUTHENTIC GUCCI JEWELRY BOX HAND-CRAFTED IN ITALY	$82.00	100 JEWELRY DISPLAY COTTON GIFT STORAGE BOXES- ON SALE!	$19.99
RARE HOTEL DES INVALIDES JEWELRY CASKET	$79.00	DB224 Deluxe SWAROVSKI CRYSTAL FABERGE EGG TRINKET BOX	$19.99

Jewelry Boxes & Supplies ▶ Tools, Findings

The median sales price in this subcategory is $5.49.

	HIGH		AVG
MEMCO INDUCTO-VAC INDUCTION CASTING SYSTEM.	$3,251.00	STERLING SILVER CURVED LOBSTER CLASPS 9mm (x10)	$5.49
5 DAY AUCTION! 5 DAY AUCTION! 5 DAY AUCTION!		Ring Sizer Stick, Finger Rings Measure US & Euro Size d	$5.49
complete jewelry - wax - mold - casting repair shop	$3,151.01	[2 of these sold for $5.49 each]	
TAIG 4 AXIS CNC MILLING MACHINE NEW mill lathe	$1,950.00	JEWELLER ROSARY PLIERS ROUND NOSE WIRE CUTTER	$5.49
TAIG 4 AXIS CNC MILLING MACHINE NEW mill lathe	$1,925.00	BEAD DESIGN BEADING BOARD GRAY FLOCK 9x12 in.	$5.49
Gemology Stereo Microscope, Used, w/Refractometer	$1,617.60	14K GOLD FILLED HEADPINS 24 GA., 2 INCHES (x25)	$5.49
TAIG CNC MILL 4 axis controller NEW not unimat lathe	$1,600.00	STERLING SILVER HEADPINS 22 ga. 1/2 inch (x100)	$5.49
[2 of these sold for $1,600.00 each]		14K GOLD-FILLED SPRING RING	$5.49
TAIG CNC MILL 4 axis controller NEW not unimat lathe	$1,521.0	ROUND CLASPS 5.5mm (x25)	
New Hermes Newest Table Top Engraving Machine, Engraver	$1,475.00	SILVER Plated HOOK & EYE CLASPS 19MM (100)	$5.49
New Hermes Vanguard 3400 Engraver	$1,326.77	Ring Sizer Stick, Finger Rings Measure US & Euro Size g	$5.49
Gemology Stereo Microscope, Used, w/Refractometer	$1,325.00	Coiled Wire Beads and Jewelry how to Book BRAND NEW	$5.49
HERMES IM3 Motorized Professional Engraving Machine	$1,200.00	STERLING SILVER Open Jump Rings 5mm (100)	$5.49
Centrifugal Casting Machine	$1,025.00	100' Beadalon 7 .015 Beading Wire	$5.49
Jewelry casting equipment - complete - ready to go!!		STERLING SILVER CURVED LOBSTER CLASPS 9mm (x10)	$5.49
Kerr centrifugal casting, GE Vacume,	$1,000.51	STERLING SILVER HEADPINS 22 ga. 1/2 inch (x100)	$5.49
JEWELERS 3 AXIS CNC BENCHTOP MILL WOW not lathe taig	$910.00	STERLING SILVER Open Jump Rings 5mm (100)	$5.49
Gemological Institute ID Kit	$820.00		
Neycraft Pro Burn Out Furnace Kiln Dental Lab Jeweler	$670.00		

Loose Beads ▶ Lampwork, Crystal & Glass

The average sales price in this subcategory is $6.44.

	HIGH		AVG
1200 6MM SWAROVSKI 5301 BICONE BEADS COMBO 50 COLORS !	$122.50	8 SWAROVSKI CRYSTAL BAROQUE	$8.10
1440 SWAROVSKI 5301 BEADS CRYSTAL AB (CLEAR) FULL PACK!	$68.45	PENDANT BEAD COLOR MIX 16MM	
300 6MM #5301 LOT SWAROVSKI CRYSTAL BICONE BEADS MIX NR	$45.00	50 pcs Swarovski 5301 6mm Crystal Beads MANY COLORS #5	$8.00
1000 Swarovski Crystal Beads 5301 4+6mm Lots Colors	$42.05	100 LIGHT GREY SWAROVSKI Crystal 5810 PEARLS 6mm Beads	$8.00
HUGE LOT 5301 Swarovski Crystal 4mm BEADS 1000+	$41.01	Vintage Swarovski 5304 ~ Crystal Comet Or ~ 6 mm Beads	$7.80
500+ SWAROVSKI CRYSTAL 4MM 6MM BICONE BEAD #5301 MIX NR	$40.00	Swarovski Crystal Beads 6mm PACIFIC OPAL (48) NO S&H	$7.66
SWAROVKSI Crystal Bead 5301 4mm (1000pc of any colours)	$40.00	20 SAPPHIRE color SWAROVSKI Crystal 5301 Beads 8mm	$7.51
Swarovski! 50 pcs 6mm Crystal Gold Plated Rondell	$36.00	Vintage Pendant, Loose Beads, Mix, Kit or Lot of Beads	$7.50
100 Swarovski Crystal Round Beads 5000 6MM Lots Colors	$35.00	Glass Fish, Loose Beads, Mix, Kit or Lot of Beads	$7.50
100 Swarovski Crystal Beads 5301 8mm - Lots of Colors	$32.64	144 COBALT SWAROVSKI CRYSTAL BICONE BEADS 5301 4MM	$7.45
600 4MM SWAROVSKI 5301 BICONE BEADS BIRTHSTONE SET!	$30.50	Swarovski Crystal Beads Round 5000 8mm CHRYSOLITE (8)NR	$7.02
600 4MM AB SWAROVSKI 5301 BICONE BEADS BIRTHSTONE SET!	$27.00	50 pcs Swarovski 5301 6mm Crystal Beads MANY COLORS #5	$7.02
200 pcs Swarovski 5301 4mm Crystal Beads U PICK Colors!	$13.00	Swarovski Crystal Beads 6mm (5301) SILK (48) NO S&H	$7.01
60 Swarovski Squaredelle Beads 6x6mm Silver/Crystal	$24.99	WONDERFUL RED CRYSTAL FACETED BEADS ASSORTED	$7.00
SWAROVSKI CRYSTAL PEARLS ROSALINE PINK 6mm (100)	$24.99	SALE! SWAROVSKI 20 4MM VITRAIL AB DIAMOND BEADS!	$6.75
[4 of these sold in a multiple item ("Dutch") auction for $8.33 each]		Swarovski Crystal Beads 6mm (5301) ROSE (48) NO S&H	$6.75

Loose Beads ▶ Stone

The average sales price in this subcategory is $10.15.

	HIGH		AVG
12 FACETED PISTACHIO YELLOW GENUINE DIAMOND BEADS	$102.50	19pc Yellow Calcite Briolette/Citrine Leaf Bead Set -PW	$12.50
BLUE PERUVIAN OPAL POTATO BEADS 6 to 9mm!~	$88.00	Aquamarine FACETED Button Beads Strand 15" A	$12.50
16" Faceted Natural Sparkling Ruby Beads Genuine SSL NR	$79.50	NEW! Lime Green Turquoise 10mm Coin Beads 16" Strand	$12.00
LARIMAR OVAL BEADS	$63.00	Gemstone Bead Assortment	$11.45
16" Peach Yellow Blue Thai Sapphire Faceted Beads SSL	$56.04	BOLD & SASSY BLUE GOLDSTONE 8MM	$11.00
APPLE GREEN Chrysoprase Teardrop/Full Briolettes 11.5mm	$56.00	GEMSTONE RD BEADS 15"!	
Two Full 15" Strands Caribbean Teal Apatite Beads SSL	$53.50	41 Green Aventurine Nugget Hand Cut Faceted Beads 15	$10.99
Genuine EMERALD 72cts Glossy Natural Nuggets 7"! SAH	$52.55	29 Ruby-Zoisite Flat Oval Beads 10 x 14mm 16"	$10.99
[5 of these sold in a multiple item ("Dutch") auction for $10.51 each]		Beautifully Patterned 30mm CARNELIAN Oval Pendant-Bead	$10.60
GLITTERING Black Spinel Pear Shaped Briolettes 12x8mm	$46.00	Glowing opalized drusy/druzy oval	$10.50
Gem Apple Green Chalcedony 8-9mm Briolette Beads	$42.50	24pc A+Soft Ivory Peach Branch/Briolette Pearl Beads-PW	$10.50
Dazzling picasso marble pendant bead	$42.00	Jewelers Blue Topaz Pear Gemstone Beads Strand 15"	$10.50

	HIGH		AVG
RHODOCHROSITE FACETED 5mm DRUM Beads !~	$41.99	9pcLilac Quartz Glass/Soft Lilac Faceted Pearl Beads-PW	$10.50
AAA Dark Blue Chalcedony 9-12mm Faceted Heart Briolette	$41.00	80 Purple Rainbow Jasper Roundel Beads 5 x 8mm 16"	$10.49
Colorful 16" Str FLUORITE 20x16mm Drilled Nugget Beads	$39.99	PERUVIAN BLUE OPAL BEADS / SQUARE 10-12 mm	$10.45
FACETED GREEN PHRENITE GEM BRIOLETTE DROP BEAD STRAND	$39.00	PERUVIAN BLUE OPAL BEADS / CUBE	$10.45

Loose Diamonds & Gemstones ▸ Diamonds

The average sales price in this subcategory is $211.19.

	HIGH		AVG
1.51 CT SI1 D PRINCESS CUT CERTIFIED DIAMOND GIA NR OS Annual Fall Sale price reduction!!!	$10,060.00	Matching Marquise Diamonds, .48cttw, VS2, G-H, Nice&NR!	$273.00
		.71ct Marquise Loose Diamond H Color, I1 Clarity	$270.00
9.77CT Certified Round Brilliant Cut Genuine Diamond	$9,999.00	.75ct Marquise Loose Diamond H-I color, I1 clarity	$265.00
Jumbo Diamond! A Beauty To be Grabbed! 100% Money Back		0.46 CT EMERALD CUT WHITE LOOSE	$253.00
1.50 CT Princess Cut H VVS2 GIA Certified Diamond!!!	$7,850.00	DIAMOND WHOLESALE PRICE	
1.01 CT PINK LOOSE ROUND DIAMOND GIA CERTIFIED	$7,600.00	killer vs CLARITY EMERALD CUT	$249.00
3.51 CT PEAR LOOSE WHITE DIAMOND J SI3 RETAIL $24,500	$7,525.00	diamond!! NO RESERVE!!	
2.10 ct Round DIAMOND Solitaire Wedding Ring or Loose	$7,400.00	.53 F/SI Emerald Cut Loose Diamond. No Reserve!	$244.49
2.01ct Pear Shape Diamond, Engagement Ring or Loose	$6,850.00	.43 CTW MARQUISE CUT DIAMOND	$227.50
GIA Certified 1.01 Carat Loose Diamond	$6,500.00	RING H VS1 14KT GOLD NR	
Color D, Clarity VVS1, Polish Very Good, Symmetry Good		LOOSE MINE CUT DIAMOND 52 POINTS	$208.00
1.51 Carat Princess Cut Diamond EGL I VVS2	$5,750.00	1/2 CT 75%BACK/RAP	
1.30ct G - SI1 ROUND LOOSE DIAMOND EGL CERTIFICATE	$5,400.00	.52ct Marquise Loose Diamond J color, SI3 clarity	$204.21
"ANY SIZE/SHAPE GUARANTEE"		0.56CT BRILLIANT C2 CHAMPAGNE NATURAL	$203.50
GIA Princess Loose Diamond G VS1! 1.02ct	$5,170.00	DIAMOND AFRICA$NR	
Appraised at $9,025! Buy a loose or as a completed ring		BEAUTIFUL C6 ORANGE COGNAC DIAMOND	$203.37
1.60 ct Round DIAMOND Solitaire Wedding Ring or Loose	$5,100.00	OCTAGON 0.75 CTS	
3.29CT Certified Princess Diamond Engagement Ring.	$4,999.00	46PT PINKISH TING CHAMPAGNE ASSCHER	$201.50
Eye Clean! Exquisite Design! Satisfaction Guaranteed!		CUT DIAMOND:COLLECT	
[2 of these sold for $4,999.00 each]		.22 VVS, D Heart Loose Engagement Diamond, NR!!!WOW	$200.50
1.20 BRILLIANT H/VS2 GIA CERT	$4,999.00	2.52 Carat Cognac Cutable Natural Uncut Rough Diamonds	$195.00
1.26 CT E VS2 WHITE PRINCESS NATURAL DIAMOND WHOLESALE	$4,944.00	.30 VS, F, Emerald Loose Engagement Diamond, NR!!!WOW	$188.50

Loose Diamonds & Gemstones ▸ Gemstones ▸ Ruby

The average sales price in this subcategory is $17.90.

	HIGH		AVG
1000ct lot rubies emeralds sapphires opals $1.99/ct	$1,999.99	NICE LARGE NATURAL BURMESE RUBY	$19.95
large gems 2ct and under cheapest price anywhere		GEMSTONES from LOVERGEM	
2+cts EXCEPTIONAL ULTRA RARE VIBRANT HOT RED RUBY	$1,892.67	[5 of these sold in a multiple item ("Dutch") auction for $3.99 each]	
FREE CERTIFICATE GLITTERING HUE&FABULOUS LUSTER-WOW!!!		NATURAL SHIMMERING RARE PINK	$19.50
AN EXCEPTIONAL 2.02CT VVS1 CHERRY RED RUBY NR	$1,826.20	RED MOGOK RUBY 2.98cts	
Fabulous Bright Red Jewel With High Sparkle & Intense F		1.95 CT Attractive Oval Facet Red Ruby	$19.50
SUPER HUGE! 69.28 CT RUBY!!! COLLECTORS MUST SEE	$1,099.99	1.19cts AWESOME PINK RED NATURAL	$19.49
COMES WITH A 3RD PARTY APPRAISAL OF $17320.00		RUBY MADAGASCAR $1NR	
SUPER HUGE! PINKISH RED RUBY 20 CT VERY RARE!	$999.99	5 PIECE 6.788 CT. RUBY OVAL CAB $1 NR	$18.99
WONDERFUL HOT PINKISH RED A REAL LOOKER!!!!!!		IMPRESSIVE 1.35CT/2P HOT RICH PINK SAPPHIRE NR	$18.50
MAGNIFICENT GIANT AUSSIE OPAL & BURMA RUBY 14K PENDANT!	$994.00	3.07ct (15pc) FABULOUS Purplish Pink BURMA RUBY $1 NR!	$18.40
Spectacular Huge 14k Semiblac k Opal & Burma Ruby		4.05 CT MARVELOUS RED STAR	$17.50
#18 LARGEST ON EBAY EMERALD-CUT MOGOK TOP RED RUBY 79CT	$736.99	RUBY OVAL (360D/52) 266/1	
10.16 CT. PIGEON BLOOD RED RUBY OVAL $1 NR	$660.00	FABULOUS BRIGHT VS1 CHERRY RED	$17.30
3.74CT FANTASTIC OVAL HOT PINK RUBY NR	$639.69	TRILLIANT CUT RUBY NR	
EXCEPTIONAL 1.95CT VVS1 EYE CLEAN CHERRY RED RUBY	$605.01	PRE-CHRISTMAS SALE 7.10 CT. DEEP RED RUBY	$17.09
NR Fabulous Flawless Burma Ruby		1200+ CARATS OF UNSEARCHED INDIAN RUBIES	$16.95
RUBY (VERY FINE) 1.15 BURMA RUBY. BURMA Ruby Pigeon blood RED	$544.50	6x4 Emerald Cut Natural Ruby	$16.60
AAA ULTRA RARE PIGEON BLOOD RED UNSEEN MOGOK RUBY 5+ct	$499.99	[2 of these sold in a multiple item ("Dutch") auction for $8.30 each]	
STUNNING-FIERY! FULL OF LUSTER--EXQUISITE BURMA RUBY		5 PIECE 2.34 CT. RUBY SQUARE $1 NR	$16.59
9.40 CT LATEST AFRICAN RED RUBY OVAL GEM (379D/33) 487	$481.79	CPD AA Gem Quality Ruby Rondell Beads Gemstone bead	$16.50
HUGE~5.11cts~VIVID PIGEON BLOOD RED RUBY ~BURMA $1	$455.00		
NR VVS~Ultimate Cut~ Deeply Saturated ~ Bid Now $1NR			
15.95 CTS OVAL SHAPE CABOCHON RED RUBY	$450.00		

Loose Diamonds & Gemstones ▸ Gemstones ▸ Other Gemstones

The average sales price in this subcategory is $15.68.

	HIGH		AVG
CHARMING 26.56ct PEACH GOLDEN YELLOW IMPERIAL TOPAZ	$305.00	2.91ct RAVISHING AAA SCISSOR CUT WATERMELON TOURMALINE	$18.50
31.75ct HUGE! EXQUISITE TOP AAA PINK&YELLOW KUNZITE NR!	$170.50	1.34ct GRACEFUL TOP YELLOWISH GREEN CHRYSOBERYL $1NR	$18.01
3.38ct., IF ,VIVID FOREST GREEN CHROME DIOPSIDE, 10mm	$145.49	Ammolite Ammonite Gemstones 11 x 9 Spinel (Feng Shui)	$17.50
MOISSANITE~CHARLES & COLVARD~Round~5.5mm LOOSE	$135.00	30.66ct SHINING PEAR TOP RICH GOLDEN LEMON QUARTZ $1NR	$17.50
1.73 CT. RED PINK SPINEL ANTIQUE CUSHION $1 NR	$112.09	3.62ct 2pcs FABULOUS ROUND RAINBOW MYSTIC TOPAZ $1NR	$17.50
$3000 2.09ct Pear Cut Emerald Loose Stone NR	$107.50	109.62CT.HUGE RARE! MARVELOUS NATURE RUTILE IN PREHNITE	$17.40
3.15ct GLARING RICH ORANGE RED SPESSARTITE GARNET $1NR	$101.99	3.66 ct ULTRARARE HOT NEON FIRE ORANGE ZINCITE	$17.00
8.39CT. PURPLE RED RHODOLITE GARNET 100% NATURAL NR!	$99.99	RARE! 4.40ct LOVELY FOREST GREEN AMETHYST BURMA! PEAR	$17.00
73.63ct GIANT RICH PURPLE & GOLDEN YELLOW AMETRINE $1NR	$88.00	7X5MM CUSHION CUT CHROME DIOPSIDE! LOOSE GEMSTONES AAA	$16.99
3.42 CT. PURPLE PINK RUBELLITE ANTIQUE CUSHION $1 NR	$82.00	2.09ct AWESOME REDDISH PINK NATURAL RUBELLITE AFRICA$1N	$16.50
Benitoite, .23ct faceted, San Benito Co, California	$81.98	6.70ct GRACEFUL TOP GOLDEN YELLOW IMPERIAL TOPAZ OVAL	$16.50
BEAUTIFUL 15.86ct VVS EMERALD CUT RARE HOT PINK TOPAZ	$76.00	1.34ct RAVISHING AAA NATURAL ORANGE RED SPESSARTITE NR!	$16.50
14.14ct 12pcs BRIOLETTE (Drilled) FANCY COLOR SAPPHIRE	$74.00	10.00ct 17pcs BRIOLETTE RASPBERRY RED RHODOLITE DRILLED	$16.05
21.80ct GORGEOUS DEEP GOLDEN ORANGE IMPERIAL TOPAZ $1NR	$67.00	1000 CARAT GEMSTONE CARVED TEAK TREASURE CHEST!	$15.50
1.3 CT. DARK GREEN TSAVORITE ROUND $1 NR	$64.99	63.70ct FANTASTIC BLUISH VIOLET CRYSTAL SAPPHIRE $1NR	$15.50

Men's Jewelry ▶ Cufflinks

The average sales price in this subcategory is $15.87.

	HIGH		AVG
VINTAGE TIGER CARVED BONE CUFFLINK CUFF LINK 503655 NR!	$121.00	UNUSUAL MOTHER OF PEARL ROMAN CHARIOT CUFFLINKS	$20.50
G.W. BUSH PRESIDENTIAL CUFF LINKS (CUFFLINKS)	$91.00	BMW Cuff Links Cufflinks. MIB. No Reserve!	$20.00
VINTAGE CUFFLINKS RHINESTONE WRAPAROUND + CUFF LINK LOT	$76.00	REVERSE PAINTED CRYSTAL 'REDDY KILOWATT' CUFFLINKS	$19.99
~ Tiffany & Co Sterling Love-knot Cufflinks 99 Cts ~	$67.50	Auth. Burberry Burberrys Men's Cufflinks Plaid Scarf	$19.99
Auth. Louis Vuitton Cuff Link Cufflinks w/ Gift Bag Men	$63.00	LOUIS VUITTON Auth CUFFLINKS Cuff Link Men Wallet GOLD	$19.99
14 K GOLD & amethyst cufflinks cuff links VERY NICE!	$61.00	NEW PINK & SILVER CATSEYE TILE CUFFLINKS CUFF LINKS NR	$19.99
AMAZING VICTORIAN PURPLE BLUE STONE ORNATE CUFFLINKS	$56.00	Auth. Burberry Cufflinks Cuff Links Matches Wallet/Tie	$19.99
HUGE LOT 36 PAIRS GORGEOUS SILVER & GOLD CUFFLINKS	$48.00	Lot of vintage Cufflinks Tie Clasps & Tacks	$19.60
HUGE LOT OF OVER 300 CUFFLINKS · MOST ARE PAIRS	$48.00	AUTH. VERSACE CUFFLINKS CUFFLINK GREAT FOR SHIRT WOW	$18.99
1923 Deco Style Baer & Wilde Kum A Part Cufflinks NR	$45.00	VINTAGE CELLULOID SNAP CUFFLINKS JEM LINK w/ Rhinestone	$18.26
GORGEOUS VINTAGE SNAP CUFFLINKS BY BAER & WILDE	$42.25	DANTE MUSEUM MASTERPIECE BLUE VIKING CAMEO CUFFLINKS	$18.07
STRIKING VINTAGE WHITE / GREEN SNAP CUFFLINKS	$38.76	Vintage Cufflinks Warrior Cameo Cuff Links	$17.50
Auth. Burberry Cufflinks Cuff Links Matches Wallet/Tie	$37.78	Presidential Seal Gold Filled Cuff Links NR Cufflinks !	$16.50
VINTAGE BLACK WITH CLEAR CENTERSTONE SNAP CUFFLINKS	$37.00	Vintage, large amber, fantastic cufflinks!	$16.49
NEW CHARCOAL, GRAY & SILVER CATSEYE CUFFLINKS CUFF LINK	$36.99	GILT STERLING TRANSLUCENT GREEN CRYSTAL CUFFLINKS	$16.13

Men's Jewelry ▶ Rings

The average sales price in this subcategory is $36.72.

	HIGH		AVG
Estate Jewelry 14K Solid Gold 4.7 Carat Emerald Ring	$399.00	weird eye ring	$45.00
NAVY VETERAN WORLD WAR 2 U.S. NAVY RING 14 KT	$375.00	Hypoallergenic Tungsten Wedding Ring Size 11 N/R $349	$44.99
8.55 Carat Citrine Estate Ring Yellow & White 14K Gold	$299.00	VINTAGE BLACK HILLS GOLD LEAF 12K GOLD MEN'S RING	$43.00
antique men's victorian cameo ring 10k gold	$227.50	Men's 9 stone gold finish Sapphire created ring	$43.00
TUNGSTEN BEVEL WEDDING RING MENS BAND RINGS BANDS NR	$199.00	MENS MANS 10K YELLOW GOLD DIAMOND ONYX SIGNET RING	$41.11
4.5ct MENS BOLD SIMULATED DIAMOND PLATINUM RING	$171.00	Hypoallergenic Tungsten Wedding Ring Size 12 N/R $349	$39.99
[6 of these sold in a multiple item ("Dutch") auction for $28.50 each]		Indian Chief Skull Silver Ring 4 Harley Chopper Biker	$39.50
Wonderful Mens 14k Solid Gold Signet Ring	$169.99	Vintage Mens Deco 10k Yellow Gold Garnet & Diamond Ring	$38.99
MENS BLACK DIAMOND RING GOLD L@@K!!!!!!!!	$150.00	High Quality Affordable CZ Masonic Mens Ring SZ 11	$36.00
vintage 14K Gold & Jade Mans Ring	$117.26	[2 of these sold in a multiple item ("Dutch") auction for $18.00 each]	
Antique Left Facing Mens Hardstone Cameo 14K Ring	$99.99	Men's 4.5c Emerald Created Ring May Birthstone	$36.00
Nice Mens 10k Solid Gold Nugget Diamond Ring	$95.00	11.4g 10K men's 1970 Deco onyx class ring $1NR	$35.51
Vintage White Gold Ring with Carnelian/Bloodstone sz 9	$89.00	ROLLED GOLD POCKET WATCH	$35.00
NEW Stainless Steel Celtic Men's Ring Wedding Bands NR	$77.00	NEW TITANIUM SILVER RING WEDDING	$34.99
MENS TIGERS EYE RING~Sz 7~10KT SOLID GOLD band,DIAMONDS	$75.02	BAND MENS RINGS $395	
RING Men's 10K Yellow Gold Tiger Eye Cameo Size 11 1/2	$72.51	FRANKLIN MINT PRIDE OF THE SOUTH CIVIL WAR RING 8.5	$33.89
MENS SCARAB RING GOLD L@@K!!!!!!!! CIRCA 1950's	$66.50	FRANKLIN MINT PRIDE OF THE SOUTH CIVIL WAR RING 11	$33.56

Necklaces & Pendants ▶ Chains

The average sales price in this subcategory is $13.36.

	HIGH		AVG
ADINA Medium Signature Circle Sterling Silver Necklace	$202.50	BRIGHTON SILVER & GOLD NECKLACE	$17.17
Authentic Tiffany & Co. Toggle Necklace & Bracelet Set	$153.51	Konstantino Treasures Sterling Silver Rope Chain 16"	$16.50
Tiffany & Co. Oval Return to Tiffany Necklace	$102.50	sterling silver 20" OMEGA NECKLACE CHAIN 2mm	$16.49
100%Authentic Gucci Twin Dogtags(0062) necklace!!	$94.99	BRIGHTON MOTHER OF PEARL & BLACK	$16.00
Authentic tiffany & Co.Heart tag toggle bracelet	$71.00	REVERSIBLE NECKLACE	
Silver CZ ICED Hip Hop 36" 5.5mm Bullet Chain Necklace	$65.99	sterling silver 16" OMEGA chain necklace 6MM	$15.99
Silpada Sterling Silver Omega Chain- Classic!	$57.56	Men's 20" Diamond Cut .925 Silver Rope Chains Necklaces	$15.77
AUTHENTIC TIFFANY ELSA PERETTI 5 OPEN HEART NECKLACE	$52.51	Native American Liquid Silver Necklace	$15.50
AUTHENTIC TIFFANY & CO. OPEN HEART NECKLACE	$51.00	.925 Sterling Silver Figaro 22" 6mm Link Necklace Chain	$13.99
Authentic Tiffany Eternal Circle Pendant Necklace	$41.00	BRIGHTON SILVER NECKLACE	$13.65
Sterling Silver Curb 300 Chain 12mm Necklace 20"	$40.95	sterling silver 18" OMEGA NECKLACE chain 4MM	$13.49
STERLING LOT NECKLACE BANGLE CHARM PENDANT BRACELET PIN	$38.07	BRIGHTON SILVER NECKLACE	$12.72
Heavy Silver Link Chain	$38.00	Vintage Tiffany Key Ring, Monogramed M E C Plus more	$12.50
[2 of these sold in a multiple item ("Dutch") auction for $19.00 each]		Sterling Silver Box Chain Necklaces 18 INCH NICE !!	$12.00
AUTHENTIC TIFFANY & CO. OPEN HEART NECKLACE	$28.55	HEART LOCKET NECKLACE 16" STERLING SILVER JEWELRY	$11.99
Men's 24" Silver Cuban Link Chains Necklaces SP Bling!	$24.00	Sterling Silver 24" Rope 2mm D/C Chain Necklace Italian	$11.99

Necklaces & Pendants ▶ Pendants, Lockets

The average sales price in this subcategory is $22.16.

	HIGH		AVG
12.6x14MM White SS Pearl 18KWG Diamond Pendant Enhancer	$360.00	$229 GENUINE RUBY AND 7MM PEARL GOLD NECKLACE	$26.49
SUPER BEAUTIFUL PURPLE PEARL AAA+ DIAMOND 14K PENT.NR	$168.00	TWIN WHITE PEARL DIAMOND YELLOW GOLD PENDANT buySAFE	$26.04
Brand New IGI Certificate Diamond and Pearl Pendant	$125.00	Rare REAL Diamond Pearl Pendant 18KWG By Tiffany Davis	$24.90
$3400 NATURAL PEACH PINK OVAL PEARL 12.3MM 14K PEN.NR$	$99.00	INCREDIBLE TWO WHITE PEARL AND DIAMOND PENDANT NO RES!!	$24.50
DANA KELLIN GREY PEARL STERLING NECKLACE & EARRINGS NR	$88.00	Genuine Marcasite Mother of Pearl Slider Pendant	$23.95
DANA KELLIN PEARL STERLING SILVER NECKLACE & EARRINGS	$86.00	Genuine Marcasite Sterling Silver Pendant Earring Set	$22.95
Exquisite real South Sea Mabe white Pearl 14KT necklace	$79.99	LARGE ESTATE VINTAGE 14K GOLD PEARL PENDANT NECKLACE NR	$22.75
DIAMOND and Pearl Pendant 14K/W/G	$79.99	CREAM TEARDROP PEARL DIAMOND PENDANT 10KT YELLOW GOLD	$20.50
$3500 GENINUE SOUTH SEA PEARL DIA.14K YG PEN NEW NR	$76.99	$210.00 GEN. PEARL & DIAMOND PENDANT ON 18" CHAIN - NWT	$20.00
14K WHITE GOLD DIAMOND PEARL NECKLACE JEWELRY $1	$71.00	RARE BIG TEARDROP MABE MOTHER OF PEARL SILVER pendant	$19.95
GORGEOUS 8MM WHITE PEARL 18K YELLOW GOLD NECKLACE	$50.00	Sterling MABE PEARL SMOKY QUARTZ Pendant FREE SHIP	$19.18

CULTURED PEARL AND SAPPHIRE PENDANT IN GOLD	$47.89	Diamond & Pearl Sliding Pendant 10K Y Gold Necklace	$18.47
$309 WHITE PCH PEARL DIAMOND 14K GOLD BUTTERFLY PENDANT	$41.00	Sterling S. Pearl & Moonstone Lace Pendant	$17.50
GORGEOUS 8MM WHITE PEARL 18K YELLOW GOLD NECKLACE	$40.00	Sterling, Pearl & Moonstone Cross Pendant NR	$17.50
DAVID YURMAN PEARL 18K VERMEIL ALBION ENHANCER PENDANT	$39.99	20mm white MABE sea salt water pearls pendant necklace	$17.49

Necklaces & Pendants ▸ Strands/Strings

The average sales price in this subcategory is $23.47.

	HIGH		AVG
Round Multi Color South Sea Pearl Necklace 11.91mm	$1,100.00	Naturally 7-8mm Akoya Pearls Necklace/Bracelet (00156)	$24.99
GORGEOUS GEM-QUALITY MULTI-COLOR PEARL NECKLACE 10MM!!	$313.00	Naturally Purple Akoya Pearls Necklace/Bracelet	$24.99
DARK GREEN SEA WATER JAPANESE AKOYA PEARL NECKLACE	$118.00	GRACEFUL NEW 7-8mm GENUINE NATURAL WHITE PEARL NECKLACE	$24.99
Akoya Pearl Necklace,RARE,UNIQUE LAVENDER PEARLS	$99.99	HUG 7rows 17"-26" 6mm turquoise necklace 925s	$24.98
ES RARE COPPER AKOYA AAA+ PEARL N. 17" 14K NR$	$99.00	huge 17" 10mm genuine cultured pearl necklace	$24.68
RARE COPPER BROWN AKOYA PEARL 2 STRAND 17/18" 14K R	$93.00	Amazing! 14mm size Golden Coin pearl Necklace	$24.50
wholease 3 strands AAA 9-10 mm freshwater pearl	$88.98	Genuine AA 10mm Slateblue Pearl Necklace-14k Gold Clasp	$23.60
ROUND 17" 12mm black genuine cultured pearl necklace	$86.00	Amazing 4Strds Barroque Golden Pearl&Red Coral Necklace	$23.37
PEARL 14K GOLD BEAD TIN CUP NECKLACE 14KT	$72.00	$1,500 Estate South Ocean pearl necklace AAA NR	$23.37
WHOLESALE LOT * MAKE A WISH LOVE PEARL PENDANT* NIB*	$59.99	RARE SILVER JAPANESE CULTURED PEARL NECKLACE 9-10 BIG!!	$22.55
RARE! 18KT WHITE GOLD DIAMOND 9mm BLACK PEARL PENDANT	$59.00	Wonderful AA 13mm Thistle Coin Pearl Necklace	$21.37
NEW MAJORICA 24" PEARL NECKLACE WITH BOX NO RESERVE	$58.77	18" 6pcs 6mm-10mm coral necklaces	$21.02
$3900 RARE LUSTER CULTURED PEARL NECKLACE 14KCLASP	$56.75	HUGE 14MM GOLDEN SOUTH SEA SHELL PEARLS NECKLACE!.	$20.50
Vintage 18Kt WG Diamond Double Strand Pearl Bead Clasp	$56.52	Swarovski Rhinestone Sahara Dessert Camel Paper Weight	$20.50
RARE UNIQUE BAROQUE TAHITI GRAY PEARL 17" NR	$52.00	50" Bead Necklace of Multi-colored FW Pearls and Quartz	$19.99

Pins, Brooches ▸ Cameos

The average sales price in this subcategory is $24.45.

	HIGH		AVG
HUGE ANTIQUE SHELL CAMEO BROOCH PENDANT 14K GOLD NR	$268.00	LOT OF RHINESTONE & VINTAGE BROACHES	$34.00
Victorian 18ct Gold Centaur and Nymph Cameo	$250.00	VINTAGE CARVED SHELL CAMEO WITH CAMEO BOX	$34.00
UNIQUE SQUARE ANTIQUE CAMEO PIN/PENDANT,14K,SAVE $$$	$201.59	LOT OF RHINESTONE & VINTAGE BROACHES	$33.00
Beautiful Large Shell Cameo With Angel	$199.00	Lovely Vintage Carved Cameo Brooch maybe stone	$32.00
VINTAGE CAMEO SHELL BROOCH FROM ESTATE	$177.50	SHELL CAMEO	$31.00
Victorian Estate ShellCameo 1800s Fountain Doves No Res	$162.51	VINTAGE CAMEO PIN/BROOCH/HAS LOOP FOR CHAIN	$30.00
10K + Diamond Carved SHELL CAMEO Brooch Pin	$154.50	BEAUTIFUL CAMEO BROOCH MUST SEE TO APPRECIATE HOBE?	$29.99
UNUSUAL RARE ANTIQUE FULL-FACE SHELL CAMEO BROOCH NR!	$153.70	STERLING SHELL CAMEO PENDANT BROOCH	$28.56
BEAUTIFUL ANTIQUE 18K CAMEO FLOWER PIN, RARE,	$151.50	Cameo Broach/Pin/Pendant BEAUTIFUL	$27.79
14K WHITE GOLD CAMEO FILIGREE BROOCH/PIN/PENDANT	$114.39	ITALIAN VINTAGE SHELL CAMEO PROFILE OF YOUNG WOMAN	$27.00
CAMEO PIN OR PENDANT PEACH BACKGROUND-OLD	$107.55	AntiqueShell Cameo Pendant Brooch	$26.01
RARE ITALIAN VINTAGE DECO ACTION SHELL CAMEO. MUST SEE	$99.00	WEDGWOOD WHITE on BLACK JASPERWARE CAMEO MEDALLION	$26.01
14K Cameo Pin Vintage Very Large & Ornate 1920's NR	$95.26	LILY of the VALLEY & FORGET-ME-NOTS CAMEO PIN/PENDANT	$26.00
Antique Three Graces Cameo: Carved Shell, C-Clasp	$86.00	OLD VINTAGE "LILY OF THE VALLEY" CAMEO PIN/BROOCH L@@K!	$26.00
White Angelskin CAMEO set in Yellow Gold	$85.00	SHELL CAMEO PENDANT/BROOCH, SIGNED	$24.99

Pins, Brooches ▸ Silver, Solid (w/o Stone)

The average sales price in this subcategory is $11.57.

	HIGH		AVG
Georg Jensen Arno Malinowski Deer Pin	$172.50	New Sterling Silver MARCASITE Humming Bird PIN Brooch	$17.99
ASCH/GROSSBARDT INLAY BUTTERFLY PIN 18K SS NEW	$67.62	Estate ETCHED STERLING PENDANT Brilliant! MEXICO Signed	$16.50
AUTHENTIC JOHN HARDY SILVER DRAGON PIN	$50.00	STERLING SILVER CAROUSEL BROOCH - HORSE MERRY-GO-ROUND	$16.00
VINTAGE ANTIQUE SIAM NIELLO STERLING SILVER PIN 1930's	$46.99	LANG STERLING SILVER PEACOCK PIN / BROOCH	$15.45
ANTIQUE STERLING SILVER HEART SHAPED PIN OR BROOCH	$40.00	LARGE VINTAGE STERLING BUCKLE STYLE BROOCH signed UB	$14.00
Large Sterling Silver Flower Brooch Pin	$39.99	QVC~Southwestern Sterling Angel Pin/Pendant~NWT	$13.50
WHITING & DAVIS VINTAGE MESH BAG	$33.03	costume jewelry 925 me elephant torquise ring disney	$11.45
vintage taxco mexico sterling silver mask brooch jade ?	$32.00	Vintage Beau Sterling Lobster Pin	$10.50
ESTATE Vintage SET 925 STERLING Brooch Earrings SIGNED	$26.51	BEAU STERLING SILVER VIOLIN PIN	$10.50
Norwegian Vintage Sterling Solje Brooch:Oslo:Jensen	$26.00	BEAUTIFUL SOLID STERLING LADY BUG BROOCH W/ ONYX INLAY	$10.50
Fantastic Sterling Silver Openwork Frog Pin!	$25.09	Vintage Sterling Danecraft Brooch	$10.49
Vintage MEXICAN STERLING Artisan Pin ROWS OF FIGURES nr	$21.50	Antique Sterling Silver Calla Lily Pin	$10.06
ZARAH STERLING ENAMEL DANGLE FISH PIN PAUL BRENT	$19.99	John Hardy Rooster Birthday Pin Sterling Silver	$10.00
SCREAMING SKULL WITH WING 100% SILVER PIN	$19.81	Vintage ENGLISH SILVER~FAIRY CHARM w/ WINGS~Moves!	$9.99
Sterling silver art nouveau lady pin!	$18.50	UNUSUAL HANDMADE STERLING SILVER ANGEL FISH BROOCH	$9.99

Rings ▸ Bands, Wedding & Anniversary

The average sales price in this subcategory is $65.35.

	HIGH		AVG
MENS 14KT WHITE GOLD AND DIAMOND RING~ 360' DESIGN	$1,025.00	Anniversary/Right Hand Ring	$99.00
14k White gold man's ring with Diamond and Black Jade	$990.00	Genuine mens gents diamond & gold anniversary ring	$91.00
1.50 CT PRINCESS DIAMOND MEN'S BAND 14W AP$ 10980 NR!	$768.00	NoRSV! SUPERB MANS WHITE GOLD DIAMOND WEDDING BAND!	$86.00
1.00 CT PRINCESS DIAMOND MEN'S BAND 14W AP$ 14600 NR!	$711.00	Wedding band 14K white gold 8mm wide starting at scrap	$86.00
MAN'S 1/2 CARAT VS2 DIAMONDS 14K WEDDING BAND 2 TONE	$603.00	10K (not 14K) White Gold Mans Diamond Wedding Ring	$79.99
3 Stone Men Round Diamond wedding Band Rings White Gold	$599.00	MENS DIAMOND CROSS WEDDING RING	$78.00
14KT WHITE GOLD MENS TRILLION DIAMOND RING / BAND	$525.00	SOLID WHITE GOLD NO RSV	
Cartier White Gold 18K Screw Motif Ring Metric 62 (10)	$459.00	Vintage Masonic Ring White Gold OB 10K	$76.99
Tiffany & Co. 14K Gold Men's Signet Ring	$379.99	Men's Wedding Ring, 14K White/Yellow, Size 7-1/2	$76.00
Mens 24K white w/Yellow, 1/2 Ctw. 5 stone Ring	$355.00	$569 MENS DIAMOND GENUINE WHITE	$76.00
1/4Ctw(0.25) Diamond Mens White Gold Wedding Band Bands	$339.00	GOLD WEDDING BAND RING	

	HIGH		
0.50 CT PRICENSS DIAMOND MEN'S BAND 14W AP$ 7220 NR!	$325.00	MENS WHITE GOLD DIAMOND WEDDING	$76.00
New Cluster Diamond Men's Rolex Band Ring Solid Gold	$250.00	RING MENS DIAMOND RING	
1/4CTW DIAMOND MENS COMFORT FIT	$239.00	MEN'S WHITE GOLD RING DIAMONDS SZ. 8?	$76.00
WEDDING BAND BANDS RING		MEN'S CHANNEL SET DIAMOND WEDDING BAND 14K YG	$75.00
BRAND NEW! MEN'S WHITE GOLD WEDDING BAND RING	$238.50	14K White Gold .33ctw Round Diamond Band Ring NR	$71.00
		BRAND NEW MEN'S 14KT WHITE GOLD BAND (NEW IN BOX)	$71.00
		Men's Diamond Wedding Band, 0.12 ctw 10K W Size 10.5 NR	$69.99

Rings ▶ Cubic Zirconia & Moissanite

The average sales price in this subcategory is $7.37.

	HIGH		AVG
HUGE 9 CARAT CZ SIMULATED DIAMOND PRINCESS BAGUETE RING	$29.00	18K GOLD BAGUETTE SIX STONE UNISEX CZ RING SIZE 10	$9.99
24k Gold GP Oval Cut CZ Simulated Diamond Cocktail Ring	$27.95	18K GOLD CITRINE EMERALD CUT LADIES CZ RING SIZE 8	$9.99
8.4 Carat Oval Cut Diamond Created 14k Gold Ring Sz 8	$26.01	DESIGNER INSPIRED TWO TONE RING WITH 23 CZ'S - Sz 7	$9.99
3.0 CT DIAMOND SIMULATED 5 STONE 14K GOLD GP RING!	$26.00	CHANNEL SET SIMULATED EMERALD ETERNITY RING CZ BAND	$9.99
Antique Design 2-tone manmade diamond Ring sz 5	$23.99	HEART SHAPED 1.3 CARAT SIMULATED DIAMOND RING SIZE 8	$9.99
24k Gold GP Oval Cut CZ Simulated Diamond Cocktail Ring	$21.95	[2 of these sold for $9.99 each]	
STUNNING cz SIMULATED DIAMOND	$17.77	Cubic Zirconia Imitation Diamond Ring	$9.99
ETERNITY RING 18K GEP 6		AVON 1997 CZ SOLITAIRE RING (SIZE 11) NIB	$8.00
Cubic Zirconia Eternity Band in White Gold Size 9	$16.99	AVON 1999 INTERCHANGEABLE RING (SIZE 11) NIB	$8.00
GORGEOUS "Baguette Fireworks" CZ RING SIZE 9	$15.00	6.54 ct CHECKERBOARD DIAMOND SIMULANT RING SIZE 6	$7.99
24k Gold GP CZ Simulated Diamond Eternity Band Ring 7	$13.95	Beautiful Diamond simulant Leaf Ring, size 11	$6.51
3.0 CT DIAMOND SIMULATED MARQUISE 14K GOLD GP RING!	$13.16	SIZE 5 18K GOLD (P) CUBIC WEDDING ETERNITY RING/RINGS	$5.99
NWT Banana Republic Aquamarine Ring -Size 6	$13.00	Exquisite Designer Style Diamond simulant Ring, sz 5	$5.99
MEN'S TWO TONE GOLD PLATED CZ RING-sz 9	$12.99	3.0 CT DIAMOND SIMULATED ART NOUVEAU 18K GOLD GP RING!	$5.50
3.15 Ct Diamond Created Cluster 14k Gold Ring Size 6	$12.49	2.0 CT DIAMOND SIMULATED ETERNITY 14K GOLD GP RING!	$5.50
14 KT GOLD OVERLAY RING W/5 20 PT SUPER CZ's SIZE 8	$12.48	LADIES MEN UNISEX CZ GOLD PLATED RING - sz 7	$4.99

Rings ▶ Diamond Engagement/Anniversary

The average sales price in this subcategory is $645.83.

	HIGH		AVG
2.45 CT PRINCESS DIAMOND ENGAGEMENT RING 14 K GOLD	$9,000.60	EGL CERT 1.75ct E/I2 Diamond SOLITAIRE Engagement RING	$900.00
2.48 CT ROUND DIAMOND SOLITAIRE RING WHITE GOLD	$5,350.00	EGL CERT 1.61ct G/I2 Diamond SOLITAIRE Engagement RING	$900.00
2.35CT NATURAL SOLITAIRE DIAMOND ENGAGEMENT RING	$5,000.00	1.16 ct EMERALD SOLITAIRE ENGAGEMENT RING	$899.99
1.50 CT F SI2 NATURAL CERTIFIED DIAMOND SOLITAIRE RING	$3,650.00	WHITE DIAMOND GOLD 9K RING $1 NR	$821.00
2.78 CT PRINCESS CUT DIAMOND ANTIQUE ENGAGEMENT RING	$3,499.00	1.20CT 3-STONE PRINCESS CUT DIAMOND ANNIVERSARY RING	$810.00
VVS2/G PRINCESS CUT DIAMOND TENSION ENGAGEMENT RING NR	$3,249.00	EGL CERT 1.07ct F/I1 Diamond SOLITAIRE Engagement RING	$720.02
3.5 CT ANNIVERSARY ENGAGEMENT DIAMOND RING MOUNT A351	$2,637.00	$3500 SIMPLY ELEGANT! 14K DIAMOND PROMISE RING NR	$720.00
1.10 CT ROUND DIAMOND SOLITAIRE RING WHITE GOLD	$2,175.00	0.53CT FSI2 CERTIFIED ROUND DIAMOND ENGAGEMENT SOLITAIR	$700.00
1.05CT ROUND CERTIFIED DIAMOND ENGAGEMENT RING SOLITAIR	$2,125.00	WHITE DIAMOND GOLD 9K RING $1 NR	$687.88
1.01CT ROUND CERTIFIED REAL DIAMOND ENGAGEMENT RING 1NR	$1,900.00	EGL CERT 1.34ct G/I2 Diamond SOLITAIRE Engagement RING	$645.00
EGL CERT 1.26ct I/SI3 Diamond SOLITAIRE Engagement RING	$1,875.00	2 Carat Round Solitaire Diamond Ring	$635.00
EGL CERT 1.70ct F/I1 Diamond SOLITAIRE Engagement RING	$1,725.00	CERTIFIED$5,100-.74 CT E/SI2 DIAMOND SOLITAIRE RING	$629.33
DIAMOND SOLITAIRE EGAGEMENT RING 1 CARAT MARQUISE	$1,699.00	EGL CERT 1.08ct I/I2 Diamond SOLITAIRE Engagement RING	$617.00
1.09 CT. ROUND CUT ENGAGEMENT WEDDING DIAMOND RING	$1,658.00	STUNNING 1.33 CT. PEAR SHAPED DIAMOND SOLITAIRE	$613.33
1.01 ct brilliant cut diamond engagement ring sz5.5	$1,500.00	EGL CERT 1.03ct H/I2 Diamond SOLITAIRE Engagement RING	$611.00

Rings ▶ Gemstone Rings

The average sales price in this subcategory is $41.96.

	HIGH		AVG
DIAMOND SOLITAIRE 0.76 CT SI1 G NR	$1,009.00	LOT OF BLUE WHITE SAPPHIRE DIAMOND YELLOW GOLD RINGS NR	$61.19
14K GOLD ESTATE 11 CARAT SAPPHIRE, 3 CARAT DIAMOND RING	$940.00	10K GOLD AQUAMARINE ANTIQUE MOUNT RING GORGEOUS	$60.00
Antique Rare Tourmaline & Diamond Platinum Ring	$431.00	N/R* 5 CARAT GENUINE AMETRINE RING 14K YELLOW GOLD	$59.95
2 CT. COCKTAIL RING , 19 DIAMONDS	$365.00	14KT GOLD DIAMOND RUBY RING ESTATE BAND BEAUTY N/R	$51.77
MENS OVAL 3CT IOLITE VS DIAMOND ACCENT GOLD PINKY RINGs	$348.38	VIBRANT DIAMOND AND PEAR CUT OPAL RING NO RESERVE	$50.00
Estate $2200 7ct Aquamarine 14kt Gold Filigree Ring	$255.00	INCREDIBLE 2.95CTW AMETHYST AND DIAMOND 14KT RING NR!!!	$48.00
HUMONGOUS SPARKLING AMETHYST SOLITAIRE 14Kt GOLD RING	$239.99	LADIES AMETHYST GOLD RING NR	$44.00
MAGNIFICENT RUBY BAGUETTE & DIAMOND ESTATE RING	$202.50	Magnificent 7.50ctw CITRINE & WHITE TOPAZ Ring SZ-7	$44.00
BEAUTIFUL WHITE GOLD EMERALD & DIAMOND RING #RG0061C	$199.00	Antique EASTERN STAR 10K Solid Gold Band VINTAG ESTATE	$42.07
10k WG ESTATE 1.08CTW TANZANITE/DIAMOND BEVEL RING 7	$184.47	10KT GOLD SAPPHIRE & DIAMOND RING	$41.00
1.75 CTW OPAL & PINK SAPPHIRE RING 14 K SOLID GOLD SZ 9	$169.38	Cat's Eye women's ring	$40.00
1.56 CT BLACK OPAL AND DIAMOND RING 14K YELLOW GOLD	$167.50	STERLING SILVER TURQUOISE STONE DESIGN RING	$39.13
Designer Sapphire Emerald Ruby Diamond Ladies 14k	$160.00	RHODOLITE GARNET & DIAMOND BYPASS RING 10K GOLD	$38.47
14K Pink Sapphire Diamond Ring	$150.00	$340.00 10K GOLD MYSTIC TOPAZ & DIAMOND RING	$37.99
14K YELLOW GOLD GENUINE BLUE ZIRCON DIAMOND RING	$139.00	$339 OVAL MYSTIC FIRE TOPAZ DIAMOND GENUINE GOLD RING	$31.55

Sets ▶ Gold, Plate/Fill (w/o Stone)

The average sales price in this subcategory is $15.13.

	HIGH		AVG
TRIFARI NECKLACE, BRACELET, EARRING SET GOLDTONE	$158.15	Set of 3 bracelets, 1 necklace, and 2 charms. 14k Gold!	$25.00
Golden Bridal Set India BellyDance Sari Salwar.gn11	$55.99	Gorgeous Genuine Pearl Ring, Necklace and Earring Set!	$24.99
VINTAGE "EMMONS" HUGE BROOCH	$55.55	MEN'S GOLD GP FIGARO BRACELET NECKLACE SET 10 MM	$24.99
& EARRING SET W/ STONES		QVC 14K GOLD LINK CHAIN SET NEW BRACELET NECKLACE	$24.50
MONTANA SILVERSMITH HEART CHOKER AND EARRINGS	$51.00	Gold & Enamel Necklace, Bracelet, Earring Set	$19.99
ITALIAN MESH BRACELET & NECKLACE	$42.99	14k GOLD BUTTERFLY NECKLACE &	$19.50

SET YELLOW GOLD BONDED		EARING SET FASHION JEWEL	
24k Gold GP Designer Omega Necklace Bracelet Hoops Set	$39.95	Coins & More Coins - Necklace & Earrings Set - SUPER!	$17.95
[2 of these sold for $39.95 each]		screw earrings, pin, necklace, black rose, VanDell	$17.50
24K GOLD DAMASCENE PARURE SET JAPAN VINTAGE	$39.00	JEWLERY SET ESTATE FIND RARE NEVADA GOLD MINER	$15.50
Beautiful 10K diamond studded tennis braclet!!	$36.00	Fun & Fabulous Circus Clown Pin & Earring Set	$15.00
Chunky Antiqued Gold Toned Necklace & Bangle Set France	$32.99	*TWEEDY BIRD* EARRINGS & BRACELET SET GOLD must see!!!!	$13.99
INDIA Sari ETHNIC Salwar 24KT GOLD PLATED Necklace SET	$31.03	PREMIER DESIGNS JEWELRY - Bracelet/Earring Set	$13.95
MENS WHITE GOLD GP FIGARO BRACELET NECKLACE SET	$30.00	PREMIER DESIGNS SILVER/GOLD BRACELETS, RING, EARRINGS	$13.00
[7 of these sold for $30.00 each]		VINTAGE NECKLACE & BRACELET COSTUME	$12.50
MEN'S GOLD GP FIGARO BRACELET NECKLACE SET 8 MM	$30.00	GREEN STONES GREAT	
[2 of these sold for $30.00 each]		Flapper Necklace the 20,s _ seeQQ	$10.99

Sets ▸ Gold, Solid (w/o Stone)

The average sales price in this subcategory is $106.57.

	HIGH		AVG
Ladies 14 carat yellow gold necklace and bracelet	$1,500.00	MEN'S SOLID GOLD 14 KARAT NECKLACE AND BRACLET ! NEW !!	$200.00
14K SOLID YELLOW GOLD NECKLACE SET 143.92 GRAMS GW NR	$1,081.11	MEN'S SOLID GOLD 14 KARAT NECKLACE AND BRACLET ! NEW !!	$199.99
Vintage Large Gold Bead Necklace 14K Scrap? 50 grams	$530.00	7 Nice 14K Gold Rings.22.6 grams as Scrap Jewelry Gold	$175.50
18K GOLD TWIST NECKLACE W/PEARL ACCENT MATCHING EARRING	$495.00	18kt Gold Chain	$135.00
14K Gold San Marco Necklace and Bracelet	$475.00	Estate 14K Yellow gold Leaf pin & Earring Set	$128.49
14k scrap/good gold lot-62.7 grams no stones!!!	$460.05	14K SOLID YELLOW GOLD NECKLACE SET(BRACELET & EARRINGS)	$128.27
14K White Gold Byzantine Necklace & Bracelet	$452.00	Unusual Style 14K Gold Pendant Necklace/ Earring Set NR	$125.00
ESTATE 14K GOLD LADIES CHOKER NECKLACE & BRACELET +NR	$415.50	GENUINE INDIAN GOLD JEWELRY 4 SETS EARRINGS 2 NECKLACE	$121.07
ALWAND VAHAN 14k GOLD & SILVER EARRINGS NECKLACE SET	$399.00	LOT QVC 14K IMPERIAL GOLD RING,PENDANT, EARRINGS NR	$117.50
22k Gold set Necklace earrings pearls Brand new	$394.00	Lot of Scrap Gold - 14-15 grams Total Weight	$100.50
Middle Eastern Gold Jewelry Set	$355.00	14K Herringbone Necklace/Bracelet Set From Friedman's	$99.99
18K GOLD TWIST NECKLACE W/PEARL ACCENT MATCHING EARRING	$330.00	Black Hills Gold Stunning Necklace	$97.51
22k Gold set Necklace dangling Earrings antique NR	$314.99	18 kt yellow/white gold necklace and bracelet set	$94.60
ESTATE SET 14K GOLD NECKLACE AND BRACELET ITALY+NR	$291.25	NEW 14K gold necklace & earring SET GORGEOUS	$89.99
SOLID 14KT GOLD NECKLACE AND BRACELET SET CUBAN LINKS !	$289.99	14K Gold Necklaces w/ Bracelet Necklace Set w/ Pendants	$89.87

Sets ▸ Silver (w/o Stone)

The average sales price in this subcategory is $59.62.

	HIGH		AVG
Tiffany & Co RTT Oval Necklace and Bracelet Set NEW	$297.33	AUTHENTIC T&Co Mesh Ring and Return to Tiffany Bracelet	$94.33
Tiffany & Co. Oval Tag Bracelet and Necklace	$281.00	AUTHENTIC TIFFANY&CO OVAL TAG NECKLACE & ROUND BRACELET	$91.08
Tiffany & Co RTT Oval Necklace and Bracelet Set NEW	$280.00	AUTHENTIC TIFFANY&CO OVAL TAG NECKLACE & ROUND BRACELET	$91.00
Tiffany & Co 1837 Lock Necklace and Bracelet Set NEW	$256.83	AUTH TIFFANY & CO VENETIAN LINK BRACELET & NECKLACE SET	$90.99
Tiffany & Co. Heart Link Bracelet and Necklace	$250.00	AUTHENTIC TIFFANY & CO TOGGLE LINK HEART NECKLACE &	$85.39
Auth Tiffany & Co. Heart Tag Toggle Bracelet Necklace	$217.51	AUTHENTIC TIFFANY & CO TOGGLE LINK HEART NECKLACE &	$78.00
Tiffany & Co. Ten-row Matching Necklace & Bracelet $680	$212.50	AUTHENTIC TIFFANY & CO TOGGLE LINK HEART NECKLACE	$76.90
AUTH TIFFANY& CO OVAL TAG NECKLACE BRACELET SET	$205.05	AUTHENTIC TIFFANY & CO TOGGLE LINK HEART NECKLACE	$76.00
Tiffany & Co Heart Toggle Necklace Bracelet Set AUTH	$205.00	TAXCO STERLING SILVERSet NECKLACE BRACELET and EARRINGS	$70.00
AUTHENTIC TIFFANY & CO TEN ROW CHAIN & BRACELET SET	$192.49	925 Sterling Silver HEART LINK Necklace Bracelet SET !!	$69.95
AUTH TIFFANY & CO LOCK NECKLACE BRACELET SET	$187.50	AUTHENTIC TIFFANY & CO HEART NECKLACE AND BRACELET	$66.00
Tiffany & Co. Oval Tag Bracelet and Necklace	$182.49	TAXCO STERLING SILVERSet NECKLACE BRACELET and EARRINGS	$65.00
Authentic Tiffany & Co Oval Tag Necklace & Bracelet Set	$177.50	Sterling Silver Necklace, Bracelet, & Earrings Set	$63.00
Tiffany & Co. Heart Link Bracelet and Necklace	$175.00	AUTHENTIC TIFFANY SILVER HEART NECKLACE+BRACELET SET	$62.05
AUTHENTIC TIFFANY AND CO. OVAL TAG NECKLACE & BRACELET	$173.49	GORGEOUS NEW BRIGHTON SAUSALITO HEART NKLC & BRAC SET!!	$61.01

Sets ▸ Other Stones, Materials

The average sales price in this subcategory is $10.73.

	HIGH		AVG
BUTTERFLY WING JEWELRY -PENDANTS BRACELET EARRINGS RING	$77.37	Premier Designs "PLAYFUL" Necklace, Bracelet & Earrings	$15.50
GLASS FLORAL NECKLACE&EARRINGS ANTIQUE ITALY	$73.50	Mthology Rachel Abroms Aphrodite Hera Bracelet Earrings	$15.38
Emerald Ring, Earrings, and necklace set	$66.00	10K ROSE/YELLOW GOLD HEART EARRING BRACELET GIFT SET	$15.25
RUBY and Diamond Set - BRACELET AND RING	$49.99	Lovely Silver Wine Grapes Pin/Pendant & Earrings Set	$15.00
NEW ~ BRIGHTON~ "DIANA PEARL" NECKLACE	$43.00	Premier Designs Jewelry MARBLE 2-pc set AFJ	$14.99
NEW ~ BRIGHTON~ "PAPILLION" EARRINGS	$30.98	COOKIE LEE AustrianCrystal Blue Flower Neck + Ears NWT	$14.00
Jewelry lot Tiger's Eye & Sterling Rings Pendant NICE	$30.00	NEW Chico's Madras Red Stones Earrings Chicos NWT	$13.99
Genuine Rose Quartz & New Jade & Nugget 2 Pc Set	$28.95	MEDIEVAL LOOK AMETHYST TOPAZ PENDANT EARRINGS SILVER NR	$13.50
NEW ~ BRIGHTON~ "PICADILLY" HEART BRACELET	$28.77	COOKIE LEE Gen Crystal Ladybug/Flower Neck & Ear SetNWT	$13.00
Premier Designs Jewelry IMPERIAL 3-pc set AFJ	$28.55	PASTEL BEAD SQUARE MEDALLION SILVER TONE JEWELRY SET	$12.99
NEW ~ BRIGHTON~ "FRENCH KISS" EARRINGS	$28.00	EXOTIC VIVID ART GLASS NECKLACE SET JAVANESE JEWELRY	$12.95
NEW ~ BRIGHTON~ "PAPILLION" REVERSIBLE NECKLACE	$27.50	Capodimonte Porcelain Necklace and Earring Set	$12.50
NEW ~ BRIGHTON~ "KASHMIR" DANGLE POST EARRINGS	$27.01	6CT MULTICUT PERIDOT DROP EARRINGS PENDANT SET SILVER	$11.51
NEW ~ BRIGHTON~ "FRENCH KISS" Necklace	$26.00	BLACK/WHITE BUTTERFLY* 3 CORD NECKLACE & EARRING SET(A	$10.75
NEW ~ BRIGHTON~ "PRINCE CHARMING" HANDBAG CHARM	$26.00	COOKIE LEE Austrian Crystal Pink Starfish Necklace NWT	$10.50

Vintage, Antique ▸ Costume

The average sales price in this subcategory is $12.34.

	HIGH		AVG
16.50CT AMETHYST, BLUE TOPAZ & MARCASITE 19 GRAMS RING	$78.00	Back To School..Pre-Teen,Teen Jewelry Lot	$15.50
Vintage BOX of over 97 pc. JEWELRY with Real CAMEO	$75.99	VERY VINTAGE MICRO-MICRO MOSAIC ESTATE PIECE	$15.00
Vintage faux Coral gold DRAGON pendant Necklace	$59.00	Vintage HOT PINK fuschia Lucite bead Necklace bracelet	$14.99

HUGE 200 PIECE LOT VINTAGE JEWELRY NO RESERVE	$56.88	FAB HAND PAINTED CAMEO- PORCELAIN-PIN-PEND-GLDTONE	$14.99
AMAZING 20CT TW CHECKERBOARD BLUE TOPAZ 19 GRAM RING-NR	$55.99	Vintage Orange Multi-Strand Glass Bead Necklace No Res	$14.99
Vintage Filigrana GLASS Necklace HAND MADE IN MURANO	$51.00	~*Lot of 8 Huge Vintage Necklaces!*~	$14.07
Bakelite Necklace-Solid Black-UnlqUe-NR- opening-$5.99	$50.00	GORGEOUS MOTHER OF PEARL & MARCASITE VINTAGE BEAUTY	$14.05
STUNNING VINTAGE BLUE & GREEN ART GLASS PARURE	$49.99	Vintage Plastic jewelry long skinny Opera beads	$13.85
Vintage MIRIAM HASKELL 30" HEART NECKLACE Pearls & Jade	$49.00	INCREDIBLE 2CT TW BOHEMIAN GARNET GOLD CROSS PENDANT-NR	$13.50
BRONZE AMETHYST CUT GLASS PEARL BROOCH ~ VOODOO	$49.00	Nice Lot of Vintage Faux Pearl Jewelry	$13.13
GLISTENING MARCASITE 19 GRAM CAT BRACELET - NR	$34.36	JEWELRY DEALER/ESTATE LIQUIDATIONS LOT 0025	$13.00
SHIMMERING ART-NOUVEAU 46 GRAM JESTER MATCH SAFE - NR	$34.13	11 Rhinestone Jewelry Pens AS IS for Repair or Parts	$12.99
Set of 55 Vintage Typewriter Keys **NICE!!**	$33.99	Vintage Bracelet & Earring Set	$12.99
breathtaking 2.5 carat garnet earrings	$33.64	Vintage Lisner Thermoset Leaf Necklace & Bracelet	$12.99
Vintage Goldette Camphor Glass Bracelet-A Super Piece!	$31.00	KRAMER Christmas Pin Lantern Style FREE POSTAGE BIN	$12.60

Vintage, Antique ▶ Fine

The average sales price in this subcategory is $1,621.55.

	HIGH		AVG
5.38 CT DIAMOND ANTIQUE ENGAGEMENT RING PLATINUM	$55,834.00	1.20 CT DIAMOND ANTIQUE ENGAGEMENT	$2,900.00
2.39 CT DIAMOND ANTIQUE ENGAGEMENT RING PLATINUM	$7,477.00	RING 14 K WHITE GOLD	
3.00 CT DIAMOND ANTIQUE ENGAGEMENT RING PLATINUM	$5,299.35	1.42 CT DIAMOND ANTIQUE ENGAGEMENT	$2,575.00
G/VS/SI 2.26CT DIAMOND VINTAGE	$5,290.00	RING 18 K WHITE GOLD	
ENGAGEMENT RING GOLD		1.43 CT PRINCESS DIAMOND ANTIQUE WEDDING RING PLATINUM	$1,536.00
1.74 CT DIAMOND ANTIQUE VINTAGE	$4,109.70	1.05 CT DIAMOND ANTIQUE WEDDING RING PLATINUM	$1,465.00
RING 18 K WNITE GOLD		1.00CT DIAMOND ANTIQUE ENGAGEMENT RING FREE SHIPPING	$1,350.00

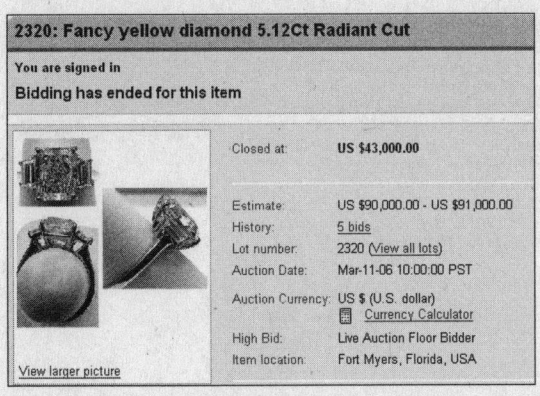

2320: Fancy yellow diamond 5.12Ct Radiant Cut

You are signed in

Bidding has ended for this item

Closed at:	**US $43,000.00**
Estimate:	US $90,000.00 - US $91,000.00
History:	5 bids
Lot number:	2320 (View all lots)
Auction Date:	Mar-11-06 10:00:00 PST
Auction Currency:	US $ (U.S. dollar) Currency Calculator
High Bid:	Live Auction Floor Bidder
Item location:	Fort Myers, Florida, USA

View larger picture

ROLEX COMEX SEA DWELLER 16600 - MINT ! - BOX &PAPERS !
Factory serviced in february 2004 !

Bidding has ended for this item

If you are a winner, Sign In for your status.

List an item like this or buy a similar item below.

Winning bid:	**US $34,100.00**
Ended:	**Mar-07-06 18:20:25 PST**
Shipping costs:	Check item description and payment instru or contact seller for details
Ships to:	N. and S. America, Europe, Australia, Japa
Item location:	Laval, Quebec Canada
History:	33 bids
Winning bidder:	djd (20 ✩)

Watches ▶ Pocket Watches

The average sales price in this subcategory is $93.09.

	HIGH		AVG
Erotic Minute Repeater Pocketwatch 18k Gold UNIQUE!!!	$5,500.00	1920's SWISS Chronograph Excelsior Pocket Watch	$126.05
*** PATEK PHILIPPE & CIE GENEVA ***	$4,450.00	3 hand,split second ,1/10 th,stop watch,complecated,40'	$125.95
RARE THE EDWARD HOWARD MOVEMENT	$2,850.00	14K SOLID GOLD LADIES HUNTER CASE POCKET WATCH	$117.50
SERIAL NUMBER 159 AS IS		Vintage 1914 Elgin Pocket Watch Size 16	$117.50
18k gold Hidden hinge Patek Philippe Pocket watch NoRSV	$1,775.00	Vintage American Waltham Pocket Watch	$112.50
SUPERB CONDITION HAMILTON RAILROAD 950B POCKET WATCH	$1,525.00	Men's New Movado watch	$110.65
Lovely Antique Tri-Color Quarter Repeater Pocket Watch	$938.00	X- 17J WALTHAM BALL -- MVT ONLY -X	$110.00
Hamilton Ball Official RR Standard 999B 16 sz 21j RARE	$850.00	Antique Pocket Watch OF KW KS 1865 #111	$107.50
14K GOLD W ENAMEL PANSY FLOWER SWISS POCKET WATCH	$735.00	OMEGA 15 JEWELS SUB SECOND .UNIQUE	$103.50
Fantastic Vacheron & Constantin Pocket Watch Hi Jewel	$685.99	HANDS & AUTHENTIC NR	
18s 999B Ball Hamilton Railroad Watch - Minty!	$640.00	HOWARD 17 JEWEL POCKET WATCH 1917	$102.83
ULYSSE NARDIN SPLIT SEC. CHRONOGRAPH ,REGIS.	$549.00	Antique Pocket Watch Sterling, Swiss Made, London #112	$102.50
18K Solid Yellow Gold Octagon Enamel Pocket Watch	$468.00	Last American Made Watch - Westclox Bullseye	$100.00
Illinois Bunn Special w/killer gothic dial 21J 18 Size	$433.00	Vintage Benedict Brothers Pocket Watch Movement NR	$99.99
HAMILTON 992E RAILROAD WATCH	$415.00	Wood Pocket watch Case Storage Display pocket watches	$99.00
GREAT CONDITION- SCARCE		13 1/2" ANTIQUE GOLD POCKET WATCH	$96.98
Hampden Special Railway 23J 18sz Killer Damaskeening	$384.00	CHAIN GREAT CONDITION	

Watches ▶ Wristwatches

The average sales price in this subcategory is $151.97.

	HIGH		AVG
New #1 18k Blancpain Tourbillon Diamond Dress Watch NR	$65,000.00	Vintage Hopalong Cassidy Watch With Original Saddle Box	$202.50
Limited Edition Blancpain Baguette Diamond Tourbillon		VINTAGE HAMM'S BEER HELBROS WATCH	$202.50
New 18k Gold Piaget Diamond Emerald Unique Piece #1 NR	$41,000.00	Genuine Movado Ladies Watch	$201.50
Limited Edition 18k Piaget #1 Unique Piece Watch Chrono		VINTAGE 1930's MICKEY MOUSE WATCH - INGERSOLL	$182.50
Rolex Daytona 18k White Gold Bracelet SODALITE 116509-D	$25,999.00	BRAND NEW LUMINOX 3101 BLACK FACE SS WATCH	$182.00
Newest D series-BNIB-Blue Dial-White Gold w/ Bracelet		Invicta Mens Watches $405 Lupah Diver 2147 Chronograph!	$177.50
2005 Rolex Lady Diamond Pearl MasterPiece MSRP $30,750	$24,850.00	Hamilton Presentation watch to a Pabst Brewery Emplye!	$175.00
Full Diamond Pearl Crown Collection Never Worn $30,750		BRAND NEW TIMEX BODYLINK HRM+GPS SYSTEM 5E671	$170.00

Ulysse Nardin SONATA - 18k - Box & Papers - UN watch	$24,690.00
18k White Gold Patek Philippe Ref 5036 Collector NEW	$24,600.00
100% NO RESERVE......GUARANTEED BEST PRICE ANYWHERE....	
PATEK PHILIPPE WATCH REF# 3945 18k YELLOW NO RESERVE	$24,600.00
100% authentic, like new, you won't find a better price	
AUDEMARS PIGUET LA BOUTIQUE NEW YORK SS/PVD LIMITED	$24,500.00
Breitling LT Ed 18K gold Perpetual Calendar Chronograph	$23,877.00
Only 50 made! Chronograph Chronometer gold band watch	
ROLEX Oyster COSMOGRAPH DAYTONA Manual SSteel MEN'S	$23,299.00
Subsidiary Seconds SILVER DIAL Circa 1978 BID NOW!	
AUDEMARS PIGUET LA BOUTIQUE PARIS TITAN LIMITED 50 PCS.	$22,000.00
Roger Dubuis "Golden Square" in 18KPG	$22,000.00
Audemars Piguet Royal Oak Alinghi Unused Watch	$21,995.00
NEW MENS ULYSSE NARDIN MAXI MARINE DIVER ROSE GOLD	$21,300.00
MENS ROLEX DAYTONA WATCH 1966 WHITE DIAL STAINLESS	$18,300.00
Seiko Master Planner Digital Alarm Chronograph Watch	$164.73
NEW Mens ESQ/Movado Centurion Chronograph watch	$162.50
EDDIE BAUER HAMILTON KHAKI MILITARY WRIST WATCH AUTO	$157.50
German Automatic Dual-Timer 2 flyback Second-hand A1207	$154.49
British Military Wrist Watch, Hamilton, Swiss 17-jewel!	$153.50
ARNEX "Swiss" HEBDOMAS Pocket Watch 15 JEWELS No Res...	$153.50
Vintage Ladies Longines Palladium Diamond Wristwatch NR	$152.51

Wholesale Lots ▸ Watches

The average sales price in this subcategory is $27.01.

	HIGH		AVG
MENS OMEGA CONSTELLATION SOLID GOLD 18-K MINT	$2,000.00	Colored Watch Faces with LOOPS-Geneva Brand-Lot of 10	$29.00
Baume&Mercier Lds Watch Diamond Bezel & Numbers	$1,035.11	WHOLESALE 4 METAL CUFF BANGLE "DIOR" WATCHES B/N	$29.00
NEW TISSOT T TOUCH ORANGE 100% AUTHENTIC	$325.00	WHOLESALE GENEVA BEADING WATCH FACES COLORED PICK 10	$29.00
GENEVA BRND SILVR WATCH FACES-SELECT 50	$145.00	WHOLESALE 5 BLING BLING ICED OUT CZ CRYSTALS WATCHES BN	$29.00
400 Sport Quest Ultimate watches	$99.99	Mars/Geneva Style Watch Faces: New 10 Piece Lot	$28.99
30 SETS OF HIS AND HER GENEVA WATCHES	$79.99	Colored Watch Faces with LOOPS-Geneva Brand-Lot of 10	$28.51
GIRARD PERREGAUX AUTOMATIC WATCH N/R	$62.88	WHOLESALE NEW GENEVA BEADING	$28.50
WHOLESALE 4 BRIGHTON SILVER	$58.00	WATCH FACES SILVER PICK 10	
BANGLE WATCHES LADIES B10		Mars/Geneva Style Watch Faces: New 10 Piece Lot	$28.50
500 BRAND NEW MENS AND WOMENS	$51.00	Geneva Elite Watch Face: New 10 Piece Lot	$28.00
DIGITAL SPORTS WATCHES!		Geneva Elite Watch Faces: New 10 Piece Lot	$28.00
WHOLESALE 5 METAL CUFF BANGLE	$51.00	WHOLESALE 4 ITALIAN CHARM WATCHES OVAL COLORED FACES	$28.00
FLOWER PRINTS WATCHES B40		Mars/Geneva Style Watch Faces: New 10 Piece Lot	$27.99
Wholesale Lot OF 20 Elegance Gent Wrist Watch wh1	$49.95	Huge Lot of Watches and Watch Parts	$27.88
50 Pcs.New Ostrich Pattern Leather Watch Bands.Band.	$48.00	WHOLESALE BEADING WATCH FACES	$27.87
160Pcs Assorted New leather Watch Bands.Band.	$46.01	TWO TONE LOOPS PICK 10	
126Pcs.Colorful Asstd. Mens Leather Watch Bands.Band.	$44.00	WHOLESALE NEW BEADING WATCH	$27.67
60 GENEVA WATCHES *30 H&H GIFT SETS* BEST PRICE!!	$42.00	FACES COLORED LOOPS PICK 10	

Wholesale Lots ▸ Mixed Jewelry Lots

The average sales price in this subcategory is $44.20.

	HIGH		AVG
Jewelry Stores Dream Wholesale Lot 14k Gold Diamonds NR	$1,009.00	WHOLESALE LOT OF 20 NEW NECKLACES	$61.00
NICE Scrap Wearable 10K 14K Gold Lot 116.1 Grams NR	$830.00	+ EARRINGS PERU ART	
HUGE STERLING SILVER JEWELRY LOT-300+ PIECES	$825.64	Lot of Vintage & New Jewelry + Supplies, New Beads +..	$61.00
Huge Lot 116gr 18K, 14K, 10K gold little scrap NR	$765.00	12 lbs of jewelry alot of nice jewelry some signed	$58.62
117 gram lot-10K 14K Gold, Wear not Scrap, Rings,Chains	$741.04	14K GOLD & DIAMAONDS WATCH CASES & 14K PENDANT	$58.10
120 GRAMS 10K+14K+18K SCRAP GOLD	$654.68	14k lot scrap or not look	$53.00
+DIAMONDS+POCKET WATCH		10+ LBD COSTUME/JUNK JEWELRY **VINTAGE TO NEW**	$52.77
10-14-18KT GOLD USABLE RINGS, CHAINS, BRACELETS 82.5grm	$528.54	LOT 84 SILVER NECKLACES EARRINGS	$52.02
Great Lot of 14kt Gold, 67.7 g, Wear or Scrap	$524.99	BRACELETS PERUVIAN NEW	
17 Pcs 46.3 grams 18k gold scrap or wear	$476.00	7 ounces Sterling Silver Jewelry Lot Wear or Scrap	$51.50
LARGE LOT OF MIXED GOLD JEWELRY & GEMSTONES	$400.00	JEWELRY SCRAPS LOT 24 14k GOLD SILVER WATCHES CZ MORE	$51.00
50+ GRAMS 14K 18K GOLD WEAR &	$384.99	Wholesale lot of 100 fantastic Necklaces&Earrings.NE257	$51.00
SCRAP (26GRM CUFFLINKS)+		Navajo Jewelry Lot (turquoise and sterling silver)	$50.99
NICE LOT 62 Grams 10k 14k 18k Gold Jewelry NO SCRAP WOW	$370.01	#15) 50 CZ RINGS SIZED PRONG SET NEW!!!	$50.00
PREMIER DESIGN HUGE LOT 70+ PIECES WORTH THOUSANDS	$365.05	Sterling Marcasite Closeout Lot FREE SHIPPING	$49.06
COOKIE LEE Fine Fashion Jewelry Cubic Zirconia huge lot	$360.00	Lot NEW Cookie Lee Necklace Bracelet Earrings +++	$46.55
jonber.com 48 TURQUOISE silver wholesale Handmade LOT	$351.57	LARGE VINTAGE JEWELRY LOT, ALL KINDS 158 PIECES	$45.00

23

MUSIC

eBay's Music category is home to one of eBay's most famous PowerSellers, if not the most famous—1 Cent CD, run by Jay and Marie Senese ("jayandmarie" on eBay, who have a feedback score in the hundreds of thousands). The husband-and-wife team has completed over a million eBay auctions, and they are the number-one seller on eBay in terms of volume. Jay and Marie have been reselling CDs on eBay since 1999, and they close some 5,000 auctions a week, according to AuctionBytes.com.

Their domination is evident when you scroll through the completed listings pages in the Music ▶ CDs subcategories; you see many auctions sprinkled throughout that start with "1 CENT CD" in their title, one of their trademarks. It's extraordinary to see so many listings from any single seller appear so frequently in eBay's pages in any category. As the Seneses say on their website, JayandMarie.com, selling on eBay is a full-time job for them, and they're not the only ones. Plenty of folks make a living selling music on eBay.

CDs vs. Vinyl vs. Cassettes

You'd probably expect that CDs would outnumber vinyl records in eBay's Music category. And they do, but not by as much as you might think. As I write this, there are about 700,000 CD listings and about 400,000 album listings, less than twice as many CDs as records, even though CDs are much more commonly played these days. No doubt this is due to the high collectibility of vinyl records—their large, colorful covers, some with famous art, such as the Peter Max painting on the Beatles' *Yellow Submarine* album, make them very desirable to many music fans, and some even hang them on their walls in special frames.

And what about cassettes—are they hanging in there? Not so much. There were only about 25,000 cassette listings in the Music category on eBay, in contrast to the 700,000 CDs. This is due to a variety of factors, not the least of which are cassettes' small size (not good for enjoying the images on the covers) and their hard-to-preserve form—how many times have you found yourself trying to wind the tape back into the case when it unspools?

Not only are there fewer cassettes on eBay than CDs or records, their prices don't hold up very well either. The highest-priced tend to land in the hundreds rather than thousands of dollars. The biggest individual cassette seller in this sample was a rap tape by Young Cellski, *Livin In The Bay*, which sold for $155.83. The median range of prices here is only around $3.00 to $4.00.

But how are CDs selling as compared with albums, and what genres, if any, stand out? Well, here those unassuming vinyl records prove their mettle: one of the highest-priced individual items in the samples below is a rock record, a "mega rare" Dutch 45 of Bruce Springsteen's "Point Blank," which sold for $7,700.00. (Indeed, this price is even greater than that fetched by many big CD lots, such as the 180 Mozart CDs that went for $1,049.99.) Other top sellers in Music ▶ Records include a rare Madonna "Lucky Star" cover art proof that went for $2,500.00, a Beatles mono red boxed set for $1,008.00; and an Elvis Presley EP for $932.00.

One of the highest prices listed in the Music ▶ Records ▶ Rock subcategory was $9,000.00 for a copy of a rare unreleased AC/DC compilation, *12 of the Best*. However, this appears to actually be a cassette tape; according to the seller, there was only one cassette and a handful of albums made, and those only for collectors. As with many rare items, it has a great story: per the seller, "In 1978 Albert music wanted to release an AC/DC 'best of' album with songs from the 3 first albums—High Voltage, Dirty Deeds and Let There Be Rock. But AC/DC refused, because the 'Powerage' album was to be released, and as [guitarist/group founder] Malcolm Young told it, 'Hits? What f****** hits?' So the project was destroyed." This kind of event—when an item is recalled, pulled, or misprinted—can equal collector gold later. In fact, the aforementioned Springsteen 45 was a recall. One of the most famous examples of this is the Beatles "butcher" *Yesterday and Today* album, where the Fab Four were featured in a scary photo with dismembered dolls. That cover was recalled and covered over with a different image, but many collectors covet the original art. (Prices for the "butcher" cover in various states range from about $50.00 to $900.00.)

Some eBayers even prefer listening to vinyl over CDs; "Vinyl is the only way to fly!" insisted one seller on the eBay Music discussion board. "Everyone has their preferences, but to me vinyl is what the Gods (Zappa and Hendrix, among others) would have wanted their music played on. The tones are warm and rich, and if properly cared for won't end up with the sound of corn popping." Another seller says 80 percent of his vinyl business is international, and that buyers pay upwards of $25.00 to "get the records here they can't get wherever they are" without blinking an eye at the cost. He ships them in padded mailers he buys on eBay. "Sell the stuff you know does well, and you can make money," is his advice. "Regular run-of-the-mill rock and roll collections from your youth are not big sellers because they are so common."

In terms of median prices, an overall keyword search for albums (using the acronym *LP*) yielded an average price of about $18.00, while a similar search for CDs (using *CD*) yielded an average price of about $9.00. This will, of course, vary depending on the genre. And remember that an "average" price will be skewed higher if there are even a few very high prices on the high end—in the Music ▶ Records ▶ Pop subcategory, the approximate median price (the price with as many prices higher as lower) is only $3.52.

If you decide to sell vinyl records on eBay, remember to be very specific about the condition of the LP and any flaws it has. As one seller put it, "The condition of the LP is GOD and just because you have, say, an LP of Sgt. Pepper does not mean it will be like the millions of other Sgt. Peppers out there. There are a myriad of different 'editions' of this LP out there, and it's the detail that people are willing to pay big money for." For example, he asks whether it was issued in the United States, the United Kingdom, or another country. Is it a first, second, third, and so on pressing; is it mono or stereo? Is there a factory mistake on the record, and does it have all the parts it came with? "The more detail you can give us the more we are able to help you sell your record for $100.00 rather than the $10.00 it may only go for when you omit a crucial point of sale in your description."

Among CDs, aside from the huge "personal collection" lots (some autographed), like the 1,700 jazz discs that sold as a lot for $3,000.00, boxed sets do very well. In this sample, the highest price in the CDs subcategory for a non-collection is a boxed set of 65 classical CDs that went for $1,074.99. Three different Phillips Complete Mozart sets (180 CDs) went for $1,049.00, $999.00, and GBP 560.00 each. High-priced individual CDs include the amusingly subtitled ("MegaRare. ButYouAlreadyKnowThisIfYouArelookingAtthis") St. Etienne fan-club-only *I Love To Paint* CD, $999.00, and *666 Ways To Love* by H.I.M. (His Infernal Majesty), $325.00. In the DJ/Dance genre, a Barbra Streisand "Night of My Life" promo remix CD went for $355.00; and in Rap, Young Gangstas' *Premeditated Gangsterism* fetched $405.00.

The UK Factor

One thing that stood out throughout all the pages of the Music category, but especially in the Pop and Jazz genres, was the large number of British sellers. Whether this is due to the popularity of eBay's UK site, a greater willingness on the part of the British to ship to the United States, the exchange rate of the British pound against the American dollar, or other reasons, there does seem to be a lot of crossover between American and UK music buyers and sellers. Or, as one eBay music fan speculated, it may be that Britain has many vinyl collectors of different genres, or that "the British were blessed with a lot of fine pressings that many U.S. collectors find desirable."

Digital Music Downloads and the Future of eBay Music

If cassettes (and even 8-track and reel-to-reel tapes) are music's past, digital music downloads may be its future. eBay announced in 2004 that it would begin experimenting with sales of digital music on the site, and there are a small number of such files available for $0.99 each as I write this. Because eBay is more associated with reselling than selling things new, it's unclear how such music will fare on the site, but I wouldn't count anything out at this point. But even if music downloads take off on eBay, you should still be able to find your vinyl here. Video may have killed the radio star, but music in all its formats will most likely go on being traded indefinitely on eBay.

Accessories

The median sales price in this subcategory is $8.99.

	HIGH		AVG
Zoom MRS-1044 MRS1044 CD Digital Recorder Make your own CD!!!	$449.99	PORTABLE CD CASE 240 DVD HOLDER ORGANIZER CASES WALLET	$8.99
table top cd player dj use(denon)	$280.00	Storage case for mini LP kami jacket CDs holds about 20.	$8.99
7" SINGLE FLIGHT CASE - IN EXCELLENT CONDITION	GBP 62.00	Intro offer thru Sept. Free P&H within USA 1 or 2 pcs.	
L/Weight 7" x 200 Aluminium Vinyl Record Storage Case	GBP 46.99	KENNY CHESNEY PROMO MUSIC POSTER	$8.99
Reason 3.0 free with a 64 Disk CD Organizer	$68.00	NEW Pro Mark Marco Minneman Signature Drum sticks	$8.99
MAILING ENVELOPES x 100 PACKAGING FOR 12" LP RECORDS	GBP 37.50	Hit Clip Micro Music clips : Classic Pack : New	$8.89
NEW Aluminium 7" x 100 Vinyl Record Storage Case	GBP 34.99	Bugs Bunny CD / DVD Zippered Hard Metal Case Excellent	$8.99
LASERLINE CD HOLDER 90-HARD TO FIND	$61.00	FREE ARMBAND+SWIVEL! BLACK IPOD MINI SKIN CASE COVER	$8.99
Sharper Image CD Power Tower 100- CD Holder-Look!!	$60.36	FREE ARMBAND+SWIVEL! IPOD 4G BLACK SILICONE SKIN CASE	$8.99
Atlantic ELF 464C47 Multimedia Storage Rack		25 LP 12" RECORD ALBUM POLY OUTER SLEEVES FREE S/H USA	$8.99
NEW IN BOX - MANUFACTURER SEALED	$60.00	FREE ARMBAND+SWIVEL! NEON WHITE IPOD MINI SKIN CASE 4GB	$8.99
VERY Rare LASERLINE 200 CD holder/rack/case laser line	$59.50	CD FLIGHT CASE	GBP 5.00
EXTREMELY RARE UNUSED 200 CD CAROUSEL/TOWER		240 Cd - DVD Carrying Case / Wallet	GBP 4.99
BCD RECORD BAG. SCOUSE/HOUSE/DANCE +NOT BOSS, AATW+	GBP 32.01	CD VISOR WALLET CASE CAR STORAGE 12 CD UNIVERSAL FIT	GBP 4.99
New Metal 600 CD DVD Storage Case MP3 Holder Box DJ	$55.00	240 Cd - DVD Carrying Case / Wallet	GBP 4.99
600 CD-R DVD Storage Case Wallet ipod Holder Box DJ MP3	$54.99	Fantastic Hip Hop Producer Software- Brand New	
RECORD BOX / CASE 100 X 7INCH VINYL	GBP 31.00	Including 600MB of Royalty Free Samples	GBP 5.00

Cassettes

The average sales price in this subcategory is $3.95.

NOTE *These results are based on a keyword search of the Cassettes subcategory for auctions with the word* cassette *in the title.*

	HIGH		AVG
500 LOT BRAND NEW CASSETTE TAPE CASES - CLEAR PLASTIC	$33.99	SWANS-Live cassette European tour 1984	$4.99
HARD KNOX Psyco's R Us Cassette Rare Glam Sleaze	$26.15	Doo Wop 45'S on Cassette: THE BEST OF THE KEYNOTES	$4.99
Tom Waits - Swordfishtrombones - Cassette - Orig Asylum	$24.99	Bon Jovi -I'LL SLEEP WHEN I'M DEAD -Cassette Single	$4.00
LOT OF 12 CHILDRENS MUSIC & AUDIO CASSETTE TAPES	$21.05	Bless The Lord - Taize Music - Cassette - NEW	$4.00
Shark Island S'cool Buss Cassette AOR!!! 1986	$20.50	NEW Jimmy Sturr CASSETTE "Pure Polka 83 Songs	$3.99
LOT of - 174 CASSETTE TAPES Rock Alternative Pop WOW!	$20.49	Lot of 6 Soundtrack Cassette Tapes	$3.99
VYPER Prepared To Strike Cassette Rare Glam xtra track	$17.50	FITNESS WALKING BEGINNER 20 MINUTE MILE CASSETTE NEW!	$3.99
John Schneider / Smallville: SEALED Cassette 1991)	$16.68	Collectible BARRY WHITE JUST FOR YOU 3 Cassette Set	$3.99
THE CURE CASSETTE TIMES SQUARE FRANCE	$15.51	NIP Wee Sing Dinosaurs Cassette and Book	$3.75
Smashing Pumpkins "Pisces Iscariot" Cassette **SEALED**	$15.50	LOT pop cassette tape MADONNA BRAXTON WHITNEY EN VOGUE	$3.25
SAM KINISON-OUT OF CONTROL(3 CASSETTE LOT)SEALED!	$14.00	Jethro Tull "20 Years Of Jethro Tull" Cassette *SEALED*	$3.25
Pink Floyd "The Wall" Cassette 1979 *****SEALED*****	$13.25	BIG COMFY COUCH CASSETTE PLUS BONUS	$3.20
HEAVYNESS Lock Me Out Cassette Mega Rare Glam Metal	$12.49	Best Of Joan C. Baez - Joan Baez (Cassette 1990)	$3.00
KEEL- LAY DOWN THE LAW-(CASSETTE) MINT	$11.99	The Blues Brothers - Original Soundtrack (Cassette 1...	$3.00
Iron Maiden "Live After Death" Cassette *****SEALED****	$11.00	Metallica Whiplash used cassette	$3.00

CDs

The average sales price in this subcategory is $9.01.

NOTE *These results are based on a keyword search of the CDs subcategory for auctions with* CD *in the title.*

	HIGH		AVG
Rare SLY FOX CD Let?s Go All The Way PRINCE, Apollonia	$560.00	Non Fiction - Mausberg (CD 2000)	$9.05
Huge CD Collection, Lot of 242 CDs Rock Pop Dance	$357.00	*NEW/SEALED* 1 CENT CD Coldplay X & Y ~ Low Ship	$9.04
PET SHOP BOYS MIRACLES MINT/SEALED JAPAN CD PLUS BONUS!	$233.50	LUNAR AURORA Welteng?er CD Nagelfar Emperor Limbonic	$9.03
MOZART - Complete Works - 170 CD BOX - SEALED	$207.50	SOUTHERN GOSPEL CD: Martha Carson Gospel Truth ^SEALED^	$9.03
240 CD Collection Music Lot Pop Rap R & B Dance Remixes	$202.50	Twiztid Cryptic Collection VOL 1 CD ICP Blaze Juggalo	$9.03
AC/DC ACDC AC DC WHOLESALE LOT CDS CD COMPACT DISCS	$200.00	Specials More Specials UK Remastered CD Bonus Videos	$9.02
W. A. MOZART COMPLETE WORKS * 170 CD SET * NEW & SEALED	$182.50	JEFFERSON AIRPLANE STARSHIP HITS - 2 CD SET	$9.01
MFSL MFCD-846 Procol Harum Broken Barricades SEALED CD	$171.09	Linkin Park-In The End NEW MINT CD SINGLE	$9.01
CD Visitors : Attention 1987 Italo / aor Ultra Rare !	$162.50	*NEW/SEALED* 1 CENT CD Damien Rice O 0 ~ Low Ship	$9.01
BEACH BOYS JAPAN 6 Mini LP CD SS + PROMO OBI + BOX SET	$159.99	DEATH IN VEGAS - Back To Mine - *XLNT+ CONDITION CD*	$9.00
LOT 10 TIME LIFE 'SWING ERA' 2 CD SETS-FIRST 10 VOLUMES	$152.95	JACK JOHNSON**BRUSHFIRE FAIRYTALES**CD	$9.00
Clay Aiken * LOOK WHAT LOVE HAS DONE * CD - Rare & Mint	$152.50	HK CD Tai Chi " Greatest Hits " RARE NEW	$9.00
BADFINGER JAPAN 5 Mini LP CD SS APPLE OBI + PROMO BOX	$144.99	WOODEN WAND... 'l'un marquer...' CD ltd six organs jomf	$9.00
Japan 3 Mini lp CD VAN DER GRAAF GENERATOR Promo Box LE	$124.50	RICK AND BUBBA SHE COMMENCED TO SHAVING 2 CD SET	$9.00
Schubert Songs Dietrich Fischer-Dieskau 21 cd box	$112.00	The First 10 Years - Joan Baez (CD 1990)	$9.00

CDs ▸ Classical

The median sales price in this subcategory is $6.32.

	HIGH		AVG
HEIFETZ COLLECTION 65 CD Classical Box Set	$1,074.99	CD:MOZART "PIANO CONCERTOS	$6.40
Philips Complete Mozart Edition - 180 CDs - NEW, SEALED	$1,049.99	#10 & 27/CURZON" IMPORT BBC	
Very RARE and Hard to Find - The Ultimate Collection!		1 CENT CD: The 5 Browns new	$6.39
Philips Complete Mozart Edition - 180 CDs - NEW, SEALED	$999.99	classsical DUALDISC SEALED	
Very RARE and Hard to Find - The Ultimate Collection!		99 Cents/MANON:La Scala '69: Freni, Pavarotti, Panerai	$6.37
Philips Complete Mozart Edition 45vols/180 CDs Pristine	GBP 560.00	The Kings Collection - Kings College Choir CD	GBP 3.64
The entire Mozart repertoire by superb artists on CD		THE 5 BROWNS CLASSICAL PIANO CD/DVD	$6.35
MAHLER No.7 Bernard Haitink Amsterdam : MINT 2 OOP CDs*	$360.00	1 CENT CD:: Berlioz 'Romeo & Juliette' Boulez 2CD SEALD	$6.35
Rubinstein Collection. 82 volumes, Book, and Box.	$750.00	GOLDSCHMIDT: Beatrice Cenci, in	$6.32
HUGE CLASSICAL & MISC 220 CD LOT! PIANO, SYMPHONY ETC.	$676.66	3 acts OOP SEALED 2 CDs	
S RICHTER - AUTHORISED RECORDINGS 21 CD SET RARE #1293	$640.00	Pavarotti - The Greatest Pavarotti Album Ever (2 CDs)	GBP 3.61
HUGE LOT OF 210 CLASSICAL CDS	$562.35	THE EARLIEST SONGBOOK IN ENGLAND(CD)	GBP 3.60
The Rubinstein Collection - Complete Recordings - NR	$456.00	NEW AND SEALED)	
Arthur Rubinstein - RCA Red Seal - Limited Edition Set		TAKEMITSU: A STRING AROUND	GBP 3.60
MOZART - COMPLETE WORKS - 170 CD SET - NEW !!	$449.99	AUTUMN, RIVERRUN ETC (NEW)	
138 CLASSICAL CD COLLECTION! BACH, MOZART, SCHUBERT	GBP 202.00	CD BEETHOVEN Cantatas on Death of Joseph II, Elevation	GBP 3.59
Choral Classics from St John's College (Boys + Men)	GBP 200.00	1 CENT CD: Luciano Pavarotti 'Live Italy' CD DVD SEALED	$6.30
75 CD collection of opera and classical music	$350.00	1 CENT CD: Berlioz 'Romeo Juliet' 2CD P Monteux SEALED	$6.30
LOT OF 81 CLASSICAL C.Ds 16 BOXED SETS, HANDEL, MOZART.	$329.51	Britten -Young Person's Guide, 4 Sea Interludes -Hickox	GBP 3.56
SYMPHONIES, OPERA BERLIOZ MANTOVANI BRUCKNER, CONCERTOS		Bartok Concerto for Orchestra - Ivan Fischer	$6.27

CDs ▸ Country

The median sales price in this subcategory is $5.50.

	HIGH		AVG
LOT OF CD'S ALL FOR ONE GOING TO HIGH BIDDER GOOD CD'S	$406.00	Under The Influence : Alan Jackson (CD 1999)	$5.50
AMERICAN COUNTRY COUNTDOWN:31 4 hr. 4:CD Shows 124 CD'S.	$399.00	Twice The Speed Of Life : Sugarland Brand New CD!!!	$5.50
"FREE" 30 CROOK & CHASE CD'S/ RADIO SHOWS:"FREE FREE"		Kenny Rogers Love Songs : Kenny Rogers (CD 2001)	$5.50

	HIGH		AVG
Lot of 232 Country CD's Big Names Chesney Garth McGraw	$365.00	Double Live : Garth Brooks (CD 1998)	$5.50
Tim McGraw CD PLUS BONUS 2 floor tickets Hard Rock Live	$325.00	The Grass Is Blue : Dolly Parton (CD 1999) NO PORTER!!!	$5.50
Lot of 250 Country CD's Big Names Garth Chesney Reba	$305.00	Chris Cagle [ECD] - Chris Cagle (CD 2003)	$5.50
Lot of 77 Country CD's Most SEALED Private Collection. Alan Jackson	$275.00	Martina - Martina McBride (CD 2003)	$5.50
Merle Haggard Dolly Parton Garth Brooks et		Garth Brooks Double Live Ltd. First Edition CD Xlnt!	$5.50
New Bob Wills 13 CDs,1 DVD Box :Bear Family :Faded Love	$234.00	See If I Care - Gary Allan (CD 2003)	$5.50
HUGE LOT of 94 Country Music CD's Tim McGraw Toby Keith	$230.27	The Greatest Hits Collection - Alan Jackson (CD 1995)	$5.50
Full List of Personal Collection - NO RESERVE, All LN!!		Fireflies - Faith Hill (CD 2005) Superb cond. *Awesome	$5.50
HUGE COUNTRY CD LOT!! 160+ CDs- -Big names ! All listed!	$228.50	At Folsom Prison [Remaster] - Johnny Cash (CD 1999)	$5.50
Miranda Lambert's FIRST CD, Very Very Rare	$227.50	Country Music Hall of Fame Package - NEW - No Reserve!!	$5.50
SARA EVANS Real Fine Place AUTOGRAPHED CD & Press Kit!	$201.56	Risin' Outlaw - Hank Williams III (CD 1999)	$5.50
Johnny Cash The Legend 4CD Plus Bonus CD & DVD - No R/S	GBP 111.00	Michael Nesmith cd Standard Ranch Stash MONKEES *Seal*	$5.50
Limited Edition - Cellophane Sealed - Brand New - Rare			
Large Lot of Old-Time Music CDs small labels obscure	$194.50		
Old Cowboy Heroes Chris LeDoux CD	$177.55		
HUGE LOT 78 COUNTRY CD'S SHANIA, TOBY, BROOKS, STRAIT	$162.01		

CDs ▶ DJ, Dance

The median sales price in this subcategory is $5.50.

	HIGH		AVG
Madonna "EROTICA BLACK LEATHER BOX CD" Limited Edition	$520.00	The Fragile : Nine Inch Nails (CD 1999)	$5.50
DJ Sasha Digweed Howells Lawler Paul Oakenfold CD lot.	$425.00	The Ambient Collection : Art of Noise (CD 1997)	$5.50
Biggest Global Underground Collection 82 Original CDs +		The Chillout Lounge 2 : Various Artists (CD 2001)	$5.50
KRAFTWERK 12345678 BOX SET 8cd very rare MINT	$405.00	1 CENT CD: M.I.A. 'Arular' fem vocs world dance 2005	$5.50
LIMITED EDITION - - - WAS NEVER FOR SALE !!!		All Nature One 2005 Live Sets CD Ferry Corsten, Armin	$5.50
110 CD LOT rare industrial electro noise wumpscut FLA. wax	$374.99	1 CENT CD: Nine Inch Nails	$5.50
trax zoth ommog haujobb pitchfork OOP metropolis		'With Teeth' 2005 industrial	
Barbra Streisand Night of My Life Promo Remix CD	$355.00	Dark Latin Groove - DLG (Dark Latin Groove) (CD 1996)	$5.50
Donna Summer Remix CD I Got Your Love	$349.99	1 CENT CD: Moby 'Ambient' electronica SEALED	$5.50
ULTIMIX BLOW OUT 45 ULTIMIX CD'S FOR $315.00	$315.00	Luxury - Fantastic Plastic Machine (CD 1999)	$5.50
DEPECHE MODE Rare 1997 "ULTRA" US Promo ADVANCE Card CD	$313.50	400 DJ 2005 Live Sets Ferry Corsten, Paul Oakenfold	$5.50
Jamiroquai Toronto Concert Tickets and Dynamite CD	$310.00	Operatica Shine CD Inva Mula	$5.50
USA CD PART 2 Remix	$299.99	Maureen O'Flynn Ying Huang	
CD COLLECTION JOB LOT CD'S ALL LISTED HOUSE TECHNO	GBP 155.00	Crazy [Maxi Single] - Andy Bell (CD 2005)	$5.50
HARDCORE POP TRANCE D&B HED KANDI INDIE		AEROBIC CARDIO STEP WORKOUT	$5.50
HUGE LOT 81 PROMO ONLY CD, DJ COPY CDS CLUB SERIES	$266.00	CD / 32 DJ PROF MIX	
Jamiroquai Toronto Concert Tickets and Dynamite CD	$255.00	WORKOUT CD /PROF 128 DJ MIX / GREAT STEP CD	$5.50
DJ Shadow Public Works Box Set Shepard Fairey Size XL	$250.00	CAFE DEL MAR vol. 9 ~ CD NEW SEALED	$5.49
5 t-shirts, mix CD, book, buttons, stickers, postcard!			
Definitive 80's NEWWAVE 12" Collection 17CD Set REMIXES	$162.99		

CDs ▶ Jazz

The median sales price in this subcategory is $6.15.

	HIGH		AVG
Over 1700 cd's some autographed	$3,000.00	Blanche Calloway - The Essential	GBP 3.50
Complete Roulette Studio Count Basie 10 CD Mosaic Box	$819.14	Coleman Hawkins/Roy Eldridge - Bean & Little Jazz	GBP 3.50
170 Jazz CD's Private Collection Coltrane Blue Note etc.	$666.99	Duke Ellington - The Brunswick Sessions Vol.3	GBP 3.50
Modern Bebop Fusion Miles Davis Impulse Blakey Mingus		Gerry Mulligan Meets Ben Webster	GBP 3.50
MFSL gold CD JS-1 JAZZ Sampler SEALED CD	$568.97	Johnny Dodds - Blue Clarinet Stomp	GBP 3.50
Thad Jones / Mel Lewis Orchestra Mosaic 5 CD Box Set!	$510.00	STEPHANE GRAPPELLI - CRAZY RHYTHM	GBP 3.49
Complete Solid State Recordings Out Of Print! RARE!		- 17 TRACKS - NEW CD	
MOSAIC MD4-114: Complete BLUE NOTE ART HODES	GBP 250.67	Elton Dean saxophone/Howard Riley piano SLAM CD 234	GBP 3.50
The Complete Master Jazz Piano Series 4 CD Mosaic Box	$470.00	CHARLES MINGUS / HIS FINAL WORK,, CD, NEW!!!	GBP 3.50
MFSL gold CD JS:1A Jazz Sampler SEALED LONGBOX	$456.66	Lee Ritenour CD OverTime	$6.15
4CD Mosaic box: Blue Note Sessions: Sidney Bechet n/r	$435.00	1 CENT CD: White Hot Odyssey	$6.15
Mosaic Complete Master Jazz Piano Series OOP 4-CD set	$380.00	ex Cherry Poppin Daddies	
COUNT BASIE/ERNIE WILKINS-Mosaic Roulette 8CD NM SET!	$325.00	Charlie Parker & Dizzy Gillespie 12 Cut CD NEW 1 CENT	$6.15
MOSAIC - The Complete CBS Jam Sessions - BUCK CLAYTON	$300.00	RAMSEY LEWIS With One Voice CD 05 Smokie Norful	$6.15
MOSAIC/CHARLES MINGUS/COMPLETE CANDID/3 CD BOX	$249.50	JOHN COLTRANE - MY FAVOURITE THINGS LIVE - NEW CD	GBP 3.49
Mosaic 150 Jackie McLean Blue Note recordings 1964- 66	GBP 135.00	MILITARY BANDS - A CONCERT PERFORMANCE - NEW CD	GBP 3.49
BUD SHANK/MEL LEWIS-Mosaic Pacific Jazz-SEALED 5CD SET!	$225.00	DJANGO REINHARDT AND STEPHANE GRAPPELLI - NEW CD	GBP 3.49

CDs ▶ Metal

The median sales price in this subcategory is $6.61.

	HIGH		AVG
Iron Maiden : The Best of the Beast : PROMO BOX SET	$865.70	1 CENT CD: DevilDriver 'Fury Of	$6.65
50 Black Metal CD Lot- Burzum, Arckanum, Arkona,	$679.69	Our Maker's Hand' 2005	
Maniac Butcher, Master's Hammer, Etc. Rare & OOP		Led Zeppelin - Led Zeppelin II (CD 1994)	GBP 3.76
IRON MAIDEN Eddie Head BOX 13 CD Set Judas Priest RARE	$500.00	BON JOVI - 7800 DEGREES FAHRENHEIT - CD *NEW	$6.63
Iron Maiden : FEAR OF THE DARK : UK PROMO BOX SET	$450.00	A Perfect Circle - Thirteenth Step CD (2003 Album)	GBP 3.75
110 Deathmetal cd lot	$439.99	1 CENT CD: Cold 'A Different Kind Of Pain' 2005	$6.62
METALLICA Nothing Else Matters/Enter Sandman (Live)	$350.00	New sealed WATCH THEM DIE Bastard Son CD	$6.61
Metallica - One Skull Box Set Limited CD Sealed	GBP 255.00	Dream Theater - Images And Words - Import	$6.61
Iron Maiden Fear Of The Dark UK Promo Box Set Very Rare	$225.00	Dream Theater - 6 Degrees Of Inner Turbulence	$6.61
number 139, date May 1992 Ultra rare UK promo box		Santana - Caravanserai (Remastered) (CD 1988)	GBP 3.75
Hybrid Theory EP	$345.00	Santana - Santana (Limited Edition) [Remastered] CD	GBP 3.75
HIM - His Infernal Majesty - 666 Ways To Love	$325.00	STARBREAKER' 2005 CD	$6.61
Iron Maiden THE FIRST TEN YEARS JAPANESE CD BOX Japan	$312.80	The Very Beast Of Dio - Dio CD	$6.60

55 CD LOT Black Metal USBM Abruptum Demoncy Ungod	$305.00	2000 MINT Condition Rock	
IRON MAIDEN THE FIRST TEN YEARS JAPAN 10 CD BOX W/OBI	$299.99	Galadriel : Empire of Emptiness CD gothic doom metal	$6.60
AC/DC - Complete Remasters 17 CD Box - Australia	GBP 165.00	1 CENT CD: Velvet Revolver 'Contraband' SEALED t	$6.60
ADX - SUPREMATIE/LA TERREUR (ORIGINAL SYDNEY PRESSING!)	$265.00	1 CENT CD: Megadeth 'Greatest Hits: Back To...' SEAL a	$6.60

CDs ▸ Pop

The median sales price in this subcategory is GBP 2.00.

	HIGH		AVG
COLDPLAY Safety ep Original CD of only 500 pressed!	GBP 469.00	Tracy Chapman CD3 Single "Fast Car"	GBP 2.00
Signed Promo CD 'A Whiter Shade of Pale' : Procol Harum		SUGABABES - STRONGER REMIX UK CD SINGLE	GBP 2.00
Limited edition numbered + signed by the song's authors	GBP 460.00	ELVIS COSTELLO-END OF THE TELESCOPE CD SINGLE	GBP 2.00
MADONNA ULTRA RARE "THE GIRLIE SHOW" BRAZIL PROMO CD	GBP 374.00	Tracy Chapman CD3 Single "baby can i hold you"	GBP 2.00
ONLY 200 COPIES WERE PRESSED FOR BRAZILIAN TOUR IN '93		Tracy Chapman CD3 Single "talkin' bout a revolution"	GBP 2.00
VMA Performer Shakira CD Plus Free Gift 2 VMA Tickets	$650.00	T'Pau CD Single "I Will Be With You" 1988	GBP 2.00
Watermelon Men - Moving Targets CD 1988 rare POP	$502.02	Talking Heads - Once In A Lifetime (The Best Of Talk...	GBP 2.00
VMA Tickets (2) Free with purchase of Shakira's CD	$450.00	Alannah Myles CD single "Black Velvet" 1989	GBP 2.00
BRAND NEW HANSON INDIE BOOMERANG & MMMBOP CD'S	$349.99	NERD - CD Album Title - FLU OR DIE	GBP 2.00
JIMMY WEBB HARSH MISTRESS NEW 5 CD RHINO HANDMADE LTD.	$297.77	Madonna the Power of goodbye rare picture disc cd	GBP 2.00
numbered limited only 2500 pressed RHINO HANDMADE		MASSIVE ATTACK - DANNY THE DOG	GBP 2.00
Pet Shop Boys Saturday Night Forever 1trk PROMO CD.	$250.00	CD - EVANESCENCE - FALLEN	GBP 2.00
Love To Infinity Radio Edit		The Doors - The Best Of The Doors - 2 x CDs	GBP 2.00
Mariah Carey UNPLUGGED RADIO SPECIAL CANADIAN PROMO '92	$499.99	Mike Oldfield - Tubular Bells Vol.2 (CD 1992)	GBP 2.00
THE RAREST MARIAH CAREY CD THAT YOU DON'T HAVE!!!		SHAKIRA - LAUNDRY SERVICE CD	GBP 2.00
Celine Dion MEGA RARE Live in Zurich 2-CD + A capella	$499.00		
TEARS FOR FEARS-GOODNIGHT SONG RARE CD SINGLE!!!	GBP 275.00		
Madonna - Like A Prayer - Promo Box Set CD RARE !!!!	GBP 254.00		
Madonna Japanese CD single collection! WOW very rare	GBP 250.00		
MADONNA WILLIAM ORBIT RARE PROMO DOUBLE CD	GBP 250.00		

CDs ▸ Rap, Hip Hop

The median sales price in this subcategory is $5.00.

	HIGH		AVG
350 Rap Cd NO DUPLICATE SEALED NEW RARE OOP NR DVD	$810.00	Touch (MCA) - John Klemmer (CD 1989) NEW SEALED	$5.00
GET THIS ONE TIME ULTIMATE COLLECTION OF RAP CD'S		Loki - Illegitimati Rap Cd	$5.00
FREE MTV VMA 2005 MIAMI tickets w/ P. Diddy CD purchase 2 seats together	$710.00	3 cds.1.Eminem Show.2.Marshall mathers.3.8 mile.	$5.00
Young Gangstas "Premeditated Gangstarism" Sircle Of Sin	$405.00	Dead Prez RBG (Revolutionary But Gangsta) CD	$5.00
+150 CD Collection - Rap,Hip Hop, and R&B - No Reserve	$400.00	The Massacre [PA] - 50 Cent (CD 2005)	$5.00
Orignally paid / Valued at over +$1700		Large lot of music CDs Country, Rock, & Rap	$5.00
Insane Clown Posse (ICP) Wicked LOT CDs, VHS, Cassettes	$390.01	The Cookbook [PA] - Missy Elliott (CD 2005)	$5.00
All original cds, t-shirts, tapes, and VHS		Lord Infamous.. Three 6 Mafia.. "Lord of Terror"	$5.00
Young Dre D Troubled Mind Bowleggs J Mack N8 Sacramento	$304.99	XZIBIT KRONDON RAS KASS PLANET	$5.00
Red Money "Il Much Red" Ultra Rare Atlanta Rap	$275.00	ASIA PHIL RARE PROMO CD	
LOT 110 Rap CD's, Real not burned, Mint Condition	$275.00	[2 of these sold for $5.00 each]	
Steady B – What's My Name CD 1987 RARE Oldschool JIVE		MADLIB SLUM VILLAGE COMMON GANG	$5.00
ORIGINAL ULTRA RARE OOP STEADY B CD TRUE GOLDEN AGE RAP	$255.00	STARR PROMO CD LOOTPACK	
DANGER MOUSE GREY ALBUM JAY-Z BLACK MF DOOM OFFICIAL	$252.49	ACEYALONE ABSTRACT RUDE FREESTYLE	$5.00
RARE MAKAVELI 'WHITE MANZ WORLD' SINGLE CD PROMO TUPAC	$203.50	FELLOWSHIP PROMO CD	
VERY RARE CD! LAST ONE ON EBAY SOLD FOR $182.50		KILLAH PRIEST WU TANG RARE	$5.00
Huge rap, hip hop, and r/b CD lot!! 100+ of the hottest rap albums!	$202.51	PROMO TRAGEDY KHADAFI CD	
allmost 150 rap cd's. mostly southern hip hop	$202.50	The Day After [PA] - Twista CD EXPLICIT BRAND NEW	$5.00
not a collection of old junk! some just came out!!!!!!!		TOO SHORT HIGH GLOSS PLASTIC POSTER FLAT RARE	$5.00
K-Rino Street Military 20-2-Life 4 Deep Z-Ro.. x40 CDS!	$202.00	Metal Fingers Presents: Special Herbs 9 & 0 MF Doom CD	$5.00
LOT "TEEN ANGEL'S" CHICANO, TATTOO, GANG ART, LOW RIDER	$199.99		
LOT,TEEN ANGELS,MAGAZINE,CHICANO RAP,TATTOO,LOW RIDER	$199.95		

CDs ▸ Reggae, Ska

The median sales price in this subcategory is $5.99.

	HIGH		AVG
SUBLIME bumS lie PSYCHO SEMANTIC POLICE CD RARE PROMO	$200.59	Bob Marley & U Brown - Reggae & Ska Twin Pack 2 CDS	$5.99
VARIOUS - TROJAN - A JAMAICAN STORY - 30 CD BOXSET NEW	GBP 102.01	APACHE INDIAN Remix Best CD JAPAN ONLY MINT 19303	$5.99
Trojan A Jamaican Story / Box Set / 500 Tracks 30 CDs.	GBP 99.99	REGGAE DISCO ROCKERS Rainbow CD JAPAN MINT 19299	$5.99
Tougher Than Tough The Story Of Jamaican Music OOP 4 Cd	$163.01	Bob Marley~~~3 CD Boxed Set~~~44 Songs~~~NEW	$5.99
Ocean 11 Rare Self Released '95 Ska CD Hepcat Reggae LP	$122.50	[5 of these sold for $5.99 each]	
DOESIA CLICK "HARD ON THE GRIND" DOJA STOCKTON RAP.	$104.00	BOB MARLEY The Legend 32 Tracks NEW SEALED 2 CD SET	$5.99
CD IS ORIGINAL 1995 RELEASE WITH NO BARCODE ON BACK		~~~DESMOND DEKKER~~~ACTION!~~~2 CD SET~~~SEALED!!!!	$5.99
4 Rare sublime cds, all oop, who wants em	$92.52	Best of Reggae~~~~54 Hits on 3 CD Boxed Set~~~~NEW	$5.99
40ozskunk2ndhandsmoke/shirtdointimeswedenblack album2		INNER CIRCLE - Bad Boys on CD - Reggae - Sweat - L@@K!	$5.99
Misty in Roots - Live at the Counter Eurovision	GBP 41.00	Big Blunts Vol. 2: More Smokin' Reggae Hits! - Vario...	$5.99
The Story of Jamaican Music, reggae, 4-CD box set	$71.00	THIRD WORLD - REGGAE AMBASSADORS (UK CD ALBUM)	$5.99
Lot of 4 Trojan Box Sets in great condition, Ska Reggae	$71.00	Live In New York City - Black Uhuru (CD)	$5.99
Whole Bob Marley Collection	$66.00	Various Artists - Island 40th Anniversary Vol.5 1972...	GBP 3.39
MADNESS AQUA FOLIES CD NEW YOUR 83 specials 2 tone ska	GBP 36.00	Live At Stubbs:... [ECD] [Digipak] - Matisyahu (CD 2...	$5.99
Slightly Stoopid Self - Titled Album 1996 (Rare)	$62.00	BROKEN SILENCE Culture Reggae	$5.99
Misty In Roots - Forward (CD 1991)	GBP 33.00	Mix CD "Safe and Secure"	
The Ultimate Trojan Skinhead Box Set / Rare / 9 x CDs.	GBP 31.00	GREGORY ISAACS The Sensational... 1996 U.K. CD oop	$5.99

CDs ▶ Rock

The median sales price in this subcategory is $6.95.

	HIGH		AVG
Pearl Jam World Tour 2003 Series. Ten Club Pakage All Unopened!!!	$1,480.00	KROQ ACOUSTIC CHRISTMAS CD	$6.95
U2 CD w/Bonus Montreal Tickets 11/26/05 Red Sec. 102	$1,025.00	Blink182/Hole/No Doubt/Bush	
45 Time Life Rock 'N Roll Era CDs Nice Condition	$1,090.89	TOMMY ROE "SHEILA" GREATEST HITS	$6.95
ST ETIENNE - I Love To Paint fanclub only cd saint.	$999.99	18TRKS CD ~SEALED/NEW~	
MegaRare.ButYouAlreadyKnowThisIfYouArelookingAtthis		CHRISTIAN DEATH "ASHES" CD Gothic	$6.95
Springsteen Ultra Rare Promo CD collection.	$870.00	Rozz Williams ~SEALED	
1988 Japanese issue : The Holy Grail!		FOGHAT "ROAD CASES" 25th ANN.	$6.95
400 CDs FOR SALE	$750.00	CD W/Bonus trks ~SEALED~	
KBCO.STUDIO C's. #2. #4. #5. #6. #8. #9. #10. #11. #12.	$737.80	NEW COAT OF PAINT CD Tom Waits	$6.95
FLAWLESS CONDITION :: 9 CD'S :: PLUS BONUSES !!!		Tribute songs CD SEALED	
1998 Evanescence EP - ULTRA RARE CD!!!	$710.00	GARY NUMAN "REMODULATE" 1984-95	$6.95
2 Free VMA TICKETS WITH CD Section Best Seats on Ebay	$700.00	- 2 CD RARE MIXES ~NEW~	
Paul McCartney JAPAN Mini-LP 17 CD Set w/OBI COMPLETE!!	$650.00	FLESHTONES, the SELF-TITLED (S/T) 1996 CD ~SEALED/NEW~	$6.95
Queen - Limited Edition 20 CD Box Set Brand New Sealed	GBP 360.00	The Beatles A Hard Day's Night CD	$6.95
MEGA COLLECTION OF CD'S 1950s-1980s TIME LIFE CDs - NR	$560.00	Three Cheers For Sweet Revenge - My Chemical Romance	$6.95
GOLD ORIGINAL Bob Dylan Genuine Live 1966 8 CD Box Set	$560.00	MICHAEL TOLCHER - I AM - NEW CD Southern Rock	$6.95
massive bob dylan collection rare deleted ones theworks.	GBP 300.00	INXS - Elegantly Wasted (CD 1997)	GBP 3.95
need to sell have to raise some fund for kids holiday		VH1 MICHAEL HUTCHENCE	
OVER 200 CDs Perfect Condition Alternative Rock RAP.	$510.00	THE ROLLING STONES Out of Our Heads [USA] + 11 bonus CD	$6.95
Soundtracks Perfect New Used Steal BIN just ask		THE ROLLING STONES Milestones + 11 bonus CD	$6.95
BRUCE SPRINGSTEEN 70'S TO 80'S JAPAN PROMO 2CD SET	$499.99	SUPERTRAMP Crisis? What Crisis? CD	$6.95
HARDEST TO FIND JAPAN BOSS's PROMO CD!![-l.,kmp0OZXcxdsw		The Beatles' Second Album CD	$6.95

CDs ▶ R&B

The median sales price in this subcategory is $5.00.

	HIGH		AVG
++ PRINCE The Work Vol.1:5 + Outtakes 1976:2001 ++.	$898.88	Late Registration [PA] : Kanye West (CD 2005)	$5.00
Rare complete set of all 20 Cds (Jill Jones, Bangles)		Let's Get It: Thug Motivation 101 [CD & DVD]	$5.00
Lot 93 Soul R&B Blues CD's Private Collection Motown. Marvin Gaye	$427.75	*NEW*. SNOWMAN DELUXE EDITION	
Isley Bros Stevie Wonder etc Many SEALED		John Mellencamp : Words and Music : Greatest Hits(2004)	$5.00
TA MARA&THE SHEEN/S.T 1985 JAPAN ONLY CD PRINCE	$330.00	Late Registration [PA] : Kanye West (CD 2005)	$5.00
177 R&B Soul Funk Blues & Jazz CD's Most are SEALED.	$320.00	Back For The First Time [Edited] : Ludacris (CD 2000)	$5.00
Popular & Obscure Titles from Old Store Stock		Aaron Neville - The Tattooed Heart CD	$5.00
Lot of 188 music cd's R&B/SOUL	$300.00	The Duprees/Skyliners/Don&Juan/Gene Chandler CD doo wop	$5.00
JEFF REDD Down Low CD 94 unreleased mega rare	$266.99	Legacy: The Greatest Hits (Deluxe) - Boyz II Men (CD...	$5.00
Dream - Reality Unreleased Album Rare Bad Boy Diddy	$234.50	CDMU0342 Fantasy Sex and Material Possessions	$5.00
Beg, Scream Shout! OOP Box Various 60s Soul NEW SEALED	$212.50	The College Dropout [PA] - Kanye West (CD 2004)	$5.00
JEFF REDD - DOWN LOW (CD)	GBP 119.00	Clarence Carter Have You Met... R&B Soul Rare Ichi-ban	$4.99
MAGIC LADY - RARE OOP MOTOWN S/T CD	$202.50	PRINCE Purple Rain (Sdtk) APOLLONIA	$4.99
SMOKEY ROBINSON * Smokey CD 1973 RARE MINT OOP	$200.50	MORRIS DAY SHEILA E	
PRINCE / JAM & LEWIS CD/CASSETTE LOT!+ VANITY PLAY BOY!	$200.00	MATERIAL Hallucination Engine - Bill Laswell Shankar CD	$4.99
THE COMPLETE MOTOWN SINGLES VOL 1: 1959-61	GBP 104.20	READY FOR THE WORLD Long	
Down Low - Jeff Redd (CD 1994) mega rare'	$172.57	Time Coming 1986 NEW SEALED CD	
CURTIS HAIRSTON/ST 1986 JAPAN ONLY CD BRAND NEW ! BB&Q	$171.50	Emergency On Planet Earth - Jamiroquai (CD 1993)	$4.99

CDs ▶ Soundtrack, Theater

The median sales price in this subcategory is $6.51.

	HIGH		AVG
Blade Runner Esper Edition MK3 - Vangelis - Full Score.	GBP 249.99	Lord Of The Rings: The Return Of The King [ECD] - Or...	$6.52
4CD Box Set: "The Definitive Collectors Edition".		Television's Greatest Hits Vol. 1 OOP Very Rare CD	$6.52
VIBES - Rare Soundtrack CD James Horner CYNDI LAUPER	$405.00	The Full Monty - Original Cast (CD 2000)	$6.52
Varèse Sarabande Club Limited Edition # 760 of 1000 !!		OST - Grease CD 1991 Travolta Newton John Frankie Valli	GBP 3.70
Lot of 204 Soundtracks, all listed, excellent condition	$350.00	CLOSE ENCOUNTERS	GBP 3.70
The Boys From Brazil Jerry Goldsmith cd SUPER RARE OOP	$255.00	1CENT CD Tarantino Connection pulp fiction true romance	$6.51
FEDORA : Soundtrack CD Miklos Rozsa VS Club Limited	$255.00	The Insider CD Soundtrack Lisa Gerrard Pieter Bourke	$6.51
EYE OF NEEDLE/LAST EMBRACE Soundtrack CD Miklos Rozsa	$255.00	Various Artists - Top Gun (CD 2000)	GBP 3.70
Eye of the Needle : Last Embrace CD Miklos Rozsa	$250.00	Mark Knopfler - Local Hero (CD 1997)	GBP 3.70
James Horner "VIBES" Varese Club Ltd-Ed CD Cyndi Lauper	$230.00	SOUNDTRACK March 1998 w/ HENRY MANCINI + M. KAMEN	$6.51
Jerry Goldsmith: BANDOLERO! (EXPANDED) OST CD.	$202.50	Cinderella Special Edition Soundtrack - Original Sou...	$6.51
OUT OF PRINT INTRADA EXPANDED CD RELEASE		BRAVEHEART : ORIGINAL SOUNDTRACK. SEALED CD	GBP 3.70
Ron Jones: STAR TREK: Starfleet Academy OST CD	$200.00	Boogie Nights - Original Soundtrack - CD Album - MINT	GBP 3.70
The core Young rare 2 cd soundtrack Intrada sealed !!!!	$199.99	MY STEPMOTHER IS AN ALIEN SOUNDTRACK CD	GBP 3.70
Jerry Goldsmith@20TH Century Fox 6 cd box set	$197.50	Original Soundtrack : Seven Years In Tibet ..NEW CD	GBP 3.69
PREDATOR Ltd. Ed. OOP CD Soundtrack (only 3,000 made!)	$192.50		
Authentic Varese CD MINT/SEALED! Glad to ship overseas!			
BLADE RUNNER Vangelis DECK Japan Import Score CD	GBP 107.00		
500 copies only, this is #255			
THE MUSICALS COLLECTION (Entire 75 CDs & Magazines)	GBP 102.08		

CDs ▶ World Music

The median sales price in this subcategory is $5.99.

	HIGH		AVG
Um Kolthoum Box Set Arabic Music CD Om Kolthoum Egypt	$456.27	ISMAEL MIRANDA & ORQ. HARLOW (CD2000) NEW Puerto Rico	$5.99
Um Kolthoum Box Set Arabic Music CD Om Kolthoum Egypt	$285.00	Andean QUICHUA MASHIS Caminante ANDES Ecuador Peru	$5.99
RARE Murmurs of Earth Voyager Record Commemorative Set	$247.77	HACIENDO PUNTO EN OTRO SON (CD) Puerto Rico	$5.99
Lot of 99 Spanish/Mexican/Latino CDs! Espanol! NEW!	$216.50	Best Of - Ricky Martin (CD 2001) IMPORT w/ Bonus VCD	$5.99
THALIA Piel Morena MEXICAN PROMO CD Megarare!!!!!!!!!!!	$169.50	UKRAINE Ukrainian CD - RUSLANA - Dyki tanzi, folk pop	$5.99
Beyond Recall: A Record Of Jewish... Bear Family 12disc.	$121.50	Flute and Guitar - Celtic Music CD Early Scottish Music	$5.99
11cds and 1 Dvd more than 14hrs of music.		Viva Cuba Libre CD (Buena Vista Social Club) CUBAN, New	$5.99
MOSTLY AUTUMN Rare PROMO Press Kit!!!!	GBP 77.00	El Otro Lado De Mi - Soraya (CD 2005) NEW CD	$5.99
THALIA No Me Enseñaste CHILE Promo CD MEGA RARE!	$112.50	New Sealed CD Fijacion Oral Vol 1 Shakira 2005	$5.99
20 Years With Turkey in the Eurovision Song Contest	GBP 63.00	Live In Belfast - The Irish Tenors (CD 2000) NEW	$5.99
FRANCK POURCEL - CONCORDE / EL CD	$105.49	INSPIRATION INDIA Vilayat Khan Duets ... NEW SEALED CD	$5.99
Live at the World Cafe Vol 1 WXPN KFOG KMTT KBCO	$103.50	UTADA HIKARU Exodus English Album+Bonus 2 CD 29 Tracks	$5.99
Sebastien Izambard (Il Divo) EXTRA RARE LIBRE CD	$100.00	\Ayumi Hamasaki ~MY STORY~ ALBUM +BONUS 2 CD J-POP	$5.99
Clara Nunes 9 CD box set samba bossa nova Brazil	$99.99	Ballroom Music - Quickstep NEW CD	$5.98
MAZZ 30 Exitos Insuperables TEJANO 2 CD'S 2004 L@@K		Grandes Exitos 91-04 Alejandro Sanz 3 CD set - HITS!	$5.98
+ 18 MAZZ CDS FROM MY PERSONAL COLLECTION L@@K	$91.00		
THE SAW DOCTORS - RED CORTINA - CD SINGLE. RARE	GBP 51.00		

Digital Music Downloads

The average sales price in this subcategory is $0.99.

NOTE *These results are based on a keyword search of the Digital Music Downloads subcategory for auctions with the word* download *in the title.*

HIGH TO LOW

Jeff O's Rockabilly Party - MP3 Download - PL0137607	$3.99	Rosita (Oldies Doo Wop) - MP3 Download - PL0070692	$0.99
Old Town Jail (Cowboy C+W) - MP3 Download - PL0071642	$0.99	Longhorn Cadillac- Free Ship - MP3 Download- PL0070840	$0.99
Thunderbird (Oldies) - MP3 Download - PL0070699	$0.99	Old Town Jail (Cowboy C+W) - MP3 Download - PL0071642	$0.99
I'm Gona Tell Ya (Oldies) - MP3 Download - PL0030357	$0.99	Ivy Jivy's Rock And Roll - MP3 Download - PL0030148	$0.99
Doo Wop Party(Friday Night) - MP3 Download - PL0070875	$0.99	Thunderbird (Oldies) - MP3 Download - PL0070699	$0.99
Old Town Jail (Cowboy C+W) - MP3 Download - PL0071642	$0.99	I'm Gona Tell Ya (Oldies) - MP3 Download - PL0030357	$0.99
Old Town Jail (Cowboy C+W) - MP3 Download - PL0071642	$0.99	Ivy Jivy's Rock And Roll - MP3 Download - PL0030148	$0.99
1959 Longhorn Cadillac - MP3 Download - PL0070840	$0.99	Doo Wop Party(Friday Night) - MP3 Download - PL0070875	$0.99
Rosita (Oldies Doo Wop) - MP3 Download - PL0070692	$0.99	Thunderbird (Oldies) - MP3 Download - PL0070699	$0.99
Doo Wop Party(Friday Night) - MP3 Download - PL0070875	$0.99	I'm Gona Tell Ya (Oldies) - MP3 Download - PL0030357	$0.99
Thunderbird (Oldies) - MP3 Download - PL0070699	$0.99	Ivy Jivy's Rock And Roll - MP3 Download - PL0030148	$0.99
Ivy Jivy's Rock And Roll - MP3 Download - PL0030148	$0.99	Doo Wop Party(Friday Night) - MP3 Download - PL0070875	$0.99
I'm Gona Tell Ya (Oldies) - MP3 Download - PL0030357	$0.99	Hound Dog Rockabilly Man - MP3 Download - PL0070889	$0.99
Hound Dog Rockabilly Man - MP3 Download - PL0070889	$0.99	[4 of these sold for $0.99 each]	

DVD Audio

The average sales price in this subcategory is $18.00.

NOTE *These results are based on a keyword search of the DVD Audio subcategory for auctions with* DVD *in the title.*

	HIGH		AVG
Orig Marty Casey Graphic - DVD & CD Rock Star INXS	$499.90	Allman Brothers Band Final Night	$18.00
[10 of these sold in a multiple item ("Dutch") auction for $49.99 each]		Beacon 2005 Nice **DVD	
US BillBoard Charts Top 100 Hits 1957-2004 on MP3 DVD	$203.00	***INXS***LIVE @ THE ROCKIES**1997 TOUR DVD	$18.00
US BillBoard Charts Top 100 Hits 1957-2004 on MP3 DVD	$202.50	Crowded House (2002) [DVD Audio] sealed	$18.00
Luther Vandross Funeral DVD & Program - FREE Shipping	$200.00	ROBERT PLANT THE GREEK LOS	$18.00
[8 of these sold in a multiple item ("Dutch") auction for $25.00 each]		ANGELES 2002 NICE**DVD	
Nick Cave "The Complete Seeds" 80 Live shows +more2 DVD	$149.99	ROBERT PLANT AUSTIN CITY 2002 NICE**DVD	$18.00
US BillBoard Charts Top 100 Hits 1957-2004 on MP3 DVD	$142.00	Allman Brothers Band Final Night Beacon 2005 Nice **DVD	$18.00
Nick Cave "The Complete Seeds" 80 Live shows +more2 DVD	$139.99	TIMBIRICHE FLANS ALASKA GIT POP &	$18.00
[2 of these sold for $139.99 each]		ROCK EN TU IDIOMA DVD	
DVD VENICE LIVE SPIN - ART TOUR 2000 RARE	$112.50	HK POP*Jacky Cheung Live Grand Performance1-3 DVD 229hi	$18.00
15,316 OLD TIME RADIO OTR LIBRARY 16 DVD	$104.97	WHITESNAKE NIGHT OF BUFFALO 1990 NICE**DVD!!	$18.00
[3 of these sold in a multiple item ("Dutch") auction for $34.99 each]		J POP*X japan dahlia tour final 1996 3 dvd New	$18.00
ROCKSTAR INXS * JD FORTUNE * DVD	$102.50	80'S NIGHT MIX VOL.2 CLUB DANCE	$18.00
NIN nine inch nails - 10 years 1989 - 1998 original DVD	$100.98	MUSIC VIDEO MIX (DVD)	
Monica Naranjo "La Colleccion" 5 DVD + Rare Remix Video	$100.00	TIMBIRICHE FLANS ALASKA GIT POP	$18.00
[2 of these sold for $100.00 each]		& ROCK EN TU IDIOMA DVD	
Stevie Ray Vaughan's TV Appearances on DVD	$99.90	Korea POP*Shinwha"Winter Story Tour 2003-2005"3 DVD New	$18.00
[10 of these sold in a multiple item ("Dutch") auction for $9.99 each]		Rolling Stones NIB Four Flicks DVD	$18.00
NIN nine inch nails - 10 years 1989 - 1998 original DVD	$91.66	ROBERT PLANT ROBIN HOOD	$18.00
Green Day Storytellers DVD Rare Limited Edition	$90.89	NEW YORK 2001 NICE**DVD	

Records

The average sales price in this subcategory is $18.00.

NOTE *These results are based on a keyword search of the Records subcategory for auctions with LP or* album *in the title, as well as searching eBay's Completed Items.*

Item	HIGH
AC/DC "12 OF THE BEST" AC DC. THE RAREST ORIGINAL MUSIC ITEM BY AC/DC	$9,000.00
BLACK AND WHITE PICTURE RECORD PRESSED BY VOGUE ONLY 2 KNOWN COPIES * DON PABLO ORCHESTRA * NO RESERVE	$4,959.09
THE RISING STORM Calm Before LP NM garage psych rare	$4,750.00
RISING STORM: Calm before MONSTER ORIGINAL. SUPER RARE PSYCH/ PROG LP, brilliant condition	$4,716.66
Pink Floyd Japan 45 See Emily Red Wax PROMO LP 7". Never has been played STONE MINT !!!	$4,650.00
4561: EXTREMELY RARE 1934 PARKER-REMINGTON SALESMAN'S P Live Auctions!	$4,000.00
northern soul-Shirley Edwards-Shrine-Dream My Heart. Super rare original Shrine release	$3,851.00
Hank Mobley-Quartet-Blue Note 5066-10"-EXCELLENT!!!	$3,450.55
Northern Soul - Yvonne Vernee on SonBert - MONSTER!!! Just Like You Did Me / I'm In Love - RARE Detroit Soul!	$3,049.00
U2 - Three (U2 - 3) Limited #539 of 1000 MEGA RARE Free // U2 - 2 SIDES LIVE // GREEN VINYL 1981 - RARE !!	$2,499.00
BEATLES-1969 YELLOW SUBMARINE LP ODEON LABEL RARE NR	$2,037.00
PARTY AFTER HOURS 10"MONO, RED WAX. SUPER RARE!! Amos Milburn, Velma Nelson, Wynonie Harris	$2,000.00
MOZART - SONATES PIANO & VIOLON - LILI KRAUS - DF	$1,970.00
Jazz Quintet 60 - Rare Danish Jazz LP - Botschinsky +++	$1,881.37
Charlie Parker-Alternate Masters 2-Dial 905-EXCELLENT!	$1,729.88

Item	AVG
Seventh Heaven SEALED LP Soundtrack Reissue	$19.37
BTO Bachman Turner Overdrive Japan Tour LP	$19.00
LP: Blowfly - In The Temple Of Doom '84 US	$19.00
Queens of the Stone Age-Lullabies 2 LP w/3 non CD traks	$18.99
Lee Morgan ~ The Sidewinder ~ Blue Note NY Mono LP	$18.01
BIOSPHERE - MICROGRAVITY APOLLO R & S AMBIENT TRANCE LP	$17.50
sounds of north american frogs FOLKWAYS LP samples	$17.15
The Beatles-Anthology III 3 LP 1968-70 SEALED	$17.00
Beastie Boys Paul's Boutique Gatefold Vinyl LP MINT	$16.07
Leroy Hutson r&b soul Lp on Curtom closer to the source	$15.60
AMERICAN NIGHTMARE 12" vinyl lp	$15.50
THE COASTERS GREATEST HITS LP	$15.50
Mandrill S/T FUNK LP PROMO	$15.49
MASON PROFFIT orig 1971 psych/rock lp	$15.39
Hi-Fi's lp on Verve V 2035	$15.00

Records ▸ Pop

The median sales price in this subcategory is GBP 1.99.

Item	HIGH
Rare undocumented MADONNA LUCKY STAR lp cover art proof. Original rejected Lucky Star LP cover art, Sire Records	$2,500.00
THE BEATLES MONO Collection Red Boxed Set	$1,008.00
Rare Vogue picture record test pressing #771 Art Kassel	$997.65
Elvis Presley PS EP original New Zealand pr SEE THE USA Picture Sleeve EP SEE THE USA THE ELVIS WAY great cond	$932.00
Beatles UK EXPORT CPCS 103 Second Album 1965 Y&B MINT-	GBP 390.00
Beatles UK LET IT BE BOX 1970 COMPLETE 1st press EX con	GBP 359.00
THAD JONES MAGNIFICENT ORIG. BLP 1527 BLUE NOTE JAZZ LP	$633.00
MIKE OLDFIELD MAGGIE REILLY Crisis RARE FLEXI 45	$600.00
APPLE ACETATE LP WISHBONE ASH UNTITLED 8 TRACK STEREO	GBP 330.00
Beatles LP MFSL Mobile Fidelity Box Set	$560.00
The Jam -Going Underground- rare test pressing	GBP 322.01
The Jam -Eton Rifles- rare test pressing	GBP 315.55
"VIRGINIA" 7" Demo written by Hank Marvin & Paul Ferris	GBP 311.00
APPLE ACETATE LP WISHBONE ASH UNIQUE DIFF TITLES RARE!!	GBP 310.00
Rolling Stones MFSL LP Box Set	$510.00

Item	AVG
GARY NUMAN CARS E REG MODEL RARE PICTURE DISC RECORD	GBP 1.99
MINT AS NEW :IKE & TINA TURNER RIVER DEEP MOUNTAIN HIGH	GBP 1.99
DAVE GAHAN : Dirty sticky... 12" DEPECHE MODE	GBP 1.99
The Lonely One EP by Duane Eddy 1958 with originalcover	GBP 1.99
Madonna Like a Prayer LP 1989 with inner sleeve (nmint)	GBP 1.99
Madonna Like a Virgin LP 1984 with inner sleeve 'exc'	GBP 1.99
ELO - A new world record.	GBP 1.99
Elton John - Madman across the water.	GBP 1.99
MICK RONSON -Love Me Tender- 7" Demo	GBP 1.99
Matthew Wilder - Break My Stride 12"	GBP 1.99
MOODY BLUES , THE OTHER SIDE OF LIFE	GBP 1.99
Cyndi Lauper - She Bop 12"	GBP 1.99
Billy Joel We Didnt Start The Fire 12" VERY GOOD COND	GBP 1.99
Novelty Instrumental 45 by the PRIVATES & The COLONELS "CHOPSTICKS CHA CHA" / "CANNONS ON BUNKER HILL"	$3.52
JACKSONS "CAN YOU FEEL IT MIXED MASTERS	GBP 1.99

Records ▸ Rock

The median sales price in this subcategory is $6.01.

Item	HIGH
AC/DC "12 OF THE BEST" AC DC THE RAREST ORIGINAL MUSIC ITEM BY AC/DC	$9,000.00
BRUCE SPRINGSTEEN POINT BLANK MEGA RARE DUTCH 45 NM	$7,700.00
BLACK AND WHITE PICTURE RECORD PRESSED BY VOGUE ONLY 2 KNOWN COPIES * DON PABLO ORCHESTRA * NO RESERVE	$4,959.09
THE RISING STORM Calm Before LP NM garage psych rare	$4,750.00
RISING STORM: Calm before MONSTER ORIGINAL SUPER RARE PSYCH/ PROG LP, brilliant condition	$4,716.66
Pink Floyd Japan 45 See Emily Red Wax PROMO LP 7" Never has been played STONE MINT !!!	$4,650.00
George Pepp NORTHERN SOUL 45 Feeling is Real / Blow Bet	$4,600.00
northern soul-Shirley Edwards-Shrine-Dream My Heart Super rare original Shrine release	$3,851.00
THE MOVE: 4 Track 7" ACETATE - all unreleased tracks!	GBP 2,171.77
SIGNED BY ELVIS PRESLEY & FRAMED 1957 RCA LP LOVING YOU AUTHENTICITY CERTIFICATE PERSONALLY AUTOGRAPHED	GBP 2,150.00
RARE GARAGE/PSYCH 45 JOHN ENGLISH & THE HEATHENS Sabra	$3,161.00
1956 ELVIS PRESLEY PHONOGRAPH & SPD:23 EP RECORD SET	$2,132.89
LEAF HOUND GROWERS OF MUSHROOM ORIG UK DECCA PROG PSYCH	$2,030.02
1964 BEATLES & FRANK IFIELD ON STAGE Portrait LP. Original : Authentic : Rare : Mono	$1,798.55
Rolling Stones 45 Lond. 9641 Stoned/I Wanna Be Your Man	$1,525.00

Item	AVG
George Clinton Funkadelic Tales of Kidd Funkadelic LP	$6.71
BEACH BOYS Tears in the morning /French pressing	$6.01
The Guess Who-45-Clap For The Wolfman/Road Food	$6.01
American Steel Rogue's March LP Crimpshrine Fifteen	$6.01
Yeats Poetry read by Siobhan McKenna & C Cusack	$6.01
Bears Records 45 Wonder Girl/ Mr. Nice G 2 track	$6.01
"VIDEO KILLED THE RADIO STAR/ KID DYNAMO" THE BUGGLES	AU $8.05
Still Bill, Bill Withers, Sussex Records, Record #SXBS	$6.01
SUNSET STRINGS & VOICES RELEASE	$6.01
ME LP WITH JIMMY BRYANT	
THE HINSONS Lighthouse RARE LP Gospel FREE SHIP OFFER	$6.01
DGG 2530185 Schumann Carnaval Wilhelm KEMPFF piano NM	$6.01
DJ SHADOW - WHAT DOES YOUR SOUL LOOK LIKE (MoWax)	$6.01
Bon Jovi Living In Sin 12" White Vinyl	GBP 3.40
DOUG SAHM SIR DOUGLAS BAND TEXAS TORNADO SEALED LP	$6.01
ANANDA PROJECT- CASCADES OF COLOR (2000 remix 2x12") Danny Tenaglia, Joe Claussell, Ben Watt, Wamdue mixes	$6.01
THE METEORS sewertime blues PSYCHOBILLY PUNK LP	GBP 3.40

Super Audio CDs

The average sales price in this subcategory is $16.63.

NOTE *These results are based on a keyword search of the Super Audio CDs subcategory for auctions with SACD in the title.*

	HIGH		AVG
15 remastered set BOB DYLAN SACD hybrid new/sealed	$132.50	SONNY ROLLINS - WAY OUT WEST Hybrid SACD Sealed New	$16.99
Jerry Goldsmith-Soundtrack-Promo Hybrid SACD OST CD	$56.00	GERSHWIN: MOBILE FIDELITY MFSL MULTICHANNEL HYBRID SACD	$16.95
Top Music McIntosh Demonstration Reference Disc SACD	$43.00	Super Audio CD SACD Stereo & Multichannel Demo Disc	$16.81
GROOVE NOTE SACD DEMO VOL. 2 DISC	$40.50	Linn Records THE TRUMPETS THAT TIME FORGOT SACD	$16.79
GROOVE NOTE SACD DEMO VOL. 1 DISC	$40.00	Mobile Fidelity John Coltrane - Soultrane SACD	$16.70
Mobile Fidelity PATRICIA BARBER - NIGHTCLUB SACD	$36.00	Top Music Jaime Valle - 'Round Midnight SACD	$16.70
Mobile Fidelity - Earth, Wind & Fire SACD	$36.00	Analogue Production KNOW WHAT I MEAN? SACD	$16.56
Meatloaf Bat Out Of Hell Sealed SACD 5.1 New	$36.00	Mobile Fidelity Ravel - Bolero SACD	$16.50
Mobile Fidelity PATRICIA BARBER - MODERN COOL SACD	$34.80	PETER GABRIEL 3 SUPER AUDIO SACD CD GENESIS SEALED	$16.50
Stevie Ray Vaughan - Couldn't Stand the Weather (SACD)	$33.16	Mobile Fidelity Smetana - Ma' Vlast SACD	$16.50
Top Music McIntosh Demonstration Reference Disc SACD	$33.00	Rounder Records ALISON KRAUSS/NEW FAVORITE SACD	$16.50
MEATLOAF Bat Out Of Hell 5.1 SACD ELLEN FOLEY MEAT LOAF	$32.99	O BROTHER, WHERE ART THOU? [SACD] – SOUNDTRACK	$16.50
CREEDENCE CLEARWATER REVIVAL CCR 20 GREATEST HITS SACD	$31.00	[3 of these sold in a multiple item ("Dutch") auction for $5.50 each]	
GROOVE NOTE SACD DEMO VOL. 1 DISC	$31.00	Analogue Production BILL EVANS/WALTZ FOR DEBBY SACD	$16.49
Mobile Fidelity PATRICIA BARBER - CAFE BLUE SACD	$30.99	Best Collection of Nature Sound Music (SACD) - New	$16.37
		DVORAK Symphonies Nos 8 & 9 Fischer BFO Philips SACD	$16.27

Other Formats (8 Track)

The average sales price in this subcategory is $8.22.

NOTE *These results are based on a keyword search of the Other Formats subcategory for auctions with 8 track in the title.*

	HIGH		AVG
LOT OF 170 EIGHT 8 TRACK TAPES 50 POUNDS O' TUNES!!!!!	$83.33	Thin Lizzy - Johnny The Fox - Vintage 8 Track Tape NEW	$9.09
2 Quadraphonic 8-track Audio Tapes The Whos Tommy	$61.00	Lot of 10- Vintage 8 Track Tapes - Classic Rock	$9.01
Live And Let Die Soundtrack - RARE Quadraphonic 8 Track	$56.55	8 Track Tapes 24 & Case Waylon George Jones Haggard	$9.00
Santana - Welcome RARE Quadraphonic 8 Track (NEW)	$56.05	Set of Two Albert King 8-track Tapes New Unused	$8.59
JOHN LENNON & YOKO ONO "WEDDING ALBUM" SEALED 8 TRACK	$51.01	George Harrison - All Things Must Pass 8-Track Tape	$8.55
8-Track Player	$50.00	David Bowie - The Man Who Sold the World 8-Track Tape	$8.50
Loggins And Messina - Debut RARE Quadraphonic 8 Track	$47.33	LOU REED - METAL MACHINE MUSIC - SEALED 8 TRACK	$8.50
Scott Joplin - Palm Leaf Rag RARE Quadraphonic 8 Track	$47.33	Shirley Bassey - Carnegie Hall OOP Quadraphonic 8 Track	$8.27
Joni Mitchell - Court & Spark RARE Quadraphonic 8 Track	$43.32	BLACK SABBATH - BLACK SABBATH 8 TRACK - HVY METAL	$8.05
Three Dog Night - Hard Labor RARE Quadraphonic 8 Track	$42.96	Marvin Gaye- Sealed 8 Track	$8.00
8-TRACK TAPES - 8TRACKS - EIGHT TRACK - ROCK 30 TAPES!!	$41.00	Hermans Hermits–Greatest Hits–8 Track Tape	$8.00
NICE LOT OF 60 TAPES Classic Rock 8 TRACK TAPE cassette	$39.00	BYRDS / YOUNGBLOODS.....CLASSIC.......8 TRACK TAPES	$7.99
Eurythmics Be Yourself Tonight Sealed 8-Track Tape OOP	$37.66	JUDY GARLAND 16 GREATEST HITS 8 TRACK TRIP RECORD CO.	$7.99
Missing Persons Spring Session M Sealed 8-Track Tape	$36.00	11 Vintage 8 Track Tapes Herb Alpert TJB Al Hirt +	$7.99
Ramones - Rocket to Russia 8-Track Tape	$33.01	Frank Sinatra 3 Box Set 8 Track Stereo Tape Cartridge	$7.77

Wholesale Lots

The median sales price in this subcategory is $10.00.

NOTE *The prices in this subcategory were obtained using eBay's Completed Items feature.*

	HIGH		AVG
45 RPM RECORDS APPROX 13,000 JUKEBOX 45's NR	$1,500.00	10 Asst. Classic/Chamber/Vocal CD's/	$10.00
Huge CD Collections 554 Albums with 4 CDs Storage boxes	GBP 763.99	NEW Factory Sealed	
No 1 R&B,Souls, Blues, Reggge,Dance etc of past years		LOT OF 100 MIXED GENRE CDS	$10.00
Huge lot 375+ Personal CD Collection ALL LISTED	$1,165.00	Lot of 5 Polydor, Siouxsie, Creatures, 7"s 45's	$10.00
All genre (Alternative/Rock/Pop/Country/Metal/etc.)		Huge lot of 45 rpm records, wide variety, good cond.	$10.00
2000+ Rolling Stones, Beatles, Elvis, 50's, 60's & 70's	$1,159.99	Kid 606 2cd lot GQ on the EQ Kill sound tigerbeat ISIS	
640 - Collection of Soul,Funk,Rock etc.. 45's	$1,102.00	LOT GREATFUL DEAD CDs MARS HOTEL,	$10.00
Lot of 10,000 Records -12" Singles - DJ -	$1,000.00	SHAKEDOWN STREET ETC.	
350 Rap Cd NO DUPLICATE SEALED NEW RARE OOP NR DVD.	$810.00	*LOOK** Lot of 11	$10.00
GET THIS ONE TIME ULTIMATE COLLECTION OF RAP CD'S		TDK - D60 cassette tapes. LOT OF 70, seventy	$10.00
(400+) 1950's & 60s LOT PROMOs 45's COLLECTION - 7".	$799.00	WHOLESALE BOX OF 30 CD'S	$10.00
DOO WOP SOUL R&B ROCK ROCKABILLY POP JAZZ		Blame It On Christmas, Vol. 1	
364 cd personal collection, 70ies-today! Great Shape!	$743.00	10 Asst. Romantic and Classical CD's/	$10.00
400+ Personal CD Collection All Listed. Pop, Rock,	$709.00	NEW Factory Sealed	
Country, Hip Hop, Classical ALL LISTED		Soul LP's-Wholesale Lot	$10.00
HUGE CLASSICAL & MISC 220 CD LOT! PIANO, SYMPHONY ETC.	$676.66	20 RAP HIP HOP UNDERGROUND RECORDS 12' MIXES	$10.00
Hip Hop/Rap Personal CD Collection LOT Awesome 219 +++	$539.99	[2 of these sold for $ 10.00 each]	
GRADE A Must SEE. Years of work put into this monster		LOT OF 45 RECORDS IN RECORD ALBUM	$10.00
Melissa Etheridge, Goo Goo Dolls & INXS Featuring JD!!!	$530.00	Kids Cds Music for Children Songs Lot of 13 Cheap	$10.00
250 CD Personal Music Collection	$510.00		
QN5 Music - Hurricane Katrina Auction Bundle #3 Giving Works Item	$510.00		

24

MUSICAL INSTRUMENTS

Musicians can find everything from instruments and cases to stands and sheet music in the Musical Instruments category. Parents who are faced with expensive purchases for their son or daughter to participate in their school's band will find some cheaper alternatives here to buying an instrument at a store, although they will need to be extremely careful about whom they buy from, and they should thoroughly vet the seller's feedback. Beyond simply looking at the feedback rating, it can be helpful to dig down into the actual feedback itself. "Look at the negative feedback and try to determine what the problems were with seller/items before bidding," counsels one eBay buyer with experience with musical instruments. "Make sure you're dealing with a seller that accepts criticism without getting hostile. I've noticed lots of sellers who go ballistic when questioned, even to neutral comments. A good, trustworthy seller will not attack anyone who is disappointed or frustrated. Don't deal with these sorts of people (or do so at your own risk)."

One of the risks that buyers discuss on the eBay Music board is the poor quality instruments that sometimes show up on the site. One way to prevent yourself from getting such an item is to check for product details: "Does the item have a serial number? Does the seller have manufacturer information/address and phone number (in case you need parts in the future)? Is there a warranty and what does it cover? How long do you have to return an item if unhappy?" asks one eBayer.

If the item does not have a serial number, he suggests, "more than likely it is a *very cheap import,* usually from China, and not many music shops are willing to repair the instrument because there are no parts available! These instruments are also very poorly made and usually break after only minimal usage. Nobody will want to help you fix even minor problems because further damage could be done during repair and they don't want the liability . . . You may think you're getting a good deal on an inexpensive instrument, but in the long run you'll lose out and have to buy a better quality one soon anyway!" (It should be noted that some eBayers defend Chinese "knock-offs" and the like, and one bought a "Chinese Telecaster knock-off" guitar that "was as good as the Mexican models.")

The same eBayer goes on to caution that some unscrupulous sellers make up bogus company or brand names that don't exist, so ask a music store or perhaps your music teacher if the company name given is a reputable one. "There are many companies online who sell reputable, well-known instruments and they can tell you whether or not they've ever heard of that instrument. Generally, beginner/student models of most musical instruments cost $300.00 to $400.00 U.S.," he says.

Getting a Fair Discount

So if most beginner instruments go for $300.00 to 400.00 in the store, what kinds of discounts can you expect on eBay, if any? Let's look at a popular instrument for student bands: the flute. Some of the most popular brand names are Yamaha, Gemeinhardt, and Selmer. In the high price range, a Yamaha "YFL-361 925-Silver flute" in its case went for $642.00. The seller says it was two years old and had only been used for two months. He also said it had been checked by a local music store and was in perfect working order, which contributed to the final sales price. The listing was accompanied by several good, clear pictures, including close-ups of the mouthpiece, the case, and the brand name inscribed on the flute. The seller had a feedback rating of 98.8 percent, which is good enough for most eBayers. A new Yamaha YFL-361 flute, part of the Yamaha Intermediate Series ("the choice of many of the world's leading players and teachers," according to a listing on the Giardinelli instruments site) goes for $1,421.00 list price, and for a sale price of $994.01 at the Giardinelli.com site.

But plenty of flutes go for $100.00 to $200.00 on eBay. In the average price range of this sample, a nickel-plated YFL-225 Yamaha flute went for $127.50. A Gemeinhardt model 2SP flute with case went for $130.50; this flute was five years old but still in mint condition, according to the seller, who had a feedback rating of 91.7 percent—not a great rating, and with only fourteen transactions, this meant two transactions went bad, one within the past six months and one within the year. The recent bad transaction, however, was for a car deal. The seller also only charged a very fair $10.00 to ship the flute, and a stand was part of the deal. In comparison, a new Gemeinhardt 2SP (student) flute currently sells for $799.00 from Music123.com, a sale price from the list price of $1,200.00.

Guitars: Your Chance to Own Rock History?

How about some bigger-ticket instruments, like electric guitars? These can go for very lofty prices on the high end, and some have wonderful rock or other musical pedigrees—one auctioned in this sample was owned by Dave Davies of the Kinks (a Gibson Les Paul, selling for GBP 12,500, or approximately $22,207.50). The auction included photos of said guitar in action with Davies, including at a 1982 Kinks concert at JFK Stadium in Philadelphia (the *Dave Davies Anthology* album cover) and at Madison Square Garden in 1981. Per the seller, "This great guitar was used on many USA and World tours and on all Kinks albums from 1977, including the hit record Come Dancing. Dave can be seen playing it on the classic video/dvd One for the Road. A true item of rock history." The auction included Dave's stage strap, as well as a letter of authenticity and a copy of the original receipt.

Other interesting high-end electric guitar auctions included a Hamer Explorer sunburst-finish guitar that was owned by Martin Barre of Jethro Tull and sold for GBP 6,000, or $10,659.60. It was believed to be the first numbered Hamer guitar, according to the seller. Barre played it on studio albums but never toured with it, "hence it [is] in mint condition," wrote the seller, and "Martin Barre has agreed to provide paperwork directly to the purchaser." Skeptics (and Jethro Tull fans) were no doubt swayed by the bonus offered: Barre agreed to hand over the guitar in person to the auction's winner.

And those prices aren't even the highest in this sample. A vintage collectible 1959 Gibson guitar ("American Electric Guitar, Gibson Incorporated, Ka.") sold for $110,000.00 in an eBay Live auction.

Average prices for electric guitars go from about $250.00 to $300.00 in this sample. An Ovation Viper went for $300.00; it was unclear from the auction how old this instrument was, but these sell for $599.00 currently on Music123.com. If you're looking for a particular brand, a good idea would be to do your own "completed items" search on eBay for that specific name. Currently, under electric guitars, Fender has the most listings of any brand, about 11,000, and Stratocaster is the most popular model, with about 7,000 listings. The final prices in that sample of eBay completed items range from $14,850.00 for a 1954 Strat (the seller says this is the first year of their issue), all the way down to about $50.00 for a used Fender Squier guitar (misspelled in some listings as "Squire"). Squiers are available from Music123.com for $99.59, a "Standard" Stratocaster goes for $369.59, and an "American Deluxe Fat Strat" goes for $1,364.99 from the site. (Prices for American Deluxe "Fat Strats" on eBay went from $700.00 for a used one to $900.00 for a "near mint" guitar, in the sample I researched.)

On the very lowest end of the price range, you will probably come across items that are accessories and not actual guitars, like neck plates and pick guards—a phenomenon at the low end of just about every eBay category, where the penny items reign supreme.

Pianos and Local Pickup Auctions

How about truly large and heavy items, like pianos? These are available, but eBay is probably not the first place people look for an item like that, because shipping would be prohibitive. However, most are sold as "local pickup" items, where the buyer drives to pick up the item in person, and many people are willing to drive across several states to pick up items. (I once had a buyer drive from Delaware to pick up a $300.00 armoire at my home in Virginia.) Not surprisingly, legendary piano-maker Steinway commands the highest prices for pianos in this sample; some are fixer-uppers, such as the Steinway Baby Grand that sold for $6,938.00. It had been damaged in Hurricane Ivan and was located in Pensacola, Florida.

There are plenty of other items in the Music category—every type of instrument, including drums, harps, and even amps and sound mixers. There are good deals here, but again, this type of purchase requires more than the usual amount of homework, so research your purchase first, and don't be afraid to look for the right item over weeks or even months. In many cases, you can save over the prices in retail and other commercial venues, but not necessarily every time; a Minimoog synthesizer sold for more on eBay than on MusiciansFriend.com: on eBay it went for $2,995.00, and on MusiciansFriend.com for a "sale" price of only $2,795.00 (the site gave $2,995.00 as its list price).

Steinway Crown Jewel Macassar Ebony Grand Piano Model M
SIGNED H. STEINWAY EXTREMELY RARE APPRAISED AT $95,000

You are signed in

Bidding has ended for this item

If you are a winner, Sign In for your status.   Learn more about

List an item like this or buy a similar item below.

Sold for:	**US $70,000.00**
	Auction ended early with Buy It Now.
Ended:	Feb-17-06 16:20:49 PST
Start time:	Feb-08-06 20:55:52 PST
History:	1 bid (US $70,000.00 starting bid)
Buyer:	User ID kept private
Item location:	MyImporters Show Room - The Finest United States

Brass ▶ Baritone, Tuba

The average sales price in this subcategory is $367.06.

	HIGH		AVG
Mirafone, 186, 5 rotary valve, BBb, Tuba	$3,525.00	KING 1124 MARCHING BARITONE / NO RESERVE	$401.51
MIRAPHONE CC TUBA 186-4U - BEAUTIFUL w/CASE !! Mirafone	$3,150.00	King 4 Valve Euphonium #2	$401.01
Mirafone BBb Tuba	$2,550.00	KING MARCHING BARITONE HORN MODEL 1124	$400.00
CERVENY PIGGY CC TUBA ,ALTIERI GIG BAG 4 valve	$2,495.00	Nice Brass Jupiter #560 marching Baritone w/Case & MP	$385.00
Yamaha YBB-641 Professional BBb Tuba/Case ***L@@K***	$2,325.00	Neat old Brass KING BBb SOUSAPHONE with mouthpiece	$379.00
Meinl Weston BB flat Tuba	$2,025.00	King Baritone - Bell forward, 3-Key	$375.00
– Miraphone Model 186-4V BBb Tuba EXCELLENT! WOW! –	$2,000.00	BESSON TUBA / NO RESERVE	$356.00
Tuba New BBb M&M Symphony Model	$1,895.00	DYNASTY SILVER MARCHING BARITONE	$335.00
Yamaha YEP-641 Professional Compensating Euphonium WOW!	$1,850.00	NEW 2006 ROTARY BRASS EUPHONIUM	$329.95
Conn 5J Bb Tuba 4 Valve	$1,820.00	HORN 4 ROTARY VALVE	
Yamaha Four Valve Euphonium Model # YEP321	$1,501.00	SUPERB NEW SILVER EUPHONIUM HORN 4	$319.95
Yamaha YBB-201 Tuba, Mint Condition, 6 Months Old	$1,500.00	PISTON VALVE W/CASE	
4 Valve Conn 24J Tuba Upright Bell * W/Cases! Nice!!!	$1,445.00	BRASS 3 ROTARY VALVE BBb TUBA WITH CASE BRAND NEW!!!!	$311.00
King BBb Sousaphone	$1,399.99	2006 MODEL BRASS EUPHONIUM HORN 4 PISTON VALVE W/CASE	$299.95
1961 Conn 20K Sousaphone Tuba w/ Naked Lady !! NICE !!	$1,325.00	[4 of these sold for $299.95 each]	

Brass ▶ Cornet, Trumpet

The average sales price in this subcategory is $121.22.

	HIGH		AVG
GETZEN 3001LE Bb TRUMPET, GOLD SEVERINSEN, not BACH	$1,375.00	Bach Trumpet	$160.07
GETZEN 3051 CUSTOM PRO MODEL Bb TRUMPET, not BACH	$1,125.00	Blessing LTML-1 Professional Trumpet	$160.01
vintage olds Flugelhorn	$950.00	2006 New Beltone Trumpet - w/ Case or Gig Bag	$159.99
Selmer Claude Gordon Trumpet	$811.56	Olds Amassador Trumpet 1950's Free Ship BIN	$150.00
trumpet F E OLDS & SON Vintage 1960 MENDEZ Mute CASE	$779.00	Bach CR 310 Cornet	$142.50
Getzen 900S Eterna Silver Professional Trumpet	$775.00	2006 GOLD Bb Band Trumpet w/ Case + YAMAHA Care Kit !	$134.95
SELMER RADIAL Bb TRUMPET, AWESOME, not BACH	$660.00	TRUMPET IN CASE - VERY UNIQUE DESIGN **TAKE A L@@K**	$125.95
Olds Recording trumpet 1960's	$617.00	BACH TR300 Bb TRUMPET	$125.00
Nice 1938 Olds Super Trumpet.... Complete and Original	$601.99	Monette Trumpet Mouthpiece Gold STC2 MF 3 Like New	$125.00
GETZEN 700 SPECIAL SILVER PLATED TRUMPET! CLEAN!!!	$450.00	Vintage Artist Model K. Blessing Trumpet & Case Clean!	$122.50
Old Antique John Heald 19thC Silver Coronet Trumpet	$449.99	NEW HIGH/MIDDLE SCHOOL SILVER BAND TRUMPET-FIRST CHAIR	$119.99
GETZEN 700 Eterna series SILVER SEMI-PRO TRUMPET Nice!	$405.00	TRUMPET-NEW 2006 SILVER MARCHING BAND TRUMPETS-MINT	$119.99
Blessing Professional Series Super Artist Trpt., Silver	$399.00	L@@K "Getzen Trumpet" L@@K	$117.51
HOLTON ST 200 Bud Brisbois .468 bore RARE Lead horn!!!	$379.99	NICE BLESSING BRASS TRUMPET W/HARD CASE AND MUZZLE	$113.50
EXCELLENT REYNOLDS CONTEMPORA TRUMPET	$365.00	Vintage Boosey trumpet in case with accessories c1920's	$112.51

Brass ▶ French Horn

The average sales price in this subcategory is $255.84.

	HIGH		AVG
KRUSPE COMPENSATING FRENCH HORN ***FREE SHIPPING***	$4,761.00	NEW DOUBLE FRENCH HORN	$325.00
French Horn: KRUSPE double, pre 1918	$3,650.00	BEAUTIFUL/NEW/DOUBLE FRENCH HORN/*2005*NKL NR	$300.00
KRUSPE DOUBLE FRENCH HORN ***FREE SHIPPING***	$2,126.00	French Horn	$300.00
Holton H379 Double French Horn!! NEW!!	$2,095.00	New Double French Horn w/ Yamaha Care Kit~BTS Sale!!!	$285.00
- Yamaha YHR-668D Professional French Horn VERY NICE! -	$1,875.00	Holton French Horn - Double - H180	$256.00
Yamaha 667 Double French Horn 'Pro'	$1,750.00	BLESSING DOUBLE FRENCH HORN	$256.00
Holton H179 Double French Horn - Excellent Shape! NR	$1,600.00	New Double French Horn w/ Yamaha Care Kit~BTS Sale!!!	$255.00
Conn 8d double French Horn	$1,600.00	Like New Silver Plate Mellophone French Horn c1975 NR	$255.00
8D CONN DOUBLE FRENCH HORN SILVER 1962 W/ CASE NR NICE	$1,442.00	MB French Horn Case-Conn,Alexander,Holton,Yamaha,King	$250.00
French Horn Conn 8D used Fantastic Condition	$1,325.00	Silver Single French Horn from USSR	$228.49
YAMAHA FRENCH HORN YHR 667,HARD CASE,3004 MOUTHPIECE	$1,300.00	NEW **2005** MODEL**DOUBLE** FRENCH HORN/NR	$224.00
1957 CONN MODEL 8D DOUBLE FRENCH HORN 4 VALVE SILVER !!	$1,251.00	BEAUTIFUL/NEW/DOUBLE FRENCH HORN/*2005*NKL NR	$224.00
Yamaha Double French Horn Intermediate YHR-567 w/ Case	$1,175.00	DOUBLE FRENCH HORN HORNS GERMAN STYLE NEW W/CASE	$202.50
Dazzaling YAMAHA DOUBLE FRENCH HORN used ONLY One Year	$1,125.00	SINGLE FRENCH HORN-CONN-EXTRAS INCLUDED-KEY OF "F"	$202.50
Holton H378 Double French Horn...Very Nice...	$1,100.00	King French Horn Cleveland Ohio...Nice...	$200.00

Brass ▶ Trombone

The average sales price in this subcategory is $184.71.

	HIGH		AVG
Nearly New Kanstul 1570 Large Bore Trombone	$1,699.00	RARE BIG BELL - BIG BORE NEW 2006 BRASS TENOR TROMBONE	$209.95
YAMAHA YBL-612R II PRO DUAL TRIGGER BASS TROMBONE exc++	$1,275.00	[2 of these sold for $209.95 each]	
GETZEN PRO CUSTOM 3047 AFR	$1,256.00	BLESSING TROMBONE W/CASE	$200.00
TROMBONE THAYER VALVE LR		RARE BIG BELL BIG BORE NEW 2006 SILVER TENOR TROMBONE	$199.95
Bach Stradivarius Trombone Model 42A w/ F Hagmann Value	$990.00	OLDS AMBASSADOR TRIGGER TROMBONE WITH CASE...	$199.95
Edwards Jazz Trombone w/ Soft Case, Great Lead Sound!!!	$836.01	Used Yamaha student trombone w/ case	$192.50
Getzen Bass Trombone w/ Double Triggers Rare!	$815.00	Maestro Bass Trombone with Case	$177.50
Olds P 24 G Bass Trombone, Very Nice, Dual Triggers	$750.00	NICE HOLTON TR602 RW TROMBONE NICE NR	$177.50
ROTH-REYNOLDS -	$733.00	Vintage Martin Committee Model Trombone - # 188980	$162.50
STERLING BELL,MINT COND!!		Nice New Trombone with trigger Bb F attachment NR	$157.50
Silver Bach Stradivarius Trombone	$703.00	Fullerton OLDS SPECIAL trombone and case, 1960s	$155.00
NEW YAMAHA Valve Trombone YSL 354V - Still in plastic!	$700.00	Blessing Trombone Excellent Cond. W/Case No RES	$153.50
KANSTUL PRO JAZZ TROMBONE Bb/F	$677.00	Holton TR401N Silver Slide Trombone N.R.	$152.70
ATTACH NOT KING OR BACH		OLDS SUPER TROMBONE READY TO PLAY	$152.50
Yamaha Trigger Trombone	$605.00	JUPITER TROMBONE W/ F ATTACHMENT JSL-536 NR	$152.50
Yamaha YSL356G Trombone...Get Your Groove On!	$600.00	REYNOLDS ADVANCE METALIST TROMBONE, NO RESERVE	$150.00
GETZEN 1025F Trombone/Open wrap F attachment	$550.00	4 Solos for Trombone or Baritone NO SHIPPING!	$4.00
Yamaha YSL 682b Trombone NICE!!!!!!	$519.00	Music - 14 Trios for Trombone or Baritone NO SHIPPING!	$4.00

Electronic ▶ Drum Machines

The average sales price in this subcategory is $295.49.

	HIGH		AVG
Akai Mpc 4000 Plus(80 gig Hard drive, digital I/O)	$2,500.00	Oberheim DX w/Factory MIDI & 20 extra eprom voices	$350.00
Roland V Session electronic kit 10 pads w module, NR	$2,499.00	Korg Electribe ES-1 Drum Machine Sampler Sequencer NEW	$329.00
** Akai MPC 4000 (3000 2000) ** Production Beat Machine	$2,250.00	AKAI ASQ-10 It's an MPC 60 without the pads! ASQ10	$324.99
AKAI MPC 4000 MINT CONDITION A STEAL!!!	$1,835.00	Hart Dynamics Prodigy Electronic Drum Set	$310.00
AKAI MPC3000LE MPC-3000 LE LIMITED EDITION MINT RARE A+	$1,745.00	KORG ELECTRIBE ER-1 drum machine & EA-1 synth PRISTINE	$305.00
Akai Mpc 3000 MIDI Production Center w/ 250mb Zip Drive	$1,500.00	Oberheim DMX Drum Machine w/original manual	$305.00
MPC 4000	$1,500.00	ALESIS DM PRO DRUM MODULE	$300.00
Roland Electric Drum Set Td-10 pd-120 pd-100 Kit td10	$1,450.00	Yamaha SU700	$300.00
HART DYNAMICS MEGA PRO ELECTRONIC DRUM SET TE3 NEW NR!!	$1,400.00	MADPLAYER beat maker drum machine digital music player	$290.00
AKAI MPC 2000xl Special Edition SE2 plus Teac CDR	$1,325.00	ION ELECTRONIC DRUM KIT - NIB	$279.99
Akai MPC 3000 - drum machine SAMPLER midi ALL ORIGINAL	$1,299.99	AKAI MPC 2000 XL IB-M208P 8 OUT EXPANDER / SPDIF	$267.00
Emu SP-1200 SP1200 Reissue Black Model	$1,175.00	<><><> Akai MPC 60 <><><>	$255.00
AKAI MPC3000 with custom FLIGHT CASE and 2 XTRA DRIVES	$1,125.00	Kawai GB4 sesson trainer music sequencer/Drum machine	$250.00
Midi Production Center MPC 3000	$1,125.00	Alesis DM Pro Expandable 20-Bit Drum Module VG! NR!	$249.00
Akai MPC 3000 - drum machine SAMPLER midi ALL ORIGINAL	$1,034.99	1980's Oberheim DX drum machine with MIDI in & out	$234.50

Electronic ▶ Samples, Samplers

The average sales price in this subcategory is $242.20.

	HIGH		AVG
AKAI MPC2000XL loaded plus custom case, and 256MB CF	$1,000.00	Yamaha SU700 SU 700 Sampler Sequencer - like AKAI MPC	$290.00
Akai MPC-2000XL 2000 Super Package 32MB+More! MINT NR!!	$1,000.00	ROLAND SP-808 STUDIO GROOVE SAMPLER (LIKE NEW)	$280.00
Roland Fantom XA 61 Key Workstation	$960.00	Kurzweil K2000R, Sampler/ Worksation/ Module	$280.00
Akai MPC 2000XL (FULLY LOADED)	$960.00	Boss SP-505 Sampling Workstation 505 Like NEW	$260.00
Akai MPC2000XL Blue MPC 2000 XL MPC2000 2000XL	$950.00	Oberheim DPX-1 Vintage Sample Player, Sound Library	$255.00
Akai MPC 2000XL w/32 Meg Ram	$925.00	Emu Orchestral ROMS Volume 1 & 2 in retail box	$251.05
AKAI MPC60 v1 ROGER LINN 3.1 O.S. DRUM MACHINE/SAMPLER	$898.88	Boss SP-505 Groove Sampling Workstation Drum Machine	$239.00
Akai MPC 2000XL w/ upgraded memory, CD & Zip Drive	$880.00	Akai VOX64 VOX 64 for Akai S5000 S 5000 Sampler	$238.00
Akai MPC2000XL Midi Production Sampler Sequencer No Res	$861.67	BOSS SP-303 SP303 Dr Sample MINT w/ Manual FREE SHIP	$235.00
Akai MPC 2000XL w/32MB of RAM and ZIP Drive Mint Cond.	$850.00	Korg Electribe ES-1 Rhythm Production Sampler	$232.50
Akai MPC2000XL Mixer Sampler	$830.00	ASR X Sampler w/ Zip 100 16mb ram & Syntaur Sound Disks	$232.50
Korg Triton 61 Key Music Workstation/Sampler	$811.00	Akai IB208-P - MPC 2000/MPC 2000XL - 8 outs - 8 outputs	$215.00
MPC 1000(never been used).............. (Brand New)	$810.00	Akai EB16 effects card - MPC 2000/MPC 2000XL	$215.00
Akai MPC2000XL Professional Drum Sampler	$799.99	ROLAND W-30 Music Workstation Sequence Sampler keyboard	$212.50
AKAI MPC2000XL DRUM MACHINE SEQUENCER SAMPLER NR	$782.11	Boss Roland SP303 SP-303 DJ Groove Sampler CLEAN	$212.50

Electronic ▶ Synth

The average sales price in this subcategory is $340.85.

	HIGH		AVG
Sequential Circuits Prophet 5 - UNTOUCHED ORIGINAL	$3,495.00	EMU XL-7 XL7 Command Station Expandable NO RES	$355.00
MOOG MINIMOOG VOYAGER ELECTRIC BLUE ANALOG SYNTH NEW!	$2,995.00	E-mu Proteus 2000 - EMU 128 Voice Synth - Excellent!	$350.00
Serge Modular music system synthesizer synth	$2,800.00	Waldorf Pulse analog synthesizer synth.	$350.00
Mint condition moog minimoog- original owner!	$2,662.11	Novation Bass Station Keyboard Analog Synth	$350.00
Mini-Moog Model D used on Johnny Carson Tonight Show	$2,400.00	Kawai K5000R Additive Synthesizer MIDI Rack Module	$350.00
Serge Modular music system sequencer synthesizer synth	$2,025.00	MOOG SYNTHESIZER MG-1 CONCERTMATE VINTAGE SYNTH	$345.00
Minimoog Voyager electric Blue '05 like New Moog $3000	$2,000.00	Alesis Micron Synthesizer Synth 3-Octave Keyboard MINT!	$340.00
SEQUENTIAL CIRCUITS PROPHET 10 KEYBOARD W/CASE	$2,000.00	Novation Bass Station Keyboard	$337.50
SEQUENTIAL CIRCUITS PROPHET 5 ANALOG SYNTH W/ CASE MIDI	$1,999.00	EMU XL-1 Turbo w/ Pure Phatt Expansion good condition	$336.00
VINTAGE ARP 2600P MODULAR SYTHESIZER & 3604P KEYBOARD	$1,925.00	Doepfer A-100G6 Analog Modular Synthesizer Shell Synth	$335.00
Moog Taurus 1, Bass Pedal Synth (Near Mint)	$1,875.00	Alesis Micron Synth	$335.00
Cherry MiniMoog Voyager in PERFECT CONDITION	$1,800.00	MOOG ETHERWAVE THEREMIN NO RESERVE!!!	$327.06
STUDIO ELECTRONICS MiDiMiNi MiDi MiNi Moog Synth RARE	$1,565.00	Technosaurus MICROCON Synth + CYCLODON Sequencer	$327.00
Vintage Minimoog Model D SN # 9476	$1,500.00	EMU World Expedition ROM for Proteus 2000 -Planet Earth	$325.00
Clavia Nord Lead 3 Performance Synthesizer - Like New	$1,475.00	E-MU PROTEUS 2000 with XTREME LEAD Expansion	$325.00

Equipment ▶ Cases

The average sales price in this subcategory is $56.09.

	HIGH		AVG
Breeders 1994 Lollapalooza Tour Drum Cases	$500.00	Gator G-901 Amplifier Head Case G901	$60.89
Accord Large Cello Case Black Hard-Shell Carbon Fiber=)	$365.00	NEW NORD LEAD KEYBOARD GIG BAG - NR [1935]	$59.99
14 SPACE ATA SHOCK MOUNT RACK CASE(BLK) 3/8" plywood	$315.00	ATA Case fits BEHRINGER UB2442FX MIXER - With FOAM! N	$59.95
Anvil Style Four Drawer Roadcase with locking wheels	$300.00	New ATA Case fits CARVIN DX2442 DX 2442 - With FOAM! K	$59.95
SKB Gig Rig Brand New	$296.00	ATA Case fits BEHRINGER EURODESK MX2442A - With FOAM! L	$59.95
SKB DS1 Drum Set Case Kit-4 Pieces-NEW!	$259.00	SITAR SOFT CASE GIG BAG Double Toomba CASES New!	$59.95
ANVIL flight case for Marshall head JMP/JCM800/JCM900	$202.50	10 SPACE ATA STYLE RACK CASE! - INCREDIBLE DEAL! NEW!	$56.00
Large Anvil type ATA Flight Road Case wheels 57x23x16	$200.00	SKB 14 x 6.5 Hard drum case w/ FOAM lining. EXCELLENT!	$55.00
Shure SM58 Cordless Microphone	$190.00	Gator G-901 Amplifier Head Case G901	$54.99
MESA BOOGIE SUS4 DEEP 4 TRIAXIS SHOCKMOUNT 8 SPACE RACK	$188.50	SKB 2U SHALLOW X RACK New in Box Great For Effects	$52.95
SKB Roto TRPX2 Trap Case-NEW!	$185.00	HARD SHELL GUITAR CASE IBANEZ V JACKSON RHOADS	$52.59
ProTec L-248 Leather Triple Trumpet no reunion blues	$177.50	SKB 3 SPACE RACK CASE LIKE NEW L@@K NICE :-)	$52.01
Fender Tweed 7 Space Guitar Stand Case	$172.50	Calzone Hard Travel Case	$51.02
MICROPHONE STANDS ATA CASE - BRAND NEW!	$169.00	skb rack case musical instrument space rack	$51.01
RARE ANTIQUE VINTAGE VIOLIN FIDDLE WITH CASE	$167.50	USA Fender Strat Tele Molded Hardshell Case	$51.00

Equipment ▸ Instrument Stands

The average sales price in this subcategory is $20.78.

	HIGH		AVG
Ultimate Support - 4 tier Apache aframe keyboard stand	$220.00	ON STAGE KS-7100 KEYBOARD STAND- VERY STURDY	$23.10
Roland V-Drum Rack! Electronic Yamaha NO RESERVE!	$152.50	Vintage MICROPHONE STAND MODEL 425 ELECTRO-VOICE E-V EV	$22.72
QUIK LOK 4 TIER KEYBOARD STAND	$129.50	Ultimate Support IQ2000 Double-Braced Keyboard Stand	$22.27
Guitar seat, adjustable stool for musicians, Brand New	$127.50	*NEW* Dual Saxophone Stand	$21.99
Ultimate Apache triple tiered keyboard stand	$100.00	Brand New Sharper Image Z Adjustable Keyboard Stand	$21.50
PRO FOLDING KEYBOARD STAND WITH	$92.03	CASIO Double Leg X-Style Keyboard Stand NEW	$21.49
2ND TIER HOLDS 500lbs		Portable Upright Bass Stand	$20.00
Ultimate Support Keyboard Stand ("A" Frame)	$91.00	NEW Double X pro line Keyboard Stand Dbl NR	$19.99
3 Double - Braced Snare Stands! Brand New! NO RESERVE!	$90.00	*NEW Heavy Duty Nylon Folding Z Keyboard Stand Bag Case	$19.99
Ultimate Support Apex 2 Tier Keyboard Stand No Reserve!	$85.00	NEW TRIPOD BASE MUSIC STAND CONDUCTOR VERY STURDY!	$19.51
On Stage Stands TWO PIANO dual KEYBOARD Stand 2 tier	$82.00	QUICK LOK Z12 RAPID SET-UP MINI "Z" KEYBOARD STAND	$19.02
[2 of these sold for $82.00 each]		*NEW Heavy Duty Nylon Folding Z Keyboard Stand Bag Case	$18.99
PRO FOLDING KEYBOARD STAND WITH 2ND TIER HOLDS 500lbs	$81.00	[2 of these sold for $18.99 each]	
NEW QUIK LOK MULTI PURPOSE ROLL AROUND STAND [2786]	$79.99	NEW TRIPOD BASE MUSIC STAND CONDUCTOR VERY STURDY!	$18.95
PRO-QUALITY 3-TIER CHROME KEYBOARD	$79.95	[2 of these sold for $18.95 each]	
TV RACK STAND NIB		15052: Z -Type Keyboard Stand: Light Duty: Piano: music	$17.50
Ultimate Support Stand Bundle - No Reserve	$77.76	NEW Pro Line DOUBLE guitar stand YLK-006 NR	$16.99
ULTIMATE 2 TIER KEYBOARD / HOME STUDIO STAND	$69.00	[3 of these sold for $16.99 each]	

Equipment ▸ Music Stands

The average sales price in this subcategory is $24.83.

	HIGH		AVG
Frank Lloyd Wright Music Stand	$390.99	Blues Harmonica 7 Pack Free Jack Daniels Guitar Picks	$29.66
Groove Tubes GT55 Microphone + Mic Stand and Cable	$300.00	Microphone Boom Stand W/ Music Stand Attached "New"	$28.13
LOT OF 6 MANHASSET MUSIC STANDS! BRAND NEW!	$156.00	*NEW* Heavy Duty Folding Tripod Sheet Music Stand *NR*	$27.99
Double MUSIC STAND Rosewood Wooden Stands Adjustable	$139.95	Microphone Boom Stand W/ Music Stand Attached "New"	$27.77
ANTIQUE WOODEN MUSIC STAND MADE BY HAMILTON	$128.50	CAST IRON MUSIC STAND~VINTAGE~HARP~LYRE~RACK	$26.00
LOT OF 5 MANHASSET SYMPHONY MUSIC	$125.00	NEW Manhasset Music Stand Model M48 Black NR	$25.00
STANDS! BRAND NEW!		*NEW* Pro Double X Keyboard Stand with Quik SQUEEZE	$24.99
[2 of these sold for $125.00 each]		[2 of these sold for $24.99 each]	
LOT OF 5 MANHASSET SYMPHONY MUSIC	$116.25	4 MUSIC STANDS BRAND NEW WITH CASES WHOLESALE	$24.96
STANDS! BRAND NEW!		VINTAGE MUSIC STAND OR BOOK STAND BY DREXEL	$24.95
Ultimate Keyboard Stand 3 Tier A Frame Black	$107.50	Manhassett M48 Music Stand	$24.95
4 Vintage Humes & Berg E-Z-Fold Music Stands Big Band	$100.00	BLACK MANHASSET MUSIC STAND! BRAND NEW! NO RESERVE!	$23.25
10 Pack of K&M Ultimate Folding Sheet Music Stand & Bag	$100.00	[4 of these sold for $23.25 each]	
ULTIMATE VERTICAL DUAL 2-TIER APEX KEYBOARD STAND	$86.00	*NEW* Pro Double X Keyboard Stand with Quik SQUEEZE	$22.99
FrederickColonial**Style**Wood**Music**Stand**	$85.00	[2 of these sold for $22.99 each]	
Brass Adjustable High Quality Music Stand	$75.00	MUSIC STAND CONDUCTOR STYLE NEW	$22.75
SOLID CAST BRASS MUSIC STAND 40-55" Tall ORNATE & HEAVY	$74.50	NEW TRIPOD BASE MUSIC STAND CONDUCTOR VERY STURDY!	$22.50
ULTIMATE Deltex Dual KEYBOARD-Synthesizer-Piano STAND	$70.00	Microphone Boom Stand W/ Music Stand Attached "New"	$22.01

Equipment ▸ Tuners

The average sales price in this subcategory is $42.58.

	HIGH		AVG
Peterson Strobe Center 5000 Tuner	$1,249.99	Chakra 7 Tuning Fork Set Natural Tones Healing SALE	$49.99
Delta 200 deluxe mixer Soundcraft - excellent w/ps	$750.00	CONN GUITAR STROBOTUNER TUBE TUNER LIKE NEW!! ST-6	$49.00
Conn Strobotuner ST-11 Everything Tuner w +2 extended	$305.00	BOSS CHROMATIC TUNER TU-12H	$45.99
Conn Strobotuner Works great	$208.99	BOSS chromatic tuner TU-12H 1 Year old	$45.01
KORG DTR-2000 1U RACK TUNER IN BOX NO RESERVE!!!	$199.99	Boss TU-12H Tuner- Xlent Cond w Power Sup & FREE 9v Bat	$45.00
CONN STROBOTUNER STROBE TUNER	$178.01	13 TUNING FORKS FORK SET 100	$44.99
ST11 GUITAR PIANO & OTHER		LOW-4096 HIGH FREQUENCIES	
CONN STROBOTUNER STROBE TUNER ST-11 GUITAR PIANO	$177.50	13 pc Tuning Fork Forks Set w Mallet Case One Octave	$42.99
CONN STROBOTUNER	$175.00	[3 of these sold for $42.99 each]	
VINTAGE KORG WT-12 CHROMATIC TUNER NO RESERVE!	$167.83	Boss TU-12 Chromatic Tuner with case; like new	$41.00
Peterson Virtual Strobe Tuner VS-1	$155.00	Boss TU-12H Chromatic Tuner	$40.00
Peterson Virtual Strobe Tuner	$152.51	TUNING FORK, OHM OCTAVE SET (68.05 low & 136.1 mid)	$39.99
Peterson Virtual Strobe Tuner VS-1 BRAND NEW	$152.50	Sabine Rack Mount Guitar Tuner	$39.00
Peterson VS-1 digital strobe tuner MINT!	$150.00	INTELLITOUCH PT-1 TUNER GUITAR BASS BRAND NEW!	$38.99
Conn Strobotuner ST-11 Guitar/Piano Tuner Strobe	$150.00	[2 of these sold for $38.99 each]	
KORG TONE WORKS DTR-1 DIGITAL RACK MOUNT TUNER	$140.50	Boss Chromatic Tuner TU-12 (digital processing)	$37.50
		ONBOARD RESEARCH (INTELLITOUCH 5 IN ONE TUNER)	$37.00
		Intellitouch PT 1 guitar,mandolin ,banjo tuner	$36.01

Guitar ▸ Acoustic

The average sales price in this subcategory is $145.52.

	HIGH		AVG
Vintage 1968 D-45 C.F. Martin acoustic guitar	$27,500.00	Classical Spanish Guitar RAMIREZ needs your help! 99?NR	$211.89
GIBSON J35, 1939 ORIGINAL	$9,000.00	Paulino Bernabe Classical Guitar and Case	$203.50
VINTAGE GIBSON ACOUSTIC ELECTRIC GUITAR-UNBELIEVABLE!!!	$8,655.00	Gretchen Wilson Autographed Acoustic Guitar	$192.50
2005 Martin Figured Koa Special. Number 21	$7,101.01	Handmade 6 String Acoustic Guitar with cutaway	$187.50
of 25 - Greven Pickguard - Geib Tweed Case		SWEET PARLOR GUITAR BY ART & LUTHERIE	$173.50
Martin D-28CWB (Clarence White Brazilian)	$6,901.00	IBANEZ AEL20 SUNBURST ACOUSTIC	$172.50
OLD GIBSON SJ-200 JUMBO GUITAR....AS-IS W/CASE	$6,500.00	ELECTRIC JUMBO GUITAR	
Manuel Contreras 1A classical guitar Solid	$6,500.00	Acoustic Weissenborn Style Lap Steel Guitar!!!	$162.50

Brazilian Rosewood back and sides	
Rare Hank Williams Sr. Martin D-28 HW ltd ed guitar	$6,102.99
1946 Blonde EPIPHONE EMPEROR gorgeous, original	$6,050.00
VINTAGE GIBSON JOHNNY SMITH GUITAR 60's Model w/ OHC	$5,100.00
Martin d-45 1996 limited edition signiture	$4,800.00
series collector d-45 ,an investment model	
VINTAGE 1971 RAMIREZ FLAMENCO 1A CLASSICAL GUITAR	$4,575.00
Lucas Concert Classical Guitar Radial braced powerhouse	$4,500.00
In European Spruce and Flamed Maple New + Case	
STAHL MODEL-6 GUITAR BY THE LARSON BROS.	$4,450.00
Built Circa 1930 - On Par w/Pre-War Martin OOO	
Taylor K-65 Acoustic Guitar - All Koa 12 String Cutaway	$4,350.00

Ventura Bruno V-44 12-String Guitar	$154.03
SEAGULL PLUS SPRUCE ACOUSTIC	$151.77
GUITAR WITH CASE	
NEW ELECTRIC JUMBO ACOUSTIC	$150.00
CARLO ROBELLI GUITAR	
Fender Guitar and Case	$125.00
Professional Rosewood Classical Guitar	$105.09
Beautiful Rosewood Classical - Project	$103.51
OAHU Hawaiian guitar...lap steel...square neck 1950's	$102.50
Vintage Gibson Dove Acoustic Guitar Copy excellent cond	$102.50

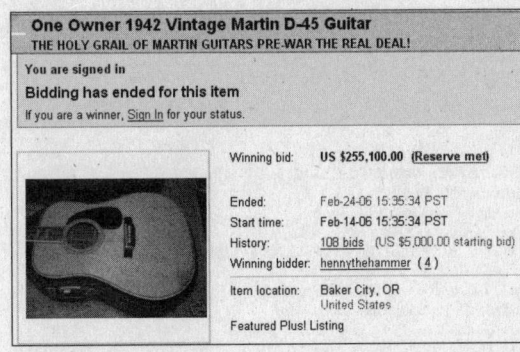

One Owner 1942 Vintage Martin D-45 Guitar
THE HOLY GRAIL OF MARTIN GUITARS PRE-WAR THE REAL DEAL!

You are signed in

Bidding has ended for this item
If you are a winner, Sign In for your status.

Winning bid: **US $255,100.00 (Reserve met)**

Ended: Feb-24-06 15:35:34 PST
Start time: Feb-14-06 15:35:34 PST
History: 108 bids (US $5,000.00 starting bid)
Winning bidder: hennythehammer (4)

Item location: Baker City, OR
United States

Featured Plus! Listing

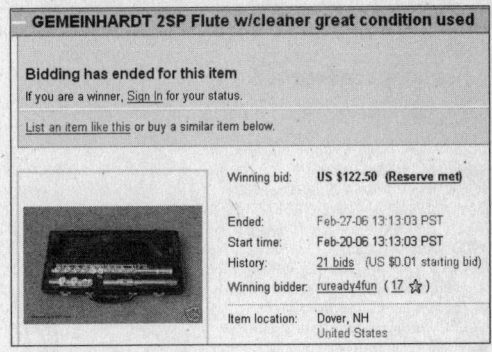

GEMEINHARDT 2SP Flute w/cleaner great condition used

Bidding has ended for this item
If you are a winner, Sign In for your status.

List an item like this or buy a similar item below.

Winning bid: **US $122.50 (Reserve met)**

Ended: Feb-27-06 13:13:03 PST
Start time: Feb-20-06 13:13:03 PST
History: 21 bids (US $0.01 starting bid)
Winning bidder: ruready4fun (17 ☆)

Item location: Dover, NH
United States

Guitar ▶ Amplifiers

The average sales price in this subcategory is $261.37.

	HIGH		AVG
MATCHLESS DC 30 A CLASS TUBE AMP !!L@@K!! LIKE NEW	$2,499.99	BOGNER SHIVA REVERB HEAD SHELL BRAND NEW	$300.00
Soldano Super Lead Overdrive SLO 100W Head NR!	$2,450.00	SILVERTONE 1333 DANELECTRO 1954 TUBE AMP AMPLIFIER	$299.99
1992 Soldano SLO 100, w/cover, loop	$1,981.00	GIBSON 30 RVS style 2x12 ext. cabinet w/ Celestions!!!	$299.00
Germino Club 40	$1,575.00	SWR GOLIATH JR JUNIOR III 8 OHM * * * NO RESERVE * * *	$280.00
Framus Cobra, Guitar Amplifier, Amp	$1,502.33	VINTAGE KAY GUITAR AMPLIFIER FENDER PRINCETON SIZE	$275.00
1950"Gibson guitar amp gt-50 with tremelo "most rare"	$1,200.00	Roland KC 300 Keyboard, Digital drum, guitar amp	$270.00
VHT Pittbull HUNDRED/CL amp- MINT/ LIKE NEW!	$1,200.00	Hartke 3500 Bass amplifier with upgrades solid amp NR	$265.00
Dr Z Maz 18 Junior with Reverb 2 X 10 class A amp	$1,183.00	2x12 Guitar Speaker Cab New CELESTION VIN 30s nu nr	$260.00
Line 6 Vetta II HD	$1,136.00	Ashdown MAGC115T Bass Combo Amp (300 watts)1x15 in spkr	$260.00
DR. Z MAZ 38 SENIOR AMP HEAD W/ REVERB NEAR MINT	$1,100.00	Vintage 60's Premier T12R tube amp for harp, guitar	$255.00
Epifani UL-502 Bass Amp, Extras, Exclnt Cond, No Rsrv!	$1,085.00	LINE 6 POD PRO RACKMOUNT UNIT! N.R.! STARTS AT A PENNY!	$255.00
Soldano Reverb-O-Sonic Guitar Amp	$1,076.00	GUILD 1960 Guitar TUBE AMP PROJECT 66-J J-66	$255.00
1960's MAGNATONE CUSTOM 460 AMP AMPLIFIER GUITAR	$1,036.00	New HARTKE Kickback 12 Bass Amplifier Amp NR	$255.00
Raezer's Edge Twin 6 Cabinet "As New" w/ orig. cover	$1,035.00	Rare 1970's GARNET TUBE Mini-Bass AMP w/ Tremelo MINTY!	$250.19
SWR Super Redhead 2x10" Bass Combo Amp	$910.00	SWR Workingman's 1x15T Speaker Cabinet 15" 15 inch	$250.07

Guitar ▶ Bass

The average sales price in this subcategory is $378.25.

	HIGH		AVG
Beautiful 6 String Ken Smith BSR6GN.Reduced no reserve!	$2,800.00	DAVID EDEN 4 X 10 XLT BASS SPEAKER CABINET	$450.00
USED MTD535 ELECTRIC BASS-MINT CONDITION	$2,700.00	[2 of these sold for $450.00 each]	
MTD 535 _5 str Bass gorgeous "Flame Mytrle Top"	$2,350.00	G&L L1500 Custom Blue Sparkle w/ matching hstock MINT!	$435.00
Sei 6 string bass 4 5 7 custom neck thru headless NR	$2,000.00	VINTAGE 1975 RICKENBACKER BASS GUITAR BODY NECK PROJECT	$420.00
Warwick Thumb 5 NT Neck Through (more pics!)	$1,650.00	Acoustic Bass Guitar	$420.00
Awesome Bass Guitar GMP! USA! MINT!	$1,599.00	DanElectro 1960 ShortHorn VINTAGE Short Scale Bass NR	$410.55
Alembic Epic 5 String Bass - NR - Excellent Condition	$1,526.00	Hohner B Bass VI six string neck-through bass guitar	$405.00
1989 Spector NS2 American Made!!! NR!	$1,500.00	Madison 810 bass guitar speaker cabinet 8 10	$405.00
1992 Rickenbacker 4001V63	$1,426.77	Ampeg 4 x 10 Bass Cabinet Model BSE410HLF	$400.68
Alembic six string bass	$1,350.00	ESP LTD Deluxe J-1005 Bass + Case	$400.00
Warwick 4string thumb bass,Genz Benz 500 amp	$1,175.00	Madison 810 bass guitar speaker cabinet 8 10	$400.00
PRE ERNIE BALL MUSIC MAN CUTLASS I MUSICMAN	$1,000.00	MTD TOBIAS GRENDEL 5	$398.53
Rickenbacker 4003 Fireglo Bass Guitar w/ case	$999.99	SCHECTER Diamond Series Custom-4 Electric BASS Guitar	$392.00
1977 RICKENBACKER 4001! RARE BLUE AZUREGLO !	$960.00	David Eden world-tour bass amp wt-1000	$384.20
Vintage 1977 Rickenbacker 4001 Jetglo Jetglow Bass	$960.00	CARVIN LB60 CUSTOM BUILT STEREO BASS GUITAR + CASE	$382.77
		Brice Prestige Z6NT 6 String Bass	$375.00

Guitar ▶ Electric

The average sales price in this subcategory is $286.05.

	HIGH		AVG
2029: American Electric Guitar, Gibson Incorporated, Ka	$110,000.00	ALVAREZ DANA SCOOP ELECTRIC	$306.76
1956 Fender Stratocaster StratGuitar original No Issues	$34,600.00	INNOVATIVE, WHITE VG, CASE	
GIBSON LES PAUL ARTISAN OWNED BY DAVE DAVIES OF KINKS. 1977	GBP 12,500.00	Vintage Sano Electric guitar thin hollow EKO Goya Italy	$305.00
USED ON MANY CLASSIC KINKS RECORDS AND TOURS		ALVAREZ DANA SCOOP!!! RARE!!!	$305.00

Vintage all original Gibson 61' sg Les Paul w/ PAF	$20,970.11
Vintage 1965 Fender Stratocaster Exceptionally Nice	
Early 1965 Green Guard About As Nice As They Come	$16,602.99
1965 Rare Hardtail Fender Stratocaster in Olympic White	$16,500.00
1954 Fender Stratocaster Not a Re-issue 1st Year Strat!	$14,850.00
Original Fender 1957 Stratocaster Blonde 57 Vintage	$13,101.00
Gibson ES-335 Crossroads Clapton 129/250 MINT NR!!!	$12,100.00
VINTAGE 1964 FENDER STRATOCASTER ORIGINAL SUNBURST! WOW	$11,101.99
LATE 1964 PRE CBS L PLATE INCREDIBLE TONE 2 OWNERS!	
Fender Stratocaster 1960. Factory Refin.(REALLY)	$11,100.00
Neck Of The Century! A Flamey Freak Of Nature!	
1968 Gibson Les Paul Custom Black Beauty W/ PAF's OHSC	$10,655.00
Hamer Explorer (Serial Number 0002) Owned by Martin Barre of Jethro Tull	GBP 6,000.00
Hank Williams Jr. Custom Eagle Guitar - Autographed	$10,600.00
Includes Two Concert Tics & Meet-N-Greet With Hank Jr.	
1958 GRETSCH CHET ATKINS 6120 with COWBOY CASE	$9,150.00

AWESOME LOOKS AND SOUND!!	
Eastwood Del Ray Guitar, 3 Mini-humbuckers, Vibrato NC	$300.00
OVATION VIPER ELECTRIC GUITAR	$300.00
Dillion DR500T guitar - Black Quilt w/PRS pickups!	$299.00
Dearmond Starfire Special Guitar	$285.99
VINTAGE KAY ELECTRIC GUITAR DEARMONDS!	$284.99
STACKPOLES! OOH!	
VINTAGE 60s NORMA ELECTRA/SUPRO	$255.00
JAPAN RARE GUITAR	
Vintage 60's 70's EKO Electric Guitar Italy Italian	$255.00
Black Schecter C 1 Elite	$250.00
Peavey USA Axcellerator Dual-Rail Excellent S****-Type	$249.00
Purple Karera electric guitar! Gibson Les Paul Strngs!	$249.00
Schecter Ultra Firebird Style Guitar	$245.00
USA made Peavey Tracer Custom II	$242.50

Guitar ▶ Parts, Accessories

The average sales price in this subcategory is $37.04.

	HIGH		AVG
THD 2X12" Accessory Speaker Cabinet	$370.00	LUTHIER GUITAR FRET WIRE RADIUS MACHINE PARTS	$47.50
Used Line 6 POD XT Pro V.2 USB Guitar Rack NR	$355.00	Scholz Rockman MIDI Pedal	$46.00
INLAID SOLID WOOD 6 STRINGS ELECTRIC GUITAR "BAT"	$310.00	Fender Red Knob Twin Output Transformer	$45.00
Dr. Z Airbrake - Dr. Z Amp.Trainwreck. Attenuator. NR!	$280.00	Lot of Guitar Parts, tons of them No Reserve	$43.00
Fender Strat WCR Wagner SR Single Coil Pickups (Fralin)	$275.00	OLD HOHNER ECHO PLUS SOUND ON SOUND REEL TO REEL NR	$42.99
GREAT INLAID CUTAWAY ACOUSTIC GUITAR "BIRDS&FLORAL"	$224.50	WIRELESS GUITAR UNIT	$39.99
Shure Wireless guitar bass UHF Diversity System UT4	$207.50	Chrome 3N3 Gibson Deluxe Tuners Guitar Parts	$39.99
Ampeg SVT DI Vacuum Tube Direct Injection Box	$177.50	Blem Strat Style Guitar Body-trem- Unfin Alder	$39.95
Gretsch Bigsby B6C Made in USA / Free Shipping	$175.00	Old Vintage Guitar Parts: Pickguard, Tuners, Bridges	$38.50
AKG Guitar Bug UHF Wireless System	$173.50	Aged Nickel Humbucking Pickup Covers (2) - New!	$38.00
Fender Strat MJ Project Guitar	$168.50	Acoustic Guitar Mic Microphone Pickup Preamp	$36.50
INTERESTING "FLORAL" INLAYS GUITAR MANDOLIN HANDWORK	$166.00	Nady Wireless One For Guitar	$36.00
SIX Jensen P10R 25W 8ohm 10" Speakers $1 NO RESERVE	$162.50	Fender Bass Precision 1997 Tuners	$35.00
AKG WMS40 wireless guitarbug UHF Diversity Guitar Bug	$162.50	Audio Technica ATW-R03 VHF Wireless System	$35.00
THD 4 OHM Hot Plate Makes you tube amp really rock	$160.01	Fender HIPSHOT TREM-SETTER for Electric Gtr - BRAND NEW	$34.79

Guitar ▶ Instruction Books, CDs, Videos

The average sales price in this subcategory is $12.98.

	HIGH		AVG
HUGE 1966 Hagelin Musical Merchandise Catalog-Guitars	$46.57	Robert Johnson's Guitar Style Blues Delta Slide Video	$13.40
12 Fake/Real Books on 1CD PDF format (No Reserve)	$39.70	Jazz Rhythm Guitar Complete Guide/Book CD	$13.40
[2 of these sold in a multiple item ("Dutch") auction for $19.85 each]		BEST OF GARTH BROOKS EASY GUITAR MUSIC BOOK	$13.00
Absolute Pitch perfect Guaranteed Or Its Free	$37.77	Pedal Steel Guitar TIPS and TRICKS "APPLE PIE SCALES"	$13.00
Electronic Music Circuits by Barry Klein	$37.00	The Beatles A-I Guitar Chord Book/100 Songs	$12.95
The Stella Guitar Book Oscar Schmidt Co. NEW	$30.95	The Complete Beatles Vol.1 A-I Piano - Vocal - Guitar	$12.95
The Paul Reed Smith Guitar Book/PRS	$26.24	Guitar World's 100 Greatest Guitarists	$12.95
GRUHN'S GUIDE TO VINTAGE GUITARS NEW BOOK	$25.95	You Can Teach Yourself FLAMENCO	$12.55
TUBE AMP TALK FOR THE GUITARIST AND TECH - GUIDE BOOK	$25.46	GUITAR–BOOK & CD!	
Play Solo FLAMENCO GUITAR Juan Martin–Book/CD/DVD!	$24.99	Play Bass Guitar Today/Ultimate Method/DVD	$12.49
BEAUTY OF THE BURST - GIBSON LES PAUL GUITAR BOOK	$24.99	Swing Jazz Guitar Book CD Combo Basics NEW	$11.95
ERIC CLAPTON Best-Guitar TAB BOOK + Backing Tracks CD.!	$24.99	First Lessons Beginning Guitar Book DVD CD Combo NEW	$11.95
BEAUTY OF THE BURST - GIBSON LES PAUL GUITAR BOOK	$24.99	George Winston for Solo Guitar/Transcriptions	$11.95
GUITAR FUZZ & FEEDBACK RARE COLLECTORS BOOK!!!	$22.50	British Blues Guitar Heroes/Beck Clapton Page	$11.70
Blue Book of Electric Guitars 9th Ed. Brand New!!	$21.95	Complete Left-Handed Guitar Method/Book & CD	$11.70
EADG 4 - Bass Guitar Player Instruction Book	$21.50	George Harrison/Brainwashed/Songbook/Beatles	$11.49

Harmonica ▶ Hohner

The average sales price in this subcategory is $25.28.

	HIGH		AVG
1898 Hohner Harmonica Revolving Dealer Display	$566.00	4 VINTAGE HARMONICAS 2 HOHNER, 1 ROY ROGERS	$26.56
RARE OLD HOHNER "HOHNERETTE" WOOD/	$229.50	Hohner Super Chromonica 270 chromatic harmonica E	$26.01
METAL- HORN * GERMANY		Hohner Chromonica I De Luxe Key of C & Case	$26.00
Vintage Harmonica Set - 13 Tombo Lee Oskar, Hohner	$182.50	M. HOHNER 64 CHROMONICA!! PROFESSIONAL MODEL!! NR!!	$26.00
Hohner Professional CBH2016 Chromatic Harmonica	$180.75	Vintage Hohner The 64 Chromonica Prof. Model "C"	$26.00
Hohner Professional 2016 CBH Harmonica	$158.05	VINTAGE HOHNER HARMONICA THE HOHNER BAND	$26.00
Vintage Harmonica Set - 13 Tombo Lee Oskar, Hohner Spec	$132.51	Hohner Chromonica	$25.00
Blues Special 20 Harmonica Set of 12 Keys Mint Cond.	$129.09	Hohner amplifier for guitar \ Harmonica ugly but plays	$25.00
Honer D40 Concertina	$128.00	Hohner 255 / 48 Chrometta 12 3 Okt Chromatic Harmonica	$24.99
RARE 1930's Hohner NO. 263 Chromatica & a Special 20	$120.00	Hohner Chrometta 12 Chromatic Harmonica, Key of C	$24.95
VINTAGE M HOHNER POLYPHONIA No 6 HARMONICA w/Orig Box	$116.50	OLDER SUPER CHOMONICA M. HOHNER HARMONICA IN CASE	$24.95
GIANT MARINE BAND HARMONICA STORE DISPLAY	$87.51	HOW TO PLAY HARMONICA BOOK, DVD,	$24.95
Hohner Echo-Luxe 'C' NEW!! very old Harmonica	$86.00	CD & HOHNER HARMONICA	
Old TRUMPET CALL Harmonica HOHNER double sided Brass	$78.00	HOHNER SPECIAL 20 HARMONICA! NEW! FREE BOOK	$24.95
1930's Hohner 14" Harmonica "Chromatica" # 263	$73.00	Hohner Chromonica 280-C Harmonica 4 Octave Professional	$24.03
Suberb Vintage Hohner Marine Band Harmonica Key Of C!	$70.99	HOHNER SPECIAL 20 MARINE BAND HARMONICA - G - FREE S/H	$23.00

Harmonica ▶ Johnson Blues King

The average sales price in this subcategory is $30.72.

	HIGH		AVG
14 PC Blues King HARMONICA SET w/	$65.00	12 Blues King Harmonicas w/case Every Key New Harps Set	$35.00
HARD CASE & FREE SHIP+		12 BLUES HARMONICAS IN ALL KEYS W/FREE CARRYING CASE!	$31.00
[2 of these sold for $65.00 each]		New set of 4 Johnson Blues King Harmonicas A C D G keys	$31.00
14 PC Blues King HARMONICA SET w/	$63.00	New set of 12 Johnson Blues Harps harmonica	$31.00
HARD CASE & FREE SHIP+		12 Blues Harmonicas w/case Every Key New Harps Set	$31.00
NEW JOHNSON HARMONICA HARMONICAS	$59.95	12 Blues Harmonicas w/case Every Key New Harps Set	$30.00
HARP SET ALL 12 KEYS		12 Blues Harmonicas w/case Every Key New Harps Set	$29.99
Diatonic Blues Harmonica Set with Case Free Ship	$49.00	12 BLUES HARMONICAS IN ALL KEYS W/FREE CARRYING CASE!	$28.50
BRAND NEW 12 key Blues King Harmonica Set w/ FREE Case!	$49.00	12 Blues King Harmonicas w/Case EVERY KEY New Harps Set	$28.00
[5 of these sold for $49.00 each]		12 BLUES HARMONICAS IN ALL KEYS W/FREE CARRYING CASE!	$27.00

Harmonica ▶ Other

The average sales price in this subcategory is $27.20.

	HIGH		AVG
OLD RARE VINTAGE ANTIQUE FRIDOLIN HARMONICA	$237.49	Cute Accent Lamp / Night Light FROG PLAYING HARMONICA	$32.90
Gregory Tiger Stripe 2 Channel Tube Amp, 60's Sweet!	$232.50	12 Key Color Blues Harmonica Set+Case+BOXES~Be A Pro~	$32.50
Antique Harmonica 1850 - 1880 Austria 2 Sided Tremolo	$103.50	P. Pohl COMET Harmonica - Art Deco Design - VINTAGE&Box	$31.50
1940 Vintage Astatic Brown Biscuit Microphone Mic	$102.50	ANTIQUE BUTTERFLY HARMONICA VIRTUOSO NEW IN BOX	$31.00
ATTENTION HARP PLAYERS Precision Electronics 10-PA amp	$100.00	New Set of 12 Keys Blues King Harps Harmonicas w/case	$31.00
[2 of these sold for $100.00 each]		Bottle 'O Blues Harmonica Microphone (Harp Mic)	$30.00
New Shure 520DX Bullet Mic Microphone Bonus CR Element	$91.00	HARMONICA SET, 6 DIFFERENT KEYS! FREE HOW-TO BOOKLET	$27.99
5164 HERING CHROMATIC HARMONICA KEY "?" NEW HOHNER PRO	$90.00	Vintage JAZZ KING HARMONICA in Original Box GERMANY	$26.00
CHORDET 20 Chord Harp Harmonica w/Instruction Manual	$89.95	YAMAHA CHROMATIC BUTTERFLY HARMONICA	$26.00
harmonium-indian/india made by tradtional artists	$75.00	*OCCUPIED JAPAN!	
RETIRED! Ltd. Ed. LIMOGES Box HARMONICA with CASE difs	$71.01	German Harmonica Mouth Organ Suprema	$25.49
VINTAGE 70'S WELTNEISTER CHROMATIC HARMONICA	$71.01	HARMONICA SET, 6 DIFFERENT KEYS! FREE HOW-TO BOOKLET	$24.99
A Trio Of Bullet Microphone Shells	$69.00	Shure harmonica harp mic element green bullet - vintage	$24.00
Vintage F.U.Bohm's Germany Silver Reeds Harmonica	$66.99	BLUES Harmonica Set New~HARMONICAS~6 KEYS~Play like Pro	$23.95
Harmonica Microphone "Mini Mojo" RED FREE SHIPPING	$65.00	12 Key Color Blues Harmonica Set+Case+BOXES~Be A Pro~	$22.50
ROLMONICA OLD HARMONICA WITH 3 PLAYER ROLLS LIKE NEW	$61.00	HOHNER MARINE BAND HARMONICA #1896 - G - FREE S/H	$22.00

Keyboard, Piano ▶ Accordion, Concertina

The average sales price in this subcategory is $146.02.

	HIGH		AVG
PIGINI Chromatic C System Accordion 120 Bass	$2,500.00	Hohner Verdi IIIM	$157.50
New "Weltmeister Cassotto" 374 Accordion	$1,800.00	Rare Paolo Rogledi Accordian Stradella Italla Accordion	$154.50
Weltmeister - Monte 41/120 Folklore Walnut Accordion	$1,449.00	ACCORDIAN PAOLO SOPRANI WURLITZER BONUS BOOKS 1939	$154.50
Sonola SS-7 Professional $4/5 Accordion	$1,000.00	FERRARI ITALY PROFESSIONAL ACCORDIAN w/ case	$152.50
Pro. Accordion/Accordian Italian and French Musette New	$899.00	ACCORDIONS-CAJUN ZYDECO ACCORDION/ACCORDIAN-H.CARVED	$152.50
GUERRINI BUTTON DIATONIC	$850.00	Cordovox CL-10 CL 10 Leslie Speaker Accordion Cabinet	$150.00
Tanzbar concertina not roller organ music box barrel	$736.00	TITANO ACCORDION Beautiful / Excellent Condition	$149.00
Main Sqeeze Beauty: Accordion. Unbeatable sound.	$700.00	Full size accordion ~ Black ~ with locking case!	$142.50
Petosa Accordian/Best Brand Excellant Condition	$685.00	Full size acordion ~ Red ~ with locking case!	$135.00
CUSTOM VINTAGE ITALIAN LASCALA	$660.00	VINTAGE CAPRI ACCORDION W/ CASE ACCORDIAN	$135.00
ACCORDION<VOCE'ORO		ACCORDIAN/ACCORDIONS AWESOME	$135.00
SUPER Anglo 30 Key Lachenal Concertina ca. 1850 RARE	$560.00	PIANO ACCORDION NEW MINT	
sonola ss 5 accordion w/case excellent shape italy ss5	$510.00	Hohner 3002 Ariette Folk/Cajun Accordion	$133.52
STAR Concertina....Vintage! Fine Condition!!	$480.00	CONTELLO ACCORDION ACCORDIAN W/KEYBOARD PEARLIZED KEYS+	$122.50
GORGEOUS DIATONIC ACCORDION "HOHNER CORSO"	$465.00	Brand New Cajun Style Accordion (C) and Case	$120.00
Hohner 3500 Corona II GCF Diatonic Accordion	$451.00	VINTAGE " RED MARBLE " ITALIAN ACCORDIAN - NO RESERVE!	$114.50

Keyboard, Piano ▶ Electronic Keyboards

The average sales price in this subcategory is $252.85.

	HIGH		AVG
EMS VCS3 SYNTHI vcs-3 Vintage Analog Modular Synth aks	$5,999.99	1970'S ARP AXXE ELETRONIC SYNTHESIZER KEYBOARD	$325.00
ARP 2600 Vintage Analog Modular Synthesizer moog 3620 !	$3,199.99	M-Audio Keystation Pro 88 Weighted Key USB Controller	$320.00
MOOG Taurus Bass Pedals Vintage and Mint!	$2,500.00	Technics SM-AC 1200 midi orchestra arranger key	$300.00
Moog Taurus 1, Bass Pedal Synth (Near Mint)	$1,875.00	Rhodes Electronic Piano Model 3363 Keyboard	$299.00
Access Virus KC 61 Note Keyboard Synth No Reserve!	$1,625.00	Alesis Micron Analog Modeling Synthesizer synth	$295.00
Sequential Circuits Prophet VS - NO RESERVE!	$1,537.00	Wurlitzer 112 Electric/Electronic Piano - tube preamp!	$280.00
Vintage Minimoog Model D SN # 9476	$1,500.00	Vintage 3 piece Gibson Keyboard Set, model G201	$250.00
Technics KN-6000 portable keyboard	$1,495.00	WHITEHALL ELECTRONIC SUITCASE COMBO ORGAN/PEAVEY AMP NR	$242.50
NEW NORD ELECTRO 2 73 KEY NEW IN BOX DEALER	$1,425.00	Akai VOX64 VOX 64 for Akai S5000 S 5000 Sampler	$238.00
OSCar Oxford Synthesizer vintage analog synth MIDI	$1,225.00	General Music S2 gem Synthesizer pro 16trk Seq keyboard	$228.50
NORD LEAD 3 /CLAVIA...LIKE NEW w/ Nord Bag...Manual..	$1,200.00	Fatar Studiologic sl-880 88 key weighted MIDI *NR*	$228.00
Waldorf Q Synth with 32 Voice Upgrade - MINT	$1,200.00	MADISON STANDARD 88 KEY ORLA ELECTRONIC PIANO KEYBOARD	$227.50
Ketron X1 Oriental, Solton, middle eastern keyboard	$1,175.50	ALESIS QS6 61 KEY SYNTH	$200.00
Clavia Nord Electro 61 V2	$1,150.00	EMU EMAX II	$200.00
Yamaha P-200 Digital Piano with stand, pedal and bench	$1,051.00	Moog Rogue	$200.00

Keyboard, Piano ▸ Organ

The average sales price in this subcategory is $194.62.

	HIGH		AVG
Lowrey Majesty Elite Series Organ Model LX/510 LX510	$6,679.00	NEW! Drawbar Organ Sound Module	$425.00
Lowrey Organ, Legacy Model SU/300	$5,427.00	Hammond xb2	$406.00
PRICE LOWER- Allen Digital Electronic Organ, Model 123C	$3,150.00	FARFISA MINI COMPACT organ antique? works!	$405.00
Vox Continental Combo Organ w/legs, pedal, cases	$2,225.00	Yamaha Electone Organ FS-300 keyboard Music NR	$324.99
Providence Model 330 Rodgers Electronic. Organ	$2,026.00	WW II ERA ARMY PUMP ORGAN BY ESTEY IN WORKING COND. NR!	$305.00
KAWAI SR7 Electronic Organ Great Sounds Play Like a Pro	$1,450.00	Yamaha Electric Organ - dual keyboard w/ matching bench	$275.00
Allen Digital Computer Organ	$1,225.00	Hammond H-111 Tonewheel Organ	$250.00
Vintage 1965 Hammond Organ Model A-122	$1,200.00	roland SUPER JV 1080	$250.00
Korg CX3 with Soft Case: Excellent Condition	$1,125.00	Crumar Trilogy: Organ, Strings and Synthesizer	$232.50
BEAUTIFUL YAMAHA FX-20 DIGITAL KEYBOARD ORGAN !!	$1,075.00	E-MU B-3 ORGAN RACK MOUNT	$203.50
Antique Mason & Hamlin Organ Circa 1870's	$999.00	Blue Chip Organ Module Drawbars	$162.50
1970 Vox Continental Organ	$950.01	4 Pipe Family - Pipe Organ Display - Desk ed.	$161.00
Electric Organ	$750.00	Farfisa Compact Duo Organ Bass Foot Pedals	$158.16
Amazing Roland VK8M Organ Module LIKE NEW!	$650.00	FARISA LIKE WHITEHALL VINTAGE ELECTRIC ORGAN	$135.81
Yamaha Electone EL7 Organ FREE SHIP/WARRANTY/NR/BENCH	$539.00	Korg 05/rw synth module	$135.00

Keyboard, Piano ▸ Piano

The average sales price in this subcategory is $212.85.

	HIGH		AVG
234: A Steinway model L grand piano with ebony finish	$25,000.00	SOLID CHERRY CABLE-NELSON UPRIGHT PIANO, LIKE NEW	$330.00
1950 BALDWIN 9' SD-10 Concert Grand MINTI #650381	$12,500.00	1986 OLMSTEAD UP-RIGHT PIANO	$300.00
Steinway Model M Grand Piano Ebony Finish	$11,500.00	CHICKERING UPRIGHT PIANO	$300.00
Yamaha, Baby Grand, G3, Black, Excellent condition	$9,901.00	Bell Upright Piano - great condition!!	$278.00
1902 Model "O" Steinway Baby Grand Piano	$9,600.00	music box, coin op, piano, nickelodeon, coin counter	$260.00
Brand New Player Piano Baby Grand / Piano Disc System. Shipped anywhere in the US	$8,299.99	Duet Size LEATHER Ebony Adjustable Concert Piano Bench	$259.90
Steinway Grand Piano!	$8,200.00	music box, coin op, piano, nickelodeon, coin counter	$255.00
FINE VINTAGE WALNUT MASON & HAMLIN GRAND PIANO MODEL A	$7,200.00	music box, coin op, piano, nickelodeon, coin counter	$250.00
VERY LOW RESERVE, SUPERB TONE AND QUALITY		Baldwin Upright Acrosonic Spinet Piano with Bench 1971	$250.00
		STUDIO UPRIGHT PIANO FOR ONLY	$202.50
YAMAHA CLAVINOVA CVP-309 CVP309 PE DIGITAL PIANO BLACK	$6,995.00	$175 NO RESERVE! $175	
Steinway & Sons "M" Baby Grand Piano 374584M Signed	$6,938.00	Piano - Beautiful Antique Upright - NR	$202.50
1880 Steinway Model A Classical Grand Piano	$6,727.00	music box, coin op, piano, nickelodeon, coin counter	$200.00
Hammond B3, Leslie 122 Mint NR	$6,651.55	music box, coin op, piano, nickelodeon, coin counter	$200.00
1916 MINT STEINWAY 5ft 10.5in Piano #650379	$6,250.00	NEW LEATHER PIANO BENCH ARTIST	$199.95
1867 chickering concert grand piano	$5,000.00	BABY GRAND PB-363-LC	
Mellotron Mark VI	$5,000.00	[3 of these sold for $199.95 each]	
		W. Gaehle & Co. Square Grand, 1800's	$199.00

Keyboard, Piano ▸ Instruction Books, CDs, Videos

The average sales price in this subcategory is $21.94.

	HIGH		AVG
GIBSON J-150	$1,199.00	GEORGE DUKE 2 VOLUME KEYBOARD INSTRUCTION DVD 2 HOURS	$23.99
yamaha djx-II everything works....power adapter	$142.50	DVD~HL~CHUCK LEAVELL~PIANO INSTRUCTION~2+HRS~$40 list	$23.88
eMedia Learn to Play Keyboard MIDI Keyboard Piano USB	$89.99	Yamaha PSR-530 Owner's Manual	$22.27
PLAY PIANO IN A FLASH with SCOTT HOUSTON DVD SET NEW	$72.00	LEARN AUTOHARP - JOHN SEBASTIAN - LOVIN SPOONFUL DVD	$21.99
Yamaha Motif instructional DVD Set	$62.00	THE BLUES/ROCK PIANO OF JOHNNIE JOHNSON *NEW* DVD	$21.99
PLAY PIANO IN A FLASH with SCOTT HOUSTON DVD SET NEW	$59.99	The JAZZ PIANO Book	$21.00
[2 of these sold for $59.99 each]		Hammond Organ Blues Rock Techniques David Cohen DVD	$21.00
Brian Auger Hammond B3 / Piano Instructional Video DVD	$45.00	DVD~BLUES/ROCK PIANO OF JOHNNIE JOHNSON~SAVE 38%~NEW! :	$20.88
Learn to Play Blues Piano DVD 1 and DVD 2 with Cohen	$44.95	LOT of 18 Piano Lesson Books BASTIEN Piano Basics	$20.50
Roland Styles CD Library E&G Series Keyboards/Organs-NR	$34.99	Piano Course in cassette tapes, books and VHS tapes	$20.00

Percussion ▸ Cymbals

The average sales price in this subcategory is $66.28.

	HIGH		AVG
Musical Instrument: Antique J.C. Deagan Xylophone	$3,050.00	20 in A Zildjian brilliant CHINA BOY LOW CYMBAL PERFECT	$75.00
Taye ProX & Zildjian K set	$1,000.00	HART E CYMBAL II HIGH HAT ROLAND V DRUMS NO RESERVE	$71.99
GONG CANNON TAIWAN GONG 30" BRAND NEW	$299.95	22" ZILDJIAN Genuine Turkish Cymbal Made in USA No Res	$71.70
FULL SIZE GONG by Xingsir Chau - 2 Feet	$285.00	Zildjian A Custom 18" Swish VGC NR china type	$71.00
FULL SIZE GONG by Xingsir Chau - 2 Feet	$285.00	Sabian 8" Mike Portnoy Max Stax China Splash Cymbal	$70.00
Paiste 22" Traditional Prototype China EX+	$265.00	ROLAND CY-6 CYMBAL WITH BOOM AND HARDWARE NO RESERVE	$67.00
Zildjian Titanium Cymbal Pack!! NR NO RESERVE!!	$264.00	ZILDJIAN ZXT MEDIUM RIDE 20" CYMBAL FOR DRUMS NO RES-!	$66.00
Paiste Tridtional 20" Swish China, WOW, no reserve .01$	$203.50	Sabian 19nch VF-X Signature Series Ride Cymbal	$66.00
Zildjian Medium Ride Cymbal $1 NO RESERVE	$202.50	Z Custom Projection Crash 19"/48cm Cymbal NR	$65.87
CONN STROBOTUNER MODEL ST 11,GUITAR STROBE TUNER	$187.50	16 Inch Zildjian china trash	$65.00
SABIAN 18" JIA CHINESE CYMBAL JOHN BLACKWELL JR. CHINA!	$170.00	Zildjian 6" ZIL-BEL	$65.00
HART E CYMBAL II 12"& 14" ROLAND V DRUMS NO RESERVE	$162.50	8 cymbal / tko percussion / gordon / sabian / 20"18" 15	$63.00
PAISTE Sound Formula 20" Thin China, NEVER USED	$152.50	Zildjian 20" ride cymbal	$62.89
Paiste traditional med. light ''22''	$152.49	Zildjian A Series Sweet Ride & Sabian Vault Cymbals NR	$62.50
VINTAGE PAISTE 2002 18"CHINA/CHINESE CRASH CYMBAL ride	$150.00	18" Sabian Crash Cymbal, Splash, China, NR	$62.00

Percussion ▸ Drums

The average sales price in this subcategory is $130.72.

	HIGH		AVG
YAMAHA ELECTRONIC DRUM SET, DTXTREME IIS, NO RESERVE!	$2,225.00	PEARL EXPORT 4 PCS DRUMS USED	$158.40
Yamaha DTXTREME Electronic Percussion/Drums System	$1,742.17	NO RESERVE MANY PICS-LOOK	
BEAUTIFUL 1941 LEEDY SET WITH HARDWARE AND ZILDJIANS	$1,699.00	Roland CY12R/C-C V-Cymbal 12" Crash/Ride - Like New!	$155.00
DW Drums - Champagne Sparkle w/ paded cases & brackets	$1,600.00	BEAUTIFUL 1965 LUDWIG 13 X 9 RED SPARKLE CLASSIC TOM	$150.00
STUNNING 1964 ROGERS SILVER GLASS GLITTER 20,12,14 SET	$1,590.00	SONOR 6.5 X 14 10-LUG SNARE DRUM-EXCELLENT	$150.00
4 Piece Noble & Cooley Drumset. DIRECT FROM FACTORY!!	$1,575.00	Drum Set	$145.00
DW Silver Sparkle 4 Piece drum kit	$1,200.00	New Sitar String Beatles Ravi Shankar Sarangi Esraj	$142.50
TENOR "C" STEEL DRUM with FREE SHIPPING	$1,050.00	BEAUTIFUL SLINGERLAND RADIO KING PLAYERS DRUM	$140.00
[2 of these sold in a multiple item ("Dutch") auction for $525.00 each]		4 piece drum set w/ maple snare & hardware	$137.50
Taye ProX & Zildjian K set	$1,000.00	Rogers 60's Swiv-O-Matic Hi-Hat w/Clutch SWIVOMATIC !!	$132.50
Mapex Pro M 8 pc ....6 Months Old	$925.00	Complete set of LUDWIG shells	$132.50
Roland TD-10 Exp TDW-1 V-Cymbal Cntrl Module TD10 *SALE	$869.99	EARLY 60'S SLINGERLAND 16 X 16 COCKTAIL BASS DRUM	$126.00
Roland TD-10 Exp TDW-1 V-Cymbal Cntrl Module TD10 *SALE	$849.99	DW 5000 double bass drum pedal	$125.00
Roland V Club TD-6 Drum Kit in Excellent Condition	$654.44	Roc N Soc Mac Saddle Drum Throne Seat Stool Never Used!	$122.50
Roland TD-3 V-Drums like NEW drumkit w/ extras !!!!!!!	$585.00	Zildjian 19" Z Custom Rock Crash	$120.00
Pearl Session Select SRX 4 Piece Jazz Kit	$535.00	PEARL 12X14 WHITE ALL BIRCH TOM FOR DRUMS-USED NR-	$119.50
NEW HART DYNAMICS PRODIGY ELECTRONIC DRUM SET	$515.00		

Percussion ▸ Parts, Accessories

The average sales price in this subcategory is $36.21.

	HIGH		AVG
ROLAND TDA 700 V DRUM AMPLIFIER	$650.00	NEW DRUM PRACTICE PADS SET SNARE TOM CYMBAL MUTE KIT	$39.50
TDW-1 WAVE AND SYSTEM EXPANSION BOARD TD-10 NR	$355.00	SKB drum case for 10 mounted tom. Hardshell Used.	$39.00
Pacific Drum Rack by DW... Super Rack. Super Sides Too.	$355.00	OLDER WOODEN SNARE DRUM FRAME, NO NAME ON IT	$39.00
ClearSonic 5 panel Drum Shield, 5.5' tall x 10' wide,	$350.00	NEW DRUM PRACTICE PADS SET SNARE TOM CYMBAL MUTE KIT	$38.00
DDRUM D-DRUM TRIGGERS WITH CABLES 5pc set	$265.00	ROGERS 1960's snare throw-off strainer & butt.	$38.00
NOMAD Drum Cases 6 piece rock case set	$179.00	Ludwig 60's baseball muffler white felt complete!	$37.01
DW 5002 Chain Drive Double Bass Drum Pedal	$155.00	LP ROCK RIDGE RIDER COWBELL&PEARL MOUNTING CLAMP	$36.52
LUDWIG 1960'S STORE LIGHTED SIGN	$150.00	2 Ludwig baseball bat style internal dampeners NICE	$36.01
roland drum dual trigger pads PD/7	$135.00	NEW DRUM PRACTICE PADS SET SNARE TOM CYMBAL MUTE KIT	$35.99
Roc-N-Soc Nitro Hydraulic Drum Throne Blue IN BOX!	$131.99	Ludwig Drum Co. Supersensitive Snare Guards	$35.06
DW 9100 Extra Heavy Duty Drum Throne Seat Stool Mint!!	$118.79	Gibraltar Bass Drum Practice Pad	$35.01
Drum Workshop 9100 Extra Heavy	$109.79	Bass Drum Trigger Pintech K3 Electronic Drum Trigger	$35.00
Duty Drum Throne DW Mint		DJEMBE CASE, ASHIKO, DRUM BAG, KACES, RBI DRUMS	$35.00
Gibraltar 9608OS Pro Oversized Motorcycle Drum Throne	$104.99	NEW Nickelworks Snare Throw-off (BLACK &CHROME finish)	$35.00
14 X 22 Radio King BD shell/Rims	$100.00	NEW DRUM PRACTICE PADS SET SNARE TOM CYMBAL MUTE KIT	$34.99
Pearl Magnesium Marching Snare Drum carrier harness NEW	$99.99	[2 of these sold for $34.99 each]	

Percussion ▸ Tambourines

The average sales price in this subcategory is $13.53.

	HIGH		AVG
Purple Rain Tour - Prince & the Revolution	$127.50	BRAND NEW! Set of 3 Tambourines - Goat Skin Heads	$13.95
VINTAGE 9-1/2" WOOD LUDWIG TAMBOURINE TAMBORINE	$91.00	[2 of these sold for $13.95 each]	
Grover Proj. Plus Tambourine + FREE grover triangle	$81.00	Lot of 12 - 5.5" Tambourines with Metal Bells	$13.95
Percussion Tambourine Grover 10" and case MINT	$72.80	[3 of these sold for $13.95 each]	
Ludwig 10" Weather Master Tambourine	$46.00	BRAND NEW! Set of 3 Tambourines - Goat Skin Heads	$13.95
All Wooden Professional Goat Skin Tambourines Lot of 3	$44.85	Remo Dove Tambourine in White, Brand New	$13.50
[3 of these sold in a multiple item ("Dutch") auction for $14.95 each]		RHYTHMTECH DST DRUM SET TAMBOURINE (USED) NR	$13.00
Vintage TAMBOURINE	$42.02	TAMBORINE HALFMOON 32 JINGLES	$12.95
Rhythm Tech Tambourine, Wood Block and Mounting Clamp	$36.00	[4 of these sold for $12.95 each]	
TUNABLE BRAZILIAN CAPOEIRA 10" TAMBOURINE PANDEIRO PRO	$32.42	Latin Percussion Mountable Tambourine	$12.50
TUNABLE BRAZILIAN CAPOEIRA 10" TAMBOURINE PANDEIRO PRO	$31.00	NICE Vintage Ludwig Wood 10" Tambourine w Skin Drum NR	$12.50
CHURCH TAMBOURINES 2 ROWS	$30.10	TAMBOURINE Black green Half Moon 2 rows Wood NEW	$12.00
JINGLE NO SKINHEADS LOW PRICE		Brand New Wooden Large size MARACA Mexican Color $12.00	$12.00
[10 of these sold in a multiple item ("Dutch") auction for $3.01 each]		All Wooden Professional Goat Skin Tambourines Lot of 3	$11.25
Ludwig Wood Tambourine Vintage-Nice	$29.00	New Laurel 8 Bell Half Moon Tambourine	$11.05
Vintage Professional Tambourine, Great sound & feel. No	$28.76	10" Wooden Professional Goat Skin Tambourines Lot of 3	$11.01
Rhythm Tech Drum Set Tambourine-Black	$26.00	3 DAY! RHTHMN TECH TAMBOURINE WITH HOLDER $1 NR	$11.00
CP HAND DRUMS * Brand New* Set Of Three (3) With Beater	$26.00	10" TAMBORINE TAMBOURINE WITH HEAD LOOK NO RESERVE!	$10.99

Pro Audio ▸ Computer Recording

The average sales price in this subcategory is $166.86.

	HIGH		AVG
Digidesign Mix Plus ! New!	$2,499.99	TC Electronic Powercore Element PCI (2 of 2) - MINT	$250.00
Digidesign Mix Plus ! New! What a Deal!	$2,499.99	EDIROL UA-25 usb interface & Cakewalk v2 studio package	$217.50
API 3124+ 4 Channel Mic Pre Mint in Box!! #2	$2,258.00	2 Removable Glyph SCSI Cheetah Drives for Trip Systems	$200.00
Pro Tools HD Accel Card	$1,625.00	M-Audio Trigger Finger USB MIDI Control Surface - NEW	$189.00
Digidesign PRO TOOLS 24 MIX System	$1,299.00	GLYPH RACK MOUNT HARD DRIVE BAY 5 DRIVES PROTOOLS	$176.99
Digidesign 002 Rack !!!	$881.00	Edirol PCR30 32 Key USB MIDI Keyboard Controller PCR-30	$159.00
Digidesign 002 Rack !!!	$840.00	6 CD Sound Effects Library Set "Original" "N/R"!!!!!	$155.00
Digidesign 002 Rack !!!	$840.00	Line 6 Guitarport w/ Rifftracker Software and 2 DVD's	$144.95
Digidesign 888/24 Interface New !	$799.99	M-AUDIO UC-33E UC33E UC 33 E UC 33 E Like New!	$125.00
KORG KARMA EXCELLENT CONDITION	$750.00	Marathon Computer Rack G rack for G4 and G3 Power Macs	$122.51
RADIKAL SAC-2.2 - B-Stock	$695.00	Alesis CD Twin in Factory Sealed Box w/No Reserve!	$103.51

MPC 60 (Classic Drum Machine!!!)	$580.00	OXYGEN8 M-AUDIO USB MIDI CONTROLLER - LIKE NEW IN BOX	$103.50
Lexicon NuVerb Effects Card with TDM - TESTED	$460.00	MidiMan M-Audio Midi Sport 4x4 Midisport Perfect!!!	$99.00
Digidesign MBOX Portable Studio W/ Pro Tools LE In Box!	$399.99	MOTU MTP AV Midi Timepiece Midi Patchbay Interface	$77.66
MOTU 828 Firewire Audio Interface - Great Condition	$395.00	Digidesign Protools III TDM nubus disk I/O card	$69.00

Pro Audio ▶ Mixers

The average sales price in this subcategory is $287.92.

	HIGH		AVG
Amek Big 44 console w/Supertrue, dynamics, more...	$9,479.00	Mackie 408M Powered Mixer, 8-Channels, 500 Watts	$365.00
Allen & Heath GL 4000 Mixer - 40 by 8 - No Reserve	$6,100.00	Soundcraft Spirit M12 Mixing Board (LIKE NEW)	$355.00
SOUNDCRAFT 6000 Console - Great Cond. with Pro Upgrades	$5,500.00	Roland VP-9000 Variphrase Processor Sampler BRAND NEW	$338.67
Soundcraft 40 Channel Spirit Monitor 2 Mixer No Reserve	$4,000.00	Shure FP410 Microphone Mixer	$338.00
Soundcraft Ghost 32x8 recording console mixer NR!	$3,360.00	Roland VM 3100 Pro - RPC-1 card	$316.00
Allen & Heath GL3300 824A Mixer w/ Power Supply & Case	$2,750.00	CRATE AUDIO G-1600X1 MIXER WITH SPEAKERS NO RESERVE	$306.01
Soundcraft Ghost 32 Channel Mixer	$2,000.00	Shure M367 six-input portable microphone mixer/amp	$305.00
Used once Digi Design 02 firewire mixer Protools digita	$1,375.00	Tascam TM-D1000 TMD1000 Digital Mixer, Mint-Exec !!NR!!	$305.00
TASCAM M-2600 32 CHANNEL PROFESSIONAL MIXING CONSOLE	$1,000.00	Roland SI-24 Studio Interface control surface, mixer	$305.00
TASCAM DM-24 DIGITAL MIXER	$930.00	Carvin PA1200 Powered Mixer NR	$285.00
Allen & Heath GL 2000 Mixing Console	$930.00	Alesis GigaMix 4CD Powered Mixer CD Player 200w $0 SH	$269.00
SOUNDCRAFT SPIRIT LX7 MIXING CONSOLE 32 IMPUTS	$885.00	Rane SM-82 8 Channel 1 Rack Stereo Line mixer Pro Tools	$265.00
Allen & Heath Mix Wizard WZ 16:2 DX mixer FREE SHIP	$825.00	Soundcraft E12 Mixer, 12 Channel + 2 Stereo (Spirit)	$249.00
Tascam M-3500 24x8 recording/live mixing board	$800.00	Tsunami 1000W (3 Channels) SMPS Powered Mixer *NIB*	$247.50
Bozak DJ Rotary Mixer CMA 10-2DL	$755.55	Kustom Profile System One PA System with BAG *NICE*	$242.50

Pro Audio ▶ Speakers

The average sales price in this subcategory is $111.96.

	HIGH		AVG
2 Mackie SWA-1501's, M-1400 Amp, Pro-M 215's, DOD430CX	$1,825.01	JBL E120-8 (JBL E-120-8) (JBL E, K, D120 Series 12")	$175.00
TANNOY System 15DMT studio monitors	$1,400.00	KLIPSCH Super Tweeter Speakers	$162.50
SHURE IEM UHF PST 700 w/ 3 PR7 RECEIVERS & ANTENNA	$1,201.00	MMTM with Crossover NR!	
1200 WATT PA DJ speakers subwoofer amp system	$675.00	UREI JBL 801 B Speaker and 2425H driver used	$152.50
Shure PSM 400 In Ear Monitor System. Wireless P4MTRE1	$672.00	YAMAHA SV-12 SV12 SPEAKER SYSTEM (1 PAIR)	$150.00
2 Madison 18" PA DJ subwoofer speakers USED	$530.00	JBL E140 Bass Guitar Speaker	$134.50
Auratone Super Sound Cube Video Shielded NICE Like 5C's	$521.00	Pair 12" Floor Monitors Studio/Stage Monitor ~ Speakers	$129.00
2 Madison 18" PA DJ subwoofer speakers USED	$510.00	JBL K-120 JBL K120 12 inch speaker	$127.50
BuzzBomb 212 2x12 Guitar amp speaker cab cabinet Black	$450.00	JBL K-110 JBL K110 10 inch speaker	$122.50
PAIR BAG END S15-D HIGH END AUDIO SPEAKERS NICE !	$436.00	Anchor LIB-6001 Unpowered Companion Speaker	$120.00
Peavey SP2G Profesional Speakers NO RESERVE!!	$428.00	NEW EDIROL ROLAND MA-10A POWERED SPEAKERS BLACK	$119.99
VINTAGE JBL D 110 D-110 10" FENDER AMP SPEAKERS RARE	$411.00	Fender Passport Tripod Speaker Stands & 2 Mic Stands	$112.95
Roland KC350 120-Watt/12 in. Speaker. 3-Band EQ	$410.00	Bass/Guitar Speaker Hartke Transporter 210 Cabinet	$110.50
Bose 802 speakers (pair) with covers NR	$405.12	212 EMPTY SLANT GUITAR SPEAKER	$110.00
JBL EON G2 PROFESSIONAL SPEAKER SYSTEM	$402.22	CAB ENCLOSURE CABINET NR	
NEW Fender Passport P-150 Sound System *NR*	$394.99	15 Bass Speaker Cabinet 300 Watt New 115 Speakers 1x15	$109.00
Klipsch Heresy speakers with stands	$380.00	JBL E140 Bass Guitar Speaker	$105.00
JBL EON G2 PROFESSIONAL SPEAKER SYSTEM	$380.00		
Fostex 6301B self powered Speakers (2)	$252.50		
NEW M-AUDIO BX5 BIAMPED PWRED SPEAKERS FREE USA SHIP	$239.99		

Pro Audio ▶ Multi-Track Recorders

The average sales price in this subcategory is $257.67.

	HIGH		AVG
Mackie HDR 24/96 24-tk HD Rec 2496 W/FREE MONITOR	$2,199.00	Fostex R8 R-8 Reel-to-Reel Recorder 1/4" 8ch - Loaded!	$299.00
HDR 24/96 Mackie	$1,925.00	Tascam DA-20 MKII Professional DAT Recorder	$299.00
Digidesign MX002 Pro Tools Digi 002 No Reserve Firewire	$1,660.00	ZOOM MRS-1044 DIGITAL STUDIO With USB	$299.00
DIGIDESIGN DIGI002 MULTI TRACK RECORDER DIGI 002 NR	$1,425.00	Zoom MRS-8 Digital 8 Track Recorder W/ Drum Machine	$282.00
Mackie HDR 2496 W 3 DIO Cards EXTRA Drive	$1,425.00	ZOOM Digital Multitrack With USB Card MRS-1044	$275.00
Boss BR1600 Multi Track Recorder BR-1600 Good Condition	$1,200.00	Teac A 6300 1/4" Reel to Reel Tape Recorder	$265.00
Otari MX5050 MKIII-8 1/2" 8track Recorder	$1,050.00	Teac X-7R Six Head Auto-Rev Reel to Reel *Warrantee*!	$255.00
Otari MTR-90 MK III	$1,025.00	Korg D12	$255.00
Tascam MX-2424 Digital Recorder 24 Tracks mx2424 NR	$999.00	ZOOM MRS-802B MRS802B MULTI TRACK RECORD CD BURNER	$255.00
Boss BR1600 Digital Recorder BR 1600	$980.43	Teac A-3300 sx vintage analog tape reel to reel	$250.01
Digi-002 Rack, Digi 002 Almost NEW with EVERTHING!!!!!!	$967.00	Boss BR-8 BR 8 BR8 Multi-Track Recording Studio	$250.00
BOSS BR1600 CD 16-TRack Recorder	$960.00	ZOOM MRS-8 MultiTrak Record. Studio w/128MB SD Card	$250.00
BOSS BR-1600 CD *EXCELLENT CONDITION*	$900.00	TEAC A-3340S 4 Channel, Reel-to-Reel Tape Deck	$247.50
TASCAM 2488 24-TRACK DIGITAL Recorder W/EXTRAS!!	$856.00	Korg D12 Digital Recording Studio w/CD-R/RW Drive	$247.50
BOSS BR1600 MULTITRACK RECORDER 4 MONTHS OLD	$835.00	BOSS BR-8 Digital Recording Studio - WITH BONUS!	$240.00

Pro Audio ▶ Power Amplifiers

The average sales price in this subcategory is $232.87.

	HIGH		AVG
QSC Powerlight 2.0 Amplifier NIB No Reserve	$1,500.00	NEW ART SLA-2 Studio Power Amp 560Watts in 1 Rack Space	$259.99
[2 of these sold in a multiple item ("Dutch") auction for $750.00 each]		Crest Audio Vs-1500 Professional Power Amplifier 800 Wa	$256.00
AVALON VT 737 SP TUBE MIC PREAMP w/COMPRESSOR & EQ NR!!	$1,425.00	Carver Cube M-400 t-mod Power Amplifier	$255.00
QSC RMX 2450 amplifier, Eminence 15" subs & PA speakers	$1,250.00	1400 Watt Mackie Power Amp FR Series M1400 *NO RESERVE*	$255.00
ROTEL RMB-1095 200WATTS x 5 THX POWER AMP	$1,200.00	Carver TFM-15CB Power Amp	$125.00
must sell to pay the rent Line6 HD147 and footswitch	$1,050.00	LINE 6 SPIDER II 112 75W GUITAR AMPLIFIER MONO AMP	$242.50
QSC MX3000a Power Amplifier 1200wrms/ch EXC	$850.00	QSC USA 1300 Rack Mount Power Amp	$242.50

QSC PLX 3402 power amp in excellent condition!	$839.00	Crate bass amplifier BFX100T bfx100 amp WOW!!	$232.51
QSC MX-3000A POWER AMPLIFIER	$821.00	MUSIC MAN 112 RD ONE HUNDRED GUITAR AMPLIFIER 100 AMP	$230.27
CREST AUDIO AMP CA-12 1200 W @4 OHM STEREO	$800.00	SoundTech S60 Portable PA System 6 Channels, 150 Watts	$227.50
QSC PLX 3402 Power Amplifier Excellent Low Reserve	$799.99	USED CREST AUDIO LA 1201 POWER AMP Amplifier like crown	$227.50
QSC EX 4000 POWER AMP	$750.00	QSC USA 900 Power Amp Amplifier Rackmount USA900 Stereo	$226.00
Leslie system 21 Rotary unit - Great for your Hammond	$705.00	QSC RMX850 RMX 850 RMX-850 Power Amplifier 6YR Warranty	$225.55
Crest Audio CA 12 Amplifier	$697.00	Crest Audio Vs900 Pro Power Amplifier VS Amp - NR!	$225.00
QSC PLX-3402 Used, But Nice	$650.00	MINT!!! MACKIE M1200 PROFESSIONAL POWER AMPLIFIER>>NR!	$218.10
MARSHALL AMP JCM 2000 AMP HEAD NO RESERVE! NOT FENDER	$649.99	crest audio power amp no reserve	$214.43

Pro Audio ▶ Rack Gear

The average sales price in this subcategory is $185.91.

	HIGH		AVG
Crane Song Ibis Equalizer - Mint Condition MSRP$4500	$3,210.99	Rane GE 60 Graphic Equalizer-NO RESERVE!!	$255.00
Audix 35102 Micpre EQ Pair. Based on Neve 33114 design	$1,800.00	RANE RA30 RA 30 RTA Real Time Analyzer w/Mic - LOOK!	$249.95
API 550 a Pair EQ's/ Not Neve/ Pultec/ Manley	$1,601.00	ORBAN Parametric Equalizer Model 622B No Reserve	$225.00
FOCUSRITE RED 2 Dual Parametric equalizer EQ MINT !!!	$1,501.00	ASHLY GQX1502 GQX-1502 STEREO 15 BAND GRAPHIC EQ	$224.95
DRAWMER 1960 Tube Mic Pre Preamp Compressor MINT!	$1,400.00	Behringer DEQ2496 Ultracurve Pro Processor EQ/RTA	$209.75
[2 of these sold for $1,400.00 each]		Behringer DEQ-2496 Ultracurve Pro (Equalizer, EQ)	$206.25
Focusrite Red Dual Channel EQ	$1,376.00	APHEX 10/4 INTERFACE MODEL	$202.50
Avalon VT-737SP Tube Mic / Instrument Preamp No reserve	$1,350.00	124A 600 OHM TERMINATE	
Drawmer 1961 Vacuum Tube Equalizer, Avalon, Focusrite	$1,325.00	SCV RE209 PRO-EQUALIZER	$202.50
(4) White Instruments 4828 and (1) 4856 Equalizers	$1,225.00	2 Rane PE 15 Parametric Equalizers EQ Sold together	$200.00
KLARK TEKNIK / EVI PRO AUDIO GROUP DN370	$1,215.00	Yamaha YDG-2030 Digital EQ	$200.00
ASHLY PROTEA DIGITAL GRAPHIC EQUALIZER	$1,050.00	Alesis DEQ230D 2-Ch Digital Graphic EQ 1/3 Octave EQ	$199.00
pair Davisound TB-4 Equalizer (not API, Pultec, Neve)	$826.00	UREI 565 Big Dipper filter set	$195.00
2 Electro-Voice EV DX38 SPEAKER PROCESOR Electro Voice	$805.00	Yamaha Q1027 Professional EQ	$195.00
BSS FCS-926 varicurve NO RESERVE	$750.00	One Yamaha Q1027 Professional EQ	$195.00
Kt DN 3600 Graphic EQ NO RESERVE	$750.00	DBX IEQ15 dual channel 15 band rackmount EQ/Limiter NR	$189.00

Sheet Music, Song Books ▶ Sheet Music

The average sales price in this subcategory is $10.30.

	HIGH		AVG
FINALE ALLEGRO 2005 - MUSIC NOTATION SOFTWARE - NEW	$146.00	1958 Moonlight In Harpswell Maine ME Music/Flora Graves	$12.26
350+ Lot Pieces of Sheet Music & Songbooks.	$130.47	Sheet Music, Songs for Praise & Worship	$11.59
Huge Lot 180+ Vintage Sheet Music & Books 30Lbs Wartime	$75.01	BIG BAND ARRANGEMENT...BAD, BAD LEROY BROWN	$11.49
Bob Zurke EYE OPENER piano solo 1939	$56.66	JAZZ MUSIC-JAMEY AEBERSOLD PLAY-ALONG V. 50	$11.05
HOLTON'S pocket edition BAND INSTRUMENT Catalog	$35.00	JAZZ MUSIC-JAMEY AEBERSOLD PLAY-ALONG V. 54	$11.05
Richard Rodgers "VICTORY AT SEA" piano solo 21 pgs	$32.19	Lot of 3 music magazines from the 1940's	$11.01
Rube Bloom NIGHTINGALE'S DREAM piano solo	$32.11	huge sheet music lot 20s 30s 40s 50s Will Rogers	$11.00
LARGE LOT (50) VINTAGE SHEET MUSIC EXCELLENT CONDITION!	$29.59	GIBSON SYSTEM FOR GUITAR PLUS SHEET MUSIC	$10.50
Lot of Vintage Sheet Music 21 Pieces No Reserve	$26.99	BIG BAND ARRANGEMENT...MAMBO #5 with vocal	$10.50
Cy Walter arr. PENTHOUSE SERENADE piano solo	$24.82	Sharpshooters March Sheet Music Accordion 1919	$10.00
Rube Bloom FIFTH AVENUE BUS piano solo	$24.50	1004 FOLK SONGS, 1700-1899~History,Sheet Music,Rags,War	$9.99
Rube Bloom AUNT JEMIMA'S BIRTHDAY novelty piano solo	$23.93	Iron Maiden Song Book includes Music notes and Lyrics	$9.99
(6) EASY PLAY SPEED EZ TODAY MUSIC BOOKS ORGAN PIANO GU	$23.50	HUGE LOT OF 100+ PCS OF SHEET MUSIC	$9.99
Lot of 4 music magazines from 1937 to 1939	$23.20	BIG BAND ARRANGEMENT..LADY MARMALADE with vocal	$9.99
Aces High Fighter Plane WWI sheet music	$22.50	BIG LOT ANTIQUE SHEET MUSIC 1930's +	$9.99

Sheet Music, Song Books ▶ Song Books

The average sales price in this subcategory is $9.92.

	HIGH		AVG
Psalmody In Miniature 3 Books-Williams-1778.	$118.00	SONGBOOK Bluegrass Gospel Music Favorites Songbook	$10.50
Jamey Aebersold 7 Volume Set Books/CDs	$94.95	HOPKINS COLLEGE SONGBOOK FROM COTILLON CLUB 1926	$9.99
Jamey Aebersold 7 Volume Set Books/CDs	$88.50	THE BIG TEN COLLEGE SONG BOOK FOR SMALL COMBOS C BOOK	$9.99
1937 Purchaser's Guide to Music Industry Trade Catalog	$88.00	THE BIG TEN COLLEGE SONG BOOK FOR SMALL COMBOS Eb BOOK	$9.99
Vocal Score to Cherubin	$56.55	SONGBOOK Old-Time Bluegrass Gospel Songbook	$9.99
W.A.S.P. wasp JAPAN RareGuitarScore w/TAB	$39.99	VINTAGE 1937 GEORGE GERSHWIN SONG ALBUM BOOK	$9.99
ULTIMATE FAKE BOOK C 3RD LATEST EDITION 1200 SONGS NR	$31.00	Collection of Hammond Organ Co sheet music books & misc	$9.99
Lot 14 Accordion Song Books & Sheet Music	$31.00	ORGAN Music - Sacred & Wedding Music ed. Roland Diggle	$9.51
Ultimate Fake Book Music Songbook Piano Vocal Guitar Nu	$29.00	Percussion Methods Books BONA, Timpani, Stick control	$9.50
65 + Organ Song Books/Sheet Music	$28.87	ORGAN Music - Hymn Int & Accompaniments Benjamin Harlan	$9.26
Organ Music Books, 65 Different , Popular Hits, More	$28.00	Dennis Chambers DRUMS Percussion Music Book / CD New	$9.00
Edition Peters J.S. Bach Organ Works 9 Vol. Complete	$26.01	Song Book Collection of Traditional Christian Music	$9.00
Best Fake Book Ever Music Songbook Piano Vocal Guitar	$24.50	* SONGBOOK~RISE UP SINGING~1200 SONGS~FOLK & MORE~NEW	$8.88
ORGAN Music - Lerner & Loewe Collection - Ashley Miller	$21.71	1970 Gospel HYMNS Sheet Music Book Instruments in C	$8.55
1869 Bk - School for Parlor Organ / Melodeon - Getze	$21.52	2 Stevie Wonder Songbooks 1976 Song Books Guitar Piano	$8.51

String ▶ Bass

The average sales price in this subcategory is $317.15.

	HIGH		AVG
NS Design US5 EUB Electric Upright Bass, Steinberger	$3,250.00	Dean Pace Bass - Electric Upright w/ Case - Met. Red	$455.00
Walter Woods Elecracoustic Ultra High Power Bass Amp!	$2,700.00	Palatino Electric Upright Bass VE-500 new in box	$450.00
American Standard Upright Bass H N White Cleveland	$2,633.99	New German Style Upright 3/4 Size Bass~Black~BTS Sale!!	$407.75
messenger electric upright bass eub e.u.b. barbera bts	$2,000.00	New Upright Bass~3/4 Size~5 Yr Wrty~BTS Sale!!	$349.99
Eminence Electric Upright Bass Portable	$1,660.00	YOU KEEP THE PROFITS! NEW 1/2 "LAMINATED" DOUBLE BASS!	$315.00

	HIGH		AVG
King SLAP KING Upright Bass Doghouse Stray Cats	$1,599.00	New German Style Upright 3/4 Size Bass~Black~BTS Sale!!	$310.00
ideal 3/4 bass - fabulous tone, no cracks, German?	$1,526.00	New Upright Bass~White~3/4 Size~NR~BTS Sale!!!	$307.00
Kay 3/4 Bass Violin 1950 Vintage Model C-1 #24107 Case	$1,525.00	Fender Jazz made in japan "No Reserve"	$300.00
Bulgarian Fully Carved 3/4 size Upright Bass New Setup	$1,525.00	Ariana Bass Guitar and Crate BX - 50 Bass Amp Combo	$300.00
Vintage KAY Bass Violin M1W w/ Bow & Case	$1,342.73	Lidl Upright Bass Size 3/4" From Luby Czech. # 5/35	$280.00
ampeg baby bass vintage electric upright	$1,200.00	KARL REISER BASS IN GREAT CONDITION	$280.00
Vintage Kay M-1 Blonde String Bass upright *No Reserve*	$1,080.00	Ibanez ATK 300 Bass	$275.00
MEISEL 8000 E FUSION ** ACOUSTIC-ELECTRIC BASS **	$869.99	2004 Ibanez Artcore Hollowbody Bass guitar	$275.00
MODULUS GVJ4F FRETLESS VINTAGE JAZZ BASS	$840.00	Double Bass CASE Upright Bass BAG gig bag BASS VIOLIN	$269.00
Fretless Yamaha TRB-5P	$800.00	a good antique french bass violin bow LAMY	$260.00

String ▶ Banjo

The average sales price in this subcategory is $216.47.

	HIGH		AVG
GIBSON Earl Scruggs Mastertone Banjo 1985 LIKE NEW!!	$4,000.00	Very Nice, Alvarez 5 String Banjo, w Soft Case, Clean!	$256.50
Concert Tone Fender Banjo	$3,556.96	Fender Banjo, brand-new condition!	$249.50
1981 Gold Star J.D. Crowe Banjo (Not Gibson)	$3,000.00	antique vintage 1904 banjo mabye fairbanks?	$242.50
Liberty Promenade Banjo, 1979, Custom, Like New	$2,794.00	FRAMUS (Germany) Long Scale 5 String Banjo & Case	$233.00
1920's Epiphone Recording Banjo w/Dragon No Res!!!	$2,700.00	SIX 6 STRING GUITAR BANJO TMG-60 NEW $0 SHIPPING L@@K	$229.95
NEW w/warranty Gibson RB-3 Wreath Banjo Mastertone	$2,585.00	Orpheum # 1 Banjo Bird's Eye Maple As-is	$220.01
New Open-Back Clawhammer Banjo by Bob Flesher	$2,325.00	NEW Oscar Schmidt OB5 5 String Banjo 30 Bracket w/ wty	$219.00
Gibson Mastertone Banjo RB-75 RB75 J.D. Crowe	$2,150.00	IMMACULATE WASHBURN B-10 BANJO & HARD CASE	$212.50
Vega long neck (Seeger-style) 5 string banjo	$1,940.00	Gold Tone MC150 W/TKL Case, Schaller Tuners, No Reserve	$208.26
A.C.Fairbanks original "WhyteLadyie"Banjo 1909	$1,500.00	TN 20 Tone Ring (fits Gibson banjo '89 to present)	$200.00
Bacon & Day Montana Silver Bell #1 Banjo Mandolin	$1,450.00	McPeake Tone Ring (fits Gibson banjo '89 to present)	$200.00
1986 Gold Star 5 String Banjo GF-100FE (Gibson Copy) NR	$1,349.00	QUALITY 5 String Deluxe Banjo New Banjos 24 Bracket	$199.00
1955 Fender Concert Tone Banjo 4-string	$1,201.52	VINTAGE REGAL 5-STRING BANJO W/CASE BEAUTY	$190.50
Gibson RB-250 - Late 1960's w/original hard shell case	$1,120.00	BRAND NEW 5 STRING BANJO(RESONATOR)FREE SHIPPING!+	$189.95
1928 TB-2 Gibson Pre War Tenor Banjo NR!	$1,100.00	[2 of these sold for $189.95 each]	
		5 STRING MAHOGONY BANJO USA REMO HEAD w HARD SHELL CASE	$188.88

String ▶ Cello

The average sales price in this subcategory is $223.84.

	HIGH		AVG
old Italian cello DAVID TECCHLER Rome 1709	$7,877.00	New FLAMED Ebony Fitted 3/4 Cello+2 Sets Strings+Stand	$249.98
Beautiful old Juzek Masterart cello (4/4) w/stamped bow	$1,790.00	New FLAMED Ebony Fitted 4/4 Cello+2 Sets Strings+Stand	$239.98
Cello Rudolf Doetsch, Bow, and Case	$1,425.00	Cello Fiberglass Hard case, Black, professional New	$239.00
full size cello -magnificent tone, no cracks, Italian?	$1,025.00	Cello Fiberglass Hard case, White 2005 New	$235.00
Yamaha Silent Cello SVC-100 Mint Condition + Extras	$910.00	[3 of these sold for $235.00 each]	
1981 4/4 John Juzec Cello	$900.00	old fine cello bow " M. Laberte "	$224.50
POULLOT cello bow, award winning French bow Artisans	$800.00	'Cello Bow stamped H.R.Pfretzschner	$217.50
Scherl & Roth Cello - Full Size - Mint Condition	$650.00	New HANDMADE Solid Wood 4/4 Cello+2 Sets Strings+Stand	$209.98
Beautiful Flamed 4/4 Cello/Sturdy Fiberglass Case (#32)	$599.99	New 4/4 Adult Size EBONY HIGHLY	$209.00
Cellos GERMAN MADE CELLO w Bow Case New NICE !	$549.99	FLAMED Solid Wood CELLO	
PROFESSIONALLY EXAMINED 4/4 CELLO AT INCREDIBLE PRICE	$500.00	[2 of these sold for $209.00 each]	
Professional Cello - Full Size - Handmade - Cornerless	$493.18	New HANDMADE Solid Wood 4/4 Cello+2 Sets Strings+Stand	$199.98
Vintage 4/4 cello by Podesva 1937	$464.00	New 3/4 Size EBONY HIGHLY FLAMED Solid Wood CELLO	$199.00
Cello bow stamped W.E. Hill & Sons	$430.00	[2 of these sold for $199.00 each]	
Cello bow stamped Albert Nurnberger	$374.00	New Solid Wood 4/4 Student Cello+2 Sets Strings+2 Cases	$189.98

String ▶ Harp, Dulcimer

The average sales price in this subcategory is $189.94.

	HIGH		AVG
Pedal Harp, Professional, 48 strings. Full size.	$9,500.00	NEW DEURA LEVERS HARPS 22 STRINGS	$250.00
Wurlitzer 940 gold leaf harp antique Starke 46 string	$7,375.00	36"CELTIC IRISH HARP	
Harp, Lyon & Healy Troubadour V	$3,400.00	Celtic Folk Harp and how to play	$233.01
Gently used Swanson Lever Harp No Reserve!	$2,034.00	Mountain Appalachian Dulcimer Hand Made by Tom Yocky	$230.00
Lyon & Healy 33 String Troubadour 2000C Lever Harp 6/70	$1,132.00	Dusty Strings Hammer Dulcimer from Seattle with stand	$227.51
Hudson Hammered Dulcimer Treble Bass Stand Case Extras	$650.00	72 STRING PERSIAN HAMMERED DULCIMER SANTOOR NEW	$212.95
HOMER LEDFORD DULCIMER	$599.95	Classic Celtic Rosewood Folk Harp Hand Carved NICE! LR!	$207.50
Dusty Strings Hand Made D35 D-35 Hammered Dulcimer	$530.00	Rare Vintage Radio-Harp Hammered Dulcimer $1 No Res!	$202.50
BRAND NEW PRO HANDCARVED	$500.00	APPALACHIAN DULCIMER	$202.50
PARAGUAYAN HARP 57" NOT GUITAR		Mountain Dulcimer	$200.00
Four String Mountain Dulcimer	$480.00	New Cherry Mountain Dulcimer	$182.50
Hammered Dulcimer with Case	$465.00	36" INCH HEATHER HARP - AMAZING!! CELTIC ROSEWOOD	$179.00
NEW HARP - 56 tall Pillar - 37 strings - NO RESERVE!	$399.00	Mountain Dulcimer Traditional Hourglass Shape	$177.50
DULCIMER HAND MADE FOLK INSTRUMENT W CASE NEVER PLAYED	$394.11	Maple / Walnut Mountain Dulcimer	$177.50
Beautiful Fahrendorff Handmade Hammer Dulcimer & Case!!	$349.99	Ben Seymour Galax-Style Dulcimer - Walnut	$175.00
George Orthey 4 string Lap Dulcimer USA #1469 9/1978	$345.00	Electric Autoharp Oscar Schmidt Classic Mod.-OS-21CE	$175.00

String ▶ Violin

The average sales price in this subcategory is $59.36.

	HIGH		AVG
Pardessus de viole, descant viol da gamba, quinton NR	$1,625.00	Vintage Conservatory Violin Germany Wood Case	$78.00
ANTIQUE GERMAN VIOLIN	$355.00	Pernambuco VIOLIN BOW w. whalebone lapping!!!	$75.00
VINTAGE VIOLIN-MUNCZI LAJOS	$299.99	Violin / Fiddle w/ Case	$69.00
NICE OLD VIOLIN FOR RESTORATION	$282.96	82% OFF NEW 4/4 VIOLIN VIOLINS FIDDLE -JUST 4 - REISEND	$65.00

	HIGH		
ANTIQUE ANTONIUS STRADIUARIUS VIOLIN Faciebat Anno 1736	$255.00	E.R. Pfretzschner Viola W/ Case	$62.01
Antique 19th Century Violin with Case and Bow Very Old	$203.74	BEWARE OF CHEAP VIOLINS NEW 4/4 FULL GEIGEN VIOLIN	$59.95
Rare paganini ? violin case bow antique vintage NR	$164.49	82% OFF NEW 4/4 FULL VIOLIN FIDDLE GERMAN JUST 4 -ADLER	$59.95
VINTAGE MINI 1/8 SUZUKI VIOLIN NAGOYA 1977 w/ BOW CASE	$121.51	3/4 VIOLIN SET VIOLINS EBONY TEACHER APPROVED ITALIAN	$59.95
NICE OLD VIOLIN AMATI MODEL	$102.50	BEWARE OF VIOLINS YOU BUY NEW 4/4 REINHART VIOLIN	$59.95
Antonius Straduarius Artisto Model Violin	$100.00	LADIES VIOLIN - E MARTIN SACHSEN GERMANY	$55.68

Woodwind ▶ Bagpipes

The average sales price in this subcategory is $99.47.

	HIGH		AVG
Gibson bagpipes (1set)	$850.00	New Full Size bagpipes, bagpipe practice chanter & book	$120.00
~ Vintage Bagpipe ~ Hardie Wooden Bagpipes	$811.00	[2 of these sold for $120.00 each]	
VINTAGE LAWRIE BAGPIPES	$750.00	Scottish Bagpipes Bag Pipes	$112.50
Bagpipes, Dunbar Imitation Blackwood, Im. Ivory Mount	$661.02	NEW IMPORTED FULL SIZE NATURAL ROSEWOOD BAGPIPES	$109.00
Full Size Scottish Bagpipes Black New	$660.00	NEW highland bagpipes and instructional book	$107.51
Uilleann Bagpipe Practice Set - Tony Hebdon - Ebony	$635.00	nice set of Bagpipes with case , no reserve	$102.50
David Naill DN2 Used	$537.50	PARLOR PIPES ! Bagpipes synthetic bag bagpipe	$102.00
Dunbar Bagpipes - Polypenco, Fully combed	$531.00	brian boru chanter for bagpipes	$100.00
Bagpipes 3-Drone John Walsh Shuttle Pipes	$500.00	Rosewood Bagpipes with Plastic Mounts and Carry Case	$99.00
SOUNDSTREAM BLACKWOOD Parlor Bagpipes	$360.00	Rosewood Bagpipes with Plastic Mounts and Carry Case	$99.00
Spanish Gaita in C - Bagpipe Bagpipes - NEW	$325.00	Highland Rosewood Bagpipes Fullsize	$95.00
Italian Bagpipes and Flute - Handmade in Italy	$307.50	Great Highland Bagpipes Like New Tartan Plaid	$91.00
rsdg dragoon guards pipe-major crossbelt kilt bagpipe	$300.00	Shepard Long Practise Chanter African Blackwood	$91.00
		Strathmore Poly Chanter	$85.00
		Bagpipes	$80.00
		NEW Fullsize Rosewood Bagpipe Royal Stewart Tartan NEW	$79.95
		[3 of these sold for $79.95 each]	

Woodwind ▶ Bassoon, Oboe

The average sales price in this subcategory is $219.87.

	HIGH		AVG
Schreiber Bassooon with Reed Tools	$2,300.00	Bundy / Selmer OBOE *VERY-NICE* w/case -NR!	$200.00
Loree Oboe: Professional Full Conservatory Model	$2,050.00	Bundy Oboe Selmer Student Resonite With Hard Case	$200.00
BRAND NEW FOX OBOE MODEL 300	$1,986.00	Linton Oboe - Student Model	$197.50
FOX OBOE MODEL 300 EXCELLENT CONDITION!!!	$1,899.00	OBOE Selmer Bundy Student Model with Case	$197.50
Renard "ARTIST" Oboe like new n.r.	$1,701.00	BUNDY SELMER CO. STUDENT OBOE # B29441 W/ CASE!! NICE!	$197.50
Fox Renard Artist Model 330 Oboe Musical Instrument	$1,557.00	HENRI SELMER PARIS OBOE	$187.50
Oboe - Fox Renard Artist Model 330	$1,525.00	Linton Student Oboe with Hard Case	$182.28
SELMER Rosewood ENGLISH HORN	$1,400.00	Guy Humphrey(Paris) "Superieur" Wood Oboe & Case	$152.50
FOX MODEL 333 RENARD PROTEGE OBOE	$1,325.00	La Margue Wood Oboe Paris France N/R	$133.50
BASSOON Conn Heckel clone #8R-1224	$1,276.00	English horn bell richly colored Grenadilla wood	$129.26
Brand New Reiger Bassoon Reed Tip Profiler	$1,175.40	Vintage Lesher Oboe in good condition	$127.53
NEW Fox Renard 333 Oboe! Great for a Beginning Student!	$1,100.00	P. Gerard (Paris) Oboe	$125.00
Fox Renard oboe - ready to play!	$999.99	A. Barre Oboe	$125.00
Buffet 4052 Grenadilla Wooden Oboe	$900.00	F. Loree English Horn Case	$122.50
Fox Renard Oboe	$886.00	Armstrong Oboe	$118.50

Woodwind ▶ Clarinet

The average sales price in this subcategory is $93.88.

	HIGH		AVG
Selmer Paris Bass Clarinet Range to Low Eb EXCELLENT!	$2,000.00	Vintage Bundy Selmer Alto Clarinet with Case	$104.37
professional " Leblanc " Paris, Wood Bass Clarinet	$1,435.00	DELUXE YAMAHA CLARINET IN NICE CASE NO RESERVE!	$102.50
BRAND NEW Vito 7166 Bass Clarinet	$969.99	JUPITER CLARINET SCL-631	$100.00
G-pitch Albert system clarinet	$822.00	Vintage Noblet Paris Wooden Clarinet	$100.00
VITO 7166 RESO-TONE USA Bass Clarinet	$799.99	Buescher Alto Clarinet	$100.00
LEBLANC CONCERTO IN A KEY PROFESSIONAL FRENCH CLARINET	$750.30	CLARINET,SELMER,USA.	$100.00
LEBLANC PARIS BASS CLARINET - VERY NICE	$660.00	85% OFF NEW PURPLE SCHILL Bb CLARINET #12142	$99.95
BUNDY SELMER BASS CLARINET IN CASE	$580.00	85% OFF NEW YELLOW SCHILL CLARINET Bb SCHOOL CLARINETS	$99.95
Selmer Series 9 Clarinet in A w/Dbl Case & Extras GC NR	$511.05	Bundy Student Clarinet (school band) w/hard case	$96.00
Yamaha YCL-34 Wood clarinet, Very Nice!	$395.00	Yamaha Clarinet & Hard Carrying Case with Mouthpiece	$93.50
HN H N White sterling Silver King Metal Clarinet horn	$370.00	Jupiter Clarinet	$93.00
Vito Reso-Tone Bass Clarinet 4740D	$363.77	VINTAGE WOOD EVETTE BUFFET Horn CLARINET PARIS #20721	$92.00
Leblanc Vito Resonite Alto Clarinet...	$285.00	Cundy Bettoney ONE PIECE ALL SILVER Clarinet Very Nice	$91.00
Selmer Clarinet 1400 Brand New!!!!!!!	$279.99	Bundy Resonite Selmer Clarinet W/Case No Reserve!	$91.00
Vito 7214 Bb Clarinet STILL IN THE FACTORY BOX!	$275.00	CLARINET Selmer 1400 w/ hard case	$90.99

Woodwind ▶ Flute

The average sales price in this subcategory is $121.93.

	HIGH		AVG
ALTUS FLUTE 1107 SRBE BRAND NEW / Split E & Low B	$2,999.00	FLUTE-BRAND NEW SILVER 18 OPEN HOLE FLUTE-B-FOOT-MINT	$195.99
Wm S Haynes Sterling Flute Mint Condition " 1957 "	$1,800.00	Antique 11-Key Wooden Flute Needs Work	$190.07
Historc E. Ritteshausen antique wood flute #2372 - LRI	$1,200.00	2006 Model Merano Bb Clarinet w/ Case+YAMAHA Care Kit!	$139.95
Grenadilla-Purpleheart Wood Flute Headjoint Head Joint	$1,200.00	[2 of these sold for $139.95 each]	
Antique Silver Flute W R Meinell w case - Boehm system	$1,009.95	GREAT DEAL!!! Gemeinhardt Flute with case and stand!!!	$130.50
NEW SILVER ALTO FLUTE , NO RESERVE, KEY OF G	$642.57	YAMAHA FLUTE YFL225 /YFL225N YFL 225 NICKEL PLATED	$127.50
YAMAHA YFL 361 925-Silver Flute in Case	$642.00	Vintage Pro Artley Flute , 4-0 , Silver	$122.50
G.H. Huller flute	$561.01	FLUTES-NEW 2005 MD. FIRST CHAIR SILVER BAND FLUTE-MINT	$119.99

GEMEINHARDT 3SB SOLID SILVER FLUTE NICE!!!!!!!!!!	$507.00	FLUTE-BRAND NEW BAND INSTRUMENT-SILVER BAND FLUTES-MINT	$119.99
Baroque Flute by Moeck - Low Pitch	$450.00	4 LEFT - NEW SCHOOL 18 KEY OPEN HOLE FLUTE C KEY #2780	$119.95
Flute Head Joint in Grenadilla, metal lined	$410.00	85% OFF NEW SCHOOL 18 KEY OPEN HOLE FLUTE C KEY #12780	$119.95
Selmer Omega Flute (PROFESSIONAL FLUTE) NO RESERVE!!!	$400.00	Unique C FLUTE - ROSE BRASS plated - Brand New	$119.37
YAMAHA YFL-285SII OPEN HOLE FLUTE! CLEAN!!! 281 285	$331.51	FLUTES-BRAND NEW SILVER BAND FLUTE-BANKRUPTCY-2006-MINT	$115.50
EARLY VINTAGE ROSEWOOD & SILVER FLUTE + CASE	$330.00	FLUTES-BRAND NEW SILVER BAND FLUTE-BANKRUPTCY-2006-MINT	$110.65
Gemeinhardt Solid Silver Piccolo	$300.52	FLUTE-BRAND NEW BAND INSTRUMENT-SILVER BAND FLUTES-MINT	$109.99

Woodwind ▶ Piccolo

The average sales price in this subcategory is $152.79.

	HIGH		AVG
Burkart Phelan Piccolo	$2,225.00	NEW CLASSIC 24K GOLD & BLACK PICCOLO & YAMAHA CARE KIT	$175.95
Zentner Piccolo Flute with Carrying Case, Cleaning Rod	$998.00	PICCOLO - VERY NICE	$175.85
Gemeinhardt 4W Wood Piccolo FACTORY BOX	$774.99	Gemeinhardt silver-plated piccolo	$169.53
Gemeinhardt 4W Wood Piccolo FACTORY BOX	$774.99	VINTAGE 1934 CONN STERLING PICCOLO MODEL 34P Db CLOSE G	$165.50
YAMAHA Piccolo YPC-62 Like NEW No Reserve	$760.00	2 Antique Unmarked Woodwind Piccolo Instruments	$156.28
YPC-32 Yamaha Piccolo (BRAND NEW) YPC32	$597.00	Gemeinhardt 4SP Piccolo	$155.73
Gemeinhardt 4S Solid Silver Piccolo FACTORY BOX	$499.99	GEMEINHARDT PICCOLO (4pmh)	$152.55
GEMEINHARDT KGB SPECIAL PICCOLO WITH GOLD LIP PLATE	$432.00	Gemeinhardt Model 4P Piccolo	$152.50
Gemeinhardt 4PSH Plastic w/ Silver Piccolo FACTORY BOX	$424.99	Piccolo, GREAT condition. Hardly used.	$152.50
Gemeinhardt 4PSH Plastic w/ Silver Piccolo FACTORY BOX	$399.99	Gemeinhardt Plastic Piccolo, w/hard case and rod NR	$151.50
H Bettoney US Military Issue Db Sterling Silver Piccolo	$380.00	NEW PICCOLO-BANKRUPTCY-2006 SILVER BAND PICCOLOS-MINT	$150.00
Gemeinhardt 4P Plastic Piccolo FACTORY BOX	$369.99	YAMAHA YPC-31 PICCOLO PLASTIC GOOD MARCHING HORN!	$150.00
BRAND NEW Armstrong 204 Piccolo!	$369.99	NEW CLASSIC SILVER and BLACK PICCOLO & YAMAHA CARE KIT	$149.95
Gemeinhardt 4S SOLID SILVER Piccolo MINT ready 2 PLAY	$365.00	l@@k! Gemeinhardt 4PSH Plastic w/ Silver Piccolo	$143.50
Gemeinhardt 4P Plastic Piccolo FACTORY BOX	$365.00	Gemeinhardt Piccolo USED	$140.00

Woodwind ▶ Recorder

The average sales price in this subcategory is $27.73.

	HIGH		AVG
YAMAHA YBS-61 F-BASS RECORDER RENAISSANCE STYLE	$510.00	Aulos Japan 3 Piece Tenor or Bass Recorder	$36.00
Woodwind Woodwind Low A Baritone Saxophone Bari Sax	$355.00	Yamaha Alto Recorder Simulated Ebony New	$35.35
Bass Recorder, Roessler Meisterbass in pearwood	$227.50	Yamaha Alto Recorder Simulated Ebony New	$35.35
Hohner Konzert Wooden Bass Recorder!!!	$222.50	Rare Wood Bamboo Shakuhachi Flutes	$35.00
Unique Set of 4 Fine Vintage German Wooden Recorders NR	$218.47	Sonata Alto German Recorder with Soft Case	$34.97
Yamaha Bass Baroque Recorder YRB302B - Brand New!	$190.00	New Age Flute like horn w/carry bag sound clip Titanic	$33.00
Kung Recorder!	$177.50	VINTAGE WEISS SUPERIOR WOOD RECORDER ALTO FLUTE W/ CASE	$31.00
Moeck Sopranino Recorder - Rosewood	$159.50	Johannes Adler Professional Recorder w Original Box	$30.95
2 MUSICAL RECORDERS ALTO & TENOR BASS GERMANY BAROQUE	$157.50	Hohner 9532 pearwood C soprano baroque recorder	$29.00
Johannes Adler Tenor Recorder - Beautiful!!!	$134.00	Recorder Books-Duets-Great Cond–NO RSV!	$27.13
Yamaha Bass Recorder Flute / plastic / 36 inch - great	$132.50	Jupiter 869SG Artist Alto Saxophone Alto Sax	$27.00
Antique Wood Keyed Recorder Neat	$132.50	SCHREIBER Recorder Made in Germany Like New RARE	$26.99
Alpine C Tenor Recorder - Made in West Germany	$99.00	Yamaha Soprano Recorder Simulated Rosewood New	$26.26
Frederick Bass RecorderSuperior Tuning-Black Satin-New	$97.00	[2 of these sold for $26.26 each]	
Nice Older England Made Alto Schott's C Recorder NoR#24	$93.99	15 NEW Yamaha Soprano Recorders (Baroque) model YRS-24B	$26.00
		Hohner Studio German Germany Wood Recorder Nice	$24.95

Woodwind ▶ Saxophone

The average sales price in this subcategory is $201.53.

	HIGH		AVG
SILVER 1913 BUESCHER SOPRANO SAX NO RESERVE!!	$1,976.00	VINTAGE C.G. CONN SILVER SAXOPHONE..*.PATD.DATE 1914*	$228.50
SAXOPHONE SELMER (PARIS) SUPER ACTION 80 SERIES II	$1,475.00	Vintage Saxaphone Pan American Elkhart Indiana	$224.50
Yamaha YSS 62 Rare Professional Model Sax	$1,325.00	New 2005 "Sky" Soprano Sax w high F# key saxophone NR!	$219.99
Yamaha Soprano Saxophone, Sax, YSS-675, part#002913	$1,300.00	90% OFF NEW "Cecilio" Gold Soprano Saxophone/Sax~SALE!!	$209.98
Vintage Buescher Saxophone with Case & Extras	$1,071.00	[4 of these sold for $209.98 each]	
YAMAHA YSS-475 Soprano Saxophone w/ C* Mouthpiece	$975.00	MEYER ALTO SAXOPHONE MOUTHPIECE	$205.50
C G CONN SAXOPHONE...OLD W/ MARTIN CASE...	$819.21	85% OFF! GOLD NEW CURVED SOPRANO SAXOPHONE #1128	$202.45
Jupiter 893SG Artist Series Baritone Saxophone Baritone	$760.00	Vintage Gold Plated Holton C Melody Sax - SN 18643	$200.00
YAMAHA YSS-475 Soprano Saxophone with Hard Case	$723.99	90% OFF NEW "Cecilio" Gold Soprano Saxophone/Sax~SALE!!	$199.98
Antique Conn tenor Ltd Saxophone Saxaphone Sax	$565.00	NICE OLD 1914 CONN C. MELODY AEGERTER SAXOPHONE	$185.00
VINTAGE LYON & HEALY LOW PITCH TENOR SAXOPHONE	$560.00	1940's Martin C-Melody low pitch	$172.50
SOPRANINO!!–Saxophone.com Eb Sopranino Saxophone	$559.00	NICE The Buescher C Melody Silver Saxophone N/R	$165.00
Beautiful Selmer New York C-Melody - Excellent Cond!	$500.00	BUNDY II 033047 Saxophone w/ Case	$162.50
1921 C.G. CONN NEW WONDER I C	$455.00	VINTAGE CONN SAXOPHONE(ATTIC FIND,NICE)	$160.50
MELODY SAXOPHONE EXC COND		Buescher True Tone C Melody Saxophone	$158.50
Vintage King Sax Saxophone with Case C Melody 1940s	$455.00	EVETTE BUFFET CRAMPON SAXOPHONE WITH CASE	$157.50

25

POTTERY & GLASS

The Pottery & Glass category on eBay is home to some very passionate collectors. Although the items in this category may have some overlap with other eBay categories, such as Home & Garden and Antiques, there are enough niches within Pottery & Glass, and devotees of each, that they warranted a separate category of their own.

In fact, the denizens of this category are sensitive enough that when eBay changed around the subcategories within it, they cried foul. "That week, I probably got a total of 3,000 or 4,000 e-mails from pottery and glass sellers saying, 'My business is down. You've done the wrong thing.' We fixed it. We rolled back the changes," said eBay CEO Meg Whitman in an August 5, 2004 interview with *The Wall Street Journal.*

Because collectors usually know their stuff so well, it pays to be well informed about the items you are buying or selling. If you sell only one kind of thing, such as Roseville pottery or Depression glass, you'll get to know what features are most desirable and valuable for your buyers. But if you are doing a one-time sale of, say, Aunt Ethel's vintage Wedgwood china, it would be a good idea to check websites and books to get an idea of the piece's age and what the identifying marks, if any, mean. Be sure to include clear photos of any signatures, dates, maker's marks, and the like, in your listing.

Many wonderful resources for identifying pottery, glass, and china have been assembled online by people who specialize in certain lines, and these can help you figure out what you have. For example, one avid collector of Riverside Glass glass has compiled photos and information about different pieces, and there is a detailed discussion on Croesus (a pattern made by Riverside from 1897 to 1919) reproductions at www.eapglass.com/croesus.htm.

Changes in Popularity over Time

While there may be some brands and patterns that have continuous popularity, there are subtle shifts and changes in the demand for different types of pottery and glass over time. For example, a list of the top "hot" subcategories in Pottery & Glass from August 2004 to August 2005, according to an About.com's Collectibles column at http://collectibles.about.com/od/ebaymonthlytoptens/a/EBpottery0805.htm, includes Arabia, Beswick, Hummel, Goebel, Herend, Bauer, and Belleek. But whereas Beswick was listed second in August 2004, it was first in August 2005. LuRay made the list in August 2004, but was not on it in August 2005.

The number of listings can change over time, as well. From March 26, 2002 to November 13, 2002, for example, the number of McCoy pottery auction listings went from 14,348 to 16,202, according to statistics on AuctionBytes.com gathered by the HammerTap DeepAnalysis tool. These changes can affect prices, too. Looking at those two months, the earlier date (which had fewer listings) had a higher sell-through rate (percentage of items that sold) than the later date (which had more listings). This roughly follows the law of supply and demand, although there are always exceptions.

Some of the highest prices in this sample are found in the Pottery & Glass ▸ Glass ▸ Art Glass ▸ North American subcategory and are designed by Dale Chihuly. Chihuly is an artist who, according to Chihuly.com, is "most frequently lauded for revolutionizing the Studio Glass movement" by expanding beyond the concept of the solitary artist working in a studio environment to the concept of working with collaborative teams. It goes on to say that Chihuly has, beyond that, influenced contemporary art in general. His pieces are "complex, multipart sculptures of dramatic beauty," and he deserves credit for pushing the envelope of the blown-glass form into an accepted vehicle for "installation and environmental art."

The top-selling Chihuly piece in this sample, a "Spectacular Maganese Blue Venetian glass" vessel that sold for $19,000.00, certainly deserves to be called sculpture. It features an intriguing coil that gradually wraps its way around and over the rim, and "a yellow lip to rim and to base," according to the item description. It appears to be a vase, but at 31 ¾ inches high, it's taller than your average flower-holder. Other high-priced Chihulys in this sample went for $16,000.00, $10,999.00, and $10,100.00, and on down to $5,400.00 for a coral "basket" vase.

But you don't have to break the bank to own a piece of North American art glass; the median price is only around $32.00. For example, a Depression-era "Fenton Topaz Opalescent Vaseline Hobnail fan vase" sold for $21.51.00. It may not be as exotic or expensive as the Chihuly, but it does glow in the dark, as shown in the seller's pictures.

$500.00 for a Burger King Mug?

When is a Burger King mug worth $480.00? When it was made by Fire-King in the mid-1900s and has a unique feature: the address of the specific Burger King in Pittsburgh, Pennsylvania, for which the mug was made. (On the other side is the Burger King logo.) Fire-King is a brand of glass made by the Anchor Hocking company starting in the 1940s, and it is now very collectible. These mugs were made for Burger King employees, and, in one recent search, sell for anywhere from $61.00 to the aforementioned $480.00 for the addressed mug, which is one of the high prices in the Pottery & Glass ▸ Glass ▸ Glassware ▸ 40s, 50s, 60s subcategory in this sample. Many Fire-King pieces are very affordable, though—some sell for as little as $0.50 and many are around $10.00. The high end is in the hundreds of dollars, with the popularity of Jadeite, a (not surprisingly) green-colored ware that Martha Stewart helped bring to people's attention.

Depression Glass

The Anchor Hocking company (makers of Fire-King) resulted from the merger of the Hocking Glass Company and Anchor Cap and Closure, two companies that had previously made Depression glass. Depression glass was inexpensive glass—plates, cups, bowls, and so on—that people used every day during the spartan era that was the Great Depression. Because people used the items so often, it's hard to find original pieces in pristine condition. That, and the fun of hunting down the many formerly mass-produced patterns, inspires collectors today.

In this sample, the highest-priced item in the Pottery & Glass ▶ Glass ▶ Glassware ▶ Depression subcategory is a "Mckee Skokie Green Vertical Lines Range Shaker Set Salt" that went for $1,001.99. Not bad for a salt and pepper shaker set! The strange thing about this set (actually four containers: salt, pepper, sugar, and flour) is that at first glance they seem fairly plain—light green shakers with simple black lettering and metal caps. But when you look closely, you realize what excellent shape they're in for their age. The seller describes them as a "very nice set of Depression age range shakers made by Mckee Glass. Three of the shakers are not marked, the flour is marked Mckee. All are in what I would call near mint condition. They do not have any chips or cracks. They do have plenty of swirls, that this glass is known for, and one has a dark spot of glass factory flaw. The rims have typical roughness, but do not have any chips or cracks. The lettering is about perfect, and has some degree of slight shine left to it . . . If you have been wanting a set of these, you would have to look real hard for a nicer looking 4 examples."

Other Depression glass that sold for high prices in this sample are a rare green horseshoe butter dish for $961.50 and a "rare vintage McKee Jadite bottoms down mug" for $395.00.

Other glass that commands very high prices in this sample is in the Glass ▶ Glassware ▶ Cut Glass subcategory: a Croesus rose bowl went for $10,650.00, and a Gorham "Sterling & American Brilliant Cut Glass Ewer" sold for $9,050.00.

The Real McCoy

But glass is only half of the Pottery & Glass category. There are also many types of pottery here, from the gorgeous art pieces to be displayed behind a glass case to the everyday pitcher. Two popular types of pottery are majolica and McCoy.

Majolica (actually a bastardization of the word *Majorca*, where some of it was made) is "earthenware with a white, tin-opacified, viscous glaze, decorated by applying colorants (often with a brush, using calligraphic brush work) on the raw glazed surface," according to an article by Linda Arbuckle that appeared on the CeramicsWeb website. Tin-glaze earthenware was brought from the Middle East to Spain and the port of Majorca, and when Italians imported it from there, they called it majolica. (The French, in turn, imported it from Faenza, and called it Faience.) The craft spread throughout the world, morphing into different styles and acquiring local flavor: in Holland it became the distinctive blue-and-white "Delft"; in Mexico it became Talavera.

High prices in the Pottery & China ▶ Art Pottery ▶ Majolica subcategory range from about $900.00 to about $8,000.00 in this sample, but average prices are an affordable $70.00. The highest-priced piece was a beautiful antique vase with swan handles, dated 1847, and the seller believed it was a piece by nineteenth century majolica maker George Jones. While that piece is truly gorgeous, several of the items in the middle of the price range are lovely as well, including a charming old French blue, yellow, and green plate with an asparagus design that went for $72.88. It was dated around 1900 but was unsigned. Another was more modern—a set of four Vietri Italian plates with wintry scenes of figures sledding and skiing. It sold for $72.00. You might draw the conclusion that an old piece of signed pottery with fine detail in nice condition will be more expensive than an unsigned piece or a more modern piece that is less detailed, and you would be right. Of course, with eBay, there are exceptions to every rule lurking somewhere, which is part of what can make it so much fun.

There is also plenty of pottery from North America. One of the most famous brands of American pottery is McCoy. According to my research, this is not *the* McCoy of the expression "the real McCoy" (which, according to WorldWideWords.org, was most likely based on American boxer and welterweight champion (1898–1900) Norman Selby, known as "Kid McCoy"), although the pottery aficionado's obsession with the authenticity of styles, signatures, and trademarks might make it seem appropriate. McCoy pottery started in 1910 when Nelson McCoy and his father J.W. McCoy founded the Nelson McCoy Sanitary Stoneware

Company in Roseville, Ohio. According to a site devoted to the company's history and collectors, McCoyPottery.com, this vaunted ware had solid but not flashy roots: "The Stoneware was functional in the beginning and consisted of such items as Jars, Jugs, and Crocks for use in food and beverage storage to items such as poultry fountains, foot warmers" and other not-so-glamorous pieces. But the styles the firm is best known for today, which were "functional but also works of art," according to the site, came after English immigrant Sydney Cope started working as a designer there in the mid-1930s.

So what are McCoys going for on eBay? The highest-priced piece in this sample is a rare "McCoy Art Deco Sphinx Sand Jar Vase" that went for $1,701.00—"one of their most sought after designs," according to the seller.

Second was a hard-to-find McCoy brown-glazed Calypso Fish jardinière/vase that sold for $341.00. It's marked "McCoy Made in USA" and dates to 1958. Another old vase, this one in the shape of a fish and from the 1940s, sold for $277.00. Others that fetched prices in the hundreds were a sunflower vase and a cookie jar with kittens on it, selling for $214.39 and $181.83, respectively. But the average price in the McCoy subcategory is only about $25.00, so there are many affordable pieces there too.

The Joys of Collecting Pottery and Glass

There is so much more to explore in Pottery & Glass. Once you start browsing, you may find a niche that captivates you and turns into an obsession. Or, like a lady whose devotion began by looking for the right ware to accent an antique sideboard, you may indirectly stumble onto a line that fascinates you.

The comments by a fan of Riverside Glass Works pieces offer insight into why people collect pottery and glass: "This glass is so beautiful that I want to share it with the world. What was inexpensive everyday tableware 100 years ago is something rare and very special today. Collecting this glass makes me long for the beauty and craftsmanship of the past . . . I am fortunate to be able to collect these pieces of history and enjoy them every day."

Glass ▸ Art Glass ▸ Bohemian/Czech

The average sales price in this subcategory is $48.06.

	HIGH		AVG
46 PIECES CZECH STEMWARE-GOLD AND POLYCHROME	$810.00	czech art glass vase * 6" tall * yellow tango spatter	$62.00
Antique Bohemian Ruby Red & White Glass Vase Lovely!	$511.00	WATERFORD CRYSTAL LISMORE SUGAR BOWL	$61.00
1900 RINDSKOPF THUMBPRINT RAINBOW IRIDESCENT VASE NR	$306.01	Super Red/Black Ruffled Cased Czech Art Glass Vase NR	$55.00
RARE Tri-Color 1860s CUT GLASS BOHEMIAN VASE MINT!	$306.00	Czechoslovakia Blue White Swirl Art Glass Trumpet VASE	$53.00
RALPH LAUREN CRYSTAL GLEN PLAID WINE GLASSES SET OF 6	$277.51	Art Deco Style Czech End Of Day Glass Vase-Stunning!	$51.01
FINE BRONZE MOUNT LARGE CRANBERRY CASKET OR BOX SUPERB	$250.00	RARE Bohemian czech ruby TOOTHPICK HOLDER ETCHED GLASS	$51.00
Cranberry Mary Gregory 7 pc water set...5DAYS....NR	$250.00	NACHTMANN LEAD CRYSTAL SMALL DECANTER RED BIRD HOFBAUER	$51.00
MOSER BOHEMIAN PITCHER SILVER OVERLAY PERSIAN MARKET	$250.00	Red, Blown Bohemian Glass Cruet, 1890s, Stag & House	$49.99
Antique Iridescent Art Glass Vase Marked Choslovakia	$224.60	Gorgeous Vintage Czech Rubina Verde Art Glass Basket NR	$49.99
Czech Hoffman Art Deco Nudes Atomizer Perfume Pair NR	$181.39	BOHEMIAN GOLD ENAMEL COBALT BLUE VASE	$49.99
FAB Moser Czech ? Glass Ptd Dresser Jar w Roses on Feet	$167.50	VINTAGE BOHEMIAN CUT TO CLEAR COBALT GLOBE WITH SOME	$49.95
c.1930 Bohemian lead crystal lamp made for Tiffany	$150.00	Juliska Crystal Smoke Olivia Pitcher-Czech/Bohemian-New	$49.95
Opaline Cut Overlay Bohemian Art Glass Decanter Estate	$145.50	Antique Art Nouveau C1900 Austrian Art Glass Vase	$49.77
6 Juliska Crystal Smoke Tessa Wine Tumblers-NIB-NR	$124.95	Vanity Set Hand painted Circa 1940's NR!	$49.00
VINTAGE CZECHOSLOVAKIA ART GLASS VASE BEAUTY	$117.50	Old Czech Glass Perfume Bottle Stopper, Frosted Flowers	$48.99

Glass ▸ Art Glass ▸ Italian

The average sales price in this subcategory is $27.18.

	HIGH		AVG
Antique Murano Venini Glass Light Chandelier Fixture	$455.00	c.1940 Venitian Italian Art Glass Table Lighter N/R	$30.00
ZANETTI Big MURANO/Italian GLASS Flamingo-NR!	$449.00	VINTAGE Italy MURANO Venetian Gold Fleck Glass BOWL	$30.00
MASSIVE EAMES ERA ITALIAN CASED GLASS DECANTER!	$260.00	Wedgewood White on Black Smoking Set (4 pieces)	$29.99
VINTAGE MURANO BAROVIER TOSO VASE W/PLATINUM N/R	$210.00	Green Depression Glass Tumblers (3)	$29.99
VINTAGE VENETIAN MURANO PERFUME VANITY SET - GOLD FLECK	$201.50	BULBOUS MINIATURE MURANO PERFUME BOTTLE GOLD FLECK N/R	$29.99
Italian Glass Vanity Tray Venini Spirals Etched Mirror	$152.50	MURANO HANDCRAFTED VASE **MUSEUM QUALITY**	$29.99
Venitian Art Glass Table Lighter Paperweight Orange N/R	$152.50	STUNNING MURANO CASED ART GLASS SWAN METALLIC COPPER	$29.75
BEAUTIFUL VINTAGE MURANO ART GLASS CAT & MOUSE - ITALY	$150.50	OLD CASED GLASS OPALINE MURANO VENINI ART GLASS BOWL	$28.99
VINTAGE VENETIAN MURANO PERFUME BOTTLE SET - SEGUSO?	$119.11	VINTAGE MURANO FRATELLI TOSO LATTICINO VASE W/STICKER	$28.03
MURANO ART GLASS DISH BOWL DECORATIVE SILVER LEAF LOOK	$114.04	NR!!! MURANO ITALIAN CRYSTAL DUCK	$28.00
Carlo Moretti Champagne Flute 1995 Signed	$105.50	ITALIAN MURANO GLASS HEART PERFUME BOTTLE LARGE A WOW!!	$26.00
VINTAGE MURANO SEGUSO RIBBED CRANBERRY SOMMERSO LAMP	$99.00	Vintage MURANO GLASS AVVENTURINA necklace Gold Leaf	$25.49
Barbini ART GLASS LIGHTER Aventurine SOMMERSO Murano	$68.00	$275 DECORATIVE MURANO TRICOLOR SOMMERSO TEARDROP	$25.45
AWESOME VINTAGE PINK Murano ITALY Glass BOWL	$57.99	Vintage MURANO GLASS AVVENTURINA necklace Gold Leaf	$24.99
MURANO NECKLACE MORETTI ARTISTI BAROVIER SALVIATI OR ?	$56.00	Real MURANO Italian VENETIAN Gold COBALT Glass BIRD	$24.99

Glass ▸ Art Glass ▸ North American

The median sales price in this subcategory is $21.51.

	HIGH		AVG
301: DALE CHIHULY Spectacular Maganese Blue Venetian gl	$19,000.00	Tiffany & Co. Crystal Bowl - New-In-Box! NR!	$21.51
300: DALE CHIHULY Large soft cylinder with random stria	$16,000.00	RARE Fenton Amethyst Waterlilly & Cattail Berry Bowl	$21.51
CHIHULY signed ART HISTORY glass & book		FENTON ART GLASS RUBY RED SMILING	$21.51
1 Only: BLUE SKY Sculpture & Pilchuck: A Glass School	$10,999.00	Happy MOUSE Mice Ret	
Early Dale Chihuly Signed & Dated Cased Cylinder Vase	$10,100.00	Fenton Topaz Opalescent Vaseline Hobnail fan vase glass	$21.51
Tiffany Studios Balance Weight Favrile Damascene lamp	$8,700.00	Fenton Cranberry Hobnail Basket	$21.50
Tiffany Studios Linen-fold lamp/ with Chinese dore base	$6,000.00	Antique Blue Bubble Creamer Pitcher BLENKO SIGNED -HTF!	$21.50
Original Dale Chihuly Coral Basket with Golden Wrap	$5,400.00	CRANBERRY OPALESCENT COIN DOT	$21.50
GREAT EARLY 20C SIGNED TIFFANY STUDIOS BRONZE BOOKEND		FENTON ART GLASS PITCHER	
RARE BEAUTIFUL ORMOLU BRONZE PATINA FOLD UP BOOKENDS	$4,300.00	Fenton vase - Charleston collection QVC /w box	$21.50
041: Quezal feathered zipper decorated art glass vase	$4,250.00	Fenton Blue/Aqua/Turquoise Fairy Light Lamp	$21.50
Rare Crown Milano Starfish Gold Hobnaill Marmalade Jar	$4,246.00	ARTIST SIGNED-SATIN GLASS-FENTON	$21.50
HUGE~Jeweled~Starfish Decor~Famous Estate~Butterfly		ANGEL-MINT COND- NR	
TIFFANY STUDIOS ZODIAC DESK LAMP BASE	$3,633.33	Rare 1937 Gold Medal Paris Exposition STEUBEN Book	$21.50
578: 47-PIECE STEUBEN CRYSTAL STEMWARE SET, Air Bubble	$3,500.00	Fenton Carnival Turtle Tree Ring Holder	$21.50
JAMES NOWAK PROTOTYPE Mercury Glass 20" AQUARIUM VASE	$3,205.00	LOT OF 4 FENTON SITTING BEARS ***MINT***	$21.50
19 PC. FENTON "HEIRLOOM COLLECTION" LIMITED EDITION	$2,999.00	FENTON WHITE MILK GLASS HOBNAIL	$21.50
NUMBERED COMPLETE SET VERY RARE ONLY 250-1000 MADE!		VANITY SUGAR CANDY JAR	
Pairpoint Table Lamp-Reverse Painted Shade w Farm Scene	$2,800.00	Fenton Cranberry Opalescent Wine Decanter - NRMT	$21.50

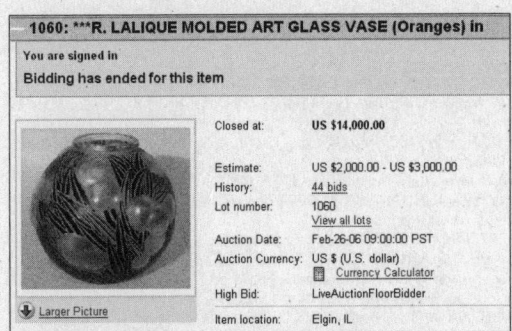

1060: ***R. LALIQUE MOLDED ART GLASS VASE (Oranges) in

You are signed in
Bidding has ended for this item

Closed at:	**US $14,000.00**
Estimate:	US $2,000.00 - US $3,000.00
History:	44 bids
Lot number:	1060
	View all lots
Auction Date:	Feb-26-06 09:00:00 PST
Auction Currency:	US $ (U.S. dollar)
	Currency Calculator
High Bid:	LiveAuctionFloorBidder
Item location:	Elgin, IL

Larger Picture

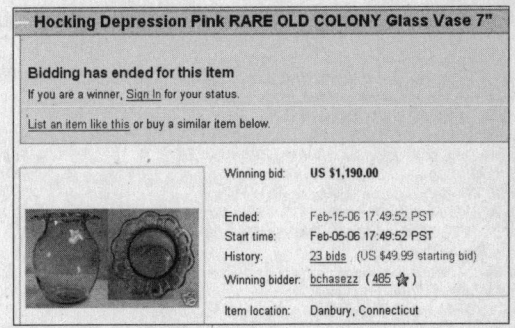

Hocking Depression Pink RARE OLD COLONY Glass Vase 7"

Bidding has ended for this item
If you are a winner, Sign In for your status.

List an item like this or buy a similar item below.

Winning bid:	**US $1,190.00**
Ended:	Feb-15-06 17:49:52 PST
Start time:	Feb-05-06 17:49:52 PST
History:	23 bids (US $49.99 starting bid)
Winning bidder:	bchasezz (485)
Item location:	Danbury, Connecticut

Glass ▸ Art Glass ▸ Scandinavian

The average sales price in this subcategory is $70.49.

	HIGH		AVG
Scandinavian Art Glass Vase NUUTAJARVI HOPEA Signed	$2,499.99	AFORS Ernest GORDON blue vase 1950s Scandinavian Glass	$86.00
1955 Scandinavian Art Glass Vase Nuutajarvi Hopea *NR*	$1,453.00	Rare Timo Sarpaneva Arkipelago Champaign Flute Iittala	$79.75
Tapio Wirkkala Comb Cut Bowl Trio Iittala Scandinavian	$1,000.00	Mats Jonasson two bear cubs art glass 5 1/2 inche	$77.55
SWEDISH CONTEMPORARY GLASS - GRAAL TECHNIQUE	$680.00	Mats Jonasson Crystal African Water Buffalo 12" Sweden	$77.51
SAARA HOPEA Nuutajarvi KUPLA Vase 1957 Pristine!	$460.00	Chartruese ! Cased glass vase Holmegaard , Eames era !	$77.00
50'S-IITALIA-TAPIO WIRKKALA-KANTARELLI LINE-FOOTED BOWL	$427.00	Old Riihimaki Nanny Still Candle Holders Finland	$77.00
Hadeland Severin Brorby Blue, Green Art Glass Vase	$356.00	FOUR IITTALA FINLAND 1970s Ultima Thule DINNER PLATES	$76.00
GIRAFFE / Mats Jonasson Crystal Glass Sculpture SWEDEN	$355.00	Vintage Scandinavian (Finland) Art Glass Vase (1960's)	$75.00
LEERDAM ? VENETIAN ? OPALESCENT WINGED GLASS VASE	$250.26	2 Riihimaki Helena Tynell SUN bottles, Riihimaen Lasi	$75.00
TAPIO WIRKKALA SIGNED ART GLASS COG VASE ITTALA FINLAND	$222.50	Kaj Franck ~ Designer-Formgivare HC Book ~ FINLAND	$71.00
EAMES ERA ART GLASS VASE HOLMEGAARD VENINI PANTON ERA	$204.50	NICE Signed Kaj Franck Iittala Art Glass Open Salt Dip	$68.54
Oiva Toikka Sign Beach Kiwi Iittala ~ FINLAND	$185.00	Sweden Lead Crystal Fish Mats Jonasson Swedish Angel	$68.00
EAMES ERA ART GLASS VASE HOLMEGAARD VENINI PANTON ERA	$181.50	Superb Horse foal Mats Jonasson Etched Crystal Block	$66.03
iittala Toikka MillenNium Birds Special Edtn *NR*MIB*	$179.00	Maija Carlson Oy Kumela Scandinavian Glass Bowl	$63.00
Notsjo Finland Green Glass Vase Signed OLD	$170.99	Iittala Tapio Wirkkala 12 Art Glass Cordial Tumbler Set	$62.00

Glass ▸ Art Glass ▸ Paperweights

The average sales price in this subcategory is $38.54.

	HIGH		AVG
Henry Clay paperweight cut New England Glass Company	$2,250.00	ANTON INTAGLIO ART GLASS PAPERWEIGHT - READ - PHOTO'S	$39.99
RICK AYOTTE--BUTTERFLY	$1,275.00	FABULOUS CRYSTAL PAPERWEIGHT BY VAL ST. LAMBERT	$39.99
Antique St. Louis Mauve Dahlia Paperweight.	$1,161.00	Sea Anemone-Paperweight, art glass, Collectors item '78	$39.98
RICK AYOTTE METAMORPHISIS	$995.69	ART GLASS SCRAMBLE MILLIFORI PAPER WEIGHT	$39.95
Vintage BACCARAT PAPERWEIGHT-Millefiori, Animals, Stars	$911.00	1973 BACCARAT HARRY TRUMAN SULPHIDE PAPERWEIGHT W/BOX	$39.00
SABINO ART GLASS BEAUTIFUL LARGE ISADORA FIGURINE	$850.00	Art Glass Artist Signed Paperweight	$39.00
STANKARD PINK WILD ROSE PAPERWEIGHT SIGNED + DATED 1974	$757.00	Beautiful 1977 Grant Studios Paperweight	$38.99
Rare St. Clair Ceramic Rose Paperweight	$750.00	Charming Pink Rose Hamon Paperweight	$38.55
JOE ST CLAIR PINK ROSE PAPERWEIGHT-MINT-ESTATE FIND	$660.00	JOSH SIMPSON PLANET PAPERWEIGHT	$37.99
AYOTTE CARDINAL PAPERWEIGHT-1978	$660.00	Vintage Art Glass Paperweight Tropical Fish	$37.66
20th C French Art Glass Clematis Latticinio Paperweight	$640.00	Collectible Glass Murano Ribbon Paperweight Italy	$37.53
Vintage Clichy Millefiori Paperweight Ex Cond NR	$632.00	HERB THOMAS BLOWN ART GLASS PAPERWEIGHT~PURPLE IRIDESCE	$37.50
Baccarat Primrose Paperweight	$599.00	Vintage Paperweight Iridescent Color Swirls Lighthouse	$37.49
BACCARAT PAPERWEIGHT BUTTERFLY ROOSTER CRANE FROG BIRD	$585.00	EYE FOOLING ABSTRACT ROLLiN KARG ART GLASS PAPERWEIGHT	$37.45
KEN ROSENFELD FLORAL PAPERWEIGHT-1987	$575.00	Art Glass Tiffany Crystal Apple Paperweight Excellent	$37.00

Glass ▸ Art Glass ▸ Stained Glass

The average sales price in this subcategory is $28.05.

	HIGH		AVG
Large Angel Stained Glass Window by Sandra St. John	$2,000.00	Stained glass panel * Rainbow *	$33.00
NEW AIM 84BD LAMPWORKING ANNEALING FUSING GLASS KILN	$1,525.00	BEVELS * UNIQUE * N.R.	
[5 of these sold for $305.00 each]		Hummingbirds and Fuschia Staind Glass FREE SHIPPING	$33.00
ANTIQUE STAINED GLASS PANEL - JESUS MARY & MARTHA	$1,226.00	Handcrafted Stained Glass Shade	$31.99
Transom Windows for Interior Doors	$912.00	STAINED GLASS WINDOW	$31.00
[4 of these sold in a multiple item ("Dutch") auction for $228.00 each]		FRAME PANEL IRIS FLORAL 19"	
Best Glass Kiln for Fusing, Bead Making SHIPS NOW!	$549.00	20"x 12"leaded stained J' suncatcher Christian Judaism	$30.00
Chili Pepper Bead Annealer Kiln Bead Making Lampworking	$449.00	Stained Glass DRAGONFLY & WATER LILIES Suncatcher	$30.00
[3 of these sold for $449.00 each]		TIFFANY WISTERIA Floral STAINED GLASS Art Panel	$27.95
Best Glass Kiln for Fusing and Bead Making by Jen-Ken	$431.56	**GEOMETRIC BEVELED DESIGN**Stained Glass Hanging	$27.00
Best Glass Kiln for Fusing and Bead Making by Jen-Ken	$407.22	HGB Dichroic COE 90 Mix Black & Clear Thin Fuser Pack	$26.97
Dichroic Glass Fusing kit & New Premium 6 inch Kiln	$395.00	Stained Glass 3-D Angel Garden Or Plant Stake	$26.12
Hot Box Kiln w Window -Glass Fusing/Slumping Supplies	$340.00	2 Panels of Stained Glass Butterfly and Bamboo!	$26.01
UNIQUE GODDESS STAINED GLASS WINDOW VINTAGE	$336.00	Hanging Stained Glass Window	$26.01
Jen-Ken Fused Glass Fusing Kiln - TLGC	$335.00	Stained Glass Kaliedoscope - Very Special Collectible	$26.00
Nortel Minor Bench Burner - Beadmaking/Lampworking Kit	$331.26	FRAMED LEADED STAINED GLASS	$26.00
Hot Box Kiln w Window -Glass Fusing/Slumping Supplies	$325.00	BUTTERFLY PANEL WINDOW	
Taurus 3 Ring Saw-Stained/Fused/Dichroic Glass+Free DVD	$312.99	**VICTORIAN FLORAL CIRCLE**Stained Glass Hanging	$26.00

Glass ▸ Glassware ▸ 40s, 50s, 60s

The average sales price in this subcategory is $24.42.

	HIGH		AVG
11 IVORY FIRE KING D HANDLE TALL 81/2 OZ COFFEE MUGS NR	$776.00	FAB VINTAGE DOROTHY THORPE LARGE SILVER WATER PITCHER	$26.00
4 Fire King Turquoise Blue Swedish Modern Mixing Bowls	$611.00	Vintage Retro Higgins Glassware Great Design MINT	$25.49
Complete 4 Bowl Set w/Original Box !		Brass ice bucket	$25.00
Ruby Glass Punch Bowl with Platter Thumbprint 35 cups	$500.00	GEORGES BRIARD, BAMBOUS D'OR	$24.99
HTF Fire-King Jadite Jadeite Tilt Ball Jug Pitcher NICE	$494.00	COVERED CASSEROLE, WHITE	
FIRE KING Addressed BURGER KING MUG	$480.00	Swirled Pink & white glass pitcher, glasses BEAUTIFUL	$24.95
Pair Dorothy Thorpe lucite double candleholders	$350.00	HTF YELLOW ORANGE DAFFODIL BOSCUL PEANUT BUTTER GLASS	$24.50
Akro Agate Type II Scalloped Top Graduated Dart Pot	$229.35	Wrought Farberware Covered Glass Dish	$24.36
DOROTHY THORPE PLATINUM RIM PUNCH BOWL SET LADLE GLASS	$212.50	~BEAUTIFUL~FENTON~HOBNAIL~MILK GLASS~EPERGNE SET~~	$24.17
6 Mini Pots or Thumb Pots	$152.50	ANTIQUE 3 PIECE GLASS COFFEE POT MAKER CORY FILTER ROD	$24.03
6 Sherbet/Champagne Glass Holmegaard/Colony? Cased	$122.59	Dorothy Thorpe Silver Water Pitcher Vintage NR Large	$22.51
Russel Wright Eclipse Shot/Small Glasses	$118.37	West Virginia Glass Blendo Pink Pitcher + 6 Tumblers	$22.50
Coral Oriental Poppy Peanut Butter Glass NAME MOVED	$111.62	Elegant AMBERINA~MOON AND STARS DIVIDED DISH-LE Smith	$22.49
Rare Purple Bunches of Violets Peanut Butter Glass	$104.27	Vintage Ripple Early Imperial Carnival Glass Vase Gold	$22.25
TIFFIN FRANCISCAN ELYSE (WATER GOBLETS) CRYSTAL	$99.95	Retro Mod Fred Press Glass Serving Tray	$21.61
NASTURTIUM PEANUT BUTTER GLASS~FILLED WITH LID NR	$89.99	Fenton Milk Glass Deviled Egg Plate~10"~40s'-60s' era	$21.50

Glass ▸ Glassware ▸ Amethyst

The average sales price in this subcategory is $16.40.

	HIGH		AVG
6 Vintage Bohemian Crystal Glass Wine Goblets Tall	$153.50	Vintage Black Amethyst Cookie Jar.	$17.50
stunning ART DECO set BOWL & TUMBLER purple GOLD band	$140.50	AMETHYST DOUBLE HANDLED ART DECO VASE 8 1/2"	$17.37
Rare Victorian Amethyst Glass Mary Gregory Glass Vase	$115.00	2 Antique 19th C Black Amethyst Hand Painted Glass Vase	$17.00
BLACK AMETHYST VASE W/GOLD ETCH+STAND-ART DECO/NOUVEAU!	$99.99	Rare PURPLE MILK GLASS Hen On Nest Salt Dish Dip LOOK!	$16.50
CAMBRIDGE Glass AMETHYST GUILDED BALL CRUET	$89.95	Black Amethyst Octagon Shape Cambridge Depression Glass	$16.49
Cambridge Caprice Amethyst Wisteria Candle Holder Stick	$86.00	Large 8" Water Pitcher Black Amethyst Glass Hob Stars	$16.45
CAMBRIDGE GLASS BALL PITCHER W/ 6 TUMBLERS *AMETHYST*	$74.99	6 Black Amethyst glasses w/sticker New, Mouth Blown	$16.00
VINTAGE RARE BLACK AMETHYST ICE BUCKET W/ 6 GLASS SET	$56.00	Oval Amethyst Glass Platter with Banded Rim	$15.50
DEEPLY DeLiCiOuS AMETHSYT! SaTiN GRaPeS. . . WOW!!!	$54.90	AMETHYST PURPLE COIN DOT THUMBPRINT GOBLET GLASS N/R	$15.50
[6 of these sold in a multiple item ("Dutch") auction for $9.15 each]		3 AMETHYST LONG STEM WINE GLASSES~MINT~	$15.50
ARCOROC FRANCE TAMPICO AMETHYST 8 PLACE GLASS SETTINGS	$52.52	Moon & and Star Amethyst 12 1/2" Boat Bowl Weishar	$15.50
Farber Bros. Cambridge Glass Amethyst pitcher	$52.35	BLACK AMETHYST BOWL WITH FLOWER FROG	$15.50
PR AMETHYST CARNIVAL SWAN CANDLE HOLDERS FENTON	$52.08	BLENKO VEINED AMETHYST VASE W/	$15.50
FENTON BLACK AMETHYST STERLING OVERLAY GLASS ICE BUCKET	$51.00	LEAF-NOT CRACKLE-MINT *	
ANTIQUE VINTAGE BEAUTUFL BLACK AMETHYST DISHES (5pc)	$51.00	Amethyst glass purple Art Deco vase - 22"	$15.50
Amethyst Carnival Glass Cambridge 10 1/2 Inch Swan Dish	$49.99	VINTAGE BLACK AMETHYST ART DECO GLASS PERFUME BOTTLE	$15.25

Glass ▸ Glassware ▸ Carnival Glass

The average sales price in this subcategory is $28.34.

	HIGH		AVG
8" Fenton Carnival Vaseline Chessie Compote 1998	$432.93	GORGEOUS Fenton opalescent carnival glass vase WOW	$29.98
FENTON "GARDEN OF EDEN" PLATE	$266.00	FENTON AMETHYST CARNIVAL 6 SIDED FERNER NR	$29.95
RARE FENTON "GARDEN OF EDEN" PLATE	$225.00	Moon & Star Cobalt Blue Carnival Fairy Lamp L.E.Smith	$29.00
ICE BLUE TOPAZ Fenton Carnival Glass ~POPPY SHOW~ Vase	$224.72	Lovely Signed Fenton "Orange Trees" Bowl	$28.99
FENTON VASELINE OPALESCENT Carnival Glass ICGA Plate~NR	$222.50	10 1/2 IMPERIAL RED CARNIVAL GLASS PULLED DIAMOND VASE	$28.77
IMPERIAL MARIGOLD HOBSTAR PUNCH SET	$200.00	Ruby Imperial Carnival Glass Pitcher - MINT - NR - #494	$28.55
Carnival Glass Pitcher Tumblers Imperial Gold Rose 7 PC	$177.50	BLACK ?- DARK RED? VINTAGE CARNIVAL GLASS ROOSTER	$28.00
7pc Imperial Purple Peacock Carnival Windmill Water Set	$175.00	Fenton Red Carnival Glass Low Compote	$28.00
DUGAN'S 5" LINED LATTICE SQUAT VASE	$174.50	Imperial Marigold OCTAGON PITCHER	$28.00
Buzz Saw Punch Bowl Stand Cups VERY RARE Carnival Glass	$164.49	Fenton Carnival Glass Purple Candy Compote Footed BIG	$28.00
Fenton Dragon and Lotus Bowl 8" Irridescent Carnival	$150.00	Carnival Glass CORNING PYREX Handled Creamer Dark Marig	$27.50
VINTAGE IMPERIAL COBALT BLUE CARNIVAL GLASS 3 SWAN VASE	$142.50	CHERRY RED FENTON CARNIVAL GLASS Stork & Rushes Tumbler	$27.00

	HIGH		AVG
PR VINTAGE IMPERIAL CARNIVAL HOBNAIL OIL/KEROSENE LAMP	$130.00	Cobalt Marigold, Rose Bowl (circa 1987) Electric colors	$26.88
Fenton Art Glass Vaseline Opalescent Carnival Epergne	$125.00	IMPERIAL GLASS IRIDESCENT COMPOTE	$26.84
Field of Flowers Water Set Black Pearl Carnival Glass	$120.00	484B FENTON CARNIVAL GLASS PEARL OPALESCENCE STAG HOLLY	$26.65

Glass ▶ Glassware ▶ Cobalt

The average sales price in this subcategory is $13.66.

	HIGH		AVG
Depression Royal Lace Toddy Cider Set, Cobalt Blue	$429.99	Czech Art Glass FLOWER in Crystal Vase COBALT BLUE ROSE	$13.99
CAMBRIDGE STATUESQUE ROYAL BLUE COMPORT 9" MINT	$168.76	4 Vintage Cobalt blue Medicine bottles	$13.65
Art Deco Cobalt Chrome Farberware Liquor Set - MINT!!	$142.53	GLASS AND SILVER=COBALT BLUE SUGAR SETIN BASKET	$13.60
VINTAGE COBALT BLUE CHAMPAGNE GLASSES - SET OF 2	$142.00	TREE FROG Pewter &Cobalt Glass Perfume Bottle (54)	$13.50
[2 of these sold in a multiple item ("Dutch") auction for $71.00 each]		COBALT BLUE GLASS PLANTERS MR PEANUT CHILDS MILK CUP	$13.49
Beautiful Cobalt Cut to Clear Crystal Electric 22" Lamp	$102.50	Vintage COBALT BLUE GLASS 7-1/2" RUFFLE VASE	$13.35
8 Old Cobalt Blue Cut Lead Crystal 4oz Cocktail Goblet	$76.00	COBALT BLUE GLASS WALT DISNEY MICKEY MOUSE CLUB BANK	$13.03
1920s Cobalt Blue Cordial Set Silver Applique 6 glasses	$67.00	Vintage cobalt blue glass Violin cello BOTTLE #2	$13.00
TIARA GLASS - COBALT BLUE HONEY BEE DISH	$51.00	Wedding Band Cobalt BLUE Sugar Bowl	$13.00
Cobalt Blue Covered Candy Dish with Metal Stand & Lid	$49.99	Cobalt Blue Crystal Cut to Clear Rose Bowl - Romania	$12.99
Vtg Mary Gregory Cobalt Blue Water Decanter & Glass	$49.99	6 Cobalt blue dessert plates NICE ground bottom	$12.99
COBALT Russian Crystal Wine Glasses SKY-BLUE VASILISA	$49.99	Gorgeous hand blown cobalt blue pitcher	$12.99
4 CRYSTAL COBALT STEMWARE GLASSES	$43.88	Cobalt Blue Glass Bowl / Dish With Deer Lid NEW	$12.99
Occupied Japan Cobalt Blue & Silver Lighter + Ashtray	$41.00	COLBALT BLUE BUTTER DISH GRAPE DESIGN	$12.95
Cobalt Blue Glass Male Head Hat Stand Art Deco NR	$40.12	ANTIQUE STYLE COBALT BLUE GLASS	$12.87
ANTIQUE COBALT BLUE DEPRESSION GLASS COVERED CANDY DISH	$37.05	COVERED DISH SHOE /BOOT	

Glass ▶ Glassware ▶ Contemporary Glass

The average sales price in this subcategory is $23.84.

	HIGH		AVG
MACKENZIE CHILDS "CIRCUS" GLASS DISHES PLATES & VASE	$550.00	Set of 4 Noritake Crystal Moodust Wine Glasses	$24.99
MacKenzie Childs circus GOBLET set / 6 PANSY PETALS	$241.99	Boyd Glass OLD 3" Hen Nest NICE Purple Ivory SLAG FUND	$24.99
4 RALPH LAUREN GLEN PLAID CHAMPAGNE GLASSES NEW NR	$169.50	Boyd Glass OLD Owl RARE Aggravation Red SLAG FUND	$24.99
ORREFORS CRYSTAL PRELUDE CHAMPAGNE GLASSES SET OF 12	$134.29	ROSENTHAL TAC 02 6" RED & BLACK GLASS BOWL NEW!!	$24.99
Levay Black Satin Raised Wing Covered Swan rare #5 of 5	$132.50	LAST SET 6 ITALIAN Shot Glasses SILVER RIMS!	$24.99
ORANGE ART DECO~Brazil MURANO ART GLASS Vase MODERN new	$123.94	8 BOYD GLASS FORGET ME NOT TOOTHPICK HOLDER	$24.50
4 RALPH LAUREN GLEN PLAID CHAMPAGNE GLASSES NEW NR	$121.00	INVERTED STRAWBERRY PALE GREEN TOOTHPICK HOLDER!	$24.04
ROGASKA GALLIA FAIRY LAMP - Candle Lit - Beautiful!	$120.99	Cobalt Blue Carnival Glass Honey Jar Pot Bee Hive Boyd	$22.99
Ruby Red Depression Pearl's Glass Cake Stand	$112.50	FOSTORIA SHEFFIELD GOBLET / WINE CRYSTAL PLATINUM	$22.83
LISA JENKS LARGE CONTEMPORARY CRYSTAL VASE ~EXQUISITE~	$102.50	Boyd Glass OLD Chick Salt Sunburst Orange SLAG HS FUND	$22.50
KINGS CROWN THUMBPRINT RUBY FLASH FOOTED CAKE SALVER	$102.50	10 COBALT BLUE LG.STYLISH water GOBLETS parfait glasses	$22.49
RALPH LAUREN HERRINGBONE 5 1/2" BRANDY SNIFTER (2)	$89.99	Boyd Glass Amethyst Heart Box made 1980	$22.00
MacKenzie Childs Hand Crafted Glass Candle Holder/Vase	$80.99	9 Pieces Crystal Glasses	$21.50
Amberina Hen Chicken 7" Covered Dish Kanawha Glass 1971	$76.00	Noritake Paris Crystal - 10oz Water Goblet	$21.00
11 Franciscan Madeira Glassware Yellow 6 5/8" Teas	$74.95	ROSELLA ORIGINAL WALTHER GLASS COUPE PLATE FROST PINK	$20.53

Glass ▶ Glassware ▶ Crackle Glass

The average sales price in this subcategory is $16.00.

	HIGH		AVG
RED BLENKO ART CRACKLE GLASS DECANTER BOTTLE W/STOPPER	$107.51	DEEP BLUE CRACKLE GLASS LEFT HANDED PITCHER	$16.49
Vintage Hand Blown Punch Bowl Set Blue Crackle Glass	$89.00	PILGRIM CRACKLE GLASS, LAVENDER (RARE COLOR) PITCHER	$16.35
CRACKLE GLASS AMETHYST SWIRLED HAND BLOWN VASE	$86.09	YELLOW CRACKLE GLASS VASE	$16.26
8 PIECE LOT OF CRACKLE GLASS ART GLASS - PITCHERS,CRUET	$86.02	Amethyst Crackle Glass Pitcher 4.5" Tall	$16.26
VINTAGE BLENKO/HAMON AMBER CRACKLE GLASS DECANTER!	$86.00	Green Footed Crackle Glass Vase	$16.25
VINTAGE RAINBOW CRACKLE GLASS DECANTER IN RARE VIOLET!	$79.00	Pink Crackle Glass Ashtray	$16.00
RAINBOW*"LONG JOHN"*MASSIVE PITCHER!*CRACKLE GLASS*WOW!	$71.22	CRACKLE GLASS BROWN CRUET WITH STOPPER	$16.00
BLENKO #546 HUSTED*AMETHYST*LARGE*CRACKLE GLASS PITCHER	$69.99	2 crackle glass pitchers TANGERINE & AMBERINA/RUBY	$16.00
BLENKO*COBALT*CRACKLE GLASS VASE*LABEL*MINT	$66.00	Set of Four Crackle Glass Pitchers Green/Amber NR	$15.99
BLENKO RAINBOW PILGRIM ART DECO RUBY CRACKLE GLASS VASE	$63.80	Tangerine CRACKLE GLASS Rainbow PITCHER - MINT w/Label	$15.99
VINTAGE RAINBOW AMBERINA CRACKLE GLASS DECANTER	$62.99	PILGRIM*"LEFT-HANDED"*PITCHER*CRACKLE GLASS*"UNIQUE"*M	$15.99
Vintage 15" Olive Green Crackle Glass Fish, not Blenko	$61.00	PAIR of CLASSIC CRACKLE GLASS pitchers Old &Mint	$15.90
Crackle Glass & Brass Candle Wall Sconces	$61.00	KANAWHA CRACKLE GLASS - PITCHER	$15.51
LOOK!!!! CRACKLE GLASS CAR VASES MARIGOLD	$61.00	Crackle Glass Pitcher Amethyst Purple Ruffled Rim	$15.50
EMERALD GREEN CRACKLE GLASS PITCHER BY RAINBOW CO.	$60.99	COBALT BLUE VASELINE URANIUM GLASS CRACKLE PITCHER EWER	$15.50

Glass ▶ Glassware ▶ Cut Glass

The average sales price in this subcategory is $81.23.

	HIGH		AVG
RARE CUT GLASS TURQUOISE CUT TO CLEAR CROESUS ROSE BOWL	$10,650.00	1800 Stiegel Intaglio Cut Glass Flint Decanter Bottle	$88.65
Gorham Sterling & American Brilliant Cut Glass Ewer NR	$9,050.00	Vintage AMERICAN BRILLIANT Cut Glass Bowl! NR!	$88.36
RARE! Apricot-Clear Cut Glass Decanter GORHAM Sterling	$5,499.00	ABCG American Brilliant Cut Glass Tuthill Intaglio Tray	$88.00
8-SIDED 15" PUNCH BOWL SINCLAIRE NO.4 ABP? CUT GLASS NR	$4,626.00	RUBY RED OVERLAY flower vase by VAL St LAMBERT Belgium	$87.55
Gorham Sterling & Engraved Crystal Martele Type Pitcher	$3,925.00	AMERICAN BRILLIANT CUT GLASS SUGAR SHAKER A35	$87.00
EXTREMELY RARE Cut Glass Rainbow Color Trumpet Vase	$2,999.00	ABP CUT GLASS EXCEPTIONAL ROLLED RIM RELISH	$86.55
Tiffany & Co Sterling Silver & ABP Cut Glass Wine Ewer	$2,905.00	NR American BRILLIANT PERIOD Cut Glass Bowl Antique	$86.00
Tiffany Sterling Brilliant Period Cut Glass 14" Pitcher	$2,545.00	Estate Antique Brilliant American Cut Glass Wine Stems	$86.00
8" Cut Glass Bowl in Theodora by Meriden	$2,049.00	Set of 10 Hawkes Glasses	$86.00
Gorham Sterling & Intaglio Grapes Cut Glass Pitcher NR	$1,801.89	Hawkes Brilliant Cut Glass Rare Perfume Bottle Amethyst	$86.00
14pcs ENGRAVED Cut Glass Wine Stems Pineapple and FAN	$1,705.00	Antique Signed Hawkes Brilliant Cut Glass Bowl NO RESER	$86.00

BOSTON & SANDWICH VASELINE CUT GLASS COLOGNES	$1,400.00
American Brilliant Cut Glass Punch Bowl by Meridan-BIG	$1,400.00
EEEnormous Am Blnt Pd Cut Glass Vase w Wide Flared Top	$1,376.00
Spectacular Hawkes "Queens" Pattern Vase	$1,250.25

SIGNED MAPLE CITY ABP CUT GLASS PUFF JAR, NR	$85.00
J. Hoare American Brilliant Cut Glass Bowl Heron Design	$84.99
Old Galway Claret by Galway Crystal, Wedgwood China	$83.00
Hawkes ABP Brilliant Cut Glass Hobstar Diamond Pitcher	$81.00

Glass ▸ Glassware ▸ Depression

The average sales price in this subcategory is $22.35.

	HIGH		AVG
Mckee Skokie Green Vertical Lines Range Shaker Set Salt	$1,001.99	Adam Pattern, Pink Depression Platter, Jeannette Glass	$22.50
RARE GREEN HORSESHOE BUTTER DISH	$861.50	FLOWER GARDEN / BUTTERFLIES - US GLASS- TIFFIN CANDLE	$22.50
Rare Vintage McKee Jadite Jadeite Bottoms Down Mug	$395.00	Hazel Atlas Starlight Depression Bowl and Sugar	$22.49
RARE FIND 19 PC ANCHOR HOCKING PINK SWIRL DINNERWARE	$350.00	Hocking BANDED RINGS Decanter + glass stopper	$22.49
Hocking Glass Ring "Banded Rings" Set of 6 & More	$330.85	VINTAGE CAMEO BALLERINA GREEN DEPRESSION GLASS BOWL	$22.49
Depression Era, U.S. Glass, Parrot Lamp	$307.52	PRETTY ORNATE CRYSTAL CAKE PLATE	$22.39
Mckee Laurel Ivory Red Trim Childs Tea Set No Reserve	$260.00	Jadite McKee 2 Cup Measuring Pitcher	$22.38
RARE MCKEE DEPRESSION GLASS BOTTOMS DOWN MUG	$250.00	Depression Glass Opalescent Vanity PUFF BOX Powder JAR	$22.38
Vintage1931 Art Deco Nude Girl McKee 3Side Jadeite Vase	$242.50	Vintage Anchor Hocking Green Glass Syrup w/Tin Closure	$22.37
PINK TEA ROOM GLASS-4 FINGER BOWLS AND BONUS-NR	$228.72	KINGS CROWN CRYSTAL 1890'S HANDLED OLIVE NAPPY	$22.27
Vintage Hocking Hoosier COFFEE Jar/Canister GREEN GLASS	$218.28	AKRO AGATE CONCENTRIC RING POWDER JAR MARBELIZED	$22.26
9 pc Pink Green Depression Glass Optic Wine and Cordial	$213.33	Pink Depression Glass (5) Button & Bows Sherbet Plates	$22.15
JEANETTE DORIC AND PANSY ULTRAMARINE COVERED BUTTER	$203.85	McKee Tappan Roman Arch Yellow Blue Salt Pepper Shakers	$22.15
Childs dish set with old box, complete, Akro Agate	$202.50	1930s Pink Depression Doric Berry Bowls Jeanette Glass	$22.13
Federal Glass Company Depression Glass	$202.49	2 LIME GREEN DEPRESSION GLASS 3 SECTION DINNER PLATES	$22.03

Glass ▸ Glassware ▸ Early American Pattern Glass

The average sales price in this subcategory is $31.83.

	HIGH		AVG
RARE -Type I Jumbo Covered Sugar	$631.00	HTF EAPG O'Hara Glass Horseshoe CAKE STAND 1880s ~ NR	$32.99
RARE!! CUSTARD **WILD BOUQUET** CRUET w/Orig STOPPER!	$475.00	19th C Miniature EAPG Acorn P&A Floral Oil Lamp, Shade	$32.89
Greentown Holly Amber 8&1/2" Bowl	$450.00	Beautiful EAPG and Brass Oil Lamp!	$32.85
Central Glass U.S. Coin 8" Frosted Coin Compote	$249.50	Vintage Duncan Block Cracker Jar	$32.50
EAPG Etched Dakota Bride's Basket	$238.16	PAIR EAPG SHAKERS DIAMOND WITH DOUBLE FAN SUN PURPLE	$32.00
EAPG Central Glass 1892 U.S. Coin PRESERVE DISH	$232.50	1896 EAPG MW STARRED BLOCK PATTERN CANDLESTICK COMPOTE	$31.99
RARE EAPG US GLASS MANHATTAN PUNCH BOWL STAND - NO RSRV	$227.50	2 ANTIQUE PEDESTAL CRYSTAL CAKE PLATES	$31.00
SANDWICH!! **HOLLY** LARGE COVERED COMPOTE!!	$225.00	Panelled Forty Four, Reverse 44, Athenian Goblet	$30.67
RARE 1877 HAND & TORCH Oil Lamp *Must See* NO RESERVE!!	$219.50	5 Pattern Glass cups with birds & Berries, clear glass.	$30.00
WoW~GoRgEoUs Antique SUN PURPLE Etched Glass EAPG BOWL!	$202.50	EAPG Frosted Pheasant Covered Dish	$29.99
Findlay Onyx Celery Vase	$200.00	EAPG "Tecumseh" Toothpick	$29.99
Early american pattern Glass BREAD PLATE Niagara falls	$177.50	HIGBEE ALFA 11" PEDESTAL CAKE STAND SALVER w/ BEE c1900	$29.99
1800 EAPG Pattern Glass Water Pitcher Thistle Pressed	$162.50	1880s EAPG Pattern Pressed Glass STIPPLED SANDBUR	$29.95
Beautiful Nova Scotia Starflower Wine Goblet	$160.55	ANTIQUE c1890 EAPG GIRL & LARGE BASKET TOOTHPICK HOLDER	$29.95
EAPG (1877) GILLINDER & SONS LION HEAD BERRY SET	$157.51	Antique Lacy Etched Long Stem Cordials Floral	$28.99

Glass ▸ Glassware ▸ Kitchen Glassware

The average sales price in this subcategory is $13.71.

	HIGH		AVG
VASELINE DEPRESSION GLASS FRUIT/CAKE KNIFE W/BOX 9 1/4"	$99.67	Wonderful Cobalt Blue Restaurant Ware Straw Holder	$14.95
REDWING SPONGEWARE YELLOWWARE PITCHER ~MINT~	$97.00	Depression Glass Cake Fruit Knife Vintage L@@K	$14.79
Vintage Honey, Candy Jar / Bee Finial EAPG Glass?	$85.67	PINK DEPRESSION GLASS CANDLE HOLDERS	$14.50
VINTAGE JEANETTE GLASS GREEN JADITE SALT BOX, RARE	$83.55	FIRE KING Turquoise Vegetable/Serving Bowl Japan OK	$14.10
PINK DEPRESSION TALL GLASSES WITH STEM	$59.00	Glass Cake Stand Plate	$14.08
PINK DEPRESSION GLASS BISCUIT JAR	$59.00	Iron City Beer Glass Pitcher Bar Glassware Pittsburg NR	$14.00
6 PIECE JADEITE JADITE ROMAN ARCH GLASS SPICE JAR SET!	$55.00	12 Hard to find Clear Scalloped Custard Cups by Pyrex	$13.99
PINK DEPRESSION GLASS BISCUIT JAR	$54.01	NICE GREEN GLASS OLD SLEEPY EYE TOOTHPICK MATCH HOLDER!	$13.75
PINK DEPRESSION GLASS COVERED DISH	$51.00	Vintage Forest GREEN Childs Miniature CREAM & SUGAR Set	$13.61
Pitcher Complementary Johnson Brothers Summer Chintz	$51.00	6 WATER/WINE WEXFORD ANCHOR HOCKING GLASSES	$13.50
GREEN STONEX GLASS KNIFE	$50.00	LOG CABIN'S WIGWAM SYRUP ADV INDIV SYRUP SERVER	$13.07
VINTAGE 10 1/2" SILVER / COBALT ART DECO 3 PART SERVER	$45.77	Vintage hand-painted syrup pitcher - beautiful!	$12.99
Vintage Large Green Glass Pickle Jar/Vase	$43.89	Jadite Cabbage Rose Sugar and Creamer! No Reserve	$12.95
2-Vintage Glass Cookie, Candy, Jar "" LARGER SIZE""	$43.32	PINK DEPRESSION GLASS OPEN LACE BOWL	$12.51
[2 of these sold in a multiple item ("Dutch") auction for $21.66 each]		Vintage Depression Clear Glass Round Butter Dish/NR	$12.50
3 TIER RUBY RED TIDBIT CAKE PLATE SERVER NIB HOCKING	$43.00		

Glass ▸ Glassware ▸ Opalescent

The average sales price in this subcategory is $72.32.

	HIGH		AVG
Northwood Cranberry Opalescent Daffodil Tankard Pitcher	$10,073.00	Rare Northwood Opalescent Glass Spooner Epergne Vase NR	$77.50
Cranberry Opalescent Drape Pitcher Ewer Northwood ?	$2,200.00	TS Victorian Vaseline Hobbs Dew Drop Celery Vase!	$77.35
Vintage 1930s Art Deco Jadeite Opalescent Nude Jadite	$810.00	Sandwich Glass Cup Plate - Fiery Opalescent	$76.83
CRANBERRY OPALESCENT VICTORIAN GLASS HOBBS SYRUP	$795.00	Rare Green Opalescent Poinsettia Tumbler Antique	$76.00
Findlay Onyx Water Pitcher White Opalescent w/Gold	$496.00	Old Fenton Daisy and Fern Cruet	$74.99
RARE BLUE OPALESCENT RING NECK STRIPE PITCHER !!!	$430.00	Daisy and Fern Cruet Old Fenton	$74.99
Rare Opalescent Dresser Vanity Set * Steuben? Baccarat?	$425.00	4 VINTAGE EARLY 19th C OPALESCENT GLASS FURNITURE KNOBS	$74.00
VASELINE OPAL SWEET MEAT COMPORT	$420.00	Vintage Pinecone & Leaves *BLUE OPAL* Ruffled Bowl ~NR	$73.79
RARE VICTORIAN CRANBERRY OPAL REVERSE SWIRL KERO LAMP	$406.77	Victorian Glass Blue Opalescent Salt Shaker Rev. Swirl	$72.00
Rare Northwood Blue Opalescent Wide Panel Epergne	$356.00	Victorian Opalescent Glass Vase Enameled Flowers NICE!	$69.99

	HIGH		AVG
TS Vintage Fenton Vaseline Opalescent Cactus Epergne!	$355.00	ANTIQU BLUE SWIRL OPALESCENT GLASS LIGHT SHADE	$69.00
COBALT CHRISTMAS SNOWFLAKE OPALESCENT WATER SET!!NR!!	$330.00	FIVE BLUE OPALESCENT COIN DOT BOWLS	$69.00
Northwood CRANBERRY SPANISH LACE / OPALINE BROCADE Vase	$280.00	Mind Blowing IRIDESCENT Signed MAYTUM Lopez PAPERWEIGHT	$68.99
RARE! 1910 FENTON VASELINE OPALESCENT COINSPOT PITCHER	$280.00	French Opalescent Dot Optic Cruet (circa early 1940's)	$68.99
EAPG Gonterman Swirl Opalescent Glass Toothpick Holder	$265.00	BEAUTIFUL VASELINE OPALESCENT CANDY DISH ?	$68.76

Glass ▸ Glassware ▸ Opaque

The average sales price in this subcategory is $26.71.

	HIGH		AVG
IT&G Co. Greentown Nile Green Wheelbarrow. Milk Glass	$411.00	1901 Greentown Leaf Bracket Chocolate Glass Spooner NR	$27.50
HEISEY CUSTARD GLASS RING BAND CRUET TRAY,C1900,NICE	$308.50	OLD SLEEPY EYE LIME SLAG TOOTHPICK MATCH HOLDER INDIAN	$27.01
6 Northwood Inverted Fan & Feather Custard Tumblers	$280.01	Old Milk Glass American Hen Eagle Covered Dish NR!!	$27.00
MODERNISTIC GREEN SATIN GLASS SUGAR & CREAMER	$268.87	Milk Glass Ruffled Scalloped Lavender & Pink Rose Bowl!	$26.99
19TH CENTURY SOWERBY 'PEA GREEN' SWAN VASE	$264.99	Lot of 6 Blue satin-finished goblets~~Must See~~	$26.99
Northwood Inverted Fan & Feather Custard Glass Pitcher	$256.00	Hazel Atlas Milk Glass Salt & Pepper Shakers	$26.78
Blue Milk Glass FLOWERS Footed Toothpick Holder VINTAGE	$255.00	Old Upside Down Tumbler - Nude	$26.52
Antique Sowerby Glass Trough - Old King Cole - Sowerby	$222.00	TARENTUM GLASS...CANE INSERT...	$26.52
six vintage BLUE OPALINE milk glass GOBLETS p & v	$202.50	Fenton Dogwood on Cameo Satin Swan and Ginger Jar! Sig	$26.16
ANTIQUE TURTLE MILK GLASS COVERED DISH*KNOBBY BACKED	$202.49	Custard glass Bell Souvenir Logan, Kansas	$26.01
Blue Milk Glass Elephant Covered Dish Paint Vallerystal	$167.50	Pink and White Glass Items Car vase? Opaline? Unique	$26.00
Custard Glass Souvenir Toothpick MACKINAC ISLAND MI	$138.49	3 1/2" Fenton Rosaline Elephant Figurine	$26.00
8 1/4" Fenton Rosaline Donkey and Cart Figurine	$137.78	Pretty Blue Milk Glass Cruet with Flower Pattern	$26.00
[2 of these sold in a multiple item ("Dutch") auction for $68.89 each]			
Green Milk Glass Rabbit white head Covered Dish McKee	$125.00	GREENTOWN CHOC GLASS LEAF BRACKET CREAMER-NR	$25.00
GREENTOWN SCARCE CHOCOLATE CACTUS LOW PLATE!	$100.00	PINK MILK Glass CUSTARD BEEHIVE HONEY BEE JAR ~ POT	$24.99

Glass ▸ Glassware ▸ Pressed Glass

The average sales price in this subcategory is $17.00.

	HIGH		AVG
Rare Boston & Sandwich? Cobalt Toy Candlestick	$609.99	EAPG Early American Pressed Glass 9" Heavy Bowl NEX	$18.99
Pair Boston & Sandwich Doric Column Canary Candlesticks	$179.39	PRESSED GLASS RESTUARANT SUGAR BOWL W/ METAL LID	$18.60
Vintage Pair of Amber Glass Dolphin Candlesticks	$158.50	VINTAGE?DOLPHIN PRESSED GLASS CANDLESTICK AMBER &CRYSTA	$18.51
Riverside Esther Glass Green Gold Table Set Butter	$126.95	ART DECO CLEAR PRESSED GLASS QUART PITCHER	$18.49
DAVIDSON ? PEARLINE PRESSED GLASS BASKET X2.	$114.50	PRESSED GLASS AMBER CHAIR	$17.50
Unique Pressed Glass Pattern Glass Blue Glass Toy Chair	$113.50	Vintage Pressed Pattern Glass Cake Stand	$16.99
ROUND GLASS PLATE, 12 3/8", Nuutajarvi, Kastehelmi	$79.00	PRESSED GLASS Higbee Thistle toothpick holder	$16.50
1890's Pressed Glass Teardrop 10" Pedestal Cake Stand	$72.99	NEW 2005 Pressed Glass ID$$ Book EAPG Pattern 1860 Up	$16.50
Antique Puce Pressed 1865 Flint Glass Plate	$69.99	Three Pressed Glass Flower Frogs-Pink-Green-Clear	$16.28
Boston & Sandwich Flint Glass Candlestick. Mid-1800s NR	$64.99	Ribbed Glass Drugstore Shelf Support Excellent 12"	$16.26
VINTAGE CLEAR GLASS PEDESTAL CAKE PLATE LILY PAD TREE	$63.99	Pink Glass Pedestal Cake Stand	$16.01
HORN OF PLENTY SANDWICH SUGAR BOWL	$60.00	Depression Era Fostoria Bon Bon Tray - Colony Pattern	$16.00
RARE Frosted Fruits Pitcher c 1896	$57.00	Vintage Pressed Blue Glass Boat. Indiana ? Exc. Cond.	$16.00
Vintage Twin Cut Crystal Perfume Bottles with Tray	$53.61	Vintage Punch bowl pressed glass	$15.75
Boston & Sandwich Dolphin Candlestick. C. Mid-1800s. NR	$52.21	2 ELEGANT PRESSED GLASS BASKETS,CUT FLOWERS MATCHED PR.	$15.51

Glass ▸ Glassware ▸ Pyrex

The average sales price in this subcategory is $13.60.

	HIGH		AVG
Pyrex Primary color mixing bowl set VINTAGE SEALED BOX	$182.50	Pyrex Turquoise Blue Dinner, Salad Plates Cups Saucers	$14.50
Pyrex 8pc PINK Refrigerator Set Excellent L@@K	$135.00	(2) PYREX FLAMEWARE CASSEROLES (2) DETACHABLE HANDLES	$14.50
12pc. PRIMARY COLORS PYREX MIXING BOWLS&STORAGE DISHES	$105.50	Pyrex Coffee Pot & Parts-4-6 cup	$14.50
VINTAGE RARE PINK Pyrex mixing/nesting bowls set of 4	$87.99	1 GREEN and 1 RED Pyrex Nesting Bowls Take a L@@K!!	$14.27
Set of 4 Vintage Polka Dot Pyrex Nesting Bowls	$86.00	3 Pyrex Casserole Dishes...2 PINK 1 BLACK... SNOWFLAKE	$14.02
Vintage Flamingo Pink Pyrex 4 - Nesting Mixing Bowls	$75.99	6 PYREX RED TRIM BREAD & BUTTER PLATES 8 INCHES LEAVES	$13.51
VINTAGE SET OF 4 PYREX NESTED BOWLS, PRIMARY COLORS-NR	$62.21	PYREX Flameware 6 CUP Teapot TEA POT Glass NIB ? NR	$13.50
Pyrex Tayli Syphon Vacuum Coffee Maker Japan	$56.00	6 pc Corning Cornflower Blue Casserole Set	$13.50
Pyrex Mug - "Only From Corning" - At Home In Your Lab	$54.99	4 Piece Vintage Pyrex Bowl Set Clear w/White Flowers	$13.50
Pink Pyrex Mixing Bowls	$54.15	VINTAGE PYREX GLASS COFFEE POT PERCOLATOR 9 CUPS NICE	$13.49
BLUE Glass Delphite Pyrex Mug Made in Canada RARE!	$54.02	VINTAGE POLKA DOTS BLUE MIXING NESTING PYREX BOWL 403	$13.45
Vintage Pyrex 6 Cup Percolator 7756 in UNOPENED BOX!	$53.00	Pyrex Square Berry Bowls White Set of Four	$13.05
VINTAGE CASSEROLE CAVITT-SHAW BY W S GEORGE	$53.00	PYREX STORAGE DELUXE 10 PIECE SET NIB NICE SET!!	$13.01
Pyrex CITRUS Refrigerator set W/bonus YELLOW ORANGE	$51.01	VINTAGE? PYREX 3 QT. COBALT BLUE LASAGNA-BAKING DISH -	$13.00
Pyrex Primary Colors Nesting Bowl Set Vintage	$51.00	PYREX SERVEWARE SIX PIECE SCULPTURED BOWL & LID SET	$13.00

Glass ▸ Glassware ▸ Ruby

The average sales price in this subcategory is $22.79.

	HIGH		AVG
Antique Ruby Butter Dish, signed & dated (1899)	$709.00	Antique Ruby Red Depression Glass Serving Bowl N/R!!	$24.01
What a Unique Find!!! Old Ruby Pitcher and 6 glasses	$525.00	8 Ruby Flash Glass Footed Cordial 4&3/4"Tall Unusual	$23.81
KINGS CROWN CRANBERRY GLASSWARE 54 piece set	$405.00	2 Antique Ruby Red Depression Glass Serving Dishes	$23.50
Ruby and White Glass Large Bulldog Doorstop NR #E27	$357.65	11 Antique Ruby Red Depression Glass 6oz. Glasses	$23.50
Paden City Ruby Glass Crows Foot Compote Etched Orchids	$227.50	RUBY RED DEPRESSION GLASS CANDLE HOLDERS	$23.49
ELEGANT RUBY & HEAVY GOLD VENETIAN DECANTER 11 GLASSES	$212.50	4 Sets Ruby Red Glass Cups and Saucers / Charm	$22.51
Set of 9 Cambridge Carmen Ruby Goblets, Aurora	$160.00	Vintage Ruby Red Depression Glass Sherbet Dishes/NR	$22.50
Victorian Castor Cruet Set , Ruby cut to Clear	$150.00	~RUBY RED GLASS PITCHER~INVERTED THISTLE PATTERN~LARGE~	$22.50
44 PC RUBY RED DEPRESSION GLASSWARE ANTIQUE GLASS	$107.50	vintage RUFFLED HOBNAIL RUBY glass 1-handle nappy bowl	$22.50

Cranberry Glass Martini & Cocktail Shaker	$102.50	*6* RUBY FLASH KINGS CROWN FTD JUICE TUMBLERS	$22.50
DEPRESSION RED RUBY GLASS COMPLETE LUNVH/TEA SET DISHES	$100.00	FENTON RUBY CRANBERRY ART GLASS DOT ROSE BOWL c1956	$22.50
RUBY PAIR WALLPOCKETS VICTORIAN STYLE	$97.99	Bohemia Glass etched A.Lederle 1853 Pre-GERMANY	$22.49
EAPG Large Ruby Red Glass Flower Frog 16 Hole	$97.00	8 Ruby Flash Glass Footed Wine Glasses 4&1/2"T Unusual	$22.40
Set of 6 Vintage Ruby Red Place Setting	$96.00	5 CORONATION RUBY RED BERRY BOWLS - NO RESERVE	$22.15
SET OF 8 HEAVY VINTAGE RUBY RED AMBERINA GOBLETS NR	$87.00	AVON RUBY RED CAPE COD PITCHER	$22.06

Glass ▶ Glassware ▶ Waterford

The average sales price in this subcategory is $53.97.

	HIGH		AVG
Eight Waterford Lismore grapefruit footed dish	$560.00	6 Waterford Iced Beverage Glasses ALLEGRA OPTIC NEW!	$56.00
WATERFORD ARAGLIN GOLD GOBLETS Free shipping	$350.00	Waterford Crystal: Lismore coasters	$56.00
VINTAGE IMPRESSIVE WATERFORD CRYSTAL HURRICANE LAMP	$312.00	new in box waterford crystal hurricane lamp,hamden.	$55.55
VINTAGE PAIR WATERFORD CANDELABRAS	$266.62	Waterford Crystal Water Pitcher	$55.00
1982 WATERFORD CHRISTMAS ORNAMENT PARTRIDGE RARE!	$260.09	Waterford Millennium Toasting Flutes - Love	$54.12
Waterford Martini Glasses (4)	$240.00	Stunning Waterford Crystal Metropolitan Clock	$54.05
12 piece set, Waterford Marquis Brookside Crystal NIB!!	$228.50	WATERFORD CHRISTMAS CRYSTAL BELL 1986	$53.05
Waterford Crystal Simply Martini Set Of 8 All 4 Colors	$219.96	Waterford Crystal Simply Lilac Martini Pair 66% Off	$52.99
6 VINTAGE WATERFORD LISMORE OLD FASHIONED GLASSES NR	$212.50	Waterford Crystal Somerset 5 x 7 Picture Frame MIB	$52.00
Waterford Crystal Celebration Champagne Bucket New	$201.99	8-1/2" SIGNED WATERFORD-IRELAND VASE	$52.00
4 Waterford Brookside Marquis Crystal Tumblers	$200.02	2 Waterford Aqua Lismore Cased Crystal DOF Glasses-MIB	$51.50
[2 of these sold in a multiple item ("Dutch") auction for $100.01 each]		ONE WATERFORD CRYSTAL CURRAGHMORE	$51.06
Waterford Powerscourt Footed Dessert Dishes (1 pair)	$192.50	WATER GOBLET,NR	
Waterford Crystal: Clarendon Ruby Cordial+Brandy Glass	$185.11	Waterford Maeve Footed Iced Tea Goblet	$51.00
4 CRYSTAL CLEAR WATERFORD KYLEMORE WATER GOBLETS $440!	$185.00	Waterford First Light Flutes - Pair $200 Value *NEW	$51.00
4 Waterford Crystal Colleen Brandy Snifters	$183.73	WATERFORD CRYSTAL LETTER OPENER NIB w/ TAGS	$50.77

Pottery & China ▶ Art Pottery ▶ American Art

The average sales price in this subcategory is $57.04.

	HIGH		AVG
Suberb PILLIN Siamese Cat & MOON Tray , Great Colors	$2,550.00	vintage florida merritt island art pottery mini pot	$62.00
HARDING BLACK Texas Studio Pottery 1957 Crater Glaze	$999.99	Glidden Saffron 2 Serving Pieces 8 Small Plates	$61.00
Crocker Rattlesnake Jug –Large Snake Jug	$800.00	Original California Art Pottery Children Figures MINT	$61.00
Nice pillin round covered box, women, mint, 6 1/2 dia	$788.00	Ephraim Faience 362 Plum Leaf Cabinet Vase	$59.85
RARE-1930 Roseville SUNFLOWER Hanging BASKET-Vintage-NR	$750.00	Louisville Stoneware, CHIPS AND DIP, 5 PIECE PLATTER	$58.95
Rare Muncie Ruba Rombic Pottery Lamp Green	$630.00	HOWARD PIERCE Raccoon, California Pottery~SUPER!!	$56.76
LARGE CLEWELL ARTS CRAFTS MISSION COPPER CLAD POTTERY	$610.00	Zanesville STONEWARE MATT GREEN #101 MINT! NO RESERVE!!	$56.51
AREQUIPA POTTERY Vase <> Handmade Arts & Crafts c1914	$609.00	Hartstone Pottery Serving Platter Reindeer	$53.79
Rare Muncie Ruba Rombic Pottery Lamp	$523.00	Matthew Adams Alaskan Teapot 1822 Eskimo Blue Wicker	$53.66
Perfect Clewell Copper Clad Pitcher Signed, mint, rare	$399.00	1963 Pennsbury Pottery Christmas Greetings Paoli Pa Pla	$53.00
Vivika+Otto HEINO art pottery vase-Eames era-WOW!	$338.33	Burley Winter Matte Gray & Mauve Mottled Lg Jardiniere	$52.99
CLIFTON CRYSTAL PATINA VASE 6-1/2"	$325.00	Old Chalkware top hat and pipe String Holder	$52.99
RARE 1950 HARDING BLACK BOWL MOTTLED- SIGNED	$320.99	Rare Gonder Sun Fish Pottery Vase Turquoise 522 NR	$51.55
c. 1957 Boehm Anna's Hummingbird Porcelain Bird 40321	$300.00	DEDHAM POTTERY ORIGINAL HORSE CHESTNUT PLATE	$51.00
Boehm Racquet-Tailed Hummingbird Porcelain Bird 40318	$300.00	Dedham Pottery Oval Flower Holder (Nash Pottery)	$51.00

Pottery & China ▶ Art Pottery ▶ Asian

The average sales price in this subcategory is $43.36.

	HIGH		AVG
Studio Pottery - Shoji Hamada: Yunomi w/Signed Box	$4,153.00	Satsuma Matte Black China Tea Set, Gold Scenic Decor	$52.75
Large Ornate Scallop Edge Satsuma Bowl	$411.09	Studio Pottery: Powerful Nezumi Shino Tokkuri	$52.00
Chinese Qing Qianlong M&P Polychrome Saucer	$405.00	Korean Ceramic vase 8.25" t. w/marks PERFECT	$51.00
Hand Painted Asian Ceramic Pillow Vase with Wax Seal	$404.00	STUNNING LARGE 20" TALL VINTAGE CHINESE VASE SIGNED	$50.00
Chinese Fish Bowl Pot/Urn/Vase-Green-Wood Stand-$1895	$401.00	GEORGES BRIARD "IMPERIAL BROCADE" SETTING	$50.00
Tea Ceremony: Magnificent Organic Kohiki Chawan	$275.50	MARUTOMO WARE JAPAN PORCELAIN TEASET PIGS COMPLETE NR	$49.99
Sumida Ware (Japan) 1880's Fish Dish NR	$227.50	Lot of 3 "Rose Medallion" Hand Painted Chinese Bowls	$49.99
Tea Ceremony: Rare Black Shino Chawan	$213.59	SIGNED Sumida Gawa Japanese POTTERY JUG VASE Ryosai ?	$45.00
ANTIQUE LARGE IMARI CHARGER	$202.50	Exquisite & RARE Old Chinese Zi Sha Teapot Purple Clay	$45.00
Japanese Red Shino Tea Bowl	$200.50	Chinese Ming Dynasty Antique Wu Cai Porcelain Vase	$44.00
Chinese Fish Bowl Pot/Urn/Vase-Floral-Wood Stand-$1695	$190.00	GORGEOUS ANTIQUE CHINESE EXPORT PLATE-CA.1880	$39.95
Vintage Japanese Hakata Samurai Doll 1950's-1960's	$189.39	PAIR ORIENTAL PORCELAIN ROSE MEDALLION VASES NR	$39.00
C1900 LARGE IMARI OVAL PLATTER	$154.05	Studio Pottery Tea Bowl - SIGNED - Japanese Earthenware	$38.75
ASIAN ANTIQUE CHINESE ROSE MEDALLION BOWL	$145.00	Antique Asian Covered Jar Exceptional! 3-day NR Auction	$36.99
Franz Butterfly Porcelain Cup, Saucer, Plate, Tea Set	$132.50	Studio Pottery: Unique Blushing ShinoYunomi/Teacup	$36.00

Pottery & China ▶ Art Pottery ▶ Blue Mountain

The average sales price in this subcategory is $21.18.

	HIGH		AVG
Blue Mountain Pottery Slate Blue Ape Monkey HTF	$168.49	Blue Mountain Pottery Penguin BLUE GLAZE Cond New !!	$29.99
BLUE MOUNTAIN POTTERY ROOSTER!	$167.99	HURONIA ? BLUE MOUNTAIN POTTERY MINIATURE COBALT VASE	$26.55
1 of RAREST Blue Mountain Pottery ROMAR PRESIDENT Horse	$152.50	Blue Mountain Pottery SMALL TROPICAL FISH - BLUE	$25.00
Blue Mountain Pottery ROMAR BEAR & CUB ~Presidents Coll	$119.59	Country Charm Blue Mountain Pottery Pitcher Bowl Set	$24.99
Blue Mountain Pottery Giraffe Olive Lik Noahs Ark	$113.49	RARE Glaze Vintage Blue Mountain Pottery Pitcher Ewer	$23.49
Pair of Blue Mountain Pottery Cat & Fox Figurines	$106.50	Blue Mountain Pottery - Mocha Squirrel with Nut	$23.40
VASE/PLANTER BLUE MOUNTAIN POTTERY ANGEL FISH MINT	$79.99	Blue Mountain Pottery BlueJay Bird Made in Canada	$23.03
Very Rare Blue Mountain Pottery Jug Muskoka Glaze w/Tag	$78.99	Blue Mountain Rearing Horse Bookends Pair	$22.50

	HIGH		AVG
Blue Mountain Pottery Tall Red Vase	$77.00	BLUE MOUNTAIN POTTERY MINIATURE - SLATE BLUE ROOSTER	$22.35
Blue Mountain Pottery RARE Figurine GEESE IN FLIGHT MT!	$69.00	Blue Mountain Pottery RED & BLACK DOG Figurine	$21.02
Rare Artist Signed Red Blue Mountain Pottery vase	$62.95	Blue Mountain Pottery Fish (3)	$21.00
Rare Large Blue Mountain/CCC Pottery Camel Planter	$58.77	Blue Mountain Pottery VASE * Granite Glaze*Different	$20.50
Blue Mountain Pottery Lilac Handmade Art Space Age Dish	$56.55	Blue Mountain Art Pottery Vase, Rare Color	$20.50
Blue Mountain Pottery LAZY SUSAN	$52.00	BLUE MOUNTAIN POTTERY EGYPTIAN / SIAMESE CAT	$20.50
Blue Mountain Pottery Large Floor Vase~Harvest/13"	$51.00	Beautiful Blue Mountain Pottery Harvest Gold Eagle	$19.99

Pottery & China ▸ Art Pottery ▸ Brush/Brush-McCoy

The average sales price in this subcategory is $30.02.

	HIGH		AVG
BRUSH MC COY JEWEL ART POTTERY VASE	$288.56	BRUSH/McCOY-- 3 VERY OLD LADY PLANTERS	$34.50
Brush McCoy Kolorkraft Blue Onyx Large Vase SUPER FORM!	$214.50	WONDERFUL HTF BRUSH McCOY SMALL FROG EXCELLENT!!	$34.00
1923 ZUNIART BRUSH MCCOY POTTERY BOWL RARE	$208.58	Amazing Rare Green Brush McCoy Nymph Vase NR!	$33.95
Brush McCoy Amaryllis Matte Finish Vase SUPER Colors!	$180.27	Huge Haeger Pottery Blue Vase or Oil Jar	$31.00
RARE BRUSH McCoy LITTLE ANGEL COOKIE JAR W/REPAIR	$168.50	Brush-McCoy Pottery - Strawberry Pot	$31.00
Vintage 1950's McCoy Brush COW COOKIE JAR with kitten	$158.50	Brush McCoy 1929 Amaryllis Pastel Bowl - L@@K - NR	$31.00
Brush McCoy Blended Glaze Basketweave jardiniere HTF	$149.99	Brush McCoy Art Vellum / Nymph Mottled Glazed Vase HTF	$29.99
BRUSH MCCOY POTTERY WISE BIRD	$149.99	MCCOY 1940'S Ceramic White Elephant Planter***Rare***	$29.99
OWL 10" Handled DECANTER		Brush McCoy Planters (2)	$29.99
BRUSH PETER PAN COOKIE JAR	$108.85	A.E. HULL DECO DESIGN CROOKSVILLE ART POTTERY VASE	$29.99
Brush McCoy Frog Figural Ashtray SUPER CLEAN!	$102.50	EXCELLENT-1940s-VINTAGE-McCOY-JARDINIERS-CALLA-LILLYS	$29.00
Brush Amaryllis Matte Green Pink Arts Crafts Pottery	$102.50	Vintage Brush McCoy Kolorkraft Vase ODD GLAZE? *NR*	$28.75
Davy Crockett Cookie Jar / Brush Pottery 1956	$100.00	Vintage Brush McCoy Pottery White 2 Dog Figurine 1939	$28.60
Brush McCoy Kolorkraft Experimental Vase SUPER HTF!	$99.99	McCoy Blue Onyx #749 Vase	$28.57
BRUSH McCoy Pottery 10" FROG Garden Ornament Figurine	$92.55	red wing ware vase	$27.75
Brush McCoy Large Brown Onyx 12+" HTF Size!	$89.99	RARE-FIND 1935-McCOY-STRAWBERRY-JAR-BLUE-TOP-QUALITY!	$27.50

Pottery & China ▸ Art Pottery ▸ Delft

The average sales price in this subcategory is $25.00.

	HIGH		AVG
Finest Huge Late 18th Century Delft Covered Urn	$462.55	RED DELFT MADE IN HOLLAND Lidded Jar	$26.25
PORCELEYNE FLES DELFT BOTTLE. CA. 1900. NOT GOUDA.	$350.00	VINTAGE DELFT BLUE LOVERS PLATE, WINDMILL, BOCH, BOAT	$26.00
ANTIQUE DUTCH DELFT DE PORCELEYNE FLES PEACOCK? VASE	$330.00	Portuguese Blue&White Delft Pottery Lidded Urn/ Unquie	$26.00
DELFT DUTCH Large Man & Woman Figures - Holland	$296.51	Vintage Lot of 22 Delft Blue Pieces Delft ware and more	$26.00
Delft Dutch figures, man+woman, charming from Holland	$270.50	Large 13 inch collector Delfts Blauw Charger Holland	$25.45
43 DUTCH KLM DELFT 'S BLUE BOLS CANAL HOUSES. LOOK !	$257.22	DELFT BLUE COLERED PLAQUET WITH SEASON SUMMER (nr.1260)	$25.00
VINTAGE DELFT 16" CHARGER SIGNED BY ARTIST A MAUVE	$255.00	SQUARE DELFT ART WALL PLATE HAND PLATED HOLLAND	$24.99
ANTIQUE ESTATE ROYAL BONN DELFT MANTLE CLOCK WINDMILLS	$229.00	DELFT LOW BOWL ASHTRAY WHITE BLUE GREEN NO RESERVE	$24.99
Vintage 16" DELFT CHARGER/Artist DU CHATTEL Signed	$227.50	@ ANTIQUE @ Little Porceleyne Fles Delft Vase 1886 !!	$24.99
c044: Huge 16?" Delft IMARI Plate Porceleyne Fles	$204.06	DELFT BLUE PORCELEYNE FLES - LITTLE WALL PLATE 1968/2	$24.99
Large Royal Delft Vase Holland Hand Painted MINT	$155.00	DELFT BLUE - WALLHANGING PORCELAIN SPOONRACK + 6 SPOONS	$24.99
Royal Delft De Porceleyne Fles Sugar, Creamer, and Tray	$129.14	Delft blue& white vase, kissing couple, pitcher,plus 1	$24.86
1883 ANTIQUE DELFT DE PORCELEYNE FLES VASE WOW	$129.00	HAND-PAINTED DELFT BLUE GILDED PORCELAIN PLATE GERMANY?	$24.50
Royal Delft De Porceleyne Fles Coffee Pot Teapot NICE!	$122.52	Beautiful Large Delft Windmill Scene Plate/Platter	$22.50
Antique Dutch Delft tea caddy, signed	$118.50	Pair of Delft Blue & White Decorative Vases Marked	$22.27

Pottery & China ▸ Art Pottery ▸ European Art

The average sales price in this subcategory is $53.80.

	HIGH		AVG
Longwy Pottery Faience Vase Chinese Dragon Cloisonne	$2,810.00	Polish Pottery NEW 4 DINNER PLATES	$55.99
RARE ZSOLNAY 20" SCENIC ART POTTERY TRAY PLATTER	$2,039.00	CA Polish Pottery 11.25" L BAKER W/ HANDLES Boleslawiec	$55.72
Amphora Teplitz? Art Nouveau Austrian Vase	$1,913.00	J Mrazek Czech Peasant Art Pottery Covered Bowl	$55.00
GUIDO GAMBONE art pottery Nude Men On Horses LAMP	$1,849.23	UNIKAT 742 CA POLISH POTTERY STONEWARE SIGNATURE BOWL	$54.99
AMPHORA AUSTRIA HUGE ART NOUVEAU VASE *DANDELIONS*	$1,800.00	CA POLISH POTTERY STONEWARE DISH WITH HANDLES	$54.99
PAIR OF RARE ANTIQUE GIEN ORIGINAL DESIGN VASES	$1,755.00	BOLESLAWIEC POLISH POTTERY STONEWARE BIRD JAR POLAND	$54.99
Rare Art Nouveau Figural Dog & Frog Amphora Swamp Vase	$1,414.00	Soup Tureen w/ Ladle UNIKAT Polish Pottery Stoneware	$54.95
Amphora Austria art nouveau maiden vase. Circa 1900.	$1,325.00	Polish Pottery Gentleman's Mugs*** 4 mixed	$54.00
1895 Amphora Teplitz.Portrait Vase Profile of a Woman	$1,250.00	4 MFT Bubble Mugs SIGNATURE UNIKAT polish pottery	$53.00
VINTAGE ITALIAN ART POTTERY FAIENCE MAJOLICA TILES !	$1,125.00	BEAUTIFUL ART DECO NUDE COVERED BOWL, GERMANY	$52.99
ROBJ POWDER JAR BONBONIERRE BOX, BOITE~FRENCH ART DECO	$1,050.34	Vintage Signed Tay Italian Pottery Scottie Dog Great!!	$52.85
Montiere's Ceramic Pottery Vase by Jean Barol	$1,025.00	Polish Pottery Stoneware - 4 MIXED BOWLS Poland	$52.35
Secessionist Ceramic Amphora Teplitz Vase, Austrian	$1,008.00	Porcelain Herend Covered Jewelry / Trinket Box 797128	$52.11
1895 Amphora Teplitz.Portrait Vase Profile of a Girl	$986.00	EUROPEAN CERAMIC hand painted MORTAR & PESTLE E941	$52.03
1895 Amphora Teplitz Female Bust 52 cm high Art Nouveau	$975.00	Polish Pottery Stoneware - 6 MIXED DESSERT PLATES	$52.01

Pottery & China ▸ Art Pottery ▸ Folk

The average sales price in this subcategory is $72.23.

	HIGH		AVG
EDWIN MEADERS GREEN ROOSTER 1987 FOLK POTTERY	$2,168.00	19thC Penna. Redware Ovoid Small Jug Manganese Superb!	$74.99
BURLON CRAIG RARE EARLY 5 GAL FACE JUG-WOW!	$1,825.00	FIESTA GARDEN~Mexican Talavera Ceramic VASE~NEW~ART	$74.95
Early DOUBLE FACE Burlon Craig North Carolina Pottery	$1,695.00	Pennsylvania Redware Pitcher Sgraffiti Decorated/Signed	$73.89
?? Lanier Meaders Face Jug circa 1979 ??	$1,425.00	Corn Face Jug Georgia Folk Pottery	$73.35
LANIER MEADERS FACE JUG WEEPING EYE	$1,200.00	Cool Carl Block Face Jug with Horns	$72.99
Awesome Edwin (Nub) Meaders Southern Pottery Rooster	$1,160.00	Super,RED Snake Wrapped Face Jug,by R.Tobias,NC	$72.27
Great 19thC American Redware Slip Decorated Charger	$685.51	Face Jug Teapot Folk Art Jeff Young Catawba Valley	$72.15

CLEATER MEADERS 1985 DOUBLE FACE JUG	$679.69	Bobby Ferguson White Whisker's Man Georgia Pottery	$71.00
Damian Quezada~ Mata Ortiz Museum Quality Pottery	$660.00	Ruby Meaders Spit Glazed Southern Folk Pottery Rooster	$71.00
EARLY MARIE ROGERS DOUBLE FACE JUG	$577.89	Very Early Edwin Meaders Southern Folk Pottery Pitcher	$70.76
OLDER CLEATER MEADERS DEVIL FACE JUG	$470.00	Cool 3-Eyed Carl Block Face Jug, Signed	$70.00
Rare!! Flossie Meaders Southern Folk Pottery Rooster	$430.00	Collectible Carl Block Face Jug, Signed	$70.00
Burlon "B.B." Craig Face Jug	$410.00	Great Carl Block Face Jug, Signed and Stamped	$70.00
1989 Signed Face Jug-C. J. Meaders/Crocker-GA	$300.00	Fab group vintage Meyer/TX souvenir folk art pottery,CI	$69.00
Wonderful Large REDWARE BIRD PLATTER - Shooner	$295.00	RED Eyed,Green DEVIL Face Jug, by Randy Tobias,NC	$66.66

Pottery & China ▶ Art Pottery ▶ Made in Japan

The average sales price in this subcategory is $15.14.

	HIGH		AVG
KUTANI CAT FIGURINE 19th CENTURY	$216.38	Vintage COWGIRL SPAGHETTI Ceramic PLANTER - Japan	$16.49
c1950s Old Holt Howard RUSSIAN DRESSING complete *CUTE*	$177.50	Norcrest fine china birthday cake topper JAPAN	$16.27
*1959 Holt Howard ITALIAN DRESSING complete PIXIE WARE	$131.47	2 CooCoo Clocks Ceramic Wall Pockets, Made in Japan	$16.08
Japanese Moriage Dragonware Lithophane Saki	$104.49	Occupied Japan Colonial Woman Bisque Figurine	$15.83
ART DECO MATCH HOLDER ASHTRAY	$103.50	JYOTO CHINA CUP AND SAUCER MADE IN OCCUPIED JAPAN	$15.50
LUSTERWARE HANDS JAPAN NR		MADE IN JAPAN HAND PAINTED CONDIMENT SET	$15.50
VINTAGE MARUHON WARE TOMATO BUTTER CANDY DISH	$90.00	VINTAGE CHRISTMAS PLANTER SANTA Made In Japan	$15.01
VINTAGE RUBENS ladies head w/ pearl earrings & necklace	$76.00	Original vintage parrot salt and pepper shakers, Japan	$15.00
ESTATE FINDIHOLT HOWARD FIGURAL OLIVE JAR (JAPAN/1958)	$73.50	MADE IN JAPAN CHUBU OCCUPIED JAPAN BUTTERFLY RARE!!	$15.00
Japanese Handpainted Nagoya Lithophane Tea Set	$72.99	[2 of these sold for $15.00 each]	
Vintage Art Deco Art Pottery Vase-Screaming Deco!	$70.00	Vintage Japan Luster Figural Bird Flower Frog-XLNT-NR	$15.00
Napco Blue Gloved Lady Head Vase	$68.00	VINTAGE 1940'S SKUNK SALT & PEPPER SHAKERS NO CHIPS	$14.99
Vintage Whippet Afghan Greyhound Dog Figurine Figure	$65.66	NORCREST JAPAN VINTAGE PHEASANT PAIR FIGURINES CERAMIC	$14.99
Head Vase-Woman-Bust-Pottery-NAPCO-1959-Japan-Vintage	$65.09	Brother Juniper Friar 1958 Shafford Birthday figurine	$14.94
Pair Noritake Bone China Vase Nippon Toki Kaisha Japan	$63.78	2-Handle Art Deco Floral Vase Made in Japan Japanese	$14.51
8 Bisque Porcelain Dolls Made in Japan-Frozen Charlotte	$62.84	PELICAN FLOWER FROG ~ Made in Japan	$14.00

Pottery & China ▶ Art Pottery ▶ Majolica

The average sales price in this subcategory is $71.08.

	HIGH		AVG
RARE George Jones Majolica Swan Vase Pond Lilies	$8,109.00	OLD FRENCH MAJOLICA ASPARRAGUS PLATE 1900	$72.88
MINTON MAJOLICA POTTERY PEDASTLE (NO RESERVE!!!!!!!!)	$4,350.00	Victorian Majolica Oval Leaf Tray	$72.50
Rare Holdcroft English Majolica 19th Century Dog	$4,050.00	6 FRENCH MAJOLICA FRUIT PLATES MARKED PV MINT NR	$72.00
Majolica Minton Hunting Dog Game Dish- No Reserve!	$3,151.99	Vietri Italian Pottery Encore Murano Glass Bowls - 4	$72.00
RARE Set of 4 Antique Wedgwood Majolica Oyster Plates	$3,100.00	Vietri Italian Pottery Ricordi Xmas Lunch Plates set 4	$72.00
George Jones Majolica Oyster Plate with Fish RARE NR	$2,551.99	Early Majolica WATER LILY High Relief Plate	$72.00
RARE ITALIAN MAJOLICA ??HERCULES??circa XVII??signed	$1,900.00	Antique Majolica Begonia Leaf Dish bowl Green NR old	$71.89
Fabulous Old Minton ? Majolica 6 Well Oyster Plate	$1,425.00	FAB~MAJOLICA BLOWN OUT ARTICHOKE JARDINIERE VASE~WELLER	$71.01
ITALIAN 1740 ARMORIAL CASTELLI MAIOLICA DISH - MAJOLICA	$1,125.00	Deruta Italian Pottery STRIKING Planter - RICCO	$71.00
George Jones Majolica 3 piece Sardine Dish Mint	$1,026.00	LARGE ANTIQUE PRETTY FLORAL MAJOLICA JARDINIERE	$71.00
George Jones Majolica 3 piece strawberry set	$990.00	VINTAGE MAJOLICA MULTICOLOR CABBAGE LEAF PLATE NR	$71.00
Mafra Majolica Palissy lizards & snake plate	$990.00	Majolica Fielding Fan and Butterfly Tray	$70.90
SARREGUEMINES FRENCH MAJOLICA BLACKAMOOR FACE JUG 3884	$981.00	LARGE PITCHER WITH TULIPS, MAJOLICA?	$70.55
Majolica Minton Quaker Woman Toby Jug- No Reserve!	$889.00	RARE DELLA ROBBIA MAJOLICA TEAPOT-VINTAGE &NR	$70.00
Majolica Samuel Lear Sunflower Oyster Plate-No Reserve!	$889.00	antique majolica corn pattern pitcher 9 inch nice	$70.00

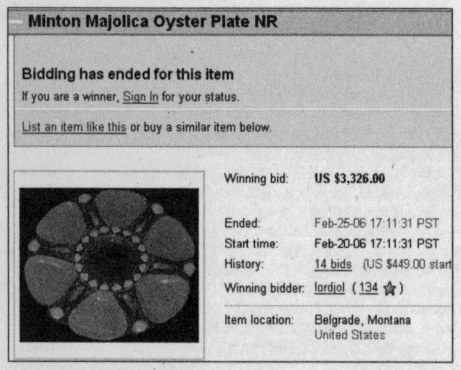

Minton Majolica Oyster Plate NR

Bidding has ended for this item
If you are a winner, Sign In for your status.

List an item like this or buy a similar item below.

Winning bid:	US $3,326.00
Ended:	Feb-25-06 17:11:31 PST
Start time:	Feb-20-06 17:11:31 PST
History:	14 bids (US $449.00 start)
Winning bidder:	lordjol (134 ☆)
Item location:	Belgrade, Montana United States

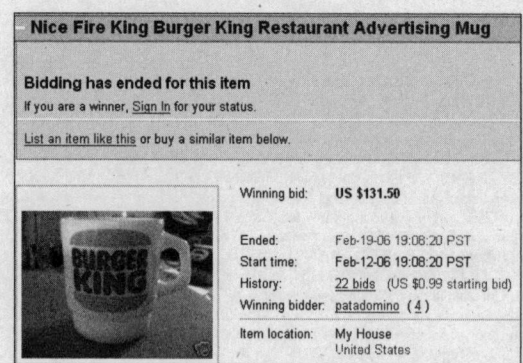

Nice Fire King Burger King Restaurant Advertising Mug

Bidding has ended for this item
If you are a winner, Sign In for your status.

List an item like this or buy a similar item below.

Winning bid:	US $131.50
Ended:	Feb-19-06 19:08:20 PST
Start time:	Feb-12-06 19:08:20 PST
History:	22 bids (US $0.99 starting bid)
Winning bidder:	patadomino (4)
Item location:	My House United States

Pottery & China ▶ Art Pottery ▶ McCoy

The average sales price in this subcategory is $25.36.

	HIGH		AVG
RARE MCCOY ART DECO SPHINX SAND JAR VASE. Early McCoy	$1,701.00	MCCOY POTTERY KITTEN KITTY CAT COOKIE JAR CANISTER!	$26.13
Art Deco at its Very Best-Great with Eames		BEAUTIFUL MCCOY SWALLOWS PLANTER W/COLD PAINT! XLNT!	$26.01
McCoy Calypso Fish Jardiniere SUPER HTF FORM! NICE!	$341.00	Rare Vintage McCoy Shawnee Blue HORSE Pitcher Planter	$26.00
Rare McCoy Miniature Fish Vase 1940 Marked USA	$277.00	Vintage McCOY TURTLE POTTERY Planter VIVID COLOR!!	$26.00
Shawnee Pottery Smiley Pig w/tulips cookie jar	$235.00	MCCOY JADITE GOLD MAMMY & CHEF SALT & PEPPER SHAKERS	$26.00
McCoy Yellow Glaze Gold Trim Sunflower Flower Form Vase	$214.39	BLACK AMERICANA MCCOY SAMBO & MAMMY S&P SHAKERS	$25.41
RARE,OLD McCOY COOKIE JAR.KITTENS IN A YARN BASKET	$181.83	Vintage McCoy Pottery Penguin Cookie Jar	$25.00

MCCOY WALT DISNEY MICKEY & MINNIE MOUSE COOKIE JAR	$174.50	Set Of Three Old McCoy Pasta Bowls-LQQK	$25.00
mccoy Jardiniere	$164.55	MCCOY TURQUOISE IVY VINTAGE VASE/PLANTER 50'S NM	$24.99
McCoy Cookie Jar=Coal Bucket with Cat/Kitten on Top	$139.38	NELSON MCCOY MATTE WHITE/	$24.99
Nelson McCoy Pink Jardiniere Base	$134.29	LEAF-BERRY HANGING PLANTER!	
MCCOY BLACK INDIAN CHIEF WARRIOR COOKIE JAR	$127.50	McCoy Pine Cone Flower Basket (1945) NR	$24.50
McCOY ELEPHANT COOKIE JAR- UNBELIEVABLE CONDITION-1953	$125.00	McCoy Goldilocks Cookie Jar #4748	$24.01
VINTAGE McCoy USA Cookie Jar COW in DOOR RED BARN ~ NR	$121.60	VINTAGE MCCOY GREEN GONDOLA BOAT PLANTER, MARKED	$24.00
Vintage McCoy Pottery Double Tulip Art Vase Yellow NICE	$107.50	McCoy Art Pottery Rustic Pine Cone Jardiniere Planter	$23.75
McCoy Green & Brown Glazed Tassel Design Jardiniere	$103.51	Mc Coy Pottery Bowl McCoy Caeerta	$23.49

Pottery & China ▶ Art Pottery ▶ Quimper

The average sales price in this subcategory is $61.41.

	HIGH		AVG
MONUMENTAL PORQUIER BLEU QUIMPER BOTANICAL CHARGER	$3,838.00	Vintage HB Quimper Hand Painted Serving Bowl NR!	$66.00
HB QUIMPER Signed FIGURAL BOOKENDS PAIR, BRETONS	$525.00	RARE Vintage Quimper Hand Painted Inkwell NR!	$62.83
Quimper, Henriot,, 1920's, 1960's, Folk Art, 27 pieces	$507.87	Antique Quimper Porringer - Man w/Pipe - NR	$62.53
QUIMPER HR HENRIOT SNUFF/ PERFUME BOTTLE BRETON	$461.30	Magnificent large French Revolution plate with lion !	$62.51
Micheau - Vernez Figure Quimper Faience	$405.00	Quimper Faience Soleil Yellow 13" Chef's Platter	$62.01
Henriot Quimper Hand Painted Signed Dishes 14 Pc. NR	$400.00	Longchamp Moustiers French pottery-set of plates/cups	$61.00
Vintage Large Quimper Serving Dish with Dolphin Handle	$315.00	Old Octagon Shape Quimper Plate, VGC, No Reserve	$61.00
VINTAGE PAIR HENRIOT QUIMPER POTTERY VASES BRETAGNE	$305.00	3 Old Henriot Quimper French Pottery Faience Plates	$61.00
HENRIOT QUIMPER FRANCE POTTERY FIGURINE	$202.50	@ FRENCH FAIENCE HB QUIMPER OYSTER PLATE @	$60.00
Vintage Henriot Quimper Plate-Paul Fouillen Artist	$200.00	SIGNED POTTERY HENRIOT QUIMPER FRANCE HANDMADE NR	$56.00
RARE QUIMPER WALL POCKET "LES SABLES" VINTAGE	$191.27	Rare HB Quimper Bowl - Exotic Bird and Flowers	$56.00
Unusual Signed HB Quimper Sailboat & Fishermen 9" Plate	$185.00	MOCHA / YELLOW WARE CUP LEFT HANDED RUSSELL HENRY	$55.21
Malicorne, not Quimper, snuff/secouette	$184.00	Old Hanging Plaque French Quimper Flute Player VCG	$55.00
HB Quimper 9" Figural of Saint Anne	$175.00	HB QUIMPER FRANCE Colorful Dinner Plate	$54.90
HB Quimper Four-Piece Breakfast Set by LaChaud	$165.00	BEAUTIFUL PAIR OF QUIMPER JARS	$52.89

Pottery & China ▶ Art Pottery ▶ Roseville

The average sales price in this subcategory is $99.79.

	HIGH		AVG
ROSEVILLE art pottery Futura 12 inch BRICK red VASE	$860.00	two ming tree conch shells	$100.00
ROSEVILLE art pottery Carnelian II 1910 TRIAL GLAZE	$850.00	Roseville Bleeding Heart Cuspidor #651-3	$100.00
35pcs green roseville raymor serving set for 6	$765.55	ROSEVILLE POTTERY ZEPHER LILLY VASE	$100.00
ROSEVILLE art pottery Brown Wisteria fat rare 9 VASE	$750.00	Roseville Pottery Blue Magnolia 2 Handled Vase 179-7	$99.99
RARE-1930 Roseville SUNFLOWER Hanging BASKET-Vintage-NR	$750.00	ROSEVILLE BLEEDING HEART HANGING BASKET	$99.99
Roseville Pottery - Gardenia Jardiniere & Pedestal Set	$735.00	Roseville Fuschia 896-8 Vase in Green	$99.51
Roseville Matte Green Large Strap Side Jardiniere	$686.58	UNUSUAL ROSEVILLE JUVENILE RABBIT HEAD CREAMER 2.25"	$97.11
12" Roseville Blackberry vase,very nice!	$675.67	LARGE ROSEVILLE WATER LILY CONSOLE BOWL 443-12	$97.00
ROSEVILLE art pottery Baneda Red VASE nice mold color	$661.00	Roseville art pottery POPPY green window box vase 878-9	$96.99
Roseville Wisteria 3pc Console Bowl & CSHs, 1933, Mint	$649.50	VINTAGE ROSEVILLE VASE, VERY SHARP CONDITION!	$96.99
ROSEVILLE art pottery Green PineCone VASE crisp 15"	$610.00	Roseville Futura Jardiniere Terrific condition!!!!!	$95.99
ROSEVILLE BLACKBERRY VASE 8"	$599.99	ROSEVILLE Pottery - Clematis Vase...Green	$93.99
Roseville 6 1/4" GREEN BANEDA #589-6 HANDLED VASE	$570.00	ROSEVILLE 45-7" FOXGLOVE RED VASE - VINTAGE -GREAT	$92.17
NO RES! 1931 Roseville Ferella, Rose & MINT! NICE!	$555.00	Roseville Imperial Vase 10 Inch Vase	$92.00
Roseville Baneda Two Handled Vase Green Blue Drip Glaze	$547.00	BEAUTIFUL BLUE ROSEVILLE FREESIA FLOWERPOT 670-5	$91.88

Pottery & China ▶ Art Pottery ▶ Scandinavian Art

The average sales price in this subcategory is $49.54.

	HIGH		AVG
Stunning SAXBO E.St.Nielsen vase mid-century eames era	$758.08	SOHOLM ceramic wall plaque Noomi Backhausen - No. 3552	$51.00
Berndt Friberg - Unique Bowl - Gustavsberg	$487.00	Arabia Ruska Dinnerware Eames Modern Ashtray Finland NR	$51.00
Stig Lindberg Stoneware Gustavesberg Textured Vase	$466.11	Book/ Magazine - Stig Lindberg	$50.00
Old Victorian Porcelain Porsgrund Commemorative Piece ?	$407.00	[3 of these sold for $50.00 each]	
Eagle B&G Royal Copenhagen	$406.00	LYNGBY PORCELAIN DENMARK LARGE RIBBED WHITE VASE!	$49.99
Stig Lindberg Gustavsberg Vase Candleholder Combined	$361.78	Rosenthal "Romanze gold rimmed large china bowl	$49.95
Vase by Rolf Palm Molle Sweden	$355.00	FANTASTIC BOWL...........................GUNNAR NYLUND	$49.00
Jorgen Mogensen stoneware sculptural vase - own studio	$355.00	Stig Lindberg Gustavsberg Sweden Reptil Carrara Vase	$48.99
Vase by J?rgen Mogensen Denmark	$330.00	Rorstrand Picknick Refrigerator Box	$48.99
Early Stig Lindberg Lg Center Bowl Gustavsberg Sweden	$308.00	Lisa Larson Cat - Gustavesberg - Sweden	$47.60
Distel Amsterdam Holland Art Pottery Vase Pair Birds	$306.00	EKEBY UPSALA ART POTTERY VASE SIGNED	$47.21
Kaj Franck - Nuutajarvi Prisma Vase signed - 1960	$305.00	royal copenhagen SHACKLED DOVES art pottery TILE	$46.67
Stig Lindberg Rare blue reptil vase Gustavsberg Sweden	$305.00	Arabia Finland - Seal - Lillemor signature -Art Pottery	$46.00
VECKLA VASE DESIGNED BY STIG LINDBERG	$299.00	Beautiful Bersa Bowl Stig Lindberg Gustavsberg	$46.00
UNUSUAL OLD ART POTTERY FINNISH	$293.00	2 EARLY DECO GERMAN BLACK FIGURES FIGURINES	$46.00
STATUE - M9802 - NR		Studio pottery female figure-Stig Lindberg/ Eames fans	$45.20

Pottery & China ▶ Art Pottery ▶ SEG/Paul Revere

The average sales price in this subcategory is $226.25.

	HIGH		
HIGH TO LOW			
SATURDAY EVENING GIRLS PAUL REVERE SCENIC TILE	$1,750.00	SEG Saturday Evening Girls GOOSE MUG/CUP Paul Revere	$131.50
SEG 1916 Plate Rabbits in Lettuce Patch Stickley Era	$765.00	Signed S.E.G 11-14 and FL for Fannie Levine NO RESERVE	
S E G SIGNED POTTERY BOOKEND	$510.00	S.E.G SMALL FLOWER FROG (SATURDAY EVENING GIRLS)	$40.00
LANDSCAPE SCENE UNUSUAL nr		Paul Revere Saturday Evening Girls Pottery Plate PRP	$33.00
RARE PAUL REVERE / SATURDAY EVENING GIRLS TRIVET	$345.00	Paul Revere American Art Pottery Teal Handled Bowl	$9.99

Pottery & China ▶ Art Pottery ▶ Staffordshire

The average sales price in this subcategory is $55.17.

	HIGH		AVG
XTREMLY RARE American view historical Staffordshire.	$950.00	1860s Staffordshire Figurine Pocket Watch Stand EX COND	$57.78
American scene historical Staffordshire potato bowl	$949.00	Set of 4 Red Pink Transferware Burgenland Plates ++++++	$57.00
American view historical Staffordshire platter. c.1830	$910.00	ANTIQUE STAFFORDSHIRE CAT WITH A MOUSE~AWESOME~NO RES	$56.55
HISTORICAL BLUE PLATE B&O RAILROAD INCLINED PLANE	$637.00	FABULOUS STAFFORDSHIRE PLATTER	$56.00
Brown Transferware Large Platter Basket Flowers Antique	$597.77	1850 16 IRONSTONE FLOW MULBERRY SAUCERS PLATES NR	$56.00
RARE Stubbs historical Staffordshire custard cup	$499.99	Pink Transferware Plate , Clyde Scenery c.1830	$55.00
Rare historical Staffordshire gravy boat.STUBBS.	$499.99	Swinnertons Hampton Ivory English Cottage Dinner Plates	$55.00
STAFFORDSHIRE DOGS ENGLISH KING CHARLES SPANIELS C 1890	$380.00	Blue Feather Edge Staffordshire Clews Leeds Soup Dish	$54.99
RARE BLUE STAFFORDSHIRE COVERED WATER PITCHER	$375.00	LIBERTY BLUE 7" PLATES WASHINGTON LEAVING CHURCH x4	$54.99
1850 4 IRONSTONE FLOW MULBERRY PITCHER & G BOAT	$374.99	English Blue Romantic Transferware Pitcher, Circa, 1860	$54.55
Mint Liberty Blue Platter Declaration Independence NIB	$354.07	ANTIQUE BLUE & WHITE RIDGWAYS ASIATIC PALACES PLATE	$53.01
FANTASTIC STAFFORDSHIRE TRANSFER PLATTER ANTIQUE SCENES	$350.01	ANTIQUE STAFFORDSHIRE DOG	$53.00
CHARMING STAFFORDSHIRE PAIR FIGURES CHILDEN ON GOATS	$345.00	Old Staffordshire Ware Poodles! ~ C.1910	$52.00
A WONDERFUL PAIR OF #2 BLACK & WHITE STAFFORDSHIRE DOGS	$300.00	Small Staffordshire Figure Bocage - NR	$51.50
A WONDERFUL STANDING STAFFORDSHIRE FIGURE OF BURNS	$295.00	5 Liberty Blue Staffordshire Old North Church Plates	$51.00

Pottery & China ▶ Art Pottery ▶ Stangl

The average sales price in this subcategory is $29.28.

	HIGH		AVG
Stangl Birds - Pair Red Headed Woodpeckers #3752D	$459.54	VINTGE STANGL POTTERY REDSTART BIRDS # 3490	$31.00
5 Pc. Set Stangl Pottery Cowboy Western Cactus Plates	$338.00	Stangl Art Pottery Vase Orange Double Handle #3106	$29.99
Stangl Birds 8" high two birds not sure which ones	$280.00	STANGL ART POTTERY c1925 German Unique Design #3784	$29.99
STANGL ART POTTERY BIRD A PAIR OF LOVEBIRDS #3404	$174.50	STANGL BIRDS - CERULEAN WARBLER - POTTERY	$29.89
Rare STANGL Art Pottery Bird BREWER'S BLACKBIRD Mint!!!	$173.08	Stangl Kentucky Warbler Bird Figurine. No Reserve	$29.50
Stangl Art Pottery Painted Signed Rooster Bird Figurine	$150.00	Stangl Bird - Red Faced Warbler.#3594	$29.01
Stangl Bird POTTERY GOLDFINCH GROUP Figurine Birds	$138.50	STANGL POTTERY JACK IN THE BOX 3 PIECE SET	$28.99
Haeger Geranium Leaf Green / Stangl Apple Handled Vase	$126.50	Trio Stangl 24kt Gold washed Ducks,1960's,EXCELLENT	$28.00
Vintage Stangl Elephant	$117.05	Very Large Art Pottery "Stangl" Vase Terra Rose Mint	$27.66
VINTAGE STANGL BIRD AND FLOWER MINT NO.5627	$112.50	Stangl Birds - Grey Cardinal #3596 (Pyrrhuloxia)	$27.00
Stangl Birds - Group of Gold finches #3635	$110.98	STANGL TWIN CANDLEHOLDER #1391-BIRD & FLOWER-1931-33	$26.99
Stangl Bird - Black-throated Green Warbler #3814	$105.98	Vintage Stangl Cigarette Box Trinket Fruit Design 3798	$26.99
STANGL DINNER PLATE PLATES BLUEBERRY 8	$103.50	STANGL ART POTTERY BOWL MAGNOLIA PATTERN - NO RESERVE	$26.98
ORIGINAL STANGL COUNTRY GARDEN DINNERWARE SET 25 PCS	$100.00	Stangl Mediterranean Blue Divided Serving Dish	$26.53
VINTAGE STANGL BIRD FIGURINE - BREWER'S BLACKBIRD 3591	$100.00	Stangl Art Pottery Vase Yellow Double Handle #3140	$26.50

Pottery & China ▶ China, Dinnerware ▶ Aynsley

The average sales price in this subcategory is $26.87.

	HIGH		AVG
Aynsley Pembroke Bone Chine Dinnerware 98pc. Teapot, soup turreen, casserole, platters, gravy WOW	$1,250.00	AYNSLEY GREEN AND FLORAL TEA CUP AND SAUCER BONE CHINA	$29.00
Aynsley EMPRESS COBALT Gilt set of 8 cream soups	$480.00	Aynsley PEMBROKE Full Size 2 Handled Covered Sugar Bowl	$28.99
AYNSLEY SUMMERTIME CHINA 5 PC/8 PLACE SET/40 PCS TOTAL	$465.00	Aynsley Art Deco Style Trio - Cup, Saucer & Tea Plate	$27.99
Aynsley EMPRESS COBALT Gilt 8 crescent salad plates	$405.00	Aynsley 1930's FLORAL ROSE BOWL - COBALT & GOLD Tea Cup	$27.84
Aynsley Pembrook 32 Pieces (Plates, Cups & Saucers)	$349.95	Aynsley HUGE PINK YELLOW RED ROSE BOWL Tea Cup NR!	$27.23
Rare & Exquisite Aynsley Cabinet Cup & Saucer	$221.50	Aynsley VIOLETTE Cup and Saucer - Mint	$26.51
Aynsley EMPRESS COBALT Gold Gilt Large Platter	$124.72	AYNSLEY LEIGHTON BLUE TEACUPS (2)	$26.50
AYNSLEY (HENLEY) FINE BONE CHINA - 4 PC SOUP BOWLS	$103.94	Aynsley Bone China Roses Biscuit Platter	$26.03
AYNSLEY ORCHARD GOLD CANDY DISH (SIGNED D. JONES)	$103.50	AYNSLEY CABINET STYLE Cup and Saucer GILDED A ++++	$26.02
UNUSUAL English AYNSLEY Cup & Saucer w/Flower Handle	$102.71	ANTIQUE 1900's AYNSLEY MIKADO DOUBLE HANDLE CUP SAUCER	$26.00
AYNSLEY HP ORCHARD TRIO	$99.99	AYNSLEY CUP SAUCER BLACK WITH POPPIES	$25.49
Aynsley Leighton 6-piece Place Setting Fine Bone China	$90.00	AYNSLEY Tea Cup Saucer: COBALT BLUE RIM ROSE SPRAY GOLD	$24.99
Vintage Aynsley Flower Handle Cup & Saucer	$80.65	Aynsley FUCHSIA ROSE BOWL - COBALT & GOLD Tea Cup	$24.99
6 ANTIQUE 1900's AYNSLEY MIKADO SALAD PLATE PLATES	$79.00	AYNSLEY 30s SPRING VIOLETS BLACK & GOLD CHINTZ Tea Cup	$24.99
LOVELY AYNSLEY "BUTTERFLY HANDLE" CUP & SAUCER	$79.00	vintage aynsley pagoda cup& saucer	$24.99

Pottery & China ▶ China, Dinnerware ▶ Blue Ridge

The average sales price in this subcategory is $22.81.

	HIGH		AVG
CHINA - SOUTHERN POTTERIES BLUE RIDGE CERAMICS	$586.00	6 Blue Ridge Southern Potteries 5" Floral Tulip Bowls	$23.94
Blue Ridge Floral Demitasse Coffee Pot	$317.47	BLUE RIDGE POTTERY CRAB APPLE LARGE OVAL PLATTER	$23.82
Magnolia Blue Ridge Pottery plate, saucers, bowl	$306.51	Beautiful Blue Ridge BUD TOP Salt 'n Pepper Shakers NR	$23.50
Blue Ridge Carillon Singing Tower Plate, Caribbean Set	$232.49	3 Blue Ridge Hand Painted "Spring Song" 9 1/4" Plates	$23.38
Blue Ridge Floral Chintz Chocolate Pot, Sugar, Creamer	$222.50	BLUE RIDGE SOUTHERN POTTERIES QUIMPER PLATE	$23.09
GREAT OLD BLUE RIDGE DINNERWARE:1930'S:55 FINE PIECES!	$192.38	Southern Potteries Blue Ridge Nappy Dish	$23.00
BLUE RIDGE CHINA 'FRENCH PEASANT' CHOCOLATE POT RARE!	$168.05	2 SOUTHERN POTTERIES BLUE RIDGE HP 10 1/4" PLATES NR	$22.51
** 88 PIECE SET SOUTHERN POTTERY -BLUE RIDGE HANDPAINTD	$152.50	6 Great Old Fruit Fantasy Blue Ridge Dinner Plates	$22.50
BLUE RIDGE POTTERY COVERED CASSEROLE	$130.49	Large Blue Ridge Pottery Poinsetta Serving Bowl Nice!!	$22.49
BLUE RIDGE CHINA FRENCH PEASANT SUGAR & CREAMER RARE!	$127.50	Blue Ridge Bluebell Bouquet Dinner Plates [2]	$22.01
BLUE RIDGE CHARM HOUSE YELLOW/PINK FLORAL CHINA TEA POT	$127.50	Blue Ridge Primrose Path Salad Dessert Plate Astor Shpe	$21.81
RARE BLUE RIDGE 8 1/4 in UGLY BIRD PLATE	$125.00	Blue Ridge Bluebell Bouquet Cups-Saucers [5]Sets	$21.69
Vintage Blue Ridge Southern Potteries Christmas Plates	$122.50	Blue Ridge Sunfire (gray) Ovide Coffee Pot Base	$21.61
Blue Ridge Jumbo Cup and Saucer	$104.00	Blue Ridge Southern Potteries Serving Bowl Signed	$21.61
Blue Ridge Rose Marie Chocolate Pot Set complete	$102.69	Three Blue Ridge Hand Painted 9.5 Dinner Plates	$21.51

Pottery & China ▶ China, Dinnerware ▶ Blue Willow

The average sales price in this subcategory is $15.86.

	HIGH		AVG
1877 JOHN MORTLOCK FLOW BLUE WILLOW PEDESTAL CAKE PLATE	$261.00	BEAUTIFUL Allerton WILLOW Rectangular Vegetable Bowl	$16.00
C1890 LARGE WILLOW SOUP TUREEN & LADLE	$200.00	Old Japan Deep Blue-Blue Willow Oval Platter	$16.00
Set of 6 Buffalo Pottery 1909 Blue Willow Tray Platters	$198.00	NIGHT LIGHT Blue Willow Theme Tea Mug Cup Nightlight	$15.99
Blue Willow dishes, Homer Laughlin, 26 pieces	$125.00	Royal Venton Blue Willow 11 1/4" x 9" Platter	$15.95
IRISH Porcelain BLUE WILLOW COVERED SERVING BOWL	$117.50	(4) FROSTED BLUE WILLOW 12 oz Beverage TUMBLERS-GLASSES	$15.95
25 pc. Child's Blue Willow Tea Set for Six	$112.50	Old Japan Deep Blue-Blue Willow Dinner Plates [2]	$15.78
Antique JOHN MORTLOCK FLOW BLUE WILLOW PLATE ~ ca 1877	$102.50	Blue Willow Ware 10" Pie Plate or Serving Dish	$15.55
Vintage Blue Willow Canisters / Japan / NR	$89.99	Blue Willow Glass Bowl..Very Different	$15.52
Blue Willow Coffee Pot and Warmer Japan	$88.00	1909 Buffalo Pottery Blue Willow Bowl No Reserve	$15.50
EXCELLENT SIGNED BLUE WILLOW MEAT PLATTER	$81.00	BLUE WILLOW TEA POT	$15.50
Vintage Blue Willow Measuring Cups with Rack / Japan	$79.99	Churchill Of England Blue Willow Large Serving Platter	$15.50
Blue Willow GAUDY TUREEN 1912 - 1930	$77.00	Blue Willow GAUDY PAGODA TEA POT STAND	$15.50
Royal Cuthbertson Blue Willow ~ 14 Pc PUNCH BOWL SET ~	$70.00	6 Blue Willow Individual Egg Holders Eggs Holder Cups	$15.50
Occupied Japan Child's Teaset 6 Cup Saucer Blue Willow	$66.00	Blue Willow Vegetable Bowl	$15.50
Unusual Blue Willow Two Drawer Spice Set	$56.99	6 CHURCHILL BLUE WILLOW SOUP/CEREAL BOWLS-mint	$15.50

Pottery & China ▶ China, Dinnerware ▶ Chintz

The average sales price in this subcategory is $31.29.

	HIGH		AVG
OLD Royal Winton GRIMWADES SUNSHINE CHINTZ TABLE LAMP	$460.23	Rosebud Chintz by Spode Cup and Saucer	$35.00
Lord Nelson "BLACK BEAUTY" Chintz Stacking Teapot	$365.00	ROYAL TUDOR CHINTZ PATTERN CAKE PLATE AND SERVER	$35.00
Rare Royal Winton Athena "Sweet Pea" Teapot	$295.00	Royal Winton Chintz Spring Glory demitasse Cup/Saucer	$34.95
VINTAGE ROYAL WINTON 6" CHINTZ PITCHER MINT	$226.00	Rosebud Chintz by Spode Square Luncheon Plate	$34.07
Royal Winton Chintz Teapot ~ Nantwich	$202.51	ROYAL COTSWOLDS FLORAL CHINA CHINTZ TEA POT TEAPOT	$33.00
ROYAL WINTON GRIMWADES CHINTZ SUMMERTIME CHEESE DISH	$188.49	Vintage Warwick - Cheery Chintz Teapot No Reserve!	$31.00
Vintage Royal Winton Chintz "MARGUERITE" Butter Dish	$165.00	Churchill CALICO Blue & White Chintz TEAPOT	$30.50
LOT OF 4! MARGUERITE~Royal Winton~CHINTZ~Tea Cup/Saucer	$156.50	Crown Ducal Harmony Chintz Dinner Plate	$29.99
Collection of antique England Chintz	$153.01	VINT. BERMUDA CHINTZ CAKE PLATE~MYOTT~MINT	$29.99
Chintz by Sango China 83 Pc. Set Rose Pattern Gold Rim	$152.50	ROYAL COTSWOLDS FLORAL CHINA CHINTZ TEA POT TEAPOT	$29.04
Gorgeous Royal Winton "June Festival" Stacking Teapot	$149.00	Vintage Chintz Lord Nelson ROSE TIME Vase - #1	$28.99
LOT OF 4! MARGUERITE~Royal Winton~CHINTZ~Tea Cup/Saucer	$138.55	Vintage Chintz Lord Nelson ROSE TIME Vase - #2	$28.99
Rare Green Tulip Chintz Cheese Keep N/R	$130.48	Empire Chintz	$28.00
OLD CLEVEDON Chintz Royal Winton Jam Pot Jampot WOW	$124.99	Lorna Doone Chintz Plant Pot	$27.99
BLACK BEAUTY LORD NELSON WARE CHINTZ CREAM SUGAR & LID	$124.50	ROYAL STANDARD BONE CHINA CHINTZ TEACUP & SAUCER	$27.89

Pottery & China ▶ China, Dinnerware ▶ Commemorative

The average sales price in this subcategory is $23.66.

	HIGH		AVG
C1850 SUNDERLAND "ENGLAND'S FUTURE KING" PLATE	$202.50	YE OLD HISTORICAL STAFFORDSHIRE POTTERY PLATE # 5	$28.50
Richard Ginori Porcelain China Urn - 2 Handled - EC	$135.83	1912 SOUVENIR PLATE RIGBY IDAHO STORE	$27.00
Grandma Moses collector plates SET OF 8 by Syracuse	$81.00	Commemorative-Coronation Mug Very Vintage	$26.01
Huge 24 pc Set Noritake Fine Ivory China Adagio 7237	$81.00	Old White Ironstone Commemorative Pitcher, Chicago Fair	$26.00
Pennoyer Sanitarium Kenosha WIS WI Wheelock Plate 1910s	$76.11	Kannapolis NC Commemorative Plate Cannon YMCA 1940s NR	$26.00
Antique Transfer Ware Pitcher For Order of Odd Fellows	$74.00	Old Small Urn Vase Souvenir China Highland Beach NJ	$26.00
Liberty Blue Pitcher-Old North Church	$70.03	Laura Knight King Edward VIII Coronation Mug Wilkinson	$22.50
TIVOLI Oak Bluffs Martha's Vineyard MA SOUVENIR CREAMER	$67.66	MINT Alaska Highway Cream & Sugar Set + BONUS	$22.02
SET OF ROYAL MUGS ENGLAND QUEENS MARY ELIZABETH KINGS	$66.00	CARLTON WARE WILTSHAW & ROBINSON CHARLES DICKENS BOWL	$20.40
Flow Blue Staffordshire Jonroth plate Mermaid Florida	$55.50	DELAND, Fl. CHina Vintage (Allen Co.)	$20.00
Old Small Mug Souvenir China Dawson Springs KY	$54.50	1919 American Flag Calendar Plate, Walnut Grove, Minn.	$19.99
1962 Eden, NY Sesquicentennial plate EXCELLENT COND!	$53.00	Old Toothpick Holder Souvenir China Watkins Glen NY	$19.99
State Prison Waupun WIS WI Wheelock Plate 1910s	$43.00	Old Volunteers Monument Halifax NS Canada Flower Vase	$19.06
FENTON STUNNING LILY TRAIL TOPAZ PITCHER/CRUET	$42.57	Souvenir of Perryville Missouri Souvenir Plate orchids	$18.88
(5) Princess Diana 8 3/4" Oval Collector Plates	$42.00	BEAUTIFUL FENTON CAT	$18.35

Pottery & China ▶ China, Dinnerware ▶ Crown Staffordshire

The average sales price in this subcategory is $33.80.

	HIGH		AVG
MINIATURE CROWN STAFFORDSHIRE HAND PAINTED TEA SET NR	$679.00	Crown Staffordshire Chelsea Manor cup and saucer	$38.77
Crown Staffordshire set - Ellesmere pattern	$350.00	CROWN STAFFORDSHIRE - HOLLYHOCK 2 LUNCH / SMALL DINNER	$37.79
Crown Staffordshire 17 Piece Hunting Scene Tea Set	$307.10	Coca Cola Numbered Crown Staffordshire Teapot Limited	$36.51
Staffordshire 42 Piece Beautiful China Dinnerware Set	$219.50	CROWN STAFFORDSHIRE MINIATURE CUP&SAUCER	$36.00
Staffordshire Chinese Willow dinner plates NEW	$162.73	Vintage Staffordshire Cup&Saucer-Fox Hunt-Bone China	$36.00
Staffordshire Chinese Willow dinner plates NEW	$159.28	Staffordshire Mr Micawber Crown Fine Bone China*RARE*	$35.99
Crown Staffordshire Coffee Can	$127.50	CR STAFFORDSHIRE ENGLAND'S BOUQUET TIER CAKE STAND	$34.99
Crown Staffordshire Coffee Can	$125.52	Crown Staffordshire Bone China Bowl of Flowers England	$33.99
[3 of these sold for $125.52 each]		Lot 11 Plates Crown Staffordshire China Golden Glory	$32.50
Crown Staffordshire Coffee Can	$125.00	CROWN STAFFORDSHIRE MINIATURE CUP AND SAUCER	$32.00
15 PC CROWN STAFFORDSHIRE TEA SET F14745	$99.99	[2 of these sold for $32.00 each]	
Vintage Crown Staffordshire Hollyhock Muffin Dish	$99.00	Royal Crownford CHINTZ Blue Calico Shakers~Unusual	$31.51
11 Pc. Bone China CROWN Staffordshire Delicate Roses	$99.00	Miniature Tea Cup and Saucer Crown Staffordshire	$31.50
CROWN STAFFORDSHIRE MINIATURE CUP AND SAUCER	$88.00	Two Crown Staffordshire Hunting Scene Luncheon Plates	$31.00
NMint 8 Piece Crown Staffordshire Miniature Tea Set WNR	$77.99	Miniature Crown Staffordshire Cup& Saucer HP	$31.00
Lot of 5 Crown Staffordshire Plates	$77.56	Two Crown Staffordshire Hunting Scene Salad Plates	$30.00

Pottery & China ▸ China, Dinnerware ▸ Dansk

The average sales price in this subcategory is $20.44.

	HIGH		AVG
DANSK Teak Tray w/ "Inlaid Brick" Design,Excellent Cond	$284.99	Dansk Ceylon Large Serving Plate 12"	$20.50
Dansk Dishes	$167.50	Dansk Teakwood Cheeseboard and Knife MINT	$20.50
Dansk Flora Bayberry Blue 6 Dinner Plates NR	$142.50	DANSK MESA TURQUOISE Serving Bowl	$20.50
Dansk Blue Mist Large Dinner Plates	$132.45	(4) DANSK BISSERUP WHITE PORTUGAL DINNER PLATES	$20.50
DANSK QUISTGAARD PEPPER MILL/SALT SHAKER EAMES ERA	$103.50	Dansk KOBENSTYLE Enamelware BLUE PAELLA PAN	$20.50
DANSK DENMARK JHQ Teak SALT	$99.00	FIVE (5) DANSK DANISH MODERN BLUE MIST LUNCHEON PLATES	$20.50
PEPPER SHAKER MILL Peugeot		2 Dansk Generation Mist Blue Soup Plates-NEW	$20.50
Dansk LARGE Blue Mesa BEAN/SOUP POT with HANDLES	$93.50	4 Dansk Design Nielstone Spice Tan Dinner Plates	$20.49
DANSK BLUE MESA PORTUGAL CANISTER SET	$89.99	4) Dansk Denmark "Brown Mist" Cups & Saucers	$20.00
Dansk Coffee Pitcher Flamestone Quistgaard Eames Era	$80.50	DANSK MESA TURQUOISE 4 CEREAL BOWLS 5.75" DIAMETER	$20.00
Dansk Cups & Saucers Demitasse Quistgaard Flamestone	$72.01	Dansk Craft Colors Rhubarb 4 piece placesetting	$20.00
Dansk Bistro Christianshavn 5 Pcs - Pots - Casserole	$71.00	DANSK Bistro Maribo - 2 Dinner Plates	$20.00
Dansk Covered Sugar Fluted Flamestone Brown	$68.99	[2 of these sold for $20.00 each]	
Danish Modern DANSK Teak Wood	$66.00	DANSK Bistro Maribo - 2 Salad/Dessert Plates	$20.00
PEPPER Grinder QUISTGAARD		DANSK BLUE MESA PORTUGAL ONION SOUP BOWL COVERED	$20.00
5 Dansk Design Nielstone Spice Tan Coupe Cereal Bowls	$64.56	[2 of these sold for $20.00 each]	
Dansk Sugar & Creamer With Oval Tray	$61.51	Pair Dansk Pottery Stoneware Candle Sticks Holders	$19.99

Pottery & China ▸ China, Dinnerware ▸ Decorative

The average sales price in this subcategory is $25.17.

	HIGH		AVG
L.W. DONATH VASE HANDPAINTED	$1,201.99	Lot 4 Bradford Exchange Ducks Unlimited Plates **Look**	$33.96
BY A. HEIDRICH FOREST DEER		Pair Porcelain Urns Vases 2 Handled Austria Vintage	$32.99
Sevres China "Candlestick" Telephone	$455.00	GAUDY IRONSTONE PLATE - ELGERS	$32.00
Beautiful Ginori Hand Painted "Roses" Vase	$299.99	6 Sided White Porcelain Covered Sugar German Vintage	$31.79
MOTTAHEDEH TORQUAY GREEN	$257.88	antique dragonware	$31.01
WINTERTHUR PORCELAIN PLATTER		RW Royal Rudolstadt Large HP Bisque Swirl Vase	$31.00
REPRODUCTION UNUSED ORMOLU	$249.99	Hand Painted Plate Bavaria Signed Peonies Antique	$31.00
PORCELAIN IMARI PUNCH BOWL		Victorian U.S. Lemonade Set Pitcher Tumblers Grape	$31.00
RARE CHINA & BRASS CHERUB	$177.50	Price Kensington Cottage Ware pitcher and 2 cups	$31.00
MUSICAL CIGARETTE DISPENSER		NORMA SHERMAN CALICO CAT BOWL ROYAL CROWNFORD ENGLAND	$30.89
2 Antique Decorative Urns Pale Green & Floral Dresden?	$112.50	Graceful Art Nouveau Gerold Porzellan Tall Ewer Vase	$30.00
LOVELY,HAND PAINTED PORCELAIN	$102.50	GORGEOUS ANTIQUE GAUDY WELSH CUP&SAUCER	$29.95
PLAQUE,FRAMED,SGND,ROSES!		MJ Art Deco Lustre Figural Bird Paradise Pheasant Bowl	$26.00
Old HndPntd R Hanke Royal Wettina Austrian Porc. Vase	$89.99	Victorian Hand Painted Signed Roses Cake Plate Charger	$26.00
Sevres Cobalt Blue White Vase w/ Gold Handles	$89.00	PRETTY SHABBY ROSE BOUQUET TEA CUP&SAUCER TRIO! ?1940	$26.00
FRENCH SEVRES SIGNED VICTORIAN LOVERS JAR 18"TALL	$89.00		
Geisha China	$86.00		
VINTAGE -MASONS - BEAUTIFUL TURKEY PLATE	$81.00		
Lynn Chase COSTA AZZURRA Seashells/Birds/Flowers Teapot	$79.00		
Vintage Richard Ginori Paradise Bird Jardiniere Vase	$67.99		

Pottery & China ▸ China, Dinnerware ▸ Dinnerware

The average sales price in this subcategory is $21.05.

	HIGH		AVG
Vintage Glidden Art Pottery 24 Pc Blue Glaze Lunch Set	$357.00	Antique Flow Blue?Furnival Old Chelsea Berry Bowls-NR	$21.82
Rare Antique Dedham Pottery 8 1/2" Swan Plate	$351.00	Four Goebel Burgund Salad Plates	$21.61
90 Pc Dinnerware Set Charlotte Edelstein Bavaria German	$299.99	Vietri Solimene 10" Dinner Plate Rare	$21.59
BIG MOTTAHEDEH HISTORIC CHARLESTON BOWL&LID~TUREEN	$271.67	Old Wachtersbach German Fish Oyster Seafood Plate	$21.50
12 x Dinner Plate LANGENTHAL BLOCK Transition WHITE	$255.25	ASST LOT OF 12 FINE CHINA STORAGE BAGS, NR!!	$21.50
8 Place settings STRAWBERRY DINNERWARE CHINA SET +++	$200.00	Corey Hill Ridgeway Polychromed Flow Blue Desert Dish 2	$21.50
SIX Richard Ginori Pots De Creme From Bonwit Teller	$154.49	Vietri Solimene 8" Salad Plate Rare	$21.49
FLINTRIDGE CHINA 43pc.PLATINUM GREY - ROSE PATTERN	$130.53	Vietri Solimene 10" Dinner Plate Rare	$21.02
New Dinnerware Set - Service for 8 plus extras!	$124.70	Blue Danube (Japan) Five-Piece Place Setting MINT	$21.00
Meissen Large Platter, Cobalt Blue, Floral, RARE, NR	$115.83	2 Hartstone Pottery Provincial Posy Handled Soup Mugs	$20.75
6 x Dessert plate LANGENTHAL BLOCK Transition WHITE	$111.02	HENN Double Sponge SALT n PEPPER Shaker Set NR	$20.57
CURRIER & IVES TRAIN MUGS RARE SET OF FOUR	$110.00	Nikko Christmastime Teddy Bear Dessert Tray & 2 Plates	$20.55
Christian Dior Gaudron Malachite, 4 Napkin Rings in Box	$103.51	GAIL PITTMAN~CREAMER & SUGAR~"MINT"~GRAPEVINE~NR!!	$20.53
4 Villeroy and Boch French Garden Cups and Saucers	$102.50	HUGE TOM TURKEY HAND PAINTED PLATTER(ITALY)MARKED	$20.50
1886 Aesthetic Brown Transfer Sauce Boat & Tray	$100.00	Cracker Barrel Red Transfer Ware Cup ~Saucer~Mint~~	$20.50
		Antique Flow Blue?Furnival Old Chelsea Berry Bowls-NR	$21.82

Pottery & China ▸ China, Dinnerware ▸ Dresden

The average sales price in this subcategory is $64.46.

	HIGH		AVG
DRESDEN LAMM BOUILLON CUPS W/UNDERPLATES SET OF 6	$1,286.10	Irish Dresden Girl with Hanky	$68.50
Dresden Lace Figurine Mother/Baby ~ EXCELLENT COND ~ NR	$685.00	NR SALE ELEGANT VICTORIAN DRESDEN LADY READING FIGURINE	$67.95
DRESDEN DINNER PLATE PLATES LAMM HEAVY GOLD SET OF 6	$617.00	Old Large Dresden 5 Arm Cherub Candlabra MINT MINT	$67.76
Vintage DRESDEN Tall PORCELAIN FIGURAL LAMP and Shade	$610.00	VERY OLD BLUE DRESDEN LACE FIGURINE COURT LADY PATTING	$67.00
Pair Large Antique Dresden Porcelain Covered Urns Vases	$561.00	Dresden Victorian Portrait Decorative Urn must see!	$67.00
1891-1914 AMBROSIUS LAMM GERMANY DRESDEN CUP & PLATE	$430.00	SUPER Hand Painted Antique Dresden Fancy Vase PAIR	$64.99
Dresden Victorian Couple Chess in Parlor Figurine lace!	$405.00	Irish Dresden Little Bluebird in Pink	$63.10
Antique Dresden Porcelain Statue Stagecoach Figurine!	$399.99	Dresden Meissen Figurine Regency Lady	$62.99
HANDPAINTED A. LAMM DRESDEN CUP & SAUCER, EXQUISITE! NR	$380.00	Vintage German Porcelain Dipped Lace Figurine Dresden?	$62.52

Vintage Irish Dresden Figurine-Beautiful,Old & MINT!!	$377.51	CALIFORNIA DRESDEN BY AVIS LACE FIGURINE "APRIL" #24102	$62.52
DRESDEN 2 VICTORIAN MAIDENS IN ELEGANT GOWNS FIGURINE	$363.78	Dresden Germany Lady Figurine Lace Victorian Woman #6	$61.00
DRESDEN LAMM 6-INCH PLATE PLATES HEAVY GOLD SET OF 6	$304.10	Dresden Germany Lady Figurine Lace Ballerina Woman #4	$61.00
Dresden Lace Porcelain Ballerina Figurine Circa 1906-30	$300.00	HAND PAINTED GERMAN DRESDEN SEATED GIRL PLAYS ACCORDIAN	$61.00
DRESDEN VICTORIAN MAIDEN FIGURAL MANTLE CLOCK 18x13x8	$260.67	1940s DRESDEN V20013 1762 PORCELAIN GIRL BALLERINA	$60.99
Dresden Porcelain Demitasse Cup&Saucer~RKlemm	$256.11	NR SALE VICTORIAN ELEGANT LADY DRESDEN FIGURINE	$60.79

Pottery & China ▸ China, Dinnerware ▸ Fiesta: Contemporary

The average sales price in this subcategory is $15.79.

	HIGH		AVG
Fiesta (Almost Vintage) Retired YELLOW Fiesta LAMP, HTF	$172.50	FIESTA WARE SET OF 8 MIXED COLORS SALAD PLATES	$15.99
New 4 piece Purple Fiestaware Sugar & Creamer Tray Set	$90.02	FIESTA WARE SET OF 4 10-1/2" MIXED COLOR DINNER PLATES	$15.99
Fiesta 60th anniversary Rose beverage set in box	$87.19	[2 of these sold for $15.99 each]	
Fiesta 60th anniversary Lilac beverage set in box	$76.05	FIESTA WARE SCARLET LIMITED EDITION MINI DISC PITCHER	$15.99
FIESTA FIESTAWARE YELLOW RETRO	$76.00	FIESTA WHITE 10" Deep Pie Baker 1st QUALITY-New In Box	$15.99
TOASTER - XLNT W/BOX		Fiesta SCARLET / RED Large 44 oz TEAPOT / TEA POT	$15.95
Fiestaware Rare SAPPHIRE Carafe - MIB - 1st quality	$70.00	FIESTA WARE SCARLET RED LARGE 1 QT BOWL	$15.75
FIESTA WARE CHARTREUSE NEW 4 PIECE PLACE SETTING	$61.00	FIESTA WARE RETIRED (2) CHARTRUE 10-1/4OZ. MUGS	$15.56
Fiesta 4 Pc. Place Setting, CHARTREUSE w/Mug, Retired	$54.00	FIESTA WARE CHARTREUSE LARGE BOWL 8-1/4"	$15.50
Fiestaware Chartreuse 5 Piece place setting	$52.00	FIESTA WARE ~ COBALT BLUE ~ SUGAR & CREAMER	$15.50
Fiesta Persimmon Millennium I Millenium Vase - NIB	$51.59	COLORFUL AND UNIQUE FIESTA FOOD PICKS	$15.50
SAPPHIRE FIESTA PLATTER- RARE RETIRED COLOR- NEW!	$51.01	~ Fiesta~ Turquiose Dinner Plate Kitchen Wall Clock	$15.50
Fiestaware Chartreuse 5 Piece place setting	$51.00	FIESTA WARE COBALT BLUE SUGAR, CREAM AND FIGURE 8 TRAY	$15.50
12- Fiesta Juniper Fruit Bowls NEW Retired! 1st Quality	$50.99	2 LOVELY FIESTA SALAD/SERVING BOWLS	$15.50
Fiesta (New) White w/ Redbird on Pine branch 10 pcs	$49.99	3 HLC Fiesta Ware Soup or Cereal Bowls-Peach Color	$15.50
FIESTA FIESTAWARE MILLENNIUM I VASE IN PEARL GRAY	$49.99	Fiesta Ware Tangerine Serving Bowl - NEW & 1st Quality	$15.50

Pottery & China ▸ China, Dinnerware ▸ Franciscan

The average sales price in this subcategory is $27.87.

	HIGH		AVG
FRANCISCAN APPLE DINNERWARE & SERVING PIECES 1970's	$406.50	Franciscan Apple Butter Dish w/Lid c1953 Mint NR	$28.76
FRANCISCAN DESERT ROSE MIXING BOWLS 3 IN ALL	$278.00	Franciscan Desert Rose Tall Salt and Pepper Shaker Pair	$28.53
56 Pieces Franciscan China Nightingale w Serving Pieces	$250.00	FRANCISCAN CHINA IVY TEA POT	$28.01
FRANCISCAN DESERT ROSE 3 pc. MICROWAVE SET U.S.A. MADE	$235.51	Franciscan Ivy 8" Crescent Salad Plate	$28.00
EL PATIO Ice Lip Pitcher, 6 Tumblers + Rack/Carrier	$225.00	[3 of these sold for $28.00 each]	
FRANCISCAN DESERT ROSE COFFEE CUP AND SAUCER - 4	$210.86	FRANCISCAN APPLE PATTERN 3-SECTION RELISH DISH	$28.00
Franciscan Starburst Atomic 5" Mugs Set of 6	$200.00	1940 Metropolitan Franciscan Ware Salad & Platter Turq	$27.99
Lot of Franciscan Desert Rose Glass Ware Bowls Compote	$164.49	Franciscan Ware Catalog Brochure Price List 1939	$27.50
IVY (Green Trim) by FRANCISCAN - Water Pitcher - 1949	$163.01	Franciscan Starburst Atomic Salt & Pepper Set	$27.50
Franciscan Desert Rose USA 9" Cookie Jar	$162.50	Franciscan Atomic Starburst Salt & Pepper Shakers	$27.10
5 California Franciscan Starburst Soup/Cereal Bowls	$157.35	Franciscan Desert Rose Spoon Rest	$27.01
FRANCISCAN DESERT ROSE 19 3/4"	$145.00	FRANCISCAN STARBURST 13" PLATTER EX COND	$27.00
TURKEY PLATTER OLD MARK		4 Franciscan Madeira Salad/Cereal/Fruit Bowls	$27.00
4 LARGE USA FRANCISCAN APPLE MUGS 4-3/8" TALL - MINT	$143.49	FRANCISCAN APPLE BLOSSOM MUG	$27.00
Franciscan Desert Rose Turkey Platter - Calif. 19 1/4"	$137.50	Vintage Franciscan Starburst Serving Bowl & Plate WOW!!	$26.51
X Lg Franciscan Ivy Juice or Milk Pitcher 50 Oz	$137.50	Franciscan Starburst Atomic Bread Plates (6)	$26.01

Pottery & China ▸ China, Dinnerware ▸ Gorham

The average sales price in this subcategory is $26.54.

	HIGH		AVG
GORHAM CHINA BRIDAL BOUQUET FOR 8 - 32 pc	$188.27	Gorham Kingsbury 1 Dinner Plate - MINT	$29.99
45 Pcs Gorham Fine China Silk Petal Service for 8	$130.25	Gorham Kingsbury 2 Salad Plates - MINT	$29.99
Gorham Kingsbury 1 Round Vegetable Bowl - MINT	$99.99	Gorham Cherrywood Cut Brandy 4 & 1/4 "	$29.99
Gorham Kingsbury 1 Oval Vegetable Bowl - MINT	$86.99	Gorham King Edward Crystal Bowl!!!! M0188	$29.95
Town & Country "Ariana" Salad Plates x 4 ~ Gorham	$86.99	Gorham Golden Sunset 6 Wine Glasses, No Res	$26.57
Gorham China Ariana 6 pieces	$83.00	3 Gorham Crystal Napkin Rings Oval Excellent Condition	$26.55
2 GORHAM CHINA "SWEET VIOLET" 8 1/2" PLATES ~ LIKE NEW!	$81.00	Gorham Fine China "Boston Tea Party" Z103	$26.00
Town & Country "Ariana" Salad Plates X 4 ~ Gorham	$72.02	4 GORHAM KING EDWARD CRYSTAL NAPKIN RINGS MINT w/BOX	$25.51
Town & Country "Ariana" Gravy Boat & Plate ~ Gorham	$66.03	GORHAM WHITE SATIN FLOWERED PORCELAIN VASE	$25.00
4 GORHAM LADY-MADISON 11" PLATES, CUPS, SAUCERS MINT	$60.00	Gorham Cut Crystal "Cherrywood" Water Goblet	$25.00
GORHAM GRAND MANOR PLATINUM OVAL PLATTER MINT!!!!!!	$58.99	Gorham Lady Anne Centerpiece Bowl	$25.00
Town & Country "Ariana" Dinner Plates x 4 ~ Gorham	$55.06	Flintridge CONTESSA BLACK Oval Vegetable Bowl	$24.95
Gorham China ROYAL BUTTERCUP set of 4 DINNER PLATES	$50.08	Gorham 2000 Annual WISHING STAR ORNAMENT Silver plated	$24.00
4 Gorham LADY ANNE CHAMPAGNE/TALL SHERBET Retired NR	$49.99	King Edward by Gorham 2 Footed Iced Beverages	$23.49
King Edward by Gorham 2 Footed WINE Goblets	$49.99	Gorham China-Florentine Lapis Gravy Boat & Under Plate	$22.19

Pottery & China ▸ China, Dinnerware ▸ Hall

The average sales price in this subcategory is $27.02.

	HIGH		AVG
HALL JEWELL TEA AUTUMN LEAF 1 LB BUTTER DISH, NR	$293.50	HALL CHINA AUTUMN LEAF NALCC RIBBED CREAMER	$28.00
Jewel Tea Autumn Leaf All-China Drip Coffee Pot	$280.01	Vintage Hall Football Tea Pot NO LID as is	$27.99
Vintage EVA ZEISEL CHINA 62 pieces CENTURY modern HALL	$255.78	HALL SUPERIOR DINNERWARE 7 LG SOUP BOWLS TEA LEAF	$27.77
VERY RARE Red Hall Carafe Coffee Pot Pitcher Tea Banded	$227.50	hall gold polka dot tea pot	$27.55
VERY HTF Hall China Birdcage Teapot Maroon Excellent	$200.00	VINTAGE HALL KITCHENWARE COBALT BLUE IRIS CASSEROLE	$27.50
HALL CHINA COLLECTIBLE TEAPOT LIPTON TEA LARGE BLACK NR	$182.45	Hall Nautilus Teapot with Mismatched Lid	$27.00
Hall China AUTUMN LEAF lid only Cookie Jar ? mint condi	$154.45	Vintage Salt Pepper Shaker Jewel Tea Hall Autumn Leaf	$27.00

MUSEUM QUALITY EVA ZEISEL TRI-TONE PITCHER, A BEAUTY	$152.60
JEWEL TEA AUTUMN LEAF ZIESEL COOKIE JAR	$152.50
Autumn Leaf Hall China Automobile Teapot UNUSUAL Colors	$151.51
Hall's Superior Jewel Tea Autumn Leaf Coffee/Teapot WOW	$137.50
Hall China #2 Chinese Red Small Ball Jug Pitcher	$135.27
Vintage Startex Hall's Jewel Tea Autumn Leaf Tablecloth	$127.50
HALL AUTUMN LEAF 1/4 POUND BUTTER DISH BEAUTIFUL	$127.50
GOLD COLORED HALL CHINA AIRFLOW TEAPOT	$127.50

HALL'S SUPERIOR QUALITY KITCHENWARE POTTERY TEAPOT NR	$26.99
HALL WESTINGHOUSE REFRIGERATOR DISH - ART DECO ORANGE	$26.57
VINTAGE HALL PITCHER NO RESERVE	$26.50
Hall China Taverne Metal Flour Sifter W Crank Handle	$26.07
HALL BLUE BOUQUET PATTERN SUGAR BOWL WITH LID	$26.01
Hall China Jewel Tea Autumn Leaf Aladin Tea Pot	$26.00
JEWEL T CASSEROLE DISH WITH LID, HALL AUTUMN LEAF	$26.00
2 Hall Jewel Tea Autumn Leaf 10" Plates	$26.00

Pottery & China ▸ China, Dinnerware ▸ Hummel, Goebel

The average sales price in this subcategory is $33.20.

	HIGH		AVG
1959 Goebel Charlot Mother w/ Baby On Knee BYJ	$610.00	# 79 Hummel Globe Trotter CM B4 Full Bee NR	$35.56
ANGEL SERENADE HUMMEL #83 RARE DOUBLE MRK	$315.00	HUMMEL CHICK GIRL # 57/0	$35.50
PRECIOUS LOT 7 M.I. HUMMEL FIGURINES WITH DEALER PLAQUE	$305.00	Hummel ~ W . Goebel Girl Wall Plaque 198	$35.00
RARE~Older Style~ Hummel "The Run-A-Way" 327 TMK-5 VGC	$299.99	VINTAGE 1965 HUMMEL GIRL ON FENCE JUST RESTING 112/4	$35.00
CROWN MARK HUMMEL #44A "CULPRITS LAMP"-SMOKE FREE HOME	$251.99	# 127 Hummel Doctor Full Bee TMK 2 ? NR	$35.00
FULL BEE HUMMEL #132 "STAR GAZER" MINT SMOKE FREE HOME	$227.50	M.I. Hummel Olszewski Mini "Accordian Boy" NR	$34.44
VERY RARE HUMMEL DUET 130 OLD CROWN MARK	$212.50	HUMMEL DUET # 130	$34.00
U.S. ZONE HUMMEL #8 "BOOKWORM" SMOKE FREE HOME	$202.50	VINTAGE HUMMEL HUM 200 LITTLE GOAT HERDER STYLIZED BEE	$34.00
Apple Tree Boy # 142 Incised Crown TMK1	$199.00	De Grazia Goebel Little Farm Boy Figurine	$33.50
Apple Tree Girl # 141 Incised Crown TMK1	$199.00	M.I. Hummel Olszewski Miniature "Baker" NR	$33.17
hummel #2133 "bashful serenade" "three sisters" $475	$184.12	Pair of Goebel Blue Birds CV73 & CV74 West Germany	$33.00
Hummel BOY & GIRL UNDER UMBRELLA - Full Bee	$180.50	50s HUMMEL 73 LITTLE HELPER Stylized Bee mark	$32.28
FULL BEE HUMMEL #123 "MAX AND MORITZ"-SMOKE FREE HOME	$177.75	De Grazia Goebel Little Maraca Indian Figurine	$31.05
FULL BEE HUMMEL #44B "OUT OF DANGER LAMP"-SMOKE FREE	$177.50	Hummel Trumpet Boy Figurine #97 wOld Hallmark	$31.02
Colorful Hummel Flower Madonna & Child 10 /1 VGC TMK-3	$175.00	1961 Goebel Porcelain JOSEPH FIGURINE West Germany	$31.01

Pottery & China ▸ China, Dinnerware ▸ Lenox

The average sales price in this subcategory is $38.68.

	HIGH		AVG
LENOX FINE CHINA	$1,000.00	Lenox (LIDO) Salt & Pepper Grinder - Beautiful	$39.99
Lenox China ~Lace Point~ Service For 8	$536.79	LENOX BROOKDALE China #11: Demitasse TEACUP + SAUCER	$39.95
Lenox Autumn Place Setting Mint Gold Banded $1700+MSRP	$510.00	Elegant Large Lenox Water Pitcher - RARE! L@@K	$39.95
Lenox China - Libery Pattern - 8 Placesettings	$400.00	LENOX HOLIDAY CUP AND SAUCER	$39.00
Lenox china moonspun cream soup	$399.00	[3 of these sold in a multiple item ("Dutch") auction for $13.00 each]	
[3 of these sold in a multiple item ("Dutch") auction for $133.00 each]		Lenox Mt Vernon Pasta SOUP BOWL NEW 8.25"	$38.95
LARGE PAIR OF LENOX VASES VASE VINTAGE	$356.01	Lenox Saybrooke Temperware Baking and Serving Dish NR	$38.00
Lenox China Windsong 5 soup bowls - NEVER USED	$300.99	LENOX AUTUMN DINNER PLATES (2).....BRAND NEW!	$37.00
Wedgwood Bone China COUNTRYWARE DINNER (12) PLATES	$276.06	LENOX ETERNAL SAUCE BOAT STAND.....BRAND NEW!	$37.00
~4~ Morning Blossom FOOTED CREAM SOUP BOWLS Lenox ~nr~	$256.00	LENOX KATE SPADE "LARABEE DOT" BUD VASE-NEW IN BOX	$36.99
3 discontinued? *LENOX * 10 1/2" Dinner Plate	$235.50	Lenox Village Tea Room (Tea Pot) New 1991	$36.26
NEW RARE QUOIZEL LUX 1st qt LENOX LAMP 33" IVORY 24k	$213.00	Lenox Spice Village 1989 24 Piece Set	$36.00
SET OF 4 LENOX CLASSIC SHELL GOLD CRYSTAL WINE GLASS	$206.01	Lenox 1982 First Annual Christmas Ornament N/R	$36.00
Lenox China Belvidere S-314 5 Cream Soups and + Saucer	$204.01	LENOX POPPIES ON BLUE CANDLESTICK HOLDERS (2) CHINA	$36.00
Lenox, Made for Tiffany Demitasse Cups & Saucers	$199.99	Lenox HAYWORTH china 5 pc place setting, Good condition	$36.00
RARE Lenox Holiday Dimension Oval Covered Butter Dish	$187.50	4 Lenox Presidential Mt Vernon Salad Plates MINT	$36.00

Pottery & China ▸ China, Dinnerware ▸ Limoges

The average sales price in this subcategory is $45.12.

	HIGH		AVG
9 GORGEOUS JPL LIMOGES DINNER PLATES GOLD & PINK ROSES	$809.99	10 Pc. Miniature Limoges Porcelain Painted w/Gold Trim	$46.50
Limoges Hand Painted Bowl	$800.00	Ornate Flow Blue w/ Gold LIMOGES OYSTER PLATES PLATE	$46.50
Raynaud Limoges Festivite Dinner Plate	$517.70	Limoges France Violet Pattern Water Milk Pitcher NM	$46.00
[10 of these sold in a multiple item ("Dutch") auction for $51.77 each]		GORGEOUS ANTIQUE LIMOGES HP GAME PLATE	$46.00
VINTAGE TRESSEMAN VOGT LIMOGES ROSE PUNCH FRUIT BOWL	$415.00	Set of 9 LIMOGES DESSERT PLATE c1895 FRANCE	$45.60
Lovely HP 18" Limoges Tray Asters T&V 1900	$386.00	19th c Victorian Limoges Porcelain Dinner Plate Rose NR	$45.00
C1890 LARGE LIMOGES PAINTED FISH PLATTER W/9 PLATES	$350.00	[2 of these sold for $45.00 each]	
FENTON WHITE HOBNAIL PUNCH BOWL WITH 12 CUPS	$330.59	Limoges Turn of the Century Peacock Charger, Signed Luc	$44.99
THEODORE HAVILAND LIMOGES Service for 8 CHINA 48 PIECES	$300.00	10 GDA FRENCH LIMOGES FLORAL CREAM SOUP & SAUCERS	$44.00
THEODORE HAVILAND LIMOGES 9 Serving Pieces CHINA	$300.00	LIMOGES HAND PAINTED HINGE AND CLASP TRINKET BOX.DM26	$43.30
LIMOGES TRAY, POWDER JAR, LOTION BOTTLE, HAIR RECEIVER	$299.00	HP Antique Limoges Charger 11" ~ Peppermint Pink Roses!	$43.12
4 LIMOGES CUP & SAUCER SETS WITH ROSES AND LOTS OF GOLD	$282.50	2 Raynaud Cristobal Limoges Porcelain Dinner Plate #2	$42.00
THEODORE R DAVIS PRESIDENTIAL CHINA HAVILAND FISH PLATE	$255.00	Vintage Fine Hand Painted Limoges Table Lamp 1920s	$41.50
HP Portrait Plaque of Moroccan Jewish Bride of Tangier	$250.00	Coffee/Tea Set Haviland Limoges	$41.00
Fabulous HP Bavarian Center Bowl Ferner Cherries 1900	$249.00	Antique cup & saucer lot SEVRES, LIMOGES, ADDERLY,	$41.00
Gorgeous HP Haviland Limoges Chocolate Pot Roses 1900	$230.00	ANTIQUE OLD GDA LIMOGES PORCELAIN BOWL CHINA DISH	$39.99

Pottery & China ▸ China, Dinnerware ▸ Made in Japan

The average sales price in this subcategory is $17.02.

	HIGH		AVG
DRAGONWARE TEA SET - 21 PIECES-KUTANI CHINA - LITHOPANE	$215.63	1940s Luster Bird SALT & PEPPER, EGG CUP HOLDER, Japan	$18.95
Rare Old Figural Porcelain QUEEN Playing Card Case	$159.50	MINIATURE GREEN DRAGONWARE CUP AND SAUCER	$17.57
HUGE SET ORIENTAL PORCELAIN DINNERWARE NR	$152.50	JAPAN DECO CAT HANDLED LUSTERWARE CREAMER	$17.50
Rare Old Figural Porcelain KING Playing Card Case	$125.00	Dragonware Saki Cups w/ Geisha Lithopane...Pair	$17.50
Double Nudes Lithopane Dragonware Cup & Saucer Royal	$111.50	Vintage Japan Figural Fez Man Lusterware Double Cache	$17.16

GorgeousThousand 1000 Faces Ginger Jar (Mount Fuji)	$102.50	Vintage Colonial Man Woman Porcelain Figurines Japan	$16.99
1000 Thousand Faces Porcelain Basket - Chikaramachi	$88.00	Floral Celery Dish w/ 4 Salt Dishes, Japan	$16.51
CROWN CORNING JAPAN - Blue/White 4 Piece Set	$66.57	Dragonware 'Moriage' C & S w/ Geisha Lithopane	$16.50
Vintage duck bird condiment Lustreware 10pc Very Rare!!	$66.00	Ardalt Strawberries & Butterflies Dish Casserole Bowl	$16.25
VINTAGE *JAPAN* EMPRESS CHINA* DINNER PLATES (9)	$65.00	Fab! Noritake Celery Dish	$16.02
SET OF 5 ORANGE CHECKERS JAPAN DIVIDED PLATES	$60.28	Nikko Christmastime Cocoa Cup w/lid & Saucer NIB	$16.01
12 PC VINTAGE 22 KT MORIAGE DRAGONWARE CUP&SAUCER SETS	$56.00	Dragonware Moriage Geisha Lithophane Cup & SAucer	$16.00
Vintage Japan Figural Red Hat Girl Cache Box	$53.99	Thames kitchen brown faux teapot with spices & rooster	$15.99
2 old Frozen Charlotte BISQUE penny Dolls vintage Japan	$53.49	MIJ Deco Bust of a Woman Ceramic	$15.76
CROWN CORNING JAPAN - Blue/White 3 Piece Set	$51.02	PAIR OCCUPIED JAPAN CUTIES,TENNIS GIRL FOOTBALL BOY	$15.65

Pottery & China ▶ China, Dinnerware ▶ Meissen

The average sales price in this subcategory is $240.01.

	HIGH		AVG
COMPLETE MEISSEN ACADEMIC PERIOD TEA/COFFEE SET c.1770	$4,050.00	Exquisite Meissen Biscuit Jar~Blue Cross swords	$256.00
Absolute very nice art from the house Meissen at 1814!	$2,651.00	19thC Meissen Porcelain Figurine Centerpiece	$250.00
Rare Meissen Ten Place Setting -	$2,650.00	Rare MEISSEN Vintage Landscape Sand Blotter	$250.00
EARLIEST MEISSEN ART NOUVEAU HENTSCHEL BOY DRINKING	$2,475.00	MEISSEN ONION PATTERN TWO HANDLED TRAY	$250.00
19 C Original Meissen Potpourri Vase With Watteau	$2,449.00	Meissen Teapot Circa 1740	$250.00
MAGNIFICENT MEISSEN FIGURAL CENTERPIECE LEUTERITZ NR	$2,436.00	Dragon Cup/Saucer set Meissen Blue sword	$234.50
EARLY MEISSEN ART NOUVEAU HENTSCHEL GIRL REACHING DOLL	$2,425.00	MEISSED CROSSED SWORDS BLUE ONION SOUP TERRINE	$229.00
18C ORIGINAL Meissen Teacaddy Chinoiserie No Reserve	$2,425.00	Vintage Meissen porcelain handpainted figurine	$225.50
VERY RARE CIRCA 1870 MEISSEN CHERUB CUPID WINTER GROUP	$2,375.00	RARE VINTAGE MEISSEN 4 PC SETTING, CROSS SWORDS	$222.50
A PAIR OF MEISSEN FIGURAL BOCAGE CANDLESTICKS C.1870	$2,222.00	TWO 18C/19C MEISSEN MARCOLINI CUP SAUCERS KAKIEMON BIRD	$218.05
Circa1800 MEISSEN Figural Group FIGURINE Trio LOVERS	$2,046.00	ANTIQUE MEISSEN PORCELAIN TRINKET BOX COBALT & FLOWERS	$216.00
ROYAL VIENNA PORTRAIT PLATE OF NAPOLEON SIGNED WAGNER	$2,025.00	DRESDEN/MEISSEN?Apple Picking Figurines,Adam/Eve?? N/R	$215.50
Meissen E249. 12" Woman with Urn Figurine 19th Century	$1,995.00	ANTIQUE MEISSEN HAND PAINTED STANDING MALE FIGURINE	$214.50
ARLEQUINO, MEISSEN, AFTER J.J. K?ler, dated 1850	$1,825.00	MEISSEN Cobalt Blue & White w/ GOLD Centerpiece BOWL	$212.50
MEISSEN, BEAUTIFUL PAIR	$1,750.00	6 MEISSEN STREWN FLOWERS DESERT PLATES, MINT	$212.50

Pottery & China ▶ China, Dinnerware ▶ Mikasa

The average sales price in this subcategory is $18.66.

	HIGH		AVG
$2,000+ Mikasa POMPADOUR RUBY ~ 9+ Place Settings	$499.00	Studio Nova~Palm Desert~4 Soup Bowls~EUC	$20.50
Mikasa Rondo Tango - Beautiful FULL SET!!	$300.00	MIKASA INTAGLIO GARDEN HARVEST PLATTER 12 3/4". NR!	$20.50
MIKASA SILK FLOWERS CASSEROLE,GRAVY & SALT/PEPPER	$112.50	Mikasa Silk Flowers Salad Plates (6) Excellent	$20.50
MINT (4) 7 Pc. Mikasa "Briarcliffe" 101 Place Settings!	$100.00	Mikasa Studio Nova Adirondack Two Tier Tidbit Tray	$19.99
Mikasa Regency Crest L3142	$100.00	12 Teacups & Saucers Mikasa Garden Club Flowerfest	$19.99
RARE China Mikasa Venetian Marble LAC82 Dinner Set 20pc	$99.00	12 Plates Mikasa Garden Club Flowerfest 8"	$19.99
Lot of Mikasa Classic Flair Plates/bowl/serving platter	$86.00	12 Dinner Plates Mikasa Garden Club Flowerfest 11"	$19.99
Mikasa Charisma Black service/8 cake plate VAL $460.00	$77.77	12 DRUMMERS DRUMMING MIKASA COVERED DISH	$18.50
62 PC SET OF BEAUTIFUL MIKASA INTAGLIO CHINA ~FANTAZZ~	$76.99	Mikasa China SILK FLOWERS QT LB Covered Butter MINT!!	$17.62
Mikasa Crown Jewel Gold 15" OVAL PLATTER MINT RARE!	$71.99	MIKASA Italian Countryside 1 QT.OVAL BAKER- NEW	$17.50
Mikasa Arabella New in Box 20 pc Dinner set Beautiful!!	$70.00	Mikasa Intaglio Annette Gravy Boat and Underdish	$17.13
MIKASA FINE CHINA TEA POT SET "MONTCLAIR" - 21 PIECES	$69.99	5 Piece Place Setting Of Mikasa Ultrastone Country Blue	$17.01
Mikasa Maxima Monet FIne China Lg Dinner Plate 12"	$67.66	MIKASA ITALIAN COUNTRYSIDE 15" OVAL PLATTER NEW!!!!!!!!	$17.00
nr MIKASA French Countryside 30 PIECE pottery CHINA nr	$61.00	Mikasa - 6 - Soup Plates - Annette CAC20 - - NICE	$16.95
MIKASA ITALIAN COUNTRYSIDE 12 FRUIT BOWLS NEW!!!!!!!!!!	$60.05	MIKASA Studio Nova ADIRONDACK 4 LARGE Plates NEW	$16.75

Pottery & China ▶ China, Dinnerware ▶ Nippon

The average sales price in this subcategory is $50.42.

	HIGH		AVG
Nippon Cobalt & Gold Moriage Scenic Vase	$2,046.60	GORGEOUS NIPPON BOWL DISH WITH PINK ROSES & GOLD NR!	$55.00
FANTASTIC NIPPON COBALT/GOLD 2 PIECE BOLTED URN! NR!	$1,706.01	Nippon Marked Hand Painted Swan Dish Handles	$53.99
Elegant Vintage Nippon 7 Inch Tapestry Vase	$995.00	NIPPON ~ 7 7/8" DIA PLATE LARGE PINK ROSES W/GOLD EDGE	$52.01
MAGNIFICENT PAIR ANTIQUE JEWELED NIPPON VASES	$825.00	Nippon Coralene Waterlily 10" charger NR!	$51.99
NIPPON hp ROSES & JEWELS BEADINGS TANKARD - No Reserve	$710.55	NIPPON GOLD ENAMELED FLORAL MELON	$51.00
RARE HAND PAINTED NIPPON PORTRAIT CUP & SAUCER SET N/R	$359.00	SHAPED CREAMER &SUGAR	
Great Nippon Cobalt&Roses footed vase	$355.00	Hand Painted Nippon Bluebird Cake Plate and Five Plates	$50.00
STUNNING BEADED NIPPON VASE W/	$330.83	LOVELY ANTIQUE ART NOUVEAU HUMIDOR,	$50.00
HANDLES HAND PAINTED WOW!		NIPPON, JAPAN, HP	
NIPPON MORIMURA Jeweled-rim Plate/Plaque	$300.00	GORGEOUS lot set 5 hand painted nippon butter pats	$49.99
Stunning gold moriage Nippon vase maple leaf VINTAGE!	$290.00	NIPPON GILDED HANDPAINTED DISH NO RESERVE	$49.99
Early Nippon Moriage Floral Inkwell Inkstand Hand Ptd	$260.52	RARE Antique/Vintage Nippon China Chamber Candle Sticks	$49.99
1911-1921 MORIMURA (Noritake) DRAGONWARE PLATTER TRAY	$255.00	Antique Nippon vase painted flowers green mark	$49.99
Beautiful Nippon Moriage Vase-Maple leaf mark	$230.25	NIPPON GREEN WREATH MARKED M RAISED NUT BOWL NR	$49.99
Beautiful Hand-Painted Nippon Vase with Farm Scene	$225.00	HAND PAINTED VINTAGE NIPPON COCOA SET FOR 5!	$49.99
NIPPON PILLOW VASE RAISED GOLD BLACKBERRIES FLOWERS NR	$202.50	Vintage Nippon Vase 1920's/Hand Painted	$49.99
NIPPON 11 1/2" LRGE COBALT GOLD ROSES SCALLOPED BOWL NR	$201.50	Nippon HP Roses Covered Bowl with Handles	$49.99

Pottery & China ▶ China, Dinnerware ▶ Noritake

The average sales price in this subcategory is $37.32.

	HIGH		AVG
Noritake Lustre Art Deco Lady / Girl Demitasse Set	$3,552.00	Noritake Rothschild Gravy Boat	$39.00
Noritake Blue Lustre Luster Plate W/ Beautiful Lady NR	$760.00	GORGEOUS NORITAKE LUSTER SUGAR BOWL WITH ROSE HANDLE	$38.78
FABULOUS NORITAKE ART DECO LUSTER PLATE RARE	$450.00	Noritake Eastfair 9171 Covered Casserole	$38.04

	HIGH		AVG
Noritake Adagio 7237 12 Piece Place Settings-83 Items	$300.00	NORITAKE ETIENNE SERVING BOWL CHINA DINNERWARE 7260 NR	$38.00
Nortake Fine China: Style Parkridge	$275.00	4 PLACE SETTING NORITAKE CHINA TEMPTATION PATTERN NR	$37.00
55 PIECE NORITAKE CHINA SET 8 PLACE SETTING "LUNCEFORD"	$275.00	Country Diary of Edwardian Lady 8 Salad Plate Noritake	$37.00
Set of 4 NORITAKE CONSERVATORY 5 piece Place Settings N	$213.50	BEAUTIFUL BLUE NORITAKE LOTUS BOWL & PLATE	$35.00
Beautiful Occupied Japan Noritake Floral Dinner Set	$205.00	4 PLACE SETTING NORITAKE CHINA TEMPTATION PATTERN NR	$34.99
VINTAGE NORITAKE no.175 cups saucers 12 sugar creamer	$190.00	Noritake ~ Roselane 5147 ~ Oval Vegetable Bowl	$34.95
/s/ Noritake DECO Blown-Out INK WELL Inkwell GORGEOUS!	$163.66	Noritake Crest 5pc Lot of Serving Pieces	$34.95
CHINA-SAVANNAH by NORITAKE-6 PLACE SETTINGS-MINT	$155.00	Elegant Covered Casserole Dish - Noritake 43061	$34.10
43 pc vintage HP Noritake Azalea tea set for 12	$155.00	Noritake Stoneware Desert Flowers Lidded Pot Dish NEW	$33.48
Noritake China EDGEWOOD #5807 Teapot	$129.99	Wedgwood Runnymede Dinner Plate Bone China	$33.00
Noritake Adagio Ivory China 67 pieces	$127.50	Noritake China Serving Bowl, Norma	$32.70
73 pc. Noritake China - Rosedale Pattern	$117.50	Large Vintage Noritake Orange Blue Lusterware Bowl	$32.00

Pottery & China ▶ China, Dinnerware ▶ Occupied Japan

The average sales price in this subcategory is $13.94.

	HIGH		AVG
Occupied Japan Bisque Chariot	$250.00	GESHIA GIRL DOLL- OCCUPIED JAPAN ?????	$14.32
DRAGONWARE COFFEE SET SERVES 12 -OCCUPIED JAPAN	$163.67	OLD MERIT OCCUPIED JAPAN PAINT FLORAL CHINA CUP SAUCER	$14.27
OCCUPIED JAPAN BISQUE AMERICAN CHILDREN "TOOTHACHE"	$125.95	BLUE WILLOW CUP & SAUCER, OCCUPIED JAPAN, 1948-52	$14.16
Miniature Tea Set - occupied Japan	$113.50	VINTAGE OCCUPIED JAPAN~TOMATO TEAPOT~EX~NR	$14.09
Miniature Tea Set - occupied Japan	$78.00	2 OCCUPIED JAPAN WALL POCKETS	$14.00
MORIAGE DRAGONWARE SET MADE IN OCCUPIED JAPAN CHINA	$66.00	Royal Sealy Moss Rose Electric coffee teapot pot	$13.99
2 Large Vintage Occupied Japan Figurines	$60.50	Occupied Japan Old Mexican Lady with Sombero VASE	$13.54
Occupied Japan Hummel Children LOT OF 8 MINT	$60.01	Vintage Woman Figurine Occupied Japan UCAGCO China	$13.50
Dragonware Tea set made in Occupied Japan	$60.00	Occupied Japan Toby Mug	$13.50
Lovely Pair of Bisque Occupied Japan Figurines 11 inch	$59.73	BLACK AMERICANA MAMMY OCCUPIED JAPAN STRING HOLDER! NR	$13.49
Miniature Tea Set - occupied Japan	$57.00	Occupied Japan Footed Demitasse Cup & Saucer N/R	$13.49
Miniature Tea Set - occupied Japan	$50.00	OCCUPIED JAPAN COLLECTIBLE MINIATURE GIRL W/CHICKEN	$13.49
OCCUPIED JAPAN DRAGONWARE-6 DEMITASSE CUPS&SAUCERS-BLUE	$48.77	2 Vintage Occupied Japan HP Imari Trinket Dish Bowl!	$13.39
29 PIECE MORIAGE DRAGONWARE CHINA SET MADE IN JAPAN	$48.17	Made in Occupied Japan Small Bird Planter	$13.16
Huge Lot set 88 Occupied Japan dinnerware floral gold t	$46.55	2 ceramic HOBO BUM figures - made in OCCUPIED JAPAN	$13.05

Pottery & China ▶ China, Dinnerware ▶ Pfaltzgraff

The average sales price in this subcategory is $13.61.

	HIGH		AVG
PFALTZGRAFF America Quilt Pattern Service for 12 EXTRAS	$331.50	PFALTZGRAFF VILLAGE CAKE PIE SERVING PLATE WITH LID	$14.95
Pfaltzgraff Tea Rose Ceiling 6 Bulb Hanging Chandelier	$149.99	Pfaltzgraff Merlot Steel Colander NEW!!	$14.50
54 Pfaltzgraff Portfolio Naturewood 10 - 5 Pcs Sets NIB	$114.50	Pfaltzgraff Tea Rose Glass Storage Jars, Set of 5, Mint	$14.50
Pfaltzgraff Tea Rose Timex Anniversary Clock-Like New!	$102.50	Pfaltzgraff Tea Rose Steel Burner Covers (4) UNIQUE	$14.44
Pfaltzgraff Rio Set of 8 Pasta Bowls, plus free gift	$96.00	PFALTZGRAFF AMERICA - 3 HEART PEDESTAL MUGS - NICE!	$14.01
Pfaltzgraff APRIL Retired Soup & Sandwich Combo - RARE	$79.96	Pfaltzgraff Cappuccino Steel Colander NEW	$13.50
[4 of these sold in a multiple item ("Dutch") auction for $19.99 each]		3 (THREE) PFALTZGRAFF VILLAGE LARGE 15-OZ MUGS	$13.49
5 Pfaltzgraff Tea Rose Pcs: Lamp, Trinket Box, Tape Dsp	$77.14	PFALTZGRAFF FOLK ART GRAVY	$13.27
Pfaltzgraff Tea Rose 20 Piece Dinnerware Set NEW IN BOX	$70.00	PITCHER & DRIP PLATE VINTAGE	
[2 of these sold in a multiple item ("Dutch") auction for $35.00 each]		PFALTZGRAFF FOLK ART 4 DINNER PLATES RETIRED 10"	$13.27
Pfaltzgraff Summer Breeze 16 Pc. Stoneware Dinner Set	$47.66	Pfaltzgraff Folk Art 2 QT Casserole - NEW	$13.06
PFALTZGRAFF VILLAGE WOOD AND STONEWARE BREAD BOX	$47.57	Pfaltzgraff Folk Art Mixer Cover-Cloth*ST	$13.04
Pfaltzgraff April Serving Tray	$47.00	Pfaltzgraff Folk Art Vegetable? Dish	$13.01
4 PIECE PFALTZGRAFF ARBOR VINE CANISTER SET	$45.99	Pfaltzgraff FOLK ART Covered Butter Dish... MINT cond.	$13.00
Pfaltzgraff Tea Rose Large Square Serving Bowl, 2 Avail	$40.66	Pfaltzgraff Pistoulet Platter Antipasto Brand New	$12.99
[2 of these sold in a multiple item ("Dutch") auction for $20.33 each]		PFALTZGRAFF YORKTOWNE ROUND	$12.99
SCARCE PFALTZGRAFF POTTERY JUG LAMP VILLAGE PATTERN	$39.99	VEGETABLE BOWL OVAL PLATTER	

Pottery & China ▶ China, Dinnerware ▶ Red Wing, Rumrill

The average sales price in this subcategory is $56.28.

	HIGH		AVG
Red Wing Nokomis Glazed 24in Floor Vase, #717, ca 1930s	$1,230.55	REDWING VILLAGE GREEN ' BROWN TEAPOT W/GREEN LID VG 6"	$58.77
SALT GLAZE CHURN 4 GALLON RED WING LEAF	$700.00	Red Wing Stoneware Rustic Women / Lyre Mug or Monk Mug	$57.99
Red Wing Salt Glazed Stoneware Beehive Jug Blue Daisy	$560.00	HTF Red Wing Mini Ad Jug - Delaney Bros Converse Ind.	$57.00
Red Wing Stoneware 8 gal Water Cooler, c. 1906-1915	$539.99	Town Country Eva Zeisel Red Wing ForGr Cereal Soup Bowl	$56.99
Redwing? Advertising Butter Crock - Grand Rapids, Minn.	$510.01	Red Wing Town & Country EVA ZEISEL Rust 3 pint jug-NRI	$56.55
RED WING Salt Glaze German Spittoon (RARE)	$500.00	MntlBRed Wing Spongeware 2001 Society Convention Bowl	$56.00
1 Gallon Red Wing Crock Stoneware Jar	$485.00	#3 Red Wing Stoneware/Crock - Perfect Oval!	$56.00
Union Stoneware 10 gallon Crock	$471.00	Adervertising mini jug, redwing?	$55.00
Altshul's Advertising Stoneware Crock Beehive Jugs	$400.00	VINTAGE RED WING SPONGE BLUE & ORANGE BOWL/MINT COND.	$55.00
Red Wing Blue White Stoneware Adv Pie Plate Crock Bowl	$383.08	VINTAGE RED WING REDWING YELLOW DUTCH GIRL COOKIE JAR	$53.99
RETRO WHITE EVA ZEISEL CREAMER GRAVY TOWN & COUNTRY? NR	$383.00	Redwing Pottery White Birch Tree Style Vase NICE	$53.16
RED WING WARE Art Pottery Large GREEN & WHITE Vase	$381.00	VINTAGE ZEISEL REDWING T&C BRONZE SCHMOO SALT & PEPPER	$52.82
Red Wing Salt Glazed Stoneware Beehive Jug Blue Redwing	$350.51	VINTAGE BRUSH RED WING DAISY PLANTER W/ GREEN GLAZE	$52.51
Red Wing Salt Glazed Stoneware Beehive Jug w/ BLUE	$345.00	7" Red Wing Stoneware Spongeware Paneled Bowl	$52.00
RED WING UNION Birch Leaf Elephant Ear #3 Butter Churn	$336.99	Vintage Turquoise RED WING Bakeware Pottery OOMPH PLATE	$52.00

Pottery & China ▶ China, Dinnerware ▶ Royal Doulton

The average sales price in this subcategory is $54.65.

	HIGH		AVG
GREAT ANTIQUE SILVER OVERLAY ROYAL DAULTON PITCHER	$885.01	White English Stoneware Royal Doulton Ting Pitcher Bowl	$56.00
HUGE 14" c1910 Royal Doulton Lambeth Artist Signed Vase	$800.00	Brand New Orchard Hill 5 piece place setting	$56.00

Antique Royal Doulton Hand Painted Vase Orchids	$663.50	ROYAL DOULTON"FATHER CHRISTMAS" LE FULL SEATED TOBY MUG	$56.00
Ca 1890 Doulton Burslem Royles Aquarius Wash Set	$500.00	ROYAL DOULTON JOSEPHINE PLATINUM 5 PIECE PLACE SETTING	$55.99
Royal Doulton The Elephant Trainer Toby Mug Jug RARE	$457.00	Royal Doulton "THE BRIDESMAID" FIGURINE Brides Maid	$55.00
1941 ROYAL DOULTON 'GOODY TWO SHOES' FIGURINE HN1889 PF	$420.00	DOULTON LAMBETH MINI STONEWARE DECANTER	$54.23
Vintage Royal Doulton English Bone China Talbot V1891	$400.00	ROYAL DOULTON FIGURINE(LORNA) HN 2311 MINT 1964	$53.52
ROYAL ALBERT "OLD COUNTRY ROSES" BONE CHINA ENGLAND	$400.00	BOY FROM WILLIAMSBURG HN 2183	$52.55
Kevin Francis Face Pot Blue Whale Mum's Edition	$370.01	ROYAL DOULTON GERMAN AIRMAN WW II TOBY STEIN MINT	$52.20
Royal Doulton Yeoman Of The Guard Toby Mug Jug	$356.00	Antique Royal Doulton Burslem Pitcher & Wash Basin	$52.12
ROYAL DOULTONS FIGURINE OLD RARE MUST SEE	$325.00	Royal Doulton Seriesware 6" Jug Jackdaw of Rheims	$52.11
ROYAL DOULTON "THE PATCHWORK QUILT" FIGURINE HN 1984	$319.50	ROYAL DOULTON BUNNYKINS BABY WARMING DISH NICE !!	$52.00
Royal Doulton Bunnykins Country Manor Coffee Teapot	$299.00	1962 "RARE" Royal Albert Old Country Roses Footed Bowl	$52.00
Royal Doulton Simple Simon Stein	$265.00	Royal Doulton The Gallant Fishers Plate	$51.01
VINTAGE ROYAL DOULTON DICKENS WARE DOUBLE HANDLED VASE	$262.00	Royal Doulton PRINCETON - LARGE Oval Platter - NEW!	$51.01

Pottery & China ▶ China, Dinnerware ▶ Spode

The average sales price in this subcategory is $46.52.

	HIGH		AVG
SPODE Staffordshire Blue Reticulated BASKET & TRAY 1805	$1,805.00	Spode Christmas Tree 5pc Pasta Set	$49.00
COPELAND-SPODE-GLOUCESTER-SERVICE 8 + SERVING PCS-MINT	$999.99	NEW SPODE Woodland Set of 2 dinners; The 2 Newest Birds	$49.00
RARE C1809 SPODE CARAMANIAN BLUE STAFFORDSHIRE PLATTER	$799.99	Spode Blue Italian Round Covered Casserole Dish	$48.99
Spode Stafford Flowers 5pc Place Setting	$600.00	SPODE -COPELAND FLORENCE	$48.10
[2 of these sold in a multiple item ("Dutch") auction for $300.00 each]		PATTERN ENGLISH CHINA	
Spode Stafford Flowers 5pc Place Setting	$598.00	Spode Blue Italian Round Covered Casserole Dish	$47.99
[2 of these sold in a multiple item ("Dutch") auction for $299.00 each]		SPODE CHELSEA GARDEN	$46.45
Rare Copeland Late Spode Large Golf Motif Pitcher 1980c	$515.00	Spode Christmas Tree Windsor Jug	$46.00
FINE CHINA PORCELAIN DINNERWARE 24 PC ROSENTHAL ETC NR	$500.00	Mint in Box Pitcher NR	
SPODE HUGE BLUE TOWER SOUP TUREEN MINT CONDITION	$330.00	SPODE BLUE ITALIAN SALT PIG NEW	$46.00
SPODE JEWEL BILLINGSLEY ROSE-32 Pieces–OLD	$319.99	Copeland Spode Blue Fitzhugh Serving Dish NR	$46.00
Vintage PELTON AUTOCLAVE FL2 TATTOO Sterlizier WORKS	$305.00	Spode Blue Italian Oven to Table Rectangular Baker Dish	$46.00
Spode Stafford Flowers 5pc Place Setting	$299.00	Spode Blue Italian 5 Piece Placesetting	$45.00
Spode THE HUNT Herring Scenes Service for 4	$250.49	c1810-15 Early Spode B&W Italian 7.25" Plate	$45.00
Spode Blue Tower - Tall Slim Square Vase -Old Mar k - NR	$222.22	SPODE TOWER PINK TIDBIT TRAY	$45.00
Spode Woodland 5pc Pasta Set	$216.50	3 TIER MUCH COLLECTED	
[2 of these sold in a multiple item ("Dutch") auction for $108.25 each]		10 early signed Copeland Spode HP Botanical Plates	$45.00
Spode Blue Colonel Large Covered Vegetable w Underplate	$208.75	Spode Wicker Lane Sugar & Creamer NR	$45.00

Pottery & China ▶ China, Dinnerware ▶ Stangl

The average sales price in this subcategory is $15.46.

	HIGH		AVG
STANGL Pitcher, Cups Happy days are here again.Kennedy?	$229.16	Stangl Kiddieware Little Bo Peep cup/mug	$15.50
STANGL POTTERY DINNER SET (THISTLE PATTERN)	$198.00	STANGL 8" CARNIVAL PLATE-NICE!!	$15.50
51 Pieces Stangl China Town and Country Hand Painted NR	$182.50	STANGL POTTERY FRUIT MUG	$15.50
STANGL HUMMING BIRD , FLOWERS # 3627	$99.99	Stangl Country Garden Pitcher Mint!	$15.50
Rare Stangl Florette Large Coffee Pot MINT	$84.88	STANGL LYRIC 10" DINNER PLATE NR	$15.49
Stangl Ladel	$76.00	VINTAGE STANGL POTTERY, COVERED CASSEROLE WILD ROSE	$15.45
Stangl reissue Kiddie Ware dolphin motif 3 pc. set	$70.99	STANGL POTTERY "STAR FLOWER" ROUND CHOP PLATTER CHARGER	$15.00
5 vintage pottery STANGL 10" dinner plates, BLUEBERRY	$64.00	Vintage Stangl Iris Creamer/Pitcher - MINT -	$15.00
6 PC STANGL POTTERY ORCHARD SONG PATTERN DINNER PLATE/S	$61.00	STANGL Charger/Platter - TULIP	$15.00
Vintage Stangl Hand Painted Butter Dish Fruit & Flowers	$57.01	3 STANGL POTTERY THISTLE 5 1/2" BOWL BOWLS	$15.00
Lot of 3 STANGL 10" dinner plates, BLUEBERRY	$56.79	STANGL SCULPTURE FRUIT LARGE COMPOTE	$15.00
2 Wonderful Tulip coffee mugs by Stangl Pottery	$56.55	Vintage Lot of 5 Stangl Thistle 8" Dinner Plates	$14.99
STANGL Pottery LUNCHEON Set HAND CARVED Painted 50's	$55.00	Beautiful Stangl Thistle 2 Qt. Pitcher	$14.99
FANTASTIC STANGL BIRD #3848 IN MINT/LIKE NEW CONDITION!	$53.00	Beautiful Stangl Thistle 12" Center/Pasta bowl	$14.99
Lot of 7 Vintage Stangl Thistle 7 1/2"Soup/Pasta Bowls	$51.00	Stangl Golden Harvest Covered Casserole Dish	$14.99

Pottery & China ▶ China, Dinnerware ▶ Steubenville

The average sales price in this subcategory is $12.96.

	HIGH		AVG
RARE RUSSELL WRIGHT STEUBENVILLE CREAM & SUGAR SET	$99.00	2 STEUBENVILLE GREEN WOODFIELD DINNER PLATES	$13.56
Vintage RUSSEL WRIGHT BY STEUBENVILLE PITCHER	$62.01	STEUBENVILLE POTTERY FAIRLANE CREAMER SUGAR BUTTER DISH	$13.01
7 Steubenville Woodfield Dinner Plates - NR!	$60.00	Woodfield Snack Set by Steubenville	$13.00
16 piece~Beautiful Grey/gray Russel Wright Steubenville	$52.00	WOODFIELD STEUBENVILLE GREEN LEAF 13" PLATTER DISH 50s	$12.95
8 Sets Luncheon Ware Cup-Woodfield by Steubenville	$44.51	(5) STEUBENVILLE VEG.BOWL U.S.A./FAIRLANE PATTERN	$12.95
27 PC STEUBENVILLE WOODFIELD CORAL & DOVE GREY CHINA NR	$37.95	4 Steubenville Dessert or Sandwich Plates NR	$12.50
A STUENVILLE PINK SALAD BOWL/KNIFE AN FORK WOODFIELD	$36.99	WOODFIELD BY STEUBENVILLE PLATTER / TRAY & SUGAR BOWL!!	$12.00
HUGE LOT STEUBENVILLE LEAF WOODFIELD PLATE CUPS BOWLS +	$34.99	Steubenville FAIRLANE 16 Pieces NR	$11.99
7 STEUBENVILLE WOODFIELD DINNER PLATES	$32.00	VINTAGE STEUBENVILLE GEORGE WASHINGTON PLATE	$11.50
RUSSELL WRIGHT SERVING BOWLS, + CELERY DISH	$32.00	Set of 6 Steubenville Plates 22K	$11.02

Pottery & China ▶ China, Dinnerware ▶ Stoneware

The average sales price in this subcategory is $63.70.

	HIGH		AVG
1800 Yellow Ware Mocha Tortoiseshell Banded Pepper Pot	$5,766.66	19TH CENTURY STONEWARE CROCK BLUE DECORATION	$66.00
Budweiser Beer W.L. Halsey Huntsville AL Stoneware Jug	$705.00	H. Krieger Sons Stoneware Advertising Jug Baltimore MD	$65.00
1800s Yellow Ware Mocha Banded Seaweed Pepper Pot	$690.00	TIN MINERS LAMP, SALESMANS SAMPLE	$64.86
HAMILTON & JONES #2 TABLETOP CHURN COBALT SNOWFLAKE	$666.00	OLD MINI POTTERY ADVERTISING CORN WHISKEY JUG NICE!	$64.63

Whites Utica stoneware crock Cobalt Blue Bird	$512.51	Rowe Pottery Miniature Salt Glaze Lidded Bean Pot	$63.99
J. C. WILBUR ZANESVILLE OHIO 19TH C STONEWARE JUG	$471.00	Miniature Mini Stoneware Jones Bros Louisville KY Jug	$63.55
VINTAGE4 GAL STONEWARE CHURN W/ COBALT GRAPE DECOR.	$455.00	Norton/Bennington 1860s Albany-Slip Glazed Syrup Jug	$63.00
MACON GA GEORGIA POTTERY SCRATCH ADV MINI JUG CHAMBLISS	$430.00	Rowe Pottery Miniature Salt Glaze Lidded Baker/Casserol	$62.99
Cobalt Blue Decorated Stoneware (crock)Water Cooler	$430.00	Rowe Pottery Miniature Salt Glaze Wide Mouth Jug 1993	$62.99
1800s Yellow Ware Mocha Banded Feather Pepper Pot	$381.98	Rowe Pottery Miniature Salt Glaze Maple Syrup Jug 1991	$62.66
Authentic Old Sleepy Eye Blue Rim 8 PitcherWOW	$364.00	old Chicago Advertising Butter/Dairy Crock	$62.52
Rare Loogootee Ind Trinity Springs Frog Mug Albany Glaz	$364.00	Stoneware Saltglaze Crock Early Ovoid	$61.99
RARE SPONGEWARE SALTBOX YELLOW WARE STONEWARE	$350.00	I. M. MEAD & CO 19TH C STONEWARE JUG 11 3/4	$61.00
A.P. DONAGHHO, Parkersburg WV Stoneware Crock 3 ZIPPERS	$331.66	Rowe Pottery Miniature Salt Glaze Pitcher 1988	$60.99
Big Blue Bird Stoneware Crock 4 Gallon WOW	$299.99	Tall Ironstone White Pitcher Antique Flower Vase	$59.97

Pottery & China ▶ China, Dinnerware ▶ Tea Pots, Tea Sets

The average sales price in this subcategory is $15.96.

	HIGH		AVG
Antique Russian Tea Caddy porcelain by Kuznetsov 1890s	$201.49	Coffee/ Tea cups with saucers set of 10 " mint"	$16.50
Tea Pot, Sugar Bowl, Creamer , S&T RS Germany, Ornate	$189.50	Lovely Gilded Chapman Porcelain Tea Cup and Saucer	$16.49
DRAGONWARE MORIAGE 23 Pc TEA SET HEAVY GOLD DECOR - MKD	$177.50	Natl Wildlife Fed Teapot Coffeepot Hummingbird Flowers	$16.29
VINTAGE 16PC DRAGONWARE? TEAPOT TEA SET JAPAN MORIAGE?	$153.67	Chinese Blue Willow Tea Pot TeaPot Asian Fable w/ Doves	$15.99
Harrods Green Tea Set with Wicker Hamper	$125.00	Tea pot, Teapot, Little Old Lady, England	$15.99
VINTAGE WEDGEWOOD JASPER TEAPOT & UNDERPLATE	$76.05	Susan Winget Teapot Rooster Chicken Avignon Morning nib	$15.95
LIGHT GREEN FIGURAL WOMAN RED-WING 260 TEA POT	$73.00	ELIZABETHAN FLORIDA ORANGES CUP, SAUCER & CAKE PLATE	$15.65
Gorgeous Pink Hand-painted Tea Set - Shabby Fab! Chic!	$66.55	COBALT BLUE HALL TEAPOT	$15.56
Vint.Palin Thorley Silver Luster Pitcher Williamsburg	$62.01	Wonderful! Art Deco Tea Set-Teapot,6 Cups &Tray	$15.50
Porcelain Bavaria Schumann Arzberg Germany Teapot Roses	$56.00	1960 Vintage Squash Calabash Pottery Michoacan Mexico	$15.50
NEW Teapottery Blue Radio Teapot mid size	$55.00	Vintage Aynsley Bone China Tea cup and saucer	$15.50
Romance Courting Limoges China Tea Set for 6 NEW	$55.00	Porcelain Teapot Blossoms & Butterflies	$15.50
22 PIECE BANARIA TEA SET	$51.02	COLLECTIBLE VINTAGE BLUE TEAPOT	$15.50
Universal Potteries Tip Top Refrig. Jug MINT CONDITION	$50.55	VERY OLD ANTIQUE BLACK ROOSTER TEAPOT~WIRE HANDLE~JAPAN	$15.50
Beautiful Lefton China Brown Heritage Teapot WOW	$49.99	CROWN WINDSOR PORCELAIN TEAPOT VIOLETS ROMANIA NEW	$15.50

Pottery & China ▶ China, Dinnerware ▶ Wedgwood

The average sales price in this subcategory is $39.59.

	HIGH		AVG
Wild Strawberry Service (144 Pieces): Service for 10	$3,000.00	2 WEDGWOOD FLORENTINE TURQ. TEACUPS	$40.00
Oyster Plate Collection	$1,225.00	W/3 SAUCERS - W2714	
RARE Wedgwood Crimson Red Dip Japserware Footed Bowl	$900.89	WEDGWOOD WEDGEWOOD PETER RABBIT EGG	$40.00
WEDGWOOD BIANCA #4499 SOUP TUREEN W/LID	$484.99	Wedgwood CORNUCOPIA 2 Salad Plates	$40.00
Wedgewood Queensware 57pc Blue on White Table service	$399.99	Wedgwood WHITEHALL RUBY 2 Bread & Butters	$39.99
VINTAGE WEDGWOOD MAJOLICA CHERUB	$332.78	WEDGWOOD CHINA BELLE FLEUR - 3 Piece Place Setting	$39.99
CANDLE HOLDER 4 MOLD		Wedgwood China PATRICIAN Gold Trim Gravy Boat	$39.99
WEDGWOOD CORNUCOPIA TEA/COFFEE	$305.00	WEDGWOOD APPLEDORE W3257 Brown Backstamp 3 Fruit Bowls	$39.97
POT SET CREAMER & SUGAR		Wedgwood Queensware Cream On Cream Shell Bread Plates	$39.95
Signed Wedgwood Fairyland Luster Vase Butterfly Pattern	$300.00	4 PC WEDGEWOOD WEDGWOOD STRAWBERRY	$39.00
PRE c1890~ Antique WEDGWOOD LARGE	$300.00	& VINE BONE CHINA	
BASALT CAMEO VASE, NR		WONDERFUL WEDGWOOD (COBALT))	$39.00
Antique Wedgwood Napoleon Ivy Lg Porcelain Punch Bowl	$299.99	DINNER PLATE RUNNEYMEDE	
Wedgwood Majolica Plate Circa 1880	$291.99	WONDERFUL WEDGWOOD (COBALT))	$39.00
WEDGWOOD CREAMWARE RIBBED	$245.00	DINNER PLATE RUNNEYMEDE	
EMBOSSED TRI COLOR VASE 1780		WEDGWOOD FLORENTINE TURQUOISE COVERED SUGAR BOWL	$39.00
Wedgewood Majolica Dessert Plate Circa 1860	$230.49	WEDGWOOD SARAH'S GARDEN BLUE 4	$38.99
BASALT WEDGWOOD DRAGON KENLOCK	$225.00	SOUP/ DESSERT BOWL (NEW)	
WARE TEA POT 1895		Wedgwood Humming Birds Gravy stand/relish dish	$38.88
Wedgwood A Holland Handpainted Cabinet Plate 1	$220.06	Wedgwood STRAWBERRY & VINE Salt & Pepper Shakers	$38.75

26

REAL ESTATE

The Real Estate category has not become the real estate broker-killer that some in the business may have feared when eBay launched the category in August 2000. But it has become an effective venue for selling some forms of real estate that are harder to sell via traditional means, from timeshares to entire towns. Yes, the tiny dale of Bridgeville, California went for $1.78 million to an anonymous bidder in 2003.

"eBay is great at making inefficient markets efficient. Residential real estate is a very efficient market," said eBay spokesman Hani Durzy, according to Classified Intelligence (www.classifiedintelligence.com) editor Peter M. Zollman in an article in Realty Times (realtytimes.com). "You'll find people are using the ad format on eBay to promote their real estate. And we're doing some selling of things where the marketplace is less efficient, such as timeshares."

Doing even better than the Real Estate category on eBay is the recent eBay acquisition Rent.com, the leading transaction-based website for apartment rentals. The site had about 20,000 listings recently, with a 90 percent increase from September 2004 to September 2005. In the 2004 eBay annual report, eBay stated, "Rent.com will complement our own Real Estate category and provide for additional growth in this area."

The Real Estate category breaks down into five core subcategories: Land (Homesite/Lot and Recreation/Acreage), Residential Homes, Commercial, Manufactured Homes, and Timeshares. As I write this, there are about 1,600 listings in Residential Homes, 1,600 in Land, 1,000 in Timeshares; 440 in Commercial, and only 27 in Manufactured Homes.

There are fewer listings in Real Estate than in most of the more-established eBay categories, but there's another difference too: Listings can be in either an auction format, where the property is bid on until there's a winner, or in ad format, where the seller simply places photos and specifics about the property and receives inquiries. Auctions can also be either binding or non-binding. As eBay explains it in the Help pages, non-binding real estate auctions do not involve commitments by users to buy and sell property. "Instead, these 'auctions' are simply a way for sellers to advertise their real estate within the auction-style environment familiar to eBay's user community." The high bidder and seller are expected to discuss entering into a contract but are not obligated to complete the transaction. (eBay explains that "non-binding auctions are used in cases where the 'binding' auction format . . . is unavailable due to legal or other restrictions.") In binding auctions of real estate, users are expected not to bid unless they intend to follow through with good faith on the purchase of the property.

Some of the most interesting items in the Real Estate category are actually in ad format. For example, one of the most expensive Land listings in a recent sample was a 155-acre residential investment property, "Rancho Mellow Yellow," which was owned by famous 1960s rocker Donovan and was advertised at $2,800,000.00. And some very expensive listings in the traditional auction format go unsold: "Puerto Rico Beach Front Land for resort . . . Turistic Development" was listed for a healthy $6,000,000.00 but didn't get any bids. Another that went unsold was "68+ Acre Equestrian Training Facility & Land" in Illinois—it was listed for $1,950,000.00.

So what is actually selling, and for how much? The highest price in the Real Estate ▶ Land ▶ Homesite, Lot subcategory was a waterfront lot in the Florida Keys (Marathon Key) that sold for $200,100.00. Was this a good value? According to the details in the listing, it certainly seemed to be. The seller said that, at .32 acres, this lot was valued at $550,000.00, and an adjacent lot with a home on it was for sale for $1,200,000.00.

Other high-price sales in the Real Estate ▶ Land ▶ Homesite, Lot subcategory included an "11 Lot Package Deal in Wakulla County, Florida" that sold for $90,000.00, a "1/2 Acre Vacant Lot In Fort Myers" that sold for $63,000.00, and a Riverside County/Quail Valley, California residential listing that sold for $50,110.00.

If you're thinking that a lot of these listings seem to be based in Florida, you're right: 12 of the top 15 prices in the Real Estate ▶ Land ▶ Homesite, Lot subcategory are for lots in Florida, and 11 of the median-priced lots are too.

The median prices for the homesite lots in this sample are between $10,500.00 and $17,100.00. For example, one of these lots is in Florida, and the seller claims its reserve price (which was met) is "much lower than what the lots are listed for with realtors on eBay." The listing title was "Punta Gorda Charlotte Co Florida Corner Lot Tee & Green. 80 X 125 Warranty Deed, Great Investment Opportunity," and it sold for $15,200.00. It certainly sounds nice: "Charlotte County is home to many golf courses and pristine beaches. The beaches provide access to the Gulf of Mexico where you can enjoy boating," writes the seller, explaining that the lot is located in the "tee and green estates." Why would this lot sell for so little? One factor may be that it's in a "scrub jay area," which, according to one Charlotte County website, can severely limit buildability.

Another residential lot didn't seem to offer any surprises: "Tellico Village-Tennessee-Prime Parcel-Oversized! Prime Lot on Cul-De-Sac with Nice Homes-Golf & Lake!!" sold for $12,500.00. The seller said, "this lot is PRIME and like lots are listed for $36,000.00 and up. It is close to the Recreation Center, the Lake, the Marinas, the Golf Courses, and the local amenities." That's about a 20-minute drive to the West suburbs of Knoxville, which include Turkey Creek, "one of the most up-to-date cities featuring the Mega-Plex type malls. Certainly the place to go for shopping, entertainment and dining." The seller offered a 30-day money-back guarantee as well as clear photos of the lot and two homes already built on the cul-de-sac.

Other land is available as simple "acreage." The high prices here range from $10,000.00 to about $60,000.00, with median prices around $2,000.00.

Gold Mining Claim Rush?

In the Real Estate ▶ Land ▶ Other subcategory, there were quite a few "gold mining claim" listings that sold for between $911.00 and $1,295.00. A listing titled "160 Acre Arizona Unpatented Gold Mining Claim/Camp, Hunt, Ride ATV's, Horses, Great Gold & Fun" generated 27 bids, with a $99.00 starting bid. The photos show a dry patch of land with part of a dirt road and a cactus. According to the seller, "unpatented" means that the government still owns the land, but you own the mineral rights; "the right to dig, rock hound, etc." The seller goes on to explain that "at this time there is a moratorium on filing for a patent. This is where you get a deed and you then own [both] the land and the mineral rights. You cannot build a summer cottage, home or other structures on any unpatented mining claim unless you are working the claim. If you are actively mining the claim you may construct a shed or building to house your equipment." The interesting thing about this land is that it's evidently located near the Vulture gold mine. The Vulture was discovered in 1863 and went on to become the most productive gold mine in the history of Arizona, producing gold worth more than $200 million, according to the item description. Whether much or any gold is still there is not clear, but apparently several folks were willing to pay about $1,000.00 to find out, judging by the several similar listings.

Residential Homes

If gold mining isn't your thing and you want an actual house to live in, the Real Estate ▶ Land ▶ Residential Homes subcategory is for you. The top seller in this sample is quite intriguing—it wasn't one but four homes, rental properties that, according to the seller, generate good income and were "all currently rented and have been for 10 years." They sold for $276,000.00, which does seem to be a song. The photos show modest one-story dwellings— they were sold "as-is," but in answer to one prospective buyer's question about whether any repairs were currently needed, the seller replied that "just minor cosmetic things on the fences and possible paint on some of the eaves" needed to be done. "The insides are in good condition. All of them have had new heaters and coolers in the last 2 years." The location was the "high desert of California," at the West end of Boron with an "unobstructed scenic view of the Mojave Desert." Is this a good deal? It might not be clear unless you saw the units in person. According to the Boron, California, page on ePodunk.com, the median home value in Boron was $56,500.00, and the median price asked for vacant housing was $45,000.00, so Boron isn't exactly Beverly Hills.

Now let's look at a big, beautiful home, a "BIG BEAUTIFUL KENTUCKY HOME with 3.3 Acres on HILL," to be precise. This one sold for $205,000.00, the next-highest price in this sample. The photo showed what appears to be a charming brown ranch house with Tudor styling. Listed as located in Leitchfield, Kentucky, the owners said they bought it in 2002 for $200,000.00 and invested nearly $50,000.00 in improvements and upgrades. It has five bedrooms, three and a half baths, a two-car attached garage, and a two-car detached garage with electrical hookup (potential workshop). "This home has excellent construction, sturdy and secure. It would cost over $400K to rebuild even before the gulf hurricanes and the increase costs in fuel and building materials," wrote the sellers. This one is a bit of a heartbreaker, as the sellers seem to have lost money on this home. (They say they had to move due to "sudden changes in employment"—hopefully good ones.) But some lucky eBayer did well.

Many of the homes in this sample were in somewhat rural or remote areas. Perhaps the real estate market is softer there, or it's harder to sell locally, so sellers decide to tap into a wider nationwide or worldwide market. But some homes are in busier areas, and they may be on eBay for other reasons, like an urgent need to sell.

This seems to be the case with the "4 Bedroom Colonial Home for Sale in Syracuse New York" that went for $48,000.00. The owner says he "MUST SELL MUST SELL MUST SELL" as he is being transferred in the Air Force. The photos show a cute, seemingly well-kept home with many charming appointments, such as a dark wood mantle, old-style door frames, new Berber carpeting, and fresh paint.

There aren't many residential homes listed, but there are some great deals if you can find one in the location you want.

Take This Timeshare—Please!

Timeshares, as mentioned before, are some of the most actively traded forms of real estate in this category. But they are a mixed bag—the nice ones in desirable locations can do very well, but some you can barely give away. Indeed, one perplexed buyer asked on the eBay

Real Estate discussion board, "Can someone explain to me how it is feasible/profitable for someone to sell timeshares at the buy it now price of one dollar? Clearly most people paid a LOT more initially . . . Is someone so desperate to get rid of their yearly fees? Or is there something wrong with these places?"

A regular seller of timeshares on eBay answered, saying that he sometimes does get timeshares deeded to him by owners who "do not want to deal with the properties anymore, for whatever reason, so we are actually getting them for free (plus recording costs). We start the bidding at $1 to attract more viewers, hoping that the bidding will end somewhere that we make a profit." Any costs that he incurs are then usually included in the closing costs that the buyer pays, and "this is where a lot of us make the money, as we have connections with closing agents or are so familiar with the process that we can do the work ourselves." He advises prospective timeshare buyers not to pay more than $400.00 in closing costs, in any case.

If you're buying, you should also make sure the photos you're looking at in the auction are of the actual unit you're bidding for and are not, for example, "stock pictures of the best units" in the club or development. When buyers who are thusly misled get to their units, "they are very disappointed that their $50.00 (plus closing costs plus maintenance fee) chalet is not the chalet with outrageous mountain views they expected. By then it's too late, of course," said the seller, who added that he usually makes about $100.00 to $150.00 profit on the units he sells, and it comes mostly from the closing costs.

While not everyone is open to the concept of timeshares, whether swapping or buying, others swear by them: "Are timeshares a good thing? My opinion is a sound yes for me. But at the same time, they are not for everyone." This buyer said he'd been to timeshares in Paris, Orlando, and Cancun, among other places, and had a good time at all of them. He "loved the resort" at Cancun, Royal Islander, and instead of paying $300.00/night (presumably at a hotel), his cost came to "$625 instead of $2,100 plus tax."

Some of the highest timeshare prices in this sample are for the Manhattan Club in New York City (200 West 56th Street), with timeshares for a week—including two weekends. According to the seller, this timeshare allows the owner to stay any week of the year, and this package "is no longer available through the Manhattan Club." The owner can use the week all at once, or can use a day or two at a time throughout the year. Evidently several folks out there want this *pied-à-terre* in the Big Apple, because in this sample a few of these timeshares sold for between $22,000.00 and $24,000.00.

Other high sellers include timeshares in Breckinridge, Colorado ($12,480.00 and $19,800.00); at the Marriott Shadow Ridge in the Palm Desert ($7,100.00–$8,400.00); in Key West, Florida ($10,801.00); and at the Marriott Kauai Beach Club in Hawaii ($10,800.00).

Median prices for most timeshares are in the hundreds of dollars, with some of the lowest in the Lakefront subcategory going for $1.00 and $2.00. A "FAIRFIELD BAY ARKANSAS GOLF 2 BD TIMESHARE" went for $2.00; the annual maintenance fee of $408.00 was due at the time of sale "since transfer will take a couple of months and usage is in January." There were also closing costs of $395.00. It's possible this may have been a timeshare the owner simply did not want anymore, due to ongoing maintenance fees.

The Real Estate category on eBay is still relatively new, but while you may not find the volume of listings here that you will in other categories, there are gems out there for those with patience or luck. One fortunate couple found this amazing deal: "Two years ago, we bought our four bedroom home, a shop, and four acres of land on eBay for under $20K! The seller was a first time lister and had only listed 'Lots for Sale' in the title. This didn't gain many lookers, and we stumbled upon it by mistake. We love our new place and are quite happy with what we got for so little! We are definitely the bargain king and queen when it comes to our real estate deal on eBay!"

NOTE   *The prices in this category were all hand-pulled, so there are no average prices to report.*

Land ▸ Homesite, Lot

	HIGH		AVG
Florida Keys Land-Waterfront Marathon Key Home Lot Residential, Watefront, Buildable Lot in FL Keys!	$200,100.00	THREE 0.73 SidexSide lots next to River...Florida...NR Well and Septic..118x270 each lot...Warranty Deed......	$17,100.00
11 Lot Package Deal in Wakulla County, Florida Warranty Deed...........Savings of $73,900	$90,000.00	Florida Property Real Estate Lot Land Investment Fl. 1.25 Acres Near Lake Rosalie Owner Financing. No Res!	$16,979.85
1/2 ACRE VACANT LOT IN FORT MYERS	$63,000.00	Pickup only. Beautiful Lakefront Property in the Poconos, PA.	$16,301.96
CA Riverside county Quail Valley Residential Lots. 40 min from San Diego County	$50,110.00	1 Acre! No Reserve! Near Lake Wallenpaupack! PUNTA GORDA CHARLOTTE CO FLORIDA CORNER	$15,200.00
Lehigh Acres 1/2 Lot Southwest Florida	$48,100.00	LOT TEE & GREEN. 80 X 125 WARRANTY DEED, GREAT INVESTMENT OPPORTUNITY	
PALM BAY, FLORIDA BUILDABLE HOMESITE. LUXURY LIVING-NEW ROADS, ELECTRIC, PHONE, CABLE, DSL	$45,000.00	2.06 Acre Lot Next to I-75 in Hamilton County, Florida.	$15,200.00
Lehigh Acres Oversized lot, Huge 1/2 lot 143x136. On preserve and canal, no neighbors ever to the S & E	$42,900.00	189x405....Winning Bid Takes Lot.....Warranty Deed..... FORT MYERS FLORIDA LOT LEE COUNTY SAN CARLOS PARK	$15,100.00
BEAUTIFUL PORT CHARLOTTE / PUNTA GORDA AREA FLORIDA LOT. WOW... WATERFRONT COMMUNITIES, $$$ LESS NR	$35,600.00	CLOSE TO BEACHES/GULF GREAT INVESTMENT OPPORTUNITY 0.23 Acre Lot Located In Central Florida...70x135...NR.	$13,000.00
0.75 ac lot borders future largest Mall Jacksonville FL. Next to coming River City Market Place & Super Wal-Mart	$35,100.00	2hrs to Daytona. Warranty Deed...Electric and Phone TELLICO VILLAGE-TENNESSEE-PRIME PARCEL-OVERSIZED!	$12,500.00
PORT CHARLOTTE, FLORIDA LAND, BUILDABLE LOT. Great Lot Flat, Minutes to Direct Gulf Access!	$32,900.00	PRIME LOT ON CUL-DE-SAC WITH NICE HOMES-GOLF & LAKE!! 2.5 ACRES -Double Lot Volusia Prime Investment Land.	$12,100.00
PORT CHARLOTTE SOUTHWEST FLORIDA LOT!!!!!! BEST INVESTMENT YOU'LL EVER MAKE !!! WARRANTY DEED !!!	$30,000.00	10 Min. to Daytona Beach. Best bang for buck land in FL WATERFRONT LOT & easy to build CABIN..BID NOW!!!!!	$11,211.11
SOUTHWEST FL., PORT CHARLOTTE, GREAT INVESTMENT !!!LOT MY OTHER OFFWATER AUCTION IS FOR LOT!!!!! !!!	$30,000.00	live, vacation, fish, swim, rent it out. GIT-R-DONE 2 BEAUTIFUL ACRES in CENTRAL FLORIDA -	$10,800.00
40 Acres! Southern CALIFORNIA Easy Access HIGH BID WINS. Dirt road frontage! 10 miles east of BARSTOW!	$25,600.00	NEAR I-4 & SR559. DEVELOPING AREA - 30 MINUTES from ORLANDO - GREEN & DRY	
.53 Acre River Front In North Florida.....75x250 No Reserve............Winning Bid Takes Lot............	$23,200.00	Florida Land-Haines City, Lakeland Area, Residential. Vacant Buildable Lot in Florida market-Invest	$10,700.00
Florida Property Real Estate Lot Land Investment Fl. 1.25 Acres Near Lake Kissimmee Owner Financing. No Res!	$22,100.00	Withlapopka Islands Citrus County, Florida RES-LOT	$10,500.00
		COLORADO ROCKY MOUNTAIN WOODED LAND IN FORBES PARK. Gated mountain development, big mountain views	$10,500.00
		5 acre Buena Vida, New Mexico Land Parcel (Cash Buyers)	$10,500.00

1-acre Washington beach neighborhood homesite
Similar beach lots nearby listed at TWICE this price

You are signed in

janinebwa won this item with a Best Offer of US $100,000.00.

Buy It Now price:	US $129,000.00
Best Offer	US $100,000.00
Ended:	Mar-05-06 09:59:16 PST
Start time:	Feb-20-06 16:52:57 PST
History:	Purchases
Buyer:	janinebwa (171 ☆)
Item location:	Bay Center, Washington United States
	Featured Plus! Listing Home Page Featured Listing
Shipping costs:	Not specified

1 of 8
Supersize

Land ▸ Recreation, Acreage

	HIGH		AVG
31 acres in Evensville, Tennessee- Rich Soil	$62,000.00	10 ACRES TEXAS, ELECTRICTY, REEVES Co LEGAL ACCESS	$2,225.00
40 Acres, California Land Deeded Access to Four Lakes. Beautiful Northern California, Minutes fromMount Shasta	$34,000.00	CASH. Just off paved rd. Near Ft. Stockton & Balmorhea S.P.#17 Resort Lot in Beautiful Central Florida.	$2,125.00
24.4 ACRES RURAL VACANT LAND	$24,100.00	You will own this lot-Its not a down payment	
PARTNERSHIP: 23,800 ACRES WYOMING RANCH Own it. Fishing, Hunting , Horseback Riding, LAKES, ATVs,	$20,000.00	NEVADA LAND 1.13 ACRE HOME SITE BEAUTIFUL,PLUS VEIW. LOT APOX 49,000SQ FTSUPER BUY NO CARRY BACK.	$2,077.00
40AC SURROUNDED BY BEAUTIFUL MNTS. NE CALIFORNIA NO RES. 2 X 20 acres lots on Racoon dr. min from Eagle Lake	$17,600.00	Smile4u Halloween Special 10 Acres Elko County Nevada. Smile4u Inc Views of Pilot Peak Beautiful Pictures	$2,075.00
28+ ACRE RETREAT LOCATED ON TUG HILL. BUCK COUNTRY, WOODS , WATERSHED, OPEN LAND	$17,100.00	Lake Havasu Parcel-NO RESERVE 1.25 Acres. Mohave Cty, AZ Large 1.25 Acre Great Investment Parcel	$2,025.00
Hot Springs Village-Golf Area Lot, across from Desoto. Large flat Lot in private golf resort $320 per month-	$17,100.00	Hudspeth County, TX-11 Acre Parcel Near Dell City. NO RESERVE! GREAT INVESTMENT OPPORTUNITY!	$2,000.01
20.2AC WITH WATER WELL TERMO, CALIFORNIA, NO RESERVE. Beautiful lot on Hummingbird dr. min from Eagle Lake	$14,850.00	Hudspeth County, TX-11 Acre Parcel Near Dell City GREAT INVESTMENT OPPORTUNITY!	$2,025.00
L@@K-2.50 ACRES FLORIDA LAND LOTS CASH @ NO RESERVE$$$$ 2 LOTS-PRICED FOR FAST CASH SALE-2 for 1--NO RESERVE!!!	$14,000.00	2.5 ACRES WITH TREES-N EAR HWY 191 ARIZONA. Witch Well Ranches-Easy Access-6,200'Elevation	$1,982.00
20.5ACRES TERMO, NE CALIFORNIA NO RESERVE. Beautiful lot on Possum dr. minutes from Eagle Lake	$12,899.00	Hudspeth County, TX-11 Acre Parcel Near Dell City. NO RESERVE! GREAT INVESTMENT OPPORTUNITY!	$1,959.00

76 ACRES NORTHERN NEVADA 300 FEET FROM I-80 CASH SALE. Mountain Views! Borders railroad! Near airport!	$12,101.00	Hudspeth County, TX-11 Acre Parcel Near Dell City. GREAT INVESTMENT OPPORTUNITY!	$1,950.00
New York 2.7 acres, close to fishing and State forest. Nice place for a Camper, Cabin or Year Round Home NR	$11,600.00	Hudspeth County, TX-11 Acre Parcel Near Dell City. GREAT INVESTMENT OPPORTUNITY!	$1,900.00
L@@K-2.5 ACRE FLORIDA LAND LOTS CASH @ NO RESERVE$$$$ 2.5 ACRES--PRICED FOR FAST CASH SALE--NO RESERVE!!!	$10,802.00	10 ACRES TEXAS, ELECTRICTY, WARD Co. LEGAL ACCESS, CASH. Cash Sale, Just Off Paved Rd. Walk to Pecos River#3	$1,870.00
Smile4u 20 Acres Humboldt County Winnemucca Nevada. Smile4u Inc Awesome Views of Santa Rosa Range	$10,099.00	11.03+/- IN BEAUTIFUL HUDSPETH COUNTY, TEXAS!!! YES, THESE ARE THE SAME ACRES SELLING FOR $2000 +	$1,850.00
40 Acres COLORADO RANCH LAND (Cash Sale) No reserve CASH SALE High Mountain Valley COLORADO	$9,600.00	10 ACRES TEXAS, ELECTRICTY, WARD Co. LEGAL ACCESS, CASH. Cash Sale, Just Off Paved Rd. Walk to Pecos River#4	$1,825.00

Land ▶ Other

	HIGH		AVG
Vacant land 10 Acres for Sale	$80,000.00	AZ Gold Mining Claim by Wickenburg & the Vulture Mine.	$1,295.00
Florida Property Real Estate Land Investment, 5.0 Acres. Hwy 60/630, Near Lake Kissimmee/River Owner Financing	$50,100.00	Enjoy the Gold, Friends, Ride ATV'S, Camp, Hunt MISSOURI-OZARKS-DIRT-CHEAP-LAND-HI BID-NO_RESERVE!! LAKE_	$1,175.00
36.50 Acre Ranch in the White Mountains of Arizona No Reserve ... Great Investment property!!!!!!	$32,400.00	LAGUNA_PALMA_CHEAP-CHEAP-FUN_INVEST-OR-RESELL_NOW! 160 Acre Arizona Unpatented Gold Mining Claim.	$1,025.00
37.03 Acre Ranch in the White Mountains of Arizona No Reserve ... Great Investment property!!!!!!	$30,500.00	Camp, Hunt, Ride ATV'S, Horses, Great Gold & Fun $L@@K-16.50 ACRES M/L IN TENNESSEE-NO RESTRICTIONS- @NR	$1,000.00
5 LOTS FLORIDA LAND-OVER 6 ACRES CLOSE TO ORLANDO !!	$30,000.00	OWNER FINANCING-NO CREDIT CHECK-PRICED FOR FAST SALE!!!	
2.5 Acre Vacant, Land Brevard Florida Investor ALERT~ No Reserve-Warranty Deed, 4 lots from I 95 RAMP.	$12,500.00	160 Acre Arizona Unpatented Gold Mining Claim. Camp, Hunt, Ride ATV'S, Horses, Great Gold & Fun	$919.00
10 LEVEL ACRES IN LANCASTER WITH ROAD FRONTAGE ELEC AND TELE ON 200TH ST, PROPERTY IN LANCASTER	$10,100.00	40 ACRE CALIFORNIA PLACER GOLD MINING CLAIM NO RESERVE! CAMP CREEK 2 BY PLACERVILLE COSUMNES RIVER MINE GOLD!!	$911.00
20 Acre Ranch 145 miles Southwest of the Grand Canyon No Reserve ... Great Investment property!!!!!!	$9,600.00	WESTMORELAND COUNTY, PA.. ROAD . NO RESERVE. About 7300 Sq. Ft. North Huntingdon TWP lot. No Reser	$830.00
HUGE 1.25 ACRE LOT- VOLUSIA COUNTY-VACANT INDUSTRIAL NEXT TO I-4 - GREAT BILLBOARD LOCATION! BUILDABLE!	$9,600.00	MISSOURI-OZARKS-DIRT-CHEAP-LAND-HI BID-NO_RESERVE!! LAKE_ LAGUNA_PALMA_CHEAP-CHEAP-FUN_INVEST-OR-RESELL_NOW!	$630.00
HUGE 1.25 ACRE LOT- VOLUSIA COUNTY-VACANT INDUSTRIAL NEXT TO I-4 - GREAT BILLBOARD LOCATION! BUILDABLE!	$9,600.00	CALIFORNIA CITY, CA-LARGE SCENIC LOT LAND PARCEL! 10,400 Square Feet + Panoramic Views + Within the City!	$610.00
20.00 Ac~Elko Nevada~Humboldt River~I-80 Frontage~NR ! Incredible Ruby Mountains & Starr Valley Views~Awesome!	$6,851.00	CALIFORNIA CITY, CA-LARGE SCENIC LOT LAND PARCEL! 7,500 Sq Ft + Amazing Scenic Area + Water + Paved!	$560.00
1.25 ACRE LOT-UNIVERSITY HIGHLANDS-CENTRAL FLORIDA HIGH DEMAND SEMI-DEVELOPED AREA - GREAT INVESTMENT OPP!	$6,600.00	2.5 ACRES NEAR BIG BEND NATIONAL PARK-TEXAS TERLINGUA- NEAR RIO GRANDE- NO RESERVE	$550.00
NR .45 Acre Florida Vacant Land Lot No House 4 LOTS No Reserve Spec Warranty Deed Recreational Corner Lots	$5,500.00	2.5 acres in Mojave(Airport), CA-Zoned Industrial 5.4 ACRE LOBO VALLEY,TEXAS RANCH- -$75MO/TERMS!	$500.00
10.0Ac~ N.E.Nevada~ Mountain Top Property ~NO RESERVE ! Soaring Peaks & Breathtaking Valley Floor Views !	$4,551.00	Almost Up Against The Van Horn Mountains!!! South Dakota Land 79.96 Acres, Butte County,Great Terms.	$370.00
DELAWARE COUNTY, PA. CHESTER CITY. NO RESERVE. About 2,400 Sq. Ft. City building lot. Build House.	$3,351.25	Monthly Payments $323 Owner Financing! Antelope Hunting Big Bend Country of West Texas Scenic and Remote.	$202.50
		Cash or Terms Read Auction BEFORE BIDDING	$202.50

Residential Homes

	HIGH		AVG
4 CALIFORNIA HOUSES FOR 1 PRICE	$276,000.00	MOVE IN CONDITION, SFH, PITTSBURGH, 4BR/2BA.	$27,100.00
BIG BEAUTIFUL KENTUCKY HOME with 3.3 Acres on HILL	$205,000.00	Great Detail, Spotless, Good Rental Income	
BANK OWNED FIXER-UPPER HOUSE/HOBBY FARM ON 34 ACRES SOUTH/CENTRAL WISCONSIN	$167,100.00	4 Units Aprt Rental Property for Auction. No Reserve! $$$$$ Annual Income. Prime Location! Large Yard.	$25,001.02
$L@@K$-.23 ACRE PORT ST. LUCIE RESIDENTIAL LOT @NR$ GOOD BUILDABLE WATERFRONT LOT-HOMESITE-WAY BELOW VALUE!	$130,000.00	Private City Hideway- Investor Cash Cow. Lovely Hilltop Home in the City	$25,000.00
FLORIDA HOUSE-EXECUTIVE BRICK HOME-3740 SQF BEAUTIFUL-TAMPA BAY-GATED COMMUNITY-RARE FIND	$101,100.00	SSO CAROLINA-4 BR 2 BA w/land-MAKE THIS YOUR HOME!!. Buy for approx $17/sq.ft.-NO RESERVE!!!!	$20,900.00
MONTANA Art Studio Home, Hunting, Horses. Blue skies, Less Stress, Wildlife, Dinosaurs	$99,000.00	Great East Baltimore Housing Investment Opportunity. Johns Hopkins and Baltimore's Redeveopment Zone	$20,655.55
Remodeled 2-3 Bedroom House In West Central Wisconsin Mississippi House and Land Cash Sale 2.2 acres NR.	$59,000.00	HOME REAL ESTATE RENTAL HOUSE INVESTMENT. GREAT RENTAL PROPERTY READY TO RENT OR MOVE IN	$20,201.00
Like new , Warranty Deed, Move in ready ! 1664sqft	$49,000.00	3 Bedroom Harrisburg Home–Low Reserve! Completely Renovated for Owner-Occupant or Investor	$20,100.00
4 Bedroom Colonial Home For Sale In Syracuse New York. Excellent Investment Investor Real Estate Katrina Rita	$48,000.00	VIRGINIA MOUNTAIN RENTAL KANSAS COUNTRY HOME OWNER 1/2 FINANCE	$20,000.00 / $19,888.00
1900 West Texas Beautiful Historic Home...NO RESERVE Gorgeous Victorian Home Perched on a Hill...	$44,800.00	FINISHED HOUSE. GORGEOUS HOME READY TO MOVE IN MANY IMPROVEMENTS	
Like New 2004 4/2.5 2 Car Garage Pool Home near Disney. Lease Option or Rent to Own No Qualify Owner Financing!	$40,000.00	WIDOW OWNED SINCE 1950 HAD HEALTH PROBLEMS NEW HOMES. BID NOW!!! NO RESERVE STARTS	$18,702.00
!!! 5 UNIT APARTMENT BUILDING 40K INSTANT EQUITY !!!!!! NO RESERVE PRICE !!!	$39,600.00	AT 1 PENNY MUST SELL FAST COMPLETELY REMODELED House!!!!! Turn Key Investment!!! .	$17,999.00
2 ACRE LOT STONE HOUSE NEW CUMBERLAND PA HARRISBURG MD MOUNTAIN TOP LOT OVERLOOKING SUSQUEHANNA RIVER WOW!	$37,000.00	Lowest Crime Area-Which Means Good Tenants Youngstown, Ohio.-DUPLEX Home Investors. No Reserve. Must sell. Youngstown, Ohio.-3 Bed/2 Bath Homes Investors. No Reserve. Must sell.	$15,600.00 / $15,300.00
Bid 4 Sale Price!! 3BR/2BA- On Market Too Long!! 2508 Cactus Drive. Killeen, TX 76549	$35,100.00	LARGE 3 UNIT FOR SALE! BIG RENTAL AREA! BIN $29,900!!! LOCATED IN ANDERSON, IN. ASSESSED AT $44,500!!!	$15,200.00
BEAUTIFUL HOUSE IN WOODBURY	$29,000.00	HOME HOUSE REAL ESTATE RENTAL PROPERTY LOT LAND WINNER. You decide Live in now or Make it a beautiful home WOW	$15,099.55

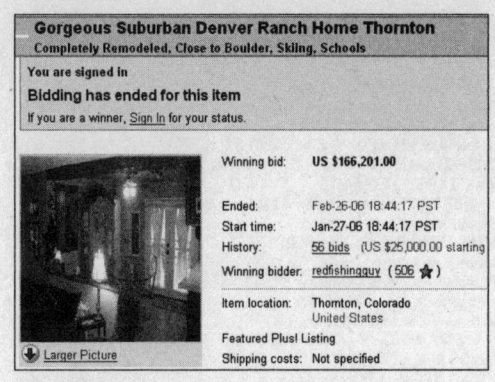

Gorgeous Suburban Denver Ranch Home Thornton
Completely Remodeled, Close to Boulder, Skiing, Schools

You are signed in

Bidding has ended for this item
If you are a winner, Sign In for your status.

Winning bid:	**US $166,201.00**
Ended:	Feb-26-06 18:44:17 PST
Start time:	Jan-27-06 18:44:17 PST
History:	56 bids (US $25,000.00 starting)
Winning bidder:	redfishingguy (506 ★)
Item location:	Thornton, Colorado United States
	Featured Plus! Listing
Shipping costs:	Not specified

Larger Picture

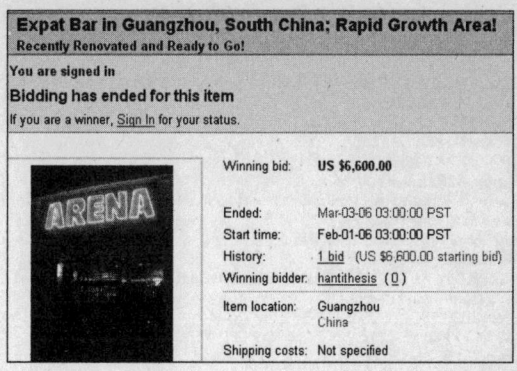

Expat Bar in Guangzhou, South China; Rapid Growth Area!
Recently Renovated and Ready to Go!

You are signed in

Bidding has ended for this item
If you are a winner, Sign In for your status.

Winning bid:	**US $6,600.00**
Ended:	Mar-03-06 03:00:00 PST
Start time:	Feb-01-06 03:00:00 PST
History:	1 bid (US $6,600.00 starting bid)
Winning bidder:	hantithesis (0)
Item location:	Guangzhou China
Shipping costs:	Not specified

Commercial

HIGH TO LOW

MINI STORAGE At Interstate Cross Roads Mini Storage Ideally Located In Prosperous Town	$200,000.00	Laundromat for sale, business and 2 buildings. You're bidding on the down payment only.	$14,600.00
APARTMENT / 18 UNITS / BRICK / FULLY OCCUPIED / NR! Decatur, IL	$199,100.00	Expat Bar in Guangzhou, South China; Rapid Growth Area! Recently Renovated and Ready to Go!	$6,600.00
FABULOUS HISTORICAL HOME- Wewoka, Okla. Bed and Breakfast/ Potential -Low Reserve-	$75,877.00	West Palm Beach Clematis Street Restaurant For Sale. Busiest area in West Palm Beach perfect for restaurant	$1,550.00
THRIVING RESTAURANT / GAS STATION IN BUSINESS FOR 25YRS. After 25 years owners are ready to retire!	$75,100.00	HISTORIC 7000sq.ft. BRICK CHURCH ~ REDKEY INDIANA ~ NR! 100% OF ALL PROCEEDS TO	$600.00
ANTIQUE SCHOOL HOUSE ON 5 ACRES-ADAMS CO. N.D. on the Cedar River-prime pheasant & deer hunting land	$15,099.00	HURRICANE KATRINA RELIEF!! $40	
$1 Starts! Brick Retail/Apartment Bldg., Marion, IN	$15,099.00	4 units on 2 c-1 lots. michigan no reserve! bank foreclosure.	$100.00
		needs work. super investment prop	$15.00

Manufactured Homes

HIGH TO LOW

FLORIDA Manufactured Mobile Trailer Home AND LAND / LOT	$30,000.00	FLORIDA Manufactured Mobile	$4,300.00
Mobile Home-Manufactured Home-Modular Home. 1990 Cavco 61' X 12'-4 Bedroom	$14,990.00	Modular Trailer Home	
5 ac Lake/Golf Arizona Land House/Manufactured-Concho. Could be next Hot Spot! Developer moving in, Title Ins	$9,000.00	1ac Lake, Golf, Concho, Arizona Land House/Manufactured. Could be next Hot Spot! Developer moving in, title ins	$4,000.00

Timeshares for Sale ▸ Attractions/Theme Parks

	HIGH		AVG
NY Manhattan Club Timeshare for sale . PLATNUM Flex Anytime 2 Weekends Per Year	$24,000.00	1 BR at Fairfield Sea Gardens, Pompano Beach, FL 1250 ANNUAL SHELL VACATIONS CLUB POINTS :	$621.00 $611.50
Manhattan Club Flexible Interest 3 weekends. 1 Bedroom 2 Bathrooms	$22,000.00	CALIFORNIA NO RESERVE : AWESOME GOLD CROWN AND FIVE STAR RESORTS	
GRAND TIMBER LODGE BRECKENRIDGE TIMESHARE CHRISTMAS. 2BR L/O 5- Christmas week, Annual Usage	$19,600.00	Arizona 5 STAR Gold Crown RED WEEK Timeshare Deed Orange Tree Golf Resort, Scottsdale, Jacuzzi, Balcony	$611.01
WORLDMARK TRENDWEST - - - - NO HOUSEKEEPING - - - - RARE "PREMIER" OWNERSHIP EXEMPT FROM HOUSEKEEPING FEES	$13,902.02	RIVIERA BEACH & SPA-BEAUTIFUL CAPISTRANO BEACH CA-L@@K! 1 OR 2-BEDROOM-NO RESERVE-2005 MAINT PD-GREAT BARGAIN-	$610.49
MARRIOTT, BRECKENRIDGE, COLORADO, TIMESHARE PLATINUM PLUS, RESERVED CHRISTMAS THIS YEAR	$12,480.00	RCI POINTS / GOLD CROWN TIMESHARE VACATION PROPERTY NR CELEBRATION WORLD / BUILD YOUR POINTS PORTFOLIO !	$610.00
Hilton HGVC at Las Vegas 7000 Points Timeshare	$11,100.00	2 BR GOLF In POMPANO BEACH Florida Timeshare Deed	$610.00
HYATT BEACH HOUSE RESORT : KEY WEST, FL. NO RESERVE : 2 BDRM PRIME RED WEEK : II 5 STAR RESORT	$10,801.00	The Fairways of Palm-Aire (Fairfield Resort) GOLD CROWN Villa del Palmar- Cabo San Lucas Mexico Timeshare RCI	$610.00
MARRIOTT KAUAI BEACH CLUB, HAWAII-PLATINUM TIMESHARE Annual Usage –1BR Lockoff –	$10,800.00	Resort of International Distinction	
		RIVIERA BEACH & SPA-BEAUTIFUL CAPISTRANO BEACH CA-L@@K! 1 OR 2-BEDROOM-NO RESERVE-2005 MAINT PD-GREAT BARGAIN-	$610.00
WORLDMARK / TRENDWEST 10,000 CREDIT PREMIER OWNERSHIP 30,000 CREDITS BANKED / UNUSED ! ! ! ! NO RESERVE	$9,469.69	Westgate Lakes Resort and Spa Villa In Orlando, FL A Vacation In Walt Disney World Sunny Florida	$610.00
WESTIN KIERLAND VILLAS SHERATON'S STARWOOD 81,000 PTS Transferable Starwood Options and Preferred Guest (SPG)	$9,410.00	NEVADA Lake TAHOE Ridge 2BR Timeshare PAYPAL-NO RESERVE	$610.00
Maximum RCI Points Trading Power 184,000 Annual Points Vacation in the Largest Units at the Finest Resorts	$9,200.00	LANDMARK HOLIDAY BEACH RESORT-PANAMA CITY BEACH, FL- 2-BD TS Week RED-05 MAINTENANCE PD-WK 44, 2006-	$599.00
Maximum RCI Points Trading Power 184,000 Annual Points Vacation in the Largest Units at the Finest Resorts	$9,200.00	- 51,400 RCI USA Points Available - Deeded USA - Yearly 25,700 RCI Points-Low Dues-Super Price..	$599.00
Worldmark / Trendwest 11,000 Annual PREMIER Membership 17K Banked. Plus a FREE gift	$8,451.00	Oregon Coast Luxury Timeshare- 180 degree View RCI-On the Beach-Wet Bar- Jacuzzi-Fireplace more	$590.00
DISNEY BEACH CLUB VILLAS! DISNEY VACATION CLUB! DVC! NO RESERVE! 100 PT Contract till 2042	$8,400.00	S. Lake Tahoe, CA Tahoe Beach & Ski Club Red Timeshare High Season Float (1-15,21-37,49&50) Annual Studio	$586.01
FIVE STAR 2BR LOCKOFF MARRIOTT'S SHADOW RIDGE TIMESHARE Palm Desert, California, One of Marriott most Desirable	$8,400.00	MAGIC TREE RESORT ORLANDO DISNEY TIMESHARE NO RES universal islands adventure city walk sea world outlets	$570.00

Timeshares for Sale ▶ Beach/Ocean

	HIGH		AVG
HYATT BEACH HOUSE RESORT : KEY WEST, FL NO RESERVE : 2 BDRM PRIME RED WEEK : II 5 STAR RESORT	$10,801.00	2 BR at Fairfield Sea Gardens, Pompano Beach, FL	$430.00
MARRIOTT KAUAI BEACH CLUB, HAWAII-PLATINUM TIMESHARE Annual Usage –1BR Lockoff –	$10,800.00	ST. MAARTEN ISLAND Summer Red Week Timeshare Deed Pelican Resort Club, NO RESERVE!!	$412.00
Kauai, Hawaii, Bali Hai Villas, Floating Red Week. Reduced to SELL.	$8,600.00	WATERSIDE BY SPINNAKER:HILTON HEAD ISLAND,SC: NO RESERVE RCI GOLD CROWN : PRIME RED GOLF WEEK : EVEN YEARS	$405.00
Kona Coast Resort Timeshare	$7,300.00	Florida Beachfront 2 BR RED Timeshare for Sale No reserve, will sell to the high bidder!	$399.00
Time Share Rental Aruba-Costa Linda Beach Resort Week 25 (High Demand)	$6,000.00	California RED WEEK GOLF Timeshare Deed L OW RESERVE! Bonus Time-RID	$357.57
Disney FAIRFIELD Points FIVE STAR Timeshare Deed Paypal-NO Reserve!!I-Star Island Resort	$5,100.00	Ormond Beach FLORIDA RED WEEK Timeshare Deed Plantation Island, Paypal-No Reserve!!	$355.01
PUEBLO BONITO RESORT LOS CABOS : CABO SAN LUCAS, MEXICO NO RESERVE : OCEANVIEW DELUXE RED WEEK : RCI GOLD CROWN	$4,596.01	Cypress Palms Resort in Orlando, Florida	$351.00
Playa Linda-Gold Crown ARUBA Top rated resort in the Carribean -MARRIOTT QUALITY	$3,750.00	2 BR 2 BTH NEW SMYRA BEACH FLORIDA TIMESHARE Sea Villas, New Smyra Beach Florida	$325.00
Maritime Beach Club Timeshare.. beach front near golf a quiet corner unit 8th floor right out over the ocean	$3,600.00	FAIRFIELD Points GOLD CROWN Timeshare Paypal-NO Reserve-Free Points!!!	$317.00
Hawaii-Large 2 bath- Kona Coast II Resort!!	$3,161.00	Florida RED WEEK Ocean front BEACH Timeshare Deed NO RESERVE-Closing includes title search & policy!	$316.00
HAWAII Kona Coast GOLD CROWN RED WEEK Timeshare Deed Kailua-Kona, GOLF, Beach, full kitchen, 2 bath, jacuzzi	$3,151.00	MYRTLE BEACH Oceanfront Red WEEK Timeshare	$305.00
HAWAII Kona Coast GOLD CROWN RED WEEK Timeshare Deed Kailua-Kona, GOLF, Beach, Paypal!!	$3,129.00	Schooner II Beach and Racquet Club,No Reserve!I- PAYPAL FAIRFIELD PEPPERTREE ATLANTIC BEACH, NC : NO RESERVE 2 BEDROOM PRIME RED SUMMER WEEK : RCI & II RESORT	$304.00
TWO Fixed Xmas Ownerships On The Beach! Gold Crown! This Is A 2 UNIT PACKAGE! Own 2 for the price of one!!!	$2,999.00	FAIRFIELD PEPPERTREE ATLANTIC BEACH, NC : NO RESERVE. 2 BEDROOM RED WEEK : HANDICAP UNIT : RCI & II RESORT	$299.00
Southern California!!!! SUMMER Beach Front! Huge 2br!	$2,999.00	VACATION VILLAGE AT BONAVENTURE: WESTON, FL: NO RESERVE 2 BDRM LOCKOUT RED WEEK : CONVERTS TO 43,500 RCI POINTS	$299.00
Luxury Hawaii 2 Bedroom Timeshare -Clearance!!	$2,850.00	WATERSIDE BY SPINNAKER:HILTON HEAD ISLAND,SC:NO RESERVE RCI GOLD CROWN : PRIME RED SUMMER WEEK : ODD YEARS	$299.00

Timeshares for Sale ▶ Lakefront

NOTE *There were only 26 complete items in this subcategory, so all the auctions are listed.*

HIGH TO LOW

TAHOE LAKE California RED Weeks 2 BR Timeshare Deed NO RESERVE! Bonus Time-SKI & Summer float-Casino	$1,581.87	New RCI USA Points Memberships-28,000 Available Now!	$249.00
Vacation Club at Shanty Creek, Michigan Timeshare RCI Gold Crown Resort ! No Reserve !	$1,350.00	Free-Silverleaf 2BR LOCKOFF LAKEFRONT Timeshare Deed Silverleaf's Ozark Mountain, Free Closing/Transfer Fee!	$207.50
Lake Arrowhead Chalets, California Timeshare	$1,026.23	BEAUTIFUL LAKEFRONT TIMESHARE VACATION	$207.50
27,500 Annual USA RCI Points – Resort Dues $270.53 – Deeded-Low Dues-USA RCI Points Memberships	$880.00	HOT SPRINGS ARK RCI RID / GREAT SUMMER RED WEEK /FABULOUS LAKE HAMILTON	
LAKE TAHOE SPRING OR FALL WEEK! TIMESHARE RID RATED Tahoe Beach & Ski, swing season	$821.13	SILVERLEAF'S FOX RIVER RESORT : SHERIDAN, IL NO RESERVE : 2 BEDROOM PRIME RED FALL WEEK : RCI RESORT	$199.00
FAIRFIELD SAPPHIRE VALLEY : SAPPHIRE, NC : RCI RESORT NO RESERVE : 105,000 FAIRFIELD FAIRSHARE PLUS POINTS	$761.50	MINNESOTA 1 BD LAKEFRONT TIMESHARE Breezy Point International, Lakefront 1bd high season	$102.50
Crown Point Resort Timeshare Arkansas RCI Gold Crown Resort 2bdrm 2 bath Summer week	$665.00	Silverleaf 2BR Missouri RED WEEK Timeshare Deed Silverleaf's Ozark Mountain, Paypal, No Reserve!!	$100.00
- 51,400 RCI USA Points Available - Deeded USA – Yearly 25,700 RCI Points-Low Dues-Super Price..	$599.00	RCI Timeshare For Sale! RARE Floating Holiday Usage!	$99.99
BRANSON /LAKE FRT/2BD LO/ GOLD CROWN/ RED FLT/TIMESHARE THIS IS A TERRIFIC RESORT/ RED FLOAT/ LOCK OFF gReAt !	$520.00	NO Reserve! Use with RCI Weeks or Points 4 Deposit! OWN 2 BR Lockoff MISSOURI Deeded Timeshare For Sale RCI-Resort Of International Distinction, RED WEEK	$56.00
TIMESHARE-POINTE RESORT & CLUB-MINOCQUA, WI free and clear-worth $8,500	$455.00	BREEZY POINT, MN GC 2BD TIMESHARE IN SPRINGTIME White Birch in Springtime! 2bd near Pelican Lake	$20.00
VILLAS AT LANTERN BAY : BRANSON, MO : SERENE II RESORT NO RESERVE : 2 BDRM LAKEFRONT FLOATING RED WEEK VILLA	$299.00	$1 SALE! FAIRFIELD BAY ARKANSAS GOLF 2 BD TIMESHARE Fairfield Bay, 2 BD GOLF RESORT, GOLD CROWN RATED	$2.00
TAHOE SEASONS RESORT : SOUTH LAKE TAHOE, CA: NO RESERVE PRIME FLOATING RED WEEK	$299.00	$1 SALE! 2 BR 2 BTH RID RATED MONTGOMERY TX TIMESHARE Sweetwater At Lake Conroe	$2.00
RCI - USA Points - Deeded-New RCI Points Memberships Low Resort Dues-No Reserve-37,400 Available Now ! $299.00- USA RCI Points Week Deeded-Resort Dues	$236.68	$1 SALE! 2 BR 2 BTH LAKE CONROE TEXAS TIMESHARE SILVERLEAF'S PINEY SHORES-RID, attractions GOLFING	$1.00
		THE VILLAS OF FOXWOOD HILLS: WESTMINSTER, SC NO RESERVE!2 BEDROOM 2 BATH TOWNHOME: RCI RED WEEK	$1.00

Timeshares for Sale ▶ Mountain/Skiing

	HIGH		AVG
GRAND TIMBER LODGE BRECKENRIDGE TIMESHARE CHRISTMAS 2BR L/O 5- Christmas season, Annual Usage	$19,600.00	TAHOE California 2br LOCKOFF Timeshare DEED No Reserve-Paypal, Tahoe Seasons Resort!!!	$922.13
MARRIOTT, BRECKENRIDGE, COLORADO, TIMESHARE PLATINUM PLUS, RESERVED CHRISTMAS THIS YEAR	$12,480.00	GREAT SUMMER TIMESHARE VACATION IN THE POCONO MOUNTAINS YOU WILL THRILL AT THE BREATHTAKING VIEWS IN THIS AREA	$736.00
FIVE STAR 2BR LOCKOFF MARRIOTT'S SHADOW RIDGE TIMESHARE Palm Desert, California, One of Marriott most Desirable	$8,400.00	FIVE STAR Sedona ARIZONA ILX Timeshare Deed ILX Premiere Vacation Club, No Reserve!!!	$710.00
FIVE STAR 2BR LOCKOFF MARRIOTT'S SHADOW RIDGE TIMESHARE Palm Desert, California, One of Marriott most Desirable	$7,100.00	S. Lake Tahoe, CA Tahoe Beach & Ski Club Red Timeshare High Season Float (1-15,21-37,49&50) Annual Studio	$586.01
THE SUMMIT@MASSANUTTEN:MCGAHEYSVILLE,VA: 4 BDRM LOCKOUT NO RESERVE : RCI GOLD CROWN RESORT: RED WEEK	$5,776.00	FAIRFIELD BLUE RIDGE VILLAGE:SUGAR MTN, BANNER ELK, NC	$560.00

FAIRFIELD SMOKEY MOUNTAINS:GATLINBURG, SEVIERVILLE, TN	$5,200.00
NO RESERVE : 300,000 FAIRFIELD POINTS : RCI GOLD CROWN	
MARRIOTT BRECKENRIDGE 5 STAR COLORADO SKI TIMESHARE!!!	$5,000.00
Platinum Winter Week Sale -President's Day Week 2006!	
Reduced 2 sell Pollard Brook 5- Resort, NH MTN/SKI RED,	$4,599.99
,,,øø-TOP-øø,,,øø-NOTCH-øø,,,øø-EBAYER-øø,,,	
Marriotts Streamside at Vail, Colorado Timeshare Ski Week!	$3,150.00
Grand Timber Lodge, Breckenridge, CO Green week with	$3,051.00
Interval International membership	
14000 (Even) Bluegreen Points at Mountain Loft	$2,710.00
Colorado AVON 2 BR FLOAT RED WEEK Timeshare Deed.	$2,651.00
Vail Valley-SKI-full kitchen-Bonus Time	
SKI Week VAIL Colorado Deeded Timeshare for sale	$2,375.10
NO RESERVE- The Wren Resort !	
MARRIOTT Streamside at Vail PRIME SKI WEEK Timeshare	$2,038.00
Five Star Resort, Ski Week, Rare Find on Ebay!	
FAIRFIELD FLAGSTAFF FIXED SUMMERTIME WEEK 27	$1,749.00

NO RESERVE: 2 BDRM FALL PRIME RED WEEK : RCI GOLD CROWN	
FAIRFIELD FLAGSTAFF ARIZONA 2BR GOLD CROWN	$533.00
TIMESHARE NO RESERVE!	
FAIRFIELD BLUE RIDGE VILLAGE:SUGAR MTN, BANNER ELK, NC	$515.00
NO RESERVE : FALL PRIME RED WEEK : RCI GOLD CROWN	
TAHOE California HOLIDAY Ski WEEK Timeshare DEED	$401.00
No Reserve-Paypal, Tahoe Seasons Resort!!!	
MARRIOTT'S MOUNTAIN VALLEY LODGE-BRECKENRIDGE,COLORADO-	$399.00
STUDIO-SLEEPS 4 -NO RESV-05 MAINTENANCE PAID-USE IN 06-	
2BR Deeded Steamboat Springs Red Timeshare	$355.00
FIVE STAR Sedona ARIZONA ILX Timeshare	$332.50
Deed For Sale NO RESERVE !!!	
COLORADO 2 BR Lockoff RED WEEK Timeshare DEED	$305.00
Celebrity Resorts Steamboat Hilltop,NO RESERVE!!	
VAIL, COLORADO! RED SEASON TIMESHARE FOR SALE	$152.50
NO RESERVE! WILL SELL TO THE HIGHEST BIDDER!	
GOLF!! COLORADO Dillon 3 BR Timeshare DEED	$152.50
Orofino by Straight Creek, Low Maintenance Fees !!	
Avon COLORADO Prime RED Summer Week Timeshare	$102.50
Deed NO RESERVE-Prime Summer Season-Bonus Time	

Timeshares for Sale ▸ Other

	HIGH		AVG
Manhattan Club Flexible Interest 3 weekends.	$22,000.00	MAYAN PALACE RESORTS-THE BEST OF MEX-10 RESORTS TO	$1,278.00
1 Bedroom 2 Bathrooms		USE BEGINS IN 06-NO RESV-LOW MAINT-GET A BONUS WEEK-	
Worldmark / Trendwest 11,000 Annual PREMIER Membership	$8,451.00	EXCELLENT GOLD CROWN DAYTONA BEACH FLORIDA TIMESHARE	$1,075.00
17K Banked. Plus a FREE gift		Tropic Shores- Daytona Beach Florida	
Timeshare Westin Palm Desert CA	$8,000.00	LOS ABRIGADOS-SEDONA AZ-NO RESERVE-2005 MAINT FEES	$911.00
Worldmark / Trendwest 8,000 Annual PREMIER Membership	$5,801.00	PAID 1-BEDROOM-RED FLOATING WEEK-A BEAUTIFUL BARGAIN	
10K Banked. Plus a FREE gift		2 BD Red French Lick Timeshare Deed	$910.00
Worldmark / Trendwest PREMIER 6K Packed with Credits!	$4,901.00	Big Bear Lake, CA Lagonita Lodge Annual 1 Bed	$500.00
FREE Ocean Vacation Included!		Timeshare Spring/Fall Floating Week Annual 1 edroom	
Worldmark / Trendwest PREMIER 6,000 credit membership	$4,451.00	PALM CANYON RESORT & SPA-111 POINTS+111 BONUS POINTS-	$490.00
Paid in Full! Free Gift Included		FOR 2006-NO RESERVE-EVERY YEAR USAGE- PALM SPRINGS-L@@K	
ARIZONA /SCOTTSDALE VILLA MIRAGE /	$4,450.00	SCOTTSDALE CAMELBACK RESORT-ONE BEAUTIFUL VACATION 4U	$399.00
TIMESHARE TWO BEDROOM LOCK-OFF UNIT		4U STUDIO LOFT-NO RESV-05 MAINTENANCE FEES PAID-USE	
HILTON GRAND VACATIONS-FLAMINGO LAS VEGAS-3400 POINTS-	$4,109.98	77,000 FAIRFIELD POINTS GC TIMESHARE Fairfield Resorts	$305.00
GOLD SEASON-NO RESERVE-05 MAINTENANCE PAID-USE IN 2006-		Points-MEXICO NOT DEEDED	
HILTON GRAND VACATIONS-FLAMINGO LAS VEGAS-3400 POINTS-	$3,700.00	VACATION VILLAGE @ PARKWAY-KISSIMMEE FL-NEAR THE ACTION	$299.00
GOLD SEASON-NO RESERVE-05 MAINTENANCE PAID-USE IN 2006-		2-BED LOCK-OUT-NO RESERVE-ODD YEAR USE-05/06 FEES PAID	
2BD ORANGE LAKE COUNTRY CLUB FLORIDA NICE!!!!	$3,158.93	ALHAMBRA @ POINCIANA-BEAUTIFUL RESORT-REMODELED	$207.50
WEEK 48! Week 48 great break week orlando attractions		2-BED LOCK-OUT-NO RESERVE-05 MAINT PAID-USE IN 2006-	
49,000 RCI Points Annual Gold Crown VERY RARE!!	$3,000.00	TAHOE SEASONS RESORT- LAKE TAHOE-JULY 4th HOLIDAY WEEK	$202.50
NO CLOSING COSTS!!! 0% financing for 9 months!		CHALET 1-BEDROOM-NO RESERVE-NEAR ALL THE ACTION-L@@K!!!	
Orlando Florida Gold Crown 2 Bed Orange Lake Timeshare Annual	$2,025.01	VACATION VILLAGE@WESTON-WESTON FLORIDA-EVEN YEAR	$199.00
2 Bed Gold Crown Fixed Week #42 Orange Lake C.C.		USE- 2-BEDROOM LOCK-OUT-NO RESERVE-05 MAINT PAID-	
164,000 Fairfield Resort Points	$1,750.00	LIKI TIKI VILLAGE-WINTER GARDEN/ORLANDO-CLUB NAVIGO RST	$199.00
STAR ISLAND RESORT-(Managed by Fairfield)-KISSIMMEE,FL-	$1,725.00	1800 POINTS-NO RESERVE-USE 12/10-17/05-05/06 MAINT.PAID	
3-BEDROOM LOCK-OUT-WEEK 51-NO RESERVE-05 FEES PAID-L@@K		5 STAR DAYTONA BEACH FLORIDA TIMESHARE OCEANFRONT	$199.00
FAIRFIELD FLAGSTAFF-126,000 FAIRSHARE POINTS-WOW-L@@K-	$1,525.00	Marine Terrace, Daytona Beach, 5 Star Rated	
NO RESERVE-MAINTENANCE FEES PAID THRU 10/31/2005		FREE-Wisconsin GOLF Float Week Timeshare Deed Telemark,	$100.00
		No Reserve!!!-FREE CLOSING!!	

Other Real Estate

HIGH TO LOW

VICTORIAN QUEEN ANNE HOUSE IN ARKANSAS	$179,100.00	Houston 2 Bedroom Furnished Condo / World Series 5 Day	$2,500.00
RUSHFORD LAKE WATER FRONT COTTAGE	$45,000.00	Rental from Oct 24th-Oct 29th	
IN NEW YORK STATE		A GORGEOUS 10 ACRES IN JEFF DAVIS COUNTY, TEXAS	$1,280.00
One Share of Stock in Davis Weber Canal Company-Water	$18,500.00	GREAT INVESTMENT OPPORTUNITY	
Log Cabin Home Kit - Cabin I	$7,840.00	Ron Legrand Complete Cash Flow System	$380.00
Free 25,000 sq/ft Nursing Home on 17 acres w/ 4bd Home.	$3,550.00	REALTOR Real Estate Agent RUBBER DUCK Ducky Duckie	$8.05
Owner will finance -Great Terms, Central Wisconsin			

27

SPECIALTY SERVICES

Specialty Services is a relatively new category on eBay, but it's one that eBay sellers may find useful, since many of the services offered apply to eBay auctions themselves. There are eBay ad auction templates, international shipping services, professional logo creation and graphic design services, promotional services, e-books about selling on eBay, and more.

Pet Projects

Although the business services look useful, some of the most interesting auctions in Special Services are in the Artistic Services subcategory. Several people bid on auctions for a custom portrait of their pet—in this sample, these sold for $99.95, $51.01, and $40.00 at the high end and $25.00, $24.99, and $10.00 in the median price range. "I paint your pet from your favorite photograph," says Sherry O., the lister of the portrait auction that closed at $99.95. "I have been painting animals for six years and I have learned to capture the essence of your pet and bring them to life on canvas!" she says, and she offers a money-back guarantee. She emphasizes the value of this custom art: "These same portraits sell for $200.00 to $400.00 at the art shows!" And she has satisfied customers: "I can't tell you how much I love the portrait that you painted of our shelties, Duffy & Casey. I was blown away by the way that you captured their personalities and their beauty. You have incredible talent; thank you so very much!" reads one of the testimonials from her auction description.

There are even a couple of auctions that were specifically for portraits of a horse. If you don't have a pet, however, you can commission a portrait of yourself or your home. The highest seller in this sample was for a "CUSTOM OIL PORTRAIT PAINTING FROM YOUR PHOTO" that went for $235.00. Other custom portraits of people sold for $225.00, $77.00,

$70.00, and on down to $10.00 for a "CUSTOM LACQUERED FAMILY PORTRAIT PAINTING ON ART CANVAS." The custom house paintings do well too—they went for $115.00, $69.99, $45.00, and $19.99.

Are paper and canvas not your thing? How about having your portrait done on a rock? Yes, a "Custom Painted Portrait on a Rock Gift Services" auction successfully closed at $16.99. (This brings a new meaning to the idea of a "pet rock.") Another artist who lists in this category chooses embroidery as her medium for pet portraits.

Finding Your Voice

Other auctions include custom costumes, hats, bags, shirts, and even tattoos. And in the Specialty Services ▶ Artistic Services ▶ Other subcategory, you can also bid on an intangible type of art: voice talent. For only $0.99 (and $4.95 in another auction), an eBayer bought a "Professional Voice Greeting / On Hold Message" from "Your eBay Voiceover Connection— Voice Talent, Inc."

Other voice-related auctions include a "COMPLETE SINGING VOICE LESSON SERIES with Shelley Kristen" that went for $22.40 in Specialty Services ▶ Advice & Instruction ▶ Lessons, Tutoring and a "VoIP VOICE MAIL, & ON HOLD RECORDING, AFFORDABLE!!" that went for $9.99 in Specialty Services ▶ Media Editing & Duplication ▶ Photo & Video.

If the professional voiceover isn't enough to promote your business, there are plenty of other business services available in this category. You can get 5,000 full-color business cards, which sold here for $149.00, or a custom logo and business ID package, which went for $169.00 in a Buy It Now auction. In the Specialty Services ▶ Graphic & Logo Design subcategory, custom original logo designs sold for between $8.99 and $99.00. Under Specialty Services ▶ Printing & Personalization ▶ Signs, Decals, business signs sold for between $49.95 and $195.00, with an auction for 24" by 30" "Custom Sandblasted Signs" going for $167.50.

Or you could try a radio ad: a commercial for one year on WTBC Radio sold for $200.00. ("Get your message out to 50,000+ monthly listeners.") Available at www.WTBCRadio.com, a "leading Christian Internet broadcast site," WTBC Radio stations receive over 2,500 logins per day, and they have listeners in every metropolitan area in the United States. The seller says, "This opportunity is especially valuable to those who have Internet-based businesses or ministry web sites," and it would be "excellent promotion for Gospel artists." The winner has the choice of six 30-second spots or four 60-second spots per day to run for one year— a $2,940.00 value, according to the seller. You can also get your commercial produced for an extra fee ($100.00 to $150.00).

Your Business in a Blog? Web Services

In the Specialty Services ▶ Web & Computer Services ▶ Internet Promotion subcategory you can find auctions for web banner ads, targeted email lists, and search engine optimization. But perhaps my favorite listing here was from the guy who sold a 30-day banner ad spot on his blog, "HRSEO"—it went for the highest price in that subcategory's sample, $700.00. Yes, Joel Cheesman offered a 250 by 250 pixel ad space within his blog's content, which discusses Internet recruiting and search engine optimization. ("Want your company, publication, event, Web site, service or whatever in front of the online recruitment industry's elite? If so, I'm confident you've come to the right place.") Cheesman admits, "I know I'm really putting myself out there with this auction. There's a chance no one will bid, making me look like a total loser." But he says, "I'm willing to take that risk. One, this is a neat experiment. And two, I'm really just too lazy and busy to actively sell real estate on my blog." Happily, his risk paid off.

Indeed, Specialty Services seems to attract risk-takers and forward-thinking business people. Be sure to troll the Specialty Services subcategories for other unique offers and opportunities: guitar repair, car decals, holiday cards, wedding and party favors, or a "U.S. Bank Account for Non-Residents." It's hard to imagine not enjoying bidding on some of these items, but if you don't, rest assured the sellers are having fun when their items sell.

A service is, after all, more personal than many eBay auctions, as the seller is putting his or her talent into it. As one seller wrote on the eBay Specialty Services discussion board, "I successfully sold a Custom Spell Writing auction, and have received terrific feedback. This is a real thrill for me. I used to publish a lot of poetry, but it didn't pay anything, so that kind of fell by the wayside after college. Now I can get paid to write poetry . . . This is so much fun!"

NOTE *There are no average price statements in this chapter because the prices were obtained using eBay's Completed Items feature.*

Advice & Instruction ▶ Business & Computer

	HIGH		AVG
Writing Service: Editing Formatting Rewriting Revising		Cash Flow Dollars in Mailbox - you just RELAX watch TV!	$6.85
I Have a Master's Degree in Professional Writing!	$50.00	$600/day Your OWN Videographer	$6.85
The Stay*at*Home Internet Millionaire	$45.25	Home Business! Video $$$	
US Bank Account for Non Residents plus FREE ATM Visa	$37.00	Increase Sales by Customer Referrals/Word*of*Mouth Book	$6.09
Easy, secure. Works with PayPal. 60 days M/B Guarantee.		2 Custom Name or word(s) Vinyl Decals CHROME!	$6.00
Process Engineering Toolkit	$29.95	US Bank Account for Non-Residents, Access Paypal!	$5.00
Knowledge Management Toolkit	$29.95	SECRETS TO MAKING MONEY NOW, Books & Tapes.	$4.99
Outsourcing Toolkit	$29.95	Learn how to make MONEY in The Information Age!!!!	
Project Management Toolkit	$29.95	PowerSeller's Secret lists.. want to on the list??	$4.99
11 CD LOT Monopolize Your Marketplace Marketing Set NR	$27.99	Wanna be PowerSeller ?? Not sure where to buy??	
Resume Writing: Editing Formatting Rewriting Revising	$25.00	Stay at Home MOMS!! Earn with Ebay Success Kit	$4.99
I Have a Master's Degree in Professional Writing!		Everything you need to know to start making money NOW	
SOFTWARE Inventory, Customer Point of Sale, Credit Card	$25.00	VIRTUAL INVESTIGATIONS 3.1 SOFTWARE*	$4.95
FREE Shipping. FREE Credit Card Software. Money Back Gy		NO SECRETS*EBOOK	
multi * purpose suggestion & drop box	$19.55	Increase Sales by Customer Referrals/Word*of*Mouth Book	$4.25
multi * purpose suggestion & drop box	$19.52	3000+ Wholesale Ebooks lot *Business resell CD kit!	$4.15
multi * purpose suggestion & drop box	$16.55	3000+ Wholesale Ebooks lot *Business resell CD kit!	$4.00
multi * purpose suggestion & drop box	$16.50	Make $1000 per Week With Your Camera *Business Report!	$4.00
I pay my BOAT with MISSPELLED ebay items!! 1000s	$12.95	3000+ Wholesale Ebooks lot *Business resell CD kit!	$3.49
of item available right now LISTEN TO MY AUCTION		Solar Products Catalog 1000's of Items to choose from	$3.00

Advice & Instruction ▶ Diet & Fitness

HIGH TO LOW

	HIGH		AVG
Drink your money away, courtesy of Bet Sig Dart Team.	$29.99	Take TOTAL CONTROL thru SELF HYPNOSIS NLP 6 CD Set	$8.95
Personalized Nutritional Consultation.	$20.50	[3 of these sold for $8.95 each]	
Your Body Tells You What It Needs!		1993 Richard Simmons Deal*A*Meal comp. like new	$7.99
The Protein Power Plan As Seen On TV Complete	$12.50	Take TOTAL CONTROL thru SELF HYPNOSIS NLP 6 CD Set	$6.95
		Gwen Shamblin EXODUS Out of Egypt Weight Program Set	$2.00

Advice & Instruction ▶ Lessons, Tutoring

	HIGH		AVG
David DeAngelo Double your Dating, Sexual Communication	$300.00	RESUMES THAT GET RESULTS. Let's Do Something	$10.00
Rosetta Stone Language Learning Sucess. Spanish * Level 1 and 2 Box Set	$255.00	with your Lifeless Resume	
DAWN LESTER National Pageant Modeling Videos	$102.50	PPAP/QS 9000/ISO 9001&9000 FORMS.TEMPLATES READY TO USE.	$10.00
Stock Market Day/Swing Trading Course ($250.00 value).	$79.00	ISO 9001: 2000 CERTIFICATION FOR $5000 OR LESS.ASK NOW!	
Learn Stock Trading Online: 5 hrs, Live Mentoring		Incredible Self Confidence, Hypnosis CD	$8.49
Dan Kennedy Collection Training Videos & Tapes	$75.33	Incredible Self Confidence, Hypnosis CD	$8.05
Horseback Riding Lessons * Angier, NC Giving Works Item	$70.00	Incredible Self Confidence, Hypnosis CD	$7.99
Tony Robbins 17 CD set Get The Edge Brand New And Personal Power	$54.99	Mortgage Elimination & Credit Repair	$6.95
Tropical Dream Stars National Finals Pageant Video	$54.00	Lazy Person's SECRETS to Overnight WEALTH! $5,000/mo!!!	$6.85
Custom Original Term Research Papers Resumes Reports	$44.85	36 Taoist Strategies to Control + Harness Human Nature!	$5.99
DAWN LESTER National Pageant Modeling Videos	$41.00	MATHEW LESKO FREE MONEY TO CHANGE YOUR LIFE	$5.97
Stock Market Day/Swing Trading Course ($97 Value).	$27.00	ACT Test Prep In*A*Flash Flash Cards English & Science	$5.50
ebook plus 1 hr Hour Live Online Mentoring Session		Lamaze Childbirth Contraction Coaching/Doula Tape	$3.99
COMPLETE SINGING VOICE LESSON SERIES with Shelley Kristen	$22.40	Ebay Business Starting Kit * Detail Step by Step Guide!	$2.99
HOOKED ON PHONICS COMPLETE SET	$21.00	Golf Package 3 Tapes & 2 Books Instr. and Humour	$2.99
Auctions for Income	$20.00	25 Things EVERY Landlord Should Know!	$2.00
Turn Your Wife/Girlfriend into Your SEX SLAVE Hypnosis	$19.95	ENGINEERING AND SCIENCE DO IT YOURSELF, TOOLBOX EDITION	$0.99

Advice & Instruction ▶ Other

	HIGH		AVG
Sammy Chua's The Way to Market Wealth Level II	$200.00	How to Heal a Broken Heart in 30 Days by Howard Bron...	$6.50
Daytrading Using the Level II Trading Windows.		EBOOKS, MEGA WHOLESALE LIST, MAKE $$$..FREE SHIP!!!!	$5.99
NFL Picks! Computer Handicaps 75% - Guaranteed Victory!	$199.00	*INSTANT ACCESS!! TO THOUSANDS OF TERM	$5.99
Advanced Computer Algorithms Utilized to Pick Over 75%!		PAPERS, ESSAYS. 60% OFF! ORIGINAL PRICE	
Underground Music Seminar (Atkins/Mackey Guests)	$152.50	OF $14.95 *EBAY EXCLUSIVE DEAL*	
Real Estate * Roger Butcher Real Estate Starter Package	$150.00	Design Your Life and DESTROY Your Problems. Do you have	$5.99
ANTHONY ROBBINS GET THE EDGE 7 DAY PROGRAM	$107.50	a PROBLEM? I got the SOLUTION.	
Color Me Beautiful Color Analysis! Personalized Colors	$52.01	A Romantic Wedding Planner ByVictoria	$5.50
There Are 12 Seasons Now!! Which One Are You?		Sports Handicapping Betting Service	$5.00
ANTHONY ROBBINS PERSONAL POWER II CDS	$52.00	1 game a day (unit based) always up at the end of week	
5 PAGE CUSTOM WRITTEN TERM PAPER / ESSAY	$50.00	Canadian Pen Pal * either letters or email	$5.00

100% ORIGINAL RESEARCH, COMPILATION, VALID CITATIONS		A True Tarot Reading	$5.00
car repair and tune*up manual passenger car Thompson	$25.00	Student Loans: Default, Wage Garnishment, Bad Credit,	$5.00
Foreclosures & Real Estate Investment Pro. Advise. No Gimmicks,	$25.00	LOW POWER FM LETTER * Radio Industry Newsletter on LPFM	$4.99
No Books, No Tapes * Real Live Help		SAVE $$$ BUILD YOUR OWN WAKEBOARD POLE / PYLON	$4.99
NFL Football Sports Handicapping Betting Picks* Winners.	$24.99	Color Me Beautiful Color Analysis! Personalized Colors.	$4.99
You get the entire NFL season & playoffs for $24.99		There Are 12 Seasons Now!! Which One Are You?	
Bible of Persuasion Closing the Sale Zig Ziglar CDs	$20.50	Living Will State Specific for ALL 50 States Legal L@@K	$4.95
NFL Week 1 Picks * Guaranteed to Break the Bank !!!!!!	$20.00	Free Football Handicapping Picks NFL 2005 Sportbetting	$4.00
Sleep Better * Self Help Sleep Kit * Overcome Insomnia	$19.95	All year =$4. Introduction to sportsbooks /online poker	
Motivation Tapes Zig Ziglar Dennis Waitley NO RESERVE!	$19.50	LEGAL - DO IT YOURSELF FORMS - DIVORCE KIT	$3.99

Artistic Services ▸ Custom Crafts

	HIGH		AVG
Embroidered portrait of your pet by Andi Zeisler	$311.99	Mustang RUNNING HORSE Vinyl	$9.50
CUSTOM OIL PORTRAIT PAINTING FROM YOUR PHOTO	$235.00	Windshield Decal LARGE 24"	
Custom Portrait Drawing From Your Photo	$225.00	Mustang Vinyl Decal BUMPER INSERT LETTERS 99*04 NEW +	$8.99
Custom Watercolor Painting of House, Home Portrait, Art	$115.00	Mustang Vinyl Decal BUMPER INSERT LETTERS 99*04 NEW +	$7.50
By Suzanne Churchill, ORDER NOW FOR CHRISTMAS!!!		john deere print towels,	$6.50
CNC ART - clipart plasmacam cutter dxf CAD CAM plasma	$89.95	Mustang Vinyl Decal BUMPER INSERT LETTERS 99*04 NEW +	$6.49
Scooter Weather Vane - Use BUY IT NOW and get free gift		Custom cut name signs, desk, room,	$6.25
Custom Scrapbook Album not premade Any theme 12X12	$76.00	door, house Gift Services	
Handmade Knit Cotton Baby Set	$48.00	Personalized Tile Coasters BEAUTIFUL GIFT!	$6.00
2 Mustang GT SPRING HOOD STRIPE FLAT BLACK Vinyl Decals	$39.50	Mustang Vinyl Decal BUMPER INSERT LETTERS 99*04 NEW +	$5.99
SCA LOTR LARP ARMOR ***HARDENED LEATHER SPAULDERS***	$38.99	CROCHET PONY TAIL BUN COVER	$5.55
REAL CARBON FIBER RAW FABRIC BY THE YARD 50" 3K 5.7oz	$32.85	SNOOD HAIR NET BROWN	
SCA LOTR LARP Leather Spaulders Armor	$30.00	Personalized Collage for Scrapbooking or Picture Frames	$5.49
Must See Unique Photo Tile Great For Christmas Custom Art Look.	$30.00	Wedding, Anniversary Personalized Name Background Print	$4.99
You supply the photo I create the art! One of a kind		Firefighter Personalized Name Print * Fire Fighter	$4.99
leopard print Christmas tree skirt	$30.00	EMS EMT Ambulance Personalized Name Background Print	$4.99
2 Mustang Vinyl Decal ROCKER SIDE PANEL STRIPE Letters	$18.99	Wedding Personalized Name Print * Bells and Doves	$4.99
NEW Mustang Vinyl Decal HOOD SPORT STRIPE Insert	$18.50	Fire Puppy Personalized Name Background Firefighter	$4.99

Artistic Services ▸ Interior Design

HIGH TO LOW			
CERAMIC ART TILE,WALLPAPER,MURAL*MOSAIC*FIELD OF DREAMS	$10.50	CERAMIC ART TILE, WALLPAPER,MURAL*MOSAIC* EMILY STRANGE	$1.35
CERAMIC ART TILE,WALLPAPER,MURAL*MOSAIC* MARILYN MONROE	$6.76	CERAMIC ART TILE, WALLPAPER,MURAL*MOSAIC* EMILY STRANGE	$0.99
CERAMIC ART TILE, WALLPAPER, MURAL* MOSAIC* GATE KEEPER	$5.83	[2 of these sold for $0.99 each]	
CERAMIC ART TILE,WALLPAPER,MURAL*MOSAIC* MARILYN MONROE	$2.25	CERAMIC ART TILE,WALLPAPER,MURAL*MOSAIC* MARILYN MONROE	$0.99

Artistic Services ▸ Music Composition & Poetry

HIGH TO LOW			
Syndicated Car Dealer Jingle/Ad Package	$69.00	Custom made romantic poetry just for your loved one	$15.00
Personalized Poems for Every Occasion	$25.00	SPECIAL PERSONALIZED ORIGINAL	$8.88
SPECIAL PERSONALIZED ORIGINAL SONG, CUSTOM FIT FOR YOU	$19.99	SONG I help U write words	
American Idol's Judges Ultimate Voice Coach	$19.95	CUSTOM SONG with free MP3 download * Guitar Songwriter	$2.00

Artistic Services ▸ Painting & Drawing

	HIGH		AVG
CUSTOM OIL PORTRAIT PAINTING FROM YOUR PHOTO	$235.00	Animal Drawings by hand from a photo of Your Pet 12x18.	$25.00
Custom Portrait Drawing From Your Photo	$225.00	THERE IS NO SHIPPING COST WILL BE PAYED BY ME.	
Custom Watercolor Painting of House, Home Portrait, Art	$115.00	DOG, CAT, HORSE, PORTRAIT DRAWING DONE FROM YOUR PHOTO	$24.99
Original paintings & Pet portraits-Dogs,Cats,Horses.	$99.95	Your custom caricature Unique, expert caricatures created from your photos	$24.95
handpainted for you by Sherry O.		Reverse Painting on Glass Book NR!! 50% OFF	$24.95
Original Custom Oil Portrait On Canvas Frm Photo JJ-Art	$77.00	Anniversary, Wedding Present, Custom Gift Print	$20.00
Custom Portrait Drawing From Your Photo	$70.00	Your HORSE'S PORTRAIT PAINTED ON CANVAS FROM YOUR PHOTO	$19.99
HOUSE PORTRAIT your home in a pen & ink drawing	$69.99	Custom Professional Caricature/Caricatures from Photos!	$18.99
Charcoal Portraits-Custom & Hand drawn Gift Services	$60.00	Perfect Gift for Anyone! Order now for Christmas!!!	
CUSTOM Animal PET PORTRAIT Original WaTeRcOLoR ART Cas.	$51.01	Anniversary, Wedding Present, Custom Gift Print	$18.95
5"x7" Painting UNIQUE, Beautiful MEMORY for the FUTURE!		Personal Pastel of You - Someone you love - GREAT GIFT!	$18.50
Jesse Lee Vaughn Tattoo Flash. Tattoo Flash	$50.00	I will take any photo and make a personal pastel !	
[2 of these sold for $50.00 each]		CUSTOM GRAPHITE PORTRAITS - OCTOBER SALE	$17.99
Custom PORTRAIT from photos, perfect GIFT, original art Gift Services.	$50.00	Custom Painted Portrait on a Rock Gift Services	$16.99
by Internationally Collected Artist Laurie Bostian		Anniversary, Wedding Present, Custom Gift Print	$16.95
ORIGINAL Custom Portrait Drawing Commission YOUR HORSE!	$45.00	[2 of these sold for $16.95 each]	
Gift Certificate for Custom Watercolor Painting (House)	$45.00	Hand Painting From Your Photos	$15.00
Good for 1 year - Makes a great Christmas Gift		Professional Caricatures From Photos Perfect Gift Idea!	$14.99
Custom Pencil Portrait in Color, from Photo JJ-Art	$41.40	CUSTOM LACQUERED FAMILY PORTRAIT PAINTING ON ART CANVAS	$10.00
Custom Pet Portrait Pastel or Acrylics 12"x16"	$40.00	Unique and Personalised Pet Portraits Your Pet, Your Art !	$10.00

Artistic Services ▸ Other

HIGH TO LOW			
CNC ART * clipart plasmacam cutter dxf CAD CAM plasma.	$89.95	PHOTEK PHOTOGRAPHIC PHOTO LIGHT FLASH UMBRELLA 4 LOT NR	$9.99
Scooter Weather Vane * Use BUY IT NOW and get free gift		Personalized Custom 8 x 10 Poem Photo Print Sisters	$5.00
WEDDING PHOTOGRAPHY in Kitchener, Waterloo, Guelph, etc	CAD $66.00	Professional Voice Greeting / On Hold Message	$4.95
Starting bid only $9.99 - NO RESERVE - Value $2,600!!!!		Your eBay Voiceover Connection - - Voice Talent, Inc.	

Pic of [HBMS]HelloKittie in a grass skirt&coconut bra	$25.00	Your Name or Phrase as A Mazes Labyrinth Puzzle Maze	$2.37
Visual Design Photoshop WEB BANNER Animation Marketing!	$19.99	Custom Posters and Banners, Printing, Flyers and Media	$1.00
Personal auction for Hhagan	$19.95	Professional Voice Greeting / On Hold Message	$0.99
Poster Printing	$14.00	Your eBay Voiceover Connection -- Voice Talent, Inc.	$0.99
CUSTOM LACQUERED PET PORTRAIT PAINTING ON ART CANVAS	$10.00	Award Winning Tattoo Artist Offers Custom Artwork	$0.01
		ULTIMATE RETURN TO SENDER SERVICE ~ MUST SEE	$0.01

Custom Clothing & Jewelry

HIGH TO LOW

Pink Heart Taggie Baby Blanket * MONOGRAM AVAILABLE.	$16.00	~INFANT CUSTOM *JIM MORRISON & THE DOORS* ONESIE~	$6.99
other colors & style available		~INFANT CUSTOM *THE ROLLING STONES* ONESIE~	$6.99
Personalized Baby NFL Steelers Seahawks Onesie + Socks	$13.99	~INFANT CUSTOM *THE NIGHTMARE BEFORE X*MAS* ONESIE~	$6.99
Personalized Baby Broncos Chargers Colts Onesie + Socks	$13.99	Personalized Toddler Drool Bib	$5.99
kids embroidered firetruck,fireman custom t*shirt	$11.99	Personalized Prince Onesie Embroidered LongSleeve Baby	$4.99

Custom Clothing & Jewelry ▸ Costumes

	HIGH		AVG
NEW Custom Made Baton Costume	$151.50	custom made monkey costume. adorable monkey	$23.50
ANAKIN OBI*WAN STAR WARS JEDI SITH CUSTOM COSTUME.	$74.99	costume for infant /toddlers	
Children's sizes 3 to 12 any color cotton		Boys Ninja halloween costume size 7*10	$20.00
BELLYDANCE SWORD all metal authentic design !	$49.00	50s Poodle Skirt Girls Size 8 Custom-Made Costume	$19.99
orange TIGER MASK halloween costume accessory	$46.00	custom made butterfly costume. adorable butterfly costume	$19.99
BOUTIQUE CUSTOM MADE SCARECROW COSTUME 2, 3,, 5, 6	$45.00	custom made kangaroo costume. adorable	$19.99
CUSTOM GIRLS STORY BOOK COSTUME 2T*4 SNOW WHITE,.	$36.01	Kangaroo costume for infant /toddlers	
SLEEPING BEAUTY, ALICE, MULAN, DOROTHY, CINDERELLA		custom made lion costume. adorable lion costume for infant /toddlers	$19.99
Aladdin Costume for Adults	$35.00	custom made penguin costume. adorable penguin costume	$19.99
RENAISSANCE MEDIEVAL CAPE DRESS BOHO HIPPIE	$31.89	Don't be a Pirate WIN THE Prize * HEADS will turn 10/31	$15.00
custom made halloween costume. adorable cat costume	$29.99	Boys batman halloween costume size medium @7*8	$10.50

Custom Clothing & Jewelry ▸ Hats, Handbags, Accessories

	HIGH		AVG
AUTH New DOONEY & BOURKE Signature IT FLAP SATCHEL Bag	$149.99	Personalized/custom WEDDING Tote Bag embroidered!	$25.00
Personalized/custom WEDDING Tote Bag embroidered	$50.00	Personalized/custom WEDDING Tote Bag embroidered!	$22.00
[2 of these sold for $50.00 each]		Personalized/custom WEDDING Tote Bag embroidered!	$21.00
Personalized/custom cool mesh Caps/ hats Embroidered	$38.00	Personalized/custom baseball Caps/ hats Embroidered	$15.99
Personalized/custom WEDDING Tote Bag embroidered!	$37.00	PINK Essential Tote Bag with Contrasting Black Handles.	$12.99
NEW 10 Custom Embroidery Your TEXT Flame Hats/Caps	$37.00	PINK Essential Tote Bag with Contrasting Black Handles.	$11.99
10 Personalized Custom Embroidered TEXT Camo Hats/Caps	$34.00	CUSTOM EMBROIDERED HAT WITH	$11.99
Custom/Personalized Hats/Caps with Embroidery	$34.00	2 LINES OF LETTERING	
Personalized/custom WEDDING Tote Bag embroidered!	$31.00	Personalized lunchbox, backpack, Free Monogram, school	$10.00
10 Personalized Your Sandwich Hats/Caps Embroidered	$31.00	Personalized Tote Bag	$9.99
Custom/Personalized Hats/Caps with Embroidery Stonewash	$31.00	Personalized lunchbox, backpack, Free Monogram, school	$8.00

Custom Clothing & Jewelry ▸ Jewelry

	HIGH		AVG
Triple Strand Mother's Bracelet 3 Strands Up to 6 Names	$60.00	3D Crystal Custom Photo Love Necklace Laser Engrave NC	$12.00
3D Crystal Custom Photo logo Laser Engraving Service AD	$50.00	3D Crystal Custom Photo Round	$12.00
3D Crystal Custom Photo logo Laser Engraving Service AA	$45.00	Necklace Laser Engrave NB	
TOPAZ NECKLACE	$36.00	Pink Swarovski Crystal Bracelet	$12.00
Antique 19thC 2/3ct Red Ruby Facet Oval Burma	$36.00	BIG Antique Cognac Baltic Amber Gold Earrings	$9.99
Personalized Gold Silver Wire Name Necklace Birthstone.	$26.45	Antique 19thC 1¼ct Handcrafted Regal Green Sapphire	$9.99
100 % Satisfaction Guaranteed – Refund if Not Satisfied		2 Antique 19thC Faceted White I Diamonds Panna India	$9.99
Personalized Gold * Silver Handmade Wire Name Necklace.	$24.95	Antique 19thC HUGE 3 3/4ct Cut Blue Topaz Emerald	$9.99
100 % Satisfaction Guaranteed – Refund if not satisfied		3 Antique 19thC Blood Red Ruby Ovals Burma	$9.99
Diamond Cut Your Personalized Name Gold Wire Necklace	$17.95	Antique 19thC Lemon*Lime Sapphire FacetedOval	$9.99
Personalized Photo Engraved Dog Tag Pendant	$14.99	Antique Lavender Amethyst Gemstone	$9.99
Personalize Your Name in Diamond Cut Gold Wire Necklace	$14.95	14kt GF French Hooks	

Custom Clothing & Jewelry ▸ Shirts

	HIGH		AVG
144 Gildan 100% cotton 6.1 oz T*shirts 1 color imprint	$510.00	New Personalized DISC GOLF T Shirt	$9.99
100 Custom Screen Printed T*shirts Jerzee Brand. WOW!	$320.00	New CUSTOM LACROSSE T Shirt	$9.99
ONLY $320.00 for 100 Pcs. 3 DAYS ONLY! 1 COLOR		New CUSTOM LACROSSE GOALIE T Shirt	$9.99
L@@K! 50 CUSTOM SCREEN PRINTED T*SHIRTS * ANY COLOR!!!	$212.50	New CUSTOM HOCKEY T Shirt	$9.99
OVER 50 SHIRT COLORS TO CHOOSE FROM! EVEN MIX THEM UP!!		New CUSTOM GO KART RACING T Shirt	$9.99
12 Quality Custom Embroidery Logo Golf or Polo Shirts.	$120.00	New CUSTOM ARCHERY T Shirt	$9.99
Free Shipping to U.S.A. destinations		New CUSTOM GIRLS FIELD HOCKEY T Shirt	$9.99
12 Custom Print Design / Logo Screen Printed T*Shirts	$59.99	New CUSTOM SOCCER GIRLS RULE T Shirt	$9.99
CUSTOM PRINTED T*SHIRTS * 1 DOZ. ASH COLOR * MIX SIZES	$49.00	New CUSTOM FENCING T Shirt	$9.99
PERSONALIZED EMBROIDERED SOON TO BE MRS HOODIE & MORE	$32.88	New Personalized BINGO T Shirt	$9.99
GRANDMA'S ANGELS CUSTOM EMBROIDERED SWEATSHIRT SWEET!.	$30.00		
Size L * Free shipping! Unique, One of a Kind, L@@K!!!!			
Yellow Ribbon Support our Troops Hooded Sweatshirt NICE	$27.00		
Fancy Denim Horse Cowboy Shirt PERSONALIZED	$22.50		

Custom Clothing & Jewelry ▸ Other

	HIGH		AVG
Joe Rocket leather jacket, pants for motorcycle riding	$300.00	Custom/Personalized Pillow/Blanket AWESOME!!!	$15.50
SafariLand Bulletproof Vest Level III*A /K*30 Trauma Pl.	$195.00	Western Shirt Ladies Plus Size Wrangler Blues 2X Beige	$15.50
Bulletproof Level III*A Vest / K*30 Steel Trauma Pl		Western Shirt Boys Wrangler Red/White/Blue Long Sleeve	$13.50
AUTH DOONEY & BOURKE 2005 All*Weather LEATHER TOTE BAG	$189.99	COWGIRL TEASE BITCH ANGEL BOYTOY name it belt buckle	$10.20
Boutique Angels Charity PRO PHOTOGRAPHY PORTRAITS	$177.49	[2 of these sold for $10.20 each]	
50 Personalized/custom t* shirts embroidered	$159.00	Custom Sewing Services For All Your Projects!	$10.00
BASIX HEAT TRANSFER MACHINE FOR IMPRINT	$157.50	Western Shirt Ladies Plus Sz 3X Wrangler Blues Beige	$9.99
Custom Cowgirl O'alls OOAK Sz.18m-6 Boutique GONE/CBD	$69.45	Western Shirt Boys Wrangler Red/White/Blue Long Sleeve	$9.00
Special Auction denim shirts embroidered	$25.00	CUSTOMIZE Your Own Silicone Bracelet! Camouflage YOUTH	$5.99
Cute Camou Wrap Scrub Top by Dickies with EMBROIDERY	$23.49	MAKE YOUR OWN!! CUSTOM Silicone Wristbands! pink youth	$5.99

eBay Auction Services ▸ Listing Services

HIGH TO LOW

	HIGH		AVG
MANNEGUIN MANIGUIN FEMALE,MANICAN	$80.00	Women's Clothing Boutiqe Auction Template Regal Design	$4.99
Custom Auction Template Design Coordinating LOGO FREE	$39.99	HACK CRACK RESET WINDOWS NT 2000 XP 2003 ADMIN PASSWORD	$4.99
The only E-Book you'll ever need instant access,no waiting	$20.50	[2 of these sold for $4.99 each]	
on the post office to deliver		Stunning Gold Fabric Auction Template attention getter!	$4.99
4 Hours of eBay Lessons or Listing Services - in L.A.	$9.99	Ebay Extreme & Entrepreneur Resell Kit Wholesale *NEW*	$2.99
100% of the proceeds go to YWCA's Week Without Violence		[2 of these sold for $2.99 each]	
EBAY CERTIFIED AUCTION SELLERS SOFTWARE * SPOONFEEDER!	$9.95	MAKE MONEY THE EASY WAY LET ME SHOW YOU $100 *$500/DAY.	$1.99
System for On*Line Auction Sellers now on CD!		JOIN THE POWERSELLERS ON EBAY, THE LIST EVERYONE WANTS	
Shaggy Cool Auction Template * Pick your Color!	$8.50	EBAY AUCTION PROTECTOR, PROTECT YOUR AD!	$0.99
AUCTION TEMPLATES: WOW 700+ BIG PROFESSIONAL DESIGNS!	$7.95	EBAY ENTREPRENUER KIT* $$$$$ * L@@K!!!!!!	$0.89
[2 of these sold for $7.95 each]		[2 of these sold for $ 0.89 each]	
NEW * RED ROSES * Custom auction template * LOOK	$5.99	Ebay Auction Image Hosting Service Free Life Membership	$0.01
Retro Blue Plaid AuctionTemplate vivid & vibrant design	$4.99	[2 of these sold for $0.01 each]	

eBay Auction Services ▸ Packing & Shipping

HIGH TO LOW

	HIGH		AVG
175' BUBBLE WRAP - 12" WIDE-SMALL BUBBLE*CHEAP*	$9.25	International Shipping Service (Store & Forwarding)	$4.99
Extra shipping	$7.50	Earning Your Trust is Our Business !!!	$0.99
		FREIGHT MOVERS FREIGHT SHIPPING 150 POUND MINIMUM.	
		SORRY NO HOUSEHOLD ITEMS OR CARS	

eBay Auction Services ▸ Shopping Assistance

HIGH TO LOW

	HIGH		AVG
Errands, groceries, travel plans, Lot more! Columbus oh	$95.00	Gallery of Style Personal Shopping gifts and personal	$5.00
Auctions For Income System, training prog for financ fr	$24.95	NEED HELP FINDING WHOLESALE LOTS, CLOSEOUTS, PALLETS???	$4.99

eBay Auction Services ▸ Other

HIGH TO LOW

	HIGH		AVG
Custom Auction Template Mystical Golden Spheres Theme	$9.99	BEAUTIFUL BABY AUCTION TEMPLATE ~ MUST sEE ~ !	$2.99
How to write books manuals and reports to sell on Ebay	$9.95	EBAY EXTREME * * MAKE YOUR FORTUNE WITH ONLINE AUCTION !	$2.99
CUSTOM Company Business Website LOGO Graphic Design!!!!	$6.95	AUCTION TEMPLATE "BLACK SATIN & GOLD SPARKLE" SALE !	$1.99
[2 of these sold for $6.95 each]		EBAY EXTREME * * MAKE YOUR FORTUNE WITH ONLINE AUCTION !	$0.99
Fall Leaves Auction Template	$5.00	DELIVERY SERVICE INFORMATION, USA, YOU CALL WE HAUL,	$0.50
AUCTION TEMPLATE ~ SWEET SHOPPING DIVA ~ LIMITED SALE!	$3.45	[2 of these sold for $0.50 each]	

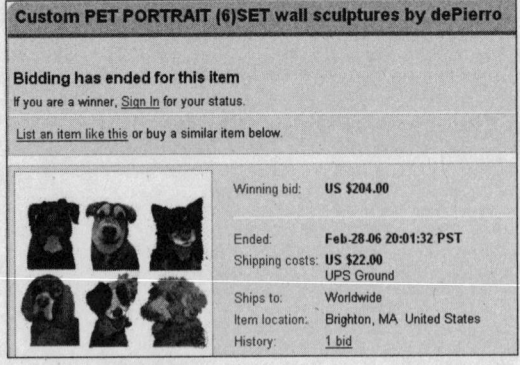

Graphic & Logo Design

	HIGH		AVG
100% Custom LOGO & BUSINESS ID PACKAGE by JORDAN DESIGN.	$169.00	CUSTOM LOGO OR BANNER DESIGN	$10.00
SEE WHAT MAKES US THE BEST CHOICE! Since 1992+Save $556		* WEBSITE,,EBAY, COMPANY.	
Vector Logo design + Flash Animated Logo + Stationary	$99.00	COME SEE WHY IT'S ONLY $10.00!!!!	
Vector Logo design + Flash Animated Logo + Stationary	$95.00	[4 of these sold for $10.00 each]	
[2 of these sold for $95.00 each]		Professional Logo Design by LogoCreek *One Day Sale*	$9.99
Logo Design by a Professional Graphic Designer.	$95.00	Primitive Folk Halloween Auction	$9.99
Includes 3 Revisions & Unlimited Colors/Plus B & W		Template 3 DAYS ONLY!	
UNIQUE LOGO DESIGN BY GRAPHIC ARTIST	$90.00	Logo Design by LogoCreek * BUY IT NOW Sale *	$8.99
[2 of these sold for $90.00 each]		Professional Web Banner Ad Design * Fast! Effective! High	$8.95
Stationery, Logo, Business Card, Letterhead & Envelope	$79.00	Quality Animated Ads * 100% Customer Satisfaction!	
Logo Design * BONUS: Letterhead, Business Card Designs.	$75.00	Vintage Art Girl and Harp Custom eBay Store Logo child	$8.95
We can Accomplish Anything! Check Out Our Samples!		Scotty Dog Gymbo Inspired BOUTIQUE Auction Template	$7.99
Custom Auction for ebay user reesiebeanskbtq	$75.00	BUTTERFLY custom auction template CUTE w/glitter!	$7.99
UNIQUE LOGO DESIGN BY GRAPHIC ARTIST	$71.00	Custom Logo or Graphic Decal Sticker.	$7.99
Professional Logo / Graphic Design Service.	$69.99	Convert any graphic into a Decal	
Complimentary Business Card/Letterhead Design included		Custom Logo or Graphic Vectorization	$7.99

Media Editing & Duplication ▸ Music

	HIGH		AVG
500 CDR 52X CD*R PRODISC SILVER INKJET HUB PRINTABLE	$89.99	100 CDR RITEK CD*R SILVER INKJET PRINTABLE GRADE A	$17.99
500 CDR RITEK CD*R SILVER INKJET PRINTABLE GRADE A	$82.99	[2 of these sold for $17.99 each]	
500 CDR RITEK CD*R SILVER INKJET PRINTABLE GRADE A	$81.99	100 CDR 52X CD*R PRODISC SILVER INKJET HUB PRINTABLE	$16.99
500 CDR RITEK 52X CD*R WHITE INKJET PRINTABLE GRADE A	$81.99	Audio Production Imaging Sweepers Radio Station Jingle.	$11.00
500 CDR RITEK CD*R WHITE INKJET PRINTABLE GRADE A	$81.99	Major Market Imaging at a VERY low price. No S&H!	
500 CDR RITEK CD*R WHITE INKJET PRINTABLE GRADE A	$80.99	100 CDR RITEK 52X CD*R SILVER INKJET PRINTABLE GRADE A	$9.99
		CD TRANSFER SERVICE * RECORD ALBUMS OR CASSETTES TO CD	$3.99

Media Editing & Duplication ▸ Photo & Video

	HIGH		AVG
Custom 8mm Film to DVD transfer for Chris Higgs	$232.00	DVD 8mm Film Conversion Copies.	$10.00
Custom 8mm Film to DVD transfer for Seng*Poh Lee	$157.00	Give A Gift Of Memories	
100 dvd duplication & printing special only $79.	$79.00	DVD PHOTO SLIDESHOW/PHOTOMONTAGE/ WEDDING	$10.00
100 dvds with printing & duplication for $79		/ MEMORY DVD! GREAT DVD SLIDESHOW	
Quasar Telecine / Film to Video Transfer Box.	$60.00	MOVIE, CUSTOMIZED FOR YOU, LOOK!!!	
Preserve your old 8MM and Super 8 home movies!		Sony Surivelance security monitor black white SSM*910	$10.00
8mm projector film convert transfer to DVD frameXframe	$60.00	VoIP VOICE MAIL, & ON HOLD	$9.99
PROFESSIONAL XFERS ARE frame x frame, INSIST ON IT!!!		RECORDING, AFFORDABLE!!!	
8mm projector film convert transfer to DVD frameXframe	$49.99	Kodak Regular 8mm Movie Film Splicing Tape	$9.99
PROFESSIONAL XFERS ARE frame x frame, INSIST ON IT!!!		Plates, Platter, Trays & Coasters made from your photo	$6.00
Vivitar UVC*1 Telecine Unit w/ Super Video Processor.	$40.00	8mm projector film convert transfer to DVD frameXframe	$6.50
Improve Your Film To Video Transfers!		8mm projector film convert transfer to DVD frameXframe	$5.99
8 mm or Super 8mm Film Transfer To DVD.	$30.00	[2 of these sold for $5.99 each]	
Preserve Your Memories Forever!			

Media Editing & Duplication ▸ Other

	HIGH		AVG
CD DVD VCD Replication Duplication Service FREESHIPPING.	$499.99	Transfer Photos, 35mm slides to DVD montage*xmas,grads	$19.99
1000 CDs shipped @ only US$0.499/ea, 1000 DVDs $0.76/ea		Six Message/Music On Hold Tracs on CD. Jazz,	$13.99
Pelco CM9760*MXB Matrix Bay {VID*CM9760MXB}	$299.00	Classical, Rock, Country, Acoustic, Holiday	
[2 of these sold for $299.00 each]		[2 of these sold for $13.99 each]	
Pelco CM9760*KBD Intelligent Key {KEY*CM9760KBD}	$177.00	Audio Production Imaging Sweepers Radio Station Jingle.	$11.00
Pelco CM9760*CDU*T Code Distribu {VID*CM9760CDUT}	$76.00	Major Market Imaging at a VERY low price. No S&H!	
CUSTOM MIXED STINGERS, JINGLES, SWEEPERS, ID'S & MORE!	$59.99	Audio production Major market mixed commercial! Save$$$	$10.49
Audio production custom mixed sweepers, jingles, radio!	$34.99	Transfer LP vinyl records 33rpm,5rpm, 78rpm to CD	$5.99

Printing & Personalization ▸ Address Labels

	HIGH		AVG
DoodleBugs TALL Funky Tree Address Labels SBELLE	$15.99	120 BABY SHOWER Envelope Seals Rubber DUCKY Favors	$7.00
Santa Flamingos Notecards & Personalized labels	$11.99	Ideal 200 Customized 6 line Self*Inking Rubber Stamp NR	$6.50
Martini Mermaid art cards and labels	$11.99	90 Diddl Mouse Return/Mailing Address Labels	$6.00
300 CLASSIC MICKEY MOUSE Address Labels Disney	$10.01	Personalized Address /Product Labels Photo /Graphic 120	$5.99
*~*YOUR PHOTO*~* Address Labels	$9.99	Ideal 5 Line FOR DEPOSIT ONLY Self*Inking Rubber Stamp	$5.99
~FREE SHIPPING!~		[2 of these sold for $5.99 each]	
300 BABY POOH PIGLET Disney Address Labels	$9.50	600 PERSONALIZED RETURN ADDRESS LABELS	$5.59
300 JIMINY CRICKET PINNOCCHIO	$9.00	[2 of these sold for $5.59 each]	
Address Labels Disney		90 Margarita Glass Cocktail Mailing Address Labels	$5.50
300 BABY POOH PIGLET Disney Address Labels	$9.00	Personalized Address Labels * Superman	$5.50
300 SEVEN DWARFS DOPEY Address Labels Disney	$8.00	120 Wedding Address or Bubble Labels Kim Anderson	$5.50
300 SNOW WHITE PRINCESS Address Labels Disney	$8.00	FAMILY FACES LABELS CHRISTMAS REGULAR SET 90	$5.50

Printing & Personalization ▸ Business Cards

	HIGH		AVG
5000 FULL COLOR BUSINESS CARDS CUSTOM PRINTED TWO-SIDED,		Engraved LEATHER BUSINESS CARD CASE Engrave Gift Wallet	$16.49
	$149.00	500 * BUSINESS CARDS * RAISED PRINTING	$15.50
HIGH QUALITY, UV COATING OR NOT - SAME PRICE		* FREE SHIPPING	
1000 FULL COLOR Business card MAGNETS	$139.00	1200 PREMIUM PERSONALIZED BUSINESS	$14.99
FULL COLOR Business Card Magnets 500	$100.00	CARDS COLORS MORE4$	
BUSINESS CARDS FULL COLOR CARD PRINTER 96 EDDIE PRINT.	$96.00	[4 of these sold for $14.99 each]	
$96.00 FOR 5000 CARDS WITH FREE DESIGN. FREE SHIPPING!		Engraved Business Silver Cigarette Case #2 wedding gift	$14.95
[2 of these sold for $96.00 each]		Awesome Business Cards Custom Personalized FREE SHIP	$14.00
5000 2 SIDED FULL COLOR UV COATED	$79.00	50 Save the Date Magnets Personalized for you	$14.00
GLOSSY BUSINESS CARDS. FREE CUSTOM DESIGNS!		1200 PREMIUM PERSONALIZED BUSINESS	$13.99
5000 2 SIDED FULL COLOR UV COATED GLOSSY	$70.00	CARDS COLORS MORE4$	
BUSINESS CARDS. FREE CUSTOM DESIGNS!		[4 of these sold for $13.99 each]	
5000 FULL COLOR BUSINESS CARDS * TWO*SIDED * 12pt.	$69.00	1100 BUSINESS CARDS COLORS!	$13.99
5000 2 SIDED FULL COLOR UV COATED GLOSSY	$69.00	PERSONALIZED MORE FOR $	
BUSINESS CARDS. FREE CUSTOM DESIGNS!		2000 PERSONALIZED REAL BUSINESS CARDS COLORS!	$12.99
5000 FULL COLOR BUSINESS CARDS * TWO*SIDED * 12pt.	$69.00	Engraved SILVER Business Card case engrave #3 wallet	$12.95
3000 Full Color Business Cards	$65.00		
FULL COLOR Business Card Magnets 500	$61.00		

Printing & Personalization ▸ Glasses, Mugs

	HIGH		AVG
8, 23oz. PILSNER GLASS PERSONALIZED	$58.00	set of 7 Engraved Flask Flasks Groomsmen Gift Gifts	$9.99
WEDDING PARTY GIFTS		[2 of these sold for $9.99 each]	
Three personalized football mugs for Jim	$35.97	Engrave Beer Mug Man Men Christmas Holiday Gifts Gift	$9.99
Engraved business SILVER SINGLE CIGAR CASE HOLDER	$32.33	set of 10 Engraved Money Clips Groomsmen Gifts Best Man	$9.99
2 Engraved Flute Champagne Glasses, Floral Arrangements	$24.95	ENGRAVED GLASS COFFEE MUG, LARGE 14 OZ.	$9.95
PAIR GLASS BEER TANKARD, MUG, CUSTOM ENGRAVED	$21.50	PERSONALIZED 15oz. BEER MUG FREE ETCHING	$9.50
Personal Wedding Toasting Glasses, Flutes, Violet Stem	$15.99	[2 of these sold for $9.50 each]	
2 ENGRAVED GLASSES Wedding or	$15.95	PERSONALIZED ETCHED LAWYER ATTORNEY JUDGE MUG GIFT	$9.45
Anniversary, Personalized		Travel Mug Stainless Steel ENGRAVED & PERSONALIZED	$9.00
2 Engraved Toasting Glasses, Champagne Wine Flutes	$15.95	PERSONALIZED ETCHED LAWYER ATTORNEY JUDGE MUG GIFT	$8.95
PHOTO MUG * TRAVEL * STAINLESS STEEL CUSTOM	$15.95	PERSONALIZED LAW ENFORCEMENT POLICE SHERIFF MUG GIFT	$8.95
Etched Wine Glasses! No Stickers! Personalized!	$15.25	CUSTOM COFFEE MUG CUP 15oz PERSONALIZED PHOTO GIFT	$8.49
		[2 of these sold for $8.49 each]	

Printing & Personalization ▸ Holiday Cards

HIGH TO LOW			
75 Personalized Handmade Stamped Christmas Tea Cards	$60.00	50 Matte Finish Custom Photo Holiday Cards CHRISTMAS	$19.99
Boutique Holiday Angel, Fairy Portraits of Your Photo	$49.99	Santa Mermaid Notecards & Personalized labels	$11.99
40 custom personalized photo holiday Christmas cards	$40.00	Personalized COUNTRY CHRISTMAS SNOWMAN Note Cards	
OOAK Custom Fairytale Portrait of Your Photo TLCD CBD	$35.99	~*FREE SHIPPING*~	$9.99
Personalized Business Christmas Holiday Greeting Cards	$25.50	FALL Personalized NOTE CARDS ~ Very Nice Must See !	$9.99
Personalized Handmade Stamped Christmas Cards 25 pack	$20.00	Christmas cards personalized Holiday card greeting	$7.99

Printing & Personalization ▸ Invitations, Announcements

	HIGH		AVG
200 WEDDING INVITATIONS DOUBLE HEARTS SCROLLS WRAPPERS.	$185.99	20 Personalized wedding Rehearsal Dinner invitations	$9.99
CHECK OUT OUR EBAY STORE FOR MORE INVITATIONS & DEALS!!		100 VELLUM WHITE SCRAPBOOK,	$9.99
[4 of these sold for $185.99 each]		WEDDING, B*DAY PAPER	
100 PERSONALIZED WEDDING PHOTO THANK YOU CARD CARDS	$99.95	20 Personalized custom Bachelorette Party invitations	$9.99
100 Fall leaf leaves autumn maple wedding invitations!!	$95.00	Cute! Halloween OR Birthday Party Invitations*6Designs!	$9.99
100 ~DOUBLE HEARTS~ WEDDING INVITATIONS FREE FAVORS	$90.00	20 Personalized Baby Shower Invitations "Boy or Girl"	$9.99
50 PINK TOILE Apple Green Accents*CUSTOM INVITATIONS	$70.00	20 Bachelorette Party Lingerie Shower Invitations	$9.99
~~STORK YARD SIGN BABY BIRTH /SHOWER ANNOUNCEMENT~~	$50.00	20 Custom Baby Shower Invitations or Birth Announcments	$9.99
OOAK Boutique 2 Fairytale Portraits Your Child TLCD CBD	$45.95	20 Personalized boy or girl Baby Shower Invitations	$9.99
25 CUSTOM PRINTED Pretty Pink Invitations*Bridal Shower.	$40.00	Pea in a Pod*Personalized Baby Shower Invitations	$9.99
Bridal Luncheon, Bachelorette party, Sweet 16....or any		Custom Baby Photo BIRTH ANNOUNCEMENTS with Ribbon!	$9.99
Wedding Programs (Personalized!) Very Elegant! Free	$35.00		
Shipping on all programs, great for any occasion!			
:: Custom Photo Baby Birth Announcements ::	$33.75		

Printing & Personalization ▸ Party Favors

	HIGH		AVG
Family Reunion Memento Favors. Great Gift for Birthday, Anniversary, Wedding	$49.99	BABY SHOWER ~ Kiss / Kisses Labels Favors ~ Many Styles	$4.99
[2 of these sold for $49.99 each]		SHOWER ~ BABY ~ CHARACTERS~ Candy Wrappers Favors	$4.99
LOT NEW CHILDRENS PLASTIC CHAIRS KIDS PARTY FAVORS NR	$36.98	SWEET SIXTEEN 16 ~ Birthday Mini Candy Wrappers Favors	$4.99
Save the Date Wedding Magnets *. Outstanding Quality.	$24.00	QUINCEANERA 15th ~ Birthday Mini Candy Wrappers Favors	$4.99
Includes up to 20 hours of custom design work		BAR / BAT MITZVAH Birthday Mini Candy Wrappers Favors	$4.99
100 Rose Wedding Table Card Place Cards	$16.99	30th 40th 50th 60 ~ Birthday Mini Candy Wrappers Favors	$4.99
[2 of these sold for $16.99 each]		30th ~ 40th ~ 50th ~ 60th ~ Kiss / Kisses Labels Favors	$4.99
100 Personalized Luncheon Napkins * S/H Included	$14.00	BIRTHDAY ~ Kiss / Kisses Labels Favors ~ Many Styles	$4.99
[2 of these sold for $14.00 each]		WEDDING ~ SHOWER ~ Kiss / Kisses Labels Favors	$4.99

Personalized 5x7n Picture Frame*FREE Engraving	$13.99
20 Customized BARNEY Magnets ~ Birthday Party Favors!	$11.95
30 "SAVE THE DATE" Magnets for your Wedding	$10.95
25 Personalized Baby Shower Soap Favors*Diaper & Pin	$10.49
25 Personalized Baby Shower Soap Favors*Baby Feet	$10.49

BABY SHOWER ~ Mini Candy Wrappers Favors ~ Many Styles	$4.99

Printing & Personalization ▸ Signs, Decals

	HIGH		AVG
Custom Printed Coroplast Yard Lawn Jobsite Realty Signs. 50 * 18"x24" 2 Side Print! With Stakes & Free Art!	$195.00	60 CINDERELLA Round Personalized Disney Stickers	$8.00
Custom Sandblasted Signs 24" x 30"	$167.50	SORCERER MICKEY Round Personalized Stickers Disney	$8.00
BANNER * commercial sign 3X8 full color CUSTOM OUTDOOR. Commercial Grade, Double Hemmed Grommets,Photo Quality	$125.00	60 JIMINY CRICKET Round Personalized Disney Stickers Jimmy Buffett "Parrothead" Decal	$8.00 $8.00
1000 Labels Custom Logo Candle Oval Kraft Gold Foil	$85.00	[2 of these sold for $8.00 each] AMERICAN FLAG STICKER DECAL W/WHITE STARS	$8.00
100pk CUSTOM URL WEBSITE Decal Decals Sticker	$69.95	20 + SKATEBOARD STICKERS	$8.00
2 vehicle magnetics and one back window decal	$68.00	CHOCALATE...CIRCA Lot#1	
25 12"x18" Full Color Coroplast Signs. FREE SHIPPING!!!	$65.00	FAIRY PRINCESS art print 4 that's mine quilt room decor	$7.99
Full Color Custom 2x4 Vinyl Outdoor Advertising Banner. Commercial Grade, Double Hemmed Grommets,Photo Quality	$54.95	Realtor Real Estate Open House Sign Kit kids AIRPLANE art print nursery decor 4 boys bedding	$7.99 $7.99
CUSTOM 3x8 BANNER INDOOR / OUTDOOR COMPANY ADVERTISING [2 of these sold for $49.95 each]	$49.95	kids nursery decor NAME art print dinosaur super saurus	$7.99
50 Custom Vinyl Decals Bumper Stickers w/ Your Logo. 4"x4" Full Color*Free Setup w/your logo photo graphic	$49.95		

Printing & Personalization ▸ Stationery

	HIGH		AVG
65 PERSONALIZED WEDDING PHOTO THANK YOU CARDS	$59.98	Personalized Mom Notepad	$7.50
Personalized Stationery, Notecard or Labels~GET 1 FREE~	$29.97	[2 of these sold for $7.50 each]	
Personalized Stationery, Notecard or Labels~GET 1 FREE~.STOCK UP NOW!!! GET 4 SETS FOR THE PRICE OF 3!!!	$29.97	Personalized Teacher Stick School Bus Note Cards Personalized MODERN Name Monogram Note Cards	$7.50 $7.50
Set of Personalized Post*it Notes: 25 pads in 5 designs	$28.00	*DoodleBugs* Halloween Personalized Note Cards SBELLE	$7.49
10 Personalized Note Pads*EACH DIFFERENT*FREE SHIPPING! [2 of these sold for $25.00 each]	$25.00	Handmade Thinking of You cards w/ envelopes FREE SHIP! Preppy Note Cards Stationery Personalized Lilly	$7.00 $7.00
25 Personalized WEDDING PHOTO Thank You Cards	$24.99	Maternity Pregnant Note Cards Stationery Personalized	$7.00
Personalized Striped Note Cards Thank you Invitation	$24.99	[2 of these sold for $7.00 each]	
DoodleBugs Personalized Note Cards BOTTLE CAPS sbelle.	$20.50	Funky Monkeys Personalized Note Card Set	$7.00
One of a Kind Personalized Boutique Note Cards		Cheerleader Personalized Note Cards ~ 2 Designs	$6.99
6 Sets of 10 (60) Personalized Note Cards*GREAT GIFTS! [2 of these sold for $19.99 each]	$19.99	Happy Pumpkins Halloween Personalized Note Cards	$6.99
Legal Size Real Estate Mortgage PRESENTATION FOLDERS [2 of these sold for $18.50 each]	$18.50		

Printing & Personalization ▸ Other

	HIGH		AVG
KINGSLEY HOT STAMP MACHINE W/ FONTS & EXTRAS!!!	$371.00	Personalized Hairdresser Cartoon	$6.95
L@@K! 50 CUSTOM SCREEN PRINTED T*SHIRTS * ANY COLOR!!! OVER 50 SHIRT COLORS TO CHOOSE FROM! EVEN MIX THEM UP!!	$212.50	Full Color Custom Personalized 15 oz. Coffee Mug/Mugs PERSONALIZED GOLD NAME NECKLACE (NECKLACES)	$6.50 $6.49
Tropical Custom Imprinted 2006 Calendars	$175.00	[2 of these sold for $6.49 each]	
Spanish Custom Imprinted 2006 Calendars	$175.00	PERSONALIZED SILVER NAME NECKLACE (NECKLACES) Gift Services	$6.49
Norman Rockwell Custom Imprinted 2006 Calendars	$175.00	[2 of these sold for $6.49 each]	
Custom T*Shirts * SJY	$172.00	Personalized Bedtime Prayer Mermaid White Asian Black	$6.49
500 PERSONALIZED CUSTOM IMPRINTED PENS W GRIP [2 of these sold for $149.00 each]	$149.00	Personalized 30 Piece Photo Puzzle for children 1 1/4 inch custom buttons made for you, pins, badges	$6.00 $6.00
Flier Printing , Flyer Printing, Postcard Printing	$139.00	[9 of these sold for $6.00 each]	
1000 ACE promotional ballpoint pens with FREE PRINTING	$120.00	Personalized Baby Kids Name Wall Print HARLEY DAVIDSON	$6.00
12 CUSTOM EMBROIDERY YOUR LOGO POLO/GOLF SHIRTS UNIFORM. FREE SHIPPING WITHIN UNITED STATES	$120.00	PERSONALIZED ENGRAVED NAME BADGES NAME TAGS NAMETAG PERSONALIZED ENGRAVED NAME BADGES NAME TAGS NAMETAG	$5.99 $5.99

Restoration & Repair ▸ Cars & Other Vehicles

	HIGH		AVG
Kwikee Step Control Unit	$101.00	OLDSMOBILE 1964*72 PARTS INTERCHANGE MANUAL CD	$14.99
"BINKS" Model 370A Glue Pot to Install Car Headliners++.	$99.95	1/4"x36"x 60" Hi Dense CLOSED CELL Foam Upholstery Foam	$13.95
Ready to Improve or Start Your Business? Make extra $$$		1/4"x31"x 60" HI DENSE Closed Cell FOAM Upholstery Foam	$12.10
Windshield repair starter kit*includes poly*lite resin [2 of these sold for $89.01 each]	$89.01	SERVICE MANUAL FOR ISUZU COMMERCIAL TRUCK Triumph Spitfire GT6 wiring diagram manual plus more CD	$10.00 $9.99
KWIKEE STEP CONTROL (BRAIN) UNIT_NIB	$60.00	HARLEY DAVIDSON WIRING DIAGRAMS ON CD	$9.99
LHS NEW YORKER INTREPID VISION CONCORDE HEATER CONTROL. FREE S&H & FREE TECHNICAL ASSISTANCE ON ALL MY AUCTIONS	$49.99	DATSUN 311 ROADSTER WIRING DIAGRAMS MANUAL Auto Upholstery FOAM BACK Headliner Fabric Black	$9.99 $6.95
1999 Buick Century Digital Climate Temperature Control	$49.99	33"x 60" Hi Dense Closed Cell Foam Upholstery Foam	$6.95
BMW 5 Series (E34) Bentley Service Manual 89*95	$46.00	27" x 60" Hi Dense Closed Cell Foam Upholstery Foam	$6.95
LHS NEW YORKER INTREPID VISION CONCORDE HEATER CONTROL. FREE S&H & FREE TECHNICAL ASSISTANCE ON ALL MY AUCTIONS	$45.99		
CHEVY PARTS INTERCHANGE MANUAL CD 1938*54 [2 of these sold for $20.50 each]	$20.50		
PACKARD PARTS INTERCHANGE MANUAL CD 1938*54	$16.00		

Restoration & Repair ▸ Jewelry & Watches

HIGH TO LOW

Bangle Bracelet/Gold Nugget/Gold Nuggets/Jewelry 8.8 gm	$49.00	JEWELRY REPAIR METHODS, TECHNIQUES $26.77
JEWELRY*REPAIR, PROFESSIONAL VIDEO* *VOLUME 1	$26.77	& TOOLS (VOLUME 2)

Restoration & Repair ▸ Computers & Electronics

HIGH TO LOW

Partner 206 and 206E Repair Service (All Releases) 1 Year Warranty on Repairs	$102.50	CELL PHONE REPAIR (ALLTEL ONLY) $15.00
Tube Amp Restoration*Fisher*Scott*Dyna*Sherwood*Eico.	$89.95	Konica Minolta Muratec manuals, parts, and CBT's $5.00
30 Day guarantee .* If it breaks I'll fix it for free!		Info how to Reset HP c9700a c9701a c9702a c9703a $3.99
DATA RECOVERY SERVICES. Recovery from Hard Drives, Floppies, CD, Flash & Other	$49.95	c9704a. LASERJET 1500 & 2500 all models
[2 of these sold for $49.95 each]		

Restoration & Repair ▸ Musical Instruments

HIGH TO LOW

Custom Guitar Refinishing! Ibanez JEM RG 550 Fender.	$140.00	Custom Guitar Refinishing! Ibanez JEM RG 550 Fender ESP. $130.00
OEM Finishes, Airbrushing, Kandies, FACTORY COLORS ALSO		FACTORY COLORS! Sunbursts, Kandies, Custom Airbrushing!

Restoration & Repair ▸ Other

HIGH TO LOW

CARPET CLEANING BANE CLENE TRUCK MOUNT Gift Service	$5,100.00	CYLINDER COMBINATING PRECISION PIN ASSORTMENT KK*80 $27.00
turbidimeter hach water analysis	$64.36	Lot of VCR Repair Parts Clips Springs O Rings Washers * $9.99
Hutchins Air File dual sander used body tools********	$56.00	New Door Jammer Body Shop Tools ***** $5.00
hach conductivity tds meter	$52.57	New Sharpe Air Pressure Gauge Body Shop Tools ***** $5.00
2 body hammers snapon cornwell used body tools	$27.56	[2 of these sold for $5.00 each]
		Antique Poreclain Bisq Pottery China Restoration Repair $0.01

Web & Computer Services ▸ Internet Promotion

	HIGH		AVG
HRSEO	$700.00	Banner Ad on Real Life Solutions Site (Over 30 Pages)	$10.50
Commercial on WTBC Radio for 1 year	$200.00	Ad spot on BaseballToaster.com * September	$10.00
Get your message out to 50,000+ monthly listeners		ADVERTISE! 6 months advertising on my HOT website!	$5.63
CBD YOUR Design in the Ad for Today's Parent Magazine!	$105.00	5,000 Website Visitors and 50,000 Banner Displays	$5.50
Alex Mandossian's WEB TRAFFIC SECRETS Complete Seminar.	$102.50	ONLINE ADVERTISING	$5.00
HARD TO FIND WEB MARKETING SEMINAR PACKAGE		PROFESSIONAL WEB SITE ADVERTISING	$5.00
Website Optimization and Promotion SEO Professional NR.	$99.95	* $5.00 FOR 2 YEARS .	
Website Marketing Expert Services for One Year!		PROFESSIONAL BANNER LINK	$4.00
Ad Space Boutique Planet 5 Spots BOYS 10/1* 10/31 CBD	$65.00	ADVERTISING * $4.00 = 2 YEARS	
Ad Space Boutique Planet 5 Spots 10/1* 31 CBD HOLIDAY	$55.00	[2 of these sold for $4.00 each]	
Top Banner on FreeTalkLive.com - Radio Show & Podcast	$43.00	5000 Quality Website Visitors	$3.00
Website Optimization and Promotion SEO Professional NR	$39.95	PUT YOUR LINK ON OUR HIGH TRAFFIC	$3.00
Ad Space Boutique Planet 5 Spots 10/1* 31 CBD HAIR	$32.00	WEB SITE FOR 2 YEARS	
Adult Website For Sale	$31.00	[3 of these sold for $3.00 each]	
Email 2.7 MILLION Targeted Prospects Everyday!. BOOST	$29.95		
your TRAFFIC today * Lifetime Membership!!!			
[3 of these sold for $29.95 each]			
Ad Space Boutique Planet 5 Spots BAGS 10/1* 10/31 CBD	$21.35		
Blank Raffle Tickets w Ticket Designer Software :411208	$19.99		

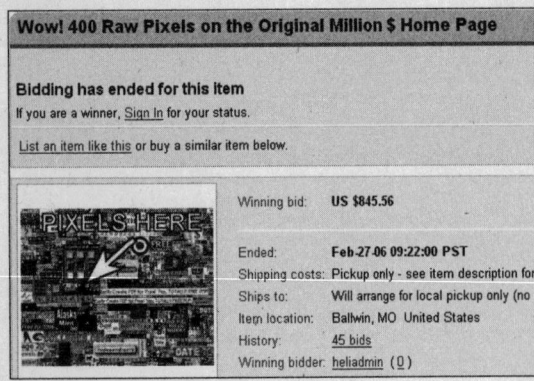

Wow! 400 Raw Pixels on the Original Million $ Home Page

Bidding has ended for this item
If you are a winner, Sign In for your status.

List an item like this or buy a similar item below.

Winning bid:	US $845.56
Ended:	Feb-27-06 09:22:00 PST
Shipping costs:	Pickup only - see item description for
Ships to:	Will arrange for local pickup only (no
Item location:	Ballwin, MO United States
History:	45 bids
Winning bidder:	heliadmin (0)

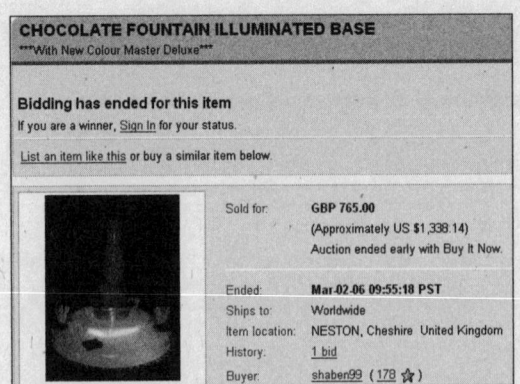

CHOCOLATE FOUNTAIN ILLUMINATED BASE
With New Colour Master Deluxe

Bidding has ended for this item
If you are a winner, Sign In for your status.

List an item like this or buy a similar item below.

Sold for:	GBP 765.00
	(Approximately US $1,338.14)
	Auction ended early with Buy It Now.
Ended:	Mar-02-06 09:55:18 PST
Ships to:	Worldwide
Item location:	NESTON, Cheshire United Kingdom
History:	1 bid
Buyer:	shaben99 (178 ☆)

Web & Computer Services ▸ Web Design

	HIGH		AVG
Web site Website Design, PHP, MySQL, Flash, E-Commerce Search Engine Placement and FREE Hosting For 2 Months	$899.00	Website LOGO design. Unlimited revisions, Guaranteed satisfaction! Vector!	$20.00
Custom Web Design - Creative, Affordable & Friendly We create CUSTOM websites to your specifications!	$275.00	Web Designer Graphic Design Flash Animation Design	$19.99
		Promo Photoshop Web Banner Design by Z3 eBay Marketing!	$19.99
Professional Web Design Services * Custom Websites!. Pay only $75.00 to have your website started [2 of these sold for $275.00 each]	$275.00	Graphic Design Web Banner by Z3 Custom PRO Animation!	$19.99
		PROFESSIONAL Website / Web site, page Design Templates	$16.55
CUSTOM 5 PAGE WEB SITE WEBSITE DESIGN w/ STORE + LOGO Giving Works Item.:QUALITY AND	$99.99	Custom BANNER DESIGN * * Great for Web Site Design!	$14.80
AFFORDABILITY:. 10% Donated to Charity! [2 of these sold for $99.99 each]		HUNDREDS of Satisfied Web Design & Banner Clients! +++	
		5 Page Web Design Package	$13.00
MACROMEDIADREAMWEAVER 4, NO BOX, JUST CD AND CODE!	$65.00	NEW *30 PHP Website Scripts ackage* Recipe's/Dating	$9.99
Quality 3 page Web Site Website Design W/ Logo + Store	$59.99	Web Page Development -pro site design website developer	$9.99
Professional Web Site Design 5 pages * website	$59.95	Custom Auction Template + Support * Fun Leopard Print	$9.99
MACROMEDIA DREAMWEAVER 4 WEB DESIGN, WINDOWS!	$51.00	Custom Designed Flash Intro For YOUR Web Site Website	$9.99
Logo.Business Card.LetterHead*Graphic Design * L@@K.	$49.99	PROFESSIONAL Web Design Templates to make your website	$9.95
Stunning Logo Design, Stationary Design FREE * SMM GD !			
Custom Business Website Flash Design 50page Web Site	$49.00		
MACROMEDIA DREAMWEAVER 4, NO BOX, JUST CD AND CODE! [2 of these sold for $40.00 each]	$40.00		
Logo Design for your website/business! Biz card, letterhead, envelope design included also!	$39.99		

Web & Computer Services ▸ Web Hosting

HIGH TO LOW

	HIGH		AVG
Unlimited Bandwidth Space & Domain RESELLER Web Hosting. cPanel WHM RVskin Fantastico Unlimited MySQL Email &FTP	$19.99	cPanel WHM RVskin UNLIMITED Domain RESELLER Web Hosting	$2.99
2 Domain cPanel UNLIMITED Web Hosting webhosting YEARLY.	$17.99	cPanel 4 Domains UNLIMITED Space Web Hosting FANTASTICO	$2.50
Unlimited Web Hosting $12.99 / YEAR, w/2 Add*Ons.	$12.99	[2 of these sold for $2.50 each]	
Unlimited Space B/W EMail Fantasico, RVskin, cPanel 10 [2 of these sold for $12.99 each]		2GB/20GB Cpanel Web Hosting webhosting w/ FANTASTICO [2 of these sold for $1.95 each]	$1.95
cPanel WHM RVskin UNLIMITED Domain RESELLER Web Hosting	$8.99	Website Template-FREE PaintShop PRO **BONUS**	$1.04
cPanel WHM RVskin UNLIMITED Domain RESELLER Web Hosting	$4.99	*NEW* Unlimited Web Hosting * Ebay Special Offer*	$0.01
cPanel 5 Domains UNLIMITED Space Web Hosting webhosting [4 of these sold for $3.99 each]	$3.99	Website Business for Sale * COMPUTER ADVERTISING SPACE [2 of these sold for $0.01 each]	$0.01

Web & Computer Services ▸ Other

HIGH TO LOW

	HIGH		AVG
juntoconsulting.com domain	$100.00	5 Hours From A Professional PHP Web Developer	$1.00
Sign Painters Font Disc Plotter, Software, 15 Fonts	$40.69	BUSINESS SUPPORT SERVICES * *	$0.99
Mail Station cordless 350	$26.00	Just Tell Me What To Do! i.e. Editing, Publishing,	
Complete Online Forum Website With Hosting And Domain	$10.45	Website, Excel, Invoices, etc	
Google Email Gmail Invitation 2G+ Storage Free Shipping	$10.01	2 GMAIL INVITES* * *2.5 GIG * * *FAST DELIVERY	$0.75
BUSINESS SUPPORT SERVICES * * Just Tell Me What To Do! i.e. Editing, Publishing, Typing, Excel, Invoices, etc.	$9.99	[2 of these sold for $0.75 each]	
		Google Email Gmail Invitation 2G+ Storage Free Shipping	$0.45
19 Rare Women History Myth Folklore Books on CD LMF09	$9.97	Google Email Gmail Invitation 2G+ Storage Free Shipping	$0.40
Catering Service Party Private Home Business! $150k/yr!	$6.85	Google Email Gmail Invitation 2G+ Storage Free Shipping	$0.35
Ultimate 2005 Fantasy Football Draft Guide/Cheat Sheet	$2.50	[8 of these sold for $0.35 each]	
10 GMAIL INVITES* * *2.5 GIG * * *FAST DELIVERY	$2.00	~500 BUISNESS LETTER TEMPLATES~ONE FOR EVERY SITUATION~	$0.22
Custom Fantasy Football Cheatsheet * Cheat Sheet * FFL [2 of these sold for $1.79 each]	$1.79	[6 of these sold for $0.22 each]	
		ANY COUNTER STRIKE HL2 HL1 CHEAP SERVER OR SLOT	$0.10

28

SPORTING GOODS

Browsing the Sporting Goods category on eBay is like walking into the largest sports store ever. Every sport imaginable seems to be represented here, from common activities like tennis, golf, and baseball, to more obscure pursuits such as go-karting and snowmobiling. And that points to one of the nicest things about this category from a buyer's perspective: In addition to getting good values, purchasing items here can save you a lot of time and gas money because some of these sporting goods are only available in specialty stores a long drive away from where you live. For example, there is no longer an ice skating supplies store less than an hour's drive round trip from my neighborhood, so I can save myself time and hassle by ordering skaters' tights and competition outfits for my daughter on eBay.

For sellers of sporting goods, this category offers a good opportunity to specialize and provide superior customer service to gain an edge over traditional bricks-and-mortar retailers. One eBay seller believes it's important to have a store presence on the site (that is, to open an eBay Store), if only because it makes you more legitimate when dealing with wholesalers: "Chances are they are not going to want to deal with you unless you have a store front," he wrote on the Outdoor Sports discussion board. "They don't want you competing with dealers that they have a long history with by under-selling them. You need to find closeouts to make any money, and you may have to deal with a liquidator."

As with other eBay categories, some buyers have concerns about determining the authenticity of items. One vendor who has been selling reconditioned Callaway, TaylorMade, and Titleist golf sets on eBay for five years said, "It's sad to see so many 'scam' golf sets being sold to an unsuspecting bidder." He suggests being wary of the following in order to get the real deal: sellers who are new eBay members with very low feedback; foreign item locations, such as Hong Kong or outside the United States; exorbitantly high shipping costs, such as $135.00;

sellers who don't accept PayPal and use only Western Union (which offers "very little buyer protection"); and items that look slightly different than the genuine article (for example, a new golf bag whose logo and lettering placement look slightly different from the real brand's bags might well be fake). "Keep in mind though, most sellers are honest and eBay is a wonderful way to buy at a great value," he adds.

Golf: Big Berthas and eBay Drop-Off Stores

Speaking of golf, *golf* and *golf clubs* are the two most popular searches in this category at this writing, so let's take a look at those prices first.

Callaway Big Bertha drivers and irons are among the most highly coveted in the sport of golf. On the high end, a "NEW Callaway Fusion Big Bertha Full Golf Club/Iron Set" sold for $1,423.98. According to the seller, these clubs were won at a raffle and were never used. (It's unclear exactly when they were won at a raffle, but one hopes it was pretty recently.) Other details from the seller: "They still have the bar codes on them. Includes irons 4 - 9, PW, SW, fairway woods 3, 5, and Titanium 454 10*. These clubs are top of the line; the fairway woods have graphite shafts and include the golf head covers. The bag is beautiful with the tags still attached." To buy these new in the store would cost over $1,500.00, according to the seller.

One other interesting thing about this auction is that it was listed by a QuikDrop franchise in New York; QuikDrop is a chain of eBay drop-off stores that allow people to bring in whatever they want to sell. The store does all the work photographing, listing, selling, and shipping the item—for a fee, of course, described on QuikDrop.com as 38 percent of the first $200.00, 30 percent of the next $300.00, and 20 percent of the remainder (over $500.00).

Perhaps a brand new set of Big Berthas are so beloved that not many people are selling them; there weren't very many available on eBay in this sample. The next two highest-priced Big Bertha auctions were both for used sets. One was a mixed set of 2002 Big Bertha irons and a TaylorMade driver, which went for $1,000.00; the other was a used set of Big Bertha irons, woods, and bag that went for $999.00 (it's not clear in what year they were made). The median price in the Golf ▶ Clubs ▶ Complete Club Set subcategory in this sample was $102.50, at which price you can find several new sets of Aspire brand clubs.

If you want a specific brand of club, you can check on eBay under the list of brands—most major brands are represented there—or just do a search for that brand within the appropriate Golf subcategory.

Different Types of Prey: Paintball, Fishing, and Hunting

The third most popular search term in Sporting Goods was, believe it or not, "paintball"—not bad for a sport that only started in the 1980s. High prices in the Sporting Goods ▶ Paintball ▶ Air Systems & Accessories subcategory include a "68/4500 2k4 MacDev Conquest Adjustable Air System," which went for $259.96, and a "MAX FLO MAXFLO REGULATOR FLOW NITRO PAINTBALL," which sold for $259.25. A new comparable MacDev Conquest air system was recently selling for $384.99 from SAKWorldPaintball.com. Average prices in this subcategory were around $59.00, and included a "Nitro Duck MiniReg 68ci 3000 psi air tank" for $63.05 and "5 Pure Energy 9 oz Co2 Tanks w/ Thread Savers NEW 3" for $60.00.

Paintballs themselves sold for an average of around $39.00, with nine auctions for "Paintball Seconds 4000 Round Case Paintballs BLOW OUT" going for $28.00 each. A case of DraXxus Midnight paintballs "Sealed and Fresh" also went for $28.00, and "4000 rounds PMI ALL STARS PAINTBALLS" went for $33.99. Two thousand rounds of "PMI All Star Paintballs" were recently selling for $60.00 from a paintball supply website, so that appears to be a good price.

Another popular sport here is fishing. There is a busy fishing folder on the Outdoor Sports discussion board called "The Tackle Box." Speaking of tackle boxes, one fishing enthusiast who posts there likes to bid on old ones: "I love to fish and have fallen in love with eBay's fishing auctions . . . the vintage tackle boxes full of tackle are like grab bags. You never know what you are getting, but I've yet to get a bad box . . . every one of them have been full of great things and a few nice surprises! Thanks to all the sellers and collectors for not picking thru them!" Indeed, the highest-priced vintage tackle box in this sample sold for more than the highest-priced new one; a "Ltd. ed. leatherbound fishing book ANGLERS CLUB OF NY" went for $600.00, while a "FISHING TACKLE BOX NEW" with 100 new lures sold for $445.00. But the average sales price of non-vintage tackle boxes was higher than the vintage ones: $25.68 for new ones versus $21.29 for used ones.

How about fishing rods and reels? Some of the most expensive reels out there are made by Penn and are for saltwater and "big game." A "PENN INTERNATIONAL 80TW ROD AND REEL COMBO" with a new in-the-box reel with "big game bent butt rod" sold for $610.00; as a comparison, a new Penn International 80TW reel sells for $749.99 from one fishing gear website. The reel and rod combination is described in the auction as "a never fished Penn International 80TW reel with the box and mounting hardware. This is the wide spool version of the famous international series, holding a massive 950 yards of line. Reel comes with a custom-made big game rod. Rod has the removable aftco ub4 80 lb curved butt and felt hand grip. The roller guides are the aftco big foot guides and are in good condition with no corrosion." The seller says this is a great combination for bluefin tuna fishing or any other big game fishing.

Archery and hunting are other popular search terms in the Sporting Goods category. Although eBay no longer allows the sale of guns or rifles, you can find other hunting items such as apparel, decoys, and game calls. In archery, bows on the high end in this sample range from about $530.00 to $845.00. Most of those are new, whereas in the average range many of the bows are used and go for around $165.00. There are exceptions, of course; a "PSE NEW 2002 BEAST W/INFERNO CAM STILL IN BOX" sold for $166.00.

Indoor Sports

Let's look at sporting goods that can be used indoors, such as tennis or fitness equipment. The prices in the high end in this sample range from $177.50 to $360.00. One new Prince O^3 Silver tennis racquet went for $179.99; these are selling new from one tennis website for $259.99, so eBay seems to offer a healthy discount. Average prices for racquets in this sample are only around $57.00, and you can get a Head racquet ("New Head i.radical intelligence tennis racket 107") for $57.00 (they are $79.95 from Tennis-Warehouse.com).

The treadmill is number 10 on the list of popular sporting goods search terms. You can pay anywhere from $350.00 for a "Proform CrossWalk Advanced 525x Treadmill" to $2,800.00 for a "Life Fitness TR9700HR Next Gen commercial treadmill!" Most likely, though, you'll want to do a search by location to find one close enough to where you live that you can pick it up in person. Even if the seller offers shipping, it ain't gonna be cheap; the shipping price for one Life Fitness model (by freight carrier) was $700.00.

"Local" pickup can be relative, of course. While I may be willing to drive an hour to fetch a bike, I want the convenience of having other things, like ice skates and skating tights, mailed to me. The nice thing about the Sporting Goods category is that it makes hard-to-find equipment accessible, and offers bargains either way you opt to receive your item. It's also one of the larger categories on eBay—three long columns of every kind of sport imaginable. If you're in the mood to find a new sport, it's a good place to browse.

Airsoft ▶ Airsoft BBs

The average sales price in this subcategory is $6.60.

	HIGH		AVG
Brand New Set of 7 Blowguns with Accessories and Stand	$137.50	AIRSOFT 8500 6MM BB,S / BB AIR SOFT NEW IN PACKAGE	$8.95
old daisy pellet gun with box	$57.99	6000 Bag .12g 6mm BBs Airsoft Air Soft BB	$7.99
WOW 40,000 6MM AIRSOFT BBs GUN RIFLE NEW good ones	$45.50	[2 of these sold for $7.99 each]	
BlackHawk Vast Commando Recon Chest Harness	$45.00	Colt Double Eagle Air Soft Hand Gun w/ Free bb's	$7.97
WOW 40,000 6MM AIRSOFT BBs GUN RIFLE NEW good ones	$44.00	5000 PREMIUM 0.12g BB AIRSOFT BulkBag BBs BB's ORANGE	$7.95
(3) Vintage BB's TINS - Daisy Special TARGETEER w/ BB's	$38.00	6000 PREMIUM 6mm 0.12g AIRSOFT BB BBs BB's 3Bottles	$7.95
Bolle Airsoft Goggle Tactical 2 lense like New L@@@@K	$31.52	5,000 Airsoft Ammo 6mm Pellet BB Air Soft BBs Gun .12g	$7.95
24000 PREMIUM 6mm .12g AIRSOFT BBs BB's 3Bags+6Bottles	$27.99	AIRSOFT STICKY TARGET 6MM BB,S AIR SOFT BB ST01	$6.95
[2 of these sold for $27.99 each]		5 Containers of Air Soft gun BBs 6 MM Pellets New SHARP	$5.99
24000 PREMIUM 6mm .12g AIRSOFT BBs BB's 3Bags+6Bottles	$24.95	Two 200 Count 6mm Paintballs Airsoft Gun Marker BBs	$5.99
DAISY SOFT AIR PELLETTS & SHOT CARTRIDGES NEW VINTAGE	$22.27	Airsoft Softair 6mm Metal Target BBs Ammo 250 pack bag	$5.99
1000 6MM AIRSOFT PAINTBALLS*BBS*6 MM BB GUN PAINT BALLS	$19.00	500 AIRSOFT PAINTBALLS - AIR SOFT - 6mm PAINT BALLS @@@	$5.99
1000 6MM AIRSOFT PAINTBALLS*BBS*6 MM BB GUN PAINT BALLS	$19.00	[2 of these sold for $5.99 each]	
MATRIX 0.20g TRACER NIGHT GLOW AIRSOFT 6mm BB 2000 RDS	$16.00	DAISY SOFT AIR PELLETTS & SHOT CARTRIDGES NEW VINTAGE	$5.50
15000 .12g premium airsoft bbs, made by Crosman	$15.95	5,000 Airsoft Ammo 6mm Pellet BB Air Soft BBs Gun .12g	$5.50
10000 Airsoft Ammo 6mm Pellet BB Air Soft BBs Gun .12g	$15.95	200 6mm Red Paintballs & 2000 6mm Orange BBs	$5.49
		[2 of these sold for $5.49 each]	
		1000-4.5 MM AIRSOFT RIFLE/GUN/PISTOL PELLETS*BBS .177	$5.00
		[4 of these sold for $5.00 each]	

Airsoft ▶ Airsoft Guns

The average sales price in this subcategory is $54.67.

	HIGH		AVG
VFC M82A1 Gas powered 8mm sniper rifle.......NR!!!!!!	$1,000.00	Smith & Wesson Sigma SW40F w/silencer	$60.00
UPGRADED JAC M16 XM177 E2 gas airsoft gun MP5	$449.00	KJW Full Metal Airsoft M9 Silver GBB	$60.00
WA Airsoft Gas Gigant gun Madbull grenade launcher MORE	$390.00	Airsoft G 26 6MM Gas BlowBack BB Gun Pistol-Pellets NEW	$59.95
RARE Tokyo Marui Walther MPL gas airsoft prop gun MP5	$375.00	KWC SMITH & WESSON SIGMA 40F C02 AIR SOFT AIRSOFT BOX	$58.00
Tokyo Marui Upgraded Steyr AUG Military and G19 AIRSOFT	$355.00	Gas .357 Magnum Revolver Airsoft BB Gun - SILVER	$57.50
Marushin Mauser Kar98 k Maxi Airsoft Rifle	$350.00	Air Soft Tokyo Marui revolver pistol M-19	$56.01
Asahi Gas Airsoft - Collectors Item	$310.00	SMITH & WESSON SIGMA SW 40F AIRSOFT GUN co2 POWER	$56.00
Western Arms FULL metal airsoft gun SV infinity 5 inch	$300.00	6 GUNS HEAVY M16 XENON LIGHT LASER RIFLE AIRSOFT LOT EQ	$56.00
AIRSOFT KJW M700 SNIPER. 450 FPS. SCOPE/RIFLE BAG	$299.99	AIRSOFT PELLET 18C VGP026 SEMI FULL AUTO GAS POWER NR	$53.00
Airsoft Western Arms MGC .45 COLT FBI Custom GBB Pistol	$275.00	Gas Heavy Weight M-2340 ABF Elite (350 FPS) Airsoft	$53.00
Airsoft Mossberg M500 8mm Pump Shotgun All Metal MIB!	$259.00	BERETTA 92FS CAMO FULL METAL GAS BLOWBACK AIRSOFTBB GUN	$52.75
Airsoft CAW M79 grenade launcher	$240.00	KJW M92F GBB Tokyo Marui ICS CA Gas Blow BackGBB Pistol	$50.99
Maruzen Ingram MAC-10 M10 full auto gas airsoft gun JAC	$227.50	AIRSOFT M92F STYLE GAS BB PAINTBALL GUN SUPER PACKAGE !	$49.99
Airsoft Paintball M79 Grenade Launcher Gas - No Reserve	$225.00	[2 of these sold for $ 49.99 each]	
Maruzen APS-2 (SV), Scope, and Custom Paint Job (OD)	$225.00	COMPLETE 5 BB GUN RIFLE M16 A2 MAC10 USP + 2 PISTOLS EN	$47.00
		KWC 1911 COMPETITION GAS BLOWBACK AIRSOFT BB GUN	$44.99

Archery ▶ Arrows

The average sales price in this subcategory is $33.56.

	HIGH		AVG
Barnett Revolution Crossbow Kit **Like New**	$330.00	BEMAN THUNDERBOLT 20 CROSSBOW ARROWS/ARCHER'S PACK	$34.99
Archery Hoyt bow, 50-60# , draw length 25.5-28.5	$234.50	@NEW@ GOLD TIP XT HUNTER 5575 CARBON BOW HUNTING ARROWS	$34.99
EASTON A/C/C SUPERLITE ARROWS	$150.00	1/2 dozen Easton Axis carbon 400 CUSTOM Made	$34.50
17 Used Easton ACE 1206 G series/370's	$125.00	2314 EASTON MAXUM SOLO ARROWS – ONE DOZEN	$34.00
Vintage Set Of 17 Cedar Fletched Arrows In Case	$124.50	Easton ACC ARROWS 349/390	$34.00
NIB 2dz Blackhawk Vapor Pro Series 5000 Arrows	$102.75	EASTON XX78 SUPERSLAM 5" VANED ARROWS 2213 6-PACK	$34.00
33 Behman carbon arrows	$100.00	Used Fiberglas Practice arrows 2 dozen	$34.00
1 DOZEN EASTON SUPERLITE A/C/C ARROWS 3-60/340	$93.60	Box of 20 old wooden arrows, real feather fletching	$33.56
ACCs Arrows Fletched and ready to shoot	$90.00	Vintage fred bear quiver + arrows !! MADE IN THE USA !!	$33.50
Lot of Aluminum Arrows	$89.88	6 PSE archery Radial X Weave 300 carbon arrows NEW	$33.00
NEW 05 EASTON ST -AXIS ARROWS 400 W/BLAZER VANES 1DZ	$86.99	6 BEMAN archery ICS Trebark 340/400 carbon arrows NEW	$33.00
1 Dz. Easton Axis 400 NR	$86.00	BEMAN ICS 400	$33.00
2018 arrows- lot of 34	$84.45	NEW 12 EASTON X 7 COSMIC ECLIPSE 2212 ARROWS	$33.00
12 Easton archery ST AXIS 340 or 400 carbon arrows NEW	$82.00	18 Nice Wood Shaft Target Arrows, 27 Inch	$33.00
12-Easton A/C/E 400 arrowscomplete 28"	$81.02	Easton 2016 Gamegetter Arrows, 1 doz, in box	$33.00

Archery ▶ Bow, Shooting Accessories

The average sales price in this subcategory is $34.45.

	HIGH		AVG
New Holographic Archery Sight and Mounting System	$275.00	Scott Archery Release	$35.00
PSE Fire Flight Compound Bow w/ accessories	$250.00	[2 of these sold for $35.00 each]	
SURE-LOC SUPREME Target sight w/ CR APEX scope	$222.50	2005 Truglo Brite Site Xteme LH	$35.00
EO-Tech Holographic Sight and Optimizer Lite Plus Mount	$215.00	HHA LIGHTABLE FIBER OPTIC SIGHT	$35.00
HHA Multiple Reticle Reddot Bow Sight With Mount Brackt	$169.99	tru-ball tornado	$34.99
CUSTOM BOW EQUIPMENT 3D XL SIGHT****	$165.00	Cobra Sidewinder Sight ~ NIB ~ NR ~ NEW ~ RH	$34.99
Toxonics Model 5200 Sight	$160.00	Cobra Mamba R1 release/hunting/archery/bow release	$34.99
Custom Bow Equipment Sight	$152.50	2005 CAROLINA FoXFIRE SP SINGLE PIN Sight RH NEW IN PKG	$34.50
BEAR QUIVER ARROWS AND ARCHERY ACCESSORIES	$152.50	New Tru Fire trufire Hurricane Buckle bow Release Aid	$34.06
TOXONICS BOW SIGHT w/FATBOY SCOPE - NO RESERVE	$152.50	Hind Sight II	$34.02
Hoyt Intruder Bow w/ 29" draw length, and soft case	$150.00	3 Quick Trigger Release for Archery Bow Hunting	$34.00

	HIGH		AVG
NEW HHA PURE N' TENSION RELEASE NIB	$139.49	New 4 Arrow Bowtech camo quiver, New in factory packge	$33.95
Trophy Ridge RHINO Sight .019 Micro	$137.50	Pendulum feather weight sight brand savage	$33.51
Pin RH RM5250 NEW!		Savage Systems Pendulum Sight - fiber optic	$33.51
SURE LOC SHORTY WITH 3 AXIS	$135.00	New Cobra Swing Away E-Z Adjust Pro Caliper Release	$33.50
CARTER JUST-B-CUZ COMPOUND RELEASE	$130.00	SCOVILL QUIVER..High Shine Leather..Loaded w/goodies	$33.50

Archery ▶ Bows

The average sales price in this subcategory is $166.66.

	HIGH		AVG
BOWTECH ALLEGIANCE VFT Loaded w/ BEST Acces 60-70lb 29"	$845.00	RIGHT HANDED, PARKER CHALLENGER	$172.50
Mathews 2005 Switchback Solocam Bow RH 28" draw 70#	$840.00	NEW PSE SPYDER SYNERGY 4 WHEEL RH & EXTRAS YOUTH BOW	$171.38
2005 Mathews Switchback LH 29" 70lb	$750.00	Martin Fury bow	$170.00
Brand New Mathews Switchback (RH)	$710.00	High Country Brute Elite RH	$170.00
Brand New Mathews Switchback (RH)	$689.00	2003 Hoyt Reflex Gamegetter cam 1/2,sights , and rest	$169.99
2005 Mathews Switchback LH 30" 70lb	$675.00	compound bow	$167.53
Brand New Mathews Switchback (RH) Bow	$660.00	NEW PSE PRO-SHOP SERIES F-2 RH 28-30 55-70#	$167.50
2005 Hoyt Ultra-Elite XT 3000	$610.00	PSE NEW 2002 BEAST W/INFERNO CAM STILL IN BOX.	$165.00
Mathews Switchback New in the box	$600.00	DARTON MX READY TO HUNT LOOK!!!!!	$163.50
Hoyt USA 2004 Ultratec Trophy Taker Sight and Rest!	$580.00	Ted Nugent autographed L/H Pro Safari Compound Bow	$162.50
Mathews Switchback, 29", 70 lb., 80% let-off	$575.00	Mathews Genesis Youth Compound Bow New RH Camo	$162.50
BOW ARCHERY RESEARCH AR 31 RAM AND HALF HYBRID CAM !!	$549.00	PSE Nova Compound Bow 2004 + Extras ($0 S/H w/BIN)	$162.50
Mathews LX LH Bow, 70#, 29" Draw, Excellent, LOOK!	$546.00	PSE AVENGER, RT HAND, BRUSH CAMO BARE BONES	$161.55
2004 Hoyt Xtec new	$535.00	PSE NOVA COMPOUND BOW 24/40 Arrows Case Quiver Guard	$161.50
BOWTECH 2005 Allegiance with newTrophy Taker rest!	$530.00	60 #, RIGHT HAND, 29", DRAW, TROPHY RIDGE SIGHT.	$160.58

Baseball & Softball ▶ Apparel & Footwear

The average sales price in this subcategory is $9.53.

	HIGH		AVG
NASCAR Roush Racing pit crew helmet	$49.99	New York Yankees 59fifty New Era Baseball Cap Hat 7 5/8	$9.99
new pink Indianapolis Colts Cheerleader hat	$37.00	CHICAGO CUBS PEEING ON CHICAGO WHITE SOX HAT / CAP	$9.99
Southwest Texas State University Hats - SWT Hats	$36.00	Chicago White Sox Baseball MLB Hat Cap White## 7 1/2	$9.99
Seattle Mariners ICHIRO Baseball Jersey New XL	$31.00	NEW LA Dodgers New Era 59 Fifty Cap Hat Fitted 7 1/8	$9.99
MLB NY Yankees MATSUI Home Baseball Jersey New 3XL	$26.49	New York Yankees Baseball MLB Trucker Hat Cap WT# 7 1/4	$9.99
new pink Chicago Bears Cheerleader hat ladies girls	$26.00	MIAMI HURRICANES HAT 7 1/4	$9.99
new Chicago White Sox South Side Hit Men t shirt XL	$26.00	New Green St. Louis Cardinals St. Patrick's Day hat	$9.99
New Era Boston Red Sox Camo hat size 7 1/8	$25.00	new pink Tampa Bay Buccaneers Cheerleader hat	$9.50
Green fitted St Louis Cardinals St Paddys Day hat 7 1/4	$23.67	CHICAGO "CUBS SUCK" WHITE SOX CARDINALS HAT / CAP	$9.50
MONTREAL EXPOS VINTAGE PINWHEEL NEW ERA HAT NWT 7 3/8	$22.50	Brand new pink Pittsburgh Steelers hat ladies	$9.10
New Era Atlanta Braves hat NR 59/50 brand new 7 5/8	$22.00	Baseball CAP KEEP Hat Washers/Protectors NEW	$9.00
Dan Harrington Poker WSOP Boston Red Sox hat 7 1/2	$21.99	BLACK BOSTON RED SOX VISOR/ BASEBALL CAP/HAT*ADJUSTABLE	$9.00
Dan Harrington Poker WSOP Boston Red Sox hat 7 1/4	$21.99	CLASSY TAN BOSTON RED SOX BASEBALL CAP/HAT*ADJUSTABLE	$9.00
BRAND NEW LA DODGERS BLACK WHITE LOGO SZ 7 1/2 60 CM	$21.50	BLACK BOSTON RED SOX VISOR/ BASEBALL CAP/HAT*ADJUSTABLE	$9.00
NEW ERA CHICAGO CUBS 5950 $35 FITTED CAP / HAT 7 5/8	$20.55	BLACK BOSTON RED SOX VISOR/ BASEBALL CAP/HAT*ADJUSTABLE	$9.00

Baseball & Softball ▶ Balls

The average sales price in this subcategory is $29.92.

	HIGH		AVG
1 Sealed Case - 6 Dozen RAWLINGS OFFICIAL NL Baseballs	$621.88	24 used LEATHER BASEBALLS-NO VINYLS OR SYNTHETICS	$30.55
Sealed Case 6 Dozen RAWLINGS A.L. Cal Ripken Baseballs	$319.00	NEW WORTH SUPERCELL LIGHTHOUSE	$30.55
10 Dozen WILSON Baseballs Little League A1074 1 CASE!!	$255.08	SOFTBALL BAT 34/26 BATS	
Diamond Baseball DOL-1 NFHS Official Baseballs 10 DOZEN	$234.50	NEW WORTH MG46 BIG BARREL BASEBALL BAT 31/28 rp=$200	$30.47
VINTAGE SPALDING BASEBALL BOX - GREAT GRAPHICS ! 1930'S	$197.50	6 Trump Softballs	$30.01
125 Used Rawlings Baseballs, Great Condition	$182.50	Dudley asa softballs 11 NEW (DOZEN)	$30.00
1 Dozen Official American League Baseballs -Bobby Brown	$172.50	Ball Cart for Baseball, Softball & Batting Cages	$30.00
1 Dozen Official RAWLINGS GOLD GLOVE BASEBALLS - NIB!!!	$158.05	wilson A1010 baseballs 1DZ	$30.00
36 - 12" Softball Yellow Dimple Pitching Machine Balls	$154.00	24 Genuine Leather **Collegiate Used** Baseball Balls	$29.89
[2 of these sold in a multiple item ("Dutch") auction for $77.00 each]		Rawlings RBRO Babe Ruth League Baseballs One Dozen New	$29.50
NEW WORTH WICKED INSANITY SLOWPITCH SOFTBALL BAT 34/30	$152.50	RAWLINGS DOZEN OFFICIAL SOFTBALLS ASA12Y47LHC NIB	$29.50
1 Dozen Rawlings Official 2004 World Series Baseballs	$149.00	20 used minor league baseballs	$29.04
5 Dz Diamond NFHS High school baseballs	$142.50	NEW WORTH MG46 BIG BARREL BASEBALL BAT 31/28 rp=$200	$29.00
VINTAGE WORTH BASEBALLS 1 DOZEN SEALED IN ORIG. BOXES	$127.53	1 Dozen 12" New DeMarini 44 375 ASA Yellow Softballs	$29.00
VINTAGE MACGREGOR BASEBALLS-1 DOZEN SEALED IN ORIG. BOX	$127.53	14 DUDLEY Offical Softballs SB-23ST RF NEW!	$29.00
1 Dozen Official RAWLINGS GOLD GLOVE BASEBALLS - NIB!!!	$124.18	WILSON OFFICIAL BASEBALL BALLS-BOX OF 12 NEW BALLS	$29.00

Baseball & Softball ▶ Bats

The average sales price in this subcategory is $43.38.

	HIGH		AVG
vintage spalding wood baseball bat axeltree model	$532.89	Louisville Slugger M9	$46.00
2004 Anderson Rocket Tech Bat - 33/24 Brand New!	$330.00	Louisville Slugger M9	$45.09
NEW MIKEN FREAK PLUS SLOWPITCH SOFTBALL BAT MODEL MSFP	$236.50	Rawlings Liquid Metal Fast-Pitch Softball Bat 34" 23 Oz	$45.00
RAWLINGS PLASMA 2006 HS/NCAA BAT 33/30 BRAND NEW	$216.50	Worth Copperhead MG46 30in. 18oz Youth Baseball Bats	$44.99
New Demarini F375 28 Oz. 34" Softball Bat	$212.51	(2) TWO PRO MODEL-LASER ENGRAVED	$44.00
[2 of these sold for $212.51 each]		WHITE ASH WOOD BATS	
MIKEN FREAK - 34/27	$210.00	Louisville Slugger Maple Powerized Wood Baseball Bat 33	$43.60
New Demarini F375 28 Oz. 34" Softball Bat	$207.50	Louisville Response Fast-Pitch Softball Bat 34" 22 Oz	$43.51

Original Mizuno Techfire Crush Softball Bat 26 Oz. 34"	$205.50	Rocky Colavito Little League Baseball Bat Excellent	$43.50
1910s Jake Daubert 14" Souvenir Mini Decal Bat Relist	$203.50	Louisville Slugger M9 Model M110 1XX MLB Timber	$43.13
EARLY UNUSUAL RING BAT, H.B. & CO. 35 INCHES 24 RINGS	$200.00	2- Hard Maple Baseball Bats–LG Flared Knob-32" & 32.5"	$43.00
New Demarini F375 28 Oz. 34" Softball Bat	$197.50	Louisville Slugger Manny Ramirez C271 Wood Baseball Bat	$42.98
New Demarini F375 27 Oz. 34" Softball Bat	$192.50	5 Louisville Slugger Wood Bats-Bench, Yaz, Clemente...	$42.77
NEW 2005 MIKEN FREAK ADULT 33/30 BASEBALL BAT	$192.50	Mizuno Wheeled Techfire Softball Or Baseball Bat Bag	$42.09
New Demarini F375 28 Oz. 34" Softball Bat	$190.72	Louisville Response Fast-Pitch Softball Bat 33" 21 Oz	$42.00
NEW 2005 MIKEN FREAK ADULT 33/30 BASEBALL BAT	$187.50	Louisville Slugger M9	$42.00

Baseball & Softball ▸ Gloves & Mitts

The average sales price in this subcategory is $37.04.

	HIGH		AVG
1930s VINTAGE BASEBALL CATCHERS GLOVE	$338.33	Mizuno GXS80 Generation catchers mitt (brand new)	$38.00
RAWLINGS RED ROLFE BASEBALL GLOVE W/ ORIGINAL BOX, RARE	$253.35	Vintage Rawlings "Stan the Man Musial" Baseball Glove!	$38.00
VINTAGE WINCHESTER REPEATING ARMS CATCHER'S MITT	$213.20	RAWLINGS RCM 45 LEFT HANDED CATCHERS MITT MIKE PIAZZA	$38.00
Rawlings HOH Bellows Web Baseball Glove Mdl XFCB	$212.00	NEW-RH A0500 FPCM 32" FASTPITCH CATCHERS MITT	$37.99
Thurman Munson catcher catchers mitt glove MINT	$202.50	*New* Rawlings RCM7 34" Baseball Catcher's Mitt RHT	$37.95
Vintage Wilson A2000 XL USA made glove - NICE!!	$200.50	NIKE SOFTBALL GLOVES 2 FOR 1 SALE	$37.75
New Rawlings Pro-Preferred PROSCM20 Catcher's Mitt	$192.50	Nokona professional catcher's mitt glove model M20	$37.50
Vintage Nokona Bob Milliken Black Baseball Glove Silver	$189.50	*New* Mizuno Vintage Pro GXC50 32.5" Catcher's Mitt RHT	$37.01
Rawlings Pro-Preferred Catchers Mitt (PROSCM20) NEW!!!!	$180.00	NOKONA lefty CM200 pro-line catchers mitt. 50s/60s	$37.00
Wilson A2044 Lefty Gomez Fielders Mitt	$178.50	Wilson Staff 700 Catchers Mitt	$37.00
70's Catchers Mitt Glove THURMAN MUNSON GOLD LETTERING	$175.00	NEW-2004 RH EASTON ULTRA LITE YOUTH CATCHERS MITT	$36.00
New Nokona Buffalo AMG175BF 12" Baseball Glove RHT	$154.49	Kelley Century Series CS-741 Infielder's Glove	$36.00
Wilson A2403 PUDGE catcher's mitt BRAND NEW WITH TAGS!	$142.50	Wilson Fast Pitch Softball Catcher's Mitt Glove 32" RH	$36.00
Rawlings Professional catchers mitt MINT	$137.50	Rawlings Left Handed Catchers Mitt	$36.00
Wilson A3000 K87 Baseball Gloves NEW . NIB	$136.01	REGENT "BIG MAN" LEATHER BASEBALL GLOVE MIT LARGE+BALLS	$36.00

Basketball ▸ Apparel & Footwear

The average sales price in this subcategory is $21.75.

	HIGH		AVG
A Lot of 13 Diffrent Rare Basketball Jerseys	$265.00	NEW Georgia Tech Yellow Jackets basketball shirt L/XL	$24.50
Air Jordan XI size sz 8.5 cool grey DEADSTOCKED DS	$227.50	TIM DUNCAN #21 Antonio Spurs NBA REEBOK jersey L-2XL	$24.49
NIKE AIR JORDAN XII RETRO NUBUCK (BLK/UNI-BLUE) DS US10	$216.00	ANTHONY DENVER NUGGETS 2005 NBA REEBOK jersey sizeL-3XL	$23.39
Nike Dunk Low SB Away Raygun sz 13 tiffany 12 prod	$175.99	BEN ROETHLISBERGER #7 NFL EQUIPMENT STEELERS JERSEY XL	$23.09
Nike Air Max CW Original sz 13 Chris Webber's dunk	$165.99	* LEBRON JAMES * CAVALIERS AUTHENTIC REEBOK JERSEY 56	$22.50
Nike air jordan 11 retro blk/red-wht 8.5 21 xi 95 xiii	$162.50	NIKE ANTI RACISM BALLER ID WRIST BAND STAND UP SPEAK UP	$22.50
Air Jordan xii 12 size sz 8.5 black / red VVVVVVVNDS	$113.50	[5 of these sold in a multiple item ("Dutch") auction for $4.50 each]	
NU JEFF HAMILTON KNICKS COWHIDE		JORDAN JUMPMAN DRI FIT B-BALL SHORTS SZ XXL	$22.50
LEATHER JACKET 2XL NBA	$103.61	6 Yellow Practice Jerseys Scrimmage Vests Shirts Youth	$21.51
MEN'S BASKETBALL UNIFORMS - FULL SET - NAVY/WHITE	$102.50	* STOJAKOVIC *#16 KINGS NBA AUTHENTIC REEBOK JERSEY 56	$21.50
Authentic 1991 Falcons Throwback Favre Jersey	$100.00	NIKE Air Jordan socks sz 10-13 **6 pair LOT	$20.51
MICHAEL JORDAN # 23 AUTHENTIC CHAMPION BULLS JERSEY 44	$99.99	* STOJAKOVIC *#16 KINGS NBA AUTHENTIC REEBOK JERSEY 58	$20.50
* MANU GINOBILI * NBA FINALS AUTHENTIC SPURS JERSEY 52	$96.00	Jock, Nike Basketball uniform satin ,PBA, Gordons gin	$20.50
NWT MICHAEL JORDAN LANEY HS THROWBACK NIKE JERSEY 2XL	$91.00	LeBron James #23 New Cleveland Cavaliers jersey L-3XL	$20.50
Air Jordan viii 8 size sz 9 white / red VNDS	$86.00	SHAQUILLE O'NEAL #32 AUTHENTIC MIAMI HEAT JERSEY L-3XL	$20.50
* MANU GINOBILI * NBA FINALS AUTHENTIC SPURS JERSEY 52	$81.00	MICHAEL FINLEY MAVERICKS AUTHENTIC NIKE JERSEY NWT 58	$20.50

Basketball ▸ Balls

The average sales price in this subcategory is $21.23.

	HIGH		AVG
Vintage Bladder Leather Laced Basketball Reach 1915	$374.00	Brand new Spalding TF-1000 28.5	$25.00
OLD VINTAGE LEATHER LACEUP J.C.HIGGINS SEARS BASKETBALL	$235.00	wide channel basketball	$24.99
Incredibly Rare Hutch Laced Basketball Official US U.S.	$178.00	8 Brand New Regulation Sized Street Basketballs	$24.99
VINTAGE RARE LEATHER LACE UP BASKETBALL BALL	$100.67	Spalding TF-1000 Basketball NEW!! TF1000	$24.99
LA Lakers Signed Basketball	$99.99	Wilson Jet Evolution basketball. Leather slightly used	$23.01
OFFICIAL SPALDING GENUINE LEATHER NBA BASKETBALL !!!!!!	$80.95	wilson evolution basketball	$23.01
Vintage Slazenger Lace Up Basketball Soccer Ball OLD	$77.56	Baden Lexum Indoor basketball. (Evolution Jet Wilson)	$23.00
OLD LACE UP LEATHER BASKETBALL	$76.99	NEW WILSON MEN'S NCCA	$21.99
Chicago Bulls 1996 Champions AUTHENTIC Spaudling Ball!	$76.00	UNDERGLASS 29.5" BASKETBALL	
[3 of these sold for $76.00 each]		Reebok VR-5000 Indoor basketball. Leather and New!	$20.50
Basketball Educational Videos not Slam Dunk film Dvd	$66.00	Brand new Spalding TF-1000 28.5 wide channel basketball	$20.50
Basketball Video DVD series 4 Seen in SLAM Magazine	$65.00	New Spalding NBA Infusion Pro Indoor/Outdoor Basketball	$20.50
Two Spalding TF-1000 basketballs. Brand new, packaged	$63.05	New Never Usd Patent Leather Detroit Pistons Basketball	$20.50
Spalding NBA Game Ball Leather Basketball 2004 Finals	$56.00	Spalding TF-1000 ZK Microfiber Composite 29.5"	$20.50
Fantastic Vintage 1940s Dubow Basketball Box with Ball	$51.01	Spalding TF-1000 ZK Microfiber Composite (Intermediate)	$20.00
Rick Fox Signed Spalding basketball NR RARE!!!	$51.00	Lebron James Basketball Jordan Brand New In Box Rare	$19.99
SPALDING NBA Official Leather Basketball	$51.00	Lebron James Basketball Jordan Cleveland New In BoxRare	$19.99

Billiards ▸ Balls

The average sales price in this subcategory is $32.89.

	HIGH		AVG
Set of Nine Antique Ivory Balls	$355.00	ELEPHANT BILLIARD BEAUTIFUL BALLS IN BOX	$35.00
Antique Ivory Billiard Balls	$225.00	8 Ball walking stick, Authentic Billiard Cue Eight	$35.00

ANTIQUE IVORY BILLIARD POOL BALLS CUE VERY NICE	$189.50	Vintage Pool/Billiard Balls Complete Set Clay?	$35.00
Licensed NFL Billiard Pool Cue Balls, Ball Set ~ NEW !	$179.95	Vintage Bumper Pool Balls - Complete Set	$34.00
BRUNSWICK CENTENNIALS	$150.00	NR Aramith Belgian Premier Billiard Balls 2 1/4"	$33.65
POKER POOL BILLIARD POOL TABLE BALLS W/ CLEAR CASE	$149.99	Never Used Set of Pool Balls, New	$33.30
POOL TABLE BALLS CLEAR PLAYBOY BILLIARD BALLS	$149.95	Vintage Bakelite Pool Billiard Balls Complete Set	$33.25
New Set of Nude (Topless) Ladies Pro Pool Balls *L@@K*	$149.95	1965 VINTAGE POOL TABLE BALLS NEW IN BOX	$32.03
POOL BALLS BILLIARD BALLS MARBLE ELEPHANT BEAUTIFUL	$149.95	NEW HALEX PREMIER BELGIAN ARAMITH BILLIARD POOL BALLS	$31.99
World Renowned FANTASY VIXENS Pool Balls * New Set *	$139.95	[3 of these sold for $31.99 each]	
BRUNSWICK VINTAGE SOLID IVORY SNOOKER BALLS	$132.50	NEW Billiard Package/Balls/Cues/Racks/Cover	$31.00
Poker Pool Balls, NIB!!! LOW RESERVE!!!	$130.00	NEW Marble/Marbled/Swirl Pool/Billiard Table Balls/Ball	$30.00
ARAMITH TV POOL BALLS BILLIARD BALLS-MEALES CUE BALL	$127.95	NEW HALEX PREMIER BELGIAN ARAMITH BILLIARD POOL BALLS	$29.99
[2 of these sold for $127.95 each]		HARLEY DAVIDSON LIVE TO RIDE BILLIARDS CUE BALLS	$29.95
BRAND NEW SUPER ARAMITH PRO TV CUP BALLS AS SEEN ON TV	$125.00	PLAIN Red or Brown Billiard/Pool ball	$29.60
Complete Centennial Brunswick Billiard/Pool Ball Set	$117.51	BILLIARD BALLS POOL BALLS BALL SET $139.00 VALUE	$29.01

Billiards ▸ Cues

The average sales price in this subcategory is $91.33.

	HIGH		AVG
2004 RUNDE IVORY JOINT & INLAYS LEATHER WRAP NEW N/R	$1,500.00	6 Custom Pool cue Sticks L2000 Canadian Maple Billiard	$99.00
Richard Harris Bluegrass cue	$1,300.00	NEW MARVEL WOLVERINE POOL CUE by Dufferin NR	$99.00
predator se 4	$795.00	NEW POOL CUE BILLIARDS TABLE STICK WALL RACK. MAHOG	$99.00
Antique pool biLLiArd old rare cue J E Came boston	$750.00	IVORY Custom Pool Cue Billiard Ebony Handmade Audrick	$99.00
Custom Pechauer Cue w/3 shafts and 2x4 case Mint	$691.00	Handmade Pool Cue Custom Billiard stick Audrick Cues	$99.00
Beautiful Richard Black Custom Cue	$673.00	3 Hand Made BIRDSEYE Custom Pool Cues Retail $540	$99.00
McDermott Harley Davidson Pool Cue Stick Used	$660.00	IVORY Custom PoolCue Billiard Rosewood Handmade Audrick	$96.00
Rare custom schon pool cue 1 of 3 made	$552.00	New Omega Custom Cue (With 2 Shafts)	$88.01
DP Pool Cue - Every Tuesday $99 Cues from Dale Perry	$515.00	Handmade Pool Stick Custom Billiard Cue - PYTHON!! NR	$85.20
Gorgeous.Coker Six Point Custom Pool Cue BEAUTIFUL	$505.00	5 Custom Pool cue Sticks L2000 Canadian Maple RBGBB	$84.00
Coker Custom Cue	$500.00	SUPER DEAL!! WHOLESALE LOT CUES poolstick billiards	$83.00
Antique pool cue rack Brunswick billiard locks	$499.00	New Helmstetter 98-3 Pool Cue, Billiards No Reserve!	$82.51
DP pool cue Billiard Dale Perry - Wrapless Beauty	$459.00	HANDMADE Custom Pool Cue 4 EBONY POINTS Retail $350 NR!	$82.05
DP pool cue Billiard Dale Perry - Sleek and Wrapless	$455.00	Handmade Pool Stick Custom Billiard Cue - Python!! NR	$81.00
SCOTT WHISLER 4/2002	$430.00	Philippine Pool Cue billiards stick REAL ELEPHANT BONES	$81.00

Billiards ▸ Tables

The average sales price in this subcategory is $574.24.

	HIGH		AVG
RARE BRUNSWICK BALKE COLLENDAR	$2,495.00	8 ft Pool Billiard Table Customized for You by You	$645.00
ANTIQUE 8 FT POOL TABLE		8ft pool table, used but in good condition must see!	$635.00
Brunswick Gold Crown III 9ft EXCELLENT CONDITION	$2,225.00	8' Slate Pool Table With Accessories	$610.00
Hard Rock Harley-Davidson 8 Foot Pool Table	$2,000.00	Valley Coin Op Pool Table 7 FT Billard Slate IOWA	$610.00
8'HOUSTON pooltables/Pool table/billiard /Billiards	$1,899.00	Pool table/Billards Bar Table	$610.00
Olhausen 8' Pool Table In Mint Condition	$1,825.00	Like NEW 44x88 1 " SLATE Pool Table	$600.00
Olhausen 8 ft. Pool Table : The Best in Billiards	$1,775.00	FABULOUS OAK GAME PUB WOOD DINING BAR TABLE SET CHAIRS	$599.00
8' Burlington 100% MAPLE Wood Billiards Pool Table	$1,599.00	Brunswick Medalist Pool Table - 8 ft.	$588.20
Pool Table Round 6ft Diameter. Coin operated or not	$1,500.00	7 ft Coin Opperated Global Pool Table Coin Op NR	$550.00
Antique, Art Deco Pool Table, manf. 1934-1947	$1,500.00	NEW Homestead 8' Cherry Pool Billiard Table Tables	$550.00
Chateau by Brunswick Regulation Pool Table, like new	$1,500.00	[2 of these sold for $550.00 each]	
BRUNSWICK BILLARD/POOL TABLE	$1,500.00	NEW Homestead 8' Oak Pool Billiard Table Tables	$550.00
FREE SHIPPING 8' POOL Billiard/billiards/pool table	$1,499.00	POOL TABLE VALLEY	$550.00
AE Schmidt 8ft Pool Table Circa 1960	$1,435.00	NEW Homestead 8' Oak Pool Billiard Table Tables	$550.00
8' Cambridge Mahogany Pool Table FREE SHIPPING	$1,425.00	8 Ft. Brunswick Billiards Pool Table	$543.33
7ft Pool Billiard Table Dinette Combo with 8 Chairs !	$1,395.00	8 Foot Pool Table !!! NEW BRAND !!!NEW ITEM!!! NEW !!!	$536.00

Bowling ▸ Apparel & Footwear

The average sales price in this subcategory is $25.55.

	HIGH		AVG
RAT PACK-retro bowling shirt-The ultimate in HIP-$19.95	$105.00	DEXTER MARSHALL BOWLING SHOES	$26.00
[5 of these sold in a multiple item ("Dutch") auction for $21.00 each]		MENS SIZE 10 NR NR NR	
The Wedge Bowling Shoes by Linds .Size 15 Right Handed	$99.88	Dexter SST 5 Black/Bronze Bowling Shoes Mens Size 7.5	$26.00
DEXTER SST 6 MENS BOWLING SHOES SIZE 8 1/2 LEFT HAND NR	$90.00	Dexter Daytona Bowling Shoes. Mens Size 14	$25.99
NEW DEXTER SST 5 SELECT CLASSIC WHITE/WHITE SZ 12 RH	$88.00	DEXTER CHARLOTTE BOWLING SHOES WOMENS SIZE 6	$25.95
DEXTER SST 5 LX Men's BOWLING SHOES SIZE 14	$87.95	DEXTER CHARLOTTE BOWLING SHOES WOMENS SIZE 7	$25.95
Dexter Mens Bowling Shoes SST6 Burgandy RH 10.5	$82.05	Dexter Charlotte Bowling Shoes. Womens Size 9	$25.95
DEXTER SST 5 LX Men's BOWLING SHOES SIZE 10 1/2	$81.01	Dexter Charlotte Bowling Shoes. Womens Size 8.5	$25.95
DEXTER SST 5 LX Men's BOWLING SHOES SIZE 9 1/2	$80.00	LINDS CLASSIC SE WOMENS BOWLING SHOES SIZE 9 RH NR	$25.49
Dexter Mens Bowling Shoes SST6 Burgandy RH 10.5	$79.05	linds mens bowling shoes	$25.00
DEXTER SST 6 MENS BOWLING SHOES SIZE 15 RIGHT HAND NR	$78.59	Mens Dexter Bowling Shoes TURBO Black 13.0	$24.95
DEXTER SST 5 LX Men's BOWLING SHOES SIZE 8 1/2	$77.95	Mens Dexter Bowling Shoes TURBO Black 9.5	$24.95
LINDS SPECIAL EDITION MENS BOWLING SHOES SIZE 10 1/2 RH	$76.95	Dexter SST 4 blue/tan Bowling Shoes Mens sz 7 RH	$24.85
Dexter BOWLING Shoes *NEW* SST 5 Comfort Mens SIZE 8	$72.01	Dexter Daytona Bowling Shoes. Mens Size 9.5	$23.99
Dexter Mens Bowling Shoes SST6 Burgandy RH 10.0	$71.05	DEXTER CHARLOTTE BOWLING SHOES WOMENS SIZE 7.5	$23.95
Dexter Mens Bowling Shoes SST6 Burgandy RH 11.0	$69.09	Dexter SST 5 Black/Gold Bowling Shoes Mens Size 7.5	$23.65

Bowling ▶ Balls

The average sales price in this subcategory is $41.13.

	HIGH		AVG
Old antique wood bowling ball two holes estate	$461.00	BRUNSWICK BLAZING INFERNO Bowling Ball 16 lb LAST LOT	$43.05
16 LB SKULL BALL, by EBONITE, UNDRILLED, NIB	$255.00	HAMMER THE BIG DEAL X OUT Bowling Ball 16 lb NIB	$43.00
BRAND NEW! LANE #1 BLACK CHERRY BOMB BUZZSAW BALL	$170.00	New 16 lb 0 oz TRACK ANIMAL UNTAMED 1st Quality	$42.95
Track ANIMALUNTAMED 1st qual. 16# one case (4 balls)	$160.00	EBONITE XXCEL X OUT Bowling Ball 16 lb NIB	$42.05
* LANE #1 - URANIUM SOLID BUZZSAW * *	$159.00	NIB! 16lb. Storm ERASER Particle Bowling Ball 4-5" pin	$42.00
BRAND NEW! LANE #1 BLACK CHERRY BOMB BUZZSAW	$152.50	Two almost new Brunswick balls 16 pounds	$42.00
BRAND NEW! LANE #1 SUPER CARBIDE BOMB BUZZSAW	$149.50	16LB EBONITE PRIME TIME PEARL BOWLING BALL NO RESERVE	$42.00
BRAND NEW! LANE #1 SUPER CARBIDE BOMB BUZZSAW	$147.50	AMF BOOGIE 7 LB KIDS BOWLING BALL W/BAG(L@@K)	$41.05
2 BALL SET COMET RUBBER DUCKPIN BALLS-PURPLE/WHITE	$141.08	16LB TRACK ANIMAL UNTAMED BOWLING BALL NO RESERVE	$41.01
1960 Brunswick Crown Jewel undrilled bowling ball 15 #	$135.49	STORM ERASER PARTICLE PEARL BRAND NEW IN BOX 16 LB!	$41.00
2 BALL SET COMET RUBBER DUCKPIN BALLS-BLUE/PURPLE	$128.34	11LB EBONITE PRIME TIME SANDED BOWLING BALL NO RESERVE	$41.00
2 BALL SET COMET RUBBER DUCKPIN BALLS-WHITE/GREEN	$127.50	HAMMER HIGH REV X OUT Bowling Ball 16 lb NIB	$41.00
16lbs Columbia NIB Blue Pearl Pulse undrilled	$127.50	[2 of these sold for $41.00 each]	
YEAH BABY!!! Legends Lane Masters 15 # NIB bowling ball	$122.00	BRUNSWICK OVERSEAS RELEASE RED ALERT 300 16 lb NIB RARE	$41.00
NIB ULTIMATE INFERNO BRUNSWICK	$122.00	16LB EBONITE PRIME TIME PEARL BOWLING BALL NO RESERVE	$41.00
BOWLING BALL 16LB NEW		16lb RotoGrip SPARE TIRE Bowling Ball REALLY NEAT	$41.00

Boxing ▶ Apparel

The average sales price in this subcategory is $19.89.

	HIGH		AVG
Muhammad Ali Fossil Limited Ed. Watch	$175.50	New 2005 TWINS Muay Thai Boxing Bow Gold Flame XL Shorts	$22.99
SHOWTIME CHAMPIONSHIP BOXING TV CREW JACKET RARE NICE!	$78.00	TWINS SPECIAL Muay Thai Boxing Black Buakaw XL Shorts	$22.99
New Everlast Men's White Satin Boxing Robe 3/4 Length	$51.00	Rare HERO Muay Thai Kick Boxing Asian Dragon XL Shorts	$22.99
Mens Adidas Brown XOB-04 Boxing Shoes Boots US 10	$46.00	EVERLAST BOXING SHORTS / TRUNKS RED W/WHITE STRIPE MED.	$20.49
EVERLAST BOXING SHORTS TRUNKS VINTAGE OLD W/ BOX BRONX	$42.50	Jock's Used Puerto Rican Flag Everlast Boxing Trunks	$19.99
Jock's Used Gold/Black Everlast Boxing Trunks Shorts	$39.99	EVERLAST BOXING BX SHOES BOOTS GLOVES ROBE NEW MENS 8.5	$19.49
Jock's Used Silver/Black Everlast Boxing Trunks Shorts	$39.99	On Sale! HERO Muay Thai Boxing Ancher Skull L Shorts	$15.99
Jock's Used Blue/White Everlast Boxing Trunks Shorts	$39.99	Original Muay Thai Boran Kick Boxing Traditional Shorts	$15.99
Everlast Boxing Jacket Large 48" Nice	$39.95	Original Muay Thai Boran Boxing Traditional Grey Shorts	$15.99
Jack Dempsey EVERLAST Boxing Jacket GOLD X-Large XL	$39.00	Promotion 3 Pairs Muay Thai Kick Boxing Ankle Guards(M)	$12.99

Boxing ▶ Gloves

The average sales price in this subcategory is $18.11.

	HIGH		AVG
GENE TUNNEY Vintage AG SPALDING Boxing Gloves NR!	$355.00	Zeepk QUALITY BOXING GLOVES size 14 OZ- 3002	$19.99
2 Pairs G&S Boxing Gloves_NR	$103.51	Zeepk QUALITY BOXING GLOVES size 12 OZ- B	$19.99
BOXING GLOVES 10 PAIR , BY RINGSIDE CONTENDER PRO 14 OZ	$99.00	Zeepk QUALITY BOXING GLOVES size 10 OZ- 3002	$19.99
EVERLAST BOXING GLOVES - CUSTOM MADE 8 OZ (CLETO REYES)	$84.00	2 PAIR EVERLAST BOXING BOXER GLOVES GLOVE #14	$19.07
GRANT 16 oz. Pro training gloves, new, special colors	$76.00	Zeepk BOXING GLOVES Top qality Gloves zw3005	$18.99
FLORES 10 oz. xxl. size fight gloves, new, red	$73.00	Vintage lot of 2 old pair of Everlast boxing gloves	$18.60
Ladies Designer PINK LEATHER Boxing Gloves COMBO!	$69.00	New TKO 16 oz/ounce All Purpose Leather Boxing Gloves	$18.54
[4 of these sold in a multiple item ("Dutch") auction for $17.25 each]		EVERLAST BOXING TRAINING BALL?! NEW!	$18.05
NEW Everlast 10-oz. Pro Fight / Boxing Gloves - Blue	$64.99	TITLE BOXING GLOVES, SZ 16, BLACK, EXCELLENT CONDITION!	$17.55
Boxing Gloves Vintage Golden Gloves Spalding	$62.00	Century Sparring/Fighting 3/4 Finger Gloves	$17.50
MUHAMMED ALI SIGNED EVERLAST BOXING GLOVE AUTOGRAPH RED	$61.00	Ringside super bag gloves	$17.50
4 PAIR VINTAGE BOXING GLOVES RAWLINGS WILSON	$56.00	New TKO 16 oz/ounce All Purpose Leather Boxing Gloves	$17.50
Ladies Designer ZEBRA Leather Boxing Gloves Free ship	$55.00	PRO TRAINING GLOVES KICKBOXING BOXING MARTIAL ARTS BLK	$16.99
Pride UFC Black SPAR MMA GLOVES 10oz Pad Free ship	$55.00	ALL Purpose BOXING Gloves and Handwraps Box Supplies	$16.50
Boxing: 16 oz Training Gloves by Ringside	$51.01	PRO TRAINING GLOVES KICKBOXING	$16.49
Mexican made pro 16oz. training gloves, new, red	$51.00	BOXING MARTIAL ARTS BLK	

Boxing ▶ Protection Gear

The average sales price in this subcategory is $16.52.

	HIGH		AVG
NEW! EVERLAST Boxing Gloves, Groin Belt and Headgear!!	$76.00	2 PAIR 16OZ BOXING GLOVES 2 HEADGEAR BRAND NEW SET GIFT	$18.99
Jock's Used Grant Pro Boxing Headguard Headgear	$52.00	PAIR COACHES GLOVES FOCUS MITTS BOXING BRAND NEW THICK	$17.99
Title Boxing Head Gear sparring kick boxing protecting	$43.50	VINTAGE U.S. ARMY WILSON BOXING HEADGEAR MUST SEE! 30'S	$17.51
EVERLAST Boxing Gloves and Headgear!! NEVER USED	$37.76	PRO FORCE BOXING HEAD GEAR PROTECTOR ADULT MED.	$17.50
2 FINGERLESS BOXING GLOVES - HEAVY CANVAS PUNCHING BAG	$29.99	PAIR COACHES GLOVES FOCUS MITTS BOXING BRAND NEW THICK	$15.99
2 PAIR 16OZ BOXING GLOVES 2 HEADGEAR BRAND NEW SET GIFT	$24.99	Top Contender groing protector, Boxing cup.	$15.50
Flextuff Full Face Boxing Martial Arts Head Guard (M)	$24.00	Zeepk Groin Protector Heavy Duty Pu Construction	$13.99
Flextuff Full Face Boxing Martial Arts Head Guard (L)	$24.00	BLACK AND RED 2 BOXING HEAD GEAR headgear SET	$13.55
[2 of these sold for $24.00 each]		[2 of these sold for $13.55 each]	
TWO EVERLAST HEAD GUARD MODEL 4022 LIKE BRAND NEW	$23.50	BLACK AND RED 2 BOXING HEAD GEAR headgear SET	$13.25

Camping, Hiking, Backpacking ▶ Backpacks

The average sales price in this subcategory is $29.66.

	HIGH		AVG
BRAND NEW~BIANCHI SPEAR UM21 BACKPACK SYSTEM~	$299.00	Camp Trails External Frame Backpacks (Lot of 5)	$30.00
[2 of these sold for $299.00 each]		Patagonia BackPack	$30.00

llama packsaddle	$202.50	HIKING CAMPING BACKPACK 5400ci Internal Frame BLK~	$29.99
VINTAGE WOVEN SPLINT PACK BASKET NICE PATINA	$192.50	Extra Large Backpack Camping 4800 Cu In BLACK BIG	$29.99
1930's Woven Splint Pack Basket ~ Back Pack	$177.50	HIKING CAMPING BACKPACK 5400ci Internal Frame BLK~	$29.99
THE NORTH FACE DUFFLE BAG *BRAND NEW W/ TAGS*	$162.50	NWT Jansport Student Backpack- TRIBAL-TM48008 Black	$29.95
Rucksack Backpack Pack ; Berghaus cyclops vulcan II	$155.00	BLACK Extra Large Backpack Camping 4800 Cu In BIG	$29.00
NEW Kelty KIDS Carrier Pathfinder	$147.50	Batch Lot 3 Three US Military Army Alice Packs Med. B	$29.00
Badlands XL Split Pack Backpack Hunting Gear NWT!!!	$140.10	BACKPACK WHOLESALE LOTOF4 COMPAR	$29.00
Blackhawk RAPTOR X1 Back Pack	$124.27	JANSPORT BACK PACK	
** PORTABLE PROPANE HOT SHOWER GIFT **	$119.90	USPS Cycling Hydration Backpack bag	$27.72
[2 of these sold in a multiple item ("Dutch") auction for $59.95 each]		large Team bladder	
Green CamelBak BFM Backpack W/ Hydration System!	$117.50	NEW 28F(-2C) SLEEPING BAG. 20% OFF	$27.00
Pop-Up Superlight Aluminum EZ set UP Canopy 17 lbs	$106.50	The North Face JESTER Back Pack BackPack BRAND NEW!!!	$26.49
Kelty Kids Backcountry backpack, Child carrier	$100.55	Black Eagle Creek Hiking Backpack NR	$26.01
Pop-Up Superlight Aluminum EZ set UP Canopy 17 lbs	$99.00	PacSafe duffle bag and backpack locking cable mesh	$26.00
Gregory Advent Pro Adventure Race Backpack Pack New!!!	$98.95		

Camping, Hiking, Backpacking ▶ Canteens, Coolers

The average sales price in this subcategory is $19.01.

	HIGH		AVG
Approximately 20 Water Jugs	$305.00	One Very cool Gatorade cooler with stand	$15.50
Dr Pepper Ice Chest Cooler	$227.50	NIP Misty Mate Cool Blast Air Cooler NEW	$15.50
COCA COLA COOLBOX ICE CHEST	$207.50	[2 of these sold for $15.50 each]	
COOLER &,AM/FM/CD STEREO		16 oz Misty Mate Pump Portable Personal Air Cooler	$15.50
Coleman Steel 50th Anniversary Cooler NEW NO RESERVE	$122.50	HOOTERS KOOZIES WHOLESALE LOTS 12 FOR 10.99	$15.39
NEW 2005 MSR WaterWorks EX Water Filter FREE SHIPPING!	$102.50	Stanley Stainless Steel Vacuum Thermos 24oz (NIB) (NEW)	$15.00
Misty Mate 16oz. Pump - 2 Pack -COOL BLAST- BLACK	$101.98	NEW *IGLOO* 5-Gallon Beverage Cooler with Cup Dispenser	$15.00
[2 of these sold in a multiple item ("Dutch") auction for $50.99 each]		VINTAGE RARE GAMBLES HIAWATHA JUG MINT!	$15.00
NIB Coleman 150 Qt Marine Cooler Holds 9.3 Cases + Ice	$99.99	WASTE MANAGEMENT INSULATED COOLER	$15.00
NIB Coleman 150 Qt Marine Cooler Holds 9.3 Cases + Ice	$95.00	[2 of these sold in a multiple item ("Dutch") auction for $7.50 each]	
COLEMAN 54 Quart Steel Belted Cooler NIB	$95.00	BUBBA KEG 128 oz Stainless Steel & Plastic COOLER	$15.00
1970s Matching COLEMAN COOLER & WATER JUG	$93.88	[2 of these sold in a multiple-item ("Dutch") auction for $7.50 each]	
Igloo Koolmate 56 Dual Electric Cooler for Car or Home	$91.00	VINTAGE COLEMAN COOLER JUG - RED - 2 GALLON/ WITH BOX	$14.99
VINTAGE VIKING PICNIC STAINLESS STEEL DRINK COOLER	$86.00	NEW! Igloo MobileMate 9 Elite Portable Electric Cooler	$14.95
Camelbak / Camelback Transalp Hydration Backpack 100oz	$81.00	NIP Misty Mate Cool Blast Air Cooler NEW	$14.76
Igloo Koolmate Electric 40 Quart Cooler/Warmer Car Home	$81.00	NEW NALGENE CXC BIG BORE BLADDER 1.75 LITER	$14.75
NEW IN BOX! MSR MIOX PURIFIER *	$79.57	Coleman Road Trip 16 Qt.Powerchill Cooler (NIB)	$14.50
AND REPLACEMENT TEST KIT		NEW WATERPROOF COOLER BAG WITH RADIO NIB	$14.25

Camping, Hiking, Backpacking ▶ Cookware, Stoves

The average sales price in this subcategory is $30.65.

	HIGH		AVG
LARGE BBQ/SMOKER/GRILL MOUNTED ON TRAILER	$399.99	Vintage Coleman 1943 WWII Military 2 Burner Camp Stove	$31.00
NEW PORTABLE ICE MAKER MACHINE WET BAR RV'S BOAT PARTY	$231.11	1 CASE 12 MEALS MRE MEALS READY TO EAT CASE A 2005	$31.00
NIB Thermos Fire & Ice Grill 2 Go	$202.50	meal, ready to eat (mre) box 12 pack	$31.00
COLEMAN ROADTRIP PORTABLE PROPANE GRILL - BRAND NEW	$152.50	Vintage BURMOS Stoves & Lamp Catalog 23 Pages 12 Models	$31.00
NIB Coleman Camp Kitchen Folding Table w/sink	$149.99	favorite mres hand picked by our troops combat tested	$31.00
[3 of these sold for $149.99 each]		Rocky Mountain Volcano cook stove	$31.00
COLEMAN HOT WATER ON DEMAND NEW W/Case,Spray&H2O Holder	$147.50	MRE UNOPENED IN ORIGINAL SEALED	$30.99
COLEMAN HOT WATER ON DEMAND NEW W/Case,Spray&H2O Holder	$145.00	CASE MENU A 05/07	
Freeze Dried Cottage Cheese 300 Portions	$140.00	NIB Coleman Roadtrip Road Trip Wheeled Carry Case Bag	$30.99
Freeze Dried Chicken Chunks 75 lb. Equiv.	$140.00	meal, ready to eat (mre) box 12 pack	$30.01
Non-Collapsible Mountaineer Wood Camp Stove wall tents	$137.50	MSR Pocket Rocket Stove BRAND NEW	$30.00
Collapsible Mountaineer Wood Camp Stove Wall Tents	$125.50	1 CASE 12 MEALS MRE MEALS READY TO EAT CASE A 1-12	$29.99
12" Pyramid Cooking System Smoker Oven Chicken Roaster	$125.00	1 CASE 12 MEALS MRE MEALS READY TO EAT CASE B 13-24	$29.99
3 Cs of MREs MRE Disaster Preparedness, Survival food	$113.50	NIB Coleman Roadtrip Road Trip Wheeled Carry Case Bag	$29.99
3 BOXES MRE MEAL READY TO EAT RATIONS CASE B	$112.50	1 CASE 12 MEALS MRE MEALS READY TO EAT CASE B 2005	$29.99
Camp Chef Tahoe Pro Triple Burner Camp Stove	$110.00	NIB Coleman Roadtrip Road Trip Wheeled Carry Case Bag	$29.99

Camping, Hiking, Backpacking ▶ Sleeping Gear

The average sales price in this subcategory is $28.81.

	HIGH		AVG
NEW SPECIAL FORCES WIGGYS BLACK BIVY TENT NEWEST YET	$231.80	2 BLUE THERM-A-REST SLEEPING PADS 1 FULL SIZE 1 3/4	$30.00
BRAND NEW!! OR OUTDOOR RESEARCH	$222.50	Girls Pink GAP Camoflauge -Camo Sleeping Bag NWT	$29.99
ADVANCED BIVY SACK 2005		Dutch Army Sleeping Bag Used with GORE-TEX Cover	$29.99
BRAND NEW!! OR OUTDOOR RESEARCH ADVANCED BIVY SACK 2005	$202.50	Raised Inflatable Air Bed Mattress Twin Airbed w/ pump	$29.99
new miltary goretex modular sleeping bag system 4piece	$199.00	[6 of these sold for $29.99 each]	
new militay modular gortex sleeping bag system 4 piece	$199.00	Therm-a-Rest Z-Lite Backpacking Mattress / Pad - NEW!	$29.75
Outdoor Research OR Delux Bivy Sack NEW NR!	$185.00	Coleman Double High Air Mattress With Electric Pump	$29.00
outdoor research advanced bivy sack	$155.00	COLEMAN 12 VOLT AIR PUMP WITH	$28.50
AERO PILLOWTOP BED AIR MATTRESS ELECTRIC AIR PUMP QUEEN	$142.50	VALVE ADAPTERS BRAND NEW	
NEW MILITARY SLEEPING BAG, BIVY COVER, AND STUFF SACK	$141.28	AEROBED PUMP + Charger Adaptor AERO AIRBED LNW	$28.50
Therm-a-rest dream time new thermarest	$123.50	Aero Sports Minute Bed Sport AirBed Air Mattress	$28.01
PAIR of ALPINE PAK Backpacker SLEEPING BAGS (Two Bags)	$118.99	Therm-a-Rest Z-Lite Backpacking Mattress / Pad - NEW!	$28.00
Hennessy Hammock EXPLORER ULTRALITE or DELUXE New $199	$118.07	Therm A Rest Matress Pad	$27.89
NORTHFACE NYLON DOWN Blanket	$118.00	Thermarest 3/4 Camping Mattress ** Explorer ** self inf	$27.88
AeroBed Deluxe QUEEN mattress bed w/recessed pump NEW	$117.50	WOOL Hudson-Bay-Type TRADE BLANKET Reenactor Camp	$27.26
Luxury Edition Long Therm-a-Rest Pad	$107.50	Coleman Quick Bed & pump NEW never used!	$27.00
[2 of these sold for $107.50 each]		COLEMAN EXPONENT Big Basin 20? Sleeping Bag NEW	$27.00

Camping, Hiking, Backpacking ▶ Tents, Canopies

The average sales price in this subcategory is $69.45.

	HIGH		AVG
Cabela's Alaskan Guide 8-Man Tent + Deluxe Vestibule	$455.00	Eddie Bauer 3-Room 8 Person Family Dome Tent NEW	$70.00
GP Army Tent Elk & Deer Hunting or Military Tent	$360.00	New Eddie Bauer 2-Room 6 - 7 person Family Dome Tent	$69.99
Eureka Tents Titan - Brand New In Package	$327.00	TRIPOD SHELTER CAMP BEACH SHADE PARK FAMILY CABANA NIB	$69.99
Eureka Kahuna-6 PERSON, 3 Season Tent-NEW 04 Model	$325.00	COLUMBIA CAMPING TENT CABIN 10 x 10 x 78	$69.99
Eureka "Kahuna" Tent - NEW!!!	$306.95	Coleman 14 x 14 Family Dome Tent NIB	$69.99
KELTY MANTRA 6 TENT-BRAND NEW TENTS!!! NR!!!	$297.50	SWISSGEAR TENT Alpine Lodge 6ft Centr 17'x13' SLEEPS 7	$69.98
KELTY MANTRA 6 TENT-BRAND NEW TENTS!!! NR!!!	$290.00	Swiss Gear Tents..Alpine Lodge 3 Room Dome Tent	$69.81
Columbia Gardner Peak 2 Room Dual Composite Dome Tent	$280.99	EDDIE BAUER 3 ROOM / 8 PERSON SPORT DOME TENT NEWINBOX!	$69.50
REI CAMP 6 - 6PERSON TENT	$267.50	Columbia Bugaboo Dome Tent-Camping Tent-4-5 person Nice	$69.01
ECWT ECWS USMC TENT 5+ 4 SEASON	$250.00	*NEW* OZARK TRAIL 12x10FT 2-ROOM DOME TENT SLEEPS 5-6	$68.01
COST MILITARY $1500		COLUMBIA CAMPING TENT CABIN 10 x 10 x 78	$68.00
Sierra Design Bedouin 6 - Brand New In Package	$233.00	Swiss Gear 13 x 17 in. Dome Tent #74115	$66.00
$1500.00 Soldier Crew Tent 10X10 Military army hunting	$225.00	Brand New 2005 5-6 Person Hex Dome Tent w/GoDry	$66.00
Eddie Bauer 10 Man Person 4 Room Family Dome Tent-NEW	$189.99	20 X 10 NORTHEAST OUTFITTERS 3 ROOM TENT "EAGLES PEAK 8	$66.00
Eureka Headquarters Luxury Family Tent	$185.07	6 Man PolarShield Camping 3 Room Cabin Tent	$66.00
GRAND SAFARI TENT 12 Persn Huge Party Canopy FAMILY NEW	$182.50	Hillary Deerlodge 4 Room Family Dome Tent Sleeps 8	$66.00

Canoes, Kayaks, Rafts ▶ Canoes

The average sales price in this subcategory is $267.38.

	HIGH		AVG
8 CANOES AND HEAVY DUTY 8 CANOE TRAILER BUSINESS	$3,200.00	Coleman 17ft canoe with paddles	$303.00
Vintage Antique 1939 16' Otca Old Town Canoe	$1,800.00	Old Town Guide 147	$295.00
20' GRAND LAKER late 60's handmade cedar "guides" canoe	$1,600.00	SEVYLOR INFLATABLE CANOE~KAYAK BOAT~BOY SCOUT DESIGN	$289.99
16' River Canoe - dates back to 1880 to 1900	$1,300.00	[2 of these sold for $289.99 each]	
NEW 16.6 ALGONQUIN KEVLAR PROSPECTOR CANOE	$1,300.00	Pelican Colorado 15'5" RAM-X Canoe	$286.52
We no nah Spirit II Canoe	$1,240.00	Used 17' Grumman Aluminum Canoe	$286.00
NEW 16.6' KEVLAR ALGONQUIN PROSPECTOR CANOE	$1,225.00	Wilderness Systems Pamlico 100 Kayak	$280.00
Mad River Express Borealis Kevlar Canoe IQ Gunwhales	$1,225.00	SEVYLOR INFLATABLE CANOE~KAYAK BOAT~BOY SCOUT DESIGN	$269.00
Clear See-Through Kayak great for FISHING free shipping	$1,100.00	Pelican DLX Explorer Canoe 15.5 feet RAMX hull~NEW	$256.00
14' Penn Yan Wooden Canoe	$1,027.00	16 foot pelican canoe, hardly been used	$255.00
Wenonah Spirit II Kevlar Canoe	$1,001.00	12FT OLD TOWN CANOE	$255.00
NEW 15ft KEVLAR PROSPECTOR CANOE	$1,000.00	Old Town Discovery Canoe 12 Feet	$255.00
Mad River Malecite Kevlar Canoe - WOW ! 51 lbs	$999.00	Coleman RAM-X 16' Scanoe	$255.00
Pasquinel 14' Canadian Stripper RARE Wood Canoe NR	$952.98	Used Pelican Explorer Deluxe 15 Foot Canoe No Reserve!	$255.00
NEW 14 FOOT KEVLAR PROSPECTOR CANOE	$900.00	16' Grumman Aluminum Canoe	$255.00
		17' Coleman Canoe (Red) 3 Person Canoe	$251.50

Canoes, Kayaks, Rafts ▶ Inflatable Canoes, Kayaks

The average sales price in this subcategory is $90.80.

	HIGH		AVG
5 Person Inflatable Boat - Zodiac Zoom 340S + Acc	$1,025.00	2 Person Self Bailing Inflatable Kayak Stearns	$202.51
Porta-Bote 12' Folding Portable Boat Duck Hunting Fish	$985.00	Innova "Junior" inflatable Kayak	$199.00
Aire Linx 1 one man inflatable whitewater kayak	$510.00	WATER SKEETER PERSONAL PONTOON WATERCRAFT RAFT BOAT	$172.50
Inflatable kayak, Hanauma, canoe, raft, ocean, NEW!!!	$425.00	Personal Fly Fishing Inflatable Pontoon Boat CIMARRON	$170.00
Used 8ft folded porta-bote,	$415.00	6.2 Feet Inflatable Kayak , Brand New !	$159.00
Aire Tomcat Solo	$399.00	(2) Used Sevylor Tahiti K79 inflatable Kayaks	$112.50
AIRE TOMCAT SOLO KAYAK "NEW"	$395.00	SEVYLOR INFLATABLE CANOE KAYAK K- 79 TAHITI WHITEWATER	$111.16
SEVYLOR RIVER SVX200 INFLATABLE	$380.00	Sevylor Fish Hunter 360 Inflatable Fishing Boat + Extra	$100.00
KAYAK - BOAT CANOE RAFT		New 11' Challenger K2 Kayak 2 Person Inflatable Kayak	$89.99
Dave Scadden Pontoon boat	$350.00	NEW Voyager 500 Boat 4-Person inflatable fishing fish	$89.01
Stearns self bailing inflatable kayak	$335.00	New 11' Challenger K2 Kayak 2 Person Inflatable Kayak	$79.99
Perception Whiplash - Low Reserve	$335.00	SEVYLOR K79 RANGER KAYAK~CANOE~INFLATABLE~ BOAT	$76.00
Sevylor SVX100 XK1 White Water Inflatable Kayak New	$330.00	NEW K1 Inflatable Deluxe Touring Kayak Set sets kayaks	$64.95
Like NEW Sea Eagle SE-9 Fisherman Dream and + (2005)	$300.01	[2 of these sold for $64.95 each]	
Sevylor SVX100 XK1 White Water Inflatable Kayak	$300.00	NEW INTEX INFLATABLE BOAT RIVER RAFT SEAHAWK 500	$61.00
Advanced Elements Inflatable Kayak	$296.00	Intex K2 Inflatable Kayak - Oars & Pump Included!	$60.95

Canoes, Kayaks, Rafts ▶ Kayaks

The average sales price in this subcategory is $253.71.

	HIGH		AVG
Klepper Expedition II Folding Kayak	$3,053.00	15' RPM Special Marathon Racing Kayak & Paddle	$258.29
QCC 500XL 16' EXPEDITION SEA TOURING KAYAK KEVLAR	$1,475.00	Feelfree Move Single Seat SOT Sit On Top Kayak NEW	$256.00
Brand New Kayak Perception Carolina 14.5 Airalite	$1,300.00	Perception Corsica S Whitewater Kayak Canoe Customized	$255.00
PADDLEYAK SEA KAYAK	$1,250.00	KAYAK WHITEWATER PERCEPTION CORSICA S COOL !!!!!!!!!!!!	$255.00
Kayak eclipse sealion 17 foot ocean going, stable& fast	$1,250.00	TRINITY BAY "MALLARD" RECREATIONAL FISHING KAYAK	$255.00
Folbot 2004 Aleut-SE Kayak plus extras –BIN!!	$1,200.00	Feelfree Dolphin Loma I Single Seat Sit In Kayak NEW	$255.00
Klepper Aerius Folding Kayak 2 Man 17 foot	$1,200.00	Feelfree Move Single Seat SOT Sit On Top Kayak NEW	$255.00
23' SINGLE FIBERGLASS ROWING SHELL	$1,159.00	Feelfree Dolphin Loma I Single Seat Sit In Kayak NEW	$255.00
HOBIE MIRAGE OUTBACK SUV KAYAK	$1,150.00	Canoe 16' Aluminum	$249.00
Clear See-Through Kayak great for FISHING free shipping	$1,100.00	Dagger Ego Whitewater Kayak NO RESERVE!!!!!	$247.52
Tempest 170 Wilderness System kayak canoe Wavesport	$1,081.00	Bell CJ solo kevlar canoe AND 3 pc. spray skirt / cover	$247.50
Folbot Aleut EXP Folding Kayak With Accessories	$1,030.00	Feelfree Dolphin Loma I Single Seat Sit In Kayak NEW	$237.50
Ocean Kayak, SOT, 2 person, complete set-up	$1,000.00	Wave Sport Kinetic	$235.00
PokeBoat (standard) Inwater 2 times Great Fishing boat	$980.00	Feelfree Dolphin Loma I Single Seat Sit In Kayak NEW	$232.50
Necky Kayak Elaho HV	$974.35	PROLINE PERCEPTION PIROUETTE KAYAK & PADDLE	$227.52

Canoes, Kayaks, Rafts ▶ Paddles

The average sales price in this subcategory is $69.18.

	HIGH		AVG
2 person Paddlewheeler Paddle boat	$665.01	Harmony Sea Passage 210cm NWT Kayak Paddle 60% off	$79.77
K&L PADDLE BOAT 5 PERSON. TWO MONTHS OLD !!	$354.00	Kayak Paddles - 2 pair - 230cm (96 in)	$76.32
Wildwood, Peter Puddicombe, 52" Bent Shaft Canoe Paddle	$270.65	Harmony Sea Passage 210cm NWT Kayak Paddle 60% off	$76.00
PELICAN DECKER 5 PERSON PEDDLE PADAL BOAT *CANOPY* LQQK	$256.99	New Sevylor 90 inch Fiberglass Lightweight Kayak Paddle	$75.99
Lendal Carbon Archipelago 220 Kayak Paddle	$238.25	Werner Kayak paddle	$72.89
Werner Little Dipper Carbon Paddle 210cm	$202.50	Aqua Bound Shred Whitewater Kayak Paddle 194cm	$71.55
VINTAGE HAWAIIAN CANOE OUTRIGGER	$202.50	WERNER SKAGIT FIBERGLASS KAYAK PADDLE PADDLES 2 PIECE	$70.99
STEERSMAN KOA PADDLE		Harmony Northwest Passage 230cm NWT Kayak Paddle	$70.00
Werner Sherpa 194cm Bent Shaft Small Shaft	$182.76	[2 of these sold in a multiple item ("Dutch") auction for $35.00 each]	
AT2 E Bent Shaft Kayak Paddle, Awesome!	$178.00	Harmony Rapid Passage 194cm NWT Kayak Paddle $140	$69.98
Epic 'Signature Series' Carbon Fiber Sea Kayak Paddle	$174.99	Werner Rec Tour Paddle 220 cm R-60degrees yellow blades	$68.00
Werner Little Dipper 220cm small diameter shaft	$162.50	Harmony Sea Passage 240cm NWT Kayak Paddle 60% off	$67.66
NEW! Speedwing S-2000 2 piece kayak wing paddle	$162.00	8'6" Carlisle Oars (set of 2)	$67.66
AT4 Play Paddle, Whitewater, Advanced Technology, NEW	$160.47	Harmony Rapid Passage 194cm NWT Kayak Paddle 4pc	$62.99
werner kayak paddle carbon	$160.00	VINTAGE ABERCROMBIE & FITCH CANOE PADDLE 5'-TED BREA	$61.00
Wildwood, Peter Puddicombe, 49" Bent Shaft Canoe Paddle	$158.07	Seven2 ISO Touring Kayak Paddle 220cm Small Grips ()	$60.99

Cycling ▶ Apparel

The average sales price in this subcategory is $13.76.

	HIGH		AVG
RARE DESCENTE SEIRYU OLYMPIC AERO	$304.00	vd-a- CAMPAGNOLO Cycling Cap / Hat – GRAY —— NEW	$14.00
SKINSUIT XL NEW NWT		(10) NIKE YOUTH Lance Armstrong LiveSTRONG BRACELETS	$13.99
rubberized cycling skinsuit rubber skin suit time trial	$132.50	[5 of these sold for $13.99 each]	
Sidi Cycling Shoes Genius 5 size 44	$124.49	HALO Headband Sweatband IT WORKS! bike bicycle cycling	$13.60
NWT Nike 10/2 Cycling Vest	$112.50	NWT Mens PEARL IZUMI Attack Shorts black sz XS	$13.49
Gary Fisher Team Mountain Bike Duffle Bag !!	$105.49	LANCE ARMSTRONG USPS TOUR DE FRANCE BIKE PIN (7X WIN?)	$13.25
Swiss National team skinsuit small brand new with tags	$104.49	Cycling Kids Youth Tinley Lycra Spandex Bike Shorts S	$13.04
Team Giant-Pearl Izumi SS Skin Suit Official Kit - NWT-	$102.50	Sugoi Jr. Cascade Short Size XL fits Youth 11/12 NR NWT	$12.56
Bailey Works Courier Bag	$96.00	SKIN SUIT by EXCELLENCE Neon Yellow "NICE" Size Small?	$12.50
NIKE USPS Armstrong Cycling Skin Suit Bib Shorts NWT M	$96.00	KEIDO SPECIALIZED Cycling Skin Suit Bib Shorts Small 2	$12.50
NWT Nike 10/2 Cycling Jersey	$88.00	CINELLI WHITE CYCLE TEE JERSEY WITH POCKETS XL CYCLE-T	$11.95
Louis Garneau Quark Pro Cycling Team LS Skinsuit Sz M	$85.00	3 Rare HOOK'EM HORNS Texas Longhorns Wrist Band UT	$11.90
Verge Used Red Padded Cycling Skinsuit Mn Euro 5 US L	$82.89	Sugoi Jr. Cascade Short Size S fits Youth 5/6 NR NWT	$11.29
Bergamo-Ritchey Short Sleeve Skin Suit	$80.00	vm-a- CAMPAGNOLO Belt Buckle Round Pewter 1980 — NEW	$11.00
NEW RLX Ralph Lauren Long Sleeve Skinsuit Med. - NR	$79.99	Sugoi Jr. Cascade Short Size XS fits Youth 3/4 NR NWT	$10.79
Lance Armstrong 10//2 Polo Shirt GRAY Large TdF NWT!	$75.00	RARE 5X LANCE ARMSTRONG USPS TOUR DE FRANCE BIKE PIN	$10.50

Cycling ▶ Helmets and Protection

The average sales price in this subcategory is $38.33.

	HIGH		AVG
2005 Troy Lee Designs D2 Bomber Downhill Helmet M/L	$185.00	Helmet Answer Adult Small	$40.00
Rossi AGV Motorcycle Helmet	$178.01	Dot Adult ATV MX Dirtbike Motorcyle Helmet New/Large	$39.99
2006 GIRO ATMOS HELMET - LANCE / DISCOVERY TEAM - M	$175.01	BMX/Motorcross FLY helmet with face shield and visor	$39.99
ARAI MOTOCROSS HELMET	$175.00	2003 Giro Helmet Animas Mtn Bike Cycle Sm Wht NIB $100	$39.99
SUPER RARE VINTAGE 1966 BUCO HELMET - MUST SEE!!!	$174.00	Bell Helmet Influx Black M MTB Reg $60 Bid Now Save $$$	$39.78
Giro Atmos Discovery Team Model Medium	$172.50	BELL Influx Med Mt .Bike helmet NEW in box!	$39.00
Rare Giro Atmos Helmet, Discovery Team, LARGE *NR*	$172.50	FLY Motocross Dirt Bike Racing Chest Protector Red NR	$39.00
NEW LG TEAM DISCOVERY GIRO ATMOS	$169.50	Bell Ghisallo Helmet Medium Red / Silver	$38.00
HELMET NIB W/ POD!!!		Six Six One full face down hill Helmet, downhill 661	$37.50
LAS 2005 Crono TT Time Trial Aero RS	$165.00	Troy Lee Designs BMX/Motocross Pants Size 32 MINT NR	$36.00
2006 GIRO ATMOS HELMET - LANCE / DISCOVERY TEAM - M	$164.99	Bell Full Face X-games helmet Fox comp elbow knee guard	$36.00
Giro Atmos Helmet Red/Blue Ltd. Edition Size Med NIB	$160.50	SIXSIXONE Chest Protector	$36.00
Dainese Shuttle Pro, downhill, dh, armor, Intense, Foes	$158.61	03 Bell Helmet X-Ray Mtn Bike Cycle Sm White NIB $100	$36.00
Troy Lee Designs Composite Flame Helmet BMX NR	$157.50	[2 of these sold in a multiple item ("Dutch") auction for $18.00 each]	
GIRO ATMOS HELMET BRAND NEW	$157.50	New Size Junior Small Kuckle Bone Full Face Helmet...	$36.00
MATTE BLACK MODEL L NR!		661 PROTECTIVE GEAR.	$35.99

Cycling ▶ Mountain Bikes & Parts

The average sales price in this subcategory is $68.24.

	HIGH		AVG
Celebrity Autographed Cannondale Bike Kidds Kids Fund	$4,601.00	Cool No Spoke Bike Rims-For 8,9 Gears	$71.00
Dakota Fanning, Kelly Clarkson, Jessica Simpson, More		Scott SE Carbon Cantilever Brakes 2 Pair not Shimano XT	$71.00
Santa Cruz Nomad Mountain Bike (updated pictures)	$3,600.00	CRANK BROTHERS EGG BEATER SL PEDALS	$70.00
Nomad w/ Race Face & Avid Juicy 7 brakes		Syntace F99 MTB Stem New 90 mm Black, Light Stiff	$69.95
Cannondale Scalpel Team Replica 2005	$3,400.00	NEW! Syntace VRO Handlebar and	$69.00
Santa Cruz Nomad *2006* Large *MINT*	$3,350.00	1 1/8" threadlessT-stem	
2003 Medium Santana Extreme MTB Tandem	$3,226.00	SUNTOUR XC COMPE PEDALS-POLISHED	$68.75
LUNA Chix Pro Mountain Bike Package Win A Week At	$3,127.00	9/16" BMX BIKE.BICYCLE	$68.67
Sea Otter Classic & Official Team Bike		NOS Campagnolo MTB Brake Levers Vintage Historical	$68.67
Santa Cruz Blur (med)	$3,001.00	BRAND NEW AVID BRAKE LEVERS,	$68.50
2006 Litespeed Pisgah Titanium mountain bike size 18	$3,000.00	ALUMINUM & TITANIUM	
SPECIALIZED ENDURO PRO 2005 SIZE MEDIUM	$2,999.00	Syntace F99 MTB Stem New 90 mm Black, Light Stiff	$67.95
BRAND NEW! retails for over $3800 NO RESERVE		Syntace F99 Road Stem New 105 mm Black, Light Stiff	$67.95

Brooklyn Machine Works Race Link #10	GBP 1,700.00	Shimano 959 pedals, used	$66.00
2005 Cannondale Scalpel Team XTR, Sm cross max mint	$2,950.00	Crank Brothers Eggbeater S pedals egg beater cx	$66.00
2004 Trek Madone 5.9 Lance Armstrong Rpl. of Mountain Storm used	$2,949.00	ROCK SHOX SID XC REAR SHOCK	$65.00
2005 Cannondale Prophet 4000 Med. Galvanized New!!!!	$2,850.00	Brooklyn Machine Works DH Downhill MTB Freeride Pedals	$65.00
Trek Top Fuel 110 Project One 17.5 Widow Maker	$2,850.00	Brooklyn Machine Works DH Downhill MTB Freeride Pedals	$65.00
2006 Santa Cruz Blur XC - Large - Blue Anodized New	$2,800.00		

Cycling ▸ Road Bikes & Parts

The average sales price in this subcategory is $50.24.

	HIGH		AVG
Softride TT7 Rocket Triathlon Racing Bike...A Beauty...	$1,825.00	Campy Road Pedals, W/ New Look Cleats & Bolts, NR!	$52.05
NEW Giant Carbon Aero bar Time Trial RARE	$356.00	Scott Aero Bars - Used	$52.00
Oval Concepts time trial, TT, tri carbon handlebars	$350.00	Nitto Moustache Handlebars	$51.01
Deda Alanera Integrated Handlebar Stem Combination	$325.00	Bontrager Race XXX Lite S-Bend Extensions, AeroBar	$51.01
Easton Attack Aerobars	$325.00	PROFILE AERO handlebars road bike triathlon training	$51.00
VISION CLIP ON CARBON BASE BAR	$319.00	FSA Chainring Set 52 x 38 Black 130bcd Shimano	$51.00
TRIATHLON TIME TRIAL FSA		New Vision TT Mini Clip-On Bar	$51.00
FSA PLASMA Integrated bar/stem size 42/120	$308.99	Profile Design Airstryke Aerobars	$50.43
BRAND NEW Profile Design "CBX Pro" aero bars	$265.00	Newton Deda Elementi Anatomic Handlebars, 7075 T6, bike	$50.00
NEW PROFILE DESIGN CARBON X AERO BARS 100MM STEM	$251.00	Vintage Campagnolo Pinarello friction shifters	$50.00
Profile Design Carbon X Aero Bar & Campy shifters	$248.40	Oval Concepts A700 SLAM Aero Bars	$50.00
Profile Carbon X Wing Aero Bar 100mm stem length NEW	$243.50	Brand NEW!! Shimano PD-R540 Pedals	$50.00
Control Tech Carbon Fiber Handlebar Drop Bar 44 cm New	$239.95	Ritchey Alloy Clip on Aero Bar, Brand New	$50.00
Deda AeroBlack Time Trial Bar w/extensions TRIATHLON	$228.50	VINTAGE SUNTOUR CYCLONE FRONT & REAR DERAILLEURS -NIB!	$49.99
Oval Concepts A700 Aluminum Aero Bar TRI NEW!	$209.99	New Vision TT Mini Clip-On Bar	$49.02

Cycling ▸ Universal Parts & Accessories

The average sales price in this subcategory is $27.21.

	HIGH		AVG
PRICE DROP LOWRIDER BIKE GET IT NOW FOR LESS	$200.00	Ritchey Spokes by DT swiss 500ct 2.0 d/butted 269mm	$28.00
Serfas Hard Bike Travel Case - No Reserve!	$180.50	Shimano Deore HG-50 Cassette 11-34 9 Speed Z Chain OEM	$27.99
Bob Bicycle Trailer Yak Bike Rubbermaid Action Packer	$180.27	[3 of these sold for $27.99 each]	
2004 NEW ROCK SHOX Duke SL	$162.50	Two New 26x2.125 Whitewall Cruiser Bicycle Tires	$27.99
BOB YAK BIKE TRAILER NO RESERVE	$154.39	Schwinn Krate Sissy Bar with Shocks New! @@	$27.95
Phil Wood Flip Flop Track Wheel	$152.50	BICYCLE 26" SPRINGER FORKS SCHWINN STYLE BIKE	$27.50
TRICO SPORTS IRON WHEELED 47x27x10	$152.50	USPS Cycling Hydration Backpack bag large Team bladder	$27.10
BICYCLE TRAVEL CASE		Sigma Sport PC-3 Heart Rate Monitor NEW 94882	$26.99
Vintage AirLite track hubs 32/40	$151.56	CARBON FIBER vinyl decal 15" x 96" + DEAL OF THE MONTH	$26.95
Shimano dura ace cassette, 12-27, 10 speed, brand new	$120.00	[4 of these sold for $26.95 each]	
YAKIMA Big Tow BICYCLE Trailer YAK	$108.01	OMAS ALUMINUM BICYCLE HEADSET MADE IN ITALY	$26.04
VW Trek mountain bike	$107.50	LOWRIDER BIKE BIRDCAGE PEDALS CHROME CRUISER BICYCLE	$26.00
Yakima, Q towers, locking, racks, Q clips	$99.00	[2 of these sold for $26.00 each]	
Cooks Cranks w/ Dust Caps and Titanium Bolts	$85.00	Profile Design Aero Bar	$25.00
Crank Brothers Egg Beater SL Clipless Pedal Pedals-New	$78.95	2 New Longhorn Style Chrome USA Bicycle Handlebars	$24.99
Vintage Campagnolo track hubs 32/40	$78.00	DT Swiss 267 Spokes Ritchey Logic Double Butted 144 ct.	$24.99
		NEW Delta Rothko Rolling Bicycle Stand bike rack ds-10	$24.99
		BURLEY CYCLING JERSEY BY NAME CLOTHIER	$24.95

Disc Golf ▸ Discs

The average sales price in this subcategory is $19.13.

	HIGH		AVG
DISCRAFT DISC GOLF ELITE Z MEGA BUNDLE @ CHARIS GAMES	$122.50	LED Light Frisbee Disc Fiber Optic - Ultimate - Red	$20.00
INNOVA DISC GOLF - CHAMPION BUNDLE 10 DISC SET @ CHARIS	$113.00	LED Light Frisbee Disc Fiber Optic - Ultimate - Blue	$20.00
1st Run CE Valkyrie golf disc	$102.52	RED Orby Mothership Brightest Light-Up Ultimate Frisbee	$19.99
~NEW~ TWO (2) 2005 CE ROC FRISBEE DISC GOLF ~ VERY COOL	$84.99	INNOVA DX DISC GOLF SET NIB FRISBEE GOLF	$19.99
LOT 16 DISC GOLF DISCS DRIVER PUTTER	$79.00	BLUE Orby Mothership BEST Light-Up Ultimate Frisbee	$19.99
INNOVA PDGA OMEGA+		INNOVA DX DISC GOLF SET NIB FRISBEE GOLF	$19.99
First Run CE Valkyrie "Mint"	$77.00	1967 WHAM O Mini FRISBEE DISC GOLF SET 2 frisbees! NICE	$19.99
EXCELLENT * USED * RARE *EARLY USDGC CE ROC GOLF DISC	$76.69	DISC GOLF JEWELRY NECKLACE CHARM~STERLING SILVER~ NEW~	$19.99
HuGe lot of 14 used disc golf disks! NO RESERVE	$76.00	Innova KC PRO Firebird Disc Golf Frisbee 175g	$19.51
2nd Run CE Valkyrie MINT	$75.00	BLUE Orby Mothership BEST Light-Up Ultimate Frisbee	$19.50
Vintage Buzzbee frisbee disc golf w/poster hemp	$75.00	Innova "Python" PDGA Golf Disc	$19.00
Champion Edition Firebird , Teebird CE Innova	$71.00	Innova KC PRO Gazelle Flying Eye Disc Golf Frisbee	$19.00
Innova First Run CE Leopard Disc Golf Frisbee 174g	$70.66	20 Disc Golf Frisbee Bag discraft innova pdga not	$19.00
Mint Virgin CE 165 Valkyrie Neon green/day-glo LQQK!	$70.00	14 Disc Golf Frisbee Bag discraft innova not	$18.99
2 Innova KC PRO TeeBird Disc Golf Frisbees 172g	$65.00	[2 of these sold for $18.99 each]	
3 Champion Edition Eagles CE 2 1ST RUNS!!!!	$61.04	SAN MARINO ROC disc golf USED	$18.56

Equestrian ▸ Riding-English

The average sales price in this subcategory is $19.02.

	HIGH		AVG
Bridle/17.5" Saddle Set- Hunter- All fittings included!	$305.00	Crops Whips - Leather Dressage Whip & Crop Set 5	$20.05
Sandwich Case/ Box/ Mini Flask - Hunt Appointments	$281.00	New leather ankle boots - fleece lined	$20.00

BRAND NEW: Pytchley Shadbelly Size US12 36R	$202.50	Hunt Saddle Carrier Bag	$20.00
NEW 17"CLOSE CONTACT SADDLE/ACESSORIES! VERY CHEAP	$172.50	New Black Rubber Reins!	$20.00
Antique BENCH Fox Hunt Horse Hand Painted Wood Seat	$161.51	Fox Hunt Foxhunt Horse Scene Kitchen, Barn, Tack Apron	$19.99
PIKEUR Full Seat Breechs Ladies size 32 long, NEW	$147.50	EQUESTRIAN STERLING TIE BAR HOLLAND HUNTING SPUR	$19.99
Antique Riding Crop Whip Eagle Snake Hunting Figural	$113.50	NIP HORSE OPEN FRONT JUMPING BOOTS-NEOPRENE-BLACK- LG.	$19.95
New Pessoa Training System	$113.50	Equestrian/Horse Jump Rail Covers (2) - Green/White	$19.95
Barnsby Leather / Sheepskin Girth 52" Like New!!!	$103.50	Troxel Riding Helmet, Black Medium	$19.50
Beval LTD Boots	$100.00	GARMENT / COAT BAG State Line Tack red MINT!!!	$18.50
WOW! C1800's Leather & Horn Figural Sword Riding Crop	$99.99	Navy/Hunter Plaid English Saddle Bag	$18.50
Kyra Kyrylund Dressage Training video english riding	$86.00	Fleece Horse Polo Leg Wraps - Polka Dot Party	$18.50
Brand New Dover's Italian Open Front Competition Boots	$86.00	Tail Brace Saddlebred or Walking Horse New w/Tags NR	$18.50
Passier Elastic Dressage Girth 24"	$65.00	Navy/Hunter Plaid English Bridle Bag	$18.02
Zilco Synthetic Deluxe Endurance Breastcollar	$64.99	BRAIDED LEATHER HORSE HALTER-HORSE TACK..FULL SIZE	$18.00

Equestrian ▸ Riding-Western

The average sales price in this subcategory is $29.42.

	HIGH		AVG
Used Cutting Saddle Gene Bader 17"	$1,825.00	Western Rear Girth Flank Strap Set	$30.00
NEW TRADITIONAL PERUVIAN PASO SHOW PELLON TACK	$699.00	Custom WESTERN Quarter Horse Head WELCOME Sign Steel	$30.00
Like New Long Haul Decker Pack Saddle Mule Tree western	$325.00	Roughout Leather Saddlebags and Rifle Scabbard	$29.99
Parelli Working bridle with Horseman's reins	$192.05	COLORADO SADDLERLY LADIES logo Spurs	$29.99
Right Handed rigging rodeo equipment gear bareback	$177.50	Roughout Leather Saddlebags and Rifle Scabbard	$29.99
rodeo vest./phoenix leather.2020 new $177.00	$177.00	Western Saddle & Boot Shelf Brackets-Metal Set of 2	$29.97
JOHN LYONS' RIDING MANUAL W/4 DVDS	$162.60	[3 of these sold in a multiple item ("Dutch") auction for $9.99 each]	
INCLUDED - BRAND NEW		**********ROPING BREAST COLLAR*********	$29.55
New show bosal 32 plait complete bridle w/mecate riens	$158.61	JOHN LYONS' EXERCISES FOR OVERCOMING RIDING PROBLEMS	$29.00
Gist Silversmith Western Trophy Belt Buckle New	$152.83	HARNESS HORSE RACING BOOTS	$28.01
YOUTH SADDLE	$152.00	Horseman's cane with hands measure in the handle	$27.99
BRAND NEW JOHN LYONS' GROUND CONTROL MANUAL	$117.55	Rawhide Bosal w/ Rawhide Core Fine Braids- Show Quality	$27.50
Broken Horn Sterling Silver Western Trophy Buckle	$107.50	LARGE LOT 105 ARKANSAS HORSE SHOW RIBBONS 1950's	$26.98
NEW Utah Panniers For A Pack Saddle	$102.50	X-FANCY* ETCHED * SILVER HAT BAND** NEW** Fancy* Sharp	$26.50
Quarter Horse Reference Books	$100.00	NEON HOT PINK Cowgirl Horse Tack~Barrel Racing~Rodeo	$26.49
NEW Saddle Pannier or Pack Saddle Panniers	$100.00	~*~HORSE TACK~*~ SPORT/TRAINING HORSE BOOTS BLACK NEW	$26.01

Exercise & Fitness ▸ Cardiovascular Equipment

The average sales price in this subcategory is $358.97.

	HIGH		AVG
PRECOR 546i "BRAND NEW IN BOX" READY TO SHIP!!!	$4,499.00	Horizon E6050 Elliptical w/ Warranty FREE Ship 4 Prgms	$375.99
PRECOR 546 NEW SERIES ELLIPTICAL - LIKE NEW!	$3,590.00	[2 of these sold for $375.99 each]	
[2 of these sold for $3,590.00 each]		NEW 2005 Professional Treadmill TX4.9 fitness exercise	$375.01
PRECOR EFX 556 (THE NEWEST SERIES) ELLIPTICAL	$3,560.00	Schwinn Johnny G Spinner PRO Exercise Bike	$375.00
[2 of these sold for $3,560.00 each]		Horizon CST3 Treadmill Warranty 2.0 CHP 6 Programs	$370.00
Precor 546 Elliptical version 3 CORDLESS! FREE SHIPPING	$3,195.00	NordicTrack CX985 Elliptical - Refurbished Dallas	$366.00
PRECOR EFX556 ELLIPTICAL CROSSTRAINER	$3,119.72	Pro-Form 740cs Treadmill - I will deliver!	$362.99
Precor EFX 5.23 Never used. Top Elliptical Crosstrainer	$2,850.00	ProForm PaceTrainer Exercise Treadmill w/ Fan - NEW	$357.00
Life Fitness TR9700HR Next Gen commercial treadmill!	$2,800.00	ProForm CrossTrainer VX iFIT Exercise Treadmill - NEW	$356.00
NuStep ? TRS 4000 Recumbent Cross Trainer Cardio NEW	$2,800.00	NordicTrack CX985 Elliptical - Refurbished Los Angeles	$355.00
Precor Treadmill 9.35 Top-of-the-Line in Box Never Used	$2,750.00	ProForm 880S Interactive Elliptical	$355.00
Life Fitness 90X Total Body Crosstrainer, Like NEW!	$2,700.00	Trainer - BRAND NEW	$355.00
CROSS TRAINER/NuStep trs 4000	$2,602.00	ProForm 800 Cardio Exercise Elliptical w/ iFIT - NEW	$355.00
Precor EFX 546 Elliptical Machine - Commercial model	$2,550.00	NordicTrack CXT 980 Elliptical Crosstrainer	$350.00
LIFE FITNESS 9500 HRR REAR-DRIVE ELLIPTICAL - NEW-REMFG	$2,375.00	Proform CrossWalk Advanced 525x Treadmill	$350.00
The Life Fitness Elliptical X3i Lifefitness, MINT COND.	$2,210.00	NordicTrack CXT 910 Elliptical Cross Trainer	$350.00
Life Fitness X5i Elliptical Cross Trainer	$2,084.62	Fantastic SCHWINN AIRDYNE Dual-Action Exercise Bike	$349.00

Exercise & Fitness ▸ Exercise Monitors, Computers

The average sales price in this subcategory is $64.21.

	HIGH		AVG
New Polar S720i Watch AND Power Output Sensor	$386.00	Oregon Scientific-Outbreaker Pro Heart rate/Altimeter	$70.00
POLAR AXN700 NEW Heart Rate Moniter	$358.00	Polar S120 Brand New Sealed	$70.00
AXN 700 Watch BLACK		[2 of these sold for $70.00 each]	
New - Polar AXN700 Hear Rate Monitor AXN 700	$335.00	Sports Instruments Pro 9 New in Box	$69.99
New Polar S625X Heart Rate Monitor NIB Exercise Running	$306.00	Sharper Image: Mio Shape Select Watch	$69.95
Polar S625X Heart Rate Monitor + Bike Sensor (Like NEW !!)	$287.00	CASIO CSP-100 HEADSET PULSE MONITOR	$69.90
NEW IN BOX POLAR S625 X Heart Rate Monitor	$275.00	RADIO & STOP WATCH	
BRAND NEW!!! Polar S625X Heart Rate Monitor	$272.55	Polar F4 Blue Ice Heart Rate Monitor NEW	$68.01
Polar S625X Heart Rate Monitor BRAND NEW **NR**	$270.00	Polar A5 Heart Rate Monitor-New In Box	$67.99
Polar Power Output Sensor Kit New In Box	$269.99	Timex ironman digital heart rate fitness monitor	$67.66
BRAND NEW!!! Polar S625X Heart Rate Monitor	$265.01	Heart Rate Monitor, by POLAR, model M21 - NEW	$66.01
Polar Power Output Sensor	$265.00	MIO Shape Heart Rate Monitor Watch	$66.00
NEW IN BOX POLAR S625 X Heart Rate Monitor	$265.00	POLAR A5 Heart Rate Monitor 2 DAY SHIPPING	$65.00
NEW POLAR S725 Heart Rate Monitor 725 S 725	$265.00	New Nike IMARA Heart Rate Monitor (HRM) Watch	$65.00
BRAND NEW!!! Polar S625X Heart Rate Monitor	$265.00	NEW Polar F4 Fitness Heart Rate Monitor	$64.60
[2 of these sold for $265.00 each]		Nautilus? ZT-300 Heart Rate Monitor (wireless)	$64.00
BRAND NEW!!! Polar S625X Heart Rate Monitor	$262.75	POLAR HEART RATE MONITOR F5 NEW IN BOX	$63.03

Exercise & Fitness ▸ Strength Training

The average sales price in this subcategory is $110.08.

	HIGH		AVG
Cybex Classic - 20 Piece Free Weight Package	$4,500.00	LIKE NEW 50lb Weight vest ! Original WEIGHTVEST.COM	$120.00
Body Solid Model EXM3000LPS Home Gym	$1,200.00	Exercise Equipment * NEW FLAT / INCLINE	$119.00
Total Gym Electra - the new MOTORIZED XL	$899.00	/ DECLINE BENCH	
Icarian Smith Machine	$800.00	Exercise Equipment NEW ROMAN CHAIR	$119.00
Hammer Strength row back lats traps shrug commercial	$800.00	* BACK HYPER BENCH	
USED COMMERCIAL GYM HEX HEAD DUMBELLS DUMBBELLS	$799.99	Body Solid Deluxe Power Bench w/bar & 230lbs of weights	$117.50
Bowflex Ultimate XTLU for pick up only in Brooklyn, NY	$780.00	Weider 148 Weight Bench/Training Station-plus weights.	$115.25
Hammer Strength shrug traps - commercial gym	$775.00	TOTAL GYM 1000 W EXERCISE BOOKLET BIN $115	$115.00
Total Gym XL - These are our lowest prices anywhere!	$700.00	Hyper Extension Roman Chair Free Ltime Warranty	$109.99
[2 of these sold for $700.00 each]		Roman Chair Hyperextension Powerline New	$104.99
Total Gym Electra - the new MOTORIZED XL	$700.00	EXTREME PERFORMANCE WEIGHT	$104.50
[2 of these sold for $700.00 each]		BENCH + ATTACHMENTS	
Maxicam Horizontal Leg Press Pre-owned	$685.00	WEIDER WEIGHT BENCH AND WEIGHTS	$104.50
Maxicam Hamstring Isolator Pre-Owned	$650.00	Bench Press, Barbell, Weights (100+ lbs.) & Stand NORES	$104.00
Total Gym XL - These are our lowest prices anywhere!	$645.00	Weider 8525 multi-station home gym	$102.70
[2 of these sold for $645.00 each]		EMS Electronic Muscle Stimulator muscle Bodybuilding	$102.50
Total Gym XL - These are our lowest prices anywhere!	$645.00	SEARS Lifestyler Toning Table	$100.01
Total Gym XL - These are our lowest prices anywhere!	$642.22	Nautilus commercial arm tricep gym	$100.00

Fishing ▸ Freshwater

The average sales price in this subcategory is $17.90.

	HIGH		AVG
1986 Sea Nymph Bass Fishing Boat - 16 .5 ft long	$1,576.00	4 New TERMINATOR T-1 Series SPINNERBAITS Each Size	$18.00
<10> FULLY GUIDED G LOOMIS EQUIPPED FISHING TRIPS	$910.00	12 Little Cleo Fishing Spoons Lures - C200 - GNR 2/5oz	$18.00
(5) FULLY GUIDED G LOOMIS EQUIPPED FISHING TRIPS	$610.00	Megabass X-80 Trick Darter GG MEGABASS-KINKURO NIP	$18.00
5000 size Abu Garcia Ambassadeur 5600 CDL Gold Plated	$550.00	Storm Wiggle Wart (Mag) Custom Painted by Tim Hughes	$18.00
Garcia Mitchell 510 Reel Fishing	$537.00	Storm Hot n Tot H72 Rare Fishing Lure Crankbait NiRedLa	$18.00
SHIMANO RODS WITH DAIWA LINE COUNTER REELS (LIKE NEW)	$485.00	12 ASSORTED CRANKBAIT LURES, NEW AND USED	$18.00
(5) FULLY GUIDED G LOOMIS EQUIPPED FISHING TRIPS	$475.00	New Handmade Wood Lures that really work! Free S/H	$18.00
L@@K (5) FULLY GUIDED G LOOMIS EQUIPPED FISHING TRIPS	$475.00	ICE FISHING JIGS ICE FISHING JIG KIT Crappie Jigs.	$17.99
NEW MOTORGUIDE 70LB-24 VOLT FISHING TROLLING MOTOR	$454.00	ICE FISHING JIGS ICE FISHING JIG KIT Crappie Jigs.	$17.99
TROLLING MOTOR MOTORGUIDE 45" 71 LB GREAT GIFT IDEA!	$454.00	ICE FISHING JIGS ICE FISHING JIG KIT Crappie Jigs.	$17.99
Fishing /Hunting Trip in Remote Northern Ontario	$417.00	Rabbit Hare Jigs Smallmouth (13) 1/8 Ounce Olive	$17.99
Fishing /Hunting Trip in Remote Northern Ontario	$410.00	Daiwa Regal 1000-4i Spinning Reel -NEW- 934685	$17.99
Fishing Trip in Remote Northern Ontario	$404.00	NEW -"2" LONG - 14 FOOT "4 SECTION" TELESCOPIC POLES	$17.95
Fishing Trip in Remote Northern Ontario	$401.51	Hugh Crumpler SPINNERBAITS 1/2 oz New 9 assorted clrs	$17.95
Fishing /Hunting Trip in Remote Northern Ontario	$396.00	Rapala Dives-To (3) DT-6 and (1) DT-4 crankbaits NEW	$17.85

Fishing ▸ Fly Fishing

The average sales price in this subcategory is $27.20.

	HIGH		AVG
Trolling Motor Trim Tabs	$700.00	Float Tube The Round Boat NEW / Never Used	$30.00
NEW! 9 FOOT COLORADO FLOAT/ PONTOON BOAT	$350.00	Orvis (fly fishing) Wader Bag (NWOT)	$29.75
NIB Creek Company ODC Jet Pack - Water Skeeter boat	$295.00	$79 Wader Waders Duffel Bag Fly Fishing Hunting	$29.00
ABEL No.1 FLY REEL	$255.00	Float Tube - Outfitters Expedition - NEW IN BOX - WOW	$28.67
Orvis MACH IV fly reel, like new!	$227.50	Brand New Fly Fishing Chest Pack! Better than Orvis $75	$28.02
ORVIS Day Tripper Float Tube Water Skeeter Fly Fishing	$226.50	Orvis Superstretch Waders for Fly Fishing MINT!!!	$27.10
Hardy Featherweight Flyfishing reel	$222.50	CLASSIC WOODEN FLY FISHING LANDING NET NEW	$27.00
Guided Fly Fishing SanJuan NM Drift Boat Orvis Rod Incl	$199.50	Brand New Sage & St. Croix Fishing Hats, & Kewl Pens	$27.00
SIMMS Guide Jacket (not the G3) Gore-Tex Excellent	$199.00	CHOTA WADING SHOES SZ 9 AND GRAVEL GAURDS	$26.99
TOP OF THE LINE WOOD RIVER FLOAT TUBE V SHAPE NR	$198.00	The ORVIS FLY TYING GUIDE Top 5 Book NEW NR	$26.95
ORVIS Day Tripper Float Tube Water Skeeter Fly Fishing	$192.50	Air Flow Twin Pak(2) Brand New Fly Lines	$26.78
PATAGONIA SST+ WADERS - BRAND NEW - SIZE M	$191.50	neoprene waders	$26.51
Simms Freestone Jacket	$170.00	Orvis, Traveler's Stripping Basket	$26.01
Water Skeeter Personal Pontoon Fly Fishing Boat	$158.55	Cortland Creel with Leather Harness-Brand New	$26.00
VINTAGE FLY FISHING FLY TIEING MATERIAL EQUIPMENT	$157.50	ORVIS JACKSON HOLE Ball Cap New w/Tags! 1 Size Fits All	$25.69

Fishing ▸ Saltwater

The average sales price in this subcategory is $54.95.

	HIGH		AVG
ACR 2744 GLOBALFIX 406 EPIRB w/INTEGRAL GPS CATEGORY II	$825.00	The Floater by Mustang-Bouyant Marine Wear SizeM	$56.99
Miya Epoch CX-4HP Electric fishing reel Made in Japan	$620.00	Okuma Magda Pro 20DX Counter Reel -2 PACK- NEW IN BOX!!	$56.00
Miya Epoch CX-4 HP Electric fishing reel Made in Japan	$613.00	6 Easy Throw Net, Joy Fish 1/4 Bait Cast Nets	$56.00
Miya Epoch CX-4HP Electric Fishing Reel 66lb Drag Japan	$610.00	USED SHIMANO CATALA 400 BAITCASTING REEL	$56.00
PENN INTERNATIONAL 80TW ROD AND REEL COMBO		PENN CAPTIVA CLL6000 LiveLiner	$55.50
NEW IN THE BOX REEL WITH BIG GAME BENT BUTT ROD	$610.00	Spinning Reel BRAND NEW!	
Fin - Nor Swedish Made 30 Light saltwater reels (two)	$520.00	Penn Slammer Rod with Penn310GTI reel	$53.50
Miya Epoch CX-4 Pro Electric fishing reel Made in Japan	$495.00	PENN 4300SS	$53.00
Penn International 80 Fishing Reel	$425.00	Like New Okuma Trolling Reel Titus PlatinumTPLD 30	$53.00
Penn International 80W Gold Series	$400.00	PENN SENATOR 4/0 FISHING REEL NO RESERVE	$52.50
Penn International II 80TW	$400.00	Okuma/Penn Rod and Reeel Comb	$52.01
ORVIS T3 908-4 SALTWATER FLY FISHING ROD	$400.00	6 Easy Throw Net, Joy Fish 1/4 Bait Cast Net	$52.00
New Shimano Calcutta TE 250 DC Casting Reel CTE-250DC	$385.00	Kidney harness and gimble belt	$51.48

Penn International 80W Gold Series	$375.00	viintage COIT ELECTRIC REEL model E $51.00
Penn International 30SW	$375.00	two 11 foot surf rods Daiwa and Ambassador $51.00
New Shimano Calcutta TE 250 DC Casting Reel CTE-250DC	$365.00	offshore gaff by aftco [nice] $51.00

Fishing ▶ Tackle Boxes

The average sales price in this subcategory is $25.68.

	HIGH		AVG
FISHING TACKLE BOX NEW with 100 new lures	$445.00	Fishing Tackle Box Loaded Lures and baits (NR) TB4	$26.00
KENNEDY TACKLE BOX FULL OF LURES, AND MISC	$310.69	NEW Flambeau 8050 Tackle Box Fishing Very Big !!	$26.00
Orange Umco Possum Belly Model 482 Tackle Box Plastech	$239.50	Huge Plano Phantom Pro 797 Tackle Box	$26.00
Antique UMCO 3500U Tackle Box with over 60 Lures	$221.39	Plano 759 Guide Series Tackle Box-Fishing Tackle	$26.00
Four Tackle Boxes..100's of Lures...Everything You Need	$202.50	Umco Fish Tackle Box Loaded Lures and Baits (NR) TB5	$26.00
PLANO TACKLE BOX LOADED LOTS OF LURES BASS FISHING LOT	$202.50	New Lot of 9 Plano 3670 CDS Stowaway Boxes (craft)	$25.49
Full tackle box Vintage? fishing reels 8 drawer LURES	$193.55	TACKLE BOX PACKED FULL 60 FLIES & FLY POPPERS + MORE	$25.38
Tackle Box With Heddon ..C.C.B.C. Pfleuger Glass eye's	$175.52	Clear Plano Box plus 20 Assorted Lures	$25.17
Nice Plano Tackle Box LOADED 95+Fishing Lures + More	$158.61	NEW FLAMBEAU TACKLE BOX WITH NEW AND OLD LURES	$25.00
FULL PLANO TACKLE BOX WITH 90+ LURES CRANKBAITS JIGS NR	$158.05	PLANO TACKLEBOX LOADED	$25.00
Vintage Umco Model 2080U Tackle Box w/120+ Lures & More	$157.50	Flambeau New Tackle Box Fully Stocked	$25.00
vintage tackle box full wooden lures duck lure	$151.97	Vintage Union Tackle Box with Tackle	$25.00
VINTAGE Umco Tackle Box full of Fishing Lures*WOW*LOOK*	$149.99	NEW FLAMBEAU TACKLE BOX W/NEW AND OLD LURES	$25.00
SIMONSEN TACKLE BOX 90+ VINTAGE FISHING LURES & MISC	$142.50	Vintage SOUTH BEND METAL TACKLE BOX	$24.99
FISHING CART LARGE ALL ALUMINUM BEACH OR PIER NEW	$132.50	Old Over & Under Plano Tackle Box with Fishing Tackle	$24.99

Fishing ▶ Vintage

The average sales price in this subcategory is $21.29.

	HIGH		AVG
Ltd. ed. leatherbound fishing book ANGLERS CLUB OF NY	$600.00	Vintage Fish Pond game, Milton Bradley	$21.50
WINCHESTER BAMBOO FOLDING FISHING NET NOT FLY ROD	$456.00	1923 FOREST AND STREAM MAGAZINE	$21.50
~ OLD BRAINERD FISH SPEAR ~ Ice Fishing Decoy L GUSTIS	$382.77	Vintage Lazy Ike Fishing Lure Booklet / Brochure 60's	$21.50
LOT OF 60 VINTAGE LURES, REELS & WOODEN TACKLE BOX 9.99	$380.00	Mitchell Half Bale 1948 Reel	$21.50
chrysler 4 hp outboard trolling motor jon boat look	$355.00	Vintage Heddon Torpedo 130 XWB &box	$21.49
OLD ALUMINUM, BARACUDA MODEL F, FISH SPEAR GUN	$317.02	Lot of Old Fishing Containers	$21.01
Early Evinrude Motor Fishing Boat Tin Advertising Sign	$228.50	Popeil's Pocket Fisherman Spin Casting Outfit w/ box	$20.73
HUGE LOT PENN REEL PARTS CLOSE TO 500 ITEMS~NR MUSTc	$199.99	OLD PAL MINNOW BUCKET vintage fishing old lures tin	$20.50
Christenson Fish Decoy - 24" Northern Pike half Plaque	$175.00	Vintage KRAFTY FISH CALLER 1960 + Box + Directions	$20.50
HAND FORGED IRON EEL GIG Fish Spear SIGNED SAG HARBOR	$172.50	vintage fishing HARDY silver spey devon bait lure	$20.50
~ FISH DECOY ~ Cadillac Ice Spear Fishing Lure * NELSON	$164.95	salt water,deep sea fishing ,photos, 6 vintage	$20.50
HEDDON SONAR STORE DISPLAY-16 LURES	$136.09	Lou J Eppinger Dardevle Vintage Fishing Parts Envelope	$20.49
Vintage Johnson Sea-Horse Boat Livery Tin Sign NR!!	$127.50	Vintage Pro Weber of Stevens Point Wood Fishing Dip Net	$20.45
8 tine J W FORDHAM eel spear, fish fishing	$101.00	Vintage Jim Harvey 23" Wood Fishing Net	$20.40
Vintage Johnson Boat Dealer Outboard Motor Stand	$86.00	Large Vintage Minnow Bucket, Falls City NO. 7820	$20.00

Football ▶ Apparel & Footwear

The average sales price in this subcategory is $30.71.

	HIGH		AVG
L.A. RAMS ROSEY GRIER AUTOGRAPHED FOOTBALL JERSEY	$112.50	PHILADELPHIA EAGLES Jevon Kearse Jersey white REEBOK M	$31.46
BO JACKSON AUTHENTIC THROWBACK RAIDERS JERSEY 60	$102.51	Authentic Ronnie Lott USC Jersey Sz 56 $250+++	$31.01
Gridiron Classics Denver Broncos Varsity Jacket	$100.00	DAN MARINO JERSEY WHITE 2XL STARTER - NEW - LOOK	$31.00
* TOMLINSON * AUTHENTIC CHARGERS PRO BOWL JERSEY sz56	$100.00	Authentic Julius Peppers Carolina Panthers Jersey 4XL	$31.00
* TOMLINSON * AUTHENTIC CHARGERS PRO BOWL JERSEY sz52	$100.00	BRIAN URLACHER BEARS AUTHENTIC RBK PROBOWL JERSEY SZ 58	$31.00
GIII NFL FOOTBAL STEELERS JACKET SIze X XL	$100.00	Ladainian Tomlinson Authentic Pro Bowl Jersey NWT sz 58	$31.00
WARREN MOON OILERS AUTHENTIC THROWBACK JERSEY 52	$99.99	Brand New Wisconsin Badger Jacket	$31.00
LAWRENCE TAYLOR AUTHENTIC GIANTS THROWBACK JERSEY 54	$99.99	RAY LEWIS MIAMI HURRICANS JERSEY SIZE 2X /54	$31.00
GIII COLLEGIATE SERIES PENN STATE FOOTBALL JCKT Sz M	$99.00	Denver Broncos Superbowl 33 jacket and hat = jersey	$30.95
GIII NFL FOOTBALL EAGLES JACKET SIze XXL	$99.00	JEVON KEARSE AUTHENTIC REEBOK EAGLES JERSEY SZ 54 SALE!	$30.01
BRIAN PICCOLO CHICAGO BEARS "THROWBACK" JERSEY	$96.00	NFL GAMEDAY SAN FRANCISCO 49ERS JACKET SIZE LARGE	$30.00
* ALEX SMITH * S.F. 49ERS AUTHENTIC REEBOK JERSEY 48	$95.00	Michael Vick Atlanta Falcons Authentic jersey SZ 60 NWT	$29.99
* MOSS *#18 AUTHENTIC OAKLAND * RAIDERS * NFL JERSEY 54	$92.25	BRIAN PICCOLO FOOTBALL JERSEY CHICAGO BEARS 2XL	$29.99
* EMMITT SMITH * COWBOYS AUTHENTIC THROWBACK JERSEY 48	$88.00	DEION SANDERS FOOTBALL JERSEY FLORIDA STATE 2XL	$29.99
LAWRENCE TAYLOR AUTHENTIC GIANTS THROWBACK JERSEY 54	$86.00	DICK BUTKUS FOOTBALL JERSEY CHICAGO BEARS 2XL	$29.99

Football ▶ Balls

The average sales price in this subcategory is $23.22.

	HIGH		AVG
Vintage Wilson Thorp Football The Duke Pete Rozelle NFL	$350.00	Brand New Wilson GST NCAA Football	$26.00
OLD LEATHER VINTAGE RUGBY FOOTBALL	$260.00	[2 of these sold for $26.00 each]	
EARLY MELON BALL WoW		OFFICIAL FULL SIZE NFL WILSON "GOLD" AUTOGRAPH FOOTBALL	$26.00
NEW High School Footballs(12) 6 in original cellophane	$170.00	VINTAGE WILSON THE DUKE JUNIOR SIZE LEATHER FOOTBALL	$26.00
NFL official football (The Duke) thorp sporting goods.	$143.49	DELUXE FULL SIZE FOOTBALL DISPLAY CASE HOLDER	$25.49
Vintage Wilson FOOTBALL "The Duke" Pete Rozelle NFL	$130.02	New WILSON Football TDY Youth	$25.00
Joe Theismann signed Notre Dame Pro Helmet W/Ins	$124.50	NEW Wilson 1003 Official College Football Leather	$25.00
Rozelle Official NFL Football Used from 1970-1989	$95.00	[5 of these sold in a multiple item ("Dutch") auction for $5.00 each]	
50 NEW YOUTH WILSON LEATHER	$88.00	DELUXE FULL SIZE FOOTBALL DISPLAY CASE HOLDER	$24.99
FOOTBALLS, N.O. SAINTS !!		RZ Trainer Football Training Tool YOUTH Joe Montana	$24.99
50 Pr. football shoes, used, not abused-high school siz	$87.01	RZ Trainer Football Throw Throwing Training Aid NEW!!!!	$24.98

WILSON OFFICIAL NFL GAME FOOTBALL!!!	$83.03	[2 of these sold for $24.98 each]	
Official NFL Leather Super Bowl XXI Football NYG v DEN	$76.98	Lot Of 5 Wilson NFL Football AFC NFC Footballs	$24.95
Wilson N.F.L. 75th Anniversary Game Football	$69.99	wilson 1003 football	$24.51
Terry Bradshaw Signed Football Steelers	$69.68	NIB DOUG FLUTIE/BUFFALO BILLS FOTOBALL FOOTBALL	$24.49
WILSON OFFICIAL NFL GAME FOOTBALL!!!	$63.00	New RAWLINGS NFHS High School Football (Practice)	$23.50
Wilson"The DUKE"L-Vintage Pro Football-70s?-MINT-NR	$61.03	WILSON N.F.L. 75TH ANNIVERSARY FOOTBALL-EX+-USA	$23.02
Wilson Official NFL Game Football A REAL GAME BALL	$56.00	Wilson Official NFL Real Game & Practice Football	$22.99
WILSON OFFICIAL NFL GAME FOOTBALL!!!	$56.00	[15 of these sold for $22.99 each]	

Football ▸ Protective Gear

The average sales price in this subcategory is $29.01.

	HIGH		AVG
RARE and EARLY Leather Football Helmet SUPERB Cond. NR	$1,040.99	BATTLE GEAR FOOTBALL PADS YOUTH 12" 13"AND ACCESSORIES	$29.99
EARLY ANTIQUE FLAT TOP FOOTBALL HELMET	$557.00	RAWLINGS MAG 16-S Shoulder Pads	$29.95
Vintage Leather Football Helmet by Draper-Maynard	$333.79	*NEW* GRID ELITE FOOTBALL HELMET - ROYAL BLUE - LARGE	$29.95
Vintage Spalding Leather Football Helmet 1930s or 1940s	$325.00	PURPLE RIDDELL FOOTBALL HELMET	$29.00
Vintage Antique Dog-Eared Leather Football Helmet	$217.50	Ridel Warior 3 Football Shoulder Pads Size 17-18 M	$29.00
Early Goldsmith Leather Football Helmet	$198.49	OAKLEY FOOTBALL VISOR!!	$29.00
3 FOOTBALL HELMETS SILVER RED SCHUTT RIDDELL L & XL!!!!	$182.50	Riddell PAC3 Helmet White	$28.00
New Football Shoulder Pads and Rib Protector.	$175.00	Vintage Riddell Football Helmet Air-Large- 7 1/4-7 3/4	$27.00
Antique Leather Football Helmet	$167.50	Football Helmet Youth Riddell M Red New	$26.99
riddell revolution black hardly used football helmet	$157.49	GTS BAD-BOY Deluxe Youth Football Shoulder Pads 30"-32"	$26.90
Riddell Revolution helmet Brand new Wht/Red	$156.49	Nokona Tomahawk Youth Football Shoulder Pads XS small	$26.89
WOW!NEVER USED RIDDELL REVOLUTION YOUTH FOOTBALL HELMET	$152.50	Football Helmet Schutt "Air" Youth Medium - Excellent!	$26.54
VINTAGE LEATHER FOOTBALL HELMET...GOOD CONDITION!	$152.50	Schutt Air Youth Football Helmet! Size S, Age 6-14 L@@K	$26.51
Antique Vintage Leather Hutch Football Helmet!!	$152.50	Youth/Kids Schutt Blocker Football Pads XL 34-36 15-16	$26.50
VINTAGE 1930'S FOOTBALL LEATHER HELMET WESTERN GOPHER	$150.00	VERY NICE YOUTH FOOTBALL HELMET, ALL-STAR, SMALL/MED	$26.50

Go-Karts, Recreational ▸ Complete Go-Karts & Frames

The average sales price in this subcategory is $533.42.

	HIGH		AVG
NEW 800cc 2 Seat OFF-ROAD GO KART CART BUGGY ATV RAIL	$4,100.00	SST Motorsports 5 HP Two Seat Go Kart / Cart 38032	$599.99
Tony Kart Mitox Shifter Racing Go Kart - No Reserve!	$3,999.00	MINI BIKE/CHOPPER ROLLING CHASSIS FRAME PLANS WHEEL HUB	$599.99
NEW 800cc 2 Seat OFF-ROAD GO KART CART BUGGY ATV RAIL	$3,995.00	KAZUMA 50 KIDS QUAD 50CC 4 WHEELER 4 STROKE GAS NEW RED	$549.99
Rotax Go-Kart 125cc	$2,550.00	KAZUMA 50 KIDS QUAD 50CC 4 WHEELER 4 STROKE GAS BLUE	$549.99
NEW 250cc 4 STROKE GO KART SANDRAIL DUNE BUGGY CART BLU	$2,325.00	90CC Off Road Go Kart Cart Dune Buggy Sand Rail Karts	$549.00
NEW 250cc 2 Seat OFF-ROAD GO KART CART BUGGY ATV RAIL	$2,130.00	USED JACKLE 90 ATV, VERY NICE, INDIANA.	$535.00
Rotax Kart	$2,125.00	Yerf-Dog Go-Kart 6 HP 35 MPH Blue Tecumseh San Jose	$525.00
2000 PHANTOM BANCHEE RACING KART	$2,025.00	GO CART - GO KART FOX 2x5 LXT 2 SEATER - 5HP	$504.00
Racing Go-Kart/ Go-Cart	$1,999.00	5.5HP SPORT GO CART 2 SEATER 163CC GOCART	$500.00
Racing Go Kart - Complete Race Ready Package	$1,995.00	GARAGE KEPT MANCO QUICKSILVER GO KART SUMMER FUN	$500.00
RACING GO KART + Accessories	$1,750.00	GO KART GO CART 5HP TECUMSEH POWER SPORT GO KART	$500.00
ULTRAMAX RACING KART, BRIGGS, CART, NEW ANIMAL ENGINE	$1,697.00	AWESOME! GO KART Bird Corporation $1800 New	$499.00
Brand New Go Cart Dune Buggy	$1,575.00	Ken-Bar 2 seater 11HP Streaker Go Cart	$481.00
Racing Go Kart 60mph + KAOS 100cc accessories	$1,526.26	Vintage 1978 Subaru Brat MINI CAR Go Cart Brown, NR	$479.00
4-Seat ELECTRIC UTILITY Vehicle	$1,465.00	9 Horse Power Go Kart Streaker	$475.00

Golf ▸ Accessories

The average sales price in this subcategory is $24.61.

	HIGH		AVG
Suunto G9 Golf Manager	$375.00	GOLF CLUBS TRAVEL VIPER BAG LIKE NEW	$25.00
BRAND NEW SkyGolf SkyCaddie SG2 GPS Rangefinder Unit	$334.01	Victorinox SwissCard Credit Card Size Multi-tool	$24.99
SkyGolf GPS - SkyCaddie SG2 Brand New! Factory Sealed!	$315.00	MENS MAGNETIC GOLF BRACELET 100% STAINLESS 40,000 GAUSS	$24.99
EZ-GO 2 & 1 Flip Seat Golf Cart Carts Yamaha Club Car	$260.00	[2 of these sold for $24.99 each]	
Nikon Laser 500G LaserCaddy Golf Rangefinder NEW 7431	$243.80	Cleveland Launcher Driver Shaft - S Flex - Excellent	$24.99
BUSHNELL YARDAGE PRO TOUR	$215.00	2 Augusta National PGA 1993 Folding Golf Chairs NR!	$24.99
LASER RANGE FINDER New!!		Avon Chamois Jumbo Soft Golf Grip / Grips	$24.50
Bushnell Yardage Pro Tour Laser Rangefinder NEW! USA!	$212.80	BRAND NEW SAMSONITE GOLF TRUNK STORAGE ORGANIZER (615)	$24.00
Revue Thommen Greenmark Golfers Watch	$202.50	Titleist Scotty Cameron Happy Smiley Face Divot Tool !	$23.99
Bushnell Yardage Pro Scout Laser Rangefinder w/batt	$175.00	TITLEIST SCOTTY CAMERON Happy Smiley Face Divot Tool !	$23.99
Bushnell Yardage Pro laser rangefinder 20-0002	$162.50	I GOTCHA EXEC. GOLF BALL RETRIEVER-NEW - FREE CASE	$23.95
NEW DELUXE GOLF CART BUGGY COVER ENCLOSURE	$158.50	(60) Sharpie markers w/MAXFLI LOGO brand NEW!	$23.01
COMPLETE TaylorMade r7 r5 TP Weight & Accessory Kit	$150.00	Johnnie Walker Golf Head Covers Unsealed	$22.50
Taylor Made R7 TP Accessory Kit EXTRA weights included	$140.00	Bag Shag Practice Golf Ball Retriever - USED	$22.06
TaylorMade r7 TP Weight Kit w/ Wrench & Launch Control	$135.01	Titleist Scotty Cameron Happy Smiley Face Divot Tool !	$21.99
TaylorMade r7 quad TP Upgrade Pack NEW	$123.50	NEW TAYLORMADE r7 ACCESSORY KIT	$21.57

Golf ▸ Apparel

The average sales price in this subcategory is $12.53.

	HIGH		AVG
Mizuno Golf Performance Rain Jacket & Pant Navy Large	$99.00	Taylor Made React Golf Glove, Left Hand, Size Medium Re	$12.95
NIKE GOLF RAIN JACKET STORM-FIT NV. LG. 100%WATERPROOF	$79.95	NEW BUTCH HARMON RIGHTGRIP GOLF GLOVES WITH VIDEO DVD	$12.95
{3} NEW ASHWORTH TOUR LOGO GOLF SHIRTS XXXL*	$69.00	NEW FOOTJOY WINTER SOF MEN'S PAIR MED- LARGE	$12.55
{3} NEW ASHWORTH TOUR LOGO GOLF SHIRTS XXXL*	$68.00	Callaway Golf Glove L and Warbird Balls	$12.51
NEW!!! NIKE SP-5 Golf Shoes still in Box 11W	$66.99	New Titleist Players Glove size men's cadet XL	$12.51

	HIGH		AVG
New from the makers of PING Italy Leather Golf Belt 44	$54.99	2 MIZUNO DOUBLE STRAP MLH GOLF GLOVES - CADET XL	$12.51
DOZ MENS LH GOLF GLOVE LEATHER / 2XL XXL/NIP	$53.99	3 NEW Maxfli Noodle Large Golf Gloves RH	$12.49
DOZ MENS LH GOLF GLOVE LEATHER / XL/NIP	$53.99	CALLAWAY WARBIRD GOLF GLOVES and BALLS GIFT PACK NEW	$12.45
DOZ MENS LH GOLF GLOVE LEATHER / CADET MEDIUM LARGE/NIP	$53.99	NWOT LizGolf/LIZ Golf Skirt, Size 14	$12.21
DOZ MENS LH GOLF GLOVE LEATHER / XL/NIP	$53.99	NEW BUTCH HARMON RIGHTGRIP GOLF GLOVES WITH VIDEO DVD	$12.00
Sharp Red washable Head Golf Knickers Size 38	$51.02	3 pk Men's US Tour Leather Sz XL Golf Gloves $9.99	$11.75
New from the makers of PING Italy Leather Golf Belt 42	$49.99	2 MAXFLI (TaylorMade) M GOLF GLOVES MEDIUM MEN'S GLOVE	$11.56
DOZ MENS LH GOLF GLOVE LEATHER / XL/NIP	$49.99	Mizuno Tech Fit Gloves Mens Reg L (3 Gloves)	$11.51
Nike Dri-Fit Tour 3 Golf Gloves White Men's Large	$49.00	3-PACK WILSON PRO FIT LEATHER GOLF GLOVES- LARGE	$11.51
Great blue washable Di Fini Golf Knickers Size 38	$46.05	LOT OF 3 K'ROOZ KANGAROO LEATHER MEN'S GOLF GLOVES XL!	$11.50

Golf ▸ Bags

The average sales price in this subcategory is $40.36.

	HIGH		AVG
MacGregor Pro BLACK Kangaroo Leather Golf Bag + Set	$480.00	New MacGregor Tourney V-Foil Stand Bag Blue/Black/Silvr	$41.00
Lilly Pulitzer Limited Edition Ladies Pink Golf Bag	$430.00	NEW PRECISE G7 DELUXE GOLF STAND BAG BLACK/RED/SILVER	$41.00
Tumi Golf bag, Black, NR Likely new	$350.00	NEW PRECISE G7 DELUXE GOLF STAND BAG BLACK/NAVY	$41.00
TOURSTAGE Japan BRIDGESTONE CBTS53 Bag NEW Item!!	$256.09	NEW PRECISE M5 DELUXE GOLF STAND BAG NAVY/BLACK	$41.00
BMW GOLF BAG FACTORY NEW OGIO	$220.00	NEW BENNINGTON ULTRA SPORTS GOLF STAND BAG GREEN	$40.99
Oakley golf bag plus free mystery oakley gifts	$202.50	NEW PRECISE G7 DELUXE GOLF STAND BAG BLACK/BLACK	$40.99
Top quality tour Golf CLubs M5 ASPIRE SERIES	$177.50	NEW ADAMS DUAL STRAP CARRY BAG WITH STAND	$40.50
$919 Dynamis Radio Golf Caddy NR	$158.45	MAXFLI - Golf stand bag - light & lots of pockets!!!	$40.25
Yonex Tour Staff Golf Bag	$127.50	NEW PRECISE G7 DELUXE GOLF STAND BAG BLACK/BLACK	$40.01
TaylorMade r7 Stand Golf Bag Black/Yellow/Silver NEW	$123.50	Cleveland Quicklite Carry Bag in Charcoal NEW!! N.R.!!!	$40.01
OAKLEY GOLF STAND BAG BLK LIKE	$119.99	NEW 2005 ADAMS TUCSON CARRY STAND GOLF CLUBS BAG	$40.00
NEW W/ RAIN COVER		[2 of these sold for $40.00 each]	
NEW! Sun Mountain Lightning ES Stand Bag!!! BLACK	$113.49	New Adams Sedona Staff Stand Bag Black/Red	$39.99
NEW! Sun Mountain Lightning ES Stand Bag!!! NAVY	$112.00	Precept Hideaway Stand Bag - Black/Green - New	$39.99
Camouflage Realtree HD Green Golf Stand Carry Bag CAMO	$110.00	NEW BENNINGTON ULTRA SPORTS GOLF STAND BAG SKY BLUE	$39.99
Cleveland Golf Stand Bag	$109.00	NEW BENNINGTON ULTRA SPORTS GOLF STAND BAG STEEL BLUE	$39.99
		NEW Precept Stand Bag (black/gold)	$39.99

Golf ▸ Balls

The average sales price in this subcategory is $23.59.

	HIGH		AVG
PING EYE Plum / Yellow golf ball / balls MINT Cond!!!!	$206.26	ALL 12 BIG 12 CONFERENCE LOGO GOLF BALLS	$24.00
90 Glow in the Dark Golfs Balls with Glowsticks and Tee	$199.00	Brand New Srixon Soft Feel Golf Balls 2 dozen	$24.00
BRAND NEW SRIXON Z-URS Z URS ZURS GOLF BALLS - 6 DOZEN	$189.99	24 TITLEIST PRO V1 GOLF BALLS AAA	$23.99
BRAND NEW SRIXON Z-UR Z UR ZUR GOLF BALLS 6 DOZEN PACK	$172.50	36 TITLEIST PRO V1 GOLF BALLS AAA/AA	$23.99
6 DOZEN BRIDGESTONE TOUR B330 GOLF BALLS BRAND NEW!!	$162.50	300 Personalized Wedding Favor Stinger Golf Tees.	$23.99
BRAND NEW SRIXON Z-URS Z URS ZURS GOLF BALLS - 6 DOZEN	$160.00	NEW VOLVIK CRYSTAL SOFT FEEL GOLF BALLS (PURPLE) 2 DZ	$23.50
BRAND NEW SRIXON Z-UR Z UR ZUR GOLF BALLS 6 DOZEN PACK	$160.00	BRAND NEW BRIDGESTONE B330 (1) DOZEN GOLF BALLS	$23.49
SRIXON Z-UR 6 DOZEN NEW.	$155.00	100 Yellow Assorted Golf Balls Very Nice MINT/AAA!!!!	$22.59
SRIXON Z-UR-S 6 DOZEN NEW.	$152.50	NEW VOLVIK CRYSTAL SOFT FEEL GOLF BALLS (GREEN) 2 DZ	$22.50
6 Dz Brand New Ben Hogan Tour Deep Golf Balls NIB	$147.50	12 New Taylor Made InerGel Pro golf balls	$22.50
New Ben Hogan "Tour Deep" golf balls 6 doz	$145.00	100 YELLOW AND ORANGE GOLF BALLS	$22.50
New Ben Hogan "Tour Deep" golf balls 6 doz	$143.51	60 **MINT** SRIXON GOLF BALLS AAAA	$22.01
6 Dozen New Ben Hogan Apex Tour Black Golf Balls .99 NR	$132.50	HUGE LOT OF 207 GOLF BALLS PLUS CALLAWAY GOLF BAG	$21.50
6 Dozen New Ben Hogan Apex Tour Black Golf Balls .99 NR	$131.27	Mayacama Golf Club logo ball balls TOP 100 COURSE	$21.02
2 Sleeves Of Vintage Jack Nicklaus Golf Balls + Box	$129.01	75 SRIXON GOLF BALLS AAA+	$20.55

Golf ▸ Clubs ▸ Complete Club Set

The median sales price in this subcategory is $102.50.

	HIGH		AVG
Collectors Q.E. 2. - ST ANDREWS GOLF CLUBS! Ltd Edition	$2,475.00	NEW ASPIRE O2 LADIES GOLF CLUB SET WOMENS CLUBS BAG RH	$102.50
Ultimate, worthy of an illuminated showcase.		BEAUTIFUL CHAMPAGNE COLOR! SUPER GIFT!	
NEW Callaway Fusion Big Bertha Full Golf Club/Iron Set	$1,423.98	NEW RAM BY TOMMY ARMOUR G-FORCE COMPLETE GOLF SET W BAG	$102.50
Ping I5 Irons 3-pw, G5 Woods best deal on ebay	$1,300.00	NEW 17 PIECE WOMENS LADIES CLUB SET GOLF CLUBS BAG RH	$102.50
Use buy it now get 6 dozen maxfli noodles balls		GUARANTEED SHIPMENT THE NEXT BUSINESS DAY!	
Callaway Big Bertha 2002 Irons/Taylor Made R7 Quad 9.5*	1,000.00	NEW ASPIRE X10 MENS CLUB SET GOLF CLUBS W/ STAND BAG RH	$102.50
A complete set of Golf Clubs w/bag Free Ship w/Buy Now		GUARANTEED SHIPMENT THE NEXT BUSINESS DAY! GREAT GIFT!	
CALLAWAY GOLF CLUBS BIG BERTHA IRONS	$999.00	LADIES PETITE GOLF CLUB SET BAG WOMENS CLUBS RH NEW -1"	$102.50
WOODS PUT BAG SET. DRIVER, WOODS,		PETITE SET (-1") PLAY WITH CLUBS THAT FIT YOU PROPERLY!	
X-16 IRONS FROM TOUR VAN, PUT, BAG, MINT		NEW Tommy Armour Golf Clubs RAM 17PC Complete Set w/Bag	$102.50
CALLAWAY GOLF CLUBS BIG BERTHA VFT IRONS PUTTER SET BAG	$999.00	2005 Model with 21 Degree Hybrid Club Included!	
VFT DRIVER 3 5 7 WOODS, VFT HAWKEYE IRONS, PUT, USA BAG		NEW 17 PIECE WOMENS LADIES CLUB SET GOLF CLUBS BAG RH	$102.50
HONMA MM45-888 Iron Complete Set w/ 320 Driver mm45 888	$925.00	GUARANTEED SHIPMENT THE NEXT BUSINESS DAY!	
13 Piece set, still in plastic, brand new made in Japan		NEW LINKSMAN GOLF MENS CLUB SET GOLF CLUBS BAG RH +1"	$102.50
LADIES CALLAWAY WOODS IRONS PUTTER BAG / 13 PC SET	$910.00	NEW +1" SET MADE FOR TALL MEN GREAT QUALITY GREAT GIFT	
"GENUINE" LADIES CALLAWAY MADE IN THE U.S.A. !		NEW ASPIRE M5 MENS CLUB SET GOLF CLUBS W/ STAND BAG LH	$102.50
New Nike Limited Edition Tiger Woods Irons & TW Driver	$850.00	STAINLESS STEEL WOODS AND IRONS! LEFT HAND SET!	
Women's Callaway '05 Gems Complete Set & Cart Bag	$850.00	NEW ASPIRE O2 LADIES GOLF CLUB SET WOMENS CLUBS BAG RH	$102.50
Driver, 7 Wood, Iron Set, Wedges & Putter		BEAUTIFUL CHAMPAGNE COLOR! SUPER GIFT!	
NIKE IGNITE SLINGSHOT COMPLETE SET $1864 RETAIL VALUE	$832.00	NEW 17 PIECE MENS CLUB SET MEN'S GOLF CLUBS WITH BAG RH	$102.50
Nike staff bag and Cameron putter alone retail for $559		GUARANTEED SHIPMENT THE NEXT BUSINESS DAY! GREAT GIFT!	
New NIKE TIGER WOODS Ignite Driver & Forged Irons	$800.01	NEW! Womens Hybrid Golf Club Set & Bag - Nice Clubs!	$102.50
Only 2004 sets were produced (LIMITED EDITION)		LIFETIME Warranty On All Shafts! 100% Graphite Set!	
Callaway Big Bertha Warbird Driver Golf Club Set	$800.00	NEW LINKSMAN GOLF MENS CLUB SET GOLF CLUBS BAG RH +1"	$102.00

NEW LADY CLEVELAND SET DRIVER, WOODS, IRONS, WEDGES CURRENT MODELS- - -ALL NEW- - -$1,800 VALUE- - -BUY IT NOW!!!	$799.99
NEW NDS NIKE IRONS 3-PW+IGNITE CUSTOM DRIVER+3 WD	$799.00
Complete Set Unused Calloway Titanium Golf Clubs	$760.00

NEW +1" SET MADE FOR TALL MEN GREAT QUALITY GREAT GIFT PING Full CUSTOM SET Golf clubs 3-PW Irons 1,3,5 Woods	$101.72
Custom Fit Clubs. Great for birthday or present	
TIGER SHARK COMPLETE SET 1,3,5 Woods 3-PW Irons	$101.50

Golf ▸ Clubs ▸ Driver

The median sales price for this subcategory is $102.50.

	HIGH		AVG
Titleist Tour Issue 905R 8.5* Fujkura Pro 95 X 460cc	$3,350.00	NEW TP TITANIUM 454 Ti DRIVER/CALLAWAY	$99.00
Fall 2005 Tour Van; Prototype from Titleist; Rare!		BIG BERTHA GRIP Callaway Big Bertha	
Taylor Made R7 TP Shallow face Diamana Matte Blue 73X	$800.00	454 Clone. 9.5, 10.5, or 11.5° loft	
Check out this TOUR issue, TXXXXX B serial #		DeLaCruz Mag Cruzer Heel Weighted Anti-Slice Driver	$99.00
TaylorMade Tour Issue R5 Dual Neutral 10.5* Driver New	$750.00	Callaway Great Big Bertha II 415 9° Tour Issue Prototyp!	$99.00
Fujikura TP Speeder 660TR S Graphite New uncut		CALLAWAY BIG BERTHA Ti 454 GRAFALLOY SHAFT RH NR	$99.00
TaylorMade R7 Tour 8.5 w/ Matte Blue Diamana	$750.00	COBRA SZ 460 TITANIUM DRIVER W/ALDILA NV SHAFT RH NR	$99.00
TaylorMade Tour Issue R7 Quad 9.5* Driver New	$699.00	NEW YONEX CYBERSTAR CT Carbon Ti 460cc Driver $549	$99.00
Fujikura Fit onl-11 Six X Graphite New uncut		Cleveland Launcher 400 Titanium 8.5 Graphite Stiff NEW	$99.00
Titleist 905T 9.5* Tour Issue 905 **MINT** ACCRA SC 75 X!!!	$650.00	Cleveland NEW Sport OS 410 Driver 10.5* Regular	$99.00
Rare New!! Callaway X18 Diamana Ion finish, not FT-3	$635.00	LH CLEVELAND LAUNCHER 460 TI 10.5* GRAF BLUE R 6305	$99.00
Taylormade r7 quad TP 9.5* Speeder 757 X RH NEW	$625.00	TaylorMade R580 XD Driver Aldila NV 65 X 10.5 USED	$99.00
Titleist 905T 8.5 Tour Tour Issue w/ Proto Mitsubishi Rayon	$599.99	Titleist 983K 10.5* Driver Pro Lite Regular Excellent	$99.00
Taylor Made R7 Quad TP TOUR ONLY 10.5 LH	$580.00	BEN HOGAN BIG BEN C-S3 9.5* DRIVER NEUTRAL GRAPH STIFF	$98.95
NEW TaylorMade r7 Quad TP 9.5* FUJI SPEEDER 757 STIFF!	$579.99	$0.99 Starting Bid and NoReserve! See Item Description.	
Free UPS 2 day shipping with Buy It Now for $579.99! NR		Ben Hogan Golf Big Ben C-S3 Driver 10.5* Aldila NV-H 70	$98.88
3 X PING G5 GRAPHITE WOODS / 1 / 3 / 5 WOODS	$563.00	CLEVELAND LAUNCHER 460 9.5* DRIVER GRAPHITE REGULAR	$98.66
Taylor Made r7 TP 9.5- Speeder 757	$549.99	$0.99 Starting Bid and NoReserve! See Item Description.	
TaylorMade r7 Quad TP 9.5 DRIVER-FUJI SIX-STIFF-NEW	$542.00	NEW 05 BEN HOGAN C-S3 TI 10.5*	$98.66
Taylor Made r7 quad TP 9.5 *S Fujikura NEW!! TP Speeder 757	$530.00	DRIVER DRAW NV-H REG	

Golf ▸ Footwear

The average sales price in this subcategory is $46.16.

	HIGH		AVG
FOOTJOY Classic Dry Premiere 10 E 2005 Model # 50582	$225.00	MENS FOOTJOY FOOT JOY CONTOUR SERIES GOLF SHOES 13 MED	$49.99
FOOTJOY FOOT JOY CLASSICS DRY PREMIERE GOLF SHOES 11.5	$215.39	MENS FOOTJOY FOOT JOY DRYJOY GOLF SHOES SZ 9 MEDIUM	$49.99
Foot joy Classic Dry Premiere New 10.5 D Black	$185.00	MENS FOOTJOY FOOT JOY CONTOUR SERIES GOLF SHOES 11 MED	$49.99
Foot joy Classic Dry Premiere New 12 E Brown	$185.00	MENS FOOTJOY FOOT JOY eCOMFORT GOLF SHOES 9.5 WIDE	$49.99
Foot joy Classic Dry Premiere New 10 D Black Lizard	$185.00	MENS FOOTJOY FOOT JOY CONTOUR SERIES	$49.99
Foot joy Classic Dry Premiere New 12 E Black Lizard	$185.00	GOLF SHOES 8.5 MED	
MENS ECCO WORLD CLASS GORETEX GOLF SHOES 45 11 11.5	$177.50	OAKLEY OVERDRIVE BLACK GOLF SHOES 11.5/NEW	$46.88
NEW Ecco World Class Golf Shoe Goretex 46 / 12 rrp$400	$174.99	NEW ECCO CLASSIC ALPHA MENS GOLF SHOES BLACK SIZE 42	$46.00
Footjoy Classics Tour Style 51651 White with Black 11	$159.50	HI-TEC "Dri-Tec Wide" Golf Shoes Size 14 W (Whi/Choc)	$46.00
Men's Footjoy Classics Dry Premiere Golf Shoes 10 D NEW	$150.00	Mens 8.0 Tommy Bahama Golf Shoes	$45.00
FOOTJOY FOOT JOY CLASSICS DRY PREMIERE GOLF SHOES 11 D	$149.99	New Mens Arnold Palmer Athletic Golf Shoes Wht/Blk 10	$45.00
FOOTJOY FOOT JOY CLASSICS DRY PREMIERE GOLF SHOES 8 E	$144.99	Footjoy Classics golf shoes size 12 D 12D white/brown	$45.00
FOOTJOY FOOT JOY CLASSICS DRY PREMIERE GOLF SHOES 9 D	$144.99	FootJoy Classic Premier 8.5 Golf Shoes, Black, NICE! NR	$45.00
[3 of these sold for $144.99 each]		Ecco Men's Cognac Dress Golf Shoe Size 7	$44.99
FOOTJOY FOOT JOY CLASSICS DRY PREMIERE GOLF SHOES 9.5 D	$144.99	Ecco Men's Casual Golf Shoe Gore-Tex Size 7	$44.99
FOOTJOY FOOT JOY CLASSICS DRY PREMIERE GOLF SHOES 8.5 C	$144.99	NEW Sergio Garcia El Nino Men Spikeless GOLF SHOES 9.5	$44.95

Golf ▸ Golf Carts, Cars

The average sales price in this subcategory is $370.87.

	HIGH		AVG
NEW! White 6-Seater Hot-Rod 'Limo' Electric Golf Cart!	$7,999.00	E-Z-Go Golf Cart, E Z GO	$499.99
2002 EZGO ST480 6" LIFTED GAS GOLF CART W/ DUMP BED	$5,000.00	ITP 12" wheels+Carlisle tires lifted Golf cart (NEW)	$465.00
Club car hot rod golf cart 34 Ford not ez go yamaha	$4,550.00	Convertible Top for your Club Car or EZGO Golf Cart!	$429.00
GEM Electric Car, Model E825 with cargo rack	$4,100.00	NFM Remote Control Electric Golf Caddy Cart Trolley NR	$415.00
Club Car Carryall Lifted Golf Cart	$4,000.00	AMF HARLEY DAVIDSON GOLF CART - YABBA DABBA DOO!	$405.00
CLUB CAR (GAS) GOLF CART	$3,600.00	Polished Wedge Golf Cart Wheels And Tires	$399.00
1998 Bombardier Electric Golf Cart LOOK!!!!!!!!	$3,550.00	REMOTE CONTROL ELECTRIC GOLF TROLLEY NEW 2006 MODEL	$389.00
2000 CUSTOM EZGO GOLF CAR/CART EZ GO	$3,000.00	CUSTOM GOLF CART WHEELS AND TIRES E-Z GO	$375.00
48 VOLT CLUB CAR GOLF CART Carts	$2,950.00	8" A-Arm Lift Kit for Club Car Golf Cart	$355.99
GOLF CART OR INDUSTRIAL VEHICLES	$2,920.69	Harley Davison Golf Cart (gas) late 60's - early 70's	$355.50
DIESEL KUBOTA CUSHMAN GATOR TURF	$2,860.00	Carter Go-cart, 2 seater with 5 hp Tecumseh motor	$305.00
TRUCKSTER GOLF GO CART		48 VOLT BATTERY CHARGER FOR CLUB CAR GOLF CART	$304.99
2003 Club Car Electric 48 Volt Golf Cart	$2,800.00	1976-1981 HARLEY DAVIDSON AMF GOLF CART	$300.00
custom lifted camo 1991 club cart gas not EZgo ,yamaha	$2,800.00	The PREDATOR High Torque 36 Volt 7.6 hp Golf Cart Motor	$299.00
2001 Club Car Golf Cart, like new, EXTRAS!! NR, LOOK!!!	$2,799.00	REAR SEAT KIT FOR CLUB CAR GOLF CART	$299.00
Royal Ride Electric Golf Cart - The Rolls Royce!!!	$2,550.00	[2 of these sold for $299.00 each]	

Golf ▸ Vintage

The average sales price in this subcategory is $50.02.

	HIGH		AVG
1930 Bobby Jones US Golf Championship grand slam ticket	$1,534.65	VINTAGE DISPLAYABLE OLD YOUTH GOLF CLUB SET & BAG	$51.01
Rolex Datejust Mdel 16030 Gray Tapestry Dial SS Jubilee	$1,376.00	Vintage Golf Seat "The Featherwate"	$51.00

1928 US AMATEUR GOLF CONTESTANT BADGE	$1,313.00	VINTAGE SPALDING BOBBY JONES Jr. IRONS/CLUBS - #7	$51.00
Vintage Wilson Betsy Rawls Golf Balls UNOPENED 4 sleeve	$625.57	Vintage Stan Thompson Old Wood Putter w/steel shaft NR	$50.75
Antique Golf Club Otto Hackbarth Putter	$500.59	WOOD SHAFT GOLF CLUB CHROMIUM 10 PUTTER (D&M IDEAL)	$50.50
STERLING GOLF MATCH SAFE (Ca. 1920)	$500.00	*3 BURR KEY BILT CLASSIC BRASS PLUG HICKORY IRONS*	$50.00
Rare Bridgestone TourStage X-Blade CB Premium Forged Ir	$425.00	MacGregor Toney Penna Driver #1 and #3 wood set	$50.00
Early Goodyear The Pneumatic bramble golf ball	$416.00	PGA - Gold Ball Award - - For Members Only	$49.99
RARE! Hugh Philp Playclub,Baffling Spoon,Putter! L@@K!	$406.50	VINTAGE ARNOLD PALMER AUTOGRAPH BOOK & STUFF 1973	$49.00
Rare Bridgestone TourStage TS-201 Athlete Spirit L.C.Fo	$367.69	ANTIQUE patent Golf Ball - Spalding Glory- c1905 -large	$48.70
Antique Golf Sand Tee Box for Tee Molds	$350.00	Wilson Putting Disc in original box (1910s-1920s)	$48.00
old antique golf balls 4 bramble balls	$345.00	1937 sport photo album Golf Pro Johnny Revolta Illinois	$46.89
Great BOBBY JONES Wins GOLF GRAND SLAM 1930 Newspaper !	$300.00	C1890 GUTTA PERCHA (GUTTY) GOLF BALL-Silvertown	$46.56
Three Antique Gutta Percha Gutty Golf Balls c.1890	$300.00	Vintage Wood Shaft Hendry & Bishop Deepface Mashie	$46.00
Rare Taylor Made 300 Forged Iron Set	$282.03	VINTAGE WOOD WAND PUTTER ......RARE	$46.00

Hunting ▶ Apparel

The average sales price in this subcategory is $31.45.

	HIGH		AVG
Scent Lok Camo Clothing Package! NO RESERVE!	$305.50	Gortex Military Camo Rain Jacket Like New Large Long	$34.75
The Heater Body Suit Hunting	$162.50	New Cordura Snake Chaps	$34.00
HEATER BODY SUIT BODY HEATER SUIT BOW HUNTING	$162.50	BIG MEN'S CAMO HUNTING BIBS OVERALLS~REAL TREE~SZ 4XLT	$33.93
ASAT 3-D Camo Leafy Suit (predator mossy oak real tree)	$132.50	CABELAS INSULATED COVERALLS	$33.00
Team Primos SCENT BLOCKER JACKET & PANTS	$127.50	Snake Chaps - Gaiters Rattlers Brand Realtree Camo L@@K	$32.66
ASAT 3-D Camo Leafy Suit (predator mossy oak real tree)	$126.00	Camo Insulated and Waterproof Bibs...Never Worn...XXL	$32.00
Complete Ghillie Suit Jacket and pants - Mossy color	$126.00	BRAND NEW with tags" SCENT BLOCKER FRONTIER PANTS	$32.00
SALE!!!,FLECTARN GORTEX GORETEX GORE-TEX XL SUIT	$124.35	Holland&Holland Womens Safari Camp Cargo Short	$31.00
Filson Outdoorsman Sweater New W/Tags Sz Lge Camel NR	$113.61	ADVANTAGE TIMBER CAMO SHIRT AND PANTS XL	$31.00
3pc. Camo Ultra-Lite Ghillie Suit	$112.65	[2 of these sold for $31.00 each]	
NEW SCENT BLOCKER PROHUNTER WATERPROOF HUNTING BIBS L	$109.49	Hunting fishing Mossy Oak camo rain gear pants L NEW	$31.00
SNIPER Ghillie Suit Jacket and pants - Desert color	$107.50	Hunting fishing Mossy Oak camo rain gear suit NEW XXXL	$30.10
Hodgman Hunting Chest Waders, Size 13 Boot, XL,Neoprene	$107.50	Holland&Holland Khaki Green Womens Safari Camp Shirt	$30.00
NEW SCENT BLOCKER PROHUNTER WATERPROOF HUNTING BIBS L	$107.50	Like new Duxbak insulated advantage timber camo bibs M	$29.99
NEW SCENT BLOCKER PROHUNTER	$107.50	NEW NWTF MENS WATCH WITH DATE -TURKEY HUNTERS SPECIAL	$29.99
WATERPROOF HUNTING BIBS XL		Mossy Oak SG Uninsulated Duck Hunting Bibs/Pants - 3XL	$29.95

Hunting ▶ Decoys

The average sales price in this subcategory is $59.44.

	HIGH		AVG
Charlie Joiner Miniature Greenwing Teal Duck Decoy Pair	$1,801.00	MOJO MALLARD DUCK DECOY MOTION DECOYS DRAKE!!!!	$60.01
George Strunk wood duck pair decoy/decoys	$1,713.00	6 NEW HERTERS CANADA GOOSE FIELD SHELL DECOYS	$60.00
PR. GEORGE STRUNK MERGANSERS - DECOY	$1,500.00	MOJO MALLARD DUCK DECOY MOTION DECOYS DRAKE!!!!	$60.00
Charlie Joiner Scaup Decoys-2001	$1,251.00	Mojo Mallard Motorized Drake	$60.00
Charlie Joiner Goldeneye Duck Decoy Pair from Betterton	$1,000.00	[2 of these sold for $60.00 each]	
MASON MALLARD DUCK DECOY DETROIT GRADE EXC.PLUS EARLY	$822.00	DOVE DECOY DECOYS BEAT THE MOJO PORTABLE POWER LINE	$60.00
Rare Old Charlie Joiner Canvasback Drake Decoy	$811.00	Duck Decoys, 1 Dz Outlaw Mallard Duck Silhouette Decoys	$59.99
ANTIQUE FOLK ART HAND-CARVED,	$665.57	[2 of these sold for $59.99 each]	
HANDPAINTED DOVE DECOYS		SUPER~DAVE RHODES~ DOWITCHER SHOREBIRD DECOY SHORE BIRD	$59.00
WORKING GEORGE STRUNK SLEEPER GOOSE DECOY OP	$650.00	DUCK DECOY ROBERT CAPRIOLA	$58.51
KEN ANGER BLUEBILL DUCK DECOY DECOYS COLLECTIBLE	$611.00	RALPH JOHNSTON...LAKE St.CLAIR...DUCK DECOY	$58.00
CANVASBACK DUCK DECOY PAIR	$430.00	24- G&H Magnum Mallards	$58.00
DELAWARE RIVER RICK BROWN NJ		MOJO MALLARD FLOATER DECOY MOTION DECOYS DRAKE!!!!!!!!!	$57.45
First Nevada Duck Stamp Print 1979 Larry Hayden	$305.00	Ron Snow Drake Canvasback Duck Decoy Michigan 82	$57.00
Ducks Unlimited Dabbler Duck Collection by John Gewerth	$300.00	MOJO MALLARD FLOATER DECOY MOTION DECOYS DRAKE!!!!!!!!!	$57.00
REDHEAD DUCK DECOY MASON? HAYS? FACTORY VINTAGE	$280.00	Cork Calling Mallard Hen Duck goose decoy	$56.98
Rig of 9 Duck Decoys,Decoy,Mallard,6-drakes&3-hens	$275.00	MOJO MALLARD DUCK DECOY MOTION DECOYS HEN!!!!	$56.50

Hunting ▶ Game Calls

The average sales price in this subcategory is $38.24.

	HIGH		AVG
Wood Hand Crafted Unique Mallard Duck Call	$762.00	RARE P.S. OLT MODEL P-17 SQUIRREL CALL	$39.53
antique mallard head duck call in org. box est.1970-72	$611.72	Custom made Duck Call Afzalia burl Wood (Very Nice!)	$39.00
LENUS O'DEAN DUCK CALL	$551.99	Trutone Duck Call	$39.00
E.L.QUINN CARVED WALNUT DUCK CALL	$399.99	J.J. Lares A-2 aluminum duck call	$38.77
VERY OLD CHECKERED HANDMADE DUCK CALL, UNKNOWN MAKER	$331.00	Oliveros Duck Call	$38.75
Melancon....last of the Turpins....duck call	$320.00	Rare Herter's "Outdoorsman" Duck Call in box	$38.51
RARE Never Used Burl Walnut Stofer Duck Call	$318.33	650 PARACORD	$38.00
Jim Crow Call Not Duck	$305.00	Wood Duck Caller On Stand With 1960 Bird Hunting Stamp	$37.88
Duck Call by Dan Crook Louisiana Call Carver.	$300.00	Scarce HERTERS model 283 Vit Glodo Duck Call & case	$37.50
E.L.QUINN CARVED & CHECKERED WALNUT DUCK CALL	$299.99	WALLY TABER SAFARI MODEL WEEMS WILD CALL WITH STICKER	$37.00
40+ DUCK AND GOOSE BANDS/LEG AND NECK COLLARS!!	$274.00	Timber Mallard Duck Call...Arkansas	$36.95
John Coats Reelfoot Style Duck Call	$272.52	P.S.Olt Model D-2 Duck Call "NIB" Not Goose	$36.88
NM RARE VINTAGE FAULKS WOODEN STORE DISPLAY DUCK CALL	$260.88	Faulks WA-33-A Adjustable Duck Call – Pat. Pend. Rare	$36.09
RARE Never Used Special Stofer Duck Call	$257.22	HAND MADE DUCK CALL by "BIG JOHNS" CUSTOM CALLS	$36.01
Painted Milkcan Turkey Call Winchester Bow Hunting	$236.60	2 LARGE OLD WOODEN GAME CALLS 1 LOHMAN DUCK CALL W BOX	$36.00

Hunting ▶ Gun Parts

The average sales price in this subcategory is $56.23.

	HIGH		AVG
WALTHER PPK BOXED MAGAZINE PISTOL CLIP-ORIGINAL	$1,250.00	270 sporter contour barrel blank	$56.36
TC Encore Barrel Package	$800.00	Thompson Center TC ML Barrel .50 Cal gun parts	$56.33
TC Encore 209x50 26" Stainless, Leupold Lots of Extra's	$445.00	BUTLER CREEK RUGER 10/22 MAGNUM FLUTED BARREL NEW NRI	$56.26
T/C Encore Virgin Valley Custom Guns .454 Casull	$405.00	Paul Jaeger Mauser Barrel	$56.05
Thompson Center Encore 209X50 w/ Burris 3-9x40 + More!	$375.00	6 MM Remington X-P 100 Barrel by Shilen N.R.	$56.00
Bullberry Contender Barrel 7-30 Improved & Redding dies	$365.85	Remington 522 Viper 10 rd. .22 rifle magazine	$56.00
Remington Model 760 Barrel in .222 Rem	$355.55	UNISSUED REMINGTON ARMS 1903-A3 30.06	$55.60
Encore TC 25-06 26" Heavy Barrel BSA Contender 8x32-50	$352.56	Winchester 94 Or ??? Pre 64 Barrel .32 WCF Rifle	$55.10
Thompson Center Encore 12 gauge, 24" rifled barrel.	$350.00	45 Caliber Muzzle Loader Barrel,Gun Parts/Part,Unused	$55.00
Thompson Center Encore Super 209X45 SS Barrel	$286.00	1911 Magazines /Holster/Mag Pouch/Ammo Boxes/No Reserve	$55.00
Thompson Center Encore 209 X 50 S/S Barrel And Stuff	$281.00	Original Martini Barrel Birmingham Small Arms Co. Rifle	$54.50
THOMPSON ENCORE CUSTOM 7MM REM MAG BARREL ONLY BLUE"24"	$275.00	Gun Parts 2 Desert Eagle Baby Eagle 45acp Magazines	$53.60
Used TC Thompson Center Carbine Barrel 7-30 Waters	$265.00	Ruger Cal..44 Mag rifle barrel, gun parts lot BI	$53.50
THOMPSON/CENTER ENCORE 26" RIFLE BARREL .25-06 S/S NEW	$260.50	3 Factory Sig P229 229 magazines exc cond 40s&w 357sig	$53.00
T/C Encore 22-250 Hvy BBL with 4-12x40 scope	$260.00	Ruger 10/22 Factory Laminated Target Stock	$53.00

Hunting ▶ Gun Accessories

The average sales price in this subcategory is $18.39.

	HIGH		AVG
Used L&R 7652 Ultrasonic Cleaner	$500.00	RUGER PADDLE HOLSTER P 90 93 94 95 97 FOBUS 9mm-45 CAL	$18.99
Winchester Deluxe Cleaning Kit w/ Walnut Case VGC	$351.00	USGI 9mm Holster Bianchi international UM84/92	$18.88
COMPLETE UNCLE MIKE'S & BIANCHI NYLON DUTY GEAR	$125.00	New Otis Gun Cleaning Kit for ar-15, .223, 5.56	$18.50
Holsters 1911 type 45 Auto pistols and mag holder	$104.56	Ankle Holster - Glock 26/27/33 & More-NEW	$18.50
OTIS Cleaning Kit for 7.62 Rifles LOT of 11 KITS	$103.50	Stephen Young Youngs .303 Gun Cleaner Oil Can	$18.50
Holster & Belt,George Lawrence Co.	$82.68	NEW REMINGTON RANGEMASTER GUN CLEANING KIT	$18.50
Antique Abercrombie Fitch Parker Hale Gun Cleaning kit	$81.00	Tactical Shoulder Gun Holster NEW AUTHENTIC SWAT ISSUED	$18.50
Otis Elite Tactical Gun Cleaning System for Field Carry	$79.00	Paddle Holster for Glock 9mm	$18.25
RARE VINTAGE MARBLE'S GUN CLEANING ROD { ANTIQUE}	$75.00	VINTAGE SEARS J C HIGGINS 22 GUN CLEANING KIT #713	$18.01
Cities Service Gun Oil Tin - Flying Geese on Front	$72.33	VINTAGE MASTER CRAFT 30 CAL GUN CLEANING KIT	$18.00
Shoulder holster for large framed semi-auto pistol H&K	$70.00	VINTAGE OUTERS SHOT GUN CLEANING KIT WITH BOX # 478	$18.00
Holster, Astra German LBPN, Police	$61.99	RARE EDWIN WELLER GUN CLEANING RODS GUN CLEANING KIT	$18.00
NEW DeSANTIS Speed Belt Gun Holster WALTHER PPK PPK/S	$61.00	M1 Garand Buttstock Cleaning Kit Combo Tool Grease Clip	$18.00
VINTAGE SAVAGE ARMS GUN GREASE WITH BOX NO RESERVE	$60.00	US Rifle Clean Kit, belt pouch, LMC M1A Springfield	$18.00
NEW DeSantis NYC Shoulder Gun Holster KAHR 9mm 40 auto	$58.00	DELUXE SHOULDER HOLSTER W/2 MAG POUCHES BERETTA TAURUS	$17.99

Hunting ▶ Hunting Accessories

The average sales price in this subcategory is $54.90.

	HIGH		AVG
HUNTING BLIND	$569.00	HUGE CAMOUFLAGE SCREENING / NETTING	$56.87
4.1 MP Digital Hunting / Trail / Scouting / Game Camera	$440.00	Easton Axis 400's new in box shafts only/ will fletch	$56.00
KIFARU LONGHUNTER BACKPACK LN NR	$415.00	Mountain Hauler Pack Frame, New by Stansport. CAMO	$56.00
Brand NEW Filson #291 Wheeled Check-In Bag Otter	$407.00	Duck Hunter's Tule Seat, Duck Hunting Padded Tule Seat	$55.99
Apple archery pro-shop kit W/adjusting arms.NEW!	$400.00	Guide Gear Pro Series Magnum Blind -NR	$55.55
Double Bull Archery Matrix 360 Degrees Hunting Blind	$366.25	AMERISTEP MODEL-814 DOGHOUSE BLIND, TANGLE-CAMO *NEW*	$54.99
Double Bull Archery Matrix 360 Degrees Hunting Blind	$360.56	NORTH AMERICAN HUNTER FEEDER KIT*DEER/TURKEY FEEDER*NIB	$54.88
Double Bull Archery Matrix 360 Degrees Hunting Blind	$356.00	Camo polar fleece Backpack w/frame by K. Kelly Design	$54.00
Double Bull Blind BS5 Recurve Blind (Like New)	$337.50	Ameristep Doghouse Blind NIB!!!!!!	$54.00
DOUBLE BULL 2005 "MATRIX" GREEN, NEW COND, DEMO MODEL	$335.00	AMERISTEP MODEL-814 DOGHOUSE BLIND, TANGLE-CAMO *NEW*	$53.99
Cuddeback Digital Camera New for 2005 3.0 NO RESERVE	$330.01	Avery Finisher Snow Cover Goose Decoy	$52.87
NEW Wiley Outdoors Boat Blind (FlexBlind) Model 17C	$310.00	3-D Leafy Camo L-XL Field Suit Turkey 3D Deer 5 Set New	$51.00
Paul Busick Layout Boat	$300.00	NEW 2005 HUNTING BLIND:hunters, camo view, archery NR!	$51.00
STEALTH CAM 2005 WD3 3.0mp COLOR	$299.00	[2 of these sold for $51.00 each]	
DIGITAL GAME CAM-NEW-		Ameristep Doghouse Blind	$51.00
New Cuddeback Digital Deer Cam Camera Stealth Scouting	$290.00	Ameristep Doghouse Blind - NR	$51.00

Hunting ▶ Knives

The average sales price in this subcategory is $40.81.

	HIGH		AVG
Original Bill Bagwell Bowie and Sheath	$1,125.00	OLD SCHRADE-WALDEN 148 HUNTING KNIFE	$41.99
Randall 1-6", many options,with sawteeth	$495.00	SCHRADE IMPERIAL DUCKS UNLIMITED STEAK KNIFE SET NIB NR	$41.11
Randall Made knives STAG HANDLE	$380.00	MEYERCO 1800's STYLE WESTERN BOWIE KNIVES / CASE NEW!!!	$41.00
HUGE, SOLID MAMMOTH IVORY TUSK SECTION 8LBS	$350.00	OLD WESTERN H40 KNIFE HUNTING SKINNING STAG 8" SHEATH	$41.00
R.H. Ruana Bonner Montana Hunting Knife	$286.00	*New* Buck 103 Skinner Hunting Knife w/Sheath	$41.00
CHRIS REEVE - GREEN BERET - KNIFE / KNIVES	$270.00	Giraffe bone handle knife from South Africa	$41.00
Rare Case Tested XX Knife & Hatchet W/Sheath, 1935	$251.59	Gil Hibbon "Dragon Lord" 1996 Edition	$40.00
BUCK BUCKMASTER 184 SURVIVAL KNIFE W/SHEATH	$228.50	BUCK SHORT NIGHTHAWK B665-ODX-0 KNIFE NEW IN BOX	$40.00
CUDA TAL 1 KNIFE NEW IN BOX	$225.00	NEW Bear MGC Double Edge Stainless Stag Boot Knife	$39.99
RANDALL STYLE KNIFE BY "GRIFFIN"	$200.00	CUSTOM ENGRAVED W.R. CASE CLASSIC LOCKBACK KNIFE!	$39.78
Beautiful Cold Steel Mini Tanto Fixed Blade in Sheath	$177.50	BUCK ALPHA HUNTER B694-BK NOT Gerber , Case , Schrade	$39.00
SCHRADE USA BT01 BOMB TECH SURVIVAL KNIFE BLADE NEW NOS	$177.25	GERBER HUNTING KNIFE BRUSH THINNER TREE STAND MACHETE	$39.00
Beautiful Gerber Mark I Tactical Model Boot Knife!	$175.00	OLD ESTWING 9 1/4" HUNTING KNIFE W/ SHEATH	$38.55
OLD PUMA 6399 WHITE HUNTER W/ ORIGINAL PUMA SHEATH	$152.50	WINCHESTER FIXED BLADE HUNTING KNIFE, KNIVES	$38.50
Barry Gallagher Investment Quality Custom Knife	$150.00	CUSTOM ENGRAVED W.R. CASE CLASSIC LOCKBACK KNIFE!	$38.00

Hunting ▶ Taxidermy, Mounts, Antlers

The average sales price in this subcategory is $59.31.

	HIGH		AVG
Buffalo/Bison Head Mount/Taxidermy/Log /Western/Hunting	$2,551.00	NICE ALLIGATOR GAR FISH - GARFISH TAXIDERMY MOUNT # 36	$61.00
Kudu trophy mount shoulder african antilope taxidermy	$1,604.55	2 pcs AFRICAN KUDU HORNS 47-48" TAXIDERMY SHOFARS K-60	$61.00
moose shoulder mount,taxidermy,wildlife,art,log home	$1,000.00	Pronghorn Antelope Shoulder Mount Taxidermy	$61.00
Authentic 2 TWO HEADED CALF!! RARE!!! Halloween	$999.99	Coyote Fur,Hides,Native American Crafts,Taxidermy,Pelt	$61.00
NEW FELTED ZEBRA RUG MOUNT TAXIDERMY HIDE PELT NEW SKIN	$950.00	DOG SKULL & Bottom Jaw! Animal Skull Mount Taxidermy	$60.95
Sheep horns/taxidermy/skull/hunting/outfitters/	$900.00	BIG 4' FT IGUANA TAXIDERMY # 47 NATURAL POSITION	$59.00
Huge Bison Buffalo Head - Shoulder Mount - No Reserve	$699.00	14" HIPPO CURVED IVORY TUSK TAXIDERMY 1.20LB H96	$57.88
MAGNIFICENT BLACK SHOULDER PEACOCK/TAXIDERMY/ MOUNTED	$599.00	EXCELLENT 60 INCH TANNED COYOTE PELT-BEAUTIFUL	$57.00
Buffalo RugHyde-not cattle hide cowboy,hair soft w/tail	$450.00	vintage jackelope license...vintage jackalope sign	$57.00
XXL WESTERN DIAMONDBACK RATTLESNAKE TAXIDERMY SNAKE	$405.00	EXOTIC GAME TROPHY - FALLOW DEER SHOULDER MOUNT	$56.00
AWESOME LEOPARD SPOTTED BOBCAT TAXIDERMY WILDLIFE ART	$365.00	XL Kangaroo Fur Skin Pelt Hide Taxidermy leather	$56.00
Summer Hair Buffalo Robe - Freshly tanned 6'1" x 7'9"	$360.53	5 PC SINGLE GEMSBOK 28 - 35" HORNS TAXIDERMY E-88	$55.00
Buffalo/Bison Head Wall Mount!!	$320.00	39" KUDU HORNS & SKULL PLATE AFRICAN TAXIDERMY # K-82	$55.00
Large Buffalo Skull Taxidermy Antlers Antler Bison	$305.00	11 - 12 POINT WHITE TAIL ANTLER RACK - TAXIDERMY MOUNT	$53.77
ARCTIC WOLF RUG TANNED WILD FUR LOG HOME HUGE 78 INCH	$299.99	Raccoon rug fur skin taxidermy	$53.55

Hunting ▶ Vintage

The average sales price in this subcategory is $34.36.

	HIGH		AVG
1970'S HUGE MALE LION PELT RUG EXCELLENT - HAVE PAPERS	$1,000.00	Used BEAR Trap Chain & Hand Forged Grapple trap traps	$36.01
VINTAGE REMINGTON -UMC CATALOG PRE 1920	$526.55	Browning Nomad, Challenger Barrel, 4 1/2", new, early	$36.00
WINCHESTER HERALD 1923 ISSUE FULL COLOR FOOTBALL COVER	$374.69	Winchester Crystal Cleaner Bottle and Box	$36.00
VINTAGE REMINGTON COUNTER 22 AMMO DISPLAY RACK	$350.00	3- Victor # 330 Conibear Trapping Traps	$36.00
ADVERTISING REMINGTON THE BULLET KNIFE - NR	$270.00	Vintage P.S. Olt Duck Calls (2), No-Name Goose Call (1)	$35.01
old Advertising Western Cowboy Colt Pistol Door Plate	$270.00	Peters & King Book-Schuetzen Sharps Borchardt-Pope!	$34.75
Allen Compund Bow, 1972 production with orig box	$265.00	Conetrol Scope mount base, lot, 18 items	$34.69
Winchester Gun Advertising Pinback-Topperwein	$258.87	WINCHESTER TUMBLER STYLE GLASSES SET OF 6 N.I.B.	$33.00
Vintage Clinton Cartridge Co.-POINTER-12ga-2pc box	$250.00	WWI ERA CARDBOARD LAFLIN & RAND GUN POWDER NAVY ADV NR!	$32.59
Rare Alabama Lynch 101 Foolproof Turkey Call	$245.83	Colt Huntsman Gun Box	$32.50
Lyman #38 Receiver Sight for Win Model 1894	$223.70	Winchester New Haven vintage copper pocket piece gun	$32.06
LEWEY LAKE HOUSE PHOTO HUNTERS	$210.50	VINTAGE WILD TURKEY 50 USPS STAMPS CALL NWTF HUNTING	$32.01
ADIRONDACK MT 1920S		Old Brass Pin-On Compass, Made by Marbles	$32.01
VINTAGE LYMAN 14 SIGHT VERNER PEEP SIGHT NEAR MINT	$205.07	WINCHESTER BATTERY FLASHLIGHT UNIT CELL 1511	$31.77
SIGN BLACK FOREST RELIEF 3-D TIN DEER HUNTER PLAQUE	$199.99	6- Victor # 2 Coil Spring Trapping Traps	$31.00
Really old shorebird decoy. OP. Nantucket? NR.	$194.50	NICE OLD PACK BASKET	$31.00

Ice, Roller Hockey ▶ Ice Hockey

The average sales price in this subcategory is $25.20.

	HIGH		AVG
FULL SET OF TEAM BLACK HOCKEY JERSEYS/SWEATERS & SOCKS	$822.51	HESPELER CLASSIC PLUS 2004 ADULT GLOVES	$24.99
Portable skate.sharpener	$305.00	New Louisville TPS R2 Ice Hockey Gloves 14" Black	$24.99
Hockey Jersey Miroslav Satan!! Game worn!! Authentic!!	$250.00	Louisville TPS HGT Team Ice Hockey Gloves Black Red 13"	$24.99
Digital Scout Team Statistical Software for Hockey	$139.95	New Louisville TPS R2 Ice Hockey Gloves 14" Black	$24.99
LOT OF 6 BAUER 2000 14" GLOVES	$127.50	Lot of NB Hockey Equipment Pads gloves pants skates BAG	$24.99
Graph pro goalie skates, 9 1/2	$127.50	Jock Worn Size 44 Hockey Varsity Jacket	$24.50
Mission S-400 Comp Hockey Skates "NEW IN BOX"sz:8EE	$123.00	Lot of Kid's Ice Hockey Gear:Jersey, Skates,Pants Etc.	$23.50
Rare Red Cooper SK 100 Hockey Hurling Helmet SR. MINT	$122.50	New Shock Doctor Men's Loose Hockey Jock and Cup	$23.50
Eagle x70 Pro Hockey gloves NEW!	$122.50	HOCKEY PLAYER PARKING SIGN sports NHL	$22.99
LOT OF YOUTH HOCKEY GEAR ALMOST NEW	$119.50	New Bauer 2000 Junior Ice Hockey Gloves Youth 12 Inch	$22.60
SERIAL KILLA HOCKEY JERSEY XL ICP TWIZTID ESHAM ABK	$110.00	Itech HG 5000 Ice/Roller Hockey Gloves 14"/Blue-Red NEW	$22.52
Brian's Airlite Matched Set of Goalie Gloves-Senior	$100.00	CCM HG 452 Radioactive Ice/Roller Hockey Gloves 14"/Red	$22.52
Graph pro goalie skates, 9 1/2	$100.00	SK8T4GOLD! Itech 4400 Gloves Navy 15" NEW!	$22.50
Easton Synergy 1300 14" Hockey Gloves Brand New	$91.00	CCM HG652 Junior Ice/Roller Hockey Gloves 12"/Red-White	$22.01
Youth Ice Hockey Equipment	$91.00	New Shock Doctor Boy's Loose Hockey Jock and Cup	$21.99

Ice, Roller Hockey ▶ Roller Hockey

The average sales price in this subcategory is $27.14.

	HIGH		AVG
Tour Beemer's 05 Inline Skates	$290.99	Hyper Roller Hockey Wheels NEW Great Deal	$29.99
Roller / Ice Hockey Goalie Equipment Set	$250.00	Franklin HX Pro Gcp 2150 Hockey Goalie Chest Protector	$29.00
Graf In Line Roller Hockey Skates Cyber Flex	$250.00	Varsity Gear Roller Hockey Skates Men's Sz 11 Like New	$28.77
Tour Beemer Roller Hockey Skates Size 10.5-NEW	$232.50	K2 Rollerblades roller blades xp 6 xp6 inline skates 12	$28.27
Tour BlueMax Inline Skates new in box only $219.99	$219.99	Sherwood Premier Street Roller Hockey Face Mask - NEW	$27.95
Nearly New! Mission D1c Roller Hockey Skates '04 model	$187.50	Mission Roller Hockey Pants	$27.00
bauer 5000 inline goalie skates size 7.5 roller hockey	$160.00	Roller Blade Wheels 82mm, 82a with abec 5 bearings NEW	$26.00
Bauer Reactor 5000 Inline Goal Skates NEW!	$152.50	CCM Tacks inline rollerblades hockey skates size 6.5	$26.00
BLACK BAUER REACTOR 1000 RH GOAL SKATES SR MENS SIZE 9D	$150.00	Itech Street Hockey Goalie Mask Riot-pictured NEW NR	$26.00
BAUER REACTOR 5000 GOALIE INLINE GOALIE SKATES 7 1/2	$140.00	CHILD/YOUTHS ROLLER HOCKEY GEAR	$26.00
Tour Beemer Roller Hockey Skates Size 9.5	$132.50	ANAHEIM BULLFROGS Roller Hockey Jersey CCM Ultra Rare	$26.00
Tour MAX 700 Inline Skates Any Size Only $110	$110.00	MISSION HOCKEY SKATES & EASTON JOFA ROLLER HOCKEY GEAR	$26.00
Tour Blue Max Size10 NIB	$109.99	RED STAR HI-LO TITANIUM CHASIS ORIGINALLY $175.00	$25.00
Riedell Lady Roller Skates size 9	$102.50	Boy's Nexed 2001 AWT M5 Inline Hockey Skates - Size 6	$25.00
Goalie Skates- Bauer 1000 Supremes	$100.00	Bauer Vapor Inline Skates - Size 6 Sr.	$25.00

Ice Skating ▸ Apparel

The average sales price in this subcategory is $24.90.

	HIGH		AVG
Baton Twirling Costume	$187.50	Skating Dress by Mary - CM 8/10 Rainbow pastel!	$25.00
CARRIE JONES FABULOUS DESIGNER SKATING DRESS Lds XSM	$160.00	NEW !!! Beautiful Ice Skating Dress Size Child XX S	$24.99
SPECTACULAR CUSTOM COMPETITION SKATING DRESS	$147.50	burgundy ICE SKATING DRESS twirling gymnastic dance	$24.99
Kim New Competition Ice Skating Dress Child 10	$132.50	NEW Glittery LIME/BLACK Velvet ICE SKATING DRESS 8/10	$24.99
FABULOUS DESIGNER SKATING DRESS CARRIE JONES LADIES SM	$129.00	NEW Capezio ice skating tights & dress Adult S Ret.$80	$24.99
DEL ARBOUR CHILD M 8/10 COMPETITION SKATING DRESS	$125.00	NEW MONDOR ICE SKATE SKATING DRESS CHILD MED 8-10	$24.95
BEAUTIFUL ICE SKATING DRESS CHILD L 10-11	$112.50	Cutest Skating Dress Ever	$24.30
BEAUTIFUL ICE SKATING DRESS CHILD MEDIUM 7	$103.93	Del Arbour Ice Figure Skating Skate Dress AS Size 4/6	$24.27
GORGEOUS Ice Skating Competition Dress sz G Med.	$101.00	Del Arbour girls size 4-6 skating dress	$24.27
Ice Stage Beautiful Designer Competition Dress CH12Tall	$99.00	Ice Skating Dress / Danielle & Co / Girls 8-10	$24.05
Very pretty competition skating dress size 10 (M)	$91.00	Duck Crossing Ice Skating Dance Dress Adult NWT	$23.99
GORGEOUS Ice Skating Competition Dress sz Girls M/L	$85.51	NEW REBEL SKATEWEAR ICE SKATE SKATING DRESS ADULT MED	$23.95
NEW ICE / FIGURE SKATING DRESS TWIRLING DANCE COSTUME	$81.00	NEW Glitter BLUE Velvet BALLET/ICE SKATING DRESS 8/10	$23.66
Yazo Original Ice Skating Dress - Be a proud skater!	$81.00	nwt BodyWrappers aqua skating dress girls 8-10	$23.51
CUSTOM CL 10/12 BLACK/RED SPANISH STYLE SKATING DRESS	$80.00	Ice Skating Dress / Duck Crossing / Girls Med 8-10	$23.50

Ice Skating ▸ Skates

The average sales price in this subcategory is $33.39.

	HIGH		AVG
Harlick figure skate boot & blade set 6.5	$385.00	Riedell child white ice skating boots size 3	$35.00
Bauer Vapor XXX (Used) Size 6.5 , (Mens 8)	$356.06	Girls Figure Ice Skates - Sz 1.5 B Sheffield, Czech Rep	$34.01
Riedell Royal ice skates 6.5 B (fits aprox 8 M) new!!	$275.00	BODYWRAPPERS COMPETITION ICE SKATING DRESS	$34.00
Baure Vapor XXX Skates Size 7.5	$255.00	Ladies JACKSON FREESTYLE Ice Skates 4.5C Nice!	$34.00
Riedell 320 size 7	$250.00	Bubble Gum Pink Sparkle Skating Dress	$33.00
Remz Limited Edition Aggressive Inline Skates Size 13	$225.00	Great Riedell Figure Skates size woman 6	$33.00
New Graf Edmonton Special Figure Skates Boots Sz 4	$189.99	Rotation Trainer / Spinner for Figure Skating	$32.10
Riedell Ice Skates w/ MK Club 2000 Blades Size 8 320B	$182.50	RIEDELL SKATES GIRLS SIZE 3 WHITE	$31.48
Riedell 320 Ladies Womans Figure Ice Skates Size 5 1/2	$182.50	Women's White Ice Skates size 7 1/2	$31.09
Mission S500 Carbon - Sz 10 - Brand New	$180.00	Sherwood Tara Girls Figure Ice Skates Size Yth 9 NEW	$31.00
COMPLETE! SP Teri Deluxe Boots+Coronation Ace Blades	$179.99	Leather RISPORT Star DANCE FIGURE SKATES & BLADE GAURDS	$31.00
Riedell Ice Skates - Gold Star - Size 3 / MK Pro blades	$175.00	Women's Ice/ Figure skates White Size 8	$31.00
Riedell Skates With wilson Dance Blade womens size 7	$172.50	New CCM Finesse Girls Ice/Figure Skates White size 3 D	$31.00
BAUER VAPOR XX ICE HOCKEY SKATES SIZE 12~NEW~	$155.00	GIRLS WHITE FIGURE SKATES SIZE 5	$31.00
GAM 080 women's competition figure skates, size 6A	$150.00	GIRLS ~SIZE 13~ ICE / FIGURE SKATES ~ GREAT CONDITION ~	$31.00

Indoor Games ▸ Air Hockey

The average sales price in this subcategory is $99.88.

	HIGH		AVG
Dynamo DH-100 Air Hockey Table!! BARELY USED!!	$1,200.00	Air Hockey Table 8 ft Like New/MUST SELL	$150.00
Classic Sport 8 ft Air Hockey Table	$510.00	8ft Air Hockey Table. Works great, looks great.	$107.50
AIR HOCKEY & POOL TABLE COMBINATION GAME ~POCKEY~ BLACK	$416.01	7 Ft. Harvard Air Hockey Table~Model# G03960	$100.00
Harvard Olympic Size Air Hockey Table	$350.00	Halex Power Glide Air Hockey Table	$100.00
7 Ft. Harvard Professional Air Hockey Table	$305.00	Voit 5-foot World COMPETITION Air Hockey Table GIFT!!!!	$99.99
POCKEY-AIR HOCKEY/POOL TABLE COMBO	$280.00	[6 of these sold for $99.99 each]	
Sport Craft 7' Air Hockey Table Great Condition	$256.00		
Sportcraft Air Hockey Table*DFW area* 4'x7'	$250.00		
LIKE NEW~TOP OF THE LINE~ HARVARD AIR HOCKEY TABLE	$203.50		
AIR HOCKEY TABLE *NO RESERVE*	$197.50		

Indoor Games ▸ Darts

The average sales price in this subcategory is $26.65.

	HIGH		AVG
Arachnid Super 6 Commercial Electronic Dart Board	$560.00	Sharper Image Electronic Dart Board Dartboard NIB!	$28.21
NEW Arachnid Electronic Dart Board Dartboard w/Cabinet	$247.50	Bottelsen 20 Gram Skinnys Soft Tip Darts 202BK	$27.99
NEW Arachnid Electronic Dart Board Dartboard w/Cabinet	$239.99	4 sets of Soft Tip Darts, Incl Sure Grips + 80%Tungsten	$27.99
NEW Arachnid Electronic Dart Board w/Cabinet Dartboard	$222.51	Solid Wood Dartboard Cabinet New in box	$27.99
Arachnid BullShooter Electronic Dartboard NEW!!!	$219.00	BRAND NEW CABINET DARTBOARD DART	$27.01
[3 of these sold for $219.00 each]		BOARDS GAME WOOD FRAME	
Arachnid Arcade Bullshooter Dartboard Bull Shooter	$199.99	BRAND NEW CABINET DARTBOARD DART BOARDS GAME WOOD FRAME	$27.00
ARACHNID BULL SHOOTER DARTBOARD	$199.00	[2 of these sold for $27.00 each]	
ARCADE GAME DART BOARD		Oxford Dart board cabinet with Cheers design new in box	$26.12
Arachnid Arcade Bullshooter Dartboard Bull Shooter	$189.99	Vintage Cheers Pub Dart Board & Wall Mount Cabinet NR	$26.00
NEW Arachnid CRICKET PRO 800 Electronic Dart Board	$174.99	*NEW* NODAR SUPAWIRE BRISTLE DART BOARD RETAIL $73	$25.56
NEW Arachnid CRICKET PRO 800 Electronic Dart Board	$174.99	Accudart Winmau Bristle Dartboard British Dart Org.	$25.55
NEW Arachnid CRICKET PRO 800 Electronic Dart Board *NR*	$170.27	two sets of harley davidson darts and electronic board	$25.50
Harley Davidson Dart Cabinet Board Darts & Line SET NEW	$162.50	NODOR Bristle Dart Board Made in Great Britain	$25.01
NEW Dart Board Game Set Custom Wood Cabinet with Darts	$158.38	NEW DARTBOARD,OAK CABINET,REGULATION-SIZE,GAME,BAR,HOME	$25.00
BRAND NEW Arachnid Cricket Pro 800 NO RESERVE	$149.99	DARTS & CASE WITH A TON OF EXTRAS !!!	$25.00
NEW Dart Board Game Set Custom Wood Cabinet with Darts	$149.95	KNOTTY PINE DART BOARD CABINET /CATHEDRAL STYLE DOORS	$25.00

Indoor Games ▶ Foosball Tables & Combos

The average sales price in this subcategory is $113.64.

	HIGH		AVG
Tornado Coin Op Professional Foosball Table	$850.00	Butcher Block Style FOOSBALL Table, P/U only DFW, TX	$152.50
Tornado T2000 coin op Professional Foosball Table	$810.52	Foosball/Soccer Game Table in Dallas,TX *WILL DELIVER*	$149.00
Tornado T2000 coin op Professional Foosball Table	$810.00	Wilson FOOSBALL TABLE. Like New! Must See!	$124.99
TORNADO CYCLONE II FOOSBALL TABLE FREE SHIPPING	$725.00	LIKE NEW FOOSBALL TABLE	$120.00
NEW Tornado Cyclone II Foosball Table Foos Ball	$655.00	Multigame table/foosball/air hockey/ping pong/10in1/NR$	$108.50
FOOSBALL & POOL TABLE COMBO GAME ~POCCER / POCKEY~ NEW!	$599.99	Refurbished Foosball Table Good Condition	$102.50
Used Tornado Storm II Foosball Table	$460.00	New Spartan 9 in 1 Combo Game Foosball Table Billiards	$100.00
TORNADO WHIRLWIND II FOOSBALL TABLE *BRAND NEW* ON SALE	$425.00	Foosball Table Harvard Used In Very Good Condition	$99.99
Tornado Twister II Foosball Table	$425.00	Tornado Foosball Complete Set of Heat Treated Rods NEW	$91.00
Oak J-S foosball soccer table	$400.00	New Spartan 54 in Regulation Size Foosball Table Soccer	$90.00

Indoor Games ▶ Shuffleboard

The average sales price in this subcategory is $148.03.

HIGH TO LOW

	HIGH		
20' Antique Shuffleboard Table - 1940's ??	$1,876.00	SHUFFLEBOARD t-shirt table puck	$14.50
SHUFFLEBOARD TABLE 12' ~BACK TO SCHOOL SPECIAL~	$695.00	SHUFFLEBOARD t-shirt table puck	$12.50
8 NEW LARGE AMERICAN SHUFFLEBOARD TABLE PUCKS	$124.99	[4 of these sold for $12.50 each]	
Vintage V shaped Shuffleboard Table great shape *L@@K*	$100.00	VINTAGE CORTLAND INDOOR SHUFFLEBOARD	$10.00
Sportcraft Rebound Shuffleboard Table Brand NEW	$69.99	GAME SET~NICE WOOD	
NEW SPORTCRAFT REBOUND SHUFFLEBOARD 6-FT GAME TABLE !	$59.99	Shuffle Wax For Shuffleboard Shuffle Bowling Alley	$9.99
SUN-GLO TOURNAMENT GOLD SHUFFLEBOARD WAX 6 PACK SUNGLO	$25.25	Sportcraft Shuffleboard table *Las Vegas P/U only*	$9.99
1986 Shuffleboard Trophy, marble base, White Oak Inn	$15.50	SUN-GLO SUPER-GLIDE SHUFFLEBOARD WAX (2 cans)	$7.00
SUN-GLO SUPER-GLIDE SHUFFLEBOARD WAX (6 cans)	$15.00	7 Old Shuffleboard Disc!	$5.51
SUN-GLO SUPER-GLIDE SHUFFLEBOARD WAX (6 cans)	$15.00	HOW TO PLAY SHUFFLEBOARD By Col P C Bullard St Pete Fl	$5.00

Inline, Roller Skating ▶ In-line Skates

The average sales price in this subcategory is $34.93.

	HIGH		AVG
Rollerblade ProBlade 100 WC size 10 US M NIB	$417.02	WOMENS NIKE IN-LINE ROLLER SKATES BLADES SIZE 9	$36.00
Rollerblade Lightning 10 Mens Inline Skates 9.5 NEW NR	$350.00	ROLLERBLADE TRS ALPHA MEN'S INLINE SKATES SIZE 10 - NEW	$36.00
Rollerblade ProBlade 100 WC size 8 US M NIB	$305.00	K2 Cadence Inline Skate Rollerblade Womens 10.5 NIB New	$36.00
Aggressive Skates, Remz, Haffeys	$295.00	Salomon In-line Skates - Womens Size 10	$36.00
Rollerblade ProBlade size 9.5 US M NIB	$272.00	Womens K2 Impulse Laceless Softboot Rollerblades Sz 9.5	$34.99
HYPER VERDUCCI BSB INLINE SPEED SKATES 84MM SIZE 2 LOOK	$250.00	*LN* ROLLER DERBY LTX-950 Womens Size 9 Roller Blades	$34.99
Bont Chameleon In-line/ Ice Speed Skating Boots Size 10	$227.50	K2 Velocity Inline Skate Rollerblade Mens 11.5 NIB New	$34.99
Rollerblade Lightnong 10 size 9 US M NIB	$202.50	K2 80 Mini Youth Aggressive Size 2-4 Inline Skates	$32.50
Xsjado Skates (sizes:6, 7, 10, 10.5, 11) FREE shipping	$202.50	K2 Softboot Mini X Junior Rollerblades Size 3-6 Skating	$32.50
Trailskates by Gateskate All-Terrain Skates, size 6-12!	$202.45	SALOMON VINNY MINTON AGGRESSIVE SKATES SIZE 10	$31.98
Remz Limited Edition, Aggressive inline skates	$193.50	Nike Women's Rollerblades with Wrist Guards; LIKE NEW	$31.01
Xsjado skates size 8.5	$182.50	K2 Exotech Rollerblades K2R101 sz 10 Mens inline skates	$31.00
New!!! Salomon Pilot 9 Pro 2 Men's USA 8	$159.99	V-Form Roller hockey skates Sz.11 roller blades street	$31.00
NEW Salomon Pilot V10 2 Men's USA 10	$159.99	ROLLERBLADE INLINE SKATES MENS 13 - NEVER USED	$31.00
RAZOR SHIMA 5 *NO RESERVE* SIZE 9	$155.00	Roces LAX LADY rollerblades/inline skates Size 9	$31.00
		Rollerblade Viablade-Parkway - Women's Size 9.5	$31.00

Inline, Roller Skating ▶ Protective Gear

The average sales price in this subcategory is $7.09.

	HIGH		AVG
NEW Salomon Aggressive/Alternative Skate Helmet - NEW!	$31.00	K2 Protective Gear. NIB. size S Knee and Wrist Guard	$8.50
Talent Sports Rib Shield Pad Youth Size Medium 10 - 12	$20.00	NEW Adult MONGOOSE Knee Elbow	$8.50
LARGE LOT OF PROTEC HELMETS SKATE ROLLER SKATEBOARD YLW	$19.50	Wrist Skate Pads XL w/Bag	
Hatch Knee and Elbow pads SWAT/ Military	$19.27	Salomon Wrist Guard Gel Hand Sliders-Size M, L OR XL	$8.50
New! Salomon Women's 3-Pack Wrist Elbow Knee Size Small	$17.49	INCREDIBLES Kids Bike/Skate Helmet/Elbow/Knee Pads NEW	$8.50
brand new pro tech knee and elbow pads	$16.62	MonGoose Protective Gear - Skating & Boarding	$7.99
Salomon X-TR Womens Wrist/Elbow/Knee 3 Pads Pack Small	$15.50	ROLLERBLADE INLINE SKATING & BIKING HELMET LG/XL	$7.95
brand new pro tech knee and elbow pads	$15.50	K2 Protective Gear. NIB. size M Knee and Wrist Guard	$7.51
NEW Knee, Elbow pads & Wrist guards/Protective Gear XL	$15.50	Knee Pads/Elbow Pads ADULT SIZE	$7.50
brand new pro tech knee and elbow pads	$15.50	2XS SPORTS IN-LINE SKATING PROTECTIVE GEAR SMALL	$6.51
Talent Sports Rib Shield Pad Chest Size Medium 38 -40	$15.00	child's XS inline skate pads protective pads new	$6.50
brand new pro tech knee and elbow pads	$15.00	Rollerblade Knee Elbow Pads Wrist Guards Sz Medium NIB	$6.25
Sabotage Aggressive In-Line knee pads, paintball, XL	$14.99	Official Rollerblade helmet, great shape	$6.02
[2 of these sold for $14.99 each]		little tikes SAFETY PAD SET NEW 3+ elbow knee gloves	$6.01
brand new pro tech knee and elbow pads	$14.51	Koho Roller Ice Hockey Elbow Pads Guards Medium	$5.99
brand new pro tech knee and elbow pads	$13.50	Protective Gear Knee, Elbow, Wrist Skating, Biking NEW!	$5.99

Inline, Roller Skating ▶ Roller Skates

The average sales price in this subcategory is $26.90.

	HIGH		AVG
Sz 9 Riedell 395 Quad Speed Skates! Laser Plates!	$295.00	NIB SKECHERS navy/hotpink ROLLERSKATES size 8.5	$28.01
Powerslide C4 Inline Speed Skate Package Sz- 11	$250.00	SKETCHERS 4 WHEEL ROLLER SKATES SIZE 8 WOMENS	$28.00

Bont Chameleon In-line/ Ice Speed Skating Boots Size 10	$227.50	NIB Salomon Profile ALU Silver Rollerblades Size 7.5	$28.00
Anitque Winchester Roller Skates Box	$178.25	NEW AIR Heelys-Style SKATE ROLLER SHOES SZ3(Black&Red)	$27.99
Skates and Outfits	$160.00	Womens Near New Riedell Roller Skates-White Size 7	$27.50
Womens SP Teri Figure Roller Skates	$157.50	Vintage, LIKE NEW roller skates LOOK ! ! ! ! N.R.	$27.00
MEN'S Riedell 395 speed SKATES with lace covers SZ 10	$153.50	NEW 4 WHEELER ROLLER SKATES SZ 8	$26.99
Risport Women's size 61/2-7 [255]Atlas Plate, Comp.	$150.00	Roller Skates 4 wheel Size 8-8.5 womens, men 7 Cruisers	$26.99
Mens Riedell Roller Skates Powell Bones Sz 10 Excellent	$146.84	Vintage Women's Chicago Roller Skates Llke New Sz 8	$26.55
Retro Riedell Speed Skates mens 8 1/2	$115.50	Rollerblade in line skates GREAT condition! 27/28.5 11	$26.05
Carrera Speed Skates - NEW - Mens size 6	$112.50	Aurora STX Men 8 two sets of wheels,stoppers	$26.01
RIEDELL SURE GRIP ROLLER SKATES MENS SIZE 13 ALMOST NEW	$105.03	MEN'S ROLLER SKATES "ROLLER DERBY" SIZE 11 (NEW COND)	$26.00
NEW SKECHERS 4Wheelers Roller Skates Women's Size 7.5	$102.50	4 Wheelers Roller Skates by Sketchers Youth 5-5.5 NIB	$26.00
Sure Grip RIEDELL Men's Invader Roller Skates Sz. 9	$102.50	ROLLER DERBY RT 4+4 Skates Men's Size 7	$26.00
ORIGINAL RIEDELL BLACK LEATHER SPEED SKATES ZINGER 7	$100.00	CHICAGO White Ladies Roller Skates Size 7? w/Box	$26.00

Lacrosse ▶ Sticks

The average sales price in this subcategory is $35.42.

	HIGH		AVG
2 ANTIQUE LACROSSE STICKS WOOD& LEATHER MADE IN ENGLAND	$320.00	New unstrung warrior razer head	$36.00
2 Vintage Wooden Lacrosse Sticks	$129.50	STX AL6000: PRO LACROSSE STICK BRAND	$36.00
Kryptopro kevlar long stick *brand new*	$100.00	NEW WITH TAGS NR	
Warrior Lacrosse Krypto Pro Kevlar Defense Shaft Stick	$91.00	STX Fuse Lacrosse Lax Complete Stick Shaft Power V Blue	$36.00
[2 of these sold for $91.00 each]		DeBeer Gait DB803 Shaft Defense WARRIOR BRINE c405	$36.00
Warrior Lacrosse Krypto Kevlar Pro Attack Shaft	$90.00	STX TURBO LACROSSE HEAD STRUNG TRADITIONAL	$36.00
2 Vintage Antique Wooden Lacrosse Sticks W/ Leather	$81.00	2 Vintage Wood Lacrosse Sticks	$35.65
Warrior Diamond Orange Krush Lacrosse Handle	$81.00	Gait Oracle Strung w/ Dura Mesh..NEW!!	$35.50
Warrior Lacrosse Krypto Pro Kevlar Defense Shaft Stick	$80.99	STX Bionic Lacrosse Stick Head with Custom Pocket	$35.00
Warrior Smokin' Silver Split Shaft Lacrosse Handle NEW!	$79.75	Warrior Razer Lacrosse head strung razor	$35.00
Warrior Lacrosse Krypto Pro Kevlar Defense Shaft Stick	$79.00	New STX Fuse Lacrosse Lax Head Strung Hard Mesh Power V	$34.05
[2 of these sold for $79.00 each]		BRINE E3 Head unstrung *NEW*	$34.00
New STX Duece Lacrosse Stick Head Custom Strung!!!	$77.99	Warrior Lacrosse Krypto Pro Kevlar Goalie Shaft Stick	$34.00
Warrior Smokin' Silver Split Shaft Lacrosse Handle NEW!	$76.75	New STX Fuse Lacrosse Lax Head Strung Hard Mesh Power V	$34.00
New 2005 HARROW SOLO One Piece Womens Lacrosse Stick NR	$76.50	STX Fuse Lacrosse Lax Complete Stick Shaft Power V Blue	$33.01
New 2005 HARROW SOLO Composite Women's Lacrosse Stick!	$76.05	BRINE MATRIX ATK Lacrosse Shaft Green/White - Sample	$33.00
Warrior Lacrosse Krypto Pro Kevlar Defense Shaft Stick	$76.00	New STX Fuse Lacrosse Lax Head Strung Hard Mesh Power V	$33.00

Martial Arts ▶ Apparel

The average sales price in this subcategory is $17.92.

	HIGH		AVG
Bruce Lee Jumpsuit Game of Death Kill Bill Jump Suit	$99.00	Sz. 2 Martial Artis Uniform-Karate-TKD	$18.00
Childrens ATA XMA Uniform	$90.85	Sz. 3 Martial Arts Uniform-Karate-TKD	$18.00
Krugans A4 Gi BJJ Jiu Jitsu Gracie UFC KOTC	$81.00	Sz. 4 Martial Arts Uniform-Karate-TKD	$18.00
Tokaido kumo #7 karate gi.	$76.00	Sz. 5 Martial Arts Uniform-Karate-TKD	$18.00
MITSUBOSHI Judo Gi Uniform Made In JAPAN Double Weave	$70.00	Black Karate Uniform Wrap Style Midweight NEW!	$17.99
ATAMA Blue Summer Weave Jiu-Jitsu Kimono/Gi Size A4	$60.00	Black Karate Uniform Wrap Style Midweight NEW!	$17.99
NEW JUDO GI UNIFORM / MARTIAL ARTS SUIT WHITE BLEACHED	$60.00	Ricardo Arona t shirt jiu jitsu bjj ufc vale tudo	$17.50
[3 of these sold in a multiple item ("Dutch") auction for $20.00 each]		Plays With Swords kendo tai chi iaido tshirt	$17.49
NEW ADIDAS ADI-LUXE TAEKWONDO MARTIAL ARTS SHOES SZ 12	$59.95	New Student Karate Uniform Size 5	$16.99
White Atama / Competition Jiu Jitsu Kimono	$57.90	NEW Martial Arts Pants TSD HKD MDK	$16.99
ATAMA kimono blue gi grappling jiu jitsu NHB MMA A3 A4	$56.50	Tangsoodo Hapkido	
Mizuno White Ichiban Gi (Aikido, Judo, Jujitsu, Kimono)	$56.00	Black Karate Uniform Wrap Style Midweight NEW!	$16.99
JIU JITSU GI - HOWARD COMBAT KIMONO - Ju Jitsu	$56.00	Brand New White Student 8 oz Karate Uniform/Gi Size 4	$16.99
Krugans Jiu jitsu Gi Kimono size A4	$51.00	Tae Kwon Do Sparring Gear Gi Belts Jacket Head Foot	$16.36
Martial arts Uniform Jiu Jitsu	$51.00	Tae Kwon Do Uniform and Gear	$16.01
NEW Shihan Jiu-Jitsu DBL Weave BLUE or WHITE Gi + Belt	$50.99	MEN'S 8 WHITE KUNG FU SHOES-COMPETITION	$16.00

Martial Arts ▶ Sticks & Swords

The average sales price in this subcategory is $24.45.

	HIGH		AVG
Sumari Sword - Ameryu Family Katana Swords	$600.00	MARTIAL ARTS BAMBOO BO TRAINING STAFF JUJITSU!	$24.99
Paul Chen Gorin Iaito Unsharpened Training Sword NEW	$269.99	Unique~ MARTIAL ARTS BAMBOO BO STAFF OKINAWAN KENPO	$24.99
KAI-GUNTO Japanese Naval officers' SWORD GOOD CONDITION	$155.25	CUSTOM Pair of Escrima Kali Arnis Fighting Sticks	$24.99
Signature Tang Unique Dragon Tsuba Japanese Tachi Sword	$152.50	Marvel Elektra's Sai Karate Comics Cosplay with Plaque	$24.99
Paul Chen Practical PLUS Wakizashi Japanese Sword #2118	$149.99	Samurai Ironwood Kamagong Bokken Katana Sword Boken tkd	$24.99
Paul Chen Practical Wakizashi Japanese Sword #2061	$129.99	BLACK SAMURAI KATANA Sword Ninja Blade Martial Arts NIB	$24.99
Cocobolo Handcrafted Bokken Aikido Iaido one of a kind	$125.00	STEEL/CHROME SAI-Sais-Daggers-Knives-Samurai-Ninja-21In	$24.96
Filipino Pinute Sword & Dagger CAS/Iberia SR526	$124.99	6 ARNIS ESCRIMA KALI SMOKED RATTAN STICKS FREE SH	$24.50
Antique furbish Blade Samurai Sword Katana	$111.50	PAIR 2 BOKKEN BOKEN JAPANESE PRACTICE TAI CHI SWORD	$23.99
South African Hippo Hide Sjambok / Whip (Pair) NEW!	$103.50	BOKEN JAPANESE PRACTICE WOODEN TAI CHI SWORD * SET OF 2	$23.99
Filipino Tausaug Barong Sword CAS/Iberia SR509 NEW ITEM	$99.99	KENDO SHINAI STICK BAMBOO SWORD * SET OF TWO	$23.99
Old gift Japanese samurai sword Tachi handmade blade	$91.00	[2 of these sold for $23.99 each]	
Cocobolo Handcrafted Suburito bokken Aikido Iaido	$90.00	Set Of 2 Stainless Steel JAPANESE SAI/SAIS 23.5" W/Plaq	$23.95
SUN&MOON COMPETITION TAICHI JIAN!	$89.95	Set of 2 Bokken Wooden Kendo Practice Sword	$22.99
SWORD-TIGER CLAW-NEW		STEEL/CHROME SAI-Sais-Daggers-Knives-Samurai-Ninja-21In	$21.95
2 Knives Marked Tang Temper Blade Samurai Sword Katana	$86.00	2 Escrima Kali Arnis Stick Weapons Bag Case Philippines	$21.00

Paintball ▸ Air Systems & Accessories

The average sales price in this subcategory is $58.69.

	HIGH		AVG
Evil Scion 68ci 5000psi N2 Paintball Tank not dye, ion	$265.00	47/3000 ACI Bulldog III Air HP Systems NEW	$66.00
68/4500 2k4 MacDev Conquest Adjustable Air System	$259.96	Nitro Duck MiniReg 68ci 3000 psi air tank	$63.05
MAX FLO MAXFLO REGULATOR FLOW NITRO PAINTBALL REG NR	$259.25	Nitro Duck Air Tank *LOW Price* 3000 PSII	$61.00
TWO CHEAP COMPRESSED AIR PAINTBALL TANKS AND EXTRAS	$257.00	Max Flow Flo Manifold Tank Regulator Smart Parts NR!!!	$61.00
NEW Evil Scion Air System *45 cu 5000 psi*	$250.00	NEW Nitro ACI 47 3000 HPA Paintball Compressed Air Tank	$61.00
45/5000 evil scion tank	$220.00	Worrgames 50/3000 PSI Air Tank Paintball HPA Not Co2	$61.00
MAX FLO MAXFLO REGULATOR FLOW NITRO PAINTBALL REG NR	$207.50	5 Pure Energy 9 oz Co2 Tanks w/ Thread Savers NEW 3	$60.00
WDP Angel AIR reg and 45/4500 tank	$202.50	PMI Pure Energy NEW Nitrogen Tank A Must See SAVE	$59.00
Evil Scion air tank paintball PMI	$202.50	BRAND NEW WORR GAS 50 CI 3000 NITRO/HPA TANK	$57.00
Tippmann 98 Custom Paintball Gun	$202.50	Crossfire 47ci 3000psi Compressed Air Tank	$57.00
Dye throttle 70 cu 4500 psi stubby peanut nitro tank	$200.00	Pure Energy brand new Nitro (N2) 3000 psi 72cu tank PMI	$57.00
Crossfire 4500 PSI Carbon Wrap lightweight nitro tank	$190.00	******WGP WORR GAS 50ci 3000psi HPA /NITRO TANK******	$57.00
Dye Throttle Paintball Air Tank 45 ci/ 4500 New in box	$190.00	CROSSFIRE 3000 psi STEEL 68cu in PAINTBALL NITRO TANK	$56.42
Angel Air nitrogen Carbon Fiber 68i 4500 psi	$189.99	Worrgames 50/3000 PSI Air Tank Paintball HPA Not Co2	$56.00
max flo	$185.00	Crossfire 47 CI 3000 PSI nitro compressed air tank	$56.00

Paintball ▸ Barrels

The average sales price in this subcategory is $30.93.

	HIGH		AVG
Autococker STO Dye Paintball Gun Hard Case 12V Hopper +	$208.00	14 inch Dye Boomstick Barrels For Automag	$31.00
Smart Parts Freak Barrel System Autococker!! 3 lengths!	$155.50	14 Inch VM-68 Rifled SNIPER Paintball Gun Barrel VM68	$31.00
Smart Parts SS Stainless Freak barrel kit paintball NR	$150.00	dye precision paintball barrel TI AC blk 14" New	$31.00
DYE 16" BOOMSTICK PAINTBALL MARKER GUN BARREL SPYDER 2P	$150.00	NEW! 3A Paintball SPYDER 2 Piece Barrel 16" Red JT	$31.00
[2 of these sold in a multiple item ("Dutch") auction for $75.00 each]		32 Degrees Whisper Barrel for Spyder 14" Black	$31.00
FREAK BARREL SYSTEM AND 2 DYE BOOMSTICKS FOR AUTOCOCKER	$147.51	i have freak back like autococker,matrix,viking,dm4	$31.00
NEW 2004 AUTOCOCKER Paintball Gun NO RESERVE	$142.50	22" Spyder Blitz 2Boku Ultralight Sniper Barrel NEW 21"	$30.69
SMART PARTS 16" PAINTBALL MARKER GUN BARREL SPYDER E-99	$140.00	Armson Stealth Barrel Tippmann A5 Pro/Carbine 13"	$30.00
[4 of these sold in a multiple item ("Dutch") auction for $35.00 each]		12" Dye Stainless Steel Autococker Auto Cocker Barrel	$30.00
Smart Parts Freak System Shocker 10" 12" Dye Front	$130.00	Smart Parts Progressive 14" Barrel Autococker threaded	$10.00
Stiffi Switch Kit Autococker/DM4/DM5/Proto/Intimidator	$125.00	Smart Parts Shocker Freak Back 1 insert .689	$30.00
HammerHead Barrel Kit - Autococker	$125.00	Paintball 21" SPYDER Sniper 3 Piece Rifled BARREL New	$30.00
NEW SUPERBOLT AUTOCOCKER Paintball Gun NO RESERVE	$122.50	NEW SMART PARTS FREAK KIT BARREL	$30.00
PAINTBALL ANGEL BARREL 4 BOOMSTICK CP BACK LCD A4 G7	$117.50	FRONT BLACK 12" TIP	
Powerlyte Scepter Barrel kit Autococker Intimidator BKO	$116.00	Spyder Piranha Rebel 21" Sniper Paintball Barrel nr NEW	$29.99
Evil Pipe Kit 14 inch autococker Silver to Black barrel	$112.50	Spyder Piranha Rebel 21" Sniper Paintball Gun Barrel	$29.99
LUCKY 15 BARREL KIT AUTOCOCKER THREAD	$110.00	[2 of these sold for $29.99 each]	

Paintball ▸ Paintballs

The average sales price in this subcategory is $30.96.

	HIGH		AVG
Paint Ball Gun DM5	$820.00	2000 PMI PREMIUM PAINTBALLS YELLOW/RED 1ST QUAL	$42.00
tippmann A-5, speedball package	$356.50	5000 Paintballs 0.68 caliber 2000 yellow 3000 blue	$41.00
PAINTBALL SET!!! TIPPMAN A-5, G8 DELTA, MASK, ETC.	$300.00	Paintball 8000 rounds Purple paintballs .68 Cliber	$41.00
Ultra EVIL paintballs 8000 rounds FREE SHIP white shell	$199.99	WoW! 4000 rounds PMI EVIL PAINTBALLS - BEST DEALS EVER!	$36.75
[3 of these sold for $199.99 each]		[4 of these sold for $36.75 each]	
Brand New Tippmann 98 Custom w/responce trigger	$175.00	WoW! 4000 rounds PMI EVIL PAINTBALLS - BEST DEALS EVER!	$34.99
Icon Z Semi- Auto Paintball Gun with acessories	$152.50	Rufus Dawg Yellow T-Balls Target Balls for Paintball	$34.99
Draxxus Inferno SFX "factory team" 4 cases FREE SHIP	$135.99	4000 rounds PMI ALL STARS PAINTBALLS 4,000	$33.99
[11 of these sold for $135.99 each]		Gameface Paintball gun E REX ELITE very nice	$31.00
spyder victor paintball gun marker,3 barrels co2,mask,	$132.50	2 Used Great Condition Brass Eagle Talon PB Guns	$30.00
PMI Big Ball paintballs 8000 rounds FREE SHIP	$125.99	1000 Pack .40 Caliber Paint Balls, FREE Blow Gun w/BIN	$29.99
[2 of these sold for $ 125.99 each]		Paintball Seconds 4000 Round Case Paintballs BLOW OUT	$28.00
Proball Blue/Pink 8000 rounds paintballs zap Free Ship	$119.99	Case of Draxxus Midnight Paintballs Sealed and Fresh	$28.00
[10 of these sold for $119.99 each]		Paintball Seconds 4000 Round Case Paintballs BLOW OUT	$28.00
ZAP Tork 8000 rounds paintballs Free Ship	$114.99	[9 of these sold for $28.00 each]	
		4000 Shrapnel / Seconds PAINTBALLS .68 Caliber	$27.99
		4000 rounds Shrapnel / Big Ball PAINTBALLS .68 Caliber	$27.99
		[3 of these sold for $27.99 each]	

Racquetball & Squash ▸ Racquetball Racquets

The average sales price in this subcategory is $57.77.

	HIGH		AVG
Head IGS Liquidmetal Racquetball Racquet - grip ss	$171.50	E-Force Radium 190 Racquet EForce 3 15/16 Grip **NEW**	$63.51
Ektelon O3 RED Racquetball Racquet Racket BRAND NEW	$170.00	Ektelon Racquetball Racquet More Attack Never Used!!!	$61.00
BRAND NEW EKTELON 03 RED Racquetball Racquet	$169.69	NEW Ektelon TT Warrior Racquetball Racquet + Eyeguard	$60.01
BRAND NEW EKTELON 03 RED Racquetball Racquet	$167.50	NEW E Force Bedlam X190 Grams Racquetball PLUS COVER	$60.00
Ektelon 03 Red Racquetball Racquet - XS grip	$165.31	E-force Bedlam Lite 170g racquet	$59.00
Brand New Head Liquidmetal IGS 165 Racquetball Racquet	$163.50	NEW E Force Bedlam X190 Grams Racquetball Racquet	$57.01
BRAND NEW HEAD LIQUIDMETAL IGS 165 Racquetball Racquet	$162.50	NEW Head Megablast 185 RACQUET & NEW $20 EYEGUARD	$57.00
HEAD LIQUIDMETAL IGS 165	$162.50	Head MegaBlast 175 Racquetball Racquet 3 5/8" Grip NEW	$57.00
Ektelon 03 Red Racquetball Racquet - ss grip	$161.06	BRAND NEW E-FORCE BEDLAM 195 RACQUETBALL RACQUET	$56.05
HEAD LIQUIDMETAL IGS 175 NEW MODEL BRAND NEW RACQUET	$158.25	NEW E Force Bedlam X190 Grams Racquetball Racquet	$56.04
Ektelon O3 RED Racquetball Racquet Racket BRAND NEW	$157.50	NEW Wilson 150 DLX Hyper Racquetball Racquet	$56.00

Ektelon 03 Red Racquetball Racquet - SS grip	$157.50	E-force Bedlam Lite 170 - NO RESERVE - free bonus	$56.00
Ektelon 03 Red Racquetball Racquet - SS grip	$155.10	Head MegaBlast 175 Racquetball Racquet 3 5/8" Grip NEW	$54.00
Brand New Ektelon 03 Red - SS!! Free Can of Balls!!	$154.77	New Head i.X160 Racquetball Racquet +CD	$53.25
NEW HEAD LiquidMetal 175 IGS Racquetball Racquet NEW	$152.57	EKTELON TRIPLE THREAT VENDETTA RACQUET	$53.09

Racquetball & Squash ▸ Squash Racquets

The average sales price in this subcategory is $61.70.

	HIGH		AVG
Head Liquidmetal Megablast 165 IGS Racquetball racquet	$155.50	HEAD I.X 120 squash racquet racket I.X120 NEW! No Reser	$78.02
New Head Liquidmetal Megablast 170 Racquetball racquet	$149.06	HEAD I.X 150 squash racquet racket I.X150 NEW! No Reser	$77.00
1 HEAD LIQUIDMETAL 140 SQUASH RACQUET	$139.00	HEAD I.X 120 squash racquet racket I.X120 NEW! No Reser	$76.00
HEAD LIQUIDMETAL 140 squash racquet NEW liquid metal LM	$129.95	PRINCE TT SOVEREIGN squash racquet racket NEW! NR	$71.00
New 05 Head Liquid Metal Liquidmetal Squash 120 racquet	$122.50	New Wilson Triad 145 Squash Racquet 3 3/4	$71.00
HEAD Liquidmetal LM 140 squash racquet NEW racket	$119.95	WILSON HAMMER 110 H110 squash racket racquet NEW! NR	$61.00
New Head Liquidmetal Megablast 180 Racquetball racquet	$112.50	Brand New Wilson 05' Hammer H145 Squash Racquet	$59.00
2 Dunlop "HOT MELT" Custom Pro Squash Racquets	$112.50	New Wilson Hammer 110 Squash Racquet 110 grams	$56.00
New Head Liquidmetal Squash 140 racquet	$110.26	HEAD I.X 140 squash racquet racket I.X140 NEW! No Reser	$56.00
Head Liquid Metal 120g Squash Racquet	$109.51	WILSON HAMMER 110 H110 squash racket racquet NEW! NR	$53.00

Running ▸ Apparel

The average sales price in this subcategory is $10.56.

	HIGH		AVG
USMC SWEAT PANT SHIRTS PT SHORTS MARINE CORPS EGA JOCK	$69.99	Disciplines Womens Running Shorts Size Small High Cut	$11.19
Men's mens N2N Ultra Runners spandex lycra tights pants	$61.00	TYR Womens Running Shorts Size Small	$11.19
1 CW-X athletic pant	$47.00	NEW JOGALITE REFLECTIVE JOGGING/RUNNING SAFETY VEST	$11.00
Assorted Running Shorts & Sport Bras	$41.01	New Mens BROOKS RUNNING Coolmax Tank Top Shirt L	$11.00
Axley Raptor Competition Eyewear Rudy Project Oakley	$40.99	brand new with tags TYR lycra singlet size medium	$10.99
N2N Jock's BLACK ULTRA RUNNERS / Sm. Workout Tights	$39.99	NIKE UNITARD TRACK SUIT PENN STATE SZ WOMENS MED	$10.99
[2 of these sold for $39.99 each]		NEW Saucony Triathlon Running top Singlet sports bra M	$10.51
Men's mens N2N Ultra Runners spandex lycra tights pants	$36.75	2 Adidas Running Tops ~ Built in Bra! Medium!	$10.51
NWT Mens Sugoi Comp Long Sleeve Shirt - Large $55	$36.00	NIKE Dri Fit Running Tank Top Jersey Size Small White S	$10.51
SPEEDO Running Jogging Pants Tights Adult 30 L@@K!	$36.00	ADIDAS LONG SLEEVE CLIMA LITE RUNNING	$10.50
LOT/3 NIKE STEVE PREFONTAINE T-SHIRT MENS MED/L	$36.00	MARATHON SHIRT M	$10.50
amphipod Run Lite SnapFlask 4 Fuel Pack Running	$33.01	Kilimanjaro Coolever Hiking Running Mesh Cap Coolmax	$10.50
SUGOI CYCLING / RUNNING JACKET womens size S	$32.72	ADIDAS Mens Polyester Running Shorts ~ Adult XL ~ NEW	$10.50
Nike Mens Running Shorts and Two (2) Singlets Size Med	$31.00	New Adidas White Running Climalite size M with tags-SS	$10.50
amphipod Run Lite SnapFlask 4 Fuel Pack Running	$28.95	BRAND NEW-RLX Ralph Lauren Technical Mesh Tee-Men's L	$10.50
NEW Orange Saucony Running Shorts Size Medium	$27.00	adidas Retro Polyester Track Warmup Jacket Sz Adult Lg	$10.50

Running ▸ Footwear

The average sales price in this subcategory is $38.97.

	HIGH		AVG
ADIDAS One 1 Intelligent Running Shoe US 8.5 UK 8 NEW	$245.00	Nike Shox NZ Red / White U.S. Size 10	$41.00
ADIDAS One 1 Intelligent Running Shoe US 10 UK 9.5 NEW	$245.00	NEW Adidas MENS Climacool II Running Shoes US 10.5 $100	$41.00
ADIDAS One 1 Intelligent Running Shoe US 10.5 UK 10 NEW	$241.50	ASICS Cumulus VI mens running shoes sz 11 NEW kayano	$41.00
Auth OG Nike AIR MAX PLUS Grey Royal Blu Sz12 Jordan	$198.88	ADIDAS Response TR 8 Trail Running Shoes Mens 9 NEW	$40.90
NiKe AiR MaX 1 87 OrIgInAl MeSh 11 us 10 uk 95 ReD	$182.50	Brooks T3 Racer 10.5 Almost New NR Men's 5.9 oz Fast!	$40.51
BRAND NEW DS MENS NIKE AIR MAX	$147.50	New Balance 717 Running Shoes – Women's Size 8, Normal	$40.00
95 SIZE US 13 SHOX NR		MEN'S NIKE AIR STRUCTURE TRIAX SZ 13 RUNNING SHOE WHITE	$40.00
NEW NIKE AIR MAX 95 MENS 10.5 U.S. AUTHENTIC	$147.50	Saucony Grid Jazz X Running Shoes Mens 11 Wide NIB	$39.99
NIKE MENS NIKE SHOX TL 2 NIB! WHITE/SILVER/RED sz 10	$112.50	[3 of these sold for $39.99 each]	
Asics Gel Kayano XI Mens Running Shoes NEW!!	$110.00	NIKE Zoom Air Spiridon Running Shoes Mens Sz 8 NEW	$39.90
Asics Gel Kayano XI Womens Running Shoes NEW!!	$110.00	ADIDAS RESPONSE TRX MENS RUNNING SHOE 9.5	$38.85
ASICS GEL KAYANO XI MENS 11 NWT	$109.00	NEW BALANCE 890 Running Shoes Womens Sz 7.5 B	$38.57
RaRe NiKe AiR MaX 95 CrEaM/OrAnGe 8us 7uk 97 1 AtMoS	$99.99	New Adidas Men's A3 Axiom Running Shoe 8.5-11 12	$38.50
NIKE MENS NIKE SHOX TL 2 NIB! BLACK/RED/SILVER sz 12	$99.95	[2 of these sold for $38.50 each]	
NIKE MENS NIKE SHOX TL 2 NIB! WHITE/SILVER/RED SIZE 8.5	$99.95	New Balance 1220 Stability Running Shoes Womens sz 6 B	$38.02
NIKE MENS NIKE SHOX TL 2 NIB! WHITE/SILVER/RED SIZE 15	$99.95	NIKE AIR GHOST RACER RUNNING FLAT SHOE SZ 10.5 NIB $80	$38.00
		NEW BALANCE 576 RUNNING SHOES 7 D UK 6.5 EUR 40 Green	$37.99

Scooters ▸ Electric

The average sales price in this subcategory is $137.87.

	HIGH		AVG
SEGWAY HT- i80	$3,700.00	500W- TIGER MODEL SHINY PINK BIGWHEEL ELECTRIC SCOOTER	$144.00
SEGWAY HT, 2004 MODEL ! 167, used less than 2 miles	$3,550.00	RAZOR E300 ELECTRIC SCOOTER BRAND NEW IN SEALED BOX 300	$143.50
Segway i167, Like New Condition FREE SHIPPING, I Series	$3,500.00	Razor E300 Electric Scooter	$140.00
Segway HT i167 - Like New - No reserve - Free Shipping	$3,450.00	Electric Bicycle / pedale or sit back & twist the grip	$140.00
SEGWAY HT i170 BRAND NEW IN BOX - NO RESERVE	$3,400.00	GT Asteroid 400w Electric Scooter Blu Ft Sus 12" Wheels	$138.50
SEGWAY HT i Series NEW IN BOX	$3,251.00	E-36 Red SCOOTER 800 WATT 36 VOLT ELECTRIC SCOOTER	$137.50
Segway Human Transporter i167	$2,325.00	600W TIGER MODEL BURGUNDY BIGWHEEL ELECTRIC SCOOTER	$136.50
SEGWAY "P" SERIES Like New at NO RESERVE!!!	$2,051.00	Brand New 2006 Tandem bike 21 speed 26" 3 color choices	$136.49
NEW $1500 Mobility PMV Electric Scooter 3 Wheel Blue NR	$680.01	SCHWINN F-18 Scooter New In Box	$135.83
SEGWAY BATTERY FOR I 170 MIDNIGHT BLUE W/CHARGER.	$510.00	500W- TIGER SHINY PURPLE BIGWHEEL ELECTRIC SCOOTER	$134.00
FOLDING MINI EBIKE E BIKE ELECTRIC BICYCLE SCOOTER NR	$500.00	600W TIGER MODEL BURGUNDY BIGWHEEL ELECTRIC SCOOTER	$134.00
EBIKE- Blue, 36 V quiet electric motor, up to 18 mph!!!	$499.00	500W-TIGER SHINY PURPLE BIGWHEEL ELECTRIC SCOOTER	$134.00
New ELECTRIC BICYCLE BIKE Scooter E-Bike w/ suspension	$469.00	[3 of these sold for $134.00 each]	

New Panterra 750w RETRO Electric Scooter Blue 6064	$405.00	600W TIGER MODEL BURGUNDY BIGWHEEL ELECTRIC SCOOTER	$134.00
2 Voy Electric Scooters Lot Moped Bike Excellent DEAL	$400.00	500W- TIGER MODEL SHINY PINK BIGWHEEL ELECTRIC SCOOTER	$134.00
		600W TIGER MODEL BLUE BIGWHEEL ELECTRIC SCOOTER	$134.00
		[3 of these sold for $134.00 each]	

Scooters ▶ Gas

The average sales price in this subcategory is $23.46.

	HIGH		AVG
GOPED Super XPED X ped GO ped Modded LOOK Awsome Now!!!	$400.00	REAL boost bottle pocket bike HP NOS X1 X2 X7 x 1 2 3 7	$24.99
Goped Sport *MANY MODS*	$200.00	47cc/49cc Pocket Bike FLYWHEEL parts clutch sprocket	$24.99
THREE HONDA MINI TRAIL 50 Z50 FRAMES L@@K!!	$161.00	47cc 49cc Pocket Bike Front Gear Box sprocket clutch HP	$24.99
22mm mikuni carb w/jets air filer 4 stroke pbu x6 x12	$160.00	47cc POCKET BIKE WHEEL AND TIRE SET 49cc SPROCKET RIMS	$24.99
GOPED TGN BF/GSR Flybars	$152.50	47cc/49cc Pocket Bike MUFFLER EXHAUST PIPE part clutch	$24.99
Go-ped NEW *GEO* FAST TUNED EXHAUST Kit	$130.00	49cc POCKET BIKE CARBURETOR! X1 X2 X6 X7 carb parts	$24.99
16.5mm Pocket Bike RACE PORTED walbro Carburetor CARB	$122.50	Performance 2-Spring Adj CLUTCH Pocket Bike Mini-Moto	$24.95
MALOSSI 70cc BIG BORE KIT FOR KYMCO ZX HONDA ELITE 50	$122.50	[2 of these sold for $24.95 each]	
NEW 49cc GAS SCOOTER POCKET BIKE COMPLETE ENGINE PARTS	$119.95	CHROME MUFFLER/EXHAUST Pocket Bike Mini-Moto NEW!	$24.95
[2 of these sold for $119.95 each]		PERFORMANCE Exhaust/Muffler 49cc Pocket Bike goFASTER!	$24.95
Comet Torq-A-Verter 3/4" Shaft 41 Chain NIB!!!!!!!!!!!!	$112.50	HONDA MINI TRAIL 50 Z50 KICK STARTER Z 50 NICE!	$24.51
ROC MID PIPE for GOPED/GO-PED	$111.50	GOPED SUPER SPORT XPED BILLET PENTAGON RIM ENGINE TRIX	$24.01
MALOSSI 70cc BIG BORE RACE KIT FOR KYMCO PEOPLE/COBRA	$111.00	GOPED BF Polished Rim - NO RESERVE	$24.00
MALOSSI#31-824 70cc LC RACE KIT MALAGUTI F12 AEROX SR50	$110.00	Air Filter Kit Chrome, Black, Blue & Red Free Shipping	$22.95
MINI BIKE	$104.50	Kryptonite Stronghold Security Anchor	$21.99
EVOLUTION 50cc RACING HIGH PERFORMANCE KIT FOR ZUMA/ATV	$100.00	47CC CAG POCKET BIKE ALUMINUM RACE CLUTCH 1.5 SPRINGS	$21.95

Scooters ▶ Kick Scooters

The average sales price in this subcategory is $15.11.

	HIGH		AVG
NEW K2 KICKBOARD SCOOTER SKATEBOARD (NIB) RARE	$152.50	High Quality GENUINE HEAVY DUTY TRI SCOOTER, triscooter	$16.00
K2 Kickboard scooter (used) "kick-two"	$86.00	[8 of these sold for $16.00 each]	
Xootr Cruz push Scooter As Is wood deck back brake NR	$80.50	TRISCOOTER 6" TRI SCOOTER TRI CYCLE 3 WHEELS BRAN NEW	$15.99
Schwinn Stingray Scooter (kick) Like New	$66.00	Barely Used STINGER Scooter	$15.50
NEW Razor A3 kick scooter clear EASY FOLD & CARRY !!	$65.00	Stinger Scooter, nice riding like razor	$15.50
Know ped by Go Ped - Red NEW	$64.03	BRAND NEW KICK SCOOTER razor thin LIGHTED WHEELS	$15.50
DYNO BMX STYLE KICK SCOOTER NICE SAFE VERY FUN & RARE	$57.82	Scooter - Twilight SC120 Royce Union (kids)	$15.50
E-Balance 4 wheel push scooter!!!Very Rare!!!	$51.00	Harley Davidson Kick Scooter	$15.50
Blue Original Razor Kick Scooter - NEW	$50.00	Razor push kick scooter LIGHTED WHEEL SET wheels tire	$15.00
CW NOPED SCOOTER FREESTYLE OLD	$45.00	[2 of these sold for $15.00 each]	
SCHOOL ODYSSEY VERT		Schwinn Sting Ray DeLuxe Scooter	$14.99
A3 Kick Scooter Razor. Brand New in Box. No reserve.	$42.95	Blue Original UFO Kick Scooter w/ EXTRA LightUp Wheels	$14.99
FX1 EZRIDER WHALINGER ELECTRIC KICK	$40.00	USED—ALUMINUM RAZOR SCOOTER	$14.99
SCOOTER NEW IN BOX		NEW KICK/PUSH SCOOTER w/ razor thin LIGHTED WHEELS	$14.75
DELUX Razor Scooters!!!	$39.99	Razor push kick scooter LIGHTED WHEEL SET wheels tire	$14.55
BLUE - Razor Pro Model Kick scooter A4	$38.00	Spider-Man classic kick scooter	$14.50
Mongoose Kick Scooter Fat Tires Hand Brakes	$37.67	SCHWINN STINGRAY DELUXE KICK SCOOTER - COMPACT	$14.48

Scuba, Snorkeling ▶ Fins

The average sales price in this subcategory is $33.60.

	HIGH		AVG
Apollo Bio SCUBA diving split fins LG BK +free shipping	$139.99	NEW TUSA Full Foot Split Fins XL 12-13	$35.00
SCUBAPRO Twin Jet Fins SCUBA Diving Black Large - NEW	$138.50	Aqua Lung V-TEK Scuba Diving Fins New Sz Large Blu.	$35.00
Scuba Pro Twin Jet Fins (Cobalt)	$137.50	US DIVERS AQUA-LUNG ORIGINAL "ROCKET.FINS" ***NICE***	$35.00
Scuba Pro Twin Jet Fins (Cobalt)	$129.99	TUSA Xpert Zoom Full Foot Split Fins Scuba Medium NEW	$35.00
Scuba Snorkel Fins Mares Volo Power - NEW	$129.00	Spring Heel Fin Straps, Scuba Spring Straps	$35.00
TUSA Xpert Zoom Split Fins Scuba Diving Snorkel Medium	$129.00	[2 of these sold for $35.00 each]	
ScubaPro Twin Jet open heel fins Twinjet Small scuba	$122.50	New Inflatable Flag N Float Scuba Diving Snorkeling	$34.95
SCUBAPRO Twin Jet Fins, Adjustable.	$121.82	[3 of these sold for $34.95 each]	
NEW Apollo Bio Fin Pro	$120.00	Oceanic Vector Fins Blue X-XL ***Brand New****	$34.00
Bio-fin Pro by APOLLO Black best fins ever!	$120.00	Spring Heel Fin Straps, Scuba Spring Straps	$34.00
TUSA XPERT ZOOM SPLIT FINS SCUBA	$119.95	Spring Heel Fin Straps, Scuba Spring Straps	$33.98
DIVING DIVE SNORKEL LG		NEW Scuba Diving Open Heel Fins Blue L-XL	$33.00
[2 of these sold for $119.95 each]		Voit Viking A6 Dive Swim Fins Size Large	$33.00
Atomic Aquatics Scuba Diving Split Fins NEW Size M	$118.55	scubapro professional twin speed FF scuba fins new	$32.23
Scuba Snorkel Fins Mares Volo Power - NEW	$115.10	Sherwood "Trek" fins, regular, NEW	$32.00
Scuba Snorkel Fins Mares Volo Power - NEW	$115.00	SWIM FINS Scubapro Jetfin antique in good condition	$32.00
ScubaPro Twin Jet Fins - Medium - Blue	$115.00	SCUBAPRO JETFIN SIZE- XL-NEW STRAPS-GREAT COND.N/R	$31.54

Scuba, Snorkeling ▶ Masks

The average sales price in this subcategory is $57.65.

	HIGH		AVG
Divator (AGA) MK II Full Face Masks (2) - SCUBA/ Dive	$2,010.00	IST Pro Ear (ProEar) SCUBA Mask, Snorkel, and Bag!!!!!	$59.99
NEW AGA FULL FACE MASK 4 SCUBA DIVING INTERSPIRO	$700.00	SEADIVE GAUGE READER SCUBA MASK +2.0 -SILICONE-USED-NR!	$59.12
[2 of these sold for $700.00 each]		TUSA Visualator Mask Scuba Diving Snorkeling NEW	$59.00
OTS AGA Diving Mask w/ Communication Wireless Like New	$605.00	NEW SeaVision 2000 Scuba Dive Mask Goggles Rose Tinted	$59.00
Scuba EXO-26 full face mask with DIVECOMM device	$499.00	TUSA Viewtrek Mask Scuba Diving Snorkeling NEW	$57.00

[2 of these sold for $499.00 each]	
Poseidon Scuba Full Face Mask w/ 2nd Stage Regulator	$499.00
AGA Interspiro Divator MKII Full Face Mask SCUBA Viking	$457.26
US Navy MK-1, KMB-10 band mask	$455.00
InterSpiro Divator Full Face Mask MK II	$445.00

Black Silicone Full Face Mask SCUBA Like New No Reserve	$53.57
Brand New Pro Ear (ProEar) SCUBA Mask & More	$53.00
SCUBA ***BRAND NEW*** Ocean Master Equalizer Purge Mask	$52.50
ScubaPro Frameless Scuba Skin Diving Mask New	$51.00
OCEANIC Shadow Mask Black *NIB* Brand New	$51.00

Scuba, Snorkeling ▸ Snorkels

The average sales price in this subcategory is $22.02.

	HIGH		AVG
TUSA Imprex Snorkels Wholesale Lot 29 Total	$145.00	New Scuba Diving Silicone Dive Mask Snorkel Fins Set M	$24.99
Scubapro Breeze Snorkels Wholesale Lot 31 Total	$94.00	Silicone New Scuba Diving Dive Mask Snorkel Fins Set L	$24.99
BODY GLOVE Snorkel Mask Fin Snorkeling Set NEW with BAG	$46.95	U.S. Divers Dry Snorkel Flex Purge Scuba Dive Diving NR	$23.51
[5 of these sold for $46.95 each]		ScubaPro Scuba Pro Twin Two Valve Snorkel Blue New	$22.51
Seac Sub Dive Mask	$45.00	New Genesis Mojave 100% Scuba Diving Dry Snorkel (Blue)	$22.50
3 SCUBA PRO SHOTGUN SNORKELs SCUBAPRO Like New Dive	$45.00	ScubaPro Scuba Pro Twin Two Valve Snorkel Yellow New	$21.10
Poseidon 3 Dee Scuba Mask, blackyellow silicone Diving	$42.00	Dive N' Surf wet sujt men's medium	$20.75
		Vintage Scubapro, Shotgun Snorkel Scuba Pro	$20.51
		ScubaPro Scuba Pro Twin Two Valve Snorkel Black New	$20.51
		Ocean Master Dry Snorkel for Diving and Snorkeling	$20.51

Scuba, Snorkeling ▸ Tanks

The average sales price in this subcategory is $86.99.

	HIGH		AVG
HONDA-POWERED SUPER SNORKEL SCUBA HOOKAH	$1,000.00	2 ALUMINUM U.S. DIVERS AQUA LUNG SCUBA DIVING TANKS	$99.99
Pressed Steel E8 HP 119 Scuba Tank 3442psi (New)	$349.99	-Left & Right (Set of 2) of PRO Valves by DiveRite-NEW-	$99.99
PST E8-119 NIB (old 95style) Nitrox ready NO RESERVE	$349.99	SCUBA Tank - Pink New Visual & Hydro Tank Aluminum 80cf	$99.00
VINTAGE 1988 US DIVERS TRIPLE 30'S SCUBA TANKS/TANK	$340.00	~~~~80CF LUXFER ALUMINUM SCUBA DIVE TANK WITH BOOT~~~~	$99.00
Pressed Steel E7-100	$325.50	LUXFER ALUMINUM SCUBA DIVING AIR TANK ***LIKE NEW***	$96.00
VINTAGE 1988 US DIVERS TRIPLE 30'S SCUBA TANKS/TANK	$303.77	6 Cubic Foot Pony Tank-SCUBA-NEW-WITH PRO DIN/"K" Valve	$95.00
Pressed Steel E7-100	$290.00	SSI Spare Air Scuba Tank 3000PSI 3 cubic Ft Capacity	$94.51
Steel 100 Faber Scuba Tank 3500 psi high pres. NITROX	$281.00	100 cf Aluminum tank w/ K valve and boot-O2 clean	$91.23
Pressed Steel Tank 120 3500 PSI AquaAire Sport	$273.01	LUXFER S80 3000 ALUMINUM SCUBA DIVING TANK - NICE	$91.00
Scuba Diving Spare Air His & Hers	$260.57	CATALINA COMPACT 80 ALUMINUM SCUBA DIVING TANK	$90.11
Steel 100 Faber Scuba Tank 3500 psi high pres. NITROX	$256.00	Luxfer SCUBA air TANK diving dive s80 ALUMINUM	$88.01
BLUE SEAS SCUBA DIVERS OXYGEN TWIN TANKS	$238.51	80 CF Aluminum Scuba Tank	$86.00
Better than Spare Air! (6 cu.ft. not 3) scuba air tank	$237.50	US Diver Twin Tank Manifold	$86.00
Better than Spare Air! (6 cu.ft. not 3) scuba air tank	$229.00	~~~80CF CATALINA ALUMINUM SCUBA DIVE TANK WITH BOOT~~~~	$86.00
100 CF steel SCUBA cylinder (tank) with boot and valve	$222.50	TigerMount Tank SCUBA Pony Bottle Mount Bracket	$85.99

Scuba, Snorkeling ▸ Wet Suits

The average sales price in this subcategory is $50.97.

	HIGH		AVG
BARE Drysuit TRILAM HD TECH DRY Display Model Large	$849.95	NEW - SCUBA DIVE SUIT - $9.99 - SIZE XXL - # 51	$51.00
Scuba Gear Scubapro Regulator, computer, BC	$435.00	BARE WET SUIT SIZE MEDIUM WITH GLOVES,BOOTS,FINS!	$51.00
DUI DRYSUIT NEW SIZE 6 SHOE UNISEX?	$300.00	Women's SSA Lycra dive skin	$51.00
Oceaner Performance Freediving Wetsuit 5mm biotherm XL	$218.05	O'NEILL WETSUIT WET SUIT MEN'S sz L NR	$51.00
New Henderson Titanium Hyperstretch 5mm Wetsuit 1pc	$217.40	Mens Deep Heet Black/Green Scuba Diving Wet/Dry Suit	$51.00
[2 of these sold for $217.40 each]		O neill Wetsuit L Reactor Series 3/2mm	$51.00
NEW SCUBAMAX 7mm hooded semi dry wet suit	$200.00	NEW XXL MENS FULL WET SUIT, SCUBA GEAR 3 MM 02	$50.99
SCUBAPRO Steamer Scuba Dive Diving 7mm Mens XL Wetsuit	$199.98	MEN'S SCUBAPRO WETSUIT- Pacific 3.0mm Steamer (Medium)	$50.00
7mm Henderson Wetsuit HYPERSTRETCH Farmer John & Coat	$192.29	used once mares size 5 8mil mens farmer john and shorty	$50.00
New Henderson Titanium Hyperstretch 3mm Wetsuit 1pc	$182.50	XXL O'Rageous 3/2 Wet Suit in Black New Item NR	$50.00
Pinnacle Aquatics Polar Men's Semi-Dry Wetsuit XL NEW	$179.00	LIKE NEW O'NEIL 7MM WETSUIT AWESOME DEAL	$50.00
New Henderson Titanium Hyperstretch 3mm Wetsuit 1pc	$177.51	Used Mares 5mm wetsuit size S mens	$50.00
MARES ISOTHERM XL	$175.00	NEW LARGE MENS FULL WETSUIT,	$49.99
New Men SCUBA Dive Diving Wetsuit 6.5mm Farmer John 2XL	$169.99	SCUBA GEAR 5 MM 02	
HENDERSON TITANIUM HYPERSTRETCH 3MM WETSUIT BRAND NEW	$168.37	NEW XXL MENS FULL WET SUIT, SCUBA GEAR 5 MM 02	$49.99
Parkway Hooded Wetsuit Simi-Dry Mens Large 7mm	$163.95	Scuba Diving Wetsuit 3mm Nylon II Back Entry Jumpsuit	$49.99

Skateboarding ▸ Apparel & Shoes

The average sales price in this subcategory is $26.88.

	HIGH		AVG
Nike Tiffany Diamond Dunk US 9.5 undefeated 35th secret	$217.50	Vintage SMA Airplane skate shirt NATAS RARE L@@K!	$28.95
LOT SALE 8pairs of 9.5 skateboard shoes mint condition	$166.08	ADIO "Optum" skateboard shoes,BrandNEW Sample size 9.5	$28.59
Nike Air Max 1 SC Curry 90 95 97 b dunk sb kid robot DS	$137.50	*NEW* ETNIES LoCut 2 SHOES skate PINK GREY womens 6.5	$28.00
NIKE SB ZOOM AIR P ROD PAUL RODRIGUEZ	$132.50	globe Skateboard Shoes decks skateboards mens 9 ramps	$28.00
9.5 WHT/BLK NIB		NEW Lakai Skateboard Shoes MJ 2 Size 5.0 NAVY FREE SHIP	$28.00
VINTAGE BONES SKATEBOARD SKATER JACKET 1970'S SATIN	$130.49	OSIRIS DAZE Skateboard Shoes Brand New M 9 SKATE SK8	$28.00
Vintage RARE! Powell Peralta BONES BRIGADE shirt - sz L	$128.76	Vintage Apple Computer shirts, iPod, iMac, OS X RARE!!	$27.89
Nike Air Jordan XX Midwest Red retro 20 xiii xiv x v DS	$122.50	OSIRIS JAY ADAMS Skateboard Shoes DOGTOWN M 9 SKATE	$27.66
HIM Long Jacket Bam Haggard Replica viva la..Ville Valo	$122.50	OSIRIS BARLETTA Skateboard Shoes Brand New M 9 SKATE	$27.00
Nike Dunk Low SB Shale Carhartt sz 9 stussy tiffany 8.5	$114.50	ALIEN WORKSHOP Skateboards "SCOUT" BACKPACK Skateboard	$26.99
Nike Air Max 1 SC Curry 90 95 97 b dunk sb kid robot DS	$108.50	[2 of these sold for $26.99 each]	
NIKE DUNK LO SB BOCA NIB 9.5 ROYAL BLUE/ LIGHTENING	$108.49	WORLD INDUSTRIES Skateboards SQUELR BackPack Skateboard	$26.99
BAM MARGERA HIM JACKET ville valo punk shirt M L goth	$107.50	OSIRIS JAY ADAMS Skateboard Shoes DOGTOWN M 9 SKATE	$26.66

	HIGH		AVG
Nike Air Max 1 Grey One kid robot huf 90 95 97 true b i	$105.61	New Dc Shoe Co Avenger Skateboard Shoes Sz 9 Emerica Es	$26.00
Vintage skate shirt Santa Cruz RIP GRIP emo punk RARE!!	$105.50	DC Shoes Skateboard JACKET Brand NEW Skate Zipper SURF	$26.00
Osiris Shoes G-Bag Backpack D3 Rare! New NR	$102.50	Adio Tony Hawk Version 1 Brown Tan NIB Sz 7 Skate Shoe	$26.00

Skateboarding ▶ Complete Skateboards

The average sales price in this subcategory is $47.88.

	HIGH		AVG
lonnie toft 8 wheeler sims kryptonics ACS 500 vintage	$495.00	BAKER COMPLETE Skateboard decks skateboards -FLIP	$49.00
Kryptonics 9.75" foam board w/ trucks & wheels	$495.00	darkstar COMPLETE Skateboard decks skateboards -KREPER	$49.00
Vintage 1978 Dogtown Bull Dog Complete, Bulldog design	$338.00	VINTAGE WOOD LONGBOARD SKATEBOARD OAK DECK WOW!	$48.77
Vintage G&S Warptail w/ Gullwing trucks & Wings wheels	$325.00	VINTAGE OLD WAYNE BROWN MODEL SKATEBOARD	$48.67
VINTAGE CHAMPION SIDEWALK SURFBOARD	$300.00	New Kryptonics Sidewalk Surfer Skateboard w/Helmet S/M	$48.50
WOOD SKATEBOARD,EX!		Hot! YOCAHER SKATEBOARDS ALUMINUM COMPLETE SKATEBOARD	$48.00
Pocket Pistols Limited Hosoi Deck #9 of 10	$300.00	[2 of these sold for $48.00 each]	
Powell Peralta Lance Mountain Primative Skateboard Comp	$276.00	almost COMPLETE Skateboard decks skateboards KREPER	$48.00
vintage sims (jeff phillips) 80's	$271.00	[2 of these sold for $48.00 each]	
MARK GONZALES Vintage 1986 Complete Skateboard Vision	$268.00	Powell Peralta Steve Caballero Venture Skateboard 80's	$47.00
LESTER KASAI SIMS VINTAGE 1983 SKATEBOARD	$265.00	OVER 10" WIDE "PIG" SKATEBOARD "LOSI" 1980 INDEPENDENT	$47.00
Sims Brad Bouman complete, vintage, old school, krypto	$255.67	BLIND Skateboards "REAPER AXE" Complete SKATEBOARD	$47.00
Collectible Metallica Zorlac Skateboard w/Pushead Art	$239.34	flip COMPLETE Skateboard decks skateboards baker	$47.00
** LUCERO ** SCHMITT STIX (vintage , old school)	$236.84	ELEMENT Skateboards SECTION Complete SKATEBOARD HOT!!	$47.00
Sims Skateboard Vintage 29 1/4"L, 91/2W Slight Wear	$225.00	Vintage "GrenTec All-American GT" FiberResin Skateboard	$46.67
Powell Quicksilver Slalom Board, Vintage	$199.06	CHRIS COLE ? SKATEBOARD	$46.01
		vintage old wood Free Former skateboard ALS industries	$46.00

Skateboarding ▶ Decks

The average sales price in this subcategory is $71.80.

	HIGH		AVG
DOGTOWN BIG FOOT - never gripped !!	$3,500.00	N.O.S. Lucero old school skateboard, Santa Cruz	$75.00
SMA SANTA MONICA AIRLINES SKATEBOARD	$1,000.00	5 BAM HEARTAGRAM SKATEBOARD DECKS 7.75 Deck + GRIP TAPE	$75.00
DECK NATAS PANTHER		Z FLEX DENNIS POLAR BEAR AGNEW TRIBUTE DECK Dogtown	$75.00
Z Flex Jay Adams Old School Skateboard NOS	$898.99	Natas Kaupas Skateboard Deck Gonz not blind, NOS, sma	$74.99
Magnusson Designs Old School Skateboard	$750.00	HOOK-UPS POCAHOOK-UPS DECK MINT CONDITION	$74.99
Tony Alva 70's Skateboard Deck owned by mike mcgill	$555.00	BULLDOG - OOP - 2004 - QUAD 10 - SKATEBOARD - dogtown	$74.00
Vintage 1978 DOGTOWN SKATES - Muir Dragon Skateboard	$450.00	44" BIG WOOD Longboards custom skateboard deck	$71.01
Ripper Team deck 80's skateboard deck powell peralta	$405.00	Z CULT COFFIN DECK NEWLY RE-RELEASED Dogtown	$71.00
Bulldog skates South Side ltd ed skateboard BDS	$370.00	POWELL PERALTA McGILL SKATEBOARD DECK	$71.00
Jay Adams 100% Skateboarder,Dogtown,Zephyr,NEW,RARE!	$355.00	BULLDOG SKATES TAIL TAP II SIGN BY P. C. DOGTOWN Z-BOY	$71.00
Corey O'Brien 80's skateboard deck Santa Cruz	$319.00	MOUNTAINBOARD BRAND COMPLTETE BETTER	$70.00
Powell Peralta TONY HAWK skateboard NOS Black	$315.00	THAN MBS BRAND NEW	
MINT 1988 Santa Cruz Sun God Skateboard Deck	$310.00	Vintage old Santa Cruz Roskopp original Skateboard deck	$70.00
Real Mark Gonzales re-vision entire set.	$305.99	FTC BIGFOOT ONE SKATEBOARD DECK.Not OBEY,FAIREY,KINSEY	$68.00
DOGTOWN - TRIPLANE - SKATEBOARD - BULLDOG - DT - BDS	$305.00	Schmitt Stix JOE LOPES oldschool deck Powell	$67.66
Tony Hawk 80's skateboard deck powell peralta	$305.00	NOS alva chris cook mini-88 skateboard deck	$67.66

Skiing & Snowboarding ▶ Apparel

The average sales price in this subcategory is $27.44.

	HIGH		AVG
New! Arcteryx Alpha SV Jacket Large ($500 MSRP)	$323.00	DUB BRAND WATERPROOF MENS XXL ULTRA HEAVY SKI PANTS	$31.00
Ski In/Ski Out Condo - Crested Butte Colorado 1Bedroom	$297.00	VINTAGE LEVIS CORDUROY PUFFY SKI COAT JACKET MENS SMALL	$31.00
[3 of these sold in a multiple item ("Dutch") auction for $99.00 each]		Columbia Tectonite Hooded Parka Jacket Kids Boys 10/12	$30.00
Arcteryx Sidewinder SV New Med Gore-tex XCR	$280.00	Ski Jacket NEW sz 2x Coats Jackets Snow Coat w/Fleece	$30.00
NEW 2005 Analog Gulag Jacket Burton Snowboard L Quarry	$210.00	Salomon Crossmax Senior / Adult Full Face Ski Helmets 5	$30.00
Spyder,NWT,Men's Ski Jacket,04-'05 Legend Series,L,Blu	$199.99	[2 of these sold for $30.00 each]	
Snowmobile\suit\helmet\bibs\snowpants	$178.23	Winter clothes, size 5 girls, lot of 10...(3 bib pants	$29.99
Spyder,NWT,Men's Ski Jacket,04-'05 Legend Series,L,Red	$173.65	Salomon Crossmax Senior / Adult Full Face Ski Helmets 5	$29.00
Mens NORTH FACE Steep Tech Ski Jacket Large Like New!	$172.50	SKI /SNOW suit, size 14, girls bibs/ matching jacket	$29.00
Spyder, Men's Ski Pants / Bib, Legend Series,Orange, L	$163.50	Salomon Mach 2 Senior Ski/Snowboard Helmet 55-56cm/Copp	$29.00
New Oakley Mace Sno Camo Ski Snowboard Pants Med Burton	$150.00	SIMS SNOWBOARDS MENS MEDIUM HEAVY SKI JACKET COAT	$28.77
SPYDER TEAM VENOM DOWN SKI JACKET MED NEW NWT	$149.99	COLUMBIA CROSS TERRA ~ Ski Jacket ~ Youth Small 7/8	$28.51
Spyder,NWT,Men's Ski Jacket,04-'05 Legend Series,L,Cob	$147.50	Burton Brown studded belt 28-30 NEW	$26.67
SPYDER PURSUIT SKI JACKET LARGE NEW NWT	$145.50	Giro Ravine SC Bomber Girl Ski and Snowboard Helmet	$26.55
THE NORTH FACE BLACK NUPTSE SKI JACKET NEW MEN'S XL	$142.50	MENS SZ XL BLACK SKI/SNOW BIBS/PANTS LIKE NEW	$26.07
SPYDER MENS DOWN JACKET Sz L	$140.00	COLUMBIA WOMANS XL FLEECE LINED SKI JACKET COAT	$26.06

Skiing & Snowboarding ▶ Cross Country Skiing

The average sales price in this subcategory is $27.20.

	HIGH		AVG
04-05 Fischer RCS Skatecut Plus 177 Med/w/bindings	$150.00	SWIX SKI VISES, brand new condition!!!	$34.00
VINTAGE ANTIQUE WOODEN SKIS SNOKRAFT, NORWAY, MAINE	$93.00	Rossignol Backcountry CrossCountry NNN BC Auto Bindings	$32.06
Cross Country Skis, Boots & Poles - Men's	$88.98	Pair of Yassa Mens Cross Country Ski Boots	$31.00
Fischer Cross Country Skis with Bindings and Poles	$81.00	Trak Spirit Cross Country Skis, Poles, Case, and Boots	$29.99
Rossignol Backcountry 83 AR Skis-Size 165	$78.25	NEW in BOX! Ladies HEIERLING Cross Country Ski Boots	$26.13
OLD WOOD SKIS WITH NORTHLAND HIGH GRADE POLES * WOODEN	$76.00	Women's Cross Country Ski Package	$26.01
$250 D Tec Pro 17 99cm Ski Blades - Grey/Black NR	$71.00	Dynastar Outland Ski's w/ Bindings	$26.00

Alpine or Cross Country Ski Waxing Table	$61.00	Salomon SR 311 Cross Country Ski Boots, LADIES - 6 2/3!	$26.00
Pinnacle/Salomon Back Country Ski Package; Nice!	$60.99	CROSS COUNTRY SKILOM SKIS	$25.00
SALOMON -SNS Pilot Equipe Skate X-Country Bindings	$51.00	Rossignol Cross Country Ski Boots	$23.50

Skiing & Snowboarding ▶ Downhill Skiing

The average sales price in this subcategory is $82.44.

	HIGH		AVG
2005 ATOMIC SX10 w/ BINDINGS - 170CM - BRAND NEW!	$479.00	SALOMON S 810 Ti NEW Performance adult bindings	$91.00
K2 Seth Morrison Pistol Skis with Salomon Bindings	$459.00	Nordica Beast	$91.00
K2 Seth Pistols w/ Salomon 912 TI bindings. NO RESERVE!	$452.00	Atomic GS11 Jr. Race Ski Boots size 25.0 - No Reserve	$89.00
2005 K2 Apache Recon 167cm BRAND NEW	$416.50	Salomon Course GT Ski Boots	$87.00
Brand New 05' Rossignol Scratch BC 188cm	$404.00	VINTAGE WOOD SKIS (71") AND BAMBOO POLES (55")	$86.50
LACROIX wood-composite Authentic 178	$400.00	New Atomic e3 Carving Skis 150 or 160 cm	$85.00
157cm new Atomic M9 Puls Metron skis with bindings	$399.00	[2 of these sold for $85.00 each]	
PRO FITTER SKI TRAINER k2-skiers-rossignol-atomic-edge	$399.00	TECNICA HOTFORM SKI BOOTS ORANGE RED SIZE 9 AVS	$82.01
2005 Nordica Dobermann Pro SC 170cm w/binding BRAND NEW	$399.00	rossignol Bandit Shape Skis 140 cm 55" long	$82.00
Brand New 05' Rossignol Scratch BC 176cm	$399.00	Silvretta 404 Backcountry Ski Bindings Good Condition!	$81.00
Line Freestyle Twintip Eric Pollard Pro Model Skis 2004	$378.00	2 SETS ROSSIGNOL SKIS SNOW SKIS + POLES + BAG 79" + 66"	$81.00
Rossignol B1 170cm skis	$349.00	ATOMIC CR 614 TD Ski Bindings, Brand NEW in Box	$80.95
2005 Nordica Speed Machine 12 162cm	$349.00	Rossignol Cut 10.4 150 cm Shaped Skis w/Bindings	$80.66
w/binding BRAND NEW		BURTON HAIL BOOTS mens size 8.5	$80.00
Rossignol B1 170cm skis	$349.00	DALBELLO VISIO 3.5 LADIES SKI BOOTS SIZE 27.5/US 10	$79.99
2005 Dalbello Krypton Pro sz 27.5 BRAND NEW!!!	$314.00	DALBELLO VISIO 3.5 LADIES SKI BOOTS SIZE 26.5/US size 9	$79.99

Skiing & Snowboarding ▶ Snowboarding

The average sales price in this subcategory is $110.64.

	HIGH		AVG
burton split board 170 snowboard w/crampons AND SKINS	$825.00	Burton Fire Alpine Race Boot size 27.5 NEW!!!	$118.51
Vintage SIMS Snowboard - 1980 +/-	$510.00	BURTON OLS Medium bindings Demo Limited Edition	$118.50
2004 Voile Backcountry Split Board 173cm	$495.00	Burton Shaun White boots new unused sz 10 mens	$117.50
BURTON FEELGOOD ES 154 cm Snowboard	$462.00	RIDE FLIGHT MIG BINDINGS SZ X-LG LIKE NEW!!	$115.00
PALMER CROWN (LE) Men's Snowboard 164 CM **NEW**	$450.00	BURTON C14 Snowboard binding DEMO Medium Precision	$113.50
Vintage snowboard, rare, swallow, collector, surf	$430.00	New 2005 Flux Super Titan 2 Snowboard Bindings Large	$112.50
BURTON SNOWBOARD SUPERMODEL 181CM USED TWICE BIG POW	$402.00	Rome Agent 160cm No Reserve!!!	$112.50
Burton T6 152cm Snowboard '05 new /unused	$395.00	'05 BURTON FREESTYLE size medium grey/navy	$112.50
BURTON CUSTOM 154 SNOWBOARD BRAND NEW- L@@K!!	$379.00	NEW 2005 SIMS X4 SNOWBOARD BINDINGS UPLINK UPGRADE	$111.50
BURTON CUSTOM 166 SNOWBOARD	$379.00	DC EMBLEM SNOWBOARD BOOTS Sz 11 CHARCOAL/STENCIL	$110.00
~NEW~ BIG MOUNTAIN RIDE!!		Burton Snow Boots "Tribute"	$110.00
burton custom le 162	$350.00	RIDE DVA WOMEN'S SNOWBOARD BINDINGS! Sz MED	$110.00
BURTON FEELGOOD ES 150 cm Snowboard	$349.99	Thirty-two Lashed boots new unused sz 13 mens	$110.00
Burton Custom LE, 158	$335.00	New 05 Ride VXn Women's Snowboard Bindings Black	$109.99
BNWT 04-05 Never Summer EVO 58 Snowboard 3 yr Warranty	$326.98	New 05 Ride LX Black Snowboard Bindings	$109.99
GNU DANNY KASS TERROR 155 SNOWBOARD 2005	$325.00	[2 of these sold for $109.99 each]	

Snowmobiling ▶ Parts & Accessories

The average sales price in this subcategory is $57.39.

	HIGH		AVG
1999 Ski Doo MXZ 670 HO & 2003 Destination Trailer	$3,500.00	VINTAGE SNOWMOBILE ARCTIC CAT OLD DRIVE BELT (NOS)	$60.00
2000 Ski Doo MXZ 700 no reserve	$2,201.00	[2 of these sold in a multiple item ("Dutch") auction for $30.00 each]	
alumunum 2 place snowmobile trailer.	$490.00	Ski-doo Blizzard Motor	$60.00
Chatterbox GMRS X1 W/NR headsets 2 NEW UNITS	$475.00	YAMAHA SRX,VIPER 700 SportPort PERFORMANCE PORTING KIT!	$59.95
[3 of these sold for $475.00 each]		Snowmobile Cover Arctic Cat ZL ZR not Firecat	$59.01
Chatterbox GMRS X1 W/NR headsets 2 NEW UNITS	$474.95	Ski-Doo X-Team Gear Bag SkiDoo	$59.00
Polaris snowmobile ultra/xcr big bore 800 kit	$450.00	Ski-Doo Tunnel Bag	$58.00
Vintage Yamaha 77 SRX 440 Factory Mod engine -LOOK	$420.00	1969 Ski-Doo Bombardier TNT 401 Twin Fan Cooled Engine	$57.82
Chatterbox FRS X2 W/NR headsets 2 NEW UNITS	$405.00	BRAND NEW YAMAHA SNOWMOBILE	$56.50
Chatterbox FRS X2 W/NR headsets 2 NEW UNITS	$397.00	292 PISTON 2ND OVERSIZE	
Ski-Doo 1+1 Seat SkiDoo	$385.00	1985 yamaha vmax 540 40MM CARBS	$56.00
[2 of these sold for $385.00 each]		Ski-Doo Tunnel Bag	$56.00
CAMOPLAST SNOWMOBILE TRACK 1.5" LUG POLARIS SKIDOO CAT	$370.00	8" Snowmobile Trailer Ski Guide 4pc Set (Slides)	$54.99
'90 Skidoo Safari LE	$350.00	BRAND NEW Aluminum Bottom Gear for Ski Doo 13 Wide	$54.00
Polaris Edge Snowmobile Electric Start Kit - NEW	$339.04	2000 Polaris 250 Trailblazer carburetor and cables	$53.85
KIMPEX SNOWMOBILE TRACK POLARIS SKIDOO CAT RIPSAW STYLE	$310.00	8" Snowmobile Trailer Ski Guide 4pc Set (Slides)	$52.99
thundercat cylinder with d/d porting	$305.00	Ski Doo RACING TRA Clutch Ramps PX Not Arctic Cat	$52.99

Soccer ▶ Apparel & Footwear

The average sales price in this subcategory is $14.27.

	HIGH		AVG
ADIDAS predator pulse soccer boots cleats NEW TRXFG	$89.00	DAVIDS #8 HOLLAND AWAY BLACK SOCCER JERSEY EURO 2004	$14.99
NEW BALANCE 1221 SN Running SHOE Mens SIZE 12- 4E	$85.00	Adidas Climacool Training soccer Jersey Size:XL	$14.99
HUMMEL SQUADRA SOCCER JERSEYS - SOCCER OUTLET	$69.00	Puma Milano Goalkeeper jersey. VERY LITE!! Size Large	$14.95
ITALY JACKET KING ZIP TRAINING SWEAT, PUMA, Sze Large	$61.00	Ukraine National SHEVCHENKO # 7 SoccerShirt Jersey.XXXL	$14.95
ADIDAS COLUMBUS CREW SOCCER JERSEY NEW LARGE BLACK/YLLW	$46.00	Llke New Adidas Goalie Shirt Kids Size M (10-12) LOOK!!	$14.56

HIGH FIVE REVERSIBLE SOCCER JERSEYS - SOCCER OUTLET	$41.03	9 RONALDO REAL MADRID SOCCER JERSEY NEW 2004	$14.50
Nike US National Soccer Team Jacket Warm Up usa jersey	$41.00	Ukraine DYNAMO KIEV Soccer SHEVCHENKO Shirt	$14.50
CAMEROON PUMA 2004 -2005 Home SOCCER JERSEY,New, Large	$38.00	AC Fiorentina Rui Costa Soccer Jersey Like New	$14.50
Diadora soccer jersey shirt lot 18 all size L Large	$36.01	3 R.CARLOS REAL MADRID SOCCER JERSEY NEW 2004	$14.00
USA White 2004 Soccer Jersey.	$36.00	9 RONALDO REAL MADRID AWAY BLACK SOCCER JERSEY NEW 2004	$14.00
NAPOLI MARADONA RETRO #10 80s RED SOCCER JERSEY SHIRT	$36.00	MARVAL L GOALIE GOALKEEPER SOCCER JERSEY SHIRT	$14.00
Ukraine National SHEVCHENKO #7 Soccer Jersey+Shorts M	$35.00	5 ZIDANE 2004 REAL MADRID SOCCER JERSEY NEW	$14.00
Ronaldinho Barcelona Home Soccer Jersey	$35.00	10 TOTTI ITALY HOME SOCCER JERSEY BLUE NEW	$14.00
CAMEROON PUMA 2004 -2005 Home SOCCER JERSEY,New, XL	$34.00	Vintage San Jose Clash (Earthquakes) Soccer Jersey MLS	$13.50
J.S.PARK # 13 Man United Home Soccer Jersey	$31.00	RONALDO #9 BRASIL HOME SOCCER JERSEY 2004 NEW	$13.46

Soccer ▶ Balls, Pumps

The average sales price in this subcategory is $31.19.

	HIGH		AVG
ADIDAS SANTIAGO MATCH BALL - CHILE FIFA WORLD CUP 1962	$412.07	14 NEW SPALDING BLUE AND WHITE	$37.51
ADIDAS QUESTRA EUROPA EURO 1996 ENGLAND + COCA COLA	$336.00	SOCCER BALLS UNINFLATED	
ADIDAS GAMARADA SYDNEY 2000 OLYMPIC OFFICIAL MATCH BALL	$266.00	6 NEW MITRE #5 DEMON SOCCER BALL BALLS WHITE	$37.00
10 NIKE TOTAL 90 TEAM 400 SOCCER BALL/BALLS/SIZE 5	$244.50	10 New Adidas TANGO TAKE OFF Soccer Balls Size 5 Ball	$36.00
10 NIKE TOTAL 90 TEAM 400 SOCCER BALL/BALLS/SIZE 5	$224.95	New Adidas Tricolore Tournoi Soccer Ball - Size 5	$35.88
adidas olympic official matchball sydney 2000 GAMARADA	$202.50	Soccer Ball VOIT Authentic Federacion Mexicana Futbol	$34.99
10 NIKE TOTAL 90 TEAM 400 SOCCER BALL/BALLS/SIZE 5	$199.95	Lot of 4 Soccer Balls - Wilson Mikasa Mitre Size 5	$33.40
50 SOCCER BALLS SIZE 5 futbol shoes pictures am #5398	$170.00	Nike Total 90 Aerow Size 5	$31.00
MITRE ULTIMAX MAJOR LEAGUE SOCCER - MLS - MATCH BALL	$152.50	6 SIZE 5 SOCCER BALLS shoes shorts goalie gloves #5332	$30.00
New Adidas Roteiro + Finale Official Match soccer balls	$142.49	6 SIZE 5 SOCCER BALLS leather ball shoes new nr #5332	$30.00
10 NIKE TOTAL 90 TEAM 250 SOCCER BALLS/BALL/Sz 4 or 5	$129.95	Nike Total 90 Aerow Size 5	$30.00
10 ADIDAS ETRUSCO WORLD CUP SOCCER BALL/BALLS/NEW!	$122.45	Nike T90 English Premier League Soccer Ball Hi vis sz 5	$27.00
[2 of these sold for $122.45 each]		6 SIZE 5 SOCCER BALLS leather ball shoes new nr #5332	$26.95
10 ADIDAS ETRUSCO WORLD CUP SOCCER BALL/BALLS/NEW!	$122.45	Five Soccer Balls - Size 3	$26.95
16 NEW MITRE #5 DEMON SOCCER BALL BALLS BLACK	$115.00	6 SIZE 5 SOCCER BALLS ball shoes shin guards new #5332	$26.95
Adidas Tricolore World Cup 98 Soccer Ball (Brand New)	$112.50	(6) SIZE 4 SOCCER BALLS - INTERNATIONAL!	$26.01
10 Brand New Yellow Nike T90 Hi-VIS Soccer Balls Size 5	$102.50	NEW! $90 VALUE	

Soccer ▶ Gloves, Socks, Shin Guards

The average sales price in this subcategory is $8.65.

	HIGH		AVG
ADIDAS Fingersave FS Titanium GOALIE GLOVES'05	$69.99	NEW NIKE Air Shield soccer shin guards mens size Large	$9.49
*NEW*Nike T90 Wired Goalkeeper Gloves Size 9 NO RESERVE	$67.00	New Brine Premiere Soccer Goalkeeper Goalie Gloves sz 9	$9.29
NEW ADIDAS FINGERSAVE EVOLUTION E3S GLOVES 8 OR 9	$61.00	New Brine Premiere Soccer Goalkeeper Goalie Gloves sz 9	$9.25
BRINE KGBCK2 B9 SOCCER GOALIE GLOVES SZ 9 - keeper	$47.00	NEW ADIDAS FINGERSAVE YOUNG PRO GOALIE SOCCER GLOVES 5	$9.01
NEW! Reusch Soccer Goalkeeper Gloves Ortho-Tec Size 10	$46.00	PARKER ATHLETIC CUSTOM FIT FIBERGLAS SOCCER SHINGUARDS	$8.95
ADIDAS FS CUP CARBON GK GLOVES - SIZE 10 - NEW!	$40.00	NIP NEW YOUTH TRI SHIELD SM SHIN GUARDS NIKE RETAIL $15	$8.95
Zeepk Fingersave glovesProfessional level performance11	$40.00	NIKE Soccer Shinguards (Sized youth small/medium	$8.50
NEW ADIDAS BLACK SCHOLASTIC	$34.99	NIKE DRI-FIT Soccer Socks, 2 PAIR , NWT, L@@K	$8.50
SOCCER SOCKS 6pk Retail $54		NIP! NEW! Nike Youth Soccer Shin Sock(Shinguard) L/XL	$8.49
Zeepk new fingersave Titanium GOALIE gloves size 10	$32.99	Brine Youth Shin Guard	$8.11
New fingersave gloves soccer goalie size 10	$32.00	Adidas:Soccer Goalie Glove "Primero"Size 4 or 5	$8.00
NEW! Reusch Soccer Goalkeeper Gloves Ortho-Sleek Size 8	$31.01	2pair of nike soccer socks size: 10-13 white and black	$8.00
Sondico Coolmax XMG soccer goalkeeper gloves size 8, NR	$31.00	Franklin PRO-TEAM Youth Shinguards For Soccer NEW!!	$7.99
SOCCER SOFTBALL ? SOCK LOT VARIETY 45 PAIR	$29.11	NIKE DRI-FIT Soccer Socks, 2 PAIR , NWT, L@@K	$7.99
New fingersave gloves soccer goalie size 9	$29.00	[2 of these sold for $7.99 each]	
7 NEW PAIRS MITRE PRO FLEX SOCCER GOALIE GLOVES #7,8,9	$28.00	PARKER ATHLETIC CUSTOM FIT FIBERGLAS SOCCER SHINGUARDS	$7.95

Surfing, Wind Surfing ▶ Apparel

The average sales price in this subcategory is $15.23.

	HIGH		AVG
VINTAGE 1980's Side Panelled QUICKSILVER Baggies	$100.99	Three Pieces of Wet Suit Gear NR! Small 5 Mil Neoprene.	$15.53
Billabong Board Shorts Teahupoo 2005 Official Surf	$51.50	ONEILL SZ M WETSUIT SHORTS PANTS SURFING DIVING MENS NR	$15.50
JOBE ADULT NEOPRENE Life Ski Vest Jacket Tri-sect XL	$48.00	NU JETPILOT MEN BOARDSHORTS SWIM SUIT TRUNKS SHORTS 38"	$15.50
VINTAGE-BIRDWELL BEACH BRITCHES-Jacket X.L.Black	$46.95	QUIKSILVER PRO STAFF Surf Contest Shirt XL	$15.50
MMYSurfboards Team Ireland Tahiti 2004 Surf Shirt L	$45.00	ROXY Pro Australia 2005 Surf Contest Staff Shirt XL	$15.50
Maui and Sons Vintage Jams/ Shorts mens medium like new	$45.00	O'NEILL RASH GUARD Surfing BODYBOARD HOT DESIGN M NEW	$15.49
VOLCOM STONE Longsleeved Sweatshirt with Hood XL	$40.00	NWT Mens Rash Guard Rash Shirt Vest Suit - ANY Sz/Color	$15.36
SUNDEK Vintage 1980s Surfer Shorts Trunks Sz 36 NWT!	$37.90	UCSB SWEATSHIRT SIZE XL HOODIE SANTA BARBARA	$15.05
VINTAGE SURFING Belt Buckle OLD L@@K	$36.56	YOUTH GOTCHA RASHGUARD RASH GUARD SZ 8/10 NWT	$15.00
BILLABONG PRO Tahiti Teahupoo 2005 Surf Contest Shirt X	$36.00	SALOMON MASTERS Australia 2005 Surf Contest Shirt XL	$15.00
Vintage KATIN Surf Trunks!! NEW!! 36-Black	$35.00	RIPCURL PRO Bells Beach Australia 2005 Surf Shirt XL	$15.00
NWT A/X ARMANI EXCHANGE MENS COMPETITION SWIM SUIT-L	$32.99	Pipeline Masters Contest Hawaii 2003 Surf Shirt XL Xbox	$15.00
[2 of these sold for $32.99 each]		OnBongo Brazilian ASP Pro Surfing Beanie	$15.00
Dragonfly KISS Destroyer Board Shorts Sz. 30	$31.95	NEW MENS QUIKSILVER BOARD SHORTS	$14.99
New BILLABONG Surf BEACH BIKINI 2 Pc Swim SUIT Womens M	$31.00	BOARDSHORTS 40 ZEN RED	
Quiksilver Pro Hebara Japan Surf Contest Shirt XL	$31.00	HURLEY BOYS/MEN CARGO PANTS NWT SZ 27	$14.99

Surfing, Wind Surfing ▸ Body Boards

The average sales price in this subcategory is $46.97.

	HIGH		AVG
New BZ Hubb Graphic 41.5 Yellow/Black BodyBoard	$285.00	NEW!!! Body Glove Titan Slick BODYBOARD 45 surf FAST	$55.95
New BZ Hubb Graphic 41.5 White/Yellow BodyBoard	$255.00	elemenohpee 2003 Elle Girls Pro bodyboard DEAL NR	$50.00
BZ BODY BOARD HUBB FUNDAMENTAL 42.5 NEW IN PACKAGE BLUE	$239.00	BZ BODY BOARD DAY TRIPPER BAG NEW IN PACKAGING	$50.00
BZ BODY BOARD HUBB GRAPHIC 41.75 NEW IN PACKAGING RED	$220.00	New Custom X Yellow 41" Python Bodyboard	$50.00
BZ HUBB BODYBOARD BODY BOARD BOOGIE BODYBOARDING	$192.50	Churchill Makapuu FINS Bodyboard swim surf divesnorkel	$45.00
NEW BZ FUNDAMENTALS BIG BRUDDAH BODYBOARD BODY BOARD NR	$177.50	MOREY MACH 25 Slick bottom BOOGIE Surf BOARD	$44.50
BZ BODY BOARD BIG BRUDDAH 45" NEW IN PACKAGING BLUE	$169.00	SALE!!! Body Glove Titan Slick BODYBOARD 42 surf FAST	$42.88
BZ 2004 HUB bodyboard	$155.00	COCA-COLA BODY BOARD COKE MUSIC BRAND NEW	$42.51
NEW UNIT X PMA 41.5 BODY BOARD BOOGIE BOARD SOLD OUT	$150.00	SALE! Wave Rebel Spectrum 42 BODYBOARD surf FAST sweet!	$41.88
Toobs body board bodyboard 44.5 NEW FREE Shipping	$149.99	NEW SURFSTER BLADE PRO SERIES INFLATABLE BODYBOARD BLUE	$41.01

Surfing, Wind Surfing ▸ Surfboards

The average sales price in this subcategory is $154.81.

	HIGH		AVG
Mint Vintage 10' David Nuuhiwa Noserider Surfboard	$5,500.00	7'4 Funboard Longboard Surfboard Fun Long Surf Board !!	$167.50
Vintage Duke Kahanamoku Longboard 9' 7" Surfboard	$1,475.00	7'5 Beginner Funboard Longboard Fun Long Surfboard !!!!	$162.50
mid to late 50s Velzy longboard	$1,058.00	Surfboard Surfing Boards 6'4 shortboard Outlaw	$162.50
CLASSIC HANSEN 50/50 SURFBOARD LONGBOARD	$1,051.00	Channel Island Surfboard - No Reserve	$160.45
Slingshot 13.0 Kite, Lite Wave 145 KiteBoard, Harness	$879.00	surfboard - 8 ft softboard - malibu shape	$160.00
Skip Frye Surfboards, Speed Egg 8'6" @@"NO RESERVE"@@	$838.00	NEW ZAP PRO SKIMBOARD W/ CUSTOM ART MEDIUM BOARD surf	$158.50
foilboard hydrofoil wakeboard surfing kitesurfing	$800.00	6'0 Small Surfboard Shortboard Fun Short Surf Board	$153.50
STARBOARD START Windsurfer board with sails and boom	$760.50	WINDANSEA SURF CLUB patch decal ect. Surfboard	$153.48
10'2 cooperfish nosedevil surfboard	$760.00	NEW ZAP WEDGE SKIMBOARD LG BOARD W/ CUSTOM ART surf	$152.50
Longboard Surf Tech Epoxy - 11' Munoz Ultra Glide	$700.00	7'6 FIXER Funboard Longboard Surfboard Long Surf Board	$152.50
Brewer Surfboard 7'8" Carbon Fiber/Epoxy Laminate	$660.00	Malibu Rum Collector Surfboard *** New***	$152.50
Cooperfish Hornet - 9'6"	$600.00	Vintage SURFBOARD LONGBOARD Barry bennett	$152.50
10'0 1964 Classic Old Vintage Longboard Surfboard !!!!!	$567.00	NEW ZAP PRO SKIMBOARD W/ CUSTOM ART MEDIUM BOARD surf	$150.01
Stewart Surfboard	$555.00	SURFBOARD 5'11" Surf Prescriptions Y2	$150.00
10' Blue Hawaii longboard surfboard SAN DIEGO used 1x	$554.78	The Real Jeff McCoy Vintage Surfboard 6' 8"	$150.00

Surfing, Wind Surfing ▸ Wetsuits

The average sales price in this subcategory is $33.40.

	HIGH		AVG
Spider Surfboard 5'-5"	$300.00	NEW JETPILOT WAKEBOARD SKI NEOPRENE WETSUIT VEST LARGE	$34.97
7'4 Pro Series Surfboard	$299.99	NEW JET PILOT WAKEBOARD WATER SKI WETSUIT VEST MEDIUM	$34.97
Bare Polarheat watersport Drysuit - New - Large	$270.00	NEW JETPILOT WAKEBOARD SKI NEOPRENE WETSUIT VEST MEDIUM	$34.97
9'3 Ultimate Beginner Longboard Surfboard Long Board !!	$270.00	BODY GLOVE Wet Suit Juniors Size 10 / 3.2 mm Fullbody	$34.49
Surfboard,Fish,Twin-Fin,Classic,Retro,Longboard-NO P.SRV	$234.50	Xcel Neoprene Sz 10S Womens Wet Suit 2 mil Scuba Diving	$34.00
O'Neill Psycho 2 3Q Zip Wetsuit - NEW	$225.00	NU JETPILOT WAKEBOARD JETSKI NEOPRENE PFD LIFE VEST LG	$34.00
NEW 2006 O'NEILL PSYCHO 2 WETSUIT SIZE MEDIUM!!	$222.50	ONEILL WETSUIT SPRINGSUIT SHORTY HAMMER NEW NR	$33.51
NEW 2006 O'NEILL PSYCHO 2 WETSUIT SIZE LARGE!!	$212.50	NU JET PILOT WAKEBOARD JETSKI NEOPRENE PFD LIFE VEST XL	$33.00
NEW 2006 O'NEILL PSYCHO 2 WETSUIT SIZE EXTRA LARGE!!	$203.68	NEW JETPILOT WAKEBOARD SKI NEOPRENE WETSUIT VEST SMALL	$33.00
Ripcurl Wetsuit Fireskin Zip free Large 4/3 Rip Curl	$195.00	Body Glove Wetsuit Wet Suit Men's Sz XL Like New	$32.99
Ripcurl Wetsuit Fireskin Zip free Large 5/4/3 Rip Curl	$187.50	O'NEILL 2.1MM WETSUIT SHORTY 3XL SURFING BODYBOARD	$32.55
Oakfoils surfboard 6'10 with FCS Fins	$182.50	NEW JETPILOT WAKEBOARD WATER SKI WETSUIT VEST XXXL	$32.50
6/5/4 New Rip Curl GB Elasto Hooded Wetsuit Sz XXL	$177.50	Aquacurl 3/2mm Men's Spring Wetsuit - ML	$32.50
New Rip Curl 3/2 Elasto Slick Skin Black Wetsuit SzXL	$168.50	O'Neill Reactor 3/2MM Full Suit - NEW	$32.50
New Rip Curl Ultimate 4/3 Stealth Steamer GB Sz XL	$162.50	NEW JETPILOT WAKEBOARD SKI NEOPRENE WETSUIT JACKET XXL	$32.44

Surfing, Wind Surfing ▸ Windsurfing

The average sales price in this subcategory is $94.86.

	HIGH		AVG
Sunfish Sailboat located in CT	$1,300.00	WINDSURFING. GAASTRA SAIL, GRIND 5.4 PROTO.. WAVE SAIL-	$104.50
NEW! Angulo Sumo Freeride Board - 125 liters	$800.00	O'BRIEN SENSATION SAIL/WINDSURFING BOARD W/SAIL & BAG	$104.19
Sunfish Sailboat & Trailer in Connecticut CT	$635.00	Windsurfing, EZZY Transformer 6.6M Sail - No Reserve!!!	$103.52
Kitesurfing Package, 1 Kite, 2 Boards, Bar, Lines, NR!	$611.00	Gaastra F1 Race 6.6 Windsurfing Sail #12	$103.50
WINDSURF BOARD MISTRAL CUSTOM FLOW120LT SUPER CONDITION	$592.00	WINDSURFING. GAASTRA-, Poison 4.7 WAVE SAIL, KP's	$103.49
11 FT Super Snark Sailboat L@@K Long Island (SUNFISH)	$535.00	Gaastra F-1 Race 5.4 Windsurfing Sail- NOSI	$102.50
Large Lot Windsurfing Gear Board Boom Mast Sail LOOK	$520.00	NEW Gaastra 5.0m windsurfing sail	$99.00
Sail Board Windsurfer Windsurfing Board	$475.00	3 WINDSURFING SAILS Up for BEST OFFER!	$89.99
Cabinha/Zero Gravity Kiteboard Package	$471.00	WINDSURFING EQUIPMENT PACKAGE: board, sails, booms, fin	$85.00
Mistral Wind Surfer Windsurfing Board and Set-up	$430.00	windsurfing mast freeride 430 cm- 15% carbon.	$82.00
NEW! Angulo Amigu 7'4" Wave Board - 80 liters	$405.00	Complete Windsurf package! Board, Sail, everything!	$81.01
Starboard Hypersonic 105 Wood - Brand New!	$405.00	windsurfing Hi Fly, freeride MAST. 465CM. carbon 30%	$81.00
NEW 14m Naish Kiteboarding Kitesurfing Kite X4	$385.00	Sail Board, 9' 10" entry level short board, high volume	$79.99
WINDSURFING. GAASTRA SAIL. NITRO 5, 7.0m PROD. NEW	$345.00	F2 Axxis 262cm windsurfing board windsurf 16.5 lbs	$79.00
Sunfish Sailfish lookalike Funfish sailboat	$338.00	NEW Gaastra 4.6m windsurfing sail 4 cams	$79.00

Tennis ▶ Apparel & Footwear

The average sales price in this subcategory is $18.52.

	HIGH		AVG
NO RESERVE.. 140 DIAMONDS IN SOLID YELLOW GOLD	$152.50	NEW BALANCE skort TENNIS SKIRT green NWT $40 sz M 8/10	$19.95
NWT $178 Nike 2 Tops + 2 Skirts Tennis Outfits! Size L	$79.99	NEW NWT ADIDAS CLIMALITE BLUE TENNIS SKIRT + SHORTS L	$19.53
* LOT OF 3 NIKE DRI FIT TENNIS SKIRTS SIZE M MEDIUM *	$72.00	NWT MENS ADIDAS Tennis/Workout/Casual Shorts Size MED	$19.50
BRAND NEW NIKE AIRZOOM VAPOR SPEED TENNIS SHOES SIZE 10	$71.00	NWT Girls XL/Womens S Nike Glam Tennis Skirt/Skort Wht	$19.49
NIKE MEN AGASSI AIR ZOOM BREATHE 2 TENNIS SHOES 12 $110	$70.00	Prince Men's Tennis Shirt Medium	$19.05
Adidas Barricade III Tennis, men many size avail 1 pair	$69.99	NEW ADIDAS WOMENS CLIMALITE TENNIS SKIRT SHORTS LARGE	$18.95
Adidas Barricade III Tennis, men , size 10 !!!!!!!!!!!!	$69.99	New XS Nike White w/Navy Border Tennis Skirt w/shorts	$18.50
[4 of these sold for $69.99 each]		NIKE DRI-FIT WOMEN'S TENNIS FITNESS SKIRT MED NWT	$18.50
NWT $86 Nike Top + Shorts Tennis Outfit! Size Small!	$67.59	NWT MENS ADIDAS Tennis/Workout/Casual Shorts Size Large	$18.50
Babolat Team All Court II Tennis Shoe New Size 9.5	$66.09	1 pair Lotto Tennis shoe Time lady ,many size !!!!!!!!	$18.00
NWT $126 Prince Tennis 2 TOPS + Skirt! Size S!	$63.99	[2 of these sold for $18.00 each]	
LILY'S tennis outfit NWT "BIG SUR " (XL)	$63.00	ADIDAS CLIMALITE TENNIS/SOCCER JERSEY, SHIRT, SIZE XL	$18.00
NIKE MEN AGASSI AIR ZOOM BREATHE II TENNIS SHOES 9.5	$61.00	NEW NWT NIKE MENS BOYS NAVY TENNIS DRI-FIT SHORTS LARGE	$17.99
NIKE MEN FEDERER AIR ZOOM VAPOR SPEED TENNIS SHOES 7	$61.00	Nike Border Ladies Tennis Jacket Medium Blue NEW w Tags	$17.77
NIKE MEN AIR VAPOR S2 TENNIS SHOES SZ 10 ($100)	$59.99	NWT NIKE Tennis Mini Skirt DRI FIT LOW RISE Size L!	$17.55
NIKE MEN AGASSI AIR ZOOM BREATHE II TENNIS SHOES 8	$59.95	NWOT Adidas White Periwinkle Blue Tennis Skirt Small	$17.51

Tennis ▶ Balls

The average sales price in this subcategory is $23.49.

	HIGH		AVG
Collection of Antique Tennis Ball Tins	$159.35	TENNIS BALLS" USED *(65)*	$25.05
Wilson US Open Tennis Balls 2 Cases (48 cans) 144 Balls	$143.72	70 Used Tennis Balls - Lots of Bounce. Only used once.	$25.00
RARE Antique Tennis Ball in SINGLE BALL Original Box !	$100.00	10 Used Tennis Balls almost new	$25.00
200 Used Tennis Balls	$84.75	lot of 16 signed tennis balls US Open Tons Of Stars!!!	$24.50
VINTAGE " TORNADO" TENNIS BALL CAN–OLD KEY WIND LID	$79.00	50 USED TENNIS BALLS - PENN, WILSON, DUNLOP,NR	$24.25
150 used tennis balls	$76.77	50 Used Tennis Balls!! Like New, Lots of Bounce	$23.50
Wilson US Open Tennis Balls - New - Bulk - 120 Count	$76.00	100 used tennis balls - Penn, Wilson, Dunlop	$23.50
Vintage Bill Tilden Tennis Ball Can with Bonus Bancroft	$76.00	50 used tennis balls	$23.50
112 Tretorn Pro-Lite Pressureless Tennis Balls - used	$68.00	60 Outdoor Used Tennis Balls ....Shipping $7.75	$23.37
Vintage Wright & Ditson tennis ball can unopend	$64.00	50 Used Tennis Balls - Good Condition - Used Indoors!	$23.01
Vintage SEALED Tennis Balls ALL METAL Can with KEY	$63.55	50 USED TENNIS BALLS - PENN, WILSON, DUNLOP,NR	$22.50
65 Used Tennis Balls	$20.57	90 Used Tennis Balls/Dogtoys, chair leg covers	$22.50
120+ Tennis Balls Used Indoors – Low Handling Fee	$60.00	21 Cans 63 Balls Lightly Used Senior Ladies Dbls	$22.50
100+ Tennis Balls Used Indoors – Low Handling Fee	$56.00	Penn Professional Tennis Balls 12 - 3 Packs (36) NIB	$22.50
Wilson US Open Tennis Balls - New - Bulk - 120 Count	$51.01	60 Brand Name Used Tennis Balls. Very Good Shape!	$22.50

Tennis ▶ Racquets

The average sales price in this subcategory is $57.24.

	HIGH		AVG
EAGNAS ELECTRONIC STRINGING MACHINE HAWK 722E - NEW	$360.00	Prince Michael Chang Tennis Racquet 4 1/2 Longbody OS	$59.00
New Ivan Lendl Mizuno Tennis Racket/Racquet	$300.00	Head Intelligence I.S 12 tennis racquet racket NEW4 3/8	$59.00
2 BABOLAT PUREDRIVE TEAM TENNIS RACQUETS GKIT4	$289.00	NEW Head Classic Midplus 4 1/4 Tennis Racquet Racket	$58.25
(3) Babolat pure control team MP plus tennis racquets	$238.00	Head Titanium Ti. S6 tennis racquet racket NEW 4 3/8	$58.03
HEAD LIQUIDMETAL PRESTIGE MID 4 3/8 (TWO) BRAND NEW	$216.50	NEW WILSON TRIAD 5.0 HAMMER 4 3/8 IN. RACKET RACQUET	$57.00
2 Fischer Pro tour Extreme New 4 3/8	$210.00	LOT OF TWO HEAD PRESTIGE 600 TENNIS RACQUETS CLASSIC NR	$57.00
Head I.Prestige MP 98 - 4 rackets! Head Tour Bag! LOT	$203.60	New Head i.radical intelligence tennis racket 107	$57.00
PRINCE O3 SILVER TENNIS RACQUET!! BRAND NEW FreeShipping	$202.50	New Head Ti.Radical Tennis Racket 107	$56.50
HEAD FLEXPOINT INSTINCT TENNIS RACUETS QTY: 2	$202.50	New Head Ti.S6 4 1/2 Tennis Racquet TiS6 Pre-Strung	$56.02
HEAD I.X16 intelligence tennis racket racquet NEW	$201.50	NEW HEAD i.Radical MP Tennis Racquet 3/8 Pre-Strung	$56.00
NEW Prince O3 Silver tennis racquet - 1/2, 3/8 or 1/4	$192.50	NEW FISCHER Pro IMPACT FT Tennis Racquet 4 3/8	$56.00
HEAD PROTECTOR MP MIDPLUS tennis racket racquet NEW NR	$189.95	Head Intelligence i.S6 OS Tennis Racquet 4-3/8 New	$56.00
NEW Prince O3 Silver OS tennis racquet 4 5/8	$179.99	Donnay Borg Pro Tennis Racquet Racket	$56.00
NEW Prince C 3 Silver (118), 4-3/8 Tennis Racket	$179.99	Agassi Donnay Pro One	$56.00
BRAND NEW Prince O3 Silver ! Many extras!!!	$177.50	NEW HEAD Ti.S5 TiS5 Tennis Racquet 1/4 NO RES	$56.00

Triathlon ▶ Bike

The average sales price in this subcategory is $172.85.

	HIGH		AVG
Cervelo P3 Fighter Jet Paint	$2,750.00	Polar 720i HeartRate Monitor/Cyclocomputer!!!BRAND NEW!	$244.51
Kuota Kalibur - Triathlon and Time Trial bike	$2,375.00	Deda AeroBlack Time Trial Bar w/extensions TRIATHLON	$228.50
FELT B2 STEALTH 60CM	$2,000.00	Oval Concepts Jetstream A900 fork full carbon 650 new	$227.50
Kuota Kalibur Medium Frame	$1,826.53	Polar S720i Heart Rate Monitor/ Triathlon Computer	$227.50
Softride TT7 Rocket Triathlon Racing Bike...A Beauty...	$1,825.00	Polar 720i HeartRate Monitor/Cyclocomputer!!!BRAND NEW!	$227.00
triathlon road bicycle softride specialized tri spoke	$1,602.00	Polar 720i HeartRate Monitor/Cyclocomputer!!!BRAND NEW!	$203.01
Trek Hilo - 56 cm, 650 cc Tri Bike Triathlon	$1,500.00	Polar S520 HeartRate Monitor/Cyclocomputer!!!BRAND NEW!	$177.50
SOFTRIDE POWERWING - GREAT DEAL	$1,375.00	Profile Designs Carbon X Handlebar	$165.02
Cannondale Multisport 4000 Triathalon Bike	$1,175.00	NEW!! '04 Deda Elementi Aeroblue TT Bars	$160.00
2003 Klein Q Carbon 55 cm	$900.00	Oval Concepts A700 Aerobars Aero bars profile fsa	$155.01
Profile Design Carbon Stryke aerobars	$870.00	Shimano Dura Ace Triathlon / TT Chainring & CrankSet	$155.00
[10 of these sold in a multiple item ("Dutch") auction for $87.00 each]		Visiontech Vision Tech aerobars time trial triathlon M	$152.50
Zipp 909, Race wheels, 650c	$850.00	SPINERGY SR-3 650C ROAD WHEELSET	$152.50
SOFTRIDE!! GREAT BIKE!	$775.00	CAMPAGNOLO TRIATHLON	
Zipp 303 tubular wheelset with cassette, tires, skewers	$711.00	New Sidi T-1 Carbon Triathlon Shoes	$140.00
Corima Carbon Fiber Bicycle bike Triathlon wheels	$710.00	NEW Team Issued USPS Cycling Vest Jersey sz Med	$128.39

Triathlon ▶ Run

The average sales price in this subcategory is $47.32.

	HIGH		AVG
BRAND NEW!!! Polar S625X Heart Rate Monitor	$265.01	BRAND NEW!!! Polar S625X Heart Rate Monitor	$252.00
BRAND NEW!!! Polar S625X Heart Rate Monitor	$265.01	ZOOT SPORTS TRI BAG	$61.00
BRAND NEW!!! Polar S625X Heart Rate Monitor	$265.00	SportCount - Lap Counter Timer Sports Watch Run Swim	$31.95
BRAND NEW!!! Polar S625X Heart Rate Monitor	$262.75	[3 of these sold for $31.95 each]	
BRAND NEW!!! Polar S625X Heart Rate Monitor	$260.02		

Triathlon ▶ Swim

The average sales price in this subcategory is $78.75.

	HIGH		AVG
NEW Triathlon Wetsuit, 2004 Orca PFlex	$389.95	QUINTANO ROO Like New - Hydrofull ~ MS	$88.00
NEW Orca Predator P-Flex Triathlon Wetsuit	$350.00	Quintana Roo QR Full Sleeve Triathlon Wetsuit, MS-Short	$86.00
Ironman Stealth 2005 Full Wetsuit – $$ goes to kids!	$300.00	Women's Xterra Ventilator Wetsuit	$86.00
NEW 2004 Orca Predator 2 Full Sleeve Wetsuit	$289.95	Warm water ProMotion triathlon wetsuit LongJohn shorty	$84.00
Ironman Stealth Full Wetsuit - 2004	$285.00	O'NEILL Wet Suit - Ex. Cond., Like New! Men's Large.	$81.00
NEW 2004 Orca Predator 2 Full Sleeve Wetsuit	$269.95	New Aqua Sphere Triathlon Wetsuit - 65-72 deg - M	$81.00
Like New Triathlon Wetsuit, Orca Pflex, Size 5	$255.00	New Aqua Sphere Triathlon Wetsuit - 65-72 deg - Small	$79.00
Orca Speedsuit Size 7 Triathlon Wetsuit	$227.50	Aqua Sphere Wetsuit Men's Large	$76.00
XTERRA VORTEX Sleeveless Wetsuit Triathlon MLA	$219.00	Hai Line Triathlon Wetsuit (Large)	$61.00
Quintana Roo SuperFull Triathlon Wetsuit, Size M/S	$217.50	TRIATHLON ZOOT WOMEN TRI RACE SUIT - M - NWT white	$53.59
Xterra Vortex wetsuit, triathlon, mens medium	$207.50	New Auth Quintana Roo Women Small Full/Ultra Wetsuit	$53.50
Orca Speedsuit Fullsleeve Triathlon Wetsuit - Sz 9	$205.00	TRIATHLON ZOOT WOMEN TRI RACE SUIT - L - NWT white	$52.00
SwiMP3, New MP3 player for Swimmers only, NEW!!	$193.00	TRIATHLON DeSoto 5-Pkt Power Skinsuit XL NWT rd De #	$51.01
NEW triathlon wetsuit Orca speedsuite full sleeve	$187.61	NEW De Soto T1 Zippered Pull Over for Triathlon Size 5	$49.00
Ironman Stealth Men's Medium Wetsuit	$185.54	TRIATHLON DeSoto WOMEN Power Skinsuit L NWT rd De #	$47.55

Wakeboarding, Waterskiing ▶ Wakeboarding, Kneeboarding

The average sales price in this subcategory is $136.10.

	HIGH		AVG
1993 Mastercraft ski boat 25th Aniversary	$11,500.00	LIQUID FORCE OMEGA 143 WAKEBOARD	$142.51
WHIPLASH WAKEBOARD TOWER BRAND NEW UNIVERSAL	$939.00	BRAND NEW 2005 MODEL	
WHIPLASH WAKEBOARD TOWER BRAND NEW UNIVERSAL	$899.00	*PIONEER* Wakeboard Tower Boat Speakers, NEW! N/R!	$142.50
Wakeboard tower custom built to your needs Low reserve	$875.00	*Kenwood* White Wakeboard Tower Boat Speakers, NEW!	$142.50
WAKEBOARD TOWER	$860.00	(((ALPINE))) - Wakeboard Boat Tower Speakers	$140.00
WAKEBOARD TOWER (by WaKe DeSgHiNgS) w/ RACKS	$787.00	NEW HYPERLITE PARKS WAKEBOARD BOOTS- XX LARGE - No rese	$139.00
Wakeboard tower custom built to your needs Low reserve	$760.00	LIQUID FORCE OMEGA 143 WAKEBOARD	$138.50
FUSION TOWER SPEAKERS T-SERIES COMBOS!!!	$749.00	BRAND NEW 2005 MODEL	
JOYSTICK UNIVERSAL WAKEBOARD TOWER	$710.00	Hyperlite Wakeskate	$137.50
/ NEW / NO RESERVE		fat sacs, straight line, launch pad, wakeboarding, pair	$135.00
JOYSTICK UNIVERSAL WAKEBOARD	$695.00	Kneeboard rack- wakeboard rack - waterski rack - knee b	$135.00
TOWER / NEW / NO RESERVE		2005 Hydroslide Pro X LT Kneeboard Wakeboard NEW	$134.49
AIR CHAIR HYDROFOIL SO YOU CAN SKI IN THE SKY	$685.00	NEW! WAKEBOARD TOWER BOAT SPEAKERS FRONT/BACK	$133.00
JOYSTICK UNIVERSAL WAKEBOARD	$610.00	*Kenwood* Wakeboard Tower Boat Speakers, NEW!	$132.50
TOWER / NEW / NO RESERVE		NEW! WAKEBOARD TOWER BOAT SPEAKERS FRONT/BACK	$131.00
AirChair Air Chair w/Training Handle & DealerOnly Video	$575.00	Fat Sac Fat Brick by Fly High - wakeboard sack	$130.00
Airchair Air Chair hydrofoil ski big sky	$510.00	[2 of these sold in a multiple item ("Dutch") auction for $65.00 each]	
Air Chair, Not Sky SKI	$455.00	Brand New Hyperlite Temet Wakeboard Bindings Mimi Med	$129.50

Wakeboarding, Waterskiing ▶ Water Skiing

The average sales price in this subcategory is $71.63.

	HIGH		AVG
2004 Sky Ski Pro ST Hydrofoil with shocktower	$1,775.00	HO Wide Trax Combo Water Skis	$74.99
Sea - Doo XP 1997	$1,500.00	66" JOBE ELIMINATOR HONEYCOMB GRAPHITE	$74.99
16' crestliner open bow runabout boat 100 hp	$1,125.00	SLALOM WATER SKI	
2004 D3 X5 SLALOM WATER SKI, 65.5"	$504.00	WATER SKI BINDINGS HO HYPERLITE SIZE 9-11	$74.99
D3 X5 2004 D3\KD\HO Inserts	$475.00	Ep XR-7 LTD Series 1 water ski's	$74.99
[2 of these sold for $475.00 each]		NEW HYDROSLIDE 45" KIDS BEGINNER WATER SKIS W/ TOW ROPE	$74.00
HO Slalom Waterski	$455.00	PAIR OF O'BRIEN TEAMCOMP COMBO WATER SKIES-almost new	$73.00
Goode Waterski "Brand New"	$450.00	NEW HYDROSLIDE 67" SLALOM WATER SKIS COMBO W/ BINDINGS	$71.01
HO Phantom Truth W/ Phantom Boots NEW Waterski, Slalom	$449.99	NEW HYDROSLIDE 48" KIDS BEGINNER WATER SKIS W/ TOW ROPE	$71.00
D3 X5 2004 D3\KD Inserts	$425.00	NEW HYDROSLIDE 59" SLALOM WATER SKIS COMBO W/ BINDINGS	$71.00
HO Monza 68" Slalom Waterski Water ski Like New	$404.99	Vintage Cypress Gardens TRIK MASTER Water Skis	$71.00
9400 Goode Ski - Slalom	$355.00	NEW HOBIE TRAINING WATER SKIS SLED 1 PIECE AGES 8 UNDER	$71.00
KD CR7 Slalom Waterski 67" Dbl Hi Wrap Bindings, new	$350.00	O'BRIEN NEW CELEBRITY WATERSKIS WAKEBOARD SLALOM	$71.00
2005 HO SYSTEM 8 SLALOM BLANK SKI 68" BRAND NEW	$335.98	NEW HYDROSLIDE 67" SLALOM WATER SKIS COMBO W/ BINDINGS	$70.00
NEW OBRIEN MAPPLE 64" SLALOM WATER SKI waterskis ski's	$330.00	O'Brien FreeCarve Performance Slalom Ski	$70.00
O'BRIEN Jumpers jump skis water ski Connelly Kidder HO	$325.00	JOBE SUPER CUT S-GLASS HONEYCOMB WATER SKI 67" NR-MINT	$69.99

Other Sports ▶ Backyard Games

The average sales price in this subcategory is $37.28.

	HIGH		AVG
SPORTCRAFT 16X12 SPORTS ARENA INFLATABLE BOUNCE HOUSE	$405.00	NEW PROFESSIONAL BOCCE BALLS SET & CASE by GOBOCCE!	$39.95
VINTAGE BOCCE BALLS LAWN BOWLING	$226.00	Classic backyard Skill game -Nice shape in original box	$39.00

SOUTH BEND Colorful Vintage Croquet Set NICE NR	$160.38	Brand New 3U/G5 NS Yonex NanoSpeed8000	$38.99
Yonex Nanospeed NS 8000 Badminton Racket Racquet 3U/G5	$149.99	badminton racket	
[2 of these sold for $149.99 each]		Bonus Bar Skill Shot Golf, WOW, like ladder golf	$38.00
Bean Bag Cornhole Baggo Game- with BOARD LIGHT	$149.99	Vintage Croquet Set, Compl set w/Stand 6clubs 6 balls	$38.00
Antique D & M Small Sized Or Childs Tennis Racquet NR	$149.50	Washer Pitching Yard Game - Great for Labor Day!	$38.00
Used Yonex Nanospeed NS 8000 US Badminton Racket	$145.00	[2 of these sold for $38.00 each]	
Chicago White Soxs Cornhole/Baggo/Bean Bags Set	$142.50	Antique Victorian Croquet Set w Box NR	$36.55
NEW YONEX ARMORTEC 800-OF Badminton Racquet*BLACK HAWK*	$135.00	Croquet Balls Vintage Set of 6 Wooden	$36.36
[3 of these sold for $135.00 each]		Brand New 3U/G5 NS Yonex NanoSpeed8000 badminton racket	$36.01
Yonex Nanospeed NS 7000 Badminton Racket Racquet 3U/G5	$129.99	New Spartan Regulation 100mm Bocce Ball Set w/Carry Bag	$36.00
Yonex Armortec 800 OF Offense Badminton Racquet Racket	$129.99	diamond horseshoes professional 30 yrs old nice pair	$36.00
[4 of these sold for $129.99 each]		BOCCE SET BY SPORTCRAFT, HARDLY EVER USED	$36.00
NEW YONEX ARMORTEC 800-OF Badminton Racquet*BLACK HAWK*	$129.99	GOOD SET OF JUVENILE YOUTH CHILDS	$36.00
NEW Prestrung YONEX NANO SPEED 7000 Badminton Racquet	$129.99	VINTAGE HORSESHOES	
NEW YONEX MP99 Badminton Racquet PRESTRUNG with BG70Pro	$129.99	New - Yonex Armortec 800 Offence 4UG5 badminton racket	$36.00
Yonex Muscle Power MP100 badminton racket/racquet new	$129.00	KUBB, VIKING LAWN GAME FOR ALL AGES, MADE IN USA	$35.95

Other Sports ▶ Cricket

The average sales price in this subcategory is $18.36.

	HIGH		AVG
SS Limited Edition Premium Eng willow Cricket bat $299	$122.50	Cricket Bat AS Sport bating gloves at Zeepk	$21.99
ALL NEW 2005 Slazenger V600 Panther Cricket Club Bat SH	$46.00	Cricket Bat Bating Gloves AS Sport	$20.50
Cricket Bat - Gunn and Moore Purest- Brand New	$39.00	Donald Bradman Box Set Radio Biography Cricket History	$19.01
Lillywhites Cricket Bat and cricket ball	$26.00	Cricket Bat (for tape ball) (Tennis Ball) AS Sport	$17.99
BDM Galaxy Cricket Batting Leg Guards, Mens Right Hand	$24.99	Cricket Bat (for tape ball) (Tennis Ball) AS Sport	$14.99

Other Sports ▶ Cheerleading

The average sales price in this subcategory is $16.73.

	HIGH		AVG
YOUTH CHEERLEADING TEAM UNIFORMS FLY AWAY SKIRT	$338.99	#110 NEW ADIDAS girls DUFFLE BAG pink/white with BONUS!	$18.99
LOT OF CDT CHEERLEADING UNIFORMS / 21 SHELLS,20 SKIRTS	$295.00	[2 of these sold for $18.99 each]	
VARSITY Cheerleading Uniform Lot 30 Pieces Total	$202.52	Cheer Mom Decals Cheerleading Cheerleader 15 for cars	$18.50
ONE TREE HILL Cheerleader Uniform!	$176.00	VINTAGE CHEERLEADER MEGAPHONE - VERY NICE	$18.45
NEW Kaepa #6346/6346Y cheerleading shoes, lot of 43	$159.51	9 Megaphone Cheerleading Socks sz. 6-9 NEW LOT	$18.00
LOT OF CDT CHEERLEADING UNIFORMS / 9 SHELLS , 8 SKIRTS	$102.50	CHEERLEADING CLOCK girls ladies school chearleader Poms	$17.99
LOT OF CDT CHEERLEADING UNIFORMS / 11 SHELLS,11 SKIRTS	$87.01	NWT Infant Girls 4 Pc Cheerleading Uniform Outfit 24 M	$17.50
LOT OF CDT CHEERLEADING UNIFORMS / 8 SHELLS , 5 SKIRTS	$71.00	3 pc High School Cheerleader Cheerleading Uniform M	$17.50
3-pc Cheerleaders Suitcase sports cheerleading girls	$70.00	THREE GREAT BATON TWIRLING BOOKS!!	$17.08
LOT OF VARSITY CHEERLEADING UNIFORMS /6 SHELLS,5 SKIRTS	$66.00	Varsity Cheerleading Cheerleader Uniform/Girls Large	$17.06
AAI Cartwheel Beam Tumbling Exercise Aerobics Floor Mat	$62.00	VARSITY Cheerleading Uniform 4 Pieces Cheer Costume	$17.00
1 LOT (14 EA.) CHEERLEADING T-SHIRTS NEW	$60.00	NWT Infant Girls 4 Pc Cheerleading Uniform Outfit 18 M	$16.99
NEW CHEERLEADING Custom UNIFORM LOT+Pom+breifs+sock LOT	$56.99	NWT Gorgeous Girls 3 Pc Cheerleading Uniform Outfit 5	$16.99
[3 of these sold for $56.99 each]		5 pc GATORS Cheerleading Uniform BUST 28" - Waist 23"	$16.82
NIB~NFINITY CHEERLEADING SHOE SZ 13 YOUTH TO 11.5 ADULT	$56.00	High School Cheerleader Cheerleading Uniform, sz Medium	$16.50
NIB~NFINITY CHEERLEADING SHOE SZ 13 YOUTH TO 11.5 ADULT	$55.00	CHEERLEADING UNIFORM DEVILS PURPLE GLD WHT YTH SMALL	$16.50

Other Sports ▶ Fencing

The average sales price in this subcategory is $27.58.

	HIGH		AVG
Complete Foil Fencing Set w/Mask/Lame/Jacket/Foils/Etc.	$301.50	Men's U.S. Size 30, Duellist 350N CE Fencing Knickers	$31.00
Costello Fencing Foil Masks & Jackets Womans/Mens 4 Pc	$107.50	Blue Gauntlet Fencing HELMET FACE MASK	$30.00
Woman Fencing Blotter ATLANTIC 1935 McCLELLAND BARCLAY	$103.49	NEW Fencing Budget Practice Jacket, zipper in the back,	$29.99
WALL MOUNT FENCING DUMMY WITH ADJUSTABLE ARMS	$91.00	$140 ELECTRIC SABRE FENCING MASK	$29.99
Pair of Vintage Fencing Swords	$91.00	[2 of these sold for $29.99 each]	
WALL MOUNT FENCING DUMMY WITH ADJUSTABLE ARMS	$85.00	Electric Fencing Foil Marked PS 93 on Blade Sword	$28.01
1855 FRENCH FENCING FOIL SWORD	$76.00	fencing mask castello RAPIER COMBAT sca large	$28.00
AWARD DIPOLMA DOCUMENT		Magnum Libre d'Escrime ~ Big Book of Fencing in English	$28.00
Fencing equipment	$75.00	MUSKETIER Fencing Mask Helmet no res low starting bid	$26.99
FENCING GEAR TWO HELMETS, JACKET	$70.00	Introduction to Foil Fencing ~ Instructors Manual	$26.99
AND UHLMANN SWORD		FENCING FOIL SABRE / SWORD / LEON PAUL SABER	$26.00
Electric Fencing Foil Marked Uhlmann Sword	$68.01	CASTELLO FENCING MASK AND JACKET	$26.00
Fencing Gear Face Prot, Outfit, Foil with Sports Bag NR	$61.54	PETMATE PET PORTER Large Dog Kennel Carrier	$25.00
SABRE LAME JACKET EUROSPORT $179 .NEW	$59.99	fencing one piece chest BREAST PROTECTOR * No Reserve*	$23.36
Fencing sculpture trophies trophy awards foil epee	$50.00	FOIL ELECTRIC PISTOL GRIP COMPETITION,NEW $99	$21.99
SABRE MASK REMOVABLE PADDING ,$150-EUROSPORT, NEW	$47.99	[3 of these sold for $21.99 each]	
Antique Pair of Fencing Foils/Swords/Rapiers/Sabers	$46.00	FENCING MASK/FACE GUARD PRIEUR	$21.51

Other Sports ▶ Field Hockey

The average sales price in this subcategory is $25.31.

	HIGH		AVG
Mercian GREAT WHITE Composite Hockey Stick Brand New	$132.50	Field Hockey Stick 38", Dita Mega 90	$30.50
BRAND NEW GRYPHON TABOO PRO COMPOSITE FIELDHOCKEY STICK	$107.50	Field Hockey Stick 37", Dita Mega 90, new, unused	$29.00
BRAND NEW TK 1.0 PLUS COMPOSITE FIELD HOCKEY STICK	$102.50	Team USA FIELD HOCKEY SHORTS stick girls Size M	$26.01
Mercian BURN Composite Hockey Stick Brand New	$100.55	STX Stealth Composite Field Hockey Stick	$23.83
BRAND NEW TK CX 1.0 COMPOSITE FIELD HOCKEY STICK	$91.00	Field Hockey Stick 36", Dita Sigma 500, new, unused	$22.01

Other Sports ▶ Rugby

The average sales price in this subcategory is $17.65.

	HIGH		AVG
LOT OF 8 VINTAGE TROPHY CUPS MADE IN ENGLAND~RUGBY	$82.00	NEW ZEALAND L/S STEINLAGER RUGBY SHIRT - Men's XL	$18.00
MALTESE NATIONAL RUGBY SHIRT UNIQUE	$49.00	NEWZEALAND BLUE RUGBY JERSEY SHIRT BRITISH LION M NEW	$17.99
NEW ALL BLACKS RUGBY JACKET SIZE LARGE	$47.00	NEWZEALAND BLUE RUGBY JERSEY SHIRT BRITISH LION L NEW	$17.99
ADIDAS EQUIPMENT BOXING SHOE 11.5	$45.00	ALL BLACKS RUGBY JERSEY SHIRT RED-BLACK L NEW	$17.99
South Africa Rugby Jersey: XL ~ NEW~	$38.53	ALL BLACKS RUGBY JERSEY SHIRT RED-BLACK M NEW	$17.99
NWT Adidas All Blacks Steinlager Training Top (2XL)	$36.00	ALL BLACKS RUGBY JERSEY SHIRT RED-BLACK XL NEW	$17.99
NEW ZEALAND ALL BLACKS 2005 TOUR	$35.00	**NEW Rugby Ball Adidas Yellow Size 5**	$17.53
ADIDAS L RUGBY JERSEY		CANTERBURY CRUSADERS RED RUGBY JERSEY SHIRT XL NEW	$16.99
Rugby Protective Headgear-Gilbert	$34.00	Rugby Shorts-Navy 42	$16.00
ADIDAS BOXING CHAMP-SPEED SHOE 10.5	$34.00	[2 of these sold in a multiple item ("Dutch") auction for $8.00 each]	
NEW ALL BLACKS RUGBY JACKET SIZE MEDIUM	$33.00	Hong Kong Sevens Rugby jersey 7S Thailand Shirts S 05	$15.99
New Zeland All Blacks Polo Style Rugby Shirt XXL	$32.57	Hong Kong Sevens Rugby jersey 7S Thailand Shirts 05 L	$15.99
NEW ALL BLACKS RUGBY JACKET SIZE XL	$32.00	Hong Kong Sevens Rugby jersey 7S Thailand Shirts 05 M	$15.99
ADIDAS BOXING CHAMP-SPEED SHOE 9.5	$30.99	Hong Kong Sevens Rugby jersey 7S Thailand Shirts 05 XXL	$15.99
ADIDAS BOXING CHAMP-SPEED SHOE 10	$29.99	Rugby Protective Headgear-Gilbert	$15.50
Argentina rugby jersey "los pumas" original "TOPPER" XL	$29.50	New Zealand All Black Hong Kong 7's Rugby Jersey (ss)	$15.05

Other Sports ▶ Snowshoeing

The average sales price in this subcategory is $45.46.

	HIGH		AVG
Atlas 1225 Snowshoes W/Case Worn One Time	$152.79	SNOW SHOES...* CUTE *.Snow Shoes INDIAN...BEAUTIFUL A06	$49.99
YUKON CHARLIE'S SNOWSHOES (2 PAIR) 930 & 825-NWT 59.99!	$130.46	YUKON CHARLIES LIGHTWEIGHT ALUMINUM SNOWSHOES CHINOOK	$49.00
Brand New Tubbs Altitude Series 30" Snowshoes	$122.50	ANTIQUE Snowshoes INDIAN 42x12 Snow Shoes TRAPS	$46.99
Great 1942 SNOWSHOES Lund Hastings MN Must See	$110.00	ANTIQUE Snowshoes INDIAN 42x12 Snow Shoes TRAPS	$46.69
pair of long old snowshoes in EXCELLENT condition	$107.50	Lightly Used Atlas 30'" Snowshoes	$46.00
Old INDIAN SNOWSHOES 41X12 Snow Shoes L@@k*!*	$105.00	ANTIQUE Snowshoes INDIAN 33x10 Snow Shoes TRAPS	$45.99
Snow Shoes-Antique-Oak-Leather-Skin? Snowshoes-NR!	$102.50	INDIAN SNOWSHOES 42X13 Snow Shoes DECOR	$45.00
Atlas 1033 snowshoes	$100.00	ANTIQUE Snowshoes INDIAN 42x16 Snow Shoes TRAPS	$45.00
NWT Northern Outfitters EXP II Boots - Extreme Outdoor	$99.00	SNOWSHOES 44X14 Snow Shoes ***L@@K****OVERLAP*****	$44.99
MSR Denali Classic Black Snowshoes & Tails Used/Nice	$86.00	VINTAGE WOODEN FABER 44X15 SNOW SHOE/SNOWSHOES	$44.99
30" Sherpa Hiker Snowshoes in EXCELLENT condition	$81.00	ANTIQUE Snowshoes INDIAN 42x14 Snow Shoes TRAPS	$44.00
Native American Indian Old Antique Wood Frame Snowshoes	$81.00	antique showshoes indian 48x14 snow shoes torpedo	$44.00
Tubbs Snowshoes 2 Pair (yes 2 pair) JUST LIKE NEW!!!	$80.00	Vermont Tubbs Classic VIntage Snowshoes 44" Long	$43.60
BEAUTIFUL 58" ANTIQUE LUND SNOW SHOES *Leather Binding	$77.50	ANTIQUE Snowshoes INDIAN 42x14 Snow Shoes TRAPS	$43.00
Women's TUBBS Adventure 21 Snowshoes Like New	$77.00	ANTIQUE Snowshoes INDIAN 33x10 Snow Shoes TRAPS	$42.52

Other Sports ▶ Volleyball

The average sales price in this subcategory is $17.07.

	HIGH		AVG
$300 NEW! COMPLETE Pro VOLLEYBALL NET Set + BADEN ball	$185.99	Lot of 4 Volleyballs - Spalding Mikasa Tachikara Baden	$19.15
Aluminum Volleyball Net Complete System NEW*w/Warranty	$115.00	New Wilson Volleyball Player Bag/Backpack w/ Ball Pouch	$18.27
BRAND NEW TRANSPORTABLE VOLLEYBALL SYSTEM - FREE SHIP!	$100.00	Silver & White VOLLEYBALL Charm - TEAM GIFT - Qty of 12	$18.01
Aluminum Volleyball Net Complete System NEW*w/Warranty	$100.00	[2 of these sold for $18.01 each]	
[3 of these sold for $100.00 each]		NEW SPALDING POWER PLAY VOLLEYBALL SET AND BALL #130 #1	$18.00
Official AVP volleyaball autographed by Karch Kiraly	$80.00	VOLLEYBALL BACKPACK BAG PERSONALIZED	$17.99
Karch Kiraly - 1980 Beach Volleyball Manhattan Open	$75.00	NEW NEBRASKA VOLLEYBALL T-SHIRT College Athlete Mens XL	$17.95
SPORTCRAFT PROFESSIONAL VOLLEYBALL SET NEW	$75.00	SPALDING CLASSIC VOLLEYBALL BADMINTON SET $228 CASE	$17.00
[2 of these sold for $75.00 each]		[2 of these sold for $17.00 each]	
SPORTCRAFT PROFESSIONAL VOLLEYBALL SET NEW	$75.00	CAUTION: VOLLEYBALL GIRL game joke new sign	$16.95
QUALITY HVY-DUTY TOURNAMENT VOLLEYBALL NET STEEL CABLES	$71.99	New Wilson Volleyball Player Bag/Backpack w/ Ball Pouch	$16.59
New Pair T2 White CHAMELEON Active Ankles size Small!!	$65.00	~WILSON AVP VOLLEYBALL REPLICA GAME BALL mcpeak NIB~	$16.50
Spotcraft Heritage Volleyball	$59.99	NEW WILSON LIQUID UNDERGLASS COMPETITIVE VOLLEYBALL AVP	$16.05
2 AMF AMERICAN VOLLEYBALL POSTS AND NET	$56.00	BORN TO PLAY VOLLEYBALL T SHIRT/NAME ADDED FREE! COOL!	$16.01
AVP VOLLEYBALL NET volley ball NO RESERVE!	$55.00	VOLLEYBALL COURT road street name sport novelty sign	$15.95
ULTIMATE KAEPA BRACE VOLLEYBALL SNEAKERS SHOES 10 NEW	$50.50	New Volleyball Official AVP Net Size Beach Pack Netting	$15.50
New Pair T2 Black CHAMELEON Active Ankles size Medium!	$50.00	NEW WILSON AVP UNDERGLASS COMPETITIVE VOLLEYBALL volley	$15.50

Other Sports ▶ Wrestling

The average sales price in this subcategory is $24.30.

	HIGH		AVG
Home wrestling mat	$390.00	Blue Wrestling or Swim Trunks.	$24.99
Home wrestling mat	$380.00	Tiger & Black Wrestling-Biker-Exercise-Swim Shorts.	$24.99
WCW Tag Team Wrestling Belts	$265.02	Dark Green Wrestling or Swim Trunks.	$24.99
WWF WCW House Show/ VHS Tapes	$183.05	Green Zebra & Black Wrestling or Swim Trunks.	$24.99
wwe wwf wcw wrestling belt	$130.00	wrestling singlet team florida new!!!!!!!!!!!!!	$24.50
WWE SMACKDOWN UNDISPUTED CHAMPIONSHIP BELT VERSION 2	$127.50	Men's ADIDAS Wrestling/Boxing Shoes Size 10	$24.50
2 Flash-Black Wet-look Vinyl & Yellow Wrestling Tights.	$122.50	Team Canada Reversible Wrestling Singlet - no shoes	$24.00
NEW Sublimated Wrestling Singlet New York (BLUE) A MED	$111.49	Team Indiana Wrestling Singlet / adult Medium, Blue/Blk	$23.69
Professional Wrestling Boots, TNA, WWE, size 12	$105.00	Men's men N2N collegiate singlet wrestling shiny NWT	$23.50
Vintage Asics Wrestling Shoes SIze 10	$102.50	Minnesota Wrestling National Singlet	$23.50
Adidas Adistar Wrestling Shoes 9 Black/Blue/White	$99.99	Team Michigan National Wrestling Singlet	$23.05
NEW Sublimated Wrestling Singlet New York (BLUE) A SM	$99.00	NEW! Size 14.0 White/Blue/Silver ASICS Wrestling Shoes	$22.72
NEW Sublimated Wrestling Singlet New York (BLUE) Y Lg	$99.00	WWF WWE WrestleMania 2001 17 X-7 X-Seven DVD The Rock	$22.50
NEW Sublimated Wrestling Singlet New York (BLUE) Y MD	$99.00	ASICS PURSUIT II 2 WRESTLING SHOES Mens SIZE 11 L/NEW	$22.50
NEW Sublimated Wrestling Singlet New York (BLUE) Y SM	$99.00	Asics Wrestling Shoes Used Size 10 Mens Black	$22.50

29

SPORTS MEMORABILIA, CARDS & FAN SHOP

The denizens of the Sports Memorabilia (or "Sports Mem," as it's known for short), Cards & Fan Shop category are an exacting and selective bunch, and there is a lot to learn from them that can be extrapolated into other eBay categories.

For example, one card aficionado on the eBay Sports Memorabilia, Cards & Fan Shop discussion board points out that he sees too many cards placed in the wrong category. (Items placed in incorrect categories can be a problem throughout eBay.) He collects Packers cards and says, "I look for a lot of cards in the 2000–now category and find that a great deal of them do not belong there. It's not so much singles that are the problem, but the lots (which really don't belong there anyway)." He adds that he will usually not even bid on cards that are in categories where they do not belong—"It's a matter of principle."

Another issue is the way lots are put together. Sellers need to look at this from the buyer's perspective, and not just lump together items according to how they want to get rid of them. "Keep your lots reasonable in size by limiting duplicates and years," advises the seller. "A 200-card lot is pretty useless to most people if 150 of them are of the punter from 1984." He says he looks for a lot of lots, and for more recent cards. "If I saw a 50-card lot of 2002–2003 cards, I'd be much more willing to bid on it than if it were part of a 200-card lot from the years 1995–2003. This will also allow you to put a more detailed description of the lot in your auction since you are not dealing with so many cards," he writes.

Another team lot buyer agrees. He says that his favorite seller does several key things: "has few duplicates, includes more star cards than scrub cards, clearly advertises the year range of the cards and distributes them fairly well, and includes plenty of cards that book for a few bucks."

The Finer Points of Cards

Another issue with sports cards is that some people collect individual cards, while others collect cards for the whole team—and sellers may want to keep that in mind when packaging lots that include athletes who have played on multiple teams. "Ahman Green rookie cards are NOT Green Bay Packers cards," protests one fan. "At least to me . . . If I see a lot for 50 Ahman Green cards but 25 of them are from Seattle, I probably won't bid, and if I do I will consider it to be a 25 card lot, as there are only 25 that mean anything to me."

He also believes that team cards should include "all the base cards in the set—not [for example] minus Brett Favre and Ahman Green. No, inserts and Parallels are not included."

Other issues that sports memorabilia fans are especially sensitive to (and that can apply to all eBay auctions) are accurate, detailed descriptions and reasonable shipping costs. "Lists definitely help," advises the aforementioned Packers fan. Although very large lots may make it very difficult to list individual cards, he suggests that "some sort of breakdown will get my attention." For example, "in a 200 card lot, you don't have to list every card, but a breakdown of how many cards for each player, or how many for each year, will get you much better results—something like 24/7 Favres with 24 being the total number of cards and 7 being the number of different cards is a great help." And repeated cards are not appreciated: "A 25-card Packers lot including seven Tony Mandarich, three Brian Noble (all the same), six Don Majkowski, four Ed West, three Robert Brown, 1 Sterling Sharpe, and 1 Brett Favre is not an awesome lot of vintage Packers cards."

How Much Can It Cost to Ship a Card?

Packing and shipping issues are also especially important in this category. Because sports memorabilia is so affected by condition, sellers need to use sturdy cardboard materials, waterproof linings, bubble wrap, and so on to ensure the item stays in the same condition as when it was listed.

And because items like trading cards are so light, at least when they're not in a very large lot, buyers don't like to be overcharged on shipping. "Shipping had better not be over $4.00 or there had better be something pretty special included," writes a buyer on the boards. "Nothing pisses me off more than paying $5.00 for shipping and having the cards arrive regular post in a simple padded envelope and the guy probably spent all of 95 cents to get the package to me."

Another buyer complains that "one of the things that is killing sports card auctions" is "baiting the buyer with a very low price and then making up for it by overcharging for shipping," which he considers unconscionable. Most buyers accept a modest charge for packing and even handling, but it's best to keep it in proportion to the cost of the item. Theoretically, if you are clear about the cost of shipping in your listing, the buyer shouldn't complain if he or she thinks it's too high. But do you really want to risk getting bad feedback from an angry buyer who didn't notice your shipping charge? You can always post a response to a negative rating or try to work it out, but that negative may stay on your record for good.

Baseball, Golf, Hockey, and Racing

For whatever reason, baseball fans seem to be among the most enthusiastic in the sports memorabilia category, and there are more baseball items than many other sports. For example, the Sports Memorabilia, Cards & Fan Shop ▸ Autographs, Original ▸ Baseball-MLB (Major League Baseball) subcategory has upwards of 20,000 listings, whereas the subcategory with the next-highest number of listings is Sports Memorabilia, Cards & Fan Shop ▸ Autographs, Original ▸ Basketball-NBA (National Basketball Association) with about 4,000 listings.

One of the highest prices in Sports Memorabilia, Cards & Fan Shop involved the signature of one of the most legendary sports heroes ever. A "Babe Ruth Cancelled Check 1942 AWESOME AUTOGRAPH" went for $6,199.99 in the Sports Memorabilia, Cards & Fan Shop ▸ Autographs, Original ▸ Baseball-MLB subcategory. Another Ruth item, a framed autograph that sold for $1,005.00, made it to the third-highest price slot in that subcategory.

The second-highest priced item was a "1927 NY Yankees Paycheck: Ruppert & Moore Signatures" that went for $1,026.00.

Average prices in Sports Memorabilia, Cards & Fan Shop ▶ Autographs, Original ▶ Baseball-MLB included a 1980s Mickey Mantle autograph that went for $87.00 and a "YANKEES DEREK JETER SIGNED AUTHENTIC #2 FOR HM JERSEY" that went for $81.00.

In the Authenticator Pre-Certified ▶ Basketball-NBA subcategory, names that pop up frequently are Michael Jordan and Magic Johnson, with signed Jordan jerseys being the top two items, selling at $900.00 and $860.00 each. Another Jordan item, a signed *Sports Illustrated* cover, went for $315.00. Magic Johnson items in this sample ranged from a "signed Michigan ST Throwback Jersery SSG" for $91.09 to a "MAGIC JOHNSON SIGNED BASKETBALL AUTOGRAPHED W/COA +CASE" for $149.99. Even higher basketball prices show up in the Autographs, Original ▶ Basketball-NBA subcategory, where a "Michael Jordan Signed UDA Autographed Auto 9/11 Jersey" went for $1,495.00, and a "KOBE BRYANT LAKERS AUTO AUTOGRAPHED SIGNED UDA UPPER DE" went for $1,300.00. Basketball great Wilt Chamberlain also shows up here in both the high and average range of prices; a "WILT CHAMBERLAIN BILL RUSSELL AUTOGRAPHED NBA BALL COA" sold for $430.00, and a "Wilt Chamberlain Signed Autographed Basketball Book" sold for $77.00.

The world of golf memorabilia on eBay seems to be dominated, in terms of volume, by legendary player Jack Nicklaus; items related to him occupy 7 out of the top 15 highest prices and 7 of the 15 average prices in the Sports Memorabilia, Cards & Fan Shop ▶ Autographs, Original ▶ Golf subcategory. Modern player Tiger Woods commands the highest prices, though: $995.00 for a signed club and $812.52 for an autographed club-head display.

The hockey subcategories are full of Wayne Gretzky and Mario Lemieux items on the high end and items for a variety of players in the average range. The highest price in the Sports Memorabilia, Cards & Fan Shop ▶ Autographs, Original ▶ Hockey-NHL subcategory is a "WAYNE GRETZKY AUTO/SIGNED OILERS BLUE M&N JERSEY WGA" that went for $599.00. The Game Used Memorabilia ▶ Hockey-NHL subcategory offers even higher prices: $1,125.00 each for a "WAYNE GRETZKY SIGNED AWAY JERSEY W/ CERTIFICATE & FRAMED" and a "Brendan Shanahan Red Wings game used jersey 0102."

In the Fan Apparel & Souvenirs subcategory, some other sports stand out: cycling and racing. The high range of prices in this sample in Fan Apparel & Souvenirs ▶ Cycling is dominated by Lance Armstrong, with the top item being a "LANCE ARMSTRONG Signed Autographed Yellow Jersey" that sold for $1,300.00. In the Fan Apparel & Souvenirs ▶ Racing-Formula 1 subcategory, a "KIMI RAIKKONEN 2005 REPLICA HELMET" went for $909.99.

You Never Forget Your First Card: Favorites

But I think my favorite subcategory is Vintage Sports Memorabilia ▶ Cereal Boxes. (Some boxes are actually unopened, including an autographed Jerry Rice Wheaties box encased in plastic, for $26.00.) There are many other Wheaties boxes here, and some box backs and tabs.

Speaking of favorites, there's a fun thread in the Sports Memorabilia, Cards & Fan Shop discussion board about traders' favorite cards. Some are fond of certain cards for purely sentimental reasons. One man's favorite is from his very first pack, bought for him when he was ten by his brother. "The top card was a 1976 Mick Tinglehoff of the Minnesota Vikings," he writes, "and thus began my collection of sports cards. I still have it today. It's worth all of about 20 cents to anyone else, but to me it is priceless and I will cherish it always."

Another, who has collected cards since he was five, says he has many cards he loves, but his absolute favorite is a 1969 Mickey Mantle. "As a nine or ten year old kid I didn't know anything about cards, but I did understand the significance of that card. Mantle had already announced his retirement, and I knew it was going to be the last card I would ever get of The Mick." So, wanting to keep the card forever and in the best shape possible, he laminated it. "I realize now I ruined the card, but I still have it."

But maybe the attitude of one Babe Ruth collector sums up how many eBayers feel about their purchases: "What would be my favorite card? That's easy! Whatever card I just bought or traded for!"

Authenticator Pre-Certified ▶ Baseball-MLB

The average sales price in this subcategory is $82.67.

	HIGH		AVG
SIGNED MICKEY MANTLE JOE DIMAGGIO YANKEES BALL PSA/DNA	$999.99	UDA KEN GRIFFEY JR AUTOGRAPHED MAJOR LEAGUE BASEBALL	$99.00
1/1? Hideki Matsui UDA Signed 2003 World Series Jersey	$787.77	RYAN 300 WIN AUTOGRAPHED COMMEM BASEBALL # 14 RANGERS	$99.00
Ichiro 51 Signed Commercial Used Pro bat PSA/DNA	$786.99	PEREZ-STEELE Postcard COOL PAPA BELL Autograph PSA/DNA	$95.99
2001 Mariners Signed GU Olerud Jersey Ichiro PSA /DNA	$561.00	WILLIE MAYS & McCOVEY AUTOGRAPHED 8x10 PHOTO wGlobalCOA	$93.50
Derek Jeter 2000 World Series Signed Steiner Jersey MVP	$355.00	GARY SHEFFIELD Auto ~YANKEES MLB BASEBALL~ PSA/DNA ~EMS	$89.99
Derek Jeter Alex Rodriguez Dual Signed Baseball STEINER	$345.00	[2 of these sold for $89.99 each]	
ALEX RODRIGUEZ Auto YANKEES Pinstripe JERSEY ~AROD HOLO	$329.99	1982 Topps Traded Cal Ripken, Jr. Orioles PSA 8	$88.09
MICKEY MANTLE SIGNED INDEX CARD~YANKEES~PSA DNA SLAB~	$316.45	1963 Topps Bob Clemente Pittsburgh Pirates PSA 7	$81.01
CAL RIPKEN JR Auto 2632 LOUISVILLE SLUGGER BAT ~PSA/DNA	$299.99	JOHNNY BENCH HOF 89 SIGNED OML BALL-PSA/DNA AUTHENTICI	$81.00
BARRY BONDS AUTO OML BASEBALL BBA, PSA/DNA & GAI/DNA	$275.00	LLOYD WANER-PITTSBURGH PIRATES AUTO/SIGNED PHOTO-PSA	$80.95
ALEX RODRIGUEZ AUTO SIGNED ML BASEBALL GRADED PSA/DNA 9	$275.00	WARREN SPAHN SIGNED ONL BASEBALL - PSA/DNA AUTHENTICI!!	$79.99
ALEX RODRIGUEZ SIGNED OML BASEBALL - PSA/DNA MINT 9!!!	$265.00	RAFAEL PALMEIRO SIGNED OAL BASEBALL - PSA/DNA AUTHENTIC	$79.99
Game Used Baseball Hideki Matsui 2nd HR Game STEINER	$260.00	NY Mets MIKE PIAZZA Auto'd Baseball BIG APPLE COA	$76.75
Alex Rodriguez Signed Baseball STEINER Auto Autograph	$232.50	1989 New York Mets Autographed Baseball GAI #171	$76.00
JOE DIMAGGIO Signed YANKEES New Era	$228.50	Reggie Jackson HOF Autographed Baseball! Pre-Certified	$75.00
Cap wGAI COA & 8x10		Cal Ripken Jr AUTOGRAPHED All Star Official Baseball LR	$74.99

Authenticator Pre-Certified ▶ Basketball-NBA

The average sales price in this subcategory is $229.69.

HIGH TO LOW

MICHAEL JORDAN SIGNED LE RED BULLS JERSEY-UDA	$900.00	Paul Pierce Autographed TN Jersey + Celts Rookie Hat	$109.00
MICHAEL JORDAN SIGNED LE BLACK BULLS JERSEY-UDA	$860.00	WILT The Stilt CHAMBERLAIN AUTOGRAPHED 8x10 Photo wCOA	$103.49
Lebron James Upper Deck Authenticated Auto jersey	$610.00	MAGIC JOHNSON SIGNED MICHIGAN ST	$102.50
Upper Deck Authenticated LeBron James auto jersey /23	$477.09	THROWBACK JERSEY SSG	
Michael Jordan autographed Sports Illustrated cover!	$315.00	MAGIC JOHNSON SIGNED MICHIGAN	$91.09
UDA Michael Jordan BULLS Auto Gatorade Dunk 16x20 Photo	$279.95	ST THROWBACK JERSEY SSG	
MAGIC JOHNSON SIGNED BASKETBALL	$149.99	UDA Kobe Auto Autograph 8 x 10 - no jersey patch SP	$89.88
AUTOGRAPHED W/COA +CASE		JULIUS "Dr. J" ERVING AUTOGRAPHED NETS 8x10 Photo wCOA	$41.00
MAGIC JOHNSON SIGNED NBA BALL	$149.95	Carmelo Anthony Signature Shots Autograph Upper Deck 04	$39.07
AUTOGRAPHED W/ OA COA +			

Authenticator Pre-Certified ▶ Football-NFL

The average sales price in this subcategory is $101.65.

	HIGH		AVG
DAN MARINO AUTOGRAPHED HOF 05 DOLPHINS PRO HELMET	$525.00	DAN MARINO AUTOGRAPHED MINI HELMET UDA	$127.50
Vikings - Daunte CULPEPPER Auto'd Game Cut Jersey	$430.00	Dolphins - Jason Taylor Auto'd Mini Helmet	$113.61
Tom Brady Autographed Patriots NFL Football Helmet	$405.00	Chargers - COCOZZO #68 Used Jersey	$108.49
Lions - Roy WILLIAMS Auto'd Game Cut Jersey	$350.00	CHARLES WOODSON AUTO MICHIGAN JERSEY HEISMAN 97 TSP WH	$103.50
Broncos - Jake Plummer Auto'd Proline Helmet	$335.00	Chargers - SINGH #72 Used Jersey	$103.50
Vikings - Michael BENNETT Auto'd Game Cut Jersey	$280.00	Bears - Brian Urlacher Auto'd Mini Helmet	$102.51
Lions - 2004 LIONS Auto'd Game Cut Jersey	$257.00	Peyton Manning UDA 16 x 20 Autographed Picture	$102.50
Donovan McNabb Autographed Eagles NFL Football Helmet	$256.02	Troy Aikman UDA 16 x 20 Autographed Picture 184/200	$100.03
Bills - Drew BLEDSOE Auto'd Game Cut Jersey	$250.01	Broncos - Tom Nalen Auto'd Mini Helmet	$100.00
Broncos - John Lynch Auto'd Proline Helmet	$242.50	MEAN JOE GREENE SIGNED JERSEY PITTSBURGH STEELERS TRI	$96.00
JEROME BETTIS SIGNED JERSEY STEELERS THE BUS INSCR PSA	$227.50	Broncos - Al Wilson Auto'd Full Size Panel Ball	$91.00
Randy Moss ROY UDA 16 x 20 Autographed Picture 87/184	$227.50	Chargers - HERBERT #35 Used Jersey	$90.98
STEEL CURTAIN SIGNED JERSEY PITTSBURGH STEELERS GAI	$192.50	Troy Aikman UDA 16 x 20 Autographed Picture 119/208	$86.25
Lions - Brock MARION Auto'd Game Cut Jersey	$180.50	Chargers - TOLTENBERG #64 Used Jersey	$81.00
MIKE SINGLETARY SIGNED CHICAGO BEARS JERSEY GAI	$177.50	Upper Deck 1993 Joe Montana Autographed Card Blow-Up!!!	$81.00

Autographs, Original ▶ Baseball-MLB

The average sales price in this subcategory is $83.43.

	HIGH		AVG
Babe Ruth Cancelled Check 1942 AWESOME AUTOGRAPH	$6,199.99	80s Mickey Mantle signed autographed 5x8 premium RARE!	$87.00
1927 NY Yankees Paycheck: Ruppert & Moore Signatures	$1,026.00	CONNIE MACK....signed page from an autograph book	$83.50
BABE RUTH FRAMED AUTOGRAPH	$1,005.00	YANKEES DEREK JETER SIGNED AUTHENTIC #2 FOR HM JERSEY	$81.00
1927 YANKEES signed payroll check TONY LAZZERI	$997.65	WYNN FELLER FORD MATHEWS SIGNED AUTOGRAPHED CACHE	$81.00
37 Baseball Team Signed St. Louis Cardinals Music Sheet	$711.99	Mickey Mantle signed book "The Mick" HTF	$80.00
Sammy Sosa Used Fielding Glove	$700.00	Wayne Gretzky UDA autographed signed hockey card set	$76.05
17 Autographed Baseballs-Mantle, Griffey Jr., DiMaggio,	$637.00	SALVINO SPORTS LEGENDS SIGNED ROY CAMPANELLA NR!!	$76.00
1927 YANKEES signed payroll check RUPPERT, MARK KOENIG	$616.66	Autographed Bob Feller Romito Figurine	$71.00
Casey Stengel signed bank check PSA/DNA Mets Yankees	$601.00	RARE HANK GREENBERG SIGNED PSA/DNA AUTO AUTOGRAPH PHOTO	$67.99
Atlanta Braves early 90's autographed bat.	$499.99	SATCHEL PAIGE AUTOGRAPHED PAPER	$66.25
1927 YANKEES signed payroll check RUPPERT, BARROW, NEE	$411.09	1999 Topps Traded #T65 Soriano Auto SCD Graded NM/EX	$66.00
WALTER JOHNSON CUT SIGNATURE!	$360.50	KEN GRIFFEY JR. SIGNED GARTLAN LIMITED EDITION STATUE	$66.00
1952 Ted Williams Contract PSA Auto	$355.54	AUTOGRAPHED New York Yankees Encyclopedia RARE	$64.97
HIDEKI MATSUI UDA RARE FS HOME PLATE AUTO W/ COA	$334.00	Autographed Brooks Robinson Orioles Figurine Statue COA	$63.00
MARK MCGWIRE AUTOGRAPH BAT BALL PIC LOT + USA TIFFANY	$330.01	DRYSDALE KALINE FELLER BROCK SIGNED AUTOGRAPHED CACHE	$61.01

Autographs, Original ▶ Basketball-NBA

The average sales price in this subcategory is $76.54.

	HIGH		AVG
Michael Jordan Signed UDA Autographed Auto 9/11 Jersey	$1,495.00	Autographed Official Steve Francis Basketball PSA DNA	$79.99
KOBE BRYANT LAKERS AUTO AUTOGRAPHED SIGNED UDA UPPER DE	$1,300.00	Large black Jersey display case frame hinged	$79.95
AUTHENTIC MICHAEL JORDAN AUTOGRAPHED BASKETBALL	$660.00	LEBRON JAMES CARMELO ANTHONY	$78.00
Lebron James UDA Autographed signed Away Jersey NEW!!!	$580.00	DWAYNE WADE KOBE SIGNED	
MICHAEL JORDAN and Wizards UDA signed basketball NR!	$563.00	KAREEM ABDUL JABBAR (L.A. LAKERS) SIGNED BASKETBALL	$77.15
UDA MICHAEL JORDAN AUTO BALL COA UPPERDECK BULLS	$550.00	Wilt Chamberlain Signed Autographed Basketball Book	$77.00
RARE* LeBron JAMES Original AUTO H.S. Basketball*	$510.00	99 new york knicks auto latrell sprewell larry johnson	$76.01
Michael Jordan UDA official NBA autographed ball!IL@@K	$485.01	Autographed Michael Jordan Basketball With Coa !	$76.00
WILT CHAMBERLAIN BILL RUSSELL AUTOGRAPHED NBA BALL COA	$430.00	'GOLDIN COA' TIM DUNCAN PLUS TWO SIGNED BASKETBALL	$75.00
04 MICHAEL JORDAN SP SIGNIFICANCE AUTO # 54/100 N/R	$404.00	Kobe Bryant and Shaq Autographed Basketball with COA!	$75.00
Dwyane 'Dwayne' Wade signed Miami HEAT white jersey	$399.95	1966 - 67 76ers Press NBA Yearbook and Signed Check PSA	$75.00
Michael Jordan signed UDA Baseball - As real as it gets	$306.00	Larry Bird autographed basketball w/COA	$72.23
Seattle Sonics 1992-93 NBA Team Signed Ball With Case	$300.00	ANDREW BYNUM SIGNED LAKERS NBA BASKETBALL W/ COA	$71.00
New Spalding Michael Jordan Autographed Basketball	$300.00	Shaq/ Dwayne Wade autographed basketball w/COA	$70.99
TRACY MCGRADY T-MAC AUTOGRAPED	$284.99	CHARLES BARKLEY AUTOGRAPHED NBA BASKETBALL COA & PROOF	$69.99
SIGNED JERSEY FRAMED COA		KNICKS SIGNED AUTO BASKETBALL BALL WALT FRAZIER Steiner	$69.99

Autographs, Original ▶ Boxing

The average sales price in this subcategory is $46.96.

	HIGH		AVG
Bear dressed and autographed by Muhammad Ali	$800.00	LOT OF (3) BOXING HALL OF FAME AUTOGRAPHED ITEMS +++	$49.95
Muhammad Ali Signed Auto 29 X 29 Photo PSA/DNA Huge	$599.00	DON KING auto OFFICIAL BOXING GLOVE HOF ** COA	$49.00
Muhammad Ali Signed Hand Painted Glove GAI/ Global	$521.00	Lennox Lewis Evander Holyfield Autographed Photo FRAMED	$49.00
UlTiMaTe aLi + FrAzleR aUto GlOvEs + TrUnKs CoLLeCtIoN	$400.00	Muhammad Ali Autographed Framed Photo Olympic Torch	$48.00
ALI FOREMAN FRAZIER HOLMES NORTON SIGNED BOXING GLOVE	$370.00	ROY JONES JR BOXING CHAMP SIGNED PIC	$48.00
MUHAMMAD ALI Signed, Autographed Gloves MM/OA COA	$338.00	FELIX TRINIDAD auto OFFICIAL BOXING GLOVE ** COA	$46.25
MUHAMMAD ALI Hand-Signed- Everlast Boxing Glove	$299.00	MUHAMMAD ALI AUTOGRAPH ,GENUINE, 1981 FUND RAISER	$46.00
PSA-DNA Muhammad Ali Autographed Sports Illustrated	$250.00	Julio Cesar Chavez Autographed Boxing Photo with COA	$46.00
JERMAIN TAYLOR SIGNED BOXING GLOVE 160 LB CHAMP	$249.99	Roy Jones Jr. signed Everlast glove PROOF	$46.00
MUHAMMAD ALI SIGNED AUTO BOXING GLOVE PSA/DNA LETTER	$214.01	Muhammad Ali signed autographed Isalm Brochure	$46.00
Muhammad Ali YELLING get up vs Liston SIGNED 16X20 LOOK	$212.50	floyd mayweather auto'd boxing glove coa nr	$46.00
JOE LOUIS AUTOGRAPHED ASSOCIATED PRESS BOXING PHOTO COA	$202.50	Autographed Sylvester Stallone Boxing Glove	$46.00
Mike Tyson Auto/Signed Everlast Glove SSG/SPORTS IMAGES	$202.50	ROY JONES JR. SIGNED/AUTO EVERLAST BOXING GLOVE *COA*	$46.00
Muhammad Ali Autographed Poster	$200.00	Roy Jones Jr. Signed Everlast Boxing Glove	$45.86
MUHAMMAD ALI AUTO SIGNED BOXING GLOVES EVERLAST	$200.00	ARCHIE MOORE Signed Auto Autograph Boxing GLOVE PSA/DNA	$45.00

Autographs, Original ▶ College-NCAA

The average sales price in this subcategory is $22.00.

	HIGH		AVG
KANSAS JAYHAWKS AUTOGRAPHED BASKETBALL COLLECTION	$899.99	DEE BROWN SIGNED 8X10 PHOTO ILLINOIS ILLINI	$23.95
UNC NORTH CAROLINA TARHEELS TEAM SIGNED AUTO PRINT	$330.11	DERON WILLIAMS DEE BROWN & LUTHER HEAD SIGNED 8X10	$23.50
John Wooden & Bill Walton UCLA Bruins AUTOGRAPHED PIECE	$249.99	Mike Krzyzewski signed/autographed photo***DUKE****	$23.50
Woody Hayes autograph / OHIO STATE with 8x10 photo WOW!	$202.50	JAMIE MORRIS University of Michigan AUTcolor 8x10	$22.50
PEYTON MANNING TENNESSEE JERSEY- SIGNED- NR	$201.50	Bobby Hurley Signed Duke Champions t shirt	$22.50
2005 UNC NORTH CAROLINA TARHEELS TEAM SIGNED BASKETBALL	$191.75	JJ REDICK SIGNED 8X10 PHOTO DUKE BLUE DEVILS	$21.99
Reggie White USFL Autograph Jersey GAI	$177.50	JOHN WOODEN Autographed Index Card PSA/DNA	$21.51
Vintage OKLAHOMA SOONER Ruf-Nek spirit paddle!	$164.38	MARVIN WILLIAMS UNC TARHEELS AUTO/SIGNED SI RIVALS-DUKE	$20.50
Brian Bosworth Signed Auto Oklahoma Sooners Jersey GAI	$157.50	Kentucky Wildcats Basketball 2004 Signed Senior Poster	$20.50
BO JACKSON AUTOGRAPHED TRISTAR AUBURN JERSEY	$122.50	N.C. State Wolfpack JULIUS HODGE SIGNED PICTURE	$20.50
Earl Campbell signed Texas Longhorns jersey #20	$122.49	XAVIER'S LIONEL CHALMERS&ROMAIN SATO AUTOGRAPHED 8X10	$20.50
David Thompson Signed NC State Wolfpack Jersey 56 COA	$109.08	DUKE BLUE DEVILS MIKE KRZYZEWSKI SIGNED 8X10 PHOTO	$20.50
Alabama Football Jay Barker Autographed Jersey	$102.50	PAUL HORNUNG SIGNED HEISMAN NOTRE DAME HELMET	$20.50
Billy Vessels autographed Oklahoma Heisman package	$100.00	UGA GEORGIA BULLDOGS DAVID GREENE SIGNED FOOTBALL!!	$20.50
CHRIS PAUL Signed Wake Forest Logo Full Size Basketball	$100.00	Lynn Swann - Pittsburgh Steelers - signed auto display	$20.50

Autographs, Original ▶ Football-NFL

The average sales price in this subcategory is $25.46.

	HIGH		AVG
DAN MARINO Auto 3 Foot Tall HOF Bobble Head LE 113 MM	$613.00	Joe Montana Signed Plate-Gartlan	$26.45
Paul Brown Autographed Goal Line Art Card HOF	$374.00	*****Walter Payton Signed Card*****	$26.12
ART OF SPORT DAN MARINO AUTOGRAPHED	$369.95	HOF Signature Series autograph of Roger Staubach	$26.05
FIGURINE HALL FAME		Bill Bergey Autopgraphed Pennant Super Bowl XV Eagles	$26.00
1935 George Halas Chicago Bears signed letter to player	$361.00	Mike Munchak Oilers Signed Gold Goal Line Art 99/100	$26.00
VINCE LOMBARDI GREEN BAY PACKERS FRAMED CHECK & PICTURE	$311.99	Don Maynard Jets signed Goal Line Art Gold #26/100	$26.00
Michael Ricker Pewter Figurine Walter Payton	$304.99	Jim Ringo Autographed Goal Line Art Card HOF	$25.50
STEVE YOUNG AUTO FULL SUPER BOWL 29 GAME TICKET! * GA	$282.00	George Musso Autographed Goal Line Art Card HOF	$25.25
	$245.00	PATRIOTS STANLEY MORGAN 85 AFC CHAMPS SIGNED	$24.99
Steel Curtain Signed Riddell Steelers Mini Helmet		FOOTBALL	
Bert Bell Double Signed 1940 Check Philadelphia Eagles	$218.39	Aramis Ramirez Chicago Cubs Signed 8x10	$24.99
Bert Bell Double Signed 1941 Philadelphia Eagles Check	$212.33	John Mackey Colts signed Goal Line Art Gold #37/100	$24.50
Don Hutson Autographed Goal Line Art Card HOF	$181.28	Gino Marchetti Colts signed Goal Line Art Gold #47/100	$24.50
McNabb Fast Pass Autograph Ticket - Eagles Carnival	$152.50	Chiefs BUCK BUCHANAN signed Super Bowl card	$24.35
Donovan McNabb Eagles Fast Pass Autograph Ticket	$150.00	Oakland Raiders Lester Hayes Auto 8x10 w/COA	$24.00
DALLAS COWBOYS EMMITT SMITH AUTOGRAPH COLLECTIBLES	$140.00	[2 of these sold for $24.00 each]	
Marion Motley Autographed Goal Line Art Card HOF	$128.25	DON SHULA SIGNED AUTO GOAL LINE ART DOLPHINS	$22.50

Autographs, Original ▶ Golf ▶ PGA

The average sales price in this subcategory is $66.67.

	HIGH		AVG
Tiger Woods and 18 other Masters Winners Autographs	$1,475.00	JACK NICKLAUS SIGNED GOLF BALL PGA	$77.55
Tiger Woods UDA signed autographed CLUB LTD 50!	$995.00	JACK NICKLAUS Autographed Golf Ball	$68.20
UDA TIGER WOODS AUTOGRAPHED AUTO	$812.52	Ben Hogan- Signed bank check from 1991	$67.00
GOLF CLUB HEAD DISPLAY		Arnold Palmer signed autographed Golf Hat	$66.00
2001 MASTERS SIGNED FLAG TIGER WOODS ARNOLD PALMER	$750.00	DENSMORE SHUTE signed presidential golf card - *RARE*	$66.00
TIGER WOODS NIKE GOLF BALL "BREAK THROUGH" PIECE	$750.00	JACK NICKLAUS HAND SIGNED AUTOGRAPHED PHOTO ~PSA DNA~	$66.00
JACK NICKLAUS+ARNOLD PALMER SIGNED MASTERS FLAG	$511.00	JACK NICKLAUS & GREG NORMAN signed 8x10C mint LEGENDS!	$65.89
Jack NICKLAUS signed 2005 British Open Flag St. Andrews	$474.00	Jack Nicklaus autographed "Good Luck" 8 X 10 Photo	$64.99
Jack NICKLAUS signed 2005 British Open Flag St. Andrews	$470.00	Autographed 2005 Masters Flag Signed By Phil Mickelson	$62.99
Jack NICKLAUS signed 2005 British Open Flag St. Andrews	$450.00	JACK NICKLAUS AUTOGRAPHED PEBBLE BEACH SCORECARD	$62.00
TIGER WOODS FRMD UDA AUTO wth PSA 9 UPPER DECK ROOKIE	$445.00	Sam Snead Auto Augusta National Scorecard	$59.99
JACK NICKLAUS signed BRITISH OPEN Flag - St Andrews	$430.00	Arnold Palmer & Gary Player Signed Color 8x10 Photo	$59.99
JACK NICKLAUS SIGNED 2005 ST.ANDREWS BRITISH OPEN FLAG	$406.00	PGA BLUE JEWELED MONEY CLIP	$59.88
GOLF MASTERS FLAG MULTIPLE SIGNITURES AUTOGRAPHS 23!! +	$399.99	Signed Phil Mickelson Masters Golf Visor W/COA	$59.01
₤5 RBS BANK NOTE JACK NICKLAUS SIGNED 2005 ST. ANDREWS	$399.00	Jack Nicklaus autographed "Jack Nicklaus" 8 X 10 Photo	$57.99
PHIL MICKELSON ARNOLD PALMER signed 2004 MASTERS FLAG	$399.00	Signed Michelle Wie Masters Golf Score Card W/COA	$57.99

Autographs, Original ▶ Hockey-NHL

The average sales price in this subcategory is $63.98.

	HIGH		AVG
WAYNE GRETZKY AUTO/SIGNED OILERS BLUE M&N JERSEY WGA	$599.00	Bob Clarke,Sami Kapanen,Sean Burke Auto. Mini Helmets	$75.00
Wayne Gretzky signed jersey with COA	$585.00	94 NY RANGERS CHAMPS AUTOGRAPH MESSIER,RICHTER,LEETCH	$72.00
AUTO WGA WAYNE GRETZKY EDMONTON OILERS JERSEY	$529.00	RAY BOURQUE SIGNED BOSTON BRUINS 8x10 TRIBUTE #Ed PHOTO	$71.00
Wayne Gretzky Autographed NY Rangers Jersey	$500.00	AVALANCHE Milan Hejduk signed PRO jersey	$67.00
Lemieux auto Limited ED Rookie Pro Jersey RPM Crosby	$480.00	Wayne Gretzky Limited Edition "Record Breaker" Plaque	$66.00
Derek Jeter STEINER Autographed Signed Collage 45/500	$440.00	ottawa senators team signed jersey	$61.01
UDA SIGNED WAYNE GRETZKY KINGS HOCKEY JERSEY 168/1000 !	$401.00	RAY BOURQUE Signed 2001 STANLEY CUP 8x10 PHOTO Auto COA	$61.00
1994 NY Rangers Team Signed 16x20 Framed Photo Steiner	$399.95	KEN DRYDEN SIGNED/AUTO 8 X10 MONTREAL	$60.66
RARE MARIO LEMIEUX AUTOGRAPH JERSEY- BLACK	$371.66	TED LINDSAY signed DETROIT RED WINGS jersey w/HHOF 66	$57.00
MARIO LEMIEUX Rookie Penguins SIGNED Hockey JERSEY RPM	$359.99	UDA Artistic Impressions Steve Yzerman Autographed Auto	$56.01
VHTF AUTHENTIC NY RANGERS 11 MESSIER 54 SIGNED! NHL CCM	$350.00	BUFFALO SABRES team signed jersey PROOF	$56.00
AHL Player Peter Horachek's Game Jersey (WORN & SIGNED)	$331.99	2005 ST LOUIS BLUES TEAM SIGNED JERSEY COA TKACHUK BY19	$56.00
Joe Sakic Signed HOME Olympic Jersey WGA COA	$310.19	TED LINDSAY signed DETROIT RED WINGS jersey w/HHOF 66	$55.32
LEMIEUX SIGNED FRAMED PENGUINS AUTHENTIC JERSEY COA	$305.00	02-03 UD Mask Collection Mini Mask Auto Nabokov	$53.05
Bobby Clarke signed Mitchell Ness home jersey FLYERS	$299.95	ISLANDERS Michael Peca signed jersey PROOF	$52.56

Autographs, Original ▶ Olympics

The average sales price in this subcategory is $27.28.

	HIGH		AVG
RARE 1980 USA OLYMPIC JERSEY SIGNED BY H. BROOKS &TEAM	$1,060.01	Olympics Track & Field, Herm Brix autographed letter	$32.00
1980 Team USA Olympic Hockey Signed Framed 16x20 Photo	$489.99	Huge Liquidation! Rare JENNIE FINCH Olympics STEINER	$31.00
1980 Miracle On Ice Signed 20x24 Photo Hori Cele Framed	$409.99	WALSH MAY AUTOGRAPHED SIGNED USA VOLLEYBALL 8X10 PHOTO	$29.99
1980 Miracle on Ice Signed 20x24 Photo Framed US Hockey	$392.00	AARON PEIRSOL AUTOGRAPHED USA SWIMMING 8X10 PHOTO	$28.00
MIRACLE ON ICE AUTO SIGNED FRAMED 16X20 PHOTO WITH COA	$355.00	Greg Louganis GOLD MEDAL WINNER SIGNED Pic WWG	$27.99
1980 Miracle on Ice Signed 20x24 Photo Framed US Hockey	$350.00	Herb Brooks auto'd 3x5(d'03)	$27.98
1980 MIRACLE ON ICE TEAM SIGNED MEDAL OLYMPIC PHOTO GS	$331.50	Huge Liquidation! Jennie Finch Softball w/Steiner COA	$27.98
RARE 16X20 1980 MIRACLE ON ICE OLYMPIC TEAM SIGNED	$299.99	2 AMANDA BORDEN AUTOGRAPHED GYMNASTIC PHOTOS 8 x 10	$26.99
DEREK JETER AUTOGRAPHED OPENING DAY BASEBALL LE/500	$219.95	Olga Korbut, Russian Gymnast, Signed Photo	$26.25
Vanessa Atler Autographed workout outfit	$155.10	Eric Heiden Signed 8x10 (1980 5X Gold Medal Skater)	$26.00
Jesse Owens- signed envelope from 1936 while at olympic	$141.60	Liquidation! 8x10 Jennie Finch COA RARE SHOT	$26.00
USA GOLD MEDAL SOFTBALL TEAM SIGNED HELMET JENNY FINCH	$112.50	FLORENCE GRIFFITH JOYNER HAND SIGNED SI MAGAZINE COA	$25.49
RYNE SANDBERG AUTOGRAPHED BASEBALL - HOF 2005	$103.50	JENNIE FINCH USA SOFTBALL SIGNED SPORTS ILLUSTRATED PIC	$25.49
1980 OLYMPIC TEAM SIGNED MIRACLE ON ICE 16X20 STEINER	$96.00	Mike Eruzione - 1980 gold Olympic Hockey auto display	$25.00
1980 OLYMPIC TEAM SIGNED MIRACLE ON ICE 16X20 STEINER	$91.00	Herb Brooks (dec) 1980 gold Olympic Hockey auto display	$25.00

Autographs, Original ▶ Soccer

The average sales price in this subcategory is $81.64.

	HIGH		AVG
FUTERA 2005 1/1 AUTOGRAPH VERON AUTO SHEVCHENKO GOLD	$1,025.00	WorldCup 2002 Champ Team Signed Soccer Ball Brazil+Pele	$99.99
D.C. United - Freddy Adu Autographed Jersey	$612.00	2005 GLASGOW RANGERS FC TEAM SIGNED JERSEY w/PROOF	$99.99
2002 UD Man United Legends David Beckham Autograph #/50	$510.00	MIA HAMM SIGNED USA SOCCER JERSEY	$91.00
Pele & Freddy Adu Dual Signed MLS Soccer Ball LE/10 WOW	$430.15	REAL MADRID DAVID BECKHAM SIGNED FOOTBALL,SOCCER,PROOF	$87.00
Pele Signed RARE Bicycle Kick 16x20 Framed Photo GS	$274.99	BRAZILIAN SHIRT SIGNED BY BEST STARS SQUAD & PELE COA	$82.00
D.C. United - Josh Gros Autographed Jersey	$250.00	ARGENTINE FOOTBALL SHIRT SIGNED BY MARADONA & STARS COA	$79.80
Signed Mia Hamm Nike Soccer Jersey Steiner Authentic	$227.50	REAL MADRID TEAM SIGNED JERSEY W/PROOF 20+ AUTOGRAPHS	$77.00
2003 Womens World Cup Autographed Soccer Ball, With COA	$202.50	DAVID BECKHAM (Real Madrid) orig. signed jersey SIZE XL	$76.50
NWT Authentic Mia HAMM Autographed Home Jersey w/ COA	$175.00	MIA HAMM SIGNED SOCCER BALL WOW!!!!!!!	$75.03
'02 BRAZIL BRASIL TEAM SIGNED AUTOGRAPHED JERSEY PELE +	$142.50	ALESSANDRO NESTA AC MILAN signed ADIDAS JERSEY SHIRT	$74.99

Autographs, Original ▶ Tennis

The average sales price in this subcategory is $28.11.

	HIGH		AVG
ANDRE AGASSI AUTOGRAPHED DONNAY TENNIS RACQUET	$374.00	CHRIS EVERET TENNIS Signed autographed 8X10 photo	$31.00
Andre Agassi Signed Photo and Tennis Outfit , Framed	$326.00	MARTINA NAVRATILOVA Signed LIMITED ED. Lithograph wCOA	$31.00
AUSTRALIAN OPEN FULLY AUTOGRAPHED 2005 OFFICIAL POSTER	$150.00	RAFAEL NADAL SIGNED WILSON TENNIS BALL	$31.00
Arnold Palmer Jack Nicklaus Signed Golf Ball Display	$100.00	Martina, Borg, Conners, Gomez, Jackson Signed Magazine	$29.99
MARIA SHARAPOVA Signed 8x10 SEXY BLACK TENNIS OUTFIT	$76.00	MARIA SHARAPOVA HOT Signed 8x10 Photo	$29.99
MARIA SHARAPOVA Signed 8x10 TRAINING PHOTO - BEAUTIFUL	$67.00	ANNA KOURNIKOVA HOT KNEES AUTOGRAPH Signed Photo	$28.95
JOHN MCENROE AUTOGRAPHED NIKE SHOES MATCH PLAYED COA NR	$62.77	ALICE MARBLE & ALTHEA GIBSON signed CARDS MATTED W/PICS	$28.90
ANDRE AGASSI SIGNED AUTOGRAPHED US OPEN TENNIS BALL	$62.00	MARIA SHARAPOVA Hot AUTOGRAPHED PHOTO SIGNED	$27.99
Tennis, Louise Brough Autographed letter	$61.00	MARTINA HINGIS SIGNED WILSON TENNIS BALL COA W/CASE	$27.00
2003 Anna Kournikova Auto Card Graded PSA 10!!	$60.00	Tennis Star ROD LAVER Hand Signed Photo~AUTOGRAPH	$26.00
MARIA SHARAPOVA SEXY Signed autographed 8X10 photo	$51.00	JOHN MCENROE HAND SIGNED AUTOGRAPH SI COA PROOF	$25.50
Maria Sharapova Signed Tennis 8x10 Photo	$45.00	Maria Sharapova Signed Photo Auto SEXY! 8x10 NR!	$25.01
BORIS BECKER HAND SIGNED AUTOGRAPH 8X10 PHOTO COA PROOF	$44.99	BJORN BORG HAND SIGNED AUTOGRAPH SI COA PROOF	$24.99
2003 Netpro Anna Kournikova AUTOGRAPH RC 1ST #/500 !	$43.76	JENNIFER CAPRIATI HAND SIGNED WILSON BALL COA W/CASE	$24.99
Bjorn Borg Signed French Open Tennis Cachet	$42.98	Signed Tennis Ball Andy Roddick Federer Andre Agassi ++	$24.99

Autographs, Original ▶ Wrestling-WWE

The average sales price in this subcategory is $12.24.

	HIGH		AVG
WWE WWF Stone Cold/Rock Wrestling Belt RARE!	$226.99	LIMITED EDITION AUTO. RVD FIGURE IN BOX wwe, ecw	$12.99
WRESTLING WWF SIGNED LP BY23 ANDRE THE GIANT HULK HOGAN	$99.99	MATT and JEFF HARDY AUTOGRAPHED Exist 2 Inspire!!!!	$12.50
Shawn Michaels signed WWE Classic Superstars figure	$75.00	ROAD WARRIOR ANIMAL autographed 8x10 color photo	$12.50
WWE HULK HOGAN SIGNED PROMO PHOTO WWF RARE HULKSTER	$59.99	AWESOME SIGNED WWE PROMO P756 OF THE GODFATHER	$12.50
JOHN CENA CHAMP SIGNED STEEL CHAIR RAW SUPERSTAR WWE	$53.00	6 WWE AUTOGRAPHS *AUSTIN*MICHAELS*	$12.50
VERY RARE SIGNED WWE PROMO P897 OF THE UNDERTAKER	$51.00	ROCK*MANKIND*KANE*+++	
EXTREMELY RARE SIGNED WWF PROMO P022 OF DAVEY BOY SMITH	$40.00	WWE WWF STONE COLD STEVE AUTIN AUTO AUTOGRAPH PICTURE	$12.50
Bill Melby- Vintage signed wrestling photo	$39.00	Miss Jackie Sexy! IP signed WWE 8x10 w/pic signing!!!	$12.00
Bill Melby and Billy Darnell vintage wrestling signed	$37.50	Victoria Sexy! IP signed WWE 8x10 w/pic signing!!!	$12.00
Old 50s 60s Male Female Wrestling Autograph book	$36.02	Kevin Nash Rare IP signed WWE WCW 8x10 w/pic signing!!!	$12.00
AWESOME SIGNED WWE PROMO P1032 OF MNM	$35.00	Edge Hot! IP signed WWE 8x10 w/pic signing!!!	$12.00
WWE RAW BELT signed by 15 HASSAN,KANE,BENJAMIN MORE!!!!	$31.00	AWESOME SIGNED 8X10 OF WWE STAR BRET THE HITMAN HART	$12.00
WWE SUPERSTAR JOHN CENA AUTOGRAPH 8 BY 10	$14.99	KIMBERLY PAGE - Signed 8x10 Photo WCW NITRO GIRL wwe	$12.00
[2 of these sold for $14.99 each]		Rowdy Roddy Piper AUTOGRAPHED Photo	$11.83
WWF/WWE Tag Team Championship 40'' Wrestling Belt COOL	$26.00	2 OLD Wrestling Medals 1924 & 1926 Copper Brass No Res	$11.61
Macho Man Randy Savage Autographed Framed Photo	$26.00	P-927 BATISTA Signed/Autograph 8x10 Promo Photo	$11.54

Cards ▶ Baseball-MLB

The average sales price in this subcategory is $12.96.

	HIGH		AVG
UNCUT SHEET ETOPPS BABE RUTH HONUS WAGNER WILLIE MAYS	$177.50	Paul Molitor 05 UD Hall Of Fame AUTOGRAPH GU #/10	$16.05
1962 Topps BB Original Card Art. Bill Short ORIOLES	$172.50	200 New York Yankees-Jeter, Rodriguez, Chien-Ming Wang	$15.99
1979 Topps Baseball Acetate Proof Set. Ty Cobb TIGERS	$132.50	Dennis Eckersly 05 UD HOF AUTOGRAPH 7 Color PATCH 7/10	$15.83
Daric Barton 2003 Prospect Premieres Auto RC BGS 9.5	$110.00	MLB 4 Uncut Baseball Card Sheets 1985 Topps	$15.10
Steve Garvey 2005 Leaf Certified AUTOGRAPH JERSEY 1/1	$87.99	Jim Palmer 2005 Leaf Certified CUTS AUTOGRAPH 7/50	$15.03
Highland Mint 24 Kt Gold Nolan Ryan 1993 Pinnacle	$87.87	Justin Verlander 2005 Fleer AUTOGRAPH 89/100	$14.48
CAL RIPKEN 04 LEAF LIMITED TRADEMARKS AUTOGRAPH 24/25!!	$82.99	Dale Murphy 2005 Absolute Triple Bat & JERSEY 21/25	$12.66
1967 Topps Baseball Orig. Card Art Larry Dierker ASTROS	$78.00	Dennis Eckersley 2005 UD Hall Of Fame AUTOGRAPH 3/5	$12.62
Philadelphia Phillies Chris Short Cut Signature	$77.06	Cal Ripken Jr 05 Timeless Dual Game Used JERSEY 83/100	$12.51
Highland Mint 24 Kt Gold Ken Griffey, Jr 1992 Topps	$71.00	David Ortiz RED SOX 2005 Leaf Certified BAT 4/5 ONLY 5	$12.50
1981 Topps Baseball Card Orig. Art. Dennis Lamp CUBS	$70.00	1979 Topps BB Acetate Proof Card Set. Tanana ANGELS	$12.50
Topps 1960 Empty 5 Cent Wax Box	$68.67	113 card Vladimir Guerrero Lot 20 inserts	$12.05
Topps 1965 Empty 5 Cent Wax Box	$68.00	9 BASEBALL ROOKIE CARDS 1969-1982! WINFIELD,NETTLES,ETC	$12.04
Highland Mint 24 Kt Gold Mike Piazza 1993 Topps	$62.13	Steve Carlton 2005 UD Hall Of Fame AUTOGRAPH 20/25	$12.03
MLB Showdown 2005 Trading Deadline Booster Box in hand!	$58.00	Andre Dawson 2004 Leaf Certified AUTOGRAPH JERSEY 35/50	$12.00

Cards ▶ Basketball-NBA

The average sales price in this subcategory is $15.76.

	HIGH		AVG
1980 Topps Basketbal Uncut Card RC Sheet. BIRD MAGIC	$510.00	Yuta Tabuse 04-05 Fleer AUTOGRAPH JERSEY 180/449	$17.50
DENNIS RODMAN 05 EXQUISITE 3 COLOR TRIPLE PATCH 3/10	$153.53	Jordan richm stack sprewell 96-97 SP SPx Force F1 1:360	$17.50
MICHAEL JORDAN 05 ULTIMATE COLLECTION 2 COLOR PATCH	$127.50	Nice 12 card rookie and star auto autograph lot	$17.05
Michael Jordan 01-02 UD Flight Team fl jersey $400 /100	$92.00	Authenticated Upper Deck 22Kt Gold Michael Jordan Set	$16.51
04-05 Finest #10 Gold X fractor 4/7—RARE—Lakers	$78.00	Baron Davis 04-05 Fleer TRIPLE PATCHES 9/13	$15.95
Tracy Mcgrady Autographics	$70.00	Nike Air Jordan 1 One XI 2 TWO Vintage Rare Retro Card	$15.50
Dennis Rodman 04 sweet shot 3 point shot jsy auto 91 EX	$67.66	KAREEM ABDUL JABBAR LAKERS GAME JERSEY #31/99	$15.50
1987-88 87 88 fleer jordan not rookie rc psa bgs 8 w/ 9	$59.50	2004-05 Finest Jalen Rose Yellow Printing Plate 1/1	$15.01
2000-01 NBA UD SP SIGN OF THE TIMES ANFERNEE HARDAWAY	$56.66	97/98 topps chrome tracy mcgrady rookie card # 125	$13.19
Dwyane Wade 04 Topps Chrome Beckett GRADED 9.5 GEM MINT	$50.90	Marvin Williams 2005 Finest DRAFT 2 X-Fractor RC 97/259	$13.00
RARE Michael Jordan / Lebron James auto # 08/23	$50.00	Childress Josh Smith 04SP double authentic auto /100 EX	$12.50
1995 LARRY BIRD HIGHLAND MINT #870/100 SILVER MT-CARD	$49.99	03/04 Exquisite Base VINCE CARTER no auto patch	$12.50
1973 Topps ABA Orig. Color Negative. George Price SPURS	$49.88	LOT OF 30 MICHAEL JORDAN CARDS	$12.27
Vince Carter 98-99 SPx Finite RC $120 1331/2500 Mt+	$46.00	1969-70 TOPPS RULER INSERT HAL GREER 76ERS NATS # 12	$11.50
Michael Jordan Topps Rookie Card	$46.00	Lakers Legends Wilt West Jabbar Magic Shaq Plaque	$11.50

Cards ▶ Boxing

The average sales price in this subcategory is $37.10.

	HIGH		AVG
1888 N332 S F HESS - JACKSON - BOXING - PSA 3 - RARE	$810.00	Vintage 1924 Franklyn Davey Boxing Complete Set NM - NR	$43.00
1948 Leaf Boxing JACK SHARKEY #38 PSA 8 (NM-MT)	$585.00	1947-66 Exhibits Rocky Marciano SGC 70 EX+ SHARPER	$42.91
1948 Leaf Gum ++ Complete Set ++ 49/49 ++ (R401) ++	$565.65	SEALED BOX RINGSIDE BOXING TRADING CARDS - AUTOS!	$41.00
PSA 9 1971 CASSIUS CLAY ALI BARRATT BK 1250.	$469.00	1938 CHURCHMAN BOXING SET 45/50	$41.00
1948 Leaf Boxing # 47 BILLY CONN PSA 7 NearMint	$380.00	Jack Johnson boxing watch fob	$40.00
1940's 1950's KID GAVILAN BREAD LABEL CUBAN BOXER	$356.00	1948 Leaf Boxing # 60 GUS LESNEVICH PSA 5 EX(mk)	$36.23
1887 N28 ALLEN GINTER - WEIR- BOXING - PSA 7 NM	$336.00	1948 Topps Magic BOXING lot JACK DEMPSEY ROBINSON PEP +	$36.05
RARE 16 CARD 1948 LEAF PROMO	$331.25	VINTAGE 1900'S BOXING STRIP CARD LOT OF (14) W/2 DUPES	$34.77
BOXING CARDS SULLIVAN TUNN		1948 Leaf Boxing # 27 TOMMY LOUGHRAN PSA 4 Vg-Ex	$33.91
36 Rare 1948 Leaf Gum Boxer Cards - Robinson, LaMotta	$330.89	1948 Leaf Boxing # 88 LOU AMBERS PSA 5 Excellent	$33.66
1887 N28 ALLEN GINTER - JEM SMITH - BOXING GAI 7.5 NM+	$325.00	SUGAR RAY ROBINSON VINTAGE RINGSIDE BOXING CARD 1950'S	$33.00
STANLEY KETCHEL TURKEY RED VINTAGE BOXING POSTCARD CARD	$274.00	James J. Jeffries Traing camp Postcard in Reno	$30.75
1956 Adventure #44 Rocky Marciano PSA MINT 9 - NR	$214.49	VINTAGE BOXING CARD LOT OF 6 OLD MECCA CIGARETTE CARDS	$30.01
1948 Leaf Boxing # 64 RAY ROBINSON PSA 7 NearMint	$213.50	1948 Leaf Boxing Cards 17 Different	$29.00
1887 N28 ALLEN GINTER - LANNON - BOXING - PSA 6	$203.38	Boxing Cards 1948 Leaf Knock-Out #15 Tony Zale	$28.99

Cards ▶ etopps

The average sales price in this subcategory is $6.67.

	HIGH		AVG
100 - Johan Santana 2005 - etopps	$457.04	3 - Vladimir Guerrero 2005 - etopps	$6.80
1 - Barry Bonds 2001 - etopps	$89.00	1 - Albert Pujols 2005 - etopps	$6.75
1 - Barry Bonds 2001 - etopps	$87.00	2 - Derek Jeter 2005 - etopps	$6.75
1 - Barry Bonds 2001 - etopps	$86.00	3 - Xavier Nady 2002 - etopps	$6.75
1 - Edgardo Alfonzo 2001 - etopps	$75.05	1 - Miguel Cabrera 2005 - etopps	$6.71
1 - Carlos Beltran 2001 - etopps	$64.02	2 - Be - Lee - Ive In Derrek - etopps	$6.62
5 - Ivan Rodriguez 2001 - etopps	$61.90	1 - Ben Sheets 2001 - etopps	$6.60
1 - Albert Pujols 2001 - etopps	$61.00	2 - Kansas City Royals 2005 - etopps	$6.60
1 - Albert Pujols 2001 - etopps	$56.00	2 - Texas Rangers 2005 - etopps	$6.59
1 - Albert Pujols 2001 - etopps	$52.13	1 - Huston Street 2005 - etopps	$6.57
1 - Albert Pujols 2001 - etopps	$52.00	1 - 10-Rod - etopps	$6.57
1 - Albert Pujols 2001 - etopps	$51.50	1 - A Young 400th - etopps	$6.55
1 - Carlos Delgado 2001 - etopps	$51.15	1 - Huston Street 2005 - etopps	$6.53
10 - Sammy Sosa 2001 - etopps	$50.50	6 - Sammy Sosa 2002 - etopps	$6.51
4 - Robinson Cano 2005 - etopps	$43.33	2 - B.J. Upton 2005 - etopps	$6.50

Cards ▶ Football-NFL

The average sales price in this subcategory is $17.23.

	HIGH		AVG
ATLANTA FALCON SEASON TICKETS (4))	$2,026.50	04 SPX DEANGELO HALL AUTO JERSEY 214/1499	$19.73
CLEVELAND BROWNS STADIUM DOUBLE SEAT / SEATS *NICE*	$355.00	1963 Topps FB Card Original Line Art. CHICAGO BEARS	$19.25
1978 Topps FB Slick Proof Card. Walter Payton BEARS	$255.00	Penn State 10 Card Autograph Lot John Cappelletti	$19.01
Dan Marino "Dropback" UDA Auto Autograph 16 x 20 Photo	$255.00	1978 Topps Football Slick Proof Card. C Waters COWBOYS	$17.50
1975 Topps Football Uncut Sheet. Many HALL OF FAME	$255.00	Robert Smith 1999 Fleer Ultra Platinum 7/99	$17.00
2005 UD CRAPHONSO THORPE 1/1 ROOKIE RC AUTO -A REAL 1/1	$222.00	Nebraska Huskers Football All Time Greats Cornhuskers	$17.00
1987 Topps Football Uncut Card Sheet. 1000 YARD CLUB	$124.60	1977 Topps Football Slick Proof Cards Bartkowski FALCON	$15.50
MARVIN HARRISON 05 CLASSICS AUTO* #03/05 COLTS SP	$114.25	1978 Topps Football Slick Proof Card. Van Horn GIANTS	$15.50
2000 Leaf Cert Cent Gear 3c jersey #d 2/21 Dan Marino	$110.00	Jamal Lewis Autographed Helmet Baltimore Ravens	$15.50
Eli Manning Autographed Helmet	$110.00	1988 1989 1990 TOPPS NFL SETS + WAX PACKS TRADED L@@K	$15.50
PEYTON MANNING CHROME ULTRA EX FINEST ROOKIE AUTO LOT I	$100.66	Terence Newman Cowboys SP Authentic RC Jersey 3 Color	$15.00
2003 Finest gold refractor Byron Leftwich BGS sgc 98	$93.77	NICE LOT OF JERSEYS AUTO'S SP AUTHENTIC SHAQ DUAL	$15.00
PEYTON MANNING 99 MVP SUPER SCRIPT #1/25	$90.00	1982 Topps FB Acetate Overlay Proof. Fred Dean 49ERS	$14.50
Lot of 32 Walter Payton Topps Cards 1977 1978 1979	$78.00	1969 Topps Original Color Negative. Don Horn PACKERS	$14.49
1963 Topps FB Card Original Art. Matt Hazeltine 49ERS	$70.00	FRED BILETNIKOFF 92 PROLINE CERTIFIED AUTOGRAPHED CARD	$14.38

Cards ▶ Golf ▶ PGA

The average sales price in this subcategory is $21.53.

	HIGH		AVG
2005 SP AUTHENTIC GOLF TIGER WOODS GLOVE REDEMPTION	$1,035.00	1981 DONRUSS GOLF SET COMPLETE 66 CARDS NRMT-MT	$22.07
2001 Sp Authentic TIGER WOODS AUTO/RC #/900	$965.00	1981 Donruss Golf Tom Watson&Lee Trevino PSA Mint 9's	$22.03
(2) 01 UD SP AUTH GOLF SEALED CASES Tiger Woods AUTO ?	$710.00	UD SP 03 MARK O'MEARA #19/25 LARGEST SWATCH CARD MADE	$22.00
SP 01 -@ TIGER WOODS @~ BAY HILL 184/273 RED AUTO L@@K	$260.01	UD SP 03 NICK PRICE #16/25 LARGEST SWATCH RARE LISTING!	$22.00
ARNOLD PALMER 04 UD SP SIGNATURE SHOTS AUTOGRAPH PHOTO	$242.50	DOTTIE PEPPER 2004 SP SIGNATURE AUTO SHIRT 1/25 LPGA	$21.75
1981 Donruss Factory Box of 36 Wax Packs Nicklaus MINT	$233.49	SI 4 Kids Michelle Wie Rookie RC ONLY INVEST NOW	$21.49
2003 SP GAME USED ARNOLD PALMER SP AUTOGRAPH #38/100	$204.83	BYRON NELSON TOURNAMENT WORN SHIRT 01 SP AUTHENTIC #500	$21.10
2005 SP Tiger Woods "Sign of the times" Autograph MINT	$202.50	2004 UPPER DECK UD GOLF BOX TIGER WOODS GEAR EAGLE AUTO	$20.55
2001 Sp Authentic MIKE WEIR GOLD Tour Swatch #5/25	$184.48	2001 SP AUTHENTIC KEN VENTURI TOUR SWATCH #238/500	$20.50
SP 03 *~ TIGER WOODS ~* BRITISH PHENOM 27/32 BGS 8.5/10	$182.50	1928 CHURCHMAN LARGE M.O.M. ABE MITCHELL # 8 RARE	$20.00
02 SP Game Used Tiger Woods AUTO BGS 9 graded	$182.50	01 SP Authentic SOTT FRED COUPLES AUTO	$19.99
Tiger Woods 1996 96 Sports Illustrated for Kids Rookie	$157.55	MIKE TIRICO 04 SP SIGNATURE GOLF AUTOGRAPH 8x10 PHOTO	$19.98
1981 DONRUSS GOLF #50 HUBERT GREEN PSA 10	$157.50	2003 03 UPPER DECK GOLF 48PK 2 BOX LOT TIGER WOODS AUTO	$19.65
1986 Masters Badge Low Number Jack Nicklaus 6th Win...	$157.49	1981 DONRUSS GOLF SET COMPLETE 66 CARDS NRMT-MT	$19.50
2003 UD SP GOLF TIGER WOODS AUTO SCOREBOARD SIGNATURE	$151.50	NATALIE GULBIS SP SIGNATURE GOLF AUTOGRAPH 8x10 PHOTO	$19.35

Cards ▶ Hockey-NHL

The average sales price in this subcategory is $17.86.

	HIGH		AVG
04/05 ITG HEROES & PROSPECTS AUTO S. Crosby	$355.00	03/04 ITG MEMORABILIA STANLEY CUP CHAMPS Friesen	$18.50
04/05 Wayne Gretzky Ultimate Auto 2 color Patch #40/50	$320.00	04/05 ITG HEROES & PROSPECTS S. Crosby	$18.50
04/05 ITG FRANCHISE COMLETE JERSEY 1/1 R. Bourque	$255.00	04/05 ITG FRANCHISE FLYERS GU MEM GOLD Parent	$18.50
1979 Topps Hockey Card Original Wax Pack Proof WRAPPER	$228.98	03/04 ITG MEMORABILIA GU GLOVE E. Shore	$18.27
05 ITG ULTIMATE MEM ARCHIVES STANLEY PLAYOFF RECORD 1/1	$176.00	98/99 ITG MEMORABILIA GU JERSEY P. Bure	$18.25
Wayne Gretzky 1998-99 Aurora Front Line Copper	$140.00	03/04 ITG PARKIE ROOKIE ROOKIE NUMBER D. Fritsche	$17.50
05 ITG ULTIMATE MEM ARCHIVES 3RD EDIT 1/1 MANIFICENT	$127.50	04/05 ITG FRANCHISE PENGUINS ORIGINAL STICK M. Lemieux	$17.50
03/04 ITG MEMORABILIA STANLEY CUP FINAL Brodeur	$102.80	01/02 ITG SIGNATURE GU JERSEY P. Turgeon	$17.50
04/05 ITG FRANCHISE AUTO LIGHTNING D. Ciccarelli	$102.50	DOMINIK HASEK GAME USED JERSEY CARDS (3) CARD LOT	$17.50
~THE HIGHLAND MINT~MARIO LEMIEUX BRONZE ROOKIE CARD	$90.00	Private Stock PATCH 3 Clr Rick DiPietro Nice!	$17.50
Wayne Gretzky 1996-97 Select Certified Mirror Gold	$86.88	2003/04 Topps Pristine Rare RC Dustin Brown /199	$17.50
Wayne Gretzky 97-98 Donruss Preferred Cut to the Chase	$86.01	03/04 ITG MEMORABILIA EMERALD M. Havlat	$17.50
Wayne Gretzky 1999-00 Upper Deck	$85.00	05 ITG ULTIMATE MEM DAY IN HOCKEY HISTORY SILVER 1/ 25	$17.49
04-05 Heroes and Prospects Mike Richards In the Numbers	$78.99	04/05 ITG FRANCHISE FLYERS DOUBLE MEM B. Clarke	$17.37
05 Ultimate Emblem attic patch silver Glenn Hall 3/5	$76.00	03/04 ITG MEMORABILIA STICK & JERSEY T. Bertuzzi	$17.28

Cards ▶ Racing-NASCAR

The average sales price in this subcategory is $17.91.

	HIGH		AVG
2 BOX LOT PRESS PASS LEGENDS RACING 2005 *HOBBY* HOT!	$225.79	3 BOXES 2004 WHEELS HIGH GEAR EARNHARDT JR. RACE CARDS	$19.99
2 BOX LOT PRESS PASS ECLIPSE 2005 *HOBBY* NASCAR NR!	$187.50	ERROR CARD, Earnhardt & Wallace Mix-Up, 1996, Nascar!	$19.95
2 BOX LOT PRESS PASS ECLIPSE 2005 *HOBBY* NASCAR NR!	$185.01	1998 UD MAXXIMUM RACING BOX - EARNHARDT SR. AUTO ?	$19.95
* 2005 WHEELS AMERICAN THUNDER RACING HOBBY 2 BOX LOT	$181.99	ELLIOTT SADLER 2005 VIP 5 CARD LOT WITH INSERT NEW!	$19.00
2 BOX LOT PRESS PASS ECLIPSE 2005 *HOBBY* NASCAR NR!	$179.55	RUSTY WALLACE 101 CARD LOT INCLUDES 27 INSERTS NO DUPES	$18.50
2 BOX LOT PRESS PASS ECLIPSE 2005 *HOBBY* NASCAR NR!	$179.01	1993 Action Packed (PREMIER) Race Cards Factory Sld Box	$17.55
2 BOX LOT PRESS PASS ECLIPSE 2005 *HOBBY* NASCAR NR!	$162.58	1992 MAXX Nascar SEALED Wax CARD Box SET Lot 4 GORDON	$17.50
* 2005 PRESS PASS VIP RACING HOBBY 2 BOX LOT	$123.99	JEFF GORDON 2005 VIP 10 CARD LOT WITH INSERTS NEW!	$17.16
2005 PRESS PASS LEGENDS RACING HOBBY BOX sealed	$114.75	RICKY RUDD 2003 PRESS PASS HAWAII CONFERENCE	$16.57
2 Box Lot Press Pass Trackside 2005 Nascar Racing Cards	$111.99	Dale Earnhardt SR 20 Cards GALLERY, RETROSPECTIVE, 10TH	$16.50
2 BOX LOT PRESS PASS PREMIUM 2005 *HOBBY* NASCAR NR!	$106.10	1995 Wheels High Gear Ser I DAY ONE Factory Sealed Box	$16.48
2 BOX LOT PRESS PASS PREMIUM 2005 *HOBBY* NASCAR NR!	$104.52	TRAKS 1994 NASCAR Trading Cards-Sealed Box	$16.00
2 Box Lot Press Pass Trackside 2005 Nascar Racing Cards	$104.49	1993 NASCAR TRAKS COLLECTOR CARDS~UNOPENED~MINT	$15.99
2 BOX LOT PRESS PASS PREMIUM 2005 *HOBBY* NASCAR NR!	$103.50	Ray Nitschke Football Card Green Bay Packers VERY RARE!	$15.50
2 BOX LOT PRESS PASS PREMIUM 2005 *HOBBY* NASCAR NR!	$102.51	500 card NASCAR lot GORDON EARNHARDT WALLACE	$15.50

Cards ▶ Soccer

The average sales price in this subcategory is $25.04.

	HIGH		AVG
05 Futera 24ct Gold Plated Jon Dahl Tomasson Auto 1/1	$678.00	2004 Manchester United SPA Jersey Roy Keane #27/99	$27.56
2002 UD Man United Legends David Beckham Autograph #/50	$510.00	05 Futera Unique ROY AITKEN 24ct Gold Film 1/1 1 of 1	$27.00
05 Futera Unique LOUIS SAHA 24ct Gold Boot Auto 1/1	$355.55	(38) 1994 Upper Deck Soccer INSERT cards *lot of 38*	$26.69
David Beckham 04 Futera Auto Jersey Patch Unopen Box	$307.85	UD SP Authentic Manchester Jersey Shirt TIM HOWARDS #99	$26.00
[5 of these sold in a multiple item ("Dutch") auction for $61.57 each]		SP Authentic Manchester Shirt OLE GUNNAR SOLSKJAER #99	$26.00
PSA 9 MIA HAMM ULTIMATE HAWAII AUTO PSA/DNA /10 1/1	$269.69	2004 UPPER DECK MLS COMPLETE SET	$25.00
02 Topps Premier League Owen Auto Rare	$202.50	WCCF European 2004-2005 CRA4 Francesco TOTTI	$25.00
05 Futera Unique DAVID BECKHAM 24ct Gold Film 1/1	$154.50	LARGE LOT 1500 CARDS SEALED WAX PACKS SOCCER SHOTS PELE	$24.99
2005 Futera Unique 24ct Gold Autograph EIRIK BAKKE #1/1	$153.85	WCCF European 2004-2005 RONALDINHO + ETO'O	$23.50
2005 UD MLS GAME WORN JERSEY COMPLETE SET!!	$149.99	JOHN TERRY REFRACTOR ETOPPS SOCCER	$23.50
05 Futera Unique GONZALEZ RAUL 24ct Gold Film 1/1	$99.00	INHAND NUMBERED 1/1	
WCCF 2001-2002 FANTASISTA Cards Complete Set	$90.00	WCCF European 2004-2005 WCN3 DECO	$23.00
Manchester United UD Legend Auto Denis Law #001/200 1/1	$89.00	Nutella Canada Soccer Set of 6 Cards 3D Lenticular	$21.16
Manchester United UD Legend Auto George Best #125/200	$89.00	2004 LANDON DONOVAN AUTOGRAPHED CARD NR	$20.78
Ronaldinho 05 Futera Unique 24ct Gold Patch #019/111	$86.00	Nutella Canada Soccer Complete Circular Card Set (8)	$20.50
05 Futera Unique JOSE ANTONIO REYES 24ct Gold Film 1/1	$85.00	2000 Merlin Premier Gold soccer card box - BECKHAM, EPL	$20.50

Cards ▶ Tennis

The average sales price in this subcategory is $15.82.

	HIGH		AVG
10 BOX SEALED 2003 NETPRO INTERNATIONAL CASE KOURNIKOVA	$300.01	NETPRO VENUS WILLIAMS AUTOGRAPHED CARD #d 365/500! RARE	$16.09
BGS 9 MICHAEL JORDAN ITALIAN PANINI ROOKIE VERY RARE	$147.50	ANNA KOURNIKOVA NETPRO INT PREVIEW CARD P10 #d 500	$16.00
JP Morgan Tennis Tickets 3 Tixs- FINALS -Aug 14- Sun.	$122.50	ANNA KOURNIKOVA 03 NETPRO JERSEY ROOKIE CARD! 10D!	$15.52
2003 Netpro Glossy Sealed Case(10) Kournikova AUTO $700	$113.50	Netpro ANNA KOURNIKOVA APPAREL CARD 10B #d 228/500 RARE	$15.50
4 NETPRO INT ANNA KOURNIKOVA JERSEY, AUTO TENNIS CARD	$99.99	*Super Rare* Andy Roddick LE Card *Only 50 Made* #9/50	$15.50
2003 Netpro Glossy Sealed Case(10) Kournikova AUTO $700	$88.88	*2 BOX LOT* 2003 NETPRO TENNIS !*ROOKIES!	$15.50
ANNA KOURNIKOVA 03 NETPRO AUTO JERSEY RC! #'d/ 100	$86.00	AUTO'D VENUS WILLIAMS 2003 NETPRO INT. 340/500 MADE	$15.50
2005 ACE AUTHENTIC TENNIS SET CASE SHARAPOVA AUTO RC	$81.80	AUTO'D DANIELA HANTUCHOVA 2003 NETPRO INT. 290/500	$15.50
NETPRO D. HANTUCHOVA AUTO/JERSEY COMBO CARD #d 60/100!!	$61.00	2005 Ace Signature Series Maira Sharapova Jersey RC	$15.49
Anna Kournikova Neptro Rookie Autograph Card 301/500	$55.06	2003 Complete NETPRO Glossy & International Series sets	$15.00
Anna Kournikova 2003 NetPro RARE PULLED Blue Dress RC	$54.00	2005 Ace Signature Series Maria Sharapova RC Jersey	$14.99
2005 Ace SIGNATURE SERIES MARIA SHARAPOVA Jersey Card	$50.99	2003 Netpro Glossy Sealed Set LE# Anna Kournikova Auto?	$14.99
AUTO'D MARTINA HINGIS 2003 NETPRO INT. MATCHWORN /100	$49.88	2005 Ace Signature Series Maria Sharapova RC Jersey	$14.99
10 Box Case 2003 NetPro Premier Edition Sealed 1st RC's	$47.66	Anna Kournikova NetPro Match Worn Dress Card #d/500	$14.51
Netpro ANNA KOURNIKOVA AUTO #d 216/500! VERY VERY RARE!	$47.26	ANNA KOURNIKOVA 03 NETPRO JERSEY ROOKIE CARD! 10D!	$14.50

Cards ▸ Wrestling-WWE

The average sales price in this subcategory is $14.04.

	HIGH		AVG
Huge WWE TNA Event Used Worn 1/1 Auto Mat Chair lot 154	$400.55	WWE RAW DEAL COMPLETE SET ROB VAN DAM FULL	$15.00
Huge WWF WWE Raw Deal Lot! Complete Sets, Foils, Belt	$270.00	WWE RAW DEAL COMPLETE SET CHYNA FULL	$15.00
2004 TNA WRESTLING HOBBY CASE 20 BOX 60X AUTO USED WWE	$217.50	WWF Topps Wrestlemania III 3 Cards Full Box 36 Packs	$15.00
2004 TNA WRESTLING HOBBY CASE 20 BOX 60X AUTO USED WWE	$200.00	THE ROCK STONE COLD WWE DUAL EVENT WORN USED CARDS LOT	$14.95
2004 TNA WRESTLING HOBBY CASE 20 BOX 60X AUTO USED WWE	$192.65	2004 PACIFIC TNA WRESTLING HOBBY BOX 3 AUTO USED WWE FS	$14.50
2004 TNA WRESTLING HOBBY CASE 20 BOX 60X AUTO USED WWE	$175.27	WWE DIVA VICTORIA "SHOWING OFF" 5 COLOR WORN SWATCH	$14.50
HULK HOGAN RARE CERTIFIED AUTOGRAPH CARD 98 TOPPS AUTO	$138.50	1987 Topps WWF George the Animal Steele Autograph GAI	$13.51
EXREAMLY RARE ECW REPLICA TITLE BELT WWE WCW ECW NR	$137.50	trish stratus ring accessories	$13.50
3 Molly Holly Cards - 1 "Kiss" and 2 Event Worn cards	$111.49	WWE DIVA TRISH STRATUS "BODY & SOUL" WORN SWATCH CARD	$13.50
02 WWF ALL ACCESS TRIPLE H OFF THE MAT AUTO AUTOGRAPH	$102.50	WWE DIVAS "MATERIAL GIRLS" TERRI 2 COLOR WORN SWATCH	$13.49
EXTREAMLY RARE ECW WORLD TAG TEAM TITLE REPLICA WWE WCW	$82.00	Fleer WWE Absolute Divas Event-Worn Top Trish Stratus	$13.38
HULK HOGAN 1987 TOPPS RARE AUTO AUTOGRAPH CARD GAII	$77.66	WWE ABSOLUTELY RAW/ULTIMATE SMACKDOWN TINS LOT OF 3	$13.26
2001 FLEER WWE RAW WAR 120 PK 6 BOX FACTORY SEALED CASE	$76.65	WWE Fleer Divas Stacy Keibler 3 Color Event-Worn Card	$12.99
VERY RARE ECW ADULT TAG TEAM TITLES WWE WCW WWF	$76.00	WWE DIVAS "W/LOVE" NIDIA 3 COLOR WORN SWATCH CARD	$12.99
WWE Divas MISS JACKIE Signed w/KISS AUTO #/50 autograph	$74.99	(3) MOLLY HOLLY WWE WWF DIVAS EVENT WORN USED CARDS LOT	$12.95

Cards ▸ Storage, Display Supplies

The average sales price in this subcategory is $13.40.

	HIGH		AVG
1 cs. 1000 ULTRA-PRO PREMIUM SILVER 9 CARD POCKET PAGES	$89.99	50 NEW SEALED REGULAR RECESSED	$14.99
[2 of these sold for $89.99 each]		4-SCREWDOWN CARD HOLDERS	
1984 TOPPS USFL #36 JIM KELLY GRADED 8.5 NM-MT+	$68.00	25 ULTRA-PRO MAGNETIC CLOSURE ONE-TOUCH CARD HOLDERS	$14.99
1/2 CASE - 1000 CARD SAVER I GRADED CARD TOP-LOADERS	$64.99	1 CASE OF 12 BINDER / NOTEBOOK BASKETBALL CARD ALBUMS	$14.99
1981TOPPS NFL SET NM-MT W/ GRADED JOE MONTANA ROOKIE	$59.88	5000 ULTRA PRO 2 5/8" X 3 5/8" POLYPROPYLENE SLEEVES	$14.99
1986 TOPPS NFL SET NM-MT W/ GRADED JERRY RICE ROOKIE	$54.07	1 CASE OF 100 NEW SEALED MINI SNAP REGULAR CARD HOLDERS	$14.99
CHERRY DISPLAY BOX FOR SPORTS CARDS, MEDALS, MILITARY	$50.00	50 NEW SEALED REGULAR RECESSED	$14.99
1000 CARD SAVER II 2 GRADED Holders TOPLOADERS 1/2 Case	$49.99	4-SCREWDOWN CARD HOLDERS	
Regular & GRADED baseball card storage case	$49.95	BASKETBALL ~ CLEAR ACRYLIC DISPLAY CASE CUBE HOLDER	$14.50
[2 of these sold for $ 49.95 each]		25 BCW 4 FOUR SCREW SCREWDOWNS RECESSED CARD HOLDERS	$13.99
1 CASE 1000 CLASSIC TOP LOADERS FREE SHIPPING	$43.00	100 CARD SAVER IV 4 x 6 TOP LOADERS CARD HOLDERS Photos	$13.99
400 ULTRA-PRO PREMIUM SILVER 9 CARD POCKET PAGES SHEETS	$39.99	1000 COLLECTOR SAFE NEW POLY TEAM SET BAGS	$13.99
ULTRA PRO SOFT SLEEVES CASE 10000 COUNT FREE SHIPPING!!	$38.99	5 Storage Shoe Boxes 2400 box 3 Rows Cards Top Loaders	$13.99
[2 of these sold for $38.99 each]		1000 NEW SELF SEALED CLEAR SOFT GRADED CARD CARD BAGS	$13.99
Sport / Trading Card Display Case Cabinet w/door	$38.95	(2000) Poly sleeves (250) Top Loads (5) 100ct Cases	$13.99
1985 TOPPS USFL SET NM-MT W/ GRADED DOUG FLUTIE ROOKIE	$38.77	(20) Ultra Pro Four Screw Card Holder for Regular Cards	$13.49
Custom Portable Baseball Card Display Case J Pearsall	$36.00	LOT OF 2 MINI HELMET ~ ACRYLIC DISPLAY CASE CUBE HOLDER	$13.00
1 CASE 10000 POLY SOFT SLEEVES FREE SHIPPING	$34.99	[3 of these sold for $13.00 each]	

Fan Apparel & Souvenirs ▸ Baseball-MLB

The average sales price in this subcategory is $24.14.

	HIGH		AVG
1906 Shoeless Joe Jackson Cabinet Photo 1919 Black Sox	$456.00	Scarce 1969 Sicks Stadium Postcard Seattle Pilots	$24.99
Rare/Vintage California Angels Bobblehead Bobble Head	$305.00	1944 St Louis Browns Vintage Collection Wool Pennant	$24.99
VINTAGE Milwaukee Braves Razor BANK	$283.99	VINTAGE Milwaukee BRAVES little boy jacket 50's NR	$24.99
EXTREMELY RARE-1955 Brooklyn Dodgers Ashtray-MINT	$275.00	1958 Milwaukee Braves Illinois Central Menu 5th Annual	$24.99
Vintage Brooklyn Dodgers BUM Cookie Jar	$275.00	RARE 1911 BROOKLYN DODGERS TEAM PANORAMIC PHOTO HUGE!	$24.95
VINTAGE Brooklyn Dodgers BUM Razor BANK	$229.38	BROOKLYN DODGERS LAST BATTERY 1957 - AUTO 34" BAT COA	$24.95
VINTAGE ST. Louis Browns Razor BANK	$220.49	Topps 1953 Roy Campanella #27-Brooklyn Dodgers	$24.10
VINTAGE Washington Senators Razor BANK	$180.00	Throwback 30's New York Giants Fitted Hat (sz 7 5/8)	$24.00
VINTAGE New York Giants Razor BANK	$175.00	ATLANTA BRAVES BLACK NEW ERA 5950 7 1/4 CAP CAPS HAT SH	$23.95
EBBETS FIELD LIGHTED SIGN Great for Your Sports Room NR	$150.00	New W/Tags Nike Brooklyn Dodgers Jersey Shirt Size XL	$23.49
Andruw Jones Game Worn Cap Hat Atlanta Braves 2004	$149.00	Lot of (5) Throwback Kansas City A's 1950's Style Hats	$23.19
WASHINGTON SENATORS Authentic 1957 Home Jersey Large	$100.00	WASHINGTON SENATORS 1963 MLB BASEBALL THROWBACK HAT	$22.95
EXCLUSIVE! WASHINGTON SENATORS	$96.00	[2 of these sold for $22.95 each]	
COOPERSTOWN JERSEY		NEW YORK GIANTS 1949 MLB BASEBALL THROWBACK HAT	$22.95
MITCHELL & NESS ST. LOUIS BROWNS #5 M&N jersey 56	$87.00	1960 Kansas City Athletics A's Team Picture	$22.72
1960 Brooklyn Dodgers Ebbets Field Demolition Negative	$86.00	AUGUST 1,1956 BROOKLYN DODGERS TICKET STUB (v. BRAVES)	$22.50

Fan Apparel & Souvenirs ▸ Basketball-NBA

The average sales price in this subcategory is $16.71.

	HIGH		AVG
MITCHELL & NESS WARRIORS WILT CHAMBERLAIN jersey 56	$109.10	Philadelphia 76ers Iverson Jersey New Era Fitted Hat	$18.50
1954 BALTIMORE BULLETS Letter From Coach CLAIR BEE	$107.51	BOSTON CELTICS NEW ERA 59 FIFTY 7 1/2 NBA CAP HAT	$18.50
Erving - 1972-73 Virginia Squires M&N Authentic Jersey	$105.00	Earl Monroe - #10 - Bullets - Bobblehead Bobble Head	$18.49
authentic LARRY JOHNSON hornets BASKETBALL JERSEY swen	$87.51	WIZARDS BULLETS AUTHENTIC JERSEY 1977 YOUTH LARGE $75	$17.99
Mitchell & Ness NBA All Star West E. Johnson Jersey 56	$82.53	BOSTON CELTICS NEW ERA 59 FIFTY 7 5/8 NBA CAP HAT	$16.95
MITCHELL & NESS WARRIORS WILT CHAMBERLAIN jersey 54	$81.00	PHILADELPHIA 76ers NEW ERA 59 FIFTY 1/2 NBA CAP HAT	$16.95
Bob McAdoo Mitchell and Ness Brand New with tags SZ56	$73.00	Philadelphia 76ers pink black New Era Fitted Hat 71/2	$16.50
MITCHELL & NESS WARRIORS WILT CHAMBERLAIN jersey 60	$69.99	CHICAGO BULLS FITTED HAT BY REEBOK SIZE 8 **	$16.10
JORDAN BULLETS NIKE THROWBACK SWINGMAN JERSEY L+2	$61.00	1970 Buffalo Braves Portland Trail Blazers 1st YR Prog	$15.55
JORDAN BULLETS NIKE THROWBACK SWINGMAN JERSEY XL+2	$59.99	LAKERS 1960 STYLE THROWBACK FITTED HAT CAP SIZE 7 3/4	$15.51
M&N Marvin Barnes St. Louis Spirits Authentic Jersey 48	$53.78	LAKERS 1960 STYLE THROWBACK FITTED HAT CAP SIZE 7 1/4	$15.51
MITCHELL & NESS DR. J VIRGINIA SQUIRES ERVING jersey 54	$49.99	NWT REEBOK CHICAGO BULLS RARE FITTED HAT CAP 7 1/4	$15.49

MITCHELL & NESS DR. J VIRGINIA SQUIRES ERVING jersey 56	$49.99	CHICAGO BULLS FITTED HAT SIZE 7 3/8 **	$15.10
MITCHELL & NESS ABA PIPERS HAWKINS M&N jersey 52	$49.00	NBA CLASSIC PHILADELPHIA 76ers FITTED 8 REEBOK HAT CAP	$15.00
MITCHELL & NESS ABA KENTUCKY COLONELS M&N jersey 56	$46.99	NBA prgm, Baltimore Bullets, 2/8/64 vs. Cincinnati	$14.99

Fan Apparel & Souvenirs ▸ Boxing

The average sales price in this subcategory is $31.31.

	HIGH		AVG
1920s Louis Firpo Boxing Wire Photo Underwood & Underw	$910.00	VINTAGE BOXING TROHPY	$34.00
* VERY RARE * Championship Ring (Boxing - New York)	$756.50	TheIncomparableFight- Jack Johnson&Jim Jeffries Poster	$33.00
Cassius Clay (Ali) Sonny Liston Boxing Ticket ~ Unused	$624.11	MUHAMMAD ALI 1997 AMATEUR BOXING 2 PIN SET	$32.55
1890S CELLULOID PINBACK BUTTON BOXING FITZSIMMONS CHAMP	$380.00	1949 Ray Robinson v Kid Gavilan Boxing Wire Photo.	$32.50
1919 Boxing full Ticket Willard vs. Dempsey PSA 6	$300.50	Muhammad Ali Doll 1976 Mego NIB Trigger Mechanism Rare	$32.00
JACK DEMPSEY (NONPAREIL) RICHARD K. FOX CABINET CARD	$262.00	Joe Louis- The Brown Bomber TIN SIGN	$31.00
Muhammad Ali Autograpgh Rice Hotel 1967 World Champ	$250.00	JULIO CESAR CHAVEZ BOXING DVD 43 FULL FIGHTS	$31.00
MUHAMMAD ALI AUTOGRAPHED Limited Ed. FOSSIL WATCH SET !	$217.50	Great Mike Tyson Limited Edition Art Lithograph	$31.00
2 MUHAMMED ALI Toothbrushes in Package-The Champ	$202.50	NEW HORIZONTAL BOXING GLOVE WALL MOUNTED DISPLAY CASE	$29.99
IKE WEIR RICHARD K. FOX POLICE GAZETTE CABINET CARD	$183.50	BENNY GOLDBERG BANTAMWEIGHT CONTENDER PHOTOGRAPH!!!	$27.99
RARE FIND EARLY GRAZIANO PROGRAM	$180.50	MARVIN HAGLER THOMAS HEARNS RARE CAESARS PALACE CARD	$27.00
1923 LUIS FIRPO PREPARES FOR DEMPSEY WIREPHOTO	$177.50	Rocky Marciano Art of Sports Figurine	$26.88
JOHN L. SULLIVAN CABINET CARD	$159.50	SONNY LISTON "ASSOCIATED PRESS" WIRE PHOTO!!! (LOOK)	$26.01
— Sugar Ray Robinson Trophy—	$158.50	NEGRO LEAGUE Jersey HOMESTEAD GRAYS LG NLBM	$26.00
YANK SULLIVAN RICHARD K. FOX POLICE GAZETT CABINET CARD	$138.45	Ali v. Liston Photogragh Signed by ALI	$26.00

Fan Apparel & Souvenirs ▸ College-NCAA

The average sales price in this subcategory is $13.15.

	HIGH		AVG
ARKANSAS RAZORBACK 1994 NCAA National Championship Ring DANIEL MOORE	$21,700.00	NEWSPAPER ALABAMA PHOTO BEAR BRYANT DIXIE HOWELL 1935	$40.95
10K 1991 NCAA University Tournament Championship Ring DANIEL MOORE	$325.00	2005 AUBURN TIGERS FOOTBALL - SIGNED PRINT & COIN	$40.00
	$280.00	AUBURN TIGERS FOOTBALL LEGENDS REUNION 2 DVD SET NEW AU	$40.00
Auburn Tigers Football 2004 Print Set of 4 Large	$255.00	Jason Kidd California Bears Sewn Nike Jersey - L	$39.99
VINTAGE BEAR BRYANT, COKE, GOLDEN FLAKE STORE POSTER	$202.51	Alabama, Tyrone Prothro auto THE CATCH"Framed	$39.99
The Tradition Continues-Daniel Moore-Alabama 1992	$202.50	Shower Curtain, University of Florida Gators	$39.95
c1910 Army Tobacco Felt Basketball Player	$187.50	AIR FORCE FALCONS ADULT MEDIUM HOCKEY JERSEY	$37.00
92 ALABAMA FOOTBALL NATIONAL CHAMPS (13-0) SEASON DVD	$177.50	Alabama Tyrone Prothro "THE CATCH" signed Daniel Moore	$37.00
2005 BAYLOR LADY BEARS NCAA CHAMPS BASKETBALL	$160.00	vintage 1953 CHEVROLET TRUCK diecast CLEMSON UNIVERSITY	$36.00
Daniel Moore Rocky Stop Large Print Alabama Football NR	$150.00	FLORIDA CATOR BASKETBALL WITH BEAR - NEW	$36.00
NEW CLEMSON UNIV TIGERS COLLEGIATE GOLF CLUB STAND BAG	$149.99	ORGIA BULLDOGS FRAMED PRINT "UGA CHILLING"	$34.99
DANIEL MOORE THE WINNING CONNECTION JAY BARKER	$129.97	1931 Cal vs Stanford Big Game Program	$34.00
University of Kansas (KU) - Brass Sandy Jayhawk Bookends	$112.50	NICK VAN EXEL Cincinnati Nike Elite Throwback Jersey XL	$33.49
Colorado CU BUFFS Hanging Neon Sign LIKE NEW! ~jb	$108.49	UNIVERSITY ARKANSAS RAZORBACKS NCAA SPARE TIRE COVER	$32.99
	$102.73	ALABAMA CRIMSON TIDE Gift NCAA Bathroom SHOWER CURTAIN	$32.99

Fan Apparel & Souvenirs ▸ Cycling

The average sales price in this subcategory is $22.56.

	HIGH		AVG
LANCE ARMSTRONG Signed Autographed Yellow Jersey	$1,300.00	USPS Cycling large golf umbrella 60" carbon rain sun	$22.83
LANCE ARMSTRONG SIGNED SPORTS ILLUSTRATED FRAMED	$499.99	Colavita Olive Oil Pro Cycling Team issue polo shirt M	$22.51
Official VIP Road Book Tour de France 2005 Lance 7th V	$227.50	COPPI '52 TOUR DE FRANCE CYCLING PHOTO BICYCLE BIKE	$22.50
RARE Lance Armstrong Racing Number from his 1999 Tour	$203.87	MERCKX 1969 TOUR DE FRANCE CYCLING PHOTO BICYCLE BIKE	$22.50
Lance Armstrong Discovery Channel Yellow Jersey XL	$182.50	Tour de France 2005 yellow Cap Hat Lance Armstrong 7th	$22.50
Lance Armstrong Signed Tour de France 1999 Certificate!	$177.50	LANCE ARMSTRONG (7) Commemorative Sports Illustrated	$22.50
Lance Armstrong Discovery Channel Yellow Jersey -Size L	$162.50	NEW NALINI CYCLING JERSEY COSTA BLANCA EURO SPORT XL	$21.52
Lance Armstrong Nike Bustin Butt Original Poster MINT	$162.50	Tour de France '93 Motorola Cycling Team Sweatshirt LRG	$21.50
LANCE ARMSTRONG POSTER IN COFIDIS UNIFORM!!!	$150.00	Lance Armstrong, Le Tour De France 2001 Red Pin	$21.49
Lance Armstrong cardboard standee/cut-out.	$138.05	Vintage Toyota Van De Heyden Cycling Jersey M	$21.01
TREK 700 MULTI-TRACK BICYCLE, COMPLETE BIKE,	$135.00	Lance Armstrong Tour de France Print NEW poster	$20.51
Lance Armstrong, Hard Rock Cafe 2003 Cyclist Pin	$129.50	2005 Tour de France Sign - Centre de Presse Permanence	$20.51
Lance Armstrong 7 time Tour Winner 2005 Oakley Poster	$122.50	NEGRO LEAGUE Multi Logo NLBM Jersey 2X WHITE	$20.50
Lance Armstrong Discovery Channel Yellow Jersey XXL	$113.50	Lance Armstrong LIVESTRONG poster and wristband	$20.50
Lance Armstrong Nike Bustin Butt Original Poster	$110.00	LANCE ARMSTRONG wins 6th Sports Illustrated NO LABEL	$20.50

Fan Apparel & Souvenirs ▸ Football-NFL

The average sales price in this subcategory is $12.59.

	HIGH		AVG
CHIPPER JONES Autographed Atlanta BRAVES Mini HELMET	$79.99	Super bowl xxiii 23 video 49ers niners bengals dvd	$14.50
Super bowl vii 7 video dolphins redskins dvd	$76.00	STEELERS 2005 COLLECTIBLE TRACTOR TRAILER	$14.50
Super bowl viii 8 video dolphins vikings dvd	$75.00	Super bowl xxiv 24 video 49ers niners broncos dvd	$13.50
NEW NFL SUPERBOWL MINI GUMBALL FOOTBALL HELMET SET 38	$49.00	1975 afc championship steelers raiders video dvd rare	$13.50
AWESOME VINTAGE POTTERY FOOTBALL PLAYER BANK, MOX '58	$46.51	TAMPA BAY BUCCANEERS AUTHENTIC FOOTBALL HELMET DECALS	$13.00
Lot of 36 NFL micro mini football helmets with rack	$46.00	OAKLAND RAIDERS AUTHENTIC FOOTBALL HELMET DECALS	$13.00
S.F. 49ers niners (5) super bowl videos dvd	$44.99	2005 PRO FOOTBALL HALL OF FAME GAME SOUVENIR T-SHIRT	$13.00
OFFICIAL NFL PRO GAME FOOTBALL(BLEM) F1000	$44.99	MIAMI DOLPHINS AUTHENTIC FOOTBALL HELMET DECALS	$13.00
20 OFFICIAL NFL GREEN BAY PACKERS PATCHES PATCH	$41.00	ST. LOUIS RAMS INTERSTATE SIGN	$12.99
ST. LOUIS BROWNS VINTAGE JACKET COOPERSTOWN COLL. LAR.	$39.99	NEW ORLEANS SAINTS INTERSTATE SIGN	$12.99
ST. LOUIS BROWNS VINTAGE JACKET COOPERSTOWN COLL. 2XL	$39.99	Chiefs football helmet decals	$12.50

BO JACKSON RAIDERS THROWBACK JERSEY	$37.50	Titans football helmet decals.....stripes included	$12.50
NFL Playoff Standings Board, NEW	$34.99	Eagles football helmet decals	$12.50
Super bowl vi 6 video dallas cowboys dolphins dvd Rare	$33.00	NFL Alumni football JACKET mens LARGE Mint	$12.50
CHICAGO BEARS Suede Leather Jacket XL, NWT	$33.00	PITTSBURGH STEELERS 4 WINNING SUPERBOWLS ON DVD + 1FREE	$12.50

Fan Apparel & Souvenirs ▸ Golf-PGA

The average sales price in this subcategory is $24.60.

	HIGH		AVG
1929 US Open Golf Bobby Jones Winged Foot RARE!!	$300.00	MASTERS GOLF TOURNAMENT HARDBACK BOOK 1991	$24.99
2005 Flags..British Open, Masters, US Open, PGA + BONUS	$280.00	John Daly 2005 PGA GOLF TOUR Bobblehead bobble head SGA	$24.99
DAVID LEADBETTER GOLF COLLECTIBLE SWING TRAINER	$250.00	MASTERS RARE CADDIE BADGE "Alonzo"#42	$24.99
TEN 10 consecutive Jack Nicklaus 5 pound notes holders	$250.00	Tiger Woods-Arnold Palmer & Jack Nicklaus 16x20 Photo	$24.99
VINTAGE BEN HOGAN 1 inch TIMEX BELT CLIP WATCH CASE ~NR	$212.50	John Daly 2005 PGA GOLF TOUR Bobblehead bobble head SGA	$24.99
1935 BRITISH OPEN GOLF BALL MARKER - 1" COIN - XX.RARE	$160.00	[2 of these sold for $24.99 each]	
TIGER WOODS SIGNED AUTOGRAPHED PGA AUGUSTA SCORECARD	$149.99	New Masters Cap / Hat (GREEN)	$24.95
2001 Masters Badge Tiger Woods 2nd Win Very Rare	$149.99	JACK NICKLAUS ₤5 FIVE POUND NOTE GOLF OPEN	$23.75
AUGUSTA NATIONAL CHINA CREAMER	$137.50	MASTERS HOWARD MILLER WOOD CLOCK AUGUSTA NATIONAL	$23.50
2005 MASTERS BADGE - TIGER WOODS 4TH WIN	$134.00	2005 U.S. Open Ticket Set Pinehurst	$22.72
LEROY NEIMAN SIGNED Valhalla, PGA 2000 TIGER WOODS	$129.99	NEW 2005 U.S. Open Ball Marker Cap Hat Pinehurst Golf	$22.50
1994 MASTERS GOLF TOURNAMENT, 1 OZ. SILVER COIN / MEDAL	$129.50	John Daly 2005 PGA GOLF TOUR Bobblehead bobble head SGA	$22.49
BEN HOGAN MEN'S STAINLESS STEEL WATCH	$128.01	VERY RARE** PINEHURST STORIES book and case	$21.99
1997 Western Open, Golf Badge Ticket, Tiger Woods Wins	$127.50	John Daly 2005 PGA GOLF TOUR Bobblehead bobble head SGA	$21.99
Jack Nicklaus 5 five pound note in USA to you in 3 days	$124.95	JACK NICKLAUS ₤5 RBS NOTE IN PRESENTATION PACK	$21.00
[5 of these sold in a multiple item ("Dutch") auction for $24.99 each]		Ltd Art Print GOLF St. Andrews Old Course "Road Hole"	$21.00

Fan Apparel & Souvenirs ▸ Hockey-NHL

The average sales price in this subcategory is $12.92.

	HIGH		AVG
Vintage Hartford Whalers Away Jersey Liut #1	$71.00	1990 Alexander Mogilny Buffalo Sabres Slide w/ Rights	$13.49
VINTAGE AUTHENTIC NHL ALL STAR JERSEY CCM XL 80'S RARE	$68.55	1989 Craig Berube Philadelphia Flyers Slide w/ Rights	$13.03
1984 Olympics Hockey Puck -Sarajevo - Sweet and Rare!	$61.61	EARLY BUFFALO SABRES GIL PERREAULT 500th GOAL PENNANT	$13.01
VLADISLAV TRETIAK RUSSIAN - C.C.C.P NIKE JERSEY * MED	$59.99	ATLANTA FALCONS AUTHENTIC FOOTBALL HELMET DECALS	$13.00
1987 Jari Kurri Edmonton Oilers Slide w/ Rights	$57.77	ROOTS NHLPA BASEBALL HAT CAP NHL HOCKEY NEW SUEDE PEAK	$12.99
Ray Bourque Souvenir Hockey Puck Bruins VS Avalanche	$50.01	Atlanta Thrashers Mascot Bobblehead & Bonus	$12.99
1988 Jari Kurri Edmonton Oilers Slide w/ Rights	$47.89	1990 John McIntyre Toronto Maple Leafs Slide w/ Rights	$12.80
1989 Adam Oates Detroit Red Wings Slide w/ Rights	$46.88	1990 Eldon Reddick Edmonton Oilers Slide w/ Rights	$12.52
VINTAGE CHICAGO BLACKHAWKS #7 JERSEY	$44.99	500 GOAL SCORERS HOCKEY POSTER GRETZKY BOSSY	$12.52
CCM 2000 NHL ALL STAR GAME HOCKEY JERSEY AUTHENTIC	$43.88	THE ORIGINAL SIX NHL HOCKEY FRAMED PICTURE NICE 30X22	$12.50
1972 Pro League Hockey MUNRO Game COMPLETE BOX NHL NR	$41.00	1984 Markus Mattsson Los Angeles Kings Slide w/ Rights	$12.50
1997 AHL ZAMBONI SET VERY RARE WHITE ROSE	$39.99	Complete 1998 Molson NHL Team Crests- Unopened	$12.00
NHL ZAMBONI SET 1997 VERY HARD TO FIND	$39.99	TORONTO MAPLE LEAFS CERAMIC COLLECTORS PLATE	$11.99
1991 Wayne Gretzky Los Angeles Kings Slide w/ Rights	$37.00	WAYNE GRETZKY VARIANT WHITE OILERS MCFARLANE LEGENDS 2	$11.99
1986 Lanny McDonald Calgary Flames Slide w/ Rights	$36.88	1984 Rollie Melanson New York Islanders Slide w/ Rights	$11.52

Fan Apparel & Souvenirs ▸ Horse Racing

The average sales price in this subcategory is $24.64.

	HIGH		AVG
1952 Hambletonian Program-Good Time Park, GOSHEN NY	$380.00	Vhs/Dvd- Very FIRST Documentary of RUFFIAN, 1980..RARE!	$24.99
HASKELL RACE WORN SADDLE CLOTH - LIKE A HERO!!!	$359.08	Vhs/Dvd-History of THOROUGHBRED...Secretariat/ALYDAR...	$24.99
1963 Hambletonian Program-DuQuoin State Fair	$338.33	KENTUCKY DERBY 1978 PROGRAM SIGNED WOODY STEPHENS ETC	$24.99
FASTNESS WINNING EDDIE READ SADDLE CLOTH	$284.99	Vhs/Dvd-RACING HIST..Lengthy MAN O'WAR Footage/Funeral	$24.99
New Horse Racing Exercise SADDLE-Race-Jockey-Silks-NR	$279.00	RUFFIAN the UNDEFEATED FILLY CHAMPION DVD 65 minutes!	$24.95
HUGE PAINTING HARNESS HORSE RACING STANDARDBRED PACER	$250.00	SARATOGA RACETRACK BLANKET-SGA-8/14/05	$24.27
1968 Hambletonian Program–NEVELE PRIDE	$250.00	1974 Kentucky Derby Souvenir Pocket Knife, NR	$23.95
1963 - 89th Kentucky Derby Official Program - Mint	$212.50	2005 Dubai $15,000,000 World Cup Race Program	$23.83
Churchill Downs Trifecta Saddle Cloth/Towel Collection	$200.02	2005 Dubai World Cup Thoroughbred Races Souvenir Book	$23.83
Antique Horse Shoe Secretariat w/1973 Belmont Photo NR	$188.05	1963 KENTUCKY DERBY / CHURCHILL DOWNS GLASS	$23.50
*Mint DAMASCUS 1967 Belmont Stakes	$187.50	*CIGAR* 7-13-96* program-mint w/(1) uncashed win ticket	$23.50
ARLINGTON MILLION - Rare Raceworn Saddle Cloth/Towel	$178.99	JOCKEY SILKS CUSTOM MADE RACE USED HORSE RACING COLORS	$22.55
Secretariat 1973 Program and Winning Ticket Original NR	$171.18	2005 SARATOGA - Red Shirt & Blue Cap	$22.09
ROYAL SPY - Firecracker Breeders' Cup Saddle Cloth	$163.16	11x14 Color photo of Smarty Jones Preakness Derby	$21.50
SECRETATRIAT Winner of the 99th Kentucky Derby Decanter	$154.49	Dan Patch porcelain plate	$21.50

Fan Apparel & Souvenirs ▸ Olympics

The average sales price in this subcategory is $13.11.

	HIGH		AVG
1952 Helsinki Olympics jury enamel badge	$431.75	2004 ATHENS Olympic "Teamwork 6" Internal pin	$14.99
2004 ATHENS Olympic Map of Greece Framed set of 37 pins	$299.99	Canadian rowing Olympic games pin	$14.00
Linfox truck olympic sydney pin brand new	$132.50	Olympic Henry Hansen bicycle shop advertising pin	$14.00
OLYMPIC pin NOC Syria? Sudan?	$82.69	2002 Hungary National Olympic Comm. Pin Salt Lake City	$13.49
ATHENS 2004 Olympic Participation Medal	$75.00	2006 Torino Hockey Helmet and Stick Olympic pin	$13.04
1936 BERLIN Summer Olympic Games Pin	$71.01	2006 Torino Olympic Monument Pin " CAVAL 'D BRONS "	$12.50
Coke Sun Production + Prototype Pins - 1996 Olympics	$68.79	4 HOCKEY Albertville 1992 Winter Olympics Hockey Pins	$12.50
Danish 1948 olympic games sterling silver pin	$67.66	32RARE Soviet Russian Olympic Games Pins MOSCOW-1980 #2	$12.50
1996 ATLANTA Olympic Collector Badge MC	$67.50	Vermeil 5000 Limited Edition Atlanta Olympics 1996 Pin	$12.50

	HIGH		AVG
Coca-Cola Salt Lake 2002 Olympics Pins Complete Set NIB	$62.00	1936 Berlin XI Olympiade Olympics Enamel Pin	$11.52
1980 Moscow Olympic Pin Badge – Water Polo!	$61.69	2004 ATHENS Olympics 1896 Silver Medal Replica pin	$11.50
Guyana Olympic Association pin	$55.00	Official Numbered Olympic Pin From Hungary 1994	$11.50
Very Rare Framed 1980 Moscow Olympic Games Pin Set 25	$49.99	2 Russia Russian Olympic Hockey Pins Olympics	$10.99
16 Cultural Olympiad Pins SOME RARE 1996 Olympics	$49.02	ATHENS 2004- OTE CHRISTMAS HAT PIN	$10.99
Coke Oval Production + Prototype Pins - 1996 Olympics	$46.77	VISA SNOWFLAKE TORINO 2006 OLYMPIC PIN	$10.55

Fan Apparel & Souvenirs ▸ Racing-Formula 1

The average sales price in this subcategory is $49.81.

	HIGH		AVG
KIMI RAIKKONEN 2005 REPLICA HELMET F1+FREESHIPP	$909.99	Official** Ferrari Marlboro F1 cap & polo ** Schumacher	$53.50
2002 FERRARI MARLBORO MICHAEL SCHUMACHER SIGNED HELMET	$900.00	Ferrari F430 spider hardback brochure 2239/05	$52.44
JUAN PABLO MONTOYA FULLSIZE BMW F1 ARAI HELMET	$850.00	Ferrari Playing cards	$52.00
1995 GERHARD BERGER FULLSIZE BIEFFE F1 FERRARI HELMET	$739.00	WEST MERCEDES BENZ MCLAREN F1 FORMULA SHIRTS SHIRT XL	$49.99
AYRTON SENNAS RACING CAR COLLECTION	$611.00	MCLAREN F1 FORMULA TRACK T-SHIRTS >KiMi< X-LARGE SHIRT	$49.99
MICHAEL SCHUMACHER SCHUBERTH REPLICA FERRARI HELMET	$575.00	2 - 1982 Detroit Grand Prix Framed Photos	$49.00
2005 MCLAREN MERCEDES HUGO BOSS CREW T SHIRT RAIKKONEN	$521.00	***FERRARI BLACK/RED BACKPACK- NEW WITH TAGS!!!***	$48.50
Michael Schumacher Helmet 1998 Formula 1	$504.00	Record car Mercedes, 1939, oryginal photo, excellent	$47.00
orig. JORDAN GP 2004 Pitcrew Suit Size XXL by PUMA	$492.00	Ayrton Senna photos from the 1994 San Marino Grand Prix	$46.00
2005 XXL MCLAREN MERCEDES BOSS CREW FLEECE RAIKKONEN	$479.00	TEAM MCLAREN MERCEDES ~ KIMI RAIKKONEN 2005 T-SHIRT	$44.00
1/1 FULL SIZE HELMET REPLICA OF FERNANDO ALONSO 2005	$478.09	TEAM MCLAREN MERCEDES ~ KIMI RAIKKONEN 2005 T-SHIRT	$42.00
AYRTON SENNA 1988 - F1 REPLICA HELMET - FULL SIZE!! 1/1	$452.15	Kimi Raikkonen 1:43 Sauber C20 Minichamps 2001 Race Ver	$42.00
AYRTON SENNA 1994 - F1 REPLICA COMMEMORATIVE HELMET 1/1	$425.00	orig. MINARDI 2003 Raceday Shirt "L"	$41.03
AYRTON SENNA 1985 COMMEMORATIVE F1 REPLICA HELMET-NR!!	$385.00	Porsche Team F1 Racing Jacket New Design M L XL XXL	$39.97
TEAM MCLAREN CREW JACKET HUGO BOSS MONTOYA RAIKKONEN	$338.00	Porsche Team F1 Racing Jacket Classic Black M-XXL	$39.97

Fan Apparel & Souvenirs ▸ Racing-NASCAR

The average sales price in this subcategory is $10.77.

	HIGH		AVG
1985 UMI NASCAR YEAR BOOK PRINTED IN 1993	$200.00	BILL ELLIOTT 2003 DODGE CLEAR RED 1:24 ACTION	$11.00
BILL ELLIOT RARE COLLECTIBLE-SOFTBALL BAT N.R.	$56.00	NASCAR CLOSE-OUT! Children's XSmall Bobby Labonte Shirt	$10.52
1994 RCCA 1/24 Car- #11 Bill Elliott/Budweiser	$52.00	Bobby Labonte #18 Nascar Silver Auto Emblem SS	$10.50
B Labonte Interstate #18 Hamilton Twill JACKET NEW 2XL	$49.99	1988 BILL ELLIOTT COORS #9 WINSTON CUP CHAMP HAT	$10.50
NEXTEL #18 BOBBY LABONTE LEATHER & WOOL JACKET LARGE	$49.99	NASCAR CLOSE-OUT! Children's XLarge Bobby Labonte Shirt	$10.50
1995 RCCA 1/24 Car- #94 Bill Elliott/Thunderbat Car	$49.95	CHASE AUTHENTICS BOBBY LABONTE JACKET	$10.50
Bill Elliot #94 NASCAR mini tool box Snap-On	$46.25	BOBBY LABONTE 1 OF 2508 TRUCK	$10.49
Bobby Labonte Nascar Nextel Uniform Twill Jacket NEW Lg	$44.95	OFFICIAL NASCAR BOBBY LABONTE #18 WATCH W/SOUND	$10.00
1/24 Bobby Labonte Slim Jim Action CWB 1 of 1,000	$41.00	4T boy girl Nascar Chase Bobby Labonte Outfit Racing	$9.99
NEGRO LEAGUE Multi Logo NLBM Jersey XL BLACK	$38.99	BOBBY LABONTE #18 INTERSTATE- BI-PLANE - RARE	$9.99
NEW NASCAR BOBBY LABONTE TEAM SHIRT ADULT L	$37.66	95 ERTL BATMAN FOREVER THUNDERBAT BILL ELLIOT 1/18 MIB	$9.99
BOBBY LABONTE HULK INTERSTATE ACTION DIE-CAST CAR	$34.00	Bill Elliott # 94 1997 Mcdonald's NASCAR	$9.99
Tony Stewart and Bobby Labonte Die-Cast Twin Pack Fr Sh	$32.00	BOBBY LABONTE INTERSTATE BATTERIES NEXTEL CUP PIT HAT	$9.99
2000 1/24 Action BOBBY LABONTE #18 Interstate NASCAR	$31.01	Bill Elliott #94 MACDONALD'S 2000 TAURUS 1/24 CAR	$9.99
BOBBY LABONTE INTERSTATE NEXTEL UNIFORM JACKET 2XLARGE	$31.00	#9 Hitch Cover Plug LIGHT Works With Brake!!	$9.99

Fan Apparel & Souvenirs ▸ Soccer-European

The average sales price in this subcategory is $19.22.

	HIGH		AVG
ADIDAS QUESTRA EUROPA EURO 1996 ENGLAND + COCA COLA	$336.00	Manchester United " The History 1878 - 2002 " DVD	$19.99
Portsmouth 1948 vintage enamel soccer football pin	$326.00	NWT OFFICIAL AC MILAN SOCCER JERSEY ADIDAS, XL, NO RES.	$19.99
90th anniversary vintage enamel soccer football pin	$234.72	Baggio " Tutte le Magie di Baggio " DVD , all 200 goals	$19.99
Antique soccer football boots shoes old vintage preWWII	$202.50	GREECE-BRAZIL EURO 2004 CONFEDERATION CUP T-SHIRT NEW-L	$19.99
Sean John Lambskin Leather Jacket 2X Retail: $475	$202.50	Mens Nike Arsenal F.C. Soccer Shorts XL	$19.99
UEFA Congress 1960 in Rome, Italy Football soccer pin	$190.26	NWT NIKE MANCHESTER UNITED AWAY SOCCER JERSEY L	$19.50
Chelsea FC tour 1946 enamel soccer football pin	$182.50	DEUTSCHER FUSSBALL- BUND #9 GERMAN SOCCER JERSEY	$18.60
Irish Football Soccer pin cumann pelle na h-Eireann	$155.28	RONALDO Brazil National Team Soccer Jersey # 9 Medium	$18.50
Centenary 1963 vintage enamel soccer football pin	$153.50	Baggio " Tutte le Magie di Baggio " DVD , all 200 goals	$18.50
UEFA Congress Paris 1959 Soccer football enamel pin	$125.00	UEFA miniature Football soccer enamel pin	$18.27
UEFA Congress Denmark 1957 Soccer football enamel pin	$125.00	18 European Soccer pins	$18.00
Sean John Lambskin Leather Jacket LG Retail: $475	$97.00	MIA HAMM SIGNED 8X10 GLOSSY COLOR PHOTO -WOMEN SOCCER-	$17.99
Birmingham City vintage enamel soccer football pin	$82.00	FOOTBALL Soccer pin Greece Referees federation	$16.50
WISLA Krakow /Poland official home jersey Nike soccer	$69.99	ADIDAS GERMANY EURO 04 REPLICA AWAY SHIRT, SIZE LARGE	$16.50
Queenspark FC vintage enamel soccer football pin	$68.87	Inter Milan - 100 Yrs of History & Goals, on DVD	$15.99

Fan Apparel & Souvenirs ▸ Soccer-World Cup

The average sales price in this subcategory is $24.07.

	HIGH		AVG
SOCCER WORLD CUP 1930.ANTIQUE AND ORIGINAL TICKET.	$500.00	1974 World Cup coins set silver in case	$28.11
ADIDAS SANTIAGO MATCH BALL - CHILE FIFA WORLD CUP 1962	$412.07	Mia Hamm Autograph ***LOOK***	$27.00
1938 FRANCE #349 WORLD CUP SOCCER MAXI POSTCARD SIGNED	$375.00	NIKE USA SOCCER YOUTH JERSEY-LARGE 14-16-NEW WITH TAGS!	$26.98
MEXICO 86 WORLD CUP TICKET; QUARTER,SEMI & FINALS -2 EA	$227.49	Argentina Soccer Football Jersey Shirt Adidas XL/LRG	$26.53
adidas olympic official matchball sydney 2000 GAMARADA	$202.50	New NIKE Authentic BRASIL RONALDO Soccer Jersey LARGE	$26.02
2002 FIFA World Cup 1 Kg Silver (0.999) Proof Coin (LOW	$164.50	RARE Penarol URUGUAY BRAND NEW NWT sealed shirt jersey	$26.00
** Guar Auth LOUIS VUITTON Eye Glass SPECTACLE Case **	$139.00	Cyanamid Italy Flag World Cup 1998 Soccer Pins Pin	$26.00
Adidas Tricolore World Cup 98 Soccer Ball (Brand New)	$112.50	Vintage adidas WC 98 France Soccer Team Shirt RARE L	$25.01

	HIGH		AVG
1994 WORLD CUP - 90 UNUSED TICKETS MINT - LOW RESERVE	$90.00	*NIKE* AUTHENTIC US WORLD CUP SOCCER SHIRT SIZE XLG	$25.00
MEXICO 70 World Cup OFFICIAL MEDIA PIN RADIO & TV BADGE	$90.00	Klinsmann Germany Authentic Adidas Jersey Size M	$22.52
1930 ORIGINAL FIRST SOCCER WORLD CUP. OFFICIAL BOOK	$89.50	PELE Starting Lineup Figure and Soccer Card	$22.00
1924 Olympic Colombes Football Official AUF Report Book	$87.00	GUADALAJARA CEMENTO TOLTECA MENS XL SOCCER JERSEY	$20.49
PUMA Cellerator Shudoh MLS Match Soccer Ball NEW sz 5	$70.00	OFFICIAL WORLD CUP 2006 LEIPZIG HOST CITY POSTER	$20.00
Rare Adidas Yugoslavia Football Soccer Jacket Shirt!	$70.00	LOT OF 3 ARGENTINA MEN'S SOCCER JERSEYS	$20.00
WORLD CUP 1994 FIFA SOCCER HUGE SPORT COLLECTION LOT	$68.00	1994 World Cup Soccer Coca Cola 6-pack Bottles-NR!	$19.99

Fan Apparel & Souvenirs ▸ Tennis

The average sales price in this subcategory is $16.75.

	HIGH		AVG
BEAUTIFUL PORCELAIN SIGN - TENNIS SHOES REQUIRED 20'S	$188.50	Reebok ANDY RODDICK Mesh Back Hat Cap US OPEN	$19.99
Vintage FILA BJ BORG Track TENNIS JACKET SUIT 80S MINT	$187.50	Nike OFFICIAL Wimbledon US Open Men's Tennis T-Shirt	$19.99
Tennis -1903 Doherty on Lawn Tennis RARE FINE BOOK	$125.00	1923 LAWN TENNIS ANNUAL. Spalding's Athletic Library	$19.99
STRING TIN BY VICTOR AND LENGTHS OF EARLY GUT	$123.01	DAVID BECKHAM SIGNED AUTOGRAPHED	$18.99
TABLE TENNIS BOXED SET c1905	$86.00	8x10 UK SOCCER CHAMP	
MARIA SHARAPOVA BOBBLEHEAD WITH UNTORN TICKET	$82.00	2005 Maria Sharapova Home	$18.00
[2 of these sold in a multiple item ("Dutch") auction for $41.00 each]		Depot Center SGA Bobble Head	
2005 Maria Sharapova Home Depot Center SGA Bobble Head	$81.75	JOHN McENROE PHOTOS x 6	$16.50
Maria Sharapova TENNIS Bobblehead Bobble Head SGA	$74.99	ILIE NASTASE PHOTOS x 5	$16.50
Maria Sharapova Bobblehead Bobble Head + Ticket SGA	$69.99	Andy Roddick 3D ACRYLIC TENNIS PHOTO SCULPTURE	$16.50
[2 of these sold for $69.99 each]		Martina Hingis Poster WTA Tennis Tour 16x20" VGC	$16.49
Maria Sharapova Bobblehead Bobble Head + Ticket SGA	$59.99	2 DVD Set Daniela Hantuchova Tennis Collection Vol. 2	$15.50
Tournament Tennis Balls in Sealed Tin Can (ENGLAND)	$59.50	NIB BALDWIN BRASS TENNIS RACQUET w/BALL ORNAMENT	$15.50
TENNIS 1930 PARIS FRANCE- DAVIS CUP CHAMPIONSHIPS	$55.00	John McEnroe Ivan Lendl Hit Hitting Tennis Balls Video	$15.40
Maria Sharapova TENNIS Bobblehead Bobble Head SGA	$55.00	Andre Agassi Vintage Nike Poster New Rare Tennis #1633	$15.00
HISTORY OF THE TENNIS RACQUET - FRAMED BEHIND GLASS	$51.00	Maria Sharapova Mug	$14.99
Maria Sharapova Bobblehead Bobble Head + Ticket SGA	$49.99	WILSON–TENNIS RACKET–OVERSIZE IMPACT–L@@K	$14.95

Fan Apparel & Souvenirs ▸ Wrestling-Professional

The average sales price in this subcategory is $15.15.

	HIGH		AVG
WWE Champion John Cena Spinner Replica Wrestling Belt	$177.50	WWF WWE TRIPLE H CLASSIC SUPERSTARS FIGURE BRAND NEW	$16.66
One Night Stand ECW Ringside Folding Chair WWE MINT WOW	$147.50	WCCW WORLD CLASS CHAMPIONSHIP WRESTLING 12/85 - 1/86	$16.48
Vintage Wrestling Poster Bobby Heenan 1950s-1960s Orig.	$128.64	Patriot Red/White/Blue w/Silver Eagle Wrestling Mask	$16.20
Authentic WCW United States Championship Belt	$125.00	WCW WWF WWE Wrestling Buddies Hulk Hogan & 2 Others	$16.00
WCW Deluxe World Championship Belt Replica	$124.50	WWE WWF WCW 1 OF A KIND RIC FLAIR	$16.00
Authentic WWE World Heavyweight Championship Belt	$122.50	CARVEDON GLASS !!!!!	
Pro Wrestling Boots WWE WCW ECW TNA ROH WWF Like New!	$88.00	WWF Million Dollar Man Wrestling Buddy	$15.50
WWE REY MYSTERIO REPLICA MASK	$85.00	WWE Backlash PPV promotional poster feat. Triple H	$15.50
REY MYSTERIO WWE REAL SIZE REPLICA MASK WHITE	$79.99	WWE New Year's Evolution PPV poster feat. Dave Batista	$15.50
[2 of these sold for $79.99 each]		La parka Grim Reaper wrestling mask lucha libre	$15.50
REY MYSTERIO WWE REALSIZE REPLICA MASK BLACK	$69.99	Masked Superstar Red/Black Wrestling Mask	$15.43
Vintage Wrestling Poster Wilbur Snyder 50s-60s orig.	$61.00	Atlantis Lucha Libre Wrestling Mask NEW wwe	$15.01
GLACIER,WCW,ARMOR,Leg Grieves,2,Ring Worn,Autograph,WWE	$60.00	EL SANTO wrestling mask lucha libre BELT BUCKLE NEW!!	$15.01
WWF WWE RAW 1997 SEASON VHS TAPES FREE WITH IVORY CARD	$56.01	3 Wrestling CD's Bad Street USA Slam Jam Hulk	$15.00
WWE REY MYSTERIO REPLICA MASK	$55.00	Atlantis Pro Wrestling Mask! Like New WWE ECW WCW TNA	$15.00
New Strongbad strong bad wrestling Mask halloween Rare	$54.99	WCW Hulk Hogan 2 Hats Bandana Tear Away shirt	$14.99

Game Used Memorabilia ▸ Baseball-MLB

The average sales price in this subcategory is $41.15.

	HIGH		AVG
Sammy Sosa Used Fielding Glove	$700.00	'04 KC ROYALS Used Locker Nameplate-JOE RANDA!	$45.44
1950 JOHNNY VANDER MEER Game Used Cubs Hat Cap *Reds	$650.00	2005 05 HALL OF FAME KIRBY PUCKETT AUTO # 1 / 25 !!!!	$45.44
Boston Red Sox Carl Yastrzemski Game Worn Cleats RARE	$606.60	2004 N.Y. YANKEES (N.Y. POST) MEDALLION SET:	$45.00
2004 ALL STAR GAME WORN JERSEY BY JEFF FRANCOEUR	$590.00	1998 New York Yankees Original Line-up card Derek Jeter	$45.00
2004 SWEET SPOT JOE DIMAGGIO AUTO! "YANKEE CLIPPER" WOW	$515.00	Boston Red Sox Original Piece of THE GREEN MONSTER	$44.00
AUTHENTIC BUSCH STADIUM SEATS~GET 'EM NOW~NO WAITING!	$465.00	DAMON MINOR Fresno Grizzlies 2004 Game-Worn Jacket #22	$41.00
Vinny Castilla game used auto Fielder's Glove Nationals	$431.00	2005 DONRUSS TONY GWYNN AUTOGRAPHED,JERSEY CARD!!	$40.00
Chad Orvella Autographed Game Used Fielding Glove	$399.99	SF GIANTS AUTHENTIC GAME USED LINEUP CARD v. DODGERS	$39.99
BIG RED MACHINE SIGNED DAVE CONCEPCION GAME-USED HAT!!!	$399.99	2003 ABSOLUTE MEMORABILIA ALEX RODRIGUEZ HR BASE CARD	$39.70
2005 Rare Detroit Tiger All Star Game Chair Tickets	$399.00	04' GAME PATCH 1/1 DEREK JETER YANKEES MUST SEE 21/22 !	$39.50
Pedro Martinez Game Used New York Mets Hat ESM	$330.01	Red Sox 2004 World Series Champions Champagne Bottle	$39.00
Phillies JOHN KRUK Game Used 1st Baseman Fielding Glove	$299.99	Shannon Stewart Minnesota Twins Game Used Hat	$38.50
GEORGE BUSH AUTOGRAPHED BOB WATSON GAME-WORN ASTROS HAT	$299.99	Edgar Renteria game worn pants St. Louis Cardinals	$37.00
c 1980 Larry Bowa Phillies Game Used Baseball Hat - Cap	$295.00	2005 05 HALL OF FAME BOB GIBSON AUTO PANTS# 3 / 5!!!	$36.99
Gavin Floyd Game Used Phillies Fielders Glove ESM	$281.87	2000 Texas Rangers Game Used Batting Helmet ESM	$36.50

Game Used Memorabilia ▸ Basketball-NBA

The average sales price in this subcategory is $66.33.

	HIGH		AVG
LeBron James Game Used Worn Highschool Shoes WOW!!	$4,050.00	04/05 UD EXQUISITE AUTO ENSHRINEMENTS YAO MING 6/25	$74.25
Dwyane Wade Auto "Game Worn/Used" PLAYOFFS Shoes! #1/11	$1,680.00	Basketball Drill Videos Series pass, shoot,dribble,DVDS	$74.01
MOSES MALONE ATLANTA HAWKS GAME	$1,326.01	Kevin Garnett MN Timberwolves game used shooting shirt	$72.00
USED/WORN NBA JERSEY		Popeye Jones Dallas Mavericks Blue Game Issued Jersey	$71.23

1987-88 ARTIS GILMORE BOSTON CELTICS GAME WORN JERSEY	$1,000.00	Minnesota Timberwolves un-used game jersey pro-cut	$71.09
Kevin Garnett Timberwolves Game Used Worn Jersey Shorts	$1,000.00	Kevin Garnett MN Twolves game used shooting shirt S/S	$69.21
Manu Ginobili 04-05 Game Shoes - Championship Season	$750.00	Pavel Podkolzin Dallas Mavericks PDiddy Game Jersey	$65.75
76ers- game worn used Allen Iverson jersey, starting $1	$560.00	2004-05 HOOPS NAMEPLATE AUTO MANU GINOBILI #d 06 /25	$61.00
CHRIS MULLIN WARRIORS GAME USED/WORN BASKETBALL JERSEY	$550.00	ERICK BARKLEY 01/02 Trail Blazers Game Issue Jersey	$60.00
KARL MALONE UTAH JAZZ GAME USED/WORN BASKETBALL JERSEY	$550.00	[2 of these sold for $60.00 each]	
LEBRON JAMES "Game Used/Worn" Nike SB Low DUNK! #1/1!!	$540.00	Abdul-Wahad Dallas Mavericks White Game Issued Jersey	$56.09
Vince Carter "Game Worn/Used" ROOKIE ROY Season Jersey!	$504.99	Penny Hardaway Practice Shorts Knicks Game Worn	$56.00
AL WOOD SEATTLE SONICS GAME USED/WORN BASKETBALL JERSEY	$402.00	Chucky Atkins Lakers 2004-05 Game Used Worn Auto Shoes	$56.00
Chris Mihm Lakers 04-05 Game Used Worn Nike Auto Shoes	$368.00	AWESOME GAMES USED BALL, FLOOR, JERSEY LOT	$55.00
2002-2003 KOBE BRYANT SP GAME USED AUTOGRAPHED PATCH	$350.02	03 KOBE/JORDAN JERSEY CARD SPX WINNING COMBOS	$54.57
Scottie Pippen Game Worn Shoes-Autographed	$350.00	Latrell Sprewell Timberwolves game used shooting shirt	$52.24

Game Used Memorabilia ▸ Football-NFL

The average sales price in this subcategory is $41.12.

	HIGH		AVG
UD Peyton Manning GAME WORN Football HELMET Colts	$2,500.00	NEW REAL GLASS FULL SIZE FOOTBALL HELMET DISPLAY CASE	$44.99
Pittsburgh Steelers Joey Porter Autographed Jersey	$910.00	BILLY YATES MIAMI DOLPHINS GAME USED WORN JERSEY RARE	$44.03
Ronnie Brown 2005 Miami Dolphins un-used game jersey	$595.00	2003 AUTHENTIC GAME ISSUED KGB PACKERS SHOES / CLEATS	$43.66
Auth Michael Vick Signed 7 Jersey Game Worn 2004 Season	$575.00	20 game used jersey auto cards lot Football ser. #d rc	$41.05
WILSON ANTIQUE LEATHER SUSPENSION FOOTBALL HELMET D291	$480.99	WASHINGTON REDSKINS GAME USED JERSEY !!	$41.00
PRIEST HOLMES KANSAS CITY CHIEFS GAME USED CLEATS ESP	$470.02	BILLS ERIC MOULDS AUTO 2004 PAIR OF GAME WORN GLOVES!	$41.00
Korey Stringer Minnesota Vikings GAME USED Jersey #77	$410.00	Indianapolis Colts game used jersey #6 name removed	$40.00
RICKY WILLIAMS NFL game worn USED autod jersey DOLPHINS	$405.00	Indianapolis Colts game used jersey # 6 Jones	$40.00
DAN MARINO 1998 GAME ISSUED MIAMI DOLPHINS JERSEY	$404.00	Indianapolis Colts game used jersey #31 J Jackson	$40.00
Indianapolis Colts game used jersey #97 Bennett	$344.51	NEW REAL GLASS FOOTBALL DISPLAY CASE w/ CHERRY BASE	$39.99
Cadillac Williams 2005 Buccaneers un-used game jersey	$338.00	Jerry Rice Authentic College Jersey 49ers Raiders	$39.99
Chicago Bears Game Used/Worn Tony Parrish Jersey PSA	$330.00	NFL New York Giants GAME USED Gloves - Lawrence Taylor	$39.99
05 Donruss Classics SS RC Matt Jones auto 4/5	$330.00	NEW REAL GLASS FOOTBALL DISPLAY CASE w/ CHERRY BASE	$39.99
Chris Collinsworth 1980's Bengals game used road jersey	$307.00	Deluxe FS NFL NCAA Football Helmet Acrylic Display Case	$39.99
OAKLAND RAIDERS CHARLIE GARNER GAME WORN USED JERSEY	$305.00	NEW REAL GLASS FOOTBALL DISPLAY CASE w/ CHERRY BASE	$39.99

Game Used Memorabilia ▸ Hockey-NHL

The average sales price in this subcategory is $71.16.

	HIGH		AVG
WAYNE GRETZKY SIGNED AWAY JERSEY W/CERTIFICATE & FRAMED	$1,125.00	Tony Amonte Signed Game Used 1999 All-Star Stick Flames	$86.00
Brendan Shanahan Red Wings game used jersey 0102	$1,125.00	Oakland Seals NHL WHA Hockey Puck	$81.50
92-93 Joe Nieuwendyk Flames Road Jersey w/ C	$1,101.00	New England Whalers NHL WHA Hockey Puck	$81.00
03-04 Belfour Leafs Alternate Set 2 / Play-Offs	$911.00	AkBars04-05 GAME WORN Jersey/SJ Sharks-KC Blades-Berlin	$81.00
1983 Calgary Flames Paul Baxter game used hockey jersey	$767.33	Quesnel Mills GAME WORN Jersey/Chevrolet-Canada/9 patch	$81.00
RARE 'TRAIL OF THE STANLEY CUP' 3 VOLUMES CHAS COLEMAN	$660.00	Kentucky Thoroughblades Game Worn/Used Enforcer Jersey	$80.00
74-75 Blues Dureen Game Used Jersey	$660.00	SIGNED RED WINGS HOCKEY STICK - CHAISSON	$75.00
brendan shanahan game worn used jersey redwings	$500.00	Trevor Linden Vancouver Canucks used Stick Signed	$75.00
MARTY TURCO MICHIGAN AUTO'D GAME WORN	$500.00	'05 SP Auth. Patch/Auto Jari Kurri-3 colors!!! #63/100	$75.00
WHA New England Whalers Jersey Game worn	$500.00	AUTHENTIC GAME ISSUED ISLANDERS JERSEY LAFONTAINE	$72.77
76-77 Blues Dureen Game Used Jersey	$460.00	Kim Johnsson game used Philadelphia Flyers Skates	$70.00
1986-87 Basil McRae Nordiques Game worn/used jersey	$449.44	NORTH BAY CENTS GAME WORN JERSEY	$66.00
Game Worn Used Danbury Trashers Jersey - Stephen Peat	$430.00	Minnesota Wild Houston Aeros Game worn jersey	$65.00
N.J.Devils: SCOTT STEVENS NHL - ALL-STAR Jersey G.I.	$397.00	2003-04 Parkhurst Rookie Antero Niittymaki JSY RC /180!	$63.00
SIDNEY CROSBY GAME USED AUTO STICK CARD 2/150 PENGUINS	$380.00	Chris Pronger Goal Scored Puck	$62.00

Game Used Memorabilia ▸ Racing-Auto

The average sales price in this subcategory is $44.22.

	HIGH		AVG
Rusty Wallace Raced Firesuit Miller Genuine Draft 1991	$1,226.00	g force single layer firesuit size XL craftsman truck	$49.99
2003 RUSTY WALLACE RACE USED FIRESUIT - AUTOGRAPHED	$999.99	TONY STEWART BRICKYARD 400 RACE WIN PIECE	$49.99
Dale Earnhardt Race Suit Worn In "Baseketball"	$999.00	Dale Earnhardt 2005 Legends Treads and Threads	$47.00
Dale Earnhardt, JR Team Crew Uniform Busch Eury NR!!	$548.00	1998 IRL champion crew shirt Tony Stewart	$46.68
NASCAR Jeff Gordon #24 race used Autometer Tachometer	$306.88	NASCAR RCR Blue Spoiler signed by Bowyer, Childress	$46.55
Johnny Benson Nascar Firesuit Sparco nomex race used	$299.99	RARE MATT KENSETH RACE USED VISINE SHEETMETAL NICE	$46.00
Blue Hollywood sparco firesuit size 56 Tony Kanaan	$199.99	STP Richard Petty Pit Crew Jacket From 1970's *LOOK*	$42.56
2005 Impact nomex firesuit IRL Monunn Fernandez Indy500	$199.99	1952 Box Seat Indy 500 Ticket Stub	$41.00
MATT KENSETH # 17 RACE USED SAW BLADES REAR BUMPER	$189.49	Sparco race cat driving shoes new size 8	$40.99
2005 Premium Matt Kenseth firesuit signature ser.14/17	$188.58	Alex Zanardi Tony Kanaan pit crew shirt size large	$40.00
RYAN NEWMAN RACE USED SPEEDPASS REAR BUMPER SHEETMETAL	$187.50	2005 DARLINGTON NASCAR GOODYEAR TIRE-DALE EARNHARDT JR	$40.00
Vintage Miss Maverick Hydroplane U-12, 00 Display Signs	$179.50	Tony Stewart Scot Brayton pit crew shirt IRL 1996	$39.99
NASCAR CREW UNIFORM(RACE USED)JEREMY MAYFIELD	$175.00	Ricky Rudd Motorcraft Sheetmetal Nose Piece	$39.55
2005 Press PAss Mark Martin Triple Burner Redemption	$162.04	Dale Earnhardt, Jr. NASCAR Race Used Tire	$39.00
RYAN NEWMAN RACE USED SHEETMETAL DOOR 2003 WIN	$154.50	Sparco race cat driving shoes new never worn	$36.59

Vintage Sports Memorabilia ▸ Baseballs

The average sales price in this subcategory is $31.43.

	HIGH		AVG
Gusset Style Baseball - Mid 1800's	$800.00	2005 Felix Hernandez MLB autographed sweetspot COA	$36.00
Mickey Mantle Signed UDA Snow White Baseball!!!! NR!!!	$732.00	VINTAGE TURN OF THE CENTURY BOUNDER BASEBALL VERY RARE	$34.88

Vintage 1890-1915 Partridge Unopened Baseball	$676.66	WILLIE NELSON & BOB DYLAN TOUR BASEBALL SEALED + BONUS	$34.00
Mickey Mantle, Joe DiMaggio, Ted Williams Signed	$455.01	COMPLETE SET 1985 TOPPS BASEBALL CARDS,CLEMENS,McGWIRE	$33.17
MICKEY MANTLE HANK AARON WILLIE MAYS +8 AUTO BASEBALL	$380.00	Rare Collectible Oakland A's Souvenir baseball	$33.00
c 1880 Figure 8 Baseball - Vintage & Antique Sm. Stitch	$338.11	antique vintage BASEBALL BAT authentic early 1900s ring	$32.00
3 DOZEN RAWLINGS OFFICIAL MAJOR LEAGUE BASEBALL NEW!!!!	$329.01	TOBER "OFFICIAL LEAGUE" BASEBALL NO BOX NOS	$31.50
Vintage Catcher's Reeded Shin Guards; great look!	$305.00	Roger Clemens Auto Ball, SLU and Topps/Leaf Rookie Lot	$31.01
Vintage 1940's Reach Official League Baseball unopened	$237.50	Lot o3 World Series Baseballs 96,98,99(YANKEES WIN)	$30.55
Mickey Mantle Autographed Baseball!!!	$207.57	2005 BOWMAN COMPLETE SET(330 IN SET)	$30.00
MICKEY MANTLE WILLIE MAYS SIGNED BASEBALL W/COA	$202.50	2005 DONRUSS TEAM HEROES COMPLETE SET (440)	$30.00
MICKEY MANTLE SANDY KOUFAX AUTOGRAPHED BASEBALL W/ COA	$187.50	3 HOF Autographed Baseballs-MUST SEE!	$30.00
Vintage Spalding Baseball & Original Box	$152.50	LARGE NEGRO LEAGUE LOT-MUST SEE!	$29.99
ICHIRO Suzuki auto baseball w/ Mariner's COA -signature	$149.50	YANKEES MICKEY MANTLE JOE DIMAGGIO AUTO 4X6 SCOREBOARD	$29.99
1940's Reach William Harridge American League Baseball	$147.50	San Francisco Giants Commemorative Baseballs	$29.95

Vintage Sports Memorabilia ▶ Bats

The average sales price in this subcategory is $51.52.

	HIGH		AVG
1950'S ROY SIEVERS SENATORS GAME USED BASEBALL BAT	$585.00	Small Old Louisville Slugger Bat Gordon Babe Phelps	$56.85
TONY CONIGLIARO LOUISVILLE SLUGGER	$504.00	OLD WOODEN KEYSTONE LEAGUE BASEBALL BAT Mfg. ELDRED, Pa	$56.00
WOODEN BASEBALL BAT		1920s 14" Lewis Hack Wilson Souvernir Mini Bat	$54.53
Napoleon Lajoie vintage decal baseball bat – rare!	$500.00	1920s 22" George Sisler Souvenir Mini Bat Louisville Sl	$53.03
Lou Gehrig Louisville Slugger H & B 34 1930's Store Bat	$431.00	THURMAN MUNSON BAT!!! H&B (GENUINE MODEL S44) BEAUTY!	$52.00
Old Original 1900's Hillerich & Son Baseball Decal Bat	$403.74	36" LS 125 JACKIE ROBINSON "AUTO" BASEBALL BAT	$52.00
Early Babe Ruth Bat Louisville Slugger 40 B.R.	$383.00	Antique Goldsmith Diamond Ball /Playground Baseball Bat	$51.00
Great Old Roberto Clemente Hillerich & Bradsby Bat MINT	$367.00	CHARLES JOHNSON GAME USED BASEBALL BAT WHITESOX	$51.00
Jorge Posada Game Used Professional Model Black Bat.	$350.00	Vintage Burke Hanna bat 34" bat logo Diamond Ball bat	$50.99
Vintage/Antique Baseball Bat Johnny Evers model	$350.00	Mickey Mantle 125 Louisville Slugger Bat Collectable	$50.00
BARRY BONDS AUTOGRAPHED BIG STICK BAT- TRI STAR	$345.00	Old 125 Louisville Slugger Bat R17 Jackie Robinson	$50.00
Tony Conigliaro Louisville Slugger Bat, NEW	$325.00	OLD MICKEY MANTLE MODEL LITTLE LEAGUE BASEALL BAT	$49.99
Antique Stall & Dean E.T.(Eddie) Collins Bat	$280.00	Deluxe Acrylic Baseball Bat Wall Mountable Display Case	$49.99
Ted Williams 1966 Hall Of Fame Induction Bat	$231.50	[2 of these sold for $49.99 each]	
Joe DiMaggio 1955 Hall Of Fame Induction Bat	$225.00	2000 WORLD CHAMPION *N.Y.YANKEES* LIMITED EDITION BAT!	$49.95
BASEBALL BAT VINTAGE BINGLER BAT DIAMOND MFG.	$224.50	Mickey Mantle bat...125S...34" MMS4..Louisville Slugger	$45.00

Vintage Sports Memorabilia ▶ Bobble Heads

The average sales price in this subcategory is $25.16.

	HIGH		AVG
MINNESOTA TWINS SGA 1965 SET OF 10 BOBBLEHEADS W COA'S	$1,184.85	Bob GIBSON Bobblehead BOBBLE HEAD SGA Cardinals W/STUB	$26.52
60's SAN FRANCISCO GIANTS mini BOBBING HEAD	$515.05	2002 BOWMAN CHROME DRAFT JHONNY PERALTA 5CT ROOKIE	$26.01
Rare/Vintage California Angels Bobblehead Bobble Head	$305.00	Ben Sheets Milwaukee Brewers Huntsville Stars Bobble	$26.00
Set of 7 SAMS 500 HR Bobblehead Mays Aaron Banks+4 More	$300.00	PAUL MOLITOR Milwaukee Brewers Bobblehead BRAND NEW	$26.00
Vintage Minnesota Twins Bobblehead Bobble Head	$227.50	WOODY HAYES BOBBLEHEAD BOBBLE HEAD RARE L@@K	$26.00
Vintage Oakland Athletics A's Bobblehead Bobble Head	$207.50	MATT TUIASOSOPO Everett Aquasox Bobble Head SGA Mariner	$24.99
Old/Vintage Baltimore Orioles Bobblehead Bobble Head	$202.50	NY METS 2005 SGA LUNCH BOX W/STUB LUNCHBOX KIDS	$24.99
SF Giants Duane Kuiper Mike Krukow Bobblehead Doll	$200.00	Rare Miguel Tejada A's SGA SGB Bobblehead With Ticket	$24.05
1961 WHITE SQUARE BASE CLEVELAND INDIAN WAHOO NODDER	$190.50	Memphis Redbirds/Cardinals So Taguchi SGA bobblehead	$23.01
1967 Washington Senators Baseball Bobblehead	$180.27	American Girl outfit, Reds Away uniform, August 6th	$22.88
VINTAGE NEW YORK YANKEES BOBBLE HEAD IN ORIGINAL BOX!	$175.00	Bob Gibson St. Louis Cardinals Bobble Head Doll N/R	$22.53
Old/Vintage Cincinnati Reds Bobblehead Bobble Head	$141.55	Jim Catfish Hunter A's SGA SGB Bobblehead With Ticket	$22.50
Vintage Chicago White Sox Bobblehead Bobble Head	$130.39	Jeter and Rodriguez Yankees Bobblehead/Bobble Head	$21.95
Lebron James bobblehead / bobble head / ERROR all star	$121.50	2005 Bobble Head SGA Felix Hernandez Mariners 66ers	$21.05
Old/Vintage New York Yankees Bobblehead Bobble Head	$113.61	Dennis Bonvie Bobblehead	$21.00

Vintage Sports Memorabilia ▶ Cereal Boxes

The average sales price in this subcategory is $8.92.

	HIGH		AVG
1935 Wheaties Box Back Lou Gehrig New York Yankees	$168.50	Cecil Travis 1937 Wheaties - Series 9 #15	$9.99
Lou Gehrig 1935 "Wheaties"	$111.50	Billy Herman 1937 Wheaties - Series 6 #10	$9.99
PETE ROSE/MARY RETTON/WALTER PAYTON/JORDAN/WHEATIES BOX	$71.00	Wheaties Redskins Cereal Super Bowl XXVI 1992	$9.99
1935 DIZZY DEAN Grape Nuts Baseball prize booklet	$58.78	BERWICK BULLDOGS 1996 PA AAA STATE CHAMPIONS CEREAL BOX	$9.97
1996 US Womens Gymnastic Autographed Wheaties Box	$52.20	1991 NFL Champions NY Giants Wheaties box	$9.38
1935 Wheaties Cereal Jimmie Foxx w/ Tab from box	$50.00	Schoolboy Rowe 1936 Wheaties - Series 4 #9	$9.19
1937 Wheaties Box Back Joe DiMaggio New York Yankees	$49.99	BABE RUTH SEALED WHEATIES SIGNED BOX W/COA!	$8.99
1935 Wheaties Cereal Pepper Martin w/ Tab from box	$49.87	Wheaties cereal box "Dan Marino's record breaker"	$8.99
1935 Wheaties Cereal Gus Mancuso w/ Tab from box	$42.89	CEREAL BOXES 6 RARE- FLUTIE FLAKES, HOT WHEELS, JORDAN	$8.99
1935 Wheaties Cereal Jack Armstrong w/ Tab from box	$33.25	San Francisco 49ERs Wheaties Box Joe Montana	$8.75
4x Michael Jordan Wheaties Boxes HBV $200 w/1st Edition	$26.59	Wheaties boxes olympics women's hockey gymnastics gold	$7.99
JERRY RICE AUTOGRAPHED WHEATIES BOX ENCASED IN PLASTIC	$26.00	Michael Jordan FIRST EDITION Wheaties Box Unopened	$7.50
Complete set of 4 Dale Earnhardt Sr. Wheaties Boxes	$25.00	lot of 13 wheaties box, chicago bulls, micheal jordan,	$7.49
ST. LOUIS RAMS SUPERBOWL CHAMPS WHEATIES BOX	$20.55	WHEATIES CEREAL BOX JIM THORPE	$7.00
Pete Rose Autographed 1986 Wheaties Box	$20.51	LARRY BIRD WHEATIES BOX (UNOPENED)	$6.50

Vintage Sports Memorabilia ▸ Gloves-Baseball

The average sales price in this subcategory is $51.89.

	HIGH		AVG
Vintage Leather Honus Wagner Baseball Glove-NR	$1,275.00	VINTAGE MICKEY MANTLE PERSONAL MODEL BASEBALL GLOVE	$78.00
Vintage Grover C. Alexander Baseball Glove	$1,000.00	1950s STAN MUSIAL HOH RAWLINGS PM BASEBALL GLOVE - RARE	$76.97
RARE-1950s WILLIE MAYS 3 FINGER USA BASEBALL GLOVE - A1	$364.99	Rawlings GJ67 Roberto Clemente Glove	$74.15
Mariano Rivera Yankees signed game-model glove Steiner	$364.00	EARLY 20TH CENTURY VINTAGE BASEBALL GLOVE	$66.99
1920's WINCHESTER Baseball Fielders Glove; 1" web	$306.00	Vintage Wilson A2000 Professional Baseball Glove $$$$	$66.97
VINTAGE FRANK MALZONE RAWLINGS FIELDING AWARD GLOVE	$304.00	SPALDING USA JIM NORTHRUP BASEBAL GLOVE NICE PRO MODEL	$60.99
VINTAGE 1950'S JOE DIMAGGIO BASEBALL MITT GLOVE REACH	$255.00	Very Unusual Baseball Glove-Macgregor Goldsmith!	$56.00
Mervyn Shea Buckleback Baseball Glove-UNLISTED!	$231.49	Lot of 4 VINTAGE ANTIQUE BASEBALL GLOVE GLOVES & MASK !	$52.00
2038 BAD NEWS BEARS Kelly's "Akadema" Baseball Glove	$189.00	Vintage Rawlings "Special" Baseball Glove-Pics	$50.99
EARLY 1900'S SPALDING BASEBALL GLOVE WITH 2" WEB	$179.50	Vintage Johnny Callison Phillies Baseball Glove 1960`s	$50.00
1940s DIXIE WALKER 2 FINGER GLOVE - EARLY- BKLYN DODGER	$177.50	Rare 50s Mint Rawlings Spalding Colavito Baseball Glove	$49.95
ROGER CLEMENS HAND SIGNED COOPER BASEBALL GLOVE / NR	$151.99	1930'S DIB WILLIAMS LEATHER BASEBALL GLOVE PHILA A'S	$47.51
Vintage AL KALINE Baseball Gloves WILSON EXCELLENT COND	$132.50	5 1950's MacGregor baseball glove endorsement photos	$46.97
VINTAGE RARE WEB FINGER SPALDING BASEBALL GLOVE 1913	$123.50	RAWLINGS 12'RH ANDRE DAWSON MODEL BASEBALL GLOVE-EX.	$46.75
OLD LEATHER ODD-STYLE BASEBALL GLOVE?	$122.50	VINTAGE BILLY HERMAN BASEBALL GLOVE HUTCH	$46.01

Vintage Sports Memorabilia ▸ Pennants, Flags

The average sales price in this subcategory is $19.03.

	HIGH		AVG
Green Bay Packers Pennant, VINTAGE, Football	$511.00	Dallas Cowboys 3x5' nylon flag	$20.30
Vintage/Antique PURDUE ROSE BOWL PENNANT FLAG from 1967	$273.63	Football Pennant Lot - 17 Different Football Pennants	$20.00
RARE 1959 NATIONAL LEAGUE ALL STARS PENNANT!! L@@K!!	$167.50	1970'S NHL ATLANTA FLAMES PENNANT - TOUGH 2 FIND!	$20.00
Baseball All Stars Pennant, VINTAGE Dimaggio, 1949	$162.27	VINTAGE KANSAS CITY ATHLETICS BASEBALL PENNANT	$19.99
New York Giants Pennant, VINTAGE, Baseball 1954	$161.39	St Louis Cardinals Football Pennant c 1960s Old Logo	$19.99
1965 MN Twins World Series Pennant and Ticket Stub	$156.40	CINCINNATI REDS 1930'S-1950'S ERA MINI-PENNANT 4" x 9"	$19.95
Los Angeles Rams Pennant, VINTAGE, Banner	$132.51	ST LOUIS CARDINALS 1930'S-1950'S ERA MINI-PENNANT 4"x9"	$19.95
1950s GREEN BAY PACKER Football Pennant NO RESERVE!!!!!	$125.50	Football Field Felt Mat/ESPN/Miller Lite Logos	$19.75
Canada Cup 1972 Pennant	$122.50	CINCINNATI REDS CHAMPIONSIP PENNANTS 1975 AND 1990	$19.48
Washington Redskins Pennant, VINTAGE, Banner	$121.49	1969 Atlanta Braves M.L.B.Pennant Near Mint	$19.05
1963 World Series Pennant Yankees vs. Dodgers EX+ Cond.	$113.50	10 PENNANT FLAG TOP LOADERS 12 x 30 HOLDERS TOPLOADERS	$18.99
VINTAGE BASEBALL PENNANT - DETROIT TIGERS - 1945 !	$111.38	[2 of these sold for $18.99 each]	
VINTAGE SAN FRANCISCO GIANTS	$106.50	NEW 3' X 5' TEXAS LONGHORN FLAG - UNIVERSITY OF TEXAS	$18.50
PENNANT /WILLIE MAYS PIN		vintage banner,pennant,washington redskins, old !	$18.50
US OPEN Golf flag, signed by Nicklaus, Palmer 1994	$104.61	5 SAN FRANCISCO Sports Pennants, 1-Warriors, 4-49ers	$18.27
Chicago Cardinals Pennant, VINTAGE Football	$104.35	1980 Philadelphia Phillies Pennant World Champs MINT	$17.99

Vintage Sports Memorabilia ▸ Photos

The average sales price in this subcategory is $13.06.

	HIGH		AVG
GREAT 1892 Sewanee, Tenn. Football Team Photo	$333.00	2 MARK MARTIN Nascar photo poster size prints NASCAR	$16.16
MICKEY MANTLE HANK AARON WILLIE MAYS +1 AUTO BASEBALL	$332.79	Dodgers Sal Maglie 1956 no-hitter wire photo!	$16.06
Ted Williams last home run 1960 wire photo!	$158.50	Dan Marino Miami Dolphins original slide with rights #2	$16.05
NY ISLANDERS STANLEY CUP FRAMED PHOTO COLLAGE	$49.99	1960s Billy Casper Wilson Staff Advisory PGA Golf Photo	$16.00
RAMBLIN RECK WRECK GEORGIA TECH WILLIAM PLANTE FRAMED	$49.00	Dan Marino Miami Dolphins original slide with rights #F	$15.50
1947 wire photo Cardinals Stan Musial Enos Slaughter!!	$42.00	Dodgers Duke Snider! 1952 Baseball magazine poster!	$15.05
Golf wire photo Gene Sarazen 1935 Ryder Cup practice!!	$39.99	Green Bay Packers Ray Nitschke Williams Print	$14.99
Steve Carlton 10 x 12 Beautiful Frame, Autographed, COA	$39.95	1976 Kroger Cincinnati Reds Set of 16 - Johnny Bench	$14.99
1986 N.Y.METS FRAMED PHOTO COLLAGE CARTER/HERNANDEZ	$38.99	Dodgers Ralph Branca ! 1947 Baseball magazine poster!	$13.16
GIANTS FRAMED PHOTO COLLAGE LAWRENCE TAYLOR+ PHIL SIMMS	$38.99	Dodgers Preacher Roe 1949 World Series wire photo!	$12.56
Forbes Field- Empty Stands	$38.00	VINTAGE EX RARE AL SCHOENDIENST CARDINAL BASEBALL PHOTO	$12.50
Boxing 1970 Muhammad Ali Jerry Quarry action wire photo	$33.03	1924 Hugh Jennings / Frank Frisch Giants Wire Photo.	$12.35
Dodgers 1949 Team pic! 1949 Baseball magazine poster!	$27.00	c. 1951 New York Giants Baseball Wire photo w/ Maglie.	$12.05
OSCAR DELAHOYA VS JULIO CESAR CHAVEZ PHOTO	$27.00	G. Burke Photo of Red Sox Max Bishop	$11.97
Dodgers Carl Furillo! 1948 Baseball magazine poster!	$26.00	Tiger Woods 11x14 matted and Framed Masters Photo	$11.55

Vintage Sports Memorabilia ▸ Pins

The average sales price in this subcategory is $17.74.

	HIGH		AVG
1920s Kolbs Bread baseball player pins Reading, PA orig	$450.00	6 Indian little league pins	$20.01
ROSE BOWL 1957 HAWKEYES BADGE PIN PASADENA CA	$418.69	Lance Armstrong Ltd.Ed. 6X Lapel Pin Set	$20.00
Ted Kluszewski's 1954 All Star Press Pin *Reds*	$330.57	1965 Twins Pinback Button. World Series v. Dodgers.	$20.00
SCARCE 1950'S MARTY MARION PM10 BASEBALL PIN BROWNS	$316.99	Parnelli Jones STP SEARS POINT PIN LOT Vintage	$20.00
1945 Cleveland Rams NFL World Championship Pin RARE	$316.00	2005 Allstate 400 Brickyard Collector Pin	$20.00
1912 Boston Red Sox - Shuman & Co Champions Pin Pinback	$292.00	COLONIAL NATIONAL INVITATION 1969 GOLF PIN D. FORSHAGEN	$19.99
Ted Kluszewski's 1956 All Star Press Pin *Reds*	$227.50	16 HYDRO HYDROPLANE BUTTONS	$19.39
Ted Kluszewski's 1955 All Star Press Pin *Reds*	$213.50	8 Older Wizzard little league pins	$18.50
1956 PM15 Yellow Base Path Baseball Pin – Kluszewski	$140.00	1933 Cracker Jack Al Simmons Pin	$18.36
1910-12 SWEET CAPORAL LOT OF 5 PINS WITH PSA 6 & 7!!	$134.06	Herman Wehmeier 1956 Topps Pin (PHILLIES)	$17.50
1910-12 SWEET CAPORAL LOT OF 5 PINS WITH PSA 6 & 7!!	$126.00	4 Fort and Indian little league pins	$17.01
1910-12 SWEET CAPORAL PINS LOT OF (6) ALL PSA 6!!	$119.50	2005 BRICKYARD Allstate 400 LIMITED EDITION PIN	$17.00
1910-12 SWEEET CAPORAL LOT OF 5 PINS ALL PSA 6!!	$108.50	1963 Minnesota Gophers Homecoming Michigan Wolverines	$16.52
1967 World Series Press Pin Boston Red Sox Fenway Park	$105.00	TRMF LITTLE LEAGUE PIN JAPAN GLOVE PINS	$16.51
1967 World Series Press Pin - St. Louis Cardinals	$104.05	Two Ducks Unlimited Auto Emblems	$16.50

Vintage Sports Memorabilia ▸ Publications

The average sales price in this subcategory is $17.48.

	HIGH		AVG
New York Baseball Club Official 1898 Scorecard	$499.00	SOCCER: Lot of Two Different New York Generals Programs	$18.29
George Foreman - Joe Frazier Program	$393.00	INDIANS JACOBS FIELD 1ST GAME PROGRAM	$17.99
Alabama Football Run in the Mud by Daniel Moore	$255.99	1988 Cubs 1st Wrigley night game program/ticket/photos	$17.99
1935 NOTRE DAME OHIO STATE Game of the Century Program	$250.00	Boxing Program :CASTILLO-CORRALES from 5/7/05 Fight	$17.50
Pittsburg Pirate Program Sept. 7 1917	$221.59	1970-71 Vancouver Canucks Yearbook Guide Program Mag	$17.49
15 State Playoff Programs TX High School Football 1950s	$197.50	SOCCER: 91/2 MISL Baltimore Blast International Program	$17.49
INGEMAR JOHANSSON - FLOYD PATTERSON III BOXING PROGRAM	$118.61	1987 Massillon Tigers Canton Bulldogs Football Program	$17.43
Tyson-Spinks 1988 Heavyweight On-Site Boxing Programs	$89.01	BIG 33 KEYSTONE CLASSIC FOOTBALL PRGM HERSHEY PA 1981	$17.30
(50) Wimbledon Palais Wrestling Programs 1959 Signed UK	$81.00	1951 Knockout Fight Program Manuel Ortiz Boxing	$16.80
1960 World Series Program Pirates @ Yankees	$71.00	1970-71 Detroit Red Wings Yearbook Guide Program Mag	$16.50
1970 Texas Notre Dame Football Program Cotton bowl MORE	$67.00	1996 Centennial Olympic Games Souvenir Program Atlanta	$16.49
1969 NBA all-star game program	$67.00	1998 Massillon Tigers Canton Bulldogs Football Program	$16.43
Hagler-Hearns 1985 Official On-site Boxing Programs 5	$67.00	Boxing Annual & Boxing Year Books - 1960's	$16.16
Vintage NFL Detroit Lions Football Program DOAK WALKER	$56.69	1936 MINOR LEAGUE HOCKEY GAME PROGRAM..RARE	$16.01
18 Different Texas State Football Championship Programs	$56.55	Fitchburg High School Waren Muir Historical LOT	$16.01

Vintage Sports Memorabilia ▸ Shirts

The average sales price in this subcategory is $20.73.

	HIGH		AVG
500 Homerun Club Atlanta Braves Jersey Mitchell & Ness	$234.02	***DAN MARINO*** HALL OF FAME POLO SHIRT MEN SZ L	$26.00
BOCA JUNIORS ARGENTINA JERSEY MATCH WORN SCHIAVI	$120.00	**DAN MARINO** HALL OF FAME POLO SHIRT MEN SZ XL	$25.49
1960's NATIONAL LEAGUE BASEBALL STARS CHILDS T-SHIRT	$103.00	embroidery Mitsubishi motor F1 Team racing Shirt M	$25.00
BOCA JUNIORS X MODEL 1907 MATCH	$95.00	**DAN MARINO** HALL OF FAME POLO SHIRT MEN SZ XL	$22.99
WORN ONLY 3 GAMES!		Eagles Terrell Owens Football Jersey (XL)	$22.50
Mitchell And Ness Throwback John Elway Jersey	$56.00	Mountain Dew Southern 500 T-Shirt- Hard to find	$20.51
1950's ROGERS HORNSBY BASEBALL CAMP JERSEY - Cardinals	$55.00	Raiders Jerry Rice Football Jersey (XL)	$20.50
Authentic Joe Montana Notre Dame Jersey size 60(5XL)	$49.00	WWF VINTAGE Cactus Jack "WANTED" SHIRT 1998 XL ECW WWE	$20.00
EARL CAMPBELL #34 OILERS THROWBACKS JERSEY SIZE 52	$40.65	***DAN MARINO*** HALL OF FAME POLO SHIRT MEN SZ L	$19.99
1930's -40's Wool Baseball Jersey ~Vincennes, IN~	$39.95	[2 of these sold for $19.99 each]	
DAN MARINO HALL OF FAME POLO SHIRT MEN SZ XL	$35.13		

Vintage Sports Memorabilia ▸ Ticket Stubs

The average sales price in this subcategory is $37.36.

	HIGH		AVG
1930 Bobby Jones US Golf Championship grand slam ticket	$1,534.65	SUPERBOWL XIV 14 ticket stub Rose Bowl RAMS/STEELERS	$39.99
Cassius Clay (Ali) Sonny Liston Boxing Ticket ~ Unused	$624.11	Vintage 1931 Michigan Stadium Football Stubs-Ohio St...	$39.99
1938 WORLD SERIES FULL TICKET DIMAGGIO HOMERS NM-MT	$611.77	1953 COTTON BOWL Football Ticket TEXAS TENNESSEE	$39.85
1932 Yankees Chicago Cubs World Series Ticket Babe Ruth	$535.01	Saint Louis Cardinals, 1968 World Series Ticket Stubs	$38.51
Superbowl I Ticket Stub- VG to Excellent Condition *NR*	$341.06	9-9-1992 FULL TICKET MINT~ROBIN YOUNT 3000 HITS	$37.99
Pair Unused Superbowl XXXIX (39) tickets w/envelope	$340.00	Japanese Baseball Hideo Nomo Debut Ticket 5/2/95 Japan	$37.00
Superbowl I Ticket Stub- VG-Excellent Condition *NR*	$320.00	1979 Ohio State at Michigan Full Unused FB Ticket	$36.78
1955 World Series Ticket Yankees @ Dodgers Game #5	$311.00	MADDUX 3000 Strikeout Full TICKET Choice Grade Cubs PSA	$36.51
1951 NFL L.A RAMS vs CLEVELAND WORLD CHAMPION TICKET	$305.00	10/3/53 Baltimore Colts vs Detroit Lions Full Ticket	$36.50
World Series Tickets stubs from 1967 - 1979	$300.00	1965 INDY 500 INTERNATIONAL TICKET IN FRAME	$36.01
1956 YANKEES & DODGERS WORLD SERIES TICKET	$282.01	1953 WORLD SERIES GAME 2 TICKET STUB..NEW YORK YANKEES	$36.00
1931 ROSE BOWL TICKET STUB	$262.57	1982 world series game four unused ticket	$36.00
1940 Indianapolis Indy 500 Original Full Ticket MINT	$251.09	Dennis Martinez Perfect Game Ticket Stub 7-28-91	$36.00
04 BOSTON RED SOX G2 MINT WORLD SERIES FULL TICKET1stub	$226.55	1962 YANKEES GIANTS GAME 5 WORLD SERIES TICKET STUB	$36.00
1947 World Series Ticket Yankees @ Dodgers Game #5	$226.27	2003 Philadelphia Eagles Inaugual Season Ticket Sheet	$35.55

Vintage Sports Memorabilia ▸ Other

The average sales price in this subcategory is $28.45.

	HIGH		AVG
1920s Vintage Coin Operated Babe Ruth Mutoscope Machine	$1,202.88	1960 World Series Ashtray – Bucs Beat Yanks	$29.99
2 TB Buccaneers @ NE Patriots LL Tickets 12/17/05	$510.00	NEW DELUXE FULL SIZE FOOTBALL CHERRY WOOD DISPLAY CASE	$29.99
Don Drysdale Original 60's Hartland Statue Dodgers	$460.00	1/18 1967 St. Louis Cardinals Chevrolet Corvette *RARE*	$29.97
1982-83 VINCE TAYLOR N.Y. KNICKS GAME WORN JERSEY	$280.00	1971 WICHITA STATE EZRA BROOKS WHEAT SHOCKER DECANTER I	$29.49
Roger Maris Original 60's Hartland Statue Yankees	$280.00	1980 ENTIRE OLYMPICS MIRACLE ON ICE USA HOCKEY TEAM DVD	$28.98
1886 BASEBALL DIE CUT H. RICHARDSON DETROIT WOLVERINES	$270.00	1979 APBA baseball card set	$28.02
1964 TOPPS STAND-UP MICKEY MANTLE..EXTREMELY NICE..RARE	$224.50	1930 Vintage Silver Trophy - Basketball	$27.99
mid 1980's RORY SPARROW N.Y. KNICKS GAME WORN JERSEY	$217.50	4 OLD 1964 CIN REDS BASEBALL STUB CROSLEY ENVELOPE	$27.55
VINTAGE METAL NHL TABLE TOP HOCKEY GAME LIKE NEW NR	$202.50	Andruw Jones 2001 Fleer Legacy AUTO Signed Hat BRAVES	$27.00
Sheila Football Figures Lead 1930s Dimestore Soldiers	$199.99	Jason Kendall bobblehead SGA Oakland A's w/ticket 7/31	$27.00
1886 BASEBALL DIE CUT F. DUNLAP DETROIT WOLVERINES	$199.16	WADE BOGGS HALL OF FAME STATUE-PAWSOX Giveaway 7/31/05	$27.00
EARLY ORIGINAL NATIONAL BALL GAME "TOFFEE WRAPPER"	$175.00	190 SPORTSCLIX COMPLETE BASIC SET & STARTER KITS 1&2 +	$26.55
Mickey Mantle Original 60's Hartland Statue Yankees	$169.50	MICKEY MANTLE - 1956 PHONOGRAPH RECORD YANKEES	$26.00
1885 BASEBALL DIE CUT CURTIS WELCH ST LOUIS	$168.50	Ultra Pro Football Helmet Display Case NEW	$26.00
Willie Mays Original 60's Hartland Statue Giants	$130.00	1972 APBA football card set	$25.99

30

STAMPS

Collecting stamps is a fun and educational hobby, and eBay has certainly broken down some barriers and helped collectors and sellers alike to connect. However, although there are some expensive and very special stamps and collections available here, you won't see the prices in general get as lofty as in other eBay categories, such as Antiques.

What's It Worth?

As one stamp collector and expert who hosted an informational workshop on eBay put it, "Every time somebody starts collecting stamps or inherits a stamp collection, the first question asked is 'What's it worth?'" As with other collectibles, the two key criteria are condition and rarity: "A well-worn, torn no. 1 stamp is going to be valued at 10 percent of catalog or even less, every time; whereas a certified, mint, well-centered, full-margin copy will realize many times catalog value."

But there aren't that many old or rare stamps around that are also in excellent condition: "Valuable collectibles are few and far between," writes the expert. While some stamps are valuable, most are not, and "few of us have the resources to put together a portfolio of very expensive stamps," or are lucky enough to inherit a stamp collection that has very valuable stamps. "Yes, it's fun to think Grandpa collected stamps in his youth that are now worth thousands of dollars, but Grandpa when he was young just enjoyed his hobby," he says.

Another eBayer, who worked for over a decade in a stamp store, suggests that for a stamp to be valuable, it needs to meet all three of these criteria: It comes from a country with a hard currency *and* a literate population; it is pre–World War II ("this is mostly to get a little age on them—allows a few collections to be lost in housefires and floods, etc., but also it gets us away from the huge numbers of 'Collectible' stamps produced to stave off national bankruptcy from tiny third world nations"); and "the day it came across the post office counter it cost most of a man's daily wage."

As to the third criterion, he points out that the cost of living has come down so much that this doesn't happen anymore. But back when the $5.00 Columbus of the United States or the $5.00 Jubilee of Canada were both produced, $1.00 a day was a very good wage that a man could raise a family on. "Only a few could afford them and they kept them in high quality albums." He points out that many stamps may meet two of the three criteria and still not have much value.

Many would-be sellers on the Collectibles discussion board say they have inherited a large stamp collection and want to know how to sell it (if not what it's worth). Some suggestions that stamp veterans give is to either sell it off as a whole collection in the Collection subcategory, or try packaging it in several boxes as "mystery" auctions so the buyers can have fun weeding through it. If the seller has more time and inclination, he or she can look up the stamps in a reference book and list them individually or in sheets.

Good packaging is, of course, also essential. When mailing anywhere from 1 to 20 stamps, use an envelope with cardboard stiffeners, advises the eBay workshop host. Bulk collections should be placed in large envelopes and sealed. Place each envelope into a larger box, use plain newsprint as packing, and "pack it well to avoid shifting," he suggests.

Hot Stamps

So which stamps are hot and selling well right now? According to eBay's What's Hot list for stamps, these categories "have experienced above-average buyer demand and interest": US stamp collections, US stamp sheets, duck stamps, Confederate US stamps, United Nations stamps, 19th century US stamps, Asia stamps, US stamps (covers), US stamps (postage), and UK stamps.

In terms of buyer's search words, these words or phrases made eBay's recent Top 10 List for the Stamps category in general: *stamps, Hong Kong, China, Israel, India, Egypt, Greece, New Zealand, Russia,* and *album.* Within the United States, these searches were hot: *sheets, US, Scott* (the name of a popular stamp catalog/reference), *USA, covers, navy, gold, block, plates,* and *lots.*

Let's look at some of the prices in these popular areas. Within the Stamps ▶ United States subcategories, it's no surprise that one of the highest prices in this sample is from an earlier century: an auction for "US Stamps # 108 15c Lincoln SUPERB MLH PFC Certificate" sold for $4,750.00 in the Stamps ▶ United States ▶ 19th Century: Unused subcategory. This stamp has a picture of Abraham Lincoln on its face and is described by the seller as "no doubt one of the finest known US Stamps, # 108 15c Lincoln in Superb, Original Gum, Lightly Hinged condition. Blazing color and stunning eye appeal, only 397 were issued so rare is not even the word. Accompanied by Philatelic Foundation certificate of authenticity that mentions part original gum but is actually a hinge. Worth more than the Scott Catalog Value - $5,000.00." The seller has 99.6 percent positive feedback, with over 20,000 transactions, so this definitely seems to be on the up and up.

The second most expensive stamp in this subcategory, interestingly, is one that meets all three of the stamp store expert's criteria, including the final one of being worth most of a man's daily wage on the day it was originally used. Entitled "US Stamps # 245 $5 Columbian Superb MLH," this stamp has an illustration of Columbus on the front, and the dates 1492–1892—this looks to be a commemorative stamp from the latter year, honoring his discovery of America. The eBay marketplace valued it at $1,550.00, which I'd say is worth more than many a man's daily wage today!

The average price in the Stamps ▶ United States ▶ 19th Century subcategory in this sample was about $68.00, so a piece of 19th century history is affordable for the average collector. One example is a "US Scott #256 Mint 6¢ Garfield VF MH Dull Brown," an 1894 series six-cent stamp with a picture of President Garfield on it, that sold for $69.75.

Because *China* was a popular search term, let's look at some stamps from there. Within the Stamps ▶ Asia ▶ China subcategory, the highest price in the sample was for a "China PRC W7 Scott 967-80 POEMS OF MAO MNH XF," which went for $905.00. This was listed by a stamps PowerSeller in the United States with 100 percent positive feedback—always a good thing to see as a buyer. The stamps have a striking bold-red background, and pictures of— yes—the poems of erstwhile Chairman Mao on them, in black Chinese writing on white. One in the set features an illustration of Mao at his desk, writing. The seller describes it as "CHINA PRC CULTURAL REVOLUTION 'Poems of Chairman Mao' complete set - mint never hinged, original gum, extra fine - PERFECT GUM: NO TONING, NO SPOTS. Listed in Michel as 995-1008. Listed in Yang as W7. Listed in Scott as 967-80. Michel catalog price in Michel is 1300 Euro = $1600. Very rare. Guaranteed genuine."

Average prices in the Stamps ▶ Asia ▶ China subcategory include several 20th century stamps that sold for around $30.00, such as the "CHINA Macau 1984 Year of the Rat. F D Cover" that went for $29.07.

European Stamps

The hottest search words in the Stamps ▶ Europe subcategory are currently *France, Portugal, Germany, sets, covers, Norway, lots, Russia, Scott,* and *cat.*

A high seller in the Stamps ▶ Europe ▶ Portugal subcategory was the "PORTUGAL-1853-D.MARIA II-AF 4-GOOD USED-CV $US 3720.00," which went for $620.00. As the description indicates, the catalog value for this stamp was $3,720.00, so it seems to have been a good deal. The seller, who was based in Spain, also offered a guarantee: If the buyer obtained a certificate from the American Philatelic Society saying that the stamp wasn't genuine (within six months of winning the lot), he would give a complete refund.

Not all collectors search for stamps by country or historical events. Some collect based on something a bit more whimsical, such as type of animal. For example, one avid stamp collector said on the eBay discussion board that he looks for stamps with wild boars on them. ("Yes, wild boars," he wrote.)

The bottom line in the hobby, he says, is having fun: "The point is, this is a hobby for pure enjoyment . . . the fun comes in completing a series of stamps," he wrote. "Sometimes it is trading or selling your duplicates. Going to stamp shows to browse the dealers' boxes for your kind of treasure. Collecting covers from the turn of the 20th century. Researching historical events related to the stamps in your collection. Learning about the world and cultures through stamps." The fun is endless in stamp collecting, he says, because it's not an expensive hobby.

United States ▶ 19th Century: Unused

The average sales price in this subcategory is $68.25.

	HIGH		AVG
US Stamps # 108 15c Lincoln SUPERB MLH PFC Certificate	$4,750.00	US #223 Pb imperf h pair cat $225	$75.00
US Stamps # 245 $5 Columbian Superb MLH	$1,550.00	Scott# 178 MINT NH w/APS Certificate SCV$ 425.00	$75.00
US Stamps # 127 10c XF MH	$1,350.00	Scott 3P vfnh	$75.00
#218 US Unused 90c Purple XF-OG-LH SCV$1200++ WOW!!	$950.00	US Stamps #290 10c 1898 Trans Miss Expo N OG LH VF	$72.70
Scott# 210 U.S. Postage Stamp, Block of 18, Mint NH	$660.00	US Stamp 157 mint VF Beauty!!	$69.99
186, Mint 6¢ VF-XF OG XXLH GEM PO FRESH Cat $1,100.00	$599.00	US Scott #256 Mint 6¢ Garfield VF MH Dull Brown	$69.75
81010 Scott #293 Trans-Mississipi Expo Issue $2.00	$565.55	scott #113 stamp 2 cent VF MINT	$69.00
US #40 - 1c Blue 1875 Reprint NG VF/XF CV $625	$560.00	# 275 MINT F-VF OG Cat.$300	$67.50
US# 98. MINT. OG. With " F " Grill. (9x13). Cat $ 4000	$555.60	#36 UNUSED CV $600.00 NR TAKE A LOOK!	$66.00
US 244 $4.00 COLUMBIAN UNUSED NO RES LOW START	$525.00	Scott 215 3c Purple Bl/4 Mint Full O.G. LHR VF XF	$66.00
81009 Trans-Missiippi Expo Issue $1.00 Scott #292	$432.77	Scott 149 Mint No Gum -VF— no reserve cat=425	$66.00
SCOTT #134 VF MINT GRILLED FRANKLIN $2300.00	$410.50	US Stamps 3¢ Locomotive 1869 Pictorial 114 MH $350.00	$66.00
SC#276A, $1 black, type II, 1895 F/VF (145)	$405.00	US #248 Mint Fresh VF MH CV$77.50	$62.00
#245 Mint $5 Columbian	$380.00	US #24; PF Certificate; Scott Catalog Val: $175.00	$61.61
U.S. Scott #25 Mint 3¢ Washington Gum Rose Centered	$355.00	Scott 290 MH -VF— no reserve cat=180	$61.01

United States ▶ 19th Century: Used

The average sales price in this subcategory is $35.52.

	HIGH		AVG
SCOTTS VERY OLD STAMPS ALBUM-OVER 15,000.00 IN CATOLOG	$1,999.99	Mr Fancy Cancel 112 STRADDLE GRILL AT ALL 4 CORNERS RAR	$37.05
US #11 CPL PLATE 3 RECONSTRUCTION 100 STAMPS	$550.00	united states commemorative postage stamp lot	$36.51
scott US Stamp # 2 10 cent Washington VF+	$530.98	US #155 Used, 90 c Perry 1871, cv $350 superb centering	$36.36
Scott 114 margin imprint copy	$433.28	LOT1300 Q1-Q12,JQ1-JQ5,QE1-QE4,WS1,S1 used/mint CV $300	$36.00
#122 90c Used Lincoln F Fancy Cancel Sm Thin Cat $2250	$381.00	SCOTT #9 VF USED 1852 FRANKLIN $130.00	$36.00
NobleSpirit~HUGE $25,000 TREASURE HUNTERS DREAM HOARD!	$368.98	SCOTT #71 - USED - 30 CENT FRANKLIN - MODERATE TARGET	$36.00
SCOTT #126 F-VF USED RE-ISSUE – RARITY $2100.00	$329.00	6c Pink Fancy Cancel Accumulation! Nice!	$36.00
SCOTT #12 F-VF USED – LIGHT RED CANCEL $1025.00	$325.00	# 112 Used F-VF Huge Bottom Margin Cat.$175	$35.00
SCOTT #118 SUPERB JUMBO - SPECTACULAR $700.00+	$325.00	US Beautiful 4 Margin copy # 11	$34.88
US #38 Used 30c orange VF/XF Sound/Small decolouration	$310.99	SCOTT #134 - VF USED - 1 CENT BANK NOTE - WITH GRILL!	$34.50
US #67 Used 5c Buff - VF/XF - CV $900	$305.00	SCOTT #152 - FVF+ USED - 15ct NATIONAL BANK NOTE ISSUE	$34.50
scott US Stamp # 9X1e 5 cent Washington VF+	$264.00	SC 112 Franklin Used SCV $245.00 (Lot #233)	$34.00
scott US Stamp # 1 5 cent Franklin VF+	$257.00	Collection of 19th Century U.S. Stamps Used	$34.00
SCOTT #120 ALMOST VF - LIGHT RED CANCEL $1075.00	$239.00	U.S. #90 Used - 12c Black with "E" Grill	$33.99
SCOTT #1 - 5 CENT FRANKLIN - RED CANCEL - FIRST ISSUE	$208.50	US USA Old United States Lot Collection Set Scott 36	$33.00

United States ▶ 1901-40: Unused

The average sales price in this subcategory is $28.26.

	HIGH		AVG
US Stamps # 364 10c XF MVLH with 2 PFCs	$1,675.00	US #297 Mint CV$95	$29.55
311, Mint $1 XF OG XXLH PO FRESH GEM Cat $750.00+	$510.00	#516 VF NH NO RESERVE	$29.49
ZEPPELIN $2.60 VLM - MAGNIFICENT EXAMPLE	$458.87	US Stamp #666 Kans Overprint Mint VF.	$29.00
533 SUPERB VF NH 2 CENT TYPE V IMPERF PAIR	$350.00	U.S. Scott # E7 Special Delivery M/VF/LH S.E. No Faults	$28.98
US #630 White Plains SS Mint VF NH	$304.56	SCOTT #528B VF NH TYPE VII STAMP $47.50	$28.85
US Stamps # 545 1c VF MNH	$277.00	US 432 MH, bright color,very well centered	$28.76
US Stamps # 392 1c Line Pair Superb MNH	$275.00	US MINT #381 Never Hinged	$28.75
SCOTT #478 F-VF MINT NH RARITY $1800.00	$261.00	US Stamps: 415 Mint, EF, VLH (cv$55.00)	$28.00
ZEPPELIN $1.30 VLM - Truly STUNNING	$260.00	Nice Collection of US Commemoratives 1907-1926 CV$250+	$27.01
571 $1 Lincoln Memorial XF/S OG NH Block/4 $480 - NR	$255.55	#753 VF NH FARLEY VERTICAL ARROW & LINE BLOCK	$27.00
SC#K16 1919 $2 ON $1 U.S. POSTAL AGENCY IN CHINA MNH-$1	$248.50	SC#370 1909 2C CARMINE ALASKA-YUKON-PACIFICE B/10 MNH	$27.00
DHE #658-679 Kansas Nebraska XF-Superb!!! CV $1809.75	$227.50	#571 VF NH NO RESERVE	$26.51
US Stamps # 459 2c VF MLH with PFC Certificate	$225.00	US 378, MNH, Magnificent stamp	$26.50
FANTASTIC AIRMAIL COLLECTION....SC# C1//C-131++++ MORE	$204.99	7—U S Precancel— Mint Plate Blocks—	$26.09
SCOTT #479 VF MINT $2 MADISON – GEM STAMP	$202.50	# 295 VF NH IMPT. SNGL NO RESERVE	$26.05

United States ▶ 1941-Now: Unused

The average sales price in this subcategory is $9.89.

	HIGH		AVG
DHE #630 White Plains Sheet Mint NH CV$600.00 NR!!!	$330.00	Commemoratives of 1987 MNH 25 different stamps	$9.99
1000 - .37 cent US Flag Postage Stamps $370.00 Face	$326.00	U.S. BICENTENNIAL STAMPS - Sheet of Individual States	$9.99
US Accumulation of Mint NH FV$105.41	$122.50	Hollywood Legends MARILYN MONROE Stamp Sheet	$9.99
400 $0.23 Cent Unused Postage Stamps	$86.99	MINT Marilyn Monroe Commemorative Stamp Souvenir Sheet	$9.99
USA 1297a to 1305Ef Untagged Precancel Coil Set **	$51.00	1981 Birds & Flowers(#1953-2002) 1/4 Priced & PP	$9.99
16diff sheets 3c MNH #1004/1108 below market price	$51.00	1981 Birds & Flowers(#1953-2002) Under Face & PP	$9.99
Celebrate The Century 10 Page Full Set Unopened	$51.00	[3 of these sold for $9.99 each]	
15 diff. sheets 3c's MNH #1015/1078 BELOW MARKET PRICE	$49.00	1460;OLYMPIC;BICYCLE;RING OUT OF ALIN.+BROKEN;	$9.99
2004 Commemorative Year Set	$48.00	1989 USPS Mint NH Commemorative US Stamps in Yearbook	$9.90
Complete Set of 5 Sheets, WWII, 20 per Sheet, Beautiful	$37.01	US 1278-95 1965-78 Prominent Americans (20) VF MLH	$9.75
USPS *1996* COMMEMORATIVE STAMP	$36.77	#667-668 KANS. OVERPRINTS OGLH $50.00	$9.50
YEAR BOOK JAMES DEAN		1982 Commerative Year Set (30 stamps)	$9.50
3 Special Issue Collections: 1970, 1971	$36.05	MarilynMonroe Leg. of Hollywood 20 stamp 32c sheet MINT	$9.50
$5 alexander hamilton 1053 MNH single	$36.05	MINT 832 & 833 SINGLES $1 & $2 PRESIDENTIAL ISSUES	$9.01
2003 Commemorative Year Set	$35.00	1980-1985 GREAT AMERICANS STAMP SET SCOTT 1844-69 NH	$9.01
100 .37 Cent Self-Adhesive Postage Stamps	$34.00	U.S. Postage Stamps 1982 MINT COMM YEAR SET	$9.01

United States ▶ 1901-Now: Used

The average sales price in this subcategory is $11.78.

	HIGH		AVG
SCOTT #313 F-VF USED $5 MARSHALL $750.00	$294.95	USED $ 14.00 EXPRESS #2542 SUPERB	$12.50
19TH CENTURY CLASSIC COLLECTION	$264.00	LIGHT CANCEL NICE	
5 Pounds 45000+ Off Paper Lot Huge SCV	$157.95	SPACE SHUTTLE Priority Mail Stamp Precancel -CALIFORNIA	$12.50
STUNNING!! MANY 1000S U.S. PRECANCELS LOADED 1" BOX!!	$139.10	3261 Priority Mail ($3.20) group of 25. $75 CV	$12.50
Precancels,100 Washington Bicentennial - DLE	$95.99	U.S. #400a and #404 Used	$12.30
SCOTT #312 VF USED SE $2 MADISON $200.00	$90.00	Commemorative Precancels from Buena Park, CALIFORNIA	$12.17
J58 BUFFALO, NY PRECANCEL- SCARCE!!	$89.00	# 614 615 616 617 USED U.S. STAMPS 1924	$12.12
Precancels,175 Conn - DLE	$83.50	#397-400A 1913 1-10c PAN. PACIFIC VF U LT CLS CV$49 $12	$11.99
1000 DIFFERENT ILLINOIS PRECANCEL TOWNS AND TYPES	$76.00	Dinosaurs Commemorative Block Precancel - CALIFORNIA	$11.39
530 DIFFERENT OKLAHOMA PRECANCEL TOWNS AND TYPES	$69.00	SPACE SHUTTLE Priority Mail Stamp Precancel -CALIFORNIA	$11.17
LOT1286 SC# 357,358 used no h fvf bluish paper CV $200.	$66.00	~~LOT OF OLD STAMPS~ESTATE SALE~~	$11.16
Scott # 331-342, Used Set	$53.61	COMPLETE SET AMERIPEX 86 S.S (4) VF POSTALLY USED	$10.78
US STAMPS: Scott 342 Used; VF; Cat. 100.00	$53.00	USA - SCOTT # 447 - USED	$10.60
690 DIFFERENT FLORIDA PRECANCEL TOWNS AND TYPES	$52.31	VERY EARLY PRECANCEL SELECTION	$10.56
Scott # 397-404 Set, Used	$51.00	# 620 621 622 623 USED U.S. STAMPS 1925-26	$10.52
Lot of thousands of stamps from 1930's, 40's and 50's	$51.00	3 HIGH VALUE STAMPS POSTALLY USED	$10.51

United States ▶ Back of Book

The average sales price in this subcategory is $24.68.

	HIGH		AVG
US Stamps # C3 24c Plate Block of 12 XF MNH	$1,575.00	SC#K9 1919 18C ON 9C U.S. POSTAL AGENCY IN CHINA—$1	$26.00
#C15 - $2.60 Graf Zeppelin Mint VF	$467.00	#c5 16c Emblem....VF-XF og NH cv$150.	$26.00
C15 - $ 2.60 Zeppelin - MLH - No Reserve!	$416.00	US C1-C6 Used Set	$25.62
SCOTT #C14 VF USED 1930 GRAF ZEPPELIN	$306.01	US AIRMAIL #C46 80c x 2 MNH PLATEBLOCKS	$25.49
US Stamps #C13 65c EF MNH Plate Number Single.	$290.00	C3 CURTISS JENNY 24¢ USED US STAMP	$25.01
#C14 - $1.30 Graf Zeppelin Mint VF+	$281.76	Special Delivery E1 "1885 10¢ Messenger issue" MOG-HR	$24.99
C3 CENTERLINE Block ogNH VF/XF SCV $675.00+++	$270.25	United States - 1918 16c Curtiss Jenny	$24.50
US C14 $1.30 MINT ZEPPELIN VF CENTERING SEE IT NO RES	$265.00	AIRMAIL TO DIE FOR ALL MINT OG NEVER HINGED	$24.50
Powerful US BOB Stamp Lot: C's, E's, J's, O's, Q's	$248.53	#E14 1925 20c SP DEL P#17185 BLK VF/XF NH CV$49 $19	$24.50
SC#K16 1919 $2 ON $1 U.S. POSTAL	$248.50	US Stamp #C5 Air Service Emblem Mint C.V. $80.00.	$24.50
AGENCY IN CHINA MNH-$1		US #C2 Mint H	$24.00
#C13 - $.65 Graf Zeppelin Mint Never hinged VF	$202.50	[2 of these sold for $24.00 each]	
US Stamps # J65 10c Plate Block of 6 with Star XF MNH	$175.00	US #C5 Mint VF Appearance H	$24.00
C6 24c Biplane BLock of 4 F/VF OG NH - $500 - NR	$169.45	US #C5 Mint VF H	$24.00
C5 16c Airmail Emblem - PLate # Block/4 F/VF OG NH $600	$151.50	US Airmail # C18 Mint	$24.00
#c18 50c Baby Zeppelin....XF-S og NH - PSE GRADE 95	$150.00	US #Q6 Mint VF HR CV$52.50	$24.00

United States ▶ Confederate States

The average sales price in this subcategory is $45.34.

	HIGH		AVG
U.S. 55 DIFFERENT CIVIL WAR PATRIOTIC ENVELOPES	$395.00	CIVIL WAR ERA POSTAL COVER - LONG BRIDGE WASHINGTON DC	$52.00
Confederate States No 5 tied to cover by Atlanta cancel	$322.77	CONFEDERATE STATES SCOTT #5 USED FAULT $500.00	$52.00
C.S.A. USED #13, STAR CANCEL	$322.00	Confederate States Stamp #1 Davis Unused CV $175.00.	$50.00
CIVIL WAR CONFEDERATE COVER CS#11e PERFORATED 12 1/2	$262.88	Confederate States Stamp #4 Davis Mint OG C.V. $180.00.	$50.00
CONFEDERATE STATES #3 Mint NG CV$500 as such	$222.49	COLLECTION OF DeLaRue CONFEDERATE STATES PRIVATE PRINTS	$49.90
Confederate Cover Headquarters Yorktown Va 1861	$202.50	GROUP OF PATRIOTIC COVERS + LETTERS	$48.80
CIVIL WAR C.S. COVER W/ VA. RAILROAD MARKINGS, #7 STAMP	$182.50	PRE CIVIL WAR ERA POSTAL COVER - FIRST EIGHT PRESIDENTS	$45.00
CONFEDERATE STATES IN A SALESBOOK	$170.19	CIVIL WAR CONFEDERATE COVER CSA#6 "FORWARDED"	$45.00
CSA TURNED COVER STONEWALL'S BRIGADE/ARMY OF VA	$163.51	Mailed Hand cancelled Confederate cover 2 5c Stamps	$44.44
VERY RARE~DISPATCH Ca. 1863 CONFEDERATE CIVIL WAR COVER	$130.27	Confederate States of America Postage Stamp block A-9	$42.58
CONFEDERATE STATES SCOTT #9 F-VF MINT $850.00	$125.50	CONFEDERATE STATES SCOTT #1 VF MINT $250.00	$41.00
On Cover CSA #4a var. Short Transfer Augusta CDS	$114.38	12 BLOCKS OF DeLaRue CONFEDERATE STATES PRIVATE PRINTS	$39.90
CIVIL WAR CONFEDERATE COVER CS#11c CONFEDERATE RR USE	$105.79	CSA #7 Pair Cover Savannah, Ga	$38.78
CSA #6 pair cover	$95.00	Confederate Scott # 4 Mint OG	$38.13
CSA #11a Richmond, Va. DUE cover	$95.00	CONFEDERATE STATES STAMPS	$37.89

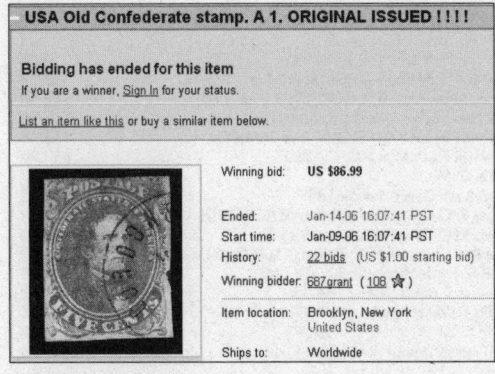

USA Old Confederate stamp. A 1. ORIGINAL ISSUED ! ! ! !

Bidding has ended for this item
If you are a winner, Sign In for your status.

List an item like this or buy a similar item below.

Winning bid:	**US $86.99**
Ended:	Jan-14-06 16:07:41 PST
Start time:	Jan-09-06 16:07:41 PST
History:	22 bids (US $1.00 starting bid)
Winning bidder:	687grant (108 ☆)
Item location:	Brooklyn, New York United States
Ships to:	Worldwide

US Stamps # 245 $5 Columbian Superb MLH

Bidding has ended for this item
If you are a winner, Sign In for your status.

List an item like this or buy a similar item below.

Find MORE great stuff
at my eBay ▪store▪
Visit Anthony's US and Worldwide Stam

Winning bid:	**US $1,550.00** (Reserve met)
Ended:	Aug-14-05 19:32:57 PDT
Start time:	Aug-04-05 19:32:57 PDT
History:	21 bids (US $1.00 starting bid)
Winning bidder:	gazwsx0_10 (105 ☆)
Item location:	New York, NY United States

United States ▶ Covers

The average sales price in this subcategory is $7.70.

	HIGH		AVG
# 4 U.S. Sub U.S.S. AMBERJACK S.S. 219 Launching	$255.00	Patriotic First Day Cover Sc# 899-901	$8.00
# 6 U.S.Sub. U.S.S. HERRING S.S. 233 Launched	$91.55	USS SNAPPER, Naval SUBMARINE, 1938, Guantanamo Cuba	$8.00
Auto Race Post Card,1917,1914 INDY 500 Winner AUTOGRAPH	$84.50	Sea-Plane Base, Hot Springs National Park,Ark., 1940	$7.99
RARE Tragedy Cover APOLLO 1 "Houston" SCCS 1/27/67	$78.77	NAMW, DeKalb,Missouri, 1938	$7.99
FORBIDDEN ATOMIC BOMB STAMP ON COVER.B29 ENOLA GAY	$56.01	Hawaii Annexed, 35th Anniversary, 1933 , Hilo Cancel	$7.99
1938 SAINT THOMAS, NEVADA +RARE CACHET PROOF SIGNED	$52.51	821 Prexie, Abraham Lincoln, Airmail, Pan American	$7.99
138 U.S. Navy Ship Covers Cachet Stamped Envelopes	$51.00	Naval Cover USS Houston CA30 Hobby Shop Cover	$7.70
C9, C11, Lindbergh, Roessler, Puerto Rico, 1929	$47.56	Naval Cover USS Astoria CA34 Mar 18, 1939	$7.60
GOLDCRAFT JUPITER 1/21/59 NASA SPACE COVER COVERS	$45.00	16 DIFFERENT U.S. NAVY SHIP COVERS 1940-1974	$7.60
USS WASHINGTON - Navy cancel Dec 7, 1941- Staehle	$42.00	ww2 patriotic; kicking mule w/ article	$7.50
ATOMIC BOMB CINDERELLA STAMP CANCELLED AUGUST 6 1995	$40.99	FIRST FLIGHT, COLUMBUS TO CHICAGO,1931,T & W.A. SERVICE	$7.50
# 5 U.S.Sub. U.S.S. DRUM S.S. 228 Launched	$37.88	2 ww2 patriotics; u.s. flag w/ mahomet pat. cancels	$7.50
FLAG AND RAILROAD COVERS:SPECIAL COLLECTIONS. JUST .49	$36.99	Naval Cover USS Massachusetts BB59 Launch Cover	$7.50
WWII Patriotic, VE DAY, U.S. Air Corps, Greetings	$32.99	2 DIFF. COVERS, POW SURVIVORS, BATAAN DEATH MARCH, U/A	$7.00
Crosby, Fleet Week,Seattle, 1935, USS MARYLAND	$32.99	ABE LINCOLN Birthday, 1945 LINCOLN, Nebraska, Heroes	$7.00

United States ▸ Errors, Freaks, Oddities

The average sales price in this subcategory is $48.24.

	HIGH		AVG
rare no orange color in 37 sheets masterworks of mint	$1,235.55	#1280 MNH VF ERROR Misperfed Full Sheet	$80.00
James Dean "Non-Perf" Framed Set	$510.01	US #114 with a major margin shift on cover Rare	$78.77
stamps with no perforation 1/2 coil	$510.00	US Architecture major color error sheet & cover	$73.42
SCOTT 2280b .25 YOSEMITE IMPERFORATE 100 STAMP ROLL	$405.00	Mr Fancy Cancel VF 119 SPLIT GRILL 4NICE MARGINS CV$350	$72.00
Errors - Wonderful Collection of US Errors	$333.99	RW6 MNH OG SUPERB COMPARE TO CAT=$800.00	$66.01
US #1b; Very Clean PF Certificate; SCV: $850.00+	$280.87	2062a, MNH BLACK COLOR SHIFTED WAY DOWN ERROR	$60.95
Error - Missing Color/Text - Mod American Architecture	$268.66	scott#1595 liberty bell bklt pane major error	$54.07
2c Carmine SMILING WASHINGTON US Stamp 634 Pl 21423 NR	$200.00	US #U646a BLUE GRAY OMITTED ERROR, CV$350.00 NO RESERVE	$52.09
Legends of the West Error & Correct Sheet w/Comm. Bk	$191.38	C25, MNH MISPERFORATED PLATE BLOCK ERROR - WoW	$49.95
Collection of 17 US Errors	$181.50	Scott 1488 8c Mint Both Stamps: Full O.G. N.H. GEM	$41.00
Recalled/Error "Legends of the West" stamp sheet & pkg	$180.27	Mr Fancy Cancel 114 HUGE STAMP BIG STRADDLE DOUBLE GRIL	$41.00
LEGENDS OF THE WEST ERROR SHEET!	$180.27	1893b BLKT PANE OF 8, IMPERF VERTICALLY, NH, CV $75	$39.99
2870 RECALLED LEGENDS ERROR SHEET - LOW PRICE!	$179.00	DOUBLE ALBINO...ENTIRE FANTASTIC DON'T MISS IT	$38.00
SCOTT #467 F-VF MINT ERROR OF COLOR $550.00	$175.05	Mr Fancy Cancel 112 STRADDLE GRILL AT ALL 4 CORNERS RAR	$37.05
Group of 19th Century US Grill Fakes Hard to Duplicate	$172.50	20 diff. ERROR & FREAK COLLECTION: COLOR, MISCUT-PERF	$34.36

United States ▸ Plate Blocks/Multiples

The average sales price in this subcategory is $16.58.

	HIGH		AVG
PB...#287 4c Trans Miss...FVFogNH - LG TOP cv$2500+	$950.00	1930-32 (lot of 5) 2c Red Plates-MNH-see descript/Sc#'s	$18.50
Powerful US Investment Mint Plate Block Collection NR	$898.88	FIRST 10 LEGENDS OF HOLLYWOOD MNH PLATE BLOCKS	$17.95
C3 CENTERLINE Block ogNH VF/XF SCV $675.00+++	$270.25	50 BEAUTIFUL 5c MNH PLATE BLOCKS GORGEOUS GUM!	$17.59
US Stamps # 324 2c Wide Top Plate Block of 4 XF MNH	$240.00	2419 $2.40 Moon Landing MNH Plate Block Less than Face	$17.59
US Stamps # 527 2c Wide Top Plate Block of 6 XF MNH	$227.50	U.S. - Small lot of Better Plate Blocks	$17.50
US Stamps # 368 2c Wide Top Plate Block of 6 XF MNH	$190.00	Older 4 Cent Plate Blocks 83 Diff. MNH Start at face	$17.09
US, 400+ MINT Plate Blocks in Harris album..NO RESERVE!	$189.97	US Plate Blocks 909-921 Overrun Flags MNH NR	$16.50
U.S. Face Lot of $235 - Mostly Plate Blocks / Strips	$184.75	13 Different MNH Matched Plate Number Sets	$16.30
US Stamps # 542 1c Plate Block of 6 VF MNH	$175.00	US Stamp #696 Liberty Mint VF-NH Plate Block.	$16.26
US Stamps # 701 50c Plate Block of 4 XF MNH	$175.00	SCOTT# 611 HARDING MEMORIAL IMPERF BLOCK OF FOUR	$16.05
MINT 1053 $5.00 PRESIDENTIAL PLATE BLOCK GEM QUALITY	$168.50	US Plate Block of 6 Airmail C21 20c OG, MNH NR	$16.00
US Block Stamp and Cover Letter Collection	$150.00	1930 Braddocks Field- Sc#688- F/VF-MNH-plate	$15.75
UNITED STATES #704-15, SET OF MINT PLATE # BLOCKS/4, NH	$150.00	US Stamps #C8 Map/Plane Mint VF-NH Plate Block.	$15.51
US #325 Unused VF Block of 4 OG HR with Top Selvage	$146.94	US PLATEBLOCK / BLOCKS 1932 - 1937 MNH/MH LOT	$15.50
SCOTT #248 F-VF NH PLATE BLOCK OF SIX $675.00	$139.00	#1557: Mariner-10 , Exploring Venus and Mercury...	$15.50

United States ▸ Possessions

The average sales price in this subcategory is $32.88.

	HIGH		AVG
US Philippine Cover HE HEACOCK Overprint REG'D 1927	$618.00	CANAL ZONE #11a Used Antique "Zone" Type CV$200	$33.77
HAWAII Sc#5 Mint NG Early Impression Nice Appearance	$495.00	US Philippines Meter Mail PHIL COLD STORAGE 1941	$33.50
HAWAII #R12, MINT REVENUE STAMPS B/4, F-VF, OG, NH	$492.00	PHILIPPINES Paid Reply Postal Card, Scott UY2	$33.00
Hawaii Cover Scott #75 2cent Brown Nice Return Cachet	$382.00	HAWAII 66 NEVER HINGED BLOCK 4 W/VARIETY	$33.00
Canal Zone Early First Day Cover Collection FDC 2 Album	$349.44	HAWAII Sc#10R Fresh Mint NG CV $60	$33.00
PHILIPPINES Official Postal Card, UZ4	$302.50	HAWAII U13 GEM	$32.77
1802) Hawaii 148 stamps mint/hinge/used since classic	$298.33	Hawaii 81 -Advert Cover Hawaii 1899	$32.55
Hawaii #U14 Blue Paper Cut Square Rare. Cats. $300	$275.00	US Philippines RPO Cover MANILA & TARLAC SOUTH 1941	$32.33
Hawaii #76 Imprint Sheet of Fifty Mostly NH	$272.30	US Philippines RPO Cover BICOL North 1941	$32.32
HAWAII SCOTT #6 F-VF USED – RARE STAMP $1100.00	$264.99	CANAL ZONE #10 VF Mint w/ Shifted & Split Ovpt Unlisted	$32.00
HIGH VALUE HAWAII CLASSIC STAMPS LOT, NO RESERVE !!!	$262.77	HAWAII Sc#72 Fresh Mint H Jumbo CV $60	$32.00
Hawaii stamp sc 30a vertical block of ten cats 600+	$260.00	Hawaii stamp sc 9 pos 3 unused cats 350.	$31.69
PHILIPPINES, Stamp Collection on Scott pages cv $1000..	$257.02	Philippines E6 Never Hinged	$31.01
HAWAII Sc#17 Used Dark Blue on Bluish CV $6750	$241.01	HAWAII UX8 GEM	$31.00
HAWAII Sc#21 Mint NG Rare!! CV $850	$239.01	Danish West Indies Stamps, lot of 12	$31.00

United States ▸ Sheets

The average sales price in this subcategory is $10.95.

	HIGH		AVG
US POSTAGE STAMPS 1000 NEW .37 CENTS	$330.01	3506 GREAT PLAINS PRAIRIE Nature of America Series	$11.00
DHE #630 White Plains Sheet Mint NH CV$600.00 NR!!!	$330.00	Scott #2162 -22 Cents "Big Brother/Sisters" Mint Sheet	$11.00
J88 1/2 postage due mint sheet	$131.00	Scott #2164 - 22 Cents "Help End Hunger" Mint Sheet	$11.00
THE FIRST 9 MINT LEGENDS OF HOLLYWOOD SHEETS	$92.95	Sc. #1937-38 Battle of Yorktown / Virginia Capes	$11.00
United States MNH Complete Space Series Stamps WOW	$86.55	1987 Delaware Statehood Stamp Sheet of 50	$10.99
13 Sheets Scott 909 thru 921 Mint NH OG	$85.00	2004 ISAMU NOGUCHI SHEET OF 20 STAMPS	$10.99
MINT UNCUT PRESS SHEET: #3178, Mars Pathfinder, FV $54	$80.99	SC 1940 - .20 Christmas Teddy Bear - Mint Sheet of 50	$10.99
GROUP OF 26 EXCELLENT STRIPS OF 16 AND 20	$80.00	NobleSpirit~ #2096 Full Mint Sheet of 50 MNH!	$10.52
Celebrate the Century - 10 SHEETS - Mint!	$69.50	2001 21c Bison (SC# 3468) MINT SHEET	$10.52
NEOPOSTAGE EARLY 34? 4STAMP SHEET CVP ATM FRAMA NEOPOST	$61.00	USPS Stamp Stamps Humphrey Bogart Full Pane Hollywood	$10.50
USPS Hologram Space Achievement and Exploration Sheet	$57.55	SC#1712-15 13c American Butterflies Full Sheet MNH@FACE	$10.50
United States Century of Progress Sheets Stamps	$50.59	3152: HOLLYWOOD LEGENDS: HUMPHREY BOGART 32c - 20 MNH	$10.50
#2481 Pumpkinseed Sunfish Mint Sheet	$50.00	2967 Marilyn Monroe Issue MNH Sheet of 20	$10.50
USPS 2001 Commemorative Stamp Yearbook w/ Stamps@FACE	$49.95	Sc# 3509 Frida Kahlo Full Sheet	$10.50
15 Sheets Commemoratives 1940's Mint NH OG	$46.00	American Comic Strips Classics US Postal Stamps MNH	$10.50

United States ▶ Collections, Lots

The average sales price in this subcategory is $52.70.

	HIGH		AVG
US COVERS, MASSIVE STOCK IN 18 BOXES, EST 10,000 ITEMS	$1,277.00	LOT OF 11 DIFFERENT US MINT BOOKLETS	$58.00
Valuable Old US Stamp Collection. Must See!	$960.00	19TH CENTURY CLASSIC COLLECTION	$57.00
19TH CENTURY CLASSIC COLLECTION	$913.00	1923-31 BUREAU PRECANCEL COLLECTION-	$57.00
Unbelievable Major Mint NH US Stamp Holding!! No Rev!	$810.00	SCOTT# C1 THUR C6 1918-1923. N.R. !!!!!!LOOK!!!!!!.	$56.75
Powerful Old US Stamp Holding, No Rev! 3 Days!	$805.00	150 UNADRESSED FIRST DAY COVERS MOSTLY MODERN PT 6	$56.05
Old Southern Dealer's Mint & Used HI Scott Hoard - NR	$801.01	96 Fisrt day covers 1930's to the1950's	$54.60
Investment Mint NH US Stamps, Face $670, More, No Rev!	$725.00	USA 1875 - 1929 Group Mint / Used Scott Cat. $1000.00+	$52.50
US Mostly Mint Accumulation CV$7300+	$649.00	19TH CENTURY CLASSIC COLLECTION	$52.37
Powerful US Stamp Collection, No Rev! 3 Day!	$545.99	NEW 2003 SCOTT MINUTEMAN US STAMP ALBUM & KIT	$52.01
Fabulous Mint NH US Stamp Collection, No Rev!	$530.00	LOT1317 SC# 11,26,63,65,68,69,71,73,78a used CV $500.00	$52.00
Fabulous US Stamp Treasure Hoard, No Reserve!	$511.00	~ Scott's International Stamp Album - Hard Cover - 1965	$51.99
Massive US Stamps in Large Carton, No Rev!	$510.99	1893 COLUMBIAN COMM.SCOTT # 230-239 N.R.	$51.00
Powerful Investment Mint US Stamps, No Rev! 3 Day!	$510.00	Lot of thousands of stamps from 1930's, 40's and 50's	$51.00
Fabulous Antique US Stamp Collection, No Rev!	$501.01	Celebrate The Century Stamp Collection 1900's-1990's	$50.95
Powerful US Back Of Book Collection, No Rev!	$478.76	United States Century of Progress Sheets Stamps	$50.59

Australia ▶ Australian States

The average sales price in this subcategory is $25.44.

	HIGH		AVG
Tasmania 6d Rouletted Chalon Blk Of 8 Mint No Gum	$461.78	WESTERN AUSTRALIA Sg#109 Fresh Mint H Wtmk CA	$31.00
SOUTH AUSTRALIA Sg#195//208 Mint HR VF Specimen Ovpt.	$439.00	A;L;2$;New Zealand lot 1862/1935 gen F/VF ;25087	$31.00
Western Australia-1854/1910 Nice SWANS Lot(67 Items)	$405.00	WESTERN AUSTRALIA Sg#144 Used VF SON CDS Wtmk Crown	$29.99
WESTERN AUSTRALIA Sg#6a Used VF Rouletted Pale Brown	$395.00	VICTORIA Sg#D19-20 Fresh Clean Used CV ?60 ($107)	$29.99
QUEENSLAND 1866-92 STAMP DUTY accumulation (many 100's)	$350.67	WESTERN AUSTRALIA Sg#41-2 Fresh Used Clean Cut Pf.14-16	$29.99
WESTERN AUSTRALIA Sg#15 Fresh Used CV ?550 ($978)	$261.00	TASMANIA 2d PICTORIAL GOLDEN VALLEY POSTMARK 1905	$29.99
TASMANIA TOWN DATESTAMP	$256.60	TASMANIA OFFICIAL COVER TULLAH to WARATAH sent FREE	$29.99
POSTMARK 240+ page COLLECTION		Tasmania 1899 Keyplate Hobart to Transvaal Rare Cover	$29.00
VICTORIA-Good 1850/1912 Lot on OLD Pages(150 Items)	$218.25	NEW SOUTH WALES 1904 SG#314 ON COLOUR PICTURE POSTCARD	$9.99
AUSTRALIAN STATES - QV - SUPERB MINT STAMP COLLECTION	$217.50	TASMANIA POSTMARKS PICTORIAL BAGDAD etc, great piece	$9.99
VICTORIA Sg#230 Used VF Appearance with Revenue Cancel	$203.60	Victoria Cover 1869, Australia	$9.99
NEW SOUTH WALES Mint & Used Collection Mostly F-VF	$199.00	[2 of these sold for $9.99 each]	
WESTERN AUSTRALIA Sg#128 Mint HR XF CV ?300 ($534)	$199.00	TASMANIA 1d PICTORIAL BISMARCK POSTMARK 1911	$9.99
NEW SOUTH WALES - 1871/1902 - RARE 1/- IMP BETWEEN PAIR	$175.50	TASMANIA 2d PICTORIAL GORMANSTON OFFICIALLY SEALED rare	$9.99
QUEENSLAND-1860/1908 USED Stamp Lot.High Cat Value (92)	$172.50	NEW SOUTH WALES AUSTRALIA #28-67 LOT OF 8 USED	$9.95
WESTERN AUSTRALIA Sg#4c Used VF Swan Pale Brown	$163.05	SOUTH AUSTRALIA #11-95 USED	$9.95

Australia ▶ Kangaroos

The average sales price in this subcategory is $43.30.

	HIGH		AVG
AUSTRALIA TWO POUND ROO USED C of A	$275.00	BCS-06, Australia Scott No. 97, 9d Roo, Superb, MUH GEM	$65.00
AUSTRALIA TWO POUND ROO USED C of A	$250.00	Australia 3rd wmk Kangaroo 5/- Perforated OS	$54.95
AUSTRALIA 9 pence MUH roo, SECOND watermark ACSC 25	$209.76	AUSTRALIA 5 SHILLING ROO SECOND WMK ACSC 43, 2/1915	$48.25
AUSTRALIA Sg#6 Mint NH VF CV ?50 ($88) for Hinged	$139.25	Australia 3rd wmk Kangaroo 9d Perforated OS pair M	$44.95
Australia CofA 2/- maroon Authority Imprint gutter blk	$124.50	AUSTRALIA – Sc#7 - MINT, LH ++	$43.00
Kangaroos Hundreds Postmarks & OS values to 5/-	$112.50	20 AUSTRALIA KANGAROO ROOS ROO to 5/-	$40.20
Kangaroo, 5/- SMWmk, MLH. Sc100 CV US$190. Sg111	$111.50	AUSTRALIA – Sc#8 - MINT, LH ++	$38.00
AUSTRALIA ONE POUND GREY ROO C of A WMK USED SG 137	$105.50	AUSTRALIA KANGAROO TEN SHILLING PINK/GREY USED C of A	$37.00
AUSTRALIA 2 pence roo Mint Never Hinged SECOND wmk !!	$99.00	Australia 6d Kangaroo 'OS' Overprint Pair Mint Hinged	$36.55
AUSTRALIA 128 Used ?1 grey Kangaroo $300.00	$96.00	AUSTRALIA SG#8-9 Mint H CV ?90 ($156) 1913-14	$36.00

Australia ▶ Collections, Lots

The average sales price in this subcategory is $24.82.

	HIGH		AVG
AUSTRALIA - SUPERB MINT STAMP COLLECTION	$426.66	Australia-Interesting Cinderellas+Revenues Lot(80+Items)	$43.05
Australia-Interesting 30s/50 Exhibition Cover+Stamp Lot	$350.00	AUSTRALIA-1918/24 M&U Stamp Lot.Good Cat Value (42).	$42.10
MINT ACCUMULATION FOR POSTAGE-FACE AU$740	$249.99	5+ pounds of Australian and New Zealand stamps on paper	$41.00
Australia-Early Collection on Pages+Better(80+Items)	$227.50	Australian Antartic Ter-1957/92 Mainly MNH Collection	$41.00
Australia-Valuable GV,Roos,GVI Lot on Pages(80+Items)	$208.50	AUSTRALIA 2000+ MIX States Roos & GV to Decimal (R066)	$36.00
NEW SOUTH WALES Mint & Used Collection Mostly F-VF	$199.00	AUSTRALIA-1931/32 M&U OFFICIAL OVPT Lot.Cat apprx ?150.	$33.02
AUSTRALIA Mint & Used Collection Sg. CV ?990 ($1761)	$175.00	NEW ZEALAND, 1500+ stamps in stbk..NO RESERVE!!	$31.00
AUSTRALIA-1932/35 M&U Lot.Incl 5/- Sydney Harbour (30).	$170.30	Australian Stamp Yearbook 1996 Collection Yearbook n/r	$31.00
VICTORIA Mint & Used Collection Much F-VF	$159.00	Australia - 1000 fine used stamps, all eras 1920's-2000	$26.00
Australia Stamp Collection 4000 Stamps Inventoried	$142.50	Australia-1966 Year MNH	$24.99
AUSTRALIA specialist decimal varieties collection,S857	$139.00	AUSTRALIA - 1927/31 - SUPERB MNH RANGE. CAT ?35+	$24.55
AUSTRALIA-Large Modern M&U Collection.MNH Face AUD$160	$123.34	Australia mint lot, F-VF	$24.26
AUSTRALIA-1913/15 M&U Stamp Lot mainly ROO's (37 items)	$122.75	A Collection of Stamps Australia & Australian States	$23.02
King George V 1.5d RED No Watermark 9 BW Varieties	$112.50	Australia 150+ stamps inc Roos & Heads	$22.05
Australia cat$295	$100.00	800 ALL DIFFERENT AUSTRALIA PICTORIALS ONLY	$22.05
		LOT OF 100+ OLD VICTORIA STAMPS FROM AUSTRALIA	$20.50
		PERFIN BS&F on 6d Engraved KOOKA RARE ?	$20.00
		Australia, 183, VF, NH, OG. Bright, Fresh ,Margin Copy	$20.00
		AUSTRALIA 800 DIFFERENT STAMPS USED	$19.95
		Older Australia Choice M/NH Stamp Collection-LOOK!	$19.21

Canada ▶ Covers

The average sales price in this subcategory is $16.57.

	HIGH		AVG
GB CANADA USA 1837 REBELLION LETTER MacKENZIE >UK	$530.00	Norway-Canada North Pole Expedition cover	$18.88
RMS Nascopie Ivigtut Greenland 7 Stamp Censor AM 1940	$281.11	Canada 1893 post card with Victoria square circle	$18.51
Canada #39 Matching Mourning Covers (2 examples)	$175.00	CANADA, ARCTIC, NWT, FORT SIMPSON, 1952	$18.38
Canada collection of over 110 mostly classic postcards	$148.50	#1362var, MISPLACED PERFORATION. RARE. Est :$250.00	$17.75
Canada 1944 Red Cross w 3 x $1 Destroyer OHMS perfins	$112.50	Canada to USA - 1899 Registered Cover w RPO, etc.	$17.50
Hawkesbury Free Stampless: Rare Ottawa & Grenville RPO	$99.88	1935 Saskatoon SK Canada 'Hudson's Bay' advert cover	$17.05
PIONEER AIRMAIL FLIGHT COVER - VICTORIA, BC TO SEATTLE	$96.56	ct6 3 1939 Canada Royal Train (Queens Visit) Covers	$16.76
CANADA, ARCTIC, NWT, EUREKA SOUND, 1947	$77.11	'40 CANADA CRAIG HARBOUR NWT+CACHET+RMS NASCOPIE ARCTIC	$16.66
Canada Caricature Landscape Issue Stamps on 23 Covers	$76.00	1898 Leaf Mourning St Joseph Street Toronto to PSD	$16.35
BC AIRWAYS 1ST FLIGHT COVER	$56.69	Canada, uprated registered stationery to Germany 1927	$16.00
SIGNED BY COMPANY ENGINEER		Canada 1894 small queens Seaside NB cancel	$16.00
FLIGHT GOLDPINES-SIOUX LOOKOUT 1928 PATRICIAN ULTRA	$56.55	Canada NS Yarmouth Square Circle cancel 1894	$15.86
Canada 1939 Royal Train Special Delivery to Postmaster	$51.99	Canada Lot 50 First Day Covers 46-49 Cents Post Office	$14.61
1845 CANADA Buckingham letter to EASDALE ISLANDS *LOOK*	$51.05	[3 of these sold for $14.61 each]	
FORTY-NINE! Canada First Flight Covers 1928-1950	$49.99	Canada Lot 50 First Day Covers 46-49 Cents Post Office	$14.60
Canada to USA - 1853 Lengthy Stampless Folded Letter	$49.99	TORONTO PIANO ADVERTISING 1932 #166 EXTENDED MOUSTACH	$14.50

Canada ▶ Mint

The average sales price in this subcategory is $20.07.

	HIGH		AVG
CANADA SCOTT #109 IMPERFORATED BLOCK OF 6,MNH,UNIQUE !!	$201.00	A;V;; Canada 85 XFNH Fresh ! ; 25388	$23.50
Canada Scott #227 Mint X.F.N.H. Block	$184.50	CANADA Un#108a Booklet Pane Mint LH CV CDN120 ($99)	$22.60
Canada Stamps # 116 XF MNH	$175.00	Canada Stamps # 68 Superb MNH	$22.00
Canada Scott #227 Mint X.F.N.H. Block	$162.50	Canada Scott #273 Mint N.H. Superb	$21.50
Canada Stamps # 101 XF MNH	$145.00	Canada Plate Blocks-MNH–21 different kinds	$21.35
Canada Scott #257-61 Mint N.H. Blocks	$114.29	CANADA Un#227 Mint VF H CV CDN90 ($74)	$21.00
CANADA Un#177 Mint VF NH CV CDN600 ($483)	$100.00	CANADA Un#302 Mint VF NH	$21.00
Canada Stamps # 80 XF MNH	$97.00	CANADA E3, Mint Never Hinged	$20.50
Canada Stamps # 99 Jumbo MNH	$90.89	CANADA Un#137 Mint Pair H CV CDN100 ($82)	$20.27
CANADA Un#176 Mint NH CV CDN600 ($483)	$90.52	Canada Stamps # 71 XF MLH	$20.00
CANADA Un#133i Mint Paste UP Pair XF LH CV CDN80 ($66)	$83.00	CANADA Un#175 Mint VF NH CV CDN100 ($81)	$20.00
Lot of 246 Mint Canada Stamps 1930s-70s, High Values	$81.00	CANADA Un#262 Mint VF LH CV CDN100 ($82)	$19.00
CANADA Un#124 Mint Pair LH/NH CV CDN437 ($360)	$81.00	CANADA Un#136 Mint Pair VF H CV CDN100 ($82)	$19.00
Canada Scott #257-61 Mint N.H. Blocks	$78.77	CANADA Un#129 Mint Pair VF LH CV CDN60 ($49)	$18.00
Large Queen 25 i Orange red Thin Paper Unused	$76.01	#1362var, MISPLACED PERFORATION. RARE. Est :$250.00	$17.75

Canada ▶ Provinces

The average sales price in this subcategory is $18.88.

	HIGH		AVG
NEWFOUNDLAND-1865/1938 M&U High Cat Stamp lot (149).	$239.26	Newfoundland #24a fine no gum cat $80	$22.26
Newfoundland 4, 1857 4d Scarlet Vermillion, Used.	$202.55	NEWFOUNDLAND Sg#59a Mint Seal Bright Blue CV ?70 ($123)	$22.00
Canada SC# 4 (Pair), Superb Condition	$181.00	Newfoundland 267 MNH 2 Sheets of 50................A909	$21.50
Canadian Prov-Interesting OLD Revenues Lot(Aprx 150+)	$144.50	NEWFOUNDLAND Sg#54 Mint RG VF Rich Color Sailing Ship	$20.50
Newfoundland-Nice OLD M&U Lot on Pages.Good Catalogue	$143.50	Prince Edward Island #13 3 Cent Rose MH	$20.50
Nova Scotia 1 used catalog $450.00	$139.00	NEWFOUNDLAND $5 Mint Revenue NH VF	$19.95
NEWFOUNDLAND Uni#114P5b Mint Trial Color Plate Proof VF	$125.00	NEWFOUNDLAND Sg#61 Fresh Mint VF Appearance Deep Brown	$19.50
NEWFOUNDLAND Sg#12 Used CV ?850 ($1494)	$107.50	NEWFOUNDLAND EARLY ISSUES	$18.94
NEWFOUNDLAND C2 Mint Alcock-Brown Airmail $190.00	$95.00	Newfoundland Proofcard Drawing by Angus H Shortt	$18.00
NEWFOUNDLAND C2a Used Alcock-Brown Airmail $200.00	$95.00	NEWFOUNDLAND Sg#177 Fresh Used CV ?48 ($84)	$17.95
newfoundland c2 1919	$86.77	Newfoundland earlies mint & used lot	$17.52
British Vancouver 6 Mint catalog $240.00	$82.10	NEWFOUNDLAND SC#28 Imp Proof Mint VF NH	$16.39
PRINCE EDWARD ISLAND Sg#2 Mint Slight Dulled OG	$80.58	1941-49 Nfld #255 3c carmine, F-VF, Broken "A", lot/4	$16.10
Stamps Newfoundland 1910 6c Unlisted Perf Error MNH	$75.00	Canada Newfoundland Airmail Sc C8 MLH	$16.06
Nova Scotia #4 XF Used	$75.00	Newfoundland #37 Mint	$16.01

Canada ▶ Used

The average sales price in this subcategory is $16.88.

	HIGH		AVG
RARE CANADA JUBILEE # 63 XF JUMBO GEM. AMAZING $1200	$449.99	UNITRADE 36vi	$18.49
Canada #7a Used On Thick Paper	$325.00	Canada 41 DEWDNEY BC split ring Jan 25 1896	$18.39
Canada #4 Used Strip Of 3 **With AIEP Certificate**	$275.00	#26i Large Queen 5 cents, Deep Olive Green VF-U, CV250	$18.05
CANADA Un#64 Used CV CDN1500 ($1236)	$199.00	1859 First Cents #19 17c blue, F, used with grid cancel	$18.00
Canada #33 Used On Laid Paper	$180.00	CANADA Sc#86 Used VF SON CDS	$17.27
CANADA Un#12 Used CV CDN1200 ($989)	$144.05	Scott 68 Halifax Squared Circle MR 27 98 tm BLANK	$17.27
CANADA Un#11 Used CV CDN2000 ($1648)	$132.50	CANADA Sc#53 Used XF Jumbo Choice!!	$16.27
CANADA Un#61 Used CV CDN1000 ($824)	$99.00	Canada Scott 26 5 C Large Queen F/VF used. Look!	$15.65
#61 Used, Cat. $475.00	$84.00	Large Queen 22 Light Brown Red Well-Centered	$15.50
#62 Used, Cat. $500.00	$82.00	CANADA SC# 17 18 USED AVE. CV; 180.00 L@@K NR	$15.15
CANADA SC#23~29 Used/F~VF Nice cancel LQ(1) HiCV	$72.99	CANADA :: 1868 QV TRIO OF LARGE FORMAT 2c, 6c, 12.5c.	$15.00
CANADA SC#55 Used XF Choice!! CV $150	$69.00	Large Queen 27, a Two Shades	$15.00
CANADA Un#4 Used VF Great Color - Brown Red?	$69.00	Large Queen 27 a With Scarce Railway CDS	$15.00
CANADA Un#62 Used CV CDN750 ($618)	$69.00	Beautiful Canada Used - SG 132 - CV ?85!	$14.99
CANADA Sc#4a Used VF Brown Red	$65.00	CANADA SC#30bx4 Used/F~VF #1 Cancel LQ(5) HiCV	$14.99

Canada ▸ Collections, Lots

The average sales price in this subcategory is $53.10.

	HIGH		AVG
Canada Early Powerhouse Stamp Collection Cat $17,000	$1,995.00	Canadian Lot of 202 Mint Never Hinged Stamps Pre-1950	$68.00
Canada great collection 1859-1951 on 82 sides with text	$1,571.70	Canadian Lot of 400+ Used Stamps. Many pre-1950s	$66.79
Canadian Booklet Hoard - Over $1000 Face Value	$767.75	CANADA - 1lb. Of 48.49.50. Cent COMMEMORATIVES ONLY !!!	$63.50
CANADA Mint & Used Collection to 1959 Safe Hingeless	$749.00	Canada 1870 Queen Victoria overprint OFFICIAL 3 stamps	$61.00
Canada and Provinces Collection Must See No Reserve	$675.00	CANADA, 3000+ stamps on stkpgs..NO RESERVE!!	$58.00
Powerful Canada Collection. Must See!	$549.00	CANADA-2 Lbs. Up To 43 Cent .MOSTLY COMMS. Great Mix !!	$57.62
Canada Early Semi-Official Air Mail Stamp Collection	$490.00	CANADA-QV/GV M&U Stamp Lot to 1935.High Values-$1 (194)	$55.12
CANADA - 1970's/1990's - MNH ACCUMULATION. FACE $542	$490.00	CANADA # 149-157 MINT ISSUES $110.00+ NICE STAMPS	$51.00
CANADA-QV/GV Lot on Early Pages(Approx 220+Items)	$465.99	Canada 1868 #26 unused, 24,29 used on scott pg	$50.02
CANADA - SUPERB PLATE BLOCKS COLLECTION . FACE VAL $468	$421.00	RARE CANADA UN/MOUNTED.MINT REVENUES .2 x SETS TO $10	$49.99
CANADA, Stamp Collection on Scott pgs..CV $3200 NO REV!	$420.00	CANADA MINT + MNH STAMPS AND STATIONERY 100'S WOW! NICE	$41.00
CANADA - MAGNIFICENT COLLECTION OF BOOKLETS. F.V $455	$360.00	Canada stamp lot 1897 Q.V. JUBILEE MINT HIGH C.V.	$41.00
Valuable Mint Canada Collection. NO Reserve!	$336.00	CANADA-BOOKLET PANES.High Cat Value apprx ?120+ (6).	$37.00
Valuable Canada Collection. No Reserve!	$260.00	England and Colonies + Canada extrem old collection	$36.00
CANADA-Good OLD/1935 M&U Lot on Pages(Approx 180 Items)	$257.00	CANADIAN POST SOUVENIR COL. OF STAMP (3) BOOKS1987-89	$35.00

UK (Great Britain) ▸ Commemorative

The average sales price in this subcategory is $5.74.

	HIGH		AVG
600 GRAMS OF HIGH AND LOW VALUE COMMEMS MODERN	$50.00	1963 BRITISH COMMEMORATIVES + PHOSPHORS, MLH	$6.50
POUND OF 2005 C0MMEMS TO JULY INC SOME CHANNEL ISLANDS	$32.00	DIANA-PRINCESS OF WALES-5 STAMPS SET-VERY RARE& RETIRED	$5.99
CLASSIC Steam LOCOMOTIVES - set of 6 stamps - MINT	$19.16	Alderney 2000 S/S The Wombles MNH h8987	$5.50
GB 1988 COMMEMORATIVE SETS COMPLETE-MNH-LOOK!!	$12.99	BEAUTIFUL 1981 ROYAL WEDDING 23 CARAT GOLD STAMP	$5.50
Charles & Di Royal Wedding Commemorative GoldStamp 1981	$10.00	Princess Diana Royal Gowns Limited Edition Stamp	$4.99

UK (Great Britain) ▸ Covers

The average sales price in this subcategory is $29.50.

	HIGH		AVG
1832 *RARE* MALACCA Officers NANING WAR letter to UK **	$2,000.00	GB - 1971 Strike Mail on OHMS Tax cover	$35.03
1846 SINGAPORE with letter to ORKNEY ISLANDS Scotland *	$322.00	1797 BRIDGE ST / WESTMINSTER on House of Commons letter	$33.66
GREAT.BRITAIN+SUPERB #1 ON COVER	$256.00	GB/France-1994 Channel Tunnel+Rail Label Benham Card	$32.75
GREAT BRITAIN 1885 Registered Cover to (Saxony) Germany	$213.50	GB 1841 wrapper from York to Fermoy Ireland	$32.33
Lundy-1940 Suspended Air Service Cover+Mini-Shhet	$180.49	1958 Commonwealth Games FDC Cardiff postmark	$32.00
1867 1d Pink Stationery lettersheet for LORD BISHOP ***	$170.50	1862 1d red POSTED SINCE 10-30 LAST NIGHT Duplex *LOOK*	$31.09
1840 Fine 1d BLACK Q/K Linlithgow to FALKIRK **LOOK**	$163.50	GB BOOK POST LABEL 2D RATE LYNN 1884 DUPLEX WITH MORE T	$28.70
India ship letter 1818 to Scotland landed DEAL in Kent	$150.00	QUEEN MARY MAIDEN VOYAGE 1936	$28.09
LUNDY-Rare Large Morocco Agenc.1940 to Lundy Air Cover	$125.95	1851 CARLISLE 1d PAID in BLACK ex Aglionby **LOOK**	$27.01
1865 1/- SG 101 On entire Liverpool to South America	$125.00	GB/France-1994 Channel Tunnel Benham+Spec.Pmk Covers(4)	$27.00
LUNDY-Morocco Agencies 1940 Lundy Rare Cover+AIR LABEL	$107.50	#28a 1856 1/- Green on Cover London to Albany, New York	$26.76
Registered cover London to Lyon 3rd Sept 1890 SG209	$94.00	GB-1940 Centenary Cover+Special Originator Letter	$26.75
1788 EDEN HALL letter to Sir P.Musgrave at Kempton Park	$92.00	GB+Channel Isl-1960s/81 Cover+Train Label+FDC+Packs Lot	$26.00
GREAT BRITAIN 1874 'SUN BURNERS' ADVERTISING COVER	$85.00	1802 Island of MULL letter to Col Maclaine of Lochbuy *	$24.99
GB-1940 Centenary FDC+Cover+Control Mint Pairs	$79.89	1788 CARLISLE p/m letter Unthank to EDEN HALL **LOOK**	$24.99

UK (Great Britain) ▸ Edward VII

The average sales price in this subcategory is $39.54.

	HIGH		AVG
GB-EVII ?1 Green High Value Used.SG266.	$210.27	GB 1902 KE7 10sh ULTRAMARINE used, sg265, S786	$51.29
GB-EDVII USED HIGH VALUE SET (3 items).2/6,5/-,10/-.	$181.00	GREAT BRITAIN SG#254 Mint VF LH CV ?80 ($140)	$40.00
GB-EVII ?1 Green High Value.Registered Used.	$150.00	GREAT BRITAIN SG#257 Mint VF LH CV ?80 ($140)	$39.99
GB-EVII 10/- High Value.Fine Used CDS.	$132.50	GB-EVII M&U Lot on Page to 5/-(36 Items)	$30.06
GREAT BRITAIN SG#265 Used VF CV ?350 ($613)	$124.50	GREAT BRITAIN SG#O103 Used VF centered CV ?55 ($96)	$27.01

UK (Great Britain) ▸ Elizabeth II

The average sales price in this subcategory is $18.24.

	HIGH		AVG
GB-1907 POSTCARDS Posted on board FAIRY QUEEN Ship(2)	$153.50	Gr. Brit, Sc# 405p//1247, MNH(-1), CV $107.05	$21.50
Great Britain: SG 536-39/ Scott 309-12 Castles 1955 MNH	$132.50	1959,2nd D.L.R. CASTLE FRESH MINT SET.	$21.50
GB-1999/2001 Millenium Presentation Packs Lot(26 Items)	$80.00	GB-1972 QE 1/2p Side Band Booklet Pane.MNH	$21.00
GREAT BRITAIN SG#540-566 Mint NH CV ?173 ($301) Sets	$78.85	GB 1990 Penny Black Anniv Book + Stamps+ M/S	$20.51
GREAT BRITAIN SG#515-531 Mint NH CV ?95 ($165)	$62.00	GB 1948 QEII SILVER WEDDING ?1 MLH 2 Stamps	$18.15
QEII Waterlow High Values SC # 309 - 312 VFLH	$50.96	GB-2000 Timekeeper Mini-Sheet Presentation Pack	$16.00
GREAT BRITAIN SG#536-9 Mint LH CV ?225 ($391)	$37.00	GB 1958 graphite 1 1/2d used SG 589	$13.01
Gr. Brit, Coll of Machins,Sc# MH1//198 MNH, CV $142.85	$36.00	GB-2000/2 Minisheet Presentation Packs Lot(3 Items)	$11.99
GB-QE 2001 2nd Class IMPERF Adhesive Stamp Pair+ALBUM	$30.50	GREAT BRITAIN- (Machins) Beautiful MNH high values	$11.90
GB-Interesting 1971 STRIKE Post Cover Lot(110+Stamps)	$28.01	Queen Elizabeth II Silver Jubilee	$9.99

UK (Great Britain) ▶ FDCs

The average sales price in this subcategory is $27.21.

	HIGH		AVG
GB 1969 CONCORE Signed BRIAN TRUBSHAW + Co-Pilots	$355.00	GB P.O in TANGIER 1957 QEII FDC to British Consulate uk	$28.50
GREAT BRITAIN 1900 COMMERCIAL FDC	$260.00	GB 1962 Productivity Year Fareham Cds FDC	$28.05
GB-1940 Centenary Illust.FDC Cover+Special Abroath Pmk	$186.35	GB 1992 Wintertime Animals Benham H/S Official 4 FDC	$27.79
GB-1940 Centenary FDC on 1890 Illustrated Jubilee Cover	$138.25	GB 2003 FDC Good Lot Special H/S 14 Items	$27.79
GB 1941 KG VI PALE COLOURS SET 1/2d - 3d ON SIX FDI	$118.29	GB 1985 TRAINS Benham Cornish Riviera Paddington ?60	$27.00
GB 1995 Good FDC Lot Special H/S 100 Items	$103.55	GB 2000 FDC Good Lot Millenium Special H/S 21 Items	$27.00
GB 1966 Westminster Ord + Phos Scarce Parliament St Pmk	$91.00	GB 1983 Fish Birmingham Anglers Bradbury Official ?50	$26.77
GB-1962 NPY Phosphor Illust.FDC Cover+Southampton T,	$91.00	GB-1993 ?10 High Value Definitive BENHAM Cover	$26.36
GB-1940 Centenary Illustrated FDC Cover.	$89.88	GB 1985 TRAINS Benham Cornish Riviera Paddington ?60	$26.15
GB-1980s/90s 1st Day Cover Lot(124)+2 R.Mail Albums	$86.00	GB-1986 RAF Benham+2002 Cats Coin+IOM+Eire Covers(11)	$26.00
GB-1940 Centenary FDC+Cover+Special Pmk Lot(13 Items)	$79.00	GB 1966 Football Slogan Stampex Cover FDC 5 Items	$26.00
GB 1957 Parliamentary Conf Block x4 Big Ben H/S	$77.80	GB 1998 DIANA Spec H/S + Benham 9 FDCs	$26.00
1951 - G. Britain - FDC - Festival of Britain	$73.00	GB-1991+94 Channel Tunnel+Train Label+France Covers(4)	$26.00
GB FDC Lot Definitive Booklets ?3 120 Items + Album	$71.00	GB 1999 FDC Lot Millenium + M/Sheets 20 Items	$25.30
GB-1975/90s Train/Channel Tunnel Spec.Pmk Covers(6)	$67.78	GB 1999-2002 FDC Lot MINI SHEET Spec H/S 9 Items	$25.05

UK (Great Britain) ▶ George V

The average sales price in this subcategory is $52.39.

	HIGH		AVG
GB-Rare GV 1929 PUC ?1.Marginal Mint.START AT $9.99 !!	$722.00	GB-GV 1913/25 Good M&U Stamp Lot.Incl Seahorses (38).	$71.00
GB-GV Nice 1929 P.U.C. ?1.00 USED.	$569.99	GB-1934 10/- Seahorse.Good Used.	$56.56
GB-GV M&U Lot on Pages.Incl.?1 SEAHORSE etc(90+Items)	$512.00	GB-Interesting M&U GV Lot on Early Pages(80+Items)	$52.06
Great Britian stamps #173, 174 & 175 MINT Cat $1,275.00	$417.67	GB 1912-24 2 1/2d BLUE BLOCK OF FOUR SG 372	$42.50
GREAT BRITAIN SG#351//395 MNH Set of 15 CV ?260 ($452)+	$229.00	GB 1911 1d wmk Crown SG333 used Die B analine scarlet	$36.00

UK (Great Britain) ▶ George VI

The average sales price in this subcategory is $42.42.

	HIGH		AVG
BRITISH POSTAL ORDER.1946.20 SHILLING x 8 PIECES.USED	$334.00	GB SG 509-512 MNH (UM) CV 90?	$45.60
GREAT BRITAIN GEORGE V1 'FOLDED PAPER' VARIETY!	$152.50	GB-1948 Royal Wedding.?1 Unmounted Mint.	$42.00
GREAT BRITAIN SG#476-478a Mint LH CV ?268 ($466)	$92.61	GB-Nice 1940 GVI Centenary FDC+Special Pmk Covers(5)	$42.00
GREAT BRITAIN SG#D19-25&24a Mint LH CV ?122 ($214)	$51.99	British George VI HIGH VALUES 2/6 - ? MNH NR	$31.00
GREAT BRITAIN SG#509-512 Mint NH CV ?90 ($156)	$49.00	Mint NH Blocks 1937-39 High Values 4p-1 shilling	$30.00

UK (Great Britain) ▶ Victoria

The average sales price in this subcategory is $51.49.

	HIGH		AVG
GB-1884 ?1 Brown-Lilac Used.Rare High Catalogued Item	$572.00	GB-QV 1840 1d Black QL on Cover/Wrapper.	$71.01
GB-QV Mainly USED OFFICIALS. High Cat Value (49 items).	$461.55	GB-QV Good USED 2d Blue.Almost 4 Margins.	$71.00
GB-QV Lovely 1858 1d RED Plates to 224 USED (152).	$355.00	Great Britain SC# 1 Used / Penny Black / 3+ Margins	$66.00
GREAT BRITAIN 1847-54 10d BROWN EMBOSSED - FINE USED!	$280.03	1893 2d REGISTERED STATIONERY + 10 x 1d Lilacs **LOOK**	$62.00
GB-1891 QV ?1 Green High Value.Used.SG212.LOW START	$223.79	GB 1858 PENNY RED PLATE 225 SA SPACEFILLER	$61.00
GB-QV Beautiful MULREADY 1d Envelope A156.	$223.50	GB-QV 1862 2/-Blue SG118/20 F.U.CDS,Wing Margin	$58.57
GB-QV 1841/1881 Range in 2 Special Padded Packs.	$223.49	GB-QV Lovely 6d PAIR + 1/-JUBILEE MINT (3 items).	$56.30
HIGH VALUE GREAT BRITAIN OLD STAMPS LOT,THE SHILLINGS !	$202.35	Penny Black World's First Postage Stamp Folio, CV$260	$55.00
GB-QV EMBOSSED 2x6d + 10d USED.High Cat Value (3).	$200.00	GB - QV Lot SG 192 4d, SG 193 5d & SG 196 1s Green	$47.75
GB-QV SURFACE PRINTED 1856/67 USED Stamp Lot (33 items)	$194.50	GREAT BRITAIN Sg#23 Fresh Used VF Small Crown Watermark	$45.00
GB-QV 1d+2d Imperfs,Perf Stars,Plates,2d,1/2d(150+Item)	$187.05	GB-QV Used in Valparaiso(Chile).10d.Cat.Val?250	$44.30
GB-QV Surface Printed USED in MALTA (11 items).	$182.50	GB-1840 2d Blue Imperf 2 to 3 Margins+Black MX.AK	$42.60
GB-QV Nice 1883/87 M&U Stamp Lot (34 items).High Cat.	$180.50	15 QV QUEEN VICTORIA 1860 to 80s	$42.50
1840 Fine 1d BLACK Q/K Linlithgow to FALKIRK **LOOK**	$163.50	GB-QV Lilac+Greens+Jubilees M&U Lot(23 Items)	$42.00
GB-QV 1840 2d Blue.4 Margins+Red MX.AH.	$162.50	GB-QV 1890 Jubilee Penny Post Illustrated Covers-M&U	$37.68

UK (Great Britain) ▶ Collections, Lots

The average sales price in this subcategory is $30.78.

	HIGH		AVG
GB-Valuable QV/EVII Lot to 10/- on Pages(130+Items)	$866.12	JERSEY + ISLE OF MAN BOX LOADED WITH MNH BOOKLETS!!!!!	$31.00
COMMONWEALTH - QE - SUPERB MNH COLLECTION . CAT ?3200+	$810.00	Great Britain - Interesting - Revenue Collection	$31.00
Great Britain Early Stamp Collection Catalog $14,500	$699.00	GREAT BRITAIN FANTASTIC LOADED 1" BOX MANY BETTER	$31.00
FANTASTIC GREAT BRITAIN OLD HUNDREDS STAMPS LOT,LOOK !!	$426.00	UK,LOT OF CLASSIC STAMPS,HIGH CV	$31.00
GB - AMAZING MINT & USED STAMP COLLECTION	$360.00	GB 1960s-80s PRESENTATION PACK 18 Items	$31.00
GB-Interesting REVENUE Specimen Overprinted Lot(41 Item	$360.00	GB 1880 1d venetian red x 176,lots numeral cancels,S113	$29.11
GB 1953-89 Mint Collection + Album 550+ Stamps	$295.00	GB-QV/EVII Officials+Other Postage Dues Lot(44 Items)	$29.06
GB, clearout sale. lots of victoria incl. Take a look..	$253.00	GB-Aviation+Cinderellas+Document+Sheet Lot	$29.00
GREAT BRITAIN 1870-80 Album Page Used CV ?2075 ($3606)	$215.00	Herm Island-Nice Mint Stamp+Cover Lot(100+Stamps+Covers	$29.00
NobleSpirit~EXTREMELY VALUABLE MINT GHANA COMPLETE!!!	$190.05	Alderney-Locals Mainly Used Lot+MNH Sheets(40 Stamps)	$29.00
GB-1958/2000 Special Albums(2) MNH Stamp,Booklet LOT	$183.51	GB/France-1994 Channel Tunnel Special Book+Covers+Pack	$28.64
GB-Interesting OLD Revenue Stamp Lot(Approx 90 Stamps)	$173.50	GB-GV/QE Land Regsitry Revenue Stamped Documents(9)	$28.51
COLLECTION PENNY RED NO.33 PLATE NO's	$152.50	Lundy,Staffa,Bardsey,Drake's-Unusual Stamp+Cover Lot	$28.25
GB Victorian lot HUGE CATALOGUE VALUE 100+ items	$148.00	GB-VICTOR SHORT Cinderellas+Labels Lot(65+Stamps)	$26.01
A;L;2$;British Colony North Borneo 1887/1931 Mint;25100	$147.50	GB-1960s/70 FDC+Cover Accumulation(30 Items)	$26.00

Asia ▶ China

The average sales price in this subcategory is $29.50.

	HIGH		AVG
China PRC W7 Scott 967-80 POEMS OF MAO MNH XF	$905.00	CHINA (12)COVERS /POSTAL STATIONARY OLD COLLECTION	$31.00
PRC China Stamps # 996a Strip of 5 XF MNH	$898.00	CHINA,SMALL LOT OF OLD STAMPS	$31.00
1979,PRC RARE,SC# 1518 S/S SCIENCE MNH.VF CONDITION.NR	$565.00	China Treaty Port Stamp Inverted O/P	$30.99
China Stamps # 1355-8 Blocks XF MNH	$446.00	~ PRC China S61 Peonies! CTO VF! ~	$30.00
CHINA PRC SC#949-56, "CULTURAL REVOLUTION", MINT!!!***	$283.66	MANCHUKUO Sc#71-4 Mint VF Block of 4 Mt. Fuji & Phoenix	$29.99
PRC China Early Mint NH Stamp Collection in Stock Book	$283.00	CHINA Formosa 1 Error Strip of 3-NH	$29.95
CHINA PRC 1979 J41M Stamp Fair in Riccione S/S MNH	$243.50	China Treaty Port Stamp	$29.35
CHINA PRC 1961 C86M S/S Table Tennis Championship MNH	$240.50	CHINA Macau 1984 Year of the Rat. F D Cover	$29.07
PRC China Stamps # 716-31 XF MNH	$232.50	1941 China Imperf Souv Sheet of Six Mint #471 *Industry	$29.01
Hong Kong-Good QV/GV M&U Lot on Pages(117 Items)	$213.61	China PRC 1983 WESTERN CHAMBER, Sc#1844, MNH $68!	$28.59
PRC One of Kind Collection # 8	$210.00	Hong Kong 1800's Lot	$27.50
~ PRC China J41M Riccione Stamp Fair! MNH! ~	$202.50	China PRC 1964 YENAN SET/6, Sc#760-5, MLH $50!	$26.88
CHINA, PRC, SC#1586 , MNH Monkey SCARCE	$202.38	China PRC Forerunner NorthEastChina Surch pair w/small5	$26.02
CHINA / TA?AN 60's Years Nice Lot MNH CV $950+	$200.00	CHINA PRC LIBERATION COVER 1950 TO USA	$26.00
China Stamps # 1091a Complete Booklet XF MNH	$192.50	Rep of China 28c Martyr Scott 436 20c Surch Retouch Var	$26.00

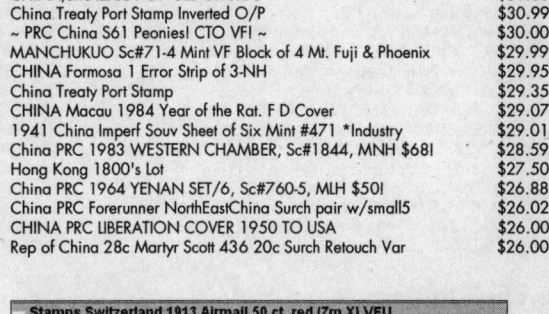

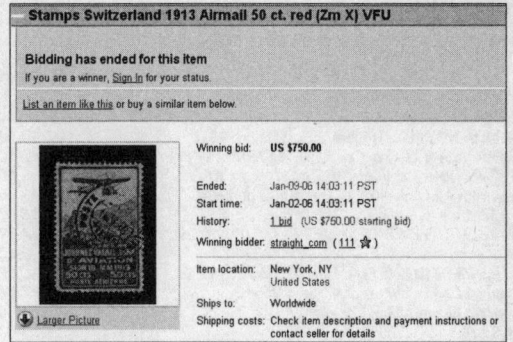

Asia ▶ Japan

The average sales price in this subcategory is $30.16.

	HIGH		AVG
CHINA PEKING TO MADAGASCAR VIA KONG-KONG... - 1908	$510.00	Japan Airs and Semipostals on 4 Pages- Mostly F-VF	$31.80
Japan Stamps # 254 XF MNH	$486.00	A;V;2$; Japan sheets lot Gen Mint/NH ; 26293	$31.28
Japan 1935 1st New Year Greeting **MINISHEET OF 20**	$442.75	Japan 1920 Sc#159-60 Census Set x2 MNH,13000y	$31.10
Japan Switzerland ca 1951 letter sheet #351,high cv	$405.00	INCREDIBLE IMPERIAL JAPAN COLLECTION ON ORIGINAL POSTER	$31.03
Korea 1891 Cover San Francisco to Incheon #177	$399.99	JAPAN - Yvert tel.10 CV u$ 200 - USED	$31.00
JAPAN 1871-1938 M&U Lot on Pages 120 Stamps	$318.20	Japan to Denmark KOFU 14y Himeji 24y Parks 1953	$31.00
Japan 1949 Moon & Geese Philatelic Week **SHEET OF 5**	$315.60	Japan 1948 Red Cross Nurse S/S	$30.27
Japan 1919 3sen Airmail Stamp With ISJP Certificate	$306.51	Japan 1936/48 Coll. on 10 Pages- Mostly F-VF Appearance	$30.00
JAPAN Sc#36 Syl.10 Used with Cross Cancel Very Scarce!!	$299.00	RYUKYU #16B VF Mint LH Type III CV$50	$30.00
Japan 1948 "Beauty" Philatelic Week **SHEET OF 5**	$275.60	1874-75 JAPAN STAMPS-3 YEL BRN GRN USED-1 BRN NOT USED	$29.53
Japan 1921 Sc#163-66 50th Anniv.UPU MNH,98400y	$260.00	Japan-Collection on stockpage U	$29.50
Japanese postcard mailed in the 1940's to the USA.	$255.00	Japan 1.5s postcard , Formosa taiwan 1901 to Japan	$29.50
Japan 1883, 1888-92 Classic Mint Group	$251.50	JAPAN Z117A, 120A, 121A,122A,125A, ALL MNH X 2,$104.00+	$29.35
Japan 1963/82 Mint Collection (Face=29,974 Yen)	$237.50	Japan #288a Nat'l Park Souv. Sheet MHG + Folder	$29.25
Japan 1919 1 1/2sen Airmail Stamp With ISJP Certificate	$225.99	Japan Selection of 4 Classical Stamps in @ (#JP1)	$29.10

Asia ▶ Korea

The average sales price in this subcategory is $43.91.

	HIGH		AVG
Korea 1902 (Kwangmu 6th) Cover Jinju-Changwon-Daegu#181	$999.99	Korea #1-2	$47.00
KOREA - 1957 2 x blocks 4 - 200 - 1000	$826.98	KOREA GENSAN - CHOSEN TO GERMANY - 1922	$46.00
KOREA, Sc #211, Industrial Reconstruction 20 Hwan MNH!!	$445.00	Korea South 1946,#74 (x21), blocks of 2 & 4, MNH OG, NR	$46.00
Korea 1891 Cover San Francisco to Incheon #177	$399.99	KS823 KOREA Stamp 50 chon x 100 Postaly Used 1946	$45.00
1955 Korea Stamp Watermark Wave CROSS Line 20 Hwan, UM	$385.00	KOREA NORTH 1953 MICHEL # 73 RARE!!!	$44.00
KOREA NINSEN - CHEMULPO - I.J.P.O - 1905	$350.00	Korea, South 1959, #290a, Mint NH OG souv.sheet, NR	$44.00
KOREA, COLLECTION OF (17) COVERS, most domestic	$334.00	Korea South,1948, #78 - 79, regular stamps, Mint NH, NR	$43.47
NORTH KOREA Postal Stationery Reply Card, 1950, RARITY	$295.00	Korea Cover, Seoul–USA, 1949	$43.01
Nice Korea Stamp Collection, No Rev!	$255.00	Korea Eagle 2R-4c (12) Mint #165	$43.00
Korea Ehwa 2wn Used #113	$249.99	1901 Imp Korea 3ch sur. cheon 34b (error based stamp)	$43.00
Korea 1899 Cover (Kwangmu 3th) Hansung to Wonsan #179	$249.99	KOREA STAMP #1-5 MOON SERIES MH & GUM 1884	$41.00
Korea 1903 2wn FALCON, Sc#51, MLH $400!	$233.71	KOREA STAMP #34 EMPEROR'S CROWN MH & GUM 1902	$40.00
Syngman Rhee Letter, Korean-American Council, 1942	$215.50	Korea North Collection of Blocks (Imperf.) #053	$39.99
KOREA - Sc #90 1st President VF OG MNH	$203.80	Vintage 1947 korea lot 10 won revenue stamp cover	$39.99
GERMANY TO KOREA NINSEN VIA NAGASAKI - 1897	$202.50	Korea South 1959, #295-6&a (x3), 6stmps&3svsht, MNH, NR	$39.12

Asia ▶ Thailand

The average sales price in this subcategory is $44.14.

	HIGH		AVG
Siam - Thailand Stamp Provisional - Fiscal Issue 1907	$2,501.01	SIAM 1887 Issue. 12 stamps. HM.	$49.21
Thailand 1908 Rama5 Jubilee issue 1 Att rare Error Mint	$543.99	SIAM 1883. 1 Solot - 1 Salung. FU.	$47.14
Thailand 36 cancels Siamese P.O. in Northern Malaya	$526.89	Thailand Royal Throne Sao Chin Cha postcard lot# 1 NICE	$47.00
Thailand-Early/Mid REVENUE Stamp Lot(66 Items)	$482.77	THAILAND - Sg 1218-21 and SG 1261-5 - 2 sets and	$46.77
Thailand 1949 5B-10B Rama IX High Values Reg Cover	$360.00	Thailand Group Rama 5 Provisional 1889-1898 and Variety	$45.01
Fabulous Thailand Stamp Collection, No Rev!	$355.00	FDI Commemorating of 2500th B.E. (Rare) 1 Cover. F.	$45.00
Thailand 1948 Tak-USA Cover w/ 20st Pair Rama IX	$241.50	THAILAND- POPE JOHN PAUL II, CHURCHILL, DISNEY,EINSTEIN	$43.95
THAILAND - Plate proofs - 1883-85 - Proofs on thick	$236.50	Thailand 1966 Asian Games, MNH	$41.00
THAILAND -SIAM 1947 COVER to USA	$222.50	1883 Thailand first issued set of 5,MLH OG,used LH,scan	$41.00
Thailand 1932 Rama VII Cover UBOL-USA	$194.50	Thailand Rama 7 Large Block of 20 with Imprinted MNH	$41.00
SIAM, THAILAND - WW I censored cover to Denmark.	$187.50	SIAM 1950 REGISTERED AIRMAIL COVER TO SWITZERLAND	$41.00
THAILAND -SIAM 1950 cover to WERNER BROS.PICTURES	$159.99	Thailand 1971 Thaipex Issue **BLOCKS OF 4**	$40.50
THAILAND 10 BAHT MICHEL 294A #MNH # $$$$$$$$$$	$142.50	Thailand 1972 75st Ruby Gemstone * SCARCE IMPERF PAIR*	$40.00
THAILAND - Sg 370-2 - 1955 Red X values - never hinged	$129.50	1889-90 Thailand issued surch. lot of 5,MLH,OG,see scan	$38.71
Thailand 1905 Multicolor Postcard Singapore Australia	$123.50	THAILAND -SIAM 1932 COVER to SWITZERLAND	$38.37

Europe ▶ Austria

The average sales price in this subcategory is $16.55.

	HIGH		AVG
AUSTRIA & Area Collection in Davo Album to 1967	$349.00	AUSTRIA, SMALL LEVANTE CLASSIC LOT	$17.67
185B Austria MNH Rare sport set	$150.50	Austria mix.german stamps cover Gludenz/Sweden 1938	$17.16
AUSTRIA Large MNH Dealer Stock Lot.................A915	$150.00	Austria B128-131 used catalog $45.00	$17.10
Austria Levant parcel 20+1pi.Constantinopel/Swiss 1909	$142.50	Austria B132-137 Mint catalog $51.00	$17.00
AUSTRIA Early Cover Card Lot Censored Hitler 44 Items	$103.50	Austria B138-141 Mint catalog $52.00	$17.00
Austria+Bosnia+Aust.Italy+KUK-OLD M&U Lot on Pages	$99.00	Belgium #374-85 nh set cat $51	$17.00
Austria 144 used catalog $275.00	$98.00	AUSTRIA 1858 2k light-yellow #6 CDS	$16.95
AUSTRIA-1929/31-VIEWS-YV 378/89(EX379/80)-MNH-CV-670.00	$94.99	AUSTRIA AIR POST STAMPS MINT/USED, C1-3, C4-11 AND MORE	$16.05
Austria(classic issues)lot	$92.00	AUSTRIA POSTAGE DUE: J10-21, J34-46, MH J19 & LOTS MORE	$16.05
A;V;; Austria lot 1910 F.VF M/U H lot of Hicv; 22193	$88.00	AUSTRIA CLASSIC , SEVERAL QUALITY (A18)	$16.00
A;V;; Austria 12 items F-VF+U CDS Hicv ; 25513	$87.56	AUSTRIA Mi#587 Used VF CV $60 ($74)	$16.00
Minkus Austria Stamp Album Copyright 1964	$83.10	Austria reg.3+4+5gr. x4+15g. Enns 1945+censor	$16.00
AUSTRIA REGISTERD LETTER 1851 (A50)	$83.00	AUSTRIA P6 AVERAGE-GOOD CONDITION SOUND $300.00+ CV	$15.60
AUSTRIA TRENTINO Sc # N49 Mint No Gum	$81.50	AUSTRIA. 3000 Used Stamp Accum. LOOK!	$15.51
Austria occ. letter Cattaro/Venezia tax. 22 1809	$78.77	AUSTRIA Very Nice Over 335 Different Stamps	$15.50

Europe ▶ Belgium & Colonies

The average sales price in this subcategory is $17.02.

	HIGH		AVG
BELGIQUE RARE LOT	$452.00	BELGIAN CONGO RUANDA URUNDI ETHNIC SET TWO VALUES	$19.50
Stamps: Belgium 1932 Cardinal Mercier Set (B114-22) M	$250.00	Belgian Congo Sc. #39 5 Francs overprint CV $24 NR	$19.49
BELGIUM CLASSIC FIRST ISSUE STAMPS I ef15	$215.50	[104] CF / SP :Nice set of stamps perfect MNH value $56	$19.16
BELGIAN CONGO 1885-1936 M&U Collection 200 Stamps	$188.05	BELGIUM SEMI POSTAL COLLECCTION ALL STAMPS SHOWN	$19.05
BELGIQUE RARE LOT	$170.00	BELGIUM very nice over 395 different stamps	$19.05
BELGIUM , classic . the first two stamps , LOOK !	$167.50	BELGIAN CONGO SECOND ISSUE 5fr GRAY USED	$19.00
Belgium Scott #B144-B150 mint NH, CV $153.35	$132.50	BELGIAN CONGO 1931 ETHNIC SET 4 VALUES WITH OVER .MINT	$18.89
Belgium Congo:The Very Extensive Collection,Cat ?400.	$126.39	BELGIAN CONGO FIRST ISSUES SMALL SELECTION MINT HINGED	$18.50
BELGIUM 1849-1935 M&U Collection 350 Stamps	$117.50	BELGIAN CONGO 1912 POST. STAT. PICTURE CARD	$18.49
BELGIUM SPECTACULAR 1850-60 COVER COLLECTION (18)COVER	$110.50	[102] Nice set of stamps MNH, face value 730Fb	$18.40
Belgium # 229 - 236 MNH	$103.50	BELGIUM PARCEL POST & AIR & OFFICIAL COLLECTION	$17.70
BELGIUM Sc 36a MINT CHOICE VF COPY SCV$350.00	$96.00	Belgium Scott 45/59 used, CV $237.75	$17.62
Switzerland+Belgium-Early/Mod+Charities Lot(850+Items)	$86.55	Belgium Scott 18/38 used, CV $237.75	$17.61
BELGIQUE RARE LOTDU MEDAILLON	$86.00	KATANGA 1960 Overprinted Issues on Cover to U.S.	$17.59
Belgium # 185 - 190 MNH	$81.72	BELGIAN CONGO 1915 ISSUE SET HINGED	$17.39

Europe ▶ Czechoslovakia, Czech Republic

The average sales price in this subcategory is $16.00.

	HIGH		AVG
CZECHOSLOVAKIA & SLOVAKIA, 5000+ stamps in 2 binders.	$330.00	Czechoslovakia: 1979/80's,MNH Collection,Cat Val ?81.	$17.50
1919 overp.post ceskoslovenska	$255.00	CZ083. CZECHOSLOVAKIA LIBERATION LOCALS 1945 KONICE	$17.49
Czechoslovakia #B97 mint	$199.99	CZECHOSLOVAKIA COMPLETE YEAR 1949 MNH LOW START	$17.00
Powerful MNH+ Czechoslovakia Minkus Specialty Album NR	$199.00	Czechoslovakia-Early/Mid Cinderellas+Blocks Lot	$16.50
Czechoslovakia Stamps Early Scout Mail Covers	$150.00	CZECHOSLOVAKIA DEALER STOCK/ACCUMULATIONI-NRIII	$16.49
Czechoslovakia Stamps 1918 Scout Post Cover	$127.50	3 CZECHOSLOVAKIA 1948-67 JUDAICA JEWISH COVER + SHEETS	$16.49
Czechoslovakia Legion in Russia Civil War Stamps. 1920.	$108.60	CZ087. CZECHOSLOVAKIA LIBERATION LOCALS 1945 SOBOTKA	$16.38
1972 MINKUS CZECHOSLOVAKIA ALBUM WITH 838 STAMPS	$97.00	CZECHOSLOVAKIA COMPLETE YEAR 1973 MNH LOW START	$16.00
1923 28.10. T.G.MASARYK jubilee, stamp collection	$81.50	Czechoslovakia: 1979/80's,MNH Collection,Cat Val ?81.	$15.51
Stamps: Czech 1925 Olympics Ovpt Set (#B137-9) MLH	$75.00	[2 of these sold for $15.51 each]	
CZECHOSLOVAKIA - AMAZING FINE	$51.00	Czechoslovakia-1918/37 M&U Lot on Early Pages(180+Items	$15.50
USED STAMP COLLECTION		Czechoslovakia MNH Hradcany blocks A	$15.50
CZECHOSLOVAKIA,1940,CENSORED AIRMAIL CVR TO ARG...	$50.10	Czechoslovakia Stamps # 707-10 XF MNH	$15.00
Czechoslovakia - Scott #B70, Mint, Hinged,	$49.95	CZECHOSLOVAKIA "REVENUE STAMP CATALOG"	$15.00
A;V;; Czechoslovachie + Germany #19 varietes ; 27049	$45.00	1941 Czechoslovak Forces in GB Commem Postcard VF!	$14.01
A COLLECTION OF RARE HISTORICAL STAMPS	$43.15	CZECHOSLOVAKIA SHEETS LOT MNH LOOK......LOW START	$14.00

Europe ▶ Denmark & Faroe Islands

The average sales price in this subcategory is $14.24.

	HIGH		AVG
DENMARK-OLD/Mod Good Collection(Approx 450+Items+ALBUM	$227.50	Denmark Post Ferry 15-3.Margin.Bl;of four. Lux Cancl;	$15.00
Denmark-Interesting OLD LOCAL Stamp Lot(Approx 120)	$191.25	Denmark Poster Stamp, Balloon.	$14.50
Denmark Post Ferry 8. Margin Bl;of four. MNH.	$132.51	Denmark Afa 304 X Var Dobb; Streik in Ship Pos 48.VFU	$14.50
001B Denmark cover 1921	$119.50	Denmark Stamps # 156-60 VF MH	$14.00
Denmark 1921 Parcel Post Labels to Hamburg	$115.50	Denmark Stamps # 192-7 VF MLH	$14.00
DENMARK , very nice classic lot , LOOK !	$113.72	Denmark Poster Stamp, Fire engine	$14.00
DENMARK-OLD Revenue/Cinderella Lot(Approx 150 Stamps)	$84.79	Denmark Stamp SC# 2, Fine Condition	$14.00
14 Denmark Revenues–Skillings & Rigsbank Dalers	$76.00	DENMARK-1854/64-YVERT 3-GOOD USED-FRESH COLOUR-CV$92.00	$13.99
DENMARK FA#PF5 Used VF CV SK2500 ($350)	$75.03	DENMARK LOT STAMPS (796)	$13.50
MNH plate no. blocks of 4 -fine to very fine denmark,	$70.00	Danish West Indies Fa 49/56 MNH (344)	$13.50
DENMARK , nice classic/semi classic lot, LOOK !	$66.00	Denmark Scott #15 used. 2005 CV is $160.00	$13.15
DENMARK , nice semi classic lot, LOOK !	$61.00	Faroe Islands - 1996 MI # 291/309 complete on FDC	$13.00
Danish West Indies #3 Used	$60.00	Faroe Islands - 1997 MI # 310/327 complete on FDC	$13.00
Denmark Collection 1851-1868, CV $725 (DENC001)	$59.99	DENMARK-1907-NEWSPAPER STAMPS-YV 1/8-P.12 1/2-FU-$79.00	$12.99
Denmark Collection 1870-1882, CV $745 (DENC002)	$59.99	13 Early Denmark Revenues–Ores and Krones	$12.51

Europe ▶ France & Colonies

The average sales price in this subcategory is $14.37.

	HIGH		AVG
NEW HEBRIDES 1903 Special Local Post PC with Pic. Rare	$199.00	FRANCE Yv#307-8 Mint LH Semipost 1935 CV ?68 ($91)	$15.00
FRANCE 1936 50 FR BANKNOTE AIRMAIL USED	$147.50	0827-Maximum Card /France 1946/Stanislas Place of Nancy	$14.99
FRANCE-Scarce YT#17A MINT. VF $ 1476.00 <jf6>	$143.50	5100a-Maximum Card /France 1952 /Viaduct of Garabit	$14.99
FRENCH INDIA 1916 Regis. Provisional Stationary Cover	$138.03	C-059) ST. PIERRE & MIQUELON , SC# J10-20, MH	$14.54
France, MH, yvert 258/62 (158)	$115.50	FRENCH COLONIES #23 USED $125.00....WOW!!!!!!!!!!	$14.50
France:1936 100th Anniversary Flight,MLH,Cat Val ?290.	$95.22	French Offices in Port Lagos Scott 3 Used	$14.50
France:1869 1F,Light Used,Catalogue Value ?1000.	$86.00	France: 1927 Merson 3F, MLH,Catalogued ?48.	$14.49
FRANCE #N1-N5, N7 X 2, ALL MINT $985.00+ CAT. VALUE!!!!	$86.00	FRANCE #N3 FANTASTIC USED GREAT CANCEL...$85.00++..WOW!	$14.19
A;V;2$; France Colonies+Monaco Special VFNH Hicv; 25273	$74.60	France China old tm117	$14.10
French Occ. Castellorizo # 12 MNH	$73.52	Older Andorra-French Admin Beautiful M/NH Collection!	$13.61
FRANCE YT 296/297 Jacques Cartier MNH CV 240	$71.99	NEW CALEDONIA USED STAMPS VERY HIGH CATALOGUE VALUE	$13.58
FRANCE Yv#76 Used CDS CV ?270 ($323)	$69.00	andorre expres card 8.12 1947 please look	$13.50
NOSSI BE J12 MINT 24 USED CV; 160.00 L@@K NR	$66.27	France colonies to290	$13.50
New Hebrides # 68 - 78 MNH	$66.00	*/** COLLECTIONS FRANCE COLONIES MN */**	$13.50
French Occ. Castellorizo # 11 MNH	$63.52	FRANCE #77 MINT $67.50+...WOW!!!!!!!!!!	$13.50

Europe ▶ Germany & Area

The average sales price in this subcategory is $16.68.

	HIGH		AVG
CHRISTIANIA NORWAY TRANS-POLAR FLIGHT EXPEDITION 1926	$401.00	DANZIG 1931 multi-franking air mail cover to Germany	$18.05
GERMANY x2 Minkus Albums, 2768 Stamps, 378 Pages - wow!	$291.00	Sudetenland Cover; Lichlowick Mixed Frank	$18.00
GERMANY OCC Belgium Sc#N24 used perfin	$214.50	Germany 5NB12-4 used	$18.00
DO-X Cover to USA with Sudamerika ZEPPELIN Franking	$206.25	German Third Reich Tunis Afrika Corp Post Stamps(3)	$17.99
A Lot of Germany 1945/ 48 Alliierte Bes. area MNH or MH	$201.00	Germany - REICH Mi 586-700 -MNH** SUPER QUALITY BARGAIN	$17.99
S.S. Bremen CATAPULT Flight Cover 1934	$190.25	German Colonies MARIANA ISL. # 18 MNH exp'd	$17.60
GERMANY Early Postal Stationary Card Used with Pic.	$149.50	German Colonies SOUTHWEST AFRICA # 24-28 MNH	$17.50
MODERN GERMANY COLLECTION INCL.THE MODERN YEARS MNH	$137.50	GERMANY FRENCH OCCUPATION SEMI POSTALS MNH NICE	$17.50
GERMANY 1923 ILLUSTR. COVER INFLATION URPATING	$130.25	Nazi Car Show 1942, VW, Grand Prix Racing Stamps, CXL!	$17.49
Shoe Box of Booklets/Germany/Netherlands/etc 100+	$124.01	German Colony Cameroun Scott 11 on pc PLANTATION sch	$17.36
Germany & Colonies Scott Album Collection	$115.50	Inflation 5 BILLION Mark Cover 1923	$16.58
Germany #C39 Zeppelin South America Pair to USA	$113.61	1922 MEMEL Plebiscite Cover	$16.50
WONDERFUL ZEPPELIN POLAR FHART MLH*	$112.50	1930s-1940s Germany Quality Mint Stamp Collection-LOOK!	$16.16
Cover posted in Libau - w Kurland and German franking	$110.50	Germany Third Reich 1938 Zeppelin Air Stamp Set Mint	$16.15
A Lot of German colony g. or MH	$103.50	1936 Building of Danzig, Winter Walfare	$16.05

Europe ▶ Greece

The average sales price in this subcategory is $43.03.

	HIGH		AVG
134B Greece 1933 Republic MNH	$1,000.00	164B Greece complete sets 1971 up to 1980 MNH 93 sets	$46.52
GREECE - 1896 - AMAZING OLYMPICS STUDY	$565.00	GREECE Flying Hermes Sc#165-78 Mint LH F-VF CV $76	$46.01
GREECE 1862-1995 Mint Collection on Scott Pages ?1575	$549.00	GREECE CLASSIC SMALL MINT AND USED COLLECTION	$46.00
101B Greece 1896 First Olympic Games MH	$547.77	Greece, 1896, #117-125, Athens First Olympics, (077)	$44.77
110B Greece 1906 second olympic games MNH	$518.88	Greece:Good Collection,Crete,P.O.'s,Locals etc.	$43.89
GREECE - 1906 Olympic set on 2 souvenir cards	$500.00	GREECE NATO 1954 MNH	$42.00
102B Greece 1896 First Olympic Games used	$382.77	GREECE Sc#C8-14 Hellas#A8-14 Mint LH VF ?82	$42.00
113B Greece 1913 Campaign (Ekstrateia) 1912 MH	$380.00	N EPIRUS Greece Sc#N219-28 Hellas#168-77 ?102	$42.00
Greece: The Valuable Collection From Imperfs.	$360.00	GREECE EARLY LOT, 36 COVERS, POSTCARDS & LETTER CARDS	$41.00
133B Greece 1933/1935 Landscapes II MNH	$350.00	GREECE EARLY COLLECTION OF 32 COVERS & LETTER CARDS.	$40.50
135B Greece 1933 Republic MH	$316.01	156B Greece 1955 Ancient Greek Art II MNH	$40.00
GREECE - 1923 - SUPERB REVOLUTION STUDY . CAT ?400+	$305.00	GREECE MIC#121 & #157 MINT HIGNED	$40.00
364A Greece MNH rare tete beche	$300.00	132B Greece 1932 Overprinted Admirals MNH	$38.00
107B Greece 1902 Metal value AM (Parcel set) MNH	$300.00	1859 Greece Ionische Isle # 1, 2, 3 hinged CV 150.00	$37.01
GREECE - 1912/13 - GREEK ADMIN. COLLECTION .CAT ?700+	$260.00	GREECE - INCREDIBLE COLLECTION OF COVERS & CARDS	$37.00

Europe ▸ Hungary

The average sales price in this subcategory is $20.49.

	HIGH		AVG
A;V;; Hungary 1,6 F-VF M OG C.V.: 1000.00 $; 29704	$560.00	Hologram Hungary 1996 MEK 101ka inter exhibition Peking	$24.99
A;V;2$; Hungary B198A-D,CB1-C XFNH Sheet of 4 ; 29741	$255.00	Hologram Hungary 1996 MEK 109ka inter exhibition Tajpej	$24.99
Hungary stamp 1871 3k Light Green 2- Extremeley Fine og	$199.99	A;V;4$; Hungary air post Mint + Used ; 29914	$24.99
Hungary old stamp 1871 10k Blue (4), Very Fine, og	$199.99	Hungary 6N14 with double overprint, Brainard & Szalay	$24.95
HUGE VALUABLE MNH HUNGARY HARRIS PAGES TO 1987	$199.99	A;V;; Hungary Franz Josef No faults hidden ; 29706	$23.10
A;V;2$; Hungary C81 XFNH perf. C.V.: 225.00$+++ ; 29716	$161.50	HUNGARY,MNH S/S LOT	$23.06
HUNGARY TOWN CANCEL COLLECTION 800+ FULL STRIKES	$153.50	Austria stationery telegraph form, mint H 3	$22.50
A;V;2$; Hungary C81 imperf XFNH Fresh ! ; 29717	$153.50	VALUABLE HUNGARY MNH SHEET ASSORTMENT, NO RESERVE !!	$22.50
HUNGARY 1947 ROOSEVELT SHEETS MNH**	$134.00	A;V;; Hungary Mint OG Fresh ! C.V.: 250.00 $; 29708	$22.50
Hungary 1921 Local issue set Golden Eagle	$132.50	WESTERN HUNGARY Lajta Banat West Ungarn 1921 LOT	$20.50
A;V;2$; Hungary Mint VFLH Fresh ! Hicv ; 29922	$113.61	HUNGARY Zeppelin Airmail Mi#478-9 Mint HR VF	$20.50
A;V;2$; Hungary occ. stamps Mint + Used Hicv ; 29920	$112.00	Hungary-Early/Mod REVENUE Stamp(65)+Documents(4) Lot	$20.50
HUNGARY - AMAZING FINE USED STAMP COLLECTION	$92.00	Hungary #1 used	$19.99
A;V;; Hungary #2,3,4,5(2) CV: 800.00 $; 29705	$88.67	HUNGARY-OLD M&U Lot on Pages(Approx 230+Items)	$19.49
A;V;2$; Hungary C66 XF LH Fresh ! CV:160.00$+++ ; 29718	$77.08	Hungary 1988 Complete Year set MNH	$19.00

Europe ▸ Ireland

The average sales price in this subcategory is $8.69.

	HIGH		AVG
IRELAND-Lovely 1922 SEAHORSE Set F.MINT.Cat apprx ?200	$216.10	Ireland-Postal stationary-Wrapper-1d red.	$9.95
IRELAND-1922/23 SEAHORSE Set MINT.Cat apprx ?265.	$177.50	Ireland - Prestige Booklet Sc#1075b Lighthouses	$9.75
IRELAND COLLECTION 1922-1989 M/U Hi-CV 49 Pages	$128.00	1957 Fr.Wadding NHM	$9.51
Ireland-Unusual Labels-Sinn Fein,Mcdonnel White etc(8)	$93.00	IRELAND CLEARANCE registered Postcards 695-8 Max	$9.50
Ireland Team of The Millennium Sheetlet Imperf Hurling	$80.00	Ireland:1997-8 birds issues MNH SC 1076-81	$9.25
Ireland-Seahorse 10/- Scott 14, v/lt hinge.	$69.95	IRELAND. 102 Different Used Incl Better. CV$75	$9.05
IRELAND-Nice 1922/34 Mint&Used Lot on Pages(64 Items)	$67.51	1997 Pacific 97 M/s NHM	$9.00
IRELAND-1922/QE Issues.Incl SG84 Seahorse 5/-MINT (89)	$63.00	Ireland Postcard with Ballinamallard Post Mark 1907	$8.70
A;V;; Ireland lot all Mint NH Fresh ! Hicv ; 23656	$61.00	Irish Hospitals Sweepstakes-OLD Sheet of 24 Stamps.MNH	$8.50
IRELAND-GV/QE Collection on pages(250+Items)	$56.00	IRELAND 1992 FRAMA LABELS FIRST DAY COVERS	$8.45
Ireland-QV/QE REVENUE Stamp Lot(50 Items)	$52.57	Europa 2000 self adhesive issue	$8.39
Ireland-Postal history-1841 entire w/octagonal PAID.	$49.95	Ireland:1998 birds issues incl self-adhesives MNH	$8.05
LOT OF 90+ OLD STAMPS FROM IRELAND	$46.77	Ireland-GV Stamped Cover+Free Ireland Labels	$8.00
Ireland 1925. Mi.No.37 II-38II 2/6, 5/- MLH, ctv 300$	$36.35	Ireland literature - The Dublin Spoon (Dulin)	$8.00
IRELAND MINT ALL DIFFERENT OLD STAMP COLLECTION	$36.05	1991 Golf Commemorations,NHm blocks of 4	$8.00

Europe ▸ Italy & Area

The average sales price in this subcategory is $25.92.

	HIGH		AVG
VATICAN CITY #35-40 USED W SISMONDO CERTIFICATE VF	$560.02	ITALY POSTAL STATIONERY	$26.99
Italy Scott #31 Unused Fine Original Gum	$426.00	Italy #518 100L Roman Republic used	$26.99
San Marino Germany combination Zeppelin cover	$299.00	1960s Vatican City Beautiful M/NH Stamp Collection!	$26.77
ITALY PRE-1940 MINT AIRMAILS CAT $829.00	$286.09	ITALY STAMPS	$26.50
TREMENDOUS ITALY HIGH VALUE LOT,THOUSANDS DOLLARS !!!	$280.95	Italian Occup. RODI INTERESTING 63.00 euro mint	$26.01
ITALY FIUME Carnaro Mi#1-19 Mint LH, 1L on 25c Sm Thin	$201.50	ITALY TRIESTE # 15 - 17 COMPLETE MLH SET $170.00+	$26.00
ITALY SARDINIA 1854 Sc. 9 used, CV 2100 $	$199.99	Italy - 1859 - Papal Cover (Pontificio)	$26.00
VATICAN ALBUM WITH STAMPS!	$197.50	Italian States: Parma,Small lot of 5 Stamps.	$26.00
ITALY 1942-1966 COLLECTION CAT $956.00	$190.05	ITALY Aegean Islands Lipso Mi#3-13 VI Mint LH	$25.51
Italy 165-70 mint	$169.16	ITALY USED SELECTION 92 gms/1350 STAMPS BARGAIN	$25.50
Italy Stamps with Advertising Labels	$155.00	R.S.I. STAMPS VARIETY	$25.05
Italy - 1856 - Papal Cover (Pontificio)	$154.17	ITALY Y1950 Small Lot Mint LH CV ?205 ($247)	$24.99
5026-Greece-Egeo 1913 Italy occupation revenue+document	$153.73	ITALY Mi#275-8 Used CV ?160 ($193)	$24.99
Italy parcel stamp 50c. block of 20 variety perforation	$149.00	1935,air cover from genova to shanghai via new york	$24.99
VATICAN C16-17 - LH - CV $300.00 - Set	$133.50	ITALIAN Oltre Giuba nice set Interesting	$24.50

Europe ▸ Netherlands & Colonies

The average sales price in this subcategory is $45.63.

	HIGH		AVG
Netherlands - MINT/MNH album with treasures	$14,950.00	Netherlands stamps, booklet # 9fF	$49.00
Netherlands - VF 1913 Wilhelmina 10 gulden (Scott 101)	$475.00	NETHERLANDS 5x maximumcard Children singing 1963	$48.00
CURACAO 1947 AIR SET MNH BARGAIN!! NR	$206.50	[3 of these sold in a multiple item ("Dutch") auction for $16.00 each]	
Japan Occ Netherlands Indies Indonesia *NICE POSTCARD*	$203.50	NETHERLANDS , nice classic lot , POSTMARKS !!	$47.60
A;V;; Netherland #3-12 XFLH Fresh ! C.V.:950.00$; 25293	$154.05	NETHERLANDS , semi classic , long set definitives !	$46.07
NETHERLAND 1852-1935 Used	$152.50	Netherlands #74 VF Mint	$46.02
Collection on Pages 180 Stamp		1951 Netherlands (HOLLAND) Air FDC,see scan	$46.00
CURACAO 1946 COMPL.SET MNH GREAT BARGAIN!! NR	$144.01	1892/97. NED- INDIE. MH. SCOTT # 232,25/25,30. N-123	$45.00
Netherlands Scott #28 Unused	$120.50	Netherlands Stamp SC# 3, Very Fine Condition	$45.00
Netherlands-Interesting Revenue+Cinderellas Lot(70+Item)	$112.50	Netherlands Catch. FDC E38 Unaddressed	$44.05
NETHERLANDS , large lot COIL stamps , VOOR HET KIND	$110.00	Netherlands Scott #3 used. 2005 CV is $110.00	$43.55
NETHERLANDS , RARE semi classic high definitives !!	$102.50	NETHERLAND ANTILLES 1949-54 FOUR SETS MNH-US. NR	$43.42
NETHERLANDS , S/S nr 1 and 2 , MNH !!	$102.50	NETHERLANDS , RARE 1 G green (coronation) and more !	$42.67
NETHERLANDS , Very rare semi classic stamp, LOOK !	$92.10	Netherlands - Early Revenue Collection.	$41.00
Netherlands Scott #J1-2 Unused O.G.	$87.51	NETHERLANDS , very rare COIL stamps , SET USED !	$41.00
NETHERLANDS , rare semi classic stamps , LOOK !	$87.23	NETHERLANDS , nice lot semi classic sets , LOOK !	$41.00

Europe ▶ Norway

The average sales price in this subcategory is $21.88.

	HIGH		AVG
NORWAY ROALD AMUNDSEN ORIG. AUTOGRAPH NORTH POLE 24/25	$450.00	Norway local Hammerfest 1888 2 on 10 ore mint H&W 5	$23.49
CHRISTIANIA NORWAY TRANS-POLAR FLIGHT EXPEDITION 1926	$401.00	Norway local Hammerfest 1888 4 on 8 ore mint H&W 6	$23.49
Norway 6 Mint catalog $900.00	$239.00	NORWAY, LOT OF OLDER STAMPS	$22.58
NORWAY-Large OLD/Mod Collection(Approx 450+ALBUM)	$163.50	NORWAY FA 12 3x with date cancellation (k16)	$22.50
NORWAY 1879-1903 POST HORN LOT 500+	$161.50	NORWAY FA 17 2x cancelled (k11)	$22.50
Norway local Namsos 1888 8 ore used H&W 3	$132.50	NORWAY 1942 COVER B52 SEMIPOSTAL HIGH CV SCARCE	$22.50
NORWAY FA 18 2x with date cancellation (k17)	$115.50	NORWAY # 177 - 80 COMPLETE MNH BLOCKS OF 4 60.00++	$22.50
Norway 41 used catalog $350.00	$112.53	NORWAY (1946) #275-278 KING HAAKON MNH CV = $67.40	$21.99
Norway 1950 FDC. Very Fine.	$102.00	NORWAY Fa#37 Used XF SON CDS	$21.59
NORWAY 1856-1935 M&U Lot on Pages 120 Stamps	$91.00	Old Norway Booklet 363a MNH Og *No Res*	$21.50
Norway 2-5 used catalog $275.00	$90.00	norway early full book 180ore 2X panes of 6-15ore vf nh	$20.70
Norway #6 // 15 Cancelled *No Res*	$77.70	Norway - Skilling values - 1856-72	$20.53
Norway #16 // 57a With Many Varieties *No Res*	$62.09	Norway #3 & 5 Cancelled *No Res*	$19.99
Norway 59-61 MH OG (Beautiful) *No Res*	$62.00	Box Lot Norway Dealer's Hoard!	$19.99
NORWAY 1855 NUMBER 1 USED [2]	$60.00	NORWAY STAMP #60 FACIT cat.$95.00 USED	$18.50

Europe ▶ Poland

The average sales price in this subcategory is $20.67.

	HIGH		AVG
POLAND Extremely Rare Mini Sheets Mi#445-7 Mint NH	$838.00	POLAND Mi#389,#398 Mint VF Overprint CV ?80 ($96)	$22.00
POLOGNE Nº 1 SUR LETTRE	$400.00	POLAND POLEN local issue TARNOW 1918	$21.57
POLAND Rare Mini Sheets Mi#1151-5 Mint NH	$248.50	Poland - WOLDENBERG - Virtuti Militari postcard	$21.50
POLAND SS Mi#1 Mint NH CV ?600 ($727)	$159.26	POLAND-Nice OLD Labels/Cinderellas+Airs Lot(48+Sheet)	$21.50
A;V;; Poland C13-18 VFHN WOW! CV:200.00$; 29969	$138.50	POLAND DEALER STOCK/ACCUMULATIONI-NR!!!	$21.50
Poland 1919 Overprinted Postal Stationery Germany	$135.83	POLAND,1939,AIRMAIL PS STAT TO ARG BY LUFTHANSA....	$21.50
A;V;; Poland occ. Italia XFNH Scarce !! WOW !! ; 27189	$125.50	Poland 1918/71 Collection on Album 446 Stamps!! Used	$21.00
Poland 1916-18 Local Post Kolo	$113.50	POLAND 672P Copernicus BLACK PRINT engr by SLANIA (43)	$20.72
A;V;; Poland Dues starps Mint VFH/LH Hicv ; 27188	$107.50	POLAND Mi#212 233//46 CV ?96 ($116) Mint LH	$20.59
Poland POW Displaced Persons Dachau Camp	$99.95	POLAND 486 First SLANIA stamp on commercial cover (3)	$20.50
A;V;; Poland 1K18,19,24 VFNH	$86.00	Poland Scarce Walbrzych Local Revenues (2)	$20.50
Signed C.V.:160.00$; 29671		[2 of these sold for $20.50 each]	
Poland Displaced Persons in Germany Bavaria Proofs	$84.00	Poland, MH, michel I/X (pol009)	$20.50
Poland 1919 Krakow Issue Poczta Polska Overprint F42	$82.57	Poland 1919 Krakow Issue Poczta Polska Overprint F54b	$20.50
1928,s/s	$82.54	Poland 1919 Krakow Issue Poczta Polska Overprint F46	$20.50
		WWII Jewish concentration LITZMANNSTADT GHETTO Postage	$20.50

Europe ▶ Portugal & Colonies

The average sales price in this subcategory is $21.43.

	HIGH		AVG
POLAND Extremely Rare Mini Sheets Mi#445-7 Mint NH	$838.00	PORT. INDIA Af#429-30 Mint NH VF Complete CV ?35 ($42)	$22.00
PORTUGAL-1853-D.MARIA II-AF 4-GOOD USED-CV $US 3720.00	$620.00	ITALY – #544-546 mint nh vf; 1950 Tobacco issue	$22.00
PORTUGAL - Album A4, loaded 1600 stamps MNH/used -3000	$305.00	MOZAMBIQUE Af#312-5 Mint NH VF CV ?42 ($52)	$21.61
PORTUGAL-1943-"CARAVELA"-1ST.ISSUE-AF 617/33-MLH	$231.50	Portugal - Angola nice telegram	$21.60
Portugal Colony:Macao,The Valuable Collection,from 1884	$218.05	Portugal - Angola nice errors	$21.50
PORTUGAL - Binder with 160 sets MNH - 1055	$202.50	Portugal - Timor nice postage due mint lot	$21.50
PORTUGAL - Red Box + 500 Heco 102 - MNH and used	$202.50	Portugal - Mozambique nice telegram	$21.50
Macau 1948 Sc#324-35 Macau Seenery Set MLH,SCV$659	$200.00	PORTUGUESE INDIA Sc#460 Sheet with 35 stamps MNH	$21.50
PORT COLONIES Collection Mostly Mint CV ?695 ($858)	$195.00	Portugal - Portuguese Guinea complete set of crowns	$21.26
Portugal - Mcau/ Macao regional fans S/ Sheet + set MNH	$160.50	EUROPA PORTUGAL CEPT 1980 (x4) MNH +++++ EXCELLENT	$21.05
Portugal - Macau/Macao nice complete sheet of 28 stamps	$150.50	Port. INDIA/REVENUES - 1920 - superb doct stamped with	$21.00
Portugal Madeira:Europa Miniature Sheets,1981/2000 (18)	$142.50	Portugal - Portuguese Guinea nice complete set	$20.50
Portugal Colony: Madeira,MLH/F/Used,Coll Cat ?650/?700	$132.49	TIMOR Af#1 Block Mint LH SS CV ?100 ($123)	$20.50
PORTUGAL Collection Mint & Used CV ?1675 ($2230)	$129.00	Portugues Stamps, Souvenir Sheet Stamps, 1992	$20.49
PORT GUINEA Af#2 Block Mint NH VF SS OG CV ?170 ($210)	$107.50	Portugal - Cabo Verde complete set MH	$20.49

Europe ▶ Romania

The average sales price in this subcategory is $13.58.

	HIGH		AVG
Romania:The Valuable Collection to the 1930's.	$236.50	A;V;3$; Romania lot WOW ! lot of scarce sheets ; 25337	$18.50
ROMANIA RUMANIA RUM?IEN FISCALS 1918 NEVER ISSUED 5L	$135.50	A;V;3$; Romania coll. Mint + Used ; 25343	$17.50
A;V;; Romania B292-303 XFLH on special paper ; 27058	$130.05	Romania-OLD M&U Lot on Pages(Apprx 100+Items)	$16.50
ROMANIA 1883 Bucuresti II Franked on weekly newspaper	$127.50	Romania 1980-96 Fencing 5 MNH compl.sets+5 SS,CV=$51	$16.50
ROMANIA #41 on COVER to NATIONAL HOTEL in VIENNA "1870"	$125.55	A;V;2$; Romania lot Mint+Used Hicv ; 25285	$15.69
A;V;; Romania B292-303 XFLH C.V.:400.00+++ Scarel;27057	$115.05	Romania Hohen Rinne local 1906 5h mint, H&W 7	$15.51
ROMANIA,nice cover,1876	$103.50	ROMANIA #C71, MINT, NH, VF, CREASE, CAT $65.00	$15.00
ROMANIA Mi#102/105F 25 for 5 on Incomplete Sheet MNH	$89.00	ROMANIA Mi#146-53Mint H CV ?110 ($136)	$14.99
Romania: Birth Centenary of Ion Creanga IMPERFORATED	$67.77	ROMANIA Mi#484-8 508-15 Mint LH Varieties on Page	$14.99
ROMANIA 1971 - Space Block Michel No: 89 FDC 350,00	$64.76	ROMANIA German Occ. OVPT incl 9th Army on Tax Stamps	$14.99
ROMANIA 1896-97 SPIC Franked two weekly newspaper	$60.00	A;V;3$; Romania coll. Mint + Used Hicv;25346	$14.50
A;V;2$; Romania Coll. 1872-1905 F-VF+U/H ; 25339	$57.51	Romania 1948 Royal Church error RPR o/p offset UMM	$13.49
ROMANIA 1862-1936 M&U Collection on Pages 250 Stamps	$56.99	ROMANIA 1864 UNISSUED 5 PA BLOCK OF 12 MINT NH L22	$12.84
ROMANIA RUM?IEN literature essais 1858-1938 RR!	$56.50	A;V;3$; Romania coll. M+U lot of imperf item Hicv;25347	$12.60
A;V;2$; Romania coll. Mint+Used WOW! Hicv ; 25356	$51.02	ROMANIA 1919 "Oradea" issue . Misplaced ovp. Nice item	$11.50

Europe ▸ Russia & Area

The average sales price in this subcategory is $22.40.

	HIGH		AVG
RUSSIA & OFFICES, 5000+ Stamps in 2 stbks..MUST SEE!!	$590.00	LATVIA - NAVIGATION EXHIBITION SLOGAN COVER	$24.17
RUSSIA Mi#4y WTMK "3" Used Signed CV ?3600 ($4442)	$444.99	Russia 1932 Sc.# E1-E3 Used & MvLH.	$24.16
RUSSIA Numeral Cancellations - Incredible Collection	$430.00	Russia, 1000 different stamps collection	$24.00
Russia Scott #C68 Mint Never Hinged Scarce Airmail	$362.50	Russia 202 Mint NH Stamps #3183 / 3687	$23.95
Russian 1961-1991 complete MNH collection.	$290.00	RUSSIA STATES WITH OVERPRINT FOR SPECIALIST RR	$23.28
RUSSIA,,1928 ,,1st FLIGHT MOSCOW TO KABUL, VIA TASHKENT	$222.00	RUSSIA Mi#313-25 Mint LH/Used on Page	$22.55
RUSSIA Mi#235 II Typo Mint LH Sgned CV ?750 ($925)	$204.01	RUSSIA 1887/1912:range 3 & 4k postal cards with uprated	$22.50
RUSSIA Mi#236 II Mint LH Signed CV ?250 ($308)	$204.01	RUSSIA Pre 1960's Very Nice over 380 Different stamps	$22.05
C7,8,9 MH with inverted surcharge	$201.50	SOWJETUNION MI 972-80+1014-22 40 EURO PLANE-AIRMAIL	$21.50
VOLUMINOUS TRAVEL BAG FROM A LAWYER - MUCH MATERIAL	$154.01	Ukraine DP Camp Stamps Education	$21.03
RUSSIA Cover Moscou local 1922.	$152.50	Russia. 1946. Medals & Orders. MNH. Sc.#1032-1046.	$21.00
Y960 - Russia, 500+ stamps, all periods	$127.50	RUSSIA FOR SPECIALIST RRR	$20.61
IMPERIAL RUSSIA. #88-194,ROMANOVS SET. MNH !	$119.00	RUSSIA Mi#450-6 72-75 Used on Page CV ?90 ($111)	$20.50
Russia, 1924, Lenin Mourning Registered Cover	$118.50	RUSSIA Mi#488-93 523-6 Used CTO CV ?62 ($77) on Page	$20.50
LATVIA, Scott #1 "Broken-Step" FLAW + BONUS	$114.72	Letterfromt with Stempelmarken from 1918(short period)	$20.50

Europe ▸ Spain & Colonies

The average sales price in this subcategory is $33.49.

	HIGH		AVG
SPAIN STAMP_1936_**_NH_EDI-801_VERY NICE	$595.00	SPAIN Souvenir Sheet Airmail Overprint NH	$34.55
SPAIN Ed#792-800 Mint NG CV ?535 ($660)	$425.00	SPAIN Ed#402-433 Mint H CV ?93 ($115)	$34.51
SPAIN Ed#NE4-NE10 Mint CV ?300 ($370)	$405.00	SPAIN #240 Used - 1878 4p Violet, Alfonso XII	$34.00
SPAIN Ed#838 Souvenir Sheet Mint H CV ?480 ($592)	$328.88	SPAIN #132 Mint VF HR CV ?41 ($51)	$34.00
SPAIN Ed#839 Souvenir Sheet Mint LH CV ?480 ($592)	$310.55	S450- SPAIN STAMPLESS TENERIFE COVER CANARIAS 1858	$34.00
SPAIN Ed#114 Mint NG Comex Certificate CV ?425 ($524)	$295.00	T202- SPAIN STAMPLESS OFFICIAL COVER CANARIAS 1857	$34.00
SPAIN Ed#129 Mint CV ?2275 ($2742)	$290.00	SPAIN Airmail Ed#782-786 Mint H CV ?87 ($107)	$34.00
SPAIN #776//C130 - 1950 Stamp Centenary Set	$276.00	SPAIN Ed#758 Souvenir Sheet Used CV ?42 ($52)	$33.99
SPAIN Mi#336-50 Mint LH VF CV ?700 ($850) for NH	$239.00	SPAIN - 1909 CORBETA NAUTILUS CACHET ON POSTCARD	$32.00
Spain 1938 Submarine Issue 6p 3 different proofs VF	$225.00	SPAIN Ed#SH836-837 Mint H CV ?44 ($54)	$32.00
SPAIN Mi#267-79 Fresh Mint LH U.P.U. CV ?900 ($1092)	$199.00	SPAIN 4 INCREDIBLE SILK POSTCARDS WOW!	$32.00
SPAIN Ed#41 Mint NG wmk loops CV ?1225 ($1512)	$199.00	T203- SPAIN STAMPLESS LAS PALMAS COVER CANARIAS 1859	$31.32
SPAIN Ed#729-730 Mint Airmail VF LH CV ?380 ($469)	$189.01	SPAIN #781-86 Mint NH - 1951 Isabella Set	$31.27
SPAIN #113 Mint XF VLH CV ?300 ($370)	$172.50	S480- SPAIN CANARIAS ICOD COVER 1870 PAIR 50 MI	$31.16
SPAIN #170 Unused - 1870 1e600m Dull Lilac, Espana	$168.80	SPAIN #201-10 Used - 1874 Justice Set	$31.01

Europe ▸ Sweden

The average sales price in this subcategory is $19.95.

	HIGH		AVG
Sweden. Special Collection. Coil Stamps.	$405.00	Sweden 1929.Facit M1. First Sw. Military Stamp.MH(NoGum	$21.00
Album used Sweden, 1855-1949, CV over 3300 USD—	$268.55	SWEDEN COMPLETE 1974 MNH	$21.00
Sweden collection 2500 different stamps	$231.50	Sweden First Issues	$20.51
Sweden. Collection. ALL MNH. High Cat.Value	$171.50	Sweden. Facit 9. Short tooth left side. MNH	$20.50
Sweden PTPO stationery letter card mint, with 14 ads	$162.50	A;V;2$; Sweden Coll. F-VF+U CDS Hicv ; 28310	$20.50
SWEDEN-Large OLD/Mod Collection on Pages(Apprx 1000+)	$154.53	Sweden 1858-61 Issue of Scott #6, 8, 9, 10, 11, 12	$20.00
SWEDEN , rarest semi classic pairs , set , LOOK !	$154.50	A;V;4$; Sweden Mint NH + Used NH Hicv + Face ; 28340	$20.00
SWEDEN BOX LOADED WITH ALL MNH BOOKLETS...HUGE $$$	$142.55	A;V;4$; Sweden Mint NH + Used NH Hicv + Face ; 28338	$19.50
SWEDEN FA 36 - MI 25B MNH (434)	$142.50	Sweden 18 Used - SCV $125.00	$19.39
A;V;; Sweden 197-211 XFLH Fresh! C.V.:700.00$++ ; 28314	$130.27	SWEDEN FA#144Acz Used VF CV SK1600 ($229)	$19.00
Sweden-Rare Early Local Post Advertising Envelope	$112.50	SWEDEN FA#156cxz Mint VF LH HR CV SK1600($224)	$19.00
A;V;; Sweden #213-28 XFLH Fresh! C.V.:750.00$+++; 28317	$112.50	SWEDEN COMPLETE YEAR 1969 MNH WITH PAIRS/PANES	$19.00
SWEDEN 1920-26 Mint Lot to 145 Ore 75 Stamps	$109.50	A;V;4$; Sweden Mint NH + Used NH Hicv + Face; 28346	$19.00
A;V;4$; Sweden Mint NH + Used NH Hicv + Face; 28345	$105.50	SWEDEN 10 MNH STAMPS FROM THE 1930's GUSTAV V SERIES	$18.90
Sweden. Collection. High Cat.Value	$103.50	Sweden. Collection. ALL MNH.	$18.50

Europe ▸ Switzerland & Liechtenstein

The average sales price in this subcategory is $16.32.

	HIGH		AVG
SWITZERLAND 1850-1935 M&U Lot on Pages 260 Stamps	$401.50	LIECHTENSTEIN 1944-6 sets/singles complete LH	$17.38
St. Helvetia 30 C. HELVETTA 1907, auf Brief, Attest	$400.00	Liechtenstein 239 MNH block of 4	$16.95
LIECHTENSTEIN, Stamps in HINGELESS alb..NO REV!!	$161.61	SMALL LOT OF OLD STAMPS,SWITZERLAND	$16.90
SWITZERLAND 1942 Fete National SS First Day Cancel	$149.99	SWITZERLAND 1923 - 1925 AIRMAIL SET MH / USED	$16.50
Stamps Switzerland 1940 Fete Day SS imperf (B105) M	$125.00	SWITZERLAND 1862-64, Scott#56, 56a USED, Cat.$223.00	$16.50
Switzerland: Embroidery miniature sheet MNH	$122.80	SWITZERLAND Scott B 21-24 USED SET	$16.50
Graf Zeppelin 1931 Liechtenstein to Lausanne cvr	$116.50	SWITZERLAND 1884-97, Scott#J21-27a USED, Cat.$167.90	$16.50
SWITZERLAND - SC 7 CV u$ 400 - FAULTLESS NICE SHADE!	$105.50	SWIZTERLAND MH AIRMAIL ACCUMULATION - CV $136.20	$16.26
SWISS POSTAGE @ 1/2 FACE>217SF- RECENT ISSUES	$104.50	SWITZERLAND SEMI POSTAL Zu#35 Mint H CV CHF130 ($100)	$16.25
SWITZERLAND 1951 LUNABA Luzern Souvenir Sheet Used	$99.99	Stehende Helvetia, Restlot Typen A, C, 1982 - 1991, ?	$16.00
SWITZERLAND 1940 Fete National Pro Patria MS Used	$96.00	J.S. Burdsal & Co. Medicine Wrapper, Scott RS44d	$16.00
SWITZERLAND Zu#32 FDC CV CHF300 ($238)	$95.25	SWITZERLAND SEMI POSTAGE ONLY?COLLECTION LOTS	$15.50
SWITZERLAND,1939,AIRMAIL CVR TO ARG + RECEP PMK.	$91.00	Switzerland 1915 Pro Juventute Fine Used 2 Stamps	$15.50
Switzerland 1923-42 Labor Officials Lot	$89.99	Switzerland Classic Collection	$15.50
Switzerland+Belgium-Early/Mod+Charities Lot(850+Items)	$86.55	SWITZERLAND PRO JUVENTUTE (Semi Postal) Zu#21-24 Used	$15.50

Latin America ▸ Caribbean

The average sales price in this subcategory is $14.76.

	HIGH		AVG
S379- CUBA SPAIN STAMPLESS LAS POZAS LINE UNDATED	$262.77	S392- CUBA IMPERFORATED AVION BLOCK 4 MNH. EDIFIL 100 e	$15.00
CUBA SPAIN STAMPLESS ARTEMISA BLACK LINE UNDATED	$205.00	S494 CUBA SPAIN STAMPLESS S CRISTOVAL BLUE BAEZA 1850	$15.00
Haiti Early Stamp Collection in Antique Stock Book	$199.99	S495 CUBA SPAIN STAMPLESS S CRISTOVAL GREEN BAEZA 1860	$15.00
S482- CUBA SPAIN STAMPLESS PUERTA GUIRA LINE 1843	$180.27	Central American Steamship Co 1886 50c mint H&W 5	$15.00
S487- CUBA SPAIN STAMPLESS ROQUE LINE UNDATED VERY RARE	$150.27	1952 Cuba Cincuentario de La Republica MNH	$14.99
T204- CUBA SPAIN REVENUE 2 & 5 REALES BLOCK 1860	$102.50	Box Lot Cuba Dealer's Hoard! Mint & Used!!	$14.99
Haiti page of errors doubles, inverts 21 singles, 1 pai	$99.95	Cuba SC#141 MH Nice	$14.95
S485- CUBA SPAIN STAMPLESS QUIVICAN RED BAEZA 1847 RARE	$99.00	Haiti 1962 WHO, Malaria, United Naions Sc486-8, C188-0	$14.95
S329- CUBA SPAIN STAMPLESS LINE BAHIA HONDA UNDATED	$88.50	CUBA COLLECTION	$14.00
S489- CUBA SPAIN STAMPLESS ROQUE RED BAEZA RARE 1847	$87.77	MODERN CUBA COLLECTION	$13.50
CUBA 1951 #C49b GUITERAS MORRILLO	$83.00	Haiti 1919-20 Sc282/308 22 items, most mint, few used	$13.00
T207- CUBA SPAIN PUERTO RICO REVENUE 1R BLUE BLOCK 1858	$82.00	1952 Cuba Sc 490-497,C73-C74 Medical Students MNH	$12.99
T206- CUBA SPAIN REVENUE 2 REALES RED BLOCK 1863	$81.00	1951 Cuba Centennial of the Flag All Stamps MNH	$12.99
Haiti 1920 Reverse ovpt TM see after 314, 10c, 15c bloc	$78.77	S387- CUBA IMPERFORATED MACEO BLOCK OF 4 MNH EDIFIL 80e	$12.50
S500- CUBA SPAIN STAMPLESS SAGUA GRANDE RED BAEZA 1846	$78.77	S389- CUBA IMPERFORATED MARTI INDEPENDENCE BLOCK 4	$12.50

Latin America ▸ Central America

The average sales price in this subcategory is $12.62.

	HIGH		AVG
Nicaragua. 1948. Set of 26 S/S & 26 stamps. $300! MNH.	$167.50	PANAMA COLLECTION OF 213 USED .GOOD VARIETY	$14.20
Costa Rica 1925 Registered Cover to Germany, Very Nice!	$94.75	EL SALVADOR PROOF "WATERLOW & SONS"	$13.99
1948,COSTA RICA ,VIA K.L.M. TO GERMANY.	$91.00	NICARAGUA 1948 PROOF "WATERLOW & SONS" b.	$13.99
A;V;3$; Peru coll. F-VF+U Look ! ; 14282	$89.88	Costa Rica interesting old lot - mainly MH	$13.52
NICARAGUA PRE-1940 COLLECTION	$85.00	Guatemala 1953 AM Natl Team SC C188-96 MOG	$12.95
A;V;2$; Panama lot 1878-1928 F.VF M/U Hicv ; 25117	$84.90	Guatemala 1902 Official Set SC O1-5 MOG	$12.95
Nicaragua 1935 Sc606-8 with signatures MOG	$77.00	Belize, olympics 1980, MNH, Sc. 451-58 imperforated	$12.51
COSTA RICA 1863 STUDY GROUP 105 STAMPS L7	$76.55	Central America lot Nicaragua gen F/VF BOB;25090	$12.50
COSTA RICA 1947 3 Col 'MUESTRA' OVERPRINT STRIP	$75.00	Panama Sc # 322-30 & C54-61 MNH	$12.00
A;V;4$; Panama coll BOB M/U F.VF Nice stamps Hicv;25125	$67.77	El Salvador, mnh collection 1964-1965, souv. sheets	$11.99
Costa Rica 1944 Censor Cover, 60c San Ramon Solo	$65.00	Honduras 1939 Airmail set Sc# C89-98 NH	$11.95
COSTA RICA Imperf Proof on Gummed Paper Mint H VF Strip	$54.00	Honduras interesting old lot - mainly MH	$11.75
A;V;3$; Peru States Coll. Hicv ; 14609	$53.00	Honduras Sc # C144-152 MNH	$11.50
1863 Costa Rica #1, 3, 4 Imperf Plate Proofs Mint	$51.00	Panama- Lot of 66 Covers	$11.50
Costa Rica Guanacaste Mi# 7 2 c. carmine MH Cv. 440	$51.00	COSTA RICA 1889 10 C CORNER BLOCK OF 4 PERF 14.5X15 L13	$11.50

Latin America ▸ Mexico

The average sales price in this subcategory is $15.96.

	HIGH		AVG
MEXICO EXPORTA 110 DIF. STRIPS OF 10. ISSUES.SHADOWS	$237.50	Memin Pinguin 5 Mexican Postal Stamp Controversial	$16.49
MEX.1861.4R black.CUERNAVACA.Sz#219.#3145	$227.50	EAGLE.2R.ZAC.102-65.Sub41.AGUASCALIENTES.Sz#1930.#673	$16.28
Juarez 1879/82: Large lot of 93 copies)	$177.50	REVENUE STAMPS FROM MEXICO	$16.06
MEX.Eagle.4R bisect.ZAC.59-65.Sub NIEVES. CERTIF.#664	$162.50	Mexico #1 1/2R Guanajunato with Great Color and Margins	$16.00
EAGLE.Pr.1R.DURANGO.141-65.Sub 16-66 CUENCAME.Sz249.#9	$152.50	117, 4ª 5082 Campeche used CV=$70	$16.00
Memin Pinguin Full Sheet of 50 Stamps Mint Condition NR	$125.99	5 MEMIN STAMPS w/Serial #1735, & #1,2&3 Comic Books	$15.95
EAGLE.1R.DURANGO.233-64.Sub19.PAPASQUIARO.Shi#57/4.#680	$125.37	5 MEMIN PINGUIN STAMPS plus #1, 2 & 3 Comic Books!	$15.95
MEMIN PINGUIN STAMPS!!!! FULL SHEET OF 50 !!!! # 3353	$125.00	Memin Pinguin Controversial 5 Mexican Postal Stamps.	$15.95
Mexico #4 4R Cuernavaca/Mexico cnl w/ Mepsi Cert NF$225	$103.92	MEXICO-Guanajuato 3 2Reales SAP GRN on cover (79)	$15.70
Memin Pinguin Mexican stamps series #9294	$102.50	Mexico #2 1R Monterrey Sz 860 Pre-Print fold + value	$15.65
Juarez 1882/83: Valuable lot of 49, (Sc. 131//144)	$100.99	Mexico Scott #774-6, C123-5 Unused V.F.O.G.	$15.50
MEMIN PINGUIN FULL SHEET OF 50 MEXICAN STAMPS	$100.00	Mexico #7 1R Guadlajara Sz292 Rare on '61s Apr '64 use	$15.50
MEMIN PINGUIN POSTAL STAMPS COMPLETE SHEET OF FIFTY !!	$99.99	Mexico Scott #642-9 Unused V.F.O.G.	$15.39
MEXICO C237A $2.75 VERY RARE FLUORESCENT MNH (125)	$99.95	1869,12 C Hidalgo PUEBLA/ATLIXCO,4-69 on cover,VF.	$15.30
Mexico Memin Penguin Stamp Full Sheet 50 Serial # 2546	$99.00	Mexico - classical lot - (kla0316)	$15.27

Latin America ▸ South America

The average sales price in this subcategory is $23.21.

	HIGH		AVG
Colombia 1920 "Cartoon" Airmail, Mint	$920.00	VENEZUELA - COLOMBIA - SCADTA CONSULAR - RARE 20c REG	$26.11
ARGENTINA, CORDOBA, SC.2, 10 CTS., CV:$2500, SEE SCAN!!	$399.99	Postcard LA PAZ Miraflores & Stadium BOLIVIA preprint	$26.00
ARGENTINA, SC.392, RENO CUTTON OF 1930, CV:$600 MH, SEE	$276.75	COLOMBIA very nice over 395 different stamps	$26.00
Peru: A Good Collection To The 1930's.	$255.00	URUGUAY SC.# 13d USED LUXE SUCURSAL!!!!!!!!!!	$24.99
Chile 5 & 10 Cent. imperfs, incredible selection	$255.00	ARGENTINA ESSAYS ORIGINAL COLOURS COMPLETE SERIE SCARCE	$24.99
GERMANY - COLOMBIA - SCADTA RARE 30c STATIONARY COVER	$202.50	PERU MLH Olympic London 1948 Stamp #458/61 DM 150	$24.00
GERMANY - COLOMBIA - SCADTA RARE 50c STATIONARY COVER	$202.50	TERRIFIC PERU CLASSIC STAMPS COLLECTION OF CANCELS !!	$23.50
Colombia Canal Zone Cover To USA + Cinderella 1941	$190.00	Brazil 1942-7 defs wmk Sc541-53 MOG	$21.95
BOLIVIA LARGE COLLECTION 500+ INCL. CLASSICS!	$167.00	CHILE (#747): "COLON" Sc.15, ovpt."SPECIMEN"	$21.63
ARGENTINA, SC.96B, YELLOW GREEN (ERROR) MH, SEE SCAN!	$158.50	1898 Brazil Newspaper Sc#131 - ERROR Two Overprt	$21.50
Uruguay: A Nice Collection, To the 1930's.	$147.50	Colombia: Antioquia, Collection From Early Issues.	$21.50
Tristan da Cunha 4 Sets Mint NH Stamps 20% Catalog	$132.50	Chile,Colombia,Canal Zone-OLD/Mod Revenue Lot(100+Items	$20.63
Paraguay: A Good Collection To the 1930's.	$120.50	BRAZIL - 1925 BILHETE POSTAL WITH HUNGARY TAX DUE STAMP	$20.50
ARGENTINA, BUENOS AIRES, SC.1, STEAMSHIP, CV:$250!	$117.51	ECUADOR PRE-1940 LOT	$20.50
VENEZUELA SC# 35 VF USED CV; 110.00 L@@K NR	$106.10	Bolivia Mint nh Sc Unlisted S/S	$20.00

Publications & Supplies ▸ Publications

The average sales price in this subcategory is $17.48.

	HIGH		AVG
Sperati Forgery Guide - 2 Vols. BPA 1955 - Forgeries	$332.00	c9823 SOUTH AFRICA 1926-28 PICTORIAL ISSUES HISTORY	$18.40
ROESSLER'S AIR PLANE STAMP NEWS Lot of 54 Issues 1920s	$261.50	MEXICO GUADALAJARA DISTRITO POSTAL 1856-1883	$18.00
2005 SCOTT CAT. VOl. 2-6 & US Spec.CD +(BONUS VOL 1)	$202.50	BOOK: Billig's Vol 40 - The Empire in Asia (Part 3)	$18.00
RR BALASSE CATALOGUE 1949 BELGIUM - CONGO / 3 VOL	$190.00	SCOTT STAMP CATALOG 2005-PART 4 J-O	$18.00
SCOTT'S 2005 CATALOGS/ VOL 1-6 LIKE NEW	$179.95	Canada Admiral Issue, A Rate Study 1912-1928, book	$18.00
003676 American Philatelic Congress #2 - 1936	$174.95	Romania 2005 T.Ataman: Ferdinand stamps Handbook & Cat.	$18.00
Complete 2004 SCOTT Catalogues + US Specialized..NO REV	$173.59	Maine Post Offices & Postal History - Dow -1976	$17.99
SCOTT 2005 STAMP CATALOGUES Full Set of 6 – Like New!	$152.50	More Stories to Collect By, Herman Herst Jr.	$17.50
Egypt Stamps and Postal History, by Peter A.S. Smith	$136.19	Literature:Austro-Hungarian A.P.O's,1914-1918	$17.05
Ferchnbaver Handbook Austria Specialized 1850-1918	$125.00	VATICAN CITY NEVER USED STAMP ALBUM	$17.00
2003 Scott Catalogs Vol. 1-6 Complete	$122.50	FELDMAN GRAND PRIX COLLECTION LARGE HERMES HEADS II	$17.00
Scott 2004 Standard Postage Stamp Catalog Vol 1,2,4,5,6	$122.50	U.S. Cancels 1890-1900	$16.79
Scotts.2004 Standard Postage Stamp Catalogue 6 Volumes	$108.63	Essays for US Adhesive Postage Stamps, Clarence Brazer	$16.50
MINKUS STAMP ALBUM FOR LUXEMBOURG 82 PAGES	$102.50	SCOTT 2003 SPECIALIZED CATALOGUE US STAMPS & COVERS	$16.50
Gen. Italo Balbo - Italian Air Armada - Ref book 1933	$98.00	ALBUM WEEDS VOL III	$16.06

Publications & Supplies ▸ Supplies

The average sales price in this subcategory is $18.04.

	HIGH		AVG
NEW SAFE Signoscope Watermk detector&adapter combo!	$229.99	Brand New HECO 8 1/2 x 5 1/2 Dealer Pages a25	$19.99
Safe Signoscope Stamp Watermark Detector	$213.51	Syzk album title page for Israel First Edition	$19.95
5 SCOTT INTERNATIONAL STAMP BINDERS	$133.50	SCOTT JUMBO GREEN SPECIALTY STAMP ALBUM DUSTCASE NICE!	$19.28
Very Clean 2 Vol Master Global Coll to 1967 NR LT7	$117.50	5 Stockbooks. Different Sizes. Hold 1000's. LOOK!	$19.10
SCOTT INTERNATIONAL #32A & B WITH BINDER	$112.50	SHOWGUARD GREEN "STRIDER" STOCKBOOK	$19.00
2 UNUSED SAFE Sheet File albums..NO RESERVE!!	$110.50	5X POWER EYESIGHT PROTECTIVE MAGNIFYING LAMP>>B	$18.90
Scott's Intl Postage Stamp Album Part I w/Dust Jacket	$78.00	Magnifying Glass 30X gold jewelers loupe/loop+FREE 10x	$18.88
SCOTT US PLATE BLOCK ALBUM SUPPLEMENTS 1945 - 1990 NEW!	$76.01	Magnifying Glass 30X gold jewelers loupe/loop+FREE 10x	$18.88
Lindner T Hingeless Album- Germany 1933-45	$74.00	SCOTT INTERNATIONAL STAMP ALBUM USED	$18.50
HUGE STAMP ALBUM & SUPPLIES LOT A MUST SEE!	$66.00	Scott Specialty 2-Post Binder (Large) - Excellent!!	$18.50
11 WHITE ACE COVER BINDERS	$64.95	Scott Specialty 2-Post Binder (Medium) - Excellent!!	$18.50
10 FIRST DAY COVER ALBUMS 1 WITH DUST COVER	$63.00	4 1" WHITE ACE JAPAN BINDERS 1 WITH DUST COVER	$18.45
Group of SHOWGARD Stamp mounts..NO RESERVE!!	$62.99	3 Packs Blank Scott Specialty Album Pages a20	$18.37
MINKUS RED NETHERLANDS AND COLONIES ALBUM WITH PAGES	$61.00	2 Harris 2 Post Brown WW Album Binders a3	$18.20
Large of Black Showgard mounts,Stamp Hinges and kit.	$60.75	NEW MINKUS SPECIALTY ALBUM PAGES THAILAND - SIAM	$18.00

Topical & Specialty ▸ Animation, Cartoons

The average sales price in this subcategory is $7.81.

	HIGH		AVG
DISNEY-Nice MNH Stamp,Mini-Sheet Collection+Album	$307.51	St Vincent Grenadines 1993-1996 Mint Never Hinged	$9.00
HIGH $$ DISNEY MINT STAMP SHEET COLLECTION ALBUM LOT F1	$158.50	Mauritania - Simpsons Stamp Sheet 7517	$9.00
## DISNEY CLASSIC MOVIES COLLECTOR PANELS STAMPS ##	$49.99	Disney 1983 Christmas S/S & Set Grenada Grenadines MNH	$8.99
St Vincent Grenadines 2254-2260 Mint Never Hinged	$16.60	Sierra-Leone 2124-2125 Mint Never Hinged	$8.07
U.S.#2096 HAND PAINTED 1st DAY COVER"SMOKEY THE BEAR"	$16.50	Sierra-Leone 2177-2127 Mint Never Hinged	$7.75
Congo - Disney Characters & Chess On Stamps M0840-3	$16.50	Lot #110-D Disney LARGE LOT OF SHORT SETS ALL MNH	$7.50
Congo - Disney Characters & Chess On Stamps M0840-3	$15.50	HORIZONTAL Disney Stamps Sheet : MICKEY'S TOONTOWN	$7.27
Disney Stamps & S/S MICKY THE FIREMAN	$15.00	Sierra-Leone 2069-2077 Mint Never Hinged	$7.25
Disney Omnibus Stamps 1988- 91 - Prinz Sheet	$15.00	Disney Stamps Sheet : ANTIGUA WINNIE the POOH 1	$7.03
Disney - Fairy Tales Souvenir Sheets - LOOK!	$14.99	Disney Stamps Souvenir Sheet: MICKEY WITH HORSE DRAGON	$7.02

Topical & Specialty ▸ Cinderellas & Fakes

The average sales price in this subcategory is $16.22.

	HIGH		AVG
ALBUM with OVER 345 GERMAN POSTER STAMPS / VIGNETTES	$213.61	2 embossed poster stamps, belgium, expo brussels 1910	$17.05
Germany-Nice OLD Poster/Advert Stamp Lot(Approx 330)	$182.50	Lesotho Set of 33 mnh gold foil Cinderella stamps	$17.00
Europe-Nice OLD Poster+Advert Stamp Lot(Apprx 450 Items	$168.50	BRITISH WW II SEALS - COMPLETE - MNH - ·	$17.00
scandinavian poster stamps soccer, golf, tennis, cricket	$163.50	CINDERELLA-G.B. POSTER STAMPS-17 DIFF EVENT PUBLICITY	$16.60
Germany-Interesting OLD Poster Stamp,Cinderellas(300+)	$140.00	GB-Jubilee Jamboree+Scout Cycle Labels Lot/Cinderellas	$16.50
Germany-1930s Advertising Labels Lot(Approx 160)	$135.15	Greece Hermes Head - Proof S/S MNH	$16.50
Germany-Nice OLD Poster/Advert Stamp Lot(330 Items+SBK)	$130.50	EKKO RADIO RECEPTION STAMP WICC BRIDGEPORT CT	$16.49
Europe-Nice OLD Poster/Advert Stamp Collection(350+Item	$130.50	22 old u.s. patriotic propaganda poster stamps	$16.30
GB-1916 War Fund Stamps+Sheets+Patriotic Label Lot	$128.05	Australia Papua New Guinea official airmail FDC	$16.10
Military-Lord Roberts Fund Labels Lot(43 Items)	$125.45	CINDERELLA-G.B. POSTER STAMPS-18 DIFF EVENT PUBLICITY	$16.10
Europe-OLD Poster/Advert Stamp Lot(Approx 325 Items)	$120.00	9 old poster stamps ed.delandre war stamps WWI u.k.	$16.01
5 old german poster stamps, nazi propaganda, swastika	$117.50	GB-Early/Modern Railway Stamps/Labels Lot(30+Sheet)	$16.01
Europe-Interesting OLD Poster Stamp Lot(Approx 300+Sbk	$113.30	2 old german poster stamps, elephant beer, worms	$16.01
Europe-Interesting OLD Poster Stamp Lot(Approx 325+SBK	$110.00	old italian poster stamp shoe polish, elephant, bologna	$16.00
Germany-OLD Poster Stamp Lot on Pages(Approx 160+Items	$103.51	Reno/Southworth's Cigar Store Advertising Label	$15.89

Topical & Specialty ▶ Nature

The average sales price in this subcategory is $8.69.

	HIGH		AVG
WWF SWAZILAND 1982 SET MNH	$110.39	Ireland 1205 - 08b "Extinct Animals" on 2 UA FDC's	$9.95
Guinea Butterflies/Scouts/Birds imperforate 1990 MNH	$102.50	China Turtle Tortoise Chelonian Thalassian Old Postcard	$9.80
CATS-M&U Stamp(250+)+FDC+Benham Cover(36) Collection	$96.00	CIRCLE GOLD FOIL—DRAGON & KING—6V.MNH BHUTAN 1966	$9.80
Malagasy Butterflies/Scouts m/sheet imperforate 1988	$89.95	China 2 Postal Card with Jilin Meteorite Pmk	$9.80
WWF IVORY COAST SET MNH	$73.89	St. Thomas, Mushroom s/sht. Owl, Frog, Orchids	$9.50
WWF GAMBIA 1984 SET MNH 011	$72.67	Guinea-Bissau – Owls & Mushrooms On Stamps GB5103a	$9.50
WWF BOTSWANA 1978 SET MNH	$51.00	ZH186 NEW ZEALAND MNH BOOKLET FAUNA BIRD VOGL DUCK	$8.67
WWF MALAWI BLOCK MNH	$49.50	ZH178 NEW ZEALAND MNH BOOKLET FAUNA BUTTERFLY $1,-	$8.51
WWF MAURITIUS BLOCK MNH	$46.00	ZH184 NEW ZEALAND MNH BOOKLET FAUNA BIRD VOGL DUCK	$8.51
WWF JAIMAICA 1984 SET MNH 019	$45.00	ZH189 NEW ZEALAND MNH BOOKLET FAUNA BIRD VOGL VOGEL	$8.51
Aitutaki Birds/OHMS 1985-90 CV 77 EURO MNH	$44.95	ZH190 NEW ZEALAND MNH BOOKLET FAUNA BIRD VOGL VOGEL	$8.51
Comores Animals/Birds Mi#332-37 Bl#76-82 MNH	$44.95	JJ AUDUBON & OWL,BIRDS–SS.+ 4V.MNH TURKS&CAICOS 1985	$8.50
WWF MALAWI SET MNH	$42.78	JJ.AUDUBON &WETLAND BIRD–SHEET+6V.MNH BELIZE 85 CAT$26	$8.50
SOUTH AFRICA 298 MNH BIRD OF PARADISE BLOCK $280	$39.99	OVPT–RARE ARAPAIMA FISH–2V.MLH BRITISH GUIANA 1954	$8.50
Togo Butterflies/Mushrooms/Scouts Mi#2160 Bl#354-55 MNH	$39.95	NEW !!! hONDURAS SEA SHELLS NEW !!!	$8.50

Topical & Specialty ▶ People, Sports

The average sales price in this subcategory is $7.39.

	HIGH		AVG
WORLD CUP - 1930/86 - COMMEMORATIVE MNH COLLECTION	$130.50	Olympics - Cook Isl. Strip of 3	$7.50
Monaco, olympics 1980, MNH deluxe sheet - SCARCE !!!	$76.22	Senegal FDC Boxing Mohamed Ali 1977	$7.50
[2 of these sold for $76.22 each]		RUGBY WORLD CUP GREAT PHOTOS SHEET 9 STAMPS	$7.50
Germany 1936 Olympics Set Of 2 S/S With Special Cancels	$72.00	Somalia - Jimi Hendrix On Stamps 222719	$7.50
LADY DIANA 21st BIRTHDAY COMMEMORATIVE STAMP ALBUM	$62.00	Rwanda - Chess on Stamps Sheets M0884-5	$7.50
Olympic Barcelona 1992 Maldives set+2s/s MNH	$41.00	St Vincent - Sinking the Bismarck Stamp Sheet SGB0506	$7.50
Olympic Barcelona 1992 Maldives set+s/s MNH	$41.00	Benin - Soccer - Real Madrid on Stamps 9508	$7.50
ITALY.1934.FOOTBALL.AIR.Set/4.Sc#.C62-5.MHR.#7140	$37.00	TENNIS Meter Slogan on Cover (F)	$7.49
2nd Olympic winter games St Moritz original seals	$36.55	Olympic Games 1993 Monaco 2 stamp booklets MNH	$7.00
ITALY.1934.FOOTBALL.Set/5.Sc#324-8.MHR.#7139	$34.33	Football Soccer 1994 Cook Isl. numiscover 10$silvercoin	$7.00
S Tome e Principe Los Angeles 84 Olympic Games 2 M/S MN	$32.00	Football Soccer 1994 Cook Isl. numiscover 5$silver coin	$7.00
Olympic Albertville 1989 Paraguay set red/silver o/pMNH	$26.00	Gambia - Marilyn Monroe On Stamps GAM0433SH	$7.00
15 Summer Olympic Official Post Cards Rome, Italy 1960	$25.00	Tanzania - Pope John Paull II Stamp Sheet TAN0506	$7.00
US PRES.STAMPS/COVERS COLLECTIONS. START .49	$23.50	Congo - Young Madonna on Stamps 9219	$7.00
SIR WINSTON CHURCHILL ADEN COVER RED OVRPR. RARE! '67	$22.70	NICE CHINA WON 2004 OLYMPIC TENNIS	$6.99
Guinea-Bissau Football Germany Silver Foil Sheet 5p05bs	$21.00	CHAMPION EVENT COVER	

Worldwide ▶ Philatelic Covers

The average sales price in this subcategory is $12.11.

	HIGH		AVG
1913 Karolinen philatelic cover German Colony Whole Set	$293.88	RED CROSS CENTRAL COMMITTEE COVER - GERMANY 1920	$13.00
ETHIOPIA - 1963/1990 - SUPERB FDC COLLECTION	$93.00	WORLDWIDE PACKED COVERS 1" BOX BIG VARIETY NICE VALUE	$12.97
1935 Catapult Flight Event Cover - Europa	$66.00	estate lot 100 old world stamp cover collection nr C6	$12.70
SPAIN - 1938/9 - CIVIL WAR COVERS RANGE	$50.00	estate lot 100 old world stamp cover collection nr C7	$12.50
Cocos Islands Malaya 1954 Royal Visit cover	$46.00	Sea Floor Bahamas Post Photosphere 1940	$12.50
Granddads exper helicopter,dedications,first flights+	$44.50	Portugal 1953 Maximum Card -Gomes Fernandez	$12.50
Granddads exper helicopter,dedications,first flights+	$42.50	1" BOX WORLDWIDE COVERS VARIETY MANY BETTER HUGE VALUE!	$11.50
GREENLAND - INTERESTING COVERS COLLECTION	$41.24	WORLDWIDE 125 PERSONAL/COMMERCIAL COVERS MANY! GREAT	$11.50
Rare and Unusual - RADIO BANGLADESH - QSL and STAMPS	$40.98	PALESTINE 4 EARLY COVERS 1940'S WOW! NICE GROUP	$11.50
DO-X First Flight Rio De Janeiro To NY 1931	$39.00	Japan 1953 Dog Maximum Card	$11.50
1931 Catapult Flight Bremen Wangerooge to PA	$34.49	Monaco 1953 Airplane triangle maximum Card	$11.05
WW2 ERA GERMAN STAMP COVER CENSOR LOT 3A NO RES	$33.75	estate lot 100 old world stamp cover collection nr C13	$10.80
Monaco c1947-49 lot of 3 Maximum cards	$32.02	LOADED WORLDWIDE 1" BOX POSTCARDS MANY BETTER!	$10.52
estate lot 100 old world stamp cover collection nr C9	$31.77	LOADED WORLDWIDE 1" BOX POSTCARDS FANTASTIC!	$10.52
1929 Catapult Flight Bremen Dresden CCL To NY	$31.49	World Federation FDC album 90 government covers F2	$10.51

Worldwide ▶ Postal History

The average sales price in this subcategory is $27.11.

	HIGH		AVG
Israel 1948 Doar Ivri Sc#1-9 Full Tabs Imaba Sheet !!!!	$1,850.00	Japan, 6 Covers, 4 PC.	$31.00
Korea 1902 (Kwangmu 6th) Cover Jinju-Changwon-Daegu#181	$999.99	1902 Costa Rica-USA Cover	$31.00
1914 NAURU WEST PACIFIC OCEAN REGISTERED COVER TO UK	$740.00	Italy 1917 Experimental Airmail Rome First Flight>Turin	$30.00
China late 1941 registered airmail cover to USA	$305.00	Germany : Munich Private Post, 1900	$29.99
USA Perfect Starter Collection MISSENT Postal History	$262.69	1883 Hamburg-Germany 80pf Buff Parcel Postal Card	$29.37
Korea 1899 Cover (Kwangmu 3th) Hansung to Wonsan #179	$249.99	GB P.O in TANGIER 1957 QEII FDC to British Consulate uk	$28.50
CHINA EXPEDITIONARY FORCE India 1918 FPO #1	$249.00	CHINA UPRATED PS CARD TO GERMANY ! SHIPS ! ec16	$27.03
GB 1840 JU 10 MULREADY PENNY ENVELOPE A131 USED	$207.50	1970 Abu Dhabi > Germany Surface Mail w/ SG68	$26.95
Ethiopia 1949 REG> NEW ZEALAND AV2 Handstamp	$199.00	LATVIA 1916 PPC WWI GERMAN OCC DESTROYED TRAIN STATION	$26.23
1934 JAPAN KARL LEWIS HANDPAINTED COVER TO FIJI	$157.51	Trading in Lion Skins in Machakos Kenya, 1908 PSC	$24.99
Israel 1948 Interim Nahariya > Haifa > Alonim Reg.Cover	$145.00	China c1935 $1.00 Sun Yat-sen Tsingtao to Switzerland	$24.99
REP OF CHINA COVER TO PEORIA IL NO RES LOW START	$140.50	1936 Germany-USA Registered Zeppelin Flight Cover	$24.99
GERMANY TO BRAZIL.1932 POLAR FAHRT ZEPPELIN COVER. LOOK	$85.85	ARGENTINA #11B 1867 ANGEL GUARELLO L1	$24.99
POLAND @1910 PPC VIEW OF LODZ BEFORE WWI UNUSED VF RARE	$81.00	G710 SWEDEN- LOCAL POST STOCKHOLM- 5 PS CARDS - 1880th.	$24.00
Aden/Yemen India + Ceylon 1910 postcard to Dutch Indies	$76.00	1911 Valparaiso Chile Revalued PC > Haiti DESTINATION	$24.00

31

TICKETS

The Tickets category is essentially broken down into two major categories—Events and Experiences—although you can filter search results in various ways. Most regular concerts, plays, sports games, and the like fall into the Events category, while special events that include some kind of "extra" or VIP access classify as Experiences.

In the Tickets ▶ Event Tickets ▶ Concerts subcategory, the highest-selling tickets package in this sample was for three tickets to a Paul McCartney concert, third row in Houston, which sold for $4,500.00. (Throughout the eBay categories, Beatles-related items sell very well.)

Another big-name old-time band, the Rolling Stones, made the top ten in the Event Tickets ▶ Concerts subcategory: four tickets to a Stones concert in Baltimore went for $3,295.00. "10 ROWS FROM BAND! TRUE FRONT FLOOR SEATS—REAL 10TH ROW—ONLY AREA SHOW!" says the seller in his description. He says the concert "sold out in minutes!" (On one online ticket site, tickets to this Stones concert in the first nine rows were going for $895.00 to $2,520.00 each for the first floor, fourth row from stage, so those tickets seem to have been bought for a decent price—it works out to $823.75 per ticket—especially considering people are often willing to pay a premium for tickets to an event that has sold out.) Other high-priced Stones tickets in the sample went for $2,860.45 and $2,000.00.

In the median price range, concert tickets are around $190.00, including various packages of Rolling Stones, Carly Simon, Gwen Stefani, and Dave Matthews Band tickets that went for $189.00 each.

The Most Overpriced Concert Ticket Ever Bought?

Tickets can either be bought at a discount or for a premium on eBay, depending on when you buy them. Paul Katcher, blogger and upper west side of Manhattan resident (www.paulkatcher.com), called this U2 ticket bought on eBay for a concert in New York City "The Most Overpriced Concert Ticket Ever Bought": "$355 for ONE ticket at the other end of Madison Square Garden from the stage. People, let me explain a phenomenon called 'getting sick.' Every day people come down with an illness. It prevents them from attending concerts and sporting events, theater performances and wet T-shirt contests. You do not buy a single ticket 200 feet from the stage for $355. If this is news to you, bookmark Craig's List right now and check back five hours from showtime," he writes.

Katcher says that eBay "has kicked 'location, location, location' in the balls," and says this is evidenced by the fact that the same seller is offering many other big-ticket concert tickets all over the United States. "eBay gives power to anyone, anywhere to be a ticket broker. I wonder if high school guidance counselors know about this," he writes.

Some artists are letting fans set prices on eBay, according to Washington Post technology columnist Leslie Walker. "In an aggressive experiment, Third Eye Blind auctioned all tickets on eBay for its 20-city spring tour," she wrote in a recent column. "The band found buyers for 97 percent of seats, more than usual, according to eBay Vice President Doug Galen." Tickets sold for $20.00 to $35.00, depending on how many people bid on any particular day, Walker wrote. "Buyers avoided service fees that ticket agencies usually charge and also shipping fees, because they printed their tickets at home."

A Hot Lunch Date with Rupert Murdoch

The highest-selling item in this sample in the entire Tickets category was for a charity lunch for five people with News Corporation chairman and CEO Rupert Murdoch that sold for $57,100.00. (The proceeds benefited the Jerusalem College of Technology.) According to the item description, "You and your guests will enjoy lunch in a private executive dining room at News Corporation's world headquarters in Manhattan with Rupert Murdoch, Chairman and CEO of News Corporation . . . The winning bidder and four (4) friends will have the unique opportunity to dine with their host, Mr. Murdoch. . . ."

A vineyard adventure with champagne-maker Krug was the next-highest selling experience in this sample, going for $12,855.95. It was auctioned as part of a "7th on Sale" charity auction that raised funds for HIV/AIDS. "It is an extraordinary and rare opportunity to truly experience Champagne Krug," read the item description. The adventure consisted of accommodations for six for one night at the Hôtel Plaza Athénée in Paris, France; transportation by chauffeur-driven car to and from Reims, France; a private luncheon for six within the renowned Clos du Mesnil vineyard; a tour of the vineyards, led by Remi and Oliver Krug, followed by a tasting of assorted Clos du Mesnil vintages; a two-night stay at the Relais & Châteaux property Les Crayères. The latter is an elegant three-story "castle hotel" situated in a private 17-acre landscaped park in Reims, France. The winner also received a case (6 bottles) of assorted Krug Champagnes hand-delivered to each participant upon his or her return. According to the seller, "This is the first time that the Krug family has ever offered the chance to visit and lunch in the Clos du Mesnil, meet the senior winemakers at the Masion, as well as to participate in a tasting led by Remi and Oliver Krug" in many years.

Median prices for Tickets ▶ Experiences ▶ Other were $50.00 to $80.00 and included such items as tickets to "Medieval Times" ($82.00), tickets to an "Arabian Nights" dinner show ($69.00), and a one-hour private helicopter flight ($51.00).

One of the most interesting items I saw in the Experiences subcategory was actually for a listing that did not sell: "A Flight into Space (Genuine Auction)." The Buy It Now price was set at GBP 250,000.00 (approximately US $428,450.00). The kicker? You have to wait until 2008, when "passenger trips into space will become a reality." The seller assures that "we will supply you with 1 genuine passenger space travel ticket and all accompanying material as soon as they are available. Departure times are subject to change. You will be kept fully updated on all developments."

Theme Parks and Sporting Events

A whole subcategory of tickets is for Theme Parks, which is dominated by Disney World and Disneyland. A common listing here is for the park "hopper" tickets, or tickets that allow you to go from park to park at Disney World during your stay. However, according to one eBayer, although she'd bought used park hoppers on eBay and didn't have a problem, "there is no way to know how many days are left until you are at the gate," and the new Disney "My Way" tickets are non-transferable. As with all auctions, be cautious and carefully examine the feedback and other information about the seller.

There are plenty of sporting events as well. The highest price in this sample in the Sporting Events subcategory was for San Francisco Giants All-Star game seats that sold for $16,498.00. ("Watch BONDS chase RUTH & AARON . . . this sale is for CHARTER SEAT LICENSES on FOUR terrific LOWER BOX SEATS in aisle 110, row 41 for the SAN FRANCISCO GIANTS at beautiful SBC Park," wrote the seller. "These tickets are right next to home plate on the first base side. You look straight up the 3rd base line . . . Just like sitting in your living room, except you're in INCREDIBLE SBC PARK, baseball's premier venue.") Other highlights included a "Philadelphia Eagles Club Box Seat" at Lincoln Financial Field (section C4, row 15, two seats together on aisle), which went for $10,500.00, and Pittsburgh Steelers "personal seat licenses," which sold for $12,650.00. The median price for Sporting Events auctions was around $150.00.

Theater: I'll Take Manhattan

The theater tickets here are dominated by Broadway tickets. The current favorites are the shows *The Odd Couple*, *Wicked*, and *Spamalot*, with the highest-priced tickets for each of those shows going for $2,026.00, $2,020.00, and $1,080.00, respectively. The median range of prices hovers around $250.00, and around this price you can find more *Wicked* tickets, some for *Spamalot*, and a Radio City holiday special.

Not all the tickets available are for Broadway, of course; the Tickets category has a drop-down menu where you can search for tickets in most major cities. I live in Washington, D.C., for example, and when I select that city, I see tickets for the Kennedy Center (and an upcoming *Wicked* performance), the National Theatre, and Ford's Theatre, among others.

There are movie tickets available here too, although most of the listings are for lots of four to ten tickets. The highest price in this sample was for ten Regal, United movie passes that sold for $61.01 (good for Regal Entertainment Group locations nationwide—Regal Cinemas, United Artist Theaters, and Edwards Theaters). With the price of movie tickets nowadays, this seems like a good deal.

The bottom line for eBay's Tickets category seems to be that you can either get a good deal or pay a premium for a last-minute ticket to a hot event. It may not be the first choice for people who plan ahead, but for people who can afford it, eBay is one more place to get an "in" to the event of your choice. For some, it replaces the traditional "scalper" market. As always, do your due diligence and try to buy only from reputable sellers.

Event Tickets ▶ Concerts

The median sales price in this subcategory is $189.00.

	HIGH		AVG
3 PAUL McCARTNEY TICKETS 11/19 HOUSTON 3RD ROW FLOOR!!! Venue Toyota Center	$4,500.00	2 BONNIE RAITT - PORTLAND - ORCHESTRA B - ROW F	$189.00
		CARLY SIMON TICKETS ~ D.A.R. CONSTITUTION HALL ~ DC	$189.00
4 U2 Vertigo Tour Tickets Miami 11/13 Sunday VIP access Venue American Airlines Arena Flagship Lounge Access, Flagship Parking, Ultimate TIX	$4,004.00	2 ~ 9TH ROW! ~ CENTER ORCHESTRA SEATS!	$189.00
		2 TICKETS INXS San Manuel Casino Highland CA bernardino	$189.00
		ROLLING STONES TICKETS SUNRISE FL BANKATLANTIC ATLANTIC	$189.00
4 U2 Vertigo Tour Tickets Miami 11/13 Sunday VIP access Venue American Airlines Arena Flagship Lounge Access, Flagship Parking, Ultimate TIX	$4,000.00	2 BONNIE RAITT - PORTLAND - ORCHESTRA C - ROW K	$189.00
		2tix Gwen Stefani Anaheim Arrowhead Pond Sec 106 Rw 22 Venue Arrowhead Pond	$189.00
PAUL McCARTNEY STAPLES CENTER LA L.A. LOS ANGELES 11/30 Venue Staples Center	$3,499.00	KANYE WEST EVERETT EVENTS CENTER FRONT ROW FLOOR	$189.00
(2) - REAL 5th ROW CENTER - FLOOR 2 ROW 5 - 11/30		BRUCE SPRINGSTEEN TRENTON NICE FLOOR FLR 6 ROW 5! Venue Sovereign Bank Arena	$189.00
ROLLING STONES BALTIMORE 4 TICKETS---10 ROWS FROM BAND! Venue 1st Mariner Arena TRUE FRONT FLOOR SEATS--REAL 10TH ROW--ONLY AREA SHOW!	$3,295.00	2 GWEN STEFANI /THE BLACK EYED PEAS GWINNETT ARENA 11/8 Venue Gwinnett Center LOWER LEVEL SECTION 109-GREAT VIEW OF SIDESTAGE!!!	$189.00

KEITH URBAN FRONT ROW TICKETS BACKSTAGE PASSES CHARITY	$3,250.00	DAVE MATTHEWS BAND-2 LOWER LEVEL SEATS-MINNEAPOLIS, MN	$189.00
Venue Richmond Coliseum		Venue Target Center	
Rolling Stones (Las Vegas)	$2,860.45	Phil Lesh 2 Tickets John Mayer Warfield San Francisco	$189.00
Venue MGM Grand Garden		Venue Warfield	
Paul McCartney Los Angeles Floor 12 rows from the stage	$2,045.00	2 GA Floor Tickets for Sold-Out Show on 12/30/05	
Venue Staples Center		2 tixs BRAD PAISLEY & SARA EVANS -TSONGAS-LOWELL,MA.	$189.00
LA Staples Center on November 29 11-29 The Best on Ebay		THE EAGLES 2 TICKETS ARROWHEAD POND ANAHEIM CA 11/17	$189.00
ROLLING STONES tickets SAN FRANCISCO SBC -- ON STAGE!!!	$2,000.00	Venue Arrowhead Pond	
Venue SBC Park		** SECTION 413, ROW P ** TICKETS IN HAND SHIP TODAY !	
2 ON STAGE TICKETS FOR SUNDAY SHOW - 11/13 --- LOOK!!!		2 JINGLE BELL BASH #8 TICKETS, TACOMA DOME	$189.00
2 PAUL MCCARTNEY TICKETS 11/19 HOUSTON 3RD ROW FLOOR!!!	$2,598.00	Venue Tacoma Dome	
Venue Toyota Center		2 FLOOR SEATS, 4 ROWS FROM THE STAGE!!	
Vans Warped Tour VIP Package	$2,325.00	# 275 MINT F-VF OG Cat.$300	$67.50
100% of the proceeds to benefit Habitat For Humanity			
TASTE OF CHAOS 2006 TICKETS & PHOTO PIT PASSES	$2,325.00		
100% of the proceeds to benefit Habitat For Humanity			
Sir Paul McCartney concert Houston Texas, Toyota Center	$2,147.09		
Venue Toyota Center			
4 FLOOR TICKETS SECTION C ROW 9. No reserve!!!			
Paul McCartney Los Angeles Floor 12 rows from the stage	$2,045.00		
Venue Staples Center			
LA Staples Center on November 29 11-29 The Best on Ebay			
KEITH URBAN FRONT ROW TICKETS BACKSTAGE PASSES CHARITY	$2,026.00		

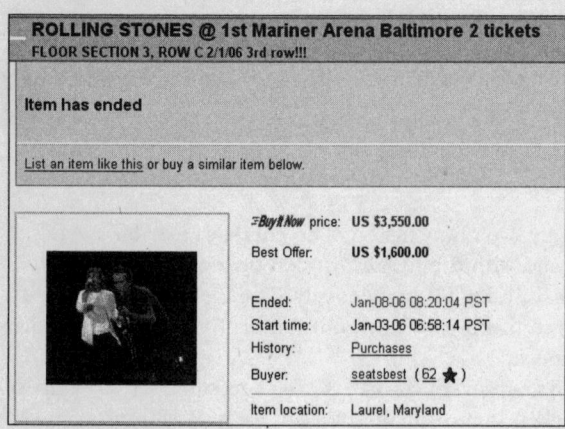

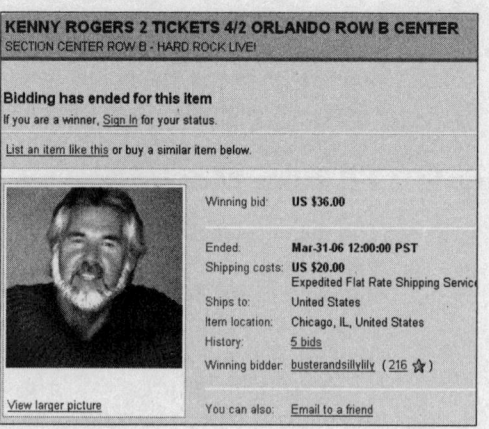

Event Tickets ▶ Movies

The median sales price in this subcategory is $18.05.

	HIGH		AVG
10 Regal, United, Free Movie Theater Ticket Passes +$10	$61.01	6 Loews Passport Movie Tickets Good Nationwide NR	$32.00
10 Regal or Edwards Movie Tickets passes FREE SHIPPING	$58.99	6 Regal Cinema's Super Saver Tickets	$30.00
10 Regal Movie Tickets	$58.37	2 passes for RENT movie ADVANCED screening	$30.00
LOT OF 8 REGAL ENT. GROUP MOVIE TICKETS(no expiration)	$53.50	4 AMC THEATRE TICKETS FREE BONUS FOR USING BUY IT NOW	$27.95
GOOD 4 ALL REGAL CINEMA/UNITED ARTIST/ EDWARDS THEATRES		ADVANCE SCREENING OF HARRY POTTER SAN DIEGO 11/13	$25.00
10 Loews Ultimate Passport Tickets Good Nationwide NR	$53.01	4 Loews Cineplex Odeon Magic Johnson Movie Tickets $19	$21.00
10 Loews Ultimate Passport Tickets Good Nationwide NR	$52.99	4 Fandango Movie Ticket Codes free shipping!	$20.51
[2 of these sold for $52.99 each]		$25 Loews Munch Money NR-Free Shipping!!	$18.05
10 Loews Ultimate Passport Movie Tickets Good Nationwid	$52.95	$25 Loews Munch Money NR-Free Shipping!!	$15.00
[2 of these sold for $52.95 each]		[3 of these sold for $15.00 each]	
10 Loews Ultimate Passport Tickets Good Nationwide NR	$52.00	2 Fandango.com movie tickets - no shipping cost	$15.00
10 LOEWS ULTIMATE PASSPORT MOVIE PASSES TICKETS	$51.00	$25 Loews Munch Money	$15.00
RENT Movie Advance Screening- -2 passes	$51.00	Free Shipping!!	
10 Loews Ultimate Passport Tickets Good Nationwide NR	$50.99	Harry Potter GoF Tickets North Canton OH 12:01 AM 11/17	$13.00
0 Loews Ultimate Passport Tickets Good Nationwide NR	$49.99	SOLD OUT 12:01 AM showing at Cinemark Tinseltown	
[7 of these sold for $49.99 each]		2 AMC movie tickets ANY MOVIE, NO RESERVE!	$12.51
LOT OF 8 REGAL ENT. GROUP MOVIE TICKETS(no expiration)	$49.03	Harry Potter Goblet of Fire Movie Ticket Tickets 5	$12.51
GOOD 4 ALL REGAL CINEMA/UNITED ARTIST/ EDWARDS THEATRES		2 Movie Tickets EDWARDS THEATRES UNITED ARTISTS REGAL	$12.50
LOT OF 8 REGAL ENT. GROUP MOVIE TICKETS(no expiration)	$48.52		
GOOD 4 ALL REGAL CINEMA/UNITED ARTIST/ EDWARDS THEATRES			
LOT OF 8 REGAL ENT. GROUP MOVIE TICKETS(no expiration)	$48.00		
GOOD 4 ALL REGAL CINEMA/UNITED ARTIST/ EDWARDS THEATRES			

Event Tickets ▶ Sporting Events

The median sales price in this subcategory is $150.00.

	HIGH		AVG
SF GIANTS CHARTER SEAT LICENSES / LOWER BOX 110	$16,498.00	2 MLS Cup tickets - behind home bench-with parking pass	$150.00
Venue SBC Park		DOLPHINS VS TENNESSEE 30YD. LOWER ROW 5 2 TIX	$150.00
Watch BONDS chase RUTH & AARON / 2007 ALL-STAR GAME		Venue Pro Player Stadium	
Pittsburgh Steelers PSL Personal Seat Licenses	$13,800.00	TENNESSEE TITANS @ JACKSONVILLE JAGUARS TICKETS + FOOD	$150.00
Venue Heinz Field		Venue Alltel Stadium	

2 PITTSBURGH STEELER P.S.L .	$12,650.00	2 LOS ANGELES KINGS@COLORADO AVALANCHE TICKETS	$150.00
Venue Heinz Field		ATAC RW1	
Philadelphia Eagles Club Box Seat License Agreement	$10,500.00	Venue Pepsi Center	
Venue Lincoln Financial Field		2 Tickets Orlando Magic Vs Miami Heat 11/26	$150.00
Section C4, Row 15 Two Seats Together on Aisle		Venue TD Waterhouse Centre	
RAVENS Club level PSL's-2 Great seats in Sec 204, Row 7	$7,500.00	(4) NOTRE DAME @ STANFORD CARDINAL TICKETS---11/26	$150.00
Venue M&T Bank Stadium		Venue Stanford Stadium	
World Cup 2006 finals 4 Tickets	$6,100.00	LOWER LEVEL-4 SEATS TOGETHER. !! DON'T MISS OUT.	
CATEGORY 1 TICKETS		Nascar Checker 500 PIR Phoenix Az Season parking Pass	$150.00
(6) 2006 BCS Rose Bowl Tickets UT Texas v USC 5th Row!	$5,150.00	Season Parking Good for all 4 days of racing!!!!!!!!!!!!	
Venue Rose Bowl		2 Denver Nuggets / N. J. Nets 11/28 MIDCOURT LOWER	$150.00
FIESTA BOWL & INSIGHT BOWL EVENT PACKAGE	$5,051.51	Venue Pepsi Center	
Venue Sun Devil Stadium		Sit just above George Karl and the Nuggets bench!!!!!!!!	
2 CINCINNATI BENGALS seat licenses GOAL LINE! LOWERS	$5,000.00	2 UK Kentucky Wildcats vs Ohio Bobcats 12/30 Cincinnati	$150.00
Venue Paul Brown Stadium		Venue US Bank Arena	
Section 116 Row 7 - FIELD LEVEL - AWESOME SEATS!		Sec 114 Row S	
2 CINCINNATI BENGALS SEAT LICENSES Field Level ROW 4	$5,000.00	2 Oregon/OSU Civil War Tickets, Sec. 18, Row 8, Nov. 19	$150.00
Venue Paul Brown Stadium		Venue Autzen Stadium	
Section 118 Row 4 - AWESOME SEATS!		2 Chiefs vs Patriots VIP Tailgate Passes FREE FOOD/BEER	$150.00
4 - Bengals Field Level Seat Licenses (COA) - Playoffs	$5,000.00	Venue Arrowhead Stadium	
Venue Paul Brown Stadium		Rockets @ Celtics Tickets Lowers Sec 14 Row 2 11/13	$150.00
MAUI INVITATIONAL BASKETBALL TOURNAMENT-Nov.21,22,23,	$4,550.00	Venue Fleet Center	
TICKETS TO ALL 12 GAMES(Mon,Tues,Wed,) FOR 2 PEOPLE		3 LA LAKERS MEMPHIS GRIZZLIES STAPLES TICKETS 12/28	$150.00
50 YARDLINE - SEC Championship Tickets !!	$4,550.00	Venue Staples Center	
Venue Georgia Dome		2 Chiefs vs Patriots VIP Tailgate Passes FREE FOOD/BEER	$150.00
Selling entire season for the Sacramento Kings, 4 seats	$4,488.00	Venue Arrowhead Stadium	
Venue ARCO Arena		Rockets @ Celtics Tickets Lowers Sec 14 Row 2 11/13	$150.00
2 Tennessee Titans Club Level PSL's	$4,257.00	Venue Fleet Center	
Venue Titans Stadium			

Event Tickets ▸ Theater

The median sales price in this subcategory is $249.99.

	HIGH		AVG
The ODD COUPLE 4 tickets - Nov. 19 VIP SEATS Row E	$2,026.00	Radio City Christmas Spectacular Dec 10 2 Tix Row GG	$250.00
Sat. Night 8pm WOW! Weekend Before Thanksgiving WOW!		Venue Radio City Music Hall The Rockettes	
8 WICKED TICKETS THANKSGIVING WEEKEND 11/26 2PM	$2,020.00	WICKED TICKETS BROADWAY NEW YORK NY 12/9	$249.99
2 The Odd Couple Tickets 12/19 @ 8 PM CENTER FRONT ROW	$1,499.00	2 WICKED Tickets Broadway FRI Nov 18th 8pm ORCH Row D	$249.99
FIRST ROW PREMIUM ORCHESTRA SEATS ROW AAA!! MUST SEE!!		WICKED Tickets NYC 2- SUN.3 PM NOV.13 ORCH Row 9	$249.99
4 The Odd Couple Tickets NY 2/7 ORCH Row C 8pm	$1,325.00	WICKED Tickets NYC 2- SUN.3 PM NOV.13 ORCH Row 8	$249.99
WICKED FORD CHICAGO 8-in-a-row!!! ORCH row L 11.27.05	$1,250.00	MONTY PYTHON'S SPAMALOT BROADWAY 2-DEC.10 MAT BOX D	$249.99
FAB SEATS, DEAD CTR, AT A GREAT PRICE, JUST COMPARE		Venue Shubert Theatre	
Odd Couple 4 Tickets Orchestra Row J Friday 12/23 2:00	$1,225.00	WICKED TICKETS BROADWAY NEW YORK NY 12/10	$249.99
Special Friday Matinee - Day before Christmas Eve		WICKED TICKETS BROADWAY NEW YORK NY 12/18	$249.99
WICKED~ 4 GREAT ORCH tix~ Kennedy Ctr, Washington DC	$1,200.00	WICKED TICKETS BROADWAY NEW YORK NY 12/9	$249.99
ODD COUPLE - NY - - BEST TICKETS IN HOUSE - - 11/12/05	$1,200.00	[3 of these sold for $249.99 each]	
BROOKS ATKINSON THEATER - ROW H, CTR SECTION, ON AISLE		MONTY PYTHON'S SPAMALOT BROADWAY 2-SAT.2PM NOV.12 ORCH	$249.99
ODD COUPLE-Sat Dec 3rd EVE. Orchestra, Row D (right)	$1,200.00	Venue Shubert Theatre	
Six rows from stage, seats 6&8 together-prime seats!!!		2 WICKED Tickets Broadway TUE NOV 29th 7pm ORCH Row DD	$249.99
(4) 700 Sundays Wilshire Theatre Crystal Tickets 2/14	$1,099.00	WICKED TICKETS BROADWAY NEW YORK NY 1/7	$249.99
ODD COUPLE-Sat DEC. 10th EVE Orchestra, Row D (right)	$1,083.00	[2 of these sold for $249.99 each]	
Six rows from stage, seats 6&8 together-prime seats!!!		WICKED TICKETS BROADWAY NEW YORK NY 1/8	$249.99
4 TIX SPAMALOT NEW YORK THANKSGIVING FRIDAY CHEAP	$1,080.00	WICKED TICKETS BROADWAY NEW YORK NY 1/14	$249.99
Venue Shubert Theatre		WICKED TICKETS BROADWAY NEW YORK NY 12/20	$249.99
2 Odd Couple Tickets 11/19 8PM VIP * ORCHESTRA *	$1,050.00		
Starting Bid at Face Value! **2 Seats together in Row D			
4 Odd Couple Tickets 11/16 8PM VIP * ORCHESTRA !	$1,000.00		
Starting Bid at Face Value! 4 Seats together in ROW C			
Odd Couple Nathan Lane Broederick Broadway Tickets!	$1,000.00		
Billy Crystal 700 Sundays Wilshire Theatre Los Angeles	$999.99		

Event Tickets ▸ Other

The median sales price in this subcategory is $107.50.

	HIGH		AVG
2 TICKETS 14 GAMES KANSAS JAYHAWKS BASKETBALL	$2,035.00	2 For 1 BILLBOARD MUSIC AWARDS 12/6 MGM GRAND LAS VEGAS	$110.05
Venue Allen Field House		Venue MGM Grand Garden	
Two (2) Crested Butte Season Ski Passes	$1,138.00	Buy One Get One FREE My Canceled Trip = $avings For YOU	
LUNCH WITH THE STARS OF SERENITY & FIREFLY!	$1,025.00	(2) Carlos Mencia Tickets Corpus Christi Front Row	$110.00
This event limited to ONLY 20 convention attendees!!		Star 94.1 Thank you party at the Hilton La Jolla	$110.00
Bon Jovi Continental Arena 12/22 first 18 rows - CENTER	$1,000.00	Detroit Opera House, La Boheme 2 tickets Nov 13th	$110.00
Venue Continental Airlines Arena		Mickey's Very Merry Christmas Party (3 Tickets)	$110.00
Absolute FRONT and CENTER FLOOR section! See BJ sweat!		WWE RAW Tickets at TD Banknorth (Boston)	$110.00
LUNCH WITH THE STARS OF SERENITY & FIREFLY!	$867.00	Venue Fleet Center	
This event limited to ONLY 20 convention attendees!!		Loge13....... Row5........ (paypal friendly)	
2 Tickets to E3 2006 & Nintendo Private Party + HOTEL	$860.00	2 One-Day One-Park Disney Tickets	$109.50
Nite-to-Unite for Kids Charity Auction		**2**WWE Raw Tickets for allstate arena in illinois	$107.50
LUNCH WITH THE STARS OF SERENITY & FIREFLY!	$812.00	Venue Allstate Arena	
This event limited to ONLY 20 convention attendees!!		*~*~*Auburn vs. Alabama Iron Bowl Ticket*~*~*	$107.50
4 JERRY SEINFELD Tickets PORTLAND 1/13 ROW 1!!!	$719.00	Las Vegas Comedy Festival, Jon Stewart. SELLING OUT!!!!	$107.00
2 CMA COUNTRY MUSIC AWARDS tickets 11/15 less then face	$715.00	Venue Caesars Palace Colosseum	
Venue Madison Square Garden			

Cirque du Soleil, Corteo, San Francisco, Nov 12, 8:00PM	$687.09	XBOX 360 ZERO HOUR LAUNCH 2 TICKETS - ACT NOW!!	$107.00
Venue SBC Park		TICKETS ARE IN HAND - ONLY CHANCE TO GET A 360!	
Two Tickets. VIP - Tapis Rouge. $200 Face Value Each		2 DAY CHILD DISNEY WORLD PARK HOPPER PLUS TICKETS FREE SHIPPING!	$105.00
BRISTOL NIGHT RACE/ 2 SEATS TOGETHER/ BUSCH AND CUP	$665.98	LOCAL PICKUP AVAILABLE FOR SAME PRICES!	
Venue Bristol Motor Speedway		[5 of these sold for $105.00 each]	
LUNCH WITH THE STARS OF SERENITY & FIREFLY!	$635.00	3 Awesome tickets to Disney Princesses on Ice	
This event limited to ONLY 20 convention attendees!!		Reunion Arena, Dalls, Texas, Nov. 17 st 7:30 pm	$105.00
2 AUBURN ALABAMA TICKETS 40 YARD LINE SEC 28 ROW 8	$635.00	4 AMERICAN MUSIC AWARDS TICKETS LOS ANGELES SHRINE AUD.	$105.00
LOWER LEVEL FREE OVERNIGHT SHIP POWER SELLER		Venue Shrine Auditorium	
2 Jerry Seinfeld Tickets Pechanga - Sold Out	$630.01	DisneyOnIce"INCREDIBLES"ContNJ Wed11/23 6LOWERS CHEAP!	$104.95
2006 SoxFest TWO 3 - Day ENTIRE WEEKEND PASSES!	$599.99	Venue Continental Airlines Arena	
SOLD OUT! See The World Champs on January 27, 28, & 29!			

Experiences ▶ Music

The median sales price in this subcategory is $41.00.

	HIGH		AVG
ALBUM DEAL!!!	$5,000.00	2 FLOOR Tix Coheed and Cambria 11/17 @Nokia Theater NYC	$66.02
LOS ANGELES RECORD DEAL	$4,550.00	4 Tickets to the GRAND OLE OPRY Nashville Tennessee	$62.00
4 U2 Concert Tickets Miami, FL 11/13/05 VIP Experience	$2,000.00	SOLD OUT - 1 Fall Out Boy Ticket - Cincinnati Bogarts	$55.00
2 Hilary Hillary Duff Tickets Toronto Ontario Canada ON	$1,999.00	Styx Waukegan Genesee Theatre	$50.00
* VIP TICKETS - MEET HILARY!!!! - CENTER FLOOR ROW 2 *		Walt Disney Concert Hall 2 Tickets Shostakovich 11/13	$49.99
Meet Rob Thomas, Attend San Diego Concert 2 Tickets	$1,525.00	WHITE CHRISTMAS AT PANTAGES THEATRE - HOLLYWOOD	$49.00
2 Def Leppard Meet & Greet passes - Las Vegas, NV 11/13	$1,000.00	4 TICKETS THRICE w/ UNDEROATH COURTYARD TAMPA FORDAMP	$41.00
Plus Early Entry to General Admission Show!		COURTYARD SHOW - GENERAL ADMISSION	
2 Def Leppard Meet & Greet passes - Las Vegas, NV 11/13	$910.00	WHITE CHRISTMAS AT PANTAGES THEATRE - HOLLYWOOD	$41.00
Plus Early Entry to General Admission Show!		Las Vegas VIP Club Passes 2 GHOSTBAR NO LINE NO COVER	$40.00
2 U2 tickets Tampa- 11/16 section GA	$811.99	6 tix -Rock and Roll Hall of Fame - below cost!	$40.00
2 Def Leppard Meet & Greet passes - Las Vegas, NV 11/13	$810.00	Las Vegas-Scintas at Rio (on 11-27-05): 2-SHOW TICKETS	$37.00
Plus Early Entry to General Admission Show!		WHITE CHRISTMAS AT PANTAGES THEATRE - HOLLYWOOD	$36.87
4 Kroq Almost Acoustic Christmas Xmas Tickets Gibson CA	$799.99	LEGENDS IN CONCERT FOR TWO - LAS VEGAS	$36.00
4 seats together! Hard to find! Loge 11! Amazing!		PAT GREEN/DIERKS BENTLEY-NOKIA THEATRE TIMES SQ	$35.00
U2 Atlanta (2) tix, CLUB LVL ACCESS on AISLE Nov. 19th	$675.00	WHITE CHRISTMAS AT PANTAGES THEATRE - HOLLYWOOD	$34.00
U2 GA FLOOR TICKET (1) Portland Rose Garden	$660.00		
2 HARD GA FLOOR U2 TICKETS HARTFORD CIVIC CENTER 12/7	$650.00		
Buy It Now Or Send Your Best Offer.			
LAST BEST CHANCE TO SEE THE ROLLING STONES IN LAS VEGAS	$637.83		
NO RESERVE! NO RESERVE! NO RESERVE!			
2 U2 U-2 Tickets Tampa St. Pete Times Forum Florida FL	$599.00		
* 2 OF 5 SEATS - SECTION 103 ROW K - AMAZING VIEW *			

LOS ANGELES RECORD DEAL

You are signed in

Bidding has ended for this item

If you are a winner, Sign In for your status.

List an item like this or buy a similar item below.

Winning bid:	**US $5,000.00**
Ended:	**Mar-19-06 17:30:00 PST**
Shipping costs:	Check item description and pay or contact seller for details
Ships to:	Worldwide
Item location:	Los Angeles, CA, United States
History:	4 bids
Winning bidder:	User ID kept private
You can also:	Email to a friend

View larger picture

Experiences ▶ Sports

The median sales price in this subcategory is $7.70.

	HIGH		AVG
2 BCS Rose Bowl Tickets USC Texas Va Tech Georgia	$3,749.99	NICKS Shirt SIGNED by Team + expert BASKETBALL CLINIC!	$415.00
VIP 2 Tickets+2 Hotel Nights+Transportation+Food		Let Coach Al Sokaitis get your game to the NBA level!!!	
Agassi! Graf! Roddick! Kournikova! Tennis! VIP Seats!	$2,201.00	NASCAR RACING EXPERIENCE	$399.00
Courtside At The Genworth Children's Advantage Classic!		Drive a REAL NASCAR 24 LAPS @ LAKELAND FLORIDA	
5 AUBURN vs ALABAMA Football Tickets	$1,750.00	Be a Ball Kid at MLS Cup 2005	$350.00
SEC 16 ROW 11 SEATS 2 & 3 ROW 10 SEATS 1, 2, &3		Richard Petty Driving Experience - "Rookie Experience"	$330.00

Denver Broncos vs New York Jets game experience 11/20	$1,625.00	STEELERS VS BROWNS December 24th 1:00pm	$320.01
Miami Dolphins game day experience November 13	$1,525.00	FREE LIMO TO GAME, GREAT XMAS GIFT	
OLE MISS 11/19/02 HONORARY CAPTAIN EXPERIENCE	$1,325.00	CELTICS Basketball Ball Boy or Ball Girl Dec 2 2005	$305.00
PGA TOUR PRO-AM LAS VEGAS GOLF EVENT GETAWAY VACATION	$1,325.00	Golf & eat w/ Saint Louis Billikens SLU Coach Soderberg	$202.50
Play with top PGA TOUR PROS and enjoy a 5-star resort!		Hurricane Relief: 18 holes + more, dinner for THREE!	
St. Louis Rams Sideline Extravaganza Experience	$1,313.00	VIP Los Angeles KINGS HOCKY Tickets in LA	$109.95
2 NASCAR HOMESTEAD MIAMI FORD 400 TICKETS CLUB SEATS	$1,225.00	VIP only!!!	
WOW, CHECK OUT WHAT IS INCLUDED IN THIS AUCTION		Copper Mountain Ski Lift 4-Pass Four Pack Free Shipping	$98.00
Killington Ski Resort - Two (2) 2005-2006 Season Passes	$1,200.00	red letter day orange experince in presentation box.	$90.00
Michigan vs. Ohio State Football Tickets! 50 Yard Line!	$1,025.00	Richard Petty Driving Experience "Ride Along"	$82.05
No, these are not student tickets! 50 yard line!		VIP Los Angeles KINGS HOCKY Tickets in LA	$81.00
Richard Petty Driving Experience Gift Certificate	$999.99	VIP only!!!	
$1500.00 Value! Great Christmas Gift for your love one.		VIP Los Angeles KINGS HOCKY Tickets in LA	$78.77
Michigan vs. Ohio State Football Tickets! 50 Yard Line!	$866.00	VIP only!!!	
No, these are not student tickets! 50 yard line!		WASHINGTON REDSKINS TAILGATE CLUB PASSES CHARGERS 11/27	$64.05
4 Detroit Lions v. Atlanta Falcons tickets & VIP Pack	$805.02	Note: Does not include game tickets!	
Includes CLUB SEATS and a Pre-Game Sideline Visit!!!		TITANS -JACKSONVILLE JAGUARS PARKING PASS LOT E!!!	$9.99
Maimi Dolphins photographer experience	$760.00		

Experiences ▶ Theme Parks

The median sales price in this subcategory is $99.00.

	HIGH		AVG
4 Premium Annual passes for California Disneyland	$1,075.00	2-Day CHILD Disney World Park Hopper Tickets+Bonus!	$100.00
These are NEW Premium passes, original price 329$ each		FREE Priority SHIPPING!! - or - Pickup at Your HOTEL!!	
Disney Meal Vouchers and More	$1,027.36	5 Disney Quick and Casual Meal Vouchers	$100.00
4 Adult Disney World Tickets (Expiration Date 2030)	$1,000.00	2 Adult 1 Day Disneyland Hopper Tickets Passes	$100.00
Disney Tickets		2-Day Child DISNEY WORLD Hopper Ticket + BONUS	$99.99
2A & 2C 7 DAY PREMIUM DISNEY WORLD TICKETS W/NO EX OPT.	$1,000.00	BRAND NEW Tickets - 4500+ Feedbacks - THANK YOU!	
Please! Read The ENTIRE description before posting ?'s 's		WALT DISNEY WORLD-BLIZZARDS	$99.99
[2 of these sold for $1,000.00 each]		BEACH PARK-4 ADULT TICKETS	
2Ad. & 2ch 7day premium Disney Tickets, NO Exp. Orlando	$930.50	DISNEYLAND $189 ticket 8-day hopper 3 days left AAA FP	$99.99
Please Read entire description before posting questions		@TWO DISNEYWORLD ONE-DAY ADULT	$99.85
2 Ad & 2 Ch 7 Day Hop W/No Ex. Opt Disney World Tickets	$885.00	TICKETS DISNEY TICKET FL	
Unused days NEVER EXPIRE! Bid With Confidence		2 Universal, 1 day, 2 Park, Theme Park Tickets (Adult)	$99.26
(2) 5-Day Adult & (2) Child Disney World Hopper Tickets	$875.00	CHILD Ticket - DISNEY WORLD 2-Day HOPPER + BONUS	$99.01
FREE USPS PRIORITY SHIPPING TO HOME OFFICE, OR HOTEL!!!		1-Day ONLY Auction - 4500+ feedbacks - FAST Shipping!	
4 - 4 Day Disney World Park Hopper Passes	$801.00	2 ADULT DISNEYLAND THEME PARK Tickets 1-Day ONLY	$99.00
4 adult - Disney world 4 day hopper passes - tickets	$800.00	Disney One Day One Park tickets	$99.00
(2) 5-Day Adult & (2) Child Disney World Hopper Tickets	$750.00	2 Disneyland or California Adventure Tickets	$99.00
FREE USPS PRIORITY SHIPPING TO HOME OFFICE, OR HOTEL!!!		4 - Busch Gardens FunCard Passes	$17.59
5 DISNEYLAND 5-DAY PARK HOPPER TICKETS 3 adult, 2 child	$700.00	FAMILY 4 PACK SIX FLAGS MAGIC MOUNTAIN TICKETS $100	$17.50
2 Disneyland Premium passes no blackout dates	$630.00	2 DISNEYLAND or CA ADVENTURE	$17.09
Parking included, original price 369$ each!!!		THEME PARK TICKETS 1DAY	
3-DISNEY WORLD 5 DAY HOPPER PASSES	$623.13		
Disney World Hopper Tickets, 4 adult 3day passes	$609.96		
2A/2C 4 Day Disneyland Park Hopper valid 11/20-12/2/05	$601.66		

Experiences ▶ Other

The median sales price in this subcategory is $56.00.

	HIGH		AVG
Charity Lunch w/ Rupert Murdoch Chairman/CEO News Corp	$57,100.00	TWO MEDIEVAL TIMES TICKETS TORONTO DINNER & SHOW	$82.00
Proceeds benefit The Jerusalem College of Technology		ATTN: SKIERS Snow Bear & Bonus Crested Butte Lift Tix	$81.00
FA 7th on Sale Champagne Krug Vineyard Adventure	$12,855.95	PLIMOTH PLANTATION HARVEST DINNER TICKETS - SOLD OUT	$72.33
A 7th on Sale Experience in France!		17TH CENTURY HARVEST DINNER - NOVEMBER 25	
FA Paul Smith & Triumph Motorcycles Adventure	$12,040.00	3 Tickets, ARABIAN NIGHTS Dinner Show, Orlando Free S&H	$69.00
A 7th on Sale Fashion Experience in England!		2 Adult, 1 Child ARABIAN NIGHTS Tickets, Orlando	$67.00
FA 7th on Sale John Hardy Balinese Adventure	$11,100.00	(2) Medieval Times Admission Certificates	$62.01
A 7th on Sale Fashion Experience		RICHARD PETTY DRIVING EXPERIENCE RIDE A LONG	$56.68
FA Roberto Cavalli Adventure @ Playboy Palms Casino	$9,200.00	XBox 360 Zero Hour Launch Party Console Preorder	$56.00
A 7th on Sale Fashion Experience		Sold on Milwaukee! Take a Spring Class at MIAD	$53.99
FA 7th on Sale Brioni Milan Adventure	$8,700.00	Milwaukee Institute of Art and Design	
A 7th on Sale Fashion Experience		Disneyland Ca Adventure Dine in the Magic Meal Vouchers	$53.73
FA 7th on Sale Burberry Adventure	$8,600.00	1 hour private helicopter flight with a Robinson R22	$51.00
A 7th on Sale Fashion Experience		Ivory-billed Woodpecker Celebration & Birthday Party!	$50.00
Galapagos "Origins of the Species Adventure" for Two	$8,000.00	Keynts-Bobby Harrison, Tim Gallagher, Pete Dunne +More!	$50.00
FA 7th on Sale Cole Haan Hawaiian Adventure	$7,800.00	[2 of these sold for $50.00 each]	
A 7th on Sale Fashion Experience		(2) One day New York Passes, The Key to the City!	$50.00
FA Diane Von Furstenberg Harbour Island Adventure	$7,600.00	Dr. Phil - Certificate for two to attend VIP Taping	
A 7th on Sale Fashion Experience		2 ski lift Tickets Nashoba Valley, MA snowboard	$48.51
Spend the day with CHAMILLIONAIRE in Houston, TX!	$6,300.00		
Lunch, In-store, Party & more celebrating the new album			
Meet and Greet with the Cast of CSI Grissom	$5,800.00		
Meet the cast at the set after watching them tape!			
Pennsylvania Ballet - A Luxury Holiday Package	$5,000.00		
Sweet and Savory			
Tony Stewart's Race for the Ronald McDonald House Pkg 5	$4,810.00		
South Africa Photo Safari for 2: For Wellness Community	$4,000.00		

32

TOYS & HOBBIES

In more than one way, eBay's roots are in the world of toys—specifically, PEZ dispensers and Beanie Babies. One of the legends of eBay's founding is that Pierre Omidyar created it as a place for his fiancée to trade her collection of PEZ dispensers (although the real reason, it has been said, was that Omidyar was interested in experimenting with auctions as a market-maker on the Internet). The Beanie Baby craze then helped spur eBay's rise in the late 1990s. And that's appropriate, because of all collectibles, toys probably have some of the most sentimental attachments. They can take us back to our childhoods and conjure cherished memories of a simpler time.

"Of all the auctions I have held, the toys hold a special place. We can never go back to our childhood, but toys are a way of being able to reconnect to that time of our lives," one eBay toy seller wrote on the Toys & Hobbies discussion board.

In fact, one of eBay's television commercials involved the joys of reclaiming a lost plaything: a little boy is playing with a toy boat on the beach in Cape Cod—the tagline says the year is 1972. His mom calls him away, he leaves the boat, and waves carry it out to sea. It winds up sinking in the ocean, and eventually we see fishermen on another continent bringing it up in their net. The boy then finds the boat listed on eBay.

Vintage Power: Toys from Old to New

You can do well as a seller by offering either vintage toys or new, hot toys. Although many modern toys show up on eBay's Top 10 List for the category, many of the highest prices in this sample come from older, "retro" toys. The eBay Top 10 List of toys as I write this contains Fisher-Price, Polly Pocket, The Simpsons, Spider-Man, Scooby-Doo, radio control helicopters, LEGO Bionicle, Care Bears, Playskool, and Traxxas. Popular searches include *star wars, fisher price, lego, Barbie, little tikes, bratz, marx, power wheels, lionel,* and *dora*.

Let's look at some of the prices for the Fisher-Price brand, which came first on the top-ten list. This may be an especially appropriate manufacturer to study, because it's been around for so long and continues to make popular toys today. Though now part of the Mattel Corporation, Fisher-Price was founded in 1930 when former Woolworth employee Irving Price teamed up with toy industry veteran Herman G. Fisher.

The highest-selling item in the Toys & Hobbies ▶ Pretend Play, Preschool ▶ Fisher Price subcategory of this sample was a lot of vintage Fisher-Price "little people" (and some Playskool toys as well) that went for $157.50. The seller wrote, "From what I can tell, there is a barn, Children's hospital, a town, a Sesame Street clubhouse, and a really old Ferris wheel and Merry-go-round," as well as a cash register and record player. The items ranged from very bad to very good condition.

Several of the highest prices in the Fisher-Price subcategory were paid for vintage items, including a 1979 "VINTAGE FISHER PRICE UNISEX SECURITY BUNNY BLANKET" that sold for $132.50 with 22 bids, and a "FISHER PRICE - MISS PIGGY & KERMIT FROG DRESS UP MUPPET" from 1982 that went for $130.69 with 19 bids. An even older Fisher-Price item, a 1932 Fisher-Price "Dr. Doodle" pull toy (not included in this sample) sold for $500.00.

But one of the highest-priced items was brand new: an "AMAZING AMANDA" interactive doll that went for $127.50. According to the seller, this doll was sold out. A variation of this doll had a retail price of $89.99 (marked down from $99.99) on Amazon.com. (In general, items that are sold out from traditional stores—and even some other online venues—can sell for a premium on eBay.)

Do You Yo-Yo? Classic Toys

Some old-fashioned, "classic" toys sold for fairly high prices in this sample. One of the highest was a lot of six Cheerios yo-yos that sold for $750.00. Titled "SIX CHEERIO YO-YO'S MINT W/ STORE DISPLAY - 1940's, 50's," it's a set of yo-yos nestled in their original store display box. The seller described it as a "great collectible—one of only a few I have seen up for auction . . . this Cheerio yo-yo store display box contain[s] 6 ea. official pro 99, wood, (maple leaf) foil sticker seal, tournament shape, glitter enamel finish, mint condition." There are two red, two sky blue, and two dark blue yo-yos, and the copyright date on the box is 1947. "A must have for the YO-YO collector," wrote the seller.

How about $320.00 for a single yo-yo? That's what the "Rare Goody Jeweled Trophy Yo-Yo Mint Condition" went for: Described as silver with a red stripe with four jewels on the front (two red and two blue), the yo-yo came out of an original box and has never been played with, according to the seller. "It is believed the jeweled Trophy yo-yos were not sold commercially but rather used as awards for yo-yo contest winners—the gold ones for first-place winners, and the silver ones for second-place winners," he wrote.

Interestingly, there weren't very many yo-yos in this sample that were not vintage, or at least not from the last year or two. Perhaps that's because they're relatively inexpensive, so not many people want to sell them. A new yo-yo titled "NEW! Special Edition HYPER RAIDER YO YO from YOMEGA" did sell for $5.50, well below the subcategory's average price of $20.80. It seems the average price in this sample spikes high due to the lofty prices on the high end.

Un-Losing Your Marbles

Marbles are some of the most beloved of toys, and there are some interesting and impressive ones here. The high seller was a lot of four antique marbles—"Four Vintage Lutz Marble" shooters that went for $450.00. Described as "Onionskin, Yellow, Green Shooters," the marbles were in very good condition; "the lutz in these marbles really shine like diamonds," wrote the seller.

A single marble—a "rare hand-made 1 1/16 inch gold mica"—sold for $405.00. The average price for marbles in this sample is about $29.00.

Another popular collectible is toy trains. The Toys & Hobbies ▶ Model RR, Trains ▶ O Scale subcategory yielded one of the highest prices in the whole sample of the Toys & Hobbies category—a "25000+ Lionel & Train Store Stock Lot - Engines, Cars +" that went for $16,100.00. There was a bit of mystery to this auction, because the seller didn't have time or space to show everything, but there are many photos of trains in new packaging. "This lot contains an amazing amount of merchandise, estimating between 25,000 to 35,000 items," wrote the seller. "There are engines, boxcars, track, buildings, transformers, people, decals, train layout accessories, kits, parts, etc. Most engines and cars are O gauge, but there are also HO and N here too."

The highest-selling single O Scale train in this sample is a "Lionel F-3 Twin Motored Diesel Locomotive #2383" that went for $250.00. The seller put the date as somewhere between the 40s and the mid-70s.

Modern Toys

One of the popular searches was for *lego*. A factory-sealed "Lego Star Wars JEDI STAR FIGHTER (#7143)" sold for $24.50 in this sample. I also found new ones on eBay for as little as $18.50 and as much as $47.20 (GBP 27.50).

There are many action figures in the Toys & Hobbies category, from "old-school" ones like G.I. Joe to Star Wars dolls that have come back into vogue since their original introduction with the first Star Wars toys (and film) in the 1970s. The high seller in this sample of Star Wars action figures is not a vintage toy—it was one of the few new toys I saw on the high end of a subcategory: an "R2D2 INTERACTIVE DROID HASBRO STAR WARS MIB – Mint in Box! When they're gone, THEY ARE GONE!" It sold for $385.01. Some of the high sellers were only a few years old, from around 2002. The average price range in the Toys & Hobbies ▶ Action Figures ▶ Star Wars subcategory was $27.00—for example, a "Disney Star Wars Tours Yoda Jedi Mickey Blue Variation" sold for $27.95.

As there is some overlap between the Toys & Hobbies category and the Dolls & Bears category, you can find several dolls, such as Barbie, Bratz, and Polly Pocket items within Toys & Hobbies. However, you may be better off doing a search to find them rather than browsing the subcategories, because they may be located in subcategories you wouldn't think to look in. For example, a "Power Wheels Barbie Cool Tunes Pink Jeep" (selling for $46.99) was located within Toys & Hobbies ▶ Outdoor Toys, Structures ▶ Ride-Ons, Tricycles—a category that might not have occurred to you as the first place to look for this Barbie item.

There are many items within Toys & Hobbies to bring a smile to your face, or your child's. Although there are other online venues in which to buy some of these toys, eBay seems to be king when it comes to vintage and collectible items, as well as new items that are harder to find—items that are sold out, or that are only sold from specialized locations, such as theme parks.

Action Figures ▶ Batman

The average sales price in this subcategory is $15.31.

	HIGH		AVG
DC Direct Batman Hush Series 1, 2 and Jason Todd	$112.50	BATMAN FIGURE LOT DC SUPERMAN JOKER	$16.49
BATMAN Super Powers mint on large card with comic	$102.50	Batman Figure Collectable with Stand Accessories New NR	$16.00
DC Direct JSA Power Girl figure - MIP	$91.58	Batman Yamato Wave 3 BANE MOC	$15.99
3 DC Comics Collector Edition Plates,Batman,Catwoman,NR	$91.00	DC Direct ClassicHeroes The Question Action Figure MIP	$15.50
DC Direct Batman Hush Loose Figure Lot!	$76.00	JLA JUSTICE LEAGUE BATMAN figure & die cast Vehicle	$15.50
Batman TAS series with 3 special collectibles	$66.76	BATMAN - MR. FREEZE NEW ACTION FIGURE	$15.50
DC Direct Loose Super-Friends Figure Lot!	$63.00	Wizard World Unmasking Batman Exclusive 2004 MINT	$15.00
Jason Todd Hush Toyfare Exclusive DC DIRECT	$61.00	DC Direct Super Friends Robin & Riddler Deluxe Fig Set	$14.99
1992 = THE PENGUIN = ANIMATED BATMAN SERIES = MOC	$54.00	Batman...Mission Masters...RIDDLER...&...Mr Freeze	$14.50
5 DC DIRECT Dark Knight BATMAN ROBIN SUPERMAN CAT WOMAN	$50.99	Mattel Batman loose lot Bat-Man Robin Variant 6 figures	$14.40
1990 Kenner BatMobile Dark Knight Collection w/box	$48.00	Batman Begins Mattel Comic-Con exclusive figure MIB	$14.27
Super Powers Hall of Justice, No Reserve! + 2 extras	$46.00	BATMAN ANIMATED BATMOBILE COMPLETE	$14.00
60s vintage Batman Robin Batmobile 1/24 tin w/ figures	$45.44	loose DC Direct JLA boxset BATMAN w/base mint	$13.55
Batman Begins Henri Ducard Brown Shirt Variant	$40.00	DC DIRECT SUPER FRIENDS GREEN LANTERN & SINESTRO MIB!	$13.51
BATMAN LARGE COOKIE JAR WB STORE MIB	$39.99	Super Powers Batman Batmobile	$13.00

Action Figures ▸ GI Joe

The average sales price in this subcategory is $24.98.

	HIGH		AVG
G.I. Joe M3 Tank Destroyer	$280.00	BBI Elite Force WW2 Pearl Harbor US Pilot Lt Doc Miller	$25.77
GI Joe Continental Guard Convention Set	$232.50	Ultimate Soldier M41 Walker Bulldog Tank MIB! 1:18	$25.50
Custom 12" Gladiator Russell Crowe	$211.41	3 - GI Joe Home For The Holidays + Airborne 12" NRFB	$25.01
GI JOE WWII Liberators Willys JEEP Vehicle! Rare! MIB!	$202.50	GI JOE Father and Son Giants baseball ultra ltd figures	$25.00
GI Joe Supersonic Test Pilot Convention Set	$167.51	Gi Joe 12" Timeless 40th Marine Communications Set MIB	$25.00
Snake Eyes DDP custom figure Marvel Legends GI JOE MOC	$162.50	2 ULTIMATE SOLDIER ARMY TANK COMMANDER + NAVY SEAL NEW	$24.99
Takara Jin-Roh Protect Gear Sexy CY Girl Figure Doll	$130.00	2 ULTIMATE SOLDIER U.S. ARMY FIGURES + 2 WEAPON SETS	$24.99
Takara Jin-Roh Protect Gear Sexy CY Girl Figure Doll	$130.00	GI Joe Flint Bust By Palisades	$24.95
GI JOE LAND ADVENTURER Ltd Ed 12" DOLL MIB Retired Club	$127.50	AUZ & TAZZ MANTRACKERS Figure Ultimate Soldier VILLAINS	$24.89
12" Halo Green Beret Hot Toys 1/6 - Dragon BBI MISB	$122.50	GI JOE GERMAN PANZER TANK SGT.-MAJOR 12" DOLL	$24.50
* COMBAT GI JOE 12" Godzilla GIJOE G I JOE	$112.50	G.I. JOE SIGMA 6 SIX SNAKE EYES 8 IN. L@@k HTF	$24.49
Jin-Roh Protect Gear Sexy CY Girl Figure German Gray	$110.00	GI Joe Little Sure Shot w/ Feathers Sgt Rock 12" NIB	$24.29
GI JOE TALKING COMMANDER w/BOX CLUB EXCL REPRO Adv TEAM	$105.49	Lot of 3 - GI Joe WWII Officers Club 12" Figures NRFB	$24.28
NEW JOES SIGMA SIX MISB WAVE 1 IN HAND	$99.99	BBI Elite Force WWII 83rd Infantry Military Police MP	$24.00
HUGE ULTIMATE SOLDIER 1:18 XD P-38 AIRPLANE MISB NEW	$99.00	GI Joe WildMan DC Comics WWII Hero DC Comics 12" NIB	$23.99

Action Figures ▸ Lord of the Rings

The average sales price in this subcategory is $14.69.

	HIGH		AVG
LOTR AOME MEGA COLLECTION, LOT, SET, NO LONGER MADE	$800.00	THE LORD OF THE RINGS LOTHLORIEN GIFT PACK (MIP)	$14.99
Lord of the Rings Action Figures/Dolls HUGE LOT	$133.50	Shagrat gorbang Orc AOME lord of the rings LOTR FIGURE	$14.99
LOTR huge action figure lot mail away Uruk Hai, Elrond	$114.99	AOME-SSW4 Elven Soldiers-Soldier #2-Bearer & Archer	$14.99
Custom Toybiz LOTR Pelennor Fields Drummer Troll MIB	$91.00	LOTR AOME - Pelennor Field Fell Beast Dlx Box Loose	$14.99
LORD Of The Rings Armies of Middle Earth Battle Helms	$79.02	EASTERLING LORD of the RINGS TWO TOWERS Figure Toybiz	$14.95
NEW Lord of the Rings 8 FIGURE CARRY CASE GIFT SET	$54.99	EASTERLING Two Towers LORD of the RINGS Figure Toybiz	$14.95
NEW Lord of the Rings 8 FIGURE CARRY CASE GIFT SET	$54.99	BATTLE TROLL 11' LORD OF THE RINGS ROTK, VERY RARE, MIB	$14.50
LOTR ROTK- HORSE+RIDERS- LEGOLAS-ARAGORN-WARG	$54.95	Lord of the Rings FOTR Orc Warrior C9 MOC	$14.27
LORD OF THE RINGS ELECTRONIC CAVE TROLL ****MIB****	$51.00	Toy Biz Lord of the Rings: Gothmog and Berserker	$14.05
Lord of the Rings Cave Troll Toy Biz BRAND NEW IN BOX	$50.00	AOME Uruk-Hai PLAY ALONG 3 Pack Ugluk Uruk Hai	$13.99
LOTR BUST FOTR High Elven Infantryman BUST SIDESHOW	$49.99	Lord of the Rings FOTR Elrond In armor Moon Box MOC C9	$13.82
LOTR FINAL BATTLE FOR MIDDLE-EARTH GIFT PACK TROLL MIB!	$39.99	1st Ringwraith w/ horse Combo Set!!!!	$13.75
ELVES OF MIDDLE EARTH 6-Figure Prologue Elven Haldir +	$39.95	Lord of the Rings FOTR ORC WARRIOR Figure RARE MINT	$13.59
KINGS OF MIDDLE EARTH 6-Figure LOTR Morgul Witch King +	$39.95	Lord of the Rings FOTR Electronic Sauron MIB red box	$13.55
Star Wars Unleashed Han Solo WOW!	$39.00	LOTR-The Two Towers-BATTLE CRY URUK-HAI WARRIOR - NIB	$13.51

Action Figures ▸ Power Rangers

The average sales price in this subcategory is $17.95.

	HIGH		AVG
Green Magiranger Helmet Power Rangers Mystic Force	$550.00	POWER Rangers LOT OF RANGER MEGAZORDS	$15.00
GIGANTIC LOT OF POWER RANGERS	$189.50	POWER RANGERS BATTLE BOOSTER MORPHER SEALED RARE ***	$15.00
1995 MOC POWER RANGERS - ALIEN RANGER (BLUE)	$153.00	ORIGINAL POWER RANGERS~1994 MM~	$15.00
Mighty Morphin Power Rangers The Movie Set	$103.51	FIGURES + BAD GUYS~MIP	$14.99
1995 MOC POWER RANGERS - ALIEN RANGER (WHITE)	$102.50	43 pc LOT Vintage POWER RANGERS 20" Plush & Vehicles	$14.99
BANDAI abaranger dinothunder DX KILLER OH MEGAZORD BNIB	$99.99	Gashapon 5 Keychains Magi Power Rangers Mystic Bandai	$14.99
1995 MOC POWER RANGERS - ALIEN RANGER (RED)	$91.00	Kamen Masked Rider Kaixa & Sidebasher 555 Faiz	$14.99
1995 MOC POWER RANGERS - ALIEN RANGER (YELLOW)	$91.00	Power Rangers Dino Thunder Brachio Staff Sounds NEW	$14.99
POWER RANGERS FIVE DINOZORDS MORPH TO MEGAZORD MIB 1993	$85.50	Great lot! POWER RANGERS! 35 pcs. Figures, Toys & Misc	$14.59
DaiRanger Encyclopedia - sentai - kamen rider - dai	$85.00	Bandai Sentai AbareKiller Morpher w/Stegozord plate	$14.51
POWER RANGERS DRAGONZORD W/	$82.00	Power Rangers Galaxy 5"Action Figure Complete set of-5	$14.50
GREEN TOMMY RANGER MIB 1993		Power Rangers LIGHTSPEED MEGAZORD MIB Ranger Rescue	$14.49
BANDAI abaranger dinothunder CEPHALO ZORD discontinued	$79.99	Lot of 2 Old 1994 POWER RANGER hb Children's Books	$14.38
POWER rangers GREEN ninja STORM ranger COSTUME chestpla	$75.00	NEW HTF Power Rangers Light Patrol *OMEGA* White Ranger	$13.99
POWER RANGERS SPD SOUND PATROL COMPLETE SET OMEGA PINK	$72.00	Wilton Cake Pan 1994 Power Ranger # 2105-5975 DEAL!	$13.50
Power Rangers 2006 DX Megazord MagiKing Rare! [new]	$69.99	POWER RANGERS - WHITE RANGER'S DELUXE FALCONZORD	$13.50

Action Figures ▸ Spider-Man

The average sales price in this subcategory is $14.03.

	HIGH		AVG
SPIDERMAN Custom 12" MEDICOM figure Dragon Hot Toys bbi	$247.00	LOT OF 10" MARVEL ACTION FIGURES RARE IRON MAN L@@K!!!!	$15.50
Sideshow 1/4 Scale Spiderman GREEN GOBLIN figure OnHand	$199.99	loose Marvel Select Black Cat action figure	$15.50
RARE MEGO 12" SPIDERMAN MINT IN US BOX MIB FLY AWAY	$165.50	New - Marvel Select Spiderman Figure	$15.00
Spider-Man Classics Marvel Legends loose lot 40 figures	$165.05	1977 SPIDERMAN VIEWMASTER PACK	$14.99
MARVEL SPIDERMAN KRAVENS LAST HUNT STATUE DIORAMA MIB!!	$145.62	AIR RESCUE CAPTAIN AMERICA SPIDERMAN AND FRIENDS HTF	$14.99
Marvel 9-inch Figure Lot Famous Covers X-Men Avengers	$118.50	Marvel Legends Series 10 1st App. Spider-Man Prototype	$14.50
1977 MIB Spider-Man Car Not Mego Remote CANADA ONLY???	$104.49	SPIDERMAN LAMP -BRAND NEW	$13.99
MEGO 8" AMAZING SPIDERMAN MINT ON US CARD MOC SPIDER	$81.00	SPIDERMAN MOVIE KIDS CHAIR BRAND NEW!!!!	$13.99
2002 NIB SPIDERMAN FLOATING HELICOPTER PLAYSET W/FIGURE	$76.00	SPIDER-MAN AND FRIENDS LASER BLAST CYCLOPS LOW SHIPPING	$13.62
Marvel Legends Spider-Man VS. the Sinister 6 Boxed Set	$51.00	SPIDER-MAN 12 INCH GREEN GOBLIN FIGURE LOOSE	$13.51
19" Knickerbocker Spider Man 1978 - New in Box	$50.00	MARVEL MINIMATES SERIES 10 6 FIGURE SET 2-PACK MIB	$13.49
Spider-man & friends HULK CAPTAIN AMERICA & MORE	$49.55	SPIDERMAN MOTION LAMP - BRAND NEW	$13.00
SPIDERMAN TWIN COMFORTER BEDDING SET BOYS ROOM MAKEOVER	$47.11	SPIDERMAN MOTION LAMP - BRAND NEW	$13.00
marvel secret wars figures lot spiderman iron man x-men	$46.00	SPIDERMAN MOVIE KIDS CHAIR BRAND NEW!!!!	$12.99
SPIDERMAN MONSTER MAYHEM 8 ACTION FIGURES SET" RARE"	$45.00	SPIDERMAN VENOM FIGURE VHTF	$12.99

Action Figures ▶ Sports

The average sales price in this subcategory is $15.89.

	HIGH		AVG
Jakks WWE Toyfare Boxing Roddy Piper 1 of 100	$405.01	RIC FLAIR WWE JAKKS INTERNET EXCLUSIVE WRESTLING FIGURE	$16.99
WWE WWF HART FOUNDATION SIGNED JAKKS CLASSIC 2 PACK	$212.51	New in Package!DALLAS COWBOYS NFL 97'MVP action figures	$16.50
73 WWF (WWE) Hasbro Wrestling Figures Inc. Dusty Rhodes	$155.00	WWE Classic Superstars Legion of Doom	$16.50
Jakks WWE Classic Superstars Legion Of Doom 2 Pack	$153.50	WWE Classic Superstars 3 Action Figure Ultimate Warrior	$16.50
WWE/WWF/WCW/ECW/NWA CLASSIC	$142.50	50 + WRESTLING AND ASSESSORIES INCLUDING SINK 100 +	$16.49
L.O.D. WRESTLING FIGURES		WWE WCW ECW WWF CUSTOM HONKEY	$16.00
wwe jakks classic superstars lot of 16 figures	$132.50	TONK MAN RA RUTHLESS	
Jakks WWE Classic Superstars Hart Foundation 2 Pack	$127.50	WWE RAW WORLD HEAVYWEIGHT TITLE BELT RARE L@@K	$15.99
WWE Classic Superstars figures series 7 set of 9 JAKKS	$109.99	CARLITO COOL RUTHLESS AGGRESSION 15 WWE JAKKS FIGURE	$15.55
New Japan Toy Wrestling Ring for Figures +Referee MIB !	$81.00	WWF Philly Spectrum house show 6/2/84 on DVD	$15.50
WWF Hasbro figure LOT all complete still packaged	$75.00	WWE Classic Superstars Legion of Doom	$15.50
66 WWF 1991 HASBRO WRESTLING FIGURES	$73.60	5 old school LJN Titan Sports Wrestling Figures Hogan	$15.50
WWE LEGION OF DOOM CLASSIC TAG	$71.00	WWE RUTHLESS AGGRESSION 11.5	$15.50
TEAMS ROAD WARRIORS RED		RANDY ORTON ACTION FIGURE	
WWF/WWE HASBRO MINT ON CARD "1-2-3 KID"	$49.99	MOC WWE CLASSIC ROWDY PIPER 1 OF 3000 TOYFARE EXCLUSIVE	$15.50
1970's NFL Action Team Mate Stadium with Accessories	$49.00	8 WWF WWE Wrestling Action Figures Lot/Stone Cold	$15.50
Remco! All Star Wrestlers! Ric Flair/Larry Zbyszko!MIB!	$46.59	6pc lot WWE Wrestling Figures New Tattoos Chyna Kane ++	$15.01

Action Figures ▶ Star Trek

The average sales price in this subcategory is $21.66.

	HIGH		AVG
Star Trek Mego THE ROMULAN MOC	$1,000.00	Star Trek Mr Spock 12 1/2"Mego Mint in Box Vintage 1979	$22.52
MOC 1974 STAR TREK 8" MEGO KLINGON RARE 5 FACED CARD	$510.00	Star Trek figures from the Voyager series	$22.50
MOC 1974 STAR TREK 8" MEGO CAPT KIRK RARE 5 FACED CARD	$357.00	STAR TREK CAPTAIN KIRK DOLL BY KNICKERBOCKER 1979	$22.50
TALOS MOC SUPER RARE MEGO ALIEN STAR TREK MINT	$315.00	STAR TREK MISTER SPOCK DOLL BY KNICKERBOCKER 1979	$22.50
MOC 1974 STAR TREK 8" MEGO MR.SCOTTIE RARE 5 FACED CARD	$305.00	Star Trek Space Talk Series USS Enterprise NCC-1701-D	$22.50
MOC 1974 STAR TREK 8" MEGO DR.McCOY RARE 5 FACED CARD	$305.00	15 STAR TREK NEXT GENERATION COLLECTIBLES PICCARD RIKER	$21.83
MIB 1974 MEGO U.S.S.STAR TREK ENTERPRISE ACTION PLAYSET	$255.00	Convention Exclusive Enterprise Tucker Limited 500 !!	$21.62
Star Trek Micro Machines Limited Set III 90s Sealed	$162.50	STAR TREK ORIGINAL TRIBBLES MIB (NEVER USED)	$21.50
K STAR TREK MICRO MACHINES LIMITED SET III 90 SEALED	$152.00	Star Trek NX-01 Enterprise 12" Discontinued Art Asylum	$21.50
Star Trek USS Enterprise Action Playset MEGO w/Box 1974	$147.50	STAR TREK ORIGINAL SERIES CLASSIC COLLECTOR FIGURE SET	$21.49
K STAR TREK MICRO MACHINES LIMITED SET II 90	$127.50	STAR TREK CHIEF ENGINEER SCOTT James Doohan Model ~MIB~	$21.00
1974 STAR TREK MEGO 5 SCOTTY Action figure NIB	$107.50	STAR TREK 1974 Playset MEGO Men/Guns ALSO on sale	$20.81
1974 MEGO Star Trek USS Enterprise Action Playset, More	$102.50	STAR TREK Classic Tricorder!!!	$20.50
NEAR MINT STAR TREK USS ENTERPRISE ACTION PLAYSET W/BOX	$102.50	Star Trek ~Amok Time Figure Set~ Kirk & Spock Mego Like	$20.50
@ Star Trek @ TNG playmates Electronic BORG CUBE_New!!	$100.00	STAR TREK, 9" COLLECTOR SERIES JAMES T. KIRK MIB !!	$20.50

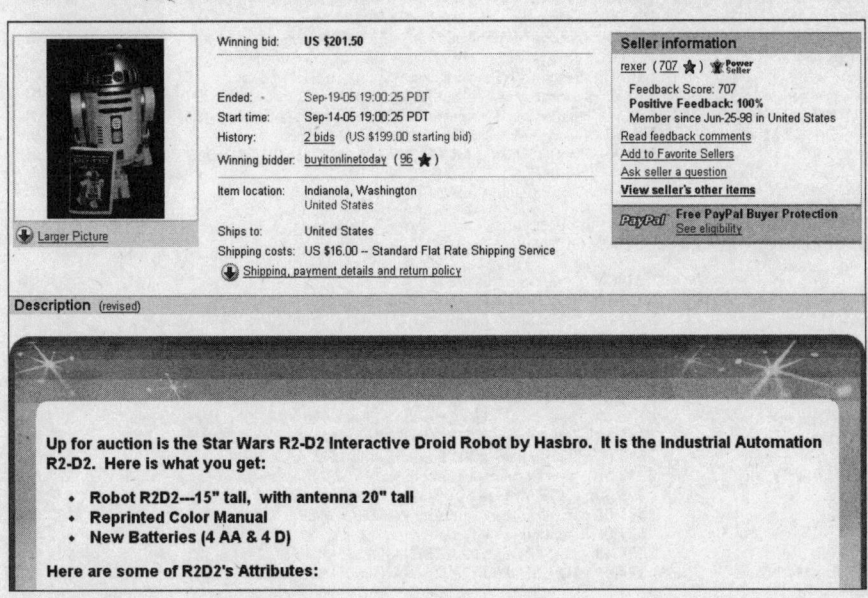

Winning bid:	**US $201.50**
Ended:	Sep-19-05 19:00:25 PDT
Start time:	Sep-14-05 19:00:25 PDT
History:	2 bids (US $199.00 starting bid)
Winning bidder:	buyitonlinetoday (96 ★)
Item location:	Indianola, Washington United States
Ships to:	United States
Shipping costs:	US $16.00 -- Standard Flat Rate Shipping Service

Shipping, payment details and return policy

Seller information

rexer (707 ★) 🏆 Power Seller

Feedback Score: 707
Positive Feedback: 100%
Member since Jun-25-98 in United States

Read feedback comments
Add to Favorite Sellers
Ask seller a question
View seller's other items

PayPal **Free PayPal Buyer Protection** See eligibility

Larger Picture

Description (revised)

Up for auction is the **Star Wars R2-D2 Interactive Droid Robot by Hasbro. It is the Industrial Automation R2-D2. Here is what you get:**

• **Robot R2D2---15" tall, with antenna 20" tall**
• **Reprinted Color Manual**
• **New Batteries (4 AA & 4 D)**

Here are some of R2D2's Attributes:

Action Figures ▶ Star Wars

The average sales price in this subcategory is $26.68.

	HIGH		AVG
R2D2 INTERACTIVE DROID HASBRO STAR WARS MIB	$385.01	STAR WARS ACTION FIGURES WITH CASE	$28.50
Master Replicas LIMITED EDITION Han Solo Blaster Ep V	$379.99	Disney Star Wars Tours Yoda Jedi Mickey Blue Variation	$27.95
Gentle Giant Clone Wars Padme Maquette FREE SHIPPING	$350.00	Disney Star Wars Tours Yoda Jedi Mickey Blue Variation	$27.95
Princess Leia Blaster Signature Edition Master Replicas	$299.99	STAR WARS Galactic Heroes PADME * MINT IN PACKAGE *	$27.00
Star Wars Miniatures Universe Complete Set	$275.00	Star Wars UNLEASHED AOTC ANAKIN SKYWALKER 1ST RELEASE	$27.00
Star Wars Huge loose lot Ep I , II , III 1 2 3 Episode	$272.00	STAR WARS GALACTIC HEROES BACKPACK HEROES HUGE LOT	$26.99

12" Star Wars Custom DARTH MAUL Medicom Marmit bbi ROTS	$267.58	Custom Star Wars Galactic Heroes Trooper Luke figure	$26.56
Star Wars Huge loose lot POTF 2 freeze frame FF	$242.83	Custom Star Wars Galactic Heroes Trooper Han figure	$26.55
AFA 90 Toy Fair 2002 Silver Anniversary Darth Vader WOW	$203.50	Custom Star Wars Galactic Heroes Qui Gon figure by OM	$26.55
Star Wars R2D2 Interactive Droid Robot by Hasbro	$201.50	STAR WARS GENTLE GIANT HAN SOLO BUST NEW	$26.02
Medicom Darth Vader Figure, Star Wars, U.S. Seller, MIB	$199.99	Star Wars Action Fleet Figures Vehicle Vaders Tie At-At	$26.00
Medicom RAH 12inch Star Wars Darth Vader	$195.00	PRINCESS LEIA STAR WARS UNLEASHED HTF BIKINI/SLAVE	$26.00
Star Wars Unleashed Vader Unmasked MOC Series 1 Rare	$187.77	Star Wars Unleashed Princess Leia Slave WOW!	$25.27
Star Wars Huge loose lot POTJ Power of the Jedi	$177.50	Star Wars UNLEASHED ROTJ SLAVE LEIA LOOSE MINT RARE!	$25.01
2002 Star Wars Silver Toy Fair Darth Vader Figure	$175.00	STAR WARS Imperial AT-ST	$25.00

Action Figures ▸ Superman

The average sales price in this subcategory is $22.49.

	HIGH		AVG
SUPERMAN WOOD JOINTED VINTAGE FIGURE IDEAL 30's - 40's	$750.00	DC DIRECT ALEX ROSS SUPERMAN & BIZARRO FIGURES	$24.99
FULL SUPER POWERS COLLECTION CYBORG RIDDLER	$500.00	9 1980's SUPER POWERS figures MINT and COMPLETE	$24.99
Superman 25 inch WB store statue RARE	$261.66	Hong Kong SUPERMAN parachute plastic figure MOC '79 AHI	$24.99
1977 Mego 8" SUPERMAN Carded Figure Unopened	$154.50	DC DIRECT BATMAN HUSH SUPERMAN JLA	$23.50
SUPERMAN JUSTICE ACTION FIGURE VARIANT AFA 90 ALEX ROSS	$149.95	DC Direct Kingdom Come Superman MIB Alex Ross	$23.00
DC DIRECT FIRST APPEARANCES-ALL 12- HAWKMAN-NIGHTWING	$142.50	Street Guardian Superman Action Figure 1995 MIB NEW	$23.00
Superman Warner Brothers Statue not Bowen Batman	$112.72	WB store superman figure with death of promo card	$22.50
SUPERMAN JUSTICE ACTION FIGURE VARIANT AFA 85 DC DIRECT	$99.99	Super Powers SUPERMAN moc 1986 UNPUNCHED no res	$21.82
Alex Ross Superman figures: Variant AND Original!	$85.00	DC Direct MON-EL LOSH MOC	$21.51
DC Direct CYBORG SUPERMAN MOC	$82.73	DC COMICS SUPER HEROES SUPERMAN & LEX MOC	$21.50
SUPERMAN JUSTICE LEAGUE VARIANT ALEX ROSS ACTION FIGURE	$80.01	DISPLAY STAND for DC Direct SUPERMAN figure	$21.50
DC DIRECT BIZARRO BRANIAC DOOMSDAY FIGURE LOT SUPERMAN	$78.00	SUPER POWER ACTION FIGURE CLARK KENT VERY RARE,SUPERMAN	$21.00
Superman Animated 4- Pack of Figures MIB! TRU Batman	$77.00	Ultra Shield Superman Action Figure 1995 MIB NEW	$21.00
STERLING SILVER SUPERMAN EMBLEM PENDANT BRAND NEW	$73.00	Superman Necklace World Wide Shipping!	$20.55
DC DIRECT - JUSTICE SUPERMAN (DEALER VARIANT)	$72.05	SUPERMAN WARNER BROS. STUDIO PEN1999, DC COMIC MAGNET	$20.51

Action Figures ▸ Teenage Mutant Ninja Turtles

The average sales price in this subcategory is $11.25.

	HIGH		AVG
Teenage Mutant Ninja Turtles Movie Figures	$91.51	Pink Panther ____ Belt _____ Buckle	$12.50
TMNT TURTLE BLIMP WACKY ATTACK AIRCRAFT	$91.00	SHREDDER *BNIB* Teenage Mutant Ninja Turtles SHREDDER	$12.00
Ninja Turtles MINI MUTANTS CYBER-ROVER PLAYSET 1995 MIB	$74.73	SPLINTER *BNIB* Teenage Mutant Ninja Turtles SPLINTER	$12.00
Ninja Turtles MINI MUTANTS PARTY WAGON PLAYSET 1995 MIB	$66.00	TMNT PLAY SHAVING SET	$11.97
Teenage Mutant Ninja Turtles Warrior Chrome Dome	$61.99	Teenage Mutant Ninja Turtles "Ace Duck w/ Hat On"	$11.51
TMNT SHOGUN SHOATE ACTION FIGURE	$56.51	Teenage Mutant Ninja Turtles "Casey Jones"	$11.50
TEENAGE MUTANT NINJA TURTLES PIZZA TOSSIN' FIGURES NR	$56.00	TEENAGE MUTANT NINJA TURTLES BUBBLE SWORD, MIB	$11.27
5 DIFF. BOXED TMNT MUTATIONS, W/ LIFT-UP LIDS, MIB 1992	$55.00	Teenage Mutant Ninja Turtles "Baxter Stockman"	$11.26
Teenage Mutant Ninja Turtles "Undercover Raphael"	$54.75	Teenage Mutant Ninja Turtles "Baxter Stockman"	$11.06
600+ Accessories, GI JOE, Teenage Mutant Ninja Turtles	$51.00	Teenage Mutant Ninja Turtles "Wingnut & Screwloose"	$11.06
Vintage Ninja Turtle Scratch MINT ! w/ accesories	$51.00	vintage TMNT ninja turtles MOC on card lot of 3 blister	$11.01
Playmates TMNT Ninja Turtles Technodrome & Turtle Van	$50.50	Teenage Mutant Ninja Turtles Turtle Bowl Dish Cereal WO	$11.01
TEENAGE MUTANT NINJA TURTLES TOON TURTLES FIGURES NR	$42.41	monster BATTRA figure GODZILLA mothra BANDAI toy TOHO	$11.01
TMNT TEENAGE MUTANT NINJA TURTLES MOC 1988 BEBOP	$41.50	Teenage Mutant Ninja Turtles "Usagi Yojimbo"	$11.00
Teenage Mutant Ninja Turtles— 88 ORIG 4— **C-9+**	$41.00	TMNT TEENAGE MUTANT NINJA TURTLES FOOT SOLDIER FIGURE	$10.99

Action Figures ▸ Transformers

The average sales price in this subcategory is $23.09.

	HIGH		AVG
VINTAGE TRANSFORMERS G1 FORTRESS MAXIMUS 100% COMPLETE	$720.00	Transformers Decepticon Thundercracker Commemorative G1	$24.99
1 CASE 1984 TONKA SUPER GOBOTS *ASST.**	$371.66	Transformers Energon OVERLOAD / ULTRA MAGNUS + Minicons	$24.99
Transformers Alternators #1-13 SET Tracks Meister Jazz	$310.00	Transformers Alternators Sideswipe Smokescreen set of 2	$24.95
Transformers Alternators lot of 9 MISB figures meister	$192.50	Swerve Transformers Alternators	$24.05
Transformers Alternators set of 11 cars!	$182.89	Transformers Alternators GRIMLOCK MISB!	$23.49
Unifive Daikyozin Daibazin Godaikin Bandai time bokan	$180.00	Transformers Alternators Shockblast - Purple Mazda	$23.49
Transformers 1995 botcon exclusive nightracer WOW! moc!	$171.49	TRANSFORMERS Commemorative Series VII RODIMUS PRIME MIB	$22.98
Transformers Takara 20th Anniversary Optimus Prime	$145.50	Transformers Alternators Shockblast Mazda RX-8 #12 MIB	$22.75
TRANSFORMERS TRU REISSUE LOT	$125.00	Transformers 2005 BotCon Exclusive Chromia Test Shot	$22.50
Transformers Wheeljack binaltech alternators custom WOW	$112.50	Rare Transformers Robot Masters GIANT Masterpiece Prime	$22.49
20th Anniversary Optimus Prime MINT IN BOX	$96.00	Lot 12 Vintage 80's Bandai Robots Transformers	$22.38
Lot of 22 Transformers Heroes of Cybertron figures	$81.00	Transformers Alternators Wheeljack MISB	$22.09
Transformers 20th Anniversary Optimus Prime	$81.00	Transformers ReIssues	$22.00
Transformers 2005 BotCon Exclusive Dark Arcee Test Shot	$78.43	TRANSFORMERS ALTERNATORS SMOKESCREEN & SIDE SWIPE SET	$21.99
TRANSFORMERS OPTIMUS PRIME 20TH ANNIVERSARY NIB	$77.01	TRANSFORMERS ALTERNATORS SMOKESCREEN & SIDE SWIPE SET	$21.99

Action Figures ▸ X-Men

The average sales price in this subcategory is $14.17.

	HIGH		AVG
custom KANG the CONQUERER figure Marvel Legends by DLC	$280.01	MARVEL LEGENDS CYCLOPS SENTINEL SERIES NEW MOC	$14.95
MARVEL LEGENDS SERIES 10 SENTINEL SERIES SET OF ALL 7	$105.00	WONDER MAN Marvel Legends FIGURE SERIES 11 IN STOCK	$14.95
MARVEL LEGENDS CUSTOM XMEN 3 FIGURE LOOSE LOT bykaz	$100.00	TASKMASTER Marvel Legends FIGURE SERIES 11 IN STOCK	$14.95
custom SASQUATCH & PUCK figure Marvel Legends by DLC	$91.00	ULTRON Marvel Legends FIGURE SERIES 11 IN STOCK	$14.95
MARVEL LEGENDS 9 SET	$90.99	ULTRON Marvel Legends FIGURE SERIES 11 IN STOCK	$14.95
MARVEL LEGENDS 10 COMPLETE SET 8 Figures MINT SENTINEL	$86.00	Marvel Legends Series 2 Dr. Doom MOC	$14.51

MARVEL LEGENDS 10 COMPLETE SET 8 Figures MINT SENTINEL	$85.05	Marvel Legends Series 3 Wolverine MOC	$14.05
SET of 7 Marvel Legends FIGURE SERIES 11 taskmaster ++	$84.95	X-Men Mutant Hall of Fame 10 Pc Figure Set #458 NIB NR	$14.00
MARVEL LEGENDS 10 COMPLETE SET 8 Figures MINT SENTINEL	$83.23	MARVEL LEGENDS SERIES II - THE THING	$14.00
SET of 7 Marvel Legends FIGURE SERIES 11 taskmaster ++	$80.95	MARVEL LEGENDS SERIES II - HUMAN TORCH (MOC)	$14.00
SET of 7 Marvel Legends FIGURE SERIES 11 taskmaster ++	$79.95	NEW MARVEL LEGENDS SENTINEL SERIES MYSTIQUE	$13.95
2005 SD Comic Con Marvel Heroclix Dark Phoenix!!!!	$79.56	MARVEL LEGENDS,10 CYCLOPS X-MEN VARIANT DC COMICS	$13.55
MARVEL LEGENDS 10 COMPLETE SET 8 Figures MINT SENTINEL	$76.00	Marvel Legends Angel blue variant sentinel figure chase	$13.54
HUGE LOT OF ART ASYLUM MINIMATES! X-MEN, SPIDEY, MORE!	$66.00	Marvel Legend Rare Chase Goliath Mint	$13.50
GIANT x-men minimates RARE mib!	$61.00	Marvel Legends Series 10 Cyclops Prototype	$13.49

Action Figures ▸ Mixed Lots

The average sales price in this subcategory is $19.41.

	HIGH		AVG
Marvel Legends Lot of 41 Figures from series 1-Galactus	$304.00	WWF WWE SMACK DOWN STAGE	$19.99
Marvel Legends Loose Lot Spiderman Movie Classics Hulk	$227.51	OF RAGE ENTRANCE W/wrestlers	$19.99
WWE JAKKS CLassic Superstars 1 - 7 MOC plus a few IE's	$220.00	Bronze Bombers 1997 3-3/4" Complete Set of Action Fig.	$19.99
MARVEL LEGENDS 8 - ALL 11- DOC OCK -STORM - BLACK WIDOW	$199.95	ACTION FIGURES..HUGE COLLECTION	$19.99
WWE JAKKS CLASSIC SUPERSTARS LOT OF SERIES 5 - 7 +	$180.00	HUGE LOTOVER 70 POWER RANGERS,	$19.99
WWE JAKKS CLASSIC SUPERSTARS SERIES THREE PACKS	$160.00	ACTION FIGURES,,ETC L@@K	
WWE JAKKS CLASSIC SUPERSTARS LOT OF SERIES 1 - 4	$160.00	70 ASSORTED ACTION FIGURES,GI JOE,WRESTLERS,HEROES	$19.99
1960's BONANZA WESTERN ACTION	$157.50	LADY DEATH SPAWN APRIL O'NEIL BATGIRL DRAGON'S LAIR	$19.99
FIGUES HORSES OVER 50 PCS		HUGE MIXED LOT OF ACTION FIGURES	$19.49
Lot of 18 Marvel Legend figure with 2 BONUS figures	$150.00	RAMBO GHOSTBUSTERS +++	
American McGee's Alice in Wonderland Figures lot RARE	$149.99	DC/Marvel SUPER HERO Action Figure LOT (10) =1984= RARE	$19.16
VINTAGE IDEAL,MEGO & MATTEL FIGURES	$107.50	BIG LOT OF ACTION FIGURES BATMAN, TMNT, X-MEN MORE	$19.00
REMCO ,AHI, UNIVERSAL MONSTER LOT!!!!!!	$102.50	MARVEL STUDIOS: BLADE, PUNISHER AND 2 DAREDEVILS	$18.71
MARVEL~LEGENDS~CUSTOM~CONAN	$100.00	ANIME ACTION FIGURES - ESCA FLOWNE AND BIG O	$18.17
~FIGURE~LOOSE~LOT~NEW~10		Marvel Alpha Flight Set of 8 figures	$17.50
MARVEL LEGENDS 9-ALL 9- PROF X- HULK- BULLSEYE-VARIANTS	$99.95	FIRST APPEARANCE SERIES 1 FIGURE DC DIRECT SET 4-FIGURE	$17.50
MARVEL LEGENDS 7 -ALL 6 - VISION - HAWKEYE - APOCALYPSE	$94.95	McFarlane SPAWN hsi.01 CLASSIC COMIC COVERS Series 24	$17.50
		WOW Lot of Figures, Selay, Minotaur, Mumm-Ra, Membros	$17.49

Beanbag Plush, Beanie Babies ▸ Disney

The average sales price in this subcategory is $8.52.

	HIGH		AVG
Lot of 53 Disney Beanie Babies	$89.99	3 NEW HALLOWEEN MICKEY MOUSE BEANS-SCARECROW/LION/TOGA	$9.99
DISNEYKINS TOY COLLECTION 40+ PCS GREAT CONDITION	$85.07	Halloween Pooh, Piglet, Tigger Bean Bag Collection	$9.50
STAR WARS MICKEY MOUSE DARTH VADER DISNEY BEANIE LE TOY	$69.95	The Disney Store....door hanger w/ 8 plush mouses.BNWT	$9.00
Disney Beanie Pooh Tigger Piglet Eyeore Astronauts	$61.00	MONGOLIA MICKEY & MINNIE Bean Bags from Hong Kong -Nice	$8.99
DISNEY STORE THE PARENT TRAP CUPPY BEANIE WITH TAGS	$52.01	5 LITTLE MERMAID BEAN BAGS Including Undersea Critters!	$8.99
The Nightmare Before Christmas Bean Bags	$42.00	Mickey & Friends Cross Dressed Halloween Bean Bag Toys	$8.99
Cuppy Bunny Bean Bag	$37.01	OZ ~ DISNEY OLYMPICS 2000 AUSTRALIA WINDSURFING POOH	$8.50
2 Disney Heffalump Lumpy plushes Large and Mini	$34.99	DISNEY PRINCE and HAG WITCH Beanies from SNOW WHITE	$8.48
Winnie the Pooh **FRIENDS!** BEANIES "LOT of 8" EEYORE	$31.00	HUGE Tigger Plush Stuffed animal Pooh friend Disney	$8.00
CHRISTOPHER ROBIN from Disney Store—MINT!!	$31.00	WINNIE THE POOH GOPHER BEANBAG DOLL 1998 MATTEL	$8.00
30 Disney & Mickey Mouse Beanies Bean Bag Beans Plush	$30.00	Disney's Tiny Kingdom The Nightmare before christmas	$7.99
2001 Disney Minnie Birthstone Bean Bag Set (12 Total)	$29.99	Disney's Tiny Kingdom The nightmare before christmas	$7.99
Disney HERBIE THE LOVE BUG Bean Bag	$28.00	Disney's Tiny Kingdom Santa Nifhtmare before christmas	$7.99
3 DISNEY STORE ROBIN HOOD BEANIES WITH TAGS	$26.53	Disney's Tiny Kingdom The nightmare before christmas	$7.99
DISNEY PARENT TRAP CUPPY MINT WITH TAGS	$26.51	Walt Disney MIckey & Minnie 12 Different Plush ALL NEW	$7.99

Beanbag Plush, Beanie Babies ▸ Ty

The average sales price in this subcategory is $13.88.

	HIGH		AVG
HUGE lot of TY Authenticated, RARE, exclusive beanies	$5,000.00	Webkinz Internet Virtual Adopt A Pet HM001 FROG	$9.95
Ty Authenticated Royal Blue Peanut Elephant	$850.00	2002 TY BIRTHDAY BEANIES BABIES COLLECTION ALL 12 MONTH	$9.95
PEANUT the ROYAL BLUE ELEPHANT Beanie Baby - MWMT	$609.00	TYS New MAY 2006 RUBY & ALANA Bear Beanies!	$9.95
Ty Billionaire (3) Three Beanie Bear #330 RARE!!!	$465.00	Webkinz Internet Virtual Adopt A Pet GOLDEN RETRIEVER	$9.95
MY DAUGHTERS BEANIE BABY - BEAR COLLECTION	$405.00	Ty Beanie Babies - Lot of 150 Teenie Beanie Babies!!	$9.95
400+ Beanie Babie Lot-Amazing Personal Collection	$400.00	Lot of 8 Retired Ty Beanie Baby Bears - MWMT	$9.95
Ty Issy Beanie Baby Bear. Santa Barbara, (Ca.) Retired	$380.05	Lot of13 Retired Ty Beanie Babies - Birds & Owls - MWMT	$9.95
Ty Beanie Rare Cranberry Old Face Teddy Museun Quality	$370.05	isa Frank Easter Bunnies Bean Bags	$9.85
TY Rare Majenta Old Face Teddy German MWMT	$362.11	Bunga Raya Ty Beanie Baby Babies	$9.79
Ty OLD FACE JADE Authenticated *PERFECT* MQ*	$355.00	Box o Beanie Babies Collector's Cards Series III 2nd Ed	$9.79
MINT 2ND GEN KOREAN OLD FACE JADE TEDDY AUTENTICATED	$355.00	Lot of 2 TY LIZZIE Lizard Beanie & McDonald TEENIE BABY	$9.77
Lot of 30 Retired Beanie Baby Cards Series 3 BBOC	$355.00	Lot of 2 TY Elephants TRUMPET Beanie BUDDY & BABY MWMT	$9.77
TY SERIES 1 BEANIE-ORIGINAL 9 SPOT THE DOG SILVER #/554	$329.00	TY Elephant PEANUT ROYAL BLUE Beanie Buddy BABY TEENIE	$9.77
AUTHENTICATED ISSY Santa Barbara Beanie Baby MUSEUM!	$326.05	TY BEANIE Baby BABIES MAGIC The DRAGON Mint TAGS WOW!	$9.76
Billionaire 7 Beanie Baby * SIGNED BY TY * #157 OF 612	$305.99	Nectar retired Bird, Hard to Find	$9.76

Beanbag Plush, Beanie Babies ▸ Other

The average sales price in this subcategory is $8.42.

	HIGH		AVG
Wizard Of Oz Warner Bros Bean Bags Complete Set	$60.99	NWT! Star Wars Beanie Buddies R2-D2, Ewok, Jawa 1997	$8.99
Target Turn on the Moon 3 animals Roarie Tallie Choobie	$58.27	TUX 6" Inch Stuffed Plush PENGUIN ~ LINUX Mascot NEW	$8.99
#2 HUGE LOT 96 BEAN BAG ANIMAL Keychains by NICI - MINT	$57.00	Boyds Collection Ltd. Reindeer	$8.99
26 Sesame Street Beanies (Complete) & 7 SS Mini Beanies	$56.00	Scooby Doo (doll,bean bag,beanie,figurine,figure)	$8.95

	HIGH		AVG
#2 HUGE LOT 96 BEAN BAG ANIMAL Keychains by NICI - MINT	$52.01	DRUG REP ITEM: ENEMAN BEANIE BABY, GAG GIFT	$8.95
Littlest Pet Shop Crab w/ Tank + Rare Notepad & Magnet	$38.88	Silly Slammers #22	$8.50
Boyds Bear puppet, retired in 2000 Charlie P Chatsworth	$34.99	ADORABLE LARGE 14" TALL LARRY BOY VEGGIE TALES PLUSHIE	$8.50
EMILY the STRANGE 8" CAT PLUSH BEANIES SET of 4 GOTH	$34.99	NWT Oscar Meyer Weinie Beanie CUTE!! UNUSUAL!! LOOK!!	$8.08
WAKO,YAKO AND DOT ANIMANIACS SET OF BEANIES. MINT	$31.00	ANNE GEDDES BUTTERFLIES LARGE BUTTERFLY NEW IN BOX	$8.00
WEBKINS Stuffed-NEW lot of 6 Virtual Reality Pets w/nr	$31.00	I Love Lucy Ep. 144 bear plush- Scottish Scotland 2004!	$8.00
Racing Greyhound Set of 8 dogs from Southland- Arkansas	$30.00	Mary Meyer Elephant Beanie for Girl Scouts still in bag	$8.00
CVS Rudolph Misfit CLARICE beanie baby plush Ornament	$30.00	Hard to Find Nintendo 64 Green YOSHI Beanbag	$7.99
BANPRESTO Nintendo Licenced BIG "TOAD" Doll	$29.99	Neopets Mini Plushie Petpet Green Warf New Release	$7.99
New Cabbage Patch Cornsilk Kids Blond Boy April 9 Bday	$26.06	AVON 2002 JEFF GORDON TEAM SPEED NASCAR BEANIE BEAR	$7.99
LOT OF 20 PINK PANTHER POSABLE STUFFED TOYS W/TAGS	$26.00	WARNER BROTHERS STUDIO STORE WITCH HAZEL PLUSH VHTF!!	$7.99

Building Toys ▸ Blocks

The average sales price in this subcategory is $16.88.

	HIGH		AVG
ANTIQUE RICHTER'S UNION STONE BLOCKS BUNGALOW BOX #206	$228.50	GIANT CARDBOARD TOY BUILDING BLOCKS! CHILD PLAY BLOCK [6 of these sold for $17.50 each]	$17.50
LITTLE TIKES BUILDING BLOCKS - LOT OF 117 - 14"x14"	$203.50	68 PIECES NEW FOAM BUILDING BLOCKS DAYCARE PRESCHOOL	$17.00
EARLY ANTIQUE RICHTER'S STONE BUILDING BLOCKS	$142.75	Pottery Barn ABC Blocks-toddler, baby	$16.54
Wood Blocks - Froebel Gifts 23456 Frank Llyod Wright	$137.51	93 PIECES NEW FOAM BUILDING BLOCKS DAYCARE SCHOOL HOME	$16.50
HUGE set antique cement building toy blocks wood box	$136.90	VINTAGE WOODEN BUILDING BLOCK LOT 45PCS (VG)	$16.50
#72- CIRCUS / WILD WEST blocks, EMBOSSING CO, Albany NY	$128.50	Ryans Room All Shapes & Sizes Geometric Blocks-New!	$16.49
#52 - Set 32 ANIMAL blocks, EMBOSSING CO, Albany NY	$107.50	better blocks child building 1201pcs instruction book	$16.49
EARLY UNION BUILDING BLOCKS F AD RICHTER NO. 6A	$96.00	Little Tikes Waffle Blocks	$16.35
WOOD UNIT BUILDING BLOCKS MAPLE HAND MADE IN KATY TEXAS	$93.00	Melissa and & Doug - Beginner Pattern Blocks - NEW	$16.25
WOOD UNIT BUILDING BLOCKS MAPLE HAND MADE IN KATY TEXAS	$89.98	50 PIECES NEW FOAM BUILDING BLOCKS DAYCARE SCHOOL HOME	$16.25
HUMONGOUS LOT OF BLOCK CITY BUILDING BLOCKS	$86.00		
Crandall's Antique Building Blocks Set with Box	$77.95		
Vintage Large Size Gemoetric Wood Blocks for School	$76.55		
86 piece hardwood maple building block set	$75.00		
HUGE "BRIK" BUILDING BLOCKS	$71.97		

Building Toys ▸ Erector Sets

The average sales price in this subcategory is $39.77.

	HIGH		AVG
Gilbert Erector 1956 No. 12 1/2 Master Builder set Exc.	$1,046.00	Antique Microscope set and chemistry set by Gilbert	$40.00
VINTAGE 1948 ERECTOR SET BY GILBERT THE WALKING GIANT !	$860.00	Old gilbert erector sets	$40.00
Antique Gilbert Erector Set Ferris Wheel Red Wooden Box	$736.00	2 Gilbert Erector #1E Square Girder Kits, Original	$40.00
RARE 1930's Meccano Bi Plane Kit w/Box Airplane RARE #2	$662.55	CONSTRUCTIONEER URBANA OHIO ERECTOR SET IN BOX	$39.99
1930's Aeroplane Constructor Meccano Bi Plane RARE #1	$611.99	Rare 1915-16 Meccano Erector Set Prize Models Booklet	$39.99
No 8 Erector Set Blimp Zeppelin +Manuel of Instructions	$585.00	ERECTOR Master Builder Fire Truck set NEW 476 parts	$39.99
1949 GILBERT ERECTOR AMUSEMENT PARK SET #10 1/2	$512.00	Antique Meccano Erector Set 1923	$39.95
1951 GILBERT ERECTOR SET & MANUAL NEVER USED, MIB	$355.00	1924 Meccano Engineering Set for Boys with Manual 1x	$39.23
HUGE LOT..50'S MECCANO....100'S OF ITEMS / MOTOR / BOOKS	$325.00	Meccano Grill and fenders for Roadster	$39.00
Antique Erector Set #4 Wooden Box Rare Lionel Motor	$266.78	4 Gilbert Erector "KW" Truck Frames, Original	$39.00
VINTAGE 1949 GILBERT ERECTOR AMUSEMENT PARK SET #10 1/2	$265.00	1930 GILBERT ERECTOR SET ELECTRIC MOTOR RUNS	$38.99
Vintage 1949 Gilbert Erector Set 10 1/2 Amusement Park	$260.55	Gilbert ERECTOR SET #7, 1926-7 Steam Shovel, Wood Box	$38.90
GILBERT ERECTOR NO 10 1/2 AMUSEMENT PARK 1946	$237.50	Very Old Gilbert Erector Set No. 4 LOOK!!!	$38.00
1959 # 12 1/2 ERECTOR MASTER BUILDER SET TOY SET MODEL	$225.95	Meccano Red 6-Volt Cricket Ball Motor	$37.60
IN THE BEGINNING THERE WAS ERECTOR AND IT WAS GOOD	$215.63	1959 Gilbert Erector Rocket Launcher Set No. 10053 NR	$37.00

Building Toys ▸ LEGO

The average sales price in this subcategory is $24.05.

	HIGH		AVG
very old lego gift set 695 mercedes,vw,fiat,austin MIB	$899.00	Harry Potter Lego Set #4705 SNAPE'S CLASS *NEW IN BOX*	$24.99
Very old LEGO gift set garage with 2 vws code 306 MIB	$665.00	Lego Star wars set: 7103 Jedi Duel New MISB Dooku Yoda	$24.85
W – A George Bush LEGO(R) Brick Mosaic REDUCED	$399.95	LEGO CAPTAIN REDBEARDS PIRATE SHIP REALLY FLOATS SEALED	$24.50
RARE Lego 19" Tall Legoman Figure - Display!!	$244.50	Lego Star Wars JEDI STAR FIGHTER 7143 Factory Sealed	$24.50
Lego Airport Shuttle 6399 MIB VERY nice set	$227.50	LEGO LOT 2+++POUNDS TAN SPECIALTY PARTS PIECES	$24.38
RARE- LEGO 19" STORE DISPLAY FIGURE, MIB	$173.50	Lego Town theme Metro PD Station 6598 w/ Box and Inst.	$24.08
LEGO Mindstorms robotics invention system 2.0 #3804	$161.00	Lego Midnight Transport & Crisis News Crew 1687 & 6553	$24.01
HARRY POTTER LEGO 4750- 4756,4758 & 4695 AZKABAN *NMIB	$157.50	Lego 4754 Harry Potter HAGRIDS HUT new MISB	$24.00
LEGO Star Wars Episode II Attack Republic Gunship	$157.50	Hundreds of Ello pieces!!!!!!	$24.00
RARE Lego 19" Tall Legoman Figure - Display!!	$157.50	STAR WARS LEGO 7131 ANAKIN'S PODRACER NEW	$23.99
18 Giant LEGO Construction Man Figure Large 1.5' LOOK	$152.50	LEGOS Harry Potter, Forbidden Corridor set #4706 NEW	$23.50
LEGO LOT 28+ LBS 47 MINI FIGS SORTED LEGOS	$150.00	Little Armory Custom ARC Trooper	$23.50
RARE- LEGO 19" STORE DISPLAY FIGURE, MIB	$147.50	Over 750 Tyco Girls Building Blocks Lego Compatible	$23.48
MISB LEGO 10144 STAR WARS SANDCRAWLER JAWA SEALED	$146.78	Lego Minifig Accessories Different themes Lot of 150	$23.00
RARE Lego 19" Tall Legoman Painter Display!!	$141.38	LGEO's Mini R2D2 & R5D4	$22.50

Building Toys ▸ Lincoln Logs

The average sales price in this subcategory is $19.81.

	HIGH		AVG
LINCOLN LOGS HUGE 50 POUNDS LOT OF LEARNING PLAYSKOOL	$124.99	Large Lot of Lincoln Logs - 350+ Pieces!	$20.00
BIG-HUGE lot 1,300+ LINCOLN LOGS:Old/Vintage/Newer: NR!	$121.11	LINCOLN LOGS GOLD MINE EXPRESS TRAIN SET M.I.B NR!!	$20.00

VINTAGE LINCOLN LOGS + FIGURES-1943-BOX-NOT CAN-NICE!	$117.50	LINCOLN LOGS	$20.00
HUGE lot of Lincoln Logs 1346 pieces vintage	$117.00	LINCOLN LOG - Bundle - Log Cabin AND Castle Sets! L@@K!	$19.99
1920's lincoln logs original box, book and logs	$114.35	Vintage Lincoln Logs w/box & 1933 design book	$19.99
LINCOLN LOGS - APPROX. 23 LBS.	$93.00	VINTAGE BUILDING LINCOLN LOGS 1969 #892 BOX INST LIKE N	$19.99
Huge Lot of Lincoln Logs Over 600 Pc. Nice Variety	$86.01	Large Lot 300+pcs Lincoln Logs/Lincoln Log	$19.95
LARGE LINCOLN LOGS DELUXE BOX 5LTF SET 1940	$80.88	LINCOLN LOGS 150 pieces Original Box Signs	$19.29
Lot of Wood Lincoln Logs 506 Pieces Great Variety	$76.00	LARGE SET OF VINTAGE LINCOLN LOGS 1950'S	$19.27
LINCOLN LOGS FROM SEVERAL SETS over 450 pieces	$72.00	HUGE LOT 215 PLAYSKOOL LINCOLN LOGS 1970'S No Reserve	$19.25
1931pc Lincoln Logs Many Accessories, Instructions HUGE	$71.00	Huge Lot Of Lincoln Logs 2 Sets 370 Pcs. Vintage 1970's	$19.00
Lincoln Logs Vintage 1000+ Pieces	$70.92	Vintage American "Lincoln" Logs by Halsam & Box 1950s	$18.50
HUGE LOT OF VINTAGE LINCOLN LOGS OVER 1,000 PIECES	$67.99	ORIGINAL LINCOLN LOGS SET, LONESOME PINE CABIN 63 PIECE	$18.50
Huge Lot of 749 Lincoln Logs neatly sorted & packed	$66.02	LINCOLN LOGS LOT - 468 Pieces - Logs/Doors/Windows/Sets	$18.50
HUGE LOT 450 PLUS LINCOLN LOGS &ACCESORIES	$66.01	Large Lot of LINCOLN LOGS - over 11 Pounds	$18.50

Building Toys ▸ Tinker Toys

The average sales price in this subcategory is $15.90.

	HIGH		AVG
Vintage Giant Tinker Toy Set In Original Box	$202.50	Playskool TINKERTOYS TINKER TOYS Tinkersaurus Dinosaur	$17.51
VINTAGE GIANT SIZE TINKER TOYS TINKERTOY 79 PIECES!	$177.50	LOT Playskool Tinkertoys Tinker Toys Plastic Building	$17.50
[2 of these sold for $177.50 each]		DIRECTION SHEET FOR SENIOR TINKER TOY	$17.49
VINTAGE GIANT SIZE TINKER TOYS TINKERTOYS 72	$152.50	Rare Vintage Tinkertoy PANEL BUILDER TINKER TOY SET	$17.05
GIANT LIFESIZE TINKER TOYS 77 PIECES VINTAGE QUESTOR	$137.50	Set of King Size Tinker Toys , Vintage, Plastic	$16.49
GIANT SIZED TINKER TOY SET-65 GIANT PIECES	$88.00	The Classic Tinkertoy Costruction Set	$16.48
Toy Tinker Puppy Tinker, Rare	$66.10	Vintage Tinker Toys Tinkertoy #150 MASTER BUILDER !!!!	$15.82
4 Never played with NOS Tinkertoy Tinker Toys Sets	$56.00	100 Pc Set of TINKER TOYS *1992* Plastic Tinkertoys WOW	$15.55
VINTAGE 1959 WOODEN TINKERTOY TINKER TOY 487 PIECE SET	$51.00	1959 TINKER TOY "CURTAIN WALL BUILDER" SET NO. 620	$15.54
Lot of 397 QUESTOR Tinkertoys, Boxes, Instructions-1972	$48.79	TinkerToys SPALDING Cannister 215pc Tinker Toys	$15.50
Playskool TINKERTOYS TINKER TOYS all PLASTIC 291 pcs	$46.00	PLAYSKOOL TINKERTOY PLASTIC BUILDING	$15.50
VINTAGE TINKER TOYS-3 CANS-395 PIECES-MUST SEE	$43.03	TOYS 1991 108 PCS!	$15.50
LOT VINTAGE WOOD TINKERTOY	$41.00	Tinker Toy Sets W/ Info Sheets	$15.50
TINKERTOYS W/ ORIGINAL BOX		Tinkertoys 236 pieces Very Old All Wood NR Tinker Toys	$15.50
Vintage Wood Tinkertoy Tinker Toy Original Can With Lid	$41.00	Jumbo Set Wooden TINKERTOYS in Canister Tinker Toy	$15.50
HUGE LOT OF WOOD & PLASTIC TINKER TOYS 1000 + PIECES	$40.00	TINKER TOY TINKERTOYS WOODEN & PLASTIC BUILDING SET	$15.50

Classic Toys ▸ Balls, Frisbees, Boomerangs

The average sales price in this subcategory is $14.03.

	HIGH		AVG
Set of 8 Brand New White Silicone Juggling Balls	$220.00	NEW AUSTRALIAN BOOMERANG [2039]	$14.99
~ BuzzBee ~ A Very Rare Pot Smoking Frisbee and Pipe ~	$147.87	Five 2 1/2"Juggling Balls Assorted Colors!!!!!!UV!!!	$14.99
Vintage pluto frisbee w/original wrapper, plus 1966	$147.38	[2 of these sold for $14.99 each]	
Vintage HACKY SACK Official Footbag in	$108.50	THE HAMMER 62p FOOTBAG - HANDMADE -	$14.99
ORIGINAL PACKAGE		TRICK HACKY SACK	
50 HOVERDISC HOVER DISC AS SEEN	$86.00	[2 of these sold for $14.99 each]	
ON TV- FUN WHOLESALE		1984 Wham-o Frisbee Odyssey NIP light purple	$14.50
~ 1959 Wham-O Frisbee ~ twirl-a-plate ~ Mint in Package	$77.87	Aspen Boomerang – Boomerangs Really Comes Back	$14.00
1977 FRISBEE GIFT SET of 3 Vintage *RARE* MIB	$76.00	100 Gliders Plane Model Kit Power Prop Wholesale Lots	$13.99
Vintage HACKY SACK Footbag Original STYLER Model NIP	$70.00	GALILEO 62-panel HANDMADE FREESTYLE	$13.99
VINTAGE WHAM-O FLYING SAUCER FRISBEE ORIGINAL 1964	$68.89	FOOTBAG HACKY SACK	
Vintage Wham-O Mini Frisbee 3 pk #671 Mint on Card 1968	$66.00	1984 Wham-o Frisbee Odyssey NIP light purple	$13.52
Set of 9 Mint Condition 2.5" Juggling Beanbags	$65.00	Vintage 1984 Wham-O 119G World Class Frisbee,Mint Pack	$13.50
1950's Vintage Whiz-eee Giant Jet Flying Saucer Frisbee	$59.00	LIGHT UP FLYING DISC RED with FREE FRISBEE NITE IZE	$13.49
VINTAGE MYSTERY Y FRISBEE 1959/60 PRE WHAM-O	$57.78	2 Wiggly Giggly Balls, 1 Lg & 1 Sm, Colorful w Giggles!	$13.47
Set of 5 Bright Blue Iluminated Glo Juggling Balls	$51.00	jim mayfield colorado boomerang vg/used/c	$13.16
Vintage 1965 Wham-O Super Mini Ball Package 6 Superball	$48.99	Five 2 1/2"Juggling Balls Assorted Colors!!!!!!UV!!!	$12.99

Classic Toys ▸ Colorforms

The average sales price in this subcategory is $11.87.

	HIGH		AVG
COLORFORMS - 3 BOXES- BATMAN - MUNSTERS - MICKEY MOUSE	$66.66	HULK MARVEL COMIC 1978 COLORFORM SET VERY NICE COMPLETE	$14.99
KISS Colorforms Toy Set 1979 - Not Mego, Makeup L@@K	$61.25	Miss Cookie's Kitchen Colorforms NRFB	$14.99
VINTAGE 1964 TAMMY DRESS-UP KIT COLORFORMS complete	$58.55	1965 WHAT'S COOKING SNOOPY COLORFORMS SET COMPLETE!	$14.25
VINTAGE 1957 "TWIGGY" DRESS-UP COLORFORMS KIT	$55.00	Raggedy Ann Play Kitchen Colorforms	$13.38
Vintage Colorforms - The Jetsons Cartoon Kit - Complete	$54.77	E.T Extra-Terrestrial Colorforms Adventure Play Set	$13.37
1966 Colorforms The Green Hornet Cartoon Kit	$54.75	VINTAGE 1963 Betsy McCall DRAWING KIT by COLORFORMS	$13.00
Vintage 1966 Green Hornet Colorforms, Complete	$52.75	vintage colorforms- Huckleberry Hound- 1960	$11.50
Jim Henson's The Muppet Show Colorforms Looks GREAT!	$51.00	Vintage Raggedy Ann Dress up Colorforms	$11.00
VINTAGE ADDAMS FAMILY COLOFORMS CARTOON KIT COMPLETE	$47.33	Vintage Snow White and the Seven Dwarfs Colorforms	$10.99
VINTAGE 1967 SPIROGRAPH COMPLETE IN BOX & INSTRUCTIONS	$46.00	3 Sets of Colorforms:Bob the Builder Spongebob,Astroboy	$10.50
Vintage Star Trek Colorforms Adventure Set 1975	$41.54	Vintage Colorforms Holly Hobby 3-D General Store Set	$10.50
VINTAGE 1977 COLORFORMS SESAME STREET PRE-SCHOOL SET NM	$36.00	Colorforms Shrinky Dinks Gremlins activity set unopened	$10.50
Vintage 1968 Liddle Kiddles Dress Up Colorforms	$31.25	Discovery Toys Colorforms Playful Patterns	$10.50
MICKEY MOUSE PUPPETFORMS THEATER 1960' COLORFORMS	$29.99	Vintage Star Trek Colorforms Adventure Set 1975	$10.50
THE BEVERLY HILLBILLIES LARGE COLORFORMS KIT ORIG. 1963	$29.98	Flintstones Fuzzy Felt by Toycraft #221 1961	$10.49

Classic Toys ▸ Etch A Sketch, Spirograph

The average sales price in this subcategory is $15.57.

	HIGH		AVG
Super Spirograph Sealed Original Box Complete	$76.00	Spirograph Kenner 1971 Vintage Educational Design Toy	$16.49
1969 KENNER'S SUPER SPIROGRAPH IN EXCELLENT COND. NR	$71.02	BOXLOT 4 SETS KENNER SPIROGRAPH DESIGN TOY 1967-'86 401	$16.28
Vintage 1959 Cherry Ames Nursing Game Complete	$71.00	SPIROGRAPH SET 1967 Kenner Great Condition	$16.00
VINTAGE 1969 Kenner's SUPER SPIROGRAPH 2400 MINT Complt	$66.06	Vintage The Dukes Of Hazzard Fun Screen Set	$16.00
1967 Spirograph 401 set in the box	$61.00	SPIROGRAPH 1967 Vintage 401 Design set COMPLETE	$15.99
1969 KENNERS SUPER SPIROGRAPH NO. 2400	$59.95	Kenner #401 Spirograph blue tray w/extra wheels 1967	$15.85
Spirograph By Kenner 1971 New In Box	$54.00	1967 KENNERS SPIROGRAPH NO. 401	$15.50
Vintage SPIROGRAPH by Kenner 1972 Complete	$50.99	2 ETCH A SKETCH STILL IN BOX	$15.50
VINTAGE SPIROGRAPH, 1967 ** 100% COMPLETE ** NEAR MINT	$47.00	1967 Kenner Spirograph Drawing Set No 401 Nice Set	$15.50
Vintage 1967 Kenner Spirograph Complete Near Mint	$46.99	1967 KENNERS SPIROGRAPH 100% COMPLETE W/ PENS	$15.50
Vintage Kenners Super Spirograph Drawing Toy Nice NR!!	$42.00	Vintage SUPER SPIROGRAPH Set Kenner 1969 Complete!	$15.50
1969 Kenner Super Spirograph 2400 set NMIB	$41.00	1967 SPIROGRAPH by KENNER ~ No. 401	$15.50
Vintage Kenners Super Spirograph and Spirofoil in Box	$40.99	SPIROGRAPH, No. 401, nice shape, 1967 Kenner	$15.50
Vintage 1967 KENNER'S 401 BLUE SPIROGRAPH Complete	$40.25	ETCH A SKETCH ANIMATOR WITH MEMORY	$15.50
Kenner's,Super Spirograph,c.1969,No.2400 Set	$40.06	VINTAGE 1968 SPIROGRAPH COMPLETE IN BOX	$15.50

Classic Toys ▸ Kites

The average sales price in this subcategory is $24.82.

	HIGH		AVG
lobster,premier,kite,3D	$430.25	Rainbow Facet Single Line Box Style Kite	$24.99
Revolution Power Blast 4-8m POWERFUL KITE	$350.00	Original Jalbert Parafoil Kite...Rare	$24.99
Flexifoil Bullet Kite 4.5 With Line & Handle NEW. NIB	$300.00	LARGE, VINTAGE 1976 BICENTENNIAL	$24.99
HQ Crossfire 6.3 Kite (New)	$290.03	PATRIOTIC KITE EAGLE!	
Flexifoil Bullet Kite 4.5 With Line & Handle NEW. NIB	$202.50	DRAGON Ripstop KITE HUGE 5.5 Ft 3D 3-Dimensional NEW	$24.99
Firebee force power traction kite (not flexifoil ozone)	$202.50	BEAUTIFUL Hand Painted Tiger Swallowtail Kite	$24.95
colorful kites of all styles	$200.00	BEAUTIFUL Hand Painted Butterfly Kites~Art, Free S & H	$24.95
Trlby Trilby Stunt Kites 6 Kite Train NEW	$195.00	HUGE F-16 FIGHTER JET DUAL LINE STUNT KITE JOEL SCHOLZ	$24.95
[3 of these sold in a multiple item ("Dutch") auction for $65.00 each]		Vintage JIN SHI Chinese Silk Kite Dragonfly with box	$24.07
flexifoil Blade III 4.9	$158.50	Giant Dual Control Stunt Kite 64" Wingspan Kites FUN	$24.00
New 12ft Powerfoil 4.0 Power Stunt Kite "FREE SHIPPING"	$149.99	Balinese Medium Dragon Kite 55" Wing Handmade & Painted	$22.99
New 05' 12'ft Powerfoil 4.0 Stunt Kite,Go Fly a Kites!!	$148.00	prism OZONE ultra light stunt kite SAIL	$22.50
HQ Beamer 5m Kite (Like New)	$135.00	Cloud Buster paper kite	$22.50
NEW 05 MIRAGE Stunt Kite with DVD by Prism Kites - Fire	$105.00	VINTAGE MAN IN THE MOON Kite 50's Topelite Paper large	$22.50
Revolution Sports Kite PACKAGE Quad Line Fun	$103.50	THE BOOMER Multi- Colored Stunt Kite Dual Control Kites	$22.00
NEW HQ KITES TRECZOKS CLASSIC BOX KITE	$99.95	Large Parrot by go fly a kite Designer Joel Scholz	$21.95

Classic Toys ▸ Magic, Magician Supplies

The average sales price in this subcategory is $16.53.

	HIGH		AVG
MR. FOX the MAGICIAN with BOX	$360.00	Lubor Fiedler - Die-A-Bolic	$19.00
1938 A C GILBERT MYSTO MAGIC MAGICIAN'S SHOW CARDS DICE	$260.00	Dan Harlan's Pack Small Play BIG VHS TRICK MAGIC TRICKS	$18.50
WIZARD MARIONETTE/PUPPET/VENTRILOQUIST FIGURE!	$150.00	Magic, Mentalism. Martin Breese Audiotape collection	$18.50
ANTIQUE VICTORIAN BOXED TRICKS AND MAGIC GAME	$132.50	3 NEW Magic Card Trick Decks Deck Tricks BICYCLE	$18.00
HUGE COLLECTION of MAGIC, amazing deal for someone!!	$127.50	On the spot Gregory Wilson's Trick Magic Tricks VIDEO	$17.00
COWGIRL OUTFIT FOR VENTRILOQUIST PUPPET! UNIQUE!	$100.00	Magic Tricks - NEW! Don't Ask, Just Look! Demo!	$16.95
Electric Balloon Pump Rechargeable Battery Powered	$99.00	Matrix God's Way coin tricks book & DVD *NO RESERVE*	$16.55
9 DVD -Card Miracles Magic Complete Set Michael Ammar	$93.00	DVD - Coin Coins Magic knock out everyone with this	$16.50
Mentalism: Impression Device Package	$90.90	Red Velvet Color Change Bag and BLENDO Magic Trick	$16.50
Mentalism: Rune Box	$87.99	JAWDROPPERS JAW DROPPERS Magic Videos & Cards	$16.50
Six Renegade Juggling Clubs well balanced and light	$79.00	1950s MAGIC TRICKs HUGE COLLECTION ANTIQUE VINTAGE TOY	$16.37
Cardio graphic + making magic video	$69.00	Magic Trick "Pass With Care" DVD - The Classic Pass	$16.02
BALLOON PUMP -MANUAL INFLATOR	$69.00	Flaming Wallet magic trick - Fire turns into money!	$15.99
1944 Tarbell Course In Magic 7 book Card Trick Magician	$62.25	On the Pass Kaufman CARD Trick Magic Tricks VIDEO	$15.51
Card Cavalcade 1-5	$62.00	Magic *** WONDER BUBBLE *** Magic Tricks	$15.95

Classic Toys ▸ Marbles

The average sales price in this subcategory is $28.74.

	HIGH		AVG
Antique Marbles Four Vintage Lutz Marble lot Shooters	$450.00	Marble: Orange Diamant Blue by PD Snell 1 1/8" 2003	$29.99
Rare Hand made 1 1/16 inch gold mica	$405.00	VINTAGE ONION SKIN PLUS 3 PONTIL MK MARBLES NR	$29.99
BOREALIS GLASS Skull & Dichro Orb Marble	$300.00	Marble: Marble Jar by Bruce Troeh 2005 Brandnew	$29.99
Rare Sulphide Marble James Garifield?	$293.00	assent of fire BIRD N FEATHERS MikeE lampwork marbles	$29.99
Marble: Paperweight by Bill Burchfield Cape Cod RARE	$275.00	Catseye Marble (1 1/8) by Anton Bodor	$29.50
Vintage Marbles: 1150+ Machine Made	$250.89	JAYGLASS marbles MULTI BIPOLAR COLOR SWIRL Marble	$29.05
Outstanding Marbles Covered JOBBER BOX, MUST SEE	$228.50	Marble Marbles Handmade 3/4 Natural Jasper Stone 17-26	$28.89
Marbles Handmade Glass James Alloway "Carnival" # 9	$203.92	CHRISTENSEN 3/4IN FLAMED SWRIL MARBLE	$28.11
lots of Lutz Indian Swirl Hand made Antique marble	$202.50	Marbles by Rick Davis, "GROUP OF THREE"	$28.07
LARGE DOUBLE RIBBON CORE HANDMADE MARBLE 2+ INCHES	$183.50	Glass Art Marbles EXOTIC ALIEN EGG MARBLE By Ferguson	$28.01
M. Gropper & Sons JOBBER BOX	$178.00	Marbles: DICRO PATTERN w/ OPAL BY SHANE CASWELL N.R.	$28.00
Marble: Dichroic Man in the Moon Murray 2" 2004	$177.50	Steve Davis Marbles 1 1/2" First Off Cane Marble '05	$28.00
aw509002 MARBLES: Fabulous Vintage Blue Clambroth, Mint	$170.00	RAZ Marbles: Racer Green Dart Frog Flower Marble	$28.00
Jobber Box with 28 Peltier Peerless Patchs	$161.38	Marbles by Steve Davis, "GROUP OF THREE"	$28.00
Outstanding Shooter Onionskin Lutz Handmade Marble	$152.50	Rick Davis Marbles 1 1/2" Flame Swirl Marble '05	$28.00

Classic Toys ▶ Rocking Horses

The average sales price in this subcategory is $51.75.

	HIGH		AVG
Stevenson Brothers Kent England Rocking Horse Hand Made	$1,800.00	VINTAGE MARVEL THE MUSTANG RIDE ON HORSE pre 1970	$56.00
TRI-ANG TOYS ENGLAND ANTIQUE WOOD ROCKING HORSE	$1,608.00	HARLEY DAVIDSONS POLICE MOTORCYCLE ROCKER	$56.00
ANTIQUE WOODEN ROCKING HORSE VINTAGE REAL HORSE HAIR	$456.50	3' Tall x 4' Long SOLID BRASS ROCKING HORSE/SCULPTURE	$56.00
ANTIQUE 19TH CENTURY FOLK-ART CARVED ROCKING HORSE	$405.00	HARLEY DAVIDSON MOTORCYCLE ROCKER, FATBOY, SOFTAIL	$55.00
RARE 1920S ANTIQUE GOULD MFG OSHKOSH WI BOSTON TERRIER	$352.47	1865 Child Riding ROCKING HORSE CDV Harlacher Waukesha	$53.99
ANTIQUE 19TH CENTURY FOLK-ART CARVED ROCKING HORSE	$300.00	Melissa & Doug #2502 Classic Rocking Horse/Plush/Sounds	$53.50
ANTIQUE CHILDS WOODEN ROCKING HORSE REAL HAIR NR	$262.87	Wooden Rocking Airplane RH-300	$52.01
ANTIQUE HORSE CHILDS RIDING TOY	$250.00	CHILD'S TOY WOODEN ROCKING HORSE GIRAFFE	$51.33
ANTIQUE ROCKING HORSE VERY OLD	$213.50	Rocking Volkswagen RH-310	$51.32
DETAILED WOOD CARVED CAROUSEL HORSE RIDEABLE SIZE	$200.01	Antique Vintage Rocking Horse	$51.01
VINTAGE ANTIQUE HOBBY HORSE 1800'S PULL TOY CHILDS NR!	$177.51	Vintage " Wonder Horse " Spring Rocking Horse	$51.00
NEW WOOD MOTORCYCLE STYLE ROCKING HORSE BABY BOY GIFT	$163.13	Melissa & Doug #2502 Classic Rocking Horse/Plush/Sounds	$51.00
NEW MOTORCYCLE STYLE ROCKING HORSE	$152.50	VINTAGE MINIATURE WOODEN ROCKING HORSE	$51.00
New Solid Wood Motorcycle Rocker by TimberRoom Customs	$150.00	Hedstrom Rocking Spring Horse	$50.00
Vintage Unique ELEPHANT Rocking Horse Hand-Carved Wood	$149.00	Harley Davidson Rocker by Kidcraft	$50.00

Classic Toys ▶ Slinky

The average sales price in this subcategory is $9.91.

	HIGH		AVG
(96) Slinky Vintage Original Metal NEW James Ind. CASE!	$139.99	1947 Slinky Original Box	$9.99
12 VINTAGE SLINKYS IN ORIGINAL BOXES PLUS DISPLAY BOX	$44.99	Very Old Slinky Cater-puller	$9.99
RARE 1955 SUSIE SLINKY WORM PULL TOY N MINT ORIG BOX	$24.99	ORIGINAL-METAL-1945-JAMES-SLINKY-GAME-	$9.99
Slinky Vintage Original Metal NEW IN BOX James Ind.	$21.50	TOY-NEW IN BOX-NR	
[10 of these sold in a multiple item ("Dutch") auction for $2.15 each]		Original James 1950's Metal Slinky w Box Philadelphia	$9.99
Slinky Dog as in Toy Story, Brand New!	$19.95	40th Anniversary Edition Brass Slinky MIB	$9.99
Gold Slinky 50th Anniversary/Wooden Box/T-Shirt	$19.05	Rainbow PSYCHEDELIC Square SLINKY - LOT of TEN (10)	$9.99
Slinky Dog as in Toy Story, Brand New!	$17.95	Vintage STEEL Slinky WITH BOX & PAPERWORK, 1960's	$9.95
[2 of these sold for $17.95 each]		Vintage Slinky Dog Early 1960s Fine Shape	$9.50
Slinky Dog as in Toy Story, Brand New!	$17.95	VINTAGE SLINKY FROG PULL TOY, MIB,	$9.00
Slinky Dog - Classic Replica - New in Box - Cute NIB	$15.00	JAMES INDUSTRIES	
Electronic Slinky W/Motion Sensors/Lights Sounds/Games	$13.55	Original Slinky Spring Toys, Remember These?	$8.95
VINTAGE 1950'S RED SLINKY FAMILY DENMARK EALC	$13.00	SLINKY SCIENCE KITS BUG HUNT SCIENCE NEW	$8.50
Slinky Vintage Original Metal NEW IN BOX James Ind.	$12.90	ORIGINAL SLINKY W/DIRECTIONS!	$8.49
[6 of these sold in a multiple item ("Dutch") auction for $2.15 each]		Perfect shape! coll. item	
Slinky Dog Collector's Edition	$12.75	Collector's Edition SLINKY DOG Pull Toy NEW IN BOX	$8.49
Neon Slinky Phone, new in box, 1999	$12.50	COLLECTOR'S EDITION OF SLINKY TOY	$8.45
Slinky: 1950's With very good box!	$10.00	SLINKY SCIENCE KITS KITCHEN CHEMISTY NIB	$8.00

Description (revised)

GREAT COLLECTIBLE--ONE OF ONLY A FEW I HAVE SEEN UP FOR AUCTION--UP FOR AUCTION IS THIS CHEERIO YO-YO STORE DISPLAY BOX CONTAINING- 6EA - OFFICIAL PRO 99, WOOD, (MAPLE LEAF) FOIL STICKER SEAL, TOURNAMENT SHAPE, GLITTER ENAMEL FINISH, MINT CONDITION. There are 2ea red, 2ea sky blue & 2ea dark blue YOYO'S. Made by CHEERIO TOYS & GAMES INC. BUFFALO NY. TRADE MARK COPYRIGHT 1947. Display Box is in great condition with a couple of fold creases but otherwise in mint condition. Fantastic graphics and must have for the YO-YO collector. Thanks for bidding and good luck!!!!

Select a picture

Classic Toys ▶ Yo-Yos

The average sales price in this subcategory is $20.80.

	HIGH		AVG
SIX CHEERIO YO-YO'S MINT W/STORE DISPLAY-1940'S, 50'S	$750.00	VINTAGE DUNCAN BEGINNERS SPIN TOP - MINT ON CARD !	$22.27
Duncan Freehand MG in mint condition!!	$410.00	Rare Autographed Bill De Boisblanc yo-yo package	$22.15
Hummingbird YoYo Clock - Like new! yo yo, yo-yo, yo	$330.00	DUNCAN GOLF BALL YO-YO 1963 NEW	$21.75
Rare Goody Jeweled Trophy Yo-Yo Mint Condition	$320.00	VINTAGE RARE DUNCAN Blue JEWEL YOYO Sealed Yo-Yo	$21.60
1940s 1950s NICE EARLY Eagle Return Top YOYO with decal	$245.50	HUMMINGBIRD Jewel Starburst Yo-Yo Rainbow Series BC New	$21.50
GENIUNE GOODY CHAMPION JEWELED FILIPINO TWIRLER YO-YO	$191.49	vintage YO-YO PLASTIMARX, MEXICO	$21.50
Vintage Huge 12" EXECTUTIVE 7.2 Pound Red Wood YO YO	$177.50	Vintage DUNCAN Satellite YO-YO Mark 1	$20.50

	HIGH		AVG
1968 BUTTERFLY IN GREAT CONDITION	$151.50	Yo-yo Case	$20.50
Rare Royal Thunderbird Yo-Yo	$146.08	YO-YO **HUGE 24 YOYO LOT** DUNCAN YOMEGA	$20.50
RARE TK YOYOS DIAMOND SPECIAL YO YO MAPLE - MINT	$139.15	Vintage Wooden Duncan Yo-Yo	$20.50
SUPER RARE TK YOYOS DIAMOND SPECIAL YO YO WALNUT MINT	$133.50	Lot of 50 Yo-Yos-great for resale	$20.50
Vintage DUNCAN Big G GENUINE DUNCAN Yo-Yo	$119.50	Buzz-On Bushido yo-yo yo yo	$20.50
Lot 23 Yo-Yos & case, belt clip Yomega Tom Kuhn YoPro +	$113.50	Vintage DUNCAN YOYO Butterfly Yo-Yo mint in package	$20.49
1978 Duncan MAGIC MOTION YO-YO DC Comics SUPERMAN MIB	$112.45	YYJ bronze enyo hitman	$20.28
VINTAGE Duncan COCA COLA MEXICAN PROMOTIONAL YO YO	$112.34	Yo-Stick by PLAYMATES TOYS INC.	$20.05

Classic Toys ▸ Other

The average sales price in this subcategory is $21.01.

	HIGH		AVG
Disney mobile phone - Dmobo M900 limited edition	$710.00	Radio Flyer Mini Red Tricycle NIB	$23.00
RARE 1938 KILGORE LONG TOM TOY CAP GUN HUBLEY RODEO RED	$391.86	Musical Jester Jack in the Box Tin Toy New Schylling	$22.95
LGB TRACK CLEANING ENGINE	$261.00	VIEW MASTERS LOT WITH CASE	$22.84
Wilesco D409 SHOWMAN?S ENGINE - NEW - UNFIRED +...BONUS	$254.99	VINTAGE TOY "CAR 54 WHERE ARE YOU?" METAL FRICTION CAR	$22.50
Super Jet Cycle Evel Knievel MIB Never Opened 1976 Look	$207.50	Lazer Tag Team Ops Deluxe 2 Player Game	$22.50
Rubber Band Gatling Gun Rare Unique One Of A Kind	$191.50	Wow! Lot of 4 Talking Elmo's!	$21.52
Water Wiggle WHAM-O 1973 Collectible Water Toy	$190.40	THINGMAKER TARZAN MOLD VERY NICE !	$21.00
John Deere 40T Precision #4 in Collector Center Series	$167.51	Schylling Classic Musical Jack-In-The-Box	$20.88
Remco Circa 1960's Long John Hook & Ladder Fire Eng.	$150.00	S3A Creepy Crawlers Goop Glow in the Dark 9 Bottles	$20.72
Mattel Creepy Crawlers Thingmaker Vintage 1964	$133.00	Lot of 19 Creepy Crawler Molds	$20.52
HUGE LOT 1983 & 1984 RAINBOW BRITE DOLLS SPRITES &CASE	$127.50	Taxi Argentina lot Fiat 125 Peugeot 504 IKA Renault	$20.50
NEW BRIGHT HOLIDAY EXPRESS ANIMATED ELECTRIC TRAIN SET	$127.50	Large Lot Of Assorted Plastic Horses Some W/Tack	$20.50
vintage Coleco Stanley Cup Playoff Hockey Game(mint)	$102.50	Western Auto	$20.50
Radio Flyer Liberty Spring Horse	$102.50	VINTAGE GAF SUPER FRIENDS TALKING VIEW-MASTER.IN CAN	$20.50
OOAK MILLEFIORI KALEIDOSCOPE BY C HARM POLYMER CLAY	$100.99	Creepy Crawlers Mold Pak Set - Gargoyles - Set 2	$20.50

Diecast, Toy Vehicles ▸ Aircraft

The average sales price in this subcategory is $34.51.

	HIGH		AVG
Steelcraft NX107 "Little Jim" Large Air Plane Must See!	$523.00	Franklin Mint Armour Luftwaffe Ju-87 STUKA "B" 1:48	$34.88
Wyandotte Streamlined Twin-Engine Airplane, Near Mint!	$385.00	Franklin Mint Armour Imperial Japanese Navy "ZERO" 1:48	$34.88
Wyndotte American Airways Passenger Plane with BOX!	$330.00	Franklin Mint Armour U.S.A.F. F-86E Sabre 1:48	$34.88
Tootsietoy 1938 Fly-N-Gyro No. 720 Airplane ~@^@~	$305.01	Franklin Mint Armour U.S.A.F. F-86F Sabre 1:48	$34.88
1930'S STRAUSS LOS ANGELES ZEPPELIN DIRIGIBLE W/P MIB	$290.00	Airplane-2-Old-Lead? Metal-Diecast? Tootsie? Vintage-NR	$34.66
Boeing 747 PAN AM Aero Mini desk model MIB	$280.00	Tin Airplane Made in Japan NO BANDAI, ICHIKO, NOMURA	$34.50
ALPS NORTHWEST AIRLINES 50s JAPAN TIN FRICTION AIRPLANE	$262.97	OLD WYANDOTTE USA DEFENSE BOMBER TOY AIRPLANE	$34.50
Y Douglas DC-7C Northwest Tin Friction Plane with BOX	$257.00	SHELL WENDELL WILLIAMS RACER DIE CAST METAL REPLICA	$33.75
LARGE VINTAGE STEELCRAFT ARMY SCOUT PLANE	$227.50	SpecCast Beechcraft Twin US Navy Wings Over Houston #4	$33.00
Dinky Aircraft 60R Empire Flying Boat Cambria G-ADUV	$194.00	U.S. AIR FORCE TOY PLANE - JAPAN - **low reserve**	$33.00
Boeing 707-320B TWA Aero Mini desk model MIP	$183.50	Vintage Hubley Camouflage Airplane	$33.00
Remco Flying Fox Passenger Airplane Battery Opt Toy!	$179.59	CORGI Lockheed C-121J Super Constellation Scale 1:144	$32.21
21" England made PRE WAR Wind-up Tin AIRPLANE as is	$155.05	vintage AIRWOLF 80's helicopter	$32.00
Franklin Mint Memphis Belle B17F signed MIB	$152.50	tootsietoy airplane, DC-2, 3 tires	$32.00
~ 1930's Tin /Steel Windup Air Mail Airplane - Girard	$152.01	Wings of Texaco #10 EAGLET PLANE - NEW	$31.05

Diecast, Toy Vehicles ▸ Bikes, Motorcycles

The average sales price in this subcategory is $37.38.

	HIGH		AVG
1950 GAMA 125 Acrobatic Motorbike Chimp in Original Box	$1,625.00	Vintage COP Motorcycle w/ sidecar	$44.05
Mint RRRumblers Boneshaker with Redline Reevers Sidecar	$850.00	RRrumblers, Torque Chop trike with 2 track guides	$43.92
1930s HUBLEY Cast Iron HARLEY 5-3/8" Toy MOTORCYCLE	$417.34	RRrumblers, Choppin' Chariot trike with 2 track guides	$43.62
1930S HUBLEY CAST IRON POLICE MOTORCYCLE W SIDECAR	$416.00	Limited Edition 1950 Starliner Die Cast Model Bicycle	$41.00
Hubley Harley Davidson 5 1/2 inch Cast Iron Motorcycle	$366.00	1954 to 56 NSU MAX by SCHUCO 1:10 SCALE	$39.95
Wells Britain 1st Place Clown Motorcycle Tin Windup Toy	$321.00	1953to 56 BMW R25/3 by SCHUCO 1:10 SCALE	$39.95
1920's Kid Special Boy on Tricycle by B&R	$317.00	VINTAGE CAST IRON MOTORCYCLE HUBLEY?	$37.01
Marx 1930's PD Police Motorcycle Sidecar Tin Wind-up	$286.00	Parcel Delivery motorcycle Barclay ? NO RES	$37.00
Tekno Toys No. 764 Black Harley w/ sidecar & box RARE	$275.00	Cast Iron Hubley Policeman On A Motorcycle	$37.00
Indian Parcel Post dispatch bike made by pride lines	$250.00	Matchbox 3 Wheeler Easy Rider Motorcycle Mint in Box	$36.59
Vintage RIP Snorter RRRumblers NICE	$206.50	FRANKLIN MINT HARLEY-DAVIDSON ELECTRIC GLIDE	$36.53
1950's MARX FIX-ALL MOTORCYCLE, HARLEY-DAVIDSON TOY	$200.00	1960 BMW R60 2 by TOOTSIETOY 1:10 SCALE	$36.01
VINTAGE SCHUCO MIRAKOMOT MOTORCYCLE #1012	$195.00	1960's COX GAS-POWERED .049 TRIKE IN RED METALLIC	$36.00
Tekno 1948 Harley Davidson Sidecar Motorcycle	$181.60	RUBBER TOY MOTORCYCLE AUBURN	$36.00
Mint in Box 1940s Goso RaceHorse w/Rider-Zone Germany	$160.50	Vintage AUBURN Toy Rubber Motorcycle~Great Condition	$35.11

Diecast, Toy Vehicles ▸ Boats, Ships

The average sales price in this subcategory is $58.60.

	HIGH		AVG
MARKLIN VIKTORIA PASSENGER STEAM SHIP	$1,875.00	AUTHENTICAST WWII JAPANESE MEDIUM TANK ID MODEL	$64.00
Vintage Japan Wooden Toy Ship T.M.Y Battery Op Gun Boat	$899.00	AUTHENTICAST WWII US SCOUT CAR #5162 ID MODEL	$63.00
Huge Denia Ocean Liner - 1940?s - Made in Spain	$855.00	1930s Tremo 1/1200 Japanese Cruiser IJN Kinugasa. Rare	$62.95
Tri-Ang Minic 709/2 Carmania Recast Ivernia 1964	$747.85	1950's Ideal Toy Boat Fire Fighter in Box	$62.16
TRI-ANG MINIC 709 CARMANIA RECAST IVERNIA 1964	$743.33	Vintage Phillips 66 Power Yacht Toy Boat in Box	$61.00
Vintage Battery Op Toy Wooden Hydroplane Speed Boat	$710.00	8 US NAVY WARSHIPS SUBMARINE DESTROYER A/C +	$59.99
RARE 1877 Reed Floating Palace Sidewheeler Boat Toy !!	$585.00	1940s WOLVERINE toy wind-up SUBMARINE works A+	$58.22

Vintage Wooden Toy Hydroplane Boat With K & O Outboard	$560.00
Johnson Toy Outboard Boat Motor Super Sea-Horse 50	$455.00
FLEET LINE DOLPHIN BOAT & SCOTT ATWATER TOY MOTOR MIB	$450.00
80MPHI27CX 1:6 BIGFOOT RADIO CONTROL RC NITRO GAS TRUCK	$369.00
FRANKLIN MINT-YORKTOWN-AIRCRAFT CARRIER LP $1250.00	$355.00
Great batle ship in tin metal	$354.00
FRANKLIN MINT-YORKTOWN-AIRCRAFT CARRIER LP $1250.00	$350.00
1950's 17" wooden boat w/ Johnson Super SeaHorse 50	$330.00
TRI-ANG MINC Queen Elizabeth Ships Presentation Set/Box	$55.00
Airship Zeppelin L 55 in glass case scale 1/1250	$55.00
WOLVERINE USA VINTAGE TIN TOY BATTLESHIP 1930'S RARE NR	$54.99
50'S JAPAN TIN TOY *NAVY TORPEDO SHIP BOAT* WIND UP	$53.58
REVELL USS SULLIVAN FLETCHER 1954 WWII DESTOYER KIT!	$53.05
Eldon 1960's Racing Sloop MIB and NO RESERVE!	$53.00
TOOTSIE TOY FREIGHTER #1038 SILVER RARE NICE CONDITION	$52.99
LARGE VINTAGE WOODEN POND BOAT	$52.01

Diecast, Toy Vehicles ▶ Cars, Trucks-Diecast

The average sales price in this subcategory is $36.33.

	HIGH		AVG
BEAUTIFUL 1925 CIJ ALFA ROMEO RACING CAR	$3,250.00	Limited Edition Die Cast White 2-155 Field Boss Farm	$41.00
Jeff Gordan and other Action Collectibles 1:24 scale	$875.00	1/18 EXACT DETAIL 1965 SHELBY R " JERRY TITUS "	$41.00
Ohlsson & Rice Gas Powered Racer low reserve	$461.99	wonderful classicwhite modelcar VOLVO PV544 in 1:18	$39.95
OLD: DIAPET YONEZAWA Nr. D-148 SUBARU 1000 1/40 MINT B	$230.50	1938 Graham Bradley Wide Front Precision Quality	$39.88
conquest models nº 104 A.C. Greyhound coupe 1960	$215.50	BREKINA ALFA ROMEO GIULIA	$38.80
1/18 UT Mclaren F1 GTR Fina BMW Presentation RARE !!!!!	$195.50	FedEx Ground Freightliner FLD 120 Double Trailer Truck	$38.06
TEKNO #318 FERRARI SPORT "ENGLAND" MIB	$173.50	1/24 GMP Pontiac GTO Judge Orange Conv. 1970,3500 pcs	$36.00
CMC Auto-Union Type D 1939 Grand Prix car	$149.99	DCP Horseshoe Express, Pete 379, 1/64, NIB, #30462	$34.99
1/43 American trolleybus Kraisler (very rare)	$149.00	KLLM, 1/64 TT, DCP stock #30319, NIB, no res, old logo	$34.99
Budgie Morestone Military Land Rover. Excellent. Rare.	$133.00	1/43 Delprado Japan 66° CHAPARRAL 2D Winner at 1000km	$34.77
1/18 Exoto Chaparral 2/2C Winner 1965 LA Times GP	$123.50	OLD TOY CAR (RACER) VERY OLD AND UNIQUE	$34.00
conquest models nº 2 Chevrolet impala convertible 1960	$123.01	1/18 CUSTOM KANSAS STATE TROOPER POLICE MUSTANG	$34.00
1\64 CUSTOM DCP PETE WITH HAY TRAILER AND PUP	$123.00	wonderful red modelcar VOLVO P 121 AMAZON in 1:18	$33.99
conquest models nº 11 Buick super convertible 1955 MIB	$122.50	CHEVROLET EL CAMINO 1970 SS 396 LTD DIECAST 1/18 BRONZE	$33.99
3 cars 1/18 F1 Ford Lotus 72D-49-49B w/display	$121.50	1/18 Minichamps BMW M3 E30 Street 1987 in Silver	$32.63

Diecast, Toy Vehicles ▶ Cars, Trucks-Plastic

The average sales price in this subcategory is $22.39.

	HIGH		AVG
Rare 30s Toy Founders Streamline Deco Car in Box COOL!	$245.00	Plastic Hubley Dump Truck & Fire Truck N/R	$24.50
SSP Smash-up derby Crazy racers/stuntcars set Sealed	$202.50	1960 Nash Metropolitan, Chevy Flatbed,Processed Plastic	$24.50
SIZZLERS STEERING TRAILER	$202.49	KEYSTONE VINTAGE SEDAN , HOOD LIFTS C. 1950 MINT	$23.41
MONSTER-SIZE Smash-UP-Derby-Kenner SSP LOT	$179.55	60s 70s Cragstan Electric Wheels Ford Mustang B/O NIB	$22.72
1961 BUICK INVICTA CONVERTIBLE PROMO CAR	$178.50	Cox Baja Bug Volkswagen VW Gas Powered Toy Car	$22.50
VINTAGE MARX BIG BRUISER TOW TRUCK BATTERY OPERATED	$177.50	1965 Rambler Classic - Red W/ White top ORIGINAL !	$22.48
OLD VINTAGE MARX BIG BRUISER TOY TONKA TOW TRUCK CAR	$175.00	2 Tootsietoy Chris Craft Capri boats with trailers	$22.35
1936 OLDS OLDSMOBILE CAST MEDAL HOOD ORNAMENT *WOW*	$170.13	F&F MOLD CEREAL PREMIUM BOATS	$22.28
VINTAGE JOHNNY EXPRESS SEMI TRUCK	$154.50	JAVELIN AMX UNBUILT PLASTIC KIT MADE BY JOHAN !!	$22.16
1975 Hess Tractor Trailer Tanker Truck MINT IN BOX NR!	$153.56	1959 DKW Junior Plastic Car (Beishe) 1/87 By Wiking	$22.00
c1960s MARX BIG BRUISER TOW TRUCK & FIX A FLAT TRUCK	$146.94	*NEW* TONKA FINS ATV Tough Truck Adventures	$21.95
1979 HESS TRUCK TRAINING VAN	$127.50	vintage redline hotwheels sizzlers Flat out pink	$21.50
MPC ~ DYNO RACER SET ~ 1969 CORVETTE ~ RED ~ OLD ~ 1/25	$125.69	4 F & F Toy Plastic Cars & 3 Plastic Century Boats	$21.50
AMT 1962 Pontiac Bonneville Convert Annual 3 in 1 Kit	$125.00	1965 Mercury Park Lane Promo - Painted !	$21.49
Vintage Pyro City Supply Plastic Truck	$106.05	Tekno Denmark Ford Taxa	$21.09

Diecast, Toy Vehicles ▶ Cars, Trucks-Pressed Steel

The average sales price in this subcategory is $161.08.

	HIGH		AVG
Vintage Kelmet White Big Boy Mobile Clamshell Crane 495	$7,700.00	Doepke American LaFrance Aerial Ladder Firetruck #2008	$177.50
50s Smith Miller Smitty Coca Cola Truck Mint w/ BOX	$4,000.00	Smith Miller Fruehauf Truck and Flatbed Trailer	$177.50
Huge Buddy L #290 Steam Road Roller 1929	$3,050.00	Buddy L #1005 Coal Car	$176.76
1926 Buddy L Aerial Fire Truck Orig Excellent Beauty	$2,650.00	VINTAGE TURNER BULLDOG MACK DUMP TRUCK 1930's	$175.00
Buddy L Locomotive Wrecking Crane	$2,200.00	MARX ROY ROGERS TRUCK & HORSE TRAILER MAGNIFICENT 1950	$170.73
Buddy L Express Line Van #204 - Outstanding Original	$2,125.00	DUNWELL TOYS TRUCK-TRAILER	$164.00
ALL AMERICAN 3 KENWORTHS 75TH ANNV TRUCKS	$2,082.00	Dunwell Metal Products Pressed Steel Toy Logging Truck!	$161.50
SMITH MILLER MAUDE'S DINER - MINT CONDITION "AS NEW"	$1,995.00	KEYSTONE RIDE 'EM DUMP TRUCK RIDE ON LIKE BUDDY L 1930S	$157.50
Antique Buddy L Keystone White Mack C cab Truck NICE **	$1,825.00	1940's Buddy L Wooden Greyhound Bus, Original NR	$157.50
Smith Miller Orginal Coca Cola Truck Minty	$1,500.00	Texaco Dealer Buddy-L Fire Engine and Box	$154.50
FANTASTIC SMITH MILLER CUSTOM MIC OWL CEMENT TRUCK-	$1,350.00	SMITH MILLER LYON TRUCK and TRAILER!!	$154.50
AMERICAN NATIONAL MACK TRUCK BUDDY L	$1,100.00	Buddy L #1006 Flatcar	$154.01
OLD BUDDY L EXPRESS TRUCK W/SCREEN SIDES 1932	$1,000.00	RARE 30's Pressed Steel 18" Truck Steam-Shovel Loader	$153.49
BUDDY L INSURANCE PATROL 205-C	$999.95	Restored Keystone Ride 'em Steamroller	$153.01
BUDDY L PUMPER FIRE ENGINE 205-A	$999.95	Renwal Pontiac Star Chief	$152.50

Educational ▶ Alphabet

The average sales price in this subcategory is $11.31.

	HIGH		AVG
Huge Lot of Learning Fisher Price..Infant/Toddler Toys	$151.50	Leap Frog little touch Leap Pad	$12.00
Anatex Mini Play Cube Toy Wooden Toys Blocks Puzzels	$129.90	School-Time Leap Top	$12.00
LEAPFROG LEAPSTER LEARNING SYSTEM PLUS 8 GAMES WOW!!	$112.50	LeapFrog Fridge Phonics Magnetic Letter Set	$12.00
Leapster L-Max Learning Game Syste NR – FREE S&H	$86.00	Mega Blocks ABC TRAIN (new) ages 1-5yrs.	$11.99
COMPACT STACKABLE ABC SORTER over 200 pieces	$72.50	FISHER PRICE BABY SMARTRONICS	$11.50
My First Leap Pad Lot by Leap Frog	$68.53	COMPUTER SYSTEM ABC	
LeapFrog Leapster Mulitimedia ** NR – FREE S&H **	$63.09	2 LEAP FROG LOT: LEARNING DRUM & DISCOVERY BALL	$11.50

My First LeapPad-Blue *HUGE LOT* comes with 6 BOOKS!	$60.01
Lot Fisher Price Leap Frog Vtech Infant/Toddler Toys	$58.00
HUGE LOT VTECH LEAPFROG INFANT/TODDLER TOYS	$56.00
LEAP FROG Pretend & Learn Shopping cart Like New W/box	$55.00
MY FIRST LEAP PAD SYSTEM WITH 8	$53.00
BOOKS 7 CARTRIDGES BLUE	
Huge Lot of Learning Fisher Price..Infant/Toddler Toys	$52.00
Lot of Fisher Price Leap Frog Vtech Infant/Toddler Toys	$51.00
Leap Pad Little Touch LeapPad Blue + FIVE Books!	$43.00
Leap Frog LeapStart Learning Table- LIKE NEW!!	$11.50
Leap Frog Alphabet Learning System Refrigerator Magnet	$11.18
Leap Frog Frig Magnetic ABCs Alphabet NR	$11.17
1940 Richmond Spelling Board LETTERS/NUMBERS	$10.99
Barbie computer with mouse	$10.99
52 pc Foam Alphabet Puzzle Floor Mat Educational Toy	$10.99
[24 of these sold for $10.99 each]	

Educational ▸ Geography, History

The average sales price in this subcategory is $20.37.

	HIGH		AVG
Montessori Wood Nienhuis Map Cabinet Puzzle Stand	$201.48	Full Set Educational Insights BrainBoosters w/DECODER!	$21.45
Leapfrog Explorer Globe	$175.00	GEOSAFARI TALKING EDUCATIONAL GLOBE QUIZ MIB	$21.00
[5 of these sold in a multiple item ("Dutch") auction for $35.00 each]		Leap Frog Leap Pad System with 8 books & Cartridges!!	$21.00
Odyssey III Interactive Globe by Leap Frog	$96.01	ExploraToy GeoSafari World Quiz Game/Globe	$20.54
1956 Renwal PANAMA CANAL Model KIT w/BOX! Hard to Find!	$93.88	Titanic Toy Lot	$20.50
GLOBE Odyssey III Leap Frog interactive world atlas NEW	$92.50	Odyssey Atlasphere Talking Globe	$20.50
Viking Spagnhelm Helmet (SCA Combat Armor)	$91.00	ODYSSEY II INTERACTIVE TALKING GLOBE	$20.49
80+ piece Men of '76 collection Revolutionary War 1776	$86.00	United States USA Map Foam Floor Puzzle EDUCATIONAL	$20.15
LEAPFROG ODYSSEY III INTERACTIVE GLOBE NO RESERVE	$81.00	Crusader Knee/Elbow Cops, Soupcan (SCA Combat Armor)	$20.00
LeapFrog Quantum Explorer Interactive Globe NIB VHTF	$81.00	PRE-1961 CRAM 10.5" SCHOLASTIC WORLD GLOBE	$20.00
Viking Spagnhelm Helmet (SCA Combat Armor)	$80.00	Crusader Knee/Elbow Cops, Soupcan (SCA Combat Armor)	$20.00
LEAP FROG GLOBE, INTERACTIVE EXPLORER	$78.89	Geo Safari 22 cards~Richard Scary, geography, puzzles	$20.00
LEAP FROG GLOBE, INTERACTIVE EXPLORER	$78.01	GeoSafari World Exploratory Talking Electronic Toy	$20.00
ODYSSEY GLOBE from LEAGFROG - Brand New	$77.55	Great States Board Game New USA Geography Map	$19.99
LEAPFROG ODYSSEY III INTERACTIVE GLOBE NO RESERVE	$76.01	LEAPFROG LEAP FROG JUNIOR EXPLORER GLOBE	$19.99
LEAP FROG GLOBE, INTERACTIVE EXPLORER	$75.35		

Educational ▸ Mathematics

The average sales price in this subcategory is $13.48.

	HIGH		AVG
AIRTECH 40 EDUCATIONAL WIND TUNNEL by PITSCO	$699.00	Leap Frog Leap Pad with 3 books Preschool - Kindergdn	$13.99
Montessori 20 Piece set	$250.00	Leapfrog Turbo Extreme School Success Ed Grades 3 4	$13.58
Educated Monkey Tin Toy Mechanical Calculator – New	$119.40	Leapster Incredibles Game Math, Spelling, Grammer *New*	$13.55
[12 of these sold in a multiple item ("Dutch") auction for $9.95 each]		Leapster Leap Frog Batman Cartridge Brand NEW Sealed	$13.51
TEXAS INSTRUMENTS TI-84 PLUS SILVER EDITION!	$99.70	Discovery Toys THINK IT THROUGH Math	$13.50
TEXAS INSTRUMENTS TI-84 PLUS! 3X THE MEMORY* BRAND NEW	$91.00	Leap Frog Twist & Shout Addition and Subtraction	$13.49
The Educated Monkey, Mathematics Toy 1918	$76.00	2 LEAP FROG TWIST AND SHOUT	$13.49
LEAP FROG QUANTUM LEAP iQUEST WITH 11 CARTRIDGES! LOOK!	$66.00	MULTIPLICATION & DIVISION	
MATH SAFARI KIT	$56.00	The Math Kit 3-D Educational Pop Up Book Van Der Meer	$13.29
TURBO TWIST MATH LeapFrog Complete Cartridge Set NEW	$56.00	VINTAGE Texas Instruments Speak and & Math appr 1980	$13.25
Huge Lot of ETA Pattern Block Math Manipulatives NEW!	$52.50	Turbo Twist Math & Spelling Quantum Leap Frog Leapfrog	$13.09
LEAPFROG I QUEST, FLASH MAGIC AND HEADPHONES NO RESERVE	$51.00	5 Decks SRA Math Cards Math Manipulatives 4th,5th,6th..	$13.08
Leapster Learning System with extras	$50.00	Hooked on Phonics Master the Math Level 3 Multiplicatio	$13.02
Montessori Introduction to Decimal Quantity Homeschool	$49.99	iQUEST - MATH - 5TH GRADE	$13.01
Montessori Constructive Triangles NEW	$49.99	1976 Texas Instruments Little Professor Calculator TI	$13.00
Tree Blocks Math Kit Set of 66	$42.00	Little Professor with Box,	$13.00

Educational ▸ Music, Art

The average sales price in this subcategory is $11.55.

	HIGH		AVG
BABY EINSTEIN AUTHENTIC 18 DVD SET +++ FREE SHIPPING!!!	$125.01	NEW Kid Kids Child Youth Acoustic Guitar PINK	$11.91
BABY EINSTEIN AUTHENTIC 18 DVD SET +++ FREE SHIPPING!!!	$119.35	[2 of these sold for $11.91 each]	
BABY EINSTEIN AUTHENTIC 18 DVD SET +++ FREE SHIPPING!!!	$104.48	NEW Kid Kids Child Youth Toy Acoustic Guitar Brown	$11.91
BABY EINSTEIN AUTHENTIC 18 DVD SET +++ FREE SHIPPING!!!	$103.50	NEW Kid Kids Child Youth Toy Acoustic Guitar Red	$11.91
Kiddie Keys Wood Baby Grand Piano IMMEDIATE SHIP	$79.99	[2 of these sold for $11.91 each]	
2 Watercolor painting VHS videos Multiple Glazes	$63.76	NEW Kid Kids Child Youth Toy Acoustic Guitar Blue	$11.91
NEW NEUROSMITH JUMBO MUSIC BALL & ROCK	$50.00	Parents Magazine Bee Bop Band Drum Set Muscial Toy	$11.51
AROUND CARTRIDGE		Neurosmith RHYTHMS OF THE WORLD	$11.50
3 RARE NEUROSMITH MUSIC BLOCKS CARTRIDGES CINDERELLA +	$47.20	Music Block Cartridge	
Large Standing Kids Easel Melissa & Doug Chalkboard +DE	$42.99	Super Art Set Studio * Lillian Vernon * $39.99	$11.50
2.0 NEUROSMITH MUSIC BLOCKS +4 NEW	$41.05	Fisher Price Vintage Musical Instruments Toy Set	$11.50
CLASSICAL CARTRIDGES		Brand New NEUROSMITH Sunshine	$11.49
LEARN HOW TO DO SPRAY PAINT ART!!! INSTRUCTIONAL DVD,IN	$39.99	Symphony Musical Baby Toy	
Emenee Guitar complete in the box	$39.30	Waldorf play STOCKMAR BEESWAX BLOCK CRAYONS	$11.49
New MELISSA And & DOUG Learn To Play Kids Piano Toy	$38.00	Musini with free Magic Wand and Cartridge - New!	$11.05
NEUROSMITH MUSIC BLOCKS BABY TODDLER TOY w/4 CARTRIDGES	$36.17	Watercolor painting VHS video A Rose is Born	$11.02
1955 You-Can-Paint Oil Paint by Numbers Set Unused	$35.00	Waldorf play STOCKMAR BEESWAX CRAYONS art toy	$11.00

Educational ▸ Reading, Writing

The average sales price in this subcategory is $14.39.

	HIGH		AVG
Leap Pad & LeapPad + Writing light & case- 20 books	$172.50	Leap Frog ALPHABET BUS Educational Toddler Children Toy	$14.95
LEAPSTER DEAL - ReCharger +7 Cartridges 48 Games + Case	$169.00	NEW LEAPFROG MIND STATION USB PC MAC IQUEST Turbotwist	$14.95

LEAPSTER SYSTEM 5 GAMES HUGE LOT LEAP FROG	$125.00	MY FIRST LEAP PAD W/ 3 BOOKS	$14.75
Speak and Spell & Math Speek n Read W/ TI Bonus Toys!	$98.00	LEAPSTER GAME CARTRIDE THE INCREDIBLES DISNEY	$14.51
Lot of 9 LeapPad books and Leap Pad cartridges	$77.01	Leap Frog Learn to Read Phonics Desk	$14.50
Leap Frog LEAPSTER System Brand New w/2 Games	$77.01	LEAP FROG LEAPSTER GAME CARTRIDGE - TOP-SECRET BEESWAX	$14.50
Leapfrog Leapster learning system, Like New with EXTRAs	$77.00	LeapFrog Leapster SpongeBob Squarepants Book/Cartridge	$14.26
Leapster L-Max Learning Game System NIB	$75.01	Leap Frog Shopping Cart Replacement Food 1,5,6,7,8 ,10	$14.25
Touch Tablet by v tech Laptop ages 9 to 15 NEW	$75.00	PINK My First LeapPad MINT with Books! Leap Pad 1st SEE	$14.06
Leapster L-Max Learning Game System NIB	$75.00	Brand New Leapster Carrying Case...Still in Box	$14.00
Leapster L-Max Learning Game System NIB	$74.00	LEAPFROG LEAPSTER–MATH BASEBALL–NEW IN BOX!!	$13.99
Leap Frog Shopping Cart New in Package Great Toy	$72.95	Pink Leap Pad W/ New Phonics Lesson 1	$13.99
Leapster L-Max Learning Game System NIB	$72.51	TEXAS INSTRUMENTS SPEAK & SPELL TI 1978 GREAT CONDITION	$13.79
Leapster L-Max Learning Game System NIB	$72.50	Leapster 2nd Grade Musical Menace ~NEW IN BOX	$13.55
LEAPSTER L-MAX <> LeapFrog <> NEW <> NR	$72.05	**LEAPSTER MR. PENCILS LEARN TO DRAW & WRITE NEW	$13.51

Educational ▶ Science, Nature

The average sales price in this subcategory is $20.18.

	HIGH		AVG
ANTIQUE BRASS BAUSCH & LOMB MICROSCOPE Pat. 1897	$209.01	Solar Swarovski Crystal Rainbow Maker - as seen on HGTV	$20.50
ELENCO 500-IN-ONE Electronic Project Science Home Lab	$155.99	Radio Shack Electronics Learning Lab Learninglab 28-280	$20.50
SOLAR PATHFINDER - THE ENERGY EVALUATOR	$152.50	Electronics Learning Lab by Radio Shack Like New	$20.50
Rock Tumbler Thumlers Model B 15 Lb. Capacity New	$149.95	Vintage Jason Venture 4000 Model 707 Microscope NR	$20.50
Rock Tumbler Thumlers Model B 15 Lb. Capacity New	$140.00	JASON MICROSCOPE #712 W/900x ZOOM,	$20.50
BRAND NEW 6" NEWTONIAN REFLECTOR TELESCOPE 1400	$130.00	&TOOLS &HARD CASE	
[2 of these sold for $130.00 each]		NEW! Nightfall Sunset in the Rockies POSTER	$20.45
BRAND NEW 6" NEWTONIAN REFLECTOR TELESCOPE 1400	$129.88	New Crayola Discover and Draw Metal Detector	$20.00
[2 of these sold for $129.88 each]		HUGH SET BRIEFCASE MICROSCOPE SET KMART FOCAL NIB WOW	$19.99
OLD VINTAGE DINOSAUR DINOSAURS	$120.21	Jason Empire Microscope Leather Case Extras Like New	$19.99
WAX FIGURE TOY SOUVENIR		MOTOR WORKS SMITHSONIAN REAL WORKING	$19.99
NEW 1400 6" NEWTONIAN TELESCOPE TELESCOPES	$117.50	MODEL ENGINE NIB	
NEW 1400 6" NEWTONIAN TELESCOPE TELESCOPES	$111.11	Solar Swarovski Crystal Rainbow Maker - as seen on HGTV	$19.97
NEW 1400 6" NEWTONIAN TELESCOPE TELESCOPES	$104.40	Potassium Nitrate (saltpeter) HighGrade 8.8lbs ExFine#	$19.97
MILLER-SIMONS JUNIOR ENGINEER	$102.50	RadioShack 300-in-1 Project Kit Like New No Reserve!!!	$19.69
STEAM ENGINE #SE100w/box		Solar Swarovski Crystal Rainbow Maker - as seen on HGTV	$19.40
NEW AUTOTRANSFORMER 20A 0-140V 50/60Hz variac	$99.99	SOLAR POWER MINI-LAB KIT - NEW (EDU-8405)	$19.00

Electronic, Battery, Wind-Up ▶ Battery Operated

The average sales price in this subcategory is $87.94.

	HIGH		AVG
1950's Wood Speed Boat Wooden Scientific Models LOOK!	$2,058.00	MARX TRICKY TOMMY FARM TRACTOR MIB	$99.99
JOLLY RABBIT&ROBIN Bird Watcher Bat Op Toy/Original BOX	$1,000.00	PAYA VINTAGE 1980 MASSIVE BMW L@@K MOTORCYCLE	$99.99
BOXED JET PLANE BASE * "Y" CO JAPAN *NO/RESERVE* LQQK *	$965.55	1950s VINTAGE Lincoln Continental Mark V Remote Japan	$99.99
1965 Gilbert, James Bond's Aston-Martin in Original Box	$917.97	TEDDY BALLOON BLOWING BOXED ALPS JAPAN w/**VIDEO**	$98.77
~*~Mickey The Magician Linemar Litho Tin Mickey Mouse~	$800.00	Tinplate Sonicon Bus Near mint TM Japan 1950s	$96.56
ORKIN CLOCKWORK TOY SPEED BOAT	$668.99	Vintage Tin ALPS Japan Hot Rod Custom T Ford B/O MIB+	$90.95
BOXED AIRCRAFT CARRIER * MARX CO JAPAN*NO/RESERVE*LQQK*	$588.00	circa 1950 wooden boat battery operated MIB never used	$88.00
RARE 50`s Directional Robot metallic grey-blue YONEZAWA	$465.00	Vintage Japan Impala Pressed Tin Police Car Battery Op	$87.00
Rembrandt The Monkey Artist Made In Japan	$446.01	Cragstan Japanese Battery Operated Musical Monkey	$86.00
The Great GARLOO ROBOT Marx Excellent w/Box NR L@@K	$405.00	Vintage battery operated S.S.TEXACO toy boat / ship	$86.00
TIN JUNGLE JUMBO WITH TEDDY ROOSEVELT HUNTER JAPAN MIB	$392.00	REMCO Bulldog Tank with Box. Very nice condition.	$84.77
RARE SNAKE CHARMER (LINEMAR TOYS) GREAT COND.! MUST SEE	$376.00	60`s MASUDAYA B/O TIN SPACE SHIP EXPLORER X-7 MIB JAPAN	$83.99
Japanese Tin Toy Car Battery Operated 1940's	$363.58	Vintage Junior Spy Walkie Talkie Attache Case radio cb	$83.00
Battery Operated Bubble Blowing Musician	$362.85	Motorific/Boaterific Blue Devil w/Outboard MIB	$81.77
MR. FOX the MAGICIAN with BOX	$360.00	Motorific/Boaterific Renegade II w/Outboard Ex	$81.77

Electronic, Battery, Wind-Up ▶ Electronic, Interactive

The average sales price in this subcategory is $20.31.

	HIGH		AVG
Sony AiBO dog ERA 110 *NO RESERVE*	$641.11	My First Leap Pad - PINK ***NIP****	$20.51
Wind Speed/Wind Direction Aerovane Sensor w/Indicator	$455.00	SUPER ARMATRON (ROBOTIC ARM) NICE ! BOXED	$20.51
MIB Worlds of Wonder Talking	$129.49	MGA Rescue Pets BLACK & GRAY Interactive Dog New	$20.51
Interactive Julie doll WOW		Talking NANO BABY electronic toy pets w/batteries RARE	$20.50
Interactive ROTS R2 D2 Robot! MISBI! New!!	$103.76	Rare TEKNO Robot Dalmation PUPPY WITH INSTRUCTIONS	$20.50
Leapster L-Max Handheld Learning Game System Leapfrog	$82.00	Interactive Disney Winnie the Pooh	$20.50
Barbie VideoCam Wireless Video Camera~NEW in Box~	$78.00	Tiger Lazer Tag Team Ops Deluxe 2-Player System Laser	$20.25
Wind Direction Indicator	$75.00	SIMON 1978 Milton Bradley Electronic Memory Game & BOX	$20.00
Wind Speed/Wind Direction Sensor	$75.00	TOMY *HIDAMARI NO TAMI* ~Onsen White Spa~ Regional JP	$19.99
Leapster L-Max Handheld Learning Game System Leapfrog	$75.00	TONY HAWK TYCO R/C Remote	$19.99
[4 of these sold for $75.00 each]		Control Xtreme Skateboard NIB	
20 pcs. LAZER LASER TAG ITEMS -	$71.00	Two NiCd 8.4V 30Amp Hi-Power AIRSOFT Battery	$19.95
WORK worlds of wonder		TYCO BEDTIME BUBBA & REAL TALKIN' BUBBA	$19.00
vtech V.Smile Pocket Learning System - Brand New	$64.00	* AURA * INTERACTOR Gaming Vest Playstation, Ninterndo	$18.50
NEW SEALED V-SMILE POCKET PORTABLE	$62.00	NIB Leapster Incredibles Game Cartridge	$18.50
SYSTEM INCLUDES GAME		Laser LAZER Tag CHALLENGE guns - vest Toymax	$18.50

Electronic, Battery, Wind-Up ▸ Wind-Up, Walking Toys

The average sales price in this subcategory is $61.68.

	HIGH		AVG
TOMBO ALABAMA COON JIGGER TIN TOY WINDUP EX.	$456.00	Frankonia Toy YO-YO Playing Bunny Tin Wind-up MIB!	$68.85
1950's Linemar Marx Donald Duck Dipsey Car Tin WU NM	$425.00	MARX GIANT REVERSING TRACTOR WITH DRIVER	$66.57
Schuco - Clown Fiddler in box - Made in Germany	$424.00	MARX MICKEY MOUSE + PLUTO RAMP WALKER	$66.00
DC3 Tinplate c/w TWA Plane Japan Pre war	$417.50	Military Police metal antique wind-up Car Early 50's	$64.50
ANTIQUE GERMAN VESPA SCOOTER MOTORCYCLE WIND-UP TIN TOY	$406.99	Schuco 3000	$63.00
N/Mint 40s Hook N Ladder 13" FireTruck-Joustra,France	$356.00	1940s RELAIBLE TOYS Charlie Chaplin Wind Up in Box	$62.53
no Marx Alps Distler rare 1930 tin car Dec? Ford? MB NR	$354.00	Small Minnie/Micky and Pig Ramp Walker	$62.00
Rosko TN Japan Louis Armstrong Trumpet Player Wind-Up	$316.00	1968 MARX WIND-UP TIN TOY WEIRD-OH GOOFY BANANA MAN !	$59.85
RARE Japan Clown Roller Skate TPS Tin Wind Up Toy MIB	$305.01	Vintage Celluoid Boy And Bunny On See Saw Wind Up	$58.79
Marx 1930's PD Police Motorcyle Sidecar Tin Wind-up	$286.00	1968 MARX WIND-UP TIN TOY WEIRD-O GOOFY CORN PERSON	$58.75
1950's TPS Japan Tin Windup POP EYE PETE! MIB NoRsv	$263.80	VINTAGE WIND UP TOY,KITTY PURSUING MOUSE	$57.00
TPS Pango Pango African Black Dancer Tin Wind-Up Toy	$256.67	1920`s TIPP&CO TIPPCO WIND-UP GERMAN PENNY TIN TOY CAR	$55.00
FANTASTIC 1930s 14" Limo W/BOX-Mettoy,England	$256.00	SCHUCO AKUSTICO 2002 U.S. ZONE GERMANY TOY WIND UP CAR	$54.56
Occupied Japan Celluloid & Tin News-Boy 1940's-Works NR	$253.50	YOSHIYA TIN WINDUP FRICTION FIRE CHIEF CAR, JAPAN, K.O.	$53.01
Circus Elephant Clowns / Japan	$237.50	Vintage Japanese "Jolly Guitarist" Wind Up (OB)	$52.56

Fast Food, Cereal Premiums ▸ Cereal & Other Premiums

The average sales price in this subcategory is $6.75.

	HIGH		AVG
ORIGINAL FREAKIES CEREAL BOX AIRPLANE ON BACK	$148.13	5 Kelloggs Disney Wobbler Mickey Thumper Jiminy Cricket	$7.50
ORIGINAL FREAKIES CEREAL BOX MYSTERY PRIZE	$138.29	3 MONSTER CEREALS FULL BOX AND FRESH OFF THE SHELVES	$7.00
Disney Kelloggs Wobblers Complete Set of 50 Free Ship	$70.00	Tinker Bell Wobbler #46 kellogs Disney Unopened	$7.00
MIB 50 Kellogg's Disney Wobblers set ON HAND!FreeShip!	$63.00	THE NABISCO THING!!!!!!!!!!!!VERY RARE!!!!!!!!!!!	$7.00
Mint COMPLETE DISNEY WOBBLERS SET in display box	$55.00	Kellogg's Wobblers ARIEL,URSULA,FLOUNDER,SEBASTIAN	$7.00
Florida Gator-Urban Meyer Gator Flakes Limited Edition	$51.00	*KELLOGGS* DONALD-PLUTO-MICKEY-GOOFY~*DISNEY WOBBLER*	$6.89
SNORKELDORF FREAKIES Cereal plastic flag	$45.50	Kellogg's Disney Wobblers Set of all 50 Order Form UPC	$6.60
PREMIUM FIGURES LOT MAGIC ROUNDABOUT,DISNEY,ASTERIX,ETC	$41.90	Kellogg Disney Wobbler mint in package LADY & TRAMP	$6.50
GARGLE FREAKIES Cereal plane cut from box	$41.90	Disney Keebler Mini Bobbles Set 12 MIP+Bonus	$6.50
DISNEY WOBBLERS IN 2-DOOR RED CASE! VERY RARE!!!!!!!!!!	$40.00	Kellogg's Wobblers MIKE AND SULLEY	$6.00
34 Vintage 1980s Post Honeycomb Cereal License Plates	$31.00	NEW Kelloggs Disney Wobblers #35 Peter, #46 Tinkerbell	$5.99
HAMHOSE FREAKIES Cereal plane from box partially cut	$28.54	Kellogg Disney Wobbler HEIMLICH #24 - A Bug's Life RARE	$5.75
Kelloggs Cereal Snap Crackle Pop figures Vintage	$24.99	KELLOGG'S SESAME STREET MINI BEANS, SET OF 8	$5.50
Kellogg's Sesame Street Mini Beans 24 Muppets + Holder	$24.50	Disney/Kelloggs #9 Cheshire Cat unopened wobbler	$5.50
Kelloggs Disney Wobblers WOODY,BUZZ,LITTLE GREEN MAN	$22.00	Mickey Mouse Mcdonalds 2005 #1 NIP	$5.50

Fast Food, Cereal Premiums ▸ Fast Food

The average sales price in this subcategory is $5.75.

	HIGH		AVG
1972 Kentucky Fried Chicken Playset MIB Child Guidance	$41.00	Dairy Queen PLAY FOOD 9 piece SET PLASTIC Playfood New!	$6.50
Big Lot of 80s Mattel FOOD FIGHTERS + Vehicles !!	$26.50	McDonald's Large Translite Win 500,000 S/H $5.75	$6.00
Lot of 6 LAND BEFORE TIME Hand Puppets Set 1988	$25.00	McDonald's Large Translite Gift Certificates S/H5.75	$6.00
12 Hanna Barbera plush toys w/tent from Dairy Queen NIB	$23.59	McDonald's 1987 Crayola HM Boxes All 4 S/H $3.00	$6.00
ARBY'S Mr Men & Little Miss , Many In Package L@@K	$23.10	Carl's Jr 2002 PEANUTS Set of Four MIB!	$5.99
@@***** REMCO McDonald's	$21.01	12 Chip & Dale & Rescue Ranger Toys + Book	$5.95
Hamburglar on Card MIB *****@@		Mayor McCheese doll - McDonald's REMCO 1976	$5.50
39 Mini Football Helmets (Dairy Queen) 1970's	$20.50	MCD McDonalds NEOPETS Neopet Plush Doll Blue SHOYRU	$5.50
2005 McDonalds Madame Alexander, SET OF 10 in hand!!!	$20.00	DQ DAIRY QUEEN ICE CREAM 22 PC PLAY	$5.50
2005 Mcdonald's Madame Alexander, SET OF 10 in hand!!!	$20.00	FOOD SET NEW IN TUB	
BK Jimmy Neutron Rocketship Set 5 MIP+Bags*COOOL	$20.00	McDonald's 1991 Barbie Hot Wheels HM Bxs all 4 S/H3.00	$5.50
2004 Mcdonalds NEOPETS SET 16 Toys	$19.95	McDonald's Mickey's B'Dayland HM U3 Donald MIP S/H1.50	$5.00
2004 Mcdonalds NEOPETS SET 16 Toys	$18.95	McDonald's Mickey's B'Dayland HM U3 Goofy MIP S/H1.50	$5.00
[2 of these sold for $18.95 each]		McDonald's Mickey's B'Dayland HM U3 Mick&Min S/H1.50	$5.00
PLASTIC PLAY FOOD FOR THE KIDS! 60+ PIECES	$15.84	Rare- McDonalds Happy Meal Toys *Batman from 1991-93*	$5.00
McDonalds Walt Disney 50TH Anniversary Happy Meal Toys	$15.50	Mix Lot Of 11 Muppets Items Jim Henson Fast Food	$5.00

Games ▸ Board, Traditional Games

The average sales price in this subcategory is $18.12.

	HIGH		AVG
COSMIC ENCOUNTER - MAYFAIR GAMES 1991 MINT/SEALED	$235.94	New & SEALED 4x4 or 5x5 Ultimate BOGGLE DELUXE game	$19.99
Rail Baron Avalon Hill New in shrink NM/Mint OOP Super	$205.27	RARE Klondike GOLD RUSH Board Game 1975 Vintage Canada	$19.99
Blackbeard Board Game Avalon Hill LIKE NEW!	$169.55	Gnip Gnop Parker Brothers Slap - Happy Game 1971	$19.49
Advanced Civilization Avalon Hill Complete unused NM	$153.50	GAME DOG OPOLY MONOPOLY DOGOPOLY NEW SEALED	$19.00
CLEVELAND BROWNS CORNHOLE GAME	$149.99	Carcassonne (Rio Grande)	$18.95
4" x 1 3/4" EBONYWOOD/BOXWOOD CHESSET SLEEK & BEAUTIFUL	$125.00	Carcassonne: Hunters/Gatherers (Rio Grande)	$18.95
1972 MYSTERY DATE Game MILTON BRADLEY Exclnt COMPLETE !	$103.50	1976 Original Mastermind Master Mind game by Invicta	$18.50
FAMILY BUSINESS Mayfair Games 454 NEW SEALED RARE!	$71.00	*Unpunched* Druid - Boudicca's Rebellion by WEG - Rare!	$17.70
Civilization Avalon Hill Complete unused EXC unpunched	$70.00	4 1/4 " KING STAUNTON Tournament Chess Set NR	$17.00
Milton Bradley Voice of the Mummy Game 1971 NO RESERVE	$57.87	[2 of these sold for $17.00 each]	
Complete Go Traveller's Set Folding Shin-Kaya Go Game	$53.00	1982 Ideal Rubik's Race Game, Complete - Irwin - Cube	$17.00
Serial Killer: The Board Game of the 90s	$52.00	Hasbro Candyland Board Game Fleece Throw Blanket New	$16.95
Vintage 67 Kenner SPIROGRAPH 401 drawing toy w/new pen	$51.00	MILTON BRADLEY HERO QUEST GAME COMPLETE-LOAD!!!	$16.02
PUBLIC ASSISTANCE by HAMMERHEAD! POLITICALLY INCORRECT!	$51.00	NIB Wooden SHOGI PIECES & GAME BOARD Japan Chess	$16.00
YS Game by Ystari game NIB sealed New!	$49.99	1980 Milton Bradley Oh What A Mountain Board Game	$15.51

Games ▸ Electronic

The average sales price in this subcategory is $28.00.

	HIGH		AVG
Rare 1978 Bally's Star Trek Pinball Machine	$755.00	Original Electronic Simon ! 1978 Milton Bradley N Mint!	$31.00
Phantom Mirage Chess Computer by Excalibur	$510.00	VINTAGE SIMON SAYS & SUPER SIMON GAMES MILTON BRADLEY	$31.00
Brand New Sony PSP for $225.00 with Spider-Man 2 movie	$225.00	N64 Nintendo 64 Game System /4 Controllers *No Reserve*	$31.00
COMPLETE Dark Tower Electronic Board Game Works 1981	$177.50	Disney PRINCESS Plug and Play TV Game New VHTF Sold Out	$29.99
1981 DARK TOWER ELECTRONIC GAME	$153.50	Great game LIGHTNING REACTION $24.99	$29.99
M.B. COMPLETE WORKING		[2 of these sold for $29.99 each]	
The Challenger Classic Skill Bar Game Electric NO RES!	$139.50	VINTAGE 1970's MB electronic game SIMON original N MINT	$28.03
Chess Challenger Vintage Electronic Game Complete w/Box	$118.50	Play TV Huntin' 2 Game by Radica	$27.58
ESPN Game Station by Fisher Price basketball home 6	$117.50	VINTAGE SIMON GAME MILTON BRADLEY	$27.00
1981 Dark Tower Game Tower Works Near complete NR!	$108.50	W/ BOX, INSTRUCTIONS	
APBA Baseball ORIGINAL Season Data Disks - L@@K NOW	$100.00	NEW DISNEY PRINCESS PLUG AND PLAY TV GAME *NO RESERVE*	$26.00
Air Hockey Table	$98.99	1978 Vintage SIMON Says ELECTRONIC GAME Milton Bradley	$25.00
Hasbro Electronic Taboo Platinum Edition	$67.00	THE GAMBIT Chess Computer Game.....Very Rare	$25.00
MINT VTECH V-Smile Learning System w/3 Games VSMILE!	$64.00	Excalibur KingMaster III Electronic Chess 911E-3 329a	$24.99
Lot of 20 Games for SNES Super Nintendo *No Reserve*	$63.00	Electronic Battleship Advanced Mission Game Hasbro	$24.95
Champion 2250XL Chess Computer game	$60.99	L@@K!! Milton Bradley Simon Electronic Game 1979	$23.01

Games ▸ Miniatures, War Games

The average sales price in this subcategory is $13.60.

	HIGH		AVG
PRIVATEER PRESS -HORDES -EXPERTLY PAINTED TROLL AXER	$260.00	Blood Bowl Star Player Dwarf Deathroller	$15.00
War in Europe SPI/Decision Games M/UP	$227.50	Warmachine Cryx Satyxis Raiders War Unit NEW!!!	$14.99
Dark Tower	$162.50	MasterFront by Columbia Games	$14.57
Game Designers Workshop GDW Europa 7 game lot	$122.50	15mm flames of war NIB BR762 Rifle Platoon (Italy)	$14.53
15mm Napoleonic Prussian Line Infantry and Artillery	$76.61	2 Renegade Legion 1/285 METAL Heavy Tanks, Deliverers	$14.00
25mm ACW old glory unpainted figures	$76.00	2 Renegade Legion 1/285 METAL Heavy Tanks, Trajans	$14.00
La Regia Marina by Simulations Canada	$72.00	Star Wars Miniatures Revenge of the Sith Starter Game	$13.50
25mm Sudan Colonial Dismounted Camel Corp	$71.00	GDW- Blood & Thunder- shrinkwrapped	$13.25
Star Wars Miniatures 239 Figure Uncommon & common Lot!!	$71.00	Foundry 25mm-The B Team (Street Violence)	$13.21
Star Smuggler by Dwarfstar Games Gd Very Rare	$61.00	Padme Amidala Very Rare Star Wars Miniatures #21/60 CS	$13.06
Game Designers Workshop - EUROPA V - Their Finest Hour	$51.00	STAR WARS Clone Strike Miniatures Starter Set NEW Tiles	$13.02
Ivanhoe by GMT Games	$46.25	Commando Speeder Bike Star Wars Miniatures Rebel Storm	$13.00
Star Wars Miniatures Revenge of the Sith Lot of 28 Yoda	$46.00	Leia Captive Star Wars miniature 12 Rebel Storm VR	$12.95
15mm Old Glory Napoleonic Prussian Uhlans	$42.00	15mm flames of war NIB GE702 Grenadier Platoon	$12.62
GUNSLINGER Avalon Hill Old West OOP RARE	$41.69	new AD&D world of greyhawk #65 monster stoppers rare	$12.62

Games ▸ Role Playing

The average sales price in this subcategory is $14.05.

	HIGH		AVG
Huge Collection Of RPG Books, Boxed Sets, Etc.	$310.65	HOW TO HOST A MURDER TEEN HOT TIMES AT HOLLYWOOD HIGH	$15.52
DEADLANDS RPG Lot of 21Books + 37 Miniatures RAIL WARS	$300.00	Rolemaster Standard System RPG Talent Law ICE 5523	$15.00
4 VINTAGE AH GAMES SQUAD LEADER CROSS OF IRON	$145.00	Rifts Dimension Book 8: Naruni Wave 2 RPG	$15.00
2 VINTAGE SPI 1976 INVASION AMERICA WAR IN THE ICE	$115.49	Goblet! Game New In Package!	$14.99
SERENITY LIMITED EDITION LEATHER HARDCOVER RPG ED HC	$98.00	Lot of 8 RPG books! L@@K!!	$14.50
4 VINTAGE GDW WAR GAMES SOUTHERN FRONT TACFORCE	$91.00	XCRAWL D20	$14.25
6 VINTAGE SPI & AH WAR GAMES BLITZKRIEG BERLIN	$81.00	Palladium Rifts China 1 World Book 24: The Yama Kings	$14.00
Three TSR games: Boot Hill, Gamma World, Divine Right	$63.00	Rifts Dimension Book 7: Megaverse Builder RPG	$13.50
7 Deadlands Hell on Earth RPG Books Bundle #2 MSRP $135	$61.00	HOW TO HOST A MURDER MYSTERY GAME **SEALED NEW**	$13.02
Lot of 5 Palladium Rifts World Source Books & More!	$56.00	MURDER MYSTERY GAME ~~BREWING TROUBLE~~ 6-8 PLAYERS	$13.00
8 Deadlands Classic RPG Adventures MSRP $124.85	$52.00	Vallejo Paints: Set 08 Panzer Colors	$12.95
Huge lot of 10 Cyberpunk adventure RPG books Retail $95	$51.00	GURPS COMPENDIUM 1 CHARACTER CREATION NEW	$12.74
How To Host a Murder/Saturday Night Cleaver/brand new	$47.27	Murder Mystery Game SATURDAY NIGHT CLEAVER disco!	$12.50
2 VINTAGE AH GAMES AIR ASSAULT ON CRETE FORTRESS EUROPA	$42.00	Murder Alacarte Game Solve mystery dinner Halloween	$12.26
2 VINTAGE AH WAR GAMES PANZER LEADER PANZER BLITZ	$38.50	The Primal Order Chessboards RPG	$12.05

Model RR, Trains ▸ N Scale

The average sales price in this subcategory is $20.96.

	HIGH		AVG
NJ International Inc.PRR BRASS R 50 B-REEFER N-Scale	$203.50	DIGITRAX DN163K0b DCC DECODER KATO F3 A/B NEW	$22.38
Fleischmann Piccolo N Nazi Streamlined Steam Loco OB	$169.56	N Scale 3 New Atlas Single Sheathed Cars - Free Ship	$22.19
MicroAce 0652 Steam Typ 9800-9801 mallet	$133.52	1998 Kato Unitrack N Scale Track Plans Book	$21.96
N BRAWA 5260 Seil Schwebebahn Cable Car Set	$129.99	Fleischmann Piccolo N 4 Steel Sided Gondolas	$21.65
Roco Electric Train Trolley rare detailed runs great!	$122.49	Kato Business Car AT$SF "Santa Fe"	$21.55
Fleischmann Piccolo N BR 011 Steam Loco OB	$102.50	1998 Kato Unitrack N Scale Track Plans Book	$21.45
TOMIX 2116 JNR ELECTRIC LOCOMOTIVE EF 15 N SCALE	$91.00	CRANES—(3) ALL THE CRANES YOU WILL EVER NEED	$21.03
N-SCALE SANTA FE WARBONNET FT AB SET BRASS DETAIL!!	$81.00	eight cabooses n/scale	$20.75
N Scale 10 New Atlas Pines Trailers - Free Ship	$76.06	Model Power ALCO RSD-15, Santa Fe, new #7550	$20.56
N-SCALE SANTA FE CAT WHISKER FT AB SET BRASS DETAIL!	$76.00	N Scale Kato 45" x 23 3/8" Loop of Unitrack Track	$20.51
N SCALE HERITAGE NO. 7465 VAN SWERINGEN BERKSHIRE	$76.00	2 COTTON BELT 3 & 4 BAY COVERED HOPPERS W/MTS	$20.51
MicroAce 9708 Steamer Typ 9600 Heavy 2 eyes	$74.00	MTR Disneyland Hong Kong Subway Diecast Disney Train	$20.50
Burlington Northern 5 Unit Maxi-Stack III DELUXE	$72.69	MRC Tech II 2500 Power supply	$20.00
N Scale Kato Undecorated F40PH DCC Ready	$71.99	Fleischmann Piccolo N 7436 Railcar Center Coach OB	$19.99
N Scale USRA 2-8-2 w/Vandy Tender UP Model Power NIB!	$69.51	MTL 100030 ATSF STEEL CABOOSE W /CUSTOM REAR LIGHTS	$19.99

Model RR, Trains ▸ HO Scale

The average sales price in this subcategory is $25.23.

	HIGH		AVG
OLD HO BRASS 2-6-6-6 LOCOMOTIVE & TENDER VINTAGE TRAINS	$355.00	Vintage Gilbert HO 420 Lackawanna Railroad Engine Train	$30.95
OMI Overland Flexi-Van Mark II Flatcar Milw, NYC others	$240.00	HO KIT WESTERFIELD - SANTA FE STOCK CAR - NIB!	$30.00
Milw. Rd. B-W Caboose by Overland in Brass HO	$203.50	Vintage Gilbert HO Scale TANKER CAR	$28.50
Milw. Rd. B-W Caboose by Overland in Brass HO	$187.50	Athearn SD Tank Car 5PK Southern Pacific.	$27.00
Milw. Rd. B-W Caboose by Overland in Brass HO	$164.05	HO Athearn U-28-B Patomac & Southern #s 3300 & 3301	$26.56
HO BRASS OVERLAND GPEX EXPRESS MILK CAR	$162.50	HO metal?steam loco train engine NO RES MDC Roundhouse	$26.00
NEW HAVEN LIGHT 4-8-2 STEAM LOCO w/SOUND TRAXX DECODER	$150.00	4 BACHMANN LOCOMOTIVES (3 F3s, 1 U36B) SEE PICS	$25.25
BROADWAY LIMITED EMD SW7 P ll UP #1800 TEST RUN ONLY	$138.00	Central Valley California Fast Freight fruit car	$25.00
Mantua PRR CAMELBACK ATLANTIC LIKE NEW W/BOX	$119.50	Ho Trains 3 Boxed Athearn Black Undec. Passenger Train	$24.99
BALBOA EMD E8 HO	$113.79	Ho Trains US Army Engine Runs Great & Caboose Train	$24.99
VINTAGE BOXED TRU-SCALE 10 CARRIAGES HO WORK TRAIN SET	$107.50	Ambroid 1 of 5,000 "Speedy" poultry car	$24.60
Vintage Gilbert HO Scale Engine & Coal Car	$106.51	HO TRAIN LOT OF 5 OLD 40' BOXCARS METAL / TIN L@@K	$23.01
Lot of misc. HO engines, train engine, locomotive RR	$77.00	Wiking #897 02 37 Menck Cable Excavator Yellow 1/87	$22.99
TRAINS LOT OF 21	$73.00	VINTAGE TT HOBBIE BERLINER BAHNEN TRAIN SET IN BOXES NR	$22.01
METRO CARS HO	$72.77	HO SCALE train sets	$21.49

Model RR, Trains ▸ O Scale

The average sales price in this subcategory is $101.08.

	HIGH		AVG
25000+ Lionel & Train Store Stock Lot - Engines, Cars +	$16,100.00	NYC WHISTLING TENDER WITH LIONEL MOTOR	$124.49
Lionel Wall Clock never used MIB 4 Christmas gift	$331.01	LIONEL O GP-7 DIESEL LOCO TRAIN ALASKA NEW 6-28857	$120.00
MTH CRUSADER READING LINES	$304.00	LIONEL O scale, HO scale, train set s A MUST SEE	$113.50
ENG & PASS CARS 73" SOUND		LIONEL O FASTRACK TRAIN TRACK SET RIGHT LEFT SWITCHES	$107.50
Lionel F-3 Twin Motored Diesel Locomotive #2383	$250.00	LIONEL O SCALE THOMAS THE TANK TRAIN ST *SPECIAL DEAL*	$103.50
LIONEL O 2-8-4 BERKSHIRE LOCO PENNSY TRAIN TMCC 6-28709	$233.50	F.M TRAINMASTER DIESEL ENG. MTH USED TALK/ YARD SOUNDS	$102.50
LIONEL O 2-8-4 BERKSHIRE LOCO PENNSY TRAIN TMCC 6-28709	$213.51	CHRISTMAS 4-6-2 DIECAST STEAM ENGINE W/CHRISTMAS TUNES	$100.00
LIONEL MISCELLANEOUS CARS - 24 CARS	$200.00	LIONEL O GP-7 DIESEL LOCO TRAIN ALASKA NEW 6-28857	$100.00
LIONEL O 2-8-4 POLAR EXPRESS TRAIN SET **SPECIAL DEAL**	$193.03	UNION PACIFIC DIESEL ENG. MTH USED CREW TAKING ++	$99.01
LIONEL O 2-8-4 POLAR EXPRESS TRAIN SET **SPECIAL DEAL**	$191.50	LIONEL O SCALE THOMAS THE TANK TRAIN ST *SPECIAL DEAL*	$96.00
LIONEL O 2-8-4 LOCO SANTA FE TRAIN RAILSOUNDS 6-28671	$177.50	MTH NYC 70ft streamlined passenger 2 car add on Lionel	$86.00
LIONEL ROTARY SNOW PLOW #58 GREAT NORTHERN N/R	$159.59	LIONEL 19559 MKT STOCK CAR (GIRLS SET)	$80.95
Lionel FASTRACK O36 REMOTE SWITCH Outer Pass Loop NEW!	$149.95	LIONEL COAL LOADER O GAUGE ~ WORKS!	$80.00
LIONEL 8687 JERSEY CENTRAL DIESEL NR	$143.53	NEW YORK CENTRAL 4-6-2 DIECAST STEAM ENGINE	$80.00
SOUTHERN PACIFIC DIESEL SWITCHER #18503	$140.00	LIONEL O FASTRACK 30 INCH STRAIGHT TRAIN TRACK 8 PIECES	$79.00

Model RR, Trains ▸ G Scale

The average sales price in this subcategory is $33.35.

	HIGH		AVG
MTH Gauge 1 Clinchfield Challenger 4-6-6-4	$839.99	MDC G-SCALE HOPPER CAR	$34.34
BRIDGEWERKS "MAG 200" 2 TRACK CONTROLLER MUST SEE	$409.75	BACHMANN BIG HAULER AT & SF LOCOMOTIVE & TENDER	$34.33
Arito-Craft PPR Pacific 4-6-2 Steam Loco G scale train	$250.01	10 PAIRS BLACK METAL WHEELS FOR LGB USA BACH	$34.15
3-foot Classic models drop gondola	$250.00	G Scale Two Handcrafted Wood Gondolas	$34.00
Kalamazoo Virginia & Truckee Passenger Set OB G SCALE	$231.40	REA C OF G - REA 46005 Box Car	$34.00
Accucraft Brass Coach	$219.50	10 PAIRS SILVER METAL WHEELS FOR LGB USA BACH	$33.99
Holiday Express Train Set G scale New Bright NEW	$175.27	Two Custom Reading Hopper Car MDC not LGB Aristo	$33.00
HARTLAND "G" SCALE 4-4-0 FIRST RUN LOCOMOTIVE NIB	$165.83	Rare Delton Dr. Pepper Silver Box Car Unused 4255D LGB	$33.00
G-SCALE Union Pacific Train (R13) Set	$160.86	10 PAIRS SILVER METAL WHEELS FOR LGB USA BACH	$32.99
AMS? DRGW Caboose NEW ITEM NIB	$159.00	10 PAIRS SILVER METAL WHEELS FOR LGB USA BACH	$32.99
A CLASSIC "G" GAUGE LOCOMOTIVE BY HEARTLAND LOCO WORK	$139.95	REA G GAUGE RAILWAY EXPRESS AGENCY CABOOSE NMIB NO RES	$32.00
G Scale Heritage Express Set	$132.45	MDC G-SCALE HOPPER CAR	$31.99
REA Diesel Locomotive - ALCO FA-1 "G" Scale	$127.51	10 PAIRS BLACK METAL WHEELS FOR LGB USA BACH	$31.01
G SCALE Old Abandoned Hotel Wood Building 1/24 scale	$112.50	BUDDY L G TRAIN LIMITED EDITION BOX CAR SANTA FE 52002	$31.00
G Scale Delton Hartland D&RGW Railbus - Doozie	$110.99	Model Masterpieces C&S 2 Story House ? Scale	$31.00

Models, Kits ▸ Air

The average sales price in this subcategory is $18.95.

	HIGH		AVG
B-50 BALSA WOOD AIRPLANE KIT BY T-M-H-K NIB	$450.00	Verlinden F-14 Super Detail Set 1/48 Scale Kit 427	$20.25
Aurora, Vintage Lightning P-38, Unbuilt, No Reserve	$147.50	Monogram B-52 Stratofortress: Kit 5709 NEW	$20.01
AURORA P-40 FLYING TIGER "NOS" 44A-69 AIRPLANE	$112.50	COX NOMAD GRAVITY RESISTANT FLYING MACHINE	$20.00
1971 MONOGRAM SKYSTICK CONTROLLER W/P-51 MUSTANG MIB	$110.91	SPACECRAFT/AIRCRAFT/AUTO PLASTIC MODEL KIT VALUE GUIDE	$19.99
KMC AA Boeing B727-200 Limited Edition 1:72 Scale model	$103.50	Fine Molds 1/48 Daimler-Benz DB601A Engine with MG17.	$19.99
1946 CLEVELAND ATC C47 AIRPLANE MODEL KIT	$102.50	DML 1/48 FOKKER Dr.1 "Knights/Sky" Model Parts	$19.50
RARE SEALED VINTAGE 1968 MONOGRAM BOEING SST MODEL KIT!	$66.00	Sky Marks American Airlines MD-80 New	$19.19
Vintage AURORA Eastern DC-9 Commercial Jet model Kit	$53.99	AURORA WWI BLACK MARIA SOPWITH TRIPLANE 1963 NIB	$17.05
Aurora F6F Hellcat kit No 40-100 unbuilt kit	$53.00	TWA MODEL DC9 AIRPLANE FOR PARTS OR ???	$17.00
DC-3 6'4" Paper Model of the World's Most Famous Plane	$51.00	Revell, Dornier Do 27, 1/32	$16.51
U-FLY-IT Piper Cherokee Instructor Pilot Set Plane Kit	$51.00	AMT A-7E Corsair II 1/48 Scale Kit 8861	$16.50
Beech Bonanza V-35 1/48 & Piper Cherokee 1/36 2 kits	$46.55	Vintage AURORA Northrop P-61 BLACK WIDOW Model Kit	$16.32
MONOGRAM CESSNA 180 FLOAT PLANE	$46.00	==> Monogram 1/48 NAA AT-6 Texan (Sealed T-6/SNJ)	$16.06
1/72 CESSNA 425 CORSAIR RESIN KIT	$46.00	Academy/Mini Craft GE F-111E 1/48 Scale Kit 1689	$16.00
1/48 Hasegawa Fine Molds Japanese KIKKA jet *Me-262	$45.00	CLEVELAND MODELS 1950's U/C KIT	$15.99

Models, Kits ▶ Automotive

The average sales price in this subcategory is $22.52.

	HIGH		AVG
1/43 BBR Ferrari F40 24H LeMans 1995 "PILOT"	$280.07	Sand Bagger Model	$25.00
1/43 Gasoline BBR Ferrari F399 GP Malaysia 1999	$270.00	BUILD AND DETAIL MODEL CARS LIKE A PRO DESIGN CUSTOM	$24.95
1/43 BBR Ferrari F310B G.P. Canada 1997 M. Schumacher	$218.50	ERTL AMT Caterpillar D8H Bulldozer Plastic Model Kit	$24.95
1/43 BBR Ferrari 412 T1 G.P. Brasile 1994 J. Alesi	$208.00	JUNKYARD OF PLASTIC AUTO MODEL KIT PARTS/TIRES/ENGINES!	$24.55
Lamborghini Gallardo - Audi - Set MR - Look Smart 1:43	$157.50	PINEWOOD DERBY SPEED KIT #1005 (SUPER FAST)	$24.51
BIG SCALE 1/12 PORSCHE 917K LEMANS 70 NOT 1/18 , 1/43	$154.00	HUBLEY MODEL A ROADSTER METAL KIT MIB	$23.00
AMT 1953 Ford Indy 500 Pace Car Promo 1/25th Built	$125.01	Garage Kit for display of 1/24 model cars, NASCAR etc.	$22.26
Pinewood Derby Car!! (250 GT LWB)	$122.50	3 Camaro models	$22.19
Revell Funster Chevy Factory Sealed	$112.79	1/25 '56 Ford Hardtop mild custom built	$22.00
Tamiya 1:12 Ferrari 312B F1 No Reserve	$112.50	1/24 shelf rack detailed for your diorama	$21.50
JAGUAR XJ-S COUPE Plastic Model Kit (1970s/1980s) Entex	$102.50	Revell 1/25 41 WILLYS Competition Coupe Plastic Model	$21.07
AMR#07 Callaway Car LM '94 Race#51 No Le Phoenix 1/43	$100.00	Testors 1/18 1934 Duesenberg Metal Model Kit NIB	$20.50
Ferrari 312 T3 SUPER KIT By Tameo 1/43 #TMK 335 WOW!!!	$92.27	1990 BLUE PRINTER SERVICE TRAILER SEALED UNBUILT KIT	$20.50
Diorama 1/24 scale tools, supplies, figurines, 4 garage	$77.07	1/25 '59 Ford Retractable Top built	$20.50
LOT OF COLLECTABLE CAR MODELS, SEALED LIMITED EDITION	$75.00	Lee Town HO Mack Truck w/Double Bottom Tank Trlrs .	$20.49

Models, Kits ▶ Military

The average sales price in this subcategory is $18.79.

	HIGH		AVG
Winchester Signal Cannon	$406.07	Pegasus 1/72 Reggiane Re2005 OOP MIB	$19.99
Built 1/32 F-105D Thunderchief	$215.50	PEGASUS 1/72 Curtiss P-40Q Bubble Top	$19.38
Pre-Aurora Saunders Swadar Fairchild XC-120 Pack Plane	$148.07	Brand New Guillows German Rumpler C5 WWI Model Kit	$19.31
Monogram B-52 Young Astronauts Issue 1/72 Scale SEALED	$131.50	Monogram, B-24D Liberator, 1/48, Model, (m11)	$19.06
Built 1/48 B-25J Mitchell "Jaunty Jo"	$130.39	GUILLOWS BALSA WOOD WWI FOKKER FLYING AIRPLANE MODEL	$19.00
Built 1/48 F-86F-30 Sabre Mike's Bird	$100.00	Zvezda 1/72 IL-4 Soviet Long- Range Bomber	$19.00
MPC Commandoes Strike at Dawn Diorama/ Playset Kit	$91.00	DID Dragon 1/6 WW2 German Infantry uniform etc. NICE	$18.99
MIG-21 Fishbed Wood Desktop Display Model Airplane	$72.00	1965 Revell 1/28 Frank Luke SPAD XIII sealed	$18.50
P-47 Thunderbolt Gabreski Wood Display Model Airplane	$69.00	LOT OF 4 BANDAI 1/48 FIELD WORK ACCESSORY SETS	$18.05
A-6 Intruder USMC Wood Desktop Display Model Airplane	$69.00	SALE! - E14Y Glen - 1/48 - Wings Models	$17.95
F-86 Sabre USAF Wood Desktop Display Model Airplane	$69.00	WANT_IT_RUSTED_&_WEATHERED?__NOTHING_DOES_IT_BETTER!	$17.94
Pre-Aurora Comet Cessna 310 mint kit # PL-25	$60.00	[3 of these sold in a multiple item ("Dutch") auction for $5.98 each]	
PBY-5A CATALINA BY MONOGRAM C/R 1955	$56.52	Aero72 1/72 Hawker Hector plastic kit	$17.50
HUGE AIRPLANE MODEL 26" WINGS	$56.00	AICHI E13A1b "JAKE" 1/48 by Nichimo.	$17.28
1960,S ERA MILITARY		MONOGRAM 1/48 SCALE F-5E TIGER II MIB	$17.27
POCHER TORINO CANNON MODEL KIT UNASSEMBLED NIB	$52.00	Revell, Dornier Do 27, 1/32	$16.51

Outdoor Toys, Structures ▶ Ride-Ons, Tricycles

The average sales price in this subcategory is $44.80.

	HIGH		AVG
Radio Flyer Bundle - Tricycles, Ride-ons, Wagons	$1,227.00	skipper barbies little sister	$49.03
VINTAGE 1930'S PLAYBOY WAGON not tricycle RIDING TOY	$649.95	Radio Flyer Town and Country Wagon Model #24 - NIB!!!	$47.00
American Tricycle 1930s	$450.00	Power Wheels Barbie Cool Tunes Pink Jeep	$46.99
Farmall 560 Tractor and Wagon (McCormick)	$280.00	Kettler Tricycle with Pushbar	$46.00
1950sMURRAY FIRE PATROL 3 WHEEL PEDALCAR NICE ORGINAL	$255.00	POWER WHEELS BARBIE BEACH PATROL 12V JEEP - SHIP	$46.00
RARE Antique 1930's "GREYHOUND DE-LUXE" Pull Wagon !	$249.00	Classic Little Red Wagon - All Terrain - NEW	$45.00
VINTAGE MOTORCYCLE PLAYGROUND BOUNCING RIDE ON TOY	$220.47	VINTAGE FOOT POWERED SCOOTER OR BICYCLE?????	$45.00
RESTORED COLSON 20" TRICYCLE - RED/GOLD W/ORIG. PARTS	$199.99	Power Wheels Yellow Volkswagon Beetle bug 6 VOLT	$43.55
John Deere Gator Peg Perego Car Truck Jeep	$177.50	Little Tikes Tykes Black PICK UP TRUCK Ride On RARE NR	$43.00
John Deere GATOR 4x2 Ride-on Peg Perego	$177.50	FISHER PR POWER WHEELS RIDE ON SAFARI JEEP! NO RESERVE!	$42.00
Big Made in England MOBO Kids Riding Horse X-CLEAN	$172.23	New Battery Kid Children Ride On Bike Train REMOTE Whte	$41.05
Peg Perego Santa Fe Express Train-RIDE-ON!–FREE SHIP	$159.99	Little Tikes Tykes Whirly Rocket discontinued	$41.01
50s? SUPPER SONDA VERY NICE ORGINAL Pedal scooter	$144.50	Todays Kids Zebra Ride On	$41.00
Rally Cart Go Kart Power Wheels Hotwheels Electric	$132.50	**NEW** DELUXE RUNABOUT STAKE WAGON (fits two toddlers)	$41.00
POWER WHEELS JEEP WRANGLER 4 TWO RIDE ON TOY CAR	$130.00	Power wheels kids go cart	$40.00

Outdoor Toys, Structures ▶ Sand, Water Toys

The average sales price in this subcategory is $48.62.

	HIGH		AVG
NEW ALUMINUM ELEVATOR BOAT LIFT 6000LB	$2,520.00	VINTAGE TIN SAND PAIL, STORY OF PETER RABBIT. J. CHEIN	$47.55
Sunray Premium Playset by Rainbow	$1,000.00	NIB Super soaker CPS 4100 squirt gun water toy	$41.57
New Jet Ski Lift PWC Lift Boat Lift	$610.50	Huge Monster redo SUPER SOAKER CPS 4100 Water Gun NEW	$40.99
Outdoor Wooden Swingset/Clubhouse Set	$350.00	Nice 30s Am. Sandpail with Children chasing Butterflies	$37.99
1950s? 60s? LASSIE WONDER DOG SWIM RING. RARE NR	$331.75	SUPER SOAKER CPS 4100 Water Gun Watergun NEW HUGE 86oz	$36.99
Six Flags Banzai Falls 19' Water Slide	$300.00	LIMITED EDITION SUPER SOAKER 7 FT TALL WATER ROCKET	$36.00
Six Flags Banzai Falls Quickset Water Slide	$256.51	OLD VINTAGE CHILDRENS OHIO ART SAND BEACH PAIL BUCKET	$33.99
Banzai Falls Wave Rider Waterslide	$157.50	INFLATABLE BEACH BALLS 24" CLOSEOUT 72 pc case 31005-S	$32.88
Nice 20's Ohio Art Sandpail with 3 Kids at the Beach	$152.83	Vintage Ohio Art Sand Pail, Farming Scenes	$32.52
super soaker water gun moster XL	$111.11	Little Tikes Sand and Water Table Toys	$32.02
Little Tikes 8 in1 playset with slides	$100.00	DOUBLE INFLATABLE FLOATING POOL BED LOUNGE FLOAT 58895	$31.95
T Cohn Childs Tin Sand Pail C1930s Children Swimming!	$98.00	The Original Tupperware Sand Pails –New!	$30.66
Little Tikes Dump Truck Sand Box Sandbox Climber	$71.00	KIDS GAZEBO 3- IN -1 POOL SANDBOX SAND BOX PLAY HOUSE	$29.99
Yoo-Hoo Chocolate Milk Ball 54 Inches Around BIG BALL	$63.00	NEW INFLATABLE CROCODILE/ALLIGATOR	$29.00
5x 250 yard water balloon launcher slingshot WHOLESALE	$55.35	3-in-1 Gazebo - Pool, Sandbox, Playcenter	$28.00

Outdoor Toys, Structures ▸ Swings, Slides, Gyms

The average sales price in this subcategory is $86.92.

	HIGH		AVG
Sunray Premium Playset by Rainbow	$1,000.00	SWING SET, wood, with 2 swings, slide, and fort	$102.50
Rainbow Play System Backyard Circus	$605.50	Step 2 Fort - Castle Climber Gym	$102.50
Swing set with Fort	$599.00	Little Tikes 8 in1 playset with slides	$100.00
Outlook II Wooden Play Center & Swing Set NIB	$566.00	Little Tikes Climber Slide	$91.00
Cedar Works Playset with Swings and Climber Unit	$561.00	SPRING SWINGS FUN RIDE SUPER-Z CABLE ZIP LINE	$89.98
Creative Playthings Wooden Swing Set	$454.93	Step 2 Slide & Playhouse, No Reserve, Columbus, OH	$89.00
Step2 Step 2 Naturally Playful Clubhouse Climber Slide	$389.95	Childrens Play House for Little Tikes-NIB-PU-Ma or Ship	$86.00
[2 of these sold for $389.95 each]		Little Tikes Tykes Jungle Climber Gym Slide	$86.00
Step2 Step 2 Naturally Playful Clubhouse Climber Slide	$389.95	Little Tikes Wave Climber Slide in Excellent Condition	$86.00
Step 2 Naturally Playful Clubhouse Climber Slide	$365.01	Little Tikes (Tykes) Playhouse Castle w/ Slide DFW area	$84.02
Step2 Step 2 Naturally Playful Welcome Home Playhouse	$364.95	Little tikes slide, gym, climber,treehouse	$80.00
Step 2 Cluhouse Climber Playhouse for Little Tikes! NR	$351.01	Vintage Saddlemate Spring Toy (Bee)	$80.00
Outdoor Wooden Swingset/Clubhouse Set	$350.00	100' Mammoth Zip Line, cable discolored- discount.	$80.00
Little Tikes Play Center Play house with Swing Set	$350.00	LITTLE TIKES 8 in 1 ADJUSTABLE	$77.50
18x16 SPORT AIRENA MOONWALK BOUNCE JUMP SLIDE NEW	$349.00	PLAYGROUND & SLIDE FL	
AirEna Sport Park BOUNCE HOUSE (MoonWalk) 16' X 12' NEW	$345.00	Vintage Saddlemate Spring Toy (Rabbit)	$77.00

Outdoor Toys, Structures ▸ Tents, Tunnels, Playhut

The average sales price in this subcategory is $138.96.

	HIGH		AVG
Lazer Maze Bounce House - Moonwalk Lazer Tag Jump House	$4,900.00	Tool King 1.0HP Blower Bounce Houses, Moonwalks Save$	$194.99
1 New Inflatable bounce house moonwalk jumper jump	$2,850.00	INFLATABLE JUMP BOUNCE OBSTACLE	$190.00
1 New Inflatable bounce house moonwalk jumper jump	$2,000.00	FUN ROOM MOONWALK NEW!	
New Obstacle Course Bounce House, Moonwalk SAVE$$	$1,449.99	inflatable bounce house moonwalk slide DOLLY FREE SHIP	$189.99
1 New Inflatable bounce house moonwalk jumper jump	$1,300.00	Bounce House Jump Castle Moonwalk	$177.50
Kid's Playhouse~Victorian~Childrens Size 8'x 10'	$1,195.00	PLAY HOUSE	$175.00
BOUNCE HOUSE/MOON BOUNCE PRINCESS JUMPER	$1,000.00	NEW B-Air 1HP Blower for Bounce Houses, Moonwalks	$169.00
BRAND NEW MOONWALK, U.S. MADE SPORTS ARENA & B-BALL HOO	$810.00	NIB BOUNCE ROUND UTLIMATE SPORTS 5 IN 1 ARENA	$132.50
moon walk	$800.00	BOUNCE ROUND JUMPER 9 X 9 KIDS BOUNCE HOUSE W/FAN	$127.50
NEW INFLATABLE BOUNCE HOUSE	$765.00	LittleTikes Tykes Patio Playhouse SD CA	$125.00
JUMPING MOONWALK NO RESERVE		LITTLE TIKES LOG CABIN BIG PLAYHOUSE house tykes! LI,NY	$122.50
HUGE Inflatable Jump Bounce Castle House Moonwalk	$560.00	Fisher Price Little Tikes Castle, Tent, Rocket Climber	$117.50
HUGE Inflatable Jump Bounce Castle House Moonwalk	$460.00	Inflatable Bouncer Castle Children Toys Daycares School	$109.99
MOONWALK dino	$415.00	Little Tikes Cottage Green Roof Playhouse PU/NJ or SHIP	$100.00
HUGE INFLATABLE JUMP BOUNCE CASTLE HOUSE MOONWALK	$405.00	SLAM-N-HOOPS INFLATABLE BOUNCER Obstacle Wall Climber	$98.90
HUGE INFLATABLE JUMP BOUNCE CASTLE HOUSE MOONWALK	$405.00	Little Tikes Playhouse COTTAGE Boy or Girl	$91.00

Pretend Play, Preschool ▸ Brio

The average sales price in this subcategory is $22.82.

	HIGH		AVG
Deluxe 150 pc Thomas - Brio Train Set	$177.50	Brio Wheelbarrow and Garden Tools	$25.00
157 PIECE BRIO TRAIN SET/SETS LIKE NEW CONDITION	$162.50	BRIO World Trains LORD OF THE ISLES GREAT WESTERN TRAIN	$24.99
220 Pc. Lot Genuine Brio Train, Farm, Firehouse Sets	$150.00	NIB BRIO Intermediate Suspension Bridge Set #33030	$24.99
Rail and Road Transportation Set - Brio - New in Box	$149.99	NIB 3 BRIO Curious George SeTs Zoo Keeper Train Wagons	$24.99
Brio Thomas The Tank Train Track LOT 110 Pieces	$127.50	NIB Bob The Builder & Muck 16 pc Starter Train SeT BRIO	$24.99
Brio train set with Nilo table	$125.00	[2 of these sold for $24.99 each]	
New! 6 SETS Brio Bob the Builder-Lofty, Muck, Travis...	$109.00	Large Set of Wood Train Track with Trains and People	$22.02
BRIO size TRAIN TABLE / FOLDING PLAY TABLE	$108.17	New Plan Toy Brio Wooden Doll Family/garden/camping/WOW	$22.02
GENUINE BRIO WOODEN TRAIN TRACK 83 PIECES THOMAS BOB	$80.01	Brio - Colored Blocks - 100 Pcs - New in Box	$22.00
119 PC. WOODEN TOY TRAIN SET - Brio, Thomas, ELC	$80.00	BRIO Pirates Wooden Railway Set, Lot of 2 items!	$21.99
LARGE ROCKING DACHSHUND DOG Brio Wooden Rocker Wood	$77.76	THOMAS & FRIENDS WOODEN RAILWAY FIGURE 8 SET	$21.95
Brio Train Table and trains	$76.00	ERTL THOMAS & FRIENDS WOOD WATERFALL TUNNEL	$21.95
145+ HUGE LOT BRIO TRACK BRIDGES TRAINS + TABLE PLANS !	$73.12	Brio Train Set - 18 pcs Wooden Track- Battery car plus	$21.63
Huge Brio Lot Curved Straight Track Tunnel Trains	$73.00	NIB BRIO Richard Scarry Lowly Worm and Apple Car #32510	$21.51
55piece Brio comp. Lot Lionel Express Track w/6Engines	$72.22	Thomas the Tank Engine Mountain Overpass	$21.50

Pretend Play, Preschool ▸ Brio Compatible

The average sales price in this subcategory is $24.41.

	HIGH		AVG
Wooden Train Set, Table & Trundles. Thomas & Brio comp.	$182.50	BRIO COMPATIBLE TRAIN TRACK, SIGNS, BUILDINGS 50+ PIECE	$26.00
HUGE LOT!! Brio, Thomas, Wood Train Table, Cars & Track	$182.50	Brio Compatible Imaginarium Wooden Train Set Wood #2	$25.99
Wooden Train Set, Table & Trundles. Thomas & Brio comp.	$175.00	THOMAS/BRIO COMP. TRAIN SET W/ STORAGE BOX	$25.00
Wooden Train Set, Table & Trundles. Thomas & Brio comp.	$175.00	SESAME STREET WOODEN TRAIN SET ~ BRIO COMP	$24.99
NEW HUGE Wood Train Table Thomas the Tank Engine / Brio	$129.99	ROUNDHOUSE TURNTABLE TRAIN TUNNEL FITS THOMAS TRAINS	$24.99
GIANT KIDKRAFT WOODEN 147	$108.99	Brio Polar Express Battery Powered Train	$24.99
PC TRAIN SET BRIO/THOMAS		Brio Compatible Wooden Train Wood Set #9	$24.25
[3 of these sold for $108.99 each]		LOT WOOD TOY TRAIN BRIO & THOMAS THE TANK ENGINE	$23.00
NEW 100 Piece Train Set Thomas the Tank & Brio + Bonus!	$105.49	Brio Compatible Imaginarium Wooden Train Set Wood #5	$22.51
New-Wooden Activity Table W/Mountain Train Set	$94.09	80 pc Lg WOODEN TRAIN Set BRIO THOMAS CARS, TRACKS MORE	$22.49
NEW BIG Wood Train Table Thomas the Tank Engine / Brio	$89.99	Large Set of Wood Train Track with Trains and People	$22.02
Britt Allcroft Thomas the Tank Toy Train Set	$77.00	Lionel Great Railway Adventure Torpedo Brio Thomas Comp	$21.62

	HIGH		AVG
55piece Brio comp. Lot Lionel Express Track w/6Engines		LOT OF 72 PIECES WOODEN TRAIN SET,BRIO/EICHHORN TRAINS	$20.50
POTTERY BARN KIDS CLASSIC TRAIN SET BRIO IN BOX $119	$72.22	100 Piece Wood Train Set Brio & Thomas Tank Compatible	$20.26
[2 of these sold for $69.99 each]	$69.99	Woody Click farm set 48 pieces new in box 3 & up nr	$20.00

Pretend Play, Preschool ▶ Dishes, Tea Sets

The average sales price in this subcategory is $14.83.

	HIGH		AVG
AKRO AGATE STIPPLED BAND CHILD'S TEASET,ORIGINAL BOX!	$149.99	Antique German Aluminum Child's Silverware Play Set	$15.50
THREE LITTLE KITTENS CHILD'S TIN TEA SET MIB 1940's	$129.49	Lot of Play Food, Dishes, Pots, Pans, etc. OVER 100 PCs	$15.50
WOLVERINE SUNNY SUZY CHILDS TIN TEA SET DELFT BLUE	$118.49	Kids Miniature Tea Set Dollhouse Pretend Play GirlsToys	$15.50
BLUE WILLOW PORCELAIN CHILD'S TEASET,ORIGINAL BOX!	$89.99	190 Pieces of Dishes/Pans~Little Tikes~Fisher Price~ +	$15.00
Ohio Art Black SquirrelTin Dishes - Vintage 1920s!	$86.99	DOLLHOUSE DISHES & COMPLETE SILVERWEAR SERVICE FOR 4	$14.99
Tin Toy Litho Art CHILDREN'S TEA SET WOLVERINE ohio USA	$70.99	Child's Tin Litho Wolverine Pretend Step-on Can Dutch	$14.99
LITTLE HOSTESS TEA PARTY SET IN ORGINAL BOX	$58.55	Two 13 Piece Raggedy Ann & Andy China Tea Sets - NIB	$14.99
Ohio Art BLUEBIRDS & BLOSSOMS tin TEASET 1920's NR	$57.52	VINTAGE MINI CHILDS TEA SET ...RED LETTER JAPAN	$14.50
LITTLE HOSTESS PARTY SET HAZEL ATLAS 1940'S	$53.01	Very unique Ceramic Childs tea set new bunnies adorable	$14.49
36 pc MY KITCHEN PLAYSET!! *NEW*	$49.99	Huge Pretend Play Food Lot - SWEETS & DESSERTS Yum Yum!	$13.51
VINTAGE GOLD MEDAL CHILDS PASTRY SET W/BOX 1950'S	$46.06	NEW! Kids Pretend Play Cash Register Food Money Kitchen	$13.51
Ohio Art Pfaltzgraff Yorktowne Childs Set 26 Pieces	$46.01	5 tin/Aluminum Child Size Pots	$13.49
Gorgeous Vintage Child's Tea Set Moss Rose Pattern, Toy	$46.00	Molly Brett Fairy Tea set 13 pc NIB	$12.99
2 Vintage Childs Tupperware Mini Serve-it & Fix It Sets	$43.50	RABBIT GARDEN PARTY TEA SET CHINA 20PC HANDPAINTED MIB	$12.99
NEW MUD PIE PRINCESS HEART 13 PC CHILDS CERAMIC TEA SET	$41.99	Chenille and Fabric ICE CREAM SHOP double dip cones!	$12.99

Pretend Play, Preschool ▶ Dress-Up, Costumes

The average sales price in this subcategory is $17.09.

	HIGH		AVG
Peanuts Plush SNOOPY Costume Halloween Toddler 4-6 NIP	$127.50	Girls Disney Cinderella Costume w/wand& Headband &Shoes	$18.50
NWT Disney THE INCREDIBLES Violet Costume L 10/12 Large	$88.00	Disney Buzz Lightyear Costume Size 4-6 FUN!!	$18.01
MULAN DRESS SIZE L 10/12 FAN,SHOES WIG CROWN DISNEY	$55.52	SHREK 2 DELUXE COSTUME CHILD S (4-6)	$17.50
NWT- Disney Store Snow White 3 Pc Costume Sz 2-3	$51.00	SHREK 2 DELUXE COSTUME CHILD MEDIUM (SIZE 8-10)	$17.50
NEW Tom Arma Ladybug Costume 6-12 months	$51.00	Girls Disney Jasmine Costume XS 4/5 Green/Gold	$17.50
DISNEY SNOW WHITE HALLOWEEN COSTUME - SZ 7/8	$49.99	Halloween Costume or Dress-up Black Cat sz 2T 3T 4T	$17.50
Tom Arma Skunk 18-24mo. Costume	$46.00	DISNEY RESORT/DISNEY STORE TINKERBELL COSTUME SM 6-6X	$17.00
HUGE LOT 8 DRESS UP COSTUME 20 + PC 4 - 6	$46.00	NEW BATMAN ROBIN DELUXE HALLOWEEN COSTUME 4-6 FREE SHIP	$17.00
Disney Cinderella LIGHT UP dress princess costume 4 5 6	$46.00	Carebear Halloween Costume size 2T-4T	$17.00
Halloween Belle Costume. Disney Store Sz 8/10 Like new	$42.05	DISNEY STORE ARIEL COSTUME W/SHOES	$17.00
NIP Disney's W.I.T.C.H. WILL costume size 7-8 M HTF!!!	$42.00	ROYAL KNIGHTS DELUXE ARMOR SET (COSTUME) KIDS	$16.85
Disney's Sleeping Beauty Costume, Size 4-6, w/Crown!!!!	$40.51	Disney Princess Belle Dress Up Costume Deluxe 3 and up	$16.75
Disney Princess lot costumes dress up clothing shoes	$40.22	DISNEY STORE PETER PAN COSTUME SIZE 4/5	$16.50
DISNEY STORE INCREDIBLES COSTUME DASH SIZE S SMALL 6 6X	$40.00	DISNEY LI SHANG Mulan Costume Boys XS NEW	$16.50
Disney Incredibles Violet Costume Size 4 / 6 SM	$39.99	Barbie Girls Dress Up Costume Tutu Fairy Wand Halloween	$16.50

Pretend Play, Preschool ▶ Fisher Price

The average sales price in this subcategory is $15.21.

	HIGH		AVG
HUGE LOT vintage Fisher Price little people Playskool	$157.50	Vintage Fisher Price Cash Register COMPLETE Retired NR	$15.50
VINTAGE FISHER PRICE UNISEX SECURITY BUNNY BLANKET - NR	$132.50	GeoTrax *Workin' Town Remote Control Train* + Cars R/C	$15.50
FISHER PRICE - MISS PIGGY & KERMIT FROG DRESS UP MUPPET	$130.69	677 Fisher Price 1975 Picnic Basket with Original Box	$15.50
BRAND NEW AMAZING AMANDA @9.99 NO RESERVE 1 DAY AUCTION	$127.50	NEW Geo Trax Sky High Suspension Bridge GEOTRAX NIB HTF	$15.50
LN HUGE LOT GEOTRAX Clocktower/Fire Station/Mt Blast+	$112.50	1974 FISHER PRICE CASH REGISTER W/ 6 COINS	$15.50
FISHER PRICE - JIM HENSON - GREAT GONZO DRESS UP MUPPET	$107.50	Fisher Price 8 Vintage Cash Register Coins	$15.50
Fisher-Price - Music Box Record Player - #995 - 1975	$104.50	GeoTrax Geo Trax Bayshore Drawbridge New NIB	$15.00
Dora's Talking Kitchen Free Ship New Item!	$90.00	geo trax OCEANSIDE FLIER ~REMOTE~ Fisher Price Geotrax	$14.99
Vintage Fisher Price Castle Set 1970's NR	$83.00	Fisher Price~Rumple Bear~Dark Chocolate Brown~1993	$14.99
Huge Lot of Geo Trax-128 pieces Mint Condition!	$82.00	FISHER PRICE COWBOYS + BRONCO BULL + HORSES!!	$14.51
FISHER PRICE WOODSEY SQUIRREL UNCLE FILBERT WITH BOX	$50.02	FISHER PRICE FLIP TRACK RAIL & ROAD 2 SETS GEOTRAX LOT	$14.50
HUGE LOT Of Fisher Price MY FRIEND Dolls & Clothes~VGC!	$41.00	Barbie Time to Cook Barbie Kitchen New	$14.50
Fisher Price Laugh and Learn Learning Home	$40.00	FISHER PRICE TOOL BOX KIT & WORKBENCH WORKSHOP STAND	$14.50
Vintage Fisher Price Sesame Street Set 1970's NR	$39.00	Fisher Price Loving Family Castle Furniture & Princess	$14.49
FISHER PRICE PIRATE SHIP GREAT ADVENTURES 100% + EXTRA	$38.00	GeoTrax Roundin Roundhouse NIB Geo Trax Fisher Price	$14.49

Pretend Play, Preschool ▶ Play-Doh, Modeling Clay

The average sales price in this subcategory is $8.69.

	HIGH		AVG
6 tubs floam-ships now-bl,grn,purple,pnk,yellow,white	$91.00	CARE BEARS "CASTLE FIGURE MAKER PLAYSET" (NEW)	$9.49
4 tubs floam-purple,yellow,green,white-ships now!	$54.57	Hot Perky Pink Floam tub NEW As Seen on TV $2 ship HTF	$9.28
PLAY DOH Vintage 1977 Fuzzy Pumper Barber Beauty Shop	$52.11	Lot of 4 Play-Doh Classic 4 Pack Flat Rate Ship	$9.00
6 Pack of FLOAM Pink Yellow Blue Green White Purple	$51.00	Play Doh Lot Camera Mr Potato Head Alphabet Eskimo Mold	$9.00
4 Tubs Packs of Floam HTF in stock yellow pink purple	$48.99	barbie dough kitchen	$8.99
4 tubs floam-purple,yellow,blue,white-ships now!	$45.00	PLAY-DOH PLAYSET BOOHBAH &	$8.99
Vintage 1976 Play Doh FUZZY PUMPER BARBER SHOP !	$41.01	USBORNE BOOK PLAYDOUGH	
BN FLOAM Pink, Blue, Green, & Yellow HTF BEAD COMPOUND	$41.00	Play-Doh Bob the Builder and Accessories + Kiddy Dough	$8.69
4 Pack of FLOAM Pink Yellow Blue Green Seen on TV Nick	$36.00	Disney PLAY-DOH It's A Small World NEW Playset Playdoh	$8.50
BNIP FLOAM Pink, Green, & Yellow HTF BEAD COMPOUND	$32.00	Play-Doh Fun Factory Vintage 3-D Farm molds	$8.00
Floam 4 Tubs Pink, Green, Blue, Yellow ready to ship!	$29.99	Play-Doh McFlurry Dessert Playshop	$7.99
Kenner Play-Doh Fuzzy Pumper Beauty and Barber Shop	$26.00	VINTAGE STRAWBERRY SHORTCAKE PLAY-DOH SET	$7.99

PLAY-DOH FUNNY PUMPER STILL IN PLASTIC NEVER USED	$20.54	Playdoh Fun Factory Playset 34 Accessory 5 Cans Playdoh	$7.57
BNIP FLOAM Green & Yellow HTF BEAD COMPOUND	$20.00	Ghoulish Green Floam tub NEW As seen on TV $2 shipping	$7.50
Purple Floam-1tub-3.5 oz size-Ready to Ship!	$19.98	69 pcs Hasbro-Play Doh Cutters - Jackknife-Rolling Pins	$7.26
[2 of these sold in a multiple item ("Dutch") auction for $9.99 each]		Play-Doh POKEMON Character Maker - NIB _ SEALED	$7.25

Pretend Play, Preschool ▶ Playmobil

The average sales price in this subcategory is $23.62.

	HIGH		AVG
Playmobil Victorian Doll House 5300 w/ Lots of Extras	$462.00	New Playmobil Adventure Tree House Play Set #5746 w/Box	$24.99
HUGE PLAYMOBIL/PLAYMOBILE VICTORIAN HOUSE 5300	$307.79	Playmobil Special 4506 Dracula, Victorian Vampire!	$24.99
Playmobil #4033 "Pacific Railroad" Steam Engine Train	$291.00	Playmobil Special 4539 Mandarin Dragon Prince! Mint!	$24.99
RARE PLAYMOBIL RC Christmas Train 4035 LIKE NEW	$255.00	Playmobil Special 4508 Blues Jazz Player & Saxophone!	$24.99
Playmobil Large Victorian Dollhouse 5300	$152.50	Playmobil Special 4515 Manly Lumberjack! He's OK! Mint!	$24.99
Playmobil 4020 Remote Control Modern Express Train	$150.00	Playmobil Indians, Horses & Rocks in LIKE NEW cond.	$24.33
PLAYMOBIL 3268 KNIGHTS' EMPIRE CASTLE - NEW IN BOX	$147.50	Playmobil #3185 Jet Airliner Plane	$23.49
Toy Playmobil 5300 Victorian Dollhouse Doll House Boxed	$137.50	Playmobil 3880 Rescue Unit 26 FACTORY SEALED MIB NR	$23.27
Playmobil 3268 Knights Empire Castle New MSRP $ 179.99	$137.50	Playmobil mix lot 36 men, Dragon much more	$23.27
Playmobil Victorian house. 5300	$124.50	Lot Of Playmobil Halloween Figures & Accessories	$23.00
Boxed Giant Playmobil Fairy Tale Fantasy Castle 3019	$117.50	Playmobil 5763 My Take Along Dollhouse Brand New box	$22.50
Playmobil fairytale castle.	$103.50	Playmobil 5324 Victorian Dollhouse Bathroom NIB	$22.25
Playmobil 5301 The grande Mansion + 7411 Ext. Floor new	$103.50	Playmobil 5312 Victorian Dollhouse Children's Bedroom	$22.25
PLAYMOBIL 5756 5760 5761 5762 UNICORN MAGIC CASTLE	$99.99	Playmobil Fairy Tale Castle dining Room #3021 MNIB	$22.09
Playmobil 3666 KNIGHT CASTLE COMPLETE LOAD W/EXTRA NICE	$96.01	Playmobil, ROYAL NAVY, Figure Lot, Pirates!!!	$22.07

Pretend Play, Preschool ▶ Playskool

The average sales price in this subcategory is $11.55.

	HIGH		AVG
Old Vintage PLAYSKOOL Bug World Toy & Original Box #409	$107.50	PLAYSKOOL "BIG, BIG TOOL BENCH" #450 - WORKBENCH -1984	$12.50
DAPPER DAN AND DRESSY BESSY DOLLS - 1970	$76.99	Playskool Talkback Picture Phone NEVER USED 1995	$12.49
1994 Playskool Dollhouse Stable & Horses Lot MINT!	$58.50	Playskool WEEBLEVILLE with MANY EXTRAS People & Animals	$12.21
1987 DEFINITELY DINOSAURS 17 PIECE HUGE SET SUPER RARE!	$57.98	PLAYSKOOL AIRTIVITY AIR-TIVITY ACTIVITY TABLE FUN TABLE	$12.00
Playskool DEFINITELY DINOSAURS Lot w/ RARE ULTRASAURUS!	$52.00	Playskool's Step Start Walk N' Ride: Two Toys in One!	$11.99
MR & MRS POTATO HEADS huge lot + MINIS 125+ pieces FUN!	$51.00	HASBRO PLAYSKOOL 6 DOLLHOUSE FAMILY FIGURES BABY PARENT	$11.75
MR POTATO HEAD SYRACUSE SKYCHIEFS CHIEFS BASEBALL SGA	$41.00	Playskool HAPPY BIRTHDAY Mr. Potato Head NIB	$11.51
Vintage Sesame Street Play skool House Store - Loaded!	$36.00	FRANKLIN THE TURTLE PHONICS PAL	$11.50
Speedstars Maximum Thrills Raceway NO BATTERIES MISB	$36.00	MR POTATO HEAD LOT OF 3 HEADS & 70 ACCESSORY PIECES	$11.50
Weeble Wobbles WOMAN BOY GIRL BEDS & CAR weebles wobble	$36.00	Set of Playskool Dollhouse People- Dad, Mom, Son & Dog	$11.11
Playskool Speedstars Maximum Thrills Raceway New Toy	$34.00	Playskool Puzzletown Set A Dr. Lion's Medical Center	$11.11
Playskool Dollhouse Doll house porch chairs umbrella	$32.00	Mr. Potato Head Christmas Holiday Dress Up Parts Set	$11.00
HUGE PLAYSKOOL Doll House & Many Accessories	$31.01	3 PLAYSKOOL LIGHT UP GLO WORMS GLOWORM 1993 SOFT CLOTH	$10.60
Playskool Dollhouse Doll house Dinning room furniture	$31.00	PLAYSKOOL MR. & MRS. POTATO HEAD	$10.52
TWO PLAYSKOOL SMART STICKS GENTLY USED	$31.00	1991 Playskool MY BUDDY Doll 21" Brown Hair Freckles !!	$10.50

Pretend Play, Preschool ▶ Puppets

The average sales price in this subcategory is $32.12.

	HIGH		AVG
Hand Carved Professional Ventriloquist Figure	$800.00	Vintage 1968 Mortimer Snerd Juro Ventriloquist Doll	$36.00
Vintage Boxed Pelham Puppet Toy Baby Bear 1963	$266.80	Pro Puppets/Ministry Puppet Mitch	$36.00
VINTAGE DILLY DALLY MARIONETTE PUPPET HOWDY DOODY SHOW	$256.01	Three Stooges Larry Hand Puppet Vintage 50s/60s	$35.03
38" Handcarved Wood Ventriloquist Character	$249.95	Pro Puppets/Ministry Puppet Jessica	$35.01
Vintage Ventriloquism Collection (8) Puppets Books	$204.84	Vintage 60s English Made Pelham Pirate Hand Puppet MIB	$33.50
MICKEY MOUSE.LTD.MUSIC BOX.ENESCO..	$197.50	Pro Puppets/Ministry Puppet Susie	$33.00
DISNEYANA.XMAS CAROL		Hansel & Gretel Composition Marionettes w/Record-1940's	$31.50
Ideal Toy Co. vinyl three faces Little Lost Baby doll	$152.50	Halloween Witch cloth hand puppet	$31.00
BOB BAKER.PINOCCHIO...DISNEYANA... MARIONETTE PUPPET	$150.00	PELHAM PUPPET-MACBOOZLE	$31.00
Pelham Puppets SL 1963 Lot of 3 Wolf, King, Queen WOW	$137.50	6 Baby Einstein Hand/Bath Puppets - New with tags	$31.00
God's Children Set Of Five Full Body Rod Arm Puppets	$135.00	2 VINTAGE HAND PUPPETS + 2 HEADS - CHARMING - NR	$31.00
Pelham Marionette Puppet - Snake Charmer with its Box	$126.00	10 Hand Puppet LOT Octopus Cricket Fish Goat Turtle +++	$30.01
JIMMY NELSONS~DOG~FARFEL~VENTRILOQUIST DUMMY~PUPPET	$115.50	CATERPILLAR PELHAM MARIONETTE PUPPET FROM ENGLAND	$30.00
Mickey Mouse Pelham Puppet, 18" Display	$113.50	HAZELLE & THE MILLIONS OF PUPPETS - VHS DOCUMENTARY	$30.00
SET OF 7 VINTAGE GERMAN HAND PUPPETS - Papier Mache	$104.03	[3 of these sold in a multiple item ("Dutch") auction for $10.00 each]	
Pelham Puppet Prince Charming circa 1956	$88.50	Vintage Ventriloquist with Original box and papers!!	$29.99

Pretend Play, Preschool ▶ Wooden, Handcrafted Toys

The average sales price in this subcategory is $26.33.

	HIGH		AVG
Kay Bojesen Rocking Horse	$500.00	Alex Toys Mini Mart Push Cart-New! Wood grocery store	$30.56
Pottery Barn Kids Chesapeake Boat Sandbox~Sold Out!	$226.50	Deluxe Mini Play Cube	$29.99
KidKraft Kitchen NIB FREE SHIP Pretend Play	$158.00	50 Unit Blocks of Fun Color by Ryan's Room - NEW	$29.99
Ryans Room Deluxe Wooden Dollhouse NIB	$157.50	SEALED Fire Station House Engine Toy Truck T212	$29.99
NEW Wood Stable Barn Corral Horse Breyer BIG!	$140.00	preschool wooden train tracks magnet trains toy thomas	$28.00
Pottery Barn Kids Toy Kitchen Stove	$135.50	Skittle-Me-Bowl Piccolo Style by Camden Rose	$28.00
Alex Toys My Playhouse Theater-New! Puppet Pretend	$132.50	Waldorf Tree Gnome Fairy Doll Set Felt Mat & Wood Acc.	$26.11
NEW NIB WOODEN TOY KITCHEN SET KIDKRAFT/DAYCARE	$132.50	Antique Kids Childs Desk Chair Easel Peg Board NICE!	$24.99
PLAY KITCHEN WOOD UNFINISHED PINE ICE BOX & CUPBOARD!!!	$125.00	Wooden Airplane Rocker Riding Toy Toddler	$24.99
HUGE WOODEN AND WALDORF TOY LOT	$120.50	Animal Zoo Playset Wooden Toy 3D Puzzle Montessori toys	$24.95

WOODEN HORSE STABLE / BARN FOR BREYER CM & STONE HORSES	$112.50	Wooden Alphabet Blocks & Tractor/Wagon ****NEW****		$22.95
WOODEN HORSE STABLE / BARN FOR BREYER CM & STONE HORSES	$112.49	STICK HORSE HOBBIE HORSE ROCKING COWBOY COWGIRL TOY		$22.51
NEW Wood Stable Barn Corral Horse Breyer BIG!	$104.99	HANDMADE WOODEN CASTLE FOLDING		$19.99
NEW Wood Stable Barn Corral Horse Breyer BIG!	$104.99	PLAYSET WOOD NOT LEGO QQ		
WOODEN HORSE STABLE / BARN FOR	$90.00	Melissa Doug WOODEN TEA SET DISHES DINING FOOD TOY PLAY		$19.99
BREYER CM & STONE HORSES		ROCKING HORSE AND CHAIR		$19.99

Puzzles ▶ Modern (1970-Now)

The average sales price in this subcategory is $12.08.

	HIGH		AVG
Isomo wooden puzzle Naef	$202.51	Slide Slider Sliding 49 Tile Puzzle SYLVESTER CAT Rare!	$12.99
1439:Lot of 3 Collectible Impossible Puzzles Rare	$142.50	Airedale Dog Wooden Amish Made Toy Scroll Saw Puzzle	$12.99
Cubicus wooden puzzle Spiel Naef	$119.13	Sterling Silver Jig Saw Puzzle Piece Design Ring- Sz 7	$12.95
T.E. BRANGS WHOLESALE LOT OF 24 BILZ OBSTACLE PUZZLE	$85.86	Melissa & Doug wooden magnetic fishing puzzle must c	$12.50
1427:Japanese Mini Secret Puzzle Box Unopened	$83.89	Playboy Playmate Puzzle 1973 Karen Christy	$12.50
1409:Lot of 4 Mini Puzzle Mugs Steins	$81.00	Lot of 5 Assorted Childrens Wooden Peg Jigsaw Puzzles	$12.50
JEFF VOLLMER KING'S SAFE WOOD BOX PUZZLE SIGNED NR OOAK	$74.99	Wood Puzzle Lot Most Playskool lot of 13	$12.01
1424:Lot of 3 "PUZZLER" Rotating Puzzles 1986	$66.00	1406:The Uptight Spider by Peterson Games 1972 Rare	$12.00
1425:Minature Key Chain Coin Wood Puzzle Impossible?	$66.00	1419:Logical Toy Tick-Tack Soviet/British Joint Venture	$11.55
1422:Wood Puzzle Bank	$58.00	1426:Int'l Puzzle Party 12th Wine Bottle & Cork Puzzle	$11.50
1418:Int'l Puzzle Party 11th Splitting Headache Cube	$57.01	Basenji Dog Wooden Amish made Scroll Saw Puzzle	$11.50
1960s GRADUAL DESPAIR Puzzle ICESKATER No Res	$54.00	4 Wooden puzzles playskool childrens	$11.50
1423:Int'l Puzzle Party 13 Explode-A-Burr Cutler	$53.88	LARGE LOT PLAYSKOOL WOOD PUZZLES SESAME ST. BARNEY	$11.50
Thirteenth Labour of Hercules wooden puzzle Pentangle	$52.50	Jack Russell Dog Wood Amish made Toy Scroll Saw Puzzle	$11.50
Japanese puzzle box, 10 movements	$46.55	WONDERFUL LOT OF 8 CHILDREN'S COLORFUL WOODEN PUZZLES	$11.50

Puzzles ▶ Vintage (Pre-1970)

The average sales price in this subcategory is $30.50.

	HIGH		AVG
Vintage STAVE PUZZLE 825 Pieces THE GOODKNIGHT	$1,475.00	Puzzle vintage Wood Jigsaw Washington & Lafayette 150pc	$32.09
OLD PARKER WOOD JIGSAW PUZZLE 612 PIECES 73 UNIQUE NICE	$592.77	2 TUCO DELUXE PICTURE PUZZLE-WWII PT BOATS+NONINTERLOCK	$32.00
Vintage 683 piece wooden jigsaw puzzle Prisoners of War	$360.77	Vtg Tuco Non Interlocking Puzzle Finny Situation Comple	$31.22
Vintage Wood Jigsaw Puzzle 62 Detailed Figurals 1930's	$346.00	SPRINGBOK PUZZLE 1965 CORAL PLANTS TO EMPEROR COMPLETE	$31.00
1930's Pastime Puzzle Jigsaw Parker Bros. 300 pieces	$296.00	SPRINGBOK 1968 THINGIE ROUND JIGSAW PUZZLE	$31.00
Parker Brothers Pastime Wood Jigsaw Puzzle (RARE ONE!)	$256.89	Vintage Perfect Picture Puzzle Dance of the Veils	$30.89
Vintage 320 Piece Wooden Pastime Puzzle	$242.49	1965 Springbok Circular Jigsaw Puzzle #C902 "The Magi"	$30.51
1930's Pastime Puzzle Jigsaw Parker Bros. 300 pieces	$237.48	Round Springbok Puzzle - Dancing Girl by Zona	$30.25
Original 1960s DRACULA Puzzle by Jaymar 6582 COMPLETE	$230.27	VINTAGE WOODEN WOOD JIGSAW PUZZLE	$30.00
1930's Pastime Puzzle Jigsaw Parker Bros. 300 pieces	$229.49	Hand Cut Wood Jigsaw Puzzle ,U.S.S. Constitution	$30.00
Madnar Antique Wood Jig Saw Puzzles	$228.76	1920's JIG PUZZLE LADY HUNTER SPANIELS DOG RELYEA	$29.99
Pastime Picture Puzzle " On the way to Market" 767 pcs	$227.50	Springbok Flirtations Puzzle Lot of 3 Hallmark 7" Boxed	$29.99
Puzzling Puzzles/Wood/Jig Saw/300 Pieces/46 Figurals	$223.39	5 VINTAGE JIG PICTURE PUZZLE-DERBY-MAYFAIR-PICCADILLY	$29.19
1930's Pastime Puzzle Jigsaw Parker Bros. 300 pieces	$191.49	VINTAGE "VICTORY" WOOD PUZZLE- MADE IN ENGLAND!!!!!!	$28.50
537 pc PANDORA WOOD JIGSAW PUZZLE-56 figurals-COMPLETE	$187.50	Vintage Plywood Puzzle Indian Prayer 2747 FAS USA	$28.00

Radio Control ▶ Vehicles

The median sales price in this subcategory is $19.99.

	HIGH		AVG
1:4 scale jet engine funny car dragster 1 of a kind	$3,495.00	NEW DragonFly King 3D Mini R/C	$19.99
1/4 scale dragster rc nitrous mopar rail	$2,200.00	RADIO CONTROL HELICOPTER	
TAMIYA BRUISER TOTALLY MINT RTR MUSEUM QUALITY !!!!!!!	$2,125.00	NEW Polaris R/C Radio Controlled ATV 4-Wheeler 1:6 Scal	$19.99
70cc QUICKDRAW TWIN brand new w/pipes,clutch	$1,900.00	XMODS™ Custom RC All-Wheel-Drive Upgrade Kit	$19.99
Traxxas Monster Buggy	$1,900.00	[2 of these sold for $19.99 each]	
VINTAGE TAMIYA SAND SCORCHER RACING BUGGY EARLY 80'S	$1,744.99	RC AIRPLANE FLIGHT / FIELD BOX PLANS	$19.99
Vario Benzin Trainer	$1,710.53	ASSOCIATED RC10GT PRO ALLOY FRONT C-HUB NEW rc10 gt	$19.99
Technopower 7 Cylinder Radial Engine R/C	$1,680.99	TAMIYA 1/14 R/C King Hauler Globe Liner Animal Guard	$19.99
VINTAGE TAMIYA MOUNTAINEER HILUX BRUISER MINT COMPLETE!	$1,675.00	NEW!! RC 1:24 JGSDF Type - 90 Battle Tank #29577	$19.99
MUSEUM QUALITY TAMIYA MOUNTAINEER READY TO ROLL LOOK!		New Super Sonic R/C Airplane~Free Shipping!!	$19.99
1/5 FG Monster Truck Brand New! RTR!! Just Add Gas!!	$1,599.00	NEW Kyosho Kanai 2/3 MP777 Front Universals CVD Axles	$19.99
www.bigboystoysandhobbies.com Paint by Zielke Racing		NEW NIB TYCO Pro Flexpak Battery+Charger Shell Shocker	$19.99
Rare Boxed Wen Mac P 38 Lighting w/ insert Like New Cox	$1,525.00	Cox Sky Cruiser radio controled jet	$19.99
FG Monster Truck Brand New RTR Just add Gas	$1,513.00	XMODS® Truck RC Top & Body Kit Ford®	$19.99
www.bigboystoysandhobbies.com Authorized FG dealer!		F-150 New "EVO" Series XMODS	
Aeromarine 48" Challenger R/C Gas DeeVee Boat w/ Zenoah	$1,500.00	THUNDER RUNNER R/C HELICOPTER!!	$19.99
Ready to Run w/ Modified Zenoah G260 and Airtronics M8		TRAXXAS REVO DIFFERENTIAL	$19.99
vintage tamiya supershot super shot NIB 4wd hotshot fox	$1,475.00	NEW T MAXX 2.5 Differential Complete Diff	$19.99
scale Raptor 60 helicopter gas helicopter	$1,460.00		
1/8 scale R/C unlimited hydro racing and parts	$1,375.00		

Robots, Monsters, Space Toys ▶ Monsters

The average sales price in this subcategory is $30.46.

	HIGH		AVG
GODZILLA VS MEGAGUIRUS POSTER ART KIT-YUJI SAKAI	$700.00	Bandai Godzilla Final Wars complete set in boxes kit	$33.00
Diecast Mecha Godzilla Bullmark Popy	$305.00	Godzilla "Final Wars" 16 Figures Set! Bandai	$32.99
HUGE 1998 21" BANDAI GAMERA Godzilla	$299.00	Bandai Baragon 2002 - godzilla	$32.58
Bandai "Godzilla Forever" MELTDOWN GODZILLA or Burning	$225.00	Offical Godzilla Compendium & G-Fan Update	$31.28

CCP 71 Godzilla & Crawling Hedorah Set of figures -2005	$210.50	Marusan glow gorosaurus- godzilla bullmark	$31.00
Bandai "Godzilla Forever" GODZILLA '62 King Goji	$202.50	Bandai UltraSeven Diorama Set - ultraman, godzilla	$31.00
95 GODZILLA latex head/bust mask figure 1:1 scale/ M1	$202.50	Godzilla vs King Kong Figures Very Cool	$30.00
Daimos Anguirus resin kit from Godzilla Final Wars new	$150.00	Marusan glow baragon - godzilla bullmark	$29.88
HUGE 1988 18" BANDAI GMS MOSU-GOJI GODZILLA	$150.00	Godzilla 2003 DX MECHAGODZILLA Figure by Banpresto MISB	$29.00
Kaiyodo 40cm Godzilla 62 vinyl kit built painted	$132.50	Bandai Baragon 2001 8 inch figure w/tag Godzilla GMK	$28.00
Bandai Godzilla HG2 set biollante destroyer mothra	$124.99	MARMIT GODZILLA LIKE VINYL PARADISE FIGURE	$27.11
RODAN Shogun Warriors Mattel 1979	$105.65	TRENDMASTERS GODZILLA BIOLLANTE MIB NO RES	$26.50
Very Rare 1977 Shogun Warrior Godzilla Figure by Mattel	$103.94	KAMEN MASKED RIDER 27 LOT GASHAPON CAPSULE TOYS BANDAI	$26.01
godzilla ghidorah destroyah collection	$102.50	Godzilla Lite Table Lighter	$26.00
CCP 2005 WCC HEDORAH 71 LTD ONLY 50 MADE!! GODZILLA NEW	$100.99	godzilla, mechagodzilla loose no tag	$26.00

Robots, Monsters, Space Toys ▶ Robots

The average sales price in this subcategory is $105.24.

	HIGH		AVG
Alps MISSILE ROBOT Near Mint C9 w/repro BOX Japan B/O	$4,629.00	Godzilla Jet Jaguar vinyls M1 Lucky Bag like bullmark	$108.49
60's Ideal Japan Zeroid Battery Robot Solar Cycle Set	$2,136.99	Shogun Warrior, Godzilla 20 inch	$107.71
RARE Daiya Japan RANGER ROBOT NMint Works with Box!!!!	$2,000.00	SOUL OF CHOGOKIN GX-05B Daiku Maryu / popy	$107.50
Chief Robotman KO Yoshia robot MIB C9+ BOXED Japan B/O	$1,999.00	SOUL OF CHOGOKIN GX-08 APHRODAI A	$107.50
1950'S JAPAN MOON SPACE SHIP WITH RARE ORIGINAL BOX	$1,875.00	i-CYBIE ROBOTIC PET BLUE DOG	$107.50
VINTAGE BATTERY OP CRAGSTAN MR. ROBOT JAPAN EXCELLENT	$923.53	1970s popy tin flying astroboy nt billiken osaka	$107.50
JUMBO MACHINDER GETTER LIGER JAPAN POPY W/ BOX	$850.00	ZOBOR & ZINTAR – TWO 1968 TOY ROBOTS - VINTAGE ROBOT	$103.53
Heathkit Hero 1 Robot Complete W/Manuals & Tech.Guide	$700.00	TIN TRACTOR ROBOT GUY	$103.50
Rare Nomura windup SPACE COMMANDO with NO RESERVE!	$660.00	1982POPY "ELECTRONIC JUSPION"	$102.50
SCARCE 50's ROBOT TORPEDO - JAPAN C9+	$649.00	Robby the Robot Space Tank tin toy robot	$102.50
Voltes V by Godaikin	$620.10	Mr. Galaxy battery operated vintage toy	$102.50
GODAIKIN VOLTRON DX GOLION POPY 100% COMPLETE BANDAI	$600.00	Trendmasters VOLTRON MACHINDER Mint in BOX DIE-CAST	$102.50
Shogun Warrior Jumbo Machinder Lot	$589.00	VINTAGE 1968 RUDY MOTORIZED ROBOT REMCO	$102.50
Daitarn 3 MACH PATROL car MIB Clover no popy, gredinzer	$581.00	STARWARS R2D2 ROBOT 17" TALL ALMOST NEW NR	$102.50
Vintage Tin Wind-Up Japanese Robot Toy	$579.00	Rudy The Robot in Original Box "1969"	$100.99

Robots, Monsters, Space Toys ▶ Space Toys

The average sales price in this subcategory is $53.37.

	HIGH		AVG
ORIGINAL MARX Flash Gordon Rocket Fighter Space Ship	$810.00	Vintage Major Matt Mason Space Rover Works!!	$56.00
HORIKAWA NEW SPACE STATION -NEAR MINT EXAMPLE	$800.00	1960s Eldon Billy Blastoff Astronaut Space Ship Vehicle	$56.00
CRAGSTAN MOBILE SATELLITE TRACKING STATION	$611.00	4 lot 1958 Mattel H2O Cap Firing Rocket Missile MIB..	$55.25
Space 1999 Eagle 1 Spaceship Mattel Model NIB Vintage	$520.00	Vintage 1950s SPACE FLYER GLIDER STORE DISPLAY	$54.99
1960 Japan tin toy large flying saucer Space Giant	$500.00	Major Matt Mason-Doug Davis Figure With Helmet-Good	$54.88
Alps Battery operated Planet Explorer space tank NMIB	$456.00	RARE! Masudaya Radar n Scope console	$53.99
Mattel Lost In Space Switch & Go PlaySet 1966	$450.00	USS Enterprise NCC-1701-D L.E. Rawcliffe Pewter	$52.75
1930's Ingraham BUCK ROGERS pocket watch works *RARE	$445.00	Vintage MAJOR MATT MASON figure ALIEN enemy CALLISTO	$52.00
Space Atomic Gun Japan MIB Tin Gun measures 8 1/2" long	$418.58	Space Pistol Thitan by Edison Giocattoli Italy BOXED	$52.00
Mattel Scorpio 1969 Matt Mason Space Toy Mint Conditio	$400.00	16 SPACE PLASTIC FIGURES, ICE CREAM PREMIUMS RAJ	$52.00
Custom Shocker Kamen Rider 12" figure + Bike Medicom	$399.99	Vintage 1950s INFLATABLE TOY ROCKET SPACESHIP MIP Ideal	$51.00
1960s LARGE 20 FIREBALL XL 5 SPACESHIP IN ORG BOX	$395.00	POPY DX JUSPION GARBIN TANK CHOGOKIN STAR WARS BANDAI	$51.00
SUPER RARE 1950's Space PATROL TANK Tin Japan! NO RSV!!	$385.00	Major Matt Mason Satellite Locker Doll & Accessories	$51.00
Friendship 7 Space Rocket—Yonezawa & Box	$373.58	Vintage Marx "Cape Canaveral" Play Set In Box	$51.00
VERY RARE VINTAGE POPY BATTLEFEVER DX BATTLESHARK MIB	$338.00	MATT MASON FIGURE W/ HELMET	$51.00

Slot Cars ▶ Modern (1970-Now)

The average sales price in this subcategory is $27.95.

	HIGH		AVG
HUGE LOTOF 45 TYCO & LIFE LIKE HO SLOT CARS	$312.78	CARRERA STARS N STRIPES 62 CORVETTE SLOT CAR *NIB	$28.99
1/24 slot cars (3) and lot.	$300.00	AURORA AFX HO SLOT CAR 31 FORD MODEL A TRUCK 1975	$28.77
1/24 SLOT CAR EUROSPORT SLICK 7 1996 IMCA WINNER	$249.10	Parma Flexi-2 Slot Car Starter Kit Set Plus More!	$28.51
GROUP 27 **ERKLE BUILT**HI END 1/4 SCALE WING CAR "	$223.50	Rare Aurora AFX Poesche 510K Can-Am, Nice	$28.51
HO Slot Cars Lot of 15 + Tyco HP7 Racin' Wheelies 440	$192.50	Parma wing Slot car,Controler,parts..	$28.06
AFX Shadow Can Am Blue/White/Red #3 NEW in JAPANESE BOX	$177.53	Tyco Magnum 440 Pro Racing F1 Slot Car Set w/ Cars	$28.00
188 AURORA SLOT CAR TRACKS, many types, straight curve	$167.55	!!! 4 1/2 " MONTE CARLO JUNIOR LOOK ALIKE !!!	$28.00
** LOOK ** 04 VETTE ROADSTER Drag Car	$160.00	Parma Big Mama braid 663	$27.55
Slot car power supply.	$152.50	Koford Box Stock 12, Feather Motor,Tri-Star Arm NEW!!!	$27.50
1/24 SLOT CAR CUSTOM PORSCHE 904 VINTAGE HARD BODY	$152.50	67 Corvette Hardbody, DRS chassis S16d	$27.00
BEUF Built Koford 6 Mag Qualifier Group 7 Motor! (Open)	$152.50	***** RJR SLOT CAR - 1/24 *********	$27.00
(3) Group 7 Motor Set-Ups. Koford & Voki 6 Mags	$142.50	**LOOK** Drag chassis	$27.00
POLISTIL LIGIER FERRARI F1 HO SLOT CAR tyco afx aurora	$139.43	Tyco-US 1-Trucking-Crate loader/unloader w/ TRAILER!!!!	$26.99
1/32 1/24 SLOT CAR MOTOR C-CAN MOTOR PARTS ASST	$137.50	TYCO CAR LOT NICE !!!!!!!!!!!!!!!!!!!!!!!!!!!!!!!!!!	$26.99
Carrera Evolution 1:32 - 1:24 Track LR not Scalextric	$137.50	Tyco HO 4 LANE TRACK LOT JUMPS *BLOWOUT SALE* BRAND NEW	$26.99

Slot Cars ▶ Vintage (Pre-1970)

The average sales price in this subcategory is $46.28.

	HIGH		AVG
AURORA THUNDERBIRD SILVER W/ TAN HARDTOP VIBRATOR!!	$1,226.00	thunderbike tjet aurora	$48.88
Case of NOS,T-Jet chassis 100 new old stock Aurora!!!!	$885.01	Vintage Atlas 1962 Chevy Impala	$48.88
Case of NOS,T-Jet chassis 100 new old stock Aurora!!!!	$885.00	aurora tjet railroad in box for ho slot cars	$48.50
HO Slot AFX Cars Aurora 65 Ft. Track Accessories Lot	$645.24	AURORA HO SLOT CAR INDIANAPOLIS RACER #2 MINT IN BOX	$48.00

	HIGH		AVG
Aurora AFX - '57 CHEVY NOMAD in Orange-Yellow - MOC	$531.99	MINT AURORA HO SLOT CAR CHAPARRAL RACER WHITE #5 in box	$47.00
Model Motoring Aurora Slot Car Train Rare Vibrator Set	$510.00	AURORA MODEL MOTORING HO SCALE SLOT CAR RACING SET	$46.98
#43 Richard Petty Superbird Tyco Pro RARE HO Slotcar	$486.00	Tyco Pro Very Rare Vintage VW Love Bus Slot Car	$46.58
Estate vintage lot of slot cars & parts! Lots of Extra	$465.00	4 Red White & Blue Tyco Slot Cars (7)	$46.00
HO Aurora T-Jet Dodge Olive Drab Charger	$405.00	3 Red White & Blue AFX Slot Cars	$46.00
RARE AURORA MIB O GAUGE DEUCE COUPE!	$395.00	AURORA HO THUNDERJET 500 FORD GT CAR MINT IN BOX	$46.00
1965 Gilbert JAMES BOND 007 Road Race set - in the BOX!	$380.00	4 Green Slot Cars - 1973 AFX	$46.00
Aurora T-Jet Lock & Joiner 4-Way Traffic Light	$376.01	M.E.V. Originals - '59 Police Car in Black - Cream MIB	$45.99
Vintage HO Slot Car Grab Box—Aurora-LOTS!!!!!	$365.00	HO Tyco Pro Trick Truck Slot Car Catalog # 8832	$45.91
Aurora AFX - '57 CHEVY NOMAD in Red-White Stripes - MOC	$358.53	Ford GT Slot Car	$45.55
RARE ORIGINAL AURORA 4 LANE SLOT CAR SET 4 OLD FORDS	$350.00	aurora tjet red Thunderbird	$45.22

Stuffed Animals ▸ Disney

The average sales price in this subcategory is $8.45.

	HIGH		AVG
Disney Store Finding Nemo Halloween Costume	$63.00	Disney Huge Winnie The Pooh Tigger	$8.99
Christopher robin stuffed toy	$61.01	STITCH AS ELVIS /(HALLOWEEN)DISNEY STORE EXCLUSIVE 14"	$8.99
ALICE IN WONDERLAND-10 PC SET-DISNEY PLUSH COLLECTIBLES	$59.00	13" Disney A-Z Winnie the Pooh plush, FUN!!***	$8.99
Aloha Stitch Talking Doll	$41.00	18 INCH CLASSIC POOH & EEYORE, LIKE NEW, DISNEY PLUSH	$8.51
LARGE HUGE BIG KANGA ROO Stuffed Animal Disney Mattel	$39.00	DISNEY'S KIM POSSIBLE "RUFUS" 9" DOLL - CUTE!!	$8.50
Disney Stuffed Kuzco Emperor's New Groove Llama	$36.00	DISNEY ALICE IN WONDERLAND PLUSH WHITE RABBIT	$8.50
36" Giant Mickey Mouse Plush, Disney	$34.99	Fisher Price Bend Me Eeyore Disney Bear Plush New	$8.50
My Name is Daisey, from Oswald,, New, Look	$31.00	Disney Store "Thumper" Small NWOT	$8.00
HUGE 25" EEYORE PLUSH STUFFED ANIMAL DISNEY STORE W/TAG	$31.00	Disney's Spirit the Horse stuffed animal	$8.00
MICKEY MOUSE LARGE STUFFED ANIMAL PLUSH DISNEY STORE	$30.99	New With Tags Snowflake Pals Mickey Mouse Plush Disney	$8.00
LOT 3 DISNEY WINNIE THE POOH & EEYORE WINTER PLUSH NEW	$29.99	disney simba stuffed toy wdw doll lion king new animal	$8.00
VINTAGE SEARS WINNIE THE POOH SET OF 5 WALT DISNEY PRO	$26.50	Baby Winnie Pooh and Eeyore Plush giggler/rattle toys	$7.99
WINNIE THE POOH DISNEY STORE LARGE STUFFED ANIMAL PLUSH	$26.00	Heffalump Lumpy Mini Bean Bag Plush Winnie The Pooh NEW	$7.99
WINNIE THE POOH MATTEL LARGE STUFFED ANIMAL PLUSH	$26.00	NWT DISNEY FINDING NEMO BRUCE SHARK BEANIE BABY PLUSH	$7.99
DISNEY STITCH FULL BODY PUPPET Plush Stuffed Animal	$26.00	LARGE MICKEY & MINNIE MOUSE SET, NEW W/ TAGS	$7.99

Stuffed Animals ▸ Gund

The average sales price in this subcategory is $11.01.

	HIGH		AVG
$400 Lot 20 Childrens Gund Stuffed Ben Dogs w/Scarf NR	$117.51	GUND WHITE BEAR–BUNKY STUFFED ANIMAL	$11.50
1992 GUND MCGUINNESS PENGUIN BY SANDRA BOYNTON	$113.50	CLASSIC WINNIE THE POOH STUFFED EEYORE BY GUND, CHARITY	$11.50
Grimsly Manor Department 56 Halloween House	$91.00	Victorias Secret 2004 Ltd Ed GUND Puppy Dog "Molly" NIB	$11.50
New! Baby Gund "Puffy Luv" Pink Kitty Stuffed Plush 8"	$82.00	VERY RARE GUND 21" POMPI BISHON FRISE PLUSH DOG W/Tags	$11.50
Rare Gund 23" Max Monkey 4756 Beanbag Plush	$71.51	$244 Lot 18 Childrens Stuffed Animals Gund Ty Toys NR	$11.49
Vintage Puppy Dog 2 Dogs Gund 1982 w/Rope Neck Tie	$61.00	WINNIE THE POOH STUFFED KANGAROO TOY BY GUND, CHARITY	$11.45
VINTAGE Walt Disney GUND Winnie The Pooh Bear	$42.09	Baby Gund SPRINKLES GIRAFFE 10" Stuffed Animal NEW	$11.00
$400 Lot 20 Childrens Gund Stuffed Ben Dogs w/Scarf NR	$36.02	Land Before Time HUGE PLUSH Littlefoot,Ducky,Cera Gund	$11.00
Karma Wilson-BEAR WANTS MORE- Book & Animal set!	$30.00	18" Bandy Bear by Gund NEW W/TAGS	$10.99
LARGE MAX & RUBY BUNNY PLUSH DOLL SET by GUND, NEW!	$29.99	ERNIE 11" SESAME STREET by GUND PLUSH NEW MINT	$10.98
$294 Lot 21 Childrens Stuffed Animals Baby Adventure NR	$29.09	Rare Gund 14" Booker Bear w/Glasses Beanbag Plush	$10.50
MINT GUND STUFFED PLUSH PINK SNUFFLES POLAR BEAR 1980	$29.00	VINTAGE 1980 GUND HAMLET THE PIG PLUSH	$10.50
$294 Lot 21 Childrens Stuffed Animals Baby Adventure NR	$27.09	Pottery Barn Allie the Alligator TOY NWT	$10.50
$400 Lot 20 Childrens Gund Stuffed Ben Dogs w/Scarf NR	$27.00	Last Elegant Bear Gund 24" with book 1983	$10.50
Max and Ruby "MAX" Plush Doll 11-1/2" New with Tags	$26.50	GUND KARITAS TENDER TEDDY COLLECTOR'S CLASSIC BEARS S/3	$10.49

Trading Card Games ▸ Magic the Gathering

The average sales price in this subcategory is $17.56.

	HIGH		AVG
Beta Black Lotus Power Nine	$819.09	ARABIAN NIGHTS Jihad	$19.50
10,000+ MAGIC THE GATHERING COLLECTION mtg L@@K huge	$463.32	Magic MTG - 4x MIRARI'S WAKE (Judgment)	$19.00
Unlimited Mox Ruby Power Nine	$315.00	Antiquities Strip Mine X4	$19.00
Unlimited Mox Jet Power Nine	$303.00	mtg Magic 1x Demonic Tutor FOREIGN BB	$18.50
Unlimited Ancestral Recall Power Nine	$286.50	Scion of Darkness X4+Dark Supplicant X3 Legions NM MTG	$17.99
MTG My Collection of 3,500 + Cards, Over 300 rares.	$250.00	Darksteel Darksteel Colossus X2 Near Mint	$17.55
MTG Magic the Gathering COLLECTION 2200+ cards Low S&H	$249.99	mtg Magic 4x Vindicate	$17.55
Unlimited Mox Emerald Power Nine	$227.50	Revised Hypnotic Specter X4	$17.50
Mishra's Workshop Antiquities NM Magic Rare MTG	$224.99	Beta Goblin King Near Mint Hard to Find	$17.26
ARABIAN NIGHTS Bazaar of Baghdad Near Mint	$152.50	mtg Magic 4x Blinkmoth Nexus	$17.22
ARABIAN NIGHTS Library of Alexandria Mint	$150.00	Magic MTG - 4x BLISTERING FIRECAT (Onslaught)	$17.10
Magic MTG Unlimited Lot 229 Uncommons -Sol Rings/Tutors	$108.49	Urza's Saga Gaea's Cradle X1	$17.00
ORIGINAL INVASION Riths Attendant ARTWORK by ADAM REX!	$100.00	Mercadian Masques Food Chain X4 Near Mint	$16.72
Legends Mana Drain Near Mint	$96.33	MTG Eternal Witness x4 - NM - INSANE!	$16.50
mtg Magic 4x Tropical Island REVISED	$90.00	Odyssey Entomb X4	$16.50

Trading Card Games ▸ Star Wars

The average sales price in this subcategory is $7.54.

	HIGH		AVG
Star Wars Decipher CCG Large Lot	$406.00	Star Wars "Jabba's Palace" Limited Booster Box	$8.00
Huge lot of Star Wars CCG Cards...700rares...70 foils	$265.00	Star Wars CCG Second Anthology	$7.99
Star Wars CCG Coruscant Complete Set 180 No AI	$135.50	Star Wars CCG Third Anthology	$7.99
Star Wars CCG: Reflections 2 (II)- sealed Booster BOX	$130.00	STAR WARS CCG ENHANCED BATTLE OF NABOO	$7.99

STAR WARS CCG REFLECTIONS III UNOPEN BOX	$122.50	Star Wars CCG Theed Palace Al Artoo, Brave Little Droid	$7.57
YOUNG JEDI Reflections Booster packs complete box	$109.16	Star Wars CCG Jabba's Palace Limited booster box	$7.50
STAR WARS CCG DEATH STAR II UNOPEN BOX	$86.01	Star Wars CCG REF 2 FOIL Flagship Executor - Destroyer	$7.50
Star Wars CCG TCG Premiere BB Complete Limited Set 362	$71.00	Star Wars CCG TCG Cloud City Limited Set (BB) Mint	$7.05
Star Wars CCG - Reflections2 Complete Premium set of 54	$61.00	Star Wars CCG Rare Endor Foil Tempest 1 URF Rare UR	$7.02
Original Star Wars CCG by Decipher Limited Ed 2000+ Set	$60.01	Star Wars CCG Rare Endor Foil Tempest Scout 4 URF UR RF	$7.02
STAR WARS CCG THEED PALACE SEALED BOOSTER BOX DECIPHER OOP	$57.99	Star Wars Light Saber spoon Green!!!	$6.70
STAR WARS CCG THEED PALACE UNOPEN BOX	$56.00	Star Wars CCG SE RARE Darth Vader Dark Lord of the Sith	$6.61
Star Wars CCG SWCCG 40 Rares from Coruscant Darth Maul	$52.66	Baron Fel Star Wars Miniatures Universe 34/60 VERY RARE	$6.51
Star Wars Tournament FOIL Imperial-Class Star Destroyer	$52.16	Star Wars CCG Death Star II - Flagship : Executor MINT	$6.50
STAR WARS CCG THEED PALACE BOOSTER BOX	$51.00	Star Wars CCG DARTH VADER BB PREMIRE SET HARD TO FIND	$6.50

Trading Card Games ▶ Yu-Gi-Oh

The average sales price in this subcategory is $22.70.

	HIGH		AVG
Yu-Gi-Oh! Lot Of Secret Rares, Ultra, Super and Regular	$193.51	YUGIOH! MASTER COLLECTION FACTORY SEALED SET	$24.95
YUGIOH 1ST EDITION CYBERNETIC REVOLUTION BOOSTER 2 box	$132.51	YUGIOH Soul Of The Duelist 24 Pack Booster Box	$24.50
(2) YU-GI-OH DARK BEGINNING 2 SEALED BOOSTER BOXES	$120.99	YU-GI-OH big 100 card lot NO DOUBLES + HOLO bonus yugio	$24.50
2BOX LOT YUGIOH BLAZE OF DESTRUCTION & FURY DEEP BOX	$119.95	YU-GI-OH GILFORD THE LIGHTNING TIN 5 PACKS-54 CARDS	$23.55
Yu-Gi-Oh Labyrinth of Nightmare Sealed Box of 36 Packs	$100.00	YUGIOH CYBER END DRAGON CRV-EN036 ULTRA HOLO NEW!	$23.39
[2 of these sold in a multiple item ("Dutch") auction for $50.00 each]		YUGIOH CYBER END DRAGON	$22.89
Yu Gi Oh/YuGiOh 2005 6 Collector Tin/Tins Complete Set	$99.00	CRV-EN036 ULTRA HOLO NEW!	
Yu Gi Oh/YuGiOh 2005 6 Collector Tin/Tins Complete Set	$97.00	Mint Yu-Gi-Oh Mechanical Chaser TP3-003	$22.53
Yu Gi Oh/YuGiOh 2005 6 Collector Tin/Tins Complete Set	$95.00	YUGIOH Flaming Eternity 24 Pack Booster Box	$22.51
Yu Gi Oh/YuGiOh 2005 6 Collector Tin/Tins Complete Set	$93.00	YU-GI-OH big 100 card lot NO DOUBLES + HOLO bonus yugio	$22.45
Limited edition Exodia with all 5 pieces and Necross	$91.00	YUGIOH ANCIENT SANCTUARY 24 Pack Booster Box	$22.01
YUGIOH YU-GI-OH 2005 TIN SET SEALED LIVE IN STOCK	$89.99	1ST EDYUGIOH Ancient Sanctuary 24 Pack Booster Box	$22.00
YuGiOh Flaming Eternity 1st Edition 2 BOXES SEALED BOX	$88.77	Sealed Yu-Gi-Oh Kaiba Blue Eyes White Dragon Tin Set	$22.00
YuGiOh The Lost Millennium 1st Edition 2 BOXES BOX	$85.98	YU GI OH Rise of Destiny 1st Ed Booster BOX (24) Packs	$21.94
YuGiOh SOUL OF THE DUELIST SOD 1st Edition 2 BOXES BOX	$81.01	1ST EDITION YUGIOH Rise of Destiny 24 Pack Booster Box	$21.50
YuGiOh Dark Revelation 2 SEALED Boxes Revelations	$81.00	CYBERNETIC REVOLUTION Box 24 Pk CRV YuGiOh 1st Edition+	$21.50

TV, Movie, Character Toys ▶ Barney

The average sales price in this subcategory is $10.13.

	HIGH		AVG
Microsoft ActiMates Interactive Barney & TV Pack (NIB)	$86.00	Childrens BARNEY & FRIENDS Car Coin Bank – NEW	$10.50
BARNEY ACTIMATES WITH TV PACK AND BONUS VIDEO **LQQK**	$59.00	Barney Sippy Cup or Mug w/ Handle! CUTE!!!!!	$10.50
21 piece Barney lot.! Movies,Books, Pillow, Chair&more!	$56.00	Barney Characters	$10.50
BARNEY MYSTERY AUCTION! Great Mystery Box 4 your child!	$56.00	BARNEY'S LEARNING LAPTOP + DRESS ME PLUSH BARNEY	$10.50
HUGE BARNEY AND FRIENDS TOYS,GAMES,VIDEOS,BARNEY HOUSE	$54.00	NWT Barney size 7 girls toddler shoes L@@K	$10.49
MICROSOFT ACTIMATES INTERACTIVE BARNEY & NEW PC PACK	$52.00	BARNEY FAUCET PROTECTOR AND SOAP DISPENSER	$10.49
MICROSOFT ACTIMATES BARNEY + INTERACTIVE PC PACK	$51.00	NWT! BARNEY LUNCHBOX LUNCH KIT THERMOS ETC	$10.16
~HUGE LOT OF "BARNEY"VIDEO[S, BOOKS,TOYS TALKING BARNEY	$49.99	8 BARNEY - B.J. - BABY BOP PVC FIGURES	$10.01
Plush Washable BARNEY CHAIR w/ 6 VHS Videos Movies LOT	$49.50	Barney - Barney and Baby Bop Lets Go T-shirt Size 3T	$10.01
Barney, BOP, BJ Toy's,Book, NEW Sheet SET NIB -Twin	$43.99	NWT Barney size 8 girls toddler shoes L@@K	$10.00
HUGE STUFFED BARNEY ▶ ▶ 39 INCHES TALL ▶ PERFECT CONDITION	$42.01	Plush Toddler BARNEY Purple Dinosaur Book Bag Back Pack	$10.00
Barney Plush foam kiddie chair NEW!! AWESOME	$40.00	BARNEY THE PURPLE DINO FIGURAL BANK - NIB!!!	$10.00
BARNEY Twin Sheet Set - New!!!	$39.99	Barney - Socktop Slippers Size 9/10	$10.00
BIG LOT BARNEY THE DINOSAUR 14 VIDEOS MOVIES WITH CASES	$36.99	BARNEY'S SCHOOL HOUSE PLAY SET PURPLE DINOSAUR FIGURES	$10.00
34 BARNEY VIDEOS ~ SOME NEVER SEEN ON TV	$36.00	Lot of Barney Books, Banjo, Train and More	$10.00

TV, Movie, Character Toys ▶ Bob the Builder

The average sales price in this subcategory is $9.26.

	HIGH		AVG
BOB THE BUILDER FULL Comforter & Sheets NEW! NR	$82.00	Bob the Builder PLAY-A-SOUND Telephone BOOK New Toy	$9.95
BOB THE BUILDER BRIO TRAIN SET AND ACCESSORIES 50 PIECE	$75.00	BOB THE BUILDER SAW,WRENCH & SCREWDRIVER BOOKS NEW	$9.95
Huge Bob the Builder Lego Duplo lot 137 pcs.	$71.00	LITTLE PEOPLE TOYS & BOB THE BUILDER	$9.95
5 Brio Bob The Builder Sets with Figures - Excell Cond!	$51.00	BOB THE BUILDER SIZE 5 TODDLER PAJAMAS NEW	$9.95
BOB THE BUILDER - 6 TALKING TRUCKS VEHICLES - FULL SET	$42.00	BOB THE BUILDER HTF TALKING DIZZY ORANGE CONCRETE MIXER	$9.58
COMPLETE SET OF 6 BOB THE BUILDER TALKING VEHICLES	$40.00	BOB THE BUILDER TOYS & PUZZLES electronic toy talking	$9.50
Bob the Builder costume sz.2-4-like NEW!!	$38.00	bob the builder VEHICLE BENNY RARE! NEW!	$9.25
BOB THE BUILDER TALKING VEHICLES, COMPLETE SET OF 6	$38.00	BOB THE BUILDER LEGO building toys with SCOOP	$9.25
BOB THE BUILDER Full Double Quilt Comforter NEW COTTON	$36.00	Bob the builder PILCHARD the cat stuffed toy RARE	$9.01
Bob The Builder Snowed Under Playset BNIB	$35.00	Lot of Bob the Builder, VHS, Vehicles, Dolls, Hammer...	$9.00
BOB THE BUILDER FARMHOUSE PLAYSET TALKING TRAVIS NIB	$34.99	Lot Of 3 Bob The Builder Dolls (Talking Toys) L@@K!!!!!	$9.00
BOB the BUILDER Sleeping Bag "Ready Bed" AIR MATTRESS	$34.33	Bob the Builder -Toolbag with Tools and Toolbelt	$9.00
Bob the Builder Electronic Talking Building Yard ++	$33.69	LARGE BOB THE BUILDER TALKING WORKSITE w/ CRANE SO COOL	$9.00
Bob the Builder Halloween Costume Size 2-4 EUC	$33.00	Lot 3 Bob the Builder Vhs kids movies videos low S&H	$9.00
BOB the BUILDER Twin Comforter/3 pc Sheet Set/Valances	$32.03	Bob the Builder 12" Stuffed Plush Doll	$8.99

TV, Movie, Character Toys ▸ Disney

The average sales price in this subcategory is $11.22.

	HIGH		AVG
Vintage Marx Toys Disney Goofy Twirling Tail Toy - Box	$127.50	Mickey Mouse Vintage Watch in Tin, by Avon *NEW*	$12.99
EARLY FISHER PRICE DISNEY DONALD DUCK POP UP PADDLE	$104.00	1/64 Mickey Mouse Disney Daytona 500 Transporter! 2004	$12.99
Vintage Disney Donald Duck Sand Sifter Pail Ohio Art	$103.50	Skating Talking Mickey And Minnie Mouse Like new.15"	$12.00
Vintage Jointed Celluloid Donald Duck Walt Disney	$77.00	DISNEY CEILING MOTION PIC PROJECTOR W MICKEY, MINNIE ++	$12.00
RARE Walt Disney DONALD DUCK Auto-Magic PROJECTOR MIB *	$76.99	11 disney GOOFY SPORTS pvc figures/toys	$11.55
DISNEY DVD CD PLAYER PORTABLE MICKEY MOUSE MOVIE DISNEY	$71.00	3 Org. 1971 MARX WDP DONALD DUCK Figures 3 Colors! MINT	$11.50
Vintage 1930's Mickey Mouse Child's Bowl RARE	$50.00	Crawling Baby Mickey and Minnie	$11.01
SUN RUBBER MICKEY MOUSE AIR MAIL	$49.99	Antique mickey mouse and hammer toy	$10.65
WALT DISNEY MICKEY MOUSE RETRO RAG DOLL 14 INCHES TALL	$49.95	5 MIP Disney Store Stuffed Animals "Peter Pan, Hook++"	$10.50
DISNEY Amusement Park TRAIN SET Mickey MOUSE & Friends	$46.00	2 Vintage Goofy Toys Tricycle & Kohner Trapeze DISNEY	$10.50
Linemar Marx Donald Duck On Tricycle–Tin Wind Up	$44.95	Donald Duck Disneykins by Marx with Box	$10.50
Composition Snow White Antique Doll	$42.99	Very Unique Skateboarding Goofy Radio Controled	$10.00
WDP Disney Japan 3 Bisque Rare Figs 2 Donald Duck Goofy	$41.00	DISNEY CLASSIC CD/RADIO DCD6000-C BRAND NEW IN PACKAGE	$9.99
Vintage Donald Duck toy pull train	$40.63	VIEW-MASTER GAF VIEW MASTER PROJECTOR WITH DISNEY TIN	$9.99
NEW Mickey Mouse Ceiling Fan 42" w/light	$39.99	Medicom Babekub Kubrick Mickey Mouse+Minnie figure doll	$9.99

TV, Movie, Character Toys ▸ Dora the Explorer

The average sales price in this subcategory is $10.68.

	HIGH		AVG
DORA THE EXPLORER TALKING HOUSE ACCESSORIES SET/LOT NIB	$74.99	DORA THE EXPLORER ~CANDYLAND GAME	$11.99
DORA THE EXPLORER TALKING HOUSE HUGE SET! OVER 20 PIECE	$65.00	DORA LUNCH BOX CAR Lunchbox NEW Bag the Explorer Auto	$11.99
14K Gold Dora The Explorer Pendant and Earrings	$54.00	Dora Explorer THROW BLANKET - NEW IN PKG!!!	$11.99
HUGE Lot of DORA the EXPLORER Party Supplies for 16	$52.00	Dora the Explorer - "Kitchen Furniture"	$11.99
FISHER PRICE DORA THE EXPLORER DORA'S TALKING HOUSE NEW	$48.99	DORA THE EXPLORER VELVETY 2 PIECE PAJAMAS NEW SZ 5T	$11.95
DISNEY PRINCESS POLLY POCKET MINI DOLLS VHTF *USA*	$45.00	DORA THE EXPLORER VALANCE FOR WINDOW	$11.95
DORA the EXPLORER DRESS AND DANCE DOLL BRAND NEW VHTF	$39.49	Dora the Explorer Purple Backpack Bag w/ Map 11"	$11.50
DORA 4 Pc Toddler Bed Sheets Set Shooting Stars Boots	$36.01	Dora the Explorer Purple Backpack Bag w/ Map 11"	$11.50
Dora the Explorer Toddler Bedding! Brand New!	$35.00	RARE 17" DORA THE EXPLORER BIRTHDAY DOLL NEW	$11.50
DORA THE EXPLORER WINTER PINK JACKET SIZE 2T NEW	$34.95	Dora the Explorer PURPLE BACKPACK purse bag & MAP RARE	$11.50
HUGE 29PIECE LOT DORA TOYS 2DOLLS,BOOKS,PURSE,BACKPACK	$34.52	Dora the Explorer Plush Dora Boots GUND & Nanco	$11.50
Dora The Explorer plush talking Boots & Swiper stuffed	$34.15	Dora the Explorer PURPLE PLUSH SHINE BACKPACK bag MAP	$11.50
Dora the Explorer We Did It Dancing Singing Doll RARE!	$33.99	Dora the Explorer BOOTS DOLL Brand New with Tags	$11.50
DORA THE EXPLORER WINTER JACKET W/HOOD SIZE 4T	$33.95	TALKING BOOTS Monkey DORA THE EXPLORER	$11.00
Dora the Explorer Flannel Sheet SET TWIN Christmas NEW	$33.53	Dora The Explorer Talking Back Pack Very Cute L@@K	$11.00

TV, Movie, Character Toys ▸ Gumby

The average sales price in this subcategory is $10.63.

	HIGH		AVG
Reboot Original Collector Edition Figure Reboot Figure	$100.00	Gumby & Pokey T-Shirt LG Blue New w/ Tag!	$12.99
Vintage 1965 Gumby Lakeside Toys No. 8101	$76.04	GUMBY 6 INCH TALL NEW IN BOX	$12.50
GUMBY'S JEEP, Gumby and Pokey Tin Car Circa 1960's	$57.69	Lot Trendmasters 2 Gumby Pokey Jeep Race Car	$12.50
GUMBY AND POKEY EMERALD DOWNS LIMITED EDITION	$53.52	GUMBY & POKEY–3 DIFFERANT SIZED SETS AND A JEEP	$12.49
Emerald Downs Gumby & Pokey SGA Limited Edition	$51.00	LOT 2 GUMBY POKEY RUBBER TYPE TOYS 1989 LIKE NEW TV	$12.00
ORIGINAL 1965 LAKESIDE GUMBY MINT ON CARD & GUMBY	$49.95	[2 of these sold in a multiple item ("Dutch") auction for $6.00 each]	
Bendable Gumby And Pokey Signed Art Clokey Blister Pack	$46.00	Lot of Gumby toy bendable figures & Space Gumby	$11.50
Vintage Gumby & Pokey bendy blister cards NEW 1968	$41.89	Gumby & Friends Figure Set	$10.50
VINTAGE GUMBY FIGURE AM FM TRANSISTOR	$40.50	VINTAGE 1986 GUMBY TELEPHONE WORKS & LOOKS GREAT	$10.50
RADIO MINT WORKS!		17" POKEY GUMBY'S HORSE PLUSH	$10.50
Gumby & Pokey Collectible Emerald Downs Limited Edition	$37.36	Vintage Gumby Poseable Toy-10 1/2 inch	$10.50
Gumby + Pokey Kumino (dressing gown) very last one!	$36.00	Large Bendy Pokey and Gumby Toys Jesco Hong Kong	$10.50
Gumby Fireman and Cowboy Costume - MINT!!!	$35.00	**** INFLATABLE BLOWUP ^^^^^ GUMBY ^^^^^ Blow up ^^^^^	$10.25
Vintage 1965 GUMBY by Lakeside on Original Card!	$27.00	Brand New! GUMBY & FRIENDS Bendable 5" Figurines Set	$10.00
Vintage Pokey Pencil Case "Gumby's Pal Pokey" 1967	$26.00	Gumby 10.5" Poseable ***NEW IN BOX***	$10.00
Super RARE 1965 Astronaut Adventure Custume for Gumby!!	$25.00	GUMBY & POKEY ART CLOKEY POKEY RUBBER KEY CHAINS X 6	$10.00

TV, Movie, Character Toys ▸ Harry Potter

The average sales price in this subcategory is $15.35.

	HIGH		AVG
HARRY POTTER FINAL CHALLENGE CHESS SET Brand New!	$360.00	Harry Potter Deluxe Costume Light-up and Sound Wand NEW	$15.99
HARRY POTTER RARE QUIDDITCH WATCH SET LE NEW	$125.00	LEGO HARRY POTTER KNOCKTURN ALLEY SET 4720	$15.60
Exclusive! Harry Potter Dumbledore Wizard Mood Watch	$119.99	LOT-Harry Potter DVD and PS2 game	$15.56
8 MIXED LOT HARRY POTTER WIZARD COLLECTION FIGURES MOC	$115.26	Harry Potter Nimbus 2000 Broom Electronic Costume $NR	$15.55
HARRY POTTER RARE QUIDDITCH WATCH SET LE NEW	$115.00	Lego Harry Potter Knight Bus #4755 NEW!!!	$15.52
LEGO HARRY POTTER #4709 HOGWARTS CASTLE NEW IN BOX	$112.50	4 HARRY POTTER MIXED LOT FIGURES MOC NEW	$15.51
BNIB HARRY POTTER HOGWARTS CASTLE LEGO SET 4709	$102.50	HARRY POTTER HAGRID DELUXE CREATURE COLLECTION NEW MOC	$15.50
LEGO HARRY POTTER #4730 CHAMBER OF SECRETS NEW IN BOX	$82.00	HARRY POTTER COSTUME ACCESSORY Green Slytherin Neck Tie	$15.05
Harry Potter Electronic Hogwarts Castle Playset + more	$76.00	HARRY POTTER black SORTING HAT	$15.00
RARE DUMBLEDORE Harry Potter & the Sorcerer's Stone	$76.00	HARRY POTTER Gryffindor NECK TIE red	$15.00
Gringotts Savings Bankbook- Harry Potter Coins Full Set	$65.00	MONKEY chimp THROW BATH RUG MAT brand new SALE	$15.00
Legos Star Wars/ Harry Potter/ HUGE LOT	$59.51	OFFICIAL HARRY POTTER black Big STUDENT HAT	$15.00
HARRY POTTER NIMBUS 2000 ELECTRONIC BROOM BROOMSTICK	$58.00	Harry Potter Party Supplies~Decorations~Prizes~Cake Pan	$15.00
harry potter QUIDDITCH pocket watch~FOSSIL #690 of 2000	$52.02	4 Harry Potter Storyteller Figurines *NEW IN BOXES*	$15.00
Harry Potter Sorcerer Stone Hogwarts Heroes Ron Figure	$51.89	Official HARRY POTTER Professor FLITWICK hat cap	$15.00

TV, Movie, Character Toys ▶ Hello Kitty

The average sales price in this subcategory is $7.63.

	HIGH		AVG
13IN COLORED HELLO KITTY TV!! GREAT CONDITION!	$78.00	HELLO KITTY school supplies stamp keychange lot	$7.99
HELLO KITTY TELEVISION TV-Now Collectible!	$76.00	Hello Kitty Music Talking Alarm Clock "Cute"	$7.99
HELLO KITTY Red RAZOR SCOOTER Rare Sanrio Exclusive NEW	$60.00	HELLO KITTY 1998 3D ICE CREAM CONE STYLE CUP W/SPOON !!	$7.99
SANRIO HELLO KITTY TOASTER WIDE SLOT COOL TOUCH	$46.00	HELLO KITTY TODDLER TRAVEL PILLOW / PINK / NEW!	$7.99
~*HELLO KITTY orig 78' SANRIO KITTY'S CHEST*~ nice! NR	$32.00	Hello Kitty 12 Party Favor Bead Necklaces Very Nice	$7.99
HELLO KITTY TOASTER + MILKSHAKE-MALT MAKER LIKE NEW	$31.00	HELLO KITTY dress up set lots of accessories	$7.99
Sanrio Hello Kitty 2 Slice Wide Slot Toaster NIB	$26.13	CUTE HELLO KITTY ACCENT TABLE LAMP LIKE NEW	$7.75
2 Chococat Hello Kitty Fleece Throws Blankets NEW NIP	$26.00	Hello Kitty Canopy - Like New!	$7.50
Hello Kitty Radio - Cd player - AM/FM radio CUTE!!	$26.00	HELLO KITTY iPod Case/MP3 Case	$7.50
JAPAN UFO Hello Kitty School Girl Blue Plush Doll Cat Q	$26.00	Hello Kitty BEST FRIEND Necklace Face PINK Silver NEW	$7.50
CHOCOCAT (HELLO KITTY) 2002 SOFT CONTACT LENS CASE NEW!	$25.99	JAPAN HELLO KITTY *STRAWBERRY NEWS* #10	$7.50
Sanrio! HELLO KITTY! TWO Strands Party Lights! NIB!!!	$25.00	Hello Kitty Hawaii Lanyard Keychain NWT	$7.50
HELLO KITTY BOOM BOX CD PLAYER AM / FM RADIO STEREO	$25.00	Hello Kitty Necklace NIP	$7.50
CINNAMOROLL (HELLO KITTY) 2003 EMBROIDERED BIG CUSHION	$24.99	Hello Kitty Hearts Tin Purse w/Beaded Handle-Mint	$6.99
New! 2 Pinky Satin Hello Kitty SEAT CUSHIONS! 2 FOR 1 !	$24.50	Sanrio Hello Kitty Pink Tool/Storage/Jewelry Box Cute!!	$6.99

TV, Movie, Character Toys ▶ Muppets, Sesame Street

The average sales price in this subcategory is $10.82.

	HIGH		AVG
Rare Steppin Out Tux Gonzo & Bernice CARDED Target N/R	$167.50	Fraggle Rock 8" Plush Doozers Set of 3	$11.51
Original 1996 Tickle Me Elmo Plush Sesame Street MIB!	$76.00	Muppets The Muppet Show Beaker 5" Push Puppet Figure	$11.50
MUPPET ANIMAL ELECTRIC MAYHEM STAGE DRUM SET NEW	$51.00	Sesame Street Cookie Monster * Christmas Musical Figure	$11.50
BNIB MY FIRST PAL ELMO BABY SESAME STREET NEW WASHABLE	$50.00	Palisades: Muppet Holiday Rizzo Retailer SIGNED	$11.50
NEW HUGE 40" SESAME STREET COOKIE MONSTER	$49.99	Brand New Chicken Dance Elmo!!!	$11.49
Shout Elmo / New 2005 / New In Box / Rare Hard To Find	$49.88	SESAME STREET BIG BIRD* 19 1/2" Chenille Stuffed Animal	$11.49
MUPPET PUPPET, SESAME STREET, VINTAGE 70'S, RARE	$48.00	MOC Muppets Collector Paradise Exclusive Animal Figure	$11.10
Muppets Henson DARK CRYSTAL 12" Kira & Pet w/ stand NR	$45.00	Big Bird Story Magic #7117 Goldilocks and the 3 Grouche	$10.60
Muppet Show Swedish Chef - Swedish Kitchen Playset NIB	$41.50	SESAME STREET PLUSH/STUFFED SNUFFLEUPAGUS * APPLAUSE	$10.51
rare SESAME STREET plush MARSHALL GROVER knickerbocker	$40.00	14" Rare Purpl Twiddle Bug Plush Sesame Street Applause	$10.51
Talking Baby Sinclair Dinosaurs Disney / Jim Henson NIB	$40.00	Animal from the muppet show	$10.50
rare MUPPET SHOW plush muppets ROWLF DOG DOLL muppet	$38.77	New Elmo Dancing, Singing, Y-M-C-A	$10.50
MUPPETS SWEDISH KITCHEN PLAYSET MIB 25 YEARS	$36.50	FRAGGLE ROCK 20TH ANNIVERSARY BOOBER 12" PLUSH DOLL	$10.50
Sesame Street: Shout Elmo	$36.00	NWT SESAME STREET COOKIE MONSTER BACKPACK BAG-CUTE!	$10.50
vintage SESAME STREET muppets COOKIE Monster PUPPET	$36.00	14" GONZO PLUSH Sesame Street With Tag MUPPETS	$10.50

TV, Movie, Character Toys ▶ My Little Pony

The average sales price in this subcategory is $15.32.

	HIGH		AVG
83 Piece Hasbro My Little Pony Lot All 1980's LOOK NR!!	$255.04	My Little Pony Show Stable w/Lemon Drop, brandy an box	$15.50
RARE 1980s MIB Lot of 12 My Little Pony BOXED Birthday	$245.07	1980's My LITTLE PONY LOT + VHS & book for CHARITY	$15.50
My Little Pony Case Stable 93 Ponies 74 MLP 19 Copycats	$218.37	Vintage My Little Pony 1983 UNICORN SUNBEAM MINT! HTF!	$15.50
My Little Pony Big Brother 4-Speed	$177.50	MY LITTLE PONY vintage BUBBLES (SITTING PONY) GRRREAT	$15.50
My Little Pony Big Brother Slugger	$177.50	My Little Pony BABY LICKETY SPLIT FIRST TOOTH+ACCES!!	$15.50
My Little Pony Big Brother Steamer	$167.50	My Little Pony PERFUME PUFF RED ROSES RARE BEAUTY	$15.50
My Little Pony Big Brother Quarterback	$155.94	My Little Pony SITTING SEA SHELL EXCELLENT RARE	$15.28
HUGE lot of 50+ My Little Pony Ponies all original 80s	$155.00	My Little Pony BIG BROTHER QUARTERBACK ACCES RARE!	$15.00
29 My Little Pony PONIES Hasbro MLP HUGE VINTAGE LOT	$153.49	RARE MAIL ORDER Snuzzle earth pony My little pony 82	$15.00
RARE 1980s MIB Lot of 6 My Little Pony BOXED Minty	$152.50	my little pony mlp lot ponies with merry go round pony	$15.00
My Little Pony Big Brother Pony Tex	$152.33	Vintage 1985 So Soft My Little Pony Taffy!	$15.00
RARE MAIL ORDER Scribbles Pretty Mane my little pony 86	$149.99	My Little Pony Twice as Fancy MERRIWEATHER ...	$15.00
Li'l Sweetcake baby pony great condition Very rare find	$115.00	Vintage my Little Pony Lot of 11, Also Megan!	$14.51
Original NSS (non so soft) Cupcake UK v/HTF, g1	$109.49	MY LITTLE PONY PONY WEAR ACCESSORIES SHOES SKATES	$14.50
'86 MY LITTLE PONY GALAXY TWINKLE-EYED, MOC	$102.50	MLP "BARNACLE" & PIRATE HAT BIG BROTHER PONY 1987-1988	$14.49

TV, Movie, Character Toys ▶ Pokemon

The average sales price in this subcategory is $8.68.

	HIGH		AVG
Super Set 215 Solid Color Pokemon Figures 2" New & Rare	$97.00	380+ Pokemon Stickers, Albums, Storages Boxes, etc. NEW	$8.99
Super Set 215 Solid Color Pokemon Figures 2" New & Rare	$84.98	Pokemon, Stickers, Series D, 35 Stick Ups, Kids Room	$8.99
Super Set 215 Solid Color Pokemon Figures 2" New & Rare	$75.00	Pokemon border Pokemon stickups -Brand new and rare!!!	$8.99
HUGE LOT OF 134 DIFFERENT POKEMON & DIGIMON PVC FIGURES	$68.00	Pokemon, Stickers, Series C, 35 Stick Ups, Kids', NEW	$8.99
41 Sealed Pokemon Pokeballs Burger King Collection	$67.75	39 Ruby & Sapphire Pokemon Figures With 2 Trainers New	$8.98
Super Set 215 Solid Color Pokemon Figures 2" New & Rare	$62.00	20 Solid Color 2 Inch Pokemon Figures (C1)	$8.98
BIG LOT OF POKEMON MARBLES *L@@K*	$59.50	pokemon advanced action figure corphish + metagross nib	$8.50
POKEMON POKEBALL KEYCHAIN COMBO	$54.00	330 POKEMON TRADING CARD GAME !!!NR!!!	$8.50
Rare 120 Pokemon Figures 2" Unique Collection! **New**	$44.00	POKEMON BACKPACK-NWO!! PIKACHU AND ASH!!	$8.50
Pokemon Twin Bed Sheets, Pillow Cases, 3 Glasses, Game	$41.00	POKEMON SUPER BOUNCING BALLS (5 PIKACHU, SQUIRTLE)	$8.50
Pokemon 27 Chapter + 3 Handbook + 3 Junior 36 Book Lot	$41.00	Nintendo Pokemon Kitty Black Backpack Bag Sling Tote	$8.49
Small rubber Pokemon figures lot Pikachu, Squirtle	$36.50	Pokemon Collector Marble Case ARCANINE #59	$8.49
Rare 120 Pokemon Figures 2" Unique Collection! **New**	$36.00	POKEMON STICKER EXTRAVAGANZA * 190 STICKERS W/ALBUM	$8.28
BURGER KING LOT OF 48 POKEMON TOYS WITH RED WHITE BALLS	$36.00	NIB Pokemon Dinnerware Set : Plate, Tumbler, Bowl	$8.01
HUGE 18 POKEMON VHS MOVIES + POKEMON DUFFLE BAG "WOW"	$35.00	New Set of 30 Pokemon Action Figures Figure	$8.00

TV, Movie, Character Toys ▶ SpongeBob Squarepants

The average sales price in this subcategory is $7.97.

	HIGH		AVG
NICKTRONICS SPONGEBOB SQUAREPANTS 13" TV	$96.99	2000 Babbling Spongebob Toy Talking Squarepants Works	$7.99
SPONGE BOB SPONGEBOB PROJECTION GLOBE ALARM CLOCK NEW	$45.00	SPONGE BOB "BIKINI BOTTOM" TALKING ALARM CLOCK	$7.99
SpongeBob Shower Curtain toothbrush cup memo board LOT	$40.99	SpongeBob Squarepants 7" MR. KRABS PLUSH ~ NWT	$7.99
GAINT SPONGE BOB SQUAREPANTS FROM BURGER KING	$40.00	Spongebob Squarepants GARY the SNAIL Plush	$7.99
SpongeBob Squarepants Poster Phone	$31.00	Spongebob Squarepants MR. KRABS Plush Doll	$7.99
SPONGEBOB KRABBY PATTY STATION GRILL NEW IN BOX	$29.99	Spongebob Squarepants Patrick door POSTER Sponge bob	$7.99
SPONGEBOB PROJECTION GLOBE ALARM CLOCK	$29.95	SPONGEBOB SQUAREPANTS SOAP LOTION DISPENSER 2 PC SET	$7.95
SPONGEBOB SQUAREPANTS ALL 5 BURGER KING WATCHES SEALED	$26.50	Spongebob Squarepants birthday party supplies a lot fun	$7.75
BIG 10" MR. KRABS PLUSH FIGURE from SpongeBob ~ NWT	$26.00	7" BIKER SPONGEBOB and 8-1/2" PATRICK PLUSH SET ~ NWT	$7.52
SpongeBob 4-Pc Toddler Bedding Set + FREE RAIN PONCHO!!	$25.95	SPONGEBOB SQUAREPANTS MAGIC 8 BALL	$7.51
SpongeBob SquarePants Bikini Bottom Hideaway Playhut	$24.99	Childs Sponge Bob Costume - Medium & Sponge Bob plush	$7.50
Sponge Bob Lot Bubble Blowing, Lamp, 2 pr Sleep pants	$22.50	SPONGEBOB SQUAREPANTS FUN ALARM CLOCK!!! MUST SEE!	$7.50
The SpongeBob SquarePants Patrick Jack in the Music Box	$21.99	Hugh Lot Of Sponge Bob Goodies Including Watch	$7.50
BRAND NEW PORTABLE SPONGEBOB CD PLAYER RADIO BOOMBOX	$20.50	SpongeBob Patrick Star Aquarium Figure New in Package	$7.50
Sponge Bob Square Pants child's Sofa, Bed, Play, Nice!	$20.50	SPONGEBOB * SQUAREPANTS WALL CLOCK NIB NO RES.	$7.25

TV, Movie, Character Toys ▶ Teletubbies

The average sales price in this subcategory is $9.37.

	HIGH		AVG
Set 4 Tummy Glow Teletubbies 1998 Mint in Box NRFB	$81.55	LOT OF HARD PLASTIC TELETUBBIES - PBS - GOOD CONDITION!	$9.51
Teletubbies Magic Dancing 16" Plush *All 4 Characters*	$51.99	Teletubbies Tinky-Winky Halloween Costume 2T	$9.50
Set of 4 teletubbies plush dolls dipsy po tinky la NEW	$51.00	TELETUBBIES COME AND PLAY PALS FIGURES PVC PLAYSET NEW	$9.50
611 ALL NEW IN PACKAGES TELETUBBIES PARTY SUPPLIES! WOW	$49.99	NIB Talking Teletubbie w/VHS "PO"	$9.50
Halloween The Crocodile Hunter Steve Costume Outfit 4-6	$49.00	EDEN Green Teletubbies DIPSY Plush! 7.5" BRAND NEW!	$9.50
SET OF 4~NEW~PLUSH~1998~TELETUBBIES	$48.50	TELETUBBIES LAA LAA HALLOWEEN COSTUME La La SZ. 18 MOS.	$9.50
DOLLS~PLAYSKOOL~NIB		TELETUBBIES SQUEEKY TOY BATH SET - BRAND NEW	$9.48
Set of 4 Teletubbies Plush Dolls Dipsy Po Tinky Laa NEW	$48.50	Teletubbies! Tinky Winky, Dipsy, LaLa, Po Talkin&glowin	$9.22
TELETUBBIES SET 4 PLUSH DOLLS TINKY DIPSY LA PO NEW	$48.00	TELETUBBIES 17" Plush TALKING TINKY WINKY Playskool	$9.07
Very Rare Teletubbies Building Mat NIB New in Box!	$43.99	NEW PBS TELETUBBIES Walking Talking BABY LA LA Girl Boy	$9.06
TELETUBBIES BEAD MAZE ROLLER COASTER EDUCATIONAL TOY	$43.32	TELETUBBIES BIRTHDAY CARD 2 YEARS PARTY	$9.03
teletubbies PLAYSET LARGE! ALL CHARACTERS! HTF NEW!!	$43.00	[3 of these sold in a multiple item ("Dutch") auction for $3.01 each]	
Teletubbies Bead Maze Roller Coaster Educational Toy	$41.00	Like New Teletubbies Laa-Laa Fleece Costume/Outfit 3T	$9.01
Very Rare Teletubbies Building Mat NIB New in Box!	$40.99	RARE Lone Ranger - Butch Cavendish & Smoke MOC	$9.00
teletubbies PLAYSET LARGE! ALL CHARACTERS! HTF NEW!!	$39.99	Teletubbies Plush NOO NOO vibrating with Tubbietoast	$9.00
[2 of these sold for $39.99 each]		ACTIMATES INTERACTIVE TELETUBBIES **LA LA **EXC	$8.99

TV, Movie, Character Toys ▶ Thomas the Tank Engine

The average sales price in this subcategory is $14.52.

	HIGH		AVG
HUGE 4x6 TRAINS Area RUG~THOMAS Tank Engine TRAIN~Rare!	$177.50	THOMAS THE TANK ENGINE BACKPACK~~~LOOK!	$14.50
THOMAS THE TANK ENGINE & FRIENDS GIANT SET 7404 TOMY **	$160.37	NWT THOMAS THE TANK/TRAIN L/S T-SHIRT-4T-"VERY COOL"	$14.50
THOMAS THE TANK ENGINE TRAIN RIDE ON W/SOUNDS & TRACK	$128.50	Thomas Tank Diaper Bag PERSONALZED child's name! Train	$14.50
Day Out with Thomas Tickets (4) Sat. Sept 24 - Colorado	$104.50	Thomas Tank sleeping bag carry PERSONALIZED! Train	$14.50
THOMAS the Tank Engine Train Halloween 3D COSTUME	$102.50	Thomas The Tank Engine Train LANTERN New In Box	$14.50
LEGO DUPLO THOMAS & FRIENDS TRAIN SET 5554 5552 5556 NW	$85.00	*NEW* Thomas the tank engine L/S T- Shirt Tee 2T	$14.50
Thomas the Tank Engine Wall Paper Border CUTE NEW	$75.26	THOMAS & FRIEND BATTERY POWERED TRAIN SMALHARD TO FIND	$14.50
Deluxe Roundhouse w/Roundabout Action Turntable	$75.00	THOMAS THE TANK ENGINE WOODEN	$14.49
HUGE LOT BRIO WOOD RAILWAY	$71.96	WATER TOWER *FREE PERCY*	
THOMAS TRAIN ROUNDHOUSE NR!!		Thomas the Train Henry Interactive Learning Railway	$14.38
Thomas the Tank Engine HUGE Lot Books VHS Videos + more	$60.00	50 Thomas Tank Engine Tattoos, Party Favors - *FREE s/h	$14.01
NEW Thomas DELUXE 3-D PUZZLE COSTUME w/hat Tank Engine	$56.00	THOMAS TRAIN Battery Operated EMILY 4 CURVED TRACK NEW	$14.00
60TH ANNIVERSARY THOMAS THE TANK, LIMITED EDITION	$49.99	NEW Thomas the Tank Engine & Friends Musical Thomas	$14.00
Thomas Interactive Learning Railway Lift and Load Crane	$48.99	Thomas Tank Engine Lamp & Plush Sounds Lights Thomas	$13.99
THOMAS THE TANK-SCOOTIN' SOUNDS THOMAS RIDE ON! **NIB**	$43.09	THOMAS TOMY TOMICA WORLD bat op BULGY THE BUS NEW	$13.99
BIG Thomas the Tank Lighted Wall Decoration! MUST C!!	$42.00	Thomas Tomy Tomica Battery DEVIOUS DIESEL w/ MILK TANK	$13.95

TV, Movie, Character Toys ▶ Winnie the Pooh

The average sales price in this subcategory is $7.58.

	HIGH		AVG
Christopher Robin From Winnie The Pooh Disney Plush Toy	$76.00	HUGE LOT Pooh & Friends Toys Books Boxes megaphone 22pc	$7.99
OLD WINNIE THE POOH LUNCHBOX AND THERMOS	$52.00	Huge Big Plush / Stuffed Disney's Tigger Doll	$7.50
LOT OF 41 TAGGED WINNIE THE POOH DISNEY STAR BEANIES	$51.00	LOT of 21 DISNEY Winnie the Pooh & Friends SOFT BLOCKS!	$7.50
Vintage Winnie The Pooh DISCO POOH Record Player WORKS	$36.00	Winnie the Pooh Wall Clock-Baby ,Tigger Childs	$7.50
WINNIE THE POOH ADORABLE 24 PC BABY DOLL PLAYSET *NIB*	$36.00	Disney Piglet 28 Talking Stuffed Doll Winnie the Pooh	$7.50
WINNIE THE POOH TOASTER-NEW IN BOX MUSICAL TOASTER	$31.00	Classic Winnie the Pooh Piglet ceramic figurine..2 cute	$7.50
POLLY POCKET DISNEY WINNIE THE POOH PLAY SET 1998	$30.99	DALE EARNHEART JR CHECKBOOK COVER NASCAR RACING CAR	$7.50
Unique Plush PIGLET Classic Winnie Pooh stuffed pig	$28.99	50 TIGGERs——— 50 TIGGERs—LOT	$7.49
NEW! DISNEY KidClips Kid Hit Clips WINNIE THE POOH 3-Pk	$25.50	Large Lot of Winnie the Pooh PVC figures playset	$7.13
7PC Russian nesting doll dolls set WINNIE THE POOH	$24.95	DISNEY WINNIE THE POOH WALL PLAQUES / HANGINGS - 5 PCS.	$6.99
CLASSIC POOH 10 INCH PIGLET AND RABBITT BY GUND NWT	$24.74	Winnie the Pooh Full Sheet Set 3 Pc GREAT Cond. 4 Tikes	$6.99
Lot of Gund Winnie the Pooh Stuffed Animals	$24.71	Disney Winnie T Pooh Eyeore Tigger Piglet Capacara TOMY	$6.99
LIKE NEW winnie the pooh DISNEY snow globe music box	$20.55	Winnie the Pooh Tigger Figures Play Set House Piglet	$6.76
RARE Winnie the Pooh toys, camping, truck treehouse	$20.00	Winnie The Pooh Piglet Eeyore Water Globe	$6.75
RARE WINNIE THE POOH HEFFALUMP MOVIE FIGURE SET BY TOMY	$18.99	Disney Classic Pooh Eeyore Tigger Piglet Cheese Spread	$6.49

Vintage, Antique Toys ▶ Cap Guns

The average sales price in this subcategory is $43.34.

	HIGH		AVG
1950's Mattel STAGECOACH Cap Gun Holster Rifle Set NMIB	$1,025.00	pair of Mattel Fanner 50 cap guns w/lone ranger holster	$46.00
RARE HOPALONG CASSIDY SCHMIDT BUCK N BRONC CAP GUN!	$406.99	RESTLESS GUN SINGLE CAP GUN HOLSTER	$46.00
Double Holster Set Hubley Cowboy Cap Gun Set	$382.00	Fanner 50 by Mattel Toymakers, Inc.	$45.99
Custom Made Holster & Guns	$375.00	1950 ERA " FRONTIER SMOKER " CAP GUN BOX	$45.00
Vintage set PALADIN CAP GUNS & HOLSTER'S	$332.00	ROY ROGERS VINTAGE SHOOTIN' IRON CAP GUN -ORIGINAL CARD	$44.44
HUBLEY ATOMIC DISINTEGRATOR CAP PISTOL TOY GUN	$331.66	MINIATURE MINI-MAG CAP GUN RIFLE / PISTOL / AS NEW	$44.00
Vintage Cowboy Rawhide Holster Set 1959 Gil Favor CBS	$325.00	TINY BERLOQUE AUSTRIA CAP GUN, GUNS NO RESER	$43.00
Gene Autry & Champion Double Holster Copper Concos Guns	$277.00	Vintage Nichols Stallion 45 Toy 12" Cap Gun	$43.00
Gene Autry Double Holster with 44 cal. Cap Guns	$261.00	MINIATURE TOY GUNS...13 IN WINDOW BOX FRAME	$43.00
BONANZA TV SERIES WESTERN CAP GUN AND HOLSTER SET	$256.00	Rare Hubley Sportsman Cap Gun Rifle 1960's	$42.99
Johnny Seven OMA One Man Army Gun Rifle	$250.00	1987 Larami #9955 Motorized MP-60 Water Gun - MIP	$42.99
Vintage Roy Rogers Cap Gun With Holster	$234.50	Hubley Cap Gun Texan 38 nice holster old Kilgore Caps	$42.89
Mattel Buffalo Hunter Shootin Shell Fanner Cap Gun Set	$229.50	OLD HUBLEY COLT .45 CAP GUN PISTOL	$42.89
Roy Rogers cap gun by Kilgore 1950's Vintage	$227.97	MATTEL SHOOTIN SHELL 30 GRAY TIPS & 3 BRASS CASES NEW	$42.00
RARE 1951 ROY ROGERS FORTY NINER CAP GUN ORIGINAL BOX	$227.50	vintage Indian Head Grip Buntline Special Cap Gun NR	$42.00

Vintage, Antique Toys ▶ Cast Iron

The average sales price in this subcategory is $64.43.

	HIGH		AVG
Original 1930 Hubley "America" Airplane >>The Big One<<	$3,427.00	ANTIQUE CAST IRON TOY CAR COUPE AC WILLIAMS	$66.99
Awesome Large Kilgore TAT Airplane >>The Rare One<<	$3,229.00	ca 1935 Hubley cast iron LARGE HORSE doorstop	$66.99
Arcade 1927 Cast Iron Buick Sedan - Nice!	$1,250.00	Vintage HUBLEY Cast Iron Washington Cars-Hard to Find	$66.00
Old CATERPILLAR tractor & plow cast iron toy	$735.00	Vintage Arcade Cast Iron Fordson Ford Tractor	$66.00
Rare Arcade National Trailways Cast Iron Toy Bus NO RES	$722.99	ANTIQUE TOYS CAST IRON CAR STREET SIGN ARCADE	$66.00
1890 Welker & Crosby Cast Iron Wood Train	$626.87	A C Williams Mack Truck Original Paint & Wheels 1920s	$65.00
1895 Ives Cast Iron Train Freight Set Rare	$538.00	1950's Big-Bang Cannon (Model 15FC)	$64.50
c.1930 Cast Iron Toonerville Trolley Toy & Original Box	$525.00	Antique toy Hubley motorcycle cop sidecar 1930 s Harley	$64.00
Arcade #1243 Cast Iron Chief Car w Balloon Rubber Tires	$500.00	Antique IDEAL Boy On Tricycle Cast Iron Plated Toy OLD!	$63.99
Extremely Rare Arcade Fageol Safety Bus/Dual Rear Wheel	$432.99	1917 HARLEY J D MOTORCYCLE & SIDECAR HUGE BY XONEX	$63.00
Cast Iron Caterpillar Tractor/Bulldozer and Motorcycle	$405.00	Cast Iron toy "Cop" motorcycle blue with sidecar c1930	$62.99
CAST IRON Toy Parlor Stove, circa 1870	$338.00	Antique Cast Iron Childs Toy Sewing Machine Hand Crank	$62.70
16" Cast Iron Baggage & Smoking Car Wilkins Floor Train	$329.99	1923 Kenton Cast Iron Train Loco	$62.00
Original Cast Iron "Home Savings Bank" Still Bank WOW!!	$306.01	Old Cast Iron Wagon Driver #4	$59.58
Hubley Cast Iron Studebaker Cast Iron Sedan Large Size	$302.00	Cast Iron 6pc. Toy Train Set Kenton (734Q)	$59.50

Vintage, Antique Toys ▶ Cowboy, Western

The average sales price in this subcategory is $37.58.

	HIGH		AVG
1950's Mattel STAGECOACH Cap Gun Holster Rifle Set NMIB	$1,025.00	Unused TopHand by TexTan Dbl Leather Cap Gun Holster	$39.99
Cowboys & Indians Toy figurines "c.c. Milano"	$743.50	Hartland Standing Western Horse 7 Inch With Chain Reins	$39.98
RARE!! VINTAGE BRITAINS DEETAIL FORT east german WOOD!	$475.00	VINTAGE 1961 TRANSOGRAM OUTLAWS TV SERIES WESTERN GAME	$39.00
Original Hartland Davy Crockett with horse	$437.99	The Lone Ranger Retailer Banner/Marx/Gabriel	$39.00
HUGE Lot~BONANZA American Character FIGURES! MUST SEE!	$436.89	CAST IRON COWBOY, BOTTLE OPENER	$38.78
Hartland Maverick Set - Excellent Condition	$400.00	Breyer Western Saddle Horse FURY PRANCER for Cowboy or	$37.73
Lone Ranger Rodeo Set No 3696 NMIB by Marx	$330.25	VINTAGE ROY ROGERS RING TOSS GAME THE REAL DEAL	$37.26
Marx Lone Ranger Boxed Range Rider - original	$330.00	Antique push toy horse cowboy wood/metal on wheels old!	$36.99
Vintage German Schleich Cowboy Indians Horse bendable	$271.00	VINTAGE RESTLESS GUN BELT & HOLSTER!	$36.78
MARX ROY ROGERS MINERAL CITY VINTAGE LITHO TIN TOY	$232.36	Vintage Roy Rogers Silk Scarf	$36.51
Mattel Buffalo Hunter Shootin Shell Fanner Cap Gun Set	$229.50	VINTAGE GONG BELL RANCH PHONE	$36.50
Leslie Henry Marshal Capgun w/ 6 bullets and wood box	$225.38	TWO VINTAGE COWBOY PREMIUM RING RALSTON TOM MIX	$36.28
Roy Rogers Cap Gun Double Holster for Cap Guns	$213.08	Vintage 9" Western Horse Saddle	$36.05
The Lone Ranger figure by Gabriel 1975 MIB	$202.50	Vintage Tin Wind Up Indian on Horse with Box	$36.00
Original Hopalong Cassidy Doll from the 1950's	$201.50	RARE 1950'S 50'S BERGEN POLICEMEN HORSE POLICE LOT MARX	$36.00

Vintage, Antique Toys ▶ Play Sets

The average sales price in this subcategory is $38.16.

	HIGH		AVG
Marx Jungle Play Set #3705 Storestock Mint in Box RARE!	$2,750.00	WOW OLD Marx Playset NAVARONE W/ ACCESSORIES	$41.00
MARX GENERAL CUSTER /MINT ORIGINAL RARE POWER BLUE	$788.00	KENNER TREEHOUSE 1975 VINTAGE TREEHOUSE COMPLETE	$41.00
1950's Marx Wells Fargo Playset, Boxed NR	$553.00	1977 Kenner Milky the Marvelous Milking Cow	$40.75
Vintage Fort Federal playset Comansi circa late 60's	$462.00	Built Rite MEDIEVEL FORT in orig. box	$40.08
Vintage Tin Grocery Store Playset	$362.57	VINTAGE ARMY JEEP AND TRUCK AND MISCELLANEOUS VEHICLES	$40.00
American Hereos Colonel Roosevelt & Rough Riders	$306.95	Rel(?) Saddle Lot	$38.77
MARX FARM tin litho BARN	$276.75	Marx Playset Type Building - DOC ADAMS	$38.00
OLD 4 LEVEL MARX PARKING GARAGE SERVICE CITY w/ EXTRAS	$227.50	6 MARX UNUSED VINTAGE BROWN PLAYSET BAGS	$37.95
REMCO ELLY & ANDY MOUSE TWINS TREE HOUSE PLAYSET	$213.08	Marx Dollhouse Playset Doll Family W Original Box Nrsv	$37.00
Vintage Walt Disney Mickey Mouse Tea Set	$208.05	MARX FARM tin litho LARGE CHICKEN COOP & CHICKENS	$37.00
MARX CONSTRUCTION CAMP 1950s TOY SET ORIG BOX UNIQUE	$202.50	5 Harem or Ladies in waiting semi nude Figures 60mm	$37.00
70's Evel Knievel Formula 1 Dragster Toy MIMB C10 evil	$202.09	MARX RARE IMAGINATION DOLLHOUSE 7 PC. DINING ROOM	$37.00
Vintage 1-12 Issues Plastic Figure & Playset Collector	$193.05	Vintage 43 piece set of WWII Army Vehicles MPC Marx?	$37.00
Vintage 1950s MARX Super Circus Tin Play Set - OB - NR!	$185.98	VINTAGE LITTLE PEOPLE BARN/SILO/LITTLE PEOPLE-COMPLETE	$36.76
Marx Split Level Doll House & Furniture Playset NIB	$181.50	Set of Vintage Weebles, horse, barn, airport and more!	$36.01

Vintage, Antique Toys ▶ Pull Toys

The average sales price in this subcategory is $39.14.

	HIGH		AVG
RARE Late 1800's Tin Goat on Cart with Bell Pull Toy!	$1,114.89	OLD TOY DOLL WAGON - 12 INCHES LONG .	$43.07
Rich Toy Company "Toy Teaming" Antique Pull Toy	$1,054.99	1926 BUCKING DONKEY PULL TOY CAST IRON WHEELS	$42.99
1989 Workshop of Gerald Henn Piggy Pull Toy	$695.00	OLD 1956 FISHER PRICE NO#777 WOOD PULL TOY & N/R	$41.00
1917 Pull Horse,real hair, great shape no res. glas i's	$550.00	RARE 1961 Fisher Price #191 Pull Golden Gulch Express	$40.99
VINTAGE TIN PULL TOY-GOATS PULLING BISON BUFFALO	$447.75	WERLICH PLAYTHINGS AIRFLOW	$39.99
HAND PAINTED LARGE WOODEN PULL CART WITH HORSE	$406.50	ANTIQUE/VINTAGE TOY WAGON	
Henn Workshops Pull Toy 1990 Clarabelle Cow	$405.00	Fisher Price Pull Toy # 52	$39.95
American Toy Corp. Horse drawn wagon, great shape 1920	$400.00	Set of Three (3) Vintage Pull-Toy Horses	$38.00
Classic 26" Zeppelin Pull Toy by "Steelcraft" - A Gem!	$341.00	1966 Fisher Price Bear With Drum Pull Toy	$37.09
CHARMING ANTIQUE GERMAN	$315.88	RARE ANTIQUE WOOD PULL TOY BOX-DECALS RED & BLUE	$36.99
HORSE & CARRIAGE W/ BISQUE DOLL		ANTIQUE BLACK SCOTTIE TERRIER DOG PULL-TOY ~ RED WHEELS	$36.99
Steelcraft Army Scout Airplane 1920's Pull Toy	$295.00	Vintage Fisher Price Pudgy the Pig Pull Toy 1962	$36.25
LEHMANN GERMAN #740 "FUTURUS" TIN BELL PULL TOY 1920	$280.01	VINTAGE WOODEN 1961 SNOOPY PULL TOY	$36.00
TIN KRAZY KAT PLATFORM TOY, NIFTY, 1920'S, VG, RARE	$271.09	1960's Marx Mystery Space Ship in Original Box	$35.00
Vintage Tin Litho German Train Pull Toy, NR!	$260.00	Fisher Price Talky Parrot #698 Pull Toy	$35.00
Reed or Bliss Wood & Paper Lithographed Ship Oceanic	$232.49	ATTIC FIND! RARE " TEDDY ZILO " Fisher Price Pull Toy!	$35.00

Vintage, Antique Toys ▶ Wind-up Toys

The average sales price in this subcategory is $88.37.

	HIGH		AVG
Fleischmann Carette Tin 1905 Liner Boat not Marklin	$5,260.00	BILLIKEN TIN PHANTOM DETECTIVE NT POPY OSAKA MASUDAYA	$96.00
rare Tin toy S. Gønthermann ZEPPELIN * German 1910	$1,999.00	VINT. WIND-UP "REMOTECONTROL" HELICOPTER - WEST GERMANY	$91.99
C I J ALFA ROMEO P2	$1,913.00	Rare 1930s Japan Celluloid & Tin Windup Girl and Goose	$91.00
WONDERFULL HANDPAINTED GøTHERMANN-GERMAN CIRCUS TOY	$1,125.00	1950s German Wind Up Huki HK Rex Dog NMIB! Tin &Plastic	$90.99
2 VINTAGE WIND UP TOYS NO RESERVE	$1,077.00	MARX HONEYMOON EXPRESS EARLY 1930's	$89.00
ANTIQUE PAIR 1930 AMOS & ANDY Tin Litho Wind-Up Walkers	$1,030.00	1950s Linemar Tin Wind-Up Bobby Bear Mint! MIB Japan	$88.77
LEHMANN NAUGHTY BOY TIN WIND-UP	$877.00	1930s Marx Fire Chief Tin Car	$87.99
RARE 1920s MARX TIN W-U CHICKEN SNATCHER NICE!!!	$876.66	MUSICAL WIND UP TIN DUCK THAT MOVES AND SINGS GERMANY	$87.00
ORIGINAL MARX Flash Gordon Rocket Fighter Space Ship	$810.00	MARX HIGHBOY CLIMBING TRACTOR TIN WINDUP MIB IN BOX	$86.00
RARE 1922 TOONERVILLE TROLLEY TIN WINDUP TOY MINT INBOX	$765.00	GODZILLA MECHANICAL TOY BY BILLIKEN	$86.00
Sparky Robot - MIB - No Res	$705.00	Vintage Tin Wind Up Santa On Sleigh Carrousel w/Box NR	$84.00
Antique Kingsbury clockwork tractor and trailor VGC	$670.00	Vintage TWA DC-3 Tin Wind Up Toy Airplane Japan	$83.50
ORKIN CLOCKWORK TOY SPEED BOAT	$668.99	Vintage Wind-up Technofix Road Track & 2 Cars VGC	$81.00
** RARE SUPERMAN ROLLOVER AIRPLANE MARX 1940s Chrome **	$648.59	VINTAGE MARX DOUGHBOY TANK-WORKING-NR	$81.00
Original Strauss Ham and Sam	$618.00	Unique Art Mfg. Co. Lincoln Tunnel wind-up	$80.00

Vintage, Antique Toys ▶ Other Vintage Toys

The average sales price in this subcategory is $32.73.

	HIGH		AVG
Circus ACROBAT TOY German 1830 ERZGEBIRGE NUREMBERG	$1,800.00	Lot 120 Vintage Toy Jacks + MIP Original Header Card	$36.00
Caterpillar 4-piece tractor set metal CAT	$1,338.35	VINTAGE 1950-60's STUFFED MONKEY HOLDING BANANA.	$35.05
Antique Car, Gas Pumps, Signal, Toy, Orig Box ! NR!	$631.11	ANTIQUE HAND PAINTED PAPER MACHE DUCK/GOOSE NOT DECOY	$35.03
Vintage 17 Piece Schoenhut Humpty Dumpty Circus Toy Set	$411.56	VINTAGE PLASTIC HANGING ANIMAL TOYS ORNAMENTS	$35.00
Johnny Reb Cannon by Remco 1960's Vintage	$330.00	ROY ROGERS PAINT SET 50'S...ROY & TRIGGER ON FRONT.LOOK	$35.00
RARE SCHOENHUT GLASS-EYED ALLIGATOR, NO RESERVE	$260.00	Marx Toys Rattlin Gattlin Shooting Gallery	$35.00
Rare Early 19th C. Tin Pig Penny Toy	$193.51	1960'S CHILD'S WASHING MACHINE FOR DOLL CLOTHES NR	$32.50
Vintage K&O Toy Outboard Motor - Scott Atwater	$191.38	Duncan Vintage Collection Twin Spin Hummer Spinning Top	$32.28
Wilesco West Germany Steam Roller/Traction Engine D 40	$189.06	1963 Mattel Music Box Cowboy Ge-Tar,Guitar, MINT in BOX	$32.09
1966 LOST IN SPACE Remco Robot blue body red arms	$188.49	Vintage Crestline Aqua Gnat Sprinkler - Water Toy - NR	$32.01
Mighty Mo Artillery Cannon 1960's by Reading	$182.51	Gilbert honey west anne francis lot2	$32.00
Antique Baby Doll in Wooden Cradle Pipsqueak Toy	$179.49	Remco Toy Screaming Mee Mee-e Rifle For Parts	$32.00
Vintage Miniature Lang Craft Outboard Boat Motor	$177.50	BING GERMANY PREWAR TIN LITHO 2 CAR GARAGE	$32.00
UNUSED Cox Dune Buggy body and trim parts	$177.50	Vintage 1950's MARX Championship HOCKEY PINBALL GAME NR	$31.54
Antique Electric Train Transformer Station Orig box NR	$174.00	VINTAGE POOSH-M-UP BASEBALL PIN BALL GAME	$31.54

33

TRAVEL

Bedeviled in the past by some fraudulent sellers, the Travel category has more stringent listing requirements than any other eBay category. Sellers must be verified by SquareTrade (www.squaretrade.com) if they plan on selling air, hotel, lodging, cruise, or vacation packages. According to eBay's "Your Simple Guide to Selling Travel on eBay" (http://pages.ebay.com/help/sell/travelsellguide.html), sellers also may not list "an item that requires or offers an additional purchase." This applies to other eBay categories as well. The guide offers this example: "travel certificates that require holder to buy or pay for something (i.e. 7 nights [in a] hotel room) as a condition of receiving the benefit of the coupon (i.e. free or discounted airfare)." For more information on restrictions in this category, see eBay's travel policies.

If you want to sell a plane ticket you can no longer use, you also must be sure it is transferable. Some airlines have rules that prohibit the reselling of tickets. Buyers should also check that before purchasing a ticket on eBay. One buyer learned this the hard way: "It is best to follow the rules of the airlines. I did not find out until I was checking in that the airlines had found that the voucher was offered on eBay. I paid $275 for the voucher and have no way of getting my money back. I will never, ever try to scam the system again," he wrote on the Travel, Vacation & Adventure discussion board.

Although the eBay restrictions, imposed in 2002, have reportedly cut down on problems in the Travel category, some sellers try to get around the new rules by listing in other categories, such as Gift Certificates, so be sure to check which category the item was listed in if you are viewing search results for travel items in eBay.

There are some other things you can do to keep from getting ripped off: research ticket prices on Travelocity.com, airline websites, or other places before buying on eBay; make your purchase with a credit card (or use your credit card through PayPal) so you have some protection from the card company if the transaction goes bad; and, as always, check the seller's feedback rating. Some buyers like to test the waters by asking the seller one or more questions before purchasing; the speed and quality of the response can give you an idea of what you're dealing with.

Good Experiences

Having said all that, there are people having good experiences buying trips on eBay. "We've rented vacation condos in a number of places—Cabo, Florida, Aspen," says one eBayer on the Travel, Vacation & Adventure discussion board. "Those ads are often time share places; they're nice usually, cookie cutter apartments," she writes.

And sellers are enjoying a new, relatively inexpensive venue in which to advertise their vacation properties. One seller with a "beautiful ocean view home with pool and all the extras" in La Jolla, California says, "We're just getting ready to list an auction for our house as a vacation rental this summer for a few different dates."

One couple has a condo in the Keystone, Colorado, area that they frequently list on eBay. "eBay is a great way to advertise, so my bet is there are several private owners like ourselves out there," they say.

Prices for Air, Land, and Sea

In the Travel ▶ Airline subcategory, a curious item sold for the highest amount: $1,800,000.00. (It was unclear who the winning bidder was, as it did not appear on the closed listing.) This was not an auction for an actual trip or airline ticket, but for a variety of Alaska travel domain names—evidently up to 71 combinations of the words *Alaska*, *travel*, and *agency* with various domains such as .com, .net, .org, .info, .biz, and .us. "Alaska is a major destination . . . the Alaska travel industry experienced accelerated growth in the wake of 9/11/2001," the seller explains in his description. "New cruise ships moved into Alaskan waters . . . The seaports, airports and roads in Alaska are rivers of tourists throughout the long Alaska summer days." He goes on to say that "to search engines and clients" the domain name AlaskaTravelAgency.com "projects authenticity" and credibility, and that those search words result in thousands of hits. It looks like some eBayer thought those potential hits were worth quite a bit. Although the auction does seem a bit odd, the seller did have a 100 percent positive feedback rating, with 117 transactions.

Other top sellers in the Airline subcategory include "2 RT Business Class Airline Tickets to Asia, Europe, Tokyo," which sold for $6,000.00; "BUSINESS CLASS Airline Ticket NEW YORK – AUCKLAND," for $3,499.00; and "BUSINESS CLASS Airline Ticket NEW YORK – TAHITI," two of which sold for $2,899.00. The average sales price in this subcategory is a low $15.31, probably because of the large number of vouchers and coupons on the lower end.

How about cruises? Caribbean cruises generally brought higher prices than Alaska cruises. The highest-priced cruise in this sample is a "New Years/Dec 31/Western Caribbean/ Balcony $1199 pp!" that sold for $2,398.00. It's described as a one-week Caribbean cruise from Galveston to Galveston, $1,199.00 per person, with stops at Majahual, Belize City, Grand Cayman, and Cozumel. The ship is the *Grand Princess*: "Taller than the Statue of Liberty and longer than three football fields, this 2,600-passenger ship features an unprecedented design with some of the most innovative amenities ever found on a cruise ship, providing its passengers with unparalleled onboard choice," according to the description. The seller, a travel agent, has 100 percent positive feedback and the SquareTrade seal, and there's even a photo of her in the description.

Alaskan cruises are increasingly popular (as the seller of the Alaska domain names claimed), and the prices in this sample range from $304.00 to $535.24.

Bed and breakfast offerings in this sample vary from a Vermont mountain inn to lodging in California. Multiple auctions for three nights with lodging for up to four people at the Vermont Cortina Inn sold for $220.00 to $280.00. Resort amenities included "two restaurants, tennis, golf nearby, fly fishing, hiking, mountain biking, indoor pool, whirlpool, saunas, game room, complimentary coffee, tea and fresh baked treats every afternoon," and "the friendliest bartenders in town." Although it was offered before ski season, this price seems to be a good deal.

Hotel offerings ranged from $4,000.00 for a "2BR/2 BA OCEANFRONT UNIT at the MARRIOTT ARUBA SURF CLUB" down to $202.50 for a "2 Night Stay at The Citadel Halifax Hotel Nova Scotia." The average price for hotels was around $212.00.

There are also a host of vacation rentals, many of them timeshares, in the Travel ▶ Lodging ▶ Vacation Rentals subcategory. Prices for California and Hawaii are among the highest, between $2,600.00 and $2,975.00.

Start Packing

You may not have thought of the Travel category as a place to find luggage, but there is some here. Not surprisingly, several of the highest-priced items within the Luggage subcategories are luxury brands, such as Louis Vuitton. For example, a Vuitton "KEEPALL 50 LUGGAGE DUFFLE CARRY ON" went for $650.00. Other brand names that pop up here include Gucci, Brighton, Chanel, and Tumi. However, there are plenty of items in the average price range that go for under $100.00, such as a "Vintage Alligator Leather Samsonite Suitcase" that sold for $76.00.

In general, although not as packed with listings as other eBay categories, the Travel category offers another set of options for vacationers and business travelers who know what they want. For sellers, it's a very cost-effective way to get their properties or vacation packages in front of people who might not otherwise see them.

NOTE *Some subcategories had relatively few completed auctions in the sample period, so there are sometimes fewer than 30 prices listed for a subcategory.*

Airline

The average sales price in this subcategory is $15.31.

	HIGH		AVG
Alaska vacation airline cruise travel fishing hunting	$1,800,000.00	NORTHWEST AIRLINES NWA COUPON VOUCHER DISCOUNT $100 OFF	$18.51
2 RT Business Class Airline Ticket to Asia, Europe, Tokyo	$6,000.00	[2 of these sold for $18.51 each]	
BUSINESS CLASS Airline Ticket NEW YORK – AUCKLAND	$3,499.00	NORTHWEST AIRLINES COUPON VOUCHER DISCOUNT $178!!!	$18.50
BUSINESS CLASS Airline Ticket NEW YORK – TAHITI	$2,899.00	LEATHER AIRLINE TRAVEL PASSPORT ID TICKET HOLDER WALLET	$18.50
[2 of these sold for $2,899.00 each]		1 United Airlines Red Carpet Club RCC Lounge Pass	$18.50
BUSINESS CLASS Airline Ticket NEW YORK – LONDON	$2,800.00	SOUTHWEST Airlines 36 Drink Coupons Booklet	$18.50
BUSINESS CLASS Airline Ticket PHILADELPHIA – MUNICH	$2,499.00	Continental airlines currency 6 vouchers coupons	$18.50
BUSINESS CLASS Airline Ticket MIAMI – SAO PAOLO	$2,190.00	Northwest airline coupon discount $100 off exp 3/31/07	$18.50
BUSINESS CLASS Airline Ticket LAX – AUCKLAND	$2,080.00	NORTHWEST AIRLINE COUPON VOUCHER	$18.50
[2 of these sold for $2,080.00 each]		CERTIFICATE TRAVEL $100	
FIRST CLASS to ASIA Eva, China airlines, United	$1,990.00	[3 of these sold for $18.50 each]	
[2 of these sold for $1,990.00 each]		Southwest airline drink coupons – 4 books – 48 coupons	$18.49
100,000 Northwest / Continental airline miles	$1,715.00	Northwest airline coupon discount $100 exp 3/31/07	$18.35
First Class award USA Europe United Airline Miles	$1,636.11	Southwest airlines drink coupon – 3 books (36 coupons)	$18.00
AIRLINE TICKET Cheap Travel NEW YORK – CHRISTCHURCH	$1,499.00	NWA NORTHWEST AIRLINES TRAVEL COUPON E-CERT RT $178!!!	$17.99
AIRLINE TICKET Cheap Travel SAN FRANCISCO – SYDNEY	$1,339.00	500 American Airlines Advantage Miles from Kellogg's	$17.87
AIRLINE TICKET Cheap Travel NEW YORK – AUCKLAND	$1,299.00	36 Southwest airlines drink coupons	$17.62
Continental Airlines 2 Round Trip Certificates	$1,125.00	300 American airlines AAdvantage Miles from Kellogg's AA	$17.58

Cruises ▶ Alaska

The average sales price in this subcategory is $382.37.

HIGH TO LOW			
Glacier Bay Alaska Cruise/7Day/Round Trip Seattle+BONUS	$535.24	Alaska Cruise to Glacier Bay Roundtrip Seattle	$306.00
Glacier Bay Alaska Cruise/7Day/Round Trip Seattle+BONUS	$455.00	Alaska Cruise to Glacier Bay Roundtrip Seattle	$304.00
Glacier Bay Alaska Cruise/7Day/Round Trip Seattle+BONUS	$450.00	[2 of these sold for $304.00 each]	

Cruises ▶ Caribbean

The average sales price in this subcategory is $508.91.

HIGH TO LOW

New Years/ Dec 31/ Western Caribbean/ Balcony $1199pp !	$2,398.50	Caribbean Cruise for 2!!! 5Day	$182.50
MSC 10N E Caribbean Christmas Cruise *3 & 4 Sail Free*	$1,980.00	4 Day Caribbean Bahamas Cruise Vacation for 2 + Bonus	$142.00
5 NT W.Caribbean for 2!MOTIVATED SALE!!!!10/17/05	$450.00	4 Day Caribbean Bahamas Cruise Vacation for 2 + Bonus	$139.00
6 DAY CARIBBEAN BAHAMAS CRUISE VACATION for 2+Kids Free	$279.00	4 Day Caribbean Bahamas Cruise Vacation for 2 + Bonus	$134.00
6 DAY CARIBBEAN BAHAMAS CRUISE VACATION for 2+Kids Free	$269.00	4 Day Caribbean Bahamas Cruise Vacation for 2 + Bonus	$131.50
Caribbean Cruise for 2/4Day/Port/Taxes Included!!	$202.50	Caribbean Cruise for 2!!! /7 Day	$100.99
4 Day Caribbean Bahamas Cruise Vacation for 2 + Bonus	$197.50		

Lodging ▶ Bed & Breakfast

The average sales price in this subcategory is $134.08.

	HIGH		AVG
Vermont Accommodations Gift Certificate at Cortina Inn	$280.00	2 NIGHTS IN FERNDALE BED & BREAKFAST, CALIFORNIA	$139.00
Vermont Accommodations Gift Certificate at Cortina Inn	$252.59	2 Nights Virginia Bed & Breakfast Inn on Poplar Hill	$132.50
Vermont Accommodations Gift Certificate at Cortina Inn	$248.09	2 Nights Virginia Bed & Breakfast Inn on Poplar Hill	$127.50
Noble residence living, Italy, Puglia, 2 Pers. 7 Nights	GBP 140.00	2 nights B&B @ Bushmills Inn Hotel, Antrim, N.Ireland	GBP 72.00
Villa Ramirez, Santa Maria di Leuca, Value £ 580.00 B/B		Bed and Breakfast in TN, Romantic Getaway for 2	$99.00
Vermont Accommodations Gift Certificate at Cortina Inn	$238.51	APPLESAUCE INN TORCH LAKE MICHIGAN GETAWAY/PRIVATE BATH	$50.50
MICHIGAN 2 NIGHT GETAWAY @ AWARD WINNING INN	$225.00	[2 of these sold for $50.50 each]	
Vermont Accommodations Gift Certificate at Cortina Inn Inn	$220.00	APPLESAUCE INN TORCH LAKE MICHIGAN GETAWAY–NO RESERVE!	$50.00
[2 of these sold for $220.00 each]			

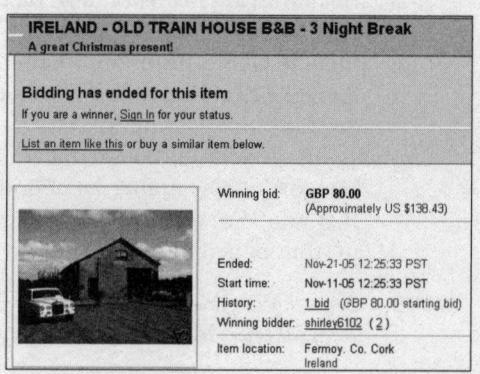

Lodging ▶ Hotel

The average sales price in this subcategory is $211.84.

	HIGH		AVG
MARRIOTT ARUBA SURF CLUB - 2BR/2 B OCEANFRONT UNIT	$4,000.00	Great Outdoors	$220.00
Romantic week at Westin St John , December 18-25, 2005	$1,025.00	2 Nts Best Western Fireside Hotel Niagara Falls Ontario	$218.60
MIAMI: Loews South Beach 5 STAR 5 nights thru Dec. 21	$995.00	Mid Winter Night's Dream	$217.51
NYC Manhattan CLUB Hotel RENTAL 10/20/05-10/23 SOLD OUT	$909.99	2 Nt Stay for 2 with Breakfast Novotel Hotel Ottawa CDN	$217.50
NEW YORK The Manhattan Club Rental Oct. 24 - 28	$885.00	2 Nts Best Western Rochester Marketplace Inn Hotel NY	$216.46
CANCUN CHRISTMAS WEEK LARGE STUDIO ON BEACH	$810.10	2 Nt Stay for 2 Best Western Fairbanks Inn Hotel Alaska	$213.50
[2 of these sold for $810.10 each]		2 Nt Best Western Adams Inn Hotel Quincy Massachusetts	$212.01
Wyndham Palms Resort & Country Club 25/12/05-1/1/06	$800.00	Mid Winter Night's Dream	$207.50
Thanksgiving Vacation (10+) Nov.19-26, 2005 Disney	$800.00	2 Night Stay at The Westin Galleria Dallas Hotel Texas	$207.50
2 Nts Best Western Hawthorne Terrace Hotel Chicago CUBS	$796.00	The Fountains Resort in Orlando - 3nts - 2BR	$207.00
DISNEY BOARDWALK timeshare rental ORLANDO DEC 11	$729.00	San Diego California family vacation	$206.01
Ski in Whistler at The Valhalla Resort 2 bedrooms	$711.00	3 Nt Stay + Dinner Loews Vanderbilt Hotel Nashville TN	$205.00
NEW YORK The Manhattan Club Weekend Rental Dec 2 to 4	$635.00	2 Nights Best Western Inn of Cobleskill Hotel New York	$203.51
[2 of these sold for $635.00 each]		2 Night Stay for 2 People Delta Ottawa Hotel & Suites	$202.51
6 Night Stay 2 People Best Western Hotel in Portugal	$634.99	2 Night Stay at The Citadel Halifax Hotel Nova Scotia	$202.50
6 Nts Best Western Hotel Dublin Campsie Dundalk Ireland	$610.00		
3 Nt Stay for 2 at Omni San Francisco Hotel California	$610.00		

Lodging ▶ Vacation Rentals ▶ US ▶ California

The average sales price in this subcategory is $771.68.

HIGH TO LOW

2 Bdrm Luxury Condo at Four Seasons Aviara in San Diego	$2,975.00	Four Seasons Aviara in San Diego 2 Bdrm Residence Club	$660.00
Marriott Newport California Timeshare Rental 2BR Dec 17	$1,000.00	Marriott's Newport Coast Villas Slps 8 Dec 9-16	$650.00
Marriott Newport California Timeshare Rental 2BR Nov26	$950.00	Marriott Newport Coast California Timeshare Rental	$615.55
Marriott Newport California Timeshare Rental 2BR Dec 3	$850.00	Marriott's Newport Coast Villas Slps 8 Dec 11-18	$600.00
Marriott Newport California Timeshare Rental 2BR Dec 2	$850.00	2 Bdrm Luxury Condo at Four Seasons Aviara in San Diego	$595.00

Four Seasons Aviara in San Diego 2 Bdrm Residence Club	$820.52	CHRISTMAS WEEK IN LAKE TAHOE! (Dec. 24 to 31, 2005)	$560.00
[2 of these sold for $820.52 each]		Capistrano Timeshare week - 1bdr	$187.50
Four Seasons Aviara in San Diego 2 Bdrm Residence Club	$811.25	Timeshare Rental in Ca, Disneyland, 1bd Deluxe	$167.50
Four Seasons Aviara in San Diego 2 Bdrm Residence Club	$799.00	2-7 nights, Embassy Vacation Resort Lake Tahoe	$50.00
Marriott Newport California Timeshare Rental 2BR Nov27	$700.00		

Lodging ▶ Vacation Rentals ▶ US ▶ Florida

The average sales price in this subcategory is $464.46.

	HIGH		AVG
2 Bedroom Deluxe Fairfield Resorts Daytona @Ocean Walk	$1,400.00	Disney Area Vacation Resort-Orlando, Florida	$485.00
Fantasy Fest Key West - Luxury - SOLD OUT!!	$1,000.00	Orlando - 7 nights Vacation Rental @ Silver Lake Resort	$455.00
CHRISTMAS AT DISNEY BEACH CLUB VILLAS WORLD ORLANDO WOW	$999.00	Daytona Condo on the beach Biketoberfest Oct. 17-22	$455.00
Orlando Vacation Rental !!!! Cristmas Week!!!!	$904.00	Christmas Week in Florida 2 Bdrm Timeshare Rental Read!	$416.00
Disney World Boardwalk Vacation Resort 5-day Package	$885.00	ORLANDO: 7 nights Sheraton Vistana Resort, 2bd 2bath	$414.51
ORLANDO/DISNEY VILLA VACATION RENTAL, MAR 12-19, 2006	$816.00	Westgate Vacation Villas getaway in Kissimme Fla Disney	$412.77
Thanksgiving Vacation (10+) Nov.19-26, 2005 Disney	$800.00	Disney Florida, 3 Bedroom 3 Bath Timeshare Rental	$400.00
Christmas in Disneyworld Orlando Marriott Grande Vista	$700.00	Port Charlotte Florida 3 Bedroom 2 Bath Pool House	$400.00
Orlando - 7 nights Vacation Rental @ Silver Lake Resort	$660.00	Disney 3 Bedroom Rental Kissim. Orlando Florida SALE!	$360.00
Port Charlotte Florida 3 Bedroom 2 Bath Pool/SPA House	$600.00	Christmas Week Ft Lauderdale, Florida	$354.00
Timeshare Rental at Orange Lake Resort, Orlando, FL	$500.00	Disney Vacation Townhouse In Kissimmee Florida L/M SALE	$350.00
Thanksgiving Vacation 7 nts 2 BR sleep 8 Wyndham Palms!	$499.00	Destin Florida Resort Rental - 10/8/05	$349.00
Disney Orlando Florida Vacation 4 Days 3 Nights Condo	$495.00	DAYTONA BEACH,FL OCEAN FRONT RESORT OCT.14-21	$327.58
Disney, Florida, Holiday week 7-night 5-star lodging	$495.00	Florida Gulf Front Vacation Rental Lido Key/ Sarasota	$300.00
Daytona Beach Condo for Biketoberfest Oct. 20-23	$495.00	For Rent Disney Timeshare 2BR Oct 29-Nov 5, 2005	$300.00

Lodging ▶ Vacation Rentals ▶ US ▶ Hawaii

The average sales price in this subcategory is $993.04.

HIGH TO LOW

	HIGH		AVG
CHRISTMAS IN MAUI (Dec 24-31) at the Westin Ka'anapali	$2,600.00	Westin Kaanapali Ocean Resort Villas!! 1 bdrm condo	$910.00
Christmas Hawaii Maui Westin Ocean Resort Villas	$2,100.00	Maui Hawaii Embassy Resort Timeshare-Holidays New Year	$900.00
Maui Hawaii Embassy Resort Timeshare-Holidays Christmas	$1,675.00	3BR Thanksgiving Orlando Disney Orange Lake 11/19 c/i	$896.00
Westin Kaanapali Ocean Resort Villas	$1,575.00	WAIKIKI BEACH - Oahu 2 WEEKS!! Nov 5-Nov 19 2005	$650.00
Christmas Hawaii Maui Westin Ocean Resort Villas	$1,500.00	Spend your December 2005 Vacation in Maui	$650.00
MAUI HAWAII EMBASSY RESORT BEACHFRONT 2BDR/ 2 FULL BATH	$1,333.03	Maui Schooner Timeshare Rental - Thanksgiving	$500.00
WESTIN KA'ANAPALI MAUI HAWAII 11/12/05-11/19/05 Veteran	$1,200.00	Maui Napili/Lahaina Ocean View 1 bedroom Condo NICE	$395.00
Maui Vacation - Kaanapali (1 week, 7 glorious days)	$1,071.77	Honolulu Hawaii Vacation Rental Panaramic Ocean Views	$325.00
KAUAI POIPU MARRIOTT WAIOHAI. 2BA-2BA. GORGEOUS!	$1,000.00	Thanksgiving wk on Hawaii's beautiful Kauai 1BR sleep 4	$300.00
Marriott Maui Hawaii Timeshare Rental Thanksgiving Wk.	$1,000.00	7 Nights in Kihei Maui at the Gold Coast, sleeps six	$161.08
Hawaii - Sands of Kahana, 3BR Week on Maui, Dec 31-Jan7	$950.00	Beautiful island and Coral Views of Kaneohe Bay	$155.00

Lodging ▶ Other

The average sales price in this subcategory is $608.23.

HIGH TO LOW

	HIGH		AVG
Vistana Disney Time Share week 37 RCI Gold Crown Resort	$2,700.00	ORLANDO~3 NIGHTS PLUS TWO '2 DAY' UNIVERSAL TICKETS!	$89.95
Ski CHRISTMAS in Breckenridge, December 23-30, 2005	$1,529.00	[2 of these sold for $89.95 each]	
Ski Heavenly @ The Ridge Tahoe in Feb or March 2006	$1,425.00	ORLANDO~3 NIGHTS PLUS TWO '2 DAY' UNIVERSAL TICKETS!	$79.95
5000 WORLDMARK/TRENDWEST ONE TIME USE POINTS	$340.01	3 Night Stay at Pigeon Forge	$61.00
7 NITE ORLANDO VACATION! 2 BDRM RESORT CONDO!	$172.45	Vacation Rental: Cabin on Otter Tail Lake Minnesota	$60.00
Vacation Rental in NEW Log Style Minnesota Lake Cabin	$143.25		

Luggage ▶ Backpacks

The average sales price in this subcategory is $29.02.

	HIGH		AVG
Osprey Crescent 85 Backpack	$275.00	New! da kine Dakine Access Surf Backpack Light Blue	$29.95
MOLLE II Comp Backpack Sys NEW! hiking auth marine's	$239.99	[2 of these sold for $29.95 each]	
Eagle Creek Switchback Max 22" Backpack Luggage NEW.NIB	$232.52	Blue ROLLING WHEELED SCHOOL LUGGAGE BACKPACK - USA NEW	$29.95
RAWLINGS LEATHER BACKPACK	$225.00	[2 of these sold for $29.95 each]	
Victorinox Swiss Parliament Leather Arch Army Briefcase	$219.99	CHE GUEVARA NWT MESSENGER BAG BACKPACK	$29.95
Eagle Creek Switchback Max 22" Backpack Luggage NEW.NIB	$202.50	Genuine Kipling extra large black backpack diaper bag	$29.50
Victorinox Swiss Parliament Wheeled Briefcase Army New	$199.00	Targus Black Matrix Notebook Backpack-Excellent Cond	$29.00
Eagle Creek Switchback Max 22" Backpack Luggage NEW.NIB	$179.99	HIKING BACKPACK INTERNAL FRAME CAMPING BACK PACK BAG KH	$28.95
Victorinox Swiss Trevi Laptop Wheeled Briefcase Army	$179.99	[2 of these sold for $28.95 each]	
Eagle Creek Switchback Max 22" Backpack Luggage NEW.NIB	$179.99	*NEW* BILLABONG SKATEBOARD BACKPACK bag skate surf NWT	$28.75
[2 of these sold for $179.99 each]		Patagonia Messenger Style Bag w/Computer Insert	$28.68
TUMI NEW COMPUTER BACKPACK BRIEFPACK	$177.50	North Face Daypack Backpack	$28.50
Victorinox Swiss Laptop Backpack Army Acropolis NEW	$177.50	JANSPORT Leather Bottom HUGE Backpack w/Side Pockets	$28.01
Brand new Filson tan rucksack bag	$152.50	Pottery Barn Teen Sport Expandable Backpack Pink Green	$28.00
USED LOUIS VUITTON BACKPACK	$150.00	**NEW** THE NORTH FACE *VAULT* BACKPACK daypack TNF NWT	$28.00
HANDBAG PURSE NO RESERVE		HIKING CAMPING BACKPACK 5400ci Internal Frame BLK~	$27.99
Dubie Travel Pack. Jandd Travel Backpacks	$149.95	[2 of these sold for $27.99 each]	
		NEW JANSPORT TE32 MADISON BACKPACK/ SINGLE STRAP BAG	$27.99
		NWT Victorinox MINI-MONOSTRAP Backpack - PALE BLUE/NAVY	$27.99

Luggage ▶ Business Cases

The average sales price in this subcategory is $74.33.

	HIGH		AVG
Louis Vuitton Taiga Leather Epicea Pallidium Briefcase	$661.00	EUROPEAN NAT. LEATHER BAG Soft Briefcase Attache Case	$76.00
RARE AUTH CHANEL Briefcase Black Quilted Lambskn	$626.00	Vintage Alligator Leather Samsonite Suitcase._SUPERB !!	$76.00
Louis Vuitton Business Case...LoVely (get it?)	$530.00	Brand New Mont Blanc Briefcase (Dark Brown Leather)	$75.00
TUMI 22018 GEN 4 Ballistic 3-in-1 Wheeled Overnighter	$500.00	Coach Leather Briefcase Black Compact Laptop	$75.00
TUMI 22018 GEN 4 Ballistic 3-in-1 Wheeled Overnighter	$495.00	Anvil Attache Road Guitar Acces Case Briefcase Key Lock	$75.00
NEW Business FILSON 252 FIELD SATCHEL Leather BriefCase	$471.00	Tumi Safecase Expandable Organizer Computer Brief #2621	$75.00
New TUMI Gen 4 Leather Expandable Brief # 96061 New	$459.00	SWISS ARMY Rolling Computer Case Briefcase + Laptop Bag	$74.89
Tumi 26103 GEN 4 Wheeled Overnight w/Computer Case	$430.00	TUMI LARGE EXPANDABLE BRIEFCASE W/ COMPUTER CASE	$72.99
LOUIS VUITTON TAIGA LEATHER BRIEFCASE - AUTHENITC	$411.00	>> NWT! TUMI DATUM SLIM SHOULDER TOTE STYLE #06412SM <<	$71.00
TUMI TU26003 Wheel-A-Way Deluxe Brief w/Computer Case	$405.00	NEW Bosca Fabric and Leather Full Function Briefcase	$70.99
New TUMI Gen 4 Leather Expandable Briefpack # 96086 New	$389.00	ZERO CENTURION ELITE CASE, SIZE 29X20X10	$69.95
New TUMI Gen 4 Leather Expandable Brief #96041 New	$359.00	Aluminum Hallburton Briefcase, Elite by Zero	$69.88
TUMI (Style 96141) Leather Briefcase - BRAND NEW! NR!	$350.00	THULE CARGO BAG CARRIER	$67.79
Coach Leather Connor Laptop Briefcase – 100% authentic	$349.00	NEW TUMI Light Expandable Compact Comp Brief, #2661	$67.00
New Tumi Exp Organizer Computer Brief Case $450 96041	$345.00	At Home America Travel Trunk!	$66.89

Luggage ▶ Carry-ons

The average sales price in this subcategory is $65.76.

	HIGH		AVG
Swaine Adeney Brigg solid leather overnight case	$711.01	ogio tote wheeled bag carry on luggage -free shipping	$69.00
NEW LOUIS VUITTON KEEPALL 50 LUGGAGE DUFFLE CARRY ON	$650.00	Tumi Leather Brown Carry On	$67.76
EXCLUSIVE TO EBAY!!!! GUCCISSIMA OVERNIGHT BAG...HOT!!!	$600.00	Vera Bradley BERMUDA PINK SATCHEL BAG - Brand New Style	$67.00
VINTAGE LOUIS VUITTON CARRY-ON LUGGAGE BAG	$510.00	VINTAGE Hat Box Train Case Suitcase Carry On	$66.26
Vintage GUCCI Carry-On Bag Luggage Bag FAB	$510.00	Hartmann Black Verticle Satche - Brand New Never Used	$66.00
NEW TUMI 22018 GEN4 WHEELED	$489.23	EXC. Hartmann Carry On Companion Tweed Luggage Rt 425	$66.00
OVERNIGHTER CARRY ON $695		AUTH LOUIS VUITTON DAMIER GEANT CANVAS SOUVERAINLUGGAGE	$66.00
NEW BRIGHTON 22" WHEELED CARRY ON LUGGAGE RED & BLACK	$480.00	VINTAGE HALLIBURTON SUITCASE LUGGAGE WITH RED LINING	$65.00
TUMI 22020 Wheeled 20" Exp. International Carry-ON NEW!	$465.00	Vera Bradley - Satchel Bag in Bermuda Pink (NWT)	$64.88
NEW BRIGHTON 22" WHEELED CARRY ON LUGGAGE RED & BLACK	$450.00	TUMI Stealth Black Carry On Duffle Bag Tote $175	$64.82
Stunning! Authentic Brighton Carry On Wheeled Luggage	$449.00	Vera Bradley HOUNDSTOOTH BROWN ~SATCHEL~ & FREE TAG,New	$63.99
TUMI 22" EXPANDABLE FREQUENT TRAVELER *NIB*	$445.00	Vera Bradley – Satchel Bag in Emily (NWT)	$63.00
TUMI 22022 Wheeled 22" Exp. Frequent Traveler CARRY ON	$425.02	[2 of these sold for $63.00 each]	
TUMI 22" ROLLING EXPANDABLE CARRY-ON TRAVELER 22022 NEW	$419.95	Vera Bradley – Satchel Bag in Sherbet (NWT)	$63.00
NEW! Auth. Louis Vuitton Keepall 55	$391.00	Vera Bradley BERMUDA BLUE SATCHEL BAG - Brand New Style	$62.25
ZERO HALLIBURTON ZR21L-SI ZR21 CARRY-ON LUGGAGE ZEROLLE	$378.00	Authentic Louis Vuitton Carry On bag with wheels	$61.66

Luggage ▶ Duffle Bags

The average sales price in this subcategory is $58.05.

	HIGH		AVG
Maison E. Goyard Paris Finest New Leather Dufflebag	$910.00	Vera Bradley LARGE DUFFEL Bag~HOUNDSTOOTH BROWN~Fall 05	$59.07
AUTHENTIC LOUIS VUITTON Largest Keepall Bandouliere 60	$665.55	Vera Bradley LARGE DUFFEL/DUFFLE Bag ~ NEW HOPE ~NWT~	$59.00
LARGE LOUIS VUITTON DUFFLE LUGGAGE BAG, KEEPALL!!!	$560.00	Vera Bradley LARGE DUFFEL BAG ~ALPINE BLACK~Fall 2005~	$59.00
BRAND NEW TUMI 22042 Extra Large Wheeled Duffel Gen 4.0	$484.00	Vera Bradley Large Duffel Piccadilly Plum NWT	$58.51
Authentic Louis VUITTON Keepall 60 Totebag NearNEW!	$480.00	Vera Bradley - Small Duffel Bag in Nantucket Red (NWT)	$58.50
Authentic Louis Vuitton Keepall - Luggage! N/R	$407.00	Vera Bradley - Small Duffel Bag in Piccadilly Plum(NWT)	$58.50
BRAND NEW TUMI 22041 Large Wheeled Duffel BLACK GEN 4.0	$405.00	Vera Bradley LARGE DUFFEL Bag~HOUNDSTOOTH BROWN~Fall 05	$58.02
AUTHENTIC LOUIS VUITTON LV MONOGRAM LARGE DUFFLE BAG	$404.99	Vera Bradley Large Duffel Bag-Piccadilly Plum	$58.00
AUTHENTIC LOUIS VUITTON KEEPALL VINTAGE DUFFEL BAG	$394.00	Vera Bradley SMALL DUFFEL//DUFFLE BAG ~ SHERBET ~ NWT ~	$58.00
NEW AUTH LOUIS VUITTON MONOGRAM KEEPALL 50 BAG LUGGAGE	$380.00	Vera Bradley Large Duffel Bag-Sherbet	$58.00
Louis Vuitton LV duffle carry on luggage bag keepall !!	$377.00	NEW SAMSONITE 32" ROLLING WHEELED DUFFEL DUFFLE BAG	$57.99
Louis Vuitton LV duffle carry on luggage bag keepall !!	$355.00	Vera Bradley HOUNDSTOOTH BROWN SATCHEL Duffel/Duffle	$57.77
Rawlings baseball glove leather duffel (new w/tags)	$349.99	Vera Bradley LARGE DUFFEL/DUFFLE BAG ~ NEW HOPE ~NWT~	$57.00
NEW TUMI 22" Wheel-A-Way DUFFLE BAG 2254 RARE $495	$349.99	48 NEW Duffel Duffle Gym Bag Mixed Colors Wholesale Lot	$57.00
HARTMANN BELTING LEATHER POLO DUFFLE (NEW)	$344.99	Vera Bradley LARGE DUFFEL BAG~CHELSEA GREEN~New Print~	$56.00

Luggage ▶ Garment Bags

The average sales price in this subcategory is $82.42.

	HIGH		AVG
LOUIS VUITTON GARMENT BAG SUITCASE LUGGAGE -100% AUTH.	$901.99	$335 Black Samsonite Silhouette 9 Garment Bag NR	$84.00
New TUMI Gen 4FXT Long Wheeled Garment Bag 22032	$689.00	Vera Bradley Blue Maison Garment Bag, NWT	$83.50
Hartmann Belting Leather Travel Bag Suitcase LTD. ED!	$610.00	Vera Bradley Chocolat Garment Bag, NWT	$83.00
BRAND NEW TUMI 22031 Wheeled Garment Bag BLACK GEN. 4.0	$535.00	Vera Bradley Emily Garment Bag, NWT	$83.00
NEW TUMI 92134 LEATHER GARMENT BAG SUITCASE GEN4 $775 !	$531.50	Vera Bradley KATHERINE Retired Large Duffel Duffle/HTF	$82.99
Hartmann Belting Leather Luggage Deluxe Mobile Traveler	$500.00	Classic All Leather Mark Cross Garment Bag Luggage	$82.98
LOUIS VUITTON GARMENT BAG + LINGERIE INSERT	$490.00	Vera Bradley Classic Black Large Duffel Bag, NWT	$82.27
NWT TUMI 42 WHEEL-A-WAY DELUXE GARMENT BAG #2231 $795.	$488.88	*NEW* Delsey Helium 2000 Trolley Garment Bag - $400	$82.01
NICE LOUIS VUITTON LUGGAGE!! TRAVEL IN STYLE!	$475.00	Vera Bradley Pink Pansy Garment Bag, NWT	$82.00
MULHOLLAND BROTHERS LARIAT LEATHER SIMPLE GARMENT BAG	$470.00	VERA BRADLEY NANTUCKET RED GARMENT BAG (NWT)	$82.00
New TUMI Gen 4FXT Ballistic Wheeled Garment Bag 22030	$444.00	EXCELLENT 40" TUMI Carry-On Garment Bag MSRP $345 NR	$81.00
New TUMI Gen 4FXT Ballistic Wheeled Garment Bag 22030	$439.00	Never Used Vera Bradley Garment Bag - Alpine Black	$81.00
NWT TUMI 42 WHEEL-A-WAY DELUXE GARMENT BAG #2231 $795.	$438.88	Vera Bradley Seaport Navy Garment Bag, NWT	$81.00
Hartmann Belting Leather Mobile Traveler Luggage Case	$432.00	[2 of these sold for $81.00 each]	
AUTHENTIC VINTAGE LOUIS VUITTON LUGGAGE GARMENT BAG	$425.00	Vera Bradley Katherine Garment Bag - NWT	$81.00
		Vera Bradley Pink Pansy Garment Bag, NWT	$81.00

Luggage ▶ Sets

The average sales price in this subcategory is $80.98.

	HIGH		AVG
Maison E. Goyard Paris Finest New Leather Garment Bag	$1,025.00	HAWAIIAN HIBISCUS EXPANDABLE 5 PIECE LUGGAGE SET TOTE	$84.00
3pc Louis Vuitton Pegase Luggage Set- NEW!! NO RESERVE	$870.00	HAWAIIAN HIBISCUS EXPANDABLE 5 PIECE LUGGAGE SET TOTE	$82.99
NWT LOUIS VUITTON MONOGRAM PEGAS SET No Reserve	$710.00	$390 Travelers Choice Amsterdam 4-pc LuggageSet Navy NR	$82.00
Ralph lauren luggage, suitcase, 5pc. , NWT $1.00 NR!!!	$621.89	Hot Pink Samsonite Luggage Set ~ 3 piece	$82.00
Louis Vuitton Garment And Duffle Bag Set	$455.00	$390 Travelers Choice Amsterdam 4-pc LuggageSet Navy NR	$81.00
Floto Italian Leather Luggage Set- tote suitcase(24,31)	$409.00	TRAVEL GEAR RED 4-PC LUGGAGE SET $600 W/ TAGS WARRANTY	$81.00
FURSTENBERG BROWN SUEDE 5-PIECE LUGGAGE SET $1240 NEW	$406.25	PIERRE CARDIN GREEN EXPANDABLE LUGGAGE SET $200 W/ TAG	$81.00
Vera Bradley Luggage Set Blue Coin Retired NWT	$356.00	Ricardo 4 pc set luggage upright Pink NEW ! NIB!	$79.99
DVF FURSTENBERG NEW PINK HEARTS LUGGAGE W/ TAGS $920	$349.95	3 Piece Hot Lips Luggage Free Cosmetic bag/ Mary Kay	$79.99
Vintage Luggage - ' 78 Corvette Pace Car / Anniversary	$330.50	Ricardo 4 pc set luggage upright Pink NEW ! NIB!	$79.99
TUMI luggage, suitcase, #2284, 26" trunk, NWT $1.00 NR	$320.00	AFRICAN SAFARI 3-PC EXPANDABLE TAPESTRY LUGGAGE SET NR!	$79.95
DVF FURSTENBERG PINK LIZARD TRIM LUGGAGE SET NWT	$306.00	Hibiscus & Turtle Print 4 PC Luggage Set Purple H150/3E	$79.00
FURSTENBERG BROWN SUEDE 5-PIECE LUGGAGE SET $1240 NEW	$305.00	NEW GASOLINE LUGGAGE 5 PC set 3 upright duffle tote	$78.00
AUTHENTIC DVF FURSTENBERG BROWN SUEDE LUGGAGE SET NWT	$300.01	$450 Traveler's Choice Villa Tierra 4-piece Luggage NR	$77.00
FURSTENBERG BLACK PINK ANIMAL TRIM LUGGAGE SET $1260	$300.00	New 3 Piece Samsonite Sandals Resort luggage	$76.00

Luggage ▶ Suitcases

The average sales price in this subcategory is $110.52.

	HIGH		AVG
fabulous louis vuitton steam ship trunk late 1800s	$6,600.00	Samsonite Ultra 3000 22" Carryon Suiter Luggage NIB!	$117.50
LOUIS VUITTON MURAKAMI 5 PIECE WHITE LUGGAGE SET	$2,950.00	Two (2) Antique Vintage Samsonite Luggage Suitcases NR	$117.23
Vintage Louis Vuitton Travel Trunk / Weekend / Suitcase	$1,725.00	Samsonite Ultra 3000 29" Suiter Luggage NIB!	$115.50
Louis Vuitton Set of Luggage Suitcase Travel Trunk !!!	$1,325.00	NEW SAMSONITE SAHORA 28" SUITER UPRIGHT SPINNER LUGGAGE	$114.99
ANTIQUE LOUIS VUITTON ALZER TRUNK SUITCASE W/ TRAY	$1,025.00	Kipling Las Vegas 24" Wheeled Upright Luggage RED NEW	$114.99
LOUIS VUITTON 4PC SET W/ DUST COVERS (NEW!!!)	$1,025.00	NEW SAMSONITE SAHORA 28" SUITER UPRIGHT SPINNER LUGGAGE	$114.99
NWT LOUIS VUITTON MONOGRAM PEGAS SET No Reserve	$935.00	Samsonite Hardside SPINNER 29" Suitcase 4 wheels NEW	$109.99
Antique LOUIS VUITTON Trunk Suitcase	$910.00	New Merrell Sprint Wheelie Full Black Suitcase Luggage	$109.00
AUTHENTIC LOUIS VUITTON DAMIER PEGASE 60	$405.00	Samsonite Ultra 3000 29" Suiter Luggage NIB!	$107.50
Louis Vuitton Cruiser 50 Luggage Bag Duffle Suitcase	$760.00	Hartmann Luggage 21" Soft Pullman Suit Case NEW w/tags	$105.95
100% Authentic Louis Vuitton Sirius 50 suitcase	$725.00	NEW Samsonite 29" Hardside 4 whls Spinner Suitcase	$104.49
NWT LOUIS VUITTON MONOGRAM PEGAS SET No Reserve	$710.00	NEW Samsonite 29" Hardside 4 whls Spinner Suitcase	$104.49
TUMI 22026 26" Wheeled Expandable Medium Trip GEN 4.0!!	$626.00	$525 Royal Blue Polo Expandable 4-piece Luggage Set NR	$103.52
100% AUTHENTIC LOUIS VUITTON PEGASE 60	$307.00	DVF BROWN SUEDE 29" EXPANDABLE LUGGAGE $400 FURSTENBERG	$103.50
LOUIS VUITTON-VINTAGE- GARMENT BAG SUITCASE W /KEYS	$611.00	Boyt Luggage - Eon Walk in Closet / Suitcase	$102.50

Luggage ▶ Other Luggage

The average sales price in this subcategory is $99.53.

	HIGH		AVG
Antique Louis Vuitton Steamer Trunk - Circa 1890	$12,600.00	ZERO HALLIBURTON ALUMINUM CASE/COMBINATION LOCK	$105.50
RARE EARLY ANTIQUE LOUIS VUITTON BROWN LEATHER TRUNK	$5,100.00	NEW Travelpro Deluxe Crew-5 Rolling Tote Bag	$105.48
Large Antique 1800's Louis Vuitton Steamer Trunk	$4,400.00	6 DURABLE CHROME LUGGAGE / SUITCASE RACK / STAND	$104.50
LOUIS VUITTON STEAMER TRUNK	$3,949.99	ZUCA MOBIL LOCKER IN RED	$102.50
LV 1910 & PURPLE CARD $1 NR		OPI Products "Nails On The Go Kit" Case on Wheels	$99.99
Vintage Louis Vuitton Trunk Suitcase, Great Size	$3,552.00	Authentic Vintage CUNARD Steamer WARDROBE SUIT TRUNK	$99.99
Rare Louis Vuitton Trunk	$3,400.00	Floto Italian Brown Leather Wheeled duffle luggage- 81v	$99.00
GEMINE SHOE CASE, TRUNK, SUITCASE	$3,020.00	AUTH LOUIS VUITTON LARGE TOILETRY TRAVEL CASE BAG - NR	$97.50
VINTAGE LOUIS VUITTON TRUNK 1920'S-1930'S	$2,382.50	Victorinox Mobilizer NXT Wheeled Cosmetic Weekend Tote	$96.00
RARE EARLY ANTIQUE LOUIS VUITTON CASE ON STAND	$2,125.00	NEW TUMI 213 EUROPEAN TRAVEL TOTE CAMERA BAG CARRY ON	$94.00
VINTAGE LOUIS VUITTON 20"x35"x20" STEAMER TRUNK NR	$2,025.00	Remin Kart-a-Bag Tri Kart 800 Luggage Cart	$92.02
GOYARD travel trunk "malle cabin"	$2,025.00	TUMI Napa leather Travel Tote	$90.00
Louis Vuitton Rare cabine trunk Champs Elysees 1930	$1,925.00	Heavy Duty ATA UTILITY TRUNK - WHEELS! Clearance Sale!	$89.00
GOYARD Malle trunk small size Vuitton quality	$1,675.00	[2 of these sold for $89.00 each]	
LOUIS VUITTON JEWELRY CASE TRUNK MURAKAMI	$1,625.00	NEW Travelpro Deluxe Crew-5 Rolling Tote Bag	$89.00
Louis Vuitton Trunk on Stand	$1,500.00	Roofbag 15 cubic ft. -cargo car top carrier luggage bag	$85.95

Vacation Packages ▶ Florida

The average sales price in this subcategory is $84.27.

HIGH TO LOW

	HIGH		
FLORIDA VACATION PACKAGE: 8 DAYS FOR 4 (UP TO 8) PEOPLE	$202.00	ORLANDO FLORIDA~5 DAYS + FREE DISNEY, TICKETS	$92.00
ORLANDO FLORIDA~5 DAYS + FREE DISNEY, TICKETS	$152.50	FLORIDA GOLF PACKAGE~ST AUGUSTINE~2 NITE~SUITE HOTEL!	$67.69
ORLANDO FLORIDA~5 DAYS + FREE DISNEY, TICKETS	$110.99	7 Nights ORLANDO/DISNEY, FLORIDA Luxury Resort Vacation	$61.00
FLORIDA GOLF PACKAGE~ST AUGUSTINE~2 NITE~SUITE HOTEL!	$102.50	6DAY DISNEY ORLANDO FLORIDA FAMILY TRAVEL VACATION FOR4	$51.59
ORLANDO FLORIDA~5 DAYS + FREE THEME PARK TICKETS	$99.00	KISSIMMEE FLORIDA, RESORT, GOLF, BEACH, LUXURY, DISNEY	$50.00
ORLANDO FLORIDA~5 DAYS + FREE DISNEY, TICKETS	$99.00	FLORIDA GOLF PACKAGE~ST AUGUSTINE~2 NITE~SUITE HOTEL!	$49.95
FLORIDA FUN~5 DAYS~SEE DISNEY & DAYTONA BEACH!	$99.00	DAYTONA BEACH FLORIDA~ FUN IN THE SUN~OCEANFRONT HOTEL	$41.00
ORLANDO FLORIDA~5 DAYS + FREE DISNEY, TICKETS	$99.00	ORLANDO FLORIDA RESORT VACATION 4 DAYS & 3 NIGHTS	$39.99
5Day/4Night Disney Florida Luxury 2 Bed Condo Sleep 6	$99.00	ST. AUGUSTINE FLORIDA~3 DAYS~SUITE HOTEL!	$39.95
[2 of these sold for $99.00 each]		COCOA BEACH-CAPE KENNEDY~FLORIDA~ 2 NIGHTS~	$29.95

Vacation Packages ▸ Hawaii

The average sales price in this subcategory is $774.50.

HIGH TO LOW

Marriott Kauai Beach Club Hawaii 7 Nights 12/11/2005	$1,000.00	HAWAII, ROMANTIC WAIKIKI BEACH!!!–8d/7n HOTEL+AIR!	$549.00

Vacation Packages ▸ Caribbean

The average sales price in this subcategory is $134.00.

HIGH TO LOW

4 Day Caribbean Bahamas Vacation for 2+Kids Free+Bonus!	$139.00	4 Day Caribbean Bahamas Vacation for 2+Kids Free+Bonus!	$129.00

Vacation Packages ▸ Mexico

The average sales price in this subcategory is $122.68.

HIGH TO LOW

5 Star Beach Front Resort! Los Cabos Mexico Vacation!!	$189.00	PALACE RESORTS, CANCUN,MEXICO-ALL INCLUSIVE	$115.00
~HOT ITEM~ CANCUN MEXICO~LUXURY RESORT VACATION~ 5 DAY	$152.50	LAST MINUTE VACATIONS ORLANDO,LAS VEGAS,MEXICO,AND MORE	$99.00
CANCUN PALACE RESORTS! MOON PALACE GOLF RESORT MEXICO	$139.99	~HOT ITEM~ CANCUN MEXICO~LUXURY RESORT VACATION~ 5 DAY	$89.00
CANCUN PALACE RESORTS! MOON PALACE GOLF RESORT MEXICO	$129.00	[3 of these sold for $89.00 each]	
CANCUN PALACE RESORTS! SUN PALACE RESORT MEXICO	$129.00		
[2 of these sold for $129.00 each]			

34

VIDEO GAMES

The Video Games category on eBay is home to both "old-school" gamers who remember some of the first systems—such as the Atari 2600—and the new generation that craves the latest gadgets.

Although there is a brisk market in vintage games and systems, most of the activity here seems to revolve around more recent video game–related items. According to eBay Pulse (http://pulse.ebay.com), the most popular products by number of listings in the Video Game category at this writing were "Microsoft Xbox 360—Game console," "Sony PSP Value Pack—Game console," "Microsoft Xbox—Game console—black," "Star Wars: Battlefront II (Playstation 2)," and "Nintendo Entertainment System—Game console."

Classic systems can fetch decent prices, but sometimes they're bought just for collector appeal. In this sample, a "Huge Atari 2600 System & Game Lot - Over 800 Titles" went for $445.00, and a "1980 ATARI 2600-A system box + Star Wars complete lot" sold for $320.00. The average price for Atari systems was $41.71, with a few average prices being $42.00 for two "ATARI 2600 SYSTEMS W/20 GAMES," and $42.00 for an "Atari 2600 System w/ 13 Games, 2 Joysticks, Paddles."

A Million-Dollar Xbox 360: Selling for a Premium

Not surprisingly, sellers can often make the most money when they are able to obtain and sell the latest, greatest stuff. When the Microsoft Xbox 360 first came out, it was hard to find, and many folks stood in long lines at stores waiting for one of the highly coveted systems. (It was also the holiday season, and some people just have to get that perfect gift for their son or daughter.)

The most expensive Xbox 360 that sold on eBay (with an apparently legitimate buyer) in this sample was a "Microsoft Xbox 360 - Game console" that fetched a whopping $1,000,010.00. Both the buyer and the seller had 100 percent positive feedback ratings, so this sale appears to have been on the up-and-up. The seller says in his listing, "I have the Xbox 360 Core System brand new. I am just trying to be a millionaire this holiday season so my wife and I can buy a nice house. All those willing and able to buy this Xbox 360 console, please place your bids." The seller's location was given as Bossier City, Louisiana, so it's possible the buyer looked at this as a Hurricane Katrina charity donation, in a sense. (It's also possible the buyer's son or daughter got on his account and tried to create trouble!)

In some cases, the completed item price on eBay can be deceiving, because the occasional prankster pops up. For example, one of the highest Xbox 360 prices I checked for this sample appeared to be an amazing boon for the seller: a listing entitled "Microsoft Xbox 360 Game console System 20GB Premium NEW; IN HAND Wireless Platinum NOT CORE Games" went for a mind-boggling $1,000,969.69. It did not appear to be a charity auction. However, on closer inspection, the bidder's eBay ID ("xbox360sucks," feedback 0) was not a good sign that this transaction went smoothly for the seller.

The next-highest Xbox price in this sample definitely was a charity sale. The $500,000.00 proceeds of this "Microsoft Xbox 360 Game Console Bundle" went to Toys for Tots. After that, the most expensive Xbox 360 went for "only" $150,000.00, and it included two controllers and "everything required to plug and play," but no box or instructions.

How about a median-priced Xbox 360? What did that include? An "Xbox 360 Premium Bundle" that sold for $686.32, a price from around the median of this sample, included a wireless controller, hard drive (20GB), headset, component HD AV cable ("This connects gamers to the world of Xbox 360 games and graphics through high-definition and standard-definition connections"), an Ethernet connectivity cable ("connects gamers to the world of Xbox Live"), and a media remote. It did not come with a box or instructions. Another Premium system sold for $686.11, did come with the box, and also included the bonus of a Halo 2 for Xbox ("played once on a different system").

Popular Newer Systems

Other than the Xbox 360, popular recent systems include the PSP and PlayStation 2. In the high end of this sample, PlayStation 2s were going for between about $250.00 and $325.00. The top seller in the Video Games ▶ Systems ▶ PlayStation 2 subcategory, a "Sony Playstation2 with Hdd and tons extra," went for $325.00. This included a hard drive and many extras "in great like-new condition"—a PlayStation 2 unit, a Sony network adapter, a Sony (Maxtor) 40GB hard drive, a stand, two dual-shock controllers, two 8MB Sony memory cards, and 2x light guns, as well as some games, cables, and other items.

PlayStation 2s from the median range were going for around $118.00: one with five games went for $120.00, and in two different auctions, a "Sony PlayStation2 Console" went for $118.50 and $120.00.

Nintendo and GameCube

Nintendo ds and *gamecube* also showed up in the eBay Pulse list of the most popular searches in the Video Games category. (The top searches were *psp, xbox, ps2, playstation 2, xbox 360, gamecube, nintendo ds, xbox games, ps2 games,* and *ps3*.)

The highest priced GameCubes in this sample were a "Nintendo GameCube/with screen-42games+accessories" that sold for $357.00, and a "Nintendo Gamecube and Gameboy Advance with 35 games" that sold for $350.00. The median price for GameCubes was around $80.00. For example, an indigo Nintendo GameCube "*Ultimate Bundle* w/ Metroid" sold for $79.99, and a GameCube with "2 controllers, games and more" sold for $80.00.

Games for the Budget-Minded

Games, and especially games bought in bulk, are generally the best value for buyers in the Video Games category. As any parent who's ever been dragged to a store to buy brand-new games knows, new games can cost a pretty penny. Currently, a brand-new PlayStation 2 game, PS2 Star Wars Battlefront II by LucasArts Entertainment, goes for between $47.99 and $49.99 on Amazon.com. On eBay, I found a recent sale for a used copy of this game for as little as $29.99.

But if you don't have to have the newest games, you can often save a lot more by buying a big lot of older games, or a mixture of old and new. For example, a "Lot of 9 Sony Playstation2, PS2 games" sold for $46.02. This included "Devil May Cry, Metal Gear Solid 2: Sons of Liberty, Tom Clancy's Ghost Recon, and The Getaway—all rated M (mature); NCAA Football 2005 and Nascar Thunder 2002—rated E (everyone); and Fire Blade, Smackdown!, Shut Your Mouth, and Kill Switch—all rated T (teen)." You can also check the Video Games ▸ Wholesale Lots ▸ Games subcategory, where larger groups of games can be found. For example, a lot of 21 Xbox games and accessories, including Halo 2 and GTA, sold for $142.50.

There are also all kinds of accessories, Internet games, and various smaller, handheld systems such as Game Boys available here. And if you find yourself spending too much money, you can always do what top video game seller, and owner of the "eGameUniverse" eBay Store, David Herzog did: start selling your games. After he lost his previous business, he bought a game on eBay just to take his mind off things, and that led to a business that now grosses over $2 million each year and is growing, according to a profile in eBay's Seller Central.

Accessories ▸ 3DO

The average sales price in this subcategory is $20.43.

HIGH TO LOW

MICHAEL JORDAN 8X10 UDA AUTHENTIC GATORADE DUNK FRAMED	$232.50	Set 2 NEW Panasonic REAL 3DO GAME CONTROL PAD FZ-JP1X	$15.00
Panasonic 3DO Memory Unit FZ-EM256 Super Rare	$123.50	**NEW** Original 3DO Controller **FREE SHIPPING**	$14.99
3DO LIGHT GUN BUNDLE (INC. 8 LIGHT GUN GAMES)	$100.00	RARE FLIGHTSTICK PRO FOR PANASONIC 3DO MINT CONDITION	$9.99
R E A L 3DO Panasonic FZ-10	$50.00	2 New, Still Shrinkwrapped in Box 3DO Controllers.	$9.51
3DO Gun Lightgun Gamegun RARE 3DO	$35.00	2 CONTROLLERS Brand NEW for the 3DO video game system	$7.50
3DO AMERICAN LASER GAMES GAMEGUN	$31.00	2 CONTROLLERS Brand NEW for the 3DO video game system	$6.99
FLIGHTSTICK PRO FOR THE 3DO GAME SYSTEM - BRAND NEW!!!	$31.00	2 CONTROLLERS Brand NEW for the 3DO video game system	$6.05
nintendo entertainment system nes	$26.00	3DO GAME SECRETS guide hint book strategy 3d0 hintbook	$6.05
2 Brand NEW 3DO Wireless controllers w/bonus demo disc	$25.49	2 CONTROLLERS for the 3DO System, By Naki w/turbo NEW	$5.99
3DO MAGIC POWER 6 BUTTON ARCADE JOYSTICK	$24.00	[9 of these sold for $5.99 each]	
2 Panasonic 3do Docs Infrared Wireless Controllers RARE	$20.50	2 CONTROLLERS Brand NEW for the 3DO video game system	$4.99
2 NEW Panasonic 3do Docs Wireless Controllers CIB Rare	$20.50	3DO Control Pad by Panasonic Joystick	$4.95
Panasonic 3do Controller & Case of Nine 3do Game Cd's	$20.50	2 CONTROLLERS for the 3DO System, By Naki w/turbo NEW	$4.24
NEW 4gb 2gb IPOD NANO Email New_ipod_Nano@yahoo.com	$20.50	2 CONTROLLERS for the 3DO System, By Naki w/turbo NEW	$3.99
Lot Of 4 Controllers & Mouse For 3DO System`LQQK~	$15.50	3DO Control Pad Panasonic - Used	$3.99
		GOLDSTAR 3DO CONTROL PAD FOR THE 3DO GAME SYSTEM - NEW!	$3.24

Accessories ▸ Atari

The average sales price in this subcategory is $12.95.

	HIGH		AVG
WICO COMMAND CONTROL JOYSTICK AND KEYPAD ATARI 5200	$216.03	Atari Lynx Battle Wheels (New Sealed)	$14.50
ATARI 2600 COMPLETE BOXED SET	$95.00	5200 Power Supply AC Adapter Plug Orig Atari New No Box	$14.00
Atari Lynx System (Mint - New Unit) (A)	$77.00	[2 of these sold for $14.00 each]	
atari 2600	$75.01	Atari Jaguar Dino Dudes Cart (New Sealed)	$13.95
4 ATARI 5200 CONTROLLERS 2 BY WICO W/ Y ADAPTER CABLES	$69.94	Atari 2600 Keyboard Controller + Basic Programming game	$13.50
Two Fully Functional Atari 5200 Joystick Controllers	$61.00	**Original** Atari 2600 with Games and Controllers	$13.00
Enhanced A/V SVideo Atari 2600 Junior System Console	$54.50	2 original Atari 2600 Joysticks controllers NR	$12.99
Large Lot ATARI 2600 game system repair parts	$45.44	Wico Command Control Joystick ~ Boxed - Nice - Atari	$12.50
ATARI 2600 WIRELESS REMOTE JOYSTICKS set *Work PERFECT*	$41.00	Atari Jaguar Pewter/Brass Lapel Pin (New)	$12.50
NES NINTENDO SYSTEM W/ 16 GAME	$41.00	Atari Lynx Paperboy (New Sealed)	$12.50
LOT KLAX TMNT MARIO NR!		REAL ATARI 2600 WIRELESS JOYSTICK	$11.61
Atari Flashback 2 Retro Video Game System New Unopened!	$39.99	GAME CONTROLLER NEW!	
BRAND NEW - Atari 5200 TRAK BALL Controller - NIB	$39.99	Atari Remote Control Wireless Joysticks Mint in Box!	$11.50
ATARI, RF, VIDEO, ADAPTOR, BEST DEAL!!! LOT OF 20	$39.99	Atari Joysticks with Top Load Thumb Fire Button ******	$11.50
JAGUAR PRO CONTROLLER ALL NEW RARE CONTROLLER !!	$38.99	Atari Jaguar Brutal Sports Football Cart New	$11.25
Lot of 2 -Original- ATARI 2600 JOYSTICKS *Near Mint*	$34.50	Atari Jaguar Checkered Flag Cart (New Sealed)	$11.25

Accessories ▶ Colecovision

The average sales price in this subcategory is $22.64.

	HIGH		AVG
Coleco Vision System w/ Atari Adapter &50+ Games	$180.00	Coleco Adam Second Digital Data Drive Great Condition	$26.00
4 Coleco Vision Super Action Controllers ColecoVision	$161.35	COLECOVISION SUPER ACTION CONTROLLERS	$26.00
Colecovision System Like New in Box Mint Condition	$112.50	Colecovision Roller Controller with 2 games	$26.00
Colecovision,coleco vision system, Roller + Games !!	$100.00	LOT 12 COLECO VISION GAMES W/BOX	$26.00
COLECOVISION VIDEO GAME SYSTEM–EXCELLENT SHAPE	$81.00	Coleco Vision Video Game System w/games and more!	$26.00
RARE 3 1/2" Disk Drive for Coleco Adam	$76.00	Coleco Colecovision Adam Software Huge Lot	$24.99
COLECO COMPLETE SYSTEM +12 COLECO GAMES	$73.00	Dukes of Hazzard COLECOVISION w/ Exp Module 2 *RARE R5*	$23.00
MIB Coleco Vision Super Action Controller* ColecoVision	$71.00	coleco vision experience 1983 video game magazine	$22.02
Enhanced A/V SVideo Colecovision System Console	$65.50	Colecovision Hand Controller Mint No Reserve	$21.50
Lot of Coleco Adam Software	$62.53	Colecovision Stuff!!! - Super Controllers and More!!!	$21.50
12 Used Software Titles for Coleco Adam	$52.00	Colecovision Adam Second Digital Data Drive Mint Coleco	$20.51
ColecoVision Console w Expansion Module + Huge Game Lot	$51.00	ColecoVision Roller Controller - Coleco Vision	$20.50
COLECO COMPLETE SYSTEM +12	$51.00	Colecovision Hand Controller ~ MINT ~ BRAND NEW!!	$19.95
COLECO GAMES (STAR WARS)		[3 of these sold for $19.95 each]	
Coleco Vision game system + organizer + 8 games Xmas	$48.00	Colecovision Roller Controller + Omega race & Victory	$18.27
LOT 12 COLECO VISION GAMES W/BOX (STAR TREK)	$46.00	COLECOVISION 4 PIN POWER SUPPLY #55416	$18.08

Accessories ▶ Commodore

The average sales price in this subcategory is $11.74.

HIGH TO AVG

	HIGH		AVG
Coleco Vision System w/ Atari Adapter &50+ Games	$180.00	Set of 2 Commodore 64 30-in-1 Plug & Play Video Game	$9.99
Amiga 1200 Tower Infinitiv	$150.00	[2 of these sold for $9.99 each]	
ZAXXON by SEGA for Commodore 64 C64 RARE!!!!Cart	$35.95	Atari Computer 800 - 800XL - 1200XL Monitor A/V Cable	$9.99
Atari 2600 Pair Of Joysticks Original Black Darth Vader	$31.00	Commodore 64 - 128 - VIC 20 Monitor Cable AV A/V Cable	$9.99
Commodore 1581 Disk Drive for C-64/128	$31.00	[2 of these sold for $9.99 each]	
Commodore 64 / C64 / 128 / C128 1764 Ram Expansion 256K	$29.99	Set of 2 Commodore 64 30-in-1 Plug & Play Video Game	$9.99
Commodore 64 / C64 / 128 / C128 Amiga 1351 mouse WORKS	$24.98	Atari Computer 800 - 800XL - 1200XL Monitor A/V Cable	$9.99
Commodore 64 / C64 / 128 / C128 1581 3.5 floppy drive	$20.50	[2 of these sold for $9.99 each]	
Commodore AMIGA TV-Modulator 520 MIB Never OPENED NR J6	$20.00	Tron 1982 Atari 2600 6"x10" VIDEO AD / MAGNET!	$9.99
Set of 2 Commodore 64 30-in-1 Plug & Play Video Game	$17.00	Vintage Commodore 64 Games Aliens Robocob Chernobyl	$9.00
Commodore 64 30-in-1 Classic Plug & Play Video Game	$13.50	Commodore 64 Keyboard Power Supply Vintage Cable NR!!!!	$8.50
Atari Computer 800 - 800XL - 1200XL Monitor A/V Cable	$9.99	Commodore 64 - 128 - VIC 20 Monitor Cable AV A/V Cable	$8.49
[2 of these sold for $9.99 each]		Commodore 64 - 128 - VIC 20 Monitor Cable A/V Cable	$7.99
Commodore 64 - 128 - VIC-20 Monitor Cable A/V Cable	$9.99	[2 of these sold for $7.99 each]	
VINTAGE COMMADORE 64 SYSTEM WITH BOX	$9.99	Atari Computer 800 - 800XL - 1200XL Monitor A/V Cable	$7.99
Commodore 64 30-in-1 Classic Plug & Play Video Game	$9.99	[2 of these sold for $7.99 each]	
Atari Computer 800 - 800XL - 1200XL Monitor A/V Cable	$9.99	NEW IN BOX !! COMMODORE MPS-803 DOT MATRIX PRINTER~	$7.99
Commodore 64 30-in-1 Classic Plug & Play Video Game	$9.99	Powerplayer Joystick (Atari,C64,Amiga) +New!+	$7.49

Accessories ▶ Intellivision

The average sales price in this subcategory is $23.76.

HIGH TO AVG

	HIGH		AVG
106 different intellivision games loose	$375.00	Intellivision system with 6 Boxed games Nice set	$15.00
Intellivision System & Game parts sealed Mattel Italy	$175.50	Mattel Intellivision Video Game and (NEW) Lock N Chase	$15.00
Intellivision Computer Module Adaptor Keyboard Mattel	$103.50	Vintage Intellivision Boxed Voice Module + 5 Games	$12.75
VINTAGE Mattel INTELLIVISION SYSTEM + 40 GAMES NR	$81.75	INTELLIVISION II vintage game system with box and games	$11.50
INTELLIVISION/INTELLIVOICE/29 GAMES/BOXS/INST/JOYSTICKS	$67.60	Intellivision intellivoice talking module voice mint bx	$11.01
Mattel Intellivision System Changer...	$51.00	Intellivision Intellivoice Voice Sythesis Module w Box	$10.50
Mattel Intellivision Computer Adapter ...	$47.89	Mattel Intellivoice Voice Synthesis Module w/ Cart	$10.50
Intellivision Music Synthesizer	$41.00	INTELLIVISION COMPUTER MODULE 4 GAMES*JETSONS*SCOOBYDOO	$10.50
INTELLIVOICE VOICE SYNTHESIS MODULE W/ GAMES THAT TALK-	$24.99	Intellivision Game console system lot w/ 17 games	$9.99
INTELLIVOICE VOICE MODULE W/ALL 4 GAMES INTELLIVISION	$20.50	Vintage Mattel INTELLIVISION Video Game System	$9.99
INTELLIVISION SYSTEM GAME PORT DEOXIDIZING PACK REPAIR	$19.99	INTELLIVISION MATTEL VOICE SYNTHESIS MODULE TRON BOMB	$9.99
INTELLIVISION SYSTEM GAMEPORT CLEANING CARTRIDGES PAIR	$19.99	Intellivision II 1982 16 Games in Boxes - Night Stalker	$9.50
INTELLIVISION 2609 W/17 VIDEO GAMES VINTAGE ATARI N/R	$16.02	Mattel Intellivision System + 5 Boxed games Star Strike	$8.09
LOT OF 21 VINTAGE INTELLIVISION GAMES PITFALL ETC.	$15.50	intellivision buzz bombers new in box	$8.00
USED INTELLIVISION MASTER COMPONET	$15.50	Intellivision instruction 4 manuals 15 overlay Truckin	$7.99

Accessories ▶ Microsoft Xbox

The average sales price in this subcategory is $23.31.

	HIGH		AVG
E3 Xbox 360 Limited Edition Faceplate New and Unopened	$305.00	Xbox Live Starter Kit 12-month Card Headset Crimson Sky	$25.75
Xbox 360 Limited Edition X05 Faceplate - VIP Only	$202.50	XBOX Action Replay 8MB MEMORY	$25.49
Microsoft Xbox - Game console - black	$158.00	CARD Cheats Codes NEW !	
XBOX SYSTEM WITH 10 GAMES **EA	$152.50	12-Month Xbox Live Subscription Card *Brand New* XBL 1	$25.00
SPORTS**/2 CONTROLLERS		12 Month Xbox Live kit! Free Mech Assault!	$25.00
custom xbox with extras	$78.00	XBOX LIVE STARTER KIT-w/CRIMSON-MECHASSAULT-NEW	$24.99
XBOX 360 HOODED SWEATSHIRT RARE COLLECTIBLE ADULT LARGE	$76.00	XBOX LIVE HEADSET Plantronics GameCom H2 Halo 2 Edition	$24.50
Working XBOX 1.0 - 1.1 Motherboard & Matched Hard Drive	$59.00	805529915442 Xbox Live 12-Month Starter Kit	$23.05
XBOX Samsung SDG-605 Original DVD Drive with Bezel	$52.00	MS XBOX Thomson TGM600 DVD Rom	$23.00
[2 of these sold for $52.00 each]		Drive X Plug n' Play NEW	

	HIGH		AVG
Xbox V 1.0 Motherboard with matching Harddrive	$50.00	Xbox Action Replay 8mb Memory Card Like New	$23.00
Microsoft XBOX Wireless G Adapter 802.11G MN-740 SAVE$$	$49.99	LOT OF 11 XBOX DVD-ROM DRIVES AS IS	$22.69
[2 of these sold for $49.99 each]		Xbox v1.0 or 1.1 Delta Electronics Power Supply	$22.52
Xbox Wireless G Adapter Model MN-740	$45.52	Xbox Live Starter Kit + 3 MONTHS Subscription NEW!*	$21.99
XBOX Live Logitech Wireless Headset Communicator	$41.00	XBox 360 Mountain Dew Hoodie Sweatshirt/Beanie/ MORE	$21.00
Logitech wireless/cordless headset for Xbox (live) *New	$41.00	XBox 360 Mountain Dew Hoodie Sweatshirt/Beanie/ MORE	$20.51
XBOX LIVE STARTER KIT-12 MONTHS FREE-CRIMSON-NEW/SEALED	$39.99	XBOX LIVE 3 - MONTH STARTER KIT	$20.50

Accessories ▸ Nintendo 64

The average sales price in this subcategory is $10.77.

	HIGH		AVG
Doctor V64 system plus several CDs of games	$122.51	Mario Kart Telephone (Nintendo)	$12.00
N64 Lot Nintendo 64 Games/Decks/System/Game Shark Pro	$71.00	N64 NINTENDO 64 SYSTEM BLUE CONTROLLER IN GREAT SHAPE!	$12.00
Nintendo 64: 4 Controllers: 11 Games: Expanded: Extras	$58.00	[3 of these sold for $12.00 each]	
Nintendo 64 system w/ 2 controllers,8 games,2mem. cards	$55.00	2 x N64 BLUE Controller NINTENDO 64 CONTROLLERS	$11.99
MINT Nintendo 64 System-4 controllers, 7 games, more!	$52.55	LOT OF 10 NINTENDO 64 VIDEO GAME BOXES	$11.50
NINTENDO 64 VIDEO GAME SYSTEM W/4 GAMES 2 CONTROLLERS	$45.00	7 NEW N64 Nintendo 64 PAK GAMESHARK 3.3 + MUCH MORE	$10.50
10 N64 Brand Nintendo 64 Controller 3D Thumbstick Part	$36.99	NINTENDO 64 TRAVEL CARRY STORAGE CASE	$10.50
10 NINTENDO 64 N64 3D THUMBSTICK REPAIR JOYSTICK PART	$35.50	N64 Nintendo 64 System Controller JUNGLE GREEN Clear	$10.50
NINTENDO 64 N64 HUGE LOT OF CONTROLLERS TESTED	$32.50	2 x N64 BLUE Controller NINTENDO 64 CONTROLLERS	$10.48
NINTENDO 64 AND 11 GAMES	$30.00	Nintendo 64 N64 Controller Blue In box	$10.01
10 N64 Brand Nintendo 64 Controller 3D Thumbstick Part	$26.00	N64 NINTENDO 64 SYSTEM GREY CONTROLLER PLAY MARIO L@@K!	$10.00
Nintendo 64 games,controllers,sharkpad,controller packs	$25.00	Nintendo Comic Book RARE! the Legend of Zelda No. 1	$9.99
2 Original Nintendo 64 Controller **TIGHT JOYSTICKS**	$22.49	4 N64 GAMES RAINBOW 6 QUAKE RESIDENT EVIL 2 FORSAKEN	$9.99
10 N64 Brand Nintendo 64 Controller 3D Thumbstick Part	$22.01	2 X NEW BLACK N64 CONTROLLER FOR NINTENDO 64 NR	$9.99
[2 of these sold for $22.01 each]		*RED* Official Nintendo 64 CONTROLLER N64	$9.99
2 Nintendo 64 Controllers green and purple	$20.50	*BLUE* Official Nintendo 64 CONTROLLER N64	$9.99

Accessories ▸ Nintendo Game Boy

The average sales price in this subcategory is $11.16.

HIGH TO AVG

POKEMON limited edition GBA SP RAYQUAZA	$139.26	NINTENDO DS INUYASHA SKIN DS VINYL SKINS NEW	$8.99
Little Sound DJ with Nintendo Game Boy	$125.00	NINTENDO DS KENSHIN SKIN KENSHIN DS VINYL SKINS	$8.99
Gameboy Micro Brand New	$87.00	Nintendogs Skin for Nintendo DS Vinyl Skins @@ SO CUTE	$8.99
game boy color good condition with lot of accessories!!	$46.00	Nintendo DS LV Pink Skin Nintendo DS Vinyl Skins ~ WOW	$8.99
Game Boy DIGITAL CAMERA~RED~Color Advance GBC GBA SP	$20.50	NINTENDO DS DARTH VADER SKIN STAR WARS VINYL SKINS	$8.99
GAME BOY CAMERA,PRINTER,PAPER,LINK CABLES	$15.77	NINTENDO DS "ONE PIECE" ANIME	$8.99
NEW Gameboy Color & Pocket Game Shark W/ Pokemon codes	$14.95	SKIN 1 PIECE VINYL SKINS	
Nintendo Game Boy Color - Handheld game system - teal	$11.61	Nintendo gameboy PRINTER PAPER 9 ROLLS NEW	$8.99
lot of VINTAGE NINTENDO GAME BOY items -no reserve nes	$10.50	Nintendo DS Star Wars Skin "STORM TROOPER" Vinyl Skins	$8.99
Nintendogs Skin for Nintendo DS Vinyl Skins @@ SO CUTE	$10.00	NINTENDO DS ZELDA LINK SKIN DS VINYL SKINS	$8.99
NEW Game Shark Pro Gameboy Color & Pocket Pokemon codes	$9.95	NINTENDO DS INUYASHA SKIN DS VINYL SKINS NEW	$8.99
NINTENDOGS SKIN for Nintendo DS Skins ~ So Cute !!	$9.50	NINTENDOGS SKIN for Nintendo DS Skins ~ So Cute !!	$8.99
Nintendogs Skin for Nintendo DS Vinyl Skins @@ SO CUTE	$9.49	Ghost In The Shell ANIME SKIN for Nintendo DS Skins	$8.99
[2 of these sold for $9.49 each]		ZELDA SKIN for Nintendo DS "Zelda The Link" Skins ~WOW	$8.99
Action Replay GBA Game Boy Advance Cheat System	$9.00	NINTENDOGS SKIN for Nintendo DS Skins ~ So Cute !!	$8.99
Nintendo gameboy PRINTER PAPER 9 ROLLS NEW	$8.99	Dragon Warrior Monsters 2	$8.00

Accessories ▸ Nintendo Game Boy Advance

The average sales price in this subcategory is $10.10.

	HIGH		AVG
GAMEBOY blue SP lot , 4 games, case and MORE **MINT**	$93.01	NINTENDO DS GAMEBOY SP MICRO ADVAN GBA MOVIE MP3 PLAYER	$12.68
NEW GAMEBOY ADVANCE SP SYSTEM COLOR: PEARL BLUE NEW	$70.99	LOT OF 3 TOAD/WAVING TOAD/"MARIO & LUIGI KART 14/16	$12.50
GAMEBOY ADVANCE SP SYSTEM COLOR: GRAPHITE NEW & SEALED	$66.00	NINTENDO DS HELLO KITTY 3M SKINS skin *CLOSEOUT PRICE*	$10.99
GAMEBOY ADVANCE SP SYSTEM COLOR: GRAPHITE NEW & SEALED	$65.08	FULLMETAL ALCHEMIST SKIN for Nintendo DS SKINS~ COOL !!	$10.50
NEW GAMEBOY ADVANCE SP SYSTEM COLOR: PEARL BLUE NEW	$62.51	NEW GAMEBOY ADVANCE E-READER & DONKEY KONG JR EREADER	$10.49
GAMEBOY ADVANCE SP SYSTEM COLOR: GRAPHITE NEW & SEALED	$59.03	NINTENDO DS LOUIS VUITTON *A* 3M SKINS skin *CLOSEOUT*	$10.49
XGflash XG2Turbo 512M for GBA SP and NDS FlashCard	$51.00	LOT OF 2 ADULT LARGE MARIO MIX/START T-SHIRTS	$10.00
Gameboy Advance Games and Accesories Kirby Mario Fire E	$36.89	Skulls Pirate Nintendo DS Skin Skins	$9.99
MARIO BROTHERS HOMEMADE CHARACTER HAT (LUIGI)	$36.50	NEW GAMEBOY ADVANCE E-READER & DONKEY KONG JR EREADER	$9.99
E3 Super Mario Kart R/C Remote Control Car Micro Sizer	$29.99	LEGEND OF ZELDA: THE MINISH CAP FULL STRATEGY GUIDE GBA	$9.99
MARIO BROTHERS HOMEMADE CHARACTER HAT (LUIGI)	$27.00	Gameboy advance game Nancy Drew Message in a Mansion	$9.99
New Intec Action Replay Max for GBA SP & Nintendo DS	$26.99	Rainbow Splat Paintball skin Gameboy Advanced SP Skins	$9.99
GBA SP TV Tuner -Use Nintendo Game Boy Advance SP as TV	$21.99	MARIO BROTHERS COIN T-SHIRT 10/12	$9.95
Nintendo DS & Game Boy Advance GBA SP Movie MP3 Player	$17.98	GameBoy PokeMon Sapphire & Ruby STRATEGY GUIDE NEW GBA	$9.95
LOT OF 4 SONIC HEY DUDE-WARIO-LINK-MARIO DS 14/16 ONLY	$15.00	NINTENDO DS SCARFACE SKIN DS VINYL SKINS	$8.99

Accessories ▸ Nintendo GameCube

The average sales price in this subcategory is $12.86.

	HIGH		AVG
DRESS UP AS MARIO & LUIGI!	$91.00	Nintendo Game Cube Travel Case	$15.00
SUPER MARIO BROTHERS HATS		New Counter Strike Game T-shirt **L@@K**	$13.99
Nintendo Gamecube, Extra Controller & Game!!!	$56.00	Gamecube Game Guide Lot. NFL, Mario, Madden.... NR	$13.50

DRESS UP AS MARIO!! SUPER MARIO BROTHERS HAT	$56.00	MARIO & WARIO BATTLE T-SHIRT X-LARGE	$13.50
BRAND NEW MOBILE MONITOR 5.4 NINTENDO GAMECUBE	$52.00	SINGLE SUPER MARIO BROS T-SHIRT 10/12	$13.50
Donkey Konga & 2 Sets of Bongos!! Perfect Condition!!	$42.25	TALES OF SYMPHONIA GAMECUBE GC STRATEGY GUIDE BOOK NEW	$13.44
Phantasy Star Online Episodes 1, 2, & 3 Official Guide	$41.01	LOT Nintendo 64 Games Action Racing NBA NIB NR	$12.53
ZELDA COLLECTOR'S EDITION	$41.00	Resident Evil Skin for Nintendo GameCube GC VINYL SKINS	$12.50
FOR GAME CUBE NEW		SUPER MARIO SKIN for Nintendo GameCube Vinyl Skins	$11.99
NINTENDO GAMEBOY PLAYER (NIB)	$36.00	RESIDENT EVIL Skin for Nintendo GameCube GC Vinyl Skins	$11.99
Nintendo Gamecube Gameboy Player - COMPLETE	$35.01	[3 of these sold for $11.99 each]	
Nintendo Gameboy Player for Gamecube Perfect!!!	$31.50	ZELDA SKIN for Nintendo GameCube ZELDA VINYL SKINS	$11.99
VERGE C30906A 5" LCD TRAVEL SCREEN FOR GAMECUBE	$31.00	[2 of these sold for $11.99 each]	
Skies of Arcadia Legends Strategy Guide for Gamecube	$30.75	NARUTO SKIN for Nintendo GameCube NARUTO Vinyl Skins	$11.99
Mario Party 4 [GameCube] NR New Factory Sealed	$29.00	[2 of these sold for $11.99 each]	
LIKE NEW NINTENDO GAMEBOYPLAYER AND 2 GAMES!!!	$28.50	Animal Crossing STRATEGY GUIDE GameCube	$11.49
NINTENDO GAMECUBE with 1 Remote	$28.01	YOSHI DAZZLE T-SHIRT—6/8	$11.45
		BRAND NEW CARRING CASE	$10.50

Accessories ▶ Nintendo NES

The average sales price in this subcategory is $13.78.

	HIGH		AVG
NINTENDO NES BIG GUN LOT OF 32 GUNS RED, ORANGE, GREY	$153.05	US Top Loading Nintendo NES System, New + 7 GAMES FREE	$15.00
45 NES BOXES nintendo BUBBLE BOBBLE metroid STAR WARS	$102.55	NEW AC ADAPTER for Nintendo 64 System /N64 power cable	$14.99
Nintendo Power * 1st 6 issues * Complete Volume 1	$79.97	Vintage Nintendo/Mario Rolling Wood Storage Cart/Case	$14.95
Mario Bros: 8 Mario T-Shirts	$78.80	Sonic Tails, Hedgehog, Knuckles - Gray Sweatshirt	$13.85
Old Nintendo Games And Controllers, LOOK!	$61.00	I Am A Frito Bandito - Gray Sweatshirt	$13.85
Lot 6 Aladdin Deck Enhancer All Factory Sealed MIB RARE	$60.00	Link with His Horse Epona Sweatshirt — T-Shirt	$13.85
[2 of these sold for $60.00 each]		7 NES nintendo game ZELDA 1 & 2 gauntlet TETRIS mermaid	$13.62
NINTENDO NES R.O.B ROBOT & GYROMITE GAME SEAL NEW	$53.00	HUGE Lot NINTENDO SUPER MARIO Brothers TOYS Figures 15	$13.50
VINTAGE NINTENDO NES ENTERTAINMENT SYSTEM STORE SIGN	$52.51	Lot of 2 Six ft Controller extension cables for the Nes	$13.00
RPG strategy guide Dragon Warrior IV nes nintendo 8-bit	$51.00	20 BLACK GAME DUST COVER S SLEEVE	$12.99
RARE NES Nintendo "MARIO CABINET / STAND"!! MUST SEE!	$49.99	S NES NINTENDO 8BIT	
R.O.B the robot In BOX NES nintendo Robby the robot	$44.02	Sonic Adventure Fans - Group Gray T-Shirt <T-Shirts>	$11.85
Lot of 25 NES Nintendo instruction manuals some RARE!	$43.77	Kirby Air Ride Head Phones Blue T-Shirt Game Boy	$11.85
Nintendo NES 9 GAMES! Zapper Gun 3 Controllers	$41.36	Animal Crossing (KK) T-Shirt GameBoy	$11.85
Nintendo NES Rob The Robot Buddy With Gyromite Game NM	$35.27	Blue Spider Tie Dye 5X Large XXXXX Large T Shirt	$11.85
NES Power Glove Game Controller Nintendo PowerGlove +	$33.00	Sonic Tails, Hedgehog, Knuckles - Gray T–Shirt	$11.85

Accessories ▶ Nintendo, Super

The average sales price in this subcategory is $9.59.

	HIGH		AVG
MARIO BROTHERS HAT LUIGI HALLOWEEN	$66.00	2 NEW ORIGINAL SUPER NINTENDO CONTROLLERS + 2 EXTENSION	$9.95
COSTUME W/ HANDS		[14 of these sold for $9.95 each]	
Super Nintendo Package Deal 6 GAMES: 2 CTRLS: &SYSTEM	$65.00	ONE (1) SNES SUPER NES NINTENDO CONTROLLER IN BOX *NEW*	$9.79
MARIO BROTHERS HAT HALLOWEEN COSTUME W/ HANDS	$55.00	10 SNES DUST COVERS FOR GAMES CLEAN SUPER NINTENDO	$8.00
Nintendo to Super Nintendo Snes converter Super 8	$53.56	OFFICIAL NINTENDO SUPER SNES CONTROLLER & EXTENSION NEW	$7.95
Nintendo Super Nintendo Complete system with games	$47.00	2 Super Nintendo SNES Controllers Boxed New in Box !!	$6.99
SUPER NINTENDO SYSTEM COMP. W/	$41.00	SEGA GENESIS AC DC POWER ADAPTER Cable Cord NEW	$6.99
2 CONT. AND 4 GAMES		Super Nintendo Game Cartridges Lot of 5	$6.95
Super Nintendo with all Accessories and Games	$41.00	Super Nintendo GAME GENIE with codebook	$6.00
SUPER NINTENDO SYSTEM COMP. W/	$39.99	SUPER NES Nintendo AC DC POWER ADAPTER Cable Cord NEW	$5.99
2 CONT. AND 4 GAMES		ORIGINAL NINTENDO SUPER SNES CONTROLLER & EXTENSION NEW	$5.95
2 x SNES Super Nintendo PC USB Controller Adapter Pack	$37.99	OFFICIAL NINTENDO SUPER SNES CONTROLLER & EXTENSION NEW	$5.95
SUPER NINTENDO GAME SYSTEM LOT W/ 2 GAMES	$36.00	[2 of these sold for $5.95 each]	
2 x SNES Super Nintendo PC USB Controller Adapter Pack	$35.99	GENUINE NINTENDO SUPER SNES CONTROLLER & EXTENSION NEW	$5.95
SUPER NINTENDO GAME SYSTEM AND ONE FREE GAME	$25.50	10 SNES DUST COVERS FOR GAMES CLEAN SUPER NINTENDO	$5.50
Origional SNES controller with Super Smartjoy Adapter	$22.00	Super NES Super Nintendo Controller Only 99 Cents!!	$5.50
Super Nintendo Super Scope 6 Accessory and Game	$19.13	NEW AC ADAPTER for Super Nintendo SNES NES SEGA Systems	$5.15
Nintendo Infrared multiple game satilite controller	$19.00	[3 of these sold for $5.15 each]	

Accessories ▶ PC Games

The average sales price in this subcategory is $20.36.

	HIGH		AVG
Thomas Racing Wheel Best Sim Wheel around	$455.00	PC Gaming l Thrustmaster Nascar Pro Force Feedback	$23.50
MOMO FORCE Steering Wheel by Logitech, RED, NIB!!	$224.00	MICROSOFT FORCE FEEDBACK STEERING WHEEL BOXED	$23.50
CH Products Flight Sim Yoke USB and Pro Pedals USB	$182.50	Logitech Freedom 2.4 Wireless joystick Brand new.	$23.15
CH Flight Sim Yoke & IPro Pedals	$142.49	Logitech Extreme Joystick with 2 Flight Games	$22.49
Nintendo gamecube ,12games,memory card,5 controllers	$131.00	Logitech Wingman Formula Force GP Steering Wheel for PC	$21.50
CH Products Flight Yoke (USB) and Pedals	$127.50	WingMan -Force Feedback -Steering Wheel- ByLogitech	$21.38
Red Logitech MOMO Force Steering Wheel	$127.50	M/SOFT SIDEWINDER 3D PRO JOYSTICK+STEERING WHEEL	$20.35
CH Products Flight Sim Yoke USB	$100.00	ThrustMaster Pro Flight Control System JoyStick	$20.00
Logitech MOMO Force Steering Wheel. Rare Leather Model	$96.00	NEW MICROSOFT SIDEWINDER PRECISION PRO JOYSTICK + GAMES	$19.99
THRUSTMASTER RUDDER CONTROL SYSTEM FOR FLIGHT SIMS PC	$91.00	Top Gun Afterburner Feedback Joystick Thrustmaster	$19.99
X-Arcade 2 Player Arcade Controller for PC & Consoles	$91.00	Top Gun Afterburner Feedback Joystick Thrustmaster	$19.50
CH Products Flight Sim Yoke USB (with Fly2 and X-Plane)	$90.00	THRUSTMASTER ENZO FERRARI FORCE FEEDBACK STEERING WHEEL	$19.28
CH Products Flight Sim Yoke	$86.75	Saitek Game Controllers 2 P3000/ 1Cyborg 3D Gold	$18.50
Thrustmaster Elite Rudder Pedals	$86.00	3in1 Controller Converter PC USB - PS2, XBOX,Game Cube	$16.99
Microsoft Force Feedback 2 with Myst3 and MS Flight Sim	$85.88	CH Virtual Pilot Pro Flight Yoke	$16.00

Accessories ▶ Sega CD

The average sales price in this subcategory is $23.21.

	HIGH		AVG
Sega CDX with BOX and Manual System Plus games	$91.00	Sega CD Backup RAM Cart w/16X Save Memory - Excellent	$34.47
SEGA GENESIS CD WITH ACCESSORIES CDS & CARTRIDGE	$67.00	Sega CD Backup RAM Cart - Complete - 16X Save Memory	$32.75
13 Sega CD Games, Mint, In Cases with Instructions	$66.00	Sega CD: CD Back-Up Ram Cart. Hard to find!!	$32.00
SEGA GENESIS GAME SYSTEM SEGA CD GAME SYSTEM BOXED +	$62.00	Lunar The Silver Star Sega CD + Official Strategy Guide	$32.00
Shining Force Sega CD RPG - Rare Game - NR	$56.00	Sega CD Back Up RAM Cart	$26.00
Sega CD Backup RAM Cart - Complete - 16X Save Memory	$50.00	Sega Saturn Backup RAM Cart - 16X Save Memory	$26.00
SEGA CD; CD BACK UP RAM CART	$47.00	CD BACK-UP RAM CART FOR SEGA CD **RARE**	$21.50
Lunar: The Silver Star (Sega CD)	$42.99	Sega CD Back Up RAM- 1 owner, Complete	$19.50
Sega CD Game Shining Force	$41.00	Sega CD: CD Back-Up Ram Cart. Hard to find!!	$18.00
Lot of 7 Sega CD games including Mortal Kombat	$41.00	SEGA CD Back UP RAM CART never used RARE	$17.39
Sega Genesis CD Backup Ram Cartridge Rare	$40.75	Sega CD 's 5 total Eternal Champions, Surgical Strike,	$15.50
Shining Force Sega CD RPG Rare	$38.50	SECRET OF MANA OFFICIAL GAME SECRETS	$14.99
Vay Sega CD + Map + Official Strategy Guide	$38.12	Final Fight with Box and Manual for Sega CD System	$12.60
Sega CD console with Sewer Shark game and bonus game!	$36.00	BACK UP RAM Cartridge MEGA-CD JP	$12.50
Sega CD Game Lunar Eternal Blue	$36.00	SUPER METROID PLAYERS GUIDE	$12.50

Accessories ▶ Sega Dreamcast

The average sales price in this subcategory is $6.00.

	HIGH		AVG
SEGA DREAMCAST BROADBAND ADAPTER AND 3.0	$70.99	NEW Sega Dreamcast 4 Extension Cables + 4 Tremor Packs	$7.95
LAN Adaptor HIT-0300 for SEGA DREAMCAST nEW	$57.00	Modem for Dreamcast lot of 10 offical by Sega	$7.50
Sega Dreamcast system with 12 games and more	$26.88	Sega Dreamcast 4 Extention Cables + 4 Rumble Paks NEW!!	$6.99
VINTAGE SEGA NEON COMMING	$22.50	DREAMCAST VMU GRAY BRAND NEW SEALED!	$6.50
SOON DRY ERASE BOARD SIGN !!!			$6.50
5x Sega Dreamcast Video Game Promo Packs NM	$20.60	LOT OF 6 VIDEONOW CASES , 2 COLOR, 4 BLACK	$6.00
NEW Sega Dreamcast SYSTEM SHELL Clear BLUE MOD Glacier	$20.50	Gameshark CDX Sega Dreamcast BRAND NEW	$5.99
sega dreamcast game lot baseball nhl and tennis 2k2 new	$20.00	SEGA DREAMCAST KEYBOARD – Like new – No Reserve	$5.50
MARINE & BASS FISHING + SEGA ROD NEW 4 Dreamcast System	$18.99	Bleem! Bleem Bleemcast Gran Turismo 2 GT2 *RARE*	$5.00
Dreamcast Light Gun!!	$15.00	Brand new Sega Dreamcast force pack	$4.99
Sega Dreamcast VGA Converter & S-Video Also!	$14.99	DREAMCAST VMU RED BRAND NEW SEALED!	$4.99
Sega Dreamcast Bleemcast for Tekken 3, NEW!	$13.00	NEW AV & AC POWER CORD CABLES FOR	$4.95
NEW SEGA DREAMCAST GAMESHARK GAME SHARK FACTORY SEALED	$12.95	SEGA DREAMCAST SYSTEM	
[2 of these sold for $12.95 each]		Bleem Bleemcast Gran Turismo 2 Dreamcast NEW!	$4.95
NEW Dreamcast CARRY CASE w/ Logo STRAP 4 system games	$10.99	NEW Sega Dreamcast AV CABLE & AC POWER Cord Set NEW	$4.95
DREAMCAST SYSTEM PLUS 2 GAMES & MORE	$10.50	SEGA Dreamcast AUDIO VIDEO CABLE & AC POWER ADAPTER NEW	$4.45

Accessories ▶ Sega Game Gear

The average sales price in this subcategory is $10.09.

	HIGH		AVG
Sega Game Gear, 11 games and accesories	$51.00	SEGA GAME GEAR PLUS 5 GAMES	$13.00
2 SEGA GAME GEARS WITH ACCESSORIES AND 15 GAMES!!!!!!!!	$51.00	DELUXE ORIGINAL Sega Game Gear BLACK CARRYING CASE	$12.50
Sega Game Gear and 12 games Cheap!!!!!!	$50.77	Sega Game Gear Handheld + 6 games NR	$12.50
Sega TV TUNER for GAME GEAR system Brand NEW NB NR	$49.15	Sega Game Gear Carrying Case	$11.50
Sega TV TUNER for GAME GEAR system Brand NEW NB NR	$44.15	SEGA GAME GEAR 7 GAMES AND ACCESSORIES! no system	$11.50
Game Gear with 4 Games	$41.01	Sega Game Gear w/ Carrying Case & Three Games	$10.50
2 Sega Game Gear - Handheld game systems!!!	$41.00	Sega Game gear and 1 game	$10.00
Sega TV TUNER for GAME GEAR system Brand NEW NB NR	$37.03	NEW 3 x Sega SONIC 8" Plush-HEDGEHOG	$9.99
SEGA GAME GEAR WITH 4 GAMES AND CARRIER	$36.56	KNUCKLES & TAILS	$9.99
SEGA GAME GEAR WITH 8 DIFFERENT GAMES!!!!!!!!	$35.00	Sega Handheld Game Gear with Games	$9.99
Sega Game Gear TV Tuner Adaptor	$32.50	Sega Game Gear w/6 games and case NR	$9.99
SEGA GAME GEAR SYSTEM WITH 5 GAMES AND EXTRAS+++	$32.20	NEW 3 x Sega SONIC 8" Plush-HEDGEHOG KNUCKLES & TAILS	$9.99
SEGA GAME GEAR like new with 7 games, and power supply	$31.00	Sega Game Gear with 4 Cartridges	$9.99
** Sega Game Gear TV Tuner w/ box and instructions **	$31.00	Sega Gamegear and 3 games	$9.99
[2 of these sold for $31.00 each]		Sega Game Gear– GAME GENIE (CHEATERS ONLY)	$8.99
Sony PSOne w/ LCD Screen, Controller, AC Adapter, Game	$31.00	Sega Game Gear POWERBACK Recharge Battery Pack w/manual	$8.99

Accessories ▶ Sega Genesis

The average sales price in this subcategory is $6.03.

	HIGH		AVG
Gunstar Heroes Sega Genesis Complete w/box,instructions	$46.00	Original Sega Genesis RF Switch Unit MK-1632	$6.99
SEGA GAME GENIE*NEW* POWER	$39.95	Sega Genesis 32X Nomad System AV Cable Cord Adapter NEW	$6.99
BASE CONVERTER AND MORE!!		[3 of these sold for $6.99 each]	
Sega Genesis System 7 Games some rare BONUS Magazine	$36.55	X BAND Modem Sega Genesis XBAND NEW FACTORY SEALED	$6.65
Sega Genesis Game System w/ 9 games / NFL / NHL / Sonic	$26.65	2 Genesis Controller Extension NEW by Sega	$6.50
TWO SONY PLAYSTATION ONE UNITS	$23.50	Sega Genesis 1 AV Audio Video Cable 1601	$5.99
W/GAMES AND ACCESSORIES		NEW Sega 32X Nomad Genesis 2 Stereo AV Cable	$5.99
Lot of 24 Sega Genesis Games—Used	$19.99	[2 of these sold for $5.99 each]	
Sega Genesis 6 Button Arcade Joy Stick Joystick	$19.52	NEW Sega 1 AV CABLE for Genesis Master systems 1601+	$5.95
6 Universal AC Adapters NES Super Nintendo Genesis NEW	$17.99	[3 of these sold for $5.95 each]	
Sega Sonic the Hedgehog 6 VHS Movie Tails Song	$17.50	NEW Sega 1 AV CABLE for Genesis Master systems 1601+	$5.95
SEGA DREAMCAST SPORTS CONTROLLER MODEL HKT - 7700	$15.50	NEW Sega 1 AV CABLE for Genesis Master systems 1601+	$5.95
7 SEGA GENESIS GAMES ALL FOR ONE PRICE	$11.00	Sega Genesis RFU RF adapter TV switch	$5.50
Lge Lot SEGA/ATARI GAME CONTROLLERS + Power & RF Switch	$10.50	Phantasy Star II Hint Book	$5.50

SEGA GENESIS ARCADE JOYSTICK	$10.00	AV CABLE CORD SEGA FOR GENESIS 1 MODEL 1601 GAME SYSTEM	$5.49
SEGA GENESIS SYSTEM , SGPROPAD6 + 12 Games	$10.00	Brand NEW AV CABLE for Sega Genesis 1 and Master System	$4.99
Sega 32 X upgrade for Genesis & 4 games & 2 genies NR!!	$9.99	AV Cable for Sega Genesis 2 & 3 MK-1631 & 1461 *NEW *	$4.99
		NEW Official Sega AC ADAPTER Genesis 2, 3 32X GameGear	$4.99

Accessories ▶ Sega Master

The average sales price in this subcategory is $16.42.

	HIGH		AVG
3 Sega Master System 3d Glasses 37 Games Extras	$102.50	THE SEGA 3-D GLASSES (LIKE NEW) 4 Sega Master System	$24.98
Excellent Sega 3-D Glasses - Boxed w/Plastics - SMS 3D!	$86.15	Sega Genesis System With 4 Games Sonic & Sports	$16.00
RARE FUN! SEGA MASTER SYSTEM 3-D GLASSES + 4 Games!	$76.76	ALEX KIDD in MIRACLE WORLD sega master system game	$15.50
SEGA Master System With 7 Games	$76.00	SEGA 3D glasses - MINT - & Space harrier 3D & Zaxxon 3D	$15.50
Sega Master System w/Gun &Controls plus 15 Games Incl.	$61.00	Y's VANISHED OMENS & AZTEC	$15.50
SEGA MASTER SYSTEM WITH 10 GAMES	$55.00	ADVENTURE sega master system	
AND 4 CONTROLLERS		Sega Genesis CD System W/7 Games & Power Plug	$15.00
Sega Genesis 32X Upgrade W/5 Games ~WORKING~	$46.55	Sega Master system 3-D Glasses plus 3-D Games	$14.99
Sega Genesis CD System W/8 Games & Programpad	$41.00	2 original Sega Master Controllers, Black	$14.50
Sega Master System 3-D Glasses	$41.00	Play Sega Master System Games on Game Gear Master Gear	$12.95
Sega Master System 3-D glasses w/ two 3-d games 3d	$31.00	[5 of these sold for $12.95 each]	
Vintage Sega Master System w/6 Games Gun 2 Controllers	$29.00	Sega Master System With Game ~WORKING~	$11.00
SMS Sega Master System 3D 3-D Glasses LOOK Boxed Nice	$29.00	SEGA MASTER SYSTEM LIGHT	$10.49
PS2 7" flat scream	$28.01	PHASER GUN FREE SHIP W BIN!!!	
Sega Master System Controller + AC Adapter + RF Switch	$26.69		
SEGA MASTER SYSTEM WITH 11 GAMES	$26.55		

Accessories ▶ Sega Pico

The average sales price in this subcategory is $17.37.

HIGH TO LOW			
Sega PICO System w/ 7 Games Storyware LOT Computer toy	$56.00	Sega Pico Games Lot of 4 (Lion King,Pooh)	$15.00
SEGA PICO SYSTEM: Unit, AC Adapter & Connector Cables	$40.51	Sega Pico with 4 games Richard Scarry Musical Zoo ++++	$13.00
SEGA PICO EDUCATIONAL COMPUTER LEARNING SYSTEM & GAMES	$28.00	ORIGINAL SEGA PICO GAME PEN "GREAT REPLACEMENT"	$10.50
NICE LOT OF 4 SEGA PICO STORYWARE GAME BOOK CARTRIDGES	$26.07	Sega Pico Game System with 1 Game !! NICE!!	$9.99
5 Sega PICO Video Games Carts I	$20.84	SEGA-PICO-REPLACEMENT=PEN-CABLES-&-ADAPTER	$8.50
Sega Pico System Computer Game Toy Educational	$17.06	Pico Game Unit W/ Three Game Cards	$5.78
SEGA PICO SYSTEM AND 7 GAMES !!!!	$17.00	SEGA PICO GAME LOT MICKEY	$5.24
PICO COMPUTER ~ SEGA ~ PLUS (4) GAMES	$15.50	POOH DALMATIONS LION KING	
SEGA PICO GAME LOT POOH BERENSTAIN BEARS MICKEY ++++	$15.50	ORIGINAL SEGA PICO AC POWER SUPPLY ADAPTOR	$5.00
Sega Pico In Box Computer Video Game Learning System	$15.50	Sega Pico POCOHONTAS + RICHARD SCARRY 2 Storybks Low$sh	$4.99

Accessories ▶ Sega Saturn

The average sales price in this subcategory is $7.27.

	HIGH		AVG
Sega Saturn Backup Memory Cart rare!	$40.00	SEGA SATURN 4in1 Storage/Memory CARD, 8190 Blocks =NEW	$8.49
Sega Saturn Virtua Cop 2 with Stunner Arcade Gun	$37.50	NEW Sega Saturn STEREO AV CABLE & AC POWER Cord Set	$7.50
sega saturn,5 games,hookups,2 controllers,mem.battery	$37.49	[5 of these sold for $7.50 each]	
RARE Sega Saturn Action Reply 4M PLUS *Brand New*	$32.95	NEW Sega SATURN Stereo AV CABLE +AC POWER Cord RCA	$7.25
[2 of these sold for $32.95 each]		[2 of these sold for $7.25 each]	
SIX SEGA SATURN GAMES IN ORIGINAL PLASTIC CASE	$28.03	NEW Sega SATURN Stereo AV CABLE +AC POWER Cord RCA	$6.99
sega saturn memory card new in box	$25.00	[2 of these sold for $6.99 each]	
2 SEGA SATURN GAME CONTROLLERS	$20.00	Sega SATURN-1 RFU-2 ST PRO -PAD- 1 FRU NOT SURE?	$6.99
Sega Saturn Official Japanese Memory Card HSS-0111	$20.00	Sega Saturn multitap 6-player adapter multi tap	$6.00
Saturn light gun and lot of 3 games: Area 51	$16.76	Sega Saturn AV Cable - (Audio Video) - New	$5.24
SEGA Saturn Cheats codes 4 in 1 Plus Memory 4MB NEW	$14.95	Lot of 5 Strike Pad Controllers, Sega Saturn Video Game	$5.00
Sega Saturn Game Shark GameShark	$14.95	Sega SATURN SVHS S Video Audio Cable Cables New!	$4.99
Memory Card NEW SEALED		[6 of these sold for $4.99 each]	
[2 of these sold for $14.95 each]		PRAYER KINGZ CHRISTIAN RAP CD (New)	$4.99
12 Lot Sega Saturn RF RFU Adapters	$12.99	NEW Sega SATURN Stereo AV RCA Cables Audio Video Cord	$4.95
BRAND NEW Wholesale		[14 of these sold for $4.95 each]	
Saturn 4 In 1 Memory Card / Play All / Action Reply NEW	$10.95	Saturn RF SWITCH (Sega Brand) Adapter Cables Cord NEW	$4.50
[2 of these sold for $10.95 each]		NEW STEREO SEGA SATURN AV AUDIO VIDEO CABLE NeW!!!	$4.49
Sega Saturn 6 Player Multi-player Adapter MINT	$10.50	[6 of these sold for $4.49 each]	
		Sega Saturn Official Game Controller	$4.15
		7 Sega Saturn Games Virtua Cop & Virtua Fighter 1 & 2	$4.09

Accessories ▶ Sony PlayStation

The average sales price in this subcategory is $9.66.

	HIGH		AVG
NEW Offical Sony LCD Screen Playstation PS1 PSOne 5"	$42.99	Playstation Gameshark Video Game Emhancer Ver.5-TF829	$9.99
Pocket station white(PS)	$42.03	SONY PSP WIRELESS EARPHONE/HEADSET FREE FM TRANSMITTER	$9.99
PS One LCD Screen 5.6 inch - Factory Sealed! Great Mod!	$39.99	SONY PSP ALUMINUM SHELL CASE [BLACK] FREE SCREEN GUARD	$9.99
[2 of these sold for $39.99 each]		PLAYSTATION ONE GAMES	$8.50
Brand New 512MB SanDisk Memory Stick PRO Duo GAMING PSP	$31.00	Sony PSP - Skin Skins Cover Shoose Your Design	$7.99
Coded Arms (PlayStation Portable)	$28.00	NEW PLAYSTATION GAME SHARK GAMESHARK PS1 PS ONE PSX NEW	$7.95
		[2 of these sold for $7.95 each]	

Accessories ▶ Sony PlayStation 2

The average sales price in this subcategory is $11.44.

	HIGH		AVG
SanDisk 2 GB Memory Stick PRO	$115.00	Arcade Stage Initial D AE86 Car Leather Wallet	$12.99
Sony PlayStation 2 with controllers and games	$72.00	NETWORK INTERNET ADAPTER W/ DISC PLAYSTATION 2 PS2 NEW	$12.49
playstation 2 hdd with final fantasyXI, and socom maps	$65.00	Gran Turismo 4 The Real Driving Simulator	$12.00
Sony PlayStation 2 Slim - Game console	$56.00	Final Fantasy ADVENT CHILDREN SKIN for Slim PS2 Skins	$11.95
Buy now! FIFA 2006, PS2 In Stock Mike @ 323-472-1302	$48.99	PS2 SCARFACE SKIN SONY PS2 VINYL SKINS NEW	$11.95
Redoctane Ignition DDR 3.0 Dance Pad PC/PS2/XBOX WOW!!!	$44.99	Devil May Cry SKIN for PS2 VINYL SKINS "DEVIL MAY CRY"	$11.95
Linksys WGA11B Wireless B Game Adaptor XBOX or PS2 NEW	$39.00	LOGITECH USB HEADSET MICROPHONE SONY PLAYSTATION 2 PS2	$10.50
New PS2 Action Replay Max EVO Edition 50000+ Cheat Code	$34.99	Resident Evil Biohazard Dog Tag Necklace	$10.00
X-PORT cheat code & save Mgmt Playstation 2 NEW PS2 USB	$31.45	NEW POWERBOARD/for playstation 2	$10.00
Delta Force Black Hawk Down PS2!!!! (Playstation 2)	$26.01	PSP Power Brick External Rechargeable Battery Pack NEW	$9.99
PS2 USB SOCOM Headset PlayStation 2 L@@K!!! Z4	$26.00	NEW AC ADAPTER POWER SUPPLY /W CORD FOR SONY PSP NR	$9.99
PC/PLAYSTATION PS2 RACING STEERING	$24.99	SONY PSP JOYSTICK SCREEN PROTECTOR SYSTEM CASE COVER	$8.95
WHEEL PADELS & SHIFT		6 NEW Eye Toy Play 2 PROMO Store Display Boxes for PS2	$8.00
Sony Play Station 2 Memory Cards (2 Pack) New Sealed	$23.01	Playstation 2 PS2 System MOD CHROME MIRROR SKIN NEW	$7.95
Katamari Damacy Cell Phone Dangler Promo For PS2	$22.50	[4 of these sold for $7.95]	
New Retrocon PS2 Controller & PS2 8MB Memory Card (Lot)	$21.50	PSP Decals Scarface Decal Skins Skin	$5.50

Accessories ▶ Other Accessories

The average sales price in this subcategory is $13.05.

	HIGH		AVG
Halo MasterChief Resin Statue Rare	$182.50	Brand New Toshiba Laptop Carrying Case Retails for $50	$19.99
Sandisk 1GB Memory Stick Pro Duo PSP	$73.26	256 MB SanDisk Memory Stick PRO DUO	$19.95
Sandisk 1GB Memory Stick Pro Duo 1 GB MS Card for PSP	$70.00	New Toshiba Red Laptop Backpack Carrying Case	$17.99
512MB Memory Stick PRO Duo for PSP BRAND NEW!!! Sandisk	$50.00	sony PSP CHARGER DOCK / Stand W/ SPEAKERS Watch Movies!	$17.50
[2 of these sold for $50.00 each]		Nyko Wireless NET EXTENDER PS2 / XBox / PC / Mac	$14.50
AK Designs Rocking Gaming Chair (400000)	$43.00	UMD PSP MOVIE "ROBOTS" (2005 UMD RELEASE)	$13.99
AK Designs Rocking Gaming Chair (400001)	$41.00	Nyko Wireless NET EXTENDER PS2 / XBox / PC / Mac	$12.50
Final Fantasy XI 11 Online Vana'diel Clock NEW! By Hori	$41.00	Xbox Live 2 month Card expires June 2006!!!! *NEW*	$11.50
Used Pyramat PM550 Sound Lounger 2.1 Stereo Sound, 80W	$37.00	Pelican All In One Case & Accessories for Sony PSP	$11.00
AK Designs Rocking Gaming Chair (400001)	$36.00	LOT: 2 Code Books made by BRADY	$9.99
AK Designs Rocking Gaming Chair (400001)	$25.00	GAMES STRATEGY GUIDES	
NINTENDO DS MANNEQUIN HAND Touching is good RARE	$25.00	VIDEO STORAGE CENTER intellivision atari playstation	$9.00
Dance Dance Revolution DDR Blue Twin TV Pad - 2 PLAYERS	$24.98	Sony PSP 16-in-1 SUPER Travel Kit Accessory Pack *NEW*	$8.99
Monster Cable Gamelink 400 CVAA-New in Box	$23.50	SONY PSP HOT PINK DELUXE LEATHER CARRYING CASE	$8.99
sony PSP CHARGER DOCK / Stand W/ SPEAKERS Watch Movies!	$22.99	Pitfall Lost Expedition Official Strategy Guide Book	$7.99
		Sony PSP Skin Skins Choose From 22 Colors	$5.99

Games ▶ 3DO

The average sales price in this subcategory is $15.33.

	HIGH		AVG
Huge Lot of Nintendo, Super NES, PS1, 3DO, Sega Nomad	$280.00	3DO game/Icebreaker/brand new	$15.50
DINOPARK TYCOON FOR THE 3DO GAME SYSTEM - SEALED!!!	$202.50	Policenauts Pilot Disc 3DO JP IMPORT.	$15.50
HUGE 3DO LOT (2) 3DO FZ-1, (1) 3DO FZ-10, (42) GAMES	$180.27	Super Street Fighter II Turbo (3DO) game PANASONIC n&c	$15.50
DINOPARK TYCOON FOR THE	$110.00	STRAHL (3DO) game PANASONIC nice & cplt	$15.50
3DO GAME SYSTEM - SEALED!!!		3DO GAME - DRAGONS LAIR - BRAND NEW!!!	$15.50
3DO Console + 11 Games (Preowned) (3DO/3D0)	$108.18	LOT OF 13 3DO by PANASONNIC GAMES - SOME COMPLETE	$15.50
Goldstar 3DO Complete With 26 Games (Rare Titles)	$103.50	LOVE BITES (3DO) game PANASONIC nice!!! adult	$15.00
Panasonic 3DO System w/ 22 games!!! Rarely Played!!!	$102.55	CHAOS OVERLORDS....RARE 3DO Classic Still in SEALED BOX	$14.99
3DO Console + 11 Games (Preowned) (3DO/3D0)	$100.99	3DO The ORIGINAL RETURN FIRE + MAPS Death ~New SEALED!~	$14.95
Panasonic REAL 3DO Interactive Multiplayer	$81.00	3DO FZI Interactive Player WIth One remote and 2 Games	$14.51
PANASONIC 3DO FZ-10 WITH 13 GAMES	$81.00	3DO The ORIGINAL RETURN FIRE + MAPS Death ~New SEALED!~	$14.50
3DO Console + 11 Games (Preowned) (3DO/3D0)	$73.01	ROAD RASH & TWISTED the game show FOR PANASONIC 3DO	$14.00
Lot of 10 Vintage 3DO Video Game System Games NOS	$65.75	3DO - Game Guru (Promotional CD)	$13.70
3DO Game LOT 25 Games + 2 gamepads 3d0 LOOK!	$65.00	[2 of these sold in a multiple item ("Dutch") auction for $6.85 each]	
>PANASONIC 3DO BUST A MOVE< CLASSIC AND RARE	$61.00	PANASONIC 3DO MURPHYS TV CD-ROM JAPAN	$13.50
Lot of 10 Vintage 3DO Video Game System Games NOS	$60.00	3DO game/Super Street Fighter II Turbo	$13.50

Games ▶ Apple

The average sales price in this subcategory is $18.43.

	HIGH		AVG
ULTIMA II MINT ~SEALED ~ RARE for Apple II by Sierra	$743.00	Sim City 4 Sims Macintosh Apple software Mac sealed	$26.00
BALDUR'S GATE II Shadows of Amn MAC GAMES AD&D Apple	$59.99	ChessMaster 9000 Mac OS X Chess Program Apple	$26.00
The Sims 2 Mac / Apple * FREE SHIPPING * NR	$45.15	Apple Seed Super Famicom/SNES JP IMPORT.	$22.00
APPLE MAC EDITION THE SIMS PARTY PACK DVD USED LIKE NEW	$39.99	Dungeon Siege for Mac Apple Used	$20.50
Total Annihilation Gold Edition for Mac Apple Macintosh	$37.01	Sim City 3000 Apple Mac Game	$16.50
New in Box DVD-ROM The Sims 2 Mac Games NIB Apple	$36.50	MAC BRAND NEW HEROES OF MIGHT & AND MAGIC 4 IV APPLE	$15.50
LIKE NEW: Rise of Nations - Gold Edition - Mac / Apple	$31.00	Icewind Dale Mac Macintosh OSX New Sealed Apple	$15.25

Games ▶ Atari

The average sales price in this subcategory is $14.98.

	HIGH		AVG
MOTO RODEO GAME FOR ATARI 2600 & 7800 NEW UNOPENED	$449.00	Atari 2600 game River Raid II - RARE and working	$15.50
Atari Jaguar Limited Edition Battle Sphere Game	$325.00	Iron Soldier (Jaguar) New Jaguar 64 Bit Cart Atari	$15.50
Huge Lot of 114 Atari 2600 Video Games and 96 Manuals	$199.00	Millipede Atari 2600 New Mint! Boxed	$15.00
IKARI WARRIORS GAME FOR ATARI 2600 & 7800 NEW UNOPENED	$181.50	Mario Brothers Atari 2600 New Mint! Boxed	$15.00
ATARI 5200 - MULTICART 94 Games	$153.53	NEW~SEALED~HOT#1ENTER~THE~MATRIX ATARI~GAME X~BOX~XBOX	$14.99
Large Lot of 78 Atari 2600 And 7800 Games!! SOME RARE!!	$117.51	Atari Jaguar Defender 2000	$14.99
ATARI Game console 2600 HUGE 97 games joystick DREAM	$113.75	Nintendo DS Retro Atari Sealed Rare New	$14.99
Atari 2600 -OBELIX- Unbelievably Rare! *R10	$103.50	Playstation 2 PS2 Game Atari Anthology ***BRAND NEW***	$14.79
Atari Jaguar Limited Edition Air Cars Game - complete	$102.50	The Destruction of E.T. The atari 2600's WORST GAME!	$14.50
Texas Chainsaw Massacre ATARI 2600 GAME *RARE 7/10*	$100.04	Tempest 2000 (Jaguar) New Jaguar 64 Bit Cartridge Atari	$14.50
Huge Lot Of 168 ATARI 2600 Video Games	$91.00	10 NINTENDO DS GAMES RETRO ATARI BRAND NEW & SEALED	$14.00
ATARI LYNX 2 SYSTEM and 4 NEW game Collection + AC/DC	$85.00	GameBoy Advance GBA SP Atari Anniversary Advance *NEW!*	$13.99
Glib Word Game ATARI 2600 bySelchow & Richter*RARE R9*	$82.00	Tax Avoiders ATARI 2600 GAME by American *RARE 5/10*	$13.79
Q*bert's Qubes Atari 2600 Rarity 9/10 Atariage Qbert's	$77.34	Pengo for the Atari 2600	$13.50
atari 2600	$75.01	ATARI JAGUAR CD GAME BALDIES MINT, COMPLETE W/ SW	$13.50

Games ▶ Colecovision

The average sales price in this subcategory is $14.60.

	HIGH		AVG
COLECOVISION - 59 VINTAGE GAME CARTRIDGES - SOME CIB!	$224.99	DUKES OF HAZZARD Colecovision Game Coleco RARE!	$16.35
COLECOVISION WITH XTRA'S	$97.00	LOT OF 16 COLECOVISION/ATARI GAMES	$16.25
ColecoVision POWER LOT! 28 GAMES + 3 MODS coleco vision	$85.01	SPY HUNTER Colecovision Game !	$14.99
Star Wars The arcade game for Colecovision	$51.00	COLECOVISION - ADAM - Mr. Do!'s Castle - Tested RARE !	$14.99
Sammy Lightfoot COLECOVISION by Sierra *RARE R8* 479+	$46.00	Electronic Games Mar 1984 ColecoVision vs 5200 - ZORK	$14.99
Coleco Vision Colecovision QBert's Qubes Q Bert's RARE	$44.99	Mr. Do!'s Castle - Colecovision	$14.49
THE DAM BUSTERS COMPLETE IN BOX COLECOVISION GAME RARE	$39.99	5 Colecovision Games-Cosmic Avenger, Smurf, Victory	$13.89
KEYSTONE KAPERS COLECOVISION COMPLETE MINT IN BOX RARE	$39.99	CHOPLIFTER Colecovision Game Coleco RARE!	$13.49
COLECOVISION XONOX Artillery Duel & Chuck Norris Coleco	$37.00	Colecovision H.E.R.O. (HERO) with box and manual	$12.50
colecovision coleco vision lady bug video game cart HTF	$36.00	RIVER RAID by Activision ~ Colecovision ~ NEW ~ NIB	$12.50
SECTOR ALPHA COLECOVISION ULTRA RARE GAME COLECO VISION	$35.99	Lot of 9 Colecovision Cartridges	$11.99
RARE Sector Alpha by SpectraVision for ColecoVision NR	$35.44	BEAMRIDER COMPLETE IN BOX COLECOVISION GAME ACTIVISION	$11.99
Q Bert's QUBES Colecovision Game Coleco RARE!	$35.44	ZENJI Colecovision Game Coleco RARE!	$11.61
TOMARC THE BARBARIAN COLECOVISION ULTRA RARE XONOX GAME	$34.99	5 Colecovision Games Coleco- Centipede, Pitfall II, etc	$11.52
Dr. Seuss Fix-up the Mix-up Puzzler - Colecovision	$34.56	Miner 2049er COLECOVISION GAME by Micro Fun *RARE R4*	$11.50

Games ▶ Commodore

The average sales price in this subcategory is $9.92.

	HIGH		AVG
Ultima IV 4 Quest of the Avatar Commodore 64	$36.00	COMMODORE VIC 20 GAMES..OMEGA RACE..RADAR RATRACE..More	$9.99
COMMODORE 64 Games KAMPFGRUPPE & GETTYSBURG Turning CIB	$31.00	COMMODORE VIC 20 GAMES..TOOTH INVADERS..MOLE ATTACK..&	$9.99
Commodore 64 - ULTIMA V complete LIKE NEW 5 c64 RPG	$28.00	COMMODORE VIC 20 GAMES..AVENGER..NUMBER NABBER..JUPITER	$9.99
Commodore 64 30-Games-in-One Joystick	$26.00	Commodore 64- Sid Meiers PIRATES –Eyepatch BONUS! c64	$9.99
Commodore 64 Rings Of Zilfin Strategy Game	$20.50	10 Factory Sealed Vintage Commodore 64/128 Games NIB	$9.99
Koronis Rift by Lucas Commodore 64 C64 Atari 400 1985	$20.00	Vintage Commodore 64/128 Patton vs Rommel NEW NR	$9.99
PuzzlePanic by Epyx Commodore 64 C64 {CIB} 1984	$18.37	Commodore 64 128 Dark Castle	$8.50
Commodore 64 Battle For Normandy Strategy Game	$18.27	Commodore 64 Battles Of American Civil War Bull Run +	$7.99
Commodore 64 30-in-1 Classis Plug & Play Video	$17.60	COMMODORE 64 " GAME COLLECTION " 5 RARE GAMES	$6.99
Dragonfire II by Magicware Commodore 64 C64 CIB 1986	$16.06	Squish'em by Sirius - Commodore 64 {NEW} C64 1983	$6.06
Amazon by Trillium Commodore 64 C64 {CIB} 1984	$15.50	Tournament Tennis by Imagic Commodore 64 C64 {CIB} 1984	$6.05
Dragonworld by Trillium Commodore 64 C64 {CIB} 1984	$15.50	Paul McCartney's Broadstreet Commodore 64 C64 CIB 1985	$6.00
Nine Princes in Amber Commodore 64 {NEW} C64 1985	$15.50	Commodore 64 / 128 Conflict in Vietnam Simulator Game	$6.00
12 cartridges Commodore 64 C64 128 C128: Lazarian, more	$15.50	Commodore 64 LOT of 4 CARTRIDGES Carts w/ JUMPMAN JR +	$5.51
Stellar 7 Commodore 64 C64 Apple II {CIB} 1984	$15.06	SKATE WARS, by UBI SOFT -NEW/RARE COMMODORE 64 GAME	$5.50

Games ▶ Intellivision

The average sales price in this subcategory is $13.90.

	HIGH		AVG
Intellicart for Intellivision	$501.00	INTELLIVISION GAMES ATLANTIS DRAGONFIRE SERPENTS RARE	$14.02
Intellivision system + 32 games, many rare + voice unit	$90.00	INTELLIVISION POLE POSITION NEW	$14.00
Turbo Coleco for Intellivision box manual HTF Rare	$87.00	3 Boxed Intellivision Games Pitfall Mission-X Dungeons	$13.99
Intellivision game lot in box Turbo Vectron B-17 Bomber	$81.00	60 GAMES Intellivision Lives Sony Playstation 2 PS2 NEW	$13.98
Super Mattel Intellivision Game System w/Tons of Games	$78.01	[3 of these sold for $13.98 each]	
Lrg. Qty Intellivision games (30) rare!!	$61.22	60 GAMECUBE GAMES INTELLIVISION LIVES BRAND NEW SEALED!	$13.97
Intellivision Game system/w 18 game cartridges	$61.00	Intellivision Venture Game Cartridge	$13.50
Intellivision Intellivoice Sega System Lots of games!	$60.99	INTELLIVISION THIN ICE BOX WITH RARE OVERLAYS	$13.49
World Series Major League Baseball - Intellivision Game	$60.00	LOT of 19 Intellivision Games!! W/BOXES Classic Coleco	$13.39
Jetsons way with words - Intellivision Game	$60.00	INTELLIVISION GAME CLUB CARD	$13.36
19 GAMES included INTELLIVISION gaming SYSTEM	$59.99	Blockade Runner for Intellivision! Complete!! RARE!!!!!	$12.51
INTELLIVISION SUPER PRO	$56.91	INTELLIVISION LOT OF CONTROLLERS FOR INTELLEVISION 2	$12.50
DECATHLON NEW W/ OVERLAYS		INTELLIVISION GAMES BEAMRIDER & THE DREADNAUGHT FACTOR	$12.50
Intellivision Thunder Castle Complete	$56.00	DUNGEONS & DRAGONS~Treasure Of Tarmin~ INTELLIVISION	$12.50
Intellivision Game OVER 42 games with boxes	$50.00	INTELLIVISION - Centipede w/ Original Box and Booklet	$12.40
Vintage Intellivision Game System w/ 48 Games	$48.00	Triple Challenge Intellivision Game	$12.00

Games ▸ Microsoft Xbox 360

The median sales price in this subcategory is $39.99.

NOTE   *The prices in this subcategory were obtained using eBay's Completed Items feature.*

	HIGH		AVG
XBOX 360 "Ultimate Game Lot " 100 GAMES	$3,999.99	Call of Duty 2 Xbox 360 Sealed Mint Condition	$39.99
XBOX 360 "Ultimate Game Lot " 50 GAMES	$1,899.99	Condemned: Criminal Origins (Xbox	$39.99
*** Eight (8) BRAND NEW SEALED XBOX 360 GAMES***	$400.00	360) SAVE $15 USED	
8 game bundle, new, in hand, w/ receipt, ready to ship!		NBA LIVE 2006, 06 MICROSOFT	$39.99
8 NEW UNOPENED XBOX 360 GAMES	$360.00	XBOX 360 ~~~LIKE NEW~~~	
6 XBOX 360 Games Wirless contol, and 12 month Live Play	$359.00	CONDEMNED: CRIMINAL ORIGINS	$39.99
6 xbox 360 games and two wireless controllers xbox 360	$330.00	XBOX 360 ~~~LIKE NEW~~~	
Madden, Tiger, Nba live, Kameo, Call of Duty 2, PGR!!!!		NBA 2K6 2006 Xbox 360 basketball video game complete	$39.99
6 XBOX 360 Games and Two Controllers	$325.00	NHL 2K6 2006 Xbox 360 hockey video game complete	$39.99
New XBOX 360 6 games bundle Call of Duty 2, NHL 2K6,	$256.00	Amped 3 (Xbox 360) Brand New Factory Sealed!!!	$39.99
Kameo, PGR 3, Ridge Racer 6, Tony Hawk Underground, NFS		Condemned: Criminal Origins (Xbox 360) Complete Mint	$39.99
6 XBOX 360 Games. Brand New. Unopened. No Reserve!	$251.51	Dead or Alive 4 (Xbox 360)	$39.99
Xbox 360 games and Harmony controller (all sealed)	$250.00	Gun (Xbox 360) *MINT*	$39.99
Perfect dark zero/Quake4/Gun/Need4speed/call of duty 2		Perfect Dark Zero (Xbox 360)	$39.99
Xbox 360 GAMES! Bundle of 5 very hot games...	$242.50	Need for Speed Most Wanted Xbox	$39.99
New XBOX 360 6 games bundle Call of Duty 2, NHL 2K6,	$242.50	360 Adult Owned FREES/H	
Kameo, PGR 3, Ridge Racer 6, Tony Hawk Underground, NFS		Project Gotham Racing 3 (Xbox 360)	$39.99
Lot of 6 Brand New XBox 360 Games - Kameo, Madden 06	$242.01	Brand New Sealed NR!	
Tiger Woods, King Kong, Ridge Racer 6, Need for Speed		GUN Xbox 360 Like New	$39.99
6 Xbox 360 Games: Perfect Dark, Call of Duty 2..	$239.49	Condemned: Criminal Origins (Xbox	$39.99
8 XBOX 360 Games for Sale	$238.49	360),COMPLETE,GREAT	

Games ▸ Microsoft Xbox

The average sales price in this subcategory is $27.44.

	HIGH		AVG
HUGE LOT 72 XBOX GAMES 72 MICROSOFT XBOX GAMES	$350.00	GRAND THEFT AUTO SAN ANDREAS MICROSOFT XBOX GAME	$29.00
Microsoft Xbox - 26 games and extras	$270.00	NEW NBA 2K6 FOR SONY MICROSOFT XBOX	$29.00
Microsoft Xbox + 10 Games + 2 controllers (1 wireless)	$270.00	NBA 2K6 - Microsoft Xbox - NEW! Basketball Game!	$28.00
Microsoft Xbox - Game console - black	$260.00	NHL 06 Microsoft XBOX game 2006 HOCKEY COMPLETE MINT	$28.00
Microsoft Xbox - Game console - black with 28 games	$250.00	NCAA 06 FOOTBALL Microsoft XBOX game COLLEGE 2006	$28.00
Microsoft Xbox- Game console	$250.00	WINNING ELEVEN 8 WORLD SOCCER Microsoft XBOX game RARE	$28.00
Microsoft Xbox - Game console - black	$234.37	Indigo Prophecy - Microsoft Xbox - NEW!	$27.20
Microsoft Xbox - Game console	$213.50	CONFLICT GLOBAL TERROR NEW SEALED MICROSOFT XBOX GAME M	$27.01
Microsoft Xbox, 2 controllers, and 16 games	$207.50	NEW NCAA Football 06 Microsoft Xbox NR	$27.00
Microsoft Xbox-Game console-W/Games-2Controllers	$200.00	GRAND THEFT AUTO SAN ANDREAS MICROSOFT XBOX GAME	$26.00
Microsoft Xbox 10 Games w/ DVD Remote No! Reserve	$192.50	Doom 3 Limited Collector's Edition for Microsoft Xbox	$26.00
Microsoft Xbox - Game console - black	$178.50	NEW Grand Theft Auto: San Andreas Microsoft Xbox NR	$25.99
Microsoft Xbox - Crystal Clear Case xbox live bundle	$177.51	Moto GP 3 Microsoft Xbox NEW SEALED!	$25.45
Microsoft Xbox - Game console - 6 controllers & 7 games	$177.50	MADDEN NFL 06 Microsoft XBOX game FOOTBALL 2006	$25.45
Microsoft Xbox - Game SYSTEM/AND 5 GAMES /HALO	$175.00	Microsoft Xbox Game: Halo 2, Used, great condition, NR	$25.00

Games ▸ Nintendo 64

The average sales price in this subcategory is $9.01.

	HIGH		AVG
Super Mario 64 DS (Nintendo DS)	$100.60	N64 MORTAL KOMBAT 4 Nintendo 64 CIB Rare Fighting Fun!	$9.50
[5 of these sold in a multiple item ("Dutch") auction for $20.12 each]		N64 Disney's A BUG'S LIFE Nintendo 64 System Game n HTF	$9.50
NEON GENESIS EVANGELION - NINTENDO 64 JAPANESE IMPORT	$91.00	Yoshi's Story (Nintendo 64) VERY RARE! BEST GAME EVER	$9.49
Huge lot of Nintendo 64 games!! – Low opening bid!!	$87.00	Nintendo 64 Bomberman 64 N64 Bomber Man Children Kids	$9.49
26 Nintendo 64 Games Package L@@k	$84.68	N64 Toy Story 2: Buzz Lightyear Rescue Nintendo 64 two	$9.42
N64 Video Game Lot (kid games) Rated E Nintendo 64	$71.00	BattleTanx (Nintendo 64)	$9.22
N64 Nintendo 64 Game Lot Doom Mario Vigilante 8 Turok +	$49.07	Mario Kart 64 (Nintendo 64) mint condition	$8.99
NINTENDO 64 SYSTEM W 2 CONTROLLERS, 10 GAMES & EXTRAS	$47.55	Diddy Kong Racing (Nintendo 64) FUN KIDS GAME	$8.99
Nintendo 64 lot NR games and controllers wheel play fun	$46.00	007 Goldeneye NINTENDO 64 N64	$8.99
N64 Video Game Lot (mature games) Rated M Nintendo 64	$43.00	GAUNTLET LEGENDS N64 NINTENDO	$8.99
HARVEST MOON Nintendo 64 CLEAN RPG "VERY RARE" FREE S&H	$36.99	64 VIDEO GAME VERY RARE!!	
N64 Nintendo 64 James Bond 007 Goldeneye-NEW-Never open	$36.00	MORTAL KOMBAT 4 N64 NINTENDO 64 FIGHTING GAME	$8.99
Nintendo 64 - Game console	$35.05	BANJO TOOIE N64 NINTENDO 64 VIDEO GAME	$8.99
Nintendo 64 System and Games	$34.50	SUPER MARIO 64 N64 NINTENDO 64 GAME	$8.95
NINTENDO 64 SYSTEM GAME MARIO KART NEW IN BOX SO SUPER!	$34.00	[2 of these sold for $8.95 each]	
N64 Nintendo 64 Game Lot Tremor Pak Memory Cards	$33.59	Super Smash Bros. (Nintendo 64)	$8.53

Games ▸ Nintendo Game Boy

The average sales price in this subcategory is $17.64.

	HIGH		AVG
40 Nintendo Gameboy Games + Game Boy Color System &More	$208.62	YOSHI TOUCH & GO NINTENDO GAMEBOY GAME BOY DS GAMES BX	$18.50
Nintendo Game Boy Advance SP system +13 games, acces...	$182.50	WOW NINTENDO GAME BOY ADVANCE - POKEMON FIRERED VERSION	$18.50
Near Mint Nintendo Game Boy Advance SP and Eleven Games	$151.03	Nintendo Game Boy Advance POKEMON LEAFGREEN game	$18.15
New Nintendo Game Boy Advance SP 5 Games & 12-in-1 Kit	$144.50	Pokemon~ SAPPHIRE VERSION Nintendo Game boy Advance,SP	$18.00
Nintendo Game Boy Advance SP - Handheld game system ...	$142.50	SUPER MARIO 64 NINTENDO GAMEBOY GAME BOY DS GAMES BX+BK	$18.00

Nintendo Game Boy Advance SP - LOTs of add-ons	$134.03	RAYMAN DS NINTENDO GAMEBOY	$18.00
Nintendo Game Boy Advance SP like new + 11 games, cases	$127.49	GAME BOY DS GAMES BOX+BOOK	
Lot of 24 Nintendo GameBoy Game Boy Games	$124.49	DONKEY KONG COUNTRY Game Boy Advance Nintendo GBA SP DS	$17.77
Nintendo Game Boy Advance SP - w/ 7 GAMES	$119.38	4 Game Boy Nintendo Games Donkey Kong Land 1,2,3 + 1!	$17.52
Nintendo DS - Handheld system GameBoy Game Boy + EXTRA	$110.00	Nintendo Game Boy Games , Dr. Mario, Tetris, etc	$17.51
Nintendo Game Boy Advance SP + 6 Games + Carrying Case	$108.49	Pokemon Yellow & Blue, for the Nintendo Game Boy	$17.50
Nintendo Game Boy Advance SP + 6 Games + 2 Videos	$107.50	LOT OF 3 SUPER NINTENDO GAMES & SUPER GAME BOY	$17.50
Nintendo Game Boy Advance with 14 games	$104.62	SPIDER-MAN 2 GAMEBOY GAME BOY NINTENDO DS GAMES GO NR	$17.50
2 Nintendo Game Boy Advance Systems & 6 Game Lot!!!	$103.35	Nintendo Game Boy Advance - Handheld game system - g...	$17.50
NINTENDO GAME BOY ADVANCE	$102.50	SUPER MARIO 64 NINTENDO GAMEBOY GAME BOY DS GAMES BX+BK	$17.50
+CASE AND THREE GAMES!!!!!!		SUPER MARIO Advance (Game Boy Advance) Nintendo MINT	$17.50

Games ▶ Nintendo Game Boy Advance

The average sales price in this subcategory is $26.97.

	HIGH		AVG
Nintendo Game Boy Advance SP system +13 games, acces...	$182.50	Nintendo Game Boy Advance Four Game Assortment	$29.00
nintendo game boy advance sp Blue with 13 games +	$170.27	Advance Wars in original box Nintendo GameBoy Game Boy	$28.50
Near Mint Nintendo Game Boy Advance SP and Eleven Games	$151.03	The Sims 2 Nintendo Game Boy Advance GBA BRAND NEW!	$28.50
Nintendo Game Boy Advance SP + 17 Games	$150.00	GOLDEN SUN Game Boy Advance Nintendo Micro GBA SP DS	$27.52
New Nintendo Game Boy Advance SP 5 Games & 12-in-1 Kit	$144.50	Nintendo Game Boy Advance - Handheld game system - g...	$27.00
Nintendo Game Boy Advance SP - Handheld game system ...	$142.50	Nintendo Game Boy Advance - Handheld game system - g...	$26.87
Nintendo Game Boy Advance SP + 5 Games + Case	$142.50	Pokemon Emerald Version Game Boy Advance Game Nintendo	$26.50
Nintendo Game Boy Advance SP - LOTs of add-ons	$134.03	Nintendo Game Boy Advance Yu-Gi-Oh! Dungeondice +3 more	$26.01
Nintendo Game Boy Advance SP like new + 11 games, cases	$127.49	NINTENDO GAME BOY ADVANCE	$26.00
Nintendo Game Boy Advance SP - w/ 7 GAMES	$119.38	The Sims 2 Nintendo Game Boy Advance GBA BRAND NEW!	$26.00
Nintendo Game Boy Advance SP with 10 games	$115.50	NINTENDO GAME BOY ADVANCE POKEMON GREEN LEAF VERSION !!	$25.85
Nintendo Game Boy Advance SP + 6 Games + Carrying Case	$108.49	The Sims 2 Nintendo Game Boy Advance GBA BRAND NEW!	$25.33
Nintendo Game Boy Advance SP + 6 Games + 2 Videos	$107.50	Tomb Raider The Prophecy Nintendo Game Boy Advance NEW!	$25.00
Nintendo Game Boy Advance with 14 games	$104.62	The Sims 2 Nintendo Game Boy Advance GBA BRAND NEW!	$24.50
Nintendo Game Boy Advance - Handheld game system - g...	$104.00	Nintendo Game Boy Advance SP Pokemon Fire Red	$23.75

Games ▶ Nintendo Game Boy Advance SP

The average sales price in this subcategory is $33.39.

	HIGH		AVG
Nintendo Game Boy Advance SP system +13 games, acces...	$182.50	Nintendo Game Boy Advance sp w cartoonnetwork speedway	$44.05
nintendo game boy advance sp Blue with 13 games +	$170.27	BLACK SP ADVANCE SYSTEM w/charger NINTENDO GAME BOY	$44.00
Near Mint Nintendo Game Boy Advance SP and Eleven Games	$151.03	BASEBALL ADVANCE Game Boy GBA Nintendo Micro SP DS	$41.00
Nintendo Game Boy Advance SP + 17 Games	$150.00	Nintendo Game Boy Advance SP - Handheld game system ...	$40.00
New Nintendo Game Boy Advance SP 5 Games & 12-in-1 Kit	$144.50	Nintendo Game Boy Advance SP	$38.00
Nintendo Game Boy Advance SP - Handheld game system ...	$142.50	Nintendo Game Boy Advance SP	$36.55
Nintendo Game Boy Advance SP + 5 Games + Case	$142.50	Nintendo Game Boy Advance SP pokemon games lot ...HTF	$34.00
Nintendo Game Boy Advance SP - LOTs of add-ons	$134.03	Nintendo Game Boy Advance SP - Handheld game system ...	$32.01
Nintendo Game Boy Advance SP like new + 11 games, cases	$127.49	Game Boy Advance SP Nintendo Game lot	$29.99
Nintendo Game Boy Advance SP - w/ 7 GAMES	$119.38	GOLDEN SUN Game Boy Advance Nintendo Micro GBA SP DS	$27.52
Nintendo Game Boy Advance SP with 10 games	$115.50	Nintendo Game Boy Advance SP Pokemon Fire Red	$23.75
Nintendo Game Boy Advance SP + 6 Games + Carrying Case	$108.49	SUPER MARIO BROS NES Game Boy Advance Nintendo SP DS	$23.50
Nintendo Game Boy Advance SP + 6 Games + 2 Videos	$107.50	DOOM Game Boy Advance Nintendo Gameboy Micro GBA SP DS	$23.49
Nintendo Game Boy Advance SP with 7 Games & Charger	$102.00	THE SIMS Bustin Out Game Boy Advance Nintendo GBA SP DS	$22.06
Nintendo Game Boy Advance SP + 6 Games + 2 Videos	$96.00	DONKEY KONG COUNTRY Game Boy Advance Nintendo GBA SP DS	$21.51

Games ▶ Nintendo Game Boy Color

The average sales price in this subcategory is $11.94.

	HIGH		AVG
40 Nintendo Gameboy Games + Game Boy Color System & More	$208.62	Game Boy Color System Nintendo game Gameboy Games	$13.00
NINTENDO GAME BOY COLOR AND POCKET 21 GAMES AND MORE	$82.88	CROC 2 Game Boy Color Nintendo Gameboy Advance SP	$12.50
2 Nintendo Game Boy Color systems and 10 games	$73.00	SCOOBY DOO Game Boy Color Nintendo Gameboy Advance SP	$12.50
3 Dragon Warrior Game Boy Color NINTENDO SAMPLE CARTS	$70.00	THE GRINCH Game Boy Color Nintendo Gameboy Advance SP	$12.50
8 Nintendo Game Boy Color/Advance Games w/Instructions	$51.00	BARBIE PET RESCUE NINTENDO GAME BOY COLOR SP	$12.02
LOT OF NINTENDO GAME BOY GAMES	$48.00	SUPER MARIO BROS DELUXE Nintendo Game Boy COLOR Gameboy	$12.00
1 GAME BOY COLOR POKEMON		~THE POWERPUFF GIRLS~ Nintendo Gameboy color game boy	$12.00
NINTENDO GAME BOY COLOR 9 GAME LOT.	$47.55	A BUG'S LIFE Complete Nintendo Game Boy Color Gameboy	$11.51
Nintendo Game Boy Color - Handheld game system - green	$46.00	Nintendo Game Boy Color - Handheld game system - purple	$11.09
NINTENDO GAME BOY COLOR SYSTEM, 8 GAMES & CASE	$46.00	FROGGER Game Boy Color Nintendo Gameboy Advance SP	$11.00
NINTENDO GAME BOY COLOR, 2 GAMES, MAD CATZ ACCESSORIES!	$45.00	Harvest Moon (Game Boy Color) Nintendo SP	$10.52
Nintendo Game Boy Advance-Glacier Color Good Condition	$43.54	Nicktoons Racing for the Nintendo Game Boy Color	$10.51
NINTENDO GAME BOY COLOR & 8 GAMES WITH CASE EXCEL COND	$42.99	FROGGER Game Boy Color Nintendo Gameboy Advance SP	$10.51
NINTENDO GAME BOY COLOR SYSTEM, 8 GAMES, CASE & LIGHT	$41.00	Pok?n CRYSTAL version Nintendo Game Boy Color/Advance	$10.50
Two Nintendo Game Boy Color handheld systems	$40.00	Nintendo GAME BOY SP DR. MARIO	$10.50
Nintendo Game Boy Color system and extras!	$36.00	ADVANCE COLOR Game VGC!!	

Games ▶ Nintendo GameCube

The average sales price in this subcategory is $18.60.

	HIGH		AVG
49 video games Nintendo GameCube WHOLESALE ! Fast Ship!	$325.00	RESIDENT EVIL 4 NINTENDO GAMECUBE MINT CON COMPLETE BIO	$19.50
Nintendo Gamecube and twenty games.	$227.50	Super Smash Bros. Melee Nintendo Gamecube	$19.28

Nintendo GameCube - 14 Games - 4 controllers - More	$212.50	3 Nintendo Gamecube games Sealed Backyard Football	$19.19
Nintendo Gamecube System with 25 games	$192.25	Starfox Assualt Nintendo Gamecube Video Game	$19.00
Nintendo Gamecube + 13 Games + Controllers + Zelda	$154.49	Super Smash Bros. Melee Nintendo Gamecube	$18.99
Nintendo GameCube-jet black–4 controllers-2 Games	$125.00	Metroid Prime 2 : Echoes Nintendo Gamecube LIKE NEW!	$18.99
Nintendo Gamecube & Games	$118.18	Nintendo Gamecube MARIO PARTY 4 Complete Like New	$18.50
Nintendo Gamecube / Game Cube, Black, Perfect Condition	$110.00	Resident Evil Zero 0 Nintendo Gamecube + Strategy Guide	$18.50
NEW IB LIMITED EDITION POKEMON	$107.50	3 Nintendo Gamecube games Godzilla Sealed Big Air Taz	$18.50
NINTENDO GAMECUBE SYSTEM		Luigi's Mansion Nintendo GameCube GAME CUBE GC LIKE NEW	$18.15
Nintendo Gamecube, steering wheel, 8 games and more!!	$107.50	NEED FOR SPEED UNDERGROUND 2 NGC	$18.00
Nintendo GameCube *Barely Used* Lot+++	$100.00	GCN NINTENDO GAMECUBE	
Nintendo GameCube - Game console - black	$100.00	NCAA Football 2005 - Nintendo Gamecube NEW Sealed	$17.99
NINTENDO GAMECUBE WITH 13 GAMES	$96.00	[2 of these sold for $17.99 each]	
NINTENDO GAMECUBE SYSTEM	$95.00	Lot of 2 Nintendo Gamecube games-The Lord of Rings	$17.52
* COMPLETE * WITH 2 GAMES		Nintendo Gamecube Game Worms 3D	$17.50
8 GAMES!! NINTENDO GAMECUBE	$86.00	SUPER SMASH BROS. BROTHERS MELEE	$17.50
HUGE LOT! ZELDA, LOTR, ETC!		NINTENDO GAMECUBE GAME	

Games ▸ Nintendo NES

The average sales price in this subcategory is $7.36.

	HIGH		AVG
Garage Cart - new for Nintendo NES - homebrew multicart	$202.50	Nintendo NES Zapper Gun with Super Mario & Duck Hunt	$7.99
88 NINTENDO NES GAMES - Ninja Gaiden TMNT Zelda Mario	$175.00	6 NINTENDO NES GAMES ZELDA JAWS PREDATOR FRIDAY 13TH	$7.99
VINTAGE COLLECTION OF 76 NINTENDO NES GAMES NICE LOT	$124.99	MANIAC MANSION WITH CASE NES NINTENDO	$7.55
48 ORIGINAL 8-BIT NINTENDO NES LOT of Video Games	$75.00	Nintendo NES Game - Double Dribble - Konami	$7.50
NES NINTENDO SYSTEM SUPER MARIO BROS. MEGAMAN 1 2 3	$74.99	NES nintendo game SPIRITUAL WARFARE	$7.50
Holy Grail RARE Nintendo MAXI-15 NEW Factory Sealed NES	$66.55	NES - Mike Tyson's Punch Out - Nintendo Video Game	$7.50
LOT OF 33 NINTENDO GAMES LOT OF 33 NES GAMES	$56.00	(Nintendo Nes) Donkey Kong Arcade Classic Series/RARE	$7.50
Nintendo Super NES Sega Genesis CLASSIC Games LOT Used	$51.00	Genghis Khan Nes Nintendo Game Very Rare hard to find !	$7.19
56 Nintendo Nes Games No Doubles Some Rare	$51.00	2 nintendo nes games Q*bert and excitebike	$7.01
34 different NINTENDO NES instruction booklets No Res.	$41.05	Wheel of Fortune (Nintendo) NES Family Edition	$7.00
NES Nintendo STARTER SET #2- 20 CLASSIC GAMES INCLUDED!	$41.00	Nintendo NES system game all-new FAMILY FEUD Rare!	$7.00
LOT 30 Nintendo NES games rare collection #1 classic	$36.00	MANIAC MANSION !!! NES / NINTENDO !! RARE !!!	$7.00
NES NINTENDO BIG NOSE FREAKS OUT SEALED BY CAMERICA!!	$35.00	NES Nintendo RBI R.B.I. BASEBALL Black Tengen Version!	$6.99
HUGE 31 NINTENDO NES GAME LOT GOOD GAMES LOOK	$34.99	NES Nintendo Game - DOUBLE DRAGON 2 II * CLASSIC *	$6.99
24 Lot "NINTENDO VIDEO GAMES" for NES Unit + Clean Kit!	$34.33	Nes Nintendo TETRIS 2 II Guaranteed RARE COMBINE SAVE $	$6.97

Games ▸ Nintendo, Super

The average sales price in this subcategory is $11.88.

	HIGH		AVG
SUPER NINTENDO CONSOLE + SUPER LOT - SNES	$300.00	Donkey Kong Country Super Nintendo Game SNES NR	$12.00
Huge SNES Super Nintendo Lot w/ System! NO RESERVE!!!	$182.50	SUPER METROID Super Nintendo Snes Game rare NR	$12.00
Big SNES Super Nintendo Lot w/ System! NO RESERVE!!!	$103.60	*ZELDA: A LINK TO THE PAST* Super Nintendo SNES game	$11.99
SUPER NINTENDO GAME SYSTEM WITH 28 GAMES	$102.50	Super Mario All-Stars (Super Nintendo) 4 in 1!!!	$11.99
Super Mario 64 DS (Nintendo DS)	$100.60	TECMO SUPER BOWL 3 III (Super Nintendo) SNES SuperBowl	$11.99
[5 of these sold in a multiple item ("Dutch") auction for $20.12 each]		SUPER MARIO ALL STARS Super Nintendo SNES AllStars Star	$11.95
LOT OF 20 SUPER NINTENDO GAME CARTRDGES –SNES GAMES	$81.00	SUPER MARIO BROS N64 NINTENDO	$11.90
NES NINTENDO SYSTEM SUPER MARIO BROS. MEGAMAN 1 2 3	$74.99	64 GAME LIKE NEW RARE NR	
Huge Super Nintendo SNES Lot w/22 Games & More Cheap!!	$66.01	NINTENDO 64 N64 ***SUPER MARIO 64*** AWESOME GAME!	$11.75
Nintendo NES complete system w/14 games; Super Mario 3	$66.00	Classic NES Nintendo Game Super Dodgeball Dodge ball	$11.51
SUPER NINTENDO SNES 15 GAMES + SUPER GAME BOY + EXTRAS	$61.09	Super Smash Bros. (Nintendo 64)	$11.50
Nintendo NES System & Super Mario Bros 1,2 and 3	$61.00	NINTENDO GAMECUBE SUPER MARIO	$11.50
Super nintendo game:MEGAMAN X3	$59.95	SUNSHINE @ $5 N/R (JWS)	
Lot of 18 Rare Super Nintendo Entertainment System Game	$59.00	Super Mario All Stars For Super Nintendo!	$11.50
SNES SUPER NINTENDO CONSOLE SYSTEM LIKE NEW w/4 Games	$57.49	SNES Kirby Superstar 8 Games in 1 Super nintendo rare!!	$11.50
[2 of these sold for $57.49 each]		Captain Commando SNES Super Nintendo Capcom SNES Title	$11.50
Super Nintendo SNES 7 game Lot Kirby Mario Tetris	$57.12	Super Mario 64 (Nintendo 64) FAST SHIPPING.. GUARANTEED	$11.50

Games ▸ PC

The average sales price in this subcategory is $11.01.

	HIGH		AVG
BIG PC Game Lot! 15+rare games!	$81.09	Bad Mojo (PC Games) the Roach Game Redux MINT! NR!	$11.53
Grand Theft Auto: San Andreas (PC Games)	$64.50	EA THE SIMS 2 SPECIAL EDITION DVD PC GAME	$11.52
X-COM: COLLECTOR'S EDITION (PC-CD)	$58.70	Star Wars Lego PC Game EIDOS	$11.50
NEW/ SEALED Grand Theft Auto San Andreas PC BANNED Ver.	$56.00	BLIZZARD WORLD OF WARCRAFT FOR PC	$11.50
Grand Theft Auto San Andreas for PC HOT COFFEE UNCUT!	$49.00	NEXUS: THE JUPITER INCIDENT * PC * NEW * LOW S&H	$11.29
The Dark Eye PC CD-ROM Adventure RARE	$39.99	NEC PC-ENGINE SCD COSMIC FANTASY 4 GEKITOTSU JAPAN	$11.16
Star Wars REBELLION pc game with Manual RARE NR	$39.95	CIVILIZATION III: GOLD EDITION PC NEW SEALED IM	$10.99
F1 CHALLENGE '99-'02 - PC CD-ROM Game - 014633146271	$39.95	New PC Video Game: LINKS 2003 - Championship Edition	$10.75
World of WarCraft (PC Games)New* No RES* LOW S/H	$36.00	MASTER LEVELS FOR DOOM II PC CDROM SHOOTER LEVELS	$10.59
PC GAME THE SIMS 2 & University & SIMS2 Night life NEW	$35.00	Sacred (PC Games) NO RESERVE!	$10.51
Battlefield 2 for PC CD-ROM, Brand New and Unopened	$34.95	Manhunt (PC Games)	$10.50
Black & White 2 For PC, NEW and IN STOCK!	$34.65	PC GAME "THE HOBBIT"...NEW...NEVER PLAYED!	$10.50
Fable: The Lost Chapters (PC Games)	$33.00	Might and Magic IX (PC Games)	$10.50
Battlefield 2 PC Game USED GREAT CONDITION!! CD retail	$32.00	Psychonauts (PC Games)	$10.50
Action PC Basketball (2005 Version)	$30.00	Guild Wars Pre-Order Box PC RARE FACTORY SEALED NIB	$10.50

Games ▸ Sega Dreamcast

The average sales price in this subcategory is $9.03.

	HIGH		AVG
HOUSE OF THE DEAD 2 w/two light guns. SEGA DREAMCAST	$61.00	Sonic Adventure 1 Original COMPLETE (Sega Dreamcast)	$9.99
Sega Dreamcast Power Stone 2	$60.00	Looney Tunes Space Race COMPLETE (Sega Dreamcast) MINT	$9.99
Sega DreamCast HOUSE of the DEAD 2 Game & 2 Guns DC NR	$51.00	Resident Evil Code: Veronica COMPLETE (Sega Dreamcast)	$9.99
NEW IN BOX SEGA DREAMCAST CONSOLE!!!!!!!!!!!!!	$51.00	Sega DREAMCAST SOLDIER OF FORTUNE Game FACTORY SEALED	$9.99
Sega Dreamcast - 4 controllers, 16 games - LOOK	$51.00	CAPCOM VS SNK Sega Dreamcast SEALED NIP Rare !!	$9.99
Multi-Regional Sega Dreamcast with 30 Bonus Games us/j	$47.00	OUTRIGGER dc SEGA DREAMCAST Out Trigger game OUTTRIGGER	$9.77
SEGA DREAMCAST COMPLETE SYSTEM PLUS 9 GAMES HUGE LOT	$45.00	Armada RARE Sega Dreamcast Space RPG Free Shipping	$9.05
Sega Dreamcast Japanese Import Cosmic Smash VERY RARE	$41.01	Bang Gunship Elite ~ Sega Dreamcast Games * BRAND NEW	$8.99
LOT OF 9 SEGA DREAMCAST GAMES ALL HAVE INSTRUCTIONS!!!!	$41.00	Tomb Raider Chronicles ~ Sega Dreamcast Games * NEW	$8.99
BANGAI-O Sega Dreamcast game EXTREMELY RARE US U.S.	$40.00	Grandia II for the Sega Dreamcast Rare RPG !!!!!!	$8.99
Bangai-O - Sega Dreamcast NEAR MINT! COMPLETE! Bangaio	$40.00	SEGA DREAMCAST NHL 2K VIDEO GAME W/ MANUAL HOCKEY FUN!!	$8.99
Ikaruga,DREAMCAST,SEGA,TREASURE,MINT,RADIANT SILVERGUN	$39.68	Lot Of 5 Official Sega Dreamcast VMU's Official rare!!!	$8.75
SEGA DREAMCAST CONSOLE SYSTEM+7 GAMES +EXTRAS	$38.00	Sega Dreamcast - Lot of 2 -Speed Devils & CODE:Veronica	$8.50
HUGE SEGA DREAMCAST GAMES ~ SHENMUE CRAZY TAXI RUSH	$37.00	SEGA DREAMCAST RUSH 2049 COMPLETE MINT	$8.50
Fatal Fury Mark of the Wolves Sega Dreamcast - COMPLETE	$37.00	THE RING: Terror's Realm Sega Dreamcast Sealed R Mature	$8.00

Games ▸ Sega Game Gear

The average sales price in this subcategory is $8.62.

	HIGH		AVG
BIG LOT OF SEGA GAME GEAR - SYSTEM LOT OF 28 GAMES	$86.00	5 SEGA GAME GEAR GAMES - Mortal Kombat, Indiana Jones..	$9.00
SEGA GAME GEAR SYSTEM MIB +8 FACTORY SEALED GAMES	$80.00	Sega Game Gear~ SUPER STAR WARS (RARE GAME)	$8.99
Sega Game Gear 2 systems 20 Games and more	$61.36	BATMAN & ROBIN for Sega Game Gear CIB Original BOX	$8.99
Sega Game Gear and 12 games Cheap!!!!!!	$50.77	GARFIELD Sega Game Gear Box, Case, Manual & Comic! NM	$8.99
Sega Game Gear Video Game Large Lot all Working GREAT	$46.00	LEGEND OF ILLUSION M.MOUSE Sega Game Gear CIB (box)	$8.99
Lot of 18 Sega Game Gear Games	$40.99	THE LOST WORLD: JURASSIC PARK Sega Game Gear CIB Box!!	$8.99
13 NEW LOT SEGA GAME GEAR GAMES + AC + BATTERY + SCREEN	$40.95	Sega Game Gear: Mortal Kombat II : Low shipping!!	$8.50
13 NEW LOT SEGA GAME GEAR GAMES + AC + BATTERY + SCREEN	$39.95	Ren & Stimpy (Game Gear) Sega Shaven Yak	$8.49
[2 of these sold for $39.95 each]		SEGA GAME GEAR GAME GAMES LOT OF 5	$8.27
10 GAMES NEW FOR SEGA GAME GEAR GAMEGEAR SYSTEM	$30.99	Sega Game Gear 4 games w/ Cases	$8.10
10 GAMES NEW FOR SEGA GAME GEAR GAMEGEAR SYSTEM	$29.99	7~SEGA~GAME~GEAR~GAMES~SONIC~2~	$7.75
Game Genie SEGA GAME GEAR CODE BOOK INCLUDED	$29.50	AERIAL~ASSAULT~TAZ	
Lot of 6 Sega Game Gear games. Box, Booklet, and Case	$29.00	Vampire Master of Darkness - Sega Game Gear RARE Japan	$7.60
SHINING FORCE THE SWORD OF HAIYA SEGA RPG GAME GEAR	$27.95	3 Sega Game Gear Disney games NEW Aladdin, Lion King +1	$7.50
NICE SEGA GAME GEAR + 9 GAMES + AC/DC ADAPTER CHARGER!!	$26.00	Sega hand held Game Gear with Sonic2 game	$7.50
		7 Sega Game Gear Games! EXC!!!	$7.50

Games ▸ Sega Genesis

The average sales price in this subcategory is $7.63.

	HIGH		AVG
231 Sega Genesis Game Lot	$137.50	Sega Genesis 6 PAK Game Sonic Golden axe Shinobi column	$8.25
HUGE VIDEO GAME LOT PLAYSTATION SEGA GENESIS GAMES	$68.67	Sega Genesis Marble Madness w/ instructions.	$8.25
Sega Genesis Console + 26 Games Disney, Sports..USED	$52.98	Sega Genesis Video Game Virtual Bart	$8.10
Nintendo Super NES Sega Genesis CLASSIC Games LOT Used	$51.00	Sega Genesis Mortal Kombat 2 with instructions.	$8.02
MENACER w/ T2 Game & 6-Game Cartridge for Sega Genesis	$51.00	MTV's Beavis and Butt-head (Sega Genesis) W/ MANUAL	$8.00
HUGE LOT OF SEGA GENESIS GAMES 41 TOTAL GAMES	$46.55	GOLDEN AXE - Sega Genesis - NEW and Sealed	$7.99
HERZOG ZWEI SEGA GENESIS NOMAD GAME *VERY RARE*	$43.20	SEGA GENESIS, SONIC 3 THE HEDGEHOG, BOOK, BOX, AND GAME	$7.75
LOT SEGA GENESIS SYSTEM w/7 GAMES, MENACER & GENISTICK	$42.00	Sega Genesis BattleToads Sonic The Hedgehog 1 & 3 Lot	$7.51
4 DIFFERENT SPIDERMAN SEGA GENESIS GAMES *	$41.00	Spider-Man (Sega Genesis) W/ CASE	$7.50
Sega Genesis Video Game ToeJam and Earl	$36.01	CASTLE OF ILLUSION,Mickey Mouse,Sega Genesis,FREE SHIP!	$7.50
SEGA GENESIS 16-BIT SYSTEM W 2 CONTROLLERS & 17 GAMES	$36.00	Sega Genesis Sonic The Hedgehog 3	$7.50
SEGA genesis Uncharted Waters New Horizons COMPLETE !	$36.00	Sega Genesis Video Game Captain America and athe Avenge	$7.50
SEGA GENESIS SYSTEM & 21 GAME SPORTS LOT - NO RESERVE !	$33.00	Sega Genesis Video Game Mega Bomberman	$7.50
Sega Genesis Limited Edition Pirates Gold Game	$31.00	Huge Lot of 11 Sega Genesis Games all Kinds no Doubles	$7.39
Sega Genesis System with 8 Games and 2 Controllers	$30.99	SEGA GENESIS GAME SPLATTERHOUSE 2 HARD TO FIND	$7.25

Games ▸ Sega Saturn

The average sales price in this subcategory is $17.10.

	HIGH		AVG
Panzer Dragoon Saga collection+ Sega Saturn! MUST SEE!	$202.50	X-Men vs Street Fighter Sega Saturn Japanese JP XMen	$19.00
ULTIMATE Sega Saturn Bundle, Like NEW!!! 31 Games	$184.27	Sonic R (Sega Saturn) US	$19.00
RADIANT SILVERGUN for Sega Saturn JP RARE!!	$172.50	VAMPIRE SAVIOR 4MB RAM BOX for Sega Saturn JP	$17.99
PANZER DRAGOON SAGA Game RARE Sega Saturn COMPLETE MINT	$149.01	POLICENAUTS ~ Limited Edition SEGA SATURN ~Import JP	$17.95
Panzer Dragoon Saga (Sega Saturn) RARE!!!!!	$137.53	FANTASY ZONE for Sega Saturn JP NTSC	$17.75
Huge Lot Sega Saturn 16 Games Virtua Fighter, X-Men EA	$118.37	Clockwork Knight 2 -Sega Saturn w/Box + Manual + Insert	$17.50
Sega Saturn Import Game: "RADIANT SILVERGUN" Rare!	$103.50	Die Hard Arcade (Sega Saturn) Complete MINT	$17.50
Lot of 23 Sega Saturn Games! $1000 value! Must See!	$99.99	GUNBIRD for Sega Saturn JP NTSC	$16.50
Shining Force III (Sega Saturn) Rare Complete US 3	$80.00	8 Sega Saturn CD video games-great condition	$16.50
LANGRISSER TRIBUTE for Sega Saturn JP REAR!	$79.99	Super Puzzle Fighter II Turbo (Sega Saturn) NR!	$16.00
Dragon Force Complete Rare(Sega Saturn)	$76.00	DRAGON FORCE - Strategy / RPG Sega Saturn Game	$16.00
SHINING FORCE III 3 Game Sega Saturn RARE + PRISTINE nr	$74.99	LAYER SECTION for Sega Saturn JP NTSC	$16.00
DRAGON FORCE + SEGA SATURN SYSTEM RARE!!	$74.00	jp import game WAKU WAKU SEVEN 7 Sega Saturn * PRISTINE	$16.00
THUNDER FORCE V Special Pack Sega Saturn JP	$73.50	Bug Too! (Sega Saturn) complete mint ship world	$15.99
Sega Saturn GUARDIAN HEROES Complete RARE - L@@K	$72.00	Sega Saturn Earthworm Jim 2 Like New Complete Rare	$15.50

Games ▸ Sony PlayStation

The average sales price in this subcategory is $29.98.

	HIGH		AVG
Sony Playstation 2 System with 22 games, MUST SEE!!!!!!	$1,525.00	NHL 2K6 Sony Playstation 2 Hockey Video Game BRAND NEW	$31.00
LOT OF 70 SONY PLAYSTATION 2	$360.00	Legend of Kay - Sony Playstation 2 - PS2 - NEW!	$30.00
GAMES PS2 COMPLETE		[2 of these sold in a multiple item ("Dutch") auction for $15.00 each]	
SONY PLAYSTATION PSP-WOW!-NO RESERVE!	$350.00	madden 06 (sony psp) playstation -preowned-	$30.00
70 video games Sony Playstation 2 PS2 WHOLESALE LOT	$326.56	VIRTUAL TENNIS FOR SONY PLAYSTATION PORTABLE PSP NEW !!	$30.00
Sony Playstation 2 - Game console- Value bundle	$300.00	[2 of these sold for $30.00 each]	
Sony (PSP) - Playstation Portable System	$224.52	Sony Playstation II Game Lot (6)	$29.99
SONY PLAYSTATION 2 WITH ONLINE	$200.00	Sony Playstation PSP Space Invaders Pocket shooter new	$29.99
PACKAGE AND 26 GAMES		Shin Megami Tensei: Nocturne Sony Playstation 2 NR	$29.55
Sony Playstation Portable - Game console - black	$193.75	VIRTUAL TENNIS FOR SONY PLAYSTATION PORTABLE PSP NEW !!	$29.00
New! Slim Sony Playstation 2 Value Pack Lot of 16 item	$189.99	[3 of these sold for $29.00 each]	
Great Deal ! Slim Sony Playstation 2 - Two controllers	$180.27	NBA 2K6 - Sony Playstation 2 - PS2 - NEW! Basketball	$28.00
New! Slim Sony Playstation 2 Value Pack Lot of 16 item	$179.99	Ridge Racer : PSP Sony Playstation Portable - LIKE NEW	$28.00
Sony Playstation 2 Slim & 3 games	$175.00	Devil May Cry 3 For Sony Playstation 2 PS2 BRAND NEW!	$28.00
Sony Playstation 2 with 25+ games plus more!	$167.50	Sony Playstation 2 PS2 EyeToy Eye Toy Antigrav New Seal	$28.00
Sony Playstation 2 console w/ 13 games 1 controller	$162.50	Need For Speed Underground 2 PS2 Sony Playstation 2	$28.00
Sony Playstation Portable - Game console - black	$162.25	Coded Arms (PlayStation Portable) Sony PSP MINT!!	$27.50
		LEGO STAR WARS PS2 Sony Playstation 2	$27.02

Games ▸ Sony PlayStation 2

The average sales price in this subcategory is $26.97.

HIGH TO AVG			
Slim Sony Playstation2 and "Old School Bundle" Games	$202.49	BROKEN SONY PLAYSTATION2	$29.01
Sony Playstation 2 ps2 playstation2 game system console	$119.50	SONY PLAYSTATION2 PS2 GAME MIDNIGHT CLUB 3 DUB EDITION	$29.00
Sony Playstation2 w/2 controllers, memory card, 4 games	$94.00	SONY PLAYSTATION2 PS2 GAME MIDNIGHT CLUB 3 DUB EDITION	$20.50
SONY PLAYSTATION 2 PLAYSTATION2 PS2 LOT OF 5 GAMES	$59.15	SONY PLAYSTATION2 PS2 VIDEO GAME GODZILLA SAVE EARTH *!	$17.00
Castlevania Curse of Darkness NEW Sony Playstation2 PS2	$47.99	SONY PLAYSTATION2 PS2 VIDEO GAME NHL HOCKYE 2K6 *NEW*	$12.50
Lot of 9 Sony Playstation2, PS2 games.	$46.02	SONY PLAYSTATION2 PS2 VIDEO GAME NHL HOCKYE 2K6 *NEW*	$12.50
Time Crisis 2 & 3 With Light Gun (Sony Playstation2)	$42.18	Sony PlayStation2 Video Games 3 Titles Cheap	$11.50
PS2 - Sony PlayStation2 - NBA Live 06 2006	$39.00	SONY PLAYSTATION2 GAMES.5 GAMES	$11.47
SOCOM 3 U.S. Navy Seals Sony Playstation2 PS2 Brand NEW	$36.03	SONY PLAYSTATION2 PS2 VIDEO GAME NHL HOCKYE 2K6 *NEW*	$9.95
ONE LOT OF SIX SONY PLAYSTATION2 VIDEO GAMES *LIKE NEW*	$36.00	SONY PLAYSTATION2 PS2 VIDEO GAME EYE TOY GROOVE *NEW*	$8.27
SOCOM 3 U.S. Navy Seals Sony Playstation2 PS2 Brand NEW	$36.00	SONY PLAYSTATION2 PS2 VIDEO GAME GODZILLA SAVE EARTH *!	$7.99
SOCOM 3 U.S. Navy Seals Sony Playstation2 PS2 Brand NEW	$33.00	SONY PLAYSTATION2 PS2 STREET FIGHTER COLLECTION *NEW*	$7.99
SONY PLAYSTATION 2 PLAYSTATION2 PS2 LOT OF 5 GAMES	$33.00	[2 of these sold for $7.99 each]	
SONY PLAYSTATION2 PS2 VIDEO GAME MADDEN 2006 *NEW*	$32.00	Baldur's Gate Dark Alliance Sony Playstation2 Gauntlet	$5.99
Six (6) Sony Playstation2 Games, GTA III, Madden.....	$31.00	Sony Playstation2 PS2 Madden NFL 2002 EASports COMPLETE	$4.95
Shadow Hearts PS2 Sony Playstation2 RPG	$29.99	Grand Theft Auto III PS2 Playstation2 Sony Playstation2	$4.00

Games ▸ Sony PSP

The average sales price in this subcategory is $43.37.

	HIGH		AVG
SONY PSP - Huge Lot - 1GB - 5 Games Madden 2 Movies NR!	$521.00	MADDEN NFL 2006 06 SONY PSP PLAYSTATION NEW $1 SHIP	$46.00
Sony PSP + 24 Movies, 4 Games & tons of accessories	$425.00	GRAND THEFT AUTO LIBERTY CITY SONY PSP NEW $1 SHIP	$46.00
VER 1.50 SONY PSP + NYKO THEATER+4	$410.00	SSX On Tour (PlayStation Portable) SONY PSP : FREE S&H	$45.00
GAMES+4 MOVIES+MORE!		Sony PSP MOBILE SUIT GUNDAM Battle Tactics umd game new	$44.99
Sony PSP Value Pack - Game console + Games... Like NEW	$400.00	FIFA Soccer 06 Sony PSP 2006 NEW SEALED!	$44.15
Sony PSP SPORTS BUNDLE Value Pk 2 Games BRAND NEW	$388.00	Sony PSP Games-UNDERGROUND 2, MLB baseball, boogeyman	$44.00
Sony PSP Value Pack - 1gig memorystick - 2games	$375.00	Death Jr. (Sony PSP) Limited Edition Rare! + 2 Bonuses!	$43.65
Sony PSP With 3 Games, 3 Movies, 1GB Card +More! Mint!	$360.00	Sony Playstation PSP Bleach Heat the Soul 2 Import UMD	$42.99
SONY PLAYSTATION PSP-WOW!-NO RESERVE!	$350.00	Sony PSP MOBILE SUIT GUNDAM Gihren's Ambition Japan new	$42.99
Sony PSP Complete With Game & Movie! Perfect condition!	$350.00	MADDEN NFL 2006 06 SONY PSP PLAYSTATION NEW $1 SHIP	$42.00
New Sony PSP Value Pk with 5 games No Reserve	$340.00	Tiger Woods PGA Tour 2006 SONY PSP New $1 SHIP	$42.00
Sony PSP Value Pack - Game console	$325.00	SONY PSP LOT OF 2 GAMES DYNASTY WARRIORS TWISTED METAL	$41.01
sony psp with 6 games & 2 movies !!!!!	$325.00	Grand Theft Auto: Liberty City Stories Sony PSP ~NEW~	$41.00
SONY PSP VALUE PACK VIDEO GAME SYSTEM	$309.99	[2 of these sold for $41.00 each]	
Sony PSP + 2 Games+Spiderman 2 movie+ accesories	$306.00	NBA LIVE 2006 06 FOR SONY PLAYSTATION PORTABLE PSP NEW	$41.00
Sony PSP Value Pack - 3 Games, 3 Movies, and more!!!!!!	$305.00	SSX On Tour PlayStation Portable Sony PSP -New & Sealed	$40.99

Internet Games ▸ Anarchy Online

The average sales price in this subcategory is $57.02.

	HIGH		AVG
220 Fixer 220 Keeper +more RK1 Anarchy Online Account	$800.00	Selling 200mils CREDITS on Anarchy Online RK1or RK2	$59.94
Anarchy Online Account RK1 220 Fixer 210 Shade	$800.00	[6 of these sold for $59.94 each]	
Anarchy Online - 220 Omni Atrox Soldier, 215+ Doc, more	$750.00	Anarchy Online AO / Atlantean RK1 - 200M Credits	$54.95
Anarchy Online RK2 212Keeper, 208Soldier,201Enforcer	$500.00	Anarchy Online AO RK1 200M CREDITS	$50.88
Anarchy Online accounts: 216 MA, 211 fix, 800mill creds	$350.00	Anarchy Online Lv 58 Doctor, with 44 Million credits	$49.99
Anarchy Online RK2 Account - 209 doc - 207 enf + More	$305.00	AO Anarchy Online 250.000.000 Credits INSTANT DELIVERY	$49.95
Anarchy Online 215+ AI lvl 10+ Soldier on RK-1	$300.00	Anarchy Online AO / Atlantean RK1 - 200M Credits	$49.95
214 shade 167 doc 79 fixer WTS rk1	$300.00	[6 of these sold for $49.95 each]	
Anarchy Online Account - RK1 - 207 MP and more	$300.00	AO Anarchy Online 250.000.000 Credits INSTANT DELIVERY	$49.95
Anarchy online 220 Sold/191 Trader No Reserve	$300.00	[2 of these sold for $49.95 each]	

Anarchy online 212adv/209enfo !!NO RESERVE!!!	$300.00	Selling 100mils CREDITS on Anarchy Online RK1 DELIVERY	$45.95
WTS 220 Neophyte Adv. RK2	$300.00	[2 of these sold for $45.95 each]	
214 Fixer 205 Engi 206 Shade credits, leets, More	$255.00	Anarchy Online AO RK1 Atlantean 150 Million Credits	$44.95
Anarchy Online Account 213 Nano Tech and 190 Engi	$250.00	[2 of these sold for $44.95 each]	
Anarchy online 215soldier	$200.00	Anarchy Online AO Rimor RK2 : 200 MILLION CREDITS Credits	$44.00
		[2 of these sold for $44.00 each]	
		Anarchy Online AO Rimor RK2 : 200 MILLION CREDITS	$42.00
		Anarchy Online RK2 lvl 160 Martial Artist	$40.00
		Anarchy Online AO Rimor RK2 : 200 MILLION CREDITS	$39.00
		[4 of these sold for $39.00 each]	
		Anarchy Online AO Rimor RK2 : 200 MILLION CREDITS	$38.00
		[2 of these sold for $38.00 each]	
		Selling 100mils Credits on Anarchy Online RK2	$37.95

Internet Games ▶ DAOC

The average sales price in this subcategory is $90.79.

	HIGH		AVG
Daoc Mordred rr11 inf 6L5 necro Lamorak 50 sham 50 hunt	$810.00	DAOC - 100 PLAT LANCELOT ISEULT PELLINOR KAY HIBERNIA	$99.99
DAOC RR11 RUNEMASTER ML8 RR9	$500.00	[11 of these sold for $99.99 each]	
HEALER ML10 PALOMIDES		Daoc Nimue, Guinevere, Percival, 3 lvl 50, Infiltrator	$99.00
** Full Reaver Bomb ** DAoC Account Alb Merlin 1mil RPs	$499.99	DAOC MLF Devon Cluster, 50 Necro, 50 Theurgist, LGMll	$99.00
DAOC Iseult Lancelot Pellinor Kay RR11L2 Berserker ML10	$460.00	Dark Age of camelot DAOC Lancelot Paladin account	$99.00
WTT/WTS 50 Infil RR 8L5, ML10, GM Alch + more	$450.00	DAOC 2 Level 50's Mid/Bedevere SM and Shammy(ML10)	$90.00
DAOC Account 10L1 Hero on the MLF / Morgan server	$425.00	Daoc Merlin Hibernia 50 Chanter 50 Druid	$90.00
DAOC 50 Shadowblade RR10l7 ML10	$425.00	Dark Age of camelot DAOC Lancelot Pole Armsman account	$90.00
Merlin Cluster With SW!		DAOC - 15 PLAT GARETH HIBERNIA GOLD $89!	$89.99
DAoC R11L2 ML10 Berserker Kay Lancelot Iseult Pellinor	$410.00	[8 of these sold for $89.99 each]	
daoc caerlon/iseult 9l2 ml10 zerker	$400.00	DAOC - 100 PLAT MERLIN BORS GAWAINE PALOMIDES ALBION	$89.99
8 50's on Morderd DAOC Vamp Friar Necro Cleric Therg	$400.00	DAOC Mordred 50 Plat Buy it now $85	$85.00
DAOC Pellinor RR11L2 ML10 Banelord LGM Armor Berserker	$400.00	L50 NS Merlin! Palomides / Bors / Gawaine / Killibury!	$85.00
DAOC Account - 7 Level 50's - DR Enabled - Secret Word	$380.00	DAOC Merlin/Palo/Bors/Gawain 50 Mana Enchanter!	$85.00
DAOC Merc , Sorc , Inf , ISEULT/GUINEVERE/PERCIVAL	$375.00	DaoC - Hibernia Lamorak: LGM Armorcraft + Level 48 Vamp	$81.00
DAOC account rr9's!!! 6 level 50's fully ToA'ed!!	$361.00	DAOC Account Level 50 nightshade ALL EXPANSIONS/bedever	$81.00
DAOC R11 Cleric Palo R9 Warrior Gawaine R6 Bard Lamorak	$350.00	DAOC Morded/Bedevere/Galahad/Merlin 4 50s + 48 w/SW	$80.00

Internet Games ▶ Diablo, Diablo 2

The average sales price in this subcategory is $13.32.

	HIGH		AVG
Diablo 2 UsEast NON LADDER 276 good items	$305.00	Diablo 2 USEAST S3 Ladder mule #LJ Occy,Tal Amy,Raven20	$13.99
DIABLO 2 UsEast 23 Godly Accounts MASS ITEMS AND CHARS!	$242.50	[4 of these sold for $13.99 each]	
Diablo 2 LOD S3 LADDER Account! GODLY Smiter/Hammerdin	$202.50	Diablo 2 USeast nl 3/10/12 Paladin Hellfire Torch grief	$13.50
DIABLO 2 LOD NON-LADDER USEAST LVL 97	$200.50	Us East Diablo 2 S3 Ladder GODLY UNID ANNI CHARM	$13.50
HAMMERDIN ACCOUNT		Diablo 2 NL Us East 3X Key sets	$13.50
DIABLO II LOD S3 LADDER GODLY LVL	$162.50	diablo 2 useast NL Fortitude, Sur Rune, Goldy Uniqs	$13.50
98 SORC ACC. USEAST		Diablo 2 NL Us East 3X Key sets	$13.50
DIABLO 2 II LOD USEAST 2 GODLY ACCOUNTS	$105.09	Diablo 2 Useast Ladder s3 NE1 rune ber jah ohm Lo zod +	$13.49
Diablo 2 USEast NL PERFECT 20/20 Paladin HellFire Torch	$100.00	Diablo 2 USeast Ladder Season 3 HOZ Herald of Zakarum	$12.99
Diablo 2 USEast Hardcore Ladder S3 FULL TRANG NECRO ACC	$89.95	Diablo2 USeast S3 ladder mule #M20 DC Ss Reaper	$12.99
Diablo 2 USEast Hardcore Ladder Season 3 Mule Account	$86.01	Diablo2 USeast S3 ladder mule #J09 Sandstorm Shaftstop	$12.99
Diablo 2 useast non-ladder GODLY 2 accounts	$86.00	Diablo 2 USEast LADDER S3 Unid Annihilus ANNI Charm	$12.99
Diablo 2 USEAST S3 Ladder Acct & Mules	$82.00	[2 of these sold for $12.99 each]	
Diablo 2 USEast Non Ladder, Godly Accounts+Items	$81.00	Diablo 2 USEast Hardcore Ladder S3 IST RUNE x1	$12.59
Diablo 2 USEast Ladder S3 Ethereal 272% Death Cleaver	$79.99	Diablo 2 useast ladder season 3 GODLY BARBARIAN COMBO	$12.50
Useast non ladder ACCOUNT soj rune anni hoto cta torch	$75.00	diablo 2 useast perf exp anni 10 exp s3 ladder	$12.50
D2 USWEST Hardcore Ladder Amazon Hellfire Torch	$69.99	DIablo 2 USEast Non Ladder GODLY Heaven's Light	$12.50

Internet Games ▶ Eve Online

The average sales price in this subcategory is $85.56.

	HIGH		AVG
EVE CHARACTER 32MIL SKILL POINTS AND 622MIL ISK	$3,050.00	Thsale EVE online 400 M ISK 24/7 Live Help	$116.99
26 Mil SKILL POINT Character, 250+ items for Eve Online	$1,525.00	ISK 400 MILLION EVE ONLINE Tranquility Fast and Safe	$109.99
Eve Online Character 27+ Mil sp's & NAVY RAVEN!!!	$1,376.23	Thsale EVE online 400 M ISK 24/7 Live Help	$108.99
Eve Online Char 21+ SP w/ TECH 2 BPO !!!!!!	$1,025.00	Eve Online Full Set Of Standard Implants (+4 modifier)	$97.00
EVE Online 5.0 BILLION ISK ***UBER BUCKS***	$955.00	Eve Online 500 Million + 50 Mill Free - NO RESERVE	$91.00
EVE Online 5.0 BILLION ISK ***UBER BUCKS***	$925.00	EVE Online 300 Million ISK (300,000,000) FAST	$86.99
EVE ONLINE ACCOUNTS CHARACTERS	$799.00	[2 of these sold for $86.99 each]	
30msp agent runner		Thsale EVE online 300 M ISK 24/7 Live Help	$81.99
EVE online 28.5mil SP char; 175mil ISK; many ships	$750.00	EVE ONLINE - FULL SET OF 5 +3 IMPLANTS + FREE IMPLANT	$76.00
THE Ultimate Character-mining, hunting, manufacturing	$750.00	Eve Online Account - MINER CHARACTER	$76.00
Eve Online Account 20.1 Mil SP Character Fighter	$685.00	with MINING BARGE	
EVE Character with 33million skillpoints (Edited)	$660.00	Eve Online character	$75.00
Eve Online Character 16.5mil SP	$644.00	7m SP Eve Character	$75.00
EVE Online 3.0 BILLION ISK ***MEGA BUCKS***	$595.00	EVE ONLINE - FULL SET OF 5 +3 IMPLANTS + FREE IMPLANT	$75.00
[2 of these sold for $595.00 each]		[2 of these sold for $75.00 each]	
EVE ONLINE 3year account 23mil+	$550.00	Eve Online 250 Million Isk	$63.00
SP 250mil+isk 1000+items			

Internet Games ▸ Sims Online

The average sales price in this subcategory is $39.77.

	HIGH		AVG
TSO Sims Online Huge Lot of Rares Pink Turk Robo Mystic	$400.00	TSO The Sims Online: Nice Saint Bernard & Pet Feeder	$40.00
The Sims Online RARE Founder Account with $4.5 mil	$365.00	The Sims Online TSO Rare St Bernard Calvin's Creek CC	$40.00
TSO SIMS ONLINE RARE 2 YEAR ACCT MYSTIC TREE ANY CITY	$260.00	The Sims Online TSO Rare St Bernard Alphaville AV	$40.00
[4 of these sold in a multiple item ("Dutch") auction for $60.00 each]		*RARE* NICE ROBODOG IN BLAZING FALLS BF	$40.00
TSO The Sims Online 50 Million Simoleans Alphaville AV	$242.50	[2 of these sold for $40.00]	
RARE Simmy SET - AV	$202.51	TSO Ripe Mystic Tree in Alphaville AV	$39.99
TSO non Founder Account Rare Sims Online 3 Mystic Trees	$200.00	TSO The Sims Online ESTABLISHED Account + 25 Days Time!	$39.56
TSO 20 million simoleans in any city xcept TC	$185.99	FIVE 5-MILLION SIMOLEANS TSO SIMS ONLINE ALPHAVILLE AV!	$39.00
TSO Sims Online - Account - Lot of Rare Items! TC&BF&JP	$183.01	4 MILL SIMOLEANS TSO The Sims Online Blazing Falls BF	$39.00
RARE COMPLETE SET OF 3 SIMMY STATUES!!	$175.00	4 MILL SIMOLEANS TSO The Sims Online Blazing Falls BF	$37.01
TSO The Sims Online 20 Million Simoleans Alphaville AV	$162.50	4 MILLION SIMOLEANS TSO The Sims Online, Jolly Pines JP	$37.00
FOUNDERS ACCOUNT ~OLD~ Founder sims online	$162.50	Established The Sims Online (TSO) Account - 427+ days	$37.00
TSO Rare non Founder Account 3 Mystic Trees Sims Online	$162.50	TSO Sims Online RARE NICE Robot Dog In Test Center TC	$37.00
THE SIMS ONLINE FOUNDER ACCOUNT WITH RARES	$155.00	TSO 5 million simoleans in any city xcept TC	$37.00
The Sims Online Rares! Blazing Falls Robo +++	$152.50	4 MILLION SIMOLEANS TSO The Sims Online, Alphaville, AV	$36.75
TSO The Sims Online - 2 ULTRA RARE GNOMES - *Any City*	$142.50	TC Rare *Robot Cat* in Test Center TSO Sims Online	$36.01

Internet Games ▸ Ultima Online

The average sales price in this subcategory is $38.41.

	HIGH		AVG
Ultima Online UO EUROPA Account *Best EVER*	$1,000.00	CHESAPEAKE Tokuno Artifacts FULL SET Ultima Online UO	$44.00
Ultima Online Accounts, 76 months and 72 months	$800.00	UO LAKE SUPERIOR 10 MILLION GOLD	$42.01
Ultima online 60 month account 40 arties! tons of 120s	$550.00	UO LAKE SUPERIOR 10 MILLION GOLD	$41.01
Ultima Online CASTLE in Fel UO Sonoma	$510.00	Napa Valley HeartWood Runic Kit	$41.00
Ultima Online UO 10 X Legendary Skills Account House ++	$488.00	UO Ultima Online Baja Tram 18x18 18 x 18 House RARE !	$40.00
Selling awesome 60 month UO lake superior account	$355.00	Ultima Online UO Atlantic Blade of Insanity Artifact	$39.99
Ultima Online Great Lakes PvP Account Legendary UO	$299.00	Ring Of The Elements ANY SHARD UO Ultima Online	$39.99
Ultima Online UO Atlantic Umbra Roadside Vendor House	$209.00	LAKE SUPERIOR Artifact Scrapper's Compendium Magery UO	$35.00
Inquisitors Resolution Inquisitors's Ulitima Online Uo	$202.50	Pendant Of The Magi ANY SHARD UO Ultima Online	$34.99
Crimson Cincture ANY SHARD UO Ultima Online	$199.99	CATSKILLS Pendant of the Magi Artifact UO Ultima Online	$34.00
[2 of these sold for $199.99 each]		UO ULTIMA ONLINE SOULSTONE !	$33.00
52 Months Vet UO Account /6 Chars/ Soulstone/ Big Tower	$199.00	NEW CODE ANY SHARD !	
UO Ultima Online Lake Superior 67+m Vet Account 120s	$165.97	LEO UO ULTIMA ONLINE EUROPA 3 MILLION GOLD	$32.99
UO Ultima Online Atlantic 51 Month WORKED Account!	$162.50	Ultima Online Chesapeake 5 mil gold Start Bid $32.00	$32.00
ULTIMA ONLINE PACIFIC, KEEP & 3000 T BODS	$153.00	Ultima Online UO Atlantic Bracelet of Health Artifact	$31.00
Ultima Online UO Ornament of the Magician, any shard!	$152.50	Ultima Online Lake Austin 42-month Veteran Account	$31.00

Internet Games ▸ Other

The average sales price in this subcategory is $50.81.

	HIGH		AVG
Everquest 2 (II) Act. 50 Guard 50 armore/ 50 temp Nek	$400.00	Guild Wars GW 1000000 Gold 1000k fast Delivery 7/24	$68.48
City of Heroes 8Lev 50s Uber pve pvp power level acct.	$280.00	[2 of these sold for $68.48 each]	
Everquest 2 (II) Account 50 Mystic (50 sage) Nek	$275.00	Guild Wars GW 1000000 Gold 1000k fast Delivery 7/24	$68.39
City of heroes 5 Lev 50s + Uber pve pvp powr lvl acct.	$227.50	TOSHIBA DVD VCR HOME THEATER SYSTEM VT55HT	$65.51
WoW Blackrock Level 60 Undead Mage	$202.50	lineage2. Teon 1M Adena (buy it now 20M) instant	$62.95
Blizzcon - World Of Warcraft Limited Edition Laser Cel	$152.50	Gunbound Latino acc Almost violet Wand great avatars	$60.00
Everquest Bard Account - 67 bard + 5 lvl 40-60 alts	$150.00	US Knight Online Ares 5 Gold Bars	$46.00
Wow Lvl 60 warlock	$150.00	MU Maya lvl 131 DK account with items MUONLINE	$39.99
Everquest Account w/ 70 Cleric, 57 War, etc. Veeshan	$150.00	lineage 2 Gustin 1M Adena (buy it now 20M) lineage2	$38.88
lineage2. Teon 1M Adena (buy it now 40M) instant	$124.95	WOW World Of Warcraft 500 Gold Any US Server	$38.00
Everquest account w/ 70 Druid, 46 SK, etc. on Veeshan	$122.50	WOW World Of Warcraft 500 Gold Any US Server	$35.99
Lineage 2 20m adena and 20m+	$99.99	EQ-1 56 gnome mage. Pottery-192	$35.00
worth of items Kain Server		WOW World Of Warcraft 500 Gold Any US Server	$34.99
Star Wars Galaxies Collectors Edition w/FREE bonus!	$86.00	[3 of these sold for $34.99 each]	
WOW World Of Warcraft 1000 Gold Any US Server	$75.01	World of Warcraft PC New Sealed Unopened & Bonus	$34.00
BLIZZCON PACKAGE ALL AUTHENTIC	$74.99	Eve Online - ANY Level 2 Battleship + FREE Bonus	$33.95
FROM 1ST BLIZZCON EVENT!		WOW World Of Warcraft 300 Gold Any US Server	$30.00

Systems ▸ 3DO

The average sales price in this subcategory is $63.60.

	HIGH		AVG
3do system, 4 controllers, plus 50 games	$291.00	Panasonic 3DO R.E.A.L FZ-1 System, MINT IN BOX +GAMES	$76.00
Huge Lot of Nintendo, Super NES, PS1, 3DO, Sega Nomad	$280.00	Panasonic REAL 3DO FZ-1 with Many EXTRAS	$75.00
NIB Panasonic REAL 3DO Interactive MUTIPLAYER FZ-1	$222.50	Panasonic FZ-10 3DO REAL with 17 games Street Fighter 2	$73.03
3DO Panasonic Interactive FZ-1 video game system	$205.00	3DO Console + 11 Games (Preowned) (3DO/3DO)	$73.01
GOLDSTAR 3DO 3D0 System Complete w/ 69 Games MINT	$185.00	Panasonic 3DO w/ 4 wireless controllers and 28 games!!	$66.50
PANASONIC 3DO 3D0 FZ-1 System Complete w/ 69 Games MINT	$175.00	PANASONIC 3DO SYSTEM CONSOLE TESTED	$64.00
PANASONIC 3DO 3D0 FZ-10 System Complete & 50 Games MINT	$165.00	WORKS NOT GOLDSTAR	
[2 of these sold for $165.00 each]		PANASONIC REAL 3DO INTERACTIVE MULTIPLAYER GAME CONSOLE	$63.00
PANASONIC 3DO 3D0 FZ-10 System Complete & 34 Games MINT	$155.00	3DO Game System, 2 Control Pads, 8 Games	$61.00
Panasonic 3DO SYSTEM W/ 11 games & Light Gun LOW SHIP!	$154.99	Panasonic 3DO Video Game System	$61.00
PANASONIC 3DO 3D0 FZ-1 System Complete	$150.00	Panasonic 3DO game system w/ 9 Games NR !!!	$58.01
w/ 33 Games MINT		Panasonic REAL 3DO Great Condition w/8 Games 1 Cntrl	$57.00

	HIGH		AVG
3DO M2 Development System RARE	$150.00	PANASONIC 3DO GAME SYSTEM W/10 GAMES	$56.00
Panasonic R.E.A.L 3DO Console FZ-1 w/BOX lot 18 Games	$147.99	Panasonic REAL 3DO Game system vintage Extras like new	$55.00
Panasonic REAL 3DO Interactive Multiplayer With Games	$132.50	Panasonic 3DO game system	$52.99
3DO Panasonic Multiplayer System + 22 Games + Bonus !!!	$127.50	Panasonic FZ-10 3DO REAL Multiplayer & 10 Games	$52.00

Systems ▸ Atari

The average sales price in this subcategory is $41.71.

	HIGH		AVG
Huge Nintendo Atari Sega SNES NES systems consoles lot	$730.00	(2) ATARI 2600 SYSTEMS W/20 GAMES	$42.00
Huge Atari 2600 System & Game Lot - Over 800 Titles NR	$445.00	atari 2600/2 controllers/37 games complete system	$42.00
1980 ATARI 2600-A system box + Star Wars complete lot	$320.00	Atari 2600 System w/ 13 Games, 2 Joysticks,Paddles...	$42.00
Atari 2600 and synthcart like LSDJ,nanoloop,or midines	$255.00	ATARI ULTRA PONG In Original Box 1977 2600	$42.00
New in Box with 23 New Games Atari Jaguar	$250.00	ATARI 2600 System Complete w 40 Games Tested & Clean !	$42.00
Atari 2600 Console System with 133 Games, 4 Controllers	$223.26	ATARI FLASHBACK 2 SYSTEM -40 games- Retro / Rare / NEW	$41.99
Atari Jaguar and Jaguar CD Complete w/M Track &13 Games	$217.50	Atari 2600 system + 15 Games Excellent Condition Boxes	$41.69
VADER Black Atari 2600 w/ 100 Games + Controls & Extras	$212.50	ATARI SYSTEM AND 20 ATARI GAMES	$41.50
Atari JAGUAR & CD &21 GAMES not nintendo sega sony xbox	$200.00	ATARI 2600 SYSTEM - complete plus 25 games	$41.12
9 SYSTEMS 101 GAMES,S&NES&64,PS1,GENESIS,G GEAR,ATARI	$199.99	Working Atari 2600 with 8 Great Games!!	$41.11
HUGE ATARI COLLECTION-2600,7800 *OVER 240 CARTRIDGES **	$193.50	Atari 7800 ProSystem! With games and extras!	$41.04
Atari JAGUAR w/CD 2 controllers 20 GAMES Team Tap	$183.00	Atari 2600 18 Games,2 Joysticks,Touch Pad,Power Plug,	$41.01
-Original- ATARI 2600 *COMPLETE* with 30 GAMES	$178.49	Atari 7800 Pro System + 14 games	$41.01
Original Atari 2600 37 Games Included Game Console Also	$175.00	1987 ATARI 7800 VIDEO GAME SYSTEM IN BOX WITH 20 GAMES	$41.01
nintendo ,nes ,snes , sega ,atari game system plus game	$152.50	Atari 7800 game system	$41.00

Systems ▸ Colecovision

The average sales price in this subcategory is $55.48.

	HIGH		AVG
Colecovision With 135 Games and Lots More	$325.00	COLECOVISION VIDEO GAME SYSTEM	$61.01
COMPLETE Colecovision Video Game System With Box Games	$177.50	COMPLETE W/ GAMES EXTRAS	$61.00
ColecoVision Console Collection	$150.00	Colecovision System with 6 Games + Instruction Tested	$61.00
EBAY'S BEST COLECOVISION SYSTEM AND GAMES COLECO VISION	$149.00	ColecoVision System with 10 games Excellent Condition	$59.99
[2 of these sold for $149.00 each]		ColecoVision System w/23 Games, Expansion Module #1 & 2	$59.88
ColecoVision w/ 22 Games & Accs. /100% Tested & Working	$132.55	Colecovision Coleco Vision w/10 Games Q-Berts Qubes	$58.75
COLECOVISION System + Original Box & 10 Games + Extras	$129.95	ColecoVision System Lot w/ 5 Games RARE Works Great!!!	$56.00
ColecoVision w/ 22 Games & Accs. /100% Tested & Working	$127.50	COLECO VISION GAME SYSTEM in box COLECOVISION	$56.00
COLECOVISION coleco vision BOXED complete + 10 GAMES	$107.50	VINTAGE COLECOVISION SYSTEM WITH 7 GAMES	$51.00
HUGE COLECO VISION COLECOVISION	$100.99	COLECOVISION W/EXP. MOD 1 W/23 CARTS	$51.00
LOT 2 CONSOLES + GAMES		Coleco Colecovision System Complete in Box! Works!	$50.00
COLECOVISION w/ATARI 2600 adaptor 5 joysticks 20 games	$100.00	Colecovision System with 5 Games + Instruction Tested	$48.53
Complete Tested Colecovision System + 10 Games + Bonus	$99.99	Like New COLECOVISION !!!IL@@K!!!!!	$48.53
Colecovision unit and more!	$91.00	ColecoVision System,Case,11 rare games,stearing wheel	$46.00
Vintage Colecovision Lot w/Roller controllers,Box &More	$89.84	COLECOVISION GAME SYSTEM 24 GAMES Atari Period	$46.00
VINTAGE COLECOVISION VIDEO GAME SYSTEM + 6 GAMES	$82.50	Vintage Colecovision System Complete W/ 6 Games! Works!	$43.87

Systems ▸ Commodore

The average sales price in this subcategory is $26.84.

	HIGH		AVG
COMMODORE SX-64 system,.tested good..cables included.	$131.50	COMMODORE 64/1541/c2n system,.software, cables. tested	$29.99
COMMODORE 128/1571 system w/cables.. clean & tested!!	$102.50	Commodore 64 Computer & Accessories (great condition)	$26.00
COMMODORE 128/1571 system w/cables.. clean & tested!!	$58.00	Commodore 64 30-Games-in-One Joystick	$26.00
COMMODORE 64/1541 system,.tested good..cables included.	$36.00	COMMODORE 64/1541 system,.tested good..cables included.	$24.99
COMMODORE 1541 disk drive cables/manual included. box	$32.59	Commodore 64 30-in-1 Classic Plug & Play Video Game	$24.50
COMMODORE vic 20/c2n game system w/games, joystick+	$31.33	COMMODORE vic20/c2n/joystick boxed near mint. collector	$24.00
Commodore 64 & Games *works great* Fun!	$31.00	COMMODORE 1541 1571 drive alignment program w/manual	$20.50

Systems ▸ Intellivision

The average sales price in this subcategory is $47.53.

	HIGH		AVG
EBAY'S BEST INTELLIVISION SYSTEM #2609 + VOICE+30 GAMES	$249.00	INTELLIVISION II SYSTEM W/ 1 GAME BURGERTIME 2 OVERLAYS	$50.00
RARE SYLVANIA INTELLIVISION SYS+VOICE+30 BOXED GAMES	$245.00	Intellivision Console System with 15 Games	$50.00
MIB ORIG MATTEL INTELLIVISION SYSTEM+RARE/HTF GAMES	$245.00	Intellivision II System (1982), INCREDIBLE !!	$50.00
Intellivision game system. New in unopened box.	$205.02	Mattel Intellivision System + 25 games	$50.00
LIKE NEW ORIG MATTEL INTELLIVISION SYS+37 BOXED GAMES	$205.00	EBAY'S BEST INTELLIVISION SYSTEM CHANGER NR	$49.99
Intellivision Games System + 16 Games in Boxes Like New	$162.50	INTELLIVISION II Game System 2 Mattel, 30 Premium Games	$49.95
Vintage INTELLIVISION Console System w. 41 Games RARE!!	$120.00	Intellivision Complete System 4 Games Box Exc Condition	$47.50
Mattel Intellivision with 35 Boxed Games!	$107.50	Intellivision vintage gaming system	$47.01
INTELLIVISION IN BOX, INCL 27 GAMES PLUS EXTRAS	$100.00	Working Intellivision console w/16 games in orig Boxes	$46.00
Intellivision 2 with 40 games, lots of extras	$99.00	INTELLIVISION 1981 SYSTEM Plus 15 Games *NICE*	$46.00
INTELLIVISION COMPLETE SYSTEM	$91.02	Original Intellivision Game System + games books inlays	$46.00
WITH 17 GAMES IN BOX!!!!!		SEARS INTELLIVISION * SYSTEM IN BOX	$46.00
Intellivision system + 32 games, many rare + voice unit	$90.00	TESTED AND WORKING	
EBAY'S BEST INTELLIVISION II SYSTEM PLUS 15 GAMES	$89.00	Mattel Intellivision System + 11 games NOT ATARI 2600	$46.00
[2 of these sold for $89.00 each]		intellivision game system super pro system original box	$43.00
Mattel Intellivision Game System Complete Mint Box 2609	$86.01	Intellivision II 2 System With 5 Classic games Rare!	$41.00

Systems ▶ Microsoft Xbox 360

The median sales price in this subcategory is $686.11.

	HIGH		AVG
Microsoft Xbox 360 - Game console	$1,000,010.00	Xbox 360 Premium Overnight Shipping No Reserve	$686.66
Microsoft Xbox 360 Game Console Bundle TOYS FOR TOTS	$500,000.00	In Hand Ready to Ship Same Day	
POWERSELLER*2000+*90% FOR GREAT CHARITY		XBOX 360 PREMIUM BUNDLE SYSTEM WITH CHOICE OF GAME!	$686.59
Microsoft Xbox 360 - Game console	$150,000.00	NIB POWER SELLER, 100% FEEDBACK! BID WITH CONFIDENCE!	
LOT OF 50 BRAND NEW XBOX 360 PREMIUM BUNDLE PRE-ORDER	$20,000.00	XBOX 360 premium package in hand not preorder	$686.52
Microsoft Xbox 360 - Game console 50 PK Premium Package	$18,000.00	Microsoft Xbox 360 Premium System Preorder Ships Nov 22	$686.50
The hottest reseller lot xbox premium system 50 PK		Xbox 360 Premium Pack- 1 Game 2 W Cont Free SHIP NR!	$686.50
EW Microsoft Xbox 360-Game system console+GAME Core	$18,000.00	Presale- You will get on or before Dec. 16th	
25,000+ FEEDBACKS+ FAST SHIPPING W/ ONLINE TRACKING #		**** XBOX 360 Premium Bundle **** WILL SHIP NEXT DAY	$686.32
Microsoft Xbox 360 Core Edition READY TO SHIP LOOOK !!!	$15,099.00	Not Preorder - I have it in hand to ship today	
WILL SHIP AS SOON AS PAYMENT IS MADE DONT MISS THIS ONE		Microsoft Xbox 360 - Game console Premium System Bundle	$686.11
50 MICROSOFT XBOX 360 PREMIUM IN STOCK! PSP NANO ALSO!	$13,750.00	******MICROSOFT XBOX 360 PREMIUM	$686.11
Microsoft Xbox 360 - Game console	$12,900.00	EDITION - IN HAND*****	
cant find in stores. Great X-mas gift		XBOX 360 Premium - New with Halo 2 and lots of extras	$686.11
Microsoft Xbox 360 - Game console Wholesale 50 UNITs	$12,150.00	wireless controller, remote, headset, cables, and game	
Microsoft Xbox 360 - Game console NIB Ready to Ship	$12,100.00	Microsoft Xbox 360 Premium. No Reserve! Buy It Now!	$686.11
LOT OF 25 BRAND NEW XBOX 360 PREMIUM BUNDLE PRE-ORDER	$11,650.00	XBOX 360 Premium Edition Bundle Everything You Need!!!	$686.01
STOCK UP FOR HOLIDAY SALES		Get Yours Before The Christmas Rush First Week of Dec.	
Xbox 360 Ultimate Premium FREE OVERNIGHT SHIPPING 11/22	$10,600.00	Microsoft Xbox 360 - Game console Premium Package NO RESERVE	$686.00
Get PERFECT DARK FREE if you 'Buy It Now'!!!		xbox 360***WILL SHIP ON WEEK OF LAUNCH***	$686.00
Microsoft Xbox 360 System (premium bundle) In Hand!!	$10,100.00	Microsoft Xbox 360 Premium Console w/ BONUS Controller	$686.00
LOT OF 25 BRAND NEW XBOX 360 PREMIUM BUNDLE PRE-ORDER	$10,000.00	Guaranteed to ship 11/22 or else it ships free! NR	
STOCK UP FOR HOLIDAY SALES		XBOX 360 W/20 GIG HARD DRIVE, UNOPENED!!! SHIPS 11/22	$686.00

Systems ▶ Microsoft Xbox

The average sales price in this subcategory is $139.46.

	HIGH		AVG
Microsoft Xbox 360 Console Autographed by Bill Gates	$3,051.00	Microsoft Xbox with 4 Games	$140.00
WOW! Microsoft Xbox 360 Kiosk with 23-Inch LCD HDTV	$1,851.64	Microsoft Xbox racing package	$140.00
Microsoft XBOX 360 Game Console	$1,045.00	Microsoft XBOX with GAMES and INCREDIBLE EXTRAS - NR!	$140.00
Microsoft XBOX 360 Game Console	$870.00	MICROSOFT XBOX 8 GAMES 2 CONTRLS	$140.00
Microsoft Xbox 360 - Game console in Hand Ready to Ship	$850.00	HD ADAP ACTION REPLAY	
[2 of these sold for $850.00 each]		Microsoft Xbox with game, 2 controllers, DvD Playback	$139.99
Microsoft Xbox 360 - Pre-Order In-Hand on the 22nd	$640.00	MIcrosoft Limited Edition Green Xbox Halo Version	$139.52
Microsoft Xbox 360 - Game console	$635.00	Microsoft Xbox HALO 2 Collector's Edition NFL 2K5 +MORE	$139.49
Microsoft Xbox 360 Console Premium Package Pre-Sale	$635.00	Microsoft Xbox - Game console - black	$138.00
Microsoft Xbox 360 Game Console - Pre-Orders Available!	$599.00	Microsoft Xbox with Halo 2, nearly NEW	$137.50
[2 of these sold for $599.00 each]		Microsoft Xbox System w/9 games, 2 controls NO RESERVE	$137.50
Microsoft Xbox 360 Game Console Receipt Available!	$599.00	Microsoft Xbox system w/ box and 6 games	$137.50
[3 of these sold for $599.00 each]		Microsoft Xbox Game console+2controllers	$137.50
Microsoft Xbox 360 - Game console Premium Package	$595.00	+8Games+ Wheel	
Microsoft Xbox 360 - Game console PREMIUM system	$587.65	Microsoft Xbox - WITH XBOX LIVE 3 MON /	$137.50
Microsoft Xbox 360 - Game console PREMIUM System	$585.00	DVD ADAPTER/REM	
MICROSOFT XBOX 360 EXCLUSIVE PREMIUM + PACKAGE	$580.09	Microsoft Xbox - Game console - black-complete	$137.50
MICROSOFT XBOX 360 EXCLUSIVE PREMIUM + PACKAGE	$560.00	Microsoft Xbox - Game console w/controller, 13 games	$137.50

Systems ▶ Nintendo 64

The average sales price in this subcategory is $36.88.

	HIGH		AVG
HUGE NINTENDO COLLECTION- 64,NES,SUPER,60+GAMES	$272.89	N64 nintendo 64 boxed 15 games nbox pokemon F1creatures	$37.01
NEW IN BOX!! Nintendo 64 Game System ***FIRE ORANGE***	$200.00	NINTENDO 64-N64 SYSTEM, CONTROLLER & 6 GAMES sweet!	$37.00
NINTENDO SYSTEMS NES,SNES,N64,Gamecube + Games Super 64	$183.50	Nintendo 64 with 3 controllers, 5 games, 1 memory card	$37.00
Nintendo 64 console - jungle neon green factory sealed	$177.50	NINTENDO 64 SYSTEM, 2 CONTROLLERS/6 GAMES/CASE/ACCES	$37.00
The Ultimate Nintendo 64 Lot With 26 Awesome Games MINT	$172.50	NINTENDO 64 - 2 CONTROLLER - FIVE GAMES	$37.00
NINTENDO DS WITH SUPER MARIO 64 DS WARIO WARE TOUCHED &	$158.51	RARE FUNTASTIC SMOKE GREY NINTENDO 64 N64 SYSTEM =GIFT!	$36.99
Nintendo 64 Bundle of 25 Games System and ETC.	$154.50	~*NINTENDO 64 GAME SYSTEM W/ RARE GOLD ZELDA GAME*~	$36.88
Nintendo 64 - Game console, 4 Controllers, 19 Games	$153.50	Nintendo 64 System plus nine games. (Perfect Dark, 007)	$36.51
2 Nintendo 64 Systems and 29 Games + Access.	$152.50	Nintendo 64+4 CONTROLLERS+ 6 GAMES+ ALL WIRING + MORE..	$36.50
Nintendo DS - Nintendogs Super Mario 64	$150.50	Nintendo 64 - Game console - 2 Controllers - 2 Games NR	$36.27
2 Nintendo 64 Game Consoles and 22 Games!!	$148.01	Nintendo 64 system and games	$36.01
Nintendo 64 System & Super Nintendo SNES Video Game Lot	$147.59	Nintendo 64 - w/ 9 Games and Accessories	$36.01
Nintendo 64 VERY RARE Fire Orange system NEW IN BOX N64	$145.00	NINTENDO 64 SYSTEM W/GAMES & NEW EXTRAS	$36.00
Used Nintendo 64, tons of games, 4 controllers!!!!!!!	$142.50	Nintendo 64 with 3 controllers and 9 games and case	$36.00
Nintendo N 64 N64 System NEW W/Extra Controller	$142.50	nintendo 64 game system with 2 controllers	$36.00

Systems ▶ Nintendo DS

The average sales price in this subcategory is $122.24.

	HIGH		AVG
Nintendo DS	$699.99	Nintendo DS - Handheld game system	$122.50
2 NINTENDO DS, 1 SP, 18 GAMES AND EXTRAS	$500.00	**NEW** Nintendo DS = 7 Colour get 1 = Case for gift	$122.50
Like new Nintendo DS + 25 Nintendo DS games!!	$450.68	Nintendo Ds electric blue/Dawn of Sorrow	$122.50

	HIGH		AVG
Used Nintendo DS w/ 24 Games & Accesories	$302.00	Nintendo DS - Handheld game system - 100% LIKE NEW!!!!!	$122.50
*LOOK!!!!! Nintendo DS + " 16 " DS games & 4 GBA ++++	$301.00	Nintendo DS - Handheld game system Black NIB	$122.50
Nintendo DS - 2 SYSTEMS - 4 GAMES - 2 CHARGERS	$275.00	Nintendo DS With EB Games Replacement Warranty	$122.50
Nintendo DS Bundle 14 Games and more NO RESERVE	$271.00	Nintendo DS Handheld game system w/ Super Mario/Pac-Man	$122.49
NINTENDO DS SYSTEM + 10 GAMES - EXCELLENT CONDITION	$249.99	Nintendo DS with Super Mario 64 and Madden 05	$121.99
UNOPENED BOX Nintendo DS - Handheld game system	$123.33	NEW Nintendo DS - Handheld game system + Bonus Game	$121.25
Nintendo DS 2 System Lot Games case extras mario	$244.50	Nintendo DS + Games	$121.21
Nintendo DS + Gameboy Advance + 12 Games + More	$242.50	NIB NINTENDO DS - NEW IN BOX- NR	$121.21
Nintendo DS - Complete -w/9 DS Games! Adult Owned NR!	$230.00	NINTENDO DS New in Open Box+Videos+Game+Acces. NO RESER	$121.00
Nintendo DS and Gameboy Micro with many extras 15 games	$229.99	Nintendo DS Handheld game system + accessories & games	$121.00
Nintendo DS - Handheld game system + games	$227.48	Nintendo DS - Handheld game system	$120.99
		Nintendo DS - Handheld game system with DS game!	$120.52

Systems ▶ Nintendo Game Boy

The average sales price in this subcategory is $45.69.

	HIGH		AVG
Nintendo Game Boy Advance SP - Handheld game system ...	$215.00	Nintendo Game Boy Color + 8 games & snake light lite!	$46.00
Nintendo Game Boy Advance SP - Used in Box w/ 12 games	$202.50	Nintendo Game Boy Advance SP - Handheld game system	$46.00
Nintendo Game Boy Advance+Game Boy Color+10 games..	$186.04	[3 of these sold for $46.00 each]	
[2 of these sold in a multiple item ("Dutch") auction for $93.02 each]		Nintendo Game Boy Advance system with 5 games	$45.99
Nintendo Game Boy Advance SP + 12 games,cords, bags	$180.50	Nintendo Game Boy Advance - Handheld game system - g...	$45.84
Nintendo Game Boy Advance SP SUPER BUNDLE - LOT!!!!!!	$173.43	Nintendo GBA GAME BOY ADVANCE Yu-Gi-Oh + Batt Pack NEW	$45.55
Nintendo Game Boy Advance SP W/ 9	$152.50	Nintendo Game Boy Advance SP - Handheld game system ...	$45.30
PERFECTLY GOOD GAMES		LIKE NEW Nintendo Game Boy Advance-Handheld W/ 3 Games	$45.00
Near Mint Nintendo Game Boy Advance SP and Eleven Games	$151.03	Nintendo Game Boy Advance SP - Handheld game system	$45.00
Nintendo DS with 4 Games + bonus, not Game Boy PSP	$150.00	[2 of these sold for $45.00 each]	
Nintendo GameCube w/Game Boy attachment and games	$150.00	Nintendo Game Boy Advance Glacier in Box + Cover/Lite	$45.00
Nintendo DS, Game Boy Advance, Game Boy Color, & More!!	$150.00	Nintendo Game Boy Advance Handheld With 3 Games	$44.99
nintendo DS with games not game boy GREAT DEAL!!!	$147.50	Nintendo Game Boy Advance system with 5 games	$45.99
New Nintendo Game Boy Advance SP 5 Games & 12-in-1 Kit	$144.50	Nintendo Game Boy Color - Handheld game system	$44.85
NINTENDO VIRTUAL BOY GAME SYSTEM	$137.50	Nintendo Game Boy Advance SP - Handheld game system ...	$44.62
Nintendo Game Boy Advance SP - W/ 11 GAMES & Case	$135.38	Super Nintendo SNES system + 4 Games + Super Game Boy	$44.02
Silver Nintendo Game Boy Advance SP+ 10 Games	$130.00	Nintendo Game Boy Advance	$44.02

Systems ▶ Nintendo Game Boy Advance

The average sales price in this subcategory is $54.57.

	HIGH		AVG
Nintendo Game Boy Advance SP - Handheld game system ...	$300.00	Nintendo Game Boy Advance gba SP Custom Unicorn+Video	$55.00
[5 of these sold in a multiple item ("Dutch") auction for $60.00 each]		Nintendo Game Boy Advance SP - Handheld game system ...	$55.00
Nintendo Game Boy Advance SP - Handheld game system ...	$215.00	[5 of these sold for $55.00 each]	
Nintendo GAME BOY ADVANCE	$205.00	NINTENDO GAME BOY ADVANCE SP ACTION PACK w/STORAGE CASE	$54.77
SP SYSTEM WITH 16 GOOD GAMES!		Nintendo Game Boy Advance SP - Handheld game system ...	$54.74
Nintendo Game Boy Advance SP - Used in Box w/ 12 games	$202.50	Nintendo Game Boy Advance - Handheld game system - i...	$54.65
Nintendo Game Boy Advance SP - Handheld game system ...	$192.50	Nintendo Game Boy Advance SP - Handheld game system ...	$54.50
Nintendo Game Boy Advance+Game Boy Color+10 games..	$186.04	Nintendo Game Boy Advance SP - Handheld game system ...	$54.01
[2 of these sold in a multiple item ("Dutch") auction for $93.02 each]		Nintendo Game Boy Advance SP - Handheld game system	$54.00
Nintendo Game Boy Advance SP + 12 games,cords, bags	$180.50	[2 of these sold for $54.00 each]	
Nintendo Game Boy Advance SP SUPER BUNDLE - LOT!!!!!!	$173.43	Nintendo Game Boy Advance SP - Handheld game system ...	$54.00
Nintendo Game Boy Advance SP W/ 9 PERFECTLY GOOD GAMES	$152.50	NINTENDO ADVANCE GAME BOY SP LIMITED EDITION LOW SHIP!	$54.00
Near Mint Nintendo Game Boy Advance SP and Eleven Games	$151.03	Nintendo Game Boy Advance SP - Handheld game system ...	$54.00
Nintendo DS, Game Boy Advance, Game Boy Color, & More!!	$150.00	[5 of these sold for $54.00 each]	
New Nintendo Game Boy Advance SP 5 Games & 12-in-1 Kit	$144.50	NINTENDO ADVANCE GAME BOY SP LIMITED EDITION LOW SHIP!	$54.00
Silver Nintendo Game Boy Advance SP+ 10 Great Games!	$136.50	Nintendo Game Boy Advance SP - Platinum + Games MINT	$53.59
Nintendo Game Boy Advance SP Bundle - Cobalt Blue	$136.49	Nintendo Game Boy Advance SP - Handheld game system ...	$53.25
Nintendo Game Boy Advance SP- W/ 11 GAMES & Case	$135.38	NINTENDO GAME BOY ADVANCE SP ACTION PACK w/STORAGE CASE	$53.05

Systems ▶ Nintendo Game Boy Advance SP

The average sales price in this subcategory is $65.29.

	HIGH		AVG
Nintendo Game Boy Advance SP - Handheld game system ...	$300.00	Nintendo Game Boy Advance SP - Handheld game system ...	$66.00
[5 of these sold in a multiple item ("Dutch") auction for $60.00 each]		Nintendo Game Boy Advance SP - Handheld game system ...	$65.99
Nintendo Game Boy Advance SP + 26 Additional Games	$267.89	GBA NINTENDO GAME BOY ADVANCE	$65.59
Nintendo Game Boy Advance SP Bundle Pack Great Deal	$224.71	SP PLATINUM MANY EXTRAS !	
Nintendo Game Boy Advance SP - Handheld game system ...	$215.00	Nintendo Game Boy Advance SP New NEW in box platinum	$65.59
Nintendo GAME BOY ADVANCE SP	$205.00	Nintendo Game Boy Advance SP - Handheld game system ...	$65.55
SYSTEM WITH 16 GOOD GAMES!		Nintendo Game Boy Advance SP - Handheld game system ...	$65.51
Nintendo Game Boy Advance SP - Used in Box w/ 12 games	$202.50	Nintendo Game Boy Advance SP with Super Mario Advance 4	$65.13
Nintendo Game Boy Advance SP - Handheld game system ...	$193.50	Nintendo Game Boy Advance SP - Handheld game system ...	$65.10
Nintendo Game Boy Advance SP - Handheld game system ...	$192.50	Nintendo Game Boy Advance SP Plus Extras	$65.03
Nintendo Game Boy Advance SP system +13 games, acces...	$182.50	Nintendo Game Boy Advance SP + charger+ 2 games + case	$65.02
Nintendo Game Boy Advance SP + 12 games,cords, bags	$180.50	Nintendo Game Boy Advance SP Cobalt Blue system BOX GBA	$65.01
Nintendo Game Boy Advance SP SUPER BUNDLE - LOT!!!!!!	$173.43	Nintendo Game Boy Advance gba SP Metallic Blue+Mario GM	$65.01
Nintendo Game Boy Advance SP - Handheld game system ...	$165.00	NINTENDO GAME BOY ADVANCE SP	$65.01
Nintendo Game Boy Advance SP + Accessories + 8 Games	$162.50	ACTION PACK w/STORAGE CASE	
Nintendo Game Boy Advance SP & Games (New)	$154.50	Nintendo Game Boy Advance SP - Handheld game system ...	$65.01
Nintendo Game Boy Advance SP W/ 9 PERFECTLY GOOD GAMES	$152.50	Nintendo Game Boy Advance SP + 2 GAMES + EXTRAS	$65.00

Systems ▸ Nintendo Game Boy Color

The average sales price in this subcategory is $22.46.

	HIGH		AVG
40 Nintendo Gameboy Games + Game Boy Color System &More	$208.62	Nintendo Game Boy Color - Handheld game system - tra...	$22.50
Nintendo Game Boy Advance+Game Boy Color+10 games..	$186.04	[2 of these sold for $22.50 each]	
[2 of these sold in a multiple item ("Dutch") auction for $93.02 each]		Nintendo Game Boy Color system "GREEN" Low Shipping	$22.50
Nintendo Game Boy Color - WITH 15 GAMES + Acessories!	$158.05	Nintendo Game Boy Color - Handheld game system - green	$22.50
Nintendo DS, Game Boy Advance, Game Boy Color, & More!!	$150.00	Nintendo Game Boy Color Pokemon	$22.50
Nintendo Game Boy Color Yellow 25 games, and Light	$142.50	Nintendo Game Boy Color with 3 great games	$22.50
Nintendo Game Boy Color & 23 Games Plus Extras	$123.88	Nintendo Game Boy Color Handheld system 3 Games	$22.49
Nintendo Game Boy Advance SP Color handheld system NEW	$105.50	Nintendo Game Boy Color - Handheld game system - tra...	$22.22
Nintendo Game Boy Advance + 2 game boy color package	$81.00	Nintendo Game Boy Color - lime green and 4 games	$22.09
Nintendo Game Boy Color Gameboy pink 11 games & extras!	$80.22	Nintendo Game Boy Color - Handheld game system - yellow	$22.02
Nintendo Game Boy Advance & Color and Games	$75.76	NINTENDO GAME BOY GAMEBOY	$22.00
Nintendo Game Boy Color Handheld System +12 Games+More	$74.35	COLOR SYSTEM ATOMIC PURPLE	
NEW Nintendo Game Boy Advance SP Flame Red Color NIB NR	$73.00	Nintendo Game Boy Color - Handheld system - yellow-LOT	$22.00
2 Nintendo Game Boy Color systems and 10 games	$73.00	Nintendo Game Boy Color - Handheld game system - purple	$21.99
Nintendo Game Boy Advance SP - RARE COBALT COLOR {NIB}	$71.69	Nintendo Game Boy Color/2 Games/Car Adapter Cable	$21.50
Nintendo Game Boy Advance SP - Pearl Blue in Color	$71.00	Game Boy Color + Croc & Caesars Palace 2 Games Nintendo	$21.50

Systems ▸ Nintendo GameCube

The average sales price in this subcategory is $79.40.

	HIGH		AVG
Nintendo GameCube/with screen-42games+accessories	$357.00	Nintendo GameCube with 4 Controllers 2x Waverbird	$80.00
Nintendo Gamecube and Gameboy Advance with 35 games	$350.00	nintendo gamecube with game	$80.00
Nintendo GameCube Game Cube Black 20 Games + Extras	$290.00	*~ NEW Nintendo GameCube - Game console Jet Black Cube	$80.00
Platinum Nintendo GameCube lot w/ 8 games Mario Kart	$261.37	Nintendo GameCube-indigo- 2 Controllers games & more	$80.00
NINTENDO GAMECUBE WITH 14 GAMES,	$256.00	Nintendo GameCube Indigo*Ultimate Bundle* W/ Metroid +	$79.99
5 CONTROLLERS+2 BONGOS		Nintendo Gamecube 3 Games Ultimate Spiderman mem card.	$79.94
Nintendo GameCube - Game console - platinum + 22 Games	$255.00	Nintendo Gamecube with Star Wars Rebel Strike New	$79.00
Nintendo Gamecube	$250.00	NINTENDO GAMECUBE WITH 5 GAMES, AFTERGLOW CONTROLLER	$79.00
Nintendo GameCube System, 23 games, memory and more	$249.50	NINTENDO GAMECUBE SYSTEM (PLATINUM) COMPLETE + 2 GAMES	$79.00
Nintendo GameCube System, 24 Games, 4 Controllers...	$237.85	Nintendo GameCube Super Smash Bros Bundle + EXTRAS!!!!	$79.00
Platinum Edition Nintendo Gamecube plus Extras	$234.77	NEW NINTENDO PLATINUM GAMECUBE	$78.77
Nintendo Gamecube and twenty games.	$227.50	SYSTEM CONSOLE GCU PACK	
Nintendo GameCube 12 games 4 controllers guides & more	$220.00	Nintendo GameCube system with 6 games LIKE NEW!!	$78.50
Nintendo GameCube - 14 Games - 4 controllers - More	$212.50	Nintendo GameCube - console - indigo, Book, Memory card	$78.00
Universal NINTENDO GAMECUBE Lot + TONS of extras LOOK!!	$212.50	Nintendo GameCube Holiday Bundle - Game console	$78.00
NINTENDO GAMECUBE WITH GAMEBOY PLAYER SUPER BUNDLE	$210.00	Nintendo GameCube - 3 controllers, 5 games, memory card	$77.00

Systems ▸ Nintendo NES

The average sales price in this subcategory is $39.49.

	HIGH		AVG
Huge Nintendo Atari Sega SNES NES systems consoles lot	$730.00	NES Nintendo System with 9 Games 4 Controllers Lot NICE	$40.18
NES NINTENDO TOP LOADER SYSTEM FACTORY SEALED RARE!!	$400.97	Nintendo NES System complete in Box with Super Mario	$40.00
NINTENDO NES HUGE SYSTEM LOT 25 SYSTEMS + ACCESSORIES!	$356.01	NES NINTENDO SYSTEM WITH GUN +GAME *TESTED*	$40.00
Nintendo Virtual Boy FACTORY SEALED BRAND NEW NES SNES	$356.00	VINTAGE NINTENDO NES SYSTEM LOT COMPLETE HOOK UPS +MORE	$40.00
Nintendo NES with 120 GAMES!!! NO DUPLICATES!!!	$265.00	NINTENDO NES SYSTEM WITH SUPER MARIO BROS NEW 72 PIN L1	$40.00
Nintendo NES Super LOT Top Loader System games MINT NR!	$238.51	COMPLETE Original NES Nintendo System~9 Games+GUN MARIO	$39.99
Nintendo NES system in box with 66 games & advantage NR	$200.00	Nintendo Nes WORKS GREAT w/ 22 games and 2 controllers	$39.50
3 NINTENDO NES GAME SYSTEMS *60 GAMES* GUNS JOY STICKS	$182.50	ORIGINAL NES NINTENDO GAME SYSTEM 8-Bit Mario !	$39.00
LOT OF 10 NINTENDO NES SYSTEMS+SNES+SUPER SCOPE!!!!!!!!	$178.49	Nintendo NES Complete with GUN, Joystick 4 Games	$39.00
AV NINTENDO FAMICOM SYSTEM + 15 GAME top loader nes jp	$164.95	Original NES Nintendo Entertainment System + ZELDA	$38.11
Super Nintendo SNES System 59 Games 2 Controllers NES	$157.50	Nintendo Entertainment System - Game console NES 4 Game	$38.00
Classic Nintendo NES Collection 31 games/Lots Extra!!	$143.50	VINTAGE NINTENDO NES SYSTEM CONTROLLERS ZAPPER, GAMES	$38.00
2 NINTENDO NES SYSTEMS, GAME GENIE, 53 GAMES AND MORE	$142.50	NES Nintendo System 2 Controllers Gun Mario New 72 Pins	$38.00
NINTENDO NES AND 67 GAMES FREE SHIPPING	$126.50	Complete NES Nintendo Entertainment Game System	$37.99
Nintendo NES Top Loader System Original NES Not FAKE !	$110.00	Nintendo Entertainment System (NES) and 16 games	$37.90

Systems ▸ Nintendo, Super

The average sales price in this subcategory is $47.33.

	HIGH		AVG
Mini Super Nintendo SNES 95 Games 3 Controller FreeShip	$318.00	SUPER NINTENDO Game System~8 Games~Super Mario	$48.01
BRAND NEW Super Nintendo System NEW Console Deck SNES	$305.00	Super Nintendo System w/10 games	$48.00
Huge Lot of Nintendo, Super NES, PS1, 3DO, Sega Nomad	$280.00	SUPER NES NINTENDO ENTERTAINMENT SYSTEM IN THE BOX	$48.00
HUGE NINTENDO COLLECTION- 64,NES,SUPER,60+GAMES	$272.89	Super Nintendo w/over 50 games SUPER WILD CARD RaRE!	$48.00
Super Nintendo System SNES 44 Games New Accessories	$242.50	Complete Super Nintendo SNES w/ 12 games Mario World	$48.00
Nintendo NES Super LOT Top Loader System games MINT NR!	$238.51	*SUPER NINTENDO SYSTEM* Complete + Controllers & Mario	$47.99
NINTENDO GAMECUBE WITH GAMEBOY PLAYER SUPER BUNDLE	$210.00	SNES Super Nintendo Entertainment System W/6 Games	$47.55
SUPER NINTENDO SNES LOT CONSOLE, CONTROLLERS, 40 GAMES	$200.00	RARE MINI Super Nintendo System SNES + 2 Games L@@K	$47.00
NINTENDO SYSTEMS NES,SNES,N64,Gamecube + Games Super 64	$183.50	SUPER NINTENDO SYSTEM + 8 GAMES	$47.00
Super Nintendo System - New & Sealed Never opened	$179.99	Super Nintendo SNES System 5 GAMES MARIO ALLSTARS More	$47.00
LOT OF 10 NINTENDO NES SYSTEMS+SNES+SUPER SCOPE!!!!!!!!	$178.49	Super Nintendo System SNES with 8 Games Complete Set	$47.00
Nintendo Game Boy Advance SP SUPER BUNDLE - LOT!!!!!!	$173.43	Nintendo SNES System & Super Mario World	$46.99
NINTENDO DS WITH SUPER MARIO 64 DS WARIO WARE TOUCHED &	$158.51	SUPER NINTENDO SYSTEM W/ 7 GAMES, METROID,MARIO, STARFO	$46.88
Super Nintendo System and 18 Games	$157.50	Super Nintendo Entertainment System + 6 Games	$46.50
Super Nintendo SNES System 59 Games 2 Controllers NES	$157.50	SNES Super Nintendo System Mario Kart World Link Donkey	$46.03

Systems ▶ Sega Dreamcast

The average sales price in this subcategory is $39.96.

	HIGH		AVG
Sega Katana Dreamcast Development Dev System	$455.02	Sega Dreamcast - Game console - gray	$40.00
Sega Dreamcast w 35 games, 4 con., 5 mem., & more	$256.00	Sega Dreamcast Lot w/ 7 Games Memory Card	$40.00
Sega Dreamcast - Game console - gray	$250.00	Sega Dreamcast System with 2 games	$39.99
SEGA DREAMCAST SYSTEM WITH GAMES BOOKS ACCESSORIES	$182.50	Sega Dreamcast with many extras	$39.99
Sega Dreamcast System with 27 games..arcade stick!!!	$156.40	Sega Dreamcast Game console + 6 Games NO RESERVE! ! !	$39.99
Sony Playstation 2 PS2 and Sega Dreamcast w/ games+more	$155.00	SEGA DREAMCAST GAME CONSOLE COMPLETE WITH BOX + GAMES	$39.99
Sega Dreamcast Hello Kitty Pink Console Japan Brand New	$149.00	SEGA DREAMCAST SYSTEM W/11 GAMES, VMU, XTRA CONTROLLER!	$39.97
Sega Dreamcast - Game console BRAND NEW IN BOX SEALED !	$145.95	SEGA DREAMCAST NICE COMPLETE AND 7 GAMES	$39.95
SEGA DREAMCAST LOT 30 GAMES FISHING ROD/GUN EXTRAS	$142.49	Sega Dreamcast With 10 Games 2 Controllers 2 Memory	$39.00
Huge Sega Dreamcast System - 3 Con, 37 Games, Lots More	$137.50	SEGA DREAMCAST SYSTEM COMPLETE WITH TONY HAWK 2	$39.00
SEGA Dreamcast Set with 17 Unopened Games	$137.25	Sega Dreamcast Game console w/ 8 games get IT here!	$39.00
Sega Dreamcast with 21 games, two controllers, vmu	$133.01	Sega Dreamcast w/ 9 Games (NFL 2K, Crazy Taxi, Sonic)	$38.25
Sega Dreamcast Console Games and Accessories	$130.25	Sega Dreamcast - Game console - gray W/Accessories	$38.01
Complete Sega Dreamcast Console System HUGE LOT 30Games	$129.99	SEGA DREAMCAST CONSOLE SYSTEM+7 GAMES +EXTRAS	$38.00
Sega Dreamcast Black R7 Console +More Japan Import	$127.50	SEGA DREAMCAST	$38.00

Systems ▶ Sega Genesis

The average sales price in this subcategory is $30.05.

	HIGH		AVG
Sega Genesis CDX Video Game System New in Box + Games	$401.00	SEGA GENESIS SYSTEM w/Games dungeons&d Lion king sonics	$31.00
Sega Nomad NEW FACTORY SEALED NEVER USED genesis nes	$326.00	Sega Genesis 3 System and 12 Great Games!	$31.00
Sega Genesis System w/ 113 Games, 3 Controllers	$224.50	Sega Genesis console, 4 controllers, and 12 games	$31.00
MINT Sega Genesis CDX System + 45 RPG Games Bundle!!!!!	$209.50	COMPLETE Sega GENESIS 2 SYSTEM +10 games Sonic/Pac-Man+	$30.99
10 Sega Genesis Systems Lot 100 Games +Bonus Rare Look!	$206.36	Huge Wholesale lot Sega Saturn Genesis Gamegear & more	$30.99
Sega Genesis/Sega CD and 32X - 42 Games - 2 Controllers	$197.50	SEGA GENESIS 16 BIT MIB WITH SONIC 1 & SONIC 2 NR!	$30.51
SEGA NOMAD PORTABLE GENESIS SYSTEM "MINT/PERFECT"	$183.50	Sega Nomad with bonuses look! Genesis	$30.00
SEGA GENESIS 3 SYSTEM FACTORY SEALED RARE UNTOUCHED	$175.00	Sega Genesis CD Console Works and Looks Great! Low s/h!	$30.00
sega genesis cd 32X MIB NIB 50+ video games game system	$168.26	SEGA GENESIS 16 BIT SYSTEM W/10 RARE GAMES EXC COND	$30.00
LARGE LOT JVC X'EYE XEYE SYSTEM SEGA CD GENESIS + GAMES	$162.50	Awesome Sega Genesis Package with Games!	$30.00
Sega Genesis CD + 32x Upgrade. 27 Games Included!!!	$152.50	Sega Genesis System with 4 Games WOW	$30.00
SEGA GENESIS 3 SYSTEM FACTORY SEALED RARE UNTOUCHED	$149.95	3 Sega Genesis console lot 5 games & game gear 1 game	$30.00
Sega Genesis CDX System COMPLETE IN BOX NEAR MINT	$145.00	Sega Genesis System Complete w/ Game Tested!	$30.00
Sega Genesis + 58 games***4 rare titles	$143.01	SEGA GENESIS SYSTEM COMPLETE WITH 12 GAMES A*	$29.99
sega megajet, mega jet, genesis, NEW, rare, ntsc-j	$134.01	Sega Genesis Huge lot System Converter 32x 5 games work	$29.99

Systems ▶ Sony PlayStation

The average sales price in this subcategory is $112.74.

	HIGH		AVG
Sony Playstation 2 System with 22 games, MUST SEE!!!!!!	$1,525.00	Sony PlayStation 2 - Game console - L@@K !!!1-DAY!!!	$117.50
NEW SONY PSP PORTABLE PLAYSTATION CERAMIC 20 GAMES	$525.00	Sony PlayStation 2 Slim - Game console - Sealed NEW	$117.00
Sony PlayStation Portable PSP W/ 6 GAMES + more!!!!!	$400.00	SONY PlayStation 2 (new design), NEW IN THE BOX!!!	$115.99
Sony PlayStation Portable - Game console - black	$380.00	SONY PLAYSTATION 2 SLIMLINE W/2 GAMES	$115.99
SONY PS2 PLAYSTATION 2 HUGE LOT SYSTEM, 48 GAMES MEMORY	$360.01	SONY PLAYSTATION 2 with GTA San Andreas & Many more!!!!	$115.95
Sony PlayStation 2 Autographed by the Cast of Alias	$358.00	Sony PlayStation 2 Slim Console SCPH-70012 PS2 Retail	$115.00
Sony PlayStation Portable - Game console - black	$350.00	SONY PLAYSTATION 2 with GRAND THEFT AUTO & CONTROLLER	$112.51
NEW Sony Playstation 2 PS2 Slim System God of War	$329.95	Sony PlayStation 2 - Game console	$112.50
Sony PlayStation 2 - Game console- Value bundle	$300.00	SONY PS2 PLAYSTATION 2 MEM CARD HSX GAME	$112.50
new Sony PlayStation Portable PSP W/ 7 MOVIES 1 GAME	$300.00	SONY PS2 SLIM PLAYSTATION 2 COMPLETE WITH WARRANTY	$112.50
Sony PlayStation 2 - Game console - charcoal black Slim	$299.99	Sony PlayStation 2 Console	$112.50
Sony PlayStation 2 - Game console - charcoal black	$287.99	Sony PlayStation 2 - Game console - black	$112.50
SONY PLAYSTATION 2 CONSOLE + ACCESSORIES + 16 PS2 GAMES	$275.00	Sony PlayStation 2 - Game console - charcoal black	$112.50
New Sony PlayStation 2 slim w/40 games ps2	$275.00	PS2 Sony PlayStation 2 Video Game System Lot !	$111.55
Sony PlayStation 2 Plus 1 Maxtor Hard Drive Combo	$270.00	Sony PS2 System PlayStation 2 Console Like New Mint A4	$111.00

Systems ▶ Sony PlayStation 2

The average sales price in this subcategory is $115.97.

	HIGH		AVG
=PS2= Sony Playstation2 with Hdd and tons extra	$325.00	SONY PLAYSTATION2 - BN CONSOLE with accessories!!!!	$120.00
Sony Playstation2-NR++30gamesPlayboyTheMansion+++more..	$300.00	Sony Playstation2 comes with 5 games	$120.00
BRANDNEW SONY PLAYSTATION2	$279.99	Sony PlayStation2 Console	$119.50
GRAND THEFT AUTO BUNDLE		Sony PlayStation2 Console	$118.50
Sony Playstation2 Linux kit PS2 LINUX with HDD NEW	$260.00	Sony PlayStation2 Console	$118.00
TV/DVD/Playstation2/SONY/IPOD/Apple/Computer	$250.00	LikeNew Sony PlayStation2+2 controllers+GTA San Andreas	$117.50
SONY PSP VIDEO GAME SYSTEM PLAYSTATION2 Value Pack	$249.99	Sony PlayStation 2 new design slim PS2 Playstation2	$116.00
[2 of these sold for $249.99 each]		SONY PS2 PS/2 PLAYSTATION	$115.00
Sony PS2 PlayStation2 Game console w/20 games+extras	$249.99	PLAYSTATION2 Console 1-Contrl	
Slim Sony PlayStation2 and "Old School Bundle" Games	$202.49	Sony PlayStation2 Console	$113.26
Sony Playstation 2 PS2 Playstation2 Game System Console	$200.00	Sony PlayStation2, Two Controllers,and Two Memory Cards	$112.53
[2 of these sold for $200.00 each]		Sony PlayStation2 Console	$112.50
Sony PlayStation2 Brand New-Charcoal	$187.50	[2 of these sold for $112.50 each]	
Black-8 Games,More		SONY Playstation2 with memory, controllers - WORKS PS2	$112.50
Sony PlayStation 2 new design slim PS2 Playstation2	$178.00	Sony PlayStation 2 PS2 Playstation2 Game System Console	$112.50
Slim sony playstation2 + many extras PS2 games like new	$177.55	Sony PlayStation 2 new design slim PS2 Playstation2	$110.77

Systems ▶ Sony PSP

The average sales price in this subcategory is $213.95.

	HIGH		AVG
Sony PSP Value Pack	$600.00	SONY PSP VALUE PACK 1001K BRAND	$215.00
NEW SONY PSP PORTABLE PLAYSTATION CERAMIC 20 GAMES	$525.00	NEW SEALED IN BOX L@@K	
SONY PSP - Huge Lot - 1GB - 5 Games Madden 2 Movies NR!	$521.00	[2 of these sold for $215.00 each]	
Sony PSP limited cream edition **20 games plus more	$500.00	Sony PSP Value Pack - NIB, Fast Shipping	$215.00
SONY PSP VALUE PACK PSP-1000KCW Ceramic White	$455.00	Sony PSP Value Pack - Game console	$214.50
[2 of these sold in a multiple item ("Dutch") auction for $227.50 each]		Sony PSP Value Pack - Game console	$214.29
Sony PSP, Barely used in box 3 Games	$450.00	Sony PSP Value Pack PSP System 1 Game/1 Movie/256 MCard	$214.10
Sony PSP * NEW * Value Pack	$403.00	NEW - Sony PSP Value Pack - Game console, No Reserve	$214.06
[2 of these sold in a multiple item ("Dutch") auction for $201.50 each]		Sony PSP Value Pack - NIB, Fast Shipping	$213.50
Sony PlayStation Portable PSP W/ 6 GAMES + more!!!!!!	$400.00	NEW - Sony PSP Value Pack - Game console, No Reserve	$213.01
SONY PSP SYSTEM AND ASSESSORIES	$400.00	Sony PlayStation Portable PSP value w/ game and movie	$213.01
SONY PlayStation Portable, PSP w/Lot of 5 Game 8 movies	$386.01	Sony PSP Game Console Value Pack PS2 Color NEW # 1001K	$213.00
Brand NEW Sony PSP "Limited Edition" pack w/accessories	$370.00	Sony PsP with 4 Games L@@K!!! Comes with everything	$212.51
SONY PLAYSTATION PSP-WOW!-NO RESERVE!	$350.00	***Ceramic White Sony PSP Value Pack with FREE GIFTS***	$212.51
Sony PSP White Edition Value Pack Japanese Release HOT!	$350.00	SONY PSP VALUE PACK BRAND NEW IN BOX NO RESERVE!!!	$212.50
Sony PSP Value Pack - Game console	$350.00	new Sony PlayStation Portable PSP Game console + vp	$212.50
SONY PSP SYS w/1GB MS DUO and LOGITECH SPKR AND MORE!!!	$350.00	Sony PSP Value Pack - NIB, Fast Shipping	$212.50

Vintage Games

The average sales price in this subcategory is $5.01.

	HIGH		AVG
Multicade 39 games-in-1 full size stand-up arcade New	$1,625.00	Atari 2600 E.T. ET Extra Terrestrial CIB MINT box game	$5.05
Mr Do Full Size Multi Arcade Machine New Monitor !	$1,345.00	MEGA MAN X Clean & Tested (Super Nintendo)	$5.04
Easy NJ pickup, delivery and shipping available!		Star Control Sega Genesis low shipping	$5.01
METAL SLUG NEO GEO AES Import JAPAN	$1,299.00	Star Wars Episode I Jedi Power Battles Playstation	$5.01
100% authentic, Great Codition ! LOOK !		NES Nintendo Game Mega Man 2 RARE	$5.01
Pinball arcade. Arcade Machine Multi Game Unit Lowest Price Ever LOOK!	$1,114.00	Dreamcast - Grand Theft Auto 2 NEW SEALED!	$5.01
NJ easy pickup , Delivery, and Shipping available NR	$995.00	Mattel Intellivision Zaxxon by Coleco Complete in Box	$5.01
FFXI Account 4 70+ jobs AMAZING Gear Remora Server	$900.00	Coleco TELSTAR MARKSMAN Light Gun Video Game with Box	$5.00
1980 Midway Galaga Standup Arcade Game	$800.00	Atari 2600 'RECONDITIONED' Video Computer System Box	$5.00
Original Galaga with raphid fire chip! Works Great!		Bentley Compu-Vision PONG System Complete with Box	$5.00
Original Star Wars Sit down video game	$800.00	ATARI 2600: Arcadia/Starpath 12-pack Dragonstomper	$5.00
24 neo geo game card aes in box !!!! don't pass it up , huge lot !! non japanese	$772.99	ColecoVision ADVENTURES IN PARK complete in box	$5.00
Super Nintendo SNES Lot Collection 47 games Ogre Battle.	$681.60	16 different Atari Games with wooden cartridge holder	$5.00
Super Mario RPG Mana FF2 FF3 Mega Man X X2 X3 MORE!		1978 Vintage Tomy Digital Derby	$5.00
Vectrex Video Game System like new in box - with games!	$660.00	Atari 2600 Spider-Man mint still sealed Parker brothers	$5.00
Lucasfilm Games LOOM FM Towns CD-ROM Game LucasArts.	$643.55		
RARE Japanese 256-color version! AUTOGRAPHED by author!			
NINTENDO Game & Watch FIRE original packaging	$643.01		
Qbert arcade machine excellent condition, NO RESERVE	$560.00		
san francisco rush driving game	$585.00		
Huge Lot - Sega Nintendo Dreamcast Playstation Gameboy	$630.00		
Huge Lot - Sega Nintendo Dreamcast Playstation Gameboy	$630.00		

Wholesale Lots ▶ Accessories

The average sales price in this subcategory is $42.28.

	HIGH		AVG
Sony PSP Value Pack Wholesale Lot of 50	$9,500.00	6 Piece Lot PS2 Memory Cards Remote Multitap Adapters	$50.00
100 NEW 72 Pin Connector Parts Nintendo NES 8bit System	$475.01	NEW 50PCS PLAYSTATION PS2 AUDIO/	$49.99
NEW LOTS OF 40 PLAYSTATION PS2	$200.00	VIDEO COMPONENT CABLE	
DUAL SHOCK 2 CONTROLLER		60PCS PS2 UNIVERSAL VCR/TV/DVD	$49.99
Brand New* LOT 40pcs PS2 D Shock2 Controllers	$200.00	REMOTE CONTROL WHOLESALE	
[6 of these sold for $200.00 each]		Xbox Logitech WIRELESS controller and headset package	$49.99
NEW LOTS OF 40 PLAYSTATION PS2 DUAL SHOCK 2 CONTROLLER	$200.00	LOT OF 15 ASSORTED MICROSOFT XBOX CONTROLLERS TYPE S	$49.00
[6 of these sold for $200.00 each]		10 NEW 72 Pin Connector Parts Nintendo NES 8-bit System	$47.99
NEW WHOLESALE LOT! 40 JET BLACK GAMECUBE CONTROLLER	$200.00	Huge collection of over 60 game guide books neat!!!	$43.75
WHOLESALE RESELL LOT SONY PSP 105 ITEM LENS CHARGER +++	$175.00	Nintendo NES Large Accessory Lot	$41.00
XBOX / PLAYSTATION 2(PS2) / GAMECUBE-HUGE BOX LOT	$157.38	SUPER NINTENDO SYSTEM COMP. W/ 2 CONT. AND 4 GAMES	$41.00
XBOX / PLAYSTATION 2(PS2) / N64 / GAMECUBE-HUGE BOX LOT	$152.50	SUPER NINTENDO SYSTEM COMP. W/ 2 CONT. AND 4 GAMES	$39.99
PS2 Fans *Ends Disk Read Errors* Wholesale Lot NEW !!	$150.00	48 New Genuine Sega Genesis controllers Wholesale Lot	$39.95
Lot of 21 xbox games and some accessories. Halo 2! GTA!	$142.50	4 Xbox Controllers BRAND NEW WHOLESALE LOT	$37.99
Microsoft Xbox (2) controllers (7) games and headset	$138.01	[4 of these sold for $37.99 each]	
NEW LOTS OF 20 JET BLACK GAMECUBE CONTROLLER *SEALED*	$120.00	Lot of 4 New XBOX Controllers	$37.99
[2 of these sold for $120.00 each]		Huge Lot of NES & Sega Genesis Systems & Accessories	$36.51
21 X-box Games Fable, Halo2, X-box Live kit, Guide	$101.99	12 NEW SUPER NINTENDO CONTROLLERS SNES WHOLESALE LOT	$36.05

Wholesale Lots ▶ Console Systems

The average sales price in this subcategory is $257.51.

	HIGH		AVG
Wholesale lof of 25 units Xbox 360 Premium-Brand New,	$9,501.00	SONY PSP VALUE PACK, NIB, IN STOCK READY TO SHIP! NR!!!	$271.00
Wholesale lot 50 units of PSP Value Pack-Brand New	$8,500.00	Sony PSP Uses w/ 4 games and 1 movie	$265.00
LOTS OF 25 BRAND NEW PSP SEALED IN RETAIL BOX!!! $$$$$	$4,890.00	Nintendo NES with 120 GAMES!!! NO DUPLICATES!!!	$265.00
BULK WHOLESALE LOTS OF 25 SONY PSP GREAT DEAL!BRAND NEW	$4,850.00	HUGE PS2 LOT LIKE NEW CONDITION GREAT X-MAS GIFT !!!	$262.00
LOT of 25 Sony PSP BRAND NEW playstation Value pack	$4,766.00	Sony PSP Value Pack + 5 Games	$262.00

LOT of 25 Sony PSP BRAND NEW playstation Value pack	$4,650.00
25 Sony PSP Value Pack - Game consoles	$4,150.00
510 GAMES 9 SYSTEMS PS2 XBOX GAMECUBE SNES PS1 N64 MORE	$4,001.00
Super Collection of Classical Systems and New Systems	$3,400.00
500 GAMES 9 SYSTEMS PS2 XBOX GAMECUBE SNES PS1 N64 MORE	$3,250.00
XBOX 360 PREMIUM SYSTEM - WHOLESALE LOT OF 5 (NEW)	$2,399.00
[4 of these sold for $2,399.00 each]	
XBOX 360 PREMIUM SYSTEM - WHOLESALE LOT OF 5 (NEW)	$2,325.00
XBOX 360 PREMIUM SYSTEM - WHOLESALE LOT OF 5 (NEW)	$2,245.00
Huge Sega Dreamcast, Genesis, CD, & Saturn Collection	$2,150.00
XBOX 360 PREMIUM SYSTEM - WHOLESALE LOT OF 5 (NEW)	$2,025.00

41 games and a xbox console and a game cube console	$255.00
Nintendo Game Cube 16 Games 2 Wavebird Controllers Lot	$250.00
XBOX IN ORIGINAL BOX W/ ACCESSORIES AND 12 GAMES	$247.50
X-box Console & Lot of Games + MANY EXTRAS L@@K!!!!	$242.50
HUGE NINTENDO NES LOT! 7 SYSTEMS GAMES N64 ATARI	$240.29
New Playstation 2 Old School Bundle	$240.00
BRAND NEW PSP CONSOLE with Full Warranty	$239.00
Nintendo NES Super LOT Top Loader System games MINT NR!	$238.51
huge ps2 lot play station 2 28 games wireless extras	$238.00
Gamecube w/17games, GameBoy Advance	$237.85
w/7 games PLUS MORE	

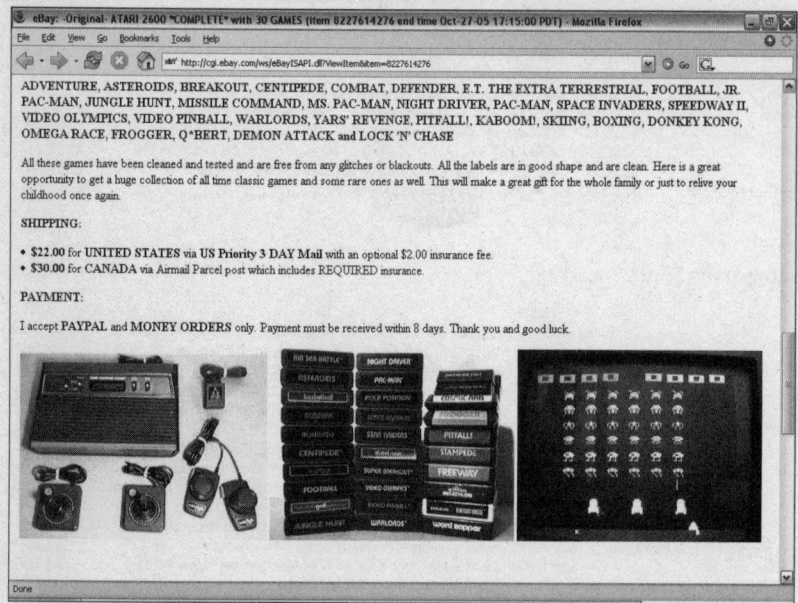

Wholesale Lots ▸ Games

The average sales price in this subcategory is $90.03.

	HIGH		AVG
525 Playstation 2, Xbox, GameCube Video Games NO DOUBLE	$3,051.00	HUGE LOT of 25 PS2 games NO DUPLICATES!!	$99.99
200 Playstation 2 Video Games, WholeSale PS2 Game Lot	$1,557.00	Lot of 10 USED Kids Gameboy Advance Games and Player	$95.00
200 Playstation 2 Video Games, WholeSale PS2 Game Lot	$1,225.99	LOT of 27 Intellivision Games!! W/BOXES Classic Coleco	$92.51
201 Xbox Video Game WholeSale Lot, NO DUPLICATES	$1,125.00	Playstation PS1 - Lot of 14 One-on-One Fighting Games	$92.09
NEW 120 PS2+XBOX+GAMECUBE WHOLESALE LOT PLAYSTATION 2	$1,105.00	15 LOT OF XBOX GAMES	$92.00
157 Playstation 2 Video Games List Lot	$910.00	Atari Jaguar 19 Game Lot Rayman Alien Vs Predator RARE	$91.11
100 Xbox Video Games with Cases & Manuals WholeSale Lot	$781.00	10 Gamecube Games GC WHOLESALE	$90.00
350 Playstation 2 PS1 PS2 Game Games HUGE LOT w/ Cases!	$776.66	10 Different Xbox Games WHOLESALE	$89.99
100 GameCube, Playstation 2, & Xbox Games NO DUPLICATES	$721.00	Lot of Playstation 2 games still in factory packaging	$88.00
100 Xbox & Playstation 2 Game Lot with Cases NO SPORTS	$699.00	10 XBOX Video Games BRAND NEW SEALED, Driver 3, Mafia +	$87.00
100 GameCube, Xbox, PS2 Video Games NO DUPLICATES!!	$698.00	15 GameBoy Color WholeSale Game Lot ReSealed NO DOUBLES	$85.93
105 Playstation 2 Video Game WholeSale Lot NO DUPLICATE	$698.00	Lot of GBA games- Castlevania 1, 2 & 3 ! Awesome!	$85.00
100 GameCube & XBOX Video Games NO DUPLICATES WholeSale	$692.00	LOT of 30 SNES Games!! No Duplicates!! Super Nintendo!!	$84.00
100 Xbox & PS2 Video Games WholeSale Lot with NO SPORTS	$686.09	SUPER NINTENDO SYSTEM & 18 HOT GAMES FOR SALE~~!!!!!!!	$83.00
100 Xbox Game Lot w/ Cases & Manuals NO DUPLICATES	$680.00	super nintendo system +40 games lot +mystery its yours	$82.00

Wholesale Lots ▸ Other

The average sales price in this subcategory is $87.88.

	HIGH		AVG
LOT of 25 Sony PSP BRAND NEW playstation Value pack	$4,766.00	PS2,FFXI,ResidentEvil2,DevilMayCry,DMC2,GTASanAndreas	$122.50
LOT of 25 Sony PSP BRAND NEW playstation Value pack	$4,650.00	Microsoft Xbox Parts Lot Motherboards dvdroms Cases Etc	$122.50
Lot of 7 Sony Playstation 2 Units AS-IS	$305.01	Barely Used Nintendo Gameboy DS W/ Wario Ware INC.	$112.50
PSP system videos and games	$247.50	Playstation 2 System w/ 5 Games + Extras! PS2	$110.00
PS2 - Bundle + 6 Games - Slim Line Playstation 2 - Used	$200.00	GAMEBOY ADVANCED SP 10 GAMES AN METAL CASE L@@k!!!!!!!	$100.00
Xbox w/ 12 games and two contrllers	$200.00	Playstation 2 System w/ 5 Games + Extras! PS2	$100.00
USED PSP! 2 GAMES INCLUDED!!!!!!!!!!!!!!!!!!!!!!!!!!	$182.50	Nintendo NES + 24 Boxed Games + Zapper + 2 controllers+	$87.05
BUNDLE OF 73 GAMES, GAMES ACC'S AND GAME SYSTEMS	$171.71	game boy/11 games,carry case.	$85.00
PS2 Playstation 2 Slim System + Extras & 7 Games Lot!	$169.99	NEW Gameboy Advance SP, Games and Accessories!	$85.00
PS2 Playstation 2 System + Extras & 7 Games Lot!	$169.99	HUGE Lot of 56 NES NINTENDO Video Games	$83.59
Xbox Crystal Limited Edition with Extras	$167.50	Sony PlayStation One - Game console plus 14 games	$83.00
Mountain Dew X-box with 5 games+3 contr. ONLY 5000 made	$164.99	HUGE LOT OF NINTENDO & SUPER NINTENDO - NO RESERVE	$82.01
Sony Playstation 2 and 14 game lot/ like new condition	$162.51	Playstation 2 with 8 games! PS2	$82.00
Nintendo 64 Bundle of 25 Games System and ETC.	$154.50	used Gamecube, 3 games 3 controllers 2 memory cards	$80.00
PS2 playstation!! 3 games!! 4 controlers!! NOT BROKEN!!	$140.00	Game Boy Advance and Games	$77.76

35

EVERYTHING ELSE

The name of the Everything Else category evokes a catchall, mishmash area, but this is such a fun category that it would be a shame if one dismissed it out of hand as auction leftovers. Although there is indeed a lot of wacky stuff here—in fact, there is an actual subcategory named Weird Stuff, with third-level subcategories ranging from Slightly Unusual to Totally Bizarre—some of the items here are actually mainstream. For example, when Halloween rolls around every year, many people don't realize that the main depository of costumes on eBay is in the Everything Else ▶ Gifts & Occasions ▶ Costumes subcategory. This is also where all the Funeral & Cemetery subcategories are (yes, there are several of them—everything from cemetery plots to mortuary supplies), as well as subcategories for Information Products, Memberships, and Mature Audiences.

Of course, there is a lot of freaky, weird stuff here too. This category probably captures the essence of the oddball eBay auctions that tend to make it into the national news. For example, the Everything Else ▶ Advertising Opportunities subcategory attracts folks who are willing to do (or sell) all kinds of outlandish things in order to get free publicity. In fact, the potential publicity brought on by these auctions is sometimes dangled by the sellers as the key draw for the items.

Unconventional Advertising

One man decided to try to use an eBay auction as a chance to get his home mortgage paid off. This auction for "Sponsor My Home Mortgage, Receive Major Media Coverage/Get Your Business or Site Mentioned on National TV" managed to get a price of $5,000.00 in a Buy It Now auction. The photo for the listing is simply a pair of hands thumbing through stacks of hundred dollar bills in a suitcase. "Free Mega Publicity for Your Web Site or Business! This is the WORLD'S first ever auction of this kind, ANYWHERE!!" touts the auction description. "How would you like to have your web site or business featured on CNN, MSNBC or ABC NEWS?" He goes on to say that major media outlets love to run stories about odd eBay auctions, giving the "house with bride" and the online casino company GoldenPalace.com as examples. (GoldenPalace.com has won several wacky auctions, such as the pregnant woman offering her belly for advertising space.) "I'd like to have you sponsor my new oddball auction called, 'Man Auctions House Payments on eBay,'" he writes in the listing description. He explains that the winning bidder will agree to sponsor six months of his mortgage payments. "Your business logo or web site will receive homepage links from my new web site for a year where I will share my story with the media and the WORLD." The only possible flaw in his offer is that these goofy eBay auctions are becoming so commonplace that the media may no longer rush to cover every one.

The mortgage auction got the second-highest price in the Everything Else ▸ Advertising Opportunities subcategory in this sample. The highest was $7,000.00 for advertising with an anonymous fraternal organization: "BUY FRATERNITY $7.3 MILLION 70,669,760 ADV IMPRESSION" touts the auction title, citing its previous advertisers as the major companies Dell, Microsoft, IBM, Sanyo, and Sony, in the auction subtitle. The seller describes it as follows: "International Fraternal Chapter will advertise your product or service as a personalized endorsed true believer with traditional marketing techniques," and claims that the buyer will gain "access to [the] $200 billion dollar college and alumni market." A bidder can "call for the name of fraternity & details!"—phone numbers are given. They also claim that "big 5 advertising agencies value for this service to be worth over $7,360,000" and list a number of other advertising media and what value they give the program. For example, *Fortune* magazine is given as $7,553,462.00, and ABC Television is given as $7,875,523.00. The advertising methods are given as "peer to peer social networking marketing" and "online peer to peer," as well as marketing at social events and road trips. The seller has a 96.4 percent feedback rating, which could be better. The most disconcerting things to me about this auction are that there are a number of grammatical mistakes in the listing, and it's a bit fuzzy concerning exactly how the organization will advertise the winning bidder's product or service.

Some of the more interesting auctions in the Everything Else ▸ Advertising Opportunities subcategory were actually for auctions that did not sell: a guy in Indianapolis offered to be your "Right-Hand Man" for the sum of $200,000.00 for the next five years: "I WILL MAKE ALL YOUR RUNS FROM 3PM TO 11PM NO MATTER WHAT THEY MAY BE…YOU NAME IT AND ITS DONE. NO JOB IS TO HARD, I WILL BE THAT ONE PERSON YOU CAN COUNT ON…AGAIN.SHERMAN WILL GET IT DONE… NO MORE WORRIES, SHERMAN IS ON THE JOB." Sherman has a can-do attitude, but he could benefit from better spelling and punctuation, and a feedback rating of higher than 0 percent.

Other ad opportunities that went unsold: sponsorship of a "NASCAR NEXTEL CUP TEAM" for $5,000,000.00; "Advertise on my Corvette" for $23,000.00; and a young woman with half-blonde, half-pink hair who would let you "Tattoo your company's name or logo on me" for a Buy It Now price of $20,000.00. She's just one of several would-be human billboards in this subcategory.

The median prices in the Everything Else ▸ Advertising Opportunities subcategory are around $9.95. One of the more popular auctions was for "Lifetime Website Submissions; Over 100K Search Engines!"—four of these auctions sold for $9.99 each. Others include assorted website banner and button ads, and even a 30-second voice-over radio advertisement for $5.99 (this is for producing the audio bit, not for the actual radio airtime).

Getting the Most out of eBay

In the eBay User Tools subcategory you can buy tools to help you use eBay. A bestseller here was an established eBay "vintage" business website (www.vintagerevolution.com) that sold for $490.00. This included all rights to the site name, all of the leftover stock of vintage clothing, and "a list of our vintage supplier and hot spots to get top-notch vintage goods," as well as two hours of phone consultation.

Another seller in the high end of the sample for eBay User Tools was a children's eBay storefront called "So Cute" for $69.99. Several custom auction packages sold for between $32.00 and $36.99, with the latter price buying a "Custom Ebay Auction Template, Logo, Store, Me Page Pack."

The middle prices in the Everything Else ▸ eBay User Tools subcategory included simpler auction templates, like the "New GRUNGE Black White auction template unique design" that sold for $4.99. Other tools that sold for $4.99 include a fee calculator, auction-tracker software, and a CD of wholesale dropshippers.

Learning New Tricks

The Education & Learning subcategories seem somewhat out of place here. Many of these auctions are for videos and books, and one wonders why they wouldn't be included in either the Books or the DVDs & Movies main categories. However, many of them are whole programs that seem to be geared toward teachers, so perhaps they aren't a perfect match for those categories. A high seller in the Everything Else ▸ Education & Learning subcategory was actually in the Adult & Career Education subcategory—an "Anthony Tony Robbins Package Valued at $36,507.97 NR" that went for $1,630.00.

Number three on the top sellers in Everything Else ▸ Education & Learning ▸ Adult & Career Education was a tax package, 2004 "JAY MITTON Total Tax Lawsuit and ASSET Protection," that sold for $1,225.00. According to the seller, this retails for $5,000.00, so that is a substantial savings. According to the description, this is a new, unopened package that teaches you how to "protect your personal and business assets today! Learn how to become judgment-proof, pay no capital gains tax and lower your income taxes!"

The mid-range of prices in the Everything Else ▸ Education & Learning ▸ Adult & Career Education subcategory is around $42.00 to $43.00, and for that you can get things like real estate courses, Quixtar CDs, and a "Double Your Dating" interview on CD.

A Tomb with a View: From Death to Life and Beyond

In a logical juxtaposition, funereal items are nestled next to genealogical records in Everything Else. The Funeral & Cemetery subcategories are Caskets, Cemetery Plots, Cremation Urns, and Mortuary Supplies.

How'd you like to stake a claim for your eternal resting place next to that of The Duke? Yes, two plots in the same Newport Beach, California, cemetery where John Wayne is buried fetched $6,000.00. "Pacific View Cemetery is located high on a hill above the City of Newport Beach, California, overlooking the blue Pacific Ocean," according to the seller, and retail prices run from $8,000.00 to $10,000.00 apiece, so for $3,000.00 each, these plots were cheap.

The lowest-priced auction sampled in this subcategory was $202.50 for two cemetery plots in Paxton, Massachusetts. Other eye-catching auctions in the Everything Else ▸ Funeral & Cemetery subcategory include the lot of 23 caskets that sold for $1,800.00 and the two six-foot stainless steel embalming tables for $1,500.00.

In the Genealogy subcategories, rare, local-based items tend to do well; a top seller was a handwritten genealogy of the Youngs family in Southold Town, Long Island, an original colony dating from 1640. Some antique local directories did well too, including an 1896 COLORADO STATE BUSINESS DIRECTORY, which sold for $872.00, an "1876 LEAVENWORTH CITY DIRECTORY W/ABERNATHY CATALOG" for $409.00, and a "1929 WASHINGTON DC CITY DIRECTORY" for $405.00.

Rounding out the Everything Else category are the Metaphysical and Religious subcategories. Things like healing crystals, feng shui, and the paranormal all have a home here. An auction for "Haunted Sapphire Ring Brings Extreme Luck & Fortune" was the high seller in the Psychic, Paranormal subcategory, going for $912.00, and second was a "possessed HAUNTED WITCHES MOTHER OF PEARL MONEY RING" for $820.00. Average-priced items included a divorce spell and a haunted doll, each for around $26.00.

Hot Memberships and Costumes

Limousine services are popular in the Memberships subcategory of Everything Else. An unlimited "while in Las Vegas" limo service went for $5,000.00 and another of these sold for $1,000.00. Several Bally's health club memberships sold here for between $660.00 and $1,300.00 in the high end of this sample. The average price in Memberships was around $20.00.

The Gifts & Occasions subcategory harbors the Costumes subcategory, as well as other party-related subcategories such as Gag Gifts, Greeting Cards, Party Supplies, and Wedding Supplies. As you can imagine, around Halloween, the Costumes subcategory is rocking. High sellers here were a "King Arthur Roman Muscle Armor Greek Spartan Cuirass" that sold for $499.99 and a Smokey Bear costume for $338.33. Average costume prices were around $33.00; a cave woman and a *Star Wars* Darth Maul costume each went for $33.00.

Mature Audiences Only

If some of the items in Gifts & Occasions, like the Gothic strait jacket, seem a bit kinky, they are nothing compared to the Wild West that is the Mature Audiences subcategory. It is broken down into lower-level categories including Adult Toys, Animation & Comics, Art: Nude, Books, Domain Names, Pin Up, Risque Novelties, Video, and, of course, Other. eBay requires users to first log in separately to this subcategory and verify that they are 18 or over.

The more artistic items here seem to sell the best, such as the "VINTAGE DEMI DIEUX Male Nude Beefcake BENNETT 11x14," two of which sold for $1,700.00 each. The Autographs subcategory here usually consists of auctions for signed centerfolds or other pictures. As one would expect, there is the usual collection of porn in Books, Magazines, and Videos, but some of the more unusual items are in Adult Toys. A "Jetaime Sex Toy - Sex Machine - Industrial Strength" sold for $510.00, and according to the seller, it retails for $1,195.00. She says, "This can be a woman's best friend!" and emphasizes, "the machine is GENTLY used." Other . . . er, machines went for between $99.95 and $380.05 in this sample. Average prices in that subcategory are around $22.00.

Taking Your Chance on a Mystery Auction

Mystery auctions have become a subculture on eBay, with buyers and sellers alike having fun with them. These are auctions that often embed clues and even incentives at different bid points (for example, the first person to bid $1,000.00 will receive a certain prize), and they can be for mystery prizes, or prizes that are described but not seen.

The highest mystery auction in this sample went for a lofty $10,000.00: "$$$ CASH Mystery BOX Auction! CASH, JEWELRY $$$$$." This auction was for a box with "100 U.S. bills, with NO 1's, NO 2's, and NO 5's!!!!!" as well as "rings, earrings, diamonds, gold, Silver!!!! They could be a mystery box worth $1000's on their own, not including the HUGE AMOUNTS OF CASH INSIDE!!!!" Six bidders took their chances on this auction. Similar mystery auctions for cash, jewelry, and combinations thereof sold for between about $5,000.00 and $10,000.00 on the high end. The median prices are around $10.00, and the auctions are for things like department store cards with undisclosed dollar amounts on them.

Weird Stuff

Finally, we get to the Weird Stuff subcategories. These are always fun to check out, just to see what's there. Some are not so weird, such as a "Movado two-tones Diamond Bezel Watch," which sold for $375.00. But then there is the 50-inch Leg Lamp, $249.00; a stripper pole, $224.00; and black leather restraints, $102.50. In the Really Weird subcategory we find a speaking role in a movie, $100.00; a "Rare Real eBay Talking and Spiting Mystery Skull," $1,000.00; and a "Weekend in a Haunted Mental Health Facility," $30.00 (well, it's cheaper than Vail).

Then there's the Totally Bizarre: "Help My Son and His Girlfriend Buy First House" for $10,000.00; "MY HUSBAND LEFT FOR ANOTHER WOMAN MYSTERY AUCTION BOX" for $761.00 ("Now that he is gone.....all of the stuff has to go too! Some of the free gifts that you may receive in your box [or boxes] are jewelry, electronics, computers, great stuff for women, great stuff for men, etc."); and a "Set of 2 Glass Prosthetic Blue Eyes Eye With Case" for $180.00. Or, if your life lacks a purpose, you can join with one eBay seller in his quest to see an auction for a Q-tip get to #1 on the eBay Pulse page. (The seller touts his ability as a high-profile seller to promote the winner as one of the draws to bidding.)

I didn't even mention the Plesiosaur skeleton that went for a whopping GBP 30,000.00, or the cave bear skeleton for GBP 15,798.60. Suffice it to say that plenty of unique and interesting things can be found here, many of them bargains. Essentially the whole human parade can be found here, from the super-luxurious to the pathetic—and in that sense, Everything Else is a microcosm of eBay itself.

Advertising Opportunities

The median sales price in this subcategory is $9.99.

	HIGH		AVG
BUY FRATERNITY $7.3 MILLION 70,669,760 ADV IMPRESSION	$7,000.00	Unlimited Website Hits For	$9.99
Dell Microsoft IBM Sanyo Sony XBox PS3 PREVIOUS ADV BUY		Your Work At Home Program!!!	
Sponsor My Home Mortgage, Receive Major Media Coverage	$5,000.00	Advertise Your Business Across The Globe For Life!!!	$9.99
Get Your Business or Site Mentioned on National TV		Black TABLE CLOTH Sprint Logo Advertising Booth	$9.99
A LAS VEGAS Advertising Opportunity So HOT, It's a SIN	$2,575.00	I WILL SELL YOUR WORK AT HOME	$9.99
Catchy Domain Name For Sale "WWW.EYECATCHER.COM"	$2,572.00	PROGRAM FOR YOU FOR LIFE!	
1 Month of Mobile Advertising Space in Downtown Chicago	$2,000.00	Lifetime Website Submissions; Over 100K Search Engines!	
Sponsorship/Advertising Open for Team USA Armwrestler	$1,150.00	[4 of these sold for $9.99 each]	
Forehead Advertising - 30 days exposure in Houston Area	$1,000.00	Your Site To Over 100,000 Search Engines For Life!	$9.99
Your company name or website on forehead for 30 days.		[2 of these sold for $9.99 each]	
INFLATABLE ADVERTISING BALLOON TUBE SIGNS 15'/20'/36'	$407.00	I'll Sell Your Home Based Business For You. For Life!!	$9.99
~Advertise On My Indoor Soccer Team~	$299.00	Car Dealer Web site,	$9.95
Reach out to the Hispanic Market, Don't miss out !!!!		Banner Ad for 3 Months-Advertise	$9.95
Advertise on My Breasts Key West Fantasy Fest	$260.00	Website UNLIMITED HITS	
Company or Website Body Painted on Me to 70,000 People!		ADVERTISE ON POPULAR TEEN WEBSITE	$8.50
NEW Email Address: XBox360_Gift@Yahoo.com HOTTT!!	$240.00	Front page Button Ad on Popular Wahm site for 90 days	$7.95
Be the One and Only Sponsor of PMOR's Christmas Station	$202.51	Banner Ad for 3 Months-Advertise	$7.00
Launches on Decmeber 11 All Xmas music thru Dec 31.		Website UNLIMITED HITS 7.00	
ELMO or RED MONSTER, mascot character, professional :)	$201.26	MAKE BIG WALL AD SIGNS BANNERS	$7.00
Exact Replica of ELMO, to make your memories memorable!		MURALS POSTERS SOFTWARE	
HUGE GIANT multi HELIUM ADVERTISING BALLOON - Wholesale	$179.00	Advertise on my website! MICHIGAN	$6.42
Promote Sales & Special Events - Special low eBay Price		365 days banners	
[3 of these sold for $179.00 each]		30 Second Voice Over Radio Advertisment Come	$5.99
Donate to Name the Police Departments canine (K9)	$125.00	on in and check out our demos.	

eBay User Tools

The median sales price in this subcategory is $4.99.

	HIGH		AVG
eBay Vintage Website Business www.vintagerevolution.com	$490.00	eBay AUCTION TRACKER 2005	$4.99
START MAKING MONEY TODAY***ESTABLISHED***		Management Software SAVE $!	
resell rights for ebay software	$100.00	Fee calculator for ebay and paypal fees by Charlestown SW	$4.99
CUSTOM Matching SET template, store, logo, me, sig tag	$74.99	EBAY AUCTIONS Auction Selling	$4.99
SO Cute Children ebay Store Front great for Kids Stuff	$69.99	POWER SELLER SOFTWARE new	
FOUND IT ON EBAY THE EBAY IT IT IS HERE GET IT WHILE SUPPLIES LAST	$49.95	Vintage Fashion Clothing Professional Auction Template	$4.99
eBay University CD - Beyond the Basics - Sell on eBay	$46.00	Cheery store logo 310x90=$4.99	$4.99
Learn how to sell on eBay by eBay!		Pink fairy dust auction template – 100% Original BHPP	$4.99
EBAY CERTIFIED SOFTWARE - SPOONFEEDER STANDARD	$39.95	ebay Fees Calc v 2.2 – Calculate ebay Fees with ease	$4.99
VERSION! System for On-Line Auction Sellers now on CD!		[4 of these sold for $4.99 each]	
[4 of these sold for $39.95 each]		Primitive house sheep crow Ebay auction template JTB	$4.99
The Invisible Clock II - Stay on top of your eBay bids	$39.95	WHOLESALE DROPSHIPPERS CD-DROP-SHIPPER SHIP SHIPPING!!!	$4.99
The best vibrating timer on the market. FREE SHIPPING!!		New GRUNGE Black White auction	$4.99
Auction Timer Invisible Clock II FREE BATTERY & POUCH	$39.95	template unique design simple!	
FREE PRIORITY SHIPPING+Battery+Travel/Storage Pouch		NEW GRUNGE red auction template unique design simple!	$4.99
eBay University Online: BEYOND THE BASICS CD-ROM	$38.52	Denim doll auction template – original design	$4.99
Custom Ebay Auction Template, Logo, Store, Me Page Pack	$36.99	ANIMATED CHRISTMAS SNOWMAN~	$4.99
[2 of these sold for $36.99 each]		SNOWFLAKES AUCTION TEMPLATE	
New To Ebay Source Code For Make Your Own Software	$35.00	NEW EBAY AUCTION WATCHER SOFTWARE + BONUSES	$4.99
EBAY University "The Basics" Instructional CD-ROM NEW!	$33.51	$39.99 Value A Must Have Tool For Sellers & Buyers!!!	
Custom Store Front Design for Mstrackvanschijndel!!	$32.00	SHABBY PINK ROSES CAMEO SOLID	$4.99
Complete Set DAVE ESPINO'S AUCTIONS FOR INCOME with DVD	$31.00	SAGE BKD AUCTION TEMPLATE	

Education & Learning ▶ Preschool-Kindergarten

The average sales price in this subcategory is $12.29.

	HIGH		AVG
LAURIE BERKNER JAMARAMA concert tickets NYC, NEW YORK	$265.00	~2~ books of Alphabet, Number, and Shape Art ~ Kdg	$12.50
7 LEVEL COMMUNICATION BUILDER by ENABLING DEVICES	$197.50	OCCUPATIONAL THERAPY LETTER ID PRE-K GRADE 2 NR	$12.50
15 DAYCARE NURSERY NAP SLEEPING COTS STACKABLE BEDS NR	$192.50	Tiny Signs: Baby Sign Language Video - VHS	$12.50
Montessori Set of 4 Sensorial Educational Products New	$189.00	~ITSY-BITSY SPIDER + BONUS!!!~Flannel Felt Board Set	$12.50
Montessori Training Realia - Complete Bead Set	$184.00	Speak Italian CD language Course Michel Thomas, WORKS!!	$12.50
BBC MUZZY FRENCH COURSE VIDEOS LEVELS 1 & 2 complete	$179.28	6' NEW KIDS CANOPY PARACHUTE PLAY TOY DAYCARE GYM KID	$12.49
BBC MUZZY Italian Level 2 II DVD Kid's Language Edu NEW	$153.51	Little Red Riding Hood Felt Board Set-Speech Therapy	$12.33
Kids Bookshelf-daycare, preschool, classroom,supplies	$134.95	FROG STREET PRESS Colors & Little Books - Kindergarten	$12.05
HOOKED ON PHONICS AGES 4-8 BRAND NEW! Homeschool BIN FS	$129.99	SNOW FAMILY FLANNEL BOARD FELT SET	$12.03
LETTER PEOPLE Reading Readiness Program	$121.50	Lot Begin to Read Phonics Kit and Books	$12.00
Brand New Motorola V330 T-Mobile Phone w/Accessories	$107.50	BEAR WANTS MORE FLANNEL BOARD FELT SET	$12.00
Letter People Childcraft Reading Readiness Program	$107.50	26 interlocking 14" foam rubber squares mat w/alphabet	$12.00
The Letter People Reading Readiness Program Complete	$104.50	Critter Counters- Traffic Signs Math Counting Game	$12.00
HOOKED ON MATH 2004 New Sealed Never Used Complete!	$103.50	COMMOTION IN THE OCEAN FLANNEL BOARD FELT SET	$12.00
CELF 3 Screening Test & Clinical Assistant Speech Lang	$102.50	Letter People CD 300 Phonics Preschool Kindergarten &up	$12.00

Education & Learning ▶ Elementary School

The average sales price in this subcategory is $19.42.

	HIGH		AVG
Edmark Reading program level 1 print Autism ABA, ESL	$315.00	Hooked on Phonics Read to Learn EUC	$19.95
Vintage Dick and Jane Flash Word Cards COMPLETE MIB	$227.50	Children Speech Therapy Illustrated Stories Home School	$19.95
Teacher Resource-SRA Reading Laboratory Kit Level 1C	$205.00	Hooked on Phonics, Cassettes, Workbooks, Cards 99%	$19.50
Switched-on Schoolhouse newer 8th gr. set - 5 subjects	$185.00	complete sets of hooked on phonics with tapes look!!!	$19.50
Switched-on Schoolhouse newer 9th gr. set - 5 subjects	$185.00	USED WRAP UPS WITH CASSETTES	$19.50
Switched-on Schoolhouse NEWEST 5th gr. set - 5 subjects	$185.00	Carson Dellosa Weather Graphing Pocket Chart new!!	$19.49
NEW SLD HOOKED on PHONICS Kindergarden 1st & 2nd grade	$179.99	NEW Magnetic Tabletop Pocket Chart (MANY USES)	$19.45
[2 of these sold for $179.99 each]		HOOKED ON PHONICS SET	$19.00
NEW 2005 HOOKED ON PHONICS LEARN TO READ SET LEVEL 1-5	$179.99	ABEKA Basic Phonics Flashcards 40517	$19.00
NEW 05/06 ALL CD LEARN TO READ HOOKED on PHONICS wGift!	$179.99	Lakeshore Phonics Fun Wheels	$18.50
Assorted Math Teaching Aids	$178.50	SRA's Hooked On Phonics Reading Power Kit	$18.50
MUZZY NEW BBC DVD / CD * SPANISH * LEVEL 1 COURSE	$177.50	CLASSROOM BULLETIN BOARD	$18.50
MUZZY BBC DVD / CD - SPANISH - LEVEL 1 - XLNT COND	$177.50	ACCENT packs, NEW	
HOOKED ON PHONICS 2005 w/CDs LEVEL 1-5 / GRADES K 1 2	$175.99	Set of 9 Portals to Reading Series Retail Value $160!!	$18.50
Like New BBC Muzzy Spanish Language DVD Level 1	$172.50	Lakeshore Alphabet Mat & 26 Alphabet Items NEW	$18.50
MUZZY DVD/CD Spanish Program *NEW* Overnight shipping only $5.00!	$169.00	God's Design for sex-Stan & Brenna Jones	$18.50

Education & Learning ▶ High School

The average sales price in this subcategory is $18.53.

	HIGH		AVG
Switched-On Schoolhouse, Complete, 10th Grade, 2004 2.0	$159.50	Award-Winning Drivers Education DVD	$24.95
School of tomorrow Chemistry videos and paces	$150.00	USED SAXON MATH ALGEBRA 1 WITH ANSWER AND TEST BOOK	$20.50
Better Basketball improvement videos dvds collection	$149.00	Math Made Easy Algebra Video Tutorial Set + Workbook	$20.50
SWITCHED ON SCHOOLHOUSE 2.0 11th GRADE	$135.00	Where There's A Will There's An A, High School	$20.49
Better Basketball Videos DVDs series with Mike Bibby	$132.50	ESSENTIALS OF BIOLOGY EXCELLENT CONDITION HIGHSCHOOL	$20.00
TI-89 Texas Instruments TI 89 graphing calculator	$85.00	McDougal Littell En Espanol Spanish TE Teacher Edition	$19.99
Driver Ed In A Box Parent Taught Driver Education CD	$84.05	KAPLAN SAT PSAT ACT 2006 Test Prep Software NEW/SEALED	$18.99
TI-84 Plus Silver Edition Graphing Calculator	$76.99	13 Computer Programs for High School Math, Science, +	$17.25
Switched on Schoolhouse 11th Grade	$76.00	Where There's a Will There's an A 6 CDs HIGH SCHOOL	$16.50
WHERE THERE'S A WILL THERE'S AN A	$66.00	Power Glide French Language Course	$15.99
HIGH SCHOOL DVD CD		Algebra 1 & 2, Geometry, Trigonometry Multimedia CD-ROM	$15.00
Early American History by The Teaching Company	$62.96	WHERE THERES A WILL THERES AN A HIGH SCHOOL CD DVD NR	$14.99
Texas Instruments TI-86 Scientific Calculator	$61.00	KAPLAN SAT PSAT ACT 2006 Test Prep Software NEW/SEALED	$14.99
Basic Math Chaulk Dust Company 6 Videos, Book, Teacher	$61.00	[4 of these sold for $14.99 each]	
Where There's A Will There's an A.	$60.95	HOYLE WORD GAMES on Sealed CD ~ 9 Favorites ~ $2 Ship	$14.99
HIGH SCHOOL-CD/VHS		[2 of these sold for $14.99 each]	
A Christian Survey of World History by R. J. Rushdoony	$60.00	TEXAS INSTRUMENTS TI-82 CALCULATOR-LIKE NEW	$14.55

Education & Learning ▶ Adult & Career Education

The average sales price in this subcategory is $42.44.

	HIGH		AVG
Anthony Tony Robbins Package Valued at $36,507.97 NR	$1,630.00	TRANSFER RITE FRISKET FILM AIRBRUSH GRAPHIC PAPER-AUTO	$44.99
Laerdal HeartSim EKG Rhythm Generator Patient Simulator	$1,600.00	Tony Robbins GET THE EDGE! New w/paper &journal FREE SH	$44.37
2004 JAY MITTON Total Tax Lawsuit and ASSET Protection	$1,225.00	David Deangelo Double Your Dating Interview CD w/ SAM	$43.30
INVESTools 2005 Advanced Technical Analysis Program NEW	$885.00	Nursing Diagnosis Cards AND Nursing Drug Cards 2004	$43.00
SCOTT SCHEEL HUGE PROFITS IN COMMERCIAL REAL ESTATE	$830.00	FRW : BARNEY ZICK-PAPER MILLIONAIRE- REAL ESTATE COURSE	$43.00
JJ John Childers Asset Protection Wealth Management LLC	$575.00	THE COMPLETE!!! ANTHONY ROBBINS COLLECTION, 17 CD'S !!!	$43.00
Laerdal HeartSim EKG Rhythm Generator Patient Simulator	$570.00	Teaching Company - After New the Testament DVD	$42.13
Investools/Sucess Magazine Advanced Options set 2005	$513.99	Real Estate Agent Training, Realtor, Realtors Success	$41.99
American Cash Flow Institute ACFI Training Program Lot	$499.99	Mega 12 Marketing Ron Legrand Dan Kennedy NEW DVDS c	$41.88
Wendy Patton 'The System; Lease Options' $1099 value NR	$480.00	GARY_HALBERT_Brian_Tracy_$1497_SEMINAR_25_CD	$41.00
LOT OF 800+ QUIXTAR / AMWAY BUS CD, TAPES, BOOKS, OTHER	$461.00	Netter's Atlas on CD ROM! Surgery & USMLE STEP 1 2 3	$41.00
Keith Cunningham Keys To the Vault Anthony Tony Robbins	$430.00	New Anatomical Bones of SKULL MODEL - Medical	$41.00
Zoll AED Plus Defib Trainer CPR Manikin Ambu Laerdal	$405.00	Quixtar/BWW Cd's PLUS More	$41.00
INVESTools Advanced Options Course *Previous Version*	$405.00	David Knox - Collection of VHS Tapes & Audio	$41.00
Steve Bigalow's Candlestick Trading Seminar DVD + Text	$400.00	Ron LeGrand Guerrilla Marketing Bootcamp Real Estate	$41.00

Education & Learning ▸ School Supplies, Equipment

The average sales price in this subcategory is $16.24.

	HIGH		AVG
Toshiba Satellite A45-S250 / 2.8 GHz Pentium 4 Like New	$798.78	Stampin' Up!*HOLIDAY FRAME*Rubber Stamps*Scrapbooking	$16.50
Elmo EV-2000AF visual presenter	$456.01	Ant Farm Ant Factory Educational Insights science lab	$16.50
Braille N Speak Scholar NIB note taker for blind	$299.99	ANT FARM VILLAGE	$16.50
Best of LED Cordless Portable Teaching Microscopes	$259.00	Little Giant Blackboard Chalk Eraser Cleaner #3364	$16.49
Vintage PERKINS BRAILLER - Works Perfectly- Looks New!!	$255.99	Box Lot of Untested School Supplies Crayola Avery NR	$16.40
6 powers! Teaching Compound Microscope	$235.00	Stampin' Up!*FABULOUS FRUITS*Rubber Stamps*Scrapbooking	$16.29
PSC PowerScan Handheld Scanner PSSR-1000	$200.00	Character Education...WITH MUSIC	$16.27
7 LEVEL COMMUNICATION BUILDER by ENABLING DEVICES	$197.50	*NEW* Case It Z-Binder 2-in-1 Zipper Binder LOOK - NR!!	$16.05
Tektronix High Voltage Oscilloscope Scope Probe P5100	$177.50	PICKETT MINI SLIDE RULE W/CASE No N1006-T	$16.01
SAND AND WATER ACTIVITY TABLE WITH TOP	$169.99	Hundreds Pocket Chart - New	$16.00
NEW! Compound Biological Light Microscope	$169.00	Standard Pocket Chart - New	$16.00
PERKINS BRAILLER TYPEWRITER WITH HARD CASE AND WARRANTY	$168.05	6' parachute/preschool/homeschool/montessori/NEW!!!	$16.00
STUDENT DESKS ! Lot of (106) Bend, Oregon	$158.50	*NEW* Case It Z-Binder 2-in-1 Zipper Binder LOOK - NR!!	$15.95
TEACHERS WIRELESS PUBLIC ADDRESS SYSTEM + 3 VHF MICS	$149.95	LOT School College Supplies Paper Pens Calculator ruler	$15.65
TEACHERS WIRELESS PUBLIC ADDRESS SYSTEM + 3 VHF MICS	$139.95	6' parachute/preschool/homeschool/montessori/NEW!!!	$15.58

Education & Learning ▸ Teaching Supplies, Resources

The average sales price in this subcategory is $17.36.

	HIGH		AVG
Wechsler Intelligence Scale Children (WISC-III) IQ Test	$926.00	Stampin' Up!*HOLIDAY FRAME*Rubber Stamps*Scrapbooking	$16.50
Wechsler Intelligence Scale Children Integ. 4 WISC-IV-I	$795.00	Ant Farm Ant Factory Educational Insights science lab	$16.50
Woodcock-Johnson III Complete Battery / All Test Kits	$745.00	ANT FARM VILLAGE	$16.50
Wechsler Presch. Primary Scale Intelligence 3 WPPSI-III	$599.00	Little Giant Blackboard Chalk Eraser Cleaner #3364	$16.49
Wechsler Adult Intelligence Scale3rd Ed (WAIS-III)	$524.00	Box Lot of Untested School Supplies Crayola Avery NR	$16.40
LETTER PEOPLE - 26 INFLATABLE LETTER CHARACTERS	$510.00	Stampin' Up!*FABULOUS FRUITS*Rubber Stamps*Scrapbooking	$16.29
By Peter Conti & David Finkel - How to Buy Foreclosures	$430.00	Character Education...WITH MUSIC	$16.27
Scott Scheel–Huge Profits In Commercial Real Estate	$365.00	*NEW* Case It Z-Binder 2-in-1 Zipper Binder LOOK - NR!!	$16.05
Clinical Evaluation Language Fundamentals 4 CELF-4	$365.00	PICKETT MINI SLIDE RULE W/CASE No N1006-T	$16.01
Wechsler Individual Achievement Test - 2nd Ed. WIAT-II	$325.00	Hundreds Pocket Chart – New	$16.00
Wechsler Intelligence Scale Children (WISC-III) IQ Test	$309.00	Standard Pocket Chart – New	$16.00
Complete WISC-III (Wechsler) Test Kit	$299.99	6' parachute/preschool/homeschool/montessori/NEW!!!	$16.00
***THE EFFECTIVE TEACHER VIDEO SERIES BY HARRY K. WONG*	$270.50	*NEW* Case It Z-Binder 2-in-1 Zipper Binder LOOK - NR!!	$15.95
Autism Boardmaker 3.6 Macintosh Mayer-Johnson	$256.71	LOT School College Supplies Paper Pens Calculator ruler	$15.65
DISCOVERY VII * D7000 ROBOTIC WORKCELL** $6,000 NEW**	$255.00	6' parachute/preschool/homeschool/montessori/NEW!!!	$15.58

Education & Learning ▸ Other

The average sales price in this subcategory is $40.02.

	HIGH		AVG
Dynavox DynaMyte Systems 3100 Communication device	$2,000.00	Teaching Company. Famous Romans. 24 lectures.	$45.44
TECHCENTER 21 - 3-AXIS CNC MILL-	$860.00	Organic Chemistry Molecular Model Kit plus bonus kit	$45.00
GREAT FOR SMALL SHOPS!!		Anyone can write Ad copy w/ this Carl Galletti Course	$44.99
InvesTools Advanced Options Trading Program	$685.05	TI-83 Plus Graphing Calculator Good Condition ,extras	$42.00
How to Buy Foreclosures by Peter Conti & David Finkel	$567.67	TI-83 Calculator by Texas Instruments	$41.23
Hofstra University Voucher Credits	$550.00	David DeAngelo/David Shade's Masterful Lover Manual	$41.00
InvesTools Advanced Technical Analysis Program	$511.47	how to blow Glass Pipe Instructional video blown glass	$40.00
05 Lease Purchase Claude Diamond	$410.00	[3 of these sold for $40.00 each]	
Wendy Patton NR Bonus		LOT PMBR REVIEW CASSETTE TAPES FOR MBE EXAM	$40.00
Michigan - Ohio State Football Tickets - U of M -	$408.00	New York Times Touch Screen Crossword Puzzle New	$39.99
David Lindahl Apartment House Riches	$396.00	Mike Ferry's Handling Objections	$39.00
Laureate Software Package Autism & Learning disability	$311.00	Gonzagarredi Montessori Inset Display Boards Set	$38.50
Forex, Stock Market Option,Day Trading ,Darlene Nelson	$300.00	BROAD STAIRS AKA BROWN STAIRS MONTESSORI DAYCARE	$38.00
Directing Commercials Seminar 2 day workshop on video	$275.17	Birth Model Kit mini pelvis/baby/uterus Doula Midwife	$37.94
David DeAngelo/Mystery Video Archive 5 DVD Set	$271.00	[5 of these sold for $37.94 each]	
Mystery Method 5 DVD Series-Pickup Artist reveals All!	$269.00	Lot 64 pcs REAL UNMOUNTED BUTTERFLIES- (D I Y)	$37.00
Werner Erhard EST Forum LOTS OF TAPES	$256.06	Destinos hardcover text book with full cd set!	$36.77

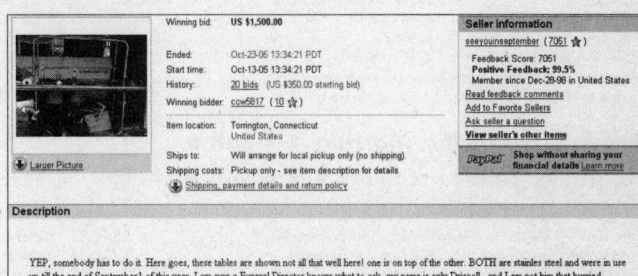

Funeral & Cemetery ▸ Caskets

The average sales price in this subcategory is $131.12.

	HIGH		AVG
23 Caskets for sale	$1,800.00	PRIME IMPORT MAHOGANY REAL	$155.16
FUNERAL CASKET - COFFIN 18 GAUGE METAL NEW!!	$499.00	CASKET COFFIN also HALLOWEEN	
Rare Antique Salesman Sample Funeral Coffin Casket	$400.00	PRIME IMPORT MAHOGANY REAL CASKET COFFIN	$127.51
Casket, White with pink trim	$300.00	Antique Childs Childrens Coffin Casket 43 Inch	$127.50
PRIME IMPORT MAHOGANY REAL CASKET COFFIN HALF COUCH	$202.50	ORIGINAL LATE 1800'S CHILDS COFFIN CASKET FUNERAL	$113.61
PRIME IMPORT MAHOGANY REAL	$199.95	Antique Childs Childrens Coffin Casket 63 Inch	$102.50
CASKET COFFIN also HALLOWEEN		PRIME IMPORT MAHOGANY REAL CASKET COFFIN HALF COUCH	$86.00
ANTIQUE CHILD'S CASKET COFFIN FUNERAL MORTUARY	$169.99	Custom Handmade Pet Caskets	$75.00

Funeral & Cemetery ▸ Cemetery Plots

The average sales price in this subcategory is $1,474.15.

HIGH TO LOW

			AVG
2 Pacific View Memorial Park Cemetery Plots NR	$6,000.00	One pair of Cemetery sites, plots, East Hanover, N.J.	$775.00
Pacific View Memorial Park Cemetery Plot NR	$3,000.00	(2) Adjacent Kensico Cemetery, Valhalla NY Grave Plots	$611.00
Cemetary Plot. Rose Hills Whittier California	$2,500.00	Ft. Lincoln Cemetery, Washington DC, Maryland	$449.00
4 CEMETERY PLOTS, ROSELAND PARK, BERKLEY MICH. CHEAP!!!	$1,200.00	2 Cemetary plots, Paxton, Massachusetts	$202.50

Funeral & Cemetery ▸ Cremation Urns

The average sales price in this subcategory is $43.84.

	HIGH		AVG
Dolpins Urn, Cast Bronze companion by Batesville	$300.00	GORGEOUS MOTHER OF PEARL FUNERAL CREMATION URN URNS	$45.00
VICTORIAN MARBLE LIDDED FUNERAL	$188.49	[2 of these sold for $45.00 each]	
CREMATION ASH BOX / URN		CLASSIC BRONZE FUNERAL CREMATION URN URNS - 9" TALL	$45.00
pet.urn.etched.engraved.marble.cremation.custom	$185.00	[2 of these sold for $45.00 each]	
New Mahogany Wood Cremation Urn	$129.00	Pet Urn - Walnut & Hard Maple	$44.99
Solid Cherry Wood Cremation Urn	$127.50	Pet Urn - Brazilian Cherry & Maple	$43.99
Solid Cherry Wood Cremation Urn	$125.00	BRZ 23 Bronze grapevine with dove cremation urn	$41.00
[3 of these sold for $125.00 each]		LIGHTHOUSE URN	$41.00
pet.urn.etched.engraved.marble.cremation.custom	$125.00	Pet Urn - One of a kind -Spalted Maple	$41.00
PEWTER ANGEL FUNERAL CREMATION URN -	$100.00	FUNERAL BLACK CERAMIC CHOKIN ART CREMATION URN	$39.95
2 NEW URNS W/CASE		PEWTER YOUTH/PET URN	$36.95
EXQUISITE FUNERAL CREMATION URN,URNS W/CASE & MEDALLION	$100.00	Customized Ceramic Cat Beloved Pet Cremation Urn	$36.00
GOING HOME FUNERAL CREMATION URN-2 NEW URNS W/CASE	$100.00	[3 of these sold for $36.00 each]	
[3 of these sold for $100.00 each]		HARDWOOD, WOOD FUNERAL CREMATION URN,	$35.99
MOTHER OF PEARL ADULT BRASS FUNERAL CREMATION URN, URNS	$100.00	WOODEN URNS HUMAN	
[2 of these each sold for $100.00 each]		Cobalt Celtic Knot Cremation Urn Urns Jewelry Necklace Urn	$35.00
EXQUISITE FUNERAL CREMATION URN,URNS W/CASE & MEDALLION	$100.00	[2 of these sold for $35.00 each]	
MAHOGANY WOOD CREMATION URN -THE ODYSSEY	$99.99	CREMATION URN ROSE URN	$35.00
CAT & BIRD SPARROW MEMORIAL SCULPTURE URN ORIGINAL	$99.00	Cobalt Angel Cremation Urn Urns Jewelry Necklace	$35.00
New Mahogany Wood Cremation Urn	$99.00	Medium Monument Style Pet Urn	$34.95

Funeral & Cemetery ▸ Mortuary Supplies

The average sales price in this subcategory is $65.34.

	HIGH		AVG
Two-(2) 6 Foot Stainless Steel Funeral Embalming Tables	$1,500.00	2 VINTAGE EMBALMING ADJUSTABLE HEAD BLOCKS - NO RESERVE	$100.00
DUO TRONIC EMBALMING MACHINE FUNERAL GOTHIC	$566.78	Over 150 vintage Mortuary, embalming supplies	$91.00
Misc. Embalming Tools Dodge Etc.	$363.99	Old Embalming Instruments and items Lot#7	$82.01
OLD EMBALMING INSTRUMENTS AND ITEMS - NO RESERVE	$330.52	Vintage Church Truck Casket Dolly	$81.00
VINTAGE PORTABLE FUNERAL EMBALMING KIT	$310.00	Embalming, History,Theory & Practice, Mayer, 1996 Book	$76.00
One set of Funeral Home Torcheres and Candles	$305.00	LOT OF EMBALMING INSTRUMENTS	$76.00
Old Embalming Instruments and items Lot#4	$304.01	DODGE Trocar-Embalming/Funeral–GLASS SIGHT TUBE Model	$66.99
Old Embalming Instruments and items Lot#9	$280.25	Old Antique Funeral Embalming Headrest	$60.01
ROYAL BOND CASKET "CHURCH TRUCK"	$275.00	Slaughter Trocar-Embalming/Funeral–HYPO or BABY TROCAR	$59.00
TURNER PORTA-BOY FUNERAL EMBALMING MACHINE	$270.00	VINTAGE EMBALMING MACHINE BY CHAMPION - NO RESERVE	$56.50
Old Embalming Instruments and items Lot#6	$258.25	Vintage Church Truck Casket Dolly	$56.00
$740 Embalming Fluid Pump Device NR	$256.79	Embalming Fluid Bottle- SATIN GLASS Art Deco Shape G40	$52.51
Embalming Instruments Funeral Home Embalmer	$255.51	EMBALMING FEATURE SETTING INJECTOR FUNERAL GOTH	$52.50
Embalming hand instruments/ Silence of the lambs	$230.00	Vintage 1930's Embalming Pump, Blood Tray,Bottle &Tools	$52.25
Vintage Undertaker Mortician Embalming Kit Early 1900's	$222.50	Hand Blown Glass Embalming Gravity Jar (Percolator)	$51.99

Genealogy ▸ Births, Marriages, Deaths

The average sales price in this subcategory is $14.62.

	HIGH		AVG
Canon MP 90 Microfilm / Microfiche Reader Printer +NICE	$549.95	History of Dauphin Co., PA & Genealogical Memoirs, 1907	$15.00
Hand Written Genealogy YOUNGS FAMILY Southold Town L.I	$228.27	Genealogies of the Families of the Presidents	$15.00
Genealogy - DELAWARE COUNTY OHIO Tombstone Inscriptions	$127.75	FTM # 502 - Massachusetts Town, Probate & Vital Records	$14.99
Genealogy Diary of Joshua Hempstead of New London, CT	$90.99	Crittenden County Kentucky KY Marriages pre-1900	$14.99
1830-1900's FAIRFIELD MAINE CHURCH HISTORY	$75.99	Canada Genealogy Source Records 1800's Canadian	$14.99
Bucks County, PA - Collection of 8 Historic books	$75.00	VIRGINIA BIBLE RECORDS GENEALOGY SOFTWARE - NEW -	$14.95
MASSACHUSETTS VITAL RECORDS MINT 9 CDS	$69.99	Marriage, Cemetery Records IN, KY, LA, MS, TN, More!!	$14.50
Family Tree Maker Disc (34)	$68.99	Giles County Virginia Marriages 1806-1850 Genealogy VA	$14.50
Franklin County, PA - Collection of 18 Historic books	$66.00	History of Cumberland & Adams Co., PA, 1886	$14.26

MICR-FICHE IGI ENTIRE RECORDS CORNWALL ENGLAND	$59.99	Adam Clarke 4v THE HOLY BIBLE 1837 1853 Coats genealogy	$13.51
OHIO SOURCE RECORDS genealogy book Family Descendants	$56.50	Genealogy and History of OSWEGO County New York	$13.50
GENEALOGY DOCUMENTS/FAMILY BIBLE	$56.00	City of St. Louis Missouri Blue Book for 1913 Genealogy	$13.47
KY KENTUCKY DEATH INDEX 1811 1986 183 MICROFICHE SET	$52.00	Maryland Families Lineage in DAR SAR Genealogy 2640+pg	$13.00
MISSOURI AREA CEMETERIES & FAMILIES OF DENT COUNTY	$51.00	MAYFLOWER QUARTERLY BINDER WITH 10 ISSUES 60'S	$13.00
Corinth, Orange County, Vermont - 9 Cemetery Listings	$51.00	Kentucky KY Court Records - 383 pages-Tons of Names!	$12.99

Genealogy ▶ Census Records

The average sales price in this subcategory is $12.50.

	HIGH		AVG
30 Rolls Microfilm Texas Federal Census 1920	$96.58	1890 Civil War census Knox County, Ohio genealogy	$12.99
1900 UNITED STATES Government 12th CENSUS Book DETAILED	$61.00	1890 Civil War census Medina County, Ohio genealogy	$12.99
Complete 1880 US Census on 35 CDs	$52.00	1890 Civil War census Muskingum County, Ohio genealogy	$12.99
1841 CHESHIRE, ENGLAND CENSUS cd set	$47.00	1890 Civil War census Portage County, Ohio genealogy	$12.99
1860 THE EIGHTH CENSUS PRE CIVIL WAR SLAVERY STATS	$37.01	1890 Civil War census Tuscarawas County, Ohio genealogy	$12.99
1880 UNITED STATES CENSUS AND NATIONAL INDEX	$36.00	1850 OH OHIO Census MUSKINGUM Genealogy 2 microfilm	$12.54
4 hrs of Family History Research! Great Gift Idea!	$30.00	1881 BRITISH CENSUS AND NATIONAL INDEX	$12.50
[3 of these sold for $30.00 each]		1908 TUFTONBORO, N. H. HISTORY-CENSUS	$12.00
1841 LANCASHIRE, ENGLAND CENSUS cd set	$26.99	1890 Civil War census Pike County, Ohio genealogy	$10.99
1905 CENSUS of WYOMING 13 p	$26.05	PAULDING COUNTY OHIO 1900's SOUVENIR NED'S SCHOOL	$10.80
Cherokee Indian Genealogy Six Books CD-Rom Research	$26.00	GENEALOGY RESEARCH UNITED STATES CENSUS THRU 1930	$10.51
[3 of these sold for $26.00 each]		1840 OH OHIO MUSKINGUM COUNTY MICROFILM	$10.50
1790 State of Maryland Federal Census for Genealogy	$26.00	New Jersey in 1773 Abstract & Index Militia Census	$10.49
1850 Census South Central Kentucky KY genealogy	$24.99	1880 OHIO Census MUSKINGUM Genealogy	$9.99
Genealogy C.D.s The London 1891 Census (38 Boxed CDs)	$24.99	NOBLE Ottawa OH	
4 hrs of Family History Research! Great Gift Idea!	$20.00	THE 1787 CENCUS OF VIRGINIA	$9.99
1800 State of Pennsylvania Federal Census for Genealogy	$19.00	MECKLENBURG COUNTY 1987	

Genealogy ▶ City, State Directories

The average sales price in this subcategory is $35.83.

	HIGH		AVG
1896 COLORADO STATE BUSINESS DIRECTORY	$872.00	1968 TAMPA FL SUBURBAN DIRECTORY	$37.00
1876 LEAVENWORTH CITY DIRECTORY W/ABERNATHY CATALOG	$409.00	Canton Ohio & Area Official City Directory ~ 1930-1931	$37.00
1929 WASHINGTON DC CITY DIRECTORY	$405.00	1943 Oakland, Alameda, Berkeley, San Leandro Phone Book	$36.09
RARE 1898-99 Los Angeles, Pasadena, Pomona, ++ BUSINES	$393.99	VINTAGE Polk's PEORIA Illinois 1963 CITY Directory L@@K	$36.01
1942 LOS ANGELES CITY DIRECTORY - TELEPHONE BOOK	$383.00	1929 Grand Rapids Holland Grand Haven Phone Directory	$36.01
RARE 1889 WICHITA KANSAS CITY DIRECTORY	$361.00	Vermont - 1881 county gazetteer & business Directory	$36.01
1875 LEAVENWORTH CITY DIRECTORY W/ABERNATHY CATALOG	$321.00	FARMERS DIRECTORY OF BALTIMORE COUNTY MARYLAND 1915	$36.00
VINTAGE CAMDEN COUNTY NJ CITY DIRECTORY MANY ADS!! 1946	$304.98	1936 TULARE COUNTY (CALIF) Directory	$35.09
1915 Summer Social Register and Dilatory Domiciles	$265.00	Crawford County Pennsylvania 'Our County & Its People'	$35.02
LARGE LEATHER 1879 HISTORY of ADAMS COUNTY ILLINOIS	$260.00	Springfield Missouri Credit Guide City Directory 1919	$35.00
1884 SOUTH BEND INDIANA CITY DIRECTORY	$256.61	1947 Directory New Brighton Rochester Beaver Falls, Pa	$35.00
Antique 1895 Boston MA City Directory Mass Genealogy	$230.39	CUSHING, IOWA CENTENNIAL BOOK 1883-1983	$35.00
1918 LOS ANGELES CITY DIRECTORY - TELEPHONE PHONE BOOK	$204.52	1932 BEVERLY HAMILTON WENHAM TOPSFIELD MA DIRECTORY	$34.99
RARE 1891 OAKLAND, ALAMEDA, BERKELEY CA CITY DIRECTORY	$196.50	1949 Huron County Ohio Directory Norwalk Willard	$34.66
1884 Manchester, NH Directory 13,000 names Maps RARE	$175.00	1927 POPLAR BLUFF MO MISSOURI TELEPHONE DIRECTORY BOOK	$34.00

Genealogy ▶ Family Trees

The average sales price in this subcategory is $17.35.

	HIGH		AVG
Genealogy "Vanessa Bell Family Album" England Photos	$102.50	Family Tree Maker 2005 COLLECTORS Edition 13 CD Set NEW	$18.89
FAMILY TREE MAKER DELUXE 24-CD SET~ BRAND NEW NR	$82.50	NEW! Family Tree Maker 2005 COLLECTORS Software 13 CD's	$18.89
[10 of these sold in a multiple item ("Dutch") auction for $8.25 each]		[3 of these sold for $18.99 each]	
1908 Debrett's Peerage Baronetage Knightage Genealogy	$66.50	GENEALOGY OF CHILD, CHILDS, & CHILDE FAMILY	$18.50
Historic Homesteads~DAR~Genealogy~ 1st Ed~1930	$66.00	Family Tree Maker Virginia Geneologies #1 & Kentucky #1	$18.00
GENEALOGY DOCUMENTS/FAMILY BIBLE	$56.00	TAYLOR Genealogy/Family History Book PDF/CD Format	$17.49
BLACK AMERICANA SCRAPBOOK:WOMANS COLLEGIATE/1920'S-BEST	$56.00	Family Tree Maker 2005 COLLECTORS Edition 13 CD Set NEW	$16.89
MISSOURI AREA CEMETERIES & FAMILIES OF DENT COUNTY	$51.00	Family Tree Maker Early Alabama, Ark., Miss. settlers	$16.00
GIDEON MACON OF VIRGINA & SOME DESCENDANTS SIGNED NR!!	$51.00	BOOTH Genealogy/Family History Book PDF/CD Format	$15.99
PEABODY (PAYBODY,PABODY,PABODIE) GENEALOGY 1909 HB NR!!	$49.95	COLEMAN Genealogy/Family History Book PDF/CD Format	$15.99
The Coffin Family Edited By Louis Coffin	$48.55	History & genealogy of the Bell Family, largely ALABAMA	$15.54
Book, The Cooley Genealogy, 1st Print, 1941	$48.00	Family Portrait Dallas Texas Pierce Byrd Pierceall Book	$15.00
Shuey Family History in America by D.B. Shuey 1919 RARE	$46.00	Thomas BEALE Genealogy/Family History PDF/CD Format	$14.99
RARE 1778 DEED - York Pa - Signed JOHN HAY & WM LEAS	$43.00	BLEDSOE Genealogy/Family History Book PDF/CD Format	$14.99
Family Medley 1842 Genealogical Talcott Grosvenor Mass	$42.00	SLAUGHTER Genealogy/Family History PDF/CD Format	$14.99
Family Tree Maker-2006	$41.25	Thomas Gaines Genealogy/Family History PDF/CD Format	$14.99

Genealogy ▶ Military Records

The average sales price in this subcategory is $20.36.

	HIGH		AVG
7 vols Georgia Roster of the Confederate Soldiers of GA	$250.00	- HUGE! Patriots at Cowpens 100's Names 156 Sources	$24.95
COLONIAL SOLDIERS Pre-Rev War Military Record genealogy	$76.00	Tennessee Court Martial - War of 1812 GENEALOGY	$24.95
FAMILY TREE MAKER GENEALOGY CD	$71.00	Muskingum Co.Ohio Zanesville-Men & Women in WWII book	$24.50
ROMS CIVIL WAR MILITARY		History Old Cheraws, St. David's Parish South Carolina	$23.95
Genealogy Soldiers North Carolina American Revolution	$67.69	DAR Patriot Index Volume 3, Indexed by Wives Names	$23.45
COLONIAL SOLDIERS Pre-Rev War Military Record genealogy	$59.78	2 LOUISA County Virginia Genealogy Books~Rev War~Land	$20.50
Very RARE MAINE ME Genealogy Revolutionary War Soldiers	$50.27	Confederate Civil War Service Record Search	$20.50

1958 U. S. Army Register, active and retired lists	$49.98	N.Y. THE REVOLUTION AS A COLONY& STATE GENEALOGY BOOK	$19.99
Czech Czechoslovakian Civil War Military Genealogy TX	$49.95	MEXICAN REVOLUTION HISTORY OF PANCHO VILLA & SAM DREBAN	$19.95
Historical Register U.S. Army 1789-1903 POW KIA Wounded	$39.00	Annals of Newberry County South Carolina genealogy	$19.95
Roster of the Confederate Soldiers of Georgia	$35.00	Confederate Civil War Service Record Search	$19.95
History of Spartanburg County, SC by Landrum	$32.95	Photographic History of the CIVIL WAR 10 Vols on CD	$19.50
Richmond Battlefields Virginia Civil War Written 1961	$30.99	[2 of these sold for $19.50 each]	
JOHNSONS ISLAND FEDERAL PRISON	$30.00	WEST VIRGINIA REVOLUTIONARY ANCESTORS by A.W. Reddy	$19.28
4 DAR Patriot Centennial Index American Revolution Book	$26.00	TEXAS REVOLUTION - SAN JACINTO - IST HAND ACCOUNT	$19.00
- HUGE! Patriots at Cowpens 100's Names 156 Sources	$24.95	ALAMO - GENEALOGY OF MEN KILLED - TEXAS REV.	$19.00
		[2 of these sold for $19.00 each]	

Genealogy ▸ Other

The average sales price in this subcategory is $16.22.

	HIGH		AVG
1800's ROOD FAMILY photo album ALLEN-PECK-ELTON—MA CT	$305.00	FTM CD 317 United States 1850 Federal Census Index	$16.50
1839 ME VT CT RI MA NH counties towns rivers WHITE MTNS	$272.09	LIST OF COLONIAL NEW YORK INHABITANTS GENEALOGY BOOK	$16.50
1914 New Ipswich New Hampshire History Genealogy Book	$132.49	Genealogy and History of YONKERS, New York	$16.50
1885 History of McDonough County Illinois Macomb Adair!	$127.40	Introduction Historic Resources In Washington County NY	$16.50
American Families of German Ancestry	$125.00	History of the Western Reserve, pub 1910 (NE Ohio)	$16.49
Genealogy Dictionary of New England 4 Vols Savage	$124.99	Tazewell County, Virginia VA Marriage Book 3 GENEALOGY	$16.47
SIGNED Massachusetts Genealogy THE ROTCHES Rare HC	$119.99	1925 BOOK:DESCENDANTS OF JOEL JONES AND LEMUEL SMITH	$16.04
THE NATIONAL BANK OF LIGONIER 1915-1920 CHECKS	$118.50	Fayette County Co History PA Pennsylvania 1882 980+pgs	$16.01
Set American Ancestry Lineages Genealogy US 1889!	$109.10	Missouri MO Pioneers Volume V GENEALOGY	$16.00
first documented history of jackson county, indiana	$105.18	Gateway to the West - Ohio Pioneers, News, Obits +++	$16.00
OLD NEW ENGLAND history mayflower founders genealogy	$104.49	Pennsylvania Genealogy and History Vol. XXI No. 4	$16.00
1941 OLD CHICAGO HOMES architecture genealogy gothic HB	$104.02	1903 Biography & History of Jackson County Michigan MI	$15.99
Historical Atlas Union County Ohio 1877	$103.50	Genealogy of Canterbury New Hampshire Merrimack Co NH	$15.99
1981 MAYFLOWER ANCESTRAL INDEX genealogy ref hb FN	$102.50	History of the Western Reserve, pub 1910 (NE Ohio)	$15.99
1850's MOULTON family HANDWRITTEN Hampton NH Newbury MA	$102.50	1896 Bio Encyclopedia of Dauphin County Pennsylvania PA	$15.99

Gifts & Occasions ▸ Costumes

The average sales price in this subcategory is $33.42.

	HIGH		AVG
King Arthur Roman Muscle Armor Greek Spartan Cuirass	$499.99	Adult Halloween costume Mystery Woman 83123 Sz M/L	$34.95
Smokey Bear mascot/costume-mint	$338.33	INFLATABLE HORSE ADULT HALLOWEEN COSTUME NEW	$34.01
SCOOBY DOO Adult Mascot Costume - Halloween Costume	$330.00	NEW ADULT AIRBLOWN INFLATABLE HORSE RIDER COSTUME GEMMY	$34.00
Brand new Brown dog professional mascot costume	$294.09	Gemmy HORSE RIDER Costume airblown Inflatable Halloween	$34.00
MINNIE MOUSE look-a-like Adult costume - Disney Mickey	$283.99	[2 of these sold for $34.00 each]	
Dora Look-A-Like Adult Costume	$269.99	Dark Vampire Slayer Costume Robe MEDIEVAL WARRIOR: Long	$33.98
Professional Brown Dog Mascot Costume	$255.01	NEW TOM ARMA INFANT TURTLE HALLOWEEN COSTUME 18-24 MON	$33.01
PROFESSIONAL CUSTOM ADULT MASCOT COSTUME	$255.00	Fred & Barney Flintstone Flintstones Costume (203)	$33.00
TEDDY BEAR MASCOT COSTUME * ADULT * ADORABLE	$247.50	Sexy Punk 5 PC Leopard Print Cave Woman Costume ML	$33.00
* MICKEY MOUSE * look-a-like Adult Costume * Disney *	$229.99	CHILDS PLAY CHUCKY ADULT OVERHEAD LATEX MASK *NEW*	$33.00
EEYORE look-a-like Adult Moscot costume *winnie pooh*	$211.75	INFLATABLE RODEO BULL ADULT HALLOWEEN COSTUME NEW	$33.00
GOLD NEW ELVIS LAS VEGAS BELT 4	$192.50	ADULT MEDUSA HALLOWEEN COSTUME FITS TO SIZE 16 NEW	$33.00
JUMPSUIT orANY COSTUME		Star Wars Darth Maul Costume	$33.00
PROFESSIONAL CUSTOM ADULT MASCOT COSTUME	$177.50	15895200 Warrior Halloween Adult Costume NEW	$33.00
Unique Pandora Paisley belly dance costume ~Peacock	$169.99	LARGE GOTHIC 32" x 34" BLACK RED Feather ANGEL WINGS	$32.99
Gene Simmons Illusive Concepts Costume	$167.50	Swashbuckler PUFFY SHIRT/PANTS PIRATE/COLONIAL COSTUME	$32.98
		[2 of these sold for $32.98 each]	

King Arthur Roman Muscle Armor Greek Spartan Cuirass

Description:

Absolutely Stunning!

Excellent Quality, Hand Forged King Arthur Muscle Curiass and Shoulder Armor

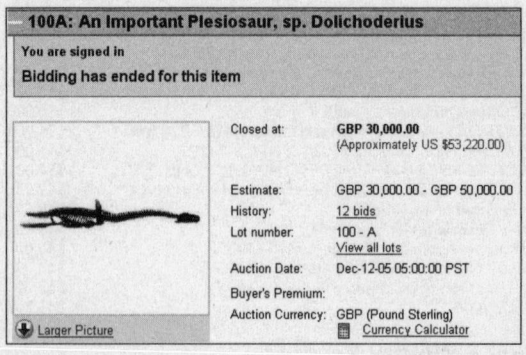

100A: An Important Plesiosaur, sp. Dolichoderius

You are signed in
Bidding has ended for this item

Closed at:	GBP 30,000.00
	(Approximately US $53,220.00)
Estimate:	GBP 30,000.00 - GBP 50,000.00
History:	12 bids
Lot number:	100 - A
	View all lots
Auction Date:	Dec-12-05 05:00:00 PST
Buyer's Premium:	
Auction Currency:	GBP (Pound Sterling)
	Currency Calculator

Larger Picture

Gifts & Occasions ▸ Gag Gifts

The average sales price in this subcategory is $10.38.

	HIGH		AVG
Adult Sissy Dress ~ Pink Flower Organza,~ BY ME	$150.00	The Original BUTT / FACE TOWEL Gag Gift Bath Beach FUN	$10.49
Adult Sissy Dress ~` Blue organza Ruffle ~Custom Fit	$150.00	[3 of these sold for $10.49 each]	
HighRisk strait straight jacket goth gothic white M/L	$95.99	2 EYE SHADES -DO NOT DISTURB/SLEEP IN BEAUTY -Blindfold	$10.49
NEW SMALL STRAIGHT STRAIT	$75.05	The Original BUTT / FACE TOWEL Gag Gift Bath Beach FUN	$10.49
JACKET RESTRAINT GOTH GOTHIC		BRAND NEW MASTER THIGH EXERCISER THIGHMASTER GREAT GIFT	$10.42

$75 BEST BUY GIFT CARD / CERTIFICATE NEVER EXPIRES NEW	$66.07	BUTT / FACE Towel Great Bachelor Gag Gift NEW ButtFace	$10.25
Strait straight jacket restraint goth gothic white L	$65.99	NOVELTY REDNECK HORN GREAT STRESS RELIEVER	$10.00
Strait straight jacket restraint goth gothic white L	$62.99	DADDY DIAPER TOOL BELT "FREE SHIPPING"	$10.00
Strait straight jacket restraint goth gothic Black L	$61.99	[2 of these sold for $10.00 each]	
NEW MEDIUM STRAIGHT STRAIT	$61.00	ANTENNA TOPPER/ COWBOY CACTUS	$10.00
JACKET RESTRAINT GOTH GOTHIC		Mr. Wonderful talking doll NIB	$10.00
Strait straight jacket restraint goth gothic Black XL	$57.99	White trash cooler	$10.00
Porn Alexus Winston Vib Pussy Ass Vagina 1st BID BUY IT	$54.99	[2 of these sold in a multiple item ("Dutch") auction for $5.00 each]	
[2 of these sold for $54.99 each]		DADDY DIAPER TOOL BELT "FREE SHIPPING"	$10.00
NEW LARGE STRAIGHT STRAIT JACKET RESTRAINT GOTH GOTHIC	$52.00	TIC TAC type mints candies Bridal Shower favors	$10.00
NEW LARGE STRAIGHT STRAIT JACKET RESTRAINT GOTH GOTHIC	$51.01	PAIR OF LIFE- LIKE BOOBS! STRESS RELIEF OR GAG GIFT!	$10.00
NEW SMALL STRAIGHT STRAIT JACKET RESTRAINT GOTH GOTHIC	$51.00	[5 of these sold for $10.00 each]	
HOOTERS @@ name tag @@ H@@TERS!...NICE!	$51.00	TUMBLEWEED POTTERY ASHES OF PROBLEM CLIENTS JAR	$10.00
		(SEXY CUTE!) HOT PINK SATIN BRA with MATCHING THONG!!	$9.99

Gifts & Occasions ▶ Gift Baskets

The average sales price in this subcategory is $21.64.

	HIGH		AVG
Allure Best of Beauty Gift Bag	$765.55	OPEN A GOURMET CANDY GIFT BASKET BUSINESS FROM HOME $$	$22.00
The Best of Scott Barnes, Celebrity Makeup Artist	$764.29	[3 of these sold for $22.00 each]	
Luxurious At-Home Spa Essentials by Cl?e Peau Beaut?	$633.00	Sigma Nu Gift Set, Retail Value $54.40	$22.00
Gift Basket supplies - $WORTH$ Thousands- BRAND NEW lot	$515.05	GODIVA CHOCOLATE GOLDEN TEMPTATION GIFT BASKET	$22.00
HUGH~ LOT~337 BASKETS~Going out of Business~	$500.00	2 sets Brown Wicker Baskets	$21.79
tarte cosmetics product collection	$459.00	24" x 500' Gift Basket Wrap Clear Cellophane CELLO Roll	$21.50
A $500 Gift Certificate to Henri Bendel	$455.00	Tri Delta Delta Delta Buttons, Retail Value $50.00	$21.49
Victoria's Secret PINK collection	$451.89	~Lot of 6~Gift Baskets~CLEARANCE~	$21.07
A LOUNGE FOR LIFE GIFT BAG	$445.00	Godiva Gift Basket - Chocolate, Candy, NEW	$21.00
HUGE GIFT BASKET BUSINESS INVENTORY	$405.00	roll of gift basket wrap CLEAR 300'x40" cello	$21.00
LOTS OF STUFF LOOK!		Cinderella basket NIB disney dvd, doll, wand, & More	$20.51
Sephora Train Case Product Collection	$373.59	Basket of Pheromones	$20.50
Victoria's Secret Beauty Gift Collection	$355.00	Beautiful Godiva Chocolate Goldent Temptati Gift Basket	$20.50
Bobbi Brown Beauty Basket	$340.00	4 Hinged Chest Box Trunk Gift Basket Supplies Lot	$20.50
Laura Mercier Product Collection	$327.79	Huge Lot of Baskets-Gift Basket Supplies & More-Nice!	$20.50
2005 DuWop Oscar Gift	$306.26	LOT 10 LATTE' BATH/BODY GIFT BASKET SUPPLIES &SHRED/BOW	$20.50

Gifts & Occasions ▶ Greeting Cards

The average sales price in this subcategory is $8.24.

	HIGH		AVG
$300 TARGET.COM ONLINE GIFT CARD	$255.00	LOT OF 50 NEW ASSORTED AMERICAN	$8.50
NEW lot of 100 Christmas Photo Cards CUSTOM	$65.00	GREETINGS CARDS $200 NR	
*** Lot 741 AMERICAN GREETINGS Cards & Envelopes ***	$61.22	HANDMADE CARDS *assortment of 10 cards Friends, etc.	$8.49
Cavalier King Charles Spaniel Christmas Cards #2	$60.00	143 vintage 60s CHRISTMAS CARDS glitter and more	$8.49
[4 of these sold in a multiple item ("Dutch") auction for $15.00 each]		Lot of 49 nw Hallmark Thanksgiving Cards-over $80	$8.40
NEW lot of 100 Christmas Photo Cards CUSTOM	$54.00	HALLMARK BARBIE CHRISTMAS CARDS	$8.37
NEW Box of 10 Christmas Photo Cards CUSTOM	$50.00	(HUMOROUS) 20 CARDS	
[5 of these sold in a multiple item ("Dutch") auction for $10.00 each]		Assortment of stamped greeting cards CTMH	$8.37
500 christmas greeting cards wholesale envelopes NIP	$50.00	36 Birds on Feeder Christmas cards Happy Holidays NIP	$8.27
Brand New Japanese Christmas/New Years Cards Mt. Fuji	$50.00	100 name brand greeting cards with env.+ more	$8.00
[2 of these sold in a multiple item ("Dutch") auction for $25.00 each]		40 Baby Duck Thank You Notes NIB	$8.00
Jukebox Holiday Cards Wurlitzer 950 Rockola Gazelle MIB	$50.00	THANK YOU CARDS Boxed Set of Art Nouveau MUDLARK	$8.00
[4 of these sold in a multiple item ("Dutch") auction for $12.50 each]		THE GRINCH and MAX Boxed CHRISTMAS CARDS - NEW!	$8.00
Crane's Christmas Cards 5 Full Boxes of 10 Cards Each	$49.00	Calico Cat with Christmas Tree Cards!! Unique cards!	$8.00
Crane's Christmas Cards 3 Full Boxes of 10 Cards Each	$45.99	BRAND NEW INK JET FEATHER EDGE	$8.00
Dalmation Inflatable Santa Dog	$44.99	GREETING CARDS BY AVERY	
CHRISTMAS BOXED CARDS	$42.00	4 NEW SEALED BOXES DISNEY WINNIE	$8.00
TIFFANY & CO. ANDY WARHOL HEAVY GRADE CHRISTMAS CARDS	$41.00	POOH CHRISTMAS CARDS	
Holly Pond Hill - Susan Wheeler Article RARE &5 cards!	$41.00	100 name brand greeting cards with env.+ more	$8.00

Gifts & Occasions ▶ Party Supplies

The average sales price in this subcategory is $12.33.

	HIGH		AVG
SALE.Sale..SALE!! Variety of 13 GIFt/FAVOR box SAMPLES	$235.00	1 Gr. of Party Poppers! #Great for Labor Day Parties#	$12.95
Classy Wrap Gift in a Balloon Machine	$511.99	Big Brother/Sister T-shirt Order to match your children	$12.95
Balloon Stuffing - Classy Wrap Machine (USED)	$217.50	IT'S A BOY 1 Ounce .999 Pure Silver Coin..GREAT GIFT!!!	$12.51
Balloon Stuffing - Classy Wrap Machine (USED)	$192.50	GORGEOUS LADYBUG BABY GIRL OUTFIT-SHOWER GIFT NWT!	$12.50
Fundue Foods Chocolate Fondue Fountain	$170.00	30th Birthday napkins, centerpiece & banner	$12.50
HORSE TIRE SWINGS 3 IN A BOX - SPECIAL DEAL	$150.00	Bachelorette Party Plates, Penis Cookie Cutters, Decor	$12.50
Classy Wrap Jiffy Wrap Balloon Stuffer Machine	$142.50	How To, Party Favors Table Decorations, DENNISON 1928	$12.40
CHRISTMAS NATIVITY YARD DECORATION	$135.99	Embossed IVY Border INVITATIONS Cards-Party/Wedding	$12.40
Classy Wrap Balloon Stuffing Machine - Gift in Balloon!	$132.50	[4 of these sold in a multiple item ("Dutch") auction for $3.10 each]	
Cool Aire II Electric Balloon Inflator Air Pump	$81.08	48 Baby Announcements , Monopoly Theme So Cute !	$12.39
PARTY WHEEL OF CHANCE-DRINKING	$76.00	[3 of these sold in a multiple item ("Dutch") auction for $4.13 each]	
GAME-BLACK HAUS BAR ITEM		50 BABY SHOWER INVITATIONS- NOAH'S ARK- ADORABLE	$12.00
WALK IN THE GARDEN - BABY DIAPER CAKE SHOWER GIFT BUGGY	$75.00	Cinderella Party Set 16 Plates Cups Napkins Invites NIP	$12.00
270 PLASTIC CHAMPAGNE FLUTES (FACETED)!!	$69.99	288 Assort Baby Shower Favor Favors Pacifiers	$12.00
[2 of these sold for $69.99 each]		40 SEED PACKETS WITH DIAPER BABY SHOWER FAVORS	$12.00
~~L@@KIE Balloon Stuffing Machine N/R~~~~	$69.00	SWEETIEHEART Baby Sock Corsage-One -of-kind	$11.99
CURIOUS GEORGE BABY SHOWER GIFT DIAPER CAKE	$65.00	PENIS Cake Pan New Great for Bachelorette B- day parties	$11.99

Gifts & Occasions ▸ Wedding Supplies

The average sales price in this subcategory is $27.28.

	HIGH		AVG
10 White Eiffel TOWER VASE 28'' W/ OSTRICH FEATHERS	$649.99	Wedding Cake Charms Ribbon Pulls STERLING SILVER **8**	$28.99
Lot 200 Banquet Wedding Chair seat Covers ball room	$345.00	Wedding Promises Lenox Wedding Cake Topper	$28.97
CINDERELLA CASTLE CARRIAGE WEDDING CARD HOLDER BOX	$225.01	HUGE MIXED LOT Wedding Bridal Supplies - MUST SEE	$28.50
10'x20' Party Wedding tent Canopy Garge Heavy Duty	$162.51	Vintage 1950's Wedding Cake Topper Lace Flowers	$28.01
10'x30' Party Wedding tent/Canopy/Gazebo/Pavilion+Walls	$162.50	Cinderella Wedding Guest book, pen, goblets, cake knif	$28.00
10'x20' Party Wedding tent Canopy Garge Heavy Duty	$157.50	Bachelor Bacheloret Party sex supplies Gift wedding	$28.00
10'x20' Party Wedding tent Canopy Garge Heavy Duty	$155.00	WEDDING DECORATIONS FANCY BALLOON DROP BAG NET DECOR	$27.45
10'x20' Party Wedding tent Canopy Garge Heavy Duty	$152.50	2 CINDERELLA & PRINCE FIGURES WEDDING DECORATION BRIDE	$27.00
10'x30' Party Wedding tent/Canopy/Gazebo/Pavilion+Walls	$151.00	Lenox Wedding Promises? First Dance Cake Topper	$27.00
10'x30' Party Wedding tent/Canopy/Gazebo/Pavilion+Walls	$150.03	Lighted DISNEY Princess Castle Wedding Cake Topper	$27.00
Large CINDERELLA Wedding Card Box Holder, Lighted	$148.50	Pottery Barn Silver Ball Glass Wedding Bubbles -6 boxes	$27.00
10'x30' Party Wedding tent/Canopy/Gazebo/Pavilion+Walls	$147.50	WEDDING BRIDE AND GROOM CAKE TOPPER WATER GLOBE NIB	$26.99
10'x20' Party Wedding tent Canopy Garge Heavy Duty	$147.00	WEDDING CARD BOX w/ Pearls Customize to your color	$26.99
10'x20' Party Wedding tent Canopy Garge Heavy Duty	$144.01	WEDDING CARD BOX w/Rhinestones Customize to your color	$26.99
10'x20' Party Wedding tent Canopy Garge Heavy Duty	$143.50	Cinderella Fairytale Castle Wedding Cake Top* Silver	$26.99

Gifts & Occasions ▸ Wholesale Lots

The average sales price in this subcategory is $19.42.

	HIGH		AVG
Wholesale lot BRAND NEW GIFT ITEMS many gifts, jewelry	$500.00	LOT 100 GLOWSTICKS 22" COLOR GLOW STICKS SAFE BRACELETS	$19.95
FLASHING LIGHT UP ICE CUBES FREE SHIPPING (glow sticks	$319.50	500 1.5" MINI GLOWSTICKS FISHING GLOW LIGHT STICKS	$19.75
[213 of these sold in a multiple item ("Dutch") auction for $1.50 each]		Lot of 40 Colgate Kid's LEGO Toothbrushes Extra Soft	$19.51
4000 Asstd glow light sticks bracelets FREE SHIPPING	$293.00	12 Disney Tinker Bell 5x7 Diary Notebook Party Favors	$19.50
400 Yard 54" wide White Tulle Wedding Decor Favor SALE!	$237.50	LOT OF WEDDING SUPPLIES	$19.50
Wholesale Lot of 1100 plus Gift Bags,Tissue, Greeter	$220.00	11 PC. BAGS OF ASSORTED ARTIFICIAL FRUIT $6.50 (3 BAGS)	$19.50
4000 Asstd glow light sticks bracelets FREE SHIPPING	$212.50	LUAU PARTY DECORATIONS 101PC Leis,Table Cover,Hibiscus+	$19.45
Haunted GreatGrandma's witches wallet, MISTERY AUCTION	$202.51	50 22" 5 COLOR GLOW STICKS NECKLACES PARTY SUPPLIES	$19.25
15 Yd: Ginger Bliss Pattern Quilting Fabric 100% Cotton	$167.52	Narcotics Anonymous Sticker LOT red NA	$19.08
Wholesale Wedding 224 Garters LAST LOT!!	$158.05	Lot of 60 Dozen USA Stars & Stripes Gliders	$19.03
FIRELIGHT OIL CANDLES, WHOLESALE LOT OF 16 MODELS	$155.00	LUAU PARTY DECORATIONS 101PC Leis,Table Cover,Hibiscus+	$18.95
400 Yard 54" wide White Tulle Wedding Decor Favor SALE!	$152.50	48PC~ HAWAIIAN SILK PETALS LEIS & LEI BRACELET LOT~LUAU	$18.95
400 Yard 54" wide White Tulle Wedding - NO RESERVE!!	$152.50	LUAU PARTY DECORATIONS 101PC Leis,Table Cover,Hibiscus+	$18.95
Warehouse Find! OLD UNOPENED Baseball packs boxes MINT!	$150.00	[2 of these sold for $18.95 each]	
[15 of these sold in a multiple item ("Dutch") auction for $10.00 each]		100 MILLION KEYCHAIN FLASHLIGHTS ## Party Favors Supplies	$18.95
400 Yard 54" wide White Tulle Wedding Decor Favor SALE!	$147.50	74 NIP GE Light Up Fiber Optic Necklaces w/Clear Cords	$18.27
400 Yard 54" wide White Tulle Wedding Decor Favor SALE!	$142.50		

Information Products ▸ How-To Guides

The average sales price in this subcategory is $28.71.

	HIGH		AVG
SCOTT SCHEEL - HUGE PROFITS IN COMMERCIAL REAL ESTATE!	$1,450.00	Dave Espino's Auctions For Income Course, NEW with VHS	$29.99
SCOTT SCHEEL'S COLOSSAL CASH IN COMMERCIAL PROPERTY	$1,425.00	Car Audio WholeSale List & IProfit Ebook with Resell !!	$29.95
Scott Scheel's Colossal Cash in Commercial Property	$1,025.00	TAX ADVANTAGES FOR YOUR HOME BASED BUSINESS	$29.50
John Reese's Traffic Secrets - $997 Value! Internet	$680.00	MAKE MONEY-BBQ FOOD BUSINESS-CONCESSION TRAILER VENDING	$29.00
John Reese 's Traffic Secrets Course - NR	$658.47	MADDEN 06' PLAYSTATION 2 PS2 NEW	$29.00
Yanik Silver Underground Online Marketing Seminar DVD	$567.00	Product Development Course on 5 set DVDs by Bill Myers	$28.99
John Reese Traffic Secrets	$475.00	DAVE ESPINO'S AUCTIONS FOR INCOME - MAKE $$$ ON EBAY!	$28.95
List Profit Secrets by Craig Perrine - Email Marketing!	$350.00	RUSS DALBY WINNING IN THE CASH FLOW BUSINESS	$28.00
INFO SUMMIT SEMINAR 2004 - DAN KENNEDY BILL GLAZER	$337.68	Light your own fire you deserve to be happy Kreidman	$28.00
MIDWEST CENTER Anxiety & Depression Kit - CD Version	$323.65	Bob Proctor's THE SCIENCE OF GETTING RICH (NEW!)	$27.97
MATT FUREY CHINESE SECRET SEXUAL KUNG FU - DVD/CD	$295.00	INVEST IN REAL ESTATE W/ NO CASH & NO CREDIT - SEMINAR	$27.78
LUCINDA BASSETT MIDWEST CENTER	$277.00	MAKE MONEY-BBQ FOOD BUSINESS-	$27.49
ATTACKING ANXIETY COURSE		CONCESSION TRAILER VENDING	
Midwest Center Anxiety Depression Kit CD Version	$255.07	Complete Carleton Sheets Real Estate Investment Program	$27.00
Midwest Center Stress Anxiety Depression KIT CD version	$255.00	Product Development Course on 5 set DVDs by Bill Myers	$26.99
Attacking Anxiety and Depression NEW Midwest Center NR!	$237.50	EFT Emotional Freedom Technique video tapes Gary Craig	$26.55

Information Products ▸ Wholesale Lists

The average sales price in this subcategory is $38.82.

	HIGH		AVG
Entire Retail Store Inventory	$17,000.00	NEW LCD COMPUTER MONITOR Wholesale List Free Shipping!!	$40.49
2005 250CC ATV QUAD FOUR WHEELER	$1,125.10	IN DASH DVD PLAYER/MP3 /CD/CAR STEREO WHOLESALE LIST	$40.00
REVERSE WHOLESALE LIST		NEW 7 INCH 16:9 PORTABLE DVD PLAYER WHOLESALE LIST	$40.00
BRAND NEW TANNING BED wholesale list!! FREE SHIPPING!!	$700.00	MP3 PLAYER WHOLESALE LIST Ipod Nano Black 4GB Free Ship	$39.99
NEW 45" FLAT SCREEN PLASMA TV	$661.00	[2 of these sold for $39.99 each]	
TELEVISION WHOLESALE LIST		1 MILLION Home Business Leads w/ Email and Phone MLM	$39.90
42" FLAT SCREEN LCD TV WHOLESALE LIST NEW!!	$610.00	[2 of these sold in a multiple item ("Dutch") auction for $19.95 each]	
BRAND NEW TANNING BED BEDS wholesale list! FREE SHIPING	$355.00	BRAND NEW LAPTOP COMPUTER! Wholesale List FREE SHIPPING	$39.00
iPOD Video 60GB Wholesale List - Free Shipping!	$330.00	NEW LCD COMPUTER MONITOR Wholesale List Free Shipping!!	$38.00
iPOD Video 60GB Wholesale List - Free Shipping!	$310.00	Abercrombie Amber Jacket Wholesale List! FREE SHIPPING	$37.99
BRAND NEW POOL TABLE WHOLESALE LIST!!! Free Shipping!	$305.30	[3 of these sold for $37.99 each]	
iPOD Video 60GB Wholesale List - Free Shipping!	$300.00	BRAND NEW SONY PSP VALUE PACK Wholesale List	$37.10
INDASH CAR AUDIO NAVIGATION/DVD STEREO Wholesale List	$268.00	BOOK Buy BELOW Wholesale From QVC To Sell On eBay!	$37.00
New iPOD Video 60GB Nano 4gb Mp3 player wholesale list	$251.59	NEW PORTABLE DVD PLAYER wholesale list FREE SHIPPING !	$37.00

	HIGH		AVG
BRAND NEW LAPTOP COMPUTER!	$230.00	INDASH CAR AUDIO NAVIGATION/DVD STEREO Wholesale List	$36.50
Wholesale List FREE SHIPPING		BRAND NEW KENWOOD IN DASH DVD CD PLAYER!!	$36.00
iPOD Video 60GB Wholesale List - Free Shipping!	$227.50	IN DASH DVD PLAYER/MP3 /CD/CAR STEREO WHOLESALE LIST	$36.00
BRAND NEW POOL TABLE wholesale list! FREE SHIPPING	$207.50	1 MILLION Business Leads w/ Email and Phone MLM	$36.00

Information Products ▶ Other

The average sales price in this subcategory is $25.32.

	HIGH		AVG
Mexico Beach Lot Bahia Kino Bay land 4 hours to Arizona	$6,000.00	*** New 2006 Wholesale Car Audio in-Dash DVD***	$26.00
MYSTERY METHOD 5 DVD & SWINGCAT 10 CD dating courses!!	$550.05	Brand NEW 2006 Hot tub wholesalelist Save HUGE!!!!!	$26.00
Ron LeGrand - Real Estate CASH FLOW SYSTEMS 2003	$405.00	Brand New DVD Camcorder Wholesale List	$26.00
Tradingmarkets With Kevin Haggerty Super Collection	$387.69	VIDEO iPod 30 GB or 60 GB Black or White plays VIDEOS	$26.00
New Car Audio TV DvD MP3 Stereo Player Wholesale list	$325.00	LAPTOP COMPUTER PC - wholesale list	$26.00
Jim Edwards Internet Marketing & Website Design Coarse	$310.00	BRAND NEW TRAMPOLINE wholesale list! Free shipping!	$26.00
COMPLETE Asset Protection System NO RESERVE!	$305.00	The FSBO Mortgage Marketing Kit for Mortgage Brokers-CD	$25.17
Jeff Kaller - Mr. Preforeclosure Real Estate Course	$305.00	LOCKSMITH ENCYCLOPEDIA 7-CD COMBO SET	$25.00
Yanik Silver & Dan Kennedy Internet Marketing Seminar	$282.07	DAVID DEANGELO- INTERVIEW with PATTY	$25.00
aL Lowwry - Real Estate CASH FLOW SYSTEMS 2003	$280.00	CAR STEREO WHOLESALE LIST FREE SHIPPING W/ BUY IT NOW!!	$24.99
MAKE A FORTUNE WITH FREE	$277.00	PORTABLE DVD PLAYER WHOLESALE LIST BUY DIRECT AND SAVE!	$24.99
PUBLICITY KIT - PAUL HARTUNIAN		CAR STEREO WHOLESALE LIST FREE SHIPPING W/ BUY IT NOW!!	$24.99
ROSS JEFFRIES MAGICK/PSYCHIC	$255.00	[3 of these sold for $24.99 each]	
INFLUENCE SEDUCTION COURSE		PORTABLE DVD PLAYER WHOLESALE LIST BUY DIRECT AND SAVE!	$24.99
Jeff Kaller - Mr PreForeclosure	$228.76	[3 of these sold for $24.99 each]	
Midwest Center Attacking Anxiety and Depression	$205.06	**BRAND NEW PLASMA TV WHOLESALE LIST - FREE SHIPPING!**	$24.99
Dan Kennedy & Ernie Kessler - public speaking & selling	$202.50	New Updated CHEAT the CHERRY MASTER CD ?	$24.99

Mature Audiences ▶ Adult Toys

The average sales price in this subcategory is $21.84.

	HIGH		AVG
Jetaime Sex Toy - Sex Machine - Industrial Strength	$510.00	*0285:Clone-A-Willy Vibrating Dildo Kit+FREE ADULT DVD!	$24.00
Hustler Virtual Girl HVG LOVE DOLL Full body vagina NEW	$380.05	Juli Ashton anal beginner kit	$23.50
The Saddle Slider !! Dildo driver SEX MACHINE!	$279.00	SHOWER SHOT DILDO KIT ~ FOR ANAL	$22.99
Nemesis - The newest thing in pleasure machines	$200.00	VAGINAL ENEMA DOUCHE	
The Full Stroke Male Masturbation Sex Machine	$189.50	TRIPLE TREAT MAUVE Rabbit vibrator anal, vaginal duel	$22.50
*1717:Love Swing With Stand+FREE SUPER HOT ADULT DVD!!	$169.99	INFLATABLE LATEX PROBE 5'' VIBRATOR	$21.99
JENNA JAMESON LOVE DOLL-MOVEABLE ARMS	$140.00	10 Inch Realistic Vibrator Feels JUST LIKE Real Thing	$21.99
ARIA's LOVE GODDESS VIBRATING DOLL ********	$139.99	DOUBLE DONG WITH HARNESS NICE STRAP ON~L@@k#040	$21.99
#1 Rated ORGASM TOOLS for Women	$125.50	Natural Contours ULTIME Vibrator Massager	$21.50
[2 of these sold in a multiple item ("Dutch") auction for $62.75 each]		Metal Shower Bidet and Enema System for men or women!	$21.25
Jana's Butterfly Ring Solo/Couples Wireless Stimulation	$119.70	#1 ORGASM TOOL for Women - The Best Rated Vibrator	$20.50
[6 of these sold in a multiple item ("Dutch") auction for $19.95 each]		Natural Contours ULTIME Vibrator Massager	$20.49
SEX MACHINE The PLEASURE CHEST Thrusting dildo	$110.00	*0285:Clone-A-Willy Vibrating Dildo Kit+FREE ADULT DVD!	$20.49
[2 of these sold for $110.00 each]		[2 of these sold for $20.49 each]	
CRYSTAL CLEAR 12" DOUBLE DILDO DONG VERY NICE	$104.65	ECLIPES OMEGA CLITORAL VIBRATOR $89.95	$20.00
[7 of these sold for $104.65 each]		Natural Contours MAGNIFIQUE Vibrator Massager	$19.99
Virtual Veronica Hi Tech Stroking Love Doll	$99.95	[2 of these sold for $19.99 each]	
10" Phallix Art Glass Dildo	$79.00	VIBRATING CLIT SUPER SUCKER WATERPROOF	$19.99
Genuine Leather Bondage Accessories	$76.01	PUMPS/SUCKS + LU	

Mature Audiences ▶ Animation & Comics

The average sales price in this subcategory is $8.26.

	HIGH		AVG
14 Adult Anime DVD's [HENTAI]	$200.00	La Blue Girl Returns Uncensored Anime DVD	$8.49
500+ HENTAI ANIME Movies, HUGE collection! & More!	$124.95	Voice of Submission 2: Gehenna 7 issue lot eros comix	$8.45
[5 of these sold in a multiple item ("Dutch") auction for $24.99 each]		Really Weird Tales of Sci-Fi Erotasy N Stuff #1 adult	$8.44
RISQUE CARTOON NOVEL TIJUANA BIBLE NUDITY SEX GRAPHIC	$104.49	New Bondage Fairies #5, Eros Comics, Adult Manga	$8.25
CARNAL COMICS mint set 72 issues PUBLSHR'S FILE COPIES	$68.89	[2 of these sold for $8.25 each]	
UNDERGROUND COMIX, SNATCH #1, PRISTINE 3RD	$68.00	New Bondage Fairies: Fairie Fetish #1, Eros Comics	$8.25
TIJUANA BIBLE RISQUE CARTOON	$66.00	[2 of these sold for $8.25 each]	
SEX NUDITY "BENNY" BANTAM		New Bondage Fairies: Fairie Fetish #2, Eros Comics	$8.25
TIJUANA BIBLE RISQUE COMIC SEX NUDITY ANDY HARDY NUDE	$66.00	A Night in a Moorish Harem Vol. 2 - quality erotica!!!	$8.13
CARNAL COMICS mint set 75 issues PUBLSHR'S FILE COPIES	$64.00	BIG HENTAI COLLECTION (vol2) 8.6+ GIGS 2 DVDS !! NEW!	$8.07
Adult PC Game - Airline 69	$60.99	Slave Nurses 1-3 Uncensored Anime DVD	$8.05
TIJUANA BIBLE RISQUE CARTOON COMIC NOVEL SEX NUDITY	$59.00	Taboo Charming Vol. 1 Uncensored Hentai Anime DVD	$8.05
TIJUANA BIBLE RISQUE CARTOON COMIC SEX NUDITY NUDE	$54.00	Kiss 92 & 99 El Vibora 232 & 239 Clowes Cooper Shelton	$8.01
TIJUANA BIBLE RISQUE CARTOON COMIC NUDITY SEX LENA	$51.00	Double Impact Suicide Run # 2 (Adult Comic)	$8.00
Adult PC Game - Wet: The Sexy Empire	$51.00	Double Impact Suicide Run Collected # 1 (Adult Comic)	$8.00
Hentai PC Game - Artificial Girl 2 English/Uncensored!	$48.00	Traci Lords: the outlaw years	$8.00
DICK TRACY RISQUE CARTOON TIJUANA BIBLE SEX NUDITY	$43.00	New Bondage Fairies #6, Eros Comics, Adult Manga	$8.00

Mature Audiences ▶ Art: Nude

The average sales price in this subcategory is $35.46.

	HIGH		AVG
VINTAGE DEMI DIEUX Male Nude Beefcake BENNETT 11x14	$1,700.00	VINTAGE 5x7 PHOTO HUNG YOUNG	$37.55
[2 of these sold for $1,700.00 each]		MAN ERECT UNCUT 1950's NR!	
50s VINTAGE URBAN Male Nude Beefcake SMOOTH Vince PERRI	$1,500.00	Dejah Thoris erotic original art by Paradis	$36.99
ORIGINAL Male Nude Beefy MAN IN MASK Exceptional 11x14	$750.00	Barry Blair /Colin Walbridge Deathwatch Agent Cassidy	$36.65

ORIGINAL ARTWORK BY CIRBY 1986, GAY INTEREST	$375.00	JORGE Male Nude Fine Art Print Gay Int NFP Breyette	$36.00
1976 EARLY TOM MILLEA NUDE STUDY 4X5 PLATINUM PHOTO	$325.00	j3038 Neg 2.4x2.4 Nude blond great body grey background	$36.00
1994 TOM MILLEA CLASSIC PORTRAIT 4X6 PLATINUM PHOTO	$325.00	Olivia- Nude signed artist print	$36.00
18" x 24" original oil painting - nudes by Steven Corry	$316.99	COED TEASERS (1978) COPPER PENNY, SPRING TAYLOR	$35.00
Original Art by Erik Drudwyn - Wild Nights -	$310.00	Solid Bronze Sculpture of Woman	$35.00
male nude, THE BASEBALL PLAYER, mixed media by kent	$305.00	Sexy Dejah Thoris bath original art by Paradis	$35.00
male nude, THE WRESTLERS, mixed media by kent	$295.00	YGRT-0082 ORIGINAL GIRLIE ARTWORK* LAUNDRY LAMENT	$34.95
Mel Roberts BOY'S 1968 (NIce)	$272.90	Barry Blair /Colin Walbridge Revenge Of The KMT	$34.95
Barry Blair /Colin Walbridge Anzio Annie Rides	$205.50	1890s CLASSIC VON GLOEDEN Male Nude Early COPY	$34.78
Barry Blair /Colin Walbridge Gothic Rider	$201.00	ORIGINAL Male Nude Oil Paintingx	$34.69
VAMPIRELLA NUDE original art by DBLACK	$153.50	Barry Blair /Colin Walbridge Kamakazai Rests	$34.00
ORIGINAL DRAWING GOTHIC BEAR	$137.50	Barry Blair /Colin Walbridge The Cave Of Doom	$33.95
HALLOWEEN MALE NUDE MURAT		[2 of these sold for $33.95 each]	

Mature Audiences ▶ Autographs

The average sales price in this subcategory is $17.83.

	HIGH		AVG
PMOY 97 Victoria Silvstedt full sig. signed Centerfold	$356.00	Playmate Miriam Gonzales Signed Nude Glossy	$17.99
CANDY LOVING signed Centerfold, 25TH ANNIVERSARY 1/79	$306.00	Playmate Debi Nicole Johnson Signed Nude Glossy	$17.99
DOROTHY STRATTEN AUTOGRAPHS PICTURE WITH HER 2 PLAYBOY	$256.51	Playmate Colleen Marie Signed Nude Photo	$17.99
Nicole Van Croft- Signed Playboy photo & ANS	$201.01	Playmate Lindsey Vuolo Signed Nude Photo	$17.99
1977 Playmate SIGNED Photos Nicki Thomas + Ashley Cox	$155.50	5/02 Playmate Christy Shake side+ lower nude Explicit	$17.99
74 PMOY Cyndi Wood wants you to pull her strings!	$135.50	7/05 Playmate Qiana Chase signed Centerfold	$17.99
Farrah Fawcett TOPLESS IN PERSON SIGNED Pic *WWG*	$127.50	Ashton Moore Signed 11x8 photo	$17.51
7/82 Playmate Lynda Wiesmeier UNPUBLISHED Centerfold!	$125.00	CAROL WAYNE SIGNED MEGA TITTIES HOT PUSSY CAT	$17.50
8/01 Playmate Jennifer Walcott signed NUDE picture!	$123.50	Kari Wuhrer-Naked-Pink Nipples-Nice Boobs-Auto 8x10	$17.50
2005 PMOY Tiffany Fallon signed NUDE picture!!! NEW!!!	$122.49	Beverly D'Angelo SEXY WET BOOBS signed pic MUST SEE	$17.50
Playmate Amanda Paige Signed Nude Glossy	$113.61	Jesse Jane & Belladonna-Touching Eachother-WOW-Auto	$17.50
Playmate Tamara Witmer Signed Centerfold	$111.01	Sexy Autographed Photograph Nude Claudia Christian	$17.50
Playmate Amanda Paige Signed Centerfold	$111.01	RAYLENE SIGNED 8x10 TOPLESS HUGE BREASTS PORNSTAR	$17.50
8/05 Playmate Tamara Witmer Full nude kneeling outside	$108.00	70's Porn Legend Carol Connors Auto Nude!	$17.50
6/00 Playmate Shannon Stewart has a "heart" on for you!	$103.61	Asian Playmate LISA MARIE SCOTT topless signed photo!	$17.50

Mature Audiences ▶ Books

The average sales price in this subcategory is $13.20.

	HIGH		AVG
Collection of 68 Erotic Novels from the 1970s-1980s	$405.00	1980 HOT WILD WIVES - GREENLEAF	$13.48
RARE STAMPED 1968 "SONS OF THE SUN" PHOTOBOOK MALE GAY	$244.75	VINTAGE ADULT PAPERBACK/AMNAL HOUSE BOOK AH1005	$13.48
Vintage Adult PB - Greenleaf Heatherpool Press - HP6293	$152.50	Greenleaf Patch Pokets 1984 Overeager Librarian PP7270	$13.45
79 NEW Variety of Adult Content Books Beeline and more	$148.59	Liverpool LB1406 Line Up for the Cheerleader 1988	$13.45
LLP-276 - Caesar Conquers Book III - Fine cond.	$147.00	GREENLEAF HP6152 Heatherpool THE TEMPTING TWO	$13.39
Vintage Adult Paperback Greenleaf Classic PB series 389	$128.50	LOT OF 2 BOOKS PAPERBACK - LIVERPOOL CORNICHE	$13.25
TWO 1997 Hardcover Bondage Books by 'Gord'-Illustrated	$123.50	Love Me, Love My Dag Vintage Erotica 1969	$13.20
LLP-272 - Caesar Comes Book I - NF cond.	$112.50	INSATIABLE by John Patrick SIGNED Gay Erotic Fiction	$13.13
LLP-274 - Caesar's Revenge Book II - Fine cond.	$112.50	Meatmen, Comic's Vol. 17-The Hun, Sean, Osze, Joe, etc.	$13.10
Bishop on Bondage - 2 Books, 2 Magazines - NR	$110.00	Benson's Bondage Art - HARDCOVER-ILLUSTRATED-FETISHI	$13.05
2 Adult NUTRIX Books, Drawings by Ande & Enege, 1959&62	$105.00	PRIVATE PAPERBACK CUSTOMER APPRECIATION SALE	$13.03
ANOTHER MAN...PHOTOGRAPHY BY JIM FRENCH	$104.14	Greenleaf RED BOND@G# BH8088 G+ to VG condition	$13.03
Set of 5 adult books	$102.51	BOY TOY by John Patrick SIGNED Gay Erotic Fiction	$13.01
Vintage Adult PB - Liverpool Book Centaur Series-LB1326	$102.50	CLASSIC LIVERPOOL DADS GIRLFRIEND 1975	$13.00
VERY ADULT COMIC BOOKS - One Long Box approx 300 Books	$100.00	YOU KITAJIMA JAPANESE IDOL PHOTO BOOK(with DVD)	$13.00

Mature Audiences ▶ Clothing, Accessories

The average sales price in this subcategory is $13.64.

	HIGH		AVG
BLACK LEATHER STRAIT JACKET~NICE QUALITY~L	$152.45	SEXY PEACH TOP / SPORT BRA MEDIUM NWOT	$14.26
BLACK LEATHER STRAIT JACKET~NICE QUALITY~MED	$149.95	HOTTIES ONE PIECE BODY STOCKING..SHEER BLACK	$14.25
EXOTIC DANCER OPEN CROTCH CRISS CROSS BODYSTOCKING	$125.86	0335:Latex Rubba Wear Corselette So Very Hot!	$13.99
[14 of these sold in a multiple item ("Dutch") auction for $8.99 each]		HOT!!! SEXY TWO PIECE RED "SHOW ME" SET	$13.99
FOR SALE! MY LITTLE PINK BOX!	$110.00	0335:Latex Rubba Wear Corselette So Very Hot!	$13.99
MONICA'S SEXY WORN BLACK RUBBER GIRDLE	$103.50	NEW Full Leather Belt Harness w/ Cock Rings!! L@@K	$13.95
Fresh, Sassy & Sexy Well Worn Coles	$103.50	TEACHER'S LITTLE SECRET all nude!!!	$13.51
Captavating Well Worn Seriously Scented Heeled Loafers	$103.50	PANTIES LIKE MINE OR SIMILAR NWOT	$13.50
Sexy NEW Canadian Booty Cotton Panties & Bonus Pictures	$87.00	SEXY WHITE BRA AND PANTIE SET SO HOT MUST SEE!!	$13.50
NEW STRAP STYLE DELUXE LEATHER BODY HARNESS MED	$82.95	Black Leather Mouth Gag Binder Restraint	$13.50
The Curve Acrylic Chastity Device w locks New $179	$81.77	SEXY NIGHT SHIRT& PANTIE SET SO HOT MUST SEE!!	$13.50
NEW STRAP STYLE DELUXE LEATHER BODY HARNESS MED	$78.95	WELL WORN SEXY FISHNET TEDDY	$13.50
USED- Lady New Balance Running Shoes- SUPER SCENTED!!!	$76.00	WITH MATCHING STOCKINGS	
BLACK LEATHER BONDAGE LEG BINDERS~LACE UP	$74.95	VERY WORN HOSE	$13.50
Male Metal Chastity	$63.85	USED WORN SEXY HIGH HEEL SHOES WHITE 9.5	$13.50
Candy's Milf NWOT Sheer Black-n-White Lace Thong Pantie	$61.00	SEXY BLACK LOWCUT TOP X-LARGE NWT	$13.26

Mature Audiences ▶ Domain Names

The average sales price in this subcategory is $11.90.

HIGH TO LOW

Earn $10,000/month Web Cams Sex Pics DVD Toy Store	$49.00	Adult Website Creation How-To CD Step-by-Step Guide $$$	$4.95
Established Adult Business Store Shop website web site	$41.00	[3 of these sold for $4.95 each]	

ADULT BANNER EXCHANGE FOR SALE!	$32.99	30 Day Membership Card to REALITY PASS Video Website	$2.95
Established Adult Business Store Shop website web site	$15.76	Adult Paid Per Sign Up WebSite. Best Money Maker On Net	$2.20
4-in-1 Flash Adult Website For Auction. Best One Yet.	$9.95	Adult website submitted to OVER 800,000 Search Engines!	$1.99
Targited Adult & Casino Traffic, Real Traffic Not Hits!	$9.95	Adult Website Business 101 - Make Best Money Quick	$1.25
Adult Website Creation How-To CD Step-by-Step Guide $$$	$6.50	Adult Website Business 101 - Make Best Money Quick	$1.04

Mature Audiences ▸ Magazines

The average sales price in this subcategory is $12.59.

	HIGH		AVG
THE BEST OF THE BEST ANTIQUE PORN MAGAZINES! LOT OF 99!	$202.52	GREAT 90'S VINTAGE MAG LATIN SPECTACULAR NO. 3	$12.99
Vintage 80's 32-pg explicit mag starring Christy Canyon	$177.50	1980s Japanese SM Bondage Fetish Magazines LOT OF 4	$12.99
VINTAGE GAY MAGAZINE MALE PICKUPS ND	$150.39	MEN OF MEN Blondes FAIR GAME Tim Kramer Jim Bentley	$12.99
Rare Vintage Private Magazine No.3 1967	$132.50	1970's LATIN STUDS Gay Porn Magazine! HCI KRISTEN BJORN	$12.99
GETTING IT Rick Donovan Dane Ford Brandon Wilde action!	$129.50	TOO HOT 2 with PETER BERLIN and 7 more	$12.95
Mel Roberts SEX FANTASY #1 1978	$126.50	GRAHAM CRACKERS BLACK BUSTY WILD 6 MAGS	$12.83
Mel Roberts Sex Fantasy 2 48 page color magazine	$112.50	The J Brian Collection Volume 4 36 page magazine	$12.55
Bishop on Bondage - 2 Books, 2 Magazines - NR	$110.00	STROKE 15.2 (1995) Brad Hunt Rip Stone Gianfranco	$12.55
VERY RARE NANCY SUITER & BALD MAN! X-RATED "BALLED"	$92.98	VINTAGE ADULT MAGAZINES	$12.55
VINTAGE GAY MAGAZINE 1969 NICKY GAY INT.	$92.00	Playguy 5/97-Nick Steel-Justin Young-Brad Whitewood-NEW	$12.51
Near-mint Very Rare COLT STUDIO MANPOWER! #1 1968	$90.00	9 Black Girls Pictorial Sable Players Mens Magazines	$12.50
1960's Gay COME ON BOYS Volume 1 #1 K&J Collectors	$81.00	STROKE 5.2 (1985) Jesse Koehler Max Montoya Chris Burns	$12.50
COLT MEN #3 Featuring Mike Davis and Al Parker RARE	$78.00	TORSO -DECEMBER 1997 NAKED GYM JOCKS JASON WEST GAY	$12.50
Bondage Fetish - HOM BREAST BONDAGE '77 1st Ed. I	$67.00	70s ~THE PRIVATE FILE #2 CATALOG from BRUCE of LA!	$12.50
Bondage Fetish - HOM BREAST BONDAGE '80 #2!	$67.00	MIXED MAGAZINE LOT Wochen End Q QUICK 1977-90 CX326 ff	$12.50

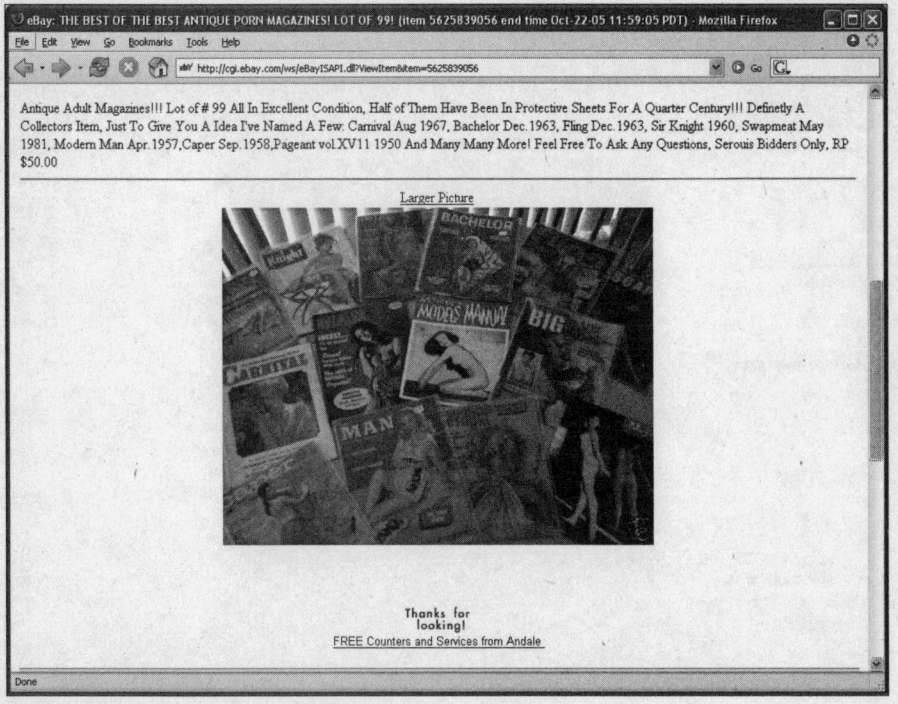

Mature Audiences ▸ Photographic

The average sales price in this subcategory is $20.60.

	HIGH		AVG
BW Gay Male Nude LON 8x10 Hot Sal SEVERINO hot pecs 40s	$1,000.00	YGNG-3929 VINTAGE 2.25 NEGATIVE DD BUSTY CANDY SAMPLES	$21.50
BW Gay Male Nude LON NY 8x10 Hot 6-Pack LargeUNCUT 40s	$760.00	RAY KELLOGG Champion vintage slide MALE GAY NUDE	$21.00
BW Gay Male Nude LON 8x10 Hot Stud Low Hanging 1940s	$760.00	[3 of these sold for $21.00 each]	
BW Gay Male Nude AI URBAN 8x10 Hot UNCUT Greek Pose	$592.22	YGNG-3267 VINTAGE 2.25 NEGATIVE DD BUSTY CHRIS SHAFFER	$20.72
BW Gay Male Nude URBAN 8x10 Hot Henry KARCZEWSKI 1940s	$500.15	BOSOMY LONGHAIRED BRUNETTE kneels on shag 8x10	$20.70
BW Gay Male Nude LON NY 8x10 Sal SEVERINO Large CUT 40s	$491.15	IT'S HOT IN INDIA!!- GAY-PHOTOS-NAKED MEN-COLOR	$20.53
BW Gay Male Nude AI URBAN 8x10	$462.53	YGR-0661: B/W 8X10* BETTIE PAGE CONTACT SHEET	$20.51
Hot John GALLAGER UNCUT		**1960's Nude Brunette On Couch-Beaver-Stockings	$20.50
BW Gay Male Nude LON NY 8x10 Hot CUT Italian Beefcake	$455.00	Lot of 3 - #860/1 Nude Photo(s) b/w 4x5 ORIGINAL	$20.50
BW Gay Male Nude LON NY 8x10 Hot Santo LEONE uncut 6pak	$455.00	Stk of 20 vintage MALE NUDE slides ~ 70s COWBOYS!	$20.50
BW Gay Male Nude LON NY 8x10 Hot Irish Lad UNCUT 6pak	$425.15	CJ 5X7 SIGNED ORIG CHAOSINAUSTIN PHOTO	$20.50
BW Gay Male Nude LON NY 8x10 Hot Joseph MASCHIO 1940s	$424.99	VINTAGE SLIDE LOT mixed original slides MALE GAY NUDE	$20.50
BW Gay Male Nude LON NY 8x10 Hot Italian LargeUNCUT 40s	$361.71	BOB MIZER amg original SLIDE MALE GAY NUDE	$20.50
BW Gay Male Nude WPG? AMG? Bruce of LA? 1950's Ed FURY	$336.50	YGG-1102 VINTAGE TOM OF FINLAND CARTOON GAY INTEREST	$20.50
BW Gay Male Nude Hot Steve WENGRYN by AI URBAN 1950's	$300.00	1985 small black and white nude of ERIC RYAN - #1010-C	$20.25
BW Gay Male Nude AMG? Bruce of LA? 1940's Beefcake	$295.00	CJ 5X7 SIGNED ORIG CHAOSINAUSTIN PHOTO	$20.00

Mature Audiences ▸ Pin Up

The average sales price in this subcategory is $12.63.

	HIGH		AVG
Marilyn Monroe- Original 1955 Golden Dream calendar	$99.99	CENTERFOLD MODEL PHOTO CD 3,000 IMAGES	$14.95
@@@ ZIMMERMAN ORIGINAL ART - The Jetson's - EATING	$78.59	RARE COLLECTABLE MARILYN MONROE Puzzle w/ NUDE POSE	$14.00
@@@ ZIMMERMAN ORIGINAL ART "Who's Yer Daddy"	$77.77	Set of 4 JENNA JAMESON POSTERS Low Price	$13.95
@@@ ZIMMERMAN ORIGINAL ART Bashful.......NOT	$69.88	[3 of these sold for $13.95 each]	
@@@ ZIMMERMAN ORIGINAL ART - BJ Elephant Sale	$68.65	HUGE 1980 Nude Pin Up Calendar Sample Spring Beauty	$12.55
@@@ ZIMMERMAN ORIGINAL ART - PopEYE & Ariel ** L@@K	$62.70	Large 16x21 poster of MARILYN MONROE from Dec '53	$12.49
JENNA JAMESON RARE LA ADULT	$61.00	1999 PLAYBOY PLAYMATE CALENDAR SEALED	$11.78
SHOW BOARD POSTER,SIGNED!		4 for 1 Bid 8x10 Color Glossies Tracy Neve	$11.55
@@@ ZIMMERMAN ORIGINAL ART - Jessica Rabbit Stockings	$56.99	5 for 1 Bid 7x10 B&W Mattes Titanic Tina	$11.50
@@@ ZIMMERMAN ORIGINAL ART - Wonder Womman	$52.99	27 assorted playboy centerfolds 1960's-80's beautiful	$11.11
32X40 Poster Of Beautiful Woman!	$52.00	MARILYN MONROE 1953 Calander, Famous Red Sheet Pose	$11.00
@@@ ZIMMERMAN ORIGINAL ART - Jessica Rabbit Weasels	$51.70	Art Fantastix Select #10 MARK ROGERS Softvcr Book PINUP	$11.00
ONE OF A KIND UNRELEASED!!! KRYSTAL STEAL POSTER PROOF!	$49.99	Lg Sexy Nude Pin Up Girl Calendar Sample Pillow Talk	$10.79
@@@ ZIMMERMAN ORIGINAL ART - Annie Fanny - HUGE BOOBS	$49.65	1978 ADVERTISING PLAYBOY PLAYMATE CALENDAR - COMPLETE	$10.75
ORIGINAL ART By Johanna, WATERCOLOR PINUP, Sunny	$40.00	Lg Sexy Nude Pin Up Girl Calendar Sample Backward Miss	$10.69
1958 PLAYBOY CALENDAR W/SLEEVE EXCELLENT SHAPE	$40.00	Art Fantastix Premiere #13 GENNADIY KOUFAY Book PinUp	$10.50

Mature Audiences ▸ Risque Novelties

The average sales price in this subcategory is $10.15.

	HIGH		AVG
1973 PLAYBOY PLAYMATE Life Size Party Puzzle COMPLETE	$108.49	ADULT PARTY GAMES - Fun for intimate parties & couples!	$10.98
adult Inflatable TRICKY DICK PENIS Halloween COSTUME	$103.51	[2 of these sold for $10.98 each]	
LOVE SWING FULLY ADJUSTABLE BRAND NEW $169	$79.95	ADULT PARTY GAMES - Fun for intimate parties & couples!	$10.97
GET THIN-GET HOT DIET PILL-COME N AND SEE WHY	$79.60	STURGIS SHOEBOX ADULT HOT WHEELS CUSTOM	$10.50
[8 of these sold in a multiple item ("Dutch") auction for $9.95 each]		WHIP - Black Leather Heavy Duty Flail Whip 21" Total	$10.50
THE SEXIEST DIET PILL EVER-COME N AND SEE WHY WHY	$49.75	MR. HAPPY-PINK STUFFED PENIS W/ BEAN BAG BALLS	$10.50
[5 of these sold in a multiple item ("Dutch") auction for $9.95 each]		Passion Pearl Thong	$10.00
Adult Love Sex Suspension Swing New adjustable	$45.80	New Erotic Dice & Naughty Ring Toss Lot, Let's Play	$10.00
Harness Leather Open Mouth Cleave Drool Ring Gag Stud	$39.99	BLACK STELTH WEENIE WARMER	$9.99
Deluxe Bed of Roses - Love Kit	$39.99	CROCHETTED PENIS BLACK W RED	$9.99
basic set of 5 Red spreader bar's Bondage	$34.95	Big Wholesale Lot Sex Drive/Breast Enhancers Etc	$9.99
The Guy Game PS2	$31.00	MUFF DIVERS Association BLACK T-Shirt	$9.99
Have an online AFFAIR with Hot, Sexy M.I.L.F. "Olivia"	$28.01	Naughty Explicit Opium Pipes from the Philippines	$9.99
Sheri's Ranch Halloween Girl Brothel Token! NEW!!!	$25.59	MUFF DIVERS Association BLACK T-Shirt	$9.99
New PEARL Blue Dolphin Vibe - A MUST HAVE - SAVE $$$	$24.99	WEIRD TIN BEST HEAD IN TOWN	$9.99
Dom/Sub/Mistress Leather Collar to Wrist Restraints	$24.99	BEER BAR ROOM SIGN	$9.99
[2 of these sold for $24.99 each]		vintage playboy pin-up doll 1960? MARILYN MONROE	$9.99
Gothic Style Black Leather Thigh Cuffs Restraints	$24.99	TURN HER ON PILL.......SHE WILL BE AN ANIMAL!!!!	$9.99

Jetaime Sex Toy - Sex Machine - Industrial Strength

Bidding has ended for this item

If you are a winner, Sign In for your status.

List an item like this or buy a similar item below.

Winning bid:	**US $510.00**
Ended:	Oct-22-05 20:40:43 PDT
Start time:	Oct-12-05 20:40:43 PDT
History:	12 bids (US $250.00 starting bid)
Winning bidder:	ckendallm (125 ☆)
Item location:	Stamford, CT United States

Mature Audiences ▸ Video

The average sales price in this subcategory is $12.03.

	HIGH		AVG
Bondage - 45 OOP Harmony Concepts Videos - No Reserve!	$126.04	Showering studs 2 - shower and locker room	$12.49
Let me make a video just for you	$113.50	Mixed sexfight in costumes! Busty blonde MIKKI TAYLOR	$12.48
30 VIDEOS-YMAC-HIS-Classics-Pre-Condoms-NR!	$93.50	BIG BUSTY CHRISTINA MODEL VIDEO 56	$12.46
Bondage - 42 Misc. Bondage/Tickling/Fetish - No Reserve	$91.00	California Spread-David Dude-Shotgun Video-RARE	$12.38
30 VIDEOS-Falcon-YMAC-Twinks-Classics-Pre-Condoms-NR!	$86.00	Forbidden Letters-Arthur Bressan-IntelligenceVideo-RARE	$12.38
Box of 100 GAY VHS VIDEOS ~ 100s of HOURS of FUN!!	$76.00	Diary of an M-VCX Video-1970's-RARE	$12.38
Bondage - 8 Natasha Flade Harmony Videos - No Reserve!	$76.00	Four Letters-RARE	$12.05
30 VIDEOS-YMAC-Cadinot-Classics-Pre-Condoms-NR!	$70.99	Wrestling Meat-Chris Burns-HIS Video-1981-RARE	$12.00
My FIRST Sexy TRICK Or TREAT Home Made Movie Video VHS	$66.00	CUCKOLD 1 Interracial Sex Femdom BLACK MALE SUPREMACY	$12.00
Amateur Tranvestite TV Elena VHS PART TWO	$59.92	Toys 3 - Jamie Summers, Carol Cummings, more...VHS	$12.00
My FIRST MILF Custom TRICK Or TREAT Home Made Video VHS	$56.00	Sexy Muscular Latino CARLOS BOTERO	$11.99
Jay Edwards Video JEV-60 Bambi	$54.00	Real * Wife Watchers * #8- INTERRACIAL !	$11.99
VHS tapes	$50.00	Twinks= Daddy's Reform School Playmate = *New In Box*	$11.99
K9 GRANNIE DENNIO, NAUGHTY ALYSHA BIG	$50.00	Best of 80's star AJA 8 hr Custom comp	$11.99
CROSS COUNTRY PARTS 1 &2 FALCON HOT!!!!!	$49.55	Falcon Jocks SERVICED vhs JVP93	$11.60

Mature Audiences ▶ Other

The average sales price in this subcategory is $20.12.

	HIGH		AVG
BILL WARD ORIGINAL SEX TO SEXTY ART	$416.00	Playboy: The Mansion (PC Games) Plus Extras (2 DVD)	$20.50
BILL WARD ORIGINAL SEX TO SEXTY ART	$380.00	I am a bad little b!tch Not a phone call CYO Fantasy	$20.50
Christy Canyon Magazine and trading card	$374.69	MY PICTURES IN HOSE AND MASK JUST FOR YOU MEEEOW	$20.50
BILL WARD ORIGINAL SEX TO SEXTY ART	$316.00	Naughty or Nice I'll let you decide....30 minute call	$20.50
BILL WARD ORIGINAL SEX TO SEXTY ART	$305.03	PHONE CHAT , PENPAL, OR EMAIL BUDDY PLUS BONUS	$20.50
NEW SOLID BODY SILICONE REAL LOVE DOLL	$305.00	Clone Your Willy Kit - Your Own Realistic!	$20.49
BILL WENZEL ORIGINAL SEX TO SEXTY ART	$263.90	Sexy Straps Kit - Colorful Ties for your Mate	$20.49
POCKET WATCH with EROTIC	$238.00	Communication....with a Naughty Naughty Girl	$20.00
AUTOMATON NAPOLEONIC DIAL		WIN A MEMBERSHIP TO MY WEB PAGE !!!!!!!!!!	$20.00
LYNN HARRISON ORIGINAL SEX TO SEXTY ART	$227.51	[2 of these sold in a multiple item ("Dutch") auction for $10.00 each]	
Christy Canyon RARE videos AND DVDs	$217.53	F. SHOCKLEY ORIGINAL SEX TO SEXTY ART	$20.00
BILL WENZEL ORIGINAL SEX TO SEXTY ART	$202.50	ROBERT STOGSDILL ORIGINAL SEX TO SEXTY ART	$20.00
Piffy is Back-Mystery Box 2-Be my Realdoll Lover Please	$177.50	Pre-Paid access to porn website	$20.00
LYNN HARRISON ORIGINAL SEX TO SEXTY ART	$177.50	FRANK SEMATONES ORIGINAL SEX TO SEXTY ART	$20.00
LYNN HARRISON ORIGINAL SEX TO SEXTY ART	$150.00	15 Minute Phone Call with Hot , Sexy M.I.L.F. "Olivia"	$20.00
BILL WENZEL ORIGINAL SEX TO SEXTY ART	$150.00	Original 1-sheet movie poster RUN SWINGER RUN 1960's	$20.00

Memberships

The average sales price in this subcategory is $20.12.

	HIGH		AVG
UNLIMITED LIMOUSINE SERVICE WHILE IN LAS VEGAS	$5,000.00	VALLARTA, MEXICO / GOLD CROWN / HIGH RED / TIMESHARE	$25.00
Mountain Lakes Campground membership Lytle Creek CA	$2,500.00	10 ACRE LUSH OCEAN FRONT - WHITE SANDS - FLOATING !!	
"R-Ranch" 1/250th OWNERSHIP of 5.119 acres ½ off	$2,081.00	COAST TO COAST I RPI NACO LTR Campground Membership	$25.00
Far Northern California, FISH,HUNT, CAMP,HORSES		$8 pr night I Full Membership Usage I Open Year Round	
Thousand Trails/ NACO/Leisure Time lifetime membership	$1,650.00	COAST TO COAST-RPI/NACO/LTR CAMPING MEMBERSHIP	$24.00
Mountain Lakes Campground Membership Lytle Creek CA	$1,526.01	$8.00 PER NIGHT NATIONWIDE" OUT CLAUSE" IN WRITING	
BALLY TOTAL FITNESS / LIFETIME OLYMPIC GOLD MEMBERSHIP	$1300.00	one year membership adult website n	$19.99
NO DUES & NO EXPIRATION/// FULL ACCESS NATIONWIDE		ude sexy hot women View similar active items	
Bally Total Fitness Bally's Presidents Membership		LIFETIME MEMBERSHIP - HOTELS ETC. SAVE 50% ON HOTELS	$19.95
$24/year for life I Paid thru 3/07, NO TRANSFER FEE !!	$1,236.00	Bally's Total Fitness Four Week Guest Pass	$15.99
******BALLY'S PREMIER MEMBERSHIP	$1,089.02	National Geographic Magazine Subscription (12 issues)	$15.50
-NO TRANSFER FEE******		HOT NEW !!! ADULT PREPAID INTERNET ACCESS CARD!! L@@K	$10.00
UNLIMITED LIMOUSINE SERVICE WHILE IN LAS VEGAS	$1,000.00	Café Latte Membership (lifetime) Coffeeclubemails $9.50	$9.50
King Limousine Platinum Membership Card		12 Months Access To Adult Webcam Site!!Jenna Pamela	$8.99
BALLY'S PREMIER PLUS MEMBERSHIP no dues till 6/08 PAY NO	$810.00	[2 of these sold for $8.99 each]	
DUES FOR 2 ½ YEARS, CURRENT RENEWAL $5.14/MONTH		Café Latte Membership (lifetime) Coffeeclubemails	$6.99
Thousand Trails Membership	$760.00	Bally 4 Week Membership PASS w/FREE Shipping ..Get Fit!	$6.01
OUTDOOR WORLD MASTER CAMPING/CAMPGROUND	$730.00	ADULT PORN FREE MEMBERSHIP SEX SITE	$5.99
MEMBERSHIP 2005 DUES PAID!!!! LOW LOW PRICE!		[3 of these sold for $5.99 each]	
Bally's Premier Plus Lifetime Membership. Bally Gym	$660.00	Trump Internat. Golf Course	$5.50
thousand trails/naco membership	$600.00	Member Phone List Exclusive Millionairs Phone List	
Gold's Gym VIP 2 Year Memberships For 2 People	$600.00	24 Hour Fitness 2 30 Day Guest Passes	$5.01

Metaphysical ▶ Astrology

The average sales price in this subcategory is $25.60.

	HIGH		AVG
The Jack Gillen Commodity Psion Computer	$1,274.00	MST3K SEASON FIVE DVDs Mystery Science Theater !!!	$30.00
The Jack Gillen Commodity Psion Computer	$1,200.00	[2 of these sold for $30.00 each]	
magick crowley ring sex tantra thelema wicca OTO occult	$250.00	10 Belgian crystal ZODIAC coasters VAL ST. LAMBERT	$29.97
ZODIAC MARBLE MOSAIC ART TILE TABLETOP OR FLOOR INLAY	$178.50	MST3K SEASON TEN DVDs Mystery Science Theater !!!	$29.00
DVD TON of MST3K Mystery Science Theater 3000 DVD	$120.00	Vintage Italian Astrology / Zodiac Pewter Globe	$28.00
[30 of these sold in a multiple item ("Dutch") auction for $4.00 each]		LOT OF 14 ASTROLOGY BOOKS New Age Past Lives Romance	$26.52
Mariner Astrolabe LARGE 12 in BRASS Antiqued	$64.15	*AWESOME CELTIC ZODIAC CIRCLE TAPESTRY~MANY USES~!*	$25.00
DVD TON of MST3K Mystery Science Theater 3000 DVD DVD	$60.00	GENERAL PRINCIPLES OF ASTROLOGY, THE - ALEISTER CROWLEY	$24.99
[15 of these sold in a multiple item ("Dutch") auction for $4.00 each]		The Astrologer by Alphonse Mucha	$24.99
MST3K SEASON EIGHT DVDs Mystery Science Theater !!!	$57.00	*CELTIC CIRCLE~ZODIAC SYMBOLS~HUGE TAPESTRY~!*	$23.50
Astrology At Work	$52.99	INTERPRETING the ECLIPSES - Rare Astrology	$22.50
Mariner Astrolabe LARGE 12 in BRASS Antiqued	$51.00	LARGE CELESTIAL Wall Clock Sun Moon Stars Clocks	$22.45
Mariner Astrolabe LARGE 12 in BRASS Antiqued	$50.99	FLEECE FABRIC/BLANKET/SUN* MOON	$21.99
Astrology At Work	$50.00	*STARS* ASTROLOGY-CUTE	
MST3K SEASON THREE DVDs Mystery Science Theater !!!	$43.00	LARGE CELESTIAL Wall Clock Sun Moon Stars Clocks	$21.95
MST3K SEASON FIVE DVDs Mystery Science Theater !!!	$41.00	[2 of these sold for $21.95 each]	
When Pigs Fly Antenna ball Guardian angel FLYING pig	$10.00	Blenko Glass Handmade Cancer Suncatcher 7.25" Orange	$21.53
[4 of these sold in a multiple item ("Dutch") auction for $10.00 each]		MST3K SEASON ONE DVDs Mystery Science Theater !!!	$21.50

Metaphysical ▶ Crystal Healing

The average sales price in this subcategory is $21.42.

	HIGH		AVG
COMPLETE SET OF 7 FROSTED QUARTZ CRYSTAL SINGING BOWLS	$875.00	PINK LEOPARDSKIN JASPER~PROTECTION, GROUNDING, INSIGHT	$21.61
LIFESIZED! Black Hills Snow Quartz Carved Crystal Skull	$721.35	*!*Australia's Laguna - Queensland Agate Creek Dznr Cab	$21.50
WOW Violet Blue Eye Naga Egg Thai Buddha Relic Talisman	$300.00	S2S Bright Blues Shattuckite Carved Crystal Skull	$21.50
AMAZINGLY RARE Strawberry Quartz Carved Crystal Skull	$289.35	BIG GREEN MOSS AGATE SPHERE ~ CRYSTAL BALL 60mm! GREAT	$21.50
Rare Colorado Phenacite crystals . 400 carats t.w.	$250.00	BIG DARK RED MAHOGANY OBSIDIAN CRYSTAL SKULL ~ STUNNING	$21.49
HUGE DARK AMETHYST QUARTZ CRYSTAL DRUZE GEODE CLUSTER	$240.38	SUNSTORM CORAL~INNER PEACE, MENTAL CLARITY, IMAGINATION	$21.49
BIG AMETHYST QUARTZ CRYSTAL CATHEDRAL GEODE CHURCH LG	$240.35	VINTAGE RHODOCHROSITE PENDANTS / TEAR DROPS CAB LOT!	$21.45

	HIGH		AVG
LG CLEAR QUARTZ CRYSTAL HEALING POINT 5lbs POLISHED	$202.50	AQUAMARINE STONE NECKLACE! HI VIBRATIONAL! SUBLIME!	$21.22
Tantra AMMONITE SHELL RING w SNOW LEOPARD HEALING W@W!	$191.49	LAPIS PENDULUM	$21.01
WOW! 4 7/8" QUARTZ CRYSTAL BALL/SPHERE - PHANTOMS	$190.50	S2S Radiant Moon Quartz Carved Mother Earth Goddess	$21.00
GIGANTIC QUARTZ CRYSTAL SPHERE	$182.50	10 Healing Hematite Magnetic Bead NECKLACES Jewelry Lot	$20.99
EXCEPTIONAL! LG. NATURAL Turquoise Carved Crystal Skull	$181.35	VERY RARE! SHIVA EYE IN *** AMETHYST *** SPHERE 48 mm	$20.59
Tantra AMMONITE SHELL AMULET Here is SUPERNATURAL POWER	$166.75	CLEAR NATURAL QUARTZ PHANTOM CRYSTAL POINT *RARE	$20.51
HUGE NATURAL QUARTZ CRYSTAL HEALING CLUSTER POINT LG	$162.50	VESUVIANITE PENDULUM	$20.51
HUGE NATURAL QUARTZ CRYSTAL HEALING CLUSTER POINT LG	$160.00	AZURITE PENDULUM	$20.51

Metaphysical ▸ Feng Shui

The average sales price in this subcategory is $10.41.

	HIGH		AVG
Rattan chair, and ottoman . brown/black lounge chair	$250.00	1920s Antique Jade 2x Dragon energy talisman Spelled	$10.50
Tibet,MrTs ULTIMATE GOOD LUCK Tibetan KALACHAKRA wood	$160.00	40mm Swarovski Crystal BALL suncatcher Prism Feng shui	$10.50
5'x2.6' RIDDLE RUG: AUSPICIOUS BATS & TIBETAN LABYRINTH	$89.00	38mm VINTAGE DIAMOND SPEAR Shape Crystal Prism 5 for $1	$10.50
36"x24"OIL REALISM ANIMAL: WHITE TIGER/feng shui animal	$61.00	[3 of these sold in a multiple item ("Dutch") auction for $3.50 each]	
Rose Quartz Lighted Fountain with Rolling Ball	$59.00	Clear Crystal Ball 110mm Globe-Sphere -Round gift box	$10.50
130MM SCRYING CRYSTAL GAZING BALL	$49.99	Zen Art Brass Feng Shuii Desktop Windbell Pavilion Styl	$10.50
Superb & Massive 'Coiling Dragon' Longevity Motif Dzi	$49.00	2 Lg. 40MM VINTAGE GOLF BALL SIZE Crystal PRISM BALLS!	$10.50
RARE 'GOLDEN DRAGON SKIN' Longevity Bottle Motif Dzi	$48.00	AUTH OLD TIBETAN AUSPICIOUS 5 EYE 5 ELEMENTS DZI BEAD	$10.30
Old Feng Shui Coin Sword w/ 130 + Coins NR	$42.01	SET 2 MINIATURE ZEN GARDENS FENG SHUI MINI GARDEN NEW!	$10.19
==5'x2.5' Tibetan Dragon & Phoenix Feng Shui Wool Rug==	$41.01	ROYAL ZEN GARDEN THE GARDEN IN A BOX! RELAX! L@@K!	$10.03
Superb & Massive 'Dual Tone' Tibetan 8 Eyed dZi Bead	$41.00	Clear Crystal Ball 110mm Globe-Sphere -Round gift box	$10.01
Ultra Fancy~Tibetan Antique Jade Tai Chi~Heart Talisman	$40.01	Feng Shui Kit:For Health,Wealth,Happiness-NIB-SHIP FREE	$10.00
Large 4" Crystal Mystic Gazing Ball Globe Wood Stand	$39.99	~BRAND NEW~ Feng Shui Candle Set ~BRAND NEW~	$10.00
50 SET of 20MM VINTAGE 32% LEAD CRYSTAL FENG SHUI BALLS	$39.95	Feng Shui Chinese Medicine Panda Bear Stress Balls Yoga 1	$10.00
[2 of these sold for $39.95 each]		[2 of these sold in a multiple item ("Dutch") auction for $5.00 each]	
LUCKY GOLDEN MONEY CAT w/ WAVING	$35.00	Silk Prayer Flags Bamboo Garden Feng Shui	$10.00
PAW GOOD FORTUNE new!!		FENG SHUI COLOR SOLID GLASS CRYSTAL BALL 80MM RUBY RED	$9.99

Metaphysical ▸ Goth

The average sales price in this subcategory is $19.46.

	HIGH		AVG
Wormwood Liquid Absinthe 12total 7.99EACH LowShip!	$96.00	BLACK GOTHIC/CELTIC Velvet VAMPIRE Princess SKIRT L/XL	$19.99
[12 of these sold in a multiple item ("Dutch") auction for $8.00 each]		[2 of these sold for $19.99 each]	
Skull & Crossbones/Lot of 38 Rings/Halloween L@@K Goth	$76.00	BLACK WICCA/VELVET Celtic MAGIC CORSET TOP/SHIRT NEW 4X	$19.99
Gothic Priest Caftan Robe & Hood Cape Black velvet Goth	$56.99	BLACK GOTHIC/GYPSY Romanian RENAISSANCE SKIRT New L/XL	$19.99
BLACK WICCA/VELVET Celtic MAGIC	$50.99	SEXY GOTH MEDIEVAL RENAISSANCE HOODED BLACK DRESS MED	$19.99
CORSET TOP/SHIRT NEW L		UNIQUE GOTHIC FACES ATHAME,CURVED BLADE DAGGER,WICCA	$19.99
Wormwood Liquid Absinthe 12total 7.99EACH LowShip! !	$47.94	TMGC- brown TIGEREYE GARGOYLE carving 59MM spotted	$18.99
[6 of these sold in a multiple item ("Dutch") auction for $7.99 each]		TMGC- brown PICTURE JASPER GARGOYLE carving 60MM gothic	$18.99
HUGE 4x6ft OOGIE BOOGIE Nightmare B4 Xmas Disney Poster	$46.96	TMGC 2.3" Green AVENTURINE GRIFFIN carving winged lion	$18.99
1967 Mag - Anton LaVey, Satanism, Hunter S. Thompson	$45.00	BLACK GOTHIC/PEASANT Plus Size CORSET TOP/SHIRT NEW 3X	$18.49
BLACK GOTHIC/CELTIC Velvet VAMPIRE Zig-Zag SKIRT 2X/3X	$44.99	Absinthe & Wormwood Liquid Instant Kit Express LowShip XL	$17.99
DYNAMITE BLACK LEATHER LOOK CLOAK/GOTH/WICCA	$39.99	[4 of these sold for $17.99 each]	
BLACK WICCA/VELVET Celtic MAGIC CORSET TOP/SHIRT NEW 4X	$36.00	BLACK GOTHIC/PEASANT Plus Size CORSET TOP/SHIRT NEW 3X	$17.99
BLACK GOTHIC/GYPSY Romanian RENAISSANCE SKIRT New L/XL	$34.99	LARGE MINERAL AMBER SPECIMEN OLD FIND NO RESV!	$17.50
BLACK 100% VELVET/LACE ~ GOTHIC/WICCA MAGIC SKIRT L/XL	$30.00	BOHEMIAN WICCAN RED CELTIC CROSS DRESS - NEW!	$16.99
BLACK WICCA/VELVET Celtic MAGIC CORSET TOP/SHIRT NEW L	$29.79	Wormwood Liquid Absinthe 12total 7.99EACH LowShip!	$15.98
Absinthe & Wormwood instant Kit Stronger LowFastShip	$28.99	[2 of these sold in a multiple item ("Dutch") auction for $7.99 each]	
PURPLE WITCH/GOTHIC SATIN Flare Cuff PEASANT TOP NEW L	$28.99	Midnight Fire Mr.Booger Lampwork Glass Bead Annealed NR	$15.50

Metaphysical ▸ Psychic, Paranormal

The average sales price in this subcategory is $26.17.

	HIGH		AVG
Haunted Sapphire Ring Brings Extreme Luck & Fortune	$912.00	PRIVATE Triquetra Spirit Board Ouija Solomon Ghost HB	$26.50
HAUNTED WITCHES MOTHER OF PEARL MONEY RING-Possessed	$820.00	[2 of these sold for $26.50 each]	
Haunted bracelet,brings love,luck,wishes,magic! LOOK!!!	$710.00	HAUNTED STERLING SILVER BRACELET Lucky! Right Place!	$26.05
HAUNTED -"DRALANA" SILVER CORD PRIESTESS	$630.00	FAST HAIR GROWTH SPELL & CUSTOM TALISMAN~by REAL WITCH!	$26.00
HAUNTED DOLL -"DRALANA" SILVER CORD PRIESTESS	$455.00	Silver skull ring found in a civil war cemetery	$26.00
1891 Wood Handpainted Ouija Game Board Fortune Telling	$405.00	HAUNTED GOLD RHINESTONE CHOKER Spirit moves items!	$26.00
HAUNTED WITCHES PURPLE PSYCHIC MONEY RING- Possessed	$366.03	*Haunted Doll - Adopt A Spirit - Who Will You Get?*	$26.00
HAUNTED TENT TRAILER?	$350.00	BREAK UP DiVoRcE SPELL & CUSTOM TALISMAN~by REAL WITCH!	$26.00
LIDIEX COBALT & CLEAR SPELLED PYRAMID ~ VOODOO ESTATE	$349.00	3 POWER BRACELET	$26.00
HAUNTED MONEY RING WICCAN SPELL.	$296.99	HAUNTED WITCH LARIMAR CONTACT SPIRITS AMULET PENDANT	$26.00
GAIN WEALTH NOW!!!!$$$		Parker Brothers OUIJA Mystifying Oracle Board Game 1972	$26.00
VINTAGE 1891 OUIJA BOARD, FORTUNE TELLING, MUST SEE!!!!	$256.66	PTTB Halloween Ghost Haunted House 13 Spook OUIJA BOARD	$25.99
VAMPIRE KILLING KIT !!!!! HAUNTED HOUSE OF HORROR!!!!!	$255.00	[2 of these sold for $25.99 each]	
HAUNTED PSYCHIC TALISMAN VISIONS	$255.00	LOVER RETURN TO ME SPELL&AMULET&MAGIC CANDLE~by WITCH!	$25.99
ESP CLAIRVOYANCE SPELL		PTTB Spooky Caribbean Pirate Ghost Ship OUIJA BOARD fun	$25.99
VINTAGE MEMBERSHIP RING Rosicrucian AMORC Jewelry	$255.00	Electromagnetic Field Detector Ghost Hunting/Paranormal	$25.71
SO POWERFUL ADARA WITCH HAUNTED ALL U NEED	$250.50	haunted**Healing Bloodstone Necklace** Owned by WITCH	$25.52

Metaphysical ▸ Reiki

The average sales price in this subcategory is $10.91.

	HIGH		AVG
Intense Rainbow Boji Alive Stone #3029	$50.99	MERKABA STAR! CRYSTAL CLEAR QUARTZ! SACRED GEOMETRY!	$14.66
Original CHAKRA Aura Abstract ART Painting BUMBLES AAM	$49.00	REIKI FOLK SPIRIT ART DOLL wwao Assemblage	$13.83

GEL Labrodorite - Mystical Earth Energies/Joy - Reiki!	$40.50	AKASHIC RECORDS ATTUNEMENT certificate, manual karma	$11.97
Indigo Star Balancing/Healing Session & Star Totem	$32.95	Crystal Grid Healing & Psychic Reading by Reiki Master	$11.00
Reiki 'Cho Ku Rei' Pure Silver & Moonstone Ring SZ 6	$29.95	Reiki Healing Lrg Quartz Wand	$10.99
3 MONTHS CONTINUOUS Reiki Energy Balancing Therapy 24/7	$29.95	MERKABA STAR! CRYSTAL CLEAR	$10.95
Reiki DVD & Attunement - Learn the secrets of healing!	$27.00	QUARTZ! SACRED GEOMETRY!	
SACRED GEOMETRY SET! BRAZILIAN CLEAR QUARTZ!	$26.50	3" CHAKRA HEALING WAND quartz crystal wicca pagan reiki	$10.95
BLUE GOLDSTONE PENDULUM COSMIC BEAUTY FREE VELVET BAG	$25.01	STERLING Silver & AMETHYST ~* OM NECKLACE ~ India Yoga	$10.53
ALTERED handpainted SKELETON KEY ART DOLL WWAO OOAK	$24.99	Reiki Meditation 2 CD Set - Strengthen Your Connection	$10.00
Karuna REIKI Session HEALING Treatment w/ ANGELS McLean	$24.95	Silver Reiki Symbol "Cho Ku Rei" Amethyst , Wicca	$9.99
SHAMBALLA MDH REIKI ATTUNEMENT manual & certificate	$23.97	1 LB Medium MIXED TUMBLED GEMSTONES wicca mojo jewelry	$9.99
SACRED GEOMETRY SET! BRAZILIAN CLEAR QUARTZ!	$23.25	Crystal Grid Healing & Psychic Reading by Reiki Master	$9.99
Distant / Distance Reiki Chakra Healing Balancing 1 hr	$22.00	1 LB Medium MIXED TUMBLED GEMSTONES wicca mojo jewelry	$9.99
[4 of these sold for $22.00 each]		Silver Reiki Symbol "Cho Ku Rei" Amethyst , Wicca	$9.99
MOONSTONE PENDULM-HIGHLY POLISHED 6 SIDED CRYSTAL	$20.05	Shamballa Multidimensional Healing (REIKI ENERGY)!!	$9.99

Metaphysical ▶ Tarot

The average sales price in this subcategory is $17.03.

	HIGH		AVG
GLASS TAROT NO. 2 - EXTREMELY RARE ART DECK!	$535.25	Manara Erotic Tarot by Milo Manara (Cards)	$17.50
The Hermetic Tarot	$350.00	THE GILDED TAROT DECK & BOOK SET	$17.50
Minotarot Tarot Cards Limited Edition Signed	$310.02	Rider Tarot Cards Deck + Waite Pictorial Key Guide New	$17.50
~ Rare Lenormand fortune telling cards - Tarot 1880 ~	$300.00	Tarot Roots of Asia Buddhist Cards Deck NEW	$17.49
Tarot Deck Collection - Huge! More than 60 Items	$275.00	Miniature Tarot "22 ARCANI - 1835"	$17.28
Rare Tibetan Tarot Cards #4/1000 first printing 1952	$263.98	THE WELL WORN PATH - WICCA/PAGAN DECK GRIMASSI ~NEW!~	$17.25
GLORIA CALDERON TAROT-Ltd. Ed #37/200, Signed, Scarce	$250.00	Builders of the Adytum Tarot Cards	$17.01
Scarce GENTILINI TAROT cards - 1976, Kaplan I, Long OOP	$250.00	1989 d'Arte TAROCCHI ERMETICI	$17.00
~ Rare Lenormand fortune telling cards - Tarot 1880 ~	$242.50	Giotto Di Bondone Tarot Cards Deck Artist MUST SEE!	$16.99
Tarot de Lasenic - Lasenicuv Tarot, Pierre de Lasenic	$212.50	Tarot Of The Imagination Cards Deck MUST SEE!	$16.99
The Tarot by Marty Yeager Tarot Cards	$158.16	Ancient Enlightened Tarot Cards Deck	$16.99
Nordic R.D. Deck Tarot Cards	$153.17	Vision Quest Shamanic Indian Tarot Cards Deck NEW!	$16.99
The Hermetic Tarot, Godfrey Dowson	$152.50	Bosch Medieval Artwork Tarot Cards Deck MUST SEE!	$16.99
Lenormand fortune telling cards-Tarot - DONDORF - 1890	$151.50	Ancient Minchiate Etruria Tarot Cards Deck Italy	$16.99
RARE ITALIAN TAROT - TAROCCHI RENATO GUTTUSO	$144.50	Vikings Pagan Tarot Cards Deck Odin Thor	$16.99

Metaphysical ▶ Wicca

The average sales price in this subcategory is $12.14.

	HIGH		AVG
Huge Lot of Wicca Magick Witchcraft Divination Supplies	$125.00	WITCH WICCA WICCAN PAGAN CIRCLE CASTING SPELL MINI KIT	$12.49
10kt 4.50ctw GREEN JADE MOON SHAPE	$100.00	Sz11 SILVER Filigree RING w/ GOLD PENTAGRAM Wiccan	$12.45
DIAMOND ACCENT RING		Wicca Witchcraft Triple Moon Goddess Silver Chalice New	$12.35
Charmed Book of Shadows Pages NEW NR	$91.00	10 Light Weight Screen Fabric Pull-String Bags	$12.00
Simple powerful spells Witchcraft pagan wicca	$91.00	[2 of these sold in a multiple item ("Dutch") auction for $6.00 each]	
SAMHAIN SALE! HUGE WICCA/GODDESS ALTAR KIT	$81.00	NEW ITEM Pewter Black Pentacle Athame Wiccan Pagan	$12.00
BIG!!! 100 mm CRYSTAL BALL & Moon Stars Stand NEW	$79.99	NIB Triple Moon Silver Chalice Wiccan Pagan Druid NICE	$12.00
Vintage WITCH'S BALL HAND BLOWN GLASS OPALESCENT SWIRL	$79.00	SALVIA APIANA not divinorum WHITE SAGE SMUDGE, 1/4 pd!!	$12.00
WITCHCRAFT, MAGIC & ALCHEMY 376 Illustrations OCCULT	$76.99	Pentacle brass screen incense burner censor wiccan	$11.99
1929 Rare WITCH History Occult Black Magic Spells Wicca	$72.00	Sz9 SILVER CAT Kitty FAMILIAR RING Wiccan MEOW Witch	$11.95
WITCHCRAFT- "THE POW-WOW BOOK!" VERY RARE!!!!!	$71.00	Clear QUARTZ Crystal Sphere MAGIC WAND Wicca Spells	$11.95
Mystery Box , MAGIC WITCH ITEMS! A Halloween A+!	$70.00	Size 9 SNAKE RING BLACK ONYX EYES Wicca Pagan Witch	$11.95
Moon~Pathworking~Occult~Magick~Wicca~Metaphysical~Witch	$69.99	Sz 7 FAIRY Dance CIRCLE RING Wicca Pagan Witch Jewelry	$11.95
Fairy Pentacle Bangle Bracelet ~WICCA, PAGAN~	$65.00	Altar Sized WILLENDORF Clay Fired GODDESS STATUE WICCA	$11.95
Samhain Fun! Huge Wiccan Pagan Lot NR 200+ Items!	$61.00	Sz7 SILVER Filigree RING w/ GOLD PENTAGRAM Wiccan Witch	$11.95
HUGE~WITCHCRAFT KIT~DRUID HERB LOT~WICCAN HERBS~SPELLS~	$60.99	Celtic PURPLE GLASS RUNE SET Elder Futhark Oracle WICCA	$11.95

Metaphysical ▶ Other

The average sales price in this subcategory is $14.41.

	HIGH		AVG
Kabbalah Zohar Holy Books English/Aramaic	$269.00	** GOTHIC 24?" GARGOYLE SHORT SWORD ** Wicca	$14.95
18K GOLD ANKH PENDANT w/ King Ankhnaton	$164.95	Silver Mists of Avalon CRESCENT MOON PENDANT Wicca	$14.95
SUPER POWERMID PYRAMID - MAGICK ORGONE MEDITATION CHI	$155.29	**** CAST IRON CAULDRON **** Wicca / Pagan	$14.95
OLD CHURCH ALTAR STONE MARBLE	$135.49	[2 of these sold for $14.95 each]	
Copper MEDITATION PYRAMID Spiritual Energy Reiki 4 ft.	$135.00	Pewter CELTIC WOLF TORC Cuff BRACELET Wiccan Wolves	$14.95
The Egely Wheel Vitality Meter - Aura Energy - Chi	$127.50	Silver RAVEN Crow PENDANT Wicca Pagan Magickal Bird	$14.95
AMAZING POWERMID PYRAMID - ASTRAL	$103.51	2 "Lavender Fluorite Sphere, Cefara & Dream Keeper	$14.40
PROJECTION LUCID MIND		33 MAGICAL ESSENTIAL OIL SAMPLER KIT wicca ritual pagan	$14.00
18K Gold ANKH with SCARAB Pendant	$99.00	CELTIC KNOT SURROUNDING PENTACLE STERLING PAGAN WICCAN	$13.99
18K GOLD ANKH with SCARAB Pendant	$95.00	Silver Wrapped AMETHYST CRYSTAL POINT NECKLACE Wicca	$13.95
Andron By Jovan - The Pheromone Based Cologne for Women	$93.99	GLASS INK WELL Silver Lid Wiccan Spell Writing BOS	$13.95
Line Carved Djembe 24" Tall X 12.25 Pro Model Hand Drum	$89.00	Tao & Zen of Self Discovery & Higher Self CD Hypnosis	$13.95
Master Chakra Stone Collection Fall 2005, 98 Stones NEW	$81.00	Art of Peace & Inner Stillness Guided Meditation CD cds	$13.95
THE TESLA PURPLE ENERGY SHIELD ultimate emf protection	$76.00	Sz9 SS Filigree RING with GOLD PENTAGRAM Wicca Pagan	$13.95
ANTIQUE WOODEN OUIJA BOARD FULD BOX AND PIECE NR	$70.00	Huge DRAGON Purple & Blue coin type boarder TAPESTRY	$13.75

Mystery Auctions

The median sales price in this subcategory is $9.49.

	HIGH		AVG
$$CASH MYSTERY AUCTION BOX$$!!CASH, JEWELRY,MUST SEE!!! HUGE BOX WITH CASH!!!! Includes other expensive jewelry	$10,000.00	* WHITE ENVELOPE WITH FREE MYSTERY BEST BUY GIFT CARD *	$9.54

Best $$$ CASH Mystery BOX Auction! CASH, JEWELRY $$$$$	$10,000.00	Mystery Gift card~Walmart Go	$9.50
LOTS OF CASH AND OTHER EXPENSIVE ITEMS! LOOK NOW! BEST$		Bananas MONKEY -TOO CUTE View	
CASH MYSTERY BOX JEWELRY RINGS DIAMONDS MUST SEE	$10,000.00	WAL-MART GIFT CARD - MYSTERY	$9.50
CONTAINS 100 U.S. BILLS: NO 1's OR 5's + JEWELRY AMAZIN		AMOUNT - $5.00 to $300.00	
An Evening in NYC with Flavia Colgan at PA Society	$8,210.00	RECEIPTS TO PROVE I BOUGHT THEM!!!!! NOT A SCAM!!	
Dinner, Governor Mifflin Party, Meet MSNBC stars		[2 of these sold for $9.50 each]	
JEWELRY BOX PACKED WITH REAL DIAMONDS, CASH &	$6,110.00	Target Mystery Gift Card	$9.50
MUCH MORE DIAMONDS......JEWELRY.....CASH		Mystery Gifts - Valued at over $250 - Christmas Sale	$9.50
JEWELLRY BOX PACKED WITH REAL DIAMONDS, CASH & MUCH MORE	$6,100.00	Mystery gift card auction Wal-Mart FUN Free Shipping	$9.50
Mystery Box Auction! Cash, Jewelry, Electronics! Look!	$6,000.00	MYSTERY BOX - CASH? YANKEE CANDLE? BATH AND BODY ?	$9.50
The best on eBay! Bidder bonuses as well!		WAL-MART GIFT CARD MYSTERY	$9.50
THE MERRY CHRISTMAS MYSTERY AUCTION! WORTH THOUSANDS!	$5,600.00	AUCTION MICKEY MOUSE $5-$300	
Im giving away more than OPRA!!!!!!!! WATCH THIS !!!!!!		* WHITE ENVELOPE WITH FREE MYSTERY BEST BUY GIFT CARD *	$9.50
$$CASH MYSTERY AUCTION BOX$$!!CASH, JEWELRY,MUST SEE!!!	$5,100.00	[2 of these sold for $9.50 each]	
HUGE BOX WITH CASH!!!! Includes other expensive jewelry		LADIES PURSE-NEW-MYSTERY AUCTION-	$9.49
CASH $$ JEWELLRT $$ ELECTRONICS $$ MYSTERY BOX	$5,100.00	BROWN -EXTRA GOODIES!!	
The Largest Bonus Payouts in Mystery Box History! L@@K!		WHEEL of FORTUNE Mystery Auction CASH BOX $$$	$9.48
CASH MYSTERY BOX JEWELRY RINGS DIAMONDS MUST SEE	$5,001.00	CASH MONEY could make you a FORTUNE BONUS $$$	
CONTAINS 100 U.S. BILLS: NO 1's OR 5's + JEWELRY AMAZIN		Card Mystery Box!!!! Non-Sport Cards	$9.48
HO,HO,HO,VERY MERRY MYSTERY AUCTION!!!WORTH $1000's!!!!	$5,001.00	What could be inside???? Not Full Of Junk!!!	
Can't Buy Me Love Mystery Auction	$5,000.12	**WHITE ENVELOPE??MYSTERY?? AMOUNT	$9.48
Diamonds, Gold, Prada, Gucci, Electronics, CASH $$$$$$		BEST BUY GIFT CARD**	
Insane Mystery Box! Guaranteed $25,000 Must See NR	$5,000.00	WAL-MART GIFT CARD - MYSTERY AMOUNT - $5.00 to $300.00	$9.46
Xbox 360 Free Ca$H, Unbelievable Gifts check feedback!!		RECEIPTS TO PROVE I BOUGHT THEM!!!!! NOT A SCAM!!	
MYSTERY ! Worth More Than $60,000+ 24k G__ Sil__ & Plati	$4,999.99	**!! MYSTERY WALMART GIFT CARD !!** !!!! Free S/H !!!!	$9.44

Personal Security ▶ Alarms

The average sales price in this subcategory is $25.66.

	HIGH		AVG
Zetron Alarm Dialer, like new, manual provided	$305.00	Strobe Motion Alarm , Portable,W / Remote, Home/Office	$31.00
[2 of these sold for $305.00 each]		HOME Security Alarm / Motion Activated W/ Dialer	$28.50
Zetron Alarm Dialer, like new, manual provided	$275.00	MOTION ACTIVATED SECURITY ALARM AUTO DIALER NIB	$27.00
Security Alarm Mini Hard Tags, Checkpoint	$150.00	MACE BRAND MOTION SENSOR	$26.00
[7 of these sold for $150.00 each]		SECURITY ALARM FOR HOME	
Wholesale Lot 50pcs Personal Alarms in Retail Package	$100.00	Gerber River Runner w/Sheath A Must Have 7in 4oz #5740	$25.95
HOME & OFFICE SECURITY SYSTEM	$80.00	[2 of these sold for $25.95 each]	
Wireless Home Security System ,Expandable ,Easy Install	$75.00	Gerber River Shorty w/Sheath A Must Have 7in 4oz #5640	$24.95
2 12/24 VDC POWER SUPPLYS ADEMCO ALTRONIX FIRE ALARM	$71.09	Safe T Alert intruder alarm SA-5300 motion detector 9V	$24.51
NAPCO Gemini 816 Performance Pak Plus Alarm System	$65.00	Federal vibratone horn 120V electric	$21.50
Western Safety Police megaphone 50 watts max output	$60.00	(48) WIRELESS DOOR & WINDOW	$20.49
HOME Security Alarm / Motion Activated W/ Dialer	$28.50	ALARMS Wholesale Lots HOME	
[3 of these sold for $28.50 each]		SMOKE DETECTORS	$20.00
Techko entry alarm(6) model S087 sold as a group	$53.00	Gerber Seat Belt Cutting Safety Knife 2.4 oz #1480	$18.95
SMART SCAN AUTO DIALER HOME SECURITY ALARM SYSTEM	$52.00	Safety Beam Area Alarm ,Chime,60 ft coverage ,Security	$18.50
Emergency Caller 10-4 Automated Call For Help System	$49.99	Gerber Seat Belt Cutting Safety Knife 2.4 oz #1480	$17.95
SPY PHONE w/ MOTION SENSOR WILL CALL YOU CAN LISTEN	$49.00	MOBIL PROXIMITY CHILD ALARM	$17.50
[2 of these sold for $49.00 each]		MOTION DETECTOR ALARM CEILING	$16.50
THREE STORY FIRE ESCAPE WINDOW LADDER–25 Feet Long!	$43.95	MOUNT w/REMOTE WIRELESS	

Personal Security ▶ Body Armor

The average sales price in this subcategory is $109.53.

	HIGH		AVG
Special Forces SPEAR Body Armor and Load Carry System	$2,000.00	BODY ARMOR, LEVEL IIIA, POINT BLANK BULLET PROOF VEST	$115.00
BRAND NEW, Multi-Hits, Body Armor, SAPI, Ceramic Plate	$500.00	POINT BLANK BODY ARMOR, BULLET PROOF	$114.50
Body armor Molle Vest, and 3A ballistic Panels NEW	$855.00	VEST SECOND CHANCE	
AMERICAN BODY ARMOR ENTRY BALLISTIC BULLETPROOF VEST	$495.00	Protech Ballistic Bullet Proof Raid Vest Size Small	$112.50
NEW GatorHawk Body Armor 3A LOOK FREE SHIP!!!	$475.00	BULLET PROOF VEST BODY ARMOR P.A.C.A. XL	$112.50
Body armor Molle Vest, and NEW	$475.00	US Military Protective Vest Body Armor Flak Jacket XL	$112.50
Body armor Molle Vest, and NEW	$450.00	PROTECTIVE PRODUCTS VIPER BULLET PROOF VEST MEDIUM	$109.50
Blackhawk Carrier + 2 XL SAPI Plates+2nd chance armor	$450.00	Kevlar Bullet Proof Flack Vest w/Metals & Care Booklet	$107.55
Bulletproof Vest Tufflex Under clothes bullet proof	$440.00	BULLETPROOF VEST BODY ARMOR SIZE XL	$107.50
[8 of these sold in a multiple item ("Dutch") auction for $55.00 each]		Safariland Drop leg holster for Glock Lined	$107.50
Safariland ZERO-G Gold IIIA Body Armor	$400.00	Safari Land Bulletproof Vest	$105.50
RBA Ranger Body Armor w/ SAPI plates Bulletproof vest	$395.00	Safariland Body Armor Bulletproof Vest Level II	$104.49
Point Blank Body Armor LARGE **NEW**	$385.00	Covert Body Armor Very thin No Reserve	$103.50
Military Issue Body Armor - LARGE molle	$365.00	Bulletproof Vest Body Armor Flak Jacket Bullet Proof	$103.49
US Ranger Body Armor	$365.00	Second Chance Level II SC229 Series Bullet Proof Vest	$102.51
Safariland bullet proof vest / body armor XXL-Long	$363.00	SECOND CHANCE MONARCH LEVEL IIA BODY ARMOR BULLET	$102.51

Personal Security ▶ Handcuffs

The average sales price in this subcategory is $12.27.

	HIGH		AVG
20 Pr REAL DOUBLE LOCKING HANDCUFFS	$153.20	New Nickel Plated Steel Leg Irons Shackles with Keys	$14.99
- CHAINED KEYS GIFT		New Pair of Black Steel Handcuffs - Double Lock w/ Keys	$14.99
Handcuffs, gangster/CAPONE era	$141.09	Double Lock Hinged Handcuffs with Case Chrome	$14.99
Handcuffs, duty belt, ASPs' and other police/security	$61.00	HANDCUFFS....personal security, fun, erotic!	$14.50
2 Sets of Handcuffs plus Bianchi Double cuff case	$43.00	REAL DOUBLE LOCKING HINGED HANDCUFFS - 2 KEYS BRAND NEW	$12.98
2 Pairs Smith & Wesson Police Handcuffs	$42.01	BIANCHI 7300 AccuMold Covered Cuff Case	$12.49
New in Box S&W Black Steel	$37.01	New Nickel Plated HANDCUFFS hand cuffs NEW	$12.00

Handcuffs - Model 300 Hinged		[11 of these sold for $12.00 each]	
2 Pairs of Peerless HANDCUFFS police issue mint	$32.01	New Nickel Plated HANDCUFFS hand cuffs NEW	$11.00
2 Pair of Smith & Wesson Model 100 Nickel Handcuffs NR	$32.00	Smith and Wesson Handcuffs S&W Model 100 NEW	$11.00
Peerless Hinged Handcuffs w/ Gould $ Goodrich case	$31.00	Chrome Double Lock Handcuffs	$10.99
Smith & Wesson Hinged Handcuffs - No Reserve	$31.00	Handcuff Case Fobus Paddle Back	$10.75
PEERLESS HINGED HANDCUFFS NICKEL COLOR	$30.88	used good quality handcuffs (with 2 keys)	$10.50
Smith & Wesson Handcuffs with 2 keys - "Hinged" cuffs	$29.50	New Nickel Plated HANDCUFFS hand cuffs NEW	$10.45
Peerless hinged handcuffs penetrate finish	$29.00	[2 of these sold for $10.45 each]	
PEERLESS HINGED HANDCUFFS	$28.00	ASP CHAINED HANDCUFFS W/KEY	$10.01
Smith & Wesson Handcuffs Hand Cuffs SW100	$28.00	VINTAGE Smith and Wesson Handcuffs Model M-100 w/ key	$10.00

Personal Security ▶ Knuckle Dusters

The average sales price in this subcategory is $9.75.

	HIGH		AVG
36 Pair Plastic Knuckle Dusters Just $3.5 ea. FREE S/H	$126.00	2 pairs BLACK PLASTIC KNUCKLES DUSTER .NOT BRASS. LEGAL	$9.95
Security And Police Leather Protective Gloves Large	$46.00	[7 of these sold for $9.95 each]	
Knuckle Dusters Plastic Martial Arts Lot of 4 New	$37.55	KNUCKLE DUSTERS/LIGHT ABS BLACK PLASTIC/NOT BRASS	$9.95
Law Enforcement Gloves with steel shot knuckles! NEW!!	$36.01	[2 of these sold for $9.95 each]	
(Nice Weight) Gold Knuckle Duster((Take A Quick Look))	$36.00	(2)PLASTIC KNUCKLES DUSTER NOT BRASS..BETTER... LEGAL	$8.99
Rare Ironwood Not Brass Knuckle Dusters Larger size	$33.00	[19 of these sold for $8.99 each]	
IRONWOOD EBONY WOOD KAMAGONG	$27.50	KNUCKLES 1 KNUCKLE DUSTERS PLASTIC (NOT brass) KNUX BRASS	$7.99
KNUCKLE KNUCKLES DUSTERS		[2 of these sold for $7.99 each]	
Law Enforcement Gloves with steel shot knuckles! NEW!!	$26.50	DTL Self Defense Knuckle LEGAL Knuckles system in COLOR	$7.95
Law Enforcement Gloves with steel shot knuckles! NEW!!	$26.00	[10 of these sold for $7.95 each]	
Knuckles dusters Plastic Skull Knuckle (not brass)	$24.18	Streetfighter bronze ring with a brass knuckle duster	$7.60
ADT YARD SIGNS **** BOX OF 3 *** LOW PRICE***	$24.00	Streetfighter bronze ring with a brass knuckle duster	$7.01
[3 of these sold for $24.00 each]		PLASTIC KNUCKLES DUSTER NOT BRASS..BETTER... LEGAL COLOR	$6.99
ironwood kamagong defense Not Brass Knuckles Dusters	$23.00	[3 of these sold for $6.99 each]	
ironwood kamagong defense Not Brass Knuckles Dusters	$22.50	Plastic Knuckle Duster Removable Spikes Self Defense GD	$6.99
GREEN/BLACK KNUCKLE DUSTER-FOLDING	$20.51	DTL Self Defense Knuckle LEGAL Knuckles system in COLOR	$6.95
KNIFE NOT BRASS BELT		2 Pair (set) Plastic Knuckles (Like Brass) Dusters Unbr	$6.51
3 KNUCKLES DUSTERS PLASTIC not brass) KNUCKLE KNUX	$20.50	KNUCKLES KNUCKLE DUSTERS ABS PLASTIC (not brass) KNUX	$6.50
		(2) PLASTIC KNUCKLES DUSTER NOT BRASS..BETTER... LEGAL	$6.50
		PLASTIC KNUCKLES DUSTER NOT BRASS..BETTER... LEGAL	$6.00
		ABS PLASTIC KNUCKLE DUSTER like BRASS KNUCKLES butLEGAL	$5.99

Personal Security ▶ Locks

The average sales price in this subcategory is $12.70.

	HIGH		AVG
LOCKSMITH BEST DOUBLE CYLINDER DEADBOLT	$61.00	NEW ONGUARD ARMOR CABLE SECURITY LOCK #100206	$19.99
locksmith kwikset deadbolt	$50.00	ADT YARD SIGNS BOX OF 3......LOW LOW PRICE !!	$17.00
KNOX-BOX 1650 SERIES KEY LOCK BOX	$39.64	U-Lock, Series 700, American Lock Co, Hardened Steel	$10.51
new pella door and window locks	$32.00	LOCKSMITH BEST RIM CYLINDERS	$10.00
DIRECTSTART REMOTE CAR STARTER SYSTEM	$31.25	LOCKSMITH FALCON BEST LOOK ALIKES	$10.00

Personal Security ▶ Pepper Spray

The average sales price in this subcategory is $6.21.

	HIGH		AVG
10 X Wholesale Police Pepper Spray, NEW, LOT	$119.99	WORLDS HOTTEST POLICE PEPPER SPRAY BIG 1/2 OZ SIZE MACE	$6.25
12 -1/2 oz key ring pepper sprays new "great resale"	$67.98	[10 of these sold for $6.25 each]	
[2 of these sold in a multiple item ("Dutch") auction for $33.99 each]		Police Magnum Mini Key Chain & Pouch Pepper Spray Mace	$6.21
Sabre Pepper Spray New In Package Free Shipping!!!	$63.92	WORLDS HOTTEST POLICE PEPPER	$6.05
[8 of these sold in a multiple item ("Dutch") auction for $7.99 each]		SPRAY BIG 1/2 OZ CAN MACE	
ASP Key Defender Mace Pepper Spray NIB	$63.00	Police Magnum 2 oz. Pepper Spray OC-17 + UV Dye ~ Mace	$6.01
[3 of these sold in a multiple item ("Dutch") auction for $21.00 each]		WORLDS HOTTEST POLICE PEPPER SPRAY BIG 2 OZ CAN MACE	$6.01
Wholesale Lot of over 140 units of Pepper Spray	$61.00	Police Magnum ORMD Pepper Spray 2oz Flip Top Unit.	$6.00
Large Lot of PEPPER SPRAY SABRE 911 Back off 74 pcs.	$50.56	WORLDS HOTTEST POLICE PEPPER SPRAY	$6.00
ASP Key Defender Mace Pepper Spray NIB	$45.81	BIG 1/2 OZ CAN MACE	
[3 of these sold in a multiple item ("Dutch") auction for $15.27 each]		Police Magnum Mini Key Chain & Pouch Pepper Spray Mace	$6.00
ASP Key Defender Mace Pepper Spray NIB	$45.00	NEW PEPPER SPRAY IN BLACK KEYCASE	$5.99
[3 of these sold in a multiple item ("Dutch") auction for $15.00 each]		.5 OZ. *ALWAYS FRESH*	
3/4 oz. Pepper Spray 17% 2 MIL. SHU 100% EFFECTIVE ! NIB	$39.50	NEW! Wholesale POLICE ISSUE PEPPER	$5.99
[10 of these sold in a multiple item ("Dutch") auction for $3.95 each]		SPRAY MACE KEYCHAIN	
Pepper spray Fox Labs 1 pound unit	$39.00	[3 of these sold for $5.99 each]	
PEPPER SPRAY 12 PACK	$30.01	2 OZ PEPPER SPRAY STREETWISE Mace 17% 2 mil SAVE$	$5.99
LOT OF 6 3/4 Oz PEPPER SPRAY IN ASSORTED COLOR KEYCASES	$29.99	NEW! Police Issue Pepper Spray Keychain 2 MILLION Mace	$5.99
Pepper Spray Ring Spy incognito Bond 007 Free Shipping	$29.00	Lot of 6 PEPPERSPRAY - Keychains - Self Defence!!!	$5.99
Pengun Tear Gas Pen	$27.47	Police OC-15 MACE Pepper Spray 15% OC Self Defense LC	$5.99
3 in 1 MACE Tear Gas Pepper Spray UV Stain Clip	$26.99	Sabre Chemical Defence/Pepper Spray, 4oz.Magnum Size	$5.99

Personal Security ▶ Safes

The average sales price in this subcategory is $32.89.

	HIGH		AVG
Brand new V-line Wall Safe	$162.51	Steel Multipurpose Drop Lock Box Safe for Money NIB	$36.00
Used large Safe in Excellent Condition!	$152.53	Brand New Cansafes Stash Safe Can Safes Dutch Auction	$35.80
MultiVault Deluxe Gun Safe by GunVault Lock GV2000-DLX	$119.99	[4 of these sold in a multiple item ("Dutch") auction for $8.95 each]	
[13 of these sold for $119.99 each]		NEW DIGITAL SAFE BOX Electronic Security home safety lg	$29.95

	HIGH		AVG
MultiVault Deluxe Gun Safe by GunVault Lock GV2000-DLX	$101.99	[5 of these sold for $29.95 each]	
[2 of these sold for $101.99 each]		NEW DIGITAL SAFE BOX Electronic Security home safety	$29.00
Personal Body Armor/ Bullet Proof Vest	$100.00	Powerful Tibetan Jade~Prosperity Fish W.Spell Talisman~	$28.77
Sentry Group Media File FireProof Safe 6720 LIKE NEW	$99.99	Authentic Shaman's Spells Engraved~Wolf Teeth~Amule	$28.50
MiniVault Deluxe Gun Safe GunVault New lock GV1000-DLX	$99.99	WFTC*Authentic Shaman's Spell Engraved~Wolf Teeth~4/4*B	$28.00
DROP SAFE FOR ANY BUSINESS	$99.95	WFTC*Authentic Shaman's Spell Engraved~Wolf Teeth~3/4*B	$26.50
[5 of these sold for $99.95 each]		NEW Electronic Digital Safe	$25.00
MultiVault GV2000 Gun Safe by GunVault Lock GV2000-STD	$96.99	Water Bottle Safe - Most Realistic Safe	$24.99
Stiffel Freeman Floor Safe Old on Wheels with Combo	$86.02	New Large Wood Tolstoy War and Peace Book Safe gift NR	$24.95
Brand New Cansafes Stash Safe Can Safes Dutch Auction	$80.55	1992 Don Alphin Oak Safe/piggy bank	$22.27
[9 of these sold in a multiple item ("Dutch") auction for $8.95 each]		(2) FAKE BOOK SAFES Secret Vault	$20.50
SAFEGUARD 2-LAYER SAFE W/ QUICK DEPOSIT "UNOPENED"	$52.50	HIDDEN Magnet Safe NEW	$20.50
LARGE SECURITY SAFE 30" TALL APPROX. 400 LB "UNOPENED?"	$52.50	NEW REAL SECRET HIDDEN COVERT	$20.50
Electronic Opening Gun Safe Box For Vehicle	$52.00	SCENTED STASH CANDLE SAFE	$20.50
Sentry 1170 Personal File Fire Safe, NEVER used	$51.00	WFTC*Authentic Shaman's Spell	$20.50
OLD Safe security lock box antiques Hall's SAFE	$36.89	Engraved~Wolf Teeth~1/4*D	

Personal Security ▶ Stun Guns

The average sales price in this subcategory is $30.94.

	HIGH		AVG
Advanced Taser Laser Sight FREE Cartridge Holster	$499.99	Small Fry 900,000 Volt Mini Stun Gun Guns with Holster	$31.00
New Taser Stun Gun	$420.00	[3 of these sold for $31.00 each]	
NEW Muscleman 100,000 Volt Stun Gun	$250.00	BC500P BLACK COBRA 500,000 VOLT STUN GUN* SELF DEFENSE	$31.00
[10 of these sold in a multiple item ("Dutch") auction for $25.00 each]		Small Fry 900,000 Volt Mini Stun Gun Guns with Holster	$30.99
STREETWISE 750K VOLT STUN BATON	$180.00	Small Fry 900,000 volt Stun Gun Stungun / Tazer & Holst	$30.99
[6 of these sold in a multiple item ("Dutch") auction for $30.00 each]		[2 of these sold for $30.99 each]	
FOUR BLACK COBRA 900,000 VOLT MICRO STUN GUN* SECURITY	$156.00	Fry Stun Gun, 900,000 Volts!!! Smallest, Most Powerful!	$30.01
Stun Gun Checkmate	$120.00	Black Cobra "Gamma" Stun Gun	$30.00
NEW Muscleman 100,000 Volt Stun Gun	$117.00	NEW MICRO WIRELESS COLOR HIDDEN	$30.00
[3 of these sold in a multiple item ("Dutch") auction for $39.00 each]		SPY CAMERA SECURITY CAM	
Black Cobra PEN-SIZE 300,000 Volts Stun Gun Guns NEW	$102.50	Brand New Stun Master SM-300SB Stun Baton	$30.00
[2 of these sold for $102.50 each]		[2 of these sold for $30.00 each]	
Black Cobra PEN-SIZE 300,000 Volts Stun Gun Guns NEW	$91.00	PEN STUNGUN 500,000 volt compact black cobra stun gun	$29.99
Black Cobra PEN-SIZE 300,000 Volts Stun Gun Guns NEW	$86.00	Small Fry 900,000 Volt Mini Stun Gun Guns with Holster	$29.99
BLACK COBRA 900,000 VOLT MICRO STUN GUN* & 500,000 PEN	$84.95	STREET WISE 600,000v,130DB SIREN, SAFEST STUN GUN EVER!	$29.95
[3 of these sold for $84.95 each]		[2 of these sold for $29.95 each]	
Black Cobra PEN-SIZE 300,000 Volts Stun Gun Guns NEW	$84.00	Stun Master 500,000 Volt Stun Baton	$29.95
Black Cobra PEN-SIZE 300,000 Volts Stun Gun Guns NEW	$80.01	500k EXTENDING STUN GUN w/FLASH LIGHT CHARGER & HOLSTER	$29.95
STREETWISE® 750K VOLT STUN BATON	$79.60	STREETWISE STUN GUN	$29.95
[4 of these sold in a multiple item ("Dutch") auction for $19.90 each]		Streetwise 900K Volt Stun Gun w/ Alarm and Holster	$29.95

Personal Security ▶ Surveillance Cameras

The average sales price in this subcategory is $41.17.

	HIGH		AVG
survielence equipment cctv dvmr monitor cameras kalatel	$1,225.00	Color Vidio Security Camera with Night Vision	$46.50
3 CCTV PANASONIC SUPER DYNAMIC II PTZ CAMERAS	$880.00	NEW WIRELESS COLOR NIGHT VISION VIDEO CAMERA SPY CAM	$46.50
CCTV/3 PANASONIC PTZ DOME CAMERAS WITH CONTROLLER	$610.00	NEW PRO WIRELESS CCTV NIGHT VISION VIDEO CAMERA SPY CAM	$46.00
Panasonic WV-CS854 PTZ Dome Surveillance Camera	$599.00	NEW WIRELESS COLOR NIGHT VISION VIDEO CAMERA SPY CAM	$46.00
Complete Survellience System-DieBold 4 cameras, etc....	$511.00	WIRELESS HIDDEN MINI PINHOLE COLOR SPY CAMERA NANNY CAM	$42.11
hidden camera and sony video walkman bundle pack	$400.00	NEW Wireless NIGHT VISION VIDEO CAMERA Security Spy Cam	$42.00
2 HONEYWELL CCTV COLOR CAMERAS PELCO ADEMCO	$244.50	WIRELESS HIDDEN MINI PINHOLE COLOR SPY CAMERA NANNY CAM	$41.01
SONY DOME CAMERA KIT, EVERYTHING TO GET YOU STARTED!!	$194.99	WIRELESS HIDDEN MINI PINHOLE COLOR SPY CAMERA NANNY CAM	$41.00
VIDEO INTERCOM SYSTEM	$182.50	NEW WIRELESS COLOR NIGHT VISION VIDEO CAMERA SPY CAM	$41.00
Color Rotating Camera W / Remote & Control Box , SECURE	$130.00	[2 of these sold for $41.00 each]	
2 Day / Night Cameras, W / Audio , B&W Monitor & Cables	$120.00	NEW WIRELESS COLOR NIGHT VISION VIDEO CAMERA SPY CAM	$40.00
Color Vidio Security Camera with Night Vision	$120.00	INFRARED WIRELESS NIGHTVISION MINI COLOR CAMERA CCTV	$39.00
[4 of these sold in a multiple item ("Dutch") auction for $30.00 each]		WIRELESS HIDDEN MINI PINHOLE COLOR SPY CAMERA NANNY CAM	$39.00
Hidden Wireless Camera Clock Radio Sony Dream Machine N	$100.00	NEW WIRELESS COLOR NIGHT VISION VIDEO CAMERA SPY CAM	$39.00
SPYCAM5 SUPER TINY WIRELESS COLOR CAMERA w/ RECEIVER	$99.00	[2 of these sold for $39.00 each]	
WORLDS SMALLEST WIRELESS COLOR	$99.00	Camera Switcher for up to 4 Security Cameras	$38.50
SURVEILLANCE CAMERA* NEW		Fake Motion Detector Surveillance Camera blinking light	$7.50

Personal Security ▶ Other

The average sales price in this subcategory is $23.06.

	HIGH		AVG
2 STAND ALONE Body Armor Bulletproof Plates Level 3 NIJ	$529.95	BOOK VAULT Diversion Hidden Covert Spy Stash Safe	$23.75
[2 of these sold for $529.95 each]		NEW WIRELESS PINHOLE HIDDEN SPY CAMERA CCTV NANNY CAM	$23.69
Stoeling lie detector/ polygraph	$460.00	KIDDE PREMIUM PLUS CARBON MONOXIDE ALARM	$23.51
COMPLETE 6 SPY CAM SET w/6 CHANNEL	$399.00	NEW WIRELESS PINHOLE HIDDEN SPY CAMERA CCTV NANNY CAM	$23.50
SURVEILLANCE RECEIVER		WIRELESS HIDDEN MINI PINHOLE COLOR SPY CAMERA NANNY CAM	$23.50
tscm kaiser 4020 mini stetho ied/locksmith/pi	$375.00	ADT YARD SIGNS * BOX OF 3 * BRAND NEW * REDUCED !	$23.00
NEW IN BOX Zero-G Level II Bullet Proof Vest/Body Armor	$355.00	[2 of these sold for $23.00 each]	
Lot of 10 Brand New Welded Chain Mail Mesh Aprons	$355.00	NIGHTHAWK CARBON MONOXIDE & EXPLOSIVE GAS ALARM	$22.99
Protect the ones you love with a Life Hammer lot#100	$328.00	Voice Changer Telephone Phone New Portable Disguiser	$22.99
Concealable Bulletproof level 3A VIP Body Armor Vest	$323.95	[4 of these sold for $22.99 each]	
Bulletproof VEST, Body Armor -BULLET PROOF POLICE III-A	$319.99	*FRESH* POLICE Duty Size MACE Pepper FOAM	$22.99
[3 of these sold for $319.99 each]		Driveway Patrol Alarm WIRELESS! drive way motion alert	$22.97
Concealable Bulletproof level 3A VIP Body Armor Vest	$319.95	[3 of these sold for $22.97 each]	
OUTLAST Concealable Bullet-proof lvl 3A Body Armor Vest	$319.95	300,000 volt STUN GUN & CASE__HIGH VOLTAGE__w/ALARM!	$22.95

	HIGH		AVG
[2 of these sold for $319.95 each]		[4 of these sold for $22.95 each]	
Concealable Bulletproof level 3A VIP Body Armor Vest	$309.95	WORLD WIDE (1) DEFIANCE DOG REPELLENT PEPPER SPRAY	$22.95
[2 of these sold for $309.95 each]		WORLD WIDE (1) DEFIANCE DOG REPELLENT PEPPER SPRAY	$22.90
Brand New New Yorker Leather Helmet N5A!!	$300.00	NEW WIRELESS PINHOLE HIDDEN SPY CAMERA CCTV NANNY CAM	$22.50
Bulletproof VEST, Body Armor -BULLET PROOF POLICE III-A	$300.00	[5 of these sold for $22.50 each]	
C CURE 800/8000 Security Management System !	$299.99	250V Stungun Stun gun guns With Real Flashlight Compact	$21.99

Religious Products & Supplies ▸ Bibles Covers & Accessories

The average sales price in this subcategory is $11.32.

	HIGH		AVG
Book Common Prayer 1928 with Hymnal 1940, red leather	$139.28	NEW!!!Embassy Genuine Leather Bible Cover FREE SHIPPING	$12.50
1866 Leather Bound Family Civil War Era Bible Apocrypha	$104.49	New Genuine Handcrafted Leather Bible Cover	$12.50
1892 Pictorial Family Bible w Civil War Family info	$62.00	BIBLE 48 AUDIO CASS KJV KING JAMES VER OLD & NEW TESTAM	$12.01
Gorgeous keepsake Bible Box-with personal Bible	$48.99	NCV New Testament on Audio CD read by women	$12.00
2005 Version Quick Verse Platium Edition	$46.00	ANGEL Bible Cover & Tote Set-NEW	$11.99
JOYCE MEYER - 6-CD Teaching Album- MINT - GIFT QUALITY!	$41.00	[2 of these sold for $11.99 each]	
Antique 1896 ROYAL SCROLL Bible Study Maps Notes Print	$36.00	New BIBLE COVER BAG PURSE Navy Blue XL ICHTHUS	$11.50
New Revised Standard Version Pulpit Bible Black NEW	$30.00	The Bible on CD, The New Testament, New	$11.06
Antique Book The Psalms of David 1816	$29.00	THOMAS KINKADE TAPESTRY WOVEN BIBLE COVER	$11.03
JESSE DUPLANTIS - A Merry Heart Like Medicene-NEW DVD	$25.95	ANGEL Bible Cover & Tote Set-NEW	$10.99
JOYCE MEYER - 6-CD Teaching	$24.50	MARILYN HICKEY - "The Tabernacle: The Pattern"	$10.50
Album- MINT - GIFT QUALITY!		Perry Stone Prophecy Book - Like New - 275 Pages!	$10.50
No Reserve!!!! Columbia Electronic Bible Model EB-1	$22.50	XL HAND CRAFTED LEATHER BIBLE COVER BIBLECOVER	$10.50
The International Inductive Study Bible	$20.50	Holy Bible, New catholic Edition 1954	$10.50
Holy Bible Old 1901 Thomas Nelson & Sons	$20.50	NEW: THE KING JAMES STUDY BIBLE	$10.49
HUGE LOT 50 RELIGIOUS JESUS BUTTONS PINS - LARGE	$20.00	Lot of 5 Bible Covers Full Zip Holds Everything ~GIFTS~	$10.00

Religious Products & Supplies ▸ Clothing

The average sales price in this subcategory is $16.41.

	HIGH		AVG
Lot Red Choir Robes Ivory/Gold Collar Whole Adult Choir	$466.98	Vintage Style RELIENT K Emo Punk Christian T-Shirt	$20.50
NEW AWANA 50 PC LOT*SHIRTS*CHILD 10 12*S M L XL 2XL 3XL	$123.50	Awana Game Director T-Shirt - sz L - Yellow - Like New!	$20.50
QUALITY BLACK &VELVET CHOIR or MINISTER ACADEMIC ROBE	$112.50	Holiday play pageant MARY COSTUME NATIVITY GIRLS MED	$18.00
NEW AWANA 25 PC LOT*SHIRTS*CHILD 10 12*S M L XL 2XL 3XL	$96.00	Awana Game Director T-Shirt - sz L - Green - Like New !	$17.50
Santa Claus suit w/bag free shipping w/ buy it now	$81.00	NEW 10 PC AWANA SHIRT LOT*MEDIUM*SPIRITUAL*PRE TEEN*	$17.01
NEW AWANA 25 PC LOT*SHIRTS*CHILD 10 12*S M L XL 2XL 3XL	$77.54	Awana Game Director T-Shirt - sz L - Red - Like New !!	$17.00
AWANA 25 PC LOT*SPIRITUAL*SHIRT*CHILD 10 12*ADULT S M L	$64.00	4 Christian Western Shirt Great Buy!!!Great Gifts!!!!	$16.51
House of Hansen Biretta Vestment	$50.00	Awana Game Director T-Shirt - sz L - Blue - Like New !!	$15.51
NEW AWANA 16 PC LOT*SPIRITUAL	$49.01	Christian T Shirt CREATED to WORSHIP (Guitar) L/S NEW	$15.50
*TRUTH & TRAINING*T&T*S M		[2 of these sold for $15.50 each]	
COLLARS !! White/ RED bow - 13- Ready for Choir robes	$48.00	2 AWANA SHIRTS - Green Leaders Polo (L) & T-shirt (M)	$15.03
21 Exquisite Vintage Choir Robes, NO RESERVE!!!!!!!!!!!	$46.98	Scrapbooking T-SHIRT PSALM96:4a XL New ! L@@K !	$15.00
NEW ~ CHURCH PRIEST VESTMENT CHASUBLE WHITE	$46.01	4 Christian Western Shirt Great Buy!!!Great Gifts!!!!	$14.99
NEW AWANA 20 PC LOT*SHIRTS*CHILD 10 12*S M L XL 2XL 3XL	$41.00	NARCOTICS ANONYMOUS NECKLACE NA IOU 1 JEWELRY	$13.00
AWANA 15 PC LOT*SPIRITUAL*TRUTH & TRAINING*T&T* 16 S M	$39.52	Christian Motorcycle T Shirt Biker Style 2XL ROADMASTER	$12.56
NEW 10 PC AWANA SHIRT LOT*MEDIUM*SPIRITUAL*PRE TEEN*	$37.07	NEVER WORN!!!! LDS Temple Honeysuckle Dress 2XL	$12.50

Religious Products & Supplies ▸ Crosses

The average sales price in this subcategory is $12.29.

	HIGH		AVG
Collection of larger old crucifixes some old & unusual	$108.05	1 Lot 13 Asst Gold & Silver Finish Crosses/Crucifixes	$14.00
VINTAGE WOOD CROSS W JESUS &	$41.01	CELTIC CROSS, Handcast IRISH Stone by Kieran Forde	$13.00
STATIONS CRUCIFIX GERMANY		28227 JESUS CRUCIFIX	$12.95
ETERNAL LIGHT ANGEL SOLAR POWERED	$36.00	12 Asst Antique Gold / Silver Crosses and Crucifixes	$12.50
ETERNAL LIGHT ANGEL SOLAR POWERED	$34.33	Jesus Wall Cross	$12.50
ETERNAL LIGHT ANGEL SOLAR POWERED	$33.01	12 Asst Antique Gold / Silver Crosses and Crucifixes	$12.00
ANTIQUE SOLID BRASS LARGE CRUCIFIX NR	$32.51	Lot of 12 New "Risen Christ" Crosses Catholic Christian	$12.00
ENTERNAL LIGHT ANGEL SOLAR POWERED	$31.57	REPLICA POPE JOHN PAUL II's PAPAL CRUCIFIX	$11.90
ENTERNAL LIGHT ANGEL SOLAR POWERED	$31.56	[2 of these sold in a multiple item ("Dutch") auction for $5.95 each]	
ETERNAL LIGHT ANGEL SOLAR POWERED	$31.00	Lot of 12 New "Risen Christ" Crosses 6 Silver 6 Gold	$11.49
ETERNAL LIGHT ANGEL SOLAR POWERED	$30.00	Jimmy Swaggart Teaching Cds	$11.00
ETERNAL LIGHT ANGEL SOLAR POWERED	$29.52	Pair of Wood Cross CRUCIFIXES - Sick Prayer Box	$10.60
Shield of Faith Sterling Silver Pin by Rom	$29.50	Ultra~Tibetan Talisman~Amulet~Fire element~W.Spells~NR~	$10.43
ENTERNAL LIGHT CROSS SOLAR POWERED	$27.75	24 piece lot Brass Gold Plated Crucifixes for Rosaries	$10.00
ENTERNAL LIGHT CROSS SOLAR POWERED	$27.50	BYZANTINE ORTHODOX CRUCIFIX	$9.99
ENTERNAL LIGHT ANGEL SOLAR POWERED	$27.25	Beautiful Crucifix - Full Colour - Nail - Must See - NR	$9.99

Religious Products & Supplies ▸ Educational Materials

The average sales price in this subcategory is $16.55.

	HIGH		AVG
THE NEW INTERNATIONAL COMM. ON OLD TESTAMENT 21 VOLUMES	$630.00	Serengeti Trek Vacation Bible School VBS by Group	$17.50
THE NEW INTERNATIONAL COMM. OF NEW TESTAMENT 16 VOLUMES	$480.00	Perry Stone: Dueling Prophets - Discerning Prophecy CD	$17.09
Lot of Goldy Play Stories	$450.00	How to Get the Most Out of Mass by Scott Hahn,4 CD's	$17.00
EDDIE WALKER Noah's Ark 19 Piece Set, Numbered New!	$331.00	Joyce Meyer Destiny CD & VHS Tape Vindicator Lot Set NR	$16.99
Fr John Corapi THE TEACHING OF JESUS CHRIST 48CD series	$204.49	Joyce Meyer VICTORY OVER DEPRESSION - 6 cassettes	$16.72
Scientology Congress Lectures on CD by L. Ron Hubbard	$127.50	The True Meaning of Christmas Fulton Sheen	$16.65
Travels Through Jewish Heritage, Berel Wein, Cassettes	$119.50	Answering Common Objections by Scott Hahn set of 6 CDs	$16.52

SHEPHERDING A CHILD'S HEART TRIPP 42 BOOKS TOTAL	$116.47	Mike Murdock The Strategy of Hourly Obedience 6 Cass...	$16.50
L. Ron Hubbard: Research and Discovery Series 1 thru 10	$112.45	LOT 3 JOYCE MEYER TAPES BOOK - ANXIETY, FEAR, STRENGTH	$16.50
SCIENTOLOGY HUBBARD SET OF 4 CONGRESS LECTURES TAPES	$104.16	Sign of Contradiction Fulton Sheen 5 set of CDs	$16.05
HUGE AWANA SPARKS BOOK LOT SKIPPER HIKER CLIMBER 24 NIV	$100.00	Caring For People Gods Way AACC Certificate WORKBOOK	$16.05
L. RON HUBBARD SCIENTOLOGY CD SET ALL NEW SEALED NO RES	$91.11	The Left Behind Series - 8 books by Tim LaHaye	$16.05
25 NEW Awana Sparks Hiker Books NIV Version	$89.99	Children's Church Lessons CD - 2 Years	$16.00
BETTY LUKENS BIBLE FELT SMALL DELUXE FLANNEL SET	$86.51	Preparing for Adolescence. Dr. James Dobson 8 Tapes	$15.65
WOMEN OF FAITH Conferences Audio,Music,VHS-Big Lot-NEW!	$76.00	Dr. Charles Stanley Teaching Series Lot of 6 Cassettes	$15.50

Religious Products & Supplies ▸ Jewelry

The average sales price in this subcategory is $16.81.

	HIGH		AVG
14 K Gold Christ Head Pendant 3- D Charm Face of Jesus	$690.00	Mary Magdalene prayer image necklace jewelry religious	$20.50
ST.FLORIAN FIREFIGHTER PROTECTON MEDAL 14KT WHITE GOLD!	$115.99	Sterling MUSTARD SEED Faith Amulet CHARM Necklace	$20.50
[2 of these sold for $115.99 each]		Sterling Silver Enameled St Christopher Medal	$20.00
18K BLESSED MOTHER YELLOW GOLD MEDAL 18K 18.4MM NR	$66.00	1-Lot (3) Red and White Enameled St Christopher Medals	$18.51
Wholesale LOT of 35 Necklaces w/Christian Cross & Fish	$55.93	BEAUTIFUL SCAPULAR ESCAPULARIO	$17.77
Like New LDS "CTR" 14K Gold Ring!* MUST SEE!!	$54.00	PEARLS + RHYNESTONE	
rare unusual silver catholic locket	$50.99	1 dozen round prayer box necklace's	$16.99
CELTIC ST. FLORIAN'S FIREFIGHTERS PROTECTION MEDAL!	$43.99	Virgin Mary prayer image necklace jewelry religious	$16.33
[2 of these sold for $43.99 each]		TRUE LOVE WAITS RING WITH	$15.95
Large Oval St Christopher Medal Antique Oxidized Finish	$32.97	VOW OF PURITY CERTIFICATE	
[3 of these sold in a multiple item ("Dutch") auction for $10.99 each]		VOW OF PURITY RING WITH VOW OF PURITY CERTIFICATE	$15.95
Sterling Silver Enameled St Christopher Medal	$26.00	Sterling MUSTARD SEED Amulet of Faith Charm NECKLACE	$15.77
[2 of these sold for $26.00 each]		Sterling MUSTARD SEED Amulet of FAITH w Verse Pendant	$15.77
ZION COVENANT VOL 1-6 BY	$25.00	[2 of these sold for $15.77 each]	
JESUS SILVER COIN DOLLAR MONEY CLIP	$24.99	Sterling MUSTARD SEED Faith Amulet CHARM Necklace	$15.77
Angel Pin Mothers Personalized Birthstone Heirloom	$24.99	[2 of these sold for $15.77 each]	
1-Lot (3) Blue & White Enameled St Christopher Medals	$24.27	St. Saint Therese Lisieux necklace jewelry religious	$15.62
1 Lot Sterling Silver Rosary Bracelets	$23.00	1-Lot (3) Green & White Enameled St Christopher Medals	$15.50
1-Lot (3) Red and White Enameled St Christopher Medals	$22.27	Eternity Bracelet Cross Christian Jewelry Religious	$15.45

Religious Products & Supplies ▸ Judaica

The average sales price in this subcategory is $17.10.

	HIGH		AVG
The Holy Zohar: English/Aramaic addition	$200.00	Bible Code Software	$20.50
1882 Russian Imperial Silver Kiddush Cup	$90.01	[2 of these sold for $20.50 each]	
Israel Ram's Horn Shofar With Display Stand- Like New	$89.88	JUDAICA 17" Seder Plate	$19.99
Brand New Tefillin-Kosher	$86.99	Beautiful Tehilim Psalms Keyring Key Chain Israel NEW!!	$18.95
LARGE COVENANT RAINBOW FLAG PRAISE WORSHIP DANCE	$75.00	The Orthodox Jewish Bible by Dr. Phil Goble Messianic	$18.07
Awesome Tallit from The Cardo in Jerusalem 51" X 70"	$58.00	Authentic Mezuzah scroll/parchment - NEW from ISRAEL	$18.02
Rams Horn Shofar-Genuine Ram	$56.00	Amber Glass Mezuzah case by Coresh, Judaica, Mezuza	$18.00
KABBALAH 7th Book MOSES Jewish HEBREW Mysticism MADONNA	$49.99	STAR OF DAVID MARCASITE STERLING SILVER NECKLACE NR	$15.99
MESSIANIC SEAL YESHUA MESSIAH PRAISE BANNER FLAG	$48.00	Purple Glass Mezuzah case by Coresh, Judaica, Mezuza	$15.00
[2 of these sold for $48.00 each]		R & B Orenstein Menorah Hand Carved wood Art Signed NR	$15.00
Brand New Stone Edition Tanach Gold edge leather bind	$46.00	PRAISE&WORSHIP GLORY HOOPS-TABRET-WORSHIP FLAGS	$15.00
Tefillin tfillin tefilin w/ embroidered case	$40.00	Jewish Headcovering Kippah,Yarmulke,Kippot, Silver Blue	$14.99
Driedel Maude 1995 Ceramic Jerusalem Art Magnificent!	$39.97	JUDAICA SEDER PLATE	$13.99
KABBALAH 6th 7th Book MOSES Jewish MYSTIC Zohar MADONNA	$37.36	Tabret Glory Hoop "Joseph's Coat" Worship Praise Dance	$12.99
KABBALAH 6th 7th Book MOSES Jewish MYSTIC Zohar MADONNA	$37.01	snoods snood hair net sca renaissance BLACK CHENILLE	$12.99
R & B Orenstein Dreidel Hand Carved wood Art Signed NR	$36.89	7 Branch Solid Brass Menorah	$12.50

Religious Products & Supplies ▸ Rosaries

The average sales price in this subcategory is $12.98.

	HIGH		AVG
48 pc. lot Assorted Antique Silver Rosary Centers	$138.49	Rudraksha & Mercury Prosperity & Health Bracelet, India	$14.99
Hand Carved Japanese Wood DARUMA Rosary/ Prayer Beads	$91.00	[3 of these sold for $14.99 each]	
Toothill McBean antique 1898 rosary box? silver plated	$67.99	Rose Quartz & Cloisonne Crystal Mala Beads 27+1	$14.99
NewGenuine Black Onyx & Sterling Silver Rosary/Necklace	$55.00	Lotus Seed & Rudraksha, Crystal 5 Elements Prayer Mala	$14.99
1950'S VERY RARE HUMMEL ' PRAYING	$51.88	1 Lot-12 Asst. Gold / Silver Crucifixes & Crosses	$14.50
VIRGIN MARY ' MINT		Gold & Green Rosary - ANTIQUE STYLE	$14.14
Beautiful moonstone & sterling silver rosary hand mount	$49.99	LOVELY SILVER & BLUE SWAROVSKI CRYSTAL ROSARY BEADS	$13.01
Heavy Vintage Sterling Crystal Rosary with Celtic Cross	$43.50	LOVELY SILVER & BLUE SWAROVSKI CRYSTAL ROSARY BEADS	$12.50
Lapis Lazuli Rosary Blessed by Pope John Paul	$40.00	Bone Goddess Rosary Beads	$12.00
1 Lot Rosary Cases with Embossed Miraculous Cover	$37.02	Gold-plated Crystal Bead Capped Rosary - ELEGANT	$11.99
48 pc. lot Asst. Antique Finished Silver Rosary Centers	$34.00	Genuine Carnelian Crystal Prayer Beads 10mm Mala	$11.99
Vintage Catholic sterling silver creed rosary	$33.01	Genuine Tiger Eye Crystal Prayer Beads 8mm Mala	$11.99
12 Assorted Rosary Crucifixes Antique Silver Finish	$30.69	Carnelian Crystal Prayer Mala Beads 6-10mm 108+1	$11.99
Christmas Rosary Swarovski Crystals	$30.00	Gold-plated Crystal Bead Capped Rosary - ELEGANT	$11.99
100 pc. lot Assorted Gold Plated Brass Rosary Centers	$30.00	Guardian Angel Rear View Mirror Rosary - St. Michael	$11.98
[2 of these sold for $30.00 each]		[2 of these sold in a multiple item ("Dutch") auction for $5.99 each]	
48 pc. lot Asst. Antique Finished Silver Rosary Centers	$30.00	Old Black/Brown Glass Bead 5 Decade Rosary	$11.48

Religious Products & Supplies ▶ Other

The average sales price in this subcategory is $20.78.

	HIGH		AVG
21 MODERN SOLID OAK PADDED CHURCH PEWS ~ REDKEY INDIANA	$3,003.00	Perry Stone -HIDDEN PROPHECIES IN GENESIS VHS 1993 used	$21.50
Scientology/Exteriorization & Phenomena of Space tapes	$750.00	Yoga / Zabuton + Zafu (Buckwheat Hulls) Meditation Set	$21.50
11 ANTIQUE PINE CHURCH PEWS 10' 10" REDKEY INDIANA, NR!	$735.00	Dr. Scott Hahn ~Mystery of Matrimony~ 3 CD's	$21.15
PADRE PIO ORIGINAL POST CARD WITH SIGNATURE	$500.00	Cherry Cremation Urn Funeral Urn (NR)	$21.02
OAK CHURCH PEWS	$500.00	NEW ELECTRONIC BIBLE CHALLENGE GAME GIFT	$20.95
Restoration of Knowing Cause,L Ron Hubbard, Scientology	$405.00	Dr. Scott Hahn ~GET THE MOST OUT OF MASS~ 4 CD's	$20.83
PDC tapes L. Ron Hubbard Scientology	$375.00	Lot of 12 Angel Worry Stones	$20.75
SLABBINCK green vestment - festive, elegant, new	$350.00	Dr. Scott Hahn ~EVANGELIZE THE BAPTIZED~ CD set	$20.58
New Acrylic Pulpit Podium Lectern "The Best on Ebay"	$330.00	Dr. Scott Hahn ~Successful Evangelization~ 4 CD's	$20.57
PULPIT CHURCH LECTERN WITH OPTIONAL COMMUNION TABLE	$260.00	WEIGH DOWN WORKSHOP: Advanced	$20.51
One (1) Ounce Salvia Divinorum Incense extract / NR!!	$222.50	*NEW!* Book & Tapes	$20.51
New Betty Lukens BIBLE IN FELT LARGE Deluxe Flannel Set	$219.95	Fulton Sheen ~Voice From Calvary~ 3 CD's	$20.50
[4 of these sold for $219.95 each]		Jehovah's Witnesses Watchtower KM Folder Blk irregular	$20.50
41extremely nice padded church pews	$212.50	A Psalm of David - The 23rd Psalm Brass Wall Hanging	$20.50
SLABBINCK white/gold chasuble, vestment	$208.05	Joyce Meyer-The Power of Hope	$20.50
early 1900's quarter cut oak church pew	$202.50	Church of Christ is offering Hymn Display Board	$20.50

Reward Pts, Incentive Progs ▶ Proof of Purchase, UPCs

The average sales price in this subcategory is $14.49.

	HIGH		AVG
1,226 VIRGINIA SLIMS UPC's ~1,000+ Proof of Purchases!	$178.49	1400 Marlboro Miles - "FIVE MILES" Type	$15.38
VIRGINIA SLIMS~1,270 UPCs plus BONUS!~Proof of Purchase	$170.00	2,000 Marlboro miles "FIVE" **NEW**	$15.26
25,000 + Marlboro Miles	$152.49	6 WENDY'S AIRTRAN FLIGHT COUPONS WENDYS AIR TRAN $1 SHI	$15.25
800 Virginia Slims UPC 's, trimmed and ready to ship!	$131.50	1 Envelope & 8 wendys airtran coupons AIR TRAN WENDY'S	$15.22
600 VIRGINIA SLIMS UPC'S / XTRA 25 !!!!	$91.00	2300 Marlboro Miles Cut and Trimmed	$15.06
12,500 NEW Marlboro FIVE MILES! Cut Ready to Ship	$81.00	240 NEWPORT UPC LOT CATALOG GOODS UPCS REWARDS POINTS	$15.00
500 VIRGINIA SLIMS UPC LABELS - GREAT GIFTS & STUFF!!!	$76.99	300 lbs purina second nature dog litter weight circles	$15.00
marlboro miles	$76.00	8 lot of Wendy's Air Tran UPC Wendys AirTran	$14.99
500+ VIRGINIA SLIMS UPC'S PROOF OF PURCHASE	$75.00	8 WENDYS AIR TRAN AIRTRAN FLIGHT COUPONS	$14.19
1027 VIRGINIA SLIMS UPC's ~ 1000+ PROOFS OF PURCHASE	$68.18	110 BTFE Box Tops for Education FREE SHIPPING	$14.06
400 VIRGINIA SLIMS UPC's	$65.00	1 ENVELOPE + 7 WENDY'S AIRTRAN COUPONS	$14.01
~10,365~ MARLBORO MILES~2073 UPC CODES	$59.00	1,750 NEW MARLBORO MILES - DON'T MISS OUT - NR	$13.50
350+ Virginia Slims UPC's Proof of Purchase FREE SHIP	$59.00	7 WENDY'S AIRTRAN COUPON CUPS !!!!!!!!!!!!	$13.50
Purina Weight Circles (1130 Lbs)	$56.51	228 Pounds of Purina ONE / Dog Chow Weight Circle	$13.06
Purina Weight Circles (1102 Lbs)	$55.77	500 NEWPORT CIGARETTE UPC	$13.01

Reward Pts, Incentive Progs ▶ Impressions, Ad Space

The average sales price in this subcategory is $12.78.

HIGH TO AVG			
Promote your site PR8 Text Link	$42.01	1000 Guaranteed International Sign Ups!!!	$15.49
1000 Guaranteed International Signups!!!	$26.00	[2 of these sold for $15.49 each]	
[2 of these sold for $26.00 each]		1000 Guaranteed International Signups!!!	$14.99
Promote your site PR8 Text Link	$21.75	[31 of these sold for $14.99 each]	
1000 Guaranteed International Sign Ups!!!	$21.50	10 shared Searchads (Themailclub)	$9.99
1000 Guaranteed International Sign Ups!!!	$20.50	30 US/CAN Search ads (Mistyandsamscash)	$9.99
[2 of these sold for $20.50 each]		GOLD membership (Themailclub)	$6.99
Promote your site PR7 Text Link	$16.50	30 days PTP ad to ALL (Mistyandsamscash)	$5.99
30 US/CAN Searchads (Themailclub)	$15.50	Promote your site PR7 Text Link	$5.50
		SUPER ad package (Mistyandsam)	$3.75

Reward Pts, Incentive Progs ▶ Other

The average sales price in this subcategory is $23.41.

	HIGH		AVG
$490 Purina Dog Food Rebate Checks 70 @ $7.00 coupons	$340.55	250 Referrals for your Favorite Program!!!!	$24.99
Worldmark / Trendwest 5,000 One-Time Use Credits	$340.00	250 Referrals for your Favorite Program!!!!	$24.50
SOUTHWEST AIRLINES SWA FREE R/T RAPID REWARDS VOUCHER	$325.00	Envelope + BONUS, 20 Mcdonald's Monopoly Pieces + Food	$24.50
SOUTHWEST AIRLINES COUPONS + FREE R/T TICKET	$320.00	2000 CAMPBELLS SOUP LABELS FOR EDUCATION/CLFE	$24.25
SOUTHWEST AIRLINES SWA FREE R/T RAPID REWARDS VOUCHER	$315.00	45 BTFE box tops for education + free 200 BONUS btfe	$23.87
Southwest Drink Coupon Book W/ free RT Voucher/Ticket	$315.00	2000 CLFE Campbells Labels for Education	$23.50
Southwest Airlines SWA FREE R/T Rapid Rewards Voucher	$305.00	200 Boxtops for Educatoin BTFE (Box Tops)	$23.49
12 Southwest Airlines Drink Coupons	$300.00	200 BTFE Boxtops for Education, Box Tops	$23.49
Southwest Drink Coupon Book W/ free RT Voucher/Ticket	$300.00	200 Camel Casino Chip Codes (10 Codes)	$22.99
Southwest Airline Drink Tickets + Free RT	$300.00	300 Boxtops For Education	$22.01
Southwest Airlines Rapid Rewards Voucher Paperless R/T	$290.16	200 box tops for education/boxtops btfe non expired	$22.00
CLICKER PRIZE WHEEL - FUN CORPORATE PMB INCENTIVE KIT !	$284.99	200 BOX TOPS FOR EDUCATION	$22.00
[3 of these sold for $284.99 each]		220 Box top for Education - FREE SHIPPING	$22.00
CLICKER PRIZE WHEEL - FUN CORPORATE PMB INCENTIVE KIT !	$279.99	2,100 CLFE Campbells Labels for Education	$21.99
[3 of these sold for $279.99 each]		200 Boxtops For Education BTFE *Free Ship*	$21.59
NEW!"CLICKER PRIZE WHEEL - SPINNING REWARDS! FREE GIFT!	$277.77		
SOUTHWEST AIRLINES SWA FREE R/T RAPID REWARDS W/ COUPON	$255.00		

Weird Stuff ▶ Slightly Unusual

The average sales price in this subcategory is $16.27.

	HIGH		AVG
MOVADO TWO TONED DIAMOND BEZEL WATCH	$375.00	Novelty Blow Up Doll/Love Piggie	$16.99
50 inch Leg Lamp A Christmas Story - Exact Replica!	$249.00	SMILE ZONE happy face joke humor NEW sign	$16.95
Removable Lil Mynx COLOR Stripper Pole Exercise Poles	$224.00	REDNECK PARKING truck beer sport NEW sign	$16.95
ALESSI HOT BERTAA kettle , design by Philippe STARCK	$222.55	NEW Swarovski Crystal Rainbow Maker AS SEEN ON TV N160	$16.50
Night Vision Goggles, made in Russia, US military issue	$215.56	The Traveling State to State Coffee Mug Collection	$16.50
stainless steel jail prison toilet sink combo	$199.00	PURPLE JELLY BALL GAG ~ WITH LEATHER BUCKLE STRAP	$16.49
Narcotics Anonymous Commemorative Edition 1 of 5000	$175.00	Hells Angels Support Red & White Sticker + 2 more	$16.39
Removable 8-10 foot adjustable Spinning Stripper Pole	$150.00	COOL TOY BEER TRUCK UNOPENED COORS	$16.00
Male chastity device / belt CB 3000 new with ksd-G2	$137.50	14" WALNUT GAVEL - BIG AND SERIOUS!!	$16.00
CHEVY TAHOE YUKON 95-99 WOOD CARBON DASH TRIM KIT	$123.00	Virgin Mary Guadalupe appears on Neon light picture	$15.99
MITSUBISHI MONTERO SPORT WOOD ALUMINUM DASH TRIM KIT	$119.00	Neon light Tiger spiral lamp picture w frame Cool ART	$15.99
1950*14K GOLD MENS RING W/ STONE*FAMILY THINKS HAUNTED	$102.50	LUSCIOUS RED JELLY BALL GAG ~ WITH LEATHER BUCKLE STRAP	$15.99
BLACK LEATHER restraints 11 pieces plus two connectors	$102.50	Key to my Secret Garden Keeper Mix media WWAO OOAK	$15.99
1 FREE Ticket FSU vs. UF Game 11/26 in Gainesville	$100.00	SEXY ATHLETIC SPORT JOCK W/ SNAP OFF POUCH	$15.99
44 inch Leg Lamp A Christmas Story Best Quality	$100.00	3 Grams Salvia Divinorum Extract Incense PREMIMUM	$15.50

Weird Stuff ▶ Really Weird

The average sales price in this subcategory is $91.43.

	HIGH		AVG
Win A Speaking role in our Movie!	$100,000.00	1956 Book True Story of Men in Black-UFOs! Signed Copy!	$97.00
All cash... How many 100's can you count ?? PLus a gift	$5,000.00	Huge Lot Animal POOPING PALS keychains gross kids	$96.96
2004 KTM 525 MXC lots of extras not crf or yzf NO Res!	$4,450.00	[8 of these sold in a multiple item ("Dutch") auction for $12.12 each]	
Rights to name a street in Lakewood NJ	$1,275.00	PREMIUM LEATHER LACED ARM BINDER RESTRAINT L/XL 2XL/3XL	$96.00
TATTOO ADVERTISEMENT ON MY FOREHEAD	$1,050.00	14K Ugly Vintage Diamond Pave Ring Size 6	$95.00
RARE REAL EBAY TALKING AND SPITING MYSTERY SKULL	$1,000.00	14K Ugly Vintage Diamond Ring Size 7 1/2	$95.00
CONVINCE MY HUSBAND THIS LOOKS RIDICULOUS!!!	$504.99	STEER SKULL 4 FT 8 IN LONG HORNS	$92.00
Churchhill`s of Londons Carousel 2 a 3000.00 mystery	$500.00	COW LONGHORNS #1724	
DISNEY MYSTERY AUCTION BIG HUGE BOX FULL OVER 50 ITMES!	$331.00	PREMIUM LEATHER LACED ARM BINDER RESTRAINT L/XL 2XL/3XL	$92.00
Weekend in Haunted Mental Health Facility	$300.00	14K Gold Vintage Diamond Men's Ring Size 10 mens	$90.00
[10 of these sold in a multiple item ("Dutch") auction for $30.00 each]		Pee Wee Herman 30" VENTRILOQUIST DOLL MIB	$89.95
Vintage go-kart mini-bike Simplex gas tank	$229.00	HEAVY LEATHER ARM SPLINTS - PADDED ARM BINDER RESTRAINT	$89.95
I HAD HIS BABY!! NOW HE WANTS A DNA TEST!!! PART 2!!	$202.50	BRAND NEW 50LB PISTOL HUNTING	$89.90
MY DAUGHTER MACKENZIE'S	$202.50	CROSSBOW GUN ARROWS GIFT	
1st MYSTERY BOX!!! FILLED W/$$$		[10 of these sold in a multiple item ("Dutch") auction for $8.99 each]	
Leather Catsuit Jacket Pants Jeans Shirt Size XL NEW	$187.50	14K Gold Vintage Diamond Men's Ring Size 9 1/2 mens	$88.77
Mystery Money Clip!! COLD HARD FOLDABLE CASH!	$171.50	Liberator Stage	$86.00
		Liberator Ramp	$86.00
		Love NEW Sex-y Spinning Swing/Sling in LEOPARD!	$85.00

Weird Stuff ▶ Totally Bizarre

The average sales price in this subcategory is $76.31.

	HIGH		AVG
Prada Mystery Bag with Mystery Boxes #4	$10,200.00	ANCIENT ANTIQUE HAUNTED PAGAN	$95.01
HELP-HELP MY SON AND HIS GIRL FRIEND BUY FIRST HOUSE	$10,000.00	WITCHES AD PENTACLE RING	
MY HUSBAND LEFT FOR ANOTHER	$761.00	1ST POWER MIX ONLINE RADIO TRAVELING T-SHIRT MYSTERY	$81.00
WOMAN MYSTERY AUCTION BOX		CAN a Q - TIP be NUMBER ONE on THE PULSE ???	$72.00
~THE ULTIMATE LUXE DIVA MYSTERY~DIVAS APPLY WITHIN~	$755.00	vampire gothic full finger armor ring jewelry wholesale	$71.00
Mystery Money Clip with $$ CASH Relisted	$630.00	vampire gothic full finger armor ring jewelry wholesale	$68.00
Mystery Witches Chest! Real 17th. Century Magic! NR!	$450.00	Svengoolie painting on canvas by EsQui halloween gothic	$64.99
LEATHER SLEEPSACK / BODY BAG NEW	$310.00	Ancient Antique Witch Doll, Handmade by Real Witch! NR!	$64.00
Set of 2 Glass Prosthetic Blue Eyes Eye With Case	$180.50	vampire gothic full finger armor ring jewelry wholesale	$61.00
Hurricane Katrina Signed by Survivors Rare 1 of a kind	$158.49	original art mask that holds you captive	$54.00
Real Fruit Bat Framed Taxidermy NR EXACT ONE SHOWN #35	$119.99	vampire gothic full finger armor ring jewelry wholesale	$51.00

Other

The median sales price in this subcategory is $5.95.

	HIGH		AVG
100A: An Important Plesiosaur, sp. Dolichoderius	GBP 30,000.00	FETISH/S&M/SEXY MENS BLACK NET/SPANDEX MIX GAY INTEREST	CAD $6.99
159: 1989 Bentley Turbo R	$30,900.00	Silky Stockings Picture CD Collection - 10,000+ pics	CAD $6.99
188: 1959 190SL Vintage Mercedes Race Car SCCA	$25,500.00	OUIJA board Awesome Mouse Pad Weird Ghost Gift	$5.99
142: 1958 190SL Mercedes	$25,000.00	SOUTH AFRICA Flag Awesome Mouse Pad XL Sharp	$5.99
171: 1967 Jaguar XKE 2+2	$18,600.00	Four Tiffany & Company Gift Boxes	$5.99
507: 1999 Regal 200 Destiny Boat w/ Mercury 21ft	$16,500.00	10 ASSORTED WOMENS LIQUOR T-SHIRTS	$5.99
147A: A COMPLETE CAVE BEAR SKELETON, Pliestocene	GBP 9,000.00	Christmas present - RADIO TOILET ROLL HOLDER	GBP 3.41
133A: A RARE "MASS MORTALITY" TRILOBITE SPECIM EN	GBP 7,500.00	Kendall Johnson Black Racing Visor	$5.95
Destiny Powered Parachute PPC airplane not nascar	$12,000.00	TRADING STOCKS INVESTMENT, ULTIMATE TRADE REVEALED	$5.95
Have You Ever Wanted To Fly, Now You Can		[2 of these sold for $5.95 each]	
154A: A MAMMOTH TUSK, Siberia	GBP 6,000.00	Iditarod Nome, Alaska Polar Bear Air T-Shirt - size M	$5.95
137A: A FORMATION OF PECTEN SHELLS, Miocene	GBP 5,000.00	auction for dietrech2005	$5.95
652: STOCK 1965 CHEVY IMPALA SS SUPER SPORT 2 DR	$8,000.00	OLD MINATURE BRASS FIRE EXTINGUISHER PRESTO CB	$5.95
1969 mach 1 clone mustang. 302 automatic.	$7,500.00	NFL Football Dallas Cowboys New Christmas Ornament	$5.95
62A: AN AMETHYST "CATHEDRAL",	$7,021.60	Kendall Johnson Black Racing Visor	$5.95
ST Dupont Limited Edition Pharoah Series	$6,319.44	RAINFALL FOREST RAIN SHOWER HEAD SHOWERHEAD	$5.95

EBAY LISTS

It can be fun and interesting to look at eBay's wide range of prices, but this vast repository of data can yield other instructive snapshots as well.

Somewhere between the first item ever auctioned on eBay—a broken laser pointer listed by eBay founder Pierre Omidyar—and the eBay "wedding dress guy" Larry Star, strange eBay auctions started to take hold of the national psyche. eBay became a place where people who were willing to take risks, or who had very offbeat items (sometimes involving their own body parts), could obtain nationwide publicity. In this chapter, we'll take a look at some of the items that worked their way into national (or worldwide) consciousness, with lists of auctions that are notable for being particularly strange, infamous, celebrity-oriented, high-priced, or that stand out in other ways.

Similarly, we'll look at some non-price facts—who are the top sellers on eBay, and what do they sell? What can you not sell on eBay? What keywords do people search for most often throughout the site? Which eBay categories have brought in $1 billion or more in worldwide annualized gross merchandise volume (GMV)?

Just as looking at price data on eBay can give us a bird's-eye look at how people value a wide range of things these days, and these lists give us a glimpse into another realm of knowledge which can be gleaned from the site, even if it's just that we're all fascinated by foods with images of the Virgin Mary, the Pope's hat, or Hello Kitty.

Most Infamous eBay Auctions

1. The "eBay wedding dress guy"

    "eBay wedding dress guy" Larry Star's auction of his ex-wife's gown, featuring Star himself modeling the dress, sold for $3,850.00.

Star was featured twice on the *Today* show. ("I've never seen anything come close to a million," said eBay's Dean of Education Jim "Griff" Griffith, who featured the wedding dress auction on his radio show.)

The auction's title was "SIZE 12 WEDDING DRESS/GOWN NO RESERVE. SURE IS A BEAUTY! CHEAP! USED ONLY ONCE!"

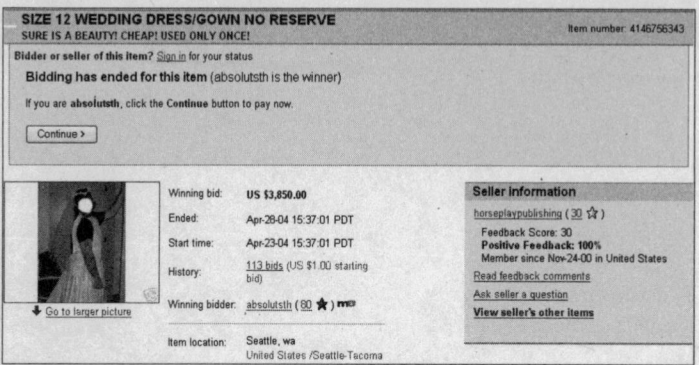

2.   Virgin Mary grilled-cheese sandwich

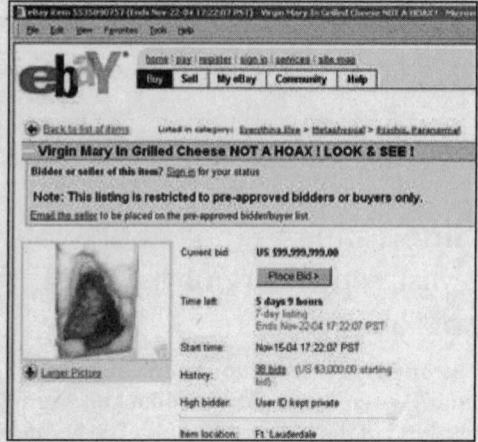

The auction of a grilled-cheese sandwich that allegedly bore an image of the Virgin Mary on it went for $28,000.00. Online casino site GoldenPalace.com was the winning bidder. Sandwich owner Diane Duyser, from Florida, said the sandwich has never gone moldy since she made it 10 years ago, according to a BBC news article.

eBay initially pulled the auction, saying it didn't post joke items, according to an MSNBC.com article. The page was restored after eBay was convinced that Duyser would deliver on the bid.

Duyser made the famous snack 10 years ago and saw a face staring back at her. She put the sandwich in a clear plastic box with cotton balls and kept it on her night stand. The sandwich has apparently never shown any signs of mold.

3.   House with bride

Deborah Hale, 48, of Denver, listed an auction for her house for $600,000.00, and threw in a bonus: herself. Yes, for the right man willing to spend his life with her, the property could be his. She also created her own website, www.housewithbride.com.

"I decided to give my best effort towards something whereby that special man could 'find me. . .'" She was attracted to eBay's "non-binding" real estate transaction, which "provides a means to advertise my house (and myself), with neither party being obligated to complete the transaction." said Hale on her site. "You might be wondering why

I have my listing at $600,000.00 plus myself for bid as 'priceless,'" she continues. "First, I estimate the value of the house with furnishings at approximately $600,000.00. When I asked my girlfriends their advice on what I (the 'bride') was worth, most responded that I was 'priceless.'"

eBay pulled the ad. Hale appeared on TV show *The Insider*, and said she received 15,000 hits an hour, and several email proposals.

4. Ad space on pregnant woman's belly

Amber Rainey sold ad space on her pregnant belly for $4,050.00. That grilled-cheese loving company Golden Palace Casino was the high bidder, and Rainey's page received more than 50,000 hits. Golden Palace officials were contemplating having her expose her belly at events such as concerts and the Super Bowl, according to an Associated Press article.

5. Ad space on man's forehead

Twenty-year-old Andrew Fischer of Omaha, Nebraska, put his forehead for sale on eBay as advertising space. The winning bid was $37,375.00 for Fischer to advertise the snoring remedy, SnoreStop.

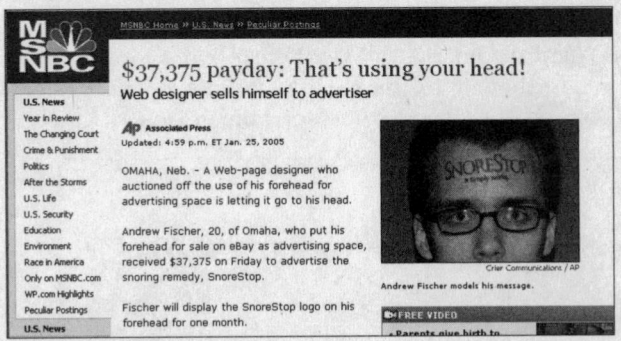

Nine Auctions Inspired by the Virgin Mary Grilled-Cheese Sandwich

1. Meg Whitman grilled cheese sandwich on a towel

A photo of this auction page was featured at eBay Live 2005 in San Jose.

2. Hello Kitty grilled cheese

The seller's description: "You are viewing an extroidinary out of this world item!! I made this sandwich 10 minutes ago, when I took a bite out of it, I saw a face looking up at me, It was Hello Kitty starring back at me, I was in total shock, I would like to point out there is no mold or disingration , The item has not been preserved or anything, It has been keep in a plastic baggie, not a special one that seals out air or potiential mold or bacteria, it is like a miracle, It has just preserved itself which in itself I consider a miracle, people ask me if I have had blessings since she has been in my home, I do feel I have, Yesterday before the sandwich was even made my wife found over $4.00 in change while cleaning out her purse, Every single sock that has gone into the laundry has come back out...."

3. ET's head on a piece of cereal—$1,035.00

Bidding started at $16.00 for the Kellogg's Nutri-Grain flake, auctioned by Australian graphic designer Chris Doyle. The auction closed at $1,035.00.

4. Howard Stern grilled cheese—$3.25, 4 bids

The description read thus: "You are bidding on a 5 x 7 picture of this miraculous event. The story is as follows: My wife is a witch and she hates when I listen to Howard Stern. She said if she caught me one more time, she would cast a spell and make me look just like Howard and then I would see what it would be like to live life looking like him.

"So the next morning I had just sat down w/ a grilled cheese sandwich I had made. I put on the radio and started to listen to Howard. In she came on her broom, screaming and waving her wand. She pointed it at me and a spark flew from it right towards me. I protected myself with the only thing I had close, my grilled-cheese sandwich. The spell hit the sandwich, and lo and behold, the Howard Stern Grilled Cheese Sandwich was born. You can see the results in the picture. Since this has happened, I find myself being followed by miscreants, lesbians and midgets. Owning this picture may bring you the same luck."

5. Virgin Mary on a pancake—bidding got as high as $75.00

The item location was listed as "The Pan in My Kitchen." Here's the seller's description: "That's right…it's a pancake…I made it myself….And before ya knew it, we had one of these newfangled eBay accounts, online and all…you know that there Intranet that Mr. Al Gore invented. So here it is…My pancake is…kinda tan in color…I reckon it measures about 6 inches one way and about 5 the other…guess it ain't quite round…. Anyways, if you're lookin' for Mystery…Guess what's in my pancake? Visions of the Virgin Mary…Gaze real hard at my pancake! Fancy advertising space…plenty of room on my pancake! Gotta million dollars you need to blow…buy my pancake!"

6. Jesus on a fish stick—the "Son of Cod"?

Fred Whan, of Ontario, had saved the fish stick for a year after burning it at dinner. His son said he thought the burn mark looked like Jesus. Others said it looked more like Jeff Daniels, Che Guevara, Jim Morrison, or Don McLean.

First loaves (the grilled cheese sandwich), now fishes —

KINGSTON, Ontario - An eastern Ontario man is hoping to make a bit of money by auctioning a fish stick he says looks like Jesus.

Fred Whan, who has kept the fish stick in his freezer since burning it at dinner a year ago, decided Tuesday that it was time to thaw it out so he could sell it on eBay.

A Florida woman recently sold a decade-old grilled cheese sandwich with the toasty visage of what's purported to be the Virgin Mary for $28,000, according to the eBay Web site.

Source: http://newmexiken.com/archives/2004/11/004259.php

7. Baby Jesus and Mary on popcorn—bidding began at $250.00

8. Mary and Jesus Funyun—sold for $609.00

West Virginian John Mize found the curiously shaped piece of snack food under his car seat. Bidding started at $0.99; Mize said the proceeds could help pay for law school.

In the Wake of Grilled Cheese Mary
Following the $28,000 sale of that Virgin Mary Grilled Cheese Sandwich, it seems like it's been loony season on eBay (if it was ever NOT loony season on eBay, that is). Among the more memorable Grilled Cheese Mary Wannabes have been the Jesus Fish Stick, the NutriGrain cereal that looks like ET, and the piece of popcorn that looks like the Virgin Mary holding Baby Jesus.
Buck Wolf, in his weekly column on ABC News, points out some miracle foods from years past that have beguiled the public, including the Tennessee Nun Bun (a cinnamon bun that looks like Mother Teresa), the Miracle Tortilla of New Mexico (a tortilla that looks like Jesus), and the Holy Eggplant of India (an eggplant that spells out 'Allah' in urdu script).
Posted: Wed Dec 01, 2004 | Total Comments: 12
Category: eBay, Food, Religion

9.   Pope's hat Dorito—sold for $1,209.00 to GoldenPalace.com

A nacho cheese–flavored Dorito shaped like the Pope's mitre went for a healthy $1,209.00 to that eBay-loving online site, GoldenPalace.com. The nacho auction received 41,000 visitors and inspired its own website, PopeHatChip.com.

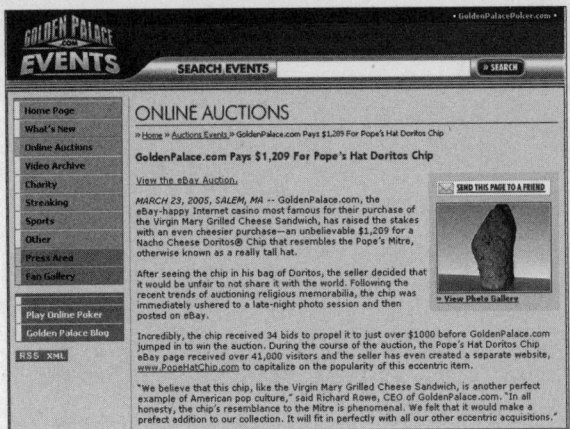

Twenty-Five Things You Can't Sell on eBay

1.   Human organs

In 1999, someone listed a "fully functional kidney" on eBay to much controversy. Bidding got up to more than $5.7 million before eBay blocked the sale.

2.   Alcohol, except for certain sellers of wine, and alcohol in certain unopened collectible containers

3.   Tobacco, except for in certain collectible containers

4.   Guns

5.   Live animals, except for tropical fish and certain snails

6.   Native American skulls or bones

7.   KKK relics

8.   Nazi helmets

9.   Fireworks

10.   Antique fire extinguishers containing carbon tetrachloride

11.   Radioactive waste

12.   FBI badges

13.   Postage meters

14.   Used lipstick

15.   Pharmaceutical drugs

16.   Contact lenses

17.   Non-pasteurized dairy products

18.   Lockpicking or locksmithing devices

19.   Used clothing that has not been cleaned

20.   Used underwear

21.   Listings containing nothing but a link to a store

22.   Auctions for "nothing"

23.   Switchblade knives

24.   Teachers' editions of textbooks

25.   Lottery tickets

Twelve Auctions That Became eBay Trading Cards

1. A broken laser pointer

   This was the first item ever listed on eBay; founder Pierre Omidyar said he was sure to ask the winner, "You know it's broken, right?"

2. Shoeless Joe's bat

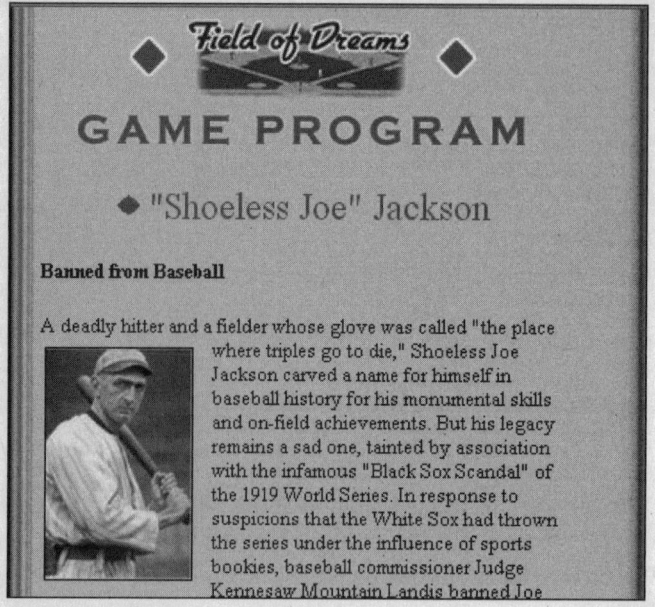

GAME PROGRAM

♦ "Shoeless Joe" Jackson

Banned from Baseball

A deadly hitter and a fielder whose glove was called "the place where triples go to die," Shoeless Joe Jackson carved a name for himself in baseball history for his monumental skills and on-field achievements. But his legacy remains a sad one, tainted by association with the infamous "Black Sox Scandal" of the 1919 World Series. In response to suspicions that the White Sox had thrown the series under the influence of sports bookies, baseball commissioner Judge Kennesaw Mountain Landis banned Joe

Source: www.fieldofdreamsmoviesite.com

Setting a record for the most valuable bat ever sold, "Shoeless Joe" Jackson's original "Black Betsy" bat sold on August 7, 2001, for $577,610.00. So named by the legendary baseball player, who played for the Cleveland Indians and later the Chicago White Sox, the "Black Betsy" was handmade out of hickory and weighs more than 40 ounces, compared to today's average bat weight of 32 to 34 ounces. (Shoeless Joe acquired his nickname in the minor leagues, when he doffed a pair of new spikes that were giving him blisters and played the rest of the game in his stocking feet.) Jackson had the third highest career batting average of .356 and was known for a swing so perfect that Babe Ruth admitted to copying it.

3. Jay Leno's Harley Davidson

   The bike was auctioned to raise money for victims of the 2004 tsunami. Bidding spiked in the last three minutes from $200,000.00 to $800,100.00.

4. Oldest known pair of Levi jeans

   Selling for $46,532.00 to Levi Strauss & Co. and setting a record for the highest priced pair of denim pants ever sold, these jeans were circa 1880s, not much older than the first pair of jeans created by Levi Strauss & Co. in 1873. Levi's planned to produce and sell an exact replica of the pants for their Levi's Vintage Clothing line, complete with original details such as the "tool pocket" located on the left thigh, the fabric, fit, buttons, and stitching.

5. Gulf Stream II business jet

   The highest-priced item to date sold on eBay; it went for $4.9 million.

6. Civil War dirt

   Listed as "Real Arkansas Civil War Dirt," the seller described it thus: "100% guaranteed to be from the Civil War era. You get 1 lb. of unchecked Civil War dirt from Arkansas, which was in the Civil War. Who knows what you may find. Comes with certificate of authenticity."

7. Virgin Mary in grilled cheese

   Inspiration to a host of auctions for "found" images in food, this sandwich was sold to GoldenPalace.com for $28,000.00.

8. The meaning of life

   "I have discovered the reason for our existence and will be happy to share this information with the highest bidder," per the seller. Someone bought it for $3.26.

9. Cathedral pickle bottle

   This pickle jar was bought at a garage sale for $3.00 and turned out to be so rare that collectors knew of only five in the world. It sold for $44,100.00.

10. Size 12 wedding dress/gown (the "eBay wedding dress guy")

11. Ghost cane

12. A human kidney

    The seller's description read: "Fully functional kidney for sale. You can choose either kidney. Buyer pays all transplant and medical costs. Of course only one for sale, as I need the other one to live. Serious bids only."

Five of the Weirdest Auctions according to eBay's Uncle Griff

1. "One Soul! Get it before the devil does."
2. "Young man's virginity, Please Look."
3. "Fully functional kidney." (eBay soon came out with a rule against selling body parts.)
4. "The Internet"—on sale for $1 million ("it's worth a trillion").
5. "Ghost in a jar"—This was just some kind of black mist that a guy had discovered coming out of a jar, and wanted to pass on to the next person . . . hmmm. This led to a rash of other "ghost" auctions, as well as some spooky doll auctions.

Four Websites Devoted to eBay Auctions or eBayers

1. AllMyLifeforSale.com

   John Freyer sold off all his possessions on eBay starting around November 2000, and ending in the summer of 2001. He also created a website devoted to the project. His endeavor generated considerable PR. He then traveled around the country to visit his items and chronicled the auctions, their new homes and owners in his book, *All My Life for Sale*. His final sales tally was $4,906.52, with a total of 1,927 bids. Items included a salt shaker and salt that went for $1.00 and a Mac PowerBook Duo 250 that brought in $102.50.

2. WeddingDressGuy.com

   The aforementioned Larry Star, who shares photos of himself from the original eBay listing, decked out in white.

3. HousewithBride.com

4. PopeHatChip.com

   The official cyber home of the nacho cheese–flavored Dorito shaped like the Pope's topper. It sold for $1,209.00 to GoldenPalace.com and received 41,000 visitors.

eBay Auction with the Most Hits

"eBay wedding dress guy"—it got about 6 million hits, 113 bids, and sold for $3,850.00.

Three "Ghost" Auctions

1. Ghost in a jar
   The original "ghost" auction that inspired the copycats
2. Ghost droppings
3. Ghost in a bra

Six of the Most Expensive Things Sold on eBay

1. A 340-year-old copy of Shakespeare's *Pericles, Prince of Tyre*, which survived the Great Fire of London in 1666 (GBP 5 million)
2. A Grumman Gulfstream II jet ($4.9 million)
3. A 1909 Honus Wagner baseball card ($1.65 million)
4. Diamond Lake Resort, western Kentucky ($1.2 million)
5. A 2003 Ferrari Enzo ($975,000.00)
6. Shoeless Joe Jackson's "Black Betsy" baseball bat ($577,610.00)

Source: Wikipedia

Five Celebrity Home Auctions and a Door

1. Eminem's Michigan home—bidding topped $1 million
   The 1,300-square foot house was appraised at $91,000.00.

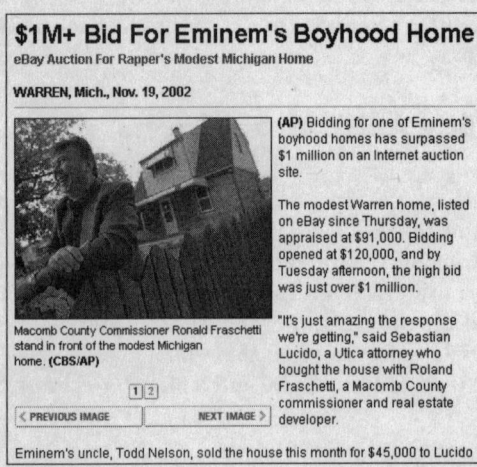

$1M+ Bid For Eminem's Boyhood Home
eBay Auction For Rapper's Modest Michigan Home

WARREN, Mich., Nov. 19, 2002

(AP) Bidding for one of Eminem's boyhood homes has surpassed $1 million on an Internet auction site.

The modest Warren home, listed on eBay since Thursday, was appraised at $91,000. Bidding opened at $120,000, and by Tuesday afternoon, the high bid was just over $1 million.

"It's just amazing the response we're getting," said Sebastian Lucido, a Utica attorney who bought the house with Roland Fraschetti, a Macomb County commissioner and real estate developer.

Macomb County Commissioner Ronald Fraschetti stand in front of the modest Michigan home. (CBS/AP)

1 2

< PREVIOUS IMAGE   NEXT IMAGE >

Eminem's uncle, Todd Nelson, sold the house this month for $45,000 to Lucido

2. Madonna's childhood home—bids as high as $99 million before it was withdrawn
   Per the description, "Madonna lived in the house with her father, stepmother and seven siblings from the time she was in sixth grade until she left for the University of Michigan. Bidding for this item begins at the actual value of the property as stated on the appraisal report at the time of its purchase." Fraudulent bidding drove the price up to a ridiculous $99 million, and the owner withdrew it from auction on the site.

3. Lucille Ball's childhood home—received at least 23,107 hits and was listed for $98,500.00

Lucille Ball's circa 1890 childhood home in Celeron, southwestern New York state, went up on eBay in 2002, starting at $98,500.00. Ball's daughter, Lucille Arnaz, was reportedly interested. The house had been an unofficial tourist attraction for years.

4. Bob Dylan's boyhood home—$94,000.00

Bob Dylan's boyhood home in Duluth, Minnesota, sold in 2001 for a reported $94,600.00. Bidding opened at $85,000.00. Dylan, who was born in 1941, lived in the house until he was 6 years old. "Rock legend Bob Dylan's first steps were taken in this charming duplex…original woodwork still shows the initials young Dylan scratched in his bedroom," wrote the seller. The house featured an unfinished attic and basement, which the seller wrote could be used for "a small cafe or gallery for fans of Dylan's to come and feel the artistic vibe within the walls."

5. Jimi Hendrix's Seattle childhood home—didn't actually sell

Bidding on the Seattle house where Hendrix spent several years apparently got up to $45,000.00 before the high bid was withdrawn, reportedly due to the terrorist attacks on the East Coast.

6. Ozzy Osbourne's door—didn't actually sell

The man who lives in Ozzy Osbourne's childhood home on Lodge Road in Birmingham was reportedly considering auctioning it off on eBay because he was sick of the rocker's fans coming by and defacing it.

Strange Human Auctions

1. Man's dignity: sold for $10.50, 7 bids

The auction's description read: "My dignity for sale. The winner will receive a piece of paper that says 'My Dignity' on it, with my signature. Warning: I may become a sad man after relinquishing my dignity. No shipping costs in U.S. Starting bid: $2.00."

2. Virginity

3. Brother: $1.50, 3 bids

"annoying little did i mention annoying brother for sale."

4. "I will kick your ass": bid up to $99,999,999.00, 63 bids.

   Description: "Winning bid will receive a butt-kicking from me personally. I guarantee that I will not break any bones or kill you, nor will I use any weapons on you, but I will give you a good beating….Do not pick me up, as I will be attacking you completely randomly. It may be when you are sleeping or showering or some other time when you are vulnerable. During this beating, I may damage one or more of your household items, if I have to break glass to get into your home or knock over furniture if you attempt to run from me. This should be expected and covered in my expenses."

5. Sense of humor: opening bid $9.99, 0 bids

   "Family and friends have been begging me to get rid of it. They says it has to go. They are just plain sick and tired of my puns, the slapstick, my pratfalls and the practical jokes. That is why I have decided to sell my sense of humor to the highest bidder. Winner gets one sheet of blank paper representing my sense of humor. Free postage. I am not responsible though if it doesn't "take" or if it returns home. AND NOW FOR THE OTHER WARNINGS: …DO NOT INGEST. NOT A TOY. DO NOT THROW IN THE AIR. NOT INTENDED AS A LIFE SAVING FLOTATION DEVISE. VOID WHERE PROHIBITED. THIS IS NOT A LADDER. PLEASE DO NOT USE FOR ONE FULL HOUR AFTER EATING A MEAL. IF YOU EXPERIENCE DIZZYNESS OR FATIGUE, DISCONTINUE USE AND SEE A DOCTOR. MAY NOT BE MACHINE WASHED. NOT RECOMMENDED FOR USE ON DOMESTIC ANIMALS. DO NOT INSERT THIS OR ANY OTHER OBJECT IN YOUR EAR CANAL. Search words: funny, fun, silly, laugh, joke, ha, ha, he, he, snicker, smile, grin, chuckle. ;-)"

Five Popular Collectibles Searches

1. Plate
2. Dog
3. Poster
4. Gold
5. Coca-Cola

Twelve eBay Categories That Delivered $1 Billion or More in Worldwide Annualized Gross Merchandise Volume (GMV)

1. eBay Motors at $9.8 billion
2. Consumer Electronics at $2.5 billion
3. Computers & Networking at $2.4 billion
4. Clothing, Shoes & Accessories at $2.2 billion
5. DVDs & Movies at $2.1 billion
6. Sporting Goods at $2.0 billion
7. Home & Garden at $1.6 billion
8. Collectibles at $1.4 billion
9. Toys & Hobbies at $1.3 billion
10. Jewelry & Watches at $1.2 billion
11. Cameras & Photo at $1.1 billion
12. Business & Industrial at $1.1 billion

Based on Q2-04 gross merchandise volume (GMV)

Top Keywords from A-Z

1. Abercrombie
2. Banana Republic
3. CD
4. DVD
5. eBay
6. Free shipping
7. Gap
8. Harley Davidson
9. iPod
10. Jersey
11. Kate Spade
12. Laptop
13. Motorola
14. Nike
15. Oakley
16. PlayStation 2
17. Quilts
18. Ralph Lauren
19. Sony
20. Tommy Hilfiger
21. U.S. Coins
22. Vintage
23. Wedding
24. Xbox
25. Yamaha
26. Zoppini

Source: eBay Home Page, July 22, 2004

Fifty Top eBayers with the Most Feedback

Rank	ID	Feedback	Prev. Rank	Country	Yr. Started
1	everydaysource	297,733	1	United States	2000
2	glacierbaydvd	265,950	2	United States	1999
3	eforcity	265,888	4	United States	2000
4	jayandmarie	264,467	3	United States	1999
5	accstation	252,657	6	United States	2001
6	itrimming	250,552	5	United States	2000
7	mancon2	216,340	9	Germany	2001
8	moviemarz	214,758	7	United States	2004
9	justdeals.com	202,697	8	United States	1997
10	mr.mobile	185,912	11	Germany	1999
11	buyessex	183,057	10	United States	2000
12	onando	179,598	12	Germany	2001
13	skshop	173,985	15	Germany	1999
14	grapevinehill	169,109	16	United States	1999
15	www.memoryworld.de	168,315	14	Germany	1999
16	casacaiman	167,882	17	United States	2002
17	abebooks-half	166,934	13	United States	2001
18	daniks-world	155,463	18	Germany	2000
19	foto-walser	145,722	19	Germany	2000
20	pugster888	144,422	20	United States	2002
21	the_sharper_image	140,116	24	United States	1999
22	bargaincell	138,552	26	United States	2001
23	alibris	138,400	22	United States	1998

24	totalcampus.com	137,894	21	United States	1998
25	papier11	137,146	23	United States	1999
26	copro-online	135,587	25	Germany	2001
27	greatdeals00	135,335	27	United States	2000
28	ebestdeal4u	134,230	29	United States	2001
29	soundcitybeaches	129,904	30	Canada	2001
30	patan01	128,610	32	United States	1999
31	restaurant.com	127,451	28	United States	2001
32	okluge_de	127,386	34	Germany	2001
33	foto-kontor	125,767	31	Germany	2002
34	dynamic-auction	122,048	40	Germany	2001
35	airbrushtower_de	121,187	36	Germany	1999
36	bargainland-liquidation	120,829	37	United States	1999
37	mombocom	120,804	33	United States	2003
38	play_it	119,256	35	Germany	2001
39	hoots-loot	119,085	38	United States	1998
40	olly_trading!	118,878	39	Germany	2002
41	cametaauctions	118,154	45	United States	2001
42	symmic	117,824	42	United States	1999
43	save-it-smart_de	117,594	41	Germany	2000
44	gothamcityonline	117,130	46	United States	1999
45	greatbuybooks	116,833	48	United States	2004
46	xcceries	115,659	44	United States	2001
47	sell2all	114,706	43	United States	1999
48	megabuys.com	112,326	52	United States	1998
49	procarparts.com	112,112	47	United States	2001
50	allshewants	110,958	49	United States	1999

Source: Nortica.com

What Ten of the Top eBay Sellers Sell

1. everydaysource—feedback of 297,733

   Cellular phone and computer accessories; "The #1 Electronics Seller on eBay," reads their store tagline.

2. glacierbaydvd—feedback of 265,950

   DVDs and CDs—movies and music.

3. eforcity—feedback of 265,888

   Electronics, including cell phones, PDAs, digital cameras, MP3 accessories, and ink cartridges.

4. jayandmarie—feedback of 264,467

   Founders of the "1 Cent CD" and "1 Cent DVD" auctions, Jay and Marie Senese are probably the most famous sellers on eBay, and at one time were the top seller. They still start some auctions at a penny.

5. accstation—feedback of 252,657

   Cell phones, DVDs, ink, MP3/PDA items, universal accessories

6. itrimming—feedback of 250,552

   Cell phones, PDAs, DVDs, digital camera accessories

7. mancon2—feedback of 216,340

   DVDs and videos

8. moviemarz—feedback of 214,758

   "Movies. Music. Madness."

9. justdeals.com—feedback of 202,697

   A wide range of electronics including cameras and digital cameras, computers and accessories, stereo equipment, Wi-Fi equipment, and more. "Multi-channel and cross-border trade solutions." One of the featured speakers at eBay Live 2005.

10. mr.mobile—feedback of 185,912

    Electronics including PDAs, camcorders, PC accessories; storefront is in German

Some Revenge Auctions

1. An early "revenge" auction was that of a man selling his wife's stash of 26 beanie babies . . . emphatically stating that he didn't know their exact value and was amazed people were so interested in them.

2. "eBay wedding dress guy" Larry Star (yes, him again) selling his ex's gown, and modeling it in the listing, complete with black T-shirt and body hair.

3. "NASTY SOCKS/ HUSBAND WON'T PICK UP"

   The seller's description read: "I HAVE HAD IT!!! I have one nerve dangling, and my husband is swinging on it!!! I asked him and I begged him TO PICK UP HIS NASTY SOCKS!! He peeled them off one evening on the living room and just dropped them on the floor right where he sits!!! That's where they've been ever since. I'm sick and tired of him and HIS SOCKS!!!The clock is ticking away and so is my patience. He steps over them EVERY DAY but won't bend down and grab them. They have been in the same spot for 4 weeks, 1 day, and I'm NOT picking them up!!!

   "I'm taking a stand! I'm fed up with husbands who disregard and disrespect everything their wives do for them. WITH ALL THAT SAID: UP FOR BID, one pair of size 9-10 men's (almost) white sport socks. Condition is very used. Join my cause, show support. Starting bid is only .50 cents. I'M DONE, I'M OVER HIM!!! Shipping is only $2.50 socks will be mailed in a sealed plastic bag for your protection. Thanks."

   With two days, one hour to go, it still had no bids. Hmm . . . this one is technically against eBay rules, as used clothing is supposed to be laundered.

4. Angriest Parent Auction: "Selling Son's Beloved Play Station 2 for Punishment!", sold for $122.50.

   "Parents please let your children read this auction.

   "It was a glory day when my son received his Play Station 2. This beloved machine was his prize possession. He played, if not for hours at a time. When he would not take care of anything else, but he took care of this little treasure of his. Ground him, take away phone privilege....anything but this PS2.

   "UP FOR AUCTION OR FOR SALE DUE TO PUNISHMENT

   "PLAY STATION 2/PS2/USED.

   "PLAYS GREAT! ASK MY SON [gives his email address]

   "COMES WITH TWO CONTROLERS SOME TYPE OF MEMORY CARD. NO GAMES. NO RESERVE

   "Here is the story: This weekend my 13-year-old son decided to be destructive, deceptive and disobedient. I had a bugle I was selling on eBay and while I was out he decided to 'play' with it. Sunday morning when the auction was to end, He picked up the bugle and asked me if I knew it was broken. He handed me the bugle which he had 'played' with and both solder joints were broken and since it was out of alignment the slide is now stiff."

   She goes on to say how her son and his friend invited someone she did not know to the house while she and her husband were not there. "I get home about 11:30 PM and find the house is wrecked. Beer was missing. Confronted son and friends about beer...Yes they had drank the beer. -$6.00 Strike one! Get up the next morning only the find the mysteriously broken bugle! -$51.00 Strike two!"

   She goes on to say her husband found a corkscrew and part of a cork on the floor, asked their son if he knew anything about it, and he confessed to drinking not only the beer but a bottle of 1995 Dom Perignon champagne they had been saving for a year, as well. "Well I hope you enjoyed that because it cost $120.00 a bottle!" said the dad.

   "I AM SELLING THIS PRIZE possession TO RECOUP WHAT I LOST," the mom sums up.

ABOUT THE CD

The CD contains a demo version of HammerTap, eBay research software, and access to the Auction Accelerator, which contains six eBay startup lessons.

To run the CD, you'll need:

- Windows XP or better
- 256MB
- Pentium III or greater
- A live internet connection

If you purchase DeepAnalysis through the demo interface, you will receive 20% off the purchase price.

Make More Money

Knowing that a product is likely to sell is valuable. But knowing how to successfully close more auctions is even better. DeepAnalysis uncovers the market trends that lead to higher auction success rates. Discover which day of the week to end your auction listing, find out whether or not to use a reserve, choose starting prices that attract more bids, and much more. DeepAnalysis provides a well of data so deep that you can discover how to make even more money than the top sellers.

Our philosophy is simple: don't mimic the competition, exceed it. Even the most successful seller occasionally lists auctions that do not sell. And the most successful sellers don't always gain the highest profit for every auction. So why study sellers with flaws when you can study flawless auctions?

Reach More Markets

Once you discover a demand for the products you sell, take the next step and use your niche and your client list as a solid basis for a web storefront.

Our Customers Say…

"I was able to achieve eBay Power Seller status after only three months of using this program!!! I recommend it to anyone!!" --Julie Norton

"I use DeepAnalysis to help me find niche markets for my websites. It shows what people are looking for in real-time data." –Paul Godfrey

"I've been using DeepAnalysis for about three years now, and it just keeps getting better and better." –Idaline Hall

"DeepAnalysis provides me with the capability to analyze if a given product is in demand before I commit to selling it. A great marketing tool!!!" –Donna Kober

Power To Profit ™

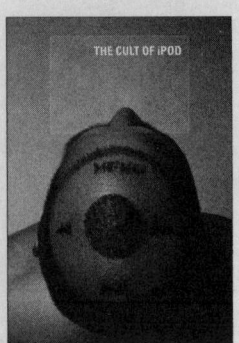

IT'S NEVER DONE THAT BEFORE!
A Guide to Troubleshooting Windows XP

by JOHN ROSS

It's Never Done That Before is a guide to troubleshooting Windows XP for people who use computers but don't necessarily feel comfortable poking around "under the hood" to make fixes. It includes basic troubleshooting techniques, specific instructions for solving the most common problems in Windows XP, and general tips for finding and fixing the more obscure ones. It also provides explanations of BIOS beep codes and blue screen errors, pointers for using the troubleshooting tools supplied with Windows XP, such as Safe Mode and the Recovery Console, and advice for dealing with device drivers, the ROM BIOS, and the Windows Registry. Viruses, spyware, and Internet connection problems are all discussed, and you'll find hints for getting the most out of the Microsoft Knowledge Base and navigating help desks and technical support centers.

MAY 2006, 288 PP., $29.95 ($38.95 CDN)
ISBN 1-59327-076-3

CREATIVE COMPUTER CRAFTS!
50 Fun and Useful Projects You Can Make with Any Inkjet Printer

by MARCELLE COSTANZA

This eye-catching book shows, step by step, how to use a computer and an inkjet printer to make fun and functional projects. Even with minimal technical skills, readers will be able to jump right in and try their hand at the projects described. All projects include easy-to-follow instructions, diagrams, and photos of the finished product. A resource list of websites and message boards provides entrée into the computer crafting community, and an exhaustive directory of crafting material suppliers makes it even easier for readers to find what they need.

MAY 2006, 208 PP., FULL COLOR, $24.95 ($32.95 CDN)
ISBN 1-59327-068-2

PHONE:
800.420.7240 OR
415.863.9900
MONDAY THROUGH FRIDAY,
9 A.M. TO 5 P.M. (PST)

FAX:
415.863.9950
24 HOURS A DAY,
7 DAYS A WEEK

EMAIL:
SALES@NOSTARCH.COM

WEB:
WWW.NOSTARCH.COM

MAIL:
NO STARCH PRESS
555 DE HARO ST, SUITE 250
SAN FRANCISCO, CA 94107
USA

COLOPHON

The eBay Price Guide was laid out in Adobe FrameMaker. The font families used are New Baskerville for body text, Futura for headings and tables, and Dogma for titles.

The book was printed and bound at Malloy Incorporated in Ann Arbor, Michigan. The paper is Abitibi 40# Abibook.

UPDATES

Visit **www.nostarch.com/ebaypg.htm** for updates, errata, and other information.